Encyclopaedia
of
Medical Astrology

Astrologically Yours,
H. L. Cornell, M.D., D.A.

Encyclopaedia

of

Medical Astrology

by

HOWARD LESLIE CORNELL, M.D., LL.D.
(Honorary Professor of Medical Astrology at the First National
University of Naturopathy and Allied Sciences, Newark, N.J.)

Author of "Astrology and the Diagnosis of Disease", 1918, a bound
volume of his "Magazine Articles on Medical and Biblical Astrology",
1924. *Member of* The New York PsychicalResearch Society; National
Geographic Society; The British Institute of Medical Astrology and
Metaphysical Science; Permanent Member of the National Eclectic
Medical Association. *Formerly* National Secretary of the National
Astrological Society of the United States, and of the American
Astrological Society.

THIRD REVISED EDITION

Introduction by Laurel Lowell

SAMUEL WEISER, INC.

York Beach, Maine

First paper edition published in 1992 by
Samuel Weiser, Inc.
Box 612
York Beach, ME 03910

This work was first published in 1933
Second edition, 1939
Third revised edition, 1972

Library of Congress Cataloging-in-Publication Data

Cornell, H. L. (Howard Leslie) , b. 1872.
   Encyclopaedia of medical astrology / by H. L.
Cornell. -- 1st paper ed.

      p.   cm.
   Originally published: 3rd, rev. ed. 1972.

   1. Medical astrology--Encyclopedias.   I. Title.
BF1718.C73   1992
133.5 ' 861 ' 03--dc20   92-26219
                                           CIP

ISBN 0-87728-753-8
EB

Printed in the United States of America

The paper used in this publication meets the minimum
requirements of the American National Standard for Perma-
nence of Paper for Printed Library Materials Z39.48-1984.

LETTER OF INTRODUCTION

FIRST NATIONAL UNIVERSITY OF NATUROPATHY

AND

ALLIED SCIENCES

143 ROSEVILLE AVENUE
NEWARK, N. J.

COMBINING
N. J. COLLEGE OF OSTEOPATHY
MECCA COLLEGE OF CHIROPRACTIC
U. S. SCHOOL OF NATUROPATHY
U. S. SCHOOL OF PHYSIOTHERAPY

February 3, 1933

COURSES
PROFESSIONAL AND POST GRADUATE
3 YEARS OF 8 MONTHS EACH
4 YEARS OF 7 MONTHS EACH
4 YEARS OF 9 MONTHS EACH

TO WHOM IT MAY CONCERN:

I have examined the preliminary sheets of the work
on Medical Astrology by Doctor H.L. Cornell, and this
work will be a monument to Doctor Cornell, and to
Astro-Science.

It is a Work that should be in every Astrologian's
Library for study and reference. As soon as this book
is off the Press, the First National University of
Naturopathy will make it one of the standard Textbooks
for the Chair in Astro-Pathological Diagnosis.

We have known Doctor Cornell for many years, and have
given him our highest Honors. He has spent the best
years of his life in research study along the lines of
Medical Astrology, and also used this knowledge to
practical advantage in his many years of Practice as a
Physician. This Encyclopaedia is the only book of its
kind ever attempted in the history of the World, as far
as we know, and it gathers together the knowledge along
the lines of Medical Astrology in a way that students
can get at it, as subjects are all arranged alphabetically.

We trust the book will be well-received, and appreciated
by the Astrological and Scientific World, and by Healers
of all Schools who are interested in Astrology as an aid
in Pathological Diagnosis, Prognosis, and in the etiological
factors in knowing more about the Philosophy of Disease, and
the Planetary Causes of Disease.

Respectfully,

F.W. Collins, M.D., A.M., Dean

Frederick W. Collins, M.D.,A.M.,Dean
FIRST NATIONAL UNIVERSITY OF
NATUROPATHY AND ALLIED SCIENCES.

ABBREVIATIONS AND SYMBOLS USED IN THIS BOOK

ABBREVIATIONS—

affl.—afflicted, afflicting.
apply.—applying, apply.
A.P.—(See Vertebrae).
Asc.—Ascendant.
asp.—aspect.
asps.—aspects.
AT.—(See Vertebrae).
AX.—(See Vertebrae).
B.—birth.
Card.—Cardinal.
Chap.—Chapter.
Coc.—Coccyx.
C.P.—(See Vertebrae).
d.—days.
Dec.—Decanate, Declination.
Decan.—Decanate.
decumb.—decumbiture.
decr.—decrease, decreasing.
deg.—degree, degrees.
Desc.—Descendant.
Dir.—Direction, Directed.
E.—East, Equinox.
Eq., Equi.—Equinox.
espec.—especially.
Fem.—Feminine, Female.
Fig.—Figure.
gd.—good.
H.—House.
Horo.—Horoscope.
Hor'y Q.—Horary Questions.
H.P.—(See Vertebrae).
incr.—increasing, increase.
infl.—influenced, influence.
ill-dig.—Ill-dignified.
1001 N.N.—1001 Notable Nativities.
K.P.—(See Vertebrae).

ABBREVIATIONS—

Lat.—Latitude.
Long.—Longitude.
L.C.P.—(See Vertebrae).
Li.P.—(See Vertebrae).
L.P.P.—(See Vertebrae).
Lu.P.—(See Vertebrae).
m.—months.
M.C.—The Midheaven.
M.C.P.—(See Vertebrae).
Mut.—Mutable.
N.—North.
N.N.—Notable Nativities.
No.—Number.
occi.—occidental.
ori.—oriental.
Per.—Periodic.
P.P.—(See Vertebrae).
Pr., Prog.—Progressed, Progression.
Q.—Question, Questions.
℞—Retrograde.
Rev.—Revolution.
S.—South.
Sac.—Sacrum.
Sec.—Section.
sepr.—separating.
Sig.—Significator.
Sigs.—Significators.
Spl.P.—(See Vertebrae).
S.P.—(See Vertebrae).
Subs.—Subluxations.
Tr., tr.—Transit.
U.P.P.—(See Vertebrae).
V.—Vertebra, Vertebrae.
W.—West.
well-dig.—well-dignified.
y.—years.

ASPECTS—

⌄—Semi-Sextile—30°.
∠—Semi-Square—45°.
⚹—Sextile—60°.
□—Square—90°.
△—Trine—120°.
⚲—Sesquiquadrate—135°.
☍—Opposition—180°.
P.—Parallel.
☌—Conjunction.

SIGNS OF THE ZODIAC—

♈—Aries.
♉—Taurus.
♊—Gemini.
♋—Cancer.
♌—Leo.
♍—Virgo.
♎—Libra.
♏—Scorpio.
♐—Sagittarius.
♑—Capricorn.
♒—Aquarius.
♓—Pisces.

PLANETS—

☉—Sun.
☽—Moon.
♆—Neptune.
♅—Uranus.
♄—Saturn.
♃—Jupiter.
♂—Mars.
♀—Venus.
☿—Mercury.

OTHER SYMBOLS—

⊕—Part of Fortune.
℞—Retrograde.
☊—Ascending Node.
    Dragon's Head.
☋—Descending Node.
    Dragon's Tail.
°—Degrees.
′—Minutes.
″—Seconds.
×—Multiplied By.
+—Plus.

THE CHART OF BIRTH

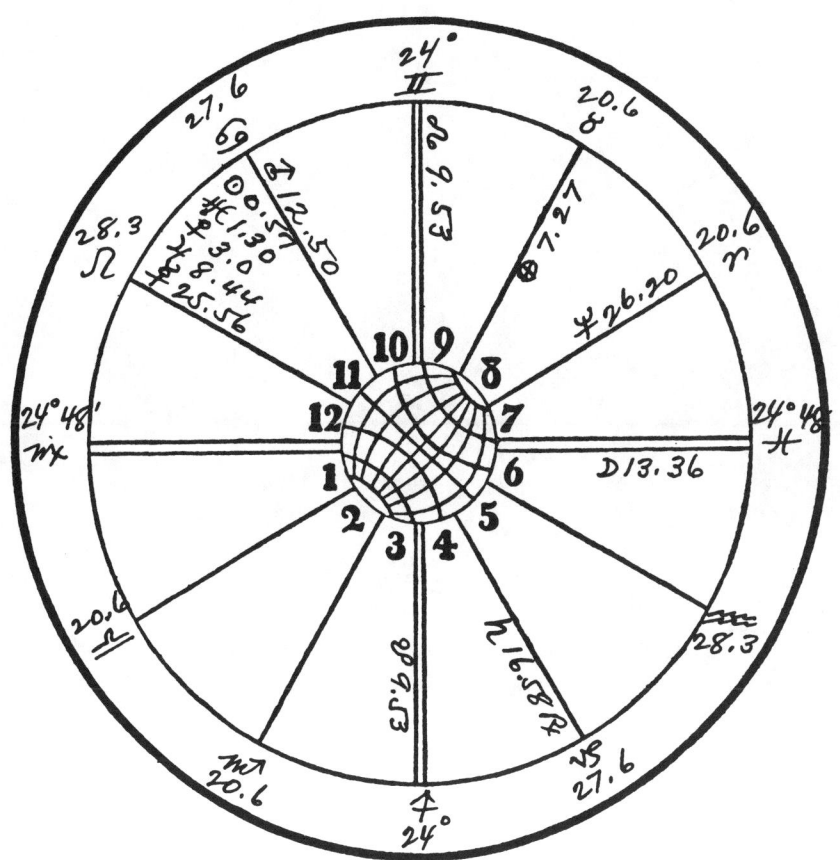

H. L. CORNELL, A.M., M.D., Ph.D.

Born July 23, 1872, 9:27 A.M.
Hartsville, Bucks County, Pennsylvania
75° W. L., 40° 12′ N. Lat.

INTRODUCTION TO THIRD EDITION

When Dr. Cornell enriched the astrological world with his *Encyclopaedia of Medical Astrology* in 1933 little was known about the planet Pluto and indeed most dedicated scholars strongly doubted the ultimate value of its effect upon our lives.

To support this disbelief Dr. Cornell quotes E. H. Bailey, Editor of the *British Journal of Astrology*. "I have no belief whatever in the alleged influence of this planet," and again, "I see no reason whatever to include it when dealing with horoscopes."

The shattering events of the early thirties coincide with the dramatic emergence of Pluto upon the scene and they were characterized by what we have since come to understand as Plutonian evolutionary and revolutionary tactics.

For the first time mass attention was focused upon the basic, individual needs—the Union of One with the Collective Whole. Established customs were challenged, laws repealed, the Federal Reserve System was reconstructed. There was belated aid to farmers, the NRA, WPA—every imaginable alphabetized tag symbolizing the results of a gigantic upheaval—the birth of Bureaucracy.

This evoluationary planet revolutionized the world to such an extent that even the most critical and discerning student must take its influence into sober account. And even before Pluto was officially added to the planetary family, his influence (Invisibility) may well account for the missing link in otherwise puzzling delineations.

As early as 1915 astronomer Percival Lowell and other astronomers observing from the Lowell Observatory in Flagstaff, Arizona, published "findings" on a new planet—a star of the 15th magnitude, its mass greater than half the Earth's Mass and approximately 1/50,000th that of the Sun, and located in the eastern part of the constellation Taurus traveling an eccentric path. However, it was not until 1930 that the planet (having been widely observed by then) was "discovered" and named Pluto.

As Man's consciousness expands, true to Cosmic Law and precisely "on cue," a new planet becomes visible and another evolutionary chapter unfolds. To better comprehend each revelation we need only refer to the point of reference bequeathed us (a veritable

Mein Kampf of the Skies)—the Encyclopedia of Life as embodied in mythological mysteries.

As we read about Pluto and his astral realm is absorbing—the subconscious implications, preoccupation with life and death, the very mystery of his Invisibility. Pluto must surely "rule" Scorpio and the Eighth House, for no other Sign has the stamina to endure the spiritual and psychological surgery Pluto employs.

The Latin translation for Pluto is *The Rich One,* and rich indeed was he, for all that is below the earth belonged to him. This fabulous and powerful god of the Underworld lived for six months of each year in his dark and well-heeled Kingdom—assessing his holdings—receiving and regenerating the souls of the dead.

Pluto was a resourceful and wily god. He saw, loved and carried off Persephone to his gloomy home. When Jupiter interceded for her release, it could not be completely effected, for Persephone had sucked the sweet pulp from a few pomegranate seeds which Pluto had cunningly offered her. So a compromise was made. Persephone was to pass half of her time with her mother (above) and the remaining half with her husband (below). This arrangement, as chronicled by Bulfinch, was probably the first recorded incidence of Equal Time!

With all due respect to Bulfinch, basic psychology today teaches us that Persephone must have elected to spend half of her time with Pluto sharing those treasures and rulings as his very powerful queen.

Along with Persephone, we are all profoundly affected by Pluto's magic (witness the lives of those who have already consciously hosted him in their Signs—Cancer, Leo and Virgo and a presently foreshadowed Libra). We have all journeyed to Tartarus (deep subconscious) and have emerged with new concepts.

Pluto is a "gutsy" god, often unscrupulous, who traditionally exemplifies Power and Will. He has much in common with Jupiter (they were brothers, and blood tells) and is noted for the same largesse. They both exert powerful influences the scope of which is immeasurable.

Fantastically adventurous Pluto excites the purest and highest potentialized energy—creative Will Power and Genius. His message is simply *love* finally realized through *Occult awareness.*

PLUTO RULERSHIP—ARIES OR SCORPIO?

The entire subject of rulership is hopelessly involved in spirited controversy but, as with all esoteric symbolism, there does appear to be deep meaning and an uncanny order to the assignment of each new planet as it appears upon the scene to impress itself upon the consciousness of the age it heralds.

The ancients held that Leo, the most regal of Signs, must surely be "ruled" by the Sun and that Cancer, the maternal Sign, was ruled by the Moon.

Moving outward from the Sun and clockwise around the Zodiac, Mercury was ascribed to Gemini and Virgo, Venus to Taurus and Libra, Mars to Aries and Scorpio, Jupiter to Pisces and Sagittarius and Saturn to Aquarius and Capricorn. To validate dual rulerships the Positive Signs (Aries, Gemini, Libra, Sagittarius and Aquarius) were considered the Day Homes, and the Negative Signs (Taurus, Virgo, Scorpio, Capricorn and Pisces) the Night Homes. Everything worked well enough under this system while only the Lights and the seven other known planets encompassed the Zodiac.

When Uranus was discovered in 1781, "modern" astrologers were hard put to find a tenable home for the newcomer. It was finally ascribed to Aquarius (and experience has proven this to be the proper choice) and so Saturn was relieved of divided allegiance.

In 1846 the advent of Neptune occasioned a similar reshuffling of rulerships, and Neptune emerged the ruler of Pisces, leaving Jupiter to reign noble and supreme in Sagittarius.

And so in 1930 Pluto's emergence necessitated one more re-evaluation, and the planet Mars, like his predecessors Saturn and Jupiter, found himself operating in a special and more concentrated area—ruling a single kingdom—and there appears to be little doubt that the potent segment of the Zodiac he so rules is Aries.

To understand the god Pluto is to comprehend the Scorpio native for, in a very real sense, Pluto *is* Scorpio and he must have come finally to claim his own. Everything within the province of the Eighth House has Plutonian overtones (astral projection, birth, death, dream consciousness, fate, magic, money belonging to others, mysticism, psychic experiences, regeneration)—a few of its characteristics, simply stated.

Wily Pluto couldn't possibly maneuver in Aries, for Aries is as naive as Scorpio is complex. Aries never needs a reason for action, Scorpio always has a nicely laid plan—a motivation and a purpose. Aries is ever young in experience, Scorpio is old and inscrutable. Aries is spelled out loud and clear and seeks the Light, Scorpio poses an everlasting riddle and prefers the Shadows. Aries (Mars) rushes into every conceivable situation unprepared, Scorpio (Pluto) moves only when the subconscious dictates absolute surrender. Aries is

Abortive—Scorpio, Conclusive. These are but a few of the countless and obvious comparisons.

John M. Allegro, in his contemporary and painstaking research of ancient Sumerian writings, (oldest known written language—5,000 years B.C.) "The Sacred Mushroom and the Cross," contributes the following definition of the name Pluto:

> *The name Pluto, Greek Plouton, is primarily a fertility word now recognizable as coming from an original Sumerian BURO-TUN "deliverer of the womb," is cognate with the Greek Bruo "teems with, be full, burst forth." The same Sumerian word appears in such names as Apollo, Aphrodite (from which comes our "aphrodisiac"), and the plant name Abrotonon, "Southern wood," a sprig of which under the pillow, Pliny tells us, "is the most effective countercheck of all to magical potions given to produce sexual impotence."*

One more interesting observation to further substantiate Pluto's rulership of Scorpio's domain is the obliquity of the planet's course. This departs from other planetary graphs in a most pronounced manner. Although Uranus usurped Saturn in the Eleventh House, and Neptune, Jupiter in the Twelfth House, Pluto arbitrarily (following its eccentricity) by-passed the First House and veered over to take a 150° stance in the Eighth House to pinpoint and resolve the struggle between Selfhood and Soul and so open the channel to Immortality.

Where else can this illuminating confrontation take place other than in Scorpio—Scorpio who is eternally preoccupied with the riddle of Life and Death?

LAUREL LOWELL

April 23, 1970
Boston, Massachusetts

PLUTONIAN CORRESPONDENCES

A new, transmuting ingredient has been added to the cosmic cauldron. In an attempt to excite further interest and deepen understanding of the potent qualities of this ingredient (Pluto), the following alphabetized categories are correlated and examined by aspect.

The information that follows has been culled from books, magazines, dictionaries, lists inherited from Astrologers' files, etc.

The delineations of aspects for Anatomy, Chemistry, and Diseases have been determined by examining accumulated birth charts from personal files, charts of contemporaries, and those of famous (or infamous) people.

Whatever limitations these sources imposed were remedied by aggressive exploration—i.e., by searching out people in circumstances under study and thereby closing the gaps in resource material.

This source material will help identify and corroborate the students' determinations—it's a Pluto Proving Ground—the launching pad for eternal questing.

ANATOMY

Target Areas	Comments	Aspects
bladder		♇aspects♂ ☽ ♋□♂
descending colon		♇♂ 6H cusp ⚹ ♂♏(♂□☉)
discolored blood		♇⚻♃ = (♃♂ Asc)
enzymes	metabolic balance	♇□☽ (☽ on Asc⚻♂)
fissures		♇aspects to ♅ and/or ♂
fluids	vital fluid at nape of neck, connects pineal gland and pituitary nerves, organs centered in the neck	♇♂ ☽⚹♄
genitals		♇to ♂ or planets in ♏
glands	digestive	♇ to ☉☽ or ♆
gland pineal	more open	♇♂ ♀10H⚹♆☽□♂ (angles)
organs	excretory and generative	♇aspects to ☽♄
nervous system	sensitized	♇⚹♆□4H planets♂☉
pancreas		♇ to ☽ or ☿ or to planets in ♋♍
prostate gland		♇aspects to planets in ♏
pulsations	heart	♇□☉☽♌
rectum		♇to 6 and 8H or planets in ♏
sacral vertebrae	pubic arch	♇to planets in ♎♏♐
sigmoid flexure	part of intestine	♇ to 6 and 7H also planets in ♍♏
solar plexus		♇to planets in ♍ or houses occupied by ☿

CHEMISTRY

Target Areas	Comments	Aspects
alchemy		♇☌ ☉☽✶♆
burning	dross sloughed off— purification	♇☌ ♂□♃
decomposition		♇☌ ♂□☉
distillation		♇□☉♀
fermentation		♇☌ ♂♏
putrefaction		♇☌ ♂♃♍✶☽♋
spagyric	separates and assembles	♇☌ ♅✶☿
transforming processes		♇✶♆□♂
transmutation		♇☌ ♀✶☽

DISEASES

Target Areas	Comments	Aspects
acidosis	chronic mineral deposits	♇☌ ♆□♀♍
adenoiditis		♇☌ ♂∠♅
arteriosclerosis		♇☍♄(♄□♀)
arthritis		♇☌☽(♀☍♄)
epidermal		♇☌♃□☽
hoarseness		♇☌♀□♄
irregular menses		♇☌☽♃♐♀
leucorrhea		♇□☽♏ and ♃
malformation	lower part of body	♇□♅☍☉♐
metabolism	male	♇□☉♅☽♈✶♂♒
nasal catarrh		♇☌☉☽♄□♂
nervous breakdown		♇✶♆♅□☿♂
ovarian		♇☌☉☽ 8H □♀
piles		♇☌♄ 8H ♐ Asc
pituitary glands		♇✶♆♐☉♂♀
plagues		♇♅☌☽ (☽□♄)
prostate structures		♇□☉ (☉ ruler 8H)

DISEASES continued

uterine	♇ □☉⚹☽♏ 5H
venereal	♇☌ ♀ₙ □☽ₚ ♍□♄ₚ ♆

PHYSIOLOGY

action	between acid and alkali
body emanation	sensitive to odor, scent, animal
	earth, human, plant, sense of touch
fluxing influences	
metabolism	balance between anabolistic and
	catabolistic phases

PHYSIQUE

build	sturdy
corpulent	
eyebrows	bushy
eyes	magnetic
expression	sensuous
face	angular—pretty
	depicts struggle matter vs. spirit
	lower half—material
	upper half—spiritual
hair	fine on scalp, little on body
robust	
skin	delicate
stature	medium

INTRODUCTION TO SECOND EDITION

The results which this book will produce on the readers and students will, of course, depend largely upon the attitude of mind and mental advancement in which they approach the subject with which it deals.

Many students approach metaphysical phenomena with ingrained disinclination, to accept facts and conclusions which interfere with their preconceived opinions and dogmatic, **youth-instilled** beliefs.

Readers of this category will be necessarily incapable of comprehending the **message** and helpful advice contained in the following pages.

Those who are ready, cosmically speaking, to study this subject with an open, unbiased and unprejudged mind will find, perhaps, that whilst they can accept factors stated, they cannot reconcile themselves to PROGRESS—progress in thought, progress in the application thereof, no matter how sane they may appear to them.

The exposition as portrayed by Dr. Cornell in his treatise of something new, that has been suppressed for the past century, is but the beginning of a NEW ERA in the field of the Healing Arts; whatever conclusions or repercussions may arise therefrom are but a step FORWARD in the RIGHT DIRECTION.

A science whose significance is so far reaching and whose influence on the entire field in the Healing Arts will be revolutionary, to say the least, is bound to have repercussions from the old, obsolete and, by demonstration, impractical methods belonging to the past.

But, we must not overlook the fact, that with all our so-called advancements of standards of living, we still have with us a daily floating hospital population of close to 2,500,000 sick and ailing people in these United States. What is the cause? Too many 'Doctors' or not enough? Maybe not the right kind that know how to CURE disease or to alleviate suffering? Something surely IS wrong! Maybe, after all, the ancients knew more about relieving pain and suffering when they used common sense remedies, such as herbs, teas, poultices, made from various roots, plants and foliage.

Everything in this world was created for a well-defined and special purpose, including the stars, which were the first LINK between Man and the Heavens. The ancients knew well how to interpret the influence of these stars, especially that of the planets, upon ALL things terrestrial, including our health.

One of the most ancient and most reliable writers on this subject, Ptolemy, in his Quadripartite on the influence of the Stars, makes special reference to the stellar influence regarding localities north or south of the equator. Nicholas Culpepper, in his treatise on English Herbs (edition of 1695) allocates not less than 369 herbs to the various planets and their correlation to the Healing Arts. L. D. Broughton, M.D., in his work on this subject (Elements of Astrology) brings out very potent and convincing factors that the stars were made for something other than for professional 'Star-gazers' to look at.

An eminent Viennese medico, Dr. Friedr. Feerhov, as late as 1914, blazed the trail in Europe by publishing an astro-medical treatise, setting forth the close relationship between physical manifestation and metaphysical influence, between chemistry and biochemistry and alchemical allocation of human types.

At that time his 'findings and observations' were ridiculed by whom? By such who "Were down on something on which they were not up on!" It is the same today, albeit in a lesser way. After all, whenever I hear 'people' talking against something they do not know anything about, I am reminded of Shakespeare's lines in Julius Caesar, act I, scene III: "And that which would appear offence in us, His countenance, like richest alchemy, will change to VIRTUE and to WORTHINESS."

All good things take time! Ever since the beginning of the Aquarian age new systems within the healing arts have been proposed and expounded. Yet, the attacks made against all and everyone by the old, intrenched and well organized medical oligarchy (serum trusts and patent medicine vendors) have wrought havoc within the ranks of progressive exponents. Yet, with all the opposition, the 'old' must give way to the 'young' and the same holds good in medicine.

Disease is caused by retention of septic matter within the body; cure can be effected only by elimination of such septic retentions. The homeopathic and naturopathic systems have done more good than all the allopaths together.

I am well aware of the consequences of this statement, but, having graduated from both schools I know whereof I speak. Anyone, who is sceptically inclined, is advised to read: "Devils, Drugs and Doctors." (Howard W. Haggard, M.D., 1929.)

At the present time, there is a revolutionary trend within the ranks of the orthodox practitioners against the dictum of the medical trust. Yet, with all their wrangling they are not able to diminish the present day, ever-increasing 2,500,000 daily floating hospital population in the United States. Something is wrong somewhere. But the guilty parties are too stubborn to admit defeat from within. It will come from without.

The natural methods of healing, when well understood and judiciously applied, bring results. They fail only when suffocated herbs are used; this latter happens quite often lately, more so since the universal use of transparent water-proof wrapping material which excludes all oxygen not only from foods, but also from therapeutics. No wonder cancer has increased by leaps and bounds since the initiation of this oxygen-excluding wrapping material.

But, we are not interested in 'health-destroying' agencies; the point is to introduce something that WILL alleviate human suffering, and Dr. Cornell's book is one link in the long chain of Real Healing.

It might not be amiss to mention that Dr. Cornell, in his later years of life, became a loyal follower of the great genius, Emanuel Swedenborg, who, albeit not having been a licentiate of any orthodox school, laid the foundation of naturopathic principles.

Undoubtedly, Dr. Cornell gleaned many valuable pointers from Swedenborg's doctrines.

Dr. Cornell, whom, unfortunately I met too late and lost too soon, has built himself an everlasting monument; the future generation will honor him alongside the great souls, such as Pasteur, Koch, Lavoisier, Roentgen, Florence Nightingale, Lord Lister, for his contribution to mankind.

R. I. P.

HENRY J. GORDON, M. D., A. M., N. D., PH. D. *h. c.*

Los Angeles, California
Easter, 1939

FOREWORD

For some years in my study of Astrology as a Physician and Surgeon, and in an effort to get at the Planetary Causes of disease, I searched through the Textbooks of Astrology to find something about the disease I was treating, but my efforts were often in vain. There are many fine things said in the Textbooks along the lines of Medical Astrology, but such statements are often made at random, and in obscure places, and are not indexed. To be sure, there are classified lists of the Planets in Signs, and the diseases they cause, but in making a study of any one disease, it is almost impossible to find in the regular Textbooks and Manuals of Astrology all that has been said about this disease, and its planetary causes, and this knowledge could only be obtained by a systematic search through my entire Astrological Library. Being so inconvenienced myself, and with a desire to get the knowledge along the lines of Medical Astrology into classified shape, about fifteen years ago I conceived the idea of making this Encyclopaedia, and of arranging the Disease Subjects alphabetically, and of gathering up the material on each subject from all the Astrological books of my Library. This has been a momentous and tedious task. To begin with, I opened up a Ledger Account for each disease subject, and began a systematic digest of my entire Library, and in reading, line by line, would post the thoughts into the Ledger under each disease subject as I would come to them. By keeping up this practice for some years I eventually had two large Ledgers filled with material. Then came the task of arranging, classifying, disentangling, and writing up these ledger Articles into readable form, as each Article was posted in as read, and like a jungled mass, and without form. It took me four years to go thru this and finish the first writing entirely in English. Then, in 1928 the idea came to me that I should retype and rearrange the entire book, and type it on an Astronomical Typewriter, and use the Symbols for the Planets, Signs, and Aspects. In this second writing it was necessary to rearrange the subjects, and place many Articles under a different letter. The system of Synonyms and cross references in the book has taken a great deal of time, and to see to it that such references were in harmony. To shorten the manuscript I have used many abbreviations, and a list of these abbreviations you can find in the front of this book.

When this mass of material was straightened out, arranged, classified, and the various influences causing a disease were gotten together and studied, it has been an interesting study to note the fundamental influence and nature of the various Planets, and how these influences were in the minds of the various Writers, from the time of Ptolemy, and on down thru the Centuries until the present time, and with these facts and data before me, it has become an easy matter for me to see what influences were missing, and which have never been listed or tabulated in any book, as far as I have been able to discover, and to fill these in, and to do my part in helping to develop the Science of Medical Astrology, and get the knowledge along this line into such shape that students can get at it quickly, and by merely turning to a subject in the alphabetical arrangement. Also in this Encyclopaedia I have given attention to the Higher and Spiritual side of Astrology, to Esoteric Astrology, and have tried to arouse the readers to an inner consciousness of their Higher Powers, to rule their stars, and not be a slave to the various planetary aspects and influences which operated over them at birth, or may be manifesting themselves along thru life.

The fundamental purpose of this Encyclopaedia is to give the planetary influences which cause the various diseases, afflictions, events, accidents, and injuries of life, and to gather such knowledge under subjects, and arrange them alphabetically. I am not attempting to repeat the Classifications to be found in the various Textbooks of Astrology, and the student is asked to use this volume in connection with his other books. Also this book does not attempt to go into the Elements of Astrology, or to be a Textbook of such Elements, although many Articles do deal with these Elements, and especially as they are related to Medical Astrology, and the Diagnosis of Disease by Astrology. The student, in order to use this Encyclopaedia intelligently, should first be a student of Astrology, and to know the Elements and Fundamentals of Astrology and Astronomy, and be familiar with the Signs and Symbols of Astronomy. Also this book is not intended to be a Treatise on the various Systems of Healing, or Schools of Treatment, but to give the planetary causes and philosophy of disease, and to allow each student to use his own methods of treatment. I honor and respect all Schools of Healing, and recognize that there is good in all, but it would be impossible in a book of this kind to go into the merits of the different Schools. The Theory of Chiropractic is closely related to Astrology, due to the planetary rulerships over the Spine and Vertebrae, and I have attempted to give and list, under various diseases, the Subluxations caused by the planetary influences. It is also my desire to have students in the various Schools of Healing, and when they are studying a certain disease, to consult this Encyclopaedia on the subject in hand, and note the planetary influences which cause such disease, and to understand the philosophy of the case, and not to be satisfied merely with the treatment of the ailment. In Ancient Times all Physicians and Healers were required to know Astrology, and its relation to disease, and to the individual afflicted, as by a study of his Star Map of Birth, and the adverse Directions which might be operating over him, and such applicants for Medical, or Healing Licenses, were not allowed to become full-fledged Physicians until they could pass a satisfactory examination in Astrology. But, for various reasons, the knowledge of Astrology became more or less suppressed during the Middle Ages, but is now being revived again, and coming into its own, and is being more and more recognized as a true and Ancient Science. Physicians and Healers should lay aside their prejudices, and investigate Astrology, prove it by observation, and when they do, I feel sure they will give it its rightful place in their Schools and Colleges of Healing, and in their daily practices among their patients. In my own practice I found Astrology of inestimable value in diagnosing my cases, and to quickly determine the seat of the disease in the patient, how long they have been sick and ailing, and to form a reasonably accurate prognosis.

In this book, the Form and Shape of the body, and the planetary influences along the lines of Form, Shape, Height, Weight, Complexion, Hair, etc., are given. Also there are many Articles along the lines of Conduct, Habits, Morals, Temperament, etc. Also the prominent Fixed Stars, and their influences, are listed. Under each subject the sub-heads are arranged alphabetically for quick reference, and the student can very quickly get at the knowledge he is seeking, on any subject, as far as they are listed and recorded in this book.

One very great difficulty I have encountered in building up this Encyclopaedia has been to determine what subjects should go in, and what should be left out, and especially along the lines of Mental Traits. The Mind and Body are so closely related, and there are so many Mental Traits which are Pathological, and practically amount to a diseased Mind, that I have listed in this volume a great number of the less desirable Mental Traits, and also for a study in contrasts, some of the more desirable ones. During my years of study in the preparation of this volume I have gathered enough material for a separate Encyclopaedia, to be known as "The Encyclopaedia of Psychological Astrology", and hope soon to begin to assemble this book, and leave it to the World as the sister book to this present volume.

In the Fall of 1918, after many years of active Practice in Medical work in this Country, and in India, I gave up the Practice of Medicine, moved my family to Los Angeles, and have lived here ever since, and given my whole time to Astrology, Writing, and in the preparation of Star Maps, Horoscopes, and Astrological Health Readings for people over the World. When this Encyclopaedia is out, circulated, and established, it is my plan to make a World Lecture Tour, and speak before the various Healing Centers and Schools in the U. S. A., and other Nations, and to make an effort to have the various Faculties make Medical Astrology one of the required studies for their students who are aspiring to be Healers. I plan to have this Encyclopaedia in the prominent Public Libraries in the large Cities over the World, and also in the Occult, Metaphysical, Astrological, and Healing Centers, and where students can have access to it. I am giving this book to the World as a labor of love, and trust it will prove of great help to you and be a fitting monument to my life work.

H. L. CORNELL, M.D.

Los Angeles, Calif.
March 21st, 1933.

Encyclopaedia
of
Medical Astrology

or injury; ♄ in the 1st H.; ♄ or ♂ in the 1st or 7th H. at B., or by tr. or dir., and espec. when in ♋, ♑, or ♓; ♄ or ♂ in all signs ascribed to animals or fishes, and the malefics ori. of the ☉, and occi. of the ☽. Sugar of Lead (Lead Acetate) Solution is a good remedy locally to relieve the irritation or inflammation from an excoriation. (See Accidents, Hurts, Injuries, Wounds).

ABROAD—Foreign Lands—Benefits or Dangers In—

Accidents Abroad—Danger of Accidents, Death, Ill-Health, or Violence Abroad—A malefic planet ruler of the 9th H. at B.; malefics in the 9th H., and affl.; the hyleg in the 9th H., and affl. by the ☌ or evil asps. of malefics; one or more malefics in the 9th H., or in ☌ in the 9th at a Solar Rev., and the hyleg affl. by a train of evil directions; lord of the 9th in the 8th, danger of death Abroad; lord of the 8th in the 9th and in ☌ lord of the Asc.; lord of the 10th in the 9th; the 2nd dec. of ♐ on the Asc., ruled by the ☽; planets ruling the anaretic places being in the cadent houses, and espec. if the ☽ be in one of the anaretic places, or in ☌ or ☍ asp. to them; the ☉ or ☽ affl., and the ☽ or lord of the 1st be near violent fixed stars, or a malefic or violent stars ascending, danger of an untimely death Abroad; the ☽ sepr. from ♂ and applying to the ☉, indicates a violent death in a strange land if Abroad at the time; ♅ in the 12th H. at B., and affl., causes the danger of detention in out-of-the-way places Abroad, by accident; ♄ or ♂ in the 9th H., and affl.; malefics in the 9th H., and affl. the hyleg. (See Sea, Ships, Shipwreck, Travel, War. See "Sickness", and the various paragraphs in this section).

Assassinated Abroad—(See Assassination).

Battle—Death or Injury in Battle and War Abroad—♂ lord of the 8th, and in the 9th H.; ♂ affl. the significators denotes death in battles Abroad, or by pirates, fire, mutiny, massacre, or lightning. (See War).

Death Abroad—(See "Accidents", and the various paragraphs in this section). Case—Death Abroad at 40 years of age—(See "Ellis", No. 830, in 1001 N. N.).

Detention Abroad—From an Accident —(See "Accidents" in this section).

Disaster Abroad—May Meet With— (See "Accidents", "Sickness", and other paragraphs in this section).

Distress Abroad—(See "Sickness" and the various subjects in this section).

Falls—Suffers from Abroad—(See Heights).

Fire—Suffers From—Death By—(See "Battle" in this section).

Foreign Travel—Unfortunate In— Meets with Accident, Death, Falls, Injury, or Sickness In—(See the various paragraphs in this section). Also see Pirates, Sea, Ships, Shipwreck, Travel).

Health—Good Health Abroad—Ill-Health Abroad—The benefics in 9th H., and this house free from affliction,

tends to good health Abroad, and may make it advisable for the native to live Abroad, but malefics in the 9th tend to ill-health, and all kinds of misfortune, injury, ill-health, or death Abroad, and the native should remain in the land of birth. (See "Native Land" under Native; the various subjects under Travel).

Ill-Health Abroad—See "Accidents", "Health", "Sickness" in this section).

Journeys Abroad—Should Take— Should Avoid—(See "Health" in this section. Also see "Abroad" under Journeys; Travel).

Lightning—(See "Battle" in this section).

Massacre—Death In Abroad—(See "Battle" in this section).

Mutiny—Death in Abroad—(See "Battle" in this section).

Native Land—Should Remain In— Should Remove—(See "Native Land" under Native; "Place of Birth" under Place).

Pirates—(See "Battle" in this section. Also see Pirates).

Residence Abroad—(See Residence).

Sickness Abroad—Lord of the 6th in the 9th, or lord of the 9th in the 6th, sickness Abroad, or at Sea; lord of the 1st, or the ☽ in the 6th, 8th, or 12th, or if combust, peregrine, or ☌ or evil asp. a malefic, much sickness or distress Abroad; the 9th H., its lord, or the ☉ or ☽ affl., denotes sickness and disaster Abroad; ♄ afflicting the Sigs. of travel, or ♄ in 9th, ruler of 9th, or affl. lord of the 9th, sickness, or chronic ill-health Abroad. (See "Accidents", "Health" in this section).

Soldiers—Death or Injury Abroad in War—(See "Battle" in this section. Also see War).

Suffering—And Distress Abroad— (See "Accidents", "Sickness", and other paragraphs in this section).

Travel Abroad—(See "Health", "Native Land" in this section. Also see Travel).

Untimely Death Abroad—(See "Accidents" in this section).

Violence—Meets with Violence, or a Violent Death Abroad—The ☽ sepr. from ♂ and applying to the ☉, a violent death in a strange land, or meets with violence; ♂ affl. in 9th H.; ♂ ruler of the 8th, and in the 9th. (See "Accidents", "Battle", in this section. Also see War).

War—Death or Injury in Abroad— (See "Battle" in this section. Also see War).

ABSCESSES—Imposthumes—A Circumscribed Cavity Containing Pus—A disease of the ☽ and ♃; a disease of the ♋ sign, and caused by afflictions in ♋; due to corrupt blood; ♃ causes abscesses due to blood changes and accumulations of fluid in a part; ♃ in ♈; ♃ affl. in ♉, abscesses of the throat or neck, and over the body due to blood disorders; ♃ in ♏ and affl., and espec. when in 6th H.; caused by afflictions to the ☽ or ♃ at B., or by dir.; ♃ in signs which rule the arms, hands, legs and feet tends to abscesses in these parts; ♄ or ♂ in angles at B., occi. of the ☉, and ori. of the ☽, and ☿ in familiarity with ♂, the frequency and number of abscesses are increased; ♂ and ☿ holding dominion at B., in familiarity with each other, and with ♂ affl. the hyleg, and elevated above the Luminaries; ♀ affl. by malefics; abscesses are denoted by afflictions in or about the 25° of ♌ or ♒, or in the 21° of ♈ or ♎. See the following subjects in the alphabetical arrangement.

Arms—Abscesses In—♃ in signs ruling the arms. (See Arms).

Aural Meatus—Abscesses In—(See Ears).

Back—(See "Abscesses" under Back).

Bladder—(See "Abscess" under Bladder).

Blood—From Blood Disorders—From Impure Blood—(See "Impure Blood" under Impure).

Body—Abscesses Over the Body—♃ affl. in ♉.

Boils—(See Boils).

Bowels—(See "Abscess" under Bowels).

Brain—(See "Abscess" under Brain).

Breasts—(See "Abscess" under Breast).

Carbuncles; Causes of Abscess—(See the first part of this Article).

Corrupt Blood—Abscesses Caused By—(See "Impure Blood" under Impure).

Ears—(See "Abscess" under Ears).

Enteritis—With Abscess—(See "Inflammation" under Bowels).

Feet—Abscess In—♃ affl. in ♓. (See Feet).

Frequency of—(See the first part of this Article).

Frontal Bone—Abscess In—♆ in ♈, and espec. when affl. by the ☉, ♄, or ♂. (See Frontal).

Generative Organs—Abscess In—(See "Abscess" under Secrets).

Hands—Abscesses In—(See Hands).

Impure Blood—Abscesses Caused By—(See "Impure Blood" under Impure).

Increased—(See the first part of this Article).

Kidneys—(See "Abscess" under Kidneys).

Liver—(See "Abscess" under Liver).

Loins—(See "Abscess" under Loins).

Mastoid; Neck—Abscess In. and on the back of the Neck—(See Neck).

Ovaries—Abscess of—(See Ovaries).

Pharynx; Phlegmonous — Phlegmonous Enteritis with Abscess—(See "Inflammation" under Bowels).

Privy Parts—(See "Abscess" under Secrets).

Pus; Pyaemia—(See Septic).

Pyonephrosis—(See "Abscess" under Kidneys).

Pyorrhoea; Reins; Retropharyngeal—(See "Abscess" under Pharynx).

Secrets; Septic; Sores; Stomach; Suppuration; Throat; Ulcers; Urethra;

Vulva—(See "Abscess" under these subjects).

ABSENT PARTY—These influences are especially to be noted in Hor'y Questions.

Cuts To—or Stabs—(See "Weapons" under Cuts).

Danger—Absent Party Has Been in Great Danger—Has Been Ill, But Will Recover—(See "Recovery" in this section).

Dead—Absent Party Is Dead—The ☉ and ☽ affl., and lord of the 8th affl. the Sig. also; the ☽ sepr. from the ☌ or evil asp. lord of the 8th, and without the assistance of any benefic ray that could save, he has been deceased for so many days or months as there are degrees between the signs; the Sig. affl., and lately in ☐ or ☍ asp. a malefic; the Sig. combust in the 8th H., or the ☉ be lord of the 8th; translation of light between the lord of the Asc. and lord of the 8th; lord of the 8th in the Asc., and lord of the Asc. in the 8th; lord of the 8th in the 4th, or lord of the 4th in the 8th, and espec. if the Sig. be affl. by evil asps., and malefic planets in angles, and the benefics cadent; lord of the Quesited's Asc. in the 4th or 8th, may be dead; Sig. of the party in the 12th, in ☐ or ☍ a malefic, or the ☉ or ☽ unfortunate in like manner; lord of the Asc. in the 4th in ☐ the ☽, the party is dead, or near great danger; an Infortune translating the light of the lord of the 8th to him is a symbol of death; lord of the 1st, or 8th ☽ in ☌ lord of the 8th in the 8th or 4th, he is dead, or if in the 6th, he will die; lord of the 1st, or the ☽ in the 8th, combust, or in the 4th, he is dead, or if in their fall or ℞, he is at the point of death; the Sigs. combust or ℞, and ☌ a malefic or lord of the 8th, indicate certain death, and that the absent party is dead. (See the various paragraphs in this section).

Death—Is at the Point of Death—(See "Dead" in this section).

Feverish—(See "Absent Party" under Fever).

Good Health—In Good Health—The ☉ in the 6th H.; the ☽ in good asp. lord of the Asc.; the ☽ in the 8th, or 12th, and not afflicted; ♃, ♀, or ♌ in the Asc.; ♃ or ♀ in good asp. the cusp of the 1st, or 6th; lord of the Asc. free from affl. by lord of the 8th; lord of the Asc. in dignity, and not affl. by ♄, ♂, or lord of the 6th; no malefics in the 6th; a benefic in the Asc., M. C., and the ☉ and ☽ well asp., and the lord of the Asc. in a good house.

Great Evil—Some Great Evil Has Overtaken the Absent Party—The Sig. combust in all Hor'y Q. of one absent.

Mind—Absent Minded—(See Mind).

Near Death—Has Been Near Death—Lord of the Asc. sepr. from lord of the 8th H.; lord of the 1st and 8th in ☌ in the 8th, or in ☍ from the 6th or 8th.

Not Dead—Absent Party Is Not Dead—The Sig. of the party strong, in a good house, and sepr. from a benefic.

Prison—Lord of the Asc., or ☽, sepr. from lord of the 12th, has been in prison, or great trouble; the Sig. of the party combust.

Recovery—(1) No Hope of—☽ Sig. applying to the ☌ or evil asp. lord of the 8th H., or in the 8th, and if no good asps. interfere, absent party will die. (See "Dead" in this section). (2) Will Soon Recover—If the ☽, or lord of the 1st sepr. from lord of the 6th or 8th, and the benefics give a good asp.

Reported Dead—But is Alive—If the lord of his Asc. be in the 9th, 10th or 11th houses, ♃ or ♀ lord of the Asc., and either in the Asc., and in no asp. to lord of the 8th.

Sick—(1) Has Lately Been Sick— Lord of the Asc. sepr. from the ill-asp. lord of the 6th; the ☽ sepr. from the □ or ☍ or ♄ or ♂. (2) Absent Party is Sick—Lords of the 1st and 8th in ☌ in the 8th, or in ☍ from the 6th or 8th. (See "Absent Party" under Fever).

Will Die—(See "Dead", "Recovery" in this section).

ABSORPTION—The Absorptive System —Absorbent Vessels—Ruled in general by ♃. The ☽ in ♉, ♊, and ♋ rules and affects the absorbent and lymphatic vessels of the Respiratory System, the throat and lungs, etc. (See Lymph, "Absorbent Vessels" under Moon).

Chyle—Abated Absorption of—(See Chyle).

Tissues—Absorption of—(See Tissues). (See Assimilation, Nutrition, Phagocytes, "Resolution of Tissues" under Resolution; Resolvent).

ABUNDANCE—Abundant—Plenty—Excessive—

Blood—Abundance of Blood in a Part —♂ in the sign ruling the part. (See Plethora, "Too Much Blood" under Blood; "Blood" under Head; "Blood Vessels" under Rupture).

Energy—(See "Abundance" under Energy).

Hair—(See "Abundance" under Hair).

Health—(See "Abundance" under Health).

Heat—(See "Abundant" under Heat).

Humours—(See "Abounding" under Humours; "Humours" under Moist).

Moist Humours—Abundance of—(See "Humours" under Moist).

Superabundance—(See Excess, Excesses, Increased, Overabundance, Plenty, Superabundance).

Vitality—Abundance of—(See "Good" under Vitality).

ACCELERATION—The work of ♂. (See Exaggerated, "Accelerated" under Motion; Rapid).

ACCIDENTS—Accident—Accidental— Casualties—Unexpected Events, etc.— This is a big subject, and there is perhaps more said along this line in the textbooks of Astrology than upon any other subject. The general planetary causes of accidents, their nature and kind, etc., will be given in the various paragraphs of this Article, and especially under the headings of "Causes", "Danger of", etc. From an Occult standpoint Accidents are not always considered as matters of

chance, but may come, and do come, upon scheduled time, according to a prearranged plan of the Higher Powers and Hierarchies, or they may come upon a Nation or individual by a special decree, all which must be considered for the good of the individual, the Nation, or for the advancement and betterment of the Planet as a whole. Some star maps of birth show practical immunity from accidents, or violence, while others contain many influences which would lead to them, or a violent death. Every part and organ of the human body may be subject to a hurt, injury, or accident, according to the planetary positions and configuations at B., and the influences by direction, transit, or progression. Many of the subjects which have to do with Accidents are considered and also listed under the subjects of "Hurts", "Injuries", and these subjects should be studied and referred to along with the study of this Article. See the following subjects in the alphabetical arrangement when not considered here, and especially look for "Accidents", "Hurts", "Injuries", "Wounds", etc., under each subject.

Abdomen; Aeroplanes; Amusements; Animals; Ankles; Arms; Bathing; Battle—(See War).

Beasts; Bites; Blindness; Blows; Bones—(See Bones, Fractures).

Breasts; Brother; Bruises; Buildings —(See "Buildings" under Falls).

Buried Alive—(See Burial).

Burns—(See Burns, Fire, Heat, Scalds).

Buttocks; Casualties—(See "Death", and the various paragraphs in this section).

Cattle; Causes of Accidents—General Causes—Ptolemy held that planets oriental at B. indicate accidents, and planets occidental, disease, but this rule does not always hold good, as the opposite is often the case. Many planets in violent signs of the zodiac at B., and espec. in angles, indicate more danger of accidents. Accidents are to be judged from the planets which may happen to be exactly rising or setting at B., and those in configuration or aspect with the ☉ and ☽, or the ascending degree. The afflictions of the malefic planets to the ☉, ☽, Asc., M.C., or hyleg at B., and by dir., and espec. when these places were affl. at B. by malefics, are common causes of accidents. The ♐ sign on the Asc., 6th or 12th H. at B.; ruler of the 8th H. at B. in the 4th H. at a Solar Rev.; Fixed Stars of the nature of ♂ ascending at B. make one more or less liable to accidents along thru life under the evil directions of these stars, or of the malefic fixed stars, to the places of the ☉, ☽, Asc., or Hyleg; the violent fixed stars, as Antares, Betelguese, etc., tend to cause accidents by their afflictions to the planets at B., or by dir. (For further influences see the various subjects in this Article).

Childbirth—(See Parturition).

Childhood—(See "Accidents" under Childhood).

Children; Clavicle; Concussions; Contusions—(See Blows, Bruises, Falls).

Cranium—(See Skull).

Crippled; Crushed; Cuts; Danger of Accidents—Liable to—Tendency to—In judging of the danger of accidents, note the Asc., the cusp of the 6th H., and whether the malefics ♄ or ♂ afflict the Luminaries at B., or by dir. The following planetary aspects and influences tend to make the native more liable to accidents, be in greater danger of, and to have a more violent map, and with greater danger of death by violence, the result of an accident. The ☉ affl. by ♂ at B., or by dir.; the ☉ or ☽ to the ♂ or ill-asp. ♂ in the zodiac or mundane; the ☉ in fixed signs at B., and coming to the ♂ or ill-asp. ♂ by dir.; the ☉ to the ♂ or ill-asp. ♆, ♄, or ♅ by dir., and espec. when in the card. or fixed signs at B., or when the directions fall in this class of signs; the ☉ or ☽ rising at B., and affl. by the ♂ or ill-asps. of ♂, or other malefics; the ☉ or ☽ in the oriental Quadrants between the Asc. and M.C., or between the Desc. and Nadir, and affl. by the ♂ or ☍ of ♂, produces accidents; the ☉ or ☽ affl. in ori. Quarters; the ☉ ori., and affl. by the malefics at B., is apt under evil directions of the malefics to the ☉ to result in an injury causing death; the prog. ☉ to the □ or ☍ the radical ☽, and the parts of the body subject to injury are ruled by the signs containing the Luminaries; the pr. ☉ or ☽ to the ♂ or ill-asp. ♂ at B.; the ☽ in asp. to ♄ or ♂ by tr. or dir., or passing the ♂ of their place at B.; the same influences and directions that apply to the ☉ will also generally apply to the ☽; the ☽ to the ♂ or ill-asp. ♂ by dir., and ♂ affl. the ☽ at B.; a Lunation, as the New or Full ☽, falling on the place of any malefic at B, and espec. if there are also evil primary directions to the hyleg at the time; the ☽ at a Solar Rev. passing over the place of ♄ or ♂ at B.; the ☽ to the ♂ or P. asp. ☿ by dir., and the ☽ hyleg, and ☿ afflicted at B.; the ☽ to the ♂ P., or ill-asp. ♅ or ♂, and the ☽ hyleg at B.; the ☽ rising at B., and affl. by ♄ or ♂; the ☽ to the ♂ or ill-asp. ♄, ♅, or ♆ by dir., and the accident will be of the nature of the afflicting planet, and espec. if the ☽ be hyleg at B., or affl. by the malefic; the ☽ ♂ ♂ in the M.C. at B., and in evil asp. to Antares; the ☽ in any evil asp. to ♂ at B. predisposes to, and to bring the danger of accident when the ☽ is affl. by the adverse directions of ♂; the pr. ☽ to the ♂ or ill-asp. any of the malefics in the radical map; the ☽ ♂, □, or ☍ ♅, ♄, or ♂ at a Solar Rev.; ♆ passing the place of ♅ at B. by tr.; ♆ coming to the ♂ or ill-asp. ♂ by dir., danger of accident on the water, or shipwreck; ♆ in the 8th H. at B., afflicted, and afflicting the hyleg by dir.; ♆ in the 9th H. at a Solar Rev., and affl. by the lord of the 8th H. (For other ♆ influences tending to accidents, see Drowning, Journeys, Shipwreck, Travel); ♅ in ♏ or ♒ at B.,

and affl.; ♅ tends to cause accidents espec. by explosions or machinery; ♅ affl. at B., and coming to the evil asps. ♂ or the Asc. by dir., or to the ill-asps. his own place at B.; ♅ exactly rising at B., or within 1 or 2° of the ascending degree, and affl. by a malefic; ♅ ♂ or P. the ☉ at a Solar Rev.; ♅ ♂ ♄ in ♈, and espec. if ♅ be affl. by an evil asp. in the M.C., or in an angle; ♅ ♂ ♂ in angles; ♅ ♂ ☿ in ♊, ♍, ♎ or ♒; ♅ in the Asc., 3rd, 9th H., or M.C. at B., and affl., and the accident is usually in that part of the body ruled by the sign containing ♅ at B.; ♅ ♂ the Asc. by dir.; a tr. of ♅, ♄ or ♂ coming to an evil asp. the places of the pr. ☉ or ☽, and espec. if these places coincide with an evil dir.; ♅ or ♂ in ♂ or ☍ asp. at B., in card. signs, or angles; ♄ to the ♂ or evil asp. the Asc. by dir., and espec. if the Asc. is hyleg; ♄ ascending at B., and afflicted, or affl. the hyleg; ♄ exactly rising on the Asc. at B. tends to serious accidents from time to time; ♄ in the Asc. at B., and ill-asps. of the ☉ or ☽ to ♄ by dir.; transits of ♄ over the places of the pr. ☉ or ☽ or in evil asp. to them, and espec. if these aspects coincide with an evil dir.; ♄ ♂ or ☍ ♂ in angles and card. signs at B., and when affl. by evil directions; ♄ ♂ or evil asp. the ☉ in fixed signs; ♄ ♂ or ill-asp. the ☽, and the planets ori.; ♄ ruler of the Asc. at B., and in ill-asp. the benefics; ♄ in the M.C. at B., afflicted, and elevated above the Luminaries; the Periodic Dir. of ♄ to the radical ♂; ♂ afflictions, transits and progressions affl. the ☉, ☽, Asc., or M.C. at B., and espec. when ♂ afflicted any of these places at B., but not so dangerous when ♂ is in good asp. to them at B.; ♂ □ or ☍ the ♂ ♂ at B., and by dir.; ♂ elevated in the East, or in the Asc., and in ♂ or ill-asp. other malefics, or affl. the ☉ or ☽; ♂ ♂, □, or ☍ the Asc.; ♂ to the ♂ or ill-asp. the Asc. by dir. ♂ ♂ ☽ in the M.C. at B., and evilly aspected by Antares; ♂ in the Asc. at B., and affl. by the ill-asps. the ☉ or ☽ by dir.; ♂ ♂ or ill-asp. ♄ in angles or card. signs at B.; ♂ at a Solar Rev. passing the radical place of ♄ or ♅; ♂ ruler of the Asc. and afflicting the benefics at B. or by dir.; ♂ □ or ☍ the ☉ or ☽ at B.; ♂ afflicting the 1st or 10th houses at B., and by dir.; ♂ afflicted in ♈ or ♌; ♂ the ruling planet, or ruler of the Asc.; ♂ pr. in ♂ or ill-asp. the ☉, ☽, Asc., M.C., or any malefic planet; ♂ in the M.C. at B., and elevated above the ☉ and ☽; ♂ rising at B., and again at a Solar Rev.; ☿ affl. at B., and the ☽ to the ill-asp. ☿ by dir.; ☿ affl. by the malefics at B., liable to accidents under the evil directions of the malefics to ☿; the Asc. a fiery sign, and containing a malefic, and afflicted; the Asc. to the ♂ or ill-asp. the malefics by dir., and espec. if the Asc. is hyleg; a planet in the Asc. at B., and affl. by the ♂ or ill-asp. a malefic, and the injury is in the part of the body ruled by the sign ascending, or that occupied by the afflicting planet, and espec. if in a card. sign; ♐ on the Asc., or planets in ♐. (See the various subjects in this Article).

Dangerous Accidents—Serious Accidents or Injuries—The ☉ or ☽ to the ☌ or ill-asp. ♂ by dir., and espec. if ♂ affl. the ☉ or ☽ at B.; the ☉ ori. at B., and affl. by the malefics; the ☽ in the 8th H. at B., and affl. by ♅, ♄, or ♂; the ☽ in the obnoxious signs at B., as in ♈, ♉, ♋, ♏, or ♑, and in her Nodes, or in extreme Lat., and the malefics brought up to the Luminaries; ♄ to the ☌ or ill-asp. ♂ by dir.; ♄ exactly rising on the Asc. at B.; ♄ or ♂ ☌ the ☉, ☽, or Asc. by dir.; ♂ in the 8th H. at B., and badly aspected by the ☉ by dir.; transits of ♂ over the places of the ☉ or ☽ at B., or in ☍ to them; the Asc. to the ☌, P., or ill-asp. ♄ by dir., and ♄ ori. at B.; the Asc. to the ☌ or P. asp. ☿ and ♀ affl. at B.; malefics in angles at B., and the ☉ and ☽ in ☌ or ☍, brought up to them. (See Excrescences).

Death by Accident—Accidental Death—Casualties—Fatalities—Causes and Indications of an Accidental Death—The ☉ or ☽ affl. by malefics at B., or by dir., and with no assistance from the benefics; the ☉ and ☽ ori., and affl. by malefics, and espec. by ♄ or ♂; the ☉ and ☽ in evil asp. to ♂ at B., or by dir., and ♂ on the Asc. at B., and afflicted; the ☉ or ☽ to the ☌, P., or ill-asp. ♂ by tr. or dir., and espec. when ♂ afflicted the hyleg at B., or was in the 8th H., or in the Asc., or M.C.; the ☉ or ☽ in evil asp. to ♂ at B., or under the directions of ♂ to the ☉, ☽, or Asc.; the ☉ or ☽ to the ☌ or ill-asps. ♂ by dir., and ♂ affl. the ☉ or ☽ at B., or be in the Asc.; the ☉ or ☽ rising at B., and affl. by ♄ or ♂; the ☉, ☽, and other planets, in the Asc. at B. with Regulus; the ☉ or ☽ Sig., and coming to the ☌ or ill-asp. ♂ by dir.; the afflictions of ♆, the ruler of the water and the Sea, tend to accidental death by drowning. (See Drowning); the afflictions of ♅ tend to accidental death by bathing at home, in pools, or at the Sea Shore, and also death by machinery in the employment, by electricity, lightning, explosions, and sudden and unexpected death. (See these subjects); ♅ in the 8th H. at B., and afflicted, or affl. the hyleg; ♄ causes an accidental death by falls, bruises, contusions, fractures, dislocations, crushes, suffocation, fall of buildings, buried alive by landslides, falls from heights or precipices; trampled by mobs, cattle or animals, strangulation, etc. (See these subjects); ♄ ☌ the Asc. by dir. when ♄ is not ruler of the Asc.; ♄ rising at B., and to the ☌ the Asc. by dir.; ♄ and ♂ both affl. the ☉ or ☽ at B., or by dir.; ♄ in the 8th H. at B., and afflicted, or affl. the hyleg at B., or by dir.; directions of ♄ falling in the 8th H., and affl. the hyleg; ♃ Sig. ☌ ♂, and ♂ ill-dignified; ♂ causes accidental death by burns, cuts, bites, stabs, assassination, loss of blood, murder, kicks, injuries, wounds, gun-shot, fury, madness, scalds, in War, by operations, knife-wounds, by iron, sharp instruments, fire-arms, fractures, abortions, miscarriages, childbirth, mob-violence, on railroads, in vehicles, etc. (See these subjects); ♂ in the 8th H. at B., and afflicted, or

affl. the hyleg by dir.; evil directions of ♂ falling in the 8th H., and affl. the hyleg; ♂ to the ☌ or ill-asps. the ☉, ☽, Asc., or hyleg by dir; ♂ rising at B., and to the ☌ of the Asc. by dir.; ♂ and ♄ both affl. the ☉ or ☽ at B., or by dir.; ♂ Sig., and ill-dig. at B., and to the ☌ the ☉, ☽, Asc., or hyleg by dir.; ♂ in particular predisposes to accidental death, and espec. by violence, and ♂ in the 8th H. at B. indicates a sudden and violent death, and by some accident. In Hor'y Questions, ♂ in the 8th H., and ruler of the 8th, or affl. the ruler of the 8th, or the cusp of the 8th., or malefic planets in the 8th, indicate an accidental death, and usually by violence of some kind; ☿ when ori., and affl. the hyleg in a train of fatal directions, the accident and the death will be of the nature of the planet with which ☿ is in asp.; many planets in violent signs at B.; a strong 6th H., and the hyleg affl. by malefics; lord of the 8th a malefic, and in the 8th, and affl. by lord of the 6th or 12th, and espec. if the lord of the Asc. and the hyleg be affl. at the same time; the 14° ♍ on the Asc.; the 28° ♐ on the Asc. at B. (For further influences along this line, note carefully each subject in this section and Article).

Deformities; Directions—(See Directions, Events).

Dislocations; Distortions; Drowning; Earthquakes; Electricity; Employment; Escapes—Narrow and Hairbreadth Escapes from Accidents, Injuries, or an Accidental Death—These are always brought about by the intervention of the benefic planets ♃ and ♀ taking part in the configuration and directions, and espec. if these planets were strong, dignified, well-aspected and placed at B., and in good asp. to the ☉, ☽, Asc., M.C., or the hyleg; ♃ and ♀ ori., in angles, and elevated above the malefics. (See "Victims" in this section. Also see Rescue).

Events—(See Directions, Events).

Excrescences; Explosions; Extraordinary Accidents—Sudden, Peculiar, and Unusual Accidents—These are caused by the afflictions of ♅, as his influence is sudden, unexpected, and acts in a peculiar, singular, strange, and unusual way. The following aspects and influences, in which ♅ takes part, are said to cause this class of accidents,—♅ affl. at B., and in ☌, P., or evil asp. the ☉, ☽, Asc., M.C., or the hyleg; ♅ in the 8th H. at B., and affl. the hyleg at B., and by dir.; ♅ in the 8th H. at the Solar Ingress of the ☉ into ♈, and affl. the ☽ or planet ascending; the ☉ hyleg, and with ♅ in the 8th H. and Anareta, and the ☉ to the ☌, P., or evil asp. ♅ by dir.; the ☽ to the ☌ or evil asp. ♅ by dir.; ♂ to the ☌ or ill-asp. the radical ♅ by dir., or vice versa. These same influences may also cause a sudden, peculiar, singular, unusual and extraordinary death, as many accidents caused by ♅ prove fatal. (See Extraordinary, Peculiar, Strange, Sudden, Unusual, etc.). Case—Of an Extraordinary Accident—See "Extraordinary", No. 192, in 1001 N.N.

Extremities; Face; Falls; Fatal Accident—Case—See "Fatal", No. 346, in 1001 N.N. (See "Death", and the various subjects and paragraphs in this section).

Father; Feet; Females; Femur; Fire; Fire Arms—(See Gunshot); **Floods; Foetus; Fractures; Fury; Genitals**—(See "Mens' Genitals" under Genitals).

Groins—(See "Injuries" under Groins).

Gunshot; Hands; Haunches; Head; Heat; Hemorrhage—(See "Lesions" under Hemorrhage).

Hips; Horary Questions—In Hor'y Questions, if the ☽, lord of the Asc., or the Asc., be applying to the ☌, P., or any ill-asp. of the malefics, and espec. to ♄ or ♂, there is danger of an accident just ahead, and espec. if the ☽ or lord of the 1st be in ♉ or ♌, unless great care and caution are used, and dangers avoided. In Hor'y Questions, if the ☽ or lord of the Asc. are separating from the ☌, or ill-asp. of a malefic, and applying to the ☌ or good asp. of a benefic, there is little danger of an accident in the near future, or on a journey contemplated. The Asc. and the ☽ have affinity in denoting the accidents of life, and become the Significators of such events. (See Horary).

Horses—(See "Hurts By" under Horses. Also see Bites, Kicks).

Houses—(See "Buildings" under Falls).

Human Hands—(See "Hand of Man" under Man).

Hurts—(See "Violent" in this section. Also see Hurts).

Husband; Illness—Illness and Disease from Accidents—Sickness and Illness may result from accidents caused by ♅, where there was great shock to the nervous system, as ♅ by his afflictions tends to greatly weaken the nervous system, and to cause collapse. ♅ strongly afflicting the ☉, ☽, Asc., or hyleg at B., and by dir.

Injuries—By Accidents—(See Hurts, Injuries. Also see "Violent", and the various subjects in this Article).

Intestines—See "Injuries" under Bowels).

Inventions—(See Employment, Machinery).

Iron; Jaws; Joints; Journeys; Kicks; Killed; Kind of Accidents—(See "Nature Of" in this section).

Knees; Knife Wounds—(See Cuts, Instruments, Stabs).

Lacerations; Lameness; Landslides—(See ♄ influences under "Death" in this section. Also see Crushed).

Left Side of Body—(See Left).

Less Liable—To Accidents—Born under the Airy Signs ♊, ♎, ♒, also known as the whole signs, and with these signs upon the Asc. at B., or with the ☉ well-aspected in these signs. These signs when strong at B., tend to keep the body more intact, and to be free from accidents, injuries, or mutilations.

Liable to Accidents—Hurts and Injuries—(See "Danger of" in this section. Also see "Liable to" under Hurts; "Tendency to" under Injuries).

Lightning; Limbs; Machinery; Madness; Maimed; Males; Mangled; Marriage Partner; Mines; Miscarriage; Mobs; Mother; Murder; Mutilated; Narrow Escapes—(See "Escapes" in this section).

Nature of Accidents—Kind of—The planets each have a specific nature of their own, and tend to produce accidents or injuries after their nature, and to injure the part, or parts of the body, ruled by the Signs or Houses in which they were posited at B., or in which they may be by tr., dir., or progression. The afflictions of ♆ tend to accidents by water, drowning, shipwreck, etc. The accidents of ♅ are sudden, extraordinary, or unusual, such as by lightning, electricity, inventions, machinery, explosions, at bathings, on railroads, and in connection with the employment. Saturn governs accidents by falls, bruises, contusions, crushes, buried alive, fall of buildings, suffocation, etc. Mars rules accidents by cuts, stabs, loss of blood, wounds, burns, scalds, injuries in quarrels, and where violence is present in some form. The ☉, ☽, ♀, and ☿ are passive, and do not usually act as the cause of accidents unless they are afflicted by one or more malefics, or are united with them in common action. (See the Introduction under "Hurts". Also see each of the planets in the alphabetical arrangement as to their special influences).

Operations—Danger of Accidental Death From—Caused by ♂. (See "Dangerous" in this section. Also see Operations).

Painful Accidents—Caused especially by ♂, and when this planet enters into the configuration, and with loss of blood, violence, etc. (See Pain).

Paralysis—Resulting from Accident—(See "Blows", "Injuries", and other subjects under Paralysis).

Parents; Parts of Body—Liable to Accident and Injury — These are known by the Sign and House containing the malefics at B., and the malefic afflicting planets by dir. The ☉ or ☽ rising at B., and affl. by the ☌ or ill-asp. ♂, or other malefics, tend to injury in those parts of the body ruled by the sign containing the Lights, or the afflicting planets. The first 10° of a sign show the upper part of an organ afflicted. The middle 10°, the middle part of an organ, or region, and the last 10°, the lower part of the organ, or part. If ♂ be in the 3rd H., it shows injury to the left side of a male, or to the right side of a female. For accidents to the various parts of the body, see the part, or organ, in the alphabetical arrangement. (See Decanates, "Left Side" under Left; Lower, Middle, "Parts of the Body" under Parts; "Right Side" under Right; Upper).

Parturition; Peculiar—(See "Extraordinary" in this section).

Pirates; Pleasure; Poison; Precipices—(See Heights).

Precipitate; Predisposes—To Accidents—(See "Danger" in this section).

Prevalent; Public; Quadrupeds; Quarrels; Railroads; Rash Acts—(See Rashness); **Relatives Reptiles; Ribs; Right Side**—Of Body—(See Right).

Scalds; Sea; Serious—(See "Dangerous" in this section).

Serpents; Ships; Shipwreck; Shocks; Shoulders; Sickness—(See "Illness" in this section).

Sister; Skull; Spine; Sports; Stabs; Steel—(See Iron); **Stings; Storms; Strange; Strangulation; Sudden; Suffocation; Suicide; Sunstroke; Surgical Operations**—(See Operations).

Sword; Teeth; Tendency To—(See "Danger" in this section).

Testes; Thieves—(See Highwaymen, Robbers, Thieves).

Thighs; Time of Accidents—The Asc. and the ☽ have affinity in denoting the accidents of life, and become Significators, and directions to the ☽ and Asc. espec. show the times of possible accidents. Accidents are indicated by directions, and espec. when the directions are formed in the Ori. Quarters of the heavens, as between the 1st and 10th houses, and the 7th and 4th, and affl. the ☉, ☽, Asc., M.C., or hyleg at B. Accidents, injuries, or illnesses usually occur when the ☉ or ☽ are transiting the places of the four malefics at B., and espec. ♄ and ♂, or when ♄ and ♂, and other malefics, are on the places of the radical ☉, ☽, or Asc., or in evil asp. to them, and at these times more care and caution are necessary, espec. if the hyleg was afflicted at the previous New or Full ☽. Fixed stars of the nature of ♂, when ascending at B., make one more liable to accidents at the times when they form evil asps. to the ☉, ☽, Asc., M.C., or hyleg in the radical map by dir. (See Directions, Events, "New Moon" under Moon; Time; "Hurts" under Travel).

Tornadoes—(See Wind).

Trampled; Travel; Treachery; Uncommon—(See "Extraordinary" in this section).

Unexpected—(See Sudden, Unexpected).

Untimely; Unusual—(See Extraordinary, Peculiar, Uncommon, Mysterious).

Vehicles; Victims—Of Accidents—The victims of accidents, and those who suffer death, or great injury from them, are those who have ♃ and ♀ weak at B., affl. the hyleg, or some vital place in the map, and also at the same time are under evil directions or transits of the malefics to the hyleg, and with no assistance from the benefics in the configurations. (See Escapes. Also see "Escapes" in this section).

Violent Accidents—Hurts, Injuries, or Death, by Violence—The ☉ and ☽ are the positive, heat-producing, and electric planets, and afflictions to them by directions, transits, or progressions, are more apt to result in accidents accompanied by hurts, injuries, violence, loss of blood, fractures, wounds, etc. People who are born under the strong influence of ♂, or who have ♂ badly affl. at B., are more subject to violent accidents. Strong ♅, ♄, and ♂ afflictions to the ☉, ☽, Asc., or hyleg at B., and by dir., and with little or no help from the benefics; the ruler of the Asc. a malefic, and evilly aspected by malefics; malefics in the 6th, 8th, or 12th houses at B., and afflicting the ☉, ☽, Asc., or hyleg. (See Hurts, Injuries; "Death" under Violent).

Volcanoes; Voyages—(See Abroad, Sea, Ships, Shipwreck, Voyages).

War; Water; Weapons; Wife; Wild Animals—(See Wild). **Wind; Women; Wounds.**

ACCOMMODATION—The Focus of the Eyes—Defects and Errors of Accommodation are ruled by the ☽, and are considered ☽ diseases. For the various errors, and disorders of Accommodation, see Astigmatism, Eyes, Hyperopia (Far-sighted); Mydriasis, Myopia (Near-sight); Presbyopia (Old Age Vision); Sight, Vision.

ACCUMULATIVE—♄ exercises a strong influence for the accumulation of wastes in the body, and the retention of waste matter which should be thrown off, and to accumulate the poisons of the body in the various tissues and organs, which wastes and deposits tend to hardening, suppressions, etc. (See Crystallization, Elimination, Hardening, Obesity, Retention, Saturn, Stoppages, Suppressions, Tumors, Wastes). ♃ tends to accumulate fluids in localized parts of the body, and in the blood vessels, causing Apoplexy, bursting of blood vessels, swellings, tumors, abscesses, etc. (See these subjects). The ☽ also has an accumulating tendency of the fluids to circumscribed parts of the body, when affl. at B., or by dir. (See Congestion, Fluids, Functions, Oedema).

ACEPHALOCYSTS—Taenia Echinococcus—The Bladder Worm—A ♀ disease. ♀ affl. in ♏. (See Worms).

ACHES—Lingering Pains—Chronic Pains—Continuous, or Throbbing Pains—The ♄ influence is the principal cause of slow, continued, and throbbing aches and pains, while ♂ tends to the more sharp and acute pains of brief duration. See the following subjects in the alphabetical arrangement.

Backache—(See Back).

Bellyache—(See Belly).

Body Suffers—From Aches and Pains—The ☽ to the ♂ or ill-asps. ♄ by dir.; ♄ rising at B., afflicted, or affl. the hyleg at B., or by dir.; ♄ to the ♂ or ill-asp. the ☉ or ☽ by dir.; ♄ tends to retard and stop the functions of the body, cause retention of the wastes and excretions, and the deposit of Uric Acid over the body, which tends to general Malaise and depression. (See Deposits, Excretion, Malaise, Uric Acid, etc.).

Earache—(See Ears).

Feet—Aches In—(See Feet).

Headaches; Heavy Aches—And Pains—All heavy and dull aches and pains are ruled by ♄, and caused by his afflictions to the ☉, ☽, Asc., or hyleg at B., or by dir. (See "Pains" under Dull).

Hips and Thighs—(See "Aches" under Hips).

Legs—(See "Aches" under Legs).

Pains and Aches—(See "Heavy" in this section).

Parts of Body—Afflicted by Aches—(See the various subjects in this Article).

Stomachache—(See "Ache" under Stomach).

Thighs—(See "Hips" in this section).

Throbbing Aches—♄ influence. (See Throbbing).

Toothache—(See Teeth).

ACHILLES TENDON—Contraction of is caused by ♄ affl. in ♒, and often resulting in Club Feet. (See "Club Feet" under Feet).

ACHONDROPLASIA—(See Cartilage).

ACIDS—Acid—Acidity—Sodium Phosphate, the Salt ruled by the ♎ Sign, is said to be connected with the Acids of the body. Acids are said to be under the rule of the negative Signs of the Zodiac, and the negative planets, and remedies to produce more acidity in the system are ruled by the negative planets, the ☽, ♅, ♄, ♀. A predominance of the planets in the negative signs at B. tends to an over-production of the acids of the body, while the positive signs tend to too much alkalinity. Also the negative planets prevailing at B., and afflicted, tend to acidity, and in those parts of the body ruled by the signs containing them at B., and the afflicting planets. For Acids not listed here look for the subject in the alphabetical arrangement.

Gastric Acidity—Acidity in the Stomach—♅, ♄, ♀ or the ☽ in ♈, ♌ or ♑ at B., and afflicted. (See Gastric, Juices, Stomach).

Hot Acids—The ♂ influence in and over the body, and over acids in general, corresponds to hot acids, and to burning astringents, pungent odors, etc. (See Pungent).

Hydrochloric Acid—(See Hydrochloric, Digestion, Stomach).

Hydrocyanic Acid—(See Hydrocyanic).

Signs—Acid Signs—(See the first part of this Article).

Stomach—Acidity of—(See "Gastric" in this section. Also see "Over-acidity", "Hydrochloric" under Stomach).

Urine—Acidity of—The ♏ sign rules the Urine, and the negative planets in ♏, and affl. at B., or by dir., and espec. ♄ in ♏, tend to acid urine. (See Alkaline, Impure, Positive, Negative).

ACNE—Inflammation of the Sebaceous Glands from Retained Secretion—A ☉ and ♈ disease; ☉ affl. in ♈; ☉ □ or ☍ ☽ or Asc. at B., or by dir.; ♂ affl. in ♉ tends to Acne Rosacea, or chronic congestion of the skin of the face; afflictions in the cardinal signs, as such signs denote the skin; ♄ affl. in ♈ or ♉, as ♄ tends to retention, and disordered functions of the glands of the skin of the face. Caused by subluxations at M. C. P., the 3rd, 4th and 5th Cervical vertebrae, and by afflictions in ♈ and ♉, the signs which influence these vertebrae. This disease is also contributed to by disturbed kidneys, and Subs at KP, Kidney Place. (See Pimples, Sebaceous, Skin, Vertebrae).

ACONITE—A ♄ remedy, and ruled by ♄, and is opposed to ♂ and ♂ diseases. Is antipyretic, diuretic, and a cardiac sedative. Aconitum Napellus is one of the 12 typical Polycrest Remedies, and corresponds to the ♈ sign. (See "Polycrest" under Zodiac).

ACQUAINTANCES—The ☽ and ☿ rule Acquaintances.

Death of—An Acquaintance—The ☽ to the place of Cor Scorpio by dir. (See Execrated, Friends).

ACQUIRED DISEASES—Those which arise after birth. Ruled by the ☽. Indicated by the condition of the ☽ at B., and her evil aspects. The ☽ is functional, while the ☉ is organic and constitutional. The ☽ denotes the acquired diseases and tendencies arising from external causes, as environment, climate, food, habits, clothing, etc. Acute diseases, and those of short duration, are generally acquired, while the chronic and lasting diseases result from organic and inherent weaknesses and defects, and the fundamental inability of an organ, or the constitution, to recover from the evil effects of an acute disease, shock or injury. (See Acute, Chronic, Congenital, Constitution, Consumption, Deformities, Environment, External, Functions, Heredity, Inherent, Organic, Structural, Susceptibility, Tendencies, etc.).

ACROMEGALY—(See "Enlargement" under Extremities).

ACTINIUM—A metal of ♅. Commercialized Zinc is obtained from it.

ACTION—Mars is the planet of action, of insistent action, and of dynamic energy. All of the planets, however, have their definite and specific modes of action in and over the mind and body, for good or ill, according to the aspects and influences at B., and by their transits, directions, and progressions. (See "Desire Body" under Desire).

Accelerated Action—♂ influence. (See Fever, Inflammation, Motion, Quick, Rapid).

Automatic Action—(See Automatic).

Coordinated Action—(See Coordination).

Cramped Action—(See "Action" under Cramps).

Disturbed Action—In Mind and Body—(See Disturbed, Disease, Erratic, Exaggerated, Incoordination, Irritable, Irritations, Mental, Mind, Motion, Movement, Rapid, Spasmodic, Slow, Walk, etc.).

Dull—(See Dull).

Erratic Action—(See Erratic, Incoordination, Jerky, Spasmodic, Tics, Walk).

Eruptive Action—(See Eruptions).

Exaggerated Action—(See Exaggerated).

Feeble Action—(See Feeble, Debility).

Feverish Action—(See Fever).

Full of Action—(See "Active Body", "Active Mind", under Active; Cardinal, Dynamic, Energy, Quick, Positive).

Hyperkinetic Action—(See Hyperkinesia, Muscles).

Incoordinated—(See Incoordination).

Inflammatory—(See Inflammation).

Lack of Action—(See Dull, Feeble, Inactive, Inertia, Languor, Lassitude, Lethargy, Listless, "Weak Body" under Weak, etc.).

Limp Action—Uncertain Action—(See Limp).

Mind—Action Of—(See the various headings in this section. Also see "Active Mind" under Active; Clogging, Clouded, Dull, Diseases and Disturbances of the Mind under Mental, Mind).

Perverted Action—(See Perversions).

Planets—Action Of—(See Benefics, Malefics, Planets, and each planet in the alphabetical arrangement).

Precipitate Action—(See Precipitate).

Quick in Action—(See "Active Body" under Active; Gait, Quick, Walk).

Rash in Action—(See Rashness).

Reflex Action—(See Reflected).

Retarded Action—(See Retarded).

Slow Action—(See Clumsiness, Retarded, Slow).

Spasmodic Action—(See Spasmodic).

Tonic Action—(See Tonic).

Uncertain Action—(See Limp).

Walk—(See the subjects under Gait, Walk).

Weak Action—(See Feeble, "Weak Body" under Weak).

Weakest Action—♋ or ♓ on Asc. at B., or many planets in watery signs, and espec. in ♋ or ♓. (For other kinds of action see the subject in the alphabetical arrangement).

ACTIVE—Activity—

Active Body—Sthenic—Active and Strong Body—Physical Activity Increased—Active Appearance—The fiery signs upon the Asc. at B., and many planets in fiery or airy signs, and rising or elevated at B.; ♐ on Asc. at B., active body, and with great desire for sports, out-door life, and athletics; the 3rd face of ♐ on Asc., an unusually active body; ♑ upon the Asc., strong and active body; cardinal signs upon the angles, or many planets in cardinal signs, and espec. rising or in angles, as the cardinal signs relate to physical activity; ☉ well-asp. in ♐; ☉ or ☽ to the good asps. ♂ by dir., and ♂ in good asp. to these bodies at B.; ☿ strong at B., and well-asp. by ♂; ☿ in ✳ or △ the Asc., active, and with quick action and movement; ☿ Sig. in ♑, active body, yet feeble and sickly. Many of the influences which tend to give an active body also produce a strong body. (See Brisk, Cardinal, Energy, "Energetic" under Gait; Exertion, Motion, Movement; "Strength" under Muscles; "Activity" under Physical; Quick, Sthenic, "Strong Body" under Strong; "Good" under Vitality; Walk).

Active Mind—Active Disposition—Active Nature—☿ is the principal ruler of the mind, and this planet when well-asp. by ♂, or in his own signs, as in ♊ or ♍, or when in the Asc., rising in the East, and well-asp. by the ☽ and ♂, tends to give an active mind; ☿ rising before the ☉; ☿ ♂ or good asp. the ☽, and free from ♄ affliction; ☿ to the good asps. ♂ by dir.; ☿ in ♊, ♍, or ♐, in good asp. to ♃, and espec. if in ♂ or P. asp. to ♃; ☿ Sig. in ♑, an active mind, but the body may be feeble thru worry; the ☉ or ☽ ♂ ♂ at B., or by dir.; the ☉ well-asp. in ♐; the ☉ in a fiery sign at B.; the ☽ ♂ or good asp. ♂ or ☿ at B., or by dir.; ☿ in the 3rd H. at B., and well-asp. tends to enhance the mental faculties; ♅ or ♂ in ♊ or ♍, and well-asp.; ♅ in ✳ to ♃ and ☿, and ☿ in ✳ or △ to ♂ at the same time; ♄ infl. and affliction tends to restrain the mind, or limit the action of the brain cells, and make the mind less active in manifestation; ♂ in ♈, ♌, or ♑ at B., well-aspected and placed in the map; ♂ rising at B.; ♂ strong at B., rising, and ruler; ♂ ♂ ☿ at B., except when in ♓; ♂ to the good asps. ☿ by dir.; ♂ ♂ the ☉ or ☽ at B.; ♂ in ♊, ♍, or ♐ at B., and well-asp.; fiery signs on the Asc. at B.; the airy signs strong, prominent, and well-occupied and placed at B., and espec. if there be one or more planets in fiery signs; ♏ on the Asc., this being the sign of ♂; lords of the nativity in S. Lat. at B., more active than when in N. Lat. Temperate climates, with alternate heat and cold produce an active mind. (See "Mental Energy" under Energy; "Quickened" under Mental).

Degree of Activity—The degree of activity in the mind and body depend largely upon the planetary positions and aspects at B., and by progression, direction, or transit. Planets rising at B., or rising and elevated, dignified, and strongly fortified by sign and aspect, tend to give greater activity of mind and body, while planets setting, below the western horizon, in weak signs, and badly aspected, tend to give less activity. The positions and aspects of the planets at B. may give too much activity, or too little, and there are very few people who are perfectly balanced in mind and body, and who do not tend to extremes in some way.

Energy—(See the various paragraphs under Energy).

Hyperactivity—(See this subject).

Mind—(See "Active Mind", "Over-Active Mind", in this section).

Muscular Activity—(See Muscles).

Over-Active Mind—Effervescent Mental Activity—Bubbling Over—The ☽ and ♂ influences when combined tend to produce, and to spend their force, by the display of temper, anger, excess of feeling, emotion, and result in the dissipation and dispersion of the brain and nerve force; ♅ in ♈ or ♊, and afflicted, and aspec. if ☿ is aspected by ♂ at the same time; ♂ in ♈; ☿ in ♈ ♂ ♂; ☿ in the 6th H. at B., and affl., and espec. ☿ in ♍ in the 6th, which tends to undermine the health also. (See Effervescent).

Perverted Activity—(See "Activity" under Perversions).

Qualities—Heat and Cold are active qualities, while dryness and moisture are passive qualities. (See Cold, Dryness, Heat, Moisture).

Sources of Activity—The ☉ and ♂ are the greatest sources of activity and energy in our Solar System, both being of a fiery nature, and having great affinity for each other. The Solar Forces are reflected upon us by ♂, to produce greater activity, and if it were not for the strong ♂ force over us there would be very little activity in the world. The ☉ and ♂ when combined in their action at birth, as the ☉ ☌ ♂ in ♈, the exalted sign of the ☉, and the sign of ♂, tend to give great activity, strong vitality, and espec. if ♈ also be on the Asc. (See Dynamic, Mars, Over-Activity, Sun).

Zest—(See Zest).

ACUTE—Acute Diseases—Acute Fevers —Short Diseases—Acquired Ailments, etc.—Diseases beginning in Summer tend to be acute, and shorter than those which begin in Winter. Acute diseases begin from the surface, and from disturbances of the Peripheral Nerves, and work toward the center, and remedies to combat acute diseases should be those which will act upon these nerves. (See Centrifugal). In chronic diseases, the cause is from within, and working outward, and caused by irritations to the ganglionic centers, and usually brought on by ♄ influence, by chilling of the surface, driving the blood inwards. (See Centripetal). Acute diseases are usually brought on by ♂ in an effort to burn up the surplus of wastes and poisons in the system, in an effort to restore the balance in the body, and to maintain normal health conditions, and are usually accompanied by a fever or inflammation. An acute disease may attack any part of the body, and instead of listing every acute disease in this Article, will ask you to see in the alphabetical arrangement the disease you have in mind if it is not listed here. Note the following general subjects concerning Acute Diseases and conditions.

Causes—General Causes of Acute Diseases—The ☉, ♃, and ♂ tend to cause acute diseases, and ♂ the acutest of all; the ☉ hyleg at B., and afflicted, and the ☉ to the ☌ or evil asps. the Asc. or ♂ by dir.; the ☉ affl. in ♌ or ♐ at B., and by transits and directions, as acute fevers are a ☉ disease, as well as diseases of ♃ and ♂; the ☉ to the ☌ or P. Dec. the Ascelli by dir. (See "Sun Diseases" under Sun); the ☽ to the ill-asps. the ☉ or ♂ by dir.; the ☽ □ or ☍ the Asc.; the ☽ in ♊, ♐, or ♓, and affl. by the ☉ or ♂ when taken ill; the ☽ in ♒ when taken ill, affl. by the ☉ or ♂, and the ☽ slow in motion and decreasing in light; ♅ causes sudden and short illnesses of an acute nature, and espec. when in the 6th H. at B., and afflicted. (See "Sudden Illnesses" under Sudden); ♃ causes acute diseases from indiscretions in eating and drink, and by cor-

rupt blood, too much blood, plethora, surfeits, etc. (See "Jupiter Diseases" under Jupiter); ♂ and the ☉ in fiery signs at B., and affl.; ♂ and the ☉ are fiery, electric, positive and heat-producing planets, and are great factors in causing fevers and acute diseases by their afflictions, or afflictions to them; an evil ♂ transit afflicting his place at B., or passing thru the birthsign, or affl. the place of the ☉, ☽, Asc., or hyleg at B. by his ☌ or ill asps.; ♂ to the ☌ or ill-asp. the ☉, ☽, or Asc. by dir.; ♂ occi. at B., and affl. the hyleg by dir.; ♂ in the 8th H. at a Solar Ingress of the ☉ into ♈, and affl. the ☽, or the planet ascending; ♂ in the Asc. at an illness causes the disease to be swift, acute and violent; ♂ in the 8th H. at B., affl. the ☉, ☽, Asc., or hyleg, or in the 8th H. by tr. or dir. at the time of the illness, ruler of the 8th, or affl. the cusp of the 8th, acute and violent sickness, and with danger of death; the Asc. to the ☌ or ill asps. ♂ by dir., and ♂ in a fiery or airy sign at B.; the Asc. to the ill-asps. the ☉ by dir., and the ☉ affl. at B.; fiery signs upon the Asc. at B., or the cusp of the 6th H., and espec. when containing the ☉ and ♂, and afflicted; many planets in fiery signs at B.; afflictions in ♌, the sign of the ☉; a ♌ disease; ♌ on the Asc. at B., or the cusp of 6th H., and containing the ☉ or ♂, and afflicted; afflictions from cardinal signs, and such diseases are usually of short duration, run their course rapidly, and leave no bad after effects unless they run into a chronic disease. (See "Illnesses" under Short).

Crises in Acute Diseases—Critical Days In—Course of—The phases and Quarters of the ☽ govern the course and crises in acute diseases, from the time of decumbency, or the taking of the patient to bed. (See "Acute Diseases" under Crises; "Course of Disease" under Course; "Moon" under Motion).

Danger Of—Liable to an Acute Disease—The ☉ to the ☌ ♂ by dir., or ♂ to the ☌ ☉. (See "Causes" in this section).

Death By—The following influences tend to cause death by an Acute Disease, and an Acute Fever—The ☉ to the ☌ or ill-asp. ♂ by dir.; ♂ afflictions tend to death after a short or sudden illness; ♂ occi. at B., and affl. the hyleg by dir.; ♂ in the 8th H., ruler of the 8th, or affl. the cusp of the 8th at the beginning of an illness; ♂ in the 8th H. at a Solar Ingress of the ☉ into ♈, and affl. the ☽, or planet ascending. See "Arguments for Death" under Death).

Duration of—Acute Diseases are of different duration, according to the severity of the disease and the afflictions, the degree of vitality, etc., and some acute diseases will resolve themselves on the 7th day, and others on the 14th, 21st or 28th days. An acute disease can last for 28 days, one complete revolution of the ☽, and if it does not resolve, or prove fatal, on the 28th day, it runs into a chronic form. (See Continuity, Duration, End).

Ease In—(See Magnetic).

Fevers—Acute Fevers—Causes of— Acute fevers are caused principally by the afflictions of the ☉ and ♂; the afflictions of ♂ to the ☉, Asc., or hyleg; by afflictions in the fiery signs, and such signs on the Asc. (See the influences of the ☉, ♂, the Asc., and fiery signs under "Causes" in this section. Also see Ephemeral, Fever).

Hot Diseases—Acute Hot Diseases— The ☽ weak and ill-dig. at B., and to the ♂ Regulus.

Liable To—Liable to Acute Disease, or Acute Fevers—(See "Causes" in this section).

Periods of Acute Disease—Subject to —Time When Apt to Come—The ☉ affl. at B. makes the native more liable to times of acute disease, and when the ☉ comes to the evil directions the Asc., or to the ♂ or ill-asps. ♂, and also when the Asc. comes to the ill-asps. the ☉ or ♂ by dir. An evil ♂ transit, affl. his place in the radical map, or passing thru the birthsign, or affl. the place of the ☉, ☽ or Asc. at B., may precipitate an acute disease, and cause a fever. (See "Periods of Bad Health" under Health).

Precipitated—An Acute Disease, or Acute Fever Precipitated—(See "Periods" in this section).

Prevalent—Acute Diseases and Sharp Fevers Prevalent—♄ lord of the year at the Vernal, in ♍, and occi. of the ☉ or ☽ in fiery signs; ♂ having sole dominion of the year at a Solar Eclipse. (See "Prevalent" under Fevers).

Quick Diseases—(See Quick).

Signs—The Cardinal Signs of the Zodiac are called the Acute Signs, and planets in them at B., and by dir., or at the time of decumbiture, tend to acute, rapid, short, and swift diseases. (See Cardinal).

Suffering—Acute Suffering—This is usually caused by the afflictions of ♂, as in injuries, wounds, and violence to the person. (See Injuries, Pain, Wounds, Violence). For the various kinds of Acute Diseases, and the parts of the body affected, see the subject, and the disease or condition you have in mind, in the alphabetical arrangement. Also see such subjects as Abatement, Acquired, Better, Cadent, Diathesis, Feelings, Fierce, Grevious. Hexis, ·Inflammation, Mild, "Acute" under Mind; Moderation, Pain, Quick, Rapid, Severe, Sharp, Short, Slight, Sudden, Swift, Vehement, Violent, Worse, etc.).

ADAM'S APPLE—Thyroid Cartilage— (See Thyroid).

ADDER—Stings By, or by some obnoxious creature, and espec. stings to Kings or Rulers—(See Bites, Kings, Rulers, Serpents, Stings, Venomous).

ADDICTS—Addicted To—For the various form of Addictions see Drink, Drugs, Drunkenness, Gluttony, Habits, Narcotics, Passion, Pleasure, Sex, Tobacco; "Solitary Vice" under Vice; Women, etc.

ADDISON'S DISEASE—(See Adrenals).

ADDRESS—(See Appearance, Manner, Speech).

ADENOIDS—A Vegetable Growth— Caused by afflictions in ♉ and ♍, and espec. in the 25° of these signs, when affl. by malefics in, or in evil asp. to this degree; ♅ or ♂ in, or affl. the 25° of ♉ or ♍; ♅ and ♂ combinations in ♉ or ♍, and also ♄ in or near the 25° ♍, and afflicted; the ☉ in the 25° ♍ or ♉, and affl. by the ♂, □, or ☌ the malefics; ♄ ♂ ♅ in ♉; ♄ affl. in ♉ or ♍; ♃ ♂ ♂ in ♉ or ♍; ♀ in ♉ or ♍ in the Asc., and afflicted; caused by Subs at LCP and SP. (See Nose, Pharynx, Throat, Tonsils, Vertebrae). Cases— See Figures 3A and 3B in "Astro-Diagnosis", and Fig. 27, in "Message of the Stars", books by Mr. and Mrs. Max Heindel.

ADENOMA—A Glandular Tumor—Quite frequent in Scrofula. The Glands are strongly acted upon by ♀,. and afflictions to this planet tend to disturbances of the glands, and to swellings and tumors. As a whole, the ☉ and ♃ rule the glands, and afflictions to these bodies may cause Adenoma, and other glandular troubles. (See Glands, Scrofula, Tumors).

Breast—Adenoma of—♀ affl. in ♋. (See Breast).

ADHESIONS—The union of two surfaces, or parts, and due to the degeneration of the parts, the restraint of the function or blood circulation in the part, the deposit of wastes and mineral substances, and is the work of ♄. The parts most liable to such affliction are those ruled by the sign containing ♄ at B. Adhesions and fusion may also result from extreme heat in a part, causing melting of the tissues, or bones, the work of the ☉ and ♂ in ♂ in a fiery sign, and possibly with other planets also in the same sign, and espec. if the sign also be on the Asc. The fiery sign ♌ rules the spine, and the ☉, ♂, and many planets in ♌, afflicted, and espec. in the 5th H., the house of ♌, may result in adhesions, and ankylosis of the vertebrae, due to melting and excess heat. (See Ankylosis, Coalition, Heat, Mars, Stricture, Sun)..

ADIPOSE—Fatty—Adipose Tissue— (See Fat).

Adiposis—(See Corpulent," Fat Body", "Fatty Degeneration" under Fat).

Adiposa Dolorosa—(See Fat).

ADJUSTMENT—(See Coordination, Incoordination).

ADOLESCENCE—Disorders at time of —(See Puberty).

ADOPTION—Of Children—Children Separated from Parents, and Adopted— (See "Death of Parents", "Separated", under Parents). The afflictions of ♆ in, or to the 5th H., often indicate the denial of children, and the necessity for adoption of children. (See Barren, Bastards; "Early Death" under Father, Parents).

ADRENALS—Suprarenal Capsules— Ruled by ♃ and the ♎ Sign. The Adrenals are Ductless Glands, and in a general way also come under the rule of ♍. When the mind has been greatly disturbed, and the poise and equilibrium lost for a time, due to the emotional disturbances caused by ♄, ♂, and the ☽, the Adrenal secretion tends to restore calm and quiet to the mind, and also when the heart action is weakened thru worry, melancholy, or sorrow, tends to act as a heart stimulant. Lack of the adrenal secretion tends to depression, dejection, despondency, gloom, and worry. (See Atrabile). During fits of anger, rage, or passion, brought on by ♂, and when the muscles are trembling and tense, the glycogen in the liver is released in larger quantities by the action of ♃, and acts as a soothing, calming influence, and to restore poise. (See Soothing). Thus the Adrenals, thru the saving and benevolent action of ♃, keep the body from being permanently weakened, destroyed, and thrown into disease, ill-health, or premature death, by the adverse action of the malefic planets ♄ and ♂ upon the mind. The Adrenals are said to be connected with the Personality. The Adrenals are quite fully discussed from an Occult and Metaphysical standpoint in the book, "The Message of the Stars", by the Heindels.

Addison's Disease—Tuberculosis, or Consumption, of the Suprarenal Capsules—Caused by ♄ affl. in ♎ or ♏.

Coma—Influence of Adrenals In— (See Coma).

Consumption of—Tuberculosis of— (See "Addison" in this section).

Diminished Secretion—Lack of Adrenal Secretion—♃ affl. in ♈ or ♎. (See Fainting).

Plexus—The Suprarenal Plexus— (See "Ductless Glands" under Ductless).

ADULTS—Adult Life—The ☽, ♀, and ☿ rule the earlier years of life, but when maturity is reached, then the ☉ and the larger, or major planets assume rule. Old age is ruled by ♄. (See Maturity, "Middle Life" under Middle; "Periods of Life" under Periods). There are diseases which are peculiar to adult life, and others to infancy, childhood, youth, middle life, and old age, etc., as the planets bear rule over the different stages of life, and the ruler of such a Period in life when affl. by directions tends to the special diseases, or afflictions, peculiar to that planet. (See Periods).

Duration of Life—Of Adults— (See "Long Life" under Life; Maturity, "Death at Middle Life" under Middle Life; Old Age).

ADYNAMIA—A Deficiency, or Loss of Vital Power—A ♄ disease. Also caused by Subs of the Atlas and Axis, and by ♄ affl. in ♈ or ♉, the signs which rule these vertebrae. (See Asthenia, Debility, Feeble, Infirm, Sickly, Vital, Vitality, Vertebrae, Weak, etc.).

AEROPLANES—Aviation—Death or Injury By—The ♒ sign, and ♅, have special rule over the Air and the Ether, and the evil directions of ♅ to the ☉, ☽, Asc., or Hyleg, tend to accidents in the air, and by machinery used in such service. Also to start an air journey when ♅ is badly afflicting the ☽ and ♂ tends to mishaps, injury,

death, and for a safe journey a propitious planetary time for the start should always be chosen. (See Accidents, Journeys, Railroads, Travel, Vehicles).

AFFECTIONS—There are some morbid and pathological deviations, or diseases of the affections and the passional nature. (See Deviations, Love Affairs, Passion, Perversions, Reins, Sex, etc.).

AFFLICTION—Afflictions—The 12th H. is known as the house of affliction, sorrow, self-undoing, confinement, restraint, limitation, etc., and planets affl. in this house at B. tend to a greater number of afflictions to mind or body. Also the planets ill-placed at B., and with many □ and ☍ asps. in the map, tend to multiply the afflictions, miseries, sufferings, ill-health, and troubles of life unless self-control, wisdom, discrimination, knowledge, and spiritual attainment enter in, and change, modify, or prevent the calamities of life on the Earth Plane. The planet ♄ is known as the Chastener, the Tester, the special Afflictor among the planets, and his afflictions tend to sorrow, trouble, delays, hindrances, restraints, worry, melancholy, and chronic forms of disease. However, Saturn people are patient under affliction. (See Saturn).

Bodily Afflictions—For the various diseases and bodily afflictions, see the subject you have in mind in the alphabetical arrangement.

Causes of Affliction—Afflictions in the 12th H., ruler of the 12th, a malefic, and espec. ♄, and in the 12th H.; the ☉ or ☽ ☌ or ill-asp. ♄ at B., and by dir.; the ☉ or ☽ joined to the Whale's Jaw, great affliction, sickness, disgrace, or ruin; ♄ or ♂ in the 12th H. (For further influences see Disgrace, Misfortune, Misery, Reversals, Ruin, Sorrow, Trouble, etc.).

Many Afflictions—The ☉ and ☽ in cadent houses at B., in weak signs, and afflicted, and espec. when in the 3rd or 6th H.; the ☽ decr. in light, and sepr. from the ☉ or ♃ at B., and applying to ♄; the ☽ at the Full, or incr., sepr. from ♀ and applying to ♂ in a day geniture; ♄ or ♂ by dir. in ☌ or ill-asp. the ☉, ☽, Asc. or M.C.; ♂ ☌ ☉ at a Solar Rev. All manner of afflictions are ruled by the 12th H. and its influences. (See Miseries).

Mental Afflictions—Mental Disorders —(See the various subjects under Mental, Mind. Also see Anguish, Anxiety, Dejection, Dementia, Depression, Despondency, Distress, Epilepsy, Fear, Frenzy, Hallucinations, Hypochondria, Idiocy, Insanity, Mania, Melancholy, Memory, Miserable, Obsessions, Paranoia, Sadness, Sorrow, Worry, etc.).

Parts of the Body—The Parts Afflicted, or Diseased—(See "Parts of the Body" under Parts; Upper, Middle, Lower).

Planets—Affliction By—(See Malefics, Planets. See each of the planets in the alphabetical arrangement).

AGARICUS—A typical drug of the ☽. (See Moon).

AGED PEOPLE—(See Old Age).

AGILE—Brisk, Nimble, Quick, Active Body—(See "Active Body" under Active; Brisk, Muscles, Nimble, Quick, Sports, etc.).

AGITATION—The ☽ affl. by ♄ at B., the mind and body are afflicted with agitation, and espec. with females. (See Excitable, Fretfulness, Nervous, Paralysis Agitans, etc.).

AGONY OF MIND—(See Anguish, Anxiety, Distress, Melancholy, Worry).

AGUE—Malaria—Intermittent Fever—Ague is threatened, and to be long-continued, when earthy signs are in the Asc., or on the 6th H., or the ☽ in an earthly sign at B., or at decumbiture, and also to threaten Consumption. (See Consumption); caused by ♄ when the dominion of death is vested in him; a ♄ disease; ♄ affl. the hyleg or the Asc.; ♄ in the 6th H.; ♄ in ♋ when ♄ is the afflictor in the disease; ♄, ♅, or ♆ in ♋, and affl. the ☉ or ☽; the ☉ or ☽ to the ☌ ♄ by dir.; ♂ too much in evidence at B. (See Intermittent, Malaria).

Death by Ague—♄ occi. at B., and affl. the hyleg by dir.; ♄ afflictions tend to; an evil dir. of ♄ to the hyleg when ♄ holds the dominion of death; fixed stars of the nature of ♄ affl. the hyleg.

Mother—The Mother afflicted by Ague—The ☽ in the 1st or 10th H., and affl. by ♄. (See Mother).

Quartan Ague—Arising from Cold—A disease and affliction of ♄; caused by ♄ when the dominion of death is vested in him; ♄ sole ruler at an eclipse of the ☉; earthy signs on the Asc. and 6th H. at B., or at decumbiture; the ☽ in ♋ ☌ or ill-asp. ♄ (or ☿ if he be of the nature of ♄) at the beginning of an illness, or at decumbiture. If the ☽ be decr., and near the body of ♄, the disease will tend to be long-continued (Hor'y). (See Quartan).

Tertian Ague—Tertian Fever—A ♂ disease, and caused by the afflictions of ♂; ♂ sole ruler at an eclipse of the ☉. (See Intermittent, "Low Fevers" under Fevers; Malaria, Miasma, Quartan, Quotidan, Remittent, Semitertian).

AILING OFTEN—Is Always Ailing—(See Feeble, "Ill-Health All Thru Life" under Ill-Health; Infirmities, Invalids, "Much Sickness" under Sickness).

AILMENTS—Indisposition of Body and Mind—(See Disease, Debility, Deformities, General, Ill-Health, Indisposition, Infirmities, Mental, Mind, Sickly, Sickness, Weak, etc.).

AIR—Atmosphere—The Air is ruled by ♅ and ☿. The Ether is ruled by ♅. The condition of the air has much to do with health and disease, and the atmosphere is much acted upon by the planetary influences each day, and so much so that the weather can be predicted a year ahead by making a study of the planetary aspects and influences that will be forming, as is done by the Hicks Almanac People, of St. Louis, Mo. The air may be corrupted and vitiated by the planetary vibrations and aspects, causing disease, epidemics, famine, pestilence, fevers, and under certain planetary influences an epidemic may spread over the World, or parts of the World ruled by the Signs of the Zodiac involved in the planetary configurations for the time. This is the reason why Cholera, a disease native to India, will spread to other shores in certain years. The germs of certain contagious diseases are developed by atmospheric conditions spontaneously in different Countries, and not spread by the transmigration of germs, as commonly supposed. See the following subjects in the alphabetical arrangement when not considered here, which have to do with the air.

Aeroplanes—Accident or Death By—(See Aeroplanes).

Air Cells—Of the Lungs—(See "Air Cells" under Cells).

Air Signs—(See "Signs" in this section).

Apparitions—In the Air—(See Phenomena).

Birds of the Air—The Body Devoured by Beasts and Birds after Death—Lack of Possible Burial—This is especially so if the malefics at B. are in Signs assigned to beasts and birds, and also when the benefics offer no assistance to the anaretic places, or to the 4th H., which house rules the end of life; ♂ in signs of human form, as in ♊, ♍, 1st half of ♐, or in ♒, or in ♎ or ⚻ the ☉ or ☽. (See "No Burial" under Burial; Fowls, Vultures).

Breath—Breathing—(See Breath; "Tidal Air" in this section).

Caisson Disease—(See Caisson, Compressed).

Cells—Air Cells of Lungs—(See "Air" under Cells).

Clear Air—(See "Healthy Air" in this section).

Cold Air—(See "Cold" under Weather; also see the Introduction under Cold).

Compressed Air—(See Caisson, Compressed, Gases).

Corrupt Air—Unhealthy Air—Stagnant Air—Dark Air—Vitiated Air—Foul Air—Impediment in the Air—Malignant Air—Mephitic Air—Pestilential Air — Impure Air — Unwholesome Air, etc.—♄ sole ruler at a Solar Eclipse makes the air turbulent, gloomy, and impure; ♄ ⚻ ♂ in Equinoctial signs, and controlling the Luminaries; ♄ in ♊, direct in motion, and angular at the Vernal Equinox; ♄ in ♋, and ori. at the Vernal, makes the air dark and unhealthy; ♄ ☌ ♂ in fiery signs; ♄, ♃, or ♂ in Perihelion. (Planets in perihelion tend to disturb the equilibrium of the gases of our atmosphere); ♄ in the ascendancy, rising in the ascendant, or lord of the year at the Vernal, tends to foul, noxious, stagnant, mephitic air, and conduces to the spread of fevers; ♂ sole ruler at a Solar Eclipse; ♂ in power at the Equinoxes or Solstices, or lord of the year at the Vernal, the atmosphere is parched by hot, blasting, and pestilential winds; ♂ in aphelion; the ☌ of malefic planets in fiery signs; the ascending sign be ♉, and ♀ affl. at a Solar Ingress into ♈; ♊ ascending at a Solar Ingress into ♈, and ☿ be affl., Countries under ♊ will suffer thru corrupt air, by high winds, tending to obstruction of the lungs and bronchial tubes; a malefic planet in power at a Summer Solstice, and affl. the ☉, ☽, or planets in the 6th H., and also a malefic in the 8th H.; the matutine rising of Sirius causes great heat and unwholesome air; coincident with the appearance of Comets, and espec. when they appear in ♋, ♑, or ♒; caused by the ♂ of several superior planets in airy signs, and due to the maximum of planetary influence. (See Cholera, Contagious, Epidemics, Miasma, Noxious, Pestilence, Plague, "Public Health" under Public, Typhus).

Dark Air—(See "Corrupt" in this section).

Dryness of the Air—(See Drouth, Dryness, Famine, Fountains, "Dry and Hot Air" under Heat; "Hot Winds" under Wind).

Epidemics—(See Cholera, Epidemics. See the Introduction to this Article).

Equilibrium—Of the Gases of the Air Disturbed—(See "Corrupt Air" in this section. Also see Gases).

Ether—The Ether is ruled by ♅. (See Ether).

Foul Air—Foul Vapors—(See "Corrupt" in this section; "Foul" under Vapors).

Fowls—Of the Air—(See "Birds" in this section. Also see Fowls).

Gas—Gases—(See Gas).

Good Air—(See "Healthy" in this section).

Healthy Air—Good Air—Pure Air—Temperate Air—Pleasant Air—Clear Air—Wholesome Air, etc.—♃ in ♉, ♋, ♎, ♏, ♐, ♑, ♒, and ♓ at the Vernal Equi., and lord of the year; ♃ in an angle at an Equinox or Solstice, and receiving the application of the ☽ at the New ☽, and espec. that nearest the Equinox, tends to temperate, good and wholesome air; ♂ in ♋, direct in motion, and lord of the year at the Vernal.

Heated and Turbulent Air—(See Comets; "Hot" under Wind; Weather).

High Winds—(See Wind).

Hot and Dry Air—Little Rain—Extreme Heat—(See Drought, Famine, Heat, Weather).

Impediment—In the Air—(See "Corrupt" in this section).

Lungs—Air Cells of—(See "Air Cells" under Cells).

Malignant Air—The ☉, ☽ and ♃ conjoined in ♎. (See "Corrupt" in this section).

Moist Air—Overmoist Air, and Suffering from—Excess of Rain—Floods—(See "Abundance" under Moisture; Rain).

Night Air—(See Miasma).

Obnoxious Air—When ♂ is in ♋, in N. Lat., or when rising or setting with Arcturus, Attair, Oculus Taurus,

Cauda Delphini, Procyon, Sirius, the bright star in the Crown, Orion, Regulus, Hyades, Antares, or Spica, causes a windy, tempestuous, sultry and obnoxious air, leading to public ill-health. (See "Corrupt" in this section).

Obscuration—Of the Air—Comets appearing in ♒. (See Comets).

Overmoist Air—(See "Moist" in this section).

Oxygenation—(See Oxygen).

Parched Air—(See "Corrupt", "Heated", "Hot" in this section; "Extreme Heat" under Heat).

Pestilential Air—Pestilential Winds—(See "Corrupt Air" in this section. Also see Epidemics, "Winds" under Pestilence).

Pleasant Air—(See "Healthy" in this section).

Pressure—Air Pressure—(See Caisson, Compressed, in this section).

Pure Air—(See "Healthy" in this section).

Signs—The Air Signs—Sweet Signs—Whole Signs—Nervous Signs—The Air signs are ♊, ♎, and ♒, which signs are in △ aspect to each other, and in harmony. The fiery and airy signs are opposed to each other in the Zodiac, as ♈ and ♎, ♊ and ♐, ♌ and ♒. The Air Signs are connected with Gases, Air Cells, Intercellular Spaces, Arteries, Veins, and the Capillaries of the body. The Airy and Earthy signs are the least excitable. They are related to the Intellect, and tend to worry and nervous troubles, and are classed as Nervous Signs. Air is co-operative, self-conscious, and impersonal. The ☉ in an airy sign gives a strong constitution, but of a refined and mental character rather than physical. These signs are next to the fiery signs in degree of vitality. The Air Signs are good for the ☽, and the ☽ is better placed in these signs than in fire signs, and tends to more normal and regular functions and secretions, as the airy signs are moist and warm, and especially ♒. The ☽ in these signs also gives a tendency to worry, anxiety, and mental strain, and liable to Anaemia, Blood, Kidney, and Skin Disorders. The Air signs tend to diseases arising from Corrupt Blood, as Gout, Leprosy, etc. Air Signs on the Asc. and 6th H. at B., or at decumbiture, or the Significators of the disease in an airy sign at the beginning of an illness, show Gout, Cutaneous Diseases, Scrofula, Corrupt Blood, etc. Afflictions in Air Signs tend to broken bones, and also to impure breath. People born under Air Signs, and with many planets in these signs, should sleep and work in well ventilated rooms, as they require more oxygen, and it is also well to live in a high altitude. Collectively the Air Signs rule the Lungs (♊), the Kidneys (♎), and the Blood (♒). They also rule the Breath, the Houses of Kin (Brethren), of Partners, Marriage, and Friends, and also give the Sanguine and Artistic Temperament. (See the subjects mentioned in this paragraph. Also see Air, Altitude, Aquarius, Atmosphere, Blood, Breath, Brethren, Eruptions, Ether, Events, External, Friends, Gases, Gemini, Introspection, Kidneys, Libra, Lungs, "Amiable" under Manners; Marriage, "Operations" under Nature; Orator, Oxygen, Partner, Pestilence, Refined, Residence, Sanguine, "Sweet Signs" under Sweet; Uranus, "Signs" under Whole, etc.).

Sultry Air—(See "Obnoxious" in this section).

Stagnant Air—(See "Corrupt" in this section).

Superabundance—Of Air—Death or Diseases From—Caused by ♃ when the dominion of death is vested in him.

Temperate Air—(See "Healthy" in this section).

Tidal Air—In the Lungs—(See Tidal).

Turbulent Air—(See "High Winds", "Tornadoes", and other subjects under Wind).

Unhealthy Air—Unwholesome Air—(See "Corrupt" in this section).

Vapors—Foul Vapors—(See Vapors).

Vitiated Air—(See "Corrupt" in this section).

Warm Air—Warm, Pestilential Air—(See "Corrupt", "Pestilential", in this section).

Weather; Wholesome Air—(See "Healthy" in this section).

Wind.

For further subjects which relate to the Air, its composition, action, etc., see Altitude, Apparitions, Carbon, Comets, Distentions, Eclipses, Emphysema, Events, Hydrogen, Lightning, Miasma, Nitrogen, "Operations" under Nature; Perigee, Perihelion, "Vital Force" under Vital; "Vocal Cords" under Voice, etc.

ALBA DOLENS—Phlegmasia Alba Dolens—(See "Milk Leg" under Legs).

ALBUMEN—Albuminuria—Albumen is ruled by the ♋ sign. (See Proteids).

Albuminuria—Albumen in the Urine—The work of ♃, and is a ♃ disease; ♃ or ♀ affl. by the □ of ♄; ♃ ☍ ♅; the ☽ affl. in ♋; fixed signs prominent, with many planets in them, and espec. in ♌, ♏, ♒; a fixed sign on the Asc. This disease is especially caused also by Subs at KP, the Kidney Place in the Spine, and by afflictions in ♎. (See Bright's Disease, Kidneys, Urine, Vertebrae).

ALCOHOL—Alcoholism—A Toxic Psychosis—Given to Alcoholic Excesses—(See "Softening" under Brain; "Delirium Tremens" under Delirium; Drink, Drunkenness, Intoxication).

ALDEBARAN—Bull's North Eye—A star of the nature of ♂, in the 2nd face of ♊. This great star when affl. the ☉, ☽, and the planets of our Solar System, tends to cause extreme suffering to humanity, sickness or death, and when directed to the angles of the horoscope produces periods of terrible stress and nervous strain. For the various influences of this star see

Blindness, Blows, Calamities, Cuts, Danger, Death, Disease, Disgrace, Enemies, Face (Injury to); Falls (Death By); Fire, Hanging, Hot Distempers, Ill-Health, Indisposition, Injuries, Military, Peril, Pestilence, Pirates, Putrid Fevers, Rashness, Red Hair, Ruin, Sickness, Sight, Soldiers, Stabs, Stars, Strain, Strangulation, Surgeons, Trouble, Untimely Death, Violence, Violent Death. For Bull's South Eye, see Oculus Taurus, Stars.

ALEXIPHARMIC—A Medicine Neutralizing a Poison. A Therapeutic Property of ♃. (See Antidotes).

ALGENIB—A Violent, unfortunate star of the 2nd magnitude, in the 2nd face of ♈, of the nature of ♂ and ♀. The M.C. directed to tends to imprisonment, and many adversaries. (See Enemies, Forgers, Imprisonment, Libel).

ALGOL—Caput Algol—Medusa's Head—Gorgon's Head—A star of the nature of ♄ and ♃, situated in the 5th face of ♉, and considered to be the most evil of all the fixed stars. The M.C. directed to Algol tends to make the native murderous, riotous, turbulent. The ☽ directed to tends to make the native dangerous and violent. Algol when in line of the R.A. of the ☉ or ☽ in a violent nativity tends to make a murderer, and to lead to an untimely end, and a tragic death. Robespierre was an example of this. (See Pearce's Text Book of Astrology, Chap. XIX, page 120). The Algol region of ♉ also tends to Apoplexy, and death by Spasms. (See Apoplexy, "Death" under Fits). In Hor'y Questions, the lord of the Asc. conjoined with Algol gives danger of death by illness or accident. (See Burns, Decapitation; Goiter; Hair, "Death by Sentence" under Judges; Operations).

ALIMENTARY CANAL—Alimentary System—Alimentary Tract—The Digestive Tube and Accessory Glands—Alimentation—Ruled by the ☽ and the ♋ Sign, and has to do with nourishment. Planets afflicted in ♋ tend to disorders of Alimentation, and of the Alimentary System. Such disorders are also caused by Subs at SP, the Stomach Place in the Spine. (See Assimilation, Digestion, Duodenum, Food, Indigestion, Nutrition, Oesophagus, Stomach, Vertebrae).

ALKALINITY—Alkaline—The positive Signs of the Zodiac, ♈, ♊, ♌, ♎, ♐, and ♒, are alkaline in a physiological way, and also the positive planets, the ☉, ♅, ♃, ♂, are alkaline in their influence. Several positive planets in positive signs, and with positive signs on the angles at B. tend to an excess of alkalinity in the body, an unbalanced body, and to lead to disease or discomfort, increased nervousness, alkaline urine, etc. Remedies under the rule of the negative planets or signs tend to neutralize alkalinity in the system. (See Acids, Electric. Also see "Drugs", "Remedies" under each of the planets ♆, ♄, ♀, ☽, the negative planetary bodies. Also see "Causes of Impure Blood" under Impure; Remedies).

ALLOPATHY—(See Antipathy, Hippocrates).

ALOPECIA—Loss of the Hair—(See Baldness; "Scanty" under Hair).

ALPHARD—A malefic Star. (See Hydra's Heart).

ALTAIR—The Eagle—Vulture—A star in 29° ♑︎, of the nature of ♅. Also listed by Pearce as being of the influence of ♄ and ☿. The ☽ to the place of gives promise of marriage and children. (See Fruitful).

ALTERATIONS—Changes—Modification—

Blood—(See "Alterations" under Blood).

Cells—Alterations In—(See "Alterations" under Cells).

Disease—Alteration In—(See Abatement, Amelioration, Better, Crises, Moderation, Modification, Recovery, Recuperation, Worse, etc.).

Tissues—Alteration In—(See "Alterations" under Cells. Also see Disintegration, Fruit, Inflammation, Metabolism, Metamorphosis, Putrefaction, Sensations, Tissues).

ALTERATIVE—Drugs which alter the processes of nutrition or excretion. Therapeutic properties of the ☽, ♂, and ☿.

ALTERNATING—Alternating, or Clonic Spasm—(See "Clonic" under Spasmodic. Also see Intermittent, Remittent, Returning).

ALTITUDE—Location—Residence—People born with the ☉, ☽, and many planets in the airy signs, ♊︎, ♎︎, or ♒︎, or with the airy signs upon the Asc. and angles of the map, should live in the higher and mountainous altitudes where the air pressure is lighter, as the airy signs rule largely over the Air and Ether, and espec. the ♒︎ sign. (See Air, Ether). Also when a cardinal sign is rising at B., the native should live upon a hill, and in a commanding situation, for the best health. People born with the ☉, ☽ and Asc. in the watery signs have better health in the low altitudes, and at Sea level, and to live near water, as rivers, lakes, or the Sea. With a common sign on the Asc. at B., live at Sea level. With a fixed sign on the Asc., live in a valley. Lung diseases are usually found in people who have the ♊︎ sign strongly afflicted at B., and by dir., and Physicians have found out by experience that such cases are benefited by high altitudes, altho they may not know the reason unless they are students of Astrology. The star map of birth shows what altitudes and locations, and whether At Home, or Abroad, and what Countries, are best suited to the native for better health or success in life. (See "Air Signs" under Air; Heights, Location, "Native Land" under Native; "Place of Birth" under Place; Residence, Travel).

ALUMINUM—A metal ruled by the ☽. Also said to be ruled by ♃.

ALZHEIMER'S DISEASE—(See "Atrophy" under Brain).

AMATIVE—Amativeness—Amative Tract.

Amativeness—A strong desire to propagate, and is largely a ♉, ♌, 5th and 7th H. influence. Is a strong ♌ characteristic, as ♌ is the sign of children, and the 5th H., the House of children. The ☉ in ♉, or ♉ on the Asc. at B., tend to make the bump of amativeness prominent. Mars in the 5th H. at B., makes one highly sexed, and espec. when in asp. to ♀. The ♉, ♌, and ♑︎ signs are strongly sex-conscious. (See Amorous, Passion, "Sex-Conscious" under Sex).

Amative Tract—Headaches In—♀ affl. in ♉. (See Headaches).

AMAUROSIS—Gutta Serena—Partial or Total Blindness—(See Gutta Serena; "Total Blindness" under Blindness).

AMBER—A color ruled by ♍. The amber color of the sky is ruled by ♅. Amber,—a yellowish, translucent Resin, is ruled by ♅. (See Colors).

AMBERGRIS—A waxy substance found floating in the Indian and Tropical Oceans. A morbid substance originating in the alimentary canal of the Sperm Whale. Ruled by ♆.

AMBIDEXTROUS—☿ in a double-bodied sign at B., and espec. in ♓; the double-bodied signs, and espec. ♊︎ or ♓, upon the Asc. or angles at B., and containing ☿, the ruler of the mind; ♆ affl. ☿ tends to; ♃ in ♊︎; the planets well-scattered out at B., and about equally divided between the positive and negative signs, which signs rule the right and left side of the body respectively. (See Right, Left).

AMBITION—The Ambitions, Hopes, and Desires are ruled by the 11th H. (See Eleventh). The fiery and cardinal signs on angles, espec. the Asc., and many planets in fiery signs at B. tend to give ambition, and an active mind and body; many planets rising and elevated in the East at B., and espec. when also in the positive, and masculine signs. The influences which give ambition also give more power and ability to resist and overcome disease, to hold on and never give up in despair as long as there is life, whereas the negative people, and those lacking in ambition, succumb to disease more easily. (See Negative, Positive, Purposes).

Of No Ambition—The ☽ or ♀ ill-dig. at B.; ♂ weak and ill-dig. at B.; many planets setting in the West at B., and espec. when below the western horizon, ill-posited, afflicted, and in signs of little or no dignity, and also with the majority of planets in the negative, or feminine signs of the zodiac, and people born under these conditions tend to succumb to disease more easily, be without hope and courage, to worry and be melancholic, and often to commit suicide. (See Carelessness, Desires, Dull, "Lack of" under Energy; "Hopes Cut Off" under Hope; Idle, Improvident, Inactive, Indifferent, Inertia, Lassitude, Lazy, Lethargy, Listless, Sedentary, etc.).

AMBUSHES—Death or Injury By—The ☉ to the place the Bull's South Horn; the ☽ to the ☌ or ill-asp. ♅ by dir.; ♆ when the afflicting planet tends to;

♂ in the 12th H., and affl., denotes violence from enemies in ambush; denoted by the 12th H., and malefic planets afflicted therein at B., and by dir. (See "Secret Enemies" under Enemies; Highwaymen, Plots, Treachery).

AMELIORATION—Of Disease, Hurts, or Injuries—The same benefic influences which tend to ameliorate and moderate disease also tend to lessen the evil effects of a hurt or injury. The good asps. of the benefics in the afflicting configuration, the afflicting planet separating from a malefic, and applying to a benefic, tend to ameliorate and modify the disease, and give a more favorable prognosis. The influences favorable for amelioration and alleviation of the evils of disease, hurts, or injury, are quite fully considered under the following subjects. (See Abatement, "Escapes" under Accidents; Alterations, Better, Continuity, Course, Crises, Curable, Curtailed, Ease, Epilepsy, "Amelioration" under Hurts; Improvement, Insanity, Minimizing, Moderation, Modification, "Action" under Morbid; Prognosis, Recovery, Recuperation, Remission, Separation).

AMENDMENT—Of Disease—(See Ameliortion).

AMENORRHEA—(See Menses).

AMNESIA—(See "Amnesia" under Memory).

AMNIOTIC FLUID—(See Foetus).

AMOEBOID MOTION—(See "Amoeboid" under Cells).

AMOROUS—

Amorous Eyes—(See "Amorous" under Eyes). (See Amative, Excesses, "Energies Wasted" under Love Affairs; "Health Suffers" under Opposite Sex; "Addicted to Women" under Men; "Loose Morals" under Morals; "Excess" under Passion; Sensuality, etc.).

Amorous Indulgence—Disease and Ill-health from Excess of—♂ in the 1st H., and affl. by ♀; ♂ affl. in the 5th H.; ♂ □ or ☍ ♀, the vitality sapped by sex excesses; lord of the 6th or 10th H. in the 5th, and afflicted. (See "Passional Excesses" under Passion; Sex, Venery).

Amours—(See this subject under Love Affairs).

AMPUTATIONS—(See "Amputations" under Operations).

AMULETS—Charms—Talismans—Amulets were worn in Ancient Times against infectious and contagious diseases, and such are in use today. Certain metals and minerals, flowers or herbs, have inherent powers to ward off disease, evils, and mischief of various kinds. Copper is worn by the natives of India, and other Countries, against Cholera. Physicians use copper internally in bowel disorders, and copper is one of the best intestinal remedies for diarrhea, dysentery, etc., and is a remedy taken from the Ancient and Oriental Peoples. In Hungary a copper plate is worn next to the skin to ward off Cholera. A Coral Necklace is worn against

Whooping Cough. (See Cholera, Contagions, Copper, Coral, Infections, "Birth Stones" under Stones; Whooping).

AMUSEMENTS—Play—Recreations—Sports, etc.—Amusements, Play, Love Affairs, Opposite Sex, Theatres, Women, etc., are ruled by the 5th H., and malefics in this house at B., a malefic ruler of the 5th, lord of the 5th H. in the 6th, 8th or 12th houses, and afflicted, or afflicting the hyleg, tend to make people less fortunate in Amusements and Recreation, and more subject to accidents, injury, or death in such pursuits. Also certain Fixed Stars, and the Nebulae, have an adverse influence in these matters, and espec. to cause injury to the eyes, and blindness from some accident to the eyes while at play. (For further influences along this line see the various paragraphs under Accidents, Blindness, Exercise, Falls, Frivolity, Hunting, Injuries, Pleasure, Recreations, Sports, Theatres, Travel).

AMYGDALITIS—(See "Tonsilitis" under Tonsils).

AMYLOID—Starch-like—(See Starches, "Amyloid Kidney" under Kidneys).

ANABOLISM—(See Constructive, Metabolism).

ANAEMIA—A Deficiency of Blood and Red Corpuscles—Impoverished Blood Anaemic—Pale—

Causes—General Causes of Anaemia—The ☉ in ♉, ♌, ♒, and affl. by the malefics ♆, ♅, or ♄; afflictions in ♌ at B., the sign which rules the heart, and also in ♒, the sign which bears strong rule over the blood, tend to, and to disturb the equilibrium of the blood; a ♌ and ♒ disease; ♒ on the Asc. at B., and afflicted; the ☉ affl. in ♊ or ♋; afflictions to the ☉ in a male nativity, and to the ☽ and ♀ in a female; the ☽ affl. in airy signs; the water signs and the ☽ influence, as well as the afflictions of ♆, tend to this disease; caused by the atonic action of the ☽; ♆ afflicted, or affl. the ☉, ☽, Asc., or hyleg at B., or by dir.; ♆ afflicting ☿ at B.; ♄ affl. in ♊, ♋, or ♒; a ♄ disease; ♄ in the 6th H., and affl. the ☉, ☽, or ♃; a ♄ disease; many planets afflicted in fixed signs, strongly characteristic of the Lymphatic Temperament; caused by improper oxygenation of the blood, and lung disturbances. (See "Beriberi" under Dropsy; Emaciation, Leukocytes, Malnutrition, "Non-Oxygenation" under Oxygen; Pale, "Blood" under Red; Sickly, Thin, Wasting, Weak. Also note the other paragraphs in this section).

Cerebral Anaemia—An ♈ disease; the ☉ or ♄ affl. in ♈ at B. (See Cerebral).

Chlorosis—Anaemia in Young Women—(See Chlorosis).

Pernicious Anaemia—The ☉ affl. in ♎ or ♒; the ☉ affl. by ♄ in males, or with females the ☽ ☌ or ill-asp. ♄; the 8° ♌ or ♒ containing the ☉, ☽, or malefics at B., and afflictions to this degree.

Women—Anaemia In—The ☉ in the sex sign ♏, affl. by ♆, ♅, or ♄, and often attended by profuse menstruation (See "Profuse" under Menses); the ☉ in ♉, ♌, ♏, or ♒, the fixed signs, and affl. by malefics; the ☽, ♏, and affl. by malefics. (See Chlorosis).

Young Women—Anaemia In—(See Chlorosis).

ANAESTHETICS—Anaesthesia—Remedies and means of producing Insensibility—Typical drugs of ♆, such as Analgesics, Anodynes, Chloroform, Ether, Hypnotics, Narcotics, Opiates, Soporifics. (See these subjects. Also see Insensibility, "Neptune Influence" under Neptune; "Sleeping Potions" under Heart).

ANALEPTIC—An agent restoring health and strength. A therapeutic property of ♃ and ♃ remedies. (See Jupiter, Restoratives).

ANALGESIA — Analgesics — Producing Insensibility to Pain and Suffering—A ♆ influence, and caused by ♆ afflictions at B., or by dir., or produced by the use of ♆ drugs and remedies, or methods and influences under the rule of ♆. Analgesic drugs are under the rule of ♆. (See references under Anaesthetics. Analgesia is also caused by Subs of the Atlas, the 1st Cervical vertebra. (See Vertebrae).

ANALYSIS—Of Tissues—(See "Absorption" under Tissues).

ANAPHRODISIACS—Remedies which lessen passion and sexual desire. A therapeutic property of ♆ remedies, such as narcotics, opiates, and sedatives. Also the remedies of ♄ act as sedatives. (See Aphrodisiac, Narcotics, Neptune, "Drugs" and "Remedies" under Saturn; Sedatives, etc.).

ANARCHISTS—Anarchy—Dangerous to the Community and Society—Destructive—Riotous—Cranks—Bomb Plotters, etc.—In the star maps of Anarchists the malefics bear sway, as a rule, are strongly fortified, usually in angles, or rising and elevated in the East, and above the Luminaries; the ☉ ☌ or ill-asp. ♅; ♆ affl. in ♈ or ♒; ♆ affl. in ♈, bomb plotters; ♅ □ or ☍ ☉ at B; ♅ ☌ or ill-asp. ♂; ♅ in the 5th H., and espec. when affl. by ♆; ♅ affl. in the 9th H. tends to make red Anarchists and Fanatics; ♅ affl. in ♎; ♅ □ or ☍ ♄; ♃ affl. in ♒; ♂ in the 3rd or 9th H., and strongly afflicting ☿, the ruler of the mind; ♂ ☌ or ill-asp. ♆; ☿ affl. by ♂ and other malefics, and espec. by ♂, the planet of violence. (See Assassins, Dangerous, Destructiveness, Enthusiasm, Fanatical, Fury, Ideals, Ideas, Imprisonment, Notions, Politics, Radicalism, Rashness, Reactionary, Reformers, Revolutionary, Riotous, Sedition, Violent, etc.).

ANARETA—The planet which destroys life, and the Anaretic Place is the sign and degree occupied by the Anareta at B. Any of the planets can act as Anareta when the dominion of death is vested in it, and when the planet afflicts the hyleg at B., and by dir., in a train of evil directions, and also occupies an Anaretic Place at B. (See Killing Place). The dominion of death is vested in the planet which occupies an Anaretic Place at B., as in the 4th,

6th, 8th, or 12th Houses, and the planets ruling the signs on the cusps of these houses are the disposers of these places. The strength of the Anareta, and of the Anaretical Places, and the rulers of these places, must be considered in passing judgment as to the duration of life. The Anareta falling in the term of a malefic greatly increases the danger, but if in the term of a benefic, almost any asp. of the benefic would save life. A malefic in the term of ♃ or ♀ would lose much of its anaretic power, and be scarcely able to kill, and a benefic in the terms of a malefic would be rendered equally unable to save. The ☉ may become Anareta when the ☽ or Asc. are hyleg, and the ☽ may become Anareta when the ☉ or Asc. are hyleg. The ☉ or Asc. may become Anareta when the ☽ is hyleg. The ☉, ☽, and ☿, being variable, may become Anareta when in asp. to ♄ or ♂, unless a benefic give testimony, and also the ☽ can operate as Anareta when in evil asp. the malefics. The ☉ can be Anareta when he is in the signs of ♄, and evilly aspected by ♄ and ♂, and acting in a train of evil directions, and cause death. The ☉, ☽, ♃, ♀ and ☿ can act as Anareta in morbid deaths. When acting as Anareta, ♆ disposes to death in a riotous manner, assassination, or a violent death. ♅ as Anareta causes death by violent accidents, explosions, machinery, or by suicide. ♄ when Anareta causes death by falls, bruises, crushes, hurts and concussions. As Anareta ♄ and ♂ are equally destructive whether by day or night in nativities. ♂ when Anareta causes death by burns, scalds, fire, cuts, stabs, explosions, etc., according to the nature of the sign he is in, and aspects to him. Planets in the 8th H. at B. can act as Anareta, and cause death by accidents or injuries when they reach the Descendant, the cusp of the 7th H. by dir. The Part of Fortune, ⊕, can become Anareta when the ☉, ☽, or Asc. are hyleg. A malefic when Anareta, and elevated above the Lights, will tend to a violent death, but if a benefic be elevated above the malefic, it will destroy or modify the anaretic tendency, and also the injurious effects of a malefic, when Anareta, will be greatly lessened if the ☉ and ☽ be elevated above the malefic at B. (See Apheta, "Arguments for Death" under Death; Directions, Hyleg. Also see the subject of "Death" under each of the planets, and note the kinds of death caused by the planets).

ANASARCA—General Dropsy—(See "Anasarca" under Dropsy).

ANATOMICAL CHANGES—♄ tends to change the body by retention of wastes, deposits, crystallization, decay, slowing up or stopping of functions, etc., and thus change the form and shape of the body, leading to deformities, disease, or death. ♂ changes the anatomy by too much heat in a part, causing fusion of parts, or the burning up of too much tissue. The ☉ also, when acting with ♂, and in a pathological way, will give a surplus of heat to a part, resulting in anatomical changes. The vertebrae of the spine being subjected to much heat thru the afflictions of the ☉ and ♂, tend to melt the bones, and cause the spine to assume many different shapes. (See Ankylosis, Spine, Subluxations, Vertebrae). Each of the planets have a beneficial and a pathological, or disease and disturbing influence, according to their sign positions, aspects to each other, and to the ☉, ☽, Asc., or hyleg at B., and by dir. (See "Action", "Influence", under each of the planets).

ANCESTRY—(See Aunts, Birth, Grandparents, Heredity, Inherent, Organic, Parents, Uncles).

ANDROGYNOUS—(See Hermaphrodite).

ANDROMEDA—Caput Andromeda—A Constellation of the nature of ♃ and ♀ in the 3rd face of ♈. (See Impalement). Zona Andromeda, in the last face of ♈, is of the nature of ♀.

ANEMIA—(See Anaemia).

ANEURYSM—A Dilatation of an Artery, The ☽ affl. in ♐; the ☽ and ♃ in signs which rule the arms, hands, legs and feet affect the vesicles and glands of these parts causing cysts, ulcers, aneurysms, and varicose veins; the ☽ in ♐, ♍, ♌, ♏, ♐, ♑, ♒, and ♓, in parts ruled by these signs; ♂ in signs which rules the arms, hands, legs and feet tends to aneurysms and inflammatory complaints in these parts; ♂ in ♌; ♂ in ♌ in the 6th H., and afflicted; a ♌ disease, and afflictions in ♌; ♌ on the Asc. at B. Aneurysm of the arch of the Aorta is caused by afflictions in ♌, and by Subs at AP, HP, and Lu.P., and which may be caused by spasmodic gushing of the blood thru the aorta, and espec. when ♅ is in ♌, and affl. by ♄ and ♂. (See Aorta, Arteries, Dilatations, Heart, "Blood Vessels" under Rupture; Varicose, Vesicles, Vessels).

Hernial Aneurysm—(See "Aneurysm" under Hernia).

Varicose Aneurysm—The simultaneous rupture of an artery and a vein—Caused by the ☽ affl. in ♐. (See Rupture, Varicose).

ANGER—Choler—Wrath—Ruled principally by ♂.

Disease Arising from Anger—Caused by ♂; ♂ in ♉ or ♏ and □ ♅; ♂ □ or ♌ ♄, and both in angles; many planets in fixed signs at B., and espec. malefics in such signs in angles, and afflicting each other, retains anger; ☽ ☌ ♂ in the Asc. when taken ill, and afflicted with spleen (Hor'y); ♅ ☌, □, ☍ ♂; ♅ in ♉ or ♏ in □ ♂; ♏ on the Asc., and espec. if ♂ be there in ♏. (See Choler, "Choleric Temperament" under Choleric; "Desire Body" under Desire; Dispersions, Effervescent, Enmity, Excitable, Fighting, Folly, Frenzy, Furious, Leukocytes, Madness, Profane, Quarrels, Rashness, Riotous, Temper, Violent, etc.).

ANGINA—A sense of suffocation—A ♉ disease; ♄ affl. in ♉ at B.; ♂ affl. in ♉ or ♌. (See Croup, Dyspnoea, Suffocation; "Quinsy" under Tonsils).

Angina Pectoris—Pain and oppression about the heart—A sense of suffocating contraction and compression about the lower part of the chest, and associated with heart disturbances—Caused by afflictions in ♌; a ♌ disease; ♂ affl. in ♌; Subs. at HP, the Heart Place, and at Lu.P., 3rd Dorsal.

Case of Angina—See "Angina Pectoris", Chap. 13, page 90, in Daath's Medical Astrology.

False Angina—Pseudo-Angina—May be caused by ♆, ♅, ♄, or ♂ in the ♉ or ♐ signs, but with lesser affliction if there be favorable asps. from the benefics and to the hyleg. Subs of the Atlas, the 1st Cervical vertebra. (See Heart, Vertebrae).

ANGLES—The angles of the star map are the 1st, 4th, 7th and 10th houses, and correspond to ♈, ♋, ♎, and ♑. Planets in angles are very strong and powerful in matters of health and disease, and are stronger than when in succedent or cadent houses, and have more power for good or ill over the life of the native. The malefic planets in the angles at B. become more powerful, and tend to disease, accidents, downfall, misfortune, or calamity to the native periodically along thru life, and when the angles are afflicted by directions, or when planets in angles at B. afflict their own places by dir., or transits. Angles show strength and vitality, and do not hasten death. In diagnosing disease by Astrology, and giving a prognosis, the student should note the influences affecting the angles, and the cardinal signs, as well as the influences of the 6th, 8th and 12th houses. (See Cardinal).

ANGUISH OF MIND—Tormented in Mind—Suffering in Mind—The ☉, ☽, or ☿ to the ill-asps. ♄ by tr. or dir.; the ☽ passing over the radical places of ♄, ♂, or ♀ at a Solar Rev., and these planets affl. at B.; the ☽ to the ☌ or ☍ P. Dec. the ☉ if the ☽ be hyleg and the ☉ affl. at B.; the ☽ to the □ or ☍ the ☉ by dir.; ♄ ruler of the 12th H., and ♄ in the 1st, 3rd or 9th houses if in these houses at B., and affl. the ☉, ☽, or ☿; anguish of mind is ruled over by the 8th H. conditions; in Hor'y Questions the dispositors of the ☉ and ☽ much afflicted and weak, and the ☽ □ the degree ascending, but with no ill-asp. of ♄ or ♂, the mind is much tormented; ☿ joined to the Anareta causes great anguish and delirium in illness. (See Anxiety, Dejected, Despondent, Depression, Despair, Fears, Hypochondria, "Low Spirits" under Low; Melancholy, Pain, Suffering, Worry, etc.).

ANGULAR—

Angular Body—(See "Angular" under Body).

Angular Face—(See "Angular" under Face).

Planets Angular—(See Angles).

Spine—Angular Curvature of—(See "Humpback" under Spine).

ANIDROSIS—Anhidrosis—Deficiency of Sweat—(See "Lessened" under Sweat).

ANIMAL—

Animal Bodies—Putrefaction of—(See Putrid).

Animal Character—Animal Expression—The Signs ♈, ♉, ♌, ♏, the 2nd half of ♐, and ♑, when on the Asc. at B. tend to give an animal expression, and more of the animal instincts to the human mind, except when ☿, the ruler of the mind, is in the Asc. and configurated with the ☽ and benefics. (See Personality).

Animal Heat—(See "Animal" under Heat).

Animal Instincts—Animal Propensities—The ☽ rules the animal instincts, and the ☽ strong at B., rising and elevated, or in the Asc., and espec. in an animal sign, tends to make the animal instincts stronger, and to give more of the primitive instincts, rash impulses, animal and passional gratifications, which, unless controlled, lead to disease, suffering, and an earlier death. (See "Atrophy" under Brain). Animal propensities depend almost wholly upon the ☽, her position and aspects, and the ☽ when afflicted tends to drink, debauchery, dissipation and gluttony. (See Desire). ♆ in evil asp. to ♀ gives larger animal propensities, and also ♆ in the 5th H. at B., and afflicted, or affl. ♀ and the ☽. The 5° ♏ on the Asc. at B. is said to make one full of animal spirits. (See "Animal Character" in this section).

Animal Magnetism—(See Magnetism).

Animal Sensations—(See Sensation).

Animal Signs—The Signs which have animals as symbols, as ♈, ♉, ♌, 2nd half of ♐, and ♑. People born with the ☉, ☽, and planets in these signs, or when they are on the Asc., are apt to be more subject to disease, live more in their lower minds until awakened into a higher spiritual life. (See Beasts; "Dogs" under Children; Quadrupeds).

Animal Tissues—(See Tissues).

ANIMALS—Beasts—Quadrupeds—Man is more or less subject to injuries, sufferings, and vicissitudes by animals acording to the positions of the planets at B., and whether they occupy animal signs or not, and are afflicted therein by ♂, or other malefic planets at B., or by dir.

Bites by Animals—(See Bites).

Cattle—Hurts and Injuries By—(See Cattle).

Death by Animals—Sickness of—♄ ♂ in animal signs, and chiefly the sickness or death of animals of the nature and form of the sign containing the ♂; the ☽ and planets in Quadrupedal Signs at the birth of an animal, or at the Equinoxes and Solstices, tend to bring disease, suffering and death to animals, and events affecting them. (See "Virus" under Pestilence).

Devoured By—The Body Devoured by after Death—(See "Birds of the Air" under Air; "Body Devoured" under Burial).

Elephants—Sickness or Death of—(See Elephants).

Ferocious Animals—Hurts By—☉ to ♂ ♂ by dir.

Good or Ill—Animals Affected for Good or Ill—The Zodiacal Constella-tions, and those of the ruling Fixed Stars out of the Zodiac, in terrestrial or quadrupedal signs at a Solar Eclipse, the effects fall upon animals of similar form. (See Quadrupeds).

Great Beasts—Attacks By—(See Beasts, Cattle, Great, Horses).

Horses—(See Horses).

Hurts by Animals—Injury or Death By—♂ by dir. to the ♂ or ill-asp. the Asc.; the Asc. to the place of the Ascelli or Capricornus; ill-asps. of ♂ to the ☉, ☽, Asc., or M.C.; the ☽ in earthy signs at B., and to the ♂ or ill-asps. ♂ by dir.; the ☉ affl. in ♐ at B., and by dir. (See Beasts, Bites, Bruises, Cattle, Distortions, Horses, Kicks, Quadrupeds).

Kicks—(See Horses, Kicks).

Large Animals—Hurts and Injuries By—(See "Great" under Beasts, Cattle; Horses, Quadrupeds).

Odors From—(See Odors).

Quadrupeds—(See Quadrupeds).

Reptiles—(See Reptiles).

Resembles Animals—(See "Dogs" under Children; Inhuman; "Animal Forms" under Monsters).

Sickness of Animals—(See "Death" in this section).

Small Animals—Ruled by the 6th H., and when the native has malefics in this house at B., he tends to be unfortunate with, and have losses of small animals, as with sheep, goats, rabbits, etc. (See Goats, Sheep).

Sterility In—(See Mules).

Venomous Animals—Bites By—Injuries By—(See Venomous).

Very Animal Like—(See "Resembles" in this section. Also see Case, "Female", Chap. 8, page 49, in Daath's Medical Astrology).

Wild Animals—Death or Injury By—Attacks By—♄ and ♂ in terrestrial signs, and affl. the ☉ or ☽; ♄ occi., in signs of bestial form, and the ☽ succedent to him, and the death will occur by day, and in public, if ♃ offer testimony and be afflicted at the same time, and such a death may occur in a public combat with wild beasts; ♄ near the Constellation of the Serpent; Comets appearing in ♌. (See Beasts, Wild).

ANIMATION—

Full Of—(See Active, Energy, Zest).

Lack Of—(See Apathy, Dull, Inactive, Inertia, Lassitude, Lethargy, Listless, Malaise, Weak, etc).

Suspended Animation—(See "Suppression" under Functions).

ANISOCORIA—(See Iris).

ANKLES—Shank—Shin Bone—Tibia—Astragalus—The Ankles are under the structural rulership of the ♒ sign, and correspond to the wrists, ruled by the ♌ sign. The ankles are also ruled and influenced by the 11th H. (See Arms, Wrists).

Affected—The ankles tend to be affected with the ☉ in ♊, and ♅ in ♐. (See Table 196 in Simmonite's Arcana).

Afflictions In—All Diseases and Afflictions In—Signified by the ♒ sign, the 11th and 12th houses, and afflictions therein; ♄ or ♂ in ♒; signified in horary questions by ♂ in ♓.

Broken Ankles—Fractures of—The ☽, ♄, or ♂ affl. in ♒; ♒ on the Asc. at B., and containing a malefic, and afflicted by an adverse direction, or a malefic coming to the ♂ or ill-asp. the Asc.

Cramps In—♅ in ♒.

Dropsy—(See "Swellings" in this section).

Injuries To—(See "Broken" in this section).

Knocking Together—Caused by ♄ influence strong at B., or ♄ affl. in ♒; ♄ ascending at B. In Horary Questions ♄ as Sig. indicates such a person. (See "Dragging" under Gait).

Lameness In—♄, ♂, ☿, or the ☽ affl. in ♒, or ♒ on the Asc. and afflicted. (See Lameness).

Operations On—Incisions, and surgical operations upon the ankles should be avoided when the ☽ is passing thru ♒. (See Operations).

Sprains—Afflictions in ♑ or ♒; ♄ in ♑ or ♒ and afflicted; ♒ on the Asc. (See Sprains).

Swollen Ankles—The ☽ or ♀ affl. in ♒; afflictions in ♒; an ♒ disease; ♃ affl. in ♌ or ♒. (See Swellings).

Weakness In—♄ affl. in ♒, weakness in or near the ankles. (See Legs, Lower Extremities, Tibia).

ANKYLOSIS—The union or fusion of the bones of a joint, resulting in a stiff joint. Is caused by the ♄ deposits of waste or excess minerals of the system. Also caused by the excess heat of the ☉ and ♂ over the part, resulting in fusion and melting of the bony tissues. (See Adhesions, Anatomical, Joints). Ankylosis can occur between the joints of any part of the body, but is more common between the vertebrae, and in the hip joint, knee joint, elbow, wrists and finger joints. ♄ in the sign ruling the affected joint tends to dry up the fluids of the joint, cause deposits, solidification, hardening, Gout in the joint, etc., resulting in a stiff joint, and ankylosis. The ☉ ♂ ♂ in a sign, both hot and fiery planets, intensifies the heat in the part, and especially if in a fiery sign in the Asc. Thus the ☉ ♂ ♂ in ♌, and with ♌ on the Asc., would tend to fusion and ankylosis of the dorsal vertebrae; ♄ affl. in ♌ or ♒ tends to ankylosis of the spine thru deposits; ♄ in ♑ would tend to a stiff knee joint, from deposits; ♄ affl. in ♋, the sign opposite ♑, would tend to stiff elbow joints; ♄ in ♍, the sign opposite ♓, would tend to ankylosis of the finger joints, etc., due to cold, deposits, whereas ♂ in the same signs would tend to fusion by excess of heat. Improper kidney action, and Subs at KP, also usually enter into ankylosis afflictions, and in addition to adjusting the vertebra, or vertebrae, thru which the nerves pass to the part afflicted, KP, the Kidney Place in the spine, should be adjusted,

to aid in elimination, secretion, and proper kidney action. (See Coalition, Crystallization, Deposits, Gout, Hardening, Heat, Stiff, etc.).

Case—A case of Ankylosis of the Hip Joint. See "Deformed", No. 689, in 1001 N.N.

ANODYNE—A drug relieving pain—A Therapeutic property of ♆. (See Anaesthetics, Analgesia, Narcotics, "Therapeutic Qualities" under Neptune; Sedatives).

ANOREXIA—Loss of Appetite—(See Appetite).

ANOSMIA—Loss of Smell—(See Smell).

ANTARES—Scorpion's Heart—Cor Scorpio—A violent fixed star of the 1st magnitude, situated in the 8° ♐, of the nature of ♃ and ♂. This star has an inimical influence on the eyesight for evil, and when the ☉ or ☽ are with it at B., tends to blindness, weak sight, eye trouble, etc. This star by its conjunctions and evil asps. tends to bring many dangers and evils upon humanity, and is one of the most mentioned stars in the textbooks of Astrology, for his evils. The good asps. of ♆ to Antares tend to give increased Spiritual Sight of a favorable nature, and the evil asps. of ♆ to Antares tend to Involuntary Clairvoyance and Mediumship, Obsessions, Spirit Controls, etc. The adverse influences of Antares when with the ☉ or ☽ at B., or afflicting them by dir., are mentioned under the following subjects, which see in the alphabetical arrangement—Accidents, Acquaintance (Death of); Assassination, Assaults (Violent); Beasts (Attacks by Great Beasts); Blindness, Blows, Burns, Calamities, Cattle, (Attacks By); Conjunctivitis, Dangers, Death (Violent Death); Demoniacal, Disease, Disgrace, Distempers (Hot); Drowning, Enemies, Eyes (Injury To and Eye Trouble); Falls (Danger From); Female Friend (Death Of); Fever (In Whole Body, and Putrid Fevers); Hanging; Hot Distempers; Ill-Health, Imprisonment; Injury (See Eyes, Right Eye, Military Life, Violence); Mediumship (Involuntary); Military Life (Injury In); Mother (Death of); Obsessions; "Over-heated" under Blood; Pestilence (Sickness or Death By); Peril, Pirates, Putrid Fevers; Right Eye (Injury to); Ruin; Scalds; Sickness (Extreme); Sight (Weak Sight and Injuries to); Spirit Controls; Strangulation; Stress (Periods of); Suffering; Suffocation, Treachery; Trouble; Vehicles (Dangers by); Violence; Violent Assaults; Violent Death; Whole Body (Fever In); Wife (Death of).

ANTENATAL—(See Conception, Foetus, Gestation, Pregnancy, Prenatal Epoch).

ANTHELMINTIC—A remedy expelling Worms. A therapeutic property of ♃.

ANTHONY'S FIRE—St. Anthony's Fire—(See Erysipelas).

ANTHRAX—(See Carbuncles).

ANTICACHECTIC—A therapeutic property of the ☉. (See Cachexia).

ANTIDOTES—An agent counteracting the action of a Poison. Each planet rules over certain drugs, herbs, minerals, metals and poisons, and as the planets are arranged in pairs of opposites in their effects, the poisons of one will be counteracted by drugs and remedies of the other. (For further consideration of this subject see Alexipharmic, Antipathy, Cure, Opposites, Poison, Remedies, Treatment).

ANTIMONY—A typical drug of ♄. (For use as a remedy, see Leprosy, Voluntary).

ANTINEPHRITIC—A remedy for inflammation of the Kidneys. ♀ remedies, and a therapeutic property of ♀. (See "Inflammation" under Kidneys).

ANTIPATHY—Contraries—Aversion—Dislike—The planets which rule opposite signs of the zodiac are in antipathy to each other. ♂ rules ♈, and ♀ rules ♎, the opposite sign. Thus ♂ is opposed to ♀, and the remedies of ♀ will oppose those of ♂. Also planets in their exalted signs are opposed to the rulers of the opposite signs. ♃ is exalted in ♋, and in vibratory, or therapeutical value, is opposed to ♄, the ruler of ♑, the sign opposite to ♋. Planets have antipathy to certain signs, which signs are their detriment or fall. ♂, a fiery planet, is weak and disturbing to the health when in ♓, a watery sign; ♄, a cold and dry planet, disturbs the body when in ♌, a fiery sign, as he is in antipathy with ♌, and has his detriment in ♌, and his fall in the fiery sign ♈. Each planet also has its especial therapeutical value, some working in harmony with each other, and some opposing, and in treating disease with medicines these values should be kept in mind. (See Drugs, Praeincipients, Remedies, Signatures, Therapeutic Properties, under each of the planets. Also see Chemical, Herbs, Medicines, Minimizing, Opposites, Remedies, Sympathy, Treatment).

Disease by Antipathy—When the afflicting planet causing the disease is opposed, or an enemy to the planet which rules the part of the body diseased or afflicted, the disease is said to arise from antipathy. Thus diseases under ♄ (♑) are treated by ☽ (♋) remedies. Disease under the ☉ (♌) are treated by ♄ (♒) remedies. Hippocrates and Galen taught antipathy and contraries in the treatment of disease. (See Hippocrates). Thus the expression, "Contraria Contrariis Curantur". Allopathy uses Contraries in the treatment of disease. (See Homeopathy). The Astrological selection of remedies has been based upon the antipathy or sympathy between the planetary influences ruling each herb, mineral or remedy. Among the planets ♄ opposes the ☉, ♂, ♀ and the ☽; ♃ opposes ♂; ♂ opposes ♄, ♃, ♀, ☿, and the ☽ in therapeutical ways, but ♂ is friendly with ♀ in helping to arouse the passions and the lower nature, and when the lower vibrations of ♂ and ♀ combine their forces in the unawakened soul, their influences tend to dissipation, debauchery, passional excesses. ♀ opposes ♄ and ♂.

A planet when passing thru its own sign is less apt to cause disease in the part ruled by such sign, but planets when passing thru signs which oppose their own strong signs are apt to produce irritation or disease, as when ♂ (♈) passing thru ♎ (♀) tends to acute inflammation of the kidneys for the time if ♎ was afflicted by ♂, or malefics at B. These rules will be easy to apply if the student will become thoroughly acquainted with the nature of each planet and sign, and then apply his knowledge to each case as it arises. A Table of the Friendships and Enmities of the Planets is given on page 241 in Dr. Broughton's Elements of Astrology. (See Kinetic).

Enemies—Antipathy Between People—Malefics in one nativity on the place of the ☉, ☽, or benefics in the other tend to antipathy and discord, and such are apt to dislike and mistrust each other, irritate each other, cause the other to weaken thru worry and discord, antagonism, etc., and to invite disease or an earlier death of the other in their natural unawakened states, and this is also the case when the Asc., or rising signs in the two maps are in □ or ☍ to each other between the two parties, and people who are contemplating marriage should see to it that their star maps blend if they would have the best of health, happiness, and contentment with each other. These rules also apply in the choosing of a Healer, Physician, or even a business associate. People also should avoid each other when the Asc. in the radix of one is on the cusp of the 6th, 8th or 12th house in the other. (For the rules in choosing a Healer, see "Compatibility" under Healers. Also see Enemies, Friends).

Healers—The Antipathy or Compatibility of a Healer to the patient—The magnetism of some Healers tends to kill the patient, while the magnetism of others, where the star maps of patient and healer blend, tends to the more quickly restore the patient to health, and thousands of lives would be saved if people knew Astrology, and would spend some time beforehand in deciding upon some one who is to be their permanent advisor and healer before sickness overtakes them. (These rules are further considered under the subjects of Healers, Polarity, Sympathy, and Treatment. Also see Hatred, Husband, Love Affairs, Marriage, Marriage Partner, Wife).

ANTIPERIODIC—(See Apiol; "Typical Drugs" under Mercury).

ANTIPERISTALSIS—An abnormal movement of the bowels towards the stomach, or of the stomach towards the oesophagus.

Of the Bowels—(See "Antiperistalsis" under Bowels).

Of the Stomach—(See "Antiperistalsis" under Stomach. Also see Emetics, Nausea, Peristalsis, Vomiting).

ANTIPHLOGISTIC—An agent reducing inflammation. A therapeutic property of ♄ remedies, as opposed to ♂, causing inflammations. (See Inflammation, Saturn Remedies).

ANTIPYRETIC—A Febrifuge—A Fever-reducing remedy—A therapeutic property of ♄ and ♄ remedies. (See Aconite, Fever, Saturn Remedies).

ANTISPASMODIC—A therapeutic property of ♃ remedies. (See Spasmodic).

ANURIA—Absence, deficiency, or suppression of Urine. (See Urine).

ANUS—Sphincter Ani Muscle—Ruled by ♏. Also under the external rule of ♎.

Condyloma—Wart-like Growth on Anus—Caused by afflictions in ♏; ♄ in ♏; Subs at LPP, the 4th and 5th Lumbar vertebrae. (See Warts).

Diseases of Anus—Troubles with the Anus—♂ in ♏ or ♐, and afflicted; ♂ in ♐ in 6th H., and afflicted. (See Fundament, Rectum).

Fissure—Afflictions in ♏, and Subs at LPP. (See Fissure, Fistula, Vertebrae).

Fistula—(See Fistula).

Hemorrhoids—(See Hemorrhoids).

Imperforate Anus—♄ affl. in ♏. Case —(See "Puzzle Horoscope", No. 273 in 1001 N.N.).

Inbreathing Thru Anus—♄ affl. in ♏ tends to a tight and constricted Sphincter Ani muscle, which disturbs the intake of air thru the Rectum, and the air pressure in the bowels, which indirectly disturbs the diaphragm and respiration. In such cases it is necessary at times to forcibly dilate the sphincter ani.

Piles—(See Hemorrhoids).

Sex Relations—By Rectum and Anus —(See Homosexuality, "Sex Perversions" under Perversions).

Ulceration Of—♄ or ♂ affl. in ♏. Caused by Subs at PP and LPP, and also at KP. (See Ulcers, Vertebrae).

Wart-like Growth—On Anus—(See "Condyloma" in this section).

ANXIETY—Anxiety Neuroses—Anxious Fears—Worry—Fixed Ideas—♅ and ♄ by their afflictions are the principal planets causing anxiety, worries, false fears, obsessions, and to give a sense of impending danger, calamity, ill-health, or reversals. The ♓ sign, and the 12th H. are also important to be considered in this connection, and espec. when occupied by malefic planets. Anxiety and worry are also more common with people born under the Mutable Signs, and who also may have many planets in such signs. Fixed Signs tend to the least worry and anxiety. Cardinal signs are usually too much absorbed in their plans and promotions to realize their dangers. Afflictions to the ☽ also tend to increase fear, apprehension, worry, and anxiety. The 12th H. is the house of tribulation; worry, anxiety, affliction, self-undoing, confinement, imprisonment, distress, trouble, and people born with this house much afflicted tend to have more than their share of what they may call "Ill-Fate". The following are some of the important planetary influences which tend to produce anxiety,—The ☉ ☌ the Asc. by dir., much anxiety; the ☉, ♄, or ♅ affl. in the 12th H.; an eclipse

of the ☉ falling on the place of ♄ at B.; the ☉ ill-aspected at B., and to the ☌ or ill-asp. the ☽, ♄, ♃, ♂, ♀, Asc., or M.C. by dir.; the ☉ or ☽ hyleg, and to the ☌ or ill-asp. ♄ by dir.; the ☽ ill-aspected at B., and to the ☌ or ill-asps the ☉, ♄, ♅, or ♂ by dir.; the ☽ affl. in ♍; the ☽ affl. in airy signs; the ☽ to Castor, Cauda Lucida, and Caput Algol, great anxiety; the ☽ to the ☌ Arcturus or Deneb, many cares and anxieties due to the native's own folly; the Prog. ☽ to the □ or 8 the Asc. or M.C.; the ☽ to the ☌ or ill-asp. ♂ by dir., strange anxieties; the Pr. ☽ to the ☌ or ill-asp. the ☉. ♄, or ♂; ♀ and ♄ afflicted in the houses of mind, the 3rd or 9th houses; ♄ in the 10th H. at a Solar Rev., and elevated above the ☉ and ☽; ♄ to the ☌ or ill-asp. the ☉, ☽, Asc., M.C., or any planet by dir.; ♄ or ♃ to the cusp the 12th H. by dir.; the transits of ♄ over the places of the ☉, ☽, and planets in the radical map, or thru the Asc., M.C., 6th or 12th houses; ♀ affl. at B., weak and ill-dignified; ♀ □ or 8 ☽, worry, anxiety and mental strain; 2nd Dec. of ♉ on Asc.; 3rd Dec. ♉ on Asc., an anxious and restless life; 3rd Dec. ♒ denotes; Asc. to the □ or 8 ☽ by dir. (See Anguish, Cares; "Anxiety" under Children; Digestion, Fears; "Irregular" under Functions; Hypochondria, Responsibility, Restless, Sorrow, Stomach, Strange, Worry).

AORTA—The main Arterial Trunk—Ruled by the ♌ Sign.

Aneurysm Of—(See Aneurysm).

Aortic Disease—Planets affl. in ♌, and espec. ♃ or ♀, as ♃ rules the arterial circulation, and ♀ the venous blood; ♅ in ♌, and affl. by ♄ or ♂, tends to spasmodic gushing of the blood thru the aorta; also caused by Subs. at HP, the Heart Place. (See Arteries, Blood, Circulation, Heart, Vertebrae, Vessels).

Aortic Plexus—(See Hypogastrium).

APATHY—A Want of Passion or Feeling—Indifference—(See Cohabitation, Dull, Feelings, Indifference, Inertia, Lassitude, Lethargy; "Free from Passion" under Passion; Rouse, Weak).

APHASIA—Loss of Speech—(See "Aphasia" under Speech).

APHETA—Giver of Life—Prorogator—(See Hyleg).

Aphetic Processes—(See Nutrition).

APHONIA—Loss of Voice due to a peripheral lesion. (See "Aphonia" under Vocal).

APHRODISIACS—Remedies which increase passion and sex desire. A therapeutic property of ♂ and ♂ remedies. Cantharides, a ♂ drug, is the principal drug used for this purpose. Also Love Potions, ruled by ♀, are used for this purpose. (See Anaphrodisiac).

APHTHAE—An Eruption—Thrush—Roundish pearl-colored flakes or specks on the lips, in the mouth, or in the gastro-intestinal tract—Small, white Ulcerous patches—

Mouth—Aphthae In—Thrush—Aphthous Stomatitis—Canker—Sore

Mouth—The ☽ or ♀ affl. in ♉; afflictions in ♋, and due to indigestion; ♂ affl. in ♎. Also occurs in adults as a result of general weakness, and a run down condition of the system; Subs at MCP, SP. (See Debility, Gangrene, "General Ill-Health" under Health; Indigestion, Mouth, Thrush, Ulcers, Vertebrae). Aphthae of the Intestines may occur when there are Subs at KP, and PP, 2nd Lumbar. Aphthae of the Rectum occurs when there are Subs at KP, and LPP, the 4th and 5th Lumbar. Look up these centers under Vertebrae.

APIOL—Parsley—Petroselinum—A typical drug of ☿. An Antiperiodic.

APOLOGETIC ATTITUDE—(See "Inferiority Complex" under Inferiority).

APOPLEXY—Apoplexies—The rupture of a blood vessel, or the oozing of blood into a part without rupture of the blood vessel. Is principally of two kinds, Cerebral and Pulmonary, but may also occur in the Spinal Cord, and also in the Spleen, in the Splenic substance.

Causes—The bad aspects of ♃, and high blood pressure, are the principal causes, and may also be the result of gluttony, gormandizing, causing plethora, and too much blood; a ♃ disease; ♃ affl. in ♉, ♌, ♏, or ♒; the ☉ in ♈ and ☌ or any asp. ♂, and afflicted by malefics; the ☉ affl. by ♃; ☉ affl. in ♉; the ☽ hyleg, and to the ☌ or ill-asps. ♄ by dir.; a ☽ disease; the ☽ afflicted at B., or by dir., by ♃ and the malefics; ♅ rising, or afflicting the Asc.; a ♄ disease; ♄ ☌ or ill-asp. the ☽ or ♃ at B., or by dir.; ♂ ☌ or ill-asp. ♃ at B., or by dir; ♂ in ♈ in the 6th H., and afflicted; ☿ at B. in P. Dec. ♄ and ♂, and in ☐ the ☽ from the 1st or 7th H.; an ♈ and ♉ disease; ♈ or ♉ on the Asc. at B., and afflicted; associated with the 16° and 24° ♉. (See Aneurysm, Plethora, Pressure, Rupture, Vessels).

Cerebral Apoplexy—An ♈ disease when the ☉, ☽, ♃, and the malefics are in ♈ at B., and afflicted; the ☉ to the ☌ or ill-asp. ♂ by dir.; the ☉ in ill-asp. ♃ at B., and by dir.; the ☽ hyleg, and to the ☌ or ill-asp. ♄ by dir.; the Prog. ☽ to the ☐ or ♉ the radical ♃; caused by ♃ when the dominion of death is vested in him; ♃ affl. in ♈; ♃ affl. in ♌ or ♒; ♂ afflicting the hyleg at B.; ☿ ☐ ☽ from the 1st or 7th houses, and ☿ at the same time afflicted by both ♄ and ♂ by ☐ or ♉; the Asc. to the place of Regulus. (See Cerebral, "Rush of Blood to Head" under Head).

Death by Apoplexy—♃ shows; ♃ much afflicted at B., and affl. the hyleg by dir.; ♃ ☌ ☉ in ♈, and affl. the hyleg; the ☉ affl. at B., and in ☐ or ♉ the ☽ or Asc., whichever may be hyleg, and the hyleg afflicted at the same time with a train of fatal directions. Case—See "Inquest on Birthday", No. 792 in 1001 N.N.

Pulmonary Apoplexy—♃ affl. in ♊ or ♐. (See Hemorrhage, Lungs).

APOTHECARY—(See Chemists).

APPARITIONS—(See Phenomena, Psychic).

APPEARANCE—The Physical and Personal Appearance—The Form and Figure—The Physical Appearance is denoted by the 1st H., and the sign upon the Asc., the Decanate rising, together with the sign occupied by the ruler of the rising sign. (See Decanates). Lilly judges the appearance from the sign ascending on the Asc., and the two signs containing the lord of the Asc., and the sign the ☽ is in, and by mixing these influences judiciously takes the greater number of testimonies. He also takes the sign descending as playing an important part. The appearance is judged by the lord of the Asc., planets in or near the Asc., planets rising, and by the positions of the ☉ and ☽, and their aspects. Planets which aspect the Asc. influence both mind and body, and tend to modify the influence of any sign, or planets in signs. When the latter part of a sign is upon the Asc., and a large part of the next sign in the Asc., and party will partake of both signs, and both will tend to influence the appearance and shape of the body. For example, a person having the latter part of ♐ upon the Asc. may have a handsome forehead, and a fine head of hair, but with ♑ also largely in the Asc. the rest of the face, and the lower part, the chin and jaw, may be very ugly. In the case of Twins, one being born with the last degrees of ♐ on the Asc. may be tall, and largely of the ♐ nature and appearance, while the second twin, born a little later, having ♑ rising, would tend to be shorter, and perhaps more sickly than the first one, and also more ugly and crooked in appearance. The subject of appearance, and the form and stature of the body, are further considered under the following subjects, which see in the alphabetical arrangement,—(1) See subjects naming the parts of the body, as Chin, Dimples, Head, Hair, Eyes, Ears, Face, Lips, Mouth, Neck, Nose, Teeth, Shoulders, etc., and on down to the feet. (2) See such subjects as Active, Animal, Aspect, Attractive, Awkward, Beautiful, Big, Blemishes, Bodily, Body, Broad, Careless, Cheerful, Color, Commanding, Commonplace, Complexion, Constitution, Consumptive, Corpulent, Countenance, Crooked, Defects, Deformities, Distorted, Dress, Dull, Dwarf, Effeminate, Erect, Expression, Extremities, Fair, Fat, Features, Feeble, Fierce, Fiery, Filthy, Flabby, Fleshy Form, Fowls, Fragile, Freckles, Full, Gait, Genteel, Giants, Good, Graceful, Grave, Great, Growth, Handsome, Harmonious, Healthy, Heavy, Height, Idiots, Ill-formed, Impairments, Imperfections, Indifferent, Infirm, Inhuman, Intellectual, Jerky, Lante, Large, Lean, Light, Limbs, Limp, Long, Look, Lumpish, Maimed, Malformed, Manner, Map, Marks, Meagre, Mean, Medium, Melancholic, Members, Middle, Misshaped, Moles, Monsters, Moping, Muscular, Mutilated, Narrow, Natural, Neat, Negro, Nervous, Normal, Obesity, Ordinary, Pale, Parts of the Body, Pensive, Personal, Physical, Pimpled, Pleasant, Plump, Pockmarked, Posture, Prepossessing (see Commanding); Prominent, Protruding, Proud, Puffing, Race, Raw, Red, Rigid, Robust, Ruddy, Rugged, Sad, Savage, Scars, Serious, Shaggy, Shape, Shiny, Short, Sickly, Size, Skeleton, Skin, Slender, Small, Smart, Smiles, Smooth, Soft, Spare, Spotted, Squab, Stature, Stiff, Stooping, Stout, Straight, Strength, Strong, Sturdy, Sunken, Swarthy, Tall, Tan, Temperament, Thick, Thin, Thoughtful, Troubled, Ugly, Uncleanly, Undersized, Undeveloped, Ungainly, Unhealthy, Unrefined, Untidy, Upright, Visage, Vulgar, Walk, Wanton, Weak, Weight, Well, White, Wide, Withered, Wrinkled, Youthful-looking, etc. There are also a class of diseases which affect the appearance, as Anaemia, Emaciation, Enlargements, Jaundice, Sores, Tumors, Ulcers, Wasting, etc. If the subject you have in mind is not listed here, look for it in the alphabetical arrangement, as these subjects mentioned are only suggestive, and to help the student to locate subjects which might be overlooked. The subject of Appearance is largely considered, and with references, under "Body", "Complexion", "Face", "Hair", and "Stature".

APPENDIX—Appendix Vermiformis— The Appendix is under the internal rule of the ♏ Sign, and is also influenced by the ♍ Sign. Some Writers say ♅ rules the Appendix. Another modern Writer says it is his opinion that ♆ rules the Appendix, and that disturbances of this organ are closely associated with Psychic, Spiritual, and Astral causes.

Appendicitis—Diseases of the Appendix—Inflamed Appendix, etc.—Afflictions in ♍ and ♏, and espec. ♂ affl. in these signs; a ♍ and ♏ disease; the ☉ affl. in ♏; ♅ is a common afflictor in this disease, and with ♅ affl. in ♍ or ♏; ♆ affl. in ♍ or ♏, and espec. with ♆ in the 6th H.; a ♆ disease; ♄ or ♂ in ♍ or ♏, and afflicted; afflictions in or to the 18° ♏; afflictions in the first three degrees, and in the 22° of the common signs; afflictions in or to the 22° of ♌ or ♒; caused by Subs at CP, KP, UPP, and PP. (See Abdomen, Bowels, Vertebrae).

Death by Appendicitis—♂ in ♍ or ♏ in the 6th H., affl. the hyleg, and ♂ holding the dominion of death. Case of Death by Appendicitis—See "Perhouse", No. 301, in 1001 N.N.

Left Side—Case of the Appendix and Caecum on the Left Side—See "Heart", No. 981, in 1001 N.N.

Operations—Do not operate upon, or remove the Appendix when the ☽ is passing thru ♍, ♎, or ♏, as increased inflammation of the surrounding tissues, infections, or death, are apt to result. (See Caecum, "Inflammation" under Bowels).

APPETITE—Appetites—The Animal Appetites—Desire for Food—Sexual Appetites—Lust, etc. The ♉ and ♋ Signs have close relationship to the appetite for food, and also the planets ♃ and ♀, and these signs and

planets when afflicted tend to abuses in eating. The sexual appetites are dominated largely by the lower vibrations of ♂, ♅, and ♆, and the afflictions of these planets to ♀. The following subjects have to do with Appetite, the Appetites, and the Desires of the physical body, and of the Lower Mind, which subjects see in the alphabetical arrangement when not considered here.

Abnormal Appetite—♄, ♃, or ♂ affl. in ♋; afflictions in ♉ and ♋; ♂ affl. in ♉. (See Abnormal, Eating, Excesses, Food, Gluttony, Obesity, etc.).

Amorous; Animal Appetites—(See Animal, Eating, Food, Gluttony, Lust, Passion, etc.).

Anorexia—(See "Loss of" in this section).

Bad Appetite—(See "Loss of" in this section).

Belly—Love Their Belly—(See Eating, Epicureans, Feasting, Food, Gluttony).

Big Appetite—(See "Excesses" under Eating and Food. Also see Gluttony).

Blood—Blood Corrupted from Overindulgence of Appetites—(See Impure).

Capricious Appetite—(See "Appetite" under Peculiar).

Chaotic—(See Chaotic, "Sensuous" under Sensuality; Unnatural).

Conviviality—(See Feasting).

Cravings; Death—From Excesses in Eating—(See Eating).

Delicate Appetite—♀ in the 6th H.

Depraved Appetites—(See Depraved).

Desire; Diet—(See Diet, Eating, Food).

Drink; Drugs—(See Narcotics).

Eating; Epicureans; Excesses; Extravagance; Fantastic Appetites—(See Peculiar).

Feasting; Food; Free Living—(See Free).

Gluttony; Gormandizing—(See Gluttony).

Gratification—Of Appetites—(See References under Gratification).

Gustativeness Large—(See "Abnormal" in this section. Also see Epicureans, Feasting, Gluttony).

Habits; Hearty Eater—(See Eating, Gluttony).

High Living—(See Free, High, Riotous).

Hunger—(See Cravings, Food)

Illicit Appetites—(See Chaotic, Drink, Drunkenness, Love Affairs, Lust, Narcotics, Perversions, Sensuous, Sex).

Illusory Appetites—(See "Appetites" under Peculiar).

Immoderate—(See Drink, Eating, Excesses, Gluttony, Lewd, Lust, Passion, Sensuous, etc.)

Indisposition—From Excessive Appetite—(See "Sickness from Over-eating" under Eating).

Indulgences; Inherent—Inherent Abnormal Appetite—Goes to Extremes in Eating—(See "Extremes" under Eating).

Large Appetite—(See "Gustativeness", and other paragraphs in this section).

Lascivious; Lewd, Licentious; Longings—(See Cravings).

Loss of Appetite—Anorexia—Bad Appetite—No Appetite—The ☽ in ♋ ♌ or evil asp. ♄, or a malefic; the ☽, ♌, and affl. by ♄ or ♂; ♄ affl. in ♋; ♀ affl. in the 6th H., a delicate appetite; Subs at SP. Orange, the color, ruled by the ☉, tends to sharpen the appetite, and rooms so papered or decorated with orange colors are good for people with little appetite.

Lower Nature—(See "Nature" under Lower).

Lust; Luxuries; Malacia—(See "Appetite" under Depraved).

Narcotics; No Appetite—(See "Loss of" in this section).

Obesity; Opiates—(See Narcotics).

Orange Color—Sharpens the Appetite —(See "Loss of" in this section).

Overeating—Sickness from Overeating—(See "Sickness" under Eating; "Excesses" under Food; Feasting; Gluttony; Impure; Obesity; Plethora, Surfeits, etc).

Over-Indulgence—Of the Appetites— (See "Overeating" in this section. Also see Amorous, Excesses, Indulgences, "Passional Excesses", and "Too Much Passion" under Passion; Sex Diseases; Venery, etc).

Passion—Excessive Passional Appetites—(See Excesses, Lewd, Lust, Passion, Sex, Venery, etc).

Peculiar Appetites—(See Peculiar).

Perversions; Pleasure; Plethora; Poor Appetite—(See "Delicate", "Loss of" in this section).

Prodigal; Ravenous Appetite—(See "Big Appetite" in this section).

Riotous Living—(See Riotous)

Sensuous Appetites—(See Lust, Sensuality).

Sex Excesses—(See Amorous, Lewd, Lust, "Passional Excesses" under Passion; "Sex Excesses" under Sex; Venery, etc.)

Sexual Appetites—Are ruled by ♌, ♏, 5th H., ♂ and ♀. (See Love Affairs, Lust, Passion, Sex, Venery).

Sharpened Appetite—(See "Loss of" in this section).

Sickness—From Overeating—(See "Sickness" under Eating).

Surfeits; Sybarites—(See Epicureans).

Tastes; Unnatural Appetites—(See Unnatural).

Venery; Voracious Appetite—An Insatiable Appetite—(See Gluttony, Voracious).

Whimsical Appetite—(See Peculiar).

Wine; Women—(See "Addicted to" under Men. Also see the various paragraphs under Women).

APPLICATIONS—
Stimulant Applications—A therapeutic property of ♂. In deficiency of circulation in a part, ♂ remedies are demanded to offset the work of ♄. (See "Deficiency" under Circulation. Also see Caustic, Rubefacient, Stimulant, Tonic, Vesicant).

AQUARIUS—The Aquarius Sign (♒). The eleventh Sign of the Zodiac, and affiliated with the 11th H. Ruled by ♅ and ♄. This Sign is classed as an airy, diurnal, fixed, fortunate, fruitful (more fruitful than barren), hot, human, masculine, mental, moist, nervous, obeying, rational, sanguine, southern, speaking, strong, sweet (a sweet disposition), vital, western, whole, wintry, etc. The Sign gives a humane and spiritual nature, when well-aspected and occupied, and when on the Asc. at B., tends to give a strong and beautiful body, with good vitality. This Sign has close affinity with the sense of Sight, as ♒ corresponds to the etheric vibrations. It is also closely associated with the blood, its composition, circulation and distribution in the tissues, and afflictions in ♒ tend to great disturbances in the circulation, and to impure blood. The pathological action of ♒ tends to gloom, nervousness, and supersensitiveness, and being a fixed sign, to make disease more enduring, and the mind and habits more fixed and set. The planet ♅ is strong in this sign, and ♒ is considered the most spiritual sign, the Sign of "The Son of Man", symbolized by the Water Pourer, pouring out blessings and alleviation upon Humanity. Some great characters have been born with the ☉ in this sign, such as Abraham Lincoln, Thomas Edison, and others of note, who have proven great Benefactors of Humanity. The Color ruled by ♒ is sky blue.

AQUARIUS RULES—Each sign has an external, internal and structural rulership. Externally the ♒ Sign rules the calves and ankles. Internally, rules the circulation, the breath, and the eyesight. Structurally rules the bones of the lower limbs, as the Tibia, Fibula, Astragalus, bones of the Ankles. As a general classification, the ♒ Sign rules the following things, which subjects see in the alphabetical arrangement,—Achilles Tendon; Ankles; Arsenicum Album (see Arsenic); Astragalus; Blood; Breath; Calves; Circulation of the Blood (see Circulation); Color,—Sky Blue; Composition of the Blood; Eyesight (see Sight); Fibula; Heart, by reflex action to ♌; Internal Saphenous Vein; Legs from Knees to Ankles; Lower Limbs; Lymph; Nations (see Nations); Shanks; Shin Bone; Sky Blue Color; Teeth; Tendo Achilles; Tibia; Vein,— Internal Saphenous Vein; Vision (see Sight).

AQUARIUS DISEASES—The Diseases and Afflictions of the ♒ Sign—See the following subjects in the alphabetical arrangement,—

Accidents—Hurts—Injuries—(See these subjects under Ankles, Calves, Legs).

Aches—In the Legs—(See "Aches" under Legs).

Anaemia; Ankles—Diseases In—Fractures—Swellings—(See Ankles).

Atmospheric Pressure—Disease from working under Increased Air Pressure —(See Caisson).

Blindness; Blood Disorders—Blood Poisoning—(See Blood, Impure, "Blood Poisoning" under Poison).

Bowels—Wind In—Wind Colic—(See "Wind" under Bowels).

Broken Ankles—(See Ankles. Also see Tibia, Fibula, "Fractures" under Legs).

Bruises—To Legs—(See "Bruises" under Legs).

Caisson Disease—(See Caisson).

Calves—Disorders and Hurts to—(See Calves).

Circulation—Of the Blood—Disorders of—(See Circulation, Blood, Impure).

Consumption; Contractions—In Legs, Ankles and Feet—(See Achilles, Contractions, Cramps, "Club Feet" under Feet; "Contractions" under Legs, Spasmodic).

Corrupted Blood—(See Impure).

Cramps—In Bowels, Legs or Feet— (See "Cramps" under Bowels, Legs, Feet).

Crawling Sensations—Over the Body —Creeping Sensations—(See Paraesthesia).

Cutaneous Diseases—(See Skin).

Disease Threatened—(See "Threatened" under Disease).

Disgrace; Dropsy—Of the Heart, Limbs, Legs, Ankles, and General— (See Dropsy. Also see "Dropsy" under Heart, Legs, Feet, and "Swellings" under Ankles).

Extraordinary Diseases—And Accidents—Caused by ♅, a strong ruler of the ♒ sign. (See "Extraordinary" under Accidents, Disease. Also see Peculiar).

Eye Diseases—(See Blindness, Eyes, Nebulae, Sight, Urn of Aquarius).

Foul Blood—(See Impure).

Fractures—Of Legs and Ankles—(See "Broken" in this section).

Gloom, Gout, Heart Disorders—Heart Dropsy—Heart Irregularities—Heart Weakness, etc.—(See Heart).

Hurts—To Legs and Ankles—(See "Accidents" in this section).

Hyperaesthesia; Impure Blood—(See Impure).

Injuries—(See Legs, Calves, Ankles).

Irregularities—(See "Irregular" under Heart. Also see Spasmodic).

Lameness—(See "Lameness" under Legs, Ankles, Feet).

Legs—Aches In—Fractures, Infirmities, Swellings—(See Legs).

Nervous Diseases—Nervousness—(See Nerves).

Peculiar Diseases—(See Extraordinary, Mysterious, Peculiar, Uncommon).

Rheumatism; Ruin; Sensations—(See Paraesthesia, Sensations).

Sickness—(See Blood Disorders, Disease, Ill-Health, Nervousness, Sickness).

Sight—Disorders of—(See Blindness, Eyes, Sight).

Skin Diseases—Causes extreme sensitiveness of the skin when the nerves are weakened and impaired. (See Skin).

Spasmodic Diseases—(See Spasmodic).

Sprains—(See "Sprains" under Legs, Ankles).

Supersensitiveness—(See Hyperaesthesia, Sensitive).

Swellings—(See "Swelling" under Legs, Ankles, Feet).

Teeth—Disorders of—(See Teeth).

Tendo Achilles—Disorders of—(See Achilles; "Club Feet" under Feet).

Ulcers—(See "Ulcers" under Legs. Also see Varicose).

Uncommon Diseases—(See Uncommon, Peculiar, Extraordinary).

Varicose Veins—(See Varicose).

Windy Disorders—Wind in Bowels— (See Wind). See "Airy Signs" under Air; "Fixed Signs" under Fixed.

AQUEOUS—

Aqueous Humor—(See Eyes).

Aqueous Tumor—(See "Aqueous" under Tumors).

Aqueous Vapors—Condensation of— (See Rain).

ARBOR VITAE—Of the Cerebellum. Ruled by ☽. (See Cerebellum).

ARCTURUS—Bootes—Star in the 5th face of ♎. The ☽ to the place of by dir. favors good health. The Asc. to place of tends to melancholy and timidity. (See Anxiety, Calamities, Melancholy, Suffocation).

AREOLAR—(See "Areolar" under Tissues).

ARGENTUM—(See Silver).

ARGO—A Southern Constellation resembling a ship. Malefic planets passing thru this Constellation tend to shipwreck, calamities at Sea, and much loss of life. (See Shipwreck).

ARGUMENTATIVE—(See Religion).

ARGYLL-ROBERTSON PUPIL—A failure of the pupil of the eye to respond to light. A symptom of Locomotor Ataxia. (See Locomotor Ataxia; "Mydriasis" under Iris).

ARIES—The Aries Sign—(♈). The first Sign of the Zodiac, ruled by ♂, and affiliated with the 1st H. Each year when the ☉ passes into ♈ is known as the Vernal Equinox. (See Equinoxes, Vernal). The ♈ Sign is known as a barren, bitter, cardinal, choleric, commanding, diurnal, dry, eastern, equinoctial, fiery, fortunate, four-footed, hoarse, hot, hurtful, inflammatory, luxuriant, masculine, mental, movable, northern, violent sign, etc. It is the day sign of ♂, the exaltation of the ☉, and the fall of ♄. (See Cardinal; "Fire Signs" under Fire). This sign gives much force, energy, and vitality when upon the Asc. at B. It is known as the

"Cerebral Pole of Paracelsus." The Sympathetic Nervous System begins with this sign, and ends with the other ♂ Sign ♏, which latter sign is known as the "Genital Pole of Paracelsus". (See Scorpio, Sympathetic). The Form of the Body given by ♈ when on the Asc. tends to be dry, spare, moderately sized, strong, red or sandy hair, a piercing eye, and a swarthy or sallow complexion. The Symbol of this sign is the Ram. The Colors ruled by ♈ are white and red, or red and white mixed. For Countries ruled by ♈, see Nations.

ARIES RULES—Some parts of the head are ruled by the ♉ and ♏ signs, but the head, taken as a whole, is ruled by the ♈ Sign. Also ♈ exerts an internal, external, and structural rulership over various parts of the head, and these will be mentioned in this section. The head is a very complicated part of the body, due to its many parts and organs, and all of the planets have a special rule over the different parts and organs of the head. The Cerebellum, base of the brain, the chin, lower lip, lower teeth, lower jaw, eustachian tubes, and the inner parts of the ears, are ruled by the ♉ sign. The right ear is ruled by ♄, and the left ear by ♂. The nose and nasal bones are ruled by ♏. The ☉ rules the right eye in a male and the left eye in a female. The ☽ rules the right eye in a female, and the ☉ the left eye in the male. The Pineal Gland, optic nerve, and the conjunctiva, are ruled by ♆. The Pituitary Body, Dura Mater, and the membranes of the brain are ruled by ♅. The skull, teeth, and skin of the head and face are ruled by ♄. The arteries, blood, and blood vessels of the head are ruled by ♃. The nose, forehead, and muscles of the head, are ruled by ♂. The complexion, cheeks, chin and upper lip, are ruled by ♀. The cerebral nerves, mouth, tongue, lower lip, and the hair, are ruled by ☿. Externally ♈ rules the head, face, nose, ears, eyes, and mouth. Internally ♈ rules the brain and nerve centers. Structurally ♈ rules the cranium and facial bones.

Alphabetical Arrangement—Of the Rulerships of ♈. See these subjects in the alphabetical arrangement,— Aconite Napellus (see Aconite); Arteries of the Head and Brain (these are especially ruled and affected by ♃ in ♈); Blood Vessels of the Brain; Bones of the Face, Skull, and Cranium, except those of the Ears and Nose; Carotid Arteries (the Internal Carotid); Cerebral Hemispheres—Cerebro-Spinal System—Cerebral Nerves, (which are especially ruled and affected by ☿ in ♈); Cheeks (ruled and affected by ♀ in ♈); Chin (ruled by ♀ in ♈); Colors—White and Red, and White and Red mixed; Complexion (ruled and affected by ♀ in ♈); Conjunctiva of the Eyes (ruled and affected by ♆ in ♈); Cranium; Dura Mater; Ears (ruled by both ♈ and ♉. The right ear is ruled by ♄, and the left ear by ♂); Eastern Parts (see Eastern); Encephalon; Externally ♈ rules the head, face, nose, ears, eyes, mouth; Eyes; Face and Facial Bones, except

the bones of the nose, which are ruled by ♏ (the skin of the face is ruled and affected by ♄ in ♈); Forehead (ruled and affected by ♂ in ♈); Hair of the Head and Face, except the hair on the chin, which is ruled by ♉ (☿ in ♈ rules and affects the hair of the head); Head and its Organs, except the Internal Ear and the Nose (♄ in ♈ rules and affects the skin of the head, and ♂ in ♈, the muscles); Internally ♈ rules the brain and nerve centers; Jaw (Upper); Left Ear (ruled by ♂ also); Left Eye (also the ☉ rules the left eye of the female and the ☽ the left eye of the male); Lips (Upper Lip is ruled and affected by ♀ in ♈, and the Lower Lip by ☿ in ♈); Mouth (ruled and affected by ☿ in ♈); Muscles of Head and Face (also ruled and affected by ♂ in ♈); Nations (see Eastern, "Aries" under Nations); Nerves (Cerebral, and which are also ruled and affected by ☿ in ♈); Nose (under the external rule of ♈, and the Nose and Nasal Bones are also ruled by the ♏ sign); Optic Nerve (also ruled and affected by ♆ in ♈); Organs of the Head, except the Internal Ears and Nose; Pineal Gland (also ruled and affected by ♆ in ♈); Pituitary Body (also ruled and affected by ♅ in ♈); Potassium Phosphate (the ♈ Sign Salt); Rams (see Sheep); Red Color (the color of ♂, and also red and white mixed); Right Ear (and also ruled by ♄); Right Eye (☉ rules right eye in males, and the ☽ the right eye in females); Scalp; Sheep; Skin of Head and Face (also ruled and affected by ♄ in ♈); Skull (also ruled and affected by ♄ in ♈); Structurally ♈ rules the Cranium and the Facial Bones; Sympathetic Nervous System (presides to); Teeth (also ♄ in ♈ rules and affects the teeth); Temples; Tongue (also ruled and affected by ☿ in ♈); Upper Lip (and also ruled and affected by ♀ in ♈); White Color (White and Red mixed).

ARIES DISEASES—And Afflictions— The pathological action of ♈ tends to excesses, dryness, heat, inflammation, excess of forcefulness and energy. Being a mental sign, afflictions in ♈ tend to produce mental diseases and afflictions, and disorders of the brain. When afflicted at B., ♈ tends to heat and disturb the system, causing inharmony. The first half of the ♈ Sign gives a stronger constitution than the second half, and also greater muscular development. Comets appearing in ♈ tend to bring sorrow to ♈ people, and Countries ruled by ♈. The health tends to be good for the time for ♈ people, and for Countries ruled by ♈, when the ☉ is lord of the year at the Vernal Equinox, and free from affliction, but the health is bad when the ☉ is afflicted at the Vernal, and when malefics are in ♈ at this time. A classified list of the diseases caused by each of the planets in the 12 Signs of the Zodiac can be found in a number of the standard textbooks of Astrology. The following are the diseases and afflictions caused and ruled by the ♈ Sign, which subjects see in the alphabetical arrangement—

Acne; Alopecia; Anger—Diseases Arising From—(See Anger).

Apoplexy; Astigmatism; Baldness; Blindness; Brain—Disorders of—(See Brain).

Catarrh; Cerebral Disorders; Coma; Complexion—Disorders of—(See Complexion, Cosmetics, Face).

Congestion—Of Brain—(See Brain).

Conjunctivitis; Cosmetics—Disorders from Improper Use of—(See Cosmetics).

Deafness—(See Hearing).

Delirium; Determination of Blood—To the Head—(See "Rush of Blood" under Head).

Dreams; Dryness and Heat—All Diseases Proceeding From—(See Dryness, Heat).

Ear—Polypus of—External Diseases of—(See Ears, Polypus).

Encephalitis—(See "Inflammation" under Brain).

Epilepsy; Epistaxis; Eruptions—On Head, Scalp and Face—(See Acne, Cosmetics, Eruptions, Face, Head, Pimples, Scalp).

Eye Diseases—(See Accommodation, Blindness, Eyes, Optic, Retina, Sight).

Face—Diseases of—(See Face).

Fevers; Fits; Giddiness—(See Fainting, Vertigo).

Glaucoma; Gumboils—(See Gums).

Harelip—(See Lips).

Head—Diseases of—(See Head).

Headaches; Heat—Heat Disturbances in the System—Heat and Dryness, and all Diseases From—(See Dryness, Fevers, Heat).

Humourous Discharges—From Eyes—(See "Humourous" under Eyes).

Hydrocephalus; Inflammations; Inharmony—In the System—Due to Fevers and High Temperatures—(See Fever).

Injuries—To Head and Face—(See Face, Head, Skull).

Insomnia; Kidney Disorders—(See Kidneys).

Measles; Megrims—(See Migraine).

Memory—Loss of—(See Memory).

Mental Disorders—(See Insanity, Mania, Mental, Mind, etc.).

Migraine; Mind—Disorders of—(See Mind).

Mouth—Diseases of—(See Mouth).

Nasal Bones—(See Nose)

Neuralgia—Of Head and Face—(See "Neuralgia" under Face, Head).

Nightmare—(See Dreams, Sleep).

Nose Bleed—(See "Epistaxis" under Nose).

Ophthalmia—(See Conjunctiva).

Palsy; Paralysis—Of Face—(See Face).

Phrenitis—(See "Inflammation" under Brain; Delirium).

Pimples; Polypus—Of Nose, Ear, or Throat—(See Polypus).

Rashes—On Face—(See Acne, "Eruptions" under Face; Pimples, etc.).

Red Face—(See "Red" under Face).

Ringworm.

Rupture—Of Blood Vessel in Brain—(See Apoplexy).

Rush of Blood—To Head—(See "Blood" under Head).

Shingles—(See Herpes).

Smallpox.

Somnambulism—(See Sleep).

Sorrow—To ♈ People—♄ affl. in ♈ at B.; Comets appearing in ♈, and to Countries ruled by ♈; malefics in ♈ in the 12th H. at B. (See Sorrow).

Spasms—Of Facial Muscles—(See "Neuralgia", "Spasmodic" under Face; Tics).

Stomach Disorders—By reflex action to the ♋ sign from ♈, and the cardinal signs—(See Stomach).

Swellings—In Head and Face—(See "Swellings" under Face; "Growths" under Head; Hydrocephalus).

Teeth—Decay and Disorders of—(See Teeth).

Temperature—High Temperature and Fevers—(See Fever).

Throat Troubles—(See "Humours" under Throat).

Tics—Of Face—(See Tics).

Toothache—(See Teeth).

Vertigo; Visions.

ARISTA—A star in the 1st face of ♎, said to be fortunate, and when ascending at B. to give good health, renown, happiness, contentment and success. This star is also known as Spica Virgo, and is of the nature of ♂ and ♀.

ARMPITS—(See Axillae).

ARMS—The arms are ordinarily said to be ruled by ☿, ♊, and the 3rd House. However, there are several divisions to the arms, the upper arms, elbow, forearm, wrists and hands, which correspond to their opposite parts, the thighs, knees, ankles, and feet. Most Authors and Writers assign the one sign ♊ to rulership of all parts of the arms, including the shoulders. The upper arms are under the external rule of ♊. The humerus, opposite to the femur (♐), is under the structural rulership of ♊. (See "Middle Cervical" under Ganglion). The elbow, opposite to the knees (♑), is under the external rulership of ♋. The forearm, consisting of the radius and ulna, opposite to the tibia and fibula (♒), is under the structural rulership of ♌. The wrists, opposite to the ankles (♒), are under the rule of ♌. The hands, opposite to the feet (♓), are under the external rulership of ♍. The nerves of the arms and legs are ruled by ☿; the veins by ♀; the arteries by ♃; the muscles by ♂; the bones and joints of the arms and legs by ♄. The arms, hands, legs and feet should be studied together, as they have many points in common, as opposite signs are complemental and affect each other, and diseases which affect the hands may also affect the feet, or vice versa, etc. The Arm Place in the Spine is the 7th Cervical and 1st Dorsal. (See Vertebrae).

Brachial Plexus—(See Brachial).

Long Arms—Slender Arms—♅ ascending at B.; ☿ ascending at B., and free from the afflictions of other planets; ⚹ gives, or □ on the Asc.; the 3rd or 4th faces of ♎ on the Asc. The ☿ influence especially tends to long arms, hands, fingers, legs and feet. □ on the Asc., when modified by planets rising, may give long arms, but with short and fleshy hands and feet.

Short Arms—The ☽ gives; the ☽ ascending at B.; ♓ influence tends to short and fin-like arms and legs; the 4th and 6th face of ♒ on the Asc.; the ♍ influence tends to brevity of members. (See "Short" under Legs).

DISEASES OF ARMS—Diseases, Infirmities and Afflictions to the Arms— See the following subjects in the alphabetical arrangement when not considered here—

Abscesses In—(See "Arms" under Abscesses).

Accidents To—Cuts, Fractures, Hurts, Injuries, Wounds, etc.—Generally caused by the afflictions of ♄ or ♂, or both, in signs which rule the different parts of the arms, as in □, ♋, ♌, or ♍; afflictions in □ or ♐; the ☽ in □ and afflicted by the ☉ or ♂; ☽ to place of the Pleiades or Praesepe; ♄ ♂ ♂ in the Asc. or M.C., in the latter degrees of □ or ♐; ♂ affl. in □ or ♐; ♂ affl. in ♐ in the 6th or 12th H.; ♂ ♂ the ☉ or ☽ in ♐ in the 6th or 12th H., and affl. by the benefics; ♂ affl. in □, ♍, or ♐, and ♂ or evil asp. the Asc. by dir.; ☿ ill-asp. by ♂; □ on the Asc., and affl. by ♂, or with ♂ in □ in the Asc., espec. tends to fractures and wounds to the arms; malefics and afflictions in the mutable signs, and with such signs on angles, as all the mutable, or common signs, as □, ♍, ♐, ♓, afflict each other, and the parts ruled by such signs. (See "Broken" in this section; "Fractures" under Legs).

Affected—The arms tend to be affected by the ☉ ♎; ☽ ♍; ♄ ♈; ♃ ♒; ♂ □ or ♑; ♀ ♐; ☿ ♌ or ♏. (See Table 196 in Simmonite's Arcana).

All Diseases In—Are signified by the 3rd H., the □ Sign, the planet ☿ and its afflictions, and also afflictions in the mutable signs and cadent houses; planets afflicted in □, or the opposite sign ♐, tend to the greatest number of diseases and afflictions to the arms, as listed in the textbooks of Astrology. Many of the influences which tend to afflict the arms also afflict the lungs, bowels, hips, thighs and feet, parts ruled by the common signs. Subs at LCP, the 6th and 7th Cervicals, and at AP, the 1st Dorsal, and at HP, the 2nd Dorsal vertebra, tend to various disorders of the arms, hands and shoulders. (See Vertebrae. Also note the various subjects in this section).

Aneurysm; Ankylosis; Armless Wonder—Case—(See "Armless Wonder", Case No. 054, in 1001 N.N. Also see "Missing" in this section).

Armpit—Tenderness In—(See Axillae).

Arthritis Deformans—In the Arms— (See Arthritis, Joints).

Atrophy of Arms—Caused by ♄, and with ♄ afflicted in signs which rule the arms; caused by Subs at LCP, the 6th Cervical, and at AP, 1st Dorsal, the Arm Place. (See Atrophy, Vertebrae).

Axillae—Tenderness In—(See Axillae).

Blood In Arms—Disordered—Impurities of—The ☉ in signs which rule the arms governs the blood in these parts, and tends to blood poisoning and blood impurities. Also ♃ in these signs tends to blood disorders in these parts.

Bones of Arm—Enlargement of Radius—Osteitis of Radius—Outgrowth of Bone (Exostosis)—The ♂ influence tends to enlargements, inflammation, and ♂ in the signs which rule the arms. The deposits of ♄ tend to enlarged parts of the bone, and outgrowth, as in ankylosis, while ♂ tends to enlargement thru heat, inflammation, etc. The ♆ influence also tends to enlargements. Also caused by Subs at LCP, the 6th Cervical, and at AP. (See Bones, Enlargement, Inflammation, Radius, Exostosis).

Broken Arms—(See "Accidents in this section). Cases—See "Broken Arm", No. 140, 141, 142, 157, in 1001 N.N. Also see Case mentioned in Daath's Medical Astrology, Chap. 13, page 97. See Fig. 22 in "Message of the Stars" by the Heindels.

Burns—Arms Contracted By—Case— See "Extraordinary Accident", No. 192, in 1001 N.N.

Carpus—Carpal Bones—(See Wrists).

Circulation—The Circulation Obstructed in the Arms and Legs—♅ ♂ ♂ in □, and ☌ ♃ in ♐, and also afflicted by □ asps. from ♍ and ♓; ♄ ♂ ♃ in □ or ♐, or in ☌ from these signs; the ♄ influence tends to obstructions in the circulation when in ♂ or ill-asps. the rulers of the circulation, ♃ and ♀; ♄ and planets in common signs. (See "Circulation" under Legs. Also see Circulation).

Clavicle—Afflictions to—(See Clavicle).

Clonic Spasm—(See "Myoclonia" in this section).

Contractions—♅ or ♄ in signs which rule the arms. (See Burns, Cramps, in this section. Also see Contractions, Spasmodic).

Cramps In—♅ afflicted in □, and signs which rule the arms. Caused by Subs at HP, the 2nd Dorsal. (See Cramps, Vertebrae).

Cuts To—(See "Accidents" in this section).

Cysts—(See Aneurysm).

Deformities—Common signs on the Asc., and containing the malefics, and espec. ♅ or ♂, and these planets in ♂ or evil asp. to each other. (See Armless, Arthritis, Missing, in this section. Also see Deformities).

Diseases Of—Infirmities In—□ signifies all diseases and infirmities in the arms, hands and shoulders, and accidents to these parts; afflictions in signs which rule the various parts of the arms, as in ♊, ♋, ♌, ♍, and also with any of these signs on the Asc. at B., and afflicted by malefics; ♄ or ♂ affl. in ♊; ♄ in ♓; the ☉ affl. in ♊, ♎, or ♐; the ☽ affl. in ♊, ♌, ♍, or ♐; ♃ affl. in ♐, ♑, or ♒; ♂ affl. in ♊, ♐, or ♈; ♀ affl. in ♊, ♋, or ♐; ☿ affl. in ♌ or ♏. Also caused by Subs at LCP, the 6th Cervical, and at AP. (See Cardia, Vertebrae).

Dislocations—♄ influence; ♄ affl. in ♊, ♋, ♌, or ♍, and in the part ruled by the Sign. (See Dislocations).

Elbows—Disorders of—Injuries To—(See Elbows).

Elephantiasis; Enlargements—(See "Bones" in this section. Also see Enlargements).

Eruptions—♂ affl. in ♊ in the 6th H., and in signs which rule the different parts of the arms; ♀ affl. in signs which rule the arms, due to wrong living. (See Eruptions).

Erysipelas—Of the Upper Arm—(See Erysipelas).

Exostosis—Abnormal Outgrowth of Bone—(See "Bones" in this section).

Extremities; Fingers—Disorders of—(See Fingers).

Forearm—Fracture of—Missing—(See Forearm. Also see Armless, Missing, in this section).

Four Arms—(See "Four" under Hands).

Fractures—(See Accidents, Broken, in this section. Also see Fingers, Fractures, Hands, Humerus, Radius, Ulna, Wrists).

Frog Child—Right Forearm Missing—(See Forearm).

Glands Of—Ruled by ♆ when this planet is in signs which rule the arms, and ♆ afflicted in these signs tends to disorders of. (See Aneurysm).

Gout—(See "Arms" under Gout).

Hands—Disorders and Afflictions to—(See Hands).

Humerus—Fracture of—(See Humerus).

Hurts—(See Accidents, Broken, Fractures, in this section).

Infirmities—(See "Diseases" in this section).

Injuries To—(See Accidents, Broken, Fractures, in this section).

Lameness In—(See Ankylosis; "Arms" under Fractures, Gout, Paralysis. Also see "Broken", "Deformities", and other paragraphs in this section).

Left Arm—Fracture of Radius Of—(See Radius).

Limbs; Lower Arm—(See Forearm).

Marks On—(See Marks).

Metacarpal Bones—(See Hands).

Missing—Both Arms Missing—(See "Armless", "Forearm", "Frog Child", in this section. Also see Malformations, Members, Missing, Prenatal Epoch).

Moles on Arms—Malefics in the 3rd H. (See Moles).

Motor Nerves—Afflicted—♅ in signs ruling the arms. (See Motor).

Movement—Of the Arms—Inability to Move Arms—♄ afflicted in ♊. Also caused by Subs at LCP, the 6th Cervical, and at AP. (See "Arms" under Gout; "Paralysis" in this section. Also see Vertebrae).

Muscles—Of Arms—Disorders of—♄ affl. in ♊. Subs at AP. (See Gout, Movement, Paralysis, Rheumatism, in this section).

Myoclonia—Of Upper Arm—♅ afflicted in ♊. (See Myoclonia; "Clonic" under Spasmodic).

Neuralgia In—☿ affl. in signs which rule the arms. (See Neuralgia).

Numbness In—(See Numbness).

Osteitis—(See "Bones" in this section).

Outgrowth of Bone—(See "Bones" in this section).

Paralysis—♅ and ☿ affl. in signs which rule the arms. (See Motor, Paralysis). Case—(See "Tunison", No. 113, in 1001 N.N.

Pains In—♂ affl. in ♊, and signs which rule the arms; the ☉ affl. in ♎; ☽ to the Bull's Horns in 5th face of ♊, of the nature of ♂; ☿ affl. in ♊, nerve pains in the arms and shoulders; ☿ affl. in ♏ tends to flying, or running pains in the arms and shoulders when ☿ is the afflictor in the disease. (See Pains).

Radius—Disorders, and Fracture of—(See Radius).

Rheumatism In—Muscular Rheumatism—Rheumatic Pains in the Arms or Shoulders—The ☉ in ♎, and ♂ or ill-asp. any of the malefics as Promittors; the ☽ affl. in ♊; ♄ ♊, occi. of the ☽, and ori. of the ☉, and affl. the ☉, ☽, or Asc.; ☿ affl. in ♏. Caused by Subs at LCP and AP. (See "Arms" under Gout; "Disease" under Extremities; Rheumatism, Vertebrae).

Right Forearm Missing—(See Forearm).

Running Pains—(See "Pains" in this section).

Scar—Malefics in 3rd H., a scar or mole on arms. (See Moles, Scars).

Shoulders—The shoulders and arms are afflicted by influences in ♊. (See Shoulders).

Skin Diseases—Of Arms—(See "Eruptions" in this section. Also see "Arms" under Skin).

Spasm—Of Muscles—(See "Myoclonia" in this section).

Swellings—(See "Arms" under Swellings).

Tenderness—In Armpits—(See Axillae)

Ulcers—(See Aneurysm; "Arms" under Ulcers).

Ulna—Fracture of—(See Ulna).

Upper Arm—Disorders In—Fracture—Afflictions in ♊ tend to disorders of the upper arm; afflictions in ♋ and ♌, in the elbow and middle arm, and afflictions in ♌ and ♍ to the lower arm, as the wrists and hands. (See

"Upper Arm" under Erysipelas; Humerus, Myoclonia).

Varicose Veins—In Arms—(See Aneurysm, Varicose).

Verruca—(See Warts).

Vesicles—(See Aneurysm, Vesicles).

Wandering Gout—(See "Arms" under Gout).

Warts—(See Warts).

Wasting—Of the Arms—(See "Arms" under Wasting).

Weakness In—The ☽ affl. in ♊, ♍, or ♐; ♄ affl. in ♊.

Wounds To—♂ affl. in signs which rule the arms; ☽ to the place of the Pleiades or Praesepe. (See "Accidents" in this section).

Wrists—Fracture and Disorders of—(See Wrists).

ARMY AND NAVY—Dangers In—Injuries, Wounds or Death In—(See Maritime, Military, Sailors, Ships, Soldiers, War).

ARNICA—A typical drug of ♂. (See "Typical" under Mars; Stimulants).

ARRESTED—Stoppage—Hindered—

Arrested Emotions—(See Emotions).

Arrested Functions—(See "Ablation", "Suppression" under Functions).

Arrested Growth—(See Deformities, Dwarf, Growth).

Arrested Mental Powers—This condition is also associated with retarded, or arrested physical growth. Also the vitality is generally reduced, and the recuperative powers may be low. (See Backwardness, "Arrested" under Mental; Recuperation, Vitality, "Weak Body" under Weak). Case—See "Never Grew Up", No. 720 in 1001 N.N.

ARROW HEAD—Of ♐. Harrow of ♐. (See "Blindness in One Eye" under Blindness. Also see Nebulous).

ARSENIC—Arsenicum Album—One of the 12 typical Polycrest Remedies, corresponding to the ♒ sign. A typical drug of ♂. (See Mucous, "Polycrest" under Zodiac).

ARSON—Tendency to Commit Arson—(See Incendiarism).

ARTERIES—The Arterial System—Ruled by the ☉ and ♃. Also under the internal rulership of the ♐ Sign. The airy signs also have much to do with the blood and circulation, and the ♒ sign especially, with morbid blood conditions. The watery signs also greatly influence the blood. ♃ dominates the arterial blood, and ♀ the venous blood. The ☉ and the ♌ Sign, and the opposite sign ♒, have much to do with the disturbances and morbid conditions of the arteries. ♃ in ♈ especially affects the arteries of the head; ♃ ♉ rules the arteries of the neck and throat; ♃ in ♊, □, and ♋ rules and affects the arteries and veins of the respiratory system; ♃ in ♋ rules the arteries of the stomach; ♃ in ♌ rules and affects the arteries and right ventricle of the heart; ♃ in ♍ rules the arteries of the bowels and abdomen, etc. (See Veins). See the following subjects in the alphabetical arrangement when not considered here—

Aneurysm; Aorta; Arterio-Sclerosis—Hardening of the Arteries—A destructive process, and the work of ♄ by abnormal mineral deposits carried by the blood, and ruled by ♄. Caused by afflictions in ♌ or ♒; ♄ ☌ or ill-asp. ♃, or ♄ ☌ both ♃ and ♀; ♄ ☌ ♃ in the 6th H.; the ☉ in ♌ or ♒; and ☌ or ill-asp. ♄, or ♄ and ♅; caused by Subs at CP, the 5th Dorsal Vertebra, ruled by ♌, and also by Subs at KP, Kidney Place. (See Crystallization, Hardening, Minerals, Vertebrae). Cases of Hardening of the Arteries—See Figures 13B and 18F in the book, "Astro-Diagnosis" by the Heindels.

Arteritis—(See "Inflammation" in this section).

Blood—Disorders of the Arterial Blood—(See "Disorders", and other paragraphs under Blood. Also see Circulation).

Carotid Arteries—(See Carotid).

Circulation—(See "Arterial Circulation" under Circulation).

Dilatation—Of Artery—(See Aneurysm; "High Blood Pressure", and "Too Much Blood", under Blood; Plethora; "Vascular Fullness" under Vascular).

Diseases of Arteries—The excess of mineral deposits laid down by the pathological action of ♄ tend to diseases of the arteries, hardening, crystallization, etc., and impair their elasticity and powers to accommodate the different volumes of the blood stream. The ☉, the ♌ Sign ruled by the ☉, and its opposite sign ♒, have much to do with the disturbances and morbid conditions of the arteries, and also the afflictions of ♄ to ♃. The good asps. of the ☽ and planets to ♃ at B., and along thru life, tend to healthy arteries, and normal replenishment of the blood flow. (See Aneurysm, Arterio-Sclerosis, and other subjects in this section).

Expansile Impulse Of—(See Pulse).

Fullness Of—(See "Dilatation" in this section).

Hardening—(See "Arterio-Sclerosis" in this section).

Head—Rupture of Artery in the Head, or Brain—(See Apoplexy; "Blood" under Head; "Blood Vessels" under Rupture).

Healthy Arteries—(See "Diseases" in this section).

Iliac Arteries—And Veins—Ruled by ♐. (See Ilium).

Inflammation—Of an Artery—Arteritis—♂ ☌ ♃.

Legs—Arterial Circulation Obstructed In—(See "Arterial" under Legs).

Mineral Deposits—Affecting the Arteries—(See "Arterio-Sclerosis" in this section).

Morbid Conditions—Of the Arteries—(See "Diseases" in this section).

Obstructed Circulation—In the Arteries—(See "Arterial" under Circulation).

Poor Circulation—(See "Obstructed" in this section).

Rupture—Of an Artery—(See "Head" in this section).

ARTHRALGIA—Pain in a Joint—(See "Arthritis", "Gout", "Pain" under Joints).

ARTHRITIS—Inflammation of a Joint—(See Joints).

ARTICULAR RHEUMATISM—(See "Rheumatism" under Joints).

ARTICULATION—Articulate—The Articulate Signs of the Zodiac are ♊, ♍, ♎, ♐, and ♒, and these signs are said to give clear articulation of words and speech. These are also called Human Signs, with the exception of ♎. The Inarticulate Signs tend to cause defects of speech. (See Dumb, Human, Inarticulate, "Hand of Man" under Man; Speech, Vocal).

ARTICULATIONS—(See Joints).

ARTIFICE—Cunning—Trickery—Strategy—Treachery—

Blindness By—(See "Artifice" and "Total Blindness" under Blindness).

Injury or Death By—(See Enemies, Mischief, Plots, Poison, Treachery).

ARTISTIC TEMPERAMENT—(See Sanguine).

ASCELLI—The Cratch—Praesepe—A Nebulous Cluster in the first decanate of ♌, of the nature of ♂ and the ☽. The Ascelli have special affinity with the Eyes and the Sight, and to cause Blindness when with the ☉ or ☽ at B. Their influence is said to be malefic, and to cause a variety of afflictions when the ☉, ☽, or malefics are near them at B. The Ascelli denote Death by fevers, fire, hanging, beheading, or some violent catastrophe, and often ruin and disgrace, when joined with the ☉ in an angle at B. Their Evils are Wounds, Hurts to the Face, Bad Eyes, Blindness, Imprisonment, Disgrace, and every evil that can befall Humanity, when directed to the ☉, ☽, or Asc. For the influences of the Ascelli, see the following subjects in the alphabetical arrangement,— "Acute Fevers" under Acute; Animals; "Bad Eyes" under Eyes; Beasts (Hurts By—See Animals; Beheaded (see Decapitation); Conjunctivitis; Crime; Defective Sight—(See Sight); Disgrace; Dissipation; Evils; Eye Disorders (see Eyes); Falls; Fevers—Death by, Inflammatory, Violent (see Fever); Gunshot; Hanging; Head—Pains In—(See Head); Honour—Loss of—(See Honour); Imprisonment; Inflammatory Fevers—(See Inflammation); Left Eye —Blindness In (see Blindness; "Left Eye" under Left); Liquids—Death by Injury By—(See Scalds, Shipwreck, "Hot Liquids" under Heat); Murderer (see "Murderous" under Murder); Pains in Head (see Head); Pestilence; Quarrels; Ruin; Scalds; Shipwreck; Sight—Danger to (see Sight, Blindness); Stabs; Violent—Violent Catastrophies, Violent Death, Violent Fevers (see Violent, and these subjects); Wounds. For collateral study see Nebulous, Praesepe, Stars.

ASCENDANT—The First House—The Sign rising upon the Eastern horizon at B. Determines largely the physical appearance, description of the body, height, weight, the degree of vitality, etc., and is very important to study in connection with health and disease. (See "First House" under First; "Passive Planets" under Passive; "Rising Sign" under Rising).

ASCETIC—(See Self-Denying).

ASCITES—Dropsy of the Abdomen— (See "Abdomen" under Dropsy).

ASH—Ashes—Waste Products in the System—The product of combustion and decay, and ruled by ♄. All influences which tend to interfere with elimination, excretion and secretion, etc., tend to deposit ash, and clog the system—(See Clogging). The body becomes heavily charged with Ash in such conditions as Impure Blood (see Impure), Gout, Kidney Trouble, Rheumatism, Uraemia, Wasting Diseases, etc. (See these subjects. Also see Elimination, Excretion, Secretion, "Influence of Saturn" under Saturn, Wastes, etc).

ASPECTS—Aspect—Appearance—Look.

Commanding Aspect—(See Commanding).

Lowering Aspect—(See "Downward Look" under Look; Stooping).

Planetary Aspects—No Planet is considered evil in itself, but it is their ever changing aspects, and angles they form with each other, that tend to make their influences and vibrations good or evil, positive or negative, contracting or expansive, etc. (See Reaction). The aspects of pathological importance are the ☌, P., □, and ☍. (See Opposition, Parallel, Square). The four Signs of any one Quadruplicity implicate each other pathologically, as by the □ and ☍. The most fortunate aspects that can be formed between the planets for good health and good fortune in life are ♃ ☌, ⚹, or △ ♀. The fortunate aspects between the planets are the ⚹ and △, and also the ☌ and P. between planets which are in harmony with each other. There are other good aspects, divisions of the ⚹ and △, which you can see listed in the Textbooks of Astrology. The evil, sinister, or adverse aspects, are the □ and ☍, and the ☌ and P. when occurring between malefics, or when a malefic afflicts the ☉, ☽, ♃, ♀, ☿, or other malefics, by a ☌ or P. As a rule only the major aspects, benefic and malefic, are listed in this book, and when the good aspects are referred to, it means not only the ⚹, △, but also all the minor good aspects, as the semi-sextile, quintile, etc. When bad aspects are referred to it means also the semi-square, the sesquiquadrate, and all sinister aspects referred to in the textbooks of Astrology. To print all minor aspects, good and bad, would involve the printing of thousands of extra symbol characters, which the Writer deems unnecessary. Many good aspects between the planets at B. tend to give better health, a stronger and better balanced mind, etc., while the evil aspects, and many of them at B. between the planets, tend to give a weaker constitution, more liable to ill-health, and also a more evil, unbalanced disposition and temperament. (See Directions, Dominion, Evil, Good, Kinetic, Opposition, Orbs, Planets, Polarity, Separation, Sextile, Square; "Perverted" under Tonic; Trine, Triplicities, etc.).

Sad Aspect—(See Sad).

Sober Aspect—(See Commanding)

Surly Aspect—♄ in ♌, in partile asp. the Asc. (See Appearance, Countenance, Expression, Face, Features, Look).

ASPHYXIA—Asphyxiation—Caused by Non-Oxygenation of the Blood—The ☉ affl. in ♒; ♅ in 6th H.; afflictions to ♃ and ♀, obstructing the arterial and venous circulation; ♄ or ♅ in ☐, or in ☐ or ☍ to ☐; ☿ affl. in ☐. (See Cyanosis, Drowning, "Non-Oxygenation" under Oxygen; Strangulation, Suffocation, etc).

Birth—Danger of Asphyxiation at Birth—Blue Baby—♄ exactly rising at B., on the Asc., or ♄ exactly on the Descendant, or ♄ ☍ the Asc. The ♄ influence also tends to delay birth. The Poet Goethe had ♄ exactly rising at B., which tended to delay his birth, and also nearly caused his death by asphyxiation at his birth. Cases—See Case of Premature Birth, and Asphyxiation soon after birth, Chap. XIV, page 102, in Daath's Medical Astrology. Also see Cases, "Strangled at Birth", No. 922 and 923, in 1001 N.N. (See "Delayed Births" under Children).

Cutaneous Asphyxiation—Suppression of the Skin Breathing—Afflictions in ♑, and espec. when also afflicting the hyleg. (See Skin). For further study see Drowning, Hanging, Strangulation, Suffocation.

ASSASSINATION—Danger of—Death By—Assassinations are ruled by the 12th H. In violent deaths the afflictions of ♆ dispose to thru treachery; ♅ affl. in ♏; ♂ afflicted, or afflicting in a human sign; ♂ in the 12th H., and affl. the ☉ or ☽; the ☽ with ♄ and Orion's Belt, or ☽ with Antares or Caput Hercules; ♄ ☌ or ill-asp. ♃, and elevated above ♃ at a Solar Ingress or Eclipse, tends to assassination of Great and Noble Men; afflictions in the 12th H., and afflicting the Hyleg; the 24° ♑ on the Asc. at B. Cases of Death By Assassination,—In 1001 N. N. see the following cases and birth data,— "Duke", No. 701; "Russia", No. 738; "Terris", No. 789; "Austria", No. 809; "Italy", No. 840; "Portugal", No. 902. (See Ambushes; "Death By" under Enemies; Kings, Stabs, Treachery; "Death" under Violent).

Assassinated Abroad—The ☽ Sig. ☌ ♂, and ♂ well-dignified, and thru a desire for travel and exploration. (See Abroad; "Journey" under Murder).

ASSASSINS—An Assassin—The following influences and afflictions tend to produce Assassins,—Caused by the ☉ and ♂ afflicted at B., which are the positive, electric and heat-producing planets; ♆ affl. in ♈; ♄ ☐ or ☍ ♂, in bad positions and angles; ♄ Sig. ☐ or ☍ ♂, or vice versa; ♂ and ☿ lords of the employment or 10th H., with ♂ strong or elevated above the Lumi-

naries, and ♂ affl. by the ☽; ♂ Sig. in ☐ or ☍ ☿; ☿ ill-posited at B., and in ☐ or ☍ ♂. (See Anarchists, Crime; "Death By" under Enemies; "Patricide" under Father; Homicide; "Murderous" under Murder; Plots, Robbers).

ASSAULTS—Batteries—Attacks—Bodily Injury—The Afflictions of the malefics ♄ and ♂ to the ☉, ☽, Asc., or hyleg at B., and espec. with the malefics in the 12th H., or in angles, and elevated above the Lights, make the native more liable to assaults and violent attacks, and many times due to his own folly or rash acts. An Eclipse of the ☉ in ♈ tends to a prevalence of Assaults and Batteries. The planetary influences which lead to assaults cover quite a large and varied field. (See the following subjects in the alphabetical arrangement,—Ambushes, Assassins, Attacks, Blows, Bruises, Cuts, Enemies, Highwaymen; "Hand of Man" under Man; Homicide, Maiming, Mobs, Murder, Pirates, Prisons, Robbers, Ruffians, Stabs, Stones, Sword, Travel, Treachery, Violence, War, Women, Wood, etc).

ASSIMILATION—Absorption of Nourishment—Distribution of Food—The Assimilative System—Assimilation is a function of the ♍ Sign. Also ♀ rules the functions of Assimilation, Nutrition and Growth until puberty, and then ♅ takes rule. The assimilation of food is regulated by ♅ thru the Pituitary Body. The ☽ is assimilative in action, as she rules the stomach, and has strong rule over the receiving and preparing of the bodily sustenance. Assimilation is aided and furthered by the good influence and aspects of ♃. (See Absorption, Alimentary, Digestion, Growth, Nutrition, Pituitary).

Imperfect Assimilation—Impaired and Poor Assimilation of Food—Disturbed Distribution of—The ☽ in ♋ or ♍ in the 6th H., and afflicted; ♅ ☌ ☽ in ♍; ♄ affl. in ♋, ♍, or ♑; ♄ ☌ ♃, ♀, or the ☽ in ♍, ♃ ☌ ♂ in ♍, disturbed assimilation in the small intestines; ♂ ☌ ☽ in ♍, the ♍ sign afflicted by the ☐ and ☍ aspects from common signs. (See Anaemia, Diet, Emaciation, Food, "Malnutrition" under Nutrition; Wasting, etc).

ASTHENIA—Asthenic—Asthenic Process—Loss of Strength—Adynamia—Asthenia is presided over by ♄ and his afflictions; the ☉ ☌ ♄; ♄ affl. in ♒. Also especially caused by Subs at AT, AX, or CP. The degree of Asthenia, and Low Vitality, will depend largely upon the severity of the afflictions of ♄ to the vital places in the map, as to the ☉, ☽, Asc., and Hyleg, and also the nature of the sign rising, etc. (See Adynamia, Anaemia, "Bad Health" under Health; Emaciation, Feeble, Infirm, Invalids, Pale, Plethora, Sickly, Vitality Low, Wasting, "Weak Body" under Weak; "Weakened" under Strength, etc).

ASTHENOPIA—Weak or Painful Vision —(See Sight).

ASTHMA—Paroxysmal Dyspnoea with Oppression—Asthmatic Diathesis—Phthisic—Asthma is considered a disease of the ☽, ☿, the ♐ and ♋ Signs, of ♐ by reflex action to ♐, and also of the common signs. Important areas in the disease are the 18° ♐ and ♐, the 4° of ♏ and ♓. Also the last few degrees of ♈ and the first part of ♉. Other causes are,—☉ □ or ☍ ☽ in common signs; ☉ affl. in 6th H. in a fixed sign; the ☽ or ☿ affl. in ♐ or ♐; the ☽ hyleg and afflicted in ♐ in a female nativity; ♓ ♐ ☌ ♄ or ☋; ♅ affl. in ♐; ♅, ♄, or ☿ in ♉, ♐, or ♋; ♅ ♋ ☌ ☽, and also affl. by ♓ or ♂, and usually due to spasmodic disturbance of the diaphragm; ♄ afflicted in ♐ or ♋; ♄ afflicted in the 3rd H.; ♄ in ♋, occi., and affl. the ☉, ☽, Asc., or hyleg; ♄ affl. in ♋ when he is the afflictor in the disease; ♄ ☌ or ☿ the ☉ in ♋ or ♑; ♄ ☌ ♃ in ♏ in the 3rd H., and in □ to bodies in the 18° ♐ or ♐; ♄ affl. in ♌, and due to heart trouble and deficiency; ♄ ☌ ♃ or ♀, by disturbance of the circulation; ♃ affl. in ♏, and ♏ on cusp of 3rd H.; ♂ affl. in ♐; ♂ in ♐ and affl. by ♃; ♂ affl. in ♉ or ♏; ♀ in ♉ ☌ or ill-asp. ♂; ♐ on the Asc., and afflicted; afflictions in the common signs, and with these signs on angles. Also caused by Subs at LCP, the 6th Cervical; at AP, the 1st Dorsal; at Lu.P, the Lung Place in the Spine, and at HP, the Heart Place. (See Breathing, Bronchial, Circulation, Consumptive, Diaphragm, Dyspnoea, Heart, Lungs, Oxygen, Respiration, Spasmodic, Stomach, Vertebrae, etc.).

Bronchial Asthma—See the first part of this Article. Also see "Congestion" under Bronchial).

Cases of Asthma—See the following case records, figures, and birth data,— Fig. 17 in "Message of the Stars" by the Heindels. Figures 10A, 20A, 20B, 20C, 20D, 20E, in "Astro-Diagnosis" by the Heindels.

Death By—Afflictions in common signs.

Hay Asthma—(See "Hay Fever" under Nose).

Heart Asthma—♄ affl. in ♌, due to disturbed heart action and deficiency.

Spasmodic Asthma—♅ affl. in ♉, ♐, or ♋; ♅ ☌ ☉ in ♐. (See Spasmodic).

Stomach Asthma—♅ affl. in ♋, due to stomach trouble and distention; ♅ ☌ ☽ ♋, and also affl. by malefics.

ASTIGMATISM—The ☉ or ☽ rising, and both in mutual affliction, and espec. by ♄ or ♂; the ☉ rising in ♈, ♉, ♌, ♑, or ♒, and afflicted; the ☉ rising in ♉ ☽ in 7th H. in ♋ and ♑; the ☽ or ☿ affl. in ♈; many planets in ♋ or ♑ in ☌ or ♉, and with ♋ or ♑ on the Asc. (See Accommodation, Eyes, Sight). Case— See "Diseases to the Eyes", page 87, Chapter 13, in Daath's Medical Astrology.

ASTRAGALUS—The Ankle Bone—Under the structural rulership of ♒. (See Ankles).

ASTRAL BODY—The Sidereal Body— One of Man's Vehicles, and an exact counterpart of the physical body. The focal point of the Astral Body is in the Spleen. The Astral Body is the seat of the Sensations. The planetary influences work upon man strongly thru his Astral Body, his Aura, his Mind, and his etheric parts, the Etheric Double, and it is thru these channels that disease and sickness gain their entrance to, and hold upon the body and mind. The afflictions of ♓ to the hyleg and mental rulers tend to make man subject to adverse Astral Influences, to obsessions, spirit controls, and death from such causes. In the Astral Body ♃ has direct relation to the Breath and the Blood, and ♂ and ♀ more especially to the sensations and passions, and as all diseases originate in, and have their counterpart in the Astral Body, it would be well for all students to study up on the subjects which have to do with the Astral Plane. The Astral Body is the mould, pattern, or counterpart, upon which the physical body is built, and when the physical body in utero is finished, and conforms to the Astral Model, birth takes place if conditions are normal. (See "Moment of Birth" under Birth; Blood, Breath, Build, "Desire Body" under Desire; Emotions, Liver, Neptune, Obsessions, Physical, Sensations, Sidereal Body, Spirit Controls, "Body" under Vital).

Astral Entities—Discarnate Spirits— Elementals, etc.—Are the Forces on the Astral Plane which greatly influence the mind of man, and to obsess, or bring diseases and troubles upon man, if they are of the evil types. (Good books to read along these lines are the Astral Plane books by Mr. Leadbeater, and also "The Message of the Stars", and "Cosmo-Conception" by the Heindels; "Realms of the Living Dead" by Dr. and Mrs Homer Curtiss).

Astral Shells—The etheric counterpart of the physical body, which separates at death, usually remains in the vicinity of the corpse, which may be seen as a "Ghost", and disintegrates with the physical body. (See "Silver Cord" under Silver).

ASTRINGENTS—Astrictives—Haemostatics—Contracting Agents—A therapeutic property of ♄, and tends to contract organic tissues and stop discharges. Acids are astringent. The influence of ♓ is also said to be astringent and contracting. (See Acids, Collyria, Contractions, Constrictions, Haemostatics, "Drugs", under Saturn).

ASTROLOGY—Study of—(See Science).

ASYLUMS—Are generally ruled by the 12th H.

Confinement In—(See Hospitals, "Asylums" under Insanity. Also see Confinement, Imprisonment, Twelfth House).

ATAXIA—An Incoordination of Muscular Action—Caused by afflictions in the ♈, ♉, and ♌ Signs, and by Subs at AT and CP. Locally caused by afflictions in the Sign ruling the part. (See Incoordination, Locomotor Ataxia, "Action" under Muscles).

ATHETOSIS—(See "Athetosis" under Fingers, Toes).

ATHLETICS—Athletic—A strong and athletic frame is given when the strong signs ♌, ♏, ♐, or ♒ are on the Asc. at B. (See Exercise, Muscles, Sports, "Strong Body" under Strong).

Pugilist—See "Sayers", No. 175, in 1001 N.N.

Wrestler—Champion Wrestler—Case See "Carkeek", No. 167, in 1001 N.N.

ATHYMIA—(See Despondency, Melancholia). Caused especially by Subs at AT, the Atlas, 1st Cervical Vetebra. (See Atlas, Vertebrae).

ATLAS—The first Cervical Vertebra, ruled and acted upon by the ♈ and ♉ Signs. (See "First Cervical" under Vertebrae).

ATMOSPHERE—Air—(See Air, Aquarius, Breath, Caisson Disease, Carbon, Compressed, Drought, Dry, Electricity, Epidemics, Ether, Famine, Floods, Gases, Heat, Hydrogen, Influenza, Lightning, Miasma, Moisture, Noxious, Oxygen, Pestilence, Pressure, Rain, Storms, Sun Spots, Thunder, Uranus, Vapor, Weather, Wind, etc).

ATONIC—Atony—Want of Tone or Power—Debility—The Atonic Planets are ♅, ♄, ♀, and the ☽. The action of planets when below normal is atonic. The minus and negative influences and aspects of the planets are atonic, while their plus and positive aspects tend to be tonic, expanding, beneficial and increasing in their effects over body and mind. (See Anaemia, Chronic, Debility, Emaciation, Feeble, Gout, Infirm, Invalids, Pale, Plethora, Sickly, Strength, Tone, Tonic, Vitality Low, Wasting, "Weak Body" under Weak).

ATRABILE — Atrabiliary — Melancholy —Suprarenal Disturbances—(See Adrenals, "Black Bile" under Bile; Depression, Hypochondria, Melancholy, Suprarenals).

ATROPHY—Wasting of a Part from Lack of Nutrition—A ♄ disease, and ♄ is the planet of atrophy; denoted by ♀; the hyleg much affl. at B., congenital atrophy. Atrophy may attack any part of the body, the organs, muscles, functions, etc., and principally in the part, parts, or organs ruled or afflicted by ♄ at B., and by dir., and by the sign and house containing ♄. (See Hemiatrophy).

Death By—Denoted by ♀ when she is the afflictor in the disease, having the dominion of death, and afflicting the hyleg; also ♄ afflicting the hyleg at B., and by dir., tends to, and espec. when taking part in a train of evil directions.

Progressive Muscular Atrophy—(See "Progressive" under Muscles). For the various matters concerning Atrophy, see Diminished, Dry, Emaciation, Growth, Nutrition, Tabes, Wasting, etc. See "Atrophy" under Arms, Brain, Congenital, Eyes, Face, Feet, Functions, Hands, Heart, Legs, Limbs, Liver, Muscles, Spine, etc).

ATROPIN—(See Belladonna).

ATTACHMENTS—(See Adhesions).

ATTACKS—Injury or Violence to the Body—Caused generally by ♂ — (See the following subjects,—Animals, Assassination, Assaults, Beasts, Beaten, Bites, Blows, Cannibals, Cattle, Cuts, Enemies, "Hand of Man" under Man; Highwaymen, Hurts, Injuries, Kicks, Kidnapped, Killed, Lynching, Maimed,

Mobs, Murder, Mutilated, Pirates, Poison, Quadrupeds, Reptiles, Robbers, Serpents, Stabs, Stings, Stones, Sword, Travel, Treachery, Venomous, Violence, "Wild Animals" under Wild; Wounds, etc).

ATTENTION—Inability to fix the mind at Attention—(See "Attention" under Mind).

ATTENUANT—Increasing the fluidity of the blood or other secretions—A therapeutic property of the ☽ remedies and herbs. (See Moon; "Moon Herbs" under Herbs).

ATTRACTIVE—Attracts—

Attractive Power—(See Healers, Magnetic, Sympathy).

Attractive Stature—(See Appearance, Beautiful, Complexion, Face, Hair, Handsome, Stature, etc.).

Attracts Disease—(See Contagions, Contracts, External, Infections, Magnetic, Negative, Passive, Scorpio, Suggestion, Susceptible, Sympathy, etc.).

AUDITORY ORGANS—The Organs of Hearing—Auditory Nerve—(See Ears, Hearing).

AUGMENTED—Increased—Enlarged—

Abundance—(See the subjects under Abundance).

Blood Augmented—In a Part—(See "Blood" under Abundance).

Cerebral Substance—Augmented—(See "Medullary Substance" under Medulla).

Death Rate Augmented—(See Mortality).

Disease—(See "Increase" under Disease).

Enlarged—(See the subjects under Enlarged).

Functions—(See "Over-functional" under Functions).

Growth—(See Giants, "Increase" under Growth).

Health—(See "Strengthened" under Health).

Increased—(See the subjects under Increase).

Motion—(See "Accelerated", "Quick" under Motion).

Nerve Force—(See "Augmented" under Vital).

Sensibility—(See "Augmented" under Sensibility).

Strength—(See "Increased" under Strength, Vitality).

Vitality—(See "Augmented", "Increased" under Vitality). Also see such subjects as Abnormal, Appetite, Corpulent, Evil, Excess, Excesses, Height, Hyper, Obesity, Over, Super, Weight, etc., and other subjects which may occur to your mind, which have to do with augmentation and increase in the body.

AUNTS—The mother's relatives in a male horoscope are ruled by the 6th H., and in a female nativity by the 12th H. The father's relatives, as his brothers and sisters, your paternal aunts and uncles, are ruled by the 6th H. in a female nativity, and by the

12th H. in a male horoscope. The mother's relations are ruled by ☿, and those of the father by ♄. Relatives in general, on both sides of the house, are ruled by ♅, and his positions and aspects tend to indicate the danger of ill-health or death among them, sudden events in connection with their lives, etc., when ♅ at B., or by dir., afflicts the parts of the native's map which rule these matters.

Case—Remarkable Similarity Between Aunt and Niece—See "Remarkable Similarity", No. 343, in 1001 N.N.

Death of An Aunt—Ill-Health or Sickness of an Aunt—The ☉ to the �, P., or ill-asp. ♅ by dir.; an eclipse falling on the radical ☿ in a child's map; ♄ ruler of the 6th or 12th H. at B., and ♄ to the � or ill-asp. the Asc. by dir., and espec. if the native be very young, and under 7 years of age.

Death of An Aged Aunt—Death of a Grandmother, or an Aged Female in the Family—The ☽ hyleg, and to the �, P., or ill-asp. ♄ by dir., and espec. if the direction fall in the 8th or 12th H.; the ☽ to the place of Rigel; ♂ to the � or ill-asps. ♄ by dir.

Maternal Aunts—Or Uncles—Death of —(See Maternal).

Paternal Aunts—Or Uncles—Sickness or Death of—Afflictions to the 6th or 12th H., according to the sex of the native, etc. (See the rules in the first part of this section. Also see Uncles). For collateral study see Family, Father, Grandparents, Maternal, Mother, Old Age, Paternal, Relations, Sixth House, Twelfth House, Uncles.

AURA—The Magnetic and Physical Aura are ruled by ♅. The conditions of the mind, body and spirit are reflected in the Aura, and can be seen by a genuine Clairvoyant or Medium. The health and disease conditions of the body and mind affect the Aura, varying its colors, etc. The magnetic aura is strengthened by the ✳ and △ aspects of ♅ to the Asc. The question of the Aura is a large and important one, and students of Healing should make a study along this line in the Occult and Metaphysical books. (See Astral Body, Desire Body).

AURAL—Pertaining to the Ears—Aural Ducts—(See Ears).

AURICLE—The External Ear—One of the upper cavities of the Heart. (See Ears, Heart).

Auricular Disease—Of the Heart—(See "Auricular" under Heart).

AURIGA'S RIGHT SHOULDER—(See Disgrace, Ruin, Violent Death).

Auriga's Left Shoulder—Capella—(See Capella).

AURUM—(See Gold).

AUSTERE—Austere Countenance—Austere Look—Stern—Severe—Characteristic of ♄ people; ♄ in ♌; ♄ Sig. □ or ☍ ♂; ♄ in ♈ or □; ♄ well-dig. in ♎, ♑, or ♒; ♄ Sig. ✳ or △ the ☉; ♄ ruler of the Asc., or horoscope at B., and aff.; the ☉ Sig. in ♐; ♂ Sig. in ♈; ♂ Sig. □ or ☍ ♄; ☿ Sig. in ♍, or ☿ ♍ partile the Asc.; ♌ gives. Austerity is a trait usually accompanied by melancholy,

and tends to invite disease unless controlled. (See Countenance, Cruel, Ferocious, Fierce, Fiery, Fulminating, Grave, Morose, "Disposition" under Severe; "High Temper" under Temper).

AUTOINTOXICATION—From wrong diet, and accumulation of poisons in the system—☽ ☌ ♅ ♍; ♄ affl. in ♋; ♃ ♋ in 12th H., and afflicted. Case—See Fig. 18D, in the book, "Astro-Diagnosis", by the Heindels. (See Autotoxic, Diet, Excesses, Food, Gluttony, Intoxication, Poisons).

AUTOMATIC ACTION—Under rule of the ☽. Tending to form habits by repetition of certain acts, whether for good or evil, for health or disease. Afflictions to the ☽ tend to interfere with the automatic action of the body and cause clumsiness. (See Clumsiness, Habits).

AUTOMOBILES—Injury or Death By—(See Vehicles).

AUTOTOXIC PSYCHOSES—(See Autointoxication, Diabetes, Psychoses, Toxic, Uremia).

AUTUMNAL—The Autumnal Signs are ♎, ♏, and ♐, and Autmnal diseases are more prevalent while the Sun is passing thru these signs, and also Kidney troubles, sex derangements or weaknesses, diseases in the hips or thighs, or accidents to these parts. (See Scurvy). For matters concerning the Autumnal Equinox see Equinox, Ingresses.

AVALANCHES—Danger, Injury, or Death By on Voyages, in Travel or Inland Journeys, etc.—Malefics in the 3rd or 9th H., and affl. the ☉, Asc., or hyleg at B., or by dir.; ♄ in the 3rd H., and affl. the hyleg at B., and by dir. (See Crushed, "Earthquakes" under Earth).

AVENA—A typical drug of ☿. (See Mercury).

AVERSIONS—Dislikes—Irrational Fears or Aversions—(See Antipathy, "Morbid" under Fears; Hatred, Misanthropic).

Marriage—Opposite Sex—Aversion to —(See Deviations; Homosexuality; "Aversions", "Indifferent" under Marriage; Perversions).

Pleasure—Averse to—(See Pleasure).

Study—Aversion to—(See "Aversion" under Study).

AVERTED—Avoided—Prevented—

Death—Death In Sickness Averted—Lord of the Asc. in the 8th H., going to combustion, intervened by a good asp. from ♃, ♀, ☿, or the ☽, and in such a case the natural strength, or the proper treatment, will modify or avert the misfortune. The interventions of the benefics, ♃ and ♀, by their good asps. to the hyleg in a train of evil directions tend to avert death, and espec. if the vitality be strong, and the hyleg favorably aspected by the benefics at B., and the patient be young. (See Crises, Curable, Escapes, Moderation, Prevented, Recovery, Recuperation, Resistance, Vitality, etc.).

Death Not Averted—(See "Arguments for Death", "Sure Death", "Time" under Death).

Disease Averted—(See Averted; Immunity; "Disease" under Prevented).

AVIATION—Death or Injury In—(See Aeroplanes).

AWKWARDNESS—Gawky—Afflictions in the mutable signs, which signs rule the limbs, and espec. afflictions to ♃ or ☿ in these signs; ♄ affl. in ♐; ♄ rising in the Asc., and espec. if ♑ is also on the Asc.; ♄ and the ♑ sign, when strong and prominent at B., tend to give a heavy and awkward appearance, and ♂ also in the configuration tends to make the native rough and careless; ♃ afflicting ☿. (See Appearance, Clumsiness, Gait, Heaviness, Posture, Stooping, Walk, etc.).

AWRY GAIT—(See Gait).

AXILLAE—Armpits—Ruled by the ♋ Sign.

  Cancer Of—♄ affl. in ♋.

  Scirrhus Of—Of the Breast or Axillae—A hard form of Carcinoma—♄ or ♂ affl. in ♋. (See Carcinoma).

  Sweating Of—Fetid Perspiration In—♂ affl. in ♋. (See Sweat).

Tenderness—In the Armpits—Caused by afflictions in ♐, ♊, ♋, or ♌, and by Subs at LCP, the 6th Cervical, and at AP and HP, the 2nd Dorsal Vertebra. (See Vertebrae).

AXIS—(See Vertebrae).

AZIMENE—The Azimene Degrees of the Zodiac—Deficient Degrees—Weak or Lame Degrees—If the Asc., or its lord, be in one of these degrees at B., the native tends to be lame, crooked, deformed, or blind. These degrees are as follows: ♈ 0°; ♉ 6, 7, 8, 9 10°; ♊ 0°; ♋ 9, 10, 11, 12, 13, 14, 15°; ♌ 18, 27, 28°; ♍ 0°; ♎ 0°; ♏ 19, 28°; ♐ 1, 7, 8, 18, 19°; ♑ 26, 27, 28, 29°; ♒ 18, 19°; ♓ 0°. (See Blindness, Crooked, Deformed, Incurable, Lameness, Weak).

AZOTE—(See Nitrogen).

AZOTH—The luminous, brilliant and fiery coloring in the Spinal Canal, seen by Clairvoyants, brighter in some than in others, according to the stage of spiritual development. Ruled by ♆. (See "Spinal Canal" under Spine. Also see Ether).

B

BACHELORS—The planetary influences at B. often tend to delay or deny marriage, or to give little or no sex desires, which conditions often lead to single life in both sexes. Malefics in the 5th or 7th H., ♂ or ill-asp. the ☽ tend to; the ☽ □ or ☍ ☉, and affl. by ♄; ☽ in the sex sign ♏ in ♂ or ill-asp. ♄; ♄ ♏ in ♂ or ill-asp. the ☉, ☽, Asc., or Hyleg, tends to deaden the passions and make the native more indifferent to the opposite sex. (See Celibacy, Deviations, Eunuchs, "Aversion" under Marriage; "Free from Passion" under Passion; Perversions; the various paragraphs under Sex; Spinsters, etc.)

BACILLUS—(See Germs).

BACK—Rear Part of the Body—The Dorsal Region—The Back is ruled by the ☉, the ♌ Sign, and the 5th H. Under the external rule of ♌. The lower part of the back (Loins), ruled by ♎ and the 7th H. (See Front). See the following subjects in the alphabetical arrangement when not considered here.

  Abscess In—Imposthumes In—A ♎ disease. (See Abscesses).

  Affected—The Back tends to be affected when the ☉ is in ♑; the ☽ ♐; ♅ ♊; ☿ ♏. (See Table No. 196 in Simmonite's Arcana). Case Record of the Back Affected—See Case 3, page 89, Chap. 13, in Daath's Medical Astrology.

  Ailments Of—(See "Diseases" in this section).

  Backache—Afflictions in ♌ or ♒; the ☉, ☽, or ♀ affl. in ♌; ♄ affl. in ♌. Case—See "Backache", page 90, Chap. 13, in Daath's Medical Astrology.

  Chronic Diseases Of—The ☉ hyleg, and to the ♂ or ill-asp. ♄ by dir.; ♄ affl. in ♌.

  Diseases Of—Ailments—All Diseases In—Distempers In—Distempered Back, etc.—Afflictions in ♌ or ♒, and also in any of the fixed signs, or many planets in the Fixed, or Succedent Houses, tend to diseases and ailments of the back; afflictions in ♐, ♌, ♏, ♒, the fixed signs, and also in the 5th H.; the ☉ affl. in ♌ or ♒, and the fixed signs; the ☉ Sig. in ♑ in horary questions; the ☉ to the ♂ or ill-asps. ♄ by dir.; diseases of the ☉ and ♀; the ☽ Sig. in ♐ (Hor'y); ♄ affl. in ♎; ♀ diseases, and afflictions to ♀; ☿ Sig. in ♏ (Hor'y); ♌, ♏, and ♒ diseases. (See the various paragraphs in this section. Also see Table on page 179, Chapter 29, in Lilly's Astrology).

  Dorsal Region—(See Dorsal).

  Imposthumes In—(See "Abscesses" in this section).

  Injuries To—The ☉ in ♌ and affl. by malefics; ♄ or ♂ in ♌, and affl. the ☉, ☽, Asc., or hyleg.

  Kidneys; Loins; Lower Part—Of the Back—All Diseases In—Injuries to, or Weaknesses In—♎ diseases and afflictions. (See Loins).

  Lumbago; Moles—Marks—Scars—Planets below the earth, and in signs which rule the back. (See "Rear Parts" under Marks).

  Muscular Rheumatism—In Back—♂ affl. in ♌ or ♒. (See Lumbago).

  Pains In—Backache—Afflictions in ♌, ♎, ♒, and all the fixed signs; the ☉ in ♐, ♌, or ♒, and to the ill-asps. any of the malefics as promittors; the ☉ affl. in ♌ when the ☉ is the afflictor in the disease; ♄ affl. in ♌, ♎, or ♒; ♄ ♂ ♃ or ♀ in ♌, due to weak heart and impaired circulation; ☿ and the ☽ in ♌, and to the ♂ or ill-asp. any of the malefics; ☿ affl. in ♌, ♑, or ♒, and to the ill-asps. the malefics; ☿ affl. in ♌, from colds caught in the feet. (See Backache, Lumbago, Muscular, in this section).

Reins of the Back—All Diseases In— (See "Back" under Reins).

Rheumatism In—(See "Muscular" in this section).

Scapula—(See Shoulders).

Scars—(See "Moles" in this section).

Spine—(See Spine, Vertebrae).

Weak Back—Weakness in the Back —A ☉ disease; the ☉ affl. in ♌ at B., or ♌ on Asc.; the ☉ to the ♂ or ill-asp. ♄ by dir.; the ☉ in 6th H. at B., in a fixed sign, and afflicted; the ☽ affl. in ♎ or ♑, and to the ♂ or ill-asps. the malefics; ☿ affl. in ♐, and to the ♂ or ill-asps. the malefics; a ♌ and ♎ disease, and afflictions in these signs. (See Dorsal, Humpback, Kidneys, Leo, Libra, Loins, Lumbar, Muscles, Reins, Rheumatism, Spine, Vertebrae). Case —Of Weak Back—See Fig. 30 in "Message of the Stars" by Max Heindel.

BACKWARDNESS—Slow in Growth and Development—Dull—Bashfulness —Retarded, etc.—The influence of ♄ tends to retard both the mental and physical growth and development; ♄ affl. in 3rd H., or the ☉ and ♄ affl. in ♉ at B., and with ☿ weak, afflicted and ill-posited, tend to backwardness of mental growth; ☿ and the ☽ afflicting each other, and in no asp. to the Asc. at B., and also ☿ ♂ ♄, or afflicted by malefics, mental growth is retarded; the conditions of the 3rd H. and ☿ give clues to backwardness along mental lines. The physical growth tends to be backward when the malefics afflict the hyleg at B., and when there are weak signs on the Asc., and the vitality low. Also caused by derangements of the Thyroid Gland. Precocity is the opposite condition to this and tends to premature development, and to Prodigies, Geniuses, etc. (See Bashful, Blushing, Dull, Genius, Giants, Growth; "Arrested" and "Deficiency" under Mental; Modesty, Precocious, Prodigies, Prudery, Retarded, "Slow" under Motion; Thyroid, etc.).

Speech—Backwardness of—(See Speech).

BACTERIA—(See Germs, Microbes).

BAD—Badly—Ill—Evil—Defective— Imperfect—Unfavorable, etc.—See the following subjects in the alphabetical arrangement—

Appetite Bad—(See "Loss Of" under Appetite).

Blood Bad—(See Corrupt, Impure).

Body—The Body Badly Made, Crooked, etc.—(See Crooked; "Ill-formed" under Ill; Ugly, etc.).

Breath Bad—(See Breath).

Children—Death Caused by Bad Children—(See "Bad" under Children).

Color—A Bad Color—(See "Bad Complexion" under Complexion; Pale, Sickly).

Complexion Bad—(See Complexion).

Conduct Bad—(See Criminal, Debauchery, Dissipation, Drink, Drunkenness, Evil, Lewd, Morals, Sex, Temper, etc.).

End—A Bad End—(See Hanging, Imprisonment, Judges, Murdered, Ruin, Suicide, Untimely Death, etc.).

Evil—(See Evil).

Gait—A Bad Gait—(See Deformed, Feet, Gait, Lameness, Legs, Walk).

Habits—Bad Habits—(See Drink, Eating, Food, Habits, Narcotics, Passion, Pleasures, Sex, etc.).

Health Bad—(See Health, Ill-Health, Invalids, Sickly, Weak, etc.).

Ill—(See Ill).

Impure Blood—(See Impure).

Legs—Bad Legs—(See Legs).

Loose Habits—Morals—(See Habits, Morals).

Magnetism—(See Healers, Incompatibility, Magnetism).

Men—Bad Men—(See the various paragraphs under Men).

Morals—Bad Morals—(See "Loose" under Morals).

Perversions; Teeth Bad—(See Teeth).

Vitality Bad—(See Vitality).

Women—Bad Women—(See Harlots, Treachery, Women). Any condition of the mind or body which is not normal may be classed as "Bad", and for subjects not listed here, look for it in the alphabetical arrangement.

BALANCE—Equilibrium—

Balance of Movement—The ♎ Sign gives grace and balance of movement. (See Coordination, Dexterity, Incoordination, "Muscular Action" under Muscular; Rhythm, Walk, "Well-Balanced" under Well).

Lack of Balance—The planetary influences and aspects at B., when not well-balanced, as when many planets are out of dignity and in evil aspect to each other, tend to cause the mind and body to be one-sided in their manifestations, and more apt to lead to mental and physical disorders until the Soul becomes awakened, and learns how to rule its stars. These evil, or negative planetary influences at B., and by transits, directions, etc., are sent upon us to try the Soul, and for experience, and no Soul can find peace, soul-growth, or any very great degree of satisfaction in earth life until it learns to conquer the "Monsters of the Zodiac" and keep its poise and balance at all times under the ever-changing planetary aspects and influences. The ♎ sign is called the Sign of "The Balance", or The Scales. (See Equilibrium, Harmony, Libra). Diseases of the Mind and Body are due to an unbalanced condition of mind and body, as a rule, and also due to sin somewhere in the life, now or in the past. The subjects in this book are taken up largely with Diseases, and the unbalanced conditions, and what you have to rule and overcome in life.

BALANITIS—Inflammation of the Glans Penis—(See Penis).

BALDNESS—Alopecia—Falling Hair— Loss of Hair—Baldness is due to an excess of heat in the system, causing a dryness, lack of proper circulation in the scalp. The fiery signs strong at B., on the Asc., and also well-occupied by planets, tend to baldness, and especially when the scalp fits tightly over the cranium. A loose scalp gives more freedom of circulation and nutrition to the part. The earthy and watery signs tend to give plenty of hair, and to retain it. The airy signs give a heavy head of hair, and tend to grayness rather than baldness. Some people are destined from birth to baldness, which is the normal condition for them, and the teachings in the Occult books are that any relief is only temporary, and massage and tonics may succeed for a time in restoring the hair, but when discontinued the hair falls out again. Some signs and influences at B. give an abundance of hair on the head and body, while others give little, or no hair. (See Beard, and the various paragraphs under Hair). The following planetary influences tend to Baldness—The ☉ in a fiery sign at B., and espec. in ♈; fiery signs upon the Asc.; many planets in a fiery sign, rising, and espec. in the Asc.; the ☉ and ♂, the fiery planets, in a fire .sign, and espec. in ♈, and in the Asc.; the ☽ ♂ the ☉ or ♂ in ♈, and espec. when in the Asc.; ♄ occi. of the ☉ at B. tends to fewer hairs on the head and body; born under the ☉, as with ♌ on the Asc., soon becomes bald; ♃ ruler of the Asc., and occidental; ♃ in ♐, and espec. with ♐ on Asc., rapid falling out of the hair early in life, and in youth; ♃ Sig. ✶ or △ ♄, and ♄ well-dignified; ♂ in ♍, and in ☐ to ♀ in ♎; ♍ influence, and with ♍ on the Asc., the sign ruled by ♄; an ♈, ♌, and ♐ disease, and with these signs upon the Asc.

Case—Loss of Hair and Eyebrows—See "Aqueous", No. 120, in 1001 N.N. (See "No Hair" under Hair).

Early in Life—Bald Early in Life—Premature Baldness—Quickly Bald—The ☉ afflicted at B.; the ☉ rising in fiery signs or fiery signs afflicted on the Asc.; ♄ or ♃ rulers of the Asc., and occi., as when between the 1st and 4th houses, or between the 10th and 7th H.; ♃ and ☿ affl. in ♐; ♂ afflicting ♀, and ♂ elevated above ♀; ♂ in ♊, ♐, or ♒, and afflicting ♀; ♐ on the Asc.; many planets in fiery signs at B., and espec. when rising in the Asc.

Forehead—Bald About the Forehead—The ☉ rising at B.; ♃ and ☿ affl. in ♐, and espec. when rising in the Asc.; ♐ on the Asc. (See Forehead. Also see "Temples" in this section).

Inhibited Growth—Of Hair—The ☉ or ♄ in the 5° ♈ or ♐; ♄ tends to inhibitions in any part of the body, according to the sign or house he is in, and espec. when affl. the ☉, ☽, Asc., or hyleg. (See Inhibitions).

Loss of Hair Increased—The high fevers of the ☉ in ♈, or ♈ on the Asc. and afflicted, tend to cause the hair to fall out rapidly, or cause complete baldness for a time after illness; the ☉ or ♂ in ♈, and espec. with ♈ on Asc., due to too much heat in the head

and scalp; ♄, the ruler of ♍, occidental; ♃ in 1st H., and affl. by ♂ or ♀, and espec. with ♃ in ♐; ♂ or ☿ holding dominion at B., and in familiarity with each other, and ♂ affl. the hyleg and elevated above the Luminaries; ♂ Sig. in ♋, without much hair; ♂ in ♍ and ☐ to ♀ ♎; ♂ ♃ ♀ tends to increased falling of hair; look to the aspects of ♂ and ♀ to the Asc., to each other, and their strength or weakness, exaltation or detriment, etc.; ♀ in 6th H., and affl. by ♂; ☿ ori. at B.; ♈ or ♐ on the Asc. at B.

Scanty Hair—Fewer Hairs on Head or Body— ♀ Sig. in ♎, scanty, but grows long. (See Beard; "Body", "Disorders", under Hair).

Temples—Bald About the Temples—Hair Growing Off the Temples—♐ on Asc. at B.; many influences in fiery signs; ♃ ♐, or ♃ ori. at B.; ♃ ♐ in Asc. (For further study see "Abundance", and the various paragraphs under Hair).

BALSAMIC—A therapeutic property of ♃. Produces an agent resembling a balsam.

BANDITS—Death or Injury By, and especially during Travel—♄ and ♂ in human signs and controlling the Luminaries. (See Highwaymen, Robbers, "Dangers", under Travel).

BANISHMENT—The ☉ directed to all Nebulous Clusters, and to Castor and Pollux, threaten banishment, and which may result in sickness and early death. (See Exile).

BAPTISM—The Planetary Baptism—The influences of the planetary vibrations stamped upon you at B., when you breathe in the magnetism of the Universe at your first cry. This is the photograph, the negative of your tendencies, possibilities, the diseases subject to, the picture of your personality, and the nature of the environment you will be apt to encounter in this day of school in earth life, and to gain experience, learn the necessary lessons for Soul-growth, etc. The map of birth is the foundation upon which you are to build a superstructure, and how you build will depend upon your degree of advancement, your spiritual insight and foresight, and your attainments, self-control, poise, balance, etc. (See "Moment of Birth" under Birth, Moment. Also see Fate, "Map of Birth" under Map; Nativity; "Free Will" under Will).

BARBERS—The ♂ influence strong at B., ♂ the ruling planet, or ♂ well-asp. in the 10th H., tend to make good Barbers, as well as Chemists, Surgeons, etc., and all who use sharp tools and instruments in their vocation. (See Chemists, Healers, Surgeons).

Barber's Itch—Inflammation of the Hair Follicles of the Face and Neck—Sycosis—Caused by afflictions in ♍, as a rule, and with ♂ in ♍ in the Asc., and also by ♂ ♈ in the Asc. or in the 6th H.; caused by Subs at MCP, the 4th Cervical, and also by Subs at KP, afflictions in ♎, as such are usually due to retained poisons, and lack of proper secretion and elimination. (See Itch, Ringworm, Vertebrae).

BARRENNESS—Sterility—Unprolific—Impotency—Unfruitful—With animals the propagative faculty is in charge of the Group Spirits presiding over the different classes of animals. The mixture of blood between animals of different species tends to sterility. The Mule is a hybrid and sterile because the horse was bred with the Ass, two different species. This displeases the Group Spirits of Horses and Asses, and sterility is imposed upon the crossed offspring to prevent its further propagation. The Human Family in its evolution is beyond the power of these Group Spirits, and Races can interbreed without the penalty of sterility, as is the case with animals. However, certain Races become sterile sooner or later, and die out when they finish a Cycle in their evolution, and are ready to enter a new Race. Thus the Bushman of Australia are being exterminated thru sterility, and in spite of all the British Government is doing to perpetuate and increase their numbers. The Occult and Inner side of this question is quite fully discussed in the book, "Cosmo-Conception", by Max Heindel. Also see the subject of "Seed Atom" in this same book.

Barren Signs—Barren Planets—In Astrology there are certain Signs of the Zodiac known as Barren Signs, as ♈ (rather barren), ♊, ♌, and ♍. The planets classed as Barren are the ☉, ♅, ♄ and ♂, which signs and planets tend to deny or kill the children when found in the houses of children, as in, or on the cusps, of the 5th or 11th houses of the parents, one or both parents. Also Cauda (☋) is classed as a barren influence, of the nature of Saturn. Both parents must have fruitful maps in order to have children, and also the Seed Atom of an incoming Ego must be implanted in the spermatozoa of the father to produce a normal child, and come with an Ego and Spirit. The Givers of children are the ☽, ♃, and ♀, when in the houses of children and well-aspected, and also the watery signs are classed as fruitful. (See Fruitful). In studying thru a library of Astrological Textbooks, I have recorded and classified the following planetary influences given as reasons for sterility, or the denial of children.

Causes of Barrenness—Children Denied—The Map of Husband or Wife Barren—Impotency—Unfruitfulness, etc.—The ☉ and malefics in barren signs, and dominating the houses of children, the 5th and 11th houses, and also the M.C., or Zenith, and the benefics below them; the ☉ and the malefics being the rulers of offspring in the map, and in barren signs, and without the good aspects of ♃ or ♀, and the malefics elevated above the benefics; the ☉ in ♑ and afflicted; the ☉ and ☿ in the 5th H., and afflicted in barren signs; the ☉ in the 5th H. causes barrenness, except he be in a watery sign, and even this doubtful;

if the ☉ be joined to ☿, and apply to the ☌, P., or ☍ of both ♄ and ♂, and angular, and espec. in ♈, ♌, ♏, ♑, or ♒, the native will be wholly unfit for generation; the ☉, ♅, ♄ or ♂ in the 5th or 11th houses, and afflicted; the ☉, ♄, and ♂ deny children, or allot but few, espec. when in the 5th or 11th houses and afflicted; the ☉, ♄, ♂, or ☋ in the 5th H., or a barren sign on the cusp of the 5th., and the ☽ in a barren sign, or if the lord of the 1st and 5th be in evil asp. to each other, or with ♄ or ♂, are all causes of barrenness; the ☉ to the ill-asps. ♀ by dir., a barren time; the ☽ in ♈, ♌, or ♑, and in evil asp. to the ☉, ♅, ♄, ♂, or ☋, denotes barrenness; the ☽ sepr. from the ☉, and applying to ♀ in a day geniture; the ☽ in a husband's horoscope, and the ☉ in the wife's, applying to ♅, ♄, or ☋ in the 5th H., there will be no family unless there be powerful testimonies for fruitfulness in both maps, and even if children are born they are subject to early death; the ☽, ♃, and ♀ weak, afflicted and unfortunate at B., and not in fruitful houses or signs, tends to deny children; one or both Lights in an angle, and espec. in the 1st or 7th houses, or in the 6th in ☌ ♄, ♂, and ♀, no children, and if a female is liable to abortion; ♅ tends to deny children, or allot but few; ♅ affl. in the 5th or 11th houses, or afflicting these houses, denial of children; ♄ in 5th H. in ♎, or ♑ denies children; ♄ in the 11th H., and ♂ in ☐ asp. to the cusp of 5th H.; ♄ affl. in ♎ or ♏; ♄ ☌ ♀ in the 7th H.; ♄ and ♀ in the western angle and afflicted; ♄ in the 5th or 11th houses, and afflicted; ♄ tends to deny children, or allot but few; ♄ in an angle and afflicting both the ☽ and ♀; ♄ or ☋ in the 5th H., or ♄ or ♂ in evil asp. to the 5th, or its lord, or the Sigs. or Benefics be in barren signs, and if any born they will not live; ♄, a cold and barren planet, in the 11th H. frustrates the hope of children in Hor'y Questions, and espec. if at the same time there are barren signs on the Asc., or cusp of the 5th; ♂ in the 5th or 11th houses, and afflicted; ♂ denies children, or allots but few, when afflicting the houses of children; ♂ in ☐ or evil asp. the cusp of 5th H., and with ♄ in the 11th H.; ♀ afflicted by the malefics; the atonic action of ♀ tends to sterility; ♀ affl. in ♑; afflictions to ♀; a ♀ disease or affliction; ♀ in a ♄ sign, and affl. by the ☽ and ♄; ☿ and the ☉ in the 5th H., in barren signs and afflicted; a cold and dry body, ruled by ☿ or ♄, tends to make the nature unprolific; ☿ denies offspring when occidental if in a barren sign and configurated with barren planets; ☿ either gives or denies children according to the planets he is configurated with at B.; malefics in the 5th or 11th houses in barren signs; the malefics ♅, ♄, ♂, and also the ☉ and ☋, when in the houses of children, and afflicted, or in barren signs, tend to deny children, allot but few, or cause their early death; the malefics and the ☉ being the rulers of offspring, and in barren signs, and without the good asps. of the benefics, and the malefics elevated above the benefics; the malefics ori. and angular, and afflicting the ruler of the 5th H., or elevated above such ruler, and also afflicting planets in the 5th, tend to deny children, and espec. when the ruler of the 5th receives no help from the benefics, and with no benefics or givers of children in the 5th H., or in fruitful signs; a malefic in a house of children, and espec. if with the ☉, the native will always be barren; ♈ is rather barren because of ♂; the ♈, ♌, or ♒ signs on the cusp the 5th H., and with no intercepted sign in the 5th, are indications of no offspring; ♊ is called a barren sign because ☿ has no particular sex; ♌ is wholly barren because the ☉ is barren; ♌ or ♒ on the Asc., 5th, or 11th houses tend to deny offspring; the ♌ sign, or the ☉ and ♂ in ♌ on the cusp of the 5th H., the human plant is scorched by excess of passion before it has time to grow; ♍ is rather barren because of its ruler ☿; ♏ is the least fruitful of the watery signs because of its ruler ♂; ♎, ♑ and ♒ are classed as indifferent signs, neither fruitful nor barren; ♑ is rather barren because it is the sign of ♄, and the exaltation of ♂; ♑ on the Asc. at the Vernal Equi., Places and Peoples ruled by ♑ suffer from great sterility; ♒ is more fruitful than barren; the lord of the 11th H. a malefic, and in the 5th H. and afflicted; planets which promise or deny children, when posited together in prolific signs, and in ♂, or afflicting each other, tend to deny children or cause their early death, or very few will be reared; a barren sign on the Asc. or cusp of 5th., and espec. on the cusps of both the 1st and 5th at the same time, as ♊ on Asc., and ♍ on the 5th; barren signs in, or on cusps of 1st and 5th, without their Sigs. being in reception, good asp., or translation, the party will not conceive; a barren sign on the cusp of the 4th H., the house denoting the end of all things, gives little hope of ever having children in Hor'y Questions. Barrenness is also caused by Subs at the Private Place, PP, the 2nd, 3rd, and 4th Lumbar vertebrae. (See Vertebrae). For collateral study, and for further influences along this line, see Abortion, Children, Conception, "Cold and Dry Body" under Dry; Fruitful, Gestation; "Anchorite" under Husband; Impotent, Maimed, Men, Pregnancy, Unprolific, Wife, Women.

BASAL GANGLIA—The Ganglia at the base of the Brain—(See "Basal" under Ganglion).

BASHFULNESS—Shy—A ♄ influence; ♄ in the 1st H. at B.; ♄ ruler of the Asc. at B., and afflicted; a characteristic of ♄ people; the ♍ influence also tends to make one "Bashful as a Virgin". (See Backwardness, Modesty, Prudery, Reserved, Retiring, Shy).

BASTARDS—Illegitimate Birth—Children Born Out of Wedlock—The 5th H. should be especially noted.

General Causes—♆ in the 5th H., or afflicting the 5th, or planets in the 5th; ♄ ruler of the 5th H. at B., and by dir. in ♂ or evil asp. the Asc., and

espec. if ♄ afflict ♂ and ♀ at B.; the ♋ in the 5th H. is an indication the child may be illegitimate if there is any doubt or question about it.

Horary Questions—In Lilly's Astrology Horary Questions are considered along the following lines: (1) Is the Child Legitimate and the Child of the Reputed Father? It is if the following conditions exist in the Horary Map,—The lord of the Asc. and the ☽, signify the Querent, and the sign of the 11th H., and its lord, signify the Issue. If these Sigs are in ⚹ or △ asp. in the hor'y map, and behold each other with reception, or not, the conception is legitimate, and the child of the supposed father. If the Sigs be in □ or ☍ asp., in close or perfect asp., and with reception; lord of the Asc., or ☽ be in the 5th H., or lord of the 5th be in the Asc., and with no evil asp. from the malefics, with one of the benefics in favorable asp. to the cusp of the 5th, or lord of the 5th, then also the child is legitimate. (2) The Child May Not be Legitimate—The Husband has Children by other Women than his Wife—Or the Wife has Children by other Men than her Husband—If none of the foregoing aspects and conditions concur; if ♄, ♂, or ☿ are in ill-asp. to the lord of the 5th, or the cusp of the 5th, there may be suspicion of adultery, or that the child is not the child of the Querent. Also if the lord of the 9th is in the 5th, and espec. if the lord of the 5th afflict the lord of the Asc., the husband may have children by other women, or the wife by other men. (See Adoption. Also see Case No. 688, "Illegitimate Birth" in 1001 N.N.).

BATHING—Bathings—The planet ♅ has special rule over bathing, swimming, etc., and his afflictions tend to bring dangers in connection with bathing and the water, and to cause the unexpected. There are times when it is dangerous to go near water, or to bathe in the Ocean, and the many deaths recorded from Sea bathing, and by drowning while bathing, have a close relation to the afflictions of ♅, and also to the afflictions of ♆ for the time. Accidents by water and bathing usually come on scheduled time unless you are forewarned of the dangers, and keep away from large bodies of water, or even be careful in your own bathtub, when these adverse planetary aspects are operating. (See "Dangerous", "Disease" in this section. Also see "Water" under Skin).

Bath House Keepers—Good influences for are ♂ and ♀ rulers of the employment and ♅ conjoined with them.

Cold Baths—Tabulated statistics show that the ♉ people are averse to taking cold baths.

Dangerous to Bathe—Dangerous to Go Near Water—Possible Death at Bathings—Drowned While Bathing— The ☽ to the ♂ or ill-asps. ♅ by dir.; ♆ by transit over the radical place of ♂, and ♂ afflicted at B. in a watery sign; ♆ in the 8th H. in ♓, and affl. by ♂; ♅ affl. in ♋ or ♓, should be warned against bathings in ponds, rivers, or at the Seashore; ♅ in the 8th H., afflicting the hyleg at B., and by dir.; ♂ by periodic direction to the ill-asps. of ♅. Here is the birth data of a case of death while bathing in the Ocean. See "Death by Drowning", Case No. 402, in 1001 N.N.

Death from Bathing—(See "Dangerous" in this section).

Demoniacal Complaints—From Bathing—(See "Bathing" under Demoniac).

Disease, Illness or Injury—From Bathing—The ☉ ruler of the 6th H. at B., and to the ♂ or ill-asp. ♅ by dir.; the ☽ to the ♂ or ill-asp. ♅ by dir. (See "Dangerous" in this section. Also see Cold, Drowning, Exposure, "Perils by Water" under Water).

Mud Baths—(See "Mud Baths" under Healers).

BATTERIES—(See Assaults, Blows).

BATTLE—Death or Injury In—(See Soldiers, War).

BEAR—Cynosura—Little Bear—(See Cynosura).

BEARD—Whiskers—The Beard is ruled by the ♉ sign, and espec. the chin beard.

Auburn Color—Sad Color—Next to Black—Typical of a ☿ person.

Barber's Itch—(See Barbers).

Color Of—(See the various paragraphs in this section).

Flaxen Beard—Sandy Flaxen—Given by ♃ influence.

Full Beard—(See "Much" in this section).

Heavy Beard—(See "Much" in this section).

Light Beard—The Beard Lighter than the Hair of the Head—♃ Sig. of the person; ♃ Sig. in ♑.

Little Beard—(See "Thin" in this section).

Much Beard—Full—Heavy—Thick—The ☉ gives much hair on the beard; the ☉ rising at B.; the ☽ gives; ♃ in ♐ in partile asp. the Asc.; ♃ in the Asc. (See "Abundance", "Bushy", "Hairy Body", under Hair).

No Beard—Often No Beard At All—☿ as Sig. in Hor'y Questions denotes.

Red Beard—Reddish—Characteristic of ♂ people; ♂ strong at B., in the Asc., or rising; ♂ in fiery or airy signs, and with fixed stars of his own nature, a deep, sandy red; in Hor'y Questions ♂ Sig. denotes reddish beard and hair, but this is according to the sign, except he be with fixed stars of his own nature. (See "Red Hair" under Hair).

Sandy Beard—(See "Flaxen", "Red" in this section).

Scanty Beard—(See "Thin" in this section).

Thick Beard—(See "Much" in this section).

Thin Beard—Little Beard—Scanty—♄ in ♈; ♄ signifies a thin, weak beard, and with the ♄ sign ♑ upon the Asc.; in Hor'y Questions ♄ or ☿ as Sigs. of the party, indicate one of a scanty, thin and spare beard; ♄ ascending at

B.; ♄ gives a thin beard when he builds the body; ♃ in ♑, in partile asp. the Asc., the beard is usually thinner and lighter than the hair of the head; ☿ people have thin beards, little beard, and often no beard at all; ☿ strong and rising at B., and free from the rays of other planets, a scanty beard, and little hair on the chin; ♑ influence, and with ♑ on Asc. (See Baldness, Hair).

BEASTS—Bestial—Beastly—The Bestial Signs, the Feral Signs, those of animal form, are ♈, ♉, ♌, ♐, ♑. (See "Brutish Signs" under Brutish). See the following subjects, which have to do with Animals, Beasts, Quadrupeds.

Animals—Attacks By—Injury or Death By—Death of, etc.—See Animals).

Attacks By—(See Animals, Cattle, Horses. Also see the various paragraphs in this section).

Beastly Form—If at conception the ☉ and ☽ are in the 6th or 12th houses in four-footed signs, and the malefics angular, the embryo will be of beastly form, but if a benefic give testimony the child will be of human shape, but of savage disposition. If ☿ be in good asp. the ☽ the faculties will be improved, altho the body will be illformed. The shape will be much better if the ☉ and ☽ be in signs of human form. (See Dogs, Foetus, Inhuman, Monsters).

Bestial Signs—(See the first part of this Article).

Bites by Beasts—(See Bites).

Cattle—Injury or Death By—(See Cattle).

Death by Beasts—♄ ori. in fixed signs, □ or ☍ the ☉ at B., or occi. in fixed signs, in □ or ☍ the ☽, and ♄ in a brutal sign. (See "Hurts", "Wild Animals" under Animals. Also see Cattle, Elephants, Horses, Quadrupeds. Note the various paragraphs in this section).

Devoured By—After Death—(See "Birds" under Air).

Dogs—The Offspring resembles Dogs, etc.—(See "Dogs" under Children; Inhuman, etc.).

Elephants—Death of—Death or Injury By—(See Elephants).

Embryo—Of Beastly Form—(See "Beastly" in this section. Also see Inhuman).

Epidemics Among—Of Cattle and Sheep—(See Epidemics; "Virus" under Pestilence; Sheep).

Form—Offspring of Beastly Form—(See "Beastly" in this section).

Furious Beasts—Injury or Death By—The ☽ to the ♂ ♂ by dir. (See "Wild Animals" under Animals).

Great Beasts—Death or Injury By—(See Cattle, Elephants, Great, Horses).

Horses—Hurts, Injuries, Kicks By—(See Horses).

Hurts by Beasts—(See "Injury", and the various paragraphs in this section. See Animals, Cattle, Elephants, Horses, etc.).

Injury By—The ☽ to the ♂ ♂ by dir.; the ☽ to the ♂ the Ascelli. (See Animals, Cattle, Elephants, Horses, etc.).

Kicks—(See Horses, Kicks).

Quadrupeds—Death or Injury By—(See Animals, Cattle, Elephants Horses, Quadrupeds, etc.).

Reptiles—Death or Injury By—(See Reptiles).

Sickness—The Sickness or Death of Beasts—(See "Death" under Animals; Epidemics, "Virus" under Pestilence; Sheep, etc.).

Signs—The Bestial Signs—(See the first part of this section).

Travel—Attacks by Beasts During Travel—(See "Wild" under Animals; "Travel" under Cattle; "Dangers" under Travel).

Venomous Beasts—Injuries By—(See Venomous).

Wild Beasts—Death or Injury By—(See "Wild" under Animals; "Dangers" under Travel; Wild, etc.).

BEATEN—(See Assaults, Blows, Iron, Lynching, Mobs; "Beaten in Prison" under Prison; "Assaults" under Stones; Sword, etc.).

BEAUTIFUL—Beauty—Elegantly Formed—Handsome, etc.—All Constellations of Human Form, both within and without the Zodiac, tend to give due proportion to the body, and a handsome shape. Also the signs of ♀ give when on the Asc., as ♉ and ♎, or with ♀ in the Asc., or rising and well-aspected. The ♒ sign on the Asc. is notable for the beauty it gives, and many times with white hair in youth, or before middle life. For further influences along this line see the following subjects,—Body, Comely, Commanding, Compact, Complexion, Dimples, Elegant, Eyes, Face, Fair, Fine, Graceful, Hair, Handsome, Harmony, Neat, Refined; "Pure Skin" under Skin; Stature; Well-composed, Well-favored, Well-proportioned, Well-shaped, etc., under "Well".

BED—Taking First to Bed in Sickness —(See Decumbiture).

Bedridden Invalids—(See Confinement, Hospitals, Invalids).

Bed Sores—Caused by the excess heat of the ☉ or ♂ in the sign ruling the part affected, or afflicting such sign and part. (See Sores).

Bed-Wetting—(See "Incontinence" under Urine).

BEES DESTROYED—♂ in ♐ at the Vernal Equinox, and espec. in Places and Countries ruled by ♐.

Droning Of—Humming Of—Said to be ruled by ♆.

BEGGING—Murmuring—(See "Exhibition of Maladies" under Exhibition).

Beggarly—Lives Beggarly and Carelessly—The ☽ ill-dignified at B.; ♃ Sig. □ or ☍ ♄. (See Poverty, Privation).

BEHAVIOR—(See the references under Conduct, Habits, Love Affairs, Marriage, Morals, Passion, Pleasures, Religion, Sex, etc.).

BEHEADED—Decapitation—Danger of Death By—The ☉ joined with the Ascelli, Castor, Pollux, Hyades, Pleiades, Praesepe; the ☉ directed to all Nebulous Clusters, and espec. to Castor or Ascelli, threatens decapitation; ♂ afflicted in Imperfect or Mutilated signs; ♂ in the 8th H., or ruler of the 8th, and with Caput Algol; ♂ near Gorgon in the 5th face of ♉, and in ♂ or ♉ the ☉ or ☽, death by, or mutilation of limb; ♂ ori., in mutilated signs, in □ or ♉ the ☉, or ♂ occi. in □ or ♉ the ☽, or with Caput Medusa; malefics in earth signs, and espec. in ♉; the hyleg ♂ Caput Algol in an angle. (See Distortions, Guillotined, Hanging, "Death by Sentence" under Judge; Maimed, Mutilated, etc.).

BELCHING—Eructations—Pyrosis—Water Brash—Burning Pains at Stomach, with Eructations—Emission of Gas Thru Mouth—A disease of the ♋ sign; ♄ or ☿ affl. in ♋; ♂ in ♋ or ill-asp. the ☽ tends to eructations and burning pains at the stomach. (See Digestion, Flatulence, Gas, "Gastric Acidity" under Acids; Heartburn, Indigestion; Stomach; "Stomach" under Wind, etc.).

BELLADONNA—Atropin—One of the 12 Polycrest Remedies, and corresponding to the ♉ Sign. Also a typical drug of ♄. (See "Polycrest" under Zodiac; "Mydriatics" under Iris).

BELLATRIX—Orion's Left Shoulder—A star of the nature of ♂ and ☿ in 19° ♊. The ☉ and ☽ to the place of tend to cause Blindness by Accident. Its influence also tends to Extreme Sickness, Dangers, Blindness, Disgrace, Drowning, Calamity, Disease, Hot Distempers, Putrid Fevers, Ruin, Violent Death, etc. (See these subjects. Also see Orion, Rigel).

BELLY—Ventral—Abdomen—The word Belly is frequently used in the text-books of Astrology, and is merely another word for Abdomen. The most of the subjects concerning the Belly you will find under Abdomen. The Belly is ruled by the ☽ and the ♍ Sign. The inferior part of the Belly, the lower Belly, is ruled by the 6th H.

Any Disease—In the Belly—A ♍ disease; afflictions in ♍.

Bellyache—Dry Bellyache—The ☽ affl. in ♍ or ♎; ♄ affl. in ♊. (See "Pain" under Bowels).

Diseases Of—Disorders—♀ diseases, and afflictions to ♀; ☽ affl. in ♍; afflictions in ♍ or the 6th H.

Fluxes Of—☽ diseases, and afflictions to the ☽; the ☽ affl. in ♍.

Large, Deep Belly—♃ in the Asc. (See "Prominent" under Abdomen).

Love Their Belly—(See Eating, Feasting, Gluttony, etc.).

Short and Lank Belly—♄ ascending at B.

Ventral Hernia—(See Hernia). See Abdomen, Bowels, Hypogastrium, Intestines, Navel, etc.

BENDING—Bent—Flexed—Flexion—Flexible—Flexure—☿ affl. in ♌ warns against bending the body.

Body Bent Forward — (See Crooked, "Downward Look" under Look; Legs, Stooping; "Round Shoulders" and "Stoop Shoulders" under Shoulders).

Flexed Signs—(See Mutable).

Womb—Flexion of—(See Flexure, Womb).

BENEFICS—The planets ♃ and ♀. These planets in ☌ or good asp. the ☉, ☽, Asc., M.C., or Hyleg at B. tend to benefit and preserve the health, and give greater vitality. The Benefics afflict only by their □ and ⚻ aspects. Heat and moisture are given by the benefics, both benevolent influences, and for this reason the Ancients called them Benefic planets. The more angular, oriental and elevated the benefics at B., the more powerful are their effects for good, and to assist in the cure and alleviation of disease. The Benefics may act as Anareta under certain circumstances. (See Anareta). They also exert a protective, preservative, nourishing influence. (See these subjects). The ☉, ☽, and ☊ are also classed as Benefics when giving their good aspects. (See these planets and Dragon's Head. Also see Horas, Malefics).

BEREAVEMENT—The general causes of a death in the family, or among relatives or friends, and to bring bereavement, are as follows,—The ☉ or ☽ to the ☌ or ill-asps. ♅, ♄, or ♂ by dir.; the ☉ to the ill-asps. the ☽ by dir.; the ☉, ♅, ♄, or ♂ by their evil directions to the hyleg, and to the vital places in the map; the progressed ☉ to the □ or ⚻ ♃ by dir.; the ☽ to the ill-asps. the ☉ by dir., and espec. to females; the ☽ to the ill-asps. ♀ by dir.; ♄ to the ☌ or ill-asp. the ☉, ☽, ♀, ☿, Asc., or M.C. by dir. (For further influences along this line see Acquaintances, Aunts, Brothers, Children, Father, Friends, Grief, Grandparents, Infants, Mother, Parents, Prevalent, Relatives, Sisters, Uncles, etc.).

BERIBERI — (See this subject under Dropsy).

BESIDE ONESELF — Frenzy — Excessively Excitable — (See Excitable, Frenzy, Fury).

BETELGEUSE—(See Orion).

BETTER—The Disease is Better—(See "Better" under Disease, Health; Improvement).

BICORPOREAL SIGNS—(See Double-Bodied).

BILE—Bilious—The Gall—Gall Bladder —Choler—Cholic—The Bile is ruled by ♄, ♂, ☿, and the ♌ and ♏ signs. The Gall Bladder, the reservoir of the Bile, is ruled by ♄, and as a receptacle, by the ☽. The Bile holds dominion from 9 A.M. to 3 P.M. The First Quarter of the ☽, which is hot and dry, acts on the Bile. The Bile is formed by ♄ in the liver, and deposited by ♄ over the body in the form of Uric Acid, causing Gout, Rheumatism, etc. (See Gout, Rheumatism). Mars portends the Gall, and also causes diseases arising from too much choler. The Bilious Signs are ♈, ♌, ♐, the fiery signs. Note the following conditions concerning the Bile, Gall Bladder, Ducts, etc., and diseases connected with them,—

All Diseases—Of the Gall—♂ diseases, and due to ♂ afflictions.

Atrabilarious Attacks — (See "Black Bile" in this section. Also see Depression, Hypochondria, Melancholy).

Biliousness—Liverishness—A disease of the ☉ and ♂, and characteristic of the Bilious, or Choleric Temperament ruled by the ☉, ♂, and the fiery signs; the ☉ ♈, ☌ or ill-asp. any of the malefics as promittors; the ☉ in ill-asp. to ♃; the ☉ in ♋ and affl. by ♃; the ☽ ♏ and to the ☌ or ill-asp. any of the malefics as promittors, and tends to great mental depression; ♆, ♅, or ♄ in ♉ or ♏, and affl. the ☉ or ☽; ♂ affl. in ♌; ♂ ♏ ☌ or ill-asp. the ☉; caused by Subs at Li.P., Liver Place, in spine.

Black Bile—Blackness of Bile—Atrabilarious Attacks—Depression—Hypochondria—Melancholy, etc.—♄ and ♂ in an angle, occi. of the ☉, and ori. of the ☽, and ☿ in familiarity with ♂; ♂ or ☿ holding dominion at B., and in familiarity with each other, and ♂ affl. the hyleg and elevated above the Luminaries, blackness of bile is increased. (See Adrenals, Atrabile).

Calculi—(See "Gall Stones" in this section).

Choler—(See Choler).

Cholera—Bilious Cholera—(See "Cholera Morbus" under Cholera).

Choleric Distempers—And Humours —(See Choleric).

Cholic—Biliary Colic—Hepatic Colic —Disturbances of the Bile—Pain in the Liver, Gall Bladder, Gall Ducts— Cramps About the Gall Bladder, etc.— A ☽ and ♏ disease; afflictions in ♏; ♄ in an angle, occi. of the ☉, and ori. of the ☽; ☿ lord of the 1st H., and applying to the □ or ⚻ ♄ or a malefic.

Complaints—Bilious Complaints— Given by the Bilious, or Choleric Temperament; diseases of the ☉, ♂, and the fiery signs; a □ disease; afflictions in ♉ or ♐; ♂ affl. in ♉; ♂ affl. in ♋ in the 6th H. (See "Choleric Temperament" under Choleric).

Cough — Bilious Dry Cough — (See Cough).

Deficiency of Bile—♄ affl. in the 6th H.

Diarrhoea—(See "Bilious" under Diarrhoea).

Diseases—And Disorders of the Bile and Gall Bladder—(See the various paragraphs in this section).

Distempers—Choleric Distempers and Humours—(See Choleric).

Disturbances—Of the Bile—(See the various subjects in this section).

Ducts—The Gall Ducts—The Bile Ducts Disordered—Stenosis of—♄ affl. in ♏, and espec. in the 6th H.; ♂ affl. in ♏; caused by Subs at Li.P., and afflictions in the signs acting thru Li.P. (See Vertebrae).

Fevers — Bilious Fevers — Burning, Hot, Fiery, Violent Fevers, and which grow worse towards sunrise—(See "High Fevers" under Fevers).

Flatulency—Bilious Flatulency—♀ affl. in ♎; ☿ affl. in ♓. (See Flatulence).

Gall Stones—Biliary Calculi—Chololithiasis—Are formed by ♄ in the Gall Bladder, and painful Gallstones are the work of ♄; ♄ ☌ or ill-asp. ♂; ♄ affl. in ♌; a disease of the ☽; afflictions in ♎; ♅ on the Asc., thru worry and brooding; caused by Subs at Li.P. For Birth Data and Cases of Gall Stones, see Figures 10A and 10B in the book, "Astro-Diagnosis" by the Heindels. (See Stone).

Headache—(See "Bilious" under Headache).

Humours—Choleric Humours—(See Choleric).

Hypochondria—(See this subject).

Jaundice—(See Jaundice).

Liver—(See the various subjects under Liver).

Liverishness—(See "Biliousness" in this section).

Melancholy—Atrabile—Black Bile—(See "Black Bile" in this section. Also see Atrabile, Melancholy).

Nausea—Bilious Nausea—(See Nausea).

Obstruction—Of the Bile Passages—♆, ♅, or ♄ in ♓, and affl. the ☉ or ☽.

Pain—In the Gall Bladder—(See "Cholic" in this section).

Stenosis—Of the Gall Ducts—(See "Ducts" in this section).

Temperament—The Bilious Temperament—(See Choleric).

Treatment—(See Signature).

Vomiting—Bilious Vomiting—(See Nausea, Vomiting).

BINDING—Limiting—Restraining—Confining—The influence and action of ♄, and also of the 12th H. (See Chronic, Confinement, Hospitals, Invalids, Limitations, Retraction, "Influence of Saturn" under Saturn; Twelfth House).

BIOCHEMISTRY—The Chemistry of Living Tissues. The study of the Chemistry of the human body in its relation to the Zodiac, and the Tissue Salts of the body under the rule of the 12 Signs of the Zodiac. (See "Salts" under Zodiac).

BIRDS—(See "Birds of the Air" under Air; Fowls, Vultures).

Bird Features—(See Monsters).

BIRTH—Births—Born—etc.—(See the following subjects in the alphabetical arrangement,—

Abnormal Births—(See Abortion, "Excision" under Foetus; Premature, Stillborn, etc. Note the various subjects in this section).

Abortion; Accident at Birth—(See "Accidents" under Infancy).

Asphyxiation—At Birth—(See Asphyxia).

Big at Birth—Very Big at Birth—See Case, "Short Life", No. 371 in 1001 N.N.

Birthday—Anniversary of Birth—The Solar Revolution—The time when the ☉ passes over the same degree of the Zodiac he was in at B. The birthday each year begins your new year, and when the vital forces of the body begin to take on new and greater activity. During the period of 105 days before the birthday the forces of the body are usually at their lowest ebb. In each life the year is divided into seven divisions, or days, corresponding to the days of the week, periods of 52 days each, and the 105 days before the birthday are the Friday and Saturday periods of the year for the native. The Friday Period is the 52 days "On the Cross", and the Saturday Period the 52 days "In the Tomb", and these are usually very difficult and trying periods of the year for the average person unless he is settled, contented, prosperous, and of good health. These Periods and Cycles are discussed in the book called "Periodicity", by Dr. James Buchanan. (See "Solar Revolution" under Solar).

Birthmarks—(See Naevus).

Birth Place—(See "Place of Birth" under Place).

Birthrate—The birthrate is increased when the ☽ is in the 5th H. at a Vernal Equinox, Ingress, or Solstice, and well-aspected by the benefics, and decreased when the ☽ is in the 5th H. at these times, and afflicted by malefics, and with no assistance from the benefics).

Birthstones—(See this subject under Stones).

Blind from Birth—(See this subject under Blindness).

Cause of Birth—From a physical standpoint the immediate cause of birth of the body into the world is due to the influence of ♂ and the ☽. The violent influence of ♂ ushers the child into the world, and normally at the 10th menstrual period, which periods are ruled by the ☽. There exists in Nature a sympathy between parent and child, and children are born at a moment when the constitution of the heavens is such as to produce one with the traits and characteristics of one or both parents. Family resemblances are thus handed down in this way. (See "Moment of Birth" under Calamity; Foetus, Gestation, Heredity, Nativity, Parturition, Prenatal Epoch).

Child—Birth of a Child Promised—(See "Birth of a Child" under Children; "Birth of a Female" under Female; "Births" under Male; "Birth of a Son" under Son).

Childbirth—(See Parturition).

Children—Birth of—(See Fruitfulness. Also see "Child" in this section).

Congenital—Existing from Birth—Innate—(See Congenital, Heredity, Innate).

Crippled—From Birth—(See Arms. Congenital, Deformed, Distortions, Excrescences, Infancy, Lame, Legs, Maimed, Monsters, Paralysis, etc.).

Daughter Born—(See "Birth of a Female" under Female).

Dead—Born Dead—(See Stillborn).

Deafness from Birth—(See "Born Deaf" under Hearing).

Death at Birth—(See "Birth", "Born Almost Dead", under Children).

Death Soon After Birth—(See "Born Almost Dead" under Children; "Nurture" under Infancy. Also see Abortion, Foetus).

Defective Births—(See "Crippled" in this section. Also see Blind, Congenital, Defects, Distortions, Freaks, Idiots, Monsters, Mute, etc).

Deformed—From Birth—(See "Crippled" in this section. Also see Deformed; "Deformed" under Infancy).

Delayed Birth—(See "Birth" under Asphyxia).

Diseases and Infections—At Birth—(See Infancy).

Distortions—From Birth—(See Distortions).

Eclipses—At Time of Birth—Danger of Death—(See Eclipses).

Embryo; Female Births—(See "Birth of a Female" under Female).

Foetus; Gestation; Heredity; Illegitimate—(See Bastard).

Incomplete—Born Incomplete—Members or Parts Missing—(See Arms, Congenital, Deformities, Incomplete, Malformations, Missing, Monsters).

Infancy—(See the various paragraphs under Infancy).

Injury at Birth—(See Parturition).

Lame from Birth—(See Lameness).

Large at Birth—(See Large).

Life—Continuance of Life After Birth—(See "Continuance" under Life).

Maimed from Birth—(See Maimed).

Male Born—(See "Births" under Male).

Miscarriage; Moment of Birth—This is counted from the time of the first cry, the first breath, when the magnetism of the Universe is breathed in. The time and moment of birth are considered fixed unless interfered with by unnatural causes. (See "Causes" in this section. Also see Baptism; Conception; Congenital; "Moment of Birth" under Moment).

Monsters; Mother—Death of In Childbirth—(See "Death of the Mother" under Parturition).

Multiple Births—(See Twins).

Normal Birth—(See Normal).

Overtime Birth—(See "Delayed", "Moment" in this section. Also see Prenatal Epoch; "Excision" under Foetus).

Paralyzed from Birth—(See Distortions).

Place of Birth—(See "Place of Birth" under Place).

Precocious Births—(See Precocious).

Premature Births—(See Abortion, Miscarriage, Premature).

Prenatal Epoch; Single Births—One Only—(See "Single Births" under Children).

Son Born—(See Son. Also see "Births" under Male).

Star Map of Birth—(See Map. Also see "Moment" in this section).

Stillborn; Strangled at Birth—(See Asphyxia).

Suffocated at Birth—(See Asphyxia, Suffocation).

Time of Birth—(See "Moment" in this section. Also see Baptism, Prenatal Epoch, Time).

Triplets; Twins.

BISEXUAL—(See Hermaphrodites).

BITES—Stings—Are usually caused by the ♂ influence, and the afflictions of the malefics.

Adder—Bites or Stings By—♄, ♂, and ♀ conjoined in ♏, Kings are stung by an Adder or some obnoxious creature. (See Adder).

Animals—Beasts—Horses—Bites By—The ☽ in an earthy sign, and to the ♂ or ill-asp. ♂ by dir.; ♄ in an animal sign, as in ♈, ♉, ♌, ♐, or ♑; the Asc. to the place of Hydra's Heart. (See "Hurts" under Horses).

Death By—The ☽ hyleg, and to the ♂ or ill-asp. ♂ by dir., and the ☽ affl. at B.; ♄ affl. in ♏, danger of death by bites of serpents; ♄ in animal signs, and afflicted, danger of death by bites of animals. (See Serpents, Stings, Venomous).

Dogs—Bites By—The ☉ to the ♂ or ill-asp. ♂ by dir., bites by dogs, mad dogs, and death by Hydrophobia. (See Dogs, Hydrophobia).

Horses—Bites By—(See "Animals" in this section).

Insects—Bites By—(See Stings, Venomous).

Journeys—Travel—Bites or Stings During Travel—Malefics in the 3rd or 9th H., in fiery signs, and affl. the ☉ or ☽. (See Venomous).

Kings—Ruler—(See "Adder" in this section).

Mad Dog—(See "Dogs" in this section).

Obnoxious Creatures—Bites By—(See "Adder" in this section. Also see Obnoxious, Venomous).

Reptiles—Bites By—(See Reptiles, Serpents, Venomous).

Serpents—Snakes—Bites By—(See "Death" in this section. Also see Serpents, Venomous).

Travel—Bites During—(See "Journeys" in this section).

Venomous Creatures—(See Adder, Death, in this section. Also see Serpents, Venomous).

Various Kinds—Of Bites—The ☉ hyleg, and the ☉ to the ♂ or ill-asp. ♂ by dir.; the ☽ to the ♂ or ill-asp. ♂ by dir.; ♄, ♂, and ♀ conjoined in ♏.

Voyages—Bites On—(See "Journeys" in this section).

BITTER—Acrid—Pungent—

Bitter Drugs—Acrid and Pungent Drugs—Are mostly ruled by ♂, as Nux Vomica, Strychnine, Quinine, etc. (See Acids, Pungent, Signature).

Bitter Signs—♈, ♌, ♐, said to be bitter, fiery and hot.

Bitter Temper—(See Sarcasm; "Nasty" under Temper).

BLACK—As a color, is ruled and signified by ♄. Is also denoted by the 6th, 7th and 8th houses. The ♍ sign signifies black spotted with blue; ♎ denotes black or swarthy; ♑ denotes black. Black, ruled by ♄, has a deadening and devitalizing influence, and black clothing should be avoided. (See Color, Colors).

Black Bile—(See Bile).

Black Death—(See Plague).

Black Eyebrows—(See Eyebrows).

Black Eyelids—(See Eyelids).

Black Eyes—(See "Black" under Eyes).

Black Figure—(See "Skin" in this section).

Black Hair—(See Hair).

Blackheads—(See "Comedo" under Sebaceous).

Black Jaundice—(See Jaundice).

Black Magic—(See Magical).

Blackmailers—(See Libel).

Black Marks—On Body—(See Marks).

Black Skin—Black Personal Figure—(See "Black" under Skin; "Dark Personal Figure" under Dark; Negro).

BLADDER— Vesica—Receptacle of the Urine—Vesical Muscle—All vesicles, or containers, which hold liquids and fluids in the body, are fundamentally ruled and influenced by the ☽ and the ♋ sign. The urinal bladder is under the internal rule of the ♍ sign. Also ♉ has affinity with the bladder. According to the various Authors and Textbooks, the Bladder is ruled by ♄, ♂, the ☽, ♎, ♍, and the 7th and 8th houses. Elimination of the urine thru the bladder is ruled by ♂ and ♍. In infants the bladder is largely ruled and dominated by the action of the ☉ and ☽ working thru the ♎ sign, and gives way to the Renal Diathesis. (See Hypogastrium). Note the following diseases and conditions concerning the Bladder:

Abscess In—Impostumes—A ♎ disease, and afflictions in ♎; ♃ affl. in ♍ in the 6th H. (See Abscesses).

All Diseases In—Are indicated by the 7th and 8th Houses, by ♎ᵣ ♍, and the afflictions of ♂, and are diseases of ♂ and the ☽.

Atony Of—♄ affl. in ♍; ♄, ♍, □ or ♉ ♅ or ♂. (See Atonic).

Bladder Troubles—(See "Diseases" in this section).

Bladder Worm—(See Acephalocyst).

Catarrh Of—(See "Cystitis" in this section).

Cloaca—(See Cloaca).

Concretions In—Gravel or Sand In—(See "Gravel", "Stone" in this section).

Cystitis—Inflammation and Catarrh of the Bladder—♂ in ♍ and affl. the hyleg; a ♍ disease, and planets affl. in ♍; ♂ affl. in ♋, and ♋ on the cusp of 8th H.; caused by Subs at PP, and LPP, and also at KP, from irritating urine. (See Catarrh, Urine, Vertebrae).

Diseases Of—Bladder Troubles—The ☉ or ☽ in the 6th H., and afflicted; the

☉ and ☽ acting thru the ♍ sign, and give way to the Hepatic Diathesis (See "Basal" under Ganglion); the ☉ or ☽ affl. in ♍; the ☽ in the 6th H., in fixed signs, and afflicted; caused by the ☽ affl. at B.; the ☽ in ♍ or ♒, and to the ☌ or ill-asps. any of the malefics by dir., and espec. if ♂ affl. the ☽ at B., or ♂ occupy the 6th H.; ♂ diseases and afflictions; ♂ ♍ ☌ or ill-asp. the ☉ or ☽; ♂ in 6th H., and affl. the ☉, ☽, or hyleg, and espec. if ♂ be in the fixed signs ♉, ♌, ♍, the ♉ or ♍ signs on the cusp of 6th H., and afflicted; caused by Subs at KP, PP, LPP. (See "All Diseases", and the various paragraphs in this section).

Gall Bladder—(See Bile).

Gravel In—Sand—(See Gravel, Sand, Stone).

Hypertrophy Of—♂ affl. in ♍. (See Hypertrophy).

Imposthumes—(See "Abscess" in this section).

Incontinence—Of the Urine—(See "Incontinence" under Urine).

Inflammation Of—(See "Cystitis" in this section).

Irritable Bladder—Constant Desire to Urinate—(See "Strangury", "Micturition" under Urine).

Micturition—(See Urine).

Neck of Bladder—Vesicae Cervis—Neuralgia of—♂, ♀, or ☿ affl. in ♍. (See "Neck" under Womb).

Neuralgia—(See "Neck" in this section).

Pains In—Violent Pains In—The ☉ affl. in ♓ when the ☉ is the afflictor in the disease, violent pains; the ☽ in ♒ and with ♍ upon the Asc. when taken ill; ♂ in ♍ when ♂ is the afflictor in the disease; ☿ affl. in ♍.

Sand—(See "Gravel" in this section).

Spasm—Stricture—♅ affl. in ♎ or ♍. (See Spasmodic).

Stone—(See Stone).

Stricture Of—(See "Spasm" in this section).

Tuberculosis Of—♄ affl. in ♍; Subs at KP and PP. (See Tuberculosis, Vertebrae).

Ulcers—A ♎ disease and afflictions in ♎. (See "Abscess" in this section).

Urine—Bladder Disorders Thru Disturbed Urine—(See the various subjects under Urine, as Micturition, Strangury, etc.

Violent Pains In—(See "Pain" in this section).

Worm—Bladder Worm—(See Acephalocyst).

Weakness Of—The ☽ hyleg in ♍ in a female nativity; ♀ affl. in ♍ in 6th H., or affl. the ☽ or Asc. (For collateral study see Elimination, Excretion, "Impar" under Ganglion; Kidneys, Secretion, Urethra, Urine).

BLEB—Bulla—(See Blister).

BLEEDING—Loss of Blood—(See Discharges, Effusions, Epistaxis, Hemorrhage, "Flooding" under Menses).

Blood - Letting— Transfusion— Withdrawing blood from the circulation should not be done in a ♃ hour, or when ♃ is affl. by the ☽, as ♃ rules the blood. (See Blood, Effusions, Jupiter).

Gums—(See "Bleeding" under Gums).
Piles—(See "Bleeding" under Hemorrhoids).

BLEMISHES—Blemished—Bodily Blemishes— External Blemishes— Ptolemy associates the words "Diseases and Blemishes", in giving the causes of Disease. (See "Causes of Disease" under Disease). The Asc. rules over Blemishes and External Complaints. The Asc. affl. by ♂ tends to hurts and blemishes; ♅, ♄, or ♂ on the cusp of the 1st, 6th, or 7th houses, or in exact evil asp. to these degrees, and espec. if the ☉ or ☽ be in ♂ or ☍ in the 1st or 7th houses; ♅, ♄, or ♂ ori. tend to blemishes or hurts; the ☽ is said to give blemishes when she is in Tropical or Equinoctial Signs, as in ♈, ♎, ♋, ♑; malefics ori., and in evil asp. the Lights, but if occi. cause diseases; malefics in angles, occi. of the ☉, and ori. of the ☽, and with no benefic configurations of the benefics to ♄ or ♂, or to the ☉ or ☽, the blemishes become permanent and can never be removed, and espec. if the malefics be fortified and elevated above the benefics. If the benefics in the foregoing configuration are elevated above the malefics, the blemishes will be mitigated, and may entirely disappear or be removed. (See Blotches, Children, Defects, Deformities, Disfigurements, Eruptions, Face, Freckles, Marks, Moles, Monsters, Naevus, Pimples, Parts, Pockmark, Scars, Sores, Teeth, Ulcers, Varicose, etc.).

Eyes—Blemish In or Near the Eyes— The ☽ at exactly New or Full ☽ at B., and in evil asp. ♂, a scar or mole; the ☽ impeded by, or evilly aspected by the ☉ at B.; the ☽ impeded by the ☉ in an angle gives a blemish in the eye, but if she be with Nebulous or violent Fixed Stars, in a succedent house, the blemish will be near the eye; the ☽ impeded in succedent houses; the ☽ ♂ or ☍ the ☉ in angles, and the ☉ or ☽ affl. by ♂: the ☽ ♂ or ill-asp. the ☉ at B. (See Cataracts, Defects, Impediments, Marks, and other paragraphs under Eyes).

Face—Blemishes On—(See Blemishes under Face).

BLEPHARITIS—(See Eyelids).

BLIGHT—Blights—Cessation of Growth —Decay— Fading— Withering, etc.— The influence of ♄, and a ♄ disease. (See Decay, Fruit, Growth, Herbs, Vegetation, Withering).

Eyes—Blight In the Eye— (See "Blight" under Eyes).

BLINDNESS—Loss of Sight in One or Both Eyes—Light Rays are transmitted by ♅, which planet rules the Ether. Thus ♅ indirectly tends to affect the eyes thru the light rays, and cause blindness or eye diseases. (See Ether, Light, Retina, Uranus). The Nebulous Spots in the heavens when found with the ☉ or ☽ at B.

also tend to blindness, and many eye disorders and weaknesses. (See Nebulous). In the Hindu System of Astrology the 2nd H. is given rule over the eyes, and afflictions in or to this house tend to impair the sight, or cause blindness. The malefics, when with the ☉ or ☽ at B., or with Nebulous Stars, increase the danger of blindness. Under the heading, "Causes of Blindness" in this section will be given the influences of the ☉, ☽, ☿, and each of the malefics in causing blindness. The Asc., or ruler of the Asc., in one of the Azimene Degrees of the Zodiac at B. also tend to Blindness. (See Azimene). Note the following conditions and influences which have to do with Blindness and its causes, and see these subjects in the alphabetical arrangement when not considered here.

Accidents—Blindness By—The ☉ or ☽ joined to Bellatrix at B., or by dir.; the ☽ or Asc. in Nebulous parts at B., or by dir., and affl. by ♂; caused principally by ♂ afflictions to the ☉ or ☽ at B., or ♂ with violent Nebulous stars; a malefic in a Nebulous place and affl. the ☉ or ☽, and espec. if the malefic be elevated above the Lights. There is more hope of relief from the accident when the malefic in a Nebulous place afflicts the ☽ rather than the ☉. (See the various paragraphs in this section. Also see "Accidents" under Eyes).

Amaurosis— Partial or Total Blindness By—(See Gutta Serena. Also see "Total Blindness" in this section).

Amusements—Sports—Blindness from Injury During—(See the ♂ influences under "Causes" in this section. Also see "Total Blindness" in this section).

Artifice—Blindness By—(See the ♂ influences under "Causes" in this section).

Azimene Degrees—(See Azimene).

Birth—Blind from Birth—(See "Born Blind" in this section).

Blind Spot of Retina— (See "Blind Spot" under Eyes; Retina).

Blows—Blindness by Blows—(See "Accidents", "Injury", under Eyes; "Eyes" under Sword).

Born Blind—Blind from Birth—The actual planetary causes of this condition are not generally shown in the natal map, but in the prenatal conditions, the Lunar Epoch, and Chart of Descent. Afflictions to the ☽ at each Lunar return during pregnancy, corresponding to the monthly period, often show the causes of congenital deformities, afflictions, blindness, and malformations which exist at B. The following conditions have existed in the maps of those born blind,—In males, ♄ on the Asc., or in the M.C., afflicting the ☉, and the ☽ sepr. from the ☉ and applying to ♂; the ☽ near a Nebulous place at B., ♂ or ill-asp. a malefic, and the ☉ also afflicted; the ☽ and ♆ conjoined in the 2nd H., and in ☐ to ♂ in the 6th (Hindu); ♆ on the Asc., and afflicting ♃, and possibly from some affection of the optic nerve; ♄ in the 2nd H., and affl. the ☉ or ☽ (Hindu). (See Azimene, Congenital,

Prenatal Epoch). Cases of Born Blind —See "Arundel", and "Seventeen Years In Bed", Cases No. 159 and 843 in 1001 N.N. See "Diseases to Eyes", Case No. 4, page 87, Chap. 13, in Daath's Medical Astrology.

Both Eyes—Blind In—(See "Total" in this section).

Bruises—Blindness By—The ☉ directed to Praesepe, Hyades, Pleiades, Castor, Pollux, or other stars of the nature of ♂ and the ☽ combined, and espec. if Praesepe be in the Asc., or with the ☉ or ☽ in an angle. (See "Total" in this section).

Burning—Blindness By—The ☉ in the Asc. or M.C., with ♂ rising before him, and the ☉ ☌ or ☍ the ☽; the ☉ in an angle in the same sign with the ☽, or in ☍, with ♄ and ♂ ori. of the ☉, ascending before him, and ♄ and ♂ occi. of the ☽. (These same influences also apply to injuries to the eyes by blows, strokes, or the sword. (See "Injuries to Eyes" under Eyes).

Cataracts;
Causes of Blindness—The ☉ or ☽ with the Pleiades, Ascelli, Antares, Praesepe, Deneb, Hyades, Castor, Pollux, or Orion's Belt, at B., or afflicted by these, and other Nebulous stars by dir., tend to blindness, or at least in one eye, or to serious injury to the eyes, and espec. when the Lights are also afflicted by ♂ from an angle; the ☉ ☌ or ☍ the ☽ in any of the Nebulous parts of the Zodiac; the ☉ with the Pleiades at B., and espec. if ♅ afflict; the ☉ or ☽ with stars of the nature of ♂ and the ☽ combined, as with the Pleiades, Praesepe, Hyades, Castor and Pollux, etc.; the ☉ ☌ ☿ in ♐ near the place of Antares; the ☉ or ☽ in the 6th H. in ☌ with Antares or the Ascelli, and in ☍ to any of the malefic planets; the ☉ or ☽ ☌ Nebulous stars, and affl. by malefics; the ☉ to the ☌ or ill-asp. the ☽ by dir., and the ☽ affl. at B.; the ☉ and ☽ in the signs of their fall, and afflicted, as the ☉ in ♎, and the ☽ in ♏; the ☉ or ☽ joined to Bellatrix; the ☉ and ☽ in ☍ from ♌ and ♒; the ☉ and ♂ in ☌ Nebulous stars, and affl. by ♅; the progressed ☉ to the bad asps. ♅; the ☉ or ☽ in the angles of the map, afflicting each other, and also afflicted by Nebulous stars; the ☉ directed to any of the Nebulous clusters threatens blindness; the ☉ and ☽ ascending, and impedited by ♄ or ♂, gives blindness, bad eyes, or scars or marks in them; the ☉ Sig. in ☌ ♄ and ♄ ill-dig; the ☉ Sig. ☍ ☽ if the ☽ be hyleg, and the ☍ close, may be blind; the ☉ to the ☌ ♂ by dir.; the ☉ to the □ or ☍ ♂ or ill-asp. ☽ by dir.; ☽ ☌ the Pleiades in the 7th H., and espec. if affl. by ♂; the ☽ to ☌ or ill-asp. ♂ by dir., and ♂ be near the Ascelli, Aldebaran, Bull's Eye, or Cor Scorpio, and affl. by the ☉ or ♄; the ☽ to the place of Praesepe, and other Nebulous stars of the nature of ♂ and the ☽, great defect in sight, and often blindness, espec. when both Lights are with Nebulous stars and affl. by malefics; the ☽ sepr. from the ☉ and applying to ♂ in a day geniture; the ☽ in an angle with the Pleiades, Praesepe, or Antares; the progressed ☽ in ☌ with malefics in ♈,

and espec. if the ☉ or ☽ were with Nebulous stars at B., and afflicted; the ☽ affl. at B., and to the ☌ or ill-asps. the ☉ by dir., and espec. if either of the Lights were near Nebulous stars at B.; the ☽ in the western angle, or 7th H., conjoined with the Pleiades, which was the case with Milton, the blind Poet; the ☽ Sig. ☌ the ☉ near the Pleiades, Hyades or Praesepe; the ☽ or Asc. in Nebulous parts, and affl. by ♄; the ☽ directed to the Pleiades, Hyades, Praesepe, or the Twins and Ascelli; the ☽ Sig. ☌ the ☉; the ☽ Sig. □ or ☍ the ☉, and espec. if sepr. from the ☍; the ☽ to the □ or ☍ the ☉ by dir.; ♀ or ♅ joined with Nebulous stars; ♀ ☌ the Ascelli; ♅ in evil asp. the ☉ or ☽ when near the Pleiades, Antares, or the Ascelli, tends to weaken the eyes, or produce blindness; ♄ causes blindness by cold, colds, cataracts, specks, films, Gutta Serena, etc., and if ☿ be with him it will be from mental exertion, reading, study, etc.; ♄ affl. the ☽ or Asc. when the latter are in Nebulous parts; ♂ causes blindness by bruises, fire, wounds, smallpox, lightning, accidents, injuries, strokes, blows, etc., when affl. the ☉ or ☽ in or near Nebulous parts, and if ♂ be with ♀ he causes blindness at some amusement, in sports, at play, by private injury, treachery, or some vile artifice; ☿ causes blindness from eye-strain, mental exertion, and from hard reading or over-study, and espec. when conjoined with the ☉ or ☽ afflicted in Nebulous spots. (For further influences see the various paragraphs in this section, and under "Eyes", "Sight", etc). Cases and Birth Data of Blindness, Acquired Blindness, Going Blind, etc.,—In 1001 N.N. see cases No. 099, 159, 684. and 843, under the headings of "Marsten", "Arundel", "Sight Defective", and "Seventeen Years in Bed". See Fig. 32 in book, "Message of the Stars" by the Heindels. See Cases 2 and 4, Chap. 13, "Diseases to Eyes", in Daath's Medical Astrology. (See Heredity).

Cold—Blindness from Cold or White Film—The ☉ in an angle ☌ or ☍ the ☽, and ♄ ascending before the ☉.

Color Blindness—Afflictions to ♀ by the malefics, and espec. by ♄, and also strong afflictions in the ☍ sign, and espec. to the 16 and 17°, tend to produce color blindness; Subs at AT and MCP, 4th C. (See Color).

Day Blindness—Nyctalopia—♆ afflictions to the ☉ or ☽, with vision best at night; ♆ with Nebulous stars, and afflicting the ☉ or ☽.

Deaf, Dumb and Blind—(See Hearing, Mutes. See Case, "Arundel", No. 159, in 1001 N.N.).

Defects—Blindness From—(See Cataracts, Film, Specks, and the various paragraphs in this section).

Exercise—Blindness By—(See "Sports" in this section).

Explosions—Blindness By—(See Explosions).

Eye Strain—Blindness By—(See "Eyestrain" under Eyes; "Mental Exertion" in this section).

Film—Blindness from White Film—(See "Cold" in this section).

Fire—By Fire—(See "Burning" in this section).

Glaucoma—Blindness By—(See Glaucoma).

Growths—Blindness By—The ☽ or Asc. in Nebulous Parts, and affl. by ♄. (See Cataract, Film, Obstructions, Specks, and other paragraphs in this section. Also see "Defects" under Eyes).

Gunshot—Blindness By—Caused by ♂, and his afflictions to the ☉ and ☽, and ♂ also with Nebulous Stars. (See Gunshot).

Gutta Serena—Blindness By—(See Gutta Serena).

Hemianopia—Blindness of One-Half the Visual Field—(See this subject under Sight).

Injury—Blindness by Injury, Wounds, etc.—(See Accidents, Artifice, Burning, Bruises, Treachery, Violence, etc., in this section).

Lame—Case of Lame, Deaf, Dumb, and Blind—See Case, "Arundel", No. 159, in 1001 N.N.

Left Eye—Blindness In—(See "Eyes" under Left). Case—See "Blind", Case No. 629, in 1001 N.N.

Lightning—Blindness By—Caused by ♂. (See ♂ influences under "Causes" in this section).

Measles—Blindness By—The Pleiades when joined with the ☉ or ☽, when rising, or when directed to the Asc.; the ☉ directed to Praesepe, Hyades, Pleiades, Castor, Pollux, and other stars of the nature of ♂ and the ☽ when combined, and espec. if Praesepe be on the Asc., or with the ☉ or ☽ in an angle; ♂ causes; the ☽ ☌ ♂ with the Pleiades, and ♄ with Regulus. (See "Total" in this section. Also see Measles).

Mental Exertion—Blindness From—Caused by ☿ entering into the configurations which otherwise cause blindness. Also caused by ♄ and ☿ afflicting the Lights. (See "Eyestrain" under Eyes; Reading, Study).

Mutes—Blind and Deaf—(See Mutes. Also see "Deaf and Dumb" in this section).

Natural Defects—Blindness By—(See "Defects" in this section).

Nearly Blind—The ☽ Sig. ☌ the ☉, and both near the Hyades, Pleiades, or Praesepe. (See Sight).

Nyctalopia—(See "Day Blindness" in this section).

Obstructing Growths—Blindness By —(See "Growths" in this section; "Growths' under Eyes).

One Eye—Blindness In—Loss of One Eye—The ☉ directed to Praesepe, Hyades, Pleiades, Castor, Pollux, and other stars of the nature of the ☽ and ♂ combined, and espec. if Praesepe be on the Asc., or with the ☉ or ☽ in an angle; the ☽ ☌ ♂, and with the Pleiades; the ☽ in an angle, in the Asc. or Desc., ☌ or ☍ the ☉, and connected with a Nebulous Spot, as the Cloudy

Spot of ♋, the Pleiades of ♉, the Sting of Scorpio, the Arrowhead of ♐, the Mane of ♌, or the Urn of ♒; the ☽ in the 1st or 7th H., in exact ☌, □, or ☍ the ☉, and affl. by ♅, ♄, or ♂, or with any Nebulous Spots, such as just mentioned; the ☽ affl. in the 22° ♊; ♄ with Regulus. (See Right, Left, in this section. Also see "One Eye" under Eyes).

One-Half Vision—(See "Hemianopia" in this section).

Optic Nerve—Inhibition of—(See Optic).

Over-Study—Blindness From—(See "Eyestrain" under Eyes; the ☿ influences under "Causes", and "Mental Exertion" in this section).

Partial Blindness—(See "Amaurosis" in this section).

Piles—Blind Piles—(See Hemorrhoids).

Private Injury—Blindness By—Caused by ♂ influence in the configuration. (See "Artifice", "Treachery" in this section).

Reading and Study—Blindness By—(See the ☿ influences under "Causes", and also "Mental Exertion", in this section. See "Eyestrain" under Eyes).

Retina—Blind Spot of—(See "Blind Spot" in this section).

Right Eye—Blind In—(See "Eye" under Right).

Searing—Blindness By—(See "Burns" in this section).

Sight—(See the various paragraphs under Sight).

Smallpox—Blindness From—Caused by ♂ in the configuration with the ☉, ☽, and Nebulous Spots; ♂ afflicted in ♈. (See the ♂ influences under "Causes" in this section. Also see Smallpox).

Specks—(See Specks. Also see "Defects" in this section).

Sports—Blindness from Injury In—(See "Amusements" under Sports; "Amusements" in this section).

Strokes—Blindness By—(See "Blows" in this section. Also see "Eyes" under Sword).

Study—Blindness from Over-study and Reading—(See "Reading" in this section).

Sword—Blindness by Injuries By—(See "Eyes" under Sword. Also see "Blows" in this section).

Total Blindness—Blind in Both Eyes —The ☉ in ♒, affl. by ♄, and espec. ☌ or ☍ ♄, tends to stone blindness; the ☉ directed to Praesepe, Hyades, Pleiades, Castor and Pollux, and other stars of the nature of the ☽ and ♂ combined, and espec. if Praesepe be on the Asc., or with the ☉ or ☽ in an angle, which tends to certain blindness; the ☽ combust and conjoined with the Pleiades and ♄, or ♂ with Regulus, sometimes total blindness ensues; the ☽ in the 1st, 4th or 7th H., in decrease, ☌ or ☍ ♅, ♄, ♂, and the malefics be occi., and at the same time ♅, ♄, or ♂ be in ☌ or ☍ the ☉, ori. of the ☉ and ascend before him, and under these circumstances ♄, ♂, (or ☿ the afflicting planet) tend to total blindness by the diseases or afflictions as set forth under "Causes" in this section; the ☽ ☌ ♂ with the Pleiades, and ♄ with Regulus. (See "Causes", and the various paragraphs in this section. Also see Gutta Serena; "Accidents" under Eyes).

Treachery—Blindness By—Caused by the combined influences of ♂ and ♀ entering into the configurations which cause blindness. (See the ♂ influences under "Causes" in this section. Also see Treachery).

Violence—Injury — Wounds —Blindness By—The ☽ in Nebulous parts, and affl. by ♂. (See Accidents, Blows, and other paragraphs in this section).

White Film—Blindness By—(See "Cold" in this section).

Wounds—Blindness By—(See Accidents, Injury, Violence, in this section).

BLISTERS—Blebs—Bulla—A ♂ disease, and caused by ♂ afflictions, as ♂ is vesicant and tends to produce blebs and blisters; the ☽ to the ☌ or ill-asps. ♂ by dir. (See Dysidrosis, Rubefacient, Serum, Vesicles).

BLIZZARDS—Much Loss of Life From —☿ in an angle, and afflicted, at a Vernal Equi., or Winter Solstice. (See Cold, Snow, Storms, Weather, Wind).

BLOATING—Flatulence—Gas in Stomach or Bowels—(See Flatulence).

Bloated Face—(See Face).

BLONDES—(See Complexion, Hair).

BLOOD—The Blood—The Sanguineous System—The Blood is ruled by ♃, altho his main activities are confined to the arterial blood. The Blood is also under the internal rule of the ♌ Sign. The Arterial Blood is ruled by ♃, and ♀ rules the Venous Blood. The ♒ sign rules strongly over the blood, its condition and circulation. All the Fixed Signs tend to rule and affect the Blood. The Blood is also ruled and strongly influenced by the Watery Signs. The Blood is one of the manifestations of the Vital Body. (See "Vital Body" under Vital). The ☉ gives oxygen to the blood, and ♂ gives the Iron and Haemoglobin. (See Iron, Haemoglobin). In the Astral Body ♃ has direct relation to the Blood. The activity of ♂ in the blood tends to Hemorrhages, Rupture of Blood Vessels, Hemorrhoids, and Excessive Menses. For the Occult significance of the Blood read what is said about the Blood in the books, "Cosmo-Conception", and "Message of the Stars" by the Heindels. This Article will be arranged in Two Sections, General Considerations, and Disorders of the Blood.

GENERAL CONSIDERATIONS—

Arterial Blood—(See Arteries).

Blood Letting — Transfusion — (S e e Bleeding).

Blood-Making—(See Haematopoiesis).

Bloodshed—(See "Shedding of Blood" in Sec. 2 of this Article. Also see War).

Blood Vessels—(See Arteries, Capillaries, Veins, Vascular, Vessels).

Carbon Dioxide—(See Carbon).

Centrifugal—Centripetal—(See these subjects).

Circulation—Of the Blood—(See Circulation).

Coloring Matter—Of the Blood—The red coloring matter of the blood is ruled by ♂ and the ♏ sign. (See "Haemoglobin", "Iron" in this section).

Composition—Of the Blood—Under the rule of ♄ and the ♒ sign.

Condition—Of the Blood—Is influenced by all the Fixed Signs.

Corpuscles—(See Leukocytes; "Blood" under Red).

Deposits In—(See Deposits, Minerals).

Enrichment—Of the Blood—The Physiological Action of ♃.

Fibrin—Of the Blood—Ruled by ♃, ♂, and the ♓ sign. (See Fiber).

Haematopoiesis—Haematosis—Blood-making—(See Haematopoiesis).

Haemoglobin—(See Haemoglobin).

Heat—Of the Blood—Is maintained by the ☉ and ♂, the iron ruled by ♂, and oxygen ruled by the ☉.

Inward—Blood is Driven Inward—(See Centripetal).

Leukocytes—White Blood Corpuscles —(See Leukocytes).

Mineral Deposits—(See Deposits, Minerals).

New Moon—Influence on the Blood—(See "New Moon" under Moon).

Outward—The Blood Driven Outward —(See Centrifugal).

Oxygen—Oxygenation of the Blood—(See Oxygen).

Portal Blood—(See Portal).

Red Blood—Red Coloring Matter—Red Corpuscles—(See "Coloring" in this section. Also see "Blood" under Red).

Rubefacients—(See this subject).

Serum—Of the Blood—Ruled by the ♋ Sign. (See Serum).

Shedding of Blood—(See Cuts, Duels, Effusions, Hemorrhage, Injuries, Menses, "Epistaxis" under Nose; Shedding; Stabs, War, Wounds, etc.).

Transfusion—Of Blood — (See Bleeding).

Venous Blood—(See Veins).

White Blood Corpuscles—(See Leukocytes).

DISORDERS OF THE BLOOD—See the following subjects in the alphabetical arrangement when not considered here—

Abscess—From Blood Disorders—(See "Impure Blood" under Impure).

Abundance of Blood—In a Part—♂ in the sign ruling the part. (See Fullness, High Blood Pressure, Plethora, Rush of Blood, Too Much Blood, in this section).

Accumulation—Of Blood In a Part or Organ—♃ when afflicted tends to, and to Obesity and Tumors. (See Obesity, Serum, Tumors, in this section).

Alterations—In the Red Blood Particles—(See "Blood" under Red).

Anaemia; Aorta—Spasmodic Gushing of the Blood Thru—(See Aorta).

Arms—Blood Disorders and Impurities In—(See "Blood" under Arms, Hands).

Arterial Blood—Disorders of—Poor Circulation of—(See Arteries, Circulation).

Asphyxia; Autointoxication—(See this subject. See "Blood Poisoning" in this section).

Bad Blood—(See "Corrupt" in this section).

Bleeding; Blood Affections — (See "Disordered", and the various paragraphs in this section).

Blood Letting—(See Bleeding).

Blood Poisoning—(See "Blood Poisoning" under Poison).

Blood Pressure—(See "Pressure" in this section).

Blood Vessels—Disorders of—(See Arteries, Capillaries, Veins, Vessels).

Bloodshed—(See "Shedding" in this section; War, etc.).

Bloodshot Eyes—(See Eyes).

Bloody Flux—(See Flux).

Boils—From Impure Blood—(See Boils).

Bowels—Hemorrhage From—(See Bowels, Dysentery, Fluxes, Hemorrhage, Typhoid).

Brain—Congestion of Blood In—Hemorrhage of—(See Apoplexy, Brain, Congestion).

Carbon Dioxide—Surplus of in Blood —(See Carbon).

Centrifugal—And Centripetal Action of the Blood—(See these subjects).

Cerebral Hemorrhage—(See Cerebral).

Changes—In the Blood Particles—(See "Blood" under Red; Corpuscles; Haemoglobin).

Circulation—Of the Blood—Disorders of—(See Circulation).

Clots—(See Clots, Embolus, Thrombus).

Coarse Blood—(See Impure).

Cold Blood—(See Cold).

Colds—Due to Chilling of the Surface, and Driving the Blood Inwards—(See Centripetal, Chills, Colds, Congestion).

Congestion of Blood—(See Congestion).

Corpuscles—(See "Blood" under Red; Corpuscles, Leukocytes).

Corrupt Blood—(See "Impure Blood" under Impure).

Cyanosis; Death—By Foul Blood—(See "Death" under Impure).

Debility—Of the Blood—(See Debility).

Defective Blood—(See Anaemia, Haemoglobin, Impure, "Blood" under Red; Leukocytes, Pale, Poor). Also see "Thin Blood" in this section).

Deficient—(See "Thin" in this section).

Deposits—In the Blood—(See Deposits, Minerals).

Depraved Blood—(See Impure).

Determination—Of Blood—Rush of—(See "Blood" under Head. Also see Aorta).

Diluted Blood—(See "Thin" in this section).

Discharges of Blood—(See Cuts, Discharges, Dysentery, Effusions, Epistaxis, Fluxes, Hemorrhage, Injuries, Menses, Stabs, Sword, Typhoid, War, Watery, Wounds, etc. Also see "Shedding" in this section).

Disordered Blood—Disorders of—Disturbances of—Caused principally by ♃, and afflictions to ♃, and also afflictions in the ♒ sign; ♃ □ or ☍ the Asc., excess of blood, and ailments from; ♃ in signs which rule the arms, hands, legs and feet, or any part of the body, tends to blood disorders and corrupt blood in these parts; the ☉ in airy signs, and espec. in ♒; the ☽ in airy signs tends to regular and normal secretions, but subject to blood disorders, anaemia, skin and kidney troubles. (See the various paragraphs in this section).

Disturbances Of—Ruled by ♒ and are principally ♒ diseases. (See "Disordered", and other paragraphs in this section).

Driven Inward—Or Outward—(See Centrifugal, Centripetal).

Dropsical Blood—(See Dropsy).

Ears—Effusion of Blood From—(See Ears).

Effusion of Blood—(See Effusions).

Embolism—(See Embolism, Thrombus).

Epistaxis—Nose Bleed—(See Nose).

Eruptions—From Bad Blood—(See Eruptions).

Evacuations; Excess of Blood—Disorders From—♃ □ or ☍ the Asc. (See Plethora, Pressure, Too Much Blood, in this section).

Excesses—Blood Disorders From—(See Excesses).

Excessive Discharges—Of Blood—(See Effusions, "Flooding" under Menses; Fluxes, Hemorrhage. Also see "Shedding" in this section).

Expectoration—Of Blood—(See Haemoptysis).

Eyes—Bloodshot Eyes—(See Eyes).

Feet—Blood In—(See "Disordered" in this section).

Feverish Blood—Hot Blood—Over-Heated Blood—(See "Over-Heated" in this section).

Fevers—From Too Much Blood—A disease of ♃. (See Plethora. Also see "Too Much" in this section).

Flooding—(See Menses).

Flow of Blood—Determination of—Rush of—etc.—(See Aorta, "Blood" under Head; Effusions, "Flooding" under Menses; Fluxes, Hemorrhage, etc. Also see Injuries, Loss of, Shedding, in this section).

Fluids; Fluxes—Bloody Discharges In—(See Dysentery, Evacuations, Fluxes).

Foul Blood—Death By—(See "Death" under Impure).

Fullness of Blood—(See Plethora, Pressure, Too Much Blood, in this section).

General Debility Of—(See "Blood" under Debility).

Good Order—(See "Pure" in this section).

Gout—From Too Much Uric Acid in the Blood—(See Gout, Uric Acid).

Gross Blood—(See Gross, Impure, Plethora. Also see "Too Much", "Rich", in this section).

Gushing—Of Blood—(See Aorta, "Blood" under Head; Effusions, "Flooding" under Menses; Hemorrhage, etc.).

Haematemesis—(See "Blood" under Vomiting).

Haematoma—Blood Tumor—(See Haematoma).

Haematopoiesis—Blood-Making—Disorders of—(See Haematopoiesis).

Haemoglobin—Disorders of—(See Haemoglobin, "Blood" under Red).

Haemophilia—Abnormal Tendency to Hemorrhage—(See Hemorrhage).

Haemoptysis; Hands—(See "Disordered" in this section).

Head—Rush of Blood To—(See "Blood" under Head).

Heated Blood—Feverish Blood—(See "Over-Heated" in this section).

Heavy Blood—(See Impure).

Hemorrhage; Hemorrhoids; High Pressure—(See "Pressure" in this section).

Hot Blood—(See "Over-Heated" in this section).

Humours—With Bloody Discharges—(See Humours, "Watery Humours" under Watery).

Hydraemia—(See "Thin Blood" in this section).

Ill-Blood—(See Impure).

Impoverished Blood—(See Anaemia; "Thin Blood" in this section; Emaciation, Malnutrition, Pale, Wasting).

Impure Blood—Impurities in the Blood—Diseases Arising From—(See Deposits, Impure, Minerals, Sores, Syphilis, Ulcers, etc.).

Indifferent Blood—(See "Poor" in this section).

Indulgence—Blood Disorders From—(See Gluttony, Impure, Indulgence, Syphilis, Venery, etc.).

Infiltration—Of Serum—(See Serum).

Inflamed Blood—The ☉ affl. in ♊, ♎, or ♏ when the ☉ is the afflictor in the disease; the Asc. to the ♂ or ill-asp. ♂ by dir., and ♂ in an airy sign. (See Inflammation).

Injuries—With Flow of Blood—Caused by ♂, but ♄ causes injuries where blood does not flow, as bruises. (See Injuries).

Insanity—From Rush of Blood to the Head—(See Insanity).

Insufficient Oxygenation—(See Oxygen).

Inward—Blood Driven Inward—(See Centripetal).

Iron—In the Blood—(See Haemoglobin, Iron; "Blood" under Red).

Kidneys—Hemorrhage of—(See "Hemorrhage" under Kidneys).

Legs—Blood In—(See "Disordered" in this section).

Letting of Blood—Transfusion—(See Bleeding).

Leukemia—(See Leukocytes).

Loss of Blood—Bloodshed—Hemorrhage—(See Accidents, Cuts, Effusions, Hemorrhage, Injuries, Menses, "Nose Bleed" under Nose; "Shedding" in this section; Stabs, Sword, War).

Low Pressure—(See "Pressure" in this section).

Melancholic Blood—(See "Blood" under Melancholy).

Menses; Mineral Deposits—In the Blood—(See Deposits, Gout, Minerals, Rheumatism, Saturn, Uric Acid, Wastes, etc.).

Morbid Blood—Morbid Changes In—The ♏ sign has much influence over morbid changes in the blood, as incomplete oxygenation, blood poisoning, impure blood, etc. (See Haemoglobin, Impure, Morbid, Oxygen, Pale, Poison; "Blood" under Red; "Sickly Looking" under Sickly; Wasting Diseases, etc.).

Much Blood—(See "Abundance", "Too Much" in this section. Also see Impure).

Non-Oxygenation—(See Oxygen).

Nose Bleed—(See Nose).

Obesity; Obstructions—Of the Blood—And From Too Much Blood—(See Clots, Thrombus; "Too Much" in this section).

Outward—Blood Driven Outward—(See Centrifugal).

Over-Heated Blood—Feverish—Hot—The heat of the blood is maintained by ♂. The ☉ affl. in ♎, and often causing skin eruptions; the ☉ in ♏ ♂ or ill-asp. any of the malefics as promittors; the ☉ ♂ ♂ in ♈, and ♈ or ♂ on the Asc., the blood may be like a hot, fiery liquid; the ☉ in ♊ or ♎, ♂ or ill-asp. any of the malefics as promittors; the ☉ directed to Cor Scorpio; the ☽ in ♌ or ♎ and affl. by the ☉ or ♂ when taken ill; afflictions in ♐; ♃ affl. in ♌; ♂ in ♌ or ♏ when ♂ is the afflictor in the disease. (See Eruptions, Exercise, Heat).

Oxygen—Lack of In Blood—(See Oxygen).

Part—Abundance of Blood in a Part—(See "Abundance" in this section).

Particles—Changes in the Blood Particles—(See Corpuscles, "Blood" under Red).

Pernicious Anaemia—(See Anaemia).

Plethora—Fullness of Blood—(See Plethora; "Too Much" in this section).

Poisoning—Blood Poisoning—Toxic Blood—Impure Blood—(See Autointoxication, Impure, Poison, Septic, Toxaemia).

Polluted Blood—(See "Stagnant" in this section).

Poor Blood—Indifferent Blood—Defective Blood—Poor State of the Blood—Watery and Thin—The ☉ in ill-asp. to ♃ at B., or by dir.; the ☉ or ☽ in ♋ or ♓, and in ♂ or ill-asp. any of the malefics as promittors; the ☽ hyleg in ♌ or ♒, and afflicted, and espec. with females; ♅, ♆, or ♄ in ♋, and affl. the ☉ or ☽; ♃ affl. in ♓, poor condition of the blood; ♀ in ♒ and affl. the ☉ or ☽; ♀ in ♒ in the 6th H. (See Anaemia, Impure, Pale, Poison, Septic, Toxic, etc. See "Thin" in this section).

Pressure—High Blood Pressure is denoted by ♃ and ♂. The bad asps. of ♃ tend to; ♄ ♂ ♃ or ♀; ♄ in ♌ ♂ ♃; ♄ ♂ ♃ in 6th H. (See "High Pulse" under Pulse; "Too Much" in this section). Low Blood Pressure is caused by ♄ affl. ♃ at B., and by dir. (See "Slow Pulse" under Pulse). ♃ causes complaints due to blood pressure.

Pure—The Blood should be kept pure, and in good order, when ♂ is affl. in ♎, and when ♀ is afflicted in ♍, or when ♃ at B., is in ♐, ♑, or ♓, and afflicted, or ♃ affl. the ☉, ☽, Asc. or hyleg from these signs. (See "Remedies" in this section).

Purpura—Hemorrhages into the Cutis—(See Purpura).

Putrefaction—In the Blood—A disease of ♃; ♃ affl. in ♐; a ♓ disease, and afflictions in ♓. (See Impure, Putrefaction).

Red Blood—(See "Coloring" in Sec. 1 of this Article. Also see Arteries, Circulation, Haemoglobin, Iron, "Blood" under Red).

Remedies—For Blood Disorders—Purple, the color ruled by ♃ in the Solar Spectrum, and purple rays, are valuable in the treatment of blood and liver disorders. The therapeutic properties of the ☉, ☽, ♅, ♂ and ☿ are classed as being favorable to the relief of blood disorders. (See Alteratives).

Renal Hemorrhage—(See "Hemorrhage" under Kidneys).

Rich Blood—Too Rich—Gross Blood—♂ ☐ or ♉ ♃. (See Impure, Too Much, in this section).

Rubefacients; Rupture—Of Blood Vessels—(See Apoplexy, Hemorrhage, "Rupture" under Vessels).

Rush of Blood—To the Head, or a Part—A ♂ influence. (See "Blood" under Head; "Abundance" in this section).

Scrofulous Blood—(See Scrofula).

Scurvy—(See Purpura, Scurvy).

Septicaemia—(See Septic. Also see "Poisoning" in this section).

Serum—Of the Blood—Disorders of—(See Serum).

Shedding—Of Blood—A ♂ influence and affliction, as in Accidents, Cuts, Injuries, War, etc. (See Accidents, Cuts, Effusions, Hemorrhage, Menses, Murder, Shedding, Stabs, Sword, War, Wounds, etc.).

Skin—Skin Disorders Thru Blood Affections—(See Centrifugal, Eczema,

Eruptions, Impure, Purpura, Scrofula, Scurvy, Skin, Syphilis, etc.).

Sluggish Blood—(See "Poor", "Sluggish", under Circulation).

Spitting of Blood—(See Haemoptysis).

Stabs—Loss of Blood From—(See Stabs).

Stagnant Blood—Polluted Blood—♄ ♂ ♃ or ♀, the rulers of the circulation; ♃ ♂ ♄, and also affl. by the ☽ and ♀. (See Impure. Also see "Sluggish" under Circulation).

Sugar—In the Blood—(See Sugar).

Surface—Blood Driven to the Surface—(See Caustic, Centrifugal, Eruptions, Rubefacients).

Surfeits—(See "Blood" under Surfeits. Also see "Too Much" in this section).

Sweat—Bloody Sweat—(See Sweat).

Syphilis—Syphilitic Blood—(See Syphilis).

Thin Blood—Hydraemia—Impoverished—Watery—Caused by the predominance of the watery signs at B., and espec. ♋ and ♓, and with these signs on the Asc. (See "Poor" in this section. Also see Anaemia, Dropsy, Emaciated, Pale, Sickly, Vitality Low, Wasting, etc.).

Thrombus—Blood Clot—(See Thrombus).

Too Much Blood—Gross Blood—Vascular Fullness—High Blood Pressure—The ☽ to the ill-asps. ♃ by dir., the blood is gross and corrupted; the ☽ in ♉ or ♌, and affl. by the ☉ or ♂ when taken ill; the ☽ or ♃ in ♎, affl. by the ☉ or ♂ when taken ill, the patient is grieved with a plenitude of blood, and feverish disorders from too much blood; a ♃ disease when ♃ is afflicted at B., and due to excesses in eating; ♃ affl. in ♎ tends to inflammatory diseases, Piles, etc., from too much blood; ♃ affl. in ♒ tends to flying pains, fevers, many diseases and complications from too much blood; the Asc. to any asp. of ♃ by dir., and with danger of pleurisy; all conditions of vascular fullness are considered ♃ diseases. (See Arteries; "Sluggish" under Circulation; Eruptions; "Blood" under Fevers; Impure, Plethora; "High Pulse" under Pulse; Surfeits, Upper, etc. Also see "Pressure" in this section).

Toxic Blood—(See Impure, Poison, Septic, Toxic, Urea, Uric Acid. Also see "Poisoning" in this section).

Treatment—Of Blood Disorders—(See "Remedies" in this section).

Tumors—Blood Tumors—(See Haematoma).

Ulcers—From Bad Blood—(See "Blood" under Ulcers).

Upper Parts—(See "Blood" under Upper).

Uremia; Uric Acid; Urine—Blood In—(See Urine).

Veins—Venous Blood—(See Veins).

Vessels—Blood Vessels—(See Vessels).

Vomiting—Of Blood—(See Vomiting).

Watery Blood—(See "Poor", "Thin" in this section).

Watery Humours—With Bloody Discharges—(See Discharges, Dysentery, Fluxes, Humours, Watery).

Weakest Part—Blood the Weakest Part—The ☉ affl. in ♐; ☽ hyleg, and affl. in a female nativity.

White—White Blood Corpuscles—(See Leukocytes).

Wind in Blood—(See Wind).

Women—(See "Blood" under Women).

BLOTCHES—Blemishes—The ☽ in ♏, and affl. by the ☉ or ♂ when taken ill, due to corrupt blood; the ☽ to the Bull's Horns by dir.; afflictions in ♓; a ♓ disease. (See Acne, Blemishes, Blisters, Eruptions, Pimples, Pustules).

BLOWS—Strokes—Concussions—The Hurtful Signs, ♈, ♉, ♌, ♏, or ♑ on the Asc. at B. make the native more liable to Blows, Falls, Wounds, and other Injuries.

Accidents—By Blows—(See "Danger" in this section).

Assaults By—Battery—(See Assaults).

Blindness—By Blows—(See "Accidents", "Injury" under Eyes; "Eyes" under Sword).

Bruises—By Blows—(See Assaults, Bruises, Falls).

Concussions—(See Concussions).

Cuts—From Blows—Caused by ♂. (See Assaults, Cuts, Duels, Hemorrhage, Stabs, Sword, etc.).

Danger of Blows—Liable to—Subject to—Accidents or Injuries by Blows—The ☉ or ☽ to the ☌ or ill-asp. ♂ by dir.; ♄ in ♈, ♌, or ♑ in ☌ or ill-asp. the Asc. by dir.; caused by ♄ or ♂, by ♄ ascending, rising or setting at B., and affl. the ☉, ☽, Asc. or hyleg; ♄ in a fiery or airy sign, and to the ill-asps. the Asc. by dir.; the ill-asps. of ♄ or ♂ by dir. to the ☉, ☽, Asc. or M.C.; afflictions in fiery signs dispose to; the Asc. to the ☌ or ill-asps. ♄ or ♂ by dir.; the Whale's Belly joined to the ☉ or ☽. (See Assaults, Bruises, Cuts, Stabs, Sword, etc).

Death by Blows—Danger of—Liable to—The ☉ joined with Castor, Pollux, Pleiades, Hyades, Praesepe, or the Ascelli; the ☉ Sig. □ or ⚹ ♄, and espec. if either be in the 10th H.; the ☽ with Antares, and ⚹ ♄ and Aldebaran, and espec. if in angles; the ☽ Sig. ☌, □, or ⚹ ♂; the ☽ directed to Capella, danger of death by blows or stabs; ♄ affl. the hyleg by dir., and holding the dominion of death, and espec. if ♄ be in the 8th H., and afflicted, which influences tend to sudden death by blows; ♄ or ♂ in the M.C., and in □ the Asc., and the ☉ afflicted; ♃ Sig. □ or ⚹ ♂; ♂ with Aldebaran, death by blows, falls, stabs, and espec. if in angles, and affl. the ☽; ♂ Sig. □ or ⚹ ♄ if either be in the Asc., or ♄ in the M.C.; those born under the hurtful signs, ♈, ♉, ♌, ♏, or ♑, are more liable to. (See Assaults, Cuts, Duels, Murdered, Stabs, Sword).

Distortions—By Blows—(See Distortions).

Duels—(See Duels, Sword).

Eyes—Blows or Strokes to—(See "Accidents", "Hurts", "Injuries" under Eyes).

Face—Blows to—(See "Cuts","Hurts" under Face).

Falls—Blows By—(See the various paragraphs under Falls. Also see "Death" in this section).

Head—Blows to—(See Head).

Hurtful Signs—(See the Introduction to this section).

Hurts—Injuries by Blows—(See the various paragraphs in this section).

Lameness—From Blows—(See "Blows" under Lameness. Also see Distortions).

Paralysis—From Blows—(See Distortions).

Severe Blows—(See "Death", Violent" in this section. Also see the Case Record on Page 97, Chap. 13, in Daath's Medical Astrology).

Skull—Blows to—(See "Blows" under Head; "Fractures" under Skull).

Stabs—(See Cuts, Duels, Stabs, Sword).

Subject to Blows—(See "Danger" in this section).

Sword—Blows By—(See Sword).

Violent Blows—Violent Death by—(See "Death" in this section. Also see "Death" under Violent).

Wounds—By Blows—(See the various paragraphs in this section.

BLUE—The color ruled by ♀ in the Solar Spectrum. In the Secret Doctrine by H.P.B., Blue is the color assigned to ♃. Blue has a soothing, uplifting, comforting, restful and religious influence over people, and is a good color where brain workers are busy. Blue flowers tend to allay fevers. It has a soothing effect upon melancholic people, Neurasthenics, the Insane, Maniacs, and is also a good color for weak eyes, as to wear blue glasses for a time. (See "Treatment" under Eyes, Insanity, Melancholy, Nerves. Also see Colors).

Blue Eyes—(See "Blue" under Eyes).

Blue Flag—(See Iridin).

Blue Marks—On the Body—(See Marks).

BLUES—(See Depression, Despondency, Hypochondria, Melancholy, Vapors, Worry, etc.).

BLUSHING—Ruled by the ☽ and ♄. (See Backwardness, Bashful, Flushings, Shame).

BODY—Bodily—Frame—Form—Figure Constitution—Physique—Stature, etc. —For the Organs, Parts, and functions of the body, and the various diseases and afflictions, see the subject in the alphabetical arrangement. Only the more abstract subjects, by way of suggestion for study and reference, will be listed in this section. Many subjects concerning the form, shape and appearance of the body are listed under Appearance, Complexion, Face, Form, Height, Shape, Stature, Weight, etc. The physical body is signified by the Asc., the 1st H., and its form, shape, etc., are largely determined by the 1st H., the degree, sign and decanate rising, by planets rising, setting, above or below the horizon, the aspects formed between the planets, the dignity or debility of planets at B., etc. (See Decanates, Physical). The directions, progressed positions of the planets and the Asc., the Transits, Lunations, Eclipses, Solar Revolutions, etc., have much to do with the condition of the body during life, its diseases, its periods of good and bad health, its debilities and weaknesses, etc., and the possible time of death, but subject to modification, according to the degree of knowledge and spiritual advancement of the native. See the following subjects in the alphabetical arrangement when not considered here—

Able Body—(See "Strong Body" under Strong).

Action; Active Body—(See Active).

Afflicted—(1) The Body Alone is Afflicted—When a malefic afflicting the lord of the Asc., or the ☽, and the part afflicted is that ruled by the sign of which the afflicting planet is lord. (2) The Affliction, or Disease, is More in the Body Than in the Mind—Lord of the Asc., and lord of the sign or house containing the ☽, be combust and afflicting the degree ascending, and the degree containing the ☽ be more afflicted than the lords of those signs. (See "Irritations" under Mind). (3) Afflicted in Both Body and Mind—(See "Afflicted in Mind and Body" under Mental). (4) The Affliction, or Disease, is Thru the Whole Body—(See "Disease" under Whole).

Agile Body—(See Agile).

Anatomical; Angular Body—☿ in ♈; ♈ on the Asc.; the ♈ influence generally gives. (See Lank, Lean, "Raw-Boned" under Bones).

Animal Propensities—(See Animal).

Appearance; Ascendant; Astral Body—(See Astral).

Athletic Body—(See Athletics).

Awkwardness; Badly Made—(See Azimene, Crooked, Deformities, "Ill-formed" under Ill; Malformations, Ugly).

Barren; Beautiful Body—(See Beautiful).

Birth; Blemishes; Body Alone Is Afflicted—(See "Afflicted" in this section).

Brisk—In Movement—(See Action, Active, Brisk, Motion, Movement, Quick, etc.).

Build; Bulky Body—(See Bulky, Corpulent, Fat, Large, Obesity, etc.).

Careful—Of the Body—(See Careful).

Carriage—(See Gait, Motion, Movement, Posture, Walk).

Cavities—(See Cavities, Receptacles, Viscera).

Changes In—(See "Body" under Changes).

Cleanly; Cleansing; Clogging; Coarse; Cold Body—(See "Body" under Cold).

Color Of—(See Color, Complexion, Face, Hair, Race, "Color" under Skin).

Comely; Commanding; Commonplace; Compact; Complete; Complexion; Composition Of—(See the various subjects in this section).

Condition—Of the Body—(See Healthy, Sickly, Strong, Vitality, Weak, etc.).

Confinements—Of the Body—(See Hospitals, Imprisonment, Insanity, Invalids, Sickness, Twelfth House, etc.).

Conformity—Of Members—(See Well-Proportioned).

Congenital; Conservation—Of the Bodily and Mental Forces—(See Conservation).

Constitution; Construction—Of the Body—Ruled over by the Asc.

Constructive Forces Of—(See Constructive).

Contracted Body—(See Diminished, Dwarf, Short, Small).

Control Of—(See Control).

Coordination In—(See Coordination).

Corpulent; Countenance; Coverings; Cravings; Crippled; Crooked; Dark; Death; Debility; Defects; Defensive Forces Of—(See Defensive).

Deficiencies In—(See Deficient).

Deformities; Degeneration Of—(See Degeneration).

Delicate; Depletions; Description; Desire Body; Destructive Processes—(See Destructive).

Deterioration Of—(See Deterioration).

Development Of—(See Development).

Devoured—After Death—(See "Birds" under Air).

Diathesis In—(See Diathesis).

Diminished—(See "Contracted" in this section).

Directions—The Effect of Primary Directions Over the Body—(See Directions).

Dirty Body—(See Filth, Unclean).

Disabilities; Disasters To—(See Disaster).

Disease; Disfigurements; Displacements; Disproportioned; Distentions; Distortions; Divisions—Of the Body—(See Divisions).

Dress; Drooping; Dry Body—(See Dry).

Dwarfed; Dying Persons—(See Dying).

Eating; Elegant; Elemental Qualities Of—(See Elemental).

Endurance; Energy; Enlarged; Entire Body—(See Whole).

Environment; Equilibrium; Escapes; Events; Evolution Of—(See Evolution).

Excitation; Exercise Of—(See Exercise, Sports).

Expansions In—(See Expansion).

Exposures; External Influences—(See External).

Fading; Fair; Fasting; Fears—Bodily Fears—(See Fears).

Feasting; Features; Feeble; Female; Filthy; Fine; First House; Flabby; Fleshy; Fluids; Foetus; Food; Forces Of—(See Forces).

Form; Frail; Frame; Freaks—Of Nature—(See Freaks, Monsters).

Fruitful; Fuel—Of the Body—(See Fuel).

Full-Bodied—(See Full).

Functions; Fundament; Gait; Genteel; Gestation; Giants; Gluttony; Good Build—(See Good).

Graceful; Gratifications Of—(See Appetites, Cravings, Gratification, Passion, Sex).

Great Body—(See Giants).

Growth; Habits; Hairy Body—(See Hair).

Handsome; Hardening; Harmony In —(See Harmony).

Health Of—(See Health).

Heat Of—(See Heat).

Heavy; Height; Helplessness; Heredity; Hermaphrodites; High Body— High Forehead—High Nose—(See High, Forehead, Nose, Tall, Giants).

Hooked Forward—(See Bending, Stooping).

Hot Body—(See Heat).

Humpback; Hurts; Ill-formed; Ill-health; Impairments; Imperfections; Imprisonment; Inactive; Incomplete; Incomposed; Incurvating; Indifferent; Inefficiency; Inferior; Infirm; Inflated; Inhuman; Injuries; Insufficiencies; Inward Parts; Juvenility; Lank; Large; Lean; Left Side—(See Left).

Lengthening; Life—Of the Body—(See Life).

Light; Limitations; Limp; Little; Local Parts—(See Local).

Locomotion; Long; Look; Loss Of— (See Loss).

Lovely; Low Stature—(See Dwarf, Low, Short, Small).

Lower Parts—(See Lower).

Lubrication; Luminous; Lumpish; Magnetic; Males; Malnutrition; Marks; Meagre; Mean Stature—(See Mean).

Medium Stature—(See Medium).

Members; Membranes; Metabolism; Mind and Body—(See Mind).

Misshaped; Moderate Stature— (See Moderate).

Moist Body—(See Moist).

Moles; Monsters; Motion; Movement; Moving Parts; Muddling Creature— (See Ill-formed).

Mulatto; Narrow; Natural; Neat; Negro; Nimble; Normal; Nutrition; Odors; Oils; Operations; Organic; Organs; Orifices; Parts of the Body— (See Parts).

Perfect; Physical; Pleasing; Plump; Portly; Posture; Powerful; Preservation; Processes; Prominent; Propensities; Proper Stature—(See Proper).

Protruding; Puffing; Pure; Quality; Quick; Quiet; Quivering; Race; Raw-Boned; Receptacles; Recuperative Powers; Refined; Relaxed; Remote Organs—(See Remote).

Reproduction; Reserve Forces—(See Reserve).

Resisting Powers—(See Resistance).

Restraints Over—(See Restraint).

Rhythm; Right Side—Of the Body— (See Right).

Rigid; Robust; Rose-Colored— (See Rosy).

Rough; Round; Ruddy; Rugged; Sallow; Sanguine; Scaly; Scars; Second Death Of—(See Twelfth House).

Sensations; Senses; Sensitive; Servitude; Sex; Shaggy; Shaking; Shallow; Shape; Sharp; Shiny; Shrunken—(See Shrinkage).

Sickly; Sickness; Sinking—Of Parts —(See Sinking).

Size; Skeleton; Skippish—In Manner —(See "Nodding" under Head).

Sleep; Slow; Sluggish; Small; Smooth; Soft; Spare; Speech; Spotted— (See "Skin Spots" under Spots).

Squatty; Staggering; Stamina; Stature; Stiff; Stinking; Stooping; Stout; Straight; Strength; Strong; Structural; Strutting; Stupor—(See Dull, Sleep).

Sturdy; Suffering; Sunken; Superabundance; Supersensitive; Susceptibilities; Swarthy; Swollen; Symmetry; System; Tall; Temper; Temperament; Temperature; Tendencies; Tender; Tension; Texture; Thick; Thin; Thirst; Tissues; Tone; Torpid; Tough; Treatment; Troubled—In Mind and Body— (See Mind, Trouble).

Ugly; Uncleanly; Uncontrolled; Undersized; Undeveloped; Unfruitful; Ungainly; Unhealthy; Unnatural; Unprolific; Unrefined; Unsound; Untidy; Upper Parts—(See Upper).

Upright; Vigor; Virile Members—(See Virile).

Vital; Vitality; Vitiated; Vulnerable Spots—(See Vulnerable).

Waddling; Walk; Wan; Wants; Warm; Wastes; Weak; Wear and Tear—(See Wear).

Weariness; Weight; Well-Composed; Well-Favored; Well-Proportioned.

Well-Descended—(See Heredity).

White; Whole Body—(See Whole).

Wide; Wild; Withered; Wretched; Yellow; Youthful; Zones.

BOILS—Risings—A ♓ disease; afflictions in ♓, and due to corrupt blood; ♃ diseases; ♂ in evil asp. the ☉, ☽, Asc., or hyleg; ♂ afflicting ♃; ♂ □ or ⚹ ☉; ♂ prog. to the ☌ or ill-asp. ♃, and arising from corrupt blood, evil habits and vices; ♂ affl. in ♐, and espec. in the 6th H.; ♂ in ♐, and affl. the ☽ or Asc.; ♂ affl. in ♊ or ♍, and ☌ or evil asp. the Asc. by dir.; the ☽ affl. in ♑, ♒, or ♓, the Winter Signs; the ☽ in ♒ ☌ or evil asp. ♄ (or to ☿ if he be of the nature of ♄) at decumbiture, or the beginning of the illness; the Asc. □ or ⚹ ♂ by dir. if in a fiery sign. Case—See "Cardan", No. 553, in 1001 N.N. (See Abscesses, Carbuncles, "Impure Blood" under Impure; Infections, Pus, Sores, Swellings, Ulcers).

Buttocks—Boils On—Afflictions in ♏ or ♐; subs at LPP, the 4th and 5th Lumbars, and at KP. (See Haunches, Vertebrae).

Face—Boils On—Afflictions in ♈ or ♉, and espec. ♃ affl. in these signs, due to corrupt blood, excessive eating, bad habits, etc.; Subs at MCP, the 4th Cervical, and at KP. (See Face, Vertebrae).

Gumboils—Afflictions in ♈. (See Gums).

Neck—Boils On—On Upper Neck, Afflictions in ♈ or ♉, and with Subs at MCP, the 3rd Cervical, and at KP; on the middle part of neck, afflictions in the latter degrees of ♈, and in ♉, and with Subs at MCP, the 4th Cervical, and at KP; ♃ afflicted in ♉.

BOLD—A ♂ characteristic; ♂ rising in the Asc. (See "Bold" under Look).

BONES—The Framework—The Osseous System—The Skeleton—The Bones, in any and all parts of the body, are ruled by ♄, and also influenced by the ♄ sign ♑. The ☉ or ☽ acting thru the ♑ sign tend to especially affect the Osseous System. The processes of hardening, crystallization, ossification, bone-building, and the deposits of the mineral substances in the bones, are carried on by ♄. An afflicted ♄, or ♄ weak at B., will tend to interfere with the normal workings of these processes, and lead to diseases of the bones and marrow. The influence of ♄ is limitation, confinement, restraint, and the bones under his rulership define the limits of the body. The Osseous structure is also connected with the Earthy Signs. The Articulations, or Joints, are also under the rule of ♄. The bones of the different parts, or zones of the body, are ruled by the Signs which rule those parts, and according to the divisions of the Grand Man. (See Osseous). The principal subjects to be considered in connection with the bones are the size, texture, diseases, dislocations, fractures, and the bones in health, etc. This Article will be arranged in two Sections. (1) General Considerations. (2) Diseases of the Bones.

GENERAL CONSIDERATIONS—

Articulation—(See Joints).

Bone Building—Ruled and denoted by ♄. A ♄ process.

Bony, Large and Strong—Given by the ☉.

Bony, Lean and Muscular—Born under ♂, and given by ♂.

Bony and Muscular—♄ in his nodes, very bony and muscular.

Bony Body—The ☉ gives a large, strong, and bony body; ♄ in N. Lat. (See Large, Long, Raw-boned, in this section).

Brittle Bones—♄ weak and affl. at B., ♄ in ♌ in many cases.

Crystallization—(See this subject).

Deposits—Mineral Deposits in the Bones—(See Deposits, Minerals).

Great Bones—(See "Large" in this section. Also see Giants).

Healthy Bones—♄ well-aspected at B., and not affl. the ☉, ☽, Asc., or hyleg; ♈ gives healthy, lusty, and robust bones.

Joints—(See Joints).

Large Bones—Given by the ☉, and the ☉ sign ♌; the ✳ and △ asps. to the ☉ tend to; ☽.♌ in partile asp. the Asc., tall, large-boned, and strong; ♄ in ♈ or ♌ in partile asp. the Asc.; ♂ in ♈ partile asp. the Asc.; ☿ in ♐ in partile asp. the Asc., well-shaped, but spare and large bones. (See "Bones" under Large).

Long Bones—Given espec. by ♓ or ♐ on the Asc.

Lusty and Robust—(See "Healthy" in this section).

Marrow—♃ and ♀, rulers of the circulation, rule strongly over the marrow, its nourishment and circulation, deposits of fat, etc., and espec. ♃. (See "Marrow" in Sec. 2 of this Article).

Minerals Of—Ruled and supplied by ♄. (See Crystallization, Deposits, Hardening, Lime, Minerals).

Ossification—The Formation of Bone —Ruled and denoted by ♄. (See "Ossification" in Sec. 2 of this Article).

Raw-Boned—Spare Body—Thin—♄ in ♑, in partile asp. the Asc.; ♄ in N. Lat. makes the body more bony; ♄ rising at B.; ♄ Sig. in ♈, ♍, or ♑. ♑ on the Asc. (See Lean, Thin).

Robust Bones—(See "Healthy" in this section).

Skeleton—(See this subject).

Small Bones—(See Diminished, Dwarf, "Short" under Arms, Legs, Limbs; "Small Body" under Small).

Spine—(See Spine, Vertebrae).

Strengthening Of—♄ in good asp. the Asc., the bodily frame is strengthened.

Synovial Membranes—And Fluids— (See Synovial).

Teeth—(See Teeth).

Vertebrae—(See Vertebrae).

DISEASES OF THE BONES—

Affected—The Bones are affected—♄ weak and affl. at B. (See "Diseases", "Disorders", and the various paragraphs in this section).

All Diseases Of—Caused by ♄ and ♄ afflictions; ♄ weak and affl. at B., and by dir.

Ankles—Broken—(See Ankles).

Ankylosis—(See this subject).

Arms—Broken Arms—(See Arms, Humerus, Radius, Ulna).

Bow Legs—(See Legs).

Break-bone Fever—(See Dengue).

Broken Bones—(See Fractures).

Caries—(See Caries).

Cell Growth—Increased Cell Growth —(See Rickets).

Clavicle—Collar Bone—Fracture of— (See Clavicle).

Cloaca; Club Feet—(See Feet).

Cranial Bones—(See Skull).

Death—From Broken Bones—(See "Death" under Falls, Fractures).

Deficiency—Of Mineral Deposits—♄ weak, afflicted, and ill-dignified at B. (See Minerals, Rickets).

Dengue—Break-bone Fever—(See Dengue).

Deposits—Osseous Deposits—(See Calculi, Crystallization, Deposits, Gravel, Hardening, Minerals, "Influence of ♄" under Saturn; Sand, Stone).

Dislocations—Luxations—(See Dislocations).

Disorders Of—♄ weak, afflicted, and ill-dignified at B.; ♄ affl. the ☉, ☽, Asc., or hyleg; the afflictions of ♄ are at the bottom of all diseases of the bones, and also of the teeth, which latter are ruled by ♄. (See the various paragraphs in this section).

Enlargements Of—(See Ankylosis, Deposits, Enlargements, Minerals, Rickets, etc. Also see "Exostosis", "Inflammation" in this section).

Exostosis—An abnormal outgrowth of bone—Exostosis in Arms—(See "Bones" under Arms).

Femur—Broken Femur—(See Femur).

Fractures—Accidents or Injuries to the Bones—Broken Bones—(See Fractures. For the fractures of the various bones of the body, see the bone, or part, in the alphabetical arrangement).

Fragile Bones—(See "Brittle" in this section).

Hardening—Hard—(1) The Bones Unusually Hard at Birth—See Case, "Short Life", No. 371 in 1001 N.N. (2) Morbid Hardening of—Morbid Ossification—A ♄ disease; ♄ affl. the Asc. or hyleg; ♄ in the 6th H. (See Hardening).

Head—Fractures To—(See Head, Skull).

Humpback—(See Spine).

Inflammation—In the Bone—Osteitis—Danger of—♂ ♂ ♄, and in the part ruled by the sign containing them. (See "Enlargements" in this section).

Injuries To—(See Fractures).

Knock Knees—(See Knees).

Legs—Fractures of—(See Ankles, Femur, Fibula, Legs, Limbs, Tibia).

Limbs—Broken—(See Arms, Legs, in this section).

Long Bones—Softening of—(See Rickets).

Luxations—(See Dislocations).

Malformations—Of the Bones—(See Arms, Deformities, Feet, Legs Malformations, etc. Also see "Misshaped" in this section).

Marrow—Disorders of—Inflammation of—(See "Osteomyelitis", "Spine" in this section. Also see Marrow).

Mineral Deposits—(See "Deficiency" in this section).

Misshaped Bones—(See Ankylosis, Caries, Deformities, "Club Feet" under Feet; "Humpback" under Spine; "Knock Knees" under Knees; "Bow Legs" under Legs; Malformations, Monsters, Rickets).

Morbid Ossification—Unnatural Ossification—Caused by ♄ afflictions; ♄ affl. the ☉, ☽, Asc., or hyleg, and espec. when ♄ is in the 6th H.

Ossification—Morbid—(See "Morbid" in this section).

Osteitis—(See "Inflammation" in this section).

Osteomyelitis—Inflammation of the Marrow—Osteomyelitis, or Pus in the bones, resulting from injury, is apt to result in any long bone when the part is afflicted by ♂, and other malefics; ♅ or ♂ ♂ ♄ in the sign ruling the part. (See "Osteomyelitis" under Femur; Marrow). Case—See Fig. 15C, in "Astro-Diagnosis", by the Heindels.

Pain in the Bones—A ♄ disease; ♄ in an earthy sign in the Asc., 6th H., or M.C., and affl. the ☉, ☽, Asc., or hyleg; the ☽ in ♉, and affl. by the ☉ or ♂ when taken ill. (See Dengue).

Periosteitis—Inflammation of the Periosteum—A ♂ affliction; ♂ in the sign ruling the part; ♂ ♂ ♄. (See "Periosteitis" under Femur).

Pus in the Bones—(See "Osteomyelitis" in this section. Also see Cloaca).

Radius—Fracture of—(See Radius).

Rheumatism—In the Bones—Born under ♄; ♄ ruler of the Asc., and affl. the ☉, ☽, or hyleg; ♄ in asp. to the Asc., and affl. the ☽ or lord of the Asc. (See Rheumatism).

Rickets—(See Rickets).

Softening Of—(See Rickets).

Spinal Marrow—Disorders of—(See "Marrow" under Spine).

Subluxations—Of the Vertebrae—(See Subluxations, Vertebrae).

Teeth—Decay and Disorders of—(See Teeth).

Tuberculosis—Of Bone—Caused by ♄ afflictions in earthy signs, and with ♄ in the Asc., 6th H., or M.C., and affl. the ☉, ☽, Asc., or hyleg (See Tuberculosis).

Ulcerous Inflammation—(See Caries, Jaws, Teeth, Ulcers).

Vertebrae—(See Vertebrae).

Wrists—Fracture of—(See Wrists). For Disorders of the Bones, with Case Records, etc., see Figures 15A, 15B, and 15C, in "Astro-Diagnosis" by the Heindels.

BOOTES—Left Shoulder of Bootes—(See Arcturus, Disgrace, Ruin).

BORBORYGMUS—(See Bowels).

BORN—(See Abortion, Birth, "Excision" under Foetus; Miscarriage, Parturition, Stillborn).

BOW-LEGGED—Bandy Leg—(See Legs).

BOWELS—Intestines—Intestinal Canal—Enteric—The Bowels are principally under the internal rule of the ♍ Sign. They are also ruled by the ☽, ☿, and the 6th H. The bowels are also influenced and affected by ♓, the sign opposite to ♍, and also by all the common signs. The 6th House is said to rule the intestines, even to the Rectum. The common signs on the 6th H., or on angles, greatly influence the bowels for good or ill, according to the nature of the planets in these signs at B., and by dir., and the aspects formed. The Large and Small Intestines are ruled by ♍. The Colon, Jejunum, Ileum, Ileo-Cecal Valve, and other parts of the Intestinal Tract, and accompanying diseases, are listed alphabetically in this section. The Bowels, as a receptacle, are ruled by the ☽. The Mesentery, or the Peritoneal Attachments of the Small Intestines, are ruled by ♍. The Colon and its different parts are ruled by ♏. (See Colon). The Lower Excretory Bowels, and the Rectum, are ruled by ♏. (See Colon, Rectum). The Intestinal Branches of the Solar Plexus are ruled by ♏. (See this influence under Ductless Glands. See Ductless). The Intestinal Ganglia and Plexuses are ruled by ♂ and the ♏ sign. The ☽ in ♍ rules the glands and functions of the bowels. ☿ in ♍ rules the nerves and nerve fibres. ♄ in ♍ rules the Spleen. ♃ in ♍ rules the Arteries. ♂ in ♍ rules the Muscles. ♀ in ♍ rules the Veins. See the following Diseases and subjects in the alphabetical arrangement when not considered here—

Abdomen; Abdominal Cramps— ♅ in ♍. (See Colic, Cramps, Flatulence, Gas, Gripings, Wind, etc.).

Abdominal Phthisis—(See Phthisis).

Abscess in Bowels—♃ affl. in ♍.

Accidents To—(See "Injuries" in this section).

Action of Bowels — (See the various paragraphs in this section).

Affected—The bowels tend to be affected with the ☉ in ♐, ♑; ☽ ♌, ♍, ♎, ♏, ♐; ♅ ♏; ♄ ♉, ♊; ♃ ♈, ♉, ♌; ♂ ♈, ♌, ♍, ♓; ♀ ♓; ☿ ♏, ♒. See Table 196 in Simmonite's Arcana. See "Disordered", and the various paragraphs in this section).

All Diseases Of—All Infirmities and Weaknesses of—All Irregularities of —Signified by the 6th H. and the ♍ sign, and planets in them.

Antiperistalsis—♃ affl. in ♓; ♄, ♂, or ♅ in ♓, and afflicted, and with the ♍ sign weak at B. and unoccupied. (See "Peristaltic" in this section).

Anus; Aphthae; Appendicitis—(See Appendix).

Arteries Of—Disordered—♃ affl. in ♍.

Asiatic Cholera—(See Cholera).

Assimilation—Impaired—(See Assimilation).

Belly—Any Disease In—(See Belly).

Biliousness—(See Bile).

Bloody Discharges — (See Dysentery, Flux, Hemorrhage, Hemorrhoids, Typhoid, Ulcers).

Borborygmus—Gas in the Bowels—Croaking and Rumbling—☿ affl. in ♍; a ♍ disease, and afflictions in ♍. (See Flatulence, Gas. Also see "Pains" in this section).

Bowel Complaints—(See the various paragraphs in this section. See "Wet Feet" under Feet).

    Caecum—Disorders of—(See Caecum).

Cancer Of—(See "Bowels" under Carcinoma).

    Catarrh Of—(See "Bowels" under Catarrh).

    Cholera; Cholera Infantum — (See Cholera).

Chyle—Disorders of—(See Chyle).

Chyme—(See Chyme).

Circulation — Obstructed, Restricted, or Sluggish—♅ ☌ ☽ in ♍, and affl. ♃ and ♀; ♄ affl. in ♍; ♄ ☌ ☽ ♍; ♄ ♍ ☌, □, or ☍ ♃ or ♀, obstructed or sluggish.

Cold in Bowels—The ☽ ♍ ☌ or ill-asp. any of the malefics as promittors, and espec. to ♄; ♄ in an angle, occi. of the ☉ and ori. of the ☽; ♄ in ♍. (See Cold).

Colic—♅ or ☿ affl. in ♍. Mucus Colic, and Flatulent Colic in Bowels are caused by Subs at KP, and PP, the 2, 3, 4 Lumbars. (See Colic, Flatulence, Gas, Gripings, Wind, etc. See Borborygmus, Cramps, Croaking, Pain, Spasm, in this section).

Colon—Disorders of—(See Colon).

Color—In the Treatment of Bowel Disorders—(See Yellow).

Congestion—In Bowels—♄ ♍. (See Congestion).

Constipation; Consumption Of—(See "Abdominal" under Phthisis).

Costiveness—(See Costiveness. See "Sluggish" in this section).

Cramps In—♅ or ☿ affl. in ♍. (See Colic, Pain, Spasmodic, Wind, in this section).

Croaking—Rumbling—(See Borborygmus, Gas, Pain, Wind, in this section).

Death—From Bowel Disorder—Common Signs show, and afflictions in them, and espec. when on angles or the 6th H.

Diarrhoea; Diet—Bowel Disorders from Wrong Diet—♃ affl. in ♍. (See "Evil Diet" under Diet).

Digestion — Disorders of Intestinal Digestion—(See Chyle, Indigestion).

Diseased Intestines—The Bowels Affected—Disordered—Afflictions in ♍, ♓, the 6th H., and in the common signs. (See "Disorders", and the various paragraphs in this section).

Disorders Of—Disordered—The Bowels Afflicted—Enteric Disorders—Distempers In—Liable to Bowel Disorders —The ☉ affl. in ♍, ♐, ♑, or ♓; the ☉ in ♍, ♑, or ♓, ☌ or ill-asp. any of the malefics as promittors; the ☉ ♍ and affl. by ♃; ☽ diseases and afflictions; born under the ☽; ☽ affl. in ♌, ♍, ♎, ♏, or ♐; ☽ affl. in ♍ or ♐, and espec. affl. the hyleg therefrom; the ☽ hyleg in ♍, and afflicted, and espec. with females; ♆ or ♅ affl. in ♍ in 6th H.; ♄ affl. in ♍ or ♏; ♄ or ♃ in ♍ and afflicted; ♄ in ♍ occi., and affl. the ☉, ☽, or Asc.; ♄ ☌ ♂ in ♍, and espec. in an angle at a Solar Ingress at an Equinox; Signified by ♄ in ♉, ♊, or ♋; ♄ or ♂ in ♍ in the 6th H.; ♄ affl. in the 6th H. in a flexed or mutable sign; ♃ affl. in ♈, ♉, ♌, ♍, or ♓; ♃ in ♐ or ♍ in the 6th H., and afflicted; ♂ affl. in ♈, ♌, ♍, or ♓; ♂ in ♍ ☌ or ill-asp. the ☉; ♂ promittor in ♓, and in ☌ or ill-asp. the ☉; ♂ in ♍ in the 6th H.; ♀ affl. in ♍ and affl. the ☽ or Asc.; ♀ affl. in ♍, ♎, or ♓; ♀ in ♍ in the 6th H., and afflicted; ☿ affl. in ♍, ♎, ♏, ♑, or ♒; ☿ affl. in ♑, due to worry and melancholy; common signs denote, and espec. afflictions in ♍, or with common signs on angles or the 6th H.; ♓ on the Asc.; earthy signs on Asc.; the malefics, or afflicting planets in common signs; a Stellium in ♍ or the 6th H.; ♍ on cusp the 6th H. (See the various paragraphs in this section. Also see Heredity).

Distempers In— (See "Disorders" in this section).

Dropsy—Of the Glands of—♄ affl. in ♍, dropsy and wasting; ☽ affl. in ♍, as the ☽ rules the glands and functions of the bowels.

Drugs— (See "Opiates" in this section).

Duodenum—Disorders of—Afflictions in ♍. (See Duodenum).

Dysentery; Eating—Bowel Disorders from Improper Eating—♀ affl. in ♍ in 6th H.; ♀ in ♍ and affl. the ☽ or Asc. (See "Diet" in this section. Also see Eating, Food).

Enema; Enteralgia— (See "Colic", "Pain" in this section).

Enteric Fever—Fever in Bowels— (See "Fever" in this section).

Enteritis — (See "Inflammation" in this section).

Enterocolitis—Caused by Subs at KP and PP; by afflictions in ♍, ♎, or ♏. (See "Inflammation" in this section. Also see Colon, Vertebrae).

Enteroptosis—(See "Prolapse" in this section).

Entozoons—Intestinal Parasites— (See Entozoons, Worms).

Eruptions—And Lesions in Bowels— (See Typhoid).

Evacuations—Bloody— (See Evacuations, Faeces, Flux).

Faeces—Disorders of— (See Faeces, Evacuations).

Feet—Bowel Complaints from Wet Feet— (See "Bowel Complaints", "Colic" under Feet).

Fever—In the Bowels—Enteric Fever —Afflictions in ♍; a ♍ disease; ♄ in ♍, occi., and affl. the ☉, ☽ or Asc.; ♂ affl. in ♍; ♂ in ♋ in the 6th H. (See Typhoid).

Flatulence—(See Flatulence. Also see Borborygmus, Colic, Cramps, Wind, in this section).

Fluxes—(See Flux).

Functions—Of the Bowels—Disordered— ☽ affl. in ♍. (See "Irregular", and the various paragraphs in this section).

Gas In Bowels— (See Colic, Flatulence, Gas, Tympanites, Wind. Also see Borborygmus, Colic, Cramps, Wind, in this section).

Gastroenteritis—Inflammation in Both the Stomach and Bowels—♂ affl. in ♍. (See Gastro).

Gastro-Intestinal Tunics— (See "Impar" under Ganglion).

Glandular Disorders— ☽ affl. in ♍; ♄ affl. in ♍, wasting of the glands of bowels. (See Glands, Wasting).

Gripings— (See Colic, Cramps, Pain, Spasmodic, Wind, in this section).

Hard Faeces—(See Faeces).

Hemorrhage Of— (See Dysentery, "Bloody Flux" under Flux; Typhoid, Ulcers).

Hemorrhoids—(See the various paragraphs under Hemorrhoids).

Hernia—Ventral Hernia— (See Hernia, Rupture).

Humours In— (See "Bowels" under Humours).

Hypogastrium; Ileum—Ileo-Caecal Valve—Disorders of—(See Ileum).

Indigestion—Intestinal—(See Indigestion).

Infarctions— (See "Obstructions" in this section).

Infections—Afflictions in ♍. (See Infections).

Infirmities In—(See "All Diseases In", and the various paragraphs in this section).

Inflammation—Enteritis—Phlegmonous Enteritis—The ☉ in ♍ or ♏, and to the ♂ or ill-asps. ♂ by dir.; the prog. ☽ in ♍ ☌, ☐, ☍ ♂; the ☽ ♍ ☌ or ill-asp. any of the malefics as promittors; ♂ affl. in ♍ or ♓; ♂ ♍ in 6th H.; ♂ in ♍ ☌ the Asc.; ♂ in watery signs and ♂ or ill-asp. the Asc. by dir.; caused by Subs at KP, UPP, PP, LPP. (See Appendicitis, Caecum; "Enteritis" under Catarrh; Dysentery, Enteritis; "Gastro-Enteritis" under Gastro).

Inguinal Hernia— (See Groins, Hernia).

Injuries—Accidents To—Afflictions in ♍, and to the ♍ sign, and espec. malefics in ♍, and afflictions in the 6th H. or Asc.

Intussusception—A ♅ disease; ♅ in ♍, or afflicted in the 6th H. in ♍.

Irregular—Bowel Action Irregular—Irregular Functions—Irregular Peristaltic Action—The ☽, ♄, or ♀ affl. in ♍; ♀ in ♍ in the 6th H., and affl. the ☽ or Asc. (See Constipation, Costiveness, Faeces. Also see "All Diseases", "Peristaltic", "Sluggish", in this section).

Irritations In—Intestinal Irritations —♂ in ♍ and affl. the hyleg; ♀ affl. in ♍.

Jejunum—Disorders of— (See Jejunum).

Large Intestines—Diseases In—Afflictions in ♍ or ♏; caused by Subs from KP to LPP. (See Colon, "Ductless Glands" under Ductless).

Lesions—(See Typhoid).

Looseness In— (See Cholera, Diarrhoea, Dysentery, Flux, etc.).

Lower Excretory Bowels—Colon—Rectum, etc.—Ruled by ♏, and diseases of caused by afflictions in ♏ and by Subs at UPP, PP, LPP.

Lumpy Faeces—(See Faeces).

Melancholy—Bowel Disorders from— (See Melancholy).

Mesentery—Disorders of— (See Mesentery, Peritoneum).

Mesocolon—(See Colon).

Mucus In—Mucus Colic—The intestinal mucus is ruled by ♓, and also influenced by ♍. Mucus in the bowels is increased and produced by ♀ in ♍, and afflicted, and espec. when ♀ is in 6th H., or affl. the ☽ or Asc.; mucus colic is caused by Subs at PP, the 2, 3, 4 Lumbar vertebrae. (See Mucus).

Muscles Of—Disorders of—♂ affl. in ♍.

Nerves Of—Nerve Fibres —Disturbances of—☿ affl. in ♍.

Neuralgia—Neuralgic Pains— ☿ affl. in ♍; Subs at PP, 2nd Lumbar. (See "Pain" in this section).

Obstructions In—Infarctions—Hard Faeces—Obstructed Circulation, etc.— ♄ affl. in ♍; ♄ ♂ ♃ or ♀ in ♍, sluggish bowels; ♄ ♍ in ♂, ☐, or ☍ ♃ or ♀; ♄ ♂ ☽ in ♍; ♅ ♂ ☽ in ♍, and also afflicted by the ☐ or ☍ of ♃ and ♀; the ☉, ☽, ♄, ♂, or ☿ affl. in ♍; ☽ affl. in ♍, and affl. the hyleg therefrom; the ☽ in ♍ ♂ or ill-asp. ♄ (or ☿ if he be of the nature of ♄) at the beginning of an illness, or at decumbiture; the hyleg in ♍ and afflicted, and espec. with females; afflictions in ♍; a ♍ disease. ♄ in ♍ tends to obstructions in the different parts of the Colon, and espec. in the Transverse Colon. (See "Circulation" in this section. Also see Colon, Ileum, Obstructions).

Omentum—(See Peritoneum).

Open—Bowels should be kept open and regular when ♄ is in ♍ at B.

Operations—The bowels, or abdomen, should not be operated upon surgically when the ☽ is passing thru the ♍, ♎, or ♏ signs. Case—Bowels Operated Upon Twice—See Case, "A Luckless Youth", No. 390 in 1001 N.N.

Opiates—Bowel Disorders from the Use of Opiates and Drugs—♆ affl. in ♍.

Pain in Bowels—Cholera Pains In— Colic—Cramps—Enteralgia—Gripings —Neuralgic Pains—Spasmodic Pains— Wind, etc.—♅ or ☿ affl. in ♍; Subs at UPP, PP, LPP. (See Borborygmus, Colic, Cramps, Neuralgia, Spasmodic, Wind, in this section. Also see Enteralgia, Flatulence, Gas).

Parasitic Diseases—(See Entozoons, Parasites, Tapeworm, Worms).

Peristaltic Action—Impeded—Sluggish—Weakened—The ♍ sign rules the peristaltic action of the bowels, and afflictions in ♍ tend to disturb this action; the ☽ ♂ ♄ in ♍; ☽ ♍ ☐ or ☍ ♄; ♄ in ♍; ♀ affl. in ♍. (See Constipation, Costiveness, Expulsion, Faeces, Impediments, Peristaltic, Sluggish).

Peritoneum—Disorders of—(See Peritoneum).

Perityphlitis—(See Caecum).

Phthisis Abdominalis—(See Phthisis).

Physic—Cathartics—Purging—(See Physic).

Piles—(See Hemorrhoids).

Prolapse—Of Bowels—Enteroptosis— ♄ influence; ♄ affl. in ♍ or ♏; Subs at PP, LPP. (See "Prolapse" under Womb. Also see Hernia).

Putrid Matter—Bowels Filled With— ♄ ♂ ♃ or ♂ in ♍, and with the ☉ or ☽ in ♎, and due to over-eating, and fermentation of food. (See Faeces).

Rectum—Disorders of — (See Anus,

Hemorrhoids, Rectum. Also see "Lower Excretory" in this section).

Regular—Bowels Should be Kept Regular—(See "Open" in this section).

Restricted Circulation—(See Circulation, Obstructed, in this section).

Retention—Of Faeces—(See Constipation, Costiveness, Faeces. Also see "Obstructions" in this section).

Rumbling—Croaking—(See Borborygmus" in this section).

Rupture—(See Hernia, Rupture).

Scybala—(See "Hard" under Faeces).

Serous Stools—(See Faeces, Serum).

Sigmoid Flexure—(See Colon).

Sluggish Bowels— (See Constipation, Costiveness, Faeces. Also see "Circulation", "Peristaltic", in this section).

Small Intestines—Ruled by ♍. All diseases in are signified by afflictions in ♍, and in the 6th and 7th houses, and by Subs at UPP and PP. Subs at UPP tend to affect the upper Small Intestines, and at PP and LPP, the lower Small Intestines. (See Assimilation, Caecum, Duodenum, Hypogastrium, Ileum, Jejunum).

Sores In—(See "Ulcers" in this section).

Spasm—Spasmodic Pains In—Gripings—Cramps—♅ or ♄ affl. in ♍; ♃ affl. in ☍ or ♑; afflictions in ♍; an ♒ disease, and afflictions in ♒. (See Borborygmus, Colic, Cramps, Gas, Pain, Wind, in this section).

Stools—(See Faeces).

Summer Complaint— (See "Cholera Infantum" under Cholera).

Suppression—Of Stools—(See Faeces. Also see "Obstructions" in this section).

Tapeworm—(See Tapeworm, Worms).

Transverse Colon—(See Colon).

Treatment—Of Bowel Disorders— Yellow Color is used in. Copper (Cuprum) is a good medicinal remedy in loose bowels and infections. The bowels should be kept regular and open by proper diet and habits, rather than by the use of physics. (See Physic).

Tuberculosis Of—♄ affl. in ♍. (See Phthisis, Tuberculosis).

Tumors In—♃, ♂, or ♀ affl. in ♍, and espec. when in the 6th H. and affl. the ☽ or Asc. (See Tumors).

Tunics— (See "Impar" under Ganglion).

Tympanites; Typhoid; Typhlitis—(See Caecum).

Ulcers— (See Duodenum, Dysentery, Ulcers).

Upper Small Intestines—(See "Small" in this section).

Veins Of—Disorders of—♀ affl. in ♍.

Ventral Hernia—(See Hernia).

Vomiting—Faecal Vomiting — (See Ileac Passion).

Wasting—Of Glands— (See "Glandular" in this section).

Weakened—(See "Peristaltic" in this section).

Weaknesses Of—(See "All Diseases", and the various paragraphs in this section).

Wet Feet—Bowel Disorders From— (See "Colic", "Wet Feet", under Feet).

Wind Colic—♅ affl. in ♍. (See "Colic" in this section. Also see Wind).

Worms — (See Entozoons, Parasites, Tapeworm, Worms).

Wrong Diet—Bowel Disorders From —(See Diet, Eating, in this section).

Yellow Color—Favorable in the treatment of Bowel Disorders—(See Yellow).

Yellow Fever—With Intestinal Derangements—Caused by afflictions in ♌ and ♍; Subs at CP, SP, and KP. (See "Yellow Fever" under Yellow).

BOYISHNESS—(See "Youthfulness" under Youth).

BOYS—(See "Births" under Male; "Birth of a Son" under Son).

BRACHIAL—The Brachial Plexus— Ruled by ☿. Innervation and nerve force to the lungs and pulmonary apparatus are given by ☿ thru the Brachial Plexus, as well as to the arms, hands and shoulders. (See Arms, "Brachial Plexus" under Plexus).

BRADYCARDIA—Abnormally Slow Pulse—(See Pulse).

BRAIN—Encephalon—Cerebrum—Cerebellum—The Brain is under the internal rulership of the ♈ Sign. The Cerebellum and Base of the Brain, however, are ruled by ♉. The degree on the Asc. also strongly rules and influences the Brain. Among the planets, ☿ is the strong ruler of the brain, in both sexes. Ptolemy says the ☉ also rules the brain. In males the ☉ is said to rule the brain. The ☉ has special affinity with the brain. The Pons Varolii is ruled by the ☉ and the ♉ sign. The brain substance is ruled by the ☽ and ☿. The Meninges, or Brain Coverings, the Dura Mater, are ruled by the ♋ Sign and ♅. In the foetus the brain development, and specialization of the nerve filaments, are ruled and carried on by ☿. The Cerebral Hemispheres, taken together, are ruled by the ♈ Sign. Separately, the right Cerebral Hemisphere is ruled by ☿, and the left Cerebral Hemisphere by ♂. The Cerebral Ventricles are ruled by ♆. The Cerebro-Spinal Nervous System is ruled by ☿. The Arbor Vitae of the Cerebellum are ruled by ♉. The functions of the brain are ruled by ☿ and the ☽. Brain balance is maintained by the secretions of the Thyroid Gland. The brain is smaller and less in weight at the New Moon, and increases in weight and size until the Full Moon, and then diminishes again. It is largely the relation between the ☉ and ☽ which determines the size and weight of the brain. The nerves of the brain are fed by the rays of the ☉. The planet ♆ has considerable action and influence over the brain and eyes. Brain workers should work in a room predominating in blue colors, as blue is restful, as well as stimulating and invigorating to the brain. The Pineal Gland

is ruled by ♆. The Pituitary Body is ruled by ♅ and the ♏ sign. The Medulla Oblongata is ruled by ♉. The Brain and Head correspond to the cardinal signs and the Mental Temperament. (See Cerebellum, Cerebrum, Cerebro-Spinal, Cortex, Medulla, Meninges, Mind, Nerves, Occiput, Pineal, Pituitary).

DISEASES OF THE BRAIN—The Brain Afflicted—Brain Disorders, etc.— See the following subjects in the alphabetical arrangement when not considered here—

Abscess Of—♅ or other malefics in ♈, or afflicting the ♈ sign; Subs at AT, the Atlas.

Absence Of—(See "Malformation" in this section).

Affected—The Brain Affected—The ☉ and ☽ acting thru the ♈ sign affect the head and its dependencies, and the Cerebro-Spinal Nervous System, and give way to the Hepatic Diathesis. The ☉ and ☽ acting thru the ♏ sign, by way of the Solar Plexus, and the different plexuses, affect the brain and the medulla. ♅ in ♈ tends especially to affect the brain and its membranes. (See Table 196 in Simmonite's Arcana. Also see the various paragraphs in this section).

All Diseases Of—Any Disease of— Diseases of ☿.

Anaemia—(See Anaemia, Cerebral).

Any Disease—Of the Brain—Encephalopathy—Caused by afflictions in ♈ or ♉; ☿ diseases. Subs at AT, CP and KP.

Apoplexy—(See Apoplexy, Cerebral).

Atrophy Of—♄ affl. in ♈. Is often found in Alzheimer's Disease, where the primitive or animal instincts prevail. (See "Animal Instincts" under Animal; Atrophy).

Balance—The Brain Balance Disturbed—(See Thyroid).

Basal Ganglia—(See Basal; "Basal" under Ganglion).

Blood—Congestion of in the Brain— Determination, or Rush of to the Head and Brain—(See "Brain" under Congestion; "Blood" under Head).

Blood Vessel—In the Brain—Rupture of—(See Apoplexy, Cerebral).

Brain Disorders — (See "Disorders", and the various paragraphs in this section).

Brain Fag—Caused by ☿ affl. by ♄, and espec. when ☿ is weak by sign or position, combust, or setting in the West at B., or unconnected with the ☽ or Asc. (See Fatigue, Reading, Study).

Brain Fever—The ☉ or ♂ affl. in ♈; ☉ ☌ ♄ by dir., in the 1st H., or to the ill-asps. of ♄; ☉ ☌ ♄ in ♎, and also □ ♂; the ☽ in the Asc. and ☌ ♂ at B.; ♂ affl. in ♈ or ♎, and espec. when ♂ is in the 6th H. or Asc.; ♂ □ or ☍ ☿; ♂ ascending, and ♂ afflicting at the Vernal, tend to a prevalence of brain fever in Countries ruled by ♈; ♄ to the ☌ or ill-asps. the ☉ in the Asc. at B.; ☿ affl. in ♈; an ♈ and ♐ disease, and afflictions in these signs. Death from brain fever is more apt to result when there are many afflictions in the cardinal signs, and espec. in ♈, and card. signs on angles, or ♈ afflicted on the cusp of 6th H. Case—See Chap. 13, page 97, in Daath's Medical Astrology.

Brain Force—Dispersion of—(See Dispersions).

Brain Storms—Violent Brain Storms —☿ affl. by ♂, and espec. when ☿ is affl. by the ☽, and unconnected with the ☽ or Asc.; the ☽ □ or ☍ ☿, and also affl. by ♂. (See Frenzy, Fury, Hysteria, Irrational, Madness, Mania, "Psychic Storms" under Psychic).

Brain Substance—(See "Substance" in this section).

Bulbar Paralysis—(See Medulla).

Cerebral Disorders—(See Anaemia, Apoplexy, Cerebral, Congestion).

Cerebro-Spinal—(See Cerebro).

Clot on Brain—Death By—♄ afflicted in ♈; ♄ ☌ ♃ or ♀ in ♈. Case—See "Birth and Death", No. 350 in 1001 N.N. (See Clots).

Concussion—Of the Brain—From Accidents and Injuries—(See Blows, Concussion, Head, "Fractures" under Skull).

Condition Of—Diseases arising from the condition of the Brain—(See such subjects as Anaemia, Apoplexy, Dizziness, Faintings, Headaches, Insanity, Insomnia, Madness, Neuralgia, Swoonings, Syncope, Vertigo, etc. Also see the various subjects in this section).

Congestions—In the Brain—Cerebral Congestion—(See Cerebral, Congestion).

Convulsions—Due to Brain Disturbances—(See Fits, Spasms).

Cortical Lesions—(See Cortex).

Curable Brain Disorders—♃ and ♀ rising and elevated, between the 1st and 10th H., while ♄ or ♂ may be in the 7th H., the disease will be curable, altho violent. (See "Incurable" in this section. Also see "Curable Diseases" under Curable).

Cyst-Like Tumor—Hydatid—Afflictions in ♈ or ♉; Subs at AT. (See Cysts, Tumors. See "Tumor" in this section).

Death—From Brain Disorders—☿ influence; ☿ occi. at B., and affl. the hyleg by dir., and espec. if ☿ be in ♈ and afflicted by malefics. (See Brain Fever, Clots, and other paragraphs in this section. Also see Apoplexy, Cerebral).

Defects—Of the Brain—The Brain Defective—The ☉ affl. in ♈ tends to structural defects of the brain; ☿ affl. at B.; ☿ affl. by the ☽ or malefics; ☿ having no relation to the ☽ or Asc., and affl. by malefics. (See Defects).

Delirium; Demoniac Affections—(See Demoniac).

Determination—Of Blood to the Brain and Head—(See "Blood" in this section).

Disordered Brain—Diseased Brain—Disturbed Brain—Distempered Brain—Brain Disorders, etc.—A ☉ disease; the ☉ □ or ☍ the Asc.; the ☉ and ☿ affl.

in ♈; the ☉ has affinity with the brain, and the sign position of the ☉, and the aspects to the ☉, largely denote the strength or weakness of the brain; the ☽ and ☿ unconnected with each other or the Asc., and affl. by malefics; the ☽ in the 6th H. and affl. by ☿; the ☽ to the ill-asps. ☿ by dir., and ☿ weak and ill-dignified at B., and espec. when ☿ is in ♈ and affl. by malefics; the ☽ hyleg, affl. in ♈, and espec. with females; the ☽ in fiery signs tends to brain disorders due to haste and excitement, and espec. when affl. in ♈; ♇ affl. in ♈, brain disorders due to the inordinate use of all drugs and opiates; ♇ in ♈, and affl. the ☉, ☽, Asc., or hyleg; ♇ affl. in ♈ in the 6th H.; ♅ affl. in ♈, and espec. to disorders of the meninges; ♄ and ♃ affl. in ♈; ♃ affl. in ♈, by rush of blood to the brain, and oftentimes apoplexy; ♂ affl. in ♈, and espec. ♂ in ♈ in the 6th H.; a ☿ disease; ☿ affl. in the 6th H., and espec. when in ♈; ☿ affl. in ♈, nervous disorders of the brain due to overwork and overstudy; ☿ □ or ☍ the Asc., brain diseases; ☿ afflicted tends to disturb the mind, brain and nerves; ☿ afflicting the hyleg tends to death by brain disorders; an ♈ and ♎ disease, and afflictions in these signs; ♈ on the Asc.; ♈ on the cusp of 6th H. and afflicted; afflictions in ♈ tend to brain exhaustion; the ♌ sign ascending at the Vernal Equi., and the ☉ afflicted, the ♌ people, and those living in Countries ruled by ♌, tend to suffer more from brain disorders, and from disorders brought on by extreme heat, drought, pestilence, and heart disturbances; Subs at AT, AX and CP. (See the various paragraphs in this section. See "Disorders Of The Head" under Head).

Distempers—Of the Brain—(See "Disordered" in this section).

Disturbed Brain—The ☽ in ♌ and affl. by the ☉ or ♂ when taken ill; ☿ affl. in ♈. (See "Disordered" in this section).

Dizziness—Lightness of the Brain—Giddiness—Swimming in the Head—(See Faintings, Vertigo).

Dropsy—Of the Brain—(See Hydrocephalus).

Drugs—The Brain Affected By, and by Opiates—♇ affl. in ♈. (See Narcotics).

Dura Mater—(See Meninges).

Encephalitis — Inflammation of the Brain—Phrenitis—(See "Inflammation" in this section).

Encephalopathy—(See "Any Disease" in this section).

Excitement—Haste, and Brain Disorders From—The ☽ affl. in fiery signs, and espec. when in ♈.

Exhaustion—Of the Brain—Afflictions in ♈.

Fagged Brain—(See "Brain Fag" in this section).

Faintings—(See "Cerebral Anaemia" under Anaemia; Coma, Delirium, Faintings, Fits, Vertigo).

Fever—(See "Brain Fever" in this section).

Functions—Disordered Brain Functions—☿ diseases.

Fury—(See Frenzy, Fury, Insanity, Madness, Mania, etc.).

Giddiness—(See Faintings, Vertigo).

Haste—And Excitement—(See "Excitement" in this section. Also see Excitable).

Headaches; Heat—Excessive Heat In the Brain—Encephalitis—(See "Inflammation" in this section).

Hemorrhage—Of the Brain—(See Apoplexy, Cerebral).

Hernia Of—(See Hernia).

Hydatids—(See "Cyst" in this section).

Hydrocephalus; Idiocy; Ill Blood In—♃ affl. in ♈ tends to ill blood in the veins of the head and brain.

Incurable Brain Disorders—♄ or ♂ alone ruling the ☽, ☿, or the 1st H.; ♃ and ♀ setting or occi., and ♄ or ♂ be angular and ori., the disease becomes more conspicuous and less liable of a cure. (See Curable, Incurable).

Inflammation—Of the Brain—Encephalitis—Phrenitis—Excessive Heat In—An ♈ disease; ♂ affl. in ♈; ☿ ill-dignified at B., and under the severe affliction of the malefics by dir.; ☿ affl., and afflicting the hyleg, tends to produce death by inflammation of the brain; malefics in ♈, and the hyleg much afflicted at B.; ♀ affl. in ♈; Subs at AT. (See "Wild Delirium" under Delirium; Encephalon).

Injuries to Brain—(See "Accidents", "Blows", "Cuts", under Head; "Fractures" under Skull).

Insanity; Insensibility; Insomnia—(See Sleep).

Intoxication—(See "Delirium Tremens" under Delirium; Drink, Drunkenness).

Leptomeningitis—(See Meningitis).

Lesions—(See Cortical).

Lightness—In the Brain—(See "Dizziness" in this section).

Madness—(See Frenzy, Fury, Madness, Mania).

Malformation—(See Idiocy. Also see Case, "Malformation", No. 921, in 1001 N.N.).

Medulla—Disorders of—(See Medulla).

Membranes—Distempers of, etc.—♅ affl. in ♈. (See Meninges. Also see "Inflammation" in this section).

Meninges—Meningitis, etc.—See Meninges).

Mental Disorders—From Brain Diseases and Defects—(See "Defects", and the various paragraphs in this section. Also see Idiocy, Insanity, Mania, Mental, Mind, etc.).

Microcephalic Head—(See Idiocy).

Mind—Disorders of the Brain Affecting the Mind—Afflictions in ♈, and Subs at AT. (See Mind. Also see the various paragraphs in this section).

Moisture—Of the Brain—(See "Brain" under Moisture).

Motor Functions—Diseases of the Brain Causing Disorders of—(See "Brain" under Motor).

Nervous Disorders—Of the Brain—☿ affl. in ♈.

Neuralgia—(See Headaches, Neuralgia).

No Brain—Merely a Frontal Mask—Case—See "Malformation", No. 921 in 1001 N.N.

Obstructions In—♄ affl. in ♈.

Opiates—(See "Drugs" in this section).

Organic Diseases—Of the Brain—The ☉ affl. in ♈; Subs at AT. (See Organic).

Over-Activity—Of the Brain—♂ in ♈.

Over-Study—Brain Disorders From—☿ affl. in ♈. (See "Brain Fag" in this section. Also see Insanity).

Over-Worked Brain—Denoted by ☿, and ☿ affl. in ♈; ♂ ☌ ☿ in ♈. (See "Brain Fag" in this section. Also see Reading, Study).

Paralysis—Bulbar—(See Medulla).

Peculiar Brain Diseases—♅ diseases; ♅ in ♈; ☿ affl. by ♅. (See Peculiar).

Phrenitis—(See "Inflammation" in this section. Also see Phrenitic).

Polioencephalitis—Inflammation of the Gray Matter of the Cortex—♂ affl. in ♈ or ♉; ☿ in ♈ and affl. by ♂.

Posterior Portion—Of the Brain Undeveloped—Case—See "Idiot from Birth", No. 742 in 1001 N.N. Also see Case, "Female", Chap. 8, page 49, in Daath's Medical Astrology.

Rattle-Brained—(See "Rapid" under Speech).

Rupture of Vessels—In Brain—(See Apoplexy, Cerebral).

Shocks—Brain Disorders from Shocks—♅ in ♈. (See Shock).

Shrinkage—Of the Brain—♄ affl. in ♈. (See "Atrophy" in this section).

Softening—Of the Brain—A ♓ disease, and with many planets in ♓ and afflicted; is often the result of Alcoholism, a ♓ affliction; Subs at AT cause acute softening of the brain. (See Alcoholism, Softening).

Spasmodic Diseases—Diseases of the Brain Causing—♅ affl. in ♈; Subs at AT. (See Spasmodic).

Spinal Cord—Diseases of the Brain and Spinal Cord—Subs at CP; afflictions in ♈ and ♌. (See Cerebro-Spinal).

Storms—(See "Brain Storms" in this section).

Strengthened—The Brain Strengthened—♅ ⚹ or △ the Asc.

Structural Defects—The ☉ affl. in ♈; Subs at AT. (See "Organic", "Substance" in this section).

Study—Brain Disorders from Over-Study—☿ affl. in ♈; ☿ affl. in ♈ in 6th H. (See "Brain Fag" in this section).

Substance—Disorders of the Substance of the Brain—☉ affl. in ♈; ☿ diseases, and ☿ affl. in ♈; diseases of the ☽; the ☽ affl. in ♈ or ♎, and espec. when in the 6th H.; Subs at AT. (See "Organic", "Structural" in this section. Also see Substance).

Swimming—In the Head—(See Vertigo).

Swoonings—(See Faintings).

Syncope—(See Fainting).

Thrombus—(See "Clot" in this section).

Tuberculosis—Of the Brain—♄ affl. in ♈; Subs at AT.

Tumor Of—Hydatid, Cyst-like Tumor—♄ affl. in ♈ tends to unusual deposits in the brain tissues, hardening of the vessels, and tumors; ♃, ♀, or the ☽ affl. in ♈, and often the result of bad living, dissipation, Alcoholism, Too Much Blood, Gluttony, etc. (See "Cyst-like" in this section. Also see Tumors).

Unconsciousness—(See Anaesthetics, Apoplexy, Catalepsy, Coma, Delirium, Dreams, Faintings, Insensibility, Sleep, Trance, etc.).

Vertigo; Vessels of Brain—Rupture of—(See Apoplexy, Cerebral).

Violent Brain Storms—(See "Brain Storms" in this section. Also see Violent).

Water—On the Brain—Dropsy of—(See Hydrocephalus).

Weight—Of the Brain—(See Introduction to this section).

BRASH—Water Brash—Eructations from Stomach—(See Belching).

BREAK-BONE FEVER—(See Dengue, Fermentation, Zymotic).

BREAKDOWN IN HEALTH—(See "Breakdown" under Health, Mental).

BREAKING—

Of Blood Vessels—(See Apoplexy, "Blood Vessels" under Vessels; Hemorrhage, Rupture, etc.). See Bursting, Lacerations.

Of Bones—(See Fractures).

BREAKINGS OUT—(See Acne, Chickenpox, Eruptions, Measles, Pimples, Rashes, Scarlatina, Skin Diseases, Smallpox, Sores, Syphilis, Ulcers, Venereal, etc.).

BREAST—Breasts—Mammae—Breast Bone—Pectoral Region—Chest—The Milk, etc.—Are denoted by the 4th H. and the ♋ Sign. Are under the external rule of the ☽ and ♀. Are also ruled by the ☽ and ♀. The Mammary Glands and the Lacteal System are ruled by the ☽ and the ♋ sign. The breasts of women are ruled by the ☽ and ♀. The Milk is ruled by the ☽, the ♋ sign, and the watery signs in general. The Sternum, or Breast Bone, the flat bone of the breast, is under the structural rulership of ♋. The Nipples, or Paps, are ruled by ♋. (See Chest, Milk). See the following subjects in the alphabetical arrangement when not considered here—

Ablation—Suppression of the Mammae—♄ in ♋ or ♑, and espec. when affl. by the ☽, the ruler of the breasts, and the ♋ sign; ♄ in ♋ in the 1st or 4th H., and affl. the ☽. (See Removal, Remote, Suppressions).

Abscess Of—Imposthumes—Ulcer—A ♋ disease, and afflictions in ♋; ♂ ♋ ☌ or evil asp. ♄, and ♂ affl. the hyleg. (See Abscesses).

Accidents To—Injuries or Hurts To—♅, ♄, or ♂ in ♋ or the 4th H., and afflicted; ♋ sign on the Asc., and containing malefics, or otherwise afflicted; afflictions in ♋. (See "Bruises" in this section).

Adenoma—Glandular Tumor of the Breast—♀ affl. in ♋. (See Adenoma, Glands, Scrofula).

Affected—The Breast tends to be affected with the ☉ in ♍; ♅ ☿; ♄ in ♈, ☿; ♃ ♊, ♌, ♓; ♂ ♊, ♋, ♒; ♀ ♌, ♑; ☿ ♍, ♐. (See Table 196 in Simmonite's Arcana).

All Diseases—In the Breast—Signified by the ♋ sign, the 4th H., and afflictions therein.

Breastbone—Protrusion of—Chicken-breasted—♋ on the Asc., and affl. by ♄ or ♂; Subs at Lu.P.

Breast Pang—(See Angina Pectoris).

Broad Chest—Or Breast—♄ lord of the Asc., and ori., as from the Asc. to M.C., or from Desc. to Nadir. (See "Stout" under Chest).

Bruises In—♄ ♋. (See "Accidents" in this section).

Caked Breasts—♄ affl. in ♋. (See Milk).

Cancer of the Breast—(See "Breasts" under Carcinóma).

Chest; Chicken-Breasted—(See "Breastbone" in this section).

Cyst Of—(See "Breast" under Cyst).

Defects—Such as Marks, Moles, Scars, etc.—♋ on the Asc. (See Marks, Moles, Scars).

Fever In—♂ affl. in ♋.

Full, Large Breasts—The ☉ or ☽ ♋; many planets in ♋; ♋ on the Asc.

Glands—Disorders of—(See "Adenoma in this section. Also see Glands, Milk).

Heat In—The ☽ in ♈, affl. by the ☉ or ♂ when taken ill; the ☽ ☌ or ill-asp. ♄ in ♌ (or ☿ if he be of the nature of ♄) at the beginning of an illness, or at decumbiture, and they frequently die when the ☽ comes to the ☍ of ♄ if no good asps. prevent it.

Heaviness—Of the Breast—The ☽ ☌, □, ☍, or P. ♄ (or ☿ if he be of the nature of ♄) at the beginning of an illness or at decumbiture (Hor'y).

Humours Falling Into—The ☽ ♋ ☌ or ill-asp. ♄ (or ☿ if he be of the nature of ♄) at the beginning of an illness or at decumbiture (Hor'y). If the ☽ be decr., and near the body of ♄, the disease may continue for a long time.

Imperfections In—A ☽ disease; a ♋ sign disease and affliction, and afflictions in ♋; ♋ on the Asc. (See "Defects" in this section).

Imposthumes—(See "Abscess" in this section).

Inflammation In—♂ affl. in ♋; ♂ in ♋ in the Asc. or 6th H., and afflicted; the ☽ in ♑ and affl. by the ☉ or ♂ when taken ill. (See Inflammation).

Injuries To—(See "Accidents" in this section).

Lacteals—(See Milk).

Large Breasts—(See "Full" in this section).

Lungs; Mammary Glands—Disorders of—Afflictions in ♍, ♋, ♌; Subs at Lu.P. (See Milk).

Marks—Moles—Scars—♋ on the Asc. (See "Imperfections" in this section).

Milk—Disorders of—(See Milk. Also see "Mammary" in this section).

Moles—(See "Marks" in this section).

Narrow Breast—(See "Narrow" under Chest).

Nipples—Disorders of—(See Nipples).

Obstructions In—♄ affl. in ♋. (See Adenoma, Milk).

Pain In—♂ affl. in ♋; ♂ in ♋ in the Asc.; the ☾ in ♈, affl. by the ☉ or ♂ when taken ill; ♋ on Asc. at the Vernal, and the ☾ weak and affl. by ♂, or ♂ in ♋. This is espec. true of people who have ♋ on the Asc. at B., and also among people in Countries ruled by ♋. (See "Pain" under Nipples).

Pang—(See "Breast Pang" in this section).

Paps—(See Nipples).

Pectoral Disorders—(See the various paragraphs in this section).

Peculiar Disorders—Of the Breasts—♅ affl. in ♋. (See Peculiar).

Phlegm—The Breast Affected With Tough Phlegm—(See "Breast" under Phlegm).

Pigeon-Breasted—(See "Breastbone" in this section).

Prominent Breasts—(See "Full" in this section).

Protrusion—(See "Breastbone" in this section).

Scars—(See "Defects", "Imperfections", in this section).

Scirrhus—A Hard Form of Carcinoma —(See Axillae, Carcinoma).

Slimy Matter—Breast Much Affected With—(See "Breast" under Phlegm).

Thorax; Tough Phlegm—(See Bronchial; "Breast" under Phlegm).

Tumors—Subs at Lu.P., 3rd Dorsal, and at KP. (See "Adenoma" in this section).

Ulcers—(See Abscess, Cancer, in this section).

Weaning—(See Weaning).

BREATH — Breathing — Respiration — Organs of Respiration—Respiratory Tract, etc. The Respiratory Tract consists of the Mouth, Nose, Throat, Larynx; Trachea, or Windpipe; Bronchial Tubes, Lungs, and Diaphragm, etc., all of which have a part in connection with the Breath, Breathing, Inhalation, Exhalation, the taking in of the Air, Oxygen, Oxygenation, and the expulsion of the Carbon and Wastes of the body. The Respiratory Tract and Organs are ruled by the ♉, ♍, and ♋ Signs. The Breath is ruled by ☿, ♃, the Airy Signs in general, and is especially under the internal rulership of ♍, as Breathing is a special function of ♍. Physiologically ☿ rules Respiration. In the Astral Body ♃ has direct relation to the Breath. (See Astral). The Throat, Windpipe, and the Larynx, are ruled by the ♉ sign. The Bronchi, the smaller Bronchial Tubes, and the Upper Lobes of each Lung, are ruled by ♍. The Pleura, the Pleural Cavity, Lower Lobe of the Left Lung, the two Lower Lobes of the right Lung, and the Diaphragm, are ruled by the ♋ sign. Neptune, ♅ and ☿ in ♉, ♍, and ♋ rule and affect the Breath, Breathing, the Respiratory System, Nerves of the Respiratory System, the Air Cells, and the Windpipe. ♅ espec. has strong rule over the Respiratory action and Breathing. The following subjects have to do with the Respiratory Tract, its action, conditions, afflictions, etc., which see in the alphabetical arrangement when not considered here—

Abnormal Breathing—Afflictions in ♉, ♍, and ♋; Subs at AP and Lu.P. (See the various paragraphs in this section).

Absorbent Vessels—(See Absorption).

Action—The ☉, ☾, ♅, or ☿ in the ♉, ♍, or ♋ sign, and afflicted, tend to disturb the respiratory action. (See the various paragraphs in this section).

Affected—The Breath and Breathing Affected—Afflictions in ♉, ♍, and ♋, and espec. the malefics in these signs. (See the various paragraphs in this section. See "Middle Cervical" under Ganglion).

Affections—Of the Breath—(General) —☿ affl. at B., and in evil asp. the Asc. by dir.; the Asc. to the evil asps. ☿ by dir., and ☿ affl. at B., and espec. if ☿ be affl. by ♄ at B. (See the different paragraphs in this section).

Air Cells—Tidal Air—☿ affl. in ♉, ♍, or ♋ tends to disturbances of the air cells in lungs, and respiration. (See "Tidal" in this section).

Anus—Inbreathing Thru—(See Anus).

Asphyxiation; Asthma; Bad Breath— (See "Foul" in this section).

Bad Respiration—Due to Tight Lacing—(See Dress, Lacing).

Breath—Breathing—Disorders and Irregularities of—(See the various paragraphs in this section).

Bronchial Disorders—(See Bronchial, Lungs).

Carbonic Acid Wastes—(See Carbon).

Chest; Cheyne-Stokes Breathing— Rhythmical Irregularity of the Breathing—♄ affl. in ♍.

Complaints—Respiratory Complains —(See the various paragraphs in this section).

Consumption; Cough; Croup; Cyanosis; Death—Disease and Death from Impure and Immoderate Respiration— Caused by ♃ when the dominion of death is vested in him.

Deep Breathing—Prevented—(See "Obstructions", "Shallow" in this section).

Defects—Of the Respiratory Organs —☿ affl. in ♍. (See Structural, Troubles, and other paragraphs in this section).

Diaphragm; Difficult Breathing—(See "Labored" in this section).

Diseases Of—The Respiratory Tract —(See "Troubles", and the various paragraphs in this section).

Disorders—Of the Breath—Of Breathing, etc.—(See the various paragraphs in this section).

Dress—Breathing Interfered With By—(See Dress).

Dust—Inhalation of and Disease From—(See "Dust" under Lungs).

Dyspnoea—(See "Labored" in this section).

Exercise—The Respiratory Organs should have proper exercise when ☿ is in ♐.

Exhalation—Expiration—Interferences With—(See "Irregular", "Labored" in this section).

Fainting; Foul Breath—Foul Tongue —Bad Breath—Halitosis—Impure Breath—Putrid Breath—Unpleasant Breath—Stinking Breath, etc.—A ☉ disease, and caused by an afflicted ☉; the ☉ affl. by ♄; a ♄ disease; a ☿ disease, and espec. when ☿ is affl. by ♄; ☿ affl. in the 6th H., and espec. by ♄; a 1st H. disease, and espec. when ♄ is there and affl. the ☉, ☿, or the hyleg; the 4th face of ♉ on the Asc., and ♄ there. In Hor'y Questions ♄ as Sig. denotes a person seldom free from bad breath. (See Carbon, Foul, Impure, Indigestion, Gangrene, Mouth; "Foul" under Tongue).

Goitre—Interfering with Breathing— (See Goitre).

Halitosis—(See "Foul" in this section).

Hiccough—Spasmodic Inspiration— (See Hiccough).

Hurried Respiration—(See "Rapid" in this section).

Immoderate Respiration—(See "Death", "Rapid", and other paragraphs in this section).

Impure Respiration—(See "Death", "Foul", in this section).

Inbreathing—Thru the Rectum—(See Anus).

Inspiration—(See Cheyne-Stokes, Hiccough, Irregular, Labored, and other paragraphs in this section).

Interference—With Breathing—Many afflictions in common signs, and espec. in ♊, ♐, and ♓; ♅ ☌ ☽ in ♋, and afflicted by ♆, ♂, and other planets, and due to gas and stomach dilatation. (See Dress, Hiccough, Labored, and the various paragraphs in this section).

Interrupted Breathing—(See Hiccough, Interference, Obstructions, and the various paragraphs in this section).

Irregular Breathing—(See Cheyne-Stokes, Hiccough, and the various paragraphs in this section).

Jerky Breathing—(See Cheyne-Stokes, Hiccough, in this section).

Labored Inspiration—Dyspnoea—Difficult Breathing—Wheezing—Caused by afflictions in ♊, to the ♐ sign, or to planets in ♊; the ☉ ☌ ♅ in ♊; the ☉ at B., or by progression, □ or ☍ ♃ or ♀, the rulers of the circulation; the

Prog. ☉ □ or ☍ planets in ♊, and espec. when a malefic transits the 6th H. at the same time; ♄ in ♊ ☍ the ☽, by insufficient tidal air; ♄ ♌ and affl. by ♅; ♄ in ♊ or ♐, by interfering with the circulation in the lungs; ♄ in ♋ or ♑, by disturbances of the diaphragm; ♃ ☍ ♀, and espec. in ♊ and ♐; ♀ in ♊ ☍ ♃, and espec. when transits or prog. influences afflict ♀. (See Angina, Asthma, Bronchial, "Convulsive" under Cough; Croup; Cyanosis, Diaphragm, Dyspnoea, Goitre, Heart, Hiccough, Oxygen, Tidal, etc. Also see "Interference", "Obstructions", in this section).

Lacing—Tight Lacing—(See Dress).

Larynx; Lungs; Lymphatic Vessels— Of the Respiratory System Affected— (See Absorption).

Membrane—Deficient Secretion of Mucus On—(See "Respiratory" under Mucous).

Mouth Breathing—(See Adenoids, Nose, Polypus, Snoring. Also see "Stertorous" in this section).

Mucous Membranes—Of the Respiratory Tract—(See "Respiratory" under Mucous. Also see Phlegm).

Muscles—Of Breathing—(See "Speech" in this section).

Nasal Polypus—(See Polypus).

Noisy Breathing—(See "Snoring", "Stertorous", in this section).

Non-Oxygenation—(See Oxygen).

Nose—Interference with Breathing— (See Adenoids, Nose, Polypus).

Obstructions—To Breathing—Deep Breathing Prevented—Obstructions in the Circulation—The afflictions of ♄ to ♃ and ♀, and also tend to non-oxygenation; ♃ or ♀ affl. in ♊, and espec. when in the 6th H., and which may also be from tight lacing. (See Adenoids, Dress, "Non-Oxygenation" under Oxygen; Nose, Polypus. Also see "Labored", "Rhythmic", "Shallow", in this section).

Organic Defects—(See "Lungs" under Structural).

Oxygen—Insufficient—(See Oxygen).

Phthisic; Phthisis; Pleura; Pneumoconiosis—(See "Dust" under Lungs).

Polypus; Putrid Breath—(See "Foul" in this section).

Rapid Breathing—Hurried—A ☿ disease, and afflictions to ☿. Also occurs in high fevers, and with high pulse. (See "High Fevers" under Fever; "High Pulse" under Pulse).

Rectal Breathing—(See Anus).

Respiratory Tract—Disorders of— (See the various paragraphs in this section).

Rhythmic Breathing—Interference With—The ☉ in ♊ or ♐, in □ or ☍ the ☽, as the ☽ governs the tidal air; ♅ ☌ ♂ in ♊; ♅ elevated in ♊ or ♋, and afflicted; ♄ ☌ ♅ in ♉ or ♏; ♄ in ♉ or ♏, by afflicting the throat region by growths or obstructions. (See Dress, Hiccough, Oxygen, Tidal. Also see the various paragraphs in this section).

Shallow Breathing—Superificial Breathing—♄ in ♏, in ♌ the ☽, lack of tidal air, and the breathing restrained; ♄ in ♏ and affl. by both ♃ and ♀ from common signs; ♄ □ ♂ or ill-asp. ♃ and ♀; ♅ ♂ ☽ ♌, due to gas and distended stomach; Subs at Lu.P. and SP. (See Oxygen. Also see Obstructions, Rhythmic, in this section).

Short Breath—(See Labored, Rapid, Shallow, in this section).

Sighs Frequently—Prolonged Deep Inspiration—The ☽ or ♅ ♂, □, or ♌ ♄ (or ♀ if he be of the nature of ♄), and espec. at the beginning of an illness, or at decumb.; the ☽ ♂ ♄ in ♏; caused by non-oxygenation, and ♄ affl. in ♏. (See Oxygen. Also see "Shallow" in this section).

Skin Breathing—Interfered With—(See "Cutaneous" under Asphyxiation).

Snoring—Usually caused by the vibrations of a long Uvula, and sleeping on the back; ♅, ♂, or ♀ in ♌ may cause excessive growth of the Uvula. (See "Stertorous" in this section. Also see Uvula).

Spasmodic Breathing—♅ affl. in ♌, ♏, or ♋. (See Cheyne-Stokes, Interference, Labored, Rapid, in this section. Also see Asphyxiation, Hiccough, Oxygen).

Speech—Improper Breathing in Speaking or Singing—Usually caused by ♄ affl. in ♏ or ♋, causing improper action of the muscles of breathing, and of the Diaphragm, and also causing disturbances of Oxygenation. (See Diaphragm, Oxygen, Speech, Vocal).

Stertorous Breathing—Noisy— Snoring—A Sonorous, Resonant, Ringing Sound in Breathing—A ♀ disease; ♀ affl. in ♏. (See "Snoring" in this section).

Stinking Breath—(See "Foul" in this section).

Structural Defects—The ☉ afflicted in ♌, ♏, or ♋, structural defects in throat, lungs, and respiratory system.

Suffocation—(See Asphyxia, Drowning, Hanging, Oxygen, Suffocation, Strangling).

Suspension—Temporary Suspension of Breathing—(See Cheyne-Stokes, Interference, Interrupted, Obstructions, Spasmodic, in this section. Also see Catalepsy, Fainting, "Stoppage" under Heart; Trance, etc.).

Swoonings—(See Fainting).

Syncope—(See Fainting).

Throat—Interferences with Breathing from Throat Disorders and Obstructions—(See Goitre, Tonsils. Also see "Swellings", and paragraphs under Throat).

Tidal Air—Insufficient—(See Carbon, Oxygen, Tidal. Also see Labored, Rhythmic, Shallow, in this section).

Tight Lacing—Interfering with Breathing—(See Dress).

Tissues Affected—Wasting of—♇ in ♌, ♏, or ♋.

Tongue—Foul Tongue—(See "Foul" in this section).

Tonsils—Enlarged, and Interfering with Breathing—(See Tonsils).

Trachea; Tract—Disorders of the Respiratory Tract—(See "Troubles", and the various paragraphs in this section).

Trance—With Suspended Breathing—(See Catalepsy, Trance).

Troubles — Respiratory Troubles — Diseases of the Respiratory Organs and Tract—Are ruled and caused principally by ♀, afflictions to ♀, and afflictions in the ♀ sign ♏; malefics in the 3rd, 6th, 9th, or 12th Houses, and in common signs; ♀ affl. in ♏; the ☽ hyleg in ♏, and espec. with females; the ☽ □ ♂ or ill-asp. ♆, ♅, ♄, or ♂ as promittors; ♄ ♂ or ill-asp. the ☽; ♄ affl. in ♏; ♂ promittor in ♓ and in ♂ or ill-asp. the ☉. (See the various paragraphs in this section. Also see Cardia; "Middle Cervical" under Ganglion).

Unpleasant Breath—(See "Foul" in this section).

Uvula—(See "Snoring" in this section).

Veins—(See "Respiratory" under Veins).

Voice—Disorders of from Respiratory Troubles—(See Voice. Also see "Mouth Breathing", "Speech", in this section).

Waste of Tissues—(See "Tissues" in this section).

Wheezing—(See "Labored" in this section).

Whooping Cough—(See Whooping).

Windpipe—(See Trachea).

Yogi Breathing Exercises—One Occult Writer says that holding the breath in deep breathing exercises poisons the system, and creates unusual physic conditions. (See Yogi).

BREECH—Breech Presentation—(See Parturition).

BRETHREN—Shown and governed by ♊ and the 3rd H., and our relations to them, their sicknesses, prospect of life, death, etc. The term Brethren as used here espec. refers to brothers and sisters. One writer says that the 3rd H. and its lord signify brethren in Hor'y Questions, but not in Nativities, and that Brethren in Nativities are signified by the sign on the M.C., and the sign following, and to these are added the maternal place of ♀ by day, and the ☽ by night. In a predominance of Textbooks the 3rd H. is said to rule brothers, sisters, cousins, neighbors, etc., and our relations to them for good or ill, according to the signs and planets ruling this house at B. The following influences should be noted in the map of birth of the native as regards his relationships to his brethren. The following subjects have to do with Brethren, Relatives, Kindred, etc., which see in the alphabetical arrangement when not considered here—

Brothers; Death—Of Brethren—(See "Death" under Brothers, Family, Relatives, Sisters, etc.).

Elder Born Brethren—Are represented by the more oriental stars, while the younger brethren are denoted by the more occidental stars.

Family; Few Brethren—(See "Few" under Brothers).

Increase Of—Many Brethren—Increase of brothers and sisters is indicated by the sign on the M.C. and 11th H., and by ♀ by day, and the ☽ by night. These places favorably aspected by benefics give increase according to the number of planets by which they are aspected, and the number is doubled if the planets be in double-bodied signs. Also the ☉ surrounded by good stars, or well-aspected by many, gives many brethren.

Length of Life Of—(See Brothers, Sisters).

Many Brethren—(See "Increase" in this section).

Marriage Partner—Brethren of—Are ruled by the 9th H. (See "Relatives" under Marriage Partner).

Relatives — Conditions Concerning — (See Relations).

Short-Lived—Sickly—If both malefics and benefics aspect the M.C., the 11th H., ♀ and the ☽, and the malefics outnumber the benefics.

Sickness Among—Lord of the 3rd H. in the 6th, or lord of the 6th in the 3rd, there is much sickness among them.

Sisters; Younger Brethren—(See "Elder" in this section). For collateral study see Aunts, Children, Father, Mother, Uncles, etc.

BREVITY—Brief—

Brevity of Members — (See Ephemeral, Limbs, Members, Short, "Brevity" under Signs of the Zodiac).

Disease Is Brief—(See Quick).

BRIGHT'S DISEASE — Nephritis — Inflammation of the Kidney—

Acute Bright's Disease—Acute Nephritis, and usually attended with Albumen in the Urine—A predominance of afflictions in the fixed signs, and a fixed sign rising; ♂ affl. in ♎; ♀ affl. by ♄, ♃, or ♂; a ♎ disease, and afflictions in ♎; ♎ on the 6th H., and espec. when ♂ is in ♎ in the 6th. (See Albuminuria; "Nephritis" under Kidneys).

Cases of Bright's Disease—See Cases on pages 92, 93, and 94, Chap. 13, in Daath's Medical Astrology. (See Kidneys, Urine).

Chronic Bright's Disease—♄ affl. in ♎; ♄ in ♎ in the 6th H.; ♄ □ or ☍ ♃ and ♀; ♃ affl. by ♅; the ☉ or ☽ in ♎, and affl. by ♄, and espec. when the ☉ or ☽ are in ♎ in the 6th H., and affl. by ♄. (See "Cirrhosis" under Kidneys).

BRISK—Brisk in Movements—(See Action, Active, Energetic, Gait, Manner, Motion, Movement, Quick, Rapid, Smart, Walk, etc.).

BRITTLE—(See Fragile, Nails).

BROAD—(See "Broad", or "Wide", under Chest, Face, Forehead, Ligaments, Nails, Shoulders, etc.).

BROKEN—Fractured—Sundered, etc.

Broken Bones—(See Fractures).

Broken Heart—Dies of Sorrow and a Broken Heart—♄ and ♑ influence; ♄ affl. ♀ at B., and by dir.; ♄ in the 1st or 10th H., and affl. the ☉, ☽, ♀, and hyleg; ♀ in ♑ and otherwise affl. by ♄; ♑ on the Asc., and espec. the 29°, and ♀ also affl. by the ☽ and ♄; lord of the 1st in the 8th, and the ☽ in evil asp. lord of the 8th by application, and without reception, or if lord of 8th be a malefic and in the 1st. (See Despondency, Melancholy, Sorrow).

Broken Signs—Of the Zodiac—♌, ♏, and ♓. Also called imperfect, or mutilated signs, as people born under them tend to be broken, or deformed in some way. (See Crooked, Deformities, Distortions, Imperfect, Mutilated).

Broken Sleep—(See Sleep). See Lacerations, Rupture, Vessels.

BROMIDROSIS—Fetid Perspiration—Caused by ♂. In the Axillae, ♂ in ♋; in the feet, ♂ in ♓; ♂ in common signs. (See Excrement, Excretion, Sweat).

BRONCHIAL—The Bronchials—Bronchial Tubes—Are ruled by ♀, the ♊ sign, and the 3rd H. One writer gives ♏ also as ruler, as the Bronchials are concerned with elimination, which function is largely under the rule of ♏. The Bronchial Tubes are ruled by ♊. The following subjects have to do with the Bronchial Tract and System, which see in the alphabetical arrangement when not considered here—

Acute Bronchitis—(See "Bronchitis" in this section).

Affections—Bronchial Affections—The ☉ affl. in ♊; the ☽ hyleg in ♊ in a female nativity; ♄ occi. in ♉, and affl. the ☉; ♀ affl. in ♐; a ♀ disease; ♀ affl. in ♊ or ♐; ♊ on the cusp the 6th H. (See the various paragraphs in this section).

Asthma—Bronchial Asthma—(See Asthma. Also see "Congestion" in this section).

Breathing; Bronchiectasis—(See "Dilatation" in this section).

Bronchioles—Disturbance of—♅ ♊, and espec. in the Summer months, and greatly disturbing in Asthma cases from pollen.

Bronchitis—Acute—Inflamed Bronchi —The ☉, ☽, ♅, ♄, ♂, or ♀ affl. in ♊ or ♐; the ☉ or ☽ in the 6th H. in fixed signs, and afflicted; ♅ in ♉ or ♊ and affl. the ☉, ☽, Asc., or hyleg; a ♄ disease; ♄ affl. in the 6th H. in a fixed sign; ♄ in ♊, ♐, or ♓; ♄ ♂ ♀ in 3rd H.; ♄ and ♀ afflictions involving the 3rd H. by rulership or occupancy; a ♃ disease; ♃ ♊ and affl. by ♂; ♂ in ♊ in the 3rd H.; ♂ in ♉, ♊, or ♐ at B., and affl. the hyleg at B., or by dir.; ♂ in ♊ or ♐ predisposes to; ♂ in ♊ in the 6th H.; ♀ affl. in ♉, ♊, or ♋; ♀ ♂ or ♂ the malefics, and the hyleg afflicted; the Asc. to the □ or ☍ ♀ and ♀ affl. at B.; a ♊ and ♐ disease; also caused by afflictions in ♉, ♏, and ♓; afflictions in ♓ predispose to quick attacks of from wet feet; caused by planets in ♊ opposed by malefics in ♐; the hyleg much afflicted at B., and espec. by malefics in ♊ and ♐; ♏ on the Asc. at B.; afflictions in the 29° ♋ or ♑; Subs at LCP, AP, and HP. (See "Chronic" in this section).

Catarrh—Bronchial Catarrh—The ☽ in ♉, ♊, or ♋ tends to. (See Catarrh).

Chest; Chronic Bronchitis—♄ affl. in ♉, ♉, or ♋; ♄ in ♓ and affl. the ☉ or ☽ in ♍; ♄ ☌ ☿ in ♍ in 3rd H.; ☉ ☌ ☽ in ♍, and in □ to ♄ in ♓; Subs at Lu.P. (See Case, "Chronic Bronchitis", Chap. 13, page 91, in Daath's Medical Astrology).

Colds; Congestion—Of the Bronchials —And tending to Asthma, and Bronchial Asthma—♃ affl. in ♏, and ♏ on the cusp the 3rd H. (See Asthma. Also see "Bronchioles" in this section).

Consumption—Bronchial Consumption —Malefics in ♉ tend to; a ♉ disease; ♄ ♉. (See Consumption).

Cough—Bronchial Cough—Afflictions in ♍ or ♐; the ☉, ♂, ♀, or ☿ in ♍ or ♐, and afflicted; the ☉ or ☽ in the 6th H., in fixed signs, and afflicted; ♅ and ♂ in ♏ on the Asc.; ♄ lord of the 3rd H., and afflicting ♀; ♄ afflicted in the 6th H. in fixed signs; afflictions in ♉. (See Cough).

Death—From Bronchitis, and Bronchial Trouble—♄ or ♂ in ♍, and affl. the hyleg at B., or by dir.; ♂ occi. at B., and affl. the hyleg at B.; afflictions in fixed signs, and espec. when on the cusp of 3rd, 6th, or 8th H., and affl. the hyleg; lord of the 8th in ♍, and affl. the hyleg at B., and by dir.

Dilatation—Of the Bronchial Tubes—Bronchiectasis—Afflictions to ♃ and ♀, causing disturbances in the circulation; ♄ or ♂ in ♍ in ☌ or ill-asp. ♃ or ♀; Subs at AP. (See Dilatations).

Dyspnoea; Hay Fever—Hay Asthma —(See Asthma, Nose).

Hemorrhage—Broncho-Pulmonary Hemorrhage—♄ or ♂ affl. in ♍; Subs at AP., 1st Dorsal, and at Lu.P. (See Hemorrhage under Lungs).

Inflammation—Of Tubes—(See "Bronchitis" in this section. Also see "Inflammation" under Lungs).

Lungs; Mucous; Obstructions—Bronchial—□ ascending at a Solar Ingress into ♈, and with ☿ afflicted, Countries and People under □ suffer thru corrupt air, by high winds, and by obstructions of the lungs and bronchial tubes; ♄ affl. in □, and espec. when in the 3rd or 6th H.; Subs at LCP, 6th Cervical, at AP and SP. (See Chest, Lungs, Obstructions, Phlegm, Pneumonia).

Phlegm; Phthisis; Pleura;

Pneumonia — Broncho-Pneumonia — The ☽ hyleg in □ or ♋, and affl. by ♄ or ♂; the hyleg afflicted at B., and with malefics in □ or the 3rd H.; Subs at LCP, the 6th Cervical, at AP and Lu.P. (See Pneumonia).

Respiration—Difficult Bronchial Respiration—Breathing Difficult—♄ affl. in □; ♄ ☌ ♃ or ♀ in □. (See "Labored" under Breathing).

Tuberculosis; Tubes—Dilatation of the Bronchial Tubes—(See "Dilatation" in this section).

Upper Bronchi—Superior Bronchi—Disorders In—Afflictions in ♉ and the first degrees of □; Subs at LCP., AP., HP.

Winds—Bronchitis-Producing Easterly Winds—♄ rising in the Asc., or lord of the year at the Vernal Equinox. (See Air, Epidemics, Wind).

BRONCHOCELE—(See Goitre).

BROODING—Introspection—Moodiness Moods—Melancholy—The ☉ in ♑ and affl. by ♄; the ☉ hyleg, and to the ☌ or ill-asps. ♄ by dir.; due to ♄ and ♆ afflictions; ♄ prog. to the ☌ or ill-asps. ☿, or vice versa; ♄ to the ill-asps. his own place by dir., or transit; ♄ Sig. □ or ☍ the ☽; ♄ in the Asc., 3rd or 9th H., and affl. ☿; ♂ affl. in ♍. (See Anguish, Anxiety, Dejection, Depression, Despondency, Fears, Gloom, Introspection, Melancholy, Retrospective, Worry, etc.).

Imaginary Diseases—Imaginary Troubles—Brooding Over—♄ to the ill-asps. his own place by dir., or tr.; ♂ affl. in ♍; ☿ in the 6th H., and affl. by ♅, ♄, or ♂. (See Hypochondria, Imaginary).

BROTHERS—Much that is said here will also apply to sisters. Our brothers and sisters are shown and ruled by the 3rd H., and our relations to them, whether for good or ill. Their sicknesses are also largely denoted by the conditions over the □ sign in your map or birth.

Brothers Indicated—Stars masculinely constituted indicate brothers. The place of brethren (brothers or sisters) in the native's map is taken from the sign on the cusp the 10th or 11th H., and the maternal places, which are the position of ♀ by day, and the ☽ by night. This refers only to children of the same mother. The signs on the 10th and 11th being maternal, are indicative of the mother and her children, and the same places may, therefore, be allotted to brothers and sisters. (See "Births" under Male. Also see Son).

Death of a Brother—An eclipse falling on the radical place of ♂ in the map. Should a hostile configuration be in the Asc., and ♂ there also, or ♂ in any angle, and espec. when in the 10th, then ♂ will tend to destroy or diminish the total number of brothers or sisters. (See Eclipse. Also see "Few", "Fratricide", in this section).

Delicate Constitution—The malefics elevated above those which promise, or give brethren; lord of the 8th in the 3rd H., and a malefic and afflicted. (See "Short-lived", "Sickness", under Brethren).

Elder-Born Brethren—(See Brethren).

Few Brothers—Or Sisters—Few Brethren—The malefics having superiority in power or numbers in the 10th, 11th, or 4th H., and espec. if the ☉ be surrounded by malefics; malefics configurated to the 10th or 11th H., or to the ☽ or ♀, or if they surround the ☉, the number is decreased; both ♄ or ♂ in the 1st or 7th show few brothers or sisters, or their early death, and also the lord of the 10th affl. in the 3rd.

First-born Brother—Death or Sickness of—♄ represents the first-born brother, and should the hostile configuration be from the Asc., would tend to his death, or a lingering illness.

(See "Elder-Born" under Brethren. Also see "Near Relatives" under Relations).

Fratricide—♂ affl. in □ or the 3rd H.

Health Poor—Lord of the 6th H. in the 3rd, and afflicted. (See "Near Relatives" under Relations. Also see Sixth House, Third House).

Hurts—Accidents or Injuries To—Malefics in the 3rd H. of the native, and afflicted; lords of the 6th, 8th, or 12th H. in the 3rd, and afflicted; lord of the 3rd H. a malefic, and afflicted, and espec. if ♄ or ♂.

Length of Life—(See the various paragraphs in this section).

Long Life—A benefic in the 3rd, or lord of the 3rd H., well-aspected, and with no malefics in the 3rd; the benefics elevated above the lord of the 3rd H., and in favorable aspect.

Possibility—Of Brothers and Sisters—(See "Several" in this section).

Several Brothers—The benefics favorably configurated with the 10th or 11th H., or in these houses.

Short-Lived—(See "Death of", "Delicate", "Health Poor", in this section).

Sickness Of—(See the various paragraphs in this section. Also see "Sickness" under Brethren).

Younger Brethren—(See Brethren). For other study, see Daughters, "Birth of a Female" under Female; Family, Relatives, Sisters, etc.).

BROW—(See Forehead).

Eye-Brows—(See Eye-Brows).

BROWN—The Color Brown—Ruled by ♏, and espec. Dark Brown. ♅ rules black, and dark brown. Brown is also ruled by the 7th H.

Complexion—Brown Complexion—Brown Skin—☿ ascending at B., and free from the rays of other planets; ☿ ori. at B.; ☿ in ♈ or ♑; ♄ indicates one of an earthy, brown, swarthy, dark, or dusky complexion; ♃ gives when rising and well-aspected; ♀ in ♏; ♈, ♏, and ♑ give. (See Olive, Sunburnt, Tan, under Complexion).

Eyes—Brown Eyes—(See "Brown" under Eyes).

Hair—Brown Hair—(See "Brown" under Hair).

Skin—(See "Complexion" in this section).

BRUISES—Contusions—Concussions—The subject of Bruises is largely considered under the subjects of Blows, and Falls.

Accidents By—Hurts and Injuries By—Liable To—♄ causes hurts and injuries by bruises, blows and falls; ♄ ascending at B.; ♄ rising or setting at B.; ♄ by transit in ☌ or ill-asp. the ☉, ☽, ♃, or ♀ in the radix; ♄ in ♈, ♌, or ♐, ☌ or ill-asp. the Asc. by dir.; ♄ affl. the ☉ at B., and by dir.; ♄ rising, and affl. the ☉ or ☽ at B.; ♄ ruler of the 4th or 8th H., and to the ill-asps. of ♂; ♄ ☌ ♂ in ♑; the ☉ affl. in ♑; the ☉ and ☽ ori., and affl. by ♄ or ♂; the ☉ directed to the Cratch (Praesepe) in the 6° ♌; ♅ to the ill-asps. his place

at B.; ♂ in the 1st H., and affl. by ♅ or ♄; ♂ or ♄ in ♑, and affl. the ☉, ☽, or Asc.; ♑ on the Asc.; the Asc. to the ☌ or ill-asp. ♄ by dir. (See Blows, Concussion, Falls).

Animals—Bruises by Large Animals—♄ in the 12th H. (See Animals).

Blindness—By Bruises—(See "Bruises" under Blindness).

Blows—Bruises By—(See Blows).

Breasts—Bruises To—(See "Bruises" under Breast).

Death by Bruises—♄ and ♂ denote death by; ♄ rising or setting at B., and affl. the hyleg; ♄ ☌ or evil asp. the Asc. when ♄ is not ruler of the Asc.; the ☉ or ☽ ori., and affl. by ♄ and ♂; ♂ in the 10th H., and □ the Asc., and the ☉ also afflicted. (See "Death" under Blows, Falls).

Falls—Bruises By—(See Falls, Fractures, Heights).

Head—Bruises To—(See "Bruises" under Head).

Hips—Thighs—Bruises To—(See Hips).

Large Animals—Bruises and Hurts By—(See "Large Animals" under Animals).

Legs—Bruises To—(See Legs).

Liable to Bruises—Predisposition To—(See "Accidents" in this section).

Thighs—Bruises To—(See "Bruises" under Hips).

BRUNETTES—(See "Dark" under Complexion; "Black" and "Dark" under Hair).

BRUTISH—Cruel—Unfeeling.

Brutish Signs—♌ and the 2nd half of ♐, and those born under them are said to be brutish, savage, and inhuman; ♌ or the 2nd half of ♐ on the Asc. at B., or the ☉ or ☽ in either of them, and the malefics in angles, render the native fierce, cruel and brutish. (See Cruel, "Human Signs" under Human; Madness).

BRYONIA—Bryonia Alba—One of the typical Polycrest Remedies corresponding to the □ sign. Also a typical drug of ♂. (See Resolvent; "Polycrest" under Zodiac).

BUBO—Bubo Inguinal Tumor—A Swelling in the lymphatic gland of the Groin—A ♏ disease, and by reflex action affecting the Parotid Gland ruled by ♉; caused by Subs at PP, the 2, 3, 4 Lumbars, and also at KP. (See Gonorrhea, Groins).

Bubo Plague—Bubonic Plague—Afflictions in ♏; a ♏ disease; ♄ ☌ ♃ in the first 6 deg. of the ♈ sign; a ♂ disease and caused by ♂ afflictions; the ☉ affl. in ♌; eclipses of the ☉ or ☽ tend to, and in Nations ruled by the Sign in which they occur. No Plague from an eclipse can affect the whole earth, nor endure more than 4 months or 4 years, according to the nature and duration of the eclipse. Caused by Subs at CP, KP, LPP. (See Eclipse, Plague).

BUDDING—Reproduction By—(See Gemmation).

BUILD—Of the Body—(See Appearance, Body, Corpulent, Defects, Deformities, Fat, Form, Good, "Ill-Formed" under Ill; "Muscular" under Muscles; Shape, Short, Stature, Strong, Tall, Thin, Weak, etc.).

Building of the Body—The body is built along the lines of its Astral Double, and each of the planets have their part in the work, according to the parts they rule. Thus ♄ builds the bones, framework, skeleton, etc. (See Blood, Bones, Cells, Processes, Tissues, etc. See the influence of each of the planets, and also of the Signs of the Zodiac). A good description of the building of the body, from an Occult standpoint, and its evolution from the earliest stages of Humanity on this planet, can be gotten from the various books on Rosicrucianism, Theosophy.

BUILDINGS—Houses—Death or Injury by Falls from Buildings, or by the Fall of Buildings—(See Crushed, "Earthquakes" under Earth; "Buildings" under Falls; Incendiarism).

BULBAR PARALYSIS—(See Medulla).

BULKY BODY—♃ in the Asc. tends to give bulk to the body. (See Corpulent, Fat, Fleshy, Lumpish, Stoutness, etc.).

Bulky Organs—Enlarged—Over-developed—(See Enlargements).

BULLA—(See Blisters).

BULLS—Oxen—Large Cattle—

Attacks By—(See Animals, Cattle, Quadrupeds).

Bull Fighter—Killed in Bull Fighting—Case—See "Bull Fighter", No. 063 in 1001 N.N.

Bull's Eyes—Bull's South Eye—(See Oculus Taurus).

Bull's North Eye—(See Aldebaran, "Death by Fire" under Fire; "Good Health" under Health; Pestilence).

Bull's Horns—Bull's North Horn—Bull's South Horn—Situated in ♊, and of the nature of ♂. The Bull's N. Horn, when crossing the Asc. of ruling signs of a Country or City, tends to great fires, calamity, and loss of life. This was the case in London in the year 1866, the year of the Great Fire, when this star was passing thru ♊, the Asc. of the City of London. (See Lilly's Astrology, page 5). For the various influences of the Bull's Horns, see Ambushes; "Pains" under Arms; Blotches, Fury, Inflammation, Intoxication, Rashness; "Strangury" under Urine; Violent.

BUNIONS—Corns—A ♓ disorder, and afflictions in ♓; ♅, ♄, ♂, ♀, or ☿ affl. in ♓; ♀ ♓ in 6th H., and afflicted; ♀ ♓, and affl. the ☉ or ☽; the ☽ hyleg in a female nativity, and afflicted. (See Crusts; "Skin" under Hardening; Scales).

BUOYANT—Vivacious—Hopeful—Cheerful—Full of Life and Activity—♃ influence; ♃ rising in the Asc. or M.C., well-aspected and dignified, and also the ☉ and ♂ in strong positions at B.; fiery signs upon the Asc. at B., and many planets in these signs; cardinal signs on the angles at B.; the majority of the planets at B. rising

and elevated in positive signs of the Zodiac. (See "Active Body", "Active Mind", under Active; Cheerfulness; "Abundance of" under Energy; "Excess of" under Force; Hope, Joy, Mirth, Optimism, Positive Nature, Power; "Strong Will" under Will, etc.).

BURGLARS—Injury or Death By—(See Highwaymen, Robbers, Thieves).

BURIAL—

Buried Alive—Danger of Premature Burial—♆ in 8th H., and due to Trance conditions simulating death; ♄ causes death, being buried alive, as by landslides, fall of buildings, etc. (See Avalanches; "Fall of Buildings" under Buildings; Crushed, Trance, etc.).

No Burial—The Body Not Interred—No Church or Regular Burial—Several malefics ruling the Anaretic places, or occupying them; ♅, ♄, or ♂ claiming prerogative in the Anaretic Places, and with no assistance from the benefics to the 4th H., or to the Anaretic Places.

Body Devoured—The body may be devoured by beasts or birds after death if the malefics are in signs assigned to beasts and birds, and also when the benefics offer no assistance to the Anaretic Places, or to the 4th H., the house which rules the end of life. (See "Birds of Air" under Air; Vultures).

Buried Under the Earth—♅ or ♄ in ♈, ♋, ♎, or ♑, in the 4th H., and in ☌, □, or ☍ the ☉ or ♂; ♄ in ♉, ♍, or ♑, ☌, □, or ☍ the Asc. by dir., and ♄ holding the dominion of death, danger of being buried alive under the earth, as by Cave-ins, Avalanches, Landslides, etc. (See "Buried Alive" in this section).

BURNS—Burning—Searing—Scalds, etc. —Burns are caused by the ☉ and ♂, the positive, electric, and heat-producing planets. The following subjects are connected with Burns, Burning, Fire, Injuries or Disorders from Intense Heat within or without the body; Scalds, Hot Liquids or Metals, Searing, etc., which see in the alphabetical arrangement when not considered here—

Accidents by Burns—(See "Danger", and the various paragraphs in this section).

Arms—Burns To—The ☉ or ♂ affl. in ♊, and signs which rule the arms. (See "Burns" under Arms).

Blindness By—(See "Burning" under Blindness).

Burned Alive—Danger of—The ☉ directed to the Ascelli; the ☽ Sig. ☌ ☉ or ♂; ♂ in fiery signs and ☌ the Asc. by dir.

Burned at Stake—(See "Stake" in this section).

Danger of Burns—Liable to Burns—Subject To—Accidents By—The ☉ or ☽ hyleg, and to the ☌ or ill-asps. ♂ by dir.; the progressed ☉ or ☽ to the ☌ or ill-asps. ♂; the ☽ ☌ ♂ in the M.C., and evilly aspected by Antares; the ☽ Sig. ☌ the ☉, subject to burns and scalds; ☽ Sig. □ or ☍ ☉, and espec. if ♂ aspect the ☉; caused by ♂ afflictions; ♂ affl. in ♈, ♌, or ♐, the fiery signs; ♂ affl. in the 6th H., and espec. in a cardinal or fiery sign; ♂ affl. in the 4th H., and espec. in a fiery sign, burns due to fire in the home; ♂ affl. in the Asc. or M.C.; ♂ □ or 8 the ☉ at B., and by dir.; ☿ Sig. ♂ the ☉ and the ☉ ill-dignified; ♈ on the Asc.; fiery signs in the Asc. or 6th H., or the ☽ in a fiery sign at B., threatens burns under the evil directions of ♂ to the ☽, or ♂ in or to the Asc. or 6th H. (See "Danger" under Fire. Also note the various paragraphs in this section).

Death by Burns—Burned to Death— Death by Burning or Searing—The ☽ affl. by ♂, and ♂ descending, and if ♂ also be configurated with ☿, it happens from an accident in sports, or by robbers; the ☽ hyleg, and to the ♂ or ill-asp. ♂ by dir.; ♂ in 8 near Caput Algol, or in ♏ in 8, and in □ or 8 to the ☉ or ☽; ♂ ori. at B., and affl. the hyleg by dir., and espec. if ♂ be in a violent sign; ♂ in 8 or ♏, and affl. the hyleg; ♂ afflicting from fiery signs. Cases—See "Burned to Death", No. 687, and No. 889, in 1001 N.N. (See "Burned Alive" and "Searing" in this section. Also see "Death" under Fire, Scalds; "Hot Liquids" under Heat).

Electricity; Explosions; Eyes—Injury to by Burns—(See "Burning" under Blindness; "Accidents" under Eyes).

Face—Burns To—♂ affl. in ♈, and espec. in the Asc. Case—Left Side of Face and Neck severely burned—See "Extraordinary Accident", No. 192 in 1001 N.N. (See "Searing" in this section).

Father—Burns To—(See "Burns" under Father).

Fevers—High, Burning Fevers—(See "High Fevers" under Fever).

Fire—Danger or Death By—(See Fire. Also see the various paragraphs in this section).

Gun Powder Burns—(See Gunshot).

Home—Burns in the Home—Danger of—♂ affl. in the 4th H. in a fiery sign. (See "Fire" under Home).

Injuries by Burns—(See "Danger", and the various paragraphs in this section).

Journeys—Travel—Voyages—Burns on Journeys or in Travel—Malefics, and espec. ♂, in the 3rd or 9th H., and afflicting the ☉ or ☽ in fiery signs.

Liable to Burns—(See "Danger" in this section).

Lightning; Liquids—Burns or Death by Hot Liquids—(See "Hot Liquids" under Heat. Also see Scalds).

Mother—Burns To—Death By—(See "Burns" under Mother).

Neck—Burns To—(See "Face" in this section).

Pains—Burning Pains in the Stomach —(See Belching).

Powder Burns—(See Gunshot).

Robbers—Burned By—(See "Death" in this section).

Scalds; Searing—Injury or Death By —♂ in 8 near Caput Algol, or in ♏ in 8 aspect, and in □ or 8 the ☉ or ☽. (See "Burning" under Eyes).

Sensations—Burning Sensations— (See Belching, "Heartburn" under Heart; Paraesthesia, Sensations, etc.).

Sports—Burned During—(See "Death" in this section).

Stake—Burned at the Stake—Case— See "Savonarola", No. 459, in 1001 N.N.

Stomach—Burning Pains At—(See Belching).

Travel—Burns During—(See "Journeys" in this section).

Voyages—Burned During—(See "Journeys" in this section).

Water—Burns by Hot Water—(See "Hot Liquids" under Heat. Also see Scalds).

BURSA—A small sac between movable parts.

Bursitis—In the Knee—♀ affl. in ♑. (See Joints, Synovial).

BURSTING—Rending—Tearing—Rupture—Laceration, etc.—

Blood Vessels—Bursting of—(See Apoplexy, Cerebral, Hemorrhage, "Blood Vessels" under Vessels).

Parts—Bursting and Rending of— (See Hernia, Lacerations, Rupture).

BUSHY—(See "Bushy" under Eyebrows, Hair; "Curly" under Hair).

BUSINESS—The Trade or Employment—

Death In—Accident, Injury or Illness In—(See Cares, Employment, Explosions, Machinery, Occupation, Partner, Ruin, Vocation).

BUTCHERS—♂ strong at B., or the ruling planet, tends to make good Butchers, Cutters and Surgeons; the ☉, ☽, or ♂ well-asp. in ♏; ♂ in the Asc. or M.C. in ♏. The ♏ influence should predominate at B. to make good Surgeons, Cutters, or Butchers. (See Surgeons).

BUTTOCKS—Nates—Gluteal Region— Rump—Haunches—Ruled by ♎ and the 7th H., and the parts adjoining the Hips, included in the Haunches, are ruled and influenced by ♐.

Boils On—(See "Buttocks" under Boils).

Diseases In—Afflictions in ♎ and ♐.

Fistulous Tumors—A ♐ disease, and afflictions in ♐.

Heats In—Humours In—A ♎ disease, and afflictions in ♎; ♂ affl. in ♎ or ♐.

Hurts To—Accidents or Wounds To— Afflictions in ♐; ♄ or ♂ affl. in ♐. (See Haunches, Hips, Ilium, Loins).

BUZZARDS—Vultures—Fowls of the Air—The Body Devoured By After Death—No Burial—(See "Birds of the Air" under Air; "Body Devoured" under Burial; Fowls; "Vultures Eat the Body" under Vultures).

BUZZING—

Buzzing Noises—In Ears—(See "Buzzing" under Ears).

Buzzing Sensations—As in the Spine or Nerves—Usually caused by pressure upon the nerves, or sublaxations of vertebrae, and should be studied locally, and the planetary afflictions noted in the sign ruling the afflicted part. (See Paraesthesia).

Droning—Buzzing—(See Humming).

C

CACHEXIA—A Depraved condition of Nutrition—(See Anaemia, Anticachectic, Assimilation, Emaciation, Nutrition, Pale, Sickly, Unhealthy; "Vitality Low" under Vitality; Wasting, Weak, etc.).

CADAVEROUS—Pale, Corpse-like, Unhealthy—(See Pale, Unhealthy, White).

CADENT HOUSES—As the 3rd, 6th, 9th and 12th H., and correspond to the Mutable Signs. These houses are identified with disease, and tend to give a weak constitution, and espec. when occupied by the ☉, ☽, and many planets at B. The 6th and 12th houses are the more evil of the cadent houses. The 6th H. is more noted for acute diseases, and the 12th H. denotes lingering and chronic diseases. (See Houses, Mutable).

CAECUM—Ruled by ♏.

Inflammation Of—Typhlitis—Perityphlitis—♂ affl. in ♏. Caused by Subs at PP, the 2nd and 3rd Lumbars. (See Appendix).

Ileo-Caecal Valve—(See Ileum).

CAESARIAN OPERATION—(See "Excision" under Foetus).

CAISSON DISEASE—Symptoms from working under increased air pressure—Compressed Air and Gases are ruled by ♅, which planet strongly rules over the ♒ sign. An ♒ disease; the ☉ affl. in ♒. (See Air, Compressed, Ether, Gases, Pressure).

CALAMITY—Catastrophies—Disaster—Misfortune—Tragedies, etc.—

Great Calamities—Are heralded by the appearance of Comets, and espec. to People, Individuals, and Countries ruled by the sign thru which the Comet is seen to pass. Great Calamities to the individual, as disgrace, ruin, scandal, breakdown in health, etc., are indicated when one has eminent fixed stars of the nature of ♄ in the angles at B., and with the ☉, or afflicting the angles or the ☉ by dir.; also caused by ♄ afflicting his own place at B. by tr. or dir., or ♄ passing the place of the ☉, Asc., M.C., or hyleg, or severely afflicting these places. ♄ is considered the planet of Calamity to those who are not living right, as he is the Tester, the Chastener, the Judge, to mete out justice, and to punish and correct the evils in the life of the native. (See Comets, Events, Disgrace, Misfortune, Ruin, Trouble, Sorrow).

Impending Calamity—Fear of—The ☉ or ☽ to the ☌ or ill-asp. ♄ by dir.; the ☽ to the ☌ or ill-asp. ♂ by dir., and espec. if ♂ afflict the ☽ at B.; the Prog. ☽ to the ☌ or ill-asp. ♄ or ♂ by dir.; ♆ afflicted at B.; ♆ □ or ☍ ♅ at B., and by dir.; ♅ affl. in ♓ or the 12th H. at B., or by dir.; ♄ affl. the ☉ or ☽ at B., and ♄ to the ☌ or ill-asps. the Lights by dir.; the transit of ♄ over the place of the ☉ at B., and espec. if ♄ afflict the ☉ at B., and have no dignity in the sign of transit. (See Anxiety, Fear, Obsessions).

Many Calamities—The ☉ to the ☌ or ill-asp. ♄, ♂, or the malefics by dir.; the ☉ Sig., and to the ☌ or ill-asp. ♄ by dir.; the ☉ to the ill-asps. ♅ by dir.; the ☉ ☌, or to the place of Aldebaran, Antares, the Ascelli, Arcturus, Cor Hydra, Fomahaut, Hircus, Markab, Pleiades, or Regulus, and espec. when culminating, tend first to great honors, to be followed by the greatest calamities; the ☽ sepr. from ♄ and applying to the ☉ at B., or by dir.; the ☽ with Antares or Aldebaran in the 1st or 10th H.; the ☽ to the place of Hercules; ♄ to his own ill-asps. by dir.; the M.C. to the place of Algenib, Antares, Bellatrix, Betelgeuse, Procyon, or any star of the nature of ♂ and ☿; Praesepe rising with the ☉ or ☽, and espec. in ☌ in an angle, causes every calamity upon the native. (See Evils, Reverses, Ruin, etc.).

Moment of Birth—Calamity From—Malefics with the ☉ or ☽ at B., and affl. the hyleg. This is espec. true of Excrescences, Distortions, Lameness or Paralysis. (See these subjects. Also see "Moment of Birth" under Birth).

Sea—Calamities at Sea—(See Maritime, Navigation, Ocean, Sea, Ships, Shipwreck, Waters).

Serious Calamities—Or Disasters—Danger of—Lord of the 6th in the 10th H., and afflicted, meets with many downfalls, or serious disasters in life, and espec. if lord of the 6th is a malefic. (See Disasters).

Strange Calamities—Or Catastrophies—Subject To—♆ or ♅ in the Asc. or M.C. at B., and affl. the ☉, ☽, or hyleg at B., or by dir.; ♀ Sig. in ♑. (See Extraordinary, Mysterious, Peculiar).

Sudden Calamity—The ☉ to the ☌ or ill-asps. ♅ by dir. (See Sudden).

Threatened—Calamity or Disaster Threatened—♆ in tr. over the place of ♄ at B.; a total eclipse of the ☉ falling on the place of the ☉ at B. (See Disaster).

Travel—Calamities During—(See Journeys, Maritime, Navigation, Railroads, Sea, Ships, Travel, Vehicles, Voyages).

Violent Calamities—Death by Violent Catastrophies—☉ to the ☌ ♂ by dir., and ♂ affl. the ☉ at B.; ☉ joined with the Ascelli at B., or by dir. (See Violent).

Wind—Calamities By—(See Wind). For collateral study see Affliction, Anguish, Anxiety, Assassination, Catastrophies, Death, Desert, Disaster, Disgrace, Dishonor, Earthquakes, Enemies, Execution, Floods, Famine, Highwaymen, Misfortune, Pirates, Prison, Reputation, Reversals, Ruin, Sickness, Sorrow, Suicide, Sudden, Storms, Thieves, Trouble, Untimely, Volcanoes, etc.

CALCES—Calx—Calcium—(See Chalk, Lime). Coral is a form of Calcium, or Lime. (See Coral).

CALCULATOR—Lightning Calculator—(See Prodigies).

CALCULUS—Stone-like Concretions in the Body—Lithiasis—(See "Gall Stones" under Bile; Concretions, Deposits, Gravel, Minerals, Sand, Stone).

CALLOUS—Hard—Indurated—(See Hard).

CALM—When a patient is nervous, excitable, and of an angry disposition, he can be more easily calmed in a ♄ hour. (See "Hours" under Planets).

Spiritual Calm—Lack of—(See Spiritual).

CALOMEL—A typical drug of ☿. (See Mercury).

CALORIC—(See Fever, Heat, Temperature).

CALVES—Fleshy part of the leg below the knee. Are under the external rule of ♒. Also ruled by ♄ and the 11th H.

Diseases Of—Afflictions in ♒ or the 11th H.

Hurts To—Accidents or Injuries To—♄ or ♂ afflicted in ♒ or the 11th H.; ♒ on the Asc., and afflicted.

Stiffness Of—♄ affl. in ♒. Subs at PP and LPP tend to the various disorders of the Calves. (See Ankles, Fibula, "Dropsy" under Legs; Tibia, Varicose).

CALX—(See Chalk, Lime).

CAMELS—Sickness or Death of—(See Cattle).

CAMP FEVER—(See Typhus).

CANALS—(See Alimentary, "Inguinal Canal" under Groins; "Intestinal Canal" under Bowels; Lachrymal Canal (see Tears); Sinus; Spinal Canal (see Spine); Tubes, etc.).

CANCER DISEASE—(See Carcinoma).

CANCER SIGN—The 4th sign of the Zodiac, the only sign of the ☽, and affiliated with the 4th H. The Symbol of this sign is the Crab. The ☉ enters ♋ at the Summer Solstice. This sign is classed as a cardinal, cold, commanding, crooked, destructful, feminine, fruitful, moist, mute, negative, phlegmatic, psychic, sensitive, unfortunate, tropical, watery, weak, sign. It is the home sign of the ☽, the exaltation of ♃, and the fall of ♂. It is considered the weakest sign of the Zodiac, along with ♓, for vitality, and espec. when upon the eastern horizon at B., and afflicted, and with the ☉, ☽, or hyleg afflicted also. This sign is considered weak owing to its receptivity to outside influences, and afflictions in ♋ tend to quickly affect the mind and the digestive organs. The ☉ well-aspected in the ♋ sign at B., and rising and elevated, tends to strengthen the constitution, to augment the recuperative powers, give better health, etc., as the ☉ in any sign tends to bring more vital force and power to that sign. The ☉ affl. in ♋ tends to a weakened constitution, and lowered vitality. The ☽ well-aspected in ♋ is strong, and tends to regular functions and good health. Ipecac, an emetic, is classed as the typical Polycrest Remedy corresponding to the ♋ sign.

Cloudy Spot of Cancer—(See Cloudy).

CANCER RULES—Externally ♋ rules the Breast, Epigastric Region, and the Elbow. Internally, ♋ rules the Stomach, Digestive Organs, and the Womb. Structurally, ♋ rules the Ribs, Sternum, Elbow Joint. In general ♋ is said to rule Albumen, the Axillae, the Bladder as a receptacle; Blood (Serum of); Brain Coverings; Breastbone (Sternum); Breasts (Mammae); Chymification; Color—Green or Russet; Diaphragm; Digestion, which is a function of the ♋ sign; the Digestive Organs and System; Elbow (Thoracic); Elbow Joint and Elbow; Epigastric Region; Ganglia (Semilunar); Green Color; Ipecac; Lacteals; Liver (Upper Lobe); Lung (lower lobe of left lung, and the two lower lobes of right lung); Mammae; Milk; Oesophagus; Pancreas; Pleura and Pleural Cavity; Ribs; Russet Color; Serum (of Blood), Sternum; Stomach, and the Peristaltic action of; Thoracic Duct; Womb. (See these subjects in the alphabetical arrangement).

CANCER DISEASES—And Afflictions—The special pathological quality of ♋ is lowered vitality. See the following subjects in the alphabetical arrangement—

Abscesses; Appetite Bad—(See "Bad", "Delicate", "Loss of" under Appetite).

Asthma; Blood—Spitting of—(See Haemoptysis).

Breath—Short Breath—(See "Labored", "Shallow", under Breath).

Cancers—(See Carcinoma).

Catarrh—Of the System—(See Catarrh).

Constitution Weak—(See "Vitality Low" under Vitality; "Weak Body" under Weak. Also see Constitution, Resistance, Recuperation).

Consumptions; Coughs; Diaphragm—Disorders of—(See Diaphragm).

Dipsomania; Dropsy; Flatulence;

Gastric Catarrh—(See "Stomach" under Catarrh).

Haemoptysis; Hiccough;

Imposthumes—(See Abscesses).

Indigestion; Inflamed Lungs—(See "Pulmonitis" under Lungs).

Lungs—Inflamed—Ulcerated—(See "Pulmonitis", "Ulceration", under Lungs).

Sclerosis; Stomach—Disorders of—(See Digestion, Gastric, Indigestion, Stomach, Vomiting).

Vitality Low—(See Vitality).

Weak Constitution—(See Constitution, Recuperation, Resistance, Sickly, Vitality, Weak).

CANDY—Misuse of—(See Sugar).

CANCRUM ORIS—Gangrene of the Mouth—(See Gangrene).

CANIS MAJORIS—☽ to the place of tends to bring pleasure and good health.

CANKER—(See Aphthae, Carcinoma, Gangrene, Sores).

CANNABIS INDICA—Canabis Sativa—Indian Hemp—A typical plant and drug ruled by ♄.

CANNIBALS—Savages—Attacks, Injuries or Death by During Travel—The afflictor to the Sig. of Travel being in the 12th H., and in □ or ♏, and espec. if ♂ or ☿ be the afflictor. (See Savage, Travel).

CANTHARIDES—A typical drug of ♂, and a strong vesicant. (See Aphrodisiac, Rubefacient, Sinapis, Vesicant).

CAPELLA—A Fixed Star in 4th face of □, of nature of ♂ and ☿. (See Auriga, Blows, Hircus, Stabs, Vices).

CAPILLARIES—Minute Blood Vessels—Tubules—Are ruled by, and associated with the □ sign in particular, and also connected with all the airy signs. The influence of ♄ (cold) tends to contract them, driving the blood inward, and causing congestions, colds, etc. The ♂ influence (heat) tends to dilate them, and make the surface circulation in them more free. Morbid dilatation of the capillaries, however, is a ♄ influence, due to deposits, wasting, and a weakened condition of the walls of the vessels. Capillary obstructions are caused by ♄ afflictions, and by the afflictions of ♄ to ♃ and ♀, rulers of the blood and circulation. For various conditions affecting the capillaries, see Acne, Centrifugal, Centripetal, Circulation, Congestion, Constrictions, Dilatation, Erythema, "Red Face" under Face; Lungs, Nose, Obstructions, Oxygen, Veins; "Blood Vessels" under Vessels.

CAPRICORN—The Goat—Capricornus—The 10th sign of the Zodiac, and affiliated with the 10th H. The ☉ enters ♑ at the time of the Winter Solstice. The night sign of ♄; the exaltation of ♂; the fall of ♃, and the detriment of the ☽. Is a cardinal, changeable, cold, crooked, domestic, earthy, egotistical, feminine, four-footed, hoarse, hurtful, melancholic, moveable, negative, nocturnal, obeying, southern, tropical, unfortunate, violent, winter sign. Is a rather weak sign as regards vitality, and espec. when upon the eastern horizon at B. However, the ♑ people do not yield readily to disease, but when once sick and diseased they become despondent and melancholic, hold onto it, and often become hypochondriacs. This sign is not strong in vitality during the early years of life, and espec. from birth to the 7th birthday, and there is much infant mortality among those born with the ☉, ☽, and other planets in ♑, and afflicted, or with ♑ upon the Asc. at B. In adult life the diseases produced by ♑ tend to become chronic, being under ♄ rule. It does not contribute much to the beauty of the human form, and espec. when rising, and often tends to ugliness, crookedness of body, deformities, and a thin, angular, awkward and ungainly physique. The ☉ is weak in ♑, but tends to longevity. The ☽ is weak in this sign, in which she is in detriment and debility, and when afflicted in this sign tends to impeded, uncertain and irregular functions, and lowered vitality, due to mental depression, worry, and anxiety. It is a strong business sign, and the ♑ people are usually full of business, promotion,

and many of their diseases result from business anxieties, cares, or losses. The accidents of ♑ are broken limbs, bruises, falls, sprains, dislocations, and hurts to the knees and lower limbs. The Symbol of this sign is the Goat. The pathological qualities of ♑ are crystallization, deliberation, dryness, and limitation. Sulphur is a typical remedy of ♑. For an illustration, and birth data, of a person born with 6 planets in ♑ in the 3rd H., see "Pasteur", No. 950, in 1001 N.N.

CAPRICORN RULES—Barrenness, Black, Bones, Brown (Swarthy or Dark Brown, and Dark Gray); Cold, Connective Tissue, Cutaneous System, Cuticle, Dryness, Epidermis, Epithelial Tissue, Goats, Hams, Hair of Pubes, Joints, Knees, Knee Cap, Legs, Limitations, Mineral Deposits in the System, Mucous Surfaces (the outer); Nations (see ♑ under Nations); Nucleolation, Patella, Peripheral Nerves (the Sympathetic Peripheral); Pubes and Pili; Resources (the husbanding of the material resources); Restraints, Russet Color, Servitude, Skin (the outer skin, cuticle, or epidermis); Sterility (♄, ruler of ♑ tends to deny or destroy children); Stomach (by reflex action to ♋ from ♑); Sulphur; Swarthy Brown; Sympathetic Nerves (the Peripheral). Externally ♑ rules the Knees and Epidermis. Structurally ♑ rules the Patella, and the bones of the Knee Joint.

CAPRICORN DISEASES—And Afflictions—See the following subjects in the alphabetical arrangement when not considered here—The ☉, ☽, planets, and afflictions in or to ♑, or ♑ upon the Asc., the 6th or 12th H., and containing malefics, or otherwise afflicted, tend to produce the following diseases and afflictions—

Accidents—The Accidents of ♑—(See the Introduction to this Article).

Animals—Hurts By—(See "Hurts" under Animals).

Antiperistalsis—Of the Stomach—(See Vomiting).

Articular Rheumatism—(See Joints, Rheumatism).

Anxiety; Bones—Diseases of—Broken Bones—(See Bones, Femur, Fractures, Knees, Legs, Limbs).

Bruises; Chest Disorders—(See Breast, Chest, Lungs).

Chronic Diseases—(See Chronic).

Cold—All Diseases Arising From—(See Cold).

Conjunctivitis; Criminal Tendencies—(See Crime).

Cutaneous Complaints — Eruptions—(See Eruptions, Skin).

Depression—Depressed—Dejection—Hypochondria—Low Spirits—Melancholy—Despondency—Worry, etc.—(See these subjects).

Despondency; Digestive Disorders—(See Digestion, Gastric, Indigestion, Stomach).

Dislocations; Dry Skin—Dry and Sallow—(See Dry; "Dry Skin" under Skin).

Eczema; Eruptions, Erysipelas; Falls; Fever; Fractures—(See "Bones" in this section).

Functions—Impeded Functions—(See "Disorders" under Functions).

Gastric Disorders—(See Digestion, Gastric, Indigestion, Stomach).

Gloom; Gout; Gunshot—(See "Danger" under Gunshot).

Hardening; Heat—Insufficient Heat in the Body—(See "Body" under Cold; "Lack of" under Heat).

Hypochondria; Hysteria; Impediments—Impeded Functions—♅ being ruled by ♄ acts in a similar manner to ♄, and the diseases of ♄ and ♅ are much the same, and whatever ♄ does, the ♅ influence will also do, and espec. when this sign is strong at B., on the Asc., or occupied by ♄ and many planets, and afflictions to ♅. (See the list of diseases under "Saturn". Also see Functions, Impediments).

Impetigo; Indurations—(See Cirrhosis, Deposits, Hardening, Minerals, Sclerosis, Thickening).

Infancy—Low Vitality In—Much Mortality In—(See Childhood, Infancy, Vitality. Also see the Introduction to this Article).

Injuries—To the Knees or Legs—(See Knees, Legs).

Itching; Knees—Accidents To—Disorders of—Weak Knees—(See Knees).

Leprosy; Liquids—Hot Liquids—Danger From—(See Liquids).

Lower Limbs—Legs—Diseases of—Injuries To—(See Extremities, Legs, Limbs, Lower).

Lowered—Lowering—Lowered Vitality—(See Low, Lowered, Vitality).

Lungs—Disorders of—(See Bronchial, Consumption, Phthisis, Pulmonary, Tuberculosis).

Luxations—(See Dislocations).

Melancholy; Mental Depression—(See Anguish, Anxiety, Depression, Melancholy, Worry, etc.).

Mucous Diseases—(See Humours, Mucous, Phlegm).

Nausea—(See Nausea, Vomiting).

Nettle Rash—(See Urticaria).

Parasitic Diseases—(See Parasites).

Pruritis—(See Itch).

Rheumatism—In Knees or Lower Limbs—(See Gout, Knees, Legs, Rheumatism).

Scabies—(See Itch, Scabies).

Scalds; Sensitive; Skin Diseases—(See Eruptions, Skin).

Sprains; Stomach—Diseases of—Antiperistalsis—Indigestion—(See Digestion, Gastric, Indigestion, Stomach).

Synovitis—(See Joints, Synovial).

Tibia—Dislocation of Head of—(See Tibia).

Tissues—Hardening of—(See Crystallization, Hardening, Tissues).

Urticaria; Vitality Lowered—(See Vitality).

Vomiting; Worry.

CAPSICUM—Red Pepper—Ruled by ♂. (See "Mars Group" under Herbs; Rubefacients).

CAPSULES—Suprarenal Capsules—(See Adrenals).

CAPTIVE—Captivity—Held in Captivity for Ransom During Travel—Possible Death or Injury In—The 12th H. strongly occupied by malefics at B., or by dir., and afflicted, tends to captivity, exile, or imprisonment, and injury therein, torture or death; the ☽ sepr. from ♃ and applying to the ☉, and espec. if the ☽ be in ♈, ♏, ♑, or ♒; the ☽ decr. in light, sepr. from ♃ and applying to ♄. (See Abroad, Exile, Pirates, Prison, Travel).

Many Held In Captivity—An eclipse of the ☽ in ♏.

CAPUT—

    Caput Algol—(See Algol).

    Caput Andromeda—(See Andromeda).

    Caput Draconis—(See Dragon's Head).

    Caput Hercules—Pollux—Of the nature of ♂. (See Assassination, Calamity, Disgrace, Drowning, Fever, Pollux, "Imprisonment" under Prison; Ruin; "Extreme Sickness" under Sickness; Suffocation; "Death" under Violent).

CARBON—Carbonic Acid—Carbon Dioxide—Carbon is ruled by ♄, and is a dominant element of the earthy signs ♉, ♍, an ♑. Carbonic acid gas is expelled from the lungs in the breath. The obstructive influences of ♄ tend to retention of the wastes within the system, and the obstruction of the circulation of the blood, and its purifying influences. (See "Operations" under Nature).

    Carbohydrates—(See Hydrocarbonates).

    Carbonic Acid Poisoning—A surplus of carbonic acid, and not sufficient cleansing from the blood—Retention of—Lack of Tidal Air—The ☉ affl. in ♒; ♄ or ☋ in ♊, and espec. when afflicting the ☽, tends to make the blood unable to throw off the carbonic acid in sufficient quantities, due to the obstructive power of ♄; ♄ □ ☍ ☽, lack of tidal air; ♄ ☌ ♃ or ♀ tends to obstruct the arterial and venous circulations, and cause carbonic acid to be retained. (See "Non-Oxygenation" under Oxygen; "Tidal Air" under Tidal).

    Elimination Of—The ♒ sign rules, and has principle charge of, the elimination of carbonic acid gas from the system. Afflictions in, or to the ♒ sign, tend to obstruct and hinder this elimination. (See Air, Elimination, Gases, Malnutrition, Miasma, Nitrogen, Oxygen, "Blood" under Poison; Tidal). See Hydrocarbonates, Sugar.

CARBUNCLES—Anthrax—♃ affl. in ♉, the result of plethora and gormandizing; a ♂ disease, and caused by ♂ afflictions; ♂ affl. in ♑; ♂ ♑, occi., lord of the year at the Vernal, tends to a prevalence of boils and carbuncles; Subs at CP and KP. (See Abscesses, Boils, Plethora, Swellings, Tumors, Ulcers, etc.).

CARCINOMA—Cancers—Malignant Tumor—Epithelioma—

Carcinoma (Cancer) is a ☽ disease, a ♋ sign disease, and caused by afflictions in the ☽ sign ♋; the ☽ affl. at B., and to the evil asps. the Asc. by dir.; the ☽ affl. in ♋, or affl. the hyleg therefrom; the ☽ affl. in ♈, ♉, or ♑; the ☉ in asp. at B. with both ♃ and ♄, or in asp. with one of them in, or from a sign, ruled by the other; caused by the ♄ influence when he enters into the configuration; ♄ ☌ ♃ or ♀; ♄ opposes ♃, and this conflict between entirely different influences tends to set up the disease in weakened constitutions; ♄ affl. in the 6th H. in mutable signs; ♄ affl. in ♋ when he is the afflictor in the disease; ♆ affl. the ☉ tends to produce the disease under evil directions of ♆ to the ☉ or hyleg; sensitive degrees in this disease are the 25° ♍ and ♓, and the ☉, ☽, or malefics in or afflicting these degrees tend to cancer; caused by Subs at CP and KP. (For further influences, and the different forms of cancer, see the various paragraphs in this section).

Axillae—Cancer and Scirrhus of— (See Axillae).

Bowels—Cancer of—The ☉ or ♄ affl. in ♍; Subs at KP and PP, the 2nd Lumbar.

Breasts—Cancer of—A ☽ disease; a ♋ disease, and afflictions in ♋; the ♋ sign on the Asc., and afflicted; ♄ affl. in ♋, afflicting the hyleg, and being the afflictor in the disease; ♄ ♋, occi., and affl. the ☉, ☽, Asc., or hyleg; ♃ ♋, and aspecting ♄, or ♄ ♋ affl. by ♃, and where one or both may be affl. the hyleg. (See Axillae, Breasts).

Canker—A Cancerous Sore— (See Canker, Gangrene).

Death by Cancer—Afflictions in the cardinal signs dispose to, and espec. in ♋; ♄ ♋ and affl. the hyleg at B., and by dir.; ♄ in a fixed sign at B. and affl. the hyleg by dir.; ♃ causes death by when afflicting the hyleg at B., and by dir., and being the afflictor in the disease; ♀ affl. the hyleg by dir., and ♀ much afflicted at B., and holding the dominion of death. Case— Death by Cancer — See "Food Reformer", No. 264 in 1001 N.N.

Epithelioma—A Cancerous growth of the skin—(See Epithelioma).

Face—Cancer of—♄ affl. in ♈ or ♉; Subs at MCP, the 5th Cervical. (See Face).

Fatty Cancer—Lardaceous—Waxy— Caused by the afflictions of ♃.

Gangrene—(See Canker, Gangrene).

Generative Organs — Sex Organs— Womb, etc.—♅ or ♄ affl. in ♏, or both in ♌, in ♏ and affl. the hyleg, and espec. when ♄ is the afflictor, or holds the dominion of death; caused by Subs at KP and PP, the 2, 3, and 4th Lumbars. (See Sex, Womb).

Hard Form Of—(See "Scirrhus" in this section).

Head—Cancer of—Afflictions in ♈ or ♉, and espec. ♄ affl. in these signs; caused by Subs at MCP, the 5th Cervical.

Lardaceous Form—(See "Fatty" in this section).

Liver—Cancer of—♄ affl. in ♋ or ♍; afflictions in the 5th H.; Subs at Li.P. and KP. (See Liver).

Oesophagus—Cancer of—♄ affl. in ♋. (See Oesophagus).

Operated Upon—For Cancer—Case— See "Unfortunate Case", No. 351 in 1001 N.N.

Pancreas—Cancer of—(See Pancreas).

Rectum—Cancer of—(See Rectum).

Scirrhus—Hard Form of—Occurs espec. in the Breasts—♄ or ♂ affl. in ♋. (See Axillae).

Sex Organs — (See "Generative" in this section).

Solanoid Form — Potato-like Formations—Caused by the afflictions of ♃.

Spleen—Cancer of—(See Spleen).

Stomach—Cancer of—A ☽ disease; a disease of the ♋ sign, and afflictions in ♋; the ☉, ♅, or ♄ affl. in ♋, and also affl. the hyleg; Subs at SP, the 7th Dorsal, and at KP. (See Stomach).

Treatment Of — Injections of Potassium are said to cure cancer, as the disease is often due to a lack of this Salt. The Grape Cure is also highly successful. For Cases of cancer cured, see birth data, and Figures 21A and 21B in "Astro-Diagnosis" by the Heindels.

Waxy Form— (See "Fatty" in this section).

Womb—(See "Generative" in this section). For collateral study see Abscesses, Sores, Tumors, Ulcers.

CARDIA—Cardiac—Pertaining to the Heart. Cardia is also an orifice of the stomach. The action of the ☉ and ☽ thru the Sympathetic Nervous System affect the Cardia, the Heart, the upper part of the Stomach, and the Dorsal Vertebrae, and give way to the Cardiac Diathesis. The therapeutic properties of ☉ remedies are cardiac and affect the heart action.

Cardiac Diathesis—(See the Introduction to this section).

Cardiac Diseases—(See Heart).

Cardiac Muscle—(See "Jupiter Group" under Muscles).

Cardiac Plexus—The ☉ and ☽ acting thru the deep Cardiac Plexuses affect the Respiratory System and the upper Limbs, and give way to the Cranian Diathesis.

Cardiac Sedative—(See Aconite).

Cardialgia—Heartburn—Pain in the Heart—(See "Heartburn" under Heart).

Carditis—(See Heart).

CARDINAL SIGNS—Moveable Signs— Acute Signs—They are ♈, ♋, ♎, and ♑, and have largely to do with physical activity. These signs are ruled by ♂, ☽, ♀ and ♄. These four signs form the cardinal cross, and are all in □ or ☍ asp. to each other, and in affliction. Thus a person born with a majority of planets in the cardinal signs may tend to have a more or less unbalanced condition of mind and body, and with less harmony in the system. The cardinal signs are mental in temperament. An affliction in one cardinal sign tends also to afflict the parts ruled by all the other cardinal signs, and this is also true of all the fixed and common signs, as all Signs of the same group afflict each other. Thus ♄ in ♋ at B. can cause stomach trouble, kidney disorders, eye infirmities, and weak and disordered knees. The cardinal sign ♈ rules the head; ♋, the stomach; ♎, the kidneys, and ♑, the knees. These signs are affiliated with the Angles of the map, the Equinoctial and Tropical Points, the 1st, 4th, 7th and 10th Houses, which are known as the cardinal houses. The cardinal signs on the angles at B. give an active nature, a restless energy, and considerable ability to throw off disease, but diseases caused by them tend to be acute, quick, severe, and to soon run their course. (See "Disease" under Nature). On the angles they also tend to lessen the chances of Insanity, or an unbalanced mind. Afflictions from the cardinal signs are moveable, and not as fixed or stationary, and can be overcome. People born with many planets in these signs, or when they are upon the angles, have more power to throw off disease or trouble, and to start life anew after failure, being hopeful, aggressive and optimistic. They try hard to get well when sick, and to cooperate with the Healer. The intensity of disease is associated with the cardinal signs. (See Severity). The cardinal signs denote the head, stomach, kidneys and skin. Cardinal signs also show death on railways, by fire, fits, scalds, gunshot, lightning, murder, and a notorious death. (See Active, Acute, Angles, Aries; Cancer, Capricorn, Curable, Energy, Functions, Head, Houses, Kidneys, Knees, Libra, Morbid, Skin, Stomach).

CAREFUL—The ☽ and ♄ influences make one careful, and give strong instincts of self-preservation and self-protection, and espec. the good asps. of the ☽ and ♄. The fiery signs tend to be lacking in caution, carefulness and prudence.

Careful of the Body—A ♍ characteristic. (See Cleanly, Neat).

Careful in Diet—(See "Careful" under Diet). See Careless.

CARELESS — Carelessness — Negligent —Slovenly—A ♓ influence; many planets in bicorporeal, or double-bodied signs at B.; the ☽ to the ♂ or ill-asp. ♇ by dir., indifferent to life's duties; the ☽ ill-dig. at B., lives carelessly and beggarly, and content in no condition of life, either good or ill; ♃ to the bad asps. of ♂ by dir.; ♂ afflicting ♀; ♀ ill-dig. at B., nothing careful of the things of this life, and tending to dissipation, sickness, or early death.

Ailments From—Diseases and Irregularities From—The ☽ affl. by ♀; ♓ on the 6th H., and afflicted, from carelessness in personal ·cleanliness; ♓ produces ailments thru carelessness and forgetfulness. (See "Of No Ambition" under Ambition; Awkwardness, Cleanly, Excesses, Filth, Folly, Forethought,

Forgetful; "Free Living" under Free; "Bad Habits" under Habits; "High Living" under High; Improvident, Imprudent, Indifferent, Indiscretions; "Requirements" under Nature; Neglect, Poverty, Slovenly♪ Uncleanly, Untidy).

CARES—

Cares Multiplied—Full of Cares—♄ ♂ or ill-asp. the ☽ at B., or by dir.; the evil directions of ♂ to the ☉, ☽, or Asc.; fixed stars of the nature of ♄ ascending. (See Anxiety, Responsibility, Worry).

Disease from Cares—The ☽ ☐ at B., in ♂ or ill-asp. ♄, and when ♄ may be affl. the natal ☽ by dir., the disease has its origin in the mind, and from the multiplicity of business cares, or fatigue from over-study, writings or literary work; the ☽ ☐ and in ☐ or ☍ ♄ (or ☿ if he be of the nature of ♄) at the beginning of an illness, or at decumbiture. (See Anxiety, "Brain-Fag" under Brain; Fatigue, Reversals, Trouble, Vexations, Worry, etc.).

CARIES—Ulcerous Inflammation of Bone—A ♄ disease. (See Bones).

Nose—(See "Caries" under Nose).

Spine—(See "Caries" under Spine).

Teeth—Caries of—Decay of—(See "Carious", "Decay", "Toothache" under Teeth). See Decay, Ulcers.

CAROTID—

Carotid Arteries—The Internal Carotid Artery is ruled by ♈, and the External Carotid Artery is ruled by the ♉ sign.

Carotid Plexus—(See "Ribes" under Ganglion).

Fullness Of—Plethora of—Increased Beating of—A ♃ disease. (See Arteries, Circulation, Plethora).

CARPUS—Carpal Bones—(See Wrist).

CARRIAGE—Of the Body—The Gait, etc.—(See Awkward, Clumsiness, Commanding, Erect, Gait, Locomotion, Motion, Movement, Posture, Quick, Slow, Stooping, Walk, etc. This subject is· mostly considered under "Gait", and "Walk").

CARTILAGE—Gristle—Ruled by ♄, and also crystallized by ♄. Cartilaginous tissue building is the work of ♄. (See Tendons).

Achondroplasia—Lack of Proper Formation of Cartilage, as in Foetal Rickets—A ♄ disease; ♄ ♂ or ill-asp. ♂, or ♂ ♂ or ill-asp. ♄, according to which is the dominating planet. (See Rickets).

Caries Of—(See "Caries" under Nose).

Chondroma—Cartilaginous Tumor—(Fibro-Cartilaginous Tumor)—♄ ♂ or ill-asp. ♃. (See Fiber).

Nose—Caries of Cartilage of—(See "Caries" under Nose).

CARUNCLE—A Small Fleshy Growth—Occurs usually on the Conjunctiva, near the inner canthus, and caused by ♄ affl. in ♈; a ♄ influence, and due to suppression of function, or of the nerve supply to the part; ♄ ♂ ♃ or ♀, due to disturbed circulation in the part. Caruncle also occurs on the posterior lip of the meatus urinarius, and caused by ♄ affl. in ♏; Subs at PP. (See Conjunctiva, Growths, Sarcoma).

CARUS—Complete Insensibility — The Last Degree of Coma—A ♆ disease. (See Analgesia, Coma, Insensibility, Neptune).

CASEIN—The Clotted Proteid of Milk. Ruled by the ☉. (See Milk).

CASTOR—A violent star of the 2nd magnitude, in the 18° ♋, of the nature of ♄, ♂ and ♀. Makes one liable to violence, and also portends mischievousness. The ☉ with at B. is indicative of evil, and liable to a violent death. The Knee of Castor and Pollux with the ☉ in an angle at B. tend to much sickness, trouble and disgrace. When directed to the ☉, ☽, or Asc., tends to Bad Eyes, Hurts to the Eyes; Blindness in One or Both Eyes; Hurts to Face; danger from Sharp Instruments; Imprisonment; Violence or a Violent Death; Wounds, and every evil and calamity that can befall humanity. The influence of Castor when with the ☉, ☽, or Asc. at B., or afflicting them by dir., also tends to Beheading, Blows, Cuts, Disgrace, Measles, Much Evil, Rape, Ruin, Stabs, Shipwreck, Shooting, Trouble, and the native also often turns out to be a murderer, or is murdered. Castor and Pollux are called "'The Twins". The star Propus is the Left Foot of Castor, and of the nature of ♂. (See Pollux. Also see these various subjects in the alphabetical arrangement).

CASTRATION—(See Testes).

CASUALTIES—See Accidents, Calamity, Death, Drowning, Earthquakes, Electricity, Fire, Floods, Lightning, Machinery, Murder, Railroads, Ships, Shipwreck, Travel; "Untimely Death" under Untimely; Volcanoes, Water, Weather, Wind, etc.

CATABOLISM—A Retrograde Change in the Tissues of the Body—♄ influence. (See Consumption, Crystallization, Decay, Emaciation, Hardening, Softening, Tuberculosis, Wastings).

CATALEPSY—A Neurosis caused by ♆; a ♆ disease; ♆ in the 8th H. In this disease there is loss of will and muscular activity, but with no change in the circulation. (See Coma, "Neurosis" under Nerves; Trance).

CATALYSIS—A Chemic Reaction or Change—Death—Decay—Dissolution—Degeneration—♄ is the principal Significator of, and by his asps. to the ☉, ☽, Asc., M.C., and hyleg; ♆ also causes catalysm when affl. the hyleg at B., and by dir. (See "Arguments for Death", "Danger of Death", and the various paragraphs under Death; Decay, Degeneration, Dissolution, Saturn).

CATAMENIA—(See Menses).

CATAPHORA — Lethargy attended by short remissions—A ♆ disease. (See Lethargy).

CATARACT—Opacity of the Crystalline Lens—A ☉ disease; the ☉ affl. in the Asc.; the ☉ in the Asc., or M.C. in ♂ or ☍ the ☽, and ♄ rising before the ☉, or evilly configurated with the ☉;

the ☽ or Asc. in Nebulous Parts, and affl. by ♄; ♆ ♈ and affl. by ♄; ♄ causes blindness by (See "Total" under Blindness); ♄ ♈; ♄ ♂ ☉ or ☽ in ♈; ♄ ♈ and ☐ the ☽ in ♋; Subs at MCP, and KP, the 11th Dorsal. (See Blindness, Eyes, Sight). Cases—See Fig. 11B in Astro-Diagnosis by the Heindels. Also see "Diseases in the Eyes", Chap. 13, page 88 in Daath's Medical Astrology.

CATARRH—Catarrhs—Defluxions—Fluxions—Rheum—Inflammation of Mucous Membranes, with Watery Discharges, etc.—Fluxions follow a Solar Periodicity. Catarrh is listed as a disease of the ☉, ☽, and ♄; ♄ ♂ the Asc. by dir.; lord of the 1st or 6th H., or the ☽, in watery signs; the watery signs strong and predominating at B., and with afflictions in such signs, predispose to. (See the various paragraphs in this section).

Bladder—Catarrh of—Subs at LPP, the 4, 5, and 6th Lumbars tend to acute catarrh of; ♂ affl. in ♏. (See "Cystitis" under Bladder).

Bowels—Catarrh of—☽ affl. in ♏; ☽ ♏ ♂ ♅ or ♄; a ♏ disease and afflictions in ♏; ♄ affl. in ♏; ♄ ♂ ♃ in ♏, and affl. by dir. or progression. (See "Enteritis" in this section).

Bronchial Catarrh—(See "Catarrh" under Bronchial).

Colds—(See Colds).

Coryza—(See "Coryza" under Nose).

Death by Catarrh—♄ in the 8th H. at a Solar Ingress into ♈, and affl. the ☽ or planet ascending, tends to be very fatal, according to the sign occupied by ♄.

Defluxions—(See Defluxion).

Discharges—(See "Catarrhal" under Discharges).

Ears—Catarrh of—(See Ears).

Enteritis—Catarrhal Enteritis—The ☉, ☽, or ♂ affl. in ♏; ♂ ♏ in the 6th H. (See "Inflammation" under Bowels).

Fever—Catarrhal Fever—(See Fluxes, Influenza).

Flux—Fluxions—(See Flux).

Gastric Catarrh—(See "Stomach" in this section).

Head—Catarrh In—(See Head).

Humours—(See Fluids, Humours).

Influenza—Catarrhal Fever—(See Influenza).

Larynx—Catarrh of—(See Larynx).

Leucorrhoea—Catarrh of Womb—(See Leocorrhoea).

Liver—Catarrh of—(See Liver).

Lungs—Catarrh of—(See Lungs).

Mucous—Mucus—(See Mucous).

Nasal Catarrh—Nose—Catarrh of—(See Nose).

Phlegm—(See Mucous, Phlegm).

Pneumonia—Catarrhal Pneumonia—(See Pneumonia).

Rheum—Catarrhal Discharge—(See Rheum).

Spleen—Catarrh of—(See Spleen).

Stomach—Catarrh of—(See "Catarrh" under Gastric, Stomach).

Subject to Catarrh—Liable To—Predisposed To—♄ people are espec. subject to; ♄ in the Asc. at B.; ♄ affl. in ♈ or ♓; a ☉ disease, and caused by an afflicted ☉; a ☽ disease; the ☽ affl. in ♈, or in watery signs; the ☽ in ♋, ♂ or ill-asp. ♄ (or ☿ if he be of the nature of ♄) at the beginning of an illness, and will tend to become chronic, and continue for a long time, if the ☽ be decr., and near the body of ♄ at the time; ♅, ♅, or ♄ in ♈ or ♓, and affl. the ☉ or ☽; ♋, ♏, or ♓ upon the Asc., and affl. at B., or by dir.; afflictions in ♏. (See the first part of this section).

Throat—Catarrh In—(See Throat).

Watery Discharges — (See Fluxes, Humours, Rheum, Watery).

Womb—Catarrh of—(See Leucorrhea, "Catarrh" under Womb).

CATASTROPHIES—Death By—Injury By—Death by a Violent Catastrophe—The ☉ joined with the Ascelli; ♀ in ♑, partile asp. the Asc., often meets with strange and sudden catastrophe. (For further influences see Calamity, Casualties).

CATHARTIC—(See Physic).

CATS—Sickness or Death of—(See Pets; "Pestilential Virus" under Pestilence).
Resembles Cats—(See "Animal Forms" under Monsters).

CATTLE—The 6th H. rules Small Cattle, and the 12th H. the Great, or Large Cattle. Many of the planetary conditions which affect Man, in health or disease conditions, also affect the Animal Kingdom. Man is also subject to attacks, injuries, and infirmities received thru Cattle, Horses, Wild Animals, Reptiles, Insects, etc.

Attacks by Cattle—Danger of Injury or Death by the Attacks of Bulls, Oxen, and Large Cattle—The ☉ to the cusp the 12th H. by dir.; the ☽ to the place of Cor Scorpio or Ceti by dir.; a malefic ruler of the 12th H. at B., and located in the 12th H. in a Solar Rev.; ♂ in the 12th H., and affl. by ♅ or ♄; Ceti joined with the Luminaries at B.; lord of the 6th H. in the 12th H.; the Whale's Jaw in the M.C. (See Animals, Beasts, Elephants; "Great Cattle" under Great; Quadrupeds).

Cattle Breeders—Death of—Presignified by ♄ lord of the year at the Vernal Equi., in ♒, and ℞.

Death of Cattle—Loss of Cattle—Loss of Camels—An eclipse of the ☉ or ☽ in a fiery sign; an eclipse of the ☉ in ♉. (See "Death" under Animals; Blizzards; "Virus" under Pestilence; "Cold" under Weather).

Destruction Among—♂ in the 6th or 12th H.; an eclipse of the ☽ in the 1st Decan. of ♉.

Diseases Among — Much Sickness Among—Lord of the 6th in the 12th, or lord of the 12th in the 6th H. of the native, tends to bad fortune with his cattle, and with small or large animals. (See the various paragraphs in this section).

Epidemics Among — (See Events; "Epidemics" under Sheep).

Great Cattle—Large Cattle—Attacks By—Disease or Death of—(See "Great Cattle" under Great; "Cattle" under Detriment).

Hurts By—Attacks or Injury By—(See "Attacks" in this section).

Injury to Cattle—To Camels and Horses—An eclipse of the ☉ in ♐; ♄ or ♂ affl. in the 6th or 12th H. (See "Destruction", and the various paragraphs in this section).

Large Cattle—(See "Great" in this section).

Loss Of—(See the various paragraphs in this section).

Much Sickness Among — (See "Diseases" in this section).

Resembles Cattle — (See "Animal" Forms" under Monsters).

Sickness Among—(See "Disease", "Epidemics", and the various paragraphs in this section).

Small Cattle—Diseases Among—Loss of—Malefics in the 6th H.; Comets appearing in ♈; afflictions and eclipses in ♈ at a Solar Ingress.

Travel—Attacks by During Travel—The afflictor to the Sig. of Travel being in the 12th H., and in ♐, and espec. if ♂ or ☿ be the afflictor.

Veterinary—Makes a Good Cow Doctor—(See Veterinary). For collateral study see Animals, Beasts, Elephants, "Nature Of" under Events; Horses, Quadrupeds, Sheep, Sixth House, Twelfth House.

CAUDA—
Cauda Draconis—Moon's South Node—(See Dragon).

Cauda Leonis—Cauda Lucida—Deneb—(See Lion's Tail).

CAUL—Born With—(See "Caul" under Face).

CAUSTIC—Escharotic—♂ influence. A therapeutic property of ♂. (See Applications, Rubefacients, Stimulant, Vesicant).

CAVERNOUS PLEXUS — (See "Ribes" under Ganglion).

CAVITIES—A Hollow—A Receptacle—There are both normal, and abnormal or disease cavities, in the body. (See Follicles, Receptacles, Sacs, Vesicles).
Pus Cavities—(See Cloaca, Pus).

CECUM—(See Caecum).

CELIBACY—The bad asps. of ♄ to the ☉, ☽, ♀, and ☿ tend to pervert, or destroy passion, and espec. when ♄ is in, or afflicts the 5th and 7th houses, and in fiery signs at B.; ♄ affl. in ♈ tends to apathy, want of feeling and passion. (See Apathy, Bachelors, Barren, "Anchorite" under Husband; "Aversion", "Indifferent", under Marriage; "Free From" under Passion; Perversions, Spinsters).

CELLS—Cell—A Small, Protoplasmic Mass, and usually Nucleated.
Air Cells—Are connected with the airy signs; ☿ in ♉, ♐ and ♋ rule and affect the air cells of the lungs. (See Air, Breathing, Lungs, Oxygen, Trachea).

Alterations—In the Cells and Tissues —The five planets, h, $\mathcal{4}$, $\mathcal{S}$, $\mathcal{Q}$, $\mathcal{Q}$, and the 5 Processes which they rule, namely, the Splenic Process, Thoracic Process, Hepatic Process, Renal Process, and the Nervous Influx respectively, have to do with the alteration and metabolism of the cells, and organic changes, and the alterations occur in the zones of the body ruled by the sign in which the respective planets may be located. In alterations the ☉ tends to structural changes; h to stenosis; $\mathcal{4}$ to hypertrophy; $\mathcal{S}$ to the Sthenic Process; $\mathcal{Q}$ to Retrogressive Metamorphosis; $\mathcal{Q}$ the Irritation and Periodicity. (See Alterations, Decay, Degeneration, Metabolism, Metamorphosis, Periodicity, Processes, Stenosis, Sthenic, Structural, Tissues, etc. Also see "Renal Process" under Kidneys; "Hepatic Process" under Liver; "Influx" under Nerves; Spleen, Thorax).

Amoeboid Motion — Nebuloid Motion —Under the rule of Ψ.

Asthenic Process—Presided over by h. (See Asthenia).

Blood Cells—(See "Corpuscles" under Blood. Also see Haemoglobin, Leukocytes).

Budding—(See "Gemmation" in this section).

Cellular Tissue — Hypertrophy of — (See Elephantiasis, Hypertrophy).

Cellular Tissue Building—(See "Tissue Building" in this section).

Cellulose—Ruled by $\mathcal{4}$.

Congestion—Cellular Congestion— The work of $\mathcal{Q}$.

Cytoplastema—A Plastic Fluid—Ψ presides over cell development in this fluid. (See Cytoplastema, Plastic).

Development—Cell Development— The physiological action of $\mathcal{4}$. Cell development in the plastic fluid, and independent of other cells, is presided over by Ψ. (See the Introduction under Jupiter).

Diseases of the Cells—The 5 Processes mentioned under "Alterations" in this section have to do with all the diseases to which the cell is liable.

Division—$\mathcal{4}$ rules cell reproduction by division of the cell. (See "Gemmation", "Reproduction", in this section).

Excitation—The ☉ and ☽ influences sum up the 5 Processes mentioned herein, and manifest them by cellular excitation, and cellular zymosis. (See Zymosis).

Filtration—(See "Substance" in this section).

Fluids—The intercellular fluids, and the organic systems thru which they circulate, are ruled by the ☽. (See Fluids, Oedema).

Gemmation—Budding—Cell reproduction by is under the rule of $\mathcal{Q}$. (See Gemmation. Also see "Division", "Reproduction", in this section).

Haemoglobin—(See Haemoglobin).

Hypertrophy—$\mathcal{4}$ rules hypertrophy, or the abnormal increase in the size of the cell. (See Hypertrophy).

Inflammation — Inflammation of the cell takes place under the action and afflictions of h, $\mathcal{4}$, and $\mathcal{S}$. (See Inflammation).

Intercellular—Interstitial—The intercellular spaces are connected with the airy signs. (See "Fluids" in this section. Also see Intercellular; "Air Signs" under Air).

Irritation Of—(See "Alterations" in this section).

Lungs—Air Cells of—(See "Air Cells" in this section).

Metabolism—(See Metabolism. Also see "Alterations" in this section).

Metamorphosis—(See Metamorphosis. Also see "Alterations" in this section).

Molecular Nutrition—(See Nutrition).

Nebuloid Motion—(See "Amoeboid" in this section).

Nucleus—Ruled and supported by the ☉ influence. (See Nucleus, Protoplasma).

Organic Changes—Structural Changes —Ruled by the ☉. (See "Alterations" in this section. Also see Organic, Structural).

Periodicity—Of the Cell — Presided over by the ☽ and $\mathcal{Q}$. (See Periodicity. Also see "Alterations" in this section).

Polarity Of—(See Polarity).

Protoplasma—(See Protoplasma).

Reproduction—(See "Division", "Gemmation" in this section. Also see Proliferation).

Reservation—(See "Substance" in this section).

Retrogressive Metamorphosis — (See "Alterations" in this section).

Salts—Cell Salts—(See Salts; "Salts" under Zodiac).

Selection — (See "Substance" in this section).

Spaces — (See "Intercellular" in this section).

Stenosis — Narrowing or Constriction of the Cell—Presided over by h. (See Stenosis).

Sthenic Process — The activity, strength, and excessive force of the cell given by $\mathcal{S}$. (See Sthenic).

Storing—(See "Substance" in this section) .

Structural Changes — (See "Organic" in this section).

Substance — The storing, filtration, reservation, selection, and transformation of the various cell substances are the work of Ψ, $\mathcal{4}$, and $\mathcal{Q}$. (See Defensive).

Thickening—The thickening of cell walls is the work of h and a h disease. (See Thickening).

Tissue Building—Cellular Tissue Building is the work of Ψ, $\mathcal{4}$, $\mathcal{Q}$, and the ☽. (See Tissues).

Walls of Cells—Changes In—Division of—Thickening of, etc.—(See the various paragraphs in this section).

Zymosis — (See "Excitation" in this section).

CENTRAL—
Central Ganglia—(See "Vaso-Dilator" under Vaso).
Central Line of Impulse— (See Prenatal Epoch).
CENTRES—Centers—Nerve Centers—Spinal Centers—Vital Centers—(See Erethism, Ganglion, "Centers" under Nerves; Spine, Vascular, Vital).
CENTRIFUGAL—Receding from the center. The ♂ influence over the body tends to drive, or draw, the blood outward towards the surface, causing fevers, inflammation, surface congestions, acute diseases, etc. (See Acute, Centripetal, Rubefacients, "Vaso-Dilator" under Vaso).
CENTRIPETAL—Traveling toward the center. The ♄ influence over the body is to drive the blood inward, leaving the surface chilled, and to cause colds, internal congestions, chronic diseases, constrictions, mortifications, etc. (See Chronic, Cold, Constrictions, Derma, Gangrene, Intropulsion, Peripheral, Saturn, "Vaso-Constrictor" under Vaso).
CEPHALIC—Affecting the Head. A therapeutic property of ☿ and ☿ remedies. (See Head).
CEPHEUS—A Northern Constellation. (See Hanging, Impalement).
CEREBELLUM—The Instrument of Co-ordination. Ruled by the ☽ and the ♉ sign. Is under the internal rulership of ♉. The Arbor Vitae of the Cerebellum are ruled by ♉. The ♎ and ♏ signs, classed as nervous signs, have a special action on the Cerebellum (vegetative life). (See Brain, Cerebral, Cerebrum, Cerebro-Spinal; Coma, Coordination).
CEREBRAL—Pertaining to the Brain. The Cerebral Hemispheres are ruled by ♈, and the ♈ sign is called the "Cerebral Pole" by Paracelsus. The right Cerebral Hemisphere is ruled by ☿, and the left one by ♂. The Cerebral Ventricles are ruled by ♆. The Cerebral Nerves are ruled by ☿, and ☿ in ♈. The Cerebro-Spinal System is ruled by ☿. (See Brain, Cerebellum, Cerebro-Spinal, Cerebrum).
Cerebral Anaemia—(See Anaemia).
Cerebral Apoplexy—(See Apoplexy).
Cerebral Congestion—(See Congestion).
Cerebral Functions—Derangement of—The ☽ affl. in ♈, and espec. with females.
Cerebral Hemispheres—Diseases of—♈ diseases, and afflictions in ♈; ♄ affl. in ♈; ♂ affl. in ♈, afflictions to the left hemisphere; ☿ affl. in ♈, afflictions of the right hemisphere. (See "Hemispheres" under Head).
Cerebral Hemorrhage—Rupture of a Blood Vessel of the Brain—The ☉ or ♂ affl. in ♈; ♂ ♈ in the 6th H. and afflicted. (See Apoplexy).
Cerebral Meningitis—(See Meninges).
Cerebral Substance—Augmented and Diminished—(See Medulla).
Cerebral Symptoms—(See Anaemia, Apoplexy, Brain, Coma, Congestion,

Delirium, Faintings, Headaches, Vertigo, etc. Also note the various paragraphs in this section).
Cerebral Syncope—♄ affl. in ♈. (See Coma, Delirium, Fainting, Fits, Vertigo, etc.).
CEREBRO-SPINAL—Relating to the Brain and Spine.
Cerebro-Spinal Meningitis—Afflictions in ♈ and ♌; ☉ affl. in ♌, and with ♂ in ♌, or ♂ affl. in ♌, and with ☉ affl. in ♈. (See Meninges, "Spotted Fever" under Spotted).
Cerebro-Spinal Nervous System—Ruled by ☿. Also ruled and influenced by the ♈ sign. The ☉ and ☽ acting thru the ♈ sign tend to affect this system. (See "Ribes" under Ganglion). The ☉ Group of Minerals and Herbs have a physiological action on it. The ♂ Group of plants and minerals have a pathological action. The Cerebro-Spinal System being ruled by ♈, is opposed to the Renal System, ruled by the opposite sign ♎. Thus malefics and afflictions in ♎ tend to affect the Cerebro-Spinal System, and afflictions in ♈, the Renal System, or Kidneys. (See Cerebral, Medulla, Pituitary, Spine).
CEREBRUM—The chief portion of the Brain. The same influences that tend to affect the Brain will also apply here. (See Brain, Cerebral).
CERVICAL—Pertaining to the Neck, or to a Cervix—
Cervical Ganglion—The Superior Cervical Ganglion are ruled by the ♉ sign. The ☉ and ☽ acting thru the Cervical Ganglion affect the Eustachian Tubes, Cervical Glands, the Throat, Neck, and their dependencies, and give way to the Renal Diathesis. (See "Cervical" under Ganglion).
Cervical Nerves—Owing to the strong relationship existing between the two opposite signs ♉ and ♏, planets in either of these signs, and espec. when afflicted, affect the Cervical Nerves, the Neck, Throat, and the Genito-Urinary System.
Cervical Vertebrae—Are under the structural rulership of ♉. Also ♄ when in ♉ espec. rules and affects them, as ♄ rules the bones. (See "Cervical" under Vertebrae).
CERVIX—Neck—
Cervix Vesicae—Neck of the Bladder—(See "Neck" under Bladder).
Uterine Cervix—(See "Cervix" under Womb).
CESSATIONS—(See Saturn, Stoppages, Suppressions, etc.).
CESTODE—Resembling a Tapeworm—
Stomach—Cestode of—(See "Worms" under Stomach. Also see Tapeworm, Worms).
CETI—Menkar—Whale's Jaw—Lucida Maxilla—A star of the nature of ♄ in the 3rd face of ♉. Tends to cause disease and sickness with the ☉ and ☽ at B. Dangers from cattle, from great beasts, and ill-fortune, disgrace, etc., are indicated when in the M.C. at B., or by dir. (See Cattle, Disgrace, Falls, Fortune, Menkar, Whale).

CHALCOLITE—A mineral ruled by ♅. (See Uranus).

CHALK—Calx—Chalk and Lime formations in the body are ruled by ♄.

Chalk Stones of Gout—The work of ♄ retaining and crystallizing the waste products of the body. (See Deposits, Gout, Lime, Minerals, Wastes, Whooping Cough).

Chalky Skin—Given by ♓. (See Pale, Sickly, Skin, White).

CHAMOMILLA—A typical drug of the ☉. One of the 12 Polycrest Remedies corresponding to the ♌ sign. (See "Polycrest" under Zodiac).

CHANCES—Endures Many Sudden and Violent Chances in Life—The ☉ or ☽ near the Bull's North Eye at B., or by dir. (See Aldebaran, Dangers, "Narrow Escapes" under Escapes; Foolhardy, Oculus Taurus, Perils, etc.).

CHANCRE—(See Syphilis).

Chancroid—Soft Chancre—(See Gonorrhea).

CHANGE—Changes— Mutations — The principle of the ☽ is change. Also ♅ is the principal planet causing changes, removals, journeys, and furnishes the sudden notions or impulses by his directions and afflictions, which lead to changes, and espec. among people who are drifting in life, who have not yet found their true calling, work or location, and where much inharmony exists in the environment. The ♅ influence espec. tends to many changes in seeking health, or business advancement. The ☿ influences also conduce to changes in life. The ☽ influence tends to changes in the body by acting upon the bodily fluids.

Better—Changes For the Better in Life—The ☽ to the ☌, or P. asp. the ☉ if the ☉ be strong and well-aspected by ♃ or ♀ at B. For change for the better or worse in disease, see Crises; "Worse" under Disease; "Better" under Disease and Health; "Improved" under Health.

Blood Particles—Changes In—(See "Blood" under Red).

Body—Changes In—Changes and mutations in the body are ruled by the ☽, and espec. thru the bodily fluids. (See Fluids, Moon, Mutations).

Change of Life—(See "Menopause" under Menses).

Changeable—(See Mutable, Signs).

Comfort—Changes Which Interfere with Comfort and Health—(See Comfort).

Disease—Changes to Some Other Form of Disease—(See Chronic, Complications, Crises, Relapses, Return, Worse).

Fluids — (See "Mutation" under Fluids).

Healers—Change of Healer Advisable—(See Healers).

Humoural Changes—(See this subject under Humours).

Life—Change of Life in Women—(See "Menopause" under Menses).

Location—Change of Location Advisable—(See Location, "Native Land" under Native; "Place of Birth" under Place; Residence).

Metabolism — Cell Changes — (See Cells, Metabolism, Metamorphosis, Processes, Tissues).

Scenery—Change of Good for the Health—(See Location, Residence, Travel).

Sudden Changes—Subject To—♅ influence and afflictions; ♀ Sig. in ♑. (See Restless, Sudden).

Worse—The Disease Changes for the Worse—(See Complications, Crises, "Worse" under Disease; Relapses).

CHANNELS—And Vents—Sex Channels —(See "Channels" under Genitals). See Passages.

CHAOTIC—Confused—Disordered—Disorganized—

Acts—Chaotic and Unnatural Acts—(See Perversions, Unnatural).

Appetites—Chaotic, Sensuous, Unnatural—(See Appetites, Food, Gluttony, Morbid, Passion, Perversions, Sensuous, Sex, Unnatural).

Confusion—Confusion of Ideas—Of Mind—(See Ideas, Projects. Also see "Mental Chaos" in this section).

Fancies—Chaotic Fancies—(See Fancies).

Mania—Chaotic Religious Mania—(See Mania, Religion).

Mental Chaos—Chaotic Mind—Confusion of Mind—Vague Mental States —Flightiness—Caused by the afflictions of ♆ to ☿, or to the Sigs., the ☉, ☽, or Asc., by dir.; ♆ in the 3rd or 9th H. in ill-asp. to the ☽ or ☿; a ♆ disease and affliction; ♆ affl. in ♊; ♆ ♊ and affl. the ☽ or ☿; ♆ ☌ ☽ or ☿, and affl. by the □ or ☍ ♅; ♆ ♈ ☌ ☽ or ☿, and □ or ☍ ♅; ♆ □ or ☍ ☿; the □ or ☍ asps. of ♆ to the ☉, ☽, ☿, Asc., or hyleg, and espec. under the evil directions of ♆ to these places in the natal map; ☽ ☌ ♆ or ♂ in ♈, and affl. by the □ or ☍ of ♅, ♄, or ♃; the 30° ♍ on the Asc. at B., and afflicted. (See Fears, Flightiness, Hallucinations, Idiocy, Imaginations, Insanity).

Religion—Chaotic Religious Mania—(See Mania, Religion).

Sex Relations—Chaotic, Irregular and Unlawful—(See "Relations" under Sex).

Unnatural—Chaotic and Unnatural Acts—(See Perversions, Sex, Unnatural, Vices). For further study see Clairaudience, Clouded, Concentration, Dreamy, Ideas, Incoordination, Obsessions, Projects, Spirit Controls, Vagaries, Vague, Vain, Weird, etc.

CHARACTER—The ☽ represents the personal character, the Personality or lower mind. The Higher Mind, or the Individuality, is denoted by the sign the ☉ is in at B. However, the real and true character of the Ego, its present stage in evolution, is difficult to determine from the star map of birth. It is said that the character of an incoming Ego is more typically shown and represented by the star map for the time of conception, the Prenatal Epoch map, and usually this map will reveal many hidden traits of the character not shown on the map of birth. The map of birth shows tendencies of the temperament, the environment and external conditions and associations which the native will encounter during the present life; shows the nature of the experiences necessary and the lessons to be learned for soul growth, but does not necessarily reveal the character, or the real nature of the Ego, or the Soul. The native may have a good reputation, yet be hypocritical and evil in his inner character, may be unawakened and unspiritualised, and not yet conscious of his inner, higher, and Divine powers. Advanced Egos have more power over disease, while the younger, negative, inexperienced, and more susceptible souls give way to disease more easily and are more bound by earth and materialistic conditions. The student can learn much about the nature and meaning of Character by making a study of the Occult and Metaphysical books, and too much space cannot be given the subject here. All the good manifestations in a person come down from the Higher Mind, the Spirit, while the evils are usually the emanations of the Personality, or Lower Mind. There are no diseases, or disease thoughts in the Higher Mind, and the afflictions, diseases, ailments, traits of temperament, etc., listed in this work are mostly those of the Lower Mind. (See Conduct, Desires, Disease, Dishonesty, Fate, Heredity, Morals, Religion, Responsibility, and the various subjects thruout this Encyclopaedia).

CHARMS—Amulets—Talismans—(See Amulets).

CHART—
   Chart of Birth—(See Map, Nativity).
   Chart of Descent — (See Prenatal Epoch).

CHARTERING—Injury or Death By—(See Contests, Duels, "Death" under Quarrels).

CHEATING—Fraudulent— A Swindler —Afflictions to ☿, ruler of the mind; ☿ ill-dig. at B.; ☿ Sig. ☌ ☿; ♂ affl. in ♓; ♂ ill-dig. at B., and affl. ☿; ♄ Sig. □ or ☍ ☿. (See Deceitful, Dishonest, Forgers, Liars, Pettifogging, Swindlers, Shrewdness, Thieves, etc.).

   Much Cheating Generally—☿ elevated above, and configurated with ♄ at a Solar Ingress or Eclipse.

CHEEKS—Sides of Face—Ruled by ♀ and the ♈ sign. (See Decanates).

   Bloated Cheeks—(See "Bloated" under Face).

   Dimples In—(See Dimples).

   Falling In Of—Hollow Cheeks—♂ Sig. in fiery signs; Subs at MCP, the 3rd Cervical. (See "Sunken" under Face).

   Moles On—(See Moles).

   Puffy—Blub-Cheeked—Caused by the ☽ influence, and espec. the ☽ in watery signs. (See "Bloated", "Lumpish", under Face).

   Red Cheeks—(See "Red" under Face; "Cheeks" under Red).

CHEERFULNESS—The ♃ influence makes one jovial, and also the ♀ influence strong at B. tends to mirth and cheerfulness; the ☽ Sig. in ♎, a cheerful face. The ♄ people tend to be lacking in cheerfulness, and to be morose and melancholic. The ♐ sign gives cheer to the nature, which is a ♃ sign, and espec. when ☿ is not affl. by ♄. Cheerfulness is a strong asset for good health and longevity. (See Contentment, Happiness, Joy, "Peace of Mind" under Mind; Optimistic, Sanguine, Smiling, etc.).

CHEMICAL ACTION—All of the planetary rays have a special chemical action of their own upon the Mineral, Vegetable and Animal Kingdoms. Some of these rays are agreeable and compatible among themselves, and others incompatible, the same as among chemicals, and a bad mixture of the planetary rays at B., or at any time or period in life, tends to explosions in the temperament, or to ill-health and disease, whereas a good mixture of planetary rays which are agreeable tend to expansion, benefits, good health, peace of mind, etc. For the subjects of planetary affinities and repulsions, see Antipathy, Opposites, Sympathy.

   Chemical Changes—(See Explosions).

CHEMISTS—Chemistry—Apothecary—Druggists—Pharmacists—

   Chemistry of the Body—There are 12 basic and fundamental chemical elements in the body, and each ruled over by one of the Signs of the Zodiac. These chemical constituents may be well-balanced in the different parts and organs of the body, or very much out of proportion, which latter condition may lead to disease unless rectified. For a further study of this subject see "Salts" under Zodiac. For the general chemical processes in the body see such subjects as Assimilation, Bone Building, Digestion, Elimination, Excretion, Gastric Juices, Haematopoiesis (Blood-Making); Nutrition, etc.

   Make Good Chemists—The ♂ and ♏ influences are said to bear strong rule over Chemists, and Chemistry, and people born with the ☉, ☽, ♃, ♂, or ☿ in ♏, and well-aspected, or with ♏ on the Asc., usually make good Chemists or Druggists, and are drawn to such study or practice. Other influences are the ☉ or ☿ in the 12th H., and well-aspected; ♂ a strong ruler at B.; ♂ in ♍ or ♏ and well-aspected; ♂ in the 10th H.; ♂ in good asp. to ☿; ♂ and ♀ together rulers of the employment make good Druggists, and espec. if ♅ be joined with them; ♂ in ✶ or △ asp. the ☉ at B.; ♂ ascending in a watery sign; ♂ ruler, and lord of the Asc.; any asp. of ♂ to the ☽ or ☿ inclines to the study of Chemistry, Dentistry, Medicine or Surgery; lord of the Asc. in his own dignities if he apply to ♂ exalted, and in an angle, honours for Chemists, Surgeons or Physicians; the ✶ or △ asps. of ♂ to the ☉, ☽, and planets; ♃ Sig. in ✶ or △ ♂, a good Chemist; ♃ Sig. ☌ ♂; ♀ Sig. ☌ ♂, and ♂ well-dignified; ♀ ruler, and in the 10th H., favors dealings in drugs, poisons, dyes, colors, and perfumes; ♀

and ☿ as joint rulers make good Apothecaries or Physicians; the ☽ Sig. in ♂ ♂, and ♂ well-dig.; the M.C. or Asc. to the ✶ or △ ♂ by dir., success as Chemists; the majority of planets in earthy signs at B.; lord of the employment in ♏ or ♐, and well-asp.; the 6th face of ♐ culminating on the M.C. at B.; the 1st or 4th faces of ♌ culminating. In Hor'y Questions, the Sig. in ♏, denotes a good Chemist, Pharmacist, Surgeon or Healer; the Sig. in fiery signs indicates a good Chemist or Apothecary. Case—Famous Chemist— See "Davy", No. 703, in 1001 N.N. (See Drugs, Dentists, Healers, Herbs, Medicine, Remedies, Surgeons).

CHESS PLAYERS—Great Ability At— Geniuses—(See Genius, Mathematical, Prodigies).

CHEST—Thorax—Upper Portion of the Body—Trunk—The Chest is ruled by the ♋ sign, and the 3rd H. The chest cavity generally is ruled by ♋. (See "Impar" under Ganglion).

Afflicted—The Chest Afflicted—(See "Disorders" in this section).

Broad Chest—(See "Broad" under Breast).

Burning Sensation In—(See "Heartburn" under Heart).

Capacious Chest—Good Lung Capacity—(See "Capacity" under Lungs).

Colds on Chest—(See "Colds on Chest" under Lungs).

Congestions—Congested and Feverish Chest—♂ affl. in ♊. (See "Congestion" under Bronchial, Lungs).

Deformities Of—Afflictions in ♊ or ♋. (See "Breastbone" under Breast. See "Hollow", "Narrow", in this section).

Disorders Of—The Chest Afflicted— The Chest Deranged—Liable to Chest Disorders—The ☉ in the 6th H., and affl. in common signs, liable to Consumption, and all kinds of chest disorders, and espec. when affl. by the ☽ or ♄; the ☉ affl. in ♋; the ☽ hyleg in ♊, and espec. in female nativities; ♃ affl. in 6th H. in ♊ or ♍; ♂ in the 6th H. at B., in common signs, and affl. by the ☉ or ☽; ☿ affl. in ♎; ♋ on the Asc.; afflictions in ♋ or ♑; Subs at Lu.P. (See Breast, Bronchial, Consumption, Dress, Lungs, Trunk, Tuberculosis).

Dropsy Of—Hydrothorax—Water in the Chest—The ☽ in ♋, and a watery sign on cusp 6th H., and with other planets in watery signs; the ☽ affl. in ♌ or ♒, with people suffering from heart trouble; the ☽ affl. in ♍ or ♓; the ☽ ♓, ♂ or ill-asp. ♂ (or ☿ if he be of the nature of ♄) at the beginning of an illness or at decumb.; ♃ affl. in ♓; Subs at H.P., Lu.P. and K.P., the 11th Dorsal. (See Dropsy).

Emphysema—Pleural and of Chest— ♅ affl. in ♊; a ♅ disease. (See Emphysema).

Feverish and Congested—(See "Congestions" in this section).

Fluids Of—(See "Chest" under Fluids).

Heartburn—(See "Heartburn" under Heart).

Hollow Chest—♄ affl. in ♊. (See "Narrow" in this section. Also see Consumption).

Hydrothorax—(See "Dropsy" in this section).

Intercostal—Intercostal Bulging—Intercostal Neuralgia—(See Intercostal, Neuralgia).

Lungs—(See Lungs).

Mediastinal Tumors—(See Tumors).

Narrow Chest—Hollow Chest—♄ and ♑ influence; ♑ on the Asc. at B., and afflicted; ♄ affl. in ♊; ♄ ♂ or ill-asp. the ☽. (See "Deformities", "Hollow", in this section).

Neuralgia—(See "Intercostal" in this section).

Pains—In Chest—♄ affl. in the 6th H., in cardinal signs; ♂ affl. in ♊ or ♋; great pains in the chest are caused when, at the beginning of a disease or at decumb., the ☽ is in ♒, slow in motion, decr. in light, and affl. by the ☉ or ♂. (See "Pain" under Breast).

Pigeon Shaped—(See "Breastbone" under Breast).

Pleura—(See Pleura).

Prevalent—Chest Disorders Prevalent —♂ lord of the year, in ♋, at the Vernal; ☿ in ♋ at the Vernal Equi., lord of the year, and affl. by ♂.

Ribs—(See Ribs).

Short and Wide—Born under ♃. (See "Wide" in this section).

Sternum—(See Breast, Sternum).

Stout Chest—Stout and Broad Chest —♄ ori. at B.; ♃ in the Asc. (See "Broad" under Breast. Also see "Short and Wide", "Wide", in this section).

Sunken Chest—(See "Hollow", "Narrow" in this section).

Thorax—(See Thorax).

Tightness Of—♄ affl. in ♊, or affl. the ☉ or ☽; also a ♃ disease. (See Bronchial, Cough, Lungs).

Tuberculosis—(See this subject).

Tumors Of—(See "Mediastinal" under Tumors).

Trunk—(See Trunk)).

Water In—The ☽ in ♓, ♂ or ill-asp. ♄ when taken ill, or when compelled to take to bed. (See "Dropsy" in this section).

Weak Chest—(See "Weak" under Lungs).

Wide Chest—♄ ori. at B.; ♄ in ♌, partile the Asc.; ♄ Sig. in ♌. (See "Broad", "Short and Wide", "Stout", in this section).

Wounds To—♂ affl. in ♊, ♋, or ♌, or other malefics and afflictions in these signs. (See "Accidents" under Breast).

CHEYNE-STOKES BREATHING—(See "Cheyne-Stokes" under Breathing).

CHICKEN-POX—Varicella—A ♂ disease; ♂ affl. in ♑; Subs at MCP., the 4th and 5th Cervicals, and at CP, KP, the 11th Dorsal. (See Infectious Diseases, Scabs, Scarlet Fever, Sloughing, Smallpox, etc.).

CHILBLAIN—Cutaneous Inflammation Due to Cold—A ♄ disease, and due to cold; a ♀ and ♓ disease; ☽, ♄, or ♀ affl. in ♓; ♀ ♓ in the 6th H., and afflicted; ♀ ♓ and affl. the ☽ or Asc. (See Cold, Feet).

CHILDBED FEVER— (See "Puerperal Fever" under Puerperal. Also see Parturition).

CHILDBIRTH—Accouchment—Labor—Confinement—(See Parturition, Puerperal).

CHILDHOOD—Early Years of Life— This subject is considered largely under Infancy, and Children, but for convenience of reference, subjects which relate to Childhood in general will be listed and considered in this section. The Period of Childhood is divided into three parts. The first 7 years are under the rule of the ☽; the period from 7 to 14 years under the rule of ☿, and the period from 14 to 21 under ♀ rule. Some Authors divide these periods differently, which divisions are given under "Periods." (See Periods). The Period from 1 to 7 years is also discussed under Infancy. (See Infancy). In the Kabala the period of childhood was dedicated to the ☽. The Vital Body, one of the human vehicles, takes charge of the child at the 7th year, at the 7th birthday, and tends to excessive growth from 7 to 14 years of age. (See "Body" under Vital). At the age of 14 comes Adolescence, and the birth of the Desire Body, another of the human vehicles. (See Desire Body, Puberty). The birth of the Desire Body gives the power of procreation, and also tends to passion. The Mind does not take full control of the body until the 21st birthday, the end of the third seven-year cycle of childhood, and at 21 the child becomes "Of Age" legally. The following influences are listed in this section, which are supplemental to those which appear under "Children", "Infancy", "Youth".

Accidents in Childhood—Accidents in the early years of life are caused by the same general influences as given in the Article on "Accidents", only these influences come to a climax sooner after birth. A child having a malefic anywhere from 1 to 15° from the vital points of the map, such as the ☉, ☽, Asc., M.C., Desc., Hyleg, etc., would be liable to an accident, injury, fall, blow, fracture, sickness etc., according to the time it took the afflicting malefic, or planet, to reach the Asc., by direction, or other vital places in the map, and the affliction would be according to the nature of the afflicting planet. The same influences which cause accidents in childhood may also cause death, according to the severity of the afflictions, and a train of evil directions to the hyleg. (See Accidents; "Accidents" under Children, and Infancy; "Children" under Hurts).

Danger in Early Years—Weak Body During Early Childhood—Not Strong in Early Years—Much Sickness in Childhood—♑ on the Asc., or the ☉ or ☽ affl. in ♑, the early years weak, and with greater danger of death; ♄ affl. in the Asc.; lord of the 6th H. in the Asc., and affl.; the 19° ♓ on the Asc. (See "Death", "Poor Health", "Vitality", under Infancy. Also note the various paragraphs in this section).

Death During Childhood—These influences are much the same as given in the section on "Arguments for Death" under Death, only that they come to a climax earlier in life. If in the 6th year of life a train of evil directions afflict the hyleg, the child will be apt to pass out in that year. Children are more susceptible to planetary afflictions, and to pass out under conditions which an adult might weather thru, as children have not yet learned the laws of mind and spirit, and also the mind does not take more complete possession of the body until the 21st year. Thus an Astrologer can make a study of the star map of a new-born infant, and usually tell whether the child will live thru the first year, or not, by the transits, afflictions, and directions that may culminate over the hyleg in that year, if any. However, it is unethical for Astrologers to predict the time of death, even if they knew, as such would only tend to worry the parents, and the child also if old enough to comprehend the meaning of it. For the planetary influences along this line see "Arguments for Death", "Early Death", "Time of Death", under Death; "Death in Infancy", and other paragraphs under Infancy; "Short Life" under Life; "Death in Early Youth" under Youth. Also note the various paragraphs in this section. Here are a few cases and Birth Data of children dying during childhood, given in 1001 N.N., and dying at ages of 5, 14, 15 and 16 years of age. See "Early Death", No. 428; "Elizabeth" No. 654; "Prince", No. 654; and "France", No. 533, all in 1001 N.N. Also under the heading of "Death" under Infancy, there are about 12 Cases, and Birth Data listed from 1001 N.N., cases of Death in Infancy.

Early Childhood—Early Years of Life —Sickness or Death In—(See the various paragraphs under Children, Infancy, and in this Article. Also see "Short Life", under Life; Youth, etc.).

Enteritis in Childhood— Inflamed Bowels In—Afflictions in ♍; ♂ affl. in ♍; Subs at UPP. (See "Inflammation" under Bowels).

Fevers in Childhood— And Early Youth—♂ coming to the ☌ or ill-asp. the Asc. in early years, tends to chickenpox, fevers, hurts, inflammations, measles, smallpox, wounds, etc. (See Fever).

Many Diseases—In Childhood—No asp. between the ☉ and ♂ at B. (See "Danger" in this section).

Much Sickness—In Childhood—The Body Weak in Early Years—(See "Danger" in this section; "Much Sickness" under Infancy; "Vitality Low" under Vitality).

Restricted and Unhappy— An Unhappy Childhood—The ☉ in ♓ in the 12th H., and affl. by ♄; ♄ ☌ ☉ or ☽ in the Asc. at B. (See Saturn, Twelfth House).

Rickets—In Childhood—(See Rickets). For other subjects, diseases or afflictions concerning Childhood and Children, see the various paragraphs under Children, Infancy, and also look in the alphabetical arrangement for the subject you have in mind.

CHILDREN — Offspring — Progeny — Issue — The 5th and 11th Houses are the principle rulers of children. The 10th H. is also strongly related to children. According to Ptolemy the 10th and 11th Houses signify children, and planets in them, or configurated with them, but if there are no planets in these houses, or in aspect to them, then take the 4th and 5th Houses. ♃, ♀, and the ☽ are the Givers of Children. ♄ and ♂ tend to deny them, and cause barrenness. ☿ is variable according to stars with which configurated. ☿ ori. tends to give children, but occi. to deny them, and cause barrenness. (See Fifth House, Eleventh House, Tenth House, Fourth House). The subjects of Childhood, Early Years, Infancy, Diseases of Infancy, Death in Infancy, Youth, etc., are considered under the subjects of Childhood, Infancy, Youth. So much has been said in the Textbooks of Astrology on the subject of Children, and I have gathered so much material, that I will arrange this Article in three Sections as follows—

Section One — General Considerations. Section Two — The Diseases of Children. Section Three — Duration of Life, and Death of Children. See the following subjects in the alphabetical arrangement when not considered more fully in this Article.

— SECTION ONE —

GENERAL CONSIDERATIONS—

Adolescence—(See Puberty).

Adoption — (See Adoption, "Early Death or Parents", "Separation from Parents", under Parents).

Advent of a Child—(See "Birth of a Child" in this section).

Amativeness In—(See Amativeness).

Anxiety to Parents — (See "Parents", "Worries", in this section).

Barren Time—No Issue—The ☉ to the bad asps. ♀ by dir. (See Barrenness).

Barrenness — No Children — (See Barrenness, Husband, Impotence, Wife. Also see "Denial" in this section).

Bastards; Birth of a Child—Time of Advent of a Child—Promise of a Child—The ☉ to the ☌ and good asps. ♀ by dir.; the ☉ to the P., and good asp. the ☽ by dir. if the ☽ be strong at B.; the ☉ to the ☌ or P. asp. ☿ by dir., and ☿ strong and well-asp. at B.; the good asps. of the ☉ by dir. to the ☽, Asc., M.C., or to the ✳ his own place; the ☽ to the good asps. the ☉ by dir. unless the ☉ be greatly affl. at B.; the ☽ or ♀ to the ✳ or △ the Asc. by dir., and a daughter reign. is promised; the ☽ to the ☌ or good asps. ♃ by dir.; the ☽ to the good asps. ☿ by dir.; the ☽ at a Solar Rev. passing over the place of ♃ at B.; the ☽ to the ☌ or good asps. of ♀ by dir., and espec. if the ☽ was in the 5th H. at B., and children were not denied; ♃ at a Solar Rev. ☌ or P. the place of the ☉ or ☽ at B.; ♃ to the ☌ the ☽ by dir., and espec. if in the 5th

H.; ♃ or ♀ to the ✳ or △ the ☉ or ☽ by dir.; ♃ by Periodic Rev. to the ☌ the place of the ☽ at B.; the good asps. of ♃ by dir. to any of the Moderators, as the ☉, ☽, Asc., or M.C.; the good directions of ♃ to the M.C., or fruitful places, or a giver of children in the map; ♂ ✳ or △ the Asc. or M.C. by dir.; ♀ in ♉, ♎, the Asc., or 7th H., and the place of ♀ ascending at a Solar Rev., a child that year if married; ♀ ☌ the Asc. by dir.; ♀ to the ☌, ✳ or △ the M.C. by dir.; the Asc. to the ☌, P., or good asp. ♃ or ♀ by dir.; the Asc. to the ✳ or △ ☿ by dir.; the M.C. to the ☌, P., ✳ or △ ♃ or ♀ by dir.; the M.C. to the good asps. the ☽ by dir. (See "Female Births" under Female; "Births" under Male; "Time" under Parturition. Also see "First Born" in this section).

Birth Delayed—(See "Delayed in this section).

Birth of Children Prevented—(See "Denial" in this section. Also see Barren).

Birthrate—(See this subject under Birth).

Black Sheep—The Black Sheep in the Fold—The house ruled by a malefic planet, in the order of children given, will tend to be the black sheep among the children, and bring sorrow, trouble, or disgrace upon himself and the parents. (See "Parents", "Worries", in this section).

Blessing—Children tend to prove a blessing to the parents—♃ or ♀ well-asp. in the 5th H., and no malefic influences over this house at B. in the maps of the parents.

Born—When Will the Child Be Born? —Probable Time of Birth—Birth usually takes place when the ☽ reaches her 10th Lunation from the time of conception. Usually when the ☉ is passing some asp. of the cusp of 5th H.; when the ☉ or ♂ reach a ☌ with lord of the 5th; at the time of the ☌ of lord of the 5th with lord of the Asc. in the 5th; when the lord of the Asc. goes out of one sign into another. These influences tend to precipitate the birth if they exist near the time of regular delivery. Note the distance of lord of the 5th H. from the cusp of the 5th., and give one month to each sign. Judge according to the majority of testimonies. (See "Moment of Birth" under Birth, and Moment; "Time" under Parturition; Premature. Also see "Delayed" in this section).

Boy Born—(See "Births" under Male. Also see Son. See "First Born" in this section).

Brothers Indicated—(See Brothers).

Child Promised — (See "Birth of a Child" in this section).

Childbirth—(See Mother, Parturition).

Childhood — (See Childhood, Infancy, Youth. Also see the various paragraphs in this section).

Childless — (See Barren, Husband, Wife. Also see "Denial" in this section).

Complexion — Fair in Youth — (See Youth).

Conception—Moment of—Signs of—(See Conception).

Creative Powers—Of the Parents—(See Barren, Creative, Fruitful, Husband, Powers, Wife).

Daughter Born—(See "Female Births" under Female).

Decreased—The Number of Children Decreased—♄ in the 5th H., and affl. The number of children will be increased or diminished according to the nature of the planets in the 5th H., and the asps. to such planets. (See "Increased" in this section).

Delayed Births—♄ rising, or on the Asc., and with danger of Asphyxiation. This was the case with Goethe, the Poet. (See "Birth" under Asphyxia). Also what some people would consider a delayed, or overtime birth may be normal according to the laws of the Prenatal Epoch, as in Epochs of the 2nd and 3rd Orders, which show 273 days + x in utero, etc. (See Prenatal Epoch).

Denial of Children—The ☉, ♅, ♄ and ♂ tend to deny children, or allot but few, or cause their death when born, and espec. if these bodies are in the 5th H. of the parents at B., and affl. (See Barrenness, Husband, Wife).

Denoted—Children Denoted—Promise of—(See Fruitful, Husband, Wife. Also see "Birth of" in this section).

Desire For Children Strong—(See Amativeness).

Directions and Children—The Primary or Secondary Directions of Childhood and Youth—In case of young children and infants, the first train of evil directions to the hyleg tend to kill, and espec. during the ☽ period from 1 to 7 years of age. Children at an older age may survive evil directions, and even have good health if born with strong vitality, but the evil directions may severely afflict the parents, cause disease, suffering, or the death of a parent. (See "Direction" in Sec. 3 of this Article. Also see "Directions" under Infancy, Parents).

Disposition Of—(See Disposition, Savage, Temperament. Also see "Savage" in Sec. 2 of this Article).

Dogs—May Resemble Dogs—(See "Dogs" in Sec. 2 of this Article).

Double Births—(See Twins).

Drink—Parents Given to Drink and Neglect of Children—(See "Drink" under Parents).

Duration of Life—(See Sec. 3 of this Article).

Dwarfs; Early Years—Conditions Affecting—(See the various paragraphs in this section. Also see Childhood, Infancy, "Short Life" under Life; Youth, etc).

Eclipses—Children Born at Time of—(See Eclipses, "New Moon" under Moon).

Eight Months Children — Children Born at the 8th month of Pregnancy—A child born at the 8th month is more apt to die because, according to the Science of Numbers, the number 8 is made up of two feminine factors,

4+4=8, the two elements making up 8 both being even, or feminine numbers. (See Climacteric). Children born at the 7th month live, it is said, because the elements making up 7, consisting of 3+4=7, combine an odd and even number, or a masculine and feminine number. (See Cases under Premature). Children born at the 9th month also have a positive and feminine combination, an odd and even number, as 4+5=9, and such combinations give force and vitality, whereas the combination of the two even numbers lack balance and the vital force necessary to sustain the child after delivery. This theory is discussed in books on the Science of Numerals, and is undoubtedly, in my opinion, the true explanation and philosophy of the matter. All Nature is founded upon the laws of Mathematics, Numbers, Vibration, etc., and the Planetary influences also work according to these rules and laws. (See Gestation).

Eleventh House—As Related to Children. (See the Introduction to this Article. Also see Eleventh).

Embryo—(See Foetus).

Faithful Children—(See "Blessing" in this section).

Family—A Large Family of Children —(See "Many Children" in this section).

Father—Conditions Affecting the Father—(See Father, Parents. Also see "Parents", "Worries", in this section).

Female—Barrenness In—(See Barrenness).

Female Births—Daughter Born—(See "Female Births" under Female).

Female Child Promised—(See "Birth of a Child" in this section. Also see "Female Births" under Female).

Female Children—Predominance of—This matter is largely judged from the sex of the horoscope. In female nativities the 5th H. is female, and the 4th H. is male. In male horoscopes the 5th H. is male, and the 4th H. is female. The conditions of these houses will show the predominating sex, and which gives the greater promise of fruitfulness, while the opposite houses show detriments. The majority of planets at B. in the feminine signs also indicate more female births, and the majority in masculine signs, more male births. (See "Female Births" under Female; "Births" under Male; Predetermination. Also see "First Born" in this section).

Female Horoscope—First Born Child In—(See "First Born" in this section).

Female or Male—During Pregnancy —(See "First Born" in this section. Also see Predetermination).

Few Children—But Few Promised—Few or No Children—One or Two Allotted—Small Family—The ☉, ♅, ♄, ♂, and ☊ allot but few, or deny children; the ☉ in ♍; the ☉ affl. in the 5th H.; the ☉ in the 5th H. of the marriage partner; the ☉, ♅, ♄, ♂ or ☿ in the 5th H. may give a few, but if afflicted, apt to see their early death; ☿ occi., in a barren sign, and configurated with barren planets; the ♌ sign on the cusp of 5th H.; a barren sign on the Asc. or cusp of 5th H., or the ☽ ruler of the Asc. in such signs; lord of the Asc. in the 5th H., and affl. by ♄, ♂, or ☋. (See Barrenness. Also see "Denial" in this section).

Fifth House—This is the principal house of children, and the conditions affecting this house in the maps of the parents indicate much along the lines of children, their fate and destiny, and whether children will be born or denied; whether they will live or die; whether they may prove a blessing to the parents, or a source of worry and anxiety, etc. (See Fifth House).

First-Born Child—In a male horoscope the 5th H. denotes the first child, and the possible sex. The 7th H. denotes the second child, and the 9th H. the 3rd child; the 11th H., the 4th child, etc., in a male horoscope. Thus if there are malefics in the 5th H. of the father the first child is apt to be sickly, or die early; if malefics in the 7th H., the second child may die; if in the 9th H., the third child, etc. Benefics in these houses would show which of the children would be more fortunate, honorable, useful, a blessing, etc. In a female nativity the first child is denoted by the 4th H.; the second child by the 6th H.; the third child by the 8th H., etc., and the nature and possible destiny of each, from the mother's standpoint, is to be judged from the nature of the planets in these houses in her map. ♅, ♄, or ♂ in the 5th H. of the father, or in the 4th H. of the mother, indicate accidents, injuries, or sickness, death, etc., of the first child. Malefics in other houses, as stated, indicate hurt, loss of, or detriment to the second or third child. (See "First Born Brother" under Brothers). Cancer, a feminine sign, on the cusp of the 5th H., and with the ☽ or ♀, feminine planets also in ♋ in the 5th H., indicate a daughter in a male nativity. The ♐ sign on cusp of 5th H., and masculine planets in the 5th, would indicate a son as the first child in a male nativity, etc. The 7th H. dominated and influenced by masculine planets, and a masculine sign, indicate that the 2nd child, in a male nativity, would be a boy, etc. These rules, of course, apply to the natural order of conceptions, and where conception has not been interfered with, or prevented in any way. (See "Female Births" under Female; "Births" under Male; Son).

Foetus—Embryo—For matters concerning the Embryo and Foetus, see Abortion, Conception, Foetus, Gestation, Miscarriage, Pregnancy, Prenatal Epoch).

Fortunate Children—(See "Blessing" in this section).

Fourth Child—(See "First Born" in this section).

Fruitful—The Parents Fruitful, and a Large Family Indicated—(See Fruitful, Husband, Wife. Also see "Many Children" in this section).

Geniuses—(See Geniuses, Prodigies).

Gestation; Givers of Children—Gives Children—♃, ♀, and the ☽ are Givers of Children, and espec. when in the 5th H., and in fruitful signs. ☿ either gives or denies children, according to the planet, or planets configurated with at B. (See Fruitful, Moon, Jupiter, Venus).

Good Health—Of Children—(See "Long-Lived" in Sec. 2 of this Article. Also see "Long Life" under Life; "Good Vitality" under Vitality).

Grandchildren—Indicated when the maps of the parents are fruitful, and when good influences in the houses of children indicate good health and long life for children. (See Fruitful. Also see "Long Life" in Sec. 2 of this Article).

Grief Through Children—Malefics in or ruling the 5th H. of a parent. (See "Directions", "Parents", "Worries", in this section. Also see Parents).

Growth of Children—(See Corpulent, Diminished, Dwarf, Enlarged, Fat, Growth, Short, Tall, Thin, etc.).

Guardians; Healthy—(See "Long Life" under Life; "Children", and "Good" under Resistance; Vitality Good. Also see "Long-Lived" in Sec. 2 of this Article).

Heredity; Houses of Children—(See the Introduction to this Article).

Human Shape—Not of Human Shape—Resembles Animals—(See Inhuman, Monsters. Also see "Dogs" in Sec. 2 of this Article).

Ill-Fortune—Children bring ill-fortune, grief and sorrow to Parents—(See Parents. Also see "Black Sheep", "Grief", "Parents", "Worries", in this section).

Illegitimate Children—(See Bastards).

Imprisonment—A Parent Imprisoned Thru the Plots of Children—Lord of the 12th H. a malefic, and in the 5th H. (See "Plots" under Prison).

Increased Number—Of Children—Several Children—The ☽, ♃, or ♀ in the 5th H., in a fruitful or double-bodied sign, as in ♋, ♏, or ♓, or in ♊ or ♐; the ☽ in the 5th or 11th H. in a fruitful sign. (See Fruitful. Also see "Decreased", "Many", in this section).

Increased Strength—(See "Strength" under Infancy; Vitality. Also see "Strength" in this section).

Infancy—For the various conditions affecting Infants see Infancy, Childhood, and also note the various paragraphs in this Article).

Injured—Children Injured—Parents Injured by Children—(See "Accidents" in Sec. 3 of this Article. See "Parents" in this section; "Injured" under Parents).

Issue—No Issue—A Barren Time—(See "Barren Time" in this section).

Kidnapped; Labor—Confinement—(See Parturition).

Lactation—(See Milk, Nursing).

Large Family—(See Fruitful, Husband, Wife. Also see "Increased", "Many", in this section).

Legitimate—Is the Child Legitimate? —(See Bastards).

Lives—The Child Will Live and be Healthy—(See "Long-Lived" in Sec. 2 of this Article).

Long-Lived—(See "Long-Lived" in Sec. 2 of this Article).

Love and Affection—Love and Affection of the Parents For—(See "Love and Affection" under Parents).

Male Children Born—(See "Births" under Male; Son. Also see "Female Births" in this section).

Male Nativity—First Child In—Second Child In, etc.—(See "First Born" in this section).

Male or Female—During Pregnancy —(See Predetermination).

Males—Two or Three Males Born at One Confinement—(See "Births" under Male; Twins, Triplets).

Many Children—A Large Family— The ☽ in ♋, ♏, or ♓, or in the double-bodied signs ♊ or ♐, in the 5th H., and well-asp. by ♃ or ♀; the ☽ in the 5th or 11th H. in a fruitful sign; the ☽ in the 5th H. in other than barren signs, and well-asp. by benefics; the ☽ in ♉, her exalted sign, in the 5th H., and well-asp.; ♃, ♀, or ☽ in 5th H., and the ☽ in good asp. to ♃ or ♀, increases their number; ♃ well-asp. in ♏; ♀ in the 5th H., and well-asp., and espec. in a watery sign; ♋, ♏, ♓, or ♉ upon cusp of 5th H. if the ☽ is well placed and aspected; planets, or ☊ in the 5th H., and well-asp. by ☽ or ♀; rulers of the 1st and 5th H. in fruitful signs, and espec. when ♃ and ♀ are in good asp. to the ☽ or ruler of the 5th; ♋ on the Asc. or 5th H. at B., strong, and with the ☉, ☽, ♃ or ♀ in ♋; lord of the 5th H. in a fruitful sign in the Asc., if not afflicted; ♋ or ♓ on cusp 5th H., and no malefics in the 5th, indicate a large family; cusp of the 5th H., and its lord, strong, or in fruitful signs, or if many planets, and espec. ♃ or ♀ be here, or in translation or reception with its lord, or if lord of the Asc. be there, or ☊, gives many children; lord of the 7th H. in the 5th. (See Fruitful. Also see "Increased" in this section). Cases of Many Children—Had Sixteen Children—See "Anne", No. 518 in 1001 N.N. Had 9 sons and 4 daughters—See "Maximillian", No. 549, in 1001 N.N.

Matricide—(See "Patricide" under Father).

Midwives; Mind—Children of—(See Creative).

Misfortune—Thru Children—(See "Parents", "Worries", in this section).

Moment of Birth—(See "Moment" under Birth).

Moon—A Female Born at Time of Eclipse of—(See Eclipses).

Mother—(For conditions affecting the Mother, see Mother).

Neglected—Children Neglected by Parents—(See "Drink" under Parents).

No Children—(See Barrenness; "Anchorite" under Husband. Also see "Denial" in this section).

Number of Children—(See Decreased, Few, Increased, Many, and the various paragraphs in this section. Also see Barrenness, Fruitful).

Numerous Children—(See "Many" in this section).

Nursing—(See Breasts, Milk, Nipples, Nursing).

Obedient Children—(See "Blessing" in this section).

One at a Birth—(See "Single Births" in this section).

One or Two Allotted—Few Children— (See "Few", "Worries", in this section).

Orphans—(See "Adoption" in this section).

Overtime Children—(See "Delayed" in this section).

Parental Love—(See "Love" under Parents).

Parents—Influences Affecting the Parents Thru the Children—(See Black Sheep, Directions, Imprisonment, Injured, Worries, etc., in this section. Also note the various paragraphs under Father, Mother, Parents).

Parturition—Childbirth—(See Parturition).

Patricide—(See "Patricide" under Father).

Perfect—Some Perfect, and Some Imperfect—(See Beautiful. Also see "Illformed", "Imperfect", in Sec. 2 of this Article).

Periods of Childhood—(See the Introduction under Childhood).

Precocious; Predetermination—Of the Sex During Pregnancy—(See Predetermination).

Predominance of Sexes—(See "Female Children" in this section).

Pregnancy—Male or Female During —(See Predetermination. Also see "First Born" in this section).

Pregnant—The Woman is With Child —The Woman is Not With Child—(See Pregnancy).

Premature Births—(See Abortion, Miscarriage, Parturition, Premature, Prenatal Epoch).

Prenatal Epoch; Prevented—The Birth of Children Prevented—Denial of Children—(See Barrenness. Also see "Denial" in this section).

Probability of Children—Fruitful signs on the cusps of 4th, 5th, 10th or 11th Houses; ♃, ♀, or the ☽ in the 4th, 5th, 10th or 11th Houses, and well-asp. Look first to the 10th and 11th Houses, and if no planets therein, look to the 4th and 5th Houses. If none there look to planets which may be in good asp. to degrees on the cusps of these Houses. (See Fruitful).

Prodigies; Promise of a Child—Children Promised—(See "Birth of a Child", and "Increased" in this section. Also see Fruitful).

Propagation—Strong Desire For— (See Amativeness).

Prosperous Children—(See "Blessing in this section).

Puberty; Quadruplets—(See Quadruplets, Twins, Triplets).

Religious Veneration—Children Resemble Animals Held in Religious Veneration—(See "Dogs" in Sec. 2 of this Article).

Second-Born Child—(See "First Born" in this section).

Seven Months Children—(See "Eight Months Children" in this section).

Several Children Promised—(See "Increased", "Many", in this section. Also see Fruitful).

Sex of Children—(See "First-Born", "Female Children", "Male Children", in this section. See Predetermination).

Short-Lived—(See Sec. 3 of this Article).

Significators of Children—♃, ♀, and the ☽. The 5th H. and its lord are Sigs. of children in Hor'y Questions only. (See "Givers" in this section).

Signs of Children—(See Fruitful. Also see "Increased", "Many", in this section).

Single Births—One Birth Only—Not Twins—Planets which give children placed singly, and unaspected, in the 4th, 5th, 10th or 11th H.; an absence of the givers of children in double-bodied signs, or absence of such signs on the cusps of the 5th or 11th H. (See Twins).

Sisters Indicated—(See Sisters).

Sixteen Children—Gave Birth To—(See "Many" in this section).

Small Family—(See "Few" in this section).

Son Born—Son Promised—(See "First Born" in this section. Also see "Births" under Male; Son).

Sorrow—Thru Children—(See "Parents", "Worries", in this section).

Stamina Of—(See "Long-lived" in Sec. 2 of this Article. Also see Stamina, Tone, Vitality).

Step Children—Ruled by the 11th H.

Strength of Children—Increased by benefics well-asp. in the 5th or 11th H., and decreased by malefics affl. in these houses. (See "Long-lived" in Sec. 2 of this Article; "Early Death", and other paragraphs in Sec. 3 of this Article. Also see "Long Life" under Life; Resistance, Stamina, Tone, Vitality).

Strong Children—(See "Strength" in this section; "Long-lived" in Sec. 2 of this Article).

Symbols of Children—(See Fruitful). Also see "Givers" in this section).

Teething—(See Teeth).

Tenth House—As Related to Children—(See Tenth House).

Third Child—(See "First-Born" in this section).

Three at a Birth—(See Triplets).

Time of Advent—(See "Birth of a Child", "Born", "Delayed", "Premature", in this section. Also see Time).

Triplets; Trouble to Parents—(See "Parents", "Worries", in this section. Also see Parents).

Twins—Two at a Birth—(See Twins, Triplets).

Two Children Allotted—One or Two Allotted—(See "Few" in this section).

Undertime Children—(See "Eight Months", "Premature", in this section).

Unfortunate with Children—(See "Parents", "Worries", in this section).

Unhappiness with Children—(See "Parents", "Worries", in this section).

Welfare and Health—Of Children—Ruled by the 5th H. (See Sec. 3 of this Article).

When Will the Child Be Born?—(See "Birth of a Child", and "Born", in this section).

Woman Is With Child—The Woman Is Not With Child—(See Pregnancy).

Worries Thru Children—Malefics in the 5th H., or rulers of the 5th; malefics in the 11th H.; the ☉, ♅, ♄, or ♂, when taken as the Givers of Children in the map, may give one or two if in the houses of children and favorably aspected by the ☽, ♃, or ♀, but those given may cause the parents much trouble, or meet with ruin, disaster, much sickness, or an early death, or prove dissolute; ☿ affl. in the 5th H.; ruler of the 5th H. in the 2nd, 6th, 8th or 12th Houses; lord of the 8th H. in the 5th H. of parent. (See "Parents" in this section).

Youth—For conditions concerning Youth, see Childhood, Puberty, Youth, and also note the various paragraphs in this section).

— SECTION TWO —

DISEASES OF CHILDREN—Afflictions to Children—The Health of Children—Children Suffer—Adverse Planetary Influences Affecting Children, etc.—The Welfare and Health of Children are ruled principally by the 5th H. See the following subjects in the alphabetical arrangement when not considered more fully here.

Abortion; Accidents To—Hurts or Injuries To—The ☉ or ☽ to the ill-asps. ♅, ♄, or ♂ by dir.; ♅, ♄, or ♂ affl. in ♌ or the 5th H.; ♅, ♄, or ♂ to the cusp the 5th H. by dir; ♅ on, or within 1° of the degree ascending at B.; ♂ in the 5th H. and affl. the ☉ or ☽. These influences may also cause death by accident if the map otherwise indicates a violent death. They also cause hurts, cuts, bruises, wounds, fractures, etc. For accidents at childbirth see Parturition. (See Hurts, Injury, in this section).

Adolescence—For disturbances at this period see Puberty.

Afflicted Children—Affliction to Children—The ☉ in the 5th H. and affl.; the ☽ in the 5th or 11th H. at B., and to the ☌, P., or ill-asps. ♅ by dir. (For further influences, see the various paragraphs in this section, and also in Sections 1 and 2 of this Article).

Amativeness; Animal Heat—Lacking in Animal Heat in Early Years—♇ influence; ♇ on the Asc. at B. (See "Animal" under Heat).

Asphyxiation—Danger of at Birth—(See "Birth" under Asphyxia. Also see "Delayed" in Sec. 1 of this Article).

Bad Children—♄ or ♂ affl. in the 5th H. at B. (See "Parents", "Worries", in Sec. 1 of this Article).

Barrenness—Children Born Barren— (See Barrenness, Impotency).

Beastly Form—(See "Beastly Form" under Beasts; Foetus; Inhuman. Also see "Dogs" in this section).

Bed Wetting—(See "Incontinence" under Urine).

Birth—(1) Delayed Birth—(See "Delayed" in Sec. 1 of this Article). (2) Disease and Infection at Birth—Unusual Diseases at Birth—(See "Infections" under Infancy). (3) Injury or Accident to Child at Birth—Injury by Instrumental Delivery — (See "Accidents" under Infancy; "Injury" under Parturition). (4) Birth Prevented— (See "Birth" under Asphyxia; Barrenness, Birth; "Excision" under Foetus; Parturition. Also see "Delayed" in Sec. 1 of this Article).

Blemishes—(See Blemishes, Congenital).

Blind from Birth—(See "Born Blind" under Blindness).

Blue Baby—Nearly Asphyxiated at B. —(See "Birth" under Asphyxia).

Body—(1) Not of Human Shape—(See "Beastly Form" in this section). (2) Strong Body — (See Strong, Vitality. Also see "Long-lived" in this section). (3) Weak Body—(See "Low" under Vitality; "Weak Body" under Weak. Also see "Animal Heat", "Sickly", and other paragraphs in this section).

Born—But Sickly and Short-lived— (See "Sickly" in this section; "Early Death" in Sec. 3 of this Article).

Bow Legs—(See Legs, Limbs).

Bowel Disorders—(See Bowels).

Breech Presentation — (See "Breech" under Parturition).

Bronchitis; Caesarian Operation—(See "Excision" under Foetus).

Calamity—From the Moment of Birth —(See "Moment of Birth" under Calamity).

Cats— Offspring Resemble— (See "Dogs" in this section).

Chickenpox; Child Will Suffer—(See "Afflicted", "Suffers", and the various paragraphs in this section and Article).

Childbirth—Accident or Injury at Time of—(See Parturition. Also see "Birth" in this section).

Childhood—See the various paragraphs under Childhood, Infancy, and also in this Article).

Cholera Infantum—(See Cholera).

Circumcision; Club Feet—(See Feet).

Colic; Congenital Defects—(See Blemishes, Blind, Congenital, Deaf, Defects, Deformities, Distortions, Idiocy, Missing, Monsters, Mute, etc.).

Constitution Poor—(See "Sickly", "Weak", in this section. Also see "Early Death" in Sec. 3 of this Article).

Convulsions—(See Convulsions, Fits. Also see "Dentition" under Teeth).

Cough; Cramps, Cretinism; Crippled —From Birth—(See "Armless" under Arms; Congenital, Crippled, Deformities, Distortions, Excresences; "Club Feet" under Feet; Lameness, Legs, Limbs, Maimed, Missing, Monsters, Paralysis; "Child" under Walk).

Croup; Danger to Children—Danger of Injury—Subject to Many Dangers— ♅ or ♂ to the cusp the 5th H. of a parent by dir.; ♅ on, or within 1° of the ascending degree at B.; ♂ affl. in the Asc. of the child at B., or ♂ here afflicting the ⊙, ☽, or hyleg. (See "Accidents" in this section, and also under Childhood, Infancy).

Daughter—Danger To—(See Daughter).

Deaf and Dumb—(See Hearing).

Defective Births—(See "Defective" under Birth; "Congenital", "Crippled", in this section).

Deformed—(See "Deformed" under Infancy; Deformities, Distortions, Inhuman, Lame, Legs, Limbs, Monsters, etc. See "Congenital", "Crippled", and the various paragraphs in this section).

Delicate—(See "Sickly" in this section).

Delivery—Injury At—(See "Accidents" under Infancy; "Injury" under Parturition).

Dentition—Spasms During Teething —(See "Dentition" under Teeth).

Detriment to Children—The ⊙ in the 5th H. at the Vernal Equinox; malefics affl. in the 5th H. at B., and affl. the 5th H. by dir. (See "Accidents", "Dangers", and the various paragraphs in this Article, and also under Childhood, Infancy).

Diarrhoea; Diminished Growth—(See Diminished, Dwarf, Growth).

Diphtheria; Disease—Liable To—The Children Diseased—Sickly Children— Diseases at Birth—(See "Sickly", "Unhealthy" in this section; "Many Diseases" under Childhood; "Infections" under Infancy, etc. Also note the various paragraphs in this Article).

Disposition—(See Inhuman, Savage, Wild. Also see "Dogs" in this section).

Distortions; Dogs—The Offspring Resembles Dogs, Cats, and other creatures held in religious veneration, and used in worship—When the ruler of the last New or Full Moon before birth, and the rulers of the ⊙ and ☽ are unconnected with the preceding New or Full ☽, and if in addition to this absence of connection, ♅, ♄, or ♂ be in angles, and the ⊙ and ☽ be in a bestial sign, as in ♈, ♉, ♌, ♐, or ♑, then the conception will be normal, and tend to resemble the animal or creature ruled by the sign predominating. If the Luminaries be so unconnected, but with support from the benefics, and be affl. by ♄ and ♂ at the same time, the offspring will then be like Dogs, Cats, or other creatures held in religious veneration. If ♃ and ♀ do not interpose with their good asps., and the ⊙ and ☽ are also disconnected, and evilly aspected by ♄ and ♂, then the creature born will be wholly wild, i n d o c i l e, and of evil nature. Also people born in extreme cold climates, as in the Arctics, tend to have a wild and indocile nature, owing to constant cold. (See "Beastly Form" under Beasts; Foetus, Inhuman; "Animal Forms" under Monsters; Savage, Wild).

Drunkards—C h i l d r e n May Become Drunkards—(See Drunkenness).

Dumb—Deaf and Dumb—(See "Deaf and Dumb" under Hearing. Also see Mute).

Dwarf; Dysentery; Early Years—Influences Affecting Children During—(See the various paragraphs in this Article. Also see Childhood; "Early Years" under Early; "Animal Heat" under Heat; Infancy, Youth, etc.).

Eclipses—Children Born at Time of—(See Eclipses).

Eight Months Children—Born at 8th month—Sickness or Death of—(See "Eight Months Children" in Sec. 1 of this Article).

Emaciation; Embryo—Of Beastly Form—(See "Beastly Form" under Beasts. Also see "Dogs" in this section).

Enuresis—(See "Incontinence" under Urine).

Epilepsy; Eruptions; Evil Children—Evil in Nature—(See "Parents", "Worries", in Sec. 1 of this Article; "Dogs" in this section; Evil, Parents).

Excision of Foetus—(See Foetus).

Excrescences; Eyes Weak—(See Blindness, Eyes, Sight).

Fat Body—(See Fat).

Feet—Disorders and Deformities of—(See Feet).

Female—Barrenness In—Disorders of—(See Barren, Females, Impotency).

Fevers—In Childhood or Infancy—♂ to the ☉ or ill-asps. the Asc., or to the ill-asps. the ☉, ☽, or hyleg by dir. (See Fever; "Fever" under Infancy).

Fierce and Savage—(See "Dogs" in this section; "Beastly Form" under Beasts).

Fits—(See Fits; "Dentition" under Teeth; Spasms).

Foetus—Disorders of—Excision of—(See Foetus).

Foolish Children—(See Foetus, Foolish, Idiocy, Imbecile).

Frog Child—(See Frog).

Gives Children—But Weakly and Short Lived—The Givers of children, ♃, ♀, or ☽ in barren signs, and the malefics more powerful by strength or number. (See "Sickly", "Short-Lived" "Weak", in this section; "Early Death" in Sec. 3 of this Article).

Growth—(See Dwarf, Diminished, Enlarged, Fat, Giants, Growth, Height, Short, Tall, Thin, etc).

Healthy—And L o n g - l i v e d — (See "Long-lived" in this section. Also see Constitution, Health, Strong, Vitality).

Hearing Affected — (See Hearing, Mute).

Heart Affections—(See Heart).

Heat—Lacking in Animal Heat—(See "Animal Heat" under Heat).

Hermaphrodites; Human Shape—Not of Human Shape—(See "Dogs", "Inhuman" in this section; "Beastly Form" under Beasts).

Hurts To—(See "Accidents" in this section and under Childhood, Infancy; "Children" under Hurts).

Hydrocephalus; Idiocy; Ill-Formed Body—(See Ill-formed, Ugly).

Ill-luck—To Children—The ☽ in the 5th H. of a parent, and to the ♂ or ill-asp. ♅, ♄, or ♂ by dir.; malefics affl. in 5th H. of parent. (See "Accidents", and the various paragraphs in this section).

Illegitimate—(See Bastards).

Imbecile; Imperfect Shape—Imperfect Children—If all the configurations are imperfect the child will be imperfect. See "Beastly Form" under Beasts; Defects; Ill-formed, Imperfect, Incomplete, Inhuman, Monsters, etc. See "Crippled", "Dogs", in this section).

Impotence; Indigestion; Indocile—(See "Dogs" in this section).

Infancy—Disorders of—(See Infancy).

Infections—At Birth—Infectious Diseases — (See Contagious, Infections; "Infections" under Infancy).

Infirmity—(See "Sickly", "Unhealthy", and the various paragraphs in this section).

Inhuman Shape — (See "Beastly Form", "Dogs", in this section. Also see Inhuman, Monsters).

Injury—Danger of—Injury at Birth—(See "Accidents", "Birth", "Dangers", in this section. See "Accidents" under Childhood, Infancy).

Insanity; Instrumental Delivery—(See "Accidents" under Infancy, Parturition).

Intestinal Troubles — (See Abdomen, Bowels, Colic, Cramps, Flatulence, Wind, etc.).

Kidney Disorders—(See Kidneys).

Knock Knees—(See Knees).

Lame—Lame from Birth— (See Congenital, Distortions, Excrescences, Feet, Lameness, Legs, Maimed, Missing, Paralysis, etc.).

Legitimate—Is the Child Legitimate? —(See Bastards).

Liable to Disease—Liable to Accidents—(See "Accidents", "Dangers", "Sickly", "Unhealthy", in this section. Also see Recuperation, Resistance, Stamina, Tone, Vitality, Weak, etc).

Lives Thru Sickness — A fiery sign rising upon the Asc. at B., as ♈, ♌, ♐, as these signs are the strongest for vitality. (See Recuperation, Resistance, Vitality).

Long-lived—Healthy and Long-lived Children—The ☉, ☽, ♃ or ♀ in the 5th H. of the parent, and well-asp.; ♃ or ♀ in the 5th or 11th H., well-asp.; lords of the 5th or 11th H. in a fruitful sign, in good houses, well-asp., and free from the affliction of malefics; no malefics in the 5th or 11th houses, or affl. the lords of these houses; lord of the 5th in the 5th H., and espec. if a benefic. (See "Long Life" under Life; "Good" under Vitality).

Luck—Good or Bad Luck to a Child—(See "Ill-luck" in this section; "Blessing" in Sec. 1 of this Article).

Lunatic—The Child a Lunatic—Born of a Lunatic Mother—(See Insanity. See Case, "Mad Mother", No. 074 in 1001 N.N.).

Maimed; Males—For conditions affecting Males, see Males, Son. Also see "First-born", "Female Children", in Sec. 1 of this Article).

Many Diseases—(See "Many Diseases" under Childhood. Also see "Sickly" in this section).

Marasmus—(See Emaciation).

Measles; Mentality—(See "Mind" in this section).

Mind—the Mind Afflicted—Weak Mind—(See Imbecile, Idiocy, the various paragraphs under Mental and Mind. Case of Mental Suppression and Childlike Mind — (See Case, "Never Grew Up", No. 720 in 1001 N.N.).

Miscarriage; Misfortune To — (See "Accidents", "Luck", and the various paragraphs in this section. Also see Misfortune).

Moment of Birth—Calamity From—(See "Moment of Birth" under Calamity, Birth).

Monsters; Morbid Sex Desires — At Puberty—(See Puberty).

Mother—The Mother as Affected By Children—(See Mother. Also see "Parents", "Worries", in Sec. 1 of this Article).

Much Sickness Among—(See "Sickly", "Unhealthy", "Weak", in this section. Also see "Much Sickness" under Sickness).

Mumps; Mutes — (See "Deaf and Dumb" under Hearing; Mutes).

Mutilated—The Foetus Mutilated—(See Foetus).

Myxoedema; Nativity Weak — But Reared—(See "Reared" in this section).

Nature—Savage and Fierce—(See "Dogs" in this section).

Neglected—By Parents—(See "Drink" under Parents).

Never Grew Up—Mental Suppression —(See "Mind" in this section).

Nursing—The Child Could Not Nurse and Died—Case—See "Born Incomplete", No. 281 in 1001 N.N. (See Breasts, Milk, Nipples, Weaning).

Nurture—Nutrition—Not Susceptible to Nurture—(See "Nurture" under Infancy; Nutrition).

Obesity—(See Fat, Fleshy, Obesity).

Orphans; Pain—(See Bowels, Colic, Cramps, and the various paragraphs under Pain).

Paralysis—From Birth—(See Paralysis).

Parents—The Parents as Affected By the Children—(See Parents. Also see "Parents", "Worries", in Sec. 1 of this Article).

Parturition—Danger to Child In—(See Birth, Foetus, Parturition).

Passional Excesses — Dies Young From—(See "Dissipation" in Sec. 3 of this Article).

Polypus; Poor Constitution—(See Constitution. Also see "Sickly", "Weak", in this section, and "Early Death" in Sec. 3 of this Article).

Prenatal Epoch—The Prenatal Period —(See Conception, Gestation, Pregnancy, Prenatal).

Prepuce—(See Circumcision).

Puberty—Dangers At—Disorders of—(See Puberty).

Puny and Sickly—(See "Sickly" in this section. Also see Emaciated; "Malnutrition" under Nutrition; Thin, Vitality, Weak).

Reared with Difficulty—Sickly, But Will Be Reared—♋, ♍, or ♓ on the Asc. at B.; the ☽ sepr. from a malefic, and applying to the ☌ or good asp. a benefic; malefics in the 5th or 11th H., but well-asp. by ♃ or ♀; ruler of the Asc. in the 6th H., affl. by lord of 8th H., but assisted by the good asps. of ♃ or ♀, or by planets in their dignities. (See "First-Born" in Sec. 1 of this Article; "Sickly" in this section. Also see Recuperation, Resistance, Sickly, Vitality, Weak).

Recuperative Powers—(See Recuperation, Resistance, Robust, Stamina, Strong, Tone, Weak, Vitality).

Resistance—To Disease—(See Resistance).

Rickets; Robust—(See Robust, Stamina, Tone, Vitality. Also see "Long-lived" in this section). Children do not tend to be robust in early years when ♑ is on the Asc. at B., and are also lacking in Animal Heat. (See "Animal" under Heat).

Savage and Fierce—(See "Dogs" in this section).

Scarlet Fever;

Separated from Parents—(See Adoption, Family, Orphans, Parents).

Sex—Sex Activity at Puberty—(See Puberty).

Sex of Children—(See "Female Children", "First-born", "Male Children", in Sec. 1 of this Article. Also see Conception, Predetermination, Pregnancy).

Shape of the Body—(See Beautiful, Crooked, Form, Handsome, Ill-formed, Monsters, Stature, Ugly, Well-formed, etc. Also see "Dogs" in this section).

Short-lived—(See "Short Life" in Sec. 3 of this Article).

Sickly Children—Vitality Low—Weak Constitution—Much Sickness Among—Unhealthy, etc.—The ☉, ♅, ♄, or ♂ in the 5th H. and affl.; the ☉ affl. in the 5th H., and espec. if benefics are not also in the 5th H., or in good asp. the ☉; the ☉, ☽, or ☿ in the 5th H., and affl. by malefics; the ☉ or malefics in the 5th or 11th H., and affl.; the ☽ in 5th H., and affl. by ♄ and ♀, and these latter two planets being in ☌; the ☽ and ♀ afflicting each other at childbirth; the ☽ in the 5th H., and affl. by ♄, and with no good asps. of the benefics, much sickness among; ψ or ♅ affl. in 5th H. of a parent; ♅, ♄, or ♂ in the fruitful, or prolific signs, in map of parent, but supported by the good asps. of benefics; ♄ in 5th H., and ill-asp. by the ☉ or ☽; ♄ or ♂ to the cusp the 5th H. by dir.; ♄ or ♂ affl. in the 5th H.; ♋ affl. in 5th H. of parent; ruler of Asc. in 6th H., and affl. by lord of 8th, and with no assistance from benefics; lord of 5th H. weak and affl.; lord of the 5th H. in the 6th or 8th, and affl.; lord of the 6th H. in the 5th H., the children are afflicted; lord of the 10th H. a malefic, and in the 5th. (See "Reared", "Short-lived", "Unhealthy", and the various paragraphs in this section. See Constitution; "Ill Health All Thru Life" under Ill-Health; Recuperation, Resistance; "Much Sickness" under Sickness; "Low" under Vitality; "Weak Body" under Weak).

Sickly, But Will Be Reared — (See "Reared" in this section).

Sickness — Lives Thru Sickness and Thrives — Fiery signs upon the Asc. at B., and the hyleg well-asp.; also Airy signs upon Asc. at B., or ♏, give good vitality and endurance, and to live thru sickness, where others with weak signs on Asc., and the hyleg badly affl., are more apt to succumb. (See Resistance, Stamina, Tone, Vitality. For the influences causing Much Sickness, see "Sickly", "Weak", in this section. Also see "Much Sickness" under Sickness).

Sickness of Children Generally — Malefic planets lord of the year at the Vernal, and posited in the 5th or 11th H. (See Childhood, Infancy, Mortality).

Skin — Diseases of — (See Eruptions, Skin).

Slow Growth — (See Diminished, Dwarf, Growth, Retarded, Slow, Suppressions).

Smallpox; Some Perfect — Some Imperfect — (See "Perfect" in Sec. 1 of this Article).

Spasms — (See Fits, Spasmodic; "Dentition" under Teeth).

Stamina; Stature; Sterility In — Born Barren — (See Barrenness, Impotency).

Stomach Trouble — (See Digestion, Indigestion, Nutrition, Stomach).

Strength — (1) The Strength Increased — Benefics or the ☽ in the 5th or 11th H. at B., and well-asp.; fiery signs upon the Asc. at B. (2) Strength Decreased — Malefics in the 5th or 11th H. of a parent, and affl.; ♋, ♑, or ♓ upon the Asc. of the child at B. (See Stamina, Recuperation, Resistance, Stamina, Strength, Strong, Vitality, Weak, etc.).

Strong — ♑ upon Asc. at B., the child is not strong in early years. Fiery signs upon Asc. give strength and greater vitality all thru life. (See "Strength" in this section).

Suckling Children — (See "Nursing" in this section).

Suffers — The Child Suffers — Health Will Suffer — A weak sign upon the Asc. at B., as ♋, ♑, or ♓, and the ruler of the Asc. or the hyleg affl. (See "Afflicted", and the various paragraphs in this section and Article).

Suffocation — (See "Birth" under Asphyxia).

Summer Complaint — (See "Cholera Infantum" under Cholera. Also see Bowels, Diarrhoea).

Suppressions — Suppressed Growth — Suppressed Mentality — Suppressed Functions, etc. — (See "Growth", "Mind" in this section. Also see Functions, Suppressions).

Teeth — Troubles with Dentition — Bad — Teeth — (See Teeth).

Thin and Puny — (See "Puny" in this section. Also see Emaciated, Thin, Weak).

Tonsils — Disorders of — (See Tonsils).

Unhealthy Children — Sickly — Planets which grant children being in barren signs and places, beneath the malefics, or in such signs as ♌ or ♍, may give children, but they will tend to be weakly, unhealthy, and short-lived; the ☉ and Givers of Children in barren and masculine signs, and the malefics elevated above them; ♄ in the 5th H. and affl. (See "Sickly" in this section; "Early Death" in Sec. 3 of this Article; "Low" under Vitality; "Weak Body" under Weak).

Unusual Diseases — ♅ in the 5th H. and affl. in map of parent. (See Extraordinary; "Infections" under Infancy; Uncommon, Unusual, etc.).

Virile Members — Excessive — (See Virile).

Vitality — For the various degrees of Vitality, see Vitality. Also see "Vitality" under Infancy; "Long Life", "Short Life", and "No Duration of Life" under Life. See Recuperation, Resistance, Stamina, Strength, Strong, Tone, Weak, etc.).

Walk — (See "Child" under Walk).

Watery Diseases — ♆ in the 5th H. of parent. (See Watery).

Weak Body — (See "Weak" under Constitution, Infancy; "Ill-Favored Body" under Ill; "Ill-Health All Thru Life" under Ill-Health; "Much Sickness" under Sickness; "Low" under Recuperation, Resistance, Vitality).

Whooping Cough — (See Whooping).

Wild Nature — Savage — (See "Dogs" in this section).

Worms; Wounds To — (See "Accidents" in this section).

Youth — Early Youth — (See Youth). For diseases and afflictions which may not be listed here, look for the subject in the alphabetical arrangement.

— SECTION THREE —

DEATH OF CHILDREN — Duration of Life, etc. —

Accident — Death By — (See "Accidents" in Sec. 2 of this Article).

Adult Life — Not Apt To Live To — (See "Death" under Childhood, Infancy, Youth; "Early Death" under Death. Also see "Early Death", "One May Live To Adult Life", and the various paragraphs in the section).

All May Die in Infancy — (See Infancy).

Birth — (1) Death at Birth — ♅ in ♏ sometimes causes death at birth by injury in delivery. Males born at an eclipse of the ☉, or females at an eclipse of the ☽, or immediately after, often die at birth, or live but a few hours. (See "Accidents" under Infancy; Eclipses). (2) Dies Soon After Birth— (See this subject under Infancy).

Born Almost Dead—Lives But a Few Hours or Days—The ☉ or ☽ in angles in ⚹ asp., and two or more malefics in □ to the ☉ or ☽, or ♄ ⚹ ♂ occupying the other two angles, and in □ to the ☉ and ☽, and the child will live as many hours or days as there are degrees between the Prorogator and the nearest malefic; the ☉ and ☽ in angles in □ asp. malefics, and the Lights receiving no help from the benefics, and also the malefics elevated above the benefics; the ☉ ☍ ☽, and malefics in □ to the ☉ and ☽, being a double ⚹, the child will live if, under such an ⚹, the ☉ or ☽ are preceded by ♃ and ♀, and the ☉ or ☽ be separating, but the child will be weakly, and be apt to die early, and when the first evil asp. occurs between the Hyleg and Anareta; benefics in the Asc., 5th or 11th H., and affl. by malefics; planets which promise children being under the Western horizon at B. (See "Death Soon After Birth" under Infancy. Also note the various paragraphs in this section).

Born Dead—(See Stillborn).

Buries His Children—(See "Loss of" in this section).

Boy Born at Solar Eclipse—May Die —(See Eclipse).

Calamity—From the Moment of Birth —(See Calamity).

Childbirth—Death of Child or Mother In—(See "Birth" in this section. Also see Parturition).

Childhood—Death In—(See Childhood. Also note the various paragraphs in this section). Does Not Live Beyond Childhood—(See "Early Death", and the various paragraphs in this section. See "Early Death" under Early; "Short Life" under Life).

Children Born But They Die—The benefic and malefic planets mixed in the houses of children; the 5th H. affl. in the mother's horoscope, and espec. if also in the Child's map the ☉ or ☽ are afflicted.

Children Die Young—(See "Early Death" in this section).

Danger of Death of a Child—The ☉ to the ill-asps. the ☽ by dir. in map of parent; the ☽ to the ill-asps. ♄ by dir.; ♅ affl. in the 5th H., and it is usually the first child; ♄ affl. in the 5th or 11th H.; ♄ to the ill-asps. ♀ by dir.; ♂ affl. in the 5th H.; the M.C. to the □ or ☍ ☿, and ☿ affl. at B. (See the various paragraphs in this section).

Daughter May Die—When born at time of an eclipse of the ☽. (See Eclipse).

Days—Lives Only a Few Hours or Days—(See "Born Almost Dead" in this section).

Death at Birth—(See "Birth" in this section).

Death Immediately After Birth—Not Susceptible to Nurture—(See "Nurture" under Infancy. Also see "Born Almost Dead" in this section).

Death of Children—♄ in the 5th or 11th H.; lord of the 5th peregrine in

the 8th H. denotes the death of the child in Hor'y Q.; a child born at the instant of a Full ☽ dies, it is said, at the next New ☽. A child born at the New or Full ☽ rarely lives unless the benefics give a favorable aspect. (See "Loss of", and the various paragraphs in this section).

Death of Some—(See "Some May Die" in this section).

Death Premature—(See "Premature", "Untimely", in this section. See "Eight Months Children" in Sec. 1 of this Article).

Death Soon After Birth—(See "Born Almost Dead" in this section; "Death Soon After Birth", and "Nurture" under Infancy).

Dentition—Child May Die from Spasms During—(See "Dentition" under Teeth).

Destroys the Children—♄ in the 5th H. in all signs except ♊, ♍, ♎, or ♑, and affl.; ♄ or ♂ ☍ ♃ destroys some; ☿ in the 5th H. in a barren sign and affl. (See "Death of", "Some May Die", and the various paragraphs in this section).

Die—Will the Child Live or Die?— (See "Signs of Death" under Infancy).

Die Before Maturity—(See Maturity. Also see the various paragraphs in this section, and under Childhood, Infancy, Youth).

Die in Infancy—Or Childhood—(See Infancy, Childhood).

Die in Womb—(See Stillborn).

Directions—Primary Directions, Secondary Directions, Progressions, Transits, New Moons, Lunations, etc., and the Death of Children—Before the age of 3 years, children are killed by the radical positions in their maps. After 3 years of age they are killed by directions. Children with weak and evil maps usually die when the ☽ by transit or direction reaches a malefic, and espec. in the 4th H., the house of the grave and close of life, or in the 6th or 8th H. Much depends upon the vitality, and also the indications in the maps of the parents as to whether the child will live or die. The signs ♋, ♑ or ♓ on the Asc. at B. tend to lower the vitality, and evil directions are more liable to kill in early life. The New ☽ is critical in infancy and tends to much infant mortality, and the Longitude of each succeeding New ☽ after birth should be noted, and the aspects it forms to the radical map. The evil directions of the ☽ should be carefully studied, and also the transits of malefics over the afflicted portions of the radical figure. (See Directions, Eclipses; "New Moon" under Moon; Transits). In the nativities of children, the influences of evil directions which do not disturb the health, fall on the parents, the Guardian, or the Family. (See Family, Guardian, Parents).

Dissipation—Children Die Young Thru Dissipation and Passional Excesses— The 9° ♓ on the Asc. at B. (See Debauched, Dissipation).

Early Death of Children—Children Die Young—Of Short Life, etc.—The ☉ and givers of children in masculine and barren signs, and malefics elevated above them; the ☉ in evil asp. to the ruler of 5th H., or to ♅ or ♄ in the 5th; the ☉ or ☽ hyleg and ♂ a malefic at B., and with no assistance to the hyleg from the benefics; children given or allotted by the ☉, ♅, ♄, or ♂ are apt to die early; the ☉ and ☽ angular and conjoined with malefics; the ☉, ♅, ♄, or ☿ in the 5th H. and affl.; rulers of the Lights in the 6th or 8th H.; the ☉ affl. by ♄, danger in early years; the ☽ in the husband's horoscope, and the ☉ in the wife's nativity, applying to ♅, ♄, or ☋ in the 5th H.; ♅ affl. the ☉, ☽, or Asc., and elevated above the Luminaries; ♄ affl. in the 5th H., the untimely death of children; ♂ affl. in the 5th H., or affl. the ☉ or ☽ from this house, some die early and suddenly; the malefics in feminine, or prolific signs, even tho supported by benefics at B., the first train of evil directions to the malefics, or to the hyleg after birth, tend to kill; the malefics angular and oriental, affl. the ruler of the 5th H., or planets in the 5th, and with no assistance from benefics to the givers of children; a malefic on the Asc., affl. by lord of the 8th, and the ☽ also affl. by the ☉, ♄, or ♂, the child soon dies; a malefic on the Asc., and affl. by lord of the 8th, and also the ☉ or ☽ affl. at B.; the hyleg at B. severely affl. by ♄, or ♂, and with no good asps. from the benefics; lord of the Asc. in the 5th, and affl. by ♄, ♂, or ☋; lord of the 7th, 11th, or 12th H. a malefic, and in the 5th H. and affl.; the 5th H. affl. in the mother's map, and the ☉ and ☽ both affl. in the child's map; ♋, ♑, or ♓ on the Asc. at B., and the hyleg severely affl. by malefics; malefics in the 5th or 11th H. at B., and affl., or afflicting the hyleg. Unless the hyleg is much afflicted an early death is not necessarily shown. (See "Death" under Infancy, Childhood; "Early Death" under Death; "Short Life" under Life, and also note the various paragraphs in this section. For the early death of Parents, see Adopted, Orphans, Parents).

Early Life—The Early Years of Life—Danger of Death In—♑ on the Asc., or the ☉ or ☽ affl. in ♑, tends to make the early years weak, lacking in animal heat, and with greater danger of death, and to give a weak body; lord of the 6th H. in the Asc., and affl., and espec. with ♑ on the Asc.; the 19° ♓ on the Asc. (See Childhood, Infancy; "Short Life" under Life. Also note the various paragraphs in this section). The hyleg must be severely affl. at B., and by dir., to cause death in early life and childhood, and a good asp. from ♃ or ♀ in the configuration will tend to save the life.

Eclipses—A male born at an eclipse of the ☉, or a female at an eclipse of the ☽, are in danger of immediate, or early death. (See Eclipses).

Eighth Month—Birth At, and Usually Resulting in Death—(See "Eight Months Children" in Sec. 1 of this Article).

Extraordinary Death—Of Children—♅ in the 5th H. of a parent, and espec. the mother. (See Extraordinary).

Father—Early Death of—(See Father).

Female Children—Death of When Born at an Eclipse of the ☽. (See Eclipses).

Few Live—But Few Live—(See "All May Die in Infancy", and "But Few Live", under Infancy).

Fifteen Years of Age—Death At—Case—See "Elizabeth", Case No. 654 in 1001 N.N.

Fifth House—This is the principal house of children in the map of parents, and malefics affl. in this house tend to death of the children, or to bring much sorrow thru them. (See Fifth House).

Five Years of Age—Death Before or at This Age—Child Apt to Die at This Age—♅, ♄, or ♂ ruling the places of the ☉ or ☽ at B., and the benefics affl.; ♅, ♄, or ♂ in the 1st H. at B., and the ☉ or ☽ ♂ a malefic in the 6th, 8th, or 12th H.; a malefic exactly midway between the ☉ and ☽, and the rulers of the ☉ and ☽ controlled by a malefic, and with no assistance from benefics in the configuration. (See "Death" under Infancy; "Early Death", in this section).

Four Years of Age—Apt to Die at About This Age—The ☽ sepr. from a benefic, and applying to the ♂, P., or ill-asp. a malefic, the child will hardly attain more than 4 years.

Fourteen Years of Age—Possible Death At—Case—See "France", No. 533 in 1001 N.N.

Fourth Child—Possible Death of—Malefics in the 10th H. of the mother, or in the 11th H. of the father. (See "First Born" in Sec. 1 of this Article).

Great Mortality Among—(See "Mortality" in this section).

Healthy and Long-lived—(See "Long-lived" in Sec. 2 of this Article).

Hours—Lives But a Few Hours or Days—(See "Born Almost Dead" in this section; "Nurture" under Infancy).

Immediately Dies After Birth—(See "Death Immediately" in this section).

Infancy—Death In—All May Die In Infancy—Some Die In Infancy—(See the various paragraphs under Infancy).

Injury at Birth—Possible Death From—(See "Accidents" under Infancy, Parturition).

Kill—Evil Directions More Liable to Kill—(See "Directions" in this section).

Life Prolonged—In weak nativities, and where the vitality is low, life may be prolonged if ♃ or ♀ are in the Asc. at B., and not severely afflicted, and also at the same time in favorable asp. to the hyleg, or if the lord of the Asc. is free from affliction and well-placed, and these influences may save the life of the child, or considerably prolong life, even tho a train of evil directions may be operating. (See Recuperation, Resistance, Vitality).

Live—Will Live and Be Healthy— (See "Long-lived" in this section). Will the Child Live or Die?—(See "Signs of Death" under Infancy).

Lives But Short Time—A Few Hours or Days—(See "Born Almost Dead" in this section; "Nurture" under Infancy).

Long Life—Healthy and Long-lived— (See "Long-lived" in Sec. 2 of this Article. Also see "Long Life" under Life).

Loss of Children—Loses Many Children—Buries His Children—The ☉ in the 5th H. and affl., and espec. unless ♃, ♀, or the ☽ be also in the 5th, or in good asp. to the ☉; the ☉ to the ill-asps. the ☽ by dir.; the ☽ in the 5th H., and affl. by ♄, ♂, or ♀; the ☽ in the 10th or 4th H., and affl. by malefics; the ☽ in the 5th H., and affl. by any planet in the 8th or 12th H.; the ☽ to the ill-asps. ☿ by dir., and the ☽ or ☿ affl. by a malefic at B.; ♅, ♄, ♂, or ♋ in the 5th H., and espec. in ♌ or ♍; ♅, ♄, ♂, or the ☉ in the 5th or 11th H., and affl.; ♄ in the 5th H., and affl., and espec. ill-aspected by the ☽; ♄ affl. in the 11th H.; ♄ affl. by ♃ threatens loss of offspring; if children are promised, yet if ♄ or ♂ be in the 5th H., and espec. in ♌ or ♍, loses many children; ♂ in the 5th H., and affl. by the ☉, ☽, ♅ or ♄; ♂ affl. in ♌ or ♍ in the 5th H.; ☿ affl. at B., and the ☽ to the ill-asps. ☿ by dir.; ☿ in the 5th H., and affl. by malefics; malefics in the 5th or 11th H.; ruler of the 5th H. in ☌ ruler of the 8th H., or affl. by malefics; lord of the 8th H. in the 5th H. (See "Death", "Destroys", and other paragraphs in this section).

Majority Will Die—Most Will Die In Early Years—Malefics in the 5th or 11th H., and affl.; lord of the 5th H. in the 6th or 8th H. and affl.; lord of the 5th in the 8th, and affl. by lord of the 8th; lord of the Asc. in the 6th, and affl. by lord of the 8th, and with no assistance from benefics. (See "All May Die in Infancy" under Infancy).

May Have Children But They Die— (See "Children Born But They Die" in this section).

Middle Life—Dies Young, or Before Middle Life—(See "Early Death" under Early; "Dies Before Middle Life" under Middle Life; "Short Life" under Life. Also see "Early Death" in this section).

Miscarriage—Death By—(See Abortion, Miscarriage, Parturition, Premature).

Moment of Birth—Calamity From— Death At—(See Calamity. Also see "Birth" in this section).

Moon—Death of Females Born at Eclipse of—(See Eclipses; "New" and "Full Moon" under Moon).

Mortality Great—Among Children and Young People—Comets appearing in ♓; ♂ in ♉ and ℞, occi., and lord of the year at the Vernal Equi., and many die from Scarlatina and Smallpox. (See "Directions" in this section, Mortality, Scarlet Fever, Prenatal Epoch, Smallpox).

Most of Those Born Will Die—(See "Majority" in this section).

Mother—Death of Mother—(See Mother).

Mysterious Death—Ψ or ♅ in the 5th H. of parent, and espec. of the mother.

New Moon—Full Moon—Death of Female Infants Born at Time of an Eclipse—(See Eclipses; "New" and "Full Moon" under Moon. Also see "Directions" in this section).

No Duration of Life—(See "Born Almost Dead", and "Birth" in this section; "Death in Infancy" and "Nurture" under Infancy; Eclipses).

Nurse—Child Could Not Nurse and Died—Case—See "Born Incomplete" No. 281 in 1001 N.N.

Nurture—Not Susceptible to Nurture —Death Soon After Birth—(See "Nurture" under Infancy).

Old Age—Children Live To—(See Old Age).

One May Live to Adult Life—Malefics in, ruling, or aspecting the 5th or 11th H., other testimonies promising children, and with ♃ or ♀ ⚹ or △ the 10th H., or in good asp. to the ruler of the 5th or 11th. (See "Adult Life" in this section).

One or More May Die Young—The ☉, ♃, ♀ or the ☽ in the 5th H., and ill-asp. by ♄ or ♂.

Parents—Death of—Death of Caused by Children—(See Adoption, Father, Mother, Orphans, Parents. Also see "Parents", "Worries", in Sec. 1 of this Article).

Passional Excesses—Dies Young From—(See Dissipation, "Dies Before Middle Life" under Middle Life; "Passional Excesses" under Passion; Venery).

Premature Death—(See Premature, Sudden, Untimely; "Early Death" under Early; "Short Life" under Life; "Death" under Infancy, Childhood. See "Sudden" in this section).

Probable Death of Those Born—♅ ☌ or bad asp. ♄ in the 5th H., and affl. the ☉, a sure indication of the death of some; malefics in the 5th or 11th H.; ruler of the 5th H. in the 6th, 8th, or 12th H., and affl. by malefics; lord of the 8th a malefic, in the 5th, and affl.; the benefic and malefic planets mixed at B. in fruitful houses. (See "Danger", "Destroys", "Loss of", "Some May Die", and the various paragraphs in this section).

Prolonged—(See "Life Prolonged" in this section).

Radical Planets and Death — (See "Directions" in this section).

Reared With Difficulty—(See "Reared With Difficulty" in Sec. 2 of this Article).

Scarlatina—Many Children Die of, and of Smallpox—(See "Mortality Great" in this section).

Second Child Will Die—(See "First-Born" in Sec. 1 of this Article).

Short Life—Short-Lived and Sickly— Barren signs on cusp the 1st or 5th H., and other testimonies favorable, and the evil ray of a malefic fall in the place; ♄ or ☋ in the 5th H., or ♄ or ♂ in evil asp. to the 5th and its lord, and other testimonies give children; ♂ affl. in the 5th H., if any children; the Sigs. or Benefics in barren signs, if any children they are short-lived (Hor'y). (See "Early Death", and other paragraphs in this section. See "Short Life" under Life; "Death" under Infancy, Childhood, Youth).

Short Time—Lives But a Short Time —Dies Within a Few Hours or Days— (See "Born Almost Dead", "Death Immediately", and other paragraphs in this section).

Shorter Will Be the Life — (See "Shorter" under Infancy).

Sickly, But Will Be Reared—(See "Reared" in Sec. 2 of this Article).

Sickness—Lives Thru and Thrives— (See "Long-Lived", "Sickness", in Sec. 2 of this Article).

Signs of Death—Of Children—(See "Signs of Death" under Infancy; "Arguments for Death" under Death).

Smallpox—Many Die of—(See "Mortality" in this section).

Solar Eclipse—Death of Males Born At—(See Eclipses).

Some May Die—The ☽ in the 10th or 4th H., and affl. by malefics; ♄ or ♂ in the 5th H., and affl. the ☉ or ☽; ♄ or ♂ ☍ ♃ destroys some; ♃, ♀, or the ☽ in the 5th or 11th H., and affl. by malefics; ♀ ☍ ♃ or ♂ tends to destroy some; malefics in fruitful signs in the 5th or 11th H. (See "Probable Death" in this section; "Some Die" under Infancy).

Son Born May Die—If Born at Time of Solar Eclipse—Male May Die if First-Born—(See Eclipses; "First-Born" in Sec. 1 of this Article).

Spasms—Death By—Death By During Dentition—(See Fits; "Dentition" under Teething).

Stillborn—(See Stillborn).

Sudden Death Of—♅ affl. in ♌ or 5th H. of the parent; ♂ in the 5th H., and affl. the ☉ or ☽. (See "Extraordinary" in this section. Also see "Sudden Death" under Death).

Sun—Males Die Born at Eclipse of— (See Eclipses).

Teething—Death During—(See "Dentition" under Teeth).

Third Child—Possible Death of—(See "First-Born" in Sec. 1 of this Article).

Three Years of Life—Possible Death Before the Third Year—Death After the Third Year—(See "Directions" in this section).

Time of Death — (See "Directions", "Early Death", and the various paragraphs in this section. See "Death" under Childhood, Infancy, Youth. See "Time" under Death).

Two Months—Death at Two Months of Age—Case—See "Born in a Flood", No. 227 in 1001 N.N. Various Cases and Birth Data of Death in Infancy are given under Infancy.

Undertime Children — Possible Death of—(See "Eight Months Children" in Sec. 1 of this Article).

Violent Death—Danger of—Lord of the 8th H. a malefic, and in the 5th H., and affl. (See Violent).

Vitality—For the various degrees of Vitality, see Constitution; "Animal Heat" under Heat; Recuperation, Resistance, Stamina, Strength, Strong, Tone, Vitality, Weak, etc. See "Vitality" under Infancy.

Weak Body—Weak Nativities and Death—(See "Directions" in this section. Also see "Weak Body" under Weak).

Will the Child Live?—Or Die?—(See "Signs of Death" under Infancy).

Womb — Dies in the Womb — (See Abortion, Miscarriage, Stillborn).

Young—Dies Young—(See "Early Death", and the various paragraphs in this section. See "Death" under Childhood, Infancy; "Short Life" under Life).

Youth—Dies in Early Youth—(See Youth).

CHILL—Chill and Cold—Chills—Cold— This subject is largely considered under COLD. (See Cold). Chill is a ♄ influence and affliction. Chill of the surface is due to cold, and ♄ influence, and drives the blood inwards, causing internal congestions, colds, and diseases resulting therefrom. The part of the body most liable to be affected by chills and cold is denoted by the sign and house of ♄ at B., and varies in severity according to the malignancy of the vibration, and the strength of the aspect in any particular case. ♄ in ♑ tends to chills and cold, and people born under this influence should wear warm clothing, and woolen underwear, if necessary, as wool helps to counteract the ♄ influence, and keep the temperature of the surface even.

Death by Chill and Cold—Denoted by ♄. (See "Death" under Cold).

Disorders Arising from Chill—And Cold—The ☽ in ♓ tends to chills and colds which fly to the lungs; denoted by the ☽ when the ☽ afflicts the ☉ or Asc. at B., or by dir.; women tend to suffer with fever from chills and colds under the asp. of the ☽ to the ☌ the ☉ by dir.; ♆, ♅, or ♄ in ♓, and affl. the ☉ or ☽; ♄ affl. in ♈, ♉, ♋, or ♑; ♄ ☌, P, ☐ or ☍ the Asc.; the ♑ sign on the Asc., or on cusp of 6th H., predisposes to chill and colds; Subs at CP, and KP, violent shaking from chill or chills. Chills also accompany Acute Fevers, Nervous Conditions, Prostration and Weakness, due to the strong afflictions of ♄. (For Irregularities of the System Arising from Chills and Cold, see "Acute Fevers" under Acute; Centripetal, Chilblain; "Epidemics" under Cholera; Chronic; "Diseases Arising from Cold", and "Cold Diseases" under Cold; Colds; "Deafness" under Hearing; "Chills" under Nerves; Saturn Diseases).

Functions—The Functions Suppressed By Cold—The ☽ affl. by ♄. (See Functions).

Internal Diseases—Arising From Chill and Cold—♄ ☌, P, ☐ or ☍ the ☉, internal disorders arising from chill, cold, neglect and privation. (See Congestion; "Congestions" under Internal). For further influences see the various paragraphs under Cold.

CHIN—The Mentum—Lower Jaw—The Chin is ruled by ♀ and the ♉ sign. Also ♀ when in ♈ rules and affects the Chin. (See Appearance, Face).

Beard—The chin beard is ruled by ♉. When ☿ is ascending at B., and free from the rays of other planets, there is little hair, or beard, on the chin. (See Beard).

Dimple in Chin—(See "Chin" under Dimples).

Face—The Face Narrows Down to the Chin—(See "Falling In" under Cheeks; Decanates; "Thin Face" under Face).

Jaws—(See "Lower Jaw" under Jaws).

Long Chin—Long, Narrow, Pointed, Protruding—♆ rising in the Asc., a pointed chin; ☿ gives a narrow chin, and with ☿ rising and free from the rays of other planets; ♑ on the Asc. at B., narrow, and often protruding like that of the Goat, which animal is the symbol of the ♑ sign.

Marks—Moles—Scars on Chin—Planets in ♉, and espec. ♄ or ♂ in ♉; the 2° ♉ on the Asc., a mark near the left side of the chin. (See Marks).

Narrow Chin—(See "Long" in this section. Also see Decanates).

Pointed Chin—Protruding—(See "Long" in this section).

Receding Chin—♍ on the Asc. at B.

Scar On—(See "Marks" in this section).

Short Chin—The ☉ influence denotes; the ☉ in ♉; the ☉ as Sig. of the person in Hor'y Questions.

Thin Chin—☿ ascending at B., and free from the rays of other planets (See Beard, Cheeks, Face, Hair, Jaws, Lips).

CHIROPRACTORS — (See Healers, Sublaxations, Vertebrae).

CHLOASMA — (See "Pigmentation" under Skin).

CHLORIDE OF POTASSIUM — (See Potassium).

Sodium Chloride—(See Sodium).

CHLOROFORM—A typical drug of ♆. (See Anaesthetics, Neptune).

CHLOROSIS—Green Sickness—A form of Anaemia common in young women, and attended with menstrual disturbances, and a greenish color of the skin. A ☽ and ♋ sign disease; ♄ affl. in ♋; attended with Subs at SP, KP 11th Dorsal), and at PP. (See Anaemia, Menses).

CHOKING — (See Asphyxia, Cough, Drowning, Hanging, Phlegm, Strangulation, Suffocation, Throat, etc.).

CHOLAGOGUE—A Remedy That Promotes the Flow of Bile—Podophyllin, ruled by ☿, and also the Mercurials, are types of this group. (See Bile, Mercury, Physic, Podophyllin).

CHOLER—Bile—The Gall—A Bilious Complaint—Cholic—etc. Anger is also spoken of sometimes as Choler. ♂ causes diseases arising from too much choler.

Choleric Temperament—The Bilious Temperament—(See Choleric). For further influences about Choler, see Anger, Bile, Cholera; "High Temper" under Temper, etc.).

Diseases Arising from Choler—Caused by the fiery signs; lords of the 1st, 6th, or the ☽ in fiery signs. (See Anger, Choleric).

CHOLERA—Asiatic Cholera—A disease characterized by diarrhoea, vomiting, cramps and pains in the bowels, and prostration. This is principally a ♍, ♏, and ♂ disease. Workers in copper mines are usually free from Cholera. The Hindus wear a copper amulet to ward off Cholera. Copper is a ♀ remedy, opposed to ♂, and a good remedy and antidote for Cholera. In Hungary a copper plate is worn next to the skin against Cholera.

Asiatic Cholera—A Malignant Form of Cholera—A ♍ disease, and afflictions in ♍; ♂ affl. in ♍. (See "Causes" in this section).

Causes of Cholera—Afflictions in ♍; a ♍ disease; the ☽ affl. in ♍, or affl. the hyleg therefrom; ♂ in ♍ in the 6th H., and affl.; ♂ in ♍, and having the sole dominion at a Solar Eclipse; ♅ in ♍ in the 8th H. at a Solar Ingress of the ☉ into ♈, and affl. the ☽ or planet ascending; ☿ affl. in ♒; the ☉ to the ☌ or ill-asp. ♂ by dir.; violent ♅ or ♂ afflictions involving the ♍ and ♏ signs; Subs at CP, SP, KP, Li.P. and PP. (See the paragraphs in this section).

Cholera Infantum — Infectious Diarrhoea—Summer Cholera—Summer Complaint—♂ or the ☽ affl. in ♍ at B., and espec. when in the 6th H. (See "Death" in this section. Also see Diarrhoea).

Cholera Morbus—Sporadic Cholera—Bilious Cholera—English Cholera—An acute catarrhal inflammation of the mucous membrane of both the stomach and intestines. Caused by ♂ affl. in ♋ or ♍, in the 6th H., and affl. by a ♂ direction. The symptoms of this disease are much the same as in Asiatic Cholera, but the Bacillus of Koch is absent.

Cholera Pains—(See "Cramps" in this section).

Cholera Prevalent—Occurs at times of a Solar Eclipse, and the ☉ or ☽ affl. by ♅, ♄, or ♂; ♅ in the 8th H. at times of great conjunctions, as ♄ ☌ ♂; ☿ affl. in ♍ at the Vernal Equi., and lord of the year, so afflicts Peoples and Places under ♍. (See "Epidemics" in this section).

Cholerine—A Mild Form of Cholera—A ♍ disease, and afflictions in ♍, but with the other configurations less violent in their effects. Caused by Subs, and other influences, as given under "Causes" in this section).

Cramps—Cholera Cramps and Pains in the Bowels—The ☉ to the ☌ or ill-asps. ♂ by dir.; the ☽ in ♈, ♍, or ♑, and affl. by the ☉ or ♂ when taken ill; ♂ affl. in ♍ in the 6th H. (See Cramps).

Death from Cholera—The ☽ affl. in ♍, or affl. the hyleg therefrom; ♅ in ♍ in the 8th H. at a Solar Ingress of the ☉ into ♈, and affl. the ☽, or planet ascending; ♂ in ♍, and having the sole dominion at a Solar Eclipse. Case of Death by Infantile Cholera—See "Short Life", No. 371 in 1001 N.N.

Diarrhoea—(See Diarrhoea).

Epidemics—Cholera Epidemics usually occur when one of the major planets is in perihelion (nearest the ☉) in its orbit. Its spread is due to vitiated atmospheric conditions. It spreads faster than human means of travel, and one Epidemic may quickly encircle the Globe when ♄ or ♃ are in perihelion, and in other years, when no planets are in perihelion, it usually remains in or near its birthplace, which is India. Its germination is dependent upon atmospheric conditions caused by planetary influences, and is not local, or due to insanitation, as commonly believed. The orbit of ♃ is 12 years, and every 12 years he is in perihelion, and Cholera has broken out in India every 12 years for Centuries, and under the influence of ♃ in perihelion. These same influences also tend to cause Floods, Volcanic Eruptions, Earthquakes, which surface changes tend to decomposition and fermentation of vegetation, to vitiate the atmosphere, and produce Chills, Fever, Typhoid, and to lower the vitality of the inhabitants. Cholera also occurs epidemically when ♂ is in perigee, and at the same time in ☍ the ☉, which is once every 15 years. (See Air).

Immunity To—(See Immunity).

Infantile Cholera—Death By—(See "Death" in this section).

Sporadic Cholera — (See "Cholera Morbus" in this section). See Epidemics, Pestilence, Plague).

Summer Cholera—Summer Complaint —(See "Cholera Infantum" in this section).

CHOLERIC—Related to the Choler, or Bile. ♈, ♌, and ♐ are classed as the Choleric Signs.

Choleric Distemper—The ☽ to the ☌ or ill-asp. ♂ by dir.; ♃ affl. in ♐, and arising from putrefaction of the blood; a ♂ disease.

Choleric Humours—A ♂ disease; ♂ affl. in ♌ or ♍; the ☽ to the ☌ or ill-asp. ♂ by dir. (See Humours).

Choleric Passion—The ☽ in ♐, and affl. by the ☉ or ♂ when taken ill.

Choleric Temperament—Bilious Temperament—A Hot and Dry Temperament—Hot and Dry Body—Ruled by the ☉, ♂, and the Fiery Signs, and is a temperament of action. Tends to make one hasty, fiery, irascible, excitable, feverish, easily angered, and subject to bilious and inflammatory affections. Produced principally by ♂, and ♂ affl. in the fiery signs at B.; ♂ in ill-asp. the ☉ at B., and by dir.; the ☉ ☌ ♂ at B.; the ☽ to the ☌ or ill-asp.

♂ by dir.; the sign ascending, or its lord, in fiery signs; ♄ in ♐ in partile asp. the Asc., rather choleric. (See Anger, Bile, Cholic, Excitable, Fevers, Imprudent, Impulsiveness, Temperament).

CHOLIC—Pertaining to the Bile. May also refer to Cramps, or Painful Affections About the Gall Bladder, or Bilious Attacks. (See Bile, Cholic, Cramps).

CHOLOLITHIASIS—(See "Gall Stones" under Bile).

CHONDROMA — A Cartilaginous Tumor—(See Cartilage).

CHOREA—(See Saint Vitus Dance).

CHOROID—The Second, or Vascular Tunic of the Eye.

Choroiditis—Inflammation of the Choroid—A ☉ disease; the ☉ affl. in ♈. (See Eyes).

CHRONIC DISEASES — Long, Tedious, Protracted, Slow, Lingering, Deep-Seated, Permanent, Enduring, Sub-Acute, Morbid Diseases, etc., and attended usually with a Decline, Low Fever, Wasting, Decay Emaciation, Crystallization, Hardening, or a Consumption in some part of the body. All Cold, Lingering, and Chronic Diseases are produced by ♄, and espec. when ♄ is in the 6th H. at B., and affl. the hyleg or Asc. Chronic Diseases usually begin in Winter, from cold and chilling of the skin, or surface, driving the blood inwards, and causing internal congestions, the result of ♄ influence, as ♄ rules Cold. (See Centripetal, Chill, Cold, Congestions). In Greek Mythology ♄ is called "Kronos", from which our word "Chronic" is taken. The 12th H. and ♄ have general rule over Chronic Diseases, and those which tend to become morbid. While Permanent Diseases proceed from ♄, their course is regulated by the motion of the ☉, and it is very essential to watch the aspects to, or afflictions to the ☉, to give a prognosis, or forecast, concerning the probable outcome of a chronic disease. The course of Acute Diseases is ruled by the ☽. (See "Crises" under Acute). Chronic Diseases begin their action in the Ganglionic Centers, and all remedies indicated in chronic diseases must begin their action in these centers. (See Ganglion). Diseases indicated by the radical map tend to become chronic, or sub-acute, and espec. when afflicting planets are in the Occidental Quarters, between the Nadir and Asc., and between the Midheaven and Descendant at B., and are usually organic, constitutional, hereditary, or structural diseases. Acquired Diseases, and those of shorter duration, are the result of Directions, rather than from the indications of the map of birth. An Acute Disease which reaches the 28th day, or the Fourth Quarter of the ☽ from the time the disease began, will either resolve itself, or go into the chronic form. Thus any acute disease may become chronic, and run on indefinitely, eventually become cured, or end in death, according to the amount of vitality, resistance, recuperating power, etc. It would consume too much time and space to list all the names of diseases in this section, which may be chronic, and will ask you to look in the alphabetical arrangement for the special disease you have in mind. The more general subjects concerning chronic diseases will be taken up in this section.

Causes of Chronic Diseases—The SUN affl. in ♍, as ♍ courts diseases, as a rule, and tends to hold onto it longer (See Virgo); the ☉ hyleg, and to the ☌ or ill-asp. ♄ by dir.; the ☉ in the 12th H. at the Vernal Equi., lord of the year, and espec. if the ☉ is in the 6th, 8th or 12th H. at B., or the ☉ or ♄ in the 12th H. at a Solar Rev.; the ☉ affl. in the 6th or 12th H.; the ☉ occi. at B., and affl. by ♄; the ☉ or ♄ in the 6th H., or either in the 6th in □ or ☍ to each other, denotes heavy affliction; the ☉ in ♋ and affl. by ♄; the ☉ affl. in ♍; the ☉ in the 6th H. unless well-aspected; the ☉, ☽, and many planets in fixed signs at B.; the ☉ and ♄ in P. asp. by Progression; the progressed ☉ to the ☌ or ill-asp. the radical ♄; the ☉ ill-asp. by the ☽ at B., and espec. when ♄ also afflicts the ☉, ☽, Asc., or hyleg in the radix; evil Solar directions to Promittors tend to cause ill-health for a period of four years, two years before the completion of the asp., and two years after, and bad Lunar asps. coinciding with adverse Solar asps. will intensify the evil. In female nativities the ☉ causes chronic troubles when affl. the hyleg. The MOON to the ☌ or ill-asp. ♄ by dir., and the ☽ hyleg at B., and affl., tends to all lingering diseases, according to the nature of ♄ and the sign he occupies; the ☽ in the 6th H. at B., and affl. by malefics; the ☽ affl. in earthy signs tends to Agues, Consumptions, and other Melancholic Diseases; the ☽ to the ☌ or ill-asp. ♆ by dir., wasting chronic diseases; the ☽ decr. at B., sepr. from ♃, and applying to ♄, frequent chronic ailments; the ☽ affl. in the 6th H. in an earthy sign; the ☽ in a fixed sign at B., and affl., and applying to ♄ in a Solar Rev.; the ☽ hyleg in ♑ in a female nativity, and affl.; NEPTUNE in the 1st, 6th, 8th or 12th houses at B., and affl.; ♆ afflictions tend espec. to wasting diseases. (See Wasting); URANUS in □ or ☍ ♄, and in parts or organs afflicted according to the Signs in at B.; ♅ ☌ ♄ in the 6th H., heavy and prolonged sickness; SATURN in the 12th H. at B., or in ♓, the 12th H. Sign, and affl. and with danger of being confined as an invalid in some Hospital, or Institution; ♄ affl. in the 6th H., chronic and deepseated; ♄ ☌, □, or ☍ the ☉, Asc., or hyleg at B., and by dir.; ♄ denotes death by chronic diseases when affl. the hyleg at B., and by dir., and holding the dominion of death; ♄ occi. at B. and affl. the hyleg by dir.; ♄ in the 6th H., and affl. the Asc. or hyleg; ♄ on the M.C. at B., in a common sign, and affl. the ☉ or ☽ by □ or ☍ asp.; ♄ ☌, P, □, or ☍ the ☉, ☽, Asc., or hyleg at B., or by dir., or to the ill-asps. these places in the radix by progression; ♄ affl. in any sign or house tends to chronic ailments and afflictions in the part ruled by such sign

or house; ♄ the sole ruler of a Solar Eclipse (see Eclipses); caused by the afflictions of ♄ to the hyleg and sensitive places of the map, when the dominion of death is vested in him; ♄ exactly rising or setting at B.; ♄ in the 12th H. at a Solar Rev., and affl.; born under the strong influence of ♄, and ♄ ill-dig., and badly aspected at B.; ♄ in the 8th H. at B., or by dir., and affl. the hyleg; ♄ lord of the 6th, R, slow of motion, and at the same time in a fixed sign at B., tends to slow and tedious diseases, and poor powers of recuperation; ♄ lord of the Asc., R, and slow motion; JUPITER to the ill-asp. ♄ by dir., and espec. if ♄ rule the 1st, 6th, 8th, or 12th H. at B.; VENUS to the ☌ or ill-asp. ♄ by dir., and espec. when ♀ holds the dominion of death and affl. the hyleg at B., and the influence of ♀ in such cases is to cause a consumption or a wasting chronic disease; ASCENDANT to the ☌ or ill-asp. ♄ by dir., and ♄ occi. at B.; the Asc. affl. by the ☌ or ill-asp. ♄ at B., and by dir.; lord of the Asc. in the 6th H., and affl. by lord of the 6th; ruler of the Asc. in the 12th H., and affl.; fixed signs on all four of the angles at B.; many afflictions from fixed signs; the Sig. in a fixed sign (see "Fixed Signs" under Fixed); ♍ on the cusp of 6th H.; earthy signs on the Asc., or cusp of 6th H., and with many planets in such signs; malefics in occi. Quarters of the map of birth indicate long and tedious sicknesses when taken ill; lord of the 6th H. a malefic, and in the 6th H.; lord of the 6th H. slow of motion, and R in a fixed sign; the afflicting planet stationary, R, or slow of motion at B., or by dir. (See the various paragraphs and references in this section).

Cold Chronic Diseases — (See "Chronic" under Cold).

Crises in Chronic Diseases—(See "Chronic Diseases" under Crises).

Dangerous Chronic Maladies—The Asc. to the ☌ or ill-asps. ♄ by dir., and ♄ occi. at B.; ♄ affl. the hyleg by dir., and also accompanied by a train of evil directions to the hyleg, or to the ☉, ☽, Asc., or M.C.

Death by Chronic Diseases—♄ occi. at B., and affl. the hyleg by dir.; ♄ in the 8th H., ruler of the 8th, or affl. the lord of the 8th, or cusp of the 8th H.; in female horoscopes the ☉ causes death by long, chronic, severe, and painful illnesses when affl. the hyleg at B., and by dir. (See "Arguments for Death", "Death More Certain", under Death; Fatal, Incurable, Lingering, Malignant, Morbid, Tedious, etc.).

Fevers — (See "Chronic" under Fevers).

Long Chronic Distempers — Fixed signs on the cusp the 6th H., or in the Moon's place; lord of the 6th a malefic, and in the 6th; lord of the Asc., or 6th H., or the ☽, be in ☌, □, or ☍ ♄ or ♂, the disease will be lasting. (See the various paragraphs and influences in this section. Also see "Fixed Signs" under Fixed; "Long Siege of Ill-Health" under Ill-Health; "Tedious Diseases" under Tedious).

Signs of a Long Disease—(See "Long" in this section). For further study, see Aches, Agues, Cold, Consumptions, Curable, Crystallization, Decay, Debility, Emaciation, Hardening, Hurts, Invalids; "Low Fevers" under Fever; Malignant, Morbid, Tuberculosis, Wastings, etc. Also see the various Organs and Parts of the Body, and also the subjects of Assimilation, Declines, Digestion, Elimination, Environment, Excretion, Functions, Fluids, Incurable, Inflammation; "Melancholic Diseases" under Melancholy; Nutrition, Organic Diseases; "Low" under Resistance; Saturn, Suppressions, Structural; "Low" under Vitality; Wastings; "Weak Body" under Weak).

CHRYSOLITE — A Mineral ruled by the ☉.

CHYLE—The Milky Fluid of Intestinal Digestion. The ♍ sign and ♄ are concerned with chylification, or chylopoiesis, the preparation, absorption and assimilation of the Chyle. As a fluid, the ☽ also rules the Chyle. Also the physiological action of the ☽ and ♀ produce Chylification, Chylopoiesis, Chyle formation, and its absorption. The afflictions of ♄ tend to have a pathological action on the Chyle. (See Chyme, Digestion).

Abated Absorption—Of the Chyle—A ♍ disease; the ☉, ☽, or ♄ affl. in ♍; ♍ on the Asc. and afflicted. (See "Intestinal" under Indigestion).

Chyluria— (See "Milky Urine" under Urine).

CHYME—Ruled by the ♋ sign. (See Digestion, Food).

CIGARETTES—Smoking of — Craving for—(See Narcotics, Tobacco).

CINCHONA—Peruvian Bark—A typical drug of ♂. Quinine, a principal alkaloid. (See Bitter).

CINNABAR— Occurs in brilliant red crystals, and is ruled by ♂.

CIRCULATION—Circulation of the Blood, and Other Fluids of the Body— The Arterial Circulation—The Venous Circulation—Circulation of the Fluids of the Body—Circulation of the Nerve Force, etc. The Circulation of the blood is under the internal rule of ♒. The ♌ and ♎ signs also are concerned with distillation and the circulation. Also ruled by Posterior Lobe of the Pituitary Body.

Arterial Circulation — Ruled by ♃. Poor Arterial Circulation—Obstructed —Restricted—Impeded—Sluggish— Spasmodic—Good Circulation of, etc.— The afflictions of ♄ to ♃; ♄ ☌, P, □ or ☍ ♃; ♄ ☌ the ☉ and planets in ♌, the heart sign; ♄ ☌ the ☽ in ♌; ♄ affl. in ♌ or ♒; ♄ in the 6th H., and afflicting ♃; ♄ ☌ the ☉ or ☽ in ♌ or ♒, etc., tend to Poor, Restricted, Obstructed, and Sluggish Arterial Circulation, and of the Circulation in general. The afflictions of ♄ to ♃ tend to increase the mineral deposits in the walls of the arteries and blood vessels, restricting circulation, and causing hardening of the arteries. Also the afflictions of ♄ to ♃ tend to over-eating, gluttony, resulting in too much blood, and Plethora, causing sluggish circulation.

Spasmodic disturbances of the Arterial Circulation are caused by the afflictions of ♅ to ♃. The good asps. of the ☽, and other planets, to ♃ at B., and by direction, favor good circulation, normal blood pressure, and to keep the blood properly replenished and in a healthy condition, as well as the arterial walls. (See Arteries, Blood, Cyanosis, Degeneration, Vessels. Also see "Good", "Poor", in this section).

Bad Circulation—(See "Poor", and the various paragraphs in this section).

Blood—Circulation of the Blood— Upon the action of the heart, and its force or weakness, depends the condition of the circulation of the blood. Therefore, the Circulatory System in general is ruled by the ☉ and the ♌ sign. The ♒ sign, in ☍ to ♌, and complementary to ♌, also has much to do with the circulation of the blood. ♄, the ruler of ♒, and ruler of the peripheral nerves, presides over the circulation and distribution of the blood in the tissues, and the surface of the body, and for this reason the pathological action of ♄, and the influences of Cold, tend to disturb the peripheral circulation, drive the blood inward, and cause internal congestion, colds, etc. (See Centripetal). Afflictions in, or to the ♒ sign, tend to disturb the blood circulation, causing corrupt and impure blood, morbid conditions of the blood, blood poisoning, and incomplete oxygenation. The Blood is of two kinds, the Arterial and Venous. (See "Arterial", "Venous", in this section. Also see "Blood Poisoning" under Poison; "Impure Blood" under Impure; "Blood" under Morbid; Oxygen). The Circulation of the Blood is assisted by the ☉, and impeded by ♄. In a physiological way, the Herbs and Plants ruled by the ☉, affect the heart and circulation in a beneficial way, strengthen and help to restore its action to normal. Gold, the mineral ruled by the ☉, is also a remedy, used in conditions of disturbed circulation and heart disorders. The drugs and remedies of ♄, such as Aconite, tend to slow up the circulation and heart action. The drugs and remedies of ♂ accelerate the heart action and circulation, such as Strychnine, and act as tonics.

Blood Vessels—(See Vessels).

Bowels—Circulation of Obstructed— (See "Circulation" under Bowels).

Capillary Circulation—(See Capillaries).

Changes in Blood Circulation—♃ affl. in ♎ or ♒.

Clots—Circulation Impeded By—(See Clots).

Congestion of Blood—In a Part—(See Congestion).

Cyanosis—(See Cyanosis).

Deficiency of Circulation—In a Part —A ♄ disease; caused by parts or organs ruled by the Sign or House in which ♄ is found at B., or by progression or direction. Is counteracted by ♂ remedies internally, as by Strychnine, or locally by a rubefacient, as by Cantharides.

Disorders—Of the Circulation—See the various paragraphs in this section. Cases and Birth Data of Disorders of the Circulation—See Figures 11A, 11B, 11D, 11E, 11F, 11G, 11H, in the book, "Astro-Diagnosis", by the Heindels.

Disturbed Circulation—The ☽ affl. in ♌; ♅, ♄, or ♂ ☌ or ill-asp. ♃ or ♀; ♄ in ♌ tends to obstruct and disturb the circulation thru the heart; ♄ or ♃ affl. in ♒, the circulation disturbed by the blood becoming too thick, impure, or by too much blood. (See the various paragraphs in this section. Also see "Too Much Blood" under Blood; Dropsy, Fainting, Heart, Impure).

Ears—(See "Circulation" under Ears).

Females—Irregular Circulation In—The ☽ to the ill-asps. ♃. (See Menses).

Fluids of Body—Circulation of Disturbed—♄ ☌ or ill-asp. the ☽. (See "Ailments of" under Fluids; Pituitary).

Good Circulation—Of the Blood—The ☉, ♃, or ♀ in the ♌ or ♒ signs, and free from affl.; ♂ in any asp. to the ☉ or ☽; airy signs and good ♃ influence; given by the Sanguine Disposition, or Temperament, and espec. when the ♌ and ♒ signs are free from the affliction of the malefics. (See "Sanguine Temperament" under Sanguine).

Head—Rush of Blood To—(See "Blood" under Head).

Heart—(See "Circulation" under Heart).

Hemorrhages—(See Hemorrhage, Menses; "Nose Bleed" under Nose).

Impeded Circulation—♄ influence and affliction; ♄ affl. in ♌ or ♒. (See "Poor", and the various other paragraphs in this section).

Infarct—(See Clots, Thrombus).

Interferred With—♆ or ♄ ☌ ♃ and ♀; ♆ and the ☽ □ or ☍ ♃ and ♀. (See the various paragraphs in this section).

Intestines—Circulation Restricted In—(See "Circulation" under Bowels).

Irregular Circulation—Mostly in Females—(See "Females" in this section).

Kidneys—(See "Renal" in this section).

Letting of Blood—(See Bleeding).

Lower Limbs—Circulation In Obstructed—(See "Circulation" under Arms, Legs).

Nerve Force—The Vital Fluid—Circulation of—(See "Fluid" under Vital).

Neuralgia—(See "Circulation" under Neuralgia).

Obstructions—In the Circulation—♄ affl. in ♌ tends to obstruct the passage of the blood thru the heart; ♄ in ♊, obstructions and poor circulation in the lungs; ♄ or ♉ in any sign tends to poor circulation at times, according to the sign they are in, and the parts ruled by such sign; ♃ affl. in ♎ tends to obstruct the circulation. (See the various paragraphs in this section. See "Too Much Blood" under Blood).

Peripheral Circulation—(See "Blood" in this section).

Poor Circulation—Of the Blood—Im-

peded—Defective—Disordered—Disturbed—Weak—Sluggish, etc.—The ☉ affl. in ♌ or ♒, defective circulation; the ☉ ☌ ♄ or ♉, and in □ or ☍ ♃ or ♀; the ☽ □ or ☍ ♃ or ♀; the ☽ hyleg in ♌ or ♒ with females, and affl.; ☽ ☌ ♄ in ♌ or ♒; a ♄ disease; ♄ in evil asp. the ☉ from common signs; ♄ ☌, □, ☍ ♃ or ♀; ♄ or ♃ in ♍ and □ the ☉ or ♅ in □; ♄ in the 6th H. and affl. ♃ or ♀; ♄ affl. in ♌ or ♒; ♄ in the Asc. in ♌; a ♃ disease; ♃ affl. in ♌ or ♒; ♃ or ♀ in the Asc., and affl.; ♃ □ or ☍ the ☉; ♃ affl. in ♑; born under ♃; ♂ □ or ☍ ♃ or ♀; caused by an afflicted ♀; ♍ or ♒ on the 6th H.; ♒ on cusp the 6th H. tends to diseases arising from bad circulation. (See "Arterial", "Impeded", "Venous", and the various paragraphs in this section).

Pressure—High Blood Pressure—(See "Pressure" under Blood).

Pulmonary Circulation—(See "Blood" under Lungs; Pulmonary. Also see "Obstructions" in this section).

Renal Circulation—(See "Circulation" under Kidneys).

Restricted Circulation—(See "Arterial", "Impeded", "Poor", and the various paragraphs in this section. See Case, 11E in "Astro-Diagnosis" by the Heindels).

Serous Circulation—Interferences With—♄ affl. in ♎ or ♏; afflictions to the ☽; Subs at KP, the 12th Dorsal. (See Dropsy, Serum).

Sluggish Circulation—♄ influence; ♄ ☌ or ill-asp. ♃ or ♀. (See "Poor" in this section. See "Too Much Blood" under Blood, Tumors).

Spasmodic Circulation—♅ ☌, □, ☍ ♃ and ♀. (See Spasmodic).

Stomach—Circulation In Impeded—(See "Circulation" under Stomach).

Thrombus; Veins—(See Veins).

Venous Circulation—Ruled by ♀. For Disorders of the Venous Blood and Circulation see Veins.

Vital Fluid—Circulation of—(See "Fluid" under Vital).

Weak Circulation—(See "Poor" in this section. Also see Pulse; "Weak Heart" under Heart). See Aquarius.

CIRCUMCISION—Male children who have ♄ in ♏ at B. should, as a rule, be circumcised, as ♄ in this sign tends to contraction of the prepuce, with its attendant sex irritations and disorders. (See Penis).

CIRRHOSIS—Thickening of the connective tissue of an organ. Occurs mostly in the liver or kidneys, and is a ♄ disease and affliction. (See Connective Tissue, Density, Fiber, Hardening; "Cirrhosis" under Kidneys, Liver; "Local Parts" under Local; Sclerosis).

CLAIRAUDIENCE—Hears voices, which may be of an undesirable character. Caused by ♆ rising and elevated in the East at B., and affl. the ☽ or ♀; ♆ affl. in the 12th H., or in the M.C.; the progressed ☽ to the ☌ or ill-asp. ♆ in the radix, and espec. if ♆ be affl. at B. (See Chaotic, Clairvoyance, Hearing, Mediumship, Obsessions, Prophetic, Spirit Controls, Weird, etc.).

CLAIRVOYANCE—Clear Sight—Insight—Divination—Crystal Gazing—Mediumship—Given by ♆ and the watery signs. There are two kinds of Clairvoyance, the genuine, or trained Clairvoyance, which can be called into action at will, and the Involuntary form of Clairvoyance which comes upon people at any time, without an act of the will, and leads to obsessions, or undesirable mediumship.

Involuntary Clairvoyance—♆ ruler of the horoscope, and afflicted; due to the pathological action of ♆; ♆ affl. in the 6th or 12th H. at B.; ♆ □ or ☍ ♅ at B.; the evil directions of ♆ to the ☉, ☽, ☿, or the Asc. tend to intensify the evil, and espec. if the radical map shows such an affliction. (See Antares, Clairaudience, Fears, Hallucinations, Illusions, Imagination, Insanity, Mediumship, Obsessions, Pituitary, Prophetic, Psychic, Spirit Controls, etc. Case—See "Clairvoyant", No. 322 in 1001 N.N.

CLAP—The popular term for Gonorrhoea. (See Gonorrhoea).

CLAUSTROPHOBIA—A morbid dread of an inclosed place, or a morbid fear of crowds, or being tightly confined in a large crowd, or jam of people. A ♅ disease and affliction, and also associated with an evil asp. of ♄ to ☿; ☿ in a sign of ♄ and affl. by ♅; ♅ □ or ☍ ♄. Also caused by the pathological action of ♆, and with ♆ afflicting ☿ at B. (See "Morbid Fears" under Fears; Neurasthenia, Obsessions).

CLAVICLE—The Collar Bone. Under the structural rulership of ♊. (See Arms, Shoulders).

Disease or Injury Of—♄ or ♂ affl. in ♊; Subs at LCP, the 6th Cervical; at AP, the 1st Dorsal.

Fracture Of—♂ affl. in ♊. Cases of Fracture—See "Saturn in the Tenth", No. 831 in 1001 N.N. Twice Broken—Case—See "A Luckless Youth", No. 390 in 1001 N.N.

Swelling—About the Clavicle—The ☽ affl. in ♊; planets affl. in ♊; Subs at LCP and AP. (See "Disease" in this section).

CLEANLINESS—Cleanly—The ♍ influence strong at B.; ♀ in ♂ or good asp. the ☽; good asps. between ♀, ☿, and the ☽. (See Careless, Dress, Filthy, Habits, Neat, Sanitation, Uncleanly, Untidy).

CLEANSING OF THE BODY—♂ cleanses the body of wastes and filth, and when the system becomes clogged thru excesses, dissipation, or gluttony, brings fevers and inflammation to quickly burn up the wastes, and thus save life. The ☽ also is cleansing and fluidic, and acts thru the fluids of the body in carrying off wastes. (See Combustion, Deposits, Destructive, Elimination, Enemas, Excretion, Fever, Inflammation; "Lease" under Life; Physic, Poisons, Retention, Wastes).

CLEAR—
Clear Complexion—Clear Skin—(See Complexion, Skin).
Clear Eyes—(See Eyes).
Clear Intellect—(See Intellect).
Clear Voice—(See Voice).

CLEFT—Cleft in the Spine—(See "Spina Bifida", and "Diseases of the Spine" under Spine. Also see Fissure, Palate).

CLERGYMEN—Ministers—Priests—
Anxiety To—Sadness To—An eclipse of the ☽ in ♓. (See Religion).
Ill-Health Of—♄, or other malefics, afflicting ♃ at B.; malefics in the 9th H.; planets in the 9th, and affl. by lords of the 6th, 8th, or 12th H.; lord of the 6th in the 9th, or lord of the 9th in the 6th; lord of the 6th as Sig. in Hor'y Questions.

CLIMACTERIC YEARS—Critical Years of Life—Every 7th and 9th year of life are called Climacterical because the ☽ then repeats her □ and △ aspects to her positions at B. by progression. The □ asps. of the ☽ to her radical place are the 7th, 14th, 21st, 28th, 35th, 42nd, 49th, 56th, 63rd years, etc., and are considered unfortunate and critical years, while her △ asps. fall in the 9th, 18th, 27th, 36th years, etc., and are more fortunate years in life. The ☉ hyleg, and to the □ or ☍ ♂ by dir. is a very evil, and often a fatal influence, when falling due in a climacteric year, or under any other fatal direction or Lunation. (See Directions). Also it takes ♄ a little more than 28 years to make one circuit in his orbit, and his first □ asp. to his radical place comes about the 7th year; his ☍ at the 14th year; his □ again at about the 21st year, and his ☌ with his radical place about the 28th or 29th years of life, which tends to make these times very critical years in life every seven years, and subject the native to ill-health, reversals, self-undoing, or a downfall, etc.

Grand Climacteric—Double Climacterical Years—The 49th and 63rd years, being 7×7, and 7×9, and the statistics of Undertakers show that the years of greatest mortality among adults are the 49th and 63rd years. In the 49th and 63rd years of life, the native usually continues to live if the ☽ at B. is well-aspected, and the directions for the year are good, but if not, death is more apt to come, especially if there is worry, anxiety and unsettledness. A fundamental rule is that the number 7 when multiplied by an odd number, as by 1, 3, 5, 7, 9, indicate the more evil and critical years in life, the climacterical years, while multiplied by an even number, as by 2, 4, 6, 8, give the more fortunate years, or years of less danger to life under evil directions. The even numbers are feminine, and the odd numbers masculine, and a masculine and feminine number when combined by addition or multiplication, according to the Science of Numbers, give greater strength and resistance to the body, whereas two masculine, or two feminine numbers combined tend to lowered vitality. (See "Eight Months Children" in Sec. 1 under Children). There are other years in life which may become critical, due to the aspects and directions, and yet not be called Climacteric. (See Crises, Critical, Cycles, Enneatical, Periodic, Periods).

CLIMATE—In considering the physical constitution and its welfare, the ☽ and her positions and aspects at B., becomes the Significator of affections which proceed from external causes, as climate, clothing, food, environment, etc. Climate is very important to good health. The different Climates, Countries, and parts of the Earth, are ruled by the different Signs of the Zodiac, and Planets, and in deciding upon the location, kind of climate, etc., for any individual, it is necessary and important to make a detailed study of the Star Map of Birth. Climates which would kill some people are beneficial for others. Some constitutions require a high altitude for good health, and others the Sea Level, or a low altitude, all which is shown and indicated by the Map of Birth. Many people suffer ill-health because they are in the wrong location and climate. Chronic diseases are often developed by people removing from their native climate, as to the Tropics, if born in a Northern Latitude, and then find a cure again by returning to their own Country. This subject of climate, location, etc., is further considered under Abroad, Altitude, Cold, Endemic, Environment, Exposure, External, Heat, Location, Nations; "Native Land" under Native; "Place of Birth" under Place; Races, Residence, Travel, Weather, etc.).

CLITORIS—The Glans Clitoris—Ruled by ♏.

CLOACA—A Cavity Containing Pus—An Opening in a Diseased Bone—A Common Outlet to the Recum and Bladder—A ♄ disease and affliction. In the Rectum and Bladder, ♄ affl. in ♏. In the Bones, ♄ affl. in an earthy sign, and principally in ♑. (See Abscesses, Malformations, Pus, Rectum, Urethra).

CLOGGING—Hindrances, Impediments, Stoppage, etc.

Clogging of the Mind—♓ on the Asc., physical condition often tends to clog the mental action. (See Dull, Languid, Lassitude, Lethargy, Listless, Stupidity, etc.).

Clogging of the System—The work of ♄ impeding and obstructing elimination; ♄ affl. in ♎, due to retention of wastes, poisons and toxins; the work of ♃ and ♀ thru excesses, gormandizing, and bad habits. (See Ash, Crystallization, Cleansing, Deposits, Elimination, Excretion, Hardening, Hearing, Impeded, Impediments, "Impure Blood" under Impure; Obstructions; "Poor Circulation" under Circulation; Retentions, Stoppages, Suppressions, Wastes).

CLONIC—(See "Clonic" under Spasmodic; Epilepsy, Muscles. Also see Myoclonus).

CLOSE OF LIFE—The 4th H. rules and denotes the conditions at the close of life, and is to be judged by the rulership of this house, and the nature of the planets in this house. Also the manner of death in old age is partly indicated by the 8th H. conditions, and planets in the 8th. (See Old Age).

CLOSURES—(See Imperforate, Orifices).

CLOTHING—(See Acquired, Cleanly, Climate, Colds, Comforts, Dress, Habits, Linen, Uncleanly, Wet).

CLOTS—Blood Clots—Coagulations in the Body—Congelation—Infarct—Thrombus—A ♄ influence. (See Congelation, Haemostatics, Infarct, Obstructions, Thrombus, Vessels). Case —Died from Blood Clot on the Brain —See "Birth and Death", No. 350 in 1001 N.N.

CLOUDED—Clouding—Cloudy—

Clouded Mind—(See "Clouded" under Mind).

Clouded Sight—(See Blindness, Cataract, Nebulous, Sight).

Clouding of Consciousness—(See Chaotic).

Cloudy Complexion—(See Complexion).

Cloudy Spot of Cancer—(See "One Eye" under Blindness. Also see Nebulous).

Cloudy Urine—(See Urine).

CLOUDS—The Clouds are ruled by ♃. The influence of ♃ in his configurations with the different planets tends to free the moisture of the clouds in superabundance, causing excessive rains and floods, which endanger human life, and cause sickness and suffering. (See Floods, Lightning, Rain, Storms, Wind).

CLUMSINESS — Awkwardness — Afflictions to the ☽ at B.; ♀ to the ill-asps. ☿ by dir. (See Automatic, Awkwardness, Gait, Motion, Movement, Walk).

CLYSTER—Clystering—Injections—(See Enema).

COAGULATION—Clotting—♄ influence. (See Clots).

COALITION—Fusions—Union of Parts —Bringing Together—In a beneficial way, as causing harmony and rhythm in the mind and body, and eliminating discordant elements, coalition is the work ♂ ♀. In a pathological way ♄ tends to coalition, union of parts, etc., thru deposits, hardening, crystallization, etc. The influences of the ☉ ☌ ♂ also tend to fusion of parts thru excessive heat. (See Adhesions, Anatomical, Ankylosis, Crystallization, Deposits, Fusions, Hardening, Harmony, Rhythm, etc.).

COARSE—Rough—Unrefined—

Body—Coarse Body—♏ on the Asc. (See Rough, Unrefined).

Features—(See "Coarse" under Features).

Hair—(See "Coarse" under Hair).

Legs—(See "Coarse" under Legs).

Manners—Coarse Manners—(See Gross, Obscene, Manners, Rough, Sensual, Unrefined).

Skin—Coarse and Rough—(See "Rough" under Skin).

Voice—(See "Coarse" under Voice).

Women—Coarse Women—(See Deviations, Effeminate, "Tomboyishness" under Females; "Coarse" under Voice).

COCAINISM—(See "Drug Habit" under Narcotics. Also see "Neptune Group" under Herbs).

COCCYX—The Os Coccyx is under the structural rulership of the ♏ sign. The Coccygeal Region of the Spine, the Coccygeal Vertebrae, are ruled by the ♐ sign. (See Vertebrae).

Coccydynia—Pain in the Coccyx—♄ or ♂ affl. in ♏ or ♐; Subs at LPP, and of the Sacrum and Coccygeal Vertebrae. (See Sacrum).

COCTION—The Coction Process—Digestion—Combustion—(See Combustion, Digestion).

COFFEE—(See "Neptune Group" under Herbs).

COHABITATION—Coition—

Little or No Desire For—The ☉ or ☽ in ♏ ♂ or ill-asp. ♄; the ☉ by progression making no asp. to planets for a long period of time; the ☽ void of course, and in the last degrees of a sign, and making no asp. to planets; ♄ influence tends to produce apathy, and espec. when in ♈, and lack of passion and feeling. (See Apathy, Bachelors, Celibacy; "Aversion" under Marriage; "Free from Passion" under Passion; "Married Women" under Sex; Spinsters).

Passional Excesses—(See Intercourse, Passion, Sex, Venery, etc.).

COHESION—Lack of Cohesion of Parts —A ♅ disease and affliction.

COLD—Chill—Saturn rules and produces Cold, and excess of cold in the body, or in the atmosphere. Cold is noxious and destructive, and all matter is dissipated by coldness and dryness. Cold and Dry are malevolent influences and tend to decay. Cold is affiliated with moisture, and heat with dryness. Cold is a negative quality, and also passive, and predominates in the left side of the body. (See Left). The watery signs, ♋, ♏, and ♓ are cold in nature. The therapeutic action of ♄, and ♄ remedies, are cooling and refrigerating, and such remedies are used to combat the high fevers given by ♂. Hydrogen, ruled by ♄, has affinity with Cold. Statistics show that about 50% of all our diseases come from cold, chill, exposure to cold, and the chilling of the skin, or surface of the body, by improper clothing, thus driving the blood inwards and causing functional disorders, internal congestions, colds, etc. (See Centripetal, Colds, Congestion, Ganglion). Cold, Lingering, and Chronic Diseases are produced by ♄. The parts of the body, or organs more liable to be afflicted with cold, colds, or chill, are those ruled by the Sign or House containing ♄ at B., and espec. when ♄ is in an earthy or watery sign, affl. the ☉, ☽, Asc., or hyleg, and when this class of Signs may also be on the Asc., or cusp of the 6th H., or the ☉, ☽, and a majority of planets in such Signs at B., tending fundamentally to give a cold body or constitution. Cold tends to contractions and obstructions in the body. There are diseases and bodily conditions which arise from Cold alone. Others from a combination of Cold and Moisture, and others from a combination of Cold and Dry causes. The following diseases and afflictions

have to do with Cold, Cold and Moisture, and with the ♄ influence. Also the diseases listed under Saturn are mostly Cold Diseases, and caused by Cold at their beginnings. (See "Cold", "Diseases of Saturn", under Saturn. Also see Chill, Dry, Moisture).

Ague—(See "Quartan Ague" under Ague).

Augmented Cold—Cold Augmented In the Body—(See "Body" in this section).

Blindness from Cold—(See "Cold" under Blindness).

Blood—Cold Blood—The ☉ or ☽ in ♓ and affl. by ♄; the ☽ affl. in ♏; the ♓ influence tends to cold blood, and ♓ on the Asc. at B.

Body—Cold Body or Constitution— Cold Augmented In the Body—The System Affected Generally with Cold —The ☉ affl. by the ☽ at B.; the ☉ or ☽ ♂ or ill-asp. ♄ at B., and by dir.; the ☉ afflicting the Asc. at B., or by dir.; the ☽ in a watery sign at B., and espec. if the Asc. is also a water sign; the ☽ from her 3rd Quarter to the New ☽ makes the constitution more cold; ♄ in an angle, occi. of the ☉, and ori. of the ☽, and espec. if ♄ be in familiarity with ☿; ♄ or ☿ holding dominion at B., and these planets being in familiarity; ♄ ♂ or ill-asp. the ☉, ☽, Asc., or hyleg at B., or by dir.; the Asc. affl. by the ☉, ☽, or ♄; earthy or watery signs in the Asc. at B., or on the cusp of 6th H., and the ☉, ☽, or ♄ also in this class of signs at the same time. Those born in the Arctic Regions and in cold climates tend to have a cold constitution. (See "Animal Heat" under Heat. Also see "Temperament" in this section).

Bowels—Cold in the Bowels—(See "Cold" under Bowels).

Chilblain—(See Chilblain).

Chill—Chills—(See Chill).

Chronic Diseases—From Cold—♄ ♂ or ill-asp. the ☉, ☽, Asc., or hyleg at B., or by dir., and espec. the ☽ affl. by ♄. (See Chronic).

Climate—Cold Climate—Suffering From—(See "Cold" under Weather; also see Blizzards, Snow, Winter).

Cold Baths—(See Bathing).

Cold Body—(See "Body" in this section).

Cold and Chill—(See Chill. Also note the various paragraphs in this section).

Cold and Dry—(See "Cold and Dry Body", "Cold and Dry Diseases" under Dry).

Cold and Heat—(See "Cold and Heat" under Heat).

Cold and Moist—(See "Cold and Moist" paragraphs under Moisture).

Cold Temperament—(See "Body", "Temperament", in this section).

Cold Water—(See Cravings).

Cold Weather—(See "Climate" in this section).

Colds—Catching Cold—(See Colds).

Constitution Cold—(See "Body" in this section).

Contractions—Due to Cold—(See Contractions).

Crystallization—The Result of Cold—(See Crystallization, Hardening, Petrifaction, Stone).

Dampness and Cold—Diseases and Fevers Arising From—Caused by ♄ and ♑. (See "Cold and Moist" under Humours, Moisture; "Humours" under Watery).

Death—By Cold, and Cold Diseases—Denoted by ♄ and the ☽, and by fixed stars of the nature of ♄; the evil directions of ♄ to the hyleg, and espec. when holding the dominion of death; when the ☉ or Asc. are hyleg, the ☽ by her evil asps. and directions to the ☉ or Asc. tends to cause death by cold and chronic diseases. (See "Arguments for Death" under Death; "Cold, Phlegmatic Diseases" under Phlegm).

Defluxions—Cold Defluxions—♄ diseases. (See Defluxions, Fluxions).

Diseases Arising from Cold—Cold Diseases—Irregularities of the System Thru Cold and Chill—All Illnesses Arising from Cold—The ♄ influence is the principal cause of all Cold diseases, and his afflictions to the vital places of the map, the ☉, ☽, Asc. or hyleg. Also watery signs on the Asc., or on cusp of the 6th H. predispose to cold diseases. Note the following influences which cause diseases arising from Cold,—The SUN affl. by the ☽, the system is generally affected with cold; the ☉, ☽, and many planets in watery signs at B.; the ☉ in ♑ at B., or ♑ upon the Asc., as ♑ is the coldest of the earthy signs; the ☉ or ☽ ☌ or ill-asp. ♄ at B., and by dir.; MOON ruler of the Asc. in an earthy or watery sign, and affl. by ♄, diseases of a cold nature, and people so born rarely suffer from hot or burning fevers; the ☽ in a watery sign at B., and a watery sign upon the Asc. or cusp of 6th H.; the ☽ ☌ or ill-asp. ♄ or ☿ at B., and by dir., or at the beginning of an illness if ☿ be of the nature of ♄; the ☽ to the ill-asps. the Asc. or hyleg by dir.; URANUS afflictions to the ☉, ☽, Asc. or hyleg, diseases arising from sudden exposure to cold, as at bathings; SATURN to the ☌ or ill-asps. the Asc. by dir.; ♄ in the 6th H., and affl. the Asc. or hyleg; ♄ the sole ruler at a Solar Eclipse, a prevalence of colds, and diseases arising from cold; ♄ having the dominion of death in the map of birth; the ASCENDANT affl. by the ☉ or ☽; the Asc. ☌ or ill-asp. ♄ at B., or by dir.; the Asc. an earthy or watery sign, and the ☽ at the same time in one of these signs; earthy or watery signs on the cusp the 6th H., and espec. if one of these signs be also on the Asc., or containing the ☽, and the ☽ affl. by ♄. (See the various paragraphs in this section. Also see Chill, Concretions).

Distempers—Cold Distempers—Cold and Moist Distempers—♓ diseases. (See "Cold and Moist" under Humours, Moisture).

Dry and Cold—(See "Cold and Dry" under Dry).

Excessive Cold—(See "Climate" in this section).

Exposure to Cold—Diseases Arising From—(See Exposure, External; "Cold" under Weather).

Externally Cold—With Internal Heats—(See "Internal Heats" under Heat).

Extremely Cold Weather—General Suffering From—(See "Cold" under Weather).

Extremes of Heat and Cold—Body Suffers From—(See "Cold and Heat" under Heat).

Extremities—Cold Extremities—(See "Cold" under Extremities, Hands, Legs, Feet).

Feet—Cold Feet—Cold Taken In—(See Feet).

Frost—Ruled by ♄. (See Frost).

Hands—Cold Hands—(See Hands).

Head—The Head Disordered by Cold—Cold In the Head—(See "Colds" under Head).

Health Suffers—From Cold—(See the various paragraphs in this section).

Heat and Cold—(See "Cold and Heat" under Heat).

Hips—Cold and Chill In—♄ ♐. (See Hips).

Humours—Cold Humours—Cold and Moist Humours—(See "Cold" under Humours).

Ice—Ruled by ♄. (See Hail, Snow).

Indigestion—From Cold, or Taking Cold—(See "Cold" under Indigestion).

Irregularities—Of the System from Cold and Chill—(See "Diseases", and the various paragraphs in this section. See "Irregular" under Functions).

Knees—Cold In—(See Knees).

Legs—Cold In—(See Legs).

Liver—Cold and Dry—(See Liver).

Lumbar Region—Cold and Chill In—(See Lumbar).

Lungs—Cold In—(See "Colds on Chest" under Lungs).

Manner—(See "Coldness" under Manner).

Moist and Cold—(See "Cold and Moist" under Moisture).

Nose—Cold In—(See Nose).

Organs—Cold Organs—(See Organs).

Phlegmatic—Cold, Phlegmatic Diseases—(See Phlegm).

Quartan Ague—Arising from Cold—(See Ague).

Rheumatic—Cold, Rheumatic Diseases—(See Rheumatism).

Rigor Mortis—The Rigidity After Death—Ruled and produced by ♄. (See Death).

Rigors—Coldness—Stiffness—(See Rigid, Rigors, Stiffness).

Skin—Cold Skin—(See "Cold" under Skin).

Snow—Ruled by ♄. (See Snow).

Stiffness from Cold—(See Rigors; "Cold Weather" under Weather).

Stomach—Cold Stomach—The Stomach Afflicted With Cold Humours—(See "Raw Humours" under Indigestion).

Stone—(See Concretions).

Superabundance—Of Cold In the System—Disease or Death Produced By—Caused by ♄, and when ♄ holds the dominion of death in the map of birth; ♑ on the Asc. at B. (See "Animal Heat" under Heat).

Susceptible to Cold—The Body Susceptible to Cold—(See "Body" in this section).

System—The System Affected Generally with Cold—(See "Body" in this section).

Taking Cold—Diseases Arising Therefrom—(See "Causes of Colds" under Colds).

Temperament—Indisposed by Cold Temperament—Fixed Stars of the nature of ♄ and ♂ ascending at B.; ♄ in the Asc. at B., in ♑, and ♑ upon the Asc.; ♓ upon the Asc., or cusp of 6th H.; an earthy sign upon the Asc., and with the ☽ in ♓. (See "Body" in this section).

Thighs—Cold In—♄ ♐. (See Thighs).

Toes—Coldness of—(See Toes).

Watery and Cold Diseases—(See "Cold and Moist" under Humours, Moisture).

Weather—Cold Weather—(See "Cold" under Weather).

COLDS—Saturn causes and rules Colds, which arise principally from Cold, and chilling of the surface of the body, driving the blood inwards, and causing internal congestions. (See Centripetal, Congestions, Constrictions). People who have ♄ weak at B., and not afflicting the ☉, ☽, Asc., or hyleg, and when the watery sign element also is not prominent, do not suffer much from Colds. People who have ♄ in an earthy or watery sign at B., and affl. the ☉, ☽, Asc., or hyleg, and when this class of Signs may also be upon the Asc., or cusp of the 6th H., should guard against Colds. Saturn people catch cold easily from wet feet, drafts, or from the slightest wetting. It is said that Colds are caused by Sidereal influences, and disturbed atmospheric conditions, as taking cold in a room, and against which no precautions seem to be available or successful. For the general influences causing Colds, see "Causes" in this section. Also the following diseases and afflictions are associated with Colds and Cold, or are the direct result of them.

Blindness from Colds—Caused by ♄; ♄ affl. in ♈. (See "Causes" and "Cold" under Blindness).

Body—Cold Taken from Over-Exertion of the Body or Mind—(See "Colds" under Exercise; "Over-Exertion" under Exertion).

Bowels—Colds In—(See "Cold" under Bowels).

Bronchitis—(See Bronchial; "Cold on Lungs" under Lungs).

Catarrh—(See the various paragraphs under Catarrh).

Catches Cold Easily—(See "Causes" in this section).

Causes of Colds—Liable to Colds—Tendency to Colds—Catches Cold Easily—Susceptible to Colds—Suffers from Colds—The ☉ or ☽ to the ♂ or ill-asps. ♄ by dir., and espec. if ♄ be strong at B., and affl. the Lights, or the ☉ or ☽ be hyleg; the ☉ or ☽ ♂ or ill-asp. ♄ at B., and espec. when occupying watery signs, or an earthy or watery sign upon the Asc. or cusp the 6th H.; the ☉ affl. in ♑; the ☉ affl. by the ☽ at B., or by dir.; the ☽ affl. in ♓, colds which fly to the lungs; the ☽ in bad asp. to the ☉ at B., and by dir.; denoted by the ☽ when the ☽ afflicts the ☉ or Asc.; the ☽ to the ill-asps. ♅ or ♆ by dir.; ♄ ♂ or ill-asp. the ☉, ☽, Asc., or hyleg at B., or affl. these places by dir.; ♄ to the ♂ or ill-asp. the ☽ if the ☽ be hyleg, or ruler of the 6th or 8th H.; ♄ by transit ♂ or ill-asp. the ☉, ☽, ♃, or ♀ in the radical map; ♄ ruler of the 6th H. at B., and the M.C. to the ♂ or ill-asp. ♄; ♄ in ♋, ♏, ♑, or ♒ warns of cold and chills to the system; ♄ in ♈, and espec. colds in the head; ♄ ♂ or ill-asp. the ☉ in common signs; ♄ in the 1st H.; ♄ in any sign or house tends to colds and chills in the parts of the body ruled by the sign containing ♄ at B.; ♄ in ♓, colds in and thru the feet; ♀ affl. in ♋ or ♌, and espec. when ☿ partakes of the nature of ♄; afflictions in ♓, and are ♓ diseases; afflictions in common signs; many planets in watery signs, or a water sign upon the Asc. or cusp of 6th H.; afflictions in ♋; ♑ on cusp the 6th H.; the Asc. to the ♂ or ill-asp. ♄ by dir. (See the various paragraphs in this section).

Chest—Colds On—(See "Bronchitis" in this section).

Chills and Colds—(See Chill).

Clothing—Colds from Wet Clothing or Linen—(See "Cold Taken" under Feet; "Colds" under Moisture; "Linen" under Wet).

Coryza—(See "Coryza" under Nose).

Cough from Colds—(See Cough).

Damp Places—Colds from Living In—(See "Colds" under Moisture).

Death from Colds—Or Coughs—(See "Death" under Cough).

Delirium—From Colds and Coughs—(See "Death" under Cough).

Exercise—Colds from Over-Exercise and Over-Exertion of the Body—(See "Colds" under Exercise).

Feet—Colds from Wet Feet—(See "Cold" under Feet).

Hay Fever—Rose Cold—(See "Hay Fever" under Nose).

Head—Colds In—(See "Colds" under Head; "Coryza" under Nose).

Hips and Thighs—Cold and Colds In—♄ ♐.

Indigestion—From Taking Cold—(See "Cold" under Indigestion).

Influenza—(See Influenza).

Knees—Cold In—(See Knees).

La Grippe—(See Influenza, La Grippe).

Lameness—From Colds—♄ affl. in signs which rule the legs, knees and feet, as in ♐, ♑, ♒ or ♓. (See "Cold" under Legs, Knees, Feet. See Lameness).

Legs—Cold and Colds In—(See Extremities, Legs, Limbs).

Liable to Colds—(See "Causes" in this section).

Linen—Cold from Wet Linen—(See "Clothing" in this section).

Lungs—Colds On—(See "Bronchitis" in this section).

Mind—Colds Taken from Over-Exertion of Mind and Body—(See "Colds" under Exercise).

Moist Places—Colds Taken from Living in Damp and Moist Places—(See "Colds" under Moisture).

Mother—Death of the Mother from Extreme Colds—(See "Cold", "Death", under Mother).

Mucus—Mucous Discharges—(See Defluxions, Discharges, Humours, Mucous, Phlegm, Rheum, Watery, etc.).

Over-Exertion — Colds Taken By— (See "Colds" under Exercise).

Phlegm — Discharges of — (See Phlegm).

Places—Damp Places—Colds from Living In—(See "Colds" under Moisture).

Pneumonia—Colds Resulting In—(See Pneumonia).

Prevalence of Colds—♄ sole ruler at a Solar Eclipse. (See "Diseases" under Cold).

Rheum — Catarrhal and Watery Discharges—(See Rheum).

Rhinitis — (See "Coryza", "Rhinitis" under Nose).

Rose Cold—(See "Hay Fever" under Nose).

Severe Colds—Death From—(See "Death" under Cough).

Sneezing—(See Nose).

Suffers from Colds—(See "Causes" In this section).

Susceptible to Colds—(See "Causes" in this section).

Taking Cold—Takes Cold Easily—Diseases Arising From—(See "Causes" in this section. Also see "Diseases Arising From" under Cold; External).

Tendency to Colds—(See "Causes" in this section).

Thighs—Colds In—♄ ♐. (See Hips, Thighs).

Wet Feet—Colds From—(See "Cold" under Feet).

COLIC—Spasmodic Pain in the Abdomen—Cholic—

Biliary Colic—(See "Cholic" under Bile).

Bowels—Colic In—(See "Colic" under Bowels).

Causes of Colic—A ♍ disease, and afflictions in ♍; ♍ on the Asc., or cusp of 6th H.; the ☉ affl. in ♍; a ♑ disease; the ☽ affl. in ♍, or affl. the hyleg therefrom; the ☽ hyleg, and to the ♂ or ill-asp. ♄ by dir.; the ☽ in ♈ or ♍, and affl. by the ☉ or ♂ when taken ill; the ☽ hyleg, and to the ill-asps. the ☉ by dir.; the ☽ weak and affl. at B., and ♂ Asc. by dir.; the ☽ ♂ ♂ in ♍ in the Asc. when taken ill; the ☽ decr. in

light, sepr. from ♄, and applying to ☿; the ☽ hyleg in ♍, and afflicted, and espec. in a female nativity; caused by fixed stars of the nature of the ☽; a ♄ disease; caused by ♄ when he is strong at B., and espec. when the dominion of illness or death is vested in him; ♄ in an angle, occi. of the ☉, and ori. of the ☽; ♄ affl. in ♍, and espec. in the 6th H.; ♃ affl. in ♌ or ♍; ♂ in ♍ in the Asc. or 6th H., and afflicted; ☿ affl. in ♍ or ♓; ☿ in ♍, and to the ♂ or ill-asp. ♆, ♅, ♄, or ♂; ☿ affl. in ♋, due to worry and anxiety; Asc. to the □ or 8 ♄ by dir.; afflictions in ♓.

Cramps—(See Cramps).

Enteralgia—(See Enteralgia; "Pain" under Bowels).

Erratic Movements — (See "Movements" under Erratic. Also see Spasmodic).

Feet—Colic Taken Thru the Feet— (See "Colic" under Feet).

Flatulence—(See Flatulence).

Gas—In Bowels—(See "Gas" under Bowels).

Hepatic Colic—(See "Cholic" under Bile).

Incoordination — In Abdomen and Bowel Tract—The ☉ or ♅ affl. in ♍. (See Incoordination).

Kidney—Colic In—Nephritic Colic—Renal Colic—(See "Colic" under Kidneys).

Lead Colic—Saturnine Colic—Painter's Colic—A ♄ disease; ♄ affl. in ♍; ☽ ♂ ♄ in ♎. (See Lead).

Nephritic Colic — (See "Colic" under Kidneys).

Pain—(See "Cramps", "Pain", under Bowels).

Painter's Colic—(See "Lead" in this Section).

Prevalent—Colic Prevalent—♄ or ♂ holding power at a Summer Solstice, and in ♍, and affl. planets in the 6th or 8th H.

Renal Colic—(See "Colic" under Kidneys).

Saturnine Colic—(See "Lead" in this section).

Stomach Colic—(See "Colic" under Stomach).

Ureters—Colic of—(See "Colic" under Kidneys).

Wind Colic — (See "Bowels" under Wind. Also see "Cramps", "Pain", under Bowels).

COLLAPSE—Complete Collapse—Failure of the Vital Powers—Nervous Collapse—Prostration—

Danger of Collapse—♆ in a prominent and powerful position in the map of birth, and affl. by the ☽ or ☿, tends to make some people nervous, excitable, neurotic, and subject to paroxysms of nervous excitation, which are often followed with complete collapse; 8 on the Asc. at B., danger of collapse. (See "Worse" under Crises; Excitable, Exhaustion, Feeble, Neurasthenia, Prostration, Vitality Low; "Weak Body" under Weak).

Muscular Collapse—Case—See "Seventeen Years in Bed", No. 843 in 1001 N.N.

Sudden Collapse—The ☉ affl. in ♌, and espec. when the ☉ is hyleg, and affl. by the ♂ or ill-asp. ♄ by dir. (See "Illness" under Accidents).

COLLAR BONE—(See Clavicle).

COLLES FRACTURE—(See "Fracture" under Wrists).

COLLIQUATIVE—Profuse—Excessive—(See Excessive; "Night Sweats" under Phthisis; Profuse; "Excessive" under Sweat).

COLLYRIA—Collyrium—A medicinal lotion for the eyes. Sugar of Lead, a ♄ remedy, a principal ingredient in, for its astrictive property. (See Astringent, Lead, Ointments).

COLOCYNTH—A typical drug of the ☽. (See "Typical" under Moon).

COLON—The superior part of the large intestine. The Colon, and its different sections, the Descending Colon, the Transverse Colon, the Sigmoid Flexure, and the Mesocolon, are ruled by ♂ and the ♏ sign.

Colitis—Inflammation of the Colon—♂ affl. in ♏; Subs at PP, the 2nd Lumbar Vertebra.

Enterocolitis—Inflammation of the Intestines and the Colon—Malefics in both ♍ and ♏; Subs at KP, and PP, the 2nd Lumbar.

Inflamed Colon—(See "Colitis" in this section).

Obstructions—In the Colon—♄ affl. in ♍ tends to obstructions in the Transverse Colon.

Sigmoid Flexure—Disorders of—(See Sigmoid).

COLOR—

Bad Color—Bad Complexion—(See "Bad Complexion" under Complexion; Pale; Sickly, White).

Blindness—Color Blindness—(See "Color" under Blindness).

Blood—Red Coloring Matter of—Ruled by ♂ and the ♏ sign. (See Haemoglobin; "Blood" under Red).

Clothing—Color of—(See Colors, Dress).

Complexion—Color of—(See "Bad Color" in this section).

Good Color—(See "Good" under Complexion).

Hair—(See "Color" under Hair).

Reddish Color—(See "Red" under Complexion).

Sense of Color—Is ruled by ♀. Also the 16° and 17° ♉, a sign of ♀, are said to strongly rule this sense.

Skin—Color of—(See Complexion, Pigment, Races, Skin). See the next Article on Colors.

COLORS—Colors, according to Astrology, are symptoms of the nature of the Stars. Fixed Stars of the color of ♂ are of the nature of ♂; those of the color of ♃, of the nature of ♃, etc. The ☉, ☽, and planets, each have a color under their rule. The colors in the Solar Spectrum are ruled by the ☉, ☽, and the five planets, excepting

♅ and ♆. For the rulership of the various colors, see "Planets", "Signs", and the various paragraphs in this section.

Clothing—Dress—Colors of Clothing in Horary Questions are said to be according to the mixture of the planets, and the Signs and Terms they are in, as follows—The ☉, saffron or sandy color; the ☉ and ☽, light yellow or green; the ☉ and ♄, dark yellow, or bronze color; the ☉ and ♃, very deep, shining red; the ☉ and ♂, deep shining red; the ☉ and ♀, olive; the ☉ and ☿, light gray; the ☽, light mixed colors, white, cream-colored, or pale green; the ☽ and ♄, deep gray or russet; the ☽ and ♃, bright green; the ☽ and ♂, light red; the ☽ and ♀, light blue, or bluish white; the ☽ and ☿, buff or fawn color; ♄, black; ♄ and ♃, dark black green; ♄ and ♂, dark brown; ♄ and ♀, whitish gray; ♄ and ☿, dark gray or blue; ♃, green, spotted, or ash colored; ♃, red mixed with green; ♃ and ♀, blue and yellow, or greenish gray; ♃ and ☿, spotted green; ♃ and ♂, tawny, with light spots; ♂, red; ♂ and ♀, light red or crimson; ♂ and ☿, red tawny; ♀, white or bluish; ♀ and ☿, purple or light mixture; ☿, gray or dove color; ♉, red mixed with citron; ♊, red and white mixed. When a planet is in the house of another planet, judge of him as mixed with that planet. Thus, ♄ in ♌, the house of the ☉, denotes the dress to be either dark yellow, or bronze color, etc. (See Mixed).

Complexion—For the various colors of the complexion, see Complexion, Face. Also see the remarks under "Signs" in this section.

Dress—Colors of—(See "Clothing" in this section).

Houses—Colors of—(See Houses).

Light Colors and White—Are ruled by the 1st H.

Mixed Colors—Ruled by ♅ and the ☽. (See "Clothing" in this section. Also see the ♅ influences under "Planets" in this section).

Planets and Color—Planetary Colors—In the Secret Doctrine by H. P. B., the colors in the Solar Spectrum are assigned to the planets as follows,—The ☉, Orange; the ☽, Violet; ♄, Green; ♃, Blue, or Purple; ♂, Red; ♀, Indigo; ☿, Yellow. Astrological Authorities seem to differ some from this classification, and in the following notes, I am using the assignments as given in the textbooks of Astrology. The ☉ rules orange in the Solar Spectrum. Orange is the color of the Pranic life forces in the blood. The ☉ rules yellow, or golden, inclined to purple, has an active power, and gives radical heat. The ☽ rules green in the Solar Spectrum. The ☽ rules white, or white spotted, or a light mixed color. The ☽ has a passive power, and is the sign of radical moisture. One Author ascribes violet to the ☽. In the Solar Spectrum ♄ rules Indigo. ♄ signifies black, and black being ruled by ♄, has a deadening and devitalizing influence, and black clothing should be avoided. ♄ rules lead color, and is a sign of intemperate coldness and dryness. One Author ascribes green to ♄. In the Solar Spectrum ♃ rules violet. ♃ opposes ♄ in nature, which makes the Violet Ray helpful in treating chronic and morbid conditions, and violet is considered a beneficent color. One Author ascribes purple to ♃. Also ♃ is listed as ruling blue, and red mixed with green. The blue and yellow of ♃ and ♀ are signs of heat and moisture united. Heat is predominant in ♃, and moisture with ♀. ♂ rules red in the Solar Spectrum. ♂ rules fiery red, the result of intemperate heat and dryness. Red being ruled by ♂ is a tonic color. Red and orange are the predominant masculine colors. Yellow in the Solar Spectrum is ruled by ♀. One Author ascribes blue and indigo to ♀. White and purple are also ascribed to ♀. In the Solar Spectrum blue is the color of ☿. Yellow is also ascribed to ☿. Azure and light blue are also ascribed to ☿. Mixed colors, checks and plaids are ruled and given by ♅. Lavender, and a smoky gray or blue, are ascribed to ♆. Color Therapy has its value by using the ray or color of one planet to oppose that of another, and the diseases caused by each. (See Antipathy, Opposites, Polarity, Sympathy, Vibration). For each of the colors of the Solar Spectrum, ruled by the planets, such as Blue, Green, Indigo, Orange, Red, Violet, and Yellow, see these subjects in the alphabetical arrangement. Also see Black, White.

Race Horses—Color, or Combined Colors of a Winning Horse—When two horses, or more, are to race, if a Horary figure is set up, the sign or planet signifying their color, which is strongest, or posited in the best house, shows which horse will win. (See the book, "The Silver Key" by Sepharial).

Sense of Color—(See this subject under Color in the section before this one).

Signs of the Zodiac—Colors Ruled By —The Colors ruled by the Signs are given under each Sign. (See "Colors" under Aries, Taurus, Gemini, etc. Also the colors ruled by each planet are given under the planets. (See "Color" under Sun, Moon, Saturn, etc.). The Colors are said to be an indication of the color of the complexion of any person signified by these signs and planets, or by the combination of sign and planet, and in Hor'y Questions to also indicate the color of their dress. (See "Clothing", "Complexion", "Skin", and the various paragraphs in this section).

Skin—For the various colors of the skin, or discoloration, normal and abnormal, see such subjects as Black, Blemishes, Brown, Complexion, Dark, Discolorations, Face, Freckles, Jaundice, Marks, Moles, Naevus, Negro, Pigment, Races, Red, Skin, White, Yellow, etc.

Solar Spectrum—(See "Planets and Color" in this section).

Therapy—Color Therapy—(See "Planets" in this section).

Vibration—Each Color has its special rate of vibration, and these vibrations

are in tune and harmony with the rate of vibration of the planet, sign, or combination of planet and sign, which rule the various colors, singly, or in mixed combinations. It is on the basis of the rate of vibration of the different colors that they can be used with success in the treatment of disease, the same as the planetary herbs or minerals are used. Thus the violet rays of ♃ oppose the vibrations given off by ♄, and assist in alleviating the symptoms produced by ♄ in chronic diseases. (See "Planets" in this section. Also see Polarity, Vibration).

Vocation and Colors—♀ ruler, and in the 10th H. favors dealing in Dyes, Colors, Perfumes, etc.

Zodiac Colors—(See "Signs" in this section). For odd colors, and the various shades of colors, look in the alphabetical arrangement for the subject you have in mind. Also many of the odd colors and mixtures are mentioned in this section under the headings of "Clothing", "Planets".

COLUMNS—Motor Columns of the Spine —(See "Spinal Cord" under Motor; "Lesions" under Spine).

COMA—Stupor—An Abnormally Deep Sleep—Comatic—Comatose—♆ is comatic, and Coma is due principally to ♆ afflictions; ♆ □ or ☍ ♅; ♆ in the 8th H., affl. the hyleg, tends to Coma, ending in death. Produced by ♆ when the Psychic Powers are in a state of hyperactivity, and the bodily energies are held in abeyance. Coma is also caused by afflictions in ♈ or ♎, and is an ♈ and ♎ disease; ♃ affl. in ♎ tends to; Subs at AT, Lu.P. and KP.

Carus—The last degree of Coma. A ♆ disease. (See Carus).

Uremic Coma—The connection of ♏ with ♈, both ♂ signs, the former influencing the Kidneys and Suprarenal Capsules, and the latter the Cerebellum, in pathological conditions tends to Uremic Coma in kidney troubles, and also to disturbed sleep. Also caused by Subs at AT, and KP, the 11th D. (See Catalepsy, Delirium, Epilepsy, Fainting, Hysteria, Insensibility, Sleep, Stupor, Trance, Uremia).

COMBUSTION—Coction Process—One of the four fundamental and essential operations of Nature. A ☉ and ♂ influence; a physical action of the ☉; ♂ tends to the combustion of the wastes of the body by his fevers and inflammations. (See "Combustion" under Tissues. Also see Cleansing, Digestion, Fevers, Inflammation, Mars, Oxygen, Sun).

COMEDO—Blackheads—(See "Comedo" under Sebaceous).

COMELY—Beautiful Body—Graceful—Handsome—The ☉ in ♐ in partile asp. the Asc.; the ☉ configurated with lord of the Asc., more comely, and the habit better; the ☉ as Sig. in Hor'y Questions, a fair and comely person is denoted; the ☽ in ♊, partile the Asc., a tall, comely, and well-made person; the ✶ or △ asps. of the ☽; ♃ in ♌, in partile asp. the Asc., rather comely; ♀ ☍ partile the Asc., comely, but with a mean stature; ♀ Sig. ✳ or △ ♄, comely, but rather pale; the ✳ or △ asps. of ♀ to the ☉, ☽, and planets. (See Beautiful, Face, Fair, Graceful, Hair, Handsome).

COMETS—From Ancient Times the appearances of Comets have had a special significance of calamity or disease in some form. They tend to affect the Regions and Places ruled by the Sign, or parts of the Zodiac, in which they appear, and in the direction of their trains, and those Parts suffer most toward which its tail points. Coincident with their appearance have occurred Famine, Pestilence, Drought, Floods, Fires, Bloodshed, War, Slaughter, Fevers, Epidemics, Endemic Diseases, Calamities, Earthquakes, Tidal Waves, The Plague; Death of Rulers, Nobles, Kings and Prominent People; the death of Children; affections of the Eyes; loss of Cattle; the death of Fish in the Rivers and Seas; Attacks upon Man by Wild Animals; Dissentions and Quarrels; the Locust Pest; Robberies, Increase of Crime, Poverty, unusual Sadness among Peoples; Treachery, Wind, Storms, Rain, Hurricanes, Dangers to Women; Derangement of the System; a prevalence of Urinary and Sex Disorders; Obscuration of the Air; Dangers in Navigation; Hot Seasons in Countries ruled by the Sign in which they appear; Troubles in Religion, and to bring every kind of evil upon Mankind. Comets appearing in the Airy Signs tend to Disturbances in the Air, as Corrupt Air, etc. In the earthy signs, Famine, Drought, Loss of Crops, Rottenness of Seeds, Pestilence, etc. Fevers are prevalent when Comets appear in ♍. In the fiery signs, Fevers, Fires, Wars, Quarrels, Hot Weather, etc. In the watery signs, Floods, Destruction of Fish, Perils, Dangers on the Seas, Tidal Waves, Disturbances of the Fluids of the Body, etc. Halley's Comet is the best known of the Comets, and the different appearances of this Comet along thru the Ages have been attended with Plague, Spotted Fever, Pestilence, Volcanic Eruptions, and great calamities of some kind, and espec. in the years when there were great conjunctions between the major planets, or many major planets in cardinal signs. Halley's Comet appeared in 1909 and 1910, and the death of King Edward, of England, followed within 12 days of its appearance. Also Revolution broke out in Portugal in 1910, and King Manuel fled to England. A good Chapter on Comets, and their influences over disease and afflictions to Humanity, is to be found in Pearce's Textbook of Astrology. (See Eclipses, Events. Also see the subjects mentioned in this Article).

COMFITS—Confections—Sweet Things —Over-indulgence In—♀ in ♎. (See Food, Sugar, Sweets).

COMFORTS—The 6th H. denotes the comforts of life, as food, clothing, servants, etc. ♆ affl. in the 6th H. tends to loss of physical comforts. ♅ affl. in the 6th H. tends to many sudden changes, and a mental restlessness,

which interferes with health and comfort. ♃ in the 8th H., and not seriously afflicted, indicates an easy and natural death, and "In comfort and order". ♀ in good asp. the ☽, the comfort and general health of the native are enhanced. (See Contentment, Dress, Food, Happiness, Luxuries; "Peace of Mind" under Mind; Poverty).

COMMANDING—Commanding Appearance—Commanding Aspect—Prepossessing Appearance—Given by the ✳ and △ asps. of the ☉, ☽, and ♀; the ☉ rising in ♌; ♂ rising in ♎, tall and commanding; ♀ Sig. ♂ ♀, prepossessing; ♌, ♎, or ♒ on the Asc., and many planets rising and elevated, and espec. in fiery or airy signs; ♌ on the Asc., tall and commanding; born under ♃, sober and commanding; one strong planet rising and elevated in the East, in good asp. the Asc., generally gives distinction of appearance. (See Appearance, Form, Giants, Portly; "Positive Form" under Positive; Stature, Tall, etc.).

Commanding Signs—The Northern Signs, ♈, ♉, ♊, ♋, ♌, ♍. (See Northern). The six Southern Signs are called Obeying Signs.

COMMON—

Common People—The Public—The Common People, and the Laboring Classes, are ruled by the 6th H. Injury by the Common People is denoted when ♃ is in □ or ☍ asp. the ☽ at B., and by dir. (See Crushed, Hanging, Humanity, Lynching, Mankind, Mobs, Poor, Public, Riots, Tumults).

Common Sense—Lacking In—(See Erratic, Judgment, Notions).

Common Signs—(See "Mutable Signs" under Mutable).

COMMONPLACE APPEARANCE—Many planets setting in the West at B., and out of dignity by Sign or House; a lack of aspects to the rising degree. (See Appearance, Stature).

COMPACT BODY—♃ ☍, partile the Asc., strong and compact; ♃ □ partile Asc., a decent-made, compact body; ♃ ♏ partile Asc., compact and corpulent; ♃ ♒ partile Asc., compact and of middle stature; ♂ ☍ partile Asc., compact, short and corpulent; ♂ ♐ partile Asc., compact, fleshy, tall and well-made; earthy signs on the Asc., or many planets in earthy signs at B., give compact forms of body, but with less physical power; ☍ on the Asc., usually compact, well-formed, or beautiful, with ♀ as ruler; ♍ on Asc., compact, neat, well-proportioned, and well-made. (See Beautiful, Corpulent, Neat, Well-Made, Well-Proportioned).

Compactness—(See Density).

COMPANIONS—Associations—Company —Friends—Social Relations—(See Environment, External, Family, Friends, Husband, Love Affairs, Low, Marriage, Men, Morals, Pleasant, Pleasures, Social Relations, Wife, Women, etc.).

COMPATIBILITY—(See Antipathy, "Chemical Action" under Chemical; Healers, Magnetism, Opposites, Polarity, Repulsion, Sympathy, Vibration).

COMPLAINING—Complaining of Their Maladies—(See Exhibition, Murmuring). The ♉ and ♍ people tend to complain much about their diseases, and to hold onto them. (See Taurus, Virgo).

Does Not Complain—Endures Disease Without Complaining—Lord of the 5th H. in the 6th H.

COMPLAINTS—(See Diseases, Disorders, Distempers, Humours, Ill-Health, Infirmities, Sickness, etc. Also see in the alphabetical arrangement the complaint, or disease you have in mind).

COMPLETE—

Collapse—Complete Collapse—(See Collapse).

Complete and Elegant Form—(See Beautiful, Form, Handsome, Stature, Well-Made, Well-Proportioned).

COMPLEX—(See "Inferiority Complex" under Inferior; "A Murderer" under Murder.

COMPLEXION—The Complexion is said to be ruled by ♀, and to be especially affected by ♀ in ♈. Venus has to do with the skin of the face, and disorders of the face and complexion by the indiscriminate use of Cosmetics. Many subjects which have to do with the Complexion are considered and listed under Eyes, Face, Hair. In a general way the Complexion may be divided into four classes, such as Dark, Light, Pale and Ruddy. The fiery signs, and the ☉ and ♂ strong at B. tend to give a red and ruddy complexion. The earthy signs give a more dull, muddy, and obscure complexion. The airy signs, a clear and rather delicate complexion. The watery signs, and espec. ♋ and ♓, give a pale and more sickly complexion when upon the Asc. at B., and due largely to a weakened and lessened vitality from birth. The following subjects have to do with the Complexion, which see in the alphabetical arrangement when not considered here.

Bad Complexion—Pale—Poor—Sickly Bad Color—♋ or ♓ upon the Asc. at B.; the ☽ in ♉ or ♑ in partile asp. the Asc.; ♂ in ♑ or ♓, partile the Asc.; ☿ in ♋ or ♍ in partile asp. the Asc.; ☿ ruler of the Asc., and occi. (See Evil, Pale, Poor, Sickly, in this section).

Beautiful Complexion—Beautiful, Sanguine—(See Clear, Fair, Good, Ruddy, Sanguine, in this section. Also see Beautiful, Fair, Handsome).

Birthmarks—(See Naevus).

Blemishes; Blond Complexion—(See "Light" in this section. Also see "Light Hair" under Hair).

Blotches; Bronzed—(See "Tan" in this section).

Brown; Brunettes—(See "Dark" in this section. Also see "Black", "Dark", under Eyes, Hair).

Cheeks; Chestnut Complexion—♃ influence. (See "Chestnut" under Hair).

Clear Complexion—Given by the airy signs, and espec. by ♒ on the Asc.; ♄ ♎ or ♐, in partile asp. the Asc., tolerably clear; ♄ or ☿ in ♒, partile the

Asc.; ♀ ♉ partile the Asc., ruddy, but not clear; ♀ ♌, partile the Asc. (See "Good" in this section).

Cloudy—(See Dull, Obscure, Sunburnt, in this section).

Colors—Of the Complexion—(See "Complexion" under Colors. Also see the various paragraphs in this section).

Cosmetics—Bad Effects of Upon the Complexion—(See Cosmetics).

Cruel Complexion—(See Cruel).

Dark Complexion—Brunettes—Made principally by ♄ and the ☽; ♄ occi. at B.; ♄ ♓ ascending; ♄ ♓, dark sanguine; denoted by ♄ as Sig. of the party in Hor'y Questions; ♄ lord of the Asc., and occi., as between the M.C. and Desc., or between the Nadir and Asc.; ♄ in the Asc. at B.; ♄ Sig. in ♊, ♍, or ♑ in Hor'y Questions; ♄ in ♉; ♄ makes the complexion paler or darker; the ☉ or ☽ in ♑, ♒, or ♓, or any of these signs upon the Asc.; The ☉ ♉, partile the Asc.; the ☽ makes the complexion darker when ruling the half sign rising at B.; the ☽ Sig. in ♋, ♍, or ♏; the ☽ in ♏ partile the Asc.; ♃ in ♓, partile the Asc., but with light brown hair; ♀ ♍ partile the Asc.; ☿ ♑ partile the Asc.; ☿ ori. at B., and espec. when ☿ is of the nature of ♄; ♍ on Asc., dark ruddy; ♏, ♑, ♒, ♓ on the Asc. (See "Black" and "Dark" under Hair; "Dark" under Eyes; "Dark Figure" under Dark. Also see Dull, Dusky, Swarthy, in this section).

Defect In—☿ ori. at B. (See Blemishes, Face, Freckles, Marks, Moles, Naevus, Pimples, Scars, etc.).

Delicate Complexion—Delicate and Clear—The airy signs give, and espec. when ♒ is on Asc. (See Clear, Fair, Fine, White, in this section).

Dull Complexion—Cloudy—Dun—Muddy—Not Clear—The ☉ Sig. in ♏, cloudy, dull, dun, or sunburnt; ♃ Sig. in ♏, or ♃ ♏ partile the Asc., dull and muddy; ☿ Sig. in ♈, ♌, or ♍. (See Sunburnt, Swarthy, in this section).

Dun Complexion—(See Dull, Smoky, Sunburnt, in this section).

Dusky—Somewhat Dark—Obscure—Swarthy—The ☽ ♋, partile asp. the Asc., pale and dusky; ♏ gives; ♃ ♊ partile the Asc., dusky and sanguine; ♀ ♏ partile the Asc.; ☿ in ♈ or ♑ partile Asc. (See Dark, Obscure, Swarthy, in this section).

Evil Complexion—♀ Sig. □ or ☍ ♄. (See Bad, Pale, Poor, Sickly, in this section).

Eyes—(See the various Colors of the Eyes under Eyes).

Face—(See "Cosmetics", "Lotions", and the various paragraphs under Face).

Fair Complexion—The ☉ and ☽ ascending, and not afflicted, make the native fair, but the ☉ never causes beauty altho he may give a good complexion; the ☉ ♈, partile Asc., good but not fair; the ☉ ♒ partile Asc.; the ☽ and ♋ give a fair, pale complexion; ♃ ruler of the Asc., and ori., but moderately fair when occi.; ♃ ♍ partile Asc., fair but not ruddy; ♃ in ♎ or ♒ partile Asc.; ♂ ♉ partile Asc., ruddy but never fair; ♀ ♊ partile Asc., rather fair; ♀ ♐ partile Asc., fair sanguine; ♀ ♒ partile Asc., and with light brown or flaxen hair; ♀ ruler of the Asc., and ori.; ☿ ruler of the Asc., and occi., but color not as good; ♊ on Asc., fair, tall and straight. (See "Fair", "Round Face", under Face; "Light Hair" under Hair; "Blue Eyes" under Eyes; also in this section see Clear, Delicate, Good, Light).

Fine Complexion—Pure—The ☽ ♎ partile Asc., fine, red and white complexion; ♃ Sig. in Hor'y Questions. ♎ on the Asc., fine in youth. (See Clear, Fair, Good, in this section).

Florid—(See "Ruddy" in this section).

Freckles; Ghastly Look—(See Pale).

Good Complexion—Good Color—Fine —Clear—The ☉ rising at B., and not affl.; the ☉ Sig. in ♈, good altho not very clear; the ☉ ruling the rising sign at B.; the ☉ ♍ partile Asc.; the ☉ or ☽ Sigs. in ♒; the ☉ ♓, well-aspected and partile Asc.; the ☽ in ♊; the ☽ Sig. in ♉ or ♍, tolerably clear; the ☽ in ♎, fine sanguine; the ☽ Sig. in ♒; ♄ Sig. in ♎, tolerably good and clear; ♄ Sig. in ♒; ♀ or ♀ ori., the skin is clear; also ♃ occi. tends to a pure and lovely complexion, but not as fair as when ori., and ruler of the Asc.; ♃ rising in the Asc.; ♃ Sig. in ♎ or ♒; ♂ Sig. in ♒, fair and clear; ♂ rising and ori. of the ☉, clear; ♀ ruler of the Asc., and ori.; ♀ in ♈, partile the Asc., good; ♀ in ♌ or ♒, clear; ♀ in ♐, clear and sanguine; ♀ in ♓, moderately good; ♀ Sig. in ♊ or ♎; ☿ in ♊ partile the Asc.; ☿ Sig. in ♐ or ♒; ♀ or ♒ on the Asc.; Northern Signs, and also ♐ and ♓, are said to give a good color; ♓ also is a mixture, and being a Winter sign, produces a bad color according to its position and aspects; ♈, the house of ♂, and a Northern sign, its color is both good and bad; ♓ on the Asc., if the ☉ be rising in ♓, gives a good complexion, and in females ♓ gives a clear, lucid, and very white skin; the Quadrant from the Asc. to the Nadir tends to produce a good complexion; Temperate climates, with alternate hot and cold Seasons, produce a good complexion; characteristic of those born in cold climates, and in the Arctic Regions. (See Clear, Fair, Light, Red, Ruddy, Sanguine, in this section).

Hair—The Colors of Hair and the Complexion—(See Hair).

Handsome Complexion—(See Beautiful, Handsome. See "Good" in this section).

Hard and Dull—(See "Dull" in this section).

High-Colored—(See Ruddy).

Honey-Colored—♃ or ☿ ori. at B.

Ill Complexion—(See Pale, Sickly. See "Bad" in this section).

Indifferent—The ☉ Sig. in ♓; ☿ in ♍; ♋, ♌, or ♍ on the Asc., signs of the Summer Quarter, or the ☉ or ☽ in these signs.

Jaundiced Look—(See Jaundice).

Lead-Colored—(See Lead).

Lean and Sallow—☿ occi. at B. (See Sallow).

Light Complexion—Blondes—Fair— The ☉ makes the complexion lighter and fairer when ruling the sign, or part of the sign rising on the Asc. at B.; the ☉ Sig. of the person in Hor'y Questions; ♃ a strong Sig. of the person; ♃ or ♂ as Sigs. in ♒; ♀ strong at B., or ruler; ♀ in ♊; ♀ in the Asc. (See "Blue Eyes" under Eyes; "Light Hair" under Hair; "Degrees" under Light).

Lovely—(See Beautiful, Good, in this section).

Lucid—(See Clear, Good, in this section).

Middle Life—Complexion In—(See "Middle Life" under Pimples).

Middling Complexion—☿ as Sig. of the party in Hor'y Questions.

Moderately Good—♀ in ♓. (See "Good" in this section).

Muddy—Obscure—(See Dull, Dark, Dusky, Olive, Sunburnt, Swarthy, Tan, in this section).

Mulatto—(See "Yellow" in this section).

Obscure—(See "Muddy" in this section).

Oily—Shiny—(See "Oily" under Face).

Old Age—Complexion In—(See "Pimples", "Ruddy", under Old Age).

Olive—☿ ascending at B., and free from the rays of other planets.

Ordinary—The Quadrant from the Summer Tropic to the Autumnal Equinox tends to give an ordinary complexion.

Pale Complexion—(See Pale, Sickly. See "Bad", "Poor", in this section).

Pasty Complexion—♍ on the Asc.

Pimpled Face—(See Pimples).

Poor Complexion—Bad—Evil—Sickly —Pale—The ☉ in ♋; the ☽ in ♑ or ♉; the ☽ Sig. in ♑; ♂ in ♑; ♂ Sig. in ♋, ♑, or ♓; ♀ Sig. □ or ♉ ♄, an evil complexion, and not very handsome; ☿ in ♋ or ♍; ♍ seldom gives a good complexion. (See Pale, Sickly. See "Bad", "White", in this section).

Pure—(See Clear, Fine, Good, in this section).

Red Complexion—Rosy—Reddish Color—Ruddy—The fiery signs, and the ☉ and ♂ strong at B.; ♃ ♎ partile Asc., fine, red and white; ♃ Sig. in Hor'y Questions, red and white mixed; ♂ or ☿ ruler of the Asc., and occi.; ♂ gives, and when born under ♂, red rather than ruddy. (See "Red" under Beard, Eyes, Face, Hair, Lips. See "Ruddy" in this section).

Rosy—(See "Red" in this section).

Ruddy Complexion—Florid—Rosy—A Healthy Glow—Tinged with a Reddish Hue—(See "Complexion" under Ruddy. Also see "Red" in this section).

Sad Brown—A ☿ person, neither black nor white, but between. (See "Sad" under Hair).

Saffron—The ⊙ gives a Saffron and Yellow Complexion. (See Orange. See "Yellow" in this section).

Sallow—An Unhealthy, Yellowish Color—♄ influence; ♄ ♑ partile the Asc.; ♈ on Asc., sallow or swarthy; ☿ occi. at B., lean and sallow. (See Bad, Jaundiced, Pale, Poor, Sickly, Swarthy, Yellow, in this section).

Sanguine—(See "Complexion" under Sanguine).

Shiny—(See "Oily" in this section).

Sickly Complexion—Given by the watery signs, and espec. by ♋ or ♓ on Asc. (See Bad, Poor, Sallow, in this section. See Pale, Sickly, Unhealthy, Vitality Low).

Smoky—(See Smoky. Also see Dark, Dull, Dun, Muddy, Swarthy, in this section).

Soft Complexion—♀ rising in the Asc.

Sunburnt Complexion—The ⊙ gives; the ⊙ Sig. in ♍, dun or sunburnt; the ⊙ ♍ partile Asc., cloudy, sunburnt; the ⊙ Sig. in ♐, olive brown, or sunburnt; ♂ Sig. in ♌; ♂ ♌ partile Asc.; characteristic of ♂; in Hor'y Questions, a person denoted by ♂; ☿ ori. as regards the ⊙ except when ☿ is in ♊; ☿ Sig. in ♉ or ♌; ☿ ♉, partile Asc., swarthy, sunburnt; ♐ gives. (See Dull, Olive, Smoky, Swarthy, Tan, in this section).

Swarthy Complexion—Dark—Cloudy—Muddy—Tawny—Tan—Obscure—Dusky—Smoky, etc. The ⊙ Sig. in ♉; in Hor'y Questions, the ⊙ Sig. of the party, sometimes swarthy or bronzed; the ☽ makes the complexion darker when ruling the half sign rising at B.; the ☽ Sig. in ♋ or ♍; the ☽ in ♍, dark ruddy; the ☽ ♍; ♄ ascending at B.; ♄ signifies one of a swarthy or lead color; ♄ makes the complexion paler or darker; in Hor'y Questions ♄ as Sig. indicates one of a dark or swarthy complexion; in Hor'y Questions, ♄ as Sig. in ♊, ♍, or ♑; ♄ in ♉, ♊, or ♍; ♄ ♊, dark sanguine; ♄ ♍ partile Asc.; ♄ ori., and lord of the Asc., as between the Asc. and M.C., etc.; denoted by ♄; ♃ ♉ partile Asc.; ♃ Sig. in ♉ or ♊; ♃ Sig. in ♓, obscure; ♂ Sig. in ♈, ♉, ♍ or ♑; ♂ ♉ ♈, swarthy; ♂ ♉ ♍, dark ruddy; ♂ rising at B., dark reddish; ♂ ♈ partile the Asc., but if ♂ be ori. the native will be tall and less swarthy; ♂ ♍ or ♏ partile Asc.; ♀ Sig. in ♍ or ♏, dusky; ♀ ♍, dark sanguine; ☿ ori. at B., swarthy brown; ♑ rules swarthy brown; ☿ in ♈, ♉, ♊, ♌, or ♍; ☿ Sig. in ♉, ♌, ♍, or ♑ partile Asc., swarthy, sunburnt; ☿ ♌ or ♏ partile Asc.; ♈ on the Asc., swarthy or sallow; ☿ ruler of the Asc., and ori.; ♉ on the Asc.; ♉ gives a large, swarthy, shining face; ♊ gives; ♊ on the Asc., dark, sanguine; ♍, ♏, ♑ give; the Quarter from the Winter Tropic to the Vernal Equinox gives a dark complexion. (See Black, Brown, Brunettes, Dark, Dull, Dusky, Lead, Muddy, Obscure, Olive, Sad, Sunburnt, in this section. Also see "Smoky Degrees" under Smoky).

Tan—Bronzed—Tawny—Brownish Yellow—Sunburnt. The ☽ Sig. in ♐, bronzed; a raw-tanned, leathery appearance is characteristic of ♂ peo-

ple; ☿ occi. at B., tawny visage. (See Brown, Dull, Olive, Smoky, Sunburnt, Swarthy, in this section).

Tawny—(See "Tan" in this section).

Thin, Pale and Sickly—Thin, Sickly Visage—(See Pale, Sickly, Thin).

Tolerably Clear—(See "Clear" in this section).

Unhealthy Complexion—Unwholesome—Sallow—(See Bad, Poor, Sallow, in this section. See Jaundice, Pale, Sickly, White, Yellow).

Unwholesome—(See "Unhealthy" in this section).

White Complexion—(See "Complexion" under White).

Women—Complexion In—(See Cosmetics, Dark, Light, in this section).

Yellow Complexion—(See "Saffron" in this section. See Yellow).

Youth—Ruddy Complexion in Youth—(See "Complexion" under Youth).

COMPLICATIONS—Complication of Diseases—The planets in the Signs show the zones of the body afflicted, but the aspects, and the influences of the planets themselves, have to be considered in complications. (See "Complications" under Disease). Ruling over the human body are three Crosses, known as the Cardinal, Fixed and Mutable Crosses in the star map of birth. The Fixed Signs ♉ and ♏, being opposites, and also the ♌ and ♒ Signs being opposites, and all four of these signs being in □ or ☍ asp. to each other, the fixed signs when occupied by many planets, and espec. malefics, tend to diseases or complications in parts or organs ruled by all four of these Signs. Thus a disease starting in the throat, ruled by ♉, may affect the Heart, Sex Organs, Lower Limbs, or the Circulation of the Blood, all of which are ruled by the fixed signs. Evil Directions, or Transits, coming into a Fixed Sign during the course of a disease may tend to involve and complicate, or extend the first disease to other parts of the body ruled over by a fixed sign. Also during the course of a disease, if the ⊙, in the case of a male, comes to an evil asp. a malefic, or some evil direction be formed to the ⊙, there is apt to be a relapse, or a complication of diseases, according to the signs occupied by the ⊙ and the afflicting planet. The same with the ☽ in the case of a female. In males, afflictions to the ⊙ rule the course of the disease, and to the ☽ in females. (See Chronic, Crises, Continuity, Course, Curable, Duration, Incurable, Moderation, Opposites, Prognosis, Prolonged, Relapses, Remote, Return, Sympathy, Tedious, Various, etc.).

Many Complications—The ⊙ to the ill-asp. his own place at B., and by dir.; ♄ in the 6th H., and affl.

Many Diseases—Many Diseases Afflict the Body—The ⊙ to the ill-asps. his own place by dir., and the ⊙ affl. by malefics at B.; no asp. between the ⊙ and ♂ at B., and espec. in childhood; ♃ affl. in ♒, due to the blood being corrupted by too much blood. (See

Impure; "Much Sickness" under Sickness; "Too Much Blood" under Blood).

Shifting of the Disease—Changes to Some Other Form of Disease—The Sig. of the disease being in a double-bodied sign; the afflictor in the disease changing signs, or passing from one house into another, and the disease will either shift to some other form, become chronic if it has been acute, or resolve itself. The strong affinity which exists between opposite signs of the Zodiac also tends to complications, and a change in the disease. Thus stomach disorders, rulder ordinarily by the ♋ sign, may have skin complications and eruptions, and espec. if there are also afflictions in ♑. (See Crises, Opposites, Praeincipients, Remote, Scope, Sympathy, Various, etc. Also note the different paragraphs in this Article).

COMPREHENSION—Is ruled by ☿.

Dull—The Comprehension Dull—(See Dull, Intellect, the various paragraphs under "Mental", "Mind"; Perception, Understanding, etc.).

Good—The Comprehension Good—(See "Active Mind" under Active; "Good Judgment" under Judgment; "Activity" under Mental; "Sound Mind", and other paragraphs under Mind; Perception; Reason, Understanding).

COMPRESSED—Compression—

Compressed Air—Ruled by ♅. (See Air, Caisson, Ether, Gases, Uranus).

Compressed Gases — (See Caisson, Gases).

Organs—Compression of—Compression of organs, or parts, is denoted by ♄; ♄ ☌ or ill-asp. ♅.

Spinal Cord—Compression of—♄ affl. in ♌ or ♒ especially, or ♄ affl. in the sign ruling the part compressed or pinched. (See Contractions, Depressions, Saturn, Spine, Subluxations, Vertebrae).

COMPULSIONS—Morbid Compulsions—(See "Compulsions" under Morbid).

CONCEALMENT — Of Disease — (See "Concealment" under Disease).

CONCEITED—(See Pretender).

CONCENTRATION—Of Mind—

Good Powers Of—Good asps. of ♄ to the ☉, ☽, or ☿; ♄ in ♎, ♑, or ♒, and well-dignified; many planets in fixed signs at B., or with fixed signs upon the angles; ♅ gives the ability to work a long time upon one subject; ☿ in a fixed sign at B., and in good-asp. to the ☽ or Asc.

Inability to Concentrate—A Wandering Mind—♆ affl. in ♊; ☿ Sig. □ or ☍ ☽, never applies very closely to any subject; many planets in common signs at B., and such signs upon the angles; ☿ in a weak sign at B., and affl. by the ☽, ♄, and ♃: ☿ in no asp. to the ☽ or Asc. (See "Mental Chaos" under Chaotic; Confusion, Dreamy, Visionary).

CONCEPTION—The Fecundation of the Ovum—Conception is under the rule of the ☽.

Abnormal Conceptions—Inhuman in Shape—Deformed, or Afflicted in Vari-

ous Ways During Pregnancy and At Birth—(See Congenital; "Beastly Form" under Beasts; "Dogs" under Children; Deformities, Foetus, Inhuman, Monsters, etc.).

Conception Has Taken Place—Conception Has Not Taken Place—(See "Woman Is With Child", "Woman Is Not With Child", under Pregnancy).

How Long Conceived?—(See "How Long Pregnant?" under Pregnancy).

Moment of Conception—A Star Map of the Heavens for the moment of conception is very important to study in helping to know the character and temperament of a person, and also to diagnose diseases which are not especially shown or indicated in the map of birth. The Moment of Conception is known as "The Epoch", and is determined by the rules of the Prenatal Epoch. The moment of birth and the moment of conception have a fixed relation, and when the moment of birth is known approximately, the moment of conception can be determined by the laws of Astronomy, as the degree on the Asc. or Descendant at B. is said to be the Longitude of the ☽ at conception. The moment of conception may occur some days, or a week after coition, and is ruled by the motion of the ☽ in the individual case. (See "Moment of Birth" under Birth; Prenatal Epoch). The Occult Side of Conception, the connection of the Ego with conception, etc., is discussed under the headings of "Conception", "The Ego", "The Seed Atom", etc. in the book entitled "Cosmo-Conception" by the Heindels.

Party Has Just Conceived—If the dispositor of the ☽, and the lord of the hour be angular, or ♂ in the 7th H. (Hor'y).

Party Will Not Conceive—(See Barrenness).

Predetermination—Of the Sex at Conception—(See "Sex of Children" under Children; Predetermination).

Pregnancy—(See Pregnancy).

Prenatal Epoch—(See this subject).

Quadruplets Conceived—(See Quadruplets).

Sex of the Conception—(See "Predetermination" in this section).

Single Conceptions — (See "Single Births" under Children).

Signs of Conception—(See Fruitfulness; "Signs of Children" under Children).

Signs of No Conception—(See Barrenness, Pregnancy).

There Is No Conception—(See Barrenness; "Woman Is Not With Child" under Pregnancy).

Time of Conception—It is said if the lord of the 5th H. be in the 1st, it will be in the first year of married life; if in the 2nd H., in the 2nd year; in the 10th H., in the 3rd year; in the 7th H., in the 4th year; in the 4th H., in the 5th year, and so on, in accordance with the preeminence of the houses. Others measure the time by the application of the lord of the Asc., or the

☽, to the lord of the 5th, or to ♃ or ♀, reckoning by degrees according to the nature of the sign the applying planet is in. (See "First-Born Child" under Children).

Triplets Conceived—(See Triplets).

Twins Are Conceived—(See Twins, Triplets. Also see "Single Births" under Children). For further study see Barren, Birth, Children, Fecundation, Female, Fruitful, Gestation, Heredity, Mother, Pregnancy, Prenatal Epoch, Wife, Women.

CONCRETIONS—A Calculus—An Osseous Deposit—Stone—Concretions are the work of ♄, by crystallization, and mineral deposits which should be eliminated. They are formed by mineral deposits carried by the blood, and are ruled by ♄. They are connected with the earthy signs. They are also the result of Cold, ♄ influence, and are associated usually with Cold Diseases. (See Chalk, Cold, Crystallization, Deposits, Elimination; "Gall Stones" under Bile; Gravel, Growths, Hardening, Lime, Minerals, Osseous, Sand, Stone, Suppressions, etc.).

CONCUSSION—A Shaking—Shock—Bruises—Hurts by Concussion, etc.—

Brain—Concussion of—(See "Blows", "Accidents", under Head; "Fractures" under Skull). Case of Concussion of Brain—See Case, "Concussion of Brain", No. 890, in 1001 N.N.

Hurts by Concussion—♄ causes concussions and contusions where blood does not flow; ♄ ☌, P, or ill-asp. the Asc. at B., and by dir.; also caused by the afflictions of ♅ or ♂ to the ☉, ☽, Asc., or hyleg. (See Blows, Bruises, Buildings, Crushed, Explosions, Falls, Fractures, Hurts, Injuries, Kicks; "Assaults by Stones" under Stones; Violence; "Storms" under Wind; Wounds).

CONDEMNED TO DEATH—(See "Death by Sentence" under Judges).

CONDENSATION—One of the four Operations of Nature. To make more dense, to harden. A ♄ influence, and the work of ♄. (See Concretions, Crystallization, Clots, Density, Hardening, Nitrogen; "Operations" under Nature; "Saturn Influence" under Saturn).

CONDUCT—Behavior—Deportment—Actions—The conduct of the individual has much to do with health and disease, of both mind and body. Therefore, a number of subjects relating to conduct, habits, morals, etc., have been considered in this work. The ☽, her sign, position, afflictions, good aspects, etc., have much to do with the conduct and habits of the native. Many of the subjects along this line you will find listed alphabetically at the end of the Article on the Mind, both good and bad traits. However, a few prominent and suggestive subjects will be listed here. For subjects not listed here, or under Mind, look in the alphabetical arrangement for what you have in mind. See the following subjects,—Anger, Amorous, Bad, Careless, Cheating, Cleanly, Companions, Criminal, Cruel, Dangerous, Debased, Debauched, Deceitful, Depraved, Disgrace, Dis-

honest, Disorderly, Dissipated, Dissolute, Drink, Drunkenness, Effeminate, Erratic, Erring, Evil, Excesses, Females, Filthy, Folly, Foolhardy, Foul Minded, Fierce, Forgers, Furious, Gambling, Gentle, Gluttony, Good, Habits, Harlots, Honest, Husband, Immoral (see Morals); Improvident, Imprudent, Indecent, Intemperate, Intoxication, Knavish, Lascivious, Lewd, Liars, Libelers, Licentious; "Loose Morals" under Morals; Love Affairs; "Low and Base" under Low; Lustful, Luxurious, Madness, Manners, Marriage, Mean, Men, Mild, Morals, Murderous, Neat, Newsmonger, Noble, Obscene, Obstinate, Passion, Perverse, Perversions, Pettifogging, Prison, Prodigal, Profligate, Quarrelsome, Rashness, Recklessness, Religion, Responsibility, Riotous, Robbers, Rough, Saucy, Savage, Scandal, Sensuous, Sex, Shameless, Shrewd, Social Relations, Strange, Swindler, Temper, Thieves, Ungovernable, Unruly, Vagabond, Venery, Vices, Vicious, Violent, Wanton, Wench, Wife, Women, etc. The references and paragraphs under these subjects will lead you to others along the lines of conduct throughout the book.

CONDYLOMA—(See Anus, Warts).

CONFECTIONS—Sweets—Given To Excess of in Eating—(See Sugar, Sweets).

CONFINEMENT—In the sense of limitations, restraints and restrictions over your liberty of action, it is principally a 12th H. influence, and the nature of the confinement is indicated by the planets therein, and the sign upon the cusp. Also ♄ tends to bind, hinder, confine and restrict, and espec. when ♄ or ☋ are in the 12th H., and affl. the ☉ or ☽.

Asylum—Insane Asylum—Confinement In—(See "Asylums" under Insanity).

Bed—Long Confined to Bed—(See "Sick Bed" in this section).

Captivity—Held In—(See Captive).

Chronic Diseases—Confined By—(See Chronic, Infirmities, Invalids, Lameness, Paralysis, etc.).

Deformities—Malformations—Confinement By—(See Deformities, Malformations, Monsters, etc.).

Exile—(See Exile).

Hospitals—Confinement In—(See Hospitals).

Invalids—Confined Upon Sick Bed—(See Invalids. Also see "Sick Bed" in this section).

Limitations—Upon the Body—(See Limitations).

Parturition—The Period of Confinement—(See Parturition).

Prison—Confined In—(See "Imprisonment" under Prisons).

Restraints—Over Mind and Body—(See Restraint).

Sick Bed—Long Confinement Upon—The ☉ ☌ ♄ or ☽ in 12th H.; many afflictions in the 12th H.; ♄ in 12th H., and affl. the hyleg therefrom. Case—See "Seventeen Years In Bed", No.

843 in 1001 N.N. Case—See Fig. 25 in "Message of the Stars" by the Heindels. (See Chronic, Invalids, Lingering, Long Diseases, Prolonged, Tedious). See "Saturn Influence" under Saturn; Twelfth House.

CONFORMITY OF MEMBERS — (See "Well-Proportioned" under Well).

CONFUSION—

Ideas—Confusion of—(See Chaotic, Dreamy, Ideas, Projects).

Mind—Confusion of—(See "Mental Chaos" under Chaotic; "Inability" under Concentration; Dreamy, Fears, Flightiness).

CONGELATION—Clotting—Thickening —A Concretion—One of the four Operations of Nature, and ruled by ♄. (See Cirrhosis, Clots; "Operations" under Nature; Nitrogen).

CONGENITAL—Existing from Birth— Innate—The derivation, causes, and explanations of congenital afflictions, defects and deformities are shown in the figure of the Prenatal Epoch, in the aspects and afflictions to the ☽ in the Chart of Descent, and are reflected in the horoscope thru the interchange of the two factors the ☽ and the Asc. at the Epoch and at birth. The horoscope influences begin with the moment of birth, and continue in power until the death of the body. The ☉, ☽, Asc., or Hyleg much afflicted by malefics at B. will account for most of the diseases and afflictions which develop after birth, or known as Acquired Ailments. Deep-seated, organic, structural, and innate ailments, can usually be located in the map of the heavens for the time of conception, or in figures erected for the time of the return of the ☽ to her place each month during gestation. This subject is further discussed under Prenatal Epoch. The list of congenital defects is a large one, and a few of them are here suggested for study, and if the subject, or disease, is not mentioned here, look for it in the alphabetical arrangement. See the following subjects,—Acquired, Atrophy, Birth, Blemishes, Blind, Constitutional, Crippled, Cyclops, Deaf, Defects, Deformities, Distortions, Dumb, Excrescences, Heredity, Hermaphrodites, Idiots, Imbecility, Imperfections, Inhuman, Infancy, Lameness, Limbs, Maimed, Malformations, Marks, Members, Mind, Monsters Mutes, Naevus, New Moon, Organic, Organs, Paralysis, Pressure, Prenatal Epoch, Savage, Structural, Triplets, etc.

CONGESTION—Congestions—Hyperaemia of a Part—A ♄ disease and condition, and often caused by Cold and Chill, and also by the deposits of the waste materials of the body, causing stoppages, retention, crystallization, hardening, suppression of function, etc.; ♄ ☌ or ☍ Asc. Also a ♃ disease, as ♃ tends to congestion, surfeit, overfunctional activity of the part of the body ruled by the sign he is in at B., by dir., or by transit. The afflictions and bad asps. of ♃ to the ☉, ☽, ♀, Asc., or the hyleg, tend to, and principally from over-eating, gluttony, etc. Also

the ill-asps. of the ☽ to ♃ by tr., progression, or dir., tend to congestion of the part of the body ruled by the sign in which ♃ was posited at B. (See Centripetal, Chill, Circulation, Cold, Complications, Constrictions, Consumption, Deposits, Eating, Erythema, Functions, Gangrene, Gluttony, Hardening, Hyperaemia, Mortification, Plethora, Retention, Stoppages, Suppressions, Surfeits, Wastes, etc.).

Bowels — Congestion In — (See Bowels).

Brain—Congestion of the Blood in the Brain—Cerebral Congestion—Encephalic Congestion—The ☉ affl. in ♈; an ♈ disease; the ☉ ☌ ♄ or ♅ in ♈, and in □ asp. to ♃ or ♀; ♄ ☌ or ill-asp. the ☽, and espec. if neither be in ♈; ♃ affl. in ♈ or ♎; ♂ in ♈, affl. the hyleg at B., or ♂ in the 6th H., and afflicted. (See Accumulative, Brain, Cerebral; "Blood" under Head).

Bronchial Congestion — (See Asthma, Bronchial; "Congestion" under Lungs).

Cellular Congestion—(See Cells).

Cerebral Congestion—(See "Brain" in this section).

Ears—Congestion In—(See "Venous Circulation" under Ears).

Encephalic—(See "Brain" in this section).

External Congestions — (See External).

Eyes—Congestion of Muscles of— (See "Crystallization" under Eyes).

Face—(See "Congestion" under Face).

Inflammation—Congestive Inflammation—(See "Congestive" under Inflammation).

Internal Congestions—(See "Congestive" under Internal).

Intropulsive Congestion—(See Centripetal, Intropulsion).

Kidneys—Congestion In—(See Kidneys).

Lungs—Congestion In—(See "Bronchial" in this section).

Stomach—Congestion In—(See Stomach).

Vascular—(See "Vascular Fullness" under Vascular).

CONIUM—Hemlock—A typical drug of ♄.

CONJUNCTION ASPECT — (See Aspects).

CONJUNCTIVA—The Mucous Membrane of the Eye—Ruled by the ♈ Sign. Also especially ruled and influenced by ♆ when this planet is in ♈.

Caruncle—(See Caruncle).

Conjunctivitis—Inflammation of the Conjunctiva—Opthalmia—Sore Eyes— Ulcer—Eyes Red and Inflamed—The ☉ affl. in ♈; the ☉ affl. in fiery signs, and ☌, □, or ☍ the Asc. by dir.; the ☉ affl. the ☽ or Asc.; the ☉ or ☽ hyleg, and the ☉ to the □ or ☍ the ☽ by dir.; the ☉ to the □ or ☍ ♂ by dir., bloodshot and inflamed; the ☉ to the place of Cor Scorpio; a ☉ disease; the ☽ affl. in ♈; the ☽ in ♐ and affl. by the ☉ or ♂ when taken ill (Hor'y); the ☽ to the place of the Pleiades or Praesepe; ♆ in ♈, and affl. the ☽, Hyleg, or Asc.;

Ψ in Υ in the 6th H.; $\male$ in Υ, lord of the year at the Vernal Equi., and affl. by $\saturn$, much conjunctivitis prevalent; $\mercury$ lord of the year at the Vernal, and $\odot$ $\male$, much inflammation of the eyes generally; a $\male$ disease; a Ω disease, and afflictions in Ω; the Asc. to the place of the Ascelli or Capricornus; Fixed Stars of the nature of $\male$ and the $\moon$ ascending at B.; Subs at MCP, the 4th Cervical, and at KP. Green, the color of $\saturn$, is good for inflamed eyes, and to wear green glasses, or work in a green room, have green lamp shades, etc. Case—An Infant—Inflammation of eyes sets in a day or two after birth—See "Sight Defective", No. 684, in 1001 N.N. (See "Eye Trouble", "Inflamed", under Eyes; "Conjunctivitis" under Infancy; "Defective Sight" under Sight).

Trachoma— (See "Granulated" under Eyelids).

CONNECTIVE TISSUE—The Binding Tissue of the Body—Interstitial—Areolar Tissue—Cellular Tissue—Dominated largely by $\saturn$ and the $\capricorn$ sign.

Anasarca—(See "Anasarca" under Dropsy).

Cells—(See "Cellular Tissue", "Thickening", "Walls", under Cells).

Cirrhosis—Thickening—(See Cirrhosis).

Fiber—Connecting Fiber—(See Fiber).

Hardening—Induration—(See Hardening, Hypertrophy, Sclerosis).

Induration—(See Hardening).

Over-Growth—Of Connective Tissue—Of Organs—The work of $\saturn$, and mineral deposits.

Parenchyma—Soft Cellular and Connective Tissue—The Functioning of—(See Parenchyma).

Sarcoma—A Connective Tissue Tumor—(See Sarcoma).

Sclerosis—(See Hardening, Sclerosis).

Soft—Soft Connective Tissue—(See Parenchyma).

Thickening—(See Cirrhosis).

Tissues—(See the various paragraphs under Tissues).

CONSCIOUSNESS—Conscious Life—The $\odot$, his position, and aspects at B., are the essential factors in our conscious life. (See Ego).

Clouding of Consciousness—(See "Confusion", "Mental Chaos", under Chaotic; "Clouded" under Mind).

Unconsciousness—(See Anaesthetics, Catalepsy, Coma, Delirium, Dreams, Epilepsy, Faintings, Fits, Insanity, Insensibility, Madness, Sleep, Subconscious, Trance, etc.).

CONSERVATION—Conservation of the Mental and Bodily forces is the work of $\jupiter$ and $\venus$, the benefic planets. $\jupiter$ exerts a conservative and preservative influence over the body. The conserving, transforming and storing functions of the body are under the influence of $\jupiter$, $\venus$, and Ψ. (See "Substance" under Cells; "Conservation" under Energy; Nutrition, Preservation).

CONSIDERABLE—Considerable Diseases Ensue—See Disease; "Ill-Health All Thru Life", "Signs of Ill-Health", under Ill-Health; "Much Sickness" under Sickness; "Vitality Low" under Vitality; "Weak Body" under Weak).

CONSISTENCY—The Degree of Density or Hardness—

Adipose Tissue—The Consistency of Increased—(See Fat). See Condensation, Crystallization, Hardening.

CONSOLIDATION—Consolidating—The consolidating influences in the body are the work of $\saturn$, as in crystallization, condensation, hardening, etc. $\saturn$ $\sextile$ or $\trine$ the $\odot$ tends to strengthen and consolidate the constitution. Consolidation in Pneumonia is ruled by $\saturn$. (See Concretions, Condensation, Consistency, Crystallization, Deposits, Hardening, Minerals, Pneumonia, Retention, Stone, Suppression, Wastes).

CONSPICUOUS DISEASES—The $\moon$ or $\mercury$ unconnected with each other or the Asc., but the benefics $\jupiter$ and $\venus$ conciliated and posited in Eastern Parts, and in angles, and the malefics in Western Parts, under these conditions the disease may be highly conspicuous, but susceptible of a cure. (See Curable, Exhibition, Incurable).

Conspicuous Marks—(See Marks, Moles).

Conspicuous Mental Diseases—$\saturn$ and $\male$ angular and ori., and $\jupiter$ and $\venus$ setting and occi. (See Demoniac, Epilepsy, Frenzy, Fretfulness, Fury, Idiocy, Imbecility, Incurable, Insanity, Madness, Mania, etc.).

CONSTANCY—Constant—Fixed—Durable—Prolonged—

Cough—Constant Cough—(See "Constant" under Cough).

Disease—The constancy and duration of the effects of disease are aggravated and prolonged by the afflicting planet being stationary in position at B., or at the beginning of an illness. Also many planets in fixed signs at B., and at the beginning of, or duration of a disease, and espec. the afflicting planet, or planets, tends to make the disease more constant. (See Chronic, Continuity, Crises, Direct, Duration, Fever; "Fixed Signs" under Fixed; Persevering, Prolonged, Retrograde, Stationary, Tedious, etc.).

CONSTELLATIONS—(See Stars).

CONSTIPATION—A Sluggish Action of the Bowels—The $\odot$ affl. in $\virgo$ or $\capricorn$; the $\moon$ hyleg in $\virgo$ or $\capricorn$ in females; Ψ, $\Uranus$, or $\saturn$ in $\virgo$, and affl. the $\odot$ or $\moon$; a $\saturn$ disease; born under $\saturn$; $\saturn$ in $\taurus$, $\virgo$, $\scorpio$, or $\capricorn$; $\saturn$ in the Asc., and $\scorpio$ rising; $\saturn$ in some asp. to the Asc., or in ill-asp. to the $\moon$ or lord of the Asc.; $\saturn$ or $\Uranus$ in $\virgo$ or $\scorpio$ and afflicted; $\saturn$ and $\male$ in $\scorpio$, by bringing piles, tending to neglect of stools, and resulting in constipation; $\saturn$ affl. in $\scorpio$, and tending to an obstructed rectal region; $\male$ in $\virgo$, $\odot$ or ill-asp. the $\odot$; $\male$, ruler of the rectum, affl. by $\saturn$; $\venus$ in $\virgo$ and affl. the $\moon$ or Asc.; $\venus$ in $\capricorn$ in the 6th H., and affl.; $\mercury$ affl. in $\capricorn$, due to worry and melancholic tendencies; a $\taurus$ disease, by reflex to $\scorpio$; a $\virgo$ disease, and $\virgo$ on the

Asc.; afflictions in ♍; ♍ or ♎ on the 6th H.; Subs at KP, Li.P. and PP, (2L). Cases — See Figures 7, 8, and 27 in "Message of the Stars", by the Heindels. (See Faeces).

Headaches of Constipation—♄ affl. in ♍ or ♏; Subs at PP (2L). (See Headaches).

Nervous Constipation—☽ in ♍ ♂ ♄ and ☿; ♄ ♂ ☿ ♍. (See "Requirements" under Nature).

CONSTITUTION — Constitutional — Organic Constitution—The Physical Constitution—Constitutional Diseases, etc. —Planets in the East at B. affect the physical constitution. The 1st H., or the Asc., rule the constitution, the peculiarities and construction of the physical body. (See the Introduction under Body). In a female nativity the asps. to the ☽ determine the strength of the constitution, and the asps. and position of the ☉ in a male horoscope. In general, however, the strength of the constitution in both sexes is denoted by the ☉ at B., his asps. and power, as the ☉ is the central source of power, and the ☽, and other planets, reflect the Sun's rays, power and influence, for good or evil for the time, according to the aspects. In judging the constitution, the ☉, ☽, Asc., and Hyleg, and their conditions, must be carefully noted. (See "Strength" in this section). Many subjects concerning the physical constitution are considered under the Articles on Appearance, Body, Complexion, Defects, Form, Height, Organs, Stature, Weight, etc. The physical body, (the constitution), is subject to two classes of diseases, those which are congenital, innate, hereditary, organic and structural, and secondly, acquired and the more temporary ailments. (See Acquired, Acute, Chronic, Congenital, Diathesis, Organic, Prenatal, Structural, etc.). The Constitutional, or Conditional Signs, are the Cardinal, Fixed and Mutable classifications, and the Constitutional Temperament is determined by the groupings of the planets in the Constitutional Signs. (See Temperament). Note the following subjects, conditions, benefits, afflictions, diseases, etc., which have to do with the Constitution. For the diseases of the Constitution, and subjects which may not be listed here, see "Diseases", and also look for the subject in the alphabetical arrangement.

Cold Constitution — (See "Body" under Cold).

Cold and Dry — (See "Cold and Dry Body" under Dry).

Cold and Moist—(See "Cold and Moist Body" under Moisture).

Consolidation Of—(See Consolidation).

Constitutional Diseases—Organic Diseases—Structural Diseases—Innate —Hereditary—Inherent, etc.—These are diseases indicated by the radical map, and prenatal conditions, are more inherent, and in contrast to Acquired Diseases. The latter class of diseases are of shorter duration, more often acute, while Constitutional diseases tend to become chronic, and

sometimes incurable. Constitutional Diseases are ruled by the ☉, and the ☉ much affl. at B. brings the danger of serious and severe constitutional, deep-seated, and organic diseases. The ☉ affl. by the ☽ at B. tends to weaken the constitution, and make one more liable to some form of Constitutional Disease. Also the sign ♄ is in tends to weaken the part of the body ruled by such sign, and to make the part, or organ ruled by the sign, more subject to inherent disease, and espec. if ♄ be severely afflicted, or weak in the sign, and also the map show weak vitality in general, and poor health conditions. The following are a few of the more serious Constitutional Diseases, which have to do with Constitutional Disorders and Defects, their cause, etc., which subjects see in the alphabetical arrangement, — Anaemia, Asthma, Atrophy, Cancer, Chronic, Congenital, Consumption, Crystallization, Decay, Defects, Deformities, Distortions, Emaciation, Epilepsy, Excrescences, Hardening, Heredity, Incurable, Insanity, Latent, Leprosy, Leukaemia, Malnutrition (see Nutrition), Organic, Palsy, Paralysis, Phthisis, Prenatal, Rickets, Sclerosis, Scrofula, Stone, Structural, Suppressions, Tuberculosis, Wastings, etc. The lists of diseases given under Chronic, the Sun, and Saturn, also suggest diseases which tend to be constitutional, inherent, and organic. Also see "New Moon", "First Quarter", "Full", "Last Quarter", under Moon; "Solar-Lunar" under Solar.

Constitutional Hurts—(See "Hurts" in this section).

Defects — Constitutional Defects — (See Defects).

Diathesis; Dry Constitution — (See "Dry Body" under Dry).

Dry and Cold — (See "Cold and Dry Body" under Dry).

Dry and Hot — (See "Dry and Hot Body" under Dry).

Dull Constitution—Dull and Effeminate—♋ gives; ♋ on the Asc. (See Dull, Effeminate).

Effeminate in Constitution — (See Effeminate).

Endurance—Of the Constitution— (See Endurance, Recuperation, Resistance, Solid, Strong, Vitality, Good).

Feeble Constitution—(See Feeble, Infirm, Weak, etc.).

Female Constitution — The Strength or Weakness of—(See "Constitution" under Female).

Fine Constitution—(See "Good" in this section).

Frail Constitution — (See "Weak" in this section).

Full — The Constitution is at Full when the ☉ at B. is between the middle of the 1st H., on around by the Mid-heaven, and on down to the middle of the 6th H., and in a Hylegiacal Place. (See Hyleg).

Functions—When there is no asp. between the ☉ and ☽ at B. constitutional defects do not disturb the functional activities, and also functional derangements do not act detrimentally upon the vitality. (See Defects, Functions).

Good Constitution—Fine Constitution—Advantageous Stature—Strong Constitution—Healthy Body—Vitality Strong—The Quadrant from the Asc. to the Nadir tends to produce, and espec. the 1st H. strong at B., and a fiery sign upon the Asc.; the ☉ in the Asc., or M.C., and well-asp.; the ☉ in ♐ unless the hyleg be affl.; the ☉ strong and dignified at B.; the ☉, ☽, and Asc. well-asp. by benefics, and free from evil asps. of malefics; the ☽ strong at B., and free from affl.; ♄ ori.; ♄ moderately fortified in the 1st H., and in good asp. to the ☉, ☽, ♃, or ♀; ♃ ascending at B., and in good asp. to the ☉ and ☽; ♃ in the 1st H., or having the same or opposite Dec. with the Asc.; ♃ ✳ or △ the ☉ and if the ☽ and Asc. be free from affl.; ♃ or ♀ in the Asc. at B., and well-asp.; ♂ ascending at B.; ♂ ☌, ✳ or △ the ☉; ♀ ascending at B., well-placed and aspected; ♈, ♌, ♏, ♎, ♏, or ♐ on the Asc.; given by the fixed signs when on the angles at B., and well-fortified and occupied; the ♒ influence when strong, or on the Asc., gives a healthy appearance. (See "Good Health" under Health; "Great Physical Powers" under Physical; Recuperation, Resistance, Robust, Ruddy, Stamina; "Body" under Strong; Tone, Vitality Good).

Harmonious Constitution—(See "Good Health" under Health; Harmony. See "Good Constitution" in this section).

Hot Constitution—(See "Hot Bodily Temperament" under Heat, Temperament).

Hot and Dry—(See Choleric; "Hot and Dry" under Heat; "Dry and Hot" under Temperament).

Hot and Moist—(See "Hot and Moist" under Moisture, Temperament).

Hurts—Constitutional Hurts—These may be in the form of disease, wounds, or injuries to the body. Planets in the 8th H. tend to, and at the time they set in ☌ with the Desc. by oblique descension. (See Accidents, Hurts, Injuries, Wounds).

Increased Strength—Of the Constitution—(See "Strengthened" in this section).

Internal Diseases—(See Internal).

Moist Constitution—(See "Bodily Temperament" under Moist).

Moist and Cold—(See "Cold and Moist Body" under Moist).

Moist and Hot—(See "Hot and Moist Body" under Moist).

Not Very Strong—(See Debility, Feeble, Infirm, Sickly, Vitality Low; "Weak Body" under Weak).

Organic Diseases—(See Internal, Organic, Structural).

Positive Constitution—(See Positive).

Powerful Constitution—Given by the ☉ in a fiery sign, and espec. when the ☉ is in a fiery sign in the Asc. (See "Strong" in this section).

Robust Constitution—Ruddy—(See Robust, Ruddy).

Sensitive Constitution—(See Sensitive).

Sickly—(See Delicate; "Ill-Health All Thru Life" under Ill-Health; Pale; "Much Sickness" under Sickness; Sickly, Vitality Low, Weak, etc.).

Signs—The Constitutional Signs—(See the Introduction to this Article).

Solid Constitution—(See Solid).

Sound Constitution—(See "Good", "Powerful", "Strong", in this section).

Stamina—(See Stamina, Tone; "Vital Force" under Vital; Vitality, etc.).

Strength—Of the Constitution—The strength and vital forces of the Constitution depend upon the position of the ☉ at B., and must be judged by the influence of the ☉, no matter in what part of the horoscope he may be in, in either a male or female nativity. (See the Introduction to this section).

Strengthened—The Strength of the Constitution Increased—The ☉ well-asp. by the ☽ at B.; the ☉ in a fiery sign; the ☉ ☌, or good asp. ♃; the ☉ well-asp. by ♂; the ☽ in ♉, ♎, ♏, or ♓; ♆ in ✳ or △ asp. the ☉ benefits the constitution psychically rather than in a physical way; ♄ ✳ or △ the ☉ tends to strengthen and consolidate the constitution. (See "Increased" under Vitality).

Strong Constitution—(See "Body" under Strong. Also see "Good", "Powerful", in this section).

Strongest Constitution—The ☉ gives the strongest constitution when in the 1st, 10th, or 7th H.; the next strongest when in the 9th or 11th H., and weaker when in the 8th or 12th H. (See "Strongest Body" under Strong).

Vital Force—(See Vital).

Vitality—(See Vitality).

Weak Constitution—(See Feeble, Invalids, Majority, Retrograde, Sickly; "Much Sickness" under Sickness; "Low" under Vitality; "Weak Body" under Weak).

Weak Parts—Of the Body—(See "Weak Parts" under Parts).

Weakened Constitution—(See Depletion, Lack of, Lessened, Weakened, under Vitality).

Weaker Constitution—The ☉ below the horizon at B., and not in a hylegiacal place, tends to give a weaker constitution. (See "Weaker" under Weak).

Weakest Constitution—The ☉ in the watery signs ♋ or ♓, and afflicted by malefics or the ☽; ♋ or ♓ on the Asc. at B. (See "Weakest" under Weak).

Weakness—Constitutional Weakness—See the various paragraphs in this section. See Vitality Low; "Weak Body" under Weak. Case—A Case of Constitutional Weakness—See "Loss of Hair", No. 121, in 1001 N.N.

CONSTRICTIONS—Stenosis—Contractions—Constrictive—Constrictor Nerves—The Blood Vessels of the surface and extremities are constricted by cold, the work of ♄, driving the blood inwards, causing internal congestions, colds, etc. The influence of ♄ is to narrow, bind, and constrict, and to cause stenosis of vessels, or parts. ♄, the ruler of ♑ and ♒, has a special pathological action over the cutaneous capillary vaso-constrictor nerves, and by cold to cause them to contract, throwing the blood inwards. Constrictions also are caused by the contracting influence of ♅, and espec. of the spasmodic variety. Constrictions may occur in any narrowed channel of the body, as in the Blood Vessels, Bowels, Capillaries, Ducts, Nose, Heart, Pylorus, Throat, Ureters, Urethra, and caused by ♄ afflictions, and with these planets in the sign ruling the afflicted part. See these parts in the alphabetical arrangement, or any other part or organ you may have in mind, and remember that ♄ especially tends to constrict, hamper, restrain, and suppress any part or organ ruled by the sign containing ♄ at B. ♆ is also referred to by some Authors as causing constrictions. (See Astringents, Capillaries, Centripetal, Cold, Colds, Congestions, Contractions, Cramps, Hernia, Spasmodic, Stenosis, Strictures; "Vaso-Constrictor" under Vaso; Vessels).

CONSTRUCTIVE — Constructive Energies—Constructive Metabolism—Anabolism—Constructive Processes—Constructive Functions—The ☉ and ♂ are constructive in the body. The principle of the ☉ is constructiveness, and the constructive energies in the body are directly under the influence and rule of the ☉. The ☽ rules the constructive functions, and the general health. In subsidiary ways ♄ and ♂ have a part in the constructive work going in the body. Bone building is carried on by mineral deposits formed by ♄. Mars has a constructive influence by burning up wastes and refuse in the body by fevers and inflammations. (See Action, Blood, Bones, Destructive, Energy, Fevers, Functions, Granulations, Haemoglobin, Inflammation, Iron, Mars, Metabolism, Muscles, Nerves, Sun, Tissues, Vital).

Constructive Mind—(See Inventive).

CONSUMPTION — Consumptions—A Consumption — Consumptive—A Consuming Disease—A Wasting Disease—Tuberculosis—Phthisic—Phthisis, etc. —Consumption is a ♄ disease, appears in many parts of the body, and is a consuming, or wasting of that part, and is not limited to the lungs. Note the following Consumptive conditions.

A Consumption—♄ ☌ or evil asp. the Asc. by dir.; ♃ affl. in ♍; the Asc. to the ☌ or ill-asp. ♄ by dir., and ♄ occi. at B.

Abdominal Phthisis—(See Phthisis).

Acquired Consumption — This affection, and also congestion of the lungs, are often caused by the afflicted bodies being in the ♒ sign.

Acute Phthisis—(See Phthisis).

Adrenals—Consumption of—(See Adrenals).

Appearance—Consumptive Appearance—The 4th face of ♊, the 2nd face of ♋ or ♌ on the Asc. at B. (See Complexion, Face, Pale, Sickly, White).

Asthma—(See Asthma).

Bones—Tuberculosis of—(See Bones).

Bowels—Consumption In—(See "Abdominal" under Phthisis).

Bronchial Consumption—(See Bronchial).

Chest—Consumption In—(See "Disorders" under Chest).

Cold In Feet—Consumption From—(See "Cold Taken In" under Feet).

Colliquative Sweats—Of Phthisis—(See "Night Sweats" under Phthisis).

Consumptions—General—Prevalent—♄ or ☿ (when ☿ partakes of the nature of ♄) sole rulers of a Solar Eclipse; a ☍ disease.

Consumptive—Liable to Consumption—Danger of—Tendency to—Predisposed to some form of Consumption, Tuberculosis, and a Wasting Disease—The ☉ affl. in common signs in the 6th or 12th H.; the ☉ in ♓ in the 6th or 12th H., and affl. by ♄ and malefics; the ☉ hyleg and affl. by ♄ in an angle, and espec. with ♄ in the Asc.; the ☉ and ☿ in the 6th H., in a common sign, and afflicted, and with ♍ rising; the ☉ or ☽ in the 6th H. in a common sign, and affl. by ♄; a ☽ disease; ☽ to the ☌ ♄ by dir.; prog. ☽ ☌ ♄ in ♊, galloping consumption; ♆ in ♉, ♊, or ♋; ♄ denotes death by; ♄ ☌ the Asc. by dir.; ♄ in ♉, ♊, ♋, or ♓; ♄ afflictions to the hyleg; ♄ on the M.C. in □ or ☍ the ☉, and espec. if ♄ is in a common sign; ♄ ☌ or ill-asp. the ☉ at B., and by dir., and espec. in common signs; ♄ affl. in the 6th H. in a common sign; ♂ affl. in ♉, ♊, or ♋; ☿ Sig. ☌ the ☉, and the ☉ ill-dig.; lords of the 1st or 6th H., or the ☽, in earthy signs, and affl.; a ☍, ♊, and ♋ disease, and afflictions in these signs; many planets in common signs; a common sign on the Asc., and espec. ♓; common signs on the cusp of 6th H.; malefics in ♊, ♐, or ♓, and espec. consumption in the lungs; afflictions from malefics in common signs, and espec. when the malefic is in the common sign division of the common sign in which placed; Subs at Lu.P. (See Lungs, Navamsa, Phthisis, Tuberculosis; "Body" under Wasting). Cases of Consumption—See "Bankruptcy", No. 093; "Consumption", No. 070, No. 348, No. 678; "Spendthrift", No. 262, all in 1001 N.N.

Danger of Consumption—(See "Consumptive" in this section. Also see "Pulmonary" under Phthisis).

Death by Consumption—♄ denotes death by; the hyleg affl. by ♄; denoted by fixed stars of the nature of ♄ or ☿; ♄ in a common sign, the afflictor in the disease, afflicting the hyleg, and holding the dominion of death; ☿ affl. in 8th H. (See "Death" under Phthisis). Cases of Death By—See the cases under "Consumptive" in this section. Also see Chap. 14, page 104 in Daath's Medical Astrology.

Diseases Proceeding From—Diseases Which Proceed from Consumption—(See the various paragraphs in this section. Also see Atrophy, Emaciation, Wasting, etc.).

Feet—Consumption from Colds Taken in the Feet—(See "Cold Taken In Feet" under Feet).

Galloping Consumption—(See "Consumptive" in this section).

Hectic Fever of Phthisis—(See Phthisis).

Inward Parts—Consumption of—(See "Consumption" under Reins).

Knees—Consumptive Pains In—(See Knees).

Laryngeal Consumption—(See Larynx).

Liable To—(See "Consumptive" in this section).

Lingering Consumption—Long Continued—Earthy signs in the Asc. or 6th H., or the ☽ in an earthy sign at B., or at decumbiture; ♄ the afflictor in the disease; ♄ in the 6th or 8th H., in a common sign, and affl. the hyleg. (See Ague, Chronic, Lingering; "Diseases" under Long; Prolonged, Slow, Tedious).

Lungs—Consumption of—Tuberculosis of—(See "Pulmonary" under Phthisis; Tuberculosis).

Lupus—A Tubercular Skin Disease—(See Lupus).

Mother—The Mother Afflicted with Consumption—Death By—(See "Consumption" under Mother).

Night Sweats Of—(See "Night Sweats" under Phthisis).

Pains—Consumptive Pains in Knees or Thighs—(See Knees, Thighs).

Phthisis—(See Phthisis).

Pulmonary Consumption—(See "Pulmonary" under Phthisis).

Reins—Consumption of—(See Reins).

Scrofula—Tubercular Tendency In—(See Scrofula).

Skin—Tubercular Skin Disease—(See Lupus).

Suprarenal Capsules—Consumption, or Tuberculosis of—(See Adrenals).

Symptoms of Consumption—Symptoms of Spleen—The ☽ in ♉, ☐ or ☍ ♄ (or ☿ if he be of the nature of ♄) at the beginning of an illness, or at decumbiture (Hor'y). (See "Consumptive" in this section).

Tendency To—(See "Consumptive" in this section).

Thighs—Consumptive Pains In—(See Thighs).

Tuberculosis—(See Tuberculosis).

Various Forms of Consumption—Caused by the afflictions of ♄ at B., and by dir.; the Asc. ☌ or ill-asp. ♄ by dir., and ♄ occi. at B.; earthy signs on the Asc. or 6th H. at B., or at decumbiture, or the Sigs. of the disease in such signs.

Wasting Away—Or Consumption—(See Emaciation, Hardening, Tabes, Wasting, etc. Also note the various paragraphs in this section).

CONTAGIOUS DISEASES—Contagions—The Process of Transfer of Specific Diseases—Infectious Diseases—Communicable Diseases—The ☉ affl. in ♏ or ♓; the ☉ to the ☌ ☋ by dir.; the ☽ people become easy subjects to contagious and infectious diseases and fevers; ♅ affl. in the Asc. at B. makes the native more subject to contagious diseases; caused and ruled by ♂ afflictions; a ♂ and ♏ disease; ♂ Sig. ☌ the ☉. The ♏ sign, having an excess of magnetic power, tends to attract disease, and espec. contagious and infectious complaints, and the ♏ people fall easy victims to epidemics. (See "Corrupt Air" under Air; Amulets, Cholera, Epidemics, Eruptions, External, Infectious, Influenza, Magnetic, Measles, Pestilence, Plague, Pox, Scarlet Fever, Smallpox, Venereal, Vesicles, etc.). For Contagious Diseases not listed here, see the subject in the alphabetical arrangement.

Death By—Death By a Contagious or Infectious Fever—The planetary influences causing contagious and infectious diseases are much the same, and death by these diseases and fevers is espec. caused by the severe afflictions of ♂ to the hyleg at B., and by dir. (See Infectious, Mars, Perihelion, Scorpio, etc.).

CONTENTMENT—Contented—Content of Mind—Health of Mind—Peace of Mind—The ☉ well-asp. at B., and espec. by the ☽ and ♂, and the ☉ to the good asps. the Asc. by dir.; the ☉ or ☽ to the ☌ or good asps. ♃ by dir.; the ☉ directed to Arista; the ☽ well-asp. at B., and to the ☌ or good asp. ♃, ♀, or the Asc. by dir.; the ☽ to the ☌ ☊ by dir.; ♃ at a Solar Rev. passing the place of the radical ☽, and the ☽ well-asp. at B., or ♃ passing over the radical ♄ if ♄ be in one of his strong signs and well-asp. at B.; the Asc. meeting the good directions of the benefics; the Asc. to the place of Crater or ⊕ by dir.; good asps. to ♀ and the ♎ sign; Arista ascending at B. The benefic asps. and influences at B., and by dir. tend to bring peace and contentment. (See Cheerfulness, Comforts, Discontentment, Fortune, Happiness; "Good Health" under Health; Hope, Jovial, Joy, "Peace of Mind" under Mind; Optimistic, Prosperity, Restlessness, etc.).

CONTESTS—Killed or Injured in Some Contest—The ☉ Sig. to the ☐ or ☍ ♂; the 26° ☐ on the Asc. at B. is said to bring such a fate. (See Disputes, Duels, Feuds, Fighting, Gunshot, Instruments, Quarrels, Sword, War, etc.).

CONTINUITY—Continuous—Continued—The Continuity of Disease is associated with the Fixed Signs. The afflicting planet stationary tends to continuity, duration of effects, and constancy of the disease. Direct motion of the afflicting planet favors continuity of the disease. A planet ℞ tends to disorganization of the disease when the afflictor, and to solution of continuity. (See Amelioration, "Better" under Disease; Chronic, Constancy, Course, Crises, Direct, Duration, Fixed Signs (see Fixed); Incurable, Interrupted, Invalids, Lingering, Long Diseases (see Long); Moderation, Prolonged, Relapse, Resolution, Retrograde, Sequence, Return, Tedious, Worse, etc.).

Continued Fever—See "Constant", "Low", under Fever; Flux).

Continued Sickness—The Disease Prolonged—The afflicting planets in fixed signs; the ♂ of the rulers of the 1st and 6th houses unless free from affliction. Continuous fevers grow worse towards sunset. (See the references in the first part of this section).

Disease Will Continue—The Disease Will Continue Until, etc.—The lord of the 1st H. in the 6th, and the lord of the 6th in the 1st H., the disease will continue until one of them quits the sign he is in, and then if he meets the □ or ☍ of ♄, ♂, or lords of the 4th or 8th, it is a symbol of death. (See Duration).

Life—Continuity of After Birth—(See "Continuance" under Life).

Muscles—Continued Contraction of—(See Contraction, Muscles, Tetanus; "Tonic" under Spasmodic).

Pains and Aches—Continuous—(See the various paragraphs under Aches, Headaches, Neuralgia, Pains).

Solution of Continuity—(See the Introduction to this section).

Spasms — Spasmodic Action — Continuous—(See "Muscles" in this section).

CONTORTIONS—Contorted—Twistings—A ♅ disease. The organ of Coordination is under the rule of ♌, and reflex afflictions in ♌ from ♏, the exalted sign of ♅, tend to contortions and twistings of parts.

Awry Gait—A Twisted Walk—(See "Awry" under Gait).

Rigid Parts—Contortions of—(See Rigid).

Wry Neck—Torticollis—(See Neck). See Congenital, Contractions, Coordination, Deformities, Distortions, Erratic, Face, Features, Genitals, Lameness, Muscles, Paralysis, Spasmodic, Spine, Subluxations, Trunk, Twistings).

CONTRACTIONS—Contracted—Contracting—♄ is contracting in his influence, and also the influence of Cold, and Astringent Drugs, which he rules. Cold Diseases, ruled by ♄, are accompanied by contractions. ♆ is contractive and astringent. ♅ tends to spasmodic contractions by his afflictions to the Center of Coordination ruled by ♌; ♅ in the 6th H. tends to contractions, spasmodic and erratic diseases; the ☽ affl. by ♅; ♄ influence; ♄ ♂ or ill-asp. ♅. Parts of the body ruled by the signs containing the malefics, ♆, ♅, and ♄ at B., or parts afflicted by the asps. of these malefics, are subject to contractions, and the list of diseases associated with contractions would be too long to list here. Look in the alphabetical arrangement for the subject you have in mind. Also see the following subjects,—Astringent, Capillaries, Clonic, Cold, Colic, Compressed, Constrictions, Contortions, Convulsions, Coordination, Cramps, Deformities, Depressions, Distortions, Dwarfed, Epilepsy; "Movements" under Erratic; Exaggerated, Expansion; "Crossed Eyes" under Eyes; "Club Feet" under Feet; Fits, Gripings; "Orifice" under Heart; Hyperkinesia, Imperforate, Incoordination, Inertia, Irregular, Jerky, Legs, Limbs, Muscles; "Wry Neck" un-

der Neck; Opisthotonos; "Spasmodic" under Pain; Retraction, Rigidity, Saint Vitus Dance; "Spasms" under Spasmodic, Tonic; Spine, Stature, Stenosis, Stiffness; "Pylorus" under Stomach; Strictures, Tetanus, Tics, Torsion, Torticollis, Tremors, Twistings, Windpipe; "Hour Glass" under Womb; "Wry Neck" under Neck, etc.

CONTRACTS—

Contracts Disease Easily—☽ people; born under the strong influence of the ☽, or with the ☽ much afflicted at B. by the ☉ and malefics, and with little assistance to the ☽ from the benefics. (See Attracts, Contagious, Magnetic, Resistance; "Low" under Vitality).

Injury Thru Contracts—Death Thru Contests, Quarrels, etc. (See Contests, Duels).

CONTRARIES—(See Antipathy, Hippocrates).

CONTROL—

Mind—Lack of Control Over—(See Anger; "Brain Storms" under Brain; Chaotic, Coma, Confusion, Delirium, Demoniac, Fears, Furious, Fury, Hypochondria, Idiocy, Insanity, Intemperate, Madness, Mania, Melancholy, Mental, Mind, Obsessions; "Self-Control" under Self; Spirit Controls, Suicide, Temper, Uncontrolled, Vicious, Violent, Worry, etc.).

Muscles—Lack of Control Over—(See Erratic, Incoordination, Involuntary, Jerky Muscles, Paralysis, Spasmodic, Tics, Twitchings, Uncontrolled, etc.).

Self-Control—(See this subject under Self).

Spirit Controls—(See this subject).

Voice—(See "Control" under Voice).

CONTROVERSIES—Death or Injury By—(See Contests, Duels, Fighting, Quarrels, etc.).

CONTUSIONS—(See Assaults, Attacks, Blows, Bruises, Falls, Fractures, Kicks, etc.).

CONVALESCENCE—Recovery from Disease—(See Abatement, Amelioration; "Better" under Disease; Continuity, Crises, Improvement, Moderation, Recovery, Resolution, etc.).

CONVERTIBLE DISEASES—(See Curable).

CONVICTS—Danger of Injury By, or Death at Hands of Fellow Prisoners—(See Prisons).

CONVULSIONS—A Spasm or Fit—Spasmodic Jerking—In Convulsions the trouble lies between the fixed and common signs, and also the fixed and common Navamsas are in full evidence. (See Navamsa). The Nervous System is ruled by the common signs, and espec. ♊ and ♐. Convulsions are a secondary complaint, and result from some other cause or complaint. They may be Epileptic in origin. Convulsions are an ♈ and ♌ disease; a ☿ disease; ♅ is also spasmodic and convulsive, and his afflictions to ☿ or the hyleg, tend to convulsions; ♅ affl. by ♆; ♅, ♄, ☿ and the ☽ in fixed signs and afflicted; the ☽ to the ♂ or ill-asp.

♂ by dir., in children, and may result in death; the ☽ and ☿ affl. by ♅ and ♄; a majority of planets in fixed signs; caused by Subs at AT, AX, CP, KP (11D), and at PP. Cases of Convulsions, Birth Data, etc., are considered on pages 85 and 86, Chap. 13, in Daath's Medical Astrology. Cases of Death by Convulsions, see "Convulsions", No. 155, and "Short Life", No. 371, in 1001 N.N.· (For further influences see Coma, Contractions, Coordination; "Dentition" under Teeth; Delirium, Eclampsia, Epilepsy, Erratic, Faintings, Fits, Hysteria, Incoordination, Infancy, Involuntary; "Spasms" under Spasmodic; Uremia, etc.).

Death by Convulsions—(See the first part of this Article. Also see "Death" under Fits).

Movements—Convulsive Movements—(See Contractions, Cough, Cramps, Erratic, Incoordination, J e r k y, Movements, Muscles, Saint Vitus Dance, Spasmodic, Tics, Twitchings, etc.).

Puerperal Convulsions—At Delivery —(See "Convulsions" under Parturition).

Uremic Convulsions—(See Uremia).

COOLING—Refrigerant—A therapeutic property of ♄. (See Cold, Refrigerant, Saturn).

Cooling Medicines—Cooling Remedies —(See Ice; "Cooling" under Medicines; Snow).

COORDINATION—Harmonious A c t i o n —The instrument of coordinated action is under the rule of the ♍ sign. The Cerebellum is the organ of Coordination. (See Cerebellum).

Coordinated Action—Harmonious Action in the Body—(See Balance, Dexterity, Equilibrium, Harmony; "Good Health" under Health; "Clear Intellect" under Intellect; "Judgment Good" under Judgment; "Good · Mind" and "Peace of Mind" under Mind; Perception, Reason, Rhythm, Understanding).

Disorders of Coordination—(See such subjects as Action, Anxiety, Ataxia, Contortions, Convulsions, Cramps, Disease, Distortions, Epilepsy, Erratic, Fits, Gait, Hiccough, Hysteria, Ill-Health, Incoordination, Insanity, Involuntary, Jerkings, Lameness, Melancholia, M o t i o n, Movement, Muscles, Nausea, Paralysis, Saint Vitus Dance, Spasmodic, Speech, Taurus, Tetanus, Tics, Tremors, Twitchings, Unbalanced, Walk, Winking, Worry, etc.).

COPIOUS—Excessive—

Discharges—Copious or Excessive Discharges—(See Blood, Bowels, Catarrh, Cholera, Defluxions, Diarrhoea, Discharges, Dysentery, Ears, Excess, Excessive, Eyes, Faeces, Fluids, Fluxes, Head, Humours, Leucorrhoea, Menses, Nose, Rheum, Sweat, Urine, etc.).

COPPER—Cuprum—Ruled by ♀. A typical drug of ♀. Copper is correlated with ♀ and the color Indigo. (See Amulets, Cholera, Therapeutics).

COPROLALIA—The insane use of obscene words. (See "Obscene" under Speech).

COR HYDRA—(See Hydra's Heart).

Cor Leonis—(See Regulus).

Cor Scorpio—(See Antares).

CORAL — (See Amulets, Lime, Whooping Cough).

CORD—Cords—

Silver Cord—(See Silver).

Spermatic Cord—(See Spermatic).

Spinal Cord—(See Spine).

Umbilical Cord—(See Navel).

Vocal Cords—(See Vocal).

CORDIALS—An Aromatic S p i r i t o u s Stimulant—Ruled by ♀. (See Stimulants, T o n i c s; "Professions" under Venus; Wines).

CORIUM—The deep layer of the Cutis. (See Derma, Skin).

CORN—

Corn Destroyed—(See Drought, Fruit, Famine; "Corn" under Scarcity; Vegetation, Wheat).

CORNEA—(See "Cornea" under Eyes).

CORNIFICATION — Making Hard or Horny — ♄ influence. (See Bunions; "Skin" under Hardening; Horny, Scales).

CORNS—Bunions—(See Bunions; "Skin" under Hardening; Scales).

CORONARY—Coronary Plexuses — (See "Middle Cervical" under Ganglion).

CORPSE—

Devoured After Death—(See "Birds of the Air" under Air; "Body Devoured" under Burial; Vultures).

Dissolution Of—(See Cremation, Decay, Disintegration, Dissolution, Matter).

Rigor Mortis—(See Rigors, Morgues).

CORPULENT—Corpulency—Largeness of the Body—Obesity—Adiposis—The ☉, ☽, and many planets in watery signs, or with such signs upon the Asc. at B.; the ☉ ♒ partile Asc., middle stature, corpulent, and well-made; the ☽ gives a smooth, corpulent and phlegmatic body; the ☽ when ori. gives a body more corpulent, tall and smooth; the ☽ ♉, partile Asc., strong, corpulent and well-set; the ☽ ♒ partile Asc., corpulent, middle-sized, but well-formed; ♄ in N. Lat. makes the body more corpulent, strong and bony; ♄ ♒ partile the Asc.; ♃ influence; born under ♃ if ♃ is ori.; ♂ ♉, partile the Asc., corpulent, short and compact; ♂ ♍ partile Asc., corpulent, well-set and middle sized; ♂ ♒ partile Asc., corpulent, well-set and tall, or middle-sized; ♀ ♏ partile Asc., short, corpulent and well-set; ♀ ♒, handsome, well-made and rather corpulent; ☿ ♉ partile Asc., corpulent, well-set, and middle stature; ♏ on the Asc., corpulent, strong, robust, middle-sized; ♒ on the Asc., sometimes corpulent. (See Bulky, Fat, Fleshy, Full, Large, Mean, Middle Life, Muscles, Obesity, Phlegmatic, Plump, Portly, Puffing, Robust, Short, Stout, Strong, Tall, Thick, Well-Set).

CORPUSCLES—Blood Corpuscles—(See Anaemia, Haemoglobin, Iron, Leukocytes; "Blood" under Red).

CORRESPONDENCES—Law of Signatures—(See Antipathy, Harmony, Signature, Sympathy).

CORROSION—To Eat Away, and Destroy—The general influence of ♄ on the tissues by his evil aspects and afflictions is to eat away, waste, and destroy, or cause decay. ♅ has an especially corrosive influence on the Nervous System, tending to Lesions and Paralysis. ☿ affl. by ♅ also tends to corrosion of the nerves. (See Decay, Destructive, Lesions, Paralysis, Saturn, Uranus, Wasting, etc.).

CORRUPT—Corruptive—Corruption—Corruptive Disorders are ♄ and ☽ diseases as a rule.

  Corrupt Air—(See Air).

  Corrupt Blood—(See Carbon; "Morbid", "Poor", "Thin", "Too Much Blood", under Blood; Foul, Impure; "Non-Oxygenation" under Oxygen; Ulcers).

  Corrupt Breath — (See "Foul" under Breath).

  Corruption of Fruit—Sickness from Eating—(See Fruit).

  Corrupt Humours—Corruptive Disorders—(See Decay, Humours, Impure, Mortification, Pus, Putrefaction).

  Corruption of Waters—Corruption of Moisture—(See Fish, Moisture, Rivers, Waters).

CORTICAL—Cortex—The external gray layer of the brain. Is ruled by ♈.

  Cortical Lesions — (See Lesions; "Aphasia" under Speech).

  Cortical Substance—Of the Kidneys—(See Kidneys).

CORYZA—Catarrhal Inflammation of the Nose—(See "Coryza" under Nose).

COSMETICS—Remedies for Beautifying the Skin—Lotions—Hair Tonics—Toilet Articles, etc.—

  Indiscreet Use Of—Injurious Use of —Venus has to do with the complexion and skin of the face, and disorders from unwise use of Cosmetics. ♀ in ♈, eruptions due to injudicious use of cosmetics; ♀ affl. in ♈ in the 6th H.; ♀ affl. in ♑ tends to misuse of skin and hair lotions, and to mar the beauty of the complexion; ♆ affl. in ♑ tends to indiscreet use of cosmetics and lotions; ♎ people are more adversely affected by their use, as ♎ is the exalted sign of ♄, and tends to skin diseases. (See Barbers, Complexion, Eruptions, Face, Lotions, Pimples, Skin, etc.).

COSTAL—Pertaining to the Ribs—(See Intercostal, Ribs).

COSTIVENESS—Hardness and Retention of the Faeces—(See "Sluggish" under Bowels; Constipation; "Hardening" under Faeces; "Requirements" under Nature; Retention).

COUGH—Tussis—Coughs—A Sudden, Forced Expiratory Noise—Caused by afflictions in ♉, ♊, ♋, ♍, ♐, and ♓, and afflictions in the common signs. The planets tending to cause coughs are the ☽, ♄, ♅, ♂, and ☿. Afflictions in ♉ and ♍, supplemental signs, cause coughs originating more in the throat, as ♍ suffers almost as much from

coughs and throat troubles as ♉. Afflictions in ♊, ♐, or ♓ tend to lung coughs. ♅ causes convulsive and spasmodic coughs when affl. in ♊. The coughs arising from weakness, lingering and chronic diseases, as from Consumption or Tuberculosis, are caused by ♄, and espec. when ♄ is in ♊ or ♓, and afflicted. Afflictions in ♋ tend to stomach coughs, and also all coughs and colds in general. Coughs are caused by ♄ when he has strong rule (and by ☿ when he is of the nature of ♄), and the dominion of death is vested in them; ♄ in an angle, occi. of the ☉, and ori. of the ☽; ♄ to the ♂ or ill-asps. the ☽ if the ☽ is hyleg, or ruler of the 6th or 8th H. at B.; ♄ ♂ the Asc. by dir.; ♄ ♂ ♂ in ♉ or ♊; ♄ ♂ ♅ or ♆ in ♊; the ☉ to the ♂ ♄ or ☿ by dir.; the ☽ hyleg, and to the ♂ or ill-asps. the ☉ or ♄ by dir.; the ☽ decr. in light, sepr. from ♄ and applying to ☿; the ☽ in ♋ and affl. by the ☉ or ♂; the ☽ to the bad asps. the ☉; the ☽ in ♋ at B., and the transit of ♄ over the place of the radical ☽, and espec. if the native is of weak constitution; the ☽ in ♋ or ♎, ♄ or ill-asp. ♄ (or ☿ if he be of the nature of ♄) at the beginning of an illness, there is cough, and if the ☽ be decr., and near the place of ♄, the cough will tend to be of long duration; ♂ affl. in ♊; ♂ ♂ ☿ in ♊; a ☿ disease; ☿ affl. in ♊ or ♐; ☿ affl. at B., and evilly aspecting the Asc. by dir.; ☿ sole ruler at an eclipse; the Asc. to the ill-asps. ♄ by dir.; the Asc. to the ill-asps. ☿ by dir., and ☿ affl. by ♄ at B.; malefics in ♊, and afflicting ♃ and ♀, rulers of the circulation, and interfering with proper oxygenation of the blood; watery signs on the Asc. and 6th H. at B., or at decumbiture, and the Sigs. in water signs at the beginning of an illness. (See the various pararaphs in this section).

Bilious Dry Cough—♂ affl. in ♋. (See Bile).

Bronchial Cough—(See "Cough" under Bronchial). Also caused by Subs at AP, L.C.P. (6th C.), and at SP.

Constant Cough—Seldom Free from a Cough—♅ ♂ ♄ in ♉, and affl. the ☉, ☽, or Asc.; denoted by ♄; ♄ strong at B., and affl. the hyleg, seldom free from a cough; ♄ in ♉ or ♊; in Hor'y Questions ♄ Sig. of the party. (See Constant).

Convulsive Coughing—Paroxysms of —♅ in ♊, from the lungs; ♅ in ♋, from stomach disorders. Also convulsive, or spasmodic coughing, results when ♅ is affl. in ♍, ♐, or ♓, due to reflex action and irritations to the bronchial tract ruled by ♊. (See Spasmodic, Violent, Whooping, in this section).

Death from Coughs—Death from Severe Colds—♄ affl. the hyleg by dir., and ♄ holding the dominion of death; ☿ affl. the hyleg by dir., and ☿ affl. by ♄ at B., and ☿ holding the dominion of death; ☿ in the 8th H. at B., and in ♂ or ill-asp. ♄, and ♄ affl. the hyleg by dir., and ♄ holding the dominion of death, and also much delirium may attend; afflictions in the common signs. (See Colds).

Dry Coughs—The ☽ to the ♂, □, or ☍ ♄ or ☿ by dir., and espec. if ☿ be of the nature of ♄; ♄ ♂ or ill-asp. ☿, due to deficient secretion of mucus on the respiratory membranes; ♂ affl. in ♋; a ☿ disease, and afflictions to ☿ at B. (See "Bilious", "Dry Hard Cough", in this section. Also see Dry).

Dry Hard Cough—♅ affl. in ♊, dry, hard lung cough; ♅ affl. in ♋, dry, hard stomach cough; ♂ ♋ ♂ or ill-asp. the ☉, dry, hard stomach cough.

Frequent Short Cough — Hacking Cough—♅ affl. in ♊.

Hacking Cough — (See "Frequent", "Throat", in this section).

Hiccough—(See Hiccough).

Long Duration—(See the first part of this section).

Lung Cough—♅ ♊ tends to a hard, spasmodic, dry lung cough; ♄ ♊, coughs from lingering or chronic lung trouble; ♂ ♊, due to acute colds on the chest; Subs at Lu.P. (See Bronchial, Consumption, Lungs, Mucus, Phlegm, Phthisis, Tuberculosis).

Paroxysms—Of Coughing—(See "Convulsive" in this section).

Pertussis — (See "Convulsive", "Whooping", in this section).

Rotten Coughs—A ☽ disease, and afflictions to the ☽ at B., and by dir.; the ☽ ♓ ♂ or ill-asp. ♄ (or ☿ if he be of the nature of ♄) at the beginning of an illness; a ♋ sign disease and afflictions in ♋. (See Rotten).

Seldom Free from Cough—(See "Constant" in this section).

Short and Frequent—♅ affl. in ♊.

Spasmodic Cough—♅ affl. in ♊, from the lungs. (See "Convulsive" in this section. Also see Spasmodic).

Stomach Cough—♅ affl. in ♋ tends to a hard, dry, spasmodic and convulsive stomach cough, and from stomach disorders; ♂ ♋ ♂ or ill-asp. the ☉; a ♋ sign disease, and afflictions in ♋; Subs at SP.

Throat Cough—♅, ♄, or ♂ affl. in ♉; a ♉ disease; ♅ affl. in ♉, a hacking, tickling, spasmodic throat cough; Subs at LCP, and SP (7D). (See Mucus, Phlegm, Throat).

Violent Cough—The ☽ ♓, and affl. by the ☉ or ♂ when taken ill; ♂ configurated with influences which tend to cause cough make the cough more severe and violent.

Whooping Cough—(See Whooping).

COUNTENANCE — Face — Expression — Look — Features — Visage, etc. — This subject is largely considered under such subjects as Appearance, Aspect, Complexion, Expression, Eyes, Face, Features, Look, etc. In this section, however, some subjects which have to do with the countenance will be considered and listed alphabetically. Disease, Conduct, Habits, Ill-Health, Pain, Suffering, etc., tend to change the countenance, and it would take considerable space and time to list here every subject related to countenance. Therefore, if the subject is not listed here, or under the subjects mentioned, look in the alphabetical arrangement for the subject you have in mind. See the following subjects,—Anaemic, Animal, Appearance, Aspect, Austere, Beautiful, Blemishes, Bold, Cheeks, Cheerful, Chin, Commanding, Complexion, Contented. Cruel, Debauched, Dimples, Dissipated, Downward Look (see Look); Effeminate, Expression, Eyes, Face, Fair, Features, Fierce, Fiery, Glances, Gloomy, Good, Grave, Handsome, Harmless, Humane, Indifferent, Intellectual, Intemperate, Jaundiced, Kind, Lean, Long, Look, Lowering, Lumpish, Lustful, Mouth, Nose, Open, Oval, Pale, Peaceful, Pensive, Piercing, Pleasant, Pimpled, Pockmarked, Red, Refined, Robust, Round, Ruddy, Sad, Savage, Scarred, Scurvy, Sensual, Serious, Severe, Sharp, Sickly, Slender, Smiling, Smooth, Solid, Sympathetic, Sober, Stern (see Austere); Strong, Surly (see Aspect); Teeth, Thin, Thoughtful (see Grave); Unhealthy, Violent, Visage, Voluptuous (see Amorous, Sensuous); White, Wicked, Wide, Wrinkled, Youthful, etc.

COUNTER-IRRITANTS—Ruled by ♂. (See Caustics, Rubefacients, Vesicant).

COUNTRIES RULED BY SIGNS—Nations—The different Countries, Nations, Cities, and Parts of our Globe, have been assigned to the rulership of the different Planets and Signs of the Zodiac. A list of these rulerships can be found in Lilly's Astrology, and other textbooks. In travel, and espec. for health, it is very important for people to avoid Countries ruled by the Signs in which they have the malefic planets at B., unless such planets have dignity and power in the sign, and are well-aspected. Under the subject of "Nations", the rulership of the different Countries and prominent Cities is given. Also see Location; "Native Land" under Native; "Place of Birth" under Place; Residence, Travel, etc.).

COURAGE—(See Bold, Mars, Positive, Resolute, Servitude).

COURSE OF DISEASE — As no two people are born exactly alike, and have varying inherent, natal and prenatal qualities, there can be almost a limitless number of ways in which a disease may manifest itself, and the course it will pursue. In making a prognosis as to the course any particular disease will pursue, you should make a detailed study of the map of birth, the prenatal epoch map, and also the map of the heavens for the time of decumbiture, the beginning of the illness, or when the patient takes to his bed, and interpret it according to the Laws of the Science. The transits, directions, and progressed influences now working over the native should be studied. The nature of the signs and houses containing the afflicting planet, or planets, should be considered, and the afflicting planet, and the times when such planet, or planets, will change signs or pass into the next house, etc. (See Continuity). Disease tends to take its course when the ☉, ♀, or ☿ are in the 8th H. at B., as there is less resistance by the mind under these conditions. Also in negative people illness is more apt to take its own course and time, as such people give up easily, and lack will-power, resistance, grit and determination.

Danger In Course Of—The lord of the Asc. in evil asp. the ☽; the malefics affl. the hyleg at B., and by dir., and espec. when the hyleg is affl. by a train of adverse directions, and without the favorable intervention of the benefics ♃ and ♀. (See "Certain", "Sure", under Death; Fatal; "High" under Fever; "Dangerous" under Ill-Health; Malignant; "Disease" under Severe; "Violent" under Sickness; Vehement, Worse).

Irregular Course—☿ diseases. (See Irregular).

Peculiar Course—(See Peculiar).

Various Course—☿ diseases. (See Erratic, Irregular, Peculiar, Various). For further study along this line see the following subjects,—Acute, Alteration, Amelioration; "Better" under Disease; Changes, Chronic, Complications, Constancy, Continuity, Convalescence, Crises, Critical, Curable, Curtailed, Cycles, Dangerous, Death, Direct, Disease, Disturbances, Duration, Ease, Elimination, Erratic, Extraordinary Fever, Grievous, Ill-Health, Improvement, Incurable, Intermittent, Lingering, Long, Mild, Moderation, Modification, Negative, Painful, Peculiar, Periodic, Periodicity, Periods, Pernicious, Positive, Prognosis, Prolonged, Quick, Recovery, Recuperation, Recurrent, Relapses, Remission, Remittent, Resistance, Resolution, Retrograde, Return, Severe, Sharp, Shifting, Short, Shortened, Sickness, Slight, Slow, Solution, Stamina, Stationary, Susceptibility, Swift, Symptoms, Tedious, Termination, Variable, Various, Vitality, Wasting, Worse, etc.

COURSES—(See Menses).

Bad Courses—(See "Conduct" under Evil; Debauched, Dissipation, Drink, Drunkenness, Men, Morals, Passion, Sex, Women, etc.).

COUSINS—Ruled by the 3rd House. (See Relations, Third House).

COVERINGS—

Of the Bowels—(See Peritoneum).

Of the Brain—(See Brain, Meninges).

Of the Lungs—(See Pleura).

Also see Membranes, Mucous Membranes, Respiratory, Serous, Skin, Spine, etc.

COWPER'S GLANDS—Ruled by ♍. (See Urethra).

COXALGIA—Pain In the Hip Joint—(See Hips).

CRAMPS—Gripings—Spasmodic Muscular Contraction with Pain—Cramps are partly caused by lack of coordination, and afflictions to the Organ of Coordination ruled by ♌. The principal planet causing cramps and incoordination is ♅, and in the part ruled by the sign containing ♅ at B. ♅ and ☿, when associated together, also tend to cause cramps, and in the parts ruled by the signs containing them. Also ♄ by his binding and restricting

influences tends to cause cramps in that part of the body, or organ, ruled by the sign he is in at B., and espec. in the limbs when in signs ruling the limbs, and afflicted, or in configuration with ♅. Also ♃ may cause cramps indirectly, due to gorging, excesses, gluttony, indigestion, etc. Cramps are also considered a ☉ disease, and espec. when the ☉ is configurated with ♅. (See Uranus). The following subjects have to do with Cramps in the various parts and organs of the body, and the causes of Cramps, which see in the alphabetical arrangement when not considered here—

Abdominal Cramps—♅ or ☿ affl. in ♍. (See "Cramps" under Bowels).

Action—Cramped Action—♆ and ♅ when afflicted tend to. (See Action, Movement).

Ankles—Cramps In—♅ ♒.

Arms—Cramps In—♅ and ☿ in signs which rule the Arms, Shoulders, Hands, Legs and Feet tend to cramps in these parts. (See "Cramps" under Arms).

Borborygmus—(See Bowels).

Bowels—Cramps In—♅ affl. in ♍. (See "Cramps", "Gas", "Pain", under Bowels).

Cholera—(See "Cramps" under Cholera).

Cholic—(See "Cholic" under Bile).

Colic; Constrictions; Contractions; Coordination; Curable Cramps—Curable when affecting the Limbs—Malefics angular, occi. of the ☽, and in the last degrees of ♑ or ♐, if the benefics are with the malefics, or ori., or angular, and cast any ray to the Lights, they will be curable, but incurable if the benefics are weak and give no assistance. (See Curable, Incurable).

Erratic Movements—(See Erratic).

Exaggerated Action—(See Exaggerated).

Exalted—Exalted Excito-Motory Function—Cramps From—(See Exaltation).

Extremities—(See "Arms", "Curable", in this section).

Eyelids—(See "Winking" under Eyelids).

Feet—(See "Arms", "Curable", in this section; "Cramps" under Feet).

Flatulence; Gas; Gripings; Hands—(See "Arms", "Curable", in this section; "Cramp" under Hands).

Heart—(See "Cramp" under Heart).

Hips—Cramps In Hips and Thighs—(See "Cramps" under Hips).

Incoordination; Incurable—(See "Curable" in this section).

Indigestion—Cramps From—(See "Cramps" under Indigestion).

Intermittent Cramp—(See Intermittent).

Intestines—(See "Bowels" in this section).

Knees—(See "Cramps" under Knees).

Legs—(See "Arms", "Curable", in this section; "Cramps" under Legs).

Limbs — (See "Arms", "Curable", in this section).

Motor Nerves—(See Motor).

Muscles — (See Contractions, Intermittent; "Cramps" under Muscles).

Neck—(See "Cramps" under Neck).

Nerves — (See "Cramps" under Nerves).

Pain; Paralysis; Saint Vitus Dance; Shoulders — (See "Arms" in this section; "Cramp" under Shoulders).

Spasmodic; Stomach — (See "Cramp" under Stomach).

Tetanus; Thighs—(See "Cramp" under Thighs).

Toes — (See "Feet" in this section; "Cramps" under Toes).

Tympanites; Wind—(See "Bowels" under Wind).

Winking—(See Eyelids).

Writer's Cramp—(See Hands).

CRANIUM — Cranial — Cranian — The Skull—The Head—The Bony Case of the Brain—For considerations concerning the bony structure of the Cranium, see Skull.

Cranian Diathesis—The ☉ and ☽ acting thru the ♊ and ♍ signs affect the Respiratory System, the Upper Limbs, the Abdominal Organs, and the Lower Part of the Stomach, and give way to the Cranian Diathesis. The elemental qualities of this Diathesis are Cold and Dry. (See "Middle Cervical" under Ganglion).

Cranio-Abdominal Diathesis — (See "Fifth Thoracic" under Ganglion).

Cranial Nerves—Ruled by ♈.

Depressions — In the Cranium, or Skull—(See "Depressions" under Skull).

Fractures—(See Skull).

Malformations—(See Skull). See the various paragraphs under Brain, Head.

CRATCH—The Cratch — (See Ascelli, Praesepe).

CRATER—A Constellation of the nature of ♃ and ♀, in the 5th face of ♍, and said to be fortunate. The Asc. to the place of tends to bring good health, happiness and contentment.

CRAVINGS — Longings — Hunger—Desires—

Cold Water—A Craving For In Illness—The ☽ in ♉ and affl. by the ☉ or ♂ when taken ill (Hor'y). (See "Craving" under Liquids; Thirsty).

Drink—Craving for Drink and Liquors — (See Dipsomania, Drink, Drunkenness, Intemperance, Intoxication, Liquors, Wines, etc.).

Drugs — Craving For — (See Narcotics).

Food — Abnormal Cravings Along Food Lines—(See "Cravings", "Eccentric", "Peculiar", under Food).

Liquids — Craving For — (See Drink; "Craving" under Liquids; Thirst).

Sex Cravings—(See Amorous, Lascivious, Lewd, Licentious, Lust; "Loose Morals" under Morals; Men, Nymphomania, Passion, Pituitary, Sensuous, Sex, Unsavory, Women, etc.).

Wine—A Foolish Craving for Wine—(See Wine). See Appetites, Desires, Eating, Epicureans, Gluttony, Habits, Luxuries, Perversions, Pleasures, Unnatural, etc.

CRAWLING SENSATIONS — (See Hyperaesthesia, Sensations).

CRAZY — (See Dementia, Demoniac, Fury, Insanity, Madness; "Unbalanced", "Unsound", under Mind).

CREATIVE—

Creative Force — Sex Force — (See "Creative Force" under Sex).

Creative Powers — Are associated with the ☉ and the 5th H., the house related to the ☉ and the ♌ sign. The 5th H. denotes the offspring, whether physical, or the creations and children of the mind. (See Children, Fifth House).

CREEPING SENSATIONS—Crawling Sensations—(See Hyperaesthesia, Sensations).

CREMATION — (See "Silver Cord" under Silver).

CRETINISM—Deficient Development of the Organism, and Accompanied by Idiocy, and also often with Goiter. Caused by degeneration of the Thyroid Gland, ruled by ☿, and by afflictions to ☿. (See Diminished, Dwarfed, Goiter, Idiocy, Myxoedema, Thyroid).

CREVICE—A Small Fissure—

Spine—Crevice In—(See "Spina Bifida" under Spine). See Fissures.

CRIMINAL TENDENCIES—Criminals— Crime — Inclined to Criminal Acts — Due to•♂ afflictions to the ☉, ☽, ♄, ☿, the Asc., M.C., and ♂ in ♏ at B.; ♂ in ♉, ♋, or ♎, and affl. by the □ or ☍ of planets; ♂ Prog. ☌, P, □ or ☍ ♄ or ♃, or vice versa; ♂ in the 7th H. at a Solstice tends to make criminals active for the following Quarter, and lead to many robberies, much violence and murder; ♅ by tr. ☌ to ☽ or ☿ at B. of ♆ also be affl. in the radical map; ♅ ☌ ♂ in ♈; ♄ Sig. to the ill-asp. ♂ by dir., and espec. if ♄ or ♂ be in the 1st, 3rd, 9th or 10th H. at B.; ☿ ruler of the horoscope and affl. by malefics; Asc. to the place of the Ascelli or Capricornus. (See Anarchists, Assassins, Cheating, Deceitful, Destructiveness, Evil, Execution, Forgers, Gamblers, Highwaymen, Incendiarism, Intercourse, Liars, Mischief; "A Murderer" under Murder; Outrages, Pirates, Prison, Robbers, Swindlers, Thieves, Violent, Wicked, etc.).

Much Crime Prevalent—♂ in ♋, ℞ at the Vernal, lord of the year; Comets appearing in ♑. (See Assassination, Assaults, Comets, Murders, Outrages, Robberies, Slaughter, Violence, etc.).

CRIPPLED —Disabled — Partial or Total Loss of Use of Limbs—

Crippled by Accident—The Prog. ☉ or ☽ to the ☌, □, ☍, or P. ♂ by dir.; ♄ to the ☌ or ill-asp. ♂ by dir., danger of being crippled for life by accident or injury. The malefics ♄ and ♂ in the signs ruling the arms, legs, knees and feet bring great danger of accidents and injuries in these parts, in loss of members, disease, fracture, ankylosis, deposits, etc., by which the members, or parts, are temporarily or permanently crippled. (See Accidents, Arms, Birth, Congenital, Contortions, Contractions, Deformities, Distortions, Falls, Feet, Fractures, Gait, Hands, Incoordination, Infancy, Injury, Joints, Lameness, Legs, Limbs, Maimed, Members, Monsters, Muscles, Mutilated, Paralysis, Parturition, Rheumatism, Rigid, Spine, Walk, etc.).

Crippled from Birth—(See "Crippled" under Birth; Congenital).

CRISES IN DISEASE—Turning Point in Disease—A Paroxysm or Increase in the Disease — Crises are brought about by the changes of the ☽, by transits, by Prog. ☽ aspects, or a New ☽, and by directions. Judgment should not be based upon any one affliction, but all are to be considered. In making a judgment about crises, for the better or worse, the fundamental vitality should be considered, the indications of the radical map. The time of death usually comes at a crisis time, but should not be predicted openly, or to a sick person, even though certain death is indicated by the planetary influences, configurations and directions. The map of birth shows the days when crises are due, and when the transits or progressed planets will affect the radical planets by aspect.

Acute Diseases—Crises In—The 7th, 14th, 21st, and 28th days from the time the patient is taken sick are crises days of the disease, being based upon the Four Quarters of the ☽. (See Critical). The ☽ makes on revolution in her orbit in about 28 days, and the 7th, 14th, 21st days, and her return to her place at the time of the New Moon, correspond to her Quarters, adverse aspects, and crises times in the disease. The First, Second, and Third Quarters of the ☽, from the time the illness began, are crises days in acute diseases and fevers. If the patient lives thru these crises, and until the ☽ returns to her place, the disease will dissolve itself, or run into a chronic form. A person taken sick with a fever exactly at the New ☽ would have the crises days on the exact Quarters of the ☽ as given in the Calendar. In Acute diseases and fevers, the crises days are the dangerous ones. The most serious crisis day in an acute disease is on the 14th day, as a rule, when the ☽ arrives at the 8 asp. to her place at the beginning of the illness, and this crisis day is called "The Criticus Primus", the one of prime importance. More patients die on the 14th day of a serious fever than on the other crises days, and if they do not die on the 14th day their chances for recovery and moderation of the disease are usually good. The patient is usually worse on the 7th and 21st days of the disease, but these crises are considered of minor importance as compared to the 14th day crisis. Improvements in the disease are due on the 9th, 10th, 18th, and 19th days of the disease, as these aspects correspond to the △ aspects of the ☽, her good aspects from the day

the illness began. (See Acute, Climacteric, Enneatical).

Better—Crisis a Turn for the Better—The Crisis Favorable—The ☽ in good asp. a benefic when she is 45, 90, or 135° from her place at the beginning of the illness; the ☽ on a crisis day in ✳ or △ asp. the lords of the Asc., 9th, 10th or 11th Houses, gives an interval of ease and relief; lord of the Asc. on a crisis day in good asp. the ☉ if the ☉ does not have the power of dominion over the disease. (See Amelioration; "Solution" under Continuity; "Better" and "Ease" under Disease; Enneatical, Moderation, Modification, Recovery, Recuperation, Remission, Resistance, etc.).

Chronic Diseases — Crises In — In Chronic Diseases the crises are Solar, and based upon the movements of, or aspects to the ☉, rather than to the ☽. Chronic disease follows the motion of the ☉, and acquires a crisis after the 40th day, and judgment, or prognosis, can be made when the ☉ arrives to the ☐ his own place in the map. Then there is a turn for the better if the ☉ is well-asp. by the benefics, but worse if configurated with malefics. The ☉ to the ✳ or △ his own place indicates improvement, but to the ☐ or 8, a change for the worse. As ♄ is the author of chronic diseases, a serious crisis usually comes, with a turn for the worse, or death, when ♄ by direction comes to the ☌ or ill-asp. the ☉, ☽, Asc., or Hyleg, and also when accompanied by a train of evil directions to the hyleg, and when there is little or no assistance, or favorable intervention, from the benefics. Crises days, crises periods, and the critical times in life in health matters can thus be somewhat predicted, and possible forecasts of the outcome made, by looking ahead in the planetary tables, and by calculating the times when evil aspects and directions form and culminate, tending to make the patient worse, and when the favorable aspects come, making moderation, convalesence, and cure possible. (See Chronic).

Eye Diseases — Crises In — (See "Crises" under Eyes).

Fevers—Crises In—(See "Acute Diseases" in this section. See Fever).

Indicative Crises—(See Indicative).

Worse—The Crisis a Turn for the Worse—The ☽ at 45, 90, or 135° from her place at the beginning of an illness, and in evil asp. a malefic, or lords of the 6th or 8th H.; the ☽ at crisis day ☌ or ill-asp. a planet which afflicted the lord of the Asc. at decumbiture; the ☽ at a crisis day ☌ or ill-asp. lord of the 6th, or planets in the 6th H., the disease runs high and relief measures do little good. (See "Acute", "Chronic", in this section. See "Increase", "Worse", under Disease; "High Fevers" under Fevers). For collateral study see Accidents, Acute, Amelioration, Better, Childhood, Chronic, Convalescence, Critical, Course, Curable, Dangerous, Death, Directions, Duration, Ease, Fatal, Fever, Improvement, Increase, Incurable, Infancy, Mild, Moderation, Modification; "New Moon", "Quarters", under Moon; "Moon" under Motion; Paroxysms, Pestilence, Quick Diseases, Recovery, Relapses, Remission, Resolution, Severe, Solution, Stamina, Termination, Tone, Vitality, Worse, etc.).

CRITICAL—Pertaining To a Crisis—
Critical Days—The critical days in acute diseases and fevers are the crises days. (See "Acute", "Fevers", under Crises). For critical days and times in Chronic diseases, see "Chronic" under Crises. Every individual meets with many critical days in life, due to transits, progressions, or directions over the radical map, and the ☽ aspects, which may precipitate an accident, injury, fever, disputes, quarrels, misfortune, reversal in business, sorrow, worry, etc., and it would take considerable time to study out beforehand all the critical days and crises each person is apt to meet during life. The person who becomes advanced, spiritualized, with balance, equilibrium, poise, self-control, wisdom, knowledge, discretion, discrimination, foresight, intuition well developed, etc., one who has found his right calling and place in the world, and who can keep quiet, work, persist and endure in his work, can usually pass thru the critical days of life unharmed, can pilot his ship of life safely thru the troubled waters of earth existence, and be a master of his destiny. The critical days and times in life, the evil planetary aspects from day to day, etc., are more apt to overtake, weaken, discourage, or ruin the one who is drifting along thru life, like a ship without control or a pilot, and who lacks knowledge of the scheme of things, the laws of the Universe, the philosophy of life and destiny, etc. The study of Astrology is one of the very important Guides in life, and to learn from it, and by a study of your own star map of birth, what the Will of the Higher Powers is for your life. (See Fate; "Free Will" under Will).
Critical Degrees—(See "Sensitive Degrees" under Zodiac. Also see Azimene, Degrees).
Critical Disposition—(See Scolding, Virgo).
Critical Epochs In Life—Are under the rule of the ☽. (See Climacteric, Periods, Years).
Critical Illnesses—(See Dangerous, Fatal, Fierce, Grievous; "High Fevers" under Fever; Heavy, Incurable, Malignant, Morbid, Mortal, Rapid, Serious, Severe, Sharp, Swift, Vehement, Violent, Virulent, Wastings etc.).
Critical Periods—In Life—(See Climacteric, Periods, Years; "Critical Epochs" in this section).
Critical Years—(See Climacteric, Periods, Years).
Hypercritical—(See Petulant).
CRITICUS PRIMUS—The 14th day of a fever, the second crisis. (See "Acute Diseases" under Crises).
CROOKED—Not Straight—Irregular—Ill-Shaped—Incurvating—Imperfect—Bent, etc.—

Crooked Body—Denoted by ♄, and the ♄ sign ♑ on the Asc.; ☽ Sig. □ or 8 ♄; the □ and 8 aspects of the ☽ tend to a badly made and ugly body; ♄ ♋ partile asp. the Asc.; ♂ ♋ partile Asc., crooked, short, and ill-made; ☿ ♑ partile the Asc., often crooked; 8, ♑, and ♓ give. For further influences see "Ill-Formed" under Ill. Also see Azimene, Bent, Broken, Contortions, Defects, Deformed, Distortions, Feet, Incurvating, Knees, Legs, Malformations, Paralysis, Spine, Stooped, Ugly.
Crooked Knees—(See Knees).
Crooked Legs—(See the various paragraphs under Legs. Also see "Knock Knees" under Knees).
Crooked Shoulders—(See Shoulders).
Crooked Signs—8, ♋, ♑, and ♓. The ☽ or Asc. in one of these signs at B., and affl. by malefics, the native tends to be crooked or imperfect. (See Azimene, Broken, Distortions; "Ill-Formed" under Ill; Imperfect, Mutilated).
Crooked Teeth—(See Teeth).
CROPS—Destruction of—(See Corn, Drought, Famine, Fruit, Scarcity, Vegetation, Wheat).
CROSSED EYES—Squint—(See "Strabismus" under Eyes).
Crosses—(See Complications).
CROTON OIL—A typical drug of ♅. (See "Typical Drugs" under Uranus).
CROUP—A 8 disease, and afflictions in 8; the ☽ hyleg in 8, and afflicted, and espec. with females; ♄ or ☿ affl. in 8; ♄ 8 and affl., membranous deposits in croup; many planets in fixed signs, and espec. in 8 or ♏; Subs at LCP (6th C), and SP (7th D). Case—See No. 1, Chap. 13, page 86 in Daath's Medical Astrology. (See Angina, Diphtheria, Dyspnoea, Larynx, Pneumonia, Trachea).
Croupous Pneumonia—(See Pneumonia).
CRUCIFIXION—Death By—(See Impalement).
CRUEL—Harsh—Severe—Pitiless—Inflicting Mental or Physical Pain—Unfeeling—Without Mercy—Brutish—The ☽ Sig. □ or 8 ♂; the ☽ at full, or incr. in light in a nocturnal geniture, sepr. from ♀ and applying to ♂, tends to cruel persons in great power, but subject to many dangers; ♂ and ☿ lords of the employment, and if ♂ be stronger than ☿, the native will be more violent and wickedly inclined, and engage in cruel practices; ♂ affl. in ♈; ♂ Sig. in □ or 8 ♄, and vice versa; ☿ Sig. □ or 8 ♂; the 8 influences, when afflicted, or containing ♂, tend to make one abusive and unfeeling; the brutish signs ♌, and the 2nd half of ♐, when on the Asc., or afflicted, tend to make the native cruel and brutish; the 22° and 28° of ♏ on the Asc.; the 2° and 6° ♑ on the Asc. (See Assassins, Beastly, Brutish, Destructiveness, Fierce, Inhuman, Irrational, Masochism, Merciless, Murderous, Prison, Profane, Pity, Raving, Savage, Violent, etc.).

Cruel Complexion—Cruel Countenance—♂ Sig. □ or ☍ ♂, and vice versa.

Death from Cruelty—Death from Cruel Treatment—Case—See "Popejoy", No. 771, in 1001 N.N.

Surgeons—(See "Unfeeling" under Surgeons).

CRUSHED—Mashed—Pressed—

Accidents By—Injury or Death By, or by Being Buried Alive—Caused by ♄; ♄ in an earthy sign, and to the ill-asp. the Asc. by dir., and ♄ holding the dominion of death; ♄ in ♉, ♍, or ♑, ♂ or ill-asp. the Asc. by dir.; ♄ affl. the hyleg by dir., or when in the M.C., or close to the Asc. at B.; ♄ the afflicting planet, and in a violent sign, and affl. the hyleg by dir.; the ☉ hyleg, and to the ♂ or ill-asp. ♄ by dir.; ♅ or ♄ in ♈, ♋, ♎, or ♑, in the 4th H., and ♂ or ill-asp. the ☉ or ♂. (See Avalanches; Burial, Earthquakes; "Buildings" under Falls; Mobs; "Death" under Suffocation; Trampled). Cases—Death by Being Crushed—See "Crushed", No. 686, and "Pressed to Death", No. 626, in 1001 N.N.

CRUSTS—A Dried Mass of Exudate on the Skin—(See Corns, Decay, Excretion, Exudate, Favus, Gangrene, Hardening, Scabs, Scales, Skin, Sloughing, Sores; "Crusts under Tissues; Wastes).

CRYING—Shedding of Tears over Sorrows or Troubles—(See "Crying" under Tears).

CRYSTAL GAZING—(See Clairvoyance, Mediumship, Psychic).

CRYSTALLIZATION—The Formation of Crystals—Hardening—The work of ♄, the ☽, and the ♑ sign. A principle of ♄. Renal Stones and Gravel are crystallizations, carried on by ♄ by virtue of his exaltation in ♎, the kidney sign. Also ♄ crystallizes Gall Stones, furnishes the mineral deposits which harden the Bones. Hardness, density, strength, and resistance in the tendons and cartilages are given by ♄. All crystallization is the effect of the electric action of the planets, whether in the body or in the mineral world. Rock, Coal, Lead, etc. are the crystallizations of ♄ in Nature. Up to a certain point the crystallizing work of ♄ in the body is normal, but ♄ also has his pathological action in the body by causing too much crystallization by his afflictions, and causing disease, such as Stone, Hardening of the Arteries, hard Tumors containing mineral deposits, such as Goiter, and also by crystallizing the Nerves and Muscles. After middle age the body begins to crystallize more rapidly, and when at last it is so hardened as to lose its elasticity, death comes to the body, and the separation of its vehicles. The action of the ☽ is also crystallizing, and the ☽ is a hard, crystal body, incapable of sustaining animal life or vegetation. Crystallization is also the result of Cold, and Cold Diseases tend to abnormal and pathological crystallization. Cauda (☋), the Dragon's Tail, also exerts a ♄ influence along this line. ♄ in any sign tends to more rapid crystallization in the part, or organ, ruled by the sign he is in, and espec. after middle life, but it may be earlier in life if ♄ is badly afflicted, and also the afflictor in the disease, holding the dominion of death, etc. Thus ♄ in □ tends to crystallization in the lungs; ♄ in ♎, to crystallizations in the kidneys; ♄ ♂ ♃, to crystallization and hardening of the arteries, etc. (See Arteries, Bile, Bones, Cold, Concretions, Condensation, Congestion, Consolidation, Density, Deposits, Elimination, Eyes, Fiber, Goiter, Gout, Gravel, Hardening, Lameness, Lime, Minerals, Muscles, Nerves, Obstructions, Optic Nerve, Osseous, Retention, Rheumatism, Rigidity, Sand, Saturn, Stone, Suppressions, Tumors, etc.). For crystallizations in the various organs and parts of the body, and as associated with the various diseases, if not mentioned in the preceding list, see the subject in the alphabetical arrangement.

CULPEPPER—"Culpepper's Herbal" is a large book giving the planetary rulership of Herbs, and is a good book for students to have, as it is quite exhaustive along the lines of Herbs, their use in the treatment of disease, and the best times to gather them to get their best medicinal values. (See Herbs).

CUPRUM—(See Copper).

CURABLE—Cure—Cured—Cure of Disease—

Curable Diseases—Convertible Diseases—A disease is more curable when the afflictions are in the cardinal or common signs, as the influences of these signs are more flexible and amenable to treatment and a cure, but when in the fixed signs tend to be incurable, or greatly prolonged. However, if a disease is allowed to run its course, no matter from what kind of signs the afflictions may be, the disease may become chronic, and espec. if the mind and temperament are too weak to throw off the trouble, as is the case with many negative people. (See Negative). Disease is more curable if the benefics are with the malefics, or ori., angular, and cast any ray to the Lights, but if the benefics do not lend any assistance, or are weak, the disease tends to be incurable. The absence of malefics with the ☉ and ☽ in angles, and the benefics giving a good aspect, tends to hope of a cure, and the alleviation of the disease. Also if the 6th H. is free from afflictions there is more hope of a cure. (For further influences as to when a disease is curable, or incurable, see in the alphabetical arrangement the disease subject you have in mind, such as "Curable" under Cramps, Epilepsy, Fits, Insanity, etc.).

Curable Mental Disease—(See Conspicuous; "Curable", and "Incurable" under Brain).

Cure of Disease—Afflictions from the fixed signs are difficult to remedy. From the common signs are more amenable to treatment. From cardinal signs are more acute and transient, and may be quickly broken or cured. (See "Curable" in this section. Also see Native Land, Prognosis; "Cure of the Sick" under Sick; Treatment).

Cured But Has Relapse—(See Relapse).

Difficult to Cure—(See Chronic, Grievous, Incurable; "Sure Death" under Death). For collateral study see Antipathy, Cardinal, Complications, Constancy, Continuity, Course, Crises, Death, Duration, Environment, Fatal, Fixed Signs, Healers, Incurable, Influenced, Lingering, Malignant Medi-, cines, Moderation, Majority, Mutable, Native Land, Nature, Negative, Opposites, Polarity, Positive, Praeincipients, Prolonged, Recovery, Relapse, Remedies, Return, Short Diseases (see Short), Subluxations, Sure Death (see Death), Sympathy, Tedious, Treatment, Vehement, Vertebrae, Violent, etc.

CURIOUS—

Curious Death—(See Extraordinary).

Curious Diseases—(See Mysterious, Strange).

Curious Forebodings—(See Forebodings).

Curious Studies—(See Occult).

CURSED—Cursed by the Multitude—(See Execrated).

CURTAILED—Shortened—Modified—

Disease—The Disease Is Curtailed—(See Amelioration, Course; "Better" under Disease; Duration, Modification, Recovery, Recuperation, Resolution, Short, Solution, etc.).

CURVATURE—Of the Spine—Kyphosis—(See Curvature, Humpback, Pott's Curvature, Tubercular, under Spine).

CUTANEOUS—Pertaining to the Skin. (See Skin).

Cutaneous Asphyxia—(See "Cutaneous" under Asphyxia).

Cutaneous Diseases—(See Eruptions, Skin).

Cutaneous Inflammation—(See "Inflammation" under Skin).

Cutaneous Spots—(See Moles).

CUTICLE—The Epidermis or Scarf Skin—Ruled by ♄. (See "Epidermis" under Skin).

CUTIS—The Derma—Corium—The True Skin—(See Derma, Skin).

Hemorrhages Into—(See Purpura).

CUTS—Incised Wounds—Knife Wounds—Stabs—Injuries by Sharp Instruments, the Sword, etc.—♂ afflictions predispose to, as ♂ is the instigator of quarrels, disputes and violence. The ☉ and ♂ both tend to incised wounds and injuries, as they are the positive, electric, and caloric-producing planets. ♂ in the Asc. at B., liable to; ♂ in the 8th H. at B., and affl. the ☉, ☽, or hyleg; ♂ □ or ⚹ the ☉; ♂ by dir. ☌ or evil asp. the ☉, ☽, Asc., or M.C.; ♂ ruler at B., ruler of the Asc.; people born under the strong influence of ♂; the ☉ or ☽ ori., and affl. by ♂; the ☉ or ☽ in fire signs; the ☉ affl. by ♂; the ☉ or ☽ to the ☌ or ill-asp. ♂ by dir.; the Prog. ☉ or ☽ to the ☌, □, or ⚹ ♂; the Asc. to the ☌ or evil asp. ♂ dir.,

and espec. if ♂ is in a fiery sign; the Asc. to the place of the Pleiades, Hyades, or Castor; Fixed Stars of the nature of ♂ ascending at B. (See the various paragraphs in this section).

Absent Party—Cuts or Stabs To—(See "Weapons" in this section).

Arms, Hands, Shoulders—Slight Cuts To—♂ in ♐; ☿ in ill-asp. to ♂. (See "Accidents" under Arms; "Cuts" under Hands).

Danger of Cuts—Liable To—Predisposed To—(See the first part of this section).

Death by Cuts—By Stabs, Daggers, Wounds, Sword, Sharp Instruments, etc.—♂ with Aldebaran, and ♂ in □ or ⚹ the ☉, and ♂ just setting at B.; ♂ the afflicting planet in a violent sign, and affl. the hyleg; the ☽ to the ☌ or ill-asp. ♂ by dir. (See "Death" under Duels, Stabs, Sword).

Face—Cuts To—(See "Cuts" under Face).

Hands—Cuts To—(See "Arms" in this section).

Hips and Thighs—Cuts To—(See Hips).

Instruments—Cuts by Sharp Instruments—(See Instruments. Also note the various paragraphs in this section).

Lameness from Cuts—Or Stabs—♂ in ♐, on the Asc., from accidents to the hips or thighs; ♂ in ♑, ♒, or ♓, from cuts to lower limbs, knees, or feet. (See Distortions).

Murdered—By Cuts or Stabs—(See Assassinated, Murdered, Stabs).

Operations—Rules for Time of, and Making Incisions—(See Operations).

Paralysis—From Cuts—Or Stabs—(See Distortions).

Severe Cuts—The ☉ or ☽ ori., and affl. by ♂. (See Severe).

Shoulders—Cuts To—(See "Arms" in this section).

Slight Cuts—To Arms or Hands—(See "Arms" in this section).

Surgery—(See Operations).

Sword—Cuts By—(See Duels, Sword, War).

Throat—Cuts His Own Throat—Suicide By—(See "Cuts" under Throat).

Travel—Journeys—Voyages—Cuts or Stabs During—♂ in the 3rd or 9th H. at B., and affl. the ☉ or ☽ at B., or by dir.

Violent Death—By Cuts—(See "Death" in this section. Also see Violent).

Voyages—Cuts On—(See "Travel" in this section).

Weapons—Cuts by Sharp Weapons—♂ in the 8th H. at B., or by dir., and affl. the ☉, ☽, Asc., or Hyleg; ♂ in the 8th H. in a Hor'y Map, and affl. the ☉, ☽, or Asc., indicates the absent party may be wounded by cuts or stabs. (See Instruments, Iron, Sword). For collateral study see Accidents, Assassination; "Shedding" under Blood; Blows, Contests, Enemies, Falls, Hurts, Injuries, Iron, Lacerations, Mobs, Murdered; "Death" under Quarrels; Riots,

Robbers, Stabs; "Flying Stones" under Stones; Suicide, Sword, Violence, War, Wounds, etc.

CYANOSIS—Blue Discoloration of the Skin and Nails—Nonoxygenation of the Blood—Afflictions in ♌ or ♒; ♄ affl. in ♌; many planets in fixed signs. (See Asphyxia, Breathing, Circulation, Nails, Oxygen. Case—See "Male", Chap. 8, page 48, in Daath's Medical Astrology.

CYCLES—(See Climacteric, Crises, Critical, Periodic, Periodicity, Periods, Years). Good books on the Law of Cycles are "Periodicity", by Dr. James Buchanan, and the book, "The Law of Cycles", published by the Aryan Theosophical Press, Point Loma, Calif.

CYCLOPS—A Monster with Eyes Fused Into One. The following influences have been noted to exist in the natal maps of these cases,—The ☉ and ☽ in the 6th or 12th H., and affl. by ♅, ♄, and ♂; ♅, ♄, and ♂ in the 5th, 6th, or 12th H., or afflicting these houses, or the cusp of Asc.; ♅, ♄, and ♂ in fixed signs in ♂ or ☍ asp.; ♌, ♏, or ♑ on the Asc.; many planets in ♍ in the 6th or 12th H., and afflicted. Case—See "Male", Chap. 8, page 48 in Daath's Medical Astrology. (See Congenital, Deformities, Monsters, Prenatal Epoch).

CYNOSURA—A Northern Constellation —Ursa Minor—The Little Bear—Is

mentioned in Wilson's Dictionary several times as having an evil influence. (See "Much Evil" under Evil; "Much Sickness" under Sickness; Thieves).

CYSTITIS—(See "Cystitis" under Bladder).

CYSTS—A Membranous Sac containing Fluid.

Arms—Cysts in the Arms, Hands, Legs and Feet—(See Aneurysm, Vesicles).

Brain—(See "Cyst" under Brain).

Breast—Cyst of—♀ affl. in ♋; ♀ in ♋ in the 6th H., and afflicted; ♀ afflicting the ☽ or Asc. (See Breast).

Disorders—Disorders Attended with Cysts—♀ diseases.

Hollow—Cystic and Hollow Tumor Formations—♀ diseases.

Hydatid Cysts—Caused by ♃ affl. in ♓. (See "Cyst" under Brain).

Sebaceous Cysts—(See Fat, Wen).

Steatoma—(See Wen).

Tongue—Cystic Tumor under the Tongue—Ranula—(See "Cystic Tumor" under Tongue).

Wen—A Sebaceous Cyst—(See Wen).

CYTOPLASTEMA—The Cytoplastema— To ♆ belongs cell development in a plastic fluid, the Cytoplasm, and independent of other cells. (See "Cytoplastema" under Cells; Plastic).

D

DAMPNESS—(See Exposure, Moisture, Vapors, Water, Wet).

DANCING—Dancing Spasm—(See "Saltatory" under ‚Spasmodic; "Dancing" under Sports).

DANGER—Dangers—Perils—The malefic planets strong at B., and affl. the ☉, ☽, Asc., or hyleg, predispose to unusual dangers all thru life, and espec. when the Asc. is afflicted by evil directions; the ☽ Sig. □ or ☍ ♂, passes thru innumerable dangers; the ☽ incr. in light, sepr. from ♃ and applying to ♂ in a nocturnal nativity; the ☽ with Antares or Aldebaran in the Asc. or M.C.; ♃ ruler of the 1st H., and to the ill-asps. ♄ by dir.; ♂ ☌ ☋; Comets appearing in ♏ tend to great perils generally. (For further influences see the various paragraphs in this section). For the dangers and afflictions which accompany the various diseases, and when the disease may become dangerous, and for the dangers which any organ, or part of the body may be subject to, see in the alphabetical arrangement the subject you have in mind. Also note the alphabetical list at the end of this Article, which deals with sources of danger, the classes of danger, and the classes of people especially subject to dangers and perils in their various phases. Death of the body is the ultimate result of all dangers, and for the various kinds and causes of death, and the dangers contributing to death, see the various

paragraphs under Death, Disease, and also in this section. Here are a few of the more abstract subjects concerning danger—

Beset with Dangers—♆ affl. in the 12th H.

Dreams of Danger—(See Dreams).

Fond of Danger—People born under strong ♂ influence, as with ♂ in the Asc. or M.C., or ♂ rising in one of his own signs in ♂ with the ☉, ☽, or Asc., or ♂ rising and ruler of the Asc., etc., such tend to be fond of danger, risks, and exposures.

Great Dangers—(See "Many" in this section).

Great Perils Generally—Comets appearing in ♏.

Has Endured Many Dangers—(See Escapes, Foolhardy).

Many Dangers—Subject To—The ☉ Sig. ♂ ♂ and ♂ ill-dig.; the ☉ or ☽ to the place of Antares; the ☽ to the □ or ☍ the ☉ by dir., great dangers; the ☽ with Antares or Aldebaran in the 1st or 10th H.; ♂ Sig. □ or ☍ ♄, meets with much danger and suffering, or a violent death, and espec. if ♄ be stronger than ♂ (see "Short Life" under Life; "Death" under Violent); Antares, Aldebaran, Regulus, Deneb, Frons Scorpio, or the Shoulders of Orion, when directed to the ☉, ☽, or Asc., bring danger, violence, trouble, or sickness. (See Perils, Precarious, Sickness, Trouble).

Near Some Danger—♄, ♂, or ☊ in the Asc. or 7th H., peregrine, ℞, or in detriment, some danger or misfortune near according to the quality of the Significators, and of the houses those planets are lords of which afflict the ☽ (Hor'y). (See Imminent; "Some Misfortune Near" under Misfortune).

Premonition of Danger—Fear of— (See Calamity; "Danger" under Fear).

Rushes Into Danger—Born under ♂. (See "Fond of" in this section).

Secret Dangers—(See Ambushes; "Secret Enemies" under Enemies; "Poison Death" under Poison; Treachery).

Sudden Dangers—(See "Danger" under Sudden).

Unknown Danger—Fear of—(See "Danger" under Fear). For further influences along the lines of Danger, see the following subjects,—Abroad, Accidents, Acquaintance, Aeroplanes, Air, Animals, Assassins, Aunts, Bathings, Beasts, Bloodshed (see Blood); Blows, Brethren, Brothers, Bruises, Buildings, Buried Alive (see Burial); Burns, Calamity, Cattle, Childhood, Children, Cold, Criminals, Crushed, Cuts, Dampness, Dangerous, Daughter, Desert, Directions, Disaster, Disease, Disgrace, Drink, Drowning, Duels, Earth, Earthquakes, Eclipse, Electricity, Employment, Enemies, Escapes, Events, Execution, Explosions, Exposures, External, Extraordinary, Falls, Father, Females, Fire, Fire Arms, Floods, Food, Foreign Lands, Friends, Great Men (see Great); Gunshot, Hanging, Heat, Heights, Highwaymen, Homicide, Honor, Husband, Impalement, Imprisonment, Infancy, Injuries, Insects, Instruments, Intoxication, Journeys, Kings, Life, Lightning, Liquids, Machinery, Males, Members, Men, Middle Life, Military, Mischief, Misfortune, Moisture, Monarchs, Mother, Murder, Navigation, Nobles, Old Age, Operations, Parents, Peculiar, Perils, Periods (Danger Periods); Pirates, Plots, Poison, Presidents, Princes, Quadrupeds, Quarrels, Railroads, Rain, Relatives, Reptiles, Reputation, Rescues, Reversals, Robbers, Ruin, Rulers, Sailors, Scalds, Scandal, Sea, Seduction, Sharp Instruments (see Instruments); Ships, Shipwreck, Short Journeys (see Journeys); Sister, Sons, Stabs, Storms, Suffocation, Suicide, Surgeons, Sword, Thieves, Travel, Treachery, Uncles, Vehicles, Venomous, Volcanoes, Voyages, War, Water, Weapons, Weather, Wife, Wind, Women, Wounds, Young, Youth, etc. (For subjects not listed here look for them in the alphabetical arrangement).

DANGEROUS—Fierce—Savage—Vicious—Violent, etc.

Accidents—(See "Dangerous" under Accidents).

Chronic Diseases—(See "Dangerous" under Chronic).

Community and Society—Dangerous To—(See Anarchists).

Dangerous Accidents—(See Accidents).

Destructiveness—Dangerous Destructiveness—(See Anarchists, Destructiveness).

Disease Not Dangerous—Lord of the Asc. strong, angular, and not afflicted, the disease is not dangerous. (See Course, Crises; "Better" under Disease).

Disposition—Dangerous—(See Beastly, Cruel, Fierce, Savage, Temper).

Fevers—Dangerous Fevers—(See "Dangerous" under Fevers).

Illness—Dangerous Illness—(See "High Fever" under Fever; Fierce, Grievous, Rapid, Severe, Sharp, Vehement, Violent, etc.).

Internal Disease—Dangerous—(See "Women" under Internal).

Lunatics—(See "Dangerous" under Insanity).

Operations—Surgical—(See "Dangerous" under Operations).

Periods—Dangerous Periods in Life— (See Climacteric, Crises, Critical; "Menopause" under Menses; Parturition, Periods, Puberty, Years, etc.).

Sickness—Dangerous Sickness—(See "Illness" in this section).

DARK—Darkened—

Air—Dark Air—(See "Corrupt" under Air).

Black—(See Black).

Brunettes—(See "Dark" under Complexion; "Black" and "Dark" under Hair).

Brown—Dark Brown—(See "Dark" under Hair).

Complexion—Dark Complexion—(See "Dark" under Complexion).

Darkened Desires—(See "Darkened" under Mind).

Degrees—The Dark Degrees of the Zodiac—(See "Dark Degrees" under Zodiac).

Eyes—Dark Eyes—(See "Dark" under Eyes).

Figure—Dark Personal Figure—♄ indicates a person of a black, earthy, or brown complexion; ♄ occi. at B. Predominant in people born under Southern Parallels, and who have the ☉ continually in their Zenith, and are scorched by his rays. (See Black, Negro).

Hair—(See "Black", "Dark", under Hair).

Marks—Dark Marks on Body—(See "Dark" under Marks).

Mind Darkened—(See Mind).

Races—Dark Races—(See "Figure" in this section).

DARKNESS—Governed by ♄.

Fear of the Dark—Fear in Solitude— ♇ affl. the ☽ or ☿; ♇ afflicted in one of the houses of mind, as in the 3rd or 9th H., and also in the 8th H., more liable to obsessions and morbid fears. (See Claustrophobia; "Morbid", "Solitude" under Fears). Case—See "Strange Case", No. 379 in 1001 N.N.

DAUGHTER—

A Daughter Born—A Daughter Promised—(See "Birth of a Female" under Female; "First-born Child" under Children).

Danger to a Daughter—Ill-Health of —Damage To—The M.C. to the illasps. the ☽ or ♀ by dir.; the ☽ to the place of Hercules by dir., damage to.

Death To—Danger of—(See Eclipse; "Death" under Females, Women).

Ill-Health Of—(See "Danger" in this section. See "Ill-health" under Females; "Women" under Misfortune).

DAY—Diurnal—The Daytime—Day Nativities, etc. The Daytime is electric, and ruled by the ☉, and the influence of the ☉ by day is to restore the vitality, and destroy morbid germs. (See Magnetic). The day is more vitalizing than the night. The ☽ rules the night. (See Elevated, Magnetic, Night).

Blindness—(See "Day Blindness" under Blindness).

Day Dreamer—(See Dreamy).

Day of Death—(See "Day", "Hour", "Time", under Death).

Death by Day—(See "Wild Animals" under Animals).

Disease by Day—The Disease Is Better or Worse by Day—♄ or ♂ by Day in Disease—♂ is more malignant by day as the ☉ adds to his heat and dryness. ♄ is less malignant by day as the ☉ moderates his coldness. Thus ♄ is less malignant in day nativities, and ♂ more so. However, as Anareta, ♄ and ♂ are equally destructive whether by day or night. (See Epilepsy, Fits, Insanity, Night).

Insanity by Day—When Caused in a Day Nativity—(See the ♄ and ♂ influences under Insanity).

Pain—The Pain Less by Day—(See "Pain" under Night).

Parents—(See "Day" under Parents).

Patient Better by Day—Better by Day—Worse at Night—(See Magnetic; "Diseases", "Pain", "Worse" under Night).

Signs—Diurnal Signs—(See "Nocturnal Signs" under Night).

DAYS—

Critical Days—(See Crises, Critical).

Days of the Week—(See Week).

Hour of the Day—Best Hour to Give Medicines—(See "Hours" under Planets).

Treatment—Best Days and Times For in Individual Cases—(See "Days of the Week" under Week).

DEAD—Deadly—

Absent Party is Dead—(See "Dead" under Absent).

Corpse—(See Corpse).

Deadly Diseases—(See "Fatal Illness" under Fatal).

Fugitive is Dead—(See Fugitive).

Tissue—Crusts of Dead Tissue. (See Crusts, Gangrene, Hardening, Scales; "Crusts" under Tissues).

Womb—Dead in the Womb—(See Stillborn).

DEAFNESS—(See "Deafness", and the various paragraphs under Hearing).

Deaf and Dumb—(See "Deaf and Dumb" under Hearing. Also see Mute.

DEATH—Dissolution—The Terminus Vitae.

The 8th H. is known as the House of Death, and the death dealing forces act the strongest thru this house. The 4th, 8th and 12th Houses are called the Terminal Houses, and have to do with the close and end of life, and the death of the physical body. (See Fourth, Eighth, Twelfth, Terminal). The ♏ Sign, affiliated with the 8th H., is said to give the death sting, and the malefic planets, ♄ and ♂ to cut the Silver Cord. (See "Silver Cord" under Silver). The general influence of ♄ especially is to bring death of the body by his afflictions to the Hyleg. ♄ is called the Planet of Death. He is The Tester, Father Time, and it is his business to ultimately separate the Soul from its earthly vehicle, and set the Soul free. ♄ is the principal Significator of death by disease, and ♂ by accident or violence. The Benefics do not of themselves cause death, and even their evil aspects will often avert death when they fall in a train of evil directions. However, the Benefics, when holding the dominion of death, do largely contribute to the causes leading to death. (See Saturn, Mars, Jupiter and Venus Influences. Also see Scorpio). The New Moon implies decay, disintegration, and death, and the preparation for a new cycle, and is the low ebb of the physical forces. (See "New Moon" under Moon). The Killing Place is called the Anareta, and death depends upon the one, or more, killing planets which occupy an Anaretic Place at B. (See Anareta). The ☐ aspect by direction from the Killing Planet to the hyleg is known as the Killing Arc. The Diseases and Afflictions which tend to cause, produce, contribute to, and be the immediate cause of death of the physical body, are legion in number, and too numerous to list here. For Death by the various diseases, see the disease subject in the alphabetical arrangement. For death by Accidents, Bruises, Blows, Hurts, Injuries, Violence, Wounds, etc., see the various headings under these subjects. Only the more abstract subjects concerning death will be listed and considered here, such as Arguments for, Causes, Kinds, Manner, Quality, etc., and also a number of subjects listed for your attention, which you might overlook. See "Death" under the following subjects in the alphabetical arrangement when not more fully considered here, which subjects have to do with death, causes of death, the manner, time or place of death, death to others, death by others, etc.—

Abortion; Abroad; Absent Party—(See Absent).

Accidents—Accidental Death—(See Accidents).

Acquaintance; Adversary—Death By —Death of—(See Enemies).

Aeroplanes; Aged People—(See Old Age).

Air—(See Air, Gases).

Ambushes; Amputations—(See Operations).

Anareta—The Killing Planet—(See Anareta. Also see "Arguments" in this section).

Animals—Death By—Death of—(See Animals, Beasts).

Arguments for Death—Danger of Death—Death Threatened—The Causes of Death—The Life in Danger, etc.— The influences in this paragraph are given in the following order,—☉, ☽, ♅, ♄, ♃, ♂, ♀, ☿, ☋, Asc., M.C., 4th H., 6th H., 8th H., 12th H., Fixed Stars, Eclipses, Hyleg, Anareta, Directions. SUN—The ☉ by his ill-aspects to the ☽ or Asc. acts like ♂, and assists in causing death; the ☉ to the □ his own place by dir., almost certain and sure death; the ☉ and hyleg both badly afflicted at same time increases the danger; the ☉ hyleg ☌ ♅ as Anareta in the 8th H., and the ☉ to the ☌ or ill-asp. ♅ by dir.; ☉ to the place of Aldebaran; the ☉ hyleg, and to the ☌ or ill-asp. ♄ or ♂ by dir., and espec. if ♄ or ♂ rule the 6th, 8th, or 12th H., and either of them be Anareta; the ☉ to the evil asps. the ☽ if the direction falls in the 8th H., or the ☉ or ☽ rule the 8th, and are radically afflicted by ♄ or ♂ ruler of the 8th; evil directions of the ☉ to the ☽ or Asc. when they are hyleg; the ☉ to the P. asp. ♄ in the Zodiac by direct or converse motion; an eclipse of the ☉ falling in the same degree held by the ☉ at B., and with the ☉ strongly afflicted at B., or by dir., and the hyleg also affl. by malefics; the ☉ lord of the 8th H. at B., and affl., and the ☉ to the evil asps. the Asc. by dir.; adverse asps. of the ☉ to ♄, ♂, ♅ or ♆ by dir., and espec. among the aged and those frail of constitution; the ill-asps. of several malefic promittors to the ☉ tend to double or treble the danger to life, cause breakdown in health, disaster, or death; the ☉ in the 6th or 8th H. at B., and to the ☌ or ill-asp. ♄ by dir.; the ☉ and ☽ both affl. by ♄ in an angle; the ☉ in the 4th H. with ♄ or the ☽ in the 4th H. with ♂; the ☉, the Light of Time, ☌ or ill-asp. ♄ lord of the 6th, in fixed signs when taken ill; the ☉ in the 8th H., or with the lord of the 7th by dir. at the time of the illness; in female horoscopes the ☉ causes death by severe illnesses and feverish disorders. (See "Death" under Sun). MOON—The ☽ hyleg and affl., and to the cusp the 8th H. by dir.; the ☽ hyleg, and in evil asp. to ♄, ♂, or ☿ threatens death; the ☽ weak and affl. at B., and ☌ the cusp the 4th H. by dir.; ☽ to the □ or 8 ♄ or ♂ by dir., and espec. if the ☽ be hyleg; prog. ☽ ☌ ♄ in 8th H., and ♄ affl. the hyleg at B.; the ☽ sepr. from the ☉ and applying to ☿ in a night nativity; the ☽ at Full, or increasing in a night nativity, sepr. from ♀ and applying to ♂ (Hor'y); the ☽ at a Solar Rev. passing the place of ♂ at B., and the ☽ affl. at the Rev.; the ☽ to the □ or 8 ☿ if the ☽ be hyleg, and ☿ affl. at B.; the ☽ applying to the 8 ♂ in the 8th H., and when in exact 8; the ☽ hyleg, and to the ☌ the ☉

by dir., and the ☉ and ☽ affl. at B.; the ☽ affl. at B., and to the ☌, P, or ill-asp. the Asc. by dir.; the ☽ hyleg, and to the ☌ or ill-asp. ♄ by dir., and espec. if the direction fall in the 6th or 12th H.; the ☽ hyleg, and to the ☌ or ill-asp. ♂ by dir.; the ☽ to the ☌ or P. Dec. the ☉ if the ☽ be hyleg and the ☉ affl. at B.; the ☽ to the ☌ or P. Dec. Aldebaran, Antares, or Regulus, if the ☽ be hyleg; the ☽ Sig., applying to the ☌ the ☉, is in danger of death, and espec. if it happen in the 8th H., or the ☉ be lord of the 8th, but if sepr., the danger is not as great; the ☽ hyleg, and directed to the ☌ a malefic, and both with the same Lat.; the ☽ hyleg and affl. by ♄ from an angle by dir.; the ☽ near the cusp of the Asc. by dir., and in □ to ♂ in the 4th H.; the ☽ in the 8th H. by dir., and combust; the ☽ lady of the 6th H., and combust in the 1st or 4th H., and espec. if lord of the 8th be affl.; the ☽ hyleg and applying to the ☌ ☉, but not so evil when in ♈, ♌, or ♌; the ☽ in the 4th H. in asp. to ♄ in the 6th, and applying to the □ the ☉; ☽ affl. by a malefic in 1st H., the house of life; the ☽ sepr. from lord of the Asc., in signs of long ascension, and transferring her light to lords of the 4th or 8th; the ☽ leaving the 8 ☉ and applying swiftly to the □ or 8 ♂, threatens a fatal end; the ☽ and lord of the Asc. in ☌ lord of the 8th, and without the interposing good asps. of ♃ or ♀; ☽ affl., and applying to a planet in the 8th; ☽ ♈ when taken ill, and espec. if the ☽ leave the ☌ ♂ and go to the ☌ or ill-asp. ♄, or if the ☽ decr. in light, or be slow of motion; the prog. ☽ to the □ or 8 her radical place, and espec. if affl. at B. by the ☌, □, or 8 malefics. (See "Death" under Moon). NEPTUNE—♆ in evil asp. the hyleg, or Giver of Life, helps to destroy life. (See "Buried Alive" under Burial; "Death" under Neptune). URANUS—♅ does not kill of himself, but assists by his evil asps., and when affl. the hyleg; ♅ passing the place of ♂ at B. by transit, if affl. the ☉ at same time; ♅, ♄, or ♂ in the 1st or 7th H. in 8 each other, or in mutual reception, or with the ☉ or ☽, death will be more certain; ♅ by Periodic Rev. to the evil asps. the hyleg; ♅ in the 8th H., and Anareta, and the ☽, and the ☉ to the ☌ or ill-asp. ♅; adverse asps. of ♅ to the ☉ by dir., and espec. among the aged and those of frail constitution; ♅ affl. the hyleg by dir. (See "Death" under Uranus). SATURN—♄ ☌, □, or 8 the radical ☉ by dir.; ♄ affl. the hyleg at B., and by dir., and ♄ holding the dominion of death; ♄ in the 8th H. at B., and near the place of violent fixed stars. (See "Death" under Saturn. Also in this paragraph see the ☉, ☽, ♅, Asc., 6th, 8th and 12th H. influences). JUPITER —(See the Introduction to this Article, and the Moon influences in this paragraph. See the Introduction and "Death" under Jupiter). MARS—♂ in the Asc. at decumb., and the ☉ and ☽ and their dispositors affl.; ♂ by dir. to the ☌ or ill-asp. the Asc., and espec. if ♂ is Anareta. (See "Death" under Mars. Also see the influences of the

⊙, ☽, ♅, and Asc. in this paragraph). VENUS—(See "Death" under Venus. Also see the Moon influences in this paragraph). MERCURY—(See "Death" under Mercury. Also see the Moon influences in this paragraph). CAUDA— ☋—The Dragon's Tail—Exerts much the same influence as ♄, and when the Sig. of death is very evil. (See Dragon). ASCENDANT—Lord of the Asc. in the 6th H., and lord of the 6th in the Asc., and one of them in changing signs meets the evil asps. of malefics, or lords of the 4th and 8th, and they slow in motion, and it be from signs in □ or ☍ to each other, the sick one usually dies (Hor'y); the Asc. to the cusp of the 4th H. by dir.; the Asc. to the □ ♄, and ♄ affl. the hyleg at same time; the Asc. to the ☌ ♄, or ♄ ☌ Asc. by primary dir.; very few deaths occur without some unusual and severe afflictions to the Asc. at B., or that which holds the Asc. by dir. at death; the Asc. affl. by ♄ by dir.; lord of the Asc. affl. by a malefic, or in ☍ the ⊙, or in ☌, □, or ☍ lord of the 8th, or in the 8th, combust or ℞, threatens death, and espec. if the Lights be afflicted; the Asc. affl. by the malefics, or having violent fixed stars near its cusp, and the nearer the cusp the greater the danger; the Asc. to the □ or ☍ ♄ or ♂ by dir.; lord of the Asc., or sign ascending, affl. by lord of the 8th, or a planet in the 8th, tends to be fatal, and death approaching; lord of the Asc. affl., and in the 8th, and the ☽ also weak and in no dignity; lord of the Asc. ☌ lord of the 4th, 6th, 8th, or 12th; lord of the Asc. combust in the Asc.; lord of the Asc. in the 4th, 6th, 8th, or 12th, and affl. by malefics; lord of the Asc. affl. by lords of the 6th or 12th, and lord of the Asc. in ♌ or ♒; lord of the Asc. conjoined with Antares, Caput Algol, Aldebaran, or with violent fixed stars; lord of the Asc. in the 8th, or with lord of the 8th, or lord of the 8th in the Asc. (See "First House" under First. Also see the ⊙, ☽, ♄, ♂, 6th, 8th, and 12th H. influences in this paragraph). MIDHEAVEN—M.C.—The M.C. affl. by the ☌ or ill-asp. ♄ by dir. (See "Tenth House" under Tenth). FOURTH HOUSE—The 4th H. is a Terminal House, and indicative of death and the end of life when severely afflicted during an illness, or at B.; lord of the 4th in the 6th, 8th, or 12th; lord of the 4th in ☍ the Asc. (See Terminal; "Fourth House" under Fourth. Also see the ⊙, ☽, Asc., 6th, 8th and 12th H. influences in this paragraph). SIXTH HOUSE— The 6th H. has no affinity with the Asc., and signifies loss of life. The ☽ lady of the 6th, and combust in the 1st or 4th, and espec. if lord of the 8th be affl.; the lord of the 4th in the 6th, and affl. (See "Sixth House" under Sixth. Also see the various influences of the ⊙, ☽, and all the planets and houses mentioned in this paragraph). EIGHTH HOUSE—Known as the House of Death, and espec. indicates the Manner, Kind, and Quality of the death. A malefic passing thru the 8th, and affl. the place of the ⊙ or ☽ at B., or the place of the prog. ⊙ or ☽; the 8th H. has no affinity with the Asc.,

and signifies loss of life; lord of the 8th angular, and lord of the Asc. cadent, and espec. if lord of the 8th be a malefic; neither of the Fortunes will save life if the lords of the 8th and 6th are in evil asp. to each other; lord of the 8th crossing the cusp of the Asc. by transit; the ☽ transferring the light of lord of the 8th to the lord of the Asc.; lord of the 8th in the Asc., and in ill-asp. to lord of the Asc. under the earth, or if lord of the 8th and lord of the Asc. be in ☌ in the 4th; lord of the 8th in the 10th, and lord of the Asc. in the 4th, 6th, 8th, or 12th, and affl. by malefics; lord of the 8th in ☌ or ill-asp. the ☽; lord of the 8th in the 8th; malefic planets in the 8th, and affl. the hyleg; the ☽ applying to the □ or ☍ asp. the lord of the 8th, or the Sig. to the evil asps. the lord of the 8th; the Sig. applying to the ⚹ the lord of the 8th, in signs of long ascension, have the same effect as the □ asp.; lord of the Asc. in the 8th, or with lord of the 8th. (See "Eighth House" under Eighth. Also see the various planetary and house influences in this paragraph). TWELFTH HOUSE — This house has no affinity with the Asc., and indicates death and loss of life. (See "Twelfth House" under Twelfth. Also see the various planetary and house influences in this paragraph). FIXED STARS— The fixed star Antares is productive of death when afflicting, or joined to the hyleg at B. (See Aldebaran, Algol, Antares, Regulus; "Fixed Stars" under Fixed; Stars. Also see the Moon influences in this paragraph). ECLIPSES —(See Eclipses. See the Eclipse influence under the Sun influences in this paragraph). HYLEG—Life is not destroyed unless the hyleg be severely afflicted, however evil the directions may be, altho the health may suffer greatly by the directions. (See the mention of the various afflictions to the hyleg under the ⊙, ☽, ♆, ♅, ♄ influences in this paragraph. Also see Hyleg). ANARETA—The △ asps. of the Anareta to the hyleg, in signs of short ascension, or the □ asps. in signs of long ascension, according to Ptolemy, will kill or threaten death; the Anareta ☌ or evil asp. the hyleg by dir. (See Anareta. Also see the mention of the Anareta among the ⊙, ♅ and Directions influences in this paragraph). DIRECTIONS—A train of evil directions afflicting the hyleg and the vital points of the map are necessary to produce death. The hyleg must be affl. by the ☌, P, □ or ☍ asp. of the killing, or Anaretical stars, and these also must be afflicted of themselves to cause death. To produce death there must be a combination of several evil directions to the hyleg, and without the aid or intervention of the Benefics to the Anaretic Places, or to the 4th H. One evil direction to the hyleg, however powerful, rarely destroys life. The hyleg evilly aspected at B., but supported by the Benefics, brings great danger of death under a train of evil directions to the hyleg, but with possibility of escape and mitigating influences, and espec. if the benefics give a good asp. to the hyleg at the time of the evil directions. (See Directions; "Danger to Life" under Life. Also see "Certain", "Symbols", in this section). Each of the Houses and Signs of the Zodiac also bear rule over certain diseases, and to contribute to death by these diseases, or afflictions, and for these influences see each of the Houses, and the Signs, in the alphabetical arrangement, in addition to the 4th, 6th, 8th, and 12th H. influences already given in this paragraph.

Asphyxiation; Assassination;

Assaults; Aunt; Automobiles—See Vehicles).

Averted — Death Averted — (See "Death" under Averted. Also note the influences of the Benefics under "Arguments" in this section).

Bad End—(See Beheaded, Execution, Hanging, Judges, Lynched, Suicide, Untimely, etc.).

Bathings; Battle—(See War).

Beasts—Death By— (See Animals, Beasts).

Beheaded; Bereavement; Birth — Death at Birth, or Soon After Birth— (See Abortion, Birth, Parturition).

Bites; Blasts of Wind—(See Wind).

Blizzards; Blows; Born Alive — Dies Soon After Birth—(See "Birth" in this section).

Broken Heart—Dies of—(See Broken).

Bruises; Buildings — By Fall of, or Falls from — (See "Buildings" under Falls).

Burglars—(See Robbers, Thieves).

Burial; Burns—Burned at Stake—(See Burns).

Calamity; Casualties; Catalysis;

Cattle; Causes His Own Death—♀ ruler of the 8th H., or ♀ in this house and afflicted, and usually caused by dissipation, debauchery, indiscretions, or quarrels in love affairs; the 2nd dec. of ♏ on the Asc.; lords of the 1st and 8th being the same planet, as when ♎ is on the Asc., and ♉ on the 8th, or when ♈ is on the Asc., and ♏ on cusp the 8th, and the death is usually the result of intemperance, dissipation, etc., when ♀ rules, or by contests, duels, quarrels, rashness, suicide, violence, etc., when ♂ rules the two cusps or houses. (See these subjects).

Causes of Death—(See "Arguments", and the various paragraphs in this section).

Certain Death—Death More Certain— Death Inevitable—Sure Death, etc.— The ☉ to the □ his own place by dir.; the ☽ and lords of the 1st and 8th in the 6th; the ☽ or lord of the Asc. apply by evil asp. to lord of the 8th, and the latter a malefic; Antares or Caput Algol ascending tends to be fatal; lord of the 1st in the 8th, and lord of the 8th in the 1st, renders death inevitable; the Anareta in the 4th H., death is certain; lords of the 4th and 6th, or lords of the 8th and 6th, in reception or in evil asp. each other denotes death. (See "Arguments", "Fatal", "Symbols", in this section; "Small Hope of Life" under Life; "Many Sicknesses" under Sickness).

Chartering; Childbirth—Death In— (See Parturition, Puerperal).

Childhood; Children — Death of — Death of Parent Caused by Bad Children—(See "Death", "Parents", "Worries", under Children).

Church—No Church or Regular Burial —(See Burial).

Condemned to Death—(See Judge).

Contempt for Death — No Fear of Death—♂ strong ruler of the horoscope. (See "Fear" in this section).

Corpse; Cremation—(See "Silver Cord" under Silver).

Crucifixion—(See Impalement).

Cruel Treatment—Death By— (See Cruel).

Crushed; Curious Death — (See Extraordinary).

Cuts; Danger of Death—(See "Arguments", "Certain", in this section; "Danger" under Life).

Daughter; Day of Death—Is apt to be on a day when the ☽ is in a sign afflicting the Asc., the M.C., or the afflicting planet. (See "Hour", "Time", in this section).

Daytime Death—Death by Day—(See "Wild Animals" under Animals).

Dead—(See Dead).

Death More Certain — (See "Certain" in this section).

Death Not Indicated—Is not indicated unless the hyleg is afflicted by a train of evil directions, and by the very evil asp. of the Anareta to the hyleg by dir. Also the good asps. of the benefics to the hyleg in a train of evil directions, and also a benefic supporting the Anareta, tend to spare life. (See "Spared" under Life).

Death Rate High—(See Mortality).

Death to Be Feared — (See "Arguments", "Certain", in this section).

Death Will Ensue—(See "Certain" in this section).

Debauchery—(See Debauchery, Dissipation. Also see "Causes His Own Death" in this section).

Decapitation—(See Beheaded).

Denotes Death—The 3rd Dec. of ♍ denotes death and dissolution, decay, weakness, infirmity and old age. (See "Arguments", "Certain", "Symbols", in this section).

Depopulation—(See Mortality).

Desert — Lost In — Death In — (See Desert).

Desire for Death—The ☉ to the □ his own place by dir., gives a desire to depart from earth life.

Devoured — Body Devoured After Death—(See Burial).

Disease—The Disease Which Is the Immediate Cause of Death—(See Immediate. Also see "Quality" in this section).

Disintegration; Dissipation — (See "Debauchery" in this section).

Dissolution—(See "Denotes Death" in this section).

Dominion of Death—Is vested in the Anareta, the planet causing death. (See Anareta).

Dreadful Death — (See "Burned at Stake" under Burns; Execution, Fire, Hanging, Ignoble, Impalement, Judges, Lynched, Murdered, Poison, Prison, Treachery, etc.).

Drink; Drought; Drowning;

Drug Habit—(See Narcotics).

Drunkenness; Duels; Dying Persons —(See Dying).

Early Death—(See Early).

Earthquakes—(See Earth).

Easy Death—Gentle, and with Little Suffering—Peaceful Ending to Life— ♃ in the 4th H.; ♃ in the 8th H., and well-asp., and usually after a long life; ♃ and ♀ in the 8th H. indicate a quiet end, and without pain or distress; ♃ and ♀ in the 8th, rulers of the 8th, or in good asp. to cusp the 8th, and with no malefics in the 8th; ♄ lord of the 4th, usually an easy departure, and expiring without a struggle; a benefic acting as Anareta, or afflicting the hyleg, if the Anareta be not near violent fixed stars; lord of the 11th in the 8th H. (See Comforts; "Natural Death" under Natural).

Eating—Death from Excess in Eating—(See Eating).

Eighth House—(See the Eighth House influences under "Arguments" in this section).

Elderly People—Death of—(See Adults, Grandparents, Old Age).

Electricity; Embryo — (See Embryo, Foetus).

Employment—(See Employment, Explosions, Machinery).

Enemy—Death of—Death By—(See Enemies).

Enmity; Epidemics; Epilepsy;

Escapes—Narrow Escapes from Death —(See Escapes).

Events; Excesses; Execution — (See Execution, Judge, Law).

Exercise—(See Exercise, Sports).

Explosions; External Causes—As by Accident, Air, Blows, Bruises, Cuts, Earthquakes, Epidemics, Fire, Heat, Hurts, Injuries, Railroads, Robbers, Travel, Water, Wounds, etc. See the various paragraphs in this section.

Extraordinary; Falls; Family—Death In—(See Family, Relatives).

Famine; Fatal; Fatality; Father;

Fear of Death—Fears His Own Death —No Fear of Death—(See "Death" under Fear).

Female Friend—Death of—(See Friends).

Female Relative—Death of—(See Aunt, Grandparents, Mother, Relatives, Sister, Wife).

Female Treachery—Death By—(See Treachery).

Females—Death of—(See "Death" under Female; Women. Also see Aunt, Mother, Sister, Wife,, etc.).

Fiancee; Fire; Fistula; Floods;

Fluxes; Flying Stones—(See "Flying" under Stone).

Foetus; Folly; Foreign Lands—Foreign War — (See Abroad, Foreign, War).

Foretold Own Death — (See "Foretold", Case No. 979, in 1001 N.N.).

Fourth House — (See Fourth, Terminal).

Fractures; Frenzy; Friends; Fury;

Gases; Grandparents; Great — Death of the Great—(See Great).

Guillotine; Gunshot; Habits; Hand of Man—Death By—(See Hand of Man, Human, Man).

Hanging; Happy Death — (See "Desire", "Easy", in this section).

Heat; Heights; Highwaymen; Home —Dies In His Own Home—Lord of the 8th in the 4th H.

Homicide; Honour—Death In Affairs of—(See Duels, Honour).

Horses—Death By—Death of—(See Horses).

Hospital—Death In—(See Hospital).

Hot—Hot Diseases—Hot Water—Hot Weather — Death By — (See Heat, Liquids, Scalds, Water, Weather).

Hour of Death — Wilson says that when the ☉ is Anareta in a train of evil directions, and affl. the hyleg, and the hour of death is imminent, that death, or an important crisis, usually occurs at about the hours of 2 A.M., or 2 P.M. when the ☉ is 1/3 of his semi-arc either beyond the N. or S. angles. The hour of ♄ is also called the hour of death. (See "Hours" under Planets).

House of Death—(See Eighth House influences under "Arguments" in this section).

Houses—Buildings—Death By Fall of —(See "Buildings" under Falls).

Human Means — Death By — (See "Hand of Man" in this section. Also note the various subjects in this Article).

Hurts; Husband; Ignoble Death — Ignominious—♄ ruler of the horoscope and affl. by malefics; ♄ in the 10th H., afflicted, and affl. the hyleg. (See Execution, Judges, Law, etc.).

Immediate Cause — Of Death — (See "Disease" in this section. Also see Accidents, Injury, and the various paragraphs in this section).

Imminent—Death Imminent—Not Imminent—(See "Arguments", "Certain", in this section. See Moderation, Recovery; "Spared" under Life).

Impalement; Imprudence;

Incised Wounds—(See Cuts).

Incurable; Indicated—Death Indicated —(See "Arguments", "Certain", in this section).

Indiscretions; Indulgences; Inevitable —(See "Certain" in this section).

Infancy; Injuries; Instruments;

Intemperance; Internal Causes—(See Congenital, Heredity, Organic, Structural).

Intoxication; Iron; Irregularities;

Journeys; Judge — By Sentence of — (See Judge).

Justice — By Hand of — (See Judge, Law).

Kicks—(See Horses, Kicks).

Killed; Killing Planet—(See Anareta, Killing. Also see Anareta influences under "Arguments" in this section).

Kinds of Death—(See the various subjects in this Article).

Kings; Law; Lethargy; Life—Danger To—Life Spared—(See Life. Also see "Arguments", and the various paragraphs in this section).

Lightning; Limb—By Mutilation of—(See Beheaded, Mutilation).

Lingering Death—Slow Death—Tedious Death—The ⊙ or ☽ ☌ ♄ in the 12th H.; caused by ♄ afflictions to the hyleg; ♄ affl. in the 6th, 8th or 12th H., and espec. when affl. the hyleg; ♆ in the 8th H., and affl. the hyleg. (See Chronic, Continuity; "Fixed Signs" under Fixed; Invalids; "Long Diseases" under Long; Prolonged, Tedious, etc.).

Loved Ones—Death of—(See Family, Loved Ones, Relatives).

Lynching; Machinery; Madness;

Males—Male In Family—(See Family, Males).

Man—Death by Hand of—(See "Hand of Man", "Human", in this section).

Manner of Death—(See "Quality", and the various paragraphs in this section).

Many Deaths—(See Mortality).

Marriage Partner—(See "Death" under Husband; Marriage Partner, Wife).

Melancholy; Men—Much Mortality Among — (See "Death of Men" under Men).

Middle Life—Death At—Death Before Middle Life—(See Middle Life).

Mines; Miscarriage; Miserable Death —The ☽ Sig. □ or ☍ ♄, usually dies a miserable death; ♃ Sig. ☌ ♄, and espec. if ♂ afflict ♃ and ☿ at the same time; ♄ Sig., ill-dignified, and ☌ the ⊙ or ♂; lord of the 12th in the 8th, and after great misfortunes. (See Miserable, Misfortune).

Mobs; Moisture — (See Floods, Moisture, Rain, Water, etc.).

Monarchs; Morbid Deaths—(See Anareta).

Morgues; Mortal Illness — (See "Certain" in this section; "Fatal Illness" under Fatal).

Mortality; Mother; Multitude — (See Mobs).

Murdered; Mutilated;

Mysterious Death—Mysterious and Sudden—Caused by ♆ or ♅; the evil asps. of ♆ or ♅ to the hyleg at B., and by dir.; ♆ affl. in the 8th H.; ♆ the afflicting planet; ♅ affl. in the 8th H., or affl. the hyleg, tends to a strange and mysterious death, and in an uncommon and extraordinary manner. (See Extraordinary, Notorious, Peculiar, Remarkable, Strange, Trance, Untimely, in this section).

Narcotics; Narrow Escapes — (See Escapes).

Natural Death—(See Natural).

Nature of the Death — (See Quality, and the various paragraphs in this section).

Nobles; Not Indicated — (See "Death Not Indicated" in this section).

Notorious Death—Cardinal signs signify, as by murder, lightning, scalds, gunshot, fire, or on railroads, etc. Also see such subjects as Execution, Hanging, Judges, Law; "Public Death" under Public.

Obscure Death—(See Obscure).

Obstructions; Occurs — (See "Hour", "Time", in this section).

Officers; Old Age—(See Old).

Operations; Own Death—Causes His Own Death—Fears His Own Death—(See "Causes", "Fear", in this section).

Ordinary Deaths — (See "Desire", "Easy", "Home", "Natural", in this section).

Painful Death — (See "Death" under Pain. For Death Without Pain, see "Easy", "Natural", in this section).

Parents; Parturition; Passion—Thru Passional Excesses — (See Amorous, Passion, Sex, Venery).

Patricide—(See Father).

Peaceful Death — (See "Desire", "Easy", "Natural", "Old Age", in this section).

Peculiar Death—(See Extraordinary. See "Mysterious" in this section).

Pestilence; Phrenzy — (See Frenzy, Phrenitic).

Pirates; Place of Death—(See Place).

Plague; Planets and Death—(See Anareta. See "Death" under each of the Planets).

Pleasures; Plots; Poison; Police—(See Officers).

Precipices—Falls From — (See Falls, Heights).

Premature Death—(See Accidents, Burial, Execution, Extraordinary, Judges, Law, Mysterious, Officers, Remarkable, Sudden, Trance, Untimely, and the various paragraphs in this section).

Presidents; Pressed — (See Crushed, Trampled).

Princes; Prison; Property — Death from Loss of—(See Property).

Public Death—Public Mortality—(See Public, Mortality).

Putrefaction; Quadrupeds; Quality of Death — Manner—Nature—Species— Any planet being in the Anaretic Place, or a planet having dignity therein, will show the quality of death, but if no planet is in this place, then the first planet which comes to the Anaretic Place by body or aspect will show it. The Manner and Quality of death are shown from that planet which follows the Anareta by ☌, or aspect, to the place of the hyleg, but if none follow it is taken from that which last preceded. Thus ♃ or ♀ can show the nature of the death altho they do not cause it. The Quality of the Death is indicated by the nature of the least prominent, or least powerful directions in a train of directions to the hyleg, and by the nature of the sign, or signs, containing them. (See "Immediate Cause of Death" under Immediate; "Death" under Nature; Species. Also note the various paragraphs in this section).

Quarrels; Quick Death—(See Quick).

Quiet Death—(See "Peaceful" in this section).

Railroads; Recreations; Relatives;

Religion—Death on Account of—(See "Persecution" under Religion).

Remarkable Death—Singular — Sudden—Unusual—Extraordinary — ♅ as the afflicting planet tends to death in some remarkable, sudden, violent, tragical, and extraordinary manner; ♄ and ♂ both in evil asp. to the ☉ and ☽, or even only one, and at the same time the Asc. be afflicted; the malefics in ♌ or ♋, and lords of the Anaretic Places, and if one or more malefics attack the ☉ or ☽. (See Extraordinary, Peculiar, Sudden, Tragical, Untimely, Unusual, Violent, in this section).

Remedy—Incapable of—(See "Hurts" under Remedy; Incurable).

Reptiles; Rescue Work—(See Rescue).

Respiration — (See "Death" under Breathing).

Riots; Robbers; Rulers; Ruptures; Sad Death—Death from Sadness—(See Sad).

Sailors—(See Maritime).

Saved—The Life Will Be Saved—Will Not Be Saved—(See "Certain Death" in this section. See "Spared" under Life).

Scalds; Sea; Searing—(See "Searing" under Burns).

Second Death—(See the Introduction under Twelfth House).

Secret Enemies — (See "Secret Enemies" under Secret).

Sentence of Law—(See Judge).

Serpents; Sharp Instruments—Sharp Diseases — (See Cuts, Duels, Instruments, Sharp, Sword).

Sheep—Death of—(See Sheep).

Ships; Shipwreck; Shock;

Short Journeys—(See Journeys, Railroads, Travel).

Short Life—(See Life).

Silver Cord—(See Silver).

Signs of Death — (See "Symbols" in this section).

Signs of Zodiac — (See each of the Signs, as Aries, Taurus, etc.).

Simulated—(See Trance).

Singular Death—(See Extraordinary, Mysterious, Remarkable, in this section).

Sister; Sixth House—(See Sixth).

Slaughter; Sleep—Death During Sleep —(See Sleep).

Slow Death—(See "Lingering" in this section).

Son; Spared — (See "Spared" under Life).

Species of Death—(See "Quality" in this section).

Spiritual Causes — Of Death — (See Astral; "Death" under Neptune; Spiritual).

Sports; Stabs; Starvation; Steel and Iron—(See Iron).

Stillborn; Stings; Stones—(See "Flying Stones" under Stones).

Storms; Strange Death—Death from Strange Causes — ♆ the afflicting planet. (See "Mysterious" in this section).

Strangers—Death in the Presence of —The ☽ in the 8th H.

Strangulation; Strokes — (See Assaults, Attacks, Blows, Stabs, Sword, Violence, etc.).

Sudden Death—(See Sudden).

Suffocation; Suicide; Sure Death—(See "Certain" in this section).

Surgical Operations — (See Operations).

Sword; Symbols of Death—Signs of Death—Arguments for Death, etc.— The ☉ in ♌, P, or ♋ by application acts as a powerful Anareta, and denotes death; if the lord of the 1st be in the 6th, and lord of the 6th in the 1st, when they leave the sign or signs they are in, and meet with the □ or ♋ asps. of ♄, ♂, or lords of the 4th or 8th, death may follow; lord of the 1st in the 4th or 8th, if he be afflicted; lord of the Asc., or the ☽ combust, but with hopes of recovery if the ☽ or lord of the Asc. dispose of the ☉; lords of the 4th or 6th, or lords of the 8th and 6th, in reception, denotes death; lord of the 1st and 8th being the same planet; in sickness lord of the 6th ♌ the Anareta, and espec. if the ♌ is in the 4th H., the house denoting the grave. (Hor'y); a malefic lord of the fatal 4th, and posited in the 6th, or 8th; lord of the disease, or of the 6th H., and lord of the 4th in mutual reception, indicate that the disease will end in death; lord of the Asc. also lord of the 8th, and espec. if ♃ and afflicted (Hor'y); the afflictors in the disease in the terms of the lords of the 4th, 6th, 8th or 12th H. (Hor'y); lord of the 4th disposing of the Anareta, or being posited in or near the cusp of the 6th H. (See Arguments, Anareta, Certain, Denotes, Quality, and the various paragraphs in this section. Also see "Signs of Death" under Infancy).

Tedious Death—(See "Lingering" in this section).

Theatres; Thieves; Threatened—Death Threatened — Threatened With Death Many Times—(See "Arguments", and the various paragraphs in this section. See "Danger to Life" under Life; "Narrow Escapes" under Escapes).

Thunder Storms—(See Thunder).

Time of Death—(See Time. See "Day of Death", "Hour", in this section).

Tornadoes—(See Wind).

Tortured to Death—(See Banishment, Beaten, Captivity, Cruel, Exile, Lynched, Pirates, Robbers, Prison; "Stake" under Burns, etc.).

Tragical Death—♅ in 8th H., and affl. the hyleg; the M.C. to the place of the Pleiades, or Pollux, tends to a tragic death by women. Caput Algol disposes to a tragic death when angular at B., and affl. the hyleg. See Algol, Beheaded; "Death" under Sudden; Enemies, Execution, Extraordinary, Hanging, Judge, Poison; "Public Death" under Public; Treachery, Untimely, etc.).

Trampled—(See Crushed, Trampled).

Trance; Travel—(See Journeys, Railroads, Travel, Vehicles, Voyages).

Trodden—(See Trampled).

Twelfth House—(See Twelfth).

Uncle; Uncommon — (See Mysterious, Peculiar, Remarkable, Strange, Tragical, in this section).

Unexpected—(See Accidents; "Death" under Sudden).

Untimely Death—(See Untimely. Also note the various paragraphs in this section).

Unusual — (See Extraordinary, Mysterious, Peculiar, Remarkable, Strange, Tragical, and the various paragraphs in this section).

Vehicles; Venomous Creatures—(See Adder, Bites, Reptiles, Serpents, Stings, Venomous, etc.).

Vexation; Violent Death — (See Violent).

Viscera—By Obstruction of—(See Obstructions, Viscera).

Voyages; War; Wasting Away—(See Wasting).

Water; Weak—Death of the Weak and Frail—(See "Death" under Weak).

Weapons; Weather; Wife;

Wild Beasts—(See Wild).

Wind; Womb—Death In—(See Stillborn).

Women — Death By — Death of — (See Women).

Wounds; Wrath; Young—Dies Young — Death of Young Men — Death of Young People—(See Young).

Youth—Dies In Youth—(See "Early Death" under Early; Youth).

DEBASED IN MIND—The ☉ conciliated with the ruler of the mind, and cadent and occidentally posited. (See Debauched, Degenerate, Dissipated, Drunkenness, Depraved; "Immoral" and "Loose Morals" under Morals; Perversions, Shameless, Wanton, etc.).

DEBAUCHERY—Debauched—Afflictions in the watery signs ♋, ♏, and ♓ tend to more of debauchery, dissipation, drunkenness, and depravity, and espec. when the malefics ♄ and ♂ are also in these signs, and afflicting the ☉, ☽, Asc., or hyleg; the malefics in the 5th H., and affl. the Asc. by dir.; the ☉ to the ☌ ♀ by dir., and ♀ peregrine or afflicted at B.; the ☉ to the □ the ☽ or ♀ by dir.; the ☉ to the ☌ ☽ by dir., and the ☽ badly affl. at B.; the ☽ to the Left Hand of Ophiucus, debauchery and infamy; ♃ Sig. □ or ☍ ♀, a countenance indicative of intemperance and debauchery; in Hor'y Questions ♂ as Sig. denotes one drunken and debauched; ♀ ☌ the Asc.

by dir.; ♀ ruler of the horoscope, and affl. by malefics; Asc. to the □ or ☍ ☽ by dir.; lord of the 8th in the 5th H.

Death from Debauchery—Lord of the 8th in the 5th, and with drinking, intoxication, etc.

Debility from Debauchery—A Debauched Look—The ☉ Sig. in ♓; the ☉ Sig. □ or ☍ ♃; the ☽ Sig. in ♍; ♄ ruler of the 5th H. at B., in ♏, and ♄ in ☌ or evil asp. the Asc. by dir., and espec. if ♏ be in the 5th H. at B.; ♄ or ♃ Sig. in □ or ☍ ♀; ♂ Sig. in ♉, ♏, or ♓, and affl.; ♂ to the ill-asps. the ☽ or ♀ by dir.; ♀ ruler of the horoscope, and affl. by malefics; ♀ ill-dignified at B.; ♀ affl. at B., and to the ☌ or ill-asps. the Asc. or ♂ by dir.; ♀ or ♀ in watery signs, and affl. by ♆, ♅, ♃, or ♂; ♀ and ♀ in bad familiarity, in weak signs, and ill-posited; ♀ Sig. in ♉; ♌ on the cusp of 5th H. at B., and afflicted. (See "Causes Own Death" under Death; Debased, Dissipated, Dissolute, Depraved, Drink, Drunkenness, Folly; "Free Living" under Free; "High Living" under High; Infamous, Intemperance, Intoxication, Pale, Profligate, Prodigal; "Riotous Living" under Riotous, etc.).

DEBILITY — Debilitated — Weakness — Denoted by ♄; a ♄ disease; ♄ ascending at B., and affl. the ☉, ☽, Asc., or hyleg; denoted by the ☽ when the ☽ afflicts the ☉, Asc., or hyleg; the ☽ affl. in ♍, or ♏ upon the Asc., and espec. in the early years of life; afflictions in ♎, and a ♎ disease; watery signs on the Asc. at B., and espec. ♋ or ♓, and afflicted. (See Feeble, Infirm, Ill-Health; "Weak Body" under Weak).

Atony — Want of Tone and Power — (See Atony, Stamina, Tone, Vitality Low, Weak).

Blood—Debility of—♀ affl. in ♒ warns against. (See Blood; "Impure Blood" under Impure).

Body—Debility of—The ☉ or ☽ hyleg, and to the ☌ or ill-asp. ♄ by dir.; the ☉ to the ill-asps. ♃ by dir.; the ☽ affl. in ♍, or affl. the hyleg therefrom; ♄ ascending at B.; ♄ to the ill-asps. his own place at B. by dir.; ♄ afflictions are responsible for debility and morbid conditions; characteristic of the Lymphatic Temperament. (See Feeble; "Bad Health" under Health; Infirm, Ill-Health, Lassitude; "Weakened" under Strength; "Low" under Vitality; "Weak Body" under Weak).

Chronic Debility—The ☉ hyleg, and to the ☌ or ill-asps. ♄ by dir.; the ☉ or ☽ in the 6th H. at B., and affl. by malefics. (See Chronic, Lingering, Prolonged, Tedious).

Countenance—Debilitated Look—(See Anaemia, Emaciated, Pale, Sickly).

Debauchery—Debility By — (See Debauchery, Dissipation, Dissolute, Drink, Intemperance, etc.).

General Debility—The ☉ afflicting the ☽; the ☽ hyleg in ♒ in a female nativity; the ☽ affl. by ♄, and espec. with females, or the ☉ affl. by ♄ in males; the ☽ affl. by ♄ tends to long, lingering and chronic complaints arising from general debility; ♆ □ or ☍ the

Asc.; ♄ in the 6th H. and affl. the hyleg; a ♀ disease, and afflictions to ♀. (See Feeble; "General Ill-Health" under Ill-Health; "Debility" under Nerves; Sickly; "Weakened" under Strength; "Weak Body" under Weak; Vitality Low, etc.).

Health—Debility of—(See "Bad Health" under Health; Ill-Health).

Heart—Debility of—(See "Weak Heart" under Heart).

Look—Debilitated Look—(See Emaciated, Pale, Sickly, White, etc.).

Males—Debility of—(See "Ill-Health" under Males; Impotency).

Men—Debility of—(See "Debility" under Men).

Mental Debility—A Diseased Mind—(See Demoniac, Insanity, Idiocy, Imbecility, Madness, Mania; "Diseased Mind" and "Weak Mind" under Mind).

Morbid Debility—Caused by ♄.

Nervous Debility—(See "Debility" under Nerves).

Physical Debility—(See "Body" in this section. Also see Disease, Ill-Health, Physical, Sickness, etc.).

Sickness—Debility Greater in Sickness—The ☽ ☌ or ill-asp. ♄ or ♂, or the place of either in the radical map, and ♄ the stronger afflicting planet at the beginning of the illness. (See Recuperation, Resistance, Recovery, Vitality, etc.).

Strength—Strength of the Body Rendered Weaker—(See "Weakened" under Strength).

Weakness—Weak Body—(See Endurance, Feeble, Infirm; "Ill-Health All Thru Life" under Ill-Health; Invalids; Vitality Low; "Weak Body" under Weak).

Women—Debility of—(See Females, Women). For other study see Consumptions, Dull, Lethargy, Nutrition, Wastings, etc.

DECANATES—The division of a Sign into three parts of 10° each. The first ten degrees are of the nature of the Sign itself; the second 10° of the nature of the next sign of the same element; the 3rd part, of the nature of the third sign of the same element. Thus the first ten degrees of ♈ are of the nature of ♈; the second ten degrees of the nature of ♌, and the last ten degrees of the nature of ♐. (See Chap. 4 in Sepharial's Manual of Astrology, on the relation of the decanates and planets, and the diseases and qualities given by each of the 36 decanates). The Decanate rising on the Asc. has a distinct influence over the height, weight, bodily development, personal appearance, facial characteristics, and also determines the natural temperament. The first Dec. of cardinal signs is mental; the second Dec. is mental-vital, and the third Dec. is mental-motive. The first Dec. of Fixed Signs on the Asc. is vital; the second Dec. is vital-motive; the 3rd Dec. is vital-mental. The first Dec. of mutable signs on the Asc. is motive; the 2nd Dec. is motive-mental; the 3rd Dec. is motive-vital. The Bodily Temperament given by the Asc. may thus be either mental, motive, or vital, or a combination of two of these, as mental-vital, mental-motive, etc. These Decanates on the Asc. also have much to do with the shape of the face. The mental type is shaped like a pear, and the head narrows down to the chin, and is wide at the temples. The vital type is widest about the cheeks, and with an oval or round face. The motive type has the head and face flatter at the sides, and the square-shaped head. Each of these types are also subject to three variations or combinations, according to the Dec. rising, such as vital, vital-motive, and vital-mental, etc. Planets rising, and the position of the ruler of the Asc., also produce other variations. Also the personal appearance is much affected by the ☽, and her sign and position. Also it is said the height of a person is partly determined by the Moon's Nodes, but this cannot always be relied upon. (See Navamsa). (See Appearance, Ascendant, Body, Face, Height, Stature, Temperament, Weight, etc.).

DECAPITATION—Danger of Death By —(See Beheaded).

DECAY—Putrefactive Changes—Decomposition—Governed by ♄ and the ☽. Cold and Dryness tend to decay, dissipation and decomposition of matter, and are malevolent influences. Organic and vegetable decay are under the rule of the ☽. (See Blight, Catalysis, Cold, Corrosion, Death, Decrepitude, Degeneration, Dissolution, Dryness, Excretions, Gangrene, Granulations, Moisture, Mortification, Moonlight, Necrosis, Noxious, Putrefaction, Rotten, etc.).

Death by Decay—♃ causes death by a decayed system, and due to corrupt blood, surfeits, and brought on by excesses of various kinds. (See Excesses, Impure, Jupiter, Plethora, Surfeits, etc.).

Decayed System—(See "Death" in this section).

Old Age—The 3rd Decanate of ♍ denotes old age, decay, infirmity, weakness and dissolution. (See Infirm, Old Age, Shrinkage, Wasting, Withering, Wrinkles, etc.).

Organic Decay—Ruled by the ☽. (See Moon, Organic).

Premature Decay—(See "Fluid" under Vital).

Teeth—(See "Decay" under Teeth).

Tissues—Decay of—(See "Decay" under Tissues. Also see Corrosion, Degeneration, Emaciation, Gangrene, Mortification, Putrefaction, Urea, Wasting, etc.).

Vegetable Matter—Decay of—(See Vegetation).

DECEITFUL — Deceptive—Duplicity—False Pretenses—Deception—Largely a ♄ influence; ♄ or ♂ Sig. in □ or ☍ ☿, or ☿ Sig. in □ or ☍ these planets; ♄ Sig. in ♋ or ♓; the ☉ or ♃ Sig. ☌ ♄; ♂ Sig. in ♓; ♂ or ☿ ill-dig. at B.; ♀ or ☿ Sig. in ♋; ☿ Sig. ☌ the ☉; ☿ Sig. □ or ☍ the ☽; characteristic of the negative signs; many planets in bicorporeal signs; a ♏ influence when this sign is badly afflicted; characteristic of bad ♏ and ♑ maps when under strong ♆ afflictions; deceptions are also ruled by ♆. (See Cheating, Dishonest, Dual, Evil, Forgers, Gambling, Hypocritical, Liars, Mischief, Mockery, Pettifogging, Shrewd, Swindlers, Thieves, Treachery, etc.).

Deceitful Relatives—Injured By—The ☽ Sig. □ or ☍ ♃; lord of the 10th in the 12th; lord of the 10th a malefic, and in the 11th H., and afflicted. (See Enemies, Plots, Treachery).

DECLINATION—(See Latitude, Nodes).

DECLINES—(See Chronic, Consumptions, Emaciation; "Malnutrition" under Nutrition; Wasting Diseases, etc.).

DECOMPOSITION—(See Decay, Degeneration, Putrefaction, Disintegration).

DECREASE—Decrease of—Decreased—(See Diminished, Lack of).

Birth Rate Decreased—(See "Birthrate" under Birth).

Death Rate Decreased—(See "Death Rate" under Mortality).

Moon—Decrease of—(See "Decrease" under Moon).

Motility—Decreased Motility—(See Motion, Motor, Movement, Neuroses, Paralysis, Retarded, Slow, etc.).

The Disease Will Decrease—(See "Decrease" under Recovery).

DECREPITUDE—S.nile Feebleness—♄ is the planet of, and of decay. (See "Senility" under Old Age. Also see Decay, Feeble, Infirm, Weak).

DECUMBITURE—This means "Lying Down", the beginning of an illness, or when the patient first takes to his bed in the illness. A Horary map made up for this time gives very valuable indications as to the nature and prognosis of the disease, and when studied along with the map of birth. The ☽ and Asc. are always taken as hyleg at decumbiture in Horary Questions. The afflicting planet, or planets, in cardinal signs at decumb. show a more rapid disease, and soon over. The afflicting planet in a fixed sign shows continuity, a prolonged or tedious disease, etc. (See Acute, Cardinal, Chronic, Continuity, Crises, Duration, Fixed Signs under Fixed; Mutable, Particular, Prolonged, Short Illnesses under Short, Praeincipients, Prognosis, Symptoms, Tedious, etc.).

DEEP—

Deep Cardiac Plexus—(See Čardiac).

Deep Forehead—(See Forehead).

Deep Lines—(See Wrinkles).

Deep Mind—(See Mind).

Deep-Pitted—Pitted or Deep Degrees of the Zodiac—(See Pitted).

Deep-Seated Diseases—(See Chronic, Heredity, Organic, Structural).

Deep-Set Eyes—(See Eyeballs).

Deep Vexation—Sickness From—(See Vexation).

Deep Voice—(See Voice).

Deep Yellow—(See Yellow).

DEFECATION—Evacuations—(See Evacuation, Faeces).

DEFECTS—Defective—Imperfections—Absence of a Part or Organ, etc.—Defects may occur in any part or organ of the body, and may be congenital, from birth, or acquired. For the various Defects of Parts of the Body, Organs, Functions, etc., see the Part, Organ, or Function in the alphabetical arrangement. The ☉ in the different Signs, if afflicted, tends to cause organic and structural defects in the part or organ ruled by such sign. Also the malefics ♄ and ♂ in the various signs at B. tend to defects, marks, deformities, and afflictions to the part, or organs ruled by the sign containing them. The planet ♄ especially causes defects in the personal appearance when he is in the Asc. at B., or rising, and afflicting the ☉, ☽, or Asc. at B. The Prenatal Influences, and the planetary afflictions during Gestation, also account for many of the bodily, physical and mental defects, which defects exist from birth, and are conspicuous thruout the life. Heredity also accounts for many defects, and which are handed down from parent to child from generation to generation, such as Birthmarks, Marks, Moles, Deformities, Insanity, etc. For the Defects which arise from disease, such as Blindness, Deafness, Lameness, Paralysis, Stiff Joints, and a multitude of subjects, look for the disease and the subject in the alphabetical arrangement if not listed here. The following subjects are suggestive along the lines of Defects, which see in the alphabetical arrangement,—Abnormalities, Accommodation, Acquired, Appearance, Arms, Atrophy, Azimene, Baldness, Barrenness, Beastly Form (see Beasts); Breathing, Births, Blemishes, Blind, Blood, Blotches, Body, Brain, Breasts, Broken, Build, Chest, Children, Circulation, Cloaca, Complexion, Congenital, Constitutional, Contortions, Contractions, Crippled, Crooked, Cyclops, Deaf, Deaf and Dumb (see Hearing, Mutes); Deficient, Deformities, Digestion, Diminished, Disabilities, Displacements, Disfigurements, Distortions, Dumb, Dwarfed, Ears, Enlargements, Eunuchs, Excrescences, Eyes, Eyesight (see Sight); Face, Faulty, Feet, Foetus, Freaks, Freckles, Gait, Growth, Hair, Hands, Heart, Heredity, Hermaphrodites, Idiocy, Ill-formed, Imbecility, Imperfections, Inefficient, Inhuman, Insanity, Insufficient, Irregularities, Joints, Judgment, Knees, Lameness, Left Eye (see Left); Legs, Limbs, Locomotion, Lungs, Maimed, Malformations, Marks, Matrix (see Womb); Members, Memory, Mental, Mind, Missing, Moles, Monsters, Mutes, Mutilated, Naevus, Natural, Nerves, Ocular, Organic, Organs, Paralysis, Personal Appearances (see Appearance); Physical, Posture, Prenatal, Pressure, Rectum, Respiratory Organs (see Breathing); Right Eye (see Right); Rigidity, Savage, Scars, Sex Organs, Sight, Skin, Speech, Spine, Stature, Stooped, Structural, Teeth, Throat, Tongue, Vision, Walk, etc.

DEFENSIVE FORCES—Of the Body— Are under the especial rule of ♃, and assisted by ♀ and ♆. (See Cells, Phagocytes, Preservation, Recovery, Recuperation, Resistance, Tissues, Vital, Vitality).

DEFICIENT — Deficiency — Deficiencies —Are ruled over strongly by ♄, as ♄ tends to slow up the functions, retard, suppress bodily activities, and espec. when he is badly afflicted at B., or afflicting the vital centers, as the ☉, ☽, Asc., or hyleg. The influence of ♆ when conjoined with ♄, and affl. the rulers of the circulation, ♃ and ♀, also tends to increase the afflictions of ♄ along this line. (See Obstructions, Retardation, Stoppages, Suppressions).

Blood—Deficiency of Red Blood Corpuscles—(See "Blood" under Red).

Circulation—Deficiency of Circulation In a Part—(See "Deficiency" under Circulation).

Degrees—Deficient Degrees of the Zodiac—(See Azimene).

Devoid Of—(See Void).

Fluids—Of the Body—Deficiency of— (See Fluids).

Functions—(See "Suppression" under Functions).

Insufficiencies—(See Insufficient).

Lack Of—(See Lack).

Loss Of—(See Loss).

Lymph—Deficiency In—(See Lymph).

Mentally Deficient—(See "Deficient" under Mental).

Mineral Salts—Deficiency of in Blood —(See "Blood" under Minerals).

Mucus—Deficiency of on Respiratory Membranes—(See "Respiratory" under Mucus).

Organism—Deficient Development of —(See Diminished; "Deficient", "Undersized", under Organs).

Red Blood Corpuscles—Deficiency of —(See "Blood" under Red).

Secretions—Deficient—(See Fluids, Glands, Secretions, Suppressions).

Stomach Juices—Deficiency of—(See Digestion; "Ailments" under Fluids; Gastric, Juices, Stomach).

Void Of—(See Void). For Deficiencies in any part of the body, of any organ, function, etc., and which may not be listed here, see the subject in the alphabetical arrangement. Also see Defects, Diminished, Imperfections, Inefficiency, Irregularities, Suppressions).

DEFLUXIONS—Catarrh—A Downward Flow of Humours—Defluxions are diseases of the ☉, ☽, and ♄. (See Catarrh, Fluxion, Humours, Mucus, Phlegm; "Watery Humours" under Watery).

Cold Defluxions—♄ diseases.

Head—Defluxions of Rheum From— ☽ affl. in ♈. (See Catarrh; "Rheum" under Head).

Rheum—Defluxions of—(See Rheum).

DEFORMITIES—Deformed—Imperfect in Body—Disablements—These may be congenital or acquired. The congenital deformities are usually the result of prenatal afflictions during gestation, assisted by strong afflictions of the malefics at birth, or with what are known as the Broken, Imperfect, or Mutilated Signs on the Asc., strong, or occupied by malefics. (See Broken, Distortions, Mutilated, Prenatal).

The following subjects have to do with deformities in the various parts, and organs of the body, and also with mental deformities, defects, and deficiencies, which subjects see in the alphabetical arrangement—

Abdomen; Accidents; Acquired;

Action; Anatomical Changes—(See Anatomical).

Animals; Amputations—(See Operations).

Ankles; Ankylosis; Antenatal—(See Prenatal).

Anus—Imperforate Anus—(See Anus).

Appearance; Arms—Armless Wonder —(See Arms).

Arthritis Deformans—(See Joints).

Atrophy; Azimene Degrees—The Lame Degrees of the Zodiac—(See Azimene).

Beastly Form—(See Beasts).

Birth—Deformed from Birth—(See Congenital, Infancy, Prenatal).

Blind from Birth—Born Blind—(See Blindness).

Body Deformed—Deformed in Body and Mind—Body Incomplete—(See "Armless" under Arms; "Deformed" under Mind; Hands, Incomplete, Legs, Members, Missing, Organs, etc. Also note the various paragraphs in this section).

Bow Legs—(See Legs).

Breast—Chicken-Breasted, Pigeon-Breasted—(See Breast).

Broken—Broken Bones—Broken Limbs—Broken Signs—(See Broken).

Causes of Deformities—The planetary influences at B. attributed to deformities are as follows,—The ☉ and ☽ affl. in the 6th and 12th H. at B.; ♆ afflictions and diseases; deformities are largely ruled and controlled by ♆; ♅, ♄, and ♂ closely associated, in ☌ or ☍ in fixed signs; ♅, ♄, or ♂ in the 5th, 6th or 12th H., or afflicting these houses or cusps by aspect, or affl. the Asc.; ♄ and ♂ joined anywhere in the map, and espec. in angles, or in their own nodes, or in the Lunar Nodes; ♀ Sig. □ or ☍ ♄; many planets in ♍ in the 6th or 12th H.; ♉, ♎, ♏, ♑, ♓, or the last part of ♈ and ♌, when on the Asc. at B., or occupied by malefics, are said to cause deformity; people born under the broken signs, ♌, ♏, and ♓, tend to be deformed in some way. (For further influences see the various paragraphs in this Article).

Channels—(See "Channels" under Genitals. Also see Cloaca).

Chest; Chicken-Breasted—(See Breast).

Children—(See "Deformed" under Birth, Children).

Chronic Deformans—(See "Ankylosis", "Arthritis", "Rheumatism", under Joints).

Cloaca; Club Feet—(See Feet).

Congenital—(See Birth, Congenital, Heredity, Prenatal).

Constitution—(See Constitution, Defects. Also note the various paragraphs in this section).

Contortions; Contractions; Crippled; Crooked; Crossed Eyes—(See Eyes).

Curvature; Cyclops; Deafness; Deaf and Dumb—(See Mute).

Defects; Deficiencies; Depressions; Diminished; Disabilities;

Disfigurements; Dislocations;

Displacements; Distortions; Dogs—Resembles Dogs, Animals, etc.—(See "Dogs" under Children).

Dwarfed; Enlargements; Eunuchs;

Excessive Members — (See Hands; "Two Heads" under Head; "United Twins" under Twins; Virile).

Excrescences; Exophthalmos — (See Eyeballs).

Eyes—Blindness—Crossed Eyes—Focussed into One—Protrusion of—(See Blindness, Cyclops, Exophthalmos, Eyeballs, Eyes, Goggle).

Face; Feet; Fingers; Form;

Fractures; Freaks; Frog Child—(See Frog).

Gait; Generative Organs; Giants;

Goiter; Gout; Growth; Hair—Little Hair—No Hair or Teeth—(See Baldness, Hair).

Hands—No Hands or Arms Below the Elbows — Four Hands — (See "Frog Child" under Frog; Hands).

Harelip; Head — (See Hands; "Deformities" under Head. Also see Excrescences, Idiocy, Skull).

Heart—Heart on Right Side—(See Heart).

Hermaphrodite; Hips; Hollow;

Humpback—(See Spine).

Hydrocephalus; Idiots; Ill-Formed; Impediments; Imperfections;

Imperforations; Incomplete;

Infirmities; Inhibitions; Inhuman;

Injuries; Joints; Knees—(See "Knock Knees" under Knees).

Lameness—Lame Degrees of the Zodiac—(See Azimene, Lameness).

Legs—Various Deformities of—(See Feet, Knees, Hips, Legs, Thighs).

Limbs; Limitations; Limping; Local Parts—(See Local).

Locomotion; Maimed; Malformations; Members; Mind and Body—Deformed In—(See "Body" in this section).

Mineral Deposits—(See Deposits, Minerals, Urea, Uric Acid).

Missing Members—(See Arms, Hands, Legs, Members, Missing).

Monsters; Motion; Movement;

Mutilated; Narrow; Neck; Operations;

Opisthotonos; Organs; Paralysis;

Pigeon-Breasted—(See Breast).

Prenatal; Protruding; Rectum;

Rheumatism—Chronic Deformans—(See Joints, Rheumatism).

Rickets; Sex Organs—(See Genitals, Sex, Womb).

Shape; Shoulders; Siamese Twins—(See "United" under Twins).

Skull; Slightly Deformed—(See Slight).

Spasmodic; Spine; Sternum; Stiff;

Stooped; Strabismus—(See Eyes).

Teeth—Crooked Teeth—No Teeth or Hair—(See Teeth).

Thorax; Toes; Treachery; Triplets;

Twelfth House—(See Twelfth).

Twins; Urethra—(See Cloaca, Urethra).

Virile; Walk; Womb; Wry Neck—(See Neck). Case of Deformity—Birth Data, etc.—(See "Deformed", No. 689, in 1001 N.N.).

DEGENERATE—Degeneracy—Base—A Low Fellow—Degraded in Character—A Vagabond—♄ Sig. □ or ⚹ ☿; ♂ Sig. □ or ⚹ ☽, a fit companion for the lowest and most unprincipled of mankind. (See Debased, Low, Unnatural, Vile).

DEGENERATION—Deterioration in the structure of a tissue or organ—Degeneration of Parts of the Body is the work principally of ♄ and ♃. Jupiter helps in degeneration by giving Fatty Tumors and Growths, increase of Adipose Tissue, and by disturbances of the Arterial Circulation over which he rules. Degeneration thru Excesses and Surfeits is generally the work of ♃, ♂, and ♀. (See Catalysis, Death, Decay, Destructive, Decomposition, Emaciation, Fat, Fatigue, Growths, Hardening, Tumors, Wasting, etc.).

Fatty Degeneration—Of the Heart, Liver, Muscles—(See "Fatty Degeneration" under Fat, Heart, Liver, Muscles).

Fibrous Degeneration—(See Fiber).

Progressive Degeneration — (See Progressive, Tabes, Wasting).

Tissues—Degeneration of—(See Tissues).

DEGLUTITION—Swallowing—The ☽ rules the swallow.

Difficulty In Swallowing—Inability to Swallow — Dysphagia — ☿ affl. in ♍, thru loss of nervous control; Subs at SP, the 7th D. (See "Control", "Obstructions", "Swellings", under Throat. Also see Glass).

DEGREE—Degrees—

Disease—Degree of Disturbance In—(See Disturbances).

Physical Strength — Degree of, and Degree of Vitality—Is largely determined by the Rising Sign and the Asc., its aspects and conditions, in both sexes. (See Physical, Strength, Vitality).

Response Against Disease—The Degree and Response by the System against Disease, Exposure, Injury, Wounds, etc.—(See Endurance, Immunity, Recuperation, Resistance, Stamina, Strength, Tone, Vitality).

Vitality—Degree of—(See "Physical Strength" in this section. Also see Vitality).

Zodiac—Degrees of the Zodiac—Each degree of the Zodiac has a different meaning and expression, and in matters of health, mind, temperament, appearance, etc., the degree rising upon the Eastern horizon at B., or the degree upon the M.C., and also the degrees occupied by planets at B., have a special significance. The meanings of these degrees are well set forth and explained in the little booklet called "The Degrees of the Zodiac Symbolised", by Charubel. The Degrees of the Zodiac which have special influence over the body and mind, in matters of health, disease, deformities, form and shape of the body, complexion, the constitution, etc., are given under the following subjects. See Azimene, Critical (see "Sensitive Degrees" under Sensitive); Dark, Deep (see Pitted); Deficient (see Azimene); Fair (see Light); Feminine, Fortunate, Lame (see Azimene); Light, Masculine, Mutilated, Pitted, Predetermination, Sensitive, Smoky, Violent, Void, Weak (see Azimene). See Signs, Zodiac.

DEJECTED—Dejection—Despondent—Cast Down—Low Spirits, etc.—The ☉ or ☽ to the ill-asps. ♄ by dir; the ☽ Sig. to the ☌ the ☉ or ♄; ♄ Sig. ☐ or ☍ the ☽; ♄ to the ill-asps. his own place by dir. or tr.; ♄ Sig. ☐ or ☍ ♂, generally lives a most dejected life; ♄ affl. in ♋ or ♓; ♃ Sig. ☐ or ☍ ♄; void of strong ♂ influence and aspects at B.; ☿ Sig. in ♑; ☿ ☍ ♑ partile asp. the Asc.; lord of the 8th H. in the Asc.; the 2° ♌ on the Asc. (See Anguish, Anxiety, Brooding, Depressed, Despair, Despondency, Fears, Gloomy, Hypochondria, Introspection, Low Spirits (see Low); Melancholia, Miserable, Moods, Morose, Peace, Repining, Peevish, Sad, Unhappy, Worry, Wretched).

DELAYS—Delayed—
   Birth Delayed—(See "Delayed Births" under Children).
   Disease Delayed—Long Illnesses—(See Chronic, Continuity, Course, Crises, Duration, Long, Prolonged, Relapse, Slow, Tedious, Worse, etc.).
   Growth Delayed—(See "Arrested", "Retarded", under Growth; Retarded).
   Mental Development—Delayed Mental Growth—(See "Arrested" under Mental).
   Puberty Delayed—(See Puberty). Saturn is the planet of delays, whether in physical ailments or conditions, mental, or in the daily affairs of life. (See Saturn influences under Saturn).

DELICATE—Delicacy—Frail—Tender—Weak—
   Delicate Appetite—(See Appetite).
   Delicate Body—(See Constitution, Pale, Sickly, Vitality Low, Weak, White).
   Delicate Children—Sickly Children—(See "Sickly" under Children).
   Delicate Complexion—(See Complexion).
   Delicate Health—(See "Bad Health" under Health; "Signs of Ill-Health" under Ill-Health; "Weak Body" under Weak).
   Delicate Skin—(See Skin).

DELIRIUM—The ☽ to the ill-asps. ☿ by dir., and ☿ affl. by malefics at B., danger of delirium and madness; the ☽ ☍ ☿ at decumb., and ☋ or a malefic in the Asc. (Hor'y); ♂ in ♈ and affl. ☿ at B., or by dir.; a ☿ disease; ☿ affl. at B., and the ☽ to the ill-asps. ☿ by dir.; ☿ joined to the Anareta causes delirium in disease; ☿ afflicting the ☽ during the course of an acute disease, and espec. if ☿ be in ♈ at B., and afflicted. (See Anguish, Coma, Epilepsy, Fainting, Hysteria, Madness,, Mania).
   Colds and Coughs—Delirium With—(See "Death" under Cough).
   Delirium Tremens—Delirium from Alcoholic Poisoning—A Toxic Psychoses—Afflictions in ♓, from drink or drugs; ♅ affl. in a watery sign; ♅ in ♓, and espec. in the 6th or 12th H. (See Drink, Narcotics, Pineal Gland).
   Typhus—Delirium of—Typhomania—(See Typhus).
   Wild Delirium—A Phrenitic Man—Phrenitic Delirium—An ♈ disease, malefics in ♈, and the hyleg much affl. at B.; ♂ or ☿ affl. in ♈; ☿ ill-dig. at B.; Subs at AT. (See "Inflammation" under Brain; Coma, Convulsions, Demoniac, Dreams, Epilepsy, Fears, Fits, Frenzy, Fury, Insanity, Madness, Mania; "Brain" under Moisture; Obsessions, Pineal Gland, Spirit Controls. Also see "Delirium Tremens" in this section).

DELIVERY—Childbirth—(See Birth, Foetus, Parturition, Puerperal).

DELUGES—Floods—Great Suffering From, and Loss of Life—(See Clouds, Floods, Rain).

DELUSIONS—A ♅ disease; ♅ in ♈; ♅ in ♈ in the 6th H., and affl.; ♅ in ♈, and affl. the ☉, ☽, Asc., or hyleg; also a ♄ disease and affliction; Subs at Atlas. (See Fears, Hallucinations, Hearing, Hysteria, Ideals, Ideas, Illusions, Imagination, Insanity, Judgment, Madness, Mania, Mental Disorders, Notions, Obsessions, Paranoia, Persecution, Spirit Controls, etc.).
   Delusive—(See Deceitful, Dual, Hypocritical, Liars, Mockery).

DEMENTIA—A Profound Mental Incapacity—A Toxic Psychoses—The influences causing Dementia are much the same as those causing Fears, Idiocy, Imbecility, Insanity, Weak Mind, etc. (See these subjects).
   Dementia Praecox—A form of Dementia occurring at the time of puberty, and thru disturbances at this period. (See "Trouble" under Puberty).

DEMONIAC—Demoniacal Affections—One supposed to be possessed with a Demon, or Evil Spirit—Imagines Himself to Be Possessed With a Demon—♅ in ♈ and affl. the ☽, Asc., or hyleg; ♅ in ♈ in the 6th H.; ♅ affl. in ♏; ♅ affl. in the 12th H.; ♅ ☍ Antares; ♅ adding his evil asps. to those of ♄ and ♂, and affl. the ☽, ☿, Asc., or hyleg; ☿ and the ☽ unconnected with each other or the Asc., and with ♄ and ♂ in angles ruling the scheme, and with ♂ the strong ruler by day, or ♄ by night, and espec. if the malefics be in ♋, ♏, or ♓; ♄ ruling the ☽ at the time of a New ☽, when the ☽ is coming to the ☌ ☉, but the ☽ ruled by ♂ when the ☽ is at Full, and espec. when it may happen in ♐ or ♓, then under these conditions if the malefics be in the Eastern Parts and in angles, and the benefics in the West, the demoniacs become furious, unmanageable, wounding themselves and uttering mysterious sayings; ♄ and ♂ in angles, elevated above ♅, ♀, and the ☽, and if ♅, ♀, and the ☽ be unconnected with each other by good asps., and affl. by ♄ or ♂, and with no assistance from ♃ or ♀, tend to demoniacal affections, and also to epilepsy; ♄ and ♂ in angles ori., and with ♃ and ♀ setting and occi., the demoniac utters mysterious sayings, becomes furious, or wounds himself; the ☽ ☌ ☉, and governed by ♄, or the ☽ ☍ the ☉ governed by ♂, and espec. when in ♎, ♐, or ♓; lords of the 1st or 6th in ♈ and affl. by ♅; Subs at AT and AX usually exist in these cases. (See "Delirium Tremens", "Wild", under Delirium; Epilepsy, Fears, Fury, Hallucinations, Imaginations, Insanity, Madness, Mania; "Brain" under Moisture; Narcotics, Obsessions, Pineal Gland, Spirit Controls).

Bathing—Demoniacal complaints as a result of bathing are caused by ♅, and espec. when the ruler of the 1st, or 6th H. is in ♈ and affl. by ♅. (See Bathing).

DEMULCENT—A mucilaginous substance allaying irritation. A therapeutic property of ♀. (See Venus).

DENEB — Cauda Leonis — Lion's Tail. (See Lion's Tail).

DENGUE — Break-Bone Fever—Sometimes called Rheumatic Fever. A zymotic disease, with pain in the bones, swollen Joints, fever, and an eruption which resembles measles. A ♂ disease; ♂ affl. the Asc. at B., and by dir. Many of the influences which cause Measles will also apply to this disease. Also ♄ usually is configurated in the afflictions, affecting the bones and joints. (See "Pain" under Bones; Eruptions, Joints, Measles; "Fever" under Rheumatism; Zymosis).

DENSITY—Compactness—The work of ♄. (See Cirrhosis, Condensation, Consistency, Consolidation, Crystallization, Fiber; "Density" under Fluids; Hardening).

DENTAL—Dentist—Dentition—Pertaining to the Teeth—

    Decay of Teeth—Disorders of—(See Teeth).

    Dentition—Teething—Convulsions at Time of—Difficult Dentition, etc.—(See "Dentition" under Teeth).

    Dentist—Makes a Good Dentist—♂ in good asp. to ♅; ♂ in the 10th H., and well-asp. by the ☉, ☽, or ♅. The influences given under Chemists and Surgeons also apply here, as ♂, and the ♂ influence, is usually predominant in the maps of those who succeed in Surgery of any kind, and the use of tools and sharp instruments. (See Butchers, Chemists, Healers, Operations, Surgeons).

DENTS—A Dent in the Body, Mark, or Scar Indicated—(See Marks, Scars).

DENUDES—Denuding — Depletion—Weakening—♄ denudes, depletes, and weakens the physical constitution, while ♂ intensifies and accelerates its action. (See Depletion, Saturn Influence under Saturn).

DEPLETION—The work of ♄ and ♅; the ☉, ☽, Asc., or hyleg affl. by ♄ or ♅ at B., and by dir. Any part, organ, or function of the body tends to be weakened and depleted when ♄ is in the sign at B. ruling such part or function, and espec. when ♄ is afflicted, or afflicting the vital parts of the map. The bodily forces are also depleted when the watery signs ♋ or ♓ are on the Asc. at B., and the constitution rendered more watery and phlegmatic. (See Constitution, Eclipses; "Quarters of the Moon" under Moon; "Moonlight" under Sleep; Strength; Vitality, Weak).

    Constitution Depleted—The Tissues Depleted—The ☉ affl. in the 6th H., the constitution and vitality are depleted. (See "Lessened", "Wasted" under Vitality. Also see the first part of this section).

    Energy Depleted—(See "Depletion" under Energy. Also note the various paragraphs in this section).

    Functions Depleted—The ☽ affl. by ♄ at B., and by dir. (See "Suppression" under Functions).

    Heart Action—♄ affl. in ♌ tends to weak and depleted heart action. (See "Weak Heart" under Heart).

    Nerve Fluids—Depletion of—♅ □ or ☍ Asc. (See Fluids, Nerves).

    Vital Fluids—Depletion of—♅ □ or ☍ Asc. (See "Fluid" under Vital).

    Vitality—Depletion of—(See "Constitution" in this section). See Atrophy, Collapse, Decay, Debility, Dissipation, Emaciation, Enervation, Exhaustion, Feeble, Neurasthenia, Weak.

DEPOPULATION—(See Mortality).

DEPORTMENT—Behavior—(See Conduct, Morals, etc.).

DEPOSITS—Sediments—Collections of Morbid Particles in the Body—Mineral Deposits—Deposit of Wastes in the Tissues, Organs, and various Parts of the Body—The various mineral deposits of the body are precipitated by ♄. Some are constructive, and help to form the bones and the normal harder structures. Others are poisonous and destructive and tend to cause disease, hardening of the arteries, articulations, joints, organs, tissues and parts, membranes, and to cause gout, rheumatism, contortions, cirrhosis, deafness, deformities, gravel, stone, sand, concretions, lameness, retentions, suppressions, tuberculosis, sclerosis, arterio-sclerosis, gall stones, congestions, disturbed functions and elimination, excretion, secretion, etc. The influence of Cold, which is ruled by ♄, also tends to abnormal and morbid deposits and precipitations over the body. See these subjects. Especially note the subjects of Cold, Concretions, Crystallization, Gravel, Growths, Hardening, Lime, Leokocytes, Minerals, Osseous, Pressure, Sand, Saturn Influence, Stone, Tumors, Urea, Uric Acid, Wastes, etc.).

DEPRAVED—Depravity—Total Depravity—Dycrasia—Depraved Tastes, Desires, and Habits—Turpitude—etc.— The ☉ conciliated with the ruler of the mind, and being cadent and occidentally posited; ♀ affl. in the 5th or 7th H.; ♀ ♓ in the 5th H., and afflicted, depraved habits and dissolute vices; ♄ ♂ or ill-asp. ♀; ♄ in ♋ or ♓ and affl.; ♄ to the ill-asps. ♂ by dir.; ♂ Sig. □ or ☍ ♀; ♀ ill-dig. at B.; ♀ to the ♂ ♂ by dir.; ♀, ♂, □, or ☍ the malefics, and ♀ ruler of the horoscope; ♀ affl. at B., and to the ♂ or ill-asps. the Asc. by dir.; the 3rd Deg. of ♎ on Asc., drunkenness, licentiousness, etc. (See Appetites, Debauched, Desires, Dissolute, Drink, Drunkenness, Habits, Harlots, Indecent, Infamous, Lascivious, Leprosy, Lewd, Licentious, Low, Lust, Morals, Obscene, Passion, Perversions, Shameless, Sottishness, Tastes, Turpitude, Vices, etc.).

Depraved Blood—(See Impure).

DEPRESSANTS—An agent reducing functional activity—(See Anaphrodisiac, Narcotics, Palliatives, Sedatives, Tobacco, etc.).

DEPRESSED—Depressions—Depressed in Mind—Depressions in the Body—
Body—Depressions In—Caused by ♄. (See Contractions, Dents, Hollow).

Compressions—(See Compressions).

Diseases—Diseases Arising from a Depressed Mind—♄ affl. in the 6th H., or affl. the hyleg or Asc. (See Aches, Functions, Melancholy).

Extreme Depression—Of Mind—Morbid Anxiety Concerning the Health—(See Hypochondria).

Mental Depression—Cast Down—Atrabilarious Attacks—Melancholy—A ♄ disease and influence, and of the ♄ sign ♑, which sign produces a depressing and lowering tendency; the transit of ♄ as promittor over the place of the radical ☽ or ☿, depressed and melancholic, and espec. when ♄ is ℞ or Stationary; ♄ in the Asc., 3rd, or 6th H., and affl. ☿ or the ☽ at B., or by dir.; ♄ affl. in ♍; ♄ to the ♂ or ill-asps. his own place by tr. or dir.; ♄, ♅, or ♆ in ♏ and affl. the ☉ or ☽; ♄ in the 6th H., or affl. the ☉ or ☽; ♄ to the ♂ or ill-asp. the ☉ or ☽ hyleg and to the ♂ or ill-asp. ♄ by dir.; the ☉ in ♑ and affl. by ♄ or ♃; the ☽ to the ♂ or ill-asp. ♄ by tr. or dir.; the ☽ or ☿ affl. in ♑; the ☽ in ♍ and ♂ or ill-asp. ♄, ♅, ♆, or ♂ promittors, depressed thru biliousness or nervous debility; ♆ afflictions to the ☉, ☽, Asc. or hyleg tend to cause illnesses of a depressive nature; ♃ affl. in ♈ or ♎; the 2° ♌ on the Asc., depressed and nerveless. Lack of the Adrenal secretion tends to depression. (See Adrenals, Anxiety, Atrobile; "Biliousness" and "Black Bile" under Bile; Dejected, Despair, Despondent, Emotions; "Morbid Fears" under Fears; Gloom, Grief, Hypochondria; "Low Spirits" under Low; Melancholy, Moods, Morose, Peace, Peevish, Sadness, Sorrow, Suicide, Worry, etc.).

Nervous Depression—(See "Debility", "Depressed", "Neurasthenia", under Nerves).

Skull—Depressions In—(See Skull).

Spinal Cord—The Cord Compressed—(See Compressions, Subluxations).

DEPRESSOR—Depressor Nerves—Are influenced strongly by ♆.

Heart—Depressor Nerves of—(See "Depressor" under Heart). See Inhibition).

DERANGED—Derangements—Disordered—Discomposed—The malefics ♄ and ♂ are the principal factors in causing physiological derangements. Mental derangements are due more to the influence of ☿ and the ☽, afflictions to them, and their relations to each other and the Asc. (See "Derangement" under Mental). Any part of the body, as well as the different parts or qualities of the mind, are subject to derangement under the various planetary afflictions at B., and by dir., and for these disorders, and the influences causing them, see the subject, and the disease, disorder, or weakness, in the alphabetical arrangement. The word "Deranged" is used very little in Astrological Literature, but has been used in connection with the following subjects.

Deranged Blood—Caused by afflictions to ♃ and ♀, the rulers of the blood. (See the various paragraphs under Blood, Circulation).

Mental Derangement—(See "Derangement" under Mental).

Physiological Derangements—Bodily Disorders—(See Disease, Disorders, Distempers, Fevers, Functions, Glands, Heaviness, Humours, Ill-Health, Imperfections, Indispositions, Infirmities, Irregularities, Irritations, Lethargy, Morbid, Sickness, etc. Also see each organ and part of the body, functions, etc., for the various derangements of such parts).

Stomach Deranged—(See Digestion, Indigestion, Stomach).

System Deranged—(See "Disordered System" under System. Also see Body, Constitution, Disease, Ill-Health, Nerves, Sickness, etc.).

DERMA—The Cutis—The Corium—The True Skin—The Derma comes under the same rulership as the Skin in general. (See Skin). The Derma is contracted by ♄ and Cold, driving the blood inwards, causing internal congestions, colds, etc., and is relaxed by the heat of ♂, which influences tend to draw the blood to the surface again. (See Centrifugal, Centripetal, Cold, Colds, Congestions, Corium, Cutis, Eruptions, Purpura, Rubefacient, Skin).

DESCENDANT—The 7th H., the Cusp of the 7th, the Western Angle, etc.— This is one of the vital and sensitive places of the map of birth, and espec. the degree on the Western horizon at B. Planets when reaching this degree after birth by direction or progression tend to cause diseases, accidents, or death, according to the nature of the planets and influences. (See Physical; "Seventh House" under Seventh).

DESCENDING COLON—Ruled by ♂ and ♏. (See Colon).

DESCENT—The Chart of Descent—(See Prenatal Epoch).

DESCRIPTION—Description of the Body—Planets in the Rising Sign modify the description of the body. (See Appearance, Ascendant; "First House" under First; Form, Height, Shape, Stature).

DESERT—The Desert—Desert Places—Ruled by ♄.

Lost in the Desert—Sickness or Death In—The afflictors to the Significators of travel being in the 12th H. at B., or by dir., and usually in one of the watery signs; malefics in the 12th H. at B.; ♄ or ♂ controlling the Luminaries, in ♋, ♏, or ♓, and espec. when in the 12th H. at B., or by dir., and affl. the hyleg; ♄ and ♂ governing the Lights, being in watery signs, and espec. when in ☍ the ☉ and ☽ during the period of travel. These same influences also apply to being lost in, starvation in, death or sickness in desolate, inaccessible, or wilderness places. (See "Dangers" under Travel).

DESIRE—Desires—Desire Body—The Desires, Hopes and Ambitions are ruled by the 11th H. The principle of ♀ is desire. Venus ill-dig. at B. leads to wrong desires, illicit affections, increase of passion, excess of amorous indulgences, etc. When ♀ is well-asp. at B., and by dir., the desires are of a higher, purer, and more spiritual nature. (See Character). There are many subjects affiliated with Desire and Desires which tend to cause ill-health and disease when illicit and perverted desires are given too much liberty, and especially along the lines of food, eating, drink, pleasure, passion, sex, etc., and for subjects which may not be included in this section, look for it in the alphabetical arrangement. (See Eleventh House).

Abnormal Desires—(See Abnormal, Appetites, Cravings, Depraved, Drink, Eating, Excesses, Food, Gluttony, Lascivious, Passion, Perversions, Sex, Unnatural, etc.).

Cravings—(See Cravings).

Darkened Desires—(See "Darkened" under Mind).

Death—Desire For—(See "Desire" under Death; Suicide).

Depraved Desires—(See Depraved).

Desire Body—This is one of Man's finer Vehicles and made of Desire Stuff. Our emotions, feelings and passions originate in this body. The Desire Body being the seat of the passions and emotions is a strong factor in causing disease and sickness. The Desire Body, also known as the Animal Soul, is ruled by the ☽ and ♂, and is also influenced by ♄, ♃, and ☿. The impulses of ♂ stir the Desire Body into action. The Animal Soul has its seat in the Liver, and the Liver is the great central vortex of the Desire Body. (See Liver). The Desire Body urges us on to Action. (See Action). Desires, and the Desire Body, are affiliated with the watery signs. The As-

tral Body is the seat of the Desires. (See Astral, Childhood, Emotions, Feelings, Impulses, Iron, Sensations).

Failure of Desires—The ☉ □ or ☍ ♄ at B., and by dir. (See Ambition, Hopes).

Faulty Desires—(See "Abnormal" in this section).

Insistent Desire—♂ influence.

Low Desires—(See Depraved, Debauched, Dissipated, Drunken, Intemperate, Low, Morals, Passion, Perversions, etc.).

No Desire—Free from Passional Desire—(See Celibacy).

Perverted Desires—(See Perverse, Perversions).

Sex Desires—(See Amorous, Passion, Sex).

Spiritual Desires—(See Spiritual).

Unnatural Desires—(See Chaotic, Perversions, Unnatural).

Violent Desires—(See "Desires" under Violent).

Wrong Desires—(See the first part of this section). See Affections, Illicit, Love Affairs, Pleasures, Recreations.

DESPAIR—Hopelessness—Despondency—Discouragement—Desperation, etc.—♄ influence; ♄ in the 11th H., the house of hopes and wishes; ☿ affl. by ♄; ☿ affl. in ♑; ☿ in ♑ ♂ or ill-asp. ♄ tends to produce death thru despair, and abandonment of hope. (See Anxiety, Anguish, Dejected, Depressed, Despondent, Distress, Gloom, Hope, Melancholy, Peevish, Suicide, Worry).

DESPONDENCY—Mental Depression—Dejection—Athymia—Melancholy, etc.—The ☉ or ☽ to the ♂ or ill-asps. ♄ by dir.; the Prog. ☽ to the ♂ or ill-asps. ♄; ♄ affl. in the 3rd or 9th Houses, the houses of mind; lord of the 6th H. in the 11th H., often despondent and gloomy, and with little hope, and espec. if the lord of the 11th afflict the lord of the Asc.; lord of the 8th in the Asc.; Subs at AT. (See Anxiety, Brooding, Dejected, Depressed, Despair, Discontentment, Gloom, Grave, Hopes, Melancholy, Moods, Peace, Peevish, Worry, etc., and the references under these subjects).

DESQUAMATION—Scaling of the Cuticle—(See Scales, Skin).

DESTINY—(See Character, Events, External, Fate; "Periods" under Health; "Free Will" under Will).

DESTROYERS OF LIFE—(See Anareta).

Destroys the Children—(See "Death of Children" under Children).

Life Destroyed—(See "Certain Death" under Death; Fatal; "Life Destroyed" under Life).

DESTRUCTIVE—Destructiveness—Pernicious—Ruinous—Noxious—Cold and Dry are destructive and noxious forces in Nature, and espec. when in excess. Cold is ruled by ♄, and excess of dryness by ♂. (See Cold, Dry). Heat and Moisture, on the other hand, are prolific and nutritive, when not in excess, and are ruled by the benefic planets ♃ and ♀. (See Heat, Moisture).

Destructive Processes—In the Body—Are the work principally of ♄ and ♂, and also of the ☉ when he is in □ or ☍ asp. to the malefics, and espec. to ♄ and ♂. Saturn is destructive by retention of wastes, deposits, h a r d e n i n g, corrosion, stagnation of functions, suppressions, i m p e d e d elimination, concretions, retention of Urea, obstructions, atrophy, crystallization, etc., and by causing fears, w o r r y, pessimism, etc. Mars is destructive for the time by causing high and violent fevers to burn up the wastes of the system, and by causing a c c i d e n t s and violence. Scorpio, one of the signs of ♂, is concerned in both the destructive and reproductive processes. Thus ♄ and ♂ are both constructive and destructive a c c o r d i n g to their different aspects and influences. Destructive energy is under the rule of ♂. (See Anaemia, Atrophy, Cells, C o n s t r u c t i v e, Corrosion, Crystallization, Decay, Degeneration, Deposits, Destructiveness, Deterioration, E m a c i a t i o n, Hardening, Impediments, Mars, Metabolism, Noxious, Obstructions, Pernicious, Processes, Retention, Saturn, Stagnation, Stone, Suppressions, Tissues, Wastes).

DESTRUCTIVENESS — P e r n i c i o u s — Ruinous—Tending to Destroy—Mental Destructiveness—A ♂ disease and affliction; afflictions to ♂ at B., and by dir.; ♂ and ♅ prominent at B., and afflicted, tend to wanton and dangerous destructiveness; the ☽ □ or ☍ ♂ at B., and by dir.; the 3rd Decanate ♌ on the Asc. In a good horoscope these same forces manifest themselves in Reforms, and in the destruction of evil, sin, w i c k e d n e s s and vice wherever they may be found. (See Anarchists, Criminal, Cruel, Dangerous, Destructive, Fierce, Furious, Murderous, Pernicious, Rashness, Reformers, Religion, Revolutionary, Riotous, Savage, Temper, Violent, etc.).

DETERIORATION—To Reduce, Degenerate, Impair, Make Worse, etc.—The work of ♄.

Emotional Deterioration — (S e e "Arrested" under Emotions).

Mental—(See Idiocy, Imbecile, Insanity, Intellect, Mental, Mind, etc.').

Physical—(See A t r o p h y, Consumptions, Death, Decay, Degeneration, Destructive, Disease, Emaciation, Wasting, etc.).

DETERMINED — Mental Resolution — (See Positive, Resolute; "Strong" under Will).

DETERMINATION—Directed to a Part or Organ—

Blood—Determination of Blood to a Part — ♂ influence. (See "Determination", "Rush of Blood", under Blood).

To the Head—Determination of Blood to the Head—Rush of to the Head—Flow of Blood to the Head — (See "Blood" under Head).

DETRIMENT—Injury—Loss—Impairment—

Cattle—Detriment to Large Cattle—The 12th H. in the map of the owner rules his cattle, and ♄ or ♂ affl. in this house indicate the death of, diseases among, injury and d e t r i m e n t to his large cattle. (See "Diseases Among", "Small Cattle", under Cattle).

Children—Detriment To—(See "Detriment" under Children).

Detriment to Everything—The ☉, ♄, ♃, and ♂ conjoined in ♋; the ☽, ♀, and ☿ conjoined in ♋.

Planets in Detriment—Planets are in detriment, and weaker in influence, and afflicting, when in the signs opposite to the signs they rule. Thus the ☉ rules ♌, and is in detriment in ♒. Planets in detriment, being weaker and less fortunate, tend to invite disease and affliction to the parts of the body ruled by the sign they are in at B., and to increase the inherent debility of that part, and espec. when such planet is very e v i l l y aspected. (See Opposites). For d e t r i m e n t to Men, Women, Children, Brother, Sister, Father, Mother, Aunts, Uncles, Grandparents, Family, R e l a t i v e s, Kings, Nobles, Monarchs, Rulers, Presidents, etc., see these subjects in the alphabetical arrangement. A l s o see Accidents, Afflictions, Blows, Bruises, Disease, Disgrace, Evils, Falls, Hurts, Ill-Health, Injuries, Mental, Mind, Miseries, Misfortune, Ruin, Suffering, Trouble, Wounds, etc. For s u b j e c t s not mentioned here look for them in the alphabetical arrangement.

DEVELOPMENT—Progression Toward Maturity—

Bodily Development—(See Body, Decanates, Growth, etc.).

Early Development—(See Precocious, Premature).

Late Development—(See Backwardness).

Mental Development—(See Dull, Geniuses, Imbecile, Intellect, Mental, Mind, Perception, Prodigies, Understanding).

Organic Development — (S e e "First Quarter" under Moon; Organic).

Over-Developed O r g a n s — (S e e Organs).

Perfect Physical Development — (See Harmony).

Tissues—Development of—(S e e Tissues). See other s u b j e c t s, such as Diminished, Dwarf, Enlarged, Giants, Height, Ill-Formed, I n h u m a n, Monsters, O r g a n s, Undersized, Undeveloped, Weight, etc.).

DEVIATIONS—Abnormalities—

Faculties—Deviation of the Passive or Sensitive Faculties — Deviation i n these faculties is discernible chiefly in the excess or, deficiency of the masculine or feminine genders, and lack of the proper balance and conformation agreeable to its own nature. Thus in a male horoscope many planets in feminine signs tend to make men effeminate, and in a female nativity many planets in masculine signs tend to make women more coarse and masculine, and to deviate from the usual limits of nature. (See Abnormal, Aversions, Bachelors, Celibacy, Effeminate, Fears, Perversions, Sex, Spinsters).

Mental D e v i a t i o n s—Morbid Mental Deviations—(See "Morbid" under Mind; Unsavory).

DEVITALIZATION—A ♄ disease and affliction. (See Consumption, Emaciation, Feeble; "Lessened", "Low", under Vitality; Wastings; "Weak Body" under Weak).

DEVOID OF—Void of—(See Deficient, Diminished, Insufficient, Lack, Loss, Void, etc.).

DEVOURED—The Body Devoured After Death—(See "Body Devoured" under Burial).

DEXTERITY—Quickness of Mind and Body—Right-Handedness—Due largely to the influence of ☿ and the ♊ sign; the good asps. of ♂ to ☿. (See Action, Balance, Coordination, Graceful, Harmony, Quick; "Right Side" under Right).

DIABETES—An Auto-Toxic Psychoses—Diabetes Insipidus—An Excessive Flow of Urine—Diabetes Mellitus—A ♎ disease, and afflictions in ♎, ♈, or ♏; the ☉, ♃, ♂ or ♀ affl. in ♎; is also a ♃, ♂, or ♀ disease; ♃ affl. in ♈ or ♎; ♃ affl. in ♎ tends to the sugar variety, Mellitus, as waste of sugar is the work of ♃; ♃ and ♀ in ♎ and affl. the ☽ or Asc.; a ♂ disease; ♂ in ♎ and affl. the hyleg; ♂ in ♏; caused by afflictions to ♀; a ♀ disease; ♀ affl. in ♎; ♀ or ♃ in ♎ in the 6th H., and afflicted; ♀ to the ♂ or ill-asps. ♂; the ☽ in ♏, ♂ or ill-asp. ♄ (or ☿ if he be of the nature of ♄) at the beginning of an illness, or at decumb. (Hor'y); ♎ on the Asc. or 6th H. at B., and containing malefics; Subs at KP (11D) in the Insipidius form; Subs at KP (11D), and at Li.P. in the Mellitus, Sugar form. (See Kidneys, Sugar; "Polyuria" under Urine).

Cases of Diabetes—See Figures 7G and 7H in the book, "Astro-Diagnosis" by the Heindels.

Death from Diabetes—♀ affl. the hyleg by dir., and ♀ much affl. at B., and ♀ holding the dominion of death; common signs show, and with common signs on the angles, or many afflictions at B. in such signs. (See Mutable).

DIAGNOSIS—The Diagnosis of Disease—Judgment of the Disease—In judging and diagnosing disease by Astrology look to the 6th H., planets in the 6th, lord of the 6th, the position of lord of the 6th, and its aspects; the rising sign; lord of the Asc., and its aspects, and the aspects to the ☉ and ☽. (For further influences see Acute, Chronic, Continuity, Course, Crises, Curable, Death, Duration, Fatal, Incurable; "Judgment of the Disease" under Judgment; "Long Diseases" under Long; Prognostication, Prognosis, Prolonged; "Short Diseases" under Short; "Sixth House" under Sixth; Tedious, etc. Also note the various paragraphs and subjects under Disease, Extraordinary, Health, Ill-Health, Recovery, Recuperation, Remedy, Resistance, Sickness, Treatment, Vitality, etc.).

Locating the Disease—The planets in the different Signs at B., and also the signs on the Asc., 6th, 8th, and 12th Houses, show what parts of the body are afflicted. The Signs containing the malefics usually show what parts of the body are most afflicted from birth, and the directions, transits, and progressed influences after birth show when the afflicted organ is more apt to become diseased, and the duration of the affliction. (For further influences along this line see each of the planets, signs, and houses in the alphabetical arrangement, and note the parts of the body, or organs, they rule. Also see Left, Lower, Majority, Malformations, Middle, Organs, Parts, Prenatal, Right, Sympathy, Symptoms, Upper, etc.).

DIAPHORETICS—An Agent Producing Perspiration—(See Sudorific).

DIAPHRAGM—Midriff—Phren—Phrenic—Ruled by the ♋ and ♍ Signs.

Affected—(See "Diseased", and the various paragraphs in this section).

Breathing—Diaphragmatic Breathing—Disorders of—Afflictions in ♋; Subs at SP (8 D). (See Breathing).

Convulsive Movements—Spasmodic Disturbances of—♅ in ♍. (See Asthma, Erratic, Spasmodic).

Diaphragmatic Plexus—The ☉ and ☽ acting thru the ♋ sign, and thru this plexus, tend to affect the diaphragm, the stomach, the digestive organs, and give way to the Cranio-Abdominal Diathesis. (See "Fifth Thoracic" under Ganglion).

Diseased—♄ afflicted in ♊ or ♋; ♂ in ♐, ♊, or ♋ rules and affects the diaphragm and intercostal muscles. Also affected by Subs at LSP (8 D).

Erratic Action Of—And Tending to Cause Hiccough—♅ afflicted in ♋ or ♍. (See Asthma; "Labored" under Breathing; Hiccough; "Convulsive" in this section).

Hernia Of—♂ influence; ♂ afflicted in ♍; Subs at SP (8D).

Hiccough—(See "Erratic" in this section).

Inflammation Of—A ♋ disease; ♂ afflicted in ♋.

Paralysis Of—Paresis—Phrenasthenia—A ♄ disease; ♄ affl. in ♍; ♄ ☌ ☉ in ♍; Subs at SP (8D). (See Paralysis).

Rhythm Of—Rhythmic Action of Disturbed—♅ afflicted in ♋, and also tends to Asthma. (See Asthma, Rhythm).

Spasmodic Disturbance Of—(See "Convulsive" in this section).

DIARRHOEA—Looseness of the Bowels—Morbidly Frequent Evacuations of the Bowels—Profuse Watery Discharges—A ☽, ♂, and ♍ disease, and caused principally by afflictions in ♍; caused by the ☉, ☽, ♂, ♀, and ☿ affl. in ♍, and espec. when these planets in ♍ afflict the hyleg at the same time; the ☉ to the ♂ or ill-asp. ♂ by dir.; the ☽ in ♓ and affl. by the ☉ or ♂ when taken ill (Hor'y); ♃ affl. in ♍; ♂ affl. in ♍ or ♓; ♂ in ♍ in the 6th H.; malefics in ♍ at B., and the hyleg much afflicted. (See "Treatment" under Bowels; Cholera, Dysentery, Evacuations, Faeces, Flux, Physic). Case of Diarrhoea—Birth Data, etc.—See "Diarrhoea", Chap. 13, page 90 in Daath's Medical Astrology).

Bilious Diarrhoea—♂ affl. in ♐; ♂ to the ☽ or ill-asps. ☿. (See Bile).

Chronic Diarrhoea — The ☉, ☽, and other planets in ♍ and affl. by ♄; ♄ in ♍, and espec. when in the 6th H., and affl. the hyleg; Subs at KP (11D), and at PP (2, 3, 4L). Case—See Chap. 13, page 90, in Daath's Medical Astrology.

Diarrhoea Prevalent— ☿ in ♍ at the Vernal Equi., lord of the year, and afflicted, and espec. among People and Places ruled by ♍.

Infectious Diarrhoea — (See "Cholera Infantum" under Cholera).

DIASTASE—(See Pancreas).

DIASTOLE—The Lunar Diastole—(See "Diastole", "Full Moon", under Moon).

DIATHESIS—A Constitutional Predisposition to Disease—The Transient Disposition in Disease—Indicated by Directions. (See Directions). The Hexis, or Permanent Habit in disease, is indicated by the radix. If the Hexis and Diathesis agree, the disease is more certain and pronounced, and of the nature produced by the strong afflicting planets at B., or by dir. (See "Disease" under Severity). For the different forms of Diathesis see Asthma, Cardiac, Cells; "Cranio-Abdominal" under Cranian; Ganglion, Hemorrhage, Hepatic, Heredity, Hexis, Metabolism, Metamorphosis, Praeincipients, Processes, Renal, Splenic, Thoracic, etc. The different forms of Diathesis, and the planetary influences working with them, are given in the different paragraphs under Ganglion).

DIET—Dietetics—Eating—Food, etc. The matter of Diet is considered mostly under the subjects of Eating and Food. The ♍ Sign rules strongly over matters of Diet, Food, etc. (See Virgo). The following subjects have to do with Diet, Habits of Diet and Eating, and Ill-Health from Indiscretions, or Wrong Diet, which see in the alphabetical arrangement when not considered here—

Ailments Due to Diet—Ailments from Wrong or Bad Diet— ♃ causes complaints from High Living and injudicious dieting; the ☉ □ or ☍ ♃, ailments from indiscretions in diet; ♃ in bad asp. the ☽, impeded functions thru injudicious diet; ♃ in ♌, ailments due to diet; ♃ or ♀ affl. in ♍, disorders due to wrong and bad diet; the ☉, ☽, ♄, or ♀ affl. in ♋, or ♋ upon the Asc., diseases from wrong diet; ♀ affl. in ♋, complaints, complications, surfeits, vomiting, from wrong diet; ♀ affl. in ♍; ♋ and ♍ diseases; ♄ affl. in ♋ tends to Scurvy due to deficient, wrong and improper diet. (See "Too Much Blood" under Blood; Digestion; "Impure Blood" under Impure; Indigestion, Indiscretions, Plethora, Scurvy, Surfeits, Vomiting, etc.).

Appetite; Appetites; Assimilation;

Bad Diet—Illness From— (See "Ailments", "Evil", in this section).

Careful in Diet—♀ in the 6th H., and well-aspected; the 3rd Dec. of ♍ on the Asc., ruled by ☿. (See "Fastidious" in this section. Also see "Eccentric" under Food).

Deficient Diet — (See "Ailments" in this section. Also see Scurvy).

Dietetics—Favorable for the Study of —The ☉ or ☽ well-asp. in ♍; planets in ♍ in the Asc. or 6th H.; ♍ influence; ♍ on the Asc. (See Hygiene).

Digestion; Drink; Eating;

Epicureans; Evil Diet—Wrong Diet—Indiscretions in Diet—Improper Diet—Errors of Diet, etc.—Diseases and Surfeits Proceeding From—The ☉ affl. by ♃ or ♀; the ☽ in the 6th H., and in ill-asp. to ♀; ♃ affl. in ♏, ♋, or ♓; a ♃ disease, as most of the ♃ diseases arise from indiscretions in diet; a ♀ disease; an afflicted ♀; ♀ in ♍ and affl. the ☽ or Asc.; ♀ affl. in ♍ in the 6th H.; ♀ affl. in ♋; the Asc. to the ill-asps. the ☽ or ♀ by dir., and the ☽ or ♀ affl. at B.; ☿ affl. in ♋. (See "Ailments", "Excesses", in this section. Also see Gluttony, Indiscretions, Scurvy).

Excesses in Diet—Diseases and Surfeits Arising From—The ☉ affl. by ♃ or ♀; the ☽ in ♎ and affl. by the ☉ or ♂ when taken ill (Hor'y); the ☽ in ♎, and in ☌ or ill-asp. ♄ (or ☿ if he be of the nature of ♄) at the beginning of the illness, or at decumb., disease arising from surfeit of wine (Hor'y); ♃ affl. in the 6th H.; ♂ affl. in ♋ or ♓; ♀ in ♎ when ♀ is the afflictor; the Asc. to the ☌ or any asp. ♀ by dir., and ♀ affl. at B. (See "Ailments", "Evil", in this section. Also see Autointoxication, Drink, Eating, Excesses, Feasting, Food, Gluttony, Obesity, Plethora, Surfeits, Toxaemia, Wine, etc.).

Extravagant in Diet—♂ in the 6th H. (See Extravagance; "Rich", "Sugar", "Sweets", under Food; Luxuries).

Fastidious in Diet—Particular—Careful—Is the result of positions and influences involving the 6th H., ☿, and the ♍ sign. The ♋ people are also very particular about their food and diet. Also a ♅ trait, and espec. with ♅ in ♊ in close asp. with ☿. Aspects between ♅ and ☿, espec. if ☿ signs are involved. (See "Careful" in this section).

Fasting — People of the Sanguine Temperament benefit by fasting. (See Sanguine).

Feasting; Feeding; Food;

Functions Impeded—By Wrong Diet —(See "Ailments" in this section).

Gluttony; Gormandizing; Habits;

High Living—(See "High Living" under High).

Hygiene—Hygiene and Diet Specialist—(See Hygiene. Also see "Dietetics" in this section).

Improper Diet — (See "Ailments", "Evil", "Excesses", and the various paragraphs in this section).

Indiscretions—In Diet—(See "Ailments", "Evil", in this section).

Injudicious Dieting—(See "Ailments", "Evil", in this section).

Intemperate in Diet—(See "Excesses" in this section. Also see Intemperance; "Officer" under Military).

Luxuries; Nutrition;

Particular About Diet—(See "Fastidious" in this section).

Rich Diet—(See "Rich Foods" under Food).

Surfeits from Diet—(See "Ailments", "Evil", "Excesses", in this section. Also see Surfeits).

Vomiting—From Wrong Diet—(See "Ailments" in this section. Also see Nausea, Vomiting).

Wrong Diet—Illness from—(See "Ailments", "Evil", "Excesses", in this section).

DIFFICULT—Difficulty—

Breathing Difficult—(See "Laboured" under Breathing).

Difficult to Cure—(See Chronic, Fatal, Grievous, Incurable, Invalids, Long Diseases, Malignant, Morbid, Slow Diseases, Tedious, Wastings, etc.).

Feminine Functions — Difficult and Slow—(See "Difficult" under Menses).

Food—Difficulty in Retaining Food—(See Food).

Micturition Difficult—(See Urine).

Swallowing Difficult — (See Deglutition). See such subjects as Constipation, Deafness, Hearing, Retardation, Sight, Slow, Speech, Suppressions, Walk, etc. Look in the alphabetical arrangement for other subjects which you may have in mind along this line).

DIFFICULTIES—See such subjects as Accidents, Disaster, Disease, Disgrace, Dishonour, Hurts, Ill-Health, Injuries, Miseries, Reverses, Ruin, Sickness, Sorrow, Trouble, Worry, Wounds, etc., and other subjects you may have in mind. The influences of ♄, and also the 12th H., are to place difficulties, delays, hindrances, obstacles, etc., in our path, and to meet with self-undoing, prolonged sickness and affliction, unless we can qualify, resist, overcome, and become Masters of our Destiny.

DIFFUSIVENESS—A Scattering—

Energy—Diffusiveness of—(See Dispersions, Dissipation, Energy, Scattering, Vacillating).

DIGESTION—Coction—Digestive Organs—Digestive System—Digestive Canal—Digestive Tract—Alimentation—The Conversion of Food into Chyle and Chyme, etc.—Digestion is a function of the ♋ sign, and the Digestive Organs and System are under the internal rule of ♋. (See "Fifth Thoracic" under Ganglion). Digestion is also ruled and influenced by ♃ and the 4th H. The Coction Process in the body is ruled by ♂. The following subjects have to do with Digestion, the Digestive System, and their activities, which see in the alphabetical arrangement when not considered here—

Absorption; Acids — The Stomach Acids—(See Acids, Fluids, Gastric, Hydrochloric, Juices).

Activity—Digestive activity is ruled by ♃ and the ☽.

Alimentation—(See Alimentary).

Anxiety—Digestive Disorders from

Anxiety and Worry—♄ in ♋ or ♑, and affl. the ☉ or ☽; ☿ affl. in ♋; ♑ on the Asc. (See Anxiety, Worry).

Appetite; Assimilation; Belching;

Bowels—Intestinal Indigestion—(See "Digestion" under Bowels).

Chronic Indigestion — (See Indigestion).

Chyle; Chyme; Cold—(See "Cold" under Indigestion).

Defect—Some Defect in the Digestive Organs—Born under ♃.

Diet; Digestive Disorders—Digestive Troubles — The ☉, ☽, or ♃ in ♋, and affl. by malefics; the ☉ or ☽ affl. in ♋; the ☉ or ☽ in the 6th H., in card. signs, and affl.; the ☉ to the ♂ or P. the ☽ by dir.; the ☉ or ☽ in ♋, and to the ♂ or ill-asp. the malefics; the ☉ to the ill-asps. ♃; the ☉ in ♉, due to rich foods; the ☉ in ♋ and affl. by ♃; the ☉ or ☽ affl. in ♍; the ☽ affl. in ♍ at B., and to the evil asps. the Asc.; the ☽ □ or ☍ ♃ or ♀; the ☽ in the 6th H., and affl. by ♃; the ☽ applying to ♂, or conjoined with him in a day geniture; ♅ or ♅ affl. in ♋ or ♑; ♄ in ♋ or ♑; ♄ ♂ ☽, and espec. with females; ♃ affl. in ♋ or ♑; ♃ □ or ☍ ☽; ♂ affl. in ♋ or ♑; ♂ □ or ☍ ☽; ♂ affl. in 4th H., and espec. by the □ or ☍ asps.; ♀ affl. in ♑; caused by ♀ when the dominion of death is vested in her; ☿ affl. in ♋. Other influences affecting the digestion are given in the various paragraphs of this section, and also under Belching, Chyle, Dyspepsia, Gastric, Indigestion, Stomach, etc. Cases of Digestive Disorders, Birth Data, etc.—See Fig. 17, 18, in the book, "Message of the Stars" by the Heindels.

Dyspepsia; Eating; Emaciation;

Eructations—(See Belching).

Fermentation—In the Stomach—(See "Fermentation" under Stomach).

Flatulence; Fluids—Of the Stomach—Digestive Juices—Disturbances of—Lacking — ♄ affl. in ♋. (See Acids, Fluids, Gastric, Juices).

Food; Functions — The Digestive Functions Disturbed—Afflictions to ♃, as ♃ rules the digestive functions; ♃ affl. in ♋ or ♑; the ☉ or ☽ affl. in ♋ or ♑, the digestive functions are weakened, causing functional derangements of the Digestive System; the ☽ hyleg in ♋, and afflicted, and espec. with females; ♄, ♅, or ♇ in ♋ and affl. the ☉ or ☽. (See Functions; "Functions" under Stomach).

Gas in Stomach—(See Gas).

Gastric Juices—Gastric Troubles—(See Gastric, Stomach. Also note the various paragraphs in this section).

Gluttony; Good Digestive Powers—♂ well-asp. in the 4th H.

Hindered — Digestion Hindered—Obstructed—♄ affl. in ♋ or ♑.

Humours—Raw Humours in Stomach—See Indigestion).

Illness from Indigestion — (See Indigestion).

Impaired Digestion—Imperfect—(See Dyspepsia, Indigestion).

Impurities of the System—Digestive Disorders Arising From—The ☉ affl. in ♓. (See Impurities, Wastes).

Inability to Digest Food—♄ in ♋ and affl. by ♅ and ♄; ♄ ♋ in ♌ ♅ ♑, and both affl. by the □ of ♄, the food is often undigested and appears in the stools in pieces; ♄ in ♋, and affl. by the ☌, □, or ☍ of ♄ and ♅. (See "Chronic Indigestion" under Indigestion).

Indigestion—(See the various paragraphs under Indigestion).

Intestinal Indigestion—(See "Digestion" under Bowels).

Irregularities—Of Digestion—♍ on the Asc. (See "Digestive Disorders", and the various paragraphs in this section).

Juices—Lack of Digestive Juices— (See "Fluids" in this section).

Malnutrition—(See Assimilation, Nutrition).

Metabolism—Metabolism of the Digestive Tract Disturbed—The Prog. ☽ in ♋ or ♍, and ☌, □, or ☍ the place of malefics at B. (See Metabolism).

Nausea; Nervous Indigestion—(See Indigestion).

Nourishment—(See Nutrition).

Obstruction—Digestion Obstructed— (See "Hindered" in this section).

Organs of Digestion—Are ruled by the ☽, ♃, the ♋ and ♍ signs, including the Stomach, Duodenum, and Intestinal Digestion. These Organs are weakened by the ☉ affl. in ♋, ♍, or ♑.

Poor Digestion—(See "Digestive Disorders" in this section. Also see Dyspepsia, Indigestion).

Powers—The Digestive Powers—(See "Disorders", "Good", "Promoted", "Weak", and the various paragraphs in this section).

Promoted — The Digestive Powers Promoted and Strengthened — The ☽ well-asp. in ♋. (See "Good" in this section).

Raw Humours—In Stomach—(See Indigestion).

Stimulated—Pineapple is a good digestive stimulant. Also ♂ remedies, such as Nux Vomica in small doses before meals. (See Stimulants).

Stomach Disorders—(See Indigestion, Stomach).

Stopped—Digestion Stopped—The work of ♄ impeding the action of the Pneumogastric Nerve; signified by ♄ in ♈ when ♄ is the afflictor in the disease; ♄ in ♈, ♉, or ♋; afflictions in ♋; a ♋ and ♍ disease, and espec. with ♄ affl. in these signs; the ☽ in ♋, ♍, ♎, or ♑, and ☌ or ill-asp. ♄. (See Stoppages).

Undigested Humours — (See "Raw Humours" under Indigestion).

Vomiting; Wastings; Weak Digestion —Weak Stomach—Afflictions in ♋; a ♋ and ☽ disease; ♋ on the Asc.; the ☉, ☽, ♄, or ♂ affl. in ♋; the ☉ in the 6th H. and in a card. sign, and affl.; cardinal signs show; the ☽ in ♋, ☌ or evil asp. a malefic; ♄ affl. in the 6th H. in a card. sign; ♄, ♅, or ♆ in □ or ♋; and

affl. the ☉ or ☽; watery signs on the Asc. or 6th H., and the ☽ in a water sign at B., or at decumb. (See "Disorders", and the various paragraphs in this section. Also see Dyspepsia, Indigestion).

Weakened — (See "Functions", "Organs", and the various paragraphs in this section).

Weakest—The digestion is weakest when the ☉ is affl. in ♋ or ♑, and these signs on cusp the 6th H.

Women—Digestive Disorders In—The ☽ hyleg in ♋, and afflicted; ♄ ☌ the ☽; ♃ □ or ☍ the ☽.

Worry — Digestive Disorders Thru Worry and Anxiety—(See "Anxiety" in this section).

DILATATIONS—Dilation—Dilated— Dilatation of a Vessel or Organ—See the following subjects—

Aneurysm; Arteries—Dilatation of— (See Aneurysm; "Dilatation" under Arteries).

Blood Vessels—Dilatation of—(See Aneurysm, Capillaries; "Dilatation" under Arteries; "Vaso-Dilator" under Vaso; Vessels).

Bronchial Tubes—(See "Dilatation" under Bronchial).

Cerebral—(See Apoplexy; "Vaso-Dilator" under Vaso).

Face—Dilatation of the Capillaries of the Face—Morbid Red Face—(See "Red Face" under Face).

Heart — Cardiac Dilatation — (See Aneurysm; "Dilatation" under Heart).

Oesophagus — Dilatation of — (See Oesophagus).

Pupils of Eyes—Dilated—(See "Mydriasis" under Iris).

Scrotal Veins—Dilatation of—(See "Varicocele" under Scrotum).

Stomach—Dilatation of—(See "Dilatation" under Stomach).

Varicocele; Varicose Veins — Dilated Veins—(See Varicose).

Vaso-Dilator Action—(See Vaso).

Veins Dilated—(See Varicose). See Distentions, Flatulence, Gas, Swellings, Tympanites, Wind, etc.

DILUTED—Dilutions—

Diluted Blood—(See "Thin Blood" under Blood).

Diluted Fluids—Of the Body—The ☽ influence tends to dilution of the fluids of the body. (See Fluids, Watery).

DIM—Dimmed—Weakened—Faded, etc.

Dim Eyes—(See Eyes).

Dim Sight—(See Sight).

Energies Dimmed—(See "Depletion" under Energy). See Clouded, Depletion, Diminished, Dull, Faded, Feeble, Weakened, etc.).

DIMINISHED—Diminishments—Diminutive—Decreased—Lessened—Reduced, etc. The evil aspects between the ☉ and ☽ at B., the afflictions of ♄ to the vital centers of the map, weak signs upon the Asc., the ☉ or ☽ affl. in the 6th H., etc., tend to greatly diminish the bodily powers, the strength and vitality, the secretions, lower the functional powers, the powers of resistance to disease, etc., all which tend to disease, chronic infirmities, or an earlier death. A few subjects along this line will be listed here, but for those not listed, look for the subject in the alphabetical arrangement.

Adrenal Secretion Diminished—(See Adrenals).

Body Diminished—(See "Body" under Large; Cretinism, Dwarf, Growth, Idiocy, Organs; "Short Stature" under Short; Undersized, etc.).

Cerebral Substance—Diminished—(See "Medullary Substance" under Medulla).

Death Rate—Diminished—(See Mortality).

Pituitary Secretion—Diminished—(See Pituitary).

Secretions Diminished—(See Secretions).

Sensibility Diminished—(See Sensibility. For other subjects along this line see Abatement, Amelioration, Apathy, Atrophy, Brevity, Condensation, Constrictions, Contractions, Curtailed, Decreased, Deficient, Depleted, Dropsy, Elimination, Emaciation, Energies, Functions, Hectic, Impairments, Insufficient, Lack of, Lessened, Little, Loss of, Lowered, Moderation, Motion, Movement, Organs, Recuperative Powers, Reduced, Resistance, Retardations, Short, Shrinkage, Slow, Small, Stature, Strength, Suppressions, Undersized, Vital Powers, Vitality, Void of, Weakened, Worse, etc.).

DIMPLES—

In Cheeks—Born under ♀, dimples in cheeks or chin; ♀ in the Asc., dimples in one or both cheeks; ♀ in ♎, partile the Asc., beautiful dimples; ♀ in ♓, a round, dimpled face; ♀ rising and elevated at B., in one of her own signs, or in ☌ with the ☉; ♀ Sig. of the person in Hor'y Questions.

In Chin—♀ strong at B.; ♀ Sig. in ♓; ♀ in ♓, in partile asp. the Asc.; ♀ in the Asc. (See Cheeks, Chin, Face).

DIPHTHERIA—A ☿ disease; associated with the fixed signs, and espec. ☿ and ♏, and the 3° of these signs; the ☉ affl. by ♅, ♄, ♂, or ♀; the ☉, ☽, and afflicting bodies in the 12th H.; the ☉ afflicted in ☿; the ☽ affl. by ♄ or ♂; the ☽ in a common sign and affl. by ♆; afflictions in the 12th H.; Subs at LCP (6C), and at SP (7C). Scarlet Fever is a predisposing cause. (See Croup, Epidemics, Exudations, Fauces, Fever, Immunity, Pharynx, Scarlet Fever, Throat). Cases of Diphtheria, Death By, etc.—See "Diphtheria", No. 163, in 1001 N.N. Also see Cases in Chap. 13, in Daath's Medical Astrology.

DIPLEGIA—Double Symmetric Paralysis—(See Paralysis).

DIPLOPIA—Double Vision—(See Sight).

DIPSOMANIA—An Uncontrollable Desire for Intoxicating and Spirituous Liquors—Vehement Thirst—A disease of the watery signs; ♋, ♏, or ♓ on the Asc. at B., and afflicted; ♆ affl. in ♋; ♆ in ♋ in the 6th H., and affl. the ☉,

♽, Asc., or hyleg; ♄, ♂, or ☿ affl. in ♋; Subs at AT, SP (7D), and at KP. (See Drink, Drunkenness, Intoxication). Case—See "Dipsomaniac", No. 287, in 1001 N.N.

DIRECT MOTION—Of Planets—The disease tends to be more continuous and intense under the direct motion of the planets when such a planet is the afflictor in the disease. (See Continuity, Disturbances, Intensity, Interrupted, Retrograde, Sequence, Stationary).

DIRECTIONS—Primary and Secondary Directions—Effects of Upon the Health, Mind, and Affairs of the Native—Diseases caused by Directions tend to be functional and temporary unless neglected and allowed to progress into morbid conditions. Diathesis and the Transient Disposition in disease are indicated by Directions, while the Radix denotes the Hexis, or Permanent Habit in Disease, Structural, Organic and Constitutional Diseases. (See Diathesis). The Time and Type of the disease are shown by Directions, but only such as are foreshadowed by the radical map. (See Events, Progression, Secondary; "Spared" under Life). Mars a strong afflictor at B., and by dir., tends to Acute and Swift Diseases, Accidents, Injuries, Death by Wounds and Violence, while ♄ the afflictor tends to Chronic Ailments, and so on with the nature of each planet. The directional strength of planets depends upon their aspect, mundane position, and their position in the Zodiac. Directions of the planets are more evil in disease when they occur during the different periods of life ruled by the planets. Thus a ♄ direction is more evil during the ♄ period of life, etc. (See Periods. Also see "Directions" under Saturn, and each of the planets). Also evil Directions to the Hyleg in the Climacterical Years of life are more dangerous in health matters. (See Climacteric).

Childhood—Directions In—During Childhood and Youth the effects of Directions are said to be transferred to the Parents or Guardian. (See "Directions" in Sec. 1 under Children).

Death—Directions and Death—It takes a train of evil Directions to the Hyleg to cause death. (See Anareta, Benefics; "Directions" in Sec. 3 under Children; "Arguments for Death", "Quality", under Death; Epidemics, Hyleg; "Death" under Immediate; Maleficics).

Evil Directions—(1) First Train of Evil Directions Destroys—(See Crises; "Directions Kill" under Infancy; "Directions" in Sec. 3 under Children; "Resistance Weak" under Resistance; "Vitality Low" under Vitality; "Weak Body" under Weak). (2) Good Powers to Overcome Evil Directions—(See "Abundance of Health" under Health; Immunity, Recuperation, Resistance, Vitality Good, etc.).

Females and Directions—When the ☽ is weak, ill-dig., and badly aspected at B., the constitutional powers are often so reduced as to be unable to withstand the shock of subsequent evil directions, and with females in infancy, under such conditions, the first train of evil directions tends to kill.

Mind Afflicted by Directions—The ☉ to the bad asps. ☿; the ☽ to the bad asps. the ☉ or ♄; the M.C. to the ♂ or P. asp. the ☽. (See Drink; "Diseases", "Irritations", under Mental).

Overcoming Directions—(See "Evil Directions" in this section).

Primary Directions—If the nativity is weak, and the constitution broken by disease or age, a primary direction will kill if the planets at B. are unfortunate, and without the assistance of benefics, or an attending good Secondary Direction. In a stronger constitution a train of evil primary directions is necessary to kill, and espec. in childhood, youth, or middle life. (See Primary, Transits).

Secondary Directions—(See Secondary).

Succumbs Easily—To Directions— (See "Evil Directions" in this section. Also see Feeble; "Ill-Health All Thru Life" under Ill-Health; Incurable; "Life Destroyed" under Life; Sickly; "Much Sickness" under Sickness; "Weakened" under Strength; "Low" under Vitality; "Weak Body" under Weak).

Train of Directions—(See "Death", "Evil Directions", "Females", "Primary", in this section. Also see "Life Destroyed" under Life; "New Moon" under Moon).

Youth and Directions—(See "Childhood", "Primary", in this section).

DIRTY—(See Careless, Filthy, Habits, Unclean, Untidy, etc.).

DISABILITIES—Disablements—

Bodily Disabilities—Caused mostly by ♄. Caused by retention of wastes, mineral deposits, concretions, crystallization, hardening, deposits of Urea and Uric Acid, resulting in rigidity, stiffness, lowered functions, deformities, infirmities, total disability, etc., all which are the work of ♄, and assisted by the afflictions of the ☽. (See Accidents, Body, Congenital, Crippled, Defects, Deformities, Form, Imperfections, Infirmities, Injuries, Lameness, Limitations, Maimed, Malformations, Monsters, Paralysis, Stature, etc.).

Mental Disabilities—Are ☿ diseases, and afflictions to ☿; ☿ afflicted, and in no good relation to the ☽ or Asc. (See Coma, Delirium, Epilepsy, Faintings, Fury, Insanity, Intellect, Judgment, Madness, Mania, Mental; "Weak Mind" under Mind; Perception, Understanding, etc.).

DISAGREEABLE—Unpleasant—Offensive—

Disagreeable Breath—(See "Foul" under Breath).

Disagreeable Temper—(See Anger, Cruel, Conduct, Manners, Savage; "High Temper" under Temper; Vicious, etc.).

DISASTER—Calamity—Catastrophies—

Disaster Threatened—A total Eclipse of the ☉ falling on the place of the ☉ at B.; ♇ passing over the place of the radical ♄ by tr.; the ill-asps. of several malefic Promittors to the ☉. (See Calamity, Disgrace, Dishonour, Misfortune, Reversals, Ruin, Treachery).

Fear Of—Fear of Impending Disaster —(See "Impending Calamity" under Calamity; Fears).

Meets with Disaster—Lord of the 6th H. in the 10th H., and afflicted, danger of meeting with serious disaster, downfall, dishonour, etc. (See Abroad, Accidents, Death, Dangers, Downfall; "His Own Worst Enemy" under Enemies; Imprisonment (see Prison); Self-Undoing, etc.).

DISCERNMENT—(See Comprehension, Intellect, Judgment; "Quickened" under Mental; Mind, Perception, Reason, Understanding, Shrewdness, etc.).

DISCHARGES—A Morbid Secretion— An Evacuation—Astringents, which are remedies of ♄, tend to stop discharges by their powers of constriction. (See Astringents). The natural discharges from the body are such as Breath, Tears, Milk, Sweat, Faeces, Urine, Mucus, Saliva, Menses, Oils of the Skin. (See these subjects). Discharges occur from the orifices of the body, organs, and membranes, as from the Eyes, Ears, Nose, Mouth, Throat, Lungs, Breasts, Navel, Rectum, Skin, Urethra, Vagina, etc., and may be natural, or morbid in disease conditions.

Bloody Discharges—(See "Discharges" under Blood; Dysentery; "Bloody Flux" under Flux; Hemorrhage, Menses; "Nose Bleed" under Nose).

Catarrhal Discharges—(See Catarrh, Colds, Defluxions, Fluxes, Humours, Mucus, Nose, Phlegm, Rheum; "Watery Humours" under Watery, etc.).

Involuntary Discharges—(See Emissions, Faeces, Incoordination, Involuntary, Menses, Nose Bleed, Semen; "Incontinence" under Urine; Vital Fluids, Urine, etc.).

Offensive Discharges—Purulent—Putrid—Morbid—Pus—Foul, etc. Caused by ♄, ♂, and the ☽. (See Abscesses, Carcinoma, Catarrh, Decay, Eruptions, Evacuations, Excretions, Exudations, Fistula, Foul, Gangrene, Hemorrhoids, Menses, Morbid, Offensive, Pus, Putrid, Rotten, Sores, Sweat, Syphilis, Ulcers, Venereal, etc.).

Profuse Discharges—(See Catarrh, Diarrhoea, Dysentery, Effusions, Flow, Fluxes, Hemorrhage, Menses, Nose Bleed, Profuse, etc.).

Unnatural Discharges—A ♍ disease, and afflictions in ♍; a ♀ disease. (See Gonorrhoea, Leocorrhoea, Salivation, and Diseases of the Bowels, Skin, and Fluids of the Body).

Watery Discharges—(See Catarrhs, Diarrhoea, Fluxes, Humours, Rheum, Serous, Watery). For other subjects not mentioned here look for the subject in the alphabetical arrangement.

DISCOLORATIONS—(See Abscesses, Blemishes, Blotches, Blows, Bruises, Burns, Carcinoma, Cataract, Complexion, Cuts, Cyanosis, Defects, Epithelioma, Eruptions, Erythromelalgia, Excrescences, Eyes, Face, Freckles, Growths, Hemorrhages, Hyperaemia,

Imperfections, Marks, Moles, Naevus, Nails, Nose, Pimples, Purpura, Scars, Skin, Smallpox, Sores, Swellings, Syphilis, Teeth, Ulcers, Varicose, etc.).

DISCOMFORT—Lack of Ease—A Feeling of Discomfort or Uneasiness, as in Disease or Plethora—♂ affl. the ☽, the functions are painful and excessive, causing discomfort; ♀ □ or ☍ ☽, the functions are painful and irregular, causing discomfort, and usually due to loose living. The various diseases and afflictions of the mind and body tend to a feeling of discomfort, and for the influences causing such, see in the alphabetical arrangement the subject you have in mind. Also see such subjects as Affliction, Anxiety, Despondency, Disease, Flatulence, Gas, Ill-Health, Malaise, Melancholy, Miseries, Nervousness, Pain, Plethora, Restlessness, Sickness, Suffering, Trouble, Worry, Worse, etc.

DISCOMPOSED— Disturbed—Derangements—Irritations, etc.—

Discomposed Body— (See Deformed, Deranged, Disease, Disturbances, Illformed, Irritations, etc.).

Discomposed Mind—(See the various paragraphs under Mental, Mind. Also see Anxiety, Dejected, Depressed, Despondent, Discontentment, Fears, Hypochondria, Insanity; "Low Spirits" under Low; Melancholy, Morbid, Worry).

DISCONTENTMENT—D i s s a t i s f i e d— Restlessness—U n e a s i n e s s—Lack of Happiness or Peace of Mind—The ☉ or ☽ to the ☌ or ill-asps. ♄ by dir.; ♅ □ or ☍ ♅; ♄ in ♑ at B., and affl. the ☉, ☽, or ☿; ♄ Sig. in ♑; ♀ affl. at B., or by dir.; ☿ Sig. in ♑; ♑ on the Asc. at B., and with ♄ as ruler; the Asc. meeting the evil directions of planets; ♊ on the Asc.; the Asc. to the place of Deneb; the 3rd Dec. of ♒ denotes. (For further influences along this line see Anxiety, Changes, Complaining, Contentment, Despondency, Erratic, Fears, Fretful, Happiness; "Low Spirits" under Low; Melancholy, Murmuring; "No Peace of Mind" under Mind; Patience, Peevish, Repining, Residence, Restlessness, Unhappy, Worry, etc.).

DISCORD—(See Contests, Duels, Emotions, Enemies; "Discord" under Mind; Quarrels).

DISCRIMINATION—Lack of—(See "Bad Judgment" under Judgment; Erratic).

DISCUTIENT—An Agent Removing a Swelling or Effusion—A therapeutic property of ♂ remedies. (See Resolvent).

DISEASE—Diseases—Ailments—Complaints—Distempers—Disordered System—Maladies—Ill-Health—Pathological Disorders—Sickness, etc.

The following influences tend to cause disease,—The ☉, ☽, and planets in the Occidental Quarters at birth show disease, and in the Oriental Quarters indicate Acute Pains and Accidents. (See "Causes" under Accidents). Malefics occidental, and affl. the ☉ and ☽, cause diseases, and when oriental cause Blemishes (see Blemishes). Disease is indicated by the planetary positions and aspects to the ☉, ☽, Asc. and Hyleg, and their positions in the 6th, 8th, or 12th Houses. Ptolemy says disease and blemishes belong to the 6th and 7th Houses, and to the Asc. Malefics when ori. to the ☉, and occi. to the ☽, cause diseases. The diseases caused by each planet are said to arise from the planet whose aspect or body first arrives at the Anaretic Place. If there be no such aspect, that planet causes the disease which last separated by body or aspect from the Anaretic Place. (See Anareta). Planets ℞, or in Perigee, tend to cause disease and distempers. Disease is caused by planets afflicting the ☉, ☽, or Asc., if they be malefics, or if the malefics and the ☉ and ☽ have the same Declination. No aspect of ♃ or ♀ alone causes disease, but only as configurated with malefics. Some say most diseases owe their origin to the ☽, and they are at least governed by the aspects and periods of the ☽ for some time if they are acute diseases, and even chronic diseases are much affected by the ☽ at her Quadratures a n d Semi-Quadratures. At the New and Full ☽ the ☽ influence is not so manifest, except with Lunatics, whose fluids are more violently disturbed at the New and Full ☽. Common Signs and cadent houses are closely identified with disease, and are weaker constitutionally. The 3rd and 9th houses, both cadent, are especially c o n n e c t e d with the Mind and Mental Disorders, and ♃ and ♀ in these houses at B. will help to overcome disease thru a good state of the mind. The 6th House and the ♍ Sign are important in the consideration of disease. In these Spirit, Mind and Matter meet, as ☿, the ruler of the mind, is also the ruler of the 6th H. It is thru the Vital Principle that disease acts upon the mind, and diseases of the mind upon the body. The power and degree of morbid action show a falling off as the planets pass from cardinal to common signs. The intensity of disease is associated with the cardinal signs, and its remission with the mutable signs. (For further influences along this line, see Health, Ill-Health; "Organic" under Functions; Sickness. Also note the various paragraphs in this section. For the various diseases to which mind and body are liable, look for the subject in the alphabetical arrangement, as only the more abstract subjects concerning disease, the causes of disease, the classification of diseases, the nature and quality of the disease; the time, duration, and possible outcome of the disease, and subjects closely affiliated with disease, will be listed in this section. See the following subjects in the alphabetical arrangement when not considered here—

Abatement; Accidents; Acquired; Acts —Disease from Rash Acts—(See Rashness).

Acute; Ailing—Is A l w a y s Ailing— (See Ailing).

Ailments; Air—Diseases from Corrupt Air, Compressed Air—(See Air).

Alteration—In the Disease—(See Alteration).

Amelioration; Amendment; Anareta; Anger—Diseases Arising From—(See Anger).

Animals—Diseased—Death of—(See Animals).

Antidotes; Antipathy; Aquarius Sign—Diseases Ruled By—(See Aquarius).

Aries Sign—Diseases Ruled By—(See Aries).

Attracts Disease—(See Attracts).

Autumnal Diseases—(See Autumnal).

Bad Blood—Diseases From—(See Blood, Impure).

Bad End—To the Disease—(See End, Termination).

Bathing—Disease or Death From—(See Bathing).

Beginning—Of the Disease—(See Directions. Also see "Event", "Time", in this section).

Benefics—The Benefics and Disease—(See Anareta, Benefics, Jupiter, Venus).

Better—Disease Turns for Better—(See Amelioration, Continuity, Course, Crises, Moderation, Modification; "Action" under Morbid; Polarity, Recovery).

Bites; Blemishes; Blood—Diseases from Blood Disorders—(See Blood, Impure).

Body—(1) Diseased Body—The ☉ Sig. ☐ or ⚹ ♄, and ♄ be in the Asc., diseased body, and short-lived unless a good asp. of ♃ intervene, which may save after a severe illness if ♃ be angular. (2) Body Alone is Affected—(See 'Afflicted" under Body). (3) The Disease is More in the Body than in the Mind—(See "Afflicted" under Body). (4) The Disease is in Both Body and Mind—(See "Afflicted in Body and Mind" under Mind). (5) The Disease is Thru the Whole Body—(See "Disease" under Whole).

Brief—The Disease is Brief—(See Quick).

Brings Disease Upon Himself—Causes His Own Illnesses—Mars people; ♂ ruler, and strong at B.; the ill-asps. of ♀ by dir. to the ☽, ♂, Asc., or M.C., and brought on by free living; ☽ in 6th H., affl. by ♀, thru disorderly conduct; ♏ on the Asc. at B., and thru anger, folly, peevishness, rash acts, etc. (See Debauchery, Dissipation, Drink, Excesses, Extravagance, Folly; "Free Living" under Free; Gluttony; "High Living" under High; "His Own Worst Enemy" under Enemies; "Loose Living" under Loose; Plethora, Rashness, Surfeits).

Brooding Over Disease—(See Brooding, Hypochondria, Imaginary).

Business Cares—Diseases Caused By—(See Business, Cares).

Cadent Houses—And Disease—(See Cadent).

Cancer Sign—Diseases of—(See Cancer).

Capricorn Sign—Diseases of—(See Capricorn).

Cardinal Signs—And Disease—(See Cardinal).

Cares—Diseases From—(See Cares).

Causes—(1) Causes of Disease—(See the Introduction to this Article). (2) Causes His Own Illnesses—(See "Brings Disease" in this section).

Certain—The Disease is More Certain and Pronounced—When evil Directions agree with the radical afflictions; when the Diathesis agrees with the Hexis, or permanent habit in disease, the disease is more certain and pronounced. Thus if the Directions agree with strong ♂ affliction at B., the disease will tend to be acute, a fever, an inflammation, or perhaps bring a surgical operation, and so on with the nature of each planet. (See Diathesis, Severity).

Changes—(1) The Disease Changed—(See "Complications" in this section). (2) The Disease Changes for the Better or Worse—(See "Better", "Worse", in this section). (3) Changes to Some Other Disease—Or a Relapse—(See Chronic, Complications, Crises, Relapse, Return, Worse).

Childhood—Children—Diseases of—(See Childhood, Children, Infancy).

Choler—Diseases Arising from Too Much Choler—(See Choler).

Chronic; Clothing; Cold; Colds; Common Signs—And Disease—(See Mutable).

Complaining; Complaints—(See the various paragraphs in this section).

Complications—In Disease—Planets in the Signs show the Zones of the body afflicted, but complications, as when inflammation and congestion attack an organ at the same time, or where Plethora accompanies a nervous condition, the aspects and influences of the planets themselves must be considered, and the nature of each planet involved in the disease condition. Each planet imparts a special type of disease to an organ, but the disease may become disguised, modified, or changed by cross aspects from other planets. (See Complications, Zones).

Concealment—Of Disease—♃ in the Asc. or M.C., in a strong sign, well-aspected and elevated above the malefics; the influence of wealth, rank, or command given by ♃ well placed at B.; ☿ well configurated with ♃ gives the addition of skillful Healers, the proper treatment and remedies. (See Exhibition).

Congestions; Considerable Diseases Ensue—(See "Many Diseases" under Childhood; Complications; "Ill-Health All Thru Life", "Signs of Ill-Health", under Ill-Health; Increase; "Much Sickness" under Sickness. Also see "Many" in this section).

Conspicuous; Constancy; Constitutional; Contagious; Continuity; Contracts Disease Easily—(See Contracts).

Convalescence; Convertible—(See Curable).

Corrupt Diseases—(See Corrupt, Foul, Impure, Pus, Putrid, Rotten, etc.).

Course of Disease—(See Course).

Courts Disease—(See Virgo).

Crises; Curable—Cure of—(See Curable).

Curious Diseases—(See Mysterious, Strange).

Curtailed; Dampness—Diseases From —(See Moisture, Vapors, Water, Wet).

Danger—Danger in Course of—Danger of Disease—(See Course. See "Threatened", and the various paragraphs in this section).

Dangerous—The Disease is Dangerous—The Disease is Not Dangerous— (See Dangerous).

Day—The Disease is Better or Worse by Day—(See Day, Night).

Death—The Disease Ends in Death— The Disease Which is the Immediate Cause of Death—(See "Certain", "Immediate", under Death).

Debauchery—Disease From—(See Debauchery).

Debility; Decay; Decrease—The Disease Will Decrease—(See "Decrease" under Recovery).

Decrepitude; Deep-Seated — (See Deep).

Degeneration; Degree—The Degree of Disturbance in Disease—(See Disturbed).

Delayed—(See Chronic; "Long Siege" under Ill-Health; Lingering, Prolonged, Tedious).

Delirium; Derangements;

Destructive Diseases—(See Destructive).

Deteriorations; Detriment;

Deviations; Diagnosis; Diathesis; Diet —Diseases from Wrong Diet—(See Diet).

Difficult to Cure—(See Cure, Difficult).

Direct Motion—Of the Planets in Disease—(See Direct).

Directions and Disease—(See Directions).

Disabilities; Discomfort—In Disease —(See Anguish, Malaise, Pain, Plethora, Suffering).

Diseased Body—(See "Body" in this section).

Disguised—(See "Complications" in this section).

Disorderly Conduct—Disease Brought On By—(See "Brings Disease" in this section).

Disorders—(See Disorders. Also note the various paragraphs in this section).

Dispersions; Disposition—The Transient Disposition in Disease—(See Diathesis, Directions).

Dissipation—Disease By—(See Debauchery, Dissipation, Drink, Excesses, Habits, etc.).

Dissipation of Forces—(See Dispersions).

Distempers; Distressful Diseases— (See Anguish; "High Fevers" under Fevers; "Diseases" under Pain; Suffering, etc. Also look in the alphabetical arrangement for the subject you have in mind).

Disturbance—The Degree of Disturbance in Disease—(See Disturbed).

Dorsal Diseases—(See Dorsal).

Dreadful Diseases — (See Dreadful, Terrible).

Dress—As a Cause of Disease—(See Clothing, Colds, Dress, Exposure; "Wet Feet" under Feet; Linen, Moisture).

Drink—Diseases from Excesses In— (See Drink, Drunkenness, Intoxication).

Drought—Diseases From—(See Drought, Dryness, Famine, Pestilence).

Dryness—Dry and Hot Diseases—Diseases Concomitant with Dryness—Dry and Cold Diseases—(See Dryness).

Duration — Of Disease — (See Constancy, Continuity, Course, Duration).

Ease—Intervals of Ease—(See Ease).

Eating—Disease from Improper Eating—(See Diet, Eating, Food).

Effects Of—Duration of the Effects of Disease—(See Constancy, Duration).

End of the Disease—(See Curable; "Certain Death" under Death; End, Fatal, Incurable, Recovery, Resolution, Termination, etc.).

Endemic; Endurance — Endurance Against Disease—(See Endurance, Immunity, Recuperation, Resistance, Vitality, etc.).

Endures Disease Cheerfully—(See Complaining, Endures).

Enemas and Disease—(See Enema).

Enlarged Scope—Of the Disease—(See Enlarged).

Entire Body Disordered—(See Whole).

Environment—And Disease—(See Environment, External).

Epidemics; Erratic Course — (See Course, Erratic, Irregular, Various).

Escape—The Sick Will Hardly Escape —(See Escape).

Event—The Event, or Time of Disease—When Due, etc.—(See Events. Also see "Time" in this section).

Every Species of Disease—Causes of —(See South Scale, Species).

Evil End To—(See "End" in this section).

Excesses—Diseases From—(See Excesses).

Excrescences; Exercise—Disease from Over-Exercise and Fatigue—(See Exercise, Fatigue).

Exhibition of Maladies—(See Exhibition).

Exopathic—(See External).

Exposure—Diseases Arising From— (See Exposure).

External Causes—Of Disease—(See External).

Extraordinary Diseases — (See Extraordinary).

Extravagance—Health Undermined By—(See Extravagance; "Undermined" under Health).

Falling Off — Of the Disease — (See Amelioration; "Action" under Morbid; Moderation, Recovery).

Famine—Disease, Suffering or Death From—(See Famine).

Fatal; Fatigue; Fear of Disease—(See Fear, Taurus).

Female Diseases—(See Female).

Fierce Maladies—(See Fierce).

Fixed Signs — And Disease — (See Fixed).

Fluidic System—Diseases of—(See Fluids).

Folly—Diseases From—(See Folly).

Food and Disease—(See Diet, Digestion, Eating, Food, Stomach).

Force of the Disease—(See Force).

Foul Vapors—Disease From—(See Vapors).

Frame—The Whole Frame Is Disordered—(See Whole).

Free Living — Disease From — (See Free).

Frequent Attacks—Of Disease—(See "Ill-Health All Thru Life" under Life; "Much Sickness" under Sickness).

Full Moon and Disease—(See "Causes" in this section; "Full Moon" under Moon).

Fulminating—Sudden Severity of Disease—(See Fulminating).

Functional Diseases—(See Directions, Functions).

Gemini Diseases—(See Gemini).

General Ailments—(See General).

Gives Up Easily—To Disease—Does Little for Himself—Drifts with the Tide of the Disease—The ☉ affl. in ♋ or ♍; ♄ in ♍ in the 6th, 8th, or 12th H.; ♄ ruler of the Asc., in ♍, and in the 6th, 8th, or 12th H.; ♄ affl. in ♋ in the 6th H.; ♋ and ♍ influence; common signs on the angles; many planets in feminine signs. (See Brooding, Hypochondria, Majority, Negative, Taurus, Virgo).

Gluttony—Diseases From—(See Gluttony).

Good End to Disease—(See Curable, End, Recovery, Resolution).

Grievous Diseases — (See Grievous, Severe, Vehement).

Habit—The Permanent Habit in Disease—(See Diathesis, Directions, Hexis).

Hard to Cure—(See Chronic, Cure, Difficult, Grievous, Incurable).

Healers; Health Bad—(See Health, Ill-Health, Invalids, Sickness, etc.).

Heat—Diseases from Excessive Heat—(See "Excessive" under Heat).

Heaviness — All Over the Body — Heavy and Sad Sickness—(See Heaviness, Whole).

Hemorrhages; Heredity; Hexis—The Permanent Habit in Disease—(See Diathesis, Directions, Hexis).

High—The Disease Runs High—(See "Worse" under Crises; High; "Diseases" under Pain).

High Living—Diseases From—(See High).

Hot Diseases—Hot and Dry Diseases—(See Fevers; "Dry and Hot", "Hot Diseases", under Heat).

Houses—Diseases Ruled by the Houses—(See Angles, Ascendant, Descendant, Houses, Midheaven, Nadir, Terminal, etc.).

Humours; Hygiene;

Hyleg and Disease—(See Hyleg).

Identified with Disease—The Common Signs and Cadent Houses are identified with disease. (See Cadent, Mutable).

Ill-Health—(See the various paragraphs under Ill-Health).

Illusory Diseases—(See Delusions, Hallucinations, Illusions, Imaginary, Insanity).

Imaginary Diseases—(See Brooding, Hypochondria, Imaginary, Psychic).

Immunity; Impairments;

Impediments; Imperfections;

Important—The Disease is Not Important—(See Mild, Slight).

Improvement; Imprudence—Diseases From—(See Folly, Imprudence, Indiscretions, Rashness, etc.).

Incipient—(See Praeincipient).

Increase—In the Disease—The Disease Will Increase—(See Crises, Increase, Worse).

Increased Resistance—To Disease—(See Resistance).

Incurable; Indicated—Disease Indicated—(See "Causes", "Threatened", in this section).

Indicators—Of Disease—(See "Significators" in this section).

Indiscretions—Diseases From—(See Indiscretions).

Indispositions; Indulgences; Infancy—Diseases of—(See Infancy).

Infectious; Infirmities; Inflammations;

Inherent Tendencies—In Disease—(See Constitutional, Diathesis, Heredity, Inherent, Organic, Structural).

Innate—Inborn—Inherited Diseases—(See Heredity, Innate).

Intemperance — Diseases Arising From—(See Debauchery, Dissipation, Drink, Drunkenness, Excesses, Intemperance, Intoxication, etc.).

Intensity—Of the Disease—Severity of—(See Cardinal; "Direct Motion of Planets" under Direct; Fulminating, Increase, Intensity, Severity).

Internal Diseases—Internal Ease in Disease—(See Ease, Internal).

Interrupted Sequence—In Disease—(See Interrupted, Sequence).

Intervals of Ease—(See Ease).

Irregular Maladies—Irregularities—(See Irregular).

Irritations; Journeys—Diseases On—(See Journeys, Travel).

Judgment — Of the Disease — (See Diagnosis, Judgment, Majority, Modification, Prognosis).

Jupiter Diseases—(See Jupiter).

Kings—Diseases To—(See Kings).

Latent Diseases—(See Constitutional, Diathesis, Hereditary, Hexis, Latent, Organic, Structural, etc.).

Left Side of Body—Diseases In—(See Left).

Length of the Disease—(See Course, Crises, Duration, Long, Prolonged, Short, etc.).

Leo Diseases—(See Leo).

Less Liable—To Disease—(See "Good Health" under Health; Immunity, Recuperation, Resistance, Strong, Vitality Good, etc.).

Less Power—To Throw Off Disease—(See Inability; "Resistance Low" under Resistance; "Slow Recuperation" under Recuperation; "Vitality Low" under Vitality; "Weak Body" under Weak, etc.).

Lethargy; Liable to Disease—(See "Causes", "Less Power", "Threatened", in this section. Also see "Bad Health", "Periods of Bad Health", under Health).

Libra Diseases—(See Libra).

Linen—Diseases from Wet Linen—(See Linen. See "Dress" in this section).

Lingering Diseases—(See Chronic, Lingering, Long, Prolonged, Slow, Tedious, Wasting, etc.).

Lives Thru Disease—Lives Thru Serious Diseases—(See Serious).

Locating the Disease—(See Diagnosis).

Long Diseases—Signs of a Long Disease—Will the Illness be Long?—(See Chronic, Consumptions, Lingering, Long, Prolonged, Slow, Tedious, Wastings).

Lower Parts—Of the Body—Diseases In—(See Abdomen, Extremities, Feet, Knees, Legs, Limbs, Lower, etc.).

Lunar Diseases—(See Moon).

Lust—Diseases from Inordinate Lust —(See Lust).

Luxuries—Health Undermined By—(See Extravagance; Food; "High Living" under High; Luxuries).

Magnetism—And Disease—(See Magnetic).

Makes Effort—To Throw Off Disease —(See "Throwing Off Disease" in this section).

Malaise—Discomfort in Disease—(See Malaise).

Malefics—And Disease—(See Anareta, Malefics, Mars, Neptune, Saturn, Uranus).

Malignant; Many Diseases — Many Complications—(See Complications; "Many Diseases" under Childhood, Impure; "Ill-Health All Thru Life" under Ill-Health; "Much Sickness" under Sickness; Various).

Mars Diseases—(See Mars).

Meat—Diseases from Ill-Digested Meat—(See Indigestion, Meat).

Medicines—Medicines Do Little Good —(See Grievous, Incurable, Medicines, Remedy, Treatment).

Melancholy—Disease Arising From—(See Melancholy).

Members—Members Affected by Disease—(See Members, Organic, Organs, Parts, Structural).

Men—Diseases of—(See Men).

Mental Diseases — (See Mental, Mind, Psychic).

Mercury Diseases—(See Mercury).

Middle Life—Diseases of—(See Middle Life).

Mild—(See Mild, Minor, Slight).

Mind—Diseases of—The Disease is Chiefly in the Mind—The Disease is in the Mind Only—The Disease is in Both Mind and Body—The Mind is Centered Upon Disease—(See "Afflicted in Body and Mind", "Disease", under Mind. Note the various paragraphs under Mental, Mind).

Minimizing — Of the Disease — (See Amelioration, Mild, Minimizing, Moderation, Recovery, Slight).

Minor Diseases—(See Colds, Mild, Minimizing, Minor, Slight).

Moderation—Of Disease—(See Moderation).

Modification—Of Disease—(See Modification; "Complications" in this section).

Moist Diseases—Moist Humours—Diseases Arising from Moisture—(See Moisture, Vapors, Water, Wet).

Moon Diseases—(See Moon).

Morals—Diseases Arising from Loose Morals—(See Excesses, Morals, Passion, Sex, Venereal).

Morbid Diseases—Morbid Action in Disease—(See Morbid).

Mortal Illness — (See "Arguments", "Certain", under Death).

Motional Strength—Of Planets in Disease— The Motion of the Planets, and Disease—(See Motion).

Much Sickness—(See "Much Sickness" under Sickness).

Murmuring—And Complaining About Their Disease—(See Complaining, Exhibition, Grief, Murmuring).

Mutable Signs—Common Signs and Disease—(See Mutable).

Mysterious Diseases—(See Mysterious).

Nature of the Disease—(See "Disease" under Nature).

Neglect—As a Cause of Disease—(See Neglect, Privation).

Neptune Diseases—(See Neptune).

Nervous Diseases—(See Nerves).

Neutralizing—Of the Disease—(See Minimizing).

New Moon—The New Moon and Disease—(See "New Moon" under Moon. Also see "Causes" in this section).

Night Diseases—Night Diseases More Prevalent — The Disease Worse at Night—(See Day, Night).

Noisome Diseases—(See Frenzy, Fury, Insanity, Madness, Mania, Noisy).

Noxious Complaints—(See Noxious).

Nutrition—Nourishment—Diseases from Disturbances of—(See Assimilation, Digestion, Food, Indigestion, Nutrition).

Obscure Diseases— (See Mysterious, Obscure, Peculiar, Psychic, Strange, Uncommon).

Obstructions; Offensive; Old Age — Diseases of—(See Old Age).

Old Maladies Return—(See Return).

Organic Diseases—(See Organic).

Origin—Of the Disease—(See "Beginning", "Causes", in this section).

Outcome—Of the Disease—(See Better, Death, End, Force, Minimizing, Termination, Worse, in this section). Also see such subjects as Amelioration, Crises, Moderation, Modification, Prognosis, Recovery, Recuperation, etc.).

Outrageous — Outrageous Diseases — Outraging Nature's Laws, and Diseases Caused By—(See "Nature's Laws" under Laws; Perversions, Scandalous, Sex, Venery).

Overcoming Disease—(1) Has Good Power to Overcome Disease—(See Immunity; "Good" under Resistance). (2) Has Little Power to Overcome Disease—(See "Ill-Health All Thru Life" under Ill-Health; "Low" under Recuperation, Resistance, Vitality; Sickly; "Much Sickness" under Sickness; "Weak Body" under Weak). (3) Makes an Effort to Overcome Disease—Fixed Signs on the Angles, and ♂ well-aspected at B. (See "Fixed Signs" under Fixed; Majority, Positive, Recuperation, Resistance, Stamina, Tone, Vitality, Will, etc. See "Throwing Off Disease" in this section).

Over-Exercise—Diseases from Over-Exercise and Over-Exertion of Mind and Body — (See "Brain Fag" under Brain; Exercise, Exertion, Fatigue, Reading, Sports, Study).

Own Illnesses—(See "Brings Disease Upon Himself" in this section).

Painful Diseases—Distressful—Poignant—Sharp—(See "Diseases" under Pain).

Pandemic; Particular Disease—The Course Any Particular Disease May Follow—(See Course, Prognosis, Various).

Parts of the Body—Parts Liable to Disease—(See Blemishes, Diagnosis, Members, Parts).

Passion—Diseases from Passional Excesses — (See Excesses, Passion, Sex, Vehement, Venery).

Pathological Action—Of Planets in Disease—(See Pathological, Planets. Also see "Pathological Action" under each of the Planets).

Patient—(1) Patient Causes the Disease — (See "Brings Disease" in this section). (2) Patient Will Die—(See "Certain Death" under Death). (3) Patient Will Recover—(See Recovery). (4) Patient In Disease—(See Patience).

Peculiar Diseases—(See Peculiar).

Peevishness—Diseases From—(See Peevish; "Brings Disease" in this section).

Periodical Diseases—(See Periodical).

Periods—Of Disease and Ill-Health—(See "Periods of Bad Health" under Health; "Long Siege" under Ill-Health; Periodical, Return).

Permanent Habit—In Disease—The Hexis — (See Diathesis, Directions. Also see "Certain" in this section).

Pernicious Diseases—(See Pernicious).

Pestilence; Phlegmatic Diseases — (See Phlegm).

Pisces Diseases—(See Pisces).

Plague; Planets and Disease—(See Anareta, Benefics, Directions, Malefics, Pathological, Planets. Also see each of the planets in the alphabetical arrangement).

Plethora; Poignant Maladies—(See Fierce, Painful, Poignant, Quick, Sharp, Swift, Vehement, Violent).

Poison—Disease and Ill-Health from —(See Deposits, Drugs, Intoxicants, Medicines, Narcotics, Poison, Septic, Stimulants, Toxic, Uric Acid, Wastes).

Poverty—Disease from Poverty, Privation and Neglect—(See Neglect, Poverty, Privation).

Power—The Power of the Disease—Has Power to Throw Off Disease—Has Little Power to Overcome Disease —(See "Intensity", "Overcoming", "Severity", in this section).

Praeincipients; Predisposition;

Prenatal; Pretended; Prevention—Of Disease—(See Hygiene, Prevention, Sanitation).

Private Diseases—(See Private).

Privation—Diseases From—(See Neglect, Privation).

Profit and Support—By Exhibition of Diseases—(See Exhibition).

Prognosis; Progress; Progression;

Progressive; Prolonged; Promissor;

Promittor; Pronounced—(See "Certain" in this section).

Proof Against Disease—(See Immunity, Resistance, Vitality).

Protracted; Psychic; Pus-Forming—(See Pus).

Putrid; Quality—Of the Disease—Nature of—(See "Disease" under Nature; Quality, Species, Type).

Quarters of the Moon—And Disease —(See Moon).

Quick Diseases—Quick Termination to Disease—(See Acute, Brief, End, Ephemeral; "High" under Fever; Fierce, Pernicious, Quick, Recovery, Sharp, Short, Swift, Termination, Vehement, Violent, etc.).

Rapid; Rashness—Diseases From— (See Anger, Folly, Imprudence, Rashness, etc. Also see "Brings Disease Upon Himself" in this section).

Ravings in Disease—(See Raving).

Reading and Study—Diseases from Overstudy, etc. — (See "Reading and Study" under Blindness; "Brain Fag" under Brain; Fatigue, Reading, Study).

Recovery; Recuperation;

Recurrent Diseases—(See Periodical, Recurrent, Remittent, Returning).

Refreshment—Disease from Lack of— (See Famine, Neglect, Poverty, Privation, Rest, Sleep, Starvation, Thirst).

Relapses; Relatives—Illnesses of— (See Family, Relatives).

Religion—Diseases Caused By—(See Religion).

Remission—Of Disease—(See Remission).

Remittent; Remove—The Disease Will Remove Shortly—(See "Decrease" under Recovery).

Resistance—To Disease—(See Resistance).

Resolution—Of Disease—(See Resolution).

Response—The Degree of Response Against Disease—(See "Response" under Degree).

Rest—Has No Rest in Disease—(See Rest).

Retrograde Planets—And Disease—(See Retrograde).

Return of Disease—Old Maladies Return—(See Periodical, Returning).

Rich Food—Diseases From—(See Diet, Extravagance, Food; "Impure Blood" under Impure; Luxuries, Plethora, Surfeits, etc.).

Right Side of Body—Diseases In—(See Right).

Sagittarius Diseases—(See Sagittarius).

Sanitation; Saturn Diseases—(See Saturn).

Scandalous Diseases—(See Scandalous).

Scope of the Disease—The Scope Enlarged—(See Enlarged).

Scorpio Diseases—(See Scorpio).

Seat of the Disease—In Hor'y Questions the seat of the disease can be judged and taken from the sign in which the ☽ is posited, or from the sign on the cusp of 6th H. (See Diagnosis, Judgment, Members, Organs, Parts, etc.).

Self-Motivated Acts—Diseases From—(See Rashness).

Sensuality—Diseases From—(See Amorous, Excesses, Passion, Sensuality, Sex, etc.).

Sequence—In Disease—Interrupted Sequence—(See Sequence).

Serious Diseases—(See Serious).

Severe Diseases—The Severity of the Disease—(See "Intensity" in this section; Fulminating, Severe).

Sex Excesses—Diseases From—(See Amorous, Excesses, Passion, Sex, Venery, etc.).

Sharp Diseases—(See Sharp).

Shifting—Of the Disease—(See Chronic, Complications, Course, Crises, Relapse, Remote, Return, Sympathy).

Short Diseases—(See Acute, Curtailed, Quick, Sharp, Short, Swift, Violent).

Sick—The Sick—(See Sick).

Sickly; Sickness; Significators—Of Disease—Indicators of Disease—Diseases come from, and are indicated by the 6th H., and planets therein, signs on cusp of 6th, lord of the 6th. In chronic and lingering diseases ♄ is the Significator. In acute diseases, accidents, violence, etc., ♂ is the Sig., and so on with each of the planets, according to their influence and nature. (See "Indicators of Health" under Health).

Signs of Zodiac—Diseases Ruled By—(See Aries, Taurus, Signs, etc.).

Sixth House—And Disease—(See Sixth).

Sleep—Diseases from Lack of—(See Debauchery, Dissipation, Neglect, Privation, Refreshment, Rest; "Insomnia" under Sleep).

Slight Disorders—(See Colds, Mild, Minor, Slight).

Slow Diseases—(See Chronic, Consumptions, Lingering, Prolonged, Slow, Tedious, Wastings, etc.).

Solution—Of Continuity In Disease—(See Continuity, Solution).

Spasmodic; Species—Causes Every Species of Disease—(See South Scale, Species).

Sports—Diseases Caused By—(See Exercise, Sports).

State of Mind—Diseases Caused By—(See Anguish, Anxiety, Dejected, Depression, Despondency, Grief, Imagination, Insanity, Melancholy, Mental, Mind, Negative, Psychic, Sadness, Sorrow, Trouble, Worry, etc.).

Stationary Planets—And Disease—(See Stationary).

Strange Diseases—(See Strange).

Strong—(1) Strong Disposition to Disease—The ☽ P ♄ at B., and by dir., and espec. if the ☽ be hyleg, shows a strong tendency to disease and premature dissolution except some benefic intervene. (See "Ill-Health All Thru Life" under Ill-Health; Invalids, Sickly; "Much Sickness" under Sickness; "Low" under Vitality; "Weak Body" under Weak, etc.). (2) Strong Drink—Diseases from Excess of—(See "Delirium Tremens" under Delirium; Drink, Drunkenness, Intoxication, etc.).

Structural; Stubborn Diseases—(See Chronic, Constitutional, Consumptions, Cure, Difficult, Hereditary, Incurable, Invalids, Long, Malignant, Medicines, Obstinate, Organic, Prolonged, Remedy, Slow, Structural, Tedious, Treatment, Wastings, etc.).

Study and Reading—Diseases from Over-Study, etc.—(See "Reading" in this section).

Succumbs Easily—To Disease—(See "Low" under Recuperation, Resistance, Vitality; Succumbs; "Weak Body" under Weak). For influences which show strong resistance to disease, and where the patient does not succumb easily, see Immunity; "Good" under Resistance, Vitality; Robust; "Body" under Strong).

Sudden Diseases—Sudden Attacks of—Sudden Distempers—Sudden Severity of Disease—(See Fulminating, Sudden, Unexpected).

Suffers Much—In Disease—(See Anguish, Pain, Suffering).

Summer Diseases—(See Summer).

Sun Diseases—(See Solar, Sun).

Support—Seeks Profit and Support by Exhibition of Disease—(See Exhibition).

Suppurative Diseases—(See Abscesses, Pus).

Surfeits; Susceptibility—To Disease—(See Constitutional, Diathesis, Heredity, Organic, Praeincipients, Predisposed, Susceptibility, Vitality Low; "Weak Body" under Weak).

Swellings; Swift Diseases—(See Swift).

Sympathy—Sympathy and Antipathy—Sympathetic Diseases—(See Antidotes, Antipathy, Attracts, Complications, Opposites, Remote, Removal, Sympathy, etc.).

Symptoms—In Disease—(See Diagnosis, Prognosis, Symptoms).

System Disordered—See Constitution, Disorders, Ill-Health, Infirmities, Sickness, System. Also note the various paragraphs in this section.

Taurus Diseases—(See Taurus).

Tedious Diseases—(See Chronic, Lingering, Long, Prolonged, Slow, Tedious).

Temporary Diseases—(See Acute, Colds, Indisposition, Mild, Slight, Temporary, etc.).

Tendency to Disease—(See Attracts, Diathesis, Feeble, Infirm, Predisposition; "Low" under Resistance, Vitality; "Weak Body" under Weak. Also see "Causes", "Susceptibility", "Threatened", in this section).

Termination—Of the Disease—(See End, Prognosis, Termination).

Terrible Diseases—Dreadful Diseases—(See Terrible).

Threatened with Disease—Liable To—Strong Disposition to Disease—The ☉ or ☽ to the ☌, P, □ or ☍ ♄ or ♂, or other malefics, by dir. in the Zodiac, or Mundane; the ☉ directed to Aldebaran, Regulus, Antares, Deneb, Betelguese, Bellatrix, or Frons Scorpio; the ☽ ☌, P, or ill-asp. ♄ at B., and by dir., and espec. if the ☽ be hyleg; the ☽ directed to the Back, Neck, or Wing of the Lion; to South Scale, Right Leg of Ophiucus; Deneb, Goat's Back, or Left Shoulder or Right Arm of Aquaries, and in those parts of the body signified by the sign in which those stars are posited; the ☽ at a Lunation on the place of the malefics at B., and espec. of ♄ and ♂; the Pr. ☽ to the evil asps. of her own place at B. if affl. by malefics at B.; the Asc. to the □ or ☍ the ☉ or ♄ by dir. (See "Causes", "Liable To", "Tendency To", in this section. Also see "Danger of Sickness" under Sickness).

Thrives and Lives—Thru Serious Diseases—(See Serious).

Throwing Off Disease—(1) Has Power to Throw Off Disease Easily and Quickly—(See Immunity; "Rapid" under Recuperation; "Good" under Resistance; "Body" under Strong; "Good" under Vitality). (2) Has Little Power to Throw Off Disease—(See "Overcoming" in this section). (3) Makes Effort to Throw Off Disease—(See "Overcoming" in this section).

Time of the Disease—Time When Disease is Apt to Come—The Event of the Disease—The ☽ sepr. from the ☍ of the ☉, the next planet she applies to decides the event of the disease. (See Directions, Eclipses, Equinoxes, Events,

Ingresses, Lunations; "New Moon" under Moon; Progression; "Solar Revolution" under Solar; Solstices, Time, Transits, Vernal, etc.).

Transient—(1) Transient Disposition in Disease—(See Diathesis, Directions). (2) Transient Diseases—(See Acute, Colds, Mild, Minor, Slight).

Transits—And Disease—(See Transits; "Time Of" in this section).

Treatment—Of Disease—(See Antidotes, Antipathy, Colors, Cure, Diet, Drugs, Healers, Herbs, Hygiene, Medicines, Opposites, Prevention, Remedies, Sanitation, Sympathy, Treatment, etc.).

Twelfth House—And Disease—(See Twelfth).

Two Diseases—At the Same Time—The ☉ affl. in ♊, and arising from congestion or inflamed blood. (See Complications, Gemini, Remote, Removal, Sympathy, etc. Also see "Many Diseases" in this section).

Type—Of the Disease—(See "Disease" under Nature; Quality, Type).

Uncleanliness—Diseases From—(See Carelessness, Cleanliness, Filth, Habits, Uncleanly).

Uncommon; Understand—The Disease is Difficult to Understand—♆ and ♅ diseases. (See Difficult, Extraordinary, Mysterious, Neptune, Obscure, Peculiar, Psychic, Strange, Uranus).

Unexpected Diseases—(See Sudden).

Unusual—(See Extraordinary, Uncommon).

Upper Parts—Of the Body—Diseases In—(See Upper).

Uranus Diseases—(See Uranus).

Vague Diseases—(See Mysterious, Obscure, Psychic, Strange, Vague).

Vapors—Diseases from Foul Vapors—(See Vapors).

Variable; Various; Vascular;

Vehement; Venereal; Venomous;

Venus Diseases—(See Venus).

Vessels; Vexation—Diseases Caused By—(See Vexation).

Vibration and Disease—(See Vibration).

Vicarious; Violent; Virgo Diseases—(See Virgo).

Virulent; Viscera; Vision—Disorders of—(See Sight).

Vital—Vital Force—Vital Principle—As Related to Disease—(See Vital).

Vitality—Disorders of—(See Vitality).

Voyages—Diseases On—(See Voyages).

Vulnerable Parts—Disorders of—(See Vulnerable).

Wandering Diseases—(See Flying, Wandering).

Wards Off Disease—(See "Overcoming", "Throwing Off", in this section).

Wasting Diseases—(See Wasting).

Water—Diseases Arising From—(See Moisture, Water, Wet).

Watery Diseases—(See Watery).

Weakness—Diseases Arising From—(See Weak).

Weather—Diseases Caused by the Weather—(See Weather).

Weird Diseases—(See Weird).

What Is The Disease?—(See Diagnosis, Judgment, Nature, Parts, Vulnerable).

Whole Body—The Disease Is Thru the Whole Body—(See Whole).

Wind—Windy Disorders—(See Wind).

Winter Diseases—(See Winter).

Withering Diseases — (See Withering).

Women—Diseases of—(See Female, Women).

Worse—The Disease Becomes Worse —(See Complications, Crises, Day, High, Increase, Night, Relapses, Worse, etc.).

Youth — Diseases of — (See Young, Youth).

Zones — Diseases of the Different Zones of the Body—(See Aries, Taurus, Gemini, etc.; "First House" under First; "Second House" under Second, etc.; Members, Organs, Parts, Signs, Zodiac, Zones).

Zymotic Diseases — (See Zymotic). For Diseases, Afflictions, and Conditions not listed here. look for the subject in the alphabetical arrangement.

DISFIGUREMENTS—Blemishes—Defects—Caused by the pathological deposits of ♄, as in the joints, causing swollen, enlarged, and stiff joints. Mars causes disfigurements by cuts, blows, scars, violence, wounds, amputations, etc. All the Constellations not of human form tend to disfigure the body and model it after their own forms, whether they be fowls or animals. (See "Beastly Form" under Beasts; Birthmarks (Naevus), Blemishes, Blotches, Contortions, Crooked, Cyclops, Defects, Deformities, Discolorations, Distortions, Dogs, Eyes, Face, Fowls, Freckles, Frog, Head, Illformed, Imperfections, Inhuman, Joints, Lameness, Marks, Members, Moles, Monsters, Naevus, Nose, Paralysis, Pimples, Scars, Smallpox, Sores, Teeth, Ulcers, etc.).

DISGRACE—Dishonour—Disrepute— Loss of Honour and Reputation—Scandal—Disease and Sickness resulting therefrom due to worry, grief, sorrow, disfranchisement, isolation, reversals, ruin, etc.

Causes of Disgrace—Planetary Causes —These influences tend especially to affect those who are drifting along in life, unawakened, unspiritualized, living in sin or wickedness, etc., and such influences need not affect the more advanced Souls, and who are living lives of wisdom, honor, discrimination, self-control, etc. Much has been said in the Astrological Textbooks along this line, and these influences usually contribute to, and go hand in hand with disease and its planetary causes. Note the following influences,—The ⊙ Sig. □ or 8 ♄; the ⊙ by Periodic Rev. to the ill-asps. ♅; the ⊙ to the □ ♀ by dir.; the ⊙ conjoined with Hercules, Antares, Hyades, Regulus, Aldebaran, or any eminent star of the nature of ♂; the ⊙ to the ♂ or P. the Ascelli by dir.; the ⊙ with South Scale and Knee of Ophiucus; the ⊙ directed to Deneb, and all others of the nature of ♅; the ⊙ or ☽ joined with the Whale's Jaw; the ⊙ directed to stars in the Lion, the South Scale, the Knee and Right Leg of Ophiucus, the Goat's Back, Left Shoulder and Right Arm of Aquaries, causes disgrace, sickness, ruin, and every evil; the ⊙ ♂ a malefic in the M.C.; the ☽ to Ceti; the ☽ decr., sepr. from ♂ and apply. to ♀, disgrace thru wantonness; the ☽ decr. in a day geniture, sepr. from ♀ and apply. to ♄, brings disgrace and ruin upon himself; the ☽ directed to Deneb, public disgrace, ultimate disgrace and ruin; the ☽ directed to the Pleiades, Hyades, Praesepe, or the Twins; the ☽ directed to the Back, Neck, or Wing of the Lion; South Scale, Right Leg of Ophiucus; Deneb, Goat's Back, or to the Left Shoulder and Right Arm of Aquaries, ruin and disgrace; the ☽ to Cor. Hydra; the ☽ weak and ill-dig. at B., and to the ♂ the M.C.; the ☽ to the Left Shoulder of Bootes; the ☽ to the □ or 8 ♂, disgrace thru women; the ☽ combust by application is fatal to position in life (Hor'y); ♄ in an angle with the ⊙ or ☽, and with no good asps. from benefics; ♄ to the ♂ or ill-asp. the ⊙ or ☽ by dir.; ♄ Sig. □ or 8 the ⊙ or ☽; ♄ to the place of ☋ by dir.; ♄ is the Sig. of disgrace and ruin in Hor'y Questions; ♄ affl. in the 10th H., danger of disgrace and downfall; ♅ affl. in the 10th H.; ♃ Sig. □ or 8 ♄; ♂ in det., and 8 the Asc.; ♀ weak at B., and affl. by ♂, much scandal and disgrace; ♀ to the ♂ ♂ or ☋ by dir., disgrace by lewd courses; ☿ affl. by malefics at B., and to the ♂ the M.C. by dir., scandal and disgrace; the Asc. to the □ or 8 ♄ or the ☽ by dir.; the M.C. to the ♂ or ill-asps. ♄ or ♂ by dir.; the M.C. to the ill-asps. the ⊙, sudden disgrace; the M.C. to the ill-asps. ♀, disgrace thru women; M.C. to the place of Cauda at B.; M.C. directed to Algol, Hydra's Heart, Ascelli, Castor. Pollux, Hyades, Praesepe, Shoulders of Orion, Markab, Auriga's Right Shoulder; M.C. to the □ or 8 ☿ by dir., disgrace thru false reports; Part of Fortune (⊕) to the ill-asps. ♀ by dir., disgrace thru females; the 12th H. is the house of disgrace and misfortune, and with malefics and afflictions in this house at B., and in or to this house by dir.; lord of the 12th in the 1st H.; lord of the 12th in the 10th, sad disgrace; lord of the 10th a malefic, and in the 10th; lord of the 11th, a malefic, and in the 11th and affl.; lord of the 6th in the 10th, sickness from disgrace or shame; lord of the 10th in the 12th; lord of the 10th a malefic, and espec. if posited in the 1st or 10th; lords of the 1st and 10th sepr. from each other by asp., or the ☽ sepr. from lord of the 10th, and apply to no benefic, but apply to malefics, tends to bring disgrace, downfall, and loss of position, and the same if lord of the 1st be ℞ or combust (Hor'y); lord of the 1st or the ☽, □ or 8 lord of the 10th, or the ⊙, and if at the same time they separate from benefics and apply to malefics without reception or translation (Hor'y); malefics in the 1st or 10th H., and affl.; malefics in the 10th H. at a Solar Rev.; a malefic ☌ the ☉ in the M.C.; the 3° ♋ on the Asc. at B.; fixed stars of the nature of ♄ ascending at B.; fixed stars of the nature of ♄ and ♂ culminating at B.; fixed stars of the nature of ♂ and the ☽ culminating at B., such as the Pleiades, and other nebulous stars of this nature; all eminent fixed stars of the nature of ♄ in an angle with the ☉ at B.; Cauda (☋) in the 8th H. in a Hor'y Map; the Pleiades, Castor, Pollux, Hyades, Ascelli, or Praesepe directed to the Asc. or Lights; the Pleiades rising, or with the ☉ or ☽, or directed to the Asc.; the Pleiades rising, and ☌ the ☉ or ☽ in an angle. (See in the alphabetical arrangement each of the Fixed Stars and Constellations mentioned in this Article. Also see such subjects as Banishment, Conduct, Dishonest, Downfall, Evil, Execrated, Executed, Exile, Fortune, Grief, Habits, Harlots, Honour, Infamous, Judge, Law, Lewd, Love Affairs, Misfortune, Morals, Prison, Reputation, Reversals, Ruin, Scandal, Self-Undoing, Sentence of Law (see Judge); Shame, Sorrow, Trouble, etc.).

Harlots—Suffers Disgrace Thru Harlots—(See Harlots).

High Position—Rises to a High Position in Life, but Soon Falls Into Disgrace—♄ Sig. □ or ☍ ☉ or ☽; ♄ in the Midheaven at B., in a weak sign, afflicted, or affl. the ☉ or ☽.

Lewd Courses—Disgrace By—(See Lewd).

Perpetual Disgrace—Perpetual Trouble and Disgrace—♄ on the Meridian, or coming to the Meridian at B.

Wantonness—Disgrace By—(See Lewd, Wanton).

Women—(1) Women Fall into Disgrace—The ☽ to the ill-asps. ♅, ♄, or ♂ by dir., and espec. if the ☽ be affl. by these planets at B.; ♂ ☌ or ill-asp. the ☽ or ♀; ♀ to the ☌ or ill-asp. ♅ by dir. if ♅ afflict ♀ at B.; malefics in the 7th H. at a Solar Rev. (2) Disgrace Thru Women—The ☽ to the □ or ☍ ♂ by dir.; the M.C. or ⊕ to the ill-asps. ♀ by dir. (See Men, Women).

DISHONESTY—Dishonorable—Cheating—Crafty—Cunning—Artful—Sly—Fraudulent—Liars—Subtle—False Pretenses—Dual—Duplicity—Wily—Shrewd—Insincere—Unfair—Unprincipled—Unscrupulous—Hypocritical—Thieving — Swindling — Underhanded, etc. Dishonesty is a disease of the Mind, and for this reason these influences are inserted here. Such influences, however, can be overcome. There are usually some good influences in every map of birth, or in the character, which tend to make a person honest, kind, balanced, good, and upright, and also some evil influences which tend to the opposite unless they are controlled and transcended. Wilson has observed that those who have a copious flow of Humours from the head are remarkable for Shallowness of Intellect, and for Dishonesty. The following influences tend to Dishon-

esty, and to the traits of mind listed in the first part of this Article.

Causes of Dishonesty—The Planetary Causes at Birth and by Direction—The Prenatal Causes, the Epochal Map, the map for the time of Conception, also show the character, and contributary fundamental causes. The ☉ Sig. ☌ ♄; the ☉ Sig. □ or ☍ ♂; the ☉ Sig. ☌ ♃, and ♃ ill-dig. and ill-aspected, espec. false and hypocritical in religion; the ☽ Sig. □ or ☍ ☿, a low cunning used for dishonest purposes, but if ☿ be in △ asp. to ☿ the evil will be lessened; the ☽ to the ☌ or ill-asp. ♂, and ♂ affl. by ☿, or in a sign or house of ☿; the ☽ Sig. in ♊, crafty and subtle to excess; ♆ and ♓ are prominent and afflicted in most cases of deception; ♆ affl. the ☉, ☽, and ☿; ♅ influences and afflictions tend to make one dishonest and deceitful in love affairs, and espec. ♅ ☌ or ill-asp. ♀; ♄ Sig. □ or ☍ ☿, schemes to deceive his most intimate friends; ♄ and ♂ afflicting ☿; ♄ Sig. □ or ☍ ♀; ♄ ☌ or ill-asp. ♀ or ☿; ♄ in the 9th H., apt to be deceitful and hypocritical in religious matters; ♄ Sig. in ♊, ♋, ♍, ♏, or ♓; ♄ affl. in ♏; ♄ Sig. ☌ ☿, subtle and crafty; ♃ Sig. ☌ ♄, mean and deceitful; ♃ Sig. in ♏, subtle and crafty, and to be very warily dealt with; ♃, ♀, ☿, and the ☽ strongly afflicted, and espec. in mutable signs, should guard against being deceitful and dishonest in money matters; ♂ ☌ ☿ and affl. by ♄, and also ♄ affl. the ☉ and ☽ at the same time; the evil asps. between the ☽, ♂, and ☿ incline the native to dishonesty; ♂ Sig. in ♑; ♂ Sig. in ♓, sly and artful if in the terms of ☿; ♂ Sig. ☌ ♄, sly and cowardly; ♂ ill-dig. at B., and affl. ☿; ♂ Sig. □ or ☍ ♄, ☿, or the ☽; ♂ ruler at B., and affl. by ♄, ☿, or the ☽; ♂ represents subtle men, and ♄ tends to dishonesty from malicious motives; ♂ in bad asp. to ♄; ♂ affl. in ♊, ♍, ♑ or ♓; ♀ Sig. ☌, □, or ☍ ♄; ♀ Sig. in ♋; ♀ Sig. □ or ☍ ♄ or ♂, full of mischief; ☿ Sig. in ♋; ☿ Sig. in ♊, cunning; ☿ ill-dig. at B.; ☿ Sig. □ or ☍ the ☽, not very sincere in their professions of friendship, and also unscrupulous in their methods by which they attain their ends; ☿ Sig. □ or ☍ ♄ or ♂; ☿ Sig. ☌ ♄, calculating and covetous; ☿ affl. in the 12th H., active in schemes, plots and intrigues; ☿ Sig. ☌ ♂; ☿ when ill-dig., and afflicted by malefics, is the author of tricks and deception; ☿ Sig. in ♈, and affl. by ♄ and ♂, often a mere knave; ☿ Sig. in ♊, and affl. by malefics and the ☽; ☿ in the Asc. in □ or ☍ ♄ or ♂, and with no good asps. to the benefics; ☿ elevated above and evilly configurated with ♄ or ♂; the Asc. to the place of Hircus, apt to defraud others; the ♏ influence in its lower vibrations, uncontrolled, not spiritualized, and as deceitful as the Scorpion; ♑ influence tends to make one subtle and witty, but capricious like the Goat; the negative, or feminine signs, prominent at birth, evilly aspected and occupied by malefics, tend to give a more deceitful and dishonest nature fundamentally; violent afflictions in common signs unless ♃ is strong and well-aspected; the bicorporeal signs strong at B., and many planets in them, tend to duplicity, hypocrisy, etc., and espec. the double-bodied signs of ♃. (For collateral study and further influences along these lines see Artifice, Character, Cheating, Criminal, Deceitful, Dual-Minded, Enemies, Evil, Gambling, Hypocritical, Kleptomaniac, Knavish, Liars, Libellers, Malevolent, Mischief, Perjury, Pettifogging, Plots, Prisoners, Principles, Religion, Responsibility, Robbers, Shrewdness, Thieves, Treachery, Wicked, etc.).

DISHONOUR—Dishonourable—(See Disgrace, Dishonest, Honour, Reverses, Ruin, Reputation, etc.).

DISINTEGRATION—The New ☽ implies disintegration. (See Death, Decay; "New Moon" under Moon).

DISLIKES—(See Antipathy, Aversions, Food, Likes).

DISLOCATIONS—Luxations—Displacements—A Displacement of Organs or Articular Surfaces—Caused by ♄ afflictions; ♄ coming to the cusp of the Asc. by a direction in the Zodiac causes; afflictions in ♐ or ♑; a ♑ disorder; ♑ on the Asc. Bones and Organs in the parts of the body ruled by the sign containing ♄ at B. are espec. subject to displacement and dislocation, or the trouble brought on by the afflictions of ♄ by dir. to the part so afflicted at B. The afflictions of ♅ also cause violent dislocations, and espec. when configurated with ♄ or ♂ at the time. Mars also tends to cause dislocations by his violent nature, as by injury in accidents, etc. Mechanical Displacements, espec. of organs, are both ♄ and ♀ disorders. Organs are often displaced due to the weakening effect of ♄ afflictions to ligaments and supports.

Displacements—(See Displacements).

Femur—Dislocation of—(See Femur).

Heart—The Heart on the Right Side—Case—(See "Right Side" under Heart).

Hip Joint—Dislocation of—(See "Joint" under Hip).

Kidneys—(See "Floating" under Kidneys).

Joints—(See Joints).

Neck—(See "Dislocations" under Neck).

Organs Displaced—(See Displacements, Organs. Also see the Introduction, "Heart", "Kidneys", in this Article).

Partial Dislocation—(See Subluxations).

Shoulder—Dislocation of—♄ affl. in ♉. (See Shoulders).

Subluxations—A Partial Dislocation—(See Subluxations, Vertebrae).

Tibia—(See Tibia).

Vertebrae—Subluxations of—(See Subluxations, Vetebrae).

Wrist—Dislocated Wrist—(See Wrist).

DISORDERLY—
Disorderly Conduct—The ☉ to the bad asps. ♀ by dir., and ♀ ill-dig. at

B. (See Conduct, Debauchery, Drink, Drunkenness, Intoxication, Quarrels).

Illness—Brought On by Disorderly Conduct—(See "Brings Disease Upon Himself" under Disease).

DISORDERS—Disordered—Ailments—Diseases—Derangements—Faulty—Ill-Health—Complaints—Sickness, etc.—This subject has been largely considered in the sections on Disease, Health, Ill-Health, Sickness, etc. The following subjects have been especially mentioned in the textbooks of Astrology as "Disordered", which subjects for convenience of reference are listed here.

Disordered Blood—(See "Disordered", "Impure", "Poor", "Thin", under Blood).

Disordered Mind—(See the various paragraphs under Imagination, Intellect, Mental, Mind, Perception, Understanding, etc.).

Disordered Stomach—(See "Disordered" under Stomach).

Disordered System—(See "Disordered" under System). For the various disorders of the Organs, Functions, and Parts of the Body, see in the alphabetical arrangement the subject you have in mind.

General Disorders—(See General).

DISORGANIZED—Disorganization—Disorganizing—The ♅ influence is disorganizing, and espec. the lower vibrations of this planet. The influence of ♄ is disorganizing and depleting. Also the influence of ♆ tends to be disorganizing and chaotic in influence over the mind until the native becomes awakened and spiritualized, and learns how to rule his stars. (See Chaotic, Interrupted).

DISORIENTATION—(See Identity).

DISPERSIONS—Dispersals—Dissipation of Forces and Energies—

Forces—Dispersion and Dissipation of Forces—♂ and the ☽ combinations (fire and water) tend to, and to angry feelings, effervescent mental activity, and dissipation of brain force. (See "Over-Active Mind" under Active; Anger, Diffusiveness, Dissipation, Effervescent, Scattering).

Functional Energy—Dissipation of—♆ diseases and afflictions. (See Energy, Functions).

Violent Dispersals—♂ with ♄, and both the afflictors in the disease at the same time. (See "Compound" under Fractures; Violent).

DISPLACEMENTS—
Mechanical Displacements—♀ diseases; ♀ afflicted, or afflictions to ♀ by the malefics. (See Dislocations).

Organs Displaced—♄ influence, due to weakening of ligaments and supports. (See Dislocations, Organs; "Falling" under Womb).

DISPOSITION—The Temper—Temperament, etc.—This work is not primarily a treatise on the Disposition, but the Disposition and Disease are so intimately bound up and interdependent that many traits of Temperament have been listed and considered. The subjects are too numerous to list here.

Look in the alphabetical arrangement for the subject you have in mind. Especially see the subjects of Conduct, Decanates, Habits, Manners, Mental, Mind, Temper, Temperament, etc. Also see each of the Signs, as Aries, Taurus, etc. See each of the Planets, as Sun, Moon, Mars, etc. There are a number of classified lists of the traits of Temperament given in the various Textbooks of Astrology, such as given by each of the Signs, Planets, etc.

Transient Disposition—In Disease—(See Diathesis, Directions).

DISPROPORTIONED—

Body—Disproportioned Body—(See Corpulent, Crooked, Fat, Fleshy, Illshaped, Short; "Tall and Thin" under Thin; Ugly, etc.).

Cold—Disproportioned Cold, Heat, Dryness and Moisture—Extremes of—Lack of—Diseases Resulting From—(See Air, Atmosphere, Cold, Diminished, Drought, Dryness, Epidemics, Famine, Floods, Heat, Increased, Moisture, Pestilence, Rain, Summer, Superabundance, Weather, Winds, Winter).

DISPUTES—Controversies—Contests—Dissentions, etc.—Danger of Injury or Death From—(See Chartering, Contests, Cuts, Duels, Enemies, Feuds, Gunshot, Misunderstandings, Poisoning, Quarrels, Treachery, Sword, War).

DISRUPTION—Disruptive Agencies—♅ and ♂ influence. (See Bursting, Explosions, Lacerations, Rupture, Perversions, Vessels, etc.).

DISSATISFIED—(See Anxiety, Despondent, Discontentment, Fears, Melancholy, Restless, Unhappy, Worry, etc.).

DISSIPATED—Scattered—(See Cold, Decay, Dispersions, Dry, Energy, Scattering, Strength, etc.).

DISSIPATION—Dissipated—Liable to Dissipated Conduct—The Energy and Strength Dissipated—Disease and Ill-Health Arising From—The ☉ Sig. to the ♂ ♀; the ☉ to the ☍ or ☌ ♀ by dir., and ♀ affl. at B.; the ☉ to the □ or ☍ ♃; the ☉ directed to the Ascelli; the ☉ to the ill-asps. the cusp of the 2nd H., or ruler of the 2nd; the ☽ affl. at B., cadent, in ♏ or ♑, and with no good asps of ♃ or ♀; the ☽ to the ♂ Procyon; the ☽ decr. in light, and carried to, or conjoined with ♀, and ♂ behold ♀; the ☽ decr. in light, sepr. from ♄ and apply. to ♀; the ☽ in ♏ or ♓ at B., and ♀ passing the radical ☽ or ♂ at a Solar Rev.; ♄ Sig. □ or ☍ ♀; ♃ Sig. □ or ☍ the ☉ or ♀; ♃ Sig. □ or ☍ the ☉ or ♀; ♃ Sig. ♂ ♂, and ♂ ill-dig. and affl.; ♂ affl. in the 4th H., and espec. in ♋ or ♓, and affl. by the □ or ☍ of planets; ♂ in ♋ or ♓ in the 12th H., and affl.; ♂ □ or ☍ ♀; ♂ in the 5th H. in ♋, ♏, or ♓, and affl. by the ☽ or ♀; ♂ affl. in the 11th H., thru the influence of friends; ♂ at a Solar Rev. passing over the radical ☽; ♂ Sig. ⚹ or △ the ☽); ♀ ♂ the Asc. by dir., and ill-health following; ♀ in the Asc., and affl. by ♄ or ♂; ♀ rising and affl.; ♀ to the □ or ☍ the M.C.; ♀ lady of the year at the Vernal, and affl. and weak, tends to a prevalence of dissipation; ♀ affl. in the 5th H., ill-health by; ♀ ill-dig. at B., much given to dissipation; ♀ Sig. □ or ☍ ♄, altho not suspected; M.C. to the □ or ☍ ♀. (See Conduct; "Brings Disease Upon Himself" under Disease; "Causes His Own Death" under Death; Debased, Debauched, Depraved, Dispersals, Dissolute, Drink, Drunkenness; "Early Death" under Early; Eating, Energy Dissipated (see Energy); Excesses, Feasting, Folly, Food, Free Living (see Free); Gluttony, Habits, Harlots, High Living (see High); Infamous, Intemperance, Intoxication, Lewd, Loose, Low and Base (see Low); Lustful, Men, Middle Life—Death At—(see Middle Life); Morals, Narcotics, Opposite Sex (see Opposite); Own Worst Enemy (see Enemies); Passion, Perverted, Prodigal, Profligate, Redundant, Sex, Shameless, Taverns, Venery, Vices, Vile, Wanton, Wine, Women).

Energy Dissipated—The Strength and Energy Dissipated—Dissipation of Energy—The ☉ in ♌ in the Asc., in ⚹ or △ ♂, great energy, but tendency to dissipate it; ♂ in ♌ in the Asc., and ☉ ruler of the Asc., and afflicted; ♂ in ♌ in the Asc., and affl. by ♃ or ♀. (See Dispersions, Dissipated, Effervescent, Energy; "Energy" under Functions; Irresponsible; "Activity" under Perversions; Roaming, Scattering; "Weakened" under Strength; Unreliable, Vacillating; "Lessened" under Vitality).

DISSOLUTE—Dissolute Habits—Dissolute Living—Caused by an afflicted ♀; ♀ to the ill-asps. the Asc., M.C., or the ☽ by dir.; the ☽ affl. in ♏ in female nativities; the ☽ ascending at B., weak, and ill-dig.; ♄ to the ill-asps. ♂ or ♀ by dir.; ♆ in ♓ in the 5th H., and affl., dissolute vices and depraved habits; ♆ affl. in the Asc. in male nativities tends to dissolute habits. (See Debauched, Depraved, Dissipation, Drink, Drunkenness, Infamous, Loose, Morals, Prodigal, Profligate, Riotous, Tumors, Vices, etc.).

DISSOLUTION—Death—The Process of Dissolving—Catalysis—(See Catalysis; "Denotes Death" under Death; Decay, Disintegration, Putrefaction, Resolution, etc.).

Dissolution of Tissues—The Dissolving of Bodily Tissue—The pathological action of the ☽, and afflictions to the ☽. The 3rd Dec. of ♍ denotes death, dissolution, decay, infirmity, and old age. (See Death, Decay, Disturbances, Infirmity, Old Age, Resolvent, Resolution, Solution, Tissues, etc.).

DISSPIRITED—(See Anxiety, Brooding, Dejected, Depressed, Despondent, Discontentment, Fears, Gloom, Hope, Hypochondria, Irritable; "Low Spirits" under Low; Melancholia, Repining, Restless, Worry, etc.).

DISTEMPERS—Distemperatures—Diseases—Ailments—Indispositions, etc. The word Distemper in Modern Therapeutics is applied more to Animals than to diseases of Man. However, the word Distemper appears very frequently in Astrological Literature, and for convenience of reference the various forms of Distempers have been gathered, listed and classified in this section. Also see the Article on Disease.

Back—The Back Distempered—(See "Diseases" under Back).

Bodily—The Distemper is Bodily—The Disease is More in the Body Than in the Mind—(See "Afflicted" under Body).

Bowels—The Bowels Distempered—(See "Disorders" under Bowels).

Brain—Distempers of the Membranes of the Brain—(See "Disordered" under Brain; Meninges).

Choleric Distempers—(See Choleric).

Chronic—Long Chronic Distempers—(See Chronic).

Cold Distempers—♓ diseases. (See Cold).

Cold and Moist Distempers—(See "Cold and Moist" under Humours, Moisture).

Disease—The Disease Changes into Some Other Form of Distemper—(See "Changes" under Disease).

Dry—Dry and Melancholic Distempers—(See "Melancholy" under Dry).

Fancies Distempered—(See Fancies).

Feet Distempered—(See "Distempers" under Feet).

Feverish Distempers—(See Fever).

General Distempers—The Distemper General Over the Body—(See "General" under Whole).

Genitals—Distempers In—(See "Diseases" under Genitals; "Distempers" under Secrets).

Gluttony—Distempers Proceeding From—(See Gluttony, Intemperance, Plethora, Surfeits).

Head—Distempers In—(See "Disorders" under Head).

Heart—The Heart Distempered—(See "Heart Trouble" under Heart).

Hot Distempers—Hot and Moist Distempers—(See Fever; "Hot Diseases" under Heat; "Hot and Moist" under Heat, Moisture).

Inflammatory Distempers—Liable To—(See "Causes" under Inflammation).

Intemperance—Distempers From—(See "Diseases" under Intemperance).

Intestines—Distempers In—(See "Disorders" under Bowels).

Kidneys Distempered—(See "Diseased" under Kidneys).

Liable to Distempers—Planets in Perigee, and also when R, tend to cause diseases and distempers. (See "Causes" under Disease; Perigee, Retrograde).

Long Distempers—Long Chronic Distempers—(See Chronic).

Mad and Sudden Distempers—(See "Sudden" under Head).

Melancholic Distempers—Melancholic and Dry Distempers—(See "Melancholy" under Dry; "Diseases" under Melancholy).

Meninges of Brain—Distempers of—(See "Brain" in this section).

Mental—Mind—The Distemper is More in the Mind Than in the Body—(See "Afflicted" under Body; Cares; "Diseased Mind" under Mind; "Disease" under Psychic).

Moist Distempers—Cold and Moist Distempers—(See "Cold and Moist" under Humours; Moisture).

Morbid Distempers—(See "Diseases" under Morbid).

Neck—Chronic Distempers About the Neck—(See "Chronic" under Neck).

Putrid Distempers—(See Putrid).

Reins—Distempers In—(See "Disorders" under Reins).

Secret Parts—Distempers In—(See "Diseases" under Genitals; "Distempers" under Secrets).

Sudden Distempers—Mad and Sudden—(See "Sudden" under Head; "Diseases" under Sudden).

Throat—Chronic Distempers In—(See "Chronic" under Throat).

Toes—Distempers In—(See "Distempers" under Feet, Toes).

Veneral Distempers—(See Venereal).

DISTENTIONS—Distention—A ♂ and ♃ disease. The Distentions of Plethora are caused by ♃, and resulting from Gluttony, and the Blood Vessels being too full. (See Gluttony, Plethora, Surfeits; "Too Much Blood" under Blood; "Vascular Fullness" under Vascular; Vessels).

Distended Abdomen—(See "Distentions", "Prominent", under Abdomen).

Distended Body—The Body Inflated—(See Bloating, Flatulence, Gas, Inflation, Swellings, Tympanies).

Distended Stomach—(See Digestion, Emphysema, Flatulence, Gas, Indigestion; "Distended" and "Wind" under Stomach; Tympanites, etc.).

Distended Vessels—(See Aneurysm, Arteries; "Too Much Blood" under Blood; Capillaries, Dilatations, Varicose, Vascular, Vessels, etc.).

DISTILLATION—Distillatory—Sublimation—The Distillatory Processes of the Kidneys are ruled by ♀ and the ♎ sign. Leo and ♎ are concerned with distillation and circulation, ♎ espec. with distillation in the kidneys, and filtration. (See Kidneys, Nutrition).

Distillation of Rheum—(See Rheum).

Distilled Water—(See "Mineral Waters" under Healers; "Water" under Skin). See Filtration, Sublimation.

DISTORTIONS—Twisted Out of Natural or Regular Shape—

Causes Of—Many planets in Imperfect or Mutilated Signs at B., or with such a sign upon the Asc., as ♌, ♏, or ♓ (some Authors include ♋ and ♑), are apt to produce distortions of body and limbs; malefics in angles, and the ☉ or ☽ in ☌, or brought up to them; the ☉ or ☽ ☌ or ☍ ♄, in angles, and espec. if the ☽ be in her nodes, or in extreme Lat., or in hurtful signs, as ♈, ♉, ♋, ♏, or ♑,—under these conditions if the ☉ or ☽ be in ☌ with ♄ or ♂, the defect will be from birth, but if ♄ or ♂ be in ☍ to the ☉ or ☽, or ♄ or ♂ in the M.C. in □ the ☉ or ☽, it will be from Cuts, Blows, Stabs, Falls from Heights, Injury by Robbers, Quadrupeds, by Shipwreck, and in Accidents;

the ☽ in obnoxious signs, as ♈, ♉, ♋, ♏, or ♑, in her nodes, or in extreme Lat., and the malefics brought up to the Luminaries, the body is afflicted with Excrescences, Distortions, Lameness, or Paralysis. The calamity takes place from the moment of birth if the malefics be with the ☉ or ☽, but if the malefics be in the 10th H., and elevated above the Lights, or in ☍ to each other, then the trouble arises from Falls from Heights, Attacks by Robbers or Quadrupeds, or by some dangerous Accident, Cut, Stab, etc. (See Excrescences).

Features Distorted—(See Features).

Gait—Awry Gait from Distortions— (See "Awry" under Gait).

Limbs Distorted— (See Limbs. Also see "Causes" in this section).

Teeth Distorted—(See Teeth).

Views Distorted—(See Chaotic, Confusion, Eccentric, Erratic, Ideals, Ideas, Judgment, Notions, etc.). See Accidents, Animals, Birth, Calamity, Congenital, Contortions, Contractions, Crippled, Cuts, Defects, Deformities, Dwarf, Excrescences, Face, Falls, Feet, Fingers, Gait, Hands, Heights, Imperfections, Infirmities, Injuries, Lameness, Legs, Limbs, Maimed, Malformations, Monsters, Mutilated, Neck, Paralysis, Quadrupeds, Robbers, Shipwreck, Spasmodic, Spine, Stabs, Twistings, Walk, etc. For Distortions of the various organs or parts of the body not listed here, look for the subject in the alphabetical arrangement.

DISTRACTION—Distracted of Mind— (See Anguish, Anxiety, Dejected, Depressed, Despondent, Distress, Grief, Hypochondria; "Low Spirits" under Low; Melancholy, Miserable, Sadness, Sorrow, Trouble, Worry, etc.).

DISTRESS—Distressful—Suffering—

Abroad—Distress and Suffering Abroad—(See "Distress" under Abroad).

Death — Death Without Distress — (See "Easy Death" under Death).

Dreams—Distressful Dreams—(See Dreams).

Every Kind—Of Distress—Ruled and Denoted by the 12th H. (See Twelfth).

Maladies—Distressful Maladies—(See Fierce, Grievous, Heavy, High, Painful, Severe, Sharp, Vehement, Violent).

Mind—Distress of Mind—The 2nd Decan. ♐ on the Asc. (See Anguish, Disgrace, Dishonour, Distraction, Reputation, Reversals, Ruin, Trouble, etc. Other references are given under Anguish. For other kinds of Distress, see in the alphabetical arrangement the subject you have in mind.

DISTURBED—Disturbances—

Brain—The Brain Disturbed—(See "Disturbed" under Brain).

Circulation—Circulation of the Blood Disturbed—(See Arteries, Blood, Circulation, Congestions, Determination, Heart, Impure, Pulse, Rush, Veins).

Degree of Disturbance—In Disease— This is greater when the tempo of the movements of the planets is slower in forming or separating from aspects,

as when the planets are ℞, Stationary, Slow of Motion, etc. The rate of progression of the planets varies from day to day, and in disease the daily motion, or rate of movement of the planets, should be studied in helping to form a judgment. Planets rapid and direct in motion, and at their normal daily rate, tend to more rapid dissolution of disease. (See Direct; "Planets" under Motion; Retrograde, Stationary).

Mind Disturbed—(See Anguish, Anxiety, Insanity; "Irritations" under Mental; "Diseased Mind" under Mind; Worry, etc.).

Sleep Disturbed—(See Refreshment, Rest; "Insomnia" under Sleep).

System Disturbed—(See Constitution, Disease, Derangements, Disorders, Ill-Health, Infirmities, Sickness; "Disordered" under System).

DISUNION—Of Cells—(See "Division" under Cells; Death, Decay, Disintegration, Dissolution, etc.).

DIURESIS — Excessive Secretion of Urine—(See Diabetes; "Excess", "Polyuria", under Urine).

DIURETICS—A Medicine Increasing the Flow of Urine—A Therapeutic Property of ♀ and ♀ remedies, and also of ♄. (See Aconite, Urine, Venus).

DIURNAL—(See Day).

Diurnal Signs — And Houses — (See "Nocturnal Signs" under Night).

DIVINATION — (See Clairvoyance, Magic, Mediumship, Necromancy).

DIVISION—Divisions—

Divisions of the Body—The 12 parts, or divisions of the body, as ruled by the 12 Signs of the Zodiac. (See each of the Signs as Aries, Taurus, etc. Also see Signs, Vertebrae, Zodiac).

Division of Cell—(See "Division" under Cell).

Divisions of Life—The Periods of Life from Infancy to Old Age, and their planetary rulerships. (See Periods).

DIZZINESS—Giddiness—Light-Headedness—Vertigo—A ☉ disease; an ♈ disease; ♄ ☌ ♃ or ♀ in ♈; ♄ ☌ ♃ in the Asc.; ♃ affl. in ♈; ☿ affl. in ♐; Subs at AT, Li.P, and SP. (See Fainting, Vertigo).

DOCTORS—Influences which tend to make good Physicians and Healers of the various Schools. (See Healers, Surgeons).

DOGS—Dog Bites—Mad Dogs—Resembles Dogs, etc. Domestic Pets are ruled by ♃. (See Pets).

Death of Dogs—(See "Virus" under Pestilence).

Dog Bites—Death, Injury, or Disease From, and from Mad Dog Bites—The ☉ to the ☌ ♂ by dir. makes one liable to dog bites whether the dog is healthy or mad; caused by ♂ afflictions. (See "Dogs" under Bites; Hydrophobia).

Dog Days—Named originally after Sirius, the Dog Star, and the ☌ of the ☉ with Sirius in July. However, they are now made to depend upon the Summer Solstice, and to have no connection with Sirius, as in Ancient Times. Dog Days begin on July 3rd, or 12 days after the Summer Solstice, and end August 14th. (See Hydrophobia).

Mad Dog Bites—(See Hydrophobia. Also see "Dog Bites" in this section).

Resembles Dogs—(See "Dogs" under Children).

Sickness of Dogs—(See Hydrophobia; "Virus" under Pestilence).

DOLEFUL—(See Grief, Imagination, Melancholy, Mournful, Sadness).

DOLENS—Phlegmasia Alba Dolens—(See "Milk Leg" under Legs).

Dolens—Grief—(See Grief).

DOMINION—

Dominion of Death—This is vested in the planet which occupies an Anaretic Place at B. (See Anareta; the Introduction, and "Quality" under Death).

Dominion of the Planets—(See Planets, and each of the planets in the alphabetical arrangement, as Saturn, Sun, Moon, Mars, etc. Also see Angles, Aspects, Benefics, Cadent, Directions, Elevated, Feminine, Majority, Malefics, Masculine, Occidental, Oriental, Rising, Setting, etc.).

DORSA LEONIS—Lion's Tail—(See Lion, Melancholy, Stars).

DORSAL—Pertaining to the Back—

Nerves—The Dorsal Nerves—The Upper Dorsal Nerves are ruled by ♍; the Middle Dorsal Nerves are ruled by ♌, and the Lower Dorsal Nerves are ruled by ♍.

Spine—The Dorsal Region of the Back and Spine—Ruled by the ☉ and the ♌ Sign. This part of the Spine is afflicted, or becomes diseased, with ♄ affl. in ♌, or the ☉ afflicted, and known as ☉ diseases. (See Back, Spine).

Tabes Dorsalis—(See Tabes).

Vertebrae—The Dorsal Vertebrae—(See "Dorsal" under Vertebrae).

DOUBLE-BODIED SIGNS—Bicorporeal Signs—These Signs are ♊, ♐, and ♓. These Signs are formed, or symbolized, by two distinct animals, or contain two distinct animals. These signs when upon the Asc., 5th, or 11th H. at B., and espec. when rising upon the Asc., or containing the ☉, ☽, and many planets, tend to Twins, and multiple births. They also tend to a dual mind, and scattering of the mental and physical energies. (See Castor, Dual, Gemini, Mutable, Pisces, Pollux, Sagittarius, Twins).

DOUBTS—The ☽ Sig. ☌ ♄, likely to doubt and deliberate too long in the moment of action; the ☽ Sig. ✶ or △ ♄, does nothing with much thought or deliberation, doubting, and with some fear of consequences; ☿ affl. by ♄; the 29° ♊ on Asc., is full of doubt, misgivings, fears, suspicions, and is pessimistic; the 21° ♐ on Asc. Neptune is also called the Planet of Doubt and Fear. (See Anguish, Anxiety, Fears, Forebodings, Hallucinations, Imaginations, Imprudent, Jealousy; "No Peace of Mind" under Mind; Mistrustful, Neptune, Obsessions, Pessimistic, Premon-

itions; "Excess Of" under Prudence; Recluse, Reserved, Scepticism, Suspicious, Thinking, Worry, etc.).

DOWN—

Downcast—(See Dejected, Depressed, Despondent, Hope; "Low Spirits" under Low; Melancholy; "No Peace" under Mind; Sadness, Worry, etc.).

Downcast Look—Downward Look—(See "Downward" under Look).

Downfall—Sudden Downfall—♂ Sig. ☌ ☉. (See Disgrace, Fortune, Honour, Reputation, Reverses, Ruin, Scandal, Trouble, etc.).

Downward Flow—Of Humours—(See Defluxion).

DRAGON'S HEAD—(☊)—Caput Draconis—The ☽'s North Node—Is said to be of the nature of the ☉, and fortunate in health, and other matters, when conjoined with the Asc., M.C., or in ☌, ✶, or △ the planets. Wilson in his Dictionary says that ☊ is equal to ♃ and ♀ in benign influence. The house, or sign, of ☊ is said to be ♉.

Dragon's Tail—(☋)—Cauda Draconis—The ☽'s South Node—Is of the nature of ♄ and ♂, corresponds to ♄, and ♎, the exalted sign of ♄, and tends to suppression and obstruction of the bodily functions, the same as with ♄, only in a lesser degree. When in ☌ with a planet it has a ♄ influence, and tends to crystallize, harden, and obstruct. In ☌ with malefics it tends to double and treble their evil. According to the Ancients it is classed as malefic in influence. Its sign, or house, is said to be ♏. Is very evil when the Sig. of Death. (See Nodes, Saturn).

DRAUGHTS—Drafts—Catching Cold By —(See Colds, Tuberculosis).

DREADFUL—Terrible—

Dreadful Death—(See "Dreadful" under Death).

Dreadful Diseases—The ☉ directed to all Nebulous Clusters, and to Castor and Pollux, threatens dreadful diseases. (See Portentous, Terrible).

DREADS—Fears—(See Darkness, Dreams, Fears, Obsessions, Premonitions; "Terrors" under Strange).

DREAMS—Visions—Dreamy—Dreams are ruled and presided over by ♆ and the 9th H. Dream Consciousness is ruled by the 9th H. Dreams and Nightmare occur mostly about 48 hours before the ☽'s Perigee, and when the ☽ is about an hour high. The Hebrew letter Lamed (L) is connected with Dreams, Sleep, and the ♎ Sign. Dreams are also caused by the ☽ in the 9th H., and aspected by ♆; ♆ ✶ or △ the ☽, ♓, or ♃; ♆ affl. in ♐, dreams of danger; ♆ ✶ or △ the ☽, prophetic dreams; ♆ ☌ or in transit over the radical ☽ or ☿; ♆ in the 9th H., strange dreams; ♆ in ♈ □ or ☍ ☽, nightmare; ♅ ✶ or △ ♆, of a prophetical and inspirational nature; ♅ in ♐; ♅ in the 8th H. predisposes to dreams and visions; ♃ affl. in ♈, strange dreams, ♂ in the 9th H., distressful dreams. Case of Strange Dreams and Premonitions—See "Dreams", No. 312, in 1001 N.N. (See

Astral, Clairvoyance, Coma, Delirium, Fears, Forebodings, Hallucinations, Premonitions, Prophetic, Psychic, Sleep; "Terrors" under Strange; Trance, Visions, etc.).

Dreamy Mind—Dreamy Manner—A Day Dreamer — Absent-Minded — Visionary—Inability to Concentrate— Mental Fantasies—♎︎, ♒︎, and ♓︎, and with many planets in these signs, and ♂ obscurely placed, indulge much in day dreams. (See Absent-Minded, Chaotic, Concentration, Confusion, Delusions, Erratic, Fancies, Fears, Flightiness, Hallucinations, Ideals, Illusions, Imagination, Obsessions, Phantasies, Psychic, Recluse, Secretive, Spirit Controls, Vagaries, Vague, Visionary, Weird, etc.).

Wet Dreams—(See Semen).

DREAMY — (See "Dreamy" under Dreams).

DRESS—Clothing—Linen—Food and Clothing are ruled by the 6th H. and the ♍ sign. Venus also rules strongly over Dress, Adornment, and the indiscretions of dress.

Adornment—Fond of Personal Adornment, Fine Clothes and Jewelry—(See Pretender).

Bad Respiration — Due to Indiscretions in Dress, Tight Lacing, etc.— (See "Indiscretions" in this section. Also see Lacing).

Colors of Dress—(See "Clothing" under Colors. Also see Black).

Extravagance—In Dress and Food— ♂ in the 6th H. (See Extravagance, Luxuries).

Indiscretions—In Dress, Illness and Disturbances From—Injudicious Dressing—♀ affl. in ♉, ♊, or ♋ tends to bad respiration due to injudicious dressing and tight lacing; ♀ in ♏ in the 6th H., and afflicted, or affl. the ☽ or Asc., tends to bad respiration from tight lacing; with ♃ or ♀ in ♊, indiscretions in dress should be avoided, as they are harmful to the health; ♀ in ♌ in the 6th H., and afflicted, or afflicting the ☽ or Asc., tends to palpitation of the heart thru indiscretions in dress, or tight lacing; malefics in ♊ also tend to harmful effects upon the chest, lungs and breathing from tight lacing. (See "Obstructions" under Breathing; Exposure, External, Indiscretions, Lacing).

Neat in Dress—(See Neat).

Peculiar Tastes—In Dress—♆ in the 6th H. (See Eccentric, Fancies, Food, Habits, Ideas, Notions, Peculiar, Tastes, etc.).

Pretentious—In Dress—(See Pretender).

Throat Disorders—From Improper Dress—(See "Dress" under Throat).

Tight Lacing—(See "Indiscretions" in this section).

Untidy—(See Untidy).

Wet Clothing—Colds and Illness From —(See "Clothing" under Colds; "Cold Taken" under Feet).

DRIBBLING — (See "Salivation" under Saliva; "Incontinence" under Urine).

DRINK—Drinking—Tendency to Drink —Danger of Excesses In—Fond of Intoxicating Drink, etc.—The watery signs ♋, ♏, and ♓, when strong and predominating the map of birth, and the ☉, ☽, Asc., or many planets in such signs at B., and affl., tend to strong drink, and dissipation therefrom; especially a ♓ disease and affliction, and with the ☉ or ☽ affl. in ♓, and many planets in watery signs also; the ☽ ill-dig. at B., given to drink; the ☽ or ♀ affl. by ♆; the ☽ to the ✶ or △ ♂ if ♂ be weak and ill-dig. at B.; the ☽ in ♉ in the 5th H., and affl.; ♆ ♂, □, or ☍ the ☽; ♆ ♂ ♀ in ♉, and affl. by the ☽; ♆ and ♂ in ♉, and with the ☽ in a water sign; ♅ ♂ ☽ in ♋, and affl. by the □ or ☍ of ♂ causes strong drink; ♃ Sig. □ or ☍ ☉; ♃ or ♀ affl. in ♋; ♂ affl. in ♉, ♋, or ♓; ♂ in ♋, □, or ☍ ♆, fond of liquids and drink; the aspects of ♂ cause when ♂ is ill-dig.; ♀ in ♓ partile asp. the Asc.; Subs at SP and KP tend to, and to create a morbid condition due to excessive use of alcohol. Cases of Given to Drink, Birth Data, etc.—See "Spendthrift", No. 262, in 1001 N.N. Also see Fig. 14 in "Message of the Stars" by the Heindels. (For further influences see the various paragraphs in this Article, and the references given).

Alcoholic Excesses — ♓ on the Asc., and tending to habitual drunkenness. (See "Excess" in this section. Also see Drunkenness, Intoxication).

Ale Houses—Saloons—Taverns—A Frequenter of—Brawling in Saloons— (See Taverns).

Bacchus—Partial to the Joys of Bacchus—The 19° ♐ on the Asc. (Charubel).

Brain—Softening Of Due to Alcoholism—(See "Softening" under Brain).

Brawling in Saloons—(See Drunkenness, Taverns).

Children—The Children May Become Drunkards—(See "Children" under Drunkards).

Craving for Drink—(See "Fond Of", and the various paragraphs in this Article).

Death from Drink—(See "Death" under Eating, Intoxication).

Delirium Tremens—(See Delirium).

Dipsomania—An Uncontrollable Desire for Drink—(See Dipsomania).

Disease—Disease and Ill-Health from Too Much Strong Drink—(See "Strong Drink" in this section).

Drunkenness—(See Drunkenness).

Excess in Drink—The ☉ and ☽ badly affl., and espec. in or from fire and water signs; a weak polarity between the ☉ and ☽; the ☉ affl. in ♉, excess in eating and drinking; the ☽ affl. by ♀, and the ☽ or ♀ in a water sign at B.; the ☽ in a water sign, and to the ♂ or ill-asp. ♂ by dir.; ♆ affl. in ♋; ♆ in ♋ in the 6th H., and affl.; ♆ in ♋ and affl. the ☉, ☽, Asc., or hyleg; ♆ in the 5th H., in a water sign, and affl.; ♄ ♂ or ill-asp. ♀ or ☿, and espec. in water signs; ♃ in the Asc. in a water sign, and affl.; ♃ affl. in ♉, over-indulgence in drinking and eating, and suffering from; ♃ □ a malefic; ♂ in the Asc. in a water sign, and affl.; afflictions in or to the 11° of cardinal signs, or to the 9° or 25° of fixed signs; the 19° ♐ on the Asc.; ♅ influence and afflictions in; ♓ on the Asc. (See Debauchery, Delirium Tremens, Dissipation, Dissolute, Drunkenness, Excesses; "Sugar" under Food; Intemperance, Intoxication, Sottishness. Also see the various paragraphs in this section).

Fits of Drink—And Sensuality—♂ ☌ or ill-asp. the ☽ or ♀ by dir., and ♂ affl. these planets at B.

Fond of Drink—Craving for Drink—The ☉ to the ☌, or any asp. ♀ in a water sign, and ♀ afflicted; the ☉ to the ☌, or any asp. ♀ by dir., and ♀ affl. at B.; the ☉ to the ill-asps. the ☽ by dir., and in water signs; the ☉ affl. in a watery sign; the ☉ in a water sign ☌ ♀, and affl.; the ☉, ☽, and ☿ in ♓; the ☉ ☌ ☽ in 12th H.; the ☽ to the ☌ or ill-asp. ♂ by dir., if the nativity shows a tendency to drink; the ☽ in ♋ or ♓ and affl. by the ☉ or ♂; the ☽ weak and affl. at B., and espec. in water signs; the ☽ to the ✳ or △ ♂ by dir., and ♂ affl. at B., and both in water signs; ♆ ♓ in the 5th H.; ♆ ♋ in the 6th H., and affl.; ♅ affl. in ♏; ♄ ☌ or ill-asp. ♀ in water signs; ♃, ♓, □ or ☍ ♂; ♃ in the 1st H. in ♓; and affl.; ♂ in ♓; ♂ ♓, ☌ ☽ or ♃; ♂ ♓, □ or ☍ ♃; ♂ ♓, ♋, or ♎, and affl. by the □ or ☍ of planets; ♂ affl. in the 12th H. in ♋ or ♓; ♂ evilly posited, and afflicting ♀; ♂ in the sign or house of the ☽, and affl.; in Hor'y Questions, ♂ Sig. of the person; ♂ ruler at B., and affl., and espec. in water signs; ♂ Sig. in ♓; ♀ ill-dig. at B.; ♀ or ♀ affl. in ♓; ♀ in the Asc. or M.C., or in water signs, and affl.; ♀ Sig. ☌ ♂; ♀ affl. in ♋ or ♓; watery signs on the Asc., and espec. ♓, and afflicted; a ♋, ♏, and ♓ disease. (See the Introduction, "Excess", and the various paragraphs in this section).

Given to Drinking—(See "Fond Of" in this section).

Habits—A Habitual Drunkard—(See Drunkenness).

Husband—The Husband Given to Drink—The Marriage Partner Drinks—(See "Drink" under Husband, Marriage Partner, Wife).

Intoxication—Intemperance—(See these subjects).

Liquids—Craving for Liquors—Spirituous Liquors—The ☽ in water signs; the ☽ affl. in ♓. (See Intoxication, Liquids, Wine. Also note the various paragraphs in this section).

Marriage Partner—Given to Drink—(See "Husband" in this section).

Meals—Drink With—(See Food).

Moderate Drinker — The □ influence strong at B., and mixed in with the evils which cause Intemperance.

Over-Indulgence in Drink—(See "Excess" in this section. Also see "Delirium Tremens" under Delirium; Drunkenness, Intoxication).

Parents—The Parents Drink and Neglect the Children—(See "Drink" under Parents).

Period of Drinking—A Period of Drinking caused by evil Directions—The Prog. ☉ □ or ☍ the radical ☽, and espec. if both are in water signs at B.; the ☉ to the bad asps. ♀ or the ☽ by dir.; the ☽ to the ☌ or ill-asps. ♂ by dir., if the nativity shows a tendency to drink; the ☽ to the ✳ or △ ♂ by dir. if ♂ be weak and affl. at B., and the radical ☽ be in a watery sign; ♄ ♏ ☌ or evil asp. the Asc. by dir.; ♃ in ♓ at B., and affl., and to the ☌ or ill-asp. ♂ by dir., and ♂ also in a water sign at B., and afflicting ♃, ♀, or the ☽; ♂ to the ☌ or ill-asp. ♀ or the ☽ by dir., and espec. if these planets be in watery signs at B. and afflicted. (See Directions).

Protracted Drinking—(See "Habitual" under Drunkenness; "Period Of" in this section).

Saloons—Frequenter of—Brawling In—(See Taverns).

Softening of Brain—(See Brain).

Sottishness—A Sot—A Toper—Habitual Drunkard—(See "Habitual" under Drunkenness; Harlots, Sottishness, Taverns).

Spirituous Liquors—An Uncontrollable Desire For—(See Dipsomania).

Stimulants—Addicted to the Use of—(See Dipsomania, Drunkenness, Intoxication, Narcotics, Stimulants, Sugar, Wine, etc. Also note the various paragraphs in this section).

Stomach Disordered—By Drink—The ☽ in ♋ and afflicted by the ☉ or ♂ when taken ill.

Strong Desire — For Intoxicating Liquors—(See Dipsomania, Drunkenness, Intoxication; "Fond Of" in this section).'

Strong Drink—Strong Coffee—Addicted To—Disease From—♆ in ♋ or ♏ in the 6th H., and affl.; ♆ in ♋ and affl. the ☉, ☽, Asc., or hyleg; ♄ ☌ ♀ in ♋; the ☽ ♓ and affl. by the ☉ or ♂ when taken ill; ♂ affl. in ♉ or ♋; ♀ affl. in ♓, in some cases; ♓ on the Asc., and with other afflictions tending to drink. (See "Softening" under Brain; Delirium Tremens, Demoniac, Intoxication, Thirst).

Surfeits — From Too Much Drink — (See "Surfeits" under Diet; Eating, Food, Surfeits; "Excess", "Strong Drink" in this section).

Temperate—In Drink—(See "Moderate" in this section).

Tendency to Drink—(See the various paragraphs in this section).

Thirst—For Drink—(See "Fond Of" in this section; "Drinks" under Thirst).

Too Much Drink—(See "Excess" in this section).

Too Strong Drink—Uses Too Strong Liquors and Intoxicants—♆ affl. in ♏, and espec. in 6th H. (See Delirium Tremens, Intoxication; "Strong" in this section).

Toper—(See "Habitual" under Drunkenness).

Uncontrollable Desire—For Strong Drink—(See Dipsomania; "Strong Drink" in this section).

Vicious Drinking—♂ affl. in ♉, ♊, ♋, ♍, ♒, or ♓, and espec. when affl. the ☉, ☽, or ♀, and with the latter in water signs.

Wife—The Wife Given to Drink—(See "Husband" in this section).

Will Power—Lack of Will to Curb Appetite for Drink—♓ on the Asc. at B., and afflicted. (See Dipsomania; "Habitual" under Drunkenness).

Wine—Addicted To—(See Wine).

Women Crave Drink—♄ ☌ or ill-asp. the ☽ at B., and by dir. (See the various paragraphs under Women). For further study along this line see Conduct, Cravings, Debauchery, Disorderly, Dull; "Free Living" under Free; Habits; "High Living" under High; Improvident; "Loose Morals" under Morals; "Low Public Houses" under Low; Madness, Morals, Pineal Gland, Pleasures, Prodigal, Profligate, Ravings, Sensuality, Temperance, Vagabonds, Vices, etc.

DROOPING—Limp Body—Bodily Action Uncertain—(See Limp, Ptosis, Relaxed, Stooping).

DROPSY — Dropsies — Dropsical Humours—Hydropical Diseases—Anasarca—Oedema—Effusion of Fluids into the Tissues—etc. Dropsy is principally a disease of the ☽, the ♋ sign, and is also closely related to the watery signs, and afflictions in them. Saturn causes Dropsy by stoppages, obstructions, retentions, suppressions, and by interfering with the bodily functions. Jupiter and ♀ afflictions cause Dropsies by surfeits, over-indulgences, etc., and ♆ causes them thru excesses of various kinds, and dissipation. The Common Signs, and afflictions in them, also show Dropsy. Dropsical swellings change for the better or worse at the changes of the ☽. (See "Full Moon" under Moon). Dropsy follows the course of the ☉ when chronic, and is worse when the ☉ reaches the □, or ill-asp. his place at B. by transit, and especially when in aspect with the malefics, and diminishes when the ☉ is in good asp. his own place, or in good asp. to the benefics. Dropsy occurs in various parts of the body, from the brain to the feet, and according to the planetary afflictions at B., and by direction. The following paragraphs have to do with Dropsy, its nature, and the parts of the body so afflicted.

Abdomen—Dropsy in the Abdominal Region and Bowels—Dropsy of the Abdomen—Dropsy of the Peritoneum—Ascites—The ☽ affl. in ♍ or ♓; ♆ affl. in ♍; ♄ in ♍ or ♓; ♓ on the Asc.; Subs at KP (11D) and PP. (See Abdomen; "Dropsy" under Bowels).

Anasarca—General Dropsy—♃ affl. in ♋; afflictions in ♎ and ♑, due to the close association of these signs in ruling the kidneys and the connective tissues; Subs at KP (11D), and at UPP (1 and 2L). (See Puffing).

Ankles—(See "Swollen" under Ankles).

Ascites—Dropsy of the Abdomen—(See "Abdomen" in this section).

Beriberi—A Disease accompanied by Acute and Anaemic Dropsy, with great Weakness, Dyspnoea, and Paraplegia—Caused by many afflictions in watery signs, and espec. ♓, and with ♓ on the Asc., and afflicted; a ♄ disease; ♄ affl. in ♓ in the Asc., 6th, or 12th houses; afflictions in the common signs; afflictions in ♐, ♑, ♒, and ♓, the signs which rule the lower limbs; Subs at KP, UPP and PP. (See Anaemia, Dyspnoea; "Paralysis" under Legs).

Blood—The ☽ hyleg in ♓, dropsical condition of the blood in women (see "Blood" under Women); ♃ affl. in ♍, dropsy arising from blood discharged with watery humours; ♃ affl. in ♓, dropsy from thin and watery blood. (See "Thin Blood" under Blood).

Bowels—Dropsy In—(See "Dropsy" under Bowels; "Abdomen" in this section).

Brain—Dropsy of—(See Hydrocephalus).

Cancer Sign—An eclipse of the ☉ in the 3rd Dec. of ♋ tends to hydropical diseases among Peoples of Africa, Armenia, and Regions under ♋. (See "Cancer" under Nations).

Cardiac Dropsy—(See "Dropsy" under Heart).

Cases of Dropsy—Birth Data, Map, etc.—(See Fig. 33 in "Message of the Stars" by the Heindels).

Chest—Dropsy In—(See "Dropsy" under Chest).

Chronic Dropsy—(See the Introduction to this section).

Circulation—The Circulation and Dropsy—Serum Collections—(See "Poor", "Weak", under Circulation; Serum).

Danger of Dropsy—Liable To—Tendency To—Dropsical Complaints—The ☉ affl. in ♋, ♍, ♒, or ♓, and espec. when in ☌ or evil asp. the Asc.; the ☉ in ♓ and affl. by ♃; the ☉ affl. in ♋; a ☽ disease; the ☽ affl. in ♋, ♍, ♒, or ♓ (♒ rules strongly over the circulation of the blood, and dropsy results from disturbance of the circulation by afflictions in ♒); the ☽ to the ☌ ♄ by dir.; denoted by the ☽ when the ☽ afflicts the ☉ or Asc.; the ☽ hyleg, and to the ☌ or evil asp. ♄ by dir.; the ☽ sepr. from ♄ and apply to the ☉; the ☽ decr. in light and sepr. from ♄ and apply. to ♀; the ☽, or lords of the 1st or 6th H. in water signs; the ☽ affl. in ♋, ♍, or ♓, and affl. the hyleg therefrom; the ☽ in ♓ and affl. by the ☉ or ♂ when taken ill; the ☽ affl. at B., and to the ill-asps. the Asc. or hyleg by dir.; the ☽ hyleg in a watery sign, and affl., and espec. in female nativities; the ☽ in ♍, ☌ or ill-asp. ♄ by dir. (or ♀ if he be of the nature of ♄) at the beginning of an illness, or at decumb.; the ☽ in ♓ and in ☌, □, or ☍ ♄; ♆ affl. in ♎; a ♄ disease, and caused by ♄ afflictions; ♄ in ♋, ♍, or ♓, ☌ or evil asp. the Asc. by dir.; ♄ in ♓, occi., and affl. the ☉, ☽, or Asc.; ♃ affl. in ♋, ♍, ♑, ♒, or ♓; ♃ in ♋ or ♍ in the 6th H., and affl.; ♂ affl. in ♓ sometimes causes dropsical affections; a ♀ disease; ♀ affl. in ♑; a disease of the watery signs ♋, ♏, and ♓, and with ♋ or ♓ on the Asc.; an ♒ disease; ♒ on the Asc., and affl.; ♒ or ♓ ascending at the Vernal Equi., tend to a prevalence of dropsy among people ruled by these signs, or in Countries ruled by them; Subs at KP and Local. (See "Aquarius", "Pisces", under Nations. Also see the various paragraphs in this section).

Death By—♄ denotes death by dropsy; caused by ♄ directions when he afflicts the hyleg and holds the dominion of death; afflictions in common signs show, and espec. ♄ in a common sign and affl. the hyleg, and ♄ in the 8th H. at B., and by dir.

Diminished—The Dropsy Is Diminished—(See the Introduction to this section).

Effusions—Serous Effusions—(See Effusions, Osmosis, Serum).

Eyeballs—Dropsy of—(See Eyeballs).

Fallopian Tubes—Dropsy of—Hydrosalpinx—(See Fallopian).

Feet—Dropsy In—(See "Dropsy" under Ankles, Feet, Legs).

Fluids—(See the various paragraphs under Fluids).

General Dropsy—Anasarca—(See "Anasarca" in this section).

Heart Dropsy—(See "Dropsy" under Heart).

Humours—Dropsical Humours—The ☉ in ♓, and affl. by ♃; the ☽ in ♏, ☌ or ill-asp. ♄ (or ☿ if he be of the nature of ♄) at the beginning of an illness or at decumb.; a ♋ disease, and afflictions in ♋, or ♋ on the Asc. (See "Danger Of", and other paragraphs in this section).

Hydrocephalus—(See this subject).

Hydronephrosis—Renal Dropsy from Obstruction—(See "Dropsy" under Kidneys).

Hydrosalpinx—Water in the Fallopian Tube—Dropsy of—(See Fallopian).

Hydrothorax—(See "Dropsy" under Chest).

Increased—The Dropsy Increased—(See the Introduction to this section).

Kidneys—Dropsy of—Renal Dropsy—Hydronephrosis—(See Kidneys).

Limbs—Dropsy of Lower Limbs—(See Ankles, Feet, Legs).

Liver—Dropsy of—(See Liver).

Mucus-Like Dropsy—(See Exudations, Mucus, Myxoedema).

Obstructions—♄ causes Dropsy by obstruction of the circulation and functions. (See Obstructions. Also see the Introduction to this section).

Oedema—(See Oedema, Serum).

Osmosis—Exosmosis—Oozings—(See Osmosis).

Ovaries—Dropsy of—(See Ovaries).

Peritoneum—Dropsy of—Ascites—(See "Abdomen" in this section).

Prevalence Of—(See "Danger" in this section).

Renal Dropsy—(See "Dropsy" under Kidneys).

Serum—Dropsical Effusions of—(See Serum).

Sleeping Dropsy—(See "Sleeping Sickness" under Sleep).

Swellings—Dropsical Swellings—(See the Introduction, and the various paragraphs in this section. Also see Incurable, Swellings).

Thorax—Dropsy In—Hydrothorax—(See "Dropsy" under Chest).

Transudations—(See Osmosis).

Watery Diseases—(See Swellings, Watery. Also note the various paragraphs in this section).

Worse—The Dropsy Is Worse—(See "Increased" in this section).

DROUGHT—Hot and Dry Air—Intemperate Heat—Famine and Suffering From—

Causes Of—General Causes—Eclipses of the ☉ or ☽ in earthy signs, and espec. when the shadow falls over the Regions under the Signs involved; the ☉ eclipsed in the 1st Dec. of ♈, drought and intemperate heat; eclipses of the ☉ in fiery signs, and espec. in those Regions under the rule of the Sign in which they occur; an eclipse of the ☽ in the 2nd Dec. of ♏, dry air; ♄ ☌ ♂ in fiery signs; ♂ in power, and lord of the year at the Vernal Equinox; Comets affect the places ruled by the Signs in which they appear; Comets appearing in the Eastern Quarters of the heavens. (See Air, Atmosphere; "Cold and Dry" under Dry; Corn; "Cold and Dry", "Diseases", "Dryness of the Air", under Dryness; Epidemics, Famine, Fountains, Fruits, Grain, Heat, Pestilence, Scarcity, Vegetation, Wheat, Weather, Winds, etc.).

Disease—Disease, Death, or Suffering from Drought—Eclipses of the ☉ or ☽ in earthy signs, and affecting those People and Places ruled over by the Signs under which they occur; ♄ near the cusp of the 4th H., and in S. Lat. at the Vernal Ingress; ♂ sole ruler at an eclipse of the ☉; ♈ ascending at a Solar or Vernal Ingress, and ♂ be afflicted, Countries and Peoples ruled by ♈ suffer from extreme heat and drought; ♌ ascending at the Vernal, and the ☉ afflicted, ♌ People and Countries under ♌ suffer thru extreme heat, drought, warm pestilential air, and diseases of the heart and brain; ♑ ascending at the Vernal, and ♄ afflicted, Places and People under ♑ suffer, and have a very dry Season.

DROWNING—Death by Water—Death by Drowning—Danger of—The ☉ to the ☌ or ill-asp. ♄ or ♂ from water signs; when the ☉ or Asc. are hyleg, the ☽ by her evil directions to them assists in causing death by drowning, and espec. when in ♋, ♏, or ♓ by dir., and the ☽ holds the dominion of death; the ☉ or ☽ affl. in the 1st Dec. of ♉, ♌, ♏, or ♒, the 2nd Dec. of ♍, or when the malefics afflict the ☉ or ☽ from these decanates, dispose to drowning; the ☽ in a watery sign at B., afflicted by ♄, and afflicting the hyleg by dir., or taking part in a fatal train of directions; the ☽ lady of the 8th H. at B., and to the evil asp. the

Asc. by dir., and the ☽ in a water sign at B.; the ☽ ☌ or ill-asp. ♅ at B., and by dir., dangerous to go near water; the ☽ in a water sign, and to the ☌, P., □ or ☍ ♂ by dir., and ♂ in a water sign at B.; the ☽ with Cor. Hydra, and ☌ or ill-asp. ♄ or ♂, and ♂ in an angle; the ☽ with Antares or ♄; the ☽ affl. in the 8th H.; caused by the □ and ☍ aspects of the ☽; the ☽ weak and afflicted at B., and ☌ the Asc. by dir.; the ☽ with ♄ and Orion's Belt, or with Antares or Caput Hercules; caused by fixed stars of the nature of the ☽; death by is denoted by the ☽; ♆ the afflicting planet; ♆ affl. in ♏, accidental drowning, or suicide by, and especially if in the 8th H.; ♆ affl. in the 8th H. at B., or afflicting the hyleg therefrom; ♆ in the 8th H. in a water sign, afflicting the hyleg at B., and by dir.; ♆ ☌ the hyleg at B., and with ♆ afflicted in a water sign; ♅ or ♄ in ♋, ♍, ♏, or ♓, and affl. the ☽; ♅ afflicting the hyleg, and concurring with other testimonies for drowning; ♄ in a watery sign and affl. the Asc. or hyleg by dir.; ♄ ♍ and affl. the ☽ hyleg; ♄ in a watery sign, or in ♍, ori. of, and □ or ☍ the ☉ at B., or occi. and □ or ☍ the ☽ at B., and if near Argo, by shipwreck; ♄ ☌ the Asc. by dir., danger of if the sign be watery, or a violent fixed star near the place; ♄ in ♋, ♍, ♏, or ♓, and configurated with the ☽; ♄ in a water sign and ☌ or ill-asp. the Asc. by dir., and espec. if the Asc. be hyleg; ♄ in the Asc. when starting on a voyage, or a fiery sign on the Asc., which usually puts a watery sign on cusp of the 8th H.; ♄ affl. in the 5th H., and ♄ also affl. the hyleg; ♄ ☌ or ill-asp. the ☉ in fixed signs; ♄ espec. tends to, and to suffocation in any form; ♂ affl. in water signs, and ☌ or evil asp. the Asc. by dir.; ♂ in the 9th H. in a water sign, and affl. the ☉ or ☽ at B., and by dir.; ♂ affl. in the 9th H. on a voyage, if in a water sign; Asc. to the ☌ or evil asp. ♂ by dir., and ♂ in a water sign; Asc. to the □ or ☍ the ☽ by dir.; the 25° ♌ on the Asc.; the 1st Dec. ♓ on the Asc., ruled by ♄; a water sign ascending, with ♆ there, and ♆ affl. the hyleg; Asc. to the ☌ or ill-asp. ♄ by dir., and both ♄ and the Asc. in water signs; lord of the 8th in 9th H.; water signs dispose to; planets in ♋, ♏, or ♓, and affl. the ☽; Cor. Hydra joined to ♂, or in evil asp. the ☉ or ☽; the fixed star Hydra's Heart joined to ♂ at B.; Scheat Pegasi produces danger from drowning; malefics in the 9th H. in fire signs, and affl. the ☉ or ☽ on voyages; fixed signs, and many afflictions from them, show danger of drowning; malefics in the 3rd or 9th H. in water signs, and affl. the ☉ or ☽, danger of drowning during travel, or on a journey; planets in ♋, ♏, or ♓ during travel, and afflicting the Sigs. of travel, danger of drowning while traveling. Cases—Of Death by Drowning—See "Death by Drowning", No. 100, No. 402; "Conder", No. 315; "A Luckless Youth", No. 390; "Medici", No. 468; "Died in Harness", No. 802, all in 1001 N.N. (For further influences along this line see Abroad, Bathing, Journeys, Liquids, Maritime, Moon, Navigation, Neptune, Scalds, Sea, Ships,

Shipwreck, Suffocation, Strangulation, Travel, Voyages; "Death", "Perils", "Tidal Waves", under Water).

DROWSINESS—Sleepiness—Stupor— (See "Drowsiness" under Sleep).

DRUGGISTS—Make Good Druggists— Good Influences For—(See Chemists).

DRUGS—Medicines—Drugs as Remedies—The Harmful Effects of Drugs, etc.—

Brain—The Brain Affected by Drugs and Opiates—(See "Drugs" under Brain).

Drug Habit—Doping—Drug Taking— (See Heart, Narcotics, Poisons).

Remedies—Drugs as Remedies—The Therapeutic Properties of Drugs—The Action of Drugs—The Various Classes of Drugs, Herbs, Metals, Minerals, Plants, etc.—See Acids, Alexipharmic, Alkaline, Alterative, Anaesthetics, Analeptics, Analgesics, Anaphrodisiac, Anodyne Anthelmintic, Anticachectic, Antidotes, Antinephritics, Antiperiodic, Antipathy, Antiphlogistic, Antipyretic, Antispasmodic, Aphrodisiac, Astringents, Attenuants, Balsamic, Bitter, Cardiac, Cathartic, Caustic, Cephalic, Cholagogue, Collyria, Cooling, Cosmetics, Demulcent, Depressants, Diaphoretics, Emetic, Emollient, Escharotic, Febrifuge, Healers, Herbs, Hypnotic Drugs (see Narcotics); Liniments, Lotions, Medicines, Metals, Minerals, Narcotics, Nervine (see Nerves); Ointments, Opiates, Opposites, Planets and Drugs (see "Drugs", "Typical Drugs", under each of the Planets); Plants, Polarity, Poisons, Refrigerants, Remedies, Resolvent, Roots, Rubefacient, Sedatives, Seeds, Soothing, Soporifics, Stimulants, Styptics, Sudorifics, Therapeutics, Tonics, Treatment, Vesicants, etc. Also look for the various Drugs, Medicines, Metals, Minerals, Plants, and Remedies, in the alphabetical arrangement.

DRUNKENNESS—Inebriation—Intoxication, etc.—Many of the influences given and listed under "Drink" will also apply here. The influences of the water signs, and afflictions in them, tend to drink, and afflictions in the ♓ sign, and the ♓ sign upon the Asc. at B., to drunkenness, inebriety, and intoxication. The ☽ rules drunkards.

Children May Become Drunkards—♄ affl. in the 5th H. in a parent's map, and espec. if ♄ be in a watery sign.

Dipsomania—An Uncontrollable Desire for Drink—(See Dipsomania).

Drink—(See Drink).

Drunkenness—Tendency to Drunkenness—The ☉ or ☽ affl. in ♓; the ☉ and ♀ affl. in a watery sign, and the ☉ to the ill-asps. ♀ by dir.; the Prog. ☉ □ or ☍ the ☽, and espec. if either be in watery signs; the ☉ and ♂ in water signs at B., or by dir., and espec. if the ☉ or ☽ are affl. by ♄ or ♂ at B.; the ☉ in ♏, or ♏ on the Asc., and afflicted; the ☽ ill-dig. at B.; the ☽ affl. in ♓; ♃ in ♓, ☉ or ☍ ♂; ♃ affl. in 1st H. in ♓; ♂ ☌ the ☽ in ♓; ♂ □ or ☍ the ☽, and espec. if ♂, the ☽, or Asc. are in ♓; ♂ Sig. in ♋ or ♓; ♂ in ♓, □ or ☍ ♃; ♂ in ☍, ♋, or ♎, and affl. by the

□ or ☍ of planets; ♂ affl. in the 12th H. in ♋ or ♓; ♂ evilly aspected and badly placed in the map; ♂ evilly posited and afflicting ♀; ♂ to the ☌ or ill-asp. ♀ by dir.; ♂ in the sign or house of the ☽, and afflicted; in Hor'y Questions ♂ Sig. of the person; ♂ in the Asc. in water signs, and afflicted; ♀ ill-dig. at B.; ♀ affl. in ♓; ♀ Sig. ☌ ♂; ♀ affl. in ♋ or ♓; a ♋ and ♓ disease, and with these signs affl. on the Asc. at B.; the 3° ♎ on the Asc. (For further influences along this line see the various paragraphs in this section. Also see the various paragraphs and references in the Article on Drink).

Father—The Father May Become a Drunkard—Ruler of the 10th or 4th H. □ or ☍ ♀ or ♂, and espec. in ♓ or water signs, or ♀ in ♉, the sign ruling the palate, throat, appetite, etc. (See "Drink" under Parents).

Habitual Drunkards—A Sot or Toper —The ☉ or ☽ affl. in ♓; ♂ Sig. in ♋ or ♓; ♓ on the Asc., and afflicted. (See Sottishness, Taverns).

Husband a Drunkard—Cases—See "Marriage", No. 295, and No. 833, in 1001 N.N. (See "Drink" under Husband).

Incurable Drunkard—♃ in the 1st H. in ♓, and afflicted.

Inveterate Drunkard—♂ □ or ☍ ☽, and espec. if ♂, the ☽, or Asc. are in ♓.

Is Yet Drunk—Frequently Shows the Person Is Yet Drunk—The ☽ in ♓, and affl. by the ☉ or ♂ when taken ill (Hor'y).

Marriage Partner—A Drunkard—May Become a Drunkard—♂ in ♋, ♏, or ♓ in the 7th H., and afflicted. (See "Drink" under Husband, Wife).

DRY—Dryness—Dried—Hot and Dry—Dry Body—Dry Diseases, etc.—Dryness is noxious and destructive, and tends to diseases accompanied by friction, and by irritation of both mind and body. Dryness is associated with the earthy signs ♉, ♍, and ♑, and when acting alone is considered passive and feminine. When associated with heat, as acting thru the fiery signs, ♈, ♌, and ♐, the combination of hot and dry becomes more positive. The fiery and earthy signs contribute the heat and dryness, while the airy and watery signs are cold and moist. Dryness and Moisture are considered passive qualities. (See Moisture). The Nocturnal Signs ♉, ♋, ♍, ♏, ♑, and ♓, excel in dryness and moisture. Excess of dryness is caused by ♂. Moderate dryness is produced by the ☉, ♄, and ♂. The ☉ produces dryness due to his heat; ♂ by his hot and fiery nature; ♄ by being remote from the ☉. When masculine, ♀ produces dryness, and moisture when femininely constituted, and as ♀ is variable, produces both dryness and moisture, according to his distance from the Earth and ☽. The ☉, ♅, ♄, ♂, and ♀ tend to dryness of the body and to dry diseases. ♅ exerts a dry influence. ♅ and ♄ are cold and dry, and ♀ so when configurated with them. ♄ causes dryness when occi., and ♂ causes dryness only when occi., and when ori. causes heat and dry-

ness. Dry and Cold are malevolent influences and tend to decay. (See Decay). The elementary qualities Dry and Hot are positive, while Dry and Cold are negative. The Dry and Cold of the left side of the body are more feeble than the Hot and Dry of the right side. (See Left, Right). The elementary qualities Dry and Moist alternate, so that the 12 divisions of the body, as ruled by the 12 Signs, are once dry and once moist, positive and negative in rotation. The following subjects have to do with Dryness, which see in the alphabetical arrangement when not considered here.

Air—A Dry Air—Unusual Dryness of the Air—Eclipses of the ☽ in the 1st Dec. ♈, or in 2nd and 3rd Dec. ♏; ♂ in an angle at the Equinoxes or Solstices, and espec. in ♈, ♋, ♌, and with N. Lat.; ♂ in ♌ at the Winter Solstice, a dry Winter; Comets appearing in the Eastern Quarters of the heavens. (See "Dry Air" under Air; Drought, Heat).

All Diseases—Proceeding from Dryness and Heat—♈ diseases. (See Fever; "Dry and Hot Diseases" under Heat; Parched).

Bellyache—Dry Bellyache—(See Belly).

Body—Dry Body—Dry Constitution—Dry Bodily Temperament—The ☉, ☽, Asc., and many planets in earthy signs at B.; the ☽ from the Full to the 3rd Quarter makes the constitution more dry; the ☽ in ♌ when taken ill, and affl. by the ☉ or ♂, the body is dry and parched (Hor'y); ♂ ori. or occi.; ♂ descending; ♂ or ♀ ruler of the Asc., and occi.; ♀ occi. as regards the ☉ except when ♀ is in ♊; ♈ gives excess of heat and dryness in the body, produces a lean and dry body, and espec. when on the Asc.; born under ♈ or ♑; ♑ on the Asc., or strong at B.; ♈ on the Asc. at B. gives a dry, spare, strong, and moderate sized body. (See "Hot and Dry", "Increased Dryness", in this section).

Cold and Dry Body—Dry and Cold Constitution—Given by the earthy signs, which are cold and dry, and earthy signs on the Asc. at B.; ♄ occi.; ♄ in the Asc. at B., and in power; a cold and dry body ruled by ♄ or ♀ tend to make the nature unprolific, as cold and dry combinations are negative; the Quadrant from the Autumnal Equi. to the Winter Solstice tends to produce a cold and dry body. (See Barren; "Cranian Diathesis" under Cranium; Nervous Temperament, Noxious).

Cold and Dry Diseases—These are diseases of ♅ and ♄, and also of ♀ when ♀ is configurated with them; diseases of the earthy signs, and espec. of ♑. (See Diseases under Mercury, Saturn, Uranus).

Cold and Dry Signs—The earthy signs, ♉, ♍, and ♑.

Cough—Bilious Dry Cough—(See Cough).

Crusts—Dry Crusts—Dried Exudate—(See Crusts).

Death—(See "Dry Habit" in this section).

Destruction—From Dryness—(See "Fountains" in this section).

Diseases Concomicant with Dryness—Diseases Which Arise from Superabundant or Disproportionate Dryness—In general, ♂ sole ruler at an eclipse of the ☉; caused by ☿ when the dominion of death is vested in this planet. (See "Dry Diseases", "Dry and Hot Diseases", in this section; "Dry and Hot Diseases", "Excessive Heat", under Heat).

Disproportionate Dryness—Diseases Arising From—(See "Diseases Concomitant" in this section; Drought, Famine).

Drought—(See Drought, Famine, Heat, etc. Also see "Fountains" in this section).

Dry Body—(See "Body" in this section).

Dry Diseases—♄ and ♈ diseases. (See "Diseases Concomitant", "Dry and Hot Diseases", in this section).

Dry Habit—☿ produces death from diseases which proceed from a dry habit. (See Habit).

Dry and Hot Body—(See "Hot and Dry Body" in this section).

Dry and Hot Diseases—(See "Dry and Hot Diseases" under Heat; Fevers, Parched).

Emaciated and Dry—The Body Dry and Emaciated—(See Emaciation).

Excess of Dryness—In the Body—(See "Body", "Increased", "Superabundance", in this section).

Eyelids—Dryness of—(See Eyelids).

Faeces—Dryness of—(See Constipation; "Hardening" under Faeces).

Fauces—Dry Fauces—(See Fauces).

Fluids—Drying Up of—♄ diseases and afflictions. (See Fluids, Saturn, Suppressions).

Fountains Dry Up—The Drying Up of Fountains, Rivers, Springs, etc.—♂ in power, and lord of the year at Equinoxes or Solstices, tends to an atmosphere parched by hot, dry, pestilential, blasting winds, accompanied by drought, lightnings, fires emitted from the sky, hurricanes, attended with shipwrecks, the failing of rivers, and the drying up of springs. (See Drought, Famine, Fountains, Weather, etc.).

Habit—Dry Habit—(See "Dry Habit" in this section).

Hair—(See "Dry" under Hair).

Head—Hot and Dry Head—(See "Feverish", "Hot Diseases In", "Hot and Dry", under Head).

Heat and Dryness—All Diseases Proceeding From—The ☉ and ♂ are hot and dry, and their diseases tend to be hot and dry; the ☉ and ♂ in asp. to each other, as ☉ ✶ or △ ♂; the ☽ during her First Quarter is hot and dry, and during this time her afflictions tend to increased heat and dryness in the body; ♂ ruler of the Asc., and ori.; ♈ diseases; fiery signs on the Asc. at B., and espec. ♈; many planets in fiery and earthy signs. (See "Hot and Dry Diseases" in this section).

Hot and Dry Air—(See "Hot and Dry" under Air; "Air" in this section).

Hot and Dry Body—Hot and Dry Bodily Temperament—Hot and Dry Constitution—(See "Choleric Temperament" under Choleric; "Hot and Dry Body" under Heat. Also see "Body", "Heat and Dryness", in this section).

Hot and Dry Diseases—(See Fevers; "Dry and Hot", "Fevers", "Hot Diseases", under Heat; Parched; "Heat and Dryness" in this section).

Hot and Dry Plants—The ☉ and ♂ Groups. (See these Groups under Herbs).

Humours—Dry Humours—Humours of the Body Generally More Dry—♂ occi. at B. (See Humours).

Increased Dryness—Of the Body—Dryness of the Body Augmented—The malefics ♄ and ♂ in angles, and ♂ in familiarity with ☿, and the malefics occi. of the ☉, and ori. of the ☽; ☿ or ♂ holding dominion at B., and in familiarity with each other. (See Augmented).

Irritations and Dryness—(See Irritations).

Lean and Dry Body—♈ gives, and ♈ on Asc. (See Lean; "Body" in this section).

Liver—Dry and Cold Liver—(See "Cold and Dry" under Liver).

Melancholy—Dry and Melancholy Distempers—(See "Dry and Melancholic" under Melancholy).

Mischief—From Dryness—(See "Fountains", and the various paragraphs in this section).

Parched and Dry Body—Parched, Dry, and Hot Diseases—(See "Body", "Hot and Dry Body", "Hot and Dry Diseases", in this section; "High Fever" under Fever; "Dry and Hot Diseases" under Heat; Parched).

Plants—Dry and Hot Group of Plants—(See "Hot and Dry Plants" in this section).

Rivers—The Drying Up of Rivers, Springs and Fountains—(See "Fountains" in this section).

Scales—Dry Scale Formations—(See Psoriasis, Scales; "Dry Skin" under Skin).

Signs—The Dry Signs—The Earthy Signs, ♉, ♍, ♑, are cold and dry. The fiery signs ♈, ♌, ♐, are hot and dry.

Skin—Dry Skin—(See "Dry Skin" under Skin).

Sloughing—Dry Sloughing—(See Sloughing).

Spare and Dry Body—(See "Body", "Lean", in this section).

Strong and Dry Body—♈ gives. (See "Body" in this section).

Superabundance of Dryness—Disease and Suffering From—Excess of Dryness In the Body—Dry and Hot Weather—(See "Body"; "Diseases Concomitant", "Excess", "Fountains", "Increased", and the various paragraphs in this section; Drought, Famine; "Extreme Heat" under Heat).

Temperament—Dry Bodily Temperament—(See "Body", "Hot and Dry Body", in this section; Temperament).

Tetter—Dry Tetter—(See Tetter).

Throat—Dry and Feverish Throat—(See "Dry" under Throat).

Tissues—Drying Up of—♄ diseases and afflictions. (See Atrophy, Tissues).

Winter—A Dry Winter—(See Winter).

Withering; Wrinkles.

DUAL-MINDED—Duplicity—The Bicorporeal Signs strong at B., or many planets in them, and espec. in ♊, the sign of The Twins; ♄ and ♂ afflicting ☿; ☿ Sig. in ♋; the ☽ □ or ☌ ☿. (See Deceitful, Dishonest, Double-Bodied, Gemini).

Dual Personality—(See Memory).

Dual-Sexed—(See Hermaphrodite).

DUCTLESS GLANDS—Organs Without Ducts—Endocrine Glands—These Glands are seven in number, and are ruled by the ♏ sign and ♂, taken as a whole. The Ductless Glands are the Pituitary Body, ruled by ♅; the Pineal Gland, ruled by ♆; the Thyroid Gland, ruled by ☿; the Thymus Gland, ruled by ♀; the Spleen, ruled by the ☉; the two Adrenals, ruled by ♃. (See these subjects in the alphabetical arrangement). The substance produced by these Glands is called Endocrine. The ☉ and ☽ acting thru the ♏ sign, and thru the Intestinal and Lumbar branches of the Solar Plexus, thru the Renal, Supra-Renal, Hepatic, Spermatic and Hemorrhoidal Plexuses, affect the Medulla, the Brain, the Pituitary Gland, the Basal Ganglia, the Ductless Glands, the Bladder, Genito-Urinary System, Uterus, Rectum, Anus, Large Intestines, and give way to the Hepatic Diathesis. (See "Basal Ganglia" under Ganglion; "Pathological Action" under Mars; "Petrification" under Stone). The effects of the Ductless Glands today are said to be mostly mental and spiritual. The Occult significance of these Glands is written up in the Chapter on Ductless Glands in the book, "Message of the Stars" by the Heindels.

Disorders Of—General Derangement of the Ductless Glands—♆ diseases and afflictions; ♆ afflicted at B.; ♆ □ or ☌ ♅. Cases of Disorders of—See Figures 17A, 17B, 17C, 17D, in the book "Astro-Diagnosis" by the Heindels. (See "Sugar" under Food).

DUCTS—A Tube Conveying a Liquid—

Bile Ducts—Gall Ducts—(See "Ducts" under Bile).

Nasal Duct—The Tear Duct—(See Tears).

Sebaceous Ducts—(See Sebaceous).

Thoracic Duct—(See Thorax). For other Ducts in various parts of the body, look in the alphabetical arrangement for the subject you have in mind.

DUELS—Affairs of Honour—Contests—Quarrels—Chartering—

Death in Duels—The 7th H. rules and concerns duels, and malefics in this house, and affl. the ☉, ☽, Asc., or hyleg make it dangerous to engage in them; the ☉ Sig. ☌ ♂, death in, or terribly wounded; ♂ just setting in □ or ☍ the ☉ or ☽, and ♃ bearing testimony to ♂;

♂ to the ☌ ☋; ♂ Sig. and affl. the ☽, or the ☽ Sig. ☌ ♂, given to duels, and with danger of death thru them; lord of the Asc. in the 8th H. at the time; the 26° ♉, or the 20° ♏ on the Asc. at B. (See "Death" under Cuts; Gunshot, Quarrels, Sword. Also see Chartering, Contests, Cuts; "Causes His Own Death" under Death; Disputes, Enemies, Feuds, Fighting, Folly, Instruments, Quarrels, Rashness, Stabs, Wounds, etc.).

Injury in Duels—The ☉ Sig. □ or ☍ ♂; ♂ in fiery signs, and ☌ or ill-asp. the Asc. by dir.; ♂ Sig. □ or ☍ the ☉; to engage in a duel when the ☽, ♄, and ♂ are joined together, or in evil aspect, tends to dangerous injury, and great effusion of blood; the 26° ♉ on the Asc.

DULL—Dullness—Dulling—Dull Mind—Lack of Animation—Hebetude—Apathy—Vapid, etc.—

Aches—Dull and Heavy Aches or Pains—(See "Heavy" under Aches).

Appearance—Dull Appearance—♓ on the Asc. at B.; the ☽ Sig. of the party in Hor'y Questions. (See Appearance).

Apprehension Dull—(See "Mind", "Understanding", in this section).

Complexion Dull—(See "Dull" under Complexion).

Comprehension Dull—(See "Mind" in this section; "Weak" under Understanding).

Constitution—The Constitution Dull and Effeminate—(See "Dull" under Constitution; Effeminate).

Disposition Dull—(See "Mind" in this section; Apathy, Lassitude, Lethargy).

Effeminate and Dull—(See Effeminate; "Dull" under Constitution).

Eyes Dull—Heavy, Languid and Sleepy Eyes—(See "Dullness" under Eyes; "Drowsiness" under Sleep).

Genius—The Genius is Dull—(See Genius).

Hebetude—Dulling of the Senses and the Intellect—(See "Mind" in this section; "Dulling" under Senses).

Husband—The Husband is Dull and Timid—(See "Dull" under Husband).

Intellect Dull—(See "Mind" in this section; Intellect; "Smoky Degrees" under Smoky).

Lassitude—(See Lassitude).

Lethargy—(See Lethargy).

Mind—Dull Mind—Dull Disposition—Hebetude—Dull Intellect—Comprehension Dull—Heavy Mind—Dull Capacity, etc.—Tropical and hot climates produce; no asp. to the ☉ or ♂ at B.; the ☽ and ☿ in no asp. with each other or with the Asc.; the ☽ Sig. in ♓; the ☽ Sig. of the person, and the ☽ affl., and ill-dig. at B.; the ☽ sepr. from ☿ and apply to the ☉; the Prog. ☽ to the ☌ or ill-asp. ♆ if ♆ be affl. at B.; the ☽ Sig. in ♑; the ☽ to the ill-asps. ☿ by dir.; ♄ in ♈, apathy and want of passion or feeling; ♄ in ♋, heavy and morose; ♄ affl. ☿ at B.; ♄ in ♋; ♄ ☌ the Asc. by dir.; ♃ affl. and ill-dig. at B.; ♃ Sig. in ♑; ♂ Sig. in water signs, and espec. in ♓; no asp. between ♂

and ☿; no asp. between ♂ and the ☉ at B.; ♀ Sig. in ♋, dull and idle disposition; ♀ in ♏, inert; ♀ affl. in ♈; ♀ ruler of the mind and badly aspected and placed; ☿ ☌ the ☉, and combust; ☿ rising in ♋ or ♓; ☿ ☌ or ill-asp ♄; the cross asps. of ♂ or the ☽ to ☿ beget stupidity; the periodic directions of ♄ to ☿; ☿ Sig. ☌ ♄; ☿ affl. by ♄ at B., a dull wit; ☿ to the ☌ the ☉ by dir.; ☿ in ♉, an inert disposition; the ♋ influence tends to make dull, and timid as the Crab; ♓ on the Asc., the physical condition often tends to clog the mental action; the Asc. to the ☌ or ill-asps. ♄ by dir. (See Action, Apathy, Backwardness; "Brain Fag" under Brain; Chaotic, Clogging, Diminished, Energy, Faculties, Fatigue, Feelings, Heaviness, Hyperaesthesia, Idle, Inactive, Indifferent, Inertia, Intellect, Labour, Languid, Lassitude, Lethargy, Listless, Melancholy, Morose, Motion, Movement, Perception, Rouse, Senses, Sensibility, Slow, Sluggish, Smoky, Stupid, Study, Timidity, Understanding, Weariness; "Weak Mind" under Mind).

Pains—Dull Pains and Aches—(See "Heavy" under Aches; "Dull Pains" under Head; Headaches, Neuralgia).

Senses — The Senses Dulled—Hebetude—(See "Mind" in this section; Senses).

Timid and Dull—♋ influence. (See Timid).

Understanding Dulled—(See "Mind" in this section; Judgment, Understanding).

Unfeeling and Dull—♉ influence.

Wit—A Dull Wit—☿ affl. by ♄ at B.

DUMB—Dumbness—Mute—Without the Power of Speech—Caused by afflictions in the Dumb, or Mute Signs, ♋, ♏, or ♓ at B., or these signs greatly afflicted at conception, or during gestation. These signs are also called Reptilian Signs, as they rule creatures which make no audible sound. The Mute Signs tend to cause impediments of speech, and espec. when ☿ is also afflicted at the same time. Other Causes of Dumbness are,—A ☿ disease, as ☿ rules the speech; caused by the □ and ☍ asps. of ☿; ☿ in a mute, or dumb sign, and affl. by ♄; afflictions to ☿ at B.; ☿ in ♉ in the 12th H., as ♉ rules the vocal organs and ears; ☿ in ♉ in the 12th H. and ☌ ♅, □ ♃, which are the aspects of a case of record; if at conception the ☉ or ☽ be in the 6th or 12th H., and ☿ with one of them in the 12th H., the child will be dumb, altho of good aspects; a mute sign on the Asc., and ☿ be afflicted, or if ☿ be afflicted by a malefic posited in a dumb sign, the native will be dumb, or have a great impediment in his speech; afflictions in the ♋ sign, a mute sign, and slow of voice; afflictions in the mute signs, as these signs are typical of creatures, animals, or insects which make no audible sound. (See Inarticulate; "Impediment", and the various paragraphs under Speech; Voice).

Deaf and Dumb—(See this subject under Hearing).

Deaf, Dumb and Blind—(See Hearing, Mutes).

Deaf, Dumb and Idiot—(See Idiots, Hearing). For further study see Foetus, Mercury, Prenatal Epoch, Speech, Twelfth House).

DUN COMPLEXION — (See "Dull", "Swarthy", under Complexion; "Smoky Degrees" under Smoky).

DUODENUM—The First Part of the Small Intestines—Ruled by the ♍ sign. (See "Small Intestines" under Bowels; "Organs of Digestion" under Digestion; Pylorus).

Inflammation—Of the Duodenum—Duodenitis—♂ affl. in ♍; Subs at SP (8D), and at Spl.P (9D). (See "Inflammation" under Bowels).

Ulcer—Of the Duodenum—♂ affl. in ♍ or ♓; Subs at SP (8D), and at Spl.P. (9D). (See Ulcers).

DURA MATER—The Outer Membrane of the Brain and Spinal Cord—Ruled by ♅, and is much affected when ♅ is in ♈. (See Brain, Meninges, Spine).

DURATION—

Duration of Disease—The Length of the Disease—This may be judged by the nature of the Signs in which the afflicting planets are found, and which cause the illness. The afflictions in cardinal signs show the disease to be very severe, but soon over. Afflictions in fixed signs show long, chronic, stubborn, tedious diseases, and with slow recovery. In common signs, difficult to cure, or incurable, due to the passive and indifferent state of the patient's mind, and amenability to adverse suggestions. For the influences along this line see the following subjects in the alphabetical arrangement—Acute, Alterations, Amelioration, Cardinal, Changes, Chronic, Convalescence, Constancy, Course, Crises, Curable, Death, Decrease; "Better" under Disease; End, External, Fatal, Fever; "Fixed Signs" under Fixed; Force, Increase, Incurable, Invalids, Lingering, Long, Moderation, Modification; "Moon" under Motion; "Mutable Signs" under Mutable; Prolonged, Quick, Recovery, Recuperation, Relapses, Remission, Remote, Resolution, Return, Short, Slow, Tedious, Termination, Violent, Worse, etc.

Duration of Fever—(See "Duration" under Fever).

Duration of Life — (See "Duration" under Life. Also see the various paragraphs under Death).

DUSKY COMPLEXION — (See "Dusky" under Complexion).

DUST — Pneumoconiosis—A Disease of the Lung from Inhalation of Dust—(See "Pneumoconiosis" under Lungs).

DUTY—

Faithful to Duty — (See Honest, Reliable, Trustworthy).

Indifferent to Duty—(See Careless, Dull).

DWARF—Dwarfed—Diminutive Body—Midgets—Arrested Physical or Mental Growth—Due to afflictions at B., or during the prenatal period, to ☿, the ruler of the Thyroid Gland. Degeneration of this Gland tends to Cretinism, and to stop and arrest the growth of the mind and body. Also caused by disturbances of the Pituitary Body, which is ruled by ♅ and the ♒ Sign, and by lack of the Pituitary secretion. An earthy sign on the Asc., and two or three planets in the Asc., tend to make Dwarfs and people under the usual stature, and espec. if ♄ is also in the Asc. At the birth of Dwarfs, the ♒, ♏, or ♑ Signs are usually rising, and also there is usually an affliction between ♄ and ♂, or between ♅ and ♂. The ☌ of the malefic planets ♅, ♄, and ♂, or their ♒ aspects, in fixed signs, tend to; the ☉ and ☽ in the 6th or 12th H., and affl. by ♅, ♄, or ♂; the malefics ♅, ♄, or ♂ in, or afflicting the 5th, 6th, or 12th H., the cusps of these houses, or the cusp of the Asc., or if they be in ♍; ♄ □ ♆; ♃ in ♋, principally in the 6th H., and below the horizon, and with ♓ on the Asc., and the ☽ in ♓; many planets in ♍ in the 6th or 12th H.; ♒, ♏, or ♑ on the Asc.; ♑ on the Asc., and containing ♄, ♀, and ♀ in ☌; the lord of the Asc., and the ☽ in the last degree of a sign, and without Latitude.

Cases of Dwarfs—Birth Data, etc.— See "Dwarf", No. 064, 622, 669, and also "Wilder", The Dwarf Humorist, No. 916, all in 1001 N.N. Also see the Cases on page 49, Chap. 8, in Daath's Medical Astrology, cases of a Dwarf Hunchback, and an Adult Dwarf with the Mind of a Child. There is also the case of the Dwarf, Darius Alden, born Aug. 14, 1842, and died Sept. 22, 1926, height 3 feet, 6 inches. No further birth data available on this case. (For further influences along this line see Arrested, Contracted, Cretinism, Decreased, Deformities, Diminished, Distortions, Growth, Idiocy, Imbecility; "Body" under Large; Malformations, Monstrosities, Myxoedema, Pituitary Body, Prenatal Epoch; "Short Body" under Short; "Small Body" under Small; "Hunchback" under Spine; Thyroid, Undersized, Undeveloped, etc).

DYES—(See Chemists; "Vocation" under Colors).

DYING PERSONS—Persons About to Die—The ruling places at a Solar Eclipse situated in the West tend to affect persons about to die, for good or ill, according to the signs, houses, and aspects, and espec. people born under the signs taking part in the influence. (See Death, Eighth House).

DYNAMIC—Sthenic—Active—Strong— Mars is called the planet of Dynamic Energy, and of Action. The ☉ is also dynamic. The ☉ and ♂ when both strong in the map of birth tend to give great vitality, force, and energy. Mars weak at B., and in no asp. to the ☉, tends to lower the vitality and energy, and to give less of the dynamic force of this planet, and tending to lassitude. Dynamic power is principally given by the Solar Forces being reflected upon us by the ♂ influence, and dynamic energy is the most salient characteristic of ♂. (See Action, Active, Endurance, Energy, Force, Lassitude, Mars, Motion, Movement, Sthenic, Strength, Vitality, etc.).

DYSENTERY—Inflammation and Ulcer-

ation of the Intestinal Mucous Membrane, and with Bloody Evacuations— Bloody Flux—A ♍ disease; ♍ on the Asc.; ♍ on the 6th H.; the ☉, ☽, or ♂ affl. in ♍, and espec. when in the 6th H.; the ☉ to the ill-asps. ♂ by dir.; the ☽ affl. in ♍, or affl. the hyleg therefrom, and espec. with females; the ☽ in ♋, and affl. by the ☉ or ♂; the ☽ in an earthy sign, and to the ☌ or ill-asp. ♂ by dir., and the ☽ hyleg; ♄ in an angle, occi. of the ☉, and ori. of the ☽; ♂ ☌ the ☉ at B., and espec. in the 6th H.; ♂ in ♑ in the 6th H., or affl. the ☽ or Asc.; ♂ in ♍ in the 6th H.; caused by ♀ when the dominion of death is vested in her, and espec. ♀ in ♍ in the 6th H., and affl. the hyleg; Subs at CP, KP (11D), and PP (2, 3, 4L); Subs at PP tend to Chronic Dysentery. (See "Inflammation" under Bowels; Diarrhoea; "Bloody Flux" under Flux).

DYSIDROSIS—Dyshidrosis—Pompholyx—A rare disease, with Bullas and impaired perspiration of the Hands and Feet—Caused by ♂; ♂ affl. in ♍ or ♓. (See Blisters, Hyperidrosis; "Anidrosis" under Sweat).

DYSMENORRHOEA—Painful Menstruation—(See "Painful" under Menses).

DYSPEPSIA—Impaired or Imperfect Digestion—Indigestion—Afflictions in ♋ tend to Dyspepsia of all kinds; a ♋ disease; a ♍ disease, and afflictions in ♍; ♍ on the Asc.; ♋ or ♍ on the Asc., and afflicted; the ☉, ☽, ♄, ♃, or ♂ affl. in ♋; the ☉ affl. in ♍; the ☽ afflicted; the ☽ and ♀ in ♋, and affl. by ♄; the ☽ affl. in ♋, or afflicting the hyleg therefrom; ♄ in ♋ or ♑; ♄ in ♋ and affl. the ☽, tends to chronic dyspepsia; ♂ in ♋ on cusp of 4th H.; ♂ in ♋ or ♑; ♀ affl. in the 6th H., arising from excessive mental or nervous action; the Asc. to the place of ☿ by dir.; Subs at SP. (See Digestion, Hydrochloric, Indigestion, Stomach). Cases of Dyspepsia—See "Stone in Kidney", and "Dyspepsia", pages 89 and 92, in Daath's Medical Astrology.

Chronic Dyspepsia—♄ in ♋, and afflicting the ☽.

Nervous Dyspepsia—♅ or ☿ affl. in the 6th H., and espec. when in ♋ or ♍; Subs at SP (7D).

DYSPHAGIA—Inability to Swallow— (See Deglutition).

DYSPHASIA—Disconnected Speech— (See "Dysphasia" under Speech).

DYSPHONIA—Difficulty in Phonation— (See "Dysphonia" under Larynx; "Aphonia" under Voice).

DYSPNOEA—Difficult or Laboured Breathing—Paroxysms in Breathing— Caused by afflictions in ♊; Subs at LCP (6C), AP (1D), LHP (3D), and Lu.P. Subs at Lu.P (3D) tend to painful and rapid Dyspnoea. (See Angina, Asthma; "Laboured Breathing" under Breathing; Croup, Diaphragm; "Beriberi" under Dropsy; Gas, Heart, Stomach, etc.).

DYSTROPHIA—Imperfect or Faulty Nourishment—Defective Nutrition— (See Nutrition).

DYSURIA—Difficult or Painful Micturition—(See "Strangury" under Urine).

E

EAGLE FEATURES—(See "Eagle" under Features).

EARLY—

Early Death—Short Life—The Life Shortened—The ☉ affl. in the 8th H.; the ☉ and ☽ in common signs, and affl. by malefics, and espec. when in ♓; the ☉, ☽, and ☿ conjoined in a sign of low vitality, and affl. by malefics; the ☽ apply. to the ☌ the ☉; the ☽ sepr. from ♄ and apply. to ♂ if the ☽ be hyleg; ♅ in the 8th H. at B., and death is apt to occur at the subsequent evil asps. of the ☉ to ♅, and cause early death if within orb of the asp. at B.; ♂ affl. in ♏, from sex excesses and loss of vitality; lord of the 10th H. in the 5th, thru feasting and dissipation; the ☌ of the rulers of the 1st and 6th H., or of the 1st and 8th, unless free from affliction; a strong 6th H., but with the hyleg badly afflicted; many planets near cusps of angles, and espec. the malefics; many planets in signs of low vitality, as in ♎, ♑, and ♓, and afflicted, and espec. with these signs on cusp of the Asc. at B.; when planets are near the cusps of angles, death is apt to take place when the afflicting planet reaches the cusp; if planets afflicting the hyleg be in the 4th, 6th, 8th, or 12th H., early death is indicated under the evil directions of these planets to the hyleg if there are no good counteracting aspects. Cases of Early Death—(See "Early Death", No. 428, in 1001 N.N. Also see the Cases and Birth Data in Daath's Medical Astrology, Chap. 14. (For further influences see Accidents, Anareta, Birth, Childhood, Children, Death, Directions, Escapes, Father, Husband, Hyleg, Infancy, Life, Maturity, Middle Life, Mother, Parents, Relations; "Short Life" under Life; Sudden Death (see Sudden); Untimely, Wife, Youth, etc.).

Early Years of Life—Danger In the Early Years—Hurts In—Accidents In—Sickness In—Disorders of—♑ on the Asc., or the ☉ and ☽ in ♑, tend to make the early years weak, and with greater danger of death, and to give a weak body; the native does not tend to be strong in the early years when the lord of the 6th H. is in the Asc., and afflicted, or when ♑ is on cusp of the Asc.; the 19° ♓ on the Asc.; the ☽ affl. in ♑; ♄ in the Asc. at B. tends to falls, bruises, or fractures when ♄ by dir. reaches the rising degree at B.; ♂ in the Asc., accidents, hurts, injuries, etc., when ♂ reaches the ascending degree by dir (See "Early in Life" under Baldness; Childhood, Children; "Animal Heat" under Heat; "Early Life" under Hurts; Infancy, Youth).

EARS—Organs of Hearing—Auditory Organs—Aural, etc.—The Ears in general, the Ossicles, Nerves, and all parts of the Ears, are ruled by the ♉ sign, the external rulership of ♉, and are also influenced by the ♈ Sign. The Ears have special affinity with ♀ and the ♉ Sign. The 12th H. also tends to affect the Ears for good or ill, as this house is closely connected with the Senses, and limitations upon them, and in cases of Deafness, ♀ and the 12th H. are usually badly afflicted, or with ♀ and other planets afflicted in the 12th H. The right ear is said to be ruled by ♄, and the left ear by ♂. In the Hindu System the 3rd H. is assigned to rulership of the ears, and in our System of Astrology, the 1st H. rules and affects the ears. The Auditory Organs are also ruled by ♄ in general, and espec. the right ear, and an afflicted ♄ in ♈ or ♉, in the 12th H. at B. tends to greatly hamper the functions of the ears. The Aural Ducts are ruled by ♀. The Eustachian Tubes leading to the ears from the nasal cavity are ruled by ♀ and ♉. The following subjects have to do with the Diseases and Afflictions of the Ears, and of parts adjacent.

Abscesses In—Accompanied by afflictions in the 3° ♈ or ♎. (See Mastoid. Also see "Discharges", "Meatus", in this section).

All Diseases In—Signified by the 1st H., and planets therein.

Auditory Nerve—Clogging of—(See "Auditory Nerve" under Hearing).

Aural Diseases—(See "Disordered", and the various paragraphs in this section).

Aural Ducts—Ruled by ♀, and an afflicted ♀ tends to disorders of.

Auricles—The External Ear—Are large and great when ♄ is in the Asc. at B., or affl. the Asc., and protruding when ♂ afflicts the Asc.

Blood Effusion—From the Ear—A ♂ disease and affliction; ♂ affl. in ♉; Subs at AT. (See Effusions).

Bony Parts—The Ossicles—The Small Bones of the Ear—Hardening of—Disorders of—Due to mineral deposits by ♄, checking vibration and causing deafness. The bones grow denser when ♀ is afflicted in any part of the map, or in the 12th H.; Subs at AT and AX. (See Hardening; "Deafness" under Hearing).

Buzzing—In the Ears—Caused usually by ♄, and the obstructions or catarrhal conditions caused by ♄, and by diseases in the Eustachian Tubes; Subs at AT. (See Buzzing, Catarrh, Eustachian. Also see Catarrh, Circulation, Clogging, Obstructions, Ringing, in this section).

Catarrh Of—♄ affl. in ♉; Subs at AT. (See "Buzzing" in this section).

Circulation—Sluggish Circulation In—The Circulation Obstructed—Obstruction of the Venous Blood in the Ears—Congestion in the Ears, etc.—The ☉ ☌ ♀ in the 12th H., and ♀ combust, lack of nerve force and vital fluid to the ears; ♄ ☌ ♀ in ♉ in the 12th H.; ♀ and other planets combust in the 12th H. (See "Poor Circulation" under Circulation; Congestion; "Obstruction" under Veins).

Clogging—Of the Auditory Nerve—(See "Auditory Nerve" under Hearing).

Congestion—Congested Circulation In—(See "Circulation" in this section).

Deafness — (See "Deafness" under Hearing).

Defects—In the Ears—♄ in ♒.

Discharges—From Ear—Perforated Drum—♄, ♂, or the ☽ affl. in ♉; Subs at AT. (See Abscesses, Meatus, in this section).

Disordered Ears—Diseased—Afflicted—Afflictions in ♈, ♉, and the 1st or 12th H.; Subs at AT and AX. (See "Ear Trouble", and the various paragraphs in this section).

Drum—The Ear Drum—Tympanum—Disorders of—Perforated Drum—Inflammation of—Tympanitis, etc.—♄ or ♂ affl. in ♉; Subs at AT and MCP tend to inflammation of, and espec. with ♂ in ♉, or ♂ affl. in ♉ in the 12th H.

Ducts—(See "Aural Ducts" in this section).

Earache—Pain In Ear—The Prog. ☽ ☌ a malefic in ♈; ♄ or ♂ affl. in ♈ or ♉; Subs at AT.

Ear Trouble—Cases—See Figures 1A, 1B, 1C, in the book "Astro-Diagnosis", and also Fig. 7, 8, 30, 31, in "Message of the Stars", books by the Heindels. (See "Disordered" and the various paragraphs in this section).

Effusion of Blood—(See "Blood" in this section).

Endolymph—Lack of—♄ in ♉, and espec. when ☌ ♃ or ♀, rulers of the circulation of the blood in the ears.

Eustachian Tubes—Disorders of—(See Eustachian).

External Ear—Auricles—The Outer Ear—(See "Auricles" in this section).

Great Ears — (See "Auricles" in this section).

Hardening—Of the Bony Parts—(See "Bony Parts" in this section).

Hearing—(See Hearing).

Inflammation—In the Ears—General and Prevalent—♂ in ♊, and lord of the year at the Vernal Equinox. (See "Drum" in this section).

Injuries To—♄ or ♂ affl. in ♈ or ♉.

Large Ears—(See "Auricles" in this section).

Left Ear—Pain and Disease In—The left ear in both sexes is ruled by ♂, and Pain, Impediments, Injuries, Hurts, Accidents To, Deafness, etc., in this ear are caused by ♂ afflictions; ♂ afflicted in ♈ or ♉; ♂ or ☿ in the 12th H., and afflicted, or ♂ ☌ ☿ in the 12th H., or ☿ in the 12th, and afflicted by ♂; afflictions in the 12th H. (See Left).

Mastoid Abscesses—(See Mastoid).

Meatus—Aural Meatus—External Auditory Canal—Abscess of—Inflammation of—♄, ♂, or ☽ in ♉, and afflicted; Subs at AT and KP. (See "Abscess", "Discharges", in this section).

Nerve—(See "Auditory Nerve" under Hearing).

Nerve Force—Lack of to Ears—(See "Circulation" in this section; "Deafness", under Hearing).

Nodes—Nodules—Tubercles In—Tophus—A ♄ disease; ♄ affl. in ♉; Subs at MCP (4C), and at KP. (See Tubercles).

Obstructions—Congestion—(See "Circulation" in this section).

Ossicles—(See "Bony Parts" in this section).

Outer Ear—(See "Auricles" in this section).

Pain In—(See Earache, Left Ear, in this section).

Perforated Drum — (See "Drum" in this section).

Polypus—(See "Ear" under Polypus).

Protruding Ears—(See "Auricles" in this section).

Pustules In—A Small Purulent Papule—♂ in ⌑ and lord of the year at the Vernal.

Right Ear—Ruled by ♄. Also strongly influenced by ♃, and with ♃ in ♈. Disease, injury, and pain in the right ear are espec. ♄ afflictions; born under ♄, or with ♄ affl. in ♈, tends to congestions, blood disturbances, and interference with the circulation in this ear. (See "Circulation", "Left", in this section. Also see Right).

Ringing in Ears—Tinnitus Aurium—♄ affl. in ♉; Subs at AX and MCP. (See "Buzzing", "Catarrh", in this section).

Throbbing—Pulsating—Beating—♅ or ♂ affl. in ♉; Subs at AT. (See Palpitation).

Tinnitus Aurium—(See "Ringing" in this section).

Tophus—(See "Nodes" in this section).

Tubercles—(See "Nodes" in this section).

Tympanitis—Inflammation of Drum—(See "Drum" in this section).

Upper Ears—Disorders of—Afflictions in ♈ or ♉; ♄ and ♂ in ♈ or ♉; Subs at AT.

Venous Blood—Obstructed Circulation of—(See "Circulation" in this section).

Vital Fluid—Lack of In Ears—(See "Circulation" in this section).

Weak Ears—Weak Hearing—(See "Weak" under Hearing).

Wounds To—(See "Injuries" in this section).

EARTH—The Earth and Mundane Conditions—Telluric Influences. In Geocentric Astrology the Earth is taken as a center in the Solar System, and all Astrological positions are Geocentric, as they relate wholly to the Earth, the life and conditions on the Earth. (See Geocentric).

Barrenness of—Failure of Crops, etc.—An eclipse of the ☽ in the 2nd Dec. of ♉; eclipses in earthy signs. (See Drought, Famine, Scarcity, Starvation, etc.).

Bloodshed—Bloodshed and Loss of Life from War and Strife Increased Over the Earth—(See "Shedding" under Blood; Shedding, War).

Buried Alive—Under the Earth—(See Burial).

Corn Destroyed—(See Corn, Scarcity).

Earthquakes—♉ and ♏ are considered the earthquake signs, and also all the fixed signs when well-occupied with planets tend to cause them. Also caused by the earthy signs. They occur when planets are in violent signs, and also at the time of, or soon after an eclipse. They are also coincident with the appearance of Comets. Caused by eclipses of the ☉ in ♒ or ♓; an eclipse of ☉ in 2nd Dec. of ♒ or ♓; the ☉ to the ☌ ♄ in an earthy sign during travel brings danger of injury or death in an earthquake; the ☉ and ☽ in fixed signs, and also with heavy afflictions from several major planets in fixed signs at the same time; an eclipse of the ☽ in ♏; ♅, ♄, ♃, and ♂ in ♉ and ♏, and with other planets in fixed signs; ♄ and ♂ in terrestrial signs, and afflicting the Lights; ♄ ☌ ♂ in ♉, ♊, ♌, or ♏, in the 4th H., and on the lower Meridian; ♄ in the 4th H., and affl. the hyleg, subject to injuries or death in an earthquake; ♃ in ♉ or ♏ in ☌, P, or ☍ ♀ or ☿; several planets on or near the Equator; eclipses in the 1st Dec. of ♏; many aspects between the planets exist at the time of; great Comets in their perihelion, and within the orbits of ♅ and ♄; the 19° ♑ on the Asc., subject to earthquake casualties. (See Avalanches, Calamity, Casualties, Catastrophies; "Epidemics" under Cholera; "Danger" under Travel; Volcanoes, etc.).

Earthy Matter—Deficiency of In the Bones—(See "Deficiency" under Bones; Deposits, Minerals).

Earthy Signs—Of the Z o d i a c—The Earthy Signs are ♉, ♍, and ♑, and are cold and dry Signs. Taken collectively they rule the neck, throat, bowels, bones, knees, skin, the flesh, the carbon in the body, and are connected with the mineral salts of the body, the osseous structures, and the concretions. They give the Nervous and Melancholic Temperament. When on the Asc. they tend to give a compact body, but with less vitality and physical power than is given by the Airy or Fiery Signs. ♑ on the Asc. tends to give low vitality, an ill-shaped body, and a melancholic temperament, being the sign of ♄. The ♉ and ♍ Signs tend to strengthen the general health when containing the ☉ and benefics, and not seriously afflicted. The earthy signs are more free from fevers than other signs. Significators in, or earthy signs on the Asc. and 6th H. tend to all chronic, long and tedious diseases, Ague, Intermittent Fevers, and such as proceed from Consumptions or Melancholy. They dispose to falls, fluxes, hanging, and death by beheading. The action of the ☽ is different in all three of the earthy signs. The ☽ well-asp. in ♉ tends to good health, regular functions, and methodical habits. The ☽ in ♍ tends to bowel disturbances and irregularities, irregular intestinal functions, and digestive disorders. The ☽ is very weak in ♑, and tends to irregular functions, and which may be impeded and uncertain. Despondency and melancholy easily result, which tends to lower the vitality and weaken the functional activities. The airy and earthy signs are the least excitable. (See in the alphabetical arrangement the various subjects mentioned in this paragraph). For other subjects which have to do with the Earth, Human Affairs, the Peoples of the Earth, etc., see the following subjects,—A i r, Animals, Calamities, Catastrophies, Cold, Crime, Epidemics, Events, Famine, Fig Trees, Fire, Fish, Floods, Frost, Fruits, Grains, Heat, Herbs, Mankind, Materials, Metals, Minerals, Miseries, Mortality, Murderers, Nations; "Operations" under Nature; Ocean, Pandemics, Perils, Pestilence, Plague, Prevalent, Public, Rain, Rationalism, Reptiles, Rivers, Sadness Everywhere (see Sadness); Scarcity, Seas, Seasons, Seeds, Serpents, Slaughter, Snow, Summer, Tides, Trouble, Vegetation, Vines, Volcanoes, War, Water, Weather, Wheat, Winter, etc.

EARTHQUAKES—(See this subject under Earth).

EASE—Interval of Ease In Acute Diseases—Takes place on the crisis days if the ☽ forms a good asp. to a benefic at the time, or if the ☽ be in good asp. to the lords of the 1st, 9th, 10th or 11th Houses. (See Amelioration; "Better" under Disease; Course, Crises, Intermittent, Interrupted, Magnetic, Moderation, Modification, Recovery, Remission, Remittent,). etc.

Fond of Ease—♉ influence. (See Dull, Idle, Inactive, Indifferent, Inertia, Lassitude, Lethargy, Listless, Sedentery).

Lack of Ease—(See Discomfort, Malaise).

EASTERN PARTS—Eastern Countries—Ruled by ♈. The fiery signs are classed as Eastern Signs.

East Winds—Ruled by ♄.

Much Mortality In—(See "Eastern" under Mortality).

Nobles—Death of In Eastern Parts—(See Nobles).

EASY—

Easy Death—(See "Easy Death" under Death).

Easy-Going—(See "Fond of Ease" under Ease).

EATING—Eater—

Abnormal Eater—(See "Excesses", "Great", "Immoderate", in this section. Also see Gluttony).

Appetite—(See Appetite).

Bowel Disorders—(See "Eating" under Bowels).

Chewing—(See "Fast Eater" in this section; Mastication).

Death—Death from Excess in Eating or Drinking—♀ much affl. at B., and affl. the hyleg in a train of evil directions. (See Drink, Intoxication).

Diet—(See Diet).

Drink—(See Drink).

Epicureans—(See this subject).

Eruptions—(See "Arms" under Eruptions).

Excesses in Eating—Overindulgence in Diet—Love Their Belly—Abnormal

Appetite—Immoderate Eater—Sickness from Overeating—A Great Eater, etc. —Characteristic of ♉ people; the ☉ affl. in ♉, or ♉ on the Asc., and afflicted; the ♉ sign strong at B.; the ☉ affl. by ♃ or ♀; the ☉ ♂ ♅ in ♋ in the 12th H., and in □ or ♂ Ψ, tendency to overeat; the ☉ in ♉, and affl. by ♃; ☉ or ☽ in ♋, ✳ or △ ♀; the ☽ or ♅ □ ♃ or ♀; the ☽ to the ill-asps. ♃ or ♀ by dir.; ♄ ☍ ♀ in ♋; ♄ in ♋, ℞ and □ or ♂ ♂; ♄ affl. in ♋; ♄ ill-dig. at B.; ♄ Sig. of the party in Hor'y Questions; a ♃ disease and affliction; ♃ in ♉, □ or ♉ the ☉; ♃ affl. in ♉, ♋, or ♈; ♃ affl. in ♋ in the 12th H.; ♃ affl. in the 1st or 6th H.; ♃ affl. by the ☽; ♃ or ♀ affl. in ♉; ♃ affl. in ♋, and ♋ on the Asc.; ♃ affl. in ♍, warns against overeating; ♃ affl. in ♉, ♋, or ♍ in the 6th or 12th H.; ♃ ☌ ♂ in ♋ or ♈; ♃ or ♂ affl. in ♋; ♃ in asp. or relation to planets or signs which rule the appetite; ♂ affl. in ♋; ♂ Sig. □ or ♂ ♃ or ♀; ♂ ♋, □ or ♂ Ψ, ♃ or ♀; ♂ affl. in ♉; ♂ ♉, □ or ♂ Ψ, ♅, ♃, or ♀; ♀ in ♉, ♋, or ♍, and affl. by ♃, ♄, ♂, or the ☽, tend to overindulgence of the appetite and indisposition therefrom; ♀ Sig. in ♈; ♀ in ♋, and affl. by the □ or ♂ ♂; ♀ affl. in ♉; ♀ affl. in ♎; ♀ in ♋ and affl. by the ☽; ♀ affl. in the 5th H.; ♀ in ♌ or ♓ warns against overeating and indiscretions in diet; the Asc. to the ill-asps. ♀ by dir., and ♀ affl. at B.; ♓ on the Asc. or 6th H. at B., and the ☉, ☽, or other planets in ♓, and afflicted; afflictions in ♍ tend to overeating, excesses in drink, food, etc., and disease from; ♉, ♋, ♍, ♈, or ♓ on the Asc., and afflicted. (For further influences along this line see "Abnormal" under Appetite; Carbuncles, Cravings, Diet, Digestion, Drink, Epicureans, Excesses, Extravagance, Feasting, Food, Gastric, Gluttony, Habits; "High Living" under High; "Impure Blood" under Impure; Indigestion, Indulgence; "Enlarged Liver" under Liver; Noxious Growths, Obesity, Overindulgence, Plethora, Stomach, Surfeits, Toxaemia, etc.).

Fast Eater—Bolts the Food—Eats Hurriedly—The ☽ or ♃ in ♋, ☌ ♂; ♅ ☌ ☽ in ♋, and affl. by the □ or ♂ ♂; fast eating should be avoided when ♅ is in ♍ and afflicted; ♄ in ♋, and □ ♂; ♂ ♂ ☽ in ♋; ruler of the Asc. ☌ ♂.

Feasting—(See Feasting).

Feeding—(See Feeding).

Food—(See Diet, Food).

Gluttony—Gormandizing—(See Gluttony).

Great Eater—Goes to Extremes In Eating—(See "Excesses" in this section; "Fondness" under Food).

Hearty Eater—Characteristic of ♉ people; ♉ on Asc., or ☉ in ♉; ♃ in ♉, □ or ♂ ☉; ♃ affl. in ♋ in 12th H. (See "Excesses" in this section).

Hurriedly—Eats Hurriedly—(See "Fast Eater" in this section).

Immoderate Eater—Abnormal Eater—(See "Excesses", "Hearty", in this section).

Indiscretions—In Eating—Due to an afflicted ♃ or ♀; ♃ affl. in ♉ or ♋; ♀ affl. in ♋. (See "Ailments", "Evil Diet",

under Diet; Feasting, Gluttony, Indiscretions, Obesity, Overindulgence, Plethora, Surfeits. Also see "Excesses" in this section).

Lives to Eat—(See Epicurean).

Moderate—In Eating and Drinking— □ influence—(See "Moderate" under Drink).

Over-Eating—Tendency To—Sickness From—(See "Excesses", "Indiscretions", "Sickness", in this section).

Sickness—From Overeating—♃ affl. in' ♉; ♃ in ♋ on the Asc., and afflicted; ♀ affl. in ♎; the ♉ sign strong at B. (See "Excesses", "Indiscretions", in this section).

Surfeits—From Excess In Eating— See "Evil Diet", "Excesses", under Diet; Obesity, Puffing, Surfeits. Also see "Excesses" in this section).

Swallowing Difficult—(See Deglutition).

Wrong Tendencies—In Eating or Feeding—Should be avoided when ♂ or ♀ are affl. in ♍, or in the 6th H. (For further influences along this line see Assimilation, Digestion, Gastric, Indigestion, Intemperance, Nutrition; "Hot Stomach" under Stomach; Tumors, Wasting, etc.).

ECCENTRIC—Eccentrics—Odd—Peculiar—Queer—Freakishness—Misunderstood By the Common People—Caused principally by the ♅ influence; ♅ ascending at B., or with the chief Significator in the nativity; ♅ in the Asc., or 1st H.; ♅ in the 10th H.; ♅ in any asp. to ♀, and espec. in □ or ♂ asp.; ♅ □ or ♂ ♄; ♅ affl. in ♊, ♐, ♑, ♒, or ♓; the ☽ to the ☌ or ill-asp. ♅ by dir.; the ☽ and ♀ unconnected with each other or the Asc., and with ♄ and ♂ angular and ori., and the benefics setting and ori., and with ♅ and ♀ also partaking in the scheme. (See "Fastidious" under Diet; Dress, Erratic, Fancies, Ideals, Ideas, Imagination, Independent, Judgment, Misunderstood, Notions, Occult, Peculiar, Persecution, Tastes, etc.).

ECLAMPSIA—An Epileptic Seizure— (See Convulsions, Epilepsy; "Puerperal Fever" under Puerperal; Spasms).

ECLECTICS—The Medical School of— (See Healers).

ECLIPSES—Eclipses affect those individuals whose maps of birth have configurations similar to those at the time of the eclipse, and who may also be living under the shadow of the eclipse, or if it is visible to them. At a Solar Eclipse the Solar activity is depleted and low. At the New Moon, if an Eclipse of the ☽, the Lunar activity is more depleted than that of the ☉. Eclipses are portends which should not be overlooked. (See Lunations). The effect of an Eclipse of the ☉ endures a year for every hour the ☉ is eclipsed, and a month for every hour the ☽ is eclipsed. An Eclipse of the ☉ especially falling on the places of malefics in the radical map tend to renew and increase the original strength of such malefic, whether it relate to trouble, sickness, or death. No effect of an Eclipse can be very good even tho falling on the place of a benefic, but the evil effects ascribed to them are very probable. The lord of an Eclipse being in a human sign, its evil effects will fall upon Mankind. (See "Human Signs" under Human). They are more important, and more serious in their effects if they happen on the birthday, and take part in the Solar Revolution. A male born at an Eclipse of the ☉ may never breathe, or expire soon after birth, and so with a female born at an Eclipse of the ☽. (For Cases and Birth Data of death of Males born at time of a Solar Eclipse, see "Austria", No. 152, and "Short Life", No. 775, in 1001 N.N.). An Eclipse of the ☉ threatens some male member of the family with sickness, hurt, or death, and an Eclipse of the ☽ some female member. An Eclipse falling on the ☽ in a child's map denotes hurt to the mother; falling on the ☉, hurt to the father; on the place of ♃, hurt to an uncle; on the place of ♂, to a brother; on the place of ♀, hurt to a sister; on the place of ☿, to an aunt. (For the further mention of Eclipses, and the diseases and afflictions they cause, see Air, Bubo, Calamity, Cattle, Childbirth, Cholera, Cough, Death, Disaster, Drought, Earthquakes (see Earth); Endemic, Epidemics, Events, Fainting, Famine, Fever, Floods, Fruit, Functions, Influenza, Mankind, Middle Life, Miseries; "Full Moon", "Metonic Cycle", "New Moon", under Moon; Mortality, Murder, Old Age; "Virus" under Pestilence; Pirates, Plague, Public, Rain, Revolutionary, Rottenness, Scarlet Fever, Sedition, Shipwreck, Storms, Trouble, Volcanoes, War, Weather, Wind).

ECSTASY—Religious Ecstasy—(See "Beside One's Self" under Excitable; "Ecstasy" under Religion).

ECZEMA—Inflammation of the Skin, with Lymph Exudation—Weeping Eczema—A ♑ disease; afflictions in ♒ and ♑, or with these signs on Asc.; ♄ or ♃ affl. in ♑; ♃ affl. in the 6th H. in ♑; ♃ in ♑, from sluggish circulation; ♃ in signs which rules the arms, hands, legs and feet tends to in these parts; ♂ in ♒ and affl. the hyleg; ♀ in ♈ or ♎, and affl. the ☽ or Asc.; ♀ affl. in ♈ or ♎ in the 6th H.; the ☽ or ♀ afflicted, weeping Eczema; the ☽ hyleg in ♏, and espec. with females.

Head and Face—Eczema of—♀ affl. in ♈; ♀ in ♈ or ♎ in the 6th H., and afflicted; ♀ in ♎ and affl. the ☽ or Asc.; Subs at KP, and Local. (See Exudations, Herpes, Ringworm, Skin Diseases, Tetter).

Salt Rheum—Chronic Eczema—♄ affl. in ♑. (See Rheum).

EDEMA—Oedema—(See Dropsy, Oedema, Serum, Swellings).

EDGED TOOLS—Sharp Tools—Injuries By—(See Cuts, Duels, Instruments, Stabs, Sword).

EDUCATION—(See "Active Mind" under Active; Dull, Genius, Intellect, Knowledge, Learning, Mental, Mind, Perception, Reading, Science, Study, Understanding, etc.).

EFFECTS—
Directions—Effects of—(See Directions).

Disease—The Constancy and Duration of the Effects of Disease—(See Constancy).

EFFEMINATE—The Luminaries in female signs, configurated together with ♂ and ♀ tend to make men effeminate, lustful, salacious, wanton, and to deviate from the limits of nature, and to make women masculine, and espec. if ♂ and ♀ be also in feminine signs; the ☉ and ☽ both in masculine signs, configurated together, and with ♂ and ♀, females will be salacious, of a masculine turn, and men will be effeminate; the ☉ Sig. ♂ ♀, soft and effeminate; ♅ in the Asc. with males; the bad asps. of ♅ to the Sigs. tend to, as to the ☉, ☽, Asc., M.C., or to ♀ or ☿; ☿ in ♓, partile the Asc., very foppish and effeminate; airy signs on the Asc., and people born under them, tend to be effeminate; the 3rd decanate of ♈ on the Asc., ruled by ♀; the ♋ and ♎ influences tend to, and with many planets in these signs, and when the positive planets, as the ☉, ♅, and ♂ are in positive, or masculine signs. (See Soft).

Appearance—Effeminate In Appearance—♂ Sig. in ♎. (See "Feminine Degrees" under Female).

Constitution—Effeminate In Constitution and Disposition—The ☉ Sig. ♂ ♀; the ☉ or ☿ Sig. in ♓; ♋ gives, and with ♋ on Asc.; the 6th face ♑ on Asc., and to have a weak and vacillating nature; the ♓ influence tends to, and with ♓ on the Asc.; the 4th face ♐ on Asc. (See "Dull" under Constitution).

Men—Men Effeminate—The Voice Effeminate In Men—Due to degeneracy, sex excesses, and afflictions to ♉ and ♏. A high and effeminate tenor voice is often produced by castration, affecting the ♉ and ♏ signs which rule the voice and larynx, and many tenor singers in Italy are eunuchs. (See the first part of this section. Also see Deviations; "Castration" under Testes; "Coarse Voice" under Voice).

Signs—Effeminate Signs—♓ is the only one so called.

Women—Masculine Women—(See the first part of this section. Also see Deviations; "Fixed Signs" under Fixed; "Degrees" under Male; "Coarse Voice" under Voice).

EFFERVESCENT—Bubbling Over—Effervescent Mental Activity—Over-Active Mind—♂ and the ☽ influences combined, being fire and water, tend to displays of feeling, anger, and the dissipation and dispersal of brain force, and eruptive conditions. (See "Over-Active Mind" under Active; Anger, Dispersals, Hyperactivity, Impulses, Riotous, Temper, Violent).

EFFLORESCENCE—Redness of the Skin—Rashes—Exanthem—(See Eruptions, Exanthema, Rashes, Red, Roseola, Rubefacient, Skin).

EFFUSIONS—Extravasation of Fluid Into the Body Tissues or Cavities—
Blood—Effusion of Blood Prevalent—

A ♂ affliction; ♂ in ♌ at the Vernal Equi., and lord of the year, and chiefly in places ruled by ♌ (see "Leo Rules" under Nations); ♂ in ♍ at the Vernal, and lord of the year, and espec. in Northern Parts, and in places subject to ♍. (See "Shedding" under Blood; "Virgo Rules" under Nations; "Northern Parts" under Northern; "War and Bloodshed" under War).

Ears—Effusion of Blood From—(See "Blood Effusion" under Ears).

Menstrual Effusions—(See "Profuse", "Vicarious", under Menses).

Profluvial Effusions—A Flowing Out —Discharges Which Leave the Body— A ☽ disease and affliction. (See Discharges, Hemorrhage, Humours, Menses, Watery, etc.).

Serous Effusions—(See Serous).

Tissues—Effusions Into—(See Dropsy, Hemorrhage, Oedema, Osmosis, Tissues). For further influences along this line see "Loss of Blood" under Blood; Catarrhs, Discutient, Evacuations, Expectoration, Fluids, Fluxes, Haemoptysis, Kicks, Rheum, Serum.

Treatment for Effusion—(See Resolvent).

EGO—
Egotistical—The influences of the fire, earth, and water signs are instinctively egotistical, while the airy signs are self-conscious. The □ and 8 aspects to ♃ tend to. In Hor'y Questions ♄ Sig. in ♎. (See Pretender).

Exaggerated Ego — Egoism — Ego Mania—♂ associated with ☿, usually by the ☌ or 8; ♂ ☌, □, or 8 ☿, in angles, or in the 3rd or 9th H.; ☿ and the ☽, the mental rulers, both afflicted, or afflicting each other. (See Character, Genius, Giants, Judgment, Opinions, Religion, Saint Vitus Dance, Selfishness, Self-Righteousness, Soul, etc.). Case—See Chap. 13, Daath's Medical Astrology.

EIGHTH HOUSE — The house of ♏, ruled by ♂, and called the House of Death, and denotes the time and manner of death. It is classed as one of the evil houses, along with the 4th, 6th, and 12th Houses. It is a Terminal House, and forms one of the angles of the Terminal Triangle. (See Terminal). This being a terminal house, it indicates the end of physical life, the sundering of soul and body, the transition from the physical to the spiritual. It concerns disease, death, the nature, kind and quality of death. The different planets in this house at B. indicate the kind and nature of death, according to the nature of the planet. It is one of the Anaretical places of the map. (See Anareta). Benefics here at B. tend to an easy and natural death, and ♃ in this house tends to long life, and a natural death. Malefics in this house tend to a more sudden, accidental, or violent death. Neptune and the ☽ in this house tend to death by drowning; ♅ here, a sudden death, as by an explosion; ♂ here, a violent death, as by accident, injury; ☿ here, death by consumption. This house also rules Fear, Anguish, the Bladder, the Privy Parts, Poisons, and Poison Death.

It is a feminine house, and denotes the Genitals and Sex Organs. Its Colors are gray and black. (See the subjects mentioned in this paragraph. Also see "Eighth House" under Death).

Diseases Ruled By—Hemorrhoids, Rectal Diseases, Stone, Strangury, Diseases of the Bladder, Genitals, Generative, Reproductive and Sex Organs. (See these subjects. Also see "Scorpio Diseases" under Scorpio).

ELASTIC FIBER—(See Fiber).

ELATION—(See "Emotional Exaltation" under Emotions).

ELBOWS—In the arms, the elbows correspond to the knees in the legs. The knees are ruled by ♑, and the elbows by ♋, the opposite sign. The Elbow is under the external rulership of the ♋ sign, and the Elbow Joint is under the structural rulership of ♋. In a general way also the ♊ sign is said to rule the arms, hands, and shoulders. (See Arms).

Ankylosis Of—Dislocation of—Fracture of—Disorders of, etc.—♄ or ♂ affl. in ♋. (See Ankylosis, Dislocations, Forearm, Fractures, Hands, Joints).

ELDERLY PEOPLE—Aged People— (See Adults, Grandparents, Maturity, Middle Life, Old Age).

ELECTRIC—The positive or electric Planets are the ☉, ♅, ♃, and ♂, and are alkaline in action. (See Alkaline). ♅ espec. is electric, and rules electricity. The electric planets produce heat in the body, and are expansive, and when well placed at B. conduce to a positive, confident and forceful state of mind, and correspond to the warmth and expansion of the physical functions. (See Day, Electricity, Environment, Magnetic, Positive, Tonic).

Electric Pains—Caused by ♅; ☿ in ♈, and affl. by ♅, electric pains in the head. (See Pain).

Electro Signs—Positive and Negative —See "Electro" under Signs).

ELECTRICITY—This is the force of the ☉ reflected thru ♅. It is ruled by ♅, and ♅ rules the Ether thru which electricity travels. (See Ether; "Operations" under Nature).

Accidents By—♅ setting in 8 to the Luminaries; ♅ afflicting the Asc. (See Lightning, Machinery).

Death By—Or by Electric Apparatus —♅ ☌ or ill-asp. the ☉; ♅ affl. the ☉ at B., or by dir.; ♅ affl. the hyleg by dir.

Electrocution—Death In the Electric Chair by Sentence of Law—In these cases ♅ is espec. strong, and usually afflicts the ☉, ☽, Asc., M.C., or hyleg at B., or by dir., which predisposes to such a death if convicted of murder. (See Judge).

Healing by Electricity—People who have ♅ strong at B., as in the Asc., or M.C., and well-aspecting the ☉, are usually susceptible to the healing influence of electricity when it is applied in the right manner, and with the proper current. (See Healing, Magnetism).

Pains—Electrical Pains—(See "Electric Pains" under Electric).

Shock by Electricity—Caused by ♅ influence and afflictions. (See "Electricity" under Shock).

ELEGANT—

Elegant Body—Elegantly Formed—(See Beautiful, Handsome).

Elegant Mind—Refined Mind—☿ Sig. ☌ ♃; ☿ Sig. ☌ or good asp. ♀; ♀ Sig. ☌ or good asp. ☿. (See "Activity", "Quickened", under Mental; "Good Mind" under Mind).

Elegant Proportions—Of Body—♃ Sig. ☌ ☿ and ☿ well-dig., angular, and free from affliction; ♀ Sig. ☌ ☿, and both well-dignified; ♀ as Sig. in Hor'y Questions; born under ♀; given by the ✶ and △ asps. of ♀ or ☿ if well-dignified; ♎ on Asc. (See Beautiful, Handsome, Well-Proportioned).

Tall and Elegant—Tall and Handsome Body—The ☉ Sig. in ♐; ♃ in ♎, partile asp. the Asc.; ☿ ♎, partile the Asc., but not thin; born under ♀ and ♀ ori.; ♎ on the Asc. (See Tall).

ELEMENTAL QUALITIES—Of the Body—(See Cold, Dry, Heat, Moisture, and note the various combinations, such as Cold and Dry, Cold and Moist, Dry and Hot, Moist and Hot, etc. Also see "Bodily Temperaments" under Temperament).

ELEMENTS—Exposure to the Elements, resulting in Ill-Health — Exposure in Travel, Causing Sickness, etc. — (See Exposure, External; "Weather" under Travel; "Wet" under Journeys).

Elemental Signs—The Elemental, or Temperamental Signs, are the Fire, Air, Earth, and Water Signs. (See "Air Signs" under Air; "Earthy Signs" under Earth; "Fire Signs" under Fire; "Signs" under Water).

The Elements — Fire, Air, Earth, Water—(See these subjects).

ELEPHANTIASIS—Chronic Oedema In the Skin—Hypertrophy of Cellular Tissue—Afflictions in ♉ or ♏, and due to disturbances of coordination; Subs at AT, KP, and Local. (See Enlargements, Hypertrophy, Oedema, Skin).

In Arms—And Hands—Afflictions in ♉; Subs at MCP (5C), LCP (6C), AP, and CP.

In Skin—Afflictions in ♉; Subs at AT, AX, CP, KP, Local. (See Hypertrophy, Oedema).

ELEPHANTS—Large Beasts—The 12th H. conditions show profit or loss thru, sickness or death of, etc.

Injuries By—Hurts or Death By—Malefics in the 12th H. (See Animals, Beasts, Cattle, Horses, Quadrupeds).

ELEVATED PLANETS — Above the Earth, or Horizon, In a Nativity—The ☉ is more powerful in a day nativity, being elevated above the Earth, and in a night nativity the ☽ is more powerful when elevated, in which case the ☉ rules by day and the ☽ by night. The ☽ to be in her power should be above the Earth by night, and below the Earth by day. The planet nearest the midheaven, the M.C., at B. is the most elevated planet, and powerful in matters of health and disease. The ☽ elevated above the Earth in a nocturnal map tends to more regular and normal functions, and to weakened functions when elevated in a day nativity. A malefic elevated above the Lights denotes sickness, misfortune, death, and if the malefic is Anareta, a violent death. If a malefic be elevated above a benefic, such benefic cannot save, but if the benefic be elevated above the malefic, it will destroy or modify its anaretic tendency, and if also both the ☉ and ☽ be elevated above the malefics, it greatly lessens the injurious effects of the malefics. (See Anareta, Majority, Power, Rising, Setting).

ELEVENTH HOUSE—This House is affiliated with ♒, the 11th Sign. It is a masculine house. It rules the Legs, Calves, Ankles. Also rules Friends, Children, Stepchildren, the Hopes, Wishes and Desires. Its Colors are Saffron and Deep Yellow. This House is called "The Good Daemon" by Ptolemy. In matters of children, and as to the indications of fruitfulness or barrenness, this house is closely associated with the 5th H., as the 5th and 11th are opposite and supplemental houses, and when the 5th H. conditions tend to deny children, they are often promised if the Benefics, or the ☽, be in the 11th H., and well-aspected. The 11th H. signifies all diseases in the legs from the knees to the ankles, and in the shin bone, shank, etc. When in this house at B., ♄ brings despair, false friends, and death of children; ♂ here brings false friends, ruin, and wicked children. (See Children, Fifth House, Friends, Fruitful, Hopes, Wishes, and other subjects mentioned in this paragraph).

ELIMINATION—Excretion—The Eliminative Organs—The Organs of Elimination and Excretion are ruled by the ♏ Sign. Elimination of Urine thru the Bladder and Urethra is ruled by ♏; elimination thru the Kidneys by ♄ and his exalted sign ♎; thru the Skin, by ♄, which planet rules the Skin. (See Cleansing, Excretion, Faeces, Fever, Inflammation, Poisons, Secretions, Sweat, Uric Acid, Urine, Wastes, etc.).

Carbonic Acid Gas—Elimination of—(See Carbon).

Disorders—Of Elimination—Caused by ♄ and his afflictions.

Faulty Elimination—Afflictions in ♏ cause faulty elimination of the kidney secretions, and the retention of calcareous and poisonous matter, tending to Stone, Sand, Gravel, Disease, Tumors, Toxaemia, etc.

Hindered — Retarded—Impeded — Stopped—Obstructed—Faulty, etc.— Due to the obstructing and retarding influence of ♄; ♄ affl. in ♉, ♏, or ♎; ♄ to the ill-asps. his own place by tr. or dir.; afflictions in ♏, and espec. ♄ affl. in this sign; ☋ in ♏. (See Accumulative, Fluids, Functions, Impeded, Obstructions, Retarded, Stoppages, Suppressions, Tumors, etc.).

Impeded — (See "Hindered" in this section).

Kidneys—(See "Faulty" in this section).

Obstructed—(See "Hindered" in this section).

Poisons—(See "Elimination" under Poisons).

Rectal Elimination—Obstructed—(See Constipation, Expulsion, Faeces, Rectum).

Retarded—(See "Hindered" in this section).

Skin—Elimination Obstructed In—(See the first part of this section).

Stopped—(See "Hindered" in this section).

Sweat—Perspiration—(See "Lessened" under Sweat).

Urine—The Elimination of Urine Retarded—(See "Elimination" under Urine).

Wastes—Elimination of—(See Wastes).

Water—Elimination of from the System—(See "Elimination" under Water).

EMACIATION—Loss of Flesh—Leanness—Tabefactions—Atrophy—Wasting—Marasmus—Thin Body, etc.—A ♄ disease; ♄ in an angle, occi. of the ☉ and ori. of the ☽; ♄ in ♓ occi., and affl. the ☉, ☽, or Asc., and the hyleg much afflicted at B. (See Assimilation, Atrophy, Decay, Degeneration, Destructive, Diminished, Flesh, Hardening, Lean, Marasmus, Tabes; "Body" under Thin; Tuberculosis, Wasting).

Body Dry and Emaciated—The ☉ in ♌ or ♒, ♂, P, □ or ☍ ♅ or ♄; ♄ ♂ ☉ or ☽ in the 6th H.; ♄ in ♑ in the Asc., and afflicted. (See Dry).

Consumption—Emaciation With a Consumption—Caused by ♀ when the dominion of death is vested in her. (See Consumption, Wasting).

Progressive Emaciation—Gradual and Progressive—(See Malnutrition, Tabes).

Skeleton—A Living Skeleton—(See Skeleton).

EMBALMING—(See "Silver Cord" under Silver; Undertakers).

EMBOLISM—The Obstruction of a Blood Vessel by a Blood Clot or Embolus—(See Clots, Infarcts, Obstructions, Thrombus).

EMBRYO—A Fecundated Germ Up To the Fourth Month—The Foetus—(See Foetus. Also see Abortion, Conception, Gestation, Miscarriage, Pregnancy, Prenatal Epoch).

Embryonic Tumor—Embryonic Connective Tissue Tumor—(See Sarcoma).

EMERALD—A Mineral under the rule of the ☽.

EMETICS—Emesis—An Agent Causing Emesis, or Vomiting—A Therapeutic Property of ♀ and the ☽. The best time to give an Emetic is when the ☽ and lord of the Asc. are above the horizon, and the ☽ in one of the ruminant, or cud-chewing signs, as in ♈, ♉, or ♑. In using a drug to produce Emesis, Apomorphine and Ipecac are standard in use among Physicians. (See Antiperistalsis, Ipecac, Medicines, Nausea, Ruminant, Vomiting).

EMISSIONS—Ejections—Ejaculations—They are greatest at the Full ☽. (See "Full Moon" under Moon).

Loss of Seed—Involuntary Losses of Semen—Wet Dreams—(See "Emissions" under Semen).

Vital Fluids—Emission of—Depletion of—(See "Fluid" under Vital). Also see Discharges, Effusions, Evacuations, Hemorrhage, Haemoptysis; "Nose Bleed" under Nose.

EMOLLIENT—An Agent which softens and relaxes the tissues to which applied, as Hot Fomentations, Poultices, Oils, Resolvents, etc. A Therapeutic Property of ♃ and ♃ Remedies. (See Jupiter).

EMOTIONS—The Feelings—The Emotions arise in the Desire Body. (See "Desire Body" under Desire). In a general way ♂ is king and ruler of the emotional nature. The ☉ rules the emotional nature in women, which makes them more liable to Hysteria. Venus has to do with all complaints which arise from disturbances of the emotions. When ♆ is strong in the map of birth people are easily swayed by their emotions, and become subject to Hysteria, Crying Spells, Psychic Storms, Fainting and Trance conditions, and espec. when ♆ is afflicted, or affl. the ☉, ☽, ☿, or the Asc. The emotions are made prominent by a predominance of the watery signs and elements in the map of birth, and many planets in water signs. Also the Fixed Signs relate to feeling and emotion. The Astral Body is the seat of the emotions and desires, which are principally connected with the watery signs. (See Astral Body, Desires, Excitable, Fainting, Feelings, Hysteria, Impulses, Psychic, Sensation, Sensational, Trance; "Signs" under Water).

Arrested Emotions—Emotional Deterioration—Lack of Emotion—Weak Emotional Nature—♄ strong at B., as in the Asc., or M.C., and affl. the ☉, ☽, ☿, or Asc.; many planets in air or earth signs at B., with an airy or earth sign on the Asc., as these signs tend to depress and restrain the emotions, while the fiery and watery signs stimulate them.

Depressed Emotions—(See "Arrested" in this section).

Discord—(See "Mind" in this section).

Disorders Of—♆ strong in the map, but severely afflicted by malefics, or ♆ affl. the ☉, ☽, ☿, Asc., or hyleg; ♂ affl. by ♆, ♅, or ♄. (See Anger, Anxiety, Dejection, Dementia, Depression, Desires, Ecstasy, Equilibrium, Exaltation, Excitable, Fear, Frenzy, Fury, Hypochondria, Hysteria, Insanity, Madness, Mania, Melancholy, Passion, Perversions, Worry, etc. Also note the various paragraphs in this section).

Disturbances Of—Complaints Arising From—Due principally to ♀ influence, and afflictions to ♀; also caused by ♆ and ♂ influences. (See the various paragraphs in this section).

Emotionalism—The ☽ influence tends to; the ☉ or ☽ in ♓; the ☽ ♂ ♅ in a fire or water sign; many planets in fire or water signs; ♀ affl. in ♏; the 25° ♌ on the Asc. (See Romance).

Exaltation — Emotional Exaltation— Elation — Devotional — Religious Awakening—Caused by the afflictions of Ψ and δ; Ψ progressed in $\ast$ or $\triangle$ h in the radical map, or vice versa. (See Ecstasy, Religion).

Instability—Of the Emotions—Afflictions in fiery signs. (See Moods).

Intensified Emotions — Over-Emotional—The $\odot$, $\mathbb{D}$, and many planets in the watery signs; Ψ affl. in $\simeq$; $\Psi \ast$ or $\triangle \delta$. (See Passion).

Lack of Emotion—(See "Arrested" in this section).

Mind and Emotions—Inner Discord Between—Afflictions to Ψ or $\simeq$, or afflictions in or to any of the airy signs, causes inharmony and maladjustment, and often resulting in a quarrelsome nature. (See Irritations, Quarrelsome).

Perversion—Emotional Perversions— (See "Desire Body" under Desire; Perversions).

Psychic—Psychic and Emotional Disturbances—(See Psychic).

Quarrelsome—(See "Mind" in this section; Quarrelsome).

Restrained — (See "Arrested" in this section).

Sensations— (See Astral Body; "Desire Body" under Desire; Sensations).

Spasmodic Emotions—$\mathbb{H}$ in Ω in the Asc., and in $\aleph$ δ in the 7th H.; $\mathbb{H}$ influence; $\mathbb{H} \circ \mathbb{D}$ in the Asc. or 10th H. (See Spasmodic).

Stimulated Emotions — (See "Arrested" in this section).

Swayed by Emotion—Ψ strong at B. (See the Introduction to this Article).

Uncontrolled Emotions—$\mathbb{H}$ in $\circ$ or evil asp. the $\odot$; $\Psi \square$ or $\aleph$ $\mathcal{U}$.

Weak—The Emotions Weak—(See "Arrested" in this section).

EMPHYSEMA—A Distention of the Tissues with Air, or Other Gases—A $\mathbb{H}$ disease and affliction. (See Air, Distentions, Flatulence, Gases, Uranus).

Chest—Emphysema of—(See Chest).

Pleural Emphysema—(See Pleura).

EMPLOYMENT—The Business—The Vocation—(See Business, Occupation, Vocation).

Accidents—In the Employment—The $\odot$ ruler of the 9th or 10th H. at B., and to the $\circ$ or ill-asp. $\mathbb{H}$ by dir.; $\mathbb{H}$ in the 6th H.; $\mathbb{H}$ affl. to the $\odot$ at B., and to the $\circ$ or ill-asp. the Asc. by dir.; δ affl. in the 6th H. (See Machinery, Mangled, Occupation).

Death—Danger of Death by Machinery in the Employment—(See Machinery). Danger of death in the trade or Employment occurs under the evil directions of $\mathbb{H}$ to the hyleg, or Giver of Life; $\mathbb{H}$ afflicted at B., and to the $\circ$ or ill-asps. the Asc. by dir., and espec. if the Asc. be hyleg at B.; the $\mathbb{D}$ to the $\circ$ or ill-asps. $\mathbb{H}$ by dir. (See Accidents, Air, Burns, Electricity, Explosions, Fire, Heat, Injuries, Liquids, Mines, Railroads, Residence, Sea, Scalds, Ships, Travel, Vehicles, Voyages, Water, etc.).

EMPTY—Empty and Void of Knowledge—(See "Void Of" under Learning; "Void Degrees" under Void).

EMUNCTORY DUCTS—And Organs— (See Excretion).

ENCEPHALON—Encephalic—The Brain —Pertaining to the Brain—

Encephalic Ailments—Afflictions in Ψ or $\simeq$. (See "Disordered" under Brain).

Encephalitis—(See "Inflammation" under Brain). Encephalitis, with great Lethargy, accompanies Influenza, and Sleeping Sickness. (See Influenza; "Sleeping Sickness" under Sleep).

Encephalocele—Hernia of the Brain— (See "Brain" under Hernia).

Encephalopathy—(See "Any Disease" under Brain).

Lethargic Encephalitis—(See "Encephalitis" in this section).

ENCYSTED—Enclosed in a Cyst—

Tumors—Encysted Sebaceous Tumors —(See Wen).

END—

Bad End—Bad End to Life—(See the various paragraphs under Death; Debauchery, Disgrace, Dissipation, Executed, Hanging, Judge, Murdered, Old Age, Prison, Reputation, Suicide; "Untimely Death" under Untimely, etc.).

End of the Disease—Termination of the Disease—Signified by the 4th H. conditions and its influences, and the planets in this house at B., and by dir. Also the 8th and 12th H. conditions should be noted. (See Acute, Chronic; "Certain Death" under Death; Fatal, Incurable, Quick, Recovery, Slow, Tedious, Termination, etc.).

Evil End to the Disease—Malefics in the 6th H., and affl. the hyleg. (See Sixth House).

The Disease Will Soon End—Benefics in the 6th H., and in good asp. the hyleg; the $\mathbb{D}$ sepr. from a malefic and apply. to the good asp. a benefic soon after decumbiture, and espec. in acute ailments. (See Acute, Mild, Quick; "Short Diseases" under Short; Slight).

The End of Life—(See the various paragraphs under Death; "Early Death" under Early; "Death" under Childhood, Children, Fourth House, Infancy; "Long Life", "Short Life", under Life; Old Age, Middle Life, Youth. Also see "Bad End" in this section).

ENDEMIC DISEASES—Those Peculiar to a Nation or People—Afflictions in $\mathcal{L}$; the $\odot$ to the $\circ$ $\aleph$ by dir. Also caused by afflictions in the Sign ruling the Country, afflictions to the lord of such Sign, and espec. at the time of Eclipses, being lord of the year at the Vernal Equinox, and afflicted. Caused by the appearance of Comets in the ruling sign of a Country. (See Cholera, Comets, Eclipses, Epidemics, Leprosy, Nations, Pandemic, Pellagra, Perihelion, Pestilence, Plague, Races).

ENDOCARDIUM — The Lining Membrane of the Heart — (See "Endocarditis" under Heart).

ENDOCRINE GLANDS—(See Ductless).

ENDOLYMPH— (See "Endolymph" under Ears).

ENDOSMOSIS—(See Osmosis).

ENDURANCE—Endures—

Endures Sickness — Without Complaining—(See Complaining).

Much Physical Endurance—Good Powers of Endurance Against Disease —Can Stand Much Wear and Tear— A ♄ influence, and also of the Fixed Signs. These influences also give more moral endurance. (See "Endurance" under Morals). The ♉ and ♏ signs espec. have much endurance.˙ The feminine signs have more perseverance and patience than the masculine signs. The ☽ influence tends tó give a weaker body, and also ♀ does not have much endurance as a planet. The masculine signs, and also ♅ and ♂, tend to sudden and forceful efforts, but do not have as much endurance. Other influences and aspects which tend to greater physical endurance are,—The ☉ in ♌, or ♌ on the Asc.; the ☉ in an earthy sign, much endurance in the constitution, and can stand wear and tear; the less the ☉ is afflicted at B. the greater is the endurance; the ☉ or ☽ may be afflicted, but if they are above the malefics the endurance is greater; the body of ☽ persons is usually weak; ♄ people have great powers of endurance; ♄ ✶ or △ ☉, endures against disease, and with strength and consolidation of constitution; ♄ ✶ or △ the Asc., much physical endurance; ♃ in the Asc. at B., and in good asp. the ☉ and ☽; ♃ in the 6th H. at B., and not afflicted; ♂ in the 1st H., even tho afflicted; ♂ ✶ or △ ♄, ♃, or the ☽; ♂ well-aspected at B.; ♂ in good asp. the ☉ at B.; ♉ or ♌ on the Asc.; the 2° ♍ on the Asc. (See "Active Body" under Active; Consolidation; Constitution (see "Good", "Endurance", "Powerful", under Constitution); Dynamic, Energy; "Fixed Signs" under Fixed; Forces; "Abundance" under Health; Immunity, Patience, Perseverance, Physical, Powerful, Prolonged, Protective, Recuperation, Resistance, Robust, Ruddy, Solid, Stamina, Strength, Strong, Tone, Vital, Vitality, etc.).

ENEMA—Clystering—A Rectal Injection of Food or Medicine—The abdominal organs, and the abdomen, ruled by ♍, are usually the beginning of most of the disturbances of the organic functions, and of diseases, and therefore purging, giving enemas, or clystering, are said to be a good beginning in the healing of many diseases, and espec. where medicines and physical and material means are used. (See Cure, Healers, Medicines, Physic, Treatment).

ENEMIES—Adversaries—Open Enemies —Secret Enemies—Open Enemies are ruled by the 7th H., and Secret Enemies by the 12th H., and its conditions. In the Hindu System of Astrology the 6th H. rules Enemies. The enemies of the native are usually those born with the ☉ and ☽ in the signs containing the malefics in the map of birth, and espec. of ♄ and ♂, which causes the malefics in one map to be on the places of the Lights in the other, an evil exchange. Various Chapters are given in the Textbooks of Astrology,

and the rules concerning Enemies, and this Article is intended more to give the evil and dangerous influences which an enemy may have over the health and life of the native. (See Antipathy, Opposites, Sympathy).

Ambushes—Violence, Death, or Injury from an Enemy in Ambush—(See Ambushes, Feuds, Treachery. Also see "Murdered", "Secret Enemies", in this section).

Asylum—Confined Unjustly in an Insane Asylum or Prison by an Enemy— (See "Danger of Imprisonment" under Imprisonment; "Asylum" under Insanity. Also see "Plots", "Treachery", in this section).

Blindness—Is Blinded by the Artifice or Treachery of an Enemy—(See Artifice; "Treachery" under Blindness).

Dangerous Enemy—The native proves a dangerous enemy, and is strong in enmity—♄ ruler of the Asc., or the horoscope, and affl. by ♂, and is very hostile when enraged. (See Anger, Enmity, Hatred).

Death by An Enemy—Danger of—Injury By—♅ ☌ ♂ in the 7th or 12th H., and espec. at the times when these planets form evil directions to each other, or to their places in the radical map. (See Ambushes, Injury, Murdered, Plots, Poison, Secret, Treachery, in this section).

Disgrace—By the Work of an Enemy, and by False Reports—The M.C. to the □ or ☍ ☿ by dir. (See Disgrace).

Enemies Do Not Live Long—Lord of the 7th H. in the 2nd; lord of the 12th in the 8th H., lives to see the death of his enemies.

Fear of Enemies—Dread of—♆ in the 12th H.; ☿ elevated above, and configurated with ♂ at a Solar Ingress or Eclipse, tends to a general prevalence of fear of enemies. (See Fear).

His Own Worst Enemy—The ☉ affl. in ♓, and generally by extravagance, indulgence and feasting; the ☽ Sig. in ♓; the ☽ decr. in a day geniture, sepr. from ♀ and applying to ♄; ♃ Sig. in ♊ and near Aldebaran, inimical to himself; the Martialist, or ♂ person, tends to bring wounds and diseases upon himself by rushing into danger and excesses; ♀ to the ☌ ♂ or ♉ by dir.; ☿ Sig. in ♐, rash in many things to his own injury; lord of the 12th also lord of the Asc. (See Debauched; "Brings Disease Upon Himself" under Disease; Disgrace, Dissipated, Drink, Excesses, Extravagance, Feasting, Folly, Foolhardy, Gluttony, Habits, Indulgence, Narcotics, Rashness, Reputation, Recklessness, Ruin, Scandal, Unfortunate, Vices, etc.).

Injured by An Enemy—Danger of, or Death By—Malefics in the 7th H., by open enemies, or by secret enemies if in the 12th H.; lords of the 7th or 12th in evil houses, as in the 4th, 6th, 8th or 12th, and affl. the lord of the Asc.; the ☽ affl. at B., and to the ☌ the cusp of 12th H. (See Ambushes, Death, Murdered, and the various paragraphs in this section).

Magistrates—Enemies Among—(See Judges).

Many Adversaries—Has Many Enemies—The ☉ to the cusp the 12th H. by dir.; born with the ☉, ☽, or ☿ much afflicted at B.; the ☽ to Cor Scorpio; ♃ by Periodic Rev. to the ☌ or ill-asp. ♄, and ♄ ill-aspected at B.; many planets in the 7th or 12th H. at B., and malefics among them; the M.C. to the place of Algenib. (See Antares, Algenib. Also see "Secret" in this section).

Murdered by Enemy—♂ Sig. □ or ☍ ☉ if the ☉ is lord of the 7th or 12th H. (See Ambushes, Death, in this section).

Open Enemies—Ruled by the 7th H. Danger of being injured or killed by them when there are malefics in the 7th H., and under the evil directions of such malefic to the hyleg, or when the malefic, or malefics, afflict the 7th H., and their own place by dir. (See Seventh House).

Own Worst Enemy—(See "His Own" in this section).

Plots—Death or Injury by the Plots of Enemies—(See Ambushes, Plots; "Enemy" under Poison; Revenge, Treachery. Also see Death, Injured, Murdered, in this section).

Poisoned by Enemies—(See "Enemy" under Poison).

Prison—Confined Unjustly in Prison by an Enemy, and False Charges— (See "Asylum" under Insanity; "Plots" under Prison).

Relatives — Enemies Among — (See Relatives).

Secret Enemies—Private and Secret Enemies are ruled and indicated by the 12th H. conditions. The Signs of the Zodiac containing the malefics at B. show the types and locations of the native's worst enemies. The 8th H. shows the influences working over, and the fate of secret enemies. Note the following paragraphs about Secret Enemies,—(a) Death or Injury by Secret Foes—Denoted by the 12th H.; ruler of the 12th H. afflicting the Significator; lord of the 7th H. a malefic, and in the 12th H., and afflicted; lord of the 8th H. a malefic, in the 8th, and affl. by lord of the 6th or 12th, and espec. if the lord of the Asc., or the hyleg, be also afflicted; lord of the 8th in the 12th, and affl. the lord of the Asc., and no benefics in the 12th; the ☽ to the cusp 12th H. by dir.; the ☽ to the ☌ or ill-asp. ♂ by dir.; the ☽ in the 12th H. at the Vernal Equi., lady of the year, and afflicted, and with no good asp. of ♃ or ♀; ♅ the afflicting planet denotes death by the treachery of secret enemies; ♅ affl. in the 1st H.; ♅ ☌ ♂ in the 7th or 12th H.; ♄ or ♂ to the cusp of 12th H. by dir.; ♄ in ♏, ☌ or evil asp. the Asc. by dir.; the 20° ♍ on the Asc. at B., and affl. by malefics. (See Ambushes, Assassination; "Tragical Death" under Death; "Deceitful Relatives" under Deceitful; "False Friends" under Friends; "Murdered" under Murder; "Secret Poisoning" under Poison; Revenge, Treachery; "Twelfth House" under Twelfth; "Violent Death" under Violent). (b) Injured by Secret Enemy—The ☽ affl. at B., and to cusp the 12th H. by dir.; malefics in the 12th H.; lord of the 12th a malefic, and espec. ♄ or ♂. (c) Secret Enemy Dying—Near Death —Lord of the 12th H. be with lord of the 4th or 8th H., or in those houses (Hor'y). (d) Sickness of—Secret Diseases of—Afflicted with Some Secret Malady—Lord of the 12th H. in the 6th H., or joined to lord of the 6th.

Treachery—Death or Injury by the Treachery of Enemies—(See Plots; "Enemy" under Poison; Treachery).

Violence—Suffers Violence from Enemies — (See Ambushes, Plots, Poison, Prison, Treachery. Also see the various paragraphs in this section).

ENERGY—Energies—Energetic—Mars is espec. the planet of dynamic energy. The energy of the system is scattered, used up and dissipated by ♂ during muscular activity. Aspects to the ☉ and ♂ tend to give energy and zest, and even the bad aspects of ♂ are better to give energy than no aspects at all. In the wide sense energy is the manifestation of ♅ and ♂, acting thru the signs and houses occupied, and the planets in aspect. A new lease on the bodily energy is given by ♂ when he brings fevers and inflammations to burn the impurities from the system. The following subjects have to do with the Energies, which see in the alphabetical arrangement when not considered here—

Abeyance—Of the Bodily Energies— (See Abeyance).

Abundance of Energy—Great Energy —The ☉ in ♌ in the Asc.; the ☉ ⚹ or ∆ ♂; the ☉ or ☽ ☌ ♂; the ☽ hyleg and in ⚹ or ∆ ♃; the Prog. ☽ ⚹ or ∆ the radical ♂ if ♂ be well-asp. at B.; the ☽, P, ⚹, or ∆ ☿; ♅ well-aspected in ♏; ♅ well-asp. in ♈; ♅ or ♄ ⚹ or ∆ ♂; ♃ well-asp. at B., and ♃ to the good asps. ♂ by dir.; ♂ in the Asc., and well-aspected, and espec. in one of his strong signs; ♂ ⚹ or ∆ the ☉ or Asc; ♂ in ♌, ♏, or ♑, and well-aspected; ♂ □ or ☍ the ☉, as the evil asps. of ♂ tend to give energy and activity as well as his good aspects, but with more danger of excesses, and misuse of the energies; ♂ Prog. to the ⚹ or ∆ the radical ♃, and vice versa; ♀ ⚹ or ∆ ♂. (See Abundance, Action, Active, Buoyant, Dynamic, Endurance, Exertion, Immunity; "Force" under Life, Powerful, Resistance, Robust, Stamina, Strength, Strong, Vitality, etc. Also see "Great" in this section).

Action—(See the various paragraphs under Action).

Active Body—Active Mind—(See Active).

Apathy; Brain Storms—(See this subject under Brain).

Conservation of Energy—♄ when in ♌, and not afflicted, tends to conserve the energies of the body, and maintain good health. (See Conservation, Preservation).

Constructive Energy—(See Constructive).

Debility; Depletion;

Destruction of Energy—(See Destructive).

Diffusiveness of Energy—♂ in a mutable sign. (See Diffusiveness).

Dispersions; Dissipation Of—(See "Energy" under Dissipated).

Dull—(See Dull, Idle, Inactive, Inertia, Lassitude, Lethargy, Listless, etc.).

Dynamic; Endurance; Ennui; Excess; Excesses; Excitation; Exercise;

Explosive; Fatigue; Feeble; Fevers—Fevers and Inflammation as Related to the Energies—(See Constructive, Destructive, Fevers, Inflammation).

Fiery Signs—Are the Most Energetic and Vital Signs. (See "Fire Signs" under Fire).

Functional Energies—(See "Dissipation of" under Functions).

Gait—(See "Energetic" under Gait).

Great Energy—A Time of Great Energy and Activity—The ☉ to the ✶ or △ ♃ by dir.; the Prog. ☉ or ☽ to the ✶ or △ ♂; ♂ Prog. in ✶ or △ the radical ♃, and vice versa. (See Activity. Also see "Abundance" in this section).

Hyperactivity; Idle;

Increase of Energy—(See "Abundance", "Great", in this section. Also see "Increased" under Vitality).

Indifferent; Inefficiency; Inertia;

Inflammation—(See "Fevers" in this section).

Lack of Energy—Lack of Enterprise—The ☽ 8 ♂; afflictions to ♀, and the ill-asps. of ♀ tend to loss of stimulus, and general relaxation; the 2nd and 4th faces of 8 on the Asc. (See "Of No Ambition" under Ambition; Dull; "Resignation" under Fate; Idle, Indifferent, Inefficiency, Inertia, Labor, Lassitude, Lazy, Lethargy, Listless, Relaxation, Retrograde; "Low", "Weak", under Vitality; "Weak Body" under Weak).

Lassitude; Lethargy; Listless; Mars—(See "Mars Influence" under Mars).

Mental Energy—Mental Activity—The ☉ or ☽ ♂ ♂; the ☉ well-asp. in ♐; the ☽ ♂, ✶, or △ ♀; ♅ ✶ ♃ or ♀, and with ☿ in ✶ or △ ♂; ♂ rising at B.; ♂ in fiery signs, or in ♏ or ♑, and espec. when rising; ♂ to the good asps. ☿ by dir.; ♀ Sig. in ♍, an active mind; ☿ well-asp. in ♊, ♍, or ♒; ☿ in ♑, an active mind, yet feeble or sickly body; ♏ or ♐ on the Asc.; Temperate climates, with alternate heat and cold, tend to produce an active and energetic mind and nature; produced by fiery and airy signs; lords of the nativity in Southern Signs give energy and activity. (See "Active Mind" under Active; "Activity", "Quickened", under Mental; "Strong Mind" under Mind; "Scattered" in this section. Also for the opposite influences which tend to a dull and inactive mind, see "Mind" under Dull).

Motion; Movement; Muscular Energy—Muscular Activity—Ruled by ♂. (See "Activity" under Muscles).

Natural Energies—Natural Abilities—(See Natural).

Nervous Energy—Is upheld, given, and ruled by ☿, and depressed or suppressed by ♄. (See Nerves).

New Lease on Energy—(See the Introduction to this Article).

Opposite Sex—Energies Wasted On—(See "Health Suffers" under Opposite Sex).

Pleasure—Energies Wasted In—(See "Energies" under Pleasure).

Power; Quick; Resistance;

Restless Energy—Cardinal signs on the angles, and many planets in cardinal signs. (See Cardinal, Restless).

Robust; Ruddy, Scattered Energy—The bodily energy is scattered by ♂ during muscular activity. The mental energies are more quickly scattered by afflictions to ☿. (See Active, Dispersions; "Energy" under Dissipation. Also see "Diffusiveness", and the various paragraphs in this section).

Sex Energies—Dissipation of—(See Amorous, Lascivious, Lewd, Licentious, Lust, Passion, Sex, Venery, etc.).

Slow; Spasmodic Energies—(See Spasmodic).

Sports; Stamina; Strength; Strong;

Superabundance—(See "Abundance" in this section; Excess, Excesses, Superabundance).

Time of Great Energy—(See "Great Energy" in this section).

Tone; Vital Energy—The ☉ and ♂ represent the vital energy. The ☉ gives the vital heat, or the vital energy to the body. Also connected with the ♓ sign, and Iron Phosphate, the ♓ Salt. (See "Energy", "Heat", under Vital).

Vital Powers Weak—(See "Weak" under Vital).

Vitality—The Vitality Strong—Weak—(See Vitality).

Void of Energy—(See "Lack Of" in this section).

Walk—(See "Energetic" under Gait).

Wasted Energies—(See Debauchery, Dissipation, Excesses, Exercise, Love Affairs, Opposite Sex, Passion, Sex, Venery, etc.).

Weak Body—(See "Weak Body" under Weak).

Weariness; Zest.

ENERVATION—Enervating—Weakening—♄ affl. the ☉, ☽, Asc., or hyleg at B., and by dir.; ♃ in evil asp. to ♀, and ♃ weak and ill-dig. in the map; ♂ weak at B., and forming no asp. to the ☉, or vice versa. (See Debility, Decreased, Decrepitude, Depletion, Diminished, Feeble, Neurasthenia, Resistance Low, Vitality Low, Weak, Weakening).

ENGLISH CHOLERA—(See "Cholera Morbus" under Cholera).

ENGORGEMENT—(See "High Pressure" under Blood; Diet, Distentions, Food, Gluttony, Plethora, Surfeits; "Vascular Fullness" under Vascular; Vessels, etc.).

ENHANCED—The Health Good and Enhanced—(See "Enhanced"; "Good", under Health).

ENJOYMENT—Given to Pleasure and Enjoyment—(See Pleasure).

ENLARGED—Enlargements—Over-size —Swollen—The following subjects have to do with Enlargements, Abnormally Large Parts, Overgrowth, etc., which see in the alphabetical arrangement when not considered here.

Abdomen—(See "Prominent" under Abdomen).

Abnormalities; Acromegaly—(See "Enlargement" under Arms, Extremities, Face, Feet, Hands).

Arms—(See "Enlargement" under Arms, Extremities).

Body—Enlarged Body—The ♌, ♍, or ♐ signs when upon the Asc. at B., or strong in their influences, tend to enlarge the body. (See Corpulent, Excessive, Fat, Fleshy, Giants, Growth, Large, Tall, etc.).

Bones—(See "Large", "Long", under Bones).

Cells—(See "Hypertrophy" under Cells).

Chest—(See "Dropsy" under Chest).

Corpulent; Deformities; Deposits; Development; Dilatations;

Distentions; Dropsy; Elephantiasis; Engorgement; Excessive; Expansion; Extremities; Face—(See "Enlargement" under Face).

Fat; Feet—(See "Enlargement", "Swollen", under Feet).

Flatulence; Fleshy; Fullness; Gas; Giants; Glands; Great; Groins; Growth; Growths; Hands—(See "Enlarged" under Hands).

Head—(See "Tumor" under Brain; "Enlarged" under Head; Hydrocephalus).

Heart—(See "Enlarged" under Heart).

Hernia; Hydrocele; Hydrocephalus—(See "Dropsy" under Brain).

Hydrothorax—(See "Dropsy" under Chest).

Hypertrophy; Increased;

Inflammations; Joints — (See "Stiff Joints" under Joints).

Large; Limbs; Liver—(See "Enlarged" under Liver).

Mineral Deposits — Enlargements From—(See Deposits, Joints, Minerals, Wastes).

Morbid Enlargements—(See Abscesses, Morbid, Swellings, Tumors, Ulcers).

Neck—(See Goiter; "Swellings" under Neck).

Oedema; Organs—♂ tends to enlargement of organs, and also ♃ by the formation of fat, adipose tissue, tumors, and growths. Enlargement of parts, or organs, as in hypertrophy and excessive growths, is due to the tonic, or plus action of ♂. (See Hypertrophy; "Over-Developed" under Organs; "Tonic Action" under Mars; "Planets" under Tonic).

Overgrowth; Prostate Gland—(See Prostate).

Rickets; Ruptures; Scope—Enlarged Scope of the Disease—The two heat-producing planets, the ☉ and ♂, when combining their influences, tend to

both febrile and inflammatory conditions. (See Fever, Inflammation).

Stomach—(See "Dilatation" under Stomach).

Swellings; Tall; Testes;

Thyroid Enlargement—(See Goiter, Thyroid).

Tissues; Tonic Action—(See "Organs" in this section).

Tonsils; Tumors; Tympanites; Uvula; Varicocele; Varicose; Veins; Vessels; Virile. For subjects which may not be mentioned here, look for them in the alphabetical arrangement.

ENMITY—Hatred—Malice—

Against the Native—♅ in the 1st H.; the ☽ to the ♂ or ill-asp. ♂ by dir. tends to enmity against the Native.

Death Thru Enmity—Death from Plots—♅ affl. in the 1st H. (See Enemies, Feuds, Plots; "Death by Poison" under Poison; Treachery, etc.).

Strong In Enmity—♄ ruler of the Asc., or horoscope, at B., and affl. by ♂. (See Anger, Contests, Duels, Feuds, Hatred, Jealousy, Malice, Murderous, Plots, Poison, Revenge, Temper, Treacherous, Vicious, Violent, etc.).

ENNEATICAL—A Climax in Disease. The 9th day of a disease or illness. Also the 9th year of life is called an Enneatical Year. The word means "Nine", and refers to the 9th of any series. The 9th day of the ☽, being the trine aspect after the New ☽, or the 9th day of a fever, are crisis days, but rather favorable, and indicate relief, ease, and more favorable conditions. In Geometry, a figure with nine faces or surfaces. (See Climacterical, Crises, Critical, Periods, Years).

ENNUI—Vapors—Mental Weariness—Lack of Interest in Life—(See Apathy, Dejected, Depressed, Despondency, Dull, Hypochondria, Lassitude, Lethargy, Listless; "Low Spirits" under Low; Melancholy, Weariness, Worry).

ENOPHTHALMOS—(See Eyeballs).

ENRICHMENT—Of the Blood—(See "Enrichment" under Blood).

ENSNARING—Enticing—♅ influence—(See Illaqueative).

ENTERALGIA—Pain In the Bowels—Neuralgia In—A ♍ disease, and afflictions in ♍; the ☽ affl. in ♍, great pain and disorder in the bowels; the ☽ in ♈ or ♓, and affl. to ☉ or ♂ when taken ill (Hor'y); the ☽ in ♎, ♂ or ill-asp. ♄ (or ☿ if he be of the nature of ♄) when taken ill (Hor'y); ♅, ♄, or ♅ in ♍, and affl. the ☉ or ☽. (See Colic, Cramps, Gripings, Pain, under Bowels; Cholera, Dysentery, Flatulence).

ENTERIC FEVER—(See "Fever" under Bowels; Typhoid).

ENTERITIS — (See "Inflammation" under Bowels; "Enteritis" under Catarrh, Childhood, Phlegmon).

ENTEROCOLITIS—(See Bowels).

ENTEROPTOSIS — (See "Prolapse" under Bowels).

ENTHUSIASM—

Enthusiasts—♂ or ☿ □ or ⊗ ♄; the 2nd Dec. of ♑ on the Asc., red hot enthusiasm.

Sudden Enthusiasms—The ♃ influence strong at B.

Temperaments — (See Choleric, Sanguine).

The Fury of Enthusiasm—The ☽ and ☿ unconnected with each other or the Asc., and with the malefics in the Eastern Parts and in angles, and the benefics in the West, and also with ♀ and ♂ taking part in the scheme; a ♂ disease and affliction; also connected with ♅ afflictions; many planets in fiery signs at B. (See Anarchists, Emotions, Frenzy, Fury, Madness, Mania, Religion, etc.).

ENTIRE BODY—(See Whole).

ENTOZOONS—Intestinal Parasites— They are more active and bursting at the Full ☽. (See "Full Moon" under Moon; Parasites, Worms).

ENURESIS—(See "Incontinence" under Urine).

ENVIRONMENT — Surroundings—The nature of the individual environment, and hereditary tendencies, are indicated by the Sign ruling the Place or Country of birth. If the sign is positive or masculine, it denotes an electro-positive environment. If the sign is negative, an electro-negative environment. In long and chronic diseases the environment of the birthplace, or of the Native Country, is often a curative agent, and espec. if there are benefics with the ☉ at B., or in the 4th H. (See Abroad, Climate, Curable, Disorientation, Employment, External, Family, Friends, Habits, Heredity, Home, Incurable, Identity, Location, Marriage, Native Land (see Native); Negative, Orientation, Parents, Place of Birth (see Place); Positive, Relations, Residence, Social Life (see Social); Susceptible, Travel, Treatment, Utopianism).

Much Affected By—Much Influenced By—♅ or the ♋ sign on the Asc.; the 4th face of ♋ on the Asc.; the 6th face of ♓ on the Asc.; mutable signs on the angles at B., and also many planets in feminine and negative signs. (See External, Influenced, Mutable, Negative, Suggestion, Susceptible).

EPHEMERAL FEVERS—Brief Fevers —Fevers Which Last for Only a Day— ♀ in a fiery sign and afflicted at a decumbiture; Subs at CP and KP. (See Acute, Indiscretions, Mild, Minor, Slight).

Ephemeral Skin Eruption—(See Urticaria).

EPICUREANS—Sybarites—Given to Luxury, Pleasure, Feasting, etc.—The ☉ Sig. in ♍, convivial and fond of feasting; the ☽ affl. in ♓, given to the pleasures of the table; ♆ afflictions to ♀ or ☿, or to the Sigs., the ☉, ☽, Asc., or M.C. at B., or by dir., a Sybarite, a luxurious person; ♃ in □ or ⊗ the ☉; the 2nd Dec. ⊗ on the Asc., ruled by the ☽, fond of dainty foods and good living; the 16° ♑ on the Asc., lives to eat; the 22° ♓ on the Asc. (See Appe-

tite, Diet, Drink, Eating, Extravagance, Feasting, Food, Gluttony; "High Living" under High; Intemperance, Luxuries, Pleasures, Prodigal).

EPIDEMICS—A Prevailing Disease, and Common to Many People—

Causes—Epidemics are caused by the major planets in perihelion, and espec. ♄ and ♃, and also by ♂ in perigee. The greatest epidemics have occurred when ♃ is perihelion, and ♂ perigee at the same time. People born under the ♏ sign are very susceptible to epidemics, and to infectious and contagious diseases, due to the magnetic nature of this sign, and they fall easy victims. When in perihelion, the planets ♆ and ♅ have also been observed to cause epidemics of various kinds. They also occur at the time of the appearance of Comets, and are coincident with Earthquakes and Earth disturbances. Fatal Epidemics can be due to general causes, as great Eclipses, and may not show fatal Directions in the cases of every individual affected. The influences of the Equinoxes and Solstices also have their effects, such as ♃ in ♊, and lord of the year at the Vernal Equi., and ♄ therein conjoined with ♂, or ♄ ☌ ♂ therein, and with ♃ ℞, and ♀ combust; ♄, ♃, and ♂ conjoined in ⊗; ♄ in ♏, ℞, occi., and ruler of the year at the Vernal Ingress; ♃ ☌ or ⊗ ♅; ♂ supreme at the Equinoxes and Solstices; a ♌ disease; afflictions in ♌, and with several superior planets in ☌ in ♌; coincident with the appearance of Comets, and espec. in ♒. (For the various kinds of Epidemics, their nature, and causes, see Air, Atmosphere, Cattle, Cholera, Comets, Contagions, Diphtheria; "Earthquakes" under Earth; Eclipses, Equinoxes, External, Fruit, Horses, Infections, Influenza, Ingresses, Measles, Moisture, Pandemics, Perigee, Perihelion, Pestilence, Plague, Putrefaction, Rottenness, Scarlet Fever, Scorpio, Sheep, Smallpox, Solstices, Sun Spots (see Spots); Susceptibility, Typhoid, Typhus, Vegetation, Vernal, Virus, Yellow Fever).

Epidemic Fevers—The ☉ affl. in ♊; the ☉ to the ☌ ☋ by dir.; ♄, ♂, and ☿ conjoined in ♑; ♂ supreme at the Equinoxes and Solstices. (See "Low Fevers" under Fever; "Fevers" under Pestilence).

Fatal Epidemics—(See the Introduction to this section).

Great Epidemics — (See "Severe" in this section).

Heat—Epidemics Thru Excess of Heat—Eclipses of the ☉ or ☽ in fiery signs. (See Famine; "Fire Signs" under Fire; Heat).

Immunity To—(See Immunity).

Low Fevers—Epidemic of—(See "Low Fevers" under Fever).

Mild Epidemics—Only two of the superior planets in ☌ or ⊗. (See Mild).

Moisture—Epidemics Arising from Too Much Moisture—Caused by ♀. (See Floods; "Superabundance" under Moisture; Rain).

Pandemics—Wide Spread Epidemics —(See Pandemics).

Severe Epidemics—Great Epidemics—Three or four of the superior planets in ♂ or ☍. The great epidemics correspond to the periodicity of the ♂ and ☍ of the superior planets.

Wide Spread Epidemics — (See "Severe" in this section).

EPIDERMIS—The Outer Layer of the Skin—The Cuticle—Scarf Skin—Ruled by ♄. Also under the external rule of ♆. (See Excoriations, Scales, Skin).

EPIGASTRIUM—Epigastric Region—The Region Over the Stomach—Under the external rule of the ♋ sign.

Disorders In—(See "Heartburn" under Heart).

EPILEPSY—Eclampsia—By Ancient Writers this was classed as a mental disease, and was called the "Holy Disease", as they considered the patient in a fit, or paroxysm of the disease, to be under the influence of a Supernatural Power. Most Astrologers consider it a mental disease, as many of the same planetary influences which cause Insanity also cause this disease. Some Writers, and also Modern Medical Authorities, class it as a Nervous Disease, with loss of consciousness, and with tonic and clonic convulsions. The major attacks of Epilepsy are called "Grand Mal", and the milder forms, "Petit Mal". Eclampsia is a milder form without loss of consciousness. Some Writers say that Epilepsy is due to an abnormality of one of the Ductless Glands, the Pineal Gland, which Gland is ruled by ♆, and as ♆ rules the Spiritual Faculties, Epilepsy, no doubt, has a spiritual, as well as a mental or psychic cause, and may also be due to some obsession, or Spirit Control. (See Neptune, Obsessions, Spirit Controls). The Planetary Causes of Epilepsy are as follows — The ☉ above the horizon (daylight horoscope), with ☿ and the ☽ unconnected with each other or the Asc., and with ♄ and ♂ in angles ruling the scheme, ♄ by day and ♂ by night. (Note—♄ ruling the scheme by night and ♂ by day, tends to Insanity (see Insanity); the ☽ rules diseases which return after a time, such as Epilepsy; the ☽, ☿, and the Asc. unconnected with each other, and affl. by ♄ and ♂ from angles, and with no assistance from the benefics, tend to Epilepsy and Falling Fits, and espec. if ♄ be so posited by day, and ♂ by night; the ☽ in ♋, ♂, or ill-asp. any of the malefics as promittors; the ☽ decr., and sepr. from ♂ and apply. to ♄; a ☽ disease; the ☽ affl. in ♋, and affl. the hyleg therefrom; patients tend to be worse at the Full ☽; ♆ afflicted; ♅ in the 6th H., and affl. ☿ or the hyleg; ♅ ♂ or ill-asp. the ☉ at B., and by dir.; ♄ in an angle, occi. of the ☉, and ori. of the ☽, and ☿ in familiarity with ♂; ♄ or ♂ in the Asc. or M.C. in ♊ or ♐; a ♄ disease, and ♄ denotes death by; ♄ and ♂ ruling ♃ and ☿, and at the same time the ☽, ☿, ♅, and the Asc. be unconnected with each other; ♄ and ♂ angular, occi. of the ☉, and ori. of the ☽, and ☿ in familiarity with ♂; the combined influence of ♄ and ♂; ♄ and ♂ in angles, elevated above ♅, ☿, or the ☽, and if

♅, ☿, and the ☽ be unconnected with each other by good asps., and be affl. by ♄ or ♂, and with no assistance from ♃ or ♀; ♂ and ☿ holding dominion at B., and in familiarity with each other, and ♂ affl. the hyleg, and elevated above the Luminaries, the Epilepsy is increased; ☿ affl. at B., and to the ♂ or ill-asps. the ☽ or hyleg by dir., or by Periodic Revolution; ☿ in the 8th H., and affl. at a Solar Ingress of the ☉ into ♈, and ☿ affl. the ☽ or planet ascending (see Madness); ☿ denotes death by; ☿ and the ☽ unconnected with each other or the Asc., and ♄ and ♂ in angles ruling the scheme, ♄ by day, and ♂ by night,— under these conditions if the malefics be in Eastern Parts and angles, and the benefics in the West, the epileptic person will be subject to constant fits, danger of death, and the epilepsy becomes conspicuous; ☿ and ♃ cooperating in the scheme contribute to epilepsy, and ☿ espec. when the dominion of death is vested in him and he is of the nature of ♄; an ♈ disease; Subs at AT, CP, KP and PP. Epilepsy also is strongly associated with the ♏ sign and sex, highly sexed people, and espec. with females. (For further influences along this line see Coma, Convulsions, Consciousness, Day, Delirium, Demoniac, Deranged, Fainting, Fits, Idiocy, Insanity, Insensibility, Madness, Mania, Night, Obsessions, Pineal Gland, Spasms, Spirit Controls, etc.). Case of Epilepsy—See "Epilepsy", No. 668, in 1001 N.N.

Ameliorated—(See "Curable" in this section).

Causes of Epilepsy—(See the first part of this Article).

Conspicuous—(See the ☿ influences in the first part of this section).

Constant Epileptic Fits—(See the ☿ influences in the first part of this section).

Curable—Ameliorated — Mitigated — Epilepsy will tend to be mitigated, or curable, if the benefics are elevated at B. above the malefics which produce it, and espec. under favorable directions to the ☽ or ☿. The more oriental and angular the benefics may be, the more powerful will their effects be for good, and espec. if the malefics are setting in the West, and out of power and dignity. The opposite to these conditions would tend to make the Epilepsy incurable ordinarily, and without the proper treatment. (See Amelioration, Curable, Incurable, Modification, Recovery).

Death by Epilepsy—Danger of—♅ in the 8th H., and affl. ☿ and the hyleg, and with the malefics ♄ and ♂ elevated in the East, and above the Luminaries at B., or in angles; ♄ occi. at B., and affl. the hyleg by dir., and holding the dominion of death; ☿ affl. the hyleg, or giver of life, by dir.; ☿ affl. by ♄ or ♂ at B., and affl. the hyleg by dir., and also holding the dominion of death. (See the ☿ influences in the first part of this Article, and also the paragraph on "Curable").

Increased—The Epilepsy Is Increased —(See the ♂ influences in the first part of this Article).

Incurable—(See "Curable" in this section).

Mitigated—(See "Curable" in this section).

Worse—Epileptic patients tend to be worse at the Full ☽. (See "Worse" under Disease; "Full Moon" under Moon).

EPIPHORA—Watery Eyes—Overflow of Tears—(See Tears).

EPISTAXIS—Nose Bleed—Hemorrhage from the Nose—(See "Epistaxis" under Nose).

EPITHELIOMA—A Cancerous Growth of the Skin—An Affection of the Epithelium—♂ affl. in ♌; also a ♑ disease, as the Epithelial tissues, or the Epithelium, are connected with ♑. (See Carcinoma; "Epithelioma" under Nose; Skin).

EPOCH—(See "Critical Epochs" under Critical; Prenatal Epoch).

EPULIS—(See "Cystic Tumor" under Tongue).

EQUATOR—(See Nadir).

EQUILIBRIUM—Poise—Balance—Ruled by the ♎ sign, the sign of "The Balance".

Disturbed—The Equilibrium and Balance of the Body Disturbed—Lack of Balance Between Mind and Body—Incoordination—♄ in ♌; many planets, or a Stellium, in ♌, afflicting the organ of coordination, and resulting in inability to walk without swaying, or pitching forward. (See Balance, Coordination, Gait, Harmony, Incoordination, Libra, Miscarriage, Rhythm, Spasmodic, Walk).

Loss of Equilibrium—Caused by the ♌ sign and influence, as this is a fiery and hot sign, heats the system when strong at B., or occupied by the ☉, ♂, and many planets, thus causing loss of equilibrium. (See "Animal Heat", "Heats the System", under Heat).

EQUINOXES—Equinoctial—These are the points in the Zodiac when the ☉ enters the Signs ♈ and ♎, which are Equinoctial Signs, and the planetary aspects and configurations at these times are very important in the consideration of disease and health, as they are very sensitive points in the Zodiac. The ☉ enters ♈ at the Vernal Equinox, as he crosses the Equator on his Northward journey from out of the Tomb of Winter, and in the Fall of the year, at the Fall, or Autumnal Equinox, the ☉ enters ♎, and begins his Southward journey. The influences which afflict the ☉ at his Ingress into ♈ or ♎ tend at times to cause Drought, Epidemics, and other evils. (See "Corrupt Air" under Air; Drought, Dry, Earthquakes, Eclipses, Epidemics, Hail, Ingresses; "Nil" under Mars; Minor Disorders, Mortality, Pestilence, Solstices, Tropical, Vernal, Weather).

ERECT—Erect In Posture—Upright—Erect and Straight—Tall and Straight—The ☉ in ♎; the ☽ Sig. in ♊; ♃ in the Asc.; ♃ in ♐; ♃ Sig. in ♎ or ♐; born under ♃; ♀ Sig. in ♊ or ♎; ♀ oriental; ☿ ascending at B., and free

from the rays of other planets; ☿ strong at B., as rising, or in the Asc. (See Straight, Tall, Upright).

ERECTIONS—Painful Erections—Priapism—(See "Chordee", "Erections", "Priapism", under Penis).

ERETHISM—Abnormal Increase of Nervous Irritability—A ♂ disease and affliction; ♂ afflicting ☿; ♂ ♂ or ill-asp. ☿ tends to increased irritability and vascular excitement of the nerve centers. (See "Centers", "Neuritis", under Nerves).

ERGOPHOBIA—Fear of Work—(See Work).

EROSIONS—(See "Ulceration" under Teeth; Ulcers).

EROTIC—Pertaining To Sexual Passion—

Erotic Disturbances—(See Amorous, Passion; "Sex Desires" under Sex).

Erotic Mania—(See "Erotic" under Mania).

ERRATIC—Irregular—Changeable—

Conduct—Erratic Conduct—(See Conduct).

Course of Disease—Erratic Course—(See Course, Irregular, Peculiar, Various).

Judgment Erratic—(See Judgment).

Mind—Erratic Mind—♅ is the principal planet which, by his afflictions, gives erratic states of mind and blind impulses; ♅ ruler of the horoscope, and afflicted; ♅ in the 1st H.; ♅ in the 3rd or 9th H., and afflicted, or affl. ☿; ♅ □ or ☍ ☽; ♅ ♂ or ill-asp. ♂; ♅ by transit ♂ ♂, ☿, or the ☽; the ☉ ♂ ☿ combust in ♓, the ☉ □ or ☍ the ☽ or ♄; the Prog. ☉ or ☽ ♂ or ill-asp. ♅; the ☽ in the Uranian sign ♒ at B., and afflicted; the ☽ □ or ☍ ☿ at B.; the ☽ ♂ ♆ or ♂ in ♈, and in □ to ♅, ♄, or ♃; ♄ ♂ or ill-asp. ☿; ♃ in ♊, □ ♅ or ♂ in ♍; ♃ affl. in ♒; ☿ ruler of the horoscope, and affl. by malefics; many planets in the signs of ☿, as in ♊ or ♍, and affl. by the □ asps. of other planets; ☿ and ♀ progressed to the ♂ or ill-asp. ♅ at B., or vice versa; ☿, the mental ruler, prog. to the ♂ or ill-asp. ♅ or ♂ at B. (See Chaotic, Deviations, Dreamy, Eccentric, Emotions, Folly, Foolhardy, Habits, Ideals, Impulses, Judgment, Perversions, Peculiar, Rashness, Reckless, Religion, Riotous, Unbalanced).

Movements—Erratic Movements—Motor Neuroses—Caused by ♅ influence, by reflex action in ♌, and afflictions to planets in ♌ where the organ of coordinated action is located; a ♌ disease; a ♅ disease; ♅ in the 6th H. (See Action, Antiperistalsis, Clonic, Colic, Contortions, Contractions, Convulsions, Coordination, Cramps, Distortions, Fits, Hiccough, Incoordination, Involuntary, Irregular, Jerkings, Motion, Movement, Organs, Saint Vitus Dance, Spasms, Tics, Tremors, Twitchings, Vomiting).

Organs—Erratic Action of Organs—Caused by ♅ afflictions. (See the various Organs of the Body in the alphabetical arrangement. Also see "Movements", "Organs", in this section).

Personality — Erratic Personality — (See Personality).

Sex Life—Erratic In—(See Amourous, Excesses, Passion, Scandal, Sex, Venery, etc.).

ERRING—Intractable—Unruly—Willfully Wrong and Erring—Refractory —♄ affl. in ♐. (See Conduct, Cruel, Erratic, Errors, Evil, Judgment, Obstinate, Perverse, Rashness, Temper, Unruly, Vicious, Violent, Wicked, etc.).

ERRORS—Diet—Errors of—(See Diet, Eating, Feasting, Food, Gluttony, Habits, Indiscretions, Intemperance).

Mind and Judgment—Errors of—(See Eccentric, Erratic, Erring, Judgment, Mind, Perception, Understanding, etc.).

ERUCTATIONS—(See Belching).

ERUPTIONS—A Breaking Out—A Rash —Eruptive Diseases—Exanthema—Efflorescence, etc. Eruptive diseases, and also contagious and infectious diseases, are caused principally by the ♂ influence, and by ♂ and the ☽ combinations. They are also a ♏ disease, the sign ruled by ♂; the ☽ to the ☌ ♂ by dir.; ♄ in any sign tends to draw to, and deposit wastes in the part, or parts, ruled by the sign he is in, and cause eruptions; ♃ afflicted by ♂; ♂ also tends to draw an excess of heat and blood to the part ruled by the sign he is in, and cause eruptions, abscesses, ulcers, and sores; the afflictions of ♂ tend to hot, fiery and burning eruptions; ♂ ☌ the Asc. by dir., eruptions of all kinds; ♀ in ♈ tends to eruptions on the face due to the wrong use of cosmetics; ♀ in signs which rule the arms, hands, legs, and feet tends to skin eruptions of these parts; the Asc. to the ☐ or ☍ ♂ by dir., if in fiery signs, pestilential eruptions; the Asc. to the ☐ or ☍ ♂ by dir., if in airy signs, violent eruptions; ♅ diseases, and cutaneous; Subs at KP and Local.

All Kinds Of—♂ ☌ the Asc. by dir.

Arms—Face—Hands—Legs—Feet— Eruptions In—♀ affl. in signs which rule these parts, and due to wrong habits of living and eating. (See "Eruptions" under these subjects).

Blood—Eruptions from Bad Blood— (See "Fevers" in this section).

Cosmetics—Eruptions Caused By— (See Cosmetics; "Lotions" under Face).

Cutaneous Eruptions—Skin Eruptions —♅ diseases. (See the various subjects under Skin).

Death By—(See "Eruptive Fevers" in this section).

Eating—(See "Arms" in this section).

Eruptive Fevers—Exanthematous Fevers—The ⊙ or ☽ hyleg, and the ⊙ to the ☐ or ☍ the ☽ by dir.; the ⊙ affl. in ♎, from overheated blood; ♂ affl. the ⊙, ☽, Asc., or his own place by dir. or tr.; ♂ ☌ or ill-asp. the ☽ at B., or by dir.; ♂ in the Asc. at B., and affl. the hyleg; ♂ occi., and affl. the hyleg by dir., brings danger of death by an eruptive fever; afflictions in ♌ or ♒, due to disordered blood; Subs at CP, KP, Local. (See "Corrupt" under Blood; Impure).

Face—(See Acne, Cosmetics; "Lotions" under Face; Pimples).

Feet—(See "Eruptions" under Feet).

Fevers—(See "Eruptive Fevers" in this section).

Generative Organs—(See "Eruptions" under Generation).

Hands — (See "Eruptions" under Hands).

Hot Eruptions—Heat Rashes—♂ the afflictor in the disease; Subs at CP and KP.

Impure Blood—Eruptions Caused By — (See Impure. Also see "Eruptive Fevers" in this section).

Legs—(See "Eruptions" under Legs).

Pestilential Eruptions—The Asc. to the ☐ or ☍ ♂ by dir., if in fiery signs. (See Pestilence).

Violent Eruptions—The Asc. to the ☐ or ☍ ♂ by dir., if in airy signs. (See "Eruptive Fevers" in this section). For further influences along the lines of Eruptions, see the following subjects in the alphabetical arrangement, —Abscesses, Acne, Aphthae, Bites, Blemishes, Blood, Blotches, Boils, Breakings Out, Carbuncles, Carcinoma, Chancre, Chancroid, Chickenpox, Contagions, Cosmetics, Dengue, Diphtheria, Eczema, Efflorescence, Epidemics, Epithelioma, Erysipelas, Exanthema, Favus, Herpes, Hives, (see Urticaria); Infections, Itch, Ivy, Lupus, Measles, Ointments, Pimples, Pox, Pruritus, Psoriasis, Purpura, Pus, Rashes, Ringworm, Roseola, Rubefacients, Sarcoma, Scabies, Scarlet Fever, Scrofula, Scurvy, Shingles, Smallpox, Sores, Stomatitis, St. Anthony's Fire (see Erysipelas); Stings, Swellings, Syphilis, Tetter; Sore Throat (see Throat); Thrush (see Apthae; Tinea, Ulcers, Urticaria, Varicella (see Chickenpox); Variola (see Smallpox); Vesicles, Zoster (see Herpes, Shingles); Zymotic. Eruptions may occur on any part of the body, and may be both external and internal, and for parts, or organs, which may not have been mentioned in this Article, look for the Part, or Subject, in the alphabetical arrangement.

ERYSIPELAS—St. Anthony's Fire—A ♑ disease, and afflictions in ♑; ♄ or ♂ in ♑; ♄ or ♂ in an angle, occi. of the ⊙, and ori. of the ☽, and ♀ in familiarity with ♂; a ♂ disease; ♂ in ♈, ♉, ♑, or ♒; ♂ denotes death by; ♂ in ♉ or ♒ in the 6th H., and afflicted; ♂ in ♒ and affl. the ☽ or Asc., erysipelas in the lower parts; the hyleg much affl. a B. by ♂; caused by ♂ when the dominion of death is vested in him; ♂ or ♀ holding dominion at B., and in familiarity with each other, with ♂ affl. the hyleg, and elevated above the Luminaries, erysipelas is increased; cardinal signs show, and espec. afflictions in ♑; fiery signs on the Asc. or 6th H.; Subs at HP (2D), KP (11D), Local.

Arm—Upper Arm—Erysipelas In—♂ affl. in ♉ and the 1st face of the ♐ sign; Subs at LCP (6C), AP, KP. (See Arms).

Death By—Caused by ♂ when the dominion of death is vested in him.

Extremities—Lower Extremities—Legs—Calves—Erysipelas In—♂ in ♒ in the 6th H., and afflicted; ♂ in ♒, and affl. the ☽ or Asc.; Subs at PP, LPP. (See Calves, Legs).

Face—Erysipelas of—♂ affl. in ♈ or ♉, and espec. when in the 1st H.; Subs at MCP (3C), AP (7C), KP.

Head—(See "Face" in this section).

Increased—The Erysipelas Increased —(See the opening paragraph in this section).

Legs—(See "Extremities" in this section).

ERYTHEMA—Erythematous—A Superficial Blush or Redness of the Skin—A Morbid Redness—Dilated Capillaries—Usually caused by ♄ afflictions. Also may be caused by ♃ or ♀, due to congestion of blood, plethora, surfeits, etc. (See Capillaries, Congestion, Dilatation, Pellagra; "Red" under Face; Red, etc.).

ERYTHROMELALGIA—A Painful Affliction of the Extremeties, with Purplish Discoloration of the Parts—(See this subject under Feet).

ESCAPE—Escapes—

Accidents—Narrow Escapes From— (See "Escapes" under Accidents).

Death—Narrow Escapes From—Configurations which otherwise indicate early or untimely death are modified, and narrow escapes intervene if ♃ or ♀ form good asps. by ✶ or △ to the afflicted planet, or lord of the 8th; the malefics attacking one or both Luminaries, and with the ✶ or △ of ♃ or ♀ intervening; the ☉ affl. in the 8th H., has many narrow escapes, and is often threatened with death; ♅ ☌ ♄ in ♈, and espec. if ♅ is in the M.C., and afflicted; ♅ ☌ ☿ in ♊, ♍, ♎, or ♒, and afflicted. (See Averted).

Prison or Bondage—Escapes From— (See "Escapes" under Prison).

Sick—The Sick Will Hardly Escape— The ☉ and ☽ with malefics, or in ☌ with them, at the beginning of an illness. (See "Arguments", "Certain Death", under Death"; "Fatal Illness" under Fatal; "Death" under Fever; "Diseases" under Grievous; "Life Destroyed", "Small Hope", under Life; "Doubtful" under Recovery; "Disease" under Severe).

Travel—Narrow Escapes from Accident or Death In Travel—(See "Escapes" under Travel).

Vital Fluids—Escape of—(See "Fluid" under Vital).

ESCHAROTIC—(See Caustic).

Eschar—A Dry Slough—A Crust of Dead Tissue—♂ disorders, and caused by ♂. (See Crusts; "Tissue" under Dead; Sloughings).

ESOPHAGUS—(See Oesophagus).

ETHER—The Ether—Ethers—Ruled by ♅ and the ♒ sign. Light is transmitted by the Ether, and thru ♅ tends to adversely affect the eyes and the sight when affl. the ☉ or ☽ at B., and cause

eye diseases or blindness. Electricity, which travels thru the Ether, tends to shock and injury under ♅ afflictions. It is said the Spinal Canal is filled with Ether during life, which is called the "Spinal Spirit Fire", which becomes condensed, and a fluid, when exposed to the air. (See Air, Azoth, Blindness, Electricity, Eyes, Gases; "Light Rays" under Light; Matter, Retina, Shock, Sight; "Spinal Canal" under Spine; Uranus).

Etheric Fluid—(See "Fluid" under Vital).

Etheric Parts of Man—(See Astral).

The Drug Ether—A typical drug of ♅. Is also classed as a drug of Neptune because of its sleep-inducing and anaesthetic effect. (See Anaesthetics).

ETHIOPIAN—(See "Black Skin" under Black; "Figure" under Dark; Negro).

EUNUCHS—♀ in an angle, configurated with ☿, and with ♄ and ♂ elevated above her, or ♉ to ♀, tends to produce Eunuchs or Hermaphrodites, or one devoid of the natural channels and vents; ♄ and ♀ in the 4th H., and afflicted. (See "Channels and Vents" under Genitals; Effeminate, Hermaphrodites; "Castration" under Testes; Virile).

EUPATORIUM—A typical drug of ♃. (See Jupiter).

EUSTACHIAN TUBES—Ruled by ♀ and the ♉ sign, and are espec. affected by the ☉ or ☽ acting thru this sign, and with afflictions in or to ♉. Also ☿ when in ♉ greatly affects the tubes, and causes disorders of when afflicted, or afflicted in the 12th H., and which may lead to deafness and ear troubles. These Tubes are affected by Subs at AT, AX, and MCP (4C). (See Catarrh; "Cervical Ganglion" under Cervical; "Deafness" under Hearing; "Diseases" under Neck; Nose).

EVACUATIONS—Defacation—Evacuations of various kinds from the body tend to be more free and profuse at the time of the Full Moon when the fluids of the body are at high tide, as those thru the nose, bowels, the urine, perspiration, etc. (See Faeces).

Bloody Evacuations—Are generally considered ♂ diseases and afflictions. (See "Bloody Discharges" under Discharges; Dysentery, Effusions, Faeces, Fistula; "Bloody Flux" under Flux; Haemoptysis, Hemorrhage, Menses; "Epistaxis" under Nose; Rectum, Sweat, Typhoid, Urine, etc.).

Morbidly Frequent—(See Diarrhoea).

EVENTS—Accidents, Calamity, Sickness, etc., are events, and are usually precipitated by the aspects and movements of the ☽, and also by progressed influences, transits, and directions over the map. The ☽ tends to bring events to pass, as she is the time marker in Human Affairs and World Conditions, and on the dial of destiny corresponds to the minute hand, while the movements of the ☉ represent the hour hand. The aspects of the ☽, Lunations, New Moons, and Eclipses, indicate the times when directions and progressed influences will culminate into action.

Events, and the time of sickness, accidents, etc., are shown by the aspects of progressed planets, transits and directions, as they affect the radical map, and thus in this way "Coming Events Cast Their Shadows Before." Obstructions and impediments can be placed in the way of the planetary influences, thus greatly diminishing their force, or preventing them altogether. Events can be altered and modified by foreknowledge of their nature, and by the use of wisdom, self-control, discretion, discrimination, will-power, spiritual attainment, mastery of the lower nature, and by ruling one's stars, conquering the Monsters of the Zodiac, etc. For this reason the Ancients instituted remedies, preventatives, preservatives, and propitiations. The time of death, injuries, accidents, and dangers, is shown by the arcs of directions to the Sig. for the event.

Accidents — The Event of — (See "Time" under Accidents. Also see the first part of this Article).

Calamity—The Event of—(See Calamity, Disgrace, Misfortune, Reversals, Ruin, Trouble, etc.).

Coming Events—Are indicated by aspects applying, and past events are shown by aspects separating.

Danger—Near Some Danger—Danger Is At Hand—(See Danger).

Death—The Event of Death—Time of —(See "Time of" under Death).

Directions and Death—(See Anareta; "Arguments for" under Death; Directions).

Disease—The Event of—(See "Time of" under Disease).

Evil Events—(See "Good and Evil" in this section).

Good and Evil Events—Good events are indicated by the ☽ forming favorable aspects to the Benefics, and evil events by the afflictions of the Malefics to the ☽. The ☽ ☌ ☉ by dir., and at the same time in □ to a malefic, indicates a very evil time in the life, illness, accidents, afflictions, reversals, and possible death, and under such a configuration a remarkably evil event usually takes place. (See "Time" under Evil).

Great Events—Are coincident with the appearance of Comets. (See Comets).

Ill-Health—The Event of—(See "Periods of Bad Health" under Health; "Long Siege of" under Ill-Health).

Injury—Event of—(See "Time of" under Accidents).

Modification of Events—(See the Introduction to this Article; Destiny, Fate, Prevention; "Free Will" under Will).

Nature of the Events—The ☽ in signs of human form tends to events affecting Mankind; in air signs, the Air; in earth signs, the Earth and its fruits; in water signs, the Waters and Seas; in quadrupedal or animal signs, cattle, horses, sheep, and all four-footed Beasts. (See "Air Signs" under Air;

Animals, Beasts, Cattle; "Earth Signs" under Earth; Floods, Fruits, Horses; "Human Form" under Human; Mankind, Nature, Public, Quadrupeds, Scarcity, Seas, Sheep, Ships; "Signs" under Water; Weather).

Past Events—(See "Coming Events" in this section).

Prevention of Events—(See the Introduction to this section. Also see Prevention).

Sickness—The Event of—(See "Ill-Health" in this section; "Time of" under Disease).

Strange Events—Sudden Events—Unexpected Events—The ☉ to the ill-asps. ♅ by dir.; the ☽ to the place of ♅ at B. by dir. or tr. tends to sudden ill; ♅ stationary near the place of the ☉ or ☽ at B., or in evil asp. to either; ♅ ascending at B.; the asps. of ♅ to the ☉, ☽, Asc., M.C. by dir.; the evil asps. of ♂ to the ☉, ☽, Asc., or M.C. also tend to sudden events, and generally of an evil or violent nature, as accidents or injuries. (See Extraordinary, Mysterious, Neptune, Peculiar, Strange, Sudden, Unexpected, Untimely, Uranus).

Sudden Events—(See "Strange" in this section).

Time of Events—(See the various paragraphs in this section. Also see Time).

Unexpected Events—(See "Strange" in this section). Life is but one succession of events from the cradle to the grave, and for subjects not mentioned here, look for the subject in the alphabetical arrangement. Especially note the following subjects,—Abroad, Accidents, Afflictions, Bereavement, Birth, Blows, Bruises, Catastrophies, Character, Climacteric, Comets, Cuts, Cycles, Danger, Death, Destiny, Directions, Disease, Disgrace, Disturbances, Drought; Earthquakes (see Earth); Eclipses, Evils, Falls, Famine, Fate, Fire, Fortune; Free Will (see Will); Hurts, Imminent, Injuries, Journeys, Judges, Lunations, Malice, Mankind, Mischief, Miseries, Misfortune; New Moon (see Moon); Murder, Periods, Prison, Prognosis, Progression, Public, Railroads, Reversals, Ruin, Scandal, Seas; Secondary Directions (see Secondary); Ships, Shipwreck, Sickness, Sorrow, Stabs, Suicide, Travel, Treachery, Trouble, Vehicles, Violence, Volcanoes, Water, Weather, Wounds, etc.

EVIL—Evils—Evilly—

Absent Party—Some Great Evil Has Overtaken the Absent Party—(See "Great Evil" under Absent Party).

Complexion—Evil Complexion—(See Bad, Evil, Poor, Sickly, under Complexion).

Conduct—Evil Conduct—Disgraceful Actions—Bad Courses—Wild Conduct —The ☉ to the ill-asps. ♀ by dir.; the ☉ Sig. □ or ☍ ♃; the ☽ Sig. in ♓, not inclined to action unless of the worst kind; the ☽ in bad asp. to ♅ does not improve the moral nature; ♄ or ♂ Sig. □ or ☍ ♀; ♂ at a Solar Rev. passing the place of the radical ☽ or ♀; ♀

Sig. in ♏, and ♀ affl. by ♄ or ♂, disgraceful actions, and with very evil propensities if ♃ or the ☉ do not assist by their good asps.; the Asc. to the ill-asps. ♀ by dir., and ♀ affl. by ♄ or ♂ at B. (See Conduct, Criminal, Cruel, Debauched, Depraved, Disgrace, Dishonest, Drink, Drunkenness, Gambling, Lewd, Licentious, Mischief; "Loose Morals" under Morals; Murderous, Perverted, Profane, Riotous, Thieving, Unnatural, Vices, Violent, Wicked, etc.).

Deeds—Delights In the Most Evil Deeds—(See "Conduct" in this section).

Directions—Evil Directions—(See Directions).

Disease—Evil End to the Disease—(See Death; "End" under Disease; "Evil End" under End; Fatal).

Drink—Evils From—(See Drink, Drunkenness, Intoxication).

Events—Evil Events—(See Events).

Every Evil—(1) Every Evil Upon Humanity—Many Evils Upon Humanity—The appearance of Comets tends to bring many evils upon Mankind, and to cause a deranged system; the Pleiades rising, or with the ☉ or ☽, or directed to the Asc., every evil that can befall Humanity; Eclipses of the ☽ in the 3rd Dec. of ♐; ♄, ♃, ♂, and the ☽ conjoined in ♌; ♏ ascending at the Vernal, and ♄ ☌ ♂ therein, and with ♃ ℞, and ♀ combust; the Ascelli conjoined with the ☉ or ☽. (See Ascelli, Calamity, Castor, Comets, Eclipses; "Public Grief" under Grief; Humanity, Mankind, Miseries, Nebulous, Pleiades, Public; "Much Sadness" under Sadness, Sorrow, etc.). (2) Every Evil Upon the Native—♄ affl. in the 12th H. denotes every evil that can befall the native except death; the ☉ directed to the Jaw of the Whale, South Scale, Cynosura, or the Twins, tends to much evil for the native; the ☽ to the ☐ or ☍ ♂ by dir., every evil; the ☽ directed to the Whale's Jaw, Knees of Castor and Pollux, Belly of the Twins, or Cynosura, many evils; the M.C. to the ☐ or ☍ ♂ by dir., many evils; lord of the 9th H. weak, ℞, or combust, denotes great evils upon the native; the Pleiades rising, or with the ☉ or ☽, or directed to the Asc. (See Ascelli, Calamity, Castor, Cynosura, Disgrace, Honour, Pleiades, Pollux, Reverses, Ruin, Trouble, Twelfth House, Whale's Jaw).

Evilly Disposed—Evil Propensities—Evil Tendencies—The ☽ Sig. in ♓; ♂ Sig. ☌ or ill-asp. ♄ or ♉, and espec. in angles, the disposition is very evil, and the person often fierce and violent; ♀ Sig. in ♏, and affl. by ♄ and ♂, and no good asps. from the ☉ or ♃, very evil propensities. (See "Conduct", "Qualities", in this section).

Excesses—Evils From—(See Excesses).

Habits—(See "Evil" under Habits).

Indicative of Evil—The ☉ with the Pleiades, Hyades, Praesepe, the Ascelli, Castor or Pollux. (See "Every Evil" in this section).

Influences—Evil Influences—Evil Aspects—The evil aspects and influences in a map, as related to the health of the body and mind, are increased when augmented by the ill-asps. of the malefics, and diminished by the good asps. of the ☉, ♃, or ♀. (See Aspects, Benefics, Malefics).

Manners—Evil Manners—The ☽ sepr. from the ☉ and apply. to ☿ in a day geniture. (See Manners).

Many Evils Upon Humanity—(See "Every Evil" in this section).

Much Evil—Upon the Native, and Upon Humanity—(See "Every Evil" in this section).

Nobles and Grandees—Evil To—(See Nobles).

Qualities of Mind—Evil Qualities—An Evil Nature—Caused by the evil asps. of ♂ to the Sigs., or the ☉, ☿, or Asc. (See "Conduct", "Evilly Disposed", in this section. Also see Malevolent).

Serious Evils In Life—The ☽ to the ill-asps. ♄ by dir. (See Saturn).

Sudden Evils—The ☉ to the ill-asps. ♅ or ♂ by dir.; ♅ weak and ill-dig. at B., or by tr. or dir. (See Sudden).

Tendencies—Evil Tendencies—(See "Evilly Disposed" in this section).

Thoughts—The Mind Disturbed by Evil Thoughts—(See "Conduct" in this section; "Unclean" under Mind).

Time—An Evil Time for the Native—The ☉ to the ill-asps. the ☽, ♄, ♃, ♅, or ♂ by dir.; the ☽ to the ill-asps. the ☉ by dir. (See Accidents, Affliction, Calamity, Climacteric, Dangers, Directions, Disease, Disgrace; "Good and Evil Events" under Events; "Periods of Bad Health" under Health; Honour, Ill-Health, Imprisonment (see Prison); Injury, Judges, Misery, Misfortune, Periodic, Reverses, Ruin, Scandal, Sickness, Sorrow, Suffering, Trouble; "Time" under Accidents and Disease; Unexpected, Worry, Wounds).

EVOLUTION—The Occult teaches that Man's Mind and Body have evolved gradually thru many stages before coming to their present efficiency. Man's early bodies were bisexed, hermaphrodites, and the separation of the sexes began in the Lemurian Epoch, and Adam and Eve are considered types of the first of the separated sexes. There are still remnants of hermaphrodites in the World to-day. Also in the early stages of the Earth, when it was hot and fiery, people could not stand upon the Earth, and their bodies were like gas bags, capable of living and floating in the air. They also had a third eye in the back of their heads so they could see approaching dangers from all sides. This eye has now been drawn inward, and is the Pineal Gland. When language was needed, and a voice, the larynx and vocal cords, ruled by the ☿ sign, were taken from ♏, the sex sign, and this is the reason why the voice and the sex organs are so closely related, and why the voice in males changes at puberty. Man's body is still far from being perfect, and is still evolving and improving, and in future Ages will be a much better, and more highly spiritualized body than now. This subject of the Evolution of Man and his Vehicles, is a big one, and only a few things can be mentioned here. If you are interested in the whole story of the Evolution of Man, and of the Earth in its various Epochs, read the books, "Cosmo-Conception", by Max Heindel, and also the book, "The Key To The Universe", by Dr. and Mrs. Homer Curtiss. These books also explain the two stories of Creation in the Bible. (See Build, Character, Larynx, Pineal Gland, Puberty; "Separation of" under Sex).

EVOLVED TYPES—(See Genius, Prodigies).

EXAGGERATED—Exaggeration—

Exaggerated Action—♅ influence, as in Cramps, Hernia, Ruptures, Shock, Spasms, etc. (See these subjects). The plus, or tonic action of ♂, also tends to exaggerated action of mind and body.

Exaggerated Ego—(See Ego).

Exaggerated Hysteria—(See Hysteria).

Exaggerated Sex Desires—(See Passion).

EXALTATION—

Emotional Exaltation—(See Ecstasy, Emotions, Religion).

Functions—Exalted Excito-Motory Function—With Pains and Cramps From—♂ ☌ or ill-asp. ♅. (See Cramps, Excitable, Motor, Pain).

Mind and Body Exalted—The good asps. of ♂ to the ☉, ☽, ☿, Asc., and the hyleg. (See Mental, Mind).

Planets—Exaltation of—Planets in their exalted signs have more power for good or evil in health matters, and espec. when aspecting the hyleg. Planets in their detriment, or fall, have less power for good, and also tend to be more unfortunate over the life, health, mind, and affairs of the native. (See the Tables of Exaltations, Detriment, Fall, etc., in the Textbooks of Astrology).

EXAMINATIONS—Fails In—Poor In Study—Loses Interest In Studies—The ☉ to the ☌ ☿ by dir., or vice versa; ☿ combust, setting in the West at B., and affl. by the ☽, and also ☿ in no good asp. to the Asc.; the ☽ to the ill-asps. ☿ by dir., loses interest in studies for the time. (See Forgetful, Learning; "Shallow" under Mentality; Reading, Study).

EXANTHEMA — Exanthematous — (See Efflorescence, Eruptions, Rashes).

Fevers—Exanthematous Fevers—(See "Eruptive Fevers" under Eruptions).

Throat—Exanthematous Sore Throat —(See "Exanthematous" under Throat).

EXCELLENT—

Abilities—Excellent Abilities—(See "Active Mind" under Active; Elegant, Examinations, Genius, Learning; "Quickened" under Mentality; "Good Mind" under Mind; Prodigies, Reading, Study).

Disposition—Excellent Disposition— Even Temper—The ☉ Sig. ⚹ or △ ♃. (See Disposition, Generous, Mild, Temper, Temperament).

Health—Excellent Health—(See "Abundance", "Good", under Health; Immunity, Recuperation, Resistance, Robust, Ruddy, Stamina, Strength, Strong, Tone, Vitality, etc.).

Qualities—Excellent Mental Qualities —Good Abilities—(See "Abilities", "Disposition", in this section).

EXCESS—Excessive—Excessively—Colliquative—Copious—Overflowing—Immoderate—Profuse—Redundant— ♂ is excessive. ♃ is overflowing. ♀ is redundant and overflowing in quality. (See Abundance, Colliquative, Copious, Increase, Jupiter, Mars, Plenty, Profuse, Redundant, Venus).

Acidity—Excessive Acidity—(See Acids).

Albumin—Excess of In Urine—(See Albumen).

Alkalinity—Excess of In System— (See Alkaline).

Animal Heat—In the Body—Excess of—(See "Animal Heat" under Heat).

Atmospheric Pressure — Excessive — Disease From—(See Atmosphere, Caisson, Compressed, Gases, Pressure).

Blood—Excess of—(See "Too Much Blood", "Pressure", under Blood; Plethora; "Fullness" under Vascular).

Cold—Excess of—Caused by ♄. (See Cold; "Lack of Animal Heat" under Heat; Saturn; "Cold" under Weather).

Colliquative Sweats — Excessive Sweats of Phthisis—(See "Night Sweats" under Phthisis).

Corpulence—Excess of—(See Corpulence, Fat, Obesity).

Discharges—Excessive—(See Discharges).

Dryness—Excess of—(See Drought; "Excess" under Dryness; Famine, Fountains, Scarcity).

Fat—Excess of—(See Fat, Obesity).

Fever—Excessive—(See "High Fever" under Fever).

Fluids—Excess of—(See Puffing).

Force—Excess of—(See "Excess" under Force).

Functions—(See Discomfort; "Excessive" under Functions).

Growth — Excessive — (See Enlarged, Giants, Growth, Large).

Heat—Excess of In the Body—Excessive Heat—(See "Excessive Bodily Heat", "Extreme Heat", "Overabundance", "Warm Weather", under Heat).

Menses—Excessive and Copious—(See Menses).

Mental Action — Excessive — (See "Over-active Mind" under Active).

Nervous Action—Excessive—☿ affl. in the 6th H. (See Erethism, Excitable; "Neurotic" under Nerves).

Neurotic Action — Excessive — (See "Highly Neurotic" under Nerves).

Passion—Excess of—(See "Passional Excesses" under Passion).

Phlegm—Excess of—(See Phlegm).

Phthisis—Excessive Sweats of—(See "Night Sweats" under Phthisis).

Pleasure—Excessive Pleasure, and Diseases From—(See Pleasure).

Saliva—Excess of—(See Saliva).

Sensibility — Excessive Sensibility—(See Hyperaesthesia).

Sugar—Excess of In Urine—(See Diabetes).

Sweat — Excess of — (See "Night Sweats" under Phthisis; Sweat).

Urates—Excess of—(See Urates).

Urea—(See "Excess" under Urea).

Uric Acid—Excess of—(See Deposits, Lithemia, Uric).

Urine — Excess of — (See Diabetes; "Excess", "Polyuria", under Urine).

Virile Members — Excessive — (See Virile).

Vitality—Excess of—(See "Excess" under Vitality).

Voluntary Power—Excess of—(See Voluntary). For further study see Abnormalities, Colds, Concretions, Deposits, Diarrhoea, Dropsies, Dysentery, Effusions, Enlarged, Expanded, Excesses, Expectoration, Excitable, Extreme, Evacuations, Flow, Fluids, Fluxes, Full, Gas, Growths,, Hemorrhage, Hermaphrodite, Humours, Hydrocephalus, Hyper (the various subjects beginning with "Hyper"); Juices, Malformations, Moisture, Monsters; "Coryza" under Nose; Over (the various subjects beginning with "Over"); Plethora, Prudence, Pseudo, Rain, Rheum, Secretions, Super (the various subjects beginning with "Super"); Surfeits, Swellings, Tears, Tumors, Wastes, Water, Wind, etc.

EXCESSES—Overindulgences—Extravagance—Luxuries—Indiscretions—Carelessness—Inordinate—Free Living—etc.—♂ is excessive in nature, and his afflictions tend to excesses, and espec. along passional lines. They are also the outcome of ♃ or ♀ afflictions, or afflictions to the ☉, ☽, and Asc. Jupiter is overflowing in action. Many maps of birth are unbalanced, full of adverse aspects, and when the lower mind is ruling and dominating, tend to many extremes, excesses, and perversions. The subject of Excesses is a large one, and would be too lengthy to list every known excess in this Article. The following subjects and references are a partial list, and suggestive, and for subjects not listed or mentioned here, look in the alphabetical arrangement for the subject you have in mind.

Acoholic Excesses — (See Alcohol, Drink, etc.).

Amorous Indulgence—Excess of—(See Amourous).

Appetites—Goes to Excesses to Gratify—(See Appetites).

Blood Disorders — Thru Excesses — (See "Diseases" in this section).

Death—Thru Excesses—(See "Causes His Own Death", and the various paragraphs under Death).

Degeneration —Thru Excesses—(See Degeneration).

Diet—Food—Ailments from Excesses and Indiscretions In—(See Diet, Eating, Food, Gluttony, etc.).

Diseases—Proceeding from Excesses—The ☉ affl. by ♀; the ☽ in water signs, to the ♂ or ill-asp. ♂ by dir.; the ☽ in ♓, and affl. by the ☉ or ♂ when taken ill (Hor'y); ♃ diseases; ♃ affl. in the Asc., or 6th H.; ♃ affl. in ♒, blood disorders thru excesses; ♂ affl. in ♓; ♀ diseases; ♀ affl. in ♏; ♀ affl. by ♂; ♀ affl. in the Asc. or 6th H.; the Asc. affl. by ♃ or ♀; the Asc. to the ill-asps. ♀ by dir., and ♀ affl. at B.; ♌ on cusp of 6th H.; the 11° ♉ on the Asc.; the 1st Dec. ♏ on the Asc., which is ruled by ♂. (See "Corrupt" under Blood; Carelessness, Cramps; "Causes His Own Death" under Death; Debauchery; "Brings Disease Upon Himself" under Disease; Dissipation, Eating, Extravagances, Gout, High Living (see High); Indigestion, Indiscretions, Indulgence, Obesity, Plethora, Rheumatism, Sex Diseases (see Passion, Sex); Sickness, Surfeits, Vitality Lessened, etc.). The afflictions arising from excesses, irregularities, indulgence of the animal appetites, etc., are legion, and tend to bring disease, death, and suffering upon humanity. Look for further subjects in the alphabetical arrangement.

Drink—Excesses In—(See Delirium Tremens, Drink, Drunkenness, Intoxication, etc.).

Drugs—Excesses In Drug Taking, Narcotics, etc.—(See Narcotics).

Early Death—Thru Excesses and Dissipation—(See "Early Death" under Early).

Eating—Excesses and Indiscretions In—(See Diet, Eating).

Exercise — Excesses In—Disorders Arising From—(See Exercise, Sports).

Fevers — From Excesses — (See "Slight" under Fevers).

Food—Excesses In—(See Diet, Eating, Indiscretions).

Genitals—Diseases of Thru Sex Excesses—(See "Diseases" under Genitals).

Indulging In Excesses—Prone To—The prog. ☉ or ☽ to the ♂ or ill-asp. ♂; the ☽ in ♋ or ♓, and affl. by the ☉ or ♂; the ☽ to the ill-asps. ♃, ♀, or ♂ by dir.; ♂ Sig. □ or ☍ ♀; characteristic of ♂ people; ♂ affl. in ♓; ♀ weak and affl. at B.; ♀ affl. in ♏; ♀ Sig. □ or ☍ ♂; ♀ lady of the year at the Vernal Equi., and espec. when ♀ is ruler, and affl. at B.; the Asc. to the ill-asps. ♀ by dir., and ♀ affl. at B.; ♌ on the cusp of 6th H.; 1st Dec. ♏ on the Asc., which is ruled by ♂; 11° ♉ or 6° ♋ on the Asc. (See "Noises" under Head. Also note the various paragraphs in this section).

Love Affairs—Excesses In—(See Amorous; "Free Love" under Free; Intercourse, Love Affairs, Opposite Sex; "Passional Excesses" under Passion; "Clandestine" under Sex; Venery).

Passional Excesses — (See Amorous; "Passional Excesses" under Passion; Venery, etc.).

Sex Excesses—(See "Love Affairs", "Passional Excesses", in this section; "Early Death" under Early; "Dies Before Middle Life" under Middle Life).

Sickness—From Excesses—(See "Diseases" in this section).

Slight Disorders—Thru Excesses—(See Indiscretions, Mild, Slight).

Stomach Disorders—Thru Excesses—The ☽ in ♋ and affl. by the ☉ or ♂ when taken ill (Hor'y). (See Drink, Eating, Indigestion; "Riotous Living" under Riotous; Stomach).

Study—And Reading—Disorders from Excesses In—(See "Brain Fag" under Brain; "Eyestrain" under Eyes; Blindness, Reading, Study). For further study along the lines of Excesses, see the following subjects, and also various other subjects which occur to your mind, and which may not be listed or mentioned in this Article,—Abnormalities, Anger; "Animal Instincts" under Animal; Bad; "Lack of Balance" under Balance; Beastly; "High Pressure", "Too Much Blood", under Blood; Carelessness, Cohabitation, Conduct, Criminal, Debased, Decay, Degenerate, Depraved, Deviations, Disgrace, Dissolute, Dress, Dropsy, Energies, Epicureans, Evils, Extravagance, Feasting, Folly, Free Living (see Free); Frenzy, Fury, Gluttony, Gratification, Habits, Harlots, Heart, Headaches, Ill-Health; Improvident, Impure, Indecent, Indiscretions, Infamous, Infirmities, Inordinate, Insanity, Intemperate, Irregularities, Lascivious, Lewd, Licentious, Lust, Luxuries, Madness, Mania, Men, Morals, Noises, Nymphomania; "Over-Indulgence" under Over; Perversions, Pleasures, Prodigal, Rashness, Recklessness, Scandal; "Self-Indulgent", "Self-Undoing", under Self; Sensuality; "Sex Relations" under Sex; Shameless; "High Temper" under Temper; Tumors, Vices, Vicious, Vile, Violent, Vital Forces (see Vital); Wanton, Wasting, Wicked, Women, etc.

EXCISION—Of the Foetus—(See "Excision" under Foetus).

EXCITABLE—Excitement—Excitation

Beside Oneself—Caused by the afflictions of ♆. Excitement, religious or otherwise, and where Frenzy is apt to accompany. Mostly manifested in emotional religious experiences, which are ruled by ♆, the ruler of the Spiritual Faculties. (See Ecstasy, Emotions, Frenzy, Hysteria, Neptune, Religion).

Body and Mind—Excitation of—♂ influence. (See the different paragraphs in this section).

Cellular Excitation—(See "Excitation" under Cells).

Excitable—High Nervous Tension—High Strung—The ☉ or ☽ in fiery signs, ☌, □, or ☍ ♂; ♆ in a prominent position at B., and affl. the ☽ or ♆, tends to paroxysms of nervous excitation; ♆ affl. in the 3rd or 9th H., or ♆ rising; ♅ or ♂ affl. ☿ tend to high nervous tension, nervous excitability, and an excited manner in speaking; ♃ affl. in ♏; ♂ in ♈, highly excitable; ♂ ☌, □, or ☍ ☿; ☿ influence is excitable,

nervous, quivering, and tends to ceaseless motion; ☿ ill-dig. at B., frantic and excessively excitable, and espec. when affl. by ♂; ♈, ♌, and ♐ are the most excitable signs, and the earthy and airy signs the least; along emotional and sensational lines, the watery signs are excitable; characteristic of the Choleric, or Bilious Temperament, which is ruled by the ☉, ♂, and the fiery signs. (See Choleric; "High Strung" under High; "Neurasthenia" and "Highly Neurotic" under Nerves. Also see "Nerves" in this section).

Exhaustion—Nervous Exhaustion from Too Much Excitement—☿ ☌, □, ☍ ♂ at B., or by dir.; Subs at AT, AX, CP (5D), and PP. (See Exhaustion, Fatigue; "Neurasthenia" under Nerves).

Function—Exalted Excito-Motory Function—(See "Functions" under Exaltation).

Hasty and Excitable—The ☉, ☽, and many planets in fiery signs; the ☉ or ☽ ☌, ♂; ♂ in the Asc., or M.C., and affl. the ☉ or ☽; fiery signs upon the Asc. (See "Excitable" in this section. Also see Rashness, Recklessness).

High Strung—(See "Excitable" in this section).

Ill-Health—From Over-Excitement—The ☉ affl. in ♈. (See the various paragraphs and references in this section).

Involuntary—Involuntary Muscular Excitement—(See "Involuntary" under Muscles).

Mental Excitement—A ☿ disturbance; caused by ♂ afflictions to the ☉, ☽, or ☿, or ♂ in the Asc. or M.C., and in one of his strong signs; malefics in the 1st H. at a Solar Rev. (See the various paragraphs in this section. Also see Anger, Choleric; "High Temper" under Temper).

Mind—Excitation of Body and Mind—Excitable Mind—♂ influence. (See "Excitable", "Mental", in this section).

Muscles—Involuntary Excitement of—(See "Involuntary" under Muscles).

Nature—Disposition—An Excitable Nature—(See "Excitable" in this section).

Nerves—Nerve Centers—Nervous Excitation—Paroxysms of Nervous Excitement—Neurotic Excitement, etc.—♆ in a prominent position, or affl. the ☽ or ☿, tends to paroxysms of nervous excitation, and which is often followed by complete collapse; ♆ a strong influence at B.; also a ♅ disease; ☿ affl. by ♅ or ♂; ☿ afflicted tends to nervous diseases arising from excitement. (See "Excitable" in this section. Also see Collapse, Erethism; "Centers", "Highly Neurotic", "Neurasthenia", "Prostration", under Nerves).

Over-Excitement—Ill-Health From—(See "Ill-Health" in this section).

Paroxysms—Of Nervous Excitation—(See "Excitable" in this section).

Reflected Excitement—A ☿ disease. (See Reflected).

Religious Excitement—Religious Frenzy—♆ tends to produce, and ♆ afflicted, as by ♅ or ♂, as ♆ rules the Spiritual Faculties, and tends to Religious Frenzy, Ecstasy, etc. (See "Beside Oneself", "Excitable", in this section. Also see Emotions, Frenzy; "Religious Mania" under Mania; "Ecstasy" under Religion). For further study along these lines see Action; "Over-Active Mind" under Active; "Brain Storms" under Brain; Demoniac, Dispersions, Effervescent, Erratic, Exaggerated, Exaltation, Explosive, Fierce, Foolhardy, Fury, Hasty, Impulses, Insanity, Irritable, Jealousy, Jerky, Madness, Mania, Motion; "Nerves" under Motor; Murderous; "Strain" under Nerves; "Psychic Storms" under Psychic; Quarrelsome, Quivering, Savage, Sensational, Spasmodic, Temper, Tension, Trembling, Uncontrolled, Vicious, Violent, Wild.

EXCORIATIONS—An Abrasion of the Epidermis—(See Abrasions).

EXCREMENT—(See Excretion).

EXCRESCENCES—An Abnormal Outgrowth on the Body—Malefics in angles, and the ☉ or ☽ in ♂ or ☍, or brought up to them; the ☽ in obnoxious signs, as ♈, ♉, ♋, ♏, or ♑, in her nodes, or in extreme Lat., and the malefics brought up to the Luminaries, then the body is afflicted with excrescences, lameness, or paralysis. The calamity takes place from the moment of birth if the malefics be with the ☉ or ☽, but if the malefics be in the 10th H., and elevated above the Luminaries, or in ☍ to each other, then the trouble arises from falls from heights, attacks by robbers or quadrupeds, or by some dangerous accident. (See Distortions).

Head—Excrescences of—♈ or ♎ on the Asc., and the ☽ therein and afflicted; cardinal signs on the angles; many planets in cardinal signs, and espec. in ♈ or ♎. (See "Excrescences", "Malformation", under Head. Also see "Skull" in this section).

Moment of Birth—Excrescences From —(See the first part of this section).

Skull—And Head—Soft, Watery, Hemispherical Excrescences on the Skull and Head—Case—See "Short Life", No. 778, in 1001 N.N. This case is also commented upon in Daath's Medical Astrology, Chap. 14, page 104. (See "Head" in this section. Also see Skull). For further study see "Moment of Birth" under Calamity; Fungus, Growths, Tubercles, Warts, Wens).

EXCRETION—Excretory System—Organs of Excretion—Emunctory Ducts and Organs—Excrement, etc.—Excretion is a function of the ♏ sign. The internal Excretory System is under the internal rulership of ♏. The Excretory Processes of the body are ruled by ♏ in general. Excretion in and from the kidneys is ruled by ♏. The lower excretory bowels are ruled by ♏. The Excrementitious Fluids, such as the Menses, Sweat, Urine, etc., are ruled by ♏. Also ♏ rules the principal excretory orifices, as the Nose, Rectum, Urethra, Vagina, etc. The Ears, and excretions from, are ruled by ♉. The Skin as an organ of excretion is ruled by ♑. The Faeces are ruled by ♄ and ♏.

Discharges—The Excretory Discharges—(See Discharges, Expulsion, Faeces, Menses, Sweat, Urine, etc.).

Disorders—Of the Excretory System —The malefics, or afflicting planets, in the fixed signs, and espec. in ♉ or ♏; the ☉ affl. in ♏ tends to disorders of a violent or inflammatory nature; afflictions in ♏, or ♏ on the Asc., and afflicted; ♉ on the Asc., by reflex action; ♉, ♌, or ♏ on cusp the 6th H.

Drugs—Alteratives—Drugs which Alter the Process of Excretion—(See Alterative).

Fluids—Excrementitious Fluids— Ruled by ♏, such as the Menses, Sweat, Urine, Wastes, etc. (See these subjects).

Obstructions Of—The afflictions of ♄ tend to obstruct the excretions, and to make it more difficult for waste food products to pass the kidneys, colon, skin and other avenues of outlet, thus accumulating obstructions in the organs of excretion. The avenues of escape being gradually checked, the poisons and wastes of the body are shut in, leading to stone, decay, decrepitude and death. (See Aches, Bowels, Concretions, Decay, Deposits, Elimination, Fluids, Functions, Gravel, Kidneys, Minerals, Obstructions, Sand, Secretions, Skin, Stone, Uric Acid (see Uric); Wastes, etc.).

Sensitive Excretory Organs—♏ on the Asc.

Strain—♅ in ♏ warns against overstraining the Excretory System.

EXECRATED—Cursed by the Multitude —♃ Sig. ☐ or ☍ the ☽; the 19° ♏ on the Asc. at B., lives a cursed life, a terror and pest to Society, acquaintances, or relatives. (See Acquaintances, Execution, Friends, Hatred, Infamous, Public, Relations, Society, etc.).

EXECUTION—Death By—(See Beheaded; "Stake" under Burns; "Electrocution" under Electricity; Guillotine, Hanging, Ignoble, Impalement, Judges, Lynched, Mobs, Murder; "Public Death" under Public; "Flying Stones" under Stones; Tragical, etc.). Cases of Execution—See "Savonarola", No. 459; "Pressed to Death", No. 626; "Princess", No. 697; "Horsford", No. 764, all in 1001 N.N.

EXERCISE—Exercises—Pastimes— Athletics—Recreations—Sports, etc.— The ♐ sign bears strong rule over Exercise, Sports, Athletics, Out-door Life, Horseback Riding, Games, Fishing, Hunting, etc.

Blindness—Injury During Sports or Exercise, Resulting In Blindness—(See "Sports" under Blindness).

Blood Overheated—Thru Sports and Violent Exercise—♃ affl. in ♐.

Colds—Cold taken after Over-Exertion, or Over-Exercise of Mind and Body—The ☽ in ♐, ♂ or ill-asp. ♄ (or ☿ if he be of the nature of ♄) at the time. (See Colds).

Death—From Accidents in Sports, or after Violent Exercise—(See "Death" under Sports; "Early Death" under Early. Also see Case, "Early Death", No. 428, in 1001 N.N.).

Eyes—Injury to the Eyes During Exercise, Athletics, or Sports—Afflictions in ♐; the ☉ in an angle, ♂ or ☍ the ☽, and also ♂ configurated with ☿; the ☉ directed to Praesepe, Hyades, Pleiades, Castor, Pollux, and other stars of the nature of ♂ and the ☽ combined, and espec. if Praesepe be on the Asc., or with the ☉ or ☽ in an angle; the ☽ ♂ ♂ with the Pleiades, and ♄ with Regulus. (See "Amusements", "Sports", under Blindness; "Accidents" under Eyes).

Falls—(See "Sports" under Falls).

Fatigue—Fatigue or Disease from Over-Exercise—(See "Inordinate" in this section; "Exercise" under Fatigue).

Fond of Exercise—Partial to Exercise and Recreations—♃ Sig. in ♎ or ♐. (See Amusements, Pleasures, Recreations, Sports).

Injuries—During Exercise or Sports, and in Riding, Hunting, etc.—Afflictions in ♐. (See Hunting, Riding; "Injuries" under Sports).

Inordinate Exercise—Over-Exercise—Violent Exercise—Fatigue, Disease or Ill-Health From—The ☽ in ♐ at the time, and also at B., and affl. by the ☉ or ♂, or by ♄ (or ☿ if he be of the nature of ♄); ♄ in ♐ at B., or by dir., warns against over-strain and over-exertion of the body in sports; ♄ in the heart sign ♌, and also in the opposite sign ♒, tends to make physical strain harmful. (See "Over-Exertion" under Exertion; Strain).

Intemperate—In Exercise and Sports—♐ diseases, and afflictions in ♐. (See "Inordinate" in this section; "Over-Exertion" under Exertion; Intemperate, Indiscretions; "Intemperate" under Sports).

Lack of Exercise—Sedentary Habits—Inclined to Take Little or No Exercise—Caused by ♄ influence; ♄ ruler at B.; characteristic of ♄ people; the ☽ also rules sedentary habits, and espec. when ♂ is weak at B. and not favorably aspecting the ☉ or ☽; ♃ ☐ or ☍ the ☉ at B., and by dir.; ♀ weak and affl. at B. (See Obesity, Sedentary, Tumors).

Mind—Over-Exercise of the Mind, and with Fatigue or Illness From—(See "Over-Active Mind", under Active; "Reading and Study" under Blindness; "Brain-Fag" under Brain; Fatigue, Reading, Study).

Out-Door Exercise—Fond of—(See "Out-Door" under Sports).

Over-Exercise—(See "Inordinate" in this section).

Over-Heated Blood—(See "Blood" in this section).

Sedentary Habits—(See "Lack of Exercise" in this section).

Sports—Over-Exercise In—Indiscretions In—(See "Inordinate", "Intemperate", in this section. Also see the various paragraphs under Sports).

Travel—Over-Exercise In, and Fatigue or Sickness—(See "Fatigue" in this section; "Sickness" under Travel).

Walking—A Fondness For—(See Pedestrianism).

Wrestling—A Champion Wrestler—Case—(See Athletics).

EXERTION—Mars is called the planet of dynamic energy, and of exertion. (See Action, Active, Energy; "Mars Influence" under Mars). The ☉ is also much of the nature of ♂ as regards exertion. The ☉ and many planets in fiery signs, or these signs upon the Asc., tend to greater activity and exertion, and apt to go to extremes. The watery signs tend to inaction, and espec. ♓, and less of exertion of body and mind. (See "Active Body", "Active Mind", under Active; Dull, Inactive, Inertia, Motion, Quick).

Blindness—From Mental Exertion—From Over-Study, Reading, Eyestrain, etc.—(See "Mental Exertion", "Over-Study", "Reading and Study", "Total", under Blindness; "Eyestrain" under Eyes).

Over-Exertion—Illness from Over-Exertion of Mind and Body—From Too Much Toil of Mind and Body—The ☽ in ♐, ♂, P, ☐ or ☍ ♄ (or ☿ if he be of the nature of ♄) at the beginning of an illness, or at decumb. (Hor'y). (See "Disease" under Cares; "Colds", "Inordinate", under Exercise; "Mind" under Fatigue).

Sickly—Too Sickly To Make Much Exertion—♀ Sig. ♂ ☉. (See Decrepitude, Dull, Feeble, Infirm, Invalids, Lassitude, Lethargy, Listless, Sickly, Vitality Low; "Weak Body" under Weak, etc.).

EXHAUSTION—Great Loss of Vital Power—The same influences which tend to low vitality, weak recuperative powers, low resistance to disease, etc., tend to exhaustion, fatigue, feebleness, debility, decrepitude, infirmity, ill-health, sickly body, weak body, etc. (See these subjects).

Brain—Exhaustion of—(See "Exhaustion" under Brain).

Coughing—Exhausting Paroxysms of—(See "Convulsive" under Cough).

Heart—Exhaustion of—(See "Exhaustion", "Weak", under Heart).

Nervous Exhaustion—(See "Exhaustion" under Excitement; "Exhaustion", "Neurasthenia", "Prostration", under Nerves. Also see Breakdown, Collapse, Debility, Depletion, Feeble, Prostration, Weak).

Vital Powers—Exhaustion of—(See "Depletion", "Loss Of", "Waste Of", under Vital; "Lessened", "Lowered", "Wasted", "Weakened", under Vitality).

EXHIBITION—Exhibitionism—

Maladies—Public Exhibition of—Begging—Complaining of—Murmuring—♄ evilly configurated with the benefics at B.; ♄ angular, ori., and elevated above the benefics, and entering into the configuration which produces the disease, hurt, or infirmity; ☿ entering into the configuration, they will exhibit for support, and beg from door to door; many planets in bicorporeal signs tend to complaining, murmuring, lamentations, repining, etc.; the ☽ Sig. ☐ or ☍ ♄, or vice versa. (See Complaining, Conspicuous, Incurable, Lamentation, Murmuring, Repining).

Sex Organs—Exhibition of—Exhibitionism—Public Exposure of the Sex Organs—(See Harlots, Immodest, Infamous, Lewd; "Licentious" under Men; Nakedness, Notoriety, Obscene, Perversions, Shameless).

EXILE—Banishment—Ruled by the 12th H.; malefics in the 12th; the ☽ sepr. from ♃ and applying to the ☉, and espec. if the ☽ be in ♈, ♏, ♑, or ♒, may become an exile; also ruled by ♅. (See Banishment, Captive, Prison, Twelfth House).

EXOPATHIC—(See External).

EXOPHTHALMIC GOITER—Exophthalmos—(See "Goggle Eyes" under Eyeballs; Goiter).

EXOSMOSIS—Under the rule of ♀. (See Osmosis).

EXOSTOSIS—An Abnormal Outgrowth of Bone—(See "Bones of Arm" under Arms).

EXPANSION—Increase in Size or Volume—The ☉, ♃, and ♂ exert an expansive influence over the body, while ♆, ♅, and ♄ are contractive.

Bodily Tissues—Expansion of—Produced by the positive and electric planets, the ☉, ♃, and ♂.

Chest Expansion—Capacious Chest—(See "Capacity" under Lungs). See Contraction, Dropsies, Enlargement, Flatulence, Functions, Gas, Growth, Growths, Hypertrophy, Prominent, Swellings, Tumors, Tympanites, Veins, Vessels, etc.

EXPECTATION OF LIFE—(See the various paragraphs under Death; "Duration" under Life).

EXPECTORATION— Spitting — Hawking—Coughing—

Blood—Expectoration of—(See Haemoptysis).

Mucus—Phlegm—Great Expectoration of—(See Mucus, Phlegm).

EXPENSE—Expensive Habits—Prodigal of Expense—(See Dress, Extravagant, Food, Habits, High Living (see High); Prodigal; "Riotous Living" under Riotous).

Expensive Food—Love of Rich and Expensive Food, and with Disease Resulting From—Fond of Dainty Foods —(See "Dainty", "Rich", under Food. Also see Diet, Epicureans, Feasting, Indigestion, Indiscretions, Luxuries, Plethora, Surfeits).

EXPIRATION—Expelling of the Breath —Death—Termination—(See "Exhalation" under Breath; "Close of Life" under Close; Death, End, Fourth House, Terminal, Termination, Time).

EXPLOSIONS— Explosives — Explosive —♅ rules Explosives, and the chemical changes in them. (See Chemical). ♅ and ♂ are explosive in nature.

Accidents By—♅ causes accidents by explosions, and thru machinery.

Anger—Explosive Anger—♅ ♂, □, or 8 ♂. (See Anger).

Blindness—By Explosions—Caused by ♂; the ☽ in the 1st, 4th, or 7th H.,

decr. in light, and affl. by ♂, and espec. if the ☽ be near Nebulous Stars. (See Blindness).

Causes of Explosions—Danger of— Injury or Death Resulting From— Caused principally by ♅, and due to nitrogen, a highly explosive and unstable base with ♅ characteristics; ♅ to the P, □, or 8 the ☉ or ☽ by dir.; ♅ affl. in the 8th H. indicates sudden death from an explosion, and espec. when affl. the hyleg; ♅ affl. the hyleg by dir.; ♅ or ♃ affl. by ♂; ♅ affl. in ♏; the Prog. ☉ or ☽ to the □ or 8 ♂ or ♅; ♂ disposes to, and is explosive; ♂ Prog. to the ☌ or ill-asp. ♅, or vice versa; the Asc. affl. by ♅ at B., and by dir.; the Asc. to the ☌ or ill-asp. ♅ by dir.; the M.C. to the ☌ ♅ by dir., or vice versa. (See Chemical, Ether, Gases, Machinery, Mars, Nitrogen, Uranus).

Death By—♅ affl. in ♏ or the 8th H. at B., and by dir.; ♅ in the 8th H. at B., and affl. the hyleg by dir., and other testimonies concurring for a violent death; ♅ or ♂ affl. the hyleg by dir.; ♂ disposes to.

Killed—By An Explosion—Case—See "Died In Harness", No. 800, in 1001 N.N.

Manner—Explosive Manner—♅ and ♂ afflictions, and espec. in ill-asp. to the ☽ or ☿; afflictions in fixed signs, and espec. to the ☽ or ☿ in a fixed sign. (See "Explosive" under Manner).

Ships—Explosions On—♅ and ♂ ascending, and affl. the ☉, ☽, or Asc. when the ship sails, or these places in the ship's map. (See Ships, Shipwreck).

EXPOSURE—Exposure to Cold, Dampness, and the Elements—

Cold and Dampness—Diseases and Illness from Sudden Exposure To— Caused by ♅ afflictions to the hyleg, or to the ☉, ☽, or Asc. by dir.; ♄ in ♈, complaints due to cold and exposure; ♄ in 8, all disorders arising from exposure and cold. (See Bathing, Climate; "Exposure" under Cold, Moisture, Weather; "Clothing" under Colds; Elements, External; "Cold Taken" under Feet; "Cold and Moisture" under Moisture; "Linen" under Wet).

Fond of Exposures—(See "Fond Of" under Danger).

The Elements—Illness Thru Exposure To—♄ in the 6th H., and affl. the hyleg. (See Elements).

Travel—Journeys—The Health Suffers from Exposure In Travel—♄ in the 3rd or 9th H., and affl. the ☉, ☽, Asc., or hyleg. (See "Wet" under Journeys; "Exposure" under Travel).

EXPRESSION—The Predominating Facial Expression—The Countenance— The Look—Gestures — Speech—Voice Expression—Expression of the Eyes, etc.—This subject is largely considered under the subjects of Appearance, Aspect, Countenance, Eyes, Face, Features, Gesticulation, Glances, Look, Speech, Voice, etc. Also note the following subjects and references.

Difficult Expression—A Very Marked Expression, and One Difficult to Gauge —♅ rising in the Asc.

Full of Expression—The Countenance Full of Expression and Vivacity—The ☽ Sig. in ♎; ♂ in ♎. (See Smiles).

Impulsive Expression—Hasty Impulses—Ill-Health By—The ☉ affl. in ♈. (See Impulses).

Marked Expression—(See "Difficult" in this section).

Much Expression—♃ Sig. in ♐.

Pleasing Expression—(See "Face" under Pleasant).

Sad Expression—♄ in ♋. (See Gloom, Melancholy, Sad).

Sex Expression—Freedom of—(See "Freedom" under Sex). For further influences along this line see Amorous, Animal, Austere, Bold, Cheerful, Commanding, Cruel, Effeminate, Fierce, Fiery, Grave, Harmless, Idiotic, Indifferent, Intellectual, Intemperate, Kind, Lips, Lustful, Melancholic, Mouth, Negative, Nose, Peaceful, Pensive, Piercing, Pleasant, Positive, Refined, Resolute, Savage, Sensual, Serious, Severe, Sharp, Sickly, Smiles, Sorrowful, Stern, Sympathetic, Thoughtful, Troubled, Wanton, Wicked.

EXPULSION—Expulsive—The ☽ represents the expulsive and natural forces over the body. (See "Influence of Moon" under Moon; "Natural Forces" under Natural).

Wastes—Expulsion of—Ruled by the ☽. (See Elimination, Emetics, Excretion, Faeces, Peristalsis, Urine, Vomiting, Wastes).

EXTERNAL — Externally — Exterior— Exopathic—Exoteric — Outside Influences Over the Mind and Body—Environment — Climate — Location — Associations, etc.—The Asc. denotes the part of the body more liable to affliction from external causes. The sign on the Asc. at B. rules a part, or organ, externally, internally, and structurally. The fiery and airy signs on the Asc. give stronger physical bodies, and less liable to external disorders. The earthy and watery signs rising make the native more liable, receptive, and susceptible to outside influences, and give a weaker constitution. The watery signs espec. give too much receptivity to outside influences, and make the native more liable to infectious and contagious diseases. The ♏ sign gives greater magnetic and attractive powers, and makes one more liable to attract diseases, or impure magnetism, from the outside. The ♋ sign on the Asc. at B. gives much receptivity to external conditions. When the 4th face of ♑ is on the Asc. at B., the native is much affected by others. Acquired tendencies are denoted by the ☽, and diseases and afflictions which come from external causes, such as climate, habits, clothing, food, etc. Man in his pilgrimage upon the Earth Plane is constantly battling with external conditions, the elements, the forces about him, which he must conquer, use for his own purposes and development, or be overcome by them, and nearly every subject in this Work has some reference to Man's external conditions, his relation to them, and their effects upon

him. There are causes from within affecting man, called innate, inherited, organic and structural disorders of the body, and also mental afflictions, etc. Look in the alphabetical arrangement for the subject you have in mind if it is not listed or mentioned here. Also see the following subjects,— Abroad, Accidents, Acquired, Air, Attracts, Blows, Climate, Clothing, Cold, Colds, Confinement, Contagious, Dangers, Death, Disease, Earth, Elements, Enemies, Environment, Epidemics, Family, Fate, Fire, Food, Friends, Habits, Hurts, Imprisonment (see Prison); Infections, Injuries, Journeys, Location, Magnetism, Marriage, Men, Native Land (see Native); Negative, Passive, Place of Birth (see Place); Positive, Public, Quarrels, Receptivity, Resistance, Residence, Sensation, Social Relations (see Social); Susceptible, Tendencies, Travel, Water, Women, Wounds, etc.

Blemishes—External Blemishes—(See Blemishes).

Cold—Externally Cold, and With Internal Heats—(See Constrictions; "Internal Heats" under Heat).

Complaints—External—(See "Disorders" in this section).

Congestions—External Congestion—(See Centrifugal, Centripetal, Cold, Colds, Congestion, Constrictions; "Internal Heats" under Heat; Rubefacients, Skin Diseases).

Disorders—External Disorders— Those originating outside the mind or body, and which do not originate in the mind or body—(See the first part of this section, and the references. Also the paragraphs in this Article).

Generative Organs—The External Generative Organs—(See "External" under Genitals).

Heat—External Heat—Much External and Internal Heat—(See "External" under Heat).

Hemorrhages—External Hemorrhages—(See "External" under Hemorrhage).

Humoural Secretions—(See "External" under Humours).

Signs of Zodiac—External and Internal Rulership of the Signs Over the Various Parts and Organs of the Body —(See "External" under Signs of the Zodiac. Also see each of the Signs in the alphabetical arrangement).

Stomach—External Lining of—(See Stomach).

Urinary Organs—External Urinary Organs—(See Urine).

EXTRAORDINARY—Unusual—Uncommon—Remarkable—Strange—Singular —Curious—Mysterious—Tragical— Violent—Psychic—Sudden—(See these subjects).

Accidents—(See "Extraordinary" under Accidents).

Death—Extraordinary or Unusual Death—Peculiar Death—Singular Death—Curious Death—♅ tends to cause, and in some uncommon and extraordinary manner, and a death which creates great public concern and interest; the afflictions of ♅ to the hyleg by dir; ♅ does not kill of himself, but assists in destroying life by his evil asps., and when they concur in afflicting the hyleg, the death is usually sudden, singular, and of an extraordinary nature; ♅ conjoined with ♄ or ♂ at B. in the 8th H.; ♅ or ♆ in the 8th H. at B.; ♅ in the 8th H., a sudden, peculiar, extraordinary, and often a violent death; ♆ affl. in the 8th H., or affl. the hyleg, a curious death. (See "Mysterious", "Remarkable", "Tragical", under Death; Execution, Strange; "Death" under Sudden; Untimely).

Diseases — Extraordinary, Remarkable, Strange and Uncommon Diseases—Caused by ♅, as this planet gives remarkable features to the sickness; ♅ afflicted in the 6th H., or affl. the hyleg from this house, gives diseases which tend to baffle the skill of Medical Men and Healers; also the Uranian sign ♒ on the Asc. (See Diagnosis, Incurable, Mysterious; "Diseases" under Peculiar; Praeincipients, Strange, Uncommon).

Ideas—Extraordinary Ideas—Extraordinary Pursuits and Objects—(See Ideas; "Unusual" under Mental; Vocation).

EXTRAVAGANCE—Luxuries—Health Undermined By—The ☉ affl. in ♓; the ☉ or ☽ to the ill-asps. ♃ or ♀ by dir.; the ☉ affl. by ♄; the ☽ affl. in ♏ or ♓ at B.; ♄ Sig. ✶ or △ ♀; ♃ to the bad asps. ♂ or ♀ by dir.; bad combinations of the ♃ and ♂ influences, or of the signs which they rule; ♃ affl. in ♑; suffers thru extravagance in eating and drink; ♂ affl. in the 6th H.; ♀ affl. at B., and to the ☌ or ill-asps. the Asc. by dir., or the Asc. to the ☌ or ill-asps. ♀; the ♌, ♎, and 5th H. influences, when containing afflictions, also tend to extravagance, prodigality, and to make the native a spendthrift. (See Conduct, Debauched, Depraved, Diet, Dissolute, Dress, Drink, Eating, Epicureans, Excesses, Expense, Feasting, Food; "Free Living" under Free; Gluttony, Habits; "High Living" under High; Imprudence, Indiscretions, Indulgence, Intemperate, Loose, Luxuries, Pleasure, Plethora, Prodigal, Riches, Riotous Living (see Riotous); Self-Indulgent, Self-Undoing, Surfeits, etc.).

EXTRAVASATIONS—(See Effusions).

EXTREMES—Extreme—Extremely—

Childbirth—Extreme Danger In—(See Parturition).

Cold—Extremes of Cold In the Body—Suffers from Extremes of Cold and Heat—(See "Cold and Heat" under Heat).

Disease—Extreme Danger In—(See "Illness" under Dangerous).

Fevers—Extreme and Dangerous Fevers—(See "High Fevers" under High).

Heat—Extreme Heat—Extremes of Heat In the Body—(See "Cold and Heat", "Excessive", "Extreme Heat", under Heat).

Mental Extremes—(See Anarchists,

Anger, Cruel, Excitable, Exertion, Fanatical, Frenzy, Fury, Ideals, Ideas, Madness, Mania, Quarrelsome; "High Temper" under Temper; Vicious, Violent, etc.).

Mouth—Extreme Heat In the Mouth and Throat—(See "Heat" under Throat).

Nervousness — Extremely Nervous — (See "Highly Neurotic" under Nerves).

Sickness—Extreme Sickness—(See Dangerous, Escape, Fatal, Fierce, Grievous; "High Fevers" under High; Severe, Sharp, Vehement, Violent).

Temperature—Rapid Extremes of—(See Fever; "Rapid Extremes" under Temperature).

Thirst—Extreme Thirst—(See Thirst).

Throat—Extreme Heat In—(See "Heat" under Throat).

EXTREMITIES—Extremities of the Body—Are ruled by the common signs.

Accidents To—Accidents, Diseases, Hurts, Infirmities, Injuries, Leprosy, or Wounds To—♄ or ♂ angular in the 1st or 7th H., and in the latter degrees of ♉, ♐, or ♓, and ori. of the ☉, and occi. of the ☽. (See "Accidents", "Hurts", "Injuries", under Arms, Feet, Hands, Legs, Limbs).

Acromegaly—(See "Enlargement" in this section).

Adiposa Dolorosa—(See Fat).

Arms—Disorders of—(See Arms).

Atrophy—(See Atrophy).

Blood Vessels—Constriction of the Blood Vessels of the Extremities—(See Constrictions).

Clonic Spasm—(See "Myoclonia" in this section).

Coldness Of—♄ in ♊ or ♓; ♀ affl. in ♓. (See "Extremities" under Cold; Constrictions).

Cramps In—(See Cramps).

Diseases In—Humours—Accidents—Leprosy—Gout—and other Infirmities in the Extremities, and espec. in the Hands and Feet—(See "Accidents" in this section. Also see Gout, Humours, Leprosy, Rheumatism).

Enlargements—Acromegaly—The ☉ and ♂ cause enlargements by drawing heat to the part; ♃ by the deposit of fat; ♄ by deposits and thickening of cell walls, and ♆ by cell development; Subs at AT and CP. (See "Bones of Arm" under Arms; Cells; "Acromegaly" under Enlargements; "Overgrowth" under Growth, etc.).

Erysipelas Of—(See Erysipelas).

Erythromelalgia—(See this subject).

Fat—(See "Adiposa Dolorosa" under Fat).

Feet—Disorders of—(See Feet).

Fingers—(See Fingers).

Fractures—(See Fractures).

Gout In—Gout In Arms, Hands, Legs, Feet—(See Gout).

Hands—Disorders of—(See Hands).

Head—Disorders of—(See Head).

Humours In—(See "Accidents" in this section. Also see Humours).

Infirmities In—(See "Accidents" in this section. Also see Arms, Feet, Hands, Legs, Limbs).

Injuries To—(See "Accidents" in this section).

Legs—Disorders of—(See Ankles, Calves, Feet, Knees, Legs, Limbs, Thighs).

Leprosy In—(See "Diseases" in this section).

Limbs—Disorders of—(See Limbs).

Long and Slender—☿ ascending at B., and free from the rays of other planets. (See "Long" under Arms, Feet, Hands, Legs).

Lower Extremities — Disorders In — (See Feet, Legs, Lower).

Muscles—Disorders of—(See "Muscles" under Arms; "Atrophy" under Muscles; "Myoclonia" in this section).

Myoclonia—Myoclonus—Paramyoclonus Multiplex—(See Myoclonia).

Pain In—(See "Pain" under Arms; Feet, Hands, Legs, Limbs).

Paramyoclonus Multiplex—(See Myoclonia).

Rheumatism In—(See "Accidents" in this section. Also see Gout, Rheumatism; "Rheumatism" under Arms, Hands, Legs, Feet).

Short—(See "Short" under Limbs).

Slender—See "Long" in this section).

Spasm—Clonic Spasm—Twitching In —(See Myoclonia, Spasmodic Diseases).

Swellings In—(See "Swellings" under Arms, Hands, Legs; "Dropsy" under Feet; Swellings).

Toes—Disorders of—(See Feet, Toes).

Twitchings In — (See Myoclonia, Twitching).

Upper Extremities — (See Arms, Hands, Head, Upper).

Wounds To—(See "Accidents" in this section).

EXTROVERSION — (See Introversion, Introspection).

EXUDATIONS—A Morbid Oozing Out of Fluids—

Dried Exudations—(See Crusts).

Fibrinous Exudations—(See Fiber).

Lymph Exudations—(See Eczema, Lymph).

Membranous Exudations — Morbid Discharges—On Mucous Surfaces, as in the Throat, Tonsils, or Pharynx—(See Diphtheria. Also see Discharges, Excretion, Fluids, Morbid, Mucous, Osmosis, Pharynx, Throat, Tonsils).

EYEBALLS—For Rulership of see Eyes. The various parts of the Eyeballs are considered under Eyes.

Abnormal Protrusion Of—Goggle Eyes—Exophthalmos—Exophthalmic Goiter —The ☉ and ☽ both in cardinal or fixed signs, or in angles; ♀ affl. in ♉ tends to the Goiter variety; the ☊ influence, or the combined ☊ and ♓ influences; ☊ gives large goggle eyes. (See "Full", "Large", under Eyes; "Exophthalmic" under Goiter).

Clonic Spasm Of—Hippus—Tremulous

Contracture of the Eyeballs—♅ affl. in ♈; Subs at MCP (4C) and SP. (See Clonic, Contractions; "Iris" under Eyes; Spasmodic Diseases, Tremors. Also see "Nystagmus" in this section).

Contracture Of—(See "Clonic" in this section).

Dropsy Of—The ☽ or ♄ affl. in ♈; Subs at KP (7D), and SP. (See Dropsy).

Exophthalmos—(See "Abnormal Protrusion" in this section).

Goggle Eyes—(See "Abnormal" in this section).

Hippus—(See "Clonic" in this section).

Nystagmus—Oscillatory Movement of the Eyeballs—Quivering—A ♅ disease and affliction; afflictions in ♉, causing incoordination; a spasmodic disease, and caused by ♅ affl. in ♈ or ♉; Subs at MCP and SP (7D). (See Incoordination, Spasmodic).

Oscillation Of—(See "Nystagmus" in this section).

Protrusion Of—(See "Abnormal Protrusion" in this section).

Quivering Of—(See "Nystagmus" in this section).

Retraction Of—♄ influence; ♄ affl. in ♈; Subs at MCP (4C), and SP. (See Retraction).

Sunken Eyeballs—Sunken Eyes—Deep-Set—Hollow Eyes—♄ ascending at B.; ♄ in ♌ in partile asp. the Asc.; ♄ Sig. in ♌ (Hor'y); ☿ occi. of the ☉ except when ☿ is in ♓.

Tremulous—(See "Clonic", "Nystagmus", in this section).

EYEBROWS—The Hair, Skin, and Tissue Above the Eye—

Beetle Brows—Hanging—Overhanging—Lowering—Projecting—Denoted by ♄; ♄ ruler at B.; ♄ or ☋ in the Asc.; the ♄ sign ♑ on the Asc.; the Sig. in a ♄ sign, or ☌ ♄ (Hor'y); ♂ in ♈.

Black Eyebrows—♈ on the Asc.

Bushy Eyebrows—Full Eyebrows—♈ on the Asc., and espec. when the ☉ is also in ♈. (See "Bushy" under Hair).

Dark—♈ or ♑ on the Asc.

Dark and Full—♈ on Asc.

Full—Bushy—Dark and Full—♈ on Asc.

No Eyebrows—Or Hair—Case—See "Aqueous", No. 120, in 1001 N.N. (See "No Hair" under Hair).

Wide Apart—Large Space Between—♃ strong at B. tends to give a large space between the eyebrows. (See Eyes).

EYELIDS—Eyelashes—

Black Eyelids—Black Lashes—Black, Yet Lovely and Graceful—The ♀ influence strong at B. signifies; ♀ Sig. of the person in Hor'y Questions. (See "Black Eyes" under Eyes; "Black Hair" under Hair).

Blepharitis—Inflammation of the Edges of the Eyelids—Thick and Inflamed Edges—Falling Out of the Lashes—Inversion of the Lashes—♄ or ♂ affl. in ♈; ♂ ☌ the ☉ or ☽ in ♈;

Subs at MCP, and KP (11D). (See Conjunctivitis; "Eyestrain" under Eyes; "Danger to Sight" under Sight).

Drooping Lids—(See "Ptosis" in this section).

Dryness Of—♄ affl. in ♈; Subs at MCP and KP (11D).

Edges—Inflamed and Thick Edges—(See "Blepharitis" in this section).

Epiphora—(See "Moisture" in this section).

Excessive Moisture Of—(See "Moisture" in this section).

Falling Lashes—(See "Blepharitis" in this section).

Glands Of—(See Racemose).

Granulated Lids—Trachoma—A Form of Conjunctivitis—♄ affl. in ♈; ♄ ♂ ☉ or ☽ in ♈; Subs at MCP and KP (11D). (See Conjunctivitis. Also "Blepharitis" in this section).

Inflammation Of—(See "Blepharitis" in this section).

Inversion—Of Lashes—(See "Trichiasis" in this section).

Lashes—(See "Black", "Blepharitis", "Trichiasis", in this section).

Moisture—Excessive Moisture of—Watery Eyes—Epiphora—(See "Watery Eyes" under Tears).

Prolapsus—Of Lid—(See "Ptosis" in this section).

Ptosis—Prolapsus of Eyelid—Drooping Lid—♅ or ♄ in ♈, and espec. when affl. the ☉ or ☽ at B., and by dir.; Subs at MCP (4C), and KP (11D). (See Drooping, Prolapse).

Saint Vitus Dance—(See Saint).

Swelling Of—(See "Blepharitis", "Granulated", in this section).

Thick Edges—(See "Blepharitis" in this section).

Trichiasis—Inversion of the Eyelashes—Usually the result of Conjunctivitis, Eye Strain, and Granulations, which go with these conditions. (See "Blepharitis" in this section).

Warts On—Verruca—(See "Eyelid" under Warts).

Winking—Spasmodic and Involuntary—A ♅ influence, due to a spasmodic incoordination; ♅ affl. in ♈ or ♉. (See Incoordination, Spasmodic Diseases). See Eyes.

EYES—The Organs of Vision—Ocular—The Eyes are under the external rulership of the ♈ sign. The Eyes are also ruled by the ☉, ☽, ♆, ♅, and the ♒ sign, as ♅ and ♒ rule the Ether, thru which Light is transmitted. It is recognized that ♆ has some action on the Eyes and Brain. The Eyes have affinity with the ☉, ☽, ♅, and the ♈ and ♒ signs, and also with the Pleiades, Antares, and the Ascelli. (See "Eyes" under Mercury). In our System of Astrology the 1st H. rules and affects the eyes. In the Hindu System, the 2nd H. rules the Eyes, and afflictions in the 2nd H. tend to seriously afflict the eyes, or cause blindness. The ☉ is concerned with the structural defects of the eyes, while the ☽ rules the Lachrymal Apparatus, its diseases,

and also errors of Accommodation, defective powers of adaptation, as Hyperopia, Myopia, Presbyopia, etc. The ☉ or ☽ at B. affl. by ♅ tends to eye trouble or blindness, and espec. if the ☉ or ☽ be near Nebulous Stars, as the Pleiades, Antares, or the Ascelli. The ☉ rules the right eye of a man, and the left eye of a woman. The ☽ rules the right eye of a woman, and the left eye of a man. Due to the large mass of material to be arranged and classified, and the many subdivisions, many subjects concerning the Eyes are handled elsewhere in the alphabetical arrangement, such as Accommodation, Blindness, Eyeballs, Sight, etc. Also much is said concerning the Eyes under such subjects as Antares, Aquarius, Ascelli, Castor, Ether, Hyades, Light, Moon, Navamsa, Nebulous, Neptune, Pleiades, Pollux, Sight, Sun, Uranus, etc. This article has been arranged in two sections. Section One considers the general conditions about the Eyes, as color, form, expression, characteristics, etc. Section Two, the Diseases and Afflictions to the Eyes, the Sight. etc. See the following subjects of both Sections in the alphabetical arrangement when not considered more fully here in this Article.

— SECTION ONE —

GENERAL CHARACTERISTICS—

Description of the Eyes—

Amorous Eyes—Full of Amorous Enticements—♀ ascending and in power at B. (See Amorous).

Aqueous Humor—(See Sec. 2 of this Article).

Beautiful Eyes—Handsome—Fascinating—Lovely—♃ in ♊, in partile asp. the Asc., full, handsome; ♃ Sig. in ♊; ♀ ascending, or in configuration with the degree ascending; ♎ on the Asc., or the ☉ and ♀ in ♎, give beautiful eyes. (See Beautiful, Handsome).

Big Eyes—(See "Goggle" under Eyeballs. Also see "Large" in this section).

Black Eyes—♄ lord of the Asc., and occi., as between the M.C. and Desc., or between the Nadir and Asc.; ♄ ascending, small, black, and deeply set; ♄ denotes small, black, leering eyes; ♀ strong at B. sometimes gives black eyes; ♀ Sig. in ♉, generally black and very expressive; ♀ in the Asc., dark hazel or black; born under ♀, sparkling black eyes; a ♀ person generally has black or gray eyes, but when ☿ ascends at B., and is free from the rays of other planets, the eyes are neither gray nor black; ☿ Sig. of the person in Hor'y Questions; ☿ in ♎, black or gray. (See "Dark Complexion" under Complexion; "Black Hair" under Hair).

Blind Spot—Of Retina—(See "Blind Spot" under Retina).

Blue Eyes—♃ ♂ or ♉ ♀ in any part of the map tends to give; ♃ gives soft blue eyes; indicated by ♀; ♀ ruler of the Asc., and ori., fine blue eyes; the ✳ and △ asps. of ♀ give fine blue eyes; the ♀ signs ♉ or ♎ on the Asc.; ♎ on the Asc., beautiful and handsome blue eyes; ☿ in ♎︎; the ☉ and ♀ in ♎︎, and espec. in the Asc.; and with ♎︎ rising, beautiful blue eyes; ♋︎ on Asc., small bluish or gray; ♐︎ on Asc., fine, clear blue or gray. (See "Light" under Complexion).

Bright Eyes — Sharp — Piercing — Sparkling—Red—Fiery—Quick—Darting—Penetrating—Characteristic of ♂ people; ♂ rising at B.; ♂ strong at B., and ruler; ♂ Sig. in ♐︎; the ♂ sign ♈︎ on the Asc.; ♂ in ♈︎ or ♏︎; ♂ in the Asc. or M.C. at B.; the ☉ gives when strong at B.; ♃ Sig. in ♈︎; ♀ in the Asc.; ♀ in ♐︎; given by the ✶ and △ asps. of ♀; ♀ occi. at B.; □ gives a sharp, piercing and penetrating eye, and with quick sight.

Brown Eyes—The ☉ or ☽ in □; ♃ rising in the Asc.; ♀ Sig. in □; indicated by ☿; □ on the Asc. (See Brown. Also see "Brown Hair", "Dark Brown", under Hair).

Choroid—(See Choroid).

Clear and Fine—When strongly occupied, given by the Quadrant between the Nadir and Asc., and its opposite; ♐︎ on Asc., clear and fine; ♃ in ♐︎, a fine, clear, good eye. (See "Fine", "Good", in this section).

Dark Eyes—♄ gives; ♄ occi. at B.; ♄ in the Asc.; □ gives; □ or ✶ on the Asc. (See Dark. In this section see "Black", "Hazel").

Darting—(See "Bright" in this section).

Deep-Set—Sunken—Hollow—(See "Sunken" under Eyeballs).

Downward Look—(See Look).

Dull Eyes—Heavy—Languid—Sleepy —Weary Look—The ☽ in ♈︎, □ or ♂ ♄ (or ☿ if he be of the nature of ♄), a weariness and dullness of the eyes; the ☽ Sig. in ♓︎, sleepy eyes; the ♓︎ influences tends to; ♓︎ on the Asc.; given by the Lymphatic or Phlegmatic Temperament, which is largely ruled by ♓︎; ♄ Sig. of the person in Hor'y Questions; ♄ in ♋︎ in partile asp. the Asc., languid, dull, and heavy. (See Dull; "Temperament" under Phlegmatic).

Earth—The Eyes Always Upon the Earth—(See "Downward Look" under Look).

Expressive and Full—The ☉ Sig. in ♎︎; ♃ Sig. in □; ♀ Sig. in ♉︎, very expressive. (See "Black", "Bright", "Full", in this section).

Eyeballs—(See Eyeballs).

Eyebrows—(See Eyebrows).

Eye Lashes—(See Eyelids).

Eye Lids—(See Eye Lids).

Fair Eyes—☿ strong at B. in the Asc., or rising. (See "Fair" under Complexion).

Fascinating Eyes — (See "Beautiful" in this section).

Ferocious and Fiery—Sharp—♂ as Sig. in Hor'y Questions; given by ♂; born under ♂. (See Fiery, Sharp, Yellow, in this section).

Fiery—Red and Fiery—♃ Sig. in ♌︎, full and fiery; ♂ ruler, and strong at B., fiery and ferocious; ☿ occi. at B., red and fiery.

Fine Eyes—Clear—Good—♃ in ♐︎, partile asp. the Asc.; ♐︎ on Asc., fine and clear; □ gives fine eyes in a woman. (See Beautiful, Blue, Clear, Good, in this section).

Full Eyes—The ☉ Sig. in ♎︎; the ☉ in ♎︎, partile asp. the Asc.; the ☽, ♀, or ☿ Sigs. in ♌︎; ♃ Sig. in □, full and expressive; ♃ in □, partile the Asc., full and handsome; ♃ in ♌︎, partile the Asc.; ♃ in ♎︎, partile the Asc., a full eye; denoted by ♃ as Sig. in Hor'y Questions; born under ♃; ♃ Sig. in ♌︎, full and fiery; born under ♃, and with ♃ ori., eyes more full; born under ♃ gives full gray eyes; ♀ Sig. in ♌︎ full and prominent; ♀ ♌︎ partile the Asc.; ♀ as Sig. in Hor'y Questions denotes full or large eyes; ☿ ♌︎ partile the Asc.; ♌︎ gives full round eyes; ♋︎ on Asc. gives full, prominent, and sleepy eyes. (See Large, Prominent, Round, in this section. Also see Expression; "Goggle Eyes" under Eyeballs).

Glances—Of the Eyes—(See Expression, Look. Also note the various paragraphs in this section).

Goggle Eyes—Protruding Eyes—(See "Goggle" under Eyeballs. Also see Full, Large, Prominent, in this section).

Good Eyes—A Good Eye—Fine and Clear—Perfect and Quick Sight—□ gives a good, piercing hazel eye, and of perfect and quick sight; □, ♍, or ♒︎ on the Asc.; ♌︎ gives a good eye, and with quick sight. (See Bright, Clear, Fine, Quick, Sharp, in this section).

Gray Eyes—The ☽ gives; the ☽ ascending at B.; the ☽ indicates greenish gray eyes; the ☽ sign ♋︎ gives, and with ♋︎ on Asc.; the ♋︎ sign on the Asc. tends to give small gray eyes; indicated by the ☉ and ☿; ♄ gives a greenish gray eye; ♃ ascending, large, gray eyes; born under ♃ gives full gray eyes; ♂ ascending at B.; ♀ Sig. in ♋︎, small gray; the ✶ and △ asps. of ♀ to the ☉, ☽, and planets; ☿ in ♋︎, gray or black; ☿ as Sig. in Hor'y Questions indicates one with gray or black eyes; a ☿ person generally has gray or black eyes, but when ☿ ascends at B., and is free from the rays of other planets, the eyes are neither gray nor black; ☿ ori. of the ☉ except when ☿ is in □; ♐︎ on Asc., fine, clear, blue, or gray eyes. (See Gray).

Great Eyes—Great and Large—Full—Prominent—(See "Goggle" under Eyeballs; "Full", "Large", "Prominent", in this section).

Greenish—The ☉ indicates greenish gray eyes; ♄ indicates greenish, or greenish gray; ♀ Sig. in ♋︎, small, greenish or gray. (See Green).

Handsome Eyes—(See "Beautiful" in this section).

Hazel Eyes—Dark Brown—□ or ♒︎ give, and with these signs on the Asc.; □ gives a good, piercing, hazel eye; ♂ rising at B.; ♂ gives sharp, piercing hazel; ♀ in the Asc., dark hazel or black; ♀ Sig. in □, hazel or brown; born under ♀, sparkling dark hazel; □ gives, and with a very quick and penetrative sight; □ on the Asc., dark hazel. (See "Brown", "Dark", in this section).

Heavy and Dull — Languid — (See "Dull" in this section).

Hollow Eyes — Deep-Set — Sunken— (See "Sunken" under Eyeballs).

Iris—(See Sec. 2 of this Article).

Keen Eyes—♅ or ☿ rising in the Asc. (See Bright, Clear, Good, Piercing, Quick, Sharp, in this section).

Lachrymal Apparatus—(See Tears).

Languid Eyes — (See "Dull" in this section).

Large Eyes—Great—Prominent—Full —The Quadrant from the Summer Tropic to the Autumnal Equi., and its opposite Quadrate, tend to produce; the ☉ rising at B.; the ☉ Sig. in ♈; the ☉ Sig. in ♌, large, staring eyes; the ☉ Sig. in ♎, full, large eyes; the ☉ in ♍; the ☉ gives large goggle eyes; the ☉ indicates large eyes, and often gray; the ☉ in ♌, partile the Asc.; the ☽ Sig. in ♌; the ☽ in ♌, partile the Asc.; ♄ Sig. in ♓; ♄ in ♓ partile the Asc., large head and eyes; ♄ lord of the Asc., and ori., as from the Asc. to M.C., and its opposite Quarter, gives great eyes; ♃ in the Asc., large gray eyes; ♃ in ♌, prominent eyes; ♃ in ♎, large; ♃ oriental; ♃ ruler of the Asc., and ori.; ♃ in ♊, full, handsome eyes; ♃ strong at B.; ♃ as Sig. in Hor'y Questions; ♂ Sig. in ♌; ♂ ♌ partile the Asc., great eyes; ♀ well-dig. at B. signifies a full, large, goggle eye; ♀ denotes full and large eyes in Hor'y Questions; ♀ Sig. in ♌; ☿ Sig. in ♌, large, prominent eyes; the ♉ and ♌ signs give, and with these signs on the Asc.; ♌ gives large goggle eyes. (See Full, Goggle, Prominent, in this section).

Larger—One Eye Larger Than the Other—The ☽ causes; the ☽ eye, the left eye in a man, and the right eye in a woman, is apt to be larger, and with more vitreous, and a greater cavity.

Leering Eyes—Malicious—♄ Sig. in ♑; in Hor'y Questions, ♄ Sig. of the party, small leering eyes; when ♄ forms the body he gives small, black, leering eyes. (See Malicious).

Left Eye—In a male, ruled by the ☽, and the ☽ in ♈. In a female, ruled by the ☉, and the ☉ in ♈. (See "Eyes" under Left).

Little Eyes—(See "Small" in this section).

Look—Glances—(See "Glances" in this section).

Lovely Eyes—(See "Beautiful" in this section; "Lovely" under Complexion).

Lowering Look—(See "Downward Look" under Look).

Malicious Eyes—(See "Leering" in this section).

Muscles Of—(See "Muscles" in Sec. 2 of this Article).

Nerves Of—(See "Optic Nerve" under Optic. Also see "Nerves" in Sec. 2 of this Article).

One Eye Larger—(See "Larger" in this section).

Optic Nerve—(See "Optic Nerve" under Optic. Also see "Nerves" in Sec. 2 of this Article).

Penetrating Eyes—♊ gives a penetrating, sharp, and piercing eye; given by ♂; born under ♂; the ✶ and △ asps. of ♀ give a bright and penetrating eye. (See Bright, Ferocious, Fiery, Keen, Piercing, Quick, Sharp, Sparkling, in this section).

Perfect—Perfect and Quick Sight— (See "Good Eyes" in this section; "Good Sight" under Sight).

Piercing Eyes—The ☉ gives; ♃ in ♈ partile the Asc., quick and piercing; ♂ gives sharp and piercing; ♈ on Asc.; ♈ gives piercing, round, and prominent eyes; ♊ gives a sharp, piercing, and penetrating eye; ♊ gives a good, piercing hazel eye. (See Bright, Fiery, Good, Hazel, Keen, Large, Penetrating, Quick, Sharp, Staring, in this section).

Prominent Eyes—♈ gives prominent, round, piercing eyes; ♉ on the Asc.; ♌ on the Asc., prominent and round; ♓ on Asc., prominent, round and piercing; ♃ in ♌; ♀ Sig. in ♌, full and prominent; ☿ Sig. in ♌, large and prominent. (See Full, Large, in this section; "Goggle Eyes" under Eyeballs).

Protruding Eyes—(See "Goggle Eyes" under Eyeballs; "Exophthalmic" under Goiter).

Pupils—Inequality of—(See Iris, Pupils, in Sec. 2 of this Article).

Quality Of—♄ ori. at B., the quality is ordinary; the ♊ and ♌ signs tend to give good quality to the eyes, and with quick slight. (See Bright, Fine, Good, Perfect, in this section. Also see "Bad Eyes" in Sec. 2 of this Article).

Quick Eye—Quick Look—Quick Sight —♊ and ♌ espec. give a quick and penetrating eye, and with quick sight; ♃ ♈ partile Asc., quick and piercing; ♂ ♐ partile Asc., a very quick eye; ☿ occi. at B. (See Bright, Good, Hazel, Keen, Penetrating, Piercing, Sharp, in this section. Also see "Good Sight", "Quick Sight", under Sight).

Red Cast—Red and Fiery—♂ strong at B., and rising; ☿ occi. of the ☉, except when ☿ is in ♊. (See Bright, Fiery, in this section. Also see "Eyes" under Red).

Retina—Rulership of—Disorders of— (See Retina).

Right Eye—Ruled by the ☉ in a male, and by the ☽ in the female. (See "Eyes" under Right).

Rolling Eyes—Rolling and Wandering—♀ strong at B., or ruler.

Round Eyes—♈ gives round, prominent and piercing eyes; ♌ on the Asc. gives round, full, prominent eyes. (See Full, Large, Piercing, Prominent, in this section).

Sharp Eyes — Sharp Sight — Sharp Look — Piercing — Penetrating—Quick —Darting—Bright—Sparkling — Keen, etc.—Characteristic of ♂ people; ♂ rising in the Asc. at B.; ♂ Sig. of the person in Hor'y Questions; the ♂ sign ♈ on the Asc. gives sharp eyes and sharp sight; ♂ gives a sharp, piercing hazel eye; the ☉ gives a sharp eye when strong at B., well-aspected, and not afflicted by malefics or Nebulous

Stars; ♃ or ♂ Sig. in ♈; □ gives a sharp, piercing and penetrating eye, and often with a wanton look. (See Bright, Ferocious, Fiery, Good, Keen, Penetrating, Piercing, Quick, Yellow, in this section. Also see "Quick Sight" under Sight).

Sight—(See Good, Quick, Sharp, in this section. Also see Sight).

Sleepy Eyes—Languid—Heavy—Dull —♓ influence; ♓ on Asc. gives full, prominent, sleepy eyes. (See "Dull" in this section. Also see "Drowsiness" under Sleep).

Small Eyes—Little Eyes—Indicated by ♄; ♄ in ♐ partile the Asc.; ♄ strong at B.; ♄ Sig. of the party in Hor'y Questions denotes small, black, leering eyes; when ♄ forms the body he gives small, black, leering eyes; ♄ ascending, small, black, and deeply set; ♂ ruler of the Asc., and occi.; ♀ Sig. in ♋, small greenish or gray; ♋ on the Asc. tends to small gray or bluish; ☿ ruler of the Asc., and ori.; ☿ in ♋ partile the Asc.; ☿ Sig. in ♋ in Hor'y Questions; ☿ ori. of the ☉ except when ☿ is in □.

Soft Eyes—♃ gives soft blue eyes.

Sparkling Eyes—Characteristic of ♂ people; born under ♂; ♀ in the Asc.; born under ♀, sparkling black, or sparkling dark hazel eyes; ♀ in ♐; ☿ occi. at B.; ♎ on the Asc. (See Bright, Fiery, Penetrating, Piercing, Sharp, in this section).

Staring Eyes—The ☉ Sig. in ♌, large, staring eyes; ♌ gives. (See "Large" in this section).

Steadfast Eye—♀ in the Asc., strong and dignified at B.

Sunken Eyes — Deep-Set — Hollow — (See "Sunken" under Eyeballs).

Tears—Given to Shedding Tears— Sheds Tears Easily—Watery Eyes— (See Tears).

Third Eye—(See Pineal).

Tunics—(See Choroid).

Visage—(See Countenance, Face).

Vision—(See Sight).

Vitreous Humor — (See "Larger" in this section. Also see "Muscae Volitantes" in Sec. 2 of this Article).

Wandering Eyes—(See "Rolling" in this section).

Wanton Look—□ gives. (See Wanton. Also see "Sharp" in this section).

Winking — (See "Winking" under Eyelids).

Women—Fine Eyes In—□ gives. (See "Fine" in this section).

Yellowish Eyes—A Yellow Tinge— Characteristic of ♂ people; ♂ as Sig. in Hor'y Questions denotes sharp, ferocious eyes, and rather yellow. (See Yellow).

— SECTION TWO —

DISEASES OF THE EYES—Afflictions to the Eyes—Ocular Disorders— **Accidents to Eyes**—Hurts or Injuries To—Blows or Strokes To—Blindness from Injury to Eyes—The ☉ or ☽ in ♈, ♉, ♋, ♌, ♑, or ♒, and affl. by ma-

lefics or Nebulous Stars; afflictions to the ☉ or ☽ by the malefics or Nebulous Stars; the ☉ with the Pleiades, Praesepe, Antares, or Deneb.; both of the Lights are generally afflicted, and with one of them rising and affl. by malefics or Nebulous places; the ☉ to the P. asp. Antares by dir.; afflictions to the ☽ at B., and by dir.; the ☽ affl. by the ☉, and the ☽ affl. at the same time by malefics, or near Nebulous Stars, such as the Pleiades; the ☽ to the bad asps. the ☉ by dir., and falling near Nebulous Stars; the ☽ in an angle with the Pleiades, Praesepe, or Antares; the ☽ directed to the Pleiades, Hyades, Praesepe, or the Twins; the ☽ ☌ or ill-asp. ♄ or ♂ at B., and the ☽ on the radical place of ♄ or ♂ at a Solar Rev.; the ☽ ☌ or ill-asp. ♂ in the ♌ sign, and ♂ aspected by the ☉ or ♄ near the place of the Bull's Eye; the ☽ in the Western Angle conjoined with the Pleiades; the Prog. ☽ ☌ ♄ or ♂ in ♈ or the Asc.; Fixed Stars of the nature of ♂ and the ☽ ascending at B.; the Asc. to the Pleiades, Hyades or Castor. Mars causes injuries to the eyes by burns, blows, strokes, explosions, wounds, gunshot, lightning, smallpox, the sword, etc., which may result in blindness, and espec. when affl. the ☉ or ☽, and the Lights near Nebulous Stars and in angles. (See these subjects. See "Accidents", "Burning", "Explosions", and these various subjects under Blindness; "Eyes" under Exercise. Also see "Hurts", "Injuries", "Robbers", "Sports", in this section).

Accommodation — Disorders of the Focus of the Eyes, as Far-Sighted, Near-Sighted, etc.—(See Accommodation, Sight).

Affected—The ☉, ☽, and planets in ♈ tend espec. to affect the eyes. Also according to the influences listed in Table 196 in Simmonite's Arcana, the eyes are affected with ♃ in ♎ or ♑; ♂ in ♈; and ☿ in ♋. (See the Introduction to this Article. Also see the various paragraphs in this section).

Affections — Eye Affections — (See "Bad Eyes", "Eye Trouble", and the various paragraphs in this section).

Afflicted—In the Eyes—(See "Eye Trouble" and the various paragraphs in this section).

All Diseases Of—All Infirmities In— Signified by the 1st H. Also diseases of the ☉ and ☽.

Amaurosis—Partial or Total Blindness—(See Gutta Serena).

Anisocoria—Inequality of the Pupils —(See Iris, Pupils).

Aqueous Humor—Is ruled by ♈ and the ☉ in ♈. Stomach Disorders and Indigestion tend to affect the humor, as by floating specks, blurring the field of vision, etc. (See "Muscae Volitantes" in this section).

Argyll-Robertson Pupil—(See Argyll).

Assaults—Injury to Eyes By—(See "Treachery" under Blindness; "Eyes" under Robbers, Sword).

Asthenopia—Weak or Painful Vision— (See "Painful", "Weak", under Sight).

Astigmatism—(See Astigmatism).

Atrophy—Of the Optic Nerve—Of the Muscles—(See Muscles, Nerves, Optic, in this section. Also see Atrophy).

Bad Eyes—Ailing Eyes—The ☉ and ☽ ascending and impedited by ♄ or ♂; the ☉ with the Pleiades or Praesepe; the ☽ Sig. ☌ ☉, in exact ☌, or applying to it; the ☽ to the ☌ ☉ or ♄ by dir.; the ☽ to the □ or ☍ ☉ or by dir.; the Pleiades when rising, and when directed to the ☉, ☽, or Asc., or when with the Lights at B.; the Ascelli, Castor, Pollux, Hyades, Pleiades, or Praesepe, directed to the Asc. or Luminaries. (See "Eye Trouble", "Injuries", "Weak Eyes", and the various paragraphs in this section).

Blemishes—Blemish On or Near One or Both Eyes—(See "Eyes" under Blemishes).

Blights In—The ☉ ☌ the Asc. by dir. (See Blights).

Blindness—(See the various paragraphs under Blindness, Sight).

Bloodshot Eyes—(See Conjunctivitis. Also see "Inflamed" in this section).

Blows To—(See Accidents, Left, Right, in this section. Also see "Accidents" under Blindness; Blows; "Eyes" under Left, Right).

Both Eyes—Injury To—The ☉ in an angle in the same sign with the ☽, or in ☍, and with ♄ and ♂ ori. to the ☉ and ascending before him, and ♄ and ♂ ori. of the ☽; the ☽ in an angle and decr. in light, and ♄ or ♂ matutine, and ascending in succession to the ☽. (See "Accidents" under Blindness. Also see Accidents, Injuries, in this section. For Blindness in Both Eyes, see "Total Blindness" under Blindness.

Burns To—Burning—(See "Burning" under Blindness. Also see "Accidents" in this section).

Cases of Eye Trouble—See Cases 1, 2, 3, 4, Chap. 13, pages 86 and 87, in Daath's Medical Astrology. See Figs. 2A, 2B, 2C, 2D, 2E, 2G, 2H, in the book, "Astro-Diagnosis" by the Heindels. See Figs. 3, 4, 5, 24, 30, 31, 32, and 34, in "Message of the Stars" by the Heindels.

Cataracts—(See Cataract).

Choroiditis—(See Choroid).

Circles Under Eyes—Dark Circles Under—♄ in the 1st H.

Clonic Spasm—Of Iris—Hippus—(See Clonic, Iris; "Clonic Spasm" under Spasmodic).

Color Blind—(See Blindness).

Congestion—Of the Muscles of—(See "Crystallization" in this section).

Conjunctivitis—Bloodshot—Ophthalmia—(See Conjunctivitis).

Cornea—Inflamed Cornea—Keratitis —Diseases of—A ☉ disease; the ☉ affl. in ♈; Subs at MCP (3rd, 4C), and at SP (7D). (See "Ulcer" in this section).

Crises—In Eye Diseases—Occur when the Prog. ☉ or ☽ pass the place of nebulous stars, and at the same time afflicted by a malefic; the ☉ or ☽ affl. at B. by malefics or nebulous stars, and passing the place of malefics by

dir.; the prog. ☉ or ☽ coming to the □ or ☍ their radical places, and affl. at B. by malefics, or near nebulous stars; the prog. ☽ ☌ malefics in ♈ tends to cause a crisis for the worse if the ☉ or ☽ are with nebulous stars at B., and affl. by malefics; malefics with nebulous stars, and affl. the ☉ or ☽ by dir., and worse when the malefics are ℞, due to passing the nebulous twice. (See Blindness, Crises, Worse).

Crossed Eyes—(See "Strabismus" in this section).

Crystalline Lens—Defects and Disorders of—Opacity of—(See Accommodation, Cataract).

Crystallization—Of the Muscles and Nerves of the Eyes—Congestion—(See Congestion, Crystallization; "Crystallization" under Sight).

Cyclops—Eyes Focussed Into One— (See Cyclops).

Danger To—The ☉ directed to Praesepe; malefics ☌ the ☉ or ☽ in ♈; the ☉ or ☽ ☌ nebulous stars at B., and to the evil asps. nebulous places by dir. (See Accidents, Blows, Injuries, in this section. Also see Blindness, Sight).

Dark Circles—Under the Eyes—(See "Circles" in this section).

Decay—Of the Optic Nerve—Inhibition of—(See "Decay" under Optic).

Defects In Eyes—Ocular Defects— Natural and Structural Defects—(a) Natural Defects—The ☽ rules defects of accommodation and of the powers of adaptation; the ☽ Sig. ☌ ☉, and espec. if near the Pleiades, Hyades, or Praesepe, and apt to be nearly blind; the ☽ or Asc. with nebulous, and affl. by ♄, tends to Cataracts, Glaucoma, Obstructing Growths, and Natural Defects. (See Accommodation, Blindness, Cataracts, Defects, Glaucoma, Growths, Natural, Obstructions, Sight. Also note the various paragraphs in this section). (b) Structural Defects—Ruled by the ☉; the ☉ affl. in ♈, and espec. when in the Asc. (See Structural).

Dilated Pupils—(See Iris, Mydriasis, Pupils).

Dim Eyes—The ☉ in earthy signs and ☌ the Asc. by dir.; the ☉ to the ☌ ☌ by dir. (See "Dim Sight" under Sight).

Discharges From—Humorous Discharge From—♀ affl. in ♈. (See Discharges, Humours).

Diseased—In the Eyes—(See "Eye Trouble", and the various paragraphs in this section).

Diseases Of—The Eyes—(See the various paragraphs in this section. Also see Blindness, Eyeballs, Eyelids, Sight).

Disordered Eyes—(See "Eye Trouble", and the various paragraphs in this section).

Double Vision—(See "Diplopia" under Sight).

Dropsy—Of the Eyeballs—(See Eyeballs).

Dullness Of—Weariness of—Heavy— Languid—Sleepy—(See "Dull Eyes" in Sec. 1 of this Article).

Epiphora—(See "Watery Eyes" under Tears).

Exercise—Injury to the Eyes During —(See "Accidents" in this section; "Eyes" under Exercise).

Exophthalmos—(See "Abnormal Protrusion" under Eyeballs. Also see "Large", "Prominent", in Sec. 1 of this Article).

Explosions—(See "Blindness" under Explosions. Also see "Accidents" in this section).

Eyeballs—Disorders of—(See Eyeballs).

Eyebrows—No Eyebrows—(See Eyebrows).

Eye Lashes—Turning In of—(See "Trichiasis" under Eyelids).

Eyelids—Disorders of—(See Eyelids).

Eyesight—Disorders of—(See Accommodation, Blindness, Sight. Also note the various paragraphs in this section).

Eyestrain—Over-Worked Eyes— Errors of Accommodation In—The eyes are weaker and easily strained when the ☉ comes to the ♂, or evil directions, of nebulous stars, as Praesepe, Hyades, Castor, Pollux, and at the same time affl. by malefics; the ☽ affl. in ♈; ☿ tends to blindness from eyestrain and hard reading or study. (See "Reading and Study" under Blindness; Reading, Study).

Eye Trouble—The Eyes Afflicted— Diseased Eyes—Disordered Eyes—The Eyes Suffer—Infirmities In the Eyes— The ☉ or ☽ affl. in ♈; the ☉ affl. at B., and by dir.; the ☉ and ☽ in □ or ☍ each other and in angles; the ☉ affl. by the ☽; the ☉ or ☽ affl. in ♉ near the Pleiades; the ☉ or ☽ in ♌ with the Ascelli; the ☉ affl. in ♒; the ☉ and ☽ are usually in mutual affliction, one of them usually rising, and affl. by ♄ or ♂, and in this respect the worst signs for the Lights are ♈, ♉, ♎, ♌ and ♒; the ☉ to the ♂ or P. asp. the ☽ by dir., and the ☽ ill-aspected; the ☉ or ☽ to the ♂ or ill-asps. ♄ by dir.; the ☉ or ☽ in transit over the place of ♆, and ♆ a promittor, and the ☉ or ☽ affl. at B.; the ☉ or ☽ affl. by ♅, ♄, or ♂, and in orb of the Pleiades, the Ascelli, or Antares, or when ♄ or ♂ are in nebulous parts, and affl. the ☉ or ☽; the ☉ in the 8° ♐ with Antares, and affl. by one or more of the malefics; the ☉ or ☽ ♂ Antares, and in □ or ☍ ♂; the ☉ ♂ ☽ or ☊ near nebulous stars; the ☉ or ☽ with nebulous stars at B., as Antares, the Ascelli, or the Pleiades, and affl. by a malefic; the ☉ affl. at B., and the ☉ by dir. to the evil asp. the Asc.; the ☉ hyleg at B., and to the ♂ or ill-asp. ♄ by dir.; the ☉ directed to the Pleiades, Hyades, Castor or Pollux; the ☽ to the ♂ or ill-asp. the ☉ or ♄ by dir., and the ☉ or ☽ affl. at B., and espec. when falling near nebulous stars; the ☽ in the Western angle and conjoined with the Pleiades; the ☽ affl. in ♌, ♑, or ♒; the ☽ hyleg in ♈ or ♒, and afflicted, and espec. with females; the ☽ in ♈ or ♉, and affl. by ♆; the ☽ ♈, ♉, ♂ in ♎, and ♂ elevated above the ☽; the ☽ with the Pleiades in ♉, and affl.

by any of the malefics; the ☽ with the Ascelli in ♌; the ☽ apply. to ♂, or conjoined with him in a day geniture; the ☽ to the bad asps. the ☉, and the aspect fall near nebulous stars; the ☽ passing over the place of the ☉ at B. at a Solar Rev., and espec. if the ☉ or ☽ be affl. by nebulous stars; the ☽ afflicted, according to sign, house, and nature of the afflicting planet; the ☽ Sig. □ or ☍ the ☉, and espec. if the ☉ be affl. by ♂, or either the ☉ or ☽ are with nebulous stars; ♆ affl. in ♈ or ☍; ♆ in ♉ in the 6th H.; ♆ in ♉ and affl. the ☉, ☽, Asc., or hyleg; ♅ in ♌ and ♂ the Ascelli, and □ or ☍ ♉ the ☽; ♅ afflicting the ☉ or ☽; ♄ in ♒; ♄ to the ♂ or ill-asps. the ☉ or ☽ by dir., and probably from taking cold; ♃ Sig. in ♎ in Hor'y Questions; ♂ in ♈ and affl. the Lights; ♂ affl. in ♒, as ♒ rules the Ether; ☿ affl. in ♋ or ♎; malefics, or a malefic, with nebulous stars, and affl. the ☉ or ☽, and espec. when the malefic is ℞, and passing over the nebulous stars, back and forth several times by direct, ℞, and redirect motion; the Asc. to the ♂ or ill-asp. the ☉ by dir., and the ☉ affl. at B.; ♌ diseases; ♒ on the Asc.; ♈ or ♒ on the cusp of the 6th H. (See "Affected", "Bad Eyes", "Cases", and the various paragraphs in this section. Also see Aquarius, Ether; "Light Rays" under Light; Nebulous; "Influence of Uranus" under Uranus).

Failing Eyes—The ☉ affl. at B., and by dir. (See Affected, Defects, Dim, Weak, and other paragraphs in this section. Also see "Nearly Blind" under Blindness; Sight).

Far-Sighted—(See "Hyperopia" under Sight).

Father—Injury to Eyes of—(See "Eyes" under Father).

Film—White Film Over the Eyes— Blindness From—(See "Cold" under Blindness).

Floating Specks—(See "Muscae Volitantes" in this section).

Fused Into One—The Eyes Fused Into One Eye—(See Cyclops).

Glaucoma—A Disease characterized by increased intraocular tension—(See Glaucoma).

Goggle Eyes—(See "Goggle" under Eyeballs).

Growths—Obstructing Growths—The ☽ or Asc. in nebulous parts and affl. by ♄. (See "Growths" under Blindness; Cataracts; "Film", in this section).

Gunshot—Eyes Injured By—Blindness By—(See "Blindness" under Gunshot).

Gutta Serena—Amaurosis—Partial or Total Blindness—(See Gutta Serena; "Total Blindness" under Blindness).

Focus—Disorders of—(See Accommodation).

Headaches—Ocular Headaches—(See "Ocular" under Headaches).

Hemianopia—Blindness of One-Half of the Visual Field—(See "Hemianopia" under Sight).

Hippus—Clonic Spasm of the Iris— (See "Clonic" in this section).

Hot Diseases—In the Eyes—Hot Humours In—The Asc. to the ☌ the ☉ by dir;. ♂ affl. in ♈. (See Heat).

Humorous Discharges—(See "Discharges" in this section).

Hurts To—The ☉ and ☽ both impedited by ♄ or ♂ in any part of the figure. (See Accidents, Blows, Injuries, in this section).

Hyperopia—Hypermetropia—Farsighted—(See "Hyperopia" under Sight).

Hypertrophy—Of the Muscles—♂ affl. in ♈; Subs at SP (7D) tend to both Hypertrophy and Atrophy. (See Atrophy, Hypertrophy).

Impediments—In One or Both Eyes—(See "One Eye" under Blindness; Impediments; "Eye" under Left, Right).

Infancy—Eyes Affected In—(See "Born Blind" under Blindness).

Infirmities In—(See "Eye Trouble", and the various paragraphs in this section).

Inflamed Eyes—Inflammation in the Eyes—Sore Eyes—Caused by an afflicted ☉; the ☉ affl. in ♈; the ☉ to the ill-asps. the ☽ by dir., and the ☽ affl. at B.; the ☉ affl. by ♄; the ☉ or ☽ in ♈ and affl. by ♂; the ☉ and ☽ in ♒ asp. from ♈ and ♎, and affl. by malefics or nebulous stars; ♂ affl. in ♈; a ♌ disease and afflictions in ♌, and espec. when the ☉ or ☽ are near the Ascelli; fixed stars of the nature of ♂ and the ☽ ascending at B. (See Conjunctivitis; "Blepharitis", under Eyelids. Also see "Eyestrain", "Ulcer", in this section).

Inhibition—Of the Optic Nerve—(See "Decay" under Optic).

Injury to Eyes—Accidents—Hurts—Wounds To—(See Acicdents, Assaults, Blows, Both Eyes, Burns, Danger, Exercise, Explosions, Father, Gunshot, Hurts, Left, Loss of, Mother, One Eye, Right, Robbers, Scars, Sports, Sword, and the various paragraphs in this section).

Iris—Pupils—Disorders of—Clonic Spasm of—Hippus—Iritis—Dilated Pupils—Mydriasis—Inequality of Pupils—Iridoplegia—Paralysis of, etc.—(See Iris).

Jerky Eyes—Oscillating—(See "Nystagmus" under Eyeballs).

Keratitis—Inflamed Cornea—(See "Cornea" in this section).

Lachrymal Apparatus—Disorders of—(See Tears).

Left Eye—Disorders of—Hurts To—Sight Affected In—(See "Eye" under Left. Also see "Left Eye" in Sec. 1 of this Article).

Lens—(See "Crystalline" in this section).

Light—Failure of the Pupil to Respond to Light—(See "Light" under Iris).

Lightning—Blindness By—(See "Lightning" under Blindness; Lightning).

Loss of Eyes—Loss of Sight In One or Both Eyes—(See "Both Eyes", "One

Eye", in this section. Also see "Total Blindness" under Blindness; "Loss Of" under Sight).

Males—Men—Men Suffer In Their Eyes—♂ in ♏ at the Vernal E., and lord of the year. (See "Eyes" under Men).

Marks—Scars—Marks or Scars In the Eyes—The ☉ or ☽ ascending and impedited by ♄ or ♂; the ☉ or ☽ Sig. ☌ ♂ and ill-dig.; the ☽ Sig. ☌ ☉ or apply. to the ☌. (See "Marks", "Scars", under Face; Marks, Scars).

Mother—Injury to the Eyes of the Mother—(See "Eyes" under Mother).

Motor Paralysis—Oculo Motor Paralysis—(See "Paralysis" in this section. Also see Motor, Paralysis).

Muscae Volitantes—Floating Spots In the Visual Field—Threads—Specks—Dots and Semi-Transparent Threads and Spots Before the Eyes from Stomach Trouble and other Indisposition—♄ the afflicting planet; ♀ in ♈. (See "Specks" in this section).

Muscles of Eyes—(a) Atrophy of—♄ affl. in ♈; Subs at SP (7D). (See Atrophy). (b) Crystallization of—Congestion of—(See "Crystallization" in this section). (c) Hypertrophy of—(See "Hypertrophy" in this section). (d) Paralysis of—Ophthalmoplegia—(See "Paralysis" in this section). ,(e) Squint—(See "Strabismus" in this section).

Mydriasis—Abnormal Dilatation of the Pupil—(See "Mydriasis" under Iris).

Myopia—Near-Sighted—(See "Myopia" under Sight).

Near-Sighted—(See "Myopia" under Sight).

Nerves—Optic Nerve—Crystallization of—(See "Crystallization", "Optic", in this section).

Nystagmus—Oscillation of Eyeballs—(See "Nystagmus" under Eyeballs).

Obstructions In—Obstructive Growths—Obstruction to the Flow of Tears—♄ influence and afflictions; ♄ in ♈; the ☽ or Asc. in nebulous parts and affl. by ♄. (See Growths, Obstructions, Tears).

Ocular—Ocular Headaches—Oculo Motor Paralysis—(See "Ocular" under Headaches; "Paralysis" in this section).

Old Age Vision—(See "Presbyopia" under Sight).

One Eye—(a) Blemish In or Near—(See "Eyes" under Blemishes). (b) Blindness In—Loss of—The ☽ in the 1st or 7th H. in exact ☌, □, or ☍ ☉, or if the ☽ be angular and ☌ ♄ or ♂, or with nebulous stars; the ☽ with Orion's Belt. Wilson has observed that those who have lost one eye, or who may have scars in or near the eyes, are extremely irascible and vicious. (See "One Eye" under Blindness). (c) Impediment In—(See "Impediments" in this section. (d) One Eye Larger—(See "Larger" in Sec. 1 of this Article).

One-Half Vision—(See "Hemianopia" under Sight).

Operations—The eyes should not be tampered with when the ☽ is in ♈ or

♒︎, or when the ☽ is in an earthy sign, or in ☌, □, ☍ the ☉, or passing the place of nebulous stars, as the Pleiades in ♉︎. The ☽ should be well-placed, incr. in light, and free from the affl. of the ☉, malefics, or nebulous stars. (See Operations).

Ophthalmia—Conjunctivitis—Inflamed or Bloodshot Eyes—(See Conjunctivitis. Also see "Inflamed" in this section).

Ophthalmoplegia—(See "Paralysis" in this section).

Optic Nerve—Atrophy of—Decay of—Crystallization—Inhibition—(See Optic).

Oscillation—Of the Eyeballs—(See "Nystagmus" under Eyeballs).

Overworked Eyes—(See "Eyestrain" in this section).

Pain In—The ☉ to the place of ☊ by dir.; the ☽ hyleg, and to the ☌ or ill-asp. ♄ by dir.

Paralysis—(a) Of the Iris—Iridoplegia—(See Iris). (b) Of the Muscles—Ophthalmoplegia—The ☉ rising in ♈︎ and affl. by ♄; ♅, ♆, or ♄ affl. in ♈︎; Subs at MCP and SP. (See Paralysis). (c) Oculo Motor Paralysis—♆ or ♂ affl. in ♈︎; Subs at SP (7D). (See Motor, Paralysis).

Partial Blindness—Amaurosis—(See "Amaurosis" under Blindness; Gutta Serena).

Presbyopia—Old Age Vision—(See "Presbyopia" under Sight).

Prevalent—Eye Diseases Prevalent—The ☉ in the 6th H. and affl. at the Vernal E., and lord of the year; ♂ in ♍︎, lord of the year at the Vernal, and espec. in places subject to ♍︎; ♀ or the ☽ lady of the year at the Vernal, weak and afflicted; Comets appearing in ♌︎.

Prominent Eyes—Protrusion of the Eyeballs—(See "Prominent", "Protruding", in Sec. 1 of this Article).

Pupils—Of the Eyes—Dilatation of—Mydriasis—Inequality of—(See Iris).

Reading and Study—Eyes Suffer From—(See "Eyestrain" in this section; Reading, Study).

Red and Inflamed—(See Conjunctivitis. Also see "Inflamed" in this section).

Retina—Disorders of—(See "Optic Nerve" under Optic; Retina; "Hemianopia" under Sight).

Rheum In—♂ in ♈︎ or ♍︎. (See Rheum).

Right Eye—Blindness In—Blows To—Hurts To—(See "Eye" under Right. Also see "Right Eye" in Sec. 1 of this Article).

Robbers—Injury to Eyes by Assaults of—The ☉ in an angle, and ☌ or ☍ ☽, and the ☉ configurated with ♀. (See Robbers).

Scars—In the Eyes—(See "Marks" in this section; "Eyes" under Blemishes; Left, Right, Marks, Scars).

Short-Sighted—(See "Myopia" under Sight).

Sight—Vision—Disorders of—(See Accommodation, Blindness, Sight. Also note the various paragraphs in this section).

Smallpox—Blindness By—(See "Smallpox" under Blindness).

Sore Eyes—(See "Inflamed" in this section).

Spasm—Clonic Spasm of the Iris—Hippus—(See Iris).

Specks—Over the Eyes—(a) Blindness From—(See "Defects" under Blindness; Specks). (b) Floating Specks in the Visual Field—(See "Muscae Volitantes" in this section).

Sports—Injuries to the Eyes During Exercise or Sports—Blindness By—(See Amusements; "Sports" under Blindness; "Eyes" under Exercise; "Amusements" under Sports).

Spots—Floating Spots Before the Eyes—(See "Muscae Volitantes" in this section).

Squint—Crossed Eyes—(See "Strabismus" in this section).

Strabismus—Squint—Crossed Eyes—Incoordination of the Eye Muscles—♄ ☌ ☽, and the ☽ near nebulous stars; ♀ occi.; ♀ ruler of the Asc., and occi.; Subs at MCP and SP (7D). (See Incoordination. Case—See "Diseases to the Eyes", "Chap. 13, page 88, Daath's Medical Astrology.

Strain—Of the Eyes—(See "Eyestrain" in this section).

Strokes To—(See "Accidents" in this section; "Strokes" under Blindness; "Eyes" under Sword).

Structural Defects—In the Eyes—(See "Defects" in this section).

Study and Reading—Eye Disorders From—(See "Eyestrain" in this section).

Suffering—In the Eyes—(See "Eye Trouble", and the various paragraphs in this section. Also see Blindness, Sight).

Sword—Injuries and Cuts to the Eyes By the Sword—Blindness By—(See "Strokes" under Blindness; "Eyes" under Sword; "Accidents" in this section).

Tampering—With the Eyes—(See "Operations" in this section).

Tears—Lachrymal Apparatus—Disorders of—(See Tears).

Tension—The Intraocular Tension Increased—(See Glaucoma).

Threads—Floating Threads and Spots In the Visual Field—(See "Muscae Volitantes" in this section).

Total Blindness—(See "Total Blindness" under Blindness; "Both Eyes" in this section).

Tract—The Optic Tract—Disorders of —(See Optic. Also note the various paragraphs in this section).

Treachery—Blindness or Injury to Eyes By—(See "Treachery" under Blindness; Treachery).

Treatment—Of the Eyes—Blue, the color of ♀, is soothing to the eyes. Green, ruled by ♄, tends to relieve inflamed eyes. Sugar of Lead, ruled by ♄, is also used as a collyria in inflamed eyes. (See "Operations" in this section. Also see Blue, Green, Lead).

Trichiasis—Inversion of the Eyelashes—(See Eyelids).

Tunics—Inflammation of the Second Tunic of the Eye—(See "Choroiditis" under Choroid).

Ulcer—Of the Conjunctiva or Cornea—Afflictions in ♈; ♄ or ♂ in ♈. (See Conjunctivitis, Ulcers. Also see Cornea, Inflamed, in this section).

Vision—Disorders of—(See Accommodation, Blindness, Sight. Also note the various paragraphs in this section).

Vitreous Humor—(See "Vitreous" in Sec. 1 of this Article; "Muscae V.", "Tension", in this section).

Watery Eyes—Epiphora—Overflow of Tears—Discharges—(See Tears. Also see "Discharges" in this section).

Weak Eyes—Weakness In the Eyes—Eyes Out of Order—The ☉ or ☽ affl. in ♈; the ☉ or ☽ ☌ nebulous stars, and in ☐ or ☍ malefics; the ☉ to the ☌ or P. asp. the ☽ by dir., and the ☽ affl. at B.; the ☉ affl. in ♎; the ☉ or ☽ to the ☌ ♄ by dir.; the ☉ or ☽ affl. at B., and by dir.; the ☽ combust and sepr. from the ☌; the ☽ Sig. ☐ or ☍ the ☉; the ☽ affl. in ♑; ♄ in ♈; ♄ posited between the 24° and 30° of ♒; ♂ in ♋ and affl. by the ☉ or ☽; the M.C. to the place of the Pleiades or Pollux; in Hor'y Questions, the Sig. with the ☽, and ♄ in ♈. (See "Bad Eyes", "Eye Trouble", and the various paragraphs in this section).

Weak Sight—(See Blindness, Sight).

Weariness Of—(See "Dull Eyes" in Sec. 1 of this Article).

White Film—(See "Film" in this section).

Winking—(See Eyelids)

Wounds To—(See "Accidents" in this section).

EYESIGHT — (See Accommodation; Blindness, Eyes, Sight).

EYESTRAIN — (See "Eyestrain" under Eyes).

F

FACE—The Visage—Countenance—Look—Expression—Aspect—Features—Complexion—etc. This Article will have to do with the description, form, shape, and diseases of the Face. For other subjects which have to do with the Face and its subdivisions, see Appearance, Aspect, Beard, Cheeks, Chin, Complexion, Cosmetics, Countenance, Dimples, Ears, Expression, Eyeballs, Eyebrows, Eyelids, Eyes, Features, Forehead, Hair, Head, Jaws, Lips, Look, Mouth, Nose, Profile, Teeth, Temples, etc. The 1st H. represents the Head and Face of Man. The Face is ruled by ♂, and is also under the external rulership of the ♈ sign. The facial bones are under the structural rulership of ♈. The skin of the Face, and the complexion, are ruled by ♀. The form, shape and characteristics of the face are largely determined by the decanate rising on the Asc. (See Decanates). This Article will be divided into two Sections. Sec. 1 will deal with General Characteristics, Description, Form and Shape of the Face, and Sec. 2, the Diseases and Afflictions to the Face. See the following subjects in the alphabetical arrangement when not considered here.

— SECTION ONE —

GENERAL CONSIDERATIONS—General Characteristics—Form and Shape—Description—Countenance—Expression—Look—Complexion, etc.—

Amorous — (See "Amorous Eyes" under Eyes).

Angular—♄ rising in the Asc. (See "Angular Body" under Body).

Animal Expression—(See Animal).

Appearance; Aspect; Austere;

Beard; Beautiful Face—Lovely Face—Fair Face—Given by ♀; ♀ in the Asc., well-dig., or ♀ ruler of the Asc.; ♀ well-dig. at B., a good, fair, and round visage; ♀ rising in ♉ or ♎, and with one of these signs on the Asc.; ♀ Sig. in ♐, fair, oval face; in Hor'y Questions, ♀ Sig. of the person, fair, round face; ♉, ♎, or ♒ on the Asc.; ♎ gives a round, lovely, and very beautiful face; the ♒ sign gives more beauty of face and form than any other sign except ♎. (See Beautiful, Complexion, Dimples, Handsome. Also see Comely, Fair, Handsome, Lovely, in this section).

Big Face—♄ in ♒ in partile asp. the Asc. (See Fat, Fleshy, Full, Large, Lumpish, Plump, Square, in this section).

Bloated—The ☽ Sig. in ♓, pale and bloated. (See Pale. Also see "Bulging", "Lumpish", "Puffy", in this section).

Blushing; Bold Face—Resolute—♂ in ♈ or ♏; ♂ in the Asc. or M.C. at B.

Bones Of—The 14 bones of the face are under the external rulership of ♈. For Disorders of, see "Bones" in Sec. 2 of this Article.

Broad — ♏ influence; ♏ on the Asc., broad and square; Martialists have; ♂ strong at B., and ♂ ruler; ♂ Sig. in ♏, broad and square; ♂ Sig. in ♉ or ♏; ♂ in ♉ or ♏ in partile asp. the Asc.; the ☉ in ♉ or ♏, in partile the Asc.; the ☉ Sig. in ♉, large and broad; the ☉ Sig. in ♏; ♀ Sig. in ♏. (See Full, Large, Round, Wide, in this section).

Brow — Lowering Brow — (See Forehead).

Bulging—♓ on the Asc., bulging and large. (See Bloated, Large, Lumpish, in this section).

Caul—The Fetal Membranes Covering the Head After Birth—Usually a ♄ influence; ♄ rising in the Asc.; ♄ rising and elevated, and in one of his own signs; ♄ well-asp. in ♑ or ♏. Case—See "Born With a Caul", No. 929, in 1001 N.N.

Characteristics—Of the Face—Are largely determined by the decanate rising.

Cheeks; Cheerful Face—Cheerful Countenance—The ☽ Sig. in ♎. (See Cheerfulness. Also see Pleasant, Smiling, in this section).

Chin; Coarse Features—(See Features).

Color—Of the Face—(See Color, Complexion, Pigment, Races, Skin).

Comely—And Fair—In Hor'y Questions the ☉ as Sig. denotes such a person. (See Comely. Also see "Fair" in this section).

Commanding; Complexion; Cosmetics—The Evil Effects of—(See Cosmetics).

Countenance; Cruel; Dark—See "Dark" under Complexion).

Debauched Look—♂ Sig. in ♓. (See Debauched).

Delicate—And Pale Face—(See "Delicate", "Pale", under Complexion).

Dimples; Dissipated Look—(See Debauched, Dissipation).

Downward Look—(See "Downward" under Look).

Drawn Face—Sad Expression—♄ in ♋. (See Gloom, Grave, Grief, Melancholy, Sadness. Also see "Drawn" in Sec. 2 of this Article).

Eagle Face—Eagle Features—♏ gives. (See "Eagle" under Features).

Ears; Effeminate; Evil Complexion—(See "Bad", "Evil", under Complexion).

Expression; Eyeballs; Eyebrows; Eyelashes—(See Eyelids).

Eyelids; Eyes; Fair—Denoted by ♀; born under ♀. (See Beautiful, Good, Lovely, Round, in this section. Also see "Fair" under Complexion).

Fat Face—(See Bloated, Bulging, Large, Lumpish, in this section).

Features; Females—Face In—♀ in the Asc., in ♉ or ♎, the face very beautiful; ♃ on Asc., plump face in females; ♑ on Asc., usually ugly and not good looking. (See Beautiful, Fair, Lovely, Plump, and the various paragraphs in this section).

Fierce Countenance—(See Fierce).

Fiery Countenance—(See "Fiery" under Eyes; "Fiery").

Fleshy Face—♓ gives. (See Fleshy. Also see Bloated, Bulging, Full, Large, Long, Lumpish, Plump, in this section).

Forehead; Form and Shape—The form, shape, and characteristics of the face are determined largely by the decanate rising on the Asc. (See Appearance, Decanates, Features, Form, Shape. Also note the various paragraphs in this section).

Freckles; Full Face—The ☉ in ♌ or ♒, full, round face; the ☉ Sig. of the person in Hor'y Questions; the ☉ Sig. in ♌, ♒, or ♓, round, full face; the ☽ ascending; the ☽ strong at B.; the ☽ in ♋, or the ☽ Sig. in ♋, full, round face; the ☽ Sig. in ♌, ♏, or ♓; the ☽ Sig. in ♏, full and fleshy face; the ☽ Sig. in ♓, full and bloated; ♄ in ♈, or ♄ Sig. in ♈; ♃ strong at B.; ♃ as Sig. of the person in Hor'y Questions; ♃ Sig. in ♏, full and fleshy; ♂ as Sig. in Hor'y Questions, full, red or sun-

burnt; born under ♂, usually a full face; ♀ Sig. in ♓, full and round; ☿ in ♈, ♉, or ♒; ☿ Sig. in ♒; ♉ gives, and with ♉ on Asc.; ♓ gives round, full face, and with ♋ on Asc.; ♍ on the Asc.; ♏, ♐, ♒, and ♓ give; ♐ on Asc. tends to a long, full face; ♓ gives a good, large and full face; ♓ on Asc., full, and usually bloated or bulging. (See Bloated, Broad, Bulging, Fleshy, Large, Oval, Plump, Round, in this section).

Ghastly Look—(See Pale, Sickly, White).

Glances—(See Expression, Eyes, Look).

Gloomy Face—(See Gloom).

Good Face—♀ well-dig. at B., a good, fair and round face; ♓ gives a good, large face. (See Beautiful, Fair, Full, Handsome, Round, in this section).

Grave Countenance—(See Grave).

Hair; Handsome Face—(See "Beautiful" under Eyes; Handsome; "Beautiful", in this section).

Harmless Looking—(See Harmless).

Head; Honest Face—(See Honest).

Humane Face—(See Humane, Kind, Sympathetic).

Idiotic—(See Idiot).

Indifferent; Intellectual Look—(See Intellect).

Intemperate Aspect—(See Intemperate).

Inviting Face—(See "Beautiful" in this section, and under Eyes).

Jaundiced Look—(See Jaundice).

Jaws; Kind Face—♃ ruler, or strong at B. (See Kind, Humane, Sympathetic).

Large Face—The ☉ Sig. in ♉, large and broad; ♄ Sig. in ♒; ♄ ♒ partile asp. Asc.; ☿ in ♒; ♓ on Asc., large, bloated, bulging, pale, fleshy. (See Big, Bloated, Broad, Bulging, Fat, Fleshy, Full, Lumpish, Plump, Round, Square, in this section. Also see "Large" under Ears, Eyes, Lips, Mouth, Nose).

Lean Face—Thin—♑ gives a lean, long and slender face; ♑ on Asc.; ♄ gives. (See Long, Slender, Thin, in this section; "Lean Body" under Lean; "Thin Body" under Thin).

Left Side—Of Face—(a) Case—Burned—Burns To—(See "Face" under Burns). (b) Marks, Moles, or Warts On—(See "Marks" in this section).

Lightness—Of Feature—(See Features).

Lips; Long Face—♄ Sig. in ♑; ♄ influence strong at B.; ♄ in the Asc.; ♄ in ♍; ♃ rising at B.; ☿ strong at B., long and narrow; a ☿ person; ☿ Sig. in ♍, long visage; in Hor'y Questions' ☿ Sig. of the person; ♈ gives, and espec. when on the Asc.; ♈ gives a long and meagre; ♈ on Asc., long face and neck; ♐ gives long visage, a long, full, and handsome face; ♐ on Asc.; ♑ on Asc., a long, lean, slender, thin face, and generally ugly; ♒ gives; ♒ on the Asc., a long and rather fleshy face. (See Full, Lean, Narrow, Oval, Slender, Thin, Ugly, in this section).

Look; Lotions—Face Lotions—(See Cosmetics).

Lovely Face—♎ gives a round, lovely face, with great beauty, and with a lovely expression; ♎ on Asc.; ♐ gives. (See "Beautiful" in this section).

Lowering Aspect—(See "Downward Look" under Look; Stooping).

Lumpish Face—Unpleasant and Lumpish—♄ ascending at B.; ♀ Sig. in ♏, nothing very pleasant in the countenance. (See "Bloated" in this section).

Lustful Face—(See Lascivious, Lewd, Lust, Wanton).

Meagre Face—Small—Thin—♈ gives a long, meagre face; ♑ gives; the ☽ Sig. in ♑. (See Lean, Small, Thin, in this section).

Melancholic Face—(See "Appearance" under Melancholy).

Misshaped—♄ and ♑ influence; ♄ in the Asc., or ruler of Asc.; ♑ on Asc. (See "Distortions" under Features; "Not Handsome" under Handsome; "Ill-Formed" under Ill; "Lumpish", "Ugly", in this section).

Mouth; Narrow Face—☿ strong at B., a narrow, long face; ☿ ascending at B., and free from the rays of other planets; ☿ gives a thin, sharp, narrow face. The Mental Type has a pear-shaped head, with wide temples, and narrows down to the chin. (See Decanates. Also see Lean, Long, Meagre, Sharp, Slender, Thin, in this section).

Nose; Oily—Shiny—♃ Sig. in ♉; ♉ gives a swarthy, shiny face. (See "Glossy" under Hair; Oils).

Open Countenance—♐ on Asc. gives an open and handsome face and countenance. (See Honest, Humane, Kind, Sincere, Sympathetic).

Oval Face—The ☉ Sig. in ♎, ♐, or ♑, or in these signs in partile asp. the Asc.; the ☉ rising in the Asc.; the ☽ Sig. in ♍, ♐, or ♑, or in partile asp. the Asc. from these signs; ♄ Sig. in ♊ or ♎, or in these signs in partile the Asc.; ♃ Sig. in ♈, ♐, ♎, ♐, or ♑, or in these signs in partile the Asc.; born under ♃; ♃ in the Asc., or ruling the Asc.; ♃ gives when rising at B.; ♃ in ♎, oval and handsome; ♂ Sig. in ♌, ♎, or ♐, or in these signs in partile asp. the Asc.; ♀ Sig. in ♍, ♎, or ♐, or in these signs in partile the Asc.; ♀ Sig. in ♐, a fair and oval; ☿ Sig. in ♈, ♍, or ♐, or partile the Asc. from these signs; ♀ in ♍, oval or thin; ♌ on the Asc., oval and ruddy; ♍ on Asc., but ♍ usually tends to a face more round than oval; ♐ on Asc., long, oval face. The Vital type of Temperament tends to an oval or round face. (See Decanates. Also see Beautiful, Pyriform, Round, in this section).

Pale Face—♓ on the Asc. tends to a pale, large, and fleshy face. (See Delicate, Pale, Sickly; "Low" under Vitality).

Peaceful; Pear-Shaped—(See Pyriform in this section).

Pensive; Piercing Look—(See "Penetrating", "Piercing", under Eyes).

Plain Face—♄ in ♏; ♂ Sig. in ♏, broad and plain; ♑ on the Asc.

Pleasant—Pleasing—The ☽ Sig. in ♎; the ☽ Sig. of the person in Hor'y Questions; ♃ rising in the Asc. (See Pleasant).

Plump Face—♓ on the Asc. gives a plump face in females; ♓ influence. (See Bloated, Bulging, Fleshy, Full, Round, in this section. Also see Plumpness).

Poor Complexion—(See "Bad", "Pale", "Poor", under Complexion).

Profile—The Outline and Contour of the Face—Side View of the Face—The profile of the face is largely determined by the sign on the Asc. at B. Aries on the Asc. tends to a profile resembling the Ram; ♑ on the Asc., resembling the Goat, etc. When there is an animal sign on the Asc. at B., the native is apt to have features similar to such animal. (See "Animal Signs" under Animals; "Beastly Form" under Beasts; Cheeks; "Dogs" under Children; Chin, Face, Features, Forehead, Fowls, Lips, Mouth, Nose, etc.).

Puffy Cheeks—(See "Puffy" under Cheeks; Puffing. Also see "Bloated", "Full", in this section).

Pyriform—Pear-Shaped Face—Narrow—☿ gives. (See Narrow, Oval, in this section).

Ram Face—Resembles the Ram—♈ on the Asc. (See "Profile" in this section; "Animal Signs" under Animals).

Red Face—The ☽ as Sig. indicates a face more white than red; ♃ Sig. in ♈ tends to a peculiar redness, and pimples; ♂ gives a general redness all over the face, but not a rosy hue; ♂ as Sig. in Hor'y Questions gives a full, red, or sunburnt face. (See Freckles, Pimples, Ruddy. Also see "Morbid Red Face" in Sec. 2 of this Article).

Refined Face—♀ Sig. ♂ or good asp. ☿; ♀ Sig. ♂ ♃, or ♀ Sig. ♂ or good asp. ♀; ♀ rising at B., and free from the rays of other planets; ♎ on the Asc. (See Elegant, Intellectual, Refined).

Resolute—(See "Bold" in this section).

Right Side—Of the Face—(See "Face" under Right, Left. Also see Marks, Moles, Scars, Warts, in Sec. 2 of this Article).

Rosy—♃ in the Asc. at B., and ♃ in ♈ or ♎, the face and complexion are rosy and handsome. (See "Red Complexion" under Complexion).

Round Face—The ☉ in ♌, ♒, or ♓, partile the Asc., or as Sig. in these signs, a round and full face; the ☉ strong at B. generally gives; denoted by the ☉ in Hor'y Questions; the ☽ gives a good, fair and round visage; the ☽ rising in the Asc; the ☽ in ♈, ♋, ♌, or ♓, in partile the Asc., or as Sig. in these signs, round and full; the ☽ Sig. in Hor'y Questions; some say ♂ gives, but it is seldom the case; Born under ♀, and ♀ well-dig. at B., a good, fair, round, smooth and beautiful face; ♀ Sig. in Hor'y Questions; ♀ in ♋, ♌, or ♓, in partile asp. the Asc., or Sig. in these signs; ♀ Sig. in ♋, round, pale, sickly or white; ♀ Sig. in ♓, round, full, fair, and dimpled; ♋ gives round and full, but usually with short or small features; ♋ on Asc., round, full, white or pale; ♉, ♌, ♎, ♒, or ♓ on Asc. The Vital Temperament gives a round or oval face. (See Beautiful, Bloated, Fair, Fat, Fleshy, Full, Large, Lumpish, Oval, Plump, in this section).

Ruddy Face—Given by the ☉ and ♂; ♌ gives an oval, ruddy face. (See "Red" in this section; "Red Complexion" under Complexion; Red, Robust, Ruddy, Sanguine; "Good" under Vitality).

Sad Face—Sorrowful Face—Pensive Aspect—♄ in ♋, or Sig. in ♋; ♀ affl. in ♈, or Sig. in ♈. (See Anxiety, Gloomy, Grave, Melancholic, Pensive, Sadness, Serious, Worry, etc.).

Savage Face—Given by ♂; ♂ affl. in the Asc. or M.C. (See Cruel, Fierce, Savage, Vicious).

Sensual Face—(See Amorous, Lewd, Lascivious, Licentious, Lust, Passion, Sensuous, Wanton, etc.).

Serious—(See "Sad" in this section).

Severe—(See Austere, Cruel, Fierce, Severe).

Shape Of—Shape and Form—(See "Form" in this section).

Sharp Face—Sharp Features—☿ gives; ☿ Sig. in ♋, sharp and thin. (See Narrow, Thin, in this section).

Shiny—(See "Oily" in this section).

Short—♋ gives; ♋ on the Asc., a short, small, round face.

Sickly—See Delicate, Emaciation, Pale, Sickly. Also see Delicate, Pale, Thin, in this section).

Sincere Face—(See "Open" in this section; Generous, Honest, Humane, Kind, Sympathetic).

Skin Of—♀ has to do with the skin of the face, and the complexion, and disorders of the face from the indiscreet use of Cosmetics. (See Complexion, Cosmetics. For Skin Disorders of the Face see Sec. 2 of this Article).

Slender Face—♍ gives a long, lean, and slender visage; ♍ on Asc. (See Lean, Long, Narrow, Thin, in this section).

Small Face—♋ gives a small, short, round face; ♋ on Asc.; ♀ strong at B. gives a round, but not large face; the ☽ Sig. in ♍ indicates one of small features. (See Round, Short, in this section. Also see Features).

Smiling Face—Pleasing Smiles—A Cheerful Countenance—♀ in the Asc., or ruler of the Asc., well-dig. and aspected; ♀ Sig. of the person in Hor'y Questions. (See Cheerful, Pleasant, in this section; Cheerfulness, Jovial, Pleasant, Smiling).

Smooth—♂ Sig. in ♈ or ♍, ruddy and smooth if ♂ be ori.; born under ♀, and ♀ well-dig. at B., a good, fair, round, smooth, and beautiful face. (See Ruddy, Smooth).

Sober Face—Born under ♃, a sober and commanding aspect. (See Sober).

Solid Countenance—♄ Sig. in ♍ in Hor'y Questions. (See Solid).

Sorrowful—(See "Sad" in this section).

Square—♍ influence; ♍ on Asc., square and broad. (See "Broad" in this section).

Stern—(See Austere).

Strong Face—(See Bold, Commanding, Positive; "Ruddy", in this section).

Sunburnt—In Hor'y Questions, ♂ as Sig. denotes a full, red, and sunburnt face. (See "Sunburnt" under Complexion).

Sunken Cheeks—Sunken Face—(See "Falling In" under Cheeks; "Sunken" in Sec. 2 of this Article).

Surly Aspect—♄ in ♌, in partile asp. the Asc. (See Cruel, Fierce).

Swarthy—♉ gives a swarthy and shiny face. (See "Swarthy" under Complexion).

Sympathetic—(See "Kind" in this section).

Tawny—(See "Tan" under Complexion).

Teeth; Thin Face—Lean—Meagre—Narrow—Long—The ☽ Sig. in ♍; the ☽ ♍, partile asp. the Asc., thin face and body; ♄ gives a lean, thin face and features; ♄ in the Asc., or ♍ on Asc., thin, and not very good looking; ♄ ascending at B.; ♄ in ♋, pale and thin; ♄ in ♍, long and thin; ♄ ☌ the Sig. of the party in Hor'y Questions; ♃ in ♍, partile the Asc., or Sig. in ♍; ♂ Sig. in ♍, or ♂ in ♍ in partile the Asc.; ♀ in ♍ in partile the Asc., or Sig. in ♍, thin, lean, pale and sickly face; ☿ gives, and ☿ Sig. of the party; ☿ gives a thin, narrow, pointed, sharp face and feature; ☿ in ♋, ♍, ♍, or ♓, in partile the Asc.; ☿ Sig. in ♋, thin and sharp features; ☿ in ♍, thin or oval; ☿ Sig. in ♍; ♈ gives, and ♈ on Asc., long, meagre and thin face; ♍ on the Asc., long, lean, thin, slender face; the Sig. of the person in ♍, or ☌ ♄. In the Mental Temperament the head is broad and wide above, and narrows down to the chin, and with a thin face. (See Lean, Long, Meagre, Narrow, Slender, in this section; "Thin Body" under Thin).

Thoughtful Face—♄ and ☿ give. (See Grave, Intellectual, Serious; "Sad" in this section).

Troubled—(See Anxiety, Cares, Fears; "No Peace of Mind" under Mind; Miserable, Sadness, Trouble, Worry).

Ugly Face—♍ gives a long, thin and ugly face; ♍ on Asc.; Sig. of the party in ♍ or ☌ ♄. (See "Not Handsome" under Handsome; Ugly).

Unattractive—(See "Ugly" in this section).

Unhealthy Aspect—Bad Complexion—(See Bad, Evil, Pale, Poor, Sallow, Sickly, White, under Complexion).

Unpleasant—(See Bloated, Lumpish, Ugly, in this section).

Violent Countenance—♂ influence; ♂ affl. in the Asc. or M.C. at B., and by dir. (See Fierce, Savage, Vicious, Violent).

Visage—(See the various paragraphs in this section. Also see Complexion, Countenance, Expression, Eyes, Features, Look, etc.).

Vivacity—Full of—(See "Full of" under Expression).

Voluptuous—The ☽ Sig. in ♎; ♂ affl. in ♎; the 17° ♏ on the Asc. (See "Sensuous" under Sensuality).

Wan Face—(See Pale, Sickly).

Wanton Look—◻ gives. (See Wanton).

Well-Favored—♍ and ♎ give. (See Beautiful, Fair, Handsome, Lovely, in this section).

White Face—The ☽ Sig. in Hor'y Questions, the face is more white than red; ♋ on the Asc., usually white and pale. (See "Good" under Complexion; Pale, Sickly, White).

Wicked Look—(See Criminal, Cruel, Deceitful, Dishonest, Evil, Fierce, Malicious, Vicious, Wicked).

Wide Face—The Vital Type of Temperament gives a wide face. A ♂ and ♏ influence. (See Decanates, Wide. Also see Broad, Square, in this section).

Wrinkles; Yellow Face—(See "Complexion", "Skin", under Yellow; "Yellew" in Sec. 2 of this Article).

Young Face—Youthful Looking—(See "Youthfulness" under Youth).

— SECTION TWO —

DISEASES OF THE FACE—Afflictions to the Face—Blemishes—Marks, etc.—See the following subjects in the alphabetical arrangement when not considered here.

Abnormalities Of—Caused by the malefics in ♈, or the ☉ and ☽ affl. in ♈ at B. Also caused by the various afflictions during the prenatal period. (See the various paragraphs in this section. Especially note the following subjects in this section, and in the alphabetical arrangement,—Birthmarks (Naevus), Blemishes, Congenital, Contortions, Contractions, Cyclops, Defects, Deformed, Disfigured, Distortions; "Dogs" under Children; Enlarged, Features, Idiots, Ill-Formed, Imperfections, Inhuman, Malformations, Marks, Misshaped, Moles, Monsters, Naevus, Prenatal, Structural, Warts, etc.).

Accidents To—(See Blows, Burns, Cuts, Hurts, Scars, in this section).

Acne, Acromegaly—(See "Enlarged" in this section).

Affected—The face is affected when ♅ is in ♓. (See Table 196 in Simmonite's Arcana. Also note the various paragraphs in this section).

Afflictions To—(See the various paragraphs in this Article).

All Diseases In—Signified by the 1st H., and afflictions in ♈. (See "Diseases" in this section).

Atrophy—Facial Hemiatrophy—♄ affl. in ♈; Subs at AT, MCP, and KP. (See Atrophy).

Barber's Itch—Sycosis—(See Barbers).

Birth Marks—(See "Naevus" in this section).

Blackheads—(See "Comedo" under Sebaceous).

Blemishes—The ☉ Sig. ☌ ♄, and ♄ ill-dig.; ♄, ♂, or ☋ ascending, but in a nativity ☋ has no effect unless ☌ ☽; ♂ in ♍ in partile asp. the Asc.; malefics affl. in ♈, or the ☉ or ☽ affl. in ♈. (See Acne, Barber's Itch, Birthmarks, Blemishes, Blotches, Burns, Carcinoma, Contortions, Contractions, Cosmetics, Cuts, Defects, Deformed, Disfigurements, Eruptions; "Blemishes" under Eyes; Freckles, Growths, Harelip, Marks, Moles, Pimples, Pitted, Pockmark, Scars, Smallpox, Sores, Ulcers, Warts, Wrinkles, etc.).

Bloated Face—(See "Bloated" in Sec. One of this Article).

Blotches—Afflictions in ♈; the ☉ or ☽ in ♈, and affl. by ♄ or ♂. (See Blotches. Also note the various paragraphs in this section).

Blows To—(See Cuts, Hurts, in this section. Also see "Blows" under Eyes, Head).

Blushing; Boils—(See "Face" under Boils).

Bones—Bones of the Face Affected—♄ affl. in ♈; Subs at MCP. (See Bones).

Burns—Sears—To the Face—(See "Face" under Burns).

Cancer On—Carninoma—(See "Face" under Carcinoma).

Capillaries—Dilatation of—Congestion of—(See Acne, Capillaries; "Red Face" in this section).

Cheeks—Disorders of—(See Cheeks).

Comedo—Blackheads—(See "Comedo" under Sebaceous).

Congenital Defects—Of the Face—(See "Abnormalities" in this section).

Congestion—(See Acne, Congestion; "Red Face" in this section).

Contortions—Twistings—Distortions—♅ affl. in ♈ or ♉; ♄ affl. in ♈; Subs at MCP. (See Contortions, Deformities; "Distortions" under Features; Incoordination, Spasmodic, Twistings).

Contractions—♆, ♅, or ♄ affl. in ♈; afflictions in ♈ or ♉. (See Contractions, Deformities, Distortions).

Cosmetics—Bad Effects of—(See Cosmetics. Also see "Lotions" in this section).

Cuts To—♂ on the Asc., cuts or hurts to the face and head; ♂ in the 1st H.; ♂ in ♈. (See Hurts, Injuries, Marks, Scars, in this section; "Cuts" under Head).

Cyclops—A Monster with Eyes Fused into One—(See Cyclops).

Defects—♄ or ♂ in the 1st H. at B.; ♄ in ♋; ☿ ori. at B.; afflictions during the prenatal period. (See Blemishes, Defects, Marks, Moles, Scars, in this section).

Deformed—Disfigured Face—Afflictions in ♈; the ☉ Sig. in ♋, or in ♋ in partile asp. the Asc.; ♅ ☌ ♄ in ♈. (See "Disfigured", and other paragraphs in this section. Also see Deformities).

Delicate Looking—(See "Delicate" under Complexion; Delicate, Pale, Sickly).

Dilated Capillaries—(See Acne, Capillaries; "Red Face", in this section).

Diplegia—Double Symmetric Paralysis In—(See "Paralysis" in this section; Paralysis).

Diseases In — The ☉ affl. at B., and the ☉ to the evil asps. the Asc. by dir.; afflictions in ♈; ♈ on the cusp of 6th H., or intercepted in the 6th; malefics in ♈; ♈ diseases; Subs at AT, MCP (4C), and SP. (See the various paragraphs in this section).

Disfigured—Evil asps. to the Asc., with malefics just setting, and with no good asps. to counteract. (See Disfigurements; Abnormalities, Blemishes, Defects, Deformities, Hurts, Marks, Moles, Naevus, Pockmark, Scars, in this section).

Distorted—(See "Distorted" under Features. Also note the various paragraphs in this section).

Eczema Of—(See Eczema).

Enlarged Face—Acromegaly—♃ or ♂ affl. in ♈; ♄ affl. in ♈, by deposits; Subs at AT and CP. (See Enlargements).

Eruptions—Rashes—Pimples—The ☽ affl. in ♈, ♉, or ♊; ♂ or ♀ affl. in ♈; Subs at MCP (4C), CP, and KP (11D). (See Acne, Cosmetics, Eruptions, Measles, Pimples, Smallpox, etc.).

Erysipelas—(See "Face" under Erysipelas).

Eyes; Father—Hurts to Face of—(See "Face" under Father).

Features—Contortions of—Distortions—(See Features. Also note the various paragraphs in this section).

Flushings; Forehead; Freckles;

Ghastly Look—(See Pale, Sickly).

Growths On—(See Cancer, Moles, Warts, in this section; Growths).

Harelip—(See Lips).

Hemiatrophy—(See "Atrophy" in this section).

Herpes—(See "Face" under Herpes).

Hurts—Accidents—Injuries—Wounds —Blows—Burns—Cuts, etc.—Afflictions in ♈; the ☉ to the ☌ ♂ by dir.; the ☽ to the ☌ or ill-asps. ♂ by dir., and the ☽ hyleg; the ☽ in the Asc., close to, or ☌ ♂, liable to a blow, cut, accident or injury to face which may require a surgical operation to relieve and remedy; the ☽ to the place of the Pleiades or Praesepe; ♂ in ♈, in the Asc. and rising; the 1st Dec. of ♈ on the Asc., ruled by ♂; the 1st face of ♊ on the Asc., and containing the ☽ with ♄ and ♂. This face contains Aldebaran, of the nature of ♂; the Pleiades rising, or with the ☉ or ☽ at B., or directed to the Asc.; the Pleiades, Hyades, Ascelli, Castor, Pollux, or Praesepe, when directed to the Asc. or Lights. (See "Cuts" in this section. Also see "Hurts" under Eyes, Head).

Idiots; Ill-Formed—(See "Misshaped" in this section).

Imperfections—(See Blemishes, Defects, Marks, Scars, and the various paragraphs in this section).

Inhuman; Injuries To—(See Blows, Burns, Cuts, Hurts, and the various paragraphs in this section).

Irritations To—(See Cosmetics, Lotions, in this section).

Itch—Barber's Itch—(See Barbers).

Jaundiced Look—(See Jaundice. Also see "Yellow" in this section).

Left Side—Of the Face—Marks, Moles, or Warts On—A feminine sign on the Asc., and a masculine planet in the Asc. A masculine sign on the Asc., and a masculine planet in the Asc., tend to affect the right side of the face similarly. (See "Face" under Burns; Left; "Location" under Moles; Marks, Moles, Right, Warts, in this section).

Lotions—Face Lotions—Irritations By—Cosmetics—The ♎ people are easily affected by, as ♎, the exalted sign of ♄, tends to skin diseases; ♀ affl. in ♈, and espec. when in the 6th H., tends to injury by face and hair lotions; ♀ affl. in ♑ tends to misuse of skin and hair lotions. (See Cosmetics).

Lumpish Face—(See "Lumpish in Sec. 1 of this Article).

Malformations; Marks—Moles—Scars —The ☉ in ♌, in partile asp. the Asc., sometimes a scar or mark on the face; the ☉ affl. in ♌; the ☉ Sig. in ♌; the ☉ in ♈, in ☌ or near ☋; the ☽ Sig., □ or ☍ ☉; the ☉ Sig. ☌ ♄ and ♄ ill-dig. at B.; the ☽ Sig. □ or ☍ ☉, or sepr. from the ☍; the ☽ Sig. ☌ ☉, or apply. to the exact ☌; the ☽ Sig. ☌ ♂, and ♂ ill-dig.; ♄ in the Asc.; ♂ Sig. of the person; ♂ ruler of the Asc., and in ☌, □, or ☍ the Sig. of the person; characteristic of ♂ people; ♂ rising in ♈; ♂ rising in the Asc., a mole or mark on the face; ♂ affl. in the 1st H.; ♂ in ♉ or ♍, partile the Asc.; ♀ in ♈, partile the Asc.; ♀ Sig. in ♈; afflictions in ♈; ♈ on the Asc.; the 2nd face of ♈ ascending; the 6th face of ♉ on the Asc.; the 1st face of ♐ on Asc.; the 4th face of ♒ on Asc.; a malefic planet a little above, or a little below the Asc. tends to a mark, mole or scar high up on the face, and when the malefic is lower down in the Asc., the mark is near the middle of the face, and when very low in the Asc., the mark is on the lower part of the face, or on the neck. There is usually a mark or mole on the right side of the face when there is a masculine sign on the Asc., and a masculine planet in the Asc., and similar conditions on the left side of the face when a feminine sign and planet ascend. (See Blemishes, Cuts, Disfigured, Hurts, Pockmark, Scars, and the various paragraphs in this section; Left, Lower, Marks, Middle, Moles, Naevus, Right, Scars, Upper, Warts).

Misfortunes—To the Face—(See Accidents, Blows, Burns, Cuts, Hurts, Injuries, Marks, Scars, and the various paragraphs in this section).

Misshaped—(See "Beastly Form" under Beasts; "Dogs" under Children; Contortions. Cyclops, Deformities, Ill-

Formed, Malformations, Monsters, etc. See Contortions, Contractions, Deformed, Distortions, and the various paragraphs in this section. Also see "Misshaped" in Sec. 1 of this Article).

Moles—(See "Marks" in this section).

Morbid Red Face—(See Congestion, Red Face, in this section).

Mother—Injury to Face of—(See "Face" under Mother).

Mouth; Naevus—Birthmarks—♂ rising in ♈. (See Naevus).

Nerves—Paralysis of—Facial Paralysis—♅ affl. in ♈. (See Neuralgia, Paralysis, in this section).

Neuralgia—Of the Facial Nerves—Spasmodic—Tic Dourouleux—Facial Paroxysms—An ♈ disease; ♅, ♂, or ☿ affl. in ♈; ♂ affl. in ♈ or ♎; a ♎ disease; Subs at MCP. (See "Neuralgia" under Head; Neuralgia, Spasmodic, Tics).

Nose—Morbid Red Nose—(See "Red Face" in this section).

Oily Face—(See "Oily" in Sec. 1 of this Article).

Pale Face—Wan—Delicate—White—Sickly—(See "Bad", "Poor", under Complexion; Delicate, Pale, Sickly, White; Bloated, Pale, Sickly, in Sec. 1 of this Article).

Palsy Of—♅ affl. in ♈; Subs at MCP (4C). (See "Paralysis" in this section. Also see Palsy, Paralysis).

Paralysis—Facial Paralysis—Diplegia—♅ affl. in ♈; ♂ in ♈, ♂ the Asc., and affl. by ♅ or ♄; ♂ in the Asc., or ♂ Asc., and also in ♐ or ♉ ☽; Subs at AT, AX, MCP (4C). Case—See Fig. 13C in "Astro-Diagnosis" by the Heindels. (See Atrophy, Diplegia, Palsy, in this section; Paralysis).

Paroxysms—Tics—Twitchings—(See Neuralgia, Spasmodic, Tics, Twitchings, in this section; Paroxysms, Spasmodic, Tics, Twitchings).

Pimples—(See Pimples; "Eruptions" in this section).

Pockmarked—Pitted Face—(See Pitted Degrees" under Pitted; "Face" under Smallpox).

Poor Complexion—(See Bad, Poor, under Complexion; Delicate, Pale, Sickly, in this section).

Psoriasis—(See "Face" under Psoriasis; Herpes, Scaly, Tetter, in this section).

Puffy Cheeks—(See "Puffy" in Sec. 1 of this Article).

Rashes—(See "Eruptions" in this section).

Red—Morbid Red Face—Congestion—Dilated Capillaries—Abnormal Redness—Red Nose—A ♄ disease; ♄ in ♈; ♃ Sig. in ♈ tends to a peculiar redness and pimples; ♎ on the Asc.; Subs at MCP (3, 4C), HP, and KP. (See Acne, Capillaries, Congestions, Dilatations, Erythema, Pimples; "Red" in Sec. 1 of this Article).

Right Side—Of the Face—(See "Face" under Left, Right; "Left Side", "Marks", in this section).

Saint Vitus Dance—Chorea—(See Saint).

Scaly Face—(See "Psoriasis" in this section; Scales).

Scars—Marks—Moles—The ☉ in ♌, partile asp. the Asc.; the ☉ Sig. in ♌; the ☉ or ☽ Sig., and ♂ ♂, and ♂ illdig.; the ☽ Sig. ♂ ☉, or apply. to the exact ♂; ♄ or ♂ in the Asc., a scar or mole on the face; ♂ in the 1st H., wounds or scars on the face or head; ♂ in ♈ in the Asc.; characteristic of ♂ people; born under ♂; ♂ in ♍, partile the Asc.; ♂ as Sig. in Hor'y Questions denotes; ♀ in ♈, partile the Asc. (See "Marks" in this section).

Scurvy; Sears—(See "Burns" in this section).

Shape—Of the Face—Abnormalities In Shape—(See Abnormalities, Bloated, Contortions, Contractions, Cyclops, Deformed, Distortions, Enlarged, Features, Idiot, Inhuman, Misshaped, and the various paragraphs in this section. Also see Sec. 1 of this Article).

Shiny Face—(See "Oily" in Sec. 1 of this Article).

Sickly Looking—(See Pale, Sickly; Pale, Thin, in this section).

Skin—Of the Face—Disorders of—Especially under the rule of ♄, ♂, and ♀. Disorders from wrong use of Cosmetics and Lotions are under ♀. Dry, scaly skin, and such disorders, under ♄. Eruptions and rashes under ♂. (See Complexion, Cosmetics, Eruptions, Pimples, Skin. Also note the various paragraphs in this Article, as Birthmarks, Blemishes, Capillaries, Congestion, Defects, Diseases, Eczema, Eruptions, Freckles, Herpes, Marks, Oily, Red, Scars, etc.).

Smallpox—In the Face—Pockmarked—(See "Face" under Smallpox).

Sores On—Fixed stars of the nature of ♂ ascending at B.; ♂ affl. in ♈. (See Sores; Blotches, Boils, Cancer, Eruptions, Ulcer, in this section).

Spasmodic Diseases—Of the Face—Facial Spasm—Tics—Twitchings—Contractions—♅ affl. in ♈; Subs at AX and LCP. (See Contortions, Contractions, Distortions, Spasmodic, Saint Vitus Dance, Tics, Twitchings; Contortions, Contractions, Neuralgia, Palsy, Paralysis, Paroxysms, in this section).

Strokes To—Violent Strokes—(See "Blows" in this section. For Paralytic Strokes, see "Paralysis" in this section).

Sunken Face—In Illness—The ☽ in ♑, and affl. by the ☉ or ♂ when taken ill (Hor'y). (See "Falling In Of" under Cheeks).

Swellings—In the Face—Swollen Face—An ♈ disease; ♃ affl. in ♓, due to dropsical conditions. (See Dropsy, Swellings; "Bloated" in Sec. 1 of this Article; Boils, Enlargement, Eruptions, in this section).

Tetter—Eczema—Herpes—Ringworm—Tetter—Afflictions in ♈, ♎, or ♑; Subs at MCP (4C), and KP. (See "Head and Face" under Eczema; "Face" under Herpes; Psoriasis, Ringworm, Scales, Skin, Tetter).

Tics—Tic Douloureux—Spasmodic Facial Neuralgia—(See Tics; Neuralgia, Spasmodic, in this section).

Tissues—Of the Face Affected—Afflictions in ♈; Subs at MCP (4C). (See the various paragraphs in this section; Tissues).

Twistings—(See "Contortions" in this section; Twitchings).

Twitchings—(See "Spasmodic" in this section; Saint Vitus, Spasmodic, Tics, Twitchings).

Ulcers—Sores—Suppuration—Afflictions in ♈; ♄ or ♂ affl. in ♈; ♂ in ♈ in the Asc., and afflicted; Subs at MCP and KP. (See Ulcers; "Sores" in this section).

Unhealthy Aspect — (See "Pale" in this section; "Poor" under Complexion; Delicate, Emaciated, Low, Pale, Sickly, Unhealthy, Vitality, Weak Body, White).

Visage—Sickly, Pale and Thin Visage —(See Pale, Sickly, in this section; Thin, Visage, in Sec. 1 of this Article).

Wan Face—(See "Pale" in this section).

Warts On—Verruca—(See Blemishes, Left Side, Marks, in this section). Also caused by Subs at MCP (4C).

White Face—(See Pale, Sickly; "Complexion" under White; "White" in Sec. 1 of this Article).

Wounds To — (See Accidents, Blows, Cuts, Hurts, Injuries, in this section).

Wrinkles; Yellow Face—In Illness— The ☽ in ♍, and affl. by the ☉ or ♂ when taken ill (Hor'y). (See "Jaundiced Look" under Jaundice; "Complexion" under Yellow).

FACULTIES—Specific Powers of the Mind and Body—The Faculties are ruled by the ☽ and ☿. The ☽ rules over the bodily or sensual faculties, and ☿ more specifically over the mental faculties. (See the various paragraphs under Intellect, Mental, Mind, Perception, Reason, Senses, Understanding, etc.).

Arrested—Arrested Faculties—(See Inhibitions; "Arrested" under Mental; Retardation, Suppressions).

Disease—Disease-Resisting Faculties —(See the various paragraphs under Recuperation, Resistance, Stamina, Strength, Tone, Vitality).

Disordered—(See Idiocy, Imbecility, Insanity, Judgment, Memory; "Faculties' under Mental; "Weak Mind" under Mind; Perception, Reason. Also note the various paragraphs in this section).

Dull—The Faculties Dull—(See Dull).

Emotion—(See Emotions).

Endangered—Signs of Danger to the Mental Faculties—(See "Faculties" under Mental).

Impaired—(See Feeble, Idiocy; "Mental" under Impaired; Insanity; "Weak Mind" under Mind, etc.).

Improved—(See "Beastly Form under Beasts; "Quickened" under Mental).

Inhibition Of—(See Inhibition, Retarded, Suppressed).

Intellectual Faculties—(See Intellect, Mental, Mind, Perception, Reason, Understanding, etc.).

Instincts—The Instinctual Faculties —(See Instincts).

Intuition; Inward Faculties—The Inward Faculties Prejudiced—Disordered —(See Phantasies).

Irrational Faculties—The Sensitive Faculties—Ruled by the ☽. (See Deviations, Irrational, Sensitive).

Judgment—(See Judgment).

Loss of Faculties—Danger of—The 17° □ on the Asc., which is a degree of impotence. (See Impotent, Loss).

Memory; Mental Faculties—☿ is the chief ruler of the Mental Faculties. In judging of the mental faculties great care is necessary to note what aspects ☿ makes with other planets, for on this chiefly depends the disposition of the native. (See Intellect, Mental; "Judging the Mind" under Mind).

Moral Faculties—(See Morals).

Natural Faculties—Are ruled by the ☽. (See Natural).

Passive Faculties—The Sensitive Faculties—Irrational Faculties—Deviation of—These Faculties are ruled by the Moon. (See Deviations, Irrational, Passive, Sensitive).

Perception; Physical Faculties—Are ruled chiefly by the ☉. (See Physical).

Quickened—(See "Quickened" under Mental).

Rational—Reasoning Faculties— Ruled by ☿. (See Rational, Reason).

Reason; Religious Faculties—(See Excitable, Neptune, Pineal Gland, Religion, Spiritual).

Retarded—The Faculties Retarded— (See Decreased, Diminished, Dwarf, Hardening, Impairments, Retarded, Suppressions, etc.).

Retentive Faculties—(See Retentive).

Senses—The Faculties of Sight, Hearing, Smell, Taste, Touch, Feeling, Color, etc. (See these subjects. Also see Senses).

Sensitive Faculties—(See Irrational, Passive, in this section).

Sensual Faculties—Ruled by the ☽. (See Sensual).

Sentient Faculties—Feeling—Ruled by the ☽, ☿, and Asc. (See Sentient).

Spiritual Faculties—(See "Religious" in this section).

Strengthened—(See "Quickened" under Mental).

Understanding; Unusual—Unusual Mental Faculties—(See "Unusual" under Mental. Also see Genius, Prodigies).

Weakened—(See Derangement, Faculties, Shallow, Weak, Weakened, under Mental).

FADING—Loss of Freshness and Color —Growing Weaker—Loss of Strength, Energy and Vitality, etc.—♄ is the planet of fading, decay, death and depletion. (See Blight, Decay, Declines, Decrease, Decrepitude, Depleted, Diminished, Dimmed, Dull, Feeble, Infirm,

Languishing, Loss Of, Old Age, Pale, Sickly, Vitality (Loss of); Weak, Withering, Wrinkles, etc.).

FAECES—Excrement—Dung—Discharge of the Bowels—Evacuations—Defacation—Waste—Ruled by ♄. Also ruled by the ♍ sign, which sign has charge largely of elimination of organic waste materials, as thru the Urine, the Faeces, and thru the Nose. The following paragraphs have to do with the Faeces, which see in the alphabetical arrangement when not more fully considered here—

Abnormal Stools — Afflictions in ♍; Subs at LPP (4, 5L). (See the various paragraphs in this section).

Bloody Evacuations—Bloody Flux—(See Dysentery; "Bloody Flux" under Flux; Typhoid).

Bowels—(See the various paragraphs under Bowels).

Cholera; Colon; Constipation—Sluggish Action—(See Constipation).

Costiveness—Hardness and Retention of Faeces—(See Costiveness; "Hardening" in this section).

Diarrhoea; Discharges; Dryness—Of the Faeces—(See Constipation, Hardening, in this section).

Dysentery; Effusions; Elimination; Evacuations; Excretion; Expulsion; Flux; Food—Undigested Food In—Pieces of Food In the Stools—(See "Intestinal" under Indigestion).

Hardening—Of the Faeces—Lumpy—Scybalum—Dryness of — Retention — The work of ♄; a ♄ disease, as ♄ is a scybalous agency; ♄ affl. in ♍, and espec. when ♄ is the afflictor in the disease. (See "Sluggish" under Bowels; Constipation, Costiveness, Hardening).

Hemorrhages—(See "Bowels" under Hemorrhage).

Impeded—(See "Bowel Action" under Impeded).

Involuntary—Involuntary Faecal Discharges—♂ weak at B. (See Involuntary).

Lumpy Faeces—(See "Hardening" in this section).

Mucus In—(See "Bowels" under Mucus).

Peristalsis—(See "Peristaltic" under Bowels).

Pieces of Food—In the Stools—(See "Food" in this section).

Piles—(See Hemorrhoids).

Putrid Matter—In Faeces—(See "Putrid" under Bowels).

Rectum; Retention—(See Constipation, Costiveness, Hernia, Retention; "Hardening", "Suppression", in this section).

Sanguineous—(See "Bloody" in this section).

Scybalum—Hardening—Lumpy—(See "Hardening" in this section).

Serous Stools—The ☽ affl. in ♍; Subs at KP, and PP (2L). (See Serum).

Sluggish Bowels—(See "Sluggish" under Bowels; "Hardening" in this section).

Suppression Of—The work of ♄ impeding the action of the terminal branches of the Pneumogastric Nerve, and by generating the emotions of fear and worry. (See Hardening, Retention, in this section; Pneumogastric Nerve, Saturn, Suppressions).

Typhoid—Bowel Lesions and Hemorrhage In—(See Typhoid).

Undigested Food—In the Stools—(See "Food" in this section).

Vomiting—Faecal Vomiting—Occurs in Ileac Passion. (See Ileac).

Wastes; Watery Stools—(See "Cholera Infantum" under Cholera; Diarrhoea, Dysentery).

FAG—Brain Fag—(See "Brain Fag" under Brain; Fatigue, Reading, Study, Weariness).

FAILURE—

Business Failure—Tending to Ill-Health and Worry—(See Reverses).

Health—Failure of—(See "Bad Health", "Periods of Bad Health", under Health; Ill-Health, Infirmities, Sickness, etc.).

Heart Failure—(See "Failure", "Heart Trouble", under Heart).

FAINT—Weak—

Faint Pulse—Faintings At the Heart—(See Feeble; "Faintings", "Weak", under Heart; Pulse, Weak).

FAINTING—Faintings—Swoonings—Falling Sickness—Syncope—Insensibility—Loss of Consciousness, etc.—Syncope, or Fainting, may be Cerebral, from Heart weakness and disturbances, disturbed Circulation of the Blood, Corrupt Blood, and also accompanies such conditions as Coma, Delirium, Fits, Epilepsy, etc. The following subjects have to do with Faintings, and loss of Consciousness, which see in the alphabetical arrangement when not considered here.

Causes of Faintings—General Causes—Afflictions in ♌ or ♒, and the fixed signs; the ☉ in ♌ or ♒, and to the ♂ or ill-asp. ♂ by dir., tends to syncope if the heart is weak; a ☉ disease; the ☉ affl. in ♈, ♉, or ♐; the ☉ affl. in ♐; the ☉ in ♐, and to the ♂ or ill-asp. any of the malefics as promittors, liable to swoonings; the ☽ in ♌ and affl. by the ☉ or ♂ when taken ill; the ☽ affl. in ♌ or ♒; the ☽ ♂ or ill-asp. ♄ in ♌ (or ☿ if he be of the nature of ♄) at the beginning of an illness (Hor'y); the ☽ hyleg in ♒, and affl., and espec. with females; the ☽ in ♏ in ♂ or ill-asp. any of the malefics as promittors, tends to swoonings after over-exertion; some people faint and remain insensible at an Eclipse of the ☽, as long as the eclipse lasts, and espec. if the ☽ be hyleg and affl. at B.; caused by afflictions to ♆, and by the afflictions of ♆ to the hyleg, or to bring on Trance conditions; ♅ affl. in ♌ or ♒, and affl. the hyleg, may cause sudden swoonings due to heart failure or disturbed circulation of the blood; ♄ afflictions tend to; ♄ affl. in ♈, ♌, or ♒; ♄ in the 6th H. at B. in fixed signs, and affl. by the ☉ or ☽; ♄ □ or ☍ ♃, due to disturbed Adrenal secretions;

♃ affl. in ♈; ♂ affl. in ♌ or ♒; ♂ in ♌ in the 6th H.; ♀ in ♌, and affl. the ☽ or Asc.; ♀ affl. in ♌ in the 6th H.; ☿ affl. in ♌; ♌ on the Asc. (See the various paragraphs in this section. Also see Adrenal, Eclipse, Heart, Neptune, Trance).

Cerebral Syncope—(See Cerebral).

Coma; Consciousness—Loss of—(See Consciousness).

Death by Syncope—♅ in the 8th H., and affl. the hyleg; ♄ afflictions tend to; ♂ affl. in ♌ in the 6th H.

Delirium; Dizziness; Epilepsy;

Falling Fits—Falling Sickness—Swooning Fits—Swoonings—A disease of the ☽, and afflictions to the ☽; the ☽ in ♐ or ♐, injury by falling sickness, and the malefics in angles, and occi. of the ☽; the ☽ affl. in ♋; is a periodic disease caused by the ☽; the ☽ affl. in ♌ or ♒, and affl. by the ☉ or ♂ when taken ill, and the ☽ slow in motion and decreasing in light; the ☽ affl. in ♏; the ☽, ☿, and the Asc. unconnected with each other, and affl. by ♄ or ♂ from angles, and with no assistance from the benefics; ♄ or ♂ angular, in the 1st or 7th H., in ♐ or ♐, ori. of the ☉ and occi. of the ☽; caused by ☿ when the dominion of death is vested in him; an ♈ disease and afflictions in ♈. (See Epilepsy, Fits, Periodic; "Sudden" in this section).

Hysteria; Insensibility;

Sudden Swoonings—The ☉ gives; a ☉ disease; ♅ affl. in ♌ or ♒, and also affl. the hyleg from these signs, and due to heart failure or disturbed circulation of the blood. (See "Falling Fits" in this section).

Swoonings—(See "Falling Fits" in this section).

Trance; Vertigo.

FAIR—Comely—Beautiful—Light Hue—Pleasing to the Eye or Mind—

Fair Complexion—(See "Fair" under Complexion).

Fair Eyes—(See "Fair" under Eyes).

Fair Face—(See "Fair" under Face).

Fair Hair—(See "Light" under Hair).

Fair Proportions—The ☉ in ♒, or ♒ on the Asc. (See Beautiful, Comely, Handsome; "Well-Formed" and "Well-Proportioned" under Well).

Fair Stature—The ☉ or ☽ give when strong at B.; the ☉ in ♒; ♌ or ♒ on the Asc. (See Beautiful, Comely, Stature).

Fair and Tall—□ on the Asc. (See Tall).

FAITH HEALING—(See "Faith" under Healers).

FALL EQUINOX—(See Equinoxes).

FALLING—Falling In—Falling Out—
Cheeks—Falling In of—(See Cheeks).

Fits—(See "Falling Fits" under Fainting).

Hair—Falling Out of—(See Baldness; "Scanty" under Hair).

Sickness—Falling Sickness—(See "Falling Fits" under Fainting).

Womb—Falling of—Prolapsus of—(See "Falling" under Womb).

FALLOPIAN TUBES—Oviducts—Salpinx—Ruled by the ♎ sign. The Womb and Ovaries are ruled by ♏, and afflictions in ♏ tend to affect the Tubes indirectly, and by sympathetic action.

Disorders Of—Inflammation of—Salpingitis—Malefics and afflictions in ♎; Subs at KP and PP (2, 3, 4L).

Dropsy Of—Hydrosalpinx—The ☽ affl. in ♎; Subs at KP and PP (2, 3, 4L). (See Dropsy, Ovaries, Womb).

FALLS—Falls are caused principally by ♄ and his afflictions, and hurts, bruises or injuries by falls.

Accidents By—Also Cuts, Hurts, or Injuries By, or by Animals, and in Sports—The ☉ in ♐ and affl. by malefics. (See the various paragraphs in this section).

Animals—Hurts By—Falls From—The ☉ affl. in ♐. (See "Hurts" under Animals; "Falls" under Horses).

Bruises—And Hurts by Falls—♅ in the 12th H., and by falls from horses; ♄ rising and affl. the ☉ or ☽ at B.; ♄ in the 8th H. in Hor'y Questions. (See "Falls" under Bruises).

Buildings—Houses—Falls From—Accidents, Injury or Death by the Fall of—The ☉ hyleg, and to the ☌ or ill-asp. ♄ by dir.; ♅ or ♄ in ♈, ♋, ♎, or ♑, and in ☌ or evil asp. the ☉ or ♂; ♅ or ♄ in quadrupedal or tropical signs, and in ☌ or ill-asp. the ☉ or ♂; ♄ rising and affl. the ☉ or ☽ at B.; ♄ in cardinal signs, and espec. when in angles; ♄ in the 10th, and in ☍ the ☉; ♄ in a quadrupedal or tropical sign, and the ☉ ☌ or ☍ ♂; ♄ ☌ ♂ in ☍, ♊, ♌, or ♏, in the 4th H., and on the lower meridian. (See Buildings, Crushed; "Earthquakes" under Earth; Quadrupedal, Tropical).

Cuts By—(See "Accidents" in this section; Cuts).

Danger Of—Liable to Falls—General Causes of—The ☉ in the ♄ sign ♑, and affl. by ♄ or ♂; the ☉ or ☽ affl. by ♄ or ♂; the ☉ or ☽ to the ☌ or ill-asp. ♄ or ♂ by dir.; the ☉ directed to the Cratch; the ☉ or ☽ affl. by ♄ ascending, and espec. if ♄ be in ☍, ♐, or ♒; the ☉ or ☽ ori., and affl. by ♄ or ♂; the ☉ or ♄ affl. in ♐; the ☉ Sig., and ☌ or ill-asp. ♄, and espec. if either be in the 10th H.; the ☽ affl. in ☍ or ♐, and the malefics angular and occi. of the ☽; the ☽ affl. at B., and to the ☌ or ill-asps. ♄, ♂, ♒, or to the place of Ceti; the ☽ to the place of Cor Scorpio; the ☽ in earthy signs, and to the ☌ or ill-asps. ♄ or ♂ by dir.; ♅ by tr. over the place of the radical ♄, and espec. if ♄ is in ♎; ♅ in the 1st H. and affl. the hyleg; ♅ to the ill-asps. his place at B.; ♄ ascending at B.; ♄ rising or setting at B.; ♄ in bad asp. the ☉; ♄ ☌ or ill-asp. the ☽, and ori.; ♄ ☌ or ill-asp. the Asc. at B., or by dir.; ♄ ☌, P, □ or ☍ the ☉ from card. signs, and ♂ with ♄, makes the effect more certain and violent; ♄ in the Asc. or M.C., and the ☉ afflicted; denoted and caused by fixed stars of the nature of ♄; ♄ in a fiery or airy

sign, and to the ill-asp. the Asc. by dir.; ♄ ☌ or ill-asp. the ☉ in fixed signs; ♄ ☌ or ill-asp. ♂, and espec. when either be ori.; ♄ by tr. in ☌ or ill-asp. the ☉, ☽, ♃ or ♀; ♄ in the M.C., or angular, holding dominion, and elevated above the Lights, and affl. the hyleg; ♄ in ♈, ♌, or ♐, and ☌ or ill-asp. the Asc. by dir.; ♄ ruler of the 4th or 8th H. at B., and to the ☌ or ill-asp. ♂; the ♄ sign ♑ on the Asc.; ♂ in the 1st H., and affl. by ♅ or ♄; ♂ affl. in ☐ or ♍, and ☌ or evil asp. the Asc. by dir.; ♂ in airy signs, ☌ or ill-asp. the Asc. by dir.; ♂ by periodic rev. to the evil asps. ♅; ♂ affl. in ♑; ♂ with Aldebaran, and espec. if in an angle and affl. the ☽; ♂ in the 7th H. in ☐ or ☍ ☉, and in a four-footed sign; ♂ Sig. ☐ or ☍ ♄, if either be in the Asc., or ♄ in the M.C.; afflictions in ♐, or ♐ on the Asc., and afflicted; born under the Hurtful Signs ♈, ♉, ♎, ♏, or ♑; the Asc. to the ☌ or ill-asp. ♄ by dir., and ♄ ori. at B.; the Asc. to the ☌, ☐, or ☍ ♂ by dir.; the M.C. to the ☌ or ill-asp. ♄ by dir.; malefics in the M.C., elevated above the Luminaries, and espec. when ♄ holds dominion; earthy signs dispose to when afflicted and containing malefics; Whale's Belly when conjoined to the ☉ or ☽. (See the various paragraphs in this section. Also see Accidents, Blows, Hurts, Injuries).
Death by Falls—Violent Death By—The ☉ hyleg, and to the ☌ or ill-asps. ♄ by dir.; the ☉ Sig. ☌ ♄, and even tho ♄ be well-dig.; the ☉ Sig. ☐ or ☍ ♄, and espec. if either be in the 10th H.; the ☐ or ☍ asps. of the ☉, ☽, ♄, or ♂; the ☽ hyleg and affl., and to the ☌ ♅ by dir.; the ☽ with Antares, and in ☍ to ♄ and Aldebaran, and espec. if in angles; ♄ ☌ or evil asp. the Asc. by dir., and when he is not ruler of the 1st H.; ♄ the afflicting planet; ♄ ☌, ☐, or ☍ ☉ from cardinal signs, and ♂ with ♄; ♄ in the M.C. in ☐ the Asc., and the ☉ afflicted; ♄ the afflicting planet in a violent sign, and affl. the ☉ or ☽; caused by fixed stars of the nature of ♄ when with the ☉ or ☽, or affl. the hyleg; ♂ in ♈, ♉, ♌, ♐, or ♑, and ☍ the Asc.; ♂ in quadrupedal signs, and in ☐ or ☍ the ☉, and ♂ just setting at B.; ♂ denotes death by falls; ♂ Sig. ☐ or ☍ ♄ if either be in the Asc., or ♄ in the M.C.; ♂ in the 7th H., ☐ or ☍ the ☉ or ☽, and in a four-footed sign, denotes death by falls or broken bones. (See Buildings, Heights, and the various paragraphs in this section).
Distortions—By Falls—Lameness or Paralysis—By Falls from Heights—(See Distortions; "Limbs", in this section).
Fractures—From Falls—(See "Falls" under Fractures).
Heights—High Places—Precipices—Falls From, and Resulting in Injury or Death—(See Distortions, Heights; "Travel"; in this section).
Horses—Falls From—(See Horses).
Houses—Injury or Death by the Fall of—(See "Buildings" in this section).
Hurts by Falls—(See Accidents, Injuries, and the various paragraphs in this section).

Infancy—(See "Fall" under Infancy).
Injuries By—♄ on the Asc., or affl. the Asc. by ☐ or ☍ aspects. (See "Accidents" and the various paragraphs in this section).
Lameness From—And Distortions—(See Distortions, Excrescences, Lameness).
Limbs—The Limbs Broken by Falls—Distorted by Falls—(See Distortions, Fractures, Legs, Limbs).
Paralysis From—(See Distortions).
Precipices — Falls From — (See Distortions, Heights).
Sports—Falls During Sports, Exercise, Amusement or Recreation—The ☉ affl. in ♐. (See Amusements, Exercise, Recreation, Sports).
Travel—Voyages—Inland or Foreign Travel—Falls During, Causing Injury or Death—Malefics in the 3rd or 9th H. at B., and affl. the ☉, ☽, Asc., or Hyleg; the afflictor to the Sigs. of Travel being in the 12th H., and in a fixed sign. (See Heights, Journeys; "Accidents", "Hurts", under Travel).
Vehicles—Falls From—(See "Falls" under Vehicles).
Voyages—Falls During—Death or Injury By—(See "Travel" in this section. Also see "Accidents" under Abroad; "Injuries" under Travel).

FALSE—Pseudo—
False Angina—(See Angina).
False Fears—(See "Morbid" under Fears).
False Friends — Injury By — (See "False" under Friends).
False Imaginations—(See "False" under Imagination).
False Ischuria—Spurious Ischuria—(See Ischuria).
False Membranes—(See Croup, Diphtheria, Pseudo).

FAMILY—The Family. The following subjects have to do with the Family, Members of the Family, and the Conditions Affecting them. See these subjects in the alphabetical arrangement when not considered here.
Aged Female—Death of Aged Female In the Family—(See "Death of An Aged Aunt" under Aunts).
Aged Person—Death of In the Family—(See Grandparents; "Long Life" under Life; Old Age).

Aunts; Bereavement; Births;
Brothers; Burial; Childhood;
Children; Daughter;

Death In the Family—A Family Loss—Afflictions to the ☉ by dir. tend to male deaths, and to the ☽ or ♀, female deaths in the family; the ☉ or ☽ to the ☌ or ill-asps. ♅ or ♄ by dir., and espec. if the ☉ or ☽ were in the 8th H. at B.; the ☽ at a Solar Rev. passing the place of ♅ at B.; ♅ ☌ or P. Dec. the ☉ at a Solar Rev.; ♅ by tr. over the radical ☽, or ☌ the ☽ at a Solar Rev.; ♅ passing over his own place at B. by tr., or affl. the ☉ or ☽ by dir.; ♅ by Periodic Rev. in evil asp. the hyleg; ♅ has special rule over the death of relatives; ♄ by tr. over the radical ♅ and ♅ affl. at B.; ♂ to cusp 8th H. by dir.; the M.C. to the ☌ or ill-asp. ♄ by dir.; the M.C. to the ☌, □, or ☍ ♅ by dir., a sudden death in the family. (See Bereavement; "Death" under Aunts, Brothers, Children, Daughter, Father, Grandparents, Husband, Infancy, Mother, Parents, Sister, Son, etc.; "Family" under Fire; Relatives. Also note the various paragraphs in this section).

Environment; Father; Female; Fire; Grandparents; Heredity; Home; Husband; Large Family—(See "Many Children" under Children; Fruitfulness).

Likenesses—Family Likenesses are caused by having the same rising sign with different members of the family, and with several planets in similar signs, or in the same aspect to the rising degree. (See Heredity).

Loved Ones—Death of—(See Loved; "Death", in this section).

Male—Death of In the Family—(See "Death" under Male).

Marriage; Mother; Neglect of Family —♅ to the ☌ or ill-asp. ♄ by dir. in the map of a parent, and liable to imprisonment. (See "Father" under Drunkenness; "Drink" under Parents).

Orphans; Parents; Relatives; Separated—From Parents—(See Parents).

Servants; Sickness—In the Family— Malefics in the 4th H. at a Solar Rev. (See "Ill-Health", "Sickness", under Children, Daughter, Father, Husband, Parents, Sister, Son, Wife, etc.).

Sisters; Small Family—(See Barren; "Few Children" under Children).

Sons; Sudden Death In—The M.C. to the ☌, □, or ☍ ♅ by dir. (See "Death" in this section).

Uncles; Wife; Youth.

FAMINE—Want of Food—Starvation— Scarcity of Crops—Suffering or Death From—♄ or ♂ sole ruler at a Solar Eclipse; ♄ lord of the year, in ♈ at the Vernal Equinox; ♄ ruler of the Asc., cadent, and the ☉ □ or ☍ ☽ at the Vernal, affects people of all Countries ruled by ♄; ♄ and ♂ in Equinoctial Signs, in ☍ to and controlling the Luminaries; ♄ in ☍ in an angle, direct in motion, and affl. by ♂ and the ☽ at the Vernal E.; ♄, ♃, and ♂ conjoined in signs after their fall; an Eclipse of the ☉ in Airy Signs; a Solar Eclipse in 2nd Dec. of ♍, and espec. among Peoples and Countries ruled by ♍; an Eclipse of ☉ in the 2nd Dec. of ♍, ♎, or ♏, or in the 3rd Dec. of ♉ or ♑; an Eclipse of the ☉ or ☽ in earth signs, and in places ruled by such signs; the ☌ of several superior planets in airy signs; coincident with the appearance of Comets; Comets in ♉ or ♑; malefics in the 9th H. in earthy signs, and affl. the ☉ or ☽, famine and privation on a voyage. (See Calamity, Comets, Corn, Drought, Dryness, Eclipses, Epidemics, Floods, Food, Fountains, Fruits, Grain, Heat, Pestilence, Scarcity, Starvation, Thirst, Travel, Vegetation, Voyages, Weather, Wheat, Winds).

FAMOUS PEOPLE—Death of a Famous or Illustrious Person, as a Ruler, King, Queen, President, etc.—An Eclipse of the ☉ or ☽ in ♉, ♌, ♎, or ♓; an Eclipse of the ☽ in the 3rd Dec. of ♉, the 1st Dec. ♌, or the 3rd Dec. of ♎. (See "Great Men" under Great; Kings, Nobles, Presidents, Queens, Renown, Rulers).

FANATICAL—Intemperate or Irrational Zeal—(See Anarchists, Crazy, Destructiveness, Insanity, Intemperate, Irrational; "Unbalanced" under Mind; Rashness, Reactionary, Reformers, Religion, Revolutionary; "Impoverished" under Riches; Violent, etc.).

FANCIES—The Fancy—Fantasies— Phantasies—Fantastic—Imaginations —Vagaries.

All Evils In the Fancy—All Imperfections of the Fancy—A ☿ and □ disease, and afflictions to ☿, or afflictions in □. (See Mental, Mind).

Appetites—Fantastic Appetites—(See "Appetites" under Peculiar).

Chaotic Fancies—And Notions—Ψ in □. (See Chaotic, Confusion, Notions).

Distempered Fancies—Strange Tastes and Fancies—Chaotic Fancies—A □ disease, and afflictions in □; the ☽ to the ☌ ☿; Ψ affl. in □, the 3rd or 9th H.; ♄ to the ☌ or ill-asp. ☿, the fancy perplexed; a ☿ disease, and afflictions to ☿; ☿ weak and ill-dig. at B., and in no relation to the ☽ or Asc. (See Chaotic, Confusion, Eccentric, Ideas, Notions, Peculiar, Strange, Tastes, etc. Also note the various paragraphs and references in this section).

Dreamy Fancies—(See Chaotic, Confusion; "Dreamy Mind" under Dreams).

Fears—Fanciful Fears—(See "Fanciful" under Fears).

Foolish Fancies—Foolish and Precipitate—The ☉ ill-dig. at B.; the ☽ □ or ☍ ☿; ♃ Sig. □ or ☍ ☽; ☿ affl. at B., and in □ or ☍ the ☽ or Asc.; fixed stars of the nature of ♂ and ☿ ascending at B.; the 7° ♑ ascending at B., carried away with foolish whims and fancies. (See "Bad" under Judgment).

Ingenious Fancy—(See Genius).

Mental Fantasies—(See "Dreamy Mind" under Dreams).

Notions—Fanciful and Chaotic Notions—(See Ideals, Notions).

Novelties—Fond of—(See Novelties).

Peculiar Fancies—(See Eccentric, Misunderstood, Peculiar, Strange).

Perplexed—The Fancy Perplexed— (See "Distempered" in this section).

Precipitate Fancies—(See "Foolish" in this section).

Prejudiced—The Phantasies Prejudiced—A ♄ disease and affliction; ☿ weak, unfortunate, and afflicted at B. (See Chaotic, Confusion, Delusions, Erratic, Fears, Hallucinations, Illusions, Imaginations; "Shallow" under Mind; Prejudiced).

Riotous Fancies—(See "Turbulent" in this section).

Strange Fancies—(See "Peculiar" in this section).

Tastes—Fanciful Tastes—(See Desires; "Fastidious" under Diet; "Peculiar" under Dress; Habits, Tastes. Also see "Distempered" in this section).

Turbulent Fancies—Riotous Fancies—♂ affl. in the 9th H., and espec. when also afflicting ☿. (See Riotous, Turbulent).

Vagaries—Full of, and of Wild Fancies—(See Vagaries).

Wild Fancies—♅ affl. by ♀. (See Vagaries). For further influences along this line see Fanatical, Flightiness, Genius, Ideas, Insanity, Intuitions, Mental, Mind, Ninth House, Obsessions, Opinions, Premonitions, Psychic, Reformers, Religion, Revolutionary; "Slights" under Sensitive; Third House, Vague, Visionary, Weird, etc.).

FANTASIES — Phantasies—(See Fancies).

FAR-SIGHTEDNESS—(See "Hyperopia" under Sight).

FASTING—People born under the Sanguine Temperament benefit by Fasting. This Temperament is Moist, and is ruled by ♃ and the Airy Signs. (See Sanguine).

FAT—The Yellowish Oily Substance of Adipose Tissue—Fatty—Lardaceous—Waxy—Suet—Adipose Tissue—Sebaceous, etc.—Fat is formed by ♃, and also ♃ largely regulates its disposition. The liver is excited to increased secretion of fat by ♃. The fatty constituents in Milk are added by ♃. Fat acts thru ♃ and ♀ influence, and frequently thru ♐, its opposite sign, and acts upon the lungs. The consistency of adipose tissue, its density and hardness, is increased in disease conditions when ♂ is with ♃ at B., or afflicting ♃ by dir. (See Consistency, Density, Hardening, Jupiter, Liver).

A Little Fat—The Body Somewhat Fat—Not Much Fat—♄ in his first station at B.; ♃ in watery signs.

Adiposa Dolorosa—Characterized by Nodular Formations—A ♄ disease; ♃ affl. by ♄; ♂ with ♃ at B., or affl. ♃ by dir.; Subs at KP. (See Tubercles).

Adiposis—(See Corpulent; "Fatty Degeneration" in this section).

Body—Fat Body—The ☽ Sig. in ♓; the ☽ in a water sign; the ☽ in ♓ in partile asp. the Asc., plump or fat, and with a mean, short stature; the ☽ in her incr. gives a full, tall, fat, plump body; ♄ in his 2nd station at B.; ♄ occi. of the ☉, and with great Lat.; ♃ Sig. in water signs, a fat body, but rather comely (Hor'y); ☿ Sig. in ♋; the first parts of ♈, ♉, or ♌ ascending make the body more fat, or the latter parts of ♊ or ♍; water signs on the Asc.; the Sig. of the party in a water sign; the Sig. of the party in N. Lat. in Hor'y Questions; the 2nd face of ♌ on the Asc., grows fat with age; the 4th or 5th face of ♑ on Asc.; the 6th face of ♓ on the Asc. (See Bulky, Corpulent, Fleshy, Large Body (see Large); Lumpish; "Corpulent" under Middle Life; Obesity, Puffing, Stoutness). Case—Birth Data of Fat Man—The birth data of Tom Ton, the fattest man on record, is as follows,—

Born March 29, 1896, 5:30 A.M., Florence, Ariz. Weight, 750 lbs. Died on May 27th, 1926, at weight of 900 lbs., having gained 150 lbs in 10 days soon before his death.

Cancer—Fatty and Waxy Carcinoma—Lardaceous—(See "Fatty" under Carcinoma).

Consistency—Of Fat—(See the Introduction to this Article).

Corpulent—(See Corpulent; "Body", in this section).

Cysts—Sebaceous Cysts — Wens—Steatoma—(See Cysts, Sebaceous, Steatoma, Wen).

Degeneration—Fatty Degeneration—A ♃ disease. (See Degeneration; "Degeneration" under Heart, Liver, Muscles).

Density—Of Fat—(See the Introduction to this Article).

Distribution—Of Fat—(See Introduction to this Article).

Face—Fat Face—(See "Fat Face" under Face).

Fat Body—(See "Body" in this section).

Fat and Plump—(See "Body" in this section. Also see Corpulent, Fleshy, Plumpness).

Fat and Short—(See "Short and Fleshy" under Fleshy; "Mean Stature" under Mean; Short, Stoutness).

Fat and Tall—♃ in water signs. (See Tall).

Fatty Degeneration—(See "Degeneration" in this section).

Fleshy Body—(See Fleshy).

Fluids—The fatty consistency of fluids is ruled by ♃. (See Fluids, Milk).

Foods—Disorders from Fatty Foods—♃ in ♍. (See Diet, Food).

Formation of Fat—Fat is formed by ♃. (See the Introduction to this Article).

Hardness—The Hardness of Fat Increased—(See Introduction to this Article).

Heart—Fatty Degeneration of—(See "Fatty" under Heart).

Lardaceous Cancer—(See "Fatty" under Carcinoma).

Lipoma—Fatty Tumor—(See Lipoma).

Liver—Fatty Degeneration of—(See "Fatty" under Liver).

Marrow—(See Marrow).

Muscles—Fatty Degeneration of—(See Muscles).

Not Much Fat—(See "A Little Fat" in this section).

Obesity—Fat Body—Corpulence—(See Corpulent, Fleshy, Obesity, Stoutness; "Body", in this section).

Plump and Fat—(See Plump; "Body", in this section).

Sarcoma—Adiposa Sarcoma—(See Sarcoma).

Sebaceous Cysts—(See Cysts, Wen).

Secretion of Fat—Ruled over by ♃. (See the Introduction to this Article; Liver).

Short and Fat — (See "Short and Fleshy" under Fleshy; Short).

Steatoma—An Encysted Sebaceous Tumor—(See Wen).

Tall and Fat—Tall, Fat, Plump and Full Body—Given by the ☽ in her increase; ♃ in watery signs. (See "Body" in this section; Tall).

Tumors—Fatty Tumors—♂ ☌ or ill-asp. ♃; caused by the afflictions of ♃. (See "Fatty" under Carcinoma; Caruncle, Lipoma, Sarcoma, Sebaceous, Wen).

Waxy—(See Ambergris; "Fatty" under Carcinoma; Waxy).

Wen—A Sebaceous Cyst—(See Wen).

FATAL—Deadly—

Accidents—Fatal Accidents—Fatalities — (See "Death by Accident", "Fatal", under Accidents).

Deadly Diseases—An Eclipse of the ☽ in the 3rd Dec. of ♍ brings deadly diseases.

Disease—The Disease May Prove Fatal—(See "Symbols of Death" under Death; "The Sick Will Hardly Escape" under Escape; "Doubtful Recovery", "Little Hope of Recovery", under Recovery).

Fatal Illness—Mortal Illness—Deadly Diseases—The ☉ hyleg, and to the ☌, □, or ☍ ♄ by dir. (See "Certain Death" under Death; "Death" under Fevers; Incurable, Malignant, Pernicious; "Impossible" under Recovery).

Fatal Imprisonment — (See "Death" under Prison).

Fatalism—(See Scepticism).

FATE—Destiny—

A Bad Fate—A Fatality Hangs Over the Native from Birth—♄ in the 10th H. at B., and espec. when ill-aspected, in a weak sign, and affl. the ☉, ☽, or hyleg. (See "Malice of Fortune" under Fortune; Miseries, Misfortunes, Unfortunate).

Fate and Free Will—(See "Free Will" under Will).

Good Fate—(See Comforts, Contentment; "Fortunate In Life" under Fortune; "Good Health" under Health; Heredity; "Peace of Mind" under Mind; Riches, etc.).

Melancholic Fate—Many cross or □ aspects to a planet, or planets ascending; the 20° ♍ on the Asc. at B. (See Melancholy, Miseries, Reverses, Sadness, Self-Undoing, Sorrow, Trouble).

Resigned to Fate—Mars obscurely placed, and afflicted, tends to take the courage out of people, and to offer less resistance to obstacles. On the other hand, a prominent ♂, or ♂ affl. by ♅, many planets in positive and masculine signs at B., tend to give more fight to the nature, and to go to extreme measures to avoid defeat. The good influences of ♀ give resignation and contentment. Also ♄ in good asp. to ♂ gives a better understanding of Divine Things, and to be resigned to fate, environment, circumstances, etc., with more grace and contentment, realizing the Divinity within themselves, and by contacting the Higher Mind. (See Bold, Character, Cheerfulness, Contentment, Destiny, Energy, Environment, External, Individuality, Optimism, Positive, Resignation, Spiritual, etc.).

Ripe Fate—This is one which the Occult Writers say cannot be avoided, and that the planetary influences and directions will act with certainty regardless of the will, conduct, or decisions, due to matured Karmic conditions. (See Character, Directions, Events, Prognosis; "Free Will" under Will).

Suffering and Fate — (See "Periods" under Health; Suffering).

The Ways of Fate — (See the two verses of Poetry at the end of the Article on "Ships").

FATHER—The Father—Paternal—The ☉ and ♄ are allotted to the person of the father. In the European System of Astrology, the 4th H. governs the father, and the 10th H. the mother. In finer detail, some Writers say the 10th H. governs the father in a male nativity, and the 4th H. the father in a female geniture. In the Hindu System of Astrology, the 10th H. governs the father, and the 4th H. the mother. In afflictions to the father, the ☉ should be principally observed by day, and ♄ by night. A planet in the 4th H. is Sig. of the father in Hor'y Questions. The ☉ and ♄ are masculine, and rule espec. over the male members of the family. The ☽ and ♀ are feminine, and rule the mother and female members of the family, as sisters, daughters, aunts, grandmother. Conditions concerning the parents are to be noted in the child's map, and espec. in the map of the first-born, and the influences in the following paragraphs and subjects concerning the afflictions to, suffering, wounds, death, etc., of the father, are to be noted in the map of the child. The maps of birth of any of the children are also permissible for such study, but may not be as typical as the map of the first-born. In day maps, the ☉ and ♀ are the chief Sigs. and representatives of the father and mother, and ♄ and the ☽ in night maps, as the ☉ espec. rules by day, and the ☽ by night. (See Day, Night).

Accidents To—Hurts, Injuries or Wounds To—The ☉ or ♄ in the 4th, 5th, 7th, or 8th H., and afflicted; ♅ or ♂ in the 4th or 10th H., and afflicted, may be killed by an accident; ♅ or ♂ to the cusp the 4th or 10th H. by dir.; ♄ or ♂ affl. the ☉ in a child's map; ♂ to the cusp the 9th H.; ♂ affl. in the 4th or 10th H.; the Asc. to the ill-asps. the ☉ by dir., and the ☉ affl. at B. by a malefic; an eclipse falling on the ☉ in a child's map; planets cadent and affl. the ☉ or ♄. (See Danger, Death, Detriment, in this section).

Afflictions To—The ☉ to the ☌ ♄ by dir., or ♄ to the ☌ the ☉ by dir. (See the various paragraphs in this Article).

Aunts—The Sisters and Brothers of the Father—Sickness or Death of—(See "Paternal" under Aunts, Uncles).

Brothers Of—(See "Aunts" in this section).

Burns To—♂ □ or ⚹ ♄ from angles or succedent houses. (See Burns).

Contractions—Of the Muscles of the Limbs — (See "Muscles" in this section).

Danger to the Father—The Father Threatened—The ☉ affl. at B., and the ☉ to the evil asp. the Asc. by dir., and espec. if the ☉ be lord of the 11th H.; the ☉ in an angle near the cusp, and in □ or ⚹ ♄ at a Solar Rev., or in the 8th H.; the ☉ to the ☌ or ill-asps. ♄ or ♂ by dir.; the ☉ in Rapt P. ♄; ♅ to the cusp 4th H. by di.·.; ♅ by tr. passing over the radical ♄; ♄, ♂, or ♅ to the cusp 4th H. by dir.; afflictions to ♄ or the ☉ in the child's map; ♄ to the ill-asps. the ☉ by dir.; ♄ in the 10th H. in a masc. nativity, or in the 4th H. in a female, and affl. by the ☉ or ☽; ♂ affl. in the 4th H.; ruler of the 4th H. at B. a malefic, and in the radical 11th or 4th H. at a Solar Rev.; the Asc. to the □ or ⚹ ☉ by dir. (See Parents, Death, Detriment, Infirmities, and the various paragraphs in this section).

Death of the Father—Danger of—The ☉ affl. at B., and the ☉ to the □ or ⚹ the Asc. by dir., and espec. if the ☉ be lord of the 11th H. at B.; the ☉ to the □ or ⚹ ♄ by dir., and espec. by the □, if the ☉ be ruler of the 4th, or in the 4th H. at B.; the ☉ hyleg, and to the ☌, □, or ⚹ ♄ by dir., and espec. if the ☉ be lord of the 4th H.; afflictions to the ☉ or ♄ in the map of the child, and espec. of the first-born; the ☉ prog. to the ⚹ ♄; ♄ to the ☌ or ill-asps. the ☉ by dir.; ♄ ruler of the 4th H. at B., or in the 4th, and to the ☌ or ill-asps. the Asc. by dir.; ♄ or ♂ affl. in the 4th or 10th H.; ♄ in the 10th H. in a male nativity, or in the 4th H. in a female, and affl. by the ☉ or ☽; ♄ at a Solar Rev. ☌ or P. Dec. the radical ☉, and if the ☉ be hyleg, the death of the father in a female nativity is indicated; ♄ by evil dir. to the cusp of 4th H., or to a malefic in the 4th H. at B.; ♄ or ♉ to the ☌ or ⚹ the radical ☉ by tr., or at a Solar Rev.; ♂ □·or ⚹ ♄ from angles or succedents; ♂ elevated above the ☉ at B., or in evil asp. the ☉, and affl. the ☉ by dir.; the Asc. to the ill-asps. the ☉ by dir., and by malefics at B.; the M.C. to the ☌ or ill-asps. the place of the radical ♂ may kill or afflict a parent; the M.C. to the ☌ ☊. (See Early Death, Sudden Death, Short Life, in this section; "Death" under Parents).

Detriment To—Misfortune To—The ☉ □ ♄ in the map of the first-born until the next child is born; malefics in the 4th H. of a child until the next child is born with a more favorable map; malefics in the 4th or 10th H. at a Solar Rev.; ☊ in the 4th H. at B., and affl. by evil directions of the Asc. (See Accidents, Afflictions, Danger, Infirmities, and the various paragraphs in this section).

Diseased—The Father Much Diseased —♂ □ or ⚹ ♄ from angles or succedent houses, the father tends to be much diseased, and to be liable to fevers, burns, wounds, sickness, death, and injuries to the eyes and eyesight.

Diseases To—(See Diseased, Infirmities, Much Sickness, Violent, and the various paragraphs in this section).

Drunkard—The Father May Become a Drunkard—(See "Father", "Husband", under Drunkenness; "Drink" under Parents).

Early Death Of—Dies Young—Short Life for the Father—The ☉ and ♄ affl. at B. in the child's map; short life of the father is espec. indicated by the ☉ or ♄ being in the 1st or 10th H. at B., and afflicted; the ☉ and ♄ affl. in cardinal houses, as the 1st or 10th, or in their succedent houses, the 2nd and 11th; and ♂ be elevated above, or rising before the ☉ and ♄; ♄ affl. in the 4th H.; the ☉ and ♄ affl. in cadent houses, and with many planets in such houses; ♄ in the 1st or 10th H. and in □ or ⚹ ☉; ♅ in the 4th H., and near the lower meridian; ♂ in the 4th H. in a female nativity, or ♂ in the 10th H. in a male geniture, and affl.; the 11° ♎ on Asc., the early death of the father, or the father unknown to the child. (See Adoption; "Early Death" under Early; Orphans, Parents; "Separated From" under Parents; Death, Short Life, Sudden Death, in this section).

Eyes—Eyesight—Eyes and Face—Disorders of—Injury To—♂ in evil asp. the ☉ at B., and elevated above the ☉; ♂ □ or ⚹ ☉ from angles or succedents. In the case of the mother, ♂ affl. the ☽ in the same manner, or ♄ and ♂ both affl. the ☽. (See "Eyes" under Mother).

Face—Disorders of—Injury To—(See "Eyes" in this section).

Father-In-Law—In a male nativity, denoted by the 10th H., and in a woman's nativity by the 4th H., and afflictions in these houses tend to affect them according to their nature.

Fevers—To the Father—(See "Infirmities" in this section).

Godfathers—Ruled by ♃. Afflictions or suffering to them is caused by afflictions to ♃ in the map of the child at B., and by dir., and espec. if ♃ is weak, ill-aspected, and badly placed at B. Godmothers are ruled by ♀, and corresponding afflictions to ♀ would result in detriment to them. (See Guardians).

Good Health—To the Father—(See "Long Life" in this section).

Health—Of the Father—Good Health —Bad Health—(See Infirmities, Long Life, Much Sickness, in this section).

Humours In—Suffers from Watery Humours—♄ affl. the ☉ at B. (See Humours; "Humours" under Watery).

Hurts To—(See "Accidents" in this section).

Husband—(See Husband).

Infirmities—The Father Full of Infirmities—Suffers Fevers and Inflammations—The ☉ and ♄ affl. in cadent houses; the ☉ affl. by ♄ or ♂; the ☉ and ♄ in the 4th, 5th, 7th, or 8th H., and affl.; the ⊙ to the cusp the 6th H. by dir.; the ⊙ to the ♂ or ill-asps. ♄ by dir.; the ⊙ in the 10th H., and affl. by ♄ or ♂; an eclipse falling on the radical ⊙ in a child's map; the ⊙ to the ♂ or P. Dec. Regulus by dir.; ♆ or ♄ passing the place of the radical ⊙ by tr., or in ♂ the ⊙ at a Solar Rev.; ♄ in the 4th H., and affl.; ♄ debilitated and in □ or ☍ ⊙; ♄ in the 10th H. in a male nativity. or in the 4th H. in a female, and affl. by the ⊙ or ☽; ♄ ascending at B., and the ⊙ to the ♂ or ill-asps. ♄ by dir.; ♄ to the ♂ or ill-asps. the ⊙ by dir.; ♂ elevated above, or rising before the ⊙ and ♄; ♂ □ or ☍ ♄ from angles or succedents, fevers to: ♂ at a Solar Rev. passing the place of the radical ⊙ or ♄; the Asc. to the ill-asps. the ⊙ by dir., and the ⊙ affl. at B. (See Afflictions, Diseased, Early Death, Much Sickness, Violent, and the various paragraphs in this section).

Inflammatory Attacks — (See the ♂ influences under "Infirmities" in this section).

Injuries To—(See "Accidents" in this section).

Killed—By An Accident—♅ or ♂ in the 4th or 10th H., and afflicted, danger of. (See "Accidents" in this section).

Limbs and Muscles—Contractions In—Pains In—(See "Muscles" in this section).

Long Life—For the Father—Good Health—Good asps. to the ⊙ and ♄ at B., and these planets strong and dignified in the map of the child; ♄ ✶ or △ the ⊙, and ♄ strongly dignified; ♃ and ♀ favorably configurated with the ⊙ or ♄; the M.C. favorably aspected by the ⊙; ♃ or ♀ in the 4th or 10th H., and in good asp. to the ⊙ and ♄, and these houses free from the afflictions of malefics; if ♃ or ♀ have any configuration with the ⊙ or ♄, or ♄ in good asp. the ⊙, or joined to the ⊙ in an angle, or beholding him from angles; lord of the 4th in the 4th, and well-asp., or lord of the 10th in the 10th H., according to the sex of the native, the father lives to an old age. (See "Long Life" under Life).

Misfortune To — (See "Detriment" in this section).

Mother—(See the various paragraphs under Mother).

Much Sickness — The Father Suffers Many Illnesses—Afflictions and much sickness for the father are espec. indicated by the ⊙ or ♄ in the 4th or 7th H.; the ⊙ hyleg at B., and to the ♂ or ill-asps. ♄ by dir.; the ⊙ and ♄ in cardinal or succedent houses, and ♂ elevated above, or rising before them; ♄ in the 4th H. of the child, and afflicted; lord of the 6th H. in the 4th, and afflicted. (See Afflictions, Early Death, Infirmities, Sickly, in this section).

Muscles and Limbs—Pains and Contractions In—♂ in evil asp. to ♄, and elevated above ♄. (See Contractions, Limbs, Muscles, Pain).

Old Age—Lives To—(See "Long Life" in this section).

Pain—In Muscles and Limbs—(See "Muscles" in this section).

Parents—(See the various paragraphs under Parents).

Paternal Aunts—And Uncles—(See "Aunts" in this section).

Patricide—Or Matricide—A Parricide —♀ ill-posited, and in □ or ☍ ♂.

Relatives Of—The father's Relatives are ruled by ♃, and the mother's Relatives by ♀. (See Aunts, Maternal, Mother, Paternal, Relatives, Uncles).

Short Life—For the Father—The father usually does not live to old age when the lord of the 4th or 10th H. is in the 8th or 12th H. in the map of the child, according to the sex of the child. (See "Early Death" in this section).

Sickly—The Father Sickly—Weakly—Vitality Low—(See Early Death, Infirmities, Much Sickness, in this section).

Sickness To—The Father Sickly—Weakly—Vitality Low—The ⊙ to the ♂ ♄ by dir.; ♄ in the 4th or 7th H., and in □ or ☍ ⊙. (See Afflictions, Diseased, Early Death, Infirmities, Much Sickness, Violent, in this section).

Sisters Of—Diseases and Afflictions To—(See "Paternal" under Aunts).

Sudden Death Of—♂ elevated above the ⊙ at B., or in evil asp. the ⊙, and affl. the ⊙ by dir., danger of sudden death of the father; ♂ □ or ☍ the ⊙ from angles or succedents; ♂ or ♅ in the 4th or 10th H. (See Death, Early Death, in this section).

Suffers—Father May Suffer—(See Detriment, Diseased, Infirmities, Much Sickness, and the various paragraphs in this section).

Threatened—The Father Is Threatened—(See "Danger" in this section).

Uncles—Paternal Uncles—(See "Paternal" under Aunts, Uncles).

Unknown—The Father Unknown to the Child—(See "Early Death" in this section).

Violent Diseases To—The ⊙ to the □ or ☍ ♂ by dir.; the ⊙ to the place of Cor Leonis, violent to both the native and the father, altho not fatal. (See the ♂ influences under "Infirmities" in this section).

Vitality Low—(See "Sickly" in this section).

Watery Humours In—(See "Humours" in this section).

Weak—Weakly—(See "Sickly" in this section).

Wife's Father—Afflicted—(See "Father" under Wife).

Wounds To—(See "Accidents" in this section).

Young—Dies Young—(See "Early Death" in this section).

FATIGUE—Tired—Weariness—Exhaustion of Strength—Languor from Excessive Toxic Materials and Tissue Disintegration — Fatigue is generally caused by the afflictions of ♄ (or ☿ if he be of the nature of ♄), and espec. with brain workers. There is also the fatigue from diseases, toxic accumulations, deposit of wastes and minerals, caused by ♄ afflictions. Physical fatigue may result from over-work, over-exercise, over-study, too much excitement, due usually to a strong ♂ influence at B., and a positive nature. Also fatigue may result from long journeys and tedious travel, confinement and lack of exercise, which is usually the result of low vitality, and the afflictions of ♄ to the 3rd or 9th H. during travel.

Brain Fag—(See "Brain Fag" under Brain; Reading, Study).

Exercise—Fatigue and Disease from Over-Exercise—(See "Inordinate", "Intemperate", under Exercise; "Over-Exertion" under Exertion; Sports, Study, Weariness).

Mind—Mental Fatigue from Over-Study, or from General Weakness—The ☽ in ♈, □ or ☍ ♄ (or ☿ if he be of the nature of ♄) at the beginning of an illness, or from long mental strain. (See Anxiety; "Brain Fag" under Brain; Cares, Exertion, Reading, Rest, Study; "Weak Body" under Weak; Worry).

Sports—Fatigue From—(See "Exercise" in this section).

Travel—Fatigue or Sickness During Travel—(See "Sickness" under Travel). (See Apathy, Dull, Feeble, Heaviness, Inactive, Inertia, Languid, Lassitude, Lethargy, Listless, Sluggish, Toxaemia.)

FATTY—Fatty Cancer—Fatty Degeneration—(See Fat).

FAUCES—The Throat from the Mouth to the Pharynx—Dryness of—Dry Throat—A ♄ disease; ♄ in ♉; ♂ affl. in ♉ tends to feverish dry fauces and throat. (See Diphtheria, Mouth, Pharynx, Throat, Tonsils).

FAULTY—Defective—Deranged—Imperfect—Disordered—The Faulty Action of Functions, Organs, Parts, etc.—Faulty Elimination—Faulty Secretion—(See Defects, Derangements, Disordered, Elimination, Functions, Hardening, Imperfect, Organs, Retarded, Secretions, Stoppages, Suppressions, etc. Also see in the alphabetical arrangement the subject you have in mind).

Fault-Finding—(See Petulant, Scolding, Virgo).

FAVORABLE—Beneficial—Helpful—Propitious—

Crises—Favorable Crises In Disease —(See "Better" under Crises).

Prognosis—The Prognosis Favorable —(See "Better" under Crises; Curable; "Disease Will Soon End" under End; Prognosis, Recovery, Termination).

Years—Favorable Years and Periods of Life—(See Cycles; "Good Health" under Health; Periods. Also note the various paragraphs under Fortunate, Good).

FAVORED—

Favored Body—(See Beautiful, Comely; "Good Constitution" under Constitution; Fair, Fine; "Good Health", and "Signs of Good Health" under Health; Robust, Ruddy; "Well-Favored", "Well-Shaped", under Well).

Favored Mind—(See Genius, Intellect; "Quickened" under Mentality; "Sound Mind" under Mind).

FAVUS—A Contagious Parasitic Disease of the Skin with Crusts—

Favus of the Scalp—Porrigo (Scald-Head)—♂ affl. in ♈. (See Crusts, Parasites).

FEAR—Fears—Fearful—Phobias—Dread—Awe—Mental Aversions—Doubts—Anxieties—The Mind Fearful —Anguish of Mind—Veneration—The Mind Disturbed by Fear, Obsessions, Worry, Delusions, Superstitions, Hallucinations, etc.—All these subjects have to do with Fear in its different manifestations. See these subjects in the alphabetical arrangement. Fears, Anguish of Mind, Anxieties, etc., are ruled principally by the 8th and 12th H., and also by ♄ and ♆. Spiritual and religious fears are ruled over largely by ♆, while ♄ rules the fears arising from physical, wordly, material, business and earthly conditions. Other influences are noted in this section. The general Causes of Fears are listed under "Fears" in this section. See the following subjects in the alphabetical arrangement when not considered here—

Anguish—Of Mind—(See Anguish; "Fears", and the various paragraphs in this section).

Anxious Fears—Morbid Fears—(See Anxiety; "Morbid" in this section).

Astral Influences—Fears Caused By—♆ influences. (See Fears, Insanity, Obsessions, Spirit Controls, in this section).

Aversions—Irrational Fears—Phobias —(See Aversions, Antipathy; "Morbid" in this section).

Beside Oneself—(See this subject under Excitable).

Bodily Conditions—The Health—The Physical Welfare—Business, Worldly and Material Conditions—Fears Arising From—Ruled by ♄, and caused by ♄ afflictions over the mind at B., and by dir., and the afflictions of ♄ to ☿ or the hyleg. (See Hypochondria, Morbid, in this section).

Brooding; Business Fears—(See Cares; "Bodily" in this section).

Calamity—Fear of An Impending Calamity—(See "Impending Calamity" under Calamity).

Cares; Causes of Fears—(See "Fears", and the various paragraphs in this section).

Chaotic Mind—(See "Mental Chaos" under Chaotic; Fears, Morbid, Vain, in this section).

Claustrophobia—A Morbid Dread of An Inclosed Space—(See Claustrophobia).

Comprehension; Confined Spaces—Fear of—(See Claustrophobia).

Crowds—Fear of Being Jammed In a Crowd—(See Claustrophobia).

Danger—Fear of An Unknown Danger —♆ in the 12th H. (See "Impending Calamity" under Calamity; "Fear under Darkness).

Darkness—Fear of the Dark—Fear In Solitude—(See Darkness; "Solitude" in this section).

Death—(1) Death To Be Feared—Death More Certain—(See "Arguments", "Certain Death", under Death). (2) Fears His Own Death—Fear of Death—The ☉ or ☽ to the cusp the 8th H. by dir.; denoted by ♄, and ♄ to the ♂ or ill-asps. the ☉ by dir. (3) Less Fear of Death—If the fatal asp. or ♂ fall in the term of ♃ or ♀, or in exact ✶ or △ to ♃ or ♀. (4) No Fear of Death—♂ a strong ruler of the horoscope; ♂ rising in the Asc. or M.C. in ♈ or ♏, well-aspected and fortified. (5) Poison Death—Fear of—(See the influences in the paragraph "Death by Poison" under Poison).

Dejected; Delirium—(See "Delirium Tremens", "Wild Delirium", under Delirium).

Delusions; Dementia; Demoniac;

Depressed; Despondent; Deviations;

Disaster—Fear of Impending Disaster —(See Calamity).

Discontentment; Disease—Fear of—Dread of—Ψ affl. in the 6th H.; a ♄ characteristic; a ♄ trait; earthy signs on the Asc. (See "Earth Signs" under Earth; Hypochondria, Imaginary Diseases, Neptune, Obsessions, Saturn, Taurus).

Dissatisfied; Doubts—(See "Fears" in this section. Also see Anxiety, Brooding, Doubts, Hallucinations, Imaginations, Obsessions, Premonitions, Worry, etc.).

Dreams—(See "Dreamy Mind" under Dreams).

Eighth House—Influences of—(See Eighth).

Emotions — (See "Disorders" under Emotions).

Enemies—Fear and Dread of—Fear of Enemies Prevalent—(See "Fear" under Enemies).

Ergophobia — Fear of Work — (See Dull, Idle, Indolent, Indifferent, Labor, Lazy, Work, etc.).

False Fears — (See "Morbid" in this section).

Fanciful Fears—The ☽ affl. in the 12th H. (See Fancies, Vagaries).

Fearful—Fearful Imaginations—Fearful and Peevish—(See "Fearful" under Imagination; Fears, Peevish, in this section).

Fearless—Bold—Courageous—♂ a strong ruler at B.; ♂ rising in the Asc.

Fears—Signs of Fear—General Causes of Fear—Caused by Ψ, ♅, ♄, the 8th and 12th H. influences. The afflictions of Ψ tend to a chaotic mind, false fears, and Astral disturbances. Fears by the suppression of the bodily functions are caused by ♄. Fear and anguish of mind are ruled over and indicated by the 8th H. conditions. The ☉ or ☽ hyleg, and to the ♂ or ill-asp. ♄ by dir.; the ☉ weak at B., and affl. by ♄; the ☉ or ♃ as Sigs., and to the ♂ or ill-asp. ♄ by dir.; the ☽ to the ♂ or ill-asp. Ψ or ♄ by dir.; the ☽ P ♄, fearful and peevish; Ψ in ♈ ♂

☽ or ☿, and in □ or ☍ ♅; Ψ affl. in the 3rd or 9th H.; the tr. of Ψ thru the 1st, 3rd or 9th H. if in these houses at B.; Ψ in 1st H. at B.; Ψ affl. in ♐; Ψ □ or ☍ ♅; Ψ in evil asp. ☿; ♄ Sig. in ♑; born under strong ♄ influence; the directions of ♄ to the ☉, ☽, Asc. or M.C.; ♄ in the Asc., and affl. by □ and ☍ asps.; ♄ rules the Pneumogastric Nerve, and by restricting the action of this nerve tends to cause fears and worries; ♄ ♂ or ill-asps. the prog. ☉, ☽, or ☿; ♄ ℞ and in tr. over the place of ☿; ♄ ♂ the Asc. by dir.; ♃ affl. in ♒; ☿ affl. in ♈ or ♓; ☿ affl. by ♄; ☋ in the Asc.; malefic planets in the 8th H. are signs of fear and death; the Asc. to the ♂ or ill-asps. ♄ by dir.; the 21° ♐ on the Asc. (See "Morbid", and the various paragraphs in this section).

Forebodings; Fright; Functions—Fear Caused by the Suppression of—Caused by ♄ afflictions. (See Functions, Suppressions; "Fears" in this section).

Gloom; Hallucinations; Hanging—Haunted by Visions of Hanging—(See Hanging).

Hauntings; Health—Morbid and Anxious Fears Concerning — (See Hypochondria).

Horrors — Nervous Horrors — (See Horrors).

Hydrophobia—Fear of Water—(See Hydrophobia).

Hypochondria—Morbid Fears About the Health—(See Hypochondria).

Imaginations—Fearful Imaginations —(See Imagination).

Impending Disaster—Fear of—(See Calamity).

Imprisonment—Fear of—(See Prisons).

Inclosed Spaces—Fear of—(See Claustrophobia).

Insanity; Introspection;

Irrational Fears — (See "Morbid" in this section).

Low Spirits—(See Low).

Madness; Mania; Melancholy;

Mental Disturbances—Thru Fears—(See the various paragraphs in this section; Mental, Mind).

Mind Darkened—Thru Fear—♄ or ☋ in the Asc., in ♂ the ☉, ☽, or ☿.

Moods; Morbid Fears—False Fears—Anxious Fears—Aversions—Phobias—Irrational Fears—The ☉ or ☽ to the ♂ or ill-asps. ♄ by dir.; the ☉, ☽, Asc., or hyleg affl. by ♄ or Ψ; Ψ affl. the hyleg, and espec. with Ψ in the 6th or 8th H.; Ψ □ or ☍ ♅; ♄ influence strong at B.; ♄ Sig. in ♑; ♄ ♂ the ☉, ☽, or ☿; ♄ ♂ ♃ or ♀ in the 12th H.; ♄ ℞ and in tr. over the radical ☿; the prog. ☽ to the ♂, □, or ☍ ♄; ♃ to the cusp the 12th H. by dir.; malefics in □ or the 3rd H., and affl. the hyleg or ☿; watery signs strong and predominating at B., and espec. ♏. Case—See Fig. 25 in Message Of The Stars" by the Heindels. (See Fears, Solitude, in this section; Anxiety, Darkness, Hypochondria, Imaginations, Melancholy; "Neurasthenia" under Nerves; Worry).

Nervous Fears—Ψ affl. in the 6th H.; ♄ in the Asc. and affl. by cross aspects; ♀ Sig. to the ♂ or ill-asps. ♄ by dir. (See "Neurasthenia" under Nerves).

Obsessions — Obsessed with Fears — The Asc. to the ♂, □, or 8 ♄ by dir. (See Obsessions).

Own Death—Fears His Own Death—(See "Death" in this section).

Peevish and Fearful—(See Peevish).

Perceptions; Perversions; Phantasies;

Phobias—(See "Morbid Fears" in this section).

Physical Conditions—Fears Arising From—(See "Bodily" in this section).

Pneumogastric Nerve—Fears Arising from Restriction of—♄ influence. (See "Fears" in this section; Pneumogastric).

Poison Death—Fear of Death by Poison—(See "Death" under Poison).

Poverty—Fear of—(See Poverty).

Premonitions—Presentiments—(See Forebodings, Premonitions, Psychic).

Prophetic; Psychic Disorders — Psychoses—(See Psychic).

Reason—Disorders of—(See Reason).

Religious Fears—Ruled by Ψ. (See "Fears" under Religion).

Reverential Fear — (See Religion, Veneration).

Sciatica—Fear of—(See Sciatic).

Signs of Fear — (See "Fears" in this section).

Solitude—Fear and Dread of—The ☽ in ♏, and affl. by Ψ; the ☉ or ☽ in the 12th H., and affl. by ♄ or Ψ; ♀ affl. by ♄, ♅, or Ψ; afflictions which combine the influences of the 3rd H., ♏, ♍, and the watery element. Case—Dread of Solitude—See "Strange Case", No. 379, in 1001 N.N. (See Darkness, Fright, Solitude).

Spirit Controls—(See this subject).

Spiritual Fears—Ruled by Ψ; Ψ affl. in 9th H. (See Religion, Spirit, Spiritual, Veneration).

Strange Fears — Strange Terrors—(See ''Terrors'', "Visions", under Strange).

Superstitions; Suppressions—Restrictions—(See Fears, Functions, Pneumogastric, in this section).

Terrors — Strange Terrors — (See "Strange" in this section).

Thinking—(See Chaotic, Confusion, Clairaudience, Erratic, Judgment, Mental; "Clouded" under Mind; Peculiar, Religion, Thinking, Weird, etc. Note the various paragraphs in this section).

Twelfth House—Influences of—(See Twelfth).

Understanding; Unknown Danger—Fear of—(See "Danger" in this section).

Vagaries; Vain Fears—Vain Imaginations—Caused by Ψ and ♄; Ψ afflictions tend to vain fears and a chaotic mind; Ψ in evil asp. to ♀; Ψ □ or 8 ♅ or ♀; afflictions in watery signs, and espec. where the influence of Ψ is involved. (See Chaotic, Clairvoyance, Forebodings, Imaginations, Medium-

ship, Melancholy, Obsessions, Premonitions, Spirit Controls, Vain, etc.).

Veneration; Visions; Want—Fear of Coming To Want and Poverty—(See Poverty).

Water—Fear of—(See Hydrophobia).

Weird; Work—Fear of—(See "Ergophobia" in this section).

Worldly Conditions—Fears Arising From—(See "Bodily" in this section).

Worry.

FEASTING—

Health Injured By—Fond of Feasting—The ☉ affl. by ♃ or ♀; the ☉ Sig. in ♏, fond of feasting; lords of the 6th or 10th H. in the 5th H.

Ruins Himself By—The ☉ Sig. in ♓; ♀ Sig. in ♎, love their belly; the 1° ♍ on the Asc.; ♓ on the Asc. (See Appetite, Cravings, Diet, Drink; "Early Death" under Early; Eating; "His Own Worst Enemy" under Enemies; Epicureans, Excesses, Extravagance, Feeding, Food; "Free Living" under Free; Gluttony, Habits; "High Living" under High; Indigestion, Indulgence, Intemperate, Luxuries; "Dies Before Middle Life" under Middle Life; Over-Indulgence, Pleasures, Plethora; "Riotous Living" under Riotous; Surfeits).

FEATURES—The Different Parts of the Face—The aspects and position of ☿ at B. sometimes express and determine the features. Many of the descriptions and paragraphs under Cheeks, Chin, Complexion, Countenance, Decanates, Ears, Eyes, Eyebrows, Expression, Head, Jaws, Mouth, Nose, Profile, Teeth, etc., will also apply here. See these subjects.

Bird Features—(See Fowls).

Coarse Features — The ♏ influence tends to coarse features, skin, and body. Case—See Coarse, Rough). "Female", page 49, Chap. 8, in Daath's Medical Astrology.

Contortions Of—♅ affl. in ♈. (See Contortions; "Contortions" under Face. Also see "Distortions" in this section).

Deformed—The Features Deformed—(See Deformities; "Abnormalities", "Disfigured", "Deformed", under Face; "Distortions" in this section).

Distorted Features—The ☉ and ☽ in the 6th. H. and heavily afflicted; ♅ affl. in ♈ or 8; ♀ affl. by both ♄ and ♂, and which may be accompanied by some mental weakness; malefics in ♈; malefics in the 5th H., and espec. in ♈; ♈ or ♑ on the Asc. and containing malefics; earthy signs on the Asc.; many planets in fixed signs. Distortions of the face, features, and body are also caused by prenatal afflictions during pregnancy. (See Contortions, Coordination, Cyclops, Deformities, Face; "Wry Neck" under Neck; Prenatal). Case—See "Male", Chap. 8, page 48, in Daath's Medical Astrology.

Eagle Features — Given by ♏. (See Scorpio).

Lightness of Feature—♂ Sig. in fiery signs indicates.

Not Very Attractive—The ☉ in 8; ♑ influence; ♑ on Asc. (See "Thin", "Ugly", under Face).

Regular—All the Features Regular—♎ on the Asc.

Sharp Features—(See "Sharp" under Face).

Small Features—(See "Small" under Face).

Thin Features—(See "Thin" under Face).

Tightness of Feature—Given by ♂; ♂ rising and strong at B.

FEBRIFUGE—An Agent that Lessens Fever—♄ herbs and remedies. ♂ is the principal cause of fevers, and the remedies of ♄ counteract. (See Aconite, Antipathy, Antipyretic, Fever, Opposites; "Remedies" under Saturn).

FEBRILE—Febrile Indisposition—(See "Over-Heated Blood" under Blood; Fever).

FECUNDATION—Fertilization—Impregnation—Conception—Is principally the work of the ♀. Also ♀ rules fecundation. (See Conception, Fertile, Fruitful, Gemmation, Moon, Ovaries, Ovum, Reproduction, Semen).

FEEBLE—Adynamic—Weak—Loss of Vital Power—Decrepitude—Asthenic—etc.—The Asthenic Process is presided over by ♄, and tends to feebleness and weakness of the constitution by his afflictions, and by retention, inhibition, suppressing the functions, etc.

Action—Feeble Action To the Body—The ☉ to the ☍ or ill-asp ♄ by dir., and the ☉ hyleg at B. In Hor'y Questions the Querent is weak and feeble if the Sig. is going out of one sign into another. (See "Body" in this section).

Body—Feeble Body—Feeble Constitution—Weak Body—The afflictions of ♄ to the hyleg at B., and by dir. tend to feebleness of body; ♀ Sig. in ♋ or ♑, feeble and sickly; the watery signs ♋ or ♓ on the Asc. at B. (For the various influences along this line see Adynamia, Asthenia, Consumptions, Debility, Decrepitude, Emaciation; "Bad Health" under Health; Imbecility, Infirm, Invalids; "Senility" under Old Age; "Low" under Recuperation; Resistance, Stamina, Tone, Vitality; Sickly; "Loss Of" under Strength, Vital; "Not Strong" under Strong; "Weak Body" under Weak).

Digestion—Feeble Digestive Powers—(See "Weak" under Digestion).

Health—Feeble Health—(See "Bad Health" under Health; "Ill-Health All Thru Life" under Ill-Health; Pale, Sickly; "Much Sickness" under Sickness. See the references under "Body" in this section.

Left Side—(See "Feeble" under Left).

Mind—Feeble Mind—(See Idiocy, Imbecility; "Weak Mentality" under Mental).

Pulse—Feeble Pulse—(See "Faint", "Weak", under Pulse).

FEEDING—Wrong tendencies in feeding, and improper feeding, should be guarded against when ♂ or ♀ are in ♍. (See Diet, Eating, Food).

FEELING—Sensation—The Sense of Touch—(See Sensation, Sensibility, Touch).

Feeling—The Emotions—(See Emotions, Feelings).

Insensibility—(See this subject).

FEELINGS—The Emotions—The Power of Feeling—The Sentiments, etc.—

Acute Feelings—Common signs on the angles, or many planets in such signs.

Intellect—Feeling and Intellect—Preponderance of Feeling Over Intellect—Indicated by many planets in fiery and fixed signs, and none in airy signs. (See Anger, Desires, Emotions, Excitable, Hatred, Impulses, Intellect, Jealousy, Reins, Romance, Temper).

Sentient Faculties—(See "Sentient" under Faculties; Sentient).

Uncanny Feelings—(See Weird).

Want of Feeling—(See Apathy).

FEET—The Feet are under the external rulership of the ♓ sign. They are also ruled by ♀ and the 12th H. The ♓ sign rules from the ankles downward to the extremities of the toes. The Plantar Nerves are ruled by ♓. The bones of the feet and toes are under the structural rulership of ♓. The Os Calcis, the Heel Bone, is ruled by ♓. This Article will be arranged into two Sections. Section One—Description of the Feet. Section Two—Diseases and Afflictions.

— SECTION ONE —

DESCRIPTION OF THE FEET—

Fleshy and Short—The ☽ gives; ♊ often gives. These influences also apply to the Hands.

Ill-Made—Irregular—(See Club Feet, Deformities, Ill-Made, Malformations, in Sec. 2 of this Article).

Left Foot—(See "Marks" in this section).

Long Feet—Slender Feet (and Hands) ♃ indicates long legs and feet; ♃ in the Asc. at B.; ♀ in ♊; ♀ ascending at B., and free from the rays of other planets; the first face of ♍ on the Asc.

Marks—Moles On—(1) On Right Foot—Born under ♃ and ♃ ori. (See "Right Foot" in Sec. 2 of this Article). (2) On Left Foot—Marks, Moles, or a Scar On—The ☉, ☽, or malefics in ♓; ♓ on the Asc.; a masculine planet in ♓ in the male, and a feminine planet in ♓ in a female nativity. (See Left, Moles, Right, Scars). (3) On One or Both Feet—A Mark, Mole or Scar on One or Both Feet—The ☉, ♄, or ♂ in ♓; ♓ on the Asc., and espec. if ♅, ♄, or ♂ be in ♓, or afflicting a planet in ♓.

Moles—(See "Marks" in this section).

One or Both Feet—Marks, Moles or Scars On—(See "Marks" in this section).

Right Foot—Mole or Mark On—(See "Marks" in this section).

Scars On—(See "Marks" in this section; Scars).

Short Feet—♊ signifies long arms, but many times short hands and feet, and fleshy. (See "Short Hands" under Hands).

Short and Fleshy—(See "Fleshy" in this section; "Fleshy and Short" under Hands).

Slender and Long—(See "Long" in this section).

Strike Together—In Walking—♄ ascending at B. (See "Dragging" under Gait).

Thick Feet—The ☽ gives thick hands and feet. (See "Broad and Thick" under Hands).

Turned In—♓ on the Asc.

Uncomely—♃ in the Asc.

— SECTION TWO —

DISEASES AND AFFLICTIONS—To the Feet—

Abscess In—(See "Feet" under Abscess).

Accidents To—Hurts, Injuries, and Wounds To—All hurts to the feet are signified by the 12th H., and afflictions in ♓, or afflicting a planet in ♓, and with ♓ on the Asc.; ♄ or ♂ in the 1st or 7th H., and in the latter degrees of ♊, ♐, or ♓, and ori. of the ☉ and occi. of the ☽; ♂ affl. in ♋ or ♓; ♂ in the 9th H. in common signs, and afflicting ☿; ♓ on the Asc., and containing malefics. (See "Accidents" under Extremities. Also see "Injuries" in this section).

Aches In—The ☽ in ♍, ☌ or ill-asp. ♄ (or ☿ if he be of the nature of ♄) at the beginning of an illness or at decumb. (Hor'y). (See Aches; "Pains" in this section).

Achilles Tendon—(See Achilles; "Club Feet" in this section).

Acromegaly—(See "Enlargement" in this section; "Enlargement" under Extremities).

Affected—The feet are affected when the ☉ is in ♋; the ☽ ♓; ♅ or ♄ in ♑; ♃ in ♏ or ♒; ♂ ♋ or ♎; ♀ ♈ or ♍; ☿ or ♌. (See Table 196 in Simmonite's Arcana).

Afflicted—(See the various paragraphs in this section).

All Diseases In—All Infirmities In—Signified by the 12th H; ♓ diseases and afflictions in ♓; the 18° ♑ on the Asc., infirmities in the legs and feet. (See "All Diseases" under Legs; "Distempers", "Humours", in this section).

Aneurysm—(See Aneurysm).

Ankles—(See Ankles).

Arches Fallen—(See "Splay Foot" in this section).

Atrophy Of—Claw Feet—A ♄ affliction; ♄ affl. in ♓; Subs at LPP (4, 5L). (See Atrophy; "Wasting" in this section).

Blisters—Bullas—♂ affl. in ♓. (See Blisters).

Blood In—Stagnation of Blood In—♄ in ♍ or ♓. (See "Feet" under Blood).

Bones Of—Disorders of—♄ affl. in ♓; Subs at LPP. (See Bones).

Bowel Complaints—From Wet, Cold and Damp Feet—A ♓ disease and afflictions in ♓. (See "Cold Taken", "Colic", in this section).

Bromidrosis—Fetid Perspiration In

Feet—♂ in ♓; ♂ in common signs. (See Bromidrosis ; "Perspiring", in this section).

Bruises To—♄ affl. in ♓. (See Bruises).

Bunions—Corns—(See Bunions).

Chilblain—(See Chilblain).

Chronic Ailments In—♄ affl. in ♓. (See Chronic).

Claw Feet—Atrophy of—(See "Atrophy" in this section).

Club Feet—Talipes Varus—Contraction—Inversion—♄ affl. in ♒, from contraction of the Tendon Achilles; ♄ or ♂ affl. in ♓; the ♏ influence tends to; caused by prenatal afflictions. Subs at LPP. Cases—See "Cripple", No. 190 and 191 in 1001 N.N. Also Placidus records a case of Club Feet where ♂ was in ♓ in mundane □ ☽, and with ♄ ♉ ☽ from ♐, while the ☽ was in the western angle in her south node. (See Deformities, Ill-Made, Malformations, in this section. Also see Achilles).

Cold Feet—The feet are naturally moist and cold with ♄ in ♓, and with ♓ upon the Asc.; ☿ in ♓, and espec. when ☿ partakes of the nature of ♄; afflictions in ♓; Subs at AP, CP, KP, LPP. Due to the close connection of the feet (♓) with the brain and cerebellum (♈), the afflictions of ♄ in ♓ in the Asc., and with ♓ upon the Asc., tend to wakefulness by cold feet, and to Insomnia. (See "Cold Taken" in this section; Cold; "Insomnia" under Sleep).

Cold Taken—In the Feet—Colds Due To Damp and Wet Feet—Afflictions in ♓; ♓ on the Asc.; the ☽ affl. in ♓, or affl. the hyleg therefrom; the ☽ in ♓, ☌ or ill-asp. any of the malefics as promittors; the ☽ in ♓, ☌, □ or ☍ ♄ (or ☿ if he be of the nature of ♄) at the beginning of an illness or at decumb.; the ☽ affl. in ♓, the body tends to become disordered thru colds taken in the feet; ♄ or ♂ in ♓; ♄, ♆, or ♅, in ♓, and affl. the ☉ or ☽, tend to consumption from colds taken in the feet; ☿ affl. in ♌ tends to pains in the back from colds caught in the feet; ☿ affl. in ♓. (See "Bowel Complaints", "Colic", "Dry", in this section; Back, Cold, Colds, Consumption, Linen, Pneumonia).

Colic Taken—Thru the Feet—A ♓ disease, and afflictions in ♓; ♄ affl. in ♓. (See Bowels, Colic).

Consumption—Taken from Colds Caught In the Feet—(See "Cold Taken" in this section).

Contractions—(See "Club Feet", "Cramps", in this section).

Corns—(See Bunions, Scales).

Corrupt Humours—In the Feet—(See "Humours" in this section).

Cramps In—♅ affl. in ♒ or ♓, cramps in the feet and toes; ♅ affl. in ♓ tends to cramps, paralysis, muscular spasms, and affections of the motor nerves of the feet; ♄ in ♓, liable to cramps in the feet and toes; ♄ or ♂ angular in the 1st or 7th H., in ♊, ♐, or ♓, ori. of the ☉, and occi. of the ☽, and ♄ or ♂ in the latter degrees of these signs; ☿ affl. in ♓; Subs at KP, LPP (4, 5L). (See Cramps).

Feet

248

Feet

Crippled In—(See "Club Feet" in this section).

Damp Feet—Colds From—(See "Cold Taken" in this section).

Deformities In—Afflictions and malefics in ♓; malefics in ♓ in the 12th H.; ♓ on the Asc. (See Atrophy, Club Feet, Ill-Made, Malformations, Splay Foot, in this section).

Disability In—♄ or ♂ affl. in ♓. (See Atrophy, Club Feet, Deformities, Splay Foot, and the various paragraphs in this section).

Discoloration—(See "Erythromelalgia" in this section).

Diseases In—(See All Diseases, Distempers, Dropsy, Humours, Weakness, and the various paragraphs in this section).

Distempers In—The Feet Diseased—Trouble With the Feet—The ☉ affl. in ♋, ♍, or ♓; the ☽ affl. in ♉ or ♓; ♄ affl. in ♓; signified by ♄ in ♍, ♐, ♑, or ♓; ♃ in ♍, ♒; ♂ in ♋, ♎, ♐, or ♓; ♂ promittor in ♓, and ♂ or ill-asp. the ☉; ♀ in ♈ or ♍; ☿ in ♉ or ♌; ♓ on the Asc.; Subs at KP, PP, LPP. (See Toes. Also see the various paragraphs in this section).

Dragging—The Feet—(See "Dragging" under Gait).

Draws and Writes—With the Feet—Case—See "Armless Wonder", No. 054 in 1001 N.N.

Dropsy In—Oedema—Swollen Feet—Swellings In—The ☽ affl. in ♓; the ☽ ♓, ☌, □, or ☍ ♄; the ☽ ♓, □ or ☍ ♆; the ☉ affl. in ♋; ♃ affl. in ♓; ♂ in ♓; afflictions in ♒ or ♓; an ♒ and ♓ disease; the connection of ♓ with the ♌ sign, and from disturbed heart action and circulation, tends to oedema in the feet; Subs at KP and LPP. (See Dropsy; "Feet" under Gout; Swellings).

Dry—Should keep the feet dry when ♄ or ☿ are in ♓ at B., to avoid taking colds thru the feet. (See "Cold Taken" in this section).

Dysidrosis—Bullas In the Feet—(See Blisters, Dysidrosis).

Enlargement—Acromegaly—The ☉, ♄, ♆, ♃, or ♂ affl. in ♓. (See "Enlargements" under Extremities).

Eruptions On—☿ affl. in ♓, and due to wrong habits of living. (See Eruptions; "Eruptions" under Arms, Legs).

Erysipelas In—(See "Extremities" under Erysipelas).

Erythromelalgia—Pain, Swelling and Purplish Discoloration of the Parts—Redness and Swelling On the Bottom of the Feet—The ☽ in ♓ and affl. by ♄ or ♂; Subs at KP and LPP. (See Neuralgia, Pain, Plantar, Swelling, in this section).

Extremities—Disorders In—Accidents To—(See Extremities. Also note the various paragraphs in this section).

Fallen Arches—Flat Feet—(See "Splay Foot" in this section).

Fat Feet—Excessive Fat In the Feet —♃ affl. in ♓; ♂ ☌ ♃ in ♓; Subs at KP. (See "Adiposa Dolorosa" under Fat).

Feet First—Born Feet First—Case—

(See "Feet First" under Parturition).

Fetid Perspiration—(See Bromidrosis, Odors, in this section).

Flat Foot—(See "Splay Foot" in this section).

Foot and Mouth Disease—A contagious disease of animals, with the formation of vesicles in the mouth and on the feet—An eclipse of the ☉ in ♍ or ♓, and with ☿ badly afflicted by malefics at the same time; an eclipse of the ☉ in ♉ or ♎, and with malefics in ♓; eclipses in ♓, and with ☿ in the configuration, and afflicted; ♂ in ♓ and lord of the year at the Vernal Equi., and configurated with and afflicting ☿, as ☿ rules the mouth; malefics in ♓ at the Equinoxes or Solstices. This disease may also attack man, and espec. in those who have the ☉, ☽, ☿, and malefics in ♓ at B., or ☿ in ill-asp. to such planets in ♓ at B., and by dir., and when eclipses of the ☉ fall in ♓ on the places of malefics in ♓, and also if ☿ enter into the configuration. In Man, the Chiropractors also find Subs at MCP, CP, SP, and KP to exist at the time of the attacks. (See Vesicles).

Gait—Disorders of—(See Gait, Walk).

Glands Of—Affected—Ruled and affected by ♆ when this planet is in ♓. (See the Introduction under Aneurysm).

Gout In—Podagra—Wandering Gout —(See "Feet" under Gout).

Granulations—In the Joints—(See "Joints" in this section).

Growths—(See "Lump" in this section).

Hands—(See the various paragraphs under Hands).

Heat—In the Feet—♂ in ♓. (See Heat).

Heel Bone—The Os Calcis—(See Lump, Os Calcis, in this section).

Humours In—Corrupt Humours In—The ☽ hyleg in ♓ in a female nativity, moist humours; ♂ affl. in ♓, corrupt humours in; afflictions in ♓, cold and moist humours in; a Stellium in ♓ or the 12th H. (See "Lameness" in this section).

Hurts To—(See Accidents, Bruises, Injuries, in this section).

Hyperidrosis—Excessive Sweating In the Feet—♂ in ♓. (See Dysidrosis, Hyperidrosis, Sweat; Bromidrosis, Perspiring, in this section).

Ill-Made Feet—Irregular—Deformed —Ill-Formed—Malformations—♄ ascending at B.; ♂ in the 9th H. in common signs, and afflicting ☿; ♍ or ♓ on the Asc., or malefics in these signs. (See Club Feet, Deformities, in this section).

Infirmities In—♄ or ♂ affl. in ♓. (See All Diseases, Distempers, Humours, Lameness, Weakness, in this section).

Inflammation In—Heat In—Fever In —♂ affl. in ♓.

Injuries To—(See Accidents, Loss Of, Right Foot, in this section). Cases of Injury—See "Foot", No. 106, and "Puzzle Horoscopes", No. 665 and No. 672, in 1001 N.N.

Insomnia—From Cold Feet—(See "Cold Feet" in this section).

Inverted—Turned Inwards—(See "Club Feet" in this section).

Inward—Turned Inward—(See "Club Feet" in this section).

Irregular—(See "Ill-Made" in this section).

Joints—Granulations In—♄ affl. in ♓.

Lameness In—A ♓ disease; afflictions in ♓; ♓ on the Asc.; a ☽ disease; the ☽ affl. in ♓; ♄, ♂, or ♀ affl. in ♓; ♄, ♂, and many planets in the 12th H.; ♂ in ♓, by corrupt humours settled there when ♂ is the afflictor in the disease. (See Club Feet, Deformities, Gout, Splay Foot, and the various paragraphs in this section).

Left Foot—Mark, Mole, or Scar On—(See "Marks" in Sec. 1 of this Article. Also see Left).

Legs—(See the various paragraphs under Extremities, Legs, Limbs).

Leprosy In—(See Leprosy).

Limbs—Disorders In—(See Extremities, Legs, Limbs).

Loss of Foot—Or Feet—♂ affl. in ♓, danger of; ♂ in ♓ at B., and afflicted, and to the cusp the 12th H. by dir. Case—Loss of Foot—See "Puzzle Horoscopes", No. 665, in 1001 N.N.

Lower Limbs—Disorders In—Accidents To, etc.—(See Extremities, Legs; "Lower" under Limbs; Lower. Also note the various paragraphs in this section).

Lump—A Lump Growing On the Back of Each Heel—♄ affl. in ♓, due to deposits; ♓ on the Asc. or 12th H., and containing malefics; many afflictions in common signs. Case—See "Unfortunate Case", No. 351, in 1001 N.N. (See Growths, Tumors).

Malformations—♄ ascending at B. (See Claw, Club Feet, Deformities, Ill-Made, Splay, in this section).

Marks—(See "Marks" in Sec. 1 of this Article).

Missing—(See "Frog Child" under Forearm).

Moist and Cold—(See "Cold Feet" in this section).

Moist Humours In—(See "Humours" in this section).

Moles—(See "Marks" in Sec. 1 of this Article).

Motor Nerves—Affected—(See "Cramps" in this section).

Muscular Spasms—(See "Cramps" in this section).

Nerves—Motor Nerves Affected—(See "Cramps" in this section).

Neuralgic Pains—Plantar Neuralgia—♀ affl. in ♓; Subs at LPP (4, 5L). (See Cramps, Pains, in this section).

Odors In—Unpleasant Odors—The ☽ or ♂ affl. in ♓. (See Bromidrosis, Hyperidrosis, Perspiring, in this section).

Oedema—(See "Dropsy" in this section).

Operations On—Surgical—Should not be made when the ☽ is in ♓, or when the ☽ is afflicted, if the ☽ was in ♓, or a common sign at B. (See Operations).

Os Calcis—Disorders of—♄ affl. in ♓. (See "Lump" in this section).

Pains In—A ♓ disease, and afflictions in ♓; the ☽ in ♓ and affl. by ♄ or ♂; the ☽ affl. in ♉ or ♓, or affl. the hyleg therefrom; ♅, ♄, or ♂ affl. in ♓; ♂ affl. in the 12th H.; ♀ affl. in ♉ or ♓. (See Aches, Cramps, Erythromelalgia, Neuralgic, in this section; "Pain" under Extremities, Legs, Limbs).

Paralysis—(See "Cramps" in this section). Case—See "Tunison", No. 113, in 1001 N.N.

Perspiring Feet—Fetid—Odors—Sweating of—Afflictions in ♓; the ☉, ♃, ♅, or ♂ affl. in ♓; the ☽ hyleg in a female nativity, and afflicted. (See Bromidrosis, Dysidrosis, Humours, Hyperidrosis, Odors, in this section).

Plantar Region—Bottom of the Foot—Sole—Affections of—(See Erythromelalgia, Heel, Neuralgic, Pains, in this section).

Podagra—(See "Gout" in this section).

Pompholyx—Bullas—Blisters—(See Dysidrosis).

Purplish Discoloration—(See "Erythromelalgia" in this section).

Redness—On Bottom of Feet—(See "Erythromelalgia" in this section).

Rheumatism In—♄ in ♐ or ♓. (See "Rheumatism" under Extremities; "Feet" under Gout; Rheumatism).

Right Foot—(1) Mark, Mole, or Scar On—Born under ♃, and ♃ ori., a mole; ♓ on the Asc., and espec. if the ☉, ♅, ♄, or ♂ be in ♓, tends to a mole on one or both feet; ♂ in ♓ tends to a scar or mark on either foot by injury. (See "Marks" in Sec. 1 of this Article). (2) Right Foot Repeatedly Injured—Case—See "Foot", No. 106, in 1001 N.N.

Scars—(See "Right Foot" in this section).

Shuffling Gait—The Feet Drag or Strike Together—♄ ascending at B. (See "Dragging" under Gait).

Sole of Foot—(See "Plantar" in this section).

Spade-Like—A Condition in Myxoedema—(See Myxoedema).

Spasms In—(See "Cramps" in this section).

Splay Foot—Flat Feet—Fallen Arches—♄ affl. in ♓; ♄ and ♂ ♂ the ☽ in ♓; the 3rd Face of ♋ on the Asc.; Subs at LPP.

Stagnated Blood—In the Feet—(See "Blood" in this section).

Standing—On the Feet—♀ affl. in ♎ warns against standing on the feet too long at a time.

Strike Together—When Walking—(See "Shuffling" in this section).

Sweating Of—(See "Perspiring" in this section).

Swelling Of—Swollen Feet—Swellings On—(See Blisters, Blood, Bunions, Bruises, Corns, Dropsy, Glands, Gout, Inflammation, Joints, Lameness, Vesicles, in this section).

Talipes Varus—(See "Club Feet" in this section).

Tender Feet—Afflictions in ♓; the ☽, ♄, ♀, or ☿ affl. in ♓; ·♀ in ♓ and afflicting the ☽ or Asc.; ♀ in ♓ in the 6th H., and afflicted; ♓ on the Asc.

Tendo Achilles—(See "Club Feet" in this section).

Tissues—Wasting of—♅ affl. in ♓. (See "Wasting" under Tissues).

Toes—Disorders of—(See Toes).

Trouble — In the Feet — (See "Diseases", and the various paragraphs in this section).

Twistings—Contortions—Torsalgia— ♅ affl. in ♓. (See Contortions; "Cramps" in this section).

Ulcers On—Afflictions in ♓; the ☽ affl. in ♓; ♄ in ♓, occi., and affl. the ☉, ☽, or Asc. (See Ulcers).

Unpleasant Odors—(See "Odors" in this section).

Varicose Veins—The ☽ affl. in ♓. (See Varicose, Vesicles).

Vesicles On—(See "Foot and Mouth" in this section).

Wakefulness—From Cold Feet—(See "Cold Feet" in this section).

Walk—Irregularities In, Due to Afflicted Feet—(See the various paragraphs under Gait, Walk).

Wandering Gout—(See "Feet", "Wandering Gout", under Gout).

Wasting—Of Tissues of—(See "Tissues" in this section).

Weakness In—A ☽ disease; a ♓ disease, and afflictions in ♓; ♄ in ♓, and espec. ♄ in the 6th or 12th H.; ☿ affl. in ♓; ♓ on the Asc., and espec. if ♅, ♄, or ♂ be in ♓, or in ill-asp. to a planet in ♓; ♓ ascending at the Vernal Equi., Peoples and Countries ruled by ♓ suffer grievous infirmities in the head, feet, and with Gout and Dropsy. (See "Diseases In" in this section).

Wet Feet—Colds Taken By—Colic—Bowel Complaints By—(See Bowel Complaints, Cold Taken, Colic, in this section).

Wounds To—(See Accidents, Hurts, Injuries, in this section).

Writes and Draws—With the Feet—No Arms—(See "Draws and Writes" in this section).

FELONS—(See "Felons" under Fingers).

FEMALE — Females — Feminine — Women—Girls—Female Children, etc. —The ☽ has great influence in the horoscopes of females, and also ♀, and the ☽ and ♀ are said to rule females, the ☽ especially by night, and ♀ by day. In this Article matters which have to do with Females of all ages, from birth to death, will be listed, and subjects which have especially to do with adult females will be found in the Article on Women in the "W" section. Study both Articles together. See the following subjects in the alphabetical arrangement when not considered here.

Abortion; Accidents To—Hurts—Injuries—Wounds—The ☽ or ♀ to the ♂ or ill-asps. ♂ by dir., and espec. if ♂

afflict the ☽ or ♀ at B.; malefics to the ♂ or ill-asp. the ☽ or ♀. (See the various paragraphs under Accidents, Hurts, Injuries, Women, Wounds).

Active Mind—And Body—♂ in good asp. to the ☽ at B., and by dir. (See "Active Body", "Active Mind", under Active).

Adolescence—(See Puberty).

Aged Female—Death of—(See Aunts, Grandparents, Old Age).

Anaemia—(See Anaemia, Chlorosis).

Astray—Young Females Liable To Be Led Astray—(See Seduction).

Aunts; Bad Health—(See Health, Ill-Health, in this section).

Barrenness; Beautiful — (See Beautiful, Comely, Complexion, Eyes, Face).

Bereavement; Birth of a Female—A Daughter Born—A Daughter Promised —In female horoscopes, the 5th H. is female, and the 4th H. is male, and the conditions of these houses will show the predominating sex, and which gives the greater promise of fruitfulness, and the opposite houses show detriment, etc. More girls than boys are shown when there are many planets in feminine signs. The wife's Significators being stronger than those of the husband in the figure indicate female births, and more girls than boys. Female births are indicated when the sign on the cusp of 5th H. is female, and if the lords of the Asc. and 5th H. be in female signs, and the ☽ also in a female sign. Other indications are,—The ☉ to the ✳ or △ ♀; if the ☉, ☽, or Asc., or planets in asp. with them, be in feminine signs, or if they are feminine by being occi., the child conceived will be a female if such conditions exist at conception; the ☽ well-aspected at B., and to the ✳ or △ the Asc. by dir.; the ☽ to the ♂ or good asps. ♀ by dir., and espec. if ♀ is in the 5th H. at B., and children are not denied; ♀ in the 5th H. at B., and espec. when in a watery sign, indicates daughters; ♀ to the ♂ or good asps. the Asc. by dir., and espec. if ♀ be ruler of the 5th H. at B.; the Asc. or M.C. to the ♂ or good asps. ♀ by dir.; the M.C. to the ♂ or good asps. the ☽ if the ☽ was well-placed at B. for fruitfulness; many planets in female signs and houses, and with the sign on the Asc. and 5th H. a female sign. (For further influences along this line see "Birth of a Child", "Female Births", "First-Born", "Sex of Children", "Single Births", "Time of Birth", all under the subject of Children. Also see Birth, Conception, Daughter; "Male Births" under Male; Predetermination; "Sisters Indicated" under Sisters; "Time of Birth" under Time; Triplets, Twins, etc.).

Births To—(See Birth, Children, Conception, Fruitful, Mother, Parents, Parturition, Wife; "Birth of a Female" in this section).

Blind—In Left Eye—Accidents To—(See "Eyes" under Left, Right; "Left Eye" under Blindness, Eyes).

Blondes — (See "Blond" under Complexion).

Blood—The Circulation of Irregular—The Blood Corrupted—Dropsical Blood —(See "Blood" under Women).

Body and Mind—Much Activity of—(See "Active Mind" in this section).

Breasts In—(See Breasts).

Brunettes — (See "Dark" under Complexion).

Cerebral Functions — Disorders of — (See Cerebral).

Cervix—Disorders of—(See "Cervix" under Womb).

Chaste—Virtuous—The ☽ and ♀ free from the afflictions of malefics. (See Virtue, Unchaste).

Childbirth — (See Parturition, Puerperal).

Childhood—Disorders of Females In —Accidents In—Death In—(See Infancy, Childhood; "Early Years" under Early).

Children—Children Given—Children Denied—Trouble and Sorrow Thru—Death of, etc.—(See Barrenness, Children, Fruitfulness, Maternity, Mother, Parents, Wife, etc.).

Chills and Fever—(See Chills).

Chlorosis—Anaemia In Young Women —(See Anaemia, Chlorosis).

Chronic Diseases — Suffer From — Death By — (See "Death" under Chronic).

Circulation Irregular — (See "Blood" in this section; "Females" under Circulation).

Clitoris; Coarse — Coarse Body — Coarse Voice—(See Coarse).

Cohabitation; Cold—Suffers from Cold and Chills—(See Chills).

Complaints — Female Complaints—☽ diseases, and the ☽ afflicted; the ☽ affl. in ♏; ♏ diseases and afflictions in ♏. (See the various paragraphs in this section, and under Women).

Complexion; Conceived—A Female Conceived—(See "Birth of a Female" in this section).

Conception; Conduct — (See Conduct; "Conduct" under Women).

Constitution—The Strength or Weakness of the Female Constitution—The ☽ and ♀ strong, well-placed, well-aspected, and in good asp. to each other, strengthen the female constitution and favor good health, but when the ☽ is in bad asp. to ♀, the health is a continual source of trouble, and especially if ♄ and ♂ also afflict the ☽ and ♀, and take part in the configuration. (See Constitution, Strength, Vitality; "Health", "Ill-Health", in this section).

Corrupt Blood In — (See Impure; "Blood" under Women).

Courses — The Female Courses — (See Menses).

Danger To—(See Accidents, Blind, Childbirth, Death, Disgrace, Ill-Health, Seduction, and the various paragraphs in this section and under Women).

Daughter Born — Promised — (See "Birth of a Female" in this section).

Death of Females—Of Women—The

☽ hyleg, and affl. by ♄ at B., and by dir.; the ☽ and ♀ much affl. at B., and by dir., and the ☽ also without the good asp. of ♀ in the radical map. A female child born at an eclipse of the ☽, and under its shadow, is apt to die immediately, or soon after birth. In female horoscopes, the ☉ causes death by long, severe and painful diseases when afflicting the hyleg. (See Eclipses. Also see "Death" under Aunts, Childhood, Children, Chronic, Fevers, Fiancee, Friends, Grandparents, Infancy, Mortality, Mother, Relatives, Sister, Wife, Women).

Death by Females—(See Poison, Treachery; "Death by Women" under Women).

Debilitated—(See Constitution, Ill-Health, and the various paragraphs in this section; Debility).

Degrees of Zodiac—The Feminine Degrees of the Zodiac—♈, 9, 22; ♉, 5, 17, 24; ♊, 5, 22, 30; ♋, 8, 12, 27; ♌, 8, 23; ♍, 8, 20; ♎, 15, 27; ♏, 14, 25; ♐, 5, 24; ♑, 10; ♒, 15, 25, 30; ♓, 20, 28. The Asc., or its lord, in any of these degrees at B., the native is more effeminate in action or appearance, even though a male. (See Effeminate, Predetermination).

Deranged System—(See Constitution, Functions, Health, Ill-Health, and the various paragraphs in this section).

Detriment to Females—To Women—(See "Detriment" under Women).

Digestive Disorders — (See "Women" under Digestion).

Directions—The Effects of Evil Directions—When the malefics afflict the ☽ and ♀ at B., and by dir., and either the ☽ or ♀ are hyleg, there is great danger of serious illness, or death to females so born, and when under a train of such evil directions. (See "Arguments for Death" under Death; "Females and Directions" under Directions).

Disappointments—To Females—To Women—The ☽ to the ill-asps. ♀ by dir.; ♄ to the ♂ or ill-asps. the ☽ or ♀ by dir.

Diseases—Female Diseases—All feminine complaints come under the rule of the ☽. The ☽ rules the female functions, and afflictions to the ☽ tend especially to upset and derange the female constitution. Also an afflicted Venus tends to female disorders, illnesses, or death. (See Health, Ill-Health, and the various paragraphs in this section; Functions, Menses, Moon, Venus, Women).

Disgrace To — Disgrace By — (See "Women" under Disgrace).

Dissolute Habits — The ☽ affl. in ♏. (See Dissolute).

Drink — Given to Drink — (See "Women" under Drink).

Dropsical Blood—(See "Blood" under Dropsy, Women).

Effeminate; Eminent Female—Death of—(See "Eminent" under Women).

Emotions In—(See Emotions).

Evil—Sudden Evil For—The ☽ or ♀ to the ♂ ♅ by dir. (See Evil).

External Influences — Susceptible To —The ☽ hyleg in ♏ or ♓. (See Environment, External, Negative, Susceptible).

Eyes — (See "Blind" in this section; "Eye Trouble", "Women", under Eyes; "Eyes" under Left, Right).

Face In—(See "Females" under Face).

Faintings—Syncope—Swoonings— (See Fainting).

Father—Death of—Detriment To— (See Death, Detriment, under Father).

Female Births—(See "Birth of a Female" in this section).

Female Child Promised—(See "Birth of a Female" in this section).

Female Complaints — (See Functions, Leucorrhoea, Menses, Ovaries, Womb; the various paragraphs in this section and under Women).

Feminine Degrees — Of the Zodiac — Feminine Signs of the Zodiac — (See Degrees, Signs, in this section).

Fevers In—Subject to Fevers—Danger of—Death By—(See "Death", "Females", under Fever).

Fiancee; First Child — The First Born To—Sex of—And also of the 2nd and 3rd Child—(See "First-Born" under Children, First; Predetermination).

Flooding—(See Menses).

Fluids — Of the System — (See "Ailments" under Fluids).

Foetus; Fond of Females — (See "Addicted To" under Men).

Freedom — Unwomanly Freedom — (See "Free Love" under Free; "Unwomanly" under Morals).

Friend—Death of a Female Friend— (See "Female Friend" under Friends).

Fruitful; Functions In—Disturbed— Difficult—Slow—The female functions are ruled by the ☽, and the ☽ affl. at B., and by dir., or the ☽ in incongenial signs, as in the fiery signs at B., tend to; the ☽ ☌ or ill-asp. ♄ at B., and by dir., tends to suppressed, slow, difficult, and retarded functions in females. The special functions in females are largely under the rule of the ☽, and the ☽ in the Asc. at B. has much effect upon the female constitution, according to the aspects to the ☽. After puberty, in female nativities, the regulation of the health, the regularity of the system, and the function of maternity, depend upon the ☽ and ♀. (See Functions, Maternity, Menses, Regularity; Constitution, Diseases, Health, Ill-Health, in this section).

Generative System — Weakness of — (See "Weakness" under Generation).

Genitals; Gestation;

Good Constitution — Good Health— (See Constitution, Health, in this section; Immunity, Vitality).

Grandmother—(See Grandparents).

Great Women—Death of—(See Famous; "Great Women" under Great; Queens).

Grief—To Females—By Females— ☽ or ♀ to the ☌ or ill-asps. ♄ by dir., grief, sorrow, and trouble to females, and women. (See Grief; "Grief" under

Men; "Women" under Misfortune; Sorrow, Trouble).

Habits—(See Dissolute, Drink, and the various paragraphs in this section; Conduct; Habits).

Hair; Harlots; Hatred Of—(See "Females" under Hate).

Headaches — (See "Women" under Headaches).

Health—(1) Bad Health—The ☽ and ♀ weak at B., in evil asp. to each other, and also affl. by malefics at B., and by dir. (See Constitution, Diseases, Ill-Health, and the various paragraphs in this section). (2) Better Health—The Health Better—Stronger —When the ☽ is above the horizon in a night nativity, or below in a day geniture, well-aspected, and espec. with the ☽ in ♋ or ♓, as these signs are watery, plastic, and more agreeable to the lunar nature. (See Day; "Better" under Health; Night). (3) Good Health—Good and Strong Constitution—The Health Strengthened— The ☽ strong at B., and well-asp.; the ☽ above the horizon at B., and well-asp.; the ☽ on the Meridian, elevated above the malefics, and well-asp.; the ☽ to the good asps. the ☉, ♃, or ♀ by dir.; the ☽ and ♀ well-placed, in good asp. to each other, and not seriously afflicted by malefics; ♄ in good asp. to the ☽; ♃ in ☌ or good asp. the ☽; ♂ in good asp. to the ☽ or ♀. (See "Constitution" in this section; "Good Health" under Health). (4) Weaker— The Health Weaker—The ☽ below the horizon in a night nativity, and afflicted. (See Constitution, Diseases, Functions, Ill-Health, and the various paragraphs in this section; "Weak Body" under Weak).

Hermaphrodites; Hips and Thighs— (See "Weakness" under Hips).

Houses—The Female Houses—(See "Odd and Even" under Houses).

Humours — Moist Humours In the Feet—(See "Humours" under Feet; Humours).

Hurts To—(See "Accidents" in this section; "Children" under Hurts).

Husband; Hyleg—The ☽ or ♀ are the natural hylegs in a female nativity. (See Hyleg).

Hysteria—(See Emotions, Hysteria).

Ill-Health—For Females—For Women —Disordered System—The ☉ to the ☌ ☽ by dir., and espec. if it occur in the 6th H.; the ☽ affl. by the ☉, ♄, or ♂ at B., or by dir.; the ☽ in the 6th or 12th H. at B., in a weak sign, and affl. by the ☉ or malefics; the ☽ to the ☌ or ill-asps. the ☉, ♄, or ♂ by dir.; the ☽ to the ill-asps. ♃ or ♀ by dir.; the Prog. ☽ to the ☌ or ill-asps. the ☉, ♄, or ♂; the ☽ ☌ ♄ in the 1st H., and in ♑ or ♏; the ☽ below the horizon in a night nativity, and afflicted, the health and functions are weakened; the ☽ to the ill-asps. her own place by dir.; the ☽ affl. in ♏, and generally from dissolute habits; ♄ or ♂ ☌ or ill-asps. the ☽ at B., and by dir.; ♀ affl. the ☽ at B., and by dir. (See Constitution, Diseases, Functions, Health, and the various paragraphs in this section and under Women).

Impotent; Impurities—Of the System —The ☽ affl. in ♏ tends to impurities in a female system. (See Impurities).

Infamous — (See Infamous, Scandalous).

Infancy — Sickness or Death of Females In — (See "Female" under Infancy).

Inflammations In—(See "Females" under Inflammation).

Injuries To—Injuries By—(See "Accidents" in this section; "Injured" under Men).

Internal Complaints—(See "Women" under Internal).

Irregularities—Of the Functions—Of the System — The ☽ affl. in ♏. (See "Functions" in this section).

Left Eye—Left Ovary—Left Side of Body—(See Left, Ovaries; "Eyes" in this section).

Length of Life — The ☽ is hyleg in female nativities, or should be taken as such when possible, and the length of life may be determined according to her strength, weakness, aspects, sign and position, etc. (See "Duration of Life" under Life; "Long" in this section).

Leucorrhoea; Libidinous—Violently Libidinous—(See Lewd, Lust, Virile).

Life—Length of Life—(See "Length of Life" in this section).

Liver Disordered—(See "Women" under Liver).

Long—(1) Long Diseases—Death By —(See Chronic, Death, in this section). (2) Long Life — For Females — The ☽ well-placed by sign and house, well-aspected by the ☉, ♃, and ♀, elevated above the malefics, and espec. free from the afflictions of ♄ and ♂. (See "Long Life" under Life; "Short Life" in this section).

Love Affairs—(See Love).

Lower Order—Of Females—Of Women —(See Harlots, Shameless; Unchaste" in this section).

Lust In—Lustful—Unbridled Lust— (See Impotent, Lascivious, Lewd, Lust, Nymphomania; "Women" under Passion; Virile).

Male Child Promised — (See "Births" under Male).

Marriage — Early Marriage — Late Marriage—No Marriage—Not Inclined to Marry—Marriage Partner—(See Marriage, Marriage Partner; "Free from Passion" under Passion; Spinsters).

Masculine—Females with Predominating Masculine Traits—(See Deviations, Effeminate; "Coarse" under Voice).

Maternity—(See Maternity; "Functions" in this section).

Matrix—(See Womb).

Menopause; Menses; Midwives; Milk; Mind and Body—Much Activity of— (See "Active Mind" in this section).

Minor Disorders—(See Colds, Leucorrhoea, Menses, Mild, Minor, Slight).

Miscarriage; Misfortune To—(See "Women" under Misfortune).

Modesty; Moist Humours—(See "Humours" in this section).

Moon — The ☽ and Females — (See Moon. Also note the Introduction, and the various paragraphs in this section).

Mortality Among—Much Mortality— The ☉, ☽, and ♃ conjoined in ♎; the ☽ or ♀ lady of the year at the Vernal Equi., weak and afflicted; ♂ in ♏ at the Vernal, and lord of the year. (See "Death" in this section; Mortality).

Mother; Murders—Many Murders of Females—(See "Women" under Murders).

Natural Functions — In Females — Ruled by the ☽. (See "Functions" in this section; Menses).

Nervous Disorders—(See Emotions, Hysteria; "Disordered" under Nerves).

Nurses; Nymphomania; Obesity;

One Female Child—At a Birth—Two Females At a Birth—Three Females At a Birth—(See "Birth of a Female" in this section; Twins, Triplets).

Opposite Sex—Dealings With—(See Opposite).

Ovaries; Painful Diseases—Much Suffering or Death By—(See "Females" under Fever; "Painful" under Menses; Pain).

Parents—Death of—Afflictions To— The ☽ to the ☌ or ill-asps. ♄ by dir. (See Father, Mother, Parents).

Parturition; Passion In—Passion in Females is ruled by ♀, and ♀ much affl. by the malefics tends to disordered and perverted passions. (See "Lust" in this section).

Peace of Mind—(See "Peace of Mind" under Mind).

Periods In—Periodic Illness—(See Menses).

Planets—The Feminine Planets—The ☽ and ♀.

Poisoned—By the Treachery of Females—(See "Women" under Poison; Treachery).

Pregnancy; Private Diseases In—(See Genitals, Gonorrhoea, Private; "Diseases" under Sex; Womb).

Property—Wastes His Property and Substance On Bad Women — (See "Health Suffers" under Opposite Sex; "Bad Women" under Women).

Prostitutes—(See Harlots).

Puberty — (See Puberty; "Functions" in this section).

Puerperal Fever—(See Puerperal, Parturition).

Quarrels — With Females — With Women—The M.C. to the □ or ☍ the ☽ or ♀ by dir. (See Quarrels).

Rape; Regularity—Of the Health and Functions — (See "Females" under Regularity; "Functions" in this section).

Relative—Death of a Female Relative —Female Relatives are ruled by ♀. (See "Female Relatives" under Relatives).

Reproductive Organs—Disorders of— (See Generation, Genitals, Genito-Urinary, Ovaries, Regeneration, Reproduction, Sex, Womb, etc.).

Right Eye—Accidents To—Blindness In—Disorders of—(See "Eyes" in this section; "Eyes" under Right).

Right Ovary—(See Ovaries).

Robust—(See Constitution, Health, in this section; Robust, Ruddy, Strong, Vitality).

Ruined—By Females—By Women— Ruins Himself Among—(See "Ruined by Women" under Love Affairs).

Salacious—(See Effeminate, Lust).

Scandalous—(See Infamous, Scandalous).

Seduction; Severe Illnesses—(See "Death" in this section; Dangerous; "Females" under Fever; Pernicious, Severe, Sharp, Vehement, Violent).

Sex Gratification In—Sex Excesses— The ☽ affl. in ♏; ♂ ☌ or ill-asp. ♀. (See Amorous, Cohabitation, Effeminate, Excesses, Lewd, Licentious, Lust, Nymphomania, Passion; "Secret Bad Habits" under Secret; Sex, Shameless; "Solitary" under Vice; Wanton, etc.).

Shameless; Short Life—The ☽ weak and ill-dig. at B., badly aspected by the ☉ and the malefics, and with the malefics elevated above the ☽ at B. (See "Early Death" under Early; "Death" under Infancy, Childhood, Children, Youth; "Short Life" under Life; Vitality Low; "Weak Body" under Weak; Constitution, Death, Diseases, Health, Sickness, in this section).

Sickness—Caused by Women—Much Sickness Among Women—(See Constitution, Diseases, Functions, Ill-Health, in this section; "Health Injured" under Men; "Much Sickness" under Sickness).

Signs—The Feminine Signs of the Zodiac—The Even Signs, as 2nd, 4th, 6th, etc. The Feminine Signs are ♉, ♋, ♍, ♏, ♑, ♓. These signs are considered weaker than the masculine, or odd signs, and are also called negative signs. (See "Negative Signs" under Negative).

Single Women—Not Inclined to Marry —(See Celibacy; "Aversion" under Marriage; "Free from Passion" under Passion; Spinsters).

Sisters; Skin—In females the ♓ sign gives a clear, lucid skin, but very white. The ♍ sign gives soft, delicate, tender and beautiful skin. (See Complexion, Face, Skin).

Son Born To — (See "Births" under Male).

Sorrow To—(See "Women" under Misfortune; Sorrow, Trouble).

Spinsters—(See "Single Women" in this section).

Sports — Indiscretions In — (See "Indiscretions" under Sports).

Sterility—(See Barrenness; "Unfruitful" under Wife).

Stomach Disorders—Digestive Disorders—(See "Women" under Digestion).

Sudden Evils—(See "Evil" in this section).

Swoonings—(See Fainting).

Syncope—(See Fainting).

System — The System Disordered — (See Impurities, Irregularities, in this section; "Disordered System" under System).

Tomboyishness—Caused by the positive, or masculine signs, being prominent, and with the ☉, ☽, ♅, ♃, and ♀ being obscurely placed. (See "Women" under Coarse; "Masculine" in this section).

Tragical Death—By Women—(See Tragical).

Treachery—Death or Injury By Female Treachery—(See "Injured" under Men; "Women" under Poison; "Female" under Treachery).

Triplets—Three Females Born— (See Triplets).

Trouble—For Females—By Females —(See "Women" under Misfortune; Tragical, Treachery, in this section).

Twins; Two Females Born — (See Twins).

Ulcers—(See "Vulva", "Womb", under Ulcers).

Unbridled Lust—(See Nymphomania; "Unbridled Passion" under Passion; "Lust" in this section).

Unchaste—Danger of—♂ affl. in the 7th H. with females; ♀ ☌ ♂ in ♏; ♄ ☌ ♀ in ♏. (See Chaste, Lust, Unbridled Lust, in this section).

Unmarried Women—(See "Single" in this section).

Vagina; Venus—Venus Figure—Venus and Females — (See Beautiful; "Brunettes" under Hair; Venus. Also note the Introduction to this Article).

Vexations — (1) By Females — By Women—The ☽ in tr. over ♋ at B., or to place of by dir.; the ☽ Sig. □ or ☍ ♀; ♀ by Periodic Rev. to the ill-asps. the radical ☉. (See "Women" under Men; "Female Treachery" under Treachery; Vexations. Also see Treachery, Trouble, in this section). (2) To Females—To Women—(See "Women" under Misfortune; Sorrows, Trouble, Vexations).

Virgin—Virginity—Chaste—(See "Chaste" in this section; Apathy, Aversions; "Free from Passion" under Passion; Spinsters).

Virile; Virtuous—(See Chaste, Virgin, in this section).

Vital Spirit In—(See "Spirit" under Vital).

Vitality In—(See Constitution, Health, in this section; "Good Health" under Health; Immunity, Resistance; "Little Sickness" under Sickness; Stamina, Strength, Strong, Tone, Vitality, etc.).

Voice — (See Coarse, Effeminate; Gifted, Melodious, Musical, under Voice).

Vulva; Weak Constitution — (See "Constitution" in this section; "Weak Constitution" under Constitution; "Low" under Vitality; "Weak Body" under Weak).

Whites—(See Leucorrhoea).

Widows; Wife; Woman with Child— Is Not with Child—(See "Woman" under Pregnancy).

Womanish—(See Effeminate).

Womanly—(See "Chaste" in this section; Modesty).

Womb; Young Women—(See Chlorosis, Love Affairs, Marriage, Puberty, Young, Youth. Also note the various paragraphs in this section).

Zodiac—Feminine Degrees of—(See "Degrees" in this section).

FEMUR—The Thigh Bone—Is under the structural rulership of ♐.

Accidents To—Injuries—Broken—Fracture, etc.—The ☽ affl. in ♐; ♄ in ♐ in the Asc.; ♂ affl. in ♐ or ♐; ♂ in ♐ and affl. the hyleg; ♂ in ♐ or ♑ in the Asc., and afflicted; ♐ on the Asc.; ♐ on or in the 6th H., and afflicted; ♐ on the Asc., 6th, or 12th H.; ♐ ruler of the 6th H., and affl. by the progressions or transits of a malefic, and espec. by ♄ or ♂; ♐ ruler of the 12th H., and containing malefics, or a malefic affl. the cusp of the 12th at B., and by dir. Cases—See Fig. 15A in Astro-Diagnosis, and Fig. 6 in Message of the Stars, both books by the Heindels. (See "Accidents" under Arms; Bones, Fractures; "Fractures" under Hips; Legs).

Dislocation—Of the Femur—♂ affl. in ♐. (See Dislocations; "Joint" under Hips; Thighs).

Inflammation—Osteitis—(See "Inflammation" under Bones; "Marrow" in this section).

Marrow Of—Inflammation of—♂ affl. in ♐. (See "Osteomyelitis" under Bones; Marrow).

Osteitis—(See "Inflammation" under Bones).

Osteomyelitis—Inflammation of the Marrow—(See "Osteomyelitis" under Bones).

Periosteitis—Of Femur—♂ affl. in ♐; Subs at PP, the 2, 3, 4 Lumbars. (See "Periosteitis" under Bones).

FERAL—(See Beasts, Brutish, Savage, Wild).

FERMENTATION—Zymosis—The Process of Fermentation—

Bowels—Fermentation of Food In—(See "Putrid" under Bowels).

Stomach—(See "Fermentation" under Stomach). This subject is considered further under Zymosis. (See "Hot and Moist Body" under Moisture; Zymosis).

FEROCIOUS—

Animals—Hurts by Ferocious Animals—(See "Ferocious", "Wild", under Animals).

Eyes—(See "Ferocious" under Eyes).

FERRUM—(See Iron).

FERTILE—Fruitful—Capable of Reproduction—The ☽ and ♀ are fertile. (See Conception, Fecundation, Fruitful, Prolific, Pregnancy).

Fertilization—The ☽ is the planet of, and of impregnation. (See Conception, Fecundation, Pregnancy).

FESTERING DISEASES—Denoted by ♄. (See Pus).

FESTINATION—The Peculiar Walk of Paralysis Agitans—(See "Festination" under Walk).

FETID—Giving Out Offensive Odors—Fetid Odors are generally the work of ♄ and the ☽. The influences of ♀ also cause fetid conditions, and usually resulting from over-indulgences, excesses, gluttony, venereal diseases, etc. Read the Articles on the Moon, Saturn, and Venus. Also see such subjects as Abscesses, Axillae, Breath, Carcinoma, Catarrh, Corrupt Air (see Air); Corruption, Decay, Decomposition, Discharges, Exudations, Faeces, Feet (see "Fetid" under Feet); Foul, Gangrene, Gases, Halitosis (see "Foul" under Breath); Humours (see "Corrupt" under Humours); Impure, Menses, Moisture, Morbid, Mortification, Necrosis, Noxious, Odors, Offensive, Pools (see "Stagnant" under Pools); Pus, Putrid, Putrefaction, Rottenness, Sores, Sordes, Sweat, Ulcers, Vapors, Vegetation, Venereal, etc.

FEUDS—Deadly Feuds and Grievous Dissentions Generally, and with Danger To Life—Eclipses of the ☉ in ♐. (See Ambushes, Contests, Disputes, Duels, Enemies, Enmity, Fighting, Gunshot, Hatred, Quarrels, Revenge, Treachery, etc.).

FEVER—Fevers—Febrile Indisposition—Hot Complaints—Pyrexia—Feverish Distempers—The ☉ and ♂, the hot, fiery, and electric bodies of our Solar System, tend to cause fevers and the combustion of tissue. Mars lights the fire of fever to burn out the poisons and impurities of the system. Fevers and Inflammation usually go together, as both are ruled by ♂, and both are processes of elimination and protection to the body to burn up excess wastes, and to rid the body of its cinders and ashes. Fevers are characteristic of the Bilious, or Choleric Temperament. (See Choleric). The ♈ people, a sign ruled by ♂, have great power to resist high fevers that would ordinarily prove fatal to others. Some people are more liable to fevers and hot diseases than others, according to the predominance of the fiery influences, the ☉, ♂, and the fiery signs at B., while other classes of people, as those born with the earthy and watery elements strong at B., are less liable to fevers and espec. high, burning, or pernicious fevers. The motion of the ☽ regulates fevers. The general causes of fever, and also the various kinds and varieties of fever, etc., will be listed in the following subjects. For the main planetary influences tending to cause fever, see the paragraph, "Liable to Fever" in this section.

Abatement Of—(See Remission).

Absent Party—An Absent Party Has Recently Been Inclined To a Feverish State—The ☽ sepr. from the ☌, □, or ☍ ♄ in a Hor'y Figure. (See Absent).

Acute Fevers—(See Acute).

Ague—Malaria—Intermittent Fever—(See Ague, Intermittent, Malaria).

Air—The Spread of Fevers Due to Noxious Air—(See "Corrupt Air" under Air; Contagions, Epidemics, Pestilence).

All Feverish Disorders—♂ affl. in ♈.

All Kinds of Fever—♂ diseases; caused by ♂ and his afflictions to the ☉, ☽, Asc., or hyleg at B., and by dir.

Antipyretics—A Fever-Reducing Remedy—A Febrifuge—(See Antipyretic, Febrifuge).

Approaching—A Fever Is Approaching—The ☽ ☌, □, or ☍ ♄ (or ☿ if he be of the nature of ♄) at the beginning of an illness or at decumb. (Hor'y).

Better—(See "Curtailed" in this section).

Bilious Fevers—(See "Fevers" under Bilious; "High" in this section).

Blood—Fevers Proceeding from Too Much Blood—Hot and Feverish Blood—(See "Fevers", "Over-Heated", and "Too Much Blood" under Blood; Sanguinary).

Bowels—Fevers In—Enteric Fever—(See "Fever" under Bowels; Typhoid).

Brain Fever—(See Brain).

Breakbone Fever—(See Dengue).

Breasts—Fever In—Milk Fever—(See "Fever" under Breasts).

Brief Fevers—Ephemeral—Lasting For a Day—(See Ephemeral).

Burning Fevers—High—Bilious—Violent—Sharp—Severe — Fierce— (See "High Fevers" in this section; Pestilence).

Camp Fever—(See Typhus).

Catarrhal Fever — (See Catarrh, Fluxes, Influenza).

Causes of Fever—(See "Liable to Fever", the Introduction, and the various paragraphs in this section).

Cerebral Fevers—Cerebro-Spinal Fevers— (See Brain, Cerebral, Cerebro-Spinal, Meninges).

Childbed Fever— Puerperal Fever—(See Puerperal).

Childhood—Fevers In—(See "Fevers" under Childhood, Children, Infancy).

Chills and Fever — (See Chills, Malaria).

Cholera—(See "Epidemics" under Cholera).

Chronic Fevers—Lingering—Constant—Continuous—Low Fevers—Are caused by ♄ afflictions and evil directions to the hyleg, as in Consumption, Phthisis, and Wasting Diseases. They usually get worse towards sunset, and during the night. (See Chronic, Complications, Consumptions, Grievous, Lingering, Wasting; Constant, Low, in this section).

Cleansing—Of the Body by Fevers—The work of ♂. (See Cleansing, Combustion, Elimination, Inflammation. Also note the Introduction to this Article).

Cold and Dampness—Fevers Arising From—Caused by ♄ and ♄. (See "Dampness and Cold" under Cold; "Cold and Dampness" under Exposure; 'Cold and Moist" under Moisture).

Combustion—A Purifying Agency Thru Fevers—(See Combustion, Cleansing, Inflammation; "Cleansing" in this section).

Constant Fever—Continuous—Low—Chronic—The ☽ in ♈ or ♉, and affl. by the ☉, ♄, or ♂ when taken ill (Hor'y); the ☽ ☌ or ill-asp. ♄ (or ☿ if he be of the nature of ♄) at the beginning of an illness or at decumb. (Hor'y); caused by ♄, and also by ♂, when the dominion of death is vested in them. (See Chronic, Duration, Low, in this section; Continuity, Duration; the Introduction under Flux).

Contagious Fevers—(See Contagious, Infectious).

Continuance—Of Fever—(See Continuity, Course, Crises, Duration; Chronic, Constant, Duration, Ephemeral, Low, Slight, in this section).

Continuous Fevers—Continuing—Synocha—(See Chronic, Constant, Fluxes, Habitual, Hectic, Low, in this section).

Corrupt Air—Fevers Arising From—(See "Air" in this section).

Crises In—Critical Days In—(See Crises, Critical).

Critical Days In—(See Crises, Critical).

Curtailed Fevers—Better—Moderated—Shortened—Aspects of the afflicting planet sepr. from the ☉, ☽, Asc., or hyleg, tend to curtail and shorten the fever; the afflicting planet changing signs, or the ☽ coming to a favorable asp. her place at the beginning of the fever. (See Abatement, Amelioration, Better, Crises, Duration, Hectic, Moderation, Recovery, Remission; "Duration" in this section).

Daily Return Of—(See "Remittent" in this section).

Dampness and Cold—Fevers Arising From—(See "Cold and Dampness" in this section).

Danger—(1) Danger by Fevers—(See Death, High, in this section). (2) Danger of—(See "Liable To", and the various paragraphs in this section).

Dangerous Fevers—(See Death, High, in this section).

Death from Fever—Fatal Fevers—Dangerous—The ☉ affl. at B., and in □ or ☍ the ☽ or Asc., whichever may be hyleg, and the hyleg affl. by a train of evil directions; the ☉ or ☽ Sig., and ☌ ♂ by dir., and affl. by ♂ at B.; an afflicted ☉ causes death by fevers and severe illnesses in a female horoscope; the ☉ to the place of Praesepe; the ☉ joined with the Ascelli; the ☽ ☌ ♂ in the Asc. at B. tends eventually under evil directions of ♂ to death by some feverish complaint; the ☽ to the ☌ or ill-asp. ♂ by dir., the fever is often fatal, and espec. if ♂ affl. the ☽ and hyleg at B.; ♂ Sig. ☌, □, or ☍ ☉ by dir.; ♂ denotes death by; ♂ affl. the hyleg by dir., and holding the dominion of death; in Hor'y Q. ♂ ruler of the 8th H., or in the 8th, or affl. the cusp of 8th; the Asc. to the place of the Pleiades, Hyades, Castor or Pollux. (See "Arguments for Death", "Certain Death", under Death; Fatal; "High" in this section).

Dengue—Breakbone Fever—Rheumatic Fever—(See Dengue; "Fever" under Rheumatism).

Diathesis—And Fevers—(See Diathesis).

Directions—And Fevers—(See Directions).

Distempers—Liable to Feverish Distempers—(See "Liable To" in this section; Distempers).

Dreadful Fevers—(See High, Portentious, in this section).

Dry and Hot Diseases—(See Dryness; "Dry and Hot" under Heat; Parched).

Duration of Fever—Continuity of—A fever beginning under a lunar sign partakes of the nature of that sign, and tends to run until the ☽ reaches a sign of opposite elementary qualities. A fever beginning when the ☽ is in ♈, a hot and dry sign, and just after the New ☽, will continue and not be naturally modified until the 1st Quarter of the ☽, when the ☽ reaches the ♋ sign, and meets with opposite qualities, cold and moist. Thus a fever is either terminated, ameliorated, or aggravated, according to the elementary qualities of the Sign and Lunar Quarter ruling at the beginning of the fever, and the qualities of the signs thru which the ☽ passes on successive days, whether of the same or opposing nature. Many of the same conditions which relate to the Duration of Disease, Crises Days, Critical Days, etc., will also apply here. (See Chronic, Continuance, Curtailed, Crises, Ephemeral, Habitual, Long, Low, Prognosis, and the various paragraphs in this section).

Ease—Intervals of Ease—(See Ease; "Fever" under Intermittent; Remittent).

Elimination—(See "Cleansing" in this section).

Energy—Fever As Related To the Energies—(See "Fever" under Energy; "Cleansing" in this section).

Enlarged Scope—Fever and Inflammation Combined—(See "Scope" under Enlarged).

Enteric Fever—(See "Fever" under Bowels; Typhoid).

Entire Body—Feverish Action Over the Whole Body—The ☉ directed to Cor Scorpio. (See Whole).

Ephemeral Fevers—Brief—One Day Fevers—(See Ephemeral).

Epidemic Fevers—(See "Corrupt", "Obnoxious", under Air; Cholera, Epidemics, Noxious, Pestilence).

Eruptive Fevers — Exanthematous— (See Eruptive).

Exanthematous Fevers—(See "Eruptive Fevers" under Eruptions).

Excesses—Indiscretions—Fevers From—(See "Slight" in this section).

Excessively High—Hyperpyrexia— Burning—Violent—(See "High" in this section).

Extremes—Rapid Extremes of Temperature—♂ with ♄, and both the afflictors at the same time.

Eyes—Hot Diseases In—(See "Hot Diseases" under Eyes).

Fatal—(See "Death" in this section).

Father—Fevers To—(See "Fevers" under Father).

Febrifuge—(See "Antipyretic" in this section).

Females—Danger of Fever, Severe and Painful Diseases To, or Death by Fever—The ☉ or ♂ to the ♂ ☽ by dir., and espec. if it take place in the 6th H.; an afflicted ☉ causes death by fevers and severe illnesses in a female horoscope; the ☉ to the ♂ the ☽ by dir.; the ☽ to the ♂ the ☉ or ♂ by dir.; the Asc. to the place of Markab. (See "Death", "Ill-Health", under Females).

Fever and Inflammation—(See "Enlarged Scope" in this section).

Feverish Conditions—Danger of—Is Liable To—(See "Liable to Fever", "Patient Is Feverish", and the various paragraphs in this section).

Feverishness—Causes of—(See "Liable To", and the various paragraphs in this section).

Fierce Fevers—High—Burning— Sharp—Severe—(See "High", "Pernicious", in this section).

Free from Fevers—Immunity—The earthy signs ♉, ♍, and ♑ are cold signs, and in themselves free from fevers, and people born with an earthy sign on the Asc., and with the ☉, ☽, and many planets in earth signs at B., are more immune to, and free from fevers. (See Immunity).

Frequent Attacks—Of Fever—The ☉ or ♂ in ♈, and ♈ on the Asc.; ♂ too much in evidence at B.; ♂ in a fiery sign in the 6th H., and affl. the hyleg; cardinal signs on the 6th H. at B. (See "Liable To" in this section).

Gastric Fever—(See "Fever" under Gastric, Stomach).

Generally—Tends to Fevers Generally —Subject to Fevers of Various Kinds —Diseases of the ☉; the ☉ hyleg at B., and affl. by ♂, tends to fevers generally; the ☉ in a fiery sign in the 6th H., and affl. by ♂.

Germs and Fever—(See Germs, Miasma; "Virus" under Pestilence).

Glandular Fever—(See Glands).

Habit—The Habit In Disease—(See Diathesis).

Habitual Fever—Hectic—Chronic— Continuous—(See Chronic, Continuous, Hectic, Low, in this section).

Hay Fever—(See Hay).

Head—Hot Humours In—Feverish Head—(See Feverish, Hot Diseases, Humours, under Head).

Heart and Lungs—Fevers from Obstructions Near the Heart or Lungs— (See "Fever" under Heart).

Hectic Fever—Habitual—Protracted —Constant—Continuous—Chronic— The Protracted Fever of Phthisis—The Hectic Fever associated with Phthisis follows the motion of the ☉ and tends to be worse when the ☉ is in □ or evil asp. his own place by Tr. or Dir., and to diminish when the ☉ is in ✶, △, and good asp. his own place; the ☉ configurated with malefics when □ his own place tends to make the fever worse, and better when configurated with benefics; the ☽ to the □ or ☍ ♄ by dir.; ♄ in fiery signs at a decumb., and when the ☉ is weak and affl.; a ♂ disease when ♂ is afflicted and associated with ♄; ♀ Sig. ♌ ☉, and the ☉ ill-dig. at B., and affl. by ♂; fiery signs on the Asc. or 6th H. at B. This condition is combatted by a ♄ remedy, a preparation of Lead, known as "Tincture Saturnina". (See Chronic, Constant, Continuous, Low, in this section; "Fire Signs" under Fire; Phthisis).

Hexis—The Hexis and Fever—The Permanent Habit In Disease—(See Diathesis).

High Fevers — Burning—Hot—Dangerous — Bilious — Fierce — Hyperpyrexia—Mischievous—Severe—Sharp—Violent—Pernicious—Raging Fevers—High Temperatures—Vehement—Swift—Quick—The Disease Runs High—Rapid, etc.—The ☉ to the ♌ or ill-asp. ♂ by dir.; the ☉ or ♂ in ♈ at B., or ♈ on the Asc., fevers rise higher than with other classes of patients; the ☉ or ☽ joined with the Ascelli, or the ☉ or ☽ directed to the Ascelli; the ☉ directed to all Nebulous Clusters, and to Castor and Pollux, threatens violent fevers; the ☉ affl. in ♌ at decumb., mischievous fevers; the ☉ to the place of Praesepe, dangerous fever; the ☽ in a fiery sign, and ♌ or ill-asp. ♂ by dir.; the ☽ to the ♌ of the Pleiades, Praesepe, or the Ascelli; the ☽ in ♐ and affl. by the ☉ or ♂ when taken ill (Hor'y); the ☽ ♌, P, □, or ☍ ♄ or ♂, or ♌ the radical place of these planets at the beginning of an illness or fever, and espec. if ♂ be the stronger afflicted planet (Hor'y); an eclipse of the ☽ in ♏ tends to high fevers generally; an eclipse of the ☽ in the 2nd or 3rd Dec. of ♏ tends to high and burning fevers; ♂ too much in evidence at B. tends to high temperatures; ♂ with ♄, and both the afflictors at the same time, tend to rapid extremes of temperature; ♂ in a fiery sign at decumb. tends to fevers of a high, burning, pernicious, vehement character, and espec. if ♂ be in the 6th H., or under the Sun's beams at decumb., and affl. the Sig. of the disease; ♂ causes pestilential burning fevers; in Hor'y Q., ♂ Sig. ♌ ☉ indicates that a high and burning fever may be present; ♂ Sig. ♌ or ☍ ☉; ♂ ♌ the Asc. by dir.; a ♌ disease, and afflictions in ♌; Subs at CP and KP. (See Bilious, Crises, Death, Frequent, Liable To, Malignant, Pernicious, Portentous, Swift, Violent, in this section; Acute, Bile, Epidemics, Eruptions, Fatal, Fierce, Grievous, Heat, Malignant, Mischievous, Pain, Parched, Pestilence, Pulse, Rapid, Septic, Severe, Sharp, Swift, Vehement, Violent, Virulent, etc.).

High Living—Fevers Arising From—(See "High Living" under High; "Fevers" under Indiscretions; "Slight" in this section).

Highest — Fevers are highest at the Full Moon.

Hot Complaints — Subject To — (See "Liable To" in this section; "Hot Diseases" under Heat).

Hot and Burning Fevers—(See "High" in this section).

Hot and Dry Diseases—(See "Dry and Hot" in this section).

Hot Flashes—(See Flushings).

Hot Humours—(See "Humours" under Heat).

Hyperpyrexia — Excessively High Temperature—(See "High" in this section).

Immunity from Fever — (See "Free From" in this section).

Increased — The Fever Is Increased and Aggravated—The Fever Is Worse—(See Chronic, Duration, Enlarged Scope, Extremes, Hectic, High, Susceptibility, in this section; "Worse" under Crises; Increase).

Indiscretions—Fevers Arising From—(See "Diseases" under Excesses; "High Living" under High; "Fevers" under Indiscretions).

Indisposition—(See "Febrile" under Indisposition).

Infancy—(See "Fevers" under Infancy).

Infectious Fevers — (See Contagions, Infections).

Inflammation and Fever — (See "Enlarged Scope" in this section).

Inflammatory Fevers — (See "Fever" under Inflammation).

Influenza—A Catarrhal Fever—(See Catarrh, Influenza).

Intermittent Fever—Occurring at Intervals — (See Ague, Ease, Malaria, Quartan, Quotidian, Relapsing, Remission, Remittent, Semi-Tertian, Tertian).

Intestines—Fever In — (See "Fever" under Bowels; Typhoid).

Irregular Fevers—Remittent—Irregular Course—(See Course, Erratic, Intermittent, Irregular, Mixed, Peculiar, Remittent, Symptoms, Variable, Various).

Journeys—Voyages—Fevers On—(See "Fever" under Voyages).

Kinds of Fever — (See the various paragraphs in this section).

Liable to Fevers — Tendency To — Danger of—Causes of—Fever Threatened—Subject to Feverish Distempers—Suffers from Hot Complaints—May Have Frequent Attacks of Fever—Not Immune to Fevers, etc.—The aspects and influences which indicate that fever is actually present are given in the paragraph "Patient Is Feverish" in this Article. The following influences make one liable to fevers, and feverish conditions—A SUN disease; the ☉ affl. in fiery signs, and fever. affl. by ♂; the afflictions of the ☉ are very productive of fevers, and espec. when ♂ is in the 1st H., and affl. by the ☉; the ☉ affl. in ♈, ♌, ♐ or ♑; the ☉ in ♐ and affl. by ♂ or ♃; the ☉ or ♂ affl. in the Asc.; the ☉ affl. in ♈, due to excess of heat; the ☉ or ♂ in ♈, and ♈ on the Asc.; the ☉ ♌ ♂ in ♈ and ♈ on the Asc., the blood is like a hot, fiery liquid; the ☉ or ☽ ♌, □, or ☍ ♂; the ☉ affl. in ♌ or ♎; the ☉ in a fiery sign at B., affl. by ♂, and the ☉ in ♌, P, □ or ☍ the Asc. by dir.; the ☉ affl. at B., and the ☉ to the evil asp. the Asc. by dir.; the ☉ to the ♌ or ill-asp. ♂, and ♂ ruler of the 6th H.; the ☉ or ☽ Sig. in ♌ ♂; the ☉ Sig. □ or ☍ ♂;

the ☉ to the ☐ or ☍ ☽ by dir.; the ☉ to the place of ☋; the ☉ in a fire sign at B., affl. by ♂, and to the ☌ or ill-asp. the Asc. by dir.; the ☉ to the ill-asps. the ☽ by dir., and the ☽ hyleg at B., and affl.; the ☉ in ♈, ♌, or ♐, in ☌ or ill-asp. any of the malefics as promittors; the ☉ affl. by ♀, and thru excesses or indiscretions; denoted by the ☉ when the ☉ afflicts the ☽ or Asc.; the ☉ with the Ascelli at B., and to the place of the Ascelli by dir.; the ☉ joined with, or to the place of Antares, Praesepe, or Caput Hercules; the MOON to the ☌ or ill-asp. the ☉ or ♂ by dir.; the ☽ hyleg, and to the ☌ or ill-asp. ♄ or ♂ by dir.; the ☽ to the ☌, P., or ill-asps. the ☉ by dir. if the ☽ be hyleg, and the ☉ affl. at B.; the ☽ in ♐ in ☌ or ill-asp. ♄ (or ♀ if he be of the nature of ♄) at the beginning of an illness or at decumb. (Hor'y); the ☽ hyleg and to the ☌ or ill-asp. ♄ by dir., espec. in ♌ and affl. by the ☉ or ♂ when taken ill, the body is dry, hot and parched (Hor'y); the ☽ in ♎ and affl. by the ☉ or ♂ when taken ill, tends to fever from too much blood (Hor'y); the ☽ ☌ or ill-asp. ♄ or ♂, or the radical places of these planets, at the beginning of an illness or fever, and espec. if ♂ be the stronger afflicting planet, tends to high, burning fever; the ☽ in fiery signs, and to the ☌ or ill-asps. ♂ by dir.; the ☽ hyleg, and to the ☌ or ill-asps. the ☉ by dir., and the ☉ affl. at B.; the ☽ affl. in ♋ at B., and the tr. of ♂ over the radical ☽, and espec. in people with a weak constitution; the ☽ affl. in an airy sign at B., and a tr. of ♂ over the radical place of the ☽, or the ☽ to the ☌ or ill-asp. ♂ by dir.; the ☽ in ♈, ♉, or ♐, and affl. by the ☉ or ♂ when taken ill (Hor'y); the ☽ to the ☌ or ill-asp. ♂ by dir., and ♂ affl. the ☽ at B., a fever which may endanger the life; the ☽ Sig. ☌ ♂ (Hor'y); the ☽ to the ☌ the Pleiades or Praesepe; SATURN occi., and affl. the hyleg by dir., tends to low fevers; ♄ causes fevers arising from cold or dampness; JUPITER affl. in ♌; ♃ affl. in ♎, from too much blood; ♃ affl. in ♐; MARS in fiery signs and affl. the ☉, ☽, Asc., or hyleg; ♂ affl. in the 1st H.; ♂ in ♈ and affl. the hyleg; ♂ to the ☌ or ill-asp. the Asc. by dir.; ♂ in ♌, ☐ or ☍ ☉; ♂ ☐ or ☍ the ☉ or ☽ at B., and by dir.; ♂ affl. in ♈, ♌, ♐, or ♒; ♂ affl. in the 4th, 6th, or 8th H., and espec. when affl. the hyleg; ♂ prog. in ☌ the Asc. or M.C.; ♂ sole ruler at an eclipse of the ☉ tends to much fever everywhere; ♂ affl. in ♍ or ♏, and with ♂ in ☌ or ill-asp. the Asc. by dir.; ♂ in a fiery sign at B., and to the ☌ or ill-asp. the Asc. by dir.; ♂ to the ☌ or ill-asp. ♅ by dir.; ♂ afflicting the ☽ by dir.; ♂ to the ill-asps. his own place by dir., or to the ☉ or ☽; ♂ causes dangerous fevers when the dominion of death is vested in him, and he afflicts the hyleg at B., and by dir.; ♂ in ♐, ☌ or ill-asp. the ☉; ♂ in a fiery sign at decumb.; ♂ in a fiery sign in the 6th H., and under the Sun's beams at decumb. (Hor'y); ♂ and ♄ both the afflictors in the disease, and affl. the hyleg; ♂ in the 6th H. in ☌ the ☉; ♂ and the ☉ both being the afflictors at

the same time tend to both fever and inflammation, and to enlarge the scope of the disease; ♂ ☌ the ☉ at B. tends to fevers under the evil directions to the ☉ or ♂; ♂ promittor in ♒ and in ☌ or ill-asp. the ☉, has feverish distempers; the tr. of ♂ over the radical ☉ or ☽, or in ☍ to them; ♂ too much in evidence at B. tends to frequent attacks of fever; the evil directions of ♂ to the hyleg if ♂ is strongly affl. at B.; ♂ in ♐ in the 6th H., and affl.; ♂ in ♐ and affl. the ☽ or Asc.; ♂ affl. the hyleg at B., and by dir., and in a train of evil directions, denotes the danger of death by a high, pernicious, and violent fever, or by an accident; MERCURY Sig. ☌ ☉, and the ☉ ill-dig. at B.; the ASCENDANT a fiery sign; the Asc. to the place of the Pleiades, the Ascelli, or Capricornus; the Asc. to the place of Markab, and espec. to females; the Asc. affl. by ♂ at B., and by dir.; ♐ ascending at the Vernal Equi., and ♃ afflicted, afflicts Peoples with fevers who are born under ♐, and in Countries ruled by this sign, and likewise with People and Countries ruled by ♈ or ♌ when these signs are upon the Asc. at the Vernal, and their rulers, the ☉ and ♂, afflicted; ECLIPSES of the ☽ in ♏, or in fiery signs, tend to high and burning fevers, and espec. among People and Countries ruled by these signs, and with greater intensity if the central line of the eclipse be over them, and they come under its shadow; cardinal signs on the 6th H. at B. tend to frequent fevers; also cardinal signs in general show fevers; fiery signs upon the Asc. at B., people born under a fiery sign, or having the ☽ or lord of the Asc. in a fiery sign, are very subject to fevers and illnesses of a hot and dry nature; fire signs on the 6th H. at B.; many planets in fire signs at B.; fixed stars of the nature of the ☉ and ♂ ascending at B.; the Ascelli directed to the ☉, ☽, or Asc. (See "Patient Is Feverish", "Suffers from a Fever", in this section. Also note the various subjects and paragraphs in this Article).

Life Endangered — By Fever — (See Chronic, Constant, Dangerous, Hectic, High, Low, in this section).

Lingering Fevers—(See Chronic, Constant, Habitual, Hectic, Low, in this section).

Liver—(See "Fever" under Liver).

Lives Thru Fevers—The ♈ people, as a rule, live thru fevers where others succumb, as ♂, the ruler of ♈, gives them greater power to resist high fevers. (See Aries).

Long Fevers—(See Chronic, Constant, Continuous, Hectic, Low, in this section).

Low Fevers — Low and Persistent — Weakening—Apt to Prove Fatal If Not Checked, and the Vitality Raised—The ☽ hyleg, and to the ☌ or ill-asp. ♄ by dir.; ♄ occi. and affl. the hyleg by dir.; ♃ in perihelion, an epidemic of low fevers, and many deaths. (See Ague, Chronic Diseases, Consumptions, Perihelion, Phthisis, Tuberculosis, Wastings; Chronic, Constant, Continuous, Hectic, in this section).

Lungs—Lung Fever—Fever from Obstructions Near the Lungs and Heart—(See "Fever" under Heart; "Lung Fever" under Lungs; Pneumonia).

Malaria Fever—(See Ague, Intermittent, Malaria).

Malignant Fevers—(See Malignant).

Malta Fever—Mediterranean Fever—The fiery signs ♈, ♌, or ♐ ascending at the Vernal Equi., and with the ruler of the sign ascending afflicted, tend to this fever, as these signs rule the Peoples and Countries surrounding the Mediterranean, as England, France, Spain, and Italy. Also this fever is attended with Subs at CP and KP. (See Nations).

Melancholic Fevers — (See "Fevers" under Melancholy).

Miasma — (See "Corrupt Air" under Air; Germs, Miasma, Noxious).

Mild Fevers—(See Colds, Ephemeral. Also see Indiscretions, Slight, in this section).

Milk Fever—Fever In the Breasts—(See "Fever" under Breasts).

Mischievous Fevers—The ☉ affl. in ♌ at decumb. (See "High" in this section).

Mixed Fevers—☿ in a fiery sign at decumb. (See Variable, Various).

Moderation — Of Fever — (See "Curtailed" in this section).

Moisture—Fevers Arising From—(See "Cold and Dampness" in this section).

Mother — Fever to the Mother—(See "Slow Fevers" under Mother).

Mountain Fever—Rocky Mountain Fever—(See Mountain).

Nature—Of the Fever—Quality of—(See "Disease" under Nature; Type).

Neck — Glandular Fever In — (See "Neck" under Glands; "Mumps" under Parotid).

Non-Contagious — Simple — Those Arising from High Living, Excesses, Indiscretions, etc.—(See High Living, Indiscretions, Slight, in this section).

Noxious Air—Fevers Arising From—(See "Corrupt", "Obnoxious", under Air; Cholera, Epidemics, Miasma, Noxious, Pestilence).

Obstructions—Fevers Arising from Obstructions Near the Heart, Lungs, or Liver—(See "Fever" under Heart, Liver).

Ominous Fevers — (See "Portentous" in this section).

One Day Fevers—Brief—(See Ephemeral).

Parched Body — The Body Parched and Dry—(See "Dry Body", "Dry and Hot Body", "Dry and Hot Diseases", under Dry; "Dry and Hot Diseases" under Heat; Parched).

Parents — Fever Attacks the Parents —(See "Fever" under Father, Mother).

Patient Is Feverish—There Is Fever —The ☉ Sig. to the ☌ or ill-asp. ♂ by dir.; the ☽ in ♐ and affl. by the ☉ or ♂ when taken ill; the ☽ or ♃ in ♎, and affl. by the ☉ or ♂ when taken ill, and caused by too much blood (Hor'y). (See "Liable to Fever", "Suffers from a Fever", in this section).

Periodic Fevers—Returning At Regular Intervals — (See Intermittent, Malaria).

Periods of Fever—Periods and Times When Fever Is Apt To Come—(See "Periods" under Acute; "Periods" and "Time of the Disease", under Disease; Directions, Events; "Periods of Bad Health" under Health).

Pernicious Fevers—Fevers of a Vehement, Venomous Nature—♂ in the 6th H. at a decumb., and under the Sun's beams, and affl. the Sig. of the disease. (Hor'y). (See "High Fevers" in this section; "Destructive Processes" under Destructive).

Pestilential Fevers — (See "Corrupt Air" under Air; Cholera, Epidemics; "Fevers" under Pestilence, Plague).

Phthisis—The Hectic Fever of—(See "Hectic" in this section).

Pneumonia—Lung Fever—(See Pneumonia; "Lungs" in this section).

Portentous Fevers — Dreadful—Ominous—The ☽ conjoined with ♄, ♃, ♂, ♀, or ☿ in fiery signs at decumb., and when the ☉ is weak and afflicted also. (See High, Pernicious, in this section).

Precipitated—An Acute Fever Is Precipitated — (See "Precipitated" under Acute).

Prevalence of Fevers—♂ sole ruler at an eclipse of the ☉, much fever everywhere; ♂ in ♋ and lord of the year at the Vernal Equinox; an eclipse of the ☽ in the 1st Dec. of ♈; ☿ in ♊ in ☌ ♂ at the Vernal, and lord of the year; Comets appearing in ♍. (See "High" in this section; "Prevalent" under Acute).

Prognosis In Fevers — Depends upon the motion of the ☽ thru the Signs, and the aspects and planets which may interfere with the course of the disease. (See Prognosis; Chronic, Curtailed, Death, High, Low, Mild, and the various paragraphs in this section).

Protracted Fevers — (See Chronic, Constant, Continuous, Hectic, Low, in this section).

Puerperal Fever — Childbed Fever — (See Puerperal).

Putrid Fevers—(See "Fevers" under Putrid).

Quality — Of the Fever — (See "Nature", and the various paragraphs in this section).

Quartan Ague—(See Ague, Intermittent, Quartan).

Quarternaries—(See Quartan).

Quotidian — Intermittent — A Daily Paroxysm—(See Intermittent, Malaria, Quotidian).

Rapid Extremes — Of Temperature — (See "Extremes" in this section).

Relapsing Fevers—The Sig. of the disease in a double-bodied sign at decumb.; Subs at CP and KP. (See Course; "Worse" under Crises; Relapses; Chronic, Constant, Continuous, Increased, Intermittent, Irregular, Remittent, Worse, in this section).

Remedies — (See "Treatment" in this section).

Remission Of—(See Remission).

Remittent Fevers — Abating and Returning—Intervals of Ease—(See Ease, Intermittent, Irregular, Malaria, Quotidian, in this section; Remittent).

Resists Fever—♈ people. (See "Lives Thru Fevers" in this section).

Returning Fever — (See Intermittent, Remittent, in this section).

Rheumatic Fever — (See Dengue; "Fever" under Rheumatism).

Rocky Mountain Fever — (See Mountain).

Runs High—The Fever Runs High—Hyperpyrexia — Burning Fever — (See "High" in this section).

Sanguinary Fevers—(See Sanguinary; "Blood" in this section).

Scarlet Fever—(See Scarlet).

Semi-Tertian Fevers—(See Ague, Intermittent, Quartan, Semi-Tertian).

Septic Fevers—(See Septic).

Sharp Fevers—Fierce — High—Burning—(See "High" in this section).

Short Fevers — (See Acute, Brief, Slight, in this section).

Shortened — The Fever Shortened — (See "Curtailed" in this section).

Simple Fevers — (See "Non-Contagious" in this section).

Slight Fevers—Small Fevers—Brief—Mild — Non-Contagious — Ephemeral — The ☉ affl. by ♀, thru Excesses or Indiscretions; the ☽ ☌ ♂ in the Asc., and ♄ ruler of the 6th H. when taken ill (Hor'y); the ☽ in ♍ and affl. by the ☉ or ♂ when taken ill (Hor'y); the ☽ in ♊, □ or ☍ ♄ (or ☿ if he be of the nature of ♄) at the beginning of an illness, or at decumb. (Hor'y). (See Colds, Ephemeral, Indiscretions, Indisposition, Mild, Minor, Slight).

Slow Fevers—(See Chronic, Constant, Hectic, Low, Mother, in this section; Slow, Tedious).

Small Fevers—(See "Slight" in this section).

Spotted Fever—(See Spotted).

Spread of Fever—(See "Corrupt Air" under Air; Cholera, Contagious, Epidemics, Infectious, Miasma, Noxious, Pestilence, Plague, etc.).

Stomach — Fever In — (See "Fever" under Stomach).

Subnormal Temperature — (See "Subnormal" under Temperature).

Sudden Fever — Denoted and caused by fixed stars of the nature of ♂.

Suffers from a Fever — Suffers Hot Complaints—Is Feverish—The ☽ in ♐, and affl. by the ☉ or ♂ when taken ill (Hor'y); the ☽ in ♐, ☌ or ill-asp. ♄ (or ☿ if he be of the nature of ♄) when taken ill (Hor'y); ♂ in a fiery sign when ♂ is the afflictor in the disease; ♂ ruler of the 8th H., or in the 8th, and affl. the cusp of 8th, danger of fever in Hor'y Q.; ♂ in fiery signs and to the ☌ or ill-asps. the Asc. by dir. (See "Liable To", "Patient Is Feverish", in this section).

Surfeits—Fevers Arising From—(See "Fever" under Heart; Surfeits).

Susceptibility—To Fever Increased—

The ☉ ☌ or ill-asp. ♂ at B., and by dir.

Swift Fevers — (See "High" in this section; "Swift Diseases" under Swift).

Synocha — (See "Continuous" in this section).

Temperature — High — Increase of — Low—Subnormal—etc.—(See Temperature; High, Increased, Low, and the various paragraphs in this section).

Tendency—To Fevers — (See "Liable To" in this section).

Tertian Fevers—(See "Tertian" under Ague; Intermittent).

There Is Fever — (See "Patient Is Feverish", "Suffers from a Fever", in this section).

Thighs—Fever and Hot Diseases In—(See "Hot Humours" under Hips; "Feverish" under Thighs).

Threatened — Fever Is Threatened — (See "Liable To" in this section).

Too Much Blood — Fevers Arising From—(See "Blood", "Patient Is Feverish", in this section).

Travel—(See "Fevers" under Travel).

Treatment of Fevers—The drugs and remedies of ♄ combat fevers, as Aconite, Tincture Saturnina. Lead, etc. Blue color, and blue flowers, ruled by ♃, tend to allay fevers. Also cold, ruled by ♄, as by cold applications, ice, snow, etc., combat the fever. (See Aconite, Antipathy, Cold, Lead; "Drugs" "Herbs", "Remedies", under Saturn; Treatment; "Hectic" in this section).

Typhoid Fever—(See Typhoid).

Typhus Fever—(See Typhus).

Variable Fevers—Irregular — (See "Irregular" in this section).

Various Kinds of Fever—Subject To —Various Course In Fevers—(See Generally, Irregular, in this section).

Vehement Fevers — (See High, Pernicious, in this section; Vehement).

Violent Fevers — High — Dangerous— The ☉ directed to all Nebulous Clusters, and to Castor, Pollux, or the Ascelli; the ☽ to the Ascelli, Pleiades, or Praesepe; the Asc. to the □ or ☍ ♂ by dir.; the Ascelli directed to the ☉, ☽, or Asc. (See High, Pernicious, in this section; "High Pulse" under Pulse; Vehement, Violent).

Virus—The Pestilential Virus—(See "Virus" under Pestilence).

Vitiated Air — Fevers Spread By — (See "Corrupt Air" under Air; Contagions, Epidemics, Miasma, Noxious, Pestilence).

Voyages—Fevers On—(See "Fevers" under Voyages).

Whole Body—The Fever Is Thru the Whole Body — (See "Entire Body" in this section).

Women—Fevers To—Death by Fevers — (See "Females" in this section; Chills; "Death" under Women).

Worse — The Fever Turns for the Worse — (See Chronic, Flux, Hectic, Increased, Prognosis, in this section; Worse).

Yellow Fever—(See Yellow).

Youth—Fevers In Childhood and Youth — (See "Fevers" under Childhood).

Zymotic Fevers — Fevers from Fermentation — (See Dengue, Fermentation, Zymosis).

FIANCE—Fiancee—

Death Of — An Ancient Aphorism in Hor'y Q. is if the ☽ be in the first 12 degrees of ♑ when engagement is made, the fiance, or fiancee, usually dies before the marriage, or within six months after marriage. (See "Death" under Husband, Marriage Partner, Wife).

Sickness Of—(See "Ill-Health" under Husband, Marriage Partner, Wife). The same rules usually apply to the Fiance, or Fiancee, as to Husband or Wife, for when Engagement results, the parties come under the 7th H. influences of each other's maps, the same as if marriage has taken place, and if marriage is delayed, any evil directions coming to a climax in either map, as related to death, sickness, or accident to either party, usually take place when the event is scheduled unless forewarned, and care is taken to forestall it.

FIBER—Fibre—Fibrous—Fibrinous—Fibrosis—Fibrin—Fibro—The Fibro-Ligamentous System—Elastic Fiber—Fibroid—Fibroma—etc.—The building of Fibrous Tissue is the work of ♂, and takes part in the building of the Tendons, Sinews, Ligaments, etc. Elastic Fiber is connected with the ♋ sign, and Calcium Fluoride, the ♋ sign Tissue Salt. The Fibrin of the Blood is ruled by ♃, ♂, and the ♓ sign. The Fibro-Ligamentous System is under the rule of the ♍ and ♓ signs, and the ☉ and ☽ acting thru the ♓ sign affect the Fibro-Ligamentous System, and give way to the Thoracic Diathesis. Also by acting thru ♍, Fibro-Ligamentous affections are caused, and accompanied by Gout in the feet (Podagra). Fibrous tissue is crystallized and hardened by ♄. The density of connecting fiber is increased when ♂ is with ♃. The Nerve Fibers, ruled by ♅, are also under the internal rulership of the ♍ sign. The anterior lobe of the Pituitary Body, ruled by ♅, also influences the nerve fibers. The nerve fibers of the bowels are ruled over, and influenced by ☿, and espec. when ☿ is in ♍.

Degeneration—Fibrous Degeneration —♂ influence at B., overlaid and intermixed with other planets, as ♆, ♅, or ♄.

Exudation—Fibrinous Exudation—♂ ☌ or ill-asp. ♃.

Fibroma—Fibroid Tumor—♂ ☌ or ill-asp. ♀ or ☿. (See "Fibroid" under Womb).

Fibrosis—♄ influence; ♄ in ♊ tends to the development of fibrous tissue in the lungs, and likewise in other organs according to the sign position of ♄ at B.

Filaments—(See Filaments).

Hardening—Crystallization of Fibrous Tissue—The work of ♄.

Laxity—Of Fiber—A ♀ disease. (See Relaxation).

Nerve Fibroma—(See Neuroma).

Phthisis — Fibroid Phthisis In Lungs —(See "Pulmonary" under Phthisis).

Tonic Fibers — Over-Braced Tonic Fibers—A ♂ disease. (See Tonic).

Tumors—Fibro-Cartilaginous Tumor —(See "Chondroma" under Cartilage; "Fibroid" in this section and under Womb). See Connective, Ligaments, Muscles, Sinews, Tendons, Tissues).

FIBULA—The Small Outer Bone of the Leg—Is under the structural rulership of the ♒ sign, and is opposite to, and corresponds to the Ulna in the arm, ruled by ♌. The Fibula is also ruled by the 11th H.

Disorders Of — Afflictions in ♒; Subs at LPP, the 4, 5L.

Fracture Of—♂ affl. in ♒. (See "Fracture" under Legs). See Arms, Radius, Ulna.

FIERCE — Ferocious —Savage—Cruel—Violent—A ♂ characteristic. (See Anger; "Dogs" under Children; Cruel, Evil, Ferocious, Savage, Wild).

Fierce Fevers — (See "High" under Fevers).

Fierce Maladies — Caused by ♂ afflictions at B., and by dir., to the ☉, ☽, Asc., or hyleg; also caused by the ☉. (See Acute, Dangerous; "High" under Fever; Fulminating, Grievous, Painful, Pernicious, Poignant, Quick, Rapid, Serious, Sharp, Sudden, Swift, Vehement, Violent).

FIERY—Characteristic of the ☉ and ♂.

Diseases—Hot and Fiery Diseases—Caused by ♂. (See Fever, Heat).

Eyes—The Eyes Red and Fiery—(See "Fiery" under Eyes).

Fiery Signs — Of the Zodiac — (See "Fire Signs" under Fire).

Fiery Temperament—(See Choleric).

Hair — Fiery Red Hair — (See "Red Hair" under Hair).

FIFTH HOUSE—This is a masculine house, and is closely affiliated with the ☉, the ♌ and ♒ signs, and the 11th H. It is principally the house of children, the creative powers, and along with its opposite house, the 11th H., denotes the state and welfare of children. Fruitful signs and planets here denote many children, and barren signs and planets here tend to deny children, give but few, or cause their early death. The ☽ and the benefics here, well-aspected, denote healthy, strong, fortunate, and long-lived children. The malefics ♄ and ♂ here denote evil, sickly children, or misfortune to or by them. This is also the house of women, the state of woman with child, and parturition. This house rules the back, heart, sides, hind part of the shoulders, the liver, stomach; the appetites, and espec. along pleasurable and sexual lines; love affairs, courtship, the legitimate or illegitimate relations of the sexes before marriage; pleasures, amusements, places of amusement, theatres, music halls, taverns, games, recreations, and the accidents or injuries which may accompany such matters; rules matters of speculation in finance for gain or loss. Its Colors are black, white, mixed black and white, sanguine, and honey color. This house is also said to rule the Soul. (See Amorous, Amusements, Aquarius, Barrenness, Bastards, Children; "Creative Powers" under Creative; Eleventh House; "Free Love" under Free; Fruitful, Leo, Licentiousness, Love Affairs, Parturition, Passion, Pleasures, Recreations, Soul, Theatres, etc., and other subjects mentioned in this section).

FIG TREES—Fig Trees Corrupted—Eclipses of the ☉ or ☽ in ♈. (See Corruption, Fruit, Trees).

FIGHTING—Quarrels—Contests—Accidents, Injuries, or Death Thru—♄ to an ill-asp. ♂ by dir., and espec. if ♄ or ♂ be in the 1st, 7th, or 10th H. at B.; ♂ to the ill-asps. the ☉, ☽, ♀, or Asc. by dir.; lord of the 6th in the 7th, sickness from fighting. (See Anger, Contests, Cuts, Duels, Feuds, Mobs; "Murderous" under Murder; Quarrels, Rashness, Recklessness, Stabs, Sword, Vicious, Violence, Weapons, Women).

FIGURE—The Body—The Form, etc.— (See Appearance, Beautiful, Body, Build, Complexion, Crooked, Dark, Form, Handsome, Height, Ill-Formed, Light, Malformed, Misshaped, Size, Stature, Ugly, Weight, Well-Formed, etc., and note the references given under these subjects).

Figure of the Heavens—The Map of Birth—(See Map).

FILAMENTS—Thread-like Structures— The filaments making up the muscles are largely ruled and developed by ♂. The nerve filaments are under the rule of ☿. The development of the nerve filaments of the foetus is carried on by ☿. (See Fibers, Foetus, Muscles, Nerves).

FILM—Blindness by White Film—(See "Film" under Blindness).

FILTH—Filthy—

Body—Filthy and Unclean Body—♄ ♂ ♀; ♄ and ♂ in the Asc., and in ♋ the ☽ and ♀; the afflictions of ♄ tend to, due to deposit of, and retention of wastes; ♀ ♂ ☽ in ♎, and in ♋ ♂ in ♏. (See Cleansing, Deposits, Elimination, Excretions, Leprosy, Retentions, Uncleanly, Wastes).

Habits—Filthy In Talk and Behavior —Filthy In Habits and Deeds—♄ ♂ or ill-asp. ♀; the 17° ♑ on the Asc. (See Carelessness, Conduct; "Bad Habits" under Habits; Obscene, Profane, Uncleanly, Untidy, Vices).

Mind—Filthy Mind—Foul Minded—A ♄ characteristic; ♄ ♂ ♀. (See Immodest, Knavish, Morals, Obscene, Profane, Shameless, Vices, Wanton, Wicked).

FILTRATION — The Process of Straining or Filtering—

Cell Substances—Filtration of— (See "Substance" under Cells).

Kidneys—Filtration In—The ♎ sign rules filtration and distillation in the kidneys. (See Distillation).

Urine—Filtration of—Sublimation of —(See Distillation, Sublimation; "Filtration" under Urine).

FINANCE—(See Money, Poverty, Property, Prosperity, Riches, Wealth, etc.).

FINE—Excellent—Beautiful—Elegant, Clear, Handsome, etc.—

Body—Fine, Tall, Upright and Well-Made Body—♃ in ♐ in partile asp. the Asc. (See Tall, Upright, Well-Made).

Complexion—Fine Complexion—(See "Fine" under Complexion).

Constitution—Fine Constitution—(See "Good Constitution" under Constitution).

Eyes—Fine Eyes—Fine Blue Eyes— Fine and Clear — (See "Fine" under Eyes).

Forehead—Fine Forehead—(See Forehead).

Stature—Fine Stature—Finely Built —♃ ruler of the Asc., and ori. (See Beautiful, Commanding, Handsome, Well-Formed, Well-Proportioned; "Body" in this section).

FINGERS—The Fingers are ruled by ♊, ♍, and the 3rd H. The feet and toes are ruled by ♓, and the fingers, being the counterpart of the toes, are naturally ruled by ♍, the sign opposite to ♓. Subs at AP, the Arm Place in the Spine, tend to disorders, afflictions, infirmities, distortions, etc., of the fingers, due to lack of proper nerve supply to the fingers. Many influences which affect the Fingers are given under the subject of Hands. (See Hands. Also for comparisons, see Feet, Toes).

Ankylosis In—♄ affl. in ♊ or ♍, due to deposits, drying up of the joints, and solidification. Also caused by ♂ in ♊, or ☉ ♂ ♂ in ♊, due to excess heat and fusion of the joints. (See Ankylosis).

Athetosis—Incoordination—Inability to keep the fingers or toes in one position for very long at a time. ♅ affl. in ♊ or ♍; Subs at AT and AP. (See "Athetosis" under Toes).

Broad Fingers—Broad, Thick and Short—♉ influence; ♉ on Asc., or the ☉ and many planets in ♉. (See Clubbed, Short, in this section).

Clubbed Fingers—Club Hands—♄ affl. in ♊ or ♍; Subs at AP, HP (2D), and KP. (See "Club Feet" under Feet).

Cold Fingers—(See "Raynaud" in this section).

Conical—Long and Slender—♍ on the Asc. (See "Long" in this section).

Cramps In—(See "Cramps" under Hands).

Diseases Of—Disorders of—Afflictions in ♊ or ♍; Subs at AT, AP, HP (2D), and KP. (See "Diseases" under Hands).

Distorted Fingers—♄ affl. in ♊ or ♍; Subs at AP (1D). (See Distortions; "Deformities" under Hands).

Felons—Inflammation About the Nails —♂ affl. in ♊; Subs at LCP (2D), AP (1D), HP (2D), KP. (See "Whitlows" in this section).

Fractures Of—♄ or ♂ affl. in ♊. (See "Fractures" under Hands).

Gout In—(See "Hands" under Gout).

Hands—Note the various paragraphs under "Hands", as such influences also tend to affect the Fingers. Also see Feet, Toes).

Horny Growths—Instead of Nails—♅ in ♊. (See Horny).

Humours In—The ☽ in ♍ and affl. by the ☉ or ♂ when taken ill (Hor'y).

Incoordination In — (See "Athetosis" in this section).

Joints—Inflamed—Swollen—Ankylosis of—(See "Ankylosis" in this section).

Long Fingers — (See "Long" under Hands).

Nails—Description of—Disorders of—(See Nails; "Felons", "Horny", in this section).

Numbness—(See "Raynaud" in this section).

Panaris—(See "Whitlows" in this section).

Phlegmonous Suppuration — (See "Whitlows" in this section).

Pointed Fingers — (See "Conical" in this section).

Raynaud's Disease — Coldness and Whiteness of the Nose, Fingers and Toes—Numbness — A Waxy Pallor of the Fingers and Toes—A ♄ disease; ♄ affl. in ♊, ♍, or ♓; afflictions in ♊ or ♎; Subs at AP (1D), and KP.

Slender Fingers—Long and Slender—☿ gives. (See "Long" under Hands).

Spasm Of—(See "Tetanus" in this section).

Suppuration—About the Nails—(See "Whitlows" in this section).

Tetanus—A Tetanic Spasm Affecting the Fingers and Toes—(See "Fingers" under Tetanus).

Thumb—The Thumb Nearly Cut Off—See Case, Chap. 13, page 97, in Daath's Medical Astrology.

Toes — (See the various paragraphs under Toes).

Waxy Pallor Of—(See "Raynaud" in this section).

White and Cold—(See "Raynaud" in this section).

Whitlows—Panaris—(See "Whitlows" under Toes).

Writer's Cramp — (See "Cramps" under Hands).

FIRE—Fires—Fire is governed by ♂. (See Combustion; "Operations" under Nature).

Abroad — Suffers Injury or Death by Fire Abroad — (See "Fire" under Abroad).

Accidents by Fire — Injury By — Wounds By—The ☉ to the ♂ or ill-asps. ♂ by dir.; the ☉ to the place of the Ascelli or Praesepe; the ☽ □ or 8 ♂ at B., and by dir.; ♂ elevated above, and affl. the Luminaries; the ill-asps. of ♂ by dir. to any of the Moderators, the ☉, ☽, Asc. or M.C.; the Asc. to the ♂ or ill-asp. ♂ by dir., and ♂ in a fiery sign at B.; malefics in the M.C., and ♂ holding dominion; ♈ on the Asc. (See "Death", "Injury", and the various paragraphs in this section).

Blindness By — By Burning — (See "Burning" under Blindness).

Burns — Burning — Searing Burns — Scalds—(See Burns; "Hot Liquids" under Heat; Scalds).

Danger by Fire—Prejudice by Fire—The ☉ hyleg, and to the ♂ or ill-asp. ♂ by dir., and espec. if ♂ be in a fiery sign at B.; the Prog. ☉ or ☽ to the ♂ or ill-asps. ♂, and the ☉ or ☽ hyleg at B.; the ☉ to the ♂ or P. Dec. the Ascelli by dir.; the ☉ at a Solar Rev. passing over the place of ♂ at B.; the ☽ to the ♂ or ill-asps. ♂ by dir.; ♄ in ♌ or ♐, ♂ or ill-asp. the Asc. by dir.; ♂ affl. in the 1st H.; ♂ to the ill-asps. his own place by dir.; the ♂ sign ♈ on the Asc. at B.; ♂ by Periodic Rev. to the ♂ or ill-asps. ♅; ♂ holding dominion, and elevated above the Lights, and affl. the hyleg; ♂ Sig. ♂ the ☉; the Asc. to the ♂ ☉, and the ☉ ♂ ♂; the Asc. to the place of the Ascelli or Capricornus; afflictions in ♐; fiery signs on the Asc. (See Accidents, Burns, Death, Injury, and the various paragraphs in this section).

Death by Fire—Danger of—The ☉ or ☽ to the ♂ or ill-asps. ♂ by dir., and espec. if ♂ be near the Ascelli, and affl. by ♄; the ☉ setting in ♌, near the Ascelli, afflicted by malefics, and the ☽ at the same time be affl. by ♂ and ♂ descending; the ☉ joined with the Ascelli; the ☉ in ♌ if other testimonies concur; the ☽ in ♌, and to the ♂ or ill-asps. ♂, with ♂ affl. by the ☉ or ♄, and ♂ near the place of the Bull's Eye; the ☽ to the ♂ or ill-asps. ♂ by dir., and espec. if ♂ be in ♌ near the Ascelli, and ill-asp. by the ☉ or ♄; the ☽ Sig. □ or 8 ♂; the ☽ Sig. □ or 8 ☉, and espec. if ♂ aspect the ☉; when the ☽ or Asc. are hyleg, the ☉ by his evil directions to them will assist to cause death by fire, as the ☉ acts like ♂ in this instance, and espec. when in ♌, and when other testimonies concur; ♂ in a fiery sign and in 8 the Asc. at B., and by dir., and espec. if near the Ascelli; ♂ affl. the hyleg by dir., and holding the dominion of death, and espec. when the radix indicates a violent death; ♂ Sig. ♂, □, or 8 ☉; ♂ ori. in ♉ or ♏, □ or 8 ☉, or ♂ occi. in ♉ or ♏ in □ or 8 ☽; ♂ causes death by; ♂ in the 7th H., □ or 8 ☉ or ☽, except he be in a four-footed sign. (See "Fire" under Abroad; "Death" under Burns; "Hot Liquids" under Heat; Incendiarism, Scalds; "Family" in this section).

Electricity—Injury or Death By—(See Electricity, Lightning, Shock).

Family—Loses His Family and Property In a Fire—Case—See "Leland", No. 813, in 1001 N.N. (See Home).

Fire Arms—Death or Injury By—(See Guns).

Fire and Energy — Are given to the Vitality by ♂. (See Energy).

Fire Signs—The Fiery Signs of the Zodiac—These signs are ♈, ♌, and ♐. They rule the head and face by ♈; the heart and back by ♌, and the hips and thighs by ♐. They give the Bilious, or Choleric Temperament. People born under these signs require more sunlight. The ☉ and ♂, the fiery planets, are closely affiliated with the Fire Signs. These signs are connected with the vital heat of the body, oxygen, and also rule the Spirit, and are known to give increased physical strength and vitality when rising on the Asc. They are the strongest signs for vitality when upon the Asc. at B., or the ☉ in them, but are not good signs for the ☽, as they are not in harmony with the nature of the ☽, as the ☽ is cold and watery by nature. The ☉ in a fire sign gives a strong constitution and vitality, with much Prana, or internal force, and great power to resist disease, but with the danger of excess of force. The ☽ in a fire sign tends to a hasty and excitable nature, and to impeded, retarded, prevented, slow and difficult functions, and espec. with females. The ☽ in ♈ tends to brain disorders; in ♌, palpitation of the heart, and in ♐, nervous debility due to too much haste and excitement in the life. When strong on the Asc. at B., or with many planets in them, these signs tend to fever, hot diseases, inflammation, diseases arising from choler; hectic fevers, eruptions, erysipelas, adhesions, fusions, and to cause injury or death by cuts, stabs, blows, gunshot wounds, fire, burns, lightning, etc. (See Aries, Choleric, Fevers, Imagination, Impulsive, Inflammation, Leo, Majority; "Operations" under Nature; Sagittarius, and the various subjects mentioned in this Article).

Fires—Conflagrations—Are governed by ♂, and happen to the individual when he is under ♂ afflictions and directions, and to a community when the ☽ is afflicted by ♂ or ♅. (For other causes of Fires see Family, Forest Fires, Great Fires, Home, Ships, Theatre, and the various paragraphs in this section).

Fires of Life—(See "Fires" under Life).

Forest Fires—An eclipse of the ☽ in ♈.

Great Fires—Injury and Loss of Life By—Eclipses of the ☉ or ☽ in fire signs, and occurring in regions under the rule of these signs, and which are under the shadow of the eclipse; ♄ lord of the year at the Vernal Equi., in ♒, and occi.; ♂ lord of the year at the Vernal, and in a fiery sign; Comets appearing in the ruling sign of a Country tend to great fires in such places. (For information concerning the causes of the great London Fire of 1866, see "Bull's Horns" under Bulls).

Heat—(See the various paragraphs under Burns, Heat).

Home—Accidents, Injury, or Death by Fire In the Home—(See Home).

Hurts by Fire—Wounds, Injury, or Accidents by Fire—(See Accidents, Injuries, in this section).

Incendiarism—Pyromania—(See Incendiarism).

Injury by Fire—Prejudice by Fire or Heat—The ☉ setting in ♌, and afflicted by malefics, and espec. if the ☉ be near the Ascelli; the ☉ or ☽ to the ☌ or ill-asps. ♂ by dir., and espec. when in fiery signs; the ☉ to the Ascelli or

Praesepe; ♂ holding dominion at B., elevated above the Lights, and affl. the hyleg; the ☽ passing the place of the radical ♂ at a Solar Rev.; ♂ Sig. ☌ the ☉ at B., or by dir.; ♂ afflicted in fiery signs and ☌ or ill-asp. the Asc. by dir.; in Hor'y Q., ♂ in the Asc., and a malefic planet with the lord of the 1st H.; the ill-asps. of ♂ by dir. to the ☉, ☽, Asc., or M.C.; afflictions in ♐; the 5° ♎ on the Asc. (See Accidents, Danger, Death, and the various paragraphs in this section).

Journeys—Fire On Short or Inland Journeys—Danger of Injury By—Malefics in the 3rd H., in a fiery sign, and affl. the ☉ or ☽. On Voyages these same conditions would prevail over the 9th H., the house of Foreign Travel. (See "Ships" in this section).

Killed—In a Fire—(See Death, Family, Music Hall, Theatres, in this section).

Life—The Fires of Life—(See "Fires" under Life).

Lightning—Death or Injury By—(See Lightning).

Liquids—Hot Liquids—Injuries By—(See "Hot Liquids" under Heat; Scalds).

Music Hall—Killed in a Fire In—Case —See "Lafayette", No. 812, in 1001 N.N. (See "Theater" in this section).

Prejudice by Fire—(See Danger, Injury, in this section).

Property Loss—By Fire—♂ affl. in the 4th H.; ♂ ☌ ♄ in the 10th or 4th H. (See "Family" in this section).

Pyromania—(See Incendiarism).

Scalds—(See "Hot Liquids" under Heat; Scalds).

Sea—Fire At Sea—(See "Ships" in this section; "Voyages" under Lightning).

Searing—(See "Burning" under Blindness; "Searing" under Burns).

Ships—Danger of Injury by Fire on Ships At Sea—Malefics in the 9th H. in fiery signs, and espec. ♂, and affl. the ☉ or ☽. There is danger of fire at Sea when a ship sails when ♂ is in the Asc., and affl. the ☽. (See Ships).

Short Journeys—Fire On, and Danger By—(See "Journeys" in this section).

Signs—The Fiery Signs of the Zodiac —(See "Fire Signs" in this section).

Spinal Spirit Fire—(See Azoth, Ether; "Canal" under Spine).

Theater Fire—188 Lives Lost In—See "Exeter", No. 717, in 1001 N.N. (See "Music Hall" in this section).

Violent Death—By Fire—(See "Death", and the various paragraphs in this section; "Death" under Violent).

Voyages—Dangers by Fire On—(See "Ships" in this section).

Wounds By—(See Accidents, Blindness, Burns, Injuries, and the various paragraphs in this section).

FIRST—

First-Born Child—(See "First-Born" under Children).

First House—The Ascendant—The Rising Sign—This is a masculine house, and corresponds to the ♈ Sign. This house is a vital center, or part, of the horoscope, and contains the dominant features of the Life that are to be expressed and worked out. The three vital centers of the map are the ☉, ☽, and Asc. This house signifies the nature, life and health of the native, and relates to all questions of life, health, external complaints, appearance, stature, shape, size, color, body blemishes, and also sickness and accidents. It becomes the Sig. in Hor'y Q. in all cases where the life and health are considered. It rules the form, constitution, the bodily temperament, the bodily stamina, animal heat, the health, the personality, general characteristics, and indicates the construction and peculiarities of the physical body; rules the head, eyes, and face. It signifies all matters which affect the physical body, the mind, sickness, travel, health, change of residence, birth or death of children, and the fortunes of the native in general, and has significance of the Life of Man. The physical appearance, description of the body, the strength and vitality of the body, the height, weight, color of the eyes and hair, etc., are largely determined by the sign and degree rising on the cusp of this house, or the Ascendant. The position of the ruler of the Asc., and planets rising, tend to modify the personal appearance. (See Decanates). The 1st H. rules light colors and white. The 1st H. shows the organic elements, the physiological factors, and the physical characteristics which determine the amount of organic resistance, and the strength of the body. It also shows the degree of receptivity to diseases, and which may affect the part of the body ruled by the sign rising. The Asc. denotes, according to the sign rising, the part of the body more liable to affliction from external causes, and is the Indicator of Disease. (See the Ascendant influences in the paragraph, "Arguments for Death" under Death). The benefics, ♃ and ♀, in the 1st H. at B. indicate a good constitution, and much vitality. The malefics in the Asc. at B. denote scars, marks, moles, and defects of the head and face. The 1st H. and its conditions at B., and by dir., signify all diseases in the head, face, eyes, ears, nose, mouth, and foul breath. This house is closely related to the Feelings, Sensations, the Emotions, the Passions, the Manners, the Disposition, the quality of the Mind, etc., according to the nature of the sign rising, signs intercepted in, or partly ruling the Asc. The planet ruling the sign on the Asc. at B. is considered the principal Ruling Planet of the horoscope. (For the nature and meaning of the different kinds of signs on the Asc. at B., see Fire, Air, Earth, Water Signs, under these subjects. Also see Cardinal, Fixed, Mutable, External; "Zodiac" under Degrees). The actual degree rising on the Asc. at B. is to be considered as though it were a planet in forming judgment of the native as to his mind, body, strength, diseases subject to, etc., and all aspects to this degree are to be noted. The degree on the Asc. governs the

brain, the body, and according to the sign rising gives a predisposition to certain afflictions and diseases of the body. Planets in the Asc., together with the planet ruling the rising sign, rule the physical body, and the sign and house position of the ruler of the Asc., the aspects to it, and the condition of its disposer, should be considered. The Asc. under certain conditions may become Hyleg. In a nocturnal horoscope the Asc. becomes hyleg if the ☽ is incr., with both the ☉ and ☽ below the horizon and not in a hylegiacal place. In a diurnal horoscope the Asc. may become hyleg if the ☉ or ☽ are not in a hylegiacal place. The Asc. may become Anareta when the ☽ is hyleg. In Mundane Astrology the 1st H., or the Asc., rules the Public Health generally. (See Anareta, Ascendant, Hyleg).

First Quarter—Of the ☽—(See "First Quarter" under Moon).

First Year—Of Life—(See Infancy).

FISH—Fishes—Fishes are ruled by the ♓ sign, which is known as the sign of "The Fishes."

Death of Fish—In the Seas and Rivers —Death of Living Creatures In the Waters—Afflictions in ♋, and espec. in the rivers, as ♋ rules rivers; afflictions in ♓ tend to destroy life in the Seas; ♄ in ♋ or ♓, ℞, lord of the year at the Vernal Equi., and affl. by ♂; ♃ in ♓, lord of the year at the Vernal, and affl. by ♄ or ♂; ♂ in ♓ and lord of the year at the Vernal; ♂ in ♌, occi., and lord of the year at the Vernal; Eclipses of the ☉ or ☽ in ♍ or ♓; an Eclipse of the ☉ in the 2nd Dec. of ♓; Comets appearing in ♋ or ♓. (See "Virus" under Pestilence).

Fishing—Fond of—(See Sports).

FISSURE—A Groove or Cleft—

Anus—Fissure of—(See Anus).

Lip—Harelip—A Congenital Fissure of the Lip—(See Harelip).

Palate—Cleft Palate—(See Palate).

Rectum—Fissure of—(See "Fissure" under Anus).

Spine—Cleft In—(See "Spina Bifida" under Spine). See Cleft, Crevice, Excrescences, Fistula, Hemorrhoids.

FISTULA—Fistulous Tumor—Fistula Near the Anus—A ♄, ♂, and ♀ disease; a ♉, ♏, ♐ disease; caused by afflictions in ♏ or ♐; caused by afflictions in ♉ by reflex action, and with ♉ or ♏ on the Asc.; the ☉ affl. in ♏ or ♐; the ☉ in ♐, ☍ or ill-asp. any of the malefics as promittors; the ☽ in ♏, ☍ or ill-asp. ♄ (or ☿ if he be of the nature of ♄) at the beginning of an illness or at decumb.; ♄ or ♂ in the Asc. or M.C., in ♋, ♑, or ♓, and in signs ascribed to animals or fishes; ♄ in ♏, occi., and affl. the ☉, ☽, or Asc.; ♃ affl. in ♏; a ♂ disease; ♂ in an angle, occi. of the ☉ and ori. of the ☽; ♂ in ♏ and affl. the ☽ or Asc.; ♂ in ♏ in the 6th H.; ♂ influence overlaid and intermixed with other planets, and espec. with the malefics; a ♀ disease, and afflictions to ♀; caused by ♀ when the dominion of death is vested in her; the malefics angular in ♋, ♏, or ♓, or in signs ascribed to animals or fishes; the Asc. to the □ or ☍ ♄ by dir.; Subs at PP, LPP. (See Anus, Discharges, Hemorrhoids, Rectum).

Buttocks—Fistulous Tumors In—(See Buttocks).

Death from Fistula—♀ affl. the hyleg by dir.; ♀ badly affl. at B., and holding the dominion of death.

Thighs—Fistulous Tumors In—A ♐ disease, and afflictions in ♐. (See Thighs, Tumors).

FITS—Convulsions—Convulsive Fits or Spasms—A Sudden Paroxysm—

Causes—Liable To—Tendency To—Fits, or Convulsions are a disease of ♓, ♀, the ☽, and of the ♈, ♋, and ♌ signs; the ☉ or ☽ hyleg, ♂ or ill-asp. ♄ or ♂, and the hyleg much affl. at B.; the ☽ hyleg in ♈ or ♌, and afflicted, and espec. in females; the ☽ to the ♂ or ill-asps. ♂ by dir., and espec. in children, and may result in death; the ☽ and ♀ receiving the evil rays from ♓ or ♄; the ☽ affl. in ♈, ♋, or ♌, and affl. the hyleg therefrom; afflictions to the ☽ at B., and espec. by ♓, ♀, or ♂; the ☽ and ♀ ♂ each other, or ♂ the Asc., and evilly aspected by ♄ or ♂ from angles, and espec. ♄ by day, or ♂ by night, liable to fits, but if ♂ by day, and ♄ by night, they are apt to be frantic or melancholic; ♄ angular, holding dominion, elevated above the Luminaries, and affl. the hyleg; ♄ or ♂ affl. the ☉ or ♀ in common signs; a ♀ disease; ♀ much affl. at B., and by dir.; ♀ affl. in ♌; ♀ affl. by ♄ or ♓; ♀ in a common sign and affl. by ♄ or ♂; malefics in the M.C., elevated above the Lights, and ♄ holding dominion; a preponderance of planets in fixed signs. (See Convulsions. Also note the various paragraphs in this section).

Children—Fits In—(See Causes, Dentition, Spasms, in this section).

Convulsions—(See Convulsions; "Causes" in this section).

Convulsive Movements—(See "Movements" under Convulsions).

Curable Fits—If ♃ or ♀ be ori., or in angles, and have any configuration with the ☽ at B., the disease is curable; if the ☽ is with ♃ the disease can be cured by medicine; if the ☽ is with ♀ it will cure itself; if the benefics are cadent or occi., and the malefics ori., they will be incurable. (See Curable; "Curable" under Epilepsy; Incurable).

Death by Fits—By Convulsions—By Spasms—♃ affl. the hyleg by dir., and ♃ much affl. at B.; ♂ in ♉ near Caput Algol, or in ♏ in ☍ to Algol, and at the same time in □ or ☍ the ☉ or ☽; cardinal signs show death by fits; mutable signs death by spasms. (See "Causes" in this section; "Death" under Epilepsy).

Dentition—Fits During—(See "Dentition" under Teeth).

Drink—Fits of Drink and Sensuality —(See "Fits" under Drink; Sensuality).

Epilepsy—Eclampsia—Constant Fits In—(See "Constant" under Epilepsy).

Falling Fits—Falling Sickness—Fainting—(See "Falling Fits" under Fainting).

Females—Women—Fits In—(See Fainting, Hysteria).

Frantic—(See "Causes" in this section; Frantic).

Fury—Alternate Fits of Fury and Melancholy—(See "Fits" under Fury; Madness, Mania, Raving).

Hysterical Fits—(See Hysteria).

Incurable Fits—(See "Curable" in this section).

Liable to Fits—(See "Causes" in this section).

Long Standing—Fits of Long Standing—A ☽ disease and affliction; the ☽ hyleg and affl. by malefics.

Mania—Fits of—(See "Fits" under Mania).

Melancholic Fits—The combined influence of ♄ and ♂ induces to alternate fits of melancholy and fury. (See Fury, Melancholy; "Causes" in this section).

Nervous Affections—Fits of—Are more frequent toward the New and Full Moon. (See Nerves; "Full Moon", "New Moon", under Moon).

Obsessions—Fits of—(See "Fits" under Obsessions).

Sensuality—Fits of—(See "Drink" in this section).

Spasms—(See Convulsions, Epilepsy; "Spasms" under Spasmodic; "Dentition" under Teeth; Causes, Death, in this section).

Strong Fits—The ☽ in ♌ and affl. by the ☉ or ♂ when taken ill (Hor'y).

Swooning Fits—(See Fainting). See Contractions, Delirium, Eclampsia, Erratic, Insanity, Paroxysms.

FIXED—

Fixed Habits—Fixed Opinions—Not Given to Changes—Many planets in Fixed Signs at B.; fixed signs on the angles; ♄ a strong ruler at B.; good asps. of ♄ to the ☉, ☽, and ♀. (See Habits, Opinions).

Fixed Ideas—(See "Anxiety Neuroses" under Anxiety; Ideals, Ideas, Judgment, Monomania, Notions, Opinions).

Fixed Signs—The Strong Signs—Constitutional Signs—Foundation Signs—The Earthquake or Seismic Signs—The four Fixed Signs are ♉, ♌, ♏, and ♒, and are ruled by ♀, the ☉, ♂, and ♄ respectively. These four signs form the Fixed Cross, and are all in □ or ☍ asp. to each other, and planets in any one of them tend to affect all the other parts under the rule of the fixed signs. The Fixed Signs correspond to the Succedent Houses. Fundamentally these signs rule the vital parts, as the throat, heart, blood, and the generative system, and all parts or organs under their rule, such as the vocal organs, nose, neck, trunk, sex organs, urinary organs, bladder, excretory system, rectum, urethra, the legs below the knees, as the calves and ankles. The fixed signs give general strength of constitution, endurance, patience of mind, and are thus called the Strong,

or Foundation Signs. They are more
robust than the cardinal and common
signs. They tend to arouse the Desire
Nature, and to give stamina and persistence in action. They relate to Feeling and Emotion; are Vital in Temperament, and correspond to the Heart
and Life. The Fixed Signs are also
called "The Vicious Circle" because of
their fixed and unyielding nature.
Fixed Sign people are strongly bound
by their habits, and are difficult to
change or influence, and when a disease gets a firm hold upon them they
usually die of it, but tend to cooperate with the Healer, and try to get
well. Afflictions from fixed signs tend
to cause deep-seated, lingering, tedious,
chronic, and permanent diseases, and
more difficult to cure or remedy. Many
planets in fixed signs at B. tend to
give greater resistance to disease, but
to prolong disease, and give less power
to throw off disease when it once
gets a deep hold on the system. A list
of the diseases ruled and given by the
fixed signs is given under these signs,
and for which see "Diseases Ruled By"
under Taurus, Leo, Scorpio, Aquarius.
Their principle diseases are those of
the throat, heart, blood, sex organs,
and lower limbs, as in the calves and
ankles. (See "Disease" under Nature).
The ♒ sign espec. rules the blood, and
afflictions in ♒ tend to blood disorders,
impure blood, disturbed circulation,
etc. These signs also rule strongly
over bronchitis, spinal complaints, suffocation, diseases of the back, diphtheria, stone, gravel, bladder troubles,
disorders of the excretory system, etc.
The throat (♉), and the sex organs
(♏) are closely related by opposite
signs, and the removal of any part of
the sex organs tends to affect the
voice, and in women tends to a masculine voice, and in men to an effeminate voice. Removal of the tonsils in
childhood tends to make the puberty
period more disturbed, and also later
childhood and parturition more difficult and painful. Afflictions in these
signs at B. tend to hereditary and
organic diseases. Saturn in a fixed
sign at B., or at the begnning of a disease, tends to be a sore afflictor. On
the angles, and espec. on the Asc., they
tend to lessen the chances of Insanity,
and make the native better able to resist trouble, and protect the mind under stress, but when once disturbed in
mind or health, the fixed signs on the
angles make equipoise more difficult.
The Fixed Signs show death by drowning, suffocation, strangling, hanging;
by blood disorders, throat and heart
trouble, disorders of the Generative
System, the Excretory and Urinary
Systems. Afflictions in fixed signs
make punishment by Law, or sentence
of a Judge, more durable, and espec.
when the radical map denotes the
danger of imprisonment. Much can be
said about the fixed signs, and their
influences are much referred to
throughout this Work. Here are two
cases of individuals who had a Stellium of planets in the Fixed Signs at
B. See "Male", Chap. 8, page 48, and
"Female", page 49, in Daath's Medical
Astrology. One was a Monster, and

the other a Dwarf and Imbecile. For
further study along this line see
Ankles, Back, Blood, Bronchitis,
Calves, Chronic, Circulation, Constancy,
Constitution, Continuity, Decanates,
Deep-Seated, Diphtheria, Drowning;
Duration; "Earthquakes" under Earth;
Emotions, Endurance, Excretion, Feel-
ings, Generation, Gravel, Habits,
Hanging; "Fixity" under Head;
Healers, Heart, Heredity, Imprison-
ment (see Prison); Incurable, Insan-
ity, Invalids, Judges, Lingering, Long;
"Monomania" under Mania; Neck;
"Negative Signs" under Negative;
Nose, Organic, Patience, Perseverance,
Prejudice, Prison, Puberty; "Changes"
under Residence; Sex Organs, Slow,
Spine, Stone, Strangulation, Structural,
Suffocation, Suicide, Tedious, Throat,
Tonsils, Trunk, Voice, Wastings, etc.

Fixed Stars — Constellations — (See
Stars).

FLABBY — Soft — Flaccid — Relaxed — A
☽ influence and disease. A weak ♂ at
B. tends to flaccidity of the muscles;
♓ on the Asc.; ♓ gives flabby skin.
(See Collapse, Consumptions, Emaciation, Laxity, Muscles, Puffing, Relaxation, Soft, Tissues, Wasting).

FLANKS — The Iliac Region — Ruled by
♏. All diseases in the Flanks are signified by the 7th H., and caused by
afflictions in 7th H., and also in ♏.
(See Iliac, Sides).

FLAT — Flatter — Flattened —

Face — The Face Flatter at the Sides
— (See Decanates).

Feet — Flat Feet — (See "Splay Foot"
under Feet).

Head — The Head Flatter On the Sides,
and Square-Shaped — (See Decanates).

FLATULENCE — Gas In the Digestive
Canal — Wind — Borborygmus — Colic —
Gas — Bloating — Distentions — Infla-
tions — Tympanies, etc. —

Bilious Flatulency — (See Bilious).

Bloating — (See "Stomach" under Gas;
"Distended" under Stomach; "Bowels"
under Wind).

Bowels — Flatulence In — Colic —
Rumbling — (See "Borborygmus",
"Colic" under Bowels; "Bowels" under
Wind).

Colic — Flatulent Colic — (See "Colic"
under Bowels).

General Flatulence — A ☽, ♃, ☿, ♊, ♍,
♍, and ♒ affliction; ♃ tends to general
flatulence thru Plethora, from over-
eating, etc., and by wind in the blood
when ♃ is afflicted in ♉; ☿ affl. in the
airy signs ♊ or ♒ tends to general
flatulence by wind in the blood, veins,
etc. (See Bloating, Distentions, Gas,
Inflation, Puffing; "Puffy Body" under
Swellings; Tympanies; "Windiness"
under Veins; "Blood" under Wind).

Inflated Body — (See Inflation).

Stomach — Flatulence In — Gas In —
Bloating — ♄ in ♋. (See Belching;
"Stomach" under Gas; Gripings, In-
digestion, Inflation; "Distended",
"Wind", under Stomach; Tympanites,
Wind).

FLESH—The Flesh—Ruled by ♀. Also ruled and influenced by the earthy signs. (See "Earthy Signs" under Earth).

Loss of Flesh—(See Anaemia, Emaciation, Malnutrition, Thin, Wasting, Weight).

Much Flesh—Corpulent—(See Corpulent, Fleshy).

FLESHY—Corpulent—Stout—(See Corpulent; "Body" under Fat; Obesity, Portly, Stoutness).

Face — Fleshy Face — (See "Fleshy" under Face).

Feet—Fleshy Hands and Feet—(See "Fleshy" under Hands, Feet).

Fleshy Body — The ⊙ in ♉ or ♓, in partile asp. the Asc., short and fleshy; the ⊙ in ♏, partile the Asc., square and fleshy body; the ⊙ ☌ ♀ in ♓, fleshy after middle life; the ⊙ strong at B., and dignified, fleshy, strong, tall, and of large frame; the ☽ Sig. of the party, short and fleshy; the ☽ in ♈, partile the Asc., middle sized, but rather plump and fleshy; the ☽ in ♋, partile the Asc., fleshy, middle sized, and well-proportioned; the ☽ in ♋, Sig. of the party, and in no asp. to the ⊙ or ♂, indicates a short and fleshy person in Hor'y Q.; the ☽ in ♏, partile the Asc., a fleshy, short, thick, and ill-made body; ♄ in S. Lat. tends to a fleshy, smooth body, but in N. Lat. to one more hairy, lean, and raw-boned; ♃ in ♋, partile the Asc., fleshy but disproportioned; ♃ in ♏ or ♓, partile the Asc., middle-sized, full, and fleshy; ♂ in ♓, partile the Asc., fleshy, mean and short body; ♂ Sig. in ♓, short and fleshy; ♀ in ♉, partile the Asc., fleshy but well-made; ♀ in ♓, partile the Asc., middle-sized, but rather plump and fleshy; ♀ in ♒, partile the Asc., middle-sized and fleshy; the first half of ♈ when on the Asc. gives more flesh; ♉ on the Asc., or the ⊙ in ♉, short, stocky and fleshy; born under ♉ or ♓, fleshy after middle life; ♋ on the Asc., short and fleshy; the first parts of ♋ or ♑ ascending make the body more fleshy than the latter parts; ♏ on the Asc., fleshy and thick body; the latter part of ♐ on the Asc. tends to a fleshy body; ♓ on the Asc., a pale, sickly, short and fleshy body; water signs on the Asc. (See Bulky, Corpulent, Fat, Full, Phlegmatic, Plump, Puffing, Squat, Stout; "Fleshy" under Swellings; Thick).

Growths — A Small Fleshy Growth— (See Caruncle, Growths. See "Tumor" in this section).

Hands—Fleshy Hands and Feet—(See "Fleshy" under Hands, Feet).

Tumors—Fleshy Tumors—(See Caruncle, Sarcoma).

FLEXED—Flexible—Flexion—Flexure —Pliable—

Flexed Signs — (See "Mutable Signs" under Mutable).

Flexible Mind—A Plastic Mind—More Easily Influenced — Changeable — (See Changes, Environment, External, Influenced, Mutable, Negative; "Many Changes" under Residence; Restless, Susceptible, Unstable, Vacillating).

Flexion—Bending—The flexion, bending, falling, or prolapsus of organs is a ♄ influence, and due to a weakening of the part. (See Bending; "Flexion" under Womb).

Hepatic Flexure—(See Liver).

Sigmoid Flexure—(See Sigmoid).

Splenic Flexure—(See Spleen).

FLIGHTINESS—Flightiness of the Mind —Flight of Ideas—Flighty—A ♅, ♅, ♂, and ♀ affl. in ♓; ♃ or ♂ affl. in ♈, and due to a rush of blood to the head. (See "Mental Chaos" under Chaotic; Concentration, Confusion; "Dreamy Mind" under Dreams; "Blood" under Head; Ideas, Imagination; "Absent Minded" under Mind; Obsessions, Scattering, Vacillating, Weird, etc.).

FLOODING — Flooding Hemorrhage — (See "Flooding", "Hemophilia", under Hemorrhage; "Flooding" under Menses; "Epistaxis" under Nose; "Hemorrhage" under Womb).

FLOODS—Inundations—Violent Rains —Deluges—Great Suffering or Loss of Life From—An eclipse of the ⊙ or ☽ in watery signs, and espec. in places ruled by such signs; the ♏ sign ascending at the Vernal E., floods and afflictions by venomous creatures. (See "Epidemics" under Cholera; Clouds, Famine, Moisture, Rain, Storms, Tempests, Thunder, Venomous, Waters, Weather; "Storms" under Wind).

FLOW—

Flow of Blood—♂ has to do with all injuries attended by a flow of blood. (See "Flow of Blood" under Blood).

Head—Flow, or Rush of Blood to the Head — (See Determination; "Blood" under Head; Rush).

Humours — Flow of Humours — (See Discharges, Defluxions, Fluxions; "Flow" under Humours).

Overflowing—(See Flooding, Overflowing).

FLOWERS—(See Herbs, Plants, Vegetation).

FLUIDS — The Fluidic System — The Liquid Secretions or Excretions of the Body — Humours — The Fluids of the system are ruled by ♅, the ☽, and the watery signs. The ☽ exerts a strong fluidic influence over fluids in the system, or anywhere in Nature, as over the Tides, Rivers, Water, etc. The ☽ is fluidic and cleansing, and tends to mutations and changes in the body by acting thru the fluids. The ☽ rules or dominates all fluids, yet her real dominion is over the neutral solution, the basic or bland humor which forms the medium thru which certain substances can act and react, and put into the forms necessary for the various functions of the body. Thus in milk the ☽ rules the basic fluid, but other ingredients are developed in milk by the action of the ⊙, ♃, and ♄. (See Milk). The ☽ rules the base of any fluid, and not fluids as a whole, in specialized forms, resulting from the action of other influences, agents or reagents. The watery signs are especially connected with fluids. For the different fluids ruled by the watery signs see Cancer, Scorpio, Pisces. Also the fluids of the body are ruled over and controlled by the posterior lobe of the Pituitary Body, ruled by ♅, and espec. the circulation of the fluids in the kidneys. The following subjects have to do with the various fluids, juices, secretions, and excretions of the body, which see in the alphabetical arrangement when not considered here—

Abdomen—Fluids of—(See Abdomen, Bowels).

Accumulations In — The afflictions of ♃ cause accumulations in the fluids themselves. (See Accumulative).

Acids—(See Acids).

Ailments Of—Disorders and Disturbances of the Fluids of the Body—Irregularities of—Disturbed Circulation of—Fluidic Derangements—The ☉ affl. in the watery signs ♋, ♏, or ♓ tends to disorders of the fluidic system; the ☽ affl. by ♆; the ☽ hyleg in ♋, ♏, or ♓, and afflicted, and espec. in females; afflictions to the ☽); ☽ diseases; ♆ in ♓, and affl. the hyleg or Asc.; ♆ in ♓ in the 6th H.; ♄ tends to impede the circulation of the fluids; ♄ angular at B., holding dominion, and elevated above the Lights; ♄ or ☿ holding dominion at B., and in familiarity with each other, tend to disturbances of the fluids in the chest, stomach, and throat; ♄ in an angle, occi. of the ☉, and ori. of the ☽, and ♄ also be in familiarity with ☿; ♂ ☌ ♃ tends to increase the density of fluids in the body; ♓ on cusp the 6th H. (Note the various paragraphs in this Article).

Amniotic Fluid—(See Foetus).

Aqueous—(See "Aqueous Humor" under Eyes; "Aqueous Vapors" under Rain; "Aqueous" under Tumors).

Arterial Blood—(See Arteries, Blood, Circulation).

Bile—Gall—(See Bile).

Blood—(See Arteries, Blood, Circulation, Veins).

Bowels—Fluids of—(See the various paragraphs under Abdomen, Bowels).

Brain—Fluids and Secretions of—(See Brain, Cerebral, Meninges, Pineal, Pituitary, etc.).

Brashes—(See Brash).

Breasts — Fluids of — (See Breasts, Milk).

Bronchial Fluids—(See Bronchial, Coughs, Lungs, Mucus).

Capillaries; Catarrhs; Cavities; Cell Fluids—(See Cells).

Changes In—(See "Mutation" in this section).

Chest — Fluids of — (See Bronchial, Chest, Lungs, Thorax; "Ailments" in this section).

Chyle; Chyme; Circulation—Of the Blood—Of the Fluids—Disorders of—(See Arteries, Blood, Circulation, Veins; "Ailments" in this section).

Collection of Fluids—In the System—(See Accumulative, Cavities, Congestion, Cysts, Humours, Receptacles, Serum, Swellings, Watery; "Accumulations" in this section).

Complaints—Fluidic Complaints—(See "Ailments", and the various paragraphs in this section).

Congestion—Of Fluids—(See Congestion).

Coryza—(See Nose).

Coughs; Crusts — Dried Exudate — (See Crusts).

Cysts; Deficiency Of — Lack of — Caused by ♄ afflictions. (See Deficient, Retarded, Stoppages, Suppressions).

Defluxions; Density Increased — (See "Ailments" in this section).

Depletion Of—Caused by ♄. (See Depletion, Diminished, Suppressed; Nerve, Vital, in this section).

Derangements Of—(See "Ailments" in this section; Deranged).

Digestive Fluids—(See Acids, Digestion, Gastric, Juices, Stomach).

Dilution Of—(See Diluted).

Discharges; Disorders Of—(See "Ailments", and the various paragraphs in this section).

Disturbances Of — (See "Ailments", and the various paragraphs in this section).

Dropsies; Drying Up—Of the Fluids—Caused by ♄, and are ♄ diseases. (See "Fluids" under Dryness).

Ebb and Tide—Of Fluids—(See "Full Moon", "New Moon", under Moon).

Effusions; Elimination; Emissions; Epistaxis—(See Nose).

Evacuations; Excessive—Excessive Secretion of—Excess of—(See the various paragraphs under Excess).

Excrementitious Fluids—(See Excrement).

Excretions; Exosmosis — (See Osmosis).

Expectorations; Exudations; Faeces; Fat—(See "Fluids" under Fat).

Females—Fluids In—(See "Ailments" in this section; Females, Menses).

Fermentation Of—(See Fermentation, Zymosis).

Flow Of—(See Flow).

Fluxions; Fullness Of—(See "Full Moon", "New Moon", under Moon).

Functions — (See the various paragraphs under Functions).

Gastric Fluids—(See Digestion, Gastric, Stomach).

Glands; Glycogen; Hemorrhages; High Blood Pressure — (See "Pressure" under Blood).

High Tide — Of Fluids — (See "Full Moon" under Moon).

Hindered — The Fluids Hindered — ♄ diseases and afflictions. (See Hindered, Retarded, Stoppages, Suppressions).

Hot Fluids — (See "Hot Liquids" under Heat).

Humours; Hydro; Hyperaemia; Impeded — (See Circulation, Impeded, Retarded, Secretions, Suppressions; "Ailments" in this section).

Increased — (See "Excessive" in this section).

Intercellular Fluids — (See "Fluids" under Cells).

Irregularities Of—(See "Ailments" in this section; Irregular).

Joints—Fluids of—(See Synovial).

Juices; Kidneys — Fluids of — (See Kidneys, Pituitary Body, Urine).

Lachrymal; Lack Of—(See Deficient, Depletion, Diminished, Lack; "Drying Up", and the various paragraphs in this section).

Lacteals—(See Milk).

Leucorrhoea; Liquids; Liver — Fluids and Secretions of—(See Liver).

Loss Of—(See "Lack" in this section).

Lymph; Membranes — Fluids and Secretions of—(See Membranes).

Menses; Milk; Moon—The Moon and Fluids — (See the various paragraphs under Moon).

Morbid Fluids—Morbid Oozing—(See Exudations, Morbid, Osmosis).

Mouth; Muscae Volitantes — Floating Specks—(See "Muscae" under Eyes).

Mucus; Mutation Of—The physiological action of the ☽. (See "Physiological Action" under Moon).

Nerve Fluids — (See "Nerve Fluids" under Depletion; "Fluids" under Nerves).

Nose — Fluids of — (See the various paragraphs under Nose).

Obesity; Obstructions Of—Caused by ♄. (See Deposits, Obstructions, Secretions, Stoppages, Suppressions; "White Fluids" in this section).

Oedema; Oils; Oozing — (See Exudations, Osmosis).

Osmosis; Pancreas—Diastase of—(See Pancreas).

Peritoneum — Serum of — (See Peritoneum).

Perspiration—(See Sweat).

Phlegm—(See Mucus, Phlegm).

Plastic Fluids—(See Plastic).

Plenitude — Fluidic Plenitude — (See "Full Moon" under Moon).

Plethora; Puffing; Pus; Receptacles;

Restricted—The Fluids Restricted— (See Depletion, Retarded, Restricted, Suppressions; "Ailments", "Lack Of", in this section).

Retarded; Retention;

Revitalization Of—(See "First Quarter" under Moon).

Rush Of—Flow of—Determination of —(See Determination, Flow, Rush).

Saliva; Secretions; Semen; Serum;

Sexual Fluids — Normal or Abnormal Fluids from the Sex Organs—(See Discharges, Genitals, Generation, Leucorrhoea, Menses, Semen, Sex, Vagina, Womb, etc.).

Skin—Fluids of—Fluids from or Thru —(See Exudations, Glands, Oils, Skin, Sweat, etc.).

Snuffling — (See "Snaffling" under Nose).

Spinal Fluids — Ruled by ♅. (See Spine).

Spitting; Sputum; Stomach—Disturb-ances of Fluids of — (See "Ailments" in this section; Digestion, Gastric, Indigestion; "Fluids" under Stomach).

Stoppages; Suppressions; Sweat;

Swellings—(See Accumulative, Cysts, Dropsies, Puffing, Swellings, Tumors).

Synovial Fluid — Joints — (See Joints, Synovial).

Tears—Lachrymal Fluid—(See Tears).

Thorax — Chest — Fluids of — (See Chest, Lungs, Thorax; "Ailments" in this section).

Throat—Fluids of—(See Diphtheria, Fauces; "Restricted" under Throat; Tonsils; "Ailments" in this Article).

Tide and Ebb Of—(See "Full Moon", "New Moon", under Moon).

Transudations—Oozing—(See Exudations, Osmosis).

Tumors—Watery Tumors—(See Blisters, Cysts, Swellings; "Aqueous" under Tumors; Watery).

Urine; Vagina—Secretions and Fluids of—(See Vagina).

Veins—Venous Blood—(See Veins).

Vital Fluid—Depletion of—(See "Depletion", and the various paragraphs under Vital).

Vitreous Humor—(See "Vitreous" under Eyes).

Vomiting; Water — Water Brash — Watery Humours, etc.—(See Belching, Humours, Watery. Also note the various paragraphs in this section).

White Fluids — Of the Body — Body Oil—(See "Fluids" under White).

Womb — Fluids of, or From — (See Menses. Also note the various paragraphs under Womb).

FLUOR ALBUS—Whites—(See Leucorrhoea).

FLUORIDE OF LIME—Calcium Fluoride—This is one of the 12 Tissue, or fundamental Salts of the Body, and is ruled by the ♋ Sign. (See Lime, Salts; "Salts" under Zodiac).

FLUSHINGS — Heated Flushings—Hot Flashes—☉ diseases; ☉ ☌ ♂; ☉ ☌ ♂ in ♈, ♌, or ♐, and espec. when in the Asc. (See Blushing, Fevers, Heat).

FLUX—Fluxes—Fluxion—A Flowing— Fluxions, Catarrhal, and Continuous Fevers follow a Solar Periodicity, grow worse towards sunset. (See Periodicity; "Solar Periodicity" under Solar; "Magnetic", "Sunrise", "Sunset", under Sun).

A Flux—Suffers from a Flux— Liable To — A Flux Threatened — The ☉ in water signs at B., and to the ☌ or ill-asp. ♂ by dir.; the ☽ to the □ or ☍ ☉ by dir., a flux is threatened; the ☽ hyleg, and to the ill-asps. the ☉ by dir.; the ☽ in ♑, and affl. by the ☉ or ♂ when taken ill (Hor'y); ♄ causes when he has dominion, and afflicts the hyleg; a ♄ disease; ♂ in water signs, and to the ill-asps. the Asc. by dir.; ♀ affl. in ♍ or ♓; ☿ affl. in ♒. (See Catarrh).

Belly — Fluxes of the Belly — In Bowels, Abdomen—(See "Fluxes" under Belly).

Bloody Flux—Dysentery—The ☉ or ♂ in ♍ when the afflictors in the disease; the ☉ or ☽ affl. in ♍, and to the ♂ or ill-asp. ♂ by dir.; the ☉ to ♂ ♂ by dir., and in watery signs; ♂ affl. in ♍; ♂ affl. in water signs, and to the ♂ or ill-asp. the Asc. by dir.; ♂ ♂ Asc. by dir. if ♂ in a watery sign; a ♂ disease, and caused by ♂ afflictions; the Asc. to the ☐ or ⚹ ♄ by dir. Bloody and sanguineous evacuations are worse at the Full ☽. (See Dysentery).

Bowels — Fluxes of — (See "Fluxes" under Belly, Bowels; Cholera, Diarrhoea, Dysentery, Typhoid).

Death by Fluxes—Caused by ♄ when he is the afflictor, holds dominion, and the dominion of death is vested in him; ♄ affl. the hyleg at B., and by dir., denotes death by; the ☉ to the place of Praesepe.

Hemorrhoids—Too Much Flux of the Hemorrhoids—(See Hemorrhoids).

Prevalent— Fluxes Prevalent—Planets in ♍ or the 6th H., and affl. at a Summer Solstice.

Rheum — Watery or Catarrhal Discharges—(See Rheum).

Violent Fluxes — ♂ affl. in watery signs, and to the ♂ or ill-asp. the Asc. by dir.; the Asc. to the ☐ or ⚹ ♂ by dir., in water signs.

Watery Flux — (See Catarrh, Defluxions, Rheum, Watery).

FLYING—

Flying Fowl—Body Devoured by After Death—Destruction of—Resembles Fowls—(See Fowls).

Flying Gout—(See Gout).

Flying Humours—(See Humours).

Flying Pains—Running Pains—Afflictions in ♒; ♃ affl. in ♒, flying pains due to corruption of blood, and overabundance of blood in the system; ☿ affl. in ♒, running pains in different parts of the body; ☿ affl. in ♏ when ☿ is the afflictor in the disease, running pains in the arms and shoulders. (See "Too Much Blood" under Blood; Running, Wandering).

Flying Stones—Injuries or Death By —(See "Assaults" under Stone).

FOCUS—Of the Eyes—Defects of—(See Accommodation, Sight).

FOETUS — Embryo — From conception, the following order of the influence of the planets is recognized. (1) The Physical Plasm is formed under ♄. (2) It becomes enveloped by the Amniotic Fluid under ♃. (3) The Limbs are developed under ♂ influence. (4) The ☉ produces Quickening. (5) Sex distinction is effected by ♀. (6) Brain development and specialization of the nerve filaments are done by ☿. The Embryo is the fecundated germ up to the 4th month. The Foetus is the product of conception after the 4th month of gestation. The following subjects have to do with the Foetus, the condition and development of the child, mentally and physically, during pregnancy, or its delivery.

Abortion Of—(See Abortion, Miscarriage).

Accidents To — Injuries To — (See "Mutilation" in this section).

Beastly Form—(See "Beastly Form" under Beasts).

Birth Of — Normal Birth of — Occurs under ♃, but the child is ushered into the world under the signature of ♂. (See Birth, Normal, Parturition).

Born Alive—Lives Only a Few Hours —Dies Soon After Birth—(See Abortion; "Death Soon After Birth" under Birth; "Born Almost Dead" under Children; Infancy).

Caul Over Face—(See "Caul" under Face).

Childbirth—(See Parturition).

Conception — (See the various paragraphs under Conception).

Death at Birth—(See "Death at Birth" under Birth, Children).

Death In Womb—(See Abortion, Stillborn).

Death Soon After Birth—(See "Born Alive" in this section).

Defective Births — (See "Defective" under Birth).

Dumb—Born Dumb—(See Dumb).

Excision of Foetus—Caesarian Operation Indicated—The ☉ or ☽ to the ♂ or ill-asp. ♂ by dir.; ♂ in ♏ at B., occi., and affl. the hyleg by dir.; ♂ in an angle, occi. of the ☉, and ori. of the ☽. (See "Mutilation" in this section).

Faculties Improved — (See "Beastly Form" under Beasts; Quickened" under Mental).

Foolish—Born Foolish—(See Foolish, Idiocy, Imbecile).

Gestation — (See Gestation, Pregnancy).

Hermaphrodite—(See this subject).

Human Shape—Is of Human Shape— (See Human).

Ill-Formed—(See "Beastly Form" under Beasts; Deformities; "Ill-Formed" under Ill; Inhuman, Monsters).

Infancy—(See the various paragraphs under Infancy).

Inhuman — Inhuman In Shape — (See "Beastly Form" under Beasts; Inhuman).

Lateral Position — Is assumed under ☽ influence.

Lives Only Few Hours — After Birth —(See "Born Alive" in this section).

Monsters—(See Monsters).

Mortification Of—♂ in an angle, occi. of the ☉, and ori. of the ☽.

Mutilation Of—The Foetus Extracted In Mangled Parts—♀ in an angle, and espec. in the Western angle, and ♄ be in ♂, or in configuration with her, or in mutual reception, and ♂ elevated above ♀, or ♂ in ⚹ with ♀,—these influences tend to impotence in the male, abortions in the female, stillbirth, mangling of the child at B., or extraction in mangled parts.

Nourishment—The Embryo, or Foetus Not Nourished—The ☉ or ☽, as Giver of Life, in an angle, and in ♂ a malefic. (See Nutrition).

Parturition — (See the various paragraphs under Parturition).

Pregnancy — (See Conception, Gestation, Pregnancy).

Premature Birth — (See Abortion; "Seven Months Children" under Children; Miscarriage, Premature).

Quickening—(See Quickening).

Rickets—Foetal Rickets—(See Rickets).

Savage — (See "Beastly Form" under Beasts; "Animal Forms" under Monsters; Savage, Wild).

Shape—(See Human, Ill-Formed, Inhuman, in this section).

Sickly — The Child Will Be Sickly — (See the Introduction under Abortion; Sickly).

Stillborn—(See Abortion, Stillborn).

Version — Of the Foetus In Utero — (See "Version" under Womb).

FOLLICLES—Follicular—A Small Secretory Cavity or Sac—

Hair Follicles—Disorders of — (See "Barber's Itch" under Barbers; "Disorders" under Hair).

Tonsilitis—Follicular Tonsilitis—(See Tonsils).

FOLLY—Foolish Conduct—

Disease and Sickness From— Death From—Injury From—The ☽ affl. in ♏; ♏ on the Asc. at B., and espec. with ♂ therein, diseases arising from folly or anger. (See Anger, Conduct, Dissipation; "His Own Worst Enemy" under Enemies; Excesses, Foolhardy, Foolish, Forethought, Hasty, Impulsive, Indiscretions, Judgment, Morals, Passion, Rashness, Recklessness, Self-Undoing, Temper, Violent; "Death" under Wounds).

Misery From—Misery and Sickness From—Lord of the 12th H. in the 1st H. (See Misery, Twelfth House).

Moral Folly—Is due to the perverted and atonic action of ♀. (See "Loose Morals" under Morals).

FOMAHAUT—A star of the 1st magnitude, in the 2° ♓, of the nature of ♀ and ☿. Is said to cause bites by venomous creatures when joined with the ☉ or ♂. Also said to bring Calamity. (See Calamity, Reptiles, Stings, Venomous).

FOMENTATIONS—Hot Fomentations—(See Emollient).

FONTANELLES—(See this subject under Head).

FOOD—Diet—Nourishment—Nutrition—Eating—Provisions, etc.—Food is ruled by ☿, the ♍ sign, and the 6th H. In a general way ☿ represents food stuff. The subject of Food is also largely considered under Assimilation, Diet, Digestion, Drink, Eating, Nutrition, etc. The following subjects have to do with Food, which see in the alphabetical arrangement when not considered here—

Abnormal Eater—(See "Excesses" under Eating).

Acquired Diseases—And Food — (See Acquired).

Albumen—Albumin—(See Albumen, Proteids).

Appetite; Assimilation;

Autointoxication; Belching;

Bolts the Food—(See "Fast Eater" under Eating).

Bowels—Decomposition of Food In—(See "Putrid Matter" under Bowels).

Careful In Diet—Fastidious—(See "Careful" under Diet; "Eccentric" in this section).

Chewing of Food—Insufficient Mastication—Bolts the Food—(See "Fast Eater" under Eating).

Chyle; Chyme; Coffee—Craves Strong Coffee and Strong Drink—(See "Strong Drink" under Drink).

Comfits; Comforts—Of Life—As Food, Clothing,.etc.—(See Comforts).

Condiments—Spiced, and Highly Seasoned Foods—Craving For—Such foods are ruled by ♂; desire for given by ♂ affl. in ♉ or ♏; ♂ in ♋ in the 1st, 5th, 6th H., and in evil asp. to ♃ or ♀; ♃ ♂ ♂ in ♋ or ♑; ♃ ♂ ♅ in the 1st or 6th H. Spices are ruled by ♀. (See "Good Things", "Rich Food", in this section).

Cooked Foods—Dr. Duz, in his book, "Astral Medicine", says that the organism needs cooked foods, as the fire in cooking them "Strikes off the noxious principles contained in raw substances, but thru the fragrancy it produces by their cooking, stimulates the gastric juice and anticipates the digestion." He also advocates the eating of meat. (See Meat).

Corn—Scarcity of—(See Scarcity).

Cravings—Abnormal Cravings Along Food Lines—♅ ♂ ☽, or ♅ □ or ♉ ♃ or ♀. (See Cravings, Drink. Also note the various paragraphs in this section).

Crops—Destruction of—(See Crops).

Dainty Foods—Fondness For—Fond of Good Living Generally—A ♉ influence; the 2nd Dec. of ♉ on the Asc., ruled by the ☽); ♃ affl. in ♉; ♃ or ♂ affl. in ♋. (See "Good Things", "Rich Foods", "Sweets", in this section).

Decay Of—Corruption of — Putrefaction of—(See "Putrid" under Bowels; Corruption, Decay, Fruit, Rotten, Vegetation).

Decomposition Of—In Stomach or Bowels—(See "Putrid" under Bowels; "Fermentation" under Stomach).

Deglutition — Swallowing Difficult — (See Deglutition).

Desert—Lost In the Desert—Without Food—(See Desert).

Diet — (See the various paragraphs under Diet).

Digestion; Dislikes—Has Strong Likes and Dislikes As To Food—♅ or ♄ affl. in ♋.

Dissipation—In Food and Drink — Principally ♉ and ♋ influence, and afflictions in these signs; ♂ affl. in ♉ or ♋; ♂ ♉ in □ ♅, ♃, or ♀; ♓ on Asc. (See Drink, Drunkenness, Eating, Excessess, Gluttony, Intoxication, etc.).

Distribution—Of Food—Assimilation of—Disturbed Distribution — (See Assimilation).

Food   274   Food

Dress and Food—Extravagant In—♂ in the 6th H. (See Dress, Extravagance, Luxuries; "Rich Food", and the various paragraphs in this section).

Drink—(See the various paragraphs under Drink).

Drinking with Meals—Excessive Drinking With—♅ ☌ ☽ in ♋, and in □ or ☍ ♂. (See Drink).

Drought—Dryness and Shortage of Food—(See Drought, Famine).

Eating—(See the various paragraphs under Eating).

Eccentric—Eccentric and Peculiar About Food—Fastidious—The ☉ ⚹ or △ ♅; ♉ in the 6th H.; ♉ or ♅ in ♍. (See Eccentric, Peculiar, Tastes; "Fastidious" in this section).

Emaciation—(See Assimilation, Emaciation; "Malnutrition" under Nutrition; Wastings).

Enema—Of Food—Rectal Feeding—(See Enema).

Epicureans; Errors In Diet—(See "Evil Diet" under Diet).

Evil Diet—Errors In Diet—Indiscretions In—Wrong Diet—(See "Evil Diet" under Diet).

Excesses In—Diseases and Surfeits Arising From—(See "Abnormal" under Appetite; "Excesses" under Diet; Eating, Feasting, Gluttony, Plethora, Surfeits).

Expensive Foods—(See Dainty, Rich, in this section).

External—Diseases Arising from External Causes, as Food, Clothing, Climate, etc.—(See External).

Extravagant—In Food—(See "Dress and Food", "Excesses", "Rich", in this section).

Famine; Fast Eater—(See "Fast Eater" under Eating).

Fastidious—In Diet—Careful—Particular—(See "Careful", "Fastidious", under Diet; "Eccentric" in this section).

Fatty Food—Disorders By—(See "Foods" under Fat).

Feasting; Feeding; Fermentation—(See "Decomposition" in this section; Fermentation, Zymosis).

Fondness—For Foods Increased—In Hor'y Q. ♄ signifies a person who is a great eater; ♉ in fixed signs, rising, or in the 3rd or 9th H., and afflicted, tends to; ♃ affl. in ♉. (See "Excesses" in this section; "Excesses", "Great Eater", under Eating).

Fruit—Cannot Eat Fruit or Vegetables—(See Case, "Cannot Eat Fruit" under Fruit).

Gluttony; Good Food—Good Things To Eat—Fond of Good Food—Rich Food—Dainty Foods, etc.—The ☉ or ☽ in ♋, and espec. if ⚹ or △ ♀; ♃ ☌ ♂ in ♋ or ♑; ♂ in ♋, ⚹ or △ ♃ or ♀. (See Condiments, Rich, Sweets, in this section; Epicureans, Feasting).

Gormandizing; Grains—(See Corn, Grain, Scarcity, Wheat, etc.).

Gustativeness; Habits—Concerning Food—(See Careful, Eccentric, Fastidious, Impulsive, Unnatural, and the various paragraphs in this section).

Hard To Please—As to Food—♅ ☌ ☽ in ♋; ♅ in ♋, in □ or ☍ ♉; ♄ affl. in ♋. (See Eccentric, Peculiar, in this section).

Health Foods—Has Success In the Preparation of—♂ well-asp. in ♍.

High Living—(See High).

Highly Seasoned Foods—Fond of—(See "Condiments" in this section).

Hygiene; Immoderate Eater—(See Excesses, Hearty, Immoderate, Over-Eating, under Eating).

Improper Foods—Given To—(See "Evil Diet" under Diet).

Impulsive Habits—Concerning Food—Unnatural Habits—♅ ☌ ☽ in ♋, and affl. by the □ of ♉ or ♂. (See Habits, Unnatural, in this section).

Indigestible Food—Desire For—♉ affl. in ♋ in the 6th H. (See Indigestion).

Indigestion; Indiscretions—In Diet—(See "Indiscretions" under Diet, Eating; Indiscretions).

Intemperate—In Eating—(See "Excesses" in this section).

Intoxication; Irregularities—In Food—Denoted by ☿, his positions and aspects.

Large Quantities—Desires Food In Large Quantities—Gluttony—♃ in asp. or relation to signs or planets which rule the appetite; ♃ ☍ ☽; ♀ in the 5th H. (See "Excesses" in this section; "Abnormal" under Appetite; Gluttony).

Likes and Dislikes—As to Food—(See "Dislikes" in this section).

Liquids with Food—Should Be Avoided—When ♅ is in ♓ at B. too much liquid with the food and meals should be avoided. (See "Drinking" in this section).

Liquids and Sweets—Strong Craving For With Meals—♂ in ♋, □ or ☍ ♉; ♀ in ♋, and affl. by the ☽. (See Drinking, Sweets, in this section).

Liquors—(See Drink, Liquids, Liquors. Also see "Drinking", "Liquids", in this section).

Luxuries—Craves Luxuries In Food—(See Dainty, Extravagant, Good Food, Rich, Sweets, in this section; Extravagance, Luxuries).

Malnutrition—(See Nutrition).

Mastication—(See "Chewing" in this section).

Meat—Meat Eating—Undigested Meat and Illness From—(See "Raw Humours" under Indigestion; Meat; "Cooked Foods", "Signs", in this section).

Minces the Food—Peculiar In Choice of—(See Fastidious, Peculiar, in this section).

Moderate In Eating—(See "Moderate" under Eating).

Nausea; Nut Butters—(See "Specialties" under Healers).

Nutrition; Obesity; Over-Eating—Over-Indulgence In Food—(See "Excesses", "Hearty", "Indiscretions", under Eating; "Fondness" in this section).

Particular—About Food—(See Careful, Eccentric, Fastidious, Peculiar, in this section).

Pastries—Starches—Sweets—Fond of—(See Dainty, Rich, Starches, Sweets, in this section).

Peculiar — About Food—Peculiar Tastes—Minces Food—�125 affl. in ♋; �125 in ♋ in the 6th H.; ♄ in ♋, minces the food. (See Careful, Eccentric, Fastidious, Tastes, in this section).

Perverted Tastes — (See "Tastes" in this section).

Please—Hard To Please—(See Careful, Eccentric, Fastidious, Hard To Please, in this section).

Plethora; Proteids—Eats Excess of—♄ affl. in ♋. (See Albumen, Starches, Sugar, Sweets, in this section; Proteids).

Provisions — Scarcity of — (See Drought, Famine, Scarcity, Starvation).

Putrid—Putrid and Decomposed Food In Bowels—(See "Decomposition" in this section).

Raw Foods—(See "Cooked Foods" in this section).

Raw Humours—(See "Raw Humours" under Indigestion).

Rectal Feeding—(See Enema).

Retention—Of Food Difficult—Difficulty In Retaining Food—The ☉ and ♂ in ♋, and affl. at B., and by dir.; the Solar-Martial action in ♋. (See Nausea, Vomiting).

Rich Food—Fond of—Expensive Food—Dainty Foods—Disease and Surfeits Arising From—The ☉ affl. by ♃ or ♀, and tending to Surfeits; the ☉ affl. in ♋; the ☉ □ or ☌ ♃; ♃ affl. in ♋, ♋, or ♏; ♃ ☌ ♂ in ♋ or ♑; ♃ or ♀ in the 5th H.; ♂ in ♋ in the 1st, 5th, or 6th H. (See Epicureans, Extravagance, Feasting, "Enlarged Liver" under Liver; Luxuries, Plethora, Surfeits; Condiments, Dainty, Excesses, Good Things, Starches, Sugar, Sweets, in this section).

Riotous Living—(See Riotous).

Rottenness—Of Food—(See "Putrid" under Bowels; "Corruption" under Fruit; Rottenness; Decay, Decomposition, in this section).

Scarcity—Of Food—(See Desert, Drought, Famine, Scarcity, Starvation; "Food" under Travel).

Scurvy—Due to Deficient and Improper Food—(See Scurvy).

Seasoned—Highly Seasoned Food—Fond of—(See "Condiments" in this section).

Signs of Zodiac—The Food Adapted to People Born Under Each Sign—Diet and the Horoscope—(1) ♈—Brain foods, wheat, cereals; fish, but little meat; no stimulants or heating foods. (2) ♉ — Avoid heating, fattening, starchy foods, and malt liquors; use stimulants moderately; plenty of lemon drinks. Be moderate in diet, as this sign tends to over-eating, gout, rheumatism, surfeits, plethora, etc. (3) ♊—A mental sign—brain food, fruit, milk, meat once a day; nerve foods. Avoid eating, or a meal, before retiring. (4) ♋—Avoid stimulants, malt liquors, pastry, and all food which tends to ferment or heat in the stomach; fish and cereals are recommended, and little meat. Drink plenty of cold water

upon arising in morning, and at bedtime. (5) ♌—A vegetable diet is best, and to avoid meats, and all heating, fattening, stimulating foods. Food which builds blood and red corpuscles is required. Study vegetable foods which contain iron. (6) ♍—Chew food well, and eat at regular intervals. Use plain, well-cooked food, and avoid foods which tend to bind or heat the bowels. Eat fruits, milk, vegetables, and foods which tend to regulate the bowels. Avoid over-eating. (7) ♎—Use a light diet; milk, game, fish, poultry, eggs, cereals, cold water upon arising and at bed time. Avoid sugars, starches, malt, intoxicants. (8) ♏—Avoid all fattening, heating, and intoxicating foods and drinks, malts, meat. Use milk, cereals, fruits, vegetables, and blood-forming diet. (9) ♐—Stimulants and intoxicants should be avoided. A moderate amount of animal food is permissible. Nerve and blood-building food should be taken, a light meal at noon, a more substantial meal at sunset, and with light exercise in the evening. (10) ♑—This is a cold sign, and meat diet, and more heat-producing food, are required, and food to enrich the blood and build red corpuscles. Malts are permissible, and foods which stimulate the bodily functions. (11) ♒—A brain and nerve building diet is required, and foods which stimulate the circulation of the blood. Milk and cereals should be used, and a meat diet at one meal of the day. (12) ♓—Intoxicants should be avoided, and a temperate life lived, as many foods do not agree with this sign, and tend to indigestion, a phlegmatic and watery body. A fish diet is helpful, animal meats once a day, and the liberal use of milk, cereals, wheat products, vegetables, fruits, etc. (See "Salts" under Zodiac).

Spiced Foods—Fond of—(See "Condiments" in this section).

Starches—Tendency to Excess of In Food—The ☉ or ☽ in ♋, or ♋ on Asc.; ♄ in ♋ or ♑; ♄ ☌ ♃ or ♀ in ♋; ♀ affl. by the ☽. (See Dainty, Rich, Sweets, in this section; Starches).

Starvation—Lack of Food—(See "Scarcity" in this section).

Stomach Disorders—From Improper Food or Indiscretions—(See Digestion, Fermentation, Indigestion, Indiscretions, Stomach; "Decomposition" in this section).

Strange Foods—Desire For—(See "Unnatural" in this section).

Strong Drink—Strong Coffee—Desire For—(See "Strong Drink" under Drink).

Sugar—Heavy Sugar Eaters—Abnormal Desire For—The ☽ ☌ ♀ in a common sign; ♀ affl. at B.; ♄ in ♋ or ♑; ♀ afflicted in ♎; ♀ conjoined with the ☽ in any part of the map; ♀ □ ☽. Sugar in excess, and excess of drink and stimulants, excites the Ductless Glands. (See Sugar; "Sugar" under Urine; "Sweets" in this section).

Surfeits; Swallowing—(See Deglutition).

Sweets—Sugar—Comfits—Pastries—Fond of—Uses to Excess—Sweets and

Sugars are ruled by ♀, and asps. to ♀ tend to increase desire for; ♀ in ♋, in ⚹ ☽, strong desire for; ♀ afflicted in ♎; ♀ □ ☽), abnormal desire for; ♀ ☌ ☽ in a common sign; ♅ affl. at B. tends to a large consumption of sugar; ♄ in ♋, eats excess of sweets, sugar, proteids, pastries, and espec. if ♀ is involved in the configuration; ♄ in ♋ or ♑, fond of pastries and sugar; ♄ ☌ ♃ or ♀ in ♋, fond of pastries, sweets, starches; ♄ affl. in ♋, overloads the system with proteids, starches and sugars; ♂ in ♋, □ or ☍ ♅, a craving for sweets and liquids with meals. (See Dainty, Good Food, Proteids, Rich Food, Starches, Sugar, in this section).

Tastes—Abnormal Tastes and Appetites with Food—Perverted Tastes—Peculiar Tastes—♄ affl. in ♋; ♄ ☌ ♀ in ♋; ♅ in the 6th H.; ♂ in ♋; ♂ in ♋, □ or ☍ ♅; ♀ in ♋, and affl. by the ☽. (See Eccentric, Hard To Please, Peculiar, Unnatural, in this section; Tastes).

Thirst; Travel—Lack of Food In— (See Desert; "Privations" under Seas; "Food" under Travel).

Undigested Food—In Stomach or Bowels—(See "Putrid" under Bowels; Digestion; "Raw Humours" under Indigestion).

Unhealthful Foods—Love of—♄ in ♋ or ♑.

Unnatural Foods—Desire For—♅ affl. in ♋; ♄ ☌ ♀ in ♋, and affl. by the ☽ or ♅; ♄ in ♋ or ♑. (See Dainty, Impulsive Habits, Rich, Starches, Sugar, Sweets, Tastes, in this section; "Evil Diet" under Diet).

Vegetables—Fruit—Cannot Eat—(See "Cannot Eat" under Fruit; Vegetables).

Vitamines—Unable to Extract the Vitamines from the Food—♄ ℞ in ♋, and □ or ☍ ♂.

Vomiting; Want—In Want of Food and Water—(See "Scarcity" in this section).

Wheat; Wine; Wrong Diet—(See "Evil Diet" under Diet; Excesses; Indiscretions, Luxuries; Dainty, Rich, Starches, Sugars, Sweets, in this section).

FOOLHARDY—Reckless—Heedless of Danger—Caused by ♂ afflictions; ♂ affl. in the 1st H.; ♂ □ or ☍ ☉; ♂ ☌, □, or ☍ ♄ affl. in ♌; due to the □ or ☍ ♂ to planets; ♂ prog. ☌ or ill-asp. ♄, and vice versa; the ☉ ☌ ♂ in ♈, and ♈ on the Asc.; the ☉ to the ☌ or ill-asp. ♂ by dir.; the prog. ☉ or ☽ to the ☌ or ill-asp. ♂; ♅ by tr. ☌ the radical ♂, ☽, or ☿; ☿ ☌ or evil asp. ♂ at B., and by dir.; fixed stars of the nature of ♂ and ☿ ascending at B.; in Hor'y Q., ♄ Sig. in ♏. (See Bold, Chances, Dangers, Own Worst Enemy (see Enemies); Escapes, Excitable, Folly, Forethought, Hasty, Imprudent, Impulsive, Perils, Precipitate, Quarrels, Rashness, Recklessness, etc.).

FOOLS—Foolish—The ☽ in ♑, full of light, and conjoined with ♂; the ☽ in ♑, void of light, and conjoined with ♄; ♀ ☌ ♄, and with ♂ ☍ the ☽, a fool, yet thinks he is a Philosopher.

Foolish Fancies—(See "Foolish" under Fancies).

Foolish Mind—The Child Born Foolish—An Imbecile, or Idiot—If at conception the ☉ and ☽ be in the 6th or 12th H., and a malefic with them, the child conceived will tend to be foolish, but if a fortune be with them, the intellect will be saved, but the child formed a hermaphrodite. (See "Beastly Form" under Beasts; Idiocy, Imbecile; "Weak Mind" under Mind; "Void of Reason" under Reason; Savage).

FORCE—Forces—Forceful—

Bodily Forces—Organic Force—Physical Strength—Are ruled over by the Asc. (See Ascendant, Body, Organic, Physical, Strength).

Creative Force—Sex Force—(See Creative; "Force" under Sex).

Disease—Force of the Disease—The horoscope as a whole should be studied in judging of the force, or outcome of the disease, and not any one aspect or influence, as the good asps. from the ☉, ☽, ♃, or ♀, will tend to modify the disease in a fortunate map. If the radical map is generally weak, the disease would tend to be more severe. (See Better, Duration, Worse, and the various paragraphs under Disease).

Dispersion—Dissipation of Force—(See Dispersion, Dissipation).

Dynamic Force—(See Dynamic).

Electric Force—(See Electric, Electricity).

Endurance—(See Endurance).

Energy—(See Energy).

Excess of Force—Danger of—The ☉ in a fiery sign; ☉ ☌ ♂ in ♈ or ♌, and espec. in the Asc. or M.C.; ♈ or ♌ on the Asc. (See Active, Energy, Strength, Vitality Good, etc.).

Expulsive Forces—Of the Body—(See Expulsion).

Internal Force—Prana—Vital Power—(See "Fire Signs" under Fire; "Force" under Vital).

Kinetic Force—(See Kinetic).

Life Force—Life Forces—Of the Body—Are ruled by the ☉, and the ☉ is the chief source and regulator of the life forces. Also ♂ aids in giving force, activity, and energy. Orange, the color of the ☉, and red, the color of ♂, are the colors assigned to the life force. (See Life, Mars, Sun, Vital).

Manner—Forceful Manner—(See Active, Energetic, Quick).

Mind—Mind Force—Forceful State of the Mind—(See "Active Mind" under Active; Electric; "Quickened", "Strong Mind", under Mind; Positive).

Natural Forces—Of the Body—(See Natural).

Negative—(See Negative, Passive).

Nerve Force—Vital Force—The Nerve Force Augmented—(See "Nerve Force" under Nerves; "Augmented", "Force", under Vital).

Organic Force—Of the Body—Ruled by the ☉ and the Asc. The sign on the Asc. rules the body and physical strength. (See Organic, Structural).

Physical Forces—Physical Strength—(See Motion, Muscles, Physical, Stamina, Strength, Tone, Vitality, etc.).

Positive Forces—Of Mind and Body—(See Active, Action, Energy, Electric, Positive, etc.).

Prana — Vital Force — (See Prana; "Force" under Vital).

Sex Force — Creative Force — (See Creative, Generation, Reproduction; "Force" under Sex).

Solar Forces—(See Solar, Sun).

Strength; Strong; Vital Force—Prana—(See Prana; "Force" under Vital).

Vitality; Weak Body—The Forces Weak, Hindered and Impaired—Weak Mind — (See Feeble, Imbecile, Infirm; "Weak" under Mind; Sickly, Vitality Low; "Weak Body" under Weak).

Will Power—The Force of the Will—(See Will).

FOREARM—Is ruled by the ♌ sign, being opposite to the calves ruled by ♒. Is also ruled by ♊.

Fractures Of — (See Arms, Radius, Ulna, Wrists).

Frog Child — (See "Missing" in this section).

Missing—One or Both Forearms Missing—Born Incomplete—The Frog Child—Caused by Prenatal afflictions. Cases —See "Armless Wonder", No. 054; "Imperfectly Formed", Case No. 267; "Born Incomplete", Case No. 281, all in 1001 N.N. The Case of the Frog Child, with right forearm missing from the elbow down, and with both legs missing below the knees, is illustrated and written up in the book, "The Prenatal Epoch", by Mr. Bailey, on page 157 of Chap. 27. (See the various paragraphs under Arms, Elbows, Hands, Shoulders, Wrists, etc.).

FOREBODINGS—Premonitions—Omens —Presentiments—

Gloomy Forebodings — ♄ affl. in the 3rd or 9th H. (See Gloom).

Vague Forebodings — Curious Forebodings—Ψ affl. in the 3rd or 9th H.; Ψ affl. in ♐. (See Chaotic, Dreams, Fears, Portentous, Premonitions, Prophetic, Visions, Weird).

FOREHEAD—The Brow—Ruled by the ♈ sign, and espec. affected by ♂ in ♈.

Accidents To—♂ affl. in ♈. (See Injury, Scars, in this section).

Baldness — About the Forehead and Temples—(See "Forehead" under Baldness).

Broad Forehead — The ☉ indicates a broad and high forehead; ♉ gives, and ♉ on the Asc., a broad forehead; ♄ gives a broad forehead.

Deep Forehead — Tall, Deep, and Straight— ☿ gives; ☿ ascending at B., and free from the rays of other planets.

Disorders Of — Afflictions in ♈; Subs at AT or AX.

Fine Forehead—♂ in ♐.

Hair — Has Light Brown Hair Near the Temples and Forehead—Born under ♃, and ♃ occi. (See "Light Brown" under Hair; Baldness, High, in this section).

Handsome Forehead—The latter part of ♐ on the Asc. (See Handsome; "Fine" in this section).

High Forehead—The ☉ rising at B.; the ☉ gives a broad and high forehead; born under ♃; ♃ in the Asc. at B.; ☿ in ♍; ☿ strong at B., and rising; a ☿ person; in Hor'y Q., ☿ Sig. of the person.

Injuries To—♄ or ♂ affl. in ♈; ♈ on the Asc. at B., and containing malefics. Case—The Forehead Split Open In An Accident—See "Strange Accident", No. 832, in 1001 N.N. (See "Accidents", "Injuries", under Head).

Large Forehead—Prominent—♄ in ♎ in partile asp. the Asc. (See Broad, Deep, High, in this section).

Lowering Brow—The ☽ ascending at Birth.

Round and Large—The ☉ gives.

Scar—On Forehead—♂ affl. in ♈. Case —See "Spinal Curvature", No. 838, in 1001 N.N. (See Marks, Scars).

Temples; Ulceration—On Forehead—♄ or ♂ affl. in ♈; Subs at AT and KP. (See Ulcers).

Upper Forehead—Disorders of—Afflictions in the 1st Dec. of ♈; Subs at AT. (See Navamsa).

FOREIGN LANDS—Abroad—

Death Abroad—(See "Death Abroad" under Abroad).

Foreign War — Death or Injury In — Malefics in the 9th H., and affl. the hyleg. (See "Battle" under Abroad; War).

Ill-Health Abroad—Sickness In a Foreign Land—Lord of the 9th in the 6th H. (See "Accidents", "Sickness", under Abroad).

Residence—In a Foreign Land—Fortunate or Unfortunate — (See Abroad, Banishment, Environment, Nations, Native Land (see Native); Place of Birth (see Place); Residence, Sea, Ships, Shipwreck, Travel, Voyages).

FOREST FIRES—Causes of—Death or Injury By—(See "Forest" under Fires).

FORETHOUGHT—Foresight—Forecast—

Lack Of—Danger By—Death, Injury, Sorrow, Trouble, etc., from Lack of—The ☉ ☌ ☿ in ♓, and at the same time in ☐ or ☍ ♅ or ♂, lack of reason and forethought, and haste and impulse predominate; the ☽ strong at B., in the Asc. or M.C., or angular at B., or in ♉ or ♋, little forecast, and providing only for the present; the ☽ ill-dig. at B., of no forecast; ♂ influence; ♂ Sig. ✶ or △ ♀, improvident and thoughtless; ♐ influence; ☿ rising before the ☉ gives forethought, but rising after the ☉, lack of it. (See Excitable, Foolhardy, Hasty, Improvident, Imprudent, Impulsive, Judgment; "Brightened" under Mind; Precipitate, Rashness, Reason, Recklessness, etc.).

Painful Complaints — And Irregularities, due to Rashness and Lack of Forethought—The ☽ affl. by ♂ at B., and by dir., tr., or progression; ♂ affl. the ☽, ☿, or Asc. at B., and by dir. (See Carelessness; "Own Worst Enemy" under Enemies; Folly, Imprudence, Rashness, Recklessness, etc.).

FORETOLD — Foretelling— Prognosti-cation — (See "Foretold His Own Death" under Death; Prognosis, Prognostication, Prophetic, etc.).

FORGERS — Given to Forgery — Tendency To—Commits Forgery—The ☽ to the ill-asps. ☿ by dir., and ☿ affl. at B.; ♅, ♄, ♃, or ♂ to the ill-asps. ☿ by dir.; ♂ and ☿ together lords of the employment; ☿ affl. by ♅, ♄, or ♂ by dir.; ☿ in the Asc., □ or 8 ♄ or ♂, and with no good asps. from ♃ or ♀; the M.C. to the place of Algenib, and with danger of imprisonment. (See Cheating, Deceitful, Dishonest, Gambling, Liars, Swindlers, Thieves, etc.).

FORGETFUL—(See Carelessness; "Forgetful" under Memory).

FORM — Shape and Description of the Body—The Form of the Body is to be judged principally from three factors,—(1) The Sign rising, the degree on the Asc., and the position of the ☽ at B. (2) Planets which exactly aspect the degree rising on the Asc., or when rising or near the Asc. (3) The position and aspects of the ruler of the Asc. The Form of the body proceeds from the Asc., the 1st H., planets in the Asc.; from the ☉ and ☽, and the asps. to the ☽. Ptolemy says the Asc. has the greatest power in forming the body, and next after the Asc., the ☽. (See Relaxation). Many modifications of form arise from the various positions of the majority of the planets, whether rising, elevated, setting, or below the horizon. Many planets in one sign tend to give the predominating characteristics of that sign, both in mind and body. Family Likenesses are caused by having the same sign rising with different members of the family. (See "Likenesses" under Family).

Significators of Form—They are the sign on the cusp of the Asc., or 1st H., or a sign intercepted in this house; their lords; planets in the Asc., or in any way aspecting the Asc.; fixed stars near the cusp of the Asc., and to these some add the Luminaries and the stars that aspect them,—all these are Sigs. of both mind and body. For further consideration of Form and Shape, see Appearance; "Beastly Form" under Beasts; Body, Build; "Dogs" under Children; Congenital, Crooked, Constitution, Defects, Deformities, Distortions, Figure, Height, Ill-Shaped, Inhuman, Monsters, Posture, Shape, Stature, Weight, etc.).

FORTUNE—The Fortune of the Native —Fortunate—Unfortunate—Malice of Fortune, etc.—

Children — Fortunate Children — Unfortunate—Misfortune To—(See "Fortunate", "Unfortunate", under Children).

Degrees — The Fortunate Degrees of the Zodiac — The Degrees Increasing Fortune—♈ 19; 8 3, 15, 27; ♊ 11; ♋ 1, 2, 3, 4, 15; ♌ 2, 5, 7, 19; ♍ 3, 14, 20; ♎ 3, 15, 21; ♏ 7, 18, 20; ♐ 13, 20; ♑ 12, 13, 14, 20; ♒ 7, 16, 17, 20; ♓ 13, 10. If ♃ be in one of these degrees at B., or if on the cusp of the 2nd H., or lord of the 2nd be in such a degree, riches

and great honors are apt to come to the native. (See "Zodiac" under Degrees).

Evil—The Fortune Too Evil to Allow the Native to Succeed—♂ Sig. □ or 8 the ☉. (See Evil, Fate, Misery, Misfortune, Reverses, Ruin, Sorrow, Trouble, etc.).

Fortunate—Very Fortunate In Life— Has Good Fortune—A Fortunate Person—The ☉, ☽, ♃, and ♀ above the earth at B., and well-asp.; the ☽ Sig. ☌ ♃; the ☽ well-asp. in 8, fairly fortunate; the ☽ well-asp. in ♋ or ♐; the ☽ sepr. from the ☉ and apply. to ♃; the ☽ sepr. from the ☉ and apply. to ♀ in a day geniture; the ☽ decr., sepr. from ♂ and apply. to ♀; the ☽ sepr. from ♂ and apply. to ♃; ♃ Sig. ✱ or △ the ☉; ♃ Sig. ☌ or good asp. the ☽; ♃ rising at B., well-asp. and dignified; ♃ Sig. ☌ ♀; ♂ Sig. in ♑; ♀ Sig. in 8, ♐, ♒, or ♓; ☿ Sig. ✱ or △ ♃. These influences also tend largely to good health. (See "Good Constitution" under Constitution; Fate, Happiness; "Good Health" under Health; Poverty, Riches, etc.).

Ill-Fortune — Meets with Much Ill-Fortune—(See Business, Cares, Children, Directions, Dishonour, Disgrace, Enemies, Events, Exile, Family, Fate, Grief, Health, Honour, Ill-Health, Imprisonment (see Prison); Injuries, Marriage, Marriage Partner, Mischief, Miseries, Misfortune, Murdered, Poverty, Relatives, Reputation, Reverses, Ruin, Scandal, Sickness, Sorrow, Suicide, Treachery, Trouble, Twelfth House, Unfortunate, etc.).

Malice of Fortune—Ill-Fortune—Misfortune—The ☽ to the place of Cetl, or the Hydra's Heart; the ☽ incr. in a night nativity, sepr. from ☿ and apply. to ♄, if malefic planets afflict them; ♄ in the 10th or 4th H., and affl. the ☉ or ☽, malice of fortune is almost certain, downfalls, reversals, ill-health, etc., and espec. under evil ♃ transits or directions to the hyleg, or to his place in the radical map; ♂ Sig. in □ or 8 the ☉; ♂ Sig. ☌ ☉, sudden failures and downfalls; ♀ Sig. □ or 8 ☽. (See "Evil", "Ill-Fortune", in this section).

Misfortune—(See "Ill-Fortune", "Malice of Fortune", in this section).

Moderately Fortunate—In Life—Not Very Fortunate—♄ Sig. ☌ ☽; ♂ Sig. ☌ ♀; ♀ Sig. in ♓; ☿ Sig. in ♐. (See the various paragraphs in this section. See Unfortunate).

Part of Fortune—(See Part).

Signs of Zodiac—The Fortunate Signs of the Zodiac are the positive, odd, and masculine, as ♈, ♊, ♌, ♎, ♐, and ♒. These Signs when rising at B., upon the Asc., and espec. when occupied by a benefic, and free from malefics, tend to make the native very fortunate in life.

Unfortunate — In Life — (See Unfortunate; "Ill-Fortune", "Malice", in this section).

FORWARD—The Body Bent Forward— (See Bending; "Downward" under Look; Stooping).

FOSSAE — Fossa — A Depression, Furrow, or Sinus—(See Depression, Frontal, Nose).

FOUL —Loathsome — Offensive — Unpleasant — Fetid — Foul Odors — Foul Diseases, etc.—See the following subjects in the alphabetical arrangement when not considered here—Foul Odors and Diseases are generally the work of ♄ and the ☽. Also ♀ tends to fetid and foul conditions in the body, resulting from excesses, dissipation, etc. (See Fetid). .

Air—Foul Air—(See "Corrupt" under Air).

Axillae—Fetid Perspiration of — (See Axillae).

Blood — Foul Blood — (See "Impure Blood" under Impure).

Breath—(See "Foul" under Breath).

Cancer — Carcinoma — (See Carcinoma).

Catarrhs—(See Catarrh, Nose).

Corrupt; Decay—Decomposition—(See Decay).

Discharges; Excretions; Exudations; Faeces; Feet—Foul Odors From—(See "Odors" under Feet).

Fetid; Gangrene; Gases; Humours— (See "Corrupt", "Offending", under Humours).

Impure; Menses; Mind—A Foul Mind —(See Obscenity).

Moisture—(See "Putrefaction" under Moisture).

Morbid; Noxious; Odors; Offensive; Perspiration—(See Sweat).

Pools—Stagnant Pools—(See Pools).

Pus; Putrid — Putrefaction—(See Putrid).

Rotenness; Sores; Stagnant — (See Pools).

Stomach—(See "Foul" under Stomach).

Sweat—(See "Fetid" under Sweat).

Tongue—A Foul Tongue—(See "Foul" under Breath, Tongue).

Ulcers—(See Gangrene; "Putrifying" under Ulcers).

Vapors—(See "Foul" under Vapors).

Vegetation; Venereal Diseases — (See "Ulcers" under Venereal).

FOUNTAINS—Springs—Drying Up of— Comets appearing in ♈ or ♎; an eclipse of the ☉ in the 2nd Dec. of ♋. (See Drought; "Fountains" under Dryness; Famine).

FOUR-FOOTED ANIMALS — Injury, Hurts, or Death By — (See Animals, Beasts, Bites, Cattle, Elephants, Events, Horses, Kicks, Quadrupeds, etc.).

Signs—The Four-Footed Signs of the Zodiac — Quadrupedal Signs—Animal Signs—♈, ♉, ♌, ♐, ♑. Those born with such signs on the Asc. at B. have many of the qualities of such animals, and especially if the ☉ or ☽ be in the 6th or 12th H. at conception, or the malefics in angles. (See "Animal Signs" under Animal; Quadrupeds).

FOURTH HOUSE — This is a terminal house, a part of the terminal triangle,

and denotes old age, the grave, decay, death, rest, the end of life, and the various conditions which affect the close of life, as its diseases, worries, the environment, wealth, poverty, etc. The nature of the death, or the end of life, will be according to the planets in this house, and the sign on the cusp denotes the part, or organ, wherein the complaint lies. The lords of the 4th and 8th H. are Significators of death. This is a feminine House, denotes the breasts and lungs, and is affiliated with the ♋ sign, and is cardinal in quality. This house is the weakest of the angles, and is also an Anaretical Place. The vital powers are at their weakest when the ☉ at B. is on the cusp of this house. This house rules the breasts, the milk, lungs, stomach; inheritance, the birthplace, place of residence, the home and domestic life generally; the mother in a male nativity and the father in a female horoscope; the mother-in-law in a male nativity, and the father-in-law in a female. In Hindu Astrology, this house rules the mother, and the 10th H. the father. Benefics in this house at B. indicate that the native should not leave his native land, but remain at his birthplace all thru his life, if possible, for good health, good fortune, and a happy and peaceful ending to life. The parents usually die before the native if he has ♄ in this house at B. Mars here gives short life to the father or mother, according to the sex of the horoscope. Malefic planets in the 4th H. indicate disease, worry, and distress in old age, and also hurt, sickness, and affliction to the father or mother. This house signifies all diseases in the lungs, breast, and stomach; the end of the disease, and diseases of the ☽ and the ♋ sign. Red is the Color ruled by this house. (See Anareta, Angles, Breast, Cancer; "Fourth House" under Death; End, Environment, Father, Heredity, Home, Inheritance, Lungs, Moon, Mother, Nadir; "Native Land" under Native; Old Age, Place of Birth (see Place); Red, Residence, Stomach, Terminal, etc.).

FOWLS—Of the Air—Birds—Vultures— **Body Devoured By** — After Death — (See "Birds of Air" under Air; "Body Devoured" under Burial; Vultures).

Death Of — Destruction of — Eclipses of the ☉ or ☽ in ♐ or ♐, espec. of such as are eaten by man, and which are brought to death by human means for edible purposes; Comets appearing in ♐; ♄ in ♐, angular, direct in motion at the Vernal Ingress. (See "Virus" under Pestilence).

Parrot Fever—(See Psittacosis).

Resembles Fowls — (See Disfigurements; "Eagle Features" under Features; "Animal Forms" under Monsters).

FRACTURES—Broken Bones— **Compound Fracture** — ♂ with ♄, and both the afflictors at the same time. (See "Violent" under Dispersions; "Scope" under Enlarged).

Death By—Caused by ♄ or ♂ when the dominion of death is vested in them; ♄ coming to the cusp. the Asc., causes a fracture, dislocation, and possible death from fracture if affl. the hyleg at the same time; ♂ in ♈, ♉, ♌, ♐, or ♑, and in ☍ the Asc. by dir.; ♂ in the 7th H., □ or ☍ the ☉, and ♂ in a four-footed, or quadrupedal sign, and with ♂ just setting at B. (See Blows, Concussions, Falls, Heights, Quadrupedal).

Falls—Fractures By—♂ by Periodic Rev. to the ♂, □, or ☍ ♅, and espec. if ♂ is in the 4th, 6th, or 8th H. (See Falls).

General Causes—Afflictions in ♐, and in ♊ by reflex action; ♐ on the Asc., 6th, or 12th H.; afflictions to planets in ♐ cause more broken bones than any other sign influence; afflictions in ♑; afflictions in airy signs dispose to; the ☽ affl. in ♐; the ☽ to the ♂ or ill-asps. ♂ by dir.; ♅ afflictions show fractures, and espec. his evil asps. to the Sigs., the ☉, ☽, Asc., or M.C.; ♄ afflictions give broken bones; ♄ ascending at B.; ♄ to the ♂ or ill-asps. ♂ by dir., and espec. if either be ori.; ♄ by tr. in ♂, □, or ☍ the ☉, ☽, ♃ or ♀ in the radix; ♄, ♅, or ♂ affl. in any sign at B., and by dir., may result in a fracture in the part, or parts, ruled by such sign at B.; ♃ affl. in □; ♂ affl. in ♐; ♂ in ♐ in the 6th or 12th H.; ♂ in the 1st H., and affl. by ♃; ♂ to the ♂ or ill-asp. ♄ by dir. (For Fracture of the various bones of the body see "Fracture" under such subjects as Ankles, Arms, Bones, Clavicle, Colles Fracture (see "Hurts" under Wrists); Elbow, Face (see "Hurts" under Face); Feet (see "Accidents" under Feet); Femur, Fibula, Fingers, Forearm, Hands, Head, Hips, Humerus, Jaws, Knees, Legs, Limbs, Radius, Ribs, Scapula (see Shoulders); Shoulder, Skull, Thighs, Tibia, Ulna, Vertebrae, Wrists, etc. Also see Dislocations, Joints).

Simple Fracture—♅, ♄, or ♂ acting alone as the afflictor, and not in combination.

FRAGILE—Brittle—

Appearance—Fragile Appearance—♃ affl. in ♋. (See Pale, Sickly).

Bones—Brittle and Fragile Bones—(See "Brittle" under Bones).

Hair—Dry and Brittle Hair—(See "Dry" under Hair).

FRAIL—Frail Body—Frail Constitution—(See "Sickly", "Weak", under Constitution).

Frail People—Death of the Frail Among the Aged—(See "Aged People" under Old Age).

FRAME—The Body—The Skeleton—

Athletic Frame—(See Athletics).

Whole Frame Disordered—(See Whole). For the various conditions and descriptions of the Frame see such subjects as Appearance, Body, Constitution, Delicate, Disease, Feeble, Form, Health, Height, Large, Long, Middle Sized, Shape, Short, Skeleton, Small, Stature, Strength, Strong, Stout, Weak, Weight, Wiry, etc.

FRANTIC—Frenzied—Excessive Excitement—(See Anger, Excitable; "Causes" under Fits; Frenzy, Fury, Madness, Mania, Raving; "High Temper" under Temper; Wild, etc.).

FRATRICIDE—(See "Fratricide" under Brothers).

FREAKS—Freaks of Nature—Mental and Bodily Freaks—Influences and Illustrations along this line with the planetary causes, etc., are given under the following subjects,—Anarchists; "Beastly Form" under Beasts; "Born Blind" under Blind; Congenital, Crazy, Cyclops, Deaf and Dumb (see Deaf, Dumb); Defects, Deformities, Demoniac, Dogs—Resembles Dogs—(see "Dogs" under Children); Dwarfs, Eccentric, Effeminate, Fanatical, Fowls—Resembles Fowls—(see Fowls); Frog Child (see Forearm); Giants, Geniuses, Glass, Growth, Hermaphrodite, Idiots, Inhuman, Insanity, Malformations, Mathematical, Monsters, Murderers, Peculiar, Perversions, Pituitary, Precocious, Prenatal Epoch (see Prenatal); Prodigies, Religion (see "Fanatical" under Religion); Savage, Twins (see "Siamese Twins" under Twins); Wild.

FRECKLES—Lentigo—Circumscribed Spots On the Skin—Freckles are due principally to a predominance of Iron in the skin (Iron ruled by ♂), and ♂ prominent at B.; ♂ in the Asc., or rising, or a ♂ influence or sign on the Asc.; ♂ rising in ♈ tends to give a face full of freckles, and fiery red hair; the ☉ in ♏; the ☽ in ♋, ♏, or ♓; the ☽ Sig. in watery signs in Hor'y Q.; ♀ Sig. in ♌ or ♎, or in these signs in partile asp. the Asc.; the 4th Face of ♈ on the Asc.; the 5th face of ♍, the 3rd face of ♎, the 1st and 4th faces of ♐ on ♑, or the 4th or 6th faces of ♓ on the Asc. Case—Red Hair and Freckled Face—See "Red Hair", No. 330 in 1001 N.N. (See Blemishes, Complexion, Defects; "Red Face" under Face; "Red Hair" under Hair; Marks, Moles).

FREE—

Free Living—Loose Living—Diseases From—The ☽ to the ill-asps. ♀ by dir.; afflictions to ♀; ♀ in bad asp. to the ☉; the ill-asps. of ♀ by dir. to the Asc. or M.C.; ♀ by Periodic Rev. to the ill-asps. the ☉; the Asc. to the ♂ or ill-asps. ♀ by dir., and ♀ affl. at B.; ♌ on cusp the 6th H. (See Debauched, Depraved, Dissipated, Dissolute, Drink, Eating, Excesses, Feasting; "High Living" under High; Indulgence, Intemperate, Loose; "Loose Morals" under Morals; Passion, Perversions; "Riotous Living" under Riotous; Sex, Vices).

Free Love—Entanglements—Liaisons—Inordinate Affection—Clandestine Love Affairs—Committed To—The ☉ ♂, □, or ☍ ♅ at B.; the ☉, ☽, or ♀ to the ill-asps. ♅ by dir., and espec. if affl. by ♅ at B.; principally a ♅ affliction when under the lower vibrations of ♅; ♅ affl. in ♌, ♏, or the 5th H.; ♅ affl. the ☉, ☽, or ♀; ♀ by Periodic Rev. in ill-asp. the ☉. (See "Free Living" in this section; "Unwomanly Freedom" under Morals; Nymphomania, Perverse; "Clandestine" under Sex).

Free from Passion—(See Apathy, Aversions, Bachelor, Celibacy, Deviations; "Free from Passion" under Passion; Perversions, etc.).

Free Will—(See "Free Will" under Will).

FRENZY—Phrenzy — Violent Mania — —Frantic—Beside Oneself—Excessively Excitable—

Causes of Frenzy—Due to religious, and other excitement, caused by ♅ and ♂ afflictions; ♅ affl. in the 12th H.; the ☉ Sig. □ or ☍ ♂; a ♂ disease, and with ♂ the afflicting planet; ♂ Sig. ☌ ☉, and with danger of the life being cut short by; ♂ Sig. □ or ☍ ☉; ☿ ill-dig. at B., and espec. when also affl. by ♅ or ♂. (See Anger; "Brain Storms" under Brain; Demoniac, Emotions, Enthusiasm; "Beside Oneself" under Excitable; Frantic, Fury, Hysteria, Impulsive, Insanity, Madness, Mania, Raving, Wild).

Death By—♂ the afflicting planet and holding the dominion of death; ♂ badly afflicted, and affl. the hyleg by dir., denotes death by Frenzy.

Delirium — Phrenitic Delirium—A Phrenitic Man—(See "Wild Delirium" under Delirium).

Religious Frenzy—Caused by ♅; ♅ affl. in the 9th H. (See "Religious Excitement" under Excitement).

FREQUENT—

Abscesses Frequent—(See "Frequent" under Abscesses).

Chronic Ailments—Frequent Chronic Ailments—The ☽ decr. at B., sepr. from ♃, and apply. to ♄. (See the ☽ influences under "Causes" under Chronic Diseases).

Fever—Frequent Attacks of—(See "Frequent Attacks" under Fever).

Headaches Frequent—(See "Women" under Headaches).

Ill-Health—Frequent Ill-Health—(See "Ill-Health All Thru Life" under Ill-Health; "Much Sickness" under Sickness).

Perspiration—Frequent Perspiration —(See "Frequent" under Sweat).

FRESH—Fresh Coloured and Handsome —Given by the ⚹ or △ asps. of ♂ to the ☉, ☽, or Asc. (See "Good" under Complexion; Handsome; "Complexion" under Ruddy).

FRETFULNESS— Peevishness—Discontentment—Worry, etc.—♄ people fret and mope; ♄ affl. in ♈; ♄ Sig. □ or ☍ ☽; ♄ in ♏, conspicuous fretfulness; ♂ to the cusp the 3rd H. by dir.; the 3rd Dec. of ♒ on the Asc., ruled by the ☽. (See Anguish, Anxiety, Dejected, Depressed, Despondent, Discontentment, Fears, Irritable, Low Spirits (see Low); Melancholy, Moping, Morose, No Peace of Mind (see "Peace" under Mind); Patience, Peevish, Petulant, Repining, Restless, Scolding, Worry, etc.).

FRICTION—Fremitus—Rubbing—Irritation—Diseases Accompanied By— (See "Dry Cough" under Cough; the various paragraphs under Dry; "Respiratory" under Mucous; "Inflammation" under Pleura).

FRIDAY—Ruled by ♀. (See Week).

FRIENDS—Ruled by the 11th H. Benefics here, and well-asp., give good and helpful friends. Malefics here tend to false friends, and injury by them. Lord of the 12th in the 11th H. tends to pretended friends, and private enemies.

Acquaintance—Death of—(See Acquaintances).

Danger—To a Friend—Ruler of the 11th H. affl. in the 6th H. at a Solar Revolution.

Death—Of a Friend or Friends—The ☉ or ☽ ☌ ♅, ♄, or ♂, or the ☌ of two malefics in the radical or revolutionary 11th H., indicate a friend lost by death or misfortune; ♄ to the ☌ or ill-asp. the ☉, death of a near friend; the 24° ♏ on the Asc. at B., sorrow thru the death of friends; malefics in the 8th H. at a Solar Rev., and espec. if malefics thru the 8th H., and espec. if they were in the 8th, afflicting the 8th, or lord of the 8th H. at B. (See "Female Friend", "Short Life", in this section).

Dissipated—Thru the Influence of Friends—♂ affl. in the 11th H. (See Dissipation).

Execrated—By Friends—(See Execrated).

False Friends—Injured By—The ☽ Sig. □ or ☍ ♃; lord of the 10th in the 12th H.; lord of the 10th a malefic, and affl. in the 11th H. (See Antipathy, Deceitful, Dishonest, Fortune, Libel, Mischief, Misfortune, Plots, Poison, Reputation, Ruin, Scandal, Treachery, Trouble, etc.).

Female Friend—Death of—The ☽ to the place of Cor Scorpio. (See Antares).

Few Friends—Unpopular—The ☉ ill-asp. by the ☽ and ♀ at B.; the ☽ in evil asp. to the ☉ or ♀; malefics in the 11th H. at B., a malefic ruler of this house, and no benefics in the 11th. (See Antipathy, Enemies, Home).

Many Friends—The ☉ well-asp. by the ☽ and ♀ at B.; the ☽ ⚹ or △ ♃, sincere in friendships; ♃ or ♀ ruler of the 11th H., or in the 11th, and with no malefics in this house, or ruler of the 11th; ♃ or ♀ ruler of the horoscope, and well-asp., and espec. when placed in the 11th H.; the malefics obscure in the map, and not badly aspecting the Significators; the ♒ sign when well-occupied and aspected, and strong at B., and with other good aspects, tends to many friends, as ♒ is related to the 11th H., and is known as the Sign of Friends. (See "Amiable", "Courteous", under Manners; Popular, Sympathy).

Short Life—Of Friends—Near and intimate friends are apt to die before middle life when the lord of the 8th H. is in the 11th H., and afflicted, unless the hyleg be strong, or the Asc. well-asp. by lord of the 1st H. (For further influences see Companions, Compatibility, Enemies, Family, Healers, Home, Incompatibility, Love Affairs, Marriage, Men, Parents, Relatives, Residence, Social Relations, Vagabond, etc.).

Sickness—On Account of Friends— Lord of the 6th in the 11th H.

FRIGHT—Easily Frightened—The ☽ strong at B., well placed and dignified. (See Darkness, Fears, Nervousness, Sensitives, Shocks).

Shocks by Fright—♅ ☌ ☽ in ♈.

FRIGID—(See Chill, Cold, Frost, Ice, Rigid, Rigors, Saturn, Snow, Winter).

FRIVOLITY—Diseases and Ailments From—(See Amusements, Carelessness, Debauchery, Dissipation, Dissolute, Drink, Eating, Excesses, Feasting, Folly, Free Living (see Free); Hasty, High Living (see High); Love Affairs, Men; "Shallow" under Mind; Opposite Sex (see Opposite); Passion, Rashness, Recklessness, Sex, Sports, Women, etc.).

FROG CHILD—Forearm Missing, and Both Legs Missing Below the Knees—(See Forearm).

FRONS SCORPIO—Fixed Star in ♐. (See Danger, Disease, Putrid, Sickness, Trouble, Violence).

FRONT—Front Part of the Body—Planets above the earth at B. tend to affect the front part of the body, and when below the horizon, the back or hinder parts. (See Back, Lower, Middle, Upper).

Marks or Moles—On Front Part of Body—(See Marks).

FRONTAL—

Frontal Bones—Frontal Sinuses—Abscess In—(See "Frontal" under Abscesses).

Frontal Headaches—(See "Frontal" under Headaches).

FROST—Ruled by ♄.

Abundance Of—♅ in an angle at the Winter Solstice; ♄ ☌ ☉ in ♈, ♑, ♒, or ♓. (See Cold, Ice, Saturn, Snow, Winter).

FRUIT—Fruits of the Earth—

Alterations In Fruit—Eclipses of the ☉ or ☽ in ♈; the ☽ and planets in earthy signs at Ingresses tend to bring events affecting the fruits of the Earth for good or evil, according to the asps. to the Lord of the Year or Quarter.

Cannot Eat Fruit—Case—See "Can't Eat Fruit", No. 365, in 1001 N.N. (See Diet, Eating, Food).

Corruption of Fruit—Causing Sickness If Eaten When Gathered—Eclipses of the ☉ or ☽ in ♋, corruption of fruit when gathered; an eclipse of the ☉ in the 2nd Dec. of ♈. (See Comets, Eclipses, Figs, Rottenness, Vegetation, Vines).

Scarcity—Of Fruit—Eclipses of the ☉ or ☽ in earthy signs; an eclipse of the ☽ in ♉; ♄ ☌ ♃ in fire, air, and earthy signs; Comets appearing in ♉, ♋, ♎, or ♏. (See Blight, Corn, Drought, Earth, Events (see "Nature Of" under Events); Famine, Figs, Grains, Herbs; Pestilential Virus (see "Virus" under Pestilence); Scarcity, Trees, Weather, Wheat, etc.).

FRUITFUL—Fruitfulness—Prolific—Fertile—Children Promised—♃, ♀, and the ☽ are the Givers of Children. The watery signs ♋, ♏, and ♓, are called the fruitful signs. Also ♉, the exalted sign of the ☽, is a very fruitful sign. Other signs are less fruitful, and ♈, ♊, ♌, and ♍ are classed as unfruitful and barren signs. The 5th and 11th H., being opposite houses, are the principal houses of children, and fruitful influences in these houses at B. promise children. The 11th H. is the 5th H. of the marriage partner by turning the map upside down, and the same conditions apply to the 11th H. as to the 5th H. when the map is reversed. The ☽ and ♀ are especially fruitful in the matter of giving children, and the ♋ sign influence tends to make women more fruitful and prolific. The horoscope of both husband and wife should be studied in judging of the matter of children, fruitfulness, and promise of children. If both are fruitful, children will result. If one is fruitful, and the other barren, children will be denied. Thus a woman denied children by her first marriage, if the husband is barren, impotent and sterile, may have them in a second marriage, if both are fruitful. The ☽ is the planet of fecundation. Heat and moisture in the body in abundance tend to make one prolific, while a cold and dry body, ruled by ♄ or ☿, tends to barrenness. When ☿ is ori. in fruitful, or seminal signs, and configurated with fruitful planets, as ♃, ♀, or the ☽, he gives offspring, but when in barren signs, and with barren planets, he denies them. The malefics also may give children when in prolific, or fruitful signs, and supported by benefics, but the children are apt to be sickly and short-lived. (See "Probability of Children", "Sickly Children", under Children). For the general influences which tend to give children, promise of children, and many children, see "Signs of Children" in this section.

Brothers Promised—Brothers and Sisters Promised—(See Brothers, Sisters).

Children Born—But They Die—(See "Death of Children" under Children).

Creative Powers—(See Creative, Generation, Reproduction; "Sex Powers" under Sex).

Females Fruitful—(See Probability, Signs, Symbols, in this section. Also see "Fruitful" under Wife).

Fruitful Signs—Of the Zodiac—♋, ♏, and ♓, the watery signs. Of these signs ♏ is the least fruitful because of its ruler ♂. The ♋ sign is fruitful because of the ☽. The ♓ sign is fruitful because of ♃, and ♓ is considered the most fruitful of all the signs. The ♉ and ♎ signs are considered rather fruitful because of their ruler ♀. The ♐ sign is rather fruitful because of its ruler ♃. The ♒ sign is considered more fruitful than barren.

Generative Powers Strong—(See Creative, Generation; "Sex Powers" under Sex. Also see "Signs of Children" in this section).

Husband Fruitful—(See "Fruitful" under Husband).

Large Family—(See "Many Children" under Children).

Male—Fruitfulness In the Male—(See "Fruitful" under Husband; "Signs of Children" in this section).

Many Children—(See "Many Children" under Children).

Mind—Fruitful Mind—(See Genius, Inventive).

Moderately Fruitful—The ☽ in ♉, ♎, ♏, or ♒.

Multiple Births—(See Double-Bodied, Multiple, Triplets, Twins).

Probability—Of Children—♃, ♀, or the ☽ in the 4th, 5th, 10th, or 11th H., and well-asp., and espec. if there are fruitful signs on the cusps of these houses. Look first to the 10th and 11th H., and if no planets therein look to the 4th and 5th H. If none there look to planets which may be in good asp. to degrees on the cusps of these houses. (See Eleventh, Fifth, Fourth, Tenth House. Also see "Signs", "Symbols", in this section).

Signs of Children—Symbols of Children—Signs of Conception—Children Promised—A Fruitful Marriage—Strong Powers of Generation—These influences should exist in the maps of both husband and wife to give promise of children—The ☽ in the 5th or 11th H. in a fruitful sign, and well-asp.; the ☽ in ♉ in the 5th H.; the ☽, ♃, or ♀ in the 5th H., in a fruitful or double-bodied sign, as in ♋, ♍, ♓, or in ♊ or ♐; the ☽ in the 11th H. in a fruitful sign; if the ☽ apply to the lord of the Asc., or lord of the 5th H. by good asp. from the 10th H., or by evil asp. if with mutual reception; the ☽ in the 5th H. in other than barren signs, and well-asp. by benefics; the ☽ essentially fortified and in reception with any planet in an angle; the ☽ in the 7th H., and beholding the lord of the 7th in the 11th, or the ☽ in the 11th and beholding the lord of the 7th H. in the 7th; the ☽, Asc., or lord of the Asc. in a fruitful sign; the ☽ to the place of Altair gives promise of marriage and children (see Altair); the ☽ in ♋ tends to make a female very prolific, and the ☽ sign ♋ on the Asc. or cusp of 5th H.; ♃ and ♀ in the 5th H., and in no ways afflicted; ♃ or ♀ in the Asc. or 11th H., there will be children, but not speedily; ♃ in the 1st, 5th, or 11th H., and in no asp. to ♄ or ♂, and the malefics be slow in motion, or ℞; ♃ in ♋ or ♍, well-asp., and espec. when in the 5th or 11th H.; ♃ and ♀, and a well-asp. ☉, ☽, or ☿, indicate children; ♃ or ♀ in the Asc., or with lord of the 5th in angles; ♃ in good asp. to the ☽, the body is fruitful and the health good; ♃ and ♀ in fruitful signs, and aspecting the houses of children, angular or succedent, and more ori. than the malefics, children will be stronger and more numerous; ♀ in the 5th H., and well-asp.; ♀ well-asp. in ♉ or ♎; the Asc. a fruitful sign; fruitful signs on the Asc., 5th, 10th, or 11th H.; lord of the Asc., or the ☽, in good asp. with the lord of the 5th, and lord of the 5th strong, or in a fruitful sign; lord of the Asc. in the 5th or 7th; benefics in the Asc., or with lord of the 5th in angles; lord of the Asc. in a good house, and beholding the cusp of the Asc. by good asp.; lord of the Asc. in mutual reception with a planet by house, sign, term, triplicity, or exaltation, with a planet which has the same reception exactly, if each be in the other's house; lord of the Asc., or the ☽, joined to lord of the 5th; lord of the Asc. or the ☽ be in the 5th, and free from affliction by malefics, ☋, or lords of the 6th, 8th, or 12th H.; a

fixed sign ascending with ♃ or ♀ therein, or if the lord of the 5th be strong in the Asc. or 10th H.; a planet, or planets, in the 5th H. in good asp. with the lord of the 5th; lord of the 5th in the Asc., or lord of the Asc. in the 5th; the 5th H. and its lord as Sigs. in Hor'y Q. indicate that there are children in the family inquired of; lord of the 5th in the Asc. or 7th H.; lord of the 7th in the 5th, or the ☽ with him; the sign on the 5th, or its lord, in a fruitful sign denote fruitfulness and children; lord of the 5th in the 1st, or lord of the 1st or the ☽ in the 5th, if lords of the 1st and 5th be in ♂; a fruitful sign on the cusp of the 1st or 5th, or their lords, or the ☽, be in a fruitful sign, or if a benefic be in the 1st, 3rd, 5th, 9th, or 11th H.; translation of light between the lords of the 1st and 5th, and particularly if made by the ☽, is a good symptom of children; lord of the 1st angular, with reception, denotes children; the fruitful signs ♋, ♍, or ♓ on the Asc. or 5th H. (See Barrenness, Increased, Many, Probability, under Children; Conception, Fecundation, Fertile, Generation; "Fruitful" under Husband, Marriage, Maternity, Mother, Pregnancy, Reproduction, Seminal, Wife; "Probability", "Symbols", in this section).

Symbols of Children—The ☽, Asc., lord of the Asc., or lord of the 5th H., being strong and well-aspected in a fruitful sign, and with fruitful signs on the 5th or 11th H. (See Probability, Signs Of, in this section).

Triplets—Quadruplets—(See Multiple, Twins).

Twins; Wife Fruitful—(See "Fruitful" under Wife).

Woman Is With Child—(See "Woman" under Pregnancy).

FRUITION—The Full ☽ is typical of fruition, fullness, plenitude of fluids, etc. (See "Full Moon" under Moon).

FUEL—Of the Body—(See Glycogen, Jupiter, Liver).

FUGITIVE—Fugitive from Justice—The Fugitive Is Dead—In Hor'y Q. if the ☽ or lord of the 7th be in the 8th, or apply to its lord by evil asp., or to the evil asp. of an infortune in the 4th H., or if the dispositor of the ☽ be in the 8th, he is dead. (See Judges, Law, Prison).

FULL—Fullness—

Abdomen—Fullness of—(See "Distentions", "Prominent", under Abdomen).

Arteries—(See "Fullness" under Arteries).

Blood—Fullness of—(See "Fullness" under Arteries; "Too Much Blood" under Blood).

Body—Full Body—The ☽ in her increase, full and tall; ♄ Sig. in ♒; ♃ Sig. in ♍, a reasonably full stature; ☿ Sig. in ♌, full and large body; ♀ Sig. in ♏, full and well-set; ♉ gives a full, short, well-set body; ♌ gives a full, tall, portly, and commanding stature. (See Corpulent, Fat, Fleshy, Large, Portly, Stout, Tall, etc.).

Breasts—Full Breasts—(See "Full" under Breasts).

Chest—Full Chest—(See Capacious, Stout, Wide, under Chest; "Capacity" under Lungs).

Constitution — The Constitution At Full—(See "Full" under Constitution).

Engorgement—(See "Fullness" under Arteries; Engorgement, Gluttony; "Vascular Fullness" under Vascular).

Eyebrows — (See "Full" under Eyebrows).

Eyes—Full Eyes—(See "Full" under Eyes).

Face—(See "Full" under Face).

Fat and Full Body—(See "Body" under Fat).

Fleshy and Full Body—(See "Fleshy Body" under Fleshy).

Fluids—Fullness of—(See "Fullness" under Fluids; "Full Moon" under Moon).

Full Habit—(See Habit).

Full Moon—(See "Full Moon" under Moon).

Full-Sized Person—(See "Body" under Large).

High Blood Pressure—Full Arteries —(See "Fullness" under Arteries; "Pressure" under Blood).

Lips—Full Lips—(See Lips).

Moon—(See "Full Moon" under Moon).

Neck—(See "Thick" under Neck).

Plenitude — Fullness — (See "Full Moon" under Moon; Plethora, Plenitude).

Short—Short and Full Stature—(See "Body" in this section).

Stature—Full-Sized Stature — (See "Body" under Large).

Stomach — Fullness At — (See "Stomach" under Gas).

System—Fullness of—⊙ diseases. (See System).

Tall and Full Body—(See "Body" in this section; Tall).

Vascular Fullness — (See Arteries, Blood, in this section; Vascular).

Vital Power At Full—(See "Hylegiacal Places" under Hyleg; "Full" under Vital; "Good" under Vitality).

FULMINATING—The Sudden Severity of Disease—Intensity of the Disease— ♂ action, and a physical quality of ♂. (See "High" under Fever; Intensity, Quick, Severity, Sudden).

FUMES—Gas—Gases—(See Gas).

FUNCTIONS—The ☽ is the chief index of functional integrity, and is at the head of the functional group. The ☽ is functional, and denotes affections and functional disturbances from external causes, as food, clothing, habits, climate, environment, etc. The nature of functional and structural disorders can be inferred from the combination of the sign, planet, house and aspects. The ☽ has chief rule over the bodily functions, and is the source of natural power, as the natural powers of each organ of the body depend upon the regular and proper functions of such part. The ☽ is more powerful and benefic over the functions when in-creasing, and more weak and malefic when decreasing in light. Functions, as ruled by the ☽, are to be designated as the particular power or activity of the organ ruled by the sign which contains the ☽ at B. For the functions ruled by each Sign see the Sign in the alphabetical arrangement, as Aries, Taurus, etc. Also for the functions of the various organs and parts of the body, their disorders and disturbances, see the part in the alphabetical arrangement, as Brain, Heart, Kidneys, Liver, Stomach, etc. The following subjects and paragraphs have to do with the various functions of the body, their normal and abnormal activities.

Ablation—Of Functions—(See Ablation, Remote, Removal, Suppression).

Activities—Functional Activities— The aspects and position of the ☽ govern the general habits of life and the functional activities. (See Habits. Also note the various paragraphs in this section).

Arrangements—The ☽ rules the functional arrangements, the functional activities, and the feminine functions, as the menses and childbirth. The functional arrangement is also governed by the cardinal signs.

Atrophy—Of Function—Atrophy of Process Thru Cessation of Function— The work of ♅ and ♄, and by their afflictions to the hyleg. (See Atrophy; "Suppressed" in this section).

Augmented—The good asps. between the ⊙ and ☽ tend to augment the functional and vital energies, but the evil asps. between them tend to disturb and retard them. (See "Increased" under Vitality).

Bowels—(See "Functions" under Bowels).

Brain—(See "Functions" under Brain).

Cells—Functions of—(See the various paragraphs under Cells).

Cerebral—(See "Cerebral Functions" under Cerebral).

Cessation — Of Function — ♄ in evil asp. to the ☽; ♄ influence and affliction. (See Atrophy, Depleted, Impeded, Slow, Suppressed, in this section).

Childbirth—The Functions of—Ruled by the ☽. (See "Causes of Birth" under Birth; Parturition).

Cold—Functions Prevented By—(See "Privation" in this section).

Congestions—Of the Functions—(See Congestion).

Conserving Of—(See Conservation).

Constitution—(See "Functions" under Constitution).

Constructive Functions — (See Constructive).

Crystallization—In the Body—Function of—The work of ♄. (See Crystallization, Deposits, Hardening).

Deficient—(See "Regular" in this section).

Depletion Of—(See Depletion; Disordered, Impaired, Low, Retarded, Suppressed, in this section).

Depressants—Functional Depressants —(See Anaesthetics, Anaphrodisiacs, Sedatives).

Deranged Functions—(See "Disordered", and the various paragraphs in this section; "Functions" under Constitution; Deranged).

Diet—The Functions Impeded by Wrong Diet—(See "Ailments" under Diet).

Difficult—The Feminine Functions Difficult and Slow—(See "Difficult" under Menses).

Digestive Functions—(See Digestion, Indigestion).

Directions—The Effects of Directions Upon the Functions—(See Directions).

Discomfort—From Painful, Excessive, Impaired and Irregular Functions— (See Discomfort; Irregular, Painful, in this section).

Disordered Functions—The Functions Disordered—Disturbed—Impaired— Impeded — Weakened — Retarded, etc. Are due to afflictions to the planets, whereas organic diseases are caused by afflictions to the signs; caused by Directions (see Directions); the ☉ affl. by the ☽; ☽ affl. in the 6th H.; the ☽ affl. in ♏ or ♑; the ☽ affl. in a fiery sign; afflictions to the ☽ or ♃; the ☽ afflicting the Asc.; ♃ in ☐ or ☍ the ☉. The nature of the functional disorder can be inferred from the combination of sign, house, and aspects. (See the various paragraphs in this section).

Dispersal—Of the Functional Energy —(See Dispersions).

Dissipation—Of the Functional Energy—A ♆ disease. (See Dispersals; "Energy Dissipated" under Dissipation; Neptune).

Disturbed Functions—(See "Augmented", "Disordered", and the various paragraphs in this section).

Dropsy—From Disturbed Bodily Functions—(See Dropsy).

Efficient—The ☽ in the water signs ♋ or ♓, the functions are more efficient, strong and regular. (See Regular, Strong, in this section).

Elimination—The Functions of—(See Elimination).

Energy—The Functional Energies— (See Dissipation Of, Strong, Weak, and the various paragraphs in this section).

Exaltation Of—(See "Excito-Motory" in this section).

Excessive—And Painful—Discomfort —The ☽ affl. by ♂ or ♀. (See "Discomfort", "Profuse", in this section).

Excito-Motory Function—Exaltation of—(See Exaltation).

Excretion—The Functions of—(See Excretion).

Expansion Of—Warmth of—(See Electric).

Fear—The Functions Suppressed Thru Fear—(See "Functions" under Fear).

Female Functions—The Feminine Functions—Disorders of—(See "Functions" under Female; "Difficult", and the various paragraphs under Menses; "Impeded" in this section).

Generative Function—Abuse of— Strong—Weak, etc.—(See Barren, Creative, Fruitful, Generation, Passion, Perversions; "Clandestine", "Sex Powers", under Sex).

Gestation—Functions of—(See Conception, Gestation, Pregnancy).

Harmony—The various functions of the body are kept in greater harmony when the ☉ or ☽ are in ☌, ✶ or △ asp. the Asc. at B., and by dir. (See Harmony).

Heart—The Functional Activities of —(See "Functions", and the various paragraphs under Heart).

Hindered—The Functions Hindered— ♄ influence. (See "Suppressed", and the various paragraphs in this section).

Impaired—♄ afflictions; the ☽ affl. by ♄. At the 1st Quarter, Full Moon, 3rd Quarter of the ☽, the functions and the constitutional activities tend to be impaired. (See Depletion, Slow, Suppressed, and the various paragraphs in this section; "Quarters" under Moon).

Impeded—The functions are impeded when the ☽ is in fiery signs, and often prevented, and the feminine functions espec. tend to be difficult and slow. (See "Ailments" under Diet; Irregular, Prevented, Retarded, Slow, Suppressed, Weakened, in this section).

Inhibited—♄ influence. (See "Functions" under Inhibitions; Retarded, Slow, Suppressed, and the various paragraphs in this section).

Irregular—And Painful—The ☉ and ☽ in bad asp. to each other; functional irregularities are ruled by the ☽, and caused by afflictions to the ☽, or the ☽ in incongenial signs; the ☽ affl. by ♄, irregular, stoppage, or suppression thru cold or privation; the ☽ affl. by ♃ or ♂, irregular and profuse; the ☽ afflicted in ♉; the ☽ affl. in ♏, irregular and painful female functions; the ☽ affl. in ♑, irregular, impeded, and uncertain, and due to depression, worry, and anxiety; the ☽ below the earth in a nocturnal nativity; the ☽ ruler of the 6th H., or in the 6th, and the planet afflicting the ☽ be ruler of the 1st, 6th, or 8th H., the functions are disturbed or irregular; ♀ ☐ or ☍ ☽, disturbed or irregular; ♀ ☐ or ☍ ☽, painful and irregular, causing discomfort, and usually due to loose living; ☿ ☐ or ☍ ☽, thru mental strain or anxiety. (See Anxiety, Depression, Discomfort; "Free Living" under Free; Irregularities, Menses. Also note the various paragraphs in this section).

Liver—Functions of—(See Liver).

Low—Lowered—The Functions Lowered—The functional activities tend to be lower at the New ☽, the 1st Quarter, Full ☽, and 3rd Quarter, and if it be an eclipse of the ☉, the Solar activity is equally depleted and low. The adverse asps. of ♄ to the ☽ tend to lower, retard, and suppress the functions for the time. (See "Full Moon", "New Moon", under Moon; Impeded, Retarded, Slow, Suppressed, in this section).

Maternity — The Functions of — (See Maternity).

Menses — Functional Disorders of — (See "Female Functions", "Irregular", in this section).

Natural Functions — The Natural Functions in the body are ruled by the ☽, and espec. in the female. (See Females, Menses, Natural; "Disordered", and the various paragraphs in this section).

Nature — Of Functional Disorders — (See "Disordered" in this section).

Normal — The Functions Normal and Regular—The ☉ well-asp. by the ☽; the ☽ well-asp. in ♋ or ♓, and free from the serious afflictions of the ☉ and planets; the ☽ elevated above the earth in a nocturnal nativity, or below the earth in a day geniture. (See Elevated, Normal, Regular; Efficient, Regular, Strong, in this section).

Obstructed — The Functions Obstructed—Caused by ♄, and ♄ afflictions to the ☽. (See Impeded, Retarded, Slow, Suppressed, and other paragraphs in this section; Obstructions).

Organic Functions—Ruled by the ☽. The ☽ rules the functions of the various organs of the body. Thus the ☽ in ♋ rules the functions of the stomach; in ♌, the functions of the heart, etc. The ♍ sign, which rules the abdomen and its organs, is recognized as being the algebraic common denominator of all organic diseases and functions, due to the different states and conditions of the digestive and bowel tracts, and their contents, and that nearly all diseases have their origin under the ♍ sign rule. For this reason purging has been held to from Ancient Times as one of the first things to do to relieve and remove the causes of disease in the bowel tract. (See Physic, Virgo). The ☉ is organic, while the ☽ is functional, and afflictions to the ☉ or ☽ in ♍, and espec. when in the 6th H., tend to serious disturbances of organic functions. (See Organic, Organs).

Over-Activity — Of the Functions — The ☽ ☌ ♂ at B. and by dir., may cause. Also ♃ tends to, and to surfeits and congestion of the parts ruled by the sign he is in at B., or by dir. or tr. (See Congestion; Augmented, Excessive, Profuse, Strengthened, in this section).

Painful — And Irregular — The ☽ affl. in ♍ with females; the ☽ affl. by ♂. (See Discomfort, Excessive, Irregular, in this section).

Painless—The ☽ well-asp. by ♂ or ♀. (See Normal, Regular, in this section).

Parenchyma—The Functioning Structure of an Organ—(See Parenchyma).

Parturition — Childbirth — The Functions of—(See Parturition).

Perfect — (See "Regular" in this section).

Perversion—Of Function—♅ □ or ☍ ☽, perversion of function of some organ, or the natural function rejected and refused, such as in Sex Perversions, Sodomy, etc. (See Perversions).

Prevented—The Functions Prevented —Retarded—Impeded—(See "Impeded" in this section).

Privation — The Functions Retarded or Suppressed thru Privation or Cold— The ☽ affl. by ♄. (See "Irregular" in this section; Privation).

Profuse — The Functions Profuse — (See "Irregular" in this section).

Properly Performed — (See Efficient, Normal, Regular, Strong, in this section).

Psychopathic Functions—(See "Functions" under Psychic).

Quarters of the Moon—As Related to the Functions—(See "Quarters" under Moon).

Recuperation—The Powers of Recuperation to Recover from Disordered Functions—(See Recuperation, Resistance, Vitality).

Regular—The Functions are Regular, Efficient, Normal, and Strong—The ☉ well-asp. by the ☽; the ☽ below the earth in a day nativity, and above the Earth in a night one; the ☽ well-asp. in ♉, ♋, or ♓; the ☽ well-asp. by ♄, ♃, ♂, and ♀; the ☽ ⚹ or △ the Asc.; the ☽ well-asp. by ♄, regular, but apt to be slow, weak, and deficient; the ☽ well-asp. by ♃, and free from adverse afflictions, the functions are regular and perfect. (See Efficient, Normal, Strong, in this section).

Resistance — The Vital Resistance Good to Disordered Functions — Well Able to Fight Against Functional Disorders—The ☉ well-asp. in ♎. (See Recuperation, Resistance, Stamina, Tone, Vitality Good, etc.).

Retarded—The Functions Retarded— The ☉ or ♃ □ or ☍ ☽; ♄ affl. the ☽. (See Difficulty, Hindered, Impaired, Impeded, Irregular, Obstructed, Slow, Stopped, Suppressed, in this section).

Revitalization—Of the Functions and Fluids—(See "First Quarter" under Moon).

Secretion—The Secreting Functions— (See Secretion).

Sedatives — Functional Sedatives and Depressants — (See "Depressants" in this section).

Sensorial Functions — Impaired—(See "Functions" under Sensation).

Slow and Difficult—And Especially In Females—The ☽ affl. in fiery signs; the ☽ affl. by ♄. (See "Difficult" under Menses; Regular, Retardations, Slow, Suppressions, etc.).

Solar-Lunar Activities — As Related to the Functions and Health—The ☉ and ☽ should be in good asp. to each other at B. to insure regular and normal functions, and general good health, and afflictions between the Lights at B., and by dir., tend to impair the functional activities, and the welfare of the constitution in general. (See "Good" under Constitution, Health, Vitality; the various paragraphs in this section).

Stagnation—Of the Functions—Caused by ♄ afflictions; the ☽ ☌ or ill-asp. ♄ at B., and by dir.; also assisted by an evil asp. between the Lights at B., and with an ill-asp. of ♄ in the configuration. (See Atrophy, Cessation, Destructive, Fear, Impeded, Irregular, Retarded, Suppressed, in this section).

Stomach — The Functions of Disordered — (See Diet, Digestion, Eating, Food, Indigestion, Stomach).

Stoppage—Of the Functions—Caused by ♄, and the ☽ affl. by ♄. (See Irregular, Suppressed, in this section).

Storing — The Storing Functions of the Body—(See Conservation).

Strengthened — The Functions Strengthened—The ☉ in good asp. to the ☽; the ☽ below the earth in a day nativity, or above the Earth in a night one; the ☽ well-asp. by the ☉, ♄, ♂, ♀, and ☿; ☿ in good asp. the ☽ acts favorably upon the functions, and with greater power of mind to control them. (See Efficient, Normal, Regular, Strong, in this section).

Strong—The Functions Strong, Regular, and Efficient—The ☽ well-asp. by the ☉ and many planets, and free from ♄ affliction; the ☽ in the congenial watery signs ♋ or ♓, and well-asp., the functional activities are strong and efficient. (See Efficient, Normal, Regular, Strengthened, in this section).

Suppressed — The Functions Suppressed — Suspended— Hindered — Retarded—Slow — Stopped, etc. — Caused by ♄ and ♄ affl. to the ☽; ♅ □ or ☍ ☽, may be complete suppression, and attended by some incurable disorder. (See Hindered, Impeded, Irregular, Retarded, Slow, Stopped, in this section; Incurable, Stoppages, Suppressions).

Suspended—The Functions Suspended — ♄ influence. (See "Suppressed" in this section).

Transforming—The Transforming Functions of the Body—(See Conservation).

Uncertain—And Irregular— (See "Irregular" in this section).

Vital Functions — The Vital Functions Suspended — (See "Suppressed" in this section. Also see the various paragraphs under Vital).

Vitality—And the Functions—The ☽ affl. in ♍ in females tends to painful, irregular functions, and to lower the tone and vitality. (See the various paragraphs under Vitality).

Warmth — The Warmth and Expansion of the Functions—(See Electric).

Wastings—Wasting—Functional Disorders Caused By — (See Emaciation, Nutrition, Wastings).

Weak—The Functions Weak and Irregular — (See Impeded, Irregular, Regular, Retarded, Slow, Suppressed, Weakened, in this section).

Weakened—The Functions Weakened — Impeded — Impaired — Retarded, etc. —The ☉ □ or ☍ ☽, the functions of the organ ruled by the sign containing the ☽ are weakened, impeded, and disturbed; the ☽ affl. in ♍, ♎, or fiery signs; the ☽ below the earth in a nocturnal nativity; the ☽ affl. by ♄, weakened, and may be suppressed and stopped by cold and privation; the ☽ well-asp. by ♄, may be regular, but weak, slow, or deficient; the ☽ affl. by the bad asps. of ♃, the functions weakened and impeded by injudicious diet; ☿ □ or ☍ ☽, weakened, impeded,

and irregular thru mental strain, anxiety and worry. (See "Ailments" under Diet; "Weak Body" under Weak; Vitality Low; Impaired, Impeded, Irregular, Slow, Suppressed, in this section).

FUNDAMENT—Of the Body—The Base — The Anus — Ruled by ♂, ☿, the ♍ sign, and the 9th H.

Disorders Of—Are ♍ diseases, and afflictions to ♂ and ☿; malefics and afflictions in the 9th H. (See Anus, Rectum).

Knots In—(See Knots).

FUNGUS GROWTHS — Vegetable Growths—Ruled by ♆. Also a ☉ disease. (See Excrescences, Growths, Mushrooms, Sponges, Tumors; "Vegetable Growths" under Vegetable).

Fungi—(See Tinea).

FURY — Furious — Madness — Frenzy — Violent— Mania — Furious Conduct— Furious Temper, etc.—The ☉ affl. in ♉, ♌, or ♏; ☉ Sig. □ or ☍ ♂; the ☽ Sig. to the ♂ or ill-asps. ♂ by dir., and ♂ ill-dignified; the ☽ to the place of the Bull's Horns by dir.; ♆ affl. in the 12th H.; ♃ Sig. □ or ☍ ♂; ♂ ill-dig. at B., and affl. by ♄ and ☿; ♂ affl. at B., and born under ♂ influence, or ♂ ruler; ☿ causes when the dominion of death is vested in him; ☿ Sig. ☌ or ill-asp. ♂ at B., and by dir.; ☿ on the Asc., furious like the Bull when provoked. (See Anger, Brain Storms, (see Brain); Cruel, Demoniac, Desire Body (see Desire); Epilepsy, Excitable, Frenzy, High Temper (see Temper); Hysteria, Impulsive, Insanity, Madness, Mania, Ravings, Riotous, Savage, Uncontrolled, Vehement, Vicious, Violent, Wild, etc.).

Beasts — Injury by Furious Beasts — (See "Furious" under Beasts).

Death by Fury—(See "Death" under Madness).

Enthusiasm—The Fury of—(See Enthusiasm).

Fits of Fury — The combined influence of ♄ and ♂ induces to alternate fits of fury and melancholy.

Soldiers — Soldiers Become Furious and Cruel—(See Soldiers).

FUSIONS—Adhesions—Union of Parts —Coalition—(See Coalition).

FUTURE EVENTS—The Times of Possible Accidents, Disease, Injury, Death, etc.—Future events are of the nature of the planet, or planets, causing them. Mars ☌ or ill-asp. the ☉, ☽, Asc., M.C., or Hyleg, by dir. tends to accidents, cuts, injury, fever, inflammations, quarrels, violent death, etc. The afflictions of ♄ tend to chronic ill-health, sorrow, trouble, misfortune, reverses, or even death, if the vitality is low thru worry. And so on with each of the planets. Raphael's Ephemeris of the Major Planets from the year 1900 to the year 2000 should be in the hands of every student who wishes to look ahead over the planetary influences for many years to come. (For further discussion of this subject see Character, Directions, Events, Fate, Prognostication, Time).

G

GAIT—Carriage—Locomotion—Step—Walk — Tread — Motion In the Body, etc.—This subject is also largely considered under "Walk", as Gait and Walk are both quite frequently referred to in the Textbooks of Astrology, and for convenience of reference some of the subjects are given here, and some under Walk. See the following subjects in the alphabetical arrangement when not considered here—

Action—(See the various paragraphs under Action).

Active Body—(See Active).

Ankles Knock—(See Ankles).

Automatic Action—(See Automatic).

Awkward Gait—Or Walk—♄ Sig. in ♑; ♑ on the Asc. (See Awkwardness, Clumsiness. Also note the various paragraphs in this section).

Awry Gait — Treading — Twisted—Turned to One Side, Distorted, etc.—♄ in the Asc. or M.C. at B., in earthy signs.

Bad Gait—♄ in ♑ in partile asp. the Asc.

Balanced Movement — (See Balance, Coordination, Dexterity).

Bow Legs — (See this subject under Legs).

Brisk Gait — (See "Energetic" in this section).

Carriage — (See the various paragraphs in this section, and under Walk).

Claw Feet—(See Feet).

Club Feet—(See Feet).

Clumsy Gait — (See Clumsiness; "Dragging", and the various paragraphs in this section).

Commanding Gait—Majestic—♌ influence; ♌ on Asc. (See Commanding).

Coordination Of — (See Coordination, Incoordination).

Crippled—In the Legs or Feet—(See Crippled, Extremities, Feet, Legs, Limbs, Lower).

Defective Gait—Defects In—♄ in the Asc.; caused by ♄ afflictions. (See Defects; "Defective" under Walk).

Deformities—In Legs or Feet—(See Deformities, Distortions, Feet, Legs).

Dexterity — In Gait — ☿ and □ influence. (See Dexterity; "Energetic" in this section).

Distorted Gait — (See Distortions; "Awry" in this section).

Downward Look — (See "Downward" under Look; Stooping).

Dragging Gait—Shuffling—♄ ascending at B. (See "Knocking" under Ankles; "Club Feet" under Feet; "Knock Knees" under Knees).

Energetic Gait—Brisk Walk—Light, Quick, Smart, and Nimble Step — □ gives; ☿ Sig. of the person in Hor'y Q.; ☿ ascending at B., and free from the afflictions of other planets. (See Ac-tion, Active, Energy, Motion, Movement, Nimble, Quick, Rapid).

Equilibrium Disturbed—(See Balance, Coordination, Equilibrium, Incoordination; "Equilibrium" under Walk).

Erect; Feet — The Feet Strike Together—♄ ascending at B. (See "Dragging" in this section).

Festination — The Peculiar Walk of Paralysis Agitans—(See "Festination" under Walk).

Firm Step—Firm, Commanding, Proud and Majestic—♌ gives; ♌ on the Asc.

Flat Feet — (See "Splay Foot" under Feet).

Forward — Pitches Forward.— (See "Equilibrium" under Walk).

Genteel Carriage—A Good Carriage—□ and ♌ give; ♀ Sig. in ♎. (See Genteel).

Gouty—(See "Feet" under Gout).

Heavy Gait—♓ gives; ♓ on Asc. (See Heavy, Stooping).

Incoordinated—(See "Equilibrium" in this section).

Intoxicated Gait — Drunken — (See Drunkenness, Intoxication).

Knock Knees—(See Knees).

Lameness—In the Legs or Feet—(See Lameness; "Lameness" under Feet, Legs).

Legs — Defects In — Crooked — Deformed—Lameness In—(See Legs).

Light Walk—Nimble—Quick—Energetic — (See "Energetic" in this section; "Active Body" under Active; Motion, Movement, Nimble, Quick, Rapid, etc.).

Limping — (See "Gout", "Lameness", and the various paragraphs under Feet, Knees, Legs, Limbs).

Locomotion — Defects of — (See Action, Locomotion, Motion, Movement, Muscles).

Majestic Gait — (See Commanding, Firm, in this section).

Malformations — In Legs and Feet — (See Crippled, Deformities, in this section; Distortions, Malformations).

Motion — Of the Body — (See Action, Motion, Movement, Quick, Rapid, Slow, etc. Also note the various paragraphs in this section).

Movement—Of the Body—(See Movement. Also see the various paragraphs in this section).

Muscles—(See "Muscles" under Legs; Muscles).

Nimble Step — Light — Quick — (See "Energetic" in this section; "Quick Motion" under Motion; Quick).

Paralysis Agitans—Peculiar Gait of—(See "Festination" under Walk).

Peculiar Gait—(See "Festination" under Walk).

Pitches Forward—(See "Equilibrium" under Walk).

Posture—(See the various paragraphs under Posture).

Proud Gait — (See Proud; Commanding, Firm, in this section).

Quick Walk—(See "Energetic" in this section).

Rough In Carriage — ♄ Sig. in ♉ (Hor'y).

Shuffling Gait — (See "Dragging" in this section).

Slow Gait—(See Dull, Feeble, Inactive, Inertia, Lassitude; "Slow Motion" under Motion; "Dragging", and the various paragraphs in this section).

Smart and Quick — (See "Energetic" in this section).

Splay Foot—(See "Splay" under Feet).

Staggering Gait — Swaying — Tottering—Due to afflictions to ☿, and Incoordination. (See Clumsy, Equilibrium, Intoxicated, in this section).

Step Firm — Majestic — (See Commanding, Firm, in this section).

Stooping — Heavy — (See Downward Look, Heavy, in this section; Stooping).

Stoppage Gait—♄ influence; ♄ affl. in ♓; Subs at LPP (4, 5L); also may be caused by ♅ influence, and due to incoordination, partial paralysis, etc. (See Coordination, Incoordination, Stoppages, Suppressions; "Festination" under Walk).

Strutting Gait—Swaggering—♅ setting at B., and not in a strong sign or house; ♄ rising and affl. at B.; ♄ Sig. of the party in Hor'y Q., and one who knocks his ankles together, or who may be bow-legged or knock-kneed. (See Dragging, Equilibrium, Proud, in this section).

Swaggering—(See "Strutting" in this section).

Swaying — Tottering — (See Equilibrium, Staggering, in this section).

Tottering—(See "Staggering" in this section).

Treading Gait — (See "Awry" in this section).

Turned to One Side—(See "Awry" in this section).

Twisted Gait — (See "Awry" in this section; Contortions, Twistings).

Unsteady—(See "Staggering" in this section).

Waddling Gait—♓ on the Asc. (See Dragging, Heavy, in this section).

GALEN—Galen taught the same theories about the cure of disease as did Hippocrates. (See Antipathy, Hippocrates).

GALL—Bile — Gall Bladder — Choler — Gall Stones, etc.—(See Bile).

GALLOWS—Death On by Sentence — (See Hanging, Judges).

GAMBLING—Gamblers are born under severe mental affliction, and Gambling is practically a mental disease. The 5th H. rules largely over gambling and speculation. The watery signs predominating at B., and also malefics in ♐ or ♐, or with these signs upon the Asc., and afflicted, tend to. The ☉ Sig. in ♓; ♅ in strong asp. to the cusp of 5th H., or a planet in the 5th;

the ☽ in the 5th H., and afflicted; ♄ Sig. ♂ ♀; ♂ ruler at B., and afflicted, and also afflicting ☿; ♂ Sig. in ♉ or ♊; ♂ or ♀ in the 5th H.; ♀ Sig. ♂ ♂; ♀ in the 5th H., and affl. by ♄ or ♂, and espec. when ☿ is in a water sign; lord of the 5th H. in the Asc., and afflicted; ♐ on the Asc., and the 5th H. affl. by ♂; the 6th face of ♌ on the Asc. (See Cheating, Deceitful, Dishonesty, Forgers, Riches, Speculative, Shrewdness, Thieves, etc.).

GAMES — Fond of Outdoor Sports and Games—Danger of Injury or Death By —(See Amusements, Exercise, Hunting, Sports).

GANGLION—Ganglia—Nerve Centers— Chronic diseases begin their action in the Ganglionic Centers, while acute diseases start with disturbances of the peripheral nerves. (See Acute, Chronic, Peripheral). The action of ♄ by cold and chill, and by causing internal congestions, disturbs the ganglionic centers. (See Centripetal, Cold, Congestions, Saturn).

Basal Ganglia — The ☉ and ☽ acting thru the ♏ sign, by way of the Lumbar and Intestinal branches of the Solar Plexus, affect and influence the Basal Ganglia of the brain, and also the Medulla, the Pituitary Body, Ductless Glands, Genito-Urinary System, Bladder, Rectum, Anus, Uterus, Large Intestines, and give way to the Hepatic Diathesis. (See Diathesis, Ductless, Liver; "Ribes", in this section).

Central Ganglia—(See "Vaso-Dilator" under Vaso).

Cerebral Ganglia — (See Brain, Cerebral).

Cervical Ganglion—The ☉ and ☽ acting thru the ♉ sign affect the Superior Cervical Ganglion, the pharyngeal plexus, the eustachian tubes, the throat and neck, and give way to the Renal Diathesis. (See "Cervical Ganglion" under Cervical; "Lumbar", "Middle", in this section).

Fifth Thoracic Ganglia — (Spinal) — Influenced by the ☉ and ☽ acting thru the ♋ sign. The 5th thoracic (spinal) ganglia, the left coronary, the hepatic, splenic, diaphragmatic, and gastric plexuses, affect the organs of digestion, the pleura and their dependencies, and give way to the Cranio-Abdominal Diathesis. (See "Middle Cervical" in this section; Diaphragm).

Impar—The Ganglion Impar (in front of the Coccyx)—Acted upon by the ☉ and ☽ in ♐. Also the ☉ and ☽ in this sign, acting thru this ganglion and the inferior hypogastric plexus, affect the heart, the bladder, the muscular system, the hips, thighs, the gastro-intestinal tunics, and give way to the Thoracic Diathesis. (See Chest, Thorax).

Lumbar Ganglia—The ☉ and ☽ in ♎ act upon this ganglia, and also by acting thru the aortic, hypogastric, and renal plexuses, affect the hypogastrium, the renal system, the bladder in infants, uterus in pregnant women, the small intestine, and give way to the Renal Diathesis. (See "Cervical" in this section).

Middle Cervical Ganglion—The ☉ and ☽ in ♊, acting thru this ganglion, and the thoracic (spinal) ganglia, the right coronary plexuses, the deep cardiac, the post-pulmonary plexuses, affect the upper limbs, the respiratory system, and give way to the Cranian Diathesis. (See "Fifth Thoracic", "Splanchnic", in this section).

Pathological Formation—Of Ganglion —♀ in ♊.

Ribes—The ☉ and ☽ acting thru ♈, thru the ganglion of Ribes, and also thru the cavernous and carotid plexuses, affect the head and its dependencies, and the cerebro-spinal nervous system, and give way to the Hepatic Diathesis. (See "Basal" in this section).

Semilunar Ganglion—Ruled by the ♋ sign.

Spinal Ganglion — (See "Fifth Thoracic", "Middle Cervical", in this section).

Splanchnic Ganglia — The ☉ and ☽ acting thru the ♍ sign, thru the Splanchnic ganglia, the solar and mesentric plexuses, affect the abdominal organs and their dependencies, the lower part of the stomach, and give way to the Cranian Diathesis. (See "Middle Cervical" in this section; Cranium, Diathesis, Nerves, Plexuses).

Vaso-Dilator Action — (See "Central" in this section).

GANGRENE—The Mortification and Death of Soft Tissue — Gangrenous Sores—A ♄ disease, and caused usually by chill and cold, driving the blood inwards, causing congestion and mortification; Subs at CP and Local. (See Carcinoma, Centripetal, Cold, Congestion, Crusts, Decay, Malignant, Mortification, Necrosis, Sores, Ulcers).

Mouth—Gangrenous Sores In—Cankers—Cancrum Oris—Aphthae—A ♄ disease; ♄ in the 6th H.; ♄ affl. the hyleg or Asc. (See "Mouth" under Aphthae).

Pus—Malignant Gangrene with Pus—(See "Gangrene" under Pus).

GAS—Gases—Fumes—Air—Atmosphere —Ether—Vapor, etc.—Gases are ruled by ♅, as this planet rules the Ether, the Air, the Atmosphere, etc. Also ruled and influenced by the Airy Signs, and espec. the ♒ sign, the strong sign of ♅. The following subjects and paragraphs have to do with Gas, Gases, their compounds, influences, and effects in and out of the human body, which subjects see in the alphabetical arrangement when not considered here.

Abdomen — Gaseous Distention of — Meteorism—♅ affl. in ♍. (See Abdomen, Bowels, Distentions, Flatulence, Inflation, Tympanites; "Bowels" under Wind).

Air; Aquarius; Asphyxia; Belching;

Bloating; Borborygmus — (See this subject under Bowels).

Bowels — Gas In — (See "Gas" under Bowels).

Caisson Disease—(See Caisson).

Carbon; Colic; Compressed Gases—Compressed Air — Ruled by ♅. (See Caisson, Compressed).

Cramps; Death — By Escaping Gas — Suffocated By — Case—See "Knights", No. 270, in 1001 N.N.

Distentions; Dyspnoea; Emphysema;

Escaping Gas—Death By—(See "Death" in this section).

Ether; Explosions; Fermentation;

Flatulence; Foul Gases—(See Foul).

Fumes; Gastralgia—(See Stomach).

Hydrogen; Indigestion; Inflations;

Meteorism — (See "Abdomen" in this section).

Miasma; Nitrogen; Noxious; Odors;

Oxygen; Poisoning — Poison Gases — Death By—♅ in the 8th H., and affl. the hyleg; also Subs at Lu.P. (3D) make the effects of Poison Gases more depressive and dangerous. (See Poison).

Pressure—Gas Pressure—Compressed Gas—Ill Effects of—(See Caisson, Compressed; "Atmosphere" under Pressure).

Puffing; Pungent; Spinal Gas — The Gas In the Spinal Canal—(See "Canal" under Spine).

Stomach—Gas In—Bloating—Indigestion—Fullness At Stomach—Caused by afflictions in ♋, ♍, and ♓; ♋ on cusp the 6th H.; the ☽ in ♋ □ or ill-asp. any of the malefics as promittors; the ☽ affl. in ♋ tends to bloating from gas; ♅ affl. in ♋ or ♍; ♄ affl. in ♋; ♃ affl. in ♌ or ♋; a ♃ disease, due to surfeits; ☿ affl. in ♋ tends to windiness in stomach, and due to worry and anxiety; ☿ affl. in ♍ or ♓; the Asc. to the place of ☊ by dir. (See Bloating, Belching, Flatulence, Indigestion, Plethora, Pressure; "Wind" under Stomach).

Suffocation—By Escaping Gas—(See "Death" in this section).

Sun Spots — And the Gases of Our Atmosphere—(See "Sun Spots" under Spots).

Swellings — Caused by Gases, Wind, etc., In the Body — (See Distentions, Flatulence, Inflations, Swellings, Tympanites, etc. Also note the various paragraphs in this section).

Tympanites—(See "Abdomen" in this section; Tympanites).

Uranus—(See "Influence of ♅" under Uranus).

Vapors; Wind—(See "Bowels"; "Stomach" under Wind).

GASTRIC—Gastro—Gastronomical—Gastro-Abdominal Disorders—Stomach Disorders—Gastro-Intestinal Disorders —The subject of Gastric is largely considered under Stomach, as Gastric means pertaining to the Stomach. A few subjects concerning the Stomach, which are especially referred to in the Textbooks as Gastric, will be listed in this section, and also referred to in the section on Stomach. See the following subjects in the alphabetical arrangement, or under Stomach, when not considered here.

Abdominal—(See "Gastro-Abdominal" in this section).

Acids — The Gastric Acids — Gastric Acidity—Hydrochloric Acid—(See Acids, Digestion, Fluids, Indigestion, Juices, etc.).

Cancer—Gastric Cancer—(See "Stomach" under Carcinoma).

Catarrh — Gastric Catarrh — (See "Catarrh" under Stomach).

Deficient—The Gastric Juices Deficient—(See "Stomach Juices" under Deficient).

Disorders — Gastric Disorders — (See the various paragraphs in this section, and under Stomach).

Fever — Gastric Fever — Fever with Gastric Derangement — The ⊙ affl. in ♋; a ♋ disease; afflictions in ♋; the ☽ hyleg, and to the ☌ or ill-asp. ♄ by dir.; ♂ in ♋ in the 6th H.; ♂ affl. in ♋ or ♍. Case—See Chap. 13, page 97, in Daath's Medical Astrology. (See Fever).

Gastralgia — Pain In the Stomach — The ⊙ to the ☌ ☽ by dir.; ♂ affl. in ♋; Subs at SP (7D). (See "Pain" under Stomach).

Gastritis—Inflammation of the Stomach—The ⊙ ☌ ♂ in ♋; the ⊙ or ♂ affl. in ♋; ♅ and ♂ action in ♋; ♂ in ♋ in the 4th H. These influences tend to Acute Gastritis. Chronic Gastritis is caused by ♄ affl. in ♋, or affl. the hyleg therefrom. Subs at SP and KP tend to the various forms of Gastritis, as the acute Catarrhal form, with excessive secretion of mucus, the Phlegmonous form, with excessive redness and swelling, the toxic form from swallowing poison. Case—See "Gastritis", Chap. 13, page 91, in Daath's Medical Astrology. (See Inflammation).

Gastro-Abdominal Disorders—Due to the combined action of planets in the ♋, ♍, and ♓ signs, and in the 4th and 6th H. (See the Introduction under Disease; "Sixth House" under Sixth; "Innervation" in this section).

Gastroenteritis—Inflammation In Both Stomach and Bowels—♂ affl. in ♍. (See "Inflammation" under Bowels; Enteritis).

Gastro-Intestinal — (See "Tunics" in this section).

Gastronomical — (See "Indiscretions" in this section).

Indiscretions — Gastronomical Indiscretions—(See "Evil Diet" under Diet; Eating, Food, Gluttony; "Diet" under Indiscretions).

Inflammation — Gastric Inflammation —(See "Gastritis" in this section).

Innervation — Gastro-Abdominal Innervation—The physiological action of the ☿ Group of Planets and Herbs tends to produce, and by acting thru the Solar Plexus. (See "Mercury Group" under Herbs).

Intestinal Tunics — Gastro-Intestinal Tunics—(See "Tunics" in this section).

Juices—Gastric Juices—Are ruled by the ♋ sign. Saturn affl. in ♋ or ♍ tends to disturbances of these juices, deficiency of, abnormality of, lack of, obstructions of, restraint of, sluggish action or production of, etc. Also Subs at SP (8D) tend to disorders of. (See "Fluids" under Digestion).

Migraine—(See Migraine).

Neuroses — Gastric Neuroses — (See "Neuroses" under Stomach).

Obstructions—Gastric Obstructions— (See "Juices" in this section; "Obstructions" under Stomach).

Pepsin — Lack of In Stomach — (See "Pepsin" under Stomach).

Plexuses — Gastric Plexuses — Ruled by the ♋ sign. (See "Fifth Thoracic" under Ganglion).

Troubles — Gastric Troubles — Afflictions in ♋ or ♍. (See the various paragraphs in this section, and under Digestion, Indigestion, Stomach. Also see Migraine).

Tumor — Gastric Tumor — Tumor In the Stomach—Afflictions in ♋; a ♋ disease; the ⊙ in ♋ and affl. by ♄; ♃ or ♀ affl. in ♋. (See Tumors).

Tunics — Gastro-Intestinal Tunics — (See "Impar" under Ganglion).

Ulcer — Gastric Ulcer — Imposthumes —Abscess or Ulcer In the Stomach— ♄ in ♋; ♂ in ♋ or ♍. (See Abscess, Ulcers).

Vein — The Gastric Vein — Ruled by the ♋ sign. (See Veins).

GEMINI—The Gemini Sign—This is the Third Sign of the Zodiac, and is affiliated with the Third House. It is ruled by ☿. The Symbol of this sign is "The Twins". Gemini is hot, moist, and mental in nature, and disturbs the nervous system. Gemini is in an airy, barren, bi-corporeal, changeable, commanding, common, dexterous, double-bodied, dual, fortunate, hot, human, masculine, mental, moist, motive, mutable, nervous, northern, positive as a masculine sign, yet given to negativeness and passivity as a common sign; restless, sanguine, speaking, sweet, vernal, western, whole sign. This sign corresponds to the atmospheric vibrations, and has affinity with the sense of hearing. The Hebrew letter Zain is connected with the ♊ sign, the sign which rules the arms and hands, the instruments by which thoughts are executed. Breathing is a function of this sign. It is a sign of Speech, along with ☿, the ruler of the sign. The ☽ directed to the Right Foot of Gemini, in the Constellation Gemini, is said to bring good health. This sign on the Asc. at B. tends to give a tall, slender body, with long fingers, a straight nose, fine expressive eyes, and with good vitality. For the Countries and Nations ruled by ♊ see "Gemini" under Nations. The Colors ruled by ♊ are white mixed with red. (See "Air Signs" under Signs).

GEMINI RULES — Each Sign of the Zodiac has an external, internal, and structural rulership over the parts of the body ruled by the sign. Externally, ♊ rules the shoulders and upper arms. Internally, the breath, nerve fibres, and upper lobes of the lungs. Structurally, the clavicle, scapula, humerus, or bones of the part. The following is an alphabetical and classified list of the parts of the body, and other matters ruled by ♊, as listed and mentioned in the various Textbooks of Astrology. See these subjects in the alphabetical arrangement—Air, Arms, Atmosphere, Blood Making (see Haematopoiesis); Breathing (Breath);

Bronchial Tubes; Bryonia Alba, a typical drug of this sign; Capillaries; Chloride of Potassium, the Zodiac Salt ruled by this sign (see Potassium); Clavicle (Collar Bone); Colors, white and red mixed; Countries (see Nations); Dorsal Nerves and Dorsal Region of the Spine; Drugs (see Bryonia, Potassium); Fingers, Function of Breathing, Gases, Haematopoeisis, Hands, Hearing, Humerus; Lungs (upper lobes of); Mentality, Mind; Nations (see "Gemini" under Nations); Nerve Fibers; Nerves in General, the upper Dorsal, the upper Spinal; Nervous System; Oxygenation of the Blood (see Oxygen); Potassium Chloride, Radius, Respiratory System; Ribs (Upper); Scapula, Shoulders and Shoulder Blades, Speech; Spine (Dorsal Region of); Thymus Gland, Trachea, Twins; Ulna, Upper Dorsal and Spinal Nerves and Upper Ribs.

GEMINI DISEASES — The Diseases and Afflictions Ruled by Gemini—The ☉ afflicted in this double-bodied sign tends to two diseases at the same time. The pathological action of ♊ tends to Negativeness, Passivity, Nervousness, and Restlessness. However, ♊ is the strongest of the common signs to control and fight off disease. See the following disease subjects in the alphabetical arrangement when not considered here—

Abdomen—Disorders In—(See "Diseases" under Abdomen).

Accidents—To the Arms, Shoulders, or Hands—(See "Accidents", "Fractures", under Arms; Clavicle, Hands, Humerus, Radius, Shoulders, Ulna).

Anaemia; Arms—Diseases of—Fractures—(See Arms).

Asthma; Bilious Complaints — (See "Biliousness", "Obstruction", under Bile).

Blood—Blood Disorders—Impure Blood—(See Blood, Impure).

Bowels—Disorders of—(See Bowels).

Brain Fever—(See Brain).

Breathing—Disorders of—(See Breath).

Bronchitis—(See Bronchial).

Capillaries—Disorders of—(See Capillaries).

Chest—Disorders In—(See Chest, Lungs).

Clavicle—Collar Bone—Fracture of—(See Clavicle).

Consumption—Of the Lungs—(See Consumption, Phthisis, Tuberculosis).

Corrupted Blood—(See "Impure Blood" under Impure).

Dorsal Region — Disorders of — (See Dorsal).

Fancy—All Disorders and Evils of the Fancy—(See Fancies).

Feet—Disorders of—(See Feet).

Flatulence; Fractures—(See "Accidents" in this section).

Gout—In the Arms—(See "Arms" under Gout).

Hands—Diseases In—Fractures, Hurts, Injuries To—(See Hands).

Head—Diseases In—Accidents To—(See Head).

Hearing—Disorders of—(See Hearing).

Hips—Disorders of—(See Hips).

Imagination—Disorders of—Deranged —(See Imagination).

Impure Blood—(See Impure).

Liver—Disorders of—(See Liver).

Lower Limbs—Disorders of—(See Feet, Legs, Thighs).

Lungs—Disorders of—Consumption— —(See Consumption, Lungs, Phthisis, Tuberculosis).

Mental Disorders—Diseases of the Mind—(See Intellect, Mental, Mind).

Muscles—Disorders of—(See Muscles).

Nervous Diseases—(See Nerves).

Oxygenation—Of the Blood—Disorders of—(See Oxygen).

Pericardium—Inflammation of—(See "Pericarditis" under Heart; Pericardium).

Phthisic—(See Asthma, Consumption).

Phthisis; Pleurisy—(See Pleura).

Pneumonia; Pulmonary Disorders— (See Lungs, Pulmonary).

Respiratory Disorders—(See Breath).

Rheumatism—In the Arms, Hands, Shoulders—(See "Rheumatism" under Arms, Hands, Shoulders. Also see Rheumatism).

Ribs—Upper Ribs—Injury or Fracture of—(See Ribs).

Scapula—Fracture of—(See Scapula, Shoulders).

Shoulders—Disorders of—Hurts, Fractures of—(See Shoulders).

Thighs—Disorders of—(See Thighs).

Thymus Gland—Disorders of—(See Thymus).

Torpid Liver—(See Liver).

Trachea—Disorders of—(See Trachea, Windpipe).

Tuberculosis; Two Diseases—At the Same Time—The ☉ affl. in ♊. (See "Two Diseases" under Disease).

Veins—Windiness In—(See Veins).

Wasting Diseases — Wasting of the Lungs—(See Consumption, Lungs, Phthisis, Tuberculosis, Wastings). For collateral study see Castor, Double-Bodied, Dual-Minded, Mercury; "Mutable Signs" under Mutable; Pisces, Pollux, Sagittarius, Third House, Triplets, Twins, Virgo.

GEMMATION—Budding—Reproduction by Gemmation is under the rule of ♀, and by division of cell, under ♃. (See "Division", "Gemmation", under Cells; Fecundation; Ovaries, Proliferation, Reproduction).

GENERAL—

Actions—General Actions—(See Conduct, Habits, Manners, Morals, etc.).

Ailments—General Ailments and Disorders—(See "Disorders" in this section).

Blood—General Debility of—(See "Blood" under Debility).

Debility—(See "General Debility" under Debility; "Debility" under Nerves; "Weakness" in this section).

Disorders—General Disorders and Ailments—Are governed by the 6th H., the sign on the cusp, or planets in the 6th. (See Ailments, Disease, Disorders, Sixth House).

Dropsy—General Dropsy—(See "Anasarca" under Dropsy).

Eruptions—General On the Face or Over the Body—(See Eruptions; "Eruptions" under Face; Measles, Scarlet Fever, Smallpox, etc.).

Headaches—General Over the Head—(See "General" under Headaches).

Health—General Health—(See "General" under Health).

Ill-Health—General Ill-Health—General Weakness—(See Debility, Feeble; "General", "Ill-Health All Thru Life", under Ill-Health; Infirm, Invalids, Sickly; "Much Sickness" under Sickness; "Low" under Vitality; "Weak Body" under Weak, etc.).

Malaise—General Malaise—(See Malaise).

Relaxation—General Relaxation— Laxity—(See Relaxation).

Weakness—General Weakness—(See "Ill-Health" in this section).

Whole Body—The Disease or Weakness Is General Over the Whole Body —(See Whole).

GENERATIVE SYSTEM—Generative Organs—Generation—Organs of Regeneration—Sex Organs—Genitals— Reproductive Organs—Privy Parts— Secret Parts, etc.—Are ruled by ♂, ♀, the ♏, ♎, and ♏ signs, and the 8th H. The external organs of generation are ruled by ♂, the ♎ and ♏ signs. The internal organs of generation are ruled by ♀ and the ♏, ♎, and ♏ signs. Malefics in ♏, and espec. in ♏ in the 6th H., tend to greatly affect and disturb the uterus and internal generative organs. The following subjects have to do with the organs of Generation, which see in the alphabetical arrangement when not considered here.

Abscess In—(See "Abscess" under Secrets).

All Diseases In—Signified by the 7th and 8th H., and the ♎ and ♏ signs; afflictions in ♏, and are ♏ diseases; ☽ diseases, and caused by afflictions to the ☽, and espec. with the ☽ in ♏; ♂ diseases, either in men or women; ♀ affl. in ♏. (See Genitals; "All Diseases" under Diseases).

Barrenness—Wholly Unfit for Generation—(See Barrenness).

Cancer Of—(See "Generative Organs" under Carcinoma).

Chancre; Chancroid; Death — From Disorders of—Afflictions in the fixed signs, and espec. in ♏.

Deformities Of—(See Eunuchs; "Sex Channels" under Genitals; Hermaphrodites, Maimed, Virile).

Diseases Of—Afflictions in ♏, ♎, ♏, the 6th, 7th or 8th H.; Subs at LPP (4, 5L). (See the various paragraphs in this section, and under Females, Genitals, Men, Privates, Reproduction, Secret Parts, Sex, Venereal, Women).

Distempers In—Infirmities In—Members of Generation Afflicted—(See "Diseases" under Genitals; "Distempers" under Secrets).

Eruptions In—♃ affl. in ♏; ♃ in ♏ in the 6th H., and affl.; ♃ in ♏ and affl. the ☽ or Asc. (See Eruptions).

Excessive Members—(See Virile).

External Organs — Of Generation — Diseases of—Afflictions To—Hurts To —Afflictions to ♂; ♂ affl. in ♎ or ♏. (See Genitals).

Female Organs—Of Generation—Diseases of—Afflictions To—(See Females, Genitals, Ovaries, Vagina, Vulva, Womb, Women, etc.).

Fruitfulness; Functions—The Generative Functions—Abuse of—(See "Passional Excesses" under Passion; Perversions; "Solitary" under Vice, etc.).

Genitals — (See the various paragraphs under Genitals).

Genito-Urinary System—Disorders of —(See Genito-Urinary).

Gestation; Glands Of — (See Glands, Glans Penis (see Penis); Muciparous, Ovaries, Testes, etc.).

Gonorrhoea; Hydrocele; Impotent;

Infirmities In—(See All Diseases, Diseases, Distempers, and the various paragraphs in this section).

Inflammatory Disorders Of—♂ affl. in ♏; ♀ in ♉ or ♏ in ♌, □, or ♉ ♂. (See "Inflammatory" under Genitals, Secrets).

Injuries To—(See Maimed).

Internal Organs—Of Generation— Disorders of—Afflictions in ♏ or ♏; ♂ affl. in ♏ with females; ♂ affl. in ♍ or ♏, and espec. when in the 6th or 8th H.; afflictions to ♀. (See Ovaries, Womb).

Leucorrhoea; Maimed; Male Organ— Of Generation—(See Penis).

Malformations—♅ and ♄ in ♉ or ♏. (See "Deformities" in this section).

Masturbation—(See "Solitary" under Vice).

Men — (See "Mens' Genitals" under Genitals).

Menses; Muciparous Glands — (See Muciparous).

Nervous Disorders Of—(See "Nerves" under Secrets).

Obstructions In—The ☉ or ♄ affl. in ♏. (See Obstructions).

Ovaries; Pains In — (See "Pains" under Secrets).

Parturition; Passional Excesses—(See Passion).

Penis; Perversions; Powers Of — Strong — Weak, etc. — (See Amativeness, Apathy, Barren; "Signs Of" under Children; Creative, Fruitful, Impotent; "Powers" under Sex).

Pregnancy; Prenatal; Privates;

Procreation; Propagation—(See Amative).

Pudic; Puerperal; Regeneration;

Reproduction; Scandalous Diseases— (See Scandalous).

Serotum; Secrets—Secret Parts—Note the various paragraphs under Genitals, Reproductive Organs, Secrets, Sex, as they are supplemental to this section).

Self-Abuse — (See "Solitary" under Vice).

Semen—Seminal—(See Semen).

Sensitive — (See "Generative Organs" under Sensitive).

Sensuality; Sex — Sex Organs — Sex Diseases—(See Sex).

Spermatozoon—(See Semen).

Sterility; Strong Powers Of — (See "Powers" in this section).

Swellings In—(See "Inflammation" in this section; "Swellings" under Secrets).

Testes; Tumors In—♃ or ♀ affl. in ♏. (See Tumors).

Ulcer In—(See "Genitals" under Ulcer).

Undeveloped—The Generative Organs Undeveloped—♄ influence; ♄ affl. in ♉ or ♏; ♄ ☌ ♅ in ♉ or ♏; the ♅ influence tends to undevelopment in the part ruled by the sign he is in at B. (See Defects, Deficient, Diminished, Undersized, Undeveloped, etc.).

Unfit—Wholly Unfit for Generation—(See Barrenness).

Urethra; Uterus—(See Womb).

Vagina; Varicocele — (See Scrotum, Varicose).

Venereal Diseases—(See Venereal).

Virile — Excessive Virile Members — (See Virile).

Vulva; Weakness—Of the Generative System—Planets in the fixed signs, and afflicted, tend to weaken the Generative System; planets in ♉ by reflex action to ♏, and in ♌ and ♒ by their □ aspects to ♏; malefics in ♏ at B., and affl. the hyleg; the ☽ hyleg in ♏, and afflicted, tends to weaknesses and afflictions of the female generative organs; ♀ affl. in ♏. (See the various paragraphs in this section).

Womb—Note the various paragraphs under Womb).

Women—See the various paragraphs under Females, Women).

GENEROUS — Generosity — ♃ influence; ♃ well-aspected in ♐ or ♓; ♃ in the Asc. or M.C.; the ☽ ☌ ♃ in ♐, ♓, the Asc., or M.C. (See Humane, Kind, Riches, Sympathetic).

GENITALS—Genital Organs—The Genitalia — Pudic — Privities — Members of Generation — Secrets — Reproductive Organs — External Sex Organs, etc. — Denoted by ♂, ♏, and the 8th H. The subjects of Generative Organs, Genitals, Secret Parts, Sex Organs, Reproductive Organs, Privates, etc., are practically one and the same, but are divided into several Sections and Articles in this book for handy reference, and under the headings mentioned prominently in Astrological Literature. See the following subjects in the alphabetical arrangement when not more fully considered here.

Accidents To—Injury—Hurts — (See "Mens' Genitals" in this section; Maimed).

Any Disease — Of the Genitals — Caused by afflictions to ♀. (See "All Diseases" under Generation).

Castration—(See Testes).

Cervix—Of the Womb—(See "Cervix" under Womb).

Chancre—(See Syphilis).

Chancroid—(See Gonorrhoea).

Channels and Vents—Lack of Proper Sex Channels—♄ and ♀ in the 4th or 7th H., and afflicted. (See Eunuchs; "Deformities" under Generation).

Circumcision; Clitoris; Contortions—♅ affl. in ♏. (See Contortions, Distortions).

Deformities — (See "Deformities" under Generative).

Diseases — Of the Genitals — Disturbances of—Distempers In—Caused principally by ♂, the ruler of the Genitals, thru passional excesses and irregularities, and also by ♀ thru excess of amorous indulgence; the ☉ affl. in ♉, ♏, ♒, or ♓; the ☉ in ♏ or ♓ in ☌ or ill-asp. any of the malefics as promittors; the ☽ affl. at B.; the ☽ affl. in ♉ or ♏, or afflicting the hyleg therefrom; the ☽ in ♋ in ☌ or ill-asp. ♄ (or ♀ if he be of the nature of ♄) at the beginning of an illness or at decumb.; the ☽ affl. in ♒; ♅ in ♏ and affl. the ☉ or ☽; ♅ affl. in ♏ in evil asp. the ☉ or ☽ tends to produce sex disorders, venereal diseases, genital disturbances, and of a deep-seated nature; ♅ affl. in ♉; ♄ or ♂ affl. in ♏; ♄ in ♋, ♌, or ♍; ♂ in ♏ ☌ or ill-asp. the ☉; ♂ diseases; ♂ □ or ♉ the ☽; ♂ affl. in ♊, ♎, or ♏; ♂ in an angle, occi. of the ☉ and ori. of the ☽; ♃ affl. in ♊, ♋, ♎, or ♏; ♀ diseases; ♀ affl. in ♉, ♏, or ♐; caused by an afflicted ♀; the diseases of ♀ are principally those of the members of generation, and of the matrix, or womb; ☿ affl. in ♎ or ♏; ☿ and the ☽ in ♏ or ♓, ☌ or ill-asp. any of the malefics as promittors; ☿ affl. in ♈, ♉, ♎, ♏, ♐, ♑, or ♓; ♉ or ♏ upon the cusps of the 6th, 8th, or 12th H.; malefics conjoined in ♉ or ♏; many planets, as a Stellium, in ♏ or the 8th H. at B., and afflicted. Diseases of the Sex Organs, or Genitals, are never as severe unless ♉ (the sign opposite to ♏), and the throat and larynx, ruled by ♉, are also afflicted, or with progressed influences in ♉. (See the various paragraphs in this section; "All Diseases In", "Weaknesses", and the various paragraphs under Generation; Secrets; "Sex Diseases" under Sex). Cases of Disorders of the Genitals—See Figures 9, 10, 11, and 34, in the book, "Message of the Stars" by the Heindels.

Disorders Of — (See "Diseases", and the various paragraphs in this section).

Distempers Of — (See "Diseases" in this section).

Erections; Eunuchs;

External Genitals — Ruled by ♂, ♏, and ♎. (See "External" under Generation).

Female Genitals—Disorders of—(See the various paragraphs under Females, Women, Vagina, Venereal, Vulva).

Generation—Generative System—Disorders of—(See Generative).

Genital Pole—Of Paracelsus—The ♏ sign. (See Paracelsus, Scorpio).

Genito-Urinary — (See the various paragraphs under Genito-Urinary System).

Gonorrhoea; Hermaphrodites;

Hydrocele; Inflammation — Inflammatory Diseases of — ♂ affl. in ♍. (See "Inflammatory" under Generative, Secrets).

Injuries To—(See "Accidents" in this section).

Leucorrhoea; Losses—Seminal Losses —(See Semen).

Maimed — (See Maimed; "Accidents" in this section).

Male Organ—(See Penis).

Mens' Genitals — Diseases of — Accidents or Injury To—♂ diseases; caused by an afflicted ♂; ♂ affl. in ♍. (See Castration, Gonorrhoea, Maimed, Penis, Scrotum, Testes, Venereal).

Menses; Nervous Affections Of—♅ or ☿ affl. in ♍. (See Pudic; "Nerves" under Secrets).

Pain In—♄, ♂, or ☿ affl. in ♍; ♍ on the Asc. and afflicted, or on the cusp of 6th or 8th H., and containing malefics.

Paracelsus—Genital Pole of—(See "Genital Pole" in this section).

Parturition — (See Parturition, Puerperal).

Passional Excesses — (See "Passional Excesses" under Passion).

Penis; Pole — (See "Genital Pole" in this section).

Priapism—(See Penis).

Pudic; Reproduction; Res Venereae; Scandalous Disease — (See Scandalous).

Scrotum; Secret Parts; Semen; Sex—Sex Channels—Sex Diseases — (See "Channels", and the various paragraphs in this section, and under Generation, Secrets, Sex).

Stricture; Swellings Of—(See "Swellings" under Secrets).

Syphilis; Testes; Trouble — With the Genitals—The ☽ affl. in ♉, by reflex action in ♍. (See "Diseases", and the various paragraphs in this section).

Ulcer—In the Genitals — (See "Genitals" under Ulcer).

Undeveloped—The Genitals Undeveloped—(See "Undeveloped" under Generative).

Urethra; Vagina; Varicocele;

Venereal; Vents—And Channels—(See "Channels" in this section).

Virile Members—(See Virile).

Vulva; Whites—(See Leucorrhoea).

Womb; Women — (Note the various paragraphs under Females, Women).

GENITO-URINARY SYSTEM—The Genito-Urinary System, Tract, or Organs, are ruled by the ♍ sign, and are strongly affected for good or evil by the ☉, ☽, and planets acting thru this sign, according to the aspects. The ♂ Group of Herbs have a pathological action on the Genito-Urinary System. The nerves of the Genito-Urinary System are ruled by ♅ and ☿, and the arteries and veins by ♃. The Glands of are ruled by ♆.

Genito-Urinary Diseases—The ☉ affl. in ♍; the ☽ affl. in ♍, or affl. the hyleg therefrom; ♄ in ♍, occi., and affl. the ☉, ☽, or Asc.; ☿ affl. in ♉; ♍ on the Asc.; a Stellium .in ♍ or the 8th H., and containing malefics; afflictions in ♉, by reflex action in ♍. (See "Cervical Nerves" under Cervical).

Nervous Affections Of—♅ in ♍; ☿ affl. in ♉ or ♍. (See Bladder, Genitals, Urine, Varicocele, Varicose).

GENIUS —Geniuses— Evolved Types— Prodigies — Precocious, etc. — The ♆ and ♅ vibrations are usually strong at B., and in good asp. to ☿, the mental ruler. The map of birth does not always account for Genius, and the Prenatal influences, the map for the time of conception, should be studied. (See Prenatal). Also the qualities inherent in the Ego have much to do with Genius, or Prodigies, such as expert Mathematicians, Lightning Calculators, Chess Players, Inventors, Cranks, Musical Geniuses, etc. (See Ego).

Calculators—Lightning Calculators—Mathematical Geniuses—Cases— (See Mathematical).

Chess Players—(See Mathematical).

Child Prodigies — (See Mathematical, Music, Precocious, Premature, Prodigies).

Dull—The Genius Is Dull—The ♓ influence predominating at B.; ☿ affl. in ♓; in Hor'y Q., the Sig. of the party in ♓. (See Dull).

Ingenious — Inventive—Clever—Skillful — Of Unusual Mental Abilities — Constructive — Original, etc. — The ☉ Sig. ☌ ☿ gives ingenuity; the ☉ Sig. in ♍ or ♍; the ☽ in ♊, ♍, ♏, or ♒; the ☽ ☌, P, and good asp. ☿; the ☽ angular at B., or in ♉ or ♋; the ☽ Sig. in ♒; ♅ configurated with ☿; ♅ ascending at B.; ♄ in ♊, ♏, ♋, or ♒; ♄ Sig. in ✶ or △ ☿; ♃ Sig. in ♋; ♂ Sig. in ♊ or ♋; ♀ Sig. in ♍ or △ ☿; ☿ ascending in ♍; ☿ Sig. in ♒; ☿ Sig. ✶ or △ ♂; ☿ Sig. in ♊, an ingenious, pregnant fancy; ♋ and ♋ influence strong at B.; ♋ on the Asc. When the ☽ is Sig. in ♋ the native is not ingenious. (See "Judgment Good" under Judgment; Learning, Mathematical, Mechanical; "Quickened" under Mental; "Good Mind" under Mind).

Inventors—(See Mathematical).

Mathematical—(See Mathematics).

Mechanical—(See Mechanical).

Musicians — Musical Geniuses — (See Music).

Not Ingenious—The ☽ Sig. in ♋. (See Dull).

Pig — A Performing Pig — Case—See "Performing Pig", No. 781, in 1001 N.N. (See Swine).

Precocious—Premature Mental Development—(See Premature).

Pregnant Genius—♄ Sig. in ♒; ♂ Sig. in ♍; ☿ Sig. in ♊, a pregnant and ingenious fancy. (See "Ingenious" in this section).

Premature—(See "Precocious" in this section).

Reading—Child Reads at three years of age, studies Darwin, Huxley, at eight years of age. See Case, "Wiener", No. 353, in 1001 N.N. (See "Child Prodigy" under Prodigy).

Two Things at Once — A Male can write a letter and solve a problem at the same time—Case—See "Neptune", No. 352, in 1001 N.N.

GENTEEL—

Genteel Body—(See Beautiful, Handsome, Well-Proportioned).

Genteel Carriage—(See "Genteel" under Gait).

Genteel In Manner—The ☉ ♂ ☿ at B.; the ☽ Sig. ♂ or good asp. to ♀.

Not of Genteel Form—(See Crooked, Deformed; "Ill-Formed" under Ill; Ugly, etc.).

GENTLE—Harmless—Peaceful—

Gentle Disposition—Harmless—People born under strong ♀ influence; ♀ Sig. in ♐, ♒, or ♓; the ☉ Sig. in ♋; the ☽ strong at B., and well-placed and aspected; the ☉ Sig. in ♑, ♋, or ♒; the ☽ Sig. ✶ or △ ♀; ♃ Sig. ♂ ☿ and free from ill-asps. of malefics; ♃ Sig. in ♓; the ♒ influence tends to. (See Harmless, Mild, Temper)..

GEOCENTRIC — The System of Astrology which takes the Earth as a center, and the movements of the planets as seen from the Earth, and in the Earth's Zodiac. The most of the influences in this Work are based upon this System. The Planetary Tables, used by Astronomers and Astrologers in general, and by the Navies of the World, are Geocentric. Also Raphael's Ephemeris gives the Geocentric positions and Longitudes of the planets for each current year. See Earth, Heliocentric).

GERMS — Microbes — Bacteria — Germinal—Pestilential Virus, etc.—(See Air, Cholera, Epidemics, Microbes, Microzymasis, Miasma; "Virus" under Pestilence; Zymotic, etc.).

Germinal—(See Protoplasma).

Morbid Germs —(See Day, Night; "Night Action" under Moon).

GESTATION—Pregnancy—The Prenatal Period—Maternity—The State of a Woman with Child—The Puerperal State, etc. — The ☽ rules the mother during Gestation. The ☉, ☽, and Asc. at B., and their relation to each other, indicate whether the period of gestation has been normal, or plus or minus, according to whether the ☽ is above or below the horizon at B., increasing or decreasing in light. (See Prenatal Epoch). The period of gestation is seven or nine months, at which times the ☽ forms the □ and △ aspects to her place at conception, and children born at these times live, but children born at the 8th month do not survive, as the ☽ forms no special aspect to her place at the 8th month. (See "Eight Months Children" under Children). The state of a woman with child is judged by the 5th H. and its influences. The subject of Gestation is also considered under Pregnancy. (See Pregnancy). The following subjects have to do with Gestation, the

Prenatal Period, Pregnancy, the Foetus, etc., which subjects see in the alphabetical arrangement when not considered here.

Abortion; Abnormal Gestation — Afflictions in ♍, ♎, or ♏, and also in the 5th H. Also caused by Subs at PP (2, 3, 4L). (See Abortion; "Death" under Children; Foetus, Pregnancy, Premature, Prenatal, Stillborn).

Birth; Children; Conception;

Eight Months Children — (See this subject under Children).

Embryo; Foetus; Fruitful; Maternity —(See Maternal, Maternity, Mother).

Miscarriage; Monsters; Moon — (See "Gestation", and the various paragraphs under Moon).

Parturition; Pregnancy;

Premature Birth—(See Abortion, Premature).

Prenatal Epoch — The Conditions Which Prevail from Conception to Birth—(See Prenatal).

Quickening; Seven Months Children— (See "Eight Months Children" under Children; Parturition, Premature).

Two Weeks Before Time—Born Two Weeks Early, etc.—Case—(See Cases under Premature).

GESTICULATION —Gestures —Characteristic of the Fixed Signs, and especially of ♉. (See Speech).

GHASTLY LOOK — (See Pale, Sickly, White).

GHOSTS — (See "Astral Shells" under Astral).

GIANTS—Abnormally Tall—The tallest people, as a rule, are produced by the ♐ sign, and espec. when this sign is upon the Asc. at B., and with the ☉ and ♃ rising in this sign. The 26° ♐ on the Asc., a physical prodigy. Also ♅ rising tends to abnormal tallness. It is not always easy to determine the height from the natal map, and the prenatal conditions should be considered, heredity, ancestry, and also the inherent qualities of the Ego may enter into the matter. (See Enlarged; "Abnormal Growth" under Growth; Height; "Body" under Large; Pituitary, Tall, etc.).

GIDDINESS—Dizziness—(See Dizziness, Fainting, Vertigo).

GIFTED —Highly Accomplished — (See Excellent, Genius; "Good Mind" under Mind; "Natural Abilities" under Natural).

GINSENG—A Typical Drug of ♃. (See "Typical Drugs" under Jupiter).

GIVER OF LIFE — Hyleg — Apheta — Prorogator—(See Hyleg).

Givers of Children — (See "Givers of Children" under. Children).

GLANCES—The Look of the Eyes—(See Expression; "Glances" under Eyes; Look).

GLANDS—Glandular System—Glans—Gonads—Organs of Secretion—The Glands are under the rulership of the ☉, ☽, ♆, the mutable signs, and the internal rulership of ♓. The glands as a whole are under the rule of the

☉ and ♃, but individual glands are also under the rule of other planets. The glandular processes generally are ruled by the ☽. Also ♀ acts strongly upon the glands, causing glandular, and other swellings, at fixed points. The Glands are one of the manifestations of the Vital Body, and are the organs of secretion. (See "Body" under Vital). The Glands are subject to the physiological action of the planets and herbs ruled by ♀. The Glands of the different parts of the body are ruled also and affected by the sign of the Zodiac ruling the part, and the lord of such sign, and are stimulated or suppressed according to the nature of the planets in such signs, and the aspects to them at B., and by dir. The principal glands of the body are listed and mentioned in this Article. See the following subjects in the alphabetical arrangement when not more fully considered here.

Addison's Disease—(See Adrenals).

Adrenals; Affected — The Glands Affected — Caused principally by afflictions to the ☉, ☽, ♃, and with afflictions in ♓ and the common signs. ♅ rules the glandular system, and when in signs which rule the arms, hands, legs, and feet, tends to shrinking and withering of the limbs, and wasting of the tissues of the parts. (See "Diseases" in this section; the Introduction under Aneurysm).

Aneurysm; Arms—Glands of Affected —(See "Affected" in this section; Aneurysm).

Bowels—The ☽ in ♍ rules the glands and functions of the bowels, and the ☽ affl. in ♍ tends to glandular troubles in the bowels. ♅ in ♍ tends to wasting of the glands of the bowels. (See "Glandular" under Bowels).

Bubo; Cervical Glands — (See Cervical).

Cervix — Glands of Affected — (See "Cervix" under Womb).

Clitoris — The Glans Clitoris — (See Clitoris).

Cowper's Glands—(See Cowper).

Cysts—(See Áneurysm, Cysts).

Develops—The Glands—♅ in ✳ or △ the Asc. develops the Glandular System.

Digestion—The Digestive Glands— (See Digestion, Gastric, Juices, Stomach).

Diseases Of—Disorders of—The ☉ in water signs tends to disorders of; afflictions to ♃ or the ☽; afflictions in ♓ and the common signs; Subs at SP (7D). (See the various paragraphs in this section).

Disorders Of—(See "Diseases" and the various paragraphs in this section).

Ductless Glands—(See Ductless).

Endocrine Glands—(See Ductless).

Feet—Glands of Affected — (See "Affected" in this section).

Fever—Glandular Fever—The ☉ or ☽ affl. by ♂; ♂ in the various signs tends to glandular fever in the part ruled by such sign; Subs at CP, KP, and Local. (See Fever).

Fixed Points — Glandular Swellings at Fixed Points — ♀ diseases. (See "Swellings" in this section).

Gastric Glands—(See Digestion, Stomach, in this section).

Genito-Urinary Organs — The glands of are ruled by ♅, and ♅ affl. in ♎ or ♏ tends to disorders of. (See Genito-Urinary).

Glans—Glans Clitoris—Glans Penis— (See Clitoris, Penis).

Gonads—(See "Reproductive" in this section).

Groins — Glands In Affected — Enlarged—(See Bubo, Groins).

Hands—Glands of—(See "Affected" in this section).

Head—Glands of—The Glands of the Head are affected and disturbed by the ☽ or ♅ in ♈. (See Pineal, Pituitary, in this section).

Inguinal Glands—(See Bubo, Groins).

Intestines—Bowels—Glands of—(See "Bowels" in this section).

Kidneys—Glands of—Afflictions in ♎ tend to disorders of. (See Kidneys).

Lachrymal—(See Tears).

Lacteals—(See Milk).

Legs—Glands of—(See "Affected" in this section).

Limbs—Glands of—(See "Affected" in this section).

Liver; Lymphatic Glands — (See Lymph).

Mammary Glands — (See Breasts, Milk).

Mesenteric Glands—(See Mysentery).

Milk Glands—Lacteals—(See Breasts, Milk).

Mouth—Glands of—(See Mouth, Salivary).

Muciparous — Mucus — (See Muciparous, Mucous).

Mumps—The Parotid Glands Affected —(See Parotid).

Neck—Glands of Affected—Glandular Swellings In the Neck and Throat— (See "Glandular Swellings" under Throat).

Ovaries; Pancreas; Parenchyma;

Parotid; Penis — Glans Penis — (See Penis).

Pineal; Pituitary; Prostate;

Racemose—(See Pancreas).

Reproductive Glands — Sex Glands — Gonads—Ruled by ♂ and the ♏ sign. (See Ovaries, Ovum, Reproduction, Semen, Sex, Testes, etc.).

Salivary; Sebaceous; Secretory—(See Secretions).

Sex Glands — Gonads — (See "Reproductive" in this section).

Skin—Glands of—Ruled by ♎ and ♑. Disorders of caused by afflictions in these signs, and also by an afflicted ♄ or ♀. (See Skin, Sweat).

Softening—Of the Glandular Tissues —A ♀ and ♓ disease. (See Softening).

Spleen; Stomach—Disorders of Glands of—The ☽ in ♋ rules the glands of the stomach. Also ♅ in ♋ rules the glands and secretions of the stomach. The ☽, ♅, ♄, and other planets afflicted in ♋ tend to disorders of the glands and secretions of the stomach. Also caused by Subs at SP (7D). (See "Digestion", "Diseases", in this section; "Glands" under Stomach).

Sudoriferous—(See Sweat).

Suprarenals—(See Adrenals; "Uremic Coma" under Coma; Suprarenals).

Sweat Glands—(See Sweat).

Sweetbread—(See Pancreas).

Swellings — Glandular Swellings— Caused by ♅ and ♀ and these planets afflicted at B., and by dir. (See Fixed Points, Neck, Throat, in this section).

Testes; Throat — Swellings of the Glands of—(See "Neck" in this section).

Thymus; Thyroid; Tissues—Softening of the Glandular Tissues—(See "Softening" in this section).

Tonsils; Tumors — Glandular Tumors —(See Adenoma, Scrofula).

Urethra — Glands of — (See "Genito-Urinary" in this section).

Vagina — Glands of — Disorders of — Ruled by ♏, and caused by afflictions in ♏. (See Vagina).

Wasting Of — ♅ influence and diseases. ♅ in any sign, and afflicted, tends to wasting of the glands of the part ruled by such sign. (See Affected, Bowels, in this section).

GLASS—Case—Swallows Glass, Iron, Nails, etc. See "Human Ostrich", No. 986 in 1001 N.N. (See Deglutition, Freaks).

GLAUCOMA—A Disease with Intraocular Tension—A ☉ disease; the ☉ affl. in ♈; the ☽ or Asc. in Nebulous parts, and affl. by ♄, tends to blindness from Glaucoma. (See "Glaucoma" under Eyes).

GLEET—Gleets—Chronic Gonorrhoea— (See "Chronic" under Gonorrhoea).

GLOOM — Gloomy — Caused principally by ♄ influence and afflictions, and by the ♄ signs ♑ and ♒, and espec. by ♄ on the Asc., and with ☿ affl. in ♑; ♄ ☌ or ill-asps. ☿, the mental ruler; ♄ afflicting the Asc. or M.C.; ♄ ℞, and in tr. over, or in □ or 8 ☿; ♄ affl. in the 3rd or 9th H.; ♄ ☌ the ☉ in the 12th H.; ♄ ☌ or ill-asp. the ☽; ♄ in ♑ or ♒ and afflicted; ♄ ☌ ☿ in ♏ in the 8th H.; the ☉ in ♑, and affl. by ♄; the ☉ hyleg, and ☌ or ill-asp. ♄ at B., or by dir.; the ☽ at B., or the prog. ☽, in ☌ or ill-asp. ♄; ☿ in ♓ and affl. by ♄; caused by afflictions in ♋; the 3rd dec. of ♑ on the Asc. (See Anguish, Anxiety, Brooding, Dejected, Depressed, Despair, Despondent, Discontentment, Fears, Forebodings, Grave, Grief, Hope, Hypochondria, Introspection, Low Spirits (see Low); Melancholy, Misery, Morose, Obsessions, Optimism, Repining, Sad, Sorrow, Suicide, Worry, Wretched, etc.).

GLOSSY — Shiny — Oily — (See "Glossy" under Hair; "Oily" under Face, Skin).

GLOTTIS—Involuntary Closure of— Spasmodic Action of—Hiccough—A ♅ affliction; ♅ affl. in ♋. (See Hiccough, Spasmodic).

GLUTEAL REGION—(See Buttocks).

GLUTTONY—A Greedy Eater—Overeating—Engorgement—Repletion—Gormandizing—Feasting—Voracity—Insatiable Appetite—Ravenous Appetite—Intemperate In Eating, etc. Gormandizing habits are given by ♃ and ♀, and also by the ☽, the ruler of ♋, the stomach sign; ♋ on the Asc., and the ☽ as ruler of the Asc., afflicted, or in evil asp. to the Asc., tends to direct the mind to the stomach and cause over-eating, gluttony, obesity, etc., and people of this type, and who also have many planets in ♋ at B., should avoid over-eating. Other causes are—the ☉ affl. by ♃ or ♀; the ☉ Sig. in ♓, ruins himself by feasting; the ☉ affl. in ♉; the ☽ affl. at B., and to the evil asps. the Asc. by dir.; the ☽ affl. in ♓, given to the pleasures of the table; the ☽ in the 6th H., and ill-aspected by ♃ or ♀; the ☽ in ♐ and affl. by the ☉ or ♂ when taken ill, tends to some violent disease caused by gluttony or repletion (Hor'y); the Prog. ☽ in □ or 8 the radical ♃; ♅ affl. in ♉; ♄ ill-dig. at B.; ♄ ☌ ♃ in ♍; ♃ affl. in ♉, ♋, ♍, ♏, or in the 1st or 6th H.; ♃ in ♋ in the Asc. and afflicted; ♃ □ or 8 the ☉; ♂ to the ☌ or ill-asp. ♀; ♂ Sig. in ♉; ♂ □ or 8 ♃ or ♀; ♂ Sig. in ♉; ♀ affl. in ♎; ♀ in ♉ or ♋, ill-asp. by ♂, and espec. if the 6th H. is involved; ♀ Sig. in ♑, love their belly; ☿ affl. in ♉, or ☿ Sig. in ♉, loves ease and gluttony; ☿ affl. in ♑; the ♉ sign strong at B. tends to make great eaters; the Asc. to the ill-asps. the ☽, and the ☽ affl. at B., tends to dire results and diseases from over-eating; the 2nd face of ♉, the 4th face of ♌, the 16° ♑, and the 22° ♓ on the Asc. (See "Causes" under Apoplexy; Appetite, Congestion, Cramps, Cravings, Diet, Distentions, Drink, Eating; "His Own Worst Enemy" under Enemies; Epicureans, Excesses, Extravagance, Feasting; "Large Quantities" under Food; Gastric; "High Living" under High; Idle and Dull (see Idle); Indiscretions, Indulgence, Intemperance; "Enlarged" under Liver; Luxuries, Obesity, Over-indulgence, Pleasure, Plethora, Puffing, Redundant, Ringworm, Stomach, Surfeits, etc.).

GLYCOGEN—Animal Starch Found In the Blood and Liver—Ruled by ♃. Glycogen is formed and stored in the Liver by ♃, and is also in the blood, and is drawn upon by ♂ for fuel during muscular activity. Under stress and strain of the body Glycogen is released in large quantities to restore the equilibrium. The wastes of the Portal Blood stream are converted into Glycogen in the Liver by ♃ to act as fuel for the body. (See Liver, Starches).

GLYCOSURIA—Sugar In the Urine— (See Diabetes; "Sugar" under Urine).

GNAWING PAINS—Over the Whole Body—☿ affl. in ♒. (See "Pains" under Whole).

GOATS—Are ruled by the 6th H. in the native's map, as this house rules small animals.

Death Of—Epidemics Among—Eclipses in ♑, or malefics in this sign at the Vernal, and lord of the year, and especially if occurring in the 6th H.;

many eclipses occurring the same year, the death of goats, sheep, and many small animals in the territory afflicted by the eclipse, and espec. if the eclipses occur in four-footed, quadrupedal signs. (See "Small Animals" under Animals; "Virus" under Pestilence; Pets, Quadrupeds, Sheep).

Goat's Back—Constellation—For the evil effects of when the ☉ or ☽ are directed to it, see "Threatened" under Disease; Disgrace, Hircus, Sickness).

GODFATHERS—Ruled by ♃. Godmothers are ruled by ♀. (See "Godfathers" under Father).

GOGGLE EYES — Large, Protruding Eyes—Exophthalmos—(See "Abnormal Protrusion" under Eyeballs; "Exophthalmic" under Goiter).

GOITER—Goitre—Enlargement of the Thyroid Gland—A Crystallization and Obstruction in the Throat and Neck, affecting the Thyroid Gland—Bronchocele—Goiter is larger during the increase of the ☽, and decreases in size during the decrease of the ☽. Goiter is a ♋ disease, and caused by afflictions in ♋; ♀ affl. in ♋; ♀ in ♋, and affl. the ☽ or Asc.; ♀ in ♋ in the 6th H.; ♄ or ♅ in ♋; ♄ occi. in ♋, and affl. the ☉, ☽, or Asc.; ♄ affl. in ♏, by reflex action; ♄ ♂ the Pleiades, and malefics in ♋;; ♂ ♂ ♄ in ♋; ♂ affl. in ♋, or affl. the ☉, ☽, or Asc. from this sign; afflictions in or to the 16°♋; a result of the Algol influence in ♋; the ☽ hyleg in ♋ with females; Subs at LCP (6C), SP (7D), and at KP. Cases—See Fig. 3D, 3E, in the book, "Astro-Diagnosis", and Fig. 29 in "Message of the Stars", books by the Heindels. (See Cretinism, Crystallization, Myxoedema, Obstructions, Thyroid, Tumors).

Exophthalmic Goiter— Exophthalmos —Goggle Eyes—♀ affl. in ♋. (See Goggle Eyes" under Eyeballs).

GOLD—Aurum—Ruled by the ☉. A Typical Drug and Metal of the ☉. (See Sun, Therapeutics).

GONADS — Reproductive Glands— (See "Reproductive" under Glands).

GONAGRA—Gout In the Knees—(See "Gout" under Knees).

GONORRHOEA—Urethritis — Gleets — Running of the Reins—Inflammation of the Urethra—Chordee—Chancroids, or Soft Chancres, often accompany Gonorrhoea, and these same influences will also apply to Chancroids. Gonorrhoea is caused principally by afflictions to ♀, and is a ♀ disease; ♀ affl. in ♎ or ♏; ♀ affl. in ♏ in the 6th H.; ♀ or ♀ affl. in ♏ or ♓; ♀ in ♏ and affl. by ♂; the ☽ affl. in ♏; the ☽ in ♏, ♂, or ill-asp. ♄ (or ♀ if he be of the nature of ♄) when taken ill (Hor'y); the ☽ affl. by ♂ when taken ill (Hor'y); the ☽ to the ♂ or ill-asp. ♂ by dir., if indiscreet; ♅ ♂ ♄ or ♂ in ♏; ♂ affl. in ♏; a ♂ disease; ♂ □ or ♂ ♀; a ♏ and ♓ disease, and with afflictions in these signs; Subs at PP (2, 3, 4L), and at KP. (See Bubo, Penis, Scandalous, Urethra, Venereal).

Chancroids—A Small Sore, or Ulcer on the Genitals Which Often Accompanies Gonorrhoea—(See the first part of this section).

Chordee—Painful, Down-Curved Erection In Gonorrhoea—Caused by the same influences as Gonorrhoea, Chordee, and Chancroids, and tends to accompany the more severe forms of Gonorrhoea. (See the Influences in the first part of this section. Also see "Chordee" under Urethra).

Chronic Gonorrhoea—Gleet—A ♀ disease; ♀ affl. in ♏ in the 6th H. Also a severely afflicted ♀ denotes death by Gleet in some cases, where unusual indiscretions are carried on over a long period of time, and where ♀ afflicts the hyleg, and also holds the dominion of death. Also caused and aggravated by Subs at PP (2, 3, 4L), and at KP (11D).

Gleet—(See "Chronic" in this section).

GOOD—The term "Good" is found in many sections and Articles in this book. Good and Evil, the Positive and Negative, the Active and Passive influences, etc., are constantly working over Humanity, and the ever changing aspects of the planets tend to expansion and contraction; tend to disease, ill-health, worries, etc., by their evil aspects, and to good health, success, peace of mind, etc., by their favorable aspects. It would require too long a list to enumerate all the good conditions here, as related to the mind and body, and you are advised to look for the paragraph "Good" under whatever subject you have in mind. (See "Good" under Chemists, Children, Circulation, Complexion, Conduct, Constitution, Digestion, Eyes, Face, Figure, Health, Journeys, Judgment, Mind, Morals, Personality, Recuperation, Resistance, Shape, Sight, Stature, Surgeons, Teeth, Understanding, Vitality, etc. Also see Aspects, Beautiful, Clear, Comely, Dishonest, Evil, Favorable, Favored, Fine, Form, Handsome, Healers, Honest, Periods, etc.).

Sudden Good or Ill—The ☽ to the place of ♅ by tr. or dir., according as to how ♅ is dignified. (See "Sudden Evils" under Evil; Sudden, Uranus).

GORGON'S HEAD—(See Algol).

GORMANDIZING — Ravenous Appetite —(See Appetite, Carbuncles, Gluttony).

GOUT—Goutish Humours—Gouty—Arthralgia—Pain In the Joints—Rheumatic Gout—Is caused by the retention of Urea by ♄, and is a periodic disease. (See Saturn).

Arms—Gout In—(See the ♄ influences under "Causes" in this section).

Arthralgia—Pain· in a Joint Due to Gout and the Deposits of Urea by ♄— (See "Pain" under Joints).

Arthritis—Inflammation of a Joint Due to Gout and Urea Deposits, etc.— (See "Arthritis" under Joints).

Atonic Gout—The ☽ to the ♂ or ill-asps. ♄ by dir. (See Atonic).

Causes of Gout — Planetary Indications—The ☉ in ♉ and affl. by ♃; the ☉ affl. in ♏; the ☽ affl. in airy signs; the ☽ affl. in ♌, or afflicting the hyleg therefrom; the ☽ hyleg, and to the ♂ or ill-asp. ♄ by dir.; the ☽ affl. in ♐: the ☽ in ♊ or ♑, ♂ or ill-asp. any of the malefics as promittors; a ☽ disease; the ☽ to the ☌ ♄ by dir.; the ☽ in ♍, ☌ or ill-asp. ♄ (or ☿ if he be of the nature of ♄) at the beginning of an illness, or at decumb. (Hor'y); ♅ in ♓ and affl. the ☉; ♆, ♅, or ♄ in ♎, and affl. the ☉ or ☽.; ♄ in ♉, ♌, ♎, ♐, ♑, or ♓, and affl. the hyleg; a ♄ disease; ♄ in ♌, gout in the heart; ♄ in signs which rule the arms, hands, legs, and feet tend to gout and rheumatism in these parts; ♄ affl. in ♍; ♄ in ♏ or ♐, occi., and affl. the ☉, ☽, or Asc.; ♄ affl. in the 6th H., or affl. the hyleg therefrom; ♄ affl. the hyleg or Asc.; ♃ affl. in ♉ or ♐; ♂ in ♏ and affl. the ☽ or Asc.; ♂ in ♏ in the 6th H.; ♂ in ♑; ♀ affl. in ♐ or ♑; ☿ in ♑, ☌ or ill-asp. any of the malefics as promittors, and due principally to worry and melancholy; a ♉, ♏, ♐, ♑, ♒, and ♓ disease, and by afflictions in these signs; the Asc. to the ☐ or 8 ♄ by dir.; lords of the 1st or 6th H. in airy signs; malefics angular and occi. of the ☽, and in the last degrees of ☐ or ♐, and if the benefics are with the malefics, or ori., or angular, and cast any ray to the Lights, they will be cured, but incurable if the benefics are very weak, and do not assist; the 25° of mutable signs is usually afflicted; the 5th H. and ♀ are frequently involved, denoting the cause; airy signs on the Asc. or 6th H., or the ☽ in airy signs at B., or at decumb.; earthy signs on the Asc.; Subs at KP and Local.

Chalk Stones—Of Gout—(See Chalk).

Curable—The Gout Is Curable—(See "Causes" in this section).

Death by Gout—Afflictions in cardinal signs dispose to.

Extremities—Gout In the Upper or Lower Extremities—♄ in signs which rule the arms, shoulders, hands, tends to gout in the upper extremities, and when ♄ is in ♐, ♑, ♒, ♓, to affect the lower extremities; also by reflex action to ☐ when ♄ is in ♐, the upper extremities are often afflicted with gout or rheumatism. The lower extremities are especially afflicted with gout when the ☽ is afflicted in ♐, and affl. the ☉, ☽, or Asc.; ♄ in ♑, and occi., and affl. the ☉, ☽, or Asc.; ♄ affl. in ♓, gout in the feet. (See Arms, Feet, Hands, Knees, Legs, Lower, Shoulders, in this section. Also see "Humours" under Extremities).

Feet—Gout In Feet and Toes—Podagra—Also the Hands are often afflicted by reflex action to ♍, the sign ruling the Hands—The ☽ affl. in ☐; ♐, or ♓; the ☽ in ♐, ☌, or ill-asp. ♄ (or ☿ if he be of the nature of ♄) at the beginning of an illness or at decumb., a spice of Gout (Hor'y); the ☽ in ♐, and affl. by the ☉ or ♂ when taken ill (Hor'y); the ☽ affl. in ☐, wandering gout in the feet; ♄ affl. in ♏, ♑, or ♓; ♄ in the Asc. or M.C., in ☐ or ♐, occi. of the ☉ and ori. of the ☽, and in the latter degrees of the sign; ♄ ☌ ♂ in the Asc. or M.C., in the latter degrees of ♓; ♂ in ♓ and affl. the hyleg therefrom; ♀ affl. in ♓; ☿ affl. in ♓; ☿ affl. at B.; a ☿, ☽, and ♄ disease; a ♓ disease, and by afflictions in ♓; ♓ on the Asc.; ♓ ascending at the Vernal Equi., People ruled by ♓, and in Countries

under ♓, suffer grievous infirmities in the head, feet, and with gout and dropsy; also caused by afflictions in ♍, and by the ☉ and ☽ acting thru ♍; Subs at LPP (4, 5L) and at KP. (See "Feet" under Dropsy; Fiber; "Disorders" under Head; "Hands", "Wandering Gout", in this section).

Fingers—Gout In—(See "Hands" in this section).

Flying Gout—(See "Wandering" in this section).

Hands—Fingers—Gout In—Also May Occur In the Feet Under These Influences—Goutish Humours In the Hands —The ☽ affl. in ☐, a wandering gout in the hands; the ☽ in ♐ and affl. by the ☉ or ♂ when taken ill (Hor'y); the ☽ in ♐, ☌, or ill-asp. ♄ (or ☿ if he be of the nature of ♄) when taken ill, or at decumb.; a ♄ disease; ♄ affl. in ☐, ♏, ♐, or ♓; ♄ ☌ ♂ in the 1st or 7th H., ori. of the ☉ and occi. of the ☽, and in the latter degrees of ☐ or ♐; ♄ in the Asc. or M.C., occi. of the ☉, and ori. of the ☽, in the latter degrees of ☐ or ♐; ♃ affl. in ♉; ♂ in ♐; a ☿ disease; ☿ affl. at B.; ☿ affl. in ☐ or ♐. (See "Arms", "Feet", in this section; "Rheumatism" under Hands, Feet).

Head—Gout In—Gouty Pains In—☿ affl. in ☐.

Heart—Gout In—♄ affl. in ♌, or affl. the hyleg therefrom. (See Heart).

Hips and Thighs—Gout In—A ♐ disease, and afflictions in ♐; the ☽ in ♐; ☌, or ill-asp. ♄ (or ☿ if he be of the nature of ♄) at the beginning of an illness, or at decumb. (Hor'y); ♄ affl. in ☐ or ♐; ♄ in ♐ in the 6th H.; ♃ affl. in ☐ or ♐; ♃ affl. in ♐ in the 6th H.; ♃ in ♐, and affl. the ☽ or Asc.; ♀ affl. in ♐, hip gout; ♀ affl. in ♑, gout in thighs; ♀ in the 6th H., and afflicted, or ♀ in this house and affl. the ☽ or Asc. (See Hips, Thighs).

Humours — Goutish Humours — (See Arms, Causes, Feet, Hands, Knees, and the various paragraphs in this section. Also see Humours).

Impure Blood—Caused by Gout—(See "Impure Blood" under Impure).

Incurable Gout—Classed as Incurable Ordinarily—(See "Causes" in this section).

Joints — Gout and Pain In — Caused principally by ♄, and in the joints and parts ruled by the sign containing ♄ at B. (See "Gout" under Joints).

Knees—Gout In—Flying Gout In the Legs or Knees—♂ affl. in ♑; ♄ in ♑, the gout or rheumatism are more endurable until the causes are removed. (See "Gout" under Knees, Legs).

Legs—Gout In—Flying Gout In—(See Causes, Knees, in this section; "Gout" under Legs).

Limbs — (See Arms, Causes, Extremities, Feet, Hands, Knees, in this section).

Lower Extremities — Lower Parts — Gout In—♅ in ♐ and affl. the ☉, ☽, or Asc.; the ☽ affl. in ♐, or affl. the hyleg therefrom; ♄ in ♑, occi., and affl. the ☉, ☽, or Asc. (See "Extremities" in this section).

Melancholy—Gout From—☿ affl. in ♑. (See Melancholy).

Pains — Gouty Pains — Generally caused by an afflicted ☿, and with ☿ in the configuration causing the gout, and where the nerves are affected by mineral deposits, etc. (See Head, Joints, Legs, and the various paragraphs in this section).

Podagra — Gout In the Feet — (See "Feet" in this section).

Rheumatic Gout—Caused principally by afflictions in ♐. (See "Causes" in this section; Rheumatism).

Shoulders—Gout In—♄ or ☿ affl. in ♊. (See "Arms" in this section) .

Spice of Gout — (See "Feet" in this section).

Surfeits—Gout Resulting From—(See "Gout" under Surfeits).

Swellings — From Gout — Principally In the Joints — (See "Joints" in this section; Swellings).

Tendency to Gout—Principally by afflictions in ♐; ♃ affl. in ♐; earthy signs on the Asc. (See "Causes" in this section).

Thighs — Gout In — (See "Hips and Thighs" in this section).

Toes—Gout In—♄ in ♓. (See "Feet" in this section; Toes).

Wandering Gout — Flying Gout — In the Arms, Hands, Legs and Feet—The ☽ affl. in ♊ when the ☽ is the afflictor in the disease; ♄ affl. in ♓, in the toes. (See Arms, Feet, Hands, Knees, Legs, in this section).

Wrists—Gout In—(See "Gout" under Wrists). For further study along the line of Gout, and its causes, see Crystallization, Deposits, Minerals, Moon, Periodic, Precipitation, Pressure, Retentions, Saturn, Urea, Uric Acid, Wastes, etc.

GRACEFUL—Graceful Body, Form, and Manner — The ♎ and ♀ influences strong at B., and well-asp. by the ☽; ♎ on the Asc. gives a tall, graceful and slender body, but the last few degrees of ♎ rising tend to a shorter and stouter body, and not as graceful or comely. The active and strong planets tend to destroy grace of body and manner, and espec. when acting thru the positive signs. (See Beautiful, Comely, Coordination, Dexterity, Form, Handsome, Harmony, Manner, Shape, Well-Formed, Well-Proportioned).

GRADUAL—Gradual Emaciation—Progressive Emaciation — (See Consumptions, Emaciation; "Malnutrition" under Nutrition; Tabes, Tuberculosis, Wasting, etc.).

GRAIN—Corn—Wheat—Scarcity of— (See Corn, Drought, Dryness, Famine, Fountains, Fruit, Rottenness, Scarcity, Starvation, Vegetation, Wheat).

GRAND—

   Grandchildren—(See this subject under Children).

   Grand Mal—(See Epilepsy).

   Grand Man — The 12 Parts, or Divisions of the Body, and as ruled by the 12 Signs of the Zodiac. Planets in the Signs at B., and by dir., and the Sign upon the Asc. at B., tend to affect the part ruled by the Sign for good or evil. (See Aries, Taurus, Gemini, etc.; Houses, Signs, Zodiac).

   Grandparents—(See this subject).

GRANDEES—Nobles—Noblemen—Suffering or Death of—(See Nobles).

GRANDPARENTS—

   Grandchildren—(See this subject under Children).

   Grandfather — Death of the Grandfather, or an Aged Male In the Family —♂ to the ♂ or ill-asp. ♄ by dir. The 7th H. rules the grandfather, according to the sex of the nativity. Male relatives are ruled by ♂. (See "Male" under Relatives; Seventh House, Uncles).

   Grandmother — Death of the Grandmother, or an Aged Female In the Family — (See "Death" under Aunts, Family, Mother; "Female Relatives" under Relatives; Sister).

GRANULATIONS—The Healing Process —The Small Elevations on a Healing Surface—This is a benevolent indication and influence, and carried on by the benefic, constructive, and healing influences of the good aspects of the ☉, ♂, and ♃. If the ♄ influence is stronger than the Benefics, and the vitality low and weak, then decay, suppuration, ulceration, or mortification may set in instead of healthy granulations. (See Curable, Incurable).

   Eyelids—(See "Granulated" under Eyelids).

   Joints — (See "Granulations" under Joints).

GRAPE — Vitis Vinifera — (See Sun Group under Herbs. Also see Carcinoma).

GRAPHITE—A Native Form of Carbon — Plumbago — A Mineral of ♄. (See "Minerals", "Metals", under Saturn).

GRATIFICATION — Of the Appetites — (See Amorous, Appetites, Drink, Eating, Excesses, Epicureans, Feasting, Food, Gluttony, Luxuries, Passion, Pleasure; "Sex Excesses" under Sex; Venery, etc.).

GRAVE — Gravity—Thoughtful—Serious—Sober—Taciturn—A ♄ and ♑ influence; ♄ Sig. in ♑; ♄ ♂ ☿; ♄ in ♍ in partile asp. the Asc., tends to a grave countenance; ♄ in the 3rd, 9th, or 12th H.; the ♄ sign ♑ on the Asc. at B.; the ☉ in ♑ and affl. by ♄; the ☉ or ☽ to the ♂ or ill-asp. ♄ by dir.; the earthy signs on the Asc., and strong at B., tend to gravity, and to make one more serious, thoughtful, and melancholic. (See Austere, Depressed, Despondent, Gloomy, Melancholic, Quiet, Reserved, Responsibility, Serious, Taciturn).

   The Grave—Ruled by ♄ and the 4th H. Also Grave Diggers are ruled by ♄. (See Burial, Corpse, Death, Terminal).

GRAVEL—A Sand-Like Deposit In the Urine—Sand—Concretions—Calculus, etc.—Gravel is crystallized in the kidneys by the ♄ influence, as ♄ has his exaltation in ♎, the kidney sign.

Bladder—Gravel In—♄ affl. in ♎ or ♏; Subs at KP, PP (2, 3, 4L). (See "Bladder" under Stone)

Causes—The ☉ affl. in ♎, ♏, or ♒; the ☉ or ☽ affl. in the 6th H. in a fixed sign; the ☽ to the ☌ or ill-asp. ♂ by dir.; the ☽ in ♉ and affl. by the ☉ or ♂ when taken ill (Hor'y); ♄ in ♎ or ♏; ♄ in the 6th H. in a fixed sign; a ♄ disease; ♂ in ♉, ♎, or ♏; ♂ in ♌ when ♂ is the afflictor in the disease; ♂ in ♌, ☌ or ill-asp. the ☉; ♂ in the 6th H. in a fixed sign; a ♎ and ♏ disease, and indicated by afflictions in these signs; fixed signs show, and espec. when in the 6th H.; ♏ on the Asc., and with the ☽ at the same time in ♒, tends to the formation and voiding of red gravel. Cases of Gravel—See Fig. 8 in "Message of the Stars" by the Heindels. Also see "Gravel", Chap. 13, page 90, in Daath's Medical Astrology. (See Calculus, Crystallization, Deposits, Elimination, Hardening, Lime, Minerals, Retarded, Retention, Sand, Stone, Suppressions, Urea, Uric Acid, Wastes, etc.).

Death by Gravel—Denoted by ♂, and when ♂ is one of the afflictors, and holding the dominion of death.

Kidneys—Gravel and Sand In—♄ affl. in ♎; Subs at KP (11D). (See "Kidneys" under Stone).

Liver—Gravel In—♄ affl. in ♍, ♎, or ♏; ♄ affl. in ♋, gravel in the upper lobes; ♄ affl. in ♍, gravel in the lower lobes; Subs at Li.P. (4D). (See Liver; "Liver" under Stone).

Red Gravel — (See "General Causes" in this section).

Sand—(See Sand).

Stone—(See Stone).

GRAY—The color Gray is ruled by the 8th H. (See Colors).

Brain—Gray Matter of—(See Cortex).

Gray Hair—(See "Gray" under Hair).

GREAT—Greatness—

Great Ability — ☿ Sig. in ♍, great mental abilities; ☿ Sig. in ♎, great natural ability; ☿ in ♍ in the Asc., and in ✶ or △ asp. ♃ and the ☽); ☿ Sig. in ☌ or good asp. the ☽ and Asc.; ♂ Sig. ☌ ☿, considerable ability; ♂ Sig. ✶ or △ the ☉, a great mind. (See Excellent, Genius, Gifted, Mathematician, Mechanical; "Abilities" under Mind; "Natural Abilities" under Natural; Prodigies, Reputation, Scholar, Science, etc.).

Great Beasts — Great Cattle — Large Animals—Danger From—Attacks By—Great Beasts and Animals are ruled by the 12th H., and ♂ in the 12th H., and affl. by ♅ or ♄, makes the native liable to injury from large beasts. Also see Ceti or Menkar joined with the Luminaries at B. (See Animals, Beasts, Cattle, Elephants, Four-Footed, Horses, Quadrupeds, etc. Also see "Great Cattle" in this section).

Great Cattle—Great Beasts—Danger From, or Attacks By—The ☉ to the cusp the 12th H. by dir.; the ☽ to the place of Ceti; lord of the 6th H. in the 12th; a malefic ruler of the 12th H. at B., and in the 12th at a Solar Rev. (See "Great Beasts" in this section; "Cattle" under Large).

Great Dangers — Subject To — (See "Great" under Danger).

Great Energy — (See "Great" under Energy).

Great Events — (See "Great" under Events).

Great Eyes — (See "Great" under Eyes).

Great Learning — (See "Great" under Learning. Also see "Great Ability" in this section).

Great Lips—(See Lips).

Great Men—Death of—An Eclipse of the ☉ or ☽ in a fiery sign signifies the death of Great Men, or of Kings and Rulers; an eclipse of the ☉ in the 2nd Dec. of ♓, death of famous and excellent men; an eclipse of the ☽ in ♊, ♌, ♎, or ♓; Comets appearing in ♉, ♋, ♌, ♎, ♏, ♑, or ♒. (See Assassination, Famous, Kingdoms, Kings, Lady; "Power" under Men; Nobles, President, Princes, Queens, Renown, Rulers, etc.).

Great Mind — (See "Great Ability" in this section; "Elegant Mind" under Elegant).

Great Mortality—(See Mortality).

Great Mouth—(See Mouth).

Great Physical Powers — (See Athletic).

Great Recuperative Powers—(See Recuperation).

Great Resistance—To Disease—(See Resistance).

Great Vitality—(See Vitality).

Great Women—Death of—(See Lady, Queens).

Greatness — Sickness by Aiming At, or Great Struggle For—Lord of the 10th H. in the 6th H. at B.

The Great—Much Mortality Among—The ☉ in the 8th H. at the Vernal, and Lord of the Year, and espec. if the ☉ is evilly aspected by lord of the 8th; the ☉ in the Asc., and afflicted, and Lord of the Year at the Vernal Equinox; an eclipse of the ☉ or ☽ in a fiery sign; ♄ Lord of the Year at the Vernal, in ♓, and oriental; ♄ in ♉ in an angle, afflicted, and direct in motion at a Vernal Ingress; ♂ in ♎, ℞, and Lord of the Year at the Vernal. (See "Great Men" in this section).

GREEN—Is the color of ♄ in the Solar Spectrum. Is represented by the 2nd, 8th, 9th, and 12th Houses. Is ruled by the ☽ in ♋ or ♌. Red mixed with green is denoted by ♃; ♋ denotes green or russet; ♌, red or green; ♐, light green or olive. Green, ruled principally by ♄, tends to relieve inflamed eyes, and is a restful color to the eyes, and to live in a green room, wear green glasses, etc. Green color predominates in Nature, and is also the color of the Human Intellect. (See Colors, Conjunctivitis; "Treatment" under Eyes; "Solar Spectrum" under Solar).

Green Sickness—(See Chlorosis).

GRIEF—Dolens—Griefs—Lamentations—Sorrow, etc.—The ☉ to the ☌ or ill-asp. ♄ by dir.; the ☉ to the ☌ ☽ by dir.; the ☽ to the ill-asps. ♄ or ♀ by dir.; the 2nd Dec. of ♊ on the Asc.;

♄ in ♌, and in evil asp. the ☽; ♄ to the bad asps. ♀ or ☿ by dir. (See Anguish, Anxiety, Bereavement, Dejected, Depressed, Despondent, Disgrace, Gloom, Melancholy, Ruin, Sadness, Sorrow, Trouble, Worry, etc.).

Death By — Denoted by ☿; ♄ ☌ ☿ in ♑, and espec. when in the 12th H., as the 12th H. rules Grief.

Females—Grief To—(See "Grief" under Females).

Full of Grief—Full of Sorrow—The ☌ or ill-asps. of ♄ to the ☉ by dir. or tr.; in Hor'y Q., ♄ afflicting the Sig. (See Complaining, Murmuring, Repining, Sorrow).

Heart Afflicted by Grief—(See "Grief" under Heart).

Legs — Phlegmatic Grief In — Phlegmatic Dolens—(See "Milk Leg" under Legs).

Men — Grief To — (See "Grief" under Men).

Mind — Grief of Mind — Lord of the Asc. and the ☽ much afflicted at B., and by dir. (See Anguish, Anxiety, Despondent, Worry; the various paragraphs in this section).

Much Grief Generally—Much Sorrow Prevalent—♄ to the bad asps. his own place at B. by tr. or dir., with people so affected; ♄ sole ruler at a Solar Eclipse; an eclipse of the ☉ in the 3rd Dec. of ♈; ♑ ascending at the Vernal, and ♄ afflicted, grief to Peoples and Countries ruled by ♑. (See "Capricorn" under Nations).

Phlegmatic Grief—In the Legs—(See "Legs" in this section).

Public Grief — Public Sadness and Sorrow—An eclipse of the ☉ in the 1st Dec. of ♒; ♀ elevated above, and configurated with ♄ at a Solar Eclipse or Ingress. (See Eclipse, Ingresses, Public; "Much Sadness" under Sadness; Sorrow; "Much Grief" in this section).

Women—Grief To—(See "Grief" under Females, Women).

GRIEVOUS—Distressful—Heavy—

Colds—Grievous Colds In the Head—(See "Colds", "Disorders", under Head).

Diseases—Grievous Diseases—Distressful—Difficult to Cure—Serious Illnesses—Heavy and Prolonged Illnesses —The ☉ to the ill-asps. the ☽ by dir., and the ☽ hyleg, or affl. at B., according to the sign the ☉ is in; the ☉ or ☽ to the ☌ or ill-asps. ♄ by dir.; ♅ ☌ ♄ in the 6th H.; lord of the 6th H. affl. by the □ or ☍ of the lord of the Asc.; lord of the 6th affl. in the 6th, 8th, or 12th H., or a malefic in the 6th, not easily cured; lord of the 1st in the 4th or 8th H., and afflicted; malefics afflicted and elevated above the ☉ or ☽. (See Chronic; "Maladies" under Distressful; "Duration of Disease" under Duration; Epilepsy; "Sick" under Escape; Extraordinary, Fatal, Fierce; "Affliction" under Heavy; Incurable, Lingering, Painful, Poignant, Prolonged, Public (see "Grievous" under Public); Serious, Severe, Sharp, Slow, Tedious, Vehement, Violent, etc.).

Feet—Grievous Infirmities In—(See "Weakness" under Feet).

Head — Grievous Colds In — (See "Colds", "Disorders", under Head).

Mortality — Grievous Mortalities — (See Mortality).

GRIPINGS—Cramps—Spasmodic Pains In the Bowels or Stomach—(See "Gripings", "Pain", "Spasmodic", under Bowels, Stomach; Colic, Cramps, Gas, Spasmodic, Wind, etc.).

GRIPPE—La Grippe—(See Influenza, La Grippe).

GRISTLE—Cartilage—(See Cartilage).

GROINS—Inguinal Region—The Inguinal Canal — The Depression between the Thigh and Trunk—Ruled by the ♏ Sign.

All Diseases In—Signified by the 8th H., and espec. in Hor'y Q.

Bubo—Tumor In—Inguinal Tumor—(See Bubo).

Diseases In—Afflictions in ♏, and are ♏ diseases; malefics in the 8th H., or affl. the lord of the 8th.

Enlarged Glands Of—Afflictions in ♏ and the 8th H.; Subs at KP and PP (4, 5L). (See Bubo, Enlarged, Glands).

Hernia — Inguinal Hernia — Rupture In the Groin—(See "Inguinal" under Hernia).

Injuries In — Accidents To — Wounds To—Afflictions in ♏ or the 8th H.; ♂ affl. in ♍, or the 6th and 8th H.

Lymphatic Glands Of—Swelling of—(See Bubo).

Pain In Groins—A ♏ disease, and afflictions in ♏; ♂ affl. in ♏.

Tumors In Groins—♄ affl. in ♏. (See Bubo).

GROOVES—(See Channels, Fissure).

GROSS—Coarse—Unrefined—

Gross Blood—(See "Too Much Blood" under Blood; "Impure Blood" under Impure).

Gross Humours—The Body Is Full of Gross Humours — (See "Gross" under Humours).

Gross Manners — Coarse Manners — Lack of Refinement — ♂ strong and prominent at B., and ♀ weak; many planets in the earthy and watery signs, and the airy signs especially weak and unoccupied. (See Manners, Rough, Unrefined).

GROWTH—Increase—Expansion—Enlargement—Increment—Growth of the Mind and Body, etc.—♅ and ♀ govern the functions of growth, and nutrition of the body. ♀ rules growth until adolescence, and then ♅ takes charge. The ☽ has much to do with the growth and development of the body. Assimilation, and the growth of the body are furthered by the work of ♃. The growth of the mind depends much upon the aspects and position of ☿ at B. The Solar Forces focussed thru the ☽ stimulate the growth of the body.

Abnormal Growth — Of the Body — Strange and Abnormal Growth — Diminished or Increased Growth of the Body — Diminutive growth is due to decreased Pituitary secretion, and enlarged growth to increase of this secretion. The Pituitary Body is ruled by ♅, and the action of ♅ by his various aspects and influences on the Pituitary secretion tends to either increase or diminish the secretion, and to produce Giants, Freaks of Nature, Dwarfs, etc. Abnormal growth and freaks of nature, are produced by ♅ ☌ ♀. (See Diminished, Dwarfed, Enlarged, Giants; "Over-Developed" under Organs; Pituitary; "Abnormally Tall" under Tall).

Arrested Growth—Cessation of—(See Arrested, Atrophy, Deformities, Diminished, Dwarfed, Obstructions, Paralysis, Pituitary, Retarded, Suppressions, Thyroid, etc.).

Bone — Outgrowth of—Exostosis—(See "Bones of Arms" under Arms).

Cessation Of—(See "Arrested" in this section).

Increase of Growth—Incrementitions—Due to the tonic, or plus action of ♂. (See "Tonic Action" under Mars).

Mind—Growth of the Mind—Arrested Mental Development — Precocious — Rapid Mental Development, etc.—The Mind is but a temporary part of Man, and is one of the Vehicles thru which he acts on the Material, or Earth Plane, and by acting thru the brain. Afflictions at B., and also during the prenatal period, tend to place limitations and restraints upon the brain cells, so that the mind is crippled and hampered in its action, and these afflictions, and espec. to ☿, the mental ruler, may cause idiocy, imbecility, a foolish mind, bad judgment, and also to give the various bad traits of temperament, whereas the favorable asps. to ☿, the ☽, the Asc., and with ☿ well-asp. by the ☽, and also in good relation to the Asc., tend to give a better brain, and a more free action of the mind thru the brain. The Pineal Gland, and the Pituitary Body in the brain, have more to do with spiritual growth than with mental growth. The 12th H. conditions at B. also indicate largely the freedom of expression that the mind will have over the brain and body, and a badly afflicted 12th H. at B. tends to restraint of the senses, to deafness, and also to bring limitations upon the brain and body for the present life, so that the native may find it impossible to make much mental progress. The same influences which tend to Deformities, Hunchback, Idiocy, Poor Judgment or Memory, etc., tend to retard the mental growth and development. (See these subjects. Also see "Active Mind" under Active; "Arrested", "Quickened", under Mentality).

Miscellaneous Subjects — The following subjects have to do with Growth in its various phases, which see in the alphabetical arrangement—Abnormalities, Acromegaly, Arrested, Assimilation, Atrophy, Augmented, Backwardness, Blight, Cells, Cessation, Congenital, Corpulent, Crooked, Decrease, Defects, Deficient, Deformed, Development, Deviations, Diminished, Dwarfed, Enlarged, Exaggerated, Exostosis, Expansion, Extremities, Fat, Fleshy, Foetus, Form, Freaks, Genius, Gestation, Giants, Hair, Height, Hermaphrodites, Hindered, Humpback, Idiocy, Ill-Formed, Imbecile, Imper-

fections, Increase, Inhuman, Irregularities, Large, Limbs, Malformations, Medium, Members, Mental, Mind, Monsters, Muscles, Nutrition, Obesity, Obstructions, Organs, Outgrowth (see Excrescences, Exostosis); Overgrowth (see Over); Perversions, Physical, Pituitary, Precocious, Premature, Prenatal, Retarded, Shape, Short, Small, Stature, Stout, Suppressions, Tall, Thin, Undersized, Undeveloped, Unnatural, Uvula, Weight, Withering, etc.

Never Grew Up — At Age of 25 Had the Mind of a Child—Case—See "Never Grew Up", No. 720, in 1001 N.N.

Normal Growth—Of the Body depends largely upon the action of the Pituitary Gland, and whether or not it is functioning properly. (See Pituitary).

Retarded Growth—(See "Arrested" in this section).

GROWTHS — New Growths—Excrescences—Lumps—Growths are caused by ♄ influence, and resulting from concretions, deposits, etc. Also caused by ♃, and ♂ afflictions to ♃; ♂ prog. ☌, P, □ or 8 the radical ♃, or vice versa, due to impurities in the blood. (See Concretions, Deposits). Growths generally appear in parts and organs of the body ruled by the Sign of the Zodiac containing malefics at B., and espec. the sign containing ♄, due to deposits, or the sign containing ♃, due to congestions, and resulting from plethora or surfeits. For Growths affecting the different organs, or parts of the body, see "Growths" under the Organ or Part, in the alphabetical arrangement, as "Growths" under Head, Face, etc.

Blindness from Growths — (See "Growths" under Blindness; "Defects" under Eyes).

Bone — Outgrowth of — (See Exostosis).

Fatty Growths — (See "Lardaceous" under Carcinoma; Cysts, Degeneration, Fat, Sarcoma, Sebaceous, Steatoma, Waxy, Wen, etc.).

Fleshy Growths — (See Caruncle; "Growths" under Fleshy).

Fungus Growths—Vegetable Growths—(See Fungus, Vegetable).

Hairy Growths—(See Moles, Naevus).

Harmful Growths — (See Malignant, Noxious, Poisonous).

Harmless Growths — (See Moles, Warts, Wens; "Non-Malignant" in this section).

Horny Growths—(See Horny).

Malignant Growths—(See Carcinoma, Malignant, Tumors).

Morbid Growths — ♂ influences overlaid and intermixed with other planets, as with ♆, ♅, ♄. Also formed by ♃, due to Plethora, Excesses, Impure Blood, etc. (See Fungus, Morbid).

New Growths — Neoplasm — (See Tumors, Warts, Wens).

Non-Malignant Growths — Ruled mostly by ♀, and are Venus diseases.

Noxious Growths — Poisonous and Harmful—♃ affl. in ♋, from overeating; ♃ □ or 8 the ☉. (See "Over-Eating" under Eating; Noxious).

Obstructing Growths—(See Cataracts; "Defects" under Eyes; Goiter, Obstructions, Tumors, etc.).

Outgrowth—(See "Bone" in this section).

Overgrowth — Excessive Growth — (See Enlarged, Giants, Overgrowth).

Poisonous Growths — (See Malignant, Noxious, in this section).

Tumors—(See Tumors).

Ulcers—(See Ulcers).

Vegetable Growths — (See Fungus, Vegetable). For further study along this line see Abnormalities, Carcinoma, Caruncle, Cataract, Cells, Concretions, Congestions, Crystallization, Cysts, Decay, Defects, Deformities, Degeneration, Deposits, Epithelioma, Excessive, Excrescences, Exostosis, Eyes, Face, Feet, Goiter, Hardening, Head, Hypertrophy; "Impure Blood" under Impure; Lipoma, Lumps, Minerals, Moles, Naevus, Plethora, Retentions, Sarcoma, Scales, Sebaceous, Skin, Steatoma, Suppressions, Surfeits, Swellings, Venereal, Warts, Wens, etc.

GUARDIANS—Godfathers—Are governed by ♃, and the aspects to ♃ at B., and by dir., indicate the conditions affecting them for good or ill. Godmothers are ruled by ♀. (See "Godfather" under Father).

GUILLOTINE — Death by Sentence of Law—Beheaded—♂ affl. in ♏. (See Beheaded, Executed, Hanging, Judge). Case of Death by Guillotine — See "Princess", No. 697, in 1001 N.N.

GULLET—(See Oesophagus).

GUMS—The Gums—Gingiva—

Bleeding Gums—Spongy—Ulcerated— ♂ afflicted in ♈ or ♉; Subs at MCP (4C). (See "Ulcerated" in this section).

Gum Boils—An ♈ disease. (See Boils).

Inflamed Gums—Sore Gums—Gingivitis—♂ afflicted in ♈ or ♉. The upper Gums are ruled by ♈, and the gums around the lower teeth by ♉. (See "Lower", "Upper", under Teeth).

Putrid Gums — ♄ afflicted in ♈ or ♉. (See Putrid).

Pyorrhoea — (See Jaws, Pyorrhoea, Teeth).

Sore Gums — (See Bleeding, Inflamed, in this section).

Spongy Gums—(See "Bleeding" in this section).

Tumor—Of the Gums—Elastic Tumor —Epulis—♃ or ♀ in ♈ or ♉, and afflicted by ♄. (See "Tumors" under Mouth).

Ulcerated Gums—♃ afflicted in ♈, of the upper gums; ♃ afflicted in ♉, of the gums of the lower jaw. (See Ulcers).

Wounds To—♂ afflicted in ♈ or ♉.

GUNSHOT — Guns — Danger by Fire Arms—Powder Burns—Pistols—Shotguns — Weapons, etc.—Guns are ruled by ♂ in general, and accidents, injury, or death by are usually caused by ♂ afflictions.

Accidents by Fire Arms—♂ affl. at B.; the ill-asp. of ♂ by dir. to the ⊙, ☽, Asc., or M.C.; fire signs dispose to.

(See the various paragraphs in this section).

Blindness — By Gunshot Wounds — (See "Gunshot" under Blindness).

Danger from Fire Arms — Danger of Injury By—The ☽ to the ♂ or ill-asps. ♂ by dir.; ♂ affl. at B.; ♂ ♂ the Asc. by dir.; the Asc. to the ♂ the ⊙, and the ⊙ ♂ ♂; the Asc. to the place of the Ascelli or Capricornus. (See the various paragraphs in this section).

Death by Gunshot—Danger of—Death by Accidental Gunshot—Suicide By— The ⊙ or ☽ hyleg, and to the ♂ or ill-asp. ♂ by dir.; ♂ in a fiery sign, and ♂ the Asc., and espec. when in ♌ near the Ascelli; ♂ affl. the hyleg at B., and by dir., and holding the dominion of death, and when a violent death is indicated by the radix. Cases—(1) Shot Himself Accidentally—See "Shot Himself", No. 177, in 1001 N.N. (2) Shot Himself—See "Puzzle Horoscope", No. 672, in 1001 N.N. (3) Death by Accidental Pistol Shot — See "Gambetta", No. 736, in 1001 N.N. (4) Shot to Death —See "Mexico", No. 758, in 1001 N.N. (5) Shot Himself to Death—See "Haydon", No. 818, in 1001 N.N. (See Suicide; "Death" under Violent).

Gunshot Wounds—Danger of—Liable To—The ⊙ hyleg, and the ⊙ to the ♂ or ill-asps. ♂ by dir.; the ⊙ or ☽ affl. by ♂ from ♊, ♐, or ♒; the ⊙, ☽, and other planets in the Asc. with Regulus, and evilly aspected; the ⊙ directed to Praesepe; the Prog. ⊙ or ☽ ♂, □, or ♂ the radical ♂; the ☽ ♂ or ill-asps. ♂ by dir.; the ☽ in an airy sign, and to the ♂ or ill-asp. ♂ by dir.; the ☽ at a Solar Rev. passing over the place of ♂ at B.; caused by the ⊙ or ♂, the positive, electric, and heat-producing planets; ♂ afflictions make liable to, and usually to the part of the body most afflicted by ♂ at B.; ♂ ♂ or ill-asp. the ⊙, ☽, Asc., or M.C. by dir.; ♂ affl. in the 6th H.; ♂ affl. in ♐, and also affl. the hyleg; ♂ affl. in ♊ or ♍, and in ♂ or ill-asp. the Asc. by dir.; ♂ by Periodic Rev. to the ♂, □, or ♂ ♅; caused and ruled by ♂; fire signs dispose to; afflictions in ♐.

Hunting — Shooting — Fond of — (See Exercise, Hunting, Sports). For further influences along this line, see Assassination, Battle, Contests, Cuts, Disputes, Duels, Fighting, Feuds, Instruments, Iron, Murder, Quarrels, Sports, Stabs, Sword, War, Weapons.

GUSTATIVENESS — Gustativeness Large—(See Diet, Eating, Epicureans, Feasting, Food, Gluttony).

Gustatory Process—Ruled by ♉. (See Taste).

GUTTA SERENA—Amaurosis—Partial or Total Blindness—The ☽ in the 1st, 4th, or 7th H., decr. in light, and in ♂ or ♉ ♅, ♄, or ♂, and the malefics ascend after her, occi., and at the same time the malefics be in ♂ or ♉ the ⊙, and ori. of the ⊙ and ascend before him,—under these circumstances, with ♄ as the special afflicting planet, Amaurosis tends to result. Saturn especially tends to cause blindness by Amaurosis. Also caused by Subs at MCP (3 and 4C). (See Amaurosis).

H

HABIT— Habits—Disposition— Habitual—Tendency to Repetition—Diathesis—Hexis—Hectic—Permanent Habit —Bad Habits—Good Habits—Tendencies—Practices—Vices—Virtues, etc.— The ♄ influence tends greatly to make people governed by habit, as ♄ rules over habits, and tends to make them fixed. Habit is also the result of automatic action by the ☽. The aspects and position of the ☽ govern the general habits of life, and the functional activities. The ☽ has an important influence over the personal habits. The ☽ well-asp. in ♉ gives methodical habits. The ☉ influence leads to tendencies which are later taken up by the ☽ action and made automatic, and result in unconscious behavior. (See Automatic). The influences of the negative signs and planets tend to the formation or habits, whether good or bad, being more related to the unconscious, or the subconscious realms of the mind. The following subjects have to do with Habits, their causes, nature, etc., which see in the alphabetical arrangement when not more rfully considered here.

Abnormalities; Acquired Habits—Are generally acquired under the action and influences of the ☽, and strong ☽ characters are greatly influenced by environment and external conditions. (See Acquired).

An Ill Habit—Of the Body—(See "Ill-Health All Thru Life" under Ill-Heath).

Appearance—The Habits As To Appearance—(See Appearance, Cleanliness, Clothing, Cosmetics, Dirty, Dress, Filthy, Neat, Uncleanly, etc.).

Appetites; Automatic Action — Tendency to Form Habits by Repetition— (See Automatic).

Bad Habits—Wrong Habits—Tendency To, and especially along the lines of Eating, Drinking, Pleasure, Appetites, etc.—♄ ☌ or ill-asp. ♂ or ♀ by dir.; ♃ □ or ♉ the ☉; ♀ affl. at B.; ♀ affl. by ♂; ♀ affl. in ♍, and espec. in the 6th H. With ♀ affl. in ♍ carelessness in the habits should be avoided. (Note the various paragraphs and subjects in this section).

Better—The Habit Better—The ☉ configurated with the lord of the Asc., the native is more comely and the habit better. (See Comely).

Blackheads — Due to Bad Habits of Living — (See "Comedo" under Sebaceous).

Body—Ill Habits of—An Ill Habit of —(See An Ill Habit, Drink, Dissipation, Narcotics, and the various paragraphs in this section).

Careless Habits — Careless of Habits and the Health—♀ affl. in ♈; common signs on the angles. (See Careless; "Bad Habits", and the various paragraphs in this section).

Conduct—(See the various paragraphs under Conduct, Manners, Temperament).

Cosmetics—Ill Habits and Indiscretions In the Use of—(See Cosmetics, Lotions).

Creatures of Habit — Fixed Habits — The ☉, ☽, and many planets in fixed signs at B., or with fixed signs on the angles; the ♉ and ♍ signs tend to make creatures of habit. (See "Fixed Habits" under Fixed).

Death—Death from Bad Habits—(See Death, Drink, Eating, Excesses, Gluttony, Passion, Pleasures, Sex; "Dry Habit" in this section).

Diathesis — The Hexis, or Permanent Habit In Disease—(See Diathesis).

Diet — Habits of — (See Diet, Eating, Epicureans, Excesses, Feasting, Food, Gluttony, Intemperate, Luxuries, Moderate, Temperate, etc.).

Directions — Temporary or Transient Habits may arise under the influence of Directions, but the influences of the radical map indicate habits of a more permanent and fixed nature. (See Directions).

Dirty—(See Dirty, Filthy, Uncleanly).

Diseases—From Bad Habits—The ☽ □ or ♉ the Asc., diseases brought on by loose living and bad habits; ♀ affl. in ♈. (See "Bad Habits", and the various paragraphs in this section; "High Living" under High; "Loose Living" under Loose, etc.).

Dress — Habits of — (See Clothing, Dress, Neat, etc.).

Drink — Dissipated Habits In — (See Drink, Drunkenness, Intoxication).

Drug Habit—(See Narcotics).

Drunkenness—Habitual Drunkenness —(See Drunkenness).

Dry Habit—Of the Body—Death From —(See "Dry Habit" under Dry).

Eating — Evil Habits In — (See Diet, Eating, Excesses, Food, Gluttony, etc.).

Environment—As Related to Habits— (See Environment, External, Negative, Positive).

Eruptions — Due to Bad Habits and Improper Living — (See Eruptions; "Eruptions" under Face; Pimples).

Evil Habits — (See Drink, Narcotics, Passion, Perversions, Secret, Vices).

Excesses — From Evil Habits — (See Excesses).

Expense — Expensive Habits — (See Expense, Extravagant, Luxuries, Prodigal, etc.).

External Conditions—As a Factor In the Formation of Habits — (See Acquired, Environment, External).

Extravagant Habits — (See Expense, Extravagance, Luxuries, Prodigal).

Fevers—Habitual Fevers—(See "Habitual" under Fever).

Filthy Habits —(See Dirty, Filthy, Uncleanly).

Fixed Habits — Creatures of Habit — (See "Creatures Of" in this section).

Food—Habits Concerning the Eating and Use of—(See Diet, Eating, Food).

Formation of Habits—(See the Introduction to this section).

Full Habit — Diseases Arising from Too Full a Habit—Denoted by ♃. (See Full, Plethora).

Good Habit and Size—♂ ruler of the Asc., and ori.

Good Habits—(See Moderate, Temperate, in this section).

Governed by Habit—♄ influence, and ♄ strong at B., and ♄ tends to make the habits fixed. (See "Creatures Of" in this section).

Habitual—(See Drunkenness, Fevers, Melancholy, and the various paragraphs in this section).

Hexis—The Permanent Habit In Disease—(See Diathesis, Directions; "Certain" under Disease; Hexis).

Ill Habit—Of the Body—Ill Habits of the Body—(See An Ill Habit, Body, Narcotics, and the various paragraphs in this section).

Immoderate Habits — (See Excesses, Intemperance).

Immoral Habits—(See "Loose Morals" under Morals; Passion, Sex, etc.).

Improper Habits — Illness From — ♀ affl. in ♍.

Impulsive Habits—Ill-Health From— ♀ affl. in ♈. (See "Careless" in this section; Impulsive, Recklessness).

Intemperate Habits—(See Drink, Excesses, Intemperance, etc.).

Irregular Habits — The ☽ to the ill-asps. ♀ by dir. (See Erratic, Irregular).

Loose Habits—(See Loose).

Luxurious Habits—(See "Expense" in this section).

Melancholy — Habitual Melancholy — (See Melancholy).

Methodical Habits—The ☽ well-asp. in ♋. (See Methods).

Moderate In Habits — (See Moderate, Temperate).

Morals—The Habits and Morals—(See Morals).

Narcotic Habit—(See Narcotics).

Natural Habits — The ☉ well-asp. in ♍. (See Natural).

Nature's Wants — Careless Concerning—(See "Requirements" under Nature).

Overcoming Bad Habits—The ☉ in ♍ gives good power and ability to overcome any undesirable habit, and to make one careful of the body. (See Virgo).

Passion—The Passional Habits—(See Excesses, Passion, Sex, Venery, etc.).

Permanent Habits — Fixed Habits — Indicated by the influences of the radical map; many planets in fixed signs at B., and with fixed signs on the angles. (See "Creatures Of" in this section).

Personal Habits—The ☽ has an important influence over the personal, acquired, and temporary or transitory habits.

Perverted Habits—(See Perversions).

Pleasures — Habits Concerning — (See Pleasure).

Plethoric Habit—(See Plethora).

Questionable Habits — (See Loose, Morals).

Regular Habits—Should be cultivated when ☿ is in ♍. (See Regular).

Repeated Action — Repetition In the Formation of Habits—(See Automatic).

Secret Bad Habits—(See Perversions, Secret, Sex, Solitary).

Sedentary Habits—(See Sedentary).

Sex Habits—(See Amorous, Excesses, Passion, Sex).

Skin Eruptions—(See "Eruptions" in this section).

Solitary Habits—(See Secret, Solitary).

Studious Habits—Not Studious—(See Dull, Examinations, Genius, Knowledge, Learning; "Quickened" under Mental; Reading, Science, Study, etc.).

Temperaments — The Various Temperaments and Habit—(See Temperament).

Temperate Habits — (See Moderate, Temperate).

Tendencies — (See Heredity, Tendencies).

Tobacco Habit—(See Tobacco).

Too Full a Habit—(See "Full Habit" in this section).

Transient Habits — Temporary — Caused by Directions. (See Directions; "Fixed" in this section).

Uncleanly Habits—(See Dirty, Filthy, Uncleanly).

Unconscious Behavior — (See the Introduction to this Article).

Unsettled Habits—(See Changes, Mutable, Restless, Residence, Travel, etc.).

Unsteady Habits—(See "Unsettled" in this section).

Vices; Women—The Habits of Women —(See Females, Women).

Wrong Habits—(See "Bad", and the various paragraphs in this section). For further study see Behavior, Celibacy, Conduct, Cosmetics, Debauched, Depraved, Dishonest, Disposition, Dissipated, Gormandizing, Health; "High Living" under High; Improvident, Indiscretions, Lascivious, Licentious, Love Affairs, Lustful, Manners, Men, Obesity, Practices, Quarrelsome, Self-Indulgent, Slovenly, Spendthrift (see "Expense" in this section); Tendencies, etc. Many other subjects may also occur to your mind as related to Habits. Look for them in the alphabetical arrangement.

HAEM — The Prefix Haem — For words not listed under "Haem", see "Hem". In present-day Medical Dictionaries, words beginning with "Haem" are usually listed under "Hem". Also words like "Anaemia" are often found under "Anemia", as the shortened spelling is becoming more prevalent.

HAEMATEMESIS — (See Haemoptysis; "Blood" under Vomiting).

HAEMATIDROSIS — Bloody Sweat — (See "Haematidrosis" under Sweat).

HAEMATOMA—Blood Tumor—A Tumor Containing Blood—Caused by ♄. (See Hemorrhoids).

HAEMATOMYELIA—Hemorrhage Into the Spinal Cord—(See this subject under Spine).

HAEMATOPOIESIS — Haematosis— Blood Making—Blood Formation—The physiological action of the ☉ contributes to blood making. This process is also presided over by ♃ and ♂. Disturbances and diseases which concern blood making and formation are the diseases of ♃ and ♂, and caused by their afflictions, and also by afflictions to these planets. Pulmonary Haematosis is aided by the physiological action of the ☿ Group of Herbs. (See Blood, Haemoglobin, Iron, Oxygen).

HAEMATOSIS—(See Haematopoiesis).

HAEMATURIA—Blood in the Urine—(See "Blood" under Urine).

HAEMOGLOBIN—The Coloring Matter of Red Corpuscles—♂ assimilates Iron from the food and turns it into Haemoglobin. (See Haematopoiesis, Iron, Mars; "Blood" under Red).

HAEMOPHILIA — Hemophilia—Abnormal Tendency to Hemorrhage — (See "Haemophilia" under Hemorrhage).

HAEMOPTYSIS—The Spitting of Blood —Expectoration of Blood — A disease of the ☽ and the ♋ sign; the ☽ in ♍ or ♋, and affl. by the ☉ or ♂ when taken ill; attacks are apt to come when the ☽ is in ☌, □, or ☍ ♂; more apt to occur at the Full ☽ when the fluids of the body are at high tide; ♂ causes when the dominion of death is vested in him, and he afflicts the hyleg; ♂ in ♉, □, or ♋, and espec. when in the 6th H.; ♂ in an angle, occi. of the ☉ and ori. of the ☽.

Death — Death from the Spitting of Blood — ♂ denotes; ♂ affl. the hyleg and holding the dominion of death; ♂ occi. at B., and affl. the hyleg. (See Effusions, Expectoration, Hemorrhage; "Epistaxis" under Nose; "Blood" under Vomiting).

HAEMOSTATICS—Styptics—Having the Property of Checking Hemorrhage —A therapeutic property of ♄ remedies. (See Astringent; "Therapeutic Qualities" under Saturn).

HAIL—Hailstorms—Furious and Tempestuous Hailstorms—An eclipse of the ☽ in ♎, and espec. in the 1st Dec. of ♎, and with suffering or loss of life, injury by, etc.; ♅ in an angle at an Equinox or Solstice; Comets appearing in ♑. (See Cold, Ice, Snow, Weather).

HAIR—The Hirsute Appendage of the Skin—Pilary—Hairy—The Hair in a general way is ruled by ☿, and ☿ in ♈ rules and affects the hair. Is also ruled by ♀. Being an appendage of the skin, is ruled by ♑. The Hair is also connected with the ♍ Sign, and Potassium Sulphate, the ♍ Salt. (See Potassium). The greater part of this Article will be taken up with the description, color, and condition of the Hair, and a few paragraphs will be given to disorders of the Hair, or Hair Follicles. (See Alopecia, Baldness, Bar-

ber's Itch, Beard, Brittle, Disorders, Follicles, Inhibited Growth, Lotions, No Hair, Shrunken, in this section).

Absence Of—(See Baldness).

Abundance of Hair—Heavy—Luxuriant—Much Hair—Plentiful—Thick— The ☉ Sig. in ♍; the ☽ gives; ♄ Sig. in ♍, plentiful and dark hair; ♄ in ♍ in partile asp. the Asc.; ♄ Sig. in ♍, usually dark, short and thick; ♄ in N. Lat. gives a body with much hair, but if in S. Lat. more smooth and fleshy; ♃ strong at B., or ♃ Sig. in Hor'y Q., denotes thick hair; ♃ in the Asc.; ♀ in the Asc., and strong at B.; ♀ Sig. in ♉ in her own term, soft and luxuriant; ♀ in ♍; ♀ strong at B. and rising; ♀ Sig. in ♉, dark, short and thick; ♍ gives much hair, and curling, crispy, or bushy; ♍ on the Asc., plentiful and curly; the earthy and watery signs give; people born under the Southern Parallels, and who have the ☉ continually in their Zenith, and constantly scorched by it, have plentiful and thick hair, which is protective from the heat and rays of the ☉. (See "Growth" in this section).

Alopecia—Loss of the Hair—(See Baldness, Falling Out, Loss Of, No Hair, in this section).

Auburn Hair—♄ in ♎; ♃ in the Asc., auburn brown; ♀ indicates auburn, or light brown; ♎ gives; ♎ on the Asc., light auburn or flaxen. (See "Red" in this section).

Baldness—(See Baldness; Falling, Little, Loss Of, No Hair, in this section).

Barber's Itch—(See Barbers).

Beard—(See the various paragraphs under Beard).

Beautiful Hair—The ☉, ☽, ♀, or ♃ in ♉, and espec. near the 18°, and Medusa's Head; the ☽ or ♀ in the 5° of ♈ or ♐. (See Beautiful; Abundant, Lovely, in this section).

. Black Hair—The ☉ in ♈, ☌ or near Cauda; the ☽ in ♉, ♍, ♏, or ♑, in partile the Asc., black or brown; the ☽ Sig. in ♏, and espec. when in the terms of ♄ or ♃; the ☽ in ♏, black and curly; the ☽ Sig. in ♉, ♍, ♏, or ♑; the ♄ influence tends to darken the hair, and with ♄ strong at B., rising in the Asc., ♄ as ruler, ♄ as Sig. of the person in Hor'y Questions, and with a ♄ sign upon the Asc. at B., such as ♑ or ♒; ♄ or ♑ ascending at B., black, lanky hair; ♄ Sig. in □, ♍, ♏, ♑, or ♓ in Hor'y Q.; ♄ Sig. in □, black or dark brown; ♄ Sig. in ♓, black or a coal, or sad black; ♄ Sig. in ♏, black or dark, and usually short or thick; ♄ lord of the Asc., ori., between the Asc. or M.C., or between the 7th H. and the Nadir; ♄ Sig. in ♎ a comely brown; ♄ in □, ♍, ♏, ♑, or ♓, in partile asp. the Asc.; ♃ Sig. in ♍; ♃ combust; ♃ in ♍ in partile asp. the Asc., blackish or brown; ♂ Sig. in ♉, □, ♍, ♏, or ♑, or in these signs in partile asp. the Asc.; ♂ in ♉ partile the Asc., black, rugged; ♂ in □ or ♍, partile the Asc., black or dark brown; ♂ in ♏, partile the Asc., or ♂ Sig. in ♏, black, curly; ♂ in ♑ partile the Asc., or ♂ Sig. in ♑, black, lank hair; ♀ Sig. in ♉, in the term of ♃, shining black; ♀ in ♍, black or sad brown; ♀ in ♑, partile the Asc., dark or black; ♀ Sig. in ♏, black, unless ♀ be in the terms of ♂ or ♀; ☿ Sig. in ♍ in the terms of ♃ or ♄; ☿ Sig. in ♌; ☿ rising at B., and with a ☿ sign upon the Asc.; ☿ in ♍ in partile asp. the Asc., black or dark brown; ☿ ruler of the Asc., and occi., long black hair; ♈, ♉, ♊, ♍, ♎, ♏, or ♑ on the Asc.; ♋ on Asc., sometimes black; ♎ on the Asc. sometimes gives jet black, glossy hair, ♎ being the exalted sign of ♄; ♉ on the Asc. gives dark or black hair; ♊ gives blackish hair; ♍ gives black hair, and espec. the latter half of the sign; ♑ gives black, lanky hair; ♑ on cusp the 7th H. Sulphur, ruled by ♄, darkens the hair, and ♄ rising produces black hair. Lilly says the hair is black when ♑ descends and light when ♑ ascends. (See Black, Dark, Sulphur. Also in this section see Brunettes, Dark).

Blondes—(See "Light" in this section; "Light Complexion" under Complexion).

Body—(a) Hairy Body—Very Hairy Body—♄ strong at B.; ♄ when ori. makes the body more hairy and tall than when occi.; ♄ in N. Lat., more hairy than when in S. Lat.; denoted by ♄ as Sig. in Hor'y Q.; the ☽ influence gives much hair on the body; ♂ rising and ori. of the ☉; ♂ ruler of the Asc., and ori.; ☿ Sig. in ♓, very hairy body when in the term of ♄; ☿ in ♓ in partile asp. the Asc.; ♏ gives a hairy body; ♏ on the Asc., a short, hairy, coarse body. (See "Abundance" in this section. (b) Little Hair On the Body— Smooth Body—The ☽ ascending at B.; ♄ or ♂ occi. of the ☉ at B.; ♄ lord of the Asc., and occi., as between the M.C. and Desc., or between the Nadir and Asc.; ♄ in S. Lat. at B., the body is more smooth, and with less hair; ♂ ruler of the Asc., and occi., little or no hair on the body; born in cold climates, as in the Arctic Regions; the Quadrant from the Winter Tropic to the Vernal Equinox tends to, and to give straight hair. (See Loss Of, No Hair, in this section). (c) Some Hair On the Body—♄ occi. of the ☉, and ♄ in N. Lat.; ♂ ori. at B.

Brittle and Dry—(See "Dry" in this section).

Brown Hair—The ☉ Sig. in ♉, ♊, ♋, ♍, ♏, ♐, or ♑; the ☉ Sig. in ♒, dark brown when in the term of ♄; the ☉ rising at B., light brown; the ☉ Sig. in ♌, ♐, ♒, or ♓, light brown; the ☉ in ♑ partile Asc., lank brown; the ☉ Sig. in ♐, light brown, but of a dark brown when in the first eight degrees of this sign; the ☉ Sig. in the first six degrees of ♑, light brown; the ☉ in ♊, ♍, ♏, or ♑, in partile asp. the Asc.; the ☉ in ♍ partile Asc., much bright brown; the ☽ Sig. in any sign except ♏ or ♑; the ☽ Sig. in ♈, ♌, ♎, or ♓, light brown; the ☽ in ♎, smooth light brown; the ☽ in ♑, lank dark brown; the ☽ in ♉, ♍, or ♏, dark brown; the ☽ in ♋ or ♍, sad brown; the ☽ Sig. in ♐ or ♓, bright brown; the ☽ in ♉, ♊, ♋, ♏, ♐, ♑, ♒, or ♓, partile the Asc.; the ☽ in ♐ or ♓, partile the Asc., bright brown; the ☽ ♑, partile Asc., brown or black;

♄ in ♋, sad brown; ♄ in ♊, ♋, ♌, ♍, ♎, ♐, or ♒, partile Asc.; ♄ Sig. in ♒, sad brown; ♄ in ♊, dark brown or black; ♄ in ♍, very dark brown; ♄ Sig. in ♎, comely brown; ♄ Sig. in ♌ or ♐; ♃ indicates dark brown or chestnut; ♃ in ♉ partile the Asc., brown rugged; ♃ in ♊, glossy brown; ♃ in ♊, ♋, ♍, ♑, or ♒, partile the Asc.; ♃ in ♋ or ♑, dark brown; ♃ Sig. in ♌, light brown, or yellowish brown and curly; ♃ Sig. in ♍, dark or sad brown; ♃ Sig. in ♎ or ♓, light brown; ♃ in the Asc., thick brown; ♃ in the Asc., auburn brown, and espec. when ♂ is also rising and strong; born under ♃, soft, thick brown; ♂ in ♉ partile Asc., brown or black rugged; ♂ Sig. in the first seven degrees of ☿, light brown; ♂ Sig. in ♊, ♋, ♌, ♍, ♎, ♒, or ♓; ♂ Sig. in ♋, or ♂ in ♋ in partile Asc., thick brown; ♂ in ♊ or ♍, dark brown; ♂ Sig. in ♌, ♎, ♒, or ♓, light brown; ♂ Sig. in ♍, very dark brown, but lighter when in the first seven degrees of ♍; ♂ in ♐ partile Asc.; ♂ Sig. of the person, and ♂ in earthy signs, dark or sad brown; ♂ in earthy signs and near fixed stars of his own nature, dark or sad brown; ♂ Sig. of the person, light brown, and espec. when ♂ is in a watery sign; ♀ in the Asc., bright brown or chestnut; ♀ in the Asc., and strong at B., light brown; ♀ indicates light brown hair; in Hor'y Q. ♀ as Sig. denotes a party with smooth, soft, brown hair; the ✶ or △ asps. of ♀ give brown, or light brown hair; ♀ in ♉, ♊, ♍, ♎, ♏, ♐, ♒, or ♓, in partile asp. the Asc.; ♀ Sig. in ♉, ♊, or ♎, soft brown; ♀ in ♍, sad brown or black; ♀ Sig. in ♍ or ♏, dark brown if in her own term; ♀ in ♏, dark brown; ♀ in ♒, light brown; ☿ Sig. in any of the signs may give brown hair, according to aspects; ☿ in ♉, ♊, ♍, ♐, ♏, ♑, or ♒, in partile Asc.; ☿ Sig. in ♈, ♌, or ♎, light brown; ☿ indicates light brown or auburn hair; ☿ in ♉ partile Asc., short, thick, brown hair; ☿ in ♊, ♌, or ♍, dark brown; ☿ in ♋, sad or dark brown; ☿ Sig. of the party, sad or dark brown; ☿ rising and strong at B., sad or dark brown; ☿ Sig. in ♏, curly, bushy sad or dark brown; ☿ in ♍ partile the Asc., brown curling; ♈ on the Asc., brown or sandy; ♊, ♋, ♍, ♎, ♏, ♐, or ♓ on the Asc.; ♊ gives dark brown; ♊ on the Asc. tends to brown or blackish hair, but the first seven degrees to a lighter brown; ♋ on the Asc. gives sad or dark brown; ♍ on the Asc., a dark brown, except lighter in the 1st Dec.; ♎ on the Asc., brown and glossy; ♏ on the Asc. gives a dark or sad brown, plentiful, curly and bushy; ♐ on the Asc., a bright brown, but darker brown in the first eight degrees. (See Brown. Also see Auburn, Chestnut, Dark, Light, Tawny, in this section).

Brunettes—♀ Sig. in ♉, often handsome brunettes, a perfect beauty, and with a Venus de Milo figure. (See Beautiful, Black, Dark, in this section).

Bushy Hair—(See "Curly" in this section).

Chestnut Hair—The ☽ Sig. in ♐, shining, oily, glossy, chestnut hair; ♃ indicates chestnut or dark brown; ♃ Sig.

in ♐, or ♃ in ♐ in partile asp. the Asc.; ♃ in the Asc., but liable to be bald, and espec. about the temples; ♂ in earthy signs and near fixed stars of his own nature; born under ♀, chestnut or light hair; ♀ in the Asc., chestnut or bright brown; ☿ in ♐, chestnut, and growing off the temples; ☿ ascending at B., and free from the rays of other planets; ♐ gives light chestnut; ♐ on the Asc., light brown or chestnut, and growing back from the temples.

Coarse Hair—Stiff—Wiry—Rough—Rugged—Harsh—Strong—♄ Sig. in ♉, rough, dark; ♃ Sig. in ♉; ♃ Sig. in ♏, dark and coarse; ♂ Sig. of the person in Hor'y Q.; ♂ tends to make the hair stiff, coarse, strong and wiry; ♂ Sig. in ♉, rough and coarse; ♂ Sig. in the last six degrees of ♎; ♂ occi. at B.; ♂ in the 5° ♈ or ♐ tends to make the hair coarse and stiff; ♈ gives wiry hair; ♉ gives harsh, dark and curling hair; ♉ on the Asc., rough and curly. (See Hard, Rough, Rugged, Wiry, in this section).

Color of the Hair—The color of the hair depends upon the planets aspecting the Asc., the sign rising, and the ruler of the term ascending. Also the color is usually that given by the planet near to, or aspecting the degree on the Asc., or in Hor'y Q. the planet on the cusp, or ruling the cusp of the house which signifies the party. The hair is of a lovely and beautiful color when the ♀ influence is strong at B. (See the various paragraphs in this section, such as Black, Brown, Dark, Light, Red, etc.).

Comely Hair—♀ gives when strong at B.; ♄ Sig. in ♎, a comely brown. (See "Beautiful" in this section).

Cosmetics—(See Cosmetics, Lotions).

Crisping—(See "Curly" in this section).

Curly Hair—Crisping—Bushy—Frizzled—Shaggy—Kinky—Given principally by the ♏ sign; ♏ gives plentiful, bushy, and curly hair, and espec. with ♏ on the Asc.; ♏ on the Asc., brown curly, or plentiful sad brown; the ☉ strong at B.; the ☉ in ♏ or ♐; in Hor'y Q. the ☉ or ♂ as Sig. of the person; the ☉ gives light, sandy, curling hair; the ☽ in ♏, black and curly; ♄ ori. at B.; ♄ lord of the Asc., and ori., as between the Asc. and M.C., or between the Desc. and Nadir; ♄, ♃, or ☿ in ♏ tend to bushy and curly hair, and espec. when rising and in the Asc.; ♃ influence strong at B., the hair curls gently, and espec. if in a fiery sign; ♃ Sig. in Hor'y Q. denotes moderate curling hair; ♃ in ♉ partile the Asc., inclined to curl, or rather frizzle; ♃ Sig. in ♉ or ♌; ♃ in ♌ partile Asc., light brown, or yellowish curling hair; ♃ in ♏, dark, curling and bushy; ♂ Sig. of the person, curling or crispy, and espec. when ♂ is in an airy sign; ♂ strong at B., and ruler; ♂ in ♈ partile Asc., light or red curling hair; ♂ in ♏ partile the Asc., black curly hair; ♂ Sig. in ♈ or ♏; ♀ in ♏; ☿ Sig. in ♈ or ♏; ☿ in ♈ partile Asc., light brown, curling; ☿ in ♏ partile Asc., brown curling; ♉ gives dark, harsh, rough

and generally curling hair; ♉ on the Asc., dark curled; ♉ on the Asc., often curly in front; ♌ gives bushy or curling yellowish hair; ♏ on the Asc., brown curling, or dark curling and plentiful; the 3rd face of ♒ on the Asc.; people born under Southern Parallels, and who have the ☉ continually in their Zenith, and who are continually scorched by it; the Quadrant from the Summer Tropic to the Autumnal Equi., and the Quadrant from the Winter Tropic to the Vernal Equi., tend to produce curly hair.

Dark Hair—Dark Brown—Dark Brown or Black—Darkish—Swarthy—Sulphur, ruled by ♄, darkens the hair, and ♄ rising produces black hair; the ☉ Sig. in ♏, dark and abundant; the ☽ in ♏ or ♏, partile the Asc., dark, dark brown, or black; the ☽ in ♉, ♏, ♏, or ♑; ♄ rising at B.; ♄ Sig. in ♈, ♉, ♊; ♋, ♏, ♏, ♑, ♒, or ♓, or in these signs in partile asp. the Asc.; ♄ Sig. in ♉, rough dark; ♄ in ♊, dark brown or black; ♄ Sig. in ♏, dark and plentiful; ♄ Sig. in ♏, short, thick, and dark; ♄ in ♑ or ♒; ♄ Sig. in ♓, dark black; in Hor'y Q. an asp. of ♄ to the Sig., or the Sig. in ☌ ♄, denotes a dark-haired person; ♃ in ♋, ♏, or ♏, partile Asc.; ♃ Sig. in ♏; ♃ Sig. in ♏, dark, coarse, curling and bushy; ♂ Sig. in ♉, ♊, ♏, ♏, or ♑, or in these signs in partile the Asc.; sometimes given by ♂; ♂ in ♊ or ♏, partile the Asc., dark brown or black; ♀ Sig. in ♈ if in the term of ♃; ♀ Sig. in ♉, often handsome brunettes; ♀ Sig. in ♏ or ♑, or in these signs in partile the Asc.; ♀ Sig. in ♏ unless ♀ be in the terms of ♂ or ♀; ☿ Sig. of the person in Hor'y Q.; ☿ Sig. in ♉, ♊, ♏, or ♏, or in these signs in partile the Asc.; ☿ Sig. in ♉ or ♏, dark, short, and thick; ♈ gives dark, wiry hair; ♉ gives dark, harsh, and generally curly; ♉ on the Asc., dark or black; ♊, ♋, ♏, or ♓, when on the Asc., give dark, or dark brown; ♊, ♏, or ♓ give when on the Asc., or strongly occupied; ♋ on the Asc., generally dark brown; ♌ gives dark yellow hair; ♏ on the Asc., darkish, dark brown, or black; ♏ on the Asc., dark, curly, and plentiful; ♑ on the Asc., dark and lanky; ♒ on the Asc., a dark flaxen; ♓ on the Asc., a soft, dark brown. (See Black, Complexion, Dark; Black, Brunettes, Hazel, in this section).

Disorders—Of the Hair—The Hair Affected—The Follicles Affected—Afflictions in or to ♈ or ♑; the Asc. afflicted; ♂ affl. in ♈ or ♑, in the Asc. or 6th H.; afflictions in cardinal signs, and espec., in the 28° of card. signs; afflictions in the 18° ♉ near Gorgon's Head (Algol); ☿ affl. in ♈ tends to affect the hair; ♃ affl. in ♐, or ♐ upon the Asc., tends to falling out of the hair. (See Baldness; "Barber's Itch" under Barbers; Follicles. Also note the various paragraphs in this section).

Dry and Brittle—♄ in ♈; Subs at AT and AX. (See Dry, Fragile).

Eyebrows—Eyelashes—(See Eyebrows, Eyelids).

Fair Hair—Light—Blondes—(See "Fair", "Light", under Complexion; "Light" in this section).

Falling Hair—Baldness—Loss of—Alopecia—♃ influence; ♃ on the Asc.; ♃ in ♐. (See Baldness; "Loss Of", "No Hair", in this section).

Fine Hair—Soft—Silky—The fiery signs give fine hair, but tend to early loss of the hair, due to their heat; the airy signs give fine hair, and tend to gray rather than baldness. (See "Soft" in this section).

Flaxen Hair—Soft—Light Golden—The ☉ Sig. in ♈; the ☉ in ♈ partile Asc., flaxen or yellow; the ☉ in ♓ partile Asc.; the ☉ Sig. in the first eight degrees of ♓, flaxen and soft; the ☽ in ♈ partile the Asc., or the ☽ Sig. in ♈; ♃ Sig. in ♈, or in ♈ partile Asc.; ♃ occi., a dark flaxen; ♂ rising at B.; ♂ gives flaxen, light brown, or red; in Hor'y Q., ♂ as Sig. in watery signs denotes hair more light and flaxen; ♂ in ♌; ♂ in water signs and near fixed stars of his own nature; ♀ in ♌ partile the Asc., light flaxen; ♀ Sig. in ♌ in the term of ♀; ♀ in ♒ partile Asc., flaxen or light brown, and with a fair complexion; ♀ Sig. in ♒ in her own term; ♀ Sig. in ♓; ♀ in ♓ partile Asc., sometimes flaxen; the ♌ sign gives a dark flaxen; ♎ gives flaxen, light yellow, or light auburn, shining, smooth, and long, and espec. when on the Asc.; ♒ gives a sandy or dark flaxen, and espec. when on the Asc. (See Golden, Light, Soft, in this section).

Follicles—The Hair Follicles—Disorders of—(See "Disorders" in this section).

Frizzled Hair—(See "Curly" in this section).

Glossy Hair—Oily—Shiny—The ☽ in ♈, and espec. in the Asc.; the ☽ in ♎, smooth and glossy; the ☽ Sig. in ♐, shining, oily, glossy chestnut; ♃ in ♊, brown glossy; ♀ in the Asc.; ♀ Sig. in ♉ in the term of ♃, often a shining black; ♎ on the Asc., shining, glossy, smooth, long, brown hair, and sometimes a glossy jet black. (See Oil).

Golden—The ☉ indicates golden hair. (See Flaxen, Light, Yellow, in this section).

Gray Hair—Hoary—Ruled by ♄, the ruler of old age; the airy signs strong at B., and many planets in them, tend to fine hair, and to gray hair early in life, and do not tend to baldness; the ♒ sign on the Asc., or the ☉ in ♒, and many planets in the signs of ♄, tend to gray hair early in life, and often before middle life the hair is a pure silvery white, considered very beautiful, and the face is young looking. (See "White" in this section).

Growth—Of the Hair—The fiery signs when strong at B., and well occupied, tend to early loss of the hair. The earthy and watery signs strong at B., to abundant and plentiful, and espec. ♉, ♋, and ♓. The growth of the hair is inhibited when the ☉ or ♄ are in the 5° of ♈ or ♐. A moderate growth of hair is given by ♂ ascending at B., and also by the Quadrant from the Autumnal Equi. to the Winter Tropic when well occupied at B. (See Abundance, Baldness, Loss Of, Scanty, in this section).

Hairy Body—(See "Body" in this section).

Hard Hair—Rugged—♄ ascending at B., hard and rugged; ♃ in ♉, brown rugged; ♉ gives black rugged. (See "Coarse" in this section).

Harsh Hair—(See Coarse,Hard,Rough, in this section).

Hazel Hair—Dark Brown—☿ ascending at B., and free from the rays of other planets; □ influence. (See Brown, Dark, in this section; "Hazel" under Eyes).

Head—Hair of the Head Darker Than the Beard—(See Beard).

Heavy — Much — Plentiful — (See "Abundance" in this section; "Heavy" under Beard).

Hoary—(See Gray, White, in this section).

Inflamed—The Hair Follicles Inflamed —(See "Barber's Itch" under Barbers).

Inhibited Growth—(See "Growth" in this section).

Kinky—(See "Curly" in this section).

Lank—Lanky—Lean—Shrunken—The ☉ in ♑ in partile asp. the Asc., lank brown; the ☽ in ♑ partile Asc., lank dark brown; ♄ ascending at B., dark brown or black lanky; ♂ in ♑ partile Asc., black lanky; ♑ on the Asc., lanky dark or black hair.

Legs—Coarse and Hairy Legs—(See "Coarse" under Legs).

Light Hair—Light Brown—Blondes—Golden—Yellowish—Flaxen—Gray—White—Bright, etc.—The ☉ indicates light, or golden hair; the ☉ gives light, sandy curly hair; the ☉ rising at B., light brown; the ☉ Sig. in ♈ or ♎; the ☉ in ♌, partile the Asc., light brown or yellow; the ☉ in ♎ partile Asc.; the ☉ in ♐, ♒, or ♓, partile Asc.; the ☉ Sig. in the first six degrees of ♑, light brown; the ☽ Sig. in ♈, ♌, ♎, or ♓, light brown; the ☽ in ♈, ♌, or ♎, partile the Asc.; the ☽ in ♎, partile Asc., smooth light brown; ♄ Sig. in ♌ in Hor'y Q.; ♄ in ♌, partile Asc., light brown; ♃ in ♈ or ♎, partile Asc., light brown; ♃ in ♌ partile Asc., light brown or yellowish curly; ♃ in ♓, partile Asc., light brown, but with a dark complexion; born under ♃, and ♃ occi., light brown near the temples and forehead; ♂ in ♈, partile Asc., light or red curly; ♂ gives flaxen, light brown or red hair; ♂ occi., light or red; ♂ Sig. in watery signs in Hor'y Q., more light and flaxen; ♂ in □ in the beginning of the sign, and in partile the Asc., light brown; ♂ Sig. in the first seven degrees of □, the term of ♀, light brown; ♂ Sig. in ♌, ♎, ♒, or ♓, light brown; ♂ in ♎, partile Asc., light brown; ♀ gives light hair; ♀ in the Asc., and strong at B., light brown; ♀ Sig. in Hor'y Q. indicates and signifies a person with light hair, or a blonde; ♀ Sig. in ♈ or ♋, or in these signs in partile the Asc.; ♀ Sig. in ♋, and the ☽ with ♀, very light; ♀ in ♌, partile Asc., light flaxen or red; ♀ in ♒, partile Asc., flaxen or light brown; born under ♀, light hair; ♀ in the Asc., a bright or light brown; the ✳ or △ asps. of ♀ give bright or light brown; ☿ indicates light brown or auburn; ☿ Sig. in ♈, ♌, or ♎, light brown; ☿ in ♈, partile the Asc., curly light brown; ☿ in ♌ or ♎, partile Asc., light brown; ☿ in ♎, partile Asc., smooth light brown; ♋ on the Asc., light brown; ♌ on the Asc., light, yellow, or tawny; ♎ on the Asc., light, flaxen, light yellow, or auburn; ♑ on the Asc., more light than dark, and may be light and fair, but Lilly says that when ♑ descends the hair is usually black; ♐ on the Asc., light brown or chestnut, and growing back from the temples; ♒ on Asc., fair, light, flaxen, sandy, or white. (See Beard, Brown, Fair, Light; "Light Complexion" under Complexion; Auburn, Brown, Chestnut, Color, Curly, Fair, Flaxen, Golden, Gray, Sandy, Tawny, White, Yellow, in this section).

Little Hair—(See Body, Scanty, in this section).

Long Hair—The Hair Grows Long— ♃ ruler of the Asc., and occi.; ♀ Sig. in ♎, the hair grows long, but is not very thick or abundant; ☿ ruler of the Asc. and occi., long black hair; ♎ on the Asc., long, smooth, light and shining hair. (See Flaxen, Glossy, Lank, in this section).

Loss of Hair—Alopecia—Baldness— Cases—See "Aqueous Tumour", No. 120, and "Loss of Hair", No. 121, in 1001 N.N. (See Baldness; "No Hair", "Scanty", in this section).

Lotions—Hair Lotions—Indiscreet Use of—(See Cosmetics; "Lotions" under Face; Lotions).

Lovely Color—♀ influence strong at B. (See Beautiful, Brunettes, Color, in this section).

Luxuriant Hair—(See "Abundance" in this section).

Moderate—Moderate Curling—Moderate Growth—(See Curly, Growth, in this section).

Much Hair—(See "Abundance" in this section).

No Hair—♄ influence and afflictions tend to; ♄ affl. in ♈; ♄ affl. in the Asc. (See "Loss Of" in this section. Also see Case, "No Hair or Teeth", Chap. 8, page 49, in Daath's Medical Astrology).

Oily Hair — Glossy — Shiny — (See "Glossy" in this section).

Plentiful—(See "Abundance" in this section).

Pubes—Hair of—(See Pubes).

Red Hair—♂ exactly rising at B., and the greater the amount of iron the redder the hair; ♂ rising in ♈ gives fiery red hair, and usually red curly; ♂ ascending, strong at B., and ruler; born under ♂, and characteristic of ♂ people; ♂ in ♈, partile asp. the Asc., light or red curly; in Hor'y Q. ♂ as Sig. of the person; ♂ occi., light or red; ♂ Sig. in ♈; ♂ Sig. in the last six degrees of ♈, wiry and reddish; ♂ near the Lion's Heart (Cor Leo) at B.; ♂ in □ if ♂ be near Aldebaran; ♂ in fiery or airy signs, and with fixed stars of his own nature, a deep sandy red; ♀ in ♌ partile Asc., red or light flaxen; ♈ on the Asc., red, brown, or sandy. (See "Red Beard" under Beard; Freckles, Iron, Red; Auburn, Curly, Sandy, in this section).

Rough Hair—♈ on the Asc., rough and wiry; ♉ on the Asc., rough and curly. (See Coarse, Hard, Rugged, Wiry, in this section).

Rugged—Coarse—Hard—Wiry— Rough—♉ gives rugged hair; ♃ Sig. in ♉, or in ♉ partile Asc.; ♂ in ♉ partile Asc., brown or black rugged. (See Coarse, Hard, Rough, Strong, Wiry, in this section).

Sad Hair—Sad Brown—Sad Black—♄ ascending at B., sad hair; ♄ in ♋ partile Asc., sad brown; ♄ Sig. in ♓, sad black; ♃ combust., very sad or black; ♃ Sig. in ♍, dark or sad brown; ♂ in earthy signs as Sig. of the person, sad brown; ♂ in earthy signs and near fixed stars of his own nature, dark or sad brown; ♀ in ♍ or ♏, sad brown or dark; ☿ rising and strong at B., sad or dark brown; ☿ Sig. of the party in Hor'y Q., sad brown or dark; ☿ in ♋ partile Asc., sad brown; ☿ Sig. in ♋ or ♏, sad or dark brown; ♋ or ♏ on the Asc., sad or dark brown; ♏ on Asc., sad brown, curling and plentiful. (See Black, Brown, Dark, in this section).

Sandy—Sandy Colored—The ☉ gives light, sandy, curling hair; the ☉ Sig. in ♈; ♂ strong at B., and ♂ ruler; characteristic of ♂ people; ♂ rising at B.; ♂ in ♌, ♒, or ♓; the ♂ sign ♈ on the Asc.; ♂ in fiery or airy signs and with fixed stars of his own nature, a deep sandy red; ☿ ori. of the ☉ except when ☿ is in □; ♈ on the Asc., red, brown, or sandy; ♒ on the Asc., a sandy or dark flaxen. (See "Red" in this section).

Scanty Hair—Baldness—Thin—Loss of—Fewer Hairs on Head or Body—♀ Sig. in ♎, scanty, but grows long. (See Baldness, Beard; Body, Disorders, Falling, Loss Of, No Hair, in this section).

Shaggy—Bushy—(See "Curly" in this section).

Shiny Hair — Oily — Glossy — (See "Glossy" in this section).

Short and Thick—Abundant—♄ Sig. in ♏, usually short and thick, black or dark; ☿ Sig. in ♉, dark, short and thick; ☿ in ♉ partile the Asc., short, thick brown hair. (See "Abundance" in this section).

Shrunken—(See "Lank" in this section).

Silky Hair—Fine Texture—(See Fine, Soft, in this section).

Smooth Hair—The ☽ or ☿ Sig. in ♎, smooth light brown; the ☽ Sig. in ♎, or ♎ on the Asc., smooth and glossy; the ☽ or ☿ in ♎ in partile Asc., smooth light brown; ♀ in the Asc., and strong at B., smooth and soft; ♎ on the Asc. gives flaxen, light yellow, light auburn, shining, smooth, long hair.

Soft Hair—Fine—Silky—The ☉ Sig. in ♑; the ☉ Sig. in the first eight degrees of ♓, soft and flaxen; ♃ in the Asc., or born under ♃, soft thick brown; ♂ Sig. in ♎, except in the last six degrees; ♀ influence strong at B., soft and smooth; ♀ Sig. in ♉, in her own term, and espec. when in the Asc., soft and luxuriant; in Hor'y Q., ♀ as Sig. denotes a party with soft, smooth, brown hair; ♀ Sig. in ♉, □, or ♎, soft brown; ♓ on the Asc., soft dark brown. (See "Fine" in this section).

Some Hair—On the Body—(See "Body" in this section).

Stiff Hair—(See "Coarse" in this section).

Straight—Straight Hair occurs with those born in cold climates, or in Arctic Regions. Produced by the Quarter between the Winter Tropic and the Vernal Equi.; the ♄ influence strong at B., and ♂ weak or setting; ♂ occi. to the ☉ tends to. (See Coarse, Hard, Lank, Rugged, Strong, Wiry, in this section).

Strong—Strong and Wiry—In Hor'y Q. ♂ Sig. of the person. (See "Wiry" in this section).

Sulphur—The Effect of On the Hair—(See Sulphur).

Swarthy—(See "Dark" in this section; Swarthy).

Sycosis—(See "Barber's Itch" under Barbers; "Disorders" in this section).

Tawny—Tan—Brownish Yellow—♌ on the Asc., light, yellow, or tawny. (See Brown, Light, Yellow, in this section).

Temples—Hair Growing Off the Temples—(See "Temples" under Baldness).

Thick Hair—(See Abundance, Curly, in this section; "Much Beard" under Beard).

Thin—Scanty—(See "Scanty" in this section).

Tonics—Hair Tonics—Cantharides, a typical drug of ♂, is one of the principal ingredients in hair tonics. For the indiscreet use of Hair Tonics, Cosmetics, and Lotions, see Cosmetics.

White Hair—Hoary—Whitish Gray—The ☉ and ♀ in the ♒ sign, or with ♒ on the Asc., tend to give a beautiful white hair in youth or middle age; ♂ in watery signs, and near fixed stars of his own nature, often tends to a bright, whitish hair; ♅ on the Asc. (See "Gray" in this section). Case—Hair Turns White In a Day—See "Strange Case", No. 405 in 1001 N.N.

Wiry and Strong—Wiry and Rough—♂ tends to make the hair strong, stiff, wiry and coarse; ♂ Sig. of the person in Hor'y Q.; ♂ in the last six degrees of ♎, wiry and reddish; ♈ on the Asc., a dark wiry and rough. (See Coarse, Hard, Rugged, Strong, in this section).

Yellow—Yellowish—The ☉ gives; the ☉ Sig. in ♈ or ♌; the ☉ rising at B.; the ☉ in ♈, partile the Asc., yellow or flaxen; the ☉ in ♌, partile Asc., yellow or light brown; ♃ Sig. in ♌, or ♃ in ♌ partile the Asc., yellowish or light brown, curly; ♂ occi.; ♂ ruler of the Asc., and occi.; the ♌ sign, and with ♌ on the Asc., gives bushy or curling yellowish hair; ♎ gives; ♎ on the Asc., light yellow, light, auburn or flaxen, and usually shining and glossy. (See Yellow; Flaxen, Golden, Light, Tawny, in this section).

HALITOSIS — Foul or Disagreeable Breath — (See "Foul Breath" under Breath).

HALLUCINATIONS — A False Perception or Image—A ♆ disease and affliction; afflictions to ♆ or ☿; ♅ in ♎, and affl. ☿ or ♆; a ♄ disease and affliction;

♂ affl. in ♌; the 3rd Decan. of ♒ on the Asc., ruled by the ☽. Mild forms, as "Imagining Things", are a ♆ and ♓ condition, and also ☿ is usually afflicted by ♆; Subs at AT. (See Anguish, Anxiety, Chaotic, Clairaudience, Clairvoyant, Delirium, Delusions, Demoniac, Dreams, Fancies, Fears, Fits, Forebodings, Hearing, Horrors, Hysteria, Ideals, Idiocy, Illusions, Imaginations, Insanity, Mediumship, Melancholy, Morbid, Notions, Obsessions, Paranoia, Perceptions, Premonitions, Spirit Controls, Superstitions, Terrors, Visions, Weird, Worry, etc.).

HALTER — Death By — Malefics in ♉. (See Execution, Hanging, Judge, Law, Suffocation).

HAMS—Hamstrings—Thighs—(See Thighs).

HAND OF MAN—Human Means—Death By — Injury By — (See Ambushes, Assassination, Assaults, Attacks, Common People, Cuts, Duels, Enemies, Execution, Homicide, Human; "Hand of Man" under Man; Mobs, Murder, Poison, Robbers, Stabs, Treachery; "Death" under Violent).

HANDS—The Hands are under the external rulership of the ♍ sign. The hands correspond to, and are opposite to the feet, ruled by ♓. Also ruled by ☿, ♃, the ♊ sign, and affected by all the common signs. Ruled and affected by the 3rd, 6th, 9th, and 12th Houses. The Bones of the hands are under the structural rulership of ♊ and ♍. The Arms, Shoulders, Hands, Legs, and Feet should be studied together, as all these parts are ruled by the common signs, and what affects one may adversely affect all to a greater or lesser degree, according to the planets and afflictions in these signs at B. Also see the Articles on Fingers, Nails, Toes, Feet, Wrists, etc. The Wrists are said to be ruled by the ♌ sign, being opposite to, and corresponding to the ankles, ruled by ♒. The hands are especially denoted by the 3rd H., the house of ☿. The Forehand is governed by ♂. This Article will be divided into two Sections. Section One, Description of the Hands. Section Two, Diseases of the Hands.

— SECTION ONE —

DESCRIPTION OF THE HANDS—

Ambidextrous—(See Ambidextrous).

Arms — Long or Short Arms usually indicate the same conditions with the hands and fingers. (See the various paragraphs under Arms).

Broad Hands—Broad, Thick and Short —Given by the ♉ influence strong at B.; ♉ on the Asc., or the ☉ and other planets in ♉, broad, plump and short hands; the ☽ gives thick hands and feet. (See Fleshy, Short, Thick, in this section).

Club Hands—(See "Clubbed Fingers" under Fingers).

Dexterity—(See Dexterity).

Elbows—The Hands Growing From—No Forearm — Cases — (See "Missing" under Forearm).

Fingers—(See the various paragraphs under Fingers).

Fleshy and Short—(See Broad, Short, in this section).

Four Hands — Case — Has two heads, four arms, and four hands, and with one body — (See "Twins", No. 236, in 1001 N.N.).

Frog Child—Right Forearm and Hand Missing from Birth — (See "Missing" under Forearm).

Gross and Large—♉ gives, and with ♉ on Asc. (See "Broad" in this section).

Large Hands — (See "Gross" in this section).

Left-Handed—(See "Left-Handed" under Left).

Long Hands — Long Fingers — ♅ ascending at B.; ☿ ascending at B., and free from the rays of other planets; ♍ gives, and with ♍ on the Asc.; ♍ on the Asc.; the 3rd or 4th face of ♎ on the Asc. (See "Long" under Arms, Legs, Feet).

Nails—The Finger Nails—(See Nails. Also see "Nails" under Fingers, Toes).

No Hands—Case — See "Born Incomplete", No. 281, in 1001 N.N. See "Missing" under Forearm.

Plump Hands — (See "Broad" in this section).

Right-Handed—(See Ambidextrous, Dexterity. Also see "Left" in this section).

Short Hands—♉ gives; ♍ tends to in many cases, and to give short and fleshy hands and feet; ♍ on the Asc., short and fleshy hands, but with long arms and legs, but some say the fingers are long. (See "Broad" in this section).

Thick Hands—And Feet—The ☽ gives. (See "Broad" in this section).

— SECTION TWO —

DISEASES OF THE HANDS—

Abscesses—♃ affl. in signs ruling the hands, as in ♍ or ♍. (See Abscesses; "Felons", "Whitlows", under Fingers).

Accidents To — All Accidents, Hurts, Wounds, or Injuries to — ♍ signifies; afflictions in ♍, ♍, or ♐; ♄ or ♂ in the Asc. or M.C. in the latter degrees of ♍, ♍, or ♐; ♂ affl. in ♍ or ♍. (See Cuts, Fractures, in this section).

Acromegaly—Abnormal Development and Enlargement of the Hands—The ☉, ♄, ♆, ♃, or ♂ affl. in ♍. (See "Enlargement" under Arms, Extremities, Feet; Enlargements).

All Diseases In—Signified by the 3rd H., and afflictions in ♍ or ♍. (See "Diseases" in this section).

All Hurts To — (See Accidents, Cuts, Fractures, in this section).

Aneurysm—In the Hands—(See Aneurysm).

Ankylosis—In the Joints—(See Ankylosis; "Ankylosis" under Fingers).

Atrophy Of—Claw Hands—♄ affl. in ♍, ♍, or the 3rd or 6th H. (See Atrophy).

Blisters — Bullas — Of the Hands and Feet—(See Blisters, Dysidrosis).

Blood Impurities — (See "Corrupt Blood" in this section).

Claw Hands — (See "Atrophy" in this section).

Cold Hands—Cold Fingers—♄ influence; ♄ in ♍ or ♍; Subs at LCP, AP and HP. (See Cold; "Cold" under Extremities; Fingers).

Corrupt Blood — Blood Impurities — Disorders In the Hands From—The ☉ or ♃ in signs which rule the Arms, Hands, Legs and Feet, govern the blood of these parts, and tend to blood poisoning, blood impurities, and blood disorders in these parts, which may lead to swellings, eruptions, and skin disturbances of the hands. (See "Blood" under Arms; "Impure Blood" under Impure).

Cramps In—Writer's Cramp—Incoordination—Spasmodic Disorders—♅ affl. in ♍ or ♍; ☿ in ♍ or ♍ in the 3rd or 6th H., and affl. by ♅; Subs at LCP, AP and HP. (See "Hands" under Cramps).

Cuts to Hands—Wounds—Injuries—♂ affl. in ♍ or ♍; ☿ in ill-asp. to ♂, slight cuts. (See "Accidents" under Arms; "Arms" under Cuts; Accidents, Fractures, in this section).

Cysts In—(See Cysts).

Deformities Of—Malefics in ♍ or any of the common signs; common signs on the angles and containing malefics; afflictions between ♅ and ♂, or between ♄ and ♂ in common signs. (See "Hands" under Deformities; "Clubbed Fingers" under Fingers; "Missing" under Forearm; "Atrophy" in this section).

Diseases In—Humours In—Infirmities In—Afflictions in ♍ or ♍, with these signs on the Asc., 3rd or 6th H., and containing malefics; many planets, a Stellium, in ♍, ♍, the 3rd or 6th H., and containing malefics; ♄ or ♂ in the 1st, 3rd, 6th, or 7th H., in the latter degrees of any common sign, and ori. of the ☉ and occi. of the ☽; signified in Hor'y Q. by ♂ in ♐; signified by the 3rd and 6th H., and afflictions therein; Subs at LCP, AP, and HP. (See "Diseases" under Extremities. Also note the various paragraphs in this section, and under Arms, Extremities, Fingers, Feet).

Dysidrosis—(See Blisters, Dysidrosis).

Eczema In—(See Eczema).

Elephantiasis — Enlargement — (See "Arms" under Elephantiasis; Enlargements, Hypertrophy, Oedema; "Acromegaly" in this section).

Enlarged — (See Acromegaly, Enlarged, Elephantiasis, Gout, Swelling, in this section).

Eruptions—♃ or ♀ affl. in ♍ or ♍. (See "Arms" under Eruptions; "Corrupt Blood" in this section).

Erysipelas — In the Hands and Extremities—♂ affl. in ♍ or ♍; Subs at LCP, HP. (See "Arms", "Extremities", under Erysipelas).

Extremities — Diseases In — (See Extremities, Feet, Legs, Limbs. Also note the various paragraphs in this section).

Feet—Due to the correspondences between the hands and feet, see the various paragraphs under Feet.

Felons—(See "Felons" under Fingers).

Fingers—(See the various paragraphs under Fingers, Nails).

Fractures—♂ affl. in ☐, ♍, or ♓; afflictions in the common signs denote. (See Fractures).

Glands—The Glands and Vesicles of the Hands Affected—Ruled and affected by ♅ when this planet is in signs which rule the hands. (See the Introduction under Aneurysm).

Gout In—Gouty Humours—Wandering Gout—(See "Hands" under Gout; Joints, Lameness, Rheumatism, Swelling, in this section).

Hand of Man—Injury or Death By—(See Hand of Man).

Humours In—(See "Humours" under Fingers; Diseases, Gout, in this section).

Hurts—(See Accidents, Cuts, Fractures, in this section).

Hypertrophy—(See Elephantiasis, Enlarged, in this section).

Incoordination—(See "Cramps" in this section).

Infirmities In—(See "Diseases" in this section).

Injury To—(See Accidents, Cuts, Fracture, in this section).

Joints—Swelling or Inflammation In —(See "Joints" under Fingers; "Gout" in this section).

Lameness In—The ☽ in ☐, ♍, or ♓, and affl. by the ☉ or ♂ at the beginning of an illness (Hor'y); ♂ in ☐, ♍, or ♓, and espec. when in the 1st, 3rd, or 6th H.; ♂ in ♑ when ♂ is the afflictor in the disease. (See Gout, Humours, Joints, Rheumatism, Swelling, in this section).

Leprosy In—(See "Leprosy" under Extremities; Leprosy).

Man—Hand of Man—Injury or Death By—(See Hand of Man).

Metacarpus—Bones of the Palms of the Hands—Disorders of—Afflictions in ☐ or ♍; Subs at AP.

Missing—One or Both Hands Missing —Congenital Deformity—(See "Missing" under Forearm; "No Hands" in Sec. 1 of this Article).

Motor Nerves—The Motor Nerves Affected or Partially Paralyzed, Causing Cramps or Spasm—♅ affl. in ☐ or ♍. (See Cramps; "Cramps" under Feet; "Nerves" under Motor; Spasmodic Diseases; "Cramps" in this section).

Muscles—The Muscles of the Hands Affected—♂ affl. in ☐ or ♍; ♅ in ☐ or ♍, due to disturbed nerve supply to the muscles; Subs at AP, HP. (See Atrophy, Cramps, Motor, Paralysis, in this section).

Nails—(See the various paragraphs under Nails; "Nails" under Fingers, Toes).

Nerves—Nerve Pains In—The ☉ affl. in ♎; the ☽ to the Bull's Horns; ♂ affl. in ☐ or ♍; ☿ affl. in ☐. (See "Pains" under Arms; "Motor" in this section).

Neuralgia In—☿ affl. in ☐ or ♍. (See Cramps, Motor, Nerves, in this section; Neuralgia).

No Hands—(See "Missing" in this section).

Oedema—(See Elephantiasis, Enlarged, Swelling, in this section; Oedema).

Pains In—(See Cramps, Motor, Nerves, Neuralgia, in this section).

Palms—Of the Hands—(See "Metacarpus" in this section).

Paralysis—Cramps—Spasms In—♅ affl. in ☐ or ♍; Subs at AP, HP (2D). Case—The Hands Paralyzed—Unable to Move Them, and Writes with Aid of the Tongue—See "Tunison", No. 113, in 1001 N.N. (See Cramps, Motor, Muscles, in this section; Paralysis).

Perspiring Hands—(See Dysidrosis).

Rheumatism—♄ in ☐ or ♍; ♄ or ♂ angular, in the 1st or 7th H., in the latter degrees of ☐ or ♓, and ori. of the ☉, and occi. of the ☽. (See "Gout" in this section).

Shoulders—(See the various paragraphs under Shoulders).

Skin—Skin Disorders and Eruptions Due to Bad Blood—(See "Corrupt Blood" in this section).

Spade-Like Hands—Accompanies Myxoedema—(See Myxoedema).

Spasms—Spasmodic Disorders In—(See Cramps, Motor, Muscles, Paralysis, in this section).

Swelling In—The ☽ in ☐, ♍, the 3rd or 6th H., and affl. by the ☉ or ♂; the ☽ in ♓, ♑ or ill-asp. ♄ (or ☿ if he be of the nature of ♄) at the beginning of an illness, or at decumb.; ♃ affl. in ☐ or ♍. (See Abscesses, Acromegaly, Corrupt Blood, Enlarged, Gout, Humours, Joints, Lameness, Oedema, Rheumatism, in this section).

Thumb—The Thumb Nearly Cut Off—Case—See Chap. 13, page 97, in Daath's Medical Astrology.

Ulcers—The ☽ affl. in ☐ or ♍. (See "Ulcers" under Feet; "Arms" under Ulcers).

Varicose Veins—(See "Arms" under Varicose).

Verruca—Warts—(See "Arms" under Warts).

Vesicles—Disorders of the Glands and Vesicles—(See Aneurysm; "Affected" under Glands; Vesicles).

Wandering Gout—(See "Gout" in this section).

Warts—(See "Arms" under Warts).

Wasting—Of the Hands—♅ in signs which rule the hands. (See Wasting).

Whitlows—Phlegmonous Inflammation—(See "Whitlows" under Fingers).

Wounds To—(See Accidents, Cuts, Fractures, in this section).

Wrists—(See Wrists).

Writer's Cramp—(See "Cramps" in this section).

Writes with Tongue—Hands Paralyzed—(See "Paralysis" in this section).

HANDSOME—Beautiful—Good Looking —Elegant Form, etc.—The ♉, ♎, and ♒ signs are the most favored for beauty and handsomeness, and also ♓ if ♀ be therein. The ♒ sign gives more beauty than any other sign except ♎. The ♍ and ♓ signs also tend to make the body well-proportioned and handsome; ♐ on the Asc., ruddy and handsome; ♎ on the Asc.; the ☉ Sig. in ♍; the ☉ Sig. in ♐, tall and handsome; the ☽ Sig. in ♊, comely; the ☽ in ♎ or ♐, partile asp. the Asc.; the ☽ Sig. in ☌ ♀, and ♀ well-dignified; ♄ in ♎, partile the Asc., rather handsome but not beautiful; ♃ Sig. ☌ ♀, great personal beauty unless ♀ be in ♏ or ♑; ♃ Sig. ☌ ☿, and ☿ well-dig., and free from affliction, and espec. if both are in angles; born under ♃; ♃ Sig. in ♌ or ♍; ♃ Sig. in ♒ with females, a perfect beauty; ♃ Sig. in ✶ or △ ♀; ♀ in the Asc. in one of her own signs; ♀ Sig. in ✶ or △ ♂, a handsome man; ♀ Sig. in ♉ or ♎; ♀ Sig. ☌ ☿, handsome and well-shaped; born under ♀, very handsome altho rather short and stout if occi.; the ✶ or △ aspects of ☿, if ☿ be well-dig., give a very handsome body if ☿ is not combust; all Constellations of human form tend to give a very handsome shape. (See Beautiful). The following subjects have to do with a handsome and beautiful body, form, appearance, face, complexion, eyes, hair, etc., which subjects see in the alphabetical arrangement when not considered here.

Appearance—(See the various subjects under Appearance).

Beautiful; Body—A Handsome Body—(See the first part of this section).

Carriage — (See Carriage, Commanding, Erect, Upright).

Comely; Complexion—Handsome Complexion—♃ in the Asc. at B., and ♃ in ♈ or ♎, the complexion is rosy and handsome. (See Beautiful, Rosy, Ruddy, under Complexion).

Countenance — A Handsome Countenance — (See "Beautiful" under Complexion, Eyes, Face; Countenance, Expression, Look; "Face" in this section).

Dimples; Elegant; Expression;

Eyes — Handsome Eyes — Full and Handsome—(See Beautiful, Full, under Eyes).

Face—(1) Handsome Face—♃ Sig. in ♎, oval and handsome; ♀ Sig. in ♉ or ♎; ♎ gives a round and lovely face; ♐ gives a long and handsome face; ♐ on the Asc., an open and handsome countenance. (See "Beautiful" under Face). (2) The Face Not Handsome—The ☽ ill-dignified at B., or in watery signs and afflicted; ♃ Sig. in ♉; ♍ on the Asc., well-favored but not handsome; ♑ on the Asc., usually an ugly face. (See Face, Freckles, Marks, Moles, Pimples, Scars; "Face" under Smallpox; Ugly, etc.).

Fair; Features; Figure; Fine;

Forehead — (See "Handsome" under Forehead).

Fresh-Colored—And Handsome—(See Fresh, Ruddy).

Genteel; Graceful; Hair—(See Beautiful, Lovely, under Hair).

Lovely; Middle Stature — And In No Way Handsome—♍ on the Asc. at B.

Neat; Not Handsome — The ☽ Sig. in Hor'y Q.; ♃ in ♉, partile the Asc., stout, well-set, but not handsome; ♍ on the

Asc., well-favored body, but not handsome; ♑ on the Asc., usually crooked body, ill-favored, and ugly. (See Crooked, Deformed, Ill-Formed, Ugly).

Pleasing Body — Attractive — (See Pleasing).

Shape—Of the Body—(See the various references under Shape).

Skin — Handsome and Pure Skin — ♒ on the Asc. Also ♍ on the Asc. gives a thin, delicate, tender and beautiful skin. (See "Beautiful" under Complexion, Face).

Stature—Note the various paragraphs and subjects under Stature).

Tall and Handsome—The ☉ Sig. in ♐; born under ♀ and ♀ ori.; ♎ on the Asc. (See "Tall and Elegant" under Elegant. Also note the various paragraphs under Tall).

Ugly — (See "Not Handsome" in this section).

Well-Composed—Well-Favored Body —Well-Formed—Well-Made and Handsome — Well - Proportioned —Well-Shaped—(See these subjects).

HANGING—Death On the Gallows—Death by the Halter or Noose—Strangulation—The ☉ Sig., □ or 8 ♄, and espec. if either be in the 10th H.; the ☉ directed to, or joined with the Ascelli; the ☽ with Antares, and 8 ♄ with Aldebaran; caused by the □ and 8 asps. of the ☽; ♄ in a fixed sign, ori., □ or 8 the ☽, and contrary in condition, or ♄ occi., and the ☽ be succedent to him; ♄ ori. in a fixed sign, and in □ or 8 the ☉, or when occi. in a fixed sign, and in □ or 8 the ☽, tends to death by suffocation, hanging, or trodden by a mob in a tumult; ♄ to the ☌ or ill-asp. ♂ by dir.; ♂ affl. the ☽ from the 10th or 4th H., or near Cepheus or Andromeda; ♂ affl. in ♉ or ♏ in the 10th or 4th H. denotes hanging; ♀ in □ or 8 ♄ at B., and otherwise affl. by malefics, the native is said to inherit the Gallows; the fixed signs and the earthy signs dispose to, and espec. when in the 10th or 4th H., and containing the malefics ♄ and ♂, and with these planets affl. the hyleg, either of them holding the dominion of death in a nativity otherwise showing a violent death. (See Beheaded, Execution, Guillotine, Halter, Homicide, Ignoble, Impalement, Judges, Lynching, Mobs, Murder, Riots, Strangulation, Suffocation, Tumults; "Death" under Violent).

Fears of Hanging—Haunted by Visions of Hanging—Case—See "Haunted", No. 299, in 1001 N.N. Also for Cases and Birth Data of people hanged for crime, see "Hanged", No. 540, and "Murderer", No. 636, both in 1001 N.N.

Overhanging Eyebrows—(See "Beetle Brows" under Eyebrows).

HAPPINESS—Happy—Happy Disposition—Contentment—Peace of Mind, etc. —The ☉ to the ☌ or P. Dec. Arista by dir.; the ☽ to the ☌ and good asps. ♀ by dir.; the ☽ ☌ ♀ or ☿ in the 3rd or 9th H., the houses of mind, and these planets free from the afflictions of the malefics; the ☽ decr., separating from ♀ and applying to ♃; the ☽ sepr. from ☿ and apply. to ♃; the ☽ Sig. ☌ ♀, a happy disposition; the ☽ at full in a nocturnal geniture, sepr. from ☿ and apply. to ♀, an increase of happiness; ♅ by his good aspects tends to favorable spiritual and interior states, religious ecstasy; ♄ by his unfavorable aspects to the Sigs. tends to destroy peace of mind, and lead to melancholy and morbid fears; ♃ in the Asc. near the cusp; ♃ Sig. ♂ ♀ promises the greatest happiness; ♀ ruler at B., and well-aspected, tends to happiness, and a joyful nature; ♀ in the 3rd or 9th H. in ♂ the ☽ or ☿; the Asc. to the place of Crater. (See Arista, Cheerfulness, Comforts, Contentment, Crater; "Fortunate" under Fortune; "Good Health" under Health; Jovial, Joy, Juvenility; Mild; "Peace of Mind" under Mind; Optimistic, Prosperity, Religion, Unhappy).

Happy Death — A Peaceful and Easy Death — (See "Easy Death" under Death).

Happy Disposition — The ☽ Sig. ♂ ♀, an easy and happy disposition, and with little care beyond the enjoyment of the present moment. (See Contentment, Ease, Smiling).

HARD— Hardening—Hardness—Indurations—Sclerosis, etc.—Hardening is the work of ♄. Also called the destructive work of ♄, and caused by the pathological deposits and wastes retained by ♄. Also the work of the ♄ sign ♑, and of ♒, which is of the nature of ♄. The hardening of the bones, also the work of ♄, may be considered an exception to the rule, and a normal process up to a certain point. Hardening is carried on by the mineral deposits carried by the blood, which minerals are ruled by ♄. These minerals, when carried to excess, become pathological, and the unusual hardening of any part of the body, of an organ, joint, tissue, membrane, etc., takes place when these minerals, wastes, and acids are deposited in excess, and where elimination is at fault. (See Saturn). The following subjects have to do with Hard, and Hardening, which see in the alphabetical arrangement when not considered here.

Adipose Tissue—Hardening of—(See "Hardness" under Fat).

Arteries — Hardening of — Arterio-Sclerosis—(See Arteries).

Articulations—Joints—Hardening of —(See Joints).

Atrophy; Bones—Hardening of—Ossification—Bone Building—The work of ♄. (See Bones, Osseous).

Bunions—Corns—(See Corns).

Calculus; Carcinoma—Hard Carcinoma—(See "Scirrhus" under Carcinoma).

Chancre—Hard Chancre—(See "Chancre" under Syphilis).

Cirrhosis—Thickening—(See Cirrhosis).

Clots; Complexion — The Complexion Hard and Dull — (See "Dull" under Complexion).

Concretions; Condensation;

Congestions; Connective Tissue — Hardening and Induration of—Thick-

ening of—The work of ♄, and ♄ afflicted in the sign ruling the part. (See Cirrhosis, Connective, Sclerosis).

Consolidation; Consumptions—As Hardening of the Lungs, or other Organs, in Tubercular Conditions—Caused by ♄, and ♄ in the sign ruling the part, or organ. (See Consumptions; "Hardening" under Lungs; Tuberculosis).

Cornification; Corns; Corrosions;

Costiveness; Cough—(See "Dry Hard Cough" under Cough).

Crusts; Crystallization; Cure — The Disease Is Hard to Cure—(See Chronic, Curable, Difficult, Grievous, Incurable, Prolonged, Slow, Tedious, Wastings).

Decay; Degeneration; Density;

Deposits; Destructive; Deterioration;

Disposition — A Hard and Cruel Nature—(See Cruel).

Ears—(See "Hardening" under Ears).

Enlargements; Faeces — Hard Faeces —(See "Hardening" under Faeces).

Fat—(See "Hardness" under Fat).

Gall Stones—(See Bile).

Gout; Gravel; Growths—Hard Growths —(See Bunions, Growths, Horny, Stone; "Hard Tumors" under Tumors; Warts).

Hair—(See "Hard Hair" under Hair).

Hemachromatosis — The Skin Turns Hard — (See Hemachromatosis; "Skin" in this section).

Horny; Inhibitions; Joints — (See "Hardening" under Joints; Synovial).

Kidneys—(See Cirrhosis, Stone, under Kidneys).

Lesions; Lithemia; Liver—(See Cirrhosis, Hardening, under Liver).

Lungs — (See "Hardening" under Lungs).

Membranes—Hardening of—(See Cirrhosis, Membranes, Sclerosis, Synovial, Thickening, Tissues. Also note the various paragraphs in this section).

Moles; Naevus; Nature—A Hard and Cruel Nature—(See Cruel, Savage, Vicious).

Nerves—(See Atrophy, Decay, Lesions, Nerves, Optic, Paralysis, Sclerosis, Spinal Cord (see Spine).

Obstructions; Optic Nerve — Hardening of — (See Crystallization, Optic, under Eyes).

Organs—Hardening of—(See Kidneys, Liver, Optic, and the various paragraphs in this section; Cirrhosis, Crystallization, Sclerosis).

Ossification—(See Bones, Osseous).

Petrifaction; Retentions;

Rheumatism; Sand; Scales; Scirrhus;

Sclerosis; Skin—Hard and Rough Skin —♄ strong at B., or ♄ Sig. of the person, represents one of a rough, hard skin; the 2nd face of ♒ on the Asc. (See Hemachromatosis; "Thick" under Skin).

Spinal Cord—Hardening of—♄ affl. in ♌. (See Sclerosis; "Cord" under Spine).

Stone — Gravel — Sand — (See Gall Stones" under Bile; Gravel, Sand, Stone).

Suppressions; Synovial Membranes— Hardening of—(See Joints, Synovial).

Thickening — (See Cirrhosis, Hypertrophy, Thickening).

Tissues — Thickening of — Hardening of—(See Adipose, Membranes, in this section; Cells, Hypertrophy, Sclerosis, Tissues).

Tumors—(See "Hard" under Tumors).

Urea; Uric Acid; Vessels—Blood Vessels — Hardening of — (See "Arterio-Sclerosis" under Arteries; Vessels).

Warts; Wastes; Wasting.

HARELIP—A Congenital Fissure of the Lip—(See Lips).

HARLOTS — Prostitutes — The Lower Order of Women—Wench—Danger of Becoming—♄ and ♀ ill-affected, or ill-dignified at B.; ♀ Sig. □ or 8 ♂; ♀ in ♏ and affl. by ♄ and ♂; ♀ Sig. ♂ ♂, and given to brawling in low public houses. (See Debased, Depraved, Disgrace, Dissolute, Drink, Immodest, Infamous, Lewd, Loose, Low, Nymphomania, Obscene, Scandalous, Shameless, Taverns, Venery, Vile, etc.).

Injured By—Disgrace Thru—♄ and ♀ both ill-dig., and ill-affected in the map; ♄ Sig. □ or 8 ♀; ♂ Sig. □ or 8 ♀; ♀ Sig. □ or 8 ♂. (See "Harlots", "Injured", under Men).

HARMFUL—

Harmful to Others — (See Brutish, Cruel, Dangerous, Destructive, Fierce, Inhuman, Murderous, Savage, Vicious, Violent, etc.).

Maladies—Harmful Maladies and Diseases — (See Fierce, Grievous, Malignant, Pernicious, Severe, Vehement, Violent, etc.).

Not Harmful—Harmless to Others— The Disease Is Slight and Mild, and Not Dangerous—(See Harmless, Mild, Slight).

To Himself — (See "His Own Worst Enemy" under Enemies).

HARMLESS—Inoffensive—A Mild and Even Disposition—Quiet—The ☽ Sig. in ♎ or ♒; ♃ Sig. in ♓; ♀ Sig. in ♐, ♒, or ♓; people born under strong ♀ influence have a quiet and mild disposition; the 4th face of ♎ on the Asc. (See Gentle, Kind, Mild, Peaceful, Quiet).

Harmless Diseases—Not Dangerous— (See Mild, Slight).

HARMONY — Harmonious — The principle of the ☽ is harmony, and also of ♀. In whatever sign or house ♀ is found in at B., it is her mission to restore harmony and balance to the affairs, or part of the body ruled by such sign or house, and to help overcome the afflictions. (See Balance, Coalition, Coordination, Correspondences, Dexterity, Equilibrium, Graceful, Libra, Rhythm, Signature, Sympathy).

Body and Mind—More Harmony Between—Given by the ✶ and △ aspects of ♀ to the Asc. at B.

Constitution — A Harmonious Constitution—The ☉ or ☽ ♂, ✶, or △ the Asc. at B., and by dir.; ♀ in the 6th H., and well-aspected, the health is good if not abused, but easy to become an invalid if excesses are engaged in. (See "Good" under Constitution, Health).

Disturbed—The Harmony of Body and Mind Disturbed—(See Disease, Fevers, Ill-Health, Insanity, Melancholy, Suffering, Sickness, Worry, etc.).

Functions—(See "Harmony" under Functions).

Muscular Action—Harmonious Muscular Action—(See Coordination, Dexterity).

Physical Harmony—Perfect Physical Development — Comes from planetary harmony and good configurations at B.; a predominance of the ✶ and △ aspects in the radical map; the benefics strong at B., and the malefics weak. (See Beautiful, Comely, Graceful; "Harmony" under Functions; Handsome, Well-Proportioned).

HARROW—The Harrow of ♐—(See Arrow Head).

HARSHNESS — Of the Voice — (See Coarse; "Hoarseness" under Larynx; Rough).

HASTY—Hasty Disposition—The ☽ in fire signs at B., hasty and excitable. (See Anger; "Brain Storms" under Brain; Choleric, Erratic, Excitable, Explosive, Fierce, Foolhardy, Forethought, Improvident, Impulsive, Quarrelsome, Precipitate, Rashness, Recklessness, Riotous; "High Temper" under Temper; Uncontrolled, etc.).

HATE — Hatred — Hated — Aversion— Animosity—Enmity—This is a ♏ characteristic, and the result of the extreme vibrations of ♂, and usually mixed with ♅ and ♄ influences. The Benefics are also usually weak and obscurely placed. The hatred, malice, and revenge tend to be retained when ♄ enters into the configuration with the ♂ influence. Violence in connection with hatred may result when ♂ is also affl. by ♅. (See Anarchists, Anger, Antipathy, Aversions, Duels, Emotions, Enemies, Enmity, Execrated, Feelings, Feuds, Jealousy, Malice, Misanthropic, Murderous, Plots, Poison, Relatives, Resentful, Revenge, Riotous, Treachery, Vicious, Violent, etc.).

Females—Has the Hatred of — The Love of a Female Turned to Hate— The ill-asps. of the ☽ to the ☉ or ♀ by dir. (See Jealousy; "Grief" under Love Affairs; "Injured" under Men; Treachery).

Hated by Others — The ☽ to the ill-asps. the ☉ by dir.; ♄ Sig. □ or 8 the ☉; ♃ Sig. ♂ ♄, generally hated by every one because of his mean and deceitful ways; ☿ Sig. □ or 8 ♂, despised by others for his infamous conduct. (See Deceitful, Dishonesty, Execrated, Infamous, Mean, Outcast, etc.).

Hatred Prevalent—An eclipse of the ☉ in ♏. (See Prevalent, Public).

HAUNCHES—The Region Including the Hips, Hip Bone (Ilium), and the Buttocks—Ruled by ♎ and the 7th H. Also influenced largely by ♐.

Boils On — (See "Buttocks" under Boils).

Diseases In — (See "Diseases" under Buttocks, Flanks, Hips).

Heats — In the Haunches — Humours In—(See "Heats" under Buttocks).

Hurts To — (See "Hurts" under Buttocks; Cuts, Fractures, Injuries, under Hips; Ilium).

HAUNTINGS — Haunted by Visions of Hanging — (See "Fears" under Hanging). See Dreams, Fears, Forebodings, Hallucinations, Imaginations, Obsessions, Premonitions, Spirit Controls, Terrors, Visions, etc.

HAY FEVER—Hay Asthma—Rose Cold —(See "Hay Asthma" under Asthma; Colds; "Coryza", "Hay Fever", under Nose).

HAZEL — Dark Brown — (See "Hazel" under Eyes, Hair).

HEAD — The Upper Part of the Body Containing the Brain—Cephalic—Cranium—Skull—The Head, and the Organs of the Head, are ruled by ♂ and the ♈ sign. (See Aries, Mars). The Head is especially under the external rule of ♈. The Encephalon, the Skull, and its contents are ruled by ♈. The Brain is under the internal rulership of ♈, and the bones of the head under the structural rulership of ♈. (See Brain, Cranium). The 1st H. represents and rules the head and face of Man. The Head is also affected and influenced by all the cardinal signs, and planets in such signs at B., and by dir. The Head and Brain correspond to the cardinal signs and the Mental Temperament. (See Decanates, Temperament). The lower back part of the head, the Occipital Region, is ruled by the ♉ sign. (See Occipital). For the various subdivisions of the Head, see the subject in the alphabetical arrangement, such as Brain, Cranium, Cerebellum, Cerebral, Cerebro-Spinal, Cheeks, Chin, Ears, Eyes, Forehead, Face, Hair, Jaws, Mouth, Nose, Scalp, Skin, Teeth, Temples, etc. This Article will be divided into Two Sections. Section One, Description of the Head. Section Two, Diseases of the Head. See the following subjects in the alphabetical arrangement (in both sections) when not more fully considered here.

— SECTION ONE —

DESCRIPTION OF THE HEAD—

Bent Forward — ♓ on the Asc. (See Crooked; "Downward Look" under Look; Stooping).

Big Head—(See "Large" in this section).

Cheeks; Chin; Complexion; Dimples; Downward Look — (See "Downward" under Look).

Ears; Expression; Eyebrows; Eyelids—Eyelashes—(See Eyelids).

Eyes; Face; Flat on Sides — (See "Square" in this section).

Forehead; Glances; Great Head—(See "Large" in this section).

Hair; Horse-Shaped Head — ♐ on the Asc. (See Horses).

Jaws; Large Head—Big Head—Great Head—Produced by the ☉ influence; ♄ Sig. in ♒ or ♓; ♄ in ♒ in partile asp. the Asc.; ♄ in ♓ in partile the Asc., large head and eyes; ♌ on the Asc., large head and round. Case of Very Large

Head—See "Dwarf", No. 669, in 1001 N.N. (See "Large" under Eyes, Face).

Lips; Little Head — (See "Small" in this section).

Long Head — ♄ in ♍ when Sig. in Hor'y Q. (See "Long" under Chin, Face).

Look; Marks—Moles—Planets in ♈ at B. indicate; ♈ on the Asc., and containing one or more planets; ♂ rising in ♈ in the Asc. (See "Marks" under Face; Marks, Moles, Naevus, Scars, Warts).

Mouth; Naevus — Birthmarks — (See Naevus).

Nodding — To One Side — Skippish Manner—The native jumps forward when speaking, and nods the head to one side like a goat when it butts—♑ influence; the ☉ in ♑, or ♑ on the Asc. at B. (See "Falls To One Side" in Sec. 2 of this Article).

Nose; Occiput; Peculiar Shaped—(See "Falls To One Side" in Sec. 2 of this Article).

Red—Ruddy—(See Complexion, Face).

Round Head—Great Round Head—♌ on the Asc.

Scalp; Scars — (See Accidents, Cuts, Pockmarked, Scars, in Sec. 2 of this Article).

Skull—(See Cranium, Skull).

Small Head—Little Head—♃ or ♂ Sig. in ♑, or in ♑ in partile asp. the Asc.; ♂ occi. For Case of Small Head of an Idiot, see "Microcephalic Idiot", No. 086 in 1001 N.N. (See Idiocy).

Square Head—Characteristics of the Motive Temperament; the 1st Decan. of mutable signs on the Asc. (See Decanates; "Square" under Face).

Stooping Head — (See "Downward Look" under Look; Stooping).

Temples; Two Heads—Has Two Heads and One Body—Case—See "Twins", No. 236 in 1001 N.N. Also see Case in British Journal of Astrology for Oct., 1931. Born June 23, 1919, 6:30 A.M., Antwerp. Died at birth. (See "United Twins" under Twins).

— SECTION TWO —

DISEASES OF THE HEAD—

Troubles in the head are largely dependent upon the ♓ sign, the Plantar System, and ♍, the Abdominal Organs, and troubles originating in these parts are quickly reacted to the head, causing a great number of head and brain disturbances.

Abscesses — (See "Brain" under Abscess).

Accidents To—Hurts—Wounds—Injuries—Cuts—Blows—Bruises—Fractures, etc.—The ☉, ☽, or malefics afflicted in ♈, and espec. when in the 1st H.; the prog. ☉ or ☽ to the places of malefics in ♈; the ☉ by dir. to the ill-asps. ♂ in ♈ in the 8th H. at B.; ♅ affl. in the 1st H., by machinery; ♅ in ♈ at B., and affl. by ♂; ♄ in ♈, ☌, □, or ☍ the Asc. by dir., and espec. if ♄ be in the Asc. at B.; ♄ ☌ ♋ in ♈; ♂ in ♈, ♎, the Asc., or 1st H. at B., and afflicted;

♂ on the Asc. at B., slight hurts or cuts to the head or face; afflictions in the 1st H. at B., and by dir.; afflictions in ♈ or ♎; ♈ or ♎ on the Asc., and containing malefics; the 1st Decan. of ♈ on the Asc., ruled by ♂; malefics in any of the cardinal signs at B., and in ☌, □, or ☍ the prog. ⊙ or ☽; the 1st face of ♈ on the Asc., and the ☽ therein with ♄ or ♂; afflictions in ♈, fractures of the head or skull; the 30° ♍ on the Asc. (See Blows, Bruises, Cuts, Fractures, Injuries, Wounded, in this section; "Accidents" under Eyes, Face, Jaws, Nose).

Acne; Acute Diseases In—Acute Neuralgic Pains In—Acute Pains In—(See Darting, Headaches, Neuralgia, Pain, and the various paragraphs in this section. Also see Acute, Brain, Eyes, Nose, and the various diseases under these subjects).

Affected—The Head Affected—The ⊙ and ☽ acting thru the ♈ sign affect the head. (See "Ribes" under Ganglion). All the cardinal signs affect the head, and planets in such signs, as they form the cardinal cross, and all the cardinal signs, of which ♈ is one, are in adverse aspect to each other. The head is affected by disorders in the abdominal organs, ♍, and in the Plantar System, ♓. Any planet when in its own sign tends to affect the head, as the sign ruled by each planet is considered as influencing the head and the ♈ sign. When in a sign next to, or following the sign it rules, it affects the throat and neck and influences the ♉ sign, and so on around thru the 12 signs. Thus the head is affected by the ⊙ in ♌; the ☽ in ♋; ♄ in ♑ or ♒; ♃ in ♐ or ♓; ♂ in ♈ or ♏; ♀ in ♉ or ♎; ☿ in ♊ or ♍, as these are the home and strong signs of these planets. (See Table 196 in Simmonite's Arcana, Chap. IX, page 68, which is a Table of these influences).

Afflicted—The Head Afflicted—(See the various paragraphs in this section).

All Diseases In—Signified by the 1st H., and afflictions in ♈, or with ♈ on the Asc.

Apoplexy; Arteries—Of the Head Affected—♃ affl. in ♈. (See "Head" under Arteries).

Baldness; Beard; Beheaded;

Blemishes—Afflictions in ♈. (See "Blemishes" under Face; "Marks" in Sec. 1 of this Article).

Blood—Rush of—Flow of—Determination of Blood to the Head—The ⊙ or ♂ in ♈ at B., or ♈ on the Asc., and accompanied by high fever when ill; the the ☽ or Asc. ☌ ♂ at B.; the ☽ to the ill-asps. ♃, the direction occurring from cardinal signs, and espec. with females; ♄ in ♌, ☌, □ or ☍ ♃ or ♀; ♃ affl. in ♈; ♃ affl. in ♈, ill-blood in the veins of the head; ♂ rising in ♈; a ♂ disease; ♂ tends to cause Insanity by a rush of blood to the head; the Asc. to the place of Regulus; an ♈ disease. (See Apoplexy).

Blows—To the Head—Strokes To—♄ or ♂ affl. in ♈; ♄ in ♈, ☌, □, or ☍ the Asc. by dir., and espec. if ♄ be in the

Asc. at B.; ♄ or ♂ affl. in ♈ in the Asc. at B., and with these planets affl. the Asc. by dir. (See Blows; Accidents, Bruises, Cuts, Fractures, in this section).

Brain—Disorders of—(See Brain, Cerebral).

Bruises To—♄ in the Asc. at B., and espec. when in ♈. (See Bruises; "Accidents" in this section).

Cancer—Carcinoma—(See "Face", "Head", under Carcinoma).

Catalepsy; Catarrh—In the Head—The ☽ in ♈, ☌, or ill-asp. any of the malefics as promittors; ♄ in ♈ or ♎; ♄ occi. in ♈, and affl. the ⊙, ☽, or Asc.; ♄, ♅, or ♃ in ♈ or ♓, and in ill-asp. to the ⊙ or ☽; ♀ affl. in ♈. (See "Frontal" under Abscesses; Catarrh; "Catarrh" under Nose).

Central Part—Of the Head—Depression In—(See "Malformation" in this section).

Cephalic; Cerebellum; Cerebral; Cerebro-Spinal; Cerebrum;

Chronic Diseases—In the Head—♅ or ♄ affl. in ♈. (See Catarrh, Chronic, Nose; "Chronic" under Stomach).

Circulation—Impeded—Disturbed—♄ in ♈, ☌ ♃ or ♀. (See Apoplexy; "Impeded" under Circulation; "Blood" in this section).

Colds In—The Head Disordered by Cold—Cold or Watery Diseases In—The Head Affected by Diseases of a Cold and Watery Nature—♅, ♃, or ♄ in ♈ in ill-asp. to the ⊙ or ☽; the ☽ ☌ the Asc. by secondary direction; the ☽ in ♏ and affl. by the ⊙ or ♂ when taken ill, stoppage in the head by grievous colds; ♄ in the Asc.; signified by ♄ in ♈ when ♄ is the afflictor in the disease; ♀ affl. in ♈ when ♀ is the afflictor in the disease. (See Catarrh, Cold, Colds, Congestion; "Coryza" under Nose; Saturn).

Coma; Complexion; Congestions;

Coryza—(See "Coryza" under Nose).

Countenance; Cranium; Cuts To—(See "Accidents" in this section; "Cuts", "Hurts", under Face).

Danger To—The ⊙ directed to Praesepe. (See "Accidents" in this section; Ascelli; "Accidents" under Eyes, Face; Praesepe).

Darting Pains In—Acute Pains—Shooting Pains—♅ in ♈, ♎, or the 1st H.; ♅ rising in ♉, darting pains; ♂ in ♈, ♎, or the 1st H. (See "Pain" in this section).

Defluxions—Of Rheum From—(See "Rheum" in this section; Defluxions).

Deformities Of—Malefics in cardinal signs and afflicting each other, and espec. from angles. (See "Small Head", "Two Heads", in Sec. 1 of this Article; Hydrocephalus, Malformations, in this section).

Delirium; Depression In—(See "Malformation" in this section).

Determination—Of Blood to the Head —(See "Blood" in this section).

Diseased—The Head Much Diseased—The ☽ in P. Dec. an Infortune tends to a disease in the head, and if ☿ also be affl. by a malefic the disease will be very severe; the ☽ in partile ☍ ☿ at decumb., the head is deeply affected (Hor'y); ☿ at B. in P. Dec. a malefic, or in ☐ to the ☽ from the 1st or 7th H.; ☋ or malefics in the Asc. at decumb. (Hor'y).

Diseases Of—(See "Diseased", "Disorders Of", and the various paragraphs in this section).

Disorders of the Head—Diseases In—Distempers In—Infirmities In—Maladies In—The Head Disturbed—The Disease Lies In the Head or Brain—The ☉ or ☽ affl. in ♈; the ☉ affl. in ♎; the ☉ evilly aspected at B., and the ☉ in bad asp. the Asc. by dir.; the ☉ to the ♂ or P. Dec. the ☽ by dir.; the ☉ to the ♂ or ill-asps. ♄ or ♂ by dir.; the ☉ or ☽ in the 6th H. in cardinal signs, and afflicted; the ☉ in ♈ in the 6th H., ♂, or ill-asp. any of the malefics as promittors; the ☉ in the 6th H., lord of the year, and afflicted at the Vernal Equi., a prevalence of head troubles; the ☽ affl. in ♈ or ♎, and espec. when in the Asc. or 6th H.; the ☽ to the ♂ or ill-asp. ♅ by dir.; the ☽ in ♎, ♂ or ill-asp. ♄ (or ☿ if he be of the nature of ♄) at the beginning of an illness, or at decumb.; the ☽ P. ♄, diseases in the head and stomach; the ☽ affl. in the 6th H.; the ☽ ♂ ♂ in the Asc. when taken ill; the ☽ hyleg, and afflicted, and espec. with females; the ☽ ♂ the Asc. by secondary dir.; the ☽ in P. asp. ♄ or ♂ at B., and by dir.; ♄ in ♈ or ♎ in the 1st or 6th H.; ♄ affl. in ♒; ♃ affl. in ♈ or ♐; ♂ affl. in ♈, ♎, the 1st or 7th H.; ♂ diseases and afflictions; ♂ in ♈ in the 6th H.; mad and sudden distempers in the head are a ♂ disease and affliction, and caused by ♂ affl. in ♈, and also ♅ in ♈; ♀ or ☿ affl. in ♈; ☿ diseases; ☿ ☐ the ☽ from the 1st or 7th H., and ☿ ♂ ♄ or ♂; born under ☿; ☿ in ♈, ♂, or ill-asp. any of the malefics as promittors; a malefic or ☋ in the Asc. denotes diseases in the head, or in the part of the body signified by the sign ascending; malefics in the 1st H., or in the sign ascending; malefics, or the afflicting planets, in cardinal signs; any malefic in the Asc. when taken ill; planets in the Asc., as the Asc. rules the head; cardinal signs show, and espec. afflictions in ♈; ♈ on the Asc., and afflicted, and cardinal signs on the angles; ♈ denotes; afflictions in ♈ or ♎; ♈ or ♎ on the Asc.; the Asc. to the ♂ ☉ by dir., and the ☉ affl. at B.; ♒ ascending at the Vernal, People and Countries under ♒ so suffer; ♐ ascending at the Vernal Equi., and ♃ afflicted, People born under ♐, and in Countries ruled by this sign, are afflicted with infirmities in the head and legs, and with fevers; ♓ ascending at the Vernal, People ruled by ♓, and in Countries ruled by ♓, suffer grievous infirmities in the head, feet, and with Gout and Dropsy. An Example—Q. if the Asc. is afflicted by a malefic, ℞, slow, combust., peregrine, or in ☐ or ☍ to the lord of the 6th, 8th, or 12th, tends to trouble in the head, or to the parts signified by the sign ascending, and the planet, or planets, in the ascending sign. An Example—♋

on the Asc. and ♄ therein, trouble in the head, or parts signified by ♋, as in the bowels, reins, secrets; also cough, as ♄ rules cough, and ♋ rules the breast. Judgment is more certain if the ☽, lord of the Asc. or 6th, or sign on the 6th, signify the same member or parts as signified by ♄. See Table in Lilly's Astrology, Chap. XXIX, page 179, showing what parts of Man's body every planet signifies in the 12 Signs. (See "Disordered Brain" under Brain. Also note the various paragraphs in this section).

Distempers In—(See "Disorders Of" in this section).

Disturbed—Disturbances Of—The Head Is Disturbed—(See "Disorders Of", and the various paragraphs in this section).

Dizziness; Downward Look—Stooping Head—(See "Downward Look" under Look; Stooping).

Dropsy Of—(See Hydrocephalus).

Dry and Hot Diseases—In the Head—(See "Hot and Dry" in this section).

Dull Pains In—A ☿ disease; ☿ affl. by ♄. (See "Pains" in this section).

Ears; Eczema Of—(See Eczema).

Electric Pains In—☿ in ♈ and affl. by ♅; ☿ affl. by ♅. (See "Pains" in this section).

Encephalitis—(See Encephalon).

Enlarged—The Head Enlarges and Swells—(See "Tumor" under Brain; Enlarged, Hydrocephalus).

Eruptions—(See Eruptions; "Eruptions" under Face).

Erysipelas—(See "Head" under Erysipelas).

Excrescences—(See "Malformations" in this section; "Head" under Excrescences).

Expression; Eyes—(See Eyeballs, Eyebrows, Eyelids, Eyes).

Face—(See the various paragraps under Face).

Faintings; Falls—Hurts to Head By —♄ affl. in ♈, and espec. in the Asc. (See Accidents, Bruises, Cuts, Fractures, in this section; "Falls" under Infancy).

Falls To One Side—(See "Heavy" in this section).

Females—The Head Afflicted In—The ☽ hyleg, and afflicted, and espec. when in ♈. (See "Women" under Headaches).

Feverish Diseases—Which Affect the Head—The ☉ affl. in ♈; ☿ affl. by ♂, fevers in the head; ♈ on the Asc. (See "Hot Diseases" in this section).

Fixity—Of the Head—♄ affl. in ♈; Subs at AT.

Flow of Blood To—(See "Blood" in this section).

Fontanelles—Slow Closure of—Lack of Ossification of—The ☽ affl. in ♈; ♄ weak and affl. at B.; many planets in watery signs, and the earthy sign influences weak at B.; Subs at AT, AX. (See Ossification).

Forehead; Fractures—(See "Fractures" under Skull).

Freckles; Giddiness—(See Dizziness).

Glands—Of the Head Affected—(See "Head" under Glands).

Gout In—Gouty Pains In—(See "Head" under Gout).

Grievous Colds In—Grievous Infirmities In—(See Colds, Disorders, in this section).

Growths In—Tumorous Growths In—♀ affl. in ♈; ♀ ♂ ♅ in ♈, and in ☐ or ♉ malefics; Subs at MCP (5C). Case—See "Tumorous Growth", Chap. XIII, page 91, in Daath's Medical Astrology. (See Growths; "Growths" under Face, Eyes, Tumors).

Guillotined; Headaches—This subject, and the various kinds and causes of Headaches, are given in the section on Headaches, just following this Article. Also see "Pain" in this section).

Headstrong—(See Obstinate).

Heaviness In—Heavy Feeling In—The ☽ in ♈, ♂, ☐, or ♉ ♄ (or ☿ if he be of the nature of ♄) at the beginning of an illness, or at decumb. (See Dull Pains, Headaches, Heavy, Pain, in this section).

Heavy—The Head Is Heavy and Falls to One Side—Case—See "Unfortunate Case", No. 351 in 1001 N.N. (See Heaviness, Hydrocephalus, Large, Nodding, in this section).

Hemicrania—Neuralgia of Half the Head—♅ affl. in ♈; Subs at AT. (See "Neuralgia" in this section).

Hemispheres—Hemispherical Excrescences—(See "Malformations" in this section).

Hemorrhage In—(See "Blood" in this section; Apoplexy).

Hot Diseases In—Hot Humours In—Feverish Diseases In—The Asc. to the ♂ the ☉ by dir.; the Asc. to the ♂ stars of the nature of ♂; ♈ on the Asc. (See "Feverish" in this section; "Hot Diseases" under Heat; "Mars Group" under Stars).

Hot and Dry Diseases—In the Head—♈ on the Asc., as the head is classed as hot and dry, being ruled by the hot and dry, masculine, and positive sign ♈. (See "Dry and Hot Diseases" under Heat).

Humours In—Humour In—The ☉ to the ♂ or P. the ☽ by dir., and the ☽ ill-asp. at B.; the ☽ in the 1st or 7th H. at B., and P. ♄ or ♂, and if ☿ also be afflicted by ♄ or ♂ the disease will tend to be very severe; ♄ affl. in ♈, copious flow of humours from the head; ♀ or ☿ affl. in ♈. Wilson has observed that those who have a copious flow of humours from the head are remarkable for shallowness of intellect and for dishonesty. (See Defluxions, Hot Diseases, Moist Humours, Rheum, in this section; Catarrh, Colds, Rheum).

Hurts To—(See Accidents, Blows, Cuts, Falls, Fractures, Injuries, Wounds, in this section).

Hydrocephalus; Idiots—Small Head—Microcephalic Head—(See Idiots).

Ill-Blood—In Veins of Head—(See "Blood" in this section).

Imaginary Diseases In—☿ affl. by ♆. (See Imagination).

Impeded Circulation—In the Head—(See "Circulation" in this section).

Infirmities—Grievous Infirmities In—(See Colds, Disorders, and the various paragraphs in this section).

Inflammations In—♂ affl. in ♈. (See Catarrh, Colds; Encephalitis; "Inflamed" under Eyes; "Coryza" under Nose; Feverish, Hot Diseases, in this section).

Injuries To—Wounds—Hurts—♄ or ♂ affl. in ♈, and espec. when in the Asc. Cases—See "Sebastian", No. 576 in 1001 N.N. See Fig. 28 in the book, "Message of the Stars", by the Heindels. (See Accidents, Blows, Bruises, Cuts, Falls, Fractures, in this section).

Insanity—From Rush of Blood to the Head—(See "Blood" in this section; Insanity).

Insomnia; Jaws; Large Head—Very Large Head—(See Hydrocephalus; "Large Head" in Sec. 1 of this Article; "Heavy" in this section).

Longitudinal Depression—(See "Malformation" in this section).

Machinery—Hurts to Head By—(See Machinery).

Mad Distempers—(See the ♂ influences under "Disorders" in this section).

Maladies In—(See "Disorders", and the various paragraphs in this section).

Malformation Of—Malformation of the Skull—Soft, Watery, and Hemispherical Excrescences—Longitudinal Depression In the Central Part—The ☉ in the Asc., and affl. by malefics; the ☽ in the 1st H., or on the cusp of the 1st, and affl. by ♅; ♈ or ♎ on the Asc. (See Deformities; "Head", "Skull", under Excrescences; Idiots, Malformations, Monsters, Prenatal Epoch; "Deformities" in this section).

Marks—Moles—Scars—Blemishes—(See "Marks", "Scars", in Sec. 1 of this Article; Accidents, Blemishes, Cuts, Pockmarked, in this section).

Medulla; Megrims—(See Migraine).

Membranes—Of the Head Disordered—(See "Membranes" under Brain; Catarrh, Cerebral, Frontal, Meninges, Nose, etc.).

Men Suffer—With Affections of the Head—♂ ℞ in ♐ at the Vernal Equi., and Lord of the Year. (See Men).

Meninges; Mercury Remedies—These remedies are cephalic, and affect the head. (See "Mercury" under Herbs; "Remedies"; Therapeutic Properties", under Mercury).

Microcephalic Head—(See "Small Head" in Sec. 1 of this Article; "Idiots" in this section).

Migraine; Mind—Disorders of—(See Mental, Mind).

Moist Humours—Watery Humours—The Head Afflicted by Abundance of Moist Humours—Snuffling—The ☽ ♂ the Asc. by secondary dir.; ♄ affl. in ♈; ♀ affl. in ♈ or ♉; ♀ affl. in ♉ when ♀ is the afflictor in the disease, and also causing swellings in the neck; a ☿ disease, and ☿ affl. at B. (See "Humours" in this section; "Humours", "Moist Humours", under Moist; "Humours" under Watery).

Moles—(See Moles; "Marks" in Sec. 1 of this Article).

Mouth; Movement — Of the Head Abnormal—(See "Nodding Spasm" in this section; Erratic, Jerky, Movements, Spasmodic).

Much Diseased — (See "Diseased" in this section).

Mucus—Mucous Discharges—The ☽ in ♀ affl. in ♈. (See Catarrh, Colds, Humours, Moist, Rheum, in this section; Mucus).

Muscles — ♂ affl. in ♈ tends to affect the muscles of the head. (See Muscles).

Naevus; Navamsa — (See "Subdivisions" in this section).

Nervous Affections—Of the Head—♅ or ☿ affl. in ♈; ☿ in ♈ and affl. by ♅ or ♂; ☿ affl. by ♂. (See Neuralgia, Nodding, Pain, Spasmodic, in this section; Headaches, Nerves).

Neuralgia—In the Head or Face—The ☉, ☽, or ♅ affl. in ♈; the ☉ affl. in ♌; a ♅ disease, as neuralgia is the province of ♅; ♅ affl. in ♈; ♂ affl. in ♈, ♉, or ♎; ☿ affl. in ♈; an ♈ disease. (See Acute, Darting, Dull, Hemicrania, Pains, in this section; "Neuralgia" under Face; Headaches, Neuralgia). Case—Of Acute Neuralgic Pains in the Head — See "Pains In the Head", Chap. XIII, page 90, in Daath's Medical Astrology.

New Growths—(See Growths, Tumors, Warts, Wens, in this section).

Nodding Spasm — The Head Nods to One Side—A ♅ affliction, and due to incoordination; ♅ affl. in ♈ or ♉; Subs at AT. (See "Heavy" in this section; "Nodding" in Sec. 1 of this Article; Erratic, Incoordination, Jerky, Spasmodic).

Noises In — Rumbling In the Head — The ☽ in ♒, ♌, or ill-asp. ♄ (or ☿ if he be of the nature of ♄) at the beginning of an illness, or at decumb.; the ☽ ♌ ♄ (or ☿ if he be of the nature of ♄) at decumb., rumbling noises in the head; ☿ in ♈, ♌, or ill-asp. any of the malefics as promittors, noises arising from indigestion, or excesses of any kind. (See Catarrh, Colds; "Tinnitus" under Ears).

Nose—Obstructions In—Stoppages In the Head—Stoppages by Colds—♄ affl. in ♈, ♎, ♑, or the Asc.; the ☽ in ♍ and affl. by the ☉ or ♂ when taken ill, stoppages in the head by grievous colds; ☿ diseases, and ☿ affl. in ♈. (See Obstructions, Stoppages; "Colds" in this section).

Obstructions In — Stoppages In the Head—Stoppages by Colds—♄ affl. in ♈, ♎, or the Asc.; the ☽ in ♍ and affl. by the ☉ or ♂ when taken ill, stoppages in the head by grievous colds; ☿ diseases, and ☿ affl. in ♈. (See Obstructions, Stoppages; "Colds" in this section).

Occiput; One Side—The Head Falls to One Side—(See Heavy, Nodding, in this section).

Operations On—Do not perform surgical operations upon the head when

the ☽ is in ♈, the sign ruling the head. (See Operations).

Organs Of—Disorders of—(See Brain, Ears, Eyes, Mouth, Nose, and the various paragraphs in this Article).

Pains In — ♅, ♂, or ☿ affl. in ♈, and espec. when in the 1st H.; ♅ affl. in ♈, acute and spasmodic pains in; ♅ rising in ♉, acute neuralgic, and darting pains in; ♅, ♆, or ♄ in ♑, or ill-asp. the ☉ or ☽; the ☉ affl. at B., and ♌ or P. asp. the Asc. by dir.; the ☉ to the ♌ the ☽ by dir., and the ☽ affl. at B.; the ☉ affl. in ♌ when the afflictor in the disease, violent pains in; the ☉ in ♌, ♌, or ill-asp. any of the malefics as promittors; ♃ affl. in ♈, and caused by ♃ when the dominion of death is vested in him; ♂ affl. in ♈, violent and distracting pains in; ♂ in ♈ or ♍, ♌, or ill-asp. the ☉; ♂ affl. in ♎; ♂ by periodic rev. to the evil asps. ♅; ♂ in the Asc., and affl. the ☉ or ☽ in ♈; ♀ affl. in ♈ or ♉; ☿ affl. in ♈, ♊, or ♓; ☿ in ♈, and affl. by ♅, electric pains in the head; ☿ in ♍ or ♓, ♌, or ill-asp. any of the malefics as promittors; ☿ affl. in ♊, gouty pains in the head; a ♎ disease, and afflictions in ♎; ♉ in the Asc.; fixed stars of the nature of ♂ ascending at B.; ♋ ascending at a Vernal Equi., and the ☽ weak and afflicted, people born under ♋, and in Countries ruled by ♋, suffer pains in the head. (See Acute, Darting, Dull, Electric, Gouty, Hemicrania, Neuralgia, Spasmodic, in this section; Headaches, Neuralgia; "Neuralgia" under Face; Pain).

Pale; Pimples; Pineal; Pituitary; Pockmarked — (See "Face" under Smallpox).

Prevalence—Of Head Disorders—The ☉ in the 6th H., and Lord of the Year at the Vernal Equi. (See "Disorders" in this section).

Remedies—Remedies Affecting the Head—(See Cephalic; "Mercury" in this section).

Rheum — Defluxions of Rheum from the Head — The ☽ affl. in ♈; a ♓ disease; ♄ affl. in ♈ or ♓. (See Defluxions, Rheum. Also see Humours, Moist Humours, in this section).

Ringing—In the Head—(See "Noises" in this section; "Tinnitus" under Ears).

Rumbling Noises — (See "Noises" in this section).

Rush of Blood — To the Head — (See "Blood" in this section).

Scalp; Scars — (See "Marks" in this section).

Sickly Looking — (See "Pale" under Face; Pale, Sickly).

Sight—(See Blindness, Eyes, Sight).

Skin — Of the Head and Face — (See "Skin" under Face; Scalp).

Skull; Small Head—(See "Microcephalic" in this section).

Snuffling — In the Head and Nose — (See "Moist Humours" in this section; "Snuffling" under Nose).

Soft Excrescences — (See "Malformation" in this section).

Spasmodic Pains In—♅ affl. in ♈. (See "Pains" in this section).

Spasms In — ♅ or ☿ affl. in ♈. (See "Nodding Spasm" in this section).

Stomach—The Head Affected by Stomach Trouble— ♂ affl. in ♋. (See Dizziness, Headaches).

Stoppages In—By Colds— (See Colds, Obstructions, in this section).

Strokes To—(See "Blows" in this section).

Subdivisions—Of the Head—Disorders of—The subdivisions of the Head, and disorders in such parts, as in the Eyes, Ears, Forehead, Nose, are shown by the sub-influences of the Navamsa divisions of the ♈ sign. (See Navamsa).

Sudden Distempers—Sudden and Mad Distempers in the Head—♅ affl. in ♈; a ♂ disease and affliction; ♂ affl. in ♈, mad and sudden distempers in the head. (See Distempers; "Diseases" under Sudden; "Disorders" in this section).

Swells—The Head Swells—Swellings In—The Head Enlarged—(See "Tumor" under Brain; Hydrocephalus).

Swoonings—(See Fainting).

Teeth; Temples; Tissues—(See "Membranes" in this section).

Tongue; Trance; Troubles — In the Head — (See "Disorders Of", and the various paragraphs in this section).

Tumors In — (See "Growths" in this section).

Two Heads—(See "Two Heads" in Sec. 1 of this Article).

Ulceration—(See "Ulcers" under Face; "Ulceration" under Forehead; Ulcers).

Veins — Of the Head — Ill Blood In— (See "Blood" in this section).

Ventricles; Vertigo; Violent Pains—In the Head—♂ affl. in ♈. (See "Pains" in this section; "Violent" under Headaches).

Visage—(See Face, Visage).

Vision — (See Accommodation, Eyes, Sight).

Warts — (See "Marks" under Face; "Marks" in Sec. 1 of this Article).

Watery Diseases—(See Excrescences, Humours, Moist Humours, Snuffling, in this section).

Wens; Wounds To — Wounded In the Head—(See Accidents, Blows, Bruises, Cuts, Fractures, Injuries, in this section).

HEADACHES — Pains In the Head — Neuralgia In—It may not always be possible Astrologically to detect or locate the cause of a headache, as the causes are many, and often complicated and mixed under various planetary afflictions. However, as a fundamental rule, the ♈ sign, the Asc., ♅ and ♂ are usually involved in the configurations, and strong afflictions from the malefics to the ☉, ☽, Asc., or hyleg. There are cases where people may have malefics in ♈ in the Asc., and afflicted by other malefics, who have never had a headache, and other influences, aspects, house and sign positions of the planets would need to be studied, and also the special idiosyncrasies, or a diathesis, be considered. Headaches may occur with most any disease, and also from Dissipation, Bad Habits, Gluttony, Excesses, Drink, Loss of Sleep, Insomnia, Irregularities, Feasting, Loose Morals, Over-Exertion, Over-Study or Reading, Eye Trouble, Indigestion, Sex Excesses, etc. (See these subjects). The various kinds and varieties of Headaches, and their planetary causes, are listed in the paragraphs which follow.

All Over the Head—General Over the Head—Many planets, or a Stellium, in ♈ at B., and scattered out thru the various faces and decanates of ♈; Subs at AT and AX.

Amative Tract — Headache In — (See Amative).

Anaemic Headaches—♄ affl. in ♈; Subs at AT, MCP, and HP. Also given by the general influences causing Anaemia. (See Anaemia; "Thin Blood" under Blood; Chlorosis).

Bilious Headache—♆, ♅, ♄, or ♂ promittors, and ♂, or ill-asp. the ☉ in ♈. (See Bile).

Blood Impure—Headaches from Corrupt and Impure Blood — The ☉ in ♈, and affl. by ♃. (See Impure).

Catarrhal—Nasal—Headaches From— ♄ affl. in ♈, ♎, or ♏; Subs at MCP (3, 4C). (See Catarrh; "Catarrh" under Head, Nose).

Causes of Headaches—The following influences have been listed in the various textbooks as causes, or as existing at the time of headaches — An ♈ disease; afflictions in ♈, or ♎ by reflex action to ♈; any planets in ♈ at B., and afflicted; ♈ on the Asc., and afflicted; ♈ on the cusp the 6th H., or in the 6th H., and containing ☉, ☽, or malefics, and affl. by □ or 8 aspects; the ☉ affl. in ♈; the ☉ to the ♂ the ☽; ♂, or the Asc. by dir.; the ☽ affl. in ♈ or ♎; the ☽ in ♈, ♂, or ill-asp. ♄ (or ☿ if he be of the nature of ♄) when taken ill, or at decumb.; the ☽ in the 6th H. in cardinal signs, and afflicted; the ☽ hyleg in ♈ and afflicted, and espec. with females; the ☽ in ♈, ♂, or ill-asp. any of the malefics as promittors; the prog. ☽ in ♈, ♂ and ♂ any planets in ♈ at B.; the ☽ directed to the Ascelli; ♅ affl. in ♈ or ♎; ♄ affl. in ♈ or ♎; ♄ in ♈ in ♂ or ♀; ♄ ♂ the Asc. by dir.; ♃ affl. in ♈; ♃ ♂ ♄ in ♈; ♂ affl. in ♈; ♂ in the 6th H. in a cardinal sign, and affl. the ☉ or ☽; ♂ affl. in ♈ in the Asc. or 6th H.; ♀ affl. in ♈, 8, or ♎; ☿ affl. in ♈ or ♎; ☿ in ♈ or □, ♂, or ill-asp. any of the malefics as promittors; a ☿ disease; born under ☿.

Center of Head—Headaches In—The ☉ in ♈.

Constipation — The Headaches of — (See Constipation).

Continual Headache—Complains Continually of Headache—The ☽ ♂ or ill-asp. ♄ (or ☿ if he be of the nature of ♄) at the beginning of an illness, or at decumb.

Darting Pains — In the Head — (See "Darting" under Head).

Frequent Headaches — In Women — (See "Women" in this section).

Frontal Headaches—♆ in ♈, and affl. by the ☉, ♄, or ♂; ♄ affl. in ♈; Subs at AT and AX. (See "Abscess" under Frontal).

General—(See "All Over the Head" in this section).

Hyperaemic Headaches—The ☉ affl. in ♈. (See Hyperaemia).

Impure Blood—Headaches From—(See "Blood" in this section).

Internal Headaches—The ☉ affl. in ♈.

Migraine — Paroxysmal Headaches — Megrims In the Head—(See Migraine).

Nasal Catarrh—Headaches From—♄ affl. in ♏. (See "Catarrh" in this section).

Nervous Headaches—Nervous Strain and Headaches From—The ☉ in ♈, ♂, or ill-asp. any of the malefics as promittors; ☿ affl. in ♈, and espec. from nervous strain, or overstudy; ☿ affl. in ♎. (See "Strain" under Nerves).

Neuralgia—In the Head—(See "Neuralgia" under Head).

Occipital Headaches—♀ affl. in ♉. (See Occiput).

Ocular Headaches — The ☽ or ☿ affl. in ♈; Subs at AT, MCP, SP, and KP. (See "Eyestrain" under Eyes; Reading, Study).

Organic Headaches—The ☉ affl. in ♈. (See Organic).

Pain—In the Head—(See "Pain" under Head).

Paroxysmal Headache—(See Migraine, Paroxysms).

Periodic Headache—Headaches at the Menstrual Periods—The ☽ or ♄ affl. in ♏; Subs at AT, and PP (2, 3, 4L). (See Menses).

Rending and Study—Headaches From —(See "Ocular" in this section).

Regular Headache—Periodic—Caused by the ☽. (See Periodic; "Periodic" in this section).

Rheumatic Headache—♄ in ♈, and affl. the ☉, ☽, or Asc. (See Rheumatism).

Shooting Pains — In the Head — (See "Darting" under Head).

Sick Headache—Afflictions in ♈ and ♎; ♄ affl. in ♎; Subs at KP, and due to retained poisons, and improper kidney action.

Spasmodic Pains—In the Head—♅ in ♈. (See "Spasmodic" under Head; Migraine).

Sudden Headaches—♅ affl. in ♈ or ♎, and espec. when in the Asc. or 6th H. (See Sudden).

Temporal Headaches — ♃ affl. in ♈; Subs at Li.P. Caused mostly by liver disorders, and afflictions to ♃, the ruler of the liver. (See Temples).

Toxaemic Headache — Uremic Headache — ☿ affl. in ♈. (See Toxaemia, Uremia).

Unilateral Headache—(See Migraine).

Uremic Headache — (See "Toxaemic" in this section).

Violent Headaches—The ☽ in ♈ and affl. by ♂; ♅ affl. in ♎; ♂ in ♈. (See "Pains", "Violent", under Head).

Women—Frequent Headaches In—The ☽ to the ill-asps. ♃ by dir.; the ☽ hyleg in ♈, and affl. by ♃; the ☽ affl. in ♏, or malefics in ♏ afflicting the ☉, ☽, or Asc., from female disorders, and disturbance of the female functions.

HEALERS—Healing—The Healing Powers — The planetary influences at the birth of individuals endow various Healing Powers, and to suit the various needs, beliefs, peculiarities, and idiosyncrasies of the twelve fundamental classes of Humanity, as represented by the 12 Signs of the Zodiac. All Schools of Healing have their place in the World, have their followers, and it is the duty of a patient to call upon the Healer in whom he has faith, no matter of what School. This Book, and also this Article, are not a treatise upon the merits of the various Schools of Healing, but merely to help you understand the causes and philosophy of disease, why people are sick, the nature of the sickness, its duration, possible termination, etc., and to list those influences which tend especially to endow one with successful Healing Powers, and also to list those influences which tend to make one a failure as a Healer. For the welfare of the patient, it is important that the Healer called upon should be compatible with the patient, for the best success, and that the star maps of the Healer and patient have agreeable exchanges. Otherwise, the Healer may injure the patient. The following subjects have to do with Healers, Healing, Treatment, the care of the Sick, and those connected with such work in various ways, or the preparation of Foods or Remedies for the Sick. The Sixth House rules strongly over the Healing Powers, and the Healing Service.

Absent Healing—(See "Metaphysical" in this section).

Allopathy—The treatment of the sick by using remedies which oppose, and are in antipathy with the planetary influences causing the disease. (See Antipathy, Hippocrates, Opposites).

Antipathy—Healing By—(See Antipathy).

Asylums—Care of the Sick In—Confined In—(See Asylums).

Avoid — Healers for the Patient to Avoid—Those who have ♄ in the Asc. or 6th H. of the patient. (See "Compatability" in this section).

Bath House Keepers—Good Influences For—(See Bathing).

Biochemists—Those who use the 12 Zodiac, or Tissue Salts, in the treatment of disease, and to supply the lacking chemical constituents of the body. (See Biochemistry; "Salts" under Zodiac).

Black Magicians—Those who use Occult Powers for evil purposes in the treatment of the sick, and to defraud —(See Magical).

Chemists—(See Chemists).

Chiropodist—One Who Treats the Feet and Hands — The ♊, ♍, and ♓ people are especially adapted to this work, and espec. the ♊ people, as ♊ gives unusual skill and ability in the use of the hands.

Chiropractors—The best Chiropractors are born under ☿ and ♊, as a rule, ♊ on the Asc., or the ☉, ☽, ♂, or ☿ in ♊. A keen and sensitive touch is needed for correct palpation by the hands, and this is given especially by the □ sign, and where the hands are to be used in a more delicate and scientific manner. (See Subluxations, Touch, Vertebrae).

Color—Healing By—(See Color).

Christian Science—(See "Spiritual" in this section).

Compatibility—Of Healer and Patient —Incompatibility of—Rules For—The Compatibility of the Healer and Patient is determined by the rising sign in each map, whether in harmony or not; by the exchanges in the 6th H. in each map, whether of benefics or malefics, and also by the relation existing between ♄ in each map. The 7th H. also rules the Physician in the case. The first important rule is that the rising signs in both maps, the signs on the Asc., should be in harmony, belong to the same triplicity, and be in ✶ or △ aspect to each other. If the patient has ♈ on the Asc. at B., his Healer, for the best success, should also have a fiery sign on the Asc., as ♌ or ♐. If the Healer employed in this case should have ♋, ♎, or ♑ upon the Asc. at B., he would tend to affect the patient adversely, or cause him to get worse. If the patient should start out with an adverse Healer, and continue to get worse, by changing to a Healer whose map is in harmony, the patient would tend to improve rapidly. The ✶ and △ aspects between the rising signs of the two maps tend to naturally inspire faith and confidence between the patient and Healer, whereas the □ or ☍ aspects between them tend to an aversion, the same as between people who marry under such conditions and separate. (See "Enemies", "Healers", under Antipathy. Also see Death, Poisoned, Sympathy, in this section).

Cure of Disease—Curable Diseases— Incurable Diseases — (See Curable, Drugs, Incurable, Medicines, Moderation, Treatment. Also note the various paragraphs in this section).

Death—The Patient May Die by Having the Wrong Healer—The rising sign of the patient being in □ or ☍ to the Asc., or rising sign of the Healer; ♄ in the Healer's map in the sign occupying the 6th H. in the patient's map of birth. (See "Compatibility" in this section).

Diagnosis—(See Diagnosis, Judgment, Prognosis).

Diet and Hygiene—♍ is the sign which rules these matters, and people who have ♂, and other planets in ♍ at B., or who are born under ♍, make good Dieticians, Teachers, Lecturers, and Healers, by the direction of a well-balanced and regulated Diet for their patients. The ♍ people, however, tend to hold onto disease when sick, and espec. if they are unenlightened, and live in their lower minds. (See Virgo). Case of a Diet Specialist—See "Wallace", No. 292, in 1001 N.N. (See Diet; "Health Foods" under Food; Hygiene, Prevented (Disease Prevented); Sanitation; "Hygiene" in this section).

Divine Healers—Faith Healers—Spiritual Healers—Metaphysical Healers— Drugless Healers—♅ strong at B., and

well-aspected; ♅ rising, in the Asc. or M.C., and in ☌ the ☉, gives strong powers for the study and practice of these forms of healing, and to go deeply into the Occult and Recondite Sciences. (See Faith, Hypnotic, Magnetic, Metaphysical, Psychic, Spiritual, in this section).

Doctors — (See "Physicians", and the various paragraphs in this section).

Drugs—(See Drugs).

Drugless Healers—(See Chiropractors, Divine, Faith, Mental, Metaphysical, Nature, Naturopaths, and other paragraphs in this section).

Eclectic Physicians — This School is quite universal in its methods and practices, and tends to choose the best from many Schools of Healing, and to not be bound by any one method. Eclectics tend to be versatile, and to have their planets at B. well-scattered out thru the Signs of the Zodiac, and with a desire to delve into many subjects, and to gather Truth wherever it may be found. In addition to this, the best Eclectic Healers usually have ♂, the ♍ and ♏ signs strong and prominent at B. (See "Physicians" in this section).

Electricity—(See "Healing" under Electricity).

Enemas—Healing By—(See Enemas).

Enemies — The general influences which would tend to make certain classes and types of people an enemy to the native also tend to make the Healer adverse to him, and the magnetic and vibratory exchanges between the two maps, and natures, rather evil, and to not benefit each other. (See Enemies; "Compatibility" in this section).

Failures As Healers—Do Not Make Good Healers—♄ in the 6th H. of the Healer at B.

Faith Healing—Spiritual Methods, as by Religious Rites, Christian Science, Prayer, Laying On of Hands, etc. — ♆ strong at B., and well-aspected, makes the Healer more susceptible to the inflow of Spiritual Powers in Healing, and also ♆ strong and favorably aspected in the map of the patient makes him more amenable to the spiritual powers of healing. Such methods, however, may become dangerous when ♆ is weak and badly afflicted in the maps of both Healer and patient, and lead to obsessions, and dangerous mental and spiritual states, black magic, etc. Also ♅ strong at B. in both the maps, of Healer and patient, tend to increase the powers, knowledge, and beliefs necessary for successful healing by faith and spiritual power. (See Divine, Metaphysical, and the various paragraphs in this section).

Foods—Health Foods—(See Diet, Hygiene, Specialties, in this section).

Good Healers — Make Good and Successful Healers—The ☉ in a fiery sign at B.; the ☉ well-aspected in ♏; born under ♏. (See "Magnetic", and the various paragraphs in this section).

Health Specialties — (See Diet, Food, Hygiene, Specialties, in this section).

Herbs—The Use of Herbs In Healing —(See Herbs).

Homeopathy — Treating Disease by Sympathy and Similars — (See Homeopathy, Sympathy).

Hospitals—(See Hospitals).

Hygiene — And Diet — (See "Diet" in this section; Hygiene).

Hypnotism — Hypnotic Powers of Healing—(See Hypnotism).

Incompatibility — Of the Healer and Patient — (See Antipathy, Compatibility, Death, Enemies, Poisoned, in this section).

Incurable Diseases—(See Curable, Incurable).

Injured—By the Healer—(See Antipathy, Compatibility, Death, Enemies, Death, Poisoned, in this section).

Judgment of Disease—(See "Diagnosis" in this section).

Laying On of Hands — A Religious Rite In Healing—(See "Faith" in this section).

Length of the Illness—(See Duration, Grievous, Incurable, Invalids, Long, Prolonged, Slow, Tedious, etc.).

Magic Powers — In Healing — (See Magic).

Magnetic Healers—Born under ♏, and the ♏ influence strong at B.; the ☉ in ♏. (See "Healers" under Magnetic).

Massage—Manipulation— Kneading— Friction— Methodic Pressure—Healers born under ♏, the ☉ in ♏, are especially adaptated to this work, due to their strong magnetism and healing powers. (See "Osteopathy" in this section).

Medicines — The Use of Medicines In Healing—(See Antipathy, Drugs, Herbs, Medical, Medicines, Remedies, Sympathy, Treatment).

Mental Healing — (See "Psychic" in this section).

Metaphysical Healing—Absent Healing—Healing at a Distance thru Prayer, Concentration, Realization, Spiritual Power, etc., or the use of these same methods in the presence of the patient —♆ and ♅ strong at B. in the maps of the Healers tend to make the best Practitioners along this line, and with those who have Occult and Metaphysical knowledge, and who understand the healing and magnetic forces and currents which are operating in the Universe. (See Divine, Faith, Prayer, Spiritual, in this section).

Midwives — (See Midwives, Obstetricians).

Mineral Waters — Healers Making a Specialty of—Healers born under ♓, the ☉ in ♓, and many planets in watery signs at B. tend to be especially fortunate in this work. Also people born under ♄ make good Healers, and Managers of Mineral Water Sanitariums, as ♄ rules strongly over minerals, and the mineral products of the Earth. The Occult Masters of Wisdom teach us that we get sufficient mineral nourishment from vegetable foods, and that after 40 years of age, distilled water is more healthful for drinking purposes, and tends to prevent the excess of minerals in the system, causing

Gout, Rheumatism, etc., later in life. One Occult Axiom is, "Internally undistilled water is Man's worst enemy, but used externally on the skin is his best friend." (See Minerals; "Water" under Skin).

Mud Baths — These baths are especially helpful to strong ♄ persons, those born under ♄, and who thru melancholy and mental depression have so lowered their vital forces as to allow poisons to accumulate in the body. Mud baths help to open the pores of the skin, and to extract the excess of mineral deposits and wastes in the system. Also Healers who practice these methods are apt to be born under ♄, and to resort largely to material and physical means of healing.

Nature—The Healing Powers of—The Defensive Forces of Nature—Nature is said to do the healing, and all we can do is to assist Nature. (See Phagocytes, Recuperation, Resistance, Stamina, Tone, Vis Conservatrix, Vitality).

Nature Cure — A Nature Cure Physician, and Author of a book on the subject. See "Kleinshrod", No. 690, in 1001 N.N. (See "Curing" under Nature).

Naturopaths—Naturopathy—Good Healers along this line are born under ♍ and ♏, and whose planets at B. also indicate versatility, adaptability, magnetic powers, and with considerable knowledge of Universal Truth, the Occult and Metaphysical Wisdom, and of the Laws of Health. The Naturopaths use what are called natural methods in healing, such as by regulating the diet, habits, and also by the use of massage, electricity, baths, waters, and the various forces in Nature, but are classed as Drugless Healers, and do not use drugs internally. (See Medical Astrology).

Nurses—Influences Which Make Good Nurses—(See Nurses).

Nut Butters—A Maker of as a Health Specialty — (See "Specialties" in this section).

Obstetricians—(See this subject).

Opposites—Healing by the Use of Opposite Forces—By Antipathy—(See Antipathy, Opposites).

Orthopedist—(See this subject).

Osteopathy—The most successful Osteopaths are born under ♏, and with the ☉ and many planets in ♏, and whose magnetic powers of healing are strong. (See Magnetic, Massage, in this section).

Patient and Healer—Compatibility of —(See "Compatibility" in this section).

Periods of Success—As Healers—The ☉, ☽, Asc., or M.C. to the good asps. ♂ by dir., and espec. as Surgeons. (See Surgeons).

Phagocytes — Healing and Defending Forces of the Body—(See Phagocytes).

Physicians—A Successful Physician— Success as a Doctor of Medicine—These influences apply largely to Healers in general, and to all who have to deal with the sick in the treatment and cure of patients, the alleviation of human suffering, no matter by what method, or by what School of Healing administered—The ☉ in ♏ at B., and well-asp. by ♃ and ♂; the ☉ Sig. in ♏; the ☉ well-asp. in ♏; the ☉ P, ⚹ or △ ♃ at B.; the ☽ incr. in light, sepr. from ♄ and apply. to ☿; the ☽ ruling the employment, or in her decr., configurated with ☿, and in ♌, ♍, ♏, ♐, ♑, or ♓, and with ♓ strong, and aspected by ☿ or the ☽; the ☽ Sig. ☌ ♂, and ♂ well-dignified; ♃ ruler of the horoscope; ♃ Sig. ☌ ♂; ♃ well-asp. in ♏; ♃ well-asp. in the 6th H., the house of health; ♂ and ♀ together rulers of the employment; ♂, ♃, or ♀ in the 6th H.; ♂ lord of the 6th, and in the 6th; any asp. of ♂ to the ☽ or ☿ inclines to the study of Medicine, Surgery, or Chemistry; to have success as a Physician ♂ should be strong at B., and in good asp. to the ☉, ☽, or ☿; ♂ a strong ruler at B.; ♂ ☌ ♀ in the 6th H. usually makes good Physicians; ♀ alone ruler makes good Medical Doctors; ♀ well-asp. in the 6th H.; ☿ in ♏, well-asp. by ♃ and ♂; in Hor'y Q., the Sig. in a fiery sign denotes; born under ♏, good healers along the lines of Diet and Hygiene, but apt to be failures in surgery, and where courage is needed; born under ♏, good Medical Doctors and Surgeons; any benefic in the 6th H. tends to make good Healers; in Hor'y Q., the Sig. in ♏; benefics in the 12th H.; lord of the employment in ♏, and well-asp.; lord of the Asc. in the 6th H.; lord of the 2nd in the 6th, may gain a fortune in the Practice of Medicine; lord of the 2nd in the 12th H., success in Hospitals, Prisons, Asylums, and Institutions of Healing where patients are confined; lord of the 4th in the 6th, and well-asp.; lord of the 5th in the 6th; lord of the 6th in the 2nd, gains as a Physician; lord of the 6th in the 6th; lord of the 7th in the Asc.; lord of the 10th a benefic, in the 6th H., and well-asp.; lord of the 12th a benefic, in the 6th, and well-asp.; the Asc. or M.C. ⚹ or △ ♂; the 6th face of ♋, the 4th face of ♌, the 2nd face of ♏, or the 2nd face of ♐ culminating on the M.C.; the 10° ♑ on the Asc., a degree of healing and sympathy, and makes strong Healers. Cases of Eminent Healers and Physicians—See "Massari", "Nunn", "Quain", in 1001 N.N. (See Chemists, Surgeons; "The Sick" under Sick. Also note the various paragraphs in this section).

Poisoned — May Be Poisoned by the Healer or Physician — Incompatibility between Healer and Patient—The patient having the lord of the 8th in the 6th H. at B.; lord of the 6th in the 11th; ♄ in the Healer's map in the 6th H. of the patient, or in the sign occupying the 6th H.; the rising signs in the maps of Healer and patient in ☐ or ⚻ asp. to each other. (See Compatibility, Death, in this section; "Ill-Treatment" under Sickness).

Powers—The Healing Powers Strengthened—♅ in ⚹ or △ asp. to ♅.

Practice of Healing—Disposed to the Study and Practice of Healing, Whether it be by Medicine, Diet, Hygiene, or any Other System—The ♍ sign and the 6th H. deal with healing matters and hygiene, and ♍ and the 6th H. strong at B., and well-occupied, tend to turn the attention to Healing. Also the ♏ sign strong at B., and containing the ☉, ♂, or ☿, disposes to healing along the lines of drugs, surgery, massage, magnetism, etc. The ☉ in ♍ or ♏, and espec. when in the 6th H.; the ☉ or ☿ in the 6th H.; the ☉ well-asp. by ♂; ♅, or ♂ in ♍ or the 6th H.; ♂ well-asp. in the 10th H.; the 3rd Decan. of ♍ on the Asc., which is ruled by ☿; any aspect of ♂ to the ☽ or ☿.

Prayer— Healing by Prayer — (See Divine, Faith, Metaphysical, Psychic, in this section).

Prevention of Disease—By the Patient, or thru the Advice of the Healer — (See Diet, Hygiene; "Disease Prevented" under Prevention; Sanitation, Spiritual Power (see Spiritual); Suggestion, Thinking, etc.).

Process—The Healing Process—(See Granulations).

Prognosis—(See this subject).

Psychic Healing — Divine Healing — Mental Healing—Healing by Faith, etc. —A Good Psychic Healer—The Patient More Susceptible To—♅ strong at B., or ruler of the horoscope. The best time for Psychic Healing is when the ☽ is in ♋ or ♓. (See Divine, Faith, Hypnotism, Metaphysical, in this section; Psychic).

Reformer— A Hygienic Reformer — Case and Birth Data of—(See Hygiene).

Religion — Religious Rites — Healing By—(See Divine, Faith, in this section).

Remedies — (See Antipathy, Color, Cure, Drugs, Herbs, Medicines, Metals, Minerals, Opposites, Sympathy, Treatment, etc. Also see the various paragraphs in this section).

Sanitariums—(See Asylums, Confinement, Hospitals, Prison, Twelfth House; "Mineral Waters" in this section).

Sanitation—(See Cleanliness, Hygiene, Prevention, Sanitation).

Sick—The Treatment and Care of the Sick — (See Cure, Hospitals, Nurses, Sick. Also note the various paragraphs in this section).

Sixth House—The House which is strongly related to Health and Healers—(See Sixth House, Virgo).

Skillful Healers—(See "Good Healers" in this section).

Specialties—Makers of Health Foods and Specialties—Nut Butters—♂ well-asp. in ♍ gives success in the preparation of Health Foods and Specialties. Case—A Maker of Health Specialties and Nut Butters—See "Mapleton", No. 1000, in 1001 N.N. (See Diet, Hygiene, in this section; "Health Foods" under Food).

Spiritual Healers—♆ is the planet which rules strongly over spiritual matters, the spiritual nature, and people born under the strong influence of ♆, and also ♅, and with ♆ ☌ the ☉, or ♆ in the 1st or 10th H., and well-asp., tend to make good Spiritual Healers. Also ♆ in ⚹ or △ asp. ♅ at B. tends to strengthen these powers, and to give greater spiritual insight, and a greater consciousness of spiritual power in the healing work. (See Divine, Faith, Metaphysical, in this section).

Strengthened—The Healing Powers Strengthened—(See "Powers" in this section).

Study of Healing—Disposed To—(See "Practice of Healing" in this section).

Success As Healers—Periods of Success As Healers—(See Good Healers, Periods, Physicians, and the various paragraphs in this section).

Suggestion—Healing By—(See Hypnotism; "Psychic" in this section).

Surgeons—Makes a Good Surgeon—(See Surgeon).

Sympathy—Healing by Methods of—(See Homeopathy, Sympathy).

Treatment of Disease—(See Cure, Remedies, Treatment. Also note the various paragraphs in this section).

Unfortunate—As Healers—♄ in the 6th H. of the Healer at B.; lord of the 7th H. a malefic, and in the 6th H., and afflicted; lord of the 12th a malefic, and in the 6th H., and afflicted. The ♍ sign people tend to take on the diseases of other, and are not good Healers in the presence of dangerous illnesses and fevers, or as Surgeons, but they make good Healers along the lines of Diet, Food, Hygiene, Prevention, Sanitation, etc.

Vibration—As a Factor In Healing—(See Vibrations).

Waters—Healing By—(See Bathing; "Mineral Waters" in this section).

Wealth—Gains Wealth As a Healer, or In the Practice of Medicine—Lord of the 2nd H. in the 6th, or lord of the 6th H. in the 2nd H. (See Periods, Physicians, in this section).

Zodiac Salts—Biochemistry—Healers Who Make Use of the 12 Tissue Salts, Known as the Schuessler Tissue Remedies—(See "Biochemists" in this section; "Salts" under Zodiac).

HEALTH—The State of the Health—The General Health—Rules for Judging the Health—Good Health—Bad Health, etc.—The 6th H. and ♍ denote the state of the health. Also the 1st H. rules the health and constitution. The ☽ governs the health, and has significance over health matters, and espec. with females, while the ☉ is a strong indicator of health with males. However, the ☉ and ☽ are important factors in the health of both sexes. The rising sign also governs the health and the life. The Part of Fortune (⊕) does not affect the health, but has more to do with finance. When ♄ or ♂ both afflict the ☉, the health is not as bad as when ♄ alone afflicts the ☉, for the aspects of ♂ to the ☉, whether good or bad, tend to strengthen the system. The planet ♅ does not exercise any great influence over the health except when in the 6th H., and there tends to nervousness, suicide, or accidents. Ill-asps. between the ☽ and ♂, and between the ☉ and ♄, tend to greatly injure the health because of their opposite and dissimilar natures. The ill-asps. between the ☽ and ♂, and between the ☽ and ♄, do not injure as much, as their natures are more in common with each other. Health is largely indicated by the ☉ and ☽ at B.,

their positions, signs, and aspects, as they are the fountains of life on the Earth. In health every cell of the body is polarized in subjection to the central will. Therefore, health is obedience, government, and order in the system, while disease is rebellion, insubordination, and disunion. Remember, the stars only incline and show tendencies, and that your health can be improved and modified by self-control, right thinking, spiritualization, and by control of the passional and sex nature. Read the various paragraphs of this Article for the many and manifold considerations concerning health, as regards yourself, your family, your relatives, and also the Public Health in general. The rules for judging the normal state of the health from the star map of birth are given in the paragraph, "Judging The Health" in this section. See the following subjects in the alphabetical arrangement when not considered here—

Absent Party—State of the Health of An Absent Party in Hor'y Questions—(See Absent).

Abundance of Health—Good Health All Thru Life—Rarely Ill—Little Sickness All Thru Life—The ☉ in ♐ and well-aspected, physical ailments rare; the ☽ hyleg with females does not conduce to many ailments; ♂ ☌, P., ✳, or △ the ☉; ♀ well-asp. in the 6th H. if the health is guarded; ♌ on the Asc., rarely ill; lord of the 8th H. in the 8th, little sickness all thru life, but slightly threatened with illness at times. (See "Good Health" in this section).

Affected—The Health Affected—The Health Suffers—(See "Bad Health" in this section. Also see the various paragraphs under Ill-Health, Sickness).

Aged—Aged People—State of the Health In—(See Old Age).

Air—Healthy Air—(See "Healthy Air" under Air).

Always Ailing—(See "Bad Health" in this section; "Ill-Health All Thru Life" under Ill-Health).

Analeptics—An Agent Restoring Health and Strength—(See Analeptic).

Anxiety—Concerning the Health—(See Hypochondria).

Asthenia—Loss of Strength—(See Adynamia, Asthenia).

Aunts—Health of—(See Aunts).

Bad Health—The Health Suffers—Ill-Health—Impaired Health—Delicate Health—Poor Health—Disordered System—Weak Constitution—The Vitality Low, etc. There are two classes of planetary influences, those which cause general ill-health and weakness from birth, and those which cause periods of bad health along thru life. In this paragraph the influences will be listed which tend to general, fundamental, and prolonged bad health, and further along, in the paragraph, "Periods of Ill-Health", will be given the Directions, Transits, etc., which tend to periods of ill-health, or temporary bad health. The following are the General Influences which tend to Bad Health, and a weak constitution from birth, and with lower vitality and resistance to disease, etc.—The SUN □ or ☍ the ☽ at B.; the ☉ or ☽ affl. by malefics; the ☉ □ ♄ and the ☉ hyleg; the ☉ or ☽ in the 6th H., and affl.; the ☉ in the 6th H., and affl. by malefics or the ☽; the ☉ or ♄ in the 6th H. in ☌, □, or ☍ each other, which is one of the worst positions for bad health; the ☉ in the 6th H. in cardinal signs, and affl. by the ☽ or ♄; the ☉ occi., and affl. by ♄; the ☉ Sig. in ♋ or ♑; in male horoscopes when the ☉ is affl. by both ♄ and ♂ the health will not be exceptionally bad, as ♂ in any asp. to the ☉ tends to increase the animal heat; the MOON sepr. from ♂ and apply. to the ☉ or ♄; the ☽ Sig. □ or ☍ ♄ (Hor'y); the ☽ hyleg and ☌ a malefic, and espec. when in the 6th H.; the ☽ (or the ☉) affl. by malefics, and the malefics elevated above the Lights; the ☽ Sig. in ♑; the ☽ weak and affl. at B., the health is rarely good, and espec. with females; the ☽ in the 6th H., and affl., the disease is in the part signified by the sign on the cusp of the 6th; the ☽ ill-asp. by ♃; the ☽ affl. in the 1st H., the health not good, and the life precarious; the ☽ affl. by ♄ at B., and tends to ill-health every seven years; the ☽ □ or ☍ the ☉ at B.; the ☽ in bad asp. to the ascending degree at B., and by dir.; in female nativities the ☽ is the strong ruler in health matters, and no matter how severely the ☽ may be afflicted, if there are good asps. of the benefics to the ☽ the health is improved, and also the health does not tend to be as bad under planetary afflictions along thru life; NEPTUNE in the 1st H., and affl. the ☉ or ☽; ♆ in the 6th H., and affl. the ☉, ☽, or hyleg; ♆ □ or ☍ ♄, bad health thru obsessions, and the taking of drugs, medicines, or narcotics; SATURN in the 6th H. at B., conjoined with the ☉, or affl. the ☉; ♄ or ♂ in the Asc. at B., and affl.; ♄ affl. in the 6th H., and espec. if the mind dwells on selfish aims; ♄ in the 6th H. in ☌, □, or ☍ the ☉.; ♄ in the 10th H., affl. the hyleg, and espec. if ♄ be affl. by ♅ and ♂, always ailing; ♄ Sig. ☌ the ☉; ♄ □ or ☍ ♃; ♄ in the Asc., bad for the health in infancy and childhood; ♄ ffl. in ♍ or ♑; ♄ rising at B.; ♄ ruler of the 6th H. at B., and in ☌ or evil asp. the Asc. by dir.; ♄ rising at B., and affl. the hyleg; ♄ in the 10th H., and affl. the hyleg; ♄ in an angle, ori. of the ☽ and occi. of the ☉; ♄ Sig. in ♋, indicates a sickly person in Hor'y Q.; JUPITER in the 6th H. at B. in a cardinal sign, and affl.; ♃ affl. in the 6th H.; ♃ affl. in the Asc., ill-health thru corrupt blood; ♃ Sig. ☌ the ☉; ♃ Sig. in ♋ or ♑; MARS affl. in the 6th H., and also affl. the hyleg; ♂ ☌ ♀, and affl. by the □ and ☍ of planets; VENUS affl. in the 6th H.; ♀ affl. in the 5th H., thru pleasure and dissipation; ♀ Sig. in ♋ or ♑, sickly and feeble; ♀ Sig. ☌ the ☉, too sickly as a rule to make much exertion; MERCURY Sig. in ♑, sickly and feeble; malefics in the 6th H. at B., and affl. the hyleg; a malefic in an angle, rising before or after the ☉ or ☽; common signs on the Asc. and angles, and containing malefics and many afflictions; FIXED STARS

of the nature or ♄ or ♂ ascending at B.; ♋, ♑, or ♓ on the Asc., and with afflictions to the hyleg and 6th H.; the ASCENDANT hyleg and ☌, □ or ☍ a malefic; lord of the Asc. in the 1st, and affl. by malefics or lords of the 6th, 8th, or 12th; lord of the Asc. in the 6th, 8th, or 12th, and affl.; lord of the 4th in the 6th, and affl.; lord of the 6th in the Asc., is seldom strong or robust in early years and has poor health, and the nature of the sickness is indicated by the planets in the 6th, the sign on the 6th, and lord of the 6th; lord of the 8th in the 6th; lord of the 11th a malefic, and in the 6th; lord of the 11th in the 6th; lord of the 12th a malefic, and affl. in the 6th H. (See Disease; "Ill-Health" under Females, Males; Ill-Health, Infirmities; "Public Health Bad" under Public; Sickness, etc. Also see "Periods of Bad Health" in this section).

Benefitted—The Health Benefitted—(See Better, Improved, in this section).

Better—The Health Better—The Health is generally better when the ☉ is rising at B., and weaker when setting. (See "Better" under Disease; Immunity, Resistance, Strong, Vitality; Good, Improved, Promoted, in this section).

Blood—Bad Health from Impure Blood—From Too Much Blood, etc.—♃ affl. in the Asc. (See Impure, Pressure, Too Much, under Blood).

Breakdown In Health—Principally caused by an afflicted ♀; ♀ in ♍ ☌ ♂ or the ☽, and thru sex abuses and sex cesses; ♀ affl. in the 6th H., thru luxuries and abuses; ♀ □ or ☍ ♂; the ☉ or ☽ to the ☌ or ill-asp. the malefics by dir., and espec. among those with weak vitality, frail constitutions, and among the aged; may be caused by a train of evil directions to the hyleg, the evil directions of malefics to the hyleg, the ☉, ☽, or Asc., and espec. among the aged and the feeble. (See Chronic, Consumptions, Directions, Dissipation, Drink, Excesses, Feasting, Habits, Ill-Health, Invalids, Sickness, Wastings, etc. Also note the various paragraphs in this section).

Brothers—Health of—(See Brothers).

Careless—Of the Health and Habits—(See "Careless" under Habits).

Changes—Changes Detrimental to Health—Changes Which Interfere with Health and Comfort—♅ in the 6th H. (See Comforts).

Cheerfulness—As An Asset of Good Health—(See Cheerfulness).

Childhood—The Health In—(See Childhood, Children, Early Years, Infancy).

Children—Health of—(See Childhood, Children, Early Years, Infancy).

Comforts and Health—(See Comforts).

Common People—The Health of the Common People—The Public Health—(See Common, Mankind; "Health" under Public).

Complexion; Constitution—(See the various paragraphs under Constitution.

Contentment; Corrupt Blood—Bad Health From—(See "Blood" in this section).

Damage—To the Health—(See "Bad Health", and the various paragraphs in this section).

Daughter—Health of—(See Daughter).

Debility; Delicate Health—(See "Bad Health" in this section; Pale, Sickly, Vitality Low; "Body" under Weak).

Depressed—Depressed Concerning the Health—(See Depressed, Hypochondria).

Detrimental—Has a Detrimental Effect Upon the Health—The ☉ ☌ or P. ♄, and especially in common signs. (See "Bad Health" in this section).

Directions—Effect of Upon the Health—(See Directions).

Diseased Body—Diseased Mind—(See "Bad Habits", and the various paragraphs in this section. Also see the various subjects under Disease, Ill-Health, Mental, Mind, Sickness).

Disordered System—(See Disorders; "Disordered" under System; "Bad Health", and the various paragraphs in this section).

Dissipation—Bad Health From—(See Dissipation).

Dissolute; Distempers; Drink;

Drug Habit—Drugs—Bad Health from Use of—(See Drugs, Medicines, Narcotics).

Drunkenness—(See Drink, Drunkenness, Intoxication).

Early Years—The Health In—(See Early, Childhood, Children, Infancy, Youth).

Eating—Disorders from Wrong Eating—(See Diet, Eating, Excesses, Food, Gluttony).

Elderly People—The Health of—(See Grandparents, Middle Life, Old Age).

Emaciation; Enemies—Health of—Death of—(See Enemies).

Enfeebled Health—(See "Bad Health" in this section; Emaciated, Feeble, Infirm, Infirmities, Invalids, Sickly, etc.).

Enhanced—The Health Enhanced—The ☽ well-asp. by ♃ and ♀. (See Abundance, Improved, Promoted, in this section).

Epidemics; Excesses—The Health Injured By—(See Excesses).

Family—The Health of—(See Family).

Father—Health of—(See Father).

Fears—About the Health—(See Hypochondria).

Feasting—Ill Health From—(See Feasting, Gluttony, etc).

Feeble Health—(See Emaciated, Feeble, Infirm, Invalids, Sickly; "Bad Health" in this section).

Females—Women—The Health of—(See Aunts, Daughter, Females, Mother, Sister, Women; the ☽ influences under "Bad Health" in this section).

Foods—Health Foods—(See "Health Foods" under Food; "Specialties" under Healers).

Friends—Health of—(See Friends).

Functions—And the Health—(See Functions).

General Debility—(See Debility; "Debility" under Nerves; "Low" under Vitality; "Body" under Weak).

General Health—The General Health and the constructive functions are governed by the ☽. The General Health is much affected by the ☽, her aspects, sign and house position. The ☽ in ♋ or ♍ are good influences for the general health, and benefit it. Also ♃ and ♀ in good asp to the ☽ enhance the general health. (See General. Also for the Rules to Judge the General Health see "Judging the Health" in this section).

General Ill-Health—(See Ill-Health).

General Malaise—(See Malaise).

Gluttony—Bad Health By—(See Gluttony).

Good Health—Very Good Health—Healthy—Strong—Robust—Rarely Ill—Vitality Good—Signs of Good Health—Marks of—Periods of Good Health, etc.—The SUN, ☽, and Asc. free from affliction; the ☉, ☽, or ♃ in the Asc. or M.C. at B., strong by sign, and in good asp. to the hyleg; the ☉ in ♐ unless the hyleg is afflicted; the ☉ well-asp. by the ☽, ♂, and the benefics, and free from the strong afflictions of the malefics; the ☉ in a fire sign in the Asc. or M.C., and well-aspected; the ☉ to the ☌ ♃ by dir.; the MOON hyleg in the 1st or 10th H., well-asp. by the ☉ and benefics, and free from the ill-asps. of the malefics, and espec. with females; the ☽ free from affliction, well-asp. by ♃ or ♀, and also the Asc. free from malefic planets; the ☽ free from affliction, angular, and espec. in the 1st or 10th, not combust or evilly aspected by the lords of the 4th, 6th, 8th or 12th; the ☽ to the ☌ ♃ by dir.; the ☽ to the ☌ ♀ by dir. if ♀ be well-dignified at B.; the ☽ (or ☉) to the ✳ or △ asps. of ♃ or ♀ by dir.; the ☽ to the place of Canis Majoris; for the best of health, and location for health, follow the direction of the ☽ at B., or the lord of the Asc.; the ☽ well-asp. in ♋ or ♍; the ☽ angular and the Lights free from affliction; the ☽ ✳ or △ the ☉ or Asc. at B.; the ☽ to the △ asp. the Asc. in the Zodiac; the ☽ directed to Markab, Bull's North Eye, or the Right Foot of ♐; ♄ △ the Asc., and in good asp to the hyleg; JUPITER in the 6th H. unless much afflicted by position and aspects; ♃ ☌ or good asp. the ☉; ♃ hyleg in the Asc. or M.C., and well-aspected; ♃ Sig. ☌ ♀, very good health; ♃ well-asp. in the 1st H.; ♃ or ♀ in the 1st H., well-aspected, and with a strong sign upon the Asc.; ♃ or ♀ in the Asc. at B., and free from □ and ☍ asps.; ♃ in good asp. to the ☽; ♃ ☌ the Asc. by dir.; ♃ or ♀ to the ☌ or good asp. the M.C. by dir.; MARS ☌ or any asp. the ☉, usually strong and healthy; VENUS well-asp. in the 6th H., the health is good if not abused; the ASCENDANT well-asp. by the ☉, ☽, and many planets; a strong sign upon the Asc., and with ♃ or ♀ in the 1st H., and well-asp.; the ruler of the Asc. strong; the sign on the Asc., and the lord thereof, free from affliction, swift in motion, not combust or adversely aspected by the lords of the 4th, 6th, 8th, or 12th, dignified, angular, as in the 1st or 10th, and if in the 9th or 11th H., to be well-asp. by ♃, ♀, or the ☉, or in the terms of ♃ or ♀; lord of the Asc. in the 1st H., and well-asp.; the Asc. ✳ or △ the ·☉, ☽, or ♃; fiery signs upon the Asc., the vitality is strong and the health tends to be good if dissipation and excesses are avoided; ♒ on the Asc., healthy and strong; the signs of the Summer Quarter on the Asc., as ♋, ♌, or ♍, or the ☉ or ☽ in these signs at B., tend to give a healthy, strong and vigorous body; ♋ on the Asc., altho classed as a weak sign, tends to give a stronger and healthier body when the ☉ is in ♋ in the Asc. at B., as the ☉ adds vitality to any sign he is in at B., and espec. when in the Asc.; the 14° ♓ on the Asc.; the Asc. to the place of Crater (see Crater); the Asc., the ☉ and ☽ free from affliction; the Asc. ♂ ♃ by dir.; the hyleg strong and well-asp. by the benefics, and free from the serious afflictions of the malefics; all good asps. to the hyleg benefit the health, but good asps. to the ☉, ☽, or Asc., espec. from the 6th or 8th Houses, or their rulers, are very efficacious; the Asc. well-asp. by the ☉, ☽, and many planets; a strong SIXTH HOUSE, even tho the hyleg be afflicted; the 6th H., the sign thereon, and its ruler, free from the presence or evil asps. of malefics; lord of the 6th in the 6th, unless much afflicted; Arista ascending at B. (See "Abundance", "Prospects", in this section; Cheerfulness; "Good" under Constitution, Recuperation, Resistance, Stamina, Tone, Vitality; Contentment; "Good Health" under Females, Males; Harmony; "Abundance of Health" under Health; "Long Life" under Life; "Peace of Mind" under Mind; Optimism; "Public Health Good" under Public; Robust, Ruddy; "Body" under Strong; Vigor, Vivacious, etc.).

Grandparents—Health of—(See Grandparents).

Habits—And the Health—(See "Careless", and the various paragraphs under Habits).

Harmony — A Harmonious Constitution—(See "Good" under Constitution; Harmony).

Health Affected—(See "Bad Health", and the various paragraphs in this section).

Health Bad—(See "Bad" in this section).

Health Foods—Health Specialties—(See "Foods" in this section).

Health Good—(See "Good" in this section).

Healthy—Healthy Air—Healthy Constitution—(See Air; "Good" under Constitution; "Public Health Good", under Public; "Good Health" in this section).

Heat—The Animal Heat—Lack of, and Tending to Ill-Health—(See "Animal Heat" under Heat).

Husband—Health of—(See Husband).

Hypochondria — Morbid Fears Concerning the Health—(See Hypochondria).

Ill-Health—Tendency To Ill-Health—(See the various paragraphs under Ill-Health; "Bad Health", in this section).

Immunity—From Illness—(See Immunity).

Impaired Health—(See "Bad Health" in this section. Also note the various paragraphs under Disease, Ill-Health, Sickness).

Improved—Improved State of the Health—The Health Promoted—The ☉, ☽, or Asc. afflicted, but well-asp. by the benefics; the ☽ in ♑ or ♋, and well-asp.; the ☽ to the P. Dec. ♃; the ☽ combust, and sepr. from ♂ the ☉, and ♃ aspect the place in any way, the health will improve, but the eyes are generally left weak and out of order; ♃ or ♀ well-asp. in the 6th H.; the mundane ✳ of ♃ or ♀ to the M.C.; the favorable asps. of the benefics to the hyleg. (See "Better" under Disease; "Increased" under Vitality; Better, Enhanced, Good, in this section).

Impure Blood — Ill-Health From—(See "Blood" in this section).

Indicators of Health—Significators of Health—The ☉, ☽, Asc., planets in the 1st H., or just above the Asc.; planets in the 6th H., and the ruler of the 6th, their signs, aspects, etc.; lord of the 6th, or the strongest or most afflicted planet in the 6th; also the M.C., the Midheaven, and how aspected at B., and by dir., and planets in the 10th H. at B. (See "Significators" under Disease, Form; "Judging the Health", and the Introduction to this Article).

Indifferent State—Of the Health—The ☽ to the ♂ or ill-asps. ♅, indifference of mind to life's duties; the Asc. to the □ or ⚹ ♃ by dir., often due to plethora. (See Apathy, Careless, Dull, Indifferent, Indisposition; "Periods of Bad Health" in this section).

Indisposition; Infancy—The Health In—(See Infancy).

Infirm; Infirmities; Injury—To the Health—The Health Menaced—Planets in their signs of detriment or fall tend to injure the health when they are the afflictors in the disease; the ☉ affl. by ♄; the ☽ affl. by ♂. (See the Introduction, Bad Health, and the various paragraphs in this Article).

Invalidism; Judging the Health—Rules For—(1) The rising sign is the first to be considered, whether strong or weak, and the aspects to the degree ascending, and judge accordingly. (2) Consider the ☉, its sign and strength, the aspects to the ☉, and whether or not the ☉ is hyleg. (3) Consider the ☽, her sign and aspects, and whether strong or weak, or hyleg. These are the three sensitive points in the map, the ☉, ☽, and Asc., and govern the constitution, physical strength, and functions, and the constitutional powers, the vitality, stamina, the regularity or irregularity of the functions, and the general health, depend upon these three vital centers. (4) Consider next the planets in the 6th and 8th H., and whether they afflict any of these three vital centers, as the parts of the body ruled by the signs in which planets are posited will tend to be disordered according to the nature of the afflicting planet. (5) If no planets in the 6th H., then consider the sign on the cusp of the 6th, as the part of the body ruled by such sign will tend to be a center of physical disturbance, and the part of the body so affected will be a center, or seat from which many other disorders may arise. (See "Indicators" in this section).

Liable—To Ill-Health—(See "Ill-Health All Thru Life" under Ill-Health; "Slow" under Recuperation; "Low" under Resistance, Vitality; Sickly; "Body" under Weak). For influences which tend to make the native less liable to Disease or Ill-Health, see "Good Health" in this section; Immunity; "Good" under Constitution, Resistance, Vitality).

Little Sickness—(See Abundance, Good Health, Immunity, in this section).

Location—Residence—The Health As Affected by Location—(See Altitude, Abroad, Foreign Lands (see Foreign); Location, Native Land (see Native); Place of Birth (see Place); Residence; "Health" under Travel).

Long Life—(See Life).

Loss of Health—Loss of Strength—The ☉ in a weak sign at B., and afflicted; ♄ affl. in ♒; afflictions to ♃; ♀ □ or ☍ ♂, due to sex excesses unless controlled; ♀ in ♏, ♂ the ☽ or ♂, thru sex excesses. (See Asthenia, Bad Health, Periods of Bad Health, Undermined, and the various paragraphs in this section).

Lust—Bad Health thru Inordinate Lust—(See Lust).

Malaise; Males—The Health of—(See Males).

Malnutrition—(See Nutrition).

Marriage Partner—The Health of—(See Marriage Partner).

Medicines—Ill-Health from the Use of—The Use of Medicines In Restoring Health—(See Drugs, Medicines, Narcotics, Poisons, Remedies, Treatment).

Men—The Health of—(See Brother, Father, Grandfather, Males, Men, Uncles).

Menaced—The Health Menaced—(See "Injury" in this section).

Middle Life—The Health In—(See Middle Life).

Mind—Disorders of—The Health and Peace of the Mind—(See the various paragraphs under Intellect, Mental, Mind).

Morbid Fears—About the Health—(See "Morbid" under Fears; Hypochondria, Morbid).

Mother—The Health of—(See Mother).

Much Sickness—(See "Many Diseases" under Disease; "Much Sickness" under Sickness).

Narcotics; Nerves—Disorders of—Health Affected By—(See Nerves).

Obsessions—Health Disordered By—(See Obsessions, Spirit Controls).

Old Age—Health In—(See Old Age).

Opposite Sex—The Health Injured Thru—(See Opposite).

Passion—The Health Injured by Passional Excesses—(See Amorous, Excesses, Lust, Passion, Sex).

Peace of Mind—The Health Benefitted By—(See Contentment, Happiness; "Peace of Mind" under Mind).

People—The Health of the People—(See "Common People" in this section).

Periodic Diseases—(See Periodic).

Periods of Bad Health—The Health Suffers—The Adverse Influences of Directions, Progressions, and Transits over the Health, etc.—Of course, the degree of suffering which may come to the native at these times will depend upon his knowledge, wisdom, self-control, spiritual understanding, etc. We are taught that we must conquer the Monsters of the Zodiac, to walk the gauntlet of the Zodiacal influences undaunted, and to not be affected by them, but at this stage of human evolution there are only a few who can do it successfully, such as the Masters, the Initiates, the Adepts, etc. The influence of ♄, for instance, in his lower vibrations, is to chastise, afflict, bring suffering and death upon all those who are living in sin, evil, and wickedness, but to those who have conquered, ♄ is our best friend, our Protector, and he is the Bridge over which we pass from this Earth Plane to higher states of spiritual consciousness. So, in considering the following influences, remember they apply only to those who are drifting in life, who are unawakened, unregenerated, and who have not as yet discovered themselves, their real mission and place in life, and who may be classed as "Misfits", failures to a large extent so far in life. A study of the Occult and Metaphysical books which we already have, and to know the plan of the Universe, why we are here, where we came from, and where we go from here, will help us all to be better Masters of our Destiny, and a good book for us all to digest is "The Tarot of the Bohemians", by Papus. Also the books, "The Key to the Universe", and "The Key of Destiny", by Dr. and Mrs. Homer Curtiss; Wilde's Chaldean Astrology, and many others. The following planetary influences tend to Periods of Bad Health—The SUN to the ☌ or ill-asp. ♄ by dir., and the ☉ hyleg at B., and with danger of a fatal illness; the ☉ to the ☌ or ill-asp. the ☽ by dir., and the ☽ hyeg and affl.; directions of the ☉ affect the health if the ☉ be hyleg, and also the father; the ☉ to the □ or ☍ ♃ or ♀ by dir.; the ☉ affl. at B., and ☌ the Asc. by dir.; the ☉ to the ☌ or ill-asp. the ☽ and the direction falling in the 8th H., and espec. if the ☉ or ☽ rule the 8th at B., and be afflicted radically by ♄ or ♂; the ☉ to the cusp the 6th, 7th, or 8th H.; the ☉ to his own ill-asps. by dir., according to the sign the ☉ is in, and in which the aspect falls; the ☉ by dir. to the ill-asps. the ☽, Asc., or M.C., or to his own place; the ☉ to the bad asps. ☿ by dir., and espec. by the □ aspect, if ☿ also be affl.; the ☉ hyleg, and the ☉ to the ☌, P., □ or ☍ any of the malefics by dir.; the ☉ in the 6th or 8th H. at B., and to the ☌ or ill-asp. ♄ by dir.; the ☉ or ☽ occupying the 6th

H. by dir., and espec. if the ☉ and ☽ were in evil asp. to each other at B., or either occupied the 6th H.; adverse asps. of the ☉ to ♆, ♅, ♄, or ♂ by dir., and espec. among the aged and those of frail constitution; the Prog. ☉ to the ☌, P., □ or ☍ the ☽, ♄, the Asc., or any malefic; the Prog. ☉ to the □ or ☍ ♃ or ♀; the ☉ directed to Antares and all stars of the nature of ♂ and ☿ combined; the ☉ hyleg, and to the ☌ or P. Dec. Regulus; the ☉ by Periodic Rev. to the ill-asps. the radical ☽; the ☉ □ or ☍ ♄ at a Solar Rev. presignifies illness; the ☉ hyleg, and ♅ ☌ or P. the ☉ at a Solar Rev., ill-health of a peculiar nature; cross aspects to the ☉ by Promittors or Non-Promittors when the horoscope is an unfortunate one; when several aspects of non-promittor malefics are formed to the ☉ simultaneously, then considerable ill-heath usually follows; a total eclipse of the ☉ falling on the place of the ☉ at B., or a malefic, and espec. when the ☉ is badly affl. at B., or by dir.; the MOON to the ☌, P., □ or ☍ the ☉, Asc., or any malefic by dir., and more so if the ☽ be badly affl. at B.; the directions of the ☽, if the ☽ be hyleg, affect the health, both mentally and physically, and also affect the family affairs, the mother, sister, or wife; the ☽ or Asc. receiving evil asps. by dir. tend to adversely affect the health whether the ☽ is hyleg or not, but when the ☽ is hyleg or within 5 degrees of a hylegiacal place, evil directions to her tend to greatly endanger the health; the ☽ to the ☌ or ill-asp. ♄ by dir., and espec. if the direction fall in the 6th H.; the ☽ in the 6th H. at B., and to the ☌, P., or ill-asp. any of the malefics by dir.; the ☽ to the ☌ or ill-asp. ♂ by dir., diseases according to the sign ♂ is in; the ☽ affl. at B., and to the ☌ or ill-asp. ♀, usually from indiscretions and excesses; the ☽ affl. the rising degree or the Asc. by dir.; the ☽ affl. at B., and to the cusp of the 6th, 8th, or 12th H.; in Hor'y Q. the ☽ Sig. in ♍ indicates bad health of the party, a thin, weak, and small body; the ☽ Sig. ☌ the ☉ by dir., and espec. if the ☽ be applying, and it happens in the 8th H., or the ☉ be lord of the 8th; the ☽ to the ☌ the ☉ by dir., and espec. if in ☌ or ill-asp. the ☉ at B., and either occupied the 6th H.; the prog. ☽ to the □ or ☍ the ☉, ♃, ♀, the Asc., or to the ☌ or ill-asp. any of the malefics; the prog. ☽ to the ☌ or ill-asp. ♂, and espec. with females; the prog. ☽ to the ☌ or ill-asp. ♆, and espec. if ♆ be affl. at B.; the ☽ by periodic rev. to the ☌ or ill-asp. ♄ or ♂; the ☽ passing over the place of ♄, ♂, or ♀ at a Solar Rev., and these planets affl. at B.; the ☽ to the place of Ceti, Rigel, or Hercules; the ☽ to the ☌ or P. South Scale or Regulus if the ☽ be hyleg; NEPTUNE ☌ or P., the ☉ at a Solar Rev. if the ☉ be hyleg; ♆ passing the place of the radical ☽ by tr., or in ☌ the ☽ at a Solar Rev.; ♆ or ♅ in evil asp. the ☉ or ☽ by dir.; ♆, ♅, or any malefic falling in the 6th H. by dir., and affl. the hyleg; ♅ affl. at B., and to the ☌ or ill-asp. the Asc. by dir.; the ill-asps. of ♅ to the ☉ by dir.; URANUS by periodic rev. to the ☌ ♄ or ♂ radical; SATURN

☌ or ill-asp. the ☉, ☽, Asc., or hyleg by dir.; ♄ ruler of the 6th H. at B., and in ☌ or evil asp. the Asc. by dir.; ♄ ori. of the ☉ at B., and in ill-asp. the Asc. by dir., and the Asc. be hyleg at B.; ♄ to the ill-asps. his own place by dir. or tr., or to the place of the ☉, ☽, or any planet; ♄ ruler of the 6th H. at B., and the M.C. to the ☌ or ill-asp. ♄ by dir.; ♄ ruler of the 6th H. at B., and to the ☌ or ill-asp. the Asc. by dir.; ♄ to the ill-asps. ♃ or ♀; ♄ to the ☌ or ill-asp. the ☉ or ☽ if the ☉ or ☽ are hyleg, or either ruler of the 1st, 6th, 8th, or 12th H.; ♄ ☌, □, or ☍ the ☉ at B., and when ♄ comes to the next evil asp. the ☉ by dir.; the prog. ♄ in ☌ or ill-asp. the ☉, ☽, ♃, ♀, ☿, or the Asc.; ♄ by tr. in the 1st, 6th, 8th, or 12th H.; transits of ♄ over the Asc., M.C., or the places of the ☉ and ☽ at B., and espec. if ♄ affl. the ☉ or ☽ at B., or the Asc. or M.C.; transits of ♄, ♅, or ♂ coming to the evil asps. the progressed places of the ☉ or ☽, and espec. if these aspects coincide with an evil dir.; the tr. of ♄ or other malefics thru the 6th H. if in the 6th at B., and afflicted, or afflicting the 6th, or lord of the 6th; ♄, ♅, or ♂ on the cusp of the 6th or 7th H. at B., and such degrees ascending at a Solar Rev.; ♄ at a Solar Rev. ☌ or P. asp. the radical ☉ if the ☉ be hyleg; ♄ passing over the place of the radical ☽ by tr., or in ☌ the ☽ at a Solar Rev.; ♄ passing over the place of ☿ at B., if ☿ be weak and afflicted, or ♄ ☌ ☿ at a Solar Rev.; the periodic directions of ♄ to the radical ☉, and espec. if the ☉ be hyleg; JUPITER ruler of the 1st H. at B., and to the ill-asps. ♄ by dir.; ♃ by periodic rev. to the ill-asps. the ☉ or ♂ at B.; the bad asps. of ♃ and ♂ to the prog. places of the ☉ or ☽; ♃ or ♀ prog. in □ or ☍ asp. the Asc.; bad asps. of the progressed ♃ or ♀ to the places of the radical ☉ or ☽; MARS to the cusp of the 1st, 6th, 8th, or 12th H.; ♂ to the ☌ or ill-asps. ♄ by dir.; ♂ to the place of ☋; ♂ ☌ the Asc. by dir.; ♂ to the ☌ or ill-asp. the ☽ or ♀, and generally thru abuses or debauchery; ♂ by periodic rev. to the evil asps. ♅; ♂ rising at B., and again at a Solar Rev.; ♂ on the cusp of the 6th or 7th H. at B., and such degree ascending at a Solar Rev.; ♂ at a Solar Rev. passing the place of the radical ☽, ♄, or ♀, and espec. if the ☽ and ♀ were affl. at B.; the tr. of ♂ as promittor over the place of the ☉ or ☽ at B., or in ☍ thereto; VENUS affl. at B., and to the ☌, P., or evil asp. the Asc. by dir.; ♀ Sig. to the ☌ the ☉, and the ☉ ill-dig. at B., tends to become unhealthy; the bad asps. of the prog. ♀ to the places of the prog. ☉ or ☽; ♀ prog. to the ☌ or ill-asps. ♄; ♀ by periodic rev. to the ill-asps. ♄, ♂, the ☽, or M.C. in the map of birth; MERCURY affl. at B., and to the ill-asps. the ☽; the ASCENDANT meeting the bad directions of planets; evil directions falling in the Asc.; directions of the Asc. affect the health if the Asc. is hyleg; the Asc. to the evil asps. ♃ by dir., and diseases according to the sign in which ♃ is placed; malefics in the Asc., or 1st H., at a Solar Rev.; the Asc. by dir. to the ☌ or ill-asps. ♅; the Asc. to the place of ☋ by dir.; transit of the ruler of the 1st H., or Asc., when a malefic, over the radical M.C., or ruler of the M.C.; the Asc. by dir. to the evil asps. the ☉ or ☽; the Asc. to the ☌ the ☉ by dir.; the Asc. to the ☌, P., ☐ or ☍ any of the malefics; the Asc. to the ☐ or ☍ ♀, ill-health thru excesses, pleasures, etc.; the directions to or by the Asc. are more powerful for good or evil when the Asc. is hyleg at B.; the Asc. to the ☌ or ill-asp. ♂ by dir., sickness of the nature of ♂ and the sign he is in, considered with that of the Asc.; a malefic ☌ the Asc. by dir.; the MIDHEAVEN to the ☌ or evil-asp. the ☽ by dir., and espec. if the ☽ be affl. at B., afflicted in both mind and body; malefics ☌ the M.C. by dir., according to the nature of the malefic and the sign on the M.C.; lord of the 10th a malefic, and falling in the 6th or 8th H. by dir.; lord of the 10th a malefic, and to the ☌ the ☉, ☽, Asc., or hyleg; MALEFICS by tr. over the place of the ☉ or ☽ at B. if they afflict the Lights in the radical map; ill-asps. of the malefics to the ☉ by dir., or by tr., even tho they do not afflict the ☉ at B.; a malefic by dir. or tr. falling on the place of another malefic, evil for the health, and according to the sign occupied, and the nature of the conjoined planets; malefics in the 1st or 6th H. at a Solar Rev.; the tr. of malefics thru the 6th H. if in the 6th at B., or lord of the 6th; a train of evil DIRECTIONS affl. the hyleg, and with little assistance from the benefics, and death may result; a train of good directions, if accompanied by a very evil dir. to the hyleg at the same time, may cause ill-health; an evil dir. to the hyleg signifies illness; an evil dir. falling in the Asc. or 6th H. usually affects the health adversely, and espec. if a malefic. (See "Bad Health" in this section; "Periods Of" under Acute; Directions; "Threatened with Disease", "Time of the Disease", under Disease; Events; "Signs of Ill-Health" under Ill-Health).

Periods of Good Health—The influences at birth, and along thru life, which tend to Good Health—(See "Good Health" in this section).

Pestilence; Pleasure—The Health Injured by Excessive and Inordinate Pleasures — (See Excesses, Lust, Passion, Pleasure, Sports, etc.).

Plethora; Poor Health — (See "Bad Health" in this section. Also see Chronic, Emaciated, Feeble, Ill-Health, Infirm, Invalid, Sickly, Sickness, Wastings; "Body" under Weak, etc.).

Premature — Premature Ill-Health — Short Life— (See "Early Death" under Early; "Short Life" under Life; "Dies Before Middle Life" under Middle Life).

Promoted — The Health Promoted — (See Better, Enhanced, Improved, Strengthened, in this section).

Prospects—Of Good Health and Long Life—The prospects of good health and long life are based upon the positions of the ☉ and ☽ at B., the hyleg and its aspects, the ☉ hyleg in a male nativity, and the ☽ hyleg in the female, and with many good asps. to the ☉, ☽, Asc., or hyleg. (See Hyleg, Immunity; "Long

Life" under Life; Vitality Good. Also see Abundance, Good Health, in this section). For Prospects and Indications along the lines of ill-health see "Bad Health" in this section; Ill-Health, Invalids; "Much Sickness" under Sickness; Vitality Low; "Weak Body" under Weak.

Public Health—(See Epidemics; Pestilence, Prevalent; "Health" under Public).

Rarely Good—The Health Rarely Good —Rarely Bad—(See "Ill-Health All thru Life" under Ill-Health; Bad Health, Good Health, Improved, Promoted, Prospects, and the various paragraphs in this section).

Recuperative Powers—(See Recuperation).

Relatives — Health of — (See Aunts, Brothers, Children, Daughter, Family, Father, Grandparents, Husband, Mother, Relatives, Sister, Son, Uncles).

Residence—The Effect of the Location and Residence upon the Health—(See "Location" in this section).

Resistance—The Powers of Resistance Against Disease—(See Resistance).

Restoratives — Of Health — (See Analeptics, Cure, Diet, Drugs, Food, Healers, Medicines, Remedies, Tonics, Treatment, etc.).

Robust Health—(See Robust, Ruddy, Strong, Vitality Good. Also see "Good Health" in this section).

Ruddy; Rugged Health—(See Robust, Ruddy).

Rules—For Judging the Health—(See "Judging the Health" in this section).

Seven Year Periods — Danger of Ill-Health Every Seven Years—The ☽ affl. by ♄ at B. tends to ill-health every seven years, due to the new evil asps. formed between them; the ☐ and ☍ of ♄ to his own place by transit occurs about every seven years, tending to ill-health, and which may become chronic for a time. (See Periods).

Short Life—(See "Death" under Childhood, Children, Infancy; "Early Death" under Early; "Short" under Life; Untimely).

Sickly; Sickness — (See the various paragraphs under Disease, Ill-Health, Sickness. Also see the various paragraphs in this section).

Significators—Of Health—(See "Indicators" in this section).

Signs — Signs of Bad Health — Signs of Good Health—Signs of Death—Signs of Long and Short Life, etc.—(See Bad Health, Good Health, and the various paragraphs in this section. Also see Death, Disease, Ill-Health, Life, Sickness, etc.).

Sister—Health of—(See Sister).

Sixth House—The House of Health—(See Sixth, Virgo).

Son — Health of — (See "First Born", "Sons", under Children; Males, Sons).

Sound Body — Sound Constitution — Sound Mind In a Sound Body — (See "Good Health" in this section; "Good" under Constitution; "Sound Mind" under Mind; Sound).

Specialties — Health Specialties — Makers of — (See "Specialties" under Healers).

Stamina—(See Endurance, Recuperation, Resistance, Stamina, Strength, Tone, Vitality, etc.).

State of the Health—The 6th H. and the ♍ sign, and the influences in each, indicate the state of the health in the ordinary course of human life. Also the ☉ and ☽, their sign, house positions and aspects, have much to do with the state of the health, and when the Lights are strong, dignified, well-placed, and free from affliction, the constitution is strong and better able to resist disease. The ☉ rising tends to a better state of health. The Lights, when afflicted, or afflicting each other at B., tend to more frequent sickness and to poorer health. (See Bad, Enhanced, Good, Improved, Strengthened, Weakened, and the various paragraphs in this section).

Strength— Loss of—Much Strength— (See "Loss Of", and the various paragraphs in this section. Also see the various subjects under Strength, Strong, Vitality, Weak).

Strengthened — The Health Strengthened—♂ in aspect to the ☉ tends to strengthen the system, and give greater vitality. (See Abundance, Enhanced, Improved, in this section. Also see "Increased" under Strength, Vitality).

Strong Body — (See "Body" under Strong).

Stronger—The health is stronger when the ☉ is elevated above the Earth, and well-aspected in a day nativity, and also when the ☽ is above the horizon in a night nativity, as the ☉ rules by day, and the ☽ by night; the ☉ rising and elevated in the East at B., and espec. when in his own sign ♌; fiery or airy signs upon the Asc. (See Day, Good Health, Improved, Night, Strengthened, in this section).

Suffers—The Health Suffers—(See Bad Health, Impaired, Opposite Sex, Weak, Weakened, in this section).

System Disordered—(See "Bad Health", and the various paragraphs in this section. Also see "Disordered" under System).

Tendency— To Ill-Health—(See "Bad Health" in this section. Also see Tendency" under Disease, Ill-Health).

Tolerably Healthy — Tolerably Good Health—♀ well-aspected in the 6th H. if the health is not abused by excesses and indiscretions; the ☽ angular, and the Lights nearly free from affliction; ♑, ♒, or ♓ on the Asc., or the ☉ or ☽ in these signs, the Winter signs. (See "Medium Vitality" under Vitality).

Tone — (See Stamina, Tone, Vitality).

Transits — The Effects of upon the Health—(See Transits).

Travel — Traveling for the Health — Where To Go—If the 9th H. of the radical map shows favorable conditions for Foreign Travel, travel Abroad in those Countries ruled by the Signs in which you have ♃ or ♀ at B., unless these planets are badly aspected. If short journeys are taken, and the 3rd

H. at B. is well-aspected and fortunate, travel in the directions in which you have the benefics at B., if they are well-aspected. Much travel will be apt to be engaged in for the health when ♀ is affl. in the 6th H. at B. (See Location; "Native Land" under Land; Residence; "Health" under Travel).

Uncertain Health—The ☽ affl. in the 6th H.

Uncles—Health of—(See Uncles).

Undermined—The Health Undermined and Injured by Abuses, Debauchery, Dissipation, Excesses, Extravagance, High Living, Sex Excesses, etc.—♂ to the ♂ or ill-asp. the ☽ or ♀; ♀ affl. in the 2nd, 5th, or 6th H.; ♀ in ♏ ♂ ♂ or the ☽, and generally thru sex excesses; ♀ affl. in the 6th H., from over-study or over-work. (See Debauchery, Depraved, Dissipation, Drink, Excesses, Extravagance, Feasting, Gluttony, High Living (see High); Passion, Pleasures, Plethora, Reading, Sex Excesses (see Sex); Sports, Study, Surfeits, Venery).

Unfortunate — As to Health and In General — (See Fate; "Ill-Health All Thru Life" under Ill-Health; "Much Sickness" under Sickness; Unfortunate. Also see "Bad Health" in this section).

Unhealthy — (See Feeble, Infirm, Invalids, Pale, Sickly, Vitality Low; "Body" under Weak. Also see "Bad Health", and the various paragraphs in this section).

Venery—Bad Health Thru—(See Venery).

Virgo Sign—The Sign of Health—(See Virgo. Also see "State of the Health" in this section).

Vital Forces — Depletion of — (See Vital).

Vitality—(See the various paragraphs under Vitality).

Wards Off Disease—(See "Wards Off" under Disease).

Weak Body — Weak Health — (See Sickly, Vitality Low; "Body" under Weak; "Bad Health" in this section).

Weakened—The Health Weakened— The Health Weaker—(See "Short Life" under Life; "Lessened" under Vitality; "Weakened", "Weaker" under Weak. Also see Bad Health, Impaired, Enfeebled, Undermined, and the various paragraphs in this section).

Wife—The Health of—(See Husband, Wife).

Will Improve — The Health Will Improve — (See "Improved" in this section).

Women — The Health of — (See Females, Mother, Opposite Sex, Sister, Women).

Worries — Is Worried and Anxious About the Health—♅ affl. in the 6th H. (See Hypochondria).

Worry — Ill-Health Thru Worry — ♀ affl. in the 6th H. (See Dejected, Depressed, Despondency; Low Spirits (see Low); Melancholy, Worry, etc.).

Worse—The Health Worse—The Disease Turns for the Worse — (See Chronic, Crises; "Worse" under Disease; Worse. Also see Bad Health, Undermined, Weakened, in this section).

Worst Position—For the Health—The ☉ ♂ ♄ in the 6th H., or in □ or ⅄ with either in this house, is one of the worst positions and aspects at B. for the health. (See "Ill-Health All Thru Life" under Ill-Health; "Much Sickness" under Sickness; Vitality Low; "Body" under Weak).

Years — Good and Bad Years for the Public Health—(See Public).

Youth—Health In—(See Youth). For other subjects concerning the health, and which may not be listed in this Article, look for the subject in the alphabetical arrangement.

HEALTHY—Strong—Robust—Ruddy—

Appearance — Healthy Appearance — (See "Good", "Red", under Complexion; Robust, Ruddy, etc.).

Body — Healthy Body — (See Robust, Ruddy, Strong, Vitality Good. Also see "Abundance", "Good Health", under Health).

Children — Healthy Children — (See "Healthy" under Children).

Constitution—A Healthy Constitution —(See "Good", and the various paragraphs under Constitution; Robust, Ruddy, Strong, etc.).

Healthy Make—Strong, Robust, Plump, and Well-Set—A Healthy Make—♒ on the Asc. at B. (See Well-Made).

Healthy and Strong — Fire Signs on the Asc. at B.; ♒ on the Asc. (See "Body" under Strong; Vitality Good).

Tolerably Healthy—(See "Tolerably" under Health).

Year—A Healthy Year for the People — (See "Public Health Good" under Public).

Unhealthy—(See Sickly, Unhealthy).

HEARING—The Sense of Hearing—The Hearing is ruled by ☿, the □ sign, and the 12th H. The sense vibrations are ruled by ☿. Also ☿ rules the speech. The □ sign, ruled by ☿, corresponds to the atmospheric vibrations, and has affinity with the sense of hearing. In the Hindu System of Astrology the Hearing is ruled by the 3rd H. The Hebrew letter Vau, which letter is connected with the ⅄ sign, is predominant in Mind and Hearing, and is also closely related to the transformation of thought into speech. The Ears are the organs of Hearing, and the Ears have special affinity with ☿ and the ⅄ sign. The 12th H., and its conditions at B., tend to especially affect the hearing, as this house is closely connected with the Senses, and limitations upon them, and in cases of deafness, ☿ and the 12th H., are usually badly afflicted. In our system of Astrology the 1st H. also rules and affects the ears, and the ♈ sign also has some influence over the ears and hearing, as ♈ rules the head. The hearing of the right ear is more especially affected by ♄, and that of the left ear by ♂. (See the various paragraphs under Ears). In this Article the Hearing, its condition, defects, impediments, deafness, etc., will be considered.

Acute—The Hearing Very Acute—☿ in □, ♎, or ♒, and well-aspected by ♂.

The hearing becomes less and less acute by the clogging of the Auditory Nerve. (See "Auditory" in this section).

Auditory Nerve — Clogging of — This nerve, and the organs of hearing, and the sense of hearing in general, are ruled by ☿. Clogging and inhibition of the Auditory Nerve are due to mineral deposits by ♄, and espec. when ☿ is affl. in the 12th H., and the hearing becomes less and less acute; Subs at AT and AX.

Blood—Deafness Due to Ill-Blood In the Veins of the Ears, or Congestion In the Blood Vessels—♃ influence; ♃ in ♈, and affl. by ♄. (See Circulation, Deafness, in this section).

Bones of the Ears—Deafness Due to Hardening of—♄ influence; ♄ affl. in ♈. (See "Deafness" in this section).

Born Deaf—Born Deaf, Dumb, Imbecile, Blind and Lame—Case—See "Arundel", No. 159, in 1001 N.N. Being born deaf is due to prenatal afflictions, as a rule. Natal aspects and conditions also may concur, as ♄ affl. in ♈ or ⅄ at B.; ♄ ♂ ☿ in ♈ in the 12th H. (See Congenital, Prenatal; "Deaf and Dumb" in this section).

Catarrh—Deafness From—Catarrhal Deafness—♄ affl. in ⅄; ♄ affl. in ⅄ in the 12th H.; ♄ affl. in ♈. (See Catarrh, Eustachian).

Circulation Obstructed — Causing Deafness—♃ in ♈, and affl. by ♄; ♀ in the 12th H., and affl. by ♄, ☿ or ♂, the venous circulation in the ears obstructed, tending to deafness. (See "Blood" in this section).

Clogging — Of the Auditory Nerve — Deafness From — (See "Auditory" in this section).

Colds or Chills — Deafness From — ♄ affl. in ♈. (See Colds).

Congestion of Blood — In the Ears — Deafness From — (See Blood, Circulation, in this section).

Danger To the Hearing—☿ affl. in the 12th H. tends to bring dangers to the ears and the sense of hearing, and denotes a limitation upon the Spirit in its manifestation thru the senses on the material plane of life. (See "Disordered" under Ears; Limitations, Twelfth House).

Deafness—Liable to Deafness—Debility of Hearing—Impediment In the Hearing—The ☉ ♂ ☿ in the 12th H. in □ or ♍, and affl. by malefics; the ☉, ♀, and ☿ in ♂ in ♓ in the 12th H., and affl. by ♄, ♅, or ♂; the ☉ or ☽ in ♂ with ☿ in any part of the map, and affl. by ♄ or ♂; the ☽ decr. in light, sepr. from ♄ and apply. to ☿; the ☽ incr. in a day nativity, sepr. from ♀ and apply. to ♄; the ☽ sepr. from ♂ and apply. to the ☉; the ☽ ♂ ☿ in the 12th H., and affl. by ♄ or ♂; ♄ afflictions tend to; ♄ in the houses or terms of ☿; ♄ □ or ♂ ☿, and espec. if ☿ be lord of the 6th or 12th H.; ♄ tends to deafness by hardening of the bones of the ears, and interfering with vibration; ♄ afflictions tend to deafness by deposits of minerals along the auditory nerve, clogging this nerve and stopping vibration; ♄ occi. in ♈ and affl. the ☉, ☽, or Asc.; signified by

♄ in ♈ when he is the afflictor in the disease; ♄ in the 6th H., and afflicting ☿; ♄ in the 12th H. in ☌ or ill-asp. ☿; ♄ affl. the hyleg or Asc.; ♄ in ♈, thru colds or chills; ♄, ♅, or ♆ in ♒ and affl. the ☉ or ☽, slight deafness; ♄ affl. in ♒; ♄ in ♉; ♆ or ♅ in ♈ or ♒, and affl. the ☉, ☽, or ☿; ♅ in the 12th H. ☌ ☿; ♃ in ♈ and affl. by ♄, due to congestion in the blood vessels, or ill blood in the head and ears, but mostly of a slight and temporary nature; ♂ in ♈ and affl. ☿, and both ♂ and ☿ affl. by ♄, and espec. when the 12th H. is also concerned in the configuration; ♀ in the 12th H. in the terms of ☿, and affl. by ♄, ♂, or ☿, the venous circulation in the ear is obstructed; ☿ affl. in ♈, ♉, ♏, or ♓; ☿ affl. in ♉ in the 12th H.; ☿ weak and affl. at B.; ☿ ☌ the ☉ in the 12th H., and affl. by malefics; afflictions to ☿ in ♓, the 12th sign; ☿ affl. in the 12th H., or combust the ☉, congestion in the ears may follow, and with lack of nerve force and the vital fluids to the ears; ☿ affl. in the 12th H.; ☿ in the 12th H. in ☌ ♆ and in ☐ or ☍ ♃, tends to poor circulation in the ears; ☿ in the 12th H., and affl. by ♄; ☿ in the 12th H., and espec. in earthy or watery signs, and affl. by ♅, ♄, or ♂; ☿ ruling the 12th H., and in ☌ the ☉, or affl. by ♅, ♄, or ♂, or with ☿ in the 12th and so afflicted (☿ ruling the intellect is thus held in bondage thru the 12th H. influence); ☿ in the 5th H. in ♋, ♏, or ♓, in the map of a parent or of the child, the infant may be deaf, insane, or deformed; ☿ lord of the 6th H., and affl. by ♄; ☿ lord of the 6th or 12th, and ☿ posited in the 6th; ☿ in a sign of ♄, and in the 10th or 12th H., and affl. by ♄, ♅, or ♂; in deafness ☿ is nearly always afflicted by a malefic, and is usually in the 12th H.; afflictions in the ♍ sign are also quite common and conspicuous in deafness, and espec. with ♍ upon the Asc., the 6th or 12th H.; ☐ or ♍ on the cusp of the 12th H., and with ☿ affl. in any part of the map. Cases—See Fig. 7, 8, 30, 31, in "Message of the Stars", and Fig. 17C, in "Astro-Diagnosis", books by the Heindels. (See "Deaf and Dumb", and the various paragraphs in this section).

Deaf and Dumb—Deaf Mute—This condition is caused by a combination of the influences which cause deafness and inability of speech, and as ☿ rules both the hearing and the speech, this planet is usually heavily afflicted either during gestation, or at birth. The 12th H., the house of limitations, is also strongly involved. The following planetary influences tend to produce this double affliction,—☿ is usually afflicted by ♄ or ♂, and also the 12th H. is involved; ☿ ruler of the Asc., and affl. in the 12th H.; ♄ and ♂ ☌ ☿ in the 12th H., and espec. when in ♈; malefics and afflictions in the mute signs ♋, ♏, or ♓. This affliction, when congenital, may be caused by afflictions to the ☽ and ☿ at the time of the monthly return of the ☽ to the central line of impulse during gestation, and the planetary positions at B. may not enter into its causes at all. Also the map for the time of conception may give some clue to the disorder, and the conditions over the 12th H. and ☿ at con-

ception, and a study of the Prenatal Epoch should be made in these cases. There is also an Occult significance back of these cases, as involved in the doctrine of Karma, the Laws of Cause and Effect, of Consequence, of Heredity, and as taught in Theosophy and Rosicrucianism, and it would be well for the advanced student to read the Chapter on "The Law of Consequence" in the book "Cosmo-Conception", by Max Heindel. Also read Chap. XXVII, on "Prenatal Abnormalities" in the book "The Prenatal Epoch" by Mr. E. H. Bailey. Cases—Birth Data of Cases of Deaf and Dumb—(1) Jan. 4th, 1834, 10:55 P.M., London, Eng. (2) See "Arundel", No. 159, and "Deaf and Dumb", No. 166, in 1001 N.N. (See Congenital, Defects, Deformities, Heredity, Imbecility, Limitations, Monstrosities, Mutes, Prenatal, Speech, Twelfth House, Born Deaf, Deafness; Deaf, Dumb and Blind; Deaf, Dumb and Idiot, in this section).

Deaf, Dumb and Blind—Caused by the combined influences which lead to Deafness, Dumbness, and Blindness, and with such configurations existing during the prenatal life, and which may also be concurred in at birth in congenital cases of this kind. May also be caused, or concurred in, when the ☉ or ☽ are in ☌ Nebulous Clusters at B., such as the Hyades, Pleiades, etc. Many afflictions in and to the 12th H. at B. or during gestation, would tend to such extreme limitations upon the senses and physical organism, as with a Stellium in the 12th H., the ☉, ☽, ☿, and malefics in the 12th H., and possibly in ♓ in the 12th, as ♓ is also the 12th sign, and the sign of limitations, sorrows, etc. Also if Nebulous Stars be there with the group in the 12th H. at the time, the sight would be greatly endangered, and the blindness be added. (See "Born Blind", "Deaf and Dumb", in this section).

Deaf, Dumb and Idiot—In Idiocy ☿ is also the principal planet to be considered, and also the 12th H., the house of limitations, and Idiocy is only another of the physical and mental limitations which can be added to deafness, dumbness, blindness, imbecility, etc., at B. Case—See "Deaf and Dumb", No. 166 in 1001 N.N. Case—Born Jan. 27, 1900, 3:50 a.m., 50.44 N., 2 deg. W. Died Jan. 16, 1902. (See Idiots, Mutes; Deafness, Deaf and Dumb, in this section).

Deaf, Dumb, Blind and Lame—In Lameness afflictions to ☿ also play an important part, and afflictions in the 12th H., which house corresponds to the 12th sign ♓, and which may result in serious disability to the lower limbs and feet, causing lameness. Such afflictions, combined with those leading to Blindness, Deafness, Mutes, etc., could cause such a combination of unfortunate limitations. Case—See "Arundel", No. 159 in 1001 N.N. (See "Born Blind" under Blindness; Imbecility, Mutes, Lameness; Born Deaf, Deaf and Dumb, in this section).

Debility of Hearing—(See "Deafness", and the various paragraphs in this section).

Defective Hearing—(See the various paragraphs in this section; "Defects" under Ears).

Delusions—Of Hearing—Hallucinations of—A ♉ disease and affliction; ♉ affl. in ♈; ♉ ♂ or ill-asp. ☿, and espec. in the 12th H.; a ♄ disease, and caused by the afflictions of ♄ to ☿. (See Clairaudience, Delirium, Delusions, Hallucinations, Illusions, Paranoia).

Destroyed—The Hearing Destroyed On One Side—Case—Run Over and Skull Fractured at Five Years of Age—See "Run Over", No. 853, in 1001 N.N. (See Deafness, Loss Of, and the various paragraphs in this section).

Dulling—Of the Sense of Hearing—(See Auditory Nerve, Deafness, Slight, in this section).

Dumb and Deaf—(See "Deaf and Dumb" in this section; Mutes).

Ears—(See the various paragraphs under Ears).

Eustachian Tubes—The Hearing Impeded Thru Disorders of—(See Eustachian).

Fever—The Hearing Affected Thru High Fevers, as in Delirium, the Hearing of Voices, etc.—(See the influences under Delirium; "High Fevers" under Fever; "Delusions" in this section).

Gestation—The Hearing Affected During—Born Deaf, etc.—(See Born Deaf, Deaf and Dumb, in this section).

Hallucinations—Of Hearing—(See Delusions, Fever, in this section).

Hardening of Bones—Of the Ears—Deafness Due To—(See "Bones" in this section).

Hears Voices—(See Delusions, Fever, Voices, in this section).

High Fevers—Disturbances of the Hearing By—(See "Fever" in this section).

Idiot—Born Deaf, Dumb, and Idiot—(See "Deaf, Dumb, and Idiot" in this section).

Ill-Blood—In the Veins of the Ears—Deafness From—(See "Blood" in this section).

Imbecility—Case—Born Deaf, Dumb, and Imbecile—(See "Born Deaf" in this section).

Impediment—In the Hearing—(See "Deafness", and the various paragraphs in this section; Impediments).

Infancy—Deafness In—(See "Deformed" under Infancy).

Inhibition—Of the Hearing and Auditory Nerve—(See Auditory, Bones, Deafness, in this section; Inhibitions).

Insanity—And the Hearing—The same ♉ influences which are involved in Insanity, and also in Epilepsy, are also listed as causes of Deafness, and the delusions of Hearing in Insanity, the hearing of voices, are usually caused by an afflicted ♉, and also where the 12th H. is afflicted at the same time, or ♉ affl. by ♄ and ♂. (See Delusions, Hallucinations; "Causes" under Insanity).

Left Ear—The left ear is ruled by ♂,

and the afflictions of ♂ to ☿ tend to deafness and impediments in this ear. (See "Left Ear" under Ears; "Ears" under Left; "Right Ear" in this section).

Liable to Deafness—Tendency To—Danger of—(See Danger To, Deafness, and the various paragraphs in this section).

Limitations—Upon the Senses, and Upon the Hearing—(See Limitations, Twelfth House; Auditory, Bones, Impediment, Inhibition, and the various paragraphs in this section).

Loss of Hearing—Case—See Fig. 7 in the book, "Message of the Stars" by Max Heindel. (See Deafness, Destroyed, and the various paragraphs in this section).

Malformations—In the Ears—Deafness Due To—♄ affl. in ♈. Also may be due to prenatal influences. (See Defects; "Defects" under Ears; Malformations; Bones, Deafness, Deaf and Dumb, in this section).

Monstrosities—Defective Births—Congenital Deformities—(See Monstrosities; Born Deaf; Deaf and Dumb; Deaf, Dumb and Blind, in this section).

Mutes—A Deaf Mute—(See "Deaf and Dumb" in this section; Mutes).

Nerves—The Auditory Nerves Affected—(See "Auditory" in this section).

Obstructed—The Circulation In the Ears Obstructed—The Auditory Nerve Clogged—Deafness From—(See Auditory, Blood, Circulation, Impediment, Inhibition, in this section).

One Ear—Loss of Hearing In One Ear—On One Side—The afflictions of ♄ tend especially to deafness in the right ear, and the afflictions of ♂ to loss of hearing in the left ear. Case—Hearing Destroyed in One Ear—See Destroyed, Left, Right, in this section).

Paranoia—The Hearing Affected In—The same influences which tend to Paranoia also tend to affect the hearing, and cause delusions of hearing. (See Paranoia; Delusions, Voices, in this section).

Partial Deafness—Slight—Temporary—♉ affl. in ♈, and resulting from an abscess in the frontal sinuses; ♉ in ♈ and affl. by the ☉, ♄, or ♂; ♉ in ♈ or ♉ in ♂ ♄; ♄ affl. in ♉; ♄, ♉, or ♅ in ♒, and affl. the ☉ or ☽), slight deafness; ☿ in ♑, ♂, □, or ☍ ♄, and espec. when in a cardinal sign. (See Left, Right, in this section).

Prenatal Epoch—Many causes of Deafness may arise during gestation, or the Prenatal Period. For a general study along this line see Congenital, Defects, Deformities, Malformations, Monstrosities, Prenatal. Also see Deafness, Deaf and Dumb, in this section).

Right Ear—Ruled by ♄, and the ♄ afflictions to ☿, the Asc., and the 12th H. tend to deafness and defects in the right ear. (See "Ear" under Right; "Left" in this section).

Sense of Hearing—Dulling of—(See "Dulling" in this section).

Slight Deafness—(See "Partial" in this section).

Speech—And the Hearing—Both are ruled by ☿. (See the Introduction, and "Deaf and Dumb" in this section; Speech).

Temporary Deafness—(See "Partial" in this section).

Tendency—To Deafness—(See Danger, Deafness, and the various paragraphs in this section).

Twelfth House—The Effect of Upon the Hearing—(See the Introduction, Deafness, and the various paragraphs in this Article).

Vibration—Vibration In the Ear Stopped, Tending to Deafness—(See Auditory, Bones, Deafness, in this section; Vibration).

Vital Fluids—Lack of In the Ears—Deafness From—(See the ☿ influences under "Deafness" in this section; "Circulation" under Ears).

Voices—Hears Voices—This may be due to highly developed clairvoyant and clairaudient faculties, and also to planetary afflictions causing disturbances in the vibratory apparatus of the ears, and may be caused by the afflictions of ♆ or ♄ in the ♈ or ♉ signs, and also with the 12th H. badly afflicted, and also ☿ involved in the configuration. (See Delusions, Fever, Vibration, in this section; Clairvoyance, Clairaudience, Insanity, Mediumship, Neptune, Obsessions, Spirit Controls).

Weak Hearing—Weak Ears—The ☉, ☽, and ☿ in ♂, and affl. by ♄ or ♂; ☿ affl. in the 12th H. (See the various paragraphs under Ears, Weak).

HEART—The Heart—Cardia—Cardiac —The Heart is ruled by the ☉, the ♌ sign, and the 5th H. Is under the internal rulership of ♌. All the fixed signs, as ♉, ♌, ♏, and ♒ tend to affect and influence the heart and its action for good or ill, as these signs make up the Fixed Cross, and all are in □ or ☍ asp. to each other. The ☉ in ♌ rules the structure of the heart. The ☽ in ♌, the functions of the heart, and the pericardium; ♆ in ♌, the depressor nerve; ♅ in ♌, the valves; ♄ in ♌, the left auricle and the endocardium; ♃ in ♌, the arteries and right auricle; ♂ in ♌, the muscles; ♀ in ♌, the veins and aorta; ☿ in ♌, the nerves. The left ventricle and the arterial blood are ruled and influenced by ♃, and ♀ rules the right ventricle and the venous blood. The ventricles are also ruled by ♌ in a general way, and the valves by ♅. The heart in the male is ruled by the ☉, and in the female is strongly influenced by the ☽, her aspects, and espec. when the ☽ is in ♌ at B., or in a fixed sign. The ☉ and ☽ acting thru the ♌ sign, and thru the Splanchnic Ganglia, tend to affect the Cardia, the Heart, the 5th, 6th, 7th, 8th, and 9th dorsal vertebrae, the upper part of the stomach, and give way to the Cardiac Diathesis. (See Cardiac). In Hor'y Q. the heart is signified by planets in the following signs—the ☉ in ♏ or ♐; the ☽ in ♎ or ♏; ♄ in ♉ or ♊; ♃ in ♈, ♋, or ♓; ♂ in ♌, ♒, or ♓; ♀ in ♌, ♍, ♑, or ♒; ☿ in ♍, ♎, ♐, ♑, or ♒. (See Table in Chap. XXIX, page 179, in Lilly's

Astrology, showing the signification of each of the planets in the 12 Signs). The ♃ Group of Herbs tend to have a pathological action on the cardiac muscle. The therapeutic properties of ☉ remedies are cardiac, and affect the heart action. The following subjects have to do with the heart, its structure, action, functions, diseases, etc., which subjects see in the alphabetical arrangement when not considered here—

Accelerated Action—Rapid Pulse—High Pulse—The ☉ ♂ or ill-asp. ♂; the ☽ in ♈ or ♊, and affl. by the ☉ or ♂ when taken ill; the ☽ in ♉, ♂, □, or ☍ ♄ (or ☿ if he be of the nature of ♄) when taken ill, or at decumb., and occasioned by surfeits, high living, etc. (See "High" under Pulse).

Action of the Heart—Good Heart Action—The Action Disturbed—(See the various paragraphs in this section).

Affected—The fixed signs, and espec. the ♌ sign, tend to affect the heart. The heart is affected when the ☉ is in ♌, ♏, and fixed signs; the ☽ in ♎; ♅ in ♊; ♄ in ♉; ♃ in ♋ or ♓; ♀ in ♌, ♍, or ♒; ☿ in ♍, ♎, or ♒. This is according to the plan as given in Table 196 in Simmonite's Arcana. For explanation of the Table see "Affected" under Head. The heart is also affected by any planet in ♌, and afflicted, and also when ♌, or a fixed sign, may be upon the Asc. at B., and afflicted. (See the various paragraphs in this section).

Afflicted — Affliction At the Heart — The Heart Afflicted—The ☉ or ☽ affl. in ♌ or ♒; afflictions in ♌ or ♒, and the fixed signs. (See "Heart Trouble", and the various paragraphs in this section).

All Diseases—Of the Heart—Are signified by ♌ and the 5th H., and afflictions therein.

Aneurysm—Of the Aorta—♂ affl. in ♌. (See Aneurysm, Aorta).

Angina—Angina Pectoris— Pain and Oppression About the Heart—(See Angina).

Aorta—Diseases of—Aneurysm—(See Aneurysm, Aorta).

Arteries—Of the Heart—Disorders of —♃ affl. in ♌. (See Aneurysm, Aorta, Arteries).

Arythmia Cordis—(See "Rhythm" in this section).

Asthma—(See "Heart Asthma" under Asthma).

Atrophy Of—♄ affl. in ♌. (See Atrophy).

Auricles—Auricular Disorders—♃ affl. in ♌ tends to disorders of the right auricle; ♄ in ♌, the left auricle, and also to organic auricular weakness. (See "Organic" in this section).

Blood Obstructions — Obstruction of the Blood Thru the Heart—♅ affl. in ♌, thru valvular trouble; ♄ affl. in ♌, due to organic heart weakness, muscular weakness, poor circulation, etc.; ♄ ♂ ♃ or ♀ in ♌. (See "Obstructions" under Blood; "Poor Circulation" under Circulation; Obstructions; Arteries, Fever, Leaky, Valves, Veins, in this section). For Spasmodic Gushing of the Blood thru the Aorta, see Aorta.

Blood Vessels — Of the Heart — (See Aneurysm, Aorta, Arteries, Auricles, Blood, Veins, in this section).

Bradycardia — Abnormally Slow Action of the Heart — Slow Pulse — (See "Slow" under Pulse).

Broken Heart — Dies of a Broken Heart — (See Broken).

Cardiac — Cardiac Diathesis — Cardiac Disease — Cardiac Dropsy — Cardiac Inhibitions — C a r d i a c Orifice — Cardiac Sedatives — (S e e Cardiac; Diathesis, Dropsy, Heart Trouble, Inhibitions, Orifice, Sedatives, and the various paragraphs in this section).

Cardialgia — (See Angina, Heartburn, Pain, in this section).

Carditis — Inflammation of the Heart —The ☽ or ♂ affl. in ♌. (See Endocarditis, Inflamed, Pericarditis, in this section).

Cases of Heart Trouble—Birth Data, etc.—See "Heart Disease", No. 082, and No. 104, in 1001 N.N. See Figures 5A, 5B, 5C, 5D, 5E, in the book "Astro-Diagnosis" by the Heindels. See Figures 19, 24, 25, 33, in "Message of the Stars", by the Heindels. See Case, Male, Chap. 8, page 48, in Daath's Medical Astrology. (See all the paragraphs in this section for the various forms and manifestations of heart trouble).

Chronic Disease — Of the Heart — The ☉ hyleg, and to the ♂ or ill-asp. ♄ by dir.; ♄ affl. in ♌. (See "Chronic" under Back; Chronic, Stomach).

Circulation—The Circulation Thru the Heart Disturbed—(See "Blood" in this section; "Poor Circulation" under Circulation).

Constrictions—(See Constrictions; "Orifice" in this section).

Contractions—(See Orifice, Valves, in this section; Constrictions, Contractions).

Coronary Plexuses — (See Coronary; "Middle Cervical" under Ganglion).

Cramps—In the Heart—♅ in ♌. (See Cramps).

Cyanosis — Due to Heart Trouble — Incomplete Heart—(See the Case under Cyanosis; "Incomplete" in this section).

Death—From Heart Trouble, or Heart Failure—Fixed signs dispose to; fixed signs on angles, and many planets in fixed signs at B.; many afflictions in fixed signs, and espec. in ♌ and affl.; ♃ much afflicted at B., and affl. the hyleg by dir., tends to death from heart failure. (See Death).

Debility—Of the Heart — (See Heart Trouble, Weak, and the various paragraphs in this section).

Deformity—Of the Heart — (See Incomplete, Malformation, in this section).

Degeneration — (See "Fatty" in this section).

Depleted Action—Weak Heart—♄ in ♌. (See Feeble, Impeded, Weak, in this section).

Depressor Nerves — Of t h e H e a r t — Ruled and affected by ♆ in ♌. (See "Nerves" in this section).

Deranged Heart — (See "Heart Trouble", and the various paragraphs in this section).

Diet — Ailments of the Heart Due to Wrong Diet—♃ affl. in ♌. (See "Ailments" under Diet).

Dilatation—Of the Heart—Cardiectasis—The ☽, ♃, ♂, or ♀ affl. in ♌. (See Aneurysm, Aorta; "Dilatation" under Arteries; "Too Much Blood" under Blood; Dilatations, Distentions).

Disease—Heart Disease—Diseases— (See "Heart Trouble", and the various paragraphs in this section).

Disorders Of — (See "Heart Trouble", and the various paragraphs in this section).

Displacement Of — (See "Right Side" in this section).

Distention Of — (See "Dilatation" in this section).

Disturbed Action — ♅ ☌ ☽ in ♋, and ☐ ♂ tends to disturbed heart action from gas in the stomach. (See Affected, Heart Trouble, Irregular, Rapid, Rhythm, Suspended, Weak, and the various paragraphs in this section).

Dorsal Region — The Dorsal Region of the Spine, and the Middle Dorsal Nerves, are ruled by the ☉ and ♌, and afflictions in ♌ tend to affect this region, the back, and the heart, and also to cause Subs of the Dorsal Vertebrae. (See Back, Dorsal, Spine).

Dropsy—Of the Heart—Dropsy from Heart Trouble — Dropsy from Weak Heart Action—An ♒ disease, and many planets affl. in ♒ at B.; the ☉ in ♒ in ♂, P., or ill-asp. ♄; ♆ affl. in ♎ or ♓ in the 6th H., or affl. the Asc., or hyleg; Subs at HP, Lu.P., KP. (See Dropsy; Blood, Weak, in this section).

Drought—♌ ascending at the Vernal Equi., tends to Drought, and suffering from heart disorders among People in Countries ruled by ♌. (See "Disease" under Drought).

Drug Heart—♆ affl. in ♌ tends to suspension of the heart action thru drugs, sleeping potions, opiates, and narcotics; ♆ in the 5th H., or on cusp the 5th, or in ♉ thereto. (See "Drug Habit" under Narcotics).

Drugs—Herbs—The Action of on the Heart — The therapeutic properties of ☉ remedies are cardiac, and affect the heart action. The ♃ Group of Herbs tend to have a pathological action on the cardiac muscle. (S e e "Jupiter Group", "Sun Group", under Herbs; "Typical Drugs" under Jupiter, Sun. Also see "Remedies" in this section).

Endocarditis — ♄ in ♌ rules and affects the endocardium; ♂ affl. in ♌; ♂ in ♋ in the 5th H. (See Carditis, Pericarditis, in this section).

Enlarged Heart—Hypertrophy of—♆ in ♌ and affl. by ♄; ♅ affl. in ♌; ♃ influence tends to an enlarged heart by the formation of fat and adipose tissue; ♃, ♂, or ♀ affl. in ♌; ♂ in ♌, and affl. the hyleg; ♂ in ♌ in the 6th H. tends espec. to hypertrophy of the heart; Subs at HP. Case—Of Enlarged Heart —See "Hypertrophied", No. 082, in 1001 N.N. (See Enlarged, Expansions, Hypertrophy).

Excesses—Palpitation, and Disturbed Heart Action Thru Excesses—♀ affl. in ♌. (See Excesses; "Palpitation" in this section).

Excitement—Palpitation Due to Haste and Excitement—The ☽ in a fire sign at B., and espec. in ♌. (See Excitable, Hasty; "Palpitation" in this section).

Exhaustion—Of the Heart—♄ affl. in ♌; afflictions in ♌. (See "Weak" in this section).

Failure—Heart Failure—(See Death, Exhaustion, Faintings, Feeble, Heart Failure, Heart Trouble, Weak, in this section. See Fig. 24 in "Message of the Stars" by the Heindels).

Faintings—At the Heart—Syncope—Swoonings—The ☽ in ♌ or ♒, ☌, □, or 𝒹 ♄ (or ☿ if he be of the nature of ♄) at the beginning of an illness, or at decumb., and death often occurs when the ☽ comes to the exact 𝒹 of ♄ (Hor'y); the ☽ in ♈, and afflicted under similar conditions, tends to a weak pulse; ♅ affl. in ♌ or ♒. (See Faintings; "Weak Pulse" under Pulse; "Weak Heart" in this section).

Fatty Degeneration—Of the Heart—Fatty Heart—A ♃ disease; ♃ affl. in ♌ or the 5th H.; ♃ in ♌ and affl. by ♂ tends to this disease; Subs at HP, Lu.P., and KP. (See Degeneration, Fat; "Enlarged" in this section).

Feeble—The Heart Action Feeble—Slow and Weak Pulse—(See "Feeble" under Pulse; Depleted, Impeded, Morbid, Weak, in this section).

Fever—Fever from Obstructions Near the Heart and Lungs—The Heart and Lungs Oppressed—The ☽ in 𝒹, ☌, □, or 𝒹 ♄ (or ☿ if he be of the nature of ♄) at the beginning of an illness or at decumb. (Hor'y). This is usually occasioned by surfeits, high living, etc., and if the ☽ be not supported by benefics there is danger of death within 14 days. (See "High Living" under High; "Fever" under Lungs; Obstructions, Surfeits).

Fifth House—This house rules the heart, along with ♌, the 5th sign, and the ☉, the ruler of ♌. Afflictions in this house tend to disturb the heart. (See Fifth House; "Heart Trouble", and the various paragraphs in this section).

Fluttering—Of the Heart—(See Rapid, Spasm, in this section).

Functions—Of the Heart—The ☽ in ♌ rules the functions of the heart, and the ☽ affl. in ♌ tends to irregular and disturbed heart functions. (See Functions; "Heart Trouble", and the various paragraphs in this section).

Gases—The Heart Disturbed by the Pressure of Stomach Gases and a Distended Stomach—(See "Disturbed" in this section).

Good Heart Action—The ☉, ☽, ♃, or ♀ in ♌, and free from affliction, and also with no malefics in or afflicting the 5th H., the cusp of the 5th, or ruler of the 5th.

Gout—In the Heart—♄ in ♌. (See "Heart" under Gout, Rheumatism).

Grief In—The Heart Afflicted by Grief, Debility, and Weakness—♄ in ♌ when

♄ is the afflictor in the disease; ♄ in ♌ and affl. the ☽. (See "Weak", and the various paragraphs in this section).

Gushing of Blood—Thru the Aorta—(See Aorta).

Haste—Palpitation from Haste and Excitement—(See Excitement, Palpitation, in this section).

Heartburn—A Burning Sensation at the Epigastrium and Lower Part of the Chest—Pain In and About the Heart—Cardialgia—A ♒ and ♌ disease; a Stellium in ♌ or the 5th H., and espec. many planets in the 5th H. in a fixed sign; a ♀ disease, and caused by afflictions to ♀; the ☽ in ♌, ☌, □, or 𝒹 ♄ (or ☿ if he be of the nature of ♄) at the beginning of an illness or at decumb. (Hor'y). (See Angina, Belching, Paraesthesia; "Burning" under Sensations; "Pain" in this section).

Heart Failure—The ☉ in ♌ or ♒, and affl. by ♄; ♄ or the ☽ affl. in ♌; many planets in ♌ or ♒; ♂ affl. in ♌. (See Death, Exhaustion, Faintings, Feeble, Heart Trouble, Weak, in this section).

Heart Trouble—Heart Disease—Disturbed Heart Action—The Heart Distempered—The ☉ gives; the ☉ affl. in 𝒹, ♌, ♏, ♐, or ♒; the ☉ affl. in ♏ tends to heart trouble of a violent or inflammatory nature; the ☉ affl. in the 5th H.; the ☉, the ruler of the heart, ☌ ☋, or a malefic in ♌ in any part of the map; the ☉ ☌ ♀ in ♌, and also affl. by the ☽ and ♄; the ☉ □ or 𝒹 the Asc.; the ☉ affl. in 𝒹, thru rich foods, gormandizing, and surfeits; the ☉ or ☽ in the 6th H. in fixed signs and afflicted; the ☉ ☌ ♄ in fixed signs at B., and espec. if the ☉ or ☽ be affl. by ♅ or ♂; the ☉, ☽, and planets in 𝒹, and other fixed signs, and afflicting the ♌ sign or the hyleg; the ☉ affl. in ♌, danger of organic heart trouble; the ☽ affl. in ♌, or affl. the hyleg therefrom; the ☽ in 𝒹, ♌, ♎, ♏, or, in ☌ or ill-asp. any of the malefics as promittors; the ☽ in ♌ on the M.C., and afflicted by malefics; the ☽ ☌ ♄ or ♂ in ♌; ♅ or ♅ in ♌ or ♏, and affl. the ☉ or ☽; ♅ affl. in ♌; ♅ in ♌ on the Asc., and affl. by the □ or 𝒹 ♂; ♄ affl. in ♌ or ♒; ♄ in ♌, occi. and affl. the ☉, ☽, Asc., or hyleg; ♄ ☌ ☽ in ♌; ♄ in 𝒹 or ♈ signifies heart trouble in Hor'y Q.; ♄ or ♂ in the 6th H., in fixed signs, and affl. by the ☉ or ☽; ♄ in ♏ and affl. the ☉ or ☽; ♄ affl. in the 5th H.; ♄ ☌ or ill-asp. the ☉ in a fixed sign; ♃ in ♈, ♒, or ♓ in Hor'y Q.; ♃ in ♌, and affl. by ♂; ♂ in ♌, ♒, or ♓ in Hor'y Q.; ♂ in the 6th H. in a fixed sign, and affl. the ☉ or ☽; ♂ affl. in the 5th H.; ♂ affl. in ♓ when ♂ is the afflictor in the disease; ♂ in ♏, ☌, or ill-asp. the ☉; ♂ in 𝒹, ♌, or ♏ in the 6th H., and affl. the ☉, ☽, Asc., or hyleg; ♂ in a fixed sign at B., and affl. the hyleg; ♀ affl. in ♌ or ♒; ♀ affl. in ♌ in the 6th H.; ♀ in ♌, ♏, ♍, ♎, or ♒ in Hor'y Q.; ♀ in ♌, and affl. the ☽ or Asc.; ☿ affl. in ♌ or ♒; ☿ in ♍, ♎, ♐, ♏, or ♒, in Hor'y Q.; caused by afflictions in ♋, by distended stomach and pressure against the heart, over-indulgence of the appetite, etc.; 𝒹, ♊, ♌, ♎, ♏, or ♒ on the Asc.; fixed signs show when on the Asc., or cusp of 6th H., and containing afflictions; fixed signs on angles, and containing many planets in □ and ⚹; the malefics, or afflicting planets, in fixed signs; malefics on the cusp the 5th H., or in exact ⚹ thereto; Subs at HP, Lu.P., and KP. ♌ rising at the Vernal Equi., and afflictions in ♌ and the fixed signs, tend to an increase of, and prevalence of heart troubles and weaknesses. For the Periods and Times when heart trouble may come, be renewed or aggravated, see "Periods", "Prevalance", in this section.

Heat—The Heart Affected by Extreme Heat—♌ ascending at the Vernal Equi., and the ☉ afflicted. (See "Extreme Heat "under Heat; "Prevalence" in this section).

Herbs—The Effect of on the Heart— (See "Drugs" in this section).

Heredity—The Heart Affected by Hereditary Transmission—(See "Organic" in this section).

High Living—The Heart Affected By —(See "Fever" in this section).

Horary Questions—The Heart Signified In—Heart Affections Denoted In— (See the Introduction to this Article. Also note the various Horary influences in the different paragraphs in this section).

Hypertrophy—(See "Enlarged" in this section; Hypertrophy).

Ill-Affected Heart — (See "Heart Trouble", and the various paragraphs in this section).

Impeded Action—Slow—Suspended— Feeble—Weak—The influence of ♄ impeding the work of the Pneumogastric Nerve; a ♌ disease, and afflictions in ♌; ♄ affl. in ♌. (See Impeded; Drug Heart, Morbid, Obstructed, Slow, Stoppage, Weak, in this section).

Incompetency — (See Leaky, Mitral, Regurgitation, Valves, in this section).

Incomplete — The Partition Between the Right and Left Side of the Heart Incomplete, Resulting In Cyanosis— Case of a Male—(See the Case under Cyanosis; "Malformation" in this section).

Incoordination—Lack of Coordination of the Heart Action—♅ in ♋ or ♌ in the 5th H., and afflicted. (See Incoordination; "Rhythm" in this section).

Indiscretions—Heart Disturbances From — (See Diet, Excesses, Fever, High Living, Lacing, Narcotics, Palpitation, in this section).

Inefficiency — Muscular — Mitral — Valvular—♄ affl. in ♌; ♅ or ♂ affl. in ♌. (See Heart Trouble, Impeded, Mitral, and the various paragraphs in this section).

Inflamed Heart — Heart Trouble of a Violent or Inflammatory Nature—The ☉ affl. in ♏. (See Carditis, Endocarditis, Myocarditis, Pericarditis, in this section).

Inhibition—Cardiac Inhibition—♄ affl. in ♌, or in fixed signs. (See Inhibitions).

Insufficiency—(See Mitral, Regurgitation, Valves, in this section).

Interrupted—The Heart-Beat Irregular—Rhythm Interrupted — (See Incoordination, Rhythm, in this section).

Irregular — The Heart Action and Functions Irregular—The ☽ affl. in ♌; the Prog. ☽ ☌ the radical ♅ in ♌; ♅ affl. in ♌; ♅ in ♌ in the Asc., and in ⚹ ♂ in the 7th H.; ♃ or ♀ in ♌, and in □ or ⚹ ♅. (See Incoordination, Functions, Rhythm, Spasms, in this section).

Jupiter Group—Of Herbs—Action of On the Heart — (See "Drugs" in this section).

Lacing—Tight Lacing—Causing Palpitation—♀ in ♌. (See Lacing; "Palpitation" in this section).

Leaky Valves—♅ affl. in ♋ or ♌, and espec. when in the 5th H.; ♄ affl. in ♌, due to blood obstruction, accumulation, and pressure; ♄ affl. in the 5th H. (See Blood, Mitral, Regurgitation, Valves, in this section; Valves).

Left Auricle—(See "Auricles" in this section).

Left Coronary Plexus—(See "Plexus" in this section).

Lesions—Valvular Lesions—♅ affl. in ♋ or ♌ in the 5th H. (See Leaky, Mitral, Regurgitation, Valves, in this section).

Lining—Inflamed Linings of the Heart —(See "Inflamed" in this section).

Lower Heart—The Lower Part of the Heart Affected—Afflictions in the 3rd Decan. of ♌; Subs at Lu.P. (See "Upper" in this section. Also see Lower, Middle, Navamsa, Upper).

Malformation Of — Many planets in fixed signs, or in the 5th H., and afflicted; malefics conjoined in ♌ or the 5th H., and afflicted; afflictions in ♒. (See "Incomplete" in this section).

Medicines—And the Heart—(See Medicines, Remedies; "Drugs" in this section).

Mitral Insufficiency—Stenosis—Leaky Valve—Regurgitation — Inefficiency— Incompetency — A ♌ disease; ♅ or ♄ affl. in ♌; malefics in the 5th H., and afflicted; Subs at HP, Lu.P. (See Leaky, Regurgitation, Valves, in this section).

Morbid Action — Of the Heart — Impeded — Slow — Caused by ♃ when the dominion of death is vested in him; ♃ affl. in ♌. (See Impeded, Slow, Weak, in this section; Morbid).

Muscular Action — The Muscular Action Weak and Inefficient—♄ affl. in ♌. (See Inefficiency, Myocarditis, in this section).

Myocarditis—Inflammation of the Cardiac Muscles—♂ affl. in ♌. (See "Inflamed" in this section).

Nails — Blue and dark discolorations of the half-moons of the finger nails indicate heart weakness, valvular trouble, and are indicative of afflictions in ♌, malefics in ♌, or ♌ on the Asc. at B., and afflicted. (See Nails).

Narcotic Drugs — The Heart Action Weak, Irregular, or Suspended By— (See "Drug Heart" in this section).

Navamsa—The different parts of the heart are shown by the Navamsa subdivisions of the ♌ sign. Thus afflictions in the different faces and degrees of ♌ locate the part of the heart afflicted, weak, or disturbed. (See Navamsa).

Nervous Affections—Of the Heart—♅ in ♌ or the 5th H., and afflicted; ♅ on the cusp the 5th H., or in ☍ thereto, and afflicted; ♀ affl. in ♌. (See Angina, Depressor, Heartburn, Neuralgia, Pain, Palpitation, Spasm, in this section).

Neuralgia Of—☿ affl. in ♌ or ♒. (See Angina, Heartburn, Nervous, Pain, in this section).

Obstructed — The Heart Action Obstructed—The ☉ in ♌, ☌, □, or ☍ ♄; ♄ affl. in ♌. (See Obstructions. Also see Blood, Fever, Impeded, Inhibition, Lacing, Mitral, Regurgitation, Stoppage, Suspended, Valves, in this section).

Opiates—Harmful Action On the Heart —(See "Drug Heart" in this section).

Oppression—About the Heart—Pain and Oppression—(See Angina, Cyanosis, Fever, Heartburn, Neuralgia, Pain, in this section).

Organic Weakness — Of the Heart — Organic Heart Trouble—Organic Weak Heart — Structural Disorder — The Heart Affected by Hereditary Transmission—The ☉ in ♌ in ☌, □, or ☍ ♄; the ☽ in the 6th H. in fixed signs, and affl. by malefics; ♅ in ♌ and affl. by ♄; ♄ in ♌, and affl. the ☉; ♄ ☌ or ill-asp. the ☉. (See Heredity, Organic, Structural; Auricles, Incomplete, Malformation, Weak, in this section. See Fig. 3 in "Message of the Stars", by the Heindels for a Case record).

Orifice—Cardiac Orifice Constricted— ♄ in the first degrees of ♋, or in the last degrees of ♊, and affl. by ♆. (See Constrictions, Contractions; "Valves" in this section).

Pain In — Cardialgia — ☉ and ♌ disease; the ☉ in ♌ and affl. by ♂; the ☽ in ♒, and affl. by the ☉ or ♂ when taken ill, and the ☽ slow in motion and decr. in light (Hor'y); the ☽ in ♓, ☌, □, or ☍ ♄ (or ☍ ♀ if he be of the nature of ♄) at the beginning of an illness or at decumb. (Hor'y); ♂ affl. in ♌; ♂ affl. in ♌ in the 5th H. (See Angina, Heartburn, Neuralgia, Oppression, in this section).

Palpitation—Trembling of the Heart — Passion of the Heart — Tremors — Violent Pulsation—Throbbing—Thrills —Caused by afflictions in ♌, ♒, and the 5th H.; the ☉ affl. in ♌ or ♒; the ☉ rising in ♌, and affl. by ♂; the ☉ in ♌, and affl. by ♃; the ☉ or ☽ in ♌ or ♒ in ☌ or ill-asp. any of the malefics as promittors; the ☉ affl. by ♄; the ☉ in ♌ or ♒ in the 6th H., and afflicted; the ☉ in ♌, and affl. by ♂ by dir. or progression, violent palpitation; a ☉ disease; the ☽ in ♌ or ♒ in the 5th or 6th H., and affl. by malefics; the ☽ affl. in ♍; the ☽ in a fiery sign, and espec. in ♌ due to haste and excitement; the ☽ ☌ ♂ in ♌; palpitation is best relieved when the ☽ is in decr., and in good asp. the radical ♃ or ♀, or when the transits of ♃ or ♀ are in good asp. to the radical ☽; ♆, ♅, or ♄ as promittors in ☌ or ill-asp. the ☉ or ☽ in ♌, or in the 5th or 6th H.; ♅ ☌ the ☽ in ♌; ♅ affl. in ♌ or ♒; ♅, ♆, or ♄ in ♌, and affl. the ☉ or ☽, and over-exertion and excitement should be avoided; ♄ ☌ ♃ and ♀ in ♌; ♄ ☌ ♃ and in ☍ ♀; ♃ affl. in ♌ or ♒; a ♃ disease; ♃ in ♌ or ♒, and in ☍ the Asc. by dir.; ♂ affl. in ♌

or ♒; ♂ in ♌, or afflicting planets in ♌ or ♒, tends to palpitation, as his dynamic action leads to tremors; ♂ promittor in ♒, ☌, or ill-asp. the ☉; ♂ in ♌ or ♒ in the 6th H., and afflicted; ♂ in ♌ or ♒, and affl. the ☉, ☽, or Asc.; ♀ in ♌ or the 6th H., and afflicted, or affl. the ☉, ☽, or Asc., and usually caused by tight lacing, indiscretions, or excesses of some kind; ☿ affl. in ♌ or ♒; ☿ in ♍, ☌, or ill-asp. any of the malefics as promittors; ♄ on the Asc., and afflicted; afflictions in ♋, from distended stomach and pressure against the heart; Subs at HP, Lu.P. Case— See Fig. 11A in "Astro-Diagnosis", by the Heindels. (See Passion, Spasm, in this section).

Partition Incomplete — (See "Incomplete" in this section).

Passion—Of the Heart—Trembling of —♃ in ♌ or ♒, and ☍ the Asc. by dir.; ♅ or ♂ in ♌; ♀ affl. in ♌. (See Palpitation, Spasm, in this section).

Pathological Action—(See "Drugs" in this section).

Pericarditis — Inflammation of the Pericardium — A ♊ disease, and afflictions in ♊; ♂ in ♌. The ☽ in ♌ has special rule over the functions of the heart and the pericardium, and the ☽ ☌ ♂ in ♌ tends to inflammation of the pericardium. Also caused by Subs at Lu.P. (See Carditis, Endocarditis, Inflamed, in this section; Pericardium).

Periods of Heart Trouble—The Times and Periods When Heart Trouble Is Apt to Come — The Directions and Transits Causing—The ☉ to the ☌ or ill-asp. ♄, or other malefics, by dir.; the ☉ in ♌ or ♒, and to the ☌ or ill-asp. ♂ by dir.; the ☉ and ♂ in fixed signs at B., and by dir., and espec. if the ☉ or ☽ be affl. by ♄ or ♂; the ☽ in ♌, and affl. by the ☉ or ♂ when taken ill (Hor'y); ♄ to the ☌ or ill-asps. the ☉ by dir.; malefics passing thru ♌ by tr. or dir., and espec. if there were malefics in ♌ at B., or affl. the ♌ sign; ♌ the prog. Asc., and containing malefics; the prog. ☉ in ☌ a malefic in the radical map, and espec. in fixed signs, and the nature of the heart disturbance may be judged according to the influence of the malefic; malefics in the 5th H. at B., and by dir. (See Heart Trouble, Prevalence, in this section).

Plexus—(See "Coronary" in this section; "Cardiac Plexus" under Cardiac).

Poison—The Heart Afflicted by Poison—♄ in ♌ when ♄ is the afflictor in the disease. (See "Gout" in this section).

Poor Action—Of the Heart—♆ in ♌, and affl. by ♄; ♅ or ♄ affl. in ♌; ♀ and ☿ in ♌, and affl. by the □ or ☍ ♄; Subs at HP. (See Blood Obstructions, Heart Trouble, and the various paragraphs in this section).

Pressure Upon—(See Pressure).

Prevalence—Of Heart Trouble—General—Due to influences at the Equinoxes. (See "Extreme Heat" under Heat).

Pulse — Rapid Pulse — Slow — (See Pulse. Also see Accelerated, Faintings, Palpitation, Rapid, Slow, Weak, in this section).

Rapid Heart Action — Tachycardia — ♅ affl. in ♌. (See Accelerated, Palpitation, Passion, Spasm, in this section).

Regurgitation — Mitral Regurgitation —Leaky Valves—Caused by afflictions in ♌; the ☉ rising in ♌ and affl. by ♄, unless strain is avoided in early years; ♅ affl. in ♋; ♅ in ♋ in the 5th H.; ♄ in ♌, due to obstruction of the blood, blood accumulation and pressure; ♄ affl. in the 5th H. (See Blood, Leaky, Mitral, Obstructions, Strain, Valves, in this section).

Remedies — Heart Remedies — Action of Drugs On the Heart—(In this section see Drug Heart, Drugs; the ☽ influences under Palpitation; Sedatives, Stimulants).

Remits — The Pulse Remits and Is Slow—(See "Slow Pulse" under Pulse; Interrupted, Irregular, Obstructed, Slow, in this section).

Restricted — The Heart Action Restricted — Obstructed — Sluggish — The ☉ in ♌ in ☌, □, or ☍ ♄. (See Impeded, Inhibition, Obstructed, Poor Action, Slow, Stoppage, in this section).

Rheumatic Heart — Rheumatism Around the Heart—♄ affl. in ♌. (See Gout, Poison, in this section).

Rhythm — The Rhythm Interrupted—Disturbed — Arythmia Cordis — Afflictions in ♌ or ♒; the ☽ afflicted in ♌; ♅ ☌ ☽ in ♌ or ♒; ♅ afflicted in ♌ or ♒; ♅ in ♌ in ☍ to planets in ♒; ♅ in ♌ or ♒, ☌, □, or ☍ ☿; ♅, ♄, ♂ and ☿ in fixed signs, and especially when in ♌ or ♒; ♃ and ♀ in ♌, and in □ or ☍ ♅; Subs at HP. (See Drug Heart, Incoordination, Irregular, Obstructed, Palpitation, Passion, Spasm, and the various paragraphs in this section).

Right Side—Of the Heart—The Heart On the Right Side — Right Auricle—Right Coronary Plexus — (See "Auricles" in this section; "Middle Cervical" under Ganglion). Case of Heart on the Right Side—See "Heart", No. 981, in 1001 N.N.

Sedative—Heart Sedative—(See Aconite, Sedatives; Drug Heart, Drugs, Remedies, Sleeping Potions, Tobacco, in this section).

Sensitive—The Heart the Most Sensitive Organ—♌ on the Asc.

Sleeping Potions — And Narcotics — Are harmful when ♆ is in ♌ or the 5th H. at B., and afflicted. (See Drug Heart, Tobacco, in this section).

Slow Action — Bradycardia — (See "Slow" under Pulse; Impeded, Morbid, Obstructed, Restricted, Stoppage, Suspended, Weak, in this section).

Smoking — Effect of on the Heart in Some Cases — (See "Tobacco" in this section).

Spasm—Spasmodic Action of the Heart —Tachycardia — Paroxysm of — Fluttering—♅ affl. in ♌ or ♒; ♅ in ♌ in ☍ to planets in ♒; ♅ ☌ ☽ in ♌, and more apt to prove fatal; ♄ in ♌ and in ☌, □, or ☍ ♅; ♀ in ♌ in □ or ☍ ♅; ☿ affl. in ♌; Subs at HP. (See Irregular, Palpitation, Passion, Rapid, Rhythm, in this section). For Spasmodic Gushing of Blood Thru the Aorta, see Aorta.

Stenosis—Of the Mitral Valve—(See Mitral, Regurgitation, Valves, in this section).

Stimulants—Heart Stimulants should be used with caution during the decr. of the ☽, and espec. if the ☽ is in evil asp. to the radical ♃ or ♀. Use heart stimulants when the ☽ is in incr., and in good asp. to the places of ♃ or ♀ at B. (See Stimulants; Drug Heart, Drugs, Remedies, in this section).

Stomach Distention—The Heart Disturbed By—(See "Gases" in this section).

Stoppage — Suspension of the Heart Action—♅ affl. in ♌; ♆ affl. in ♌, due to the action of a drug, opiate, narcotic, tobacco, etc.; ♆ in ♌, and affl. the ☉, ☽, Asc., or hyleg; ♆ affl. in the 6th H. in ♌. (See "Drug Heart" in this section).

Strain — Damage to the Heart from Strain or Over-Exercise—♂ on the cusp of 5th H.; ♂ affl. in ♌. (See "Regurgitation" in this section).

Strength—Of the Heart—The ☉ has affinity with the heart, and the strength or weakness of the heart is largely denoted by the sign position of the ☉ at B., and the aspects to the ☉.

Structural Disorders—(See "Organic" in this section).

Sudden Death—From Heart Trouble —The ☉ or ♂ in fixed signs at B., or by dir., and afflicted, and especially if the ☉ or ☽ at B. were affl. by ♄ or ♂.

Suspension — (See Impeded, Obstructed, Stoppage, in this section).

Swoonings—(See "Faintings" in this section. Also see Fainting).

Syncope—From Heart Trouble—(See "Faintings" in this section).

Tachycardia — (See "Spasm" in this section; "Troubled" under Pulse).

Thrills — (See "Palpitation" in this section; Spasmodic, Uranus).

Throbbing—(See "Palpitation" in this section; "High Pressure" under Blood).

Tight Lacing—Heart Disturbed By—(See "Lacing" in this section).

Tobacco Heart—♆ affl. in ♌ or in the 5th H. at B., and also when in ♌ or the 5th H. by dir. or tr., tends to affect the heart action adversely under the strong and persistent use of tobacco or narcotic drugs of any kind. (See "Drug Heart" in this section).

Treatment — (See "Remedies" in this section).

Trembling — Tremors — (See Palpitation, Passion, Spasm, in this section).

Trouble — Heart Trouble — Troubled Heart and Pulse — (See Drug Habit, Heart Trouble, and the various paragraphs in this section; "Troubled" under Pulse).

Uncertain Action—The ☉ in ♌ or ♒, ☌, P., □, or ☍ ♅. (See "Heart Trouble", and the various paragraphs in this section).

Upper Part—Of the Heart—The upper part of the heart is more affected when planets are in the 1st Dec. of ♌, and with Subs. at UHP, the 1st Dorsal;

the middle part affected with malefics and afflictions in the 2nd Decan. of ♌︎, and with Subs at HP, the 2nd Dorsal. (See Lower, Navamsa, in this section).

Valves — Valvular Trouble — Weak Valvular Action—♅ rules the valves of the heart, and ♅ in ♌︎ tends to valvular trouble, leaky valves, mitral insufficiency, regurgitation, etc., and espec. if ♄ also afflict ♌︎ or the 5th H.; the ☉ rising in ♌︎ and affl. by ♄; ♄ affl. in ♌︎ or the 5th H., or affl. the lord of 5th, or cusp of 5th H. (See Leaky, Lesions, Mitral, Nails, Orifice, Regurgitation, in this section).

Veins Of—♀ affl. in ♌︎ tends to affect the veins of the heart, and the venous blood. (See Aorta).

Ventricles — (See the Introduction to this Article).

Violent Inflammation — Of the Heart —(See "Inflamed" in this section).

Weak Heart — Weakened Heart Action—Depleted Heart Action—Debility of the Heart—Exhaustion of—Feeble Action—Morbid Action—Afflictions in ♌︎ or ♒︎, and in the 5th H., or to the cusp of the 5th; a ☉ disease; born with the ☉ as ruler; the ☉ rising in ♌︎ at B., and affl. by ♄, and to the ♂ or ill-asp. ♄ by dir.; the ☽ affl. in ♌︎ or ♏︎, or affl. the hyleg therefrom; the ☽ affl. in fixed signs; ♄ on the cusp of 5th H., or in exact ☍ the cusp; ♄ affl. in ♌︎, organic weakness, and weak and depleted heart action; ♃ affl. in ♌︎; a ♌︎ and ♒︎ disease, and with afflictions in these signs; malefics in ♌︎ or ♒︎; planets in ♌︎ in the 5th or 6th H., and afflicted; afflictions in the 5th H., or to the cusp of 5th. (See Depleted, Exhaustion, Feeble, Heart Trouble, Impeded, Morbid, Obstructed, Organic, Weakness, Valves, and the various paragraphs in this section; "Weak Pulse" under Pulse).

Weakness—Of the Heart—Denoted by the sign position of the ☉ at B., and the aspects to the ☉. (See Auricles, Organic, Strength, Valves, Weak, in this section).

Wind—Around the Heart—☿ affl. in ♌︎.

HEARTBURN—(See this subject under Heart).

HEAT—Hot—Warm—Warmth—Heats— Heated—Caloric—Parched—The ☉ and ♂ are hot, denote heat, and are caloric, while ♃ and ♀ are warm. Heat and expansion in the body are produced by the positive and electric planets, the ☉, ♃, and ♂. The ☽ also reflects the heat from the ☉. A warm influence is exerted over the body by ♃ and ♀, and not a hot influence. Heat and moisture are prolific, nutritive, and benefic influences, while cold and dry are more malefic. Heat and cold are active, and masculine qualities. Dryness and Moisture are passive and feminine. The distribution of heat in the body is ruled by the ☉ and ♂. Heat predominates in the right side of the body, and cold in the left side, and espec. in males. (See Benefics, Cold, Dryness, Fire, Jupiter, Left, Malefics, Mars, Moisture; "Operations" under Nature; Right, Sun, Venus).

Abundant Heat — Diseases Arising from Excessive Heat—(See Excessive, Extreme, Over-Indulgence, Plenty, in this section).

Accidents By—(See Burns. Fire, Liquids, Scalds).

Acids—(See "Hot" under Acids).

Acute Hot Diseases—Acute Fevers— (See "Hot Diseases" under Fever).

Adhesions — Due to Melting and Excessive Heat—(See Adhesions).

Air — Hot and Dry Air — (See "Corrupt Air", "Hot and Dry", under Air; Drought, Famine, Pestilence; "Warm" under Weather; "Hot Winds" under Wind).

All Hot Diseases—And Inflammations —Are diseases of the ☉ and ♂, and also of the fiery signs, and espec. of ♌︎.

Animal Heat — The animal heat is ruled over by the Asc. (1) Increased— The Animal Heat Increased—♂ in good asp. the ☉ or the Asc. (2) Excess Of— ♂ ♂, P.☐ or ☍ Asc. (See "High Fever" under Fever). (3) Lack of—The Animal Heat Lacking in the Earlier Years —The ☉ or ☽ in ♑︎; ♑︎ on the Asc. The earthy signs are cold, and many planets in them at B. tend to lower the heat of the body, and give a cold body, and also make the native more affected by cold, and diseases arising from cold. (See "Cold Body" under Cold; "Early Years" under Early; Excessive, Heats the System, Lack Of, Over-Abundance, Plenty, in this section).

Blasting Hot Winds—(See "Hot Blasting Winds" under Wind; "Extreme Heat" in this section).

Blood—Overheated Blood—Hot Blood —Feverish Blood — (See "Overheated" under Blood).

Body—The Bodily Heat—Hot Bodily Temperament—(See Animal Heat, Disposition, Excessive Bodily Heat, Hot Bodily Temperament, in this section).

Breast—Heat In—(See "Heat" under Breast).

Burns—(See Burns, Fire, Scalds; "Hot Liquids" in this section).

Buttocks — Heats In — (See "Heats" under Buttocks).

Center—The Heat Center In the Spine —CP, the 5th Dorsal, is the Heat Mere, and also corresponds to the ♌︎ sign. To reduce fever, Chiropractors adjust this vertebra. (See "Fifth Dorsal" under Vertebrae; "Excessive Bodily Heat" in this section).

Cholera—(See Cholera, Epidemics).

Climate — (See Excessive Heat, Extreme Heat, Summers, Tropical, Warm, Weather, Winds, in this section).

Cold and Heat—Suffers from Extremes of Heat and Cold — Heat and Cold — The ☽ in ♐︎, ♂, or ill-asp. ♄ (or ☿ if he be of the nature of ♄) at the beginning of an illness, or at decumb. (Hor'y); the ☽ in ♐ and affl. by the ☉ or ♂; the ☽ affl. by ♄ or ♂ in airy signs; ♆, ♅, or ♄ in ♒︎, and affl. the ☉ or ☽. (For the influences of Internal Heats and Externally Cold, see "Internal Heats" in this section; Centrifugal, Centripetal).

Danger by Heat — Prejudice by Heat —(See Burns; "Injury by Fire" under Fire; Scalds).

Death by Heat—By Hot Diseases—♂ causes death of all hot diseases, high and burning fevers. Also caused by the ☉, as in sunstroke, and with the ☉ and ♂ affl. in ♈. (See "Death" under Burns; Electricity; "High Fevers" under Fever; "Death by Fire" under Fire; Lightning, Scalds; "Sunstroke" under Sun; Excessive Heat, Extreme Heat, Hot Diseases, Hot Liquids, in this section).

Decrease—Of the Heat In the Body— Low Caloric—(See Animal Heat, Lack Of, in this section).

Diseases from Heat—(See Epidemics; "Hot Eruptions" under Eruptions; Fever, Excessive Heat, Extreme Heat, Sunstroke, and the various paragraphs in this section).

Disposition—Hot In Disposition—(See "Choleric Temperament" under Choleric; "Hot and Dry Body" in this section).

Distempers—Hot Distempers—(See Blood, Hot Diseases, and the various paragraphs in this section).

Distribution of Heat—In the Body— Is carried on by the ☉ and ♂.

Drought — Suffering from Extreme Heat and Drought—(See Drought; "Extreme Heat" in this section).

Dry and Hot Air—(See Drought, Epidemics, Famine, Fountains, Summer; "High Temperature" under Weather; "Hot Blasting Winds" under Wind; "Extreme Heat" in this section).

Dry and Hot Body—(See "Hot and Dry" in this section).

Dry and Hot Diseases—Subject To— People born under a fiery sign, with a fiery sign upon the Asc., or the ☽ or lord of the Asc. in a fire sign, the illnesses are of a hot and dry nature; diseases of the ☉ and ♂; the ☽ in ♌, and affl. by the ☉ or ♂ when taken ill, the disease is of a hot and dry nature, and with high fever. (See "Dry Body" under Dryness; Fevers; "Fevers" under Moon; Heats, Hot Bodily Temperament, Hot Diseases, Humours, in this section).

Epidemics—Thru Excess of Heat— (See "Corrupt Air" under Air; Atmosphere, Cholera, Epidemics, Pestilence).

Eruptions—Hot Eruptions—(See "Fevers", "Hot", under Eruptions).

Excessive Heat—Immoderate Heat— Intemperate Heat — Diseases Arising From—The ☉ denotes when the ☉ afflicts the ☽ or Asc., as in fevers, sunstroke; caused by ♂ when the dominion of death is vested in him. (See "Extreme Heat" in this section).

Excessive Bodily Heat—The ☉ and ♂ are heating pathologically, and their afflictions tend to fevers and rise of temperature. The ♂ influence especially tends to focussed heat in the body, and to localized inflammation. Excess of bodily heat is given with ♈ on the Asc. at B. The Bilious Temperament is hot in quality. Subs at CP, the 5th Dorsal vertebra, the Heat

Mere, tend to excessive heat in a part, general excessive heat over the body, and with Subs also at KP to excessive heat with Rash. (See "Choleric Temperament" under Choleric; Fever, Inflammation; Animal Heat, Body, Heats, Hot Bodily Temperament, Hot Diseases, Humours, Internal, Over-Abundant, Plenty, in this section).

External Heat—Suffers from Much External and Internal Heat—The ☽ in ♌ ♂ or ill-asp. ♄ (or to ☿ if he be of the nature of ♄) at the beginning of an illness or at decumbiture, and they frequently die when the ☽ comes to the ☍ ♄ if no good asp. prevents it (Hor'y); ♂ in aspect to the ☉ at B., and by dir.; fiery signs upon the Asc. (See Heats, Internal Heats, in this section).

Extreme Heat—Violent Heat—Suffering from Extremely Hot and Dry Weather—An eclipse of the ☉ in ♈; ♄ ♂ ♂ in fiery signs; ♂ in ♊, and lord of the year at the Vernal Equinox.; ♈ ascending at a Solar or Vernal Ingress, and ♂ be afflicted, then Countries and People ruled by ♈ suffer from extreme heat and drought; ♌ ascending at the Vernal Equi., and the ☉ afflicted, ♌ people, and Countries under ♌, suffer from extreme heat, drought, pestilential air, and from diseases of the heart and brain. (See Dry and Hot Air, Excessive Heat, in this section). For Extreme Heat in the Mouth and Throat see "Heat" under Mouth, Throat. For Extreme Heat in a localized part of the body see "Excessive Bodily Heat" in this section. Also see Inflammation.

Extremes of Heat and Cold—Suffers From—(See "Cold and Heat" in this section).

Eyes—Hot Diseases In—Hot Humours In—(See "Hot Diseases" under Eyes).

Famine—From Extreme Heat and Drought—(See Drought, Famine, Fountains, Pestilence, Rivers, Weather, Winds).

Fevers—Hot Diseases—(See Fever; Hot Diseases, Overheated, in this section).

Fiery—Hot and Fiery Diseases— Caused by ♂. (See Burning, High, Pernicious, under Fever).

Fire—Injury or Death By—(See Burns, Fire).

Flushings—Hot Flashes—☉ diseases; the ☉ affl. by ♂; the ☉ ☌ ♂ in ♈; ♈ on the Asc. (See Flushings).

Focussed Heat—In the Body—♂ Influence. (See Inflammation; "Excessive Bodily Heat" in this section).

Fomentations—Hot Fomentations— (See Emollient).

Full of Heat—The Body Full of Heat —(See Animal Heat, Excessive Bodily Heat, Over-Abundance, Plenty, in this section).

Functions—The Warmth and Expansion of the Functions—(See Electric).

Fusions — Resulting from Extreme Heat In a Part—(See Adhesions).

General Excessive Heat — (See "Excessive Bodily Heat" in this section).

Haunches—Heats In—(See "Heats" under Buttocks).

Head—Hot Diseases In—Hot Humours In—(See "Hot Diseases" under Head).

Heart—The Heart Affected by Extreme Heat—(See "Extreme Heat" in this section; "Heat" under Heart).

Heat and Cold—Suffers from Extremes Of—(See "Cold and Heat" in this section).

Heat of the Body—(See Animal Heat, Excessive Bodily Heat, in this section).

Heat Prostration—(See "Sunstroke" in this section).

Heated Flushings—(See "Flushings" in this section).

Heats—Hot Humours—♂ affl. in the sign ruling the part. (See "Heats", "Humours", under Buttocks, Eyes, Head, Hips, Reins, Thighs; Animal Heat, Excessive Bodily Heat, Heats the System, Humours, Internal Heats, in this section).

Heats the System—♌ influence; fiery signs on the Asc. (See Animal Heat, Heats, in this section).

Hips and Thighs—Heats In—(See "Heats" under Hips).

Hot Blasting Winds—(See "Blasting" in this section).

Hot Bodily Temperament—Hot Body—Hot In Disposition—This is a positive temperament. It is given by the ☉ in a fiery sign at B., or a fiery sign upon the Asc.; many planets in fiery signs at B.; ♂ strong and rising at B., or in the Asc. or M.C.; ☿ oriental at B. The Choleric, or Bilious Temperament is hot in quality. Those born in the Tropics and hot climates, born under the Southern Parallels, and who have the ☉ continually in their Zenith, and who are continually scorched by it, have a hot bodily temperament. (See Animal Heat, Dry and Hot Diseases, Excessive Bodily Heat, Hot and Dry Body, in this section).

Hot and Dry Air—(See "Air" in this section).

Hot and Dry Body—Hot and Dry Bodily Temperament—Heat and Dryness are positive. The Quadrant from the Summer Tropic to the Autumnal Equinox tends to produce a bodily temperament abounding in heat and dryness. Given by the ☉ and many planets in fiery signs at B., or with a fiery sign upon the Asc.; ♂ strong and rising at B., as in the Asc. or M.C. The ☉ and ♂ are hot and dry, and the ☉ and ♂ Groups of Planets and Herbs are hot and dry. The Choleric Temperament is hot and dry. (See "Choleric Temperament" under Choleric; "Mars Group", "Sun Group", under Herbs; "Dry and Hot Diseases", "Hot Bodily Temperament", in this section).

Hot and Dry Diseases—(See "Dry and Hot Diseases" in this section).

Hot and Dry Head—(See "Hot and Dry" under Head).

Hot and Fiery Diseases—(See "Fiery" in this section).

Hot and Moist Body—(See this subject under Moisture).

Hot and Moist Diseases—Hot and Moist Distempers—The ☉ or ☽ Sig. ♂ tends to putrid and hot distempers; the ☽ ♂ ♂ during the increase and First Quarter of the ☽, as the ☽ is considered hot and moist from the New ☽ to the 1st Quarter; ♃ diseases; ♃ when ori. causes heat and moisture, hot and moist diseases; ♀ causes when ori. (See "Hot and Moist" under Moisture; "Moist and Warm" in this section).

Hot Body—(See "Hot Bodily Temperament" in this section).

Hot Diseases—Hot Distempers—The ☉ directed to Aldebaran, Antares, Regulus, Deneb, Betelguese, Bellatrix, and Frons Scorpio; the ☉ or ☽ Sig. ♂ ♂, and danger of death by; caused by ♂, and the ☉ affl. by ♂; ♈ or ♌ on the Asc.; Subs at CP. (See "Overheated Blood" under Blood; Fever; "Hot Bodily Temperament" under Temperament; Dry and Hot Diseases, Heats, in this section).

Hot Flashes—(See "Flushings" in this section).

Hot Humours—♂ diseases; ♂ affl. in the sign ruling the part. (See Fevers, Heats, Hot Diseases, Humours, in this section).

Hot Liquids—Hot Water—Hot Fluids—Danger By—Injury or Death By—The ☉ to the ♂ or ill-asp. ♂ by dir.; the Asc. to the place of the Ascelli or Capricornus. (See Burns, Liquids, Scalds).

Hot Signs—Hot and Moist Signs—(See "Signs" in this section).

Hot Weather—(See Blasting, Excessive Heat, Extreme Heat, in this section; Drought, Epidemics, Famine, Fountains, Pestilence, Weather).

Humours—Hot Humours—♂ diseases. (See Heats, Hot Diseases, Hot Humours, in this section; "Heats", "Humours", under Buttocks, Eyes, Head, Hips, Loins, Thighs).

Ilium—Heats In—The same as for "Heats" under Buttocks.

Immoderate Heat—Ills Arising From—(See Excessive Heat, Extreme Heat, in this section).

Increased Animal Heat—(See Animal Heat, Excessive Bodily Heat, in this section).

Inflammation—Excessive Heat In a Part—Localized Heat—(See Inflammation; "Excessive Bodily Heat" in this section).

Injuries by Heat—(See Burns, Fire, Scalds; "Hot Liquids" in this section).

Insufficient Heat—In the System—(See Animal Heat, Lack Of, in this section).

Intemperate Heat—Ills Arising From—(See Dry and Hot Air, Excessive Heat, Extreme Heat, in this section).

Internal Heat—(See "External" in this section).

Internal Heats—And Externally Cold—The ☽ in ♈, ♑ or ♋ (or ♋ if he be of the nature of ♄) when taken ill, or at decumb. (Hor'y). (See Cold and Heat, External Heat, Heats, in this section).

Lack of Animal Heat—Decreased—Low Caloric—The earthy signs are cold, and these signs on the Asc., and espec. ♑, or with the ☉ or ☽, and many planets in these signs at B., tend to lack of animal heat, and espec. in the early years of life; ♄, and the ♄ sign ♑, tend to unusual coldness in the body, and to cause ills arising from cold, such as chills and internal congestions. (See "Animal Heat" in this section; "Diseases Arising from Cold" under Cold; "Congestions" under Internal).

Left Side of Body—Cold predominates in the left side of the body, and heat in the right side, and espec. in male nativities. (See Left, Right).

Liquids—Danger by Hot Liquids—(See "Hot Liquids" in this section).

Localized Heat—In a Part—(See "Inflammation" in this section).

Loins—Heats In—(See "Heats" under Buttocks, Loins).

Low Caloric—(See "Lack of Animal Heat" in this section).

Melting—Of the Tissues by Excessive Heat—(See Adhesions, Ankylosis, Coalition).

Moist and Hot—(1) Moist and Hot Bodily Temperament—(See "Hot and Moist" under Moisture. (2) Hot and Moist Diseases—(See "Hot and Moist Diseases" in this section).

Moist and Warm—(1) Moist and Warm Diseases—♅, ♃, and ♀ diseases, as these planets are warm and moist in influence. (See "Relaxation and Moisture" under Moisture). (2) Moist Warmth In Body—☽ influence, and the ☽ well-asp. by ♃ or ♀. (See "Warmth" under Moisture). (3) Moist and Warm Signs of the Zodiac—♎ and ♒. (See Moisture; "Moist and Hot" in this section).

Mouth—Extreme Heat In—(See "Heat" under Mouth).

Much Heat—(See Animal Heat, Excessive Heat, Excessive Bodily Heat, Extreme Heat, External Heat, in this section).

Over-Abundance of Heat—Sharp and Sudden Diseases Caused from An Over-Abundance of Animal Heat—♂ diseases; ♂ in the 6th H., and affl. the ☉ or ☽. (See Excessive Bodily Heat, Fevers, Hot Diseases, in this section).

Over-Heated—The Asc. to the □ or ☍ ♂ by dir., and with violent fever. (See Blood, Excessive Bodily Heat, Sunstroke, in this section).

Parched—Parched Air—Parched Body—(See "Parched" under Air; Fevers; Air, Excessive Bodily Heat, Extreme Heat, Hot Diseases, in this section).

Part—Excessive Heat In a Part—(See "Inflammation" in this section).

Pestilential Warm Air—(See "Pestilential Air" under Air).

Plenty of Heat—In the Body—The ☉, ☽, and many planets in fiery signs at B.; fiery signs on the Asc. (See Animal Heat, Excessive Bodily Heat, in this section).

Prejudice by Heat—(See "Injury by Fire" under Fire).

Prostration—By Heat—(See Excessive Heat, Sunstroke, in this section).

Putrid Hot Diseases—(See "Hot and Moist Diseases" in this section).

Pyrexia—(See Fever).

Rashes—Heat Rashes—♂ the afflictor in the disease; Subs at CP and KP. (See Eruptions).

Reins—(See "Heat" under Reins).

Right Side of Body—(See "Left Side" in this section).

Scalds—(See Scalds; "Hot Liquids" in this section).

Searing Burns—(See "Searing" under Burns).

Sensations—Heat Sensations—(See "Flushings" in this section; "Sensations" under Burning).

Signs—The Hot Signs—♈, □, ♌, ♐. The □, ♎ and ♒ signs are classed as moist and warm, and hot and moist.

Stomach—Overheated Stomach—(See "Hot" under Stomach).

Suffering from Heat—(See Excessive Bodily Heat, External Heat, Extreme Heat, in this section; "High Fever" under Fever; Sunstroke).

Summers Warm—(See Excessive Heat, Extreme Heat, in this section; Summer).

Sunstroke—Heat Prostration—(See "Sunstroke" under Sun; Excessive Heat; Extreme Heat, in this section).

Super-Abundance of Heat—In the Body and Externally—(See Animal Heat, Excessive Heat, Excessive Bodily Heat, Extreme Heat, Hot Diseases, Overheated, Sunstroke, in this section).

Thighs—Heats In—Hot Humours In—(See "Heats", "Hot Humours", under Hips, Thighs).

Throat—Extreme Heat In—(See "Heat" under Mouth, Throat).

Tropical Heat—In Cold Climates—(See Tropical).

Urine Hot—(See "Hot Urine" under Urine).

Violent Heat—(See "Extreme Heat" in this section; "Death" under Burns).

Vital Heat—(See "Heat" under Vital).

Warm—(1) Moist and Warm—(See "Moist and Warm" in this section. (2) Warm Pestilential Air—(See "Pestilential" under Air). (3) Warm Signs—(See "Signs" in this section). (4) Warm Summers—(See "Summers" in this section).

Weather—Hot Weather—Warm Weather—The ☉ ☌, or in any strong asp. to ♃, except when the ☉ is also in asp. with ♄ or ♅. (See Drought, Dry and Hot Air, Epidemics, Excessive Heat, Extreme Heat, Famine, Sunstroke, in this section).

Winds—Hot and Blasting Winds—(See "Blasting" in this section).

HEAVY—Heaviness—Dull—The afflictions of ♄ tend to deaden the Senses, and slow up the functions of the body, causing a feeling of heaviness and weight in different parts of the body, and to cause dullness, lethargy, lassitude. See the following subjects in the alphabetical arrangement when not considered here—

Aches—Heavy Aches and Pains—(See "Heavy Aches" under Aches).

Affliction—Heavy Afflictions—(See "Sad Sickness" in this section; Affliction).

Apathy; Appearance—Heavy Appearance—In Hor'y Q. ♃ Sig. in ♉. (See Appearance).

Beard—Heavy Beard—(See "Much Beard" under Beard).

Blood—The Blood Heavy with Wastes —(See "Foul", "Gross", under Blood; "Impure Blood" under Impure).

Body—Heavy Body—♏ on the Asc., a strong and heavy body. (See Corpulent, Fat, Fleshy, Giants, Large, Obesity, Stout).

Breast—Heaviness of the Breast— (See "Heaviness" under Breast).

Dull—Dull and Heavy Appearance— Dull and Heavy Mind—(See the various paragraphs under Dull; Appearance, Mind, in this section).

Eyes—Heavy, Dull, and Sleepy Eyes —(See Dull Eyes, Sleepy Eyes, under Eyes).

Functions—The Functions Dull and Heavy—(See Hindered, Retarded, Slow, under Functions).

Gait—Heavy Gait—(See "Heavy" under Gait).

Hair—Heavy Head of Hair—Heavy Beard—Much Hair On the Body—(See "Much Beard" under Beard; Abundance, Body, under Hair).

Head—Heavy Feeling In—The Head Heavy and Falls to One Side—(See Heaviness In, Heavy, under Head).

Heaviness All Over Body—The ☽ in ♌, and affl. by the ☉ or ♂ when taken ill. (Hor'y).

Heavy Sickness—The Sickness Heavy and Prolonged—♅ ☌ ♄ in the 6th H. (See Chronic, Grievous; "Long Diseases" under Long; Prolonged, Severe, Slow, Tedious, Wastings; "Heavy and Sad" in this section).

Heavy and Sad Sickness—The ☉ or ♄ in the 6th H., and in ☌, □, or ☍ each other; ♄ affl. in the 6th H. (See "Heavy Sickness" in this section).

Inactive; Indifferent; Inertia;

Jaw—Heavy Jaw—(See Chin, Jaws).

Lassitude; Lethargy; Listless;

Melancholy; Mind—The Mind Is Heavy and Dull—Habitual Drowsiness and Sleepiness—Mental Lethargy—♄ influence; ☿ affl. by ♄ at B.; ☿ in ♑ in ☌ or ill-asp. ♄; ☿ affl. by ♄ at B., and by dir.; the Asc. to the ☌ or ill-asp. ♄ by dir. (See "Mind" under Dull; "Drowsiness" under Sleep).

Pains—Heavy Pains—(See "Body Suffers", "Heavy", under Aches).

Repletion; Retarded; Retentions;

Sad and Heavy Sickness—(See "Heavy and Sad" in this section).

Senses—The Senses Heavy and Dull— (See Dull; "Dulling" under Senses; "Mind" in this section).

Sickness—Heavy Sickness—(See Heavy Sickness, Heavy and Sad, in this section).

Sleepiness—(See Drowsiness, Sleepiness, under Sleep; "Mind" in this section).

Slow; Sluggish; Stomach—Heaviness of—(See "Heaviness" under Stomach).

Suppressions; Tired Feeling—(See Apathy, Dull, Fatigue, Inactive, Inertia, Lassitude, Lethargy, Listless, Malaise, Rouse, Tired, Weariness, etc.).

Weariness—(See Weariness; "Tired Feeling" in this section).

Weak—(See "Weak Body" under Weak).

HEBETUDE—Dulling of the Senses and of the Intellect—(See Apathy, Dull; "Mind" under Heaviness; Lethargy; "Dulling" under Senses).

HECTIC—Habitual—The Hectic Fever of Phthisis—Hectic Fever—(See "Hectic Fever", "Low Fever", under Fever).

HEELS—Heel Bone—The Os Calcis— Ruled by ♓.

Bruises To—♄ affl. in ♓. (See "Accidents", "Bruises", "Hurts", under Feet).

Disorders Of—(See "Os Calcis" under Feet).

Lump Growing On—Case—(See "Lump" under Feet).

HEIGHT OF BODY—The position of the Nodes of the ☽ are said to partly determine the height of a person. Height is also largely influenced and determined by the Decanate rising. A tall Sign upon the Asc. at B. tends to give a tall body, and a short sign rising, a short body, etc. The planetary influences causing the various heights of the body are given under the subjects referred to in this section.

Abnormal Growth—(See Growth).

Abnormally Tall—(See Giants, Tall).

Above Average Height—♈, ♌, or ♐ on the Asc. at B. (See Giants, Tall).

Above Middle Height—The ☉ Sig. in ♊ or ♌ (Hor'y); the ☽ Sig. in ♊, ♌, ♍, ♎, or ♐ in Hor'y Q.; ♄ Sig. in ♌ or ♎; ♃ Sig. in ♊; ♃ in the Asc. at B.; ♂ rising or ori. of the ☉ at B.; ♀ Sig. in ♈, ♊, ♌, ♍, ♎, or ♐; ♀ in the Asc., or rising; ☿ ascending at B.; ☿ Sig. in ♍; ♈, ♌, ♐, or ♒ on the Asc. (See "Stature" under Middle).

Diminished Stature—(See Diminished, Dwarf, Growth, Mean, Medium, Middle, Short, Small).

Low Stature—(See Diminished, Dwarfed, Mean; "Short Body" under Short; Small).

Mean Height—(See Mean, Middle).

Medium Height—(See Mean, Medium, Middle).

Middle Stature—(See Middle).

Short Body—(See Short). For further influences along the lines of Height, see Appearance, Commanding, Contracted, Decanates, Diminished, Dwarf, Enlarged, Erect, Figure, Form, Giants, Growth, High, Large, Long, Mean, Medium, Middle, Portly, Shape, Short, Size, Small, Stature, Tall, Undersized, Weight, etc.

HEIGHTS—High Places—Precipices— High Buildings—

Buildings—Falls From—Death or Injury By—(See "Buildings" under Falls).

Death — By Falls from Heights or Precipices—♄ in the M.C. in ☌ or ☍ the ☉ or ♂, and espec. if in an airy sign and affl. the hyleg; malefics in the 9th H., and affl. the ☉, ☽, or hyleg, death by falls from heights during a voyage, or in Foreign travel; malefics in the 3rd H., affl. the ☉ or ☽ in airy signs, danger of on an inland, or short journey. (See "Heights" in this section; "Travel" under Falls).

Distortions—By Falls from Heights—(See Distortions).

Excrescences—By Falls from Heights —(See Excrescences).

Heights—High Places—Precipices—Danger of Falls From — Death or Injury By—The ☉ hyleg at B. and to the ☌ or ill-asp. ♄ by dir.; the ☽ in an airy sign, hyleg, and to the ☌ or ill-asp. ♂ by dir.; the ☽ to the ☌ or ill-asp. ♅ by dir.; ♅ or ♄ in the M.C., in ♈, ♎, ♌, or ♒, and in ☌ or ☍ the ☉ or ♂; ♅ to the ☌ or ill-asp. ♄ by dir.; ♄ in quadrupedal or tropical signs in ☌ or ☍ the ☉ or ♂, and with ♄ in the M.C.; ♄ in an airy sign ☌ or evil asp. the Asc. by dir.; ♄ and ♂ controlling the Lights, the malefics being in fixed signs and distant from each other; ♄ in the M.C. in ☌ or ☍ the ☉ or ♂, and espec. if in an airy sign and affl. the hyleg; the malefics ♄ and ♂ in the M.C., and elevated above the Luminaries; the Asc. to the ☌ or ill-asp. ♂ by dir., and ♂ in an airy sign at B.; malefics in the 3rd or 9th H., and affl. the ☉ or ☽, falls from heights during inland travel, short journeys, or on voyages and in Foreign travel; if during travel the Sigs. of travel are in the 12th H., in a fixed sign, and afflicted, there is danger of falls from heights, and with great danger of fatal injuries and death. (See "Death", and the various paragraphs in this section).

Lameness — By Falls from Heights — (See Distortions).

Paralysis — By Falls from High Places—(See Distortions).

Travel — Journeys — Danger of Falls from High Places During Home or Foreign Travel—(See Death, Heights, in this section; "Travel" under Falls; "Danger", "Death", under Travel).

HELIANTHUS—Sun Flower—A typical plant and drug of the ☉. (See "Sun Group" under Herbs; "Typical Drugs" under Sun).

HELIOCENTRIC—The Heliocentric System of Astrology takes the ☉ as a center, and the indications of the planets, including the Earth, in the great Zodiac around the ☉. These influences are important, and often help to explain the nature and cause of diseases and afflictions which are not clearly shown or accounted for by merely consulting the Geocentric map of birth, or the planets as they move in the Earth's Zodiac. It is well for the student of Medical Astrology to understand the Heliocentric System, and to have a Heliocentric Table of the planets for each year. Compare your star map of birth also with a Heliocentric map for your time and year of birth, and also the directions, transits, and movements of the planets during the current year, in both systems. This Book and Work is based upon the Geocentric System of Astrology, using the Earth's Zodiac. A study of the Heliocentric System would require a separate large treatise. The System of Solar Biology, as taught by Hiram Butler, of the Esoteric Brotherhood of Applegate, California, is a good System of the Heliocentric Method, and they also can furnish you with the Heliocentric Tables of Planets for any year. (See Geocentric). The Heliocentric map for the day of your birth is said to especially show the Soul, its stage of advancement, and the problems to be faced in Earth Life for further development. The Geocentric Map of Birth shows this Soul with its limitations, acting thru the prison house of the physical body, and the relation of the native to the outer and material world for an Incarnation. Some Writers also claim that the map for the time of Conception shows the Soul, the Character, and the nature of the incoming Ego, and the student of Advanced Astrology should study all three maps if he wishes to investigate the spiritual phases of the native, as well as the physical and mental. This book, however, is limited more to the planetary influences as they affect the individual in a physical body (the diseases, afflictions, and experiences he is apt to encounter in Earth life), and we cannot take the time or space to go into the various and important matters on the spiritual side of life, or out of Incarnation, as would be indicated by the Heliocentric Map for the time of birth. It is the hope of the Author, however, that such matters and study may be added to future Editions of this Volume.

HELLEBORUS — A typical drug of ♄. (See "Saturn Group" under Herbs; "Drugs" under Saturn).

HELPLESSNESS—Helpless Creature—♂ weak at B., and considerably out of power and dignity; ♃ Sig. in ♒; many planets at B. in the negative, feminine, and mutable signs of the Zodiac; mutable signs on the angles at B., and also with the ☉ and the majority of the planets setting below the western horizon, and with many also in common signs. (See Mutable, Negative).

HEM — For words not listed under "Hem" see "Haem".

HEMACHROMATOSIS—The Skin Turns Hard, Cold, Yellow, and Leathery—A ♄ disease. (See Cold, Hardening, Skin).

HEMATEMESIS — (See "Blood" under Vomiting).

HEMATOSIS — Hematopoiesis— Blood Making—Blood Formation—(See Haematopoiesis).

HEMIANOPIA — Blindness of One-Half of the Visual Field — (See "Hemianopia" under Sight).

HEMIATROPHY—Impaired Nutrition of One Side of the Body—Facial Hemiatrophy—(See Atrophy; "Atrophy" under Face).

HEMICRANIA — Neuralgia of Half of the Head — (See "Hemicrania" under Head).

HEMIPLEGIA — Paralysis In One Side of the Body—(See "Hemiplegia" under Infancy, Paralysis).

HEMISPHERES—(See "Cerebral Hemispheres" under Cerebral, Head).

HEMLOCK—Conium—A Typical Drug of ♄. (See "Saturn Group" under Herbs; "Drugs" under Saturn).

HEMOPHILIA—Abnormal Tendency to Hemorrhage—(See "Haemophilia" under Hemorrhage).

HEMORRHAGE—Loss of Blood—Flow of Blood—Effusion of Blood—Bleeding — Bloodshed — Caused by ♂; a ♂ disease and affliction; ♂ too much in evidence at B., and by dir. or tr., and worse at the full ☽; ♂ tends to the rupture of blood vessels; ♂ causes death by violent hemorrhage; ♂ affl. in any sign brings greater danger of hemorrhage in the part, or parts, ruled by such sign; ♂ □ or 8 the ☉; ♂ in ♌, □ or 8 the ☉; ♂ ori. at B., and affl. the hyleg by dir.; ♂ sole ruler at an eclipse; ♂ ☌ the ☉ at a Solar Rev.; both internal and external hemorrhages are denoted by ♂; the ☉ afflicted tends to; a ☉ disease; the ☉ hyleg, and the ☉ to the ☌, □, or 8 ♂ by dir.; the ☽ to the ill-asp. ♂ by dir.; the Prog. ☽ to the ☌ or ill-asp. ♂ by dir.; ♄ in ♏, occi., and affl. the ☉, ☽, or Asc.; a ♃ disease, due to plethora of the blood vessels; ☿ sole ruler at an eclipse. (See "Loss of Blood" under Blood; "Blood" under Effusions. Also note the various paragraphs in this section).

Abnormal Tendency To—Haemophilia —Due to ♂ afflictions to the ☉, ☽, Asc., or hyleg; also caused indirectly by ♃ in cases of Plethora and abnormal fullness of the blood vessels; Subs at AT, CP, KP, and Local. (See "Pressure", and "Too Much Blood", under Blood; Flooding, Plethora; "Vascular Fullness" under Vascular).

Accidents— Injuries—Wounds—Cuts —Hemorrhages By—(See "Lesions" in this section; "Shedding" under Blood; Cuts, Effusions, Stabs, Wounds, etc.).

Apoplexy—Cerebral Hemorrhage— (See Apoplexy).

Arteries — Danger of Hemorrhage From—(See Aneurysm, Apoplexy, Arteries, Plethora; "Abnormal Tendency" in this section).

Bleeding—Blood Letting—(See Bleeding, Effusions; "Epistaxis" under Nose; the various paragraphs in this section).

Blood Letting—(See Bleeding).

Bloodshed — (See "Shedding" under Blood).

Blood Vessels—Rupture of—(See Apoplexy; "Rupture" under Vessels).

Bloody Discharges—(See Discharges, Flux, Spitting, in this section).

Bowels—Hemorrhage of—(See "Hemorrhage" under Bowels).

Bronchial—Broncho-Pulmonary Hemorrhage — (See "Hemorrhage" under Bronchial, Lungs).

Cerebral Hemorrhage — (See Apoplexy, Cerebral).

Childbirth—Excessive Hemorrhage At Time of—Fever or Death From—The ☽ affl. by ♂ at B., and with the ☽ hyleg, or in the 8th H. (See "Hemorrhage" under Parturition).

Clots—(See Clots).

Cutis—The Derma—Hemorrhage In— (See Purpura, Scurvy).

Death by Hemorrhage — Death by Loss of Blood—♂ shows; ♂ the afflicting planet in violent signs and affl. the hyleg; ♂ causes death by violent hemorrhage; ♂ in ♌ in the 8th H., and affl. by the □ or 8 of the ☉ or ☽; the ☉ or ☽ to the ☌ or ill-asp. ♂ by dir.; afflictions in fixed signs; afflictions in ♒, as this sign rules the blood. Case— Case of Death by Internal Hemorrhage after a Miscarriage—(See "Death from Hemorrhage", No. 168, in 1001 N.N. (See "Loss Of" under Blood; Cuts, Effusions, Flooding, Stabs, Sword, Weapons, etc.).

Diathesis — The Hemorrhagic Diathesis—Given by the Sanguine Temperament, which is ruled by ♃ and the Airy Signs. (See Diathesis, Sanguine).

Discharges—Bloody Discharges—Sanguineous Discharges—Caused by ♂, the afflictions of ♂, and ♂ entering into the configuration. The discharges are more profuse at the Full ☽. (See "Bloody Discharges" under Discharges. Also note the various paragraphs in this section).

Duels — Hemorrhage From — (See Duels, Sword).

Effusion of Blood — (See "Shedding" under Blood; Effusions).

Epistaxis—Nose Bleed—(See "Epistaxis" under Nose).

Expectoration of Blood — Spitting of Blood—(See Haemoptysis).

External Hemorrhage—Denoted by ♂; the ☉ or ☽ to the ☌ or ill-asp. ♂ by dir., both external and internal hemorrhages may result. (See Cuts, Epistaxis, Flooding, Injuries, Menses, Stabs, Weapons, Wounds, etc.).

Flooding Hemorrhage — Of Women During Menses—(See "Flooding" under Menses; Miscarriage, Parturition).

Flux—Bloody Flux—(See Flux).

Fracture — Hemorrhage With — (See "Compound" under Fracture).

Full Moon — Bloody Discharges, or a Hemorrhage, are more profuse at the Full ☽. (See "Full Moon" under Moon).

Haematemesis — (See Haemoptysis; "Blood" under Vomiting).

Haematomyelia — Hemorrhage Into the Spinal Cord—(See "Spine" in this section).

Haemophilia — (See "Abnormal Tendency" in this section).

Haemoptysis—Spitting and Expectoration of Blood—(See Haemoptysis).

Haemostatics—Agents to Arrest Hemorrhage—Styptics—Astringents—(See Astringents, Haemostatics).

Hemorrhagic Diathesis—(See "Diathesis" in this section).

High Blood Pressure—As a Cause of Hemorrhage and Rupture of Blood Vessels — (See Apoplexy; "Pressure" under Blood).

Incised Wounds — Hemorrhage From —(See Cuts).

Injuries—Lesions—Loss of Blood from Accidents or Injuries—(See Accidents, Lesions, in this section; Cuts, Stabs, Weapons, etc.).

Internal Hemorrhage — (See Death, External, in this section).

Kidneys — H e m o r r h a g e of — Renal Hemorrhage—(See "Hemorrhage" under Kidneys).

Lesions—Hemorrhage from Accidents, Injuries, Cuts, etc. — ♂ influence and afflictions; ♂ affl. in the 1st H. at B., and ☉ the Asc. by dir. or tr.; the ☉ or ☽ to the ☉ or ill-asp. ♂ by dir., and espec. in watery signs. (See "Loss Of", "Shedding", under Blood; Cuts, Effusions, Instruments, Sharp Instruments (see Sharp); Weapons).

Loss of Blood—(See "Loss Of" under Blood; "Lesions", and the various paragraphs in this section).

Lungs—Hemorrhage of—(See "Hemorrhage" under Bronchial, Lungs).

Menses — Flooding of — (See "Flooding" under Menses).

Miscarriage — Excessive Hemorrhage Attending—(See Miscarriage; "Death" in this section).

Much Bloodshed—(See "Blood" under Effusions; "Much Slaughter Everywhere" under Slaughter).

Nose Bleed — (See "Epistaxis" under Nose).

Operations—Greater Loss of Blood In — Blood Letting — Hemorrhage from the incisions of operations are greater if performed at the time of the Full ☽. (See Bleeding; "Rules For Operations" under Operations).

Parturition—Much Hemorrhage During—(See "Childbirth" in this section).

Piles—Bleeding Piles — (See Hemorrhoids).

Plethora—Hemorrhage Due To—(See Plethora; "Abnormal Tendency" in this section).

Prevalent—Effusion of Blood Prevalent—Much Bloodshed Prevalent—(See "Shedding" under Blood; "Blood" under Effusion; Shedding, Slaughter, War, etc.).

Profuse Hemorrhage—Hemorrhage is more profuse at the Full ☽, which is the time of high tide of the fluids of the body. (See Discharges, Effusions, Flooding, Full Moon, Violent, in this section).

Purpura—Hemorrhage Into the Skin —(See Purpura).

Remedy—To Help Stop Hemorrhage— (See "Haemostatics" in this section).

Renal Hemorrhage — (See "Hemorrhage" under Kidneys).

Rupture—Of Blood Vessels—(See Abnormal Tendency, Blood Vessels, Plethora, in this section).

Sanguinary Discharges—(See Bloody Discharges, Discharges, Lesions, and the various paragraphs in this section).

Scurvy — Hemorrhage In — (See Purpura, Scurvy).

Sharp Instruments — Cuts by and Hemorrhage—(See Cuts, Duels, Instruments, Sharp, Stabs, Sword, Weapons).

Shedding of Blood—(See "Shedding" under Blood; Cuts, Effusions; Shedding, Slaughter, Stabs, War. Also note the various paragraphs in this section).

Skin — Hemorrhage into — (See Purpura, Scurvy).

Spine—Haematomyelia—Hemorrhage Into the Cord—♂ afflicted in ♌.

Spitting of Blood—(See "Expectoration" in this section).

Stabs—Hemorrhage From—(See Cuts, Duels, Stabs, Sword).

Stomach — Hemorrhage of — (See "Hemorrhage" under Stomach).

Styptics—(See "Haemostatics" in this section).

Sword—Stabs and Cuts By—Hemorrhage From—(See Duels, Stabs, Sword).

Tendency To—(See "Abnormal Tendency" in this section).

Veins—The Abstraction of Blood by Opening a Vein—(See Bleeding).

Vessels—Rupture of Blood Vessel— (See Apoplexy, Plethora; "Rupture" under Vessels; "Abnormal Tendency" in this section).

Vicarious Hemorrhage—(See "Vicarious" under Menses; "Epistaxis" under Nose; "Blood" under Vomiting).

Violent Hemorrhage—Death From— ♂ causes death by violent hemorrhage. (See "Death" in this section).

Vomiting of Blood—(See Haemoptysis; "Blood" under Vomiting).

War—Bloodshed In—(See "Shedding of Blood" under Blood; Slaughter; Sword, War).

Womb — Flooding of — (See Flooding Hemorrhage, Profuse, in this section; "Hemorrhage" under Womb).

Women — Suffer Hemorrhages — (See "Womb" in this section).

Worse—Hemorrhages Worse and More Profuse—(See Flooding, Profuse, in this section).

Wounds—The Hemorrhages of—(See the various paragraphs under Cuts, Injuries, Stabs, Wounds).

HEMORRHOIDS—Piles—A Small Blood Tumor at the Anal Orifice—Ruled by ♏ and the 8th H.; a ♏ disease, and afflictions in ♏ or the 8th H.; a common ♏ disease, and almost any planet affl. in ♏ tends to; on the Asc. or 6th H.; a ♉ disease, and espec. with ♉ on the Asc. and affl. by ♂; afflictions in ♉, the sign opposite to ♏; the ♍ and ♒ signs are often involved; a ♐ disease, and caused by afflictions in this sign; the ☉, ☽, and other planets afflicted in ♏; the ☽ affl. in ♏, and espec. affl. by the ☉ or ♂ when taken ill; the ☽ in ♏, and in ☌ or ill-asp. ♄ (or ☿ if he be of the nature of ♄) at the beginning of an illness or at decumb.; ♅, ♃, or ♄ in ♏ and affl. the ☉ or ☽; ♅ ☌ ♄ in ♉ or ♏, painful hemorrhoids; ♄ affl. in ♏, and espec. when also affl. the ☉, ☽, Asc., 6th, or 8th H.; a ♄ disease;

♄ in ♏ tends to obstruct the blood circulation, which combined with the dynamic energy of ♂ in ♏ causes bleeding piles; ♄ in ♌ or ♏, and affl. ♀, tends to too much flux of the hemorrhoids; ♃ affl. in ♏, or affl. a planet in ♏, a common cause; ♃ affl. in ♎, from too much blood; a ♂ disease; caused by ♂, the ruler of the ♏ sign, and shows the activity of ♂ in the blood; ♂ affl. in ♏; ♂ in an angle, occi. of the ☉, and ori. of the ☽; ♂ influence at birth overlaid and intermingled with the influence of the other malefics ♅, ♇, and ♄; ♂ in ♏ in the 6th H., and affl. the ☽ or Asc.; ♂ in ♏ and affl. by malefics, danger of hemorrhage, and the likelihood of an operation; ♂ taking part in any configuration causing piles, and with danger of hemorrhage, and the necessity of an operation; Subs at KP. LPP (4, 5L), and at Sac. and Coc. (See Anus, Constipation, Fistula, Haematoma, Rectum).

Bleeding Piles—Hemorrhage From— Caused by the combined influences of ♄ and ♂ in ♏; ♄ in ♏ and □ ♂.

Blind Piles—Itching Piles—Protruding Piles—Caused by ♄ affl. in ♏, due to congestion and stagnation of blood in the parts. Also caused by Subs at LPP (4, 5L).

Cases of Hemorrhoids—Birth Data, etc.—See Figures 7 and 32 in Message of the Stars, and Fig. 18D in Astro-Diagnosis, books by the Heindels.

Discharges From—The Discharge More Profuse—They are more profuse at the Full ☽. (See "Full ☽" under Moon).

Flux—Too Much Flux of the Hemorrhoids—♄ in ♌ or ♏ and afflicting ♀.

Hemorrhage Of—(See "Bleeding", and also the opening part of this Article).

Itching Piles—(See "Blind" in this section).

Operations On—Hemorrhoids should not be operated on while the ☽ is passing thru the ♏ sign. Mars in ♏ and afflicted by malefics, or ♂ in any configuration causing piles, and with danger of hemorrhage, may make an operation necessary. (See "Rules" under Operations).

Painful Hemorrhoids—♅ ♂ ♄ in ♉ or ♏.

Plexus—The Hemorrhoidal Plexus— (See "Ductless Glands" under Ductless).

Protruding Piles—(See "Blind" in this section).

Too Much Blood—Hemorrhoids From —♃ affl. in ♎. (See "Too Much Blood" under Blood).

HEMP—Indian Hemp—(See Cannabis; "Saturn Group" under Herbs).

HEPATIC DIATHESIS—(See "Basal Ganglia" under Ganglion; the Introduction under Liver).

Hepatic Plexus—(See "Fifth Thoracic" under Ganglion).

Hepatic Process—(See "Alterations" under Cells; the Introduction under Liver).

HERBS—Plants—Trees—Roots—Bulbs —Berries—Vegetation—Seeds—Flowers —Leaves—Barks—Fruit—Nuts—Resins, etc.—

Herbs as Remedies—In every locality on the Earth, Nature has provided an Herb, Plant, Flower, Leaf, Root, etc., with medicinal properties to combat the diseases peculiar to that locality. Herbs to be highly efficient as remedies should be gathered during the Planetary Hour ruled by the planet which rules the Herb, and when the Herb is at its prime, green, and juicy. Read the Chapter on "Medicines and Planetary Influence" in Pearce's Textbook of Astrology, which gives the rulership of Herbs, and the rules for gathering them. The large textbook known as "Culpepper's Herbal", very fully treats of Herbs, their rulerships, and as remedies. Also see Chapters IV, V, and VI, on "Herbal Remedies", in Raphael's Handbook of Medical Astrology. Also read Chap. V, in Daath's Medical Astrology, on "How the Planets Crystallize in Organic and Inorganic Life". Herbs are used as remedies on the principles of sympathy or antipathy. Thus diseases caused by ♂ may be combatted by the Herbs and Remedies of ♄, by antipathy, or if the Herbs of ♂ are used, by sympathy. (See Antipathy, Culpepper, Cure, Drugs, Healers, Hippocrates, Homeopathy, Medicines, Polarity, Remedies, Sympathy, Treatment). The Physiological Action, the Pathological Action, the General Action, the Elementary Qualities, the Chemical Affinities, the Therapeutical Affinities, the Diathesis, etc., of the Planets and Herbs are very nicely arranged in the book called "Astral Medicine" by Dr. Duz, of Paris, France, and on pages 130 to 141 of the said book. In this Article will be listed the principal Herbs of each Planet, and the Therapeutic Properties given at the end of each Group. Also see "Drugs", Therapeutic Properties", "Typical Drugs", under each of the planets as given in the Articles on each planet. A more exhaustive list of the Herbs ruled by each planet is to be found in the book, "Culpepper's Herbal", which is quite a large volume in itself. A most interesting little Booklet on Herbs, their Therapeutic Qualities and value as remedies, is published by Heath and Heather, Herb Specialists, of St. Albans, England, which booklet is sent free to those writing for it. This Firm claims to gather Herbs at the right time, and to prepare them for the Market in their most valuable and efficient form. Their booklet contains a list of Herbs for sale, with Price List, etc. Raphael's Ephemeris and Almanac annually carries the advertisement of this Firm, and they are, no doubt, reliable.

Jupiter Group—Typical Herbs Ruled by ♃—Acer Campestre, Agrimonia Eupatoria, Alexander, Aloe (American), Aniseed, Apricots, Asclepias Vincetoxicum, Asparagus Officinalis, Avens, Balm, Balsam, Beet (White), Beta Vulgaris, Betonica Officinalis, Betony, Bilberry, Bloodwort, Borago Officinalis (Borage), Blue Flag, Castanea Vesca, Chaerophyllum Sativum, Chervil, Chestnut Tree, Cichorium Endivia, Cinnamon, Cinquefoil, Cochlearia Officinalis and Anglica, Costmary, Crithmum Maritumum, Dandelion, Dianthus Caryophyllus, Dock, Dog Grass, Endive, Eupatorium, Ficus Carica, Fig Tree, Flag (Blue), Fumitoria Officinalis, Geum Urbanum, Gilliflowers, Ginseng, Hart's Tongue, Hissopus Officinalis (Hyssop), Houseleek, Iceland Moss, Iris, Jessamine, Lapsana Communis, Lichen Caninus and Islandicus, Lime Tree, Liverwort, Lungwort, Maple, Marchantia Polymorpha, Melilotus Officinalis, Melissa Officinalis, Melitot, Moss (Iceland), Myrrh, Nailwort, Oak, Peppermint, Pinks (Wild), Polybody, Potentilla Reptans, Pulmonaria Officinalis, Roses (Red), Saccharum Officinalis, Sage, Salvia Officinalis, Samphire (Small), Scurvy Grass, Sempervivum Tectorum, Smyrnium Olusatrum, Succory (Wild), Swallow-wort, Tanacetum Vulgare, Taraxacum Densleonus (Dandelion), Thistle, Thorn Apple, Tomato, Tormentil, Triticum Repens, Vaccinium Myrtillus, Wild Pinks, Wild Succory. The Therapeutic Properties of the ♃ Group are Alexipharmic, Analeptic, Anthelmintic, Antispasmodic, Balsamic, Emollient. (See "Therapeutic", "Typical Drugs", under Jupiter).

Mars Group—Typical Herbs Ruled by ♂—Ajuva Chamaepitys, Alexandrian Senna, All-heal, Allium Sativum, Aloes, American Centaury, Anemone, Arnica, Arsmart, Artemisia Absinthium, Arum Maculatum, Barberry, Basil, Bayberry, Berberis Vulgaris, Boxtree, Briony, Brooklime, Broom, Broomrape, Bryonia Dioica, Butcher's Broom, Capsicum, Capers, Carduus Benedictus, Cassia Obovata, Catmint, Cayenne Pepper, Centaurea Calcipitra, Centaury (American), Cinchona, Civet, Cochlearia Armoracia, Cooko-pint, Corlander, Cotton Thistle, Cranesbill (Wild), Crataegus Oxyacantha, Cresses (Various), Crowfoot (Marsh), Daisy (English), Dove's-foot, Dragon's Flaxweed, Dyer's-weed, Flaxweed (Dragon's), Furzebush, Garden Cress, Garlic, Gentian (Yellow), Geranium Robertianum and Columbinum, Gratriola Officinalis. Hawthorn, Honeysuckle, Hope, Hops, Horseradish, Horsetongue, Humulus Lupus, Hyssop (Hedge), Juniperus Sabina, Lady's Thistle, Lead Wort, Leeks, Linum (Various Species of), Madder, Marsh Crowfoot, Masterwort, Mousetail, Mustard, Myrtle (Wax), Nettles (Small Stinging), Ocymum Basilicum, Onions, Oregon Grappe, Pepper (Red), Peppermint, Peruvian Bark, Peucedanum Ostruthium, Pine, Pineapple, Plantain, Poison Nut, Quaker Button, Ranunculus Aquatilis, Rheum Rhaponticum and Undulatum, Rhubarb, Rocket, Rubia Tinctorum, Sarsaparilla, Savin, Senna (Alexandrian), Sisymbrium Sophia, Savin, Smilax, Snake Root (White), Star Thistle, Strychnos Nux Vomica, Thistle (Lady's), Tobacco, Ulex Europaeus, Urtica (Urens, Dioica, and Pilulifera), Valeriana Officinalis, Wakerobin, Wax Myrtle, White Snake Root, Witch-hazel, Wormwood (Common), Yellow Gentian. The Therapeutic Properties of the ♂ Group are

Aphrodisiac, Caustic, Escharotic, Resolvent, Rubefacient, Stimulant, Tonic, Vesicant. (See "Therapeutic", "Typical", under Mars).

Mercury Group—Typical Herbs Ruled by ☿—Amara-dulcis, Anethum Graveolens, Anise, Aniseed, Apium Gravolens, Artemisia Abrotantum, Avena, Azaleas, Balm (or Melissa), Bitter Sweet, Bryonia Alba (ruled by ♅), Calamintha Officinalis, Caraway, Carrot,(Wild), Carum Carui, Celery (Wild), Convallaria Majalis, Coraline, Corylus Avellana, Cow Parsnip, Cynoglossum Officinale, Daucus Carota, Dill, Elecampane, Elfwort, Endive, Fennel, Fern, Foeniculum Vulgare, Germander, Glycerrhiza Glabra and Enchinata, Hare's Foot, Hazel Nut, Horehound (White), Hound's Tongue, Inula Helenium, Lavandula Vera, Lavender of Our Gardens, Lily of the Valley, Liquorice, May Apple, Maidenhair (White and Golden), Male Fern, Mandrake, Marjoram (Common, Wild and Sweet), Marrubium Vulgare, Melissa, Mulberry, Myrtle, Nailwort, Nephrodium Felix Mas, Nux Vomica, Oats, Olive Spurge, Organum Vulgare, Parietaria Officinalis, Parsley (Wild), Pastinaca Sativa, Pellitory of the Wall, Petroselinum Sativum, Podophyllin, Satureia Hortensis, Savory, Savoy, Scabiosa Succisa, Smallage, Southern Wood, Starwort, Teucrium Scorodonia, Trefoil, Valerian, Wild Carrots, Winter Savory. The Therapeutic Properties of the ☿ Group are Alterative, Antiperiodic, Cephalic, Nervine. (See Haematopoiesis, Innervation; "Innervation" under Gastric; "Therapeutic", "Typical Drugs", under Mercury).

Moon Group—Typical Herbs Ruled by the ☽—Acunthus Mollis, Adder's Tongue, Agaricus, Anthemis Pyrethrum, Betony Stone-crop, Brassicae, Buck's Meat, Cabbage, Caltrops, Cardamine Pratensis, Cheiranthus Cheiri, Chickweed, Clary, Cleavers Coralwort, Colewort, Colocynth, Convolvulus Coeruleus, Cress, Cuckoo Flowers, Cucumbers, Cucumis Sativis, Cucurbito Pepo, Daisy Dogtooth, Duck's Meat, Duckweed, Flaf (Sweet), Geranium Triste, Honey-Suckle, Iris, Lactucas, Ladysmock, Lemnae, Lettuce, Lily (Meadow). Livelong, Loose-strife, Mercurialis Annua, Mercury, Moonwort, Mouse-ear, Ophioglossum Vulgatum, Orpine, Pearlwort, Pellitory, Peplis Portula, Portulaca Oleraceae, Privet, Pumpkin, Purslane, Pyrethrum, Rattle Grass, Salices (many of the Salices), Salvia Verbenaca, Saxifrage (Winter), Spunk, Stellaria Media, Stonecrop, Trefoil, Utricularia Vulgaris, Wallflowers, Water Arrowhead, Watercress, Waterflag, Water Lily (Yellow), Water Violet, White Lily, White Poppy, White Rose, White Saxifrage, Whitlow Grass, Wild Wallflower, Willows, Wintergreen, Woodbine. The Therapeutic Properties of the ☽ Group are Alterative, Attenuant, Emetic. (See "Therapeutic", "Typical Drugs" under Moon).

Neptune Group — (♆). This planet is said to have rule over Herbs which are of a narcotic, soporific and sleep-producing, anaesthetic nature, such as Opiates, Tobacco, Cocaine, Morphine,

Heroin, etc. The Therapeutic Properties assigned to ♅ are Analgesic, Anodyne, Hypnotic, Soporific, and Suggestive. The Poppy Plant, Papaver Somniferum, from which Opium is made, is undoubtedly strongly ruled or influenced by ♅. The Poppy is also listed under the ♀ Group. Cocaine is the alkaloid taken from the Coca Plant (Cuca), known as Erythroxylon Coca, and is similar in its action to Caffeine, the active alkaloid of Coffee, altho Cocaine is much stronger in its deleterious effects upon the nervous system. Coffee also undoubtedly comes under the rule of ♅. Mosses, Mushrooms, Sponges, and Vegetable Fungus Growths, are also ruled by ♅. (See "Drugs", "Therapeutic", "Typical Drugs", under Neptune; Narcotics).

Rottenness of Herbs — And Seeds — (See Decay, Fruit, Rottenness).

Saturn Group — Typical Herbs Ruled by ♄ — Aconite, Aegopodium, Podagraria, Amaranthus Blitum, Aspen Poplar, Asplenium Ceterach, Atropa Belladonna, Barley, Barrenwort, Beach Tree, Beet, Belladonna, Birdsfoot, Bistort, Black Hellebore, Blackthorn, Blue Bottle, Boneset, Bucksthorn, Cannabis Sativa, Capsella Bursa-pastoris, Carduus Heterophyllus, Centaurea Nigra, Clown's Woundwort, Comfrey, Conium Maculatum, Crosswort, Cydonia Vulgaris, Equisetum Vulgaris, English Oak, Fagus Sylvatica, Flaxweed, Fleawort, Fumitory, Gladwin, Goutwort, Ground Moss, Hawkweed, Heartsease, Hedera Helix, Helleborus Niger, Hemlock, Hemp (Indian), Henbane, Holly, Hordeum Species, Horsetail, Hyoscyamus Niger, Ilex Aquifolium, Illecebrum Verticillatum, Indian Hemp, Isatis Tinctoria, Ivy (Common), Jew's Ear, Knapweed, Knotgrass, Lolium Parenne, Mangel, Medlar, Mespilus Germanica, Mosses, Mullein (Great), Navelwort, New Jersey Tea, Oak (English), Onion, Ornithopus Perpusillus, Pansies, Persicaria Urens, Plantago Psyllium, P. Coronopus, Plantain (Plantago), Polygonatum Multiflorum, Polypod (Rock), Polypodium Dryopteris, Poplar (Aspen), Populus Nigra, Prunus Spinosa, Purus Torminalis, Quince, Rhus Toxicodendron, Rock Polypod, Rupture Wort, Rushes, Rye, Sciatica Wort, Service Tree, Shepherd's Purse, Sloes, Solomon's Seal, Spleenwort, Symphytum Officinalie, Tamarix Anglica, Taxus Baccata, Tea (New Jersey), Thistle, Tulsan, Ulmus Campestris, Verbascum Thapsus, Wolfsbane. The Therapeutic Properties of the ♄ Group are Antiphlogistic, Antipyretic, Astringent, Febrifuge, Refrigerant, Sedative, Styptic. (See "Drugs", "Therapeutic", under Saturn).

Sun Group — Typical Herbs Ruled by the ☉ — Almond, Anagallis Arvensis, Angelica Sylvestris, Anthemis Nobillis, Ashtree, Bay Tree, Calendula Officinalis, Celandine, Centaurea Nigra, Chamomile, Chelidonium Majus, Citrus Aurantium, Colchicum Autumnale, Corn Hornwort, Drosera Rotundifolia, Echium Vulgare, Euphrasia Chamomilla, Eyebright, Fraxinus Excelsior, Grape (Vitis Vinifera), Heart Trefoil, Helianthus, Hypericum Androsaemium,

Juniperus Communis, Laurel, Lemon, Ligusticum Scoticum, Male Peony, Marigold, Meadow Rue, Mistletoe, Mustard, Olive, Orange, Passion Flower, Peppermint, Petasites Vulgaris, Pimpernel, Potentilla Tormentilla, Rice, Rosmarinus Officinalis, Rue, Saffron, Sanguisorba Officinalis, Sinapis Nigra and Alba, St. John's Wort, St. Peter's Wort, Sun Dew, Sun Flower, Tormentil, Turnsole, Vine (Vitis Vinifera), Viper's Bugloss, Walnut. The Therapeutic Properties of the ☉ Group are Cardiac, Anticachectic, Sudorific. (See "Drugs of the ☉" under Sun).

Uranus Group—(♅). The rulerships of the more distant planets ♅ and ♆ over Plants and Herbs, if they have such rulership on the Earth Plane, have not as yet been very clearly defined or listed. Their influences are observed so far as being mainly mental, or spiritual, and to affect the mind and nervous system. The Therapeutic action of the drugs and herbs of ♅, or the effects of ♅ action, are observed to be electric and vibrational. Of the Herbs, Croton Oil, the oil expressed from the seed of the Croton Tiglium tree, is listed as a typical herb of this planet. More of the minerals and metals are listed than herbs, as being ruled by ♅. (See "Therapeutic", "Typical", under Uranus. Read carefully the entire Article on Uranus).

Venus Group — Typical Herbs Ruled by ♀ — Acillea Ptarmica, Ajuga Reptans, Alder Tree (Black and Common), Alehoof, Alkanet, Alnus Glutinosa, Althaea Officinalis, Apples, Archangel (Wild and Stinking), Arctium Lappa, Arrack, Artichoke, Asparagus, Beans, Bear Berry, Bellis Perennis, Birch, Bishop's Weed, Black Alder, Blites, Bramble, Bugle Holly, Bunium Flexuosum, Burdock, Cherry, Chestnut (Earth), Chickpease, Cloves, Cock's-Head, Coltsfoot, Columbines, Couchgrass, Cowslip, Crabsclaw, Cranesbill, Crosswort, Cudweed, Daisy, Devil's-Bit, Dipsacus Sylvestris, Dropwort, Elder, Eryngium Maritimum, Featherfew, Figwort, Foxglove, Fumitory, Galium Cruciatum, Golden Rod, Gooseberry, Gromel, Ground Ivy, Groundsel, Herb Robert, Holly (Sea), Ivy (Ground), Indigo Plant (Indigofera), Kidney Bean, Kidney Wort, Ladies' Bedstraw, Ladies' Mantle, Leonurus Cardiaca, Ligustrum Vulgare, Lithospermum Arvense, Little Daisy, Mallow (Common), Marshmallow, Matricaria Parthenium, Mentha Pulegium, Mercury (Dog and French), Meum Athamanticum, Mint-money-wort, Mints, Motherwort, Mugwort, Nepeta Cataria, Nepeta Glechoma, Obione Portulacoides, Okro Gombo Pods, Orchis, Oxalis Acetosella, Parsley, Peachtree, Peartree, Penny Royal, Penny Wort, Peppermint, Plantago Major, Plantain (Greater), Plums, Poppy, Primula Veris, Prunella Vulgaris, Pulsatilla, Queen of the Meadows, Ragwort, Red Cherries, Rose (Damask), Rubus Fruticosis, Rye, Sanicle, Sanicula Europaea, Saponaria Officinalis, Scrophularia Nodosa and Aquatica, Sea Holly, Secale Cereale, Selfheal, Senecio Jacobaea, Sibthorpia Europaea, Silverweed, Soapwort, Sonchus Arvensis, Sorrel, Sow-thistle, Spearmint, Spignel, Strawberry, Tansy, Teasel, Throatwort, Thyme, Tussilago Farfara, Verbena Officinalis, Vervain, Violets, Wheat, Yarrow. The Therapeutic Properties of the ♀ Group are Antinephritic, Diuretic, Demulcent, Emetic. (See "Therapeutic", "Typical Drugs", under Venus).

For further and collateral study along the lines of Herbs, their use, etc., see Antipathy, Cure, Drugs, Fruits, Healers, Medical, Medicines, Metals, Minerals, Plants, Remedies, Rotten, Seeds, Sympathy, Treatment, Vegetation, etc.

HERCULES—The Star—Caput Hercules—Pollux—(See Pollux).

HEREDITY — Hereditary — Inherent—Innate—Inherited Tendencies—Constitutional, Organic, and Structural Tendencies of Body — Hereditary Transmission is often explained by the Figure of the Heavens for the moment of Conception rather than by the Figure for the moment of birth, and in this connection you should make a thorough study of the Prenatal Epoch, and how to erect Maps for the time of conception when the birth hour is known approximately. In the Natal Map the ☉ is the Sig. of the inherent tendencies and hereditary transmissions, while the ☽ denotes acquired conditions, as the ☉ is Organic, and the ☽ Functional. In many diseases the Map of Birth does not fully account for the condition, whereas the map for the time of conception does explain and account for the disease condition more fully. A person may be bothered with bowel and abdominal disorders, and the map of birth not show any afflictions in ♍ or the 6th H., but in the map for the time of conception, ♄ or ♂, or both, may be in ♍ in the 6th H., which would account for such an inherent tendency. So also in cases of Deafness, Blindness, Idiocy, and many congenital conditions, the map for the time of conception, and the influences of the ☽ at the time of her monthly return to the central line of impulse during gestation, account for many defects and congenital deformities. Inherent Mania is an affliction especially indicated by the map of conception, and may not be shown by the map of birth. In making a study of the star maps of birth of many individuals in the same family, considering their Aunts, Uncles, Grandparents, Cousins, etc., there is a noted similarity between the maps, and the same Rising Sign, or some particular Sign of the Zodiac, is usually prominent in all of them, and all are similarly afflicted or benefitted, and either the ☉, ☽, or the Asc., are in the same sign or triplicity. (See "Likenesses" under Family). However, an inherited trait may be represented by any part of the nativity, and by antenatal maps from the time of conception, and on down to birth. Heredity also must be considered to account for the differences in people born at the same time, and in the same vicinity, although the times, seasons, and appointments of their lives will be very similar. The 4th H. in the map of birth also denotes and shows heredi-

tary tendencies. The Occult side of heredity is a big subject, the incoming Ego, the effects of Karma, the age of the Soul, the stage in Evolution, etc., and these subjects are well-discussed in the book, "Cosmo-Conception", by Max Heindel, and also in the books, "The Key to the Universe", and "The Key of Destiny", by Dr. and Mrs. Homer Curtiss. Also in the book, "The Tarot of the Bohemians", by Papus, the plan of Destiny, Fate, Heredity, and how the Universe is builded and conducted; the Past, Present, and Future of the Human Race, are well defined and explained. (For collateral study see the references at the end of this section).

Hereditary Diseases—And Tendencies—These are especially indicated by the ☉, his position and afflictions at B. Also indicated by the fixed signs, and with many planets and afflictions in them at B. The 4th, 8th, and 10th H., the Lights and ♄, are espec. concerned with hereditary influences and transmissions. (See Eighth House; "Fixed Signs" under Fixed; Fourth House, Moon, Saturn, Sun, Tenth House).

Well-Descended Body—♃ in an earthy sign at B.; the Ruler or Sig. in his own triplicity, and well-aspected, one well descended. Nature and the Higher Powers so rule, arrange and manage the incarnation of an individual, and by the Law of Attraction and Similars, lead an incoming Ego to parents, ancestors, and a line of descent, which is more or less bound up with the native from out of the Past, and to cause the birth to take place at a time and place which gives a star map of birth considerably in harmony with such relationships. The parents give to the maturing embryo and child a body much like their own, as a rule, or similar to some relative or ancestor in the line, but the Occult Masters and Initiates teach that the mind and character of the child are not directly transmitted from the parents, but that the incoming Ego, or Spirit, brings such character with it. It is said that the star map of birth shows the character and attainments which the native had at his death in the physical body in his material incarnation previous to this one, and that in the present life he is forming and building the map which will be his star map of birth at his next incarnation. Also by right living, right thinking, attainment, wisdom, knowledge, understanding in the present life, by obeying the laws of health, the native is also largely determining the kind and quality of his next physical body. People who are ignorant, negative, passive, receptive, given to worry, brooding, and who are constantly thinking in terms of disease, tend to attract disease, ill-health, and to be born into a family with weak and sickly bodies, as into a family afflicted with Consumption, Asthma, Tuberculosis, and various constitutional and organic diseases, whereas a native now given to right and constructive thinking, thoughts of good and perfect health, is gradually building a body, a prototype, for his next body, and a more perfect, healthful, handsome, strong and efficient body. These matters are discussed in the books mentioned in this section, and it is well for all students of Astrology to study deeply into the Occult side of life, know The Mysteries, if you ever expect to understand the Philosophy of Life and Destiny, and not follow along ignorantly in the trails of Exoteric Schools of Thought, Religion, or Philosophy, or allow yourself to be governed by the superstitions and false traditions, and false interpretations of Truth, such as prevail over the Earth today. (For further and collateral study along this line see Acquired, Ascendant, Astral, Birth, Blindness, Character, Children, Conception, Congenital, Constitutional, Deafness (see Hearing); Deaf and Dumb (see Hearing); Defects, Deformities, Destiny, Deviations, Diathesis, Ego, Environment, Epilepsy, Events, External, Family, Fate, Father, Form, Functions, Genius, Gestation, Hexis, Idiocy, Idiosyncrasies, Imperfections, Innate, Insanity, Latent, Mania, Map, Monsters, Mother, Mutes, Nativity, Natural, Organic, Parents, Personality, Praeincipients, Prenatal, Prodigies, Remarkable, Soul, Spirit, Structural, Susceptibility, etc., and other subjects which you may have in mind which may be connected with heredity).

HERMAPHRODITES — Androgynous— Dual-Sexed — Bisexual — Male and Female Organs Developed In the Same Body — The human body in the early stages of its evolution was bisexual, hermaphrodite, and with the male and female organs equally developed in the one physical body. Then came the separation of the sexes into two bodies, a more distinct male and female body, of which Adam and Eve are regarded as the first types of the separated sexes. (See the book, "Cosmo-Conception", by Max Heindel, on this subject of the Separation of the Sexes). Remnants of this early hermaphrodite type still appear on Earth. In the remote future it is said by the Occult Masters that the male and female bodies will again be reunited into one form, or body. The word Hermaphrodite originated from the word "Harpocrates", the God of Silence, and Ptolemy used the word at times to refer to Stammerers, those who had some defect of speech, and were silent and unable to speak. The common signs strong at B. are said to predominate at the birth of a hermaphrodite. Also the ☽ in the 1st H., with ♄ and ☿, and espec. if ♂ also give testimony, a hermaphrodite, or perhaps have but one passage. (For further planetary influences which tend to this condition see Eunuchs; "Foolish Mind" under Foolish; "Hermaphrodites" under Men; "Excessive Virile Members" under Virile).

HERMES — The Greek name for Mercury, the Messenger of the Gods—(See Mercury).

HERNIA—Rupture—The Protrusion of a Viscus from Its Normal Position— Hernia is classed as a ♄, ♂, ♏, and ♍ disease. Also a ♀ disease when ♀ is affl. by ♄; afflictions in ♍ or ♏, and

espec. when these signs occupy the 6th H.; ♄ in ♍ or ♏ in the 6th H.; ♂ affl. in ♍ or ♏, and espec. in the 6th H.; ♀ in ♍ or ♏, and affl. by ♄; the Asc. to the □ or ☍ ♄ by dir.; Subs at PP. (See the various paragraphs in this section).

Abdominal Hernia—♄ or ♂ affl. in ♍; ♂ in ♍ in the 6th H.; ♀ affl. in ♍, in some cases, and espec. if affl. by ♄; Subs at PP (2, 3, 4L). (See Abdomen).

Aneurysm — Hernial Aneurysm—The ☽ affl. in ♏. (See Aneurysm).

Brain—Hernia of—Encephalocele — ♄ or ♂ affl. in ♈; Subs at AT. (See Brain).

Death by Hernia — ♂ the afflicting planet.

Diaphragm—(See "Hernia" under Diaphragm).

Encephalocele—Hernia of the Brain— (See "Brain" in this section).

Exaggerated Action—Hernia Resulting From—(See Exaggerated; Influence Of" under Mars, Uranus).

Groin—Hernia In—(See "Inguinal" in this section).

Inguinal Hernia—Hernia In the Groin, and Thru the Abdominal Ring — A ♏ disease, and afflictions in ♏; ♏ on the Asc. at B.; the ☉ or ☽ in ♏, and affl. by ♂ at B., and by dir.; a ♅ disease; ♅ affl. in ♏, and espec. in the 6th H.; a ♄ disease; ♄ affl. in ♌ or ♏, or ♄ in evil asp. to ♀; denoted by ♂; a ♂ disease and affliction; ♂ exactly rising in ♏; ♂ ☌ or ill-asp. ♅, and espec. when in ♏ and fixed signs; ♂ in ♍, ♏, or ♐, and affl. the hyleg; ♂ affl. in ♍ in the 6th H.; a ♀ disease, and espec. when ♀ is affl. by ♄; ♀ in ♏ in ☌ or ill-asp. ♄; ♀ in ♏ in the 6th H., and affl. by ♄; Subs at PP (3, 4L). (See Groins).

Lacerations—(See Lacerations).

Motion — (See "Accelerated Motion" under Motion).

Rupture—(See the various paragraphs under Rupture. Also see Bursting, Lacerations, Pressure. Note the various paragraphs in this section).

Scrotal Hernia—(See "Hernia" under Scrotum).

Strangulated Hernia — A ♄ disorder and affliction; ♄ affl. in ♍ or ♏, and espec. in the 6th H., and with danger of constriction of the bowel, and interferring with the passage of faeces; Subs at PP (2, 3, 4L). (See Inguinal, Ventral, in this section; Scrotum).

Umbilical Hernia—(See Navel).

Ventral Hernia—Hernia Thru the Abdominal Wall—♂ affl. in ♍ or ♓, and espec. in the 6th H. (See Belly; "Abdomen" in this section).

HERPES—A Skin Disease with Patches of Distinct Vesicles—

Face—Herpes On—The ☽ or ♂ affl. in ♈; an ♈ disease; ♈ on the Asc. at B., and espec. when ♂ or the ☽ are in ♈ in the Asc., and afflicted; Subs at MCP (4C), and at KP. (See Face).

Herpes Zoster—Shingles—The ☽ affl. in ♋, ♌, or ♍; a ♂ disease; ♂ affl. in ♌; an ♈ disease, and afflictions in ♈, or ♈ on the Asc., and afflicted.

Ringworm — The Circling Tinea or Herpes—(See Ringworm).

Tetter— A Form of Herpes — Ringworm — Eczema — (See Eczema, Ringworm, Tetter). For collateral study see Barber's Itch (see Barbers); Eczema, Eruptions, Psoriasis, Skin, Spotted Fever (see Spotted); Tinea, Vesicles.

HEXIS — The Permanent Habit In Disease—(See Diathesis, Directions; "Certain" under Disease; Heredity, Organic, Praeincipient, Structural).

HICCOUGH—Hiccup—Involuntary Closure of the Glottis — An Interrupted Spasmodic Inspiration—Caused by afflictions in ♋; a ♋ disease; a ☽ and ♅ disease; ♅ affl. in ♋ or ♍, and due to the erratic action of the Diaphragm; ♅ ☌ ☽ in ♋; ♅ affl. in ♉, and afflicting the organ of Coordination, located in ♉; Subs at SP (7, 8D), and at Spl.P. (9D). (See "Interference" under Breathing; Diaphragm, Glottis, Spasmodic).

HIGH—Highly—

Altitudes — High Altitudes — Falls From—(See Heights).

Blood Pressure—High Blood Pressure —(See "Pressure" under Blood).

Body — A High Body — (See Giants, Tall).

Disease Runs High—(See "High" under Fever).

Excitable — Highly Excitable — (See Excitable).

Fever — High and Burning Fever — (See "High Fever" under Fever).

Forehead — A High Forehead — (See Forehead).

High Strung—(See "Strung" in this section).

Living—High Living—Disease, Fever, or Plethora From—The ☉ affl. by ♃ or ♀; the ☉ □ or ☍ ♃; the ☽ affl. by ♃; the ☽ in ♉ at B., and to the ☌ or ill-asp. ♄ by dir. (or to ☿ if he be of the nature of ♄), at the beginning of an illness, or at decumb., fevers from; ♃ causes complaints from high living and injudicious diet; ♃ □ or ☍ the Asc.; ♃ affl. in ♉, ♍, or ♎; ♃ affl. in ♉, or ♃ affl. the ☉, ☽, or ♀ from this sign, plethora from; ♀ diseases; ♀ affl. at B., and to the ☌ or ill-asp. the Asc. by dir.; ☿ affl. in ♌; ♌ on the cusp the 6th H. tends to disorders from inharmonious living; lord of the 6th or 10th H. in the 5th H., and afflicted. (See Appetites, Debauched, Depraved, Diet, Dissipation, Dissolute, Drink, Drunkenness, Eating, Epicureans, Excesses, Extravagance, Feasting, Fever (see "Slight Fever" under Fever); Food; Free Living (see Free); Gluttony, Indigestion, Indiscretions, Indulgences, Inflation, Intemperance, Luxuries, Obesity, Plethora, Riotous Living (see Riotous); Surfeits, etc.).

Mortality High—High Death Rate— (See Mortality).

Nervous Tension—High Nervous Tension—High Strung—Highly Neurotic— (See "Nerves" under Excitable; "Neurotic" under Nerves; Tension; "Strung" in this section).

Nose—A High Nose—(See "High" under Nose).

Places—High Places—Heights—Falls From—(See Heights).

Pulse — High Pulse — (See "Accelerated" under Heart; "High" under Pulse).

Sensitive — Highly Sensitive — (See Hyperaesthesia, Sensitive).

Strung — High Strung — The ☉ in ♊; the ☉ in any asp. to ♅, or vice versa; ♆, ♅, ☿, and the ☽ tend to make the body high strung and nervous. (See "Nerves" under Excitable; "Full Moon" under Moon; "Neurotic" under Nerves).

Temper—(See Anger; "Even Temper", "High Temper", under Temper).

Tension — High Nervous Tension — (See "Nervous Tension" in this section).

Tides—Tide—High Tide—The Fluids of the Body At High Tide—(See Fluids; "Full Moon", under Moon).

Urine — Highly Loaded Urine — (See "Highly Loaded" under Urine).

Winds—High Winds—Suffering From —(See "High" under Winds).

HIGHWAYMEN—Injury or Death By— ♄ Lord of the Year, and afflicted at the Vernal Ingress, causes many highway robberies, and thieves to be active generally, and with much public anxiety, sadness, and tribulation; Comets appearing in ♎. (See Bandits, Crime, Rapine, Robbers, Thieves).

HINDER PARTS — Of the Body — (See Back, Buttocks, Dorsal, Loins, Rear, Spine, etc.).

HINDRANCES — Hindered — The influence of ♄ by his afflictions is to hinder, impede, retard, suppress, and to slow up the functions of the body, and to do so by retaining the wastes of the body, by hardening, crystallization of the tissues, suppressions of the fluids of the body, etc. (See Arrested, Clogging, Crystallization, Deposits, Functions (see "Hindered" under Functions); Hardening, Impeded, Impediments, Minerals, Obstructions, Restrictions, Retarded, Retention, Rigid, Slow, Stoppages, Suppressions, Wastes, etc.).

HINDU ASTROLOGY — This System of Astrology differs somewhat from the European System of Astrology, as used in this Work, and it would take a separate volume to go into the Hindu Methods. There is a good Treatise on Hindu Astrology in the book, "Sepharial's Manual of Astrology". Also the British Journal of Astrology, of London, and edited by Mr. E. H. Bailey, is devoting a large amount of time and space to the Hindu Methods. Also see Alan Leo's New Dictionary of Astrology. It is very evident that the Hindu interpretations of Astrology are very valuable in explaining the planetary and Zodiacal causes of many diseases and afflictions, and are an aid in diagnosis, and it is well for the student of Medical Astrology to study into the Hindu System. In future Editions of this Encyclopaedia, an elaborate treatise of the Hindu System will, and should be added, as well as many other subjects which may not appear in the First Edition. My desire is to see this Work added to as the years and Generations go by, and until it becomes a large Library of Volumes on the subject of Medical Astrology, but such a great and complete Work is too much to be done by any one person, and during the lifetime of one individual. In the Hindu System, the rulership of the Eyes and Ears is placed under different Houses than in our System. Also the rule concerning the Father and Mother is different, and is not elastic, according to sex, as in our System. (See Ears, Eyes, Father, Mother). Also, in the Hindu System, each Sign of the Zodiac is divided into nine equal parts, known as "Navamsa", and this finer division helps to locate the part of an organ afflicted, and to account for the various deteriorations of a complicated organ, such as the Heart. In this Work, I am giving you a brief Article on Navamsa, which should be enlarged upon in future Editions. (See Hyleg, Memory, Navamsa, Senses).

HIPPOCRATES—Called the "Father of Medicine". Born about 460 B.C., and died about 357 B.C. He advocated Antipathy in the cure of disease, which System is now advocated by Allopathy. (See Antipathy, Cure, Galen, Healers, Homeopathy, Medicines, Opposites, Paracelsus, Remedies, Sympathy, Treatment).

HIPPUS — Clonic Spasm of the Iris — (See "Hippus" under Eyeballs, Iris).

HIPS—The Upper Part of the Thigh— Hip Joint — The Hips are ruled by ♐ and the 9th H. They are under the external rulership of ♐. The arteries and nerves of this region are under the internal rulership of the ♐ sign. The hip bones, and the femur, are under the structural rulership of ♐. (See Sagittarius). The Locomotor Muscles of the Hips and Thighs are ruled by ♐.

Accidents To—Hurts, Injuries, Wounds To—♄ or ♂ affl. in ♐; ♄ ♂ ♂ in ♐; afflictions in ♐; ♐ on the Asc. (See Bruises, Cuts, Fractures, in this section).

Aches—In the Hips and Thighs—Old Aches In—♄ in ♐ when ♄ is the afflictor in the disease; the ☽ in ♍ in ♂ or ill-asp ♄ (or ☿ if he be of the nature of ♄) at the beginning of an illness, or at decumb. (Hor'y). (See Aches).

Ailments In—(See "Diseases", and the various paragraphs in this section).

All Diseases In—Signified by the 9th H. and ♐, and afflictions therein.

Ankylosis—Of the Hip Joint—The ☉ or ♂ affl. in ♐, or the ☉ ♂ ♂ in ♐, by excess of heat; ♄ affl. in ♐, by deposits. (See "Case" under Ankylosis).

Arthritis — Of Hip Joint — Hip Joint Disease—♄ ♂ ♂ in ♐, and also otherwise afflicted by the ☉, ☽, or malefics. (See "Arthritis" under Joints; "Hip-Joint Disease" in this section).

Bones Of — Are under the external rulership of ♐. Disorders and injuries of the hip bones are caused by afflictions in ♐, and also Subs at PP (4L). (See Dislocation, Fracture, Joint, in this section).

Broken Hip—(See "Fracture" in this section).

Bruises To—Contusions—♄ affl. in ♐. (See Bruises).

Circulation Poor In—♄ in ♐, ♂ or ill-asp. ♃ or ♀.

Cold In — Cold and Chill In the Hips and Thighs—♄ in ♐. (See Cold).

Cold and Moist Humours—In the Hips and Thighs—♀ affl. in ♐ when ♀ is the afflictor in the disease. (See "Cold and Moist" under Humours).

Contusions — (See "Bruises" in this section).

Coxalgia—(See "Pain" in this section).

Cramps In—♅ in ♐. (See Cramps).

Cuts To—Afflictions in ♐; ♂ affl. in ♐; ♐ on the Asc. (See Cuts).

Diseases In—Hip Diseases—Diseases in Hips, Thighs, and Haunches—Afflictions in ♐; ♐ diseases; ♐ on the Asc.; malefics in the 9th H.; a Stellium in the 9th H., or in ♐; the ☉, ☽, ♄, ♂, or ♀ affl. in ♐; ♄ affl. in ♊, by reflex action; ♄ in ♐ in the Asc., and afflicted. (See "Hip Joint", and the various paragraphs in this section; "Impar" under Ganglion).

Dislocation—Of the Hip Joint—Afflictions in ♐, or ♐ on Asc.; ♄ or ♂ affl. in ♐. (See Dislocations).

Drying Up—(See "Synovial Fluid" in this section).

Feverish Ailments In—♐ on the Asc.; ♂ in ♐. (See "Hot Humours" in this section).

Fluid—Of the Hip Joint—(See "Synovial" in this section).

Fracture—Broken Hip—♄ or ♂ affl. in ♐; the ☽ affl. in ♐; ♂ affl. in ♊, by reflex action; ♐ on the Asc., 6th, or 12th H.; ♐ ruler of the 6th or 12th H., and afflicted by the progression or transit of planets. (See Femur, Fractures).

Gout In—(See "Hips and Thighs" under Gout).

Hams—Hamstrings—(See Thighs).

Haunches—(See Buttocks).

Heats In—Hips and Thighs—The ☉ or ♂ afflicted in ♐; ☉ ♂ ♂ in ♐; ♐ on the Asc., and espec. if the ☉ or ♂ are also in ♐ in the Asc. (See "Heats" under Heat).

Hip-Joint Disease — Arthritis — A ♐ disease, and afflictions in ♐; ♐ on the Asc.; the ☉ in ♐, ♂ or ill-asp. ♄; the ☉ ♂ ♂ in ♐; the ☉ and other important planets in ♐, and affl. by the ♂, □, or ⚼ of ♄ and ♂; ♄ in ♐, occi., and affl. the ☉, ☽, or Asc.; ♄ afflicting the ☉, or other important body, in ♐, and with ♂ usually forming an aspect; ♄ ♂ the ☉ in ♐, and the ☉ also affl. by ♂; ♄ and ♂ both in ♐ in ♂ ☉; ♄ affl. in ♐ may result in some permanent disability of the hip joint, causing lameness, and inability to walk. Case—Hip Joint Disease—See Chap. XIII, page 85, Daath's Medical Astrology. (See Accidents, Ankylosis, Arthritis, Dislocation, Fracture, Gout, Heats, Lameness, Pain, Synovial, in this section; "Inability" under Walk).

Hot Humours—In Hips and Thighs— The ☉ or ♂ affl. in ♐ when either of these planets are the afflictors in the disease; ♐ on the Asc. (See Feverish, Heats, Humours, in this section).

Humours In—In Hips or Thighs—♂ affl. in ♐, pain and ulcers in the hips and thighs by humours settled in those parts. (See Cold and Moist, Hot Humours, Pain, in this section).

Hurts—To Hips and Thighs—♄ or ♂ affl. in ♐; malefics affl. in the 9th H., or in the Asc. in ♐. (See Accidents, Bruises, Cuts, Dislocation, Fracture, Lameness, in this section).

Ilium—The Upper Part of the Innominate, or Hip Bone—Injuries and Afflictions to this part of the Hip Bone tend to result when malefics are in the last face of ♏, and in the 1st Decan. of ♐. (See Ilium; Bone, Fracture, Ischium, Pubes, in this section).

Injuries To—Hips and Thighs—(See Accidents, Bruises, Cuts, Dislocation, Fracture, in this section).

Innominate Bone—The Hip Bone, and including the Ilium, Ischium, and Pubis—The Pelvis—Injuries To—Ruled by ♐, and also partly influenced by ♏. Afflictions and malefics in ♐ tend to injuries to. (See Ilium, Ischium, Pelvis, Pubes, in this section).

Ischium—The Inferior Part of the Hip Bone—Accidents and Injuries to may result when the afflictions are in the 3rd Decan. of ♐, or in the first face of ♑. (See Ischium, Pubes. Also see Ilium, Innominate, in this section).

Joint—The Hip Joint—Disorders of—(See Ankylosis, Arthritis, Dislocation, Gout, Heat, Hip-Joint Disease, Lameness, Pain, Synovial, in this section).

Lameness—In the Hips and Thighs—The ☽ affl. in ♐. (See Dislocation, Fracture, Gout, Hip-Joint Disease, Rheumatism, Swellings, Weakness, and the various paragraphs in this section).

Locomotor Muscles—Of the Hips and Thighs—Ruled by ♐. Disorders of are caused by afflictions in ♐.

Men Suffer—With Hip and Thigh Diseases—♂ in ♐, ℞, and Lord of the Year at the Vernal Equinox. (See Men).

Moist and Cold Humours—In the Hips —(See "Cold and Moist" in this section).

Muscles—(See Locomotor, Rheumatism, in this section).

Narrow Hips—(See "Small" in this section).

Nervous Pains In—(See "Pains In" under Thighs; "Pain" in this section).

Old Aches In—(See "Aches" in this section).

Operations On—Should not be made when the ☽ is passing thru ♐. (See Operations).

Pain—In the Hips and Thighs—Coxalgia—Nervous Pains In—The ☽ in ♎ or ♐, ♂, or ill-asp. ♄ (or ♀ if he be of the nature of ♄) at the beginning of an illness, or at decumb. (Hor'y); ♃ affl. in ♐; ♂ in ♐ and affl.. the ☉; ♂ affl. in ♐ tends to pains and ulcers in the hips or thighs due to humours settled in those parts; ♀ affl. in ♌ or ♐; nervous pains in. (See "Pain" under Thighs).

Pelvis—Disorders In—(See Pelvis; "Innominate" in this section).

Pubes—Pubis—The Anterior Portion of the Innominate Bone—(See Pubes; "Innominate" in this section).

Restrictions—In the Region of the Hips and Thighs—♄ affl. in ♐. (See Restrictions. Also note the various paragraphs in this section).

Rheumatism In—Hips or Thighs—Rheumatic Pains In—Afflictions in ♉ or ♐; ♐ on the Asc.; the ☽ affl. in ♐; ♅, ♄, or ♇ in ♐, and affl. the ☉, ☽, or Asc.; ♄ affl. in ♐; ♄ in ♐ in the 1st or 6th H.; ♃ affl. in ♉ or ♐; Subs at PP (2L). (See Gout, Lameness, in this section; Gout, Rheumatism).

Sacrum—(See Sacrum).

Small Hips—Narrow Hips—♄ ascending at B.

Strong Hips—Strong and Well-Proportioned Hips, Thighs, and Legs—♃ in the Asc.; ♐ in the Asc.

Swellings—In the Hips or Thighs—The ☽ in ♐, ♂, or ill-asp. ♄ (or ♀ if he be of the nature of ♄) at the beginning of an illness, or at decumb. (Hor'y); ♃, ♂, or ♀ affl. in ♐; ♃ affl. in ♐ in the 6th H.; ♀ affl. in ♑. (See Swellings).

Synovial Fluid—Drying Up of In Hip Joint—♄ affl. in ♐. (See Ankylosis, Arthritis, Hip Joint Disease, Lameness, in this section; Joints, Synovial).

Tumors—In Hips or Thighs—A ♐ disease, and afflictions in ♐; ♄ or ♀ affl. in ♐; ♂ affl. in ♋. (See the ☽ influence under "Swellings" in this section; Tumors).

Ulcers In—(See Humours, Pain, in this section; Ulcers).

Walk—Inability to Walk Due to Hip Diseases or Injury—(See "Hip-Joint Disease" in this section; Walk).

Weakness—In Hips or Thighs—The ☽ hyleg in ♐, and afflicted, and espec. with females; ♄ affl. in ♍ or ♐; ♂ or ♀ affl. in ♐; ♐ on the Asc. or 6th H., and containing malefics, and espec. ♄. (See "Lameness" and the various paragraphs in this section).

Well-Proportioned—Hips and Thighs —Well Formed—Strong—♃ in the Asc.; ♐ on the Asc. (See Well-Proportioned).

Wounds—To Hips or Thighs—(See Accidents, Cuts, Dislocation, Fracture, Hurts, in this section).

HIRCUS—Capella—The Goat—An eminent fixed star of the 1st magnitude in 20° ♊, of the nature of ♂ and ♀. (See Calamity, Capella, Dishonest).

HIVES—Urticaria—Nettle Rash—A Vesicular Cutaneous Eruption—(See Urticaria, Vesicles).

HOARSENESS—Dysphonia—(See "Hoarseness" under Larynx).

Hoarse Signs—Of the Zodiac—♈, ♉, ♌, ♑. Those born under them are said to have a hoarseness, or roughness of the voice, and those born under ♑ to be more weak and feminine, and to have a whistling sound in speaking. (See Throat, Voice).

HOGS—Swine—Ruled by the 6th H. in the map of the native. (See Swine).

A Performing Pig—See "Performing Pig", No. 781, in 1001 N.N.

HOLLOW—Sunken—(See "Hollow" under Cheeks, Chest; "Sunken" under Eyeballs).

Tumor — Hollow Tumor and Cystic Formations — (See "Hollow" under Cysts).

HOME—The Home—Ruled by the ☽ and the 4th H.

Death — Dies In His Own Home — Lord of the 8th H. in the 4th H. at B.

Fire—Burns, Scalds In the Home—♂ in the 4th H. at B., and by dir., in a fiery sign, and affl. the ☉, ☽, or Asc. (See Burns, Fire, Scalds).

No Home — No Home or Friends — A Wanderer—Vagabond—The ☉ Sig. in ☐ or ☍ ☽. (See "Many Changes" under Residence; Roaming; Wandering; "Wandering" under Travel; Vagabond).

Worry—Thru Home Conditions—☿, or malefics, affl. in the 4th H. (See "Worries" under Children; Environment, Family, Love Affairs, Marriage).

HOMEOPATHY — A School of Medicine founded by Dr. Hahnemann, and on the theory of treating disease by Sympathy and Similars. Thus ♄ diseases are treated by ♄ remedies; ♂ diseases by ♂ remedies, etc. Their Motto is "Similia Similibus Curantur". However, Paracelsus, a Swiss Physician and Astrologer, born in 1493, was the first to advocate the doctrine of treating by Similars. Most of the Astrological Doctors and Writers on Medical Astrology in Modern Times have been Homeopaths, and say much in support of the Homeopathic Theory. (See Antipathy, Cure, Galen, Healers, Opposites, Paracelsus, Sympathy, Treatment; "Zodiac Salts" under Zodiac). For the birth data of a leading Homeopathic Physician, see "Kali, Dr. C. S.", No. 894, in 1001 N.N.

HOMICIDE—Homicidal—Tendency To —Danger of—♄ Sig. ☐ or ☍ ♂, or vice versa; the Asc. to the ☌, P., ☐ or ☍ ♂ by dir., and ♂ in a sign of human form at B., as in ♊, ♍, the 1st half of ♐, and in ♒. The ☉ is also usually severely afflicted, and the ♈ and ♌ Signs, the strong signs of the ☉. The 0° of ♌ and ♒; the 5° of ♈ and ♎, and the 9° of mutable signs, are often involved and afflicted by malefics. (See Assassination, Criminal; "Patricide" under Father; Murder). Case of a Homicide— See "Who Was This", No. 560, in 1001 N.N.

HOMOSEXUALITY—Sodomy—The Attraction of Persons of the Same Sex— Caused by ♅ influence, and afflictions of ♅ to the ☉, ☽, or ♀ at B. Even the good aspects of ♅ to the ☉ or ♀ may lead to sex perversions and abnormalities. Also caused by ♆ affl. in 7th H. (See "Licentious" under Men; Perversions, Unnatural, Vices).

HONEST—Honesty—Upright—Honourable—Frank—Sincere—Open-Minded— Trustworthy, etc.—The ☉ in ♌, or the ☉ Sig. in ♌, and well-aspected; the ♌ influence tends to, being the sign of the ☉; ♌ on the Asc., and with the ☉ as ruler; the ☉ Sig. in ♒; the ☽ incr. in light, and apply. to ♃, unless ♂ be in ☐ or ☍ ♃, which would modify; ♄ Sig. in ♐; ♃ rising at B., well-aspected and

dignified; ♃ ruler and well-aspected; ♃ in the Asc., well-aspected and dignified; ♃, ♄, and ☿ well-placed and well-aspected; ♃ in the M.C., near the Meridian, well-aspected, and in a strong sign, honourable, and also confers honors and dignity; ♀ Sig., and in ✶ or △ ♃; ♀ on the Meridian, dignified and well-aspected, unless affl. by ♄; ♀ Sig. in ♊; the 1st face of ♎ or ♐ on the Asc. (See Character, Cheating, Conduct, Criminal, Deceitful, Dishonest, Evil, Forgers, Gambling, Good, Honour, Hypocritical, Liars, Libelers, Morals, Noble, Principles, Recreations, Reliable, Responsibility, Robbers, Sincere, Trustworthy, etc.).

Honourable Things—Strives After— ☿ Sig. in ♐, but seldom attains them.

Tolerably Honest—The ☽ Sig. ☐ or ☍ ☿, and ☿ well-asp. by ♃. (See Dual, Miserly, Selfishness).

HONOUR — Honor — Honorable — The Honour is ruled by the 10th H. (See Tenth).

Death — In Affairs of Honor — (See Contests, Duels).

Honorable—The Native Is Honest and Honourable—(See Honest).

Loss of Honour—The Honor is affected by the directions to the Midheaven, and the M.C. afflicted by the evil aspects of planets tends to loss of honor; the ☉ directed to the Ascelli; ♄ or ♂ to the cusp the 10th H. by dir.; ♄ to the ☌ or ill-asp. the radical ☉ by dir.; the periodic direction of ♄ to the radical ☉; ♃ by periodic revolution to the ill-asps. the radical ☉. (See Anxiety, Disgrace, Misfortune, Renunciation, Reputation, Reversals, Ruin, Scandal, Sorrows, Trouble, etc.).

HOOKED FORWARD — (See Bending; "Downward Look" under Look; "Stoop Shoulders" under Shoulders; Stooping).

HOPE—Hopes—Hopeful—Ambitions— Desires—Hope is ruled by the 11th H. conditions. (See Ambition, Desires, Eleventh House).

Hopeful—Sanguine — Cheerful—Optimistic—(See Cheerfulness; "Peace of Mind" under Mind; Optimistic; "Sanguine Temperament" under Sanguine).

Hopes Cut Off—Lack of Hope—In a Weak and Hopeless State—Malefics in the 11th H.; lord of the 11th a malefic, and espec. ♄, and in the 12th H. (See Dejected, Despair, Despondency, Insanity, Invalids, Low Spirits (see Low); Melancholy, Mutable Signs (see Mutable); Optimism, Worry, etc.).

Life—Small Hope of Life—The Sick Will Hardly Escape—(See "Hope" under Life; "Sick" under Escape).

HORARY QUESTIONS—A Horary Map is a Map of the Heavens made up for the time of an incident, a worry, an anxiety, or the beginning of a disease, at decumbiture, at the taking to bed in illness, etc., and the aspects, sign and house positions of the planets at such a time usually give the key to the situation, and the possible outcome for good or ill. Many of the influences listed in this Encyclopaedia are Horary. The Rules of Horary Astrology are given in Lilly's Astrology,

Wilson's Dictionary of Astrology, Simmonite's Horary Astrology, Alan ·Leo's New Dictionary of Astrology. Also a short Article in Sepharial's New Dictionary of Astrology. (See Cardinal, Course, Cure, Decumbiture, Diagnosis, Duration; "Fixed Signs" under Fixed; Long Diseases (see Long); Mutable Signs (see Mutable); Prognosis; Querent, Quesited, Recovery; "Diseases" under Short).

HORAS—These are the positive and negative halves of Signs, and are known as the Solar and Lunar Horas. The Solar Horas are the positive halves, and the Lunar Horas are the negative halves. Malefics in the positive, or Solar Horas, are very powerful, and weak when in the negative, or Lunar Horas. Benefics are stronger when in the Negative Signs, and Negative Horas, and weaker when in the positive, or Solar Horas. In the odd, or positive signs, the first half is positive, or Solar, and the second half negative, or Lunar. In the even, or negative signs, the first half is negative, or Lunar, and the second half positive, or Solar. It is well to bear these distinctions in mind in judging of the force of the benefics or malefics in disease or health, and in the matter of the duration of disease, prognosis, etc. Mr. E. H. Bailey, in his Journal, The British Journal of Astrology, is devoting considerable time and space to the subject of Horas, and their influences. (See "Negative Signs" under Negative; "Positive Signs" under Positive).

HORNY GROWTHS—Cornifications—♄ influence. (See Bunions, Cornifications, Corns, Growths, Hardening, Nails, Scales).

Venereal—Horny Venereal Growths— (See Venereal).

HOROSCOPE—The Star Map, or Figure of the Heavens, made up for the time, place, year, day, month, and hour of birth. It shows what is hidden in our auric atmosphere; shows our weaknesses of mind and body, as well as our tendencies and strong points, our talents, possibilities, suitabilities, likes and dislikes, antipathies, aversions, sympathies; shows what diseases are liable to come from birth to death, their nature and possible time, or the event; the parts of the body more liable to be afflicted, and the possible outcome of any diseases; shows the crises in disease, when they are due; shows our relation to Nature, environment, and the Will of The Higher Powers for us during the present life in the physical body. To follow the leadings of the Natal Map, its good and strong points, insures greater success with less effort, and to avoid failures and unnecessary illnesses, sorrows, reversals, downfalls, etc. The influences of the Horoscope begin at birth, and endure until the death of the body. Congenital defects belong to the Antenatal Period. The Map, or Figure of the Heavens, for the time of Conception, also indicates and shows the tendencies of the native, and the Prenatal Map, the map for time of Conception, should also be studied along with the Natal Map. (See Conception, Character, Destiny, Fate, Map, Medical Astrology, Natal, Nativity, Power, Prenatal Epoch, Radix).

HORRORS—Terrors—Fears—

Nervous Horrors—The Asc. to the □ or ⚹ ♄ by dir. (See "Nervous Fears" under Fears). For collateral study along the lines of the Horrors that can come to mind and body, see Darkness; "Delirium Tremens" under Delirium; Demoniac, Dreadful, Dreams, Fears, Forebodings, Hallucinations, Insanity, Mania, Nightmare (see Dreams); Obsessions, Portentous, Premonitions, Solitude, Spirit Controls, Terrors, Visions, Weird, etc.).

HORSES—Mules—Horses are denoted by, and ruled by the 12th H. in the map of the native, and this house shows his relation and fortune with them, and also with all large animals. Mules (Hybrids), a cross between the Horse and Ass, are barren. (See Barren). Horses are also ruled by ♃ and the ♐ sign, and people born under ♐ are usually fond of horses, and horseback riding, and all sports wherein horses are used.

Accidents—Caused by Horses, or In Their Use—Injuries By—Death By—Falls From, etc.—(See "Injuries" and the various paragraphs in this section).

Bites By—(See "Animals" under Bites).

Danger By—(See the various paragraphs in this section).

Death Of—(See "Many Horses Die" in this section).

Falls from Horses—Hurts, Injury or Death By—Afflictions in ♐; the ☽ in ♐, and affl. by the ☉ or ♂; ♅ or ♂ in the 12th H. (See Falls).

Head—The Native Has a Horse-Shaped Head—♐ on the Asc.

Hurts By—(See "Injuries", and the various paragraphs in this section).

Hybrids—(See Barrenness).

Injury By—Accidents, Hurts, Injuries by Horses—Injury by Large Animals—The ☉ or ☽ affl. by ♂ at B., and the Lights to the ☌ or ill-asp. ♂ by dir.; the ☉ or ☽ ☌ ♂ in ♐ in the Asc.; the ☽ in ♐ and affl. by the ☉ or ♂; the ☽ affl. at B., and to the ☌ cusp of 12th H. by dir.; the Prog. ☽ ☌ ♄ or ♂ in ♐; ♅ or ♂ affl. in the 12th H. at B., and affl. the cusp of 12th H. by dir., or planets in the 12th; ♄ in ♐, and affl. by ♅ or ♂; ♂ in ♊, ♍, or ♐, and ☌ or ill-asp. ♅ or ♂ by dir.; ♂ ☌ the Asc. by dir.; ♂ in ♐ in the Asc., and afflicted; ♂ in ♐ in the Asc., 6th, 8th, or 12th H., and afflicted; ♂ ruler of the 5th H. and affl. in ♐; ♐ on the Asc., 6th, 8th, or 12th H., and afflicted; ♐ on the Asc., and ♃ ruler in the 6th, 8th, or 12th H., and in ☌ ♄ or ♂. (See Bites, Falls, Kicks, Thrown, and the various paragraphs in this section; Animals, Beasts, Bites, Cattle, Elephants; "Great Beasts" under Great; Quadrupeds).

Kicks By—Thrusts—(See Kicks).

Large Animals—Horses, Cattle, Elephants, Great Beasts, etc.—Injuries By —(See "Injuries" in this section).

Many Horses Die—Destruction of—Horses and Mules Die—An eclipse of the ☉ in the 3rd Decan. of ♐, or an eclipse of the ☽ in 2nd Decan. of ♐; an eclipse of the ☉ in ♐; ♂ in ♋ at the Vernal Equi., and lord of the year; ♂ in ♐, direct in motion, at the Vernal, and lord of the year. (See "Death of Animals" under Animals; "Virus" under Pestilence).

Mules—Hybrids—(See Barrenness).

Races—The Winning Horse In Races—(See the Article on "Colours" in Wilson's Dictionary of Astrology. Also see "Race Horses" under Colors in this book. Also see the book, "The Silver Key", by Sepharial).

Riding—Fond of Horseback Riding—Fond of Horses and Outdoor Sports—The ☉ or ☽ in ♐; ♃ Sig. in ♐; a ♐ influence; ♐ on the Asc. at B. Malefics in ♐ add to the dangers, and may result in injury or death. (See Falls, Injury, Thrown, in this section; Exercise, Hunting; "Death" under Sports).

Thrown—Thrown From a Horse While Riding—Injury or Death By—The ☉ or ☽ ☌ ♂ in ♐ in the Asc.; the Prog. ☽ ☌ ♄ or ♂ in ♐; ♂ in ♐ in the Asc., and afflicted; ♐ on the Asc., and ♃ ruler in the 8th H. in ☌ ♄ or ♂. (See Falls, Injury, Riding, in this section).

Thrusts—Kicks—(See Kicks).

Veterinary Surgeon — Adapted To—(See Veterinary).

HOSPITALS — Sanitariums — Asylums—Are ruled by ♆ and the 12th H. The same influences which tend to place people in an Asylum, or Hospital, with illness or mental derangement, also tend to self-undoing, and to make the native his own worst enemy, and to undermine the health by dissipation and wrong living, and if people would live right, and obey the Laws of Health, there would be little need for Hospitals. Perfect health can only be attained when people become spiritualized, and more conscious of their Inner and Divine Powers, and of the presence of The Christ within them. It would be a strange sight to see one of the Great Masters, Adepts, or Initiates, lying sick in a Hospital, as they have learned how to conquer and prevent disease, and to rule their Stars, instead of being ruled by them.

Confinement In—Danger of Being Confined In a Hospital—The 12th H. prominent at B., and probably containing the ☉, ☽, ♄, or an afflicting planet; the ☉ or ☽ affl. in the 12th H.; the ☉ is usually affl. by ♀, and the ☽ by ♄; the Prog. ☽ ☌ or ill-asp. ♆ by dir., if ♆ is afflicted at B.; ♄ in ♓, or in the 12th H., and afflicted, danger of being confined by some chronic disease; ♆ affl. at B.; ♆ or ♅ affl. in the 12th H.; ruler of the Asc. in the 12th H.; afflictions in the 12th H. (See "Causes" under Chronic; Confinement; "Asylums" under Insanity; Invalids, Pisces, Prisons, Twelfth House).

Death In Hospital—Liable To—The ☽ affl. in the 8th H. at B., and also affl. by ♄ by dir. (See "Death" under Prison).

Employment In—Successful In Hospital Work—The ☉, ☽, ♄, ♃, or ♀ in the 12th H., and well-aspected; ♃ well-asp. in ♓; ♂ in ♓ in the 12th H., and well-aspected, tends to success as a Surgeon in Hospitals, Asylums, or Prisons. (See Healers, Nurses, Prisons, Surgeons, Twelfth House).

HOT—Heat—Warmth—(See the various paragraphs under Fire, Heat, Warmth).

HOUR—Hours—

Hour of Death—Probable Time of—(See "Hour" under Death).

Planetary Hours—(See "Hours" under Planets).

Womb—Hour-Glass Contraction of—(See "Hour-Glass" under Womb).

HOUSES—The Twelve Mundane Houses of the Heavens—The Houses have an effect on the body in accordance with their correspondence with the Signs of the Zodiac. Thus ♈ and the 1st H. rule the head; ♉ and the 2nd H., rule the neck and throat, and so on around thru the signs and houses. The Houses rule the same parts of the body as ruled by its corresponding Sign, but in a secondary way. In matters of health, diagnosis, and prognosis, it is important to know the house position of planets, and the influence of each house at B., and especially of the 6th H., the house of health, and also of the 1st H., or Asc., the house which rules largely over the physical form. The Houses are positive and negative, masculine and feminine, the same as the Signs. The Odd Houses, as the 1st, 3rd, 5th, etc., are positive and masculine. The Even Houses, as the 2nd,, 4th, 6th, etc., are negative and feminine. The Houses are also classed as Angular, Succedent, and Cadent. (See Angles, Cadent, Cardinal; "Fixed Signs" under Fixed; Mutable, Negative, Positive, Signs, Succedent; "Odd and Even" in this section). Good Articles on the influences of the Houses are to be found in Wilson's Dictionary of Astrology; Sepharial's New Dictionary of Astrology; Alan Leo's New Dictionary of Astrology; Sepharial's Manual of Astrology; Lilly's Astrology.

Angles—The 1st, 10th, 4th, and 7th Houses, the houses on the East, South, North and West places of the map. (See Angles).

Ascendant—The sign rising on the Eastern horizon at B., and also known as the 1st H. (See Aries, Ascendant, First House).

Cadent Houses—The 3rd, 6th, 9th, and 12th H. (See Cadent).

Eighth House—Known as the House of Death. Corresponds to the ♏ sign. (See Eighth House, Scorpio, Terminal).

Eleventh House—The House of Friends, Children, Hopes, Wishes, etc. (See Eleventh).

Even Houses—(See "Odd and Even" in this section).

Feminine Houses—The Even Houses, as 2nd, 4th, etc. (See "Odd and Even" in this section).

Fifth House—The House of Children, Amusements, Speculation, Love Affairs, Women, Pleasure, etc. (See Fifth).

First House—(See Angles, Aries, Ascendant, First House.

Fourth House—The House of the Close of Life, a Terminal House—(See Fourth, Nadir, Terminal).

Masculine Houses—The Odd numbers, as the 1st, 3rd, 5th, etc. (See "Odd and Even" in this section).

Negative Houses—The Even Houses —(See "Odd and Even" in this section).

Ninth House—The House of the Higher Mind, of Philosophy, Religion, and also of Foreign Travel or Residence. (See Ninth).

Odd and Even Houses—The Positive and Negative—The Masculine and Feminine—The 1st, 3rd, 5th, 7th, 9th, and 11th Houses are the odd, positive, and masculine houses, and rule the left side in a male, and the right side in a female. The even, negative, and feminine houses are the 2nd, 4th, 6th, 8th, 10th, and 12th Houses, and rule the right side in a male, and the left side in the female. The house position of the afflicting planet shows which side of the body is afflicted, according to the sex of the native. (See Feminine, Left, Masculine, Negative, Positive, Right).

Positive Houses—(See "Odd and Even" in this section).

Second House—(See Second House).

Seventh House—(See Descendant, Seventh).

Signs of the Zodiac—The Signs As Related To the Houses—(See each Sign in the alphabetical arrangement, as Aries, Taurus, Gemini, etc.).

Sixth House—The House of Health, and related to the ♍ Sign. (See Sixth).

Succedent Houses—The 2nd, 5th, 8th, and 11th Houses, those following an Angle. (See Angles, Cadent, Succedent).

Tables of Houses—The Tables by Joseph G. Dalton are much in use, showing the cusps of the houses for places between the Latitudes of 22° to 56° North. Also a Table of Houses for the same degrees of Latitude is published by the Rosicrucian Fellowship, of Oceanside, Calif. A Table of Houses published by Raphael gives the cusps for each degree of Latitude from the Equator to 50° North, and also for 59° 56′ N.

Tenth House—The Midheaven—(See Tenth).

Terminal Houses—Those having to do with Death, and the End of Life. They are the 4th, 8th, and 12th Houses. (See Eighth, Fourth, Terminal, Twelfth).

Third House—(See Third).

Twelfth House—(See Confinement, Limitations, Terminal, Twelfth).

HUMAN—

Human Form—Signs of—Articulate Signs—(See Articulate; "Nature of Events" under Events; Mankind; "Human Shape" in this section).

Human Hands—Human Means—Accident, Death, or Injury By—(See "Hand of Man" under Man).

Human Ostrich—Eats Glass, etc.— Case—See "Human Ostrich", No. 986 in 1001 N.N.

Human Race—Humanity—Every Evil To—(See "Every Evil" under Evil; Humanity).

Human Shape—Of Human Shape, Yet of Beastly Form and Savage In Disposition—(See "Resembles Animals" under Animals; "Beastly Form" under Beasts; Inhuman, Monsters, Savage, Wild).

Human Signs—Signs of Human Form —Speaking Signs—♊, ♍, ♒, and the 1st half of ♐. Also ♎ is included by some Authors. The Airy Signs are especially classed as Human Signs because they give a kinder and more human, or humane disposition, and this is especially true of the ♒ sign. When the lord of the geniture, or the Asc., is in one of these signs at B., the native is of humane disposition. The lord of an eclipse falling in a Human Sign, its evil effects will fall upon Humanity. (See Articulate; "Air Signs", "Whole Signs", under Signs).

HUMANE—Kind—Sympathetic—Spiritual—A special characteristic of the ♒ sign. Abraham Lincoln, the Emancipator, was born with the ☉ in this sign. Also given by ♃ when this planet is ruler at B., strong and well-aspected. (See Aquarius, Ideals, Jupiter, Noble, Philanthropic, Pity, Sympathy).

HUMANITY—Mankind—The Public—

Every Evil Upon—(See Calamities, Comets, Drought, Earthquakes (see Earth); Epidemics; "Every Evil" under Evil; Famine, Floods; "Human Signs" under Human; Mankind, Pestilence, Plague, Prevalent, Public, Storms, Volcanoes, etc.).

HUMERUS—The Large Bone of the Upper Arm—Is under the structural rulership of the ♊ Sign.

Atrophy Of—♄ affl. in ♊; Subs at LCP (6C), and at AP. (See Atrophy).

Exostosis Of—♄ or ♂ affl. in ♊; Subs at LCP (6C), and AP. (See "Bones of Arm" under Arms).

Fracture Of—♄ or ♂, or both, affl. in ♊. (See "Accidents", "Broken Arms", under Arms).

HUMIDITY—Humid—Moisture—Humidity is ruled by the ☽.

Much Affected by Humidity—Increased Moisture In the Body—Denoted by the ☽, and when the ☽ afflicts the ☉ or Asc. (See "Bodily Temperament", and the various paragraphs under Moisture).

HUMMING—Droning—Buzzing—A Low, Murmuring, Monotonous Sound—Ruled by ♆. (See Singing, Speech, Voice).

Humming Bird—The Humming of Bees—Buzzing—Said to be ruled by ♆. (See Bees).

HUMOURS—Humors—Humor—Any Fluid of the Body—Ruled by the ☽ in general, as the ☽ rules the Fluids of the body. Corrupt and Disease Humors are ruled by ♄ and ♂, and also caused by the afflictions of the malefics to the ☉, ☽, and Asc. (See Fluids).

Abounding—Humours Abounding— Brings Humours by Directions—The ☉ to the ☌, P., □, or ☍ the ☽ by dir., and the ☽ hyleg or afflicted at B.; the ☽ to the ☌ or ill-asp. ♄ by dir.

Aqueous Humor—(See Aqueous; "Aqueous Humor" under Eyes).

Bloody Humour—(See "Bloody Flux" under Flux).

Bowels—Humours In—The ☉ affl. in ♍ when the ☉ is the afflictor in the disease. (See Bowels, Diarrhoea, Dysentery, Flux).

Breast—Humours Falling Into—(See "Humours" under Breast).

Brings Humours—(See "Abounding" in this section).

Choleric Humours—(See Choleric).

Cold Humours—Caused by ♄, and are ♄ diseases. (See Cold. For Cold Humours in the Stomach see "Raw Humours" under Indigestion).

Cold and Moist Humours—Diseases Which Proceed from Cold and Moisture—Cold and Moist Distempers—Cold and Watery Diseases—The ☉ or ☽ to the ♂ or ill-asps. ♄ by dir., and the Lights affl. at B.; the ☽ to the ♂ or ill-asp. ♅ by dir.; the ☽ ♂ the Asc. by secondary dir.; ☽ diseases; watery signs on the Asc. and 6th H. at B., or at decumb., or the Sigs. of the disease in them at the beginning of an illness; afflictions in ♓, as the feet are cold and moist; ♀ affl. in ♐. The right or left sides of the body are more subject to, according to the sex. (See Cold; "Odd and Even" under Houses; Left; "Cold and Moist" under Moisture; Right).

Corrupt Humours—The ☽ affl. at B., and to the evil asps. the Asc. by dir.; ♄ diseases; ♂, and other afflictions in ♓, corrupt humours in the feet. (See Corrupt, Decay, Discharges, Gangrene, Impure, Mortification, Putrefaction).

Defluxion of Humours—Downward Flow of—(See Defluxion).

Dropsical Humours — (See "Danger Of", "Humours", under Dropsy).

Dry Humours—(See "Humours" under Dry).

Dysentery—(See Dysentery).

External Humours—Internal Humours—The External and Internal Humoural Secretions—♂ and the ♍ sign preside over the plexuses and the intestinal ganglia which rule the external and internal humoural secretions. The Humoural Secretions are also especially affected by the physiological action of the ♀ Group of Plants. (See "Venus Group" under Herbs; "Physiological Action" under Venus).

Extremities—Humours In—(See "Humours" under Extremities).

Eyes—Humourous Discharges From—(See "Discharges", "Hot", under Eyes).

Father—The Father Suffers From—(See "Humours" under Father).

Feet—Corrupt Humours In—(See "Humours" under Feet).

Fingers—Humours In—(See "Humours" under Fingers).

Flow of Humours—A ♓ disease; the Asc. to the ♂ the ☉ by dir., and the ☉ in a watery sign. (See Catarrh; "Humours" under Flow, Head).

Fluids—(See the various paragraphs under Fluids).

Fluxes—(See Flux).

Flying Humours— ☿ diseases. (See Flying).

Gross Humours—The Body Full of—The ☽ in ♓ and afflicted by the ☉ or ♂ when taken ill (Hor'y). (See "Gross Blood" under Blood).

Goutish Humours—(See "Humours" under Gout).

Hands — Humours In—(See "Gout", "Humours", under Fingers, Hands).

Head—Humours In—(See "Humours" under Head).

Hips and Thighs—Humours In—(See "Humours" under Hips; "Hot" in this section).

Hot Humours—In the Head, Eyes, Hips, Thighs—♂ influence; ♂ in the sign which rules the part. (See "Hot Humours" under Eyes, Head, Heat, Hips).

Humoural Changes—Those which interfere with the economy of the system are ruled over by the ☽.

Internal Humours—(See "External" in this section).

Lachrymal Humours—(See "Humours" under Tears).

Legs—Humours In—(See Gout, Humours, Rheumatism, under Legs).

Moist Humours—Moist and Cold Humours—(See "Moist Humours" under Moisture; "Cold and Moist" in this section).

Morbid Humours—(See "Offensive" in this section).

Nose—A Humour In—(See Catarrh, Colds; "Coryza", "Humour", under Nose).

Offending Humours—The principal Humour offending is indicated by the 6th H., planets in the 6th, the rulership of the cusp of the 6th at B., or at decumb. (See Sixth House).

Offensive Humours—Peccant—Morbid—Unhealthy—Those which accompany infections, and the presence of ptomaines, leucomaines, toxins, etc. The ♄ influence and afflictions encourage such action, and accompanied by lowered vitality. (See Offensive).

Peccant Humours—(See "Offensive" in this section).

Principal Humour Offending—(See "Offending" in this section).

Raw Humours—(See "Raw Humours" under Indigestion).

Rheum—Watery or Catarrhal Discharge—(See Rheum).

Secretions—Humoural Secretions—(See "External", and the various paragraphs in this section; Secretions).

Splenic Humour—(See Spleen).

Stomach—Raw Humours In—(See "Raw" under Indigestion).

Thighs—Humours In—(See "Humours" under Hips).

Throat—Humours Falling Into—(See "Humours" under Throat).

Undigested Humours—(See "Raw Humours" under Indigestion).

Unhealthy Humours—(See "Offensive" in this section).

Vitreous Humor—(See "Vitreous" under Eyes).

Watery Humours—(See Catarrhs, Colds, Discharges, Fluxes, Rheum; "Humours" under Watery).

HUMPBACK—Hunchback — Angular Curvature of the Spine—(See "Humpback" under Spine).

HUMUS—A Dark Material from Decaying Vegetable Matter—(See "Decay" under Vegetation).

HUNGER—Cravings—Desire for Food —(See Appetite, Cravings, Diet, Drink, Eating, Epicureans, Excesses, Feasting, Gluttony, High Living (see High); Indulgence, Intemperate, Obesity, Plethora, Surfeits, etc.).

HUNTING—Injury In, and In Sports While Hunting, and Especially While Riding Horses—Afflictions in ♐. (See Gun-shot; "Riding" under Horses. Also see Amusements, Exercise, Pleasure, Recreation, Shooting, Sports, etc.).

HURRICANES—Tornadoes—Wind Storms—Suffering, Injury, or Death From—(See High Winds, Storms, Tornadoes, under Wind).

HURRIED—Rapid—Accelerated—

Heart Beats—Hurried Heart Beats— (See "Accelerated" under Heart; "High Pulse" under Pulse).

Respiration Hurried—(See "Rapid" under Breath).

Speech—Hurried Speech—(See "Rapid" under Speech). See Accelerated, Exaggerated, Intense, Rapid.

HURTFUL—Causing, or Tending to Cause, Hurt or Injury—The result of the adverse action of the malefic planets, and of the evil aspects between the ☉, ☽, and planets, afflictions to the Asc., and Hyleg. (See Accidents, Affliction, Blows, Bruises, Burns, Cuts, Hurts, Injuries, Wounds, etc.).

Hurtful Signs—Of the Zodiac—Obnoxious Signs—♈, ♉, ♋, ♏, and ♑. Planets in them at B. tend to Distortions. These Signs on the Asc. at B. make the native more liable to Blows, Falls, Wounds, and other Injuries. (See Distortions, Lameness, Obnoxious).

Hurtful to No One—Harmless—Inoffensive—(See Harmless).

HURTS—Trauma—Injury—Wounds, etc. —This word covers a wide range of subjects, as disease, affliction, accidents, injuries, wounds, etc., which are classed as Hurts in Astrology. The various Hurts that can occur to the native are also listed largely under Accidents, Disease, Injury, etc. The influences and afflictions of the malefic planets, and especially when they are afflicting the ☉, ☽, Asc., or Hyleg at B., and by direction, tend to Hurts and Injuries. Hurts by Drowning, Plots, Trance, Treachery, Water, are caused by ♆. Sudden Hurts, as by bathings, water, electricity, explosions, machinery, etc., are caused by ♅. Hurts by falls, bruises, contusions, are caused by ♄. Hurts by violence, cuts, stabs, injuries, loss of blood, wounds, etc., are caused by ♂. There are also the many sources of Hurts, as by the hand of Man, by beasts, animals, hurts in battle, war, hurts by insects, reptiles; by bites, kicks; by machinery, in travel and on railroads or on ships; by burns, scalds, fire, chemicals, liquids, etc. Then the Hurts to the different parts of the body. If you do not find in the following list the particular injury, or part of the body hurt, look in the alphabetical arrangement for the subject, or part, you have in mind, and look for "Accidents", "Hurts", "Injuries", "Wounds", under the part, as under Arms, Head, Face, Hips, Legs, etc. The following list of subjects is more abstract, and giving the causes, the sources, and kinds of Hurts. People born with the Hurtful Signs on the Asc., or with planets in them, are more liable to hurts and violence. (See "Hurtful Signs" under Hurtful, the Article before this one). In judging of the liability to Hurts, Wounds, Accidents, Disease, Injury, etc., the Asc., or the 1st H., and its opposite house, the 7th H., and the planets afflicting the Hyleg, are to be considered, and judgment given by their general character. See the following subjects in the alphabetical arrangement when not considered here—

Accidents—Note the various paragraphs under Accidents).

Acids; Aeroplanes; Air; Amelioration of Hurts—The benefics elevated above the malefics which produce them, and also to cause a moderation in disease. (See Amelioration).

Amusements; Animals—(See Animals, Beasts, Quadrupeds).

Assassination; Assaults, Automobiles —(See Vehicles).

Bathing—(See Bathing, Drowning).

Battle—(See War).

Beasts—(See Animals, Beasts, Four-Footed, Quadrupeds).

Bites; Blemishes—From Hurts—(See Blemishes, Blindness, Crippled, Deformities, Disfigurements, Lameness, Limbs, Scars, etc.).

Blood—Loss of Blood by Hurts—(See Cuts; "Loss of Blood", under Blood; Hemorrhage, Stabs, etc.).

Blows; Brother—Hurts To—(See Brother).

Bruises; Buildings—Hurts by the Fall Of—(See Buildings).

Burns; Calamities; Carelessness;

Casualties; Catastrophies; Cattle— (See "Attacks By" under Cattle).

Chemical Action—Hurts By—(See Acids, Chemical, Drugs, Narcotics, Poisons, etc.).

Childhood—Hurts In—(See Childhood).

Children—Hurts to Women and Children—The ☽ to the ☌ or ill-asp. ♂ by dir., and the ☽ affl. by ♂ at B., and hurts to women especially. (See "Accidents" under Childhood, Children, Females, Women).

Chronic Hurts—Given by ♄, and espec. to that part of the body ruled by the sign or house in which ♄ was placed at B. (See Chronic).

Cold—Hurts By—(See Cold).

Concussion; Constitutional Hurts—(See "Hurts" under Constitution).

Contests; Contusions—(See Bruises).

Curable Hurts—(See Curable; "Amelioration" in this section).

Cuts; Danger of Hurts—(See "Liable To" in this section).

Dangerous Hurts—(See "Dangerous" under Accidents; "Violent" in this section).

Death by Hurts—(See "Death" under Accidents, Injuries, Violence. Also note the various paragraphs in this section, and under Death).

Diseases—Hurts By—(See the various paragraphs under Disease, Ill-Health, Sickness).

Dislocations; Distortions; Drink; Duels; Early Years—Hurts In—The ☉ or ☽ to the ☌ or ill-asp. ♂, or other malefics, by dir. during childhood; ♂ coming to the ☌, □, or ☍ the Asc. or Desc. in early life usually causes hurts, wounds, injuries, or fevers if the nativity denotes them. (See "Accidents" under Childhood, Children; "Early Years of Life" under Early; "Early Youth" under Youth).

Earthquakes—(See this subject under Earth).

Eating—Hurts from Wrong Eating—(See Diet, Eating, Food).

Electricity—(See Electricity, Lightning).

Employment—Hurts In—(See Employment).

Enemies—Hurts By—(See Enemies).

Escapes—Narrow Escapes from Hurts—(See Escape).

Exercise—Hurts During—(See Exercise, Sports).

Falls; Family—Hurt to Some Member of the Family—(See Family).

Father—Hurts To—(See Father).

Females—Hurts To—(See "Accidents" under Females, Women; "Children" in this section).

Fire—Hurts By—(See Burns, Fire).

Fire Arms—(See Gunshot).

Floods—Hurts By— (See Floods).

Four-Footed Beasts—Hurts By—(See Animals, Beasts, Four-Footed, Quadrupeds).

Fractures; Friends—Hurts To—(See "Absent Party" under Absent; Friends).

Gases; Gunshot; Habits; Hand of Man—Hurts By—(See Hand of Man).

Healers—Hurts By—(See "Injured By" under Healers).

Heat—Hurts By—(See Burns, Fire, Heat, Scalds).

Heights—Hurts by Falls From—(See Heights).

Hemorrhage; Highwaymen—Hurts By—(See Highwaymen).

Homicide; Horses—Hurts By—(See Horses, Kicks).

Human Hands—Human Means—Hurts By—(See "Hand of Man" in this section).

Hunting—Hurts and Injuries While Hunting—(See Hunting).

Hurtful Signs—(See "Hurtful Signs" under Hurtful).

Husband—Hurts To—(See Husband).

Ill-Health—(See the various paragraphs under Ill-Health).

Incisions—(See Cuts, Duels, Instruments, Stabs, Sword, Weapons).

Incurable Hurts—Without Remedy—Permanent In Effects—(See Crippled, Incurable, Permanent).

Indiscretions; Infancy—Hurts In—(See "Accidents" under Infancy).

Injuries—(See the various paragraphs under Injuries).

Insects—Hurts By—(See Adder, Bites, Insects, Stings, Venomous).

Instruments—Hurts By—(See Instruments).

Iron—And Steel—Hurts By—(See Iron).

Judging of Hurts—(See the Introduction to this Article).

Kicks; Lacerations; Lameness—From Hurts—(See Crippled, Lameness).

Liable to Hurts—Danger of—Tendency To—Susceptible To—The malefics oriental tend to hurts and injuries, and when occi. to disease. A planet in evil asp. to a Sig. at B. promises hurt, and espec. when by transit or dir. it thereafter affects the same Significator; the ☉ or ☽ affl. by ♂, or other malefic, at B., and to the ☌ or ill-asp. ♂ by dir.; the ☉ to the ill-asps. ☿ by dir., and ☿ afflicted at B.; ♆ or ♅ affl. the ☉, ☽, Asc., or hyleg at B., and by dir.; ♄ rising at B., and affl. the ☉ or ☽; ♄ ☌ or ill-asp. ♂, and espec. if either planet be oriental; ♂ □ or ☍ the ☉ or ☽ at B.; ♂ in evil asp. to ♄ at B.; ♂ on the Asc. at B., and affl. the ☉, ☽, Asc., or hyleg by dir.; the transits of ♂ as promittor over the place of the ☉ and ☽ at B.; ♂ to the ☌ or evil asp. of ♄ by tr. or dir., and espec. when ♂ was affl. by ♄ at B., and the danger is increased if ♂ be stationary or ℞ at the time; malefics in the 8th H. at B., and to the ☌ the Desc. by Oblique Descension. (See "Danger Of", "Tendency To", under Accidents, Injuries).

Lightning—Hurt, Injury or Death By—(See Lightning).

Liquids—Hurts By—(See Acids, Bathings, Drowning; "Hot Liquids" under Heat; Liquids, Scalds).

Loss of Blood—From Hurts or Accidents—(See "Loss Of" under Blood; Cuts, Duels; "Lesions" under Hemorrhage; Instruments, Stabs, Sword, Weapons, etc.).

Machinery—Hurts By—(See Employment, Machinery; "Accidents" under Uranus).

Maiming; Males—Hurts To—(See Brother, Father, Husband; "Accidents" under Male; Men, Son, Uncle).

Maritime Pursuits—Hurts In—(See Drowning, Maritime, Navigation, Sea, Ships, Shipwreck).

Men—Hurts To—(See the various paragraphs under Men).

Mobs—Hurts By—(See Mobs).

Mother—Hurts To—(See Mother).

Murdered—(See Murder).

Navigation — Hurts In — (See "Maritime" in this section).

Operations — Surgical Operations—Hurts By—(See Operations, Surgeons).

Parents — Hurts To — (See Father, Mother, Parents).

Permanent Hurts—The Effects Incurable—(See Incurable, Permanent).

Pleasure—Hurts In the Pursuit of—(See Amusements, Exercise, Hunting, Pleasure, Recreations, Sports, Theatres).

Plots—Hurts By—(See Plots).

Poison—Hurts By—(See Poison, Plots, Treachery).

Quadrupeds—Hurts By—(See "Four-Footed" in this section).

Quarrels — Hurts In — (See Assaults, Blows, Contests, Cuts, Duels, Enemies, Gun-Shot, Quarrels, Stabs, etc.).

Railroads — Hurts On — (See Railroads).

Rash Acts—Hurts From—(See Hasty, Rashness).

Recreations — Hurts During — (See Bathings, Exercise, Hunting, Pleasure, Recreation, Sports, Theatres, Travel).

Relatives — Hurts To — (See Family, Relatives).

Remedy — Hurts Without Remedy — (See Blemishes, Crippled, Deformed, Distortions, Incurable, Maimed, Permanent, Remedy, etc.).

Reptiles; Reputation — Hurts To — (See Disgrace, Honour, Reputation, Ruin, Scandal, etc.).

Riding—Hurts In—(See Horses).

Robbers—Hurts By—(See Robbers).

Ruptures; Scalds; Sea—Hurts On the Sea—(See "Maritime" in this section).

Searing—(See "Searing" under Burns).

Serpents; Sharp Instruments — (See Cuts, Duels, Instruments, Stabs, Weapons).

Ships — Hurts On — (See Sea, Ships, Shipwreck).

Shipwreck; Signs—The Hurtful Signs of the Zodiac — (See "Hurtful Signs" under Hurtful; Obnoxious).

Sister—Hurts To—(See Sister).

Snow—Suffering From—(See Snow).

Sports—Hurts In—(See Amusements, Exercise, Horses, Hunting, Sports).

Stabs; Steel and Iron — Hurts By — (See Iron).

Stings; Stones—Hurt by Flying Stones —(See "Assaults" under Stone).

Storms—(See Blizzards, Floods, Lightning, Rain, Storms, Thunder, Weather, Wind).

Strange Hurts — Sudden and Unexpected—Extraordinary—Unusual—Denoted by ♅ and his afflictions to the ☉, ☽, Asc., or hyleg at B., and by dir. Also caused by ♆. (See Extraordinary, Mysterious, Peculiar, Strange, Sudden, Tragical, Uncommon, Unusual).

Strangulation; Sudden Hurts — ♅ influence. (See "Strange" in this section).

Suffocation; Surgeons — Danger To — (See Surgeons).

Susceptible—To Hurts—(See "Liable To" in this section).

Sword; Tendency — To Hurts — (See "Liable To" in this section).

Theatres—Hurts, Injury, or Death In —(See Theatres).

Thieves—Hurts By—(See Highwaymen, Pirates, Robbers, Thieves).

Time of Hurts — When Apt to Occur —The Periods by Directions and Transits Which Bring Such Dangers—The ☉ or ☽ to the ☌ or ill-asp. ♂ or other malefics by dir.; ♂ ☌ the Asc. by tr. or dir.; malefics to the ☌ or ill-asp. the ☉, ☽, Asc., M.C., or hyleg by dir. (See "Time" under Accidents, Death, Disease, Evil. Also see Comets, Crises, Critical, Directions, Eclipses, Epidemics, Escapes, Events, Ingresses, Periods, Prognosis, Prognostication, Progression, Secondary Directions (see Secondary); Time, Years).

Tornadoes—Hurricanes—Hurts By—(See "Tornadoes" under Wind).

Trampled—(See Crushed, Mobs, Trampled).

Trance; Travel—(See "Accidents" under Abroad, Journeys, Travel, Voyages).

Treachery; Unexpected Hurts — (See "Strange" in this section; Unexpected)'.

Vehicles—Hurts By—(See Vehicles).

Violent Hurts—(See Violent).

Volcanoes; Voyages—Hurts On—(See Maritime, Navigation, Sea, Ships, Shipwreck, Travel, Voyages).

War; Water — Hurts By — (See Bathing, Drowning; "Hot Liquids" under Heat; Scalds, Sea; "Accidents" under Water).

Weapons; Weather; Wife — Hurts To — (See Husband, Marriage Partner, Wife).

Wild Animals—Hurts By—(See "Wild Animals" under Animals; Beasts; "Dangers" under Travel; Wild).

Wind — (See "High Wind", "Tornadoes", under Wind).

Women—Hurts By—Hurts To—(See "Injured by Women" under Men; Treachery; "Injuries To" under Women).

Wounds—(See the various paragraphs under Accidents, Injuries, Wounds, and also the paragraphs in this section).

Youth — Hurts In — (See Childhood, Children; "Early Years" under Early; Youth).

HUSBAND — Fiance — The ☉ rules the husband, or fiance, in a female nativity, and also the 7th H., the house of marriage, the marriage partner, and partnerships, and afflictions to the ☉, or to planets in the 7th H., indicate his fate, health, etc. Remember that all the influences in this section are in the wife's map, and affect her relations to the husband, and in the Article on "Wife", the influences given there will be taken from the map of the Husband.

Accident to Husband—Danger of—♂, or other malefics, to the ☌ or ill-asp.

the ⊙ by dir., and espec. those falling in the 7th H.; the ⊙ in a female nativity to the ☌ or ill-asp. ♂, or other malefic, and the accident or hurt will be of the nature as given by the malefic; ♂ to the ☌ or ill-asp. the ⊙ by dir., and espec. if it fall in the 7th H., there is danger of a serious accident to the husband, death by the accident, or to have an illness with a very high fever; ♂ or ♅ affl. in ♎ or the 7th H. in a female nativity. (See "Accident" under Wife).

Afflicted—The Husband Afflicted—The directions of the ⊙ in the wife's map afflict and affect the husband for good or ill; ♄ affl. in ♎ or the 7th H. (See "Afflicted" under Wife).

Anchorite—The Husband An Anchorite — A Celibate — Averse to Having Children—The ⊙ affl. by ♄ in a female nativity; ♄ in the 11th H.; ♀ affl. by the ☽ and ♄, and ♀ in a sign of ♄, and the ☽ in the sign of ♀. This may also lead to sterility. (See Barren, Celibacy).

Barrenness In—Sterility—(See Barrenness).

Celibacy Of—(See "Anchorite" in this section).

Children — Averse To — Children Not Wanted—(See "Anchorite" in this section).

Danger To — The ⊙ in the 7th H. in the wife's map, and eclipsed at a Solar return, and the ⊙ also afflicted by malefics; ♄ in the 7th H. at B., and near the cusp, and again in the 7th H. at a Solar Revolution. (See "Danger To" under Wife).

Death Of—Danger of Death of Husband, or of Fiance—The ⊙ affl. by ♅, ♄, or ♂ at B., and by dir.; the ⊙ to the ☌ or ill-asp. ♄ by dir., or other malefics; the ⊙ affl. by malefics, and a malefic in the 7th H. at B.; the ⊙ apply first to ♃, and then to ♅, and espec. if ♅ or ♄ be in the 7th H.; the ⊙ to the ☌ or ill-asp. ♅ by dir., the husband may die within the following year; ♅ affl. in the 7th H., danger of sudden death of; ♄ ☌, □, or ☍ the ⊙ at B., or by dir.; ♄ affl. in the 7th H. at B.; ♄ at a Solar Rev. passing the place of the radical ⊙, and espec. if the ⊙ be hyleg, and ♄ be stationary; ♂ in the 7th H. at B., danger of death by violence, accident, or fever; ♂ in evil asp. the ⊙ at B., and under the adverse direction of ♂ to the ⊙ after marriage; lord of the 6th or 8th H. in the 7th H. (See Dies Before Wife, Pleurality, Sudden, in this section; "Death Of" under Fiance, Marriage Partner, Wife; Widows).

Delicate In Health—Sickly—(See "Ill-Health Of" in this section).

Dies Before Wife—Will the Husband Die Before the Wife?—One of the best ways to get at this question is to erect a Horary Figure unless the Artist is thoroughly familiar with the age, constitution, habits, and stamina of the Querent, but the information should not be revealed. In Hor'y Q., the lord of the 1st H. and the ☽ are taken for the man, and the lord of the 7th and the ⊙ for the woman, and judge of the nature of the aspects to them. An-

other method is to measure the distance in degrees between the lords of the 1st and 7th H., and the lord of the 8th, and then predict that the one will die first whose Sig. is nearest the lord of the 8th. The following influences, if they exist in the map of the wife, indicate the death of the husband before the wife,—Malefics in the 7th H. at B.; the planet to which the ⊙ first applies being a malefic; malefics afflicting the ⊙, or the Sig. of the wife; ruler of the 7th a malefic, and ℞. For a woman to marry when the ☽ is combust is a bad sign, and indicates the possible death of the husband within two years after marriage. (See Widowers, Widows; "Dies Before Husband" under Wife).

Drink— Drunkard— Dissolute Habits — Husband May Be Given To — The Husband Improvident and Profligate— ♂ in the 11th H. in map of wife; ♂ in a watery sign and affl. the ⊙; ♂ ☌ or ill-asp. the ⊙; ♄ □ or ☍ the ⊙ in the wife's map, the husband improvident. (See "Husband" under Drunkenness; "Dissolute", "Drink", under Wife).

Dull and Timid—♀ connected with ♄ in the wife's horoscope. (See Dull).

Early Death Of—Malefics in the 7th H. in map of wife, danger of; lord of the 6th in the 7th, and espec. if ♂ be in the 7th H. (See "Early Death" under Wife).

Fever—The Husband Subject to Fevers—Death by High Fever—♂ affl. in the 7th H.

Fiance — Death or Illness of — (See Fiance).

Fruitful — The Husband Fruitful — Signs of—♃ in the 11th H. of the wife. The wife's nativity must also show fruitfulness. (See Fruitfulness; "Fruitful" under Wife).

Grave and Morose — Troublesome — The ⊙ applying to ♄ in the wife's map. (See "Grave" under Wife).

Habits—(See "Drink" in this section).

Hasty—Unfaithful—Untrue—♅ in the 7th H. in wife's map, and in □ or ☍ the ⊙, danger of; ♂ ☌ or ill-asp. ♀ in wife's map. (See "Free Love" under Free; "Liaisons" under Love Affairs; "Clandestine" under Sex).

Ill-Fortune To — The ⊙ to the ☌ or ill-asp. malefics by dir. in wife's map.

Ill-Health Of—The Husband Delicate In Health—The ⊙ at B., or the Prog. ⊙, in ☌ or P. ♄ in the map of the wife; the ⊙ affl. by malefics, and a malefic in the 7th H. at B.; the ⊙ to the ☌ or ill-asp. malefics by dir.; to marry when ♅, ♄, or ♂ are in the Asc. of the wife's nativity; ♅, ♄, or ♂ in the 7th H. of the wife. Directions of the ⊙ in the wife's horoscope affect the husband for good or ill. (See "Sickly" under Marriage Partner; "Ill-Health" under Wife).

Imprisoned Thru Wife — (See "Wife" under Prison).

Improvident — (See "Drink" in this section).

Killed by Accident — (See "Accident" in this section).

Marriage—Bad Time For, and the Health Affected—To marry when the ☉ is badly aspected by directions in the wife's map, or when malefics are in the Asc. or 7th H. of her map. Also the husband should not marry when the directions of ♄ badly afflict the ☉, ☽, Asc., or hyleg in his own map. (See "Best Time to Marry" under Marriage).

Marriage Partner—(See the various paragraphs under Marriage Partner).

Men—Males—(See the various paragraphs under Males, Men).

Murders His Wife—Murders His Wife, Fiancee, or Sweetheart—Danger of—♂ □ or ⚹ ♀ in the map of the lady. Case—See "Holloway", No. 189, in 1001 N.N. (See "Strangles" in this section).

Older Than Himself—Marries a Lady Older Than Himself—(See "Older Than Himself" under Marriage).

Plurality of Wives—The ☽ applying to several planets at the same time in the map of the man. Also ♀ and many planets in the double-bodied signs at B. tend to, and espec. ♀ affl. in ♊; ♄ affl. in the 7th H. of the husband may result in the death of several wives. The tendency is for the wife to share the fate of the husband's map, and if a woman does not want to die an early death by marriage, she should know the map of the fiance beforehand, and not go into the marriage relation blindly, and in ignorance of his horoscope. These same influences also indicate several marriages for the wife, and a wife so born may separate from, or bury several husbands. (See Widowers, Widows).

Poison—Husband Commits Suicide by Poison—Case—See "Husband", No. 162, in 1001 N.N.

Profligate—(See "Drink" in this section; "Dissolute" under Wife).

Relatives—The Husband's Relatives—The Relatives of the marriage partner, with both husband and wife, are said to be ruled by the 9th H. of the map. The male relatives are ruled by ♂, and the female relatives by the ☽ and ♀. Malefics in the 9th H., or lord of the 9th a malefic, indicates trouble with the marriage relatives, or their ill-health. Benefics in the 9th, good relations, and good health for them. (See Relatives; "Relatives" under Marriage Partner, Wife).

Several Marriages—(See "Plurality" in this section).

Sickness Of—(See "Ill-Health" in this section).

Sterile—(See Barrenness, Impotent; "Anchorite" in this section).

Strangles Wife—Death of Wife—Case—See "Beach Murder", No. 134, in 1001 N.N.

Sudden Death—The ☉ to the ☌ or ill-asp. ♅ or ♂ in the wife's map; ♅ or ♂ afflicting the 7th H.; ♂ afflicting the ☉ by ☌, P., or ill aspect. (See "Death" in this section).

Suffers—The Husband Suffers—(See Accident, Afflicted, Drink, Ill-Health, in this section).

Suicide Of—(See "Poison" in this section).

Timid and Dull—(See "Dull" in this section).

Unfaithful—Untrue—(See "Liaisons" under Love Affairs; "Hasty" in this section).

Unfruitful—(See "Anchorite" in this section).

Unsteady—(See Drink, Hasty, in this section).

Untrue—(See "Hasty" in this section).

Widowers—(See Widowers; "Plurality" in this section).

Wife—Note the various paragraphs under Wife).

Wives—May Have Several Wives—(See "Plurality" in this section).

HYACINTH—A Mineral or Stone ruled by the ☉. (See "Metals and Minerals" under Sun).

HYADES—Seven stars of the 3rd magnitude, a Nebulous cluster, in the first part of ♉, in the Bull's Head, violent in nature, and of the nature of ♂ and the ☽, and said to bring most every evil upon the native when directed to the ☉, ☽, or Asc. Their influences when with the ☉ or ☽ at B., or afflicting the Lights, tend to eye disorders, weak sight, blindness, hurts to the eyes or face, to measles, death from fevers, or a violent death. The ☉ with the Hyades at B. is indicative of evil, and liable to a violent death. The ☉ directed to them brings the danger of blindness in one or both eyes. The ☽ Sig. in ☌ the ☉ near the Hyades, likely to be nearly blind. The ☽ to the place of, great defect in the sight, and often blindness. The Asc. to the place of, wounds or hurts to the eyes, cuts, danger from sharp instruments, and often death from fever. The Fixed Stars and Nebulous Groups of the nature of ♂ and the ☽ are the Ascelli, Castor, Pollux, Hyades, Deneb, Pleiades, Praesepe. The Hyades are frequently listed and mentioned in this book. See such subjects as Beheaded, Blindness, Blows, Disgrace, Evil, Eyes, Face, Ill-Health, Imprisonment (see Prison); Murder, Nebulous, Pirates, Ruin, Shipwreck, Stabs, Stars, Violent Death (see "Death" under Violent); Wounds.

HYBRIDS—Mules—(See the Introduction under Barrenness. Also see Horses).

HYDATID CYSTS—A Cyst of the Tenia in its Larval State—(See "Cyst-Like Tumor" under Brain; Cysts).

HYDRAEMIA—Hydrohaemia—(See "Thin Blood" under Blood).

HYDRA'S HEART—Cor Hydra—Alphard—A star of the 2nd magnitude in the 1st face of ♌, and of the nature of ♄ and ♀. Tends to bring many evils upon the native when directed to the ☉, ☽, Asc., or hyleg. For some of the influences of this star see "Animals" under Bites; Calamity, Disgrace, Drowning; "Malice of Fortune" under Fortune; Intemperance; "Injured by Women" under Men; "Ill-Fortune" under Wife and Mother; "A Murderer" under Murder; "Death" under Poison; Riotous, Ruin.

HYDROCARBONATES—Carbohydrates, Starches, Sugars, Cellulose, etc.—Ruled by ♃. (See Jupiter, Starches, Sugar).

HYDROCELE—Caused by the ☽ affl. in ♏. (See Scrotum, Testes).

HYDROCEPHALUS — Dropsy of the Brain—Water On the Brain—A ☽ disease; the ☽ affl. in ♈, and espec. when in the Asc. or 6th H.; a ♅ disease; ♅ affl. in ♈; ♅ in ♈ and affl. by ♄; ♅ in ♈, ☌ the ☉ or ♂, and affl. by ♄; lords of the 1st or 6th, or the ☽, in watery signs; Subs at AT, KP (11D). Cases— See "Hydrocephalus", Nos. 147, 148, in 1001 N.N. See Fig. 17C in "Astro-Diagnosis", by the Heindels. (See Dropsy, Enlarged; "Large Head", "Swells", under Head).

HYDROCHLORIC ACID — One of the principal Digesting Juices of the Stomach. A lack of is caused by ♄ affl. in ♋, and resulting in Indigestion. Also caused by ♄ ☌ ☽ in ♋, as the ☽ rules the juices of the stomach in general. (See Acids, Digestion, Fluids, Indigestion, Juices; "Hydrochloric" under Stomach).

HYDROCYANIC ACID—A Typical Drug of ♄. (See Acids; "Drugs" under Saturn).

HYDROGEN — Ruled by ♄, and has affinity with Cold. (See Cold, Gases, Saturn). Hydrogen is also related to the 4th Ternary of the Signs of the Zodiac, the ♋, ♏, and ♓ Signs, the watery signs, and is the dominant element of these signs. (See "Operations" under Nature; "Signs" under Water).

HYDROHAEMIA—(See Hydraemia).

HYDRONEPHROSIS—(See this subject under Kidneys).

HYDROPHOBIA—Fear of Water. Also a Symptom of Rabies.

Fear of Water—A ♅ influence; ♅ ☌ or ill-asp. ♄ at B., and by dir.; ♅ affl. in the 8th H., and may cause death by water, as by drowning; Subs at AT, SP, and KP. (See Fears).

Hydrophobia—Rabies—Death or Injury from Mad Dog Bite—The ☉ or ☽ to the ☌, □, or ☍ ♂ by dir.; ♂ afflicting the hyleg by dir.; afflictions in common signs show, and espec. by evil aspects to the ☉ or hyleg. (See Bites, Dogs, Lock-Jaw).

HYDROSALPINX—(See "Dropsy" under Fallopian).

HYDROTHORAX—Water On the Chest —(See "Dropsy" under Chest).

HYGIENE — Disposed to the Study of Hygiene, Diet, Sanitation, Medicine, etc.—The ♍ Sign strong at B.; ♍ upon the Asc. or 6th H.; the ☉ or ♂ well-asp. in ♍, and also with increased interest in Sanitation; the ☉ in the 6th H., the house of ♍, and espec. with the ☉ in ♍. (See Cure, Diet, Food, Healers, Prevention, Remedies, Sanitation).

Hygienic Reformer — See "Lybeck", No. 212, in 1001 N.N.

Hygiene Specialist — See "Wallace" No. 292, in 1001 N.N. See "Health Foods" under Food; "Diet and Hygiene", "Specialties", under Healers.

HYLEG—The Giver of Life—Apheta—Prorogator — The ☉, ☽, and Asc. are the principal Prorogators, or Givers of Life. Also ♃, ♀, and the Part of Fortune (⊕) may become the Hyleg if they are in a hylegiacal place at B., strong, dignified, and well-aspected, and the ☉, ☽, or Asc. are not in such places. The ☉ is the Giver of Life in a day nativity if in a hylegiacal place, dignified, and well-aspected, and the ☽ is the Prorogator by night if similarly strong by sign, aspect, and house position. The Significator should be in one of the Aphetical places in order to be strong. In a male nativity the ☉ or Asc. should be taken as Hyleg if they are so situated, and in a female horoscope, the ☽ or Asc. are the first to be considered for hyleg, and if the ☽ is not strong, then ♀ should be taken as hyleg in a female nativity if in an aphetic place. In a male horoscope, ♃ may well be taken as hyleg if this planet is in dignity, and qualified for such a position, and the ☉ or Asc. are out of proper dignity. In cases of extreme emergency for a hyleg, the Part of Fortune is mentioned by some Authors as permissible to be taken as Hyleg if in a hylegiacal place, and all the other Significators are weak, and not in such places. The Asc. may be taken as Hyleg with either sex. It is advocated by some Writers that the ☉, ☽, or Asc. may become Hyleg at some time after birth by progressing into one of the hylegiacal places soon after birth, but this theory is not very strongly upheld, and does not account for the death in many instances where the supposed progressed ☉, ☽, or Asc. have been so taken. The degree rising on the Asc. at B. is always a most vital place, and is usually afflicted and badly involved in every death, whereas any other degree which may be taken after birth does not show such vital importance in accounting for death. The duration of life depends upon the Hyleg, the Hylegiacal Places, and the rulers of these places, for long life, and the ☉, ☽, Asc., or Benefics in such a place indicate long life, and strong vitality, whereas the malefics in such places weaken the strength and prospect of long life. (See Anareta; "Long Life", "Short Life", under Life). The question of death is ruled over by the afflictions to the Hyleg, the Terminal Houses, and the planets therein. (See Terminal). The Hyleg when coming to the ☌ of malefics is always weakened, and with danger of disease or death. A Hyleg which is badly afflicted by malefics at B., or in an Anaretic Place, should be avoided, and some other one chosen, as ♃, ♀, the Asc., or ⊕, if the ☉ or ☽ cannot be taken as Hyleg. When the Hyleg sets, death ensues, and the West Angle becomes Anareta. It usually takes a train of evil directions to the Hyleg to produce death, and one adverse direction is rarely considered as strong enough to cause death. (See "Arguments for Death" under Death; Directions).

Hylegiacal Places—These are the parts of the map, or Houses of the Heavens at B., which give greater vitality and endurance to the native

when the ⊙, ☽, Asc., or Benefics, are
found in these places. The majority
of Writers ascribe the following places
and degrees to be the Hylegiacal
Places,—(1) From 25 degrees below
the Asc. (rising degree), to 5 degrees
above the Asc. (2) From 5 degrees below the cusp of the 9th H. to the
middle of the 11th House. (3) From 5
degrees below the cusp of the 7th H.
to 25 degrees above the Descendant.
There is a picture of the Hylegiacal
Places in Sepharial's New Dictionary
of Astrology, in the Article on Hyleg, showing the Hylegiacal Places in
black, but with a little variation from
the figures and degrees given for the
11th H. Sepharial gives the 2nd Hylegiacal Place as extending from 5
degrees below the cusp of 9th H. to
extend over to the 25th degree of the
11th H. The student should also read
the Articles on the Hyleg in the various standard Textbooks and Dictionaries of Astrology.

The Hindu Hyleg — T h e Hylegiacal
Places In the Hindu System—These
differ some from those used in the
Western Astrology, but are strongly
advocated by Mr. Bailey, the Editor of
the British Journal of Astrology, and
Mr. Bailey considers them more correct than the ones given as authentic
in this Article. In the Hindu Astrology the Hylegiacal Places are as follows,—(1) From the middle of the Asc.
to the middle of the 12th House. (2)
From the middle of the 11th H. over to
the middle of the 8th H. (3) From the
middle of the 7th H. down to the middle of the 6th H. In any event, in
either System, these places are calculated by Oblique Ascension. Mr. Simmonite, in his Arcana of Astral Philosophy, says that "No degrees under
the Earth are eligible to the rule of
Hylegiacal locus." The 6th and 8th
Houses are classed as evil houses in
the Western Astrology, and to allow
one-half of these Houses to stand as a
Hylegiacal Place, as is done in the
Hindu System, would seem to be contrary to the facts in cases of disease
and death. (For further study along
this line see such subjects as Ascendant, Decumbiture, Descendant, Incurable, Jupiter; "Duration of Life" under
Life; Moon, Part of Fortune, Prognosis, Sun, Terminal, Venus; "Centers"
under Vital; Vitality; "Weak Body"
under Weak, etc.).

HYMEN—Imperforate Hymen—(See
"Hymen" under Vagina).

HYOID BONE—The Bone at the Root
of the Tongue—(See "Hyoid" under
Tongue).

HYOSCYAMUS—A Typical Drug of ♄.
(See "Saturn Group" under Herbs;
"Drugs" under Saturn).

HYPERACIDITY—An Abnormal Amount
of Acid In the Body—Excess Deposits
of Wastes and Poisons—Caused by the
afflictions of ♄, and especially after
middle life, and in old age. Also this
condition is more common and prevalent with people born under negative
Signs, and who have many planets at
B. in the negative Signs and Houses,
and with an earthy or watery sign

upon the Asc., and also with the negative planets ♅, ♄, ♀, and the ☽ strong
and predominant. A certain amount of
acidity in the body is normal, but with
age, under the influences and afflictions of ♄, the tissues begin to harden,
crystallize, and deposits of Urea, Uric
Acid, and other waste minerals, are
made by ♄ in order to gradually bring
on the death of the body, otherwise
people would live too long, and over-
populate the Earth. Threescore years
and ten are long enough for people to
live in a physical body unless they are
enlightened, highly spiritualized, and
have some special mission to teach and
help Humanity. An alkaline body, if
not too excessively alkaline, is a
healthy body, and when an excess of
acidity predominates, and the body is
no longer able to keep the balance
between acidity and alkalinity, death
ensues. The negative people, who are
more susceptible to this condition,
tend also to conditions of hyperacidity
by worry, brooding, introspection, and
morbid states of mind, which tend to
lower the vital forces, and the resistance against disease, and negative
people who are also born under the
strong influence of ♄, tend to die an
earlier death, and many of them commit suicide, and such people usually
are over-charged with acidity, whether
they be young or old. Acid conditions
in the body are also hastened, and
brought on, by excesses in diet, and
the use of too much sweets and pastries, starches and sugars. This condition can be remedied by living upon
a non-starchy diet, and the free use of
fruit juices, such as of the lemon,
orange, and grapefruit. Also the daily
use of a soda drink, such as Upjohn's
Citrocarbonate Effervescent Powder,
helps to neutralize the over-acid conditions in the body, and to prolong
life, and to keep the body in a healthy
and balanced condition. (See Acids,
Alkaline, Crystallization, Death, Decay,
Deposits, Elimination, Gout, Hardening, Minerals; "Negative Nature",
"Negative Planets", "Negative Signs",
under Negative; Retention, Rheumatism, Saturn, Stoppages, Suppressions,
Urea, Uric Acid, Wastes, etc.).

HYPERACTIVITY — Excessive — Exaggerated—

Body—Hyperactivity of—♂ influence,
and ♂ strong at B.; due to the plus or
tonic action of ♂. (See Accelerated,
Action, Active, Energy, Enlarged, Exaggerated, Excessive; "Over-Exercise"
under Exercise; Exertion, Growth, Increase, Motion, Movement, Muscles;
"Over-Activity" under Over, etc.).

Disease—Fevers—Inflammations—The
Hyperactivity of—(See "Causes" under
Disease, Fever, Inflammation, Spas-
modic, etc.).

Mind—The Psychic Powers—Hyperactivity of—(See "Over-Active Mind"
under Active; Hypnotism; "Hyperactivity" under Psychic).

HYPERAEMIA—A Condition of Plethora—Due to the tonic, or plus action,
of the ⊙; a ⊙ disease; the ⊙, ♃, and
afflictions in ♌; the ⊙ ☌ or ill-asp. ♂;
a ♃ disease; ♃ affl. in ♌; afflictions in

♌, general hyperaemia. (See "Too Much Blood" under Blood; Congestion, Dilatations, Distentions, Plethora, Surfeits, Swelling; "Vascular Fullness" under Vascular; "Pressure" under Vessels, etc.).

Headaches—Hyperaemic Headaches—(See Headaches).

Liver — Plethora Of — (See "Hyperaemia" under Liver).

Lungs—(See "Hyperaemia" under Lungs).

HYPERAESTHESIA — Excessive Sensibility —Hypersensitive—Supersensitive —Due principally to afflictions to ☿, as ☿ rules vibration, and afflictions to ☿ tend to increase the rate of mental and nerve vibrations, causing hypersensitiveness and nervous affections, or to cause a slower vibration, resulting in dullness, lethargy, lassitude, dulling of the senses, crawling and creeping sensations, etc. The ☉ □ or ☍ the ☽ tends to make one hypersensitive, quick to take offense; the ☉ affl. in ♐ or ♒; ☿ afflicted; ☿ affl. in the 6th H., hypersensitive to the condition of others, and liable to worries thru servants and subordinates, tending to affect the health. (See Augmented, Emotions, Excitable, High Strung (see "Strung" under High); Irritable, Mercury; "Neurotic" under Nerves; Sensation, Senses, Sensibility, Sensitive, Strain, Tension, Vibration, etc.).

HYPERAMNESIA—(See "Amnesia" under Memory).

HYPERCHLORHYDRIA—(See this subject under Stomach).

HYPERIDROSIS — Hyperhidrosis — Excessive Sweating—(See "Sweating" under Axillae, Feet; Dysidrosis; "Night Sweats" under Phthisis; "Excessive Sweating" under Sweat).

HYPERKINESIA—Exaggerated Muscular Contraction—(See "Hyperkinesia" under Muscles).

HYPEROPIA—Hypermetropia—Far-Sighted—(See "Hyperopia" under Sight).

HYPERPYREXIA—(See "High Fevers" under Fever).

HYPERSENSITIVENESS — (See Hyperaesthesia).

HYPERTROPHY — Abnormal Increase in the Size or Part of an Organ—♂ influence; a ♂ disease, and due to the tonic or plus action of ♂. Also ♃ presides to the Hypertrophic Process, and conditions of Plethora. (See Cirrhosis, Elephantiasis; "Organs" under Enlarged; Expansion, Plethora, Thickening; "Planets" under Tonic).

Cells—(See "Hypertrophy" under Cells).

Heart—(See "Dilatation", "Enlarged", under Heart).

Skin—Hypertrophy of Papillae of—(See Papilloma).

HYPNOTISM — Hypnotic — Odic Force —A Predominance of the Psychic Powers Over the Physical—The State of Artificial Somnambulism—Mesmerism—Magnetism—Ψ is hypnotic in Nature, and Hypnotic is a Therapeutic Property of this planet. Also Ψ gives

hypnotic powers. (See Clairvoyance, Magic, Magnetism, Mediumship, Negative, Neptune, Occult Powers (see Occult); "Sleep-Walking" under Sleep; Uranus).

Best Time to Hypnotize—When the ☽ is in airy sign, and especially in ♒.

Hypnotic Drugs—(See Anaesthetics; "Neptune Group" under Herbs; Narcotics).

Hypnotic Subject—Easily Hypnotized —Born under the strong influence of Ψ, and also being a negative person; Ψ ☌ the ☉, ☽, or ☿ at B., or by progression; Ψ in the Asc., 10th, or 12th H.; the afflictions of Ψ to the ☉, ☽, Asc., or hyleg tend to; Ψ progressed to the ☌, P., □ or ☍ ♀, or vice versa; the Prog. ☉ or ☽ to the ☌ or ill-asp. Ψ by dir., and espec. if Ψ is afflicted at B. People who have many planets in the positive and masculine signs of the Zodiac at B., and who are highly individualized, are usually not hypnotic subjects. (See Impressionable, Mediumistic, Negative, Obsessions, Passive, Prophetic, Psychic, Spirit Controls, Suggestion, Susceptibility).

Hypnotic Troubles—Subject To—Born under the strong influence of Ψ; Ψ affl. in the Asc., 6th, 8th, 10th, or 12th H.; Ψ affl. in ♓ in the 12th H.

Mesmerist—A Phrenologist and Mesmerist—Case—Birth Data of—See "Moores", No. 816 in 1001 N.N.

Practices Hypnotism—And Black Magic—♂ ☌ or ill-asp. Ψ, and espec. the ☌, the native practices hypnotism or black magic, or may become the victim of such. (See "Black Magic" under Magic).

Treatment—Successful In Giving Hypnotic Treatment—Has Hypnotic Powers of Healing—The Hypnotic Powers of Healing are ruled by Ψ, as Ψ is hypnotic in nature, and people who are born under the strong influence of Ψ, and with Ψ well-aspected by ♂, and who also have fortunate influences in ♏, ♓, and the 8th or 12th Houses, make fortunate Hypnotic Healers, and in the use of Hypnotism for the treatment of Obsessions, Insanity, Spirit Controls, etc., and to use White Magic in their work. Also ♅ strong at B. gives such powers, and espec. when ♅ is well-aspected by Ψ and ♂; also ♅ ☌, ⚹, or △ the ☽. (See "Magnetic Healers" under Magnetic).

HYPOCHONDRIA — Hypochondriasis — Extreme Depression, and with Morbid Anxiety Concerning the Health—Brooding Over Disease and Ill-Health —Atrabiliary—Low Spirits—Vapors—Melancholy, etc.—The ☉ affl. in ♍ or the 6th H.; the ☉ hyleg, and to the ☌ or ill-asp. ♄ by dir.; a ☽ disease and afflictions to the ☽; the Prog. ☽ to the ☌ or ill-asp. ♄; a Ψ disease; Ψ affl. in ♊, ♋, ♍, or the 6th H.; Ψ in ♋ in the 6th H.; Ψ in ♋ and affl. the ☉, ☽, Asc., or hyleg; ♅ affl. in ♍; a ♄ disease; ♄ ruler of the Asc. at B.; ♄ to the ill-asps. his own place by tr. or dir.; ♄ ascending and affl. the ☉, ☽, Asc., or ☿; ♄ afflicting the ☽ or ☿; ♄ affl. in ♍ or ♑; a ♋ disease, and afflictions in ♋, or ♋ on the Asc.; a ♑ disease; ♑ upon the Asc. The color Red has a curing effect upon Hypochondria, and patients enclosed in a room surrounded by red glass have been greatly benefitted, and soon take on a more hopeful and cheerful spirit, and with increased appetite. (See Anxiety, Atrabile, Brooding, Dejected, Delusions, Depressed, Despondency, Fears, Gloom, Illusions, Imagination, Introspection, Melancholy, Morose, Obsessions, Stone, Suicide, Worry, etc.).

HYPOCRITICAL — Hypocrites — Hypocrisy — Presenting a Good Outside — Insincere — Deceitful — Duality, etc. — ♄ Sig. in ♓; ♄ in the 9th H.; ♄ ♂ or ill-asp. ♀ or ☿, and espec. when ♄ is in the 9th H.; ♀ Sig. in ♋, puts best side outward, and seems to be in earnest when not; ☿ Sig. □ or 8 ☽. (See Deceitful, Dishonest, Dual-Minded, Liars, Mockery, Treachery, etc.).

Religion — Hypocritical In — False Religionists — The ☉ Sig. ♂ ♃ and ♃ ill-dignified and badly aspected at B.; ♄ ♂ or ill-asp. ♀; ♄ affl. in the 9th H.; ♄ Sig. in ♓; ♂ affl. in the 9th H.; ☿ affl. by ♂; malefics in the 9th H.; the 4th face of ♊ on Asc. (See "False Religionists", "Fanatical", under Religion; "Impoverished" under Riches).

HYPOGASTRIUM — The Lower Anterior Portion of the Abdominal Region — Ruled and influenced principally by the ♎ sign.

Affected — The Hypogastrium Affected — (See Abdomen, Belly, Bowels; "Lumbar Ganglia" under Ganglion).

HYPOPHYSIS CEREBRI — (See Pituitary).

HYSTERIA — H y s t e r i c s — Hysterical — Vapors — The ☉ rules the emotional nature in women, and afflictions to the ☉ tend to this trouble. A ☉ disease; the ☉ ♂, □, or 8 ♅ at B., and by dir.; the ☉ afflicted denotes hysterics in women; a ☽ disease; afflictions in the ☽ sign ♋; the ☽ □ or 8 ☿; the ☽ hyleg in ♒ in female nativities, and afflicted; the ☽ affl. in ♒, or affl. the hyleg therefrom; the ☽ in ♒, ♂, or ill-asp. any of the malefics as promittors; the ☽ in ♒, ♂, or ill-asp. ♄ (or ☿ if he be of the nature of ♄) at decumb., or the beginning of an illness, and tends to the danger of suffocation in hysterical fits (Hor'y); hysterical patients are worse at the Full ☽; a ♆ disease; ♆ □ or 8 ♃; ♆ in evil asp. to ☿; afflictions to ☿; ♆ in ♈ in the 9th H., and in □ or 8 ♅, ♄, or ♂; ♆ in ♈ in ♂ ♅ or ♂, exaggerated hysteria; ♆ in ♈ in □ ♄, for selfish reasons; ♅ affl. in ♒; ♄ denotes death by; a ♂ disease; ♀ affl. in ♒ in the 6th H.; ♀ in ♒ and affl. the ☽ or Asc.; ☿ affl. in ♒; a ♑ disease, and afflictions in ♑, Subs at AT, AX, CP, and PP. Cases — See "Nymphomania", No. 306 in 1001 N.N. See Fig. 14E in "Astro-Diagnosis" by the Heindels. (See "Brain Storms" under Brain; Coma, Delirium, Delusions, Emotions, E x a g g e r a t e d, Excitable, Fainting, Fits, Frenzy, Fury, Hallucinations; "Low Spirits" under Low; "Neurotic" u n d e r Nerves; "Psychic Storms", u n d e r P s y c h i c; Vapors; "Spirit" under Vital).

Mother — The Mother Afflicted with Hysteria — The ☽ in the 4th or 7th H., and affl. by ♄. (See Mother).

I

ICE — Ruled by ♄. (See Cold, Frost, Hail, Saturn, Snow, Winter).

ICTERUS — (See Jaundice).

IDEALS — Idealism — The Idealistic Temperament — The fiery signs, and especially ♐, tend to give Ideals, and the Idealistic Temperament, and to be interested in Utopianism. The earthy signs and ♄ have least to do with Ideals. As a rule ♉ and ♍ are the least Idealistic.

High Ideals — A special trait of the more spiritual sign ♒, and with the ☉ well-aspected in ♒ at B., or with ♒ on the Asc.; the 1st face of ♑ on the Asc. (See Honest, Humane, Noble; "Pious" under Religion).

Impractical Ideals — The afflictions of ♆ tend to, and to give wild-cat, radical, extreme ideals and notions, and to influence people to try the impossible and unreasonable way of doing things, and to lead the imagination beyond the limitations of reason. Where the horoscope indicates Humanitarian tendencies, the action of ♆ often leads to Utopianism, and espec. if the malefics ♄ and ♂ are obscurely placed, and weak in influence at B. The ♆ and ♂ influences combined tend to discontent with the present conditions in the World, and with a desire to create an ideal condition, or Utopianism. The ♅ influence combined with that of ♆ tends to a desire for rapid and sweeping Reforms. The earthy signs and ♄ give a more practical idea of things, but with tendency to endurance, and a more slow and plodding existence, get and keep what they can of material things, and to put up with things and World Conditions as they are. The ♓ sign in regard to Ideals is considered dreamy and impractical, and people with ☿ affl. in ♓ tend to be fanatical, scattering of their mental forces, and full of vagaries. (For collateral study see Anarchists, Chaotic, Conduct, Confused, Delusions, Destructiveness, D r e a m y, Eccentric, Enthusiasm, Erratic, Fanatical, Fancies; "Fixed Ideas" under Fixed; Flightiness, Habits, Hallucinations, Ideas, Illusions, Imagination, Incoherent, Incoordination, J u d g m e n t, Misunderstood, Morals, Neptune, Notions, Novelties, Obsessions, Opinions, Peculiar, Reactionary, Reformers, Religion, Riotous, Strange, Uranus, Utopianism, Vagaries, Visionary, etc.).

IDEAS — Notions — Ideals —

Extraordinary — In Their Ideas — Extraordinary Pursuits and Objects — ♅ influence; ♅ strong at B., ascending, rising; ♅ ♂ the ☉ or ☿ in the 10th H.

Fixed Ideas—Many planets in the fixed signs at B., and not easily changed. (See "Anxiety Neuroses" under Anxiety; Fixed; "Fixed Signs" under Fixed; Monomania, Obstinate).

Flight of Ideas—Confusion of Ideas—Mixed Ideas—(See "Chaotic Mind" under Chaotic; Confused, Dreamy, Erratic, Flightiness, Impulsive, Incoherent; "Bad" under Judgment; "Shallow Mentality" under Mental; Projects).

Revolutionary Ideas—(See Anarchists, Ideals, Nations, Reformers, Revolutionary, Riotous, etc.).

IDENTITY—Loss of—Disorientation—The ☉ affl. in ♈. Subs at AT or AX. (See Memory).

IDIOCY—Idiots—Phrenasthesia—Imbecility—Extreme Mental Deficiency—Feeble-Minded—Loss of Reason—

Born an Idiot—Congenital Idiocy—This is caused by lack of proper adjustment in prenatal life between the Vital Body and the Physical Body, and the head of the Vital Body may be several inches above the skull, and very noticeable after birth to one who is clairvoyant. The angle of the Stellar Ray is thrown out of proper adjustment to the mother's body during gestation in cases of congenital idiocy. During the prenatal period there are also very serious afflictions in the ♈ sign, the sign which rules the head and brain, and which tend to stop, hinder, and suppress the proper growth and development of the encephalon. head, and skull, etc. There is also an Occult cause for congenital Idiocy, which the deeper students of the Occult Mysteries will find in their reading. Some Idiots are only human animals, and with no human soul. The book, "Cosmo-Conception" goes into these matters, and from the Rosicrucian standpoint, written by Max Heindel. The planetary aspects and influences at B. usually also conform to prenatal conditions, but do not always account for the condition if it existed at B. The configurations at B. indicate conditions which may arise after birth, as a rule, and to loss of mind or reason after birth, and to imbecility. Cases—Birth Data of Congenital Idiots—See "Idiot from Birth", No. 742, in 1001 N.N. See Fig. 12 in "Message of the Stars", by the Heindels. Case—Male Born Nov. 28, 1910, 1 p.m., New York City, N.Y. Other cases are listed under "Deaf and Dumb", and "Microcephalic" in this section. (See Congenital, Hereditary, Organic, Prenatal Epoch, Structural).

Causes at Birth—Influences which conduce to Idiocy at B., or after, or which may concur with prenatal conditions, are as follows,—☿ is the principal planet to be considered, and afflictions to ☿, the houses of ☿, as the 3rd and 6th H., and also the house position of ☿; ☿ unconnected with the ☽ or Asc. at B., and afflicted (see Epilepsy and Insanity, in which diseases these influences also predominate); ☿ ☌ ♂, and with the ☽ in ☍ ♄ culminating may tend to; ☿ combust and affl. by malefics, the ☽ also weak and afflicted, the Asc. afflicted by the presence or ill-asps. of malefics, no good asp.

between the ☽ or ☿, or between them and the Asc., the native is apt to be an Idiot or go insane. This may also happen when ☿ is not combust; ☿ ruler of the Asc., and in the 12th H., and affl. by ♂ (see Case of "Deaf, Dumb and Idiot" under Hearing); ☿ affl. at B., "a very idiot or ass", says one Author; ♃ in good asp. to ☿ at B. may preserve the faculties for some years, but with the danger of losing the reason under evil directions if the foregoing conditions exist at B.; ♆ affl. in the 3rd H.; ♅ affl. in the 6th H., danger of Idiocy, and if other afflictions to ☿ concur; ♅ ☌ the ☽ at B., and by tr. or dir., tend to a mild form of Idiocy for the time if other conditions in the map of birth so indicate; the 28° ♑ on the Asc.; Subs at AT and AX. Degeneration of the Thyroid Gland, ruled by ☿, also tends to Idiocy. (For other influences along this line, and collateral study, see Cretinism, Dwarf, Epilepsy, Foolish, Hallucinations, Imbecility, Incoordination, Insanity, Irrational; "Mental Deficiency", "Weak Mentality", under Mental; Myxoedema; "Loss of Reason" under Reason; Saint Vitus Dance, Thyroid; "Body" under Vital, etc).

Deaf, Dumb, and Idiot—Influences and Case Record — (See this subject under Hearing).

Microcephalic Idiot—With a Very Small Head—Case Record—See "Microcephalic", No. 086, in 1001 N.N. (See "Small Head" under Head).

Unfortunate Case—To a Great Extent An Idiot—Head Falls to One Side—See "Unfortunate Case", No. 351, in 1001 N.N.

IDIOPATHY—An Inborn Peculiarity—A Primary Disease—A Morbid State of Mind or Body—An Idiosyncrasy—An Individual Characteristic or Affection—(See Idiosyncrasies; "Morbid Mind" under Mind).

IDIOSYNCRASIES—Peculiarities of Constitution or Temperament—(See Congenital, Constitution, Diathesis, Heredity, Idiopathy, Morbid, Organic, Peculiar, Praeincipients, Structural, Susceptibility, Temperament, etc.).

IDIOTS—(See Idiocy).

IDLE AND DULL—Indolent—Easy Going—Ergophobia—Slothful—Lazy—Inert—Lassitude, etc.—The ☉ weak at B., and badly aspected; the ☉ or ☽ as Sigs. in ♋ or ♓ in Hor'y Q.; the ☽ weak and affl. at B., and in no asp. with ♂; the ☽ or ♃ Sigs. in ♑, the ☽ ill-dig. at B.; the ☽ cadent and afflicted, and with no good aspects from ♃, ♂, or ♀; ♆ in the 3rd or 9th H., and in asp. to the ☽ or ☿, indolent; ♄ ☌ the Asc. by dir.; a weak ♂ at B., of no spirit; ♂ affl. in ♓, or Sig. in ♓; ♀ ill-dig. at B., a lazy companion; ♀ Sig. in ♋; ☿ Sig. in ♉, idle, slothful, loves ease and gluttony; the ♉ influence strong at B., a lover of ease; ♓ influences tend to a dull and indolent disposition, and espec. ♓ on the Asc., or planets as Sigs. in ♓; the earthy and watery signs strong at B. tend to an inactive and indolent nature; the 22° ♋ on the Asc.; the 4th face ♑ on the Asc.; the cardinal signs weak at B. (See "Of No Ambition" under Ambition; Apathy, Careless, Dull, Ease; "Lack of Energy" under Energy; Exertion; "Resigned to Fate" under Fate; Gluttony, Imbecility, Improvident, Inactive, Indifferent, Inertia, Labour, Lassitude, Lazy, Lethargy, Listless, Negative, Neglect, Procrastination, Rouse, Sedentery, Work, etc.).

IGNOBLE DEATH—Ignominious Death —♄ ruler of the horoscope and afflicted by malefics; ♄ affl. in 10th H. (See Banishment, Beheaded, "Burned At Stake" under Burns; "Eloctrocution" under Electricity; Execution, Exile, Fugitive, Guillotine, Hanging, Impalement, Judges, Lynching, Mobs, Murdered; "Death In Prison" under Prison; "Public Death" under Death).

Ignoble Life— (See Conduct; "Low and Base" under Low; Morals).

Ignominious and Violent Death—The ☉ or ☽ Significators in ☌ ♂, and ♂ illdignified; the ☽ weak and ill-dig. at B., and to the ☌ the M.C., if there be symptoms of a violent death in the radix; a malefic in the 10th H., in □ or ⚹ the Lights, if there are signs of a violent death in the figure. (See "Causes His Own Death" under Death; "Death" under Violent).

ILEAC PASSION—A Disease with Pain In the Abdomen, Faecal Vomiting, and Spasm of the Abdominal Muscles — Caused by ♄, and also ♄ causes death by; ♄ affl. in ♍; a ♍ disease, and afflictions in ♍; ♀ affl. in ♌ or ♍. (See Abdomen, Spasmodic).

ILEUM—The Lower Half of the Small Intestine. Ruled by ♍.

Obstructions In—Disorders of—♄ affl. in ♍; afflictions in ♍; Subs at PP. (See "Small Intestines" under Bowels; Obstructions).

Ileo-Caecal Valve—Obstruction In—♄ affl. in ♍.

ILIAC— Pertaining to the Ilium or Flanks. (See Flanks, Ilium, Sides).

ILIUM— Iliac — The Upper Part of the Innominate Bone—Hips—The Iliac Regions are ruled by ♍. The Iliac Arteries and Veins are ruled by ♐.

Diseases In — Afflictions in ♏, ♐, and the 7th H. (See Buttocks, Flanks; "Ilium" under Hips).

ILL—Bad — Evil—Misfortune—Not Advantageous, etc.—Due to its many subdivisions, the subject of "Ill-Health" is made up separately in the Article following this one. (See the various paragraphs under Bad, Evil, Fate, Fortune, Good).

Ill-Affected—(See Disease, Ill-Health, Indisposed, Sickness, etc.).

Ill Blood— (See Corrupt, Foul, Poor, under Blood).

Ill Company — Fond of Low and Bad Company—(See "Low Company" under Low).

Ill Complexion — (See "Bad" under Complexion).

Ill-Disposed—A Bad Disposition—The ☽ Sig. in ♍ or ♏; ♃ Sig. in ♏. (See Conduct, Cruel, Hatred, Judgment, Malicious, Revengeful, Temper; "Ill-Natured" in this section).

Ill Events—(See Directions, Events).

Ill Fame — (See Disgrace, Honour, Reputation, Scandal, etc.).

Ill-Fated—See Fate; "Malice of Fortune" under Fortune; Unfortunate).

Ill-Favored Body — ♄ in his second station at B. (See Crooked, Deformed, Ill-Health; "Much Sickness" under Sickness; "Ill-Formed" in this section).

Ill-Formed Body—Ill-Made Body—Ill Figure—Ill-Shaped — Ill-Proportioned — Crooked — Ugly — Misshaped — Ungainly—Ill-Composed—Disfigurements, etc.—All Constellations of human form tend to give a handsome shape and due proportions to the body. Constellations not of human form tend to vary the proportions, and incline towards their own shape by making the body larger, smaller, crooked, unshapely, stronger, or weaker. The ♄ and ♋ influences especially tend to give a crooked and misshaped body, and with ♄ in the Asc. at B., or with ♋ on the Asc. However, ♄ lord of the Asc. and occi., as between the M.C. and Desc., or between the Nadir and Asc., tends to give a good shape. In Hor'y Q. any planet as Sig. in ♋ indicates that the person inquired of is usually of an ugly, crooked, bony, thin, ungainly, and rather unpleasant appearance, stooped, and usually not handsome. The ♋ sign also tends to a misshaped body, and espec. when the ☉, ♄, ♃, or ♂ are Sigs. in this sign; ♄ Sig. in ♋ in partile asp. the Asc.; ♄ Sig. in ♉, an ill-made body, and awkwardly formed; ♄ Sig. in ♋ or ♓; ♄ Sig. in ♋, or with ♋ on the Asc., tends to make one thin and ungainly; the ☉ in ♋ partile the Asc., a mean and ill-made body; the ☽ ill-dig. at B., not handsome, but apt to be a muddling creature; the ☽ Sig. in ♏ or ♋; the ☽ Sig. in ♏, an ill-shaped, thick and short person; the ☽ □ or ⚹ ♄; the ☽ when occi. gives a lean, short, and ill-formed body; ♂ in ♋ in partile asp. the Asc., short, crooked, and ill-made; ♂ Sig. in ♋, ill-made and misshaped body, and espec. if ♂ is afflicted by the ☉ or ☽; ☿ in ♏ or ♋ in partile the Asc.; ♋ on the Asc., an ill figure, crooked, stooping, and with head bent forward. (See Abnormal, Awkward; "Beastly Form" under Beasts; Blemishes; "Dogs" under Children; Contortions, Crooked, Defects, Deformities, Disfigurements, Distortions, Face; "Club Feet" under Feet; Imperfections, Incomposed, Incurvating, Inhuman; "Knock Knees" under Knees; "Bow Legs" under Legs; Malformations, Missing, Monsters, Stooping, Teeth, Ugly, etc.).

Ill-Fortune — (See Directions, Disgrace, Events; "Malice of Fortune" under Fortune; Miseries, Misfortune, Reputation, Reversals, Ruin, Sorrow, Trouble, Unfortunate, etc.).

Ill Habits of the Body—Thru the Use of Drugs or Narcotics—♆ diseases and afflictions. (See Disease, Habits, Hexis, Ill-Health, Narcotics, Sickness, Vices).

Ill-Health—(See the next Article after this one).

Ill-Humour — Out of Sorts — (See Irritable, Temper; "Ill-Natured" in this section).

Ill-Health — 378 — **Ill-Health**

Ill-Made Body—(See "Ill-Formed" in this section).

Ill-Mannered—(See Manners).

Ill-Natured—Ill-Disposed—Ill Temper—Bad Disposition—Turbulent Nature, etc.—The ☽ Sig. in ♈, ♍, ♏, ♑, or ♓; the ☽ Sig. □ or ☍ ♄; ♄ Sig. in ♈ in Hor'y Q.; ♄ Sig. □ or ☍ the ☽; ♄ Sig. ☌, □, or ☍ ♂, or vice versa, and espec. when in angles; ♄ ☌ the Asc. by dir.; ♂ Sig. in ♉; ☿ affl. at B., and in evil asp. the Asc. by dir.; ☿ Sig. in ♈, ♋, ♌, ♑, or ♓. (See "Ill-Disposed" in this section; "High Temper" under Temper).

Illness — (See Disease, Health, Ill-Health, Sickness).

Ill-Placed — (See "Right Side" under Heart; "Floating" under Kidneys; Organs; "Ill-Placed" under Teeth).

Ill-Proportioned — (See "Ill-Formed" in this section).

Ill-Treated—(See Beaten, Cruel; "Injured By" under Healers; "Ill Treatment" under Sickness).

ILL-HEALTH — Illness — Illnesses — Sickly—Diseased, etc.—The subject of Ill-Health is also largely treated and considered under "Disease", and "Sickness", and the subjects in this Article are largely a repetition, but arranged for ready reference, as disease, sickness, suffering, etc., are so often referred to as "Ill-Health" in the Textbooks of Astrology. See the following subjects in the alphabetical arrangement when not considered more fully here—

Abroad — Ill-Health Abroad — (See Abroad, Foreign, Travel).

Absent Party—Ill-Health or Death of —(See Absent).

Accidents—Ill-Health Due To—(See "Illness" under Accidents).

Acute Diseases—(See Acute).

Ailing—Is Always Ailing—(See Ailing).

Ailments; Air — Ill-Health from Bad Air—(See "Corrupt" under Air).

Anxiety—Ill-Health Thru—(See Anxiety).

Attracts Disease—(See Attracts).

Aunts—Ill-Health of—(See Aunts).

Bad Health — (See Chronic; "Bad Health" under Health; Invalids, Sickly, Sickness, Vitality Low; "Weak Body" under Weak; the various paragraphs in this section).

Begins — Ill-Health Sets In — (See "Time Of" in this section; "Time" under Disease; "Periods of Bad Health" under Health).

Better — The Health Is Better — (See "Better" under Disease, Health).

Blood—Ill-Health from Impure Blood —(See Impure).

Bodily Ailments—(See Ailments, Disease, Infirmities, Sickness; the various paragraphs in this section).

Brings Disease Upon Himself — (See "Brings Disease" under Disease).

Brother—Ill-Health of—(See Brother).

Business Cares — Ill-Health From — (See Cares).

Cares — Ill-Health From — (See Anxiety, Cares, Troubles, Worry).

Causes—Causes of Ill-Health—Causes His Own Illnesses — (See "Causes", "Brings Disease", under Disease).

Childhood—Ill-Health In—(See Childhood, Children, Infancy).

Children — Ill-Health of — (See Childhood, Children, Early Years, Infancy, Youth).

Chronic Ill-Health — ♄ rising at B. tends to chronic ill-health, and espec. in the latter part of life. (See Chronic, Invalids, Lingering; "Ill-Health" under Old Age; Prolonged, Sickly, Tedious, etc.).

Cold Water—Craving for In Illness—(See Cravings).

Colds—Illness From—(See Colds).

Complaints; Complications — Ill-Health from a Complication of Diseases—(See Complications).

Contagious Diseases—Ill-Health By—(See Contagions).

Continued Ill-Health — (See Chronic, Continuity, Duration, Incurable, Invalids, Lingering, Permanent, Prolonged, Slow, Tedious, Wastings, etc.).

Course—The Course of Disease In Ill-Health—(See Course).

Crises; Critical—The Critical Periods of Life, Tending to Ill-Health — (See Critical, Periods, Years).

Curable; Dampness—Ill-Health By—(See Dampness, Moisture).

Dangerous Illnesses — (See Dangerous, Fatal, Fierce, Grievous, Severe, Sharp, Violent, etc.).

Days — Crises and Critical Days In Disease—(See Better, Crises, Critical, Days; "Worse" under Disease).

Death—Danger of Death from the Illness—(See "Arguments for Death" under Death; "Danger to Life" under Life).

Debauchery—Ill-Health From—(See Debauchery, Dissipation, Drink, Excesses, Intemperance, etc.).

Decay — Ill-Health Due to Decay In the System—(See Decay).

Decrepitude; Delirium; Diet — Ill-Health Due to Wrong Diet—(See Diet, Eating, Excesses, Food, Gluttony, Indigestion, Indiscretions, etc.).

Directions—As the Cause of Ill-Health —(See Directions).

Disease—(See the various paragraphs under Disease, Sickness, and also in this Article).

Disorders — (See Disease, Disorders, Sickness, etc.).

Dissipation — Ill-Health From — (See Dissipation).

Distempers—Ill-Health By—(See Distempers).

Distress — Suffering and Ill-Health Thru — (See Anguish, Anxiety, Cares, Distress, Trouble, Worry, etc.).

Drink; Drunkenness; Early Years — Ill-Health In—(See Early).

Eating — Ill-Health Thru Wrong Habits of Eating—(See Diet, Eating, Food, Gluttony, etc.).

Emaciation; Enemies—Ill-Health of—(See Enemies).

Enneatical—The 9th day of an Illness. (See Enneatical).

Entire Body—The Ill-Health Is Thru the Entire Body — (See "Whole Body" under Whole).

Events — The Event of Ill-Health — Time of—(See Directions; "Time" under Disease; Events).

Excesses — Ill-Health Due To — (See Excesses).

Excitement — (See "Ill-Health" under Excitement).

Exercise — Ill-Health from Over-Exercise—(See "Inordinate" under Exercise).

Exposure—Ill-Health From—(See Exposure).

Family—Ill-Health of—(See Family).

Fatal Illness—(See "Certain", "Sure", under Death; Fatal).

Father—Illness of—(See Father).

Feasting — Ill-Health From — (See Feasting).

Feeble; Females—Ill-Health of—(See Aunts, Daughters; "Ill-Health" under Females, Mother, Sister, Wife, Women).

Fevers; Fiance—Fiancee—Ill-Health of—(See Fiance).

Folly—Ill-Health By—(See Folly).

Food—Illness from Improper or Rich Food—(See Diet, Eating, Food).

Frequent Ill-Health—(See "Ill-Health All Thru Life" in this section; "Much Sickness" under Sickness).

Friends—Ill-Health of—(See Friends).

General Ill-Health — General Weakness—The ☉ or ☽ hyleg at B., and to the ☌ or ill-asp. ♄ by dir.; the ☽ affl. in ♑, and espec. when young; ☿ affl. in ♓; ♍ on the Asc., general weakness and debility from dyspeptic action. (See Debility, Dyspepsia, Sickly; "Much Sickness" under Sickness; Vitality Low; "Weak Body" under Weak; "Ill-Health All Thru Life" in this section).

Gluttony — Illness From — (See Gluttony).

Grandparents — Ill-Health of — (See Grandparents).

Grievous Illness—(See Grievous).

Growths — Ill-Health By — (See Growths, Tumors).

Habits — Ill-Health From — An Ill Habit of Body—(See Habits; "Ill-Health All Thru Life" in this section).

Health — (See "Bad Health" and the various paragraphs under Health).

Heat—Ill-Health from Excess of Heat —(See Fevers; "Suffering" under Heat).

High Living—Ill-Health Thru—(See "Living" under High).

Humours; Husband — Ill-Health of — (See Husband).

Ill-Health All Thru Life — Is Always Ailing — Frequent Ill-Health — Much Sickness — An Ill Habit of Body — Liable to Ill-Health — Sicky — The ☉ in the 6th H. unless well-aspected; the ☉, ☽, or Asc. hyleg, and ☌ or ill-asp. a malefic, and espec. with ♄; the ☉ ☌

♄ in the 6th H., or in ☐ or ☍ if either are in this house; the ☉ and ☽ much afflicted at B.; the ☽ affl. in ♑, often ailing, and espec. in childhood; the ☽ hyleg in ♑, and afflicted, the health is seldom good, and espec. with females; ♄ in the 10th H. in evil asp. to the hyleg, the native will always be ailing unless very powerful aspects counteract; ♄ in the 10th H. in ☐ asp. the hyleg, and ♄ evilly aspected by ♅ or ♂, except the Benefics favorably aspect both ♄ and the hyleg; the malefics ♅, ♄, or ♂ joined with the hyleg, and espec. if ♅ and ♂ also afflict ♄; a malefic planet joined with the hyleg; a malefic tends to afflict all thru life that part of the body ruled by the sign and house of the malefic, and espec. if afflicted by one or more of the other malefics, in which case the special ailments tend to be aggravated, and to predominate all thru life under evil transits and directions, and to eventually be the cause of death. Good aspects from the Benefics to ♄ and the hyleg will tend to bring much relief, and mitigate the disease. (See "Unhealthy" under Health; Incurable; Sickly; "Much Sickness" under Sickness; Vitality Low; "Weak Body" under Weak).

Imaginary Ills—(See Imagination).

Imbecility of Body—(See Imbecility).

Immunity to Disease — (See Immunity).

Imprudence—Ill-Health By—(See Imprudent).

Impulsiveness — Ill-Health From—(See Impulsive).

Incurable; Indifferent; Indigestion;

Indiscretions—Ill-Health From—(See Conduct, Diet, Excesses, Habits, Indiscretions, etc.).

Indisposition; Indulgences; Infants—Ill-Health of—(See Infancy).

Infirmities; Inflammation;

Intemperance—Ill-Health From—(See Intemperance).

Invalids; Journeys—Travel—Voyages—Ill-Health During, or the Results of—(See Abroad, Foreign Lands, Journeys, Railroads, Travel, Voyages).

Less Liable to Ill-Health—(See "Good Health" under Health; Immunity, Recuperation, Resistance, Stamina; "Body" under Strong; Tone, Vitality Good).

Liable to Ill-Health—(See Directions; "Bad Health", "Periods of Bad Health", under Health; Ingresses, Lunations, Pale, Progressions; "Low" under Resistance; Sickly, Sickness, Transits, Vitality Low; "Ill-Health All Thru Life" in this section).

Lingering Illness—(See Chronic, Lingering, Long, Prolonged, Slow, Tedious, Wastings).

Lives Thru Illness—(See "Lives Thru Serious Illnesses" under Serious).

Location — Ill-Health Due To—(See "Ill-Health" under Residence).

Long Siege—Of Ill-Health—The ☉ to the ☌, P, ☐ or ☍ ♄ by progression or dir., and espec. if the nativity shows weak vitality, and the patient is given to worry, fear, bad thinking; the ☉ in P. asp. to ♄ by progression may bring ill-health for a period of ten years; the ☉ progressed to the □ or ⚹ ♄, ill-health for three years. (See Chronic, Consumption, Invalids; "Long Illnesses" under Long; Prolonged, Tedious, etc.).

Low Spirits—Ill-Health Due To—(See "Low Spirits" under Low).

Lust—Ill-Health From—(See Amorous, Excesses, Lust, Passion, Venery).

Luxuries — Ill-Health Due To — (See Extravagance, Luxuries).

Maladies—(See Disease).

Malaise; Males—Ill-Health of—(See Father, Grandfather, Husband; "Ill-Health" under Males; Son, Uncles).

Malice of Fortune—Ill-Health Due To —(See "Malice" under Fortune).

Many Illnesses—Many Long Illnesses —(See "Ill-Health All Thru Life" in this section; "Long Illnesses" under Long; "Much Sickness" under Sickness).

Meat—Ill-Health Due to Use of—(See "Cooked Foods" under Food; "Raw Humours" under Indigestion; Meat).

Melancholy—Ill-Health Due To—(See Melancholy).

Men—Ill-Health of—(See Men).

Middle Life—Ill-Health At Time of— (See Middle Life).

Mild Illnesses—(See Colds, Mild, Slight).

Mind—Ill-Health Due to Mental Disorders, Bad Thinking, Overstudy, etc. —(See the various paragraphs under Mental, Mind, Reading, Study).

Moisture—Moist Humours—Ill-Health Due To — (See Exposure, Humours, Moisture, Water, Wet).

Mortal Illness—Danger of—(See "Arguments for Death", "Certain", "Sure", under Death; Fatal; "Small Hope of Life" under Life).

Mother—Ill-Health of—(See Mother).

Much Sickness—(See "Much" under Sickness; "Ill-Health All Thru Life" in this section).

Nature of the Ill-Health—(See "Disease", "Nature of the Disease", under Nature).

Neglect—Ill-Health From—(See Neglect, Poverty).

Nervous Disorders—(See Nerves).

Old Age—Ill-Health In—(See Adults, Grandparents, Old Age).

Old Maladies Return—(See Return).

Opposite Sex—Ill-Health Thru—(See Amorous, Excesses, Harlots, Lascivious, Lewd, Licentious, Lust; "Injured" under Men; Opposite Sex; "Passional Excesses" under Passion; "Diseases" under Sex).

Over-Eating—Ill-Health From—(See Diet, Eating, Feasting, Food, Gluttony).

Over-Excitement—Ill-Health From— (See Excitable).

Over-Exertion—Of Mind or Body, and Ill-Health From—(See Exercise, Exertion, Reading, Study).

Pain; Pale—(See Pale, Sickly).

Passional Excesses—Ill-Health From —(See "Passional", "Sex", under Excesses).

Periodic Illnesses—(See Periodic).

Periods of Ill-Health—(See Aspects, Directions; "Periods of Bad Health" under Health; Ingresses, Lunations, Periods, Progressions, Secondary, Solstices, Transits, Vernal, Years).

Plethora; Poison—(See "Sickness" under Poison).

Poverty—Ill-Health From—(See Neglect, Poverty).

Privation — Ill-Health From — (See Neglect, Poverty, Starvation).

Prolonged Illness—(See Chronic, Long, Prolonged, Tedious).

Rash Acts — Ill-Health From — (See Anger, Rashness).

Reading—Ill-Health from Too Much Reading and Study—(See "Brain Fag" under Brain; Fatigue, Reading, Study).

Recovery from Illness—(See Crises; "Better" under Disease; Moderation, Recovery, Recuperation).

Recuperation—From Illness—(See "Recovery" in this section).

Relapses; Relatives—Ill-Health of— (See Family, Relatives).

Resistance—To Disease—(See "Good Health" under Health; Immunity, Resistance, Strong, Vitality, Weak, etc.).

Serious Illnesses—(See Grievous, Incurable, Pernicious, Serious, Severe, Vehement, Violent, etc.).

Seven-Year Periods — Tending to Chronic and Lingering Illness Every Seven Years—(See "Seven-Year Periods" under Periods).

Severe Illness—(See "Serious" in this section).

Short Life—(See "Short" under Life).

Sick—The Sick—State of the Sick— (See Sick).

Sickly—The Health Not Good—(See "Bad Health" under Health; Sickly).

Sickness—(See the various paragraphs under Sickness).

Signs of Ill-Health—The Native Is Apt To Suffer Much Ill-Health If These Conditions Exist at Birth, and by Direction—The ☉ or ☽ in the 6th H., and affl. by malefics; the ☉ or ☽ on or near the cusp. of the 7th H. at B., and afflicted; the ☉ conjoined at B., or by dir., with Antares, Aldebaran, Hercules, Hyades, Regulus, or any eminent star of the nature of ♂; ♄ in the 6th H. at B., and affl. by the ☉ or ☽); ♄ or ♂ affl. the ☉, ☽, or Asc. by body or aspect, or by dir.; ☿ affl. in the 6th H.; lord of the 1st H. in the 6th, 8th, or 12th H., and afflicted, combust, □ or ⚹ lords of the 4th, 6th, 8th, or 12th H., slow in motion, out of dignity, and with no assistance from Benefics Hor'y). (See "Causes of Disease" under Disease; "Bad Health", "Periods of Bad Health", under Health; "Much Sickness" under Sickness; "Ill-Health All Thru Life" in this section).

Sister—Ill-Health of—(See Sister).

Slight Indisposition—(See Mild, Slight).

Slow Diseases—(See Chronic, Lingering, in this section; Slow).

Sores; Sports—Ill-Health By—(See Exercise, Sports).

Stamina; Study—Ill-Health from Overstudy—(See "Brain Fag" under Brain; "Eyestrain" under Eyes; Reading, Study).

Succumbs Easily—To Disease—(See "Succumbs Easily" under Disease, Sickness; Negative, Succumbs; the Introduction under Virgo; "Low" under Vitality).

Suffering—(See the various paragraphs under Suffering).

Surfeits; Symptoms; Tedious Illness—(See Tedious).

Ten Years of Ill-Health—Danger of—(See "Long Siege" in this section).

Tendency to Ill-Health—(See "Liable To" in this section).

Three Years of Ill-Health—Danger of—(See "Long Siege" in this section).

Time of Ill-Health—Time When Due Under Ordinary Conditions—(See "Time" under Disease).

Tone; Travel—Ill-Health During Travel—(See "Journeys" in this section).

Treatment—Various Lines of Treatment for Ill-Health—(See Antipathy, Cure, Drugs, Healers, Medicines, Opposites, Remedies, Sympathy, Treatment).

Tumors; Ulcers; Uncles—Ill-Health of—(See Uncles).

Vexations—Ill-Health Due To—(See Cares, Disgrace, Reversals, Ruin, Sorrow, Trouble, Vexations, Worry, etc.).

Violent Diseases—(See Pernicious, Severe, Sharp, Vehement, Violent, etc).

Vitality—Ill-Health Due to Low Vitality—(See "Low" under Vitality; "Weak Body" under Weak).

Vitiated In Body—(See "Low" under Vitality; Vitiated).

Voyages—Ill-Health On—(See Abroad, Foreign Lands, Ships, Shipwreck, Travel, Voyages).

Wards Off Disease—(See "Wards Off" under Disease).

Wastings; Weak Body—Invites Disease. (See "Attracts Disease" under Attracts; "Low" under Vitality; "Weak Body" under Weak).

Weather—Ill-Health Due to Weather—(See Cold, Heat, Storms, Weather, Wind, etc.).

Wet Feet—Colds, Disease, and Ill-Health Due To—(See "Wet Feet" under Feet).

Whole Body—The Illness Is Over the Whole Body—(See Whole).

Wife—Ill-Health of—(See Wife).

Wine—Ill-Health from Surfeit of Wine—(See Wine).

Women—Ill-Health of—(See Aunts, Females, Mother, Sister, Wife, Women).

Worse—The Health Is Worse—(See "Worse" under Disease).

Young Men—Ill-Health of—(See "Young Men" under Young).

Youth—Ill-Health In—(See Youth).

ILLAQUEATIVE—Ensnaring—Enticing—♆ influence. (See "Action Of" under Neptune).

ILLEGITIMATE—Illegitimate Children—(See Bastards).

ILLICIT—Illicit Appetites—Illicit Practices—Given To—(See "Ilicit" under Appetites).

ILLNESS—Illnesses—(See the various paragraphs under Disease, Ill-Health, Sickness).

ILLUSIONS—A False Perception of An External Object—Illusions are under the rule of the ☽.

Illusory Appetites—(See "Appetites" under Peculiar).

Illusory Diseases—And Troubles—Brooding Over—♂ affl. in ♍. (See Brooding, Hypochondria, Imaginary).

Mental Illusions—♅ affl. in ♋; ☿ affl. by ♅; Subs at AT and AX. (See Anguish, Anxiety, Brooding, Chaotic, Delirium, Delusions, Demoniac, Dreams, Fancies, Fears, Forebodings, Hallucinations, Horrors, Ideals, Imaginations, Insanity, Mania, Mental; "Diseased Mind" under Mind; Obsessions, Phenomena, Premonitions, Pseudo, Spirit Controls, Strange, Terrors, Worry).

ILLUSTRIOUS MAN—Death of—(See Famous; "Great Men", "The Great", under Great; Kings, Lady, Nobles, President, Princes, Queens, Rulers).

IMAGINATION—Imaginary—Imaginative—Imaginations—The Imagination is ruled by ♆, ♂, ☿, and the ☽. The Hebrew letter Heth is connected with the ♋ sign, and also rules the Imagination. Artistic, or Poetic Imagination, is largely the influence of the fiery and watery signs, but ♎ and ♒ may also be included. The influences of ♆ and the ♓ sign tend to Imaginations bordering on Hallucinations, and the afflictions of ♆ to Involuntary Clairvoyance. The afflictions of ♆ also tend to imaginations which may be classed as false fears, obsessions, a chaotic mind, and mental perversions, etc. The influence of ♅ has to do more with the Intuitions than with the Imagination, altho the afflictions of ♅, when configurated with ♆ or ☿, tend to disordered imaginations, eccentricities, and peculiarities of Temperament.

Deluded Imagination—(See "Disordered" in this section).

Deranged Imagination—A Diseased Imagination—A ☐ affliction, and afflictions in ♋; the ☽ affl. at B., and espec. if the ☽ is in ♋, and ☿ in ♓ at the same time; ☿ affl. at B.

Disordered Imagination—Weak or Deluded—♋ influence, and afflictions in ♋; the ☽ affl. in ♋, the ☽ in the 6th H., and affl. by ☿. (See Ideals).

False Imagination—The ☽ in bad asp. to ♂.

Fancies—(See Fancies).

Fearful Imaginations—☿ affl. at B., and in ☐ or ☍ the Asc.

Flighty Imagination—(See "Vain" in this section).

Fond Imaginations—(See Flighty; "Vain" in this section).

Head—Imaginary Diseases In—(See "Imaginary" under Head).

Imaginary Diseases—Imaginary Ills—Illusory—Pretended—The ☉, ♅, ♄, or ♂ affl. in ♍; ☿ in ♊ ♊ ♅ or ♄ in ♍; ☿ affl. in ♓; ☿ affl. by ♅, imaginary diseases in the head, and pretended ailments; ♂ affl. in ♍ tends to brooding over illusory diseases and troubles; ♋ on the Asc., and afflictions in ♋, imagine themselves suffering from ailments which may not exist; ♄ affl. in ♑. (See Brooding, Hypochondria, Illusions, Pseudo).

Imagination Runs Away—Inclined to Strange Methods, and Outside the Limitations of Reality—♅ prominent at B., and afflicted, or the ☉, ☽, ☿, or the Asc. affl. by ♅. (See Peculiar, Strange, in this section).

Imaginative—The ☽ influence strong at B.; a ♅ trait; ♅ in ♈, ♋, or ♒.

Lugubrious Imagination—(See "Melancholy" in this section).

Melancholy Imagination—Lugubrious—Doleful—Sad—The ☉, ☽, or ☿ in the signs of ♄; the ☽ in ♑ or ♒ and affl. by ♄; ♅ in ♒ and affl. by the ☽; ♄ strong at B., and afflicting ☿. (See Doleful, Gloom, Grief, Melancholy, Sadness).

Morbid Imaginations—Perverted—Unhealthy—The ☉ or ☽ ☍ ♅, and espec. along sex lines; ♅ afflicted in ♋ or ♒, the imagination should be kept pure, and morbid tendencies fought against; ♅ affl. in ♍; ♅ in the 12th H., and in ☍ ☽ in the 6th; ♂ ☌ ♀, and espec. in sex, social, and love affairs; ☿ affl. in ♋. (See "Erotic" under Mania; "Morbid" under Mind; Morbid, Nymphomania, Perversions; "Imaginations" under Puberty).

Peculiar Imagination—♅ in ♈ or ♋; the 3rd Decan. of ♒ on the Asc., ruled by the ☽. (See Peculiar).

Perverted—(See "Morbid" in this section).

Powerful Imagination—Strong—♄ in ♎, ♑, or ☿, well-dignified and aspected; ♊ gives; the 2nd Decan. of ♑, or the 3rd Dec. of ♋ on the Asc., which are ruled by the ☽.

Sensuous Imaginations—The ☽ affl. by ♀, and espec. at the age of puberty; the ☽ in ♑ and in ☍ ♄ in ♋, and espec. if ♄ afflict ♀ at the same time, or ♀ afflict ♄. (See Amorous, Lascivious, Lewd, Licentious, Lust, Nymphomania, Passion; "Imaginations" under Puberty; Sensuality, Sex).

Strange Imaginations—♅ in ♈, ♋, or ♒; ♃ affl. in ♈. (See "Peculiar" in this section; Demoniac, Peculiar, Strange).

Strong Imagination—(See "Powerful" in this section).

Unhealthy Imagination—(See "Morbid" in this section).

Vain Imaginations—Fond Imaginations—Flighty—A ☿ disorder; afflictions to ☿ at B. (See "Vain Fears" under Fears; Flighty).

Weak—The Imagination Weak and Deluded—(See "Disordered" in this section). In addition to the references already given in this Article, see An-

archists, Chaotic, Clairvoyant, Dejection, Delirium, Delusions, Depressed, Despondent, Dreamy, Eccentric, Emotions, Erratic, Hallucinations, Hypnotism, Hysteria, Ideas, Insanity, Intuition, Jealousy, Mania, Mediumship, Memory, Mental Disturbances (see Mental, Mind); Notions, Obsessions, Paranoia, Perceptions, Persecution, Pretenses, Psychic, Reformers, Religion, Sensitive, Spirit Controls, Vagaries, Visions, Worry, etc.

IMBECILITY—Imbecile—Feeble In Mind or Body—Phrenasthesia—Weak Mind, etc.—

Imbecility of Body—Weakness of—Ill-Health—If the sign of the radical 6th, 8th, or 12th H. be in the 1st H. in a Revolutionary Figure, then sickness and trouble during the year to follow is apt to come, and imbecility of body. Also when the Asc. of a Revolutionary Figure is in evil asp. to the Angles of the Radix. (See Feeble; "Periods of Bad Health" under Health; Ill-Health; "Low" under Vitality; "Weak Body" under Weak).

Imbecility of Mind—Phrenasthesia—The ☽ affl. in ♑; the ☽ in ♑ in partile asp. the Asc., one who is imbecile, idle, dull and mean. CASES of Imbecility—Birth Data, etc.—See "Arundel", No. 159; "Seventeen Years In Bed", No. 843; "Weak Mind", No. 673, all in 1001 N.N. Also see "Female" in Chap. 8, page 49, in Daath's Medical Astrology. (See Congenital, Dementia, Deranged, Dwarf, Foolish, Growth, Idiocy, Insanity; "Arrested Mental Powers" under Mental; "Weak Mind" under Mind; Monstrosities, Prenatal; "Void of Reason" under Reason; Retarded, Thyroid).

Moral Imbecility—(See "Imbecility" under Morals).

IMMEDIATE—Immediate Causes of Death, Disease, Events, Accidents, Hurts, Injuries, etc.—

Death—Immediate Cause of—When the train of Directions which cause death fall together, and none follow, for the quality of the death, and the disease which may cause it, observe those directions which precede, although at a distance; the aspects and positions of the malefics, and especially as they affect the hyleg. Also notice the positions and aspects of the Benefics, as the Benefics, altho they tend to preserve life when concurring in a train of directions, often specify the disease which is the immediate cause of death. In death by violence observe the Genethliacal positions of the ☉ and ☽, how they are affected by the malefics, and how the ☉ and ☽ are concerned in the quality of the death. (See "Quality of the Death" under Death; Directions; "Fatal Illness" under Fatal; Quality, Species; "Death" under Violent).

IMMINENT—Impending—Dangerous and Close at Hand—

An Accident Imminent—(See Accidents).

Death Imminent—(See "Arguments for Death", "Certain", "Sure", under Death; "The Sick Will Hardly Escape" under Escape; "Fatal Illness" under

Fatal; "Danger to Life", "Small Hope of Life", under Life; "Impossible" under Recovery).

Death Not Imminent—(See Amelioration; "Better" under Disease; "Spared" under Life; Moderation; "Patient Will Recover" under Recovery).

Disease Imminent — (See Directions; "Time Of" under Disease; "Periods of Ill-Health" under Ill-Health). For the various kinds of afflictions and events which may be impending and imminent see the subject in the alphabetical arrangement. See "Danger Of" under Accidents; Blows, Cuts, Dangers, Directions, Events, Hurts, Injuries, Misfortune, etc.

IMMOBILITY—Of the Body—(See Action, Cold, Locomotion, Motion, Movement, Paralysis, Rigid, Rigors, Stiff).

IMMODERATE — Excessive—Exceeding Reasonable Bounds—

   Eating—Immoderate Eater—(See "Immoderate" under Eating).

   Habits—Immoderate In Habits—(See Diet, Drink, Eating, Excesses, Feasting, Habits, Indulgence, Intemperance, Pleasure, Sports, etc.).

   Heat—Diseases Which Proceed from Immoderate Heat — (See "Excessive Heat" under Heat; "Hot Blasting Winds" under Wind).

   Menses—Immoderate Catamenial Discharges — (See "Profuse" under Discharges, Menses).

   Pulse—Immoderate Pulse—(See "High Pulse" under Pulse).

   Respiration — (See "Immoderate" under Breathing). For other study and subjects see Abnormalities, Amorous, Drunkenness, Excess, Excesses; "High" under Fever; Inordinate, Intoxication, Over-Exertion, Passion, Rapid, Rashness, Venery, etc.

IMMODEST—♄ ☌ or ill-asp. ♀ at B., and the immodesty becomes more pronounced and shameless under the afflictions of ♄ to ♀ by dir. if ♀ was affl. by ♄ at B. (See "Sex Organs": under Exhibition; Harlots, Indecent, Lewd, Modesty; "Loose Morals" under Morals; Notoriety, Obscene, Shameless, etc.).

IMMORALITY — Immoral — (See Conduct; "Loose Morals" under Morals).

IMMUNITY — Proof Against Attacks of Disease — Wards Off Disease Easily — Less Liable to Disease—Vitality Strong —Resistance to Disease Strong, etc.— The ☉ well-aspected in ♈ or ♌; the ☉ well-asp. in ♌, less liable to disease than in any other sign; the ☽ hyleg in ♐ in female nativities does not conduce to many ailments; ♃ and ♀ both rising, and supporting the Lights by good aspects, such often pass unharmed thru Pestilence, Plague, Cholera, Yellow Fever, or Diphtheria Epidemics; ♃ well-asp. in the 6th H., and not afflicted by malefics. (See "Less Liable To" under Accidents; "Immunity" under Fevers; "Abundance of Health", "Good Health", under Health; "Long Life" under Life; Recuperation, Resistance, Resources, Scarlet Fever, Smallpox, Stamina, Strong, Vitality Good, etc.).

IMPAIRMENT — Impairments — Impaired—

   Eyes Impaired — (See "Eye Trouble", and the various paragraphs under Eyes; Sight).

   Functions—The Bodily Functions Impaired—(See Functions).

   Head Impaired—(See "Disorders" under Head).

   Health Impaired—(See Disease; "Bad Health" under Health; Ill-Health, Invalids, Sickly, Sickness, etc.).

   Mental Abilities Impaired—☿ ℞ at B., and otherwise weak and afflicted; ☿ combust, some Authors say; ☿ affl. by the ☽; ☿ in no asp. to the ☽ or Asc.; ☿ setting and out of dignity, less apt to be studious. (See Comprehension; "Mind" under Erratic; Faculties, Foolish, Idiocy, Imbecility, Intellect; "Bad" under Judgment; "Shallow", "Weak", under Mentality; "Weak Mind" under Mind; Perception, Study, Understanding).

   Mental Faculties Impaired—The ☉ ☌ or P. ☿; ☿ rising after the ☉ at B.; ♒ on the 6th H. (See "Mental Abilities" in this section).

   Sensorial Functions Impaired — (See "Functions" under Sensation).

   Vitality Impaired—(See Vitality). For the various impairments of the different organs and parts of the body, or of the Mind, see in the alphabetical arrangement the subject you have in mind. Also see Blemishes, Decay, Defects, Deformities, Degeneration, Deterioration, Detriment, Disabilities, Disease, Hurts, Ill-Health, Impediments, Imperfections, Injuries, Mental, Mind, Sickness, etc.

IMPALEMENT—Death By, or by Crucifixion—Danger of Such a Death—♂ in the 10th or 4th H., near the places of Andromeda or Cepheus (within 5°), and ♂ in □ or ☍ the ☉ or ☽. (See Aldebaran, Cepheus, Hanging).

IMPAR — The Ganglion Impar — (See "Impar" under Ganglion).

IMPEDIMENTS — Impeded — Impeded Action of Mind or Body — The influences and afflictions of ♄ tend to impede and suppress the functions, and the action of the various organs of the body. The influence of ♄ with ☿, the mental ruler, is to make the mind dull, melancholic, and with fears. Saturn in any sign or house tends to impediments and weakness of the parts or organs ruled and influenced by such sign or house, and worse at times according to the aspects, transits, and directions of ♄ in afflicting his own radical place. Also ♄ afflicted in the 6th H., or ♄ afflicting the ☉, ☽, Asc., or Hyleg, tends to many impediments in the body which may adversely affect the health and mind. Nearly every subject in this book has to do with some impediment, detriment, hurt, or injury to the body and mind, and it would take too much space to list them here. (See "Hindered", "Impeded", "Impediment", "Inhibitions", "Obstructions", "Retarded", "Suppressed", etc., under each Organ, or Part of the Body, and look in the alphabetical arrangement for the subject you have in mind. However, the more general and abstract subjects along this line are listed here, which also see in the alphabetical arrangement when not more fully considered here.

Action — Impeded Action In the Body —(See Action, Motion, Movement, Retarded, Slow, etc.).

Air—(See "Impediment" under Air).

Arrested Growth — Arrested Mental Powers—(See Arrested).

Blindness—Due to Impediments—(See Blindness, Cataract; "Growths" under Eyes).

Blood — The Blood Impeded — (See "Corrupt", "Pressure", "Too Much Blood", under Blood).

Bowel Action Impeded—(See Bowels, Constipation, Costiveness, Faeces).

Circulation Impeded — (See Circulation; "Circulation" under Heart).

Disease—Note the various paragraphs under Disease).

Ears—Impediments In—(See "Left", "Right", under Ears; "Deafness" under Hearing).

Fluids—(See "Impeded" under Fluids).

Functions— (See "Impeded" under Functions).

Growth—The Growth Impeded — (See Diminished, Dwarf, Growth).

Head—Circulation In Impeded — (See "Circulation" under Head).

Hearing—The Hearing Impeded—(See "Deafness", "Deaf and Dumb", under Hearing).

Heart—(See "Impeded" under Heart).

Memory Impeded — (See "Forgetful" under Memory).

Mind—Impediments to the Mind—(See Chaotic, Dull, Idiocy, Insanity, Intellect, Judgment, Memory, Mental, Mind, Perceptions, Understanding).

Mineral Deposits — The System Impeded By — (See "Gall Stones" under Bile; Concretions, Deposits, Gout, Gravel, Joints, Minerals, Sand, Stone, Uric, Wastes, etc.).

Secretions Impeded — (See Fluids, Glands, Secretions).

Senses—The Senses Limited and Impeded—(See Hearing, Limitations, Senses, Sight, Smell, Taste, Touch, Twelfth House).

Speech—Impediments of—(See Dumbness, Mutes; "Impediment", "Stammering", under Speech; Tongue). For further study see the following subjects,—Cirrhosis, Clogging, Clots, Condensation, Congestions, Consolidation, Corrosion, Crippled, Crystallization, Deafness (see Hearing); Decay, Defects, Deficiencies, Deformities, Delayed, Density, Destructive, Elimination, Embolism, Excretion, Growths, Hardening, Hurts, Idiocy, Ill-Health, Imbecility, Imperfections, Indigestion, Infarcts, Inhibitions, Injuries, Irregular, Lameness, Motion, Movement, Mutes, Obstructions, Ossification (see Osseous); Poisons, Prevented, Retarded, Retentions, Rheumatism, Rigidity, Sand, Saturn Influence (see Saturn); Sclerosis, Sickness, Slight, Slow, Sluggish, Stiffness, Stomach (see "Stopped"

under Stomach); Stone, Stoppages, Suppressions, Teeth (see "Impediments" under Teeth); Thickening, Thrombus, Tumors, Twelfth House, Wastes, Weak, etc.

IMPERFECT—Imperfections—This is a very broad and large subject, and practically every subject in this book is related to some imperfection of the mind or body. For the Imperfections which may exist in any Part, or Organ of the body, see "Defects", "Imperfect", "Imperfections", etc., under the Part, Organ, and Subject you may have in mind, as the list and references would be too many to incorporate here in this Article. However, the more abstract subjects which are related to Imperfections, and also some of the more prominent Imperfections over the body, will be listed here in the paragraphs which follow. People born under the Imperfect Signs, ♌, ♏, or ♓, are apt to be broken, imperfect, or mutilated in some way. (See Broken, Mutilated). Imperfections are also caused by the influences and afflictions of the Malefics, and especially of ♄ and ♂, and the imperfection, defect, deformity, disease, affliction, blemish, weakness, etc., is usually in that part, or parts of the body, ruled by the Signs containing the malefics. The Signs ☉ or ☽ are in may also indicate the source and location of imperfections and weaknesses when the Lights at B. are seriously afflicted by the malefics.

All Over the Body—Imperfections All Over the Body—The ♋ sign gives, and when strongly afflicted at B. (See Whole).

Children — Imperfect Children — (See "Imperfect" under Children).

Conception — The Conception Imperfect and Defective — (See Conception, Inhuman).

Congenital—The Imperfection Is Congenital, and Exists from Birth — (See Congenital, Diathesis, Heredity).

Deafness — Deaf and Dumb — Deaf, Dumb and Blind — Deaf, Dumb and Idiot—(See Blindness, Hearing, Idiocy, Mutes).

Imperfect Signs — ♌, ♏, and ♓. (See Broken, Mutilated).

Imperfectly Formed—Case—See "Imperfectly Formed", No. 303 in 1001 N.N. (See "Beastly Form" under Beasts; "Ill-Formed" under Ill; Incomplete, Inhuman, Missing, Monsters, etc.).

Incomplete — Born Incomplete — (See "Incomplete" under Birth; Incomplete, Missing, Monsters, etc.).

Inhuman — Inhuman In Shape — (See "Beastly Form" under Beasts; Inhuman, Monsters).

Legs—Case—The Legs Imperfect, and Also Without Rectum — (See "Bad Legs", "Crooked", "Imperfect", under Legs).

Limbs Imperfect — (See Arms, Congenital, Feet, Hands, Knees, Legs, Limbs, Malformations).

Menstruation — (See "Imperfect" under Menses).

Missing Members — (See "Armless Wonder" under Arms; "Missing" under Forearm; Incomplete, Missing).

Mutes—(See "Deaf and Dumb" under Hearing; Mutes).

Mutilated Signs — (See "Imperfect Signs" in this section).

Prenatal Epoch—Many Imperfections are accounted for by prenatal conditions, and afflictions during Gestation. (See Conception, Congenital, Foetus, Gestation, Prenatal).

Signs — The Imperfect Signs — (See "Imperfect Signs" in this section).

Speech — Imperfections In — (See "Stammering", and the various paragraphs under Speech).

Stomach—(See "Imperfections" under Stomach).

Teeth—Imperfections In—(See Teeth).

Tongue — (See "Imperfections" under Tongue).

Walk—Gait—Imperfections In—(See Gait, Walk). For further study along this line see Animals (see "Resembles" under Animals); Birthmarks (see Naevus); Blemishes, Blindness (see "Born Blind" under Blindness); Blotches, Breasts (see "Imperfections" under Breasts); Broken Signs (see Broken); Cloaca, Club Feet (see Feet); Crooked, Defects, Deficient, Deformities, Disfigurements, Distortions, Dogs (see "Resembles" under Dogs); Dumb, Dwarf, Excrescences, Eyes, Face, Fancies, Feet, Fissures, Foolish, Freckles, Genitals, Head, Hermaphrodites, Humpback (see Spine); Hurtful Signs (see "Hurtful Signs" under Hurtful); Idiocy, Imbecility, Impairments, Impediments, Incomplete, Insanity, Irregular, Lameness, Marks, Members, Mind, Moles, Nipples, Organs, Peculiar, Pockmarked (see "Face" under Smallpox); Savage, Scars, Spine, Triplets, 'Ugly, Warts, Wild, etc.

IMPERFORATE — Without Opening — Closure of the Different Orifices of the Body, either Congenital or Acquired— Caused by ♄ influence, as this planet contracts and limits. Saturn in any sign may cause imperforate conditions in any orifice, or opening ruled by that sign, according to the aspects and afflictions of ♄. (See Contractions, Limitations, Orifices, Saturn).

Imperforate Anus — (See "Imperforate" under Anus).

Imperforate Hymen — (See "Hymen" under Vagina).

IMPETIGO—Acute Pustular Inflammation of the Skin—A ♏ disease; ♏ on the Asc. (See Pimples; "Pustular Diseases" under Pus; Skin).

IMPETUOUS—Choleric—Hasty—Impulsive—(See Anger, Choleric, Excitable, Hasty, Impulses, Rashness).

Impetuous Winds — High Winds and Suffering From — (See "High" under Winds).

IMPORTANT—

The Disease Is Important—(See Grievous, Serious, Severe, etc.).

The Disease Is Not Important — (See Mild, Slight).

IMPOSSIBLE—Recovery Almost Impossible — (See "Arguments For Death", "Certain", "Sure", under Death; Escape (see "Sick" under Escape); Fatal,

Grievous, Incurable; "Hope" under Life; Malignant, Pernicious, Recovery, Recuperation, Resistance, Serious, Severe, Vehement; "Diseases" under Violent; Vitality Low).

IMPOSTHUMES — Imposthumations — Abscesses—(See Abscesses, Ulcers).

IMPOTENT—Impotency—Barrenness— Sterility—The general influences causing Impotency are listed in the Article on Barrenness. Impotency may largely be considered a ♀ disease, and caused by afflictions to ♀. Also the 17° ♉, a barren sign, on the Asc. at B. is a degree of Impotency and loss of Faculties. Also caused by Subs at PP.

Females—Barrenness In—Impotency In—Lack of Sexual Power In—These influences are given under "Causes" in the Article on Barrenness. For influences which tend to cause Females to remain childless and unprolific see "Males Born Maimed" under Maimed; "Never Occur" under Menses; "Unfruitful" under Wife.

Males—Impotency In the Male—Sexual Debility In — ♀ in an angle, and espec. in the Western angle, and ♄ be in ♂, or in configuration with her, or in mutual reception, and ♂ elevated above ♀, or ♂ 8 ♀, tends to produce impotence in the male; ♀ in a feminine sign alone; ♄ and ♀ in the 7th H., and ♂ elevated above them. (See "Causes" under Barrenness; "Mutilation Of" under Foetus; "Unfruitful" under Husband).

Males Nearly Impotent—If the ☉ and ☽ be configurated together in feminine signs with ♂ and ♀, and ♀ be in a feminine sign, if a male, will be nearly impotent, but if a female very lustful, but if ♂ be feminine and ♀ masculine, males will have more strength and vigor. Mars and ♀ so configurated, when ori. and diurnal, make men more robust, but if vespertine and occi., more debilitated. If ♄ be configurated with them all, they are more prone to unnatural and violent desires. Their lust is added to by ♀, but ♃ configurated with them also moderates the desires and makes them more circumspect.

IMPOVERISHED—

Impoverished Blood — (See Anaemia; "Thin Blood" under Blood; "Impure Blood" under Impure).

Impoverished Body — (See Consumption, Decrepitude, Emaciation, Feeble, Infirm, Invalids, Malnutrition (see Nutrition); Pale, Sickly, Thin, Vitality Low; "Weak Body" under Weak).

IMPRACTICAL — (See Erratic, Ideals; "Bad" under Judgment; Notions, Practical).

IMPREGNATION — (See Conception, Fecundation, Fertilization (see Fertile); Pregnancy).

IMPRESSIONABLE — (See Influenced, Negative, Receptive).

IMPRISONMENT—Danger of—Fear of —Long Imprisonment—Time of—(See these subjects under Prison. Also see Banishment, Confinement, Exile, Fugitive; "Asylums" under Insanity; Limitations, Punishment, Restraint, etc.).

IMPROPER—

Associates—Improper Associates and Companions—Given To—(See Companions, Criminals, Environment, Gambling, Harlots; "Liaisons" under Love Affairs; "Low Company" under Low; Sex Relations (see Sex); Social Relations).

Conduct — Improper Conduct — (See Conduct).

Eating—Feeding—Improper Feeding —(See Appetite, Diet, Eating, Feeding, Feasting, Food, Gluttony, Indigestion, Indiscretions, Plethora, Surfeits, etc.).

Habits — Improper Habits — (See Habits).

Living—Improper Living—(See Appetites, Conduct, Drink, Eating, Excesses; "Free Living" under Free; Habits; "High Living" under High; "Loose Morals" under Morals; Passion, Sex, Vices, etc.).

IMPROVED—Improvement—

Conditions In Life—A Change for the Better In Life — (See "Better" under Change).

Constitution — The Constitution Improved — (See "Strengthened" under Constitution).

Disease—The Disease Is Improved— Changes for the Better — (See Abatement, Amelioration, Crises; "Better" under Disease; Moderation, Modification, Recovery, Recuperation, Resolution).

Health Is Improved — (See "Good Health", "Improved", "Promoted", under Health).

Mind Is Improved — (See Character, Destiny, Events, Fate, Fortune; "Good" under Judgment; "Quickened" under Mentality; "Sound Mind" under Mind; Riches, Wealth, etc.).

Vitality Improved — (See "Strengthened" under Constitution; "Increased" under Vitality).

IMPROVIDENT — Lack of Foresight or Thrift—The ☉ to the ☌ or P. asp. the ☽; the Prog. ☽ to □ or ☍ ♃; the ☽ afflicted and cadent, in ♍ or ♏, and with no good asps. of ♃ or ♀; ♂ ⚹ or △ ♀, thoughtless and improvident. (See Careless, Drink, Drunkenness, Dull, Idle, Judgment Bad (see Judgment); Erratic, Folly, Foolhardy, Forethought, Hasty; "Improvident" under Husband; Imprudent, Inactive, Indifferent, Lazy, Lassitude, Lethargy, Neglectful, Poverty, etc.).

IMPRUDENT — Imprudence—Rashness — Heedless — Lacking Discretion — Characteristic of the Choleric, or Bilious Temperament, ruled by the ☉, ♂, and the fiery signs; the ☉ to the ☌ or P. the ☽; the ☉ to the ☌, P., □ or ☍ ♂; the periodic direction of ♄ to the radical ♀; ☿ affl. in ♐; lord of the 1st and 8th H. being the same planet (Hor'y). (See Anger, Careless, Choleric, Cruel, Erratic, Excitable, Folly, Foolhardy, Forethought, Hasty, Improvident, Impulsive, Judgment Bad (see Judgment); Rashness, Recklessness, High Temper (see Temper); Unchaste, Uncontrolled, etc.).

Death from Imprudence—☿ affl. in ♐; lord of the 1st and 8th being the same planet (Hor'y).

Disease from Imprudence — (See "Brings Disease Upon Himself" under Disease; "His Own Worst Enemy" under Enemies; "Diseases" under Excesses; "Disease and Sickness" under Folly; Indiscretions, Rashness).

Excess of Prudence — (See "Excess" under Prudent).

Females—Imprudent Conduct of—The Asc. to the place of Markab. (See Markab; "Conduct" under Women).

Not Remarkable for Prudence—♀ Sig. ⚹ or △ ♂, not remarkable for prudence or principle; ♀ Sig. □ or ☍ ♃, void of prudence and virtue. (See Companions, Conduct, Debauched, Depraved, Disgrace, Drink, Excesses, Forethought, Love Affairs, Low Company (see Low); Passion, Principles, Sex, Shameless, Wanton, etc.).

IMPUDENT — ♂ influence; ♂ rising in the Asc. (See "Bold" under Look; Saucy).

IMPULSE — The Central Line of Impulse—(See Prenatal Epoch).

IMPULSES — Impulsiveness — ♅ and ♂ have special rule over the Impulses.

Accidents — From Impulsiveness and Precipitated Rash Actions — ♂ in the 1st H., afflicted, and in □ or ☍ the ☉ or ☽. (See Anger; "Animal Instincts" under Animal; Foolhardy, Forethought, Hasty, Imprudent, Judgment, Rashness, Recklessness).

Blind Impulses—Governed by Impulse Rather Than by Reason—The ☉ to the ☌, P., □ or ☍ ♂ by dir.; ♅ affl. in ♌; ♆ ☌, P., □ or ☍ ♂; ♅ influences tend to.

Habits — (See "Impulsive" under Habits).

Ill-Health — From Outbursts of Impulsive Expression—The ☉ affl. in ♈; ♀ affl. in ♈, ill-health from impulsive habits. (See Expression, Hasty, Precipitate, Rashness).

Impulsiveness—The ☉ ☌ or ill-asp. ♅; ♆ affl. in ♌; ♅ in ♈; ♅ affl. the ☉; ♅ or ♂ influences, and espec. when acting thru the cardinal signs; ♄ when prominent and strong at B. tends to counteract impulsiveness, and to steady the nature; ♃ affl. in ♈; ♂ affl. in the 1st H.; ♂ afflicting ♅ affl. in ♏, ♐, or ♒; ♂ ☌, □, or ☍ ♀; ♂ in ♈; ♂ to the cusp the 1st H. by dir.; ♂ ☌ ♅ by dir.; ♂ progressed ☌ or ill-asp. ♄ or ♀ in the radix, or vice versa; ☿ in ♐; ☿ progressed ☌ or ill-asp. ♂ or ♅ in the radix, or vice versa; the 3rd Decan. of ♈ on the Asc.; the 16° ♌ on the Asc.; a ♐ influence. The fire and water signs and elements incline to impulsiveness, due to emotional excitement. Fixed signs, as a class, are not as impulsive. (See Emotions, Excitable, Feelings).

Morbid Impulses — ♄ influence; ♄ strong at B.; ♄ affl. the ☉, ☽, ☿, or Asc. at B., and by dir. (See "Morbid" under Fears and Imagination; Morbid).

Nerve Impulses — (See Innervation, Nerves).

Sudden Impulses—The ☉, ☽, or ♂ affl. in ♈; the ☉ ☌ ♅ or ♂; ♅ ☌ or ill-asp. ♂; ♅ in the Asc. or 10th H.; ♂ in the 1st H. in evil asp. to the ☉ or ☽ tends to accidents, injuries, wounds, etc., from impulsive, precipitate, sudden and rash actions.

Uncontrolled Impulses—♅ afflicting ☿.

Violent Impulses — (See "Murderous" under Murder; "Tendency to Violence" under Violence). For further study along this line see Chaotic, Choleric, Dangerous, Desires, Dispersions, Eccentric, Effervescent, Erratic, Fire Signs (see Fire); Folly, Frenzy, Furious, Ideas, Notions, Peculiar, Reason, Temper, Uncontrolled, Vicious, Water Signs (see Water); etc.

IMPURE—Impurities—Corrupt—Foul—Impure Blood—Impure Conduct—Impure Morals, etc.—See "Blood", "Causes of Impure Blood", and the various paragraphs in this Article, with reference to Impure Blood, and Disorders Arising therefrom.

All Diseases — Arising from Impure Blood—Ruled by ♃, and are ♃ diseases; ♄ in □ when ♄ is the afflictor in the disease; ♀ diseases.

Arms—Hands, Legs, and Feet—Corrupt Blood In—The ☉, ♃, or ♀ afflicted in signs which rule these parts. (See "Blood" under Arms; "Blood" under Feet, Legs; "Corrupt Blood" under Hands).

Blood—Impure Blood—Corrupt Blood — Foul Blood — Gross Blood — Heavy Blood—Coarse Blood—Depraved Blood —Stagnant Blood—Poisoned Blood—Polluted Blood — Ill Blood, etc. — Corrupt Blood is due principally to the influence of ♃, and afflictions to or from this planet, as ♃ rules strongly over the blood. Impure blood is also caused by various other planetary and sign influences, which are listed under "Causes of Impure Blood", and the various paragraphs in this Article.

Boils—From Corrupt Blood—(See Abscesses, Boils).

Brain—Ill Blood In Veins of the Brain and Head — (See "Ill Blood" under Brain, Head; "Brain" under Congestion).

Causes of Impure Blood — Corrupt Blood—Foul Blood—Ill Blood—Heavy and Coarse Blood — Polluted Blood — Poisoned Blood — Toxic Blood — Blood Impurities, etc.—The ☉ in ♈, □, ♋, ♎, ♐ ♒, or ♓, and affl. by ♃; the ☉ in ♋ ☌ or ill-asp. any of the malefics as promittors; the ☉ ill-aspected by ♃ in any part of the map; the ☉ to the ill-asps. ♃ by dir.; the ☉ in ♌ or ♒, ☌, P., □ or ☍ ♅ or ♄, the blood is heavy and poisoned with waste materials; the ☽ in □, ♏, or ♑, and affl. by the ☉ or ♂ when taken ill, or at decumb. (Hor'y); the ☽ affl. in an airy sign at B., or at decumb., indicates corrupted blood, Gout, or Cutaneous affections; the ☽ hyleg and affl. in ♎ in female nativities; the ☽ to the ill-asps. ♃ by dir., the blood is gross or corrupted; ♇ or ♅ in □, ♋, ♍, ♎, or ♒, and affl. the ☉ or ☽; ♅ in the 6th H.; ♅ ☌ ♂ in □, and in □ or ☍ ♃ and ♀; ♄ in □, ♍, ♎, or ♒, and affl. the ☉ or ☽; ♄ to the ☌ ♃ by dir.; ♄ ☌ ♃ or ♀, stagnant and polluted blood; ♄ in □, ☌, □, or ☍ ♃ ♀; ♄ affl. in ♎, or ♄ in ♎ in □ or ☍ ♃ and ♀, the blood and body are charged with impurities; ♃ affl. in ♋, the result of over-eating, surfeits and plethora; a ♃ disease; ♃ causes death by im-

pure and foul blood; ♃ on the Asc. at B., and afflicted, the result of over-eating; ♃ affl. the ☉ at B., and by dir.; caused by the pathological action of the ♃ Group of Herbs (see "Jupiter Group" under Herbs); ♃ affl. in ♉, □, ♋, ♍, ♎, ♐, or ♒, or affl. the ☉ or ☽ from these signs; ♃ affl. in ♉, □, or ♋ tends espec. to foul and corrupt blood, and blood heavy with poisons and waste materials; ♃ affl. in ♎, from too much blood; ♃ affl. by ♂; ♃ affl. in ♒, the blood abounds too much, and is thereby corrupted; ♃ affl. in the Asc.; ♃ in the 6th H. at B., and affl. by the ☉; ♃ ☌ ♄, and in ♉ the ☽ and ♀; ♂ affl. in □, ♒, or ♓; ♂ to the ☌ or ill-asp. ♃ by dir., or by progression; ♂ in □, ☌, or ill-asp. the ☉; ♂ in □ in the 6th H.; ♀ affl. in □ or ♒; ♀ is nearly always afflicted by a malefic in bad blood conditions, leading to excesses in pleasures, habits, eating, and conduct; ☿ affl. in ♎ or ♒; the airy signs □, ♎, or ♒ on the Asc. at B., and afflicted; a □, ♎, and ♒ disease, and afflictions in these signs; airy signs on the Asc. or 6th H. at B., or the ☽ in an airy sign at B., or at decumb., or the Sigs. in airy signs at the beginning of an illness; a □ disease, and afflictions in □; ♐ on the Asc. at B., and afflicted; an ♒ disease, as ♒ rules the blood, and afflictions in this sign tend to impure and foul blood, disturbed circulation of the blood, to blood poisoning and morbid changes in the blood, and also insufficient oxygenation; afflictions in ♓; afflictions in or about the 25° ♌ or ♒, or the 21° ♎; lords of the 1st, 6th, or the ☽ in airy signs; Subs at SP and KP. Cases of Impure Blood—See Fig. 11G in "Astro-Diagnosis", by the Heindels. For other subjects along this line, and for the effects of Impure, Foul, and Corrupt Blood, see Abscesses, Acidity, Alkalinity, Anaemia, Aneurysm, Aquarius, Arteries, Auto-intoxication, Blood (see the various paragraphs under Blood); Boils, Breathing, Chlorosis, Circulation (see the various paragraphs and references under Circulation); Corrupt, Deposits, Dizziness, Elimination, Eruptions, Excretions, Faintings, Fetid, Fevers, Foul, Gout, Headaches, Heart (see the various paragraphs under Heart); Inflammation, Jupiter, Minerals, Obstructions, Oxygenation, Pimples, Plethora, Poisons, Pulse, Rheumatism, Septic, Skin Diseases, Sores, Stiffness, Stomach (see "Blood" under Stomach); Toxaemia, Ulcers, Urea, Uric, Varicose, Veins, Venus, Vessels, Wastes, etc. Also see other subjects you have in mind, and which are not listed here. Impure blood is usually acid blood, and too much acidity in the body means the death of the body. Pure blood is more alkaline than acid, and alkaline blood is maintained by proper diet, by avoiding excess of starches and sugars, and by eating plenty of fruits, oranges, lemons, grapefruit, vegetables, etc. Also a good and quick way to make the blood, urine, and other secretions of the body alkaline, is to take frequent doses of Citro-Carbonate (Upjohn), which is an effervescing drink, and also to take daily Epsom Salts Baths, one pound of Epsom Salts to half a tub of water in the bath tub, and soak in this solution for 10 or 15 minutes. Also, after 40 years of age, drink distilled water. Every student should make a scientific study of Diet, and the nature and food value of each article of food, in order to feed the body properly, and to maintain health, and avoid acidity of the blood, and corrupt and foul blood, etc. When the body is wholly acid, death results. Remember that excessive acidity of the body is injurious, and alkalinity of the right proportion is health and life. (See Hyperacidity).

Death from Impure Blood—♃ causes; ♃ afflicting the hyleg by dir., and ♃ much afflicted at B., and holding the dominion of death.

Digestive Disorders — From Impurities In the Blood and System—(See "Impurities" under Digestion).

Feet—(See "Feet" under Blood).

Flying Pains—From Corrupt Blood—(See "Flying Pains" under Flying).

Foul Blood—Especially an ♒ disease, and caused by afflictions in ♒. (See "Causes" in this section).

Hands — Corrupt Blood In — (See "Arms" in this section).

Head—Ill Blood In Veins of the Head —(See "Brain" in this section).

Headaches — From Bad Blood — (See "Blood" under Headaches).

Impoverished Blood — (See Anaemia, Haemoglobin, Oxygenation).

Impure Blood — (See Blood, Causes, Foul, in this section).

Impurities — Blood Impurities—The Body Charged with Impurities—♄ affl. in ♎, and due to inactive and disordered kidney action; ♄ in ♎, □ or ☍ ♃ or ♀. (See "Causes" in this section).

Legs—(See "Arms" in this section).

Many Diseases — From Impure Blood —♃ affl. in ♒, due to the blood being corrupted by too much blood, and by plethora, surfeits, etc. (See "Too Much Blood" under Blood; "Many Diseases" under Diseases; "Ill-Health All Thru Life" under Ill-Heath; Plethora; "Much Sickness" under Sickness; Surfeits).

Morals — Impure In Morals — Lewd Conduct—(See Lewd, Licentious; "Loose Morals" under Morals).

Morbid Blood—Morbid Changes In the Blood—(See "Morbid" under Blood).

Pains — Flying Pains from Corrupt Blood—(See "Flying Pains" under Flying).

Poisoning — Blood Poisoning — Poisoned Blood — Toxic Blood — (See "Causes" in this section; "Blood Poisoning" under Poisons; Toxaemia).

Poor Blood — (See Anaemia; "Poor Blood", "Thin Blood", under Blood).

Putrefaction—In the Blood—A ♃ disease. (See "Putrefaction" under Blood; Putrefaction).

Reins — Bad Blood In — (See "Blood" under Reins).

Sex Relations — (See "Impure" under Sex).

Sickness — The Illness Arises from

Corrupt Blood—The ☽ ☌ or ill-asp. ♄ in ♌ (or ☿ if he be of the nature of ♄) at the beginning of an illness, or at decumb., and they frequently die when the ☽ comes to the ☍ ♄ if no good aspects prevent (Hor'y).

Sluggish Blood — (See "Sluggish" under Blood).

Stagnant Blood—(See "Stagnant" under Blood).

Stomach Trouble — From Corrupt Blood—(See "Blood" under Stomach).

Too Much Blood — And with Corruption of the Blood — (See "Too Much Blood" under Blood).

Ulcers—Proceeding from Bad Blood—(See "Corrupt Blood" under Ulcers).

Veins—Ill Blood In Veins of the Head —(See "Brain" in this section).

Women — Corrupt Blood In — (See "Blood" under Women).

INABILITY—Lack of Power or Ability—

Concentration — Inability to Concentrate—(See Concentration).

Disease—Inability to Throw Off Disease — A characteristic of the ♍ sign class of people. (See "Low" under Recuperation, Resistance, Vitality; Virgo; "Weak Body" under Weak).

Study—Inability to Do Deep Study—(See Dull, Examinations, Imbecility; "Mental Abilities Impaired" under Impaired; "Incapable" under Learning; "Deficiency", "Incompetency", "Shallow", "Weak", under Mentality; "Weak Mind" under Mind; Study, etc.).

INACTIVE—Inaction—Inactive State of the Body or Mind—♄, ♅, or ♆ in □ at B., and affl. the ☉ or ☽; lack of strong ♂ influence at B.; the water signs strong at B.; Subs at AT, AX, SP. (See Action, Ambition, Apathy, Careless, Clumsiness, Debility, Dull, Energy, Exertion, Feeble, Idle, Indifferent, Inertia, Labour, Languid, Lassitude, Lazy, Lethargy, Listless, Low Spirits (see Low); Malaise, Motion, Movement, Retarded, Rouse, Sedentary, Sickly, Slow, Sluggish, Suppressed, Torpor, Vitality Low, Walk, Weak Body, etc.).

INARTICULATE — Incapable of Proper Articulation—Mute—Dumb—

Inarticulate Signs — ♈, ♉, ♌, and ♑. (See Articulate).

Inarticulate Speech — (See Dumb, Mutes; Impediment, Inarticulate, Stammering, under Speech; Tongue).

INCAPABLE—Incapacity—

Mental Incapacity — (See Dementia, Idiocy, Imbecile; "Study" under Inability; Insanity).

Physically Incapacitated—(See Feeble, Inefficiency, Infirm, Invalids, Sickly, Vitality Low, Weak Body).

Remedy—Incapable of Remedy—(See Incurable, Permanent; "Incapable" under Remedy).

INCENDIARISM—Pyromania—Arson— The Malicious Burning of a Building —☿ in □ and affl. by ♂; ☿ in □ ☌ ♂ at the Vernal Equinox tends to a prevalence of fires by Incendiarism.

Death by Incendiarism—♅ in a human sign at B., setting, and in ☍ to a Luminary, tends to under the evil directions of ♅ to the ☉ or ☽, and espec. when the 8th H. is involved in the configuration. (See "Death" under Fire.)

INCEST — (See "Incest" under Perversions).

INCIPIENT — Incipient Diseases — (See Praeincipients).

INCISED WOUNDS — Danger of Injury By — (See Cuts, Duels, Instruments; "Accidents" under Iron; Operations, Stabs, Sword).

INCISORS—(See "Incisors" under Teeth).

INCLINED — Incline — Inclined To — Tendencies — The Star Map of Birth, and also the Prenatal Epoch Map for the time of Conception, show the inclinations and tendencies of the body and mind. These influences show the more natural lines of expression for the native, but, of course, the evils in any map can be resisted, overcome, transcended, and controlled. The Stars only incline, and do not rule the human Will. The inclinations of the Native may be congenital, or acquired. For the various inclinations and tendencies, which operate over, and thru the native, see Acquired, Conduct, Character, Congenital, Destiny, Diathesis, Directions, Disease, Excesses, Fate, Habits, Idiosyncrasies, Ill-Health, Mental, Mind, Passion, Perversions, Propensities, Temper, Temperament, Tendencies, Vices, etc. Also look in the alphabetical arrangement for the subject you have in mind.

INCOHERENT— Incongruous—Confused — Disconnected — Lack of Coordination, etc.—(See Chaotic, Confused, Coordination, Delirium, Delusions, Dementia, Deviations, Disease, Dreamy, Erratic, Fears, Gait, Hallucinations, Ideals, Ideas, Idiocy, Imaginations, Incoordination, Insanity, Involuntary, Mania, Mind (see the various paragraphs under Mental and Mind); Notions, Paralysis, Perversions, Reason, Spasmodic, Unnatural, Walk, etc. Also look in the alphabetical arangement for the subject you have in mind).

INCOMPATIBILITY — Discordant — Antagonistic—Inharmonious, etc.—(See Antipathy, Aversions, Balance, Compatibility, Cure of Disease (see Cure); Enemies, Equilibrium, Friends, Harmony, Hatred, Healers (see "Incompatibility" under Healers); Incurable, Magnetism, Medicines, Opposites, Quarrels, Remedies, Resentful, Sympathy, Temperaments, Treatment, etc.).

INCOMPETENCY — Inability — Lack of Capacity—

Bodily Incompetency — (See Debility, Decrepitude, Deformities, Feeble, Infirm, Invalids, Sickly, Vitality Weak (see Vitality); "Weak Body" under Weak, etc).

Mental Incompetency — (See Idiocy, Imbecility; "Study" under Inability; Inefficiency, Insanity).

Mitral Incompetency — (See "Mitral" under Heart). For other parts or organs of the body which may be affected with incompetency, look in the alphabetical arrangement for the subject you have in mind.

INCOMPLETE — Imperfect — Not Fully Developed—

Born Incomplete — (See "Incomplete" under Birth; "Born Blind" under Blindness; Cloaca, Congenital, Cyclops, Deaf and Dumb (see Hearing); Defects, Deformities, Distortions, Dwarf, Frog Child, Hermaphrodites, Idiocy, Imbecile, Imperfect, Inhuman, Malformations, Members, Missing, Monsters, Organs, Prenatal Epoch, Toes, etc.).

Mental Development Incomplete — Mental Defects — (See Foolish Mind (see Foolish); Idiocy, Imbecile, Insanity; "Arrested", "Deficiency", under Mental; "Weak Mind" under Mind).

Oxygenation Incomplete — (See Oxygen).

Physical Development Incomplete — (See Diminished, Dwarf, Growth, Idiocy, Members, Organs, Undersized, etc. Also note the references under "Born Incomplete" in this section).

INCOMPOSED—Disturbed— Disordered

Body—The Body Incomposed—The 5th face of ♋ on the Asc. (See Deranged, Disease, Disordered, Ill-Health, Infirm, Weak, etc.).

Mind — The Mind Incomposed — (See Anger, Anguish, Anxiety, Despondency; "Irritations" under Mental; "High Temper" under Temper).

INCONSTANT — (See Changes; "No Home" under Home; "Light In Mind" under Mind; Mutable, Negative, Residence, Restless; "Wanderer" under Travel; Unstable, Vacillating, Vagabond).

INCONTINENCE — (See "Incontinence" under Urine).

INCOORDINATION — Of Action—Incoherent—Lack of Coordination—Caused by ♅ influence and afflictions to the organ of Coordination situated in the ♎ region of the body, and also caused by reflex action from ♍, the caudal sign of ♅; ♅ ☌, □, or ☍ the ☉ at B., and by dir.; a ☿ disease; afflictions to ☿, the mental ruler, or to a ☿ sign, or the malefics in evil asp. to the ☉ in a ☿ sign, as in ♊ or ♍.

Heart Action — Incoordination of — (See "Incoordination" under Heart).

Muscles — Incoordinated Action of — Ataxia—Case—See Fig. 1 in the book, "Message of the Stars", by the Heindels. (See Ataxia; "Incoordination" under Muscles).

Nerve Action — Incoordination of — (See such subjects as Contractions, Cramps, Involuntary, Jerky, Nausea, Nerves, Paralysis, Rhythm, Saint Vitus Dance, Spasmodic, Speech, Strabismus (see Eyes); Tetanus, Tics, Tremors, Twitchings, Vomiting, Walk, Winking (see Eyelids). Also, for further study along this line, see Action, Balance, Chaotic, Confused, Contraction, Coordination, Disease, Elephantiasis, Energy, Equilibrium, Erratic Movements (see Erratic); "Athetosis" under Fingers; Gait, Harmony, Ideals, Ideas, Idiocy, Ill-Health, Incoherent, Insanity, Mental, Mind, Motion, Movement, Nystagmus (see Eyeballs); Opisthotonos, Sickness, Spine, Subluxations, Unbalanced, Vertebrae, etc. Nearly every subject in this book is related to lack of proper coordination and harmony between mind and body, and between the various parts and functions of the body, and for subjects not listed here look in the alphabetical arrangement for the subject you have in mind.

INCREASE — Increased — Increasing — Augmentation, etc.—The plus, or tonic action, of the planets, when operating favorably, and by their good aspects, tends to increase of health, strength, vitality, and mental power. The unfavorable influences of the planets, by their plus or tonic action, tend to increase of disease, ill-health, fevers, inflammations, mental unbalance, etc. The great majority of the subjects in this book have to do with some increased or abnormal and pathological action of the planets, and all subjects which have to do with Increase cannot be listed here in this Article, but only the more important and suggestive ones, and for subjects not listed, look for it in the alphabetical arrangement.

Abscesses Increased—(See Abscesses).

Abundance—(See the various paragraphs under Abundance).

Acidity—The Acidity of the Body Increased—(See Acidity, Deposits, Gout, Hyperacidity; "Impure Blood" under Impure; Minerals, Uric, Wastes, etc.).

Action—The Action of the Mind or Body Increased—(See Accelerated, Action, Active, Hasty, Motion, Movement, Quick, Rapid, etc.).

Augmented—(See the various paragraphs under Augmented).

Bile—Blackness of Bile Increased—(See "Black Bile" under Bile).

Birth Rate—(See "Increased" under Birth).

Blood Increased—(See "Too Much Blood" under Blood).

Cold—Cold In the Body Increased—(See "Body" under Cold).

Death Rate Increased—(See Mortality).

Discharges Increased—(See Discharges, Exudations, Fluids, Flux).

Disease—The Disease Will Increase—The Disease Is Increasing—The ☽ or lord of the 6th applying to the ill-asps. the lord of the Asc.; lord of the 6th stronger than the lord of the 1st; lord of the 6th in the 8th or 12th H.; when the afflicting planets are angular and out of their dignities. (See Chronic, Crises, Directions, Fatal; "Increased" under Fevers; Grievous, Lingering, Prolonged, Relapses, Serious, Severe, Sick (see "Sick" under Escape); Vehement, Violent Maladies (see Violent); Worse).

Dropsy—(See "Increased" under Dropsy).

Dryness—The Dryness of the Body Increased—(See "Increased" under Dryness).

Energy—Increase of—(See "Increase" under Energy).

Enlargements—(See the various paragraphs under Enlarged).

Epilepsy Increased—(See Epilepsy).

Erysipelas Increased—(See Erysipelas).

Evils Increased—(See "Much Evil" under Evil).

Exaggerated Action—(See Exaggerated).

Excess Of—(See the various paragraphs under Excess, Excesses).

Expansion—Of the Bodily Tissues—(See Expansion).

Fat—Increase of—(See Fat, Obesity).

Fever Increased—(See "High Fever" under Fever).

Flesh—Increase of—(See Corpulent, Fat, Fleshy, Stoutness).

Fluids—The Fluids of the Body Increased—(See "Excessive", "High Tide", under Fluids).

Flux—Increase of—(See "Violent" under Flux).

Functions—The Functional Activities Increased—(See "Over-Activity" under Functions).

Growth—Growth of the Body Increased—(See Enlarged, Expansion, Giants, Growth).

Hair—Abundance of—Loss of Hair Increased—(See Baldness; "Abundance" under Hair).

Health—The Health Increased—(See "Good Health" under Health; Immunity; "Body" under Strong; Vitality Good).

Heat—The Heat of the Body Increased —Fevers—(See Fever; "Body" under Heat).

Height—Height of the Body Increased —(See Giants, Height, Tall).

Hyperaesthesia—Excessive Sensibility—(See Hyperaesthesia).

Hypertrophy—Abnormal Increase In the Size of An Organ—(See Hypertrophy).

Improved—(See the various paragraphs under Improved).

Incrementations—Increase or Growth —(See Enlarged, Growth).

Inflammation Increased—(See "Increased" under Inflammation).

Insanity Increased—(See "Increased" under Insanity).

Mobility Increased—(See Accelerated, Action, Exaggerated, Motion, Movement, Rapid, Spasmodic, etc.).

Moisture—The Moisture of the Body Increased—(See "Moist Constitution" and the various paragraphs under Moisture).

Moon—Increase of—(See Fluids, Functions; "Increase Of" under Moon).

Mortality Increased—Death Rate Higher—(See Mortality).

Motion—Movement—(See these subjects).

Mucus—The Mucus In the Body Increased—(See Catarrhs, Colds, Expectoration, Mucus, Phlegm).

Nervousness Increased—(See Erethism; "Increase", "Neurasthenia", under Nerves).

Over-Abundance—(See the various paragraphs under Hyper, Over, Super).

Pain Increased—(See Pain).

Phlegm—Increase of—(See "Mucus" in this section).

Plentiful—(See the paragraphs under Plenty).

Promoted—(See the paragraphs under Promoted).

Recuperation — The Recuperative Powers Increased—(See Recuperation).

Relapses—The Danger of a Relapse In Disease Increased—(See Relapse).

Resistance—The Powers of Resistance to Disease Increased—(See Resistance, Stamina, Tone, Vitality).

Rheumatism Increased—(See "Promoted" under Rheumatism).

Secretions Increased — (See Discharges, Fluids, Glands, Juices, Secretions).

Sensibility Increased—(See Hyperaesthesia, Sensibility, Sensitive).

Spasmodic Action Increased — (See Convulsions, Exaggerated, Fits, Hyperactivity, Spasmodic, Tics, Twitchings).

Strength—The Strength of the Constitution Increased—(See "Increased" under Constitution; "Improved" under Health; Strength, Vitality).

Suffering Increased—(See Pain, Suffering, Worse).

Superabundance—(See the various paragraphs under Superabundance).

Sweat—(See "Excessive" under Sweat).

Swellings—(See Swellings, Tumors).

Temperature—Increase of—High—(See "High" under Fevers; Temperature).

Tetters Increased—(See Tetter).

Thickening—(See the paragraphs under Thick).

Too Much — (See the various paragraphs under Abundance, Excess, Hyper, Over, Superabundance).

Tumors—(See the various paragraphs under Growths, Tumors).

Ulcers Increased—(See Ulcers).

Urine Increased—(See "Polyuria" under Urine).

Vitality Increased—(See Vitality).

Wastes—Of the Body Increased—(See Deposits; "Impure Blood" under Impure; Minerals, Urea, Uric, Wastes).

Weakness Increased—(See "Body" under Weak).

Weight—The Weight Increased—(See Corpulent, Fat, Fleshy, Stout, Weight).

Worry—Increase of—(See Cares; "Low Spirits" under Low; Miseries, Reversals, Ruin, Troubles, Worry, etc.).

Worse—The Disease Is Worse or Increased—(See "Worse" under Disease; Relapses, Worse). Also see such subjects as Abnormal, Anger, Appetites, Conduct, Corpuscles, Decreased, Deposits, Diminished, Dissipation, Drink, Gluttony, Habits; "High Living" under High; Immoderate, Intemperate, Passion, Pleasures, Riotous, Sex, Temper, etc.

INCREMENTATIONS—Increase or Growth—(See Enlarged, Expansion, Growth, Increase, Large, etc.).

INCURABLE—Incurable Diseases—The Disease, Affliction, or Malady Is Incurable, or Without Apparent Remedy—Many planets in the fixed signs, 8, ♌, ♏, or ♒ at B., and afflicted, tend to deep-seated and incurable diseases. The influences of the malefics, and their afflictions, are the principal causes of prolonging a disease and making it incurable, and especially the influence of ♄ at B., and by dir. If the malefics are angular, ori., and elevated above the Lights, and the benefics are occi., weak, and lend no assistance, the disease tends to be tedious, prolonged, or incurable, and the more ori. or angular the planet is, whether malefic or benefic, the more powerful will be its effects. The malefics in angles at B., well fortified, and in elevation above the Lights and Benefics, and the latter in weak signs; malefics in angles at B., occi. of the ☉, and ori. of the ☽, and the benefics in no way connected with the malefics, nor with the ☉ or ☽; the malefics strong, and holding dominion in angles, or above the Lights, and evilly aspected by ♃ or ♀, or the malefics with the ☉ or ☽ in angles, and the Luminaries receiving no help from the benefics; the malefics holding dominion, and afflicting the hyleg, and with no assistance to the hyleg from benefics, and the malefics elevated above the Luminaries at B., provided the ☉ or ☽ are not in angles, and the malefics receive no good asp. from ♃ or ♀; when a malefic in a sign and house is afflicted by two or more malefics at B., then the part of the body afflicted is apt to develop an incurable malady, and predominate more or less all thru life, and eventually cause death under a train of evil directions, and especially if at B. the malefic is in the 6th, 8th, or 12th H.; the ☉ or ☽ in the 6th H. at B., and affl. by malefics; the ☉ or ☽ in angles, and affl. by malefics elevated above them; the ☽ and many planets in fixed signs at the beginning of an illness (Hor'y); ♅ affl. in the 1st or 6th H.; ♅ diseases are mostly nervous, and often incurable; ♅ □ or 8 ♄ in fixed signs; ♅ □ or 8 the ☽, and often with complete suppression of the functions; ♅ □ or 8 the Asc.; ♄ afflicted in fixed signs; ♄ in the 6th H., and afflicting the hyleg; ♃ afflicted in ♓, due to tendency to dropsy and swellings; indicated by the 6th H. conditions; lord of the 6th affl. by the □ or 8 the lord of the Asc., grievous and hard to cure; lord of the 8th in the 6th; lord of the 1st in an Azimene degree, and affl. by lord of the 6th. (For further influences along this line see Azimene, Birth (note the various paragraphs under Birth); Blemishes, Blindness, Changes, Chronic, Complications, Congenital, Continuous, Course of Disease (see Course); Crippled, Crises, Cure, Deafness, Death (see "Arguments for Death", "Certain", "Sure", under Death); Decay, Defects, Deformities, Dementia, Directions, Distortions, Duration of Disease (see Duration); Epilepsy, Escape (see "The Sick Will Hardly Escape" under Escape); Extraordinary, Fatal, Fixed Signs (see Fixed); Functions (see

"Suppressed" under Functions); Gangrene, Grievous, Healers (see "Death" under Healers); Hereditary, Ill-Health (see "Ill-Health All Thru Life" under Ill-Health); Invalids, Lameness, Latent Diseases (see Latent); Lingering, Long Diseases (see Long); Malformations, Malignant, Malnutrition, Mania, Monsters, Morbid, Mysterious, Narcotics, Negative, Organic, Paralysis, Passive, Peculiar, Prolonged, Recovery, Recuperation, Resistance, Saturn, Sick (see the paragraphs under Sick); Sickly, Slow Diseases (see Slow); Strange Diseases (see Strange), Structural, Suppressions, Tedious, Treatment, Uranus, Wastings, Weak Body (see Weak); Worse, etc.).

Conspicuous Diseases—The Disease Is Conspicuous and Less Liable of a Cure—(See Chronic, Conspicuous, Deformities, Dementia, Demoniac, Epilepsy, Exhibitionism, Face, Feet, Foolish Mind (see Foolish); Head, Hydrocephalus, Idiocy, Imbecility, Insanity, Lameness, Leprosy, Limbs, Malformations, Monsters, Siamese Twins (see Twins); Skull, Spine, Walk, etc.).

Deep-Seated—The Disease Is Deep-Seated and Incurable—(See Chronic, Death, Fatal, Lingering, Malignant, Morbid, Tedious, etc.).

Difficult to Cure—(See Chronic; "Difficult" under Cure; Environment, Extraordinary, Grievous, Invalids, Long, Malignant, Native Land, Prolonged, Residence, Slow, Tedious, Wastings).

Drunkards—(See "Incurable" under Drunkenness).

Hurts Incurable—(See Crippled, Permanent; "Hurts" under Remedy).

Incapable of Remedy—(See Fatal, Incapable, Permanent; "Hurts" under Remedy. Also see the first part of this Article, and the various references herein).

Mental Diseases—Incurable Diseases of the Mind — The ☽ and ☿ unconnected with each other or the Asc., and with ♄ and ♂ in angles ruling the scheme, but the disease will not be conspicuous or openly displayed. The ☽ and ☿ unconnected with each other or the Asc., and the malefics in the Eastern Parts, and in the Asc. or M.C., and the benefics occi., then the disease becomes incurable and also conspicuous. (See "Curable", "Incurable", under Brain; Chaotic, Conspicuous, Dementia, Demoniac, Fears, Foolish, Frenzy, Idiocy, Imbecility, Insanity, Madness, Mania; "Derangement" under Mental; "Diseased Mind" under Mind; Obsessions, Paranoia, Spirit Controls).

Old Age — Incurable Infirmity In — (See "Incurable" under Old Age).

Remedy — The Disease or Hurt Is Without Remedy — (See "Certain", "Sure" under Death; Fatal, Permanent; "Hurts" under Remedy).

Rheumatism Incurable—(See "Death", "Incurable", under Gout, Rheumatism).

Sudden and Incurable Diseases—♅ ☐ or ☍ the ☉ at B., and by dir. For further subjects along this line, and which may not be listed here, look for the subject in the alphabetical arrangement. Also remember that many diseases are classed as "Incurable" in the ordinary sense, which may become curable when the native becomes awakened, more highly spiritualized, and learns how to think correctly, and to live in accordance with the Laws of God, and of Health, Longevity, etc.

INCURVATING BODY—Crooked — Not Straight—♄ strong at B., in the Asc., or rising; a ♄ sign on the Asc., as ♑; ☿ Sig. in ♑, a crooked make; ♓ gives a body not very straight, but incurvating. (See Crooked; "Ill-Formed" under Ill; Stooped).

INDECENT — An Abandoned Person — Profligate—Unrestrained—Morally Perverted — Without Virtue — Shameless, etc. — (See Debauched, Depraved, Lascivious, Lewd, Licentious, Lustful; "Loose Morals" under Morals; "Unbridled Passion" under Passion; Perversions, Profligate, Shameless, Virtue, Wanton, etc.).

INDEPENDENT — Independence of Thought and Opinion—♆ and ♅ influence; ♅ ascending at B.; ♅ in the 3rd or 9th H.; ♅ ☌ the ☉, ☽, or ☿ at B.; ♅ in the Asc. or 10th H. at B., in ☌ the ☉, ☽, or ☿; the ☽ applying to the ☌ or any aspect of ♆ or ♅. These influences tend to make the native unorthodox, to be much misunderstood in life, persecuted, and to be fond of Astrology, the Esoteric, Occult, Metaphysical, and Ancient Wisdom, and with a deep desire to know the Truth about Life, Death, Destiny, The Hereafter, The Mysteries, The Secret Doctrines, Religion, The Soul, Salvation, Redemption, etc. (See Eccentric, Ideals, Ideas, Metaphysics, Misunderstood, Occult, Opinions, Peculiar, Persecution, Philosophy, Positive, Nature, Reactionary, Reformers, Religion, Revolutionary, Saucy, Science, Truth, etc.).

INDIAN HEMP—A Typical Drug of ♄. (See Cannabis; "Saturn Group" under Herbs).

INDICATIVE CRISES — In Disease — Those which occur at the half aspects in every Quadrate of the ☽ from her place at seizure or decumbiture, as at 45°, 135°, 225°, or 315°. (See Crises).

INDICATORS OF DISEASE—Indicators of Health — (See Anareta; "Significators" under Disease; "Indicators" under Health; Hyleg, Malefics, Significators, Sixth House).

INDIFFERENT—Indifference—Neutral—Disinterested—Ill or Sick—Poorly—

Blood — Indifferent State of — (See "Poor", "Thin", under Blood).

Complexion — (See "Indifferent" under Complexion).

Disposition — An Indifferent Disposition — Indifference — Many planets in bicorporeal signs at B. tend to an indifferent disposition; lack of strong ♂ influence at B.; mutable signs on the Angles at B.; many planets cadent. (See Dreamy, Dull; "Lack Of" under Energy; Idle, Inactive, Inertia, Labour, Lassitude, Lethargy, Listless, Manner, Negative; "Temperament" under Phlegmatic; Rouse).

Duty — Indifferent To — (See "Of No Ambition" under Ambition; Carelessness, Debauched, Improvident, Neglectful, etc.).

Expression—Indifferent Expression of the Face—Born under ♄; ♄ rising at B.; ♄ in the Asc. (See Countenance, Dull; "Dull" under Eyes; "Sad" under Face; Grave, Melancholic; "Mind" in this section).

Face—An Indifferent Face—(See "Expression" in this section).

Health—(See "Indifferent State" under Health).

Marriage—Indifferent To—(See "Indifferent" under Marriage).

Mind—Indifferent State of Mind—Indifferent Expression — Apathy — Dull, etc.—The ☽ to the ☌ or ill-asp. ♆ by dir., indifference of the mind to life's duties; the 3rd face of ♉ on the Asc., careless and indifferent. (See Apathy, Dull, Languid, Lethargy, Listless, Procrastination; "Disposition", "Expression", in this section).

Passion — Indifferent Passions — (See Apathy, Bachelors, Celibacy; "Free from Passion" under Passion).

Signs of Zodiac—The Indifferent Signs —(See "Indifferent" under Signs).

Stature—Indifferent Stature—Not Distinctive—The ☽ Sig. in ♈; ☿ in ♒. (See Crooked, Form, Mean, Small, Stature, Stooping, Ugly, etc.).

Teeth—Indifferent Teeth — (See "Indifferent" under Teeth).

INDIGENT—Destitude—Without Comforts—In Poverty—(See Comforts, Idle, Improvident, Misery, Penurious, Poverty, Property, Reversals, Riches, Ruin).

INDIGESTION — Indigested — Undigested — Caused ordinarily by afflictions in ♋, or its opposite sign ♑ by reflex action. Also afflictions in cardinal signs show, or cardinal signs upon the angles, as the cardinal signs ♈, ♋, ♎, and ♑, are all in adverse aspect to each other, and form the cardinal cross. Also caused by the ☉ affl. in ♋, and espec. when affl. by ♄; the ☽ in ♋, and affl. by ♄; the ☽ in ♋ or ♏, and in ☐ or 8 ♃ or ♀; the ☽ ☌ ♅ in ♋ or ♍; the prog. ☽ in ♋ or ♍, and in ☌, ☐, or 8 malefics; ♆ in ♋ in the 6th H.; ♄ affl. in ♋ or ♏; ♃ or ♂ affl. in ♋; Subs at SP. (See Acids, Alimentary, Aphthae, Diet; "Digestive Disorders", "Inability to Digest Food", "Weak Digestion", under Digestion; Dyspepsia, Flatulence, Food, Gas (see "Stomach" under Gas); Gastric, Hydrochloric, Juices, Nutrition, Stomach; the various paragraphs in this section).

Anxiety — Indigestion from Anxiety and Worry—(See "Anxiety" under Digestion).

Chronic Indigestion—Inability to Digest Food—♄ affl. in ♋; ♄ in the 6th H. at B., in a cardinal sign, and affl. by the ☉ or ☽. (See "Inability" under Digestion; Emaciation; "Malnutrition" under Nutrition; Wasting).

Cold—Indigestion from Taking Cold —A ☽ disease; the ☽ affl. in ♋. (See Cold, Colds).

Cramps—From Indigestion—♅ affl. in ♋ or ♍. (See Cramps).

Food—Indigestible Food—Desire For —(See "Indigestible" under Food).

Head — Noises In the Head Arising from Indigestion—(See "Noises" under Head).

Illness from Indigestion—The ☽ in ♍, ☌, ☐, or 8 ♄ (or ☿ if he be of the nature of ♄) at the beginning of an illness or at decumb., and the patient is apt to be sick for a long time (Hor'y).

Impaired Digestion—Imperfect—(See Digestion, Dyspepsia; the various paragraphs in this section).

Inability to Digest Food — (See "Chronic" in this section).

Intestinal Indigestion—♅ in ♑ in 8 ♆ in ♋, and also in ☐ ♄, the food is often undigested and appearing in pieces in the stools; ♄ affl. in ♍; ♀ in ♍, and affl. the ☽ or Asc.; ♀ affl. in ♍ in the 6th H.; ☿ affl. in the 6th H., and due to overwork or overstudy; ♍ on the cusp the 6th H.; afflictions in the 6th H. (See Chyle).

Meat — Ill-Digested Meat and Illness From—(See Meat; "Raw Humours" in this section).

Nervous Indigestion—♅ affl. in ♋; ♅ ☌ ☽ in ♋; ☿ affl. in ♋ or ♑. (See Nerves).

Poor Digestion — Suffers from Indigestion—The ☉ affl. in ♋; the ☉ in ♋ and affl. by ♃; the ☽ affl. in ♋; a ☽ disease; the ☽ in ♍ ☌ ♄, etc. (See "Illness" in this section); ♆, ♅, or ♄ in ♋ or ♑, and affl. the ☉ or ☽; ♄ in ♋ in the Asc. or 6th H., and espec. when affl. the ☉ or ☽; ♃ affl. in ♋; ♂ in the 6th H. in card. signs, and affl. the ☉ or ☽; ♂ in ♋, ☌, or ill-asp. the ☉; ♂ ☐ or 8 ☉ at B., and by dir.; ♀ affl. in ♋ in the 6th H., and affl. the ☽ or Asc.; ☿ in ♋, ♐, ♑, ☌ or ill-asp. any of the malefics as Promittors; cardinal signs on the 6th H.; card. signs show, and afflictions in them; afflictions in ♋; ♋ on the Asc. or 6th H., and containing malefics and afflictions. (See "Chronic" in this section).

Raw Humours — The Stomach Offended with Cold, Raw, and Undigested Humours—♄, ♅, or ♆ in ♋, and affl. the ☉ or ☽; ♄ affl. in ♋, a cold stomach; ♀ affl. in ♋ when ♀ is the afflictor in the disease; the Asc. affl. by the ☉ or ☽. (See Meat).

Stomach — (See the various paragraphs under Digestion, Stomach).

Weak Digestion—(See "Weak" under Digestion).

Worry and Anxiety—Indigestion From —(See "Anxiety" under Digestion). For collateral study see Acids, Alimentary, Belching, Cachexia, Diet, Digestion, Dyspepsia, Emaciation, Emetics, Feasting, Fermentation, Fluids, Gastric, Gluttony, Juices, Nausea, Nutrition, Vomiting, etc.).

INDIGO—A color ruled by ♄ and ♀. Indigo is not blue, but a color in itself, and represents Spiritual Mind, and Intellect over-shadowed by Divine Mind. (See Colors, Copper; "Venus Group" under Herbs).

INDISCRETIONS—Indiscreet—Tending to Injure the Health—

Actions—Indiscretions In—(See Conduct, Habits; the various paragraphs and references in this section).

Conduct—Indiscretions In—(See Conduct).

Cosmetics — Indiscretions In the Use of—(See Cosmetics, Lotions).

Death—From Indiscretions—(See "Causes His Own Death" under Death; Debauchery; "Death" under Eating; "His Own Worst Enemy" under Enemies; Folly, Imprudence, Intemperance, Intoxication, Narcotics, Rashness, etc.).

Diet—Indiscretion In—Gastronomical Indiscretions—Due to an afflicted ♃ or ♀, or afflictions by these planets; ♃ and ♀ diseases; ♃ affl. in ♉ or ♋; ♃ or ♀ in the 6th H., and afflicted; ♀ affl. in ♋ or ♓; the Asc. affl. by ♃ or ♀. (See "Evil Diet" under Diet; Drink, Eating, Excesses, Food, Gluttony, Indigestion, etc.).

Diseases Arising From—♀ □ or ☍ the Asc. (See "Fever", and the various paragraphs in this section).

Drugs—Indiscretions In the Use of—(See Drugs, Narcotics).

Fever and Sickness—From Indiscretions—The ☉ affl. by ♃ or ♀; the ☽ affl. by ♀, irregularities and ailments arising from indiscretions, excesses, and carelessness; the ☽ affl. by ♃; ♃ diseases, and indiscretions in diet especially. (See "Ailments" under Diet; Excesses; "Indiscretions", "Slight", under Fever; Folly; "Free Living" under Free; "High Living" under High; Plethora, Surfeits, etc.).

Gastronomical Indiscretions—(See "Diet" in this section).

Habits—Indiscreet Habits—(See Conduct, Drink, Drunkenness, Gambling, Habits, Luxuries, Morals, Narcotics, Passion, Perversions, Vices, etc.).

Sex Life—Indiscretions and Excesses In—(See Amorous, Harlots, Intercourse, Lascivious, Lewd, Licentious; "Loose Morals" under Morals; "Excesses" under Passion; Sex, Venery).

Slight Disorders—From Indiscretions —♀ affl. the ☉ at B., and by dir. (See Ephemeral, Mild, Slight).

Sports — Indiscretions In and Suffering From — (See Amusements, Exercise, Pleasure, Sports).

Volitional Power — Will-Power — Indiscretions Thru Loss of, or Weakness of—Ψ influence; Ψ affl. in ♐. (See Involuntary, Volition, Will).

Wounds — Accidents, Hurts, Injuries or Wounds from Indiscretions — (See Accidents, Blows, Cuts, Falls, Folly, Foolhardy, Hasty, Hurts, Injuries, Quarrels, Rashness, Stabs, Violence, Wounds, etc.). For further and collateral study see Anger, Appetites, Carelessness, Cravings, Deposits, Depraved, Disease, Disgrace, Dissipation, Dissolute, Epicureans, Erratic, Feasting, Ill-Health, Improvident, Imprudent, Indulgences, Irregularities, Judgment, Love Affairs, Meat, Neglectful, Obesity, Poisons, Poverty, Prodigal, Profligate, Recklessness, Recreations, Riotous, Ruin, Sickness, Temper, Tumors, etc.).

INDISPOSITION—Indisposed—Ailing—

Cold Temperament—Indisposed By—(See "Temperament" under Cold).

Febrile Indisposition—♂ affl. in ♒; ♂ to the ill-asps. his own place at B., or by dir., or to the place of the ☉ or ☽. (See "Liable To" under Fever).

Indisposed — The transits of malefics over the place of the ☉ or ☽ at B. if they afflict the Lights in the radix; the ☉ directed to Aldebaran; the ☽ affl. in ♋ at B. and by dir.; ♄ to the ill-asps. his own place by tr. or dir., or to the place of the ☉ or ☽, or any planet; ♂ to the cusp the 1st H. by dir.; ♀ Sig. in ♌, frequently indisposed, altho not seriously. (See "Bad Health" under Health; Ill-Health, Mild, Sickly, Slight).

Lingering Indisposition—(See Chronic, Lingering, Long, Prolonged, Slow, Tedious, Wastings).

Mental Indisposition — (See "Low Spirits" under Low; Melancholy; "Irritations" under Mental; Worry, etc.).

Occasional Indisposition — ♀ affl. the ☽ at B., and by dir. or tr.; ♀ affl. in the 5th or 6th H. at B., and thru pleasures, dissipation, or wrong eating; ♀ affl. in ♌.

Parents Indisposed — (See "Afflicted" under Parents).

Slight Indisposition — Temporary Indisposition—Ill aspects of the ☉ to the malefics if the malefics did not afflict the ☉ at B.; the tr. of the ☉ over the radical Ψ when Ψ is Promittor; the ☽ to the ill-asps. her own place at B.; the ☽ to the ill-asps. Ψ or ♅ by dir., as by Colds; the ☽ to the bad asps. ♀ by dir., temporary disorders; ♄ ♂ or ill-asp. the ☽, and both occi., temporary derangement of the health; caused by directions which are brief in duration; benefics in the 6th H., and well-aspected, the indisposition will be slight and soon overcome. (See Colds, Fatigue, Headaches, Mild, Minor, Recovery, Slight, Temporary, etc.).

INDIVIDUALITY—The Sign the ☉ is in at B. represents the Individuality, or the Higher Mind. Also many planets in the positive and masculine signs at B. give a strong Individuality, and the native is not as liable to worry and brood so much over disease or trouble. People who are strongly individualized at B. have more resistance, will-power, and ability to overcome disease and obstacles, and do not give up as easily. (See Character, Fate, Negative, Personality, Positive).

INDOCILE—Child Born With a Wild, Indocile, and Savage Nature — (See "Beastly Form" under Beasts; "Dogs" under Children; "Animal Forms" under Monsters; Savage, Wild).

INDOLENT — (See Carelessness, Dull, Idle, Inactive, Improvident, Inertia, Labour, Lassitude, Lazy, Lethargy, Listless, Lymphatic, Neglectful, Poverty, Uncleanly, etc.).

INDULGENT — Indulgences — Improper Living, and Tending to Disorders of Mind and Body—

Amorous Indulgences — Excess of — (See Amorous).

Blood Disorders — Through Excesses and Indulgences — ♃ affl. in ♒. (See "Poor Blood", "Too Much Blood", under Blood; Excesses, Impure, Plethora).

Drink and Intoxicants—Too Much Indulgence In — (See Alcoholism, Drink, Drunkenness, Intoxication, Wine).

Drugs— Narcotics — Over-Indulgence In—(See Drugs, Narcotics).

His Own Worst Enemy—Thru Indulgence and Extravagance — (See "His Own" under Enemies).

Over-Indulgences — (See Over-Indulgence).

Passional Nature—Sickness from Excessive Indulgence of—(See Amorous, Excesses, Passion, Sex, Venery).

Pleasure — Excessive Indulgence In, and With Injury to the Health—(See the various paragraphs under Pleasure).

Self-Indulgent—(See this subject).

Sports — Exercise — Excessive Indulgence In—(See Exercise, Sports). For collateral study see such subjects as Debauched, Depraved, Diet, Dissipated, Extravagance, Feasting, Free Living, Food, Gluttony, High Living, Imprudent, Indiscretions, Luxuries; "Loose Morals" under Morals; Perversions, Profligate, etc.

INDURATIONS — The Hardening of a Tissue or Part—(See Hardening, Sclerosis).

INEBRIATION — A Drunken Condition —(See "Delirium Tremens" under Delirium; Drink, Drunkenness, Intoxication).

INEFFICIENCY—Incapacity—Want of Sufficient Power or Energy—

Heart—Muscular Inefficiency of—(See "Inefficiency" under Heart).

Lungs — Pulmonary Inefficiency — ♀ affl. in ♌. (See Lungs, Pulmonary). See Defects, Deficient, Incapable, Incompetent, Insufficiency, Lack Of, Loss Of).

INEQUALITY—Of the Pupils—(See Iris, Pupils).

INERTIA — Inert —Apathy— Sluggishness—Inactivity—Absence of Contractility—The ☽ gives; lack of strong ♂ influence at B.; ♂ setting in the West, weak, and ill-dignified, and in no aspect to the ☉ or ☽. (See Apathy, Dull, Idle, Inactive, Lassitude, Lethargy, Listless, Sluggish).

Inactive and Indolent—(See Carelessness, Duty Energy, Exertion, Fatigue, Improvident, Indifferent, Labour, Malaise, Vitality Low, Weak Body; the references in the first part of this section).

Mind — Inactive State of Mind — (See Chaotic, Clogging, Clouded, Dreamy, Dull, Inactive; "Arrested" under Mental; "Weak" under Mind).

System — Inactive and Inert State of the System — (See Apathy, Debility, Dull, Feeble, Inactive, Infirm, Lassi-

tude, Lethargy, Retardations, Sedentary, Sluggish, Suppressions, Weak, Weakened).

INFAMOUS—Base—Vile—Shameless—The ☽ Sig. in ♏, infamous in her desires if a female, and openly scandalous if the ☽ be affl. by the □ or ☍ of ♄ or ♂; the ☽ Sig. in the 10th H. in ♑, and affl. by ♄, ♂, or ♀; the ☽ to the left hand of Ophiucus, given to debauchery and infamy; ♄ Sig. □ or ☍ the ☉, the aspect of infamy, and to be held in contempt; ♄ and ♂ in the 4th H.; ♀ Sig.—□ or ☍ ♂, despised by every one for his infamous life. (See Debased, Debauched, Depraved, Disgrace, Dissolute, Drink, Drunkenness, Execrated, Hatred, Honour, Lewd, Low; "Loose Morals" under Morals; Obscene, Passion, Perversions, Profligate, Reputation, Scandalous, Sex, Shameless, Vile, Wanton, Wench, etc.).

INFANCY — Infants — Infantile — The Early Years of Childhood—Life from the cradle to the grave is divided into Planetary Periods, and each period ruled by a different Planet. (See Periods). The first to fourth years of life are ruled by the ☽, and during this period the evil directions of the ☽, or afflictions to the radical ☽ by transits or directions, make this period especially dangerous to the native, or to cause sickness or early death. Therefore, it is well to make a study of the star map of every infant, and note the influences of and to the ☽ during the first few years of life, and if any evil directions are found, or a train of evil directions, to be forming and culminating during this period, greater care and protection should be given the child during the infantile stage. With every new-born child the prospect of life is an important thing to know, for if early death is indicated, and the directions forming soon after birth are of a fatal nature, and also the vitality weak at B., then all else in the life of the child comes to naught as far as the physical and Earth life is concerned for the time. The death of infants, the causes of early death, their destiny, the future course of the Ego, etc., are explained from an Occult standpoint in the book, "Cosmo-Conception", by Max Heindel. Some Writers and Authorities also say that the first seven years of life in childhood are ruled by the ☽. In the Kabala, Infancy was dedicated to the ☉. The following paragraphs and subjects have to do with the beginnings, birth, the early life, diseases and afflictions of the child, and during the period of Infancy, which subjects see in the alphabetical arrangement when not considered here. Also many of the subjects along this line are listed and considered under the subjects of Birth, Childhood, Children, Conception, Congenital, Early Years (see Early); Foetus, Gestation, Pregnancy, Prenatal Epoch, etc. See these subjects.

Accidents at Birth—In Delivery, and Perhaps by the Use of Instruments—♅ in ♏; ♅ or ♂ in the 5th H. of the mother. (See "Accidents" under Childhood, Children, Parturition; "Early Years" under Hurts).

Adopted — Separated from Parents — (See Adoption).

Afflicted In Infancy—(See Poor Health, Sickly, Weak, and the various paragraphs in this section).

All May Die In Infancy — Or Early Life — But Few Live — Malefics in the 5th or 11th H. of the parents, and afflicted; lord of the 5th in the 6th or 8th H., and afflicted; lord of the 5th in the 8th, and affl. by lord of the 8th; lord of the Asc. in the 6th, and affl. by lord of the 8th, and with no assistance from the benefics. (See "Death of Children", under Children; "Early Death" under Early).

Animal Heat—Lack of In Infancy and Early Years—(See "Animal Heat" under Heat).

Asphyxiated at Birth—(See Asphyxia; "Delayed Births" under Children).

Beastly Form—(See "Beastly Form" under Beasts).

Birth — (See the various paragraphs under Birth; Accidents, Death Soon After Birth, Infections, in this section).

Bladder In Infants—(See Bladder).

Blindness In—Born Blind—Blind from Birth—(See "Born Blind" under Blindness).

Blue Baby—(See Asphyxia).

Born Alive—Lives But a Few Hours —(See "Death Soon After Birth" in this section).

Born Almost Dead—(See "Death Soon After Birth" in this section).

Born Dead — (See Abortion, Miscarriage, Stillborn).

Bowel Complaint—(See "Cholera Infantum" under Cholera; Diarrhoea).

Boys—Male Infants—(See Male, Males, Son, in this section).

Bronchitis In—(See Bronchitis).

Buries His Children — (See "Buries His Children" in Sec. 3 under Children).

But Few Live — Lord of the 10th a malefic in the 5th H. (See "All May Die" in this section).

Childhood — (See the various paragraphs under Childhood, Children, Early Years; also see the subjects in this section).

Children—(See the various paragraphs under Childhood, Children).

Cholera Infantum—(See Cholera).

Club Feet—(See Feet).

Colic; Conception; Congenital Defects —(See Birth, Congenital, Defects, Deformities, Malformations, Monsters, Prenatal Epoch).

Conjunctivitis—Case of In Infancy— (See Conjunctiva; "Ophthalmia" in this section).

Constitution In—(See Good Constitution, Poor, Sickly, Weak, under Constitution; Stamina, Strength, Strong, Weak, and the various paragraphs in this section).

Continuance of Life — After Birth — (See "Continuance" under Life; "Nurture", and the various paragraphs in this section).

Convulsions — (See Convulsions, Fits; "Dentition" under Teeth).

Cough; Cramps — (See Colic, Cramps, Flatulence; "Stomach" under Gas).

Crippled from Birth — (See Crippled, Deformities, Distortions, Lameness, Missing).

Daughter Born — (See Daughter; "Birth of a Female" under Female).

Deaf—Deaf and Dumb—Deaf, Dumb and Blind — Deaf, Dumb and Idiot — (See Blindness, Deaf, Dumb, Hearing, Idiocy, Mutes).

Death At Birth—(See "Birth" in Sec. 3 under Children; "Death Soon After" in this section).

Death by Accident — Danger of — ♂ coming to the ☌ the Asc. or Desc. soon after birth. (See "Death" under Accidents; "Accidents" in this section).

Death In Infancy — Danger of — The Premature Death of Infants—Signs of Death In Infancy—In death in Infancy, it is necessary, in order to understand the causes, to study the Prenatal Epoch Chart, and the Chart of Descent, in connection with the Natal Map. For the Rules which indicate death in Infancy see "Signs of Death" in this section. Also note the following general influences—The hyleg much afflicted by malefics; one of the malefics in ☌ the ☉ or ☽ in an angle; the malefics in angles, and with ☉, ☽, and Asc. afflicted, and with no assistance from the benefics; the ☉, ☽, Asc., and hyleg all afflicted, and with malefic planets in angles, and their evil aspects close, and with no assistance to the hyleg from benefics; those born with the ☉ ☍ ♄ live thru infancy with difficulty, and espec. if both are in angles, and the hyleg severely afflicted; the ☽ between ♂ and the ☉, or the ☽ ☌ ♂ and the ☉, will almost exchange the cradle for the grave; ♅, ♄, or ♂ near the rising degree, and affl. by the ruler of the 8th H., and the ☽ at the same time affl. by the ☉; ♄ in power and elevation at B., and affl. the hyleg, and such almost invariably die in infancy, and thus the Fable that "Saturn Devours His Own Children." In the map of the parent, if the 5th H. promises children and the 11th H. deny them, or if the 11th H. promises them and the 5th H. deny, the children are more apt to die in infancy; ♄ afflicted in the 5th H. of a parent; ♄ or ♂ in ☍ ♃ in the map of a parent destroys some; ☿ in the 5th H. in a barren sign, and afflicted. (See "Death" under Childhood; Destroys, Early Death, First-Born Child, Short Life, under Children; "Early Death" under Early; Eclipses; "Full Moon" and "New Moon", under Moon; "Death Soon After Birth", "Signs of Death", and the various paragraphs in this section). Cases—Birth Data and Cases of the Death of Infants and Children at Various Ages— (1) Death at Birth — (See "Death at Birth" in this section). (2) Death Soon After Birth—(See this subject in this section). (3) Lives 12 Hours — (See "Short Life", No. 775, in 1001 N.N. (4) Lives Three Weeks — (See "Short Life", No. 786, in 1001 N.N.). (5) Lives Two Months—(See "Born In a Flood", No. 227, in 1001 N.N.). (6) Lives Three Months—(See "Convulsions", No. 155;

"Morrison", No. 188; "Short Life", No. 776, all in 1001 N.N.). (7) Lives Four Months—(See "Short Life", No. 371, in 1001 N.N.). (8) Lives Six Months—(See "Heart", No. 981, in 1001 N.N. (9) Lives Nine Months— (See "Short Life", No. 778, in 1001 N.N.). (10) Lives Fourteen Months—(See "Short Life", No. 777, in 1001 N.N.). (11) Lives Twenty Months —(See "Short Life", No. 779, in 1001 N.N.). (12) Lives Seven Years — Or Dies During the First Seven Years— (See "Signs of Death" in this section). Also see Case, "Strangled at Birth", No. 922 and No. 923, in 1001 N.N. See Daath's Medical Astrology, Chap. 14.

Death Soon After Birth—Born Almost Dead—Lives Only a Few Hours—The ☉ or ☽ hyleg, and ♄ afflicting both the ☉ and ☽, lives but a short time, and the closer the aspects the shorter the life; the ☉ and ☽ both affl. by malefics, and one of them the hyleg; the Asc. hyleg, and with ♄ on the Asc., M.C., Desc., or Nadir, and with no assistance from the benefics to the hyleg, seldom lives long; ruler of the Asc. in the 6th or 8th H., and malefics in the Asc., and with ♋, ♑, or ♓ on the Asc.; ♋, ♑, or ♓ on the Asc., and the hyleg affl. by malefics. (See "Born Almost Dead" under Children; "Early Death" under Early; "Continuance of Life", "Short Life", under Life; "Incapable of Nurture" under Nutrition; "Low" under Vitality; "Weak Body" under Weak; "Death In Infancy", "Signs of Death", in this section).

Defective Births — (See "Defective Births" under Birth; Congenital, Defects, Deformities, Hearing, Idiocy, Inhuman; "Birth" under Lameness, Paralysis; Malformations, Missing, Monsters, Prenatal Epoch, Savage, Virile).

Deformed from Birth — ☿ in the 5th H. in ♋, ♏, or ♓ in the map of a parent, or of the child, and espec. if ♄ or ♂ afflict ☿, may be deaf, deformed, or insane. (See Blindness, Congenital, Crippled, Deformities, Distortions, Feet, Hearing, Idiocy, Insanity, Limbs, Malformations, Monsters, Parturition, Prenatal Epoch; "Defective" in this section).

Delivery—Birth—Injuries at Birth—Unusual Delivery—(See "Excision" under Foetus; "Injury", "Mangled", and the various paragraphs under Parturition).

Dentition—Fits During—(See "Dentition" under Teeth).

Destroys the Children — (See "Destroys" under Children; "Death In Infancy", "Death At Birth", "Death Soon After Birth", in this section).

Diarrhoea — (See "Bowel Complaint" in this section).

Die Before Maturity — (See "Death" under Childhood; Early Death (see Early); "Short Life" under Life; Maturity; "Death In Youth" under Youth).

Dies Soon After Birth — (See "Death Soon After" in this section).

Dies Young — (See "Death" under Childhood; "Early Death" under Children; "Short Life" under Life; "Death Before Maturity" under Maturity).

Directions Kill — The First Train of Evil Directions Kill—The ☉, ☽, or ♄ affl. in the 6th H. at B., and the hyleg severely afflicted. (See Directions; "Low" under Vitality; "Weak Body" under Weak).

Diseases and Infections—(See "Infections" in this section).

Diseases of Infancy—(See "Disease", and the various paragraphs under Children. Look for the name of the disease in the alphabetical arrangement, such as Cholera Infantum, Colic, Convulsions, Diarrhoea, Eruptions, Measles, Mumps, Scarlet Fever, etc. Also note the various paragraphs in this section).

Distortions—(See "Moment of Birth" under Calamity; Contortions, Deformities, Distortions, Excrescences).

Duration of Life — (See Duration; "Early Death" under Early; "Continuance", "Long", "Short", under Life; the various paragraphs in this section).

Early Death Of—(See "Death In Infancy", "Death Soon After Birth", and the various paragraphs in this section; "Death" under Childhood, Children; "Early Death" under Early; "Short Life" under Life).

Early Years—Accidents, Hurts, Sickness In — (See "Early Years" under Early).

Eclipses — Death of Infants Born at Time of—(See Eclipses; "Full Moon", "New Moon", under Moon).

Eleventh House — One of the Houses of Children—(See Eleventh).

Embryo — (See Conception, Embryo, Foetus, Gestation).

Eyes—Affections of the Eyes In Infants—(See "Born Blind" under Blindness; Conjunctivitis, Infections, Ophthalmia, in this section).

Fall In Infancy—See Case, "Religious Melancholia", No. 976, in 1001 N.N.

Female Infant—Birth of a Female—Death of At Birth—(See "First-Born Child" under Children; Daughter, Eclipses; "Birth Of", "Death Of", under Females).

Females Predominate — (See "Sex of Children" under Children; "Birth of a Female" under Females).

Fevers In Infancy—♂ coming to the ☉ or ill-asp. the Asc. tends to fevers, hurts, inflammations, wounds, or injuries, if the nativity denotes such, (See "Fevers" under Childhood, Children).

Few Children — (See "Few" under Children).

Few Live—(See "All May Die" in this section).

Fifth House—The House of Children —(See Fifth House).

Fits—(See Convulsions, Fits; "Dentition" under Teeth).

Foetus — (See Abortion, Conception, Embryo, Foetus, Gestation, Miscarriage, Pregnancy).

Fontanelles — Slow Closure of — (See this subject under Head).

Foolish — The Child Born Foolish — (See Foolish, Idiocy, Imbecile, Inhuman, Savage).

Gestation; Girls— A Girl Born — Daughters—(See "Female", "Females", in this section).

Good Constitution—Good Health of— Stamina and Vitality Good — Weak Constitution — (See "Constitution" in this section).

Health Poor—(See Poor, Sickly, Weak, in this section).

Healthy Infants—Healthy and Long-Lived Children — (See "Long-Lived" under Children; "Good" under Constitution, Health; Immunity, Vitality).

Heat—Lacking In Animal Heat—(See "Animal Heat" under Heat).

Hemiplegia — Infantile — The ☉ or ♄ affl. in ♈; the ☉ coming to the ♂ ♅ soon after birth; Subs at AT, AX, and CP. (See Hemiplegia; "Hemiplegia" under Paralysis).

Hermaphrodites; Hurts — (See "Accidents" in this section; "Accidents", "Hurts", under Children; "Early Years" under Early, Hurts).

Husband An Anchorite—Does Not Desire Children—(See "Anchorite" under Husband).

Hydrocephalus; Idiocy;

Ill-Formed Body—(See "Beastly Form" under Beasts; "Dogs" under Children; Crooked, Deformed; "Ill-Formed" under Ill; Inhuman, Monsters, etc.).

Ill-Health—(See Poor, Sickly, Weak, in this section; "Sickly", "Unhealthy", under Children).

Imbecility; Infant May Not Survive—(See Death In Infancy, Death Soon After Birth, Early Death, Eclipses, and the various paragraphs in this section).

Infantile Paralysis—(See Hemiplegia, Paralysis, in this section; Distortions, Excrescences).

Infections at Birth—Unusual Diseases at Childbirth—♅ afflicted in the 5th H. of the mother. (See the various paragraphs under Parturition).

Inflammations—Inflamed Eyes — (See Conjunctivitis, Eyes, Fevers, Ophthalmia, in this section; "Fevers" under Childhood; Inflammation).

Injury At Birth—(See "Accidents" in this section; "Injury At Birth" under Parturition).

Instrumental Delivery—(See "Injury" in this section).

Lame from Birth — (See Congenital, Crippled, Deformities, Distortions, Excrescences, Feet, Lameness, Legs, Paralysis).

Liable to Disease — (See Ill-Health, Poor, Sickly, Weak, in this section; "Ill-Health All Thru Life" under Ill-Health; "Low" under Recuperation, Resistance, Vitality; "Weak Body" under Weak).

Life Spared—(See "Spared" under Life; "Signs of Death", "Will Live", in this section).

Lives But a Short Time—(See Death In Infancy, Death Soon After Birth, Nurture, in this section).

Lives Thru Sickness—(See "Stamina" in this section; "Lives Thru" under Serious).

Long Life—(See "Long-Lived" under Children; "Long Life" under Life).

Maimed At Birth—Males Born Maimed —(See Maimed).

Male Infant—A Male Born—Death of a Male—(See "Male Children Born" under Children; Eclipses; "Births" under Males).

Males Predominate—(See "Male Children Born", "Sex", under Children; Predetermination, Triplets, Twins).

Maturity—Will Live To—Will Not Live To—(See Maturity; the various paragraphs in this section).

Measles; Middle Life—Will Live To— (See Middle Life).

Miscarriage; Monsters;

Mortality Among—(See "Mortality Great" under Children).

Mother—The Infant Affected by the Conditions of the Mother—(See Mother, Parents, Parturition).

Mouth—Cankerous Sores In—(See Aphthae; "Thrush" under Mouth).

Much Sickness—In Infancy—The ☉ or ☽ affl. in ♋; the ☽ affl. in the 6th H.; the hyleg much afflicted by malefics; ☿ on the Asc. (See Poor, Sickly, Weak, in this section; "Sickly", "Unhealthy", under Children; "Early Years" under Early; "Ill-Health All Thru Life" under Ill-Health; "Much Sickness" under Sickness).

No Duration of Life—(See Death At Birth, Death In Infancy, Death Soon After Birth, Dies Young, in this section; "Death" under Chidhood, Children; Duration; "Early Death" under Early; "No Duration", "Short Life", under Life; "Incapable of Nurture" under Nutrition).

Not Strong or Robust—(See Ill-Health, Much Sickness, Sickly, Weak, in this section; "Low" under Resistance, Vitality; Robust, Strength; "Not Strong" under Strong; "Weak Body" under Weak).

Nursing Of—(See Milk).

Nurture—Incapable of Nurture—Dies Immediately After Birth—(See "Incapable of Nurture" under Nutrition; Death At Birth, Death Soon After Birth, in this section).

Ophthalmia—Inflamed Eyes—Conjunctivities—Case of Inflamed Eyes two days after birth and Defective Sight— See "Sight Defective", No. 684 in 1001 N.N. (See Conjunctiva; "Inflamed" under Eyes).

Paralysis—Infantile Paralysis—Paralyzed from Birth—(See Distortions; Excrescences; "Birth", "Infantile", under Paralysis).

Parental Love—And Affection—(See "Love and Affection" under Parents).

Paroxysms—Fits During Dentition— (See "Dentition" under Teeth).

Parturition—Childbirth—Accident, Hurt, Disease, Infection, or Death to Child During—(See the various paragraphs under Parturition; Accidents, Delivery, Infection, Injury, in this section).

Poor Constitution—(See "Weak" under Constitution; Vitality Low; "Weak

Body" under Weak; Poor Health, Sickly, Weak, and the various paragraphs in this section).

Poor Health—Weak signs on the Asc. at B., as ♋, ♑, or ♓, and the hyleg afflicted by malefics; the ☉ or ☽ angular, and affl. by a malefic; the ☽ affl. in the 6th H.; ♄ affl. in the Asc., bad health during infancy and childhood. (See Ill-Health, Poor Constitution, Much Sickness, Sickly, Weak, in this section; Childhood, Children; "Early Years" under Early).

Premature Birth—Premature Death— (See Abortion; "Death under Childhood; "Death", "Eight Months Children", under Children; "Early Death" under Early; Foetus; "Short Life" under Life; Miscarriage, Premature, Prenatal Epoch, Untimely; "Death" in this section).

Prenatal Epoch—(See Prenatal).

Resistance to Disease—Good and Bad —(See Immunity, Recuperation, Resistance, Stamina, Tone, Vitality; "Weak Body" under Weak).

Rickets; Robust—The Infant Robust —Not Robust—(See Robust; "Not Strong", and the various paragraphs in this section, and under Children).

Savage—Of a Savage and Wild Disposition—(See "Beastly Form" under Beasts; Inhuman, Savage, Wild).

Scarlet Fever—Scarlatina—(See Scarlet).

Separated from Parents—(See Adoption).

Seven Years of Life—Or Dies During First Seven Years—(See "Signs of Death" in this section).

Sex of Children—Predetermination of —(See "Sex of Children" under Children; Predetermination).

Short Life—(See "Death" under Childhood, Children, Youth; "Early Death" under Early; "Short Life" under Life; "Death In Infancy" in this section. See Chap. XIV in Daath's Medical Astrology).

Shorter Will Be the Life—The greater the affliction of the Significators of Life, as the ☉, ☽, Asc., or lord of the Asc., the shorter will be the life.

Sickly—(See "Sickly" under Children; Poor Health, Much Sickness, in this section).

Sickly But Recovers—If the ☽ separate from a malefic and apply to a benefic at B., the child may be sickly for a time after birth, if the map otherwise indicated weakness, but will recover. (See Recovery, Recuperation, Resistance).

Sight—Defective Sight—(See "Born Blind" under Blindness; Conjunctivitis, Eyes, Sight; "Ophthalmia" in this section).

Signs of Death—In Infancy—Rules for Judging—Will the Child Live or Die?—Indications in the map of a parent are—Lord of the 5th H. ℞, combust, in fall or detriment, and affl. by lord of the 8th or 12th H., signs of an early death; lord of the 5th weak, affl. by a malefic in the 8th or 12th H., unless opposite testimonies concur, the child will speedily die; lord of the Asc. in the 5th H., and afflicted, or ♅, ♄, or ♂ be in the 5th H., and ℞, or ☋ in the 5th H., are signs of death. Also notes the following RULES and Influences—Signs of Death—

(1) the ☉ just below the Asc. or Desc., malefics in the ♓ Navamsas of signs, and with the negative Hora of a sign rising. (See Navamsa, Horas).

(2) The ☽ ♂ a malefic, with no assistance from a benefic, and with malefics in the Asc. or Desc.

(3) Three malefics in three angles, and the ☽ in the 4th angle, and the ☽ and malefics all in evil aspect to each other.

(4) The ☽ afflicted, and also the ruler of the 8th H. afflicting a malefic in the Asc., or just above the Asc.

(5) The ruler of the 4th or 8th H. afflicting the ruler of the Asc. in the 6th H., and with no good asp. from the benefics.

(6) The ☉ or ☽ in an angle in ♂ a malefic, or if the malefic be an equal distance from the ☉ and ☽, and without the assistance of good asps., and the rulers of the Lights also in malefic places, the child will die immediately or soon after birth.

(7) The ☉ or ☽ angular in ♂ or ill-asp. a malefic, and without the assistance of good asps.

(8) The ☽ in the 12th H., decr. in light, with no benefics in angles, with malefics rising, and also malefics in the 8th H.

(9) The ☉, ☽, and Asc. afflicted, malefics in angles, and the hyleg without assistance from the benefics.

(10) The ☉ and ☽ in 8 asp., and in ☐ asp. to malefics which are also in 8 to each other.

(11) Malefics in the 1st, 7th, 8th or 12th H. in ♂ or ill-asp. the ☽, with no good asps. to the ☽, and no benefics angular.

However these rules will not hold good, and the infant will be spared if—

(A) If the benefics ♃ and ♀ are in the Asc., in strong signs, well-aspected, and not afflicted by malefics.

(B) Lord of the Asc. strong, not afflicted, and well-aspected.

(C) The benefics in good asp. to, and ruling the hyleg.

(D) The hyleg assisted by the good asps. of ♃ or ♀.

(E) The ☽ in the decanates of ♃ or ♀ in the 6th or 8th H.

(F) The positive horas of signs rising, and espec. those of positive signs. If these last six rules, or conditions, prevail, the child will live beyond the 7th year, but may not live a long life. If the first eleven rules prevail, and with no offsetting good influences, the child generally dies during the first seven years of life. An old Kabalistic rule is that the 7th hour after birth indicates and decides whether or not the child will live, and a star map erected for a time exactly seven hours after the moment of birth, and studied as to the aspects and positions of the planets, and judged accordingly, will give valuable information as to the prospect of life. These rules apply to the map of birth only, and the Prenatal Epoch map should also be studied along with the map of birth. (See Death At Birth, Death In Infancy, Death Soon After Birth, in this section; "Death" under Childhood, Children; "Symbols of Death" under Death; "Early Death" under Early; "Short Life" under Life).

Snuffles—(See Nose).

Some Will Die In Infancy—If the 5th H. promises children, and the 11th H. deny them, and vice versa, some will die in infancy. (See "Death In Infancy" in this section).

Sons — The Birth or Death of — (See Male, Males, in this section).

Spared—The Life of Is Spared—(See the six rules, A, B, C, etc., under "Signs of Death" in this section; "Spared" under Life).

Stamina Good—In Infancy—The fiery signs on the Asc. at B., and next to them are the airy signs, and ♍ and ♏, and children born under these signs live thru illnesses that would ordinarily prove fatal to those born under weaker signs. (See Stamina, Tone, Vitality; "Healthy", "Long Life", in this section).

Stillborn; Strangled At Birth—Cases —(See Asphyxia, Strangulation).

Strength Increased — The benefics or the ☽ in the 5th or 11th H., and with fiery signs on the Asc. in the map of parent; ♂ in the Asc., and well-aspected, and in a strong sign in the map of the child, has much power to bring them thru infancy even tho the map is otherwise weak. (See "Strength" under Children; Strength).

Strong In Infancy—(See Constitution, Stamina, Strength, Vitality, in this section; Strength, Strong).

Suffers Much — (See Much Sickness, Poor Health, in this section).

Suffocated At Birth—(See Asphyxia, Suffocation).

Summer Complaint — (See "Cholera Infantum" under Cholera).

Survival—May Not Live—Will Live—(See Death, Spared, Will Live, and the various paragraphs in this section).

Teething—(See "Dentition" under Teeth).

Thrives and Lives — (See Long Life, Stamina, and the various paragraphs in this section).

Thrush — (See "Mouth" in this section).

Triplets; Twins; Ulcers—Of the Mouth —(See "Mouth" in this section).

Unhealthy—(See Ill-Health, Much Sickness, Poor Health, Sickly, Vitality, Weak, and the various paragraphs in this section).

Untimely Death—(See Death At Birth, Death In Infancy, Death Soon After Birth, and the various paragraphs in this section).

Unusual Diseases — At Birth — (See "Infections" in this section).

Vitality — (a) Good Vitality — (See Constitution, Healthy, Long Life, Stam-

ina, Strength, in this section; "Good" under Vitality). (b) Vitality Less — Low In Infancy—Born with ♋, ♑, or ♓ on the Asc.; the ☉ affl. in ♑; many evil directions to the ☉, ☽, Asc., or hyleg at B., and during infancy. (See Death, Ill-Health, Much Sickness, Poor Health, Sickly, Weak, in this section; "Sickly Children" under Children; "Low" under Vitality; "Weak Body" under Weak).

Weak—Weak Body—Weak Constitution — Weak and Sickly — (See Death In Infancy, Ill-Health, Much Sickness, Poor Health, Sickly, Vitality, in this section; "Weak Body" under Weak).

Weaning; Wild Disposition — (See "Savage" in this section).

Will Live—And Be Healthy—Thrives and Lives Thru Disease — (See Long Life, Spared, Stamina, Strong, Vitality, in this section; "Long-Lived" under Children; Endurance; "Little Sickness" under Health; Immunity; "Lives Thru" under Serious).

Will the Child Live or Die? — (See Death In Infancy, Healthy, Long Life, Short Life, Sickly, Spared, Stamina, Strength, Strong, Weak, Vitality, and the various paragraphs in this section).

Worms In Children—(See Worms).

INFARCTS — A Plug or Obstruction — Clot—Embolus— (See Clots, Embolus, Obstructions, Thrombus).

INFECTIONS—Infectious Diseases—Contagions—Invasions, etc.—Amulets were worn by the Ancients as a protective measure against Infections, and Infectious and Contagious diseases. The moderate use of Tobacco, if it does not debilitate the system, is also said to be a protection against Infections. The pathological action of the ♃ Group of Herbs tends to Infection and Toxaemia. (See Amulets, Contagions; "Jupiter Group" under Herbs; Tobacco, Toxaemia).

Birth—Infections At—(See Infancy).

Death from Infections—And Infectious Fevers—(See "Death" under Contagious).

Diarrhoea—Infectious Diarrhoea—(See "Cholera Infantum" under Cholera).

Eyes—(See "Infections" under Infants).

Infectious Diseases—Infectious and Contagious Fevers — Liable To — Predisposed To — The ☽ people contract these diseases easily. Also the ♏ people, those born under ♏, as ♏ is a magnetic sign and attracts infectious complaints. The ☉ affl. in ♏ or ♓; the ☉ affl. in ♓ gives much receptivity to infectious complaints; the ☉ Sig. to the ☌ ♂; the ☽ hyleg in ♏ or ♓, and espec. with females; ♂ diseases and afflictions, and the ♂ influence tends to death from such, and very violent and severe attacks; ♂ affl. in ♋, ♍, ♎, ♏, or ♓, infectious and contagious diseases and fevers should be guarded against; ♂ in ♓ and affl. the ☽ or Asc.; ♂ affl. in ♓ in the 6th H.; ♂ Sig. ☌ the ☉; ♀ affl. in ♏; a ♏ disease; ♏ or ♓ on the Asc. and afflicted. (See Chickenpox, Cholera, Endemic, Epidemics,

Eruptions, External, Germs; "Offensive" under Humours; Leprosy, Magnetic, Measles, Mumps, Pandemic, Perihelion, Pestilence, Plague; "Blood Poisoning" under Poison; Pus, Scarlatina, Scorpio, Smallpox, Septic, Syphilis, Toxaemia, Venereal, etc.).

INFERIOR—Inferiority—

Belly—Inferior Part of—(See Abdomen, Belly, Bowels, Groins, Hernia).

Inferiority Complex—A Strong Feeling of Inferiority—The Apologetic Attitude—♄ prominent at B., and strong afflictions of ♄ to the ☉, ☽, ☿, or Asc.; preponderance of the ☽ and ♀ influences over the more forceful planets; ♋ sign influence, as this sign tends to timidity, over-sensitiveness, and dreads disturbing and discordant conditions; ♎ influence, from a desire for agreement and concord. (See Fears, Mind, Negative, Obsessions, Self-Confidence).

Inferior Hypogastric Plexus — (See "Impar" under Ganglion).

Inferior Mentality — (See Arrested, Dwarfed, Foolish, Idiocy, Imbecility, Insanity; "Inferior" under Mentality; "Weak Mind" under Mind).

Inferior Parts of Body—(See Lower).

Inferior Physique—(See Body, Crippled, Crooked, Defects, Deformed, Dwarfed, Form; "Ill-Formed" under Ill; Infirm, Invalids, Monsters, Stature; "Weak Body" under Weak).

Inferior Planets—♀, ☽, ☿.

Inferior Vena Cava—(See "Vena Cava" under Veins).

INFILTRATIONS — (See Effusions, Osmosis, Serum).

INFIRM—Infirmities—Infirmity—

Bodily Infirmities — Infirm Body — ♅, ♄, and ♂ occi. at B. tend to disease and bodily infirmities; ♅, ♄, or ♂ on the cusp of the 1st, 6th, or 7th H. at B., or in exact evil asp. to these degrees, and espec. if the ☉ is ☌ the ☽, or ☍ the ☽ in the 1st or 7th H. If only one Luminary be with ♅, ♄, or ♂ in the 1st or 7th H. the infirmities will be produced in those parts of the body ruled by the signs on the cusps of the 1st and 7th; ♄ in ♋ and in bad asp. to the Asc.; the 3rd Decan. ♍ on the Asc. (See Adynamia, Asthenia, Death, Debility, Decay, Decrepitude, Delicate, Disease, Emaciation, Fading, Feeble; "Health Bad" under Health; "Ill-Health All Thru Life" under Ill-Health; Invalids; "Low" under Resistance; Sickly; "Much Sickness" under Sickness; "Low" under Vitality; "Weak Body" under Weak, etc.).

Grievous Infirmities — Grievous Infirmities Generally — Much Sickness Generally — (See Grievous; "Public Health Bad" under Public).

Mental Infirmities—Liable To—The ☉ or ☿ in common signs, and affl. by the ☌ or ill-asps. the malefics; the ☉ or ☽ to the ☌ or ill-asp. ♄ by dir.; mental infirmities are produced by afflictions to the ☽ and ☿, or both, in certain signs of the Zodiac, as in ♍ or ♓; ♆ affl. in the 9th H.; born under the strong and adverse influence of ♄; ☿ diseases and afflictions; ☿ in no asp.

to the ☽ or Asc. at B.; ♒ on the cusp the 6th H., and afflicted. (See Idiocy, Imbecility, Insanity, Intellect, Memory; "Deficiency", "Diseases", and the various paragraphs under Mental; "Weak Mind", and the various paragraphs under Mind; Perception, Understanding).

Much Infirmity—Often Ailing—The ☽ sepr. from ♄ and applying to ♂ at B. (See Ailing, Chronic; "Ill-Health All Thru Life" under Ill-Heath; "Much Sickness" under Sickness; "Low" under Vitality; "Weak Body" under Weak). Infirmities may occur in any organ or part of the body, and in the mind, and for the subject, or disease, you have in mind, look for it in the alphabetical arrangement, as nearly every subject in this book has to do with some Infirmity of Body or Mind. Also see such subjects as Brothers, Congenital, Defects, Deformities, Dissolution, Enemies, Extremities, Father, Females, Friends, Heredity, Limbs, Males, Men, Mother, Nobles, Old Age, Parents, Reins, Relatives, Secrets, Serious, Severe, Sister, Women, etc.

INFLAMMATION — Inflammatory — Inflammations — The termination "Itis" to words indicates Inflammation. The Inflammatory Process without alteration of tissues is presided over by ♃. The Inflammatory Process with degeneration of tissues is presided over by ♄. Inflammation and Fever are the work of ♂ to cleanse and burn out the accumulated wastes and filth of the body, and in this way ♂ is untimately constructive in his work, altho destructive for a time in the process. (See Cleansing, Combustion, Constructive, Destructive, Energy, Fever). Inflammation is brought on by ♂, and mostly because of rash and uncontrolled thinking. Also ♂ is rubefacient, reddening, and inflammatory, and tends to bring the blood to the surface. (See Centrifugal, Congestion, Rubefacient). Acute diseases under ♂ are inflammatory. (See Acute). The ☉ is also inflammatory, and tends to inflammation, and especially when afflicting ♂ in the 1st H. Inflammation is produced by the ☉ and ♂, the positive, electric, and heat-producing planets. (See Mars, Sun). People born under the Bilious and Choleric Temperaments are more subject and susceptible to inflammations and fevers. (See Bilious, Choleric). In any sign ♂ tends to inflammation in the part of the body ruled by the sign he is in at B., or is now passing thru by transit, progression, or direction. The same influences which tend to inflammations also tend to fevers. (See Fever). Inflammation may attack any organ or part of the body, and for inflammation in the part, or organ, you have in mind, see the subject in the alphabetical arrangement. The following subjects are related to inflammation, and when not more fully considered here, see the subject in the alphabetical arrangement. (See "Causes" in this section).

Abscesses; Accidents—(See Accidents, Blows, Cuts, Falls, Fractures, Hurts, Injuries, Stabs, Wounds, etc., as Inflammation may attend any of these conditions).

Acute Diseases—(See Acute).

All Kinds—Of Inflammation—A ☉ disease and affliction. Also ♂ diseases; ♌ diseases. (See the various paragraphs in this section).

All Over the Body — The ☽ in ♎ and affl. by the ☉ or ♂ when taken ill (Hor'y). (See "Whole Body" under Whole).

Aneurysm; Antiphlogistic—An Agent Reducing Inflammation — (See Antiphlogistic).

Appendicitis—(See Appendix).

Arteritis—(See "Inflammation" under Arteries).

Arthritis—(See Joints, Synovial).

Bites; Blepharitis—(See Eyelids).

Blood Inflamed — (See "Inflamed" under Blood).

Bronchitis—(See Bronchial).

Bruises; Business Partner — Suffers Inflammatory Disease—(See Partner).

Carditis—(See Heart).

Catarrhal—(See Catarrh).

Causes of Inflammation—Liable To— Susceptibility To — Inflammatory Distempers—Danger of—Subject to Inflammatory Complaints—In addition to what is said in the first part of this Article, the following influences are listed,—The ☉ or ☽ affl. by ♂ at B., and by dir.; the ☉ or ☽ to the ♂ or ill-asp. ♂ by dir., and affl. by ♂ at B.; the ☉ ♂ ♂ at B., and espec. in the 6th H.; the ☉ or ♂ affl. in the Asc.; the Prog. ☉ or ☽ to the ♂ or ill-asp. ♂; the ☉ or ☽ to the ♂ or ill-asp. ♂ by dir., and ♂ ruler of the 6th H. at B.; the afflictions of the ☉ tend to fever and inflammation; the ☽ in the 6th H. in a cardinal sign, and affl. by ♂; the ☽ to the Bull's Horns; ♅ to the ♂ or ill-asp. the ☉; ♃ affl. in ♎, from too much blood; ♂ □ or ☍ the ☉; ♂ in ♌, □, or ☍ the ☉; ♂ diseases; ♂ in a watery sign, and to the ill-asps. the Asc. by dir.; ♂ in the 6th H., and affl. the ☉ or ☽; ♂ in common signs and affl. the ☉, ☽, or Asc.; ♂ affl. in the 1st, 4th, or 6th H.; ♂ affl. in ♈ or ♌; ♂ to the ♂ or ill-asp. the ☉, ☽, or Asc., and espec. if affl. by ♂ at B.; ♂ affl. in fiery signs, and to the ♂ or ill-asp. the Asc. by dir.; ♂ to the ♂ or ill-asps. ♅ by dir.; ♂ ♂ the ☉ at B., and espec. in the 6th H.; the transits of ♂ over the places of the radical ☉ or ☽, or in ☍ to them; the evil directions of ♂ if ♂ is strongly afflicted at B.; ♂ too much in evidence at B.; ♂ in the 6th H., in bowels, and in parts ruled by the sign ♂ is in; the Asc. to the place of Cor Leonis (Regulus); Asc. to the □ or ☍ ♂ by dir.; fiery signs on the Asc.; ♈ is especially inflammatory when on the Asc.; a ♌ disease, and afflictions in ♌. (See the Introduction and the various paragraphs in this section).

Caustics; Cells and Tissues—(See "Inflammation" under Cells).

Chronic Inflammation — A ☉ disease. The inflammatory action of the ☉ is of the chronic type. (See Chronic).

Cleansing; Colitis—(See Colon).

Color—(See "Treatment" under Red).

Congestive Inflammation—♄ ♂ or ill-asp. ♃, and espec. if ♃ be more dominant. (See Congestion).

Conjunctivitis—(See Conjunctiva).

Constructive; Cuts; Cystitis — (See Bladder).

Danger of Inflammation—(See "Causes" in this section).

Death By — Caused by the afflictions of ♃. (See "Death" under Jupiter).

Destructive; Diathesis — (See Diathesis; "Causes" in this section).

Diseases—Inflammatory Diseases— (See "Causes," and the various paragraphs in this section).

Distempers—Inflammatory Distempers — (See "Causes" in this section; Distempers).

Elimination; Encephalitis — (See "Inflammation" under Brain).

Endocarditis—(See Heart).

Energy—(See Constructive, Destructive).

Enteritis—(See "Inflammation" under Bowels).

Entire Body—Inflammation In—(See "All Over" in this section).

Eruptions; Excretory System—(See "Disorders" under Excretion).

Eyes Inflamed—(See Conjunctiva; "Inflamed" under Eyes).

Face—(See Eruptions; "Red" under Face; Irritated).

Fallopian Tubes — Salpingitis — (See "Disorders" under Fallopian).

Falls; Father — (See "Inflammatory Attacks" under Father).

Females—Inflammatory Troubles In —The ☉ to the ♂ the ☽ by dir.; the ☽ to the ♂ the ☉ by dir. (See Females).

Fevers—Inflammatory Fevers—The ☽ directed to the Ascelli; ♂ □ or ☍ the Asc. by dir.; a ♌ disease and afflictions in ♌, and they grow worse towards sunrise. (See Fever).

Fever and Inflammation—The Two Combined — (See "Scope" under Enlarged).

Fingers—Toes—(See "Whitlows" under Toes).

Folliculitis—(See "Hair Follicles" under Follicles).

Gastritis—(See Gastric).

Genitals—(See "Inflammatory" under Genitals).

Glands—(See "Swelling" under Glands).

Gums—(See "Inflamed" under Gums).

Heat; Hemorrhoids; Hepatitis—(See "Inflammation" under Liver).

Hexis; Hot Diseases — (See Fever, Heat).

Hurts; Increased—The Inflammation Is Increased—The ☉ ♂ or ill-asp. ♂, the susceptibility to inflammation is increased.

Infections; Injuries; Intestines—(See "Inflammation" under Bowels).

Iritis—(See Iris).

Kicks; Kinds of Inflammation—(See the various paragraphs in this section).

Laryngitis—(See Larynx).

Left Side—Inflammations and Disorders In—(See Left).

Liable To—(See Causes, Increased, in this section).

Lower Parts—(See Lower).

Lymphangitis—(See Lymphatics).

Mastitis—(See Breasts).

Mastoiditis—(See Mastoid).

Membranes; Meningitis—(See Meninges).

Middle Parts—(See Middle).

Mother—(See "Inflammations" under Mother).

Mucous Membranes—(See "Inflammation" under Mucous).

Mumps—(See Parotid).

Naso-Pharynx—Inflammation In—(See Nose, Pharynx).

Nephritis—(See Kidneys).

Neuritis—(See Nerves).

Ophthalmia — Conjunctivitis — (See Conjunctiva).

Osteitis—(See Bones).

Ovaritis—(See Ovaries).

Pain; Parents—(See "Inflammation" under Father, Mother).

Parotiditis—Mumps—(See Parotid).

Pericarditis—(See Heart).

Peritonitis—(See Peritoneum).

Pharyngitis—(See Pharynx).

Phlegmonous—(See Phlegmon).

Piles—(See Hemorrhoids).

Pleuritis—(See Pleura).

Pneumonia; Poisons—(See "Body" under Poison).

Predisposition To—(See Causes, Increased, in this section).

Privates; Process—The Inflammatory Process—(See the first part of this Article).

Prostatitis—(See Prostate).

Pustular Inflammation—(See Phlegmon, Pus).

Red Color—(See "Treatment" under Red).

Reins—(See "Inflammation" under Reins).

Remedies For—(See Anodyne, Antiphlogistic; Emollient; "Treatment" under Red; Resolvent).

Right Side—Inflammations and Disorders In—(See Right).

Rubefacients; Salpingitis—(See Fallopian).

Secrets—Inflammations In—(See Generative, Genitals, Privates, Secrets, Sex Organs, Venereal, Womb).

Skin; Sores; Sthenic Inflammation—Strong and Active Inflammation—♂ ☌ or ill-asp. ♃. (See Sthenic, Strong).

Stomatitis—(See Aphthae).

Suppurative Inflammation — (See Phlegmon, Pus).

Susceptibility To—(See Causes, Increased, in this section).

Swellings; Tendency To—(See "Causes" in this section).

Tissues—(See "Cells" in this section).

Toxaemia; Treatment Of—(See "Remedies" in this section).

Ulcers; Upper Parts—(See Upper).

Vascular—(See Vascular, Vessels).

Veins—(See "Phlebitis" under Veins).

Venereal; Vesicants; Vessels — See Vascular; "Inflammation" under Vessels).

Violent Inflammation—The Asc. □ or ♌ ♂ by dir., if ♂ is in airy or earthy signs, threatens violent inflammation. (See Violent).

Whole Body—(See "All Over the Body" in this section).

Wounds — (See Hurts, Injuries, Wounds).

For subjects along this line, and which may not be included in this Article, look in the alphabetical arrangement for the subject you have in mind.

INFLATION—The Body Inflated—The ☽ in ♉, ♋, or ill-asp. ♄ (or ☿ if he be of the nature of ♄) when taken ill, or at decumb., and caused by surfeits, high living, etc. (Hor'y). (See Distentions, Flatulence, Gas, Puffing, Tympanites, etc.).

INFLEXIBLE—Rigidity—Stiffness—(See Cold, Rigid, Rigors, Stiff). Many planets at B. in fixed signs, or fixed signs upon the angles, tend to give an inflexible, unbending, uncompromising temperament. (See "Fixed Signs" under Fixed; Obstinate).

INFLUENCED EASILY—Impressionable—More Difficult to Cure—More Susceptible to Disease—Convinced on Slight Evidence—Negative—Receptive, etc.—♃ Sig. ☌ the ☉; ☿ weak and afflicted at B., and often in a watery sign; ♋ on the Asc., and the ☽ remote in a common sign, tends to make the native light, credulous and inconstant. (See "Difficult to Cure" under Cure; "Light In Mind" under Mind; Negative, Plastic, Receptive, Sensation, Susceptible).

INFLUENZA—Grippe—La Grippe—Contagious and Epidemic Catarrhal Fever—First called Influenza in Italy in the Seventeenth Century because attributed to the "Influenze of the Stars", and this name has passed into Medical use. This disease occurs in Countries at the time of an Eclipse, and where the Eclipse is visible, and espec. in Parts under the Central Line of the Shadow. Occurs when three or four superior planets are in ☌ or ♌. Said to be caused by electrical conditions in the atmosphere, due to planetary influence. Caused by cross aspects of Promittors, or Non-Promittors, to the ☉ when the horoscope is an unfortunate one. Catarrhal Fevers grow worse towards sunset. Also caused by the ☉ and ☽ badly aspected at B., or by dir.; the ☉ in ♉, and affl. by malefics; an eclipse of the ☉ in ♊, and the ☉ badly afflicted by malefics; the ☽ ☌, □, or ♌ ♄ at a Solar Rev.; the ☽ hyleg, and to the ☌ or ill-asp. ♄ by dir.; a ♆ disease; ♆ ☌, □, or ♌ ☉; ♄ □ ♅, and this aspect existed in 1918 during the great Influenza Epidemic of that year; ♄ □ ♆; ♄ ☌ ♃ if in the same Lat., or ♄ have higher Lat. than ♃, and tends to a malignant form; a ♅ disease, and caused by the afflictions of ♅; ♉ and ♏ are frequently afflicted, showing infection thru the throat; afflictions in ♉ at B., or by dir.; afflictions in common signs, or these signs upon the angles; Subs at MCP, CP, SP, and KP. (See Atmosphere, Catarrh, Colds, Epidemics, La Grippe, Lethargy, Nose; "Sleeping Sickness" under Sleep).

Malignant Influenza—Caused by ♃ ☌ ♄ if of the same Lat. If ♄ have higher Lat. than ♃, and these planets in ☌, Influenza and terrible diseases prevail. (See Malignant).

Nose—The Nose Affected In Influenza —(See "Influenza" under Nose).

INFORTUNES—Malefics—(See Malefics).

INGRESSES—These are the times when the ☉ passes the Equinoxes and Solstices, and the positions of the planets in the Signs and Houses at these times are very important to note in health matters, as they are times when disease is apt to come. Ingresses are frequently referred to in this book. Students of Medical Astrology should make a careful study of Ingresses, Equinoxes, and Solstices in the Textbooks of Astrology. (See Air, Catarrh, Cholera, Enemies, Epidemics, Epilepsy, Equinoxes, Fruit, Mania, Mutilated, Prevalent, Rheumatism, Scarlatina, Solar, Solstices, Tropical, Vernal).

INGUINAL—(See Groins).

Inguinal Hernia—(See Hernia).

INHARMONY—(See Antipathy, Discord, Enemies, Incompatibility, Quarrels).

INHERENT—Innate—Hereditary—(See Heredity, Innate).

INHERITANCE—Sickness from Loss of —Lord of the 6th in the 4th H., and much vexation from. (See Property, Reversals, Riches).

INHIBITIONS—Restraint of Organic Activity—Due to ♄ influence and afflictions; ♄ tends to bind, hinder, retard, and suppress the functions of both body and mind by his afflictions, or to dwarf and disorganize the different organs of the body and cause disease, improper elimination and excretion, etc. (See "Saturn Influence" under Saturn).

Auditory Nerve—Inhibition of—(See "Auditory" under Hearing).

Faculties Inhibited—♄ afflictions to the ☉, ☽, ☿, or Asc., and the Faculties inhibited or restrained are those ruled over by the sign ♄ is in at B., or by the planet, or planets, which are especially afflicted by him, and according to the signs they occupy. (See Dull, Faculties; "Arrested" under Mental).

Functions Inhibited—♄ influence, and to the parts ruled by the sign he is in at B., or in temporarily by tr. or dir.. and tends to lack of vital activity and circulation of vital forces in the part. (See Functions, Stoppages, Suppressions).

Growth—Growth of Body and Mind Inhibited—(See Dwarfed, Growth, Idiocy, Imbecility; "Arrested" under Mental; "Weak Mind" under Mind; Undersized, etc.).

Hair—Growth of the Hair Inhibited— (See Hair).

Hearing—The Hearing Inhibited— (See "Deafness", "Inhibition", under Hearing).

Heart—The Heart Inhibited—(See "Inhibition" under Heart).

Memory—The Memory Inhibited— (See Memory).

Mental Inhibitions—(See Apathy, Arrested, Dull, Examinations, Foolish, Idiocy, Imbecility, Insanity, Intellect, Memory, Mental, Mind, Perception, Understanding, etc.).

Optic Nerves—Inhibition of—(See Blindness, Optic, Sight). For further and collateral study see Atrophy, Binding, Cessation, Confinement, Crystallization, Defects, Deficient, Difficult, Diminished, Elimination, Excretion, Hardening, Hindrances, Limitations, Morbid, Restraint, Retarded, Shrinkage, Twelfth House, etc. Inhibitions can occur in any part or organ of the body, due to the presence of ♄, or other malefic, in the sign ruling the part afflicted, and for subjects not listed here, look in the alphabetical arrangement for the subject, part, or organ you have in mind.

INHUMAN—Not Perfectly Human In Shape—When the ruler of the last New or Full ☽ before birth, and the rulers of the ☉ and ☽ are unconnected with the preceding New or Full ☽, tends to unnatural conformities, and monstrous births. If in addition to this absence of connection, ♅, ♄, or ♂ be in angles, and the ☉ and ☽ be in ♈, ♉, ♌, ♐, or ♑, in Quadrupedal and Bestial Signs, then the conception will tend to be defective. (See "Beastly Form" under Beasts; "Dogs" under Children; Conception, Congenital, Deformities, Disfigurements, Distortions, Monsters, Savage, Wild, etc.).

Inhuman Disposition—♂ ill-dignified at B., and afflicted by ♄. (See Brutish, Criminal, Cruel, Merciless, Pity, Savage; "High Temper" under Temper; Vicious, Violent, Wicked, etc.).

INIMICAL TO HIMSELF—(See "Brings Disease Upon Himself" under Disease; Disgrace; "His Own Worst Enemy" under Enemies; Reversals, Ruin, Scandal, Self-Undoing).

INJECTIONS—(See Enema).

INJUDICIOUS—Indiscreet—Imprudent —Heedless—Void of Discretion—

Cosmetics—Injudicious Use of—(See "Indiscreet" under Cosmetics).

Diet—Sickness from Injudicious Diet —(See "Evil Diet" under Diet; Digestion, Excesses, Gluttony, Habits, Imprudent, Indigestion, Indiscretions).

Judgment—(See "Bad Judgment" under Judgment).

INJURIES—Traumatism—Wounds— Hurts—Accidents—Detriment—The subject of Injuries is also largely considered in this book in the Articles on Accidents, Hurts, Wounds. For Injuries to the various parts, or organs of the body, see the subject in the alphabetical arrangement. For convenience of reference many subjects are relisted here. In a general way malefics oriental at B. tend to Injuries, Accidents, Hurts, etc., and when occidental to disease. The malefics in the signs at B. indicate danger of accidents, hurts, and injuries to the part, or parts, of the body ruled by the signs containing them, and especially when under the directions or transits of the malefics to such signs. (See "Danger of Injuries", and the various paragraphs in this section. Also see the Introduction under Accidents, Hurts, Wounds). See the following subjects in the alphabetical arrangement when not considered here—

Abortion; Abrasions; Accidents—And Attended with Injury—(See the various paragraphs under Accidents, Hurts, Violence, Wounds).

Aeroplanes; Air—(See the various paragraphs under Air).

Ambushes; Anarchists; Animals—(See the various paragraphs under Animals, Beasts, Bites, Cattle, Horses, Kicks, Quadrupeds).

Assassins; Assaults; Athletics—Injuries In—(See Athletics, Exercise, Sports).

Authority—Injured by One In Authority—(See Kings, Rulers).

Automobiles—Injury By—(See Vehicles).

Avalanches; Badly Injured—But Lives—♂ or ☋ in the Asc., and ♄ affl. the lord of the 1st H., may be badly injured and nearly killed; a malefic with the lord of the Asc., and a benefic in the Asc. (Hor'y).

Bathings—(See Bathing, Drowning, Water).

Battle—Injured In—(See Contests, Duels, Quarrels, Slaughter, War).

Beasts—(See "Animals" in this section).

Bites; Blasts of Wind—(See the various paragraphs under Wind).

Blindness—From Injury—(See "Injury" under Blindness).

Blood—Injuries with Loss of Blood—(See "Injuries" under Blood; Cuts, Stabs, etc.).

Blows; Brother—Injury To—(See Brother).

Bruises; Buildings—Injury by Fall of—Falls From—(See Buildings, Crushed, Falls, Heights).

Burglars—Injury By—(See Burglars, Highwaymen, Robbers, Thieves).

Buried Alive—(See Avalanches, Burial, Crushed).

Burns; Calamities; Cattle—Injury By—(See Cattle).

Causes of Injury—♂ tends to cause all injuries which are attended by a flow of blood; ♂ ☌, □, or ☍ the ☉, ☽, Asc. or hyleg by dir., and the radical map a violent one, showing tendency to injuries, accidents, or a violent death; ♄ causes injuries where blood does not flow, as blows, bruises, concussions, falls, etc. (See the Introduction, "Danger Of", "Tendency To", and the various paragraphs in this section).

Childbirth—Injury In—(See Birth, Infancy, Parturition).

Childhood—Injury In—(See Childhood, Children, Infancy).

Children—Injury To—(See Children).

Cold—Injuries By—(See Blizzards, Cold, Snow, Storms, Winter).

Common People—Injury To—(See Common).

Concussions; Contests—Injured In—(See Contests, Duels, Quarrels, Sword).

Contusions—(See Bruises).

Convicts—Prisoners—Injured By In Prison—(See Prison).

Crippled—By Injury—(See Crippled, Fractures, Lameness, Limbs).

Crushed; Cuts; Daggers—Injured By—(See Cuts, Stabs).

Danger of Injury—Tendency To—Liable To—Predisposed To—Susceptible to Injuries—Injuries are caused principally by the ☉ and ♂, the positive, electric, and caloric-producing planets; the ☉ or ☽ hyleg, and to the ☌ or ill-asp. ♂ by dir.; the ☽ to Aldebaran by dir.; the ☽ to the ☌ or P. Dec. Regulus if the ☽ be hyleg; ♅ causes injuries by shock, electricity, accidents by machinery, explosions, sudden events; ♅ ☌ ♂ in the 7th H.; ♅ ☌ ♂ in ♈, or in angles; ♄ causes injuries by falls, blows, bruises, concussions, fractures, revenge, treachery, etc.; ♄ ☌ or ill-asp. ♂, and espec. if either planet be ori.; ♄ or ♂ in the Asc. or 7th H., or in □ or ☍ to these houses, and also the ☉ be in □ or ☍ the ☽, and either of them in angles; ♂ causes injuries by cuts, burns, violence, loss of blood, by attacks of enemies or robbers, by recklessness, gun-shot, stabs, the sword, and in battles or war; ♂ coming to the Asc. or Desc. early in life causes injuries and accidents; ♂ and the ☉ by their afflictions cause injuries by rash and self-motived acts; caused by the malefics ori. at B., and affl. the ☉, ☽, Asc., or hyleg; a malefic rising in an angle, going before or after the ☉; the 22° ♌ on the Asc. tends to; fiery signs on the Asc., and affl. by ♂; the airy signs on the Asc. at B. make the native less liable to injuries and accidents. Those born under the Hurtful Signs ♈, ♉, ♋, ♏ or ♑ are more liable to injuries. (See "Danger Of" under Accidents, Hurts, Wounds. Also in this section see the Introduction, "Causes", "Tendency To", and the various paragraphs.)

Dangerous Injuries—Or Accidents—(See "Dangerous" under Accidents).

Daughter—Injury To—(See Daughter).

Death By—The ☉ and ☽ in evil asp. to ♂ at B., and by dir.; ♂ on the Asc., and afflicted. (See "Death" under Accidents, Hurts, Violent, Wounds; "Death" under the various subjects listed in this Article).

Demoniacs—Injure and Wound Themselves—(See Demoniac).

Detriment; Diet—Injury by Wrong Diet—(See Diet, Food, Indigestion).

Directions—As the Cause of Injury—(See Directions, Events).

Disablements — From Injury — (See Disabilities).

Disease—Injury By—(See the various paragraphs under Disease).

Distortions; Dreadful Injury — Terrible—Meets With—♂ affl. the ☉ at B., and by dir., and the ☉ weak and ill-dignified.

Drugs — Injured by Use of — (See Drugs, Medicines, Narcotics).

Duels; Early Years—Injury In—(See Early).

Earthquakes—(See Earth).

Eating—Injured by Wrong Eating—(See Diet, Eating, Food).

Effusion of Blood—Injured By—(See "Loss of Blood" under Blood; Effusions).

Electricity; Elements—Injured By, as by Storms, Weather, etc. — (See Air, Cold, Electricity, Elements, Fire, Heat, Lightning, Storms, Weather, Wind).

Elephants — Injured By — (See Elephants).

Employment—Injured In—(See Employment, Machinery).

Enemies—Injured By—(See Enemies).

Enmity; Escapes — Has Narrow Escapes from Injury—(See Escapes).

Events; Excesses; Excoriations—(See Abrasions).

Exercise — (See Athletics, Exercise, Hunting, Sports).

Explosions; Extraordinary Injuries—(See Extraordinary, Peculiar, Unusual).

Extravagance; Extremities—Injuries To—(See Ankles, Arms, Extremities, Feet, Hands, Legs, Limbs, Wrists).

Falls; Father—Injury To—(See Father).

Females — Injury To — (See Aunts, Daughter, Females, Mother, Sister, Wife, Women).

Feuds; Fire—(See Burns, Fire, Heat, Liquids, Scalds).

Fire Arms—(See Gun-Shot).

Folly; Food—Injured by Wrong Use of—(See the various paragraphs under Diet, Drink, Eating, Food).

Foreign Land—Injured In— (See Abroad, Foreign).

Four-Footed Beasts — Injured By — (See Animals, Beasts, Cattle, Elephants, Four-Footed, Horses, Quadrupeds).

Fractures; Friends — Injury To — Injury By—(See Friends).

Gases; Genitals; Groins; Gun-Shot;

Habits; Hand of Man — Injured By — (See Ambushes, Assassins, Assaults, Blows, Cuts, Hand of Man, Murder, Stabs, etc.).

Harlots—Injured By—(See Harlots).

Haunches; Healers—Injured By—(See Healers).

Heat—(See Burns, Fire, Heat, Scalds).

Heights—Falls From—(See Heights).

Hemorrhage; High Places—Injury by Falls From—(See Buildings, Heights).

Highwaymen—Injured By—(See Highwaymen).

Himself—Injures Himself—♂ people. (See Demoniac, Inimical, Suicide).

Homicide; Honour — Injured In Affairs of—(See Contests, Duels, Honour).

Horary Maps—Horary Questions—Injury Indicated In — ♄, ♂, or ☋ in the 8th H.

Horses — Injured By — (See Bites, Horses, Hunting, Kicks).

Hunting — Injury In — (See Horses, Hunting).

Hurtful Signs—(See Distortions, Hurtful, Obnoxious).

Hurts — (See the various paragraphs under Hurts).

Husband—Injury To—(See Husband).

Ill-Health—Injury By—(See the various paragraphs under Ill-Health).

Immunity — Less Liable to Injury or Accident — (See "Less Liable" under Accidents; Immunity).

Incised Wounds — (See Cuts, Duels, Instruments, Sharp, Stabs, Sword).

Incurable — The Injury Is Without Remedy—(See "Incapable of Remedy" under Remedy).

Infants — Injury To — (See Birth, Infancy, Parturition).

Insects — Injury By — (See Bites, Insects, Obnoxious, Stings, Venomous).

Instruments—Injury By—(See Blows, Cuts, Duels, Instruments, Machinery, Parturition, Sharp, Stabs, Sword, Weapons).

Inventions — Injuries By — (See Employment, Inventions, Machinery).

Iron and Steel—Injury By—(See Instruments, Iron, Sharp, Steel, Weapons).

Journeys—Injuries On—(See Abroad, Foreign Lands, Journeys, Railroads, Ships, Travel, Vehicles, Voyages).

Kicks; Kings—Injury To—Injury By —(See Kings, Rulers).

Lacerations; Lack Of—(See the various paragraphs under Lack).

Lameness; Landslides — (See Avalanche, Crushed; "Earthquakes" under Earth; "Landslides" under Land).

Left Side—Of the Body—Accidents or Injuries To—(See Left).

Less Liable—To Injuries—Airy signs on the Asc. at B. (See "Less Liable" under Accidents; Immunity).

Liable to Injury—In Greater Danger of—(See Danger Of, Tendency To, in this section; "Liable To" under Accidents, Hurts).

Lightning; Liquids—(See Acids, Liquids, Poisons, Scalds).

Loss of Blood — Injuries By — (See "Loss Of" under Blood; Cuts, Effusions, Flow, Hemorrhage, Instruments, Shedding, Stabs, Sword).

Lower Order of Mankind—Injured By —(See Mankind).

Luxuries — Injured By — (See Appetites, Extravagance, Habits, Luxuries).

Machinery — (See Employment, Machinery).

Maimed; Males — Injury To — (See Brother, Father, Grandfather, Husband, Males, Son, Uncle).

Mankind—Injured by Lower Order of —(See Mankind).

Maritime People—Sailors—Injury To —(See Maritime, Navigation, Sailors, Ships, etc.).

Marriage Partner — Injury To — (See Husband, Marriage, Marriage Partner, Wife).

Medicines—Injured By—(See Drugs, Medicines, Narcotics).

Men — Injury To — (See the various paragraphs under Men).

Middle Life—Injuries In—(See Middle Life).

Middle Parts—Of Organs—Injury To —(See Middle, Navamsa).

Mind—Injuries To—(See Idiocy, Imbecile, Insanity; the various paragraphs under Mental, Mind).

Mindful of Injuries—Retains Anger— (See Anger, Enmity, Revenge, Treachery).

Mines—Injuries In—(See Mines).

Mischief; Mob — Injured By — (See Mobs).

Mother—Injury To—(See Mother).

Murder; Narcotics; Narrow Escapes— From Injury—(See Escapes).

Navigation — Injured In — (See Maritime, Navigation, Sea, Ships, Shipwreck, etc.).

Neglect — Injury By — (See Neglect, Poverty, Privation, Starvation).

Nobles—Injury To—(See Nobles).

Obnoxious — Injury by Obnoxious Creatures—(See Obnoxious).

Paralysis — From Injury — (See Distortions, Paralysis).

Parents — Injury To — (See Father, Mother, Parents).

Part of Body Injured—(See "Parts of Body" under Accidents).

Parturition — Injury to Mother or Child In—(See Birth, Infancy, Parturition).

Peculiar Injury—(See Extraordinary, Peculiar, Unusual).

Perils; Permanent In Effect — (See Permanent).

Pirates—Injury By—(See Pirates).

Plots — Injury and Treachery By — (See Enemies, Enmity, Plots, Poison, Treachery).

Popular Tumult — (See Lynching, Mobs, Tumults).

Poverty; Power — Injured by One In Power and Authority — (See Judges, Kings; "Power" under Men; Princes, Rulers).

Precipices — Falls From — (See Heights).

Predisposed—To Injuries—(See Danger Of, Liable To, Tendency To, in this section).

Prison—Injured In—(See Prison).

Private Injury — Blindness From— (See, "Total" under Blindness; Treachery).

Private Members—Injured In—(See Genitals, Maimed, Privates, Secrets, Testes).

Prostitutes — Injured By — (See Harlots).

Quadrupeds—Injured By—(See Animals, Beasts, Cattle, Elephants, Four-Footed, Horses, Quadrupeds).

Quarrels—Injured In—(See Contests, Duels, Enemies, Feuds, Quarrels, War).

Railroads—Injured On—(See "Short Journeys" under Journeys; Railroads, Travel).

Rash Acts — Injured As Result of — (See "Rash In Action" under Action; Folly, Hasty, Imprudent, Rash).

Recklessness — Injured Because of — (See Recklessness).

Reins—Injury In—(See Reins).

Relatives — Injury To — (See Family, Relatives).

Religion—Injured Because of—(See "Injured" under Religion).

Remedy — The Injury Incapable of Remedy — (See "Incurable" under Hurts; Incurable, Permanent; "Incapable" under Remedy).

Reptiles; Retains An Injury — (See "Mindful Of" in this section).

Reversals; Riding — Injured While Riding—(See Horses).

Right Side—Of the Body—Injury To —(See Right).

Robbers—Injured By—(See Robbers, Thieves).

Ruin; Rulers — Injured By — (See Kings; "Power" under Men; Princes, Rulers).

Ruptures; Sailors—Injury To—(See Maritime, Navigation, Sailors, Ships, Shipwreck).

Scalds; Scandal; Sea—Injured At Sea —(See Sea, Ships, Shipwreck, Voyages).

Secret Enemies — Injured By — (See Ambushes; "Secret" under Enemies; Feuds, Plots, Revenge, Treachery).

Secret Parts—Injury To—(See Genitals, Privates, Secrets).

Self-Inflicted Injury—(See "Himself" in this section).

Self-Motived—Injury from Rash Acts —(See "Rash Acts" in this section).

Serious Injury — (See "Dreadful" in this section; "Dangerous" under Accidents).

Serpents; Sharp-Edged Tools—Injured By — (See Cuts, Duels, Instruments, Stabs, Sword, etc.).

Ships—Injured On—(See Ships).

Shipwreck; Shock — (See Electricity, Fright, Shock, Uranus).

Sickly; Sickness — (See the various paragraphs under Sickness).

Sister—Injury To—(See Sister).

Slander—(See Disgrace, Libel, Reputation, Ruin, Scandal, Slander, etc.).

Slight Injury—(See Ameliorated, Mild, Mitigated, Moderation, Slight, etc.).

Snakes; Son—Injury To—(See Son).

Spontaneous Injury — Sudden — (See Spontaneous; "Accidents" under Sudden).

Sports — Injury In — (See Exercise, Gunshot, Horses, Hunting, Sports).

Stabs; Steel—(See Cuts, Instruments, Iron, Stabs, etc.).

Stings; Stones — Injured by Flying Stones—(See "Flying" under Stones).

Storms — (See Lightning, Storms, Wind).

Strokes—(See Blows).

Sudden Injury — (See Spontaneous, Sudden).

Suicide; Sword; Tendency to Injuries —Or Accidents, Hurts, Wounds, etc.— The ☽ to the ill-asp. the ☉ by dir., or transit; the Prog. ☽ to the ♂ or ill-asp. ♂; ♅ to the ♂ or ill-asp. ♂ by dir.; ♂ □ or ☍ the ☉, ☽, or ♅; ♂ affl. in □ or ♍, and ♂, P., □, or ☍ the Asc. by dir. (See Causes, Danger Of, Liable To, in this section).

Terrible Injury—(See Dreadful, Serious, in this section).

Thieves—Injured By—(See Highwaymen, Pirates, Robbers, Thieves).

Time of Injuries — (See "Time Of" under Accidents; Directions, Events, Time).

Tornadoes—(See Wind).

Trampled; Travel — Injury During — (See Abroad, Foreign Lands, Journeys, Railroads, Ships, Shipwreck, Travel, Vehicles, Voyages, etc.).

Treachery — Injured By — (See Ambushes, Enemies, Enmity, Feuds, Plots, Poison, Treachery).

Treatment Of—(See Resolvent).

Tumults—(See Lynching, Mobs; "Flying Stones" under Stones; Tumults).

Uncle—Injury To—(See Aunts, Uncle).

Unusual Injury—(See Extraordinary, Mysterious, Peculiar, Strange, Sudden, Unusual).

Upper Parts—Of the Body or Organs —Injury To—(See Navamsa, Upper).

Various Injuries—♂ affl. in ♓, and ♂, □, or ☍ the Asc. (See Various).

Venomous Injuries—(See Adder, Bites, Obnoxious, Reptiles, Serpents, Venomous).

Violent Injuries — (See Violent; "Death", and the various paragraphs in this section).

Volcanoes — Injury By — (See Volcanoes).

Voyages — Injury On — (See "Long Journeys" under Journeys; Maritime, Navigation, Sea, Ships, Shipwreck, Travel, Voyages).

War—Injury or Death In—(See War).

Water—Injury By—(See Bathing, Drowning, Floods; "Hot Liquids" under Heat; Liquids, Rain, Scalds, Sea, Ships, Shipwreck, Storms, Water).

Weakness—Injured by Weakness and Low Vitality—(See "Low" under Vitality; "Weak Body" under Weak).

Weapons — Injury By — (See Blows, Contests, Cuts, Duels, Gunshot, Instruments, Sword, Weapons, etc.).

Weather—Injured By—(See Drought, Famine; "Excessive Heat" under Heat; Storms, Weather, Wind).

Wife—Injury To—(See Wife).

Wild Beasts—Injury By—(See "Wild" under Animals; "Danger" under Travel; Wild).

Wind — (See the various paragraphs under Wind).

Women — Injured By — Injury To — (See "Women" under Men; also the various paragraphs under Females, Women).

Wood — Injured by Wood or Stone — (See "Assaults" under Stone).

Wounds—Injury By—(See Accidents, Cuts, Hurts, Stabs, Wounds; the various paragraphs in this section).

Young Men—Injury To—(See Young).

Youth—Injury In—(See Youth).

INNATE — (See Congenital, Constitution, Diathesis, Heredity, Natural, Organic, Structural, Temperament, etc.).

INNER PARTS—All Diseases In—(See Inward, Kidneys, Reins).

INNERVATION — The Function of the Nervous System—A Discharge of Nervous Force — Nerve Impulses — Principally under the rule of ☿, and influenced by the ☿ Group of Herbs, which are Nervine and Periodic. The physiological action of the ☿ Herbs, by their action on the Solar Plexus, tend to Gastro-Abdominal Innervation. By their action thru the Brachial Plexus, and by Pulmonary Haematosis, Pulmonary Innervation takes place. The ☿ Herbs tend to Periodicity and the Nervous Influx by their physiological action. (See Enervation; "Innervation" under Gastric; Haematopoiesis; "Mercury Group" under Herbs; "Full Moon" under Moon; Nerves, Periodic, Periodicity; "Solar Plexus" under Plexus).

INNOMINATE BONE — The Hip Bone, including the Pubis, Ilium, and Ischium —Ruled by ♐. (See Haunches, Hips, Ilium, Ischium, Pelvis, Pubes).

INOFFENSIVE—(See Gentle, Harmless, Humane, Kind, Quiet, etc.).

INORDINATE—Immoderate—Excessive —Unrestrained—

Affections — Inordinate Affections — (See Affection, Amorous, Excesses, Free Love, Passion, etc.).

Drugs — Inordinate Use of — (See Drugs, Narcotics).

Exercise—Inordinate Exercise—Disease Resulting From — (See Exercise, Exertion, Fatigue, Sports).

Growth—Inordinate and Excessive— (See Corpulent, Enlarged, Giants, Growth, Large, Stout, Tall, etc.).

Lust — Inordinate Lust, and Diseases Therefrom—(See Lust).

Pleasures — Inordinate and Lustful Pleasures, and Ill-Health From—(See Debauchery, Dissipation, Drink, Excesses; "High Living" under High; Lust; "Loose Morals" under Morals; Pleasure, Venery, etc.).

Pulse—Inordinate Pulse—(See "High Pulse" under Pulse). For further study see Abnormal, Appetites, Deportment, Eating, Habits, Immoderate, Indiscretions, Morals, Passion, Perversions, Sex, etc.

INSANITY—Lunacy—Mental Derangement — Madness — From a planetary standpoint this disease is very closely related to Epilepsy, varying according as to whether ♄ or ♂ are the afflictors in a day or night nativity. In a disease of this magnitude the configurations and aspects in the natal map must necessarily be very severe, and also during prenatal life. In studying this disease the ☽ and ☿ should be primarily considered, their afflictions, their relation to each other and to the Asc. Mental weakness is more apt to result when there is no aspect at B. between the ☽ and ☿, and also when neither form an asp. to the Asc., and at the same time be severely afflicted by malefics. In this case if ♄ be the afflictor in a day nativity, Epilepsy is more apt to occur, but in a night nativity, if ♄ be the afflictor, Insanity may follow, and espec. if the ☽, ♄, ♂, and ☿ be found in ♋, ♍, or ♓. On the other hand when ♂ is the afflicting planet, there tends to be Insanity by day, and Epilepsy by night. Also when the ☉ and ☽ are conjoined, and ill-aspected by ♄, or opposed and afflicted by ♂, Insanity may occur, and espec. if the Lights be found in ♎, ♐, or ♓, and such infirmities will tend to be incurable if there are no good asps. to the ☉, ☽, or ☿ from the benefics. In Insanity the Asc. is not necessarily afflicted, but in cases of Epilepsy the Asc. is usually badly aspected and afflicted by the ☽, ☿, and malefics. (See "Causes" in this section).

Agitated—The Insane More Agitated —(See "Full Moon" under Moon).

Asylums—Insane Asylum—Confined In An Insane Asylum or Prison, and Often by the Work of An Enemy—Ψ, Ħ, or ♂ affl. in the 12th H.; Ψ affl. in the 4th H., and apt to end days in an Asylum; Ψ in the 12th H., in □ or 8 ☿; ♄ affl. in the 12th H.; afflictions in the 12th. Case—See "Obsession", No. 130, in 1001 N.N. (See Confinement, Hospitals, Limitations, Prison, Restraint, Twelfth House).

Cases of Insanity—(1) Insane At Age of 40, and Committed Suicide—See "Suicide", No. 137, in 1001 N.N. (2) Insane At Age of 27 from Self-Abuse and Smoking—See "Self-Indulgence", No. 229, in 1001 N.N. (3) Committed Suicide When Insane—See "Bavaria", No. 823, in 1001 N.N. (4) Other Cases— Figures, Birth Data, etc.—See Figures 13, 14, and 23, in "Message of the Stars", and Figures 19A, 19B, and 19C, in "Astro-Diagnosis", both books by the Heindels. (See Cases under Lunacy).

Causes of Insanity—In addition to what has been said in the Introduction to this Article, note the following planetary influences—The SUN is also generally afflicted; the ☉ above the horizon at B., and ☿ affl. by ♂; the ☉ below the horizon and ☿ affl. by ♄; the ☉ and ☿ in common signs, and affl. by the ☌ or ill-asps. the malefics, and espec. afflictions from angles, or by planets out of dignity; the ☉ and ♂ contribute to Insanity when they rule Ħ, ☿, the ☽, or 1st H., and espec. if the ☽, ☿, and Asc. be unconnected with each other or the Asc.; the MOON, ☿, and the Asc. in no relation or aspect to each other, and ☿ affl. by the ☌ or ill-asp. the malefics, and espec. if the affliction is from angles; the Prog. ☽

☌ ♄ or ♅ in the 12th H.; the ☽ and ☿ both badly aspected by ♄, Ħ, or ♂; a ☽ disease; NEPTUNE in the configuration plays an important part in this disease, and espec. when his ill-aspects are added to those of ♄ or ♂, in which case Obsessions and Demoniacal affections may also occur; an afflicted Ψ; Ψ affl. in the 12th H.; Ψ □ ☿, and espec. if Ψ is in the 12th H.; Ψ ☌ ♂ in ♈, and affl. by Ħ and the ☽, and the map otherwise indicating mental weakness; Ψ in ♈, and in □ asp. the ☉, Ħ, ♂, and ☿; Ψ affl. in ♈ in the 12th H.; a Ψ disease; Ψ affl. in the 4th H., may end life in an Insane Asylum; Ψ affl. in the 3rd or 9th H.; URANUS elevated above, and afflicting the ☽ and ☿ at the same time; Ħ afflicting one or both Luminaries, and ♄ or ♂ afflicting the mental rulers; Ħ and ♂ afflictions tend to produce violent forms of Insanity, and where there is great muscular activity; Ħ affl. in the 6th or 12th H.; Ħ affl. in ♓; Ħ by transit in ☌ ♂, ☿, or the ☽ in the radical map, almost to the point of Insanity in some cases; Ħ in ♒ and affl. by the ☽, danger of, and espec. when other configurations indicate the disease; SATURN the afflictor in a night nativity; ♄ and ♂ in an angle, occi. of the ☉, and ori. of the ☽, and ☿ in familiarity with ♂; ♄ ☌, □, or 8 the Asc. in a night nativity, and espec. when in ♋, ♍, or ♓, and with ☿ and the ☽ in no relation to each other, or to the Asc.; ♄ ☌ ♃ in or near the 22° ♍, and affl. by Ψ, and other configurations concording; MARS affl. in the 12th H.; ♂ □ or 8 ☿; ♂ 8 ☿ from the 6th and 12th H.; a ♂ disease; ♂ afflictions tend to the violent forms; ♂ the afflictor in the configuration in a day nativity tends to, and to epilepsy in a night map; ♂ affl. in the 3rd H., and espec. when in a water sign; ♂ in ♏ in the 3rd H., and in □ to the ☽ if other aspects and afflictions concur; ♂ ☌, □, or 8 the Asc. in a day nativity, with other influences in accord, as stated; ♂ and ☿ holding dominion at B., and in familiarity with each other, and ♂ affl. the hyleg and elevated above the Luminaries, the Insanity is increased; ♂ afflicts the mental rulers, and espec. in a day nativity; MERCURY and the ☽ unconnected with each other or the Asc.; a ☿ disease; ☿ affl. in the 12th H.; ☿ badly afflicted at B., ☌, or evil asp. the malefics, and with no assistance to ☿ from the benefics; ☿ in 8 in 8 Ħ, ♄, and the ☽ in ♏; ☿ combust and affl. by malefics, etc. (This sentence and configuration is finished in full under Idiots). Mutable signs on the angles, and also greatly afflicted, tend to insanity, and also to lack of hope; cardinal and fixed signs on the Asc. and the angles lessen the chances of insanity; the 22° ♍ or ♓ on the Asc., or containing afflictions, tend to, and are sensitive degrees for this disease, and also sometimes by the exact □ aspects of the malefics, or of ☿ and the ☽ to these degrees; the 12th H. is also generally prominent and afflicted, as this house indicates confinement, limitation, restriction, and suppression of the faculties; the 12th H. is more afflicted in Insanity, while the 3rd H. is more prominent in Epilepsy, which helps to differentiate the two diseases; the Asc. unconnected with ☿ or the ☽, and otherwise afflicted by the malefics ♄ or ♂, as stated; the 28° ♑ on the Asc. tends to, and to give a weak mind or intellect; Lunations falling on the place of a badly afflicted radical ☽ tend to, and to give a temporary attack of insanity. (See Lunacy). The following paragraphs give classified conditions concerning Insanity and further influences not listed in this one, and in the Introduction to this Article. For Cases of Insanity, Birth Data, etc., see "Cases" in this section.

Children — Children May Become Insane—☿ in the 5th H. in the map of a parent, afflicted in ♋, ♏, or ♓, and espec. if ♄ or ♂ afflict ☿ at the same time. (See "Deformed" under Infancy).

Confined In Asylum—(See "Asylums" in this section).

Curable Cases—Hope of Remedy—The Insanity will tend to be mitigated, or curable, if the benefics are elevated at B. above the malefics which produce it, and espec. under favorable directions to the ☽ and ☿. The more oriental and angular the benefics or malefics may be, the more powerful their effect for good or evil. There is also hope of remedy when ☿ is in good asp. to the ☽ or Asc. (See Curable, Incurable, Lunacy).

Dangerous Lunatics — Violent Lunatics — Those under ♂ influence, and where ♂ is the causative agent. (See Fury, Madness; "Violent" under Mania; Causes, Outrageous, Violent, in this section).

Day—Insanity In a Day Nativity—♂ is the cause and afflicting planet. (See the Introduction to this Article).

Delusions—Insanity with Delusions—(See Paranoia).

Immunity From — Cardinal or Fixed Signs on the angles of the map lessen the liability to. (See Immunity; "Curable" in this section).

Increased—The Insanity Is Increased—(See the ♂ influences under "Causes" in this section).

Incurable — Lasting — The afflictions causing the affliction being in the Fixed Signs. (See "Fixed Signs" under Fixed; Incurable, Lunacy).

Mitigated — (See "Curable" in this section).

Muscular Activity In — Produced by the afflictions of ♅ and ♂. (See "Causes" in this section).

Night — Insanity In Night Nativities —♄ the afflictor in a night nativity. (See the Introduction to this Article).

Not As Susceptible To — Less Liable To—The cardinal or fixed signs on the Asc. or angles of the map at B.

Outrageous — The Patient Becomes Outrageous, Unmanageable—☿ and the ☽ unconnected with each other or the Asc., with ♄ and ♂ in angles ruling the scheme, ♂ by day or ♄ by night, and espec. if the malefics be in ♋, ♏, or ♓, and under these conditions if the malefics be in the Eastern Parts in angles, and the benefics in the West,

the insane become unmanageable, outrageous, raving, breaking away from their homes, and wandering in nakedness. (See Demoniac; "Violent" in this section).

Periodic—Insanity At Periods—♅ afflicting the ☽ and ☿ at the same time, and elevated above them. (See "Temporary" in this section).

Postponed—☿ and the ☽ at B. unconnected with each other or the Asc., but having the good asps. of the benefics, the insanity may not appear as early in life, but wait for a train of evil directions to ☿ and the hyleg.

Puberty — Insanity sometimes occurs at puberty if at birth the sex sign ♏ was afflicted by ♂, and the ☽ and ☿ in evil aspect and afflicted by malefics. (See Puberty).

Raving—The Insane Rave—(See "Outrageous" in this section).

Rush of Blood to Head — Insanity Caused By—A ♂ disease. (See "Blood" under Head).

Self-Abuse — Insanity From — Case— See "Self-Indulgence", No. 229, in 1001 N.N. (See "Solitary" under Vice).

Suicide — Commits Suicide While Insane—(See "Cases" in this section).

Surgeon — Successful As Surgeon In Asylum—(See "Hospitals" under Surgeons).

Temporary Insanity—♅ ☌ ☽ in 9th H., and in □ or ☍ ☿ and ♆. (See Periodic, Violent, in this section; "Delirium Tremens" under Delirium; Frenzy, Fury, Madness, Mania, Temporary).

Treatment Of — The Blue Color, and to be confined in a Blue Room, with blue window panes, tends to soothe the most violent maniac or insane person. Also Insanity is caused by Obsessions, Evil Spirit Controls, Morbid Fears, Fixed Ideas, etc., which could be largely relieved or mitigated, and possibly cured, by Suggestion in the Hypnotic State, or by commanding the Evil Spirit to depart, as did The Christ in some cases. (See Curable, Incurable, in this section).

Unmanageable—(See "Outrageous" in this section).

Violent Forms—Caused by ♅ and ♂ afflictions; Subs at AT and AX, and attended also with ♅ or ♂ affliction, often causes violent temporary insanity. (See Lunacy; Dangerous, Outrageous, Temporary, in this section). For further and collateral study, and in which many of the same influences predominate as in Insanity, see Anxiety, Congenital, Coprolalia, Delusions, Demoniac, Derangements, Dreamy, Emotions, Epilepsy, Fanatical, Fancies, Fears; "Fixed Ideas", "Fixed Signs", under Fixed; Foolish, Frenzy, Fury, Hallucinations, Heredity, Idiocy, Illusions, Imbecile, Intellect, Irrational, Irresponsible; "Low Spirits" under Low; Lunacy, Madness, Mania, Melancholy, Memory, Mental Derangement (see Mental, Mind); Morbid, Noisy, Obsessions, Paranoia, Perceptions, Permanent, Prenatal, Reason, Spirit Controls, Suicide, Terrors, Understanding, Unsound Mind (see Mind); Weak Mind (see "Weak" under Mind); Worry, etc.

INSATIABLE—Insatiable Appetite—(See Appetites, Diet, Eating, Feasting, Gluttony, Hunger, etc.).

INSECTS—

Insect Bites—(See Adder, Bites, Obnoxious, Stings, Venomous).

Insect Pests—(See Comets, Floods, Venomous, Vermin).

INSENSIBILITY—See Anaesthetics, Analgesia, Carus, Catalepsy, Coma, Consciousness, Delirium, Dreams, Epilepsy, Fainting, Feelings, Fits, Hypnotism, Narcotics, Neptune (the influences and afflictions of ♆ tend to conditions of Insensibility—See Neptune); Paralysis, Sleep, Trance, etc.

INSOLATION—(See "Sunstroke" under Sun).

INSOMNIA — Sleeplessness — Wakefulness—(See "Insomnia" under Sleep).

INSPIRATION—Inhalation —Inbreathing—(See "Inspiration" under Breathing).

INSTABILITY—Unstable—Changeable

Emotions—Instability of — (See Emotions).

Health—Instability of—(See the various paragraphs under Health, Ill-Health, Sickness).

Mind—Instability of — (See Changes, Chaotic, Confusion; "Dreamy" under Dreams; Flightiness; "Instability", "Unstable", under Mind; Mutable, Negative, Receptive, Restless, Roaming, Susceptibility, Unstable, Vacillating, Vagabond, Wandering, etc.).

INSTINCTS—The ☽ is instinctive and rules the Instincts. (See Faculties).

Animal Instincts—(See "Animal Instincts" under Animal).

Maternal Instincts—(See Maternal).

Self-Preservation—Instincts of—(See Self-Preservation).

INSTITUTIONS — Confinement In— Afflictions in the 12th H. (See Hospitals; "Asylums" under Insanity; Prison).

INSTRUMENTS—Weapons—

Instrumental Delivery — Injury At Birth by Instruments — (See "Accidents" under Infancy; Parturition).

Sharp Instruments—Danger By—Injury By—Wounds By—The ☉ and ♂ afflictions tend to, they being the positive, electric, and caloric-producing planets; ♂ afflictions to the ☉, ☽, Asc., or Hyleg at B., and by dir.; ♂ in the 8th H., and affl. the ☉, ☽, or Hyleg; the Asc. to the place of the Pleiades, Hyades, or Castor. (See Cuts, Duels, Iron, Stabs, Sword, Weapons).

INSUFFICIENT—Insufficiency—

Heat—Insufficient Heat In the System—(See "Animal Heat" under Heat).

Mitral Insufficiency—(See Inefficiency, Mitral, under Heart).

Oxygenation — Insufficient Oxygenation—(See Oxygen).

INTELLECT—Intellectual—Intelligence — Intelligent—Mind—Understanding, etc.—This subject is mostly considered under the subjects of Mental, Mind. See the various paragraphs under Mental, Mind. The Intellect is ruled by ☿, which planet is designated as the Mental Ruler in general. The ♈ sign also rules the Intellect. The Asc. is said to rule the brain, and to have great influence over the mind and intellect, and each of the planets as they aspect and influence the ☽, ☿, and the Asc., tend to give their peculiar qualities to the mind for good or evil. Green is the color of the Human Intellect. (See Green). The study of intellectual ability is a deep and far-reaching one, and with many things to be considered which are not always shown and indicated by the map of birth. Heredity, the Age of the Soul, past experiences and causes, the aspects and influences of the prenatal period, etc., and others, are factors which have to be considered, and which play an important part in the state and quality of the Intellect. (See "Judging the Mind" under Mind).

All Evils—Of the Intellectual Parts—All evils of these parts, and diseases of the Mind proper, are ☿ diseases fundamentally, with ☿ weak and afflicted at B., or afflictions to the parts of the natal map partaking of the ☿ influences, etc. (See "Diseases of the Mind" under Mind).

Diseases of the Intellect—Disordered Mind—(See the various paragraphs under Mental, Mind. Also note the various references at the end of this Article).

Dull Intellect—(See Dull, Smoky).

Good Intellect—A Strong and Powerful Intellect—A Good Mind—A Clear Intellect—☿ well-aspected by the ☽ at B., and also in favorable relation to the Asc., and in one of his own signs, as in ♊ or ♍, or with one of these signs on the Asc. at B., and also the 3rd and 9th Houses, the houses of mind, strong and well-aspected at B., tend to give a good and strong intellect, whereas the opposite conditions tend to give a weaker understanding, or poor judgment, a shallow mind. However, ☿ may be rather weak at B., and yet the native have a strong intellect, or be a Genius, if the 3rd H. and Asc. be strongly influenced by ☿, or a ☿ sign. This was the case with some very great men and scholars, as Sir Isaac Newton, Spencer, Huxley, and others. In some cases a strong 9th H. gives a great intellect, as with Kant. Mars in the Asc. in △ asp. the ☉ tends to give a powerful intellect. (See "Active Mind" under Active; Genius; "Good" under Judgment; "Quickened" under Mental; "Sound Mind", "Strong Mind", under Mind).

Powerful Intellect—(See "Good" in this section).

Shallow Intellect—(See "Humours" under Head; "Shallow" under Mental).

Solidarity—Of the Intellect—Any aspect of ♄ to ☿ tends to give solidarity of intellect.

Sound Intellect—The 3rd Decan. of ♑ on the Asc. at B. denotes. (See "Sound Mind" under Mind).

Strong Intellect—(See "Good" in this section).

Weak Intellect—A weak Intellect, Insanity, Imbecility, Mental Defects, etc., usually result from a weak and afflicted ☿, ☽, and Asc. at B., and with ☿ in no aspect with the ☽ or Asc., and also with weak and afflicting influences over the 3rd, 9th, and 12th Houses. The weaknesses of the Intellect are governed by ☿ and the ☽, their relation to each other and the Asc., and the aspects to them. (See Foolish, Idiocy, Imbecility, Insanity; "Weak" under Mental, Mind). For further and collateral study along the lines of Intellect and Mind see such subjects as Chaotic, Comprehension, Confusion, Congenital, Defects, Deficiencies, Dull, Eccentric, Emotions, Epilepsy, Erratic, Examinations, Expression, Faculties, Fancies, Feelings, Fury, Hebetude, Ideals, Ideas, Knowledge, Learning, Look, Mania, Mathematical, Memory, Mental, Mind, Monsters, Notions, Perception, Precocious, Prenatal, Prodigies, Psychic, Reading, Reason, Senses, Study, Talents, Temper, Temperament, Understanding, Will, etc.).

INTEMPERANCE—Intemperate—Immoderate and Excessive In Eating, Habits, Conduct, Drink, Pleasures, Sex Matters, etc.—

Causes of Intemperance—General Causes of—The ☉ ☌ ♀ in ♏ or ♓, and afflicted; the ☉ Sig. in ♓; the ☉ to the ill-asps. the ☽, ♂, or ♀ by dir.; the ☉ afflicting ♀ by asp. at B.; the ☽ affl. at B., and to the evil asps. the Asc. by dir.; the ☽ to the evil asps. ♀ by dir.; ♆ afflictions tend to make one exceedingly intemperate, and liable to moral lapsing; ♄ ☌ or ill-asp. ♀ at B., or by dir., and espec. if ♄ is out of dignity; ♃ Sig. in □ or ☍ ♀ at B., and by dir., given to all kinds of intemperance and debauchery; ♂ affl. in ♓, intemperance should be guarded against; ♂ to the ☌ or ill-asp. ♀ by dir.; ♀ affl. in ♎; ♀ affl. in ♓ in the 6th H.; ♀ in ♓ and affl. the ☽ or Asc.; ♀ affl. in ♏; caused espec. by an afflicted ♀; ♀ affl. by the ☉ at B., and by dir.; ♀ affl. at B., and to the ☌ or ill-asp. the Asc. by dir.; ♀ ill-posited and in □ or ☍ ♂; the Asc. to the ill-asps. ♀ by dir., and ♀ afflicted at B.; the Asc. to the ill-asps. the ☽ by dir., and the ☽ affl. at B.; the 10 and 11° ♌ on the Asc., given to intemperance. (See Appetites, Conduct, Cravings, Debased, Debauched, Depraved, Diet, Dissipation, Drink, Drunkenness, Eating, Epicureans, Excesses, Fanatical, Feasting, Food, Gluttony, Habits, Immoderate, Indiscretions, Indulgent, Intoxication, Lascivious, Lewd, Lust; "Loose Morals" under Morals; Passion, Perversions, Pleasures, Plethora, Profligate, Sex, Sports, Surfeits, Temperance, Venery, Wanton, etc.).

Death—Death by Intemperance—Danger of—(See "Causes His Own Death" under Death; "Brings Disease Upon Himself" under Disease; "His Own Worst Enemy" under Enemies).

Diseases Proceeding From—Distempers From—Caused principally by afflictions to ☿; ♀ affl. in ♓ in the 6th H.; ♀ in ♓ and affl. the ☽ or Asc.; ♀ ∠ ☉ at B., and by dir.; the ☽ in the 6th H., and in ill-asp. to ♀; diseases of ♃, due largely to over-eating, excesses, and plethora; ♃ Sig. □ or ☍ ☉; ♂ affl. in ♓, and espec. when ♂ is in the 6th H., or affl. the ☽ or Asc.; the Asc. to the ill-asps. the ☽ by dir., and the ☽ affl. at B., according to the sign the ☽ is in at B.; many planets in watery signs, and espec. in ♓. (See "Death" in this section).

Heat—Intemperate Heat—Diseases and Suffering From—(See "Excessive Heat" under Heat).

Ruins Himself—By Intemperance—The ☉ Sig. in ♓. (See Ruin).

Sex Life—Intemperate In—(See Amorous; "Passional Excesses" under Passion).

Sports—Intemperate In—Injuries or Disease Caused By—(See Exercise; "Intemperate" under Sports).

INTENSE—Intensity—Intensive—Intensification—♂ tends to intensify and accelerate the actions in body and mind. The opposite effect is produced by ♄, as his action tends to slow up, denude and deplete, yet the action of both ♄ and ♂ are needed in the human economy to give balance. (See Malefics, Muscles, Nerves, Temper).

Intensive Action—Over the Body—♂ influence. (See Accelerated, Action, Violent).

Intensity of Disease—Severity of—(See Direct, Fulminating; "Disease" under Increase; Severity).

Intense Itching—(See Itching). For other phases of Intensity, or Excess, see Desire, Emotion, Exaggerated, Excess, Excesses, Passion, etc.).

INTERCELLULAR—Intercellular Spaces—Are connected with the Air Signs. (See Cells; "Air Signs" under Signs).

INTERCHANGE—The ♌ sign is significant of interchange of the forces of the body. (See Leo).

INTERCOSTAL—Between the Ribs—Affected by the ♉, ♊, and ♋ signs. (See Breathing, Chest, Diaphragm, Ribs).

Bulging—Intercostal Bulging—The ☉, ♃, or ♂ affl. in ♊; Subs at Lu.P., and KP. (See Expansion).

Muscles—The Intercostal Muscles Affected—♂ affl. in ♉, ♊, or ♋. (See "Diseased" under Diaphragm).

Neuralgia—Intercostal Neuralgia—♅, ♂, or ☿ affl. in ♉, ♊, or ♋; Subs at Lu.P. (3D). (See Neuralgia).

Pain—In the Intercostal Muscles—Pleurodynia—♂ affl. in ♉, ♊, or ♋; Subs at Lu.P., and CP. (See Pain).

INTERCOURSE—Sex Relations—

A Criminal Intercourse—♄ ruler of the 5th H at B., and by dir. in ☌ or evil asp. the Asc., and espec. if ♄ afflict ♂ and ♀ at B. (See Love Affairs; "Loose Morals" under Morals; Perversions).

Little or No Desire—(See Apathy, Aversion, Celibacy, Cohabitation, Deviations; "Indifferent" under Marriage; "Free from Passion" under Passion).

Sickness from Excesses In—(See Amorous, Excesses, Indulgent, Passion, Sex, Venery, etc.).

Social Intercourse—(See Companions, Environment, Friends, Love Affairs, Marriage, Social, etc.).

INTERFERENCES—In the Functions and Parts of the Body—Usually ♄ influences. (See Deformities, Functions, Hardening, Interrupted, Lameness, Paralysis, Retarded, Rhythm, Spasmodic, Suppressions, etc.).

INTERMITTENT—Occurring at Intervals—

Cramps—Intermittent Cramps—♂ affl. in ♒, and espec. in the 6th H.; ♂ in ♒ and affl. the ☽ or Asc. (See Cramps, Erratic, Muscles, Organs, Spasms, Tetany, Tics, etc.).

Fever—Intermittent Fever—Ague—Malaria—Periodic Fever—Fever at Intervals, etc.—♂ in ♌ or ♒, and espec. in the 6th H., and afflicted, or affl. the ☽ or Asc.; earthy signs on the Asc. and 6th H. at B., or at decumb., or Significators in, signify in Hor'y Q. (See Ague, Ease, Malaria, Quartan, Quotidian, Relapsing, Remission, Remittent, Semitertian, Tertian).

Organs—Intermittent Action of—Irregular Action of—(See "Irregular" under Heart; Incoordination, Irregular; "Intermittent" under Kidneys; Spasdomic).

INTERNAL—Internal Parts of the Body—The ☉ rules all internal, organic, and constitutional diseases. The Internal Generative and Excretory System are under the internal rulership of the ♍ sign. The Internal Generative System and Organs are ruled by ♀. The sign on the Asc. at B. rules the part, or organ of the body designated by such sign, both internally, externally, and structurally. (See External, Organic, Structural).

Carotids—The Internal Carotid Arteries—(See Carotid).

Chill—Cold—Internal Diseases Arising from Chill, Cold, Neglect, or Privation—(See "Internal Diseases" under Chill).

Congestions—Internal Congestions—Caused by ♄ influence, chilling the surface of the body by the influence of cold, which is ruled by ♄, and by constricting the blood vessels of the extremities and surface, being centripetal in influence. (See Centripetal, Cold, Congestions, Saturn).

Constitutional—Internal Constitutional Diseases—Ruled and presided over by the ☉, and by the ☉ afflicted at B., and by dir. (See Constitution).

Diseases—Disorders—Internal Disorders—The ☉ affl. in ♎ tends chiefly to internal disorders. (See the various paragraphs in this section. Also see Constitution, Functions, Organic, and the various diseases affecting the Internal Organs and Tissues).

Ears—Internal Disorders of—(See Deafness, Ears, Hearing).

Ease—Internal Ease In Disease—(See Ease).

Excretory System—Disorders of the Internal Excretory System—Afflictions in ♍. (See Excretion).

Force—(See "Internal" under Force).

Generative Organs—Disorders of the Internal Generative Organs and System—(See "Internal" under Generative).

Headaches—(See "Internal" under Headaches).

Heats—Internal Heats—(See "Internal" under Heat).

Hemorrhages—Internal—Denoted by ♂. (See "Internal" under Hemorrhage).

Humoural Secretions—(See "Internal" under Humours).

Neglect—Internal Disorders From—(See "Chill" in this section).

Organic Diseases—Internal and Organic—(See Organic).

Privation—Internal Disorders From—(See "Chill" in this section).

Sex Organs—Internal—Ruled by ♀, and afflictions to ♀ tend to disorders of. (See "Internal" under Generative).

Structural Diseases—Internal — (See Organic, Structural).

Women—Females—Internal Complaints of—The ☽ to the □ or ☍ ♀ by dir.; the Asc. to the ☌, P, □, or ☍ ♄ by dir., and ♄ occi. at B., dangerous internal complaints. (See the various paragraphs under Females, Women).

Zodiac Signs—Internal Rulership of—(See "Internal" under Signs).

INTERRUPTED—Interrupted Sequence In Disease—A planet turning ℞ during the course of a disease tends to somewhat disorganize the disease for the time, cause interrupted sequence until it becomes direct in motion again. Planets direct in motion tend to continuity of the disease. (See Amelioration, Better, Continuity, Course, Crises, Ease, Retrograde, Sequence, Worse). Also interruptions may take place in the action of any organ of the body. See the different organs in the alphabetical arrangement, as Bowels, Heart, Kidneys, Lungs, Stomach, etc. Also see Breathing, Elimination, Excretion, Fever, Functions, Motion, Movement, Pulse, Retention, Rhythm, Secretion, Spasmodic, Stoppages, Suppression.

INTERSTITIAL—(See Connective; "Cornea" under Eyes; Intercellular, Tissues).

INTERVALS—Of Ease and Amendment In Disease—(See Amelioration, Better, Course, Crises, Ease, Moderation, etc.).

INTESTINES—Intestinal Canal or Tract—Enteric—(See Bowels).

INTOXICATION—Intoxicating—Intoxicants—Intoxicating Liquors—

Auto-Intoxication—(See this subject).

Danger from Intoxication—The ☽ affl. in ♓, or affl. the hyleg therefrom; the ☽ to the place of the Bull's Horns.

Death by Intoxication—Death from Drink—♅ or ♄ in ♋, ♍, ♏, or ♓, and affl. the ☽; ♓ on the Asc. (See Drink; "Death" under Eating).

Strong Intoxicants—Strong Liquors—Given to the Use of—♅ affl. in ♍ or the

6th H., or afflicting the hyleg there-from. (See "Delirium Tremens" under Delirium; Diet, Dipsomania, Drink, Drunkenness, Eating, Excesses, Food, Intemperance).

INTRACTABLE—

Intractable Diseases—Difficult to Cure (See "Difficult to Cure" under Cure, Difficult).

Intractable Disposition—(See Erring).

INTROPULSION—Intropulsive—Intropulsive Congestion — The action of Cold, ruled by ♄, tends to chill the surface, drive the blood inwards, causing internal congestions by Intropulsion. Also caused by ♄ ♂ or ill-asp. the ☽ at B., or by dir. (See Centripetal, Cold, Congestion).

INTROSPECTION—Subjectivity—Introversion—The watery signs tend to an active inner life, introspection, subjectivity, brooding, melancholy, etc., and also the airy signs. The earthy and fiery signs tend more to fix the mind and attention upon outer and material things, as in extroversion, and to brood more over worldly cares, business, finance, and earthly things. Ill-Health and mental disturbances result from either of these courses if the ideas become too fixed, or the nature be unadaptable to environment. (See Brooding, Dejected, Depressed, Despondent, Fears; "Fixed Ideas" under Fixed; Gloom, Hallucinations, Hypochondria; "Low Spirits" under Low; Melancholy, Moods, Retrospective, Self-Absorbed, Worry, etc.).

INTROVERSION—Turning Inward— (See "Squint" under Eyes; "Club Feet" under Feet; Introspection).

Moral Introversion—The bad aspects of ♆ to the Significators tend to. (See Morals).

INTUITION—Intuitions—Intuitive—♆ rules the psycho-physical processes which induce to intuitive perception. Also ♅ gives intuitive powers, and intuition is the principle of ♅. (See Uranus).

Impaired Intuitions—Heavy afflictions to ♆, ♅, ♃, or ☿ at B.

Intuitive—The ☽ in the 1st H.; ♆ or ♅ in the 3rd or 9th H., and in good asp. to ☿, or the Significators; ☿ strong at B., and well-aspected, and espec. when in the 3rd H.; the 1st decan. of ♑ on the Asc., which is ruled by ☿; the 3rd face of ♎ on the Asc.; the 1st face of ♏ on the Asc.

Spiritual Intuition—♆ or ♅ strong at B., and favorably aspected. (For further and collateral study see Dreams, Faculties, Fancies, Ideals, Ideas, Imagination, Judgment, Mental, Mind, Perception, Pineal, Prophetic, Retrograde, Spirit, Spiritual, Understanding).

INTUSSUSCEPTION—(See this subject under Bowels).

INUNDATIONS — (See Floods, Rain, Storms, Waters).

INVALIDS—Invalidism—

Chronic Invalidism—The ☉ affl. in ♏, or with ♏ on the Asc. or cusp the 6th H., apt to court and hold onto disease; the ☉ or ♄ in the 6th H., and afflicted;

♀ in the 6th H., and afflicted, if excesses are indulged in; ☿ in the 6th H., and affl. by ♄; ♐, ♏, or ♑ on the Asc., thru fear of disease. (See Asthenia, Chronic, Confinement; "Constitution" under Harmony; Hospitals, Ill-Health, Lingering; "Long Illnesses" under Long; Prolonged, Sickly, Slow, Tedious; "Low" under Vitality; Wastings; "Weak Body" under Weak).

Hopeless Invalids—The ☉ ♂ ♄ at B., and by dir.; the ☉ ♂ ♄ in the 6th H., danger of many years of ill-health or invalidism, and espec. if there is a fixed sign on the cusp the 6th H. at B.; many planets in common signs at B.; common signs on the Asc. and angles. (See "Sick Bed" under Confinement).

INVASIONS—The Onset of a Disease— (See Decumbiture, Directions; "Beginning" under Disease; Events, Infections, Progression, Time, Transits).

INVENTIONS — Devices — Machinery— Danger of Accident, Injury, or Death By — (See Employment, Machinery, Weapons, etc.).

Inventors — (See Genius, Learning, Mathematical, Novelties).

INVERTED—Inverted Feet—(See "Club Feet" under Feet).

INVIGORATION — The Invigoration of the System Increased—♂ in good aspect to the Asc. at B., and by dir. (See "Good Health" under Health; Robust, Stamina, Strong, Tone, Vigor, Vitality, etc.).

INVOLUNTARY — Independent of the Will — Involuntary disorders in the body are caused by ♅ or ♂, such as contractions, spasmodic action of muscles, twitchings, etc. For the Involuntary Processes and Functions of the body, such as Assimilation, Digestion, Elimination, Excretion, Functions, Growth, Heart Action, Nutrition, etc., see these subjects in the alphabetical arrangement.

Clairvoyance—Involuntary Clairvoyance—(See Clairvoyance).

Contractions — Involuntary Contractions of Muscles — (See Contractions, Erratic, Hiccough, Jerky, Movements, Muscles, Saint Vitus, Spasmodic, Tics, Vomiting, etc.).

Discharges — (See "Involuntary" under Discharges).

Faeces — Involuntary Discharge of — (See Faeces).

Glottis—Involuntary Closure of—See Glottis, Hiccough).

Mediumship — Involuntary — (See Clairvoyance, Mediumship).

Muscular Excitement—Involuntary— (See Muscles).

Nervous System — Involuntary Nervous System—(See Sympathetic).

Trance—Involuntary—(See Trance).

Urine — Involuntary Discharge of — (See "Incontinence" under Urine). For other study along this line see Accelerated, Action, Breathing, Clonic, Constrictions, Contortions, Coordination, Cough, Cramps, Epilepsy, Exaggerated, Fainting, Fits, Gait, Incoordination, Insanity, Irregular, Motion, Pain, Pulse, Rapid, Rigidity, Spasmodic, Strictures, Tetanus, Tonic, Tremors, Twistings, Twitchings, Winking, etc.

INVOLUTION — A Rolling or Turning Inward—The Principle of ♅. (See Neptune).

INWARD PARTS — The Reins — (See Reins).

Inward Faculties—The Phantasies or Inward Faculties Prejudiced — (See "Prejudiced" under Fancies).

IODINE — Ruled by ♅. (See "Typical Drugs" under Neptune).

IPECAC — A typical Polycrest Remedy corresponding to the ♋ Sign. Used much as an Emetic. (See Cancer Sign, Emetics; "Therapeutic" under Moon).

IRASCIBLE— Vicious — High-Tempered —Wilson has observed that people who have lost one eye are usually very vicious and irascible. (See "One Eye" under Eyes; "High Temper" under Temper; Vicious).

IRIDIN — Iris — Blue Flag — A Typical Drug of ♃. (See "Typical Drugs" under Jupiter).

IRIS—The Colored Membrane of the Anterior Part of the Eye—Pupils—The Aperture, or Opening In the Iris — The Iris comes under the influence of the ♈ and ♉ Signs.

Anisocoria—(See "Inequality" in this section).

Aperture—Pupil—Disorders of—(See the various paragraphs in this section).

Argyll-Robertson Pupil — Failure of the Pupil to Respond to Light—Paralysis of the Iris — A Condition In Locomotor Ataxia—A ♄ disease. (See Mydriasis, Paralysis, in this section; Locomotor Ataxia).

Blue Flag—Iris—Iridin—(See Iridin).

Clonic Spasm—Of the Iris—Hippus— ♅ affl. in ♈ or ♉; Subs at MCP (4C), and at SP (7D). (See "Clonic" under Spasmodic).

Dilatation—Of the Pupils—(See "Mydriasis" in this section).

Disorders Of—(See the various paragraphs in this section).

Hippus — Clonic Spasm of the Iris — A Spasmodic Pupillary Movement, and Independent of Light — (See "Clonic" in this section, and under Eyeballs).

Inequality—Of the Pupils—Anisocoria —♄ ☌ the ☉ or ☽ in ♈, and may tend to a permanent contraction in the pupil of the eye affected. (See "Left Eye", "Right Eye", in Sec. 1 under Eyes).

Inflammation—Of the Iris—(See "Iritis" in this section).

Iridoplegia—(See "Paralysis" in this section).

Iris—The Plant Blue Flag—(See Iridin).

Iritis—Inflammation of the Iris—A ☉ disease; the ☉ affl. in ♈, and usually in the eye ruled by the ☉, according to the sex. (See "Left", "Right", under Eyes).

Light — Lack of Adaptation to Light —Iridoplegia — (See Argyll-Robertson, Mydriasis, Paralysis, in this section).

Mydriasis — Abnormal Dilatation of the Pupils—A ♄ disease; ruled by ♄ and the ♑ Sign, which influences rule the Peripheral Nerves, and their afflictions tend to morbid manifestations in the action of these nerves. (See Peripheral). Large and dilated pupils occur in the later stages of Locomotor Ataxia, and are known as the "Argyll-Robertson Pupil", and due to paralysis of the centers of Accommodation for the eye. (See Locomotor Ataxia). The Argyll-Robertson pupil, in the early stages of the disease, as in Locomotor Ataxia, responds to accommodation, but not to light, but in the more advanced stages of the disease does not respond either to light or accommodation, due to the strong influence of ♄ afflictions, as ♄ tends to retard function, crystallize and harden the tissues, deposit wastes, etc. (See "Saturn Influence" under Saturn). The general planetary influences listed under Locomotor Ataxia tend to Mydriasis, and abnormalities of the pupils as to accommodation, or failure to react to light. (See "Light Rays" under Light).

Mydriatics—An Agent causing Mydriasis, or Dilatation of the Pupil—Belladonna and Atropin, which are ruled by ♄, are the principal Mydriatics used. (See Belladonna).

Paralysis—Of the Iris—Iridoplegia— ♅ or ♄ ☌ the ☉ or ☽ in ♈; Subs at MCP (4C), and SP (7D). (See "Argyll", "Mydriasis", in this section; Paralysis).

Pupils—Disorders of — (See the various paragraphs in this section).

Spasm of Iris — (See "Clonic" in this section).

Tremulous Contraction—Of the Iris— Spasm of—(See Clonic, Hippus, in this section).

IRON—Ferrum—Steel—Iron is ruled by ♂, along with Oxygen, ruled by the ☉. The Iron in the blood is ruled by ♂. Iron and the ♂ influences maintain the heat of the blood. Also Iron Color is ruled by ♂. Mars assimilates the iron from the food and converts it into Haemoglobin. (See Haematopoiesis, Haemoglobin; "Fires of Life" under Life; "Mars Influence" under Mars). In the child, from birth to puberty, the Thymus Gland has charge of the work of assimilating iron from the food, and forming Haemoglobin for the blood. At adolescence ♂ and the Desire Body take charge of the work. Mars in the Asc. at B. tends to increase the iron in the system, giving a ruddy complexion, and usually red hair. (See "Red" under Hair; "Blood" under Red). Iron is a stock remedy in ♄ complaints. (See Therapeutics).

Accidents by Iron—Accidents, Injury, or Death by Iron or Steel — Wounds, Hurts, or Cuts By, etc.—The ☉ to the ♂, P., □, or ☍ ♂ by dir.; a ♂ influence; in Hor'y Q., ♂ in the Asc., and a malefic planet with the lord of the 1st H. (See Cuts, Instruments).

Blood—The Iron In the Blood—(See the first part of this Article).

Death by Iron—Danger of—The ☉ to the ♂ or ill-asp. ♂ by dir.; the ☉ to the place of Praesepe.

Injury By—(See Accidents, Death, in this section).

Iron Phosphate — The ♓ Sign Zodiac Salt, and supplies the blood and vital energy. (See "Vital Energy" under Energy; "Salts" under Zodiac).

Irons—Put In Irons In Prison—(See "Beaten In Prison" under Prison).

Marcassite—Crystallized Iron Pyrites —Ruled by the ☽.

Swallows Iron—Swallows Iron, Nails, and Glass—Case—(See Glass).

IRRATIONAL — Impaired Reason — Weakened Understanding—The ☽ and ☿ have strong rule over the rational faculties, and the ☽ and ☿ afflicted, afflicting each other, and also have no aspect or relation to the Asc., tend to impairments of the rational and reasoning faculties, and to irrational manifestations. The Sensitive, or irrational faculties are ruled by the ☽. The ☽ Sig. in ♏ in Hor'y Q. indicates one who tends to be brutish, gross, sensuous, or irrational. (See Brain Storms, Brutish, Chaotic, Confusion, Cruel, Delirium, Erratic, Erring, Faculties, Fanatical, Foolish, Frenzy, Fury, Idiocy, Imbecile, Insanity, Intellect, Judgment, Madness, Mania, Mental, Mind, Perception, Reason, Understanding, etc.).

Irrational Fears — (See Anxiety, Dejected; "Morbid Fears" under Fears; Hypochondria, Melancholy, Morbid, Worry, etc.).

IRREGULAR — Irregularities — Irregularities of the system are denoted by the ☽ when the ☽ afflicts the ☉ or Asc.; caused by an afflicted ♅; the Asc. afflicted by the ☉ or ☽.

Bowels — Bowel Action Irregular — (See "Irregular" under Bowels).

Breathing — The Breathing Irregular —(See "Irregular" under Breathing).

Circulation—Of the Blood—(See "Irregular" under Circulation).

Course of Disease—Irregular Disease — ☿ diseases. (See Course, Erratic, Peculiar, Variable, Various, etc.).

Death—By Irregularities—Lord of the 8th in the 1st, death by irregularities or suicide. (See "Death" under Indiscretions).

Disease—Irregular Course of—Disease from Irregularities — Irregular Maladies — (See Carelessness, Course, Debauched, Depraved, Diet, Dissipation, Drink, Eating, Excesses, Food, Imprudent, Indiscretions, Love Affairs, Lust, Morals, Passion, Variable, Venery, etc.).

Erratic—(See the various paragraphs under Erratic).

Feet—Irregular and Ill-Made Feet— (See "Ill-Made" under Feet).

Females — Irregular Functions In — (See "Functions", "Irregular", under Females; "Irregular" under Functions, Menses).

Fevers—Irregular Fevers — (See "Irregular" under Fevers).

Fluids — Of the Body — Irregularities of—(See Fluids).

Food — Irregularities In — (See Diet, Drink, Eating, Food, Gluttony, etc.).

Forethought — (See "Painful Complaints" under Forethought).

Functions — (See "Irregular" under Functions).

Habits—(See "Careless", "Irregular", under Habits).

Heart Action—(See "Irregular" under Heart).

Kidneys—(See "Irregular Action" under Kidneys).

Maladies—Irregular Maladies—Irregular Course of—Maladies from Irregularities — (See "Disease" in this section).

Menses—(See "Functions" under Females; "Irregular" under Functions, Menses).

Movements — Irregular — (See Movement).

Organs—Irregular and Spasmodic Action of—♅ influence. (See Action, Erratic, Intermittent, Jerky, Spasmodic).

Painful Irregularities — (See Forethought).

Parts—Of the Body—Irregular Action of—♅ influence. (See "Organs" in this section; Uranus).

Periodic Irregularities — (See Periodic).

Pulse — Irregular — (See "Irregular" under Heart; "Troubled" under Pulse).

Rash Acts—Illness from Irregularities and Rash Acts—(See Foolhardy, Rashness, Recklessness).

Sickness — Due to Irregularities — Lord of the 6th H. in the 1st, much sickness thru Irregularities. (See "Disease" in this section).

Spasms — Spasmodic Action — (See Contractions, Cramps, Spasmodic).

Stomach—(See "Irregularities" under Stomach).

Womb — Irregular Contractions of — (See "Hour Glass" under Womb).

Women—Irregular Functions In— (See "Females" in this section).

IRRESPONSIBLE—Disregardful of the Consequences of Action — Caused by the □ and ☍ aspects of ♅; also caused by the afflictions of ♂ to the ☽ and ☿, and espec. when ♂ is rising at B., and with the map otherwise weak as to mentality; the 3rd Decan. of ♓ on the Asc. (See Idiocy, Imbecility, Insanity, Irrational; "Weak Mind" under Mind; Respect, Responsibility).

Irresponsible Medium—(See Mediumship).

IRRITABLE—Irritability—

Mental Irritability — Out of Sorts — Ill-Humor — Peevish — Fretful — The ☉ ☌ ☽ at B., or within three degrees of the ☌, out of sorts, listless, and disspirited at every New ☽; the Prog. ☉ to the ☌ or ill-asp. ♅; the ☽ □ ♂; the ☽ to the ☌ or ill-asp. ♂ by dir.; the ☽, espec. if ♂ afflict the ☽ at B.; the Prog. ☽ to the □ or ☍ ♅, ♄, or ♂ in the radical map; ♅ affl. in ♋ or ♍; ♄ ☌ the Asc. by dir., ill-humored; ♂ afflicted in ♌ or ♍; the bad aspects between ♂ and ♅, and espec. when ☿, the ☽ and Asc. are also involved; pronounced in the fiery and watery signs. (See Anger, Choleric, Excitable, Fretful; "High Strung" under High; Irascible, Peevish, Quarrelsome, Sensitive; "Sun Spots" under Spots; "High Temper" under Temper).

Nervous Irritability — Irritability of the Nerves—(See Erethism, Hyperaesthesia; "Irritability", "Neurasthenia", under Nerves).

Stomach—Irritability of the Stomach Walls — (See "Irritable" under Stomach). See Irritations.

IRRITANTS—Agents, Producing Irritation — ♂ drugs and remedies. Also some Herbs of the ☉ are irritant. Counter-Irritants are ruled by ♂. (See Applications, Cantharides, Caustics; "Typical Drugs" under Mars; Mustard, Rubefacient, Stimulants, Vesicant).

IRRITATIONS—Dryness in the body is attended with diseases causing friction and irritation, as the diseases of the ☉, ♅, ♄, ♂, and ☿. (See Dryness, Friction).

Allaying Irritation—(See Demulcent).

Bronchial Irritation—(See Bronchial, Cough).

Cellular Irritation—(See Cells).

Cosmetics—Irritations Due To—(See Cosmetics).

Diarrhoea— Irritative Diarrhoea— (See Diarrhoea, Dysentery).

Intestinal — (See "Irritations" under Bowels).

Irritants—(See Irritants).

Mental Irritations—(See "Mental Irritability" under Irritable; "Irritations" under Mental).

Renal Irritations — (See "Irritation" under Kidneys).

Skin Irritations—(See Eruptions, Itch, Skin).

Stomach Irritations—(See "Irritable", "Irritations", under Stomach).

Sympathetic Irritations—(See Sympathetic).

Throat Irritations—(See Throat). The influences of the malefics, and the evil aspects of the planets tend to cause irritations to the various organs, and parts of the body. For other subjects along this line, look in the alphabetical arrangement for the subject you have in mind.

ISCHIUM—The Inferior Part of the Hip Bone — Ruled by ♐. Also under the structural rulership of ♏.

Ischiatic Affections—The ☽ affl. in ♐.

Ischiatic Pains—And Rheumatism—♄ affl. in ♐. (See "Ischium" under Hips).

ISCHURIA — Retention or Suppression of Urine—(See "Ischuria" under Urine).

ISSUE—Children—(See Children).

No Issue—(See Barren, Impotent).

ITCH—Itching—Generally considered a ♏ disease.

Barber's Itch—(See Barbers).

Intense Itching — (See "Pruritis" in this section).

Nettle Rash—Urticaria—An Ephemeral Skin Eruption with Itching—(See Urticaria).

Piles — Itching Piles — (See "Blind Piles" under Hemorrhoids).

Pruritis — Intense Itching — A ♏ disease; ♂ or ☿ afflicted in ♏; ♂ in ♍ when ♂ is the afflictor in the disease. The itching is more intense at the Full ☽. (See "Full Moon" under Moon).

Scabies — The Itch — A Contagious Parasitic Disease—(See Scabies).

The Itch—Scabies—(See Scabies).

Thighs — Itching In — (See "Itching" under Thighs).

Urticaria — Nettle Rash — (See Urticaria). See Eruptions, Exanthema, Paraesthesia, Skin Diseases.

IVY POISON—Poison Ivy—Rhus Toxicodendron—Ruled by ♄, and Ivy Poisoning is caused by ♄. One person in 18 is susceptible to it.

J

JAUNDICE—Icterus—A Yellow Coloration of the Skin—Caused by functional disturbance of the Liver. Is principally a disease of the ☽, ♄, and ♂.

Black Jaundice—A ♄ disease; ♄ in ♍ when ♄ is the afflictor in the disease, and dark brown or greenish black in exceptional cases; the ☽ in ♌, ♂ or ill-asp. ♄ (or ☿ if he be of the nature of ♄) at the beginning of an illness, or at decumb. (Hor'y). (See "Black Bile" under Bile).

Causes—Afflictions in ♋, and to the ☽, the ruler of the ♋ sign; ♄ affl. in ♊, ♋, ♌, or ♑; ♄, ♅, or ♆ in ♊, and affl. the ☉ or ☽; ♄ in an angle, occi. of the ☉ and ori. of the ☽; ♃ affl. in ♋, ♍, ♑, or ♓; ♂ in ♐, and affl. the ☽ or Asc.; a ♂ disease; ♂ affl. in ♐ in the 6th H.; a ♌ disease, and caused by afflictions in ♌; connected with the 7th degree of ♈ and ♎, and espec. if the ☽ is therein,

and affl. by ♄ or ♃; Subs at Li.P. (See Bile; "Yellow" under Complexion, Face; Liver; "Complexion" under Yellow).

Death By—Caused by ♃, his adverse aspects, and afflictions to ♃.

Jaundiced Look—In Hor'y Q., ♄ Sig. indicates such a person. (See "Yellow" under Face).

Obstructive Jaundice — Toxaemic — A ♄ disease; ♄ afflicted in ♐; ♄ ☌ ♃, and espec. when in signs which affect the liver; Subs at Li.P.

Toxaemic Jaundice — (See "Obstructive" in this section).

Weil's Disease—Enlarged Spleen, with Jaundice—(See "Weil's Disease" under Spleen).

Yellow Jaundice — The ☽ in ♑, and affl. by the ☉ or ♂ when taken ill; a ♂ disease; a ♌ disease, and afflictions in ♌.

JAWS — Maxillary — The upper Jaw is ruled by ♈. The lower Jaw, or Mandible, is ruled by ♉. (See Appearance, Face).

Accidents To — Injuries, Fracture, Hurts, or Wounds To — ♄ or ♂ affl. in ♈ or ♉ at B., and by dir., and espec. when these signs were on the Asc. at B.

Diseases Of — (See Gums, Necrosis, Pyorrhoea, Teeth).

Lock-Jaw—(See Lock-Jaw).

Lower Jaw — Mandible — Ruled by ♉, and afflictions in ♉ tend to disorders of, and to decay of the teeth of the lower jaw. (See Chin, Gums, Teeth).

Swollen Jaw — ♂ afflicted in ♉ or ♏; afflictions in ♉ or ♏.

Upper Jaw — The Superior Maxillary —Ruled by ♈, and afflictions in ♈ tend to disorders of. The upper jaw tends to overhang the lower jaw when the 5th face of ♒ is on the Asc. at B.

JEALOUSY—A ♄ affliction; ♄ Sig. in ✶ or △ the ☽; ♄ Sig. in ♎; ♄ ☌, P., □, or ♉ ♀, a demon of jealousy in the married life; the evil directions of ♄ to the ☉, ☽, ☿, Asc., or M.C.; the ☉ affl. in the ♄ sign ♑; ♅ affl. in ♉ or ♏; ♂ in the 6th H. in ♉, ♌, or ♏, and affl. by the ☉, ☽, or ♄; ♀ affl. in ♏; ♀ well-dig. at B. tends to jealousy, and often without cause; ⊕ to the ill-asps. ♀ by dir., jealous of his wife; the 2nd face of ♈ on the Asc. (See Delusions, Doubts, Fears, Hallucinations, Hate; "Grief", "Jealousy", under Love Affairs; Malice; "Injured" under Men; Mistrustful, Obsessions, Poison, Suicide, Suspicious, Treachery, etc.).

JEJUNUM — The Upper Two-Fifths of the Small Intestine—Ruled by ♍. Obstructions in are caused by ♄ in ♍, and espec. when ♄ is in the 6th H. in this sign; Subs at UPP. (See "Small Intestines" under Bowels; Colon, Ileum).

JERKINGS — Spasmodic Movements — Incoordinations, etc.—

Jerky Movements — A ♅ disease; caused by ♅ influence, and afflictions to the Organ of Coordination situated in ♉, and ruled by the ♉ Sign. Also caused by ♅ affl. in the 6th H. (See Contractions, Convulsions, Coordination, Cramps, Epilepsy, Erratic; "Nystagmus" under Eyeballs; Fits, Hiccough, Incoordination, Involuntary, Irregular, Motion, Motor, Movements, Muscles, Nerves, Spasmodic, Tics, Twitchings, etc.).

Jerky Respiration—Irregular Respiration or Breathing—(See "Jerky" under Breathing).

JOINTS—Articulations—The Joints in general are ruled by ♄ and the ♑ Sign. The subjects in this Article have to do more with the abstract conditions which affect the Joints, Diseases of the Joints, etc. For the various Joints of the body, such as those of the Arms, Ankles, Elbows, Feet, Fingers, Hands, Hips, Knees, Legs, Shoulders, Wrists, etc., see these subjects in the alphabetical arrangement.

Accidents To—Injuries To—Hurts To, etc.—Caused generally by ♄ afflictions, and to a joint, or joints, in the part of the body afflicted by ♄ at B., and by dir. (See Bones, Dislocations, Fractures).

Ankylosis — (See Ankylosis; "Inflammation", "Stiff", in this section).

Arthralgia — (See "Gout", "Pain", in this section).

Arthritis—Inflammation of a Joint— Pain In—Excessive Heat In—Gout In — Arthritis Deformans — Rheumatoid Arthritis—♄ ☌ or ill-asp. ♂; ♂ ☌ or ill-asp. ♄ or ♃. Arthritis Deformans, and also Rheumatoid Arthritis, are caused by ♄, and in the part afflicted by ♄ at B., and thru the retention of wastes, by mineral deposits, by crystallization, thickening, and hardening. (See Deformities, Gout, Inflammation, Pain, Rheumatism, in this section; "Arthritis" under Hips).

Articular Rheumatism—(See "Rheumatism" in this section).

Atrophy—Articular Muscular Atrophy of the Legs—(See Atrophy, Legs).

Bones — Of the Joints — Ruled by ♄, and the afflictions of ♄, or afflictions to ♄, tend to disorders of the bony structure of the joints. Also the bones of the joints are affected by the excessive heat of ♂, tending to melting of the joint, adhesions, and ankylosis, resulting in a stiff joint. (See Ankylosis).

Bursa—Bursitis—A Small Sac Formation In the Joint—(See Bursa).

Chronic Inflammation — In a Joint — (See "Inflammation" in this section).

Deformities Of—Arthritis Deformans — Chronic Inflammation of a Joint, with Deformity — Caused by mineral deposits, and the retention of Urea by ♄. (See Arthritis, Gout, Rheumatism, in this section).

Diseases Of — Joints In the Different Parts of the Body Are Liable to Disease—The ☉, ☽, or ♄ affl. in ♑, or ascending at the Vernal Equinox, and ♄ afflicting People and Countries under ♑, great sufferers with the joints. (See the various paragraphs in this section).

Dislocations—Luxations—(See Dislocations).

Elbow Joints—(See Elbows).

Enlarged Joint — (See Deformities, Gout, Rheumatism, Swollen, in this section).

Fingers — (See "Ankylosis" under Fingers).

Fluids Of—(See Synovial).

Fracture Of—(See Fractures).

Gout In—Pains In—Afflictions to the ☽; ♄ strong at B., as in the Asc. or M.C., or in one of his own signs, as in ♑, and affl. the ☉, ☽, Asc., or hyleg. (See Arthritis, Deformities, Inflammation, Rheumatism, in this section; "Joints" under Gout).

Granulations In — ♄ influence. (See "Joints" under Feet).

Hardening—Crystallization—The work of ♄ by pathological and abnormal mineral deposits and the retention of wastes. A destructive process of ♄. The ♄ influence and afflictions tend to the hardening of the synovial membrane, and lack of secretion of the synovial fluid, tending to stiffen and dry up the joints. (See Crystallization, Fluids, Hardening, Synovial).

Heat—Excessive Heat In the Joints—(See Ankylosis, Arthritis, Bones, in this section).

Hip-Joint Disease—Arthritis of—(See "Hip-Joint Disease" under Hips).

Inflammation Of — Arthritis — (See "Arthritis" in this section). Chronic Inflammation in the Joints is due to ♄ afflictions, and with ♅ especially strong and afflicted at B. (See "Arthritis" in this section).

Injuries To—(See "Accidents" in this section).

Knee Joint—(See Knees).

Large Joints—Well-Set—(See "Body" under Large; "Large" under Limbs).

Leg Joints — Arthritis of — Arthritic Muscular Atrophy In—(See "Arthritis" under Legs).

Lubrication; Luxations—(See Dislocations).

Muscles—Arthritic Muscular Atrophy In Legs—(See "Arthritis" under Legs).

Pain In—Arthralgia—The ☽ in airy signs and affl. by ♄ or ♂; the ☽ in ♊ and affl. by the ☉, ♄, or ♂; the ☽ in ♎ or ♐, in ☌ or ill-asp. ♄ (or ☿ if he be of the nature of ♄) at the beginning of an illness or at decumb.; ♄, ♅, or ♆ in ♒ and affl. the ☉, ☽, or Asc. The pains tend to be in the joints over the entire body if at decumb., or when first taking sick, the ☽ is under the Sun's beams, or in ☌ with ♄, ♅, or ♂. (See Arthritis, Dengue, Gout; "Pains" under Whole; Arthritis, Gout, Inflammation, in this section).

Rheumatism In — Articular Rheumatism — Chronic Deformans — A ♄ disease; the work of ♄ deposits of Urea in the joints; a ♅ disease, and afflictions in ♅; ♄ in ♅; the ☽ affl. in ♅; the ☉ affl. in ♐. (See Gout, Rheumatism; Arthritis, Gout, in this section).

Sac—A Small Sac Formation In the Joint—(See Bursa).

Shoulder Joint — Disorders of — (See Shoulders).

Stiff Joints—Ankylosed—Hardened—Enlarged—Swollen—Crystallization of —♄ influence. Caused by the retention and deposit of Urea in the joints by ♄. (See Ankylosis; Arthritis, Deformities, Gout, Hardening, Inflammation, Rheumatism, in this section).

Subluxations—A Partial Dislocation —(See Subluxations).

Swollen Joints—Enlarged—Inflamed —Gout In—Stiff Joints, etc.—(See Dengue; Arthritis, Gout, Inflammation, Rheumatism, Stiff, in this section).

Synovial Fluid—Synovial Membranes —Disorders of—(See Lubrication, Synovial; "Hardening" in this section).

Thickening—(See "Arthritis" in this section).

Union of Bones—(See "Bones" in this section).

Well-Jointed Body—☿ oriental at B.

Well-Set Joints—(See "Large" in this section).

Whole Body—Pains In the Joints Over the Whole Body—(See "Pain" in this section).

Wrists—(See Wrists).

JOURNEYS—Short Journeys—Long Journeys—Travel—Inland Journeys— Travel In the Native Land—♅ is the principal planet causing journeys. Also the 3rd and 9th H. are the houses of Travel and Journeys, the 3rd H. indicating inland travel and short journeys, and the 9th H. Foreign Travel, Voyages, etc. Malefic planets in these houses at B., or a malefic as lord of these houses, indicate danger in travel, while the benefic planets in these houses tend to benefits and gain by travel, either in business or health matters. These matters are further considered under the subjects of Abroad, Foreign Lands, Location, Native Land, Railroads, Residence, Ships, Travel, Vehicles, Voyages, etc. The following subjects and paragraphs are listed here, as they have to do with the welfare of the native, the health, environment, business success, the mental and spiritual welfare, etc., and to assist with fore-knowledge to avoid dangers which may lead to accidents, injuries, ill-health, sickness, or death thru journeys, by traveling or locating in a wrong direction from the birthplace. Some people, according to their maps of birth, should remain at their birthplace all thru life for the best of success and health, while others should remove, or even locate in a Foreign Land. People born in Northern Latitudes, and who have nearly all their planets below the horizon at B., can, by removing to the South Latitudes, reverse their maps and bring their planets above the Earth, and near the Zenith, and into greater power, and thus a career which would have been obscure in the land of birth may become very notable, powerful, and successful in the opposite Hemisphere.

Abroad—(1) Avoid Journeys Abroad —The ☉ hyleg, and the ☉ to the ☌ or ill-asp. ♂ by dir.; the ☽ in the 9th H. in a Solar Rev., and affl. by ♄ or ♂; the ☽ to the ☌ or ill-asp. ♂ by dir., and ♂ affl. the ☽ at B., or ♂ occupying the 9th H.; ♆, ♅, ♄, or ♂ ruler of the 8th H. at B., and any of them in the 9th H. at a Solar Rev.; ♄ ascending at B., and the ☉ to the ☌ or ill-asp. ♄ by dir.; ♂ ☌ the ☉ at a Solar Rev.; malefics in the 9th H. unless they be strong by sign and aspect; ruler of the 9th H. at B. in the 4th H. at a Solar Rev., and afflicted; the M.C. to the ☌ or evil asp. the ☽ if the ☽ be weak and afflicted at B.; lord of the 2nd H. in the 9th H., and afflicted. (See Abroad, Drowning, Foreign Lands, Shipwreck; the various paragraphs in this section). (2) Should Take Journeys Abroad, or Live Abroad—Benefics in the 9th H. at B., and with malefics in the 4th H., or in the Sign ruling the Native Land. (See "Health" under Abroad; Foreign Lands, Location, Native Land; "Place of Birth" under Place; Residence, Travel, Voyages).

Accidents On Journeys—Danger of—Injuries—Hurts—Malefics in the 3rd or 9th H. at B. (See "Travels" under Falls; Railroads, Robbers, Ships, Shipwreck; "Accidents" under Travel; "Injuries" under Voyages; Long Journeys, Short Journeys, Voyages, in this section).

Avoid Journeys—A Bad Time for Journeys—The ☽ to the ill-asps. ☿ by dir.; ♑ to the bad asps. the ☽, and espec. if either rule the 3rd or 9th H.; ♄ to the ill-asps. ♃ if either be ruler of the 3rd or 9th H.; the M.C. to the ♂, P, □, or ☍ the ☽ if the ☽ be weak and afflicted at B. (See "Abroad", and the various paragraphs in this section; "Avoid", "Bad Time For", under Travel; "Danger" under Voyages).

Bad Time For—(See "Avoid", and the various paragraphs in this section).

Bites—On Journeys—(See "Journeys" under Bites).

Brings a Journey—Or Voyage—The M.C. to the ✳ or △ ♂. (See "Disposes To", "Voyage Soon Follows" under Voyages).

Burns—On a Journey—(See "Journeys" under Burns).

Cuts—On a Journey—(See "Travel" under Cuts).

Dampness—(See "Wet Journeys" in this section).

Danger On Journeys—(See Maritime, Navigation, Ships, Shipwreck; "Danger" under Travel; Voyages; "Accidents", and the various paragraphs in this section).

Death On a Journey—Death During Travel—(See Drowning; "Death" under Railroads, Sea, Ships, Shipwreck, Travel, Voyages).

Drowned—On a Journey—(See Drowning, Shipwreck; "Death" under Sea, Voyages, Water).

Exposure—On Journeys—And the Health Suffers From—(See "Travel" under Exposure).

Fatigue—(See "Sickness" under Travel).

Fever—(See "Fever" under Voyages).

Fire—On Short Journeys or At Sea—(See "Ships", "Short Journeys", under Fire).

Food—Lack of On Journeys—(See Desert; "Privations" under Sea; "Food" under Travel).

Good Time—For Journeys—Good Time for Short Journeys and Inland Travel—The ☉ to the good asps. ♂, and the ☉ or ♂ ruler of the 3rd H. at B.; the ☉ to the P. or good asps. the ☽; the ☉ to the cusp the 3rd H. by dir.; the ☉ by Periodic Rev. to the good asps. ☿; the ☽ by dir. to the good asps. the Asc. if the ☽ was well-aspected at B.; the ☽ incr. in light, and free from affliction of malefics, and well-aspected by ♃ or ♀; the ☽ in the 3rd H. at B., and to the good asps. the ☽ by dir.; the ☽ in the 5th H., and well-aspected by benefics; the ☽ to the good asps. the ☉, and espec. if the direction fall in the 3rd H.; the ☽ to the ♂ ☿ by tr. or dir., and the aspect fall in the 3rd H., or the ☽ or ☿ be in the 3rd H. at B.;

the ☽ to the ♂ or good asp. ⊕; the ☽ to the cusp the 3rd H. by dir.; the ☽ to the ♂ ♃ by tr. or dir.; the Periodic Direction of ♄ to the good asps. the radical ♂; ♃ to the ♂ the ☽ in the 3rd H.; ♃ by Periodic Rev. to the ♂ the radical ☽; ♂ by Periodic Rev. to the good asps. the ☽; the M.C. to the ♂ or P. asp. the ☽ if the ☽ rule the 3rd H. at B.; the M.C. to the good asps. the ruler of the 3rd H.; the M.C. to the ♂, P., or good asp. ☿; ☿ to the good asps. the ☽ by dir. or tr.; the ruler of the 1st H. by tr., when a benefic, to the cusp the 3rd H., or to the good asp. the ruler of the 3rd H. at B.; when ♂, the ☽ or ☿ are in the 3rd H. at B., a journey is usually made when the ☽, or planet, comes to the cusp the 3rd H. by Periodic Direction in Mundo; a benefic in the Asc. or an angle. (See "Good Time For" under Voyages).

Health—(1) The Health Suffers On a Journey—The native is liable to sickness and a fever on a journey if it is started in a ♄ or ♂ hour, or with ♄, ♂, or other malefics in the 3rd or 9th H. at B., or by dir., and the malefic afflicting the ☉, ☽, Asc., M.C. or Hyleg; taking, beginning, or returning from a journey when the ☽ is in the Asc. (See "Sickness" under Travel). (2) Journeys On Account of Health—Travels for His Health—☿ affl. in the 6th H. at B., travels on account of the health. Travel for the health should be made in the directions in which ♃ and ♀ are posited at B., and avoid the directions and Countries indicated by the directions and sign positions of malefics at B. (See "Travel" under Health).

Illness On a Journey—(See "Health" in this section).

Injury On a Journey—(See "Accidents" in this section).

Inland Journeys—Land Journeys—Short Journeys by Rail or Other Vehicle—Are governed principally by ☿. The ☽ to the ♂ ♃ inclines to. (See "Short Journeys" in this section).

Land Journeys—(See "Inland", "Short", in this section).

Long Journeys—Are governed by ♃; ♃ in the 9th H., and favorably aspected, tends to success and good health on long journeys. There is danger of accidents or death on long journeys when the ruler of the 8th H. at B. is in the 7th at a Solar Rev., and espec. if the nativity be a violent one. (See "Accidents", "Sickness", under Abroad; Drowning, Foreign, Sea, Ships, Shipwreck; "Foreign Travel" under Travel; "Good Time" under Voyages).

Many Journeys—(See "Many Changes" under Residence; "Love Of", "Wanderer", under Travel).

Ocean Journeys—(See Sea, Ships, Shipwreck, Voyages; "Fortunate", "Perils", under Water).

Pirates—Danger or Death By On Journeys—(See Pirates).

Privation On Journeys—(See "Privations" under Seas).

Railroad Journeys—Injury or Death By—(See "Short Journeys" in this section).

Ships—Journeys By—Injury, Death, or Discomfort By—(See Maritime, Navigation, Sea, Ships, Shipwreck, Voyages).

Short Journeys—Inland Journeys—Railroad Travel—Danger of Injury or Death By—The 3rd H., and planets therein, rule short journeys. Short journeys should not be made at these times, or under the following aspects and influences—The ☽ to the ☌ or ill-asp. ♅ by dir., and the ☽ in the 3rd H. at B.; the ☽ in the 3rd H. at the Vernal Equi., lady of the year, and afflicted; ♅ in the 3rd H. at B., and afflicted; ♅ afflicted in ♓; ♅ affl. at B., and to the ☌ or ill-asp. the Asc. by dir.; ♅ influence and afflictions in the 3rd H. at B., and by dir., tend to death on railways or following stock if the map of birth shows a violent end; ♅ setting at B., and in ☍ the Luminaries, and when ♅ again afflicts the Lights by dir.; ♄ by tr. or dir. in ☌, □, or ☍ the radical ☿; ♃ in the 3rd H., and afflicted, may be in an accident, but escapes injury (see "Escapes" under Travel); ♂ in the 3rd H., and afflicted; ♂ in the 1st H., and affl. by ♃; ♂ affl. in ♓; ♂ in the 3rd H., and affl. the ☉ or ☽; ♂ to the cusp the 3rd H. by dir.; ♂ by Periodic Rev. to the ill-asps. the ☽, or to the ☌ or ill-asp. ♅, and espec. if ♂ be in the 3rd or 9th H. at B.; ♂ progressed to the ☌ or ill-asp. ☿, or vice versa; ☿ in the 8th H. at B., and afflicted, avoid short journeys; ☿ in the 3rd H. at B. in ☌ ♄, ♅, or ♂, and otherwise afflicted by the ☽, ♃, or ♀; malefics in the 3rd H., and afflicted, or afflicting the ☉ or ☽; lord of the 8th or 11th H. a malefic, in the 3rd H., and afflicted; the 2nd Decan. of ♓, ruled by ♂, on the cusp of the Asc. at B. (See Railroads, Travel, Vehicles; Accidents, Avoid, Inland, and the various paragraphs in this section).

Sickness—On Journeys—(See "Health" in this section).

Stings—Bites or Stings On Journeys—(See "Journeys" under Bites).

Sudden Journeys—The ☽ by Periodic Rev. to the aspects of ♅ in the radical map.

Travel—(See the various paragraphs under Maritime, Navigation, Sea, Ships, Shipwreck, Travel, Voyages; "Brings a Journey", "Health", and the various paragraphs in this section).

Unfavorable Journeys—(See "Avoid", and the various paragraphs in this section; Railroads, Sea, Ships, Shipwreck, Travel, Voyages).

Voyages—(See the various paragraphs under Sea, Ships, Shipwreck, Voyages).

Wet Journeys—Health Suffers By—♄ in the 3rd H. at B. (See "Journeys" under Moisture).

Wind Storms—Danger From On Journeys—(See "Storms" under Wind).

JOY—Joviality—Jolly—Mirth—Gladness—Cheerfulness—Joy and life come from the ☉. Also ♀ is the author of mirth and cheerfulness, and espec. with ♀ in the Asc. or M.C. at B., or in ☌ with ☿. Jupiter rising at B. also gives a cheerful disposition, and joviality is

a ♃ trait. Other influences which produce joy and gladness are the ☽ in ♎ or ♓, and well-aspected; the ☽ incr. in light, and applying to ♃ unless ♂ be in □ or ☍ to ♃; ♃ Sig. in ♒; ♂ well-aspected in ♐; ♐ on the Asc. (See Cheerfulness, Contentment, Happiness, Life, Mild, Mirth; "Peace of Mind" under Mind; Optimistic, Sanguine).

Life Robbed of Its Joy—The ☉ or ☽ in the 12th H., and affl. by malefics; the ☉ or ☽ ☌ ♄; the ☉ ☌ ♄ in 12th H.; the ☽ in ☍ ♄ or ♀; ♇ □ ☿, due to obsessions, hallucinations, morbid fears, and adverse Astral influences; ♄ □ the ☉, ☽, or ♀; ♄ affl. in the 12th H.; ♃ or ♀ affl. in the 12th H. (See Confinement, Dejected, Depressed, Despondent, Hypochondria; "Low Spirits" under Low; Melancholy, Morbid, Obsessions, Sadness, Smiles, Sorrow, Worry).

JUDGES—Magistrates—The Law—Sentence by Law—Punishment by Law—Judicial Condemnation—Death or Imprisonment by Sentence of Law—See the following subjects in the alphabetical arrangement when not considered here—

Beheaded; Burned At Stake—(See "Stake" under Burns).

Death—By Sentence of Law—Judicial Condemnation—Judicial Execution—Judicial execution is strongly denoted by the 17° ♊ and ♐, and planets which may occupy these degrees, or degrees also in □ to them. Death by Law is denoted when ♃ is involved in configurations otherwise indicating a violent death, as ♃ is said to rule Judges and the Law. The mutable signs, and espec. ♊ and ♐, indicate the homicidal tendency, or Judicial Execution. Fixed signs also indicate such a death, and espec. when ♄ is in a fixed sign, such as ♉, and afflicting the hyleg. Other testimonies are as follows—The ☉ Sig. □ or ☍ ♂; the ☽ to the ill-asps. ☿ by dir., and ☿ or the ☽ afflicted by malefics at B.; the ☽ incr., or at Full, sepr. from ☿ and applying to ♂; ♅ ☌ ♂ in ♈; ♄ or ♂ with Caput Algol, and the ☽ with Deneb.; ♄ in a fixed sign □ or ☍ the ☉, and contrary in condition, or ♄ occi. of the ☽, and the ☽ be succedent to him; ♃ bearing testimony to ♂, and ♃ afflicted at B.; ♃ affl. the hyleg by dir.; ♃ affl. at B., and afflicting the hyleg by dir., and holding the dominion of death, and espec. where a violent death is indicated; ♂ in a human sign, and afflicting ♃; ♂ just setting in ♉ the Asc.; ♂ Sig. in □ or ☍ the ☉, and ☿ □ ♂, death by a Public Executioner, and espec. if the ☉ is in the 10th H.; lord of the 8th H. a malefic, and in the 10th, and espec. if the lord of the 8th or 10th afflict the lord of the Asc. from fixed signs; lord of the 10th in the 12th H.; the M.C. to the ill-asps. the ☉, ☽, or ♂ by dir. (See the various paragraphs in this section).

Decapitation—(See Beheaded).

Electrocution—(See Electricity).

Enemies—Has Many Enemies Among Magistrates—♀ Sig. □ or ☍ ♃.

Execution—(See the various subjects and references under Execution).

Fortunate Among Magistrates—The ☽ Sig. ☌ ♃.

Fugitives; Gallows—Sentenced to Death On—(See Hanging).

Guillotine; Halter—Death By—(See Hanging).

Hand of Man—Death By—(See "Hand of Man" under Man).

Hanging; Ignoble Death—(See Ignoble).

Impalement; Imprisonment—(See Prison).

Law—Sentenced and Punished by the Law—(See the various paragraphs in this section).

Many Enemies—Among Magistrates—(See "Enemies" in this section).

Murderer—Convicted and Sentenced for Murder—(See Assassins, Homicide, Murder).

Officers of the Law—(See Officers).

Prisons—(See "Imprisonment", and the various paragraphs under Prison).

Public Death—Public Execution—♂ Sig. □ or 8 the ☉, and ☿ also □ ♂, and espec. if the ☉ be in the 10th H. (See "Death" in this section; Execution; "Public Death", under Public).

Punishment—By Law—(See Punishment; the various paragraphs in this section).

Strangulation—Suffocation by Law—(See Hanging).

Tragical Death—(See Tragical).

Untimely Death—(See Untimely).

Violent Death—(See Execution, Hanging; "Death" under Violent; the variour paragraphs in this section. Also for other influences which contribute to sentence and punishment by Law, see Cheating, Criminal, Depraved, Disgrace, Dishonest, Downfall, Drunkenness, Evil, Gambling, Highwaymen, Honour, Liars, Libelers, Perjury, Perversions, Pirates, Plots, Poison, Reputation, Reverses, Robbers, Ruin, Scandal, Sedition, Self-Undoing, Thieves, Treachery; "Tendency to Violence" under Violent, etc.

JUDGMENT—The Act of Judging—The Decisions—The Mental Faculties—Discrimination, etc.—

Bad Judgment—Errors of Mind—Erratic Judgment—Void of Solid Judgment—Poor Judgment—Lack of Discrimination and Foresight—Lack of Tact—A Prejudiced or Biased Mind—The ☉ ♂ ☿, combust, or in □ or 8 ♅, ♄, ♃, or ♂; the ☉ afflicted and ill-dignified at B.; the ☉ Sig. ♂ ☿, not much sound judgment; the ☽ □ or 8 ☿; the ☽ and ☿ unconnected with each other or the Asc.; the ☽ Sig. ♂ ♄, commits many errors of judgment; ♃ Sig. □ or 8 ☿; ♃ to the ill-asps. ☿ by dir., wrong opinions; ♂ afflicted in the 10th H., lacks discrimination; ☿ alone ruler of the mind, and also tends to be ill-disposed; ☿ □ or 8 ♄, weak judgment, and views things thru a false medium; ☿ ♂ or combust the ☉, and ☿ receiving no assistance from the benefics; ☿ Sig. ♂ ☉; ☿ ill-dignified at B., of little judgment, and lacking in tact; ☿ in evil asp. to ♂ tends to false judgment; the 1st Decan. of ♊ on the Asc. tends to perverted judgment. (See Anarchists, Chaotic, Confused, Cruel, Delu-

sions, Deviations, Dull, Eccentric, Emotions, Erratic, Examinations, Faculties, Fanatical, Fancies, Forethought, Hallucinations, Hasty, Ideals, Ideas; "Ill-Disposed" under Ill; Illusions, Imaginations, Imbecility, Impairments, Impractical, Improvident, Impulsive, Incompetency, Indiscretions, Injudicious, Intellect, Memory, Mental (see "Shallow" under Mentality; Mind (see "Weak" under Mind); Notions, Opinions, Peculiar, Perception, Perversions, Reason, Temper, Uncontrolled, Understanding, Vicious, Violent, Void Of).

Body—Judging the Body—(See Appearance, Body, Form, Physical, Shape, Stature, etc).

Disease—The Judgment and Diagnosis of Disease—In order to judge of the disease, its mildness or severity, and its possible outcome, the following parts and influences of the map of birth should be considered—The ☉, ☽, and Asc., and their strength and afflictions; the Hyleg, its strength, aspects and afflictions; the power of the malefics and their afflictions to the Hyleg; the mutual afflictions among the planets; planets elevated, rising, or setting; malefics elevated above the benefics or hyleg (which tend to make the disease more forceful); planets in the 6th H., the House of Health; the house position of the lord of the 6th H., his nature, whether benefic or malefic, and aspects. Also the degree of the vitality should be studied, the powers of recuperation and resistance to disease, and the quality of the disease; the Significator of the disease; the nature of the planet causing the disease, and the transits, progression, directions, house and sign position of such planet at birth and now, and how the afflicting planet affects the radical map, etc. Diseases not shown, indicated, or accounted for by the radical map, can oftentimes be found and indicated in the prenatal map, the map for the time of conception, or the aspects to the ☽ at the monthly periods during gestation. Also the Heliocentric positions of planets may help to explain the nature and cause of the disease. (See Acquired, Acute, Anareta, Chronic, Constitution, Course, Curable, Diagnosis, Diathesis, Directions; "Causes" under Disease; Disturbances, Duration, Events, Fatal, Heredity, Hyleg, Incurable, Long, Majority, Mild, Modification, Nature, Organic, Parts, Prenatal, Prognosis, Quality, Recovery, Recuperation, Remedy (see "Incapable" under Remedy); Resistance, Severe, Short, Sixth House, Slight, Structural, Type, Vitality, etc.).

Good Judgment—Sensible—Sound Judgment—Tactful—Has Good Foresight, Forethought, and Discrimination—Practical—An Accurate Reasoner—The ☉ well-dignified at B.; the ☽ well-aspected, dignified, and in good relation to ☿ and the Asc.; ♃ strong at B., and well-aspected; ♃ Sig. in 8; ♃ Sig. ⁎ or △ ☿; ☿ Sig. ⁎ or △ ♃, possesses solid sense; ☿ in the Zodiac in P. asp. ♄, accurate judgment; the 3rd face of ♏ on the Asc.; ♂ a strong ruler at B., and well-aspected, gives moderately good judgment. (See "Active Mind" under Active; "Mental Energy" under Energy; Learning; "Quickened" under Mentality; "Brightened", "Clear", "Judging", "Quality", "Sound", "Strong", under Mind; Practical, Prudent, Sagacious).

Health — Judging the Health — (See "Judging the Health" under Health).

Mind—Judging the Mind—(See "Judging the Mind" under Mind).

JUGULAR VEINS—Ruled by the ♌ sign. (See Veins).

JUICES—Fluids—

Digestive Juices — (See "Fluids" under Digestion; "Juices" under Gastric). See Acids, Fluids, Glands, Secretions.

JUMPING SPASM — (See "Jumps Forward" under Manner; "Jumping" under Spasmodic).

JUPITER — The Planet Jupiter — The Greater Benefic. The general influence of ♃ is benevolent, and his aspects never kill unless configurated with malefics in a train of evil directions. By nature he is positive, masculine, electric, warm and moist. (See "Qualities" in this section). He is the Author of Justice, and when the ruling planet at B. tends to make the native just, generous, kind, jovial, and religious. In order that the student can the more quickly refer to the various influences of this planet, I have arranged this Article into three Sections. Section One—The Influences of Jupiter; Section Two—Jupiter Rules; Section Three—The Diseases of Jupiter.

— SECTION ONE —

THE INFLUENCES OF JUPITER—In this section the influences with which ♃ has to do, and over which he presides, are arranged alphabetically under subjects for quicker reference.

Activity — Seat of — The Liver is the seat of ♃ activity. There he forms Glycogen which is used as fuel for the body during muscular activity. (See Glycogen, Liver).

Afflictions Of—Evil Aspects of—♃ afflicts only by his □ and ☍ aspects, but the good influence of ♃ is vitiated by his ☌ with ♄. By his bad aspects, ♃ has the evil effect of producing congestion, undue blood pressure, apoplectic conditions, diseases arising from surfeits, gormandizing habits, clogging of the system, and indicates overfunctional activity of the parts ruled by the sign he is in at B., or by tr. or dir. The evil aspects of ♃ to the ☉, ☽, and planets tend to have a very evil and detrimental influence. (See "Aspects" in this section; "Death" in Sec. 3 of this Article).

Anareta — ♃ can act as Anareta in morbid deaths. (See Anareta).

Angel Of—Zadkiel.

Aspects Of—For the influences of his evil aspects see "Afflictions Of" in this section. The good influences of ♃, by his favorable aspects, are the preservation of life, restoration of health, elaboration, conservation of energies, and to insure fruitfulness, temperateness, etc. No aspects of ♃ or ♀ alone

cause disease, but only as configurated with malefics. In diseases caused by ♄ the good aspects of ♃ help more than those of ♀. (See "Directions" in this section).

Assimilation—And Growth—Are aided and furthered by the work of ♃. (See Assimilation, Growth).

Astral Body—In the Astral Body, ♃ has direct relation to the breath, lungs, liver, and Blood. (See Astral).

Author Of—♃ is the author of justice, temperance, and moderation.

Benefics—♃ and ♀ are called the benefic planets. (See Benefics).

Births—Normal births are ruled by ♃. (See Birth).

Children — ♃ is fruitful, and a giver of children. His good directions to the Midheaven, or to the fruitful places in the map, promise a child. (See "Birth of a Child" under Children; Fruitfulness).

Classification Of — ♃ is classed as a hot, airy, moist, fruitful, positive, masculine, and benefic planet. (See "Qualities" in this section).

Cold and Dry—♃ exerts a temperate influence between the extremes of cold and dry, and tends to warmth and moisture.

Colors — ♃ rules violet in the Solar Spectrum. Also said to rule blue, purple; red mixed with green. (See Color).

Conservation—♃ and ♀ both have to do with the nourishing, supporting, conserving, and aphetic processes, the storing of various cell substances, selection, transformation, filtration, and reservation.

Directions Of — The good directions of ♃ to the M.C. promise a child. The good directions of ♃ to the hyleg at B., and by dir. tend to good health, and also to spare life in a severe sickness. (See Benefics, Directions; "Good Health" under Health; "Spared" under Life).

Dominates—♃ dominates the Arterial System. (See Arteries).

Dry and Cold — (See "Cold" in this section).

Energies — The influence of ♃ is to conserve the energies by his good aspects.

Evil Aspects Of—(See "Afflictions Of" in this section).

Expansion and Heat—♃ being a positive and electric planet tends to produce heat and expansion in the body, and to give a positive, confident, forceful state of mind.

Fat—♃ has charge of the disposition and distribution of Fat in the body. Also, ♃ adds the fatty constituents to the milk, and other fluids. (See Fat).

Filtration — (See "Substance" under Cells).

Foetus — The Foetus becomes enveloped with the Amniotic Fluid under ♃ influence. (See Foetus).

Fuel — Of the Body — (See "Activity" in this section).

Full Effects Of — The full effects of the ♃ influence for good or ill are not felt until middle life, and especially when he is in ♋ or the 4th H. at B. (See Middle Life).

Glycogen—♃ forms the Glycogen in the Liver. (See "Activity" in this section).

Good Influences Of — (See "Aspects" in this section).

Greater Fortune—Greater Benefic—♃ is called the Greater Fortune, or Greater Benefic, and ♀ is called the Lesser Benefic. (See Benefics).

Growth and Assimilation—(See "Assimilation" in this section).

Heat and Expansion — (See "Expansion" in this section).

Herbs — The Herbs Ruled by ♃ — Typical Plants of — (See "Jupiter Group" under Herbs, Muscles; "Typical Drugs" in this section).

Hour — ♃ Hour — (See Bleeding; "Hours" under Planets).

Hyleg — ♃ as Hyleg — (See Hyleg). When ♃ is not Hyleg, his good aspects to the ☉, ☽, Asc., or Hyleg are a powerful protective agent.

Justice—(See "Author Of" in this section).

Life-Saving Power — Neither of the Benefics will save life if the lords of the 6th and 8th Houses are in evil aspect to each other. (See "Aspects", "Directions", in this section).

Metal Of—Tin. (See Therapeutics).

Middle Life — (See "Full Effects Of" in this section).

Milk — ♃ adds the fatty constituents to milk. (See Milk).

Mind—The positive and good aspects of ♃ tend to give a forceful state of mind.

Moderation—♃ is the Author of. (See "Author Of" in this section).

Moisture and Warmth — (See "Cold and Dry" in this section).

Muscular Activity — (See "Activity" in this section).

Normal Births—(See "Births" in this section).

Nourishing — (See "Conservation" in this section).

Pathological Action — (See "Pathological" in Sec. 3 of this Article).

Physiological Action—The Physiological Action of ♃ is Cell Development. (See Cells).

Plants and Herbs—(See "Herbs" in this section).

Preservation—The Principle of ♃. (See Preservation).

Principle Of—Preservation.

Processes Of—(See "Conservation" in this section).

Protective Agent — (See "Hyleg" in this section).

Qualities — Aggregative, Airy, Alexipharmic, Alterative, Analeptic, Anthelmintic, Antispasmodic, Apoplectic, Balsamic, Benefic,, Beneficient, Benevolent, Buoyant, Clogging (by evil aspects), Confident, Conservative, Cor-

pulent, Diurnal, Elaborating, Electric, Emollient, Enriching, Expansive, Forceful, Fortunate, Fruitful, Fullness (gives Fullness), Generous, Guttonous (by evil aspects), Gormandizing, Health-Restoring, Heat-Producing, Hot, Just, Masculine, Moderation, Moist, Nourishing, Optimistic, Opulent, Overflowing, Plethoric, Positive, Preserving, Redundant, Religious, Reverent, Sanguine, Self-Indulgent, Sociable, Supporting, Temperate, Warm, etc.

Reservation—(See "Conservation" in this section).

Seat of Activity — (See "Activity" in this section).

Selection—(See "Conservation" in this section).

Sidereal Body—Relation of ♃ To— (See Astral Body).

Signs—Of the Zodiac—For the influence of ♃ in each of the Signs see the classified lists of ♃ in Signs in the various Textbooks and Dictionaries of Astrology.

Social Planet—♃ is called the Social Planet, due to the joviality and good nature he gives when well-placed, well-aspected, and strong at B.

Storing—(See "Conservation" in this section).

Supporting — (See "Conservation" in this section).

Teeth — ♃ gives good teeth when strong and well-aspected at B. Also distorted teeth are attributed to his evil aspects. (See "Foreteeth" under Teeth).

Temperament — The Sanguine Temperament is given by ♃. (See Sanguine).

Temperance—(See Temperance; "Author Of" in this section).

Therapeutic Qualities—Therapeutic Properties of ♃ — Alexipharmic, Analeptic, Anthelmintic, Antispasmodic, Balsamic, Emollient. (See these subjects).

Tonic Action Of—(See Plethora).

Transformation—(See "Conservation" in this section).

Typical Drugs — Of Jupiter — Eupatorium, Ginseng, Iridin, Peppermint (Mentha), Stannum. (See "Jupiter Group" under Herbs).

Warmth — ♃ tends to warmth and moisture. (See "Cold and Dry" in this section).

— SECTION TWO —

JUPITER RULES — Governs—Dominates—See the following subjects in the alphabetical arrangement—Absorption; Adipose Tissue (see Adipose, Fat); Adrenals, Aluminum, Amniotic Fluid (see Foetus); Aphetic Process (see "Conservation" in Sec. 1 of this Article); Arms, Arteries, Arterial Blood and Circulation (see Arteries); Assimilation; Auricle, the Right Auricle of the Heart (see "Auricles" under Heart); Births, Normal Births; Blood, the Arterial Blood and Circulation, Blood Enrichment, Blood Making, the Fibrin of the Blood (see Blood, Fibrin, Haematopoiesis); Blue Color; Blue Flag (see Iridin); Bowels—Arteries of

— (see Bowels); Breath; Carbohydrates (see Hydrocarbonates); Cells—Cell Development, Cell Division, Cell Reproduction by Division, Storing of Cell Substance, Cellular Tissue Building, Cellulose (see Cells); Circulation —Of the Arterial Blood (see Arteries, Circulation); Clergymen; Colors (see "Colors" in Sec. 1 of this Article); Conservation of Energies and Tissues; Defensive Forces of the Body (see Defensive, Phagocytes); Devotion (see Religion); Digestive Organs and Functions (see Digestion); Domestic Pets; Duties; Ear—♃ in ♓ rules the Right Ear; Energy—Conservation of Energy; Eupatorium; Fat — Disposition of In the Body, the Fatty Constituents of Milk and other Fluids of the Body (see Fat); Father's Relatives; Feet; Fibrin of Blood; Filtration; Generosity; Genito-Urinary Organs — the Arteries and Veins of; Ginseng; Glycogen; God Fathers; Good Fortune; Green Color mixed with Red; Growth; Guardians; Haematopoiesis; Hams (see Thighs); Hands; Heart—♃ in ♌ rules the Arteries of the Heart (see Heart); Herbs of ♃ (see "Jupiter Group" under Herbs); Hydrocarbonates; Increase; Iridin; Journeys (Long Journeys); Legal Affairs; Legs (Arteries of); Life from 45 to 57 Years of Age (see Periods); Liver; Long Journeys (see Journeys); Lungs; Metal (Tin); Nutrition; Peppermint; Pets — Domestic Pets; Phagocytes; Pisces Sign; Plants (see "Jupiter Group" under Herbs); Pleura; Processes—(see "Conservation" in Sec. 1 of this Article; Purple Color (see Colors); Red Mixed with Green; Reins; Relatives of the Father (see Father); Religion; Reservation (see Cells); Ribs; Right Ear; Ritual; Sagittarius Sign; Sanguine Temperament (see Sanguine); Seed (see Seed, Semen); Selection (see Cells); Sides of the Body; Signs—♃ in Signs Rules (see "Signs" in Sec. 1 of this Article); Stannum; Starches; Stomach—Arteries of (see "Arteries" under Stomach); Storing Functions of the Body (see Conservation; "Storing" under Cells); Sugar In the Body (see Sugar, Sweets); Support of the Body (see "Conservation" in Sec. 1 of this Article); Suprarenal Capsules (see Adrenals); Sweets — Sweet Foods — Sweet Things In Merchandise (see Sugar, Sweets); Teeth; Thursday; Tin; Tissues—Conservation of (see Conservation); Transforming Functions In the Body (see Conservation, Transforming); Veins of the Genito-Urinary Organs (see Genito-Urinary); Violet Color In the Solar Spectrum (see Colors); Vis Conservatrix; Viscera; Wealth, etc.

— SECTION THREE —

THE DISEASES OF JUPITER — The most of the diseases of ♃ arise from indiscretions in eating or drink, causing indigestion, distempers, distentions, plethora, fullness, too much blood, corrupt blood, etc. No aspects of ♃ or ♀ cause disease, but only as configurated with malefics. Jupiter does not in himself cause any disease, but afflictions to ♃ affect the Blood, Lungs, Liver, and indirectly the Heart, as ♃ rules the Blood. Also afflictions to

♃ cause Apoplexy, Abscesses, Boils, Cramps, Pleurisy, etc. (See the Introduction, "Afflictions", "Aspects", "Directions", in Sec. 1 of this Article). The following diseases and conditions are attributed to the afflictions of ♃, and when this planet is ill-dignified at B., or afflicting the ☉, ☽, Asc., or Hyleg, and the various houses of the map of birth. See these subjects in the alphabetical arrangement when not more fully considered here—

Abscesses; Adipose Tissue—Adiposis —Formation of Adipose Tissue In Excess—Adipose Sarcoma—(See Adipose, Fat, Sarcoma).

Adrenals—Suprarenals—Disorders of —(See Adrenals).

Air — Diseases from Superabundance of—Diseases from Corrupt Air—(See Air).

Albumen—Waste of, and Excess of In the Urine — Albuminuria — (See Albumen).

Alterations—In the Red Blood Particles, and in the Tissues—(See Alterations, Blood; "Alterations" under Cells; "Blood" under Red).

Aneurysm; Apoplexy; Arms — Disorders In—(See "Circulation", "Diseases Of", under Arms).

Arteries — Arterial Blood — Disorders of — (See Arteries; "Arterial Circulation" under Circulation).

Assimilation—Imperfect Assimilation —(See Assimilation).

Back—Disorders In—♃ afflicted in ♌. (See "Pains" under Back).

Backbone—Disorders In—(See Spine, Vertebrae).

Bladder—Stone In—Abscess In—(See Bladder, Stone).

Blood—Alterations In—Corrupt Blood —Determination of Blood to the Head —Discharges of Blood with Watery Humours—Disorders of the Blood, and especially the Arterial Blood—Fevers Due to Too Much Blood—Foul Blood— High Blood Pressure — Impure Blood and All Diseases Arising From—Low Blood Pressure — Blood Making, Disturbances of—Morbid Changes In the Blood — Obstructions from Too Much Blood—Changes In the Blood Particles; Poisoning of the Blood—Putrefaction In the Blood — Red Blood Particles, Changes In — Sugar In the Blood and Urine—Thin and Watery Blood — Too Much Blood, Fevers and Obstructions From—Urine, Sugar In—Blood Vessels, Fullness of—Watery and Thin Blood— (See the various paragraphs under Blood).

Boils; Bowels — (See Arteries, Circulation, Gripings, Spasm, under Bowels).

Breast—Cancer of—(See "Breast" under Carcinoma).

Breathing — (See Immoderate, Labored, Obstructed, under Breathing).

Bronchitis—(See Bronchial).

Calculus — (See "Stone" in this section).

Cancer — Carcinoma — Cancer of the Breast—Death by Cancer—Fatty, Lardaceous, and Waxy Cancer—Cancer of the Pancreas—(See Carcinoma).

Carotid Arteries—Fullness of — (See Carotid).

Cellular Inflammation—(See "Inflammation" under Cells).

Cerebral Congestion — (See "Brain" under Congestion).

Changes—In the Red Blood Particles —(See "Blood" under Red).

Chest—Tightness of—(See Chest).

Choleric Distemper—(See Choleric).

Circulation—Of the Blood—Disorders of—(See Arteries, Circulation).

Clogging—Of the System—(See Clogging).

Cold and Dry Liver—(See Liver).

Colic; Congestions—Cerebral Congestion — Congestion of the Blood — Congestion In the Lungs — (See Blood, Circulation, Congestion, Lungs).

Consumption; Corpulence;

Corrupt Blood—(See Impure).

Cramps; Cysts—In the Arms, Hands, Legs and Feet—(See the Introduction under Aneurysm).

Death—♃ causes death by Apoplexy, Cancers, Decayed System, Enlarged Heart, Foul Blood, Foul System, Heart Disorders (Enlarged Heart), Impure Blood, Inflammations, Inflammation of Lungs, Jaundice, Judge (By Sentence of), Liver Diseases, Lung Diseases, Morbid Deaths (♃ as Anareta In), Plethora, Quinsy, Spasms, Stomach (Foul Stomach), Surfeits, Swellings, Toxaemia, Tumors. (See these subjects).

Decayed System—♃ Causes Death By — (See Decay).

Degeneration—Fatty Degeneration of the Muscles of the Heart—(See Degeneration; "Fatty Degeneration" under Heart).

Dental Maladies—(See Teeth).

Deposits — Of Fat Over the Body — (See Fat).

Determination of Blood—To the Head — Rush of Blood to the Head — (See "Blood" under Head).

Diabetes Mellitus—(See Diabetes).

Diathesis — (See "Thoracic" in this section).

Diet—Improper Diet and Diseases Arising From—(See Diet).

Digestive Disorders — Defects In the Digestive Organs — (See Defect, Disorders, under Digestion; Indigestion).

Distempers—Choleric Distemper— Distempers In the Throat—(See Choleric, Distempers, Throat).

Distentions—(See Distentions, Flatulence, Fullness, Plethora).

Dreams — Strange Dreams — (See Dreams).

Dropsy; Dry and Cold Liver — (See Liver).

Ear — Affections of the Right Ear — (See "Right Ear" under Ears).

Eating — Excesses In — (See Diet, Drink, Eating, Excesses, Food, Gluttony, Indiscretions).

Eczema; Enlargements — (See Enlarged; "Enlarged" under Heart).

Epidemics — (See Epidemics; "Sun Spots" under Spots).

Epistaxis — (See "Epistaxis" under Nose).

Excesses — In Diet and Eating, and Diseases Proceeding From—(See "Eating" in this section).

Face—Swellings In—(See Face).

Faintings; Fat — Fatty Deposits In Excess Over the Body—Fatty Degeneration of the Heart and Muscles— Fatty, Sardaceous Cancer—(See Fat).

Feet—Cysts In—(See "Arms" in this section).

Fever—From Too Much Blood—(See "Too Much Blood" under Blood).

Flatulence; Fluids — The Accumulation of In the Different Parts of the Body—(See Accumulative, Fluids).

Flying Pains—(See Flying).

Food — Excesses and Indiscretions In the Use of—(See "Eating" in this section).

Foul Blood — Foul Stomach — (See Foul, Impure; "Foul" under Stomach).

Fullness — Of the Arteries and Blood Vessels—Of the System—(See Fullness, Plethora).

Functions — Over-Activity of — (See Functions).

Habit—The Plethoric Habit—Hyperaemia—(See Plethora).

Hands — Cysts In — Eczema In — (See Cysts, Eczema).

Head — Determination of Blood To — Rush of Blood To—Fullness of Veins of—(See "Blood" under Head).

Heart—Enlarged Heart and Death By —Fatty Degeneration of—Morbid Action of—Trembling of—(See Heart).

Hemorrhoids; High Blood Pressure— (See "Pressure" under Blood).

High Living—Diseases Arising From —(See "Living" under High).

Hot and Moist Diseases — (See "Hot and Moist" under Heat).

Imaginations — (See "Strange" under Imagination).

Immoderate Breathing—(See "Breathing" in this section).

Impure—Impure Blood and Death By — Impure Respiration — (See "Impure" under Breathing; Impure).

Indigestion; Indiscretions—In Diet— (See Eating, Injudicious, in this section).

Inflammation — Death by Inflammation—Inflammation of the Lungs—Inflammatory Process—(See "Bronchitis" under Bronchial; the Introduction under Inflammation; "Inflammation" under Lungs).

Injudicious Diet—Diseases Arising From—(See Injudicious; "Eating" in this section).

Inward Parts—Disorders of—(See Reins).

Jaundice—And Death By—(See Jaundice).

Judges—Sentenced to Prison or Death by a Judge, The Law—(See Judges).

Kidneys—Disorders of—Tumor of— (See Kidneys).

Knees—Pains and Swelling In—(See Knees).

Lardaceous Cancer—(See "Fatty" under Carcinoma).

Lithiasis—(See Calculus, Stone).

Liver—All Diseases In—Cold and Dry Liver—Congestion In—Death by Liver Diseases—Inflammation and Death By — Derangements and Infirmities In — Obstructions In and Torpid Liver — (See Liver).

Localized Swellings — (See Plethora, Swellings).

Low Blood Pressure—(See "Pressure" under Blood).

Lumbago; Lungs — Congestion In — Inflammation In, and Death By—Obstructions In—(See Lungs).

Mammary Cancer—(See "Breast" under Carcinoma).

Many Diseases—Due to Corrupt Blood, or Too Much Blood—(See "Many Diseases" under Complications, Diseases).

Melancholy; Metal—The Metal ruled by ♃ is Tin, or Stannum. The Pathological action of Tin is poisonous if absorbed in too large quantities. Albumen, Milk, and Oils, are antidotes for Tin Poisoning. (See "Pathological" in this section).

Milk Glands — Disturbances of — (See Breasts, Milk).

Moist and Hot Diseases — (See "Hot and Moist" under Heat).

Morbid Conditions — Morbid Changes In the Blood—Morbid Deaths—Morbid Growths—Morbid Action of the Heart —(See "Morbid" under Blood, Death, Growths, Heart).

Muscles — Fatty Degeneration of — (See Degeneration, Fat; "Degeneration" under Muscles).

Neck—Disorders of—(See Neck).

Obstructions — In the Liver, Lungs, and Throat—(See "Obstructions" under Liver, Lungs, Throat; Obstructions).

Organs — Enlargement of — Excessive Functional Activity — (See Enlargements; "Over-Activity" under Functions).

Pains — In the Backbone (Spine) — In the Bowels—Spasmodic Pains In the Bowels— Pains In the Head, Knees— Flying Pains — (See "Spasm" under Bowels; Flying; "Pain" under Head, Knees).

Palpitation—Trembling of the Heart —(See Heart).

Pancreatic Cancer—(See Pancreas).

Pathological Action — Of ♃ Herbs — Tend to have a pathological action on the heart muscle and the Pulmonary Parenchyma. (See "Drugs" under Heart; "Jupiter Group" under Herbs; "Metal" in this section).

Piles—(See Hemorrhoids).

Plethora— Plethoric Habit—Plethoric and Sthenic Distentions—(See Plethora).

Pleurisy—(See Pleura).

Pneumonia; Poisoning—Of the Blood —(See "Poisoning" under Blood).

Potato-Like Cancer—(See "Solanoid" under Carcinoma).

Pressure—High and Low Blood Pressure—(See "Pressure" under Blood).

Process—Thoracic and Inflammatory Process of the Tissues — (See Inflammation, Thorax).

Putrefaction — In the Blood — (See Blood, Putrefaction).

Quinsy—And Death By—(See Tonsils).

Red Blood—Changes In the Red Blood Particles — (See "Red Blood" under Blood; "Blood" under Red).

Reins—Inward Parts—Disorders of— (See Reins).

Renal Calculi—Stone In the Kidney— (See "Kidneys" under Stone).

Respiration — Disorders of — Immoderate and Impure Respiration — (See Breath).

Ribs—All Diseases Lying In the Ribs —(See Ribs).

Rush of Blood—To the Head—Flow of To—(See "Blood" under Head).

Sarcoma — Adipose Sarcoma — (See Sarcoma).

Scrofula; Scurvy; Sentence of Judge —And Death By—(See Judges).

Short Diseases — (See "Illnesses" under Short).

Signs—Diseases of ♃ in Signs—(See "Signs" in Sec. 1 of this Article).

Solanoid Cancer—(See Carcinoma).

Spasmodic Pains — In the Bowels — (See "Spasm" under Bowels).

Spasms—Death By—(See "Death" under Fits).

Spine—Backbone—Vertebrae—Pains In—(See "Pain" under Spine).

Sthenic Plethora—(See Plethora).

Stomach—Disorders of—Foul Stomach and Death By—Stomach Surfeits— Tumors of—(See Gastric, Stomach).

Stone—In the Bladder—In the Kidney —Renal Calculi—(See Stone).

Strange Dreams—And Imaginations— (See Dreams, Imagination).

Strangury— (See Strangury; "Micturition" under Urine).

Sugar—Waste of In the Body—Excess of In the Blood and Urine—(See Diabetes, Sugar; "Sugar" under Urine).

Superabundance—Of Air, and Diseases Arising From — Superabundance of Blood and Diseases Arising From — (See "Superabundance", under Air; "Too Much Blood" under Blood).

Surfeits—Death By—Diseases Arising From—(See Surfeits).

Swellings — Death By — Localized — Swellings In the Arms, Face, Feet, Knees, Legs, Throat—(See "Swellings" under these subjects; also see Plethora, Swellings).

Swoonings—(See Fainting).

Thin Blood—Thin and Watery—(See "Poor Blood" under Blood).

Thoracic Diathesis—Thoracic Process —(See Thorax).

Throat—Distempers In—Obstructions and Swellings In—(See Throat).

Tightness—Of the Chest—(See Chest).

Tissues — Alterations In — Inflammatory Process of—(See Alterations, Inflammation, Tissues).

Too Much Blood — (See "Too Much" under Blood).

Torpid Liver—(See Liver).

Toxaemia—And Death By—(See Toxaemia).

Trembling—Of the Heart—(See Heart).

Tumors — Death By — Tumor In the Kidneys — (See "Tumor" under Kidneys; "Death" under Tumors).

Urine—Urinary Disorders—Excess of Albumen or Sugar In—(See Albumen, Diabetes, Sugar, Urine).

Vascular Fullness—(See Vascular).

Veins—All Diseases Lying In—Fullness of the Veins In the Head—Disorders of the Veins of the Respiratory System — (See "Blood" under Head; Veins).

Vertebrae—Pains In—(See "Pain" under Spine).

Vessels—Fullness of Blood Vessels—(See "Dilatation" under Arteries; "Pressure", "Too Much Blood", under Blood; Distentions; Fullness, Plethora, Vascular, Vessels).

Viscera—Diseases of—(See Viscera).

Vomiting; Waste — Of Albumen and Sugar In the Body — (See Albumen, Diabetes, Sugar).

Watery Blood—Watery Humours with Discharges of Blood—(See "Poor" under Blood; "Humours" under Watery).

Waxy Cancer — (See "Fatty" under Carcinoma).

JUSTICE—Just—

Death—Death by the Hand of Justice —By The Law—(See Judges, Law).

Fugitive—The Fugitive from Justice Is Dead—(See Fugitive).

Just Men — Much Mortality Among — (See "Just Men" under Mortality; Noble; Nobles).

Just Nature — (See Honesty; "Good Morals" under Morals; Noble, Sincere).

JUVENILITY—Young Looking—Youthful—Well-Preserved—The ☉ hyleg, and ☌ or good aspect ♃. Venus keeps one youthful thru a placid, calm, joyful, and cheerful mind. The adverse influences of ♄ tend to age both mind and body, and this planet strong at B. tends to premature old age, and the contraction and drying up of the body. The ♊ Sign strong at B. tends to preserve the mental faculties to an extreme age, and to keep the mind young and buoyant. The influences of the ♐ Sign tend to preserve the freshness of youth even to an advanced age. (See Well-Preserved; "Youthfulness" under Youth).

K

KARMA — Law of — (See "Ripe Fate" under Fate; Monsters; "Deaf and Dumb" under Hearing).

KEEN—Sharp—

Keen Sight—(See "Keen" under Eyes, Sight).

Keen-Edged Tools—Cuts and Injuries By — (See Cuts, Duels, Instruments, Sword).

KEPLER—The Great Astronomer. After his study of Astrology and the effects of the Planetary influences, he said—"A most unfailing experience of the excitement of sub-lunary natures by the conjunctions and aspects of the planets has instructed and compelled my unwilling belief." He believed in the influence of Comets over human affairs, and at the time of the appearance of a Comet predicted the rise and fall of Wallenstein. Kepler was born at Weil on Dec. 7th, 1571, and died Nov. 15th, 1630, at Regensberg.

KERATITIS — (See "Cornea" under Eyes).

KICKS — The Kicks of Animals — Thrusts—

Kicks by Animals — Thrusts — The ☽ to the ☌ or ill-asps. ♂ by dir.; ♂ afflicted in the 12th H., and usually attended with effusion of blood. (See "Hurts" under Animals; "Injury By" under Horses).

Kicks by Horses — ♄ or ♂ affl. in ♐; ♐ on the Asc. or 6th H., and afflicted. (See "Animals" under Bites; "Injury By" under Horses).

Kicked by Husband—Woman Kicked by Husband, Rendering Her Unfruitful — Case — See "Human Document", No. 929, in 1001 N.N.

Kicks On Voyages — Or In Travel — Malefics in fiery signs in the 3rd or 9th H., and affl. the ☉ or ☽. (See "Journeys" under Bites; "Kicks" under Voyages).

KIDNAPPED — A planet, or malefic, in the 12th H. at B., and afflicting the ☽; ♆ affl. in the 12th H.; the ☽ ☌ or ill-asp. ♆, and the ☽ otherwise afflicted by malefics at the time of the disappearance. The influence of ♆ is that of mystery, and also of treachery. (See Neptune, Plots, Seduction, Twelfth House).

KIDNEYS—The Renal System—Renal Nerves — Renal Circulation — Reins — The Kidneys are under the internal rule of the ♎ Sign. They are also ruled by ♀ and the 7th H. Libra rules the outer and upper part of the kidneys, the medullary and cortical substance, distillation, filtration, and the functional activity of secreting urine. The Distillatory Processes of the kidneys are under the joint rule of ♀ and ♎. (See Distillation, Filtration). The Medullary and Cortical substances are also under the rule of ♀. The renal papillae are ruled by ♀. Venus adds to or subtracts from the Renal Process, modifying the influence of the ☉ or ☽ over the kidneys. Being strongly under the influence of ♀, the kidneys play an important part in the nutrition of the body, as well as in the elimination of wastes. The ☉ and ☽ in ♎ act upon the Lumbar Ganglia, and also by acting thru the Renal Plexuses affect the Renal System, and give way to the Renal Diathesis. (See "Lumbar Ganglia" under Ganglion). The Circulation in the kidneys is ruled and controlled largely by ♅ acting thru the posterior lobe of the Pituitary Body. (See Pituitary). The ♍ Sign rules the under and lower portion of the kidneys, the Sinus, or Pelvis, and also indirectly affects the kidneys by ruling the bladder and urethra, thru which the elimination of urine takes place. Excretion in the kidneys is ruled by ♍. All of the fixed signs rule and affect the kidneys by planets in them, by their internal government. The cardinal signs also greatly influence the kidneys, and denote the kidneys, as they are in □ and ⚹ aspect to ♎, and form the cardinal cross, of which ♎ is a part. Wilson, in his Dictionary of Astrology, also says that ♂ has rule over the kidneys, as ♂ rules the ♍ Sign. The ♂ Group of Herbs and Metals tend to have a pathological action on the kidneys, and Gentian, a ♂ remedy, is one of the principle ingredients in kidney medicines and diuretics. Mars is opposed to ♀ therapeutically, and ♂ remedies combat ♀ diseases. (See Opposites). The following subjects have to do with the Diseases, Disorders, and Afflictions of the Kidneys.

Abscess of Kidneys—Imposthumes—Pyonephrosis—A ♎ disease, and afflictions in ♎; the ☽ or ♃ affl. in ♎; Subs at KP. (See Abscesses).

Action—Of the Kidneys—(See Intermittent, Sluggish, Spasmodic, in this section).

Acute Bright's Disease—(See Bright's Disease; Inflammation, Nephritis, in this section).

Affected—The Kidneys Affected—(See the various paragraphs in this section; "Affected" under Reins).

Albuminuria—(See Albumen).

All Diseases Of—All Diseases In the Reins of the Kidneys—Signified by ♎ and the 7th H., and afflictions therein. Also ♂ diseases.

Amyloid Kidneys—♃ affl. in ♎; Subs at KP (11D).

Anasarca—(See Dropsy).

Antinephritic—A Remedy for Inflammation of the Kidneys—(See Antinephritic).

Anuria—(See "Suppression" under Urine).

Back—Disorders of—(See Back).

Bladder—(See "Abscess", "Ulcers", and the various paragraphs under Bladder).

Brick Dust Deposit—In Urine—(See Urine).

Bright's Disease—(See Bright's Disease; "Diseased", "Inflammation", "Nephritis", in this section).

Calculus—Renal Calculus—(See "Kidneys" under Stone).

Cases—Of Kidney Trouble—Birth Data, etc.—(See "Diseased Kidneys" in this section).

Chronic Bright's Disease—Chronic Kidney Trouble—♄ affl. in ♎. (See "Chronic" under Bright's Disease; "Nephritis" in this section).

Circulation—The Renal Circulation Disturbed—The ☽ in ♎, □ or ⚹ ♃ or ♀; ♄ affl. in ♎; ♄ in ♎, ☌, □, or ⚹ ♃ or ♀. The renal circulation is ruled and controlled largely by ♅ acting thru the posterior lobe of the Pituitary Body, which ♅ rules, and an afflicted ♅ may tend to disturb the renal circulation, and also produce various other incoordinations. (See Circulation).

Cirrhosis—Of the Kidneys—Thickening—♄ affl. in ♎, and especially in the 6th H.; ♄ ☌ ♀, and with ♃ also afflicting ♀ by □ or ⚹; many afflictions in fixed signs, and with a fixed sign rising. (See Cirrhosis). Case of Cirrhosis of Kidney—See Case No. 4, Chap. XIII, page 93, in Daath's Medical Astrology.

Colic—Renal Colic—Nephritic—Calculus In Ureter—The Ureter Obstructed—♄ or ☿ affl. in ♎; ♄ affl. in ♎ or ♍; usually ♄ afflicted in the last degree of ♎; Subs at KP. Case—See Fig. 7D in the book, "Astro-Diagnosis", by the Heindels. (See Colic).

Coma—Uremic Coma—(See "Uremic" under Coma).

Congestion—Of the Kidneys—The ☉ affl. in ♉, from rich foods and gormandizing; ♀ affl. in ♈, by reflex action in ♎. (See Congestion).

Death—From Kidney Diseases—Afflictions in cardinal signs dispose to, and espec. ♄ in these signs and affl. the hyleg.

Deranged Kidneys—(See "Diseased", and the various paragraphs in this section).

Desquamative Nephritis—(See "Nephritis" in this section).

Diabetes—Diabetes Insipidus—Diabetes Mellitus—(See Diabetes).

Diathesis—The Renal Diathesis—(See "Lumbar Ganglia" under Ganglion).

Diseased Kidneys—Deranged Kidneys—Renal Affections—Kidney Trouble—Distempered Kidneys—Diseases of ♎ and the 7th H., and ♈ diseases by reflex action to ♎; ♎ on the Asc.; ♎ on the cusp the 6th H., and afflicted; afflictions in all the cardinal signs show, ♎ being included in the cardinal cross; cardinal signs on angles and containing malefics; the ☉ affl. in an airy sign, and espec. in ♎; the ☉ affl. in ♍, ♏, or ♓; the ☉ in ♌, ♎, ♏, or ♒, ☌ or ill-asp. any of the malefics as promittors; the ☉ ☌ ♄ in ♎, and in □ or ⚹ ♅; the ☽ affl. in an airy sign; the ☽ affl. in ♎, or affl. the hyleg therefrom; the ☽ in ♉, and affl. by the ☉ or ♂ when taken ill (Hor'y); the ☽ in the 6th H., in cardinal signs, and affl. by ♂; the ☽ hyleg in ♎, and afflicted, and espec. with females; the ☽ in ♎ or ♑, ☌, or ill-asp. any of the malefics as promittors; the ☽ to the ☌ or ill-asp. ♂ by dir., and espec. if ♂ afflict the ☽ at B., or ♂ occupy the 6th H.; ♅ affl. in ♎; ♄ affl. in ♈ or ♎; ♄ in ♎ in an angle, and espec. in the Asc.; ♄ in ♎, ☌, □, or ⚹ the ☉ or ☽; ♄ in ♎, occi., and affl. the

⊙, ☽, or Asc.; ♄ in ♎, ☍ ☽; ♄ in ♎, ☌, □, or ☍ ♃; ♄, ♅, or ♆ in ♌, and affl. the ⊙ or ☽; ♄ in ♎ when ♄ is the afflictor in the disease; ♄ affl. in the 6th H. in a mutable sign; ♄ or ♂ in ♎ tend to upset the kidneys; ♃ affl. in ♎, and espec. in the 6th H.; ♃ in ♎, and affl. the ☽ or Asc.; ♂ in ♎ when ♂ is the afflictor in the disease; ♂ in ♎, □ or ☍ ♄; caused by ♂ when the dominion of death is vested in him; ♂ in ♌ and affl. the hyleg; ♂ in ♉, ♌, or ♎, ☌, or ill-asp.-the ⊙; ♂ in the 6th H. in a cardinal sign; ♂ ☌ or ill-asp. ♀; ♀ diseases and afflictions; caused by afflictions to ♀; ♀ affl. in ♎; ♀ affl. in the Asc.; ♀ affl. in ♎ in the 6th H.; ♀ in ♎, and affl. the ☽ or Asc.; born under ♀ as ruler; ♀ in ♎, □ or ☍ ♄; ♀ is usually associated with ♄ in kidney diseases; ☿ in ♎, ♐, or ♓, ☌, or ill-asp. any of the malefics as promittors; ♎ on angles and afflicted; ♈, ♊, ♎, or ♒ on the Asc.; cardinal signs on the 6th H.; the malefics or afflicting planets in cardinal signs; many planets, or a Stellium, in ♎ or the 7th H.; Subs at KP (10, 11, 12D). Cases—Of Kidney Trouble—Birth Data, etc.—See Figures 5B, 6B, 6D, 7A, 7B, 7C, 7D, 7E, 7F, 7G, 7H, 18B, in "Astro-Diagnosis", by the Heindels; Figuers 3, 8, 21, 25, and 36, in "Message of the Stars", by the Heindels; "Marriage", No. 834, in 1001 N.N.; Chap. XIII in Daath's Medical Astrology. (See the various paragraphs in this section).

Distempered Kidneys—(See "Diseased Kidneys" in this section).

Diuretics — A Medicine to Act Upon the Kidneys and Increase the Flow of Urine—(See Diuretics).

Dropsy—Hydronephrosis—Dropsy of the Kidneys by Obstruction—Urine In the Pelvis of the Kidneys—♄ affl. in ♎; Subs at KP (11D). (See Dropsy).

Dysuria—(See "Strangury" under Urine).

Elimination — Faulty Elimination of Urine—Suppression of Urine — (See "Elimination" under Urine).

Eruptions—Skin Eruptions Due to Faulty Elimination of Urine, and Retention of Poisons—♄ affl. in ♎. (See Eruptions).

Excretion—Of Urine—Disorders of—(See "Excretion" under Urine).

Faulty Secretion — Of Urine — (See "Suppression" under Urine).

Fevers—From Kidney Diseases—♂ affl. in ♎; ♂ in ♎ and afflicting the ☽ or Asc.; ♂ in ♎ in the 6th H. (See Fever).

Floating Kidney—A ♀ disease, and caused by afflictions to ♀, and espec. ♀ affl. by ♄; ♅ affl. in ♎.

Glands—Of the Kidneys—Disorders of —(See "Kidneys" under Glands).

Gravel—(See Gravel).

Hemorrhage—In the Kidneys—♂ affl. in ♈ or ♎.

Hydronephrosis — (See "Dropsy" in this section).

Imposthumes—(See "Abscess" in this section).

Inflammation—Of the Kidneys—Nephritis—Inflamed Pelvis—A ♎ disease, and afflictions in ♎; ♎ on the Asc.; ♂

affl. in ♈ or ♎; ♂ in ♎ in the 6th H.; ♂ in ♎ and afflicting the ☽ or Asc. (See Bright's Disease; "Chronic", "Nephritis", in this section).

Intermittent Action—Irregular—Spasmodic—♅ affl. in ♎.

Irritation Of—♂ ☌ or ill-asp. ♀.

Ischuria — (See "Ischuria" under Urine).

Kidney Trouble—(See "Diseased Kidneys" and the various paragraphs in this section).

Libra—Diseases of—(See Libra).

Lithiasis—(See "Kidneys" under Stone).

Loins—(See the paragraphs and influences under Loins).

Lower Part—Of the Kidneys—Affected by planets in the 3rd face of ♎, and by Subs at KP (11, 12D).

Lumbar Region—Also ruled by ♎. (See Lumbar).

Nephritis—Inflammation of the Kidneys — Desquamative, Interstitial, or Parenchymatous Nephritis—Bright's Disease—May be Acute or Chronic—♂ in ♎ tends to acute forms, and ♄ in ♎ to chronic forms of nephritis; a ♎ disease, and afflictions in ♎, or ♎ on the Asc. or 6th H., and containing malefics; the ⊙ badly aspected by ♃; the ☽ afflicted in a watery sign; ♃ □ or ☍ the ⊙; ♀ badly aspected by ♄ or ♃; fixed signs prominent, and espec. ♌, ♏, and ♒; a fixed sign rising on the Asc.; Subs at KP (11D). (See Bright's Disease; Colic, Inflammation, Pyelitis, in this section).

Nephrolithiasis—(See "Kidneys" under Stone).

Nephroptosis — (See "Prolapsed" in this section).

Nervous Disorders Of—☿ affl. in ♈ or ♎.

Neuralgia Of—A ♎ disease; ☿ affl. in ♎. (See "Pain" in this section).

Obstructions—♄ affl. in ♎, and espec. when in the Asc. or 6th H.; ♃ or ☿ affl. in ♎; ♃ in ♎ in the 6th H., and afflicted, or afflicting the ☽ or Asc. (See Obstructions; Colic, Dropsy, Suppression, Stone, in this section).

Operations On—Avoid when the ☽ is in ♎. (See Operations).

Over-Worked—The Kidneys Overworked, and Elimination Retarded—♃ in ♎, ☌, □, or ☍ ♄. (See "Elimination" under Urine).

Pain In—The ☽ in ♉ and afflicted by the ⊙ or ♂ when taken ill (Hor'y). (See Colic, Neuralgia, in this section).

Parenchymatous Nephritis—(See "Nephritis" in this section).

Paroxysms—Renal—☿ afflicted in ♎. (See Paroxysms, Spasmodic).

Pathological Action—On the Kidneys —The ♂ Group of Herbs has such action. (See "Mars Group" under Herbs; "Pathological Action" under Mars).

Pelvis—Of the Kidney—Inflammation of—Pyelitis—Urine In—(See Dropsy, Inflammation, Pyelitis, in this section).

Polyuria — Excessive Secretion of Urine—(See Diabetes; "Polyuria" under Urine).

Prolapsed Kidney — Nephroptosis— ♄ affl. in ♎; Subs at KP (11D).

Ptosis Of—(See "Prolapsed" in this section).

Pyelitis—Pyelonephritis— Inflammation of the Pelvis of the Kidney—♂ affl. in ♎; Subs at KP (11D). (See Inflammation, Nephritis, Pyelonephritis, in this section).

Pyelonephritis—Inflammation of the Kidney and Its Pelvis—(See "Pyelitis" in this section).

Pyonephrosis — Suppuration Within the Kidney—Pus In the Kidney—Abscess In—Inflammation In—Ulceration In—A ♎ disease, and afflictions in ♎; a ♄, ☿, and ♃ disease; ♄ ♂ ♃ in ♎, due to disturbed circulation; · ♄ affl. in ♎, due to suppression of function, or obstructions; ♂ affl. in ♎, from inflammation; Subs at KP (11D). (See Abscesses, Inflammation, in this section).

Reins—Of the Kidneys—Disorders of —(See "All Diseases Of" in this section; Reins).

Remedies—Kidney Remedies— (See Antinephritic, Diuretics, and the Introduction to this Article).

Renal—Pertaining to the Kidneys— Renal Affections—Renal Calculi—Renal Circulation—Renal Colic—Renal Diathesis—Renal Hemorrhage—Renal Paroxysms—Renal Process—Renal Stones —(See the Introduction, and the various paragraphs in this Article).

Retarded—The Kidney Action Retarded—(See Elimination, Obstructions, Over-Worked, Retention, Stone, Suppression, in this section).

Retention — Of Urine — (See "Retention" under Urine).

Sand—In the Kidneys—(See Sand).

Secretions—Faulty Secretion of Urine —Excessive Secretion— Secretion Obstructed—(See Diabetes; Excess, Obstructions, Polyuria, Suppression, under Urine).

Skin Diseases—Due to Kidney Trouble —(See Eruptions, Pimples, Skin).

Sluggish Kidney Action—♄ or ♃ afflicted in ♎; ♄ ♂ ♃ in ♎. (See Sluggish).

Spasmodic Action—Irregular—Intermittent—The ☉ ♂ ♅ in ♎; ♅ affl. in ♎; ♅ in ♎, ♂, P., □, or ☍ ♂. (See Spasmodic).

Spurious Ischuria— (See "False Retention" under Urine).

Stone—Renal Calculus—(See Gravel, Sand; "Kidneys" under Stone).

Stoppage—Of the Urine—(See "Suppression" under Urine).

Strangury— (See "Strangury" under Urine).

Sugar—In the Urine—Waste of Sugar —(See Diabetes, Sugar; "Sugar" under Urine).

Suppression—Of Urine— (See "Suppression" under Urine).

Suppuration—In the Kidneys— (See "Pyonephrosis" in this section).

Supra-Renals — Adrenals—Disorders of—(See Adrenals).

Thickening—Of the Kidneys— (See "Cirrhosis" in this section).

Tuberculosis Of—Planets afflicted in ♎; the ☽ in ♎, □, or ☍ ♄ and ♂; ♄ afflicted in ♎; Subs at KP. (See Tuberculosis).

Tumor—Of the Kidneys—♃ affl. in ♎. Case—Died after an Operation for Tumor of the Kidney—See "Marriage", No. 834, in 1001 N.N. (See Tumors).

Ulceration—(See "Pyronephrosis" in this section).

Upper Kidneys—Afflictions in the first face of ♎ tend to disorders of; Subs at KP (10D).

Uremia—Uremic Coma— (See Coma, Uremia).

Ureters—Obstruction of—Colic In— Stone In—(See Colic, Obstructions, Stone, in this section; Ureters).

Urethra—Disorders of—(See Urethra).

Uric Acid—Excess of Over the System—Afflictions in ♎. (See Uric).

Urine—Retention of—Suppression of —(See "Suppression" under Urine).

Wastes—Deposit of Over the System Due to Disordered Kidneys—♄ affl. in ♎. (See Deposits, Poisons, Toxaemia, Wastes).

Weak Kidneys—Cardinal signs on the 6th H.; ♄ affl. in ♎. (See "Diseased", and the various paragraphs in this section).

Weakest Part — The Kidneys the Weakest Part, or Organs—The ☉ affl. in ♎, or ♎ on the Asc. at B.; ♄ affl. in ♎.

KILL—Killing—

Primary Directions Kill—(See "Primary Directions" under Directions).

The Killing Planet—(See Anareta).

KILLED—Danger of Being Killed— Meeting with a Violent End—See such subjects as Accidents, Ambushes, Animals, Assassination, Avalanches, Battle, Beasts, Bites, Blows, Buildings, Burns, Contests, Cuts, Death, Disputes, Duels, Earthquakes, Enemies, Electricity, Execution, Falls, Fire, Foreign Lands, Gunshot, Heat, Heights, Highwaymen, Homicide, Hurts, Injuries, Instruments, Journeys, Lightning, Liquids, Machinery, Mangled, Mobs, Murdered, Pirates, Poison, Prison, Quadrupeds, Railways, Robbers, Scalds, Sentence of Judge (see Judges); Stabs, Stings, Stones (Flying Stones); Storms, Sudden, Sword, Thieves, Travel, Treachery, Untimely Death (see Untimely); Violent Death (see Violent); Water (see Bathing, Drowning, Liquids, Scalds, Shipwreck, Voyages); Wild Animals (see Wild); Wind, Women (see Treachery, Women); Vehicles, Venomous, Volcanoes, Voyages, etc.

KILLING—

Killing Directions — (See "Primary Directions" under Directions).

Killing Illnesses—(See "Arguments for Death" under Death; Fatal; Malignant, Pernicious, Severe, etc.).

Killing Planet—Anareta—The Killing Planet is the one forming the most malevolent directions in a train of evil directions, and especially if it is the Anareta at birth, and severely afflicting the Hyleg. (See Anareta).

KIND—

Kind of Death—(See the various subjects listed under Death, Disease, Killed; "Nature of the Death" under Nature; "Death" under Quality, Species).

Kind of Disease—(See "Nature of the Disease" under Nature; Quality, Type).

Kind Disposition — K i n d F a c e and Countenance—Warm-Hearted—♃ ruler, strong, and well-aspected at birth. (See Generous, Humane; "Obliging" under Manner; P r o m i s e s, Smiling; "Even Temper" under Temper).

KINDRED — (See B r e t h r e n, Family, Relatives).

KINETIC—

Kinetic Force — Motor Power — Producing Motion—(See Energy, Motion).

Kinetic Points—Of the Planets in the Map—For Figure, Map, Case Record, and Explanations of the Static and Kinetic Points in the Nativity, see Daath's Medical Astrology, Chap. XII. (See "Kinetic" under Planets).

KINGDOMS—The Destruction of Kingdoms, etc.—Danger of—The appearance of a Comet in the Sign of the Zodiac ruling the Kingdom. (See Assassination; "Death of Great Men" under Great; "Death of Kings" under Kings; Misery, Nobles, Princes, Public, War).

KINGS—Queens—Princes— Monarchs— Rulers—Presidents—Great Men, etc.— Are ruled and denoted by the 10th H. Also the ♌ sign rules Kings. At Ingresses and Eclipses the conditions affecting the 10th H. should be especially noted and studied, as it is at such times that some calamity is apt to overtake a King, Kingdom, Nation, or Republic, according to the rulership of the Sign in which the Eclipse occurs. (See Comets, Eclipses, Ingresses, Kingdoms).

Assassination—Danger of—♄ ascending at B., and the ☉ to the ☌ or ill-asp. ♄ by dir.; ♄, ♃, or ♂ conjoined in ♓; ♄ ℞ in ♋ or ♌, and lord of the year at a Vernal Equinox; ♂ elevated above, and configurated with the ☉ at a Solar Ingress or an Eclipse; ♂ in ♓, lord of the year at the Vernal, and ori., presignifies the slaughter of Great Men. (See Assassination; "Death of Great Men" under Great; Nobles, President, Queens, Roman, Rulers).

Bites To—♄, ♂, and ♀ conjoined in ♏. (See "Adder" under Bites).

Danger to Kings—The ☉ in the 10th H., or ♌ on the M.C., and the ☉ affl. by ♄ or ♂ at a Solar Ingress or Vernal Equinox.

Death of Some King—Or Reigning Monarch—Danger of Untimely Death of—An Eclipse of the ☉ or ☽ in a fiery sign; an eclipse of the ☉ in ♌, ♍, or ♎, and in Countries ruled by the Sign falling under the central line and shadow of the eclipse; an eclipse of the ☉ or ☽ in ♌, as ♌ rules Kings, Princes, Rulers; an eclipse of the ☉ in the 2nd Decan. of ♈, the 1st Dec. of ♍, the 2nd Dec. of ♎, or the 3rd Dec. of ♑, and in a Country ruled by these Signs; ♌ on the 10th H. at a Vernal Equi., and the ☉ afflicted by the ☌, □, or ☍ ♂, and ♂ in the 8th H., or ruler of the 8th, or ♂ in

☌ or ☍ ♄; Comets appearing in ♌, ♑, or ♒; the ☽ to the □ or ☍ ☉ by dir., death of some King who may be under such a direction. (See Anarchists, Assassination, Famous; "Great Men" under Great; Monarchs, Nobles, President, Princes, Roman, etc.).

Death by Wrath Of—By Wrath of Kings, Princes, or Rulers—♂ just setting at B., ☍ the Asc., and ♃ bearing testimony to ♂, and ♃ afflicted at B.

Dethroned and Murdered—The ☉ to the ☌ ♂ by dir., murdered or poisoned, or death by treachery; ♂ afflicted at B., and to the ☌ the M.C.

Diseases to Kings—An eclipse of the ☽ in ♍; the 1st Decan. of ♍ on the Asc., diseases and infirmities to the King in Countries ruled by ♍.

Injury To—♃, ♂, ♀, and the ☽ conjoined in ♍; ♄, ♂, and ♀ conjoined in ♏, wounds to.

King's Evil—(See the next section after this one).

Stings To—Bites To—(See "Bites" in this section).

War Amongst Kings—Comets appearing in ♌.

Wounds To—(See "Injury" in this section).

KING'S EVIL—S c r o f u l a—S t r u m a— Scrofulous Tumors—(See Scrofula).

KLEPTOMANIAC—L i g h t - F i n g e r e d — Having a Morbid Desire to Steal—♂ afflicted in ♊; ☿ Sig. in ♋; ☿ afflicted by ♂. (See Cheating, Criminal, Deceitful, Dishonest, Forgers, Gambling, Robbers, Thieves).

KNAVISH—A Knave—Trickster—Dishonest—Unprincipled—A Rogue—♄ ill-dignified at B. indicates a foul, nasty, slovenly knave; ♄ to the body or ill-asp. ☿ by dir. (See Conduct, Dishonesty, Habits, Mischief, Morals, Obscene, Unclean, etc.).

KNEES—Knee Joint—Knee Cap—Patella—The Knees are under the external and structural rulership of the ♑ Sign, and are also ruled by the 10th H., the house of ♑. In the lower limbs the knees correspond to the elbows, ruled by the opposite sign ♋. (See Elbows). The Knee Joint and the Knee Cap (Patella) are ruled by ♑. The Hebrew letter "Ayin" (GH) is connected with the ♑ sign, the sign which rules the knees. The ☉ and ☽ acting thru the ♑ sign, thru the connective tissues and the peripheral nerves, affect the knees, thighs, cutaneous system, the osseous and mucous systems, and give way to the Splenic Diathesis. (See Capricorn, Tenth H.).

Accidents to Knees—Hurts To—Injuries—Wounds—♅, ♄, or ♂ affl. in ♑; a ♑ affliction, and with afflictions in this sign; ♑ on the Asc., and containing malefics, and espec. when ♂ is afflicted in ♑ in the Asc.; ♂ afflicted in ♑ in the 6th H. These influences also tend to fractures of the knees. Saturn in ♑ tends to bruises and contusions in the knees, hurts, falls on the knees, blows to the knees, and also to some weakness, deformity, or permanent injury to the knees. (See "Accidents" under Knees).

Affected—The Knees Affected—Afflictions in ♑, or ♑ on the Asc.; affected by the cardinal signs, to which class ♑ belongs; affected when the ☉ is in ♉; the ☽ in ♈; ♅ in ♏; ♄ in ♎; ♃ in ♌, ♍, or ♐; ♀ in ♋ or ♒; ☿ in ♊. See Table 196 in Simmonite's Arcana. (See the various paragraphs in this section).

All Diseases In—Affected At the Knees —Signified by ♑ and the 10th H., and afflictions in them; a Stellium in the 10th H.; ♑ on the Asc. (See "Diseases In", and the various paragraphs in this section).

Ankylosis—Of the Knee Joint—♄ affl. in ♑, due to deposits; ♂ afflicted in ♑, or ♂ ☉ in ♑ in the Asc., due to excess of heat in the joint, and melting of the joint. (See Ankylosis).

Blows To — Contusions — Bruises— ♄ affl. in ♑; ♑ on the Asc.

Bruises To—Contusions— (See Accidents, Blows, in this section; Bruises).

Bursitis—(See Bursa).

Capricorn—(See "Capricorn Diseases" under Capricorn).

Castor and Pollux—Knee of—(See Castor).

Chronic Trouble In—In the Knee Joint—♄ affl. in ♑, and espec. when ♑ is on the Asc., M.C., or 6th H.

Cold In—Colds In—♄ affl. in ♑; ♀ affl. in ♒; ☿ affl. in ♋. (See Cold).

Consumptive Pains In—♄ in ♎ when ♄ is the afflictor in the disease. (See "Consumptive" under Thighs).

Contusions— (See Blows, Bruises, in this section.

Cramps In—♅ in ♑ or ♒. (See Cramps).

Crooked Knees—♑ on the Asc. (See Ill-Made, Knock-Knees, in this section).

Cuts To—♂ affl. in ♑; ♂ in ♑ in the Asc. (See "Accidents" in this section).

Decayed Bone Cells—(See "Knee Cap" in this section).

Defects In — ♄ or the ☽ affl. in ♑; ♑ on the Asc.

Deformities In—♅ or ♄ affl. in ♑; ♑ on the Asc.

Diseases In—Trouble with the Knees —The ☉ affl. in ♉ or ♑; the ☽ affl. in ♈ or ♑; signified by ♄ in ♎, ♏, or ♑; ♃ affl. in ♌, ♍, ♐, or ♑; ♂ affl. in ♌ or ♑; ♂ in ♑, ♂, or ill-asp. the ☉; ♀ affl. in ♋, ♑, or ♒; ♀ in ♑, and afflicting the ☽ or Asc.; ☿ affl. in ♊, ♋, ♑, or ♓; ♑ on the Asc.; Subs at LPP. (See the various paragraphs in this section).

Falls On—♄ or ♂ affl. in ♑, and espec. when in the Asc. (See "Accidents" in this section).

Fractures—Afflictions in ♑; ♄, ♅, or ♂ affl. in ♑. (See "Accidents" in this section).

Gout In—Gonagra—Goutish Humours Above the Knees—The ☽ affl. in ♑; ♂ in ♑ and affl. the hyleg; ♂ in ♑, ♂, or ill-asp. the ☉; ♄ or ♀ affl. in ♑; ☿ affl. in ♑, Gout in, or above the knees; ♑ on the Asc., and espec. if ♄ is also afflicted. (See Gout).

Humours In—Goutish Humours—(See "Gout" in this section).

Hurts To — (See "Accidents" in this section).

Ill-Made — Crooked — ♄ ascending at B.; ♑ on the Asc. (See "Knock-Knees" in this section; "Crooked Body" under Crooked; "Ill-Formed Body" under Ill; "Crooked Legs" under Legs).

Inflammation In—♂ in ♑; ♂ in ♑ in the Asc. or 6th H., and afflicted; ♂ in ♑ or ♒, and afflicting the ☽ or Asc. (See Bursitis, Gout, Joint, Lameness, Pain, Rheumatism, Swellings, Synovitis, in this section).

Injuries To — (See Accidents, Cuts, Fractures, in this section).

Joint—The Knee Joint—Diseases of— Bursitis— Synovitis— Inflammation of —♄ affl. in ♑ tends to chronic inflammation in the knee joint; ♄ and ♂ both in ♑, and afflicted, tend to painful affections in the knee joint and knees in general; ♂ affl. in ♑. (See Ankylosis, Bursitis, Inflammation, Synovitis, in this section).

Knee Cap — Patella — Decayed Bone Cells of — Slaughter's Disease — Fracture of—♄ affl. in ♑ tends espec. to a decayed and chronic ailment in the Patella, and also to possible fracture of by blows, falls, accident, etc.; ♂ affl. in ♑, to fracture of by injury, accident. (See "Accidents" in this section).

Knee Jerk—Absence of—A ♄ disease; ♄ affl. in ♌ or ♎. This affliction is usually present in cases of paralysis of the legs, and in Tabes Dorsalis, or Locomotor Ataxia. (See Locomotor Ataxia).

Knee Joint—(See "Joint" in this section).

Knock-Knees—Overlapping of the Knees—A ♄ affliction; ♄ ascending at B.; ♄ in ♑ in the 6th H.; the ☉ or ♄ in ♑; ♑ on the Asc. In Hor'y Q. ♄ as Sig. indicates a person knock-kneed, bow-legged, or one who knocks the knees or ankles together, or who shuffles in his gait. (See Gait; "Bow-Legged" under Legs; Crooked, Defects, Ill-Made, in this section).

Lameness In—Lameness In or About the Knees—The ☉ affl. in ♑; the ☉ in ♑, ♂, or ill-asp. any of the malefics as promittors; ♄ or ♂ affl. in ♑; ☿ affl. in ♋, lameness from colds, or cold in the knees. (See "Lameness" under Legs).

Legs — (See the various paragraphs under Legs).

Limbs—(See the subjects and references under Limbs).

Lower Extremities—(See Lower).

Mark or Mole — On the Knee — ♑ on the Asc., and a malefic therein. (See Marks, Moles).

Operations On—Avoid when the ☽ is passing thru ♑. (See Operations).

Overlapping Knees — (See "Knock-Knees" in this section).

Pains In—The ☽ affl. in ♈, or afflicting the hyleg therefrom; the ☽ in ♎, ♂, or ill-asp. ♄ (or ♀ if he be of the nature of ♄) at the beginning of an illness or at decumbiture (Hor'y); ♆, ♅, or ♄ in ♎, and affl. the ☉ or ☽; ♂ in ♌, ♂, or ill-asp. the ☉, and caused thru the spinal nerve; ♂ affl. in ♑ in the 6th H.; ♃ affl. in ♐; ♀ affl. in ♒, pain and swellings in the knees from a cold cause; ☿ in ♑, ♂, or ill-asp. any of the malefics as promittors. (See Consumptive, Gout, Inflammation, Joint, Rheumatism, Swellings, in this section).

Patella—(See "Knee Cap" in this section).

Pollux—Knee of—(See Castor).

Rheumatism In—♄ affl. in ♑; ♂ affl. in ♑ in the 6th H.; ☿ affl. in ♑; ♑ on the Asc. (See Gout, Inflammation, Joint, in this section).

Rickety Knees — Weak or Wobbly Knees—♑ on the Asc. (See "Weak" in this section).

Saturn — (See the influences under Saturn).

Scars On—♂ affl. in ♑; ♂ in ♑ in the Asc. or 6th H. (See Scars; "Marks" in this section).

Slaughter's Disease—(See "Knee Cap" in this section).

Stiff Knee—(See Ankylosis, Gout, Inflammation, Joint, in this section).

Strains In — A ♑ disease, and afflictions in ♑; ♄ or ♂ affl. in ♑.

Strike Together—(See "Knock-Knees" in this section).

Swellings In—♄ or ♂ affl. in ♑; ♃ affl. in ♐; ♀ affl. in ♒, from a cold cause or an afflicted heart. (See Gout, Inflammation, Joint, Pain, in this section).

Synovitis—♂ affl. in ♑. (See Synovial; Bursitis, Inflammation, Joint, Pain, in this section).

Tenth House — Rulerships and Influences of—(See Tenth).

Tumors In—The ☉ afflicted in ♍ when the ☉ is the afflictor in the disease. (See Tumors; "Affected" in this section).

Weak Knees—Weakness In—A ♑ influence, and afflictions in ♑, or ♑ on the Asc.; the ☉, ☽, ♄, or ♂ affl. in ♑; the ☽ Sig. in ♑; ♄ ♂ ♂ in ♑; ♄ affl. in ♑ in the 6th H.

Wounds To—(See Accidents, Cuts, in this section).

KNIFE WOUNDS—Caused by ♂ afflictions. (See Cuts, Incised, Instruments, Stabs).

KNOCKING — Knock—(See "Knocking" under Ankles; "Knock-Knees" under Knees).

KNOTS — In the Fundament — ♂ in an angle occi. of the ☉, and ori. of the ☽. (See Fundament). For Knotted Veins see Varicose.

KNOWLEDGE—Learning—

Acquires Knowledge Easily — Has Depth of Mind — ☿ in ♊, ♍, or ♒, and well-aspected by the ☽, or in good relation to the Asc.; ☿ Sig. in ♎; ☿ Sig. ☌, ⚹, or △ the ☽; ♃ in good asp. to ☿; ♃ Sig. in ♊; ♃ Sig. ☌ ☽; ♂ Sig. ☌ ☿, has considerable mental ability; ♂ Sig. ⚹ or △ the ☉, a great mind. (See "Active Mind" under Active; Learning; "Quickened" under Mentality; "Sound", "Strong", under Mind; Reading, Scholar, Study).

Little Desire for Knowledge—Of Dull Mental Capacity—(See Dull, Idle, Inactive, Inertia; "Void Of" under Learning; "Arrested Mentality", "Shallow", under Mentality; "Weak Mind" under Mind; Pretender; "Void Degrees" under Void).

KNUCKLES—Joints of the Phalanges—(See Fingers, Toes).

KYPHOSIS—Humpback—Angular Curvature of the Spine—(See "Humpback" under Spine).

L

LABOR—

Childbirth—Parturition—(See Parturition).

Labor—Labour—Work—Fear of Work —Hating Work—Ergophobia—The influences which tend to Fear of Work, or Ergophobia, are the ☉ Sig. in ♋; the ☽ ill-dignified at B. (See Dull, Idle, Inertia, Lassitude, Lazy, Lethargy, Rouse).

Labored — Labored Breathing — (See "Labored" under Breath).

Laborious — Plodding — Tends to a Laborious and Plodding Life—♄ strong at B., as in the Asc. or M.C.; ♄ in any aspect to ☿; ☿ combust, well-fitted for any kind of plodding business, but with little ability for Science or the Higher Learning.

LACERATIONS — Tears — Rending — Rupture of Tissues—The Bursting and Rending of Parts—Caused by the tonic action of ♅, and by ♂ in ☌ or ill-asp. ♅. (See Bursting, Cuts; "Exaggerated Action" under Exaggerated; Hernia, Rupture).

LACHRYMAL—The Lachrymal Apparatus—Pertaining to the Tears—(See Tears).

LACING — Tight Lacing, and Diseases From—♀ afflicted in ♍, ♊, or ♋; ♀ affl. in ♌ in the 6th H., or afflicting the ☽ or Asc., and tends to palpitation of the heart. (See "Indiscretions" under Dress; "Palpitation" under Heart; Tight).

LACK OF—Deficiencies—Diminished—Insufficient—Void of, etc.—Any part or organ of the body is subject under the afflictions of the planets to a lack of secretion, or to have its functions disturbed, and the afflictions of the planet ♄ have much to do with these disturbances. It would take too much space here in this Article to list all these conditions, and you are asked to look in the alphabetical arrangement for the subject you have in mind. Many of these conditions are listed and considered under such subjects as Defects, Deficient, Diminished, Insufficient, Loss Of, Missing, Void Of, etc. See these subjects. Some of the more abstract subjects along this line are listed here, or which the student may overlook.

Adrenal Secretion — Lack of — (See Adrenals).

Animal Heat—Lack of In Early Years —(See "Animal Heat" under Heat).

Circulation—Lack of Circulation In a Part — (See "Deficiency" under Circulation).

Cohesion—Lack of Cohesion of Parts —(See Cohesion).

Energy—Lack of—(See "Lack Of" under Energy).

Feeling — Want of — (See Apathy, Cruel, Feeling, Feelings).

Firmness — Lack of Firmness, Courage, Decision, Resolution, etc. — (See Fears, Negative; "Lacking" under Resolution; "Weak Will" under Will).

Fluids — Lack of In the Body — (See "Lack Of" under Fluids).

Gastric Juice—Lack of—(See "Stomach Juices" under Deficient; Gastric).

Health—Lack of Good Health—(See "Bad Health" under Health; Invalids, Sickly; "Much Sickness" under Sickness).

Heat — Lack of Animal Heat — (See "Animal Heat" under Heat).

Men—Lack of Firmness and Resolution In—(See Effeminate; "Resolution" under Men).

Mental Power — Lack of — (See Dull, Feeble, Idiocy, Imbecile; "Weak Mind" under Mind).

Moisture — Diseases Arising from a Lack of Sufficient Moisture In the Body—(See "Dry Body" under Dry; "Excessive Bodily Heat" under Heat; Moisture).

Moral Balance—Lack of—(See "Balance", and the various paragraphs under Morals).

Muscles—Lack of Control of—Muscular Power Weak—(See Muscles).

Nerve Force—Lack of—(See "Nerve Force" under Nerves; "Force" under Vital).

Passion—Lack of—(See Apathy, Aversions, Celibacy, Deviations; "Free from Passion" under Perversions).

Resolution — Lack of — (See "Firmness" in this section).

Sports—Want of Care In—(See Exercise, Sports).

Tone—Lack of—(See Atonic, Debility, Feeble, Sickly, Stamina, Tone, Vitality; "Weak Body" under Weak).

Vital Fluid—Lack of—(See Vital).

Vitality—Lack of—(See Vitality).

Void—Of—(See Void).

Will Power — Lack of — (See "Firmness" in this section; Will).

LACTATION — Lacteals — The Milk — Mammary Glands—(See Milk).

LADY—Death of a Prominent and Eminent Lady—An eclipse of the ☉ in the 3rd Decan. of ♈; the appearance of a comet in ♒. (See Queens).

LA GRIPPE — Influenza — This disease usually travels around the world once in about every fifteen years when ♃ is in his perihelion, and ♂ in perigee at the same time. The disease may also travel around the world once or twice in a year or two until ♃, or some other planet, gets out of perihelion. It is

caused by disturbed and vitiated atmospheric conditions, and is more prevalent when the major planets, and especially ♄ or ♃, are in perihelion, and these same influences also tend to cause Typhus Fever. (See Colds, Epidemics, Influenza, Pestilence, Typhus).

LAKES—(See Rivers, Sea).

LAMENESS—Limping—Impediments In the Gait or Walk — Crippled In the Limbs—Certain Degrees of the Zodiac, known as the Azimene or Mutilated Degrees, when rising on the Asc. at B., or the ☽ in, or ruler of the Asc. in, cause lameness. (See Azimene, Mutilated). If the malefics are in angles ☌ or ☍ the Lights, and the ☽ in her node in a hurtful sign, as in ♈, ♉, ♋, ♏, or ♑, the native will be lame or distorted. The defect will be from birth if the malefics are joined to the Lights, but if in ☍ to them, or if they have a □ to them from the 10th H., it will be by falls, blows, or stabs. Caused by the □ or ☍ aspects of the ☽; ♄ and ♂ joined anywhere in the map, and especially in angles, or in their own nodes, or in the Lunar nodes, tend to. Lameness is also caused by afflictions, or the malefics, in the signs which rule the legs, as in ♐, ♑, ♒, or ♓, or when these signs are on the Asc. at B., and afflicted; a ♐, ♑, ♒, and ♓ disease; ♄ in one of the signs which rule the legs, knees, ankles, or feet, and also where ☿, ♊, and the 3rd H. are also involved by afflictions at the same time, is a very common indication of this disability; afflictions to ♊, the 3rd H., to ♐ and the 9th H., and where ☿ is also afflicted, tend to lameness; ☿ affl. in ♑. (See the various paragraphs in this section).

Accidents—Lameness Resulting From — (See Fractures; "Injuries" under Ankles, Arms, Extremities, Feet, Hands, Knees, Legs, Limbs, Lower, Thighs).

Action—Of the Body—(See the various paragraphs under Action, Motion, Movement).

Ankles—Lameness In—(See Ankles).

Ankylosis—Stiff Joint—Lameness By —(See Ankylosis).

Arms—Lameness In—(See Arms).

Atrophy — Lameness By — (See Atrophy).

Azimene Degrees—The Lame Degrees —(See Azimene, Mutilated).

Birth—Lame from Birth—Born Lame — Distortions from Birth — Ptolemy gives a number of influences under this heading, which are listed in this book under "Distortions", and "Excrescences". Also see Congenital, Deformities, Malformations. Case—Born Lame—See "Arundel", No. 159, in 1001 N.N.

Blows—Lameness By—(See "Causes" under Distortions; the Introduction to this Article).

Born Lame—(See "Birth" in this section).

Burns—Lameness By—♂ afflicted in signs which rule the limbs. (See Burns).

Case — Born Lame — (See "Birth" in this section).

Club Feet—(See Feet).

Colds—Lameness From—(See "Lameness" under Colds).

Congenital Lameness—(See Congenital; "Birth" in this section).

Coordination—Lameness Due to Lack of—(See Coordination, Incoordination).

Crystallization—Lameness Due To—(See Ankylosis, Crystallization, Deposits, Hardening, Joints, etc.).

Cuts—Lameness From—(See "Lameness" under Cuts).

Defects—Lameness Due To—(See Defects, Missing).

Deficiencies—(See Deficient).

Deformities—(See Deformities).

Degrees—The Lame Degrees of the Zodiac—(See Azimene, Mutilated; "Signs" in this section).

Disabilities—(See "Bodily" under Disabilities).

Disablements—(See Disabilities).

Distortions—(See "Causes" under Distortions).

Excrescences—Lameness By—(See Excrescences).

Falls from Heights—Lameness By—(See Distortions, Excrescences, Heights).

Feet—Lameness In—(See Feet).

Fractures—Lameness By—(See Fractures).

Gait—Walk—(See the various paragraphs under Gait, Walk).

Gout—Lameness By—(See Gout).

Hands—Lameness In—(See "Lameness" under Hands).

Hardening—Lameness By—(See "Crystallization" in this section).

Heights—Falls from, and Resulting In Lameness—Falls from High Places—(See "Falls" in this section).

High Places—Falls From—(See "Falls" in this section).

Hips—Lameness In—(See "Lameness" under Hips).

Hurtful Signs—Planets and afflictions in them at B. tend to lameness and distortions. (See the Introduction to this Article; Distortions; "Hurtful Signs" under Hurtful).

Impediments—(See Hindrances, Impediments, Limitations).

Imperfections—(See Defects, Impairments, Imperfections).

Incised Wounds—Lameness From—(See Cuts, Incised).

Incoordination—Lameness By—(See Coordination, Incoordination, Paralysis).

Injuries—Lameness By—(See Accidents, Blows, Cuts, Hurts, Injuries, Wounds; the various paragraphs in this section).

Knees—Lameness In—(See Knees).

Legs—Lameness In—(See Ankles, Calves, Knees, Legs, Thighs).

Limbs—Lameness In—(See Arms, Extremities, Legs, Limbs, Lower).

Locomotion—Disorders of—(See Gait, Locomotion, Motion, Movement, Walk).

Malformations—(See Deformities, Malformations, Missing, Monsters).

Missing—Limbs Missing—Congenital Deformities—(See Missing).

Monsters—Monstrosities—(See Monsters).

Motion—Disturbances In Motion—(See Action, Motion, Movement).

Movement—Disturbances of—Lameness From—(See Action, Gait, Locomotion, Motion, Movement, Walk, etc.).

Mutilated Degrees—Planets in them at B. tend to Lameness. (See Azimene; "Broken Signs" under Broken; "Degrees" under Mutilated).

Paralysis—Lameness From—(See Paralysis).

Prenatal Epoch—Lameness Due to Prenatal Conditions—Congenital Defects—Born Lame, etc.—(See "Birth" in this section; Congenital, Prenatal).

Quadrupeds—Lameness Due to Injuries By—(See Distortions, Quadrupeds).

Rheumatism—Lameness From—(See Rheumatism).

Robbers—Lameness from Injuries By—(See Distortions, Robbers).

Shipwreck—Lameness from Injury In—(See Distortions, Shipwreck).

Shoulders—Lameness In—(See Shoulders).

Signs—Of the Zodiac—The Broken Signs—Imperfect Signs—Planets in them at B. tend to Lameness. (See "Broken Signs" under Broken; "Signs" under Imperfect; "Degrees" in this section).

Stabs—Lameness From—(See the Introduction to this Article; Cuts, Stabs).

Thighs—Lameness In—(See Thighs).

Walk—A Lame Walk—(See Gait, Walk).

Wounds—Lameness Due To—(See "Injuries", and the various paragraphs in this section).

LAMENTATIONS—Lamenting—(See Complaining, Exhibition, Grief, Murmuring; "Lamentations" under Public; Satire).

LAND—Journeys by Land—(See "Land" under Journeys).

Landed Interests—(See Property, Riches).

Landslides—Death or Injury By—Caused by ♄ afflictions at B., and by dir., and with ♄ affl. the hyleg. (See Avalanches; "Buried Alive" under Burial; Crushed, Earthquakes).

LANGUAGE—(See Speech).

LANGUID—Languor—Languishing—(See Apathy, Dull, Idle, Inactive, Inertia, Lassitude, Lazy, Lethargy, Listless, Weak, etc.).

Languid Eyes—(See "Dull Eyes" under Eyes).

Languishing—The ☽ to the ☌ or ill-asp. ♄ by dir.; the 3rd Decan. of ♉ on the Asc., ruled by ♄. (See Apathy, Dull, Fading, Feeble, Invalids, Lassitude, Lethargy, Sickly, Weak, etc.).

LANK—Thin—Lean—Spare—

Lank Body—(See "Thin Body" under Thin).

Lank Hair—(See "Lank" under Hair).

LAPSING—A Falling Away—
Moral Lapsing—Diseases Arising From—♇ diseases, and caused by afflictions of ♇ to the ☉, ☽, ♀. (See Excesses, Morals).
LARDACEOUS—Fatty—Waxy—(See "Fatty Cancer" under Carcinoma; Fat).
LARGE—Big—Great—
Abdomen—Large and Prominent—(See Abdomen).
Animals—Large Animals—Hurts, Injury, or Death By—(See Animals, Beasts, Elephants; "Great Beasts" under Great; Horses, Quadrupeds).
Birth—Large at Birth—Case—See "Short Life", No. 371 in 1001 N.N.
Body—Large Body—Large Stature—Of Full Size—Large Frame—Large Limbs and Joints—Cold climates and the Arctic Regions tend to. Many planets matutine, or strong in the Asc., in signs of dignity, or conspicuous; a tall sign on the Asc., and many planets rising just before the dawn; the Quadrant from the Asc. to the Nadir tends to produce a large, strong and healthy body; ♌, ♍, and ♐ tend to enlarge the body; the influence of the Constellations not of human form, both within and without the Zodiac, tend to enlarge the body, diminish its size, increase or diminish its strength. In Hor'y Q. the party is of large body and stature if the Sig. be ori., and in ♌, ♍, or ♐. The ☉ strong at B., and dignified, usually presents a person of good, strong, tall, fleshy, large frame and corporature; the ☉ gives a large, strong and bony body; the ☉ Sig. in ♌; the ☉ rising at B.; the ☽ Sig. in ♌; the ☽ gives a full-sized person, and with full stature; ♄ in ♐ or ♒ in partile asp. the Asc.; ♄ Sig. in ♐ in Hor'y Q.; ♃ in ♊, ♌, ♍, ♎, or ♐; ♃ in an airy sign, and rising, large and strong body; ♃ in ♍ in partile asp. the Asc., a full-sized person; ♃ as Sig. in Hor'y Q. denotes a person of a large make; ♃ as Sig. in earthy signs in Hor'y Q. denotes a large body; ♃ in the Asc., or a ♃ sign on the Asc., tends to add to the bulk of the body, and also to increase the vitality; ♂ ascending at B.; ♂ when close to the horizon tends to give a larger body than that indicated by the rising sign; ♂ Sig. in ♌; ♂ in ♌ in partile asp. the Asc., large, tall, and strong body; ♀ Sig. in ♒; ☿ in ♌, partile the Asc.; ☿ Sig. in ♌, a large, full body; ♈ on the Asc. gives a large, strong, and bony body. (See Commanding, Corpulent, Enlarged; "Fat Body" under Fat; Fleshy, Full, Giants, Growth; "Large" under Limbs; "Body" under Strong; Tall, etc.).
Bones—Large-Boned—The ☽ Sig. in ♌; ♄ Sig. in ♌ in Hor'y Q; ♂ Sig. in ♈; Martialists have large bones; born under the strong rule of ♂ and ♂ ruler; ☿ Sig. in ♐; ♈ gives, and espec. when on the Asc., and with the ☉ in ♈. (See "Large" under Bones; "Body" in this section).
Cattle—Large Cattle—Hurts, Injuries, or Death By—The ☉ to the ☌ ♂ by dir.; the ☽ affl. at B., and to the ☌ the cusp the 12th H. by dir.; malefics in the 12th H. (See Cattle; "Injury By" under Horses).

Chest—Large Chest—(See Chest).
Ears—Large Ears—(See Ears).
Eyes—Large Eyes—(See Eyes).
Face—Large Face—Big Face—(See Face).
Family—Large Family—(See "Many" under Children; Family, Fruitful, Husband, Wife).
Feet—Large Feet—(See Feet).
Forehead—(See "Large" under Forehead).
Hands—(See "Large" under Hands).
Head—A Large Head—(See Head).
Hips—Large Hips—(See "Strong" under Hips).
Intestines—The Large Intestines—(See Bowels).
Joints—Large Joints—(See Joints; Body, Bones, in this section).
Legs—Large Legs—(See Legs).
Lips—(See "Thick" under Lips).
Moderately Large—In Size—(See Mean, Medium, Middle, Moderate, Moderately).
Mouth—Large Mouth—(See Lips, Mouth).
Muscles—(See "Large" under Muscles).
Nose—(See "Large" under Nose).
Shoulders—(See Broad, Large, under Shoulders).
Size—Large Size—(See Fat, Giants, Tall; "Bones" in this section).
Stout and Large—Oriental planets in their first orientality cause large and stout bodies. (See Corpulent, Fat, Fleshy, Stout).
Strong and Large—♌ gives; ♌ on the Asc.; the ☽ or ♃ in ♌ in partile asp. the Asc., and also to give a tall body. (See Strong; "Bones" in this section).
Strong, Large and Tall—(See "Strong and Large" in this section; Tall).
Tall, Large and Strong—(See "Strong and Large" in this section; Strong, Tall).
Upper Parts of Body—Upper Parts Large—(See "Body" under Upper).
LARVAL STATE—(See Hydatid).
LARYNX—Organ of Voice—The Vocal Organ and Containing the Vocal Cords—The Upper Part of the Windpipe—Under the internal rulership of the ♉ sign. Also ruled by ☿. Also ruled and affected by the ♏ sign by reflex action, as ♉ and ♏ are opposite and complementary signs. The Laryngeal Plexus is ruled by the ♉ sign. It is said the Larynx was taken from ♏, and built by taking from the sex force. The earliest types of humanity did not have a larynx. The origin of the Larynx is quite thoroughly discussed in the book, "Cosmo-Conception", by Max Heindel. The Larynx being so closely connected with the sex nature is the reason the voice changes at puberty, and especially in the male. Sex abuses in either sex change the voice, and affect the larynx and vocal cords. (See Effeminate, Voice). The air which stirs the vocal cords into action is ruled by

☿, and ☿ well-placed in a sign of Voice, and well-aspected by benefics, gives good voice expression, and even though ♉ is afflicted, and throat trouble exists.

Aphasia—Loss of Speech—(See "Aphasia" under Speech).

Aphonia—Whispering Voice—(See "Aphonia" under Voice).

Castration—The Larynx and Vocal Organs Affected By—(See Castration).

Catarrh Of—♄ affl. in ♉; Subs at LCP and SP. (See Catarrh).

Consumption—Of the Larynx—Phthisis of—Laryngeal Consumption—♅ ☌ ♄ in ♉ in the 8th H., and affl. the hyleg, and possible death from this disease.

Cords—The Vocal Cords—Disorders of —(See Vocal).

Croup—(See Croup; "Laryngitis" in this section).

Diseases Of—Laryngeal Affections— —♄ in ♉, occi., and affl. the ☉, ☽, or Asc. (See the various paragraphs in this section).

Dysphonia—Difficulty In Phonation—(See "Hoarseness" in this section; Speech; "Aphonia" under Voice).

Dyspnoea—(See Croup, Dyspnoea).

Expression—Difficulties In Speech—(See Expression, Speech, Voice).

Functional Disorders—Afflictions to ☿.

Glottis—Disorders of—(See Glottis).

Hoarseness — Dysphonia —Harshness of Voice from Disease In the Larynx—The ☉ affl. in ♋; the ☽ in ♉ and affl. by the ☉ or ♂ when taken ill (Hor'y); the ☽ in ♋ or ♎, ☌, or ill-asp. ♄ (or ☿ if he be of the nature of ♄) at the beginning of an illness, or at decumb., and if the ☽ be decreasing, or near the body of ♄, the disease may continue for a long time (Hor'y); ♄ affl. in ♉, due to an obstructed throat; ♄ affl. in ♏; a ☿ disease, and caused by afflictions to ☿ at B., and by dir.; ☿ affl. in ♉ or ♏; ☿ in ♉, ☌, or ill-asp. any of the malefics as promittors; afflictions in ♉ or ♏; many planets in ♉ or ♏, and in fixed signs; ♉ or ♏ on the Asc. or 6th H., and containing afflictions; born under one of the hoarse signs of the Zodiac, as under ♈, ♉, ♌, or ♑; Subs at LCP. (See "Hoarse Signs" under Hoarseness).

Inflammation—Of the Larynx—Laryngitis—A ♉ and ♏ disease, and with these signs on the Asc., and afflicted; the ☽ affl. in ♉; ♅ in ♉ and affl. the ☉, ☽, or Asc.; ♄ in ♉ in the 6th H.; ♂ affl. in ♉ or ♏; Subs at LCP and KP. (See Croup).

Laryngismus—A Spasmodic Affliction of the Larynx—♅ or ☿ affl. in ♉.

Laryngitis—(See "Inflammation" in this section).

Organic Diseases Of—Afflictions in or to ♉ and ♏; the ☉ affl. in ♉ or ♏.

Phlegm—In the Larynx—♄ affl. in ♉; the ☽ hyleg in ♉ with females. (See "Catarrh" in this section; Mucus, Phlegm).

Puberty—The Larynx and Vocal Cords

Affected at Time of—(See the Introduction to this Article; Puberty, Voice).

Spasmodic Affections—(See "Laryngismus" in this section).

Speech—(See the various paragraphs under Speech).

Suffocation—Thru Closure and Swelling, or Obstruction In the Larynx—♄ or ♂ affl. in ♉. (See Croup, Dyspnoea).

Swollen Larynx—The ☽ ☌ ♂ in ♉; ♂ afflicted in ♉ or ♏; afflictions in ♉ or ♏.

Throat—(See the various paragraphs under Throat).

Trachea—(See Trachea, Windpipe).

Tumors Of—Afflictions in ♉; ♄ affl. in ♉; Subs at LCP. (See Tumors).

Vertical Larynx—(See "Vertical" under Spine).

Vocal Cords—Voice—(See Voice. Also note the various paragraphs in this section.

Windpipe—(See Trachea, Windpipe).

LASCIVIOUS—Lascivious Habits—The ☉ ill-dignified at B., privately lascivious and prone to many vices; in Hor'y Q. the ☉ Sig. of the person, and ill-dig. and afflicted, one outwardly decent but secretly vicious and lascivious; ☿ affl. the ☽ or ♀; ♂ ☌ or ill-asp. ♀, or ♀ affl. by ♂. (See Desire, Lewd, Licentiousness, Lust; "Loose Morals" under Morals; Wanton).

LASSITUDE — Languor — Dullness —Debility — Flagging of Energy — Relaxation — Tired Feeling — Weariness — Lethargy, etc.—The Lymphatic Temperament tends to give Lassitude; the 8th deg. of ♉ on the Asc., a degree of lassitude; the ☽ ☌ or ill-asp. ♂ or ♄ by dir.; the Prog. ☽ to the ☌ or ill-asp. ♆ in the radical map, and espec. if ♆ is afflicted at B., and produces both mental and physical lassitude; ♄ ☌ the Asc. by dir.; ♃ □ or ☍ ☉ at B. and by dir. (See Apathy, Debility, Dull, Dynamic, Energy, Ennui, Fatigue, Feeble, Hyperaesthesia, Idle, Inactive, Indifferent, Inertia, Languid, Lethargy, Listless, Negative, Procrastination, Weariness, etc.).

LATENT DISEASES—Constitutional Diseases—Hereditary—Organic, etc.—Are usually caused by the ☉, and afflictions to the ☉ with the male, and by the ☽ and ♀ afflicted in female nativities. (See Constitutional, Heredity, Organic).

Mother — Death of the Mother from Some Latent Disease — (See "Latent" under Mother).

LATITUDE—Of the Planets—In disease the influence of the planets, and especially of the malefics, is more pronounced when the afflictors in the disease have the same Latitude, North or South of the Ecliptic, as the hyleg, or the planets afflicted. A wide Latitude between them lessens their evils. (See Nodes).

LATTER PART OF LIFE—(See Fourth House, Old Age; "Terminal Houses" under Terminal).

LAUGHTER—Is said to be ruled by ♆. (See Cheerfulness, Happiness, Joy, Mirth, etc.).

LAVENDER COLOR—Ruled by ♓. (See Colors).

LAW — Laws — The Law— Sentence by Law — Social and Moral Laws — Laws of Nature, etc.—
Death — By Sentence of Law — (See Execution, Judges).
Fugitive—From the Law—(See Fugitive).
Imprisonment—By Law—(See Prison).
Judge — Sentenced by a Judge — (See Judges).
Justice—Death by the Hand of Justice—Fugitive from Justice—(See Fugitive, Judges, Justice).
Lawsuits—Many Lawsuits Generally — (See "Lawsuits" under Public; Riches).
Lawyers—(See Pettifogging).
Moral Laws—Breaks the Moral Laws —(See "Moral Laws" under Love Affairs; "Loose Morals", and the various paragraphs under Morals).
Nature's Laws — Outrages Nature's Laws and Suffers Disease Thereby— The ☽ affl. in ♍.
Officers—Killed by Officers of the Law —(See Officers).
Prison—Imprisoned by Law—(See Prisons).
Sentence of Law—(See Judges).
Social Laws — Disregard For — (See Love Affairs, Low, Morals, Society).
Success At Law—♂ Sig. ◿ ♃.

LAX—Laxity—
Fibre—Laxity of Fibre and the Tissues—(See Fibre, Flabby, Relaxation, Tissues).
Laxatives—(See Psychic).
Laxness — (See Carelessness, Dull, Idle, Indifferent, Lethargy, Listless).
Morals—Lax Morals—(See Debauched, Depraved, Dissipated, Low, Lust; "Loose" under Morals; Wanton, etc.).

LAZY—(See Apathy, Carelessness, Dull, Filthy, Idle, Improvident, Inactive, Inertia, Lassitude, Lethargy, Procrastination, Rouse, Sedentary, Slovenly, Uncleanly, etc.).

LEAD—The Metal Lead — Plumbum— Ruled by ♄, and is a typical drug of ♄. (See Therapeutics). Tinctura Saturnina is a preparation of Lead, ruled by ♄, and is used in Hectic Fevers, and the Low Fever of Phthisis. (See "Hectic Fever" under Fever; Mucous; "Night Sweats" under Phthisis; "Remedies" under Saturn).
Lead Colic—Painter's Colic—A ♄ disease, and caused by strong ♄ afflictions at B., and by dir. (See "Lead Colic" under Colic).
Lead Colour Complexion — ♄ strong at B. indicates such a person, and ♄ Sig. in Hor'y Q. (See "Swarthy" under Complexion).
Marks—Pale, Lead-Colored Mark On the Body—(See Marks).
Poisoning—Lead Poisoning—Susceptible To — Born under the strong affliction of ♄; Subs at KP (11D), and at PP (3, 4L). (See Poison).
Sugar of Lead—Lead Acetate—Ruled by ♄. Used as a Collyria in inflamed

eyes, and as an ingredient in liniments and ointments for ulcers, skin diseases, excoriations, etc. (See Abrasions, Collyria, Ointments, Resolvent).

LEAKAGES — (a) Nervous Leakage — (See "Leakage" under Nerves). (b) Urine — Leakage of — (See "Incontinence" under Urine). (c) Valves—Leakage of—(See "Leaky" under Heart; Valves).

LEAN—Leanness—Thin—Slender, etc.—
Body—Lean Body—Denoted by ♄; ♄ in ♌ in partile asp. the Asc., rather lean; ♄ in ♑, partile the Asc.; ♂ in ♑, partile the Asc., small, lean and thin; ☿ ruler of the Asc., and occidental; the second, or latter parts of ♈, ♉, or ♌ ascending make the body more lean; the latter parts of ♋ or ♑ ascending make the body more lean than the first parts; the first part of ♐ on the Asc. gives a lean and spare body. (See Slender, Spare, Thin).
Bony—Bony, Lean and Muscular Body —Born under ♂, and given by ♂. (See "Bony", "Raw-Boned", under Bones).
Complexion—(See "Lean and Sallow" under Complexion).
Dry and Lean Body—(See "Lean and Dry Body" under Dry).
Face—(See "Lean" under Face).
Ill-Formed — Lean, Ill-Formed and Short—The ☽ gives when occi. at B. (See "Ill-Formed" under Ill).
Legs — When ♄ builds the body he gives lean, thin and small legs. (See "Lean" under Legs).
Middle-Sized — A Lean and Middle-Sized Body—♃ in ♈ in partile asp. the Asc. (See "Middle Stature" under Middle).
Muscular—Lean, Muscular, and Bony —(See "Bony" in this section).
Short—Lean, Ill-Formed and Short— (See "Ill-Formed" in this section).
Small—Lean, Thin and Small—♂ in ♑, partile the Asc.; ☿ in ♐, partile the Asc., some Writers say small, lean, and thin; the latter part of ♌ on the Asc. makes the body more thin and small. (See Small, Thin).
Thighs — Lean and Small Thighs — (See "Small" in this section).
Thin — Lean, Small and Thin — (See "Small" in this section).
Visage — Lean Visage — (See "Lean", "Long", under Face). For further study along this line see "Long Arms" under Arms; Atrophy, Emaciation; "Long Hands" under Hands; Sickly, Slender, Tabes, Tall, Thin, Wasting.

LEAPING SPASM — Jumping Spasm — (See "Saltatory" under Spasmodic).

LEARNING— Research— Knowledge— Reading—Study, etc.—
Acquires Knowledge — (See Knowledge, Reading, Study).
Arts and Sciences — Fondness For — Proficiency In—The ☽, ♄, or ☿ Sig. in ♒; ☿ Sig. in ⚹ or △ ♄ or ♀. (See Science).
Aversion to Study — (See "Fails" under Examinations; "Aversion" under Study).

Bad Aspects — For Learning — (See Dull, Examinations; "Shallow" under Mentality; "Weak Mind" under Mind; "Void Of" in this section).

Depth of Mind—(See Genius, Knowledge, Mathematical; "Quickened" under Mental; Metaphysics; "Deep and Profound" under Mind; Occult, Reading, Science, Study; the various paragraphs in this Article).

Examinations—Fails In—(See Examinations).

Fond of Learning — (See "Studious", and the various paragraphs in this section).

Great Learning—Has Great Learning and Knowledge — ♄, ♃, or ♂ as Sigs., and in ♂ ☿; ♃ or ♂ as Sigs., in ✶ or △ ☿. (See "Great Ability" under Great; "Good Mind" under Mind; Renown; the various paragraphs in this section).

Incapable of Learning — Wholly Unqualified for Study—☿ Sig. ♂ ☉, unqualified for study, and has a contracted and superficial mind; ☿ Sig. ♂ ♄, gains knowledge with great difficulty. (See "Bad Aspects" in this section).

Inventive Mind—Ingenius—Constructive—Original—The ☽ or ☿ Sigs. in ♒; the ☽ Sig. ♂ or good asp. ☿; the ☽ well-asp. in ♍; ♅ configurated with ☿; ♅ ascending at B., inventive, and strikes out many novelties; ♄ or ♀ Sigs. in ✶ or △ ☿. (See Genius).

Learns Easily — Quickly Acquires Many Sciences Without a Teacher— The ☽ Sig. ✶ or △ ☿, or vice versa, the best aspects for learning and scientific speculation and investigation. (See "Quickened" under Mentality; "Good Mind" under Mind; "Depth of Mind" in this section).

Literature—Addicted To—☿ Sig. ♂ ♃; ☿ in the Asc. or M.C. at B., and well-asp. and dignified; ♀ Sig. ♂ ☿, fond of the elegant branches of Literature if free from the afflictions of malefics. (See Reading, Study).

Little Depth of Mind—Small Desire for Knowledge—(See Apathy, Dull, Examinations, Idle, Inactive, Indifferent; "Shallow" under Mentality; "Incapable", "Void Of", in this section).

Loses Interest—In Studies and Learning—(See Chaotic, Dreamy, Examinations; "Little Depth" in this section).

Lover and Promotor — Of Learning — ♂ Sig. ✶ or △ ☿; ☿ Sig. in ♎.

Metaphysics—Occult Learning—Given To—♅ strong at B.; ♅ in the Asc. or M.C.; ♅ in ♒; ♅ ♂ or good asp. the ☉, ☽, ♀, or the Asc.

Much Attached — To Learning — (See "Great Learning", "Studious", in this section).

Novelties—Creates Many—(See "Inventive" in this section; Novelties).

Occult Learning—(See "Metaphysics" in this section).

Reading — Fond of — (See Reading, Study).

Science — Little Ability For — (See Science).

Scientific Mind—(See Science).

Studious Mind — Fond of Learning — Given to Study—♐ and ♍ influence; ☿

strong at B., and well-aspected; ♃ at a Solar Rev. passing the place of the radical ☿. (See "Quickened" under Mentality; "Cultivation", "Good Mind", under Mind; Scholar, Study; "Great Learning" in this section).

Superficial In Learning—A Contracted and Shallow Mind—(See "Shallow" under Mentality; "Little Depth", "Void Of", in this section).

Uncommon Pursuits — Seeks Unusual Learning — ♅ ascending at B. (See "Metaphysics" in this section).

Void of Solid Learning — The ☉ ♂ or P. Dec. ☿ at B., and both in ♓, and is usually a pretender to all kinds of knowledge; ☿ ill-dig. at B.; ☿ Sig. ♂ the ☉ or ♄. (See "Incapable", "Little Depth", in this section; "Void Degrees" under Void).

Well Informed — Has a Wide Range of Learning — (See "Great Learning", "Metaphysics", "Studious", in this section). For further and collateral study along this line see "Active Mind" under Active; Comprehension, Faculties, Intellect, Intuition, Judgment, Mathematical, Mechanical; "Educational Mind" under Mind; Perception, Precocious, Prodigies, Profound, Scholar, Talents, Truth, Understanding, etc.

LEATHERY SKIN — (See Hemachromatosis).

LEAVES — (See Herbs, Plants, Trees, Vegetation).

LEERING EYES—(See "Leering" under Eyes).

LEFT — The Left Side of the Body — Taken as a whole, the ☽ rules the left side of the body. It is also ruled by Cold, and the Cold and Moist Elements. The odd, positive, and masculine signs and houses correspond to the left side of the body in a male, and the even, negative, and feminine signs and houses to the left side of the body in a female. (See Cold, Houses, Negative, Positive, Right, Signs).

Appendix—The Appendix Vermiformis On the Left Side — Case — (See "Left Side" under Appendix).

Arm—Left Arm—Fracture of—Case— (See "Left" under Radius).

Auricle—The Left Auricle—(See "Auricles" under Heart).

Blindness — In the Left Eye — (See "Eyes" in this section; "Left Eye" under Blindness).

Caecum — On the Left Side — Case — (See "Left" under Appendix).

Cerebral Hemispheres—The left ruled by ♂ (See Cerebral).

Chin—A Mark Near the Left Side of the Chin—(See "Marks" under Chin).

Cold and Moist Humours—In Left Side of Body—(See "Cold and Moist" under Humours).

Coronary Plexus—The Left Coronary — (See "Fifth Thoracic" under Ganglion).

Diseases of Left Side — In the male they are diseases of the ☉, and ruled by the ☉. In the female they are diseases of the ☽, and ruled by the ☽.

Ears—Left Ear—Pain and Disease In —(See "Left" under Ears).

Eyes—The Left Eyes—The left eye of a woman is ruled by the ☉, and the left eye of a man by the ☽.

(a) Abscesses of Left Eye—The ☉ or ☽ near the Ascelli, and coming to the ☌, and the ☉ or ☽ affl. by the ☌, □, or ☍ malefics.

(b) Accidents to Left Eye—Hurts—Injuries—Wounds—Danger To—Loss of Sight—Blindness In—The ☉ or ☽ near Nebulous Stars at B., and affl. by ♄ or ♂; the ☉ to the ☌ malefics by dir., danger of blindness in the left eye of a female, or in the right eye of a male; the ☉ or ☽ to the ☌ malefics by dir.; the ☉ or ☽ ʼto the ☌ ♂ by dir, and espec. if ♂ be in ♈ at B., and affl. the Lights; the ☉ or ☽ in an airy sign at B., and afflicted, and espec. when affl. the Asc. by dir.; the ☉ or ☽ in the 12th H., and afflicted by Nebulous stars, or malefics (the 12th H. is said to rule the left eye); the ☉ or ☽ affl. at B., and in evil asp. the Asc. by dir, and espec. if the Lights were near Nebulous Stars at B., and otherwise afflicted by malefics; the ☽ to the ☌ the Pleiades, Praesepe, or Ascelli; ♀ ruler of the 12th H., and in the 2nd H., and affl. by ♅ or ♃ (the 2nd H. rules the eyes in Hindu Astrology). Case—See "Left Eye" under Blindness.

(c) Blindness—In the Left Eye—(See "Accidents" (b) in this paragraph).

(d) Danger—To Left Eye—(See (b) in this paragraph).

(e) Defects — In Left Eye — Impediments In—Born under the ☉ or ☽ as rulers, to the left eye of a woman when the ☉ is ruler, and to the left eye of a male when the ☽ is ruler at B.; the ☉ or ☽ affl. at B., and to the ☌ ☋ by dir. (See "Defects" under Eyes).

(f) Hurts to Left Eye—(See (b) in this paragraph).

(g) Impediments—In Left Eye—(See "Defects" (e) in this paragraph).

(h) Larger — The Left Eye Larger Than the Right—(See "Larger" under Eyes).

(i) Marks — Moles — Scar Near Left Eye — The ☉ Sig. of the party, and near, or in ☌ the ☽ or ♂ in a female nativity, and the ☽ likewise in a male horoscope.

(j) Sight—Of the Left Eye—Loss of, or Sight of Affected — ♄ between the 24° and 30° of ♒. (See (b) in this paragraph).

(k) Women—Hurts to Left Eye of—Afflictions to the ☉ at B., and by dir.; the ☉ to the ☌ ♄ or ♂ by dir., and by blows, accident, falls, etc.; the ☉ to the place of Antares. (See (b) in this paragraph). See Antares, Ascelli, Nebulous, Pleiades; "Right Eye" under Right; Sight.

Face—Left Side of—Marks, Moles, or Warts On — Burns To — (See "Face" under Burns; "Left Side" under Face).

Feeble — On the Left Side — The dry and moist elements are more feeble on the left side of the body, and also cold, while the right side of the body is hot. Planets, signs, and houses which predominate in the cold elements at B.

therefore tend to affect the left side more. Saturn is cold in nature, and when in a positive sign at B. tends to affect the left side of a male, and when in a negative and feminine sign, the right side of a male, etc. (See the Introduction to this Article).

Feet—The Left Foot—Marks, Moles, or Scar On—(See "Marks" under Feet).

Females—Accidents, Hurts, or Injury to Left Side—Blindness In Left Eyes— (See "Eyes" in this section; "Blind", "Eyes", "Hurts", "Left", under Females).

Fracture—Of the Left Arm—Case— (See "Left Arm" under Radius).

Heart — Left Auricle of — (See "Auricles" under Heart).

Humours — In the Left Side — (See "Cold and Moist" in this section). .

Hurts—To Left Side of Body—♄ or ♂ afflicted in the positive and masculine signs or houses with a male, and in the negative and feminine signs or houses with females. (See the Introduction, "Eyes", "Feeble", and the various paragraphs in this Article).

Left-Handed—A predominance of planets in the masculine signs in male nativities, or such signs on angles, or the majority of planets at B. in the feminine signs with females. The opposite of these conditions tends to right-handedness. (See Dexterity, Right).

Left Side—Of the Body—Disorders In — Hurts To — Peculiarities of — (See "Eyes", "Feeble", "Hurts", and the various paragraphs in this section).

Leg — Left Leg — (a) Fracture of — Hurts To—♄ or ♂ afflicted in a positive and masculine sign with males, as in ♐ or ♒, and in a feminine sign with females, as ♄ affl. in ♑ or ♓. (See "Hurts" in this section). (b) Left Leg Shorter Than Right—Case—See "Unfortunate Case", No., 351, in 1001 N.N.

Lungs — Lower Left Lobe of — Ruled by ♋. (See Lungs).

Males — Left Eye of — Left Side of — (See the Introduction, Eyes, Feeble, Hurts, and the various paragraphs in this section).

Marks — Moles — Scars On the Left Side—Marks or Scar On the Left Eye — Feminine planets and signs when prominent at B. tend to Marks, Moles, and Scars on the left side of the body in females, and in males when masculine signs and planets predominate. (See Marks, Moles, Scars; Eyes, Face, Feet, in this section).

Moisture — Moist and Cold Humours In Left Side — (See "Cold and Moist" under Humours). Moisture is more feeble in the left side of the body. (See Moisture).

Moles—On the Left Side—(See "Marks" in this section; Moles).

Neck — Left Side of Face and Neck Burned — Case — (See ʼʼFaceʼʼ under Burns).

Ovary—The Left Ovary—Ruled by the ☽. (See Ovaries).

Radius—Of the Left Arm—Fracture of—Case—(See "Left" under Radius).

Scars—On Left Eye—On Left Side—(See "Eyes", "Marks", in this section; Marks, Moles, Scars).

Side—Left Side of Body—Afflictions To—(See "Left Side" in this section).

Sight — Of the Left Eye — Loss of — (See "Eyes" in this section).

Testicle—Left Testicle—Ruled by the ☽. (See Testes).

Toes—Missing On Left Foot—(See Toes).

Women—Hurts to Left Eye of—Hurts to Left Side—(See "Eyes", "Hurts", in this section; "Left Eye" under Blindness).

LEGITIMATE—Is the Child Legitimate? (See "Horary" under Bastards).

LEGS—Lower Limbs—Lower Extremities — The Legs from the hips to the feet are divided into Thighs, Knees, Calves, Ankles, Feet, etc., and are ruled by the different planets and signs which rule these parts. The Thighs are ruled by ♃, ♐, and the 9th H. The Knees are ruled by ♄, ♑, and the 10th H. The Calves, and the Tibia, Fibula, Ankles, and the parts of the leg between the knees and feet, are ruled by ♒, the 11th H., and also influenced by ♄, the ruler of the ♒ sign. The Feet are ruled by ♓ and the 12th H. The Legs as the lower extremities correspond to the arms as the upper extremities, and each part of the arms is ruled by the sign in opposition to the corresponding parts of the lower limbs. (See Arms). The legs correspond to the common, or mutable signs, and to Motion and the Motive Temperament.

— SECTION ONE —

DESCRIPTION OF THE LEGS—

See the following subjects in the alphabetical arrangement when not more fully considered here.

Achilles Tendon—(See Achilles).

Action Of—(See Gait, Lameness, Locomotion, Motion, Movement, Quick, Slow, Walk, etc.).

Ankles; Arteries — Of the Legs — ♃ rules the Arteries of the Legs, and ♀ the Veins.

Bad Legs—Unsound Legs—Caused by ♄ afflictions; ♄ affl. in the 6th H. in a mutable sign. (See Bent, Crooked, Ill-Formed, Knock-Knees, in this section).

Bandy Legs—(See "Bow Legs" in this section).

Bent Legs—The 5th face of ♈ on the Asc. (See Bow Legs, Ill-Formed, Knock-Knees, in this section).

Bones and Joints—Ruled by ♄.

Bow Legs—Bandy Legs—Caused principally by ♄ affliction; the ☉ or ♄ in ♑ and afflicted; ♑ on the Asc.; ♄ as Sig. in Hor'y Q. denotes one bow-legged, or one who knocks his knees or ankles together, or has a shuffling gait; ♃ in ♏ in □ to planets in ♒; ♀ Sig. in ♑; ♏ gives; ♏ on the Asc.; common to natives of ♏; the 1st face of □ on the Asc. (See Bad, Bent, Crooked, Ill-Formed, Knock-Knees, in this section).

Calves; Coarse and Hairy — ♏ gives, and with ♏ on the Asc. (See "Hairy Body" under Hair).

Crooked Legs—♄, ♑, and ♏ influences; ♑ or ♏ on the Asc. (See Bent, Bow Legs, Ill-Formed, Knock-Knees, in this section).

Extremities; Feet; Femur; Fibula;

Fin-Like and Short—(See "Short" in this section).

Foetus—Limbs of—Developed by ♂. (See Foetus).

Frog Child — Both Legs Missing Below the Knees—(See Frog).

Gait; Hairy and Coarse—(See "Coarse" in this section).

Hams;—(See Thighs).

Hips; Ill-Formed — ♑ influence; ♏ or ♑ on the Asc.; the 3rd face of ♋ on the Asc. (See Bent, Bow Legs, Crooked, Knock-Knees, in this section).

Imperfect and Distorted—Case—See "Twins", No. 241, in 1001 N.N.

Joints—Ruled by ♄. (See Joints).

Knees; Knock-Knees—(See "Knock-Knees" under Knees).

Large and Well-Set — (See "Large" under Limbs).

Lean—Small, Lean, Thin and Slender Legs—♄ ascending at B.; ♄ gives when he builds the body; denoted by ♀ in Hor'y Q. (See "Slender" in this section).

Left Leg Shorter — (See "Leg" under Left).

Legless — Both Legs Missing Below the Knees—Case—(See "Missing" under Forearm).

Length of Limbs — (See "Long", "Short", under Bones, Limbs; Brevity, Dwarfed, Giants; "Body" under Short; Tall).

Limbs; Locomotion; Long Legs—Long and Slender — ♀ ascending at B., and free from the rays of other planets; ♀ gives, and shorter if ♀ is ori.; ♃ indicates long legs and feet; □ on the Asc.; the 1st or 4th faces of ♍ on the Asc. (See "Long" under Arms, Bones, Feet, Limbs; Giants; Tall).

Lower Extremities — Lower Limbs — (See Lower; the various paragraphs in this section).

Malformations — (See Sec. 2 of this Article).

Marks—Moles—Scars—(See "Marks" under Left, Right; Marks, Moles, Scars).

Members; Missing; Moles — (See "Marks" in this section).

Motion; Muscles—Of Legs—Ruled by ♂. (See Muscles).

Nerves—Of Legs—Ruled by ♀. (See Nerves).

One Leg Shorter—Case—(See "Leg" under Left).

Patella—Knee Cap—(See Knees).

Quick Walk—(See "Energetic" under Gait).

Scars — On Legs — Caused especially by ♂ in the signs which rule the legs. (See Cuts, Scars).

Shank—(See Tibia).

Shin Bone—(See Tibia).

Short Legs—Short and Fin-Like—Short and Thick — Brevity of Limb — The ☿ and ♍ influences tend to short legs; the 2nd face of ♏ on the Asc., short and thick; ♓ on the Asc., short and fin-like. (See Brevity, Dwarfed; "Body" under Short).

Shorter—Left Leg Shorter—(See "Leg" under Left).

Shuffling Gait—Dragging Gait—(See Gait).

Slender Legs—Thin— Lean—Slender and Small Legs—♄ ascending at B.; a ☿ person; ☿ Sig. of the person in Hor'y Q.; ☿ occidentally posited as regards the ☉ except when ☿ is in ♊. (See Lean, Long, in this section; "Tall and Thin" under Tall, Thin).

Slow Movement—(See "Slow" under Motion).

Small Legs—Small and Slender—Small and Lean—(See "Slender" in this section).

Stout Legs—Stout and Strong—♃ in the Asc.; ♂ in ♌ in partile asp. the Asc.; ♈ gives, and ♈ on the Asc.

Strikes Legs Together—♄ influence and affliction. (See "Knocking Together" under Ankles; "Knock-Knees" under Knees).

Strong Legs—(See "Stout" in this section).

Tendo Achilles—(See Achilles).

Thick and Short—Given by ♏, and with ♏ on the Asc. (See "Short" in this section).

Thighs; Thin Legs—Thin and Lean—Thin and Long—(See Long, Slender, in this section).

Tibia; Toes; Veins Of—Ruled by ♀.

Walk—(See Gait, Walk).

Well-Proportioned—Large and Well-Set—♃ in the Asc. (See "Large" under Limbs; "Stout" in this section).

— SECTION TWO —

DISEASES OF THE LEGS—

Accidents To — Injuries — Hurts — Fractures—Wounds, etc.—The ☉ or ☽ in ♑ or ♒ and afflicted by ♄ or ♂; ♅, ♄, or ♂ in ♐, ♑, or ♒, and afflicted. (See "Accidents" under Extremities).

Aches In—Leg-ache—An ♒ disease and affliction; ♄ affl. in ♒. (See Aches; "Pain" under Limbs, and in this section; Pain).

Action Of—The Action Disabled or Abnormal—(See "Action" in Sec. 1 of this Article; Deformed, Distortions, Lameness, Weak, and the various paragraphs in this section).

Affected—The Legs tend to be affected when the ☉ is in ♑; the in ♈ or ♒; ♅ in ♒; ♄ in ♏ or ♐; ♃ in ♑; ♂ in ♑ or ♒; ♀ ♌; ☿ in ♈ or ♋. (See Table 196 in Simmonite's Arcana of Astral Philosophy. Also see "Affected" under Head).

Affections—Of the Legs—♄ in ♑ or ♒; afflictions in ♒, or ♒ on the Asc. (See "All Diseases", and the various paragraphs in this section).

All Diseases In—All Infirmities In—Afflictions in ♑ or ♒, or with these signs upon the Asc., and containing malefics; the 18° ♑ on the Asc., unfortunate in the legs. (See "Affections", and the various paragraphs in this section).

Amputations—Operations—Avoid Amputations of the legs when the ☽ is passing thru ♐, ♑, or ♒. (See Operations).

Aneurysm—(See Aneurysm).

Ankles—Disorders of—Injuries To—(See Ankles).

Arterial Blood—Obstructions of the Circulation of In the Legs—Caused by afflictions to ♃ when ♃ is in signs at B. which rule the legs; ♄ ☌ ♃ in ♐; ♄ in ♐ in □ or ☍ ♃; ♃ ☌ ♅ in ♐, and affl. by the □ or ☍ ♄. (See Arteries).

Arthritis — Of the Joints — Arthritic Muscular Atrophy—♄ in ♐, ♑, or ♒, ☌ ♂, and affl. also by ♆; ♄ and ♂ afflicted in signs which rule the legs. Case—See Fig. 15B in the book "Astro-Diagnosis" by the Heindels. (See Arthritis, Atrophy).

Atrophy—Arthritic Muscular Atrophy—(See Arthritis, Muscles, Paralysis, in this section).

Bad Legs—Unsound Legs—(See "Bad Legs" in Sec. 1 of this Article).

Bent Legs—(See "Bent Legs" in Sec. 1 of this Article).

Beriberi—(See "Beriberi" under Dropsy).

Blood In—(a) Arterial Circulation Obstructed — (See "Arterial" in this section). (b) Corrupt Blood In—(See "Corrupt Blood" under Hands; "Arms" under Impure). (c) Lack of Blood In—Poor Circulation In—♄ afflicted in signs which rule the legs; few or no planets in signs which rule the lower half of the body. (See "Arterial Blood" in this section). (d) Blood Vessels—Constriction of—♄ in ♐, ♑, or ♒, and resulting from Cold, a ♄ affliction. (See Cold, Constrictions).

Bones Of—Ruled by ♄, and ♄ afflicted in signs which rule the legs tends to affections and diseases of the bones. Also they are affected by Subs at LPP, the 4, 5 Lumbar Vertebrae. (See Bones).

Bow Legs—(See "Bow Legs" in Sec. 1 of this Article).

Broken Legs—(See "Fractures" in this section).

Bruises In—♄ or ♂ in ♑ or ♒. (See Bruises).

Calves—Disorders of—(See Calves).

Circulation Obstructed—Poor Circulation—(See "Blood" in this section).

Cold In—Cold and Numb—♄ affl. in ♐, ♑, or ♒; ♄ affl. in ♒; ☿ affl. in ♋. (See Cold; "Numbness", in this section).

Congenital Defects—(See Crippled from Birth" under Birth; Congenital, Deformities, Distortions; "Club Feet" under Feet; "Birth" under Lameness; "Deformities" in this section).

Constriction—Of the Blood Vessels—(See "Blood" in this section).

Contractions In—♄ affl. in ♐, ♑, or ♒. (See Contractions).

Control—Lack of Control Over—♆ in ♑ or ♌ in □ ☉, and with ♄ affl. in ♐,

♌, or ♒; ♅ in ♐ ♌ ♊; ♄ affl. in ♑, and espec. if ♄ afflict ♆ at the same time, and may be due to spinal complications; ♄ □ or ☍ ♆, and the Prog. ♊ ♌ ♄, sometimes loses control of the legs. (See "Paralysis" in this section).

Corrupt Blood In— (See "Blood" in this section).

Cramps In—♅ in signs which rule the legs; ♄ affl. in ♒; afflictions in ♒. (See Cramps).

Crippled In—(See Accidents, Atrophy, Congenital, Deformities, Lameness, Paralysis, and the various paragraphs in this section).

Cuts—Danger of—♂ afflicted in signs which rule the legs. (See Cuts).

Deformities—♉, ♏, or ♑ on the Asc.; afflictions between ♅ and ♂, or ♄ and ♂, and these planets in common signs; ♄ in the Asc., and afflicted, and espec. if ♄ be in one of the signs ruling the legs. (See Deformities, Distortions; "Frog Child" under Frog; Malformations; "Paralysis" in this section).

Diseases Of—(See "All Diseases", and the various paragraphs in this section).

Distortions— (See Distortions; "Deformities" in this section).

Drawn Up—Under the Body— (See "Paralysis" under Limbs).

Dropsy Of—Afflictions in ♌ or ♒, and often due to a weak heart, and disturbed circulation. (See "Dropsy" under Ankles, Feet; Dropsy; "Swellings" in this section).

Enlarged Veins—(See Varicose).

Eruptions On— ♀ afflicted in signs which rule the legs, and due to wrong habits of eating and living. (See Eruptions; Sores, Ulcers, in this section).

Erysipelas—♂ afflicted in ♒. (See Erysipelas).

Extremities—(See Extremities, Feet, Limbs, Lower).

Falls—The Limbs Distorted by Falls —The ☉ Sig. ♌ ♄, and ♄ ill-dignified, the limbs distorted and broken; ♄ affl. in ♑ or the 10th H.; ♑ on the Asc. (See Distortions; "Limbs" under Falls; "Fractures" in this section).

Feet—(See the various paragraphs under Feet).

Femur—Fracture of—(See Femur).

Fibula—Fracture of—(See Fibula).

Fractures— Broken Legs—Broken Limbs—Afflictions in ♐, ♑, or ♒; ♄ affl. in ♐, ♑, or ♒; ♂ affl. in ♊, ♏, ♐, ♑, or ♒, and ♂ ♌ or evil asp. the Asc. by dir.; ♂ in ♐ in the 6th or 12th H.; ♐ on the Asc. or cusp of 6th or 12th H., or intercepted in these houses. (See Fractures; "Fractures" under Arms, Feet, Knees, Limbs; Accidents, Falls, in this section).

Frog Child—(See Frog).

Gait—Walk—Disorders of—(See Gait, Locomotion, Movement, Walk).

Glands—Vesicles of—Disorders of— ♆ rules and affects the glands of the legs when in signs which rule the legs.—(See Aneurysm; "Affected" under Glands).

Gout—In the Legs—The ♊ affl. in ♐, or afflicting the hyleg therefrom; the ♊ affl. in ♊ when the ♊ is the afflictor in the disease, wandering gout in; ♅ in ♐, and affl. the ☉, ♊, or Asc.; ♄ in ♑, occi., and affl. the ☉, ♊, or Asc.; ♄ affl. in ♓, wandering gout in; ♂ in the Asc. or M.C., and in the latter degrees of ♊, ♐, or ♓; ♂ affl. in ♑, flying gout in the legs; ♂ in ♒ and afflicting the hyleg; ♃ afflicted in ♐; ♃ in ♐ in the 6th H., and afflicted. (See Gout).

Hams—Disorders of—(See Thighs).

Hips — Disorders of — (See Hips, Thighs).

Humours In—♂ in ♍ when ♂ is the afflictor in the disease. (See Humours).

Hurts To—(See Accidents, Fractures, in this section).

Hypertrophy—Of the Muscles—♃ or ♂ afflicted in signs which rule the legs; Subs at LPP (4, 5L). (See Hypertrophy; "Muscles" in this section).

Ill-Formed—(See Sec. 1 of this Article).

Impure Blood In—(See "Blood" in this section).

Incoordination In — (See "Incoordinated" under Gait; "Walk" in this section).

Infirmities In— (See "All Diseases", and the various paragraphs in this section).

Injuries To—(See Accidents, Fractures, in this section).

Jerk—Knee Jerk—Absence of—(See "Knee Jerk" under Knees; Locomotor Ataxia).

Joints—Disorders of—(See "Arthritis" in this section; Joints, Synovial).

Knees—Disorders of—(See Knees).

Knock-Knees—(See Knees).

Lack of—Lack of Blood In—Lack of Control Over—(See Blood, Control, in this section).

Lameness In—The ☉ or ♊ in ♑, ♒, or ♓, and afflicted; ♄ or ♂ in ♐, ♒, or ♓, and afflicting the ☉, ♊, or Asc.; ♀ affl. in ♋ or ♑, and usually from colds settling in the legs; ♐, ♑, ♒, or ♓ on the Asc., and containing malefics, or the Asc. afflicted by them by aspect; malefics in ♐, ♑, ♒, or ♓, and affl. the ☉, ♊, or Asc. (See "Lameness" under Feet, Knees; "Gout", and the various paragraphs in this section).

Legless—(See Sec. 1 of this Article).

Leprosy In—(See Leprosy).

Locomotion—Disorders of—(See Gait, Lameness, Locomotion, Motion, Movement, Paralysis, Walk; "Lameness", and the various paragraphs in this Article).

Locomotor Ataxia—Absence of Knee Jerk In—(See "Knee Jerk" under Knees; Locomotor Ataxia; "Paralysis" in this section).

Lower Limbs—Lower Extremities— The Legs—(See Ankles, Calves, Extremities, Feet, Knees, Limbs, Lower, Thighs. Also note the various paragraphs in this Article).

Malformations—(See "Malformations" under Limbs).

Members—Parts of the Lower Members Missing—Disorders of the Lower Members — (See Extremities; "Frog Child" under Frog; Limbs, Members, Missing. Also note the various paragraphs in this Article).

Milk Leg—Phlegmasia Alba Dolens —Venous Obstruction and Oedema In the Leg—The ☉ afflicted in ♏ when the ☉ is the afflictor in the disease; ♃ affl. in ♒.

Missing—The Legs Missing Below the Knees—Case—(See "Frog Child" under Frog).

Monstrosities—(See this subject).

Motion—In the Legs—Disorders of— (See Gait, Motion, Movement, Walk; Lameness, Paralysis, in this section).

Motor Nerves—♅ in signs which rule the legs tends to cramps, spasms, paralysis, and affections of the motor nerves of the legs. (See Motor).

Movement—Disorders of the Movement of the Legs—(See "Motion" in this section).

Moving Parts—(See Moving).

Muscles—Of the Legs—Ruled by ♂. Afflictions to ♂ when he is in signs which rule the legs tend to disorders of the muscles of the legs. Saturn in signs which rule the legs tends to atrophy of the leg muscles, stiffness of, gout and rheumatism in. The leg muscles are also affected and disturbed by Subs at PP (4, 5L). (See Arthritis, Atrophy, Gout, Hypertrophy, Lameness, and the various paragraphs in this section).

Mutilation Of—(See "Degrees", "Limbs", under Mutilated).

Nerves Of—Disorders of—♅, ♄, or ☿ in signs which rule the legs; afflictions in ♒. (See Aches, Neuralgia, Pain, Paralysis, and the various paragraphs in this section).

Neuralgia In—Pain In—Aches In—☿ afflicted in ♐, ♑, or ♒. (See Aches, Pain, in this section; Neuralgia).

Numbness In—♅ in signs which rule the legs tends to a numbness and prickling sensation in the legs; ♄ affl. in ♐, ♑, ♒, or ♓ tends to a numbness in the lower limbs, and accompanied by a coldness of the parts, and lack of circulation and the proper supply of nerve force at times; ♄ ☌ ♃ or ♀ in ♐, ♑, or ♒, numbness and disturbed circulation. (See Cold, Numbness; "Cold" in this section.

Obstruction In—(See Blood, Numbness, in this section; "Obstructions" under Limbs; Obstructions).

Operations On—(See "Amputations" in this section).

Pain In—The ☉ affl. in ♊; the ☽ affl. in ♉ or ♒, or afflicting the hyleg therefrom; the ☽ in ♒, ☌, or ill-asp. any of the malefics as promittors; ♃ in the 6th H., and afflicted; ♂ in the 12th H.; ♂ promittor in ♒, ☌, or ill-asp. the ☉; ♂ affl. in ♐, ♑, or ♒; ♀ affl. in ♌ or ♒; ♀ affl. in ♒ tends to pain and swelling in the legs from a cold cause. (See "Pain" under Extremities, Feet, Knees, Limbs, Thighs; "Neuralgia" in this section).

Paralysis In—Paraplegia—♅ afflicted in signs which rule the legs. (See "Beriberi" under Dropsy; "Paralysis" under Limbs; Paralysis).

Paraplegia—(See "Paralysis" in this section).

Patella—Fracture of—(See Knees).

Phlegmasia Alba Dolens—(See "Milk Leg" in this section).

Poor Circulation In—(See Blood, Numbness, in this section).

Rheumatism In—Caused by ♄, and with ♄ afflicted in ♐, ♑, or ♒. (See "Gout" in this section; "Rheumatism" under Extremities; Rheumatism).

Rigidity—Of Muscles—♄ affl. in ♐, ♑, or ♒, the result of cold, or excess of mineral deposits and wastes. (See Gout, Lameness, Muscles, Numbness, Pain, Rheumatism, Swellings, in this section; Rigid, Stiff).

Scars On—(See "Scars" in Sec. 1 of this Article).

Sciatica—(See Sciatic).

Shins—(See Tibia).

Skin Diseases—Eruptions—♄ and ♑ rule the skin, and ♄ affl. in ♑ tends to skin disorders of the legs; ♂ affl. in ♑ or ♒, and with eruptions; ♀ affl. in ♐, ♑, or ♒. (See "Eruptions" in this section; Eruptions, Skin).

Sores On—♄ affl. in ♒, and usually due to impure blood, obstructed circulation. (See Sores; Eruptions, Ulcers, in this section).

Spasms In—Spasmodic Diseases of— ♅ affl. in signs which rule the legs. (See Contractions, Cramps, Incoordination, Motor, Nerves, Numbness, Paralysis, in this section; Spasmodic).

Sprains—♄ in ♑ or ♒; afflictions in ♑ or ♒; ♒ on the Asc. (See "Sprains" under Ankles; Sprains).

Stand—Inability to Stand or Walk— Legs Drawn Up Under Body—(See "Paralysis" in this section; "Inability" under Walk).

Stiffness In—(See "Rigidity" in this section; Ankylosis; "Stiffness" under Calves; Joints).

Swellings In—The ☽ affl. in ♒ or ♓; ♄ affl. in ♒; ♃ affl. in the 6th H. in ♐; ♃ in ♐, and affl. the ☽ or Asc.; ♀ affl. in ♒, from a cold cause or heart trouble; ♀ affl. in ♓. (See Blood, Dropsy, Gout, Pain, in this section).

Synovial Fluid—Disturbances of—♄ affl. in ♐, ♑, or ♒. (See Joints; "Joint" under Knees; Synovial).

Tendo Achilles—(See Achilles).

Thighs—Disorders of—(See the various paragraphs under Thighs).

Tibia—Shin Bone—Fracture of—(See Tibia).

Torsion—Torsalgia—(See "Twistings" in this section).

Tumors In—♄ in signs which rule the legs, and the Asc. to the □ or 8 ♄ by dir. (See Tumors).

Twistings In—Torsion—Torsalgia— Contortions—♅ afflicted in signs which rule the legs; Subs at LLP (4, 5L). (See Contortions).

Ulcers In—The ☉ in ♐, ♐, or ill-asp. any of the malefics as promittors; the ☽ affl. in ♒, or afflicting the hyleg therefrom; ♂ in ♒ in the 6th H., and afflicted, or afflicting the ☽ or Asc. (See Ulcers; "Milk Leg" in this section).

Unable to Stand—(See "Stand" in this section).

Unfortunate—In the Legs—(See "All Diseases In", and the various paragraphs in this Article).

Unsound Legs—The ☽ affl. in ♑, ♒, or ♓; ♑ on the Asc. (See "Bad Legs" in Sec. 1 of this Article).

Upper Parts Of—Behind the Knees—All diseases in are signified by the 10th H.

Useless—The Legs Useless—(See "Paralysis" in this section; "Inability to Walk or Stand" under Walk).

Varicose Veins—(See Varicose).

Veins Enlarged—(See Varicose, Veins).

Vesicles Of—Glands of—Disorders of —(See "Glands" in this section).

Walk — Unable to Walk or Stand — (See "Stand" in this section).

Wandering Gout—(See "Gout" in this section).

Wasting Of — ♆ in signs which rule the legs. (See "Legs" under Wasting).

Weak Legs — Weakness In — The ☉ affl. in ♊; the ☽ affl. in ♑; the ☽ in ♍, and afflicted by the ☉ or ♂; ♄ or ♃ affl. in ♑; ☿ affl. in ♓; ♑ or ♒ on the Asc. Case—See Fig. 30 in the book "Message of the Stars", by the Heindels. (See "Weak" under Limbs).

Wounds To—(See "Accidents" in this section).

LENGTH—Lengthening—
Body—Length of—Lengthening of—(See Diminished, Dwarfed, Giants, Growth, Height, Medium, Short, Tall).

Disease — Length of — (See Acute, Chronic, Course, Crises, Duration, Long, Prolonged, Short, Slow, Tedious).

Life—Length of—(See "Death" under Childhood, Infancy, Youth; "Early Death" under Early; "Long Life", "Short Life", under Life).

LENTIGO—(See Freckles).

LEO—The Leo Sign—The Fifth Sign of the Zodiac, and is affiliated with the 5th H. Leo is ruled by the ☉, and is the day and night house of the ☉. The symbol of this sign is the Lion. Leo is classed as a fixed, fiery, electric, positive, masculine, active, vital, constructive, barren, hot and dry sign. This sign is classed as barren because the ☉ is barren. The ☉ is strong in this sign, and ♌ on the Asc. at B. gives great vitality. Leo represents the heart of the physical organism, and is significant of vital force, vital power, generation, interchange and ardency, and the sphere of ♌ is a deep-seated and extensive one. As ♌ is a hot sign, it heats the system, and also under affliction tends to cause loss of equilibrium in mind and body. Leo belongs to the trinity of fiery signs, as ♈, ♌, and ♐, and these are considered the signs of greatest vitality when on the

Asc. at B., and also well-occupied by planets, and especially when rising and elevated in the East at B. Leo draws its strength largely from and thru the Spleen, which is ruled by the ☉. Leo on the Asc. at B. tends to give a tall, commanding figure, strong vitality, fiery and expressive eyes, a good complexion, strong and broad shoulders, a fearless and proud nature. (See Cor Leonis, Lion, Mane of Leo). The Hebrew letter Teth (T) is connected with the ♌ sign, and Teth is predominant in love. Gold is the Metal ruled by ♌. The Colors of ♌ are Gold, Red and Gold, Red and Green. For the Countries and Nations ruled by ♌, see "Leo" under Nations. The Typical Remedy of ♌ is Gold. Magnesium Phosphate is the Salt ruled by ♌. (For further details about the ♌ sign see the classified Articles on Leo in the various Textbooks and Dictionaries of Astrology).

LEO RULES—For a classified list of the influences of each of the planets in ♌, see the Textbooks of Astrology. The principal rulership of ♌ is over the Heart, and the Circulation thru the Heart. Also, ♌ rules the Back, and that part of the Spine back of the Heart, and the Heart Place in the Spine, HP, the 2nd Dorsal Vertebra. Each sign has an external, internal, and structural rulership. Externally, ♌ rules the Back and Forearm. Internally, ♌ rules the Heart. Blood, and Liver. Structurally, ♌ rules the Dorsal Vertebrae, the Radius and Ulna of the Arm, and the Wrists. The following is an alphabetical and classified list of the parts of the body, and other matters ruled by ♌, as listed and mentioned in the various Textbooks of Astrology. See these subjects in the alphabetical arrangement—Aorta; Ardency (see Amorous); Back; Blood; Chamomilla; Children; Circulation of the Blood (♌ and ♎ are concerned with Circulation and Distillation); Circulatory System; Constructive Forces of the Body, along with ♂; Creative Powers; Distillation; Dorsal Region of the Back and Spine; Dorsal Nerves (Middle); Dorsal Vertebrae; Equilibrium in the Body; Fifth House; Forearm; Gall and Gall Bladder; Generation; Gold; Heart; Inferior Vena Cava; Interchange of Forces in the Body; Liver; Magnesium Phosphate Salt; Marrow of the Spine; Middle Dorsal Nerves; Nerve Sheaths; Nerves of the Spine; Offspring; Radius; Salt (Magnesium Phosphate); Spinal Cord; Spine — Dorsal Region of — Marrow and Nerves of); Spleen; Superior and Inferior Vena Cava; Ulna; Vena Cavae; Vital Fluids, Vital Forces, and Vital Power of the Body; Wrists. By aspect and reflex action, the ♌ sign also influences all of the other fixed signs, and the parts of the body ruled by them, and is a part of the Fixed Cross, made up of ♉, ♌, ♏, and ♒.

Leo Qualities — Active, Affectionate, Amorous, Animal, Ardent, Arrogant, Autocratic, Barren, Bitter, Broken, Brutish, Changeable, Choleric, Commanding, Conjugal, Constructive, Convulsive, Diurnal, Dry, Eastern, Electric, Eruptive, Feverish, Fierce, Fiery,

Fixed, Fortunate, Four-Footed, Hasty, Hoarse, Hot, Hot and Dry, Impulsive, Inflammatory, Masculine, Northern, Oppressive, Passionate, Positive, Romantic, Savage, Sharp, Strong, Summer, Violent, Vital.

LEO DISEASES — The Diseases and Afflictions Ruled by Leo—
The Pathological Qualities of ♌ are Ardor, Arrogance, Fixity of Purposes, Impulse, Vitality. Gold is the Typical Remedy of the ♌ Sign, and of the ☉. (See "Sun Diseases" under Sun). The principal diseases of ♌ are those of the Heart and Circulation, and diseases resulting from heart and blood disturbances. Also diseases resulting from Excesses, Pleasures, Amusements, Love Affairs, Passional Excesses, etc. The following are Diseases ruled by the ♌ Sign, which see in the alphabetical arrangement—

Acute Fevers—Acute Diseases—(See Acute).

Anaemia; Aneurysm; Angina Pectoris —(See Angina).

Apoplexy; Arterio-Sclerosis—(See Arteries).

Back—All Diseases and Affections of —Injuries To—(See Back, Spine).

Blood Disorders—The Blood and Circulation Disturbed—(See Blood, Circulation).

Burning Fevers—High Fevers—Sharp — Violent — (See "High Fever" under Fever).

Cardialgia— (See "Heartburn" under Heart).

Carditis—(See "Carditis" under Heart).

Circulation of Blood—Disorders of— (See Arteries, Blood, Circulation, Veins).

Convulsions; Curvature of Spine—(See Curvature, Spine).

Cutaneous Affections — Due to Blood Disorders — (See "Skin" under Blood; Cutaneous; "Skin Diseases" under Skin).

Dizziness; Dropsy; Effusion of Blood —(See Effusions).

Endocarditis—(See Heart).

Enlargement — Of the Heart — (See "Enlarged" under Heart).

Epidemics; Eruptions — Eruptive Fevers—(See Eruptions).

Eyes—Sore and Inflamed Eyes—(See Eyes).

Fainting; Fatty Degeneration—Of the Heart—(See "Fatty" under Heart).

Fevers — High, Violent and Burning Fevers—(See "High" under Fever).

Gout—In the Heart—(See "Gout" under Heart).

Hardening—Of the Arteries—(See Arteries).

Heart Troubles—Various Forms of— (See Heart).

Heartburn—(See Heart).

High Fevers—(See "High" under Fever).

Hot Diseases—(See Fevers; "Dry and Hot Diseases" under Heat).

Hydraemia—(See "Thin Blood" under Blood).

Hyperaemia; Hypertrophy — Of the Heart—(See Heart).

Inflamed Eyes — (See "Inflamed" under Eyes).

Inflammations—Inflammatory Fevers —(See "Fevers", and the various paragraphs under Inflammation).

Injuries—To the Back or Spine—(See Back, Spine).

Jaundice — Yellow Jaundice — (See Jaundice).

Locomotor Ataxia— (See Locomotor).

Marrow of Spine—Diseases of—(See "Marrow" under Spine).

Measles; Meningitis — Spinal — (See Meninges).

Mitral Disorders — (See "Mitral" under Heart).

Neuralgia—Of the Heart—(See "Neuralgia" under Heart).

Oppression — About the Heart — (See "Oppression" under Heart).

Palpitation — Of the Heart — (See Heart).

Passion — Of the Heart — (See Palpitation, Passion, under Heart).

Pericarditis—(See Heart).

Pestilence; Plague; Pleurisy;

Regurgitation—(See Heart).

Rheumatism — In the Back — (See Back).

Ribs—Pains In—(See Ribs).

Sclerosis—Arterial—(See Arteries).

Sharp Fevers — (See "High" under Fever).

Shingles—(See Herpes).

Sides — All Diseases of — (See Ribs, Sides).

Slow Heart Beat—(See Impeded, Slow, under Heart).

Smallpox; Sore Eyes—(See "Inflamed" under Eyes).

Spine — Disorders of — (See Back, Spine, Subluxations, Vertebrae).

Sunstroke — (See this subject under Sun).

Swoonings—(See Fainting).

Syncope—Swooning—(See Fainting).

Tachycardia—(See Heart).

Trembling — Of the Heart — (See Heart).

Valves—Of the Heart—Disorders of— (See Heart, Valves).

Vertigo; Violent Fevers — (See High, Violent, under Fever).

Weak Back—(See Back).

Weak Heart—(See "Weak" under Heart).

Yellow Fever—(See Yellow).

Yellow Jaundice—(See Jaundice).

LEPROSY — This disease is caused by disorders of the Pituitary Body, ruled by ♅, and by a disordered Thyroid Gland, ruled by ☿. The disease is caused by filth of body, uncleanness, sex excesses, moral depravity, and venereal diseases, which disturb the functioning of the Pituitary Body. It is also an endemic, chronic, and infectious disease.

General Causes—The ☽ in the Autumnal Equinox at B., and afflicted by ♄; the ☽ in the sign of the Vernal Equi. at B. tends to white leprosy; the ☽ affl. in ♈, ♉, or ♐, white leprosy; the ☽ affl. in ♎, ♏, or ♐; ♆ in ♑ in the 6th H., or afflicting the hyleg or Asc. from this sign; ♅ afflicted at B., and by dir.; a ♄ and ♑ disease; ♄ or ♂ in the 1st or 7th H. in ♋, ♑, or ♓, in signs ascribed to animals or fishes, and especially when in the latter degrees of the signs containing them; ♄ ☌ ♂ in the 1st or 7th H., in the latter degrees of ♐, ♐, or ♓, ori. of the ☉ and occi. of the ☽, tends to leprosy in the extremities, as in the hands, legs and feet; ♄ in the latter degrees of ♐, ♐, or ♓, and one of them in the 1st or 7th H., and espec. when ♄ is occi. of the ☉ and ori. of the ☽, tends to leprosy in the extremities; ♀ affl. at B., and by dir.; lords of the 1st, 6th H., or the ☽ in airy signs; Subs at CP and KP. Cases— See "Child of a Leper", No. 355 in 1001 N.N. Also see Fig. 12A in the book, "Astro-Diagnosis", by the Heindels. (See Depraved, Endemic; "Diseases" under Extremities; Filth, Infections; "Loose Morals" under Morals; Pituitary; "Sex Excesses" under Excesses, Passion, Sex; Thyroid, Uncleanly, Venereal).

Treatment of Leprosy—The use of Chaulmoogra Oil is said to be a cure for this disease. In Guayaquil, Ecuador, 300 cases are said to have been cured by the use of Colodial Salts of Antimony. For information as to the Cure, write to the Department of Agriculture, Washington, D.C.

LEPTOMENINGITIS—(See Meninges).

LESIONS—Structural Tissue Changes from Disease or Injury, and caused principally by ♅ influence. Also, ♄ and ♂ are prominent in causing Lesions.

  Bowels—Lesion In—(See Typhoid).

  Corrosions—(See Corrosions).

  Cortical Lesion—(See Cortical).

  Heart—Valvular Lesion of—(See "Lesions" under Heart).

  Nerves—Nervous System—Lesion of —(See Corrosion; "Lesions" under Nerves; Paralysis).

  Paralysis—Nerve Lesions—(See "Nerves" in this section).

  Peripheral Lesion—(See "Aphonia" under Vocal).

  Valvular Lesions—(See "Lesions" under Heart).

LESS—Lessened—

  Less Liable to Disease—(See "Less Liable" under Disease).

  Less Power—To Throw Off Disease— (See "Less Power" under Disease).

  Resistance Less—To Disease—Recuperative Powers Low—(See Recuperation, Resistance, Vitality Low).

  Vitality Lessened—(See Vitality).

LETHARGY—A Condition of Drowsiness—The ☉ and ♂ unaspected at B.; the ☽ affl. in ♈ with females; the ☽ affl. in ♈, or afflicting the hyleg therefrom; the ☽ in ♈, ☌, or ill-asp. any of the malefics as promittors; the ☽ Sig.

in ♑ or ♓; the ☽ in ♓, an easy-going and inactive disposition; the ☽ to the ☌ or ill-asp. ♄ by dir.; a ♆ disease; caused by ♆ when the bodily powers are in abeyance, and the psychic powers are in a state of hyperactivity; ♄ ☌ the Asc. by dir., and to cause drowsiness; ♃ Sig. in ♑; ♀ affl. in ♈; a ♀ disease, and caused by afflictions to ☿ as ☿ rules vibration, and a lessened rate of vibration tends to dull the senses; ☿ denotes death by lethargy; ♋ on the Asc. at B. tends to give a lethargic disposition. Encephalitis, with great lethargy, accompanies Influenza and Sleeping Sickness. Lethargy, attended by short remissions, is caused by ♆. (See Apathy, Cataphora, Depressed, Dull, Encephalon; "Lack Of" under Energy; Ennui, Fatigue, Hyperaesthesia, Idle, Inactive, Indifferent, Inertia, Influenza, Lassitude, Lazy, Listless, Pituitary, Rouse; "Drowsiness", "Sleeping Sickness", under Sleep; Weariness).

LEUCEMIA—(See Leukocytes).

LEUCO—See words beginning with Leuko.

LEUCOMAINES—Leokomain—(See "Offensive" under Humours).

LEUCORRHOEA—Leukorrhea—Fluor Albus—Whites In Women—Catarrh of the Womb—A ♍ disease, and caused by afflictions in ♍; the ☽ affl. in ♎, ♏, or ♑; the ☽ in ♎ or ♑, ☌, or ill-asp. any of the malefics as promittors; the ☽ in any of the fixed signs and afflicted by ♆, ♅, or ♄; the ☽ in the 6th H. in evil asp. to ♀ in ♍, in Hor'y Q. denotes a person suffering with this trouble; the ☉ in ♉, ♌, or ♒, and afflicted by ♆, ♅, or ♄ when attended by profuse menstruation; ♄ affl. in ♋ in the 8th H.; ♄ affl. in ♏; a ♀ disease; ♀ affl. in ♍; Subs at KP, and PP (2, 3, 4L). (See "Profuse" under Menses; Vagina; "Catarrh" under Womb).

LEUKEMIA—(See Leukocytes).

LEUKOCYTES—Leukemia—Leucaemia —White Blood Corpuscles. These are said to be destroyers of the body, and to form a nucleus for mineral deposits. They are manufactured in the Spleen, and are principally the work of ♄. During anger, and also during disease and various afflictions, they pass thru the walls of the blood vessels, and deposit themselves in weakened or diseased tissues, and form a nucleus for the increased deposit of mineral wastes of the body, forming tumors, ulcers.

  Increase Of—Leukemia—Leukocytosis —Caused by ♄ afflicted at B., or ♄ afflicting the hyleg; ♄ affl. in ♍, as ♍ rules the Spleen; ♄ in ♍ and afflicting the ☉, ☽, Asc., or Hyleg; ♄ afflicted at B., and ♂ weak; Subs at CP, SP, and KP. (See Anaemia, Deposits, Lymph, Minerals, Spleen, Tumors, Wastes).

LEUKOCYTOSIS—(See Leukocytes).

LEOKOPLASIA BUCCALIS—(See Tongue).

LEWD—Libidinous—Lustful—Lascivious—Given to Lewd Companies of Women or the Opposite Sex—The ☉ afflicted in watery signs; the ☽ afflicted in ♏ or ♑; the ☽ decr., separating from

♂ and applying to ♀, disgrace thru wantonness; ♂ ill-dig. at B., and affl. the ☽ or ♀; ♂ in the house of ♀; ♂ Sig. ☌ ♀, often associates with women of no respectability; ♂ Sig. ✶ or △ ♀; ♂ ☌ or afflicting ♀; ♂ and ♄ to the ill-asps. ♀ by dir.; ♀ in bad asp. to ♂ at B., and by dir; ♀ to the ill-asps. ♄ by dir.; ♀ in ♈, ♍, ♏, or ♑, and afflicted by ♂, and espec. ♀ in ♏; ♀ to the ☌ ♂ or ♂ by dir., disgrace thru lewd courses; ♀ ill-dig. at B. (See Debauched, Depraved, Disgrace, Dissipated, Excesses, Exhibitionism, Harlots, Improvident, Lascivious, Licentious, Lust; "Loose Morals" under Morals; Nymphomania, Parents; "Passional Excesses" under Passion; Perversions, Sex, Shameless, Virile, Wanton, Wench).

LIABLE—Liability To—Tendency To—Danger of, etc.—

Accidents—Hurts, Injuries, Wounds—Liable To — (See "Danger Of", "Liable To", "Tendency To", etc., under Accidents, Hurts, Injuries).

Disease—Liable To—(See Directions; "Liable To" under Disease; "Bad Health", "Periods of Bad Health", under Health; Invalids, Lunations, Progressed; "Low" under Resistance, Vitality; Sickly; "Much Sickness" under Sickness; Sixth House; Transits; "Weak Body" under Weak).

Less Liable to Disease — (See "Good Health" under Health; Immunity; "Strong" under Recuperation; "Good" under Resistance, Vitality; Robust, Ruddy, Stamina; "Body" under Strong; Tone). The ills to which humanity are subject are legion, and too numerous to list here. Look in the alphabetical arrangement for the subject you have in mind. See Character, Destiny, Disgrace, Dishonour, Fate, Pain, Reversals, Ruin, Sorrow, Suffering, Trouble; "Free Will" under Will. A person may be liable to many evils, according to the indications of their star maps, especially if they are drifting in life, lacking in wisdom, self-control, discretion, discrimination, and the knowledge of Astrology, but the student of the Occult, of Astrology, the Metaphysical, etc., can usually by his foreknowledge forestall many evils that would naturally overtake the ignorant, the uninitiated, and those who are not ruling their stars. Ripe Fate may be the exception, which is discussed under "Fate".

LIARS—Lying—Falsifiers— ☿ affl. at B., and the ☽ to the ☌ or ill-asp. ☿; ☿ ill-dig. at B.; ☿ □ or ☍ ☽); ☿ Sig. in ♈; ☿ to the ☌ or ill-asp. ♂ by dir., and ♂ weak; ♄ and ♂ afflicting ☿; ♄ Sig. □ or ☍ ☿; ♂ to the ☌ or ill-asp. ☿; ♂ Sig. □ or ☍ ☿, his most solemn protestations are not to be believed. (See Artifice, Character, Cheating, Deceitful, Dishonest, Dual, Forgers, Gambling, Hypocrites, Knavish, Libel, Mischief, Perjury, Pettifogging, Principles, Shrewdness, Swindlers, Thieves, Treachery, Truth).

LIBEL — Libellers — Given to Libel — Blackmailers — Slanderers — Defames the Character of Others — Writers of Libel—Liars, etc.— ☿, the mental ruler, ill-dig. at B., afflicted by malefics, and the ☽ to the ill-asps. ☿ by dir.; ☿ at a

Solar Rev. passing the place of the radical ♂; ☿ Sig. □ or ☍ ♄, much given to villifying the character of others, and is apt to suffer lawsuits for libel and blackmail; the ☽ incr. in light, sepr. from ♄ and apply. to ☿; ♃ to the ill-asps. ☿ by dir., and ☿ afflicted by ♃ at B.; ♂ to the ill-asps. ☿ by dir., and ☿ affl. by ♄ or ♂ at B.; the M.C. to Algenib, danger of imprisonment thru libel. (See Character, Dishonesty, Liars; "Scandalmongers" under Scandal).

LIBERTY—At Liberty to Travel Where You Will—(See "Home or Abroad" under Travel).

LIBIDINOUS—Violently Libidinous—(See Lewd, Lust, Nymphomania, Virile).

LIBRA — The 7th Sign of the Zodiac, the day and home sign of ♀, and is related to the 7th H. Libra is classed as an airy, cardinal, positive, masculine, hot, warm, moist, humane, and nervous sign. It is the exalted sign of ♄, and the fall of the ☉. When afflicted it causes inharmony and want of tone by disturbances in the system, and disordered kidneys. Libra implies sublimation, which is vaporization and recondensation. The Symbol of this sign is "The Balance", and the influence of the sign is to help keep the balance in the system by the work of secretion, excretion, elimination, and separating the poisons which are carried off in the urine. Libra and ♒ are considered the weakest of the positive signs. Externally, ♎ rules the external Generative and Urinary Organs, and the Anus. Internally, it rules the Kidneys. Structurally, this sign rules the Lumbar Vertebrae. Libra rules the outer or upper portion of the Kidneys, the Medullary and Cortical Substances. Libra and ♌ are concerned with Distillation and Circulation, and ♎ especially rules Distillation and Filtration. Libra and ♏ are closely associated in the work of the kidneys, secretion and excretion of urine. (See Kidneys, Scorpio, Urine). Libra is a rather fruitful sign because of ♀. For the Nations and Countries ruled by ♎ see "Libra" under Nations. The Colors ruled by ♎ are Black, and Dark Crimson. The Hebrew letter "Lahmed" (L) is connected with the ♎ sign, and also with Sleep and Dreams. When on the Asc. at B. the ♎ sign gives a tall, graceful, slender body, but the last few degrees rising, the body is shorter and stouter due to the influence of the next sign ♏. The Pathological Qualities of ♎ are Jealousy, Melancholy, Self-Centeredness, Sensitiveness. (See Seventh House, Venus). The following are the Qualities ruled over, or given by ♎ —Airy, Artistic, Autumnal, Beauty, Cardinal, Changeable, Diurnal, Equinoctial, Fortunate, Fruitfulness, Graceful, Hot, Humane, Masculine, Moist, Moveable, Musical, Nervous, Obeying, Positive, Sanguine, Southern, Speaking, Sweet, Warm, Western, Whole, etc.

LIBRA RULES—For the external, internal and structural rulerships of ♎ see the Introduction to this Article. The following is an alphabetical list of the parts of the body, and other matters ruled by ♎. Look for these subjects in the alphabetical arrangement—Adrenals; Anus; Back — Lower Part of; Balance — Poise and Equilibrium; Black or Dark Brown in Hor'y Q; Black or Dark Crimson Colors; Bladder; Blue and Dark Crimson; Circulation; Colors—Black or Dark Brown —Black or Dark Crimson—Swarthy or any Dusky Color—Blue and Dark Crimson—Tawny; Cortical Substances of the Kidneys; Crimson Color; Dark Brown Color in Hor'y Q.; Dark Crimson or Black; Distillation of Urine; Dusky Colors; Equilibrium, Equipose; Fallopian Tubes; Filtration, Distillation and Sublimation of Urine; Functional Activity of Secreting Urine; Generative Organs — External; Haunches to the Buttocks; Hypogastrium; Jealousy; Kidneys—Outer and Upper Parts of; Liver; Loins; Lower Part of the Back; Lumbar Region in General, Including the Lumbar Nerves, the Lumbar Vertebrae, Lumbar Region of the Spine, and the Kidneys; Medullary and Cortical Substances of the Kidneys; Melancholy; Mouth (Duz); Nerves (Lumbar); Outer and Upper Part of the Kidneys; Ovaries; Poise; Recondensation; Reins of the Back; Remedy —Rhus Toxicodendron; Renal System (see Kidneys); Rhus ˙ Toxicodendron (see "Saturn Group" under Herbs); Secretion of Urine; Self-Centeredness; Sensitiveness; Skin; Sodium Phosphate Salt; Spine (Lumbar Region of); Sublimation of Urine; Suprarenals; Tawny Color; Tongue (Duz); Upper Part of Kidneys; Ureters; Urinary Organs (External); Urine — Distillation, Filtration, Secretion, and Sublimation of; Vaporization; Vaso-Motor System; Veins; Vertebrae (Lumbar).

LIBRA DISEASES—The Afflictions of —Pathological Effects of—See the following subjects in the alphabetical arrangement when not considered here—

Abscess—(Imposthumes)—Of the Bladder—Of the Kidneys—Of the Reins —(See "Abscess" under Bladder, Kidneys, Loins, Reins).

Anuria—Suppression of Urine—(See Urine).

Atrophy—Wasting— (See Atrophy, Wasting).

Back—All Diseases In—Injuries or Weakness In the Lower Part of the Back—Disorders In Reins of the Back —(See Back, Reins).

Bladder—Disorders of—All Diseases In — Abscess, Imposthumes, or Ulcers In—(See Bladder).

Blood—Corrupt Blood—(See Impure).

Bright's Disease—(See Bright's).

Calculus — Renal — In thé Kidneys — (See "Kidneys" under Stone).

Colic—Renal—(See "Colic" under Kidneys).

Coma; Corruption—Of the Blood—(See Impure).

Debility—Weakness—(See Debility).

Diabetes; Diseased Kidneys—Distempered Kidneys—(See Kidneys).

Distillation—Of Urine—Disturbances of—(See Distillation, Filtration, Sublimation, Urine).

Eczema; Emaciation — (See Emaciation, Tabes).

Filtration — Of Urine — Disturbances of — (See Filtration, Distillation, Sublimation, Urine).

Floating Kidney—(See Kidneys).

Functions — Functional Disturbances of the Kidneys — (See "Diseased Kidneys" under Kidneys; "Suppression" under Urine).

Gravel—In the Bladder or Kidneys— (See Gravel).

Haunches—Heats In—(See Buttocks, Haunches).

Head — Pains In or Injury To — (See Head).

Health—Of Libra People—The Health of ♎ People, and in Countries ruled by ♎, tends to be good when the ☉, ☽, ♃, or ♀ are in ♎ at the Autumn Quarter, and free from affliction, but poor and afflicted in health when the malefics so occupy ♎.

Heats—(See "Heats" under Buttocks).

Imposthumes—(See "Abscess" in this section).

Inflammation — Of the Kidneys and Ureters—(See Kidneys, Ureters).

Inharmony—In the System—And Disturbances—Afflictions in ♎. (See "Disordered" under System).

Insomnia—(See Sleep).

Ischuria—False Ischuria—(See Ischuria).

Kidneys—All Diseases In—(See Kidneys).

Liver—Disorders of—(See Liver).

Loins — Abscess In — Pains and Diseases In—(See Loins).

Lower Part of Back—Pains and Diseases In—(See Back).

Lues—(See Syphilis).

Lumbago; Lumbar Region — Of the Spine—Diseases In—(See Lumbar).

Malnutrition—(See Nutrition).

Nephritis—(See Kidneys).

Neuralgia—Of the Kidneys—(See Kidneys).

Pains — In the Back and Kidneys — (See "Pain" under Back, Kidneys).

Pathological Action—Of the ♎ Sign— (See the Introduction to this Article).

Polyuria — (See Diabetes; "Polyuria" under Urine).

Poor Health — (See "Health" in this section).

Pyelitis—(See Kidneys).

Reins — All Diseases In — Abscesses, Imposthumes, and Ulcers In — (See Reins).

Renal Disorders — Renal Calculus — Renal Colic—(See Kidneys).

Sand—(See Gravel, Sand, Stone).

Skin Diseases—(See Skin).

Sores; Spurious Ischuria—(See "Ischuria" under Urine).·

Stone — In the Bladder or Kidneys — (See Stone).

Suppression of Urine—(See Urine).

Syphilis; Tabes; Tone—Lack of—(See Tone).

Tumors—Of the Kidneys—(See Kidneys).

Ulcers—In the Bladder or Reins—(See "Ulcers" under Bladder, Reins).

Uremia; Ureters—Inflammation and Obstruction In—(See Ureters).

Urine—Disturbances of—(See Urine).

Veins—All Diseases of—(See Veins).

Wasting Diseases—(See Atrophy, Consumptions, Emaciation, Tabes, Wasting).

Weakness—In the Back—General Weakness and Debility—(See "Weak" under Back; Debility, Weak).

LICENTIOUSNESS—Lascivious—Lewd —Wanton—Loose—Dissolute, etc.— Ruled and indicated by the 5th H.; the ☽ sepr. from ♄ and applying to ♀; ♀ affl. in the 5th H., licentious habits; ♅ in ☐ or ☍ to planets, and espec. to ♀; ♂ with ♀ alone, and ♄ absent; ♂ Sig. ☐ or ☍ ♀; in a female horoscope ♂ and ♀ in masculine signs, and in ☌, or evilly configurated, tend to make women licentious beyond nature, and espec. if the Luminaries also be in masculine signs at B.; ♀ ill-dig. at B.; ♀ affl. at B., and to the ☌ or ill-asp. the Asc. or ♂ by dir.; ♀ Sig. ☐ or ☍ ♂; the 3rd Decan. of ♎ on the Asc. (See Amorous, Debauched, Depraved, Dissipation, Dissolute, Harlots, Indecent, Lascivious, Lewd; "Licentious" under Men; "Loose Morals" under Morals; Nymphomania, Obscene, Passion, Perversions, Scandal, Shameless, Wanton, etc.).

LIFE—Prospects of Life—Length of Life, etc.—The expression of life, continuity, and the giving of life, are the most salient characteristics of the ☉, and the ☉ has significance of life and the constitution. The 1st H. also has signification of the life of Man, and his physical body and appearance. The ☉ gives the life force, and life and joy are said to come from the ☉. The fiery signs are life-giving signs. Life also corresponds to the fixed signs, and to the heart and Vital Temperament. Life manifests as motion, or vibration. Saturn afflicts and suppresses life and joy by his evil aspects to the ☉, ☽, Asc., or Hyleg. The following subjects have to do with life, and the planetary influences as they affect and influence life for good or ill, which subjects see in the alphabetical arrangement when not considered here—

Accidents; Anareta—The Destroyer of Life—(See Anareta).

Average Life—The ☉ well-aspected in the Asc. at B. indicates an average length of life, and a strong constitution in Hor'y Q. (See "Long Life" under Life; Middle Life).

Benefics—The Benefics As Givers and Preservers of Life—(See Benefics).

Birth—Continuance of Life After Birth—(See "Continuance' in this section).

Change of Life—(See "Menopause" under Menses).

Changeable Life—(See Changes, Instability, Location, Residence, Restless, Roaming, Travel, Unstable, Wandering).

Childhood—Life In—(See Childhood).

Close of Life—(See Close, Fourth House, Old Age, Terminal).

Conscious Life—(See Consciousness).

Continuance of Life—Continuity of Life—The continuance and continuity of life after birth are expressed by the ☉; the ☉, ☽, and Asc., and one of them hyleg, well-aspected by benefics, and with good aspects among them, and free from the evil asps. of malefics, promote life and give a strong constitution; the benefics ♃ and ♀ angular, free from affliction, and in good asp. to the hyleg, as by ☌, ⚹, △, or P., is a good sign of the continuance of life; the ☉ hyleg in a male nativity, and well-aspected, and the ☽ hyleg in a female nativity, well-aspected, and free from the afflictions of malefics, indicate a continuance of life, and long life. The last aspect formed between the ☉ and ☽ before birth, whether a good or evil asp., is important to be considered when judging of the influences as to continuance and duration of life. Also, in considering whether the child will live, the Asc., its ruler, and the ruler of the 8th H., the house of death, should be noted, and their aspects and relations to each other, whether good or bad. The lord of the 8th H., and especially when a malefic, and afflicting the lord of the Asc. at B., is not favorable for a continuance of life, and the child may soon die. (See "Death" under Childhood, Children, Infancy; "Early Death" under Early; "Nurture" under Infancy; "Long Life", "Short Life", and the various paragraphs in this section).

Corresponds To—Life Corresponds To—(See Introduction to this Article).

Danger to Life—The Life In Danger —Danger of Losing the Life—In Danger of Death—May Cause Death— Death Threatened, etc.—The ☉ to the ☌ or ill-asp. ♄ or ♂ by dir., and the ☉ hyleg at B.; the adverse asps. of the ☉ to ♄, ♆, ♅, or ♂ by dir., and espec. among the Aged, or those of a frail constitution; the ill-asps. of several malefic promittors to the ☉ tend to double or treble the danger to life, cause a breakdown in health, disaster or death; a total Eclipse of the ☉ falling on the place of the ☉ at B., and espec. when the ☉ is badly afflicted at B., or by dir.; the ☉ in the 6th or 8th H. at B., and to the ☌ or ill-asp. ♄ by dir.; the ☽ hyleg and to the ☌ or ill-asp. ♄ by dir.; the ☽ Sig. in ☌ the ☉ by dir., and espec. if the ☽ be applying, and it happens in the 8th H., or the ☉ be lord of the 8th; the ☽ hyleg and afflicted, and to the cusp the 8th H. by dir.; the ☽ to the ☌, P., or ill-asp. ♂ by dir., and the danger is by accident, blow, cut, stab, fever, or violence; the ☽ sepr. from the ☉ and apply. to ☿ in a night nativity; the ☽ at Full, or incr. in a nocturnal nativity, sepr. from ♀ and apply. to ♂; the ☽ at a Solar Rev. passing over the place of ♂ at B., and the ☽ afflicted at the Revolution; the ☽ to the ☐ or ☍ ☿ if the ☽ be hyleg, and ☿ afflicted at B.; the ☽ apply. to the ☍ ♂ in the 8th H., and when in exact ☍; the ☽ hyleg and to the ☌ the ☉ by dir., and the ☉ and ☽ afflicted at B.; the New ☽ implies death, disintegration, and preparation for a new Cycle, and a New ☽, or Lunation, badly afflicted just previous to birth, or just before a disease sets in, is very evil for a continuance of life; ♅ afflicting the hyleg by dir.; ♅ passing over the place of ♂ at B. by transit, and if afflicting the ☉ at the same time; taken sick in a ♄ hour; operating evil primary and secondary directions bring danger of death when the hyleg is evilly aspected at B., but supported by the benefics. (See "Danger of Death" under Children; Danger; "Arguments for Death" under Death; Directions, Eclipses, Fatal, Lunations; "New Moon" under Moon; Old Age, Transits, etc.).

Death — (a) Death Threatened — See "Arguments for Death", "Threatened", under Death. (b) Death Not Imminent —(See "Spared" in this section).

Destiny — (See Character, Destiny, Events, Fate).

Destroyed—Life Destroyed—The hyleg setting on the Western Angle, death ensues; the hyleg ☌, □, or 8 ♄ or ♂ in the Zodiac or Mundane P. when they are equally distant from any angle, is said to destroy life. It takes a train of evil directions to the hyleg to destroy life, and one evil direction seldom kills, and espec. if the native be young, vigorous and healthy. (See "Certain Death", "Sure Death", under Death; Directions, Fatal).

Destroyers of Life — (See Anareta, Malefics).

Dies Soon After Birth — (See Abortion, Birth, Infancy, Parturition).

Directions—The Effect of Directions On Life—(See Directions).

Does Not Live to Old Age — (See "Death At Middle Life" under Middle Life; "Old Age Seldom Attained" under Old Age).

Duration of Life — (See Continuance, Long Life, No Duration, Probable, Short Life, and the various paragraphs in this section; "Death" under Childhood, Children, Early, Infancy, Middle Life, Old Age, Youth, etc.).

Early Death—(See Early).

Early Life — (See Childhood; "Early Years" under Early; Infancy).

End of Life—Ruled principally by the 4th H. (See Death, Eighth House, End, Fatal, Fourth House, Old Age, Terminal, Twelfth House).

Evils of Life—(See Evil).

Excess of Life Force — (See "Life Force" in this section).

Expression of Life — (See Introduction to this Article).

Extravagant Life—(See Extravagant, Luxury).

Fatal to Life—(See Fatal).

Father — The Father Long-Lived — Short Life For—(See Father, Parents).

Few Hours of Life—Lives But a Few Hours—(See "Death Soon After Birth" under Infancy).

Fires of Life—They are kept burning by the life-giving ☉, and the Iron

given by ♂, and the cleansing power of ♂ in eliminating wastes and filth. (See Iron; "Constructive" under Mars).

First Half of Life—Is said to be ruled by the ☽. (See Periods).

Force—Forces—The Life Force—(See "Excess", "Life Force", under Force; Vital).

Giver of Life — Giving of Life — (See Hyleg; the Introduction to this Article).

Hazards Life — To Rescue Others — (See Rescue).

Hope of Life—Small Hope of Life— The Sick Will Hardly Escape—The ☽ in ♈, afflicted by the ☉ or ♂ when taken ill, and espec. if the ☽ leaves the ☌ of ♂ and goes to the ☌ or 8 ♄ during the illness, or if the ☽ decr. in light and be slow in motion (Hor'y). (See "Destroyed", "Spared", in this section; "Certain Death" under Death; "Sick" under Escape; Fatal).

Hyleg—The Giver of Life—(See Hyleg).

Idle Life—(See Idle).

Ill-Health All Thru Life — (See this subject under Ill-Health).

Indigent Life—(See Indigent).

Infancy — Dies In — (See "Death" under Infancy).

Joy and Life—Come from the ☉. (See Joy).

Judging of Life—Judging the Length of Life—(See "Length" in this section).

Killed — Sudden End to Life — (See Killed).

Lease On Life—A New Lease On Life —Is given by the fevers and inflammations brought by ♂ to burn out the dross and accumulated impurities, provided the system has enough fundamental vitality to withstand his severe cleansing fires. (See Cleansing; "Constructive" under Mars).

Length of Life—Judgment on this is formed on the ☉, ☽, Asc., and lord of the Asc., their aspects, etc., and also the strength of the hyleg. (See Duration, Length; Continuance, Duration, Long, Probable, Short, in this section).

Life Destroyed—(See "Destroyed" in this section).

Life Force — The ☉ gives the life force. Also ♂ aids in giving force, activity, and energy. The ☉ ☌ ♄ at B., the life forces are obstructed, sapped and undermined. (See "Force" in this section).

Life-Giving Signs—The Fiery Signs— (See "Fire Signs" under Fire).

Life Saved—The Life Will Be Spared —Will Not Be Saved—(See "Spared" in this section).

Long Life—Signs of—Marks of—Dies In Old Age—Marks of Long Life—The SUN, ☽, Asc., and hyleg strong at B., well-aspected, and free from evil asps. of malefics; the ☉ rising in ♈, ♌, or ♒, well-placed, and not afflicted; the ☉ well-aspected in 8 at sunrise; the ☉ in the 1st H., well-aspected and dignified; the ☉ or ☽ in the 1st, 10th, 11th, or 2nd H., and well-aspected by ♃ and ♀; the less the ☉ is afflicted at B., and espec. with males, and the less the ☽ is afflicted with females, the greater the prospects of long life; the ☉ hyleg and well-aspected with males, and the ☽ hyleg, and well-asp. with females, promises long life; the ☉ strong in male nativities; the ☉ in ♑ gives longevity, and to cling to life to the very last; the ☉ and ☽, and the ♌ and ♋ signs, the signs of the ☉ and ☽, well-placed in the map, long lease of life is assured; the ☉ elevated, ♃ and ♀ angular, and in greater power than the malefics; the ☉ well-aspected by the ☽ and benefics, and free from the affliction of malefics; the ☉, ☽, Asc., or hyleg not vitiated by malefics, or lords of the 6th or 8th H.; the ☽ sepr. from the △ of ♀, and applying to the △ of ♃, and with ♃ in the Asc. or M.C., and well-aspected by malefics; the MOON in good asp. to the ☉; the ☽ free from affliction, and well-aspected by ♃ or ♀, and also the Asc. free from malefic planets; the ☽ free from affliction, not combust, or evilly aspected by lords of the 4th, 6th, 8th, or 12th H.; the ☽ and lord of the Asc. direct in motion, swift, angular, and especially in the 1st or 10th H., or in the 8th or 11th., well-aspected by ♃, ♀, and the ☉, or in terms of ♃ or ♀; the ☽ well-asp. in the 8th H., but with danger of drowning; SATURN in ♎ or ♏, and well-aspected; ♄ well-asp. in the 8th H., and espec. when in ♎ or ♑ in the 8th; ♄ moderately fortified in the 1st H., and well-asp. by the ☉, ☽, ♃, or ♀; JUPITER or ♀ in the 8th H. and well-aspected; ♃ and ♀ in good asp. to the hyleg, and not afflicted by malefics; ♃ ☌ or good asp. the ☉, usually long life; ♃ in the 1st H. near the cusp, long life and happiness; MARS ✶ or △ the ☉, usually long life; the ASCENDANT, its lord, and planets there, be well-dignified, free from affliction, well-posited, and increasing in light and motion; if the Asc., lord of the Asc., and the ☉ or ☽, or the majority of them, are strong, free from affliction, not combust or ℞, not near any violent fixed stars, not besieged by malefics, or having the declinations of malefics, and not impeded by the lords of the 4th, 6th, 8th, or 12th H., these are signs of long life, and most or all of these conditions reversed denote short life or great danger to the native; the Asc., and the ☉ and ☽ free from affliction; lord of the 1st H. and the ☽ in no way afflicted, and no malefic, nor the lord of the 8th, nor ☋ ascending, are considered marks of a long life; lord of the 1st and the ☽ in ☌, or well-aspected by a benefic, or a benefic in the Asc.; the distance between the lords of the 1st and 8th H., allowing one degree for a year, indicate the length of life of the native, as a rule, or the event of some serious illness or accident, but as the body of the ☉ may be considered Anareta, if the lord of the 1st become combust before he reaches the lord of the 8th, then reckon according to the number of degrees between him and the ☉ (Hor'y); lord of the Asc. in the 1st H.; lord of the 8th a benefic, in the 8th, and not afflicting the hyleg; lord of the 8th in the 8th H., even if a malefic, and not afflicted; the 1st Decan. of ♍

on the Asc., ruled by the ☉; the 3rd face of ♐ on the Asc.; the 6th face of ♒ on the Asc.; the 4° ♍, the 3° ♑, the 2° ♒, the 10° ♓ on the Asc. indicate long life. (See Duration; "Long Life" under Females, Males; "Good Health", "Prospects", under Health; Hyleg, Immunity; Majority, Maturity, Old Age, Recuperation, Resistance, Stamina; "Body" under Strong; Vitality; "Continuance", "Seldom", and the various paragraphs in this section).

Maintenance of Life — Life Is Maintained by the ☉, the giver of life, and by ♂, the giver of iron in the blood. (See "Fires of Life" in this section).

Malefics — Destroyers of Life — (See Anareta, Malefics).

Man — Life of Man — The 1st H. has significance of the life of man, his body, and physical appearance.

Manifests—Life Manifests as Motion and Vibration. (See Motion, Vibration).

Manner of Life—Manner of Living— (See Conduct, Habits, Manner, Morals).

Many Illnesses—All Thru Life—(See "Ill-Health All Thru Life" under Ill-Health; "Much Sickness" under Sickness).

Maturity — Lives To — (See Maturity, Middle Life).

Middle Life — Lives To — (See Middle Life).

Military Life — Injury or Death In — (See Military).

Miserable Life—(See Miserable).

Mother — Long Life For — Short Life For—(See Mother).

Motion and Life—(See "Manifests" in this section).

Night Life—Disposed To—(See "Nocturnal" under Night).

No Duration of Life—(See "Death At Birth" under Birth; "Early Death" under Early; Eclipses; "Death", "Death Soon After Birth", under Infancy; "Incapable of Nurture" under Nutrition; "Short Life" in this section).

Nurture—Incapable of—(See "Incapable" under Nutrition).

Obstructed Life Forces—Caused by ♄ influence and affliction; the ☉, ☽, Asc., or hyleg ☌ ♄ at B., and by dir.; the ☉ in ♌, ☌, □, or 8 ♄. (See Obstructions, Retarded, Suppressions; "Life Force" in this section).

Old Age—Lives To—Seldom Lives To —(See Old Age).

Parents — Long or Short Life For — (See Parents).

Periods of Life—(See Critical, Cycles, Periods, Years).

Poverty—A Poverty-Stricken and Indigent Life—(See Idle, Indigent, Poverty).

Precarious Life — The ☽ affl. in the Asc., the health not good, and the life precarious (Hor'y).

Preserved—The Life Preserved—(See "Spared" in this section).

Preservers of Life — (See Benefics, Preservation).

Probable Length of Life—Of the Querent (Hor'y)—Observe the Asc., lord of the Asc., and the ☽; also lord of the 8th, and malefics in the 8th; the planet to whom the ☽, or lord of the 1st H. be joined by a ☌, □, or ☍ aspect. The time of death and the duration of life may be determined by the number of degrees between the Significator and the aspect of the afflicted planet. Years are denoted if the lord of the Asc. be in ☌ the lord of the 8th in an angle. Angles show strength and vitality and do not hasten death. Half years and half months of life are denoted if the Sig. be in fixed signs; if in succedent houses, months; if in cadent houses, weeks. In this case, the lord of the Asc. is more to be considered than the ☽, and the ☌ of the lord of the Asc. with the ☉ or lord of the 8th is to be feared the most. The lord of the Asc. being sorely afflicted in this question does not denote health or life. Only aspects by application are to be considered. (See Continuity; "Time of Death" under Death; Duration; Continuance, Duration, Length, Long, Short, in this section).

Prolonged — Life Prolonged — (See "Life Prolonged" in Sec. 3 under Children; Endurance, Prolonged).

Regulator—Of the Life Forces—The ☉ is the chief source and regulator of the life forces. (See Sun).

Rescues Life of Others—(See Rescue).

Roaming Life—Leads a Roaming and Wandering Life — (See "Changeable" in this section).

Sad Life—(See Sadness).

Sapped—The Life Forces Sapped and Undermined—(See "Life Force" in this section).

Saved—The Life Saved—Not Spared—(See "Spared" in this section).

Second Half of Life—Ruled by the ☉. (See "First Half" in this section).

Seldom of Long Life—The ☉, ☽, Asc., or hyleg afflicted by malefics at B. (See "Death" under Early; "Short Life" in this section).

Short Life—Signs of—Early Death—The SUN and ☽ both afflicted at B.; the ☉ badly aspected by the ☽ at B.; the ☉ or ☽ in the 6th H. at B., afflicted, and the rising sign a weak one; born at the time of a total eclipse of the ☉ with males, or an eclipse of the ☽ with females, seldom of long life or strong constitution (see Eclipses); the ☉ or ☽ Sig. ☌ ♂, and ♂ ill-dig., and usually early death thru quarrels, fury, accident, etc.; the ☉ Sig. □ or ☍ ♄ if he be in the Asc., unless a good asp. of ♃ intervene, the native is diseased and short-lived; the ☉ Sig. □ or ☍ ☽ if the ☽ be hyleg, and the aspect close; if the ☉, ☽, Asc., or lord of the Asc., or the most of them, are weak, afflicted, besieged by malefics, or occupying the same declination as malefics, if they be combust or ℞, and impeded by lords of the 4th, 6th, 8th, or 12th H., these are signs of short life or of great danger; the ☉ besieged by ♄ and ♂, cadent, and afflicted by lords of the 6th or 8th, or stars of their nature; the ☉ or ☽ affl. in common signs, and espec. in ♓; the ☉ afflicted in signs of low vitality, as

in ♋, ♑, or ♓; the ☉ ☌ several malefics in ♑; the ☉, ♆, ☽, and ☿ conjoined in a sign of low vitality; the MOON nearly in ☌ with the ☉ at B., not well-aspected, and also the hyleg weak and afflicted by malefics; the ☽ sepr. from ♂ and apply. to the ☉; the ☽ ruler of the 1st H., being in the 6th, 8th, or 12th H., and afflicted, combust, ☌, □, or ☍ lords of the 6th, 8th, 12th, or 4th H., and also being slow in motion, out of dignity, and with no assistance from benefics; the ☽ cadent and unfortunate, and afflicted by lords of evil houses; the ☽ or ☉ Significators, in □ or ☍ ♄, according to the sex of the native (see Males, Females); the greater the affliction of the Significators of life, as the ☉, ☽, or Asc., the shorter the life will be; the ☽ ☌ or evil asp. a malefic in the 4th, 6th, 8th, or 12th H., or besieged by ♄ and ♂; the ☽ Sig. ☌ the ☉, very close to the ☉, combust, or applying to the exact ☌; the ☽ Sig. □ or ☍ ♂, and the ☽ hyleg; born at exactly the New or Full ☽ except the ☽ have great Lat.; NEPTUNE culminating and afflicted; URANUS, ♄, or ♂ near the rising degree, afflicted by lord of the 8th, and the ☽ afflicted by the ☉ at the same time; SATURN rising, and the ☉ afflicting the ☽ at the same time; ♄ and ♂ both afflicting the ☽ in female nativities, or the ☉ in male horoscopes; ♄ or ♂ afflicting the ☉, ☽, or Asc. by body or aspect; ♄, ♂, or ☊ in the Asc. or 7th H., peregrine, ℞, or in detriment (Hor'y); ♄ Sig. ☌ the ☉, seldom healthy or of long life; ♄ or ♂ in the Asc., and afflicting the hyleg; ♄ in the 1st H. near the cusp; ♄ in the 7th H.; ♄ culminating and affl. the hyleg; ♄ near the cusp of the 4th H. at B.; MARS afflicted in the 1st H. near the cusp generally cuts the life short, and smallpox is apt to occur when he arrives at the horizon; VENUS Sig. ☌ ☉, and the ☉ ill-dig., and usually due to prodigality; ♀ afflicted at B. tends to short life; born under ♀ influence, and with ♀ afflicted, tends to ill-health, excesses, bad habits which shorten life; ♀ Sig. ☌ ☉; lord of the Asc. combust, ℞, or peregrine, and the cause will be shown by the house that the afflicting planet is lord of, and in which he is posited; ruler of the ASCENDANT in the 6th or 8th H., and malefics in the Asc., and with ♋, ♑, or ♓ on the Asc.; lord of the Asc. under the beams of the ☉, or going to combustion if hyleg; lord of the 6th H. in the 8th or 12th, and afflicted, and espec. if the lord of the Asc. apply to the □ or ☍ lord of the 6th; lord of the 8th in the Asc. if a malefic and afflicted; many planets, and espec. malefics, near cusps of angles at B.; many planets afflicted in signs of low vitality, as in ♋, ♏, or ♓, or these signs on the Asc., and afflicted; the Significators, the lord of the 1st, or the ☽, afflicted by malefics, or by the lords of the 4th, 6th, 8th, or 12th H., or jointed to ☊, denotes short life according to the degree of affliction, and the degrees between the Sig., and the chief afflicting planet, are said to denote the weeks, months, or years of life for the Querent, and as the Promittor may be in Cardinal, Fixed, or Common Signs (Hor'y); the life tends to be short, or with some grave danger or misfortune near, according to the quality of the Significators, and of the houses those planets are lords of, and which afflict the ☽ (Hor'y). A number of Cases and birth data of Short Life, and Death in Infancy, are given under Infancy. (See "Death" under Childhood, Children, Infancy; "Early Death" under Early; "No Duration of Life" in this section).

Shorter—The Shorter Will Be the Life—(See "Shorter" under Infancy).

Signs—Life-Giving Signs—The fiery signs ♈, ♌, and ♐.

Signs of Long Life—Of Short Life—(See "Long", "Short", in this section).

Small Hope of Life—(See "Hope" in this section).

Source of Life—(See "Regulator" in this section).

Spared—(a) The Life Is Spared—Death Not Imminent—The Life Saved—Life Preserved, etc.—Life will not be destroyed, or end in death from disease, unless the hyleg is sorely afflicted. The life is spared when there is no train of evil directions, as one direction rarely kills, no matter how malevolent it is. Life is always spared as long as the hyleg remains strong. When the ☽ is hyleg and directed to the ☌ of a malefic planet, if her Lat. when the aspect is completed differs greatly from that of the afflicting planet at B., life will generally be spared, altho a serious illness may result. A good direction of ♃ or ♀ to the hyleg in an otherwise train of evil directions, the life will be spared if the benefics were not badly aspected at B.; a benefic in good asp. to the Anareta; ♃ or ♀ within orb of the Anareta, and with ♃ within 12°, or ♀ within 8° the anaretic point, life is spared; a malefic in the term of a benefic; the Anareta in the term of a benefic; a benefic in the term of a malefic will do less good, and renders it vicious; if an evil direction of ♃ or ♀ are within the orb of the anaretic point they help to save life; when the hyleg is ☌ the Anareta, but differing widely in Declination, life will be saved; in the World, or Mundane, even one degree of difference in Lat. between the hyleg and Anareta may save if the Anareta is in the term of a benefic, and espec. if the native has a good constitution, but severe indisposition may follow for a time; if the benefics cast a ray of any kind, good or evil, to the anaretic point, the life will be saved unless they are outnumbered by the malefics, and if two malefics are opposed to one benefic there is little hope except the benefics be strong in an angle, and the malefics cadent; if the Anareta falls in the term of a benefic almost any aspect of a benefic will save life. Ptolemy says a ray of either ♃ or ♀, of any kind, falling on the Anareta will save life, but Wilson in his Dictionary thinks ♀ cannot do so alone unless ♃ assists. (See Amelioration, Crises, Directions, Moderation, Recovery, Recuperation).

(b) Life May Not Be Spared—The hyleg ☌ the Descendant, death usually

results, and espec. if the hyleg is under evil directions of malefics; an assisting benefic in the term of a malefic, or the place of the anareta in the term of a malefic; a benefic is vitiated by being in the house, exaltation, or triplicity of a malefic, but most vitiated when in the term of a malefic; a benefic alone, not strong or dignified, has little power to save when threatened by two malefics. Life may be prolonged for a time, but the two malefics will prevail in time.

(c) Life Not Spared—Death Certain—A benefic in the term of a malefic; the anareta in the term of a malefic; a benefic in the term, house, exaltation, or triplicity of a malefic, death is practically certain unless both benefics intervene with good asps. to the hyleg; a benefic alone, afflicted and undignified, and threatened by two malefics; the hyleg and anareta in ☌, yet differing greatly in declination. (See "Arguments for Death", "Certain Death", "Fatal", "Sure Death", "Threatened", under Death; "Destroyed", "No Duration", in this section).

Sudden End to Life—(See Accidents, Assassination, Killed, Murdered; "Death" under Sudden; Suicide; "Death" under Violent).

Suppressed—Life Suppressed, Retarded and Hindered—♄ influence. (See Saturn, Suppressions).

Sustains Life—The Hyleg is the Giver of Life, and when well-placed and strong, sustains and upholds life. (See Hyleg).

Terminal Houses—Houses Which Denote the End of Life—(See Terminal).

Trials of Life—(See Adversity, Affliction, Anxiety, Fate, Misery, Misfortune, Reverses, Ruin, Sadness, Sickness, Sorrow, Trials, Trouble, Worry, etc.).

Troubles of Life—(See "Trials" in this section).

Undermined—The Life Forces Undermined—(See "Life Force" in this section).

Unsettled Life—(See "Changeable" in this section).

Upholds Life—(See "Sustains" in this section).

Vibration—(See "Manifests" in this section).

Vital Forces—Life Force—Vital Spark of Life—(See "Force" in this section; "Force", "Spark", under Vital).

Vitality—The Vital Principle of Life—(See Vitality).

Wandering Life—(See "Changeable" in this section).

Will Not Live—Will Not Live to a Great Age—Early Death—Short Life, etc.—(See "Seldom" in this section).

Youth—Death In—Life In—(See Youth).

LIGAMENTS—Sinews—Tendons—The Ligaments are ruled by ♄ and ♂, and ♄ tends especially to harden and crystallize them, and to cause loss of strength in the ligaments, and ♄ in any sign tends to affect the ligaments in the part ruled by the sign he is in at B. Thus ♄ afflicted in ♌ tends to loss of strength and elasticity in the ligaments of the spine. The ligaments are affected also by the ♓ sign, and the ☉ or ☽ in ♓, and acting thru ♓ and the Plantar Nerves tend to influence and affect the fibro-ligamentous system, the respiratory and synovial systems, the os calcis, the feet, toes, etc., and give way to the Thoracic Diathesis. Uranus in ♎ warns against over-straining of the sinews. (See Fiber, Muscles, Sinews, Tendons).

LIGHT—Lightness—Fair—Light Color, etc.—

Action — Light In Action — Quick In Action — (See "Quick" under Action; Active, Agile, Athletics, Brisk, Gait, Motion, Movement, Nimble, Quick, Sports, Walk, etc.).

Adaptability—Lack of Adaptability to Light—(See "Light" under Iris).

Beard—Light Beard—(See Beard).

Brain—Lightness In—(See Dizziness, Fainting; "Shallow" under Mentality; Vertigo).

Colors — Light Colors and White are ruled by the 1st H. (See Colors).

Complexion—Light Complexion—(See "Light" under Complexion).

Degrees — Light or Fair Degrees of the Zodiac—If the Asc., or its lord, are in one of these degrees at B. the native tends to be of fair and light complexion—♈ 8, 20, 29; ♉ 7, 15, 28; ♊ 4, 12, 22; ♋ 12, 18; ♌ 30; ♍ 8, 16; ♎ 5, 18, 27; ♏ 8, 22; ♐ 9, 19, 30; ♑ 10, 19; ♒ 9, 21, 30; ♓ 12, 22, 28. (See Degrees).

Eyes—Light-Colored—(See Blue, Gray, under Eyes).

Feature—Lightness of—(See "Lightness" under Features).

Fingered—Light-Fingered — (See Kleptomaniac).

Hair—Light Hair—(See "Light Hair" under Hair).

Mind—Light In—Shallow Mind—(See "Fails In" under Examinations; "Shallow" under Mentality; "Weak Mind" under Mind).

Rays — Light Rays — Light Rays are transmitted by ♅, which planet rules the Ether. Uranus thus indirectly tends to affect the eyes thru the light rays, and cause eye diseases or blindness. (See Ether, Mydriasis; "Operations" under Nature; Uranus).

Time—Light of Time—The ☉ is called The Light of Time. (See Sun).

Walk — Light Walk — Quick Walk — (See "Action" in this section; Gait; "Quick" under Walk).

Weight—Light In—(See Diminished, Dwarfs, Emaciated; "Small Body" under Small; Thin, etc.).

LIGHTNING—

Blindness By — (See "Lightning" under Blindness).

Calculator—Lightning Calculator—(See Mathematical).

Casualties — By Lightning — ♃ in ♊, lord of the year at the Vernal, and in asp. with ♂, many casualties by lightning; ☿ in ♊ ☌ ♂ at the Vernal Equi., and lord of the year; Comets appearing in ♒. (See Thunder).

Child—Struck by Lightning—Case—See "Struck by Lightning", No. 796, in 1001 N.N.

Death By — ♅ setting in ☍ to the Luminaries at B. shows danger of, and espec. under evil directions of ♅ to the ☉ or ☽. Also cardinal signs predominant and prominent at B. show, and espec. when they contain several malefics afflicting the hyleg by dir.; ♂ afflicting the Significators. (See "Battle" under Abroad; "Injury" in this section).

Injury By—Accidents By—Death By—The fiery signs strong at B. dispose to; ♅ afflicted in ♏; ♅ ☌ or ill-asp. the ☉; ♅ afflicting the hyleg by dir.; the ♅ influences cause accidents by electricity, as ♅ rules the Ether; ♄ in ♉, direct in motion and angular at the Vernal E., much lightning and danger from; ♂ afflicted in fiery signs, and ☌ or ill-asp. the Asc. by dir.; ♂ sole ruler at an eclipse of the ☉; ♂ Sig. ☌ the ☉. (See Clouds; "Fountains" under Dry; Electricity, Ether, Rain, Thunder, Weather, etc.).

Sea—Shipwrecks—Damage by Lightning At Sea—(See "Fountains" under Dry; "Lightning" under Ships; "Voyages" in this section).

Voyages — Danger by Lightning On Voyages — Malefics in the 9th H. in airy signs, and afflicting the ☉ or ☽. (See "Sea" in this section; "Ships" under Fire).

LIKES AND DISLIKES—♅ in ♌ tends to. (See Antipathy; "Dislikes" under Food; Hate, Opposites, Sympathy, etc.).

LILLY — William Lilly, the Astrologer, and Author of Lilly's Grammar of Astrology. One of the great Astrologers of his day. For a Biography of Mr. Lilly see Sepharial's Dictionary of Astrology.

LIMBER — Nimble — (See Athletics; "Quick In Motion" under Motion).

LIMBS—The Legs and Arms—The Extremities—In the Textbooks of Astrology many influences which affect or describe the Arms and Legs are referred to as "Limbs", and this Article is arranged for convenience of reference. These subjects are also considered in the Articles on Arms, Calves, Extremities, Feet, Fingers, Hands, Knees, Legs, Lower, Members, Motion, Movement, Moving Parts, Thighs, Upper, Walk, etc. (See these subjects). Also see the following subjects in the alphabetical arrangement when not more fully considered here—

Accidents To — Hurts — Injuries — Wounds—(See "Accidents" under Arms, Extremities, Legs).

Afflictions In—(See "Diseases" under Arms, Extremities, Legs).

Amputations—Avoid when the ☽ is in ♊ or ♐. (See Operations).

Ankles—Disorders of—Injuries To—(See Ankles).

Arms—Disorders In—♆ in signs which rule the arms, hands, and feet tends to wasting of the tissues, shrinking, and withering of the limbs. (See the various paragraphs under Arms).

Atrophy In — ♄ in signs which rule the limbs. (See "Atrophy" under Arms, Feet, Hands, Legs).

Birth — The Limbs Distorted from Birth — Lame from Birth—(See Birth, Congenital, Crippled, Deformities, Distortions, Lameness, Paralysis; "Paralysis" in this section).

Blood Vessels—Constriction of—Impure Blood In—Lack of Circulation In —(See "Blood" under Arms, Legs).

Brevity of Limbs—♍ influence. (See Brevity, Short).

Broken Limbs—(See "Fractures" under Arms, Legs).

Calves—Disorders of—(See Calves).

Circulation In — (See Circulation; "Blood Vessels" in this section).

Cold Limbs—♄ in ♉, ♐, ♑, ♒, or ♓; ☿ afflicted in ♓. (See Cold, Constrictions; "Coldness" under Extremities, Legs).

Congenital Defects—(See Birth, Congenital, Deformities, Malformations; "Birth" in this section).

Constriction—Of Blood Vessels—(See "Blood" under Legs; "Cold" in this section).

Contractions In — ♄ influence. (See Contractions; "Father" in this section).

Cramps In — (See "Arms" under Cramps; "Cramps" under Legs).

Crippled In—(See "Birth" in this section).

Crooked Limbs — (See "Ill-Formed" under Ill; Knees; "Crooked" under Legs).

Defects In — Defective from Birth — (See "Birth" in this section).

Deformities—Of Limb—(See the various paragraphs under Arms, Feet, Hands, Knees, Legs, Thighs; Birth, Congenital, Deformities, Malformations, Paralysis, and the various paragraphs in this section).

Diseases Of — (See "Afflictions", and the various paragraphs in this section).

Distortions — From Birth — Common signs rising at B., and usually with an adverse aspect between ♅ and ♂ in common signs. (See "Causes" under Distortions; Excrescences).

Drawn Up Under Body—(See "Paralysis" in this section).

Dropsy Of — (See "Dropsy" under Legs).

Elbows—Disorders of—(See Elbows).

Erysipelas In—(See Erysipelas).

Extremities — Disorders In — (See Arms, Extremities, Feet, Legs).

Falls — The Limbs Fractured or Distorted by Falls—The ☉ Sig. ☌ ♄, and ill-dignified; ♄ affl. in ♑ or the 10th H.; ♑ on the Asc. (See Distortions, Falls, Fractures).

Father—Contractions of the Limbs of the Father — (See "Muscles" under Father).

Feet — Disorders In — Afflictions To — (See the various paragraphs under Feet; "Arms" in this section).

Femur—Fracture of—(See Femur).

Fibula—Fracture of—(See Fibula).

Foetus—The Limbs of are developed by ♂. (See Foetus).

Fractures Of—(See "Fractures" under Arms, Knees, Legs, Thighs).

Gait—Disorders of—(See Gait, Walk).

Glands Of — (See "Affected" under Glands).

Gout In — (See "Extremities" under Gout).

Hands—Disorders In—(See Hands).

Humerus — Fracture of — (See Humerus).

Humours In — (See "Humours" under Extremities, Hands, Legs).

Hurts To — (See "Accidents" in this section).

Ill-Shaped — (See "Crooked" in this section; "Knock-Knees" under Knees; "Bow Legs" under Legs).

Immobility—(See "Rigidity" in this section).

Imperfect — Imperfections In — (See Arms, Feet, Forearms, Hands, Knees, Legs; Birth, Crooked, and the various paragraphs in this section).

Infirmities In—(See the various paragraphs under Arms, Extremities, Legs, and in this section).

Injuries To—(See "Accidents" in this section).

Knees—Disorders In—Hurts To—(See Knees).

Lameness In — (See Crippled, Gout, Paralysis, and the various paragraphs in this section).

Large Limbs — Large Joints — Well-Set and Large—☿ orientally posited of the ☉ except when ☿ is in ♉. (See "Large" under Joints, Legs; "Bones" under Large; "Long" in this section).

Legs—Disorders In—Hurts To—(See Legs).

Length of Limb—(See Long, Short, in this section; "Body" under Length).

Leprosy In — (See "Diseases" under Extremities; "General Causes" under Leprosy).

Long Limbs—♅ or ☿ ascending; ♅ in the Asc., or close thereto, tends to give length of limb, and a slender body. (See "Long" under Arms, Extremities, Legs; Slender, Tall).

Loss Of — Malefics afflicted in signs which rule the limbs, and especially ♂ in such a sign, and making amputation necessary. (See "Amputations" under Legs).

Lower Limbs — Disorders In — Afflictions To — (See Ankles, Calves, Extremities, Feet, Knees, Legs, Lower, Thighs; "Paralysis", and the various paragraphs in this section).

Malformations — ♂ in the 3rd or 9th H. in common signs, and afflicting ☿; ♓ on the Asc., and espec. if ♅, ♂, or ♉ afflict the Asc. (See Arms, Crippled, Deformities, Feet; "Ill-Formed" under Ill; Legs, Malformations; "Paralysis" in this section).

Members — Brevity of — Length of — Disorders of, etc.—(See Arms, Brevity, Legs, Members; Long, Short, and the various paragraphs in this section).

Missing—Part of Limbs Missing from Birth—(See "Missing" under Forearm).

Motion In — (See Action, Crippled, Lameness, Locomotion, Movement, Quick, Slow, Walk; Birth, Distortions, Paralysis, in this section).

Movement In — (See "Motion" in this section).

Moving Parts — Ruled by ☿. (See Moving).

Muscles — Of the Limbs — (See "Muscles" under Arms, Extremities, Legs, Thighs; Muscles).

Mutilation of Limb — (See Beheaded, Mutilation).

Nerves of Affected — ☿ affl. in signs which rule the limbs. (See "Neuralgia" under Arms; "Nerves" under Feet, Hands, Legs).

No Limbs—No Arms or Legs—There are such cases, as I saw such a lady in a Museum, and her trunk and head were set up on a pedestal for view. Her birth data I did not obtain. Such cases of congenital deformity are caused by prenatal conditions, and afflictions in ♊, ♐, the 3rd and 9th H. at the time of the return of the ☽ to the central line of impulse during gestation. Also such deformity is said to be caused by ♊ or ♐ on the Asc., the common signs on the angles at such a time during pregnancy, and containing malefics, and also the ☉, ☽, and Asc. being badly afflicted at the same time. The case of the Frog Child has the forearms missing, both legs missing below the knees. (See Forearm, Prenatal Epoch).

Obstructions In—Weakness In—Weak Limbs—The ☉ in ♊ or ♐, and to the ♂ or ill-asp. any of the malefics as promittors; the ☉ or ☽ in the Asc. in ♑, ♒, or ♓, and afflicted; the ☽ affl. in ♊ or ♐. (See "Obstructions", "Weak", under Legs).

Operations On — (See "Amputations" in this section).

Pain In — The ☽ in ♒, ♂, or ill-asp. any of the malefics as promittors; ♄ in ♐, ♑, or ♒, ♂, □, or ☍ ♃ or ♀; ♂ promittor in ♒, ♂, or ill-asp. the ☉; ♂ in the 12th H. (See "Pain" under Arms, Feet, Hands, Legs).

Paralysis In—Paraplegia—The ☉ affl. in ♐; ♅ and ☿ affl. in signs which rule the limbs; ♄ affl. in ♐ or ♑ on the M.C., or in the Asc., and affl. the ☉; ♄ in ♑ on the upper Meridian, and affl. the ☉, tends to paralysis, defective limbs from birth, or the lower limbs to be drawn up under the body in some cases, and espec. where afflicting prenatal conditions concur. Cases of Paralysis in Limbs—See "Tunnison", No. 113, in 1001 N.N., a case of Paralysis in every Limb; "Seventeen Years In Bed", No. 843, in 1001 N.N., a case of Partial Paralysis; "Von Kothen", No. 211, in 1001 N.N., a case of Legs Paralyzed; Figures 13 A, B, C, D, F, G, and 14A, in the book, "Astro-Diagnosis", by the Heindels. (See "Paralysis" under Arms, Hands, Legs; Lameness, Motor, Palsy, Paralysis; "Festination" under Walk).

Radius—Fracture of—(See Arms).

Rheumatism In—Rheumatic Pains In —♄ in signs ruling the limbs. (See "Rheumatism" under Extremities; Gout, Rheumatism).

Rigidity Of—Stiff Limbs—Caused by the afflictions of ♄ in signs which rule the limbs, and by the hardening of the synovial membranes. (See Hardening, Immobility, Rigidity, Stiffness).

Short Limbs — (See "Short" under Arms, Legs; Brevity, Dwarfed; "Body" under Short).

Slender Limbs—(See "Small" in this section).

Small Limbs—Small and Slender—☿ occidentally posited as regards the ☉ except when ☿ is in ♊. (See "Slender" under Legs).

Stiffness Of—(See "Rigidity" in this section).

Stout Limbs—Strong Limbs—♂ in ♌ in partile asp. the Asc. (See "Strong" in this section).

Strong Limbs — Stout — Muscular—♃ in the Asc.; ♂ Sig. in ♌; ♈ on the Asc. (See "Stout" under Legs; "Body" under Strong).

Swellings In—(See "Swellings" under Arms, Extremities, Feet, Hands, Legs).

Thick Limbs — (See "Thick" under Hands, Legs).

Thighs—Disorders In—Accidents and Hurts To—(See Thighs).

Throbbing In — ♃ affl. in ♑. (See "Pain" in this section; Throbbing).

Tissues — Wasting of — (See "Wasting" in this section).

Ulcers In—(See "Arms" under Ulcers).

Ulna—Fracture of—(See "Ulna" under Arms).

Upper Limbs—(See Arms, Hands, Upper).

Varicose Veins—(See Varicose).

Walk — Disorders of — (See Gait, Walk).

Wasting—Of the Limbs—Of the Tissues—(See "Arms" in this section).

Weak Limbs—(See "Obstructions" in this section). Case of Weak Limbs— See Fig. 30 in the book, "Message of the Stars", by the Heindels.

Well-Proportioned — Well-Set Limbs —♃ in the Asc. (See "Strong" in this section).

Withering Of — (See "Arms" in this section).

Wounds To—(See "Accidents" in this section).

Wrists—Fracture of—(See Wrists).

LIME — Calcium — Chalk — Calcareous Substances — Coral is a form of Calcium. Lime Fluoride, or Calcium Fluoride, is ruled by the ♋ sign, and supplies the teeth and elastic fibre. (See Calces, Coral, Fiber). Calcium Phosphate is ruled by ♑ and supplies the bones. (See Bones, Minerals, Phosphate; "Salts" under Zodiac). Calcium Sulphate is ruled by the ♏ sign, and is connected with tissue cleansing. Lime and Chalk formations in the body are ruled by ♄. (See Chalk, Crystallization, Deposits, Gout, Hardening, Osseous, Rheumatism, Saturn, Sclerosis, Stone, Sulphates, Suppressions, Wastes).

LIMITATIONS — Restrictions — Impediments—Hindrances, etc.—Limitation is the principle of ♄, the ♄ sign ♑, and of the 12th H.

The Body—Limitations Upon the Body —The ☉, ☽, ♄, or ☿ afflicted in the 12th H. (See Asylums, Barren, Binding, Birth, Blindness, Confinement, Congenital, Deafness, Defects, Deformities, Disease, Dumb, Hearing, Hindrances, Hospitals, Idiocy, Ill-Health, Imbecile, Impediments, Imperforate, Invalids, Malformations, Missing, Monsters, Mute, Paralysis, Prison, Restraint, Saturn Influence, Senses, Servitude, Sickness, Sight, Speech, Tongue, Twelfth House, etc.).

The Mind—Limitations Upon—The ☉, ☽, ♄, or ☿ in the 12th H., and afflicted. Conditions become worse under the evil directions of these planets, and espec. when afflicted at the Vernal Equinox, and Lord of the Year. (See Anguish, Anxiety, Dejection, Depression, Despondency, Fears, Idiocy, Imbecility, Insanity, Melancholy; "Weak Mind" under Mind; Worry, etc.).

LIMP BODY—Drooping—Relaxation— Caused by the ♂ influence weak at B.; the 20° ♓ on the Asc. at B.; ♓ on the Asc. tends to weak bodily action, and uncertain walk. (See Action, Apathy, Drooping, Feeble, Inactive, Indifferent, Inert, Lethargy, Motion, Movement, Prolapse, Ptosis, Relaxation, Slow, Stooping; "Weak Body" under Weak; "Low" under Vitality, etc.).

LIMPING — (See Crippled, Deformities, Feet, Gait, Hips, Knees, Lameness, Legs, Paralysis, Thighs, Walk, etc.).

LINE—The Line of Central Impulse— (See Pranatal Epoch).

LINEN — Diseases from Wet Linen — Colds, etc.—(See "Linen" under Colds; "Wet Feet" under Feet; "Colds" under Moisture; "Pain" under Nipples; "Linen" under Wet).

LINGERING—Slow—Prolonged—Tedious—

Lingering Death—♄ causes a lingering death; ♄ affl. in the 8th H., and espec. afflicting the hyleg; ♄ in the 6th H., death by a lingering disease; ♅ in the 8th H., and affl. the hyleg. (See "Lingering" under Death).

Lingering Diseases—Lingering Pains —The ☉ or ☽ affl. by ♄; ♄ diseases and afflictions; ♄ affl. the hyleg at B., and by dir.; ♄ ☌ the ☉ or ☽ in the 6th H. (See Aches, Chronic, Consumptions; "Low Fever" under Fever; Grievous; "Long Siege" under Ill-Health; Incurable, Invalids; "Diseases", "Long Ascension", under Long; Prolonged, Slow, Tedious, Wasting).

LINIMENTS—(See Collyria, Lead, Lotions, Rubefacients).

LION—The Lion is the Symbol of the ♌ Sign.

Lion's Heart—Cor Leonis—Regulus— A Fixed Star—(See Regulus).

Lion's Tail—Cauda Leonis—Deneb—A Star of the nature of ♄ and ♅, and brings disgrace and ruin by adverse aspects. The ☉ directed to tends to danger of putrid fevers, and public disgrace; the ☽ directed to, danger of misfortune, mischief and great anxiety; the Asc. to the place of, melancholy, trouble, and discontent. (See "Death by Sentence" under Judge; Putrid; "Defect In Sight" under Sight; Vehicles). For influences of the Back, Mane, Neck, or Wing of the Lion, see Blindness; "Threatened" under Disease; Disgrace, Melancholy, Military, Ruin; "Fixed Stars" under Stars).

Mane of Leo—(See Mane).

LIPOMA—Fatty Tumor—♂ ☌ or ill-asp. ♃. (See "Tumors" under Fat).

LIPS — Labia — The Upper Lip is ruled by ♈ and ♊, and is especially influenced by ♀ in ♈. The lower lip, the lower teeth, and the chin, are ruled by ♉. Also the under lip is influenced by ☿ in ♈.

Diseases — Of the Lips — Planets afflicted in ♈ and ♉; Subs at MCP, and SP (7D). (See Mouth).

Full Lips—Given by ☿.

Harelip—A Congenital Fissure of the Lip—An ♈ affliction.

Large Lips—(See "Thick" in this section).

Lower Lip—(a) Drawn to One Side— Case — See "Extraordinary Accident", No. 192, in 1001 N.N. (b) The Lower Lip Thicker, or Larger Than the Upper One—In Hor'y Q. ♀ as Sig. of the party; ♀ influence at B. signifies; ☿ in ♑, thick lower lip.

Mouth—(See "Broad", and the various paragraphs under Mouth).

Plump Lips — ♀ Sig. of the person signifies.

Red Lips — Ruddy—Ruby—Cherry—♀ in the Asc. at B., and well-dignified; ♀ as Sig. of the party in Hor'y Q.

Rolling Lips—♓ on the Asc.

Scabbed Lips—The ☽ in ♑, ♒, or ♓.

Thick Lips—Large Lips—Great Lips —♄ signifies great lips like those of the Negro; in Hor'y Q. ♄ signifies; ♄ ascending at B.; given by ♄ when he forms the body; ☿ in ♑, thick lower lip; ♉ on the Asc.

Thin Lips—☿ gives; ☿ ascending at B. and free from the rays of other planets.

Upper Lip — Ruled by ♈, and especially affected and influenced by ♀ in ♈. (See Articulate, Inarticulate, Speech).

LIQUIDS—Liquors—♆ and the ☽ have strong influence over liquids. In the body the ☽ rules liquids and fluids in general.

Burns—By Hot Liquids—(See "Hot" in this section).

Craving for Liquors—The ☽ affl. in ♓ and water signs. (See Alcoholism; "Drink" under Cravings; Dipsomania, Drink, Thirst, etc.).

Death by Liquids—The ☉ to the ☌ or ill-asp. ♄ by dir., and one or both in watery signs. (See Bathing, Drowning, Scalds, Water).

Delirium Tremens — From Excessive Drink—(See Delirium).

Drink — (See the various paragraphs under Drink; "Liquids" under Food).

Drunkenness—(See this subject).

Excesses — Excessive Use of Liquors and Drink — (See "Excess" under Drink).

Fluids—(See Fluids).

Hot Liquids—Burns, Injury, or Death By—(See "Hot Liquids" under Heat; Scalds).

Intoxication—(See this subject).

Meals—Liquids with Meals and Food —(See Drinking, Liquids, under Food).

Pursuits—Liquid Pursuits—Are ruled and indicated by the ☽; the ☽ in the 10th H. at B., or a watery sign on cusp of 10th; many planets in watery signs. (See Business, Employment, Vocation).

Scalds — (See "Hot Liquids" under Heat; Scalds).

Strong Liquids — Uses Too Strong Liquids — (See "Strong Drink" under Drink).

Sweets and Liquids — (See "Liquids and Sweets" under Food).

Thirst—(See Cravings, Drink, Thirst).

Water — (See the various paragraphs under Bathing, Floods, Fountains, Ocean, Rain, Rivers, Sea, Water).

Wine — (See Wine). For collateral study, see Blood, Fluxes, Glands, Humours, Juices, Milk, Moisture, Moon, Neptune, Osmosis, Saliva, Secretions, Serums, Ships, Shipwreck, Sweat, Tears, Tides, Urine; "Signs" under Water).

LISPING — Imperfect Pronunciation of Letters and Words—♂ gives the lisp and ♄ the stammer. In Hor'y Q. ♄ in ♈ or a bestial sign, afflicting ☿ when the Significator, and the ☽ also be afflicted; ☿ in a weak sign, as in ♌, ♐, or ♓, and affl. by ♄ or ♂, in which case ♂ gives the lisp and ♄ the stammer; ☿ ruler of the 6th H., in a watery sign, and affl. by ♂; ☿ in a watery sign, in any house, and affl. by ♄ or ♂, lisps and pronounces words badly. (See "Stammering" under Speech).

LISTLESS—Dull—Vapid—Apathetic— Inactive—No Animation, etc.—The ☉ ☌ ☽ at B., and within 3°, listless all thru life at each New ☽; the ☉ and ♂ unaspected at B.; the ☽ in ♓, easy and inactive disposition; the ☽ Sig. in ♓, not inclined to action unless of the worst kind; the ☽ Sig. in ♑, inactive and dull; the ☽ Sig. in ♒; ♀ in ♏, inert; ☿ in ♉, inert disposition; ♓ on the Asc.; earth and water signs tend to give inactive and indolent natures; lords of the nativity in N. Lat. (See Apathy, Dull, Ennui, Fatigue, Idle, Inactive, Indifferent, Inertia, Irritable, Lassitude, Lethargy; "Low Spirits" under Low; Moping, Rouse, Slow, Sluggish, Weariness, etc.).

LITERATURE — Addicted To — (See "Literature" under Learning).

LITHEMIA—Excess of Uric Acid In the Blood — ♄ influence. (See Deposits, Gout, Rheumatism, Stone, Urates, Urea, Uremic, Uric).

LITHIASIS — The Formation of a Calculus — ♄ influence. (See Calculus, Lime, Stone).

LITTLE—

Little Bear — A Star — When joined with the ☉ in an angle is said to cause much sickness, disgrace, great affliction, and trouble. (See "Much Sickness" under Sickness).

Little Beard—(See Beard).

Little Body — (See Diminished, Dwarfed, Short, Small).

Little Eyes—(See Eyes).

Little Head — (See "Small" under Head; Idiots).

Little Mind—(See Idiocy; "Shallow" under Mentality; "Light", "Weak", under Mind).

Little Recuperative Power—(See Recuperation; "Low" under Vitality; "Weak Body" under Weak).

Little Resistance—To Disease—(See Resistance).

Little Sickness — Rarely Ill — (See "Good Health" under Health; Immunity; "Good" under Recuperation, Resistance, Vitality).

Little Slender Body—(See Slender).

Little Stature—(See "Little Body" in this section).

Little Stamina—(See Stamina).

Little Suffering — At Death — (See "Easy Death" under Death).

Little Vitality — (See "Low" under Vitality). See Lack Of, Loss Of, Void Of.

LIVELIHOOD—Lives In a Mean Way— Exercises Wits For a Livelihood—♂ Sig. in ♊, but the good aspects of the ☉, ♃, and ♀ mitigate. (See Gambling, Poverty).

LIVELY—Active—Spirited—Healthy—

Lively Complexion—(See "Red" under Complexion).

Lively Disposition—(See Action, Active. Brisk, Energy, Quick, etc.).

LIVER—Hepatic—The Liver is an organ and gland which is acted upon and influenced by a number of planets and Signs of the Zodiac. The liver is the largest gland in the body, and is the seat of the Animal Soul, or Desire Body. (See "Desire Body" under Desire). In the Astral Body ♃ has direct relation to the liver, and the liver is also the central vortex of the Desire Body, and the seat of the passional desires. (See "Astral Body" under Astral). Jupiter is the main ruler of the liver. It is also under the internal rulership of the ♌ sign. The liver is affected by planets in any of the cardinal signs, as in ♈, ♋, ♎, ♑. The liver is also ruled by ♎, ♏, ♐, and presided over by ♍. The 5th H. denotes the liver. Ptolemy and Wilson say that ♀ rules the liver. Mars also rules the liver, the bile and gall. The upper lobes of the liver are ruled by ♋, and the lower lobes by ♍. The Liver Place in the spine is the 4th Dorsal vertebra, designated as Li.P. The waste products of the Portal Blood Stream are converted into Glycogen in the liver by ♃. (See Glycogen). Saturn forms Uric Acid, Urea, and the Gall in the liver. (See Bile, Urea, Uric). The afflictions of ♄ have an adverse influence over the action of the liver, and infirmities in the liver are given by ♃, while the 5th H., its ruler, and planets therein, signify all diseases in the liver. Mars adds or subtracts to the Hepatic Process, and the ♂ group of herbs act upon and modify the Hepatic Diathesis, and oppose the ♄ diseases of the liver. (See Hepatic). Also the remedies of ☿ have a specific action upon the liver, and relieve its congestion, and especially of the Gall Bladder. Podophyllin (May Apple Blossom), a ☿ remedy, is one of the best remedies to act upon the liver, and to relieve biliousness. Calomel, a ☿ remedy, has also been greatly used as a liver remedy. The ☉ and ☽ acting thru the ♈ sign, thru the ganglion of Ribes, and thru the cavernous and carotid plexuses, affect the cerebro-spinal nervous system, the head and its dependencies, and give way to the Hepatic Process, and also acting thru the ♏ sign. (See Ductless Glands, Fifth House, Ganglion, Hepatic, Jupiter, Mars, Mercury, Saturn, Venus). The following are the diseases and afflictions of the liver, as mentioned in the various Textbooks of Astrology, which see in the alphabetical arrangement when not more fully considered here.

Abscess of Liver—♃ affl. in ♍; Subs at Li.P. and KP. Case—See Fig. 10A in "Astro-Diagnosis" by the Heindels. (See Abscesses).

Affected — The liver is affected by planets in any of the cardinal signs. (See the various paragraphs in this section).

All Diseases Of—Signified by the 5th and 6th H., and by ♄ and ♃ afflictions.

Amyloid Liver—Caused by ♃ afflictions; ♃ affl. in ♋ or ♍. (See Amyloid).

Asiatic Cholera—The Liver Afflicted In—A ♍ disease; ♂ affl. in ♍. (See Cholera).

Atrophy Of—♄ affl. in signs which rule the liver; Subs at Li.P. (See Atrophy).

Bile—Disorders of—(See Bile).

Biliousness—(See Bile).

Cancer Of—(See "Cancer" under Carcinoma).

Catarrh Of—The ☉, ☽, or ♄ affl. in ♋ or ♍; ♄ affl. in ♍ in the 5th or 6th H.; Subs at Li.P. (See Catarrh).

Cirrhosis Of—Hardening—Thickening —♄ affl. in ♍; Subs at Li.P. (See Cirrhosis).

Cold and Dry Liver—♃ affl. in ♍. (See "Cold and Dry" under Dry).

Colic Of—♂ affl. in ♍ in the Asc. or 6th H. (See "Cholic" under Bile).

Congestion Of—♄ affl. in ♍; ♃ affl. in ♍, due to bad circulation. (See Congestion).

Death — From Liver Trouble — ♃ shows; ♃ affl. the hyleg by dir., and ♃ much afflicted at B., and holding the dominion of death; ♀ much afflicted at B., and affl. the hyleg in a train of fatal directions; cardinal signs dispose to.

Degeneration Of—(See "Fatty" in this section).

Deranged Liver—Disorders of the Liver—Liver Complaints—Infirmities In the Liver—Diseased Liver—The ☉ in ♍ and affl. by ♃; the ☉ to the ill-asps. ♃ by dir.; the ☉ affl. in the 6th H. in cardinal signs; the ☉ in ♋ and affl. by malefics; ☽ diseases and caused by the ☽ affl. at B.; the ☽ to the ill-asps. ♃ by dir., and espec. if ♃ be in ♌ or the 6th H. at B.; the ☽ in the 6th H., and affl. by ♃; ♄ people are subject to, brought on by worry, fretting and moping; ♄ in ♌ or ♍; ♄ in ♌, occi., and affl. the ☉, ☽, or Asc.; ♄ or ♃ in ♎; ♄ affl. in ♎ in the 6th H., great derangement of the liver; ♄, ♅, or ♄ in ♏, and affl. the ☉ or ☽; ♄ affl. in ♈; ♃ affl. in ♉, ♋, ♍, or ♏; ♃ affl. in the 6th H.; ♃ □ or ☍ ☽, and espec. with women; ♃ affl. the ☉; ♃ affl. in ♍, and espec. in the 6th H.; ♃ on the 6th, and with afflictions in ♐; ♃ in ♌ or the 6th H. at B., and affl. the ☽ by dir.; ♃ afflicted by ♂; ♂ □ or ☍ ♃; ♂ affl. in ♍; caused by ♀ when the dominion of death is vested in her; ♀ affl. in ♍; the Asc. to the ☌ or any aspect ♃ by dir., and ♃ affl. at B., and espec. if ♃ be in ♌ or ♒; cardinal signs show, and espec. afflictions in ♎; Subs at Li.P. The ☉ affl. in ♎ tends to diseases which affect the liver. (See the various paragraphs in this section).

Diseased Liver—Diseases of—(See "Deranged", and the various paragraphs in this section).

Dropsy Of—The ☽, ♄, or ♃ affl. in signs which rule the liver; Subs at Li.P., and KP. (See Dropsy).

Dry and Cold Liver—(See "Cold" in this section).

Enlarged Liver—The ☉ affl. in ♉, thru the use of rich foods; ♃ affl. in ♋ in the Asc., the result of gluttony; ♃ affl. in ♍ or ♓; ♃ affl. in the 6th H., caused by overeating. (See Eating, Enlargements, Feasting, Food, Gluttony).

Fatty Degeneration—Of the Liver— Fatty Liver—Fatty Transformation of —A ♃ disease; ♃ affl. in ♊, ♍, or ♑; Subs at Li.P. (See Degeneration, Fat).

Fever—From Obstructions Near the Liver—Arising from Surfeits, High Living, etc.—The ☽ ☌ or ill-asp. ♄ (or ☿ if he be of the nature of ♄) when one is first taken ill, or compelled to take to his bed, and if the ☽ be not supported by benefics there is danger of death within 14 days (Hor'y). (See "Fever" under Heart).

Flexure—Hepatic Flexure—♄ affl. in ♍, and in signs which rule the liver, due to weakening of the parts; Subs at PP (3L). (See Flexure).

Gall—Gall Bladder—Gall Stones— (See Bile).

General Diseases Of — Afflictions in cardinal signs, and in signs which rule the liver; Subs at Li.P.

Glands—The Liver is a Gland, and for disorders of the Glands in general see Glands.

Glycogen—Disorders of—Formation of—(See Glycogen).

Gravel In—(See "Liver" under Gravel).

Hardening Of — (See "Cirrhosis" in this section).

Hobnail Liver—The Result of Atrophic Cirrhosis—♄ affl. in ♍; Subs at Li.P. (See Atrophy, Cirrhosis, in this section).

Hyperaemia Of—A ♃ disease; ♃ affl. in ♍; Subs at Li.P., and KP. (See Hyperaemia).

Inactive Liver—(See "Torpid" in this section).

Infirmities In—Given especially by an afflicted ♃, and with ♃ affl. in ♍. (See "Deranged", and the various paragraphs in this section).

Inflammation Of — Hepatitis — The ☽ in ♈ and afflicted by the ☉ or ♂ when taken ill (Hor'y); ♂ affl. in ♍; Subs at Li.P. tend to an inflamed liver, and also Perihepatitis, inflammation of the Peritoneal Covering of the Liver.

Jaundice—(See Jaundice).

Liver Complaints — (See "Deranged", and the various paragraphs in this section).

Liverishness — (See "Biliousness" under Bile).

Lobes—Disorders In—Afflictions in ♋, in the upper lobes, and in the lower lobes by afflictions in ♍.

Nerves—Nerves of Affected — ♅ or ☿ afflicted in signs which rule the liver. (See Colic, Pain, in this section; "Hepatic Plexus" under Hepatic).

Obstructions — (See "Fever" in this section; "Obstructive Jaundice" under Jaundice).

Pain In — (See "Nerves" in this section; "Cholic" under Bile).

Perihepatitis—(See "Inflammation" in this section).

Peritoneal Covering—Of the Liver—Inflammation of—(See "Inflammation" in this section).

Portal Blood Stream—(See Portal).

Remedies—For Liver Diseases—(See "Treatment" in this section).

Rickets — The planetary influences and afflictions which cause Rickets tend to changes in the liver and spleen. (See Rickets, Spleen).

Sluggish Liver—Torpid—Inactive—♄ affl. in ♍; ♄ ☌ or ill-asp. ♃; ♃ affl. by ♅; ♃ affl. in the 6th H.; Subs at Li.P. (See "Torpid" in this section).

Spots — Liver Spots—Cholasmus—Caused by ♄; ♄ affl. in ♍; afflictions in cardinal signs. (See "Biliousness" under Bile; Constipation, Jaundice).

Stenosis — Of the Bile Ducts — (See "Ducts" under Bile).

Thickening Of — (See "Cirrhosis" in this section).

Torpid Liver — Inactive—Sluggish—The work of ♄; ♄ affl. in ♍; caused by the excessive use of any drug ruled by ☿ and ♐, as ♐ is the opposite sign to ♐, the sign which rules the liver. (See "Sluggish" in this section).

Toxaemic Jaundice—(See Jaundice).

Transformation—(See "Fatty" in this section).

Treatment — Of Liver Disorders — In the use of Colors the purple is a good remedy for blood and liver disorders. Also in the way of drugs, use podo-

phyllin. Adjustments of the 4th Dorsal Vertebra, Li.P., are also quite necessary to give fuller and complete nerve supply to the liver. (See the Introduction to this Article).

Tuberculosis Of — ♄ afflicted in signs which rule the liver; Subs at Li.P. (See Tuberculosis).

Ulcerated Liver—♃ affl. in ♍, and also to Abscess. (See Ulcers; "Abscess" in this section).

Urea—(See Urates, Urea, Uric Acid).

Uric Acid—(See Uric).

Wasting Of—♄ affl. in ♌. (See Wasting).

Waxy Liver—Waxy, or Fatty Degeneration—(See "Fatty" in this section).

Women — Liver Disorders of — ☽ diseases, and by afflictions to the ☽ at B.; ♃ ☐ or ☍ ☽. Afflictions to the ☉ would tend more to liver disorders in males.

Wort — Liverwort — A ♃ herb. (See "Jupiter Group" under Herbs).

Yellow Jaundice—(See Jaundice).

LIVES—Lives Thru Disease—The Disease Is Not Fatal—(See "Spared" under Life; "Lives" under Serious).

LIVING — (See Conduct, Debauchery, Dissipation, Drink, Eating, Excesses, Food; "Free Living" under Free; Habits, Life, Loose, Luxuries, Men; "Loose Morals" under Morals; Passive, Pleasures, Poverty, Prodigal, Riotous, Sports, Women, etc.).

LOADED—Highly Loaded Urine—(See Urine).

LOATHING — At the Stomach — (See "Loathing" under Stomach).

LOBES—A Rounded Division of An Organ—(See "Lobes" under Liver, Lungs).

LOCAL PARTS—

Deformities Of — The work of ♄ by retention and crystallization of wastes, and thickening of tissue. (See Crystallization, Gout, Hardening, Joints, Wastes).

Localized Swellings — (See Abscess, Boils, Carbuncles, Cysts, Fullness, Hyperaemia, Infections, Inflammation, Plethora, Tumors, Ulcers, etc.).

LOCATION—Residence—Locality, etc.—It is said for good health and success, locate in the direction of the ☽ at B., or lord of the Asc. Also locate in places ruled by signs which contain the benefics at B., or in the direction of the benefics. This subject is more fully discussed under Abroad, Altitude, Foreign Lands, Nadir, Native Land, Place of Birth (see Place); Polarity, Residence, Travel, etc. Also see Changes, Climate, Discontentment, Environment, External, Removals, Roaming, Wanderer, etc.).

Disease — Location of — (See Diagnosis).

LOCK-JAW — Trismus — Spasm of Muscles of Mastication—Malefics in ♉ at B., and affl. the ☽ sign by dir.; the ☉ or ☽ in ♉, and affl. by ♅ or ♄ at B., and by dir.; ☽ on the Asc. at B., and containing malefics by dir.; Subs at MCP (4C). Case—See "Lockjaw", No. 913, in 1001 N.N. (See Hydrophobia, Jaws, Spasmodic).

LOCOMOTION — Disorders and Defects of—♄ influence; ♄ ♂ or ill-asp. the ☉ or ☽ at B.; ♄ rising and affl. the ☉, ☽, or Asc.; ♄ in ♐, ♑, ♒, or ♓. (See Action, Ankles, Carriage, Crippled, Deformities, Deposits, Feet, Gait, Gout, Knees, Legs, Limbs, Locomotor Ataxia, Motion, Movement, Paralysis, Rheumatism, Swellings, Walk, etc.).

LOCOMOTOR ATAXIA—Tabes Dorsalis —A ♄ disease; ♄ in ♌ or ♎; a ♌, ♎, and ♐ disease, and caused by afflictions in these signs; a ☿ disease, and caused by afflictions to ☿, and by the afflictions of ☿, and espec. when ☿ partakes of the nature of ♄. This disease is the result of Tabes Dorsalis of the spine, a disease of the posterior columns of the spinal cord, attended by incoordination, and lack of sensation. The Knee-Jerk is also absent. Also caused by Subs at AT, AX, CP, and KP. Case — See "Locomotor Ataxia", No. 255, in 1001 N.N. (See Ataxia, Argyll; "Argyll Pupil' under Iris; Paralysis, Tabes).

  Locomotor Muscles — (See "Locomotor" under Hips).

LOCUST PEST—(See Comets).

LODESTONES—Magnetized Iron Ore— Ruled by ♅. (See Iron, Magnetism).

LOGORRHOEA—Abnormally Rapid Speech—(See "Rapid" under Speech).

LOINS—Lower Part of the Back—Reins —Ruled by ♎ and the 7th H.

  Disorders In—Diseases In—♀ diseases, and caused by afflictions to ♀, the ruler of ♎ and the 7th H. Also the afflictions of ♄ tend to as ♄ has his exaltation in ♎; Subs at UPP and PP. (See "Diseases" under Back; "Disorders" under Reins).

  Heats In—♂ afflicted in ♎ or the 7th H. (See "Heats" under Buttocks, Reins).

  Imposthumes In — A ♎ disease, and afflictions in ♎. (See "Abscess" under Back).

  Pain In — (See "Pains" under Back; Lumbago).

  Ulcers In—A ♎ disease. (See Ulcers).

  Weak Loins — Weakness In — Weak Back — The ☉ affl. in the 6th H. in a fixed sign; ♂ in ♉ when ♂ is the afflictor in the disease. (See "Weak" under Back, Kidneys; "Lumbar Region" under Lumbar).

  Wounds In—♂ affl. in ♎ or the 7th H.

LONELINESS—♄ influence; ♄ strong at B., rising, in the Asc. or M.C., and especially afflicting the ☉, ☽, or ☿. (See Recluse, Secretive, Solitude).

LONG—Lengthy—Prolonged—

  Arms—Long Arms—(See Arms).

  Ascension — Signs of Long Ascension —The ♋, ♌, ♍, ♎, ♏, ♐ signs, and so-called because they take longer in ascending. The signs of short ascension are ♑, ♒, ♓, ♈, ♉, ♊, and these signs take less time in ascending. A ✳ aspect in a sign of long ascension has the same effect as a ◻, and the disease is prolonged when the afflictors are in signs of long ascension, and shorter when in signs of short ascension.

Body — Long Body — ♈, ♉, ♎, and ♏ when on the Asc. give a rather long body, but moderate in stature. (See Giants, Growth, Height, Length, Tall).

  Chin—(See "Long" under Chin).

  Diseases—Long Diseases—Long Distempers — Signs of a Long Disease — The Disease Will Be Long — Diseases related to the ☉ usually become chronic and of long duration, and resist treatment; caused by the afflictions of ♄ to the hyleg at B., and by dir.; ♄ in the 6th, or lord of the 6th, and afflicting the hyleg; ♄ ♂ ☽ at the beginning of a disease; ♄ ♂, P., ◻ or ☍ ☉; the ☽ in a fixed sign (Hor'y); all the Significators in fixed signs, or if they be slow of motion. (See Chronic, Consumptions, Continuity, Course, Crises; "Long" under Disease, Ill-Health; Duration; "Low" under Fever; Incurable, Invalids, Lingering, Prolonged; "Low" under Recuperation, Resistance, Vitality; Rising Sign, Slow, Tedious, Wasting, etc.).

  Face—Long Face—(See Face).

  Father—Long Life For—(See Father).

  Feet—Long Feet—(See Feet).

  Fingers — Long Fingers — (See Fingers).

  Hair—(See "Long" under Hair).

  Hands—(See "Long" under Hands).

  Head—(See "Long" under Head).

  Illnesses—Long Illnesses—(See "Diseases" in this section).

  Imprisonment—(See "Long Imprisonment" under Prison).

  Journeys — (See "Long" under Journeys, Voyages).

  Legs — (See "Long" under Legs, Thighs).

  Life — Long Life — (See "Long Life" under Life).

  Limbs — (See "Long" under Arms, Legs, Limbs, Thighs).

  Mother—Long Life For— (See "Long Life" under Mother).

  Nails—Long Nails and Fingers—(See "Long" under Fingers, Hands, Nails).

  Neck—(See "Long" under Neck).

  Nose—(See "Long" under Nose).

  Sight — Long-Sighted — (See "Hyperopia" under Sight).

  Thighs — (See "Long" under Legs, Thighs).

  Upper Half of Body — Upper Part Longer—(See "Body" under Upper).

  Uvula—(See "Long" under Uvula).

  Visage — Long Visage — Long Face— (See "Long" under Face).

LONGINGS — (See Appetites, Cravings, Desires, Wishes, etc.).

LOOK—Glances—Expression—Aspect— Visage—

  Active Look—Sharp Look—◻ on the Asc.

  Angry Look—Fierce Look—♂ Sig. in fiery signs. (See Anger).

  Austere Look—(See Austere).

  Bold Look—♂ rising in the Asc. (See Boldness, Resolute).

Commanding Look — (See Commanding).

Countenance — (See the various subjects under Countenance).

Debauched Look—(See Debauched).

Dissipated Look — (See Debauched, Dissipated).

Downward Look—Lowering Aspect—Eyes Looking Downward — Stooping Forward — A strong ♄ characteristic; ♄ in the Asc.; ♄ Sig. □ or ☍ ☽, and tends to stoop forward; the ☽ strong at B., a little lowering; ♅ influence tends to hold the head down when walking, and to a stooping, heavy gait. (See Bent, Downcast, Stooping).

Dull and Idle Look — (See Dull; "Sleepy Eyes" under Eyes; Idle, Weariness).

Effeminate Look—(See Effeminate).

Enquiring Look— ☿ rising in the Asc.

Expression—(See the paragraphs under Expression).

Eyes — Expression of — (See Dull, Glances, Piercing, Quick, Sharp, Sleepy, and the various paragraphs under Eyes).

Face — (See the various paragraphs under Complexion, Countenance, Expression, Face, Features).

Features—(See Chin, Face, Features, Jaws, Lips, Mouth, Nose, etc.).

Fierce Look — (See "Angry" in this section).

Foolish Looking—(See Fools).

Gentle Look—(See Gentle, Kind).

Ghastly Look — (See Pale, Sickly, White).

Inquiring Look— ☿ rising in the Asc.

Intellectual Look — Refined Expression— ☿ in □ or ♍; ☿ Sig. in □; ☿ rising in the Asc., and espec. when in his own signs, and well-aspected by the ☽; ♀ in □. (See "Strong Mind" under Mind).

Jaundiced Look—(See Jaundice).

Lowering Look — Lowering Aspect — (See "Downward" in this section).

Penetrating Look—(See "Penetrating" under Eyes).

Piercing Look—(See Piercing, Sharp, under Eyes).

Quick and Active Look — Quick Sight —(See "Quick" under Eyes).

Sardonic Look—♆ rising in the Asc.

Saucy Look—♂ rising in the Asc. (See Boldness, Independent).

Sharp Look — □ on the Asc. (See "Sharp" under Eyes).

Sickly Look — (See Anaemia, Chlorosis, Pale, Sickly).

Smart and Active Look — □ on the Asc.

Sober Look—Grave Aspect—♄ influence; ♄ in the Asc. (See Despondent, Grave, Melancholic, Serious, Worry).

Stern Look—(See Austere).

Surly Look—♄ in ♌ in partile aspect the Asc.

Visage — (See Complexion, Countenance, Expression, Face).

Wanton Look — □ gives. (See Wanton).

Weary Look — (See Depressed, Dull, Fatigue, Weariness, etc.).

LOOSE—Looseness—

Loose Habits — Loose Living — Free Living—The ☉ or ☽ to the bad aspects ♀ by dir.; ♄ to the bad asps. ♂ by dir.; ♀ on the Meridian at B., and ill-aspected by ♂; the ☽ to the □ or ☍ the Asc. by dir., illnesses from loose living and bad habits; ♃ afflicted also tends to loose living, bad habits, and espec. along lines of eating, causing plethora and bad blood. (See Debauchery, Dissipation, Drink, Eating; "Free Living" under Free; Gluttony; "High Living" under High; "Loose Morals" under Morals).

Loose Morals — (See "Loose" under Morals).

Loose Women — (See Harlots, Nymphomania, Shameless).

Looseness In Bowels — (See Cholera, Diarrhoea, Dysentery).

LOSS OF — Detriment— Losses—There are quite a number of paragraphs throughout this book indicating the loss of something, as loss of health, of comforts, of friends, of loved ones, or property, fortune, honour, etc., and subjects too numerous to list here, and you are requested to look in the alphabetical arrangement for the subject you have in mind. However, the following are prominent suggestions as to subjects along this line. The afflictions and adverse aspects of the planets at B., and by dir., usually tend to the loss of something as regards the individual, while the good aspects of the planets by transit, progression, and direction tend to the restoration of that which was lost, if restorable, as health, wealth, comforts, ease, peace of mind, success, etc. Look for the heading, "Loss Of", under the following subjects, or others you may have in mind—Appetite, Arms, Aunt, Blood, Character, Cheer, Children, Citizenship (see Banishment, Exile); Comforts, Credit (see Cheating, Deceitful, Dishonesty, Forgers, Thieves, etc.); Daughter, Death, Equilibrium, Eyes, Faculties (see Idiocy, Imbecility, Insanity); Family, Father, Feeling, Feet, Finger, Flesh, Fluids, Fortune, Friend, Hair, Hands, Happiness, Health, Hearing, Honour, Husband, Identity, Infant, Inheritance, Integrity (see Cheating, Criminal, Deceit, Disgrace, Dishonour, Forgers, Liars, Libel, Reputation, Ruin, Thieves, etc.); Joy, Legs, Liberty (see Prison); Limbs, Manhood (see the various paragraphs under Men); Marriage Partner, Memory, Modesty, Money, Mother, Passion, Peace of Mind (see "No Peace" under Mind); Position (see Disgrace, Dishonour, Poverty, Property, Reverses, Ruin, Wealth); Property, Reason, Relatives, Reputation, Riches, Seed (see Semen); Sex Desire (see Apathy, Celibacy; "Free From" under Passion); Sight (see Blindness, Sight); Sister, Smell, Son, Speech, Stamina, Stimulus, Strength, Taste, Teeth, Tone, Uncle, Virtue, Vitality, Voice, Volitional Power, Wealth, Weight, Wife, Womanhood (see Harlots, Shameless). Also see Detriment, Diminished, Lack Of, Less, Lessened, Void Of, Wasting, etc.

LOTIONS—Face and Hair Lotions—Ill Effects of—(See Cosmetics; "Lotions" under Face).

LOUD SPEAKING — (See "Loud" under Speech, Voice).

LOVE AFFAIRS—Love—Dealings with the Opposite Sex—The 5th H. and the ♌ sign are predominant in love affairs, and also ♎ and the 7th H. Venus is the principle of love, and it is afflictions to ♀ that tend to disturbances in the love nature, and to diseases and ill-health by its abuses. The afflictions of ♅, ♓, and ♂ to ♀ tend to excesses, abuses, and irregularities of the love nature, leading to weakness, exhaustion of the vital forces, sorrow, suffering, or death. The afflictions of ♄ to ♀ also cause carelessness in love affairs, or make one unnatural, or given to excessive illegal practices, or abnormal affections. The good aspects of the planets to ♀ tend to make the affections and love nature true and genuine, and to be properly used, and also restrained. The question of love affairs is a large one, and cannot be gone into here except along lines where the love nature is afflicted, abnormal, perverted, and which tends to ill-health, suffering, injury, or death. The unrestrained use of the love and sex nature, and passional displays, excesses, and the use of the sex nature for pleasure and gratification, are undoubtedly the causes of much of the sin, suffering, sorrow, and misery in the World today, and often lead to an untimely death, whereas if the vital forces were saved, used only for propagation, and the nature spiritualized, people would live longer, have better health, and be spared much of the suffering that now overtakes them. The Occult side of love, and love affairs, is very fully considered in the books, "The Key of Destiny", by Dr. and Mrs. Homer Curtiss, and also the book, "Cosmo-Conception" by Max Heindel.

Addicted To Women—(See "Addicted" under Men).

Adulterous Tendencies — Covets Unlawful Beds—The lower vibrations of ♅ tend to irregularities of the affections and passions, and lead to unconventionalities, chafing under vows and restraints. The afflictions of ♅ to the ☽ in a male horoscope, and the afflictions of ♅ to the ☉ in a female nativity, tend to make one adulterous. Also ♅ in, or afflicting the 7th H., the house of marriage; ♅ affl. ♀ at B., and by dir., tends to many irregularities among young people; ♀ ill-dignified at B.; ♀ with, or afflicted by the malefics at B.; the ☽ sepr. from ♂ and applying to ♀ by aspect; ♂ and ☿ lords of the employment. (See Amorous; "Free Love" under Free; Intercourse, Lascivious, Lewd, Lust, Passion, Sex, etc.).

Affections—(See Affections, Inordinate; "Unlawful" in this section).

Amativeness—(See Amative).

Amorous—(See Amorous).

Amours—Illicit Amours—Precipitancy in, and unrestrained impetuosity, caused by the evil directions of ♀; the ☉ or ☽ to the ill-asps. ♀ by dir.; ♓ affl. in the 5th H.; ♓ affl. the ☽ or ♀; ♅ to the ill-aspects ♀ by dir.; ♅ to the good asps. ♀ by dir., but escapes detection. (See "Free Love" under Free; Adulterous, Clandestine, Liaisons, in this section).

Ardent—Over-Ardent—Ardency is given by the ☉, the ♌ sign, ♀, and ♀ afflicted or aspected by ♂; ♂ afflicting ♀ tends to ardent passions, and ♂ influence gives ardency; the 3rd decan. of ♈ on the Asc., ruled by ♀. (See Affections, Amorous, Passion).

Astray—Women Liable to Be Led Astray—(See Seduction).

Attachments—Indiscreet In—Keeps Bad Company—Fond of Low Company—(See Harlots; "Low Company" under Low).

Bohemian Pleasures—Fond of—(See "Bohemian" under Pleasures).

Celibacy—(See Apathy, Bachelors, Celibacy, Deviations; "Free From" under Passion).

Chastity—(See "Chaste" under Females).

Clandestine Affairs—(See "Clandestine" under Sex).

Cohabitation—Excesses In—Little Desire For—(See Amorous, Celibacy, Cohabitation, Excesses, Passion).

Covets Unlawful Beds—(See Adulterous, Amours, in this section).

Death—Sudden Death Thru a Love Affair—The ☽ at Full, or incr., sepr. from ♀, and applying to ♂ in a day geniture. (See "Causes His Own Death" under Death).

Disease—Thru Love Affairs—(See "Health Suffers" under Opposite Sex).

Energies Wasted—Energies and Substance Wasted On the Opposite Sex—♂ afflicting ♀. (See Amorous; "Wasted" under Energies; "Passional Excesses" under Passion; "Ruined" in this section).

Engagement—(See Fiance).

Entanglements—Has Many Unwise Entanglements With the Opposite Sex—♀ affl. at B. by the malefics ♅, ♄, or ♂.

Fiance—Fiancee—(See Fiance).

Fickle—The Affections Fickle and Changeable—♀ weak at B., and afflicted, and espec. with ♀ in ♋ or ♍; the ☽ in the Asc. at B., or ruler of the Asc., and afflicted; the ☽ □ or ☍ �t; the ☉ by Periodic Rev. to the ill-asps. the radical ☽; ♄ Sig. in ♓; ♃ in ♊; ♂ affl. in ♊ or ♎; ☿ rising in ♍ and afflicted; ♊ or ♍ on the Asc.; the influences of the bicorporeal signs strong at B.

Fixation—Mother Fixation—Tendency of a Man to Marry a Woman Like His Mother, and Much Older Than Himself —(See "Mother Fixation" under Marriage).

Flirting—(See "Fickle" in this section; "Unwomanly Freedom" under Morals).

Foolish In Love Affairs—Fixed Stars of the nature of ♄ and ♃ ascending at B., easily mislead by their love nature and passions.

Fornication—(See "Adulterous" in this section; "Clandestine" under Sex).

Free Love—Free Living—(See Free).

Genuine—The Affections True and Genuine, Fixed and Stable—Depth of Affection—♀ well-aspected in ♉; ♀ in the Asc. in a strong sign, and well-aspected. (See "Affections" in this section).

Grief—Trouble, Grief, Scandal, or a Downfall Thru the Opposite Sex—♅, ♄, ♂, or the ☽ to the ill-asps. ♀ by dir., and espec. if ♀ or the ☽ be greatly afflicted by malefics at B.; the ☽ to the place of Hydra's Heart; the periodic direction of ♄ to the radical ♀; Fixed Stars of the nature of ♂ and the ☽ ascending at B.; the ill-asps. of the ☽ to ♀ at B. tend to give males the hatred or ill-favor of the fair sex, and the ill-asps. of the ☽ to the ☉ by dir. tend to turn the love of some female to hate. (See Jilted, Ruined, in this section; "Females" under Hate; "Grief", "Women", under Men; Treachery).

Hate—The Love of a Woman Turns to Hate—(See "Grief" in this section).

Health Suffers—Thru the Opposite Sex—(See "Injury", "Women", under Men; "Health" under Opposite Sex; "Energies" in this section).

Illicit Amours—(See Adulterous, Amours, Clandestine, Free Love, in this section).

Imaginations—(See "Morbid" under Imagination).

Immorality—(See "Loose Morals" under Morals; Perversions, Shameless, Vices).

Incest—Inclined To—(See "Incest" under Perversions).

Indiscreet Attachments—(See Harlots; "Low Company" under Low).

Intrigues—(See Adulterous, Clandestine, Fornication, Liaisons, in this section).

Jealousy—In Love Affairs—The ☉ affl. in ♑; ♅ affl. in ♉ or ♍; ♄ ☌ or ill-asp. ♀; ♄ Sig. in ♒; ♄ Sig. ✶ or △ the ☽; the ill-asps. of ♄ to the ☉, ☽, ♀, the Asc. or M.C. by dir.; ♂ in the 6th H. in ♉, ♌, or ♍, and affl. by the ☉, ☽, or ♄; ♀ affl. in ♍; ♀ greatly afflicted at B., and espec. by ♄; ♀ also well-aspected and dignified at B. may tend to jealousy, and often without cause; the ⊕ to the ill-asps. ♀ by dir., jealous of his wife. (See Jealousy).

Jilted—By the Opposite Sex—♄ to the ☌ or ill-asps. ♀ by dir., and may tend to great weakness, sorrow, and ill-health at the time.

Liaisons—Illicit Intimacy—Intrigue—The ☉, ☽, or ♀ to the ill-asps. ♅ by dir., and espec. if afflicted by ♅ at B. (See Adulterous, Clandestine, Free Love, in this section).

Love Passion—♀ affl. in ♌, and often of bad consequence. (See Amorous, Amours; "Passional Excesses" under Passion).

Love Potions—Philtres—Ruled by ♀.

Low Company—Fond of—(See "Low Company", "Low Pleasures" under Low).

Many Love Affairs—(See "Fickle" in this section).

Moral Laws—Little Respect for Social or Moral Laws—♆ afflicted in the 5th or 7th H.; ♂ ruler at B., and afflicted, and espec. when they interfere with his liberty of action. (See "Free Love" under Free; "Loose Morals" under Morals; Unconventional, Vows, in this section).

Mother Fixation—(See "Fixation" in this section).

Opposite Sex—Dealings With for Good or Ill—(See the various paragraphs under Opposite Sex, and also in this Article).

Passion—Passional Excesses—Free from Passion—(See Apathy, Celibacy; "Excesses", "Free From", under Passion).

Philtres—(See "Love Potions" in this section).

Platonic Love—(See Marriage).

Pleasures—Fond of Bohemian and Low Pleasures—(See Low, Pleasures).

Prostitutes—(See Harlots).

Promiscuity—(See "Clandestine" under Sex).

Respect—Has Little Respect for Moral Laws or Social Customs—(See "Moral Laws" in this section).

Romance—Love of—Born under ♅; ♅ ☌ or afflicting ♀ at B.; ♅ in the 5th H. (See Romantic).

Ruined by Women—♂ ☌ or ill-asp. the ☽ or ♀ at B., and by dir.; ♂ Sig. in ♌ or ♎; ☿ Sig. in ♉, ruins himself among the female sex. (See Energies, Grief, Health, in this section; "Injured", "Women", under Men).

Scandal—Danger of—(See Disgrace, Dishonour; "Loss of Honor" under Honor; Scandal).

Scatters the Affections—(See "Fickle" in this section).

Seduction—(See Seduction).

Seeks Female Company—♀ to the good aspects the ☽ by dir. or transit. (See "Addicted To Women" under Men).

Sex Disorders—Thru Excesses and Love Affairs—(See Genitals, Private, Scandalous; "Sex Diseases" under Sex; Venereal, Venery).

Sexual Immorality—(See Adulterous, Amours, Fornication, Illicit, in this section; Harlots, Lewd; "Loose Morals" under Morals; Perversions, Shameless, Vices, etc.).

Social Laws—Little Respect For—(See Moral Laws, Unconventional, Vows, in this section).

Substance Wasted—(See "Energies" in this section).

Sudden Death—Thru a Love Affair—(See "Death" in this section).

Suffers In Health—Thru Love Affairs—(See Grief, Health, in this section).

Suicide—On Account of a Love Affair—(See Suicide).

Trouble — Thru the Opposite Sex— (See "Grief", and the various paragraphs in this section).

True Affections—(See "Genuine" in this section).

Unconventional — In Love Affairs— Little Respect for Vows, Restraints, and Social Laws—♅ affl. in the 5th or 7th, or in ♎; ♅ affl. in ♌ or ♎; ♅ ☌ or ill-asp. ♀. (See "Free Love" under Free; "Moral Laws" in this section; Perverse).

Unfaithful—In Love Affairs and Sex Relations—♅ or ♂ affl. in ♎; ♅ to the ☌ or ill-asp. ♀ by dir. (See Adulterous, Amours, Clandestine, Fickle, Unconventional, in this section).

Unlawful Affections—The ☉ to the ☌ ♀ if ♀ be weak at B. (See "Free Love" under Free; Adulterous, Clandestine, Liaisons, Moral Laws, in this section).

Unwise Entanglements — (See "Entanglements" in this section).

Unwomanly Freedom — (See "Unwomanly" under Morals).

Vows and Restraints—Chafes Under —♅ affl. in the 5th or 7th H.; ♅ ☌ or ill-asp. ♀. (See Moral Laws, Unconventional, in this section).

Wandering Affections—(See "Fickle" in this section).

Wastes Energies — (See Energies, Health, in this section).

Women — (See Addicted To, Astray, Fond Of, Grief, Hate, Health, Jealousy, Opposite Sex, Ruined, Scandal, Seduction, and the various paragraphs in this section; "Poison Death" under Poison; Treachery).

Zealous—In Love Affairs and In Affection—♀ in ♌ or the 5th H. (See Amorous, Ardent, in this section). For further and collateral study along this line see Companions, Conduct, Debauched, Depraved, Dissipated, Drink, Excesses, Expense, Females, Habits, Harlots, Husband, Immodest, Indecent, Indiscretions, Lascivious, Licentious, Lust, Marriage, Marriage Partner, Obscene, Prodigal, Renunciation, Riotous, Social Relations, Suicide, Virile, Wanton, Wench, Wife, Wine, Women, etc.).

LOVED ONES—Death of—♄ progressed ☌, P, □ or ☍ the radical ♀, and vice versa. (See "Death" under Brother, Children, Daughter, Family, Father, Husband, Mother, Relatives, Sister, Son, Wife, etc.).

LOVELY—Beautiful—Elegant, etc.—

Lovely Body—♍ gives, but not necessarily beautiful. (See Beautiful, Comely, Elegant, Handsome).

Lovely Complexion — (See Complexion).

Lovely Eyes—(See Eyes).

Lovely Face — (See "Beautiful", "Lovely", under Complexion, Face).

Lovely Hair — (See Brunettes, Color, Lovely, under Hair).

LOW—

Low Altitudes—Residence In—(See Altitude).

Low and Base — Vile — Miscreant— Sordid—♂ Sig. □ or ☍ ☽; ♀ Sig. □ or

☍ ♂; ☿ Sig. ☌ ♂, a treacherous miscreant; ♄ Sig. □ or ☍ ☿. (See Degenerate, Depraved, Infamous, Treachery, Vile).

Low and Cunning—The ☽ Sig. □ or ☍ ☿. (See Cheating, Deceitful, Dishonest, Forgers, Thieves, Treacherous, etc.).

Low Blood Pressure—(See "Pressure" under Blood).

Low Business — Follows Some Low Business—♄ Sig. ☌ ♂, engages in some public calling of the lowest order, and often ends days in prison; ♂ Sig. in ♎, usually employed in some low business, and incapable of better. (See Character, Cheating, Deceitful, Dishonest, Evil, Forgers, Libel, Morals, Murderous, Prison, Thieves, Wicked).

Low Caloric—Low Animal Heat—(See "Lack of Animal Heat" under Heat).

Low Character — (See Low and Base, Low Business, in this section; "Loose Morals" under Morals).

Low Company—Fond of—Keeps Bad Company — The ☽ sepr. from ♀ and apply. to the ☉; ♄ to the ill-asps. ♀ or ☿ by dir.; the periodic direction of ♄ to the radical ♀; ♂ by periodic direction to the ill-asps. the ☽ or ♀; ♂ Sig. □ or ☍ the ☽ or ♀; ♂ to the ill-asps. the ☽, ♀, or ☿ by dir.; ♀ Sig. in ♎; ♀ Sig. ☌ ♂; ♀ to the ☌ ♂ by dir.; ♀ Sig. in ♓, and affl. by ♄ or ♂. (See Low and Base, Low Business, Low Women, in this section; Depraved, Debauched, Dissipated, Harlots, Lewd, Lust; "Harlots" under Men; Prodigal, Venery).

Low Desires—(See Desires; Low and Base, Low Company, and other paragraphs in this section).

Low Fellow — (See "Low and Base" in this section).

Low Fevers—(See "Low Fevers" under Fever).

Low Mentality—Mind of a Low Order—(See "Low and Base", and other paragraphs in this section; Criminal, Deviations; "Low" under Mind; "Loose Morals" under Morals; Obscene, Perversions, etc.).

Low Morals—(See "Low and Base" in this section; Depraved, Infamous; "Loose" under Morals; Obscene, Perversions, Shameless, etc.).

Low Pleasures — Given to Low and Sensuous Pleasures — (See "Low" under Pleasures).

Low Public Houses—Frequenter of— (See Harlots, Taverns).

Low Resistance — To Disease — (See "Low" under Recuperation, Resistance, Vitality).

Low Spirits — Sad — Dispirited — Dejected — Cast Down — Melancholic — Vapours—The ☉ ☌ ☽ at B., within 3 degrees, disspirited all thru life at each New ☽; the ☉ or ☽ to the ☌ or ill-asps. ♄ by dir. or tr.; the ☽ Sig. □ or ☍ ♄; ♄ to his own bad asps. by dir.; ♄ Sig. □ or ☍ ☽; ♄ by tr. in ☌, □, or ☍ ☉, ☽, ♃, ♀, or ☿ radical; ♀ afflicted, and espec. by ♄ or ♄ sign influence, tends to ennui, dissatisfaction, discontentment, languor of spirits, lack of interest in life, weariness, etc.; ☿ Sig. in ♑; ♓ on the Asc., and affl. by

♄, or with ♄ rising at B. and afflicting the hyleg. (See Anguish, Anxiety, Apathy, Brooding, Chaotic, Dejected, Depressed, Despondent, Discontentment, Dissatisfied, Doleful, Ennui, Fears, Fretful, Hope, Hysteria, Imaginations, Indifferent, Introspection, Irritable, Joy, Languid, Lassitude, Lethargy, Listless, Melancholia; "No Peace of Mind" under Mind; Morbid, Peevish, Pensive, Psychic, Restless, Sadness, Suicide, Vapors, Weariness, Worry, etc.).

Low Stature—The ☽ in her decrease tends to give a low, short, and squat stature. (See Decreased, Diminished, Dwarf, Growth, Height; "Short Body" under Short; Squab).

Low Vitality—(See "Low" under Vitality).

Low Women—Given To—(See "Low Company" in this section; Harlots, Lewd; "Women" under Men). See Lack Of, Less, Lessened, Loss Of, Lower, Lowered, Lowering, Lowest, Void Of.

LOWER—

Arm — The Lower Arm — (See Forearm, Hands).

Back—Lower Part of the Back—(See Back, Loins, Lumbar).

Belly—Lower Belly—(See Belly).

Bowels—The Lower Excretory Bowels — (See ''Lower Excretory'' under Bowels).

Desires—Lower Desires—(See Animal, Desires, Instincts, Passion, etc.).

Dorsal Nerves—Lower Dorsal Nerves —(See Dorsal).

Extremities — Lower Extremities — Lower Limbs — Disorders In — (See Ankles, Calves, Extremities, Feet, Femur, Fibula, Fractures, Gout, Knees, Legs, Limbs; "Neuritis" under Nerves; Rheumatism, Sprains, Swellings, Thighs, Tibia).

Gout — In the Lower Limbs — (See Gout; "Gout" under Extremities, Feet, Knees, Legs, Limbs).

Head—The Lower Back Part of the Head—(See Occipital).

Jaw—Lower Jaw—(See Jaws).

Kidneys — The Lower Portion of — Ruled by ♏. (See the Introduction under Kidneys).

Limbs—Lower Limbs—Disorders In— Accidents or Hurts To—(See the references under "Extremities" in this section).

Lip—Lower Lip—(See Lips).

Lobes — Lower Lobes — (See "Lobes" under Liver, Lungs).

Mankind—Lower Order of Mankind— (See Mankind).

Mind—The Lower Mind—(See "Animal Instincts" under Animal; "Lower Mind" under Mind; Personality).

Nature — The Lower Nature — (See "Mind" in this section; Conduct, Desires, Habits, Low, Passion, etc.).

Organs—Lower Parts of—(See "Parts of Body" under Accidents; "Marks" under Face; Marks; "Organs" under Middle; Moles, Navamsa; "Lower Part" under Organs; Upper).

Parts — Lower Parts of the Body — Diseases and Suffering In—♀ rules the lower part of the body in general; ♀ diseases and afflictions; born under ♀; ♄ affl. in ♏ in the 6th H. The ♋ sign on the Asc., the lower part of the body is shorter and smaller, and the upper part rounder. (See References under "Extremities" in this section; Abdomen, Belly, Bladder, Bowels, Genitals, Marks, Organs, Rectum, Sex Organs).

Passions—The Lower Passions—(See Amorous, Amours, Animal, Appetites, Desires, Excesses, Love Affairs, Passion, Sex, Venery, etc.).

Teeth — Lower Teeth — (See "Lower Jaw" under Jaws; Teeth).

Women—Lower Order of—(See Harlots, Nymphomania, Shameless, Treachery, etc.).

LOWERED — The Vitality Lowered — (See Recuperation, Resistance, Stamina, Tone; Lessened, Lowered, under Vitality).

LOWERING—

Lowering Brow — (See "Lowering" under Forehead).

Lowering Look—Lowering Aspect— Downward Look—♄ gives. (See "Downward" under Look).

LOWEST—Vitality At Its Lowest—(See "Force" under Vital; "Lowest" under Vitality).

LUBRICATION — Is carried on by the Synovial Fluid, ruled by the ☽. The afflictions of ♄ to a part tend to lack of, and a dry condition of the joints. Thus ♄ affl. in ♑ tends to dryness, pain, and trouble in the knee joint. Saturn affl. in ♌ tends to lack of lubrication between the dorsal vertebrae, which may result in ankylosis. (See Ankylosis, Fluids, Joints, Juices, Mucous Membranes, Oils, Serums, Synovial, etc.).

LUCIDA MAXILLA — Ceti — A Star of the nature of ♄. (See Ceti).

LUCK—(a) Bad Luck—(See Accidents, Banishment, Calamity, Disgrace, Enemies, Execution, Exile, Fate, Fire; "Malice" under Fortune; Honour, Hurts, Ill-Fortune, Ill-Health, Injury, Judges, Miseries, Misfortune, Plots, Poverty, Prison, Reputation, Reverses, Ruin, Scandal, Shipwreck, Sorrow, Treachery, Trouble, Unfortunate, Vehicles, Water, Wounds, etc.). (b) Good Luck — (See Comforts; "Good Fate" under Fate; "Fortunate" under Fortune; "Good Health" under Health; "Popular" under Reputation; Wealth).

LUES—Lues Venereae—Syphilis—(See Syphilis).

LUGUBRIOUS—Sad—Solemn—Mournful — (See Imaginations, Melancholy, Mournful, Sadness).

LUMBAGO—Pain In the Loins—Pain In the Back—The ☉ in ♉, ♊, or ill-asp. a malefic; the ☉ in ♒ and affl. by ♃; the ☽ hyleg in ♎ with females; ♅ affl. in ♎, spasmodic lumbago; a ♎ disease; ♄ affl. in ♎; ♃ affl. in ♒; ☿ affl. in ♈ or ♎; afflictions in ♎; ♌ or ♎ on the Asc.; the 7th H. involved, and ♄ afflicting ♀, provided the map otherwise shows a rheumatic constitution. (See "Pain" under Back; Gout, Loins, Lumbar, Rheumatism).

LUMBAR—The Lumbar Region—Lumbar Vertebrae—The Lumbar Region is ruled by ♎. The Lumbar Vertebrae are under the structural rulership of ♎. The bones and nerves of this region are ruled by ♎. For influences concerning the Lumbar Ganglia, and also the Lumbar branches of the Solar Plexus, see Ductless Glands (see Ductless); "Basal Ganglia", "Lumbar Ganglia", under Ganglion.

Circulation In — Obstruction of — ♄ affl. in ♐; ♄ in ♐, ☌, □ or ☍ ♃ or ♀; Subs at PP, UPP, LPP.

Cold and Chill In—Organic Weakness In—♄ affl. in ♎.

Diseases Of—♎ diseases, and afflictions in ♎.

Fifth Lumbar Nerve—Obstruction of —♄ in ♐ in □ or ☍ ♃.

Neuralgia In — ♅, ♂, or ☿ affl. in ♎; Subs at PP, and LPP.

Organic Weakness In — (See "Cold" in this section).

Pain In—♂ in ♎ in the 6th H., or affl. the ☽ or Asc. (See "Neuralgia" in this section).

Vertebrae—(See "Lumbar" under Vertebrae).

Weakest Part—Lumbar Region Weakest Part—The ☉ or ♃ affl. in ♎, or ♎ on the Asc.

LUMINOUS — Luminous Gas In the Spinal Canal—(See Ether; "Canal" under Spine).

LUMPISH APPEARANCE—In Hor'y Q. ♄ Sig. in ♉. (See Corpulent, Fat, Fleshy, Plump, Short, Stout).

LUMPS — Lump — Lumpy — Generally caused by the afflictions of ♄ and ♂, and in the parts ruled by the Signs containing these planets at B. Also caused by ♃ or ♀, due to disturbed circulation in a part. (See Abscesses, Boils, Bruises, Cysts, Deposits, Enlargements; "Hardening" under Faeces; "Lump" under Feet; Growths, Hurts, Injuries, Stone, Swellings, Tumors, Wart, Wen, etc.).

LUNACY — Insanity — The subject of Lunacy is more fully considered under the subject of Insanity, and the influences given here are supplemental to those in that Article. Lunacy is a disease of the ☽, and is called Lunacy after Luna, Lunar, the ☽, and lunacy patients are more affected, agitated, restless, or raving at the time of the Full ☽. (See "Full Moon" under Moon). If ♃ or ♀ are ori. or angular, and have any configuration with the ☽, it is curable. If the ☽ is with ♃ it can be cured by medicine. If the ☽ is with ♀ it will cure itself. If the Benefics be cadent or occidental, and the malefics oriental, the disorder will be incurable. Other influences causing Lunacy are ♂ in evil asp. the ☽ at the Full, or ♄ at a change in ♐ or ♓; ♂ afflicting the ☽ and ☿, and the ☽ in □ or ☍ ☿, causes violent lunacy. Epilepsy and Insanity are very closely associated. (See Epilepsy, Insanity). Case—Child Born of a Mad Mother In a Lunatic Asylum—See "Mad Mother", No. 074; "Obsession", No. 130, in 1001 N.N.

LUNAR — From the Latin word Luna, the Moon.

Lunar Activities Depleted—This is so at the time of the New ☽, the First Quarter, at the Full, and at the Last Quarter. (See Eclipses; Decrease, Full Moon, New Moon, Quarters, under Moon).

Lunar Diseases — (See "Lunar Diseases" under Moon).

Lunar Eclipses — (See Eclipses; Full Moon, New Moon, under Moon).

Lunar Epoch—(See Prenatal Epoch).

Lunar Functions—(See "Action" of the Moon", and the various paragraphs under Moon).

Lunar Horas—(See Horas).

Lunar Power Weakened — (See "Lunar Activities" in this section).

Semi-Lunar—(See Ganglion).

Solar-Lunar Activities—(See Solar).

LUNATICS—(See Insanity, Lunacy).

LUNATIONS—These are a New or Full ☽ which coincide with, or immediately precede, a dangerous accident or severe illness, and are important influences to study in connection with an illness, or the nature and immediate cause of an accident, hurt, or injury. When a Lunation falls on the place of one of the malefics in the radical map, trouble, anxiety, or illness are apt to result, and especially if there is an adverse primary direction operating over the nativity at the same time. (See Directions; "Threatened", "Time", under Disease; Eclipses, Insanity; Full Moon, New Moon, under Moon).

Periodic Lunation—(See Periodic).

LUNGS—Organs of Respiration—Respiratory System — Pulmonary — Bronchial — Pleura, etc. — The Lungs are ruled principally by ☿ and the ♊ sign, the 3rd and 4th Houses, and are influenced, or afflicted by all the common signs, and by the four cadent houses, when such are occupied by planets at B. The common signs, as ♊, ♍, ♐, and ♓, all affect the lungs, and rule them by their internal government. The upper lobes of the lungs are ruled by ♊, are under the internal rulership of ♊, and the lower lobes are ruled by the ♋ sign. Jupiter also rules the lungs, and in the Astral Body ♃ has direct relation to the lungs. The Bronchial Tubes are especially ruled by ♊. (See Bronchial). The Chest Cavity as a whole, and as a receptacle, is ruled by the ☽. (See Chest Trunk). The Arteries of the lungs are ruled by ♃, and ♀ rules the veins. The Pleura, the lung coverings, are ruled by ♃ and the ♋ sign, and also influenced by afflictions in ♊, and other common signs. The ♉, ♊, and ♋ signs rule the Respiratory System, and afflictions in any of these signs tend to affect the organs of Respiration. The 3rd Dorsal Vertebra, Lu.P., is the Lung Place in the Spine. (See Breath, Pleura, Pulmonary, Throat). The Tidal Air in the lungs is ruled by the ☽.

Absorbent Vessels—Of the Lungs Affected—(See Absorption).

Acute Disorders—(See "Acute" under Bronchial, Phthisis; "Pleurisy" under Pleura; Pneumonia, Psittacosis).

Afflictions In — (See "Pulmonary Affections", and the various paragraphs in this section).

Air—(a) Air Cells of the Lungs—☿ in ♋, ♌, or ♏ rules and affects the air cells, the breath, windpipe, and nerves of the Lungs and Respiratory System. (See "Air Cells" under Cells). (b) Tidal Air—Of the Lungs, ruled by the ☽. (See Tidal).

All Diseases In—Signified by the 4th H.

Altitude — The Lungs as Affected by Altitude—(See Altitude).

Anaemia — As a Cause of Lung Disorders—(See Anaemia).

Angina—(See Angina).

Apoplexy Of—Pulmonary Apoplexy—(See "Pulmonary" under Apoplexy).

Asthma—Phthisic—(See Asthma).

Blood In Lungs—Poor Circulation of —♄ or ☋ ☌ ♃ in ♌ tends to poor circulation of the arterial blood in the lungs, and ♄ or ☋ ☌ ♀ in ♌, poor circulation of the venous blood. (See "Poor Circulation" under Circulation; Congestion). Jupiter afflicted in ♋, ♌, or ♏ tends to Pleurisy and Blood Impurities of the Respiratory System. (See "Impure Blood" under Impure).

Breath — Breathing — Disorders of — (See the various paragraphs under Breath).

Bronchial Affections—(See Bronchial).

Capacity—Good Lung Capacity—Good Lung Expansion—Full Chest—♃ well-aspected in the Asc. (See Chest).

Capillaries—Of the Lungs—(a) Contracted and Spasmodic Action of—♅ in ♌. (See Oxygenation). (b) Obstruction of—Afflictions in ♌; ♄ affl. in ♌; afflictions of ♄ to ♃ or ♀ in ♌; the prog. ☽ ☌ ♄ in ♌ in the radix; a New ☽ in ♌ ☌ ♄ in ♌; a New ☽ afflicting the ♌ sign, and malefics in ♌ or ♊ to ♌. (See Capillaries, Obstruction). (c) Oxygenation — Capillary Oxygenation Disturbed—♅ affl. in ♌. (See Oxygenation). (d) Restricted—Spasmodic Contraction of—♅ in ♌. (See Oxygenation).

Cases of Lung Trouble — Birth Data, etc.—See Fig. 4A, 4B, 4C, 6A, 9C, 19C, in the book "Astro-Diagnosis" by the Heindels; Fig. 16, 25, 26, 35, in the book, "Message of the Stars" by the Heindels. Also see Chap. XIII in Daath's Medical Astrology.

Catarrh Of — The ☽ affl. in ♌. (See "Catarrh" under Bronchial; Catarrh).

Cells—Air Cells of Lungs—(See "Air" in this section).

Chest—Colds In—Congested and Feverish—(See Colds, Congestion, Feverish, in this section).

Chronic Disorders In — (See Asthma; "Chronic" under Bronchial; Consumption, Phthisis, Pleurisy, Tuberculosis).

Circulation In — Poor Circulation — (See "Blood" in this section).

Colds On Chest—Cold In—♅ in ♌; ♅, ♆, or ♄ in ♓ and afflicting the ⊙ or ☽; the ☽ affl. in ♓; ♄ or ♂ affl. in ♌ or ♐. (See "Bronchitis" under Bronchial; "Tightness" under Chest; Cold, Colds, Cough, Expectoration, Pleurisy, Pneumonia).

Congestion of Lungs — Pulmonary Congestion—The ☽ in ♌, ☌, or ♊ ♄; ♄ affl. in ♉, ♌, or ♏; ♄ ☌ ♃ or ♀ in ♌; ♃ or ♀ affl. in ♌; ♂ affl. in ♌, congested and feverish; many planets in lung signs and affl. by ♄; the afflicted bodies in ♒, as ♒ rules largely over the circulation. (See Asthma; "Congestion" under Bronchial; Consumption; Blood, Pulmonitis, in this section). Case of Congestion—See Chap. XIII in Daath's Medical Astrology.

Consumption Of—Pulmonary Consumption—(See Consumption, Phthisis, Tuberculosis, Wasting). Case — See Daath, Chap. XIII.

Convulsive Movements—Spasmodic Lung Cough—♅ in ♌. (See "Convulsive" under Cough).

Cough — Lung Cough — Hard, Dry, Spasmodic Lung Cough—♅ in ♌. (See "Cough" under Bronchial; "Lung Cough" under Cough; "Spasmodic" in this section).

Crystallization — Hardening — Of the Lung—♄ affl. in ♌. (See Consumption, Crystallization, Hardening).

Death — From Lung Disease — Death by Inflammation of the Lungs—♃ affl. the hyleg by dir., and ♃ much afflicted at B. and holding the dominion of death; ♃ shows; afflictions in common signs, and espec. in ♌; ♄ in the 8th H., and affl. the hyleg, and ♄ in ♌. (See "Death" under Bronchial, Consumption).

Defect—Some Defect In the Lungs—Born under ♃. (See Defects; "Structural" in this section).

Deficient Respiration—Due To Tight Lacing and Indiscretions In Dress—♀ affl. in ♉, ♌, or ♋. (See "Indiscretions" under Dress).

Diseased Lungs—Disordered Lungs—Trouble In the Lungs—The ⊙ ☌ ♄ in ♓; ♄ affl. in ♌ in the 6th H.; ♌ on the Asc. at B., and containing malefics; common signs on the angles, and espec. ♌, ♐, and ♓; Subs at Lu.P. (See "Cases", "Pulmonary Affections", and the various paragraphs in this section).

Dress — The Lungs Disturbed by Improper Dress—(See "Deficient" in this section).

Dropsy—Of the Chest—Hydrothorax—(See "Dropsy" under Chest).

Dry Lung Cough — (See "Cough" in this section).

Dust Inhalation — (See "Pneumoconiosis" in this section).

Dyspnoea—(See "Labored Breathing" under Breath; Dyspnoea).

Expansion Good — (See "Capacity" in this section).

Expectoration — Great Expectoration —(See Expectoration, Mucus, Phlegm).

Feverish and Congested—♂ affl. in ♌; the ☽ in ♉ and affl. by ♄, due to obstructions near the lungs, and caused by plethora from high living. (See "Fever" under Heart; "Lung Fever" in this section).

Fibrosis In—♄ affl. in ♌. (See "Fibrosis" under Fiber).

Gas Poisoning—Death By—(See "Poisoning" under Gas).

Gemini—Diseases of the Gemini Sign —(See Gemini, Third House).

Haematosis — Pulmonary Haematosis —Disturbances of — (See Haematopoiesis).

Haemoptysis — The Expectoration of Blood—(See Haemoptysis).

Hard Lung Cough — (See "Cough" in this section).

Hardening—Of the Lungs—♄ or ♅ in ♉. (See Consumption, Hardening).

Hemorrhage — In the Lungs — The ☉ or ♆ in ♉ ♉ ♂; ♄ or ♂ in ♉, and afflicted; the prog. ☽ ☌ ♄ in ♉, the capillaries obstructed; Subs at Lu.P. (See "Hemorrhage" under Bronchial; "Vicarious" under Menses; "Capillary" in this section).

Hydrothorax — (See "Dropsy" under Chest).

Hyperaemia — Of the Lungs — The ☉ affl. in ♉, ♉, or ♋. (See Hyperaemia).

Impaired Breathing—(See Breath, Deficient, in this section).

Impurities — Blood Impurities In — (See "Blood" in this section).

Inefficiency — Pulmonary Inefficiency —(See "Lungs" under Inefficiency).

Inflammation — Of the Lungs — Pulmonitis—(See "Pulmonitis" in this section).

Inhalation of Dust — Lung Disorders From—(See "Pneumoconiosis" in this section).

Innervation—Pulmonary Innervation —(See Innervation).

Interlobar Pleurisy — (See "Pleurisy" under Pleura).

Irritations — (See Congestion, Cough, Dust, Inflammation, Obstructions, and the various paragraphs in this section).

Lacing—Bad Effects from Tight Lacing — (See "Deficient Respiration" in this section).

Left Lung—The Lower Lobes of are disturbed by afflictions in ♋. (See "Lobes" in this section).

Lobes — Of the Lungs — The upper lobes of the lungs are ruled by ♉, and the lower lobes by ♋, and the lobes are affected by afflictions in these signs. The upper lobes are more affected by Subs at Lu.P. (3D), and the lower lobes by Subs at Li.P. (4D).

Lung Cough — (See "Cough" in this section).

Lung Disease — (See "Pulmonary Affections", and the various paragraphs in this section).

Lung Fever—Croupous Pneumonia— (See "Croup"; "Croupous Pneumonia" under Pneumonia; "Feverish and Congested" in this section).

Lungs Weak—Lungs Weakest Part— (See Weak, Weakest, in this section).

Motion — Spasmodic Motion of the Lungs—(See Cough, Spasmodic, in this section).

Mucus In—Phlegm—(See "Bronchitis" under Bronchial; Consumption, Cough, Mucus, Phlegm, Tuberculosis).

Nerves Of — The Nerves Affected — (See "Air Cells" in this section).

Obstructions In—(a) In Bronchials— (See "Obstruction" under Bronchial). (b) Capillary — (See "Capillaries" in this section). (c) In Lungs—The ☽ or ♄ affl. in ♉; ♃ affl. in ♍; ♉ ascending at the Vernal Equi., and ☿ afflicted, Countries and Peoples under ♉ will suffer thru corrupt air, obstructions of the lungs and bronchial tubes, and by high winds. (See "Corrupt Air" under Air; "Irritations" in this section). (d) Near the Lungs, and with Fever Resulting — (See "Feverish" in this section). (e) In Windpipe—The Trachea Obstructed with Phlegm — (See "Breast" under Phlegm; Trachea).

Oedema—Of the Lungs—The ☽ affl. in ♉, ♉, or ♋; Subs at Lu.P., and KP. (See "Catarrh" under Bronchial; Oedema).

Oppressed — The Lungs Oppressed — The ☽ in ♉ or ♉, ☌, or ill-asp. ♄ (or ☿ if he be of the nature of ♄) at the beginning of an illness or at decumb., and also causes obstructions. (See Congestion, Dyspnoea, Feverish, Inflammation, Obstructions, Pain, and the various paragraphs in this section).

Organic Defects — (See "Defect" in this section).

Osmosis In — Morbid Osmosis — (See Osmosis).

Over-Activity—The ☽ in ♐, and coming to the ♉ ♃ in ♉, tends to over-activity of the lungs, stomach and nerves; the ☉ in ♐. (See Over-Activity).

Oxygenation — Disturbances of—(See Oxygen; "Capillaries" in this section).

Pain In — (See Angina; "Bronchitis" under Bronchial; "Pains" under Chest; Dyspnoea, Pleurisy, Pneumonia; "Pulmonitis" in this section).

Parenchyma—The Pulmonary Parenchyma Affected—(See Parenchyma).

Paroxysmal Dyspnoea—With Oppression—(See Asthma, Breath, Dyspnoea).

Phlegm — Phlegm and Mucus In the Lungs—(See "Bronchitis" under Bronchial; Mucous, Phlegm).

Phthisic—(See Asthma).

Phthisis — Wasting — Consumption— (See Consumption, Phthisis, Tuberculosis, Wasting).

Pleura — The Serous Membrane Enveloping the Lungs — Disorders of — Pleurisy, etc.—(See Pleura).

Plexus — Pulmonary Plexus — (See "Middle Cervical" under Ganglion).

Pneumoconiosis—The Lungs Diseased from Inhalation of Dust — ♅ or ♄ afflicted in ♉; Subs at Lu.P.

Pneumogastric Nerve—(See Pneumogastric).

Pneumonia—(See "Pneumonia" under Bronchial; Pneumonia).

Poisoning — Gas Poison — (See "Gas" in this section).

Poor Circulation — (See Blood, Congestion, Obstructions, in this section).

Prevalent — Lung Diseases Prevalent —(See "Public Health Bad" under Public).

Pulmonary Affections—Lung Trouble —Diseased Lungs—Liable to Lung Diseases—The Lungs Afflicted—Pulmonary Complaints, etc.—The ☉, ☽, ♄, ♃, or ☿ in ♓ and afflicted; the ☉ or ☽ in the 6th H. in common signs, and afflicted by malefics; the ☉ affl. in ☐ or ♐; the ☉ in ♍ and affl. by ♃; the ☉ prog. to the ☐ or ☍ the ☐ sign, and afflicting any planets in ☐ at B., and also at the same time a malefic in the 6th H. by transit; the ☽ in the 6th H. in common signs and afflicted; the ☽ hyleg in ☐ or ♐, and afflicted, and espec. with females; the ☽ in ♐ in ☍ to ♃ in ☐; the ☽ afflicted in ♓; ♅ ☌ ☽ in ☐ or ♐; ♄ affl. in ☐, ♐, or ♓; ♄ in ☐, angular, and direct in motion at a Vernal Ingress, tends to a great prevalence of lung disorders; a ♃ disease; ♃ in the 6th H. at B. in common signs,. and affl. by the ☉ or ☽; ♃ affl. in ☐ or ♓; ♃ in ☐ in ☍ to the ☽ in ♐; ♂ in ☐ in the 6th H., and afflicted; ♂ in an angle and occi. of the ☉, and ori. of the ☽; ♂ promittor in ♓, and ☌ or ill-asp. the ☉; ♀ affl. in ☐ or ♐; ♀ in ♐ and affl. the ☽ or Asc.; ♀ affl. in ♐ in the 6th H.; ☿ affl. in ♎; ☿ in the 6th H. in common signs, and afflicted; the Asc. to the ☌ ♃ by dir., and ♃ afflicted at B.; airy signs on the Asc. and afflicted by malefics; ☐, ♐, or ♓ on cusp the 6th H.; many planets (a Stellium) in the 3rd H.; planets in ☐ in ☍ to planets in ♐; afflictions in common signs, and espec. in ☐; the malefics, or afflicting planets, in flexed or common signs; ♐ on the Asc.; afflictions in ☐, ♋, ♐, ♑, ♒, and ♓; a ☍, ☐, ♋, ♐, and ♓ disease; Subs at Lu.P., Li.P., and KP. Lung diseases and affections depend largely upon the peripheral sympathetic nerves and circulation, ruled by ♑, and upon the abdominal organs ruled by ♍. Thus chill of the skin, causing internal congestions and bowel disorders, are usually at the beginning, and the preliminary causes of lung disturbances. By keeping the bowels in proper order, and the surface of the body at an even temperature, many lung disorders and congestions can be prevented. (See Centripetal, Colds, Congestions; the various paragraphs in this section).

Pulmonitis—Inflammation of the Lungs—Pain In the Lungs—Congestion—The ☉ in ☐ or ♐, and to the ☌ or ill-asps. ♂ by dir.; the ☉ or ♂ in ☐ or ♐ at B., or by dir., and espec. if the ☉ or ☽ are afflicted by ♂ or ♂ at B.; the ☉ or ♂ afflicted in ☍, ☐, or ♋; a ♃ disease; ♃ shows death by inflammation of the lungs when much afflicted at B., and afflicting the hyleg by dir.; caused by ♃ when the dominion of death is vested in him; ♂ affl. in ☍, ☐, or ♋; ♂ affl. in ☐ or ♐, and espec. with ♂ in the 6th H. in these signs; ♂ in ♐ and affl. the ☽ or Asc.; a disease of the ♋ sign and afflictions in ♋; the ☽ in ♋ at B., and the tr. of ♂ over the radical ☽ if the ☽ is afflicted at B., and espec. if the constitution is weak; Subs at Lu.P. (See "Bronchitis" under Bronchial; "Pleurisy" under Pleura; Pneumonia).

Rapid Breathing—Rapid Dyspnoea— (See Breathing, Dyspnoea).

Residence—Lung Trouble Benefitted By—(See Altitude).

Respiratory Troubles—(See Breath).

Restricted Capillaries — (See "Capillaries" in this section).

Right Lung—Disorders In Lobes of— (See "Lobes" in this section; Left, Right).

Sclerosis—Hardening, Induration, and Thickening of the Connective Tissue of the Lungs — (See "Hardening" in this section; Sclerosis).

Spasmodic Affections — Of the Lungs —♅ affl. in ☐; ♅ in ☐ or ♐, ☌ the ☉ or ☽. (See Capillaries, Convulsive, Cough, in this section; "Spasmodic" under Breathing; Spasmodic).

Stenosis—Pulmonary Stenosis—Constriction—♄ affl. in ☐. (See "Capillaries" in this section; Constrictions, Stenosis).

Structural Defects—The ☉ in ☐ and afflicted. (See "Defect" in this section).

Suffocation—A Feeling of—(See Angina; "Labored" under Breath; Dyspnoea; Suffocation).

Tidal Air — Of the Lungs — Ruled by the ☽. (See Tidal).

Tight Lacing — Lungs and Breathing Affeeted By—(See "Deficient Respiration" in this section).

Tightness—Of the Chest—(See "Tightness" under Chest).

Tissues—Wasting of—♆ affl. in ☍, ☐, or ♋, and also to Consumption. (See Wasting).

Trachea—Obstructed — (See "Breast" under Phlegm; Trachea).

Trouble—Lung Trouble—(See "Pulmonary Affections", and the various paragraphs in this section).

Trunk — (See Chest, Thorax, Trunk).

Tuberculosis — (See Consumption, Phthisis, Tuberculosis, Wasting).

Ulceration — Of the Lungs — ♄ in ♋ when ♄ is the afflictor in the disease; the ☽ in ☍, ☌, or ill-asp. ♄ (or ☿ when of the nature of ·♄) at the beginning of the disease, or at decumbiture (Hor'y). (See Ulcers).

Upper Lobes — (See "Lobes" in this section).

Wasting—Of the Tissues—(See "Tissues" in this section).

Weak Lungs — Lungs the Weakest Part—Weak Chest and Lungs—The ☉ in the 6th H. in a cardinal sign and afflicted, weak chest; the ☽ affl. in ♓, weak lungs; ♄ ☌ or ill-asp. the ☉ in mutable signs; ♄ affl. in ☐; ♄ ☌ ☉ in ☐; ♄ in the 6th H. at B., in common signs, and affl. by the ☉ or ☽; ♄ affl. in ♓; ♃ affl. in ☐ if the native be dark in complexion; ♂ ☌ ☿ in ☐; ♂ in the 6th H. in common signs; ☿ affl. in ☐ in the 6th H.; ☿ ruler of the Asc., and in the 6th H. in ♐ or ♓, and afflicted; ☿ in ♓, ☌, or ill-asp. any of the malefics as promittors, sometimes a little lung weakness; ☐ on cusp the 6th H., and afflicted, and with malefics in ☐ in the 6th. (See Consumption, Phthisis, Pulmonary, Tuberculosis, and the various paragraphs in this section).

Windpipe Obstructed—(See "Trachea" in this section).

Winds — Easterly Winds Which Produce Bronchitis—(See "Winds" under Bronchial).

LUPUS—A Chronic Tuberculous Skin Disease—Caused by ♄; ♄ affl. in ♎ or ♑; ♄ rising and affl. the ☉ or ☽. Red color, the color of ♂, and the remedies of ♂, are good in the treatment of Lupus, as ♂ opposes, and tends to remedy and alleviate the diseases of ♄; Subs at MCP (4C), and KP. (See Red, Skin, Tuberculosis). Case of Lupus—See "Lupus", No. 363, in 1001 N.N.

LUST—Lustful—Inordinate Lust—Salacious—Wanton—Libidinous, etc.—The ☉ to the ill-asps. ♀ by dir.; the ☽ decr. and sepr. from ♂ and applying to ♀, disgrace thru wantonness; the ☽ to the ill-asps. ♀ by dir., and ♀ badly afflicted at B.; ♂ ☌ or afflicting ♀; ♂ Sig. ☐ or ☍ ♀; ♂ to the ☌ or ill-asp. ♀ by dir.; ♀ in ♏ and affl. by ♂; ♀ in ♏ ☌ the ☽ or ♂, unbridled or violent lust; ♀ afflicted by ☐ and ☍ aspects tends to turn love to lust, and espec. when afflicted by malefics; ♀ ruler of the horoscope and afflicted by malefics; ♀ in a feminine sign alone, and in ☌, ☐, or ☍ ♂; ♀ affl. at B., and to the ☌ or ill-asp. the Asc.; ♀ and ♂ both in masculine signs tends to make females more lustful; Fixed Stars of the nature of the ☽ and ♂ ascending at B. tend to wantonness. (See Amorous, Amours, Debauched, Degenerate, Depraved, Deviations, Disgrace, Effeminate, Excesses, Impotent, Infamous, Lascivious, Lewd, Licentious; "Adulterous" under Love Affairs; Low; "Loose Morals" under Morals;; Nymphomania, Obscene, Passion, Perversions, Pleasure, Scandal, Sex, Shameless, Virile, Wanton).

Females Lustful — (See Effeminate; "Males Nearly Impotent" under Impotent; Nymphomania, Shameless, Virile).

Health Injured—By Inordinate Lust—♂, ♅, or ♆ in the 5th H. and afflicted; ♂ ☌ or ill-asp. ♀; ♀ afflicting the Asc. at B.; ♀ in the 5th H. and afflicted by malefics; lord of the 6th in the 5th H.; lord of the 10th in the 5th H., by pleasure, or too much indulgence in improper living. (See Amorous, Harlots; ''High Living'' under High; "Health Injured" under Men; "Health Suffers" under Opposite Sex; "Passional Excesses" under Passion; Venereal, Venery).

Lusty Bones — (See "Healthy Bones" under Bones).

Men Lustful — (See Effeminate; "Licentious" under Men; Virile; the various references in this section).

LUXATIONS—(See Dislocations).

LUXURIANT — Luxuriant Hair — (See "Abundance" under Hair). The ♈ sign is Luxuriant. (See Aries).

LUXURIES—Luxury—Extravagance—Lavish—

Fond of Luxuries — Luxuriant Living —The ☉ afflicted in ♎ or ♓; the ☉ affl. in ♉, fond of luxuries in food, indulgence in rich foods; the ☽ Sig. ☌ ♀;

the ☽ to the ☐ or ☍ ♃ by dir.; ♄ in ♎; ♄ Sig. in ♎, prodigal of expense (Hor'y); ♃ afflicted in ♉; ♂ affl. in ♎, a luxurious disposition; ♀ afflicted at B.; ♀ in aspect with ☿, fond of luxury; ♀ affl. in the 6th H., and ill-health from. (See Amusements, Appetites, Comforts, Conduct, Diet, Dress, Drink, Eating, Epicureans, Expense Extravagance, Feasting, Food; "Free Living" under Free; Gluttony, Habits; "High Living" under High; Ornaments, Pleasure, Prodigal, Riches, Sports, etc.).

Health Undermined — By Luxuries — (See Extravagance; "Undermined" under Health).

LYING—Liars—(See Liars).

LYMPH—Lymphatics—The Lymphatic System—Lymphatic Glands—Absorbent Glands—The Lymph is ruled by the ☽, and the ♒ and ♓ signs. Under the internal rule of ♓. The watery signs are lymphatic, and especially ♓. Venus is also lymphatic. The lymph is carried principally by the Thoracic Duct, ruled by ♋. The ☉ and ☽ acting thru the ♒ sign, and thru the Sanguineous System, affect the Lymphatic System, the nutrition of the tissues, the legs and ankles, and give way to the Splenic Diathesis. The ☽ in her last Quarter acts especially on the lymph. The ☽ in ♉, ♊, and ♋ rules and affects the absorbent and lymphatic vessels of the throat, lungs, and respiratory system. (See Absorption).

Circulation—The Circulation Is Impeded—♄ ☌, ☐, or ☍ ☽.

Deficiency In — ♄ or ♆ ☌ ☽; ♆ ☌ ☽, and in ☐ or ☍ ♃. Case—See Fig. 18A in the book, "Astro-Diagnosis", by the Heindels.

Diseases Of—Disorders of—The ☉ afflicted in watery signs; ☽ diseases, and afflictions to the ☽; the ☽ ☌ or ill-asp. ♄ or ♆ at B., and by dir.; many afflictions in watery signs at B. on the Asc., and afflicted. (See "Diseases Of" under Glands).

Disturbed—The Lymphatics Disturbed —♂ ☌ ☽ in ♏.

Exudation — Lymph Exudation — Occurs in Eczema. (See Eczema).

Functions Of — The ☽ well-aspected in ♋ or ♓, the lymphatic and absorbent vessels are regular in their functions, and the ☽ afflicted tends to disturbed functions.

Impeded Circulation — (See "Circulation" in this section).

Inflamed—The Lymphatic Glands Inflamed, and with Fever—♂ ☌ ☽ in ♏.

Lacteals—Disorders of—♄ affl. in ♏. (See Chyle).

Leukemia—Lymphatic Leukemia—♄ affl. in ♏. (See Leukocytes).

Lungs — Lymphatic Vessels of Disordered—The ☽ affl. in ♉, ♊, ♋.

Obstructed—Impeded—(See "Circulation" in this section).

Respiratory System — Lymphatics of Disordered—☽ affl. in ♉, ♊, ♋. (See Absorption).

Signs — The Lymphatic Signs are ♋, ♏, ♓, the watery signs. (See "Signs" under Water).

Swelling—In Lymphatic Glands In the Groin—(See Bubo).

Temperament — The Lymphatic Temperament—Indolent Temperament—Ruled and given by the ☽. Also ruled by the water signs and ♀. Also ♅ is strongly associated with this Temperament, and adds his influence to the ☽, ♀, and the watery signs. This is a temperament of thinking and feeling rather than action. There is a lack of brisk vascular action in this temperament. Lethargy of the Pituitary Body is also given by this temperament. Serous discharges are also characteristic of this temperament. Also a lack of tone is given by the lymphatic temperament. This is also called the Phlegmatic Temperament, and is classed as cold and moist. (See Anaemia, Dropsy, Dull, Lassitude, Lethargy; "Cold and Moist Body" under Moisture; Pale; "Temperament" under Phlegmatic; Pituitary; "Blood" under Red; Serous; "Lymphatic" under Temperament; Tone, etc.).

Throat — Lymphatic Vessels of Affected—☽ affl. in ♉, ♊, ♎. (See Throat).

Vesicles—(See Vesicles).

LYNCHING — Lynched — Death By— ♄ afflicting the hyleg, and in signs of human form. (See "Common People" under Common; Hanging; "Human Signs" under Human; Mobs, Riots).

M

MACHINERY—Inventions—Ruled by ♅.

Accidents By—Danger By—Hurts or Injury by In the Employment—Danger of Death By—♅ afflicted at B., and by dir.; the ☉ ruler of the 9th or 10th H. at B., and the ☉ to the ☌ or ill-asp. ♅ by dir.; the ☉ to the □ or ☍ ♅ or ☌ by dir.; the ☉ directed to Praesepe or The Cratch; the ☽ to the ☌ or ill-asp. ♅ by dir. (See Electricity; "Accidents" under Employment).

Death By—In the Employment—(See "Death" under Employment; "Accidents" in this section).

Head—Hurts or Injuries To the Head by Machinery—♅ in the 1st H., and afflicted. (See "Accidents" under Head).

MADNESS — Mad — Mania — Rabid — Insane—Raving—Fury, etc. This subject is also considered under the subjects of Delirium, Frenzy, Fury, Insanity, Mania, Raving, etc. See these subjects.

Cases of Madness—Became Mad—See "Mexico", No. 824; "Mad Mother", No. 074 in 1001 N.N.

Death by Madness—Death by Fury—Accident or Injury By—☿ afflicting the hyleg, the Giver of Life, by dir.; ☿ affl. by ♂ at B., and holding the dominion of death.

Distempers—Mad and Sudden Distempers—Caused by ♂. (See Fulminating; "Sudden Distempers" under Head; Noisome; "Diseases" under Sudden).

Mad Acts—Mad and Brutish—♂ afflicted in ♈. (See Anger; "Brain Storms" under Brain; Brutish, Cruel, Excitable, Feelings, Fierce, Frenzy, Fury, Ravings, Savage; "High Temper" under Temper).

Mad Dog Bites—(See Hydrophobia).

Mad Mother—(See "Cases" in this section).

Mad with Pain — (See "Mad" under Pain).

Madness Plague—♂ affl. in □ or ♍, and ♂ ☌ or evil asp. the Asc. by dir.

Madness Threatened — Tendency to Madness or Mania—Causes of Madness —♂ afflictions tend to Madness and Mania, and also afflictions to ☿, and espec. ♂ afflicting ☿, the mental ruler; ♂ afflicting the ☉, and espec. ♂ □ ☉; ♂ □ ☿; ♂ ☌ the Asc. by dir.; the ☉ affl.

in ♌ when the ☉ is the afflictor in the disease; the ☉ hyleg and the ☉ to the □ or ☍ ♂ by dir.; the ☽ to the ill-asps. ☿ and ☿ greatly afflicted at B., a disease of the ☽, and espec. if afflicted by malefics, and the malefics strong and dominant; the ☽ hyleg, and affl. by ♄, or by ♂ and ☿, threatens madness and death; the ☽ to the □ or ☍ ♂ or ☿ by dir.; ♅ affl. in the 12th H. (see Hallucinations, Obsessions); ♅ in the 6th H., and affl. by the ☽ or ☿; ♄ and ♂ in angles, elevated above ♅, the ☽ or ☿, and if ♅, ☿, the ☽ and Asc. be unconnected with each other by good aspects, but are afflicted by ♄ and ♂, and with no assistance from the benefics; ♃ Sig. ☌ ☉, and the ☉ ill-dignified, and espec. if the ☽ and ☿ be afflicted; a ☿ disease; caused by ☿ when the dominion of death is vested in him, and ☿ affl. by ♂; ☿ affl. at B., and the ☽ to the ill-asps. ☿ by dir.; ☿ in the 8th H., and afflicted at a Solar Ingress of the ☉ into ♈, and ☿ afflicting the ☽ or planet ascending; ☿ □ or ☍ ♄, and with ♂ also afflicting ☿; ☿ and ♂ □ or ☍ ♄; ☿ ☌ ♂, and affl. by the ☽, ♅, or ♄; fixed stars of the nature of ☿ denote death by madness; the phantasies are often prejudiced when ☿ is weak, afflicted and unfortunate at B., and under evil directions. (See "Prejudiced" under Fancies). Also caused by Subs at AT and AX. The Asc. to the □ or ☍ ♀ or ☿ by dir. (See Anger, Anguish; "Delirium Tremens" under Delirium; Drink, Enthusiasm, Epilepsy, Fears, Frenzy, Fury, Insanity, Irrational, Mania, Melancholy, Noisome, Raving, Suicide, Worry, etc.).

MAGIC—Magical Powers—Ruled largely by ♅ and the ♏ sign, and also the 8th and 12th H. are usually involved.

Black Magic—♆ affl. by ♂ gives tendency to, and espec. where the 8th or 12th H. are involved in the configuration, or the 8th and 12th signs, as ♏ and ♓; the 13° ♓ on the Asc. (See "Black Magic", "Faith Healers", under Healers; "Low Grade" under Psychic; Science, Spirit Controls, Witchcraft).

Ceremonial Magic—Ritual—Presided over by ♃, and is also ascribed to the 6th H. (See "Ritual" under Religion).

White Magic—Ruled by the same influences as govern Black Magic, only with the good aspect of ♂ to ♅, and fortunate influences in the 8th and 12th H., or in ♏ and ♓. (See "Treatment" under Hypnotism; Magnetism, Necromancy).

MAGISTRATES—(See Judges, Law).

MAGNESIA PHOSPHATE—Ruled by the ♌ sign. This Salt supplies the Nerve Sheaths. (See "Salts" under Zodiac).

MAGNETISM—Magnetic—The ♏ sign tends to give much magnetic and attractive power, and for this reason also attracts disease and infectious complaints. (See Contagious, External, Infections). Magnetism is strongly allied with Electricity, and ruled by ♅. (See Electric, Electricity; "Native Country" under Native). Terrestrial Magnetism is ruled by ♅. (See "Operations" under Nature; Uranus). In disease the magnetic influences are stronger at night due to the ☽ influences, and hence diseases are usually more raging at night, and espec. with acute fevers. (See "Diseases" under Night). During the daytime the electric forces of the ☉ tends to diminish the fevers, and ease the disease. Also ♄ is cold and magnetic. (See Saturn).

Animal Magnetism—Under the rule of ♂ and ♅. (See Animal).

Aura—The Magnetic Aura—(See Aura).

Body — Magnetic Body — ♃ well-aspected in the 12th H.

Healers — Magnetic Healers — The ♏ influence strong and prominent at B.; ♏ on the Asc.; the ☉ well-asp. in ♏; ♀ ♂ ♀ and in ✶ or △ ☿; ♃ in ✶ or △ ☽; ♂ in the 12th H., free from affliction, in his exalted sign ♑, or in ♌ or ♐; the 24° ♓ on the Asc. (See "Magnetic Healers" under Healers; Hypnotism, Incompatibility, Magic, Mesmerism; "Curing" under Nature; Psychic, Scorpio).

Iron — Magnetized Iron — (See Lodestones).

Man—A Magnetic Man—Case—See "Magnetic Man", No. 849 in 1001 N.N.

Nature—Magnetic Nature—Born under the strong influence of ♅; the ☽ to the ✶ or △ ♅ by primary or secondary dir., the magnetic power is increased; ♅ in 6th H., and well-asp. by ♆ and ☿; ♂ in good asp. the ☉; the 24° ♓ on the Asc.

Negative Signs—The negative signs are divided into two parts, called Horas, which are alternately magnetic, and magneto-electric. (See Horas; "Signs" under Negative, Positive).

Planets—The Magnetic Planets—(See "Negative Planets" under Negative).

Signs—Magnetic Signs—♏ is classed as the principal magnetic sign. The feminine, or negative signs, are considered magnetic. (See "Negative" in this section; "Attracts Disease" under Attracts; "Signs" under Feminine, Negative; Scorpio).

MAIMED—Maiming—Mayhem—

Maiming of the Body—♄ to the ☌ or ill-asp. ♂ by dir.; ♄ casting an evil

asp. to ♃ or ♀,.and ♂ in ☐ or ⚹ ☿ at the same time; ♂ ☐ or ⚹ the ☉ at B., and by dir. (See Mutilated).

Males Born Maimed—Crippled from Birth—Defective In the Private Members—♀ in an angle, with ♄ and ♂ ascending after ♀, and configurated with the ☉ and ☿, the ☉, ☽, and ♀ being in masculine signs, and the ☽ in her decrease,—then males are born maimed, crippled, or injured in their private members, especially under ♈, ♌, ♏, ♑, or ♒, and females will remain childless and unprolific. (See "Crippled" under Birth; Congenital).

Males Maimed by Castration—Violent Castration—(See "Violent Castration" under Testes). See Eunuchs.

MAINTENANCE—Of Life—(See "Maintenance" under Life).

MAJESTIC—Majestic Carriage—(See "Majestic" under Gait).

MAJOR—

Major Bodily Disorders—(See Chronic, Constitutional, Consumptions, Invalids, Lingering, Malignant, Morbid, Organic, Serious, Severe, Structural, Tedious, Wastings, etc.).

Major Planets—Superior Planets—♆, ♅, ♄, ♃ and ♂. Diseases ruled by these planets are of greater consequence, and more severe in their effects, and espec. when they also hold the dominion of death. (See Severe). The diseases of ♀ and ☿, the minor planets, are less serious unless they hold power at B., hold the dominion of death, or greatly afflict the hyleg both at birth and by direction. (See Perihelion).

Major Subluxations—Of the Vertebrae —(See Subluxations, Vertebrae).

MAJORITY—Majorities of the Planets In a Nativity, and Their Effects—In the diagnosis, prognosis, and consideration of disease, the majorities of the planets in Signs, Houses, Rising, Setting, Elevated or Below the Horizon, Retrograde, etc., should be taken into account. Many planets, or a Stellium, in one sign or house, tend to greater afflictions of the parts of the body ruled by such sign and house. The majority of the planets in the positive signs gives greater will-power, and the ability to overcome disease, obstacles and the limitations of life. (See Positive, Negative). The ☉, and a majority of the planets rising at B. usually give greater vitality and resistance to disease, while a majority setting at B. tend to weaken the physical powers, and give less power to overcome obstacles and make life come your way, as the planets when setting are weaker, and deprived of much of their power, unless greatly dignified by sign, house, and aspect. The majority of planets in fiery signs tend to increased vitality, whereas a majority below the Earth at B. tend to weaken the constitution, and espec. when the majority is in the 6th H., and below the western horizon at B. A study along these lines will help you in judging the map along the lines of health and disease, and to better analyze the case. Life also tends to be longer when the majority of the planets are rising and elevated, and in fiery signs, regardless of many other evil influences of the map. (See "Signs" under Air, Cardinal, Earth, Fire, Fixed, Mutable, Water; Cure, Diagnosis, Elevated, Life, Prognosis, Recuperation, Resistance, Rising, Setting, Stellium, Vitality, Will, etc.).

MAL—Sickness—(See Disease, Ill-Health, Sickness).

Mal-Adjustment—(See Saint Vitus Dance).

Mal-Assimilation—(See Assimilation, Digestion; "Malnutrition" under Nutrition).

Petit and Grand Mal—(See Epilepsy).

MALACIA—Malacosis—Málacoma—A Morbid Softening of the Tissues—A ♀ and ♓ disease; ♀ affl. in ♓. (See Softening).

Malacia—A Depraved Appetite—(See "Abnormal", "Depraved", under Appetite).

MALADIES—Malaena—(See Disease, Ill-Health, Sickness).

Exhibition of Maladies—(See Exhibition).

MALAISE—A Feeling of Uneasiness and Discomfort—(See Discomfort, Restlessness).

General Malaise—Attacks of Malaise Arising from Plethora—♄, ♅, or ♆ in ♏, and affl. the ☉ or ☽, general malaise; ♄ affl. in the 6th H. (See Aches, Debility, Discomfort, Dull, Lassitude, Listless, Plethora, Weak).

MALARIA—Ague—Intermittent Fever —♂ affl. in ♌, ♍, ♐, or ♒. (See Ague, Intermittent, Miasma, Moonlight, Noxious, Quartan, Remittent, Spleen, etc.).

MALE—Males—Masculine—The ☉ is the strong ruler in a male nativity, and also ♂ rules the male sex generally, and the ☽ and ♀ rule females. Afflictions to the ☉ tend to cause disease and affliction to the male, and afflictions to the ☽ or ♀ to the female. The ☉ is considered hyleg in a male nativity, and the ☽ hyleg in a female, unless they are greatly out of dignity and afflicted, when one of the Benefics, or the Asc., may be taken as hyleg. The following subjects have to do with Males, Masculine. Also see Brother, Father, Husband, Men, Son, Uncle.

Accidents to Males—Hurts—Injuries —Wounds—Danger of—Malefics to the ♂ or ill-asp. the ☉. (See "Hurts" under Brother; "Accidents" under Father, Husband).

Afflictions To—(See the various paragraphs in this section).

Appearance—Women Masculine In Appearance—Masculine Women—(See Deviations, Effeminate; "Coarse" under Voice).

Bad Health For—(See Disease, Ill-Health, Short Life, in this section).

Barrenness—In the Male—(See Barren; "Anchorite" under Husband; Impotent).

Births—Male Births—A Male Child Is Promised—In male nativities the 5th H. is male, and the 4th H. female, and the conditions of these houses will show the predominance of sex, and which gives the greater promise of fruitfulness, and the opposite houses show detriments, etc. Planets which promise children, when posited in the 10th, 11th, 4th or 5th H., in male signs, or in aspect to the ☉, promise male children. Mars in ✳ or △ asp. the Asc. by dir., birth of a male child is promised. If the ☉, ☽, or Asc., or planets in aspect with them, or with the Asc., be in masculine signs, or are masculine by being oriental, the child conceived will be a male if such conditions exist at conception. Jupiter in ✳ or △ the ☉ by dir., if ♃ is strong and well-dig. at B., promises a male child. Mercury is masculine or feminine as he is aspected. He is also masculine when ori. of the ☉, and feminine when occidental. If the dispositor of the ☽, and the lord of the hour be angular, and ♃ in the 7th H., the mother has quickened and the child will be a male, and if ♐ or ♓ be in the 7th H. under these conditions the child is a female (Hor'y). If the 1st or 5th, their lords, the ☽ and the planet to which she applies, be all or most of them, in masculine signs, or in aspect with masculine planets or stars of a masculine nature, the child will be a male, and vice versa. (Hor'y). For Cases of three males conceived, two males and one female, one male and two females, see Triplets; for two males, see Twins. (See "First-Born Child" under Children; "Birth of a Female" under Female; Predetermination, Son).

Brain—In the male, ruled by the ☉. (See Brain).

Brother—(See the various paragraphs under Brother).

Children—Male Children Born or Conceived—(See "Births" in this section).

Colors—Orange and Red, colors of the ☉ and ♂, are the predominant masculine colors.

Conceived—Male Child Conceived—(See "Births" in this section; Conception).

Constitution—(a) Strong Constitution —The ☉ in a strong sign and house, free from afflictions, and well-asp. by ♃. (See "Strong" under Constitution). (b) Weak Constitution—(See "Sickly", "Unhealthy", under Children; "Death" under Infancy; "Low" under Vitality; "Weak Body" under Weak).

Crippled—Born Crippled or Maimed —(See Crippled; "Males Born Maimed" under Maimed).

Danger to Males—Afflictions to the ☉ at B., or by dir.; born at time of eclipse of the ☉, may die at B. (See Eclipse. Also note the various paragraphs in this section).

Death of a Male—In the Family—The ☉ directed to Cor Scorpio; the ☉ badly afflicted by malefics at B., and by dir.; born at time of an eclipse of the ☉, may die soon after birth. (See "Death" under Brother, Father, Husband; "First-born" under Children; Eclipses; "Male" under Infancy, etc.).

Debility In—(See Impotent; "Ill-Health", "Weak", in this section).

Degrees—Masculine Degrees of the Zodiac—♈ 8, 15, 30; ♉ 11, 21, 30; ♊ 16, 26; ♋ 2, 10, 23, 30; ♌ 5, 15, 30; ♍ 12, 30; ♎ 5, 20, 30; ♏ 4, 17, 30; ♐ 2, 12, 30; ♑ 11, 30; ♒ 5, 21, 27; ♓ 10, 23, 30. If the ascendant or its lord be in one of these degrees the native will be more masculine in appearance even tho a female. (See "Appearance" in this section; Predetermination).

Disease In the Male—In a male horoscope afflictions to the ☉ tend to cause disease, or an earlier death, and the ☉ also in a weak sign or house, and much afflicted by malefics; the ☉ hyleg and much afflicted tends to give a weaker constitution, and more subject to disease and ill-health all thru life; ♄ affl. the ☉ at B., and by dir. The ☉ is general Significator of health in the male, and the ☽ in the female. In an adult nativity the ☉ rules the male, and the ☽ the female. (See "Ill-Health" in this section).

Effeminate—Males Effeminate—(See Effeminate).

Eyes—In the Male—(See Eyes; "Eyes" under Left, Right).

Father—(See the various paragraphs under Father).

Females—(a) Injury to Males By—(See Grief, Health, Injured, Treachery, Women, under Men). (b) Masculine Women—(See Appearance, Degrees, in this section).

First Child—In a Male Nativity—(See "First-Born" under Children).

Fruitfulness—In the Male—(See Fruitful; "Fruitful" under Husband).

Genitals—In the Male—(See Genitals).

Good Health—For Males—The Health Strengthened—Men More Robust—The ☉ strong at B., and well-aspected; the ☉ well-aspected by the ☽ and ♂; the ☉ in a fiery sign, better prospect of good health and long life; ♂ in good asp. to the ☉, as ♂ always augments the ☉; ♂ in a female sign and ♀ in a masculine sign, and both oriental. (See "Constitution" in this section; "Good Health" under Health; "Body" under Strong; "Good" under Vitality).

Grandfather—(See Grandparents).

Health—The ☉ is the Sig. of health with males, and the ☉ weak and ill-dig. at B., and afflicted, tends to impair the health, and espec. under evil directions to the ☉. (See Good Health, Ill-Health, and the various paragraphs in this section).

Heart Disease—In the Male—The ☉ affl. in ♌; afflictions to the ☉, as the ☉ rules the heart in the male. (See Heart).

Hermaphrodites—(See this subject).

Horoscope—The ☉ has great influence in a male horoscope, and to judge of the prospects of a male in health, and other matters, study the position, aspects, sign and house position of the ☉ at B., and also the directions to the ☉ after birth, and when they culminate. (See Horoscope).

Houses—The Masculine Houses—The odd numbers, as the 1st, 3rd, 5th Houses, etc., as these houses correspond to the masculine and positive signs, as ♈, ♊, ♌, etc. (See "Masculine" under Houses).

Hurts To—(See "Accidents" in this section).

Husband—(See the various paragraphs under Husband).

Hyleg—In the Male Nativity—The ☉, as a rule, unless the ☉ is weak and badly afflicted at B. (See Hyleg).

Ill-Health—For Males—The ☉ rules the health in males. The ☉ affl. at B., as by ♄; the ☉ ☌, □, ☍ or P. ♄; the ☉ hyleg at B., and much afflicted; the ☉ in the 6th or 12th H. at B., and affl. by malefics, unless the laws of health and hygiene are observed, and the vital powers conserved; the ☉ ☌ ♄ in ♋ or ♑ in the 1st H.; the adverse aspects of the ☉ to any of the malefics by dir., and espec. among the aged, feeble, and those of frail constitution; the prog. ☉ to the ☉ or ☍ the Asc.; the prog. ☉ to the ☌ or ill-asp. ♄; the afflicting planet a malefic, and elevated above the ☉, and the health will be worse than it would be if the ☉ was elevated above the malefic; the ☉ affl. in ♓, and with ♓ or ♋ on the Asc. at B. The health will not tend to be exceptionally bad if ♂ is in favorable asp. to the ☉, even tho ♄ afflict the ☉, as the good asp. of ♂ tends to augment the animal heat. (See "Disease", and the various paragraphs in this section; "Sickly Children" under Children; Eclipses; "Bad Health", "Periods of Ill-Health", under Health; "Low" under Vitality; "Weak Body" under Weak).

Impotency In—(See Barren; "Unfruitful" under Husband; Impotent).

Infant—Death of a Male Infant—(See Eclipses; "Death" under Infancy).

Injuries To—(See Accidents, Females, in this section).

Left Eye—In Male—Hurts To—Afflictions to the ☽ at B., and by dir., as the ☽ rules the left eye of a male, and the ☉ the right eye. (See "Eyes" under Left).

Length of Life—For Males—The ☉ is usually taken as hyleg and Giver of Life in a male nativity, and the length of life may be forecasted according to the sign, house, and strength of the ☉ at B., and the aspects to him, whether good or bad, etc. (See Long Life, Short Life, and the various paragraphs in this section; "Death" under Childhood, Children, Infancy, Middle Life, Old Age, Youth; "Early Death" under Early, etc.).

Long Life—For Males—Prospect of—The ☉ in a fiery sign at B., and favorably aspected by benefics; the ☉ strong at B., and not much afflicted; the ☉ hyleg, strong, and well-aspected. (See "Long Life" under Life; "Good" under Vitality; "Good Health" in this section).

Maimed—Males Born Maimed—(See Maimed).

Male Births—(See "Births" in this section).

Male Organ—Penis—Disorders of—(See Genitals, Penis, Urethra, Venereal).

Marriage Of—(See Fiance, Husband, Marriage, Marriage Partner, Wife).

Masculine—(a) Masculine Degrees of the Zodiac—(See "Degrees" in this section). (b) Masculine Houses—(See "Houses" in this section). (c) Masculine Planets—(See "Masculine" under Planets). (d) Masculine Signs—(See "Masculine" under Signs). (e) Masculine Women—(See Appearance, Degrees, in this section).

Men — (See the various paragraphs under Men).

Mixture of Sex — (See Hermaphrodites).

One Male Conceived—(See "Births" in this section; "Single Births" under Children; Conception; "Birth" under Son). For two males, or three males conceived, or born, see Twins, Triplets).

Organ—The Male Sex Organ—(See "Male Organ" in this section).

Penis—(See "Male Organ" in this section).

Planets — Masculine Planets—(See "Masculine" under Planets).

Predominate—Males Predominate In the Family—(See "Female Children" under Children; "Births" in this section).

Quadrants—The Male Quadrants In the Star Map of Birth — (See Quadrants).

Recuperation—Augmented or Slow for Males—(See "Males" under Recuperation).

Relatives—(See "Male Relations" under Relations).

Right Eye—Of a Male—Ruled by the ☉, and the ☉ to the ♂ or ill-asp. a malefic by dir. tends to hurts, injuries, or blindness in the right eye, and espec. if the ☉ is badly afflicted at B., or with Nebulous Stars. The ☉ afflicted at B., and to the ♂ or ill-asp. the Asc. by dir. tends espec. to hurts to the right eye. (See Blindness; "Eyes" under Left, Right; "Left Eye" in this section).

Robust—Males Robust—(See "Good Health" in this section; Impotent, Robust, Ruddy; "Good" under Vitality).

Scrotum—(See Scrotum).

Sex — (a) Mixture of Sex In — (See Hermaphrodites). (b) Male Sex Organ —(See "Male Organ" in this section).

Sharp Illnesses In—Severe But Soon Over—The ☉ in a fiery sign at B. (See Severe, Sharp).

Short Life—For Males—Note especially the aspects to the ☉ at B., and by dir. A train of primary directions culminating soon after birth, and espec. where the ☉ is badly afflicted, or in childhood, tend to early death of males. The ☉ hyleg at B., and afflicted by directions soon after birth, tends to death. (See "Death" under Childhood, Children, Infancy, Youth; "Early Death" under Early; Eclipses; "Short Life" under Life).

Significator—In Hor'y Q. the ☉ is taken as the Sig. in dealing with males, and espec. in health matters.

Signs—Masculine Signs of the Zodiac —(See "Masculine" under Signs).

Sons—(See "First-Born" under Children; Son; "Births" in this section).

Sterility In—(See "Barrenness" in this section).

Strength and Vigor—Males Have— (See Constitution, Good Health, Long Life, Robust, in this section).

Strong Constitution—(See "Constitution" in this section).

Sun — The ☉ is the Sig. of health in male nativities. (See Sun).

Testes—(See Testes).

Three Males Born—(See Triplets).

Triplets — Three Males — Two Males and One Female — One Male and One Female—One Male and Two Females— (See Triplets).

Twins — Two Males — One Male and One Female—(See Twins).

Two Males Born—(See Twins).

Uncles—(See Uncles).

Venereal Diseases—(See Venereal).

Vigor and Strength—For Males—(See "Strength" in this section).

Virile Members — Excessive Virile Members—(See Virile).

Vitality In — (a) Good Vitality—The ☉ well-asp. in a fiery sign. (See "Good Health" in this section). (b) Weak Vitality—The ☉ in a water sign, and espec. in ♋ or ♓, afflicted, and with one of these signs on the Asc. at B.; the ☉ ♂ ♄ in the 6th H. (See "Sickly" under Children; "Low" under Vitality; "Weak Body" under Weak).

Voice — The Voice Masculine and Rough In Women — (See Appearance, Degrees, in this section).

Weak Constitution — (See Constitution, Vitality, in this section).

Wife — (See the various paragraphs under Wife).

Women — Males Injured By — Masculine Women — (See Appearance, Females, in this section).

Wounds To—(See "Accidents" in this section).

Zodiac — Masculine Signs of — (See "Masculine" under Signs).

MALEFICS—The Malefics—The Infortunes—♆, ♅, ♄, and ♂ are called the malefic planets. Also ☋ (Cauda) is considered malefic, and of the nature of ♄. Saturn tends to give excess of cold in the system, and ♂ excess of heat, and are malevolent in this regard, and espec. in health matters. However, ♄ is said to exert a good influence by his favorable aspects, but is very evil by his adverse aspects, and tends to afflict any sign he is in at B., or after by dir. or tr., and to afflict the part of the body ruled by such sign. The places occupied by the malefics at B. are always considered points of affliction, or weakness, in the body, or in the mind if a mental sign is so occupied; or the mental rulers afflicted by malefics. The signs and houses occupied by the malefics at B. indicate the weak parts of the constitution. The malefics afflict by their ♂,

P., □, and ☌ aspects, but their good aspects, as the ✳ and △, tend to assist in health matters for the time, and to give more peace of mind. The more angular, oriental, or elevated a malefic may be at B., or elevated above the ☉, ☽, or benefics, the more evil are their effects, and to make disease more tenacious, severe, or incurable. A malefic elevated above the Lights denotes misfortune, sickness, or death, and when Anareta tends to a violent death if the map is a violent one. Any of the malefic planets may become the Anareta, or the killing planet. These matters, and the nature of the influence of each of the malefics, is discussed under these planets. The malefics are stronger when in the positive, or Solar Horas of the Signs. (See Horas). In Perigee or Zodiacal Parallel ♃ lessens the evil of a malefic, but ♃ when in ☌ ♄ or ♂ increases their evil when of the same, or near Latitude, but less so when of widely different Latitude. (See Anareta, Angles, Benefics, Elevated, Evils, Incurable, Malevolent, Malignant, Mars, Neptune, Oriental, Saturn, Severe, Uranus, etc.).

MALEVOLENT — Evil — An Evil Disposition Toward Others — Malicious — The ☉ or ♂ Significators in □ or ☍ ♄; the ☽ afflicted in ♏; the ☽ in ♏ and affl. by ♄ or ♂; the ☽ Sig. in ♏; the ☽ or ☿ Significators □ or ☍ ♂; the Full ☽ sepr. from ♂ and applying to ☿ in a nocturnal geniture; ♄ as Sig. denotes a malicious person; the influence of ♄ strong at B.; ♄ Sig. □ or ☍ ☿; caused by the evil aspects of ♄; ♄ ☌ or ill-asp. ♂, and espec. in angles; in Hor'y Q. ♄ Sig. in ♋ or ♓; ♂ in evil aspect to ♄; ♂ Sig. □ or ☍ ♄. (See Cruel, Evil, Malice; "Mean-Spirited" under Mean; Mischief, Revengeful, Treachery, Vicious).

MALFORMATIONS — An Abnormal Shape or Structure — Deformities — Irregularities In Form, Whether Congenital or Acquired —

Acquired Malformations — Some malformations are acquired after birth, and may be the result of disease and various afflictions. They may be caused by the hindrances, retentions, excess deposits, stoppages, and suppressions of the ♄ afflictions. Also ♂ can cause them by an accident, violence, or an excess of heat to a part, as in Ankylosis, the melting of a part, and result in a deformity and abnormality in shape. This subject is largely dealt with in the Articles on Deformities, and also listed under Saturn Diseases, Mars Diseases, etc. The planet ♆ also causes malformations thru wasting of the tissues. (See the Diseases listed under Neptune, Wasting). The following is a list of some of the Acquired Malformations, and abnormalities of shape, due to conditions arising after birth. See these subjects in the alphabetical arrangement — Ankylosis (see Ankylosis, Joints); Atrophy; Contractions; Fractures (the result of); Gout (from Mineral Deposits); Kidney (Floating); Joints (Ankylosis, and Enlarged Joints); Lameness; Paralysis; Rheumatism (from Deposits of Min-

erals, Wastes, Urea); Rickets; Swellings; Twistings; Wastings; Wry Neck (see Neck), etc. For subjects not listed here, look in the alphabetical arrangement for the subject you have in mind.

Congenital Malformations — And Deformities — If malformations exist at B. they are caused by prenatal conditions and afflictions during the period of gestation, and the prenatal map for the time of conception, and for each month during pregnancy, should be studied to trace the causes of malformations which exist at B. The following are some of the influences which have been observed to exist at B. in congenital malformations — the ☉ or ☽ in ♉, ☌ a malefic; the ☉ ☍ ☽ in angles, and □ ♄ or ♂, with no help from benefics, with benefics in a weak sign, or below the Western Horizon at B.; ♄ □ ♆; ♂ ☌ or ill-asp. ♄ at B., and espec. in angles, and affl. the ☉, ☽, Asc., or hyleg. Congenital Malformations are legion, and too numerous to mention and list here in this Article, but you will find them in the alphabetical arrangement. Consult the Articles which deal with the parts and organs of the body, and the defects, malformations, and irregularities of such parts, or organs, will be found listed in such Articles, and giving both the congenital and acquired malformations. Also see the Articles on Deformities, Extremities, Limbs, Members, Organs, Parts. The following are some of the more prominent congenital malformations, and also the more obscure ones, and which are listed here that they may not be overlooked. See the following subjects in the alphabetical arrangement — Abdomen (Prominent, Rickets); Abnormalities; Arms (Forearm Missing); Barrenness; Beastly Form (see Beasts); Birth (Born Blind, Deaf, Dumb — Paralyzed from Birth — See the paragraphs under Birth); Blind from Birth (see Birth, Blindness); Breastbone (Pigeon-Breasted); Chest (Hollow); Cloaca; Club Feet (see Feet); Conception; Crooked Body (see Crooked); Congenital; Contortions; Contractions; Crippled; Cyclops; Deafness — Deaf and Dumb — (see Dumb, Hearing); Defects; Deformities; Diminished; Distortions; Dogs — Resembles Dogs — (see "Dogs" under Children); Dwarfed; Enlargements; Eunuchs; Excrescences; Extremities; Eyes — Born Blind — Crossed Eyes — (see Eyes); Feet (Club Feet); Foetus; Forearms (Missing); Frog Child (see Forearm); Generative System; Genitals; Gestation; Growth; Harelip (see Lips); Hearing (Deaf and Dumb); Heart (see "Partition", "Right Side", under Heart); Hermaphrodites; Humpback (see Spine); Hydrocephalus; Idiocy; Ill-Formed; Incomplete; Inhuman; Limbs; Maimed; Members; Misshaped; Monsters; Mutes; Organs; Paralysis — From Birth (see Distortions, Excrescences); Parts; Prenatal Epoch; Rectum (see Cloaca); Sex Organs (see Hermaphrodites, Virile); Siamese Twins (see "United" under Twins); Undersized; Undeveloped; Urethra; Virile, Void Of, etc. For a better understanding of the prenatal conditions which tend to congenital malformations, the student should make a thorough study of the book, "The Prenatal Epoch", by Mr. E. H. Bailey, Editor of the British Journal of Astrology, at 10 and 11 Red Lion Court, Fleet St., London, E.C.4, England. (See the Article on Prenatal Epoch in this book).

MALICE—Malicious—Revengeful—Signified by ♄; a ♄ characteristic; ♄ to the ☌ ☋ by dir. (See Cruel, Malevolent, Revengeful, Treachery, Vicious). Malice is also one of the low forms of the ♂ action, and espec. when acting thru his night sign ♏. Also people born under ♅ and ♅, and afflicted by the evil aspects of these planets, tend to malice. The Mercurial Temperament also when afflicted tends to petty malice and vindictiveness. (See Ambushes, Aversions, Enemies, Enmity, Feuds, Hate, Jealousy, Mischief, Murderous, Plots, etc.).

Malice Aforethought—♄ Sig. in ♓.

Malicious Eyes — (See "Leering" under Eyes).

Malice of Fortune—(See "Malice" under Fortune).

MALIGNANT—Virulent—Fatal—Poisonous—The malefic planets ♄ and ♂ are quite malignant at times by their afflictions. Mars is more malignant in day nativities, and ♄ in night ones. (See Day, Night, Noxious, Poisonous). Jupiter in ☌ ♄ increases the malignancy of ♄, and ♃ in close ☌ with ♂ increases the malignancy of ♂ except where ♂ differs widely in Latitude.

Air — Malignant Air — (See "Malignant" under Air).

Chronic Diseases — Malignant Forms —The ☽ in a fixed sign at B., and afflicted, and applying to ♄ in a Solar Revolution. (See "Death By" under Chronic; "Fatal Illness" under Fatal).

Diseases — Malignant Diseases — Caused by the hyleg much afflicted at B., and by dir., and espec. if affl. by ♄; ♄ Sig. □ or 8 ♂. (See Carcinoma, Chronic; "Constitutional Diseases" under Constitution; Decay, Gangrene, Influenza, Latent, Morbid, Mortification, Organic, Structural, Wastings, etc.).

Fevers — Malignant Fevers — Danger of Death From—♃ Sig. □ or 8 ♂. (See "Low", "Pernicious", under Fever).

Gangrene—Malignant Gangrene with Pus—(See "Gangrene" under Pus).

Growths — (See "Malignant", "Non-Malignant", under Growths).

Influenza — (See "Malignant" under Influenza).

Scars—Malignant Scars—(See Scarlatina).

Tumors — Malignant Tumor — (See Carcinoma; "Malignant" under Tumors).

Vesicle — A Malignant Vesicle — (See Carbuncle).

MALNUTRITION—(See Nutrition).

MAMMARY—The Mammae—Mammary Glands — The Breasts — (See Breasts, Glands, Lacteals, Milk, Secretions).

MAN—
Hand of Man—Death by Human Means, as by Accident, Assassination, or in War—Death by Human Hands—The afflicting planets in human signs, and espec. ♂, as in ♊, ♍, ♒, and the 1st half of ♐; the ☽ in an airy sign and to the ☌ or ill-asp. ♂ by dir. (See Ambushes, Assassination, Assaults, Duels, Enemies, Events, Gunshot, Hand of Man; "Human Signs" under Human; Judges, Killed, Murdered, Plots, Poison, Stabs, Sword, Treachery, War, etc.). Violent death by human hands is apt to result when the ☉ or ☽ are in human signs, in angles, in □ or 8 ♂ from angles, and espec. in the 10th or 4th H.

Life of Man—(See "Man" under Life).

Odors from Man—(See Odors).

MANDIBLE—(See Jaws).

MANE OF LEO—A Nebulous Cluster—The ☉ or ☽ with at B., or by dir. tend to blindness, and the loss of one eye. (See "One Eye" under Blindness; Eyes).

MANGLED —Torn—Mutilated—The afflictions of ♅ tend to cause accidents with machinery in the employment, and whereby the native may be mangled, torn, mutilated, or killed. Also ♅ is the cause of many Railroad accidents, explosions, sudden and unexpected events, injuries, etc. (See Accidents; "Wild Animals" under Animals; Beasts, Employment, Explosions, Lacerations, Machinery, Maimed, Mutilated, Railroads, Uranus).

MANHOOD — The Age of Manhood or Womanhood — (See Adults, Husband, Marriage, Men, Middle Life, Old Age, Puberty, Wife, Women, etc.).

MANIA—Maniacal—Madness—Frenzy—Fury—Phrenitic—An Insane Person—Furious Madness — Toxic Psychosis—Delirium, etc.—Mania is usually caused by afflictions to ☿, the mental ruler, and espec. when afflicted by ♂ or ♅. The ♅ influence tends to Obsessions, Evil Spirit Controls, Delirium Tremens, Demoniacal Demonstrations, etc., and espec. when ♅ is afflicted in the 12th H. at B., and by dir.; ♅ □ or 8 ♅ at B., danger of obsessions, abnormal fears, dreads, etc.; ♅ in ♈ at B., and greatly afflicted by the other malefics at B., and by dir., and espec. if ♅ is in the 6th, 8th, or 12th H.; afflictions at a Solar Ingress of the ☉ into ♈, the brain sign, and ☿ afflicting the ☽ at the same time, or the planet ascending, tends to outbursts, or a return of maniacal attacks, and espec. if Mania is indicated in the radix. (See Fury, Insanity, Madness; the various paragraphs in this section). See the following subjects in the alphabetical arrangement when only listed here—

Acute Mania — ☿ afflicted by ♂ at B., and by dir.

Alcoholic Mania—(See "Delirium Tremens" under Delirium).

All Forms Of — Caused by ♅ and his afflictions, and are ♅ diseases. (See Neptune).

Anarchists — The ♅ and ♅ influences and afflictions tend to make Anarchists, and a mania for certain lines of destructive action. (See Anarchists).

Aversions; Blues—The Blues—Melancholy—(See Blues, Depression, Despondency, Melancholy).

Brainstorms—(See Brain).

Cases of Mania—(See Religious, Sexual, in this section).

Chaotic Religious Mania — (See "Religious" in this section).

Confusion—The Mind Confused—Ideas Confused—(See Confusion).

Dangerous Maniacs—♂ afflicting ☿ at B., and by dir., and ☿ weak and otherwise afflicted at B., and in no relation to the ☽ or Asc. (See "Dangerous" under Insanity; "Violent" in this section).

Death From—(See "Death" under Madness).

Delirium—Mania with Delirium—(See Delirium Tremens, Wild Delirium, under Delirium).

Delusions; Dementia; Demoniacs;

Deranged—Mentally Deranged—(See Insanity; "Derangement" under Mental).

Deviations—Of the Mental Faculties—(See Deviations).

Dipsomania—An Uncontrollable Desire for Strong Drink—(See Dipsomania).

Ego Mania—(See Ego).

Emotions—Extreme Disturbances of—(See Emotions, Feelings).

Enthusiasm—The Fury of—(See Enthusiasm).

Epileptic Mania—(See Epilepsy).

Erotic Mania—Morbid Sex Desires—Ψ afflicted in the 5th H.; Ψ affl. in ♍; the ☽ or ♀ affl. by ♄. (See Amorous; "Morbid" under Imagination; Nymphomania; "Passional Excesses" under Passion; Perversions; Unsavory).

Excitement—Extreme Mental Excitement—(See Excitable).

Fanatical—Irrational Zeal—(See Fanatical).

Fancies—Turbulent Fancies—(See Fancies).

Fears; Feelings—(See Anger, Emotions, Feelings).

Fits of Mania—Ψ afflicted, and espec. by ♅ and ♂ at B., and by dir. (See "Fits of Fury" under Fury).

Fixed Ideas—(See Anxiety; "Fixed Ideas" under Ideas).

Frenzy; Fury; Hallucinations;

Hereditary Mania—Latent—Inherent—Is usually caused by the severe afflictions or Ψ or ♂ to ☿ at time of conception, and the Prenatal Epoch map should be studied. (See Heredity).

High Temper—(See "High" under Temper).

Homicidal Mania—(See Homicide).

Ideas—Fixed Ideas—(See Ideas).

Illusions; Imaginations—Disordered Imagination—(See the various paragraphs under Imagination).

Inherent Mania—(See "Hereditary" in this section).

Insanity—(See Dangerous, Outrageous, Violent, under Insanity).

Intoxication—Mania From—(See "Strong Intoxicants" under Intoxication).

Irrational; Kleptomania—Morbid Desire to Steal—(See Kleptomaniac).

Latent Mania—(See "Hereditary" in this section).

Lunatics—(See Insanity, Lunacy).

Madness; Mentally Deranged—(See "Deranged" in this section).

Mind—Disorders of—(See "Derangement" under Mental; "Diseased Mind" under Mind. Also note the various paragraphs in this section).

Moisture of Brain—Causing Fury or Mania—(See "Brain" under Moisture).

Monomania—Insanity on One Subject—☿ in a fixed sign, and affl. by the ☽ and ♂; many afflictions in fixed signs, causing Mania, and with fixed signs also on the angles. (See Delusions; "Fixed Signs" under Fixed; Hallucinations; "Fixed Ideas" under Ideas).

Morbid Mind—(See "Morbid" under Mind; "Compulsions" under Morbid).

Morphomania—(See Narcotics).

Murderous—A Mania to Murder and Kill—(See Murder).

Neurotic Mania—Mania of a Neurotic Character—Ψ afflicted by ♂. (See "Highly Neurotic" under Nerves).

Noisome Diseases—With Loud and Maniacal Demonstrations—(See Noisome).

Notions—Chaotic Notions—(See Chaotic; Notions).

Nymphomania; Obsessions; Paranoia—Insanity with Delusions—(See Paranoia).

Persecution—Delusions of, and Bordering on Mania—(See Paranoia).

Perversions—(See Perversions).

Phantasies; Phrenitic Man—(See "Wild Delirium" under Delirium).

Phrenzies—(See Frenzy).

Prenatal Epoch—Often Explains the Causes of Mania, as Inherent Mania—(See Prenatal).

Prevalence—Of Mania—Of a Neurotic Nature—(See "Neurotic" in this section).

Psychic Disturbances—(See Psychic).

Puerperal Mania—(See Puerperal).

Pyromania—(See Incendiarism).

Ravings; Religious Mania—Chaotic Religious Mania—Caused by Ψ; Ψ in the 9th H., and afflicting ☿; ☿ ☌ or Par. ♄, and afflicted by the □ or ☍ ♂, and with ☿ in a weak sign, as in ♓; ☿ or the ☽ afflicted by Ψ. (See Ecstasy, Exaltation, Excitable, Fanatical, Frenzy, under Religion). Cases of Religious Mania—See "Marriage" No. 834; "Mentally Defective", No. 408, in 1001 N.N.

Return of Mania—(See the Introduction to this Article).

Sex Mania—(See "Licentious" under Men; Nymphomania).

Spirit Controls—Demoniacal Obsessions—(See Demoniac, Spirit Controls).

Suicidal Mania—(See Suicide).

Temper—(See Cruel; "High Temper" under Temper).

Terrors—Strange Terrors—(See Demoniac, Hallucinations, Imaginations, Obsessions, Spirit Controls; "Terrors" under Strange; Visions).

Transitory Mania—Of Short Duration—☿ weak at B., afflicted by ♂, disconnected with the ☽ or Asc., and with ☿ afflicted by the evil transit of ♂, or by an adverse secondary dir. of the ☽. (See Transient).

Treatment of Mania — The blue color is soothing to Maniacs, and violent Maniacs when confined in a blue room, with the walls and all colorings blue, are soon calmed. A suggestive treatment under Hypnosis is also often successful, and reaches the subconscious mind, removing the disturbing influences there, or the obsessing spirit, if it is such, is driven out. See the account in Matt. 8:28-32.

Typhomania—The Delirium of Typhus Fever—(See Typhus).

Violent Mania — Violent Maniacs — Caused by the afflictions of ♂ to ☿, and where ☿ is weak at B., and otherwise afflicted by malefics, and espec. when ☿ is disconnected with the ☽ or Asc. at B., and where the radical map shows a tendency to Insanity, Epilepsy, or Madness. (See Frenzy, Fury; "Violent" under Insanity; Madness).

MANKIND — Humanity — The Human Race—The ☽, and planets in signs of human form, tend to affect mankind for good or ill, and to bring disease, suffering, and sorrow upon human beings. At a Solar Eclipse, when the Zodiacal Constellations, and those of the ruled Fixed Stars out of the Zodiac, are in signs of human form, the effects fall upon the human race, for good or evil, according to the signs occupied. For influences and afflictions which tend to affect Mankind in general, or a part of Humanity, according to location, etc., see Air, Atmosphere, Birthrate, Blizzards, Calamity, Casualties, Catastrophies, Cholera, Climate, Cold, Common People, Countries, Crime, Crops, Disasters, Drought, Earth, Earthquakes, Eclipses, Endemic, Epidemics, Events, Evils, Famine, Fevers (see "Prevalance" under Fever); Fire (see "Great Fires" under Fire); Floods, Fruit; Great (Death of the Great—see Great); Grief, Hail, Heat (see "Extreme Heat" under Heat); Human, Humanity, Influenza, Kingdoms, Kings, Miseries, Misfortune, Mortality, Mourning, Nations, Nobles, Pandemics, Perigee, Perihelion, Pestilence, Pests, Plague, Prevalent, Princes, Public, Rain, Robberies, Rulers, Sea, Ships, Snow, Sorrow, Storms, Summer, Vermin, Volcanoes, War, Water, Weather, Winds, Winter, etc.

Lower Order of Mankind—Always In Trouble With — Receives Many Injuries From—The ☽ Sig. □ or ☍ ♄. (See "Low Company" under Low).

MANNER—Manners—The Manners are ruled by the ☽ and the Asc., or chiefly influenced by them. See the following subjects in the alphabetical arrangement when only listed here—

Abrupt—In Manner—Ⅲ ascending at B., or with the chief Sig. of the nativity; a prominent and afflicted Ⅲ; fixed sign influences tend to terse and sudden expression. (See Cruel, Eccentric, Fierce; "High Temper" under Temper).

Accomplished Manners — Accomplished Mind—♃ Sig. in ♐; ♀ Sig. ☌ or good asp. ☿, or vice versa, a refined and accomplished mind and manner. (See Genteel; "Great Ability" under Great; "Popular" under Reputation).

Action—(See the various paragraphs under Action, Conduct, Movement, Walk, etc.).

Address — (See "Manly" in this section; Appearance, Speech).

Agreeable — The ☽ on the Meridian, or coming to, and well-aspected by ♀. (See Accomplished, Obliging, in this section).

Amiable — Even Temper — Good Disposition—The airy signs produce, and with the ☉ or ☽ well-aspected in them, or with an airy sign on the Asc.; the airy signs are known as the Sweet Signs, and tend to give a sweet, kind, and affable disposition when well occupied and aspected at B.; the ☽ Sig. ☌ or good asp. ♀, or vice versa; the ☽ sepr. from ♀ and apply. to ♃; ♃ in the Asc.; ♃ ☌ ♀ in the Asc.; ♃ well-asp. in ♌, ♏, or ♓; ♃ in the M.C., and ♀ in the Asc., and in good asp. to each other, and if the ☉ and ☽ are free from ♄ affliction; ♃ Sig. in ♈; ♄ Sig. in ♒; ♄ in ♐ or ♒, affable, courteous and obliging; ♀ having chief dominion over the mind and disposition; ♀ in ♉, ♍, ♎, ♐, or ♒; ♀ Sig. in ♒, very courteous and affable; ♀ Sig. ⚹ or △ ♃; ♀ in good asp. with ☿. (See "Many Friends" under Friends; Mild; "Popular" under Reputation; Agreeable, Genteel, Pleasing, and the various paragraphs in this section).

Blunt—(See "Abrupt" in this section).

Breezy—Brisk—Animated—Sprightly—A ♌ characteristic if ♃ is also well-placed and aspected; ♃ strong at B., or born under a ♃ sign, as ♐ or ♓. (See Brisk).

Brisk — (See Brisk; "Breezy" in this section).

Coarse — In Manner — Rough — (See Coarse, Gross, Rough, Unrefined).

Coldness—Of Manner—♄ influence; ♄ strong at B., and espec. acting thru the negative signs; lack of planets in the fiery signs; planets obscurely placed, out of dignity, and espec. in the mutable, watery and earthy signs. These influences tend to reserve. (See Indifferent, Recluse, Reserved, Secretive).

Commanding — (See Commanding, Proud).

Conduct—(See the various paragraphs under Conduct).

Courteous — (See Amiable, Genteel, Obliging, in this section).

Cross—(See Abrupt, Gruff, in this section; Anger; "High Strung" under High; Irascible; Irritable; "High Temper" under Temper; Vicious).

Death — Manner of Death — (See the various paragraphs under Death).

Disagreeable—The ☉ Sig. in ♏; the ☉ Sig. ☌ ♄; ♄ Sig. ☐ or ☍ the ☉, or ☌ ☿; ♃ Sig. in ☐ near Aldebaran; ♂ Sig. in ♋, unamiable; ☿ Sig. in ♑. (See Abrupt, Coldness, Cross, Gruff, Ill-Mannered, Rough, in this section).

Disposition; Dreamy; Elegant — Refined and Engaging In Manner—The ☽ in an angle, or in ♉ or ♋ at B.; ☿ Sig. ✶ or △ ♀; ♂ ascending at B., and free from the rays of other planets. (See Agreeable, Amiable, Obliging, in this section).

Engaging—(See Amiable, Elegant, in this section).

Evil—(See "Manners" under Evil).

Excellent—(See "Elegant" in this section).

Excitable—(See Excitable; "Cross" in this section).

Explosive—(See "Abrupt" in this section; Anger; "Manner" under Explosive; Fierce; "High Temper" under Temper).

Fascinating — (See Agreeable, Amiable, Elegant, Obliging, in this section; Beautiful, Complexion, Countenance, Expression, Eyes, Face, Glances, Hair, Look, etc.).

Fierce—♂ people. (See Anger, Cruel, Fierce, Vicious, Violent).

Forceful — (See Active, Energetic, Forceful, Quick).

Genteel—(See Genteel; Amiable, Elegant, in this section).

Good Manners — (See Accomplished, Agreeable, Elegant, Genteel, Obliging, in this section).

Graceful Manner — (See Graceful; "Good" in this section).

Gross Manners—(See Gross; "Coarse" in this section).

Gruff—Cross—Rude—Surly—In Hor'y Q. ♄ Sig. in ♌. (See "Cross" in this section; Rough).

Habits—(See the various paragraphs under Habits).

Haughty—(See Breezy, Proud, in this section).

Highly Accomplished — ☿ Sig. in ♎. (See "Accomplished" in this section).

Ill-Mannered—The ☽ Sig. ☌ ♄. (See "Disagreeable" in this section).

Indifferent Manner — (See Apathy, Dull, Indifferent, Inert, Lassitude).

Jerky and Nervous — (See Jerky; "Nervous" in this section).

Jumps Forward — (See "Skippish" in this section).

Life—Manner of Life—(See Active, Ambition, Careless, Companions, Conduct, Criminal, Drink, Dull, Dishonest, Extravagant, Gamblers, Gluttonous, Habits, Happy, Honest, Idle, Immodest, Improvident, Inactive, Indulgent, Intemperate, Lazy, Low, Miserable, Miserly, Men, Morals, Neglectful, Poverty, Prodigal, Reckless, Riches, Riotous, Shameless, Social Relations, Thieves, Women, Wretched, etc. Also look in the alphabetical arrangement for the subject you have in mind).

Mad and Fierce—(See "Fierce" in this section; "Angry Look" under Look; "High Temper" under Temper).

Manly and Sober — In Address and Manner—♃ in the Asc.; ♃ ruler and well-aspected; born under ♃, sober and commanding. (See Commanding, Grave, Serious).

Meek; Mild; Modest—Retiring—(See Bashfulness, Immodest, Meek, Modesty, Reserved, Retiring, Shy).

Nervous Manner—♄ in the 1st H; ♄ ruler and afflicted at B. (See Jerky, Nerves, Restlessness).

Obliging — Polite—Courteous—Agreeable — Decorous — Excellent Manners, etc.—The ☉ influence tends to great decorum outwardly, and also the ♌ influence; the ☉ Sig. in ☐, affable, courteous and kind; ♄ well-asp. in ♒, courteous; ♃ in the Asc.; ♃ Sig. in ♈, ☐, or ♐; ♃ in ♎, obliging; ♃ in ♐, courteous; the ☽ Sig. in ♒, affable, courteous and inoffensive (see Harmless); ♀ Sig. in ♉, ☐, or ♐; ♀ Sig. in ♒, affable and courteous; ♀ Sig. ☌ ☿; ♌ gives a courteous and free disposition. (See Accomplished, Agreeable, Amiable, Elegant, Genteel, in this section).

Pleasing; Polite—(See "Obliging" in this section).

Profane; Proud—(See "Breezy" in this section; Proud).

Quarrelsome—(See Quarrels).

Refined—(See "Elegant" in this section; "Elegant Mind" under Elegant; Refined).

Reserved—(See Meek, Modest, in this section).

Retiring—(See "Modest" in this section; Grave, Melancholic, Prudery, Quiet, Recluse, Retiring; "Secretive under Secret; Serious, Shy).

Rough — (See Coarse, Brutish, Pity, Rough; Disagreeable, Gruff, Ill-Mannered, Violent, in this section).

Rude — (See Disagreeable, Gruff, Rough, in this section).

Skippish Manner — Jumps Forward When Speaking—(See "Nodding" under Head; Skippish).

Sober and Manly — (See "Manly" in this section; Sober).

Speech — Manner of Speaking — (See Speech).

Stately—(See Commanding).

Stiff In Manner—(See Coldness, Disagreeable, Reserved, Retiring, in this section).

Surly—(See "Gruff" in this section).

Taciturn—Silent—Reserved—Not Inclined to Converse—♄ influence. (See Melancholic, Reserved, Retiring, Secretive, Serious).

Temperament—(See Temper, Temperament).

Unpleasant Manner—(See Coarse, Disagreeable, Gruff, Violent, in this section).

Unrefined—(See Coarse, Disagreeable, Gruff, Ill-Mannered, Rough, Violent, in this section; Unrefined).

Untidy; Violent—In Manner—Rough
—Rude—Disagreeable—Repulsive, etc.
—♅ ascending at B., or with the chief
Sig. of the map; ♂ in the Asc. or M.C.,
and affl. by ♄; ♂ in ♈ or ♏ in the Asc.
or M.C., and afflicted; the ♏ influence
strong at B.; the ☉ or ☽ in ♏ and affl.
by ♂. (See Anger, Brutish, Cruel,
Pity, Vicious, Violent).

Walk—Manner of—(See Gait, Stooping, Walk). Also for other study see
such subjects as Appearance, Countenance, Expression, Gestures, Glances,
Expression, Eyes, Face, Look, Motion,
Movement, Quick, Slow, etc.

MANSLAUGHTER—Danger of Commit-
ting—The ☽ to the ♂ Caput Algol.
(See "Fratricide" under Father; Homicide, Murder).

MANUBRIUM—(See Sternum).

MANY—

Many Calamities—(See Calamities).

Many Children—(See Children).

Many Complications—In Disease—
(See Complications; "Complications"
under Disease).

Many Dangers — Subject To — (See
"Many Dangers" under Dangers;
Perils).

Many Diseases—(See Diseases).

Many Enemies—(See Enemies; "Hated
by Others" under Hate).

Many Friends—(See Friends).

Many Long Illnesses—(See "Many Illnesses" under Ill-Health; "Long Illnesses" under Long).

Many Sicknesses—(See Sickness).

MAP—The Star Map of Birth—The Nativity—Geniture—The Radix—Chart of
Birth—The Figure of the Heavens for
the actual Moment of Birth, at the
time of the first cry, when the magnetism of the Universe is breathed
into the lungs, shows the stamp which
is put upon the native, and the tendencies of temperament he will be apt
to follow during his lifetime, the rate
of his vibrations, etc. This figure is
like a flashlight picture, and the native
is really a miniature picture, or photograph, of the Universe for that moment, and as seen from the place of
birth, and he will partake of the vibrations, forces, and influences that were
operating in the Universe, and the
Planetary forces that were reflected
and focussed to the place of birth. In
Astrology, the moment the child is
ushered into the world, or when the
cord is cut, are not considered a basis
for the map of birth, but the time is
taken for the first cry, or breath, when
the vibrations of the Universe are in-
drawn and stamped upon the native.
Thus, by a study of the Map of Birth,
and the Signs, Houses, and Aspects of
the Planets at birth, forecasts can be
made about the Health, the Mind, the
Diseases liable to, the Temperament,
Prospect of Life, the Degree of the Vitality, the best Location for Health,
the Shape of the Body, the Physical
Constitution, the Complexion, the Financial Prospects, the Business Suit-
ability, whether Positive or Negative,
a Leader or Follower, the Religious
Propensities, about Friends, Enemies,
Marriage, Love Affairs, Travel, Residence, etc., and about every subject
that is vital to human life, and in the
affairs, fate, destiny, character, success or failure, good health or ill-
health of the native, etc. This map,
however, does not necessarily show
the inner, or real character, but only
tendencies, the environment and possible contacts with the outer world,
the problems to be worked out during
the present life. The real character,
the Ego, the Spirit, its nature, present
stage of Evolution, etc., are better
shown and indicated by the map for
the time of Conception, known as the
Prenatal Epoch Map, for such map indicates the nature of the incoming
Ego, its past, and also much of the
fate that is overhanging the native,
the causes and effects, the sowing and
reaping, the difficulties of life and temperament that must be overcome if
the native would advance, and not
stand still, or fall behind, or become a
straggler in the Universe. Every student should make a deep study of Astrology, the Secret and Esoteric Doctrines, that he may the better understand the plan of life, destiny, why
you are here, where you came from,
and where you go from here, and these
matters are well discussed in the various textbooks and writings of the Occult and Metaphysical Societies of the
World, and also in various Religious
Organizations. The Map of Birth is
said to reveal the secrets of the Soul,
and if you do not want these to be
known, and your true nature revealed,
your weaknesses, as well as your
strong points, do not give your birth
data to a qualified Astrologer. Every
student should make a thorough study
of the mathematics of star map work,
and be able to erect a map for any
time and place on Earth. To learn to
make Star Maps, purchase the book,
"Casting the Horoscope" by Alan Leo.
This book can be purchased from Occult Book Centers, or direct from the
"Modern Astrology" Office at 42 Im-
perial Buildings, Ludgate Circus, London, E. C. 4, England. This Office also
sends out a very reliable Correspondence Course of Lessons in Star Map
Work, and on Esoteric Astrology, and
the writer of this Encyclopaedia took
this Course many years ago, and got a
good start in Map and Horoscope
work. Other Lesson Courses in Star
Map work, and Astrology in general,
are sent out by "The Church of Light",
(formerly "The Brotherhood of Light"),
at 818 Union League Bldg., Los Angeles, Calif. Also a Lesson Course is
sent out by the Llewellyn College of
Astrology, at 8921 National Blvd., Los
Angeles. The A. F. Seward & Co., Astrological Publishers and Book Dealers,
3620 Rokeby St., Chicago, Illinois,
also send out a Lesson Course in Astrology, and Star Map work. The
practicing student also needs a set of
Raphael's Ephemeris for the years
from 1860 to the present time, so as to
have the Planetary Tables at hand to
look up the planetary influences at
birth among his clients and friends,
and from which to make Star Maps of

Birth. The student also needs Dalton's Tables of Houses, to get the Signs and Degrees of the Zodiac on the cusps of the Houses for the various degrees of Latitude over the Earth, and at the birthplaces of people born in the different Nations and Countries of the World, and at any hour of the day or night, whether in the Northern or Southern Hemispheres. With this equipment, and a thorough knowledge of the Elements of Astrology, Physicians and Healers should be able to become very proficient in Medical Astrology, Diagnosis, Prognosis, etc.

For further study along this line see such subjects herein as Aspects, Baptism, Benefics, Birth, Character, Conception, Congenital, Day, Destiny, Diagnosis, Diathesis, Directions, Dominion, Elevated, Evil, Fate, Free Will (see Will); Geocentric, Good, Heredity, Horoscope, Houses, Majority, Malefics, Moment of Birth (see "Moment" under Birth); Natal, Nativity, Negative, Night, Occidental, Oriental, Planets, Positive, Powerful, Prenatal, Prognosis, Radix, Rising, Sensitive, Setting, Signs, Vulnerable, etc. Also look in the alphabtical arrangement for subjects you may have in mind.

MARASMUS—A Wasting or Emaciation —Tabefaction—(See Assimilation, Atrophy, Consumptions, Decay, Degeneration, Emaciation, Lean, Nutrition, Phthisis, Tabes, Thin, Tuberculosis, Wasting, etc.).

MARCASSITE—(See Iron).

MARITIME—Pertaining to the Sea—

Loss of Life — Much Loss of Life Among Maritime People—Much Injury to Sailors—Shipwrecks and Much Loss of Life At Sea, etc.—♄ in ♏, lord of the year at the Vernal Equinox, and occidental; ♄ in S. Lat. in ♓, and lord of the year at the Vernal E. (See "Long Journeys" under Journeys; Navigation, Ocean, Sailors, Sea, Ships, Shipwreck, Travel, Voyages, Water).

Maritime Pursuits—Fond of—♃ in ♋ or ♓; ♃ Sig. ☌ ☽. (See "Fortunate Upon the Seas" under Sea).

MARKAB—A violent star of the 2nd magnitude, in the 5th. Face of ♓, of the nature of ♂ and ♀. Said to threaten a violent death when with the Asc., and to bring great dangers and sufferings to the native when joined with the ☉, ☽, ♂, or the Asc. (See Disgrace; "Females" under Fever, Imprudent; Ruin; "Death by Soldiers" under Soldiers; "Death" under Violent; "Death by Wild Beasts" under Wild). The ☽ when directed to Markab by good aspect is said to give good health. (See "Good Health" under Health).

MARKS—Marked—Marks of — Personal Marks On the Body—Blemishes—Moles —Scars, etc. — Marks, Moles, or some kind of a Blemish, usually are found on those parts of the body ruled by the Signs or Houses containing Planets at B., and especially on the parts ruled by the Asc., Midheaven, or 6th H. Marks may occur on any part of the body, and under the different parts, as Head, Face, Arms, Legs, etc., look for "Blemishes", "Marks", "Moles",

"Scars", etc., under these parts, or any part you may have in mind. The influences of the two malefic planets ♄ and ♂ are largely responsible for Marks, Scars, or Blemishes other than Moles, while the ☉ influence away from ♂, and not afflicted by ♂, tends to Moles. Marks tend to be Moles when the part is not afflicted by ♂. The malefics indicate Marks according to their positions. The part ruled by the sign ascending is also subject to Marks, Moles, or a Scar, and also on the part ruled by the sign containing the lord of the Asc., lord of the 6th H., or on the part ruled by the sign on cusp of the 6th. The sign or planet signifying the Mark, when much afflicted, makes the Mark more eminent, obvious, conspicuous, and prominent. The color of Marks is largely determined by the Planets, and the color given by each planet. Thus the ☉ gives a chestnut or olive mark; the ☽ one of a whitish hue, or partly of the color of the planets she aspects; ♄ gives a dark, black, or obscure mark; ♃ a purple of bluish mark; ♂ a red mark, a red mole, or a red birthmark, and a blemish of a reddish color; ♀ gives a yellow or yellowish mark; ☿ one of a pale or lead color. The Mark is on the right side of the body if the sign or planet are masculine, and on the left side if the sign or planet are feminine. If the Significators of the Mark or Mole be above the Earth, or horizon, the Mark is on the forepart of the body, and visible. If the planet be below the horizon, the Mark is inside and invisible, or on the hinder part of the body. The Marks are on the upper, middle, or lower parts of the part ruled, according to whether the first, middle, or last part of a sign ascend, or a planet be in the first, middle, or last part of a sign. (See Left, Lower, Middle, Right, Upper). Saturn in ☌ ♂ in any sign or house tends especially to a mark on the part ruled by such sign or house. Thus ♄ ☌ ♂ in ♈, or in the 1st H., a mark on the head or face; ♄ ☌ ♂ in ♉ or the 2nd H., a mark on the neck, etc. For further examples of the location of Marks or Moles see "Location" under Moles. Peculiar personal Marks are due to the rising of ♄ or ♂. The subject of Marks, Moles and Scars, etc., and their location, kind, color, description, etc., is dealt with very extensively in the books on Horary Astrology, which books are listed in the Article on "Horary Questions" in this book. (See Colors, Horary). The following subjects have to do with Marks, their location, description, causes, etc., which subjects see in the alphabetical arrangement when not considered here.

Accident—The Mark May Be Congenital, or the Result of An Accident—♂ rising in the Asc.

Arms—♄ or ♂ in ♊ or the 3rd H., or ♄ ☌ ♂ in these positions. (See "Moles" under Arms).

Back Part—Of the Body—Marks On— Indicated by planets below the horizon at B.

Birthmarks—(See Moles, Naevus).

Black Marks—Given by ♄.

Blemishes; Bluish Mark—Given by ♃.

Breasts—(See "Marks" under Breast).

Chestnut Color—Given by the ☉.

Chin—(See "Mark" under Chin).

Congenital Marks—(See Birth, Congenital, Naevus; "Accident" in this section).

Conspicuous—The sign or planet signifying the mark being much afflicted. The Sig. of the mark above the Earth at B.

Cuts—(See Lameness, Paralysis, under Cuts).

Dark Marks—Given by ♄.

Defects; Deformities; Dents — ♂ the afflicting planet in a fiery sign tends to a dent or scar.

Expression—A Marked Expression— (See "Difficult" under Expression).

Eyes—A Mark or Scar Near the Eyes — (See Marks, Scars, under Eyes; "Eyes" under Blemishes, Left, Right; "Right Eye" under Scars).

Face—(See Marks, Scars, under Face).

Feet—(See "Marks" under Feet).

Forepart of the Body—Marks On— The Planet or Sign causing the Mark being above the Earth at B.

Foreteeth—(See Teeth).

Front Part—Of the Body—Marks On —(See "Forepart" in this section).

Good Health—Marks of—(See "Good Health" under Health).

Head—(See "Marks" under Head).

Hinder Parts—Marks On—(See "Back Part" in this section).

Horary Questions—The Kind, Location, Color, and Nature of Marks Indicated In — The general influences given in the various paragraphs in this Article also apply to Horary Indications, as many of them are gathered from the Textbooks on Horary Astrology.

Incisors—Marks On — (See "Foreteeth" under Teeth).

Injury—Marks From—Caused usually by ♂, and ♂ rising in the Asc. (See Burns, Cuts, Scars, Stabs, etc.).

Inside — The Marks Inside and Invisible—Given by planets below the horizon at B.

Invisible—Hidden—Inside—(See Back Part, Inside, in this section).

Knees—(See "Scars" under Knees).

Lead Color—Pale and of a Lead Color —Given by ☿.

Left Side—Of the Body—Marks On— The sign or planet causing the mark being feminine. (See "Eyes" in this section).

Location—Of Marks—(See the Introduction, and the various paragraphs in this Article; "Location" under Moles).

Long Life—Marks of—(See "Long Life" under Life).

Lower Parts—Marks On—Caused by the last part of a sign ascending, or a planet in the last few degrees of a sign. In such case the mark is on the lower part of the organ, or part, ruled by such sign. Also malefics in signs which rule the lower parts of the body, as the Legs, Knees, Thighs, Ankles, Feet, etc., cause marks on these parts. (See Lower).

Middle Parts—Of an Organ or Part— Marks On—(See "Organs" under Middle; the Introduction, Lower Parts, Upper Parts, in this Article).

Moles—(See Blemishes, Marks, Moles).

Naevus—Birthmarks—(See Naevus).

Neck—Marks On—Malefics in ♉, the 2nd H., or very low in the Asc. at B. (See "Marks" under Face, Neck).

Obscure—(See "Invisible" in this section).

Obvious—(See "Conspicuous" in this section).

Olive Color—Given by the ☉. Also gives chestnut color.

Pale—Lead Color— ☿ influence.

Parts of Body—Moles On the Various Parts—(See the Introduction, and the various paragraphs in this section).

Peculiar—♄ or ♂ rising tend to peculiar personal marks.

Personal—(See "Peculiar" in this section).

Pitted Degrees—Of the Zodiac—The Asc. or its lord in any of these degrees make the native subject to deep marks, scars, pockmarks, etc. (See Pitted).

Pockmarks—(See "Face" under Smallpox).

Prominent — (See "Conspicuous" in this section).

Purple Marks—Given by ♃.

Rear Parts—Of the Body—Marks On —(See "Back Part" in this section).

Red Marks—And Moles—Given by ♂.

Right Foot — (See "Marks" under Feet).

Right Side—Of the Body—Marks On —The Planet or Sign causing the Mark being Masculine, marks on the right side of the body, or of a member. (See "Left" in this section; Left, Right).

Scars—(See the various paragraphs under Scars).

Shoulders—Marks On—(See "Marks" under Shoulders).

Upper Parts — Of the Body — Upper Parts of an Organ—The 1st face or decanate of a sign rising, or planets in the first part of Signs, marks on the upper part of a part or organ. (See Upper; Arms, Breast, Face, Head, Neck, Shoulders, in this section.

Visible—(See "Conspicuous" in this section).

Whitish Hue—Given by the ☽. (See White).

Wounds—Marks From—Caused by ♂, with ♂ rising, or in the Asc. at B., and by dir.

Yellow Marks—Given by ♀. (See Yellow).

MARRIAGE—The ♎ Sign and the 7th H. rule over Marriage and the Marriage Partner. Marriage affairs are also governed by the ☽. Due to the many paragraphs, or subdivisions, the subject of "Marriage Partner" is made into a separate Article, and just following this one. The following paragraphs have reference to Marriage, the Husband, Wife, their Joys, Happiness, Afflictions, Sorrows, Weaknesses, Health Matters, etc.

Adultery—(See "Adulterous" under Love Affairs).

Antipathy—(See Antipathy, Aversions, Likes, Opposites, Sympathy; "Unhappy" in this section).

Aversion from Marriage—Indifferent to Marriage — The Significators of Marriage in sterile signs, cadent, combust or ℞, as in ♈, ♊, ♌, or ♍; the lord of the 7th H., planets in the 7th, the planet to which the appropriate Luminary first applies, or ♀, the ☽, or lord of the Asc. in a barren sign; the 7° ♍ on the Asc.; ♄ in the 7th H., or in □ or ☍ ♀, tends to, or to delay or deny marriage, or cause separation after marriage. (See Apathy, Bachelors, Celibacy, Deviations; "Free from Passion" under Passion; Perversions, Spinsters).

Bachelors—(See Bachelors; "Aversions" in this section).

Bad Time—For Marriage—(See "Marriage" under Husband).

Barrenness—Sterility—No Promise of Children — (See Barrenness; "Anchorite" under Husband; Impotent; "Unfruitful" under Wife).

Best Time To Marry—The Athenians married at the time of the New ☽, or just after, in the increase and light of the ☽, and the ☽ free from affliction, which was considered the best time. Marry between the New ☽ and her 1st Quarter. The ☽, the Asc., or lord of the Asc. should be in ♊, ♍, ♐, or ♓ at the time of engagement or marriage, for the best results. Let the rulers of the Asc. and 7th H. be in good asp. to each other. Let the ruler of the 10th H., or a benefic in the 10th, be in good asp. with the lord of the Asc., or the ☽. (See the various chapters on Marriage in the Textbooks of Astrology).

Celibacy In—(See Celibacy; "Chaste" under Females; "Anchorite" under Husband).

Children—Death of—Many Children—No Children—Sickness of—Children Not Wanted, etc.—(See Barren, Birth, Children, Fruitful; "Children" under Husband; "Childbirth" under Wife).

Clandestine—Given to Clandestine Love Affairs—(See "Free Love" under Free; "Unfaithful" under Husband; Adulterous, Liaisons, Unconventional, Unfaithful, Unlawful, under Love Affairs; "Clandestine" under Sex; "Untrue" under Wife).

Death—Of the Marriage Partner—Of Fiance or Fiancee—(See "Death" under Fiance, Husband, Marriage Partner, Wife). Case—See "Death on Eve of Marriage", No. 677 in 1001 N.N.

Delayed Marriage—Marriage May Be Denied—Born under ♄; ♄ in the 7th H., or ruler of the 7th; ♄ ☌ ☉ or ♀ in a female nativity, and ♄ ☌ ☽ in a male nativity; ♄ ☌ ♀ in ♑; the ☽ in an Occidental Quarter at B., as between

the Nadir and Asc., or between the M.C. and Descendant. These rules are more fully given and elaborated upon in the chapters on Marriage in the various Textbooks and Dictionaries of Astrology. (See Apathy, Aversions, Bachelors, Deviations; "Free From Passion" under Passion).

Denied—Marriage Denied—The ☽ or ♀ affl. by ♄, if ♄ is strong and the Significators of Marriage weak at B.; the ☽ or ♀ in barren signs and afflicted by ♄; the ☽ in the occidental quarters and affl. by the ☉ and ♄; the ☽, ♀, and ruler of the 7th H. in barren signs and affl. by ♄ or ♅. (See the chapter on Marriage in Sepharial's Manual of Astrology, and other Textbooks).

Deviations—(See Apathy, Aversions, Celibacy, Deviations, Perversions).

Divorce—Separation—(See "Unhappy" in this section).

Early Marriage—The ☉, ☽, ♀, and lord of the 7th H. well-aspected, and free from ♄ affliction; no malefic influence over the 7th H.; the ☽ in an oriental quarter at B. Early marriage is before the 28th birthday, and a late marriage after that age, as considered in Astrology. The ☉ ☌ ♀ with females usually leads to a very young marriage, and espec. if ♄ does not afflict these bodies, or the 7th H.

Elderly Person—Marries One Older Than Himself—(See "Older" in this section).

Fiance—Fiancee—Death of—(See Fiance).

Fickle—The Affections Changeable—(See "Fickle" under Love Affairs).

Free Living—Free Love—Free from Passion—(See Free; "Free From" under Passion).

Fruitful Marriage—♃ or ♀ in the 5th or 11th H. in maps of both parents. (See Fruitful; "Fruitful" under Husband, Wife).

Gains by Marriage—♃ Sig. ☌ the ☽ or ♀; the 8th H. fortunate, occupied by a benefic, and free from the affliction of malefics, apt to gain wealth by marriage; the 4th H. free from malefics, lord of the 4th a benefic, or a benefic in the 4th, the home life is more happy and beneficial.

Happy Marriage—Benefics in the 7th H., or lord of the 7th a benefic and free from affliction of malefics; absence of malefic influence over the 7th H.; the ☉, ☽, and ♀ free from the affliction of ♄ and malefics at B.; ♀ well-aspected in ♉, ♎, or ♓, her strong signs.

Husband—(See the various paragraphs under Husband).

Ill-Health—Of the Marriage Partner — (See "Death", "Unhappy", in this section; "Ill-Health" under Husband, Wife; "Sickly" under Marriage Partner).

Incompatibility—(See Antipathy, Unhappy, in this section).

Indifferent — To Marriage — (See "Aversion" in this section).

Late Marriage—(See "Delayed" in this section).

Length of Marriage—The Sig. of marriage coming to the ☌ or ill-asp. a malefic after marriage usually terminates the marriage, either by separation or death of the marriage partner. Thus if ♀ were in the 1° ♎, and ♄ in 10° ♎, the length of the marriage would ordinarily be 10 years, etc. (See the Chapter on "Length of Marriage" in Sepharial's Manual of Astrology).

Liaisons—(See "Clandestine" in this section).

Libra—The Sign of Marriage—(See Libra, Seventh House).

Loose Morals—(See Morals).

Many Marriages—The ☉, ☽, and many planets in the double-bodied signs at B.; the ☽ in ♊, ♐, or ♓, and aspected by several planets from bicorporeal signs, tends to plurality of wives; the ruler of the Asc. in the 7th H. in a double-bodied sign, or in ☌ the ruler of the 7th in such a sign, plurality of marriages. (See Double-Bodied).

Marriage Partner — (See the next Article after this one. Also see Husband, Wife).

Mother Fixation—Tendency to Marry a Woman Older Than Himself, and a Replica of His Mother—Caused by the ♋ sign prominent at B., or the ☽ strongly afflicted by ♄. In a female nativity the ♑ sign strong or prominent, and with the ☉ affl. by ♄, a tendency to marry a man older than herself, or one who resembles her father in mind, temperament, and body.

No Marriage—(See "Denied" in this section).

Not Inclined to Marry—(See "Aversion" in this section).

Nymphomania—Unbridled Passion In Women In the Married Life or Single —(See Nymphomania).

Occult Views On—Born under the strong influence of ♆ or ♅. (See Celibacy; "Anchorite" under Husband; "Vows and Restraints" under Love Affairs; Unconventional; "Platonic" in this section).

Older Than Himself—Marries An Elderly Person—Born under the strong influence of ♄, or who have ♄ as ruler; ♄ affl. the ☉, ☽, or ♀, and where the love nature is grave, sedate, and rather mournful, and not frivolous, joyous, or careless. (See "Mother Fixation" in this section).

Opposites—Marrying Opposites—(See Opposites).

Passion—Excess of—Free From—(See Amorous, Apathy, Aversions, Bachelors; "Free From", "Passional Excesses", under Passion; Spinsters; "Aversions" in this section).

Perversions—(See this subject).

Platonic Unions—♆ in or afflicting the 7th H.; ♆, ♅, or ♄ in the 5th H., or affecting this house or the lord of the 5th; ♆, ♅, or ♄ in the 5th or 7th H., or divided between these houses, and aspecting each other; ♂ afflicting ♀, and espec. where ♆, ♄, or ♅ may also enter into the configuration, giving advanced or occult views as to marriage and sex life. (See Apathy, Celibacy, Co-

habitation; "Chaste" under Females; "Free from Passion" under Passion).

Plurality of Marriages—(See "Many Marriages" in this section).

Quarrels In—Malefics in ♎ or the 7th H.; ♄ or ♂ ☌ ♀; ♀ affl. in ♏. (See Antipathy, Clandestine, Deviations, Fickle, Occult, Unhappy, in this section; "Unfaithful" under Husband, Love Affairs; "Untrue" under Wife).

Restless In—The ☽ afflicted in the 7th H.; many planets in double-bodied signs at B.; ♀ afflicted in ♋ or ♏. (See "Fickle" under Love Affairs; "Many Marriages" in this section).

Second Marriage—The ☽ in ♊, ♋, ♏, ♐, or ♓, and aspected by many planets, and espec. if there is a planet in the 7th H. which does not aspect the ☽; the ☽ in a double-bodied sign, and aspected by several planets from signs of this nature. (See "Many Marriages" in this section).

Separation—Or Divorce—(See "Unhappy" in this section).

Seventh House—The House of Marriage—(See Seventh House).

Several Marriages—(See "Many" in this section).

Sex Disturbances—In Marriage—(See Aversion, Celibacy, Deviations, Passion, Unhappy, and the various paragraphs in this section).

Sickness In—(See "Ill-Health" in this section).

Sorrows In—(See "Unhappy" in this section).

Spinsters—(See Spinsters; "Denied" in this section).

Sympathy In—(See "Happy" in this section).

Time of Marriage—(See Early, Late, in this section. Also see the Chapter on "The Time of Marriage" in Sepharial's Manual of Astrology).

Troubles In—(See "Unhappy", and the various paragraphs in this section).

Unconventional Views—(See "Occult" in this section).

Unfaithful—(See "Clandestine" in this section).

Unfortunate Marriage—(See Antipathy, Clandestine, Unhappy, in this section).

Unhappy Marriage—Unfortunate— Troubles In Marriage—Danger of Separation or Divorce—The ♅ influence and affliction seems to be inimical to a happy marriage, and espec. when in the 7th H. at B., and tends to separation, to make one less conventional, to chafe under vows and restraints, more apt to favor free love, and to have some peculiar views about sex; ♀ afflicted by ♅, and ♀ ☌ ♅, tend to many troubles in marriage, and with possible ill-health resulting therefrom; malefics in the 7th H., or ruling this house. (See Antipathy, Clandestine, Fickle, Quarrels, Restless, in this section; Husband, Incompatible, Marriage Partner, Opposites; "Law Suits" under Public; "Married Women" under Sex; Sympathy, Wife, Widowers, Widows).

Unlikely—Case—See "Marriage Unlikely',, Nos. 246 and 278, in 1001 N.N.

Vows—Chafes Under Vows and Restraints—♅ influence; ♅ in the 7th H., or afflicting ♀. (See "Occult" in this section).

Widower; Widows; Wife—(See the various paragraphs under Wife).

Women—Married Women—(See Marriage Partner; "Married Women" under Sex; Wife).

MARRIAGE PARTNER—This subject is also considered under Husband, Wife, and Marriage. The influences in this section may apply to either husband or wife unless qualified.

Accident To—♅ or ♂ afflicted in ♎ or the 7th H.

Death Of—The ☽ in a male nativity applying first to ♃, and then to ♅, or the ☉ in the same way in a female geniture, and espec. if ♅ or ♄ be in the 7th H.; ♅ or ♄ affl. in the 7th H., according to aspects; ♅ in the 7th H. in □ or ☌ ♄ or ♂; ♄ affl. in the 7th H. in a mutable sign; malefics in the 7th H.; lords of the 6th or 8th in the 6th H., and afflicted; lord of the 7th a malefic, and afflicted in the 12th H., does not live to be old. The marriage partner usually dies before the native when he (or she) has ♄ afflicted in the 7th H. in the radix. (See "Death" under Husband, Wife; Early Death, Sudden, Violent, in this section).

Drink—Drunkenness—Marriage-Partner Given to Drink or Drunkenness—(See "Husband", "Marriage Partner", under Drunkenness; "Drink" under Husband, Wife).

Early Death Of—Short Life—The ☉ ☌, □, or ☍ ♄ at B.; ♆, ♅, or ♄ in the 7th H. and afflicted; ♄ in the 7th H. whether afflicted or not; ♄ affl. in ♎; lord of the 8th H. a malefic, and afflicted in the 7th. (See "Early Death" under Early, Husband, Wife).

Fiancee—Death of—(See Fiance).

Husband—(See the various paragraphs under Husband).

Ill-Health Of—(See "Sickly" in this section).

Neurotic—Neurotic Wasting of the Marriage Partner—♆ affl. in the 7th H. (See Wasting).

Relatives Of—Kindred—Ruled by the 9th H., lord of this house, planets occupying the house, and the aspects affecting this house or its lord, show their state and condition, and their attitude toward the native. (See "Relatives" under Husband, Wife).

Self-Indulgent—♃ afflicted in the 7th H. (See Self-Indulgent).

Sex Addict—♂ in ♋, ♏, or ♓ in the 7th H., and espec. ♂ affl. in ♏, or ♂ ☌ ♀ or the ☽ in ♏. (See Amorous, Nymphomania; "Passional Excesses" under Passion).

Short Life—(See "Early Death" in this section).

Sickly—♄ in the 7th H., and espec. if afflicted by the ☉ or ☽; lord of the 7th a malefic, and in the 12th H. and afflicted. (See "Early Death" in this section; "Ill-Health" under Husband, Wife).

Sudden Death Of—♅ or ♂ afflicted in the 7th H.; ♅ affl. in ♎, by accident, or some sudden, strange and mysterious malady; ♂ affl. in ♎, by accident or acute disease. (See "Sudden Death" under Husband, Wife).

Violent Death Of—♂ afflicted in the 7th H. (See "Death" under Violent).

Wasting Disease Of—Neurotic Wasting—(See "Neurotic" in this section).

Which Will Die First—(See "Dies Before Wife" under Husband; "Dies Before Husband" under Wife).

Wife—(See the various paragraphs under Wife).

MARROW—The Fatty Substance in the Cavity of a Long Bone—

Inflammation Of—Osteomyelitis—Caused by ♂, and in the part ruled by the sign containing ♂ at B.; ♂ affl. in ♐ tends to inflammation of the marrow in the femur of the leg. Fracture of the femur may occur when ♄ is ☌ ♅ in ♐, and inflammation of the marrow in the femur result. Also osteomyelitis in the marrow of the bones, and with pus development, may follow an injury caused by ♂ in the part ruled by the sign containing ♂, and when there are also other malefics in the same sign with ♂. Case—A Case of Osteomyelitis—See Fig. 15C in the book "Astro-Diagnosis" by the Heindels. (See "Marrow", "Osteomyelitis", under Bones; Femur).

Osteomyelitis—(See "Inflammation" in this section).

MARS—The Red Planet, and known as "The God of War". In size ♂ is smaller than the Earth. Mars is, perhaps, the most written about Planet in Astrological Literature, and has more to do with human ills than any other planet, and creates more disturbances in human affairs by his afflictions than any other planet. However, ♂ has a good and powerful influence also, and along with the ☉ is constructive, gives energy, heat, and force to the body, as well as courage and stimulus to the mind. For convenience of reference this Article is arranged in three Sections. Section One, about the General Influences of Mars; Section Two, what Mars Rules, and Section Three, the Diseases and Afflictions of Mars.

— SECTION ONE —

GENERAL INFLUENCES OF MARS—Mars is known as "The Lesser Infortune", and ♄ as "The Greater Infortune", and both are considered as malefic planets, and especially by their afflictions. The action of ♂ is more acute and violent, while that of ♄ is more slow and chronic. The following paragraphs, arranged alphabetically, give briefly the various influences of Mars. For his special Qualities see the paragraph "Qualities" in this section.

Action of Mars—The action of ♂ is inflammatory, hot, dry and barren, and corresponds to pungent odors, burning astringents and hot acids. The action of ♂ is centrifugal, from the center out, tending to redden the surface, cause congestions of the surface of the body, being rubefacient in action, and is not circumferential in circles like the ☉, but a violent expulsion along the lines of the radii. Mars is rubefacient, inflaming, and reddening, and brings the blood to the surface. (See Caustic, Centrifugal, Rubefacient). The plus, or tonic action of ♂, tends to exaggerated action. Mars is an energetic, dynamic, positive, inflammatory, acute, excessive, destructive, constructive by bringing fevers to burn up poisons in the system, is generally an antagonistic influence, and one of the most potent forces among the planets. Mars occidental causes dryness only, and when oriental both heat and dryness. Mars is sudden and intense, while ♄ is slow, tardy, and restrained. Together ♄ and ♂ act as heat and cold, acute and chronic. Mars influence may be compared to a fever, very severe for a time, but not lasting. The basic forms of ♂ action are inflammatory, intensive, poignant, and centrifugal. Mars accelerates and intensifies, and tends to hurts or illnesses by excesses. Mars tends to action, and to make people assertive, and to do and say what they think and believe, and he never makes hypocrites as ♄ does. (See "Planets" under Tonic. Also for the various actions of ♂ see the different paragraphs in this Article).

Afflicted—An afflicted ♂ tends to cause excess of heat, eruptions, fevers, inflammations, excessive action, and violence.

Anareta—♂ may become the Anareta, or the Killing Planet. (See Anareta).

Angel of Mars—Samael.

Aries Sign—Ruled by ♂, and also ♏ is the night sign of ♂. (See Aries, Scorpio). Mars is strong in ♈, ♏, ♑. He has his exaltation in ♑ and his fall in ♋.

Author of Strife—♂ is the author of strife, quarrels, and contentions, as well as of War.

Blood—Takes Part In Blood Making—Draws Blood To the Surface—(See Centrifugal, Haematopoiesis, Haemoglobin, Iron).

Burns Up Impurities—By Fevers and Inflammation—(See Constructive, Fever, Inflammation).

Causes—♂ causes hot diseases, such as Measles, Smallpox, Scarlatina, Fevers, Erysipelas, Inflammations, Typhus Fever, Eruptive Diseases, etc. The ☉ or ☽ joined with ♂ at B. cause the same diseases as if ♂ were in the Asc. (See the Diseases of ♂ in Sec. 3 of this Article).

Centrifugal Action—(See "Action" in this section).

Classification Of—♂ is classified as positive, masculine, electric, hot, dry, fiery, barren, inflammatory, heating, active, forceful, accelerating, intensifying, etc. (See "Qualities", and the various paragraphs in this Article).

Cleansing—♂ cleanses the system by bringing fevers to burn up the excess of poisons and wastes. (See Constructive, Fever, Inflammation).

Color—♂ is known as the "Red Planet", and rules red as a color. Also ♂ rules red in the Solar Spectrum. (See Red). Mars produces a fiery red color, the result of intemperate heat and dryness. Also ♂ rules Iron color, and rules Iron, Steel, etc. (See Color, Iron).

Constructive—The ♂ force is very useful and constructive when properly harnessed and controlled, but destructive when allowed to run wild in our natures. Mars is pathologically constructive by bringing inflammation and rapid fevers to burn up and eliminate the wastes and poisons from the system. (See "Cleansing" in this section).

Day—The Influence of Mars In a Day Nativity—(See Day, Night; "Day" in Sec. 3 of this Article).

Denotes—♂ denotes high blood pressure, sharp pains, rapid fevers, external and internal hemorrhages, heat, inflammation, swellings, sores, ruptures, effusion of blood, etc. Mars denotes, or shows death by fevers, burns, injuries, violence, etc. (See "Death" in Sec. 3 of this Article).

Destructive—The ♂ influence, and especially his afflictions, are very destructive and pernicious over the average person who is drifting in life, and uncontrolled, and leads to much strife, to quarrels, contentions, bloodshed, etc. His influence is also constructive in many ways, by making blood, haemoglobin, cleansing the body, and by giving daring, courage, and fortitude to meet the battles of life. (See Action, Cleansing, Constructive, Pernicious, in this section).

Directions of Mars—The Directions of ♂ are more dangerous during the ♂ Period of Life, from the 42nd to 56th years, a 14-year period. (See Directions, Periods).

Diseases Of—(See Sec. 3 of this Article; "Denotes" in this section).

Drugs Of—(See Herbs, Remedies, Typical Drugs, in this section).

Eighth House—The House of ♏ and ♂. (See Eighth House).

Emotional Nature—♂ is King of the Emotional, Sense, and Passional nature. (See Desire, Emotions, Passion).

Exaltation—♂ has his exaltation in the ♑ sign.

Exerts—♂ exerts a quick, hot, positive, electric, heating, and infectious nature.

Fall—♂ has his fall in the ♋ sign.

First House—The House of ♈ and ♂. (See First House).

Focuses Heat—♂ focuses heat and draws an abundance of blood to the part ruled by the sign he is in at B.

Friendly To Nothing—♂ is classed as a violent planet and is said to be friendly to nothing, and ♂ people are usually very blunt, abrupt, quarrelsome, and unfriendly.

Geometrically—Geometrically ♂ is the angle, the acute angle, sharp and piercing.

Glycogen—The ♂ Influence Over Glycogen—(See Glycogen).

Heat—♂ is hot and fiery and produces and focuses heat. (See Fevers; "Animal Heat" under Heat; "Focuses" in this section).

Heat and Dryness—♂ is hot and dry by nature. (See "Heat and Dryness" under Dry).

Herbs Of—(See "Mars Group" under Herbs).

Hot In Nature—♂ is the planet of action, and stirs life into action, is hot in nature and sets everything to boiling. (See Action, Heat, in this section).

Hour of Mars—(See "Hours" under Planets).

Houses of Mars—The 1st and 8th Houses are especially affiliated with ♂, which houses correspond to the ♈ and ♏ signs, the signs ruled by ♂, and ♂ when in these houses is very strong and powerful in health matters, disease, accidents, hurts, etc., according to his aspects, or the afflictions to ♂ at B., and by dir. The house and sign occupied by ♂ at B. are centers of activity, energy, and augmentation. (See Eighth House, First House).

Impurities—♂ burns up the impurities of the system. (See "Constructive" in this section).

Indicates—♂ afflicted indicates involuntary muscular action. (See Afflicted, Tends To, and the various paragraphs in this section).

Influence of Mars—This subject is covered largely by the various paragraphs in this Article. Note especially the adjectives under "Qualities" in this section. Mars is dynamic energy, which is said to be the most salient characteristic of ♂. Mars by reflecting the Solar Forces gives dynamic power, but the dynamic energy of ♂, unless directed and controlled, tends to palpitation, to accelerated motion, and to tear everything into pieces. Mars tends to give an active, hasty, and intensive life, and is just the opposite of the ♄ influence, which tends to delays, hindrances, decay, defects, denuding, stoppages, and to slow down the powers and forces of the native by his afflictions. Mars gives some of our worst faults, as well as some of our best virtues, for without his influences at B. we would tend to be cowards, very timid, weaklings, without courage, bravery, and resolution. (See Action, Constructive, Destructive, Qualities, Zest, and the various paragraphs in this Article).

King Of—(See "Emotional Nature" in this section).

Lesser Infortune—♂ is the Lesser Infortune, and ♄ is called the Greater Infortune, but some Authorities think and say that ♂ should be called the Greater Infortune, for his damage and destructive powers are almost without parallel when he is afflicting the native, and especially in a violent map. (See Action, Destructive, in this section; Malefics).

Life—♂ being the planet of action stirs life into action. The ☉ and ♂ are friendly, and both play their part in giving life, blood, vital force and energy to the system, and also courage, daring, and fortitude to the mind. (See "Fires of Life" under Life).

Malefics—The Malefic Planets are ♆, ♅, ♄, ♂. (See Malefics).

Martial—♂ tends to make people martial, bellicose, beligerent, warlike, and fond of Martial Exploits, and to be a good Soldier. (See War).

Mental Qualities—Given by ♂—Antagonistic, Courageous, Energetic, Impetuous, Quarrelsome, Rash. (See "Qualities" in this section).

Metal Ruled by ♂—Iron and its products, as Steel, Sharp-Edged Tools, Weapons made of Iron and high-tempered Steel. (See Iron, Therapeutics).

Minerals Ruled by ♂—Trap Rocks, Cinnabar.

Motion—♂ quickens, accelerates, and increases motion, movement, and action in body and mind. (See "Accelerated" under Motion).

Night—♂ influence by night, and in Night Nativities—(See Day, Epilepsy, Insanity, Night; "Night" in Sec. 3 of this Article).

Occidental—♂ when occidental produces dryness only. (See Occidental, Oriental; "Action", "Oriental", in this section).

Oriental—♂ when oriental causes both heat and dryness. (See "Action", "Occidental", in this section; Oriental).

Own Worst Enemy—People born under ♂ tend to be quarrelsome, and their own worst enemy. (See "Own Worst Enemy" under Enemies).

Passion—♂ is the King of the Passional Nature. (See Passion).

Pathological Action—Of Mars, and of the ♂ Group of Herbs and Minerals—Pathologically ♂ is Caustic, Vesicant, Eruptive, Febrile, Heating, Inflammatory, Rubefacient. Mars also by his afflictions, or by the action of a ♂ Drug or Remedy, tends to affect, disturb, or change the action of the Cerebro-Spinal and Sympathetic Nervous Systems, the Ductless Glands, the Genito-Urinary and Renal Systems, and Vaso-Dilatation. The pathological action of ♂ is both constructive and destructive. (See Constructive, Destructive, Tonic, in this section).

People—Mars People are usually quick and active, and move about freely. (See "Martial", and the various paragraphs in this section, for the various characteristics of ♂ people).

Period—The Mars Period of Life—(See "Directions" in this section).

Pernicious—♂ is very pernicious and destructive in his influences when following or succeeding the ☉. (See "Destructive" in this section; Pernicious).

Plants and Herbs—(See "Mars Group" under Herbs; Therapeutic, Typical Drugs, in this section).

Predisposes To—Accidents, Anger, Cuts, Excitability, High Fever (see Fever); Foolhardiness, Fractures, Gunshot Wounds, Haste, Hurts, Inflammations, Injuries, Murder, Rashness, Recklessness, Scalds, High Temper (see Temper); Violence, etc. (See these subjects).

Presides Over—Mars presides over the Haematopoiesis, or Blood Making; the Red Blood Corpuscles and the Haemoglobin in the Blood; the Iron in the Food and Blood; the Hepatic Process (see Liver); the Sthenic Process. (See Haematopoiesis, Haemoglobin, Iron, Sthenic).

Principle Of—Anger, Energy, Expansion, Inflammation.

Produces—♂ produces the heat and dryness of the body, fevers, inflammations, accidents, injuries, wounds, rashness, etc.

Professions Ruled By—Vocations of —The Employments of—Chemists, Surgeons, Dentists, Pharmacists, Butchers, Military People, Warriors; Workers with Sharp-edged Tools, Metals and Fire; Hazardous and Dangerous Callings.

Qualities Of—Abrupt, Abusive, Accelerating, Accentuating, Acidy, Action, Active, Acute, Aggravating, Aggressive, Amorous, Anger, Antagonistic, Aphrodisiac, Argumentative, Assertive, Astringent, Augmentative, Barren, Bellicose, Belligerent, Boiling, Bold, Brave, Burning, Caloric-Producing, Caustic, Centrifugal, Choleric, Coalescent, Coarse, Combative, Combustive, Congestive, Constructive, Contagious, Contemptuous, Contentional, Courageous, Cruel, Dangerous, Delusive, Derisive, Destructive, Discordant, Disdainful, Disorderly, Disruptive, Domineering, Drastic, Dry, Dynamic, Electric, Eliminating, Emotional, Energetic, Energizing, Enhancing, Enlarging, Eruptive, Escharotic, Evolutionary, Exaggerating, Excessive, Exciting, Expansive, Explosive, Expulsive, Fearless, Febrile, Festering, Feverish, Fierce, Fiery, Foolhardy, Forceful, Frenzied, Fulminating, Furious, Harmful, Harsh, Hasty, Heating, Hot, Hot-Tempered, Hurtful, Impetuous, Impulsive, Incisive, Infectious, Inflammatory, Injurious, Intemperate, Intensive, Jealous, Kinetic, Lacerating, Lascivious, Life-Giving, Loosening, Lustful, Malefic, Malevolent, Malicious, Malignant, Martial, Masculine, Militant, Mischievous, Mocking, Murderous, Nocturnal, Offensive, Painful, Passionate, Pathological, Penetrating, Pernicious, Poignant, Poisonous, Positive, Pungent, Quarrelsome, Radiating, Rapid, Rash, Reckless, Red, Reddening, Resolute, Resolvent, Revolutionary, Robust, Rough, Rubefacient, Ruddy, Savage, Scornful, Self-Preservative, Sensuous, Severe, Sharp, Stimulant, Sudden, Tonic, Torturing, Turbulent, Uncompromising, Uncontrolled, Unfriendly, Unreasonable, Unruly, Vesicant, Vicious, Violent, Vital, Volcanic, Wanton, Warlike, Warring, Willful, Worrisome, Wounding, Zestful, etc.

Red Planet—♂ is known as the Red Planet, as his color is red as he appears in the sky. He rules the color Red. (See Red).

Remedies Of—(See "Mars Group" under Herbs; "Treatment" under Red; Therapeutic Qualities, Typical Drugs, in this section).

Representative Of—♂ is representative of Courage and Animal Strength.

Represents—♂ .represents the Male Sex generally, Doctors, Surgeons, Military Men, and all who use force and energy, and who are positive, assertive, and aggressive.

Ruler—♂ as Ruling Planet tends to give force, energy, boldness, aggressiveness, courage, etc., to the native. (See "Mental Qualities", and the various paragraphs in this section).

Salient Characteristic—Dynamic Energy. (See Dynamic).

Saturn and Mars—These planets act in an opposite manner. Mars is acute, and ♄ chronic; ♂ is accelerating, while ♄ slows up the action and functions of the body. The diseases of ♂ are relieved by the remedies of ♄. Mars is hot and ♄ is cold. Mars is centrifugal, working from the center out, driving blood to the surface, while ♄ is centripetal, chilling the surface, and driving the blood inwards, causing internal congestions. (See "Action", and the various paragraphs in this Article; Saturn).

Scorpio Sign—The Night Sign of ♂. (See Scorpio).

Sense Nature—♂ is King of. (See "Emotional Nature" in this section).

Significator Of—♂ is Sig. of Violence and Murder; of High Fevers and Inflammations; of Acute Diseases; of Quarrels, Disputes, War, etc.

Signs Ruled by Mars—♈ and ♏.

Stars of Mars Nature—Fixed Stars and Nebulous—Aldebaran, Antares, Bull's North Horn, Castor, Cor Leo, Crater, Deneb, Hyades, Hydra's Heart, Markab, Pleiades, Pollux, Regulus, Sirius. (See these subjects. Also see Nebulous; "Mars Group" under Stars).

Strife—♂ is the Author of—(See "Author Of" in this section).

Strong—♂ is strong in ♈, ♏, ♑, and in the Asc. or 10th H. (See "Aries Sign" in this section).

Sun and Mars—These two bodies are sympathetic in nature, both fiery, life-giving, constructive. Mars aids the ☉ in maintaining life, and by bringing fevers and inflammations to burn the refuse and impurities out of the system. In this way ♂ has a constructive influence over the body. Mars transmutes the Solar Forces into passion, anger, and animal spirits, and is ever a dangerous and consuming fire unless controlled by the Will, the Reason, and by Spiritual Attainment. Mars working with the ☉ tends to aggravate and accentuate the ☉ diseases. The aspects of ♂ to the ☉ are necessary to give zest to life, and his bad aspects are better than none at all. (See Sun).

Surgery—♂ the planet of. (See Operations, Surgeons).

Temperament—♂ gives the Choleric Temperament. (See Choleric).

Tends To—Mars influences tend to exaggerated action, violence, disputes, quarrels, destructiveness, bleeding, effusions of blood, cuts, burns, high fevers; short, quick, and violent diseases and affections. (See the various paragraphs in this Article).

Therapeutic Qualities—Aphrodisiac, Caustic, Escharotic, Resolvent, Rubefacient, Stimulant, Tonic, Vesicant. (See these subjects).

Tonic Action Of—The plus, or Tonic Action of ♂, tends to exaggerated action of mind and body. (See Exaggerated, Motion, Tonic).

Typical Drugs Of — Arnica, Arsenic, Bryonia, Cantharides, Capsicum, Cinchona, Iron, Nux Vomica, Quinine, Sarsaparilla, Strychnine, Sulphur, Tonics. (See "Mars Group" under Herbs; "Therapeutic Qualities" in this section).

Vocations Of—(See "Professions" in this section).

War and Quarrels—♂ is the Author and Instigator of. (See Quarrels, War).

Zest—The aspects of ♂ are necessary to give Zest. (See Zest).

— SECTION TWO —

MARS RULES—The different subjects over which Mars rules are here listed alphabetically. See these subjects in the alphabetical arrangement—Accelerated Motion in the Body; Accidents; Acids (Hot Acids); Action and Insistent Action; Adventures; Aggravations; Aggressiveness; Ambitions; Anger; Animal Lust and Passion; Animal Magnetism; Animal Spirits; Animal Strength; Antagonisms; Aries and Scorpio Signs; Arms (Muscles of); Arnica; Arsenic; Assertiveness; Assimilation; Astringents; Augmented Mobility and Sensibility; Barbers; Battle; Bile; Blood Corpuscles (Red); Blood Fibrin; Blood (Hemorrhages of); Blood-Making (Haematopoiesis); Bloodshed; Boldness; Bowels (Muscles of); Bryonia; Burns; Butchers; Cantharides; Capsicum; Centrifugal Action in the Body; Cerebral Ganglia; Cerebral and Genital Poles of Paracelsus; Cerebral Hemisphere (Left); Chemists; Childbirth; Choleric Temperament; Cinchona; Cinnabar; Coction Process in the Body (Combustion, Digestion); Color (Red and Iron Color, Scarlet Red and Shot Crimson); Combativeness (Mental); Combustion (Coction Process); Condiments; Constructive Energy in the Body; Contests; Controversies; Counterirritants; Courage; Criminal Tendencies; Cuts; Dangers and Dangerous Callings; Death by Sharp Fevers, Injury, Violence, etc.; Desire and Insistent Desire; Destructive Energy; Diaphragm; Digestion (Coction Process); Dilator Action (see Vaso); Dissentions; Doctors (Surgeons); Drugs (see "Typical Drugs" in this Article); Dryness of the Body, Earth, and Atmosphere; Ductless Glands; Duels; Dynamic Energy; Ear (Left Ear); Effusion of Blood; Elation and Elevation of Spirits; Elimination of Wastes and Poisons; Emotions; Energy; Enlargements; Eruptions and Eruptive Action; Exaltation and Elation of Spirit; Excesses; Excretion of Urine; External Genitals; External and Internal Humoural Secretions; Face; Fevers; Fibrous Tissue Building; Fire and Fires; Focussed Heat in the Body; Foetus (Growth and Development of Limbs of); Food (Highly Seasoned Food and Condiments); Foolhardiness; Force; Forehead; Forethought (Lack of); Fundament; Gall and Gall Bladder; Ganglia (see "Vaso-

Dilator" under Vaso, and the Introduction under Bowels); Generative Organs (External Genitals); Genital and Cerebral Poles of Paracelsus (see Aries, Scorpio); Growth (Increase of); Guns and Gunshot; Haematopoiesis (Blood-Making); Haemoglobin; Head, and Hurts To; Heart (Muscles of); Heat in the Body, and Fevers, and the Heat in the Body Given by Iron and Haemoglobin; Hepatic Process (Adding to or Subtracting from); Herbs of Mars (see "Mars Group" under Herbs); High Death Rate (see Mortality); High Temper (see Temper); Highly Seasoned Food and Condiments; Hot Diseases; Hot-Headedness; Hour of Mars (see "Hours" under Planets); Houses of Mars (see First House, Eighth House); Humoural Secretions (External and Internal); Hurts by Violence; Imagination; Impulses and Impulsiveness; Incisions; Increase of Growth (Enlargements); Inflammations; Injuries; Insistent Action, Desire, and Will; Intemperance; Intemperate Heat and Dryness; Intercostal Muscles; Internal and External Humoural Secretions; Intestinal Ganglia and Plexuses (see the Introduction under Bowels); Iron Metal and Color, and the Iron in Food and the Blood; Jealousies; Kidneys (Pelvis of and the Parts where Stones are Formed); Left Cerebral Hemisphere, and Left Ear; Legs (Muscles of); Life from 42 to 56 Years (see Periods); Liver; Lust; Madness; Magnetism (Animal); Male Relatives; Mental Combativeness; Military People; Mobility (Augmentation of); Motor Nerves; Motor Segment of Spinal Cord; Movement in the Body; Murder; Muscles (Muscular Force and the Muscular System Generally, and the Muscular and Destructive Energy); Naso-Pharynx; Nerves (The Motor Nerves, and the Sympathetic Nervous System); Nose; Operations (Surgical); Organs (External Genitals); Pain (Sharp, Acute and Violent); Palpitations and Accelerated Motion in the Body; Paracelsus (Cerebral and Genital Poles of); Parturition; Passion and Passional Excesses; Pepper (Red); Pharmacists; Pineapple; Plants and Herbs of Mars (see Herbs); Plexuses (see Introduction under Bowels); Poison, Poisoning, and Poison Death; Privates; Prowess; Pungent Odors (see Acids); Quarrels; Quick Action; Quinine; Rashness and Uncontrolled Thinking; Rectum; Red (Red Blood Corpuscles and Increase of, Red Color in the Solar Spectrum, Red Hair); Reins; Relatives (Male); Reproductive Organs; Resolution; Respiratory System (Diaphragm of); Rubefacients; Sarsaparilla; Scalds; Scarlet Color; Scorpio Sign; Secretions (External and Internal Humoural); Sense Nature; Sensibility (Augmentation of); Sensuality; Severe and Violent Diseases; Sex Organs (External, and the Uterus, Vagina); Sharp (Sharp-Edges Tools, Sharp Fevers and Sharp Pains); Signs of Zodiac (Aries and Scorpio); Sinews; Smell (Sense of); Soldiers; Spinal Cord (Motor Segment of); Stabs; Steel; Sthenic Process in the Body; Stimulants; Strife; Strychnine; Sudden Death; Sulphur; Surgeons; Sympathetic Nervous System;

Tar; Taste (Sense of); Temper (High Temper); Tension in the Body; Testicles; Tonics; Trap Rock; Tuesday (Day of the Week); Typical Drugs (see Sec. 1 of this Article); Uncontrolled Thinking; Unfriendliness; Urethra; Urine (Excretion of); Uterus; Vagina; Vaso-Dilator Action of the Cerebral Ganglia; Veins; Viciousness; Violence (Violent Death, Violent Actions, Violent Diseases); Vital Energy; Vitality; War; Warriors; Wastes and Poisons in the Body (Elimination of); Will (Insistent Will and Desire); Witch Hazel; Womb; Wounds; Youth (The Flourishing Time of); Zest.

— SECTION THREE —

MARS DISEASES AND AFFLICTIONS—Here are a few general considerations concerning the action of ♂ in disease, health matters, and his efforts to vitalize, cleanse, and restore the balance to the system. The ☉ and ♂ act together in sympathy in disease, and the diseases of the ☉ are accentuated by ♂. The ☉ joined with ♂ causes the same diseases as when ♂ is in the Asc. The fevers and inflammations caused by ♂ are of a more destructive, quick, burning, and contagious type, while those produced by the ☉ are slower, but severe. Mars by his fevers and inflammations burns up the impurities of the system, and in this regard is constructive. Mars is rubefacient, caustic, centrifugal, and draws or drives the blood to the surface. Mars causes hot diseases, such as Measles, Smallpox, Scarlet Fever, Fevers, Inflammations, Erysipelas, Typhus Fever, etc. Mars is less malignant at night, as his heat is moderated by the moisture of the night. An afflicted ♂ tends to cause heat, eruptions, and excessive action. Also ♂ afflictions indicate involuntary muscular action. Mars diseases tend to be relieved when the Prog. ☽ forms a good aspect to ♀. Mars focusses heat, and draws an abundance of blood to the part ruled by the sign he is in. Mars exerts a quick, hot, positive, electric, heating, and infectious nature. The plus, or tonic action of ♂, tends to exaggerated action of the mind and body. For the Pathological Action of ♂, his Therapeutic Properties, and Typical Drugs of, Remedies of, see these paragraphs in Sec. 1 of this Article. The following are listed as Diseases and Afflictions of Mars, which see in the alphabetical arrangement when not more fully considered here—

Abortion—Death By—(See Abortion).

Abrasions; Absent—♂ Diseases Absent—(See "Nil" in this section).

Accidents; Action—Excessive Action—(See Action, Exaggerated, Rapid).

Acute Diseases—(See Acute).

All Feverish Diseases—And Inflammatory Disorders—(See Fever, Inflammation).

Alteration of Tissues—(See the Introduction under Inflammation).

Amusements—Injury In—Blindness By—(See Amusements, Blindness).

Aneurysm; Angina; Ankylosis;

Artifice—Blindness By—(See Artifice).

Augmentation—(See Augmented).

Battle—Wounds or Death In—(See War).

Bile—Disorders of—(See Bile).

Bladder—Disorders of—Pain In—Stone In—(See Bladder).

Bleeding—Loss of Blood—(See Bleeding; "Loss of Blood" under Blood; Effusions, Hemorrhage).

Blindness—By Amusements, Artifice, Burns, Explosions, Fire, Gunshot, Smallpox—(See Blindness; "Blindness" under these subjects).

Blisters; Blood—The activity of ♂ in the Blood tends to Hemorrhages, Rupture of Blood Vessels, Hemorrhoids, and Excessive Menses. Also ♂ has a centrifugal action on the blood, causing it to rush to the surface, producing congestions and reddening, inflammations, Hyperaemia, etc. Other ♂ disturbances in the Blood, or relating to the Blood, are—Bloody Flux, Corrupt Blood, Determination of Blood to the Head or a Part, Rush of Blood, Flow of Blood, Expectoration of Blood, High Blood Pressure, Hot Blood, Loss of Blood, Shedding of Blood, etc. (See the various paragraphs under Blood).

Blood Vessels—Rupture of—(See Apoplexy, Hemorrhage; "Rupture" under Vessels).

Boils; Bowels—Inflammation and Obstructions In—(See "Muscles" under Bowels; Inflammation, Obstructions).

Brain Fever—(See Brain).

Breakings Out—(See Eruptions).

Breast—Affections and Pains In—(See Breast).

Bruises; Burning Fevers—(See "High" under Fever).

Burns; Bursting Blood Vessels—(See "Rupture" under Vessels).

Calculi—In Kidneys and Bladder—(See Stone).

Carbuncles; Cells—Inflammation of—(See Cells).

Centrifugal Action—(See Centrifugal).

Cerebro-Spinal Disorders—(See "Pathological Action" in Sec. 1 of this Article).

Chickenpox; Childbirth—Dangers, Injury, or Death In—(See Parturition).

Children—Worms In, and Various Diseases of—(See Children, Worms).

Cholera; Choleric Distempers—(See Choleric).

Colliquative Sweats—(See "Night Sweats" under Phthisis).

Congestion of Blood—On the Surface—(See Centrifugal).

Conjunctivitis—(See Conjunctiva).

Constant Fevers—(See "Constant" under Fever).

Consumption—Liable to Consumption—(See "Consumptive" under Consumption).

Contagious Fevers—(See Contagions, Epidemics, Infections).

Corrupt—Corrupt Blood—Corrupt Humours—(See Humours, Impure).

Cough—Dry Cough—(See Cough).

Courses Overflowing—(See Menses).

Crusts—Of Dead Tissue—(See Eschar; "Skin" under Hardening; Sloughing; "Crusts" under Tissues).

Cutaneous Eruptions—(See Eruptions, Skin).

Cuts; Day—The Diseases Caused by ♂ in a Day Nativity—Mars is more malignant by day, due to his increased heat, and augmented by the heat of the ☉, and ♂ is less malignant at night, at his heat is moderated by the coolness and moisture of the night. (See Day, Epilepsy, Insanity, Night).

Dead Tissue — (See "Crusts" in this section).

Death — Mars rules, or causes Death in the following ways. See "Death" under these subjects—Abortion, Accidents, Acute Diseases, Assassination, Battle, Bruises, Burns, Bursting of Blood Vessels (see Vessels); Childbirth (see Parturition); Contagions, Contests, Cuts, Daggers (see Stabs); Dog Bites (see Dogs); Epidemic Diseases; Erysipelas, Excesses, Falls, Fatty Degeneration of the Heart, Fevers, Fire and Fires, Fire Arms, Fractures (Compound); Frenzy, Fury, Gunshot, Hemorrhages, Hot Diseases, Incised Wounds, Infections, Inflammations, Injuries, Lacerations, Loss of Blood, Mad Dog Bites (see Dogs); Madness, Mania, Miscarriage, Mortification, Murder, Operations, Passional Excesses, Ruptures, Scalds, Short and Sudden Illnesses, Smallpox, Spitting of Blood, Stabs, Stone in the Kidney or Bladder, Strangury, Sudden Death, Suicide, Sword, Syphilis, Venery, Violence, Violent Hemorrhage, War, Wounds, etc. (See the various paragraphs under Death).

Degeneration—Fatty Degeneration of the Heart, and Death By—(See Degeneration, Fat, Heart).

Delirium; Depletion—Of the Vitality—(See "Wasted" under Vitality).

Determination of Blood—To the Head or a Part—(See Determination, Flow; "Blood" under Head).

Diabetes; Diaphragm — (See Hernia, Inflammation, under Diaphragm).

Diarrhoea; Diphtheria;

Disfigurements; Distempers—Choleric Distempers, Distempers In the Head, Mad and Sudden Distempers, Venereal Distempers—(See Distempers).

Distentions; Dog Bites—(See Dogs).

Drought; Dry Cough—(See Cough).

Dry and Hot Diseases—(See Fevers; "Dry and Hot Diseases" under Heat).

Dry Sloughing—(See Sloughing).

Dryness—Diseases Concomitant With —Diseases from Excessive Dryness In the Body, or In the Atmosphere—(See Dryness).

Ductless Glands—Disturbed Action of —(See Ductless; "Pathological Action" in Sec. 1 of this Article).

Duels—Injury or Death By—(See Duels).

Dysentery; Dysuria—(See "Strangury" under Urine).

Ear—Left Ear—Pain and Disease In —(See "Left Ear" under Ears).

Effusion of Blood—(See Effusions).

Elation — Undue Exaltation of the Feelings and Emotions—(See "Exaltation" under Emotions).

Enlargements; Enteric Fever—(See "Fever" under Bowels).

Epidemics; Epilepsy — (See "General Causes" under Epilepsy).

Erethism; Eruptions; Erysipelas;

Eschar—(See Eschar, Sloughing).

Exaggerated Action — (See Exaggerated).

Exaltation — Of the Feelings and Emotions—Elation—(See "Exaltation" under Emotions).

Excesses — Hurts or Illness From — Passional Excesses — (See Excesses, Passion, Venery).

Excessive Action—(See Action, Exaggerated; "Hyperkinesia" under Muscles).

Excessive Disorders—(See the various paragraphs under Excess).

Excitation—Unduly Excitable—(See Excitable).

Excoriations; Expansions;

Expectoration of Blood—(See Haemoptysis).

Explosions—Blindness, Death, or Injury By—(See Explosions).

External — External and Internal Hemorrhages—Disorders of the External Genitals — (See Genitals, Hemorrhage).

Eyes — Inflamed — Rheum In — (See Conjunctiva; "Inflamed", "Rheum", under Eyes).

Face — Hurts To — Pockmarked — Smallpox In—Scars On—(See "Hurts", "Scars", under Face; "Face" under Smallpox).

Falls; Famine; Fatty Degeneration— Of the Heart—(See Heart).

Feet — Accidents To — Corrupt Humours In—Excessive Sweats In—Lameness In—(See Feet).

Fevers — All Kinds — Acute — Burning — High — Constant — Habitual — Epidemic —Contagious—Eruptive—Hectic — Rapid — Intermittent — Sharp — Violent—Pestilential—Semitertian—Death By, etc. (See the various paragraphs under Fever).

Fibers — Over-Braced Tonic Fibers — (See Fiber).

Fierce Disorders—And Fevers—(See Fierce, Rapid, Sharp).

Fiery and Hot Diseases—(See Fiery).

Fire — Fires — Blindness, Injury, or Wounds By—(See Blindness, Fire).

Fire Arms—Injury or Death By—(See Gunshot).

Fistula; Flightiness; Fluxes;

Flying Gout—(See Gout).

Focussed Heat — In the Body — (See Fevers, Inflammation; "Focuses Heat" in Sec. 1 of this Article).

Forehead—Hurts To—(See Forehead).

Fractures; Frenzy; Functions—Excessive or Painful—(See Functions).

Fundament—Disorders of—(See Fundament).

Fury; Gall—Gall Bladder—Bile—Disorders of—(See Bile).

Gastric Disorders—(See Gastric).

Generative Organs—Disorders of—(See Generative, Genitals, Privates, Secrets, Sex, Womb, etc.).

Genitals—Disorders of—(See Genitals).

Genito-Urinary System—Disorders of—(See Genito-Urinary).

Gonorrhoea; Gravel; Guns—Gunshot—Injury or Death By—(See Gunshot).

Habitual Fever—(See "Hectic" under Fever).

Haemoptysis; Hands—Lameness In—(See Hands).

Head—Accidents and Hurts To—Rush of Blood To—Violent Pains In—(See Head).

Heart—Disorders of—Fatty Degeneration of—(See Heart).

Heat—Abundant—Excessive Heat In the Body—Focussed Heat In Body—Fevers, etc.—(See Fever, Heat).

Hectic Fever—(See "Hectic" under Fever).

Hemorrhages; Hemorrhoids;

Herbs of Mars—And their Therapeutic Properties—(See "Mars Group" under Herbs). The remedies and herbs of ♄ and ♀ combat and oppose ♂ diseases, as they are soothing and quieting to the quick and fiery diseases of ♂. (See Antipathy, Opposites, Sympathy).

Hernia; Herpes; High Blood Pressure—(See "Pressure" under Blood).

High Death Rate—(See Mortality).

Hips—Humours In—Pains In—(See Hips).

Hot Diseases—Fevers—Hot Body—Hot Eruptions—Hot and Dry Diseases—Hot Urine, etc.—(See Eruptions, Fevers, Heat, Urine).

Hot Liquids—Death or Injury By—(See "Hot Liquids"under Heat; Scalds).

Humours—Choleric—Corrupt Humours In the Feet—Humours In the Hips, Legs and Thighs—(See Humours).

Hurts; Hydrophobia; Hyperaemia; Hyperkinesia—(See "Excessive Action" in this section).

Hypertrophy; Hysteria;

Ideas—Flightiness of Mind and Ideas—(See Flightiness, Ideas).

Illness—From Excesses, Fevers, Hurts, Unbridled Passion, etc.—(See Excesses, Fevers, Hurts, Passion).

Illnesses—Sharp and Sudden—(See "High Fever" under Fever; Sharp, Sudden).

Imaginations; Immoderate Heat—Illness From—(See "Excessive Heat" under Heat).

Incised Wounds—Danger or Death By (See Cuts, Incised, Operations).

Incrementations; Infections;

Inflammations—Inflammatory Diseases—(See the various paragraphs under Inflammation).

Injuries—(See the various paragraphs under Accidents, Cuts, Hurts, Injuries, Wounds, etc.).

Inner Parts—All Diseases In—(See Reins).

Insanity; Instruments—Wounds By—(See Instruments).

Intemperance; Intermittent Fevers—(See Intermittent).

Internal Hemorrhage—(See Hemorrhage).

Involuntary—Involuntary Muscular Excitement—(See "Involuntary" under Muscles).

Inward Parts—All Diseases In—(See Reins).

Iron or Steel—Injuries, Wounds, or Death By—(See Iron).

Irregularities—(See "Painful Complaints" under Forethought; "Disease or Injury" under Rashness).

Itch; Jaundice; Kidneys—All Diseases In—Stone In—(See Kidneys, Stone).

King's Evil—(See Scrofula).

Knees—Injuries To—Lameness In—Pains, Inflammation, and Swellings In—(See Knees).

Lameness—In the Arms, Hands, Knees, Feet—(See Lameness; "Lameness" under these subjects).

Left Ear—Pain and Disease In—(See "Left Ear" under Ears).

Legs—Humours, Lameness, Pains In—(See Legs).

Lightning—Blindness or Injury By—(See Lightning).

Lithiasis—(See Stone).

Liver—Disorders of—(See Deranged, Inflammation, under Liver).

Loins—Weakness In—(See Loins).

Loss of Blood—And Death By—(See "Loss of Blood" under Blood; Effusions; "Death" under Hemorrhage).

Lues—(See Syphilis).

Lungs—Hemorrhage of—Inflammation of—(See Lungs).

Madness—Mad—Mad Distempers—Mad Dog Bites, etc.—(See Madness).

Malaria; Malignant Diseases—Malignant Scarlatina—(See Malignant).

Mania; Measles; Megrims—In the Head—(See Migraine).

Mens' Genitals—Diseases In and Injury To—(See Genitals).

Menses—Excessive—(See Menses).

Metorrhagia—(See Menses).

Migraine; Miscarriage—Death By—(See Abortion, Miscarriage, Parturition).

Mobility Augmented—(See "Accelerated" under Motion).

Mortification—Death By—(See Mortification).

Motor—Motor Nerves—Motor Segment of the Spinal Cord—Disorders of—(See Motor; "Motor" under Spine).

Mouth—Extreme Heat In—(See Mouth).

Murderous—(See Murder).

Muscles—Disorders of—(See Muscles).

Nasal Disorders—(See Nose).

Naso-Pharynx — Inflammation In — (See Nose).

Neck — Inflammation and Pains In — (See Neck).

Nephritis—(See Kidneys).

Nerves—Nerve Centers—Disorders of — Inflammation and Vascular Excitement of the Nerve Centers — Nervous Irritability, and Abnormal Increase of —Disorders of the Motor Nerves, etc.— (See Centres, Erethism, Nerves; "Motor" in this section).

Night—Night Sweats—The Action of ♂ In Night Nativities and Disease At Night—(See Day, Night; "Night Sweats" under Phthisis; "Day" in this section).

Nil — ♂ diseases are almost entirely absent, and are not epidemic, when ♂ has little power and is not elevated above, or configurated with the ☉ or ☽ at an Eclipse, Equinox, or Solstice, and ♂ neither ℞ nor in perigee. (See Eclipse, Perigee).

Nose—Disorders of—(See Nose).

Obstructions — (See "Bowels" in this section).

Operations — Danger of Death By — (See Operations).

Organs — Enlargement or Inflammation of—(See Enlargement, Inflammation, Organs).

Over-Braced Tonic Fibers — (See Fiber).

Over-Heated Blood—And Diseases From — (See "Over-Heated" under Blood).

Pain— Pains—Painful Complaints—♂ tends to cause acute, sharp, darting, cutting, sudden and severe pains in almost every part of the body, according to the sign he is in at B., his aspects, afflictions by dir., transits, etc. Mars also causes painful complaints due to rashness and want of forethought. (See "Pain" under the various parts and organs of the body, such as under Arms, Bladder, Breasts, Head, Hips, Legs, Neck, Reins, Shoulders, Stomach, Thighs, Throat, etc. See Forethought, Rashness, and note the various paragraphs under Pain).

Palpitations; Part—Determination of Blood to a Part—(See "Determination" in this section).

Parts of Organs—Enlargement or Inflammation of—(See Enlarged, Inflammation, Parts).

Parturition — Childbirth — Fever, Injury, or Death In—(See Parturition).

Passion — Passional Excesses, and Diseases From — (See Amorous, Passion, Venery).

Pathological Action— Of Mars — (See "Pathological" in Sec. 1 of this Article).

Pectoral Affections—(See Breast).

Penis—Ulceration, and Diseases of— (See Genitals, Penis, Urethra, Venereal).

Perityphlitis—(See Caecum).

Pernicious Diseases; Pestilence;

Pharynx — Naso - Pharynx — Disorders of—(See Pharynx).

Phrenzies—(See Frenzy).

Phthisis; Piles—(See Hemorrhoids).

Plague; Pneumonia; Pock-marked;

Poisoning—Death By—(See Poison).

Private Diseases — Private Injury — Private Parts—(See Private).

Privates — Genitals — Disorders In — (See Genitals, Generative, Genito-Urinary, Penis, Private, Reproduction, Sex, Urethra, Vagina, Venereal, Vulva, Womb, etc.).

Process—The Hepatic and Inflammatory Process — (See "Alterations" under Cells; the Introduction under Inflammation, Liver).

Prodigality; Puerperal Fever — (See Parturition, Puerperal).

Pyelitis—(See Kidneys).

Quarrels; Quick Diseases—(See Acute, Quick).

Quinsy—(See Tonsils).

Rapid Fevers — And Diseases — (See Rapid).

Rash Acts—Injury or Death By—(See Anger, Folly, Foolhardy, Forethought, Fury, Rashness, Recklessness, Violent).

Recklessness; Rectum — Disorders of —(See Rectum).

Reddening — (See Caustic, Rubefacient).

Regenerative Organs — Diseases In— Ulcer In — (See Generation, Genitals, Privates, Regeneration, Reproduction, Secrets, Sex Organs, Venereal, Womb).

Reins—Disorders In—(See Reins).

Religious Frenzy—(See Excitable).

Renal Calculi — (See "Stone" under Kidneys).

Respiratory System — Disorders of — (See Breath, Bronchial, Diaphragm, Lungs).

Rheum In Eyes — (See "Rheum" under Eyes).

Rheumatism—(See "Tendency" under Rheumatism).

Ringworm; Rubefacient; Rupture — Hernia, and Death By — Rupture of Blood Vessels—(See Hernia, Rupture, Vessels).

Rush of Blood — To the Head — To a Part—(See Determination).

Scabies; Scalds; Scarlatina;

Scars On Face — (See "Scars" under Face).

Sciatica; Scrofula; Secret Parts—Diseases In—(See Secrets).

Semitertian Fevers — (See Semitertian).

Sensibility Augmented — (See Sensibility).

Sex Organs—Diseases In—Injuries To —(See "Regenerative Organs" in this section; Sex).

Sharp Fevers—Sharp Illnesses—Sharp Pains—Sharp Instruments and Injuries By—(See Sharp).

Shingles—(See Herpes).

Shock—Violent Shock—(See Shock).

Short Illnesses — Short and Sudden and Death By—(See Acute; "High Fevers" under Fever; Rapid, Sharp, Short, Sudden, Swift, Violent).

Signs—Diseases of ♂ in the Signs of the Zodiac — ♂ in each of the signs tends to inflammations, hurts, injuries to the part, parts, or organ ruled by such sign, and also to cause an excessive supply of blood to be drawn to the part at times. (See the list of Diseases under each of the Signs, as "Aries Diseases" under Aries; "Taurus Diseases" under Taurus, etc. For a classified arrangement of the diseases of ♂ in each of the Signs, see the regular Textbooks and Dictionaries of Astrology).

Skin Eruptions — (See Eruptions, Skin).

Sloughing — Dry Slough — Crusts of Dead Tissue—(See Sloughing).

Smallpox—Blindness From—Smallpox In the Face, and Pockmarks — (See "Smallpox" under Blindness; "Face" under Smallpox).

Smell—Disorders of—(See Smell).

Sores—(See Plague, Sores).

Spinal Cord—Disorders of Motor Segment of—(See "Motor" under Spine).

Stabs; Steel and Iron—Hurts, Cuts, Injury or Death By—(See Iron).

Stomach—Disorders of—Ulcer of—Inflammation—(See Gastric, Stomach).

Stone—Stone In the Reins, Kidneys, Bladder—(See Stone).

Strangury—(See Urine).

Sudden Illnesses—Sudden Death—Sudden Distempers—Sudden and Short Illnesses—(See "Short" in this section; Sudden).

Suicide; Sunstroke; Surfeits;

Surgical Incisions—(See Operations).

Sweats—Night Sweats of Phthisis—(See Phthisis).

Swellings; Swift Diseases — (See Swift).

Sword—Injury or Death By—(See Duels, Sword).

Sympathetic Nervous System—Disorders of—(See "Pathological Action" in Sec. 1 of this Article; Sympathetic).

Syncope—(See Fainting).

Syphilis; Temper—(See "High" under Temper).

Temperament—(See Choleric).

Temperature—Increase of—High—(See "High Fever" under Fever).

Tension—In the Body—High Nervous Tension—(See Excitable, Tension).

Tertian Fevers — (See Intermittent, Tertian).

Tetter; Thighs—Humours In—Pains In—Tumors In—(See Thighs).

Thinking — Uncontrolled and Rash Thinking—(See Anger, Rashness, Vicious, Violent).

Throat—Disorders of—Extreme Heat In—Pains In—(See Throat).

Tissue—Alteration of—Hypertrophy of—Crusts of Dead Tissue—(See "Alterations" under Cells; Hypertrophy, Sloughing, Tissues).

Tone—Of the Body—Disturbances of —(See Recuperation, Resistance, Stamina, Tone, Vitality).

Tonsils—Tonsilitis—(See Tonsils).

Tonic—Tonic Action and Disorders of — Tonic Color (Red) — Tonic Fibers Over-Braced — Tonic Medicines — (See "Organs" under Enlarged; Tonic).

Treatment—Of ♂ Diseases—The Herbs and Remedies of ♀ are very favorable, as ♀ opposes ♂, and are used on the principle of Antipathy. Also the Herbs and Remedies of ♂ can be used to combat ♂ diseases, on the principle of Sympathy, as in Homeopathy. Also the Remedies and Herbs of ♄, the cold planet, can often be used to relieve the heat, fever, and congestion of ♂ diseases. The color Blue may be used to soothe and quiet the exciting qualities of ♂ diseases, and especially where the mind is affected. (See Blue; "Mars Group", "Saturn Group", "Venus Group", under Herbs; "Remedies", "Therapeutic Qualities", "Typical Drugs", in Sec. 1 of this Article, and also under Mars, Saturn, Venus).

Tumors In Thighs — (See "Tumors" under Hips).

Tympanies; Typhoid Fever; Typhus;

Ulcers—In Genitals, Vagina, Womb, Secret Parts, Stomach, etc.—(See Ulcer).

Uncontrolled Thinking—Disease or Injury By—(See "Thinking" in this section).

Urethritis—(See Urethra).

Urine—Hot Urine—(See "Scalding" under Urine).

Uterus—Ulcer of—(See Womb).

Vagina—Ulceration of—(See Vagina).

Vascular Excitement—Of Nerve Centers—(See Erethism).

Vaso-Dilatation—(See "Vaso-Dilator Action" under Vaso).

Venereal Diseases—(See Venereal).

Vessels—Rupture of Blood Vessels—(See Vessels).

Violence—Injury or Death By—(See Assassination; "Death" under Injuries; Murdered, Violence).

Violent Disorders—Violent Hemorrhage—Violent Tendencies—(See Fierce, Hemorrhage, Pernicious, Rapid, Severe, Sharp, Violent).

Vital Force—Wasting of—(See "Health Suffers" under Opposite Sex; "Waste" under Vital; "Wasted" under Vitality).

Vitality Wasted—(See "Wasted" under Vitality).

Voluntary Power — Excessive — (See Voluntary).

Vulva — Abscess or Ulceration of — (See Vulva).

Wasting—Of the Vital Forces—(See "Vital" in this section).

Weakness—In Loins—(See Loins).

Womb—Inflammation of—Ulcer of—(See Womb).

Worms—In Children—(See Worms).

Wounds—In Battle—Blindness By—Death By—By Fire, Burns, Scalds, Iron and Steel, Sharp Instruments—Sudden and Spontaneous, etc.—(See the various paragraphs under Accidents, Blows, Cuts, Hurts, Injuries, Instruments, Iron, Violence, Weapons, Wounds, etc.).

Yellow Jaundice—(See Jaundice).

Zoster—Herpes—(See Herpes).

MASCULINE—Male—Pertaining to the Male Sex—Masculine Qualities—Masculine Appearance—Masculine Births —Masculine Children—Masculine Degrees—Masculine Houses—Masculine Colors—Masculine Nativity—Masculine Planets—Masculine Sex Organs—Masculine Signs of the Zodiac—Masculine and Coarse Voice In Women, etc.— (See "Masculine", and these various paragraphs under Male.

MASOCHISM—A Form of Sexual Perversion which Delights in Cruel Treatment—♂ ♂ or ill-asp. ♀ at B.; ♂ ♂ ♀ in ♏; a ♂ influence, and with ♂ configurated with ♄ and ♀; ♂ ♂ ♄ and ♀ in ♏; malefics in the sex sign ♏, and especially ♂ afflicted in this sign. (See Cruel, Perversions).

MASSACRE—Danger of Death In Massacre Abroad—(See "Massacre" under Abroad).

MASSAGE—(See Healers).

MASTICATION—The Process of Chewing—

Fast Eater—Does Not Chew the Food Well—(See "Fast Eater" under Eating).

Spasm of Muscles Of—(See Lock-Jaw).

MASTOID—The Mastoid Bone, Process, Cells and Sinuses—

Mastoid Abscess—Mastoiditis—Inflammation of the Mastoid Cells—The Mastoid Cells in the interior of the Mastoid Process, and which are lined with mucous membrane, open on the posterior wall of the middle ear, and are affected by afflictions in ♉, which sign rules the Ears generally. Saturn or ♂ in ♉, and espec. when in the 12th H., and affl. the ☉, ☽, or ☿ tend to Mastoid Abscess. Also afflictions in ♈ or ♎ may cause the trouble, and the extension of Ear Abscess over into the Mastoid Process. The right or left Mastoid Processes are affected according to sex, and whether ♄ or ♂ are the afflictors. Also this trouble is sometimes caused by the Prog. ☽ in ♂ with planets in the radical map, and espec. if in ♂ with ♄, ♂, ♀, or ☿ in this sign. (See Abscesses, Left Ear, Right Ear, under Ears). Case of Mastoiditis—See Fig. 7B in the book, "Astro-Diagnosis" by the Heindels.

Sterno-Mastoid Region—The Sterno-Mastoid Muscle—Disorders of—Afflictions in the latter part of the ♉ sign, or in first few degrees of ♊; Subs at LCP (6, 7C).

MASTURBATION—Self-Abuse—(See "Solitary Vice" under Vice).

MATERIA MEDICA—The Branch of Medical Science Treating of Drugs—Many Drugs, Herbs, Plants, Metals, and Minerals are listed alphabetically in this book, and giving their Planetary Rulership, Action, Therapeutic Value, etc. Look in the alphabetical arrangement for the subject you have in mind. Also under each of the Planets see such subjects as "Drugs", "Herbs", "Metal", "Remedies", "Therapeutic Qualities", "Typical Drugs", "Treatment", "Pathological Qualities", etc. Also see the general subjects of Antipathy, Cure, Drugs, Healers,

Herbs, Medicines, Metals, Minerals, Narcotics, Opposites, Pathological, Poisons, Remedies, Salts (see "Salts" under Zodiac); Signs of the Zodiac (under each of the Signs note the Drugs and Herbs each Sign rules); Sympathy, Therapeutics, Treatment.

MATERIALISM—A ♄ influence; ♄ strong at B., ruler, or in the Asc.; ♄ in the 9th H., the house of the Higher Mind and Religion; many planets in earthy signs at B.; earthy signs on the Angles. People born with many planets in the earthy signs tend to be more earth-bound, materialistic, and to have a more slow, plodding, and laborious career, and also to be more given to Melancholy, Despondency, Hypochondria, Mental Depression and Dejection, and to have a greater desire for wealth and the things of this World, and to the possible neglect of their spiritual welfare. Brooding over worldly matters may tend to ill-health, and to weaken the vitality. The negative earth sign people, as ♉, ♍, ♑, tend to Materialism, and to diseases, such as Gout, Rheumatism, Crystallization, Hardening, Suppression of the Functions, Excess Deposit of Wastes and Poisons in the system, which are ♄ diseases, and these diseases usually go with a Materialistic Mind, as the mind is turned downward toward the Earth, and earthly things, in most cases, rather than upward toward the higher and more spiritual Truths, and the Secret Doctrines and Mysteries. The good aspects of, and the higher influences of the planets ♆ and ♅, tend to uplift the native, and away from Materialism. (See Metaphysical, Neptune, Occult, Rationalism, Saturn, Scepticism, Spirituality, Uranus).

MATERNITY—Maternal—Pertaining to the Mother and Motherhood—In these matters the positions and aspects of the ☽ and ♀ are to be considered. The supreme function of maternity depends almost wholly upon the positions and affections of the ☽ and ♀, and the conditions of these two bodies in the horoscope of the mother. The wife may be fruitful, and have a fruitful map of birth, yet may not become a mother unless she also has a fruitful husband, as many men are impotent and sterile from birth. Therefore, if a prospective bride wishes to make sure that she is fruitful, and will have children, she also should know beforehand that her intended husband has a fruitful map, or she may make a mistake, and be sorely disappointed. Also there are women who are fruitful, but who have the malefics ♄ and ♂ in the 5th H., the house of children in their maps, which would indicate unfortunate children, or their early death, and it would be well for a woman to know of these things before she marries, so as to know what to expect, what to prepare for, and how to the better understand her children, and early take them in hand, and give them the proper care and training. Some women, while fruitful, tend to be unfortunate as to children, and make very undesirable mothers.

Aunts and Uncles—Maternal Aunts, Uncles, and Relatives—The mother's relations are ruled by ☿ in your map, and the aspects to, or by ☿, and the position and strength of ☿ at your birth will determine your relation largely to your relatives on your mother's side, and also their condition, illnesses, or possible death. Aunts and Uncles on the mother's side are also ruled by the 6th H. in a male nativity, or on the father's side in a female geniture. The 12th H. rules the opposite conditions. (See Aunts, Brethren; "Aunts", "Relatives", under Father; Relatives, Uncles).

Death of Maternal Relatives—Death of Maternal Aunts and Uncles—Suffering and Illness of—♄ ruler of the 12th H. at B., and ♄ ☍ or ill-asp. the Asc. by dir. (See "Death" under Relations; Sixth House, Twelfth House).

Functional Trouble—In Maternity—The ☽ in the 5th or 6th H. at B., and afflicted; ♀ afflicted in the 6th H. (See Functions).

Instincts—Maternal Instincts—These are strong when the ♋ sign, or the 5th H. are well and favorably occupied and aspected at B. Mars in the 5th H., and well-aspecting the ☽, gives a strong desire for children, but danger of accidents and sickness to them. The maternal instincts are lessened when ♆, ♅, or ♄ occupy the 5th H. at B., and also many planets in the positive and masculine signs at B. (See the influences under "Amativeness", which give a strong desire for children, and to propagate the Race. Also see Barren, Fruitfulness, Instincts).

Maternal Place—In the Map of Birth—The place of ♀ by day, or the ☽ by night, in the map of the mother. (See Conception, Family, Foetus, Moon, Mother, Parturition, Paternal, Pregnancy, Prenatal Epoch, Puerperal, Venus, Wife, etc.).

Maternal Relatives—(See "Aunts and Uncles" in this section).

MATHEMATICAL—A Good Mathematician—Mathematical Prodigy—Lightning Calculator—The ♉ sign is said to give good mathematical ability. Also ♂ is associated with ☿, either by ☌ or ☍. The □, P., or any aspect of ♂ to ☿, tends to make the mind more keen for mathematics. In Hor'y Q. ♂ Sig. ☌ ☿, or in ✶ or △ ☿, indicate a good mathematician. Mars and ☿ in angles, in aspect, or in houses of mind, the 3rd or 9th H. Some of the greatest Mathematical Geniuses, Lightning Calculators, Chess Players, Mechanical Geniuses, Inventors, etc., and even as Child Prodigies, have ♂ ☌ or ♉ ☿ in the 3rd or 9th H., and also with ♅ lending a good and strong aspect to ☿. Neptune also in good asp. to ☿ at the same time gives a higher, intuitional, inspirational, and spiritual trend to the mind, and capable of great mental and spiritual feats. The greatest Mathematicians are usually Advanced Souls. It is said also that high attainments and gifts in mathematics are indications of a genuine and highly developed spiritual nature, but not necessarily an emotional nature, or relig-

ious fervor, which may be mistaken for spiritual power. (See Freaks, Genius; "Great Ability" under Great; Learning, Mechanical; "Quickened" under Mentality; Precocious, Premature, Prodigies, Scientific, Spiritual).

MATRICIDE—(See "Patricide" under Father).

MATRIX—The Womb—(See Womb).

MATTER—Substance—Material Things—The ☽ is typical of Matter, and the ☉ of Spirit. Matter is condensed Ether, or condensation of the etheric and gaseous particles which float in the Ether. During the great Cosmic Nights of the Universe all Matter, Planets, and Bodies in space, are dissolved back into their etheric and gaseous state. It is said that "Matter is Condensed Spirit". No matter is ever lost in the Universe, but merely changes form. The influence of ♄ tends to decay, or resolution of matter into its primary elements and gases, and to bring on the "Death", or separation, of living cells and organisms, such as the human organism. A corpse is much alive as the cells becomes disorganized, their leader, master, and organizer, the Ego, having departed, and each cell struggles for its freedom that it may enter into other organized forms and combinations. (See Ether, Spirit, Substance).

MATURE—Maturation—Maturity—Ripening—Is typified by the full ☽. In the Kakala mature age was dedicated to ♃. (See "Full Moon" under Moon).

Dies Before Maturity—Will Not Live to Maturity—Rarely Lives to Maturity—The ☉ or ☽ in an angle at B., ☌, or ill-asp. a malefic, and with no good aspects from the Benefics; a malefic rising and afflicting the lord of the 8th H.; ruler of the Asc. in the 6th H., and afflicted by lord of the 8th H., and with no assistance from Benefics. For other influences along this line see "Death" under Childhood, Children, Infancy; "Early Death" under Early; "Short Life" under Life; "Dies Before Middle Life" under Middle Life; "Death In Youth", "Early Youth", under Youth).

Rarely Lives to Maturity—(See "Dies Before Maturity" in this section).

Reason—Lack of Mature Reason—(See "Lack Of" under Forethought; Irrational, Irresponsible; "Bad Judgment" under Judgment; "Weak Mind" under Mind; Reason).

Tubercle—Maturation of—(See Tubercle).

Will Live to Maturity—Prospects of Long Life—A strong sign on the Asc. at B., and the ruler well-placed and free from affliction, and at the same time the hyleg free from affliction, the child will live to maturity, have good powers to withstand disease, and to recuperate rapidly from illness. (See Adults; "Good" under Constitution, Health, Recuperation, Resistance, Stamina, Tone, Vitality; Immunity; "Long Life" under Life; "Death" under Middle Life).

Youth—The Time of Adolescence and Maturity—(See Manhood, Puberty, Youth).

MAXILLARY—Pertaining to the Jaws —(See Jaws).

MAYHEM—(See Maimed, Mutilated).

MEAGRE— Thin—Emaciated—Inadequate—Scanty, etc.—♄ and ♀ influence.

Meagre Body—(See Emaciated, Thin).

Meagre Face—(See "Meagre" under Face).

Meagre Hair—The Hair Scanty or Thin—No Hair—(See Baldness; "No Hair", "Scanty", under Hair).

MEALS—Eating—Food—(See Assimilation, Diet, Digestion, Drink, Eating, Epicureans, Feasting, Food, Gluttony, Indigestion, etc.).

MEAN—Medium—Middle—Mean Stature —Mean Actions, etc.—

Mean Abilities—The Mind, Talents, and Abilities More Mediocre—Not Especially Brilliant—(See Dull; "Fails In Examinations" under Examinations; "Lack Of" under Forethought; Idle, Improvident, Indifferent; "Bad" under Judgment; Lassitude, Lethargy; "Shallow" under Mental).

Mean Actions—Hating All Sordid and Mean Actions—♃ in the Asc. at B., and free from the affliction of malefics. (See Honest, Honorable, Humane; "Popular" under Reputation). For the influences which tend to a mean disposition and temper see Anger, Cruel, Hate, Revengeful; "High Temper" under Temper; Vicious, Violent; Mean-Spirited in this section.

Mean Creature—♂ Sig. in ♋, mean, servile, and unfortunate; ☿ Sig. in ♋, a mean little wretch if ☿ is afflicted.

Mean-Spirited— Mean Disposition — The ☽ Sig. ⚹, △, □, or ☍ ♄, mean in actions; the ☽ in ♑ in partile asp. the Asc.; ♃ Sig. ☌ ♄, mean and deceitful disposition; persons devoid of ♂ influence at B.; ☿ Sig. ☌ ♄; ♀ on the Meridian at B., and affl. by ♄. (See Anger, Choleric, Conduct, Cruel, Deceitful, Dishonest, Evil, Hatred, Jealous, Malevolent, Malice, Revengeful, Secretive, Savage; "High Temper" under Temper; Thieving, Vicious, Violent, etc.).

Mean Stature—Middle Stature—Short —The ⊙ in ♋ or ♑, a mean and ill-made body; the ☽ in ♑ partile the Asc., a mean, small, weak figure; the ☽ in ♓ partile the Asc., a short, mean stature, but plump or fat; ♄ shortens the body, and the ♄ sign ♑ when strong at B., tends to a medium, mean, or short stature; ♃ in ♑ partile the Asc.; ♂ in ♑ partile Asc.; ♂ in ♓ partile Asc., mean, short, and fleshy body; ♀ in ♉ partile Asc., comely, but with a mean stature; ♀ in ♑ partile Asc., mean, short stature; ☿ in ♈ partile Asc., thin, mean stature; ☿ Sig. in ♏; ☿ in ♏ partile the Asc., mean stature, but well-set and broad-shouldered; ☿ in ♑ partile the Asc., a mean figure, crooked, often bow-legged, and with a thin face; ☿ in ♓ partile Asc., a mean, short stature, and some Writers say this influence gives a short, thin body. The ♉, ♋, and ♓ influences produce small persons, and of mean stature. The ♑ sign gives a short, slender, and ill-formed person, and often corpulent.

(See Corpulent, Fat, Fleshy; "Middle Stature" under Middle; "Moderate Stature" under Moderate; "Body" under Short).

MEASLES — Rubeola— Principally a ♂ disease; ♂ exactly rising or setting at B. tends to; ♂ coming to the ☌ or ill-asps. the Asc. early in life causes smallpox, measles, or scarlatina; ♂ in the 1st H.; ♂ affl. in ♑; ♂ afflicted in ♓, and ☌ or ill-asp. the Asc. by dir.; ♂ afflicting the Asc. at B.; ♂ ☌ the Asc. by dir.; the hyleg much afflicted by ♂; the ⊙ to the □ or ☍ the ☽ by dir.; the ⊙ afflicted in ♋; the ⊙ to the ill-asps. the ☽ by dir., and the ☽ affl. by ♂ at B.; attacks occur under the directions of the ⊙, ☽, or Asc. to ♂, or to the ⊙ or ♃ if either be afflicted by ♂ at B.; the ⊙ coming to the ill-asps. the Asc. early in life; the ill-asps. and directions of the ⊙ to the hyleg if the ⊙ be afflicted by ♂; afflictions to the ☽, and espec. by ♂; the ☽ to the ☌ or ill-asp. ♂ by dir.; a disease of the ☽; the ☽ in ♋ at B., and the transit of ♂ over the ☽ if the ☽ is afflicted, and espec. in children of a weak constitution; the ☽ in ♏, and afflicted by the ⊙ or ♂ when taken ill (Hor'y); the ☽ to the □ or ☍ ♀ by dir., with ♀ in a watery sign, and espec. in children; ♄ in ♋, ♏, or ♓, ☌, or ill-asp. the Asc. by dir.; ♃ peregrine in an airy or watery sign in ☌ the Asc. by dir.; ♀ afflicted in a watery sign at B., and the ☽ to the ill-asps. ♀ by dir.; a pustular disease denoted by ♀; an ♈ disease when there are malefics in ♈; a ♌ disease, and afflictions in ♌; the Asc. to the □ or ☍ ♃ by dir., and ♃ afflicted by ♂; the Asc. to the place of ☋ by dir.; Subs at MCP (5C) and CP, KP. (See Chickenpox, Eruptions, Exanthema; "Pustular Diseases" under Pus; Scarlet Fever, Smallpox; "Vascular Tissues" under Vascular).

Blindness from Measles—(See "Measles" under Blindness).

Epidemic of Measles — ♂ is supreme in years of Measles and Smallpox Epidemics, and of other Eruptive Diseases, as Chickenpox, Scarlatina, and Scarlet Fever. These Epidemics occur when ♂ is perigee, and the major planets ♄ or ♃ in perihelion. Mars supreme at the Equinoxes and Solstices; ♂ predominating at the ☌ of three or four of the superior planets, and is severe in type, but milder when ♂ is in ☌ or ☍ only one other superior planet, and ♂ holding power; ♂ Lord of the Year in ♈ at the Vernal Equi., and afflicted by ♄. (See Dengue, Epidemics, Perigee, Perihelion, Pestilence, Plague, etc.).

MEAT—

Ill-Digested Meat — Illness From — The ☽ in ♎, ☌, □, or ☍ ♄ (or ☿ if he be of the nature of ♄) at the beginning of an illness or at decumbiture. (See "Meat" under Indigestion).

Meat Eating — One Astrological Authority advises that people who have ♂ in ♈ at B. should avoid meat as food. Meat is somewhat heating, it is said, and does not agree very well with people born with many planets in fiery signs. Also meat contains the passion, vibrations, and poisons of the animal, and with people badly afflicted by ♄ at B., or born under ♄, tends to Gout and Rheumatism, excess of deposits and wastes, and would tend to have better health to live on nuts, vegetables, fruits, fruit juices, etc., and avoid meat. The question of Meat Eating is a large one, and many Authorities advise the eating of Meat, while others are against it. The Occult Writers in general seem to be against Meat Eating, and the killing of animals for food, and say that it is not right to take the life of animals. The Religions of the Orient are especially strong against taking the life of animals, birds, or even insects. Blood is strongly related to the Astral Plane, and the Occult Masters teach that the eating of the blood of animals tends to violent vibrations in the body, and to increase the passion, and also to incorporate the poisons and wastes of the flesh of the animal into the human body. Dr. Duz, the famous French Medical Astrologer, strongly advocated meat eating. The question of Meat Eating, both from an Occult and Physiological standpoint, and also Vegetarianism, are discussed in the book, "Cosmo-Conception", by Max Heindel, of the Rosicrucian Fellowship. (See Diet, Eating, Food, Fruit, Vegetables).

MECHANICAL—

Mechanical Displacements—(See Displacements).

Mechanical Genius—Mechanical Skill —Is due to the combination of the ♂ and ☿ influences, and ♂ configurated with ☿; ♂ ruler of the horoscope at B.; ♂ Sig. ☌ ☿; ☿ Sig. ✳ or △ ♂. The Fixed Star Rigel also tends to give mechanical ability when culminating or setting at B. (See Genius, Inventive, Mathematical, Prodigies).

MEDDLERS — Triflers — Prattlers — Busy-Body—♃ Sig. in ♋; ☿ ill-dignified at B.

MEDIASTINUM — The Septum of the Thoracic Cavity — Tumor of — (See Chest, Thorax; "Mediastinum" under Tumors).

MEDICAL ASTROLOGY — The Branch of Astrology which has to do with the Planetary Causes of Disease, and also the Planetary Rulership of Herbs, Metals, Minerals, Plants, etc., and their Therapeutic value. In every Nation and Tribe there is a remedy, an Herb or Mineral, for the cure and alleviation of every disease known to such locality, and the Medicine Men of such communities generally know of such Remedies. Every Herb is governed by a Planet, but the highest efficacy of such herbs depends largely upon the time they are gathered, and under the right planetary influence. Medical Astrology deals with the Star Map of Birth from the health standpoint, showing tendencies, weaknesses, the parts of the body most afflicted from birth, the probable degree of vitality, and the times along thru life, under directions, progressions, transits, etc., when accidents, disease and ill-health

are apt to come in the life of the ordinary individual, and the time of the duration of such indisposition, when it may begin, and when it will end in the course of Nature, the quality and nature of the disease, and the planetary aspects be more favorable again for normal health, peace of mind, and freedom from worry and anxiety. In Ancient Times, all Physicians were required to be Medical Astrologers, and to know the Planetary Causes of Disease, and the Philosophy of Disease, before they were permitted to Practice upon, or Treat the Sick. This practice should be revived today, and the subject of Medical Astrology taught in every School of Healing, whether it be in Schools which teach the use of Drugs, or in the Drugless Healing Schools. The First National University of Naturopathy, and the Mecca College of Chiropractic, located at 143 Roseville Ave., Newark, N. J., under the able leadership of their Founder and President, Dr. Frederick W. Collins, A.M., M.D., have already established a Chair of Medical Astrology, and other Schools should speedily follow their example. It is my desire to spend the remaining years of my life visiting the various Schools of Healing over the World, to Lecture, and bring before the Faculties the value of Medical Astrology as an aid in Diagnosis and Prognosis, and to have them establish such study in their Curriculums. In my years of Practice as a Physician, I have, by the use of Astrology, been able to very quickly locate the seat of the disease, the cause of the trouble, the time when the patient began to feel uncomfortable, as based upon the birth data of the patient, and this without even touching or examining the patient, and my intense desire to get this knowledge and wisdom before students and Healers in a classified form, is the reason for this Encyclopaedia, as such knowledge is today in a rather scattered and unclassified condition, and not available for the student unless he spends years in going thru a large library of books on Astrology. When once you have discovered the cause of the disease, and understand its philosophy and the relation of the patient to the great Scheme of Nature, the matter of Treatment I leave to you, and according to the System and Methods you may be using. Read the Books, "Astro-Medicine" by Dr. Duz; "Daath's Medical Astrology"; "Elements of Astrology", by Dr. Broughton; "The Textbook of Astrology", by Dr. Pearce. These books are especially strong along the lines of Medical Astrology. Also, Mr. E. H. Bailey, the Editor of the British Journal of Astrology, has issued a course of brief lessons on Medical Astrology to send out as Mail Order Lessons. Also read the book, "The Prenatal Epoch", by Mr. Bailey, which deals with the Prenatal causes of disease, Congenital Defects, the time of Conception, etc. Medical Astrology is one of the very important Branches of Astrology, and should be carefully and scientifically studied by every student.

In this volume see Cure, Drugs, Healers, Herbs, Map, Medicines, Nativity, Prenatal Epoch, Prognosis, Remedies, Surgeons, Therapeutics, Treatment. Also under each of the Planets see "Drugs", "Pathological", "Remedies", "Therapeutic", "Treatment". "Typical Drugs", etc.

MEDICINES—Medicine—Drugs—Remedial Agents—Medicine As a Profession, etc.—Drugs have a local action on the body, and in order to be remedies must operate on the same organs the disease affects, as each organ has an affinity for a certain drug, whether it be a mineral or herb. (See Chap. V in Pearce's Textbook of Astrology). For a list of the Therapeutic Values of the different Medicines see the Article on Drugs. The names of the various Medicines and Remedies mentioned in this Encyclopaedia will not be listed or mentioned in this Article, and for such see the Articles on Herbs, Metals, Minerals, Poisons, etc., and also see the paragraph on "Typical Drugs" under each of the Planets. The names of drugs, and also their Therapeutic Qualities, are listed alphabetically in this book. Look in the alphabetical arrangement for the subject you have in mind.

Best Time to Take Medicine — When the ☽ is in ♋ or ♓, as these signs are moist and have strong absorbing powers; when the ☽ is on the place of ♃ or ♀ at decumbiture; when ♃ or ♀ are in the Asc.; in a ♀ or ☿ hour. (See "Hours" under Planets).

Care In Taking Medicine — The Star Map of Birth should be carefully studied before giving medicines, to know what organs are especially afflicted, and what dangers there are to combat in the use of drugs. Be careful what medicines are taken when the Asc. has come to the place of Cor Leo by direction, as they are more liable to disturb the heart action.

Cooling Medicines—♄ remedies. They should be taken when the Asc. comes to the place of The Ascelli, or Capricornus. Externally, Ice or Snow, ruled by ♄, may be used. (See Refrigerant).

Dealing In Medicines—♀ ruler of the Profession favors dealing in Medicines, Perfumes, Cordials, Wines, etc., and if ♄ gives testimony, to deal in poisons. (See "Make Good Chemists" under Chemists).

Herbs—Herbs Ruled by the Planets—(See Herbs).

Ill-Health—From Taking Medicines— ♆ influence strong at B.; ♆ afflicted in the 6th H.; ♆ □ or ☍ ♄. (See Narcotics).

Improper Medicines—Injured By— When the lord of the 6th H. is in the 4th H. at B. The 10th H. signifies the medicine given in sickness. The medicines and their nature, and whether they are proper or not, are shown by the 5th H. and its lord. When the lord of the 8th is in the 6th H., there is danger of the Physician giving the native a wrong medicine by mistake. (See "Injured By" under Healers; "Sickness from Poisoning" under Poison).

Medicines Do Little Good—(See "Worse" under Crises; Fatal; Incurable; Relapses; Worse).

Medicines Ruled by Planets — (See Herbs, Metals, Minerals; "Drugs", "Remedies", "Typical Drugs", under each of the Planets).

Metals—(See Metals, Therapeutics).

Minerals—(See Minerals).

Narcotics — Drug Habit — (See Narcotics).

Ointments; Opening Medicines — Physic — Catharsis — (See Physic; "Bowel Disorders" under Yellow).

Pathological Action—Of Medicines and Herbs of the Planets—(See "Pathological Action" under each of the Planets; Pathological).

Physic—(See "Opening Medicines" in this section).

Poisons—(See Poisons).

Practice of Medicine—Success or Failure In — (See "Failures", "Success", under Healers).

Salts—Zodiac Salts—Tissue Remedies —(See "Salts" under Zodiac).

Sickness — The medicine given in is indicated by the 10th H. (See "Improper Medicines" in this section).

Signature—The Law of Signature In Drugs—(See Signature).

Study — Given to the Study of Medicine and Surgery—(See "Practice of Healing" under Healers; Surgery).

Therapeutic Qualities — Of Drugs — (See Herbs; "Therapeutic Qualities" under each of the Planets).

Tonic Medicines—Ruled by the ☉ and ♂. (See Stimulants, Tonics).

When to Give Medicine — (See "Best Time" in this section).

When Not to Give Medicine — When the ☽ is passing thru a Ruminant Sign, thru a sign symbolic of an animal which chews the cud, as ♈, ♉, or ♑. Medicines taken in a ♄ hour tend to do more harm than good. Do not give when the 1st face of ♊ is on the Asc. Emetics are best given when the ☽ is passing thru a ruminant sign, as vomiting is more easily induced at such times. (For further study, see Antipathy; "Chemical Action" under Chemical; Compatability; "Cure of Disease" under Curable; Drugs, Emetics, Explosions; "Curable" under Fits; Incompatibility, Incurable, Moderation; "Medicines" under Obsessions; Opposites, Remedies, Roots, Ruminant, Sympathy, Treatment).

MEDIUM—

Medium Coeli — The M.C. — The Midheaven — Tenth House — (See Tenth House).

Medium Stature — Medium Height — Middle Stature — ☿ indicates people who are of medium height, and also tall and thin; ♈, ♎, ♍, and ♏ give a medium stature; ♍ on the Asc., medium, slender, and well-made; ♓ on the Asc. (See "Mean Stature" under Mean; "Middle Stature" under Middle; Moderate).

Medium Vitality—(See Vitality).

MEDIUMSHIP — Mediumistic—The influences and aspects of ♆ at B., and by dir., are largely responsible for the powers of Mediumship, for good or evil, and whether it is voluntary or involuntary, under control, or irresponsible).

Cases of Mediumship — Birth Data, etc.—See "Medium", No. 966, and also "Suicide", No. 171, both in 1001 N.N.

Dangers Thru Mediumship—♆ affl. in the 12th H. at B.; ♆ ruler of the horoscope, and afflicted; caused by the evil aspects of ♆; ♆ afflicted in the Asc., 10th, 12th, or 6th H.; ♆ affl. in ♍ or ♓; ♆ □ or ☍ ♅, ♄, or the ☽; ♆ ☌, P., □ or ☍ ♂; ♆ prog. in ☌, P., □ or ☍ ♅, and vice versa; ♆ by transit in ☌ the ☽ or ☿ if ♆ is afflicted at B.; the □ or ☍ aspects of ♆ are especially evil; the ☽ or ☿ afflicted by ♆; the ☽ in ♓ and afflicted by ♆; the prog. ☽ ☌, P., □, or ☍ ♆ if ♆ be afflicted at B.; ♅ in the 6th H., and affl. by ♆; ♅ affl. in ♓; ♓ on the Asc. (See Forebodings, Hypnotism, Obsessions, Spirit Controls).

Genuine Mediumship — (See "Voluntary" in this section).

Involuntary — Irresponsible Mediumship — Intermittent — Not Under Control—Undesirable Phases of, and with Vain Fears and Obsessions—♆ □ or ☍ ♅ at B.; the ill-aspects of ♆ to Antares (see Antares); ♆ afflicted in the 12th H.; ♆ ☌ the Asc., and afflicted. (See Clairvoyance, Fears, Obsessions, Prophetic, Spirit Controls).

Voluntary Mediumship — Under Control—Genuine—Responsible—The good aspects of ♆ to ♅, the ☽ or Asc.; ♆ △ the ☽, ♅, ♄, or ☿; the 4° ♓ on the Asc., Mediumship of a high order. (See Pituitary).

MEDULLA—Bulbar—Medullary—

Bulbar Paralysis — ♄ afflicted in ♉; several planets in ♉ in ☌, and afflicted by the □ and ☍ aspects of other planets; ♉ or ♏ on the Asc., and afflicted. (See Brain; "Cord" under Spine). Case of Bulbar Paralysis—See Case One, in Chap. XIII, of Daath's Medical Astrology.

Kidneys — Medullary Substance of — Ruled by ♀ and ♎. (See the Introduction under Kidneys).

Medulla Oblongata—The Lowest Division of the Brain, and the enlarged portion of the Spinal Column in the Cranium—Is located in the Zone of Taurus, and ruled largely by ♉, and affected by the ♏ sign thru reflex action to ♉. (See Occiput). Is also influenced by the ♌ sign, which sign rules the Spinal Cord. Authorities seem to be uncertain at present as to what Planet rules the Medulla. The ☉ and ☽ acting thru the ♏ sign tend to affect the Medulla. (See "Basal Ganglia" under Ganglion).

Medullary Substance—The Medullary and Cerebral Substance and Juices are augmented at the Full ☽, and suffer diminution at the New ☽. The Brain is also smaller at the New ☽. (See "Full", "New", under Moon).

Medullary Substance Inflamed—Neuromyelitis— ☿ afflicted by malefics at B., and by dir.; afflictions in ♌; ♂ af-flicted in ♉ or ♏; ♉ or ♏ on the Asc., and afflicted. (See "Neuritis" under Nerves).

MEDUSA'S HEAD—(See Algol).

MEEK—In Manner—The ☉ Sig. in ♍. (See "Modest" under Manners).

MEERSCHAUM—A Mineral under the rule of ♆. (See "Metals and Minerals" under Neptune).

MEGRIMS — In the Head — (See Migraine).

MELANCHOLY — Melancholia—Melancholic Temperament—Atrabiliary—Vapours—The Nervous Temperament — Saturnine—Black Bile—Blues—Athymia, etc.—The earthy signs ♉, ♍, and ♑ are known as the Melancholic Signs, and people born under these signs are more given to melancholy.

Afflicted with Melancholy—(See Melancholia, Tendency To, in this section).

All Tendencies To—(See "Tendency" in this section).

Appearance—Melancholic Appearance —Sad Appearance—Melancholic Face —Given by ♄, born under ♄, and ♄ rising in the Asc. or M.C., and strong at B.; ♄ ☌ the ☉, ☽, or Asc. at B.; ♄ or ♀ Sig. in ♈; ♄ in ♍; the 2nd face of ♑, or the 5th face of ♒ on the Asc. (See Grave, Pensive, Sad, Serious).

Black Bile—Atrabilarious Attacks— (See "Black Bile" under Bile).

Blood—Melanchoic Blood—The ☽ afflicted in ♍ when the ☽ is the afflicter in the disease.

Blues—Attacks of the Blues — (See "Vapours" in this section).

Bowels—Bowel Disease from Melancholy— ☿ afflicted in ♑.

Death by Melancholy—♄ and ☿ denote death by; ♄ occi. at B., and afflicting the hyleg by dir.; ☿ affl. by ♄ at B., and ☿ holding the dominion of death; ☿ afflicting the hyleg, the Giver of Life, by dir.; ☿ in ♑, and afflicted by ♄, ♃, and the ☽, tending to poor judgment, worry, and bad thinking.

Diseases—Melancholic Diseases—Diseases Which Proceed from Melancholy —A Melancholic Disease—Melancholic Distempers—The ☽ ☌ or ill-asp. ♄ (or ☿ if he be of the nature of ♄) at the beginning of an illness, or at decumb. (Hor'y); the ☽ to the ☌ ☋, a melancholic disease proceeding from Phlegm; ♄ to the ill-asps. his own place by tr. or dir.; ♄ afflictions tend to dry and melancholic diseases; ♄ to the ill-asps. the ☉, ☽, Asc., or hyleg by dir.; lords of the 1st or 6th H., or the ☽ in earthy signs, cause melancholy, or melancholic diseases, such as Agues, Consumptions, and all Chronic diseases. (See "Tendency To" in this section).

Disposition—Melancholic Disposition or Temperament—Also called the Nervous Temperament—Born under strong ♄ influence; ♄ ruler at B., and with ♄ in the Asc. or M.C., and afflicting ☿; ♄ Sig. □ or ☍ the ☽; ♄ Sig. in ♑; ♄ in ♍; ♄ promittor in transit over the radical ☽, or in ill-asp. the ☽ by dir.; the ☽ Sig. in ♍; the ☽ Sig. □ or ☍ ♄; ☿ afflicted in ♑; ♉ influence tends to melancholy; the Asc. to the place of

Arcturus. (See Arcturus; "Nervous Temperament" under Temperament; "Tendency", and the various paragraphs in this section).

Dry and Melancholic Distempers—Caused by ♄, and are ♄ diseases; ♄ afflicting the ☉, ☽, Asc., or hyleg by dir. (See "Diseases" in this section).

Face—Melancholic Face—(See "Appearance" in this section).

Fears—(See "Morbid" under Fears).

Fevers—Melancholic Fevers—♄ mixing signification with ♂ in fiery signs at a decumbiture.

Fits of Melancholy—(See "Melancholic Fits" under Fits).

Gout from Melancholy—☿ afflicted in ♑. (See Gout).

Habitual Melancholy—♄ ruler and afflicted; ♑ on the Asc.

Health—Melancholic About the Health—(See Hypochondria).

Imagination—A Melancholic Imagination—(See "Melancholy" under Imagination).

Inclined to Melancholy—(See Disposition, Tendency, in this section).

Joy—Life Robbed of Its Joy—(See Joy).

Little—A Little Melancholic—☿ Sig. ⚹ or △ the ☽, and espec. if ☿ partake of the nature of ♄.

Low Spirits—(See Low).

Melancholia—Vapours—Much Depression of Spirits—Gloominess—(See Disposition, Tendency, in this section; Dejected, Depressed, Despair, Despondency, Gloom, Grave, Hypochondria; "Low Spirits" under Low; Worry, etc.).

Melancholic Temperament—(See "Disposition" in this section).

Much Melancholy—The Patient Is Melancholic—The ☉ or ☽ to the ☌ or ill-asp.; the ☽ in ♐, ☌, P., ☐ or ☍ ♄ (or ☿ if he be of the nature of ♄) at the beginning of an illness, or at decumb. (Hor'y); ♄ Sig. in ♑; ♄ ruler of the year at the Vernal Equi., and afflicting the ☉ or ☽, much melancholy everywhere, sadness, bereavement, and sorrow. (See Prevalent; "Sorrow" under Public).

Nervous Temperament — The Melancholic Temperament — (See "Disposition" in this section).

Patient Is Afflicted—With Melancholy—(See "Much Melancholy" in this section).

Religious Melancholy— (See "Melancholia" under Religion).

Repining—(See Regretful, Repining).

Rheumatism — From Melancholy— ☿ affl. in ♑. (See Gout, Rheumatism).

Sadness—Sorrow—Melancholy From—(See "Much Melancholy" in this section; Sadness, Sorrow).

Signs—The Melancholic Signs of the Zodiac—The earthy signs ♉, ♍, ♑.

Temperament—The Melancholic Temperament—(See "Disposition" in this section).

Tendency to Melancholy—The ☉, ☽, or ☿ in ♑, and afflicted; the ☉ hyleg, and to the ☌ or ill-asp. ♄ by dir.; the ☉ or ☽ afflicted in earthy signs; the ☉

or ☽ in the 12th H., and affl. by the ☌, ☐, or ☍ ♄; the ☉ in ♒ and afflicted by ♄; the ☉ or ☽ to the ☌ ♄ ☊; the ☽ afflicted in ♍ or ♑; the ☽ to the ☌ or ill-asp. ♄ by dir.; the ☽ in ♍ in partile asp. the Asc.; the prog. ☽ to the ☌ or P. ♄; the ☽ ☌ ♄ in the Asc., and in an earthy sign; the ☽ and ☿ ☐ or ☍ ♄; ☿ afflicted in ♑; ♄ ruler of the horoscope; caused by ♄ influence and afflictions; ♄ ☌, P., ☐ or ☍ the ☉, ☽, or ☿; ♄ in the Asc. or M.C.; ♄ in the 12th H. in ☌ the ☉ or ☽; ♄ affl. in the 1st H., melancholic, and with many sorrows; ♄ in ♉, ♍, or ♑, in partile asp. the Asc.; the afflictions of ♄ to the hyleg and mental ruler denote death by melancholy; ♄ ☌ the Asc. by dir.; ♄ in the 3rd or 9th H., and afflicted; ♄ ruler of the Asc.; ♄ in ♎, ☌, ☐, or ☍ the Asc. by dir., and ♄ ruler of the 1st H. at B.; signified by ♄ in ♈ when ♄ is the afflicter in the disease; ♄ Sig. in ♑; ♄ afflicted in ♉; ♄ in ♈, ♉, ♍, ♏, or ♑, and affl. the ☉, ☽, ☿, Asc., M.C., or hyleg; ♄ prog. ☌ or ill-asp. ☿, or vice versa; ♄ by tr. ☌ or ill-asp. the ☉, ☽, ♃, ♀, or ☿; ♄ to his own bad aspects by dir.; fixed stars of the nature of ♄ ascending at B.; ♄ in the 12th H.; ♄ in ♌ in bad asp. the ☽; ♄ or ☊ in the Asc. or M.C., and with ♑ on the Asc.; the ♄ sign ♑ on the Asc. or 6th H.; ♃ Sig. ☌ the ☉ and the ☉ ill-dignified; ♃ Sig. ⚹ or △ ♄; ♃ affl. in ♎, due to deficient Adrenal secretion (see Adrenal); ♃ affl. in ♍ or ♑; ♃ in ♒ and affl. by ♄; ♀ affl. by ♄; ♀ affl. in ♑; ♀ in ♓ and affl. by ♄; ☿ in the 6th or 12th H., ☌ or ill-asp. ♄; ☿ affl. in ♌; caused by ☿ when the dominion of death is vested in him; ☿ ☐ or ☍ ♄ from common signs or ♑; ☿ in the 1st H., and affl. by ♄; fixed stars of the nature of ☿ cause melancholy; afflictions in ♍, and a ♍ disease; Asc. to the ☌ Rigel, Arcturus, Orionis, Deneb, or North Scale; ♉, ♍, ♑ on the Asc.; the Asc. to the ☌, ☐, or ☍ ♄ by dir., and ♄ occi. at B.; lord of the Asc. in the 8th H., and afflicted; a ♎ disease, as this is the exalted sign of ♄; caused by the star Dorsa Leonis, the Lion's Back; the 27° ♊ on the Asc.; the 12° ♋ on the Asc., melancholic and taciturn; the 20° ♍ on the Asc., a melancholic fate; the 30° ♍ on the Asc.; the 2nd, 8th, 13th, or 30° ♎ on the Asc.; the 3rd decan. of ♑ or ♒ on the Asc. Case—Of Melancholy—See Figures 12 and 25 in the book, "Message of the Stars" by the Heindels. (See Death, Diseases, Disposition, and the various paragraphs in this section).

Treatment of Melancholy—Blue, the color of ♀, has a soothing effect upon a melancholic person, and to live and study in a room with blue colorings. (See Blue). The best way to prevent melancholy is to seek Truth, have an understanding of the Universe, its plan, about the Secret Mysteries, to Know Yourself, and how to rule and shape your destiny, and to find your true calling in life, and do your work. This entails study and research along Occult, Mystical, and Metaphysical lines. You must find the God in you, and discover your Higher Self, conquer your lower nature, strike at the source of the evil in your nature and tear it out of your heart, and fight daily the battle against evil, depression, failure, and be optimistic. Advanced and enlightened Souls are not given to melancholia, but know how to conquer the conditions of their environment, rise above, and not be affected by them in an adverse manner. There are many Books, and Systems of Teaching, which will bring you this Light, and these you will find for yourself when you are ready for them. "When the Pupil is ready, the Teacher appears", is an Occult Maxim. Medicines and lines of physical treatment do not cure Melancholy, and if you do not relieve the cause, and get your Understanding broadened and enlightened, you will not make much progress. Keep your Personality, or Lower Mind, under control, and let your Ego, your Spirit, your Higher Mind, which is Divine, rule you. Know first your Star Map of Birth, your tendencies, your weak and strong points, and thus know what the plan of God over you is for the present life, then keep down the evils of your Map, let the good in you predominate, and do the work to which you have been called. (See Character, Destiny, Fate, Horoscope, Map, Nativity, Star Map).

Vapours — Vapors—The Blues—Low Spirits—Hysteria—The ☽ to the ☌ or ill-asp. ♄ by dir. or transit; ♄ in ♈ or ♌; signified by ♄ in ♈ when ♄ is the afflicter in the disease; ♄ to the evil aspects his own place by direction. (See "Tendency" in this section). For further influences, and collateral study along this line see Anguish, Anxiety, Brooding, Chaotic, Delusions, Discontent, Disgrace, Distress, Ennui, Expression, Fears, Fretfulness, Grief, Hallucinations, Helplessness, Hope, Ideas, Illusions, Imaginations, Introspection, Irritable, Look (see "Downward Look" under Look); "Mind Threatened", "No Peace of Mind", under Mind; Miserable, Moods, Morose, Mournful, Negative, Obsessions, Peevish, Pensive; "Quality of the Disease" under Quality; Restless, Reverses, Ruin, Serious, Suicide, Suffering, Stone, Trouble, Unhappy, Worry, Wretched.

MELTING—Of the Tissues—(See Adhesions, Ankylosis; "Heat" under Mars).

MEMBERS—Of the Body—

Brevity Of—A ♍ influence. (See Brevity; "Short Limbs" under Limbs; "Body" under Short).

Conformity—In the Members—(See Beautiful, Comely, Handsome, Harmony, Well-Proportioned).

Disease—The Members, or Parts of the Body Affected by Disease, or Other Affliction—The Member, or Part, apt to be so afflicted is shown by the Sign in which the Significator of the disease is placed. (See "Locating the Disease" under Diagnosis; Organs; "Afflicted Parts" under Parts).

Generation—Members of—Diseases of —(See Generation, Genitals, Privates, Regeneration, Reproduction, Secrets, Sex, etc.).

Long Members—(See "Long" under Arms, Bones, Hands, Legs, Thighs; also see Tall).

Missing Members—(See "Armless" under Arms; "Missing" under Forearm, Legs; "No Hands" under Hands).

Short Members—(See "Brevity" in this section).

Virile Members—(See Strong, Virile).

Weak Members—(See Weak).

MEMBRANES—Membranous—Tunics—

Affected—The planet ♅ in the different signs tends to affect, or rule, the membranes of the sign ruling such part. Thus ♅ in ♈ rules and affects the membranes of the Brain; ♅ in ♋ rules and affects the membranes of the stomach, etc. (See "Membranes" under the various organs and parts of the body).

Brain—Membranes of—(See "Membranes" under Brain; Meninges).

Deposits—Membranous Deposits—(See Croup).

False Membranes—(See Croup, Diphtheria).

Mucous Membranes—(See Mucous).

Respiratory Membranes—(See Breath, Bronchial, Lungs, Pleura).

Sacs—Membranous Sacs—(See Cysts).

Serous Membranes—(See Serous).

Spinal Cord—Membranes of—(See Spine).

Synovial Membranes—(See Synovial).

Tunics—(See Tunics). For the inflammations and diseases of the membranes of the various parts, and organs of the body, such as of the Bowels, Eyes, Head, Heart, Lungs, Nose, Stomach, Throat, etc., see "Membranes" under the part, or organ, you have in mind. (See Cells, Exudations, Peritoneum, Tissues).

MEMORY—The Retentive Faculty of Mind—Recollection—The Memory is ruled by ♄ and ☿, but principally by ☿. Also ruled by the ☉. A ♄ person has a strong memory for injuries done him, as malice and revenge are ♄ traits. In the Hindu System of Astrology the 1st H. rules the Memory.

All Defects In—☿ diseases and afflictions to ☿.

Amnesia—Loss of Memory for Words —☿ afflicted by ♄ and the ☽, and ☿ in no aspect or relation to the Asc.; ☿ affl. in ♈; ☿ combust, and afflicted by ♄ and the ☽, and also setting in the West, out of dignity, and in a weak sign; Subs at AT. (See Forgetful, Impaired, and the various paragraphs in this section).

Defective Memory—☿ badly afflicted at B., and by dir.; Subs at AT and AX. (See the various paragraphs in this section).

Dual Personality—Many planets in double-bodied signs at B., and such signs also on the angles; ☿ in a double-bodied, or bicorporeal sign, as ♊, ♐, or ♓, and afflicted by ♄ and the ☽. The influence of ♄ is to restrain the mind when afflicting ☿, and to limit the mental faculties, and to cause disturbances of, and an unbalanced mental state. (See Double-Bodied, Dual, Personality).

Forgetfulness — Defective Memory — Poor Memory — ☿ alone having dominion over the mind, and ill-disposed; ☿ Sig. ☌ the ☉, combust; a ☿ disease, and with ☿ weak, ill-dignified, and badly afflicted at B., in ☐ or ☍ the ☽, and in no aspect with the Asc.; ☿ afflicted in ♓; ☿ affl. in ♏, carelessness and forgetfulness of Nature's requirements, and to be neglectful of the body, as in eating, habits, bowel movements, etc.; the ☽ ☐ or ☍ ☿, and in no aspect the Asc.; ♄ ☐ or ☍ ☿; a ♓ disorder, and with ☿ afflicted in ♓, and ♓ produces ailments thru forgetfulness and carelessness. (See Carelessness; "Fails In" under Examinations; "Incapable" under Learning; "Shallow" under Mentality; "Weak Mind" under Mind).

Identity — Loss of — Disorientation — (See Identity).

Impaired Memory — ☿ in mutable signs or cadent houses, and afflicted by malefics; ☿ affl. by the ☽, ♄, and ♃, and in no aspect to the Asc.; the ♓ element strong in the nativity.

Inhibited — The Memory Inhibited — Never Had Any Memory — No Trace of a Memory — ☿ in ♊, ☌ the ☉ or ♂, and in ☐ the ☽, and ☿ in no aspect to the Asc. and benefics.

Lack of Memory — (See Inhibited, No Memory, Poor, in this section).

Little or No Memory — Case of a Female — This case is written up, with birth data, in Chap. VIII in Daath's Medical Astrology.

Loss of Memory — (See "Amnesia" in this section).

Mindful of An Injury — Never Forgets An Injury — (See Enmity, Hatred, Jealousy, Malice, Revenge, Treachery).

Never Had Any Memory — (See "Inhibited" in this section).

Poor Memory — Forgetful — Defective Memory — (See "Forgetfulness", and the various paragraphs in this section).

Retentive Memory — The ☽ strong at B., dignified and well aspected, and espec. when in good asp. to ☿ and the Asc.; ♃ ☌ or good asp. ☿; ☿ strongly posited and well aspected at B.; the ♋ sign strong at B., and free from malefic afflictions. (See Genius, Intellect; "Good" under Judgment; Learning, Mathematical; "Quickened" under Mentality; "Good Mind" under Mind; Reading, Scholar, Study; "Wonderful" in this section).

Weakened Memory — ☿ weak and afflicted at B., in evil asp. the ☽, and in no relation to the Asc., and also not fortified by benefics; ☿ ☌, P., ☐, or ☍ ♄; ♆ ☌ or ill-asp. ♄, and also with ☿ out of dignity and afflicted; ♆ ☐ or ☍ ☿. (See Forgetful, Impaired, in this section).

Wonderful Memory — Case — See "De" (Mr. H. De), No. 266 in 1001 N.N. (See "Retentive" in this section).

Words — Loss of Memory for Words — (See "Amnesia" in this section). For collateral study see Apathy, Chaotic, Confusion, Dull, Idiocy, Imbecile, Insanity; "Clouded Mind", "Weak Mind", under Mind.

MEN — Conditions Which Affect Adult Males — The ☉ rules the male in adult Nativities, and the ☽ and ♀ in the female. Many of the planetary influences affecting adult males are also given under "Male", but for convenience of reference the conditions listed here are especially referred to in the Textbooks of Astrology as having to do with Men. (See the various paragraphs under Father, Husband, Male). See the following subjects in the alphabetical arrangement when not more fully considered here—

Accidents to Men — Or Males — (See "Accidents" under Male).

Addicted to Women — Fond of Females — The ☉ Sig. in ♋, ♑, or ♓; ♄ Sig. ☌ ♀; ♃ Sig. in ♋; ♃ Sig. in ☐ near Oculus Taurus (see Oculus Taurus); ♂ Sig. ☌ ♀; ♂ Sig. in ♉, ♌, ♎, or ♓; ☿ Sig. in ♉, ♏, or ♓. (See Amorous; "Free Love" under Free; "Low Company" under Low; "Loose Morals" under Morals; "Passional Excesses" under Passion; Fascinating, Harlots, Women, in this section).

Apathy Of — Free from Passion — (See Apathy, Bachelors, Celibacy; "Anchorite" under Husband; "Indifferent" under Marriage; "Free from Passion" under Passion).

Bachelors; Baldness;

Barrenness — (See Barren, Impotent).

Beard; Blindness — Hurts to the Eyes — (See Left Eye, Right Eye, under Male).

Brain In — Ruled by the ☉. (See Brain).

Constitution — Strong Constitution — The ☉ in a fiery sign and well-aspected; the ☉ in a strong sign and house, and well-aspected by ♂ and benefics. The ☉ in a weak sign, and afflicted tends to a weak constitution. (See "Good", "Strong", "Weak", under Constitution, and note especially the ☉ influences).

Crippled from Birth — (See "Crippled" under Birth).

Danger to Men — The ☉ afflicted by malefics at B., and by dir.

Death by Hand of Man — (See "Hand of Man" under Man).

Death of Men — Many Deaths Among Men — Great Mortality Among — The ☉ ☌ or ill-asp. ♄ at the Vernal Equinox, and ♄ lord of the year; ♄ passing thru a fixed sign; ♄ in a fixed sign at the Vernal, or a Solar Ingress, and afflicting the lord of the year; ♂ in ♎ at the Vernal, and lord of the year; Comets appearing in ♊. (See "Death" under Father, Husband, Male; "Young Men" under Young).

Debauched; Debility of Men — Men Debilitated — ♆ in the Asc. at B.; ♀ in a masculine sign, and ♂ in a feminine sign at B., and both occidental. (See Debility, Impotent).

Deportment of Men — (See the various subjects listed under Conduct).

Depraved; Desires — The Desires Unnatural, Obscene, and Impure — (See Desires, Lewd, Obscene, Perversions, Shameless, Unnatural, etc.).

Detriment to Men—(See "Danger" and the various paragraphs in this section).

Disease In Men — (See "Disease In" under Male).

Diseases Peculiar to Men—(See Penis, Perversions, Scrotum, Testes, Urethra, Venereal).

Drink; Drunkenness; Effeminate;

Eunuchs; Excellent Men—Death of—(See "The Great" under Great; Kings, Nobles, Princes, Rulers).

Excesses In—(See Eating, Excesss, Gluttony, Intoxication; "Passional Excesses" under Passion; Sports, etc.).

Excessive—Excessive Virile Members —(See Virile).

Eyes—Blindness In—Hurts To—(See "Blindness" in this section; "Males" under Eyes).

Famous Men—Death of—(See Famous, Great; "Excellent" in this section).

Fascinating — To Women—Favorites with Women—Has the Love and Favor of Women—Seeks Female Company— Fond of Women — Successful by the Help of Women, etc.—Men born under the strong influence of ♀; ♀ in the Asc. or M.C., or in ☌ the ☉ or ☽ at B.; ♀ Sig. ☌ ☿; ♀ Sig. ✶ or △ the ☽; ♀ on the Meridian at B., and well-aspected; the ☉ Sig. ✶ or △ the ☽; the ☉ ☌ ♀; the ☽ ✶ or △ ♀; the ☽ Sig. in ♎; the ☽ on the Meridian, or culminating, and well aspected by ♀; ♄ Sig. ☌ ♀; ♃ Sig. ☌ the ☽ or ☿; ♃ Sig. ✶ or △ ♀; ♂ Sig. in ♎, much beloved by women, but also ruined by them; ♂ Sig. ☌ ☽; ♂ Sig. in ♎, but generally to his prejudice or undoing; ♂ Sig. ✶ or △ ☽, receives much assistance from females; ♂ Sig. ✶ or △ ♀, exerts his fascinating influence over females to the utmost. (See "Addicted To" in this section; Love Affairs).

Female Company — Seeks Female Company—(See Addicted, Fascinating, in this section).

Female Friends — Has Many — (See 'Fascinating" in this section).

Females — Grief Thru — Ill-Health Thru Associations With—Injured By— Poisoned By—Treachery By, etc.—(See Grief, Hate, Health, Injured, Poison, Treachery, in this section).

Firmness—Lacking In—(See "Resolution" in this section).

Fruitfulness In—(See Fruitfulness; "Fruitful" under Husband).

Genitals of Men—Diseases and Injuries To—(See Genitals, Penis, Testes, Venereal).

Gonorrhoea—Among Men—(See Gonorrhoea).

Good Health—For Men—The ☉ strong and well aspected at B. (See "Good Health" under Males).

Great Men—Death of—(See Great).

Grief—Thru Women—The ☽ to the ill-aspects her own place by dir.; the ☽ or ♀ to the ☌ ♄, ♅, or ♂ by dir. (See "Females" in this section).

Habits—In Men—(See the various subjects under Conduct, Habits).

Handsome Man — ♀ Sig. ✶ or △ ♂. (See Commanding, Handsome).

Harlots—Liable to Associate With— May Associate with Low Women—♀ ill-dignified at B.; ♀ afflicted by ♂; ♂ Sig. ☌ ♀. (See Harlots, Lewd, Licentiousness; "Low Company" under Low; Lust, Obscene, Passion, Perversions, Sensuality, Shameless, Wanton).

Hated—By a Female—(See "Females" under Hate).

Head—Affections of—(See "Men Suffer" under Head).

Health—Good or Bad Health for Men —(See Constitution, Good Health, Injured, in this section).

Health Injured—Thru Women—Lord of the 6th in the 5th or 7th H. (See "Injured" in this section; Debauchery; "Passional Excesses" under Passion; Venereal, Venery).

Health Not Bad—Not Exceptionally Bad—The ☉ afflicted by both ♄ and ♂, as any aspect of ♂ to the ☉ helps to increase the vitality and resistance. (See "Bad" under Health).

Health Worse—The Health Worse Than Otherwise—An afflicting malefic elevated above the ☉ at B. tends to more ill-health than if the ☉ were elevated above the malefic. (See "Ill-Health" under Males).

Heart—The Heart In Man—Ruled by the ☉. The ☉ afflicted in ♌ tends especially to heart diseases and disturbances in men. (See "Heart Disease" under Male).

Hermaphrodites — In Males—A Mixture of Sex In Males—♂ and ♀ both in masculine signs, apt to cause such manifestations. (See Hermaphrodite; Virile).

Hips—(See "Men" under Hips).

Hurts—To Men—The ☉ afflicted at B., and by dir., by ♅, ♄, or ♂. (See "Accidents" under Male).

Hyleg—In a Male—The ☉ is to be taken as Hyleg when strong, and not badly afflicted. Also ♃ or the Asc. can be taken. (See Hyleg).

Ill-Health — For Men — (See "Ill-Health" under Male; "Public Health Bad" under Public; "Injured", and other paragraphs in this section).

Ill-Health Thru Women—(See "Health Injured", "Injured", in this section; Venereal).

Impotence; Impurity—Among Men— (See Lewd, Licentious; "Loose Morals" under Morals; Obscene, Passion, Perversions, Shameless, etc.).

Infirmities Among — (See "Public Health Bad" under Public).

Injured Thru Women—The Health Injured—Meets with Bodily Injury or Violence By—Lord of the 6th H. in the 5th or 7th H., the health injured; the ☽ to the place of Hydra's Heart (see Hydra's Heart); the ☽ in the 12th H. in ♏ or ♑, and afflicted; ♂ ☌ or ill-asp. the ☽ or ♀ at B., and by dir.; ♂ Sig. in ♌ or ♎; ♀ afflicted in the 1st H.; caused by fixed stars of the nature of ♀. (See Harlots, Jealousy; "Passional Excesses" under Passion; "Poison Death" under Poison; Treachery).

Left Eye—Blindness In, or Injury To —(See "Left Eye" under Male).

Left Side of Body—In Males—Afflictions To—(See "Males" under Left).

Length of Life—(See "Length of Life" under Males).

Licentious—Men Highly Licentious, Obscene, and Lustful—Sex Gratification In Men—If the Luminaries be in feminine signs in a male horoscope, and also ♀ in a female sign and afflicted by ♂, men will tend to be wanton, licentious, soft, and seek connection contrary to nature, but in privacy, and not openly. If ♂ also be in a feminine sign, and afflicting ♀, men will tend to shamelessness and publicity in their sex practices. Mars with ♀ alone and ♄ absent. Mars rules the passions in men, and ♀ in women. Venus in a feminine sign alone and afflicted by ♂. (See Deviations, Exhibitionism, Lasciviousness, Lewd, Licentiousness, Lust, Obscene; "Violence" under Passion; Perversions, Sadism, Scandalous, Sex, Shameless, Sodomy, Unnatural, Wanton, etc.).

Long Life—For Men—The ☉ well-aspected in a fiery sign. (See "Long Life" under Males).

Loved by Females—(See "Fascinating" in this section).

Low Women—May Associate With—(See "Harlots" in this section).

Lustful—(See Lascivious, Lewd, Lust; "Licentious" in this section).

Maimed—(See "Males" under Maimed).

Male In Family—Death of—(See "Death" under Father, Husband, Male, Son).

Male Organ—Disorders of—Injuries To—(See Genitals, Penis).

Manly—Sober—(See Honest; "Manly and Sober" under Manners; Noble, Upright).

Manners—(See Manners).

Marriage—(See Fiance, Husband, Love Affairs, Marriage, Marriage Partner, Wife).

Men—Death at the Hands of Men—(See "Hand of Man" under Man).

Men In Power—(See Great, Kings, Rulers; "Power" in this section).

Middle Life—Men At Middle Life—(See Middle Life).

Mortality Among—(See "Death of Men" in this section; "Just Men" under Mortality).

Neck—The Neck Afflicted with Men—(See "Men" under Neck).

Obscenity—Given To—(See Obscene; "Licentious" in this section).

Opposite Sex—Health Suffers By—Injured By—Little Attraction For—(See "Health", "Injured", in this section; Apathy, Bachelors, Celibacy; "Anchorite" under Husband; "Indifferent" under Marriage; Opposite Sex; "Free from Passion" under Passion).

Passion—In Men—Ruled by ♂. For Excess of Passion in Men, or Lack of, see Amorous, Apathy, Celibacy, Excesses; "Free from Passion", "Passional Excesses", under Passion; "Licentious" in this section).

Penis—Male Organ of Generation—(See Genitals, Penis, Urethra).

Perversions—Sex Perversions—(See Deviations, Indecent, Obscene, Perversions, Shameless).

Poisoned—Death by Poison—By the Treachery of Women—(See Poison, Treachery).

Power—Men In Power—(a) Gains Much by Patronage of—♂ Sig. in ✶ or △ the ☉. (b) Incurs Displeasure of—Often Ruined By—Oppressed By—♄ Sig. □ or ☍ ☉; ♃ or the ☽ Sig. ♂ the ☉. (See Judges, Kings, Princes, Rulers). (c) Death of Men In Power—(See "Death" under Great, Kings, Rulers).

Prostate Trouble—(See Prostate).

Recuperation Slow—Or Rapid—(See "Males" under Recuperation).

Regenerative Organs—Reproductive Organs—Diseases of In Men—(See "Genitals" in this section).

Relatives—Men, or Male Relatives—Conditions Affecting—(See "Relatives" under Male).

Resolution—Firmness—Lack of—The ☉ in ♊; ♂ weak and ill-dignified at B.; born under the strong influence of ♀. (See "Mutable Disposition" under Mutable; Negative).

Right Eye—Blindness In—Hurts To—(See "Right Eye" under Male).

Right Side—Of the Body—(See "Left Side" under Left; "Right Side" under Right).

Robust—Men More Robust—(See "Good Health" under Males; Robust).

Ruined by Women—(See "Ruined by Women" under Love Affairs).

Seminal Fluid—Disorders of—(See Semen).

Senility—(See Old Age).

Severe Illnesses—Sharp Illnesses In Men—The ☉ afflicted in fiery signs, but soon over. (See "High Fevers" under Fever; Severe, Sharp).

Sex Gratification—In Men—(See "Licentious" in this section; "Violence" under Passion).

Sex Organs—Diseases of—Injuries To—(See "Genitals" in this section).

Shameless Practices—(See "Licentious, Lustful, Perversions, in this section).

Sharp Illnesses—(See "Severe" in this section; Pernicious, Sharp).

Sober and Manly—(See "Manly and Sober" under Manners; "Manly" in this section).

Sterility In—(See Barrenness).

Stricture of Urethra—(See Urethra).

Strong Constitution—(See "Constitution" in this section, and under Male).

Syphilis; Testicles; Thighs—The Hips and Thighs Affected In Men—(See "Men" under Hips).

Treachery—Suffers Treachery by Women—(See Poison, Tragical, Treachery).

Unnatural Desires—And Practices—(See Desires, Licentious, in this section; Unnatural).

Untimely Death Of—(See "Early Death" under Early; "Death" under Middle Life; Untimely).

Urethra—Disorders of—(See Urethra).

Valiant Men—♂ strong at B., or ruler. (See Bold; "Qualities" under Mars; Warrior).

Varicocele; Venereal Diseases—(See Genitals, Gonorrhoea, Privates, Sex, Syphilis, Venereal).

Violent—In Sex Gratification—Given to Violent Actions—(See Cruel, Sadism; "Shameless Practices" under Shame; Violent).

Virile Members Excessive—(See Hermaphrodite, Virile).

Vitality In—(See "Vitality" under Male; "Good", "Low", under Vitality).

Widowers; Women—Wastes His Money and Substance On—♄ Sig. ✶ or △ ♀. (See Debauched, Dissipation, Expense; "Energies Wasted" under Love Affairs; Opposite Sex, Passion, Prodigal, Venery, etc.). For the various dealings of men with women see in this section,—Addicted To, Fascinating to Women, Females, Grief, Harlots, Hated, Health Injured, Injured Thru Women, Licentious, Marriage, Opposite Sex, Poisoned, Ruined by Women, Treachery, etc.

Worse—The Health Worse—The ☉ afflicted at B., and by dir. (See "Ill-Health" under Males).

Wounds To—(See "Accidents" under Males).

Young Men—Great Mortality Among —(See "Young Men" under Young). For further study along this line see the various paragraphs under Brothers, Father, Females, Grandparents, Husband, Love Affairs, Marriage, Marriage Partner, Son, Uncles, Wife.

MENIDROSIS — Bloody Sweat— (See "Haematidrosis" under Sweat).

MENINGES—Membranes of the Brain —Dura Mater, the Outer Membrane of the Brain and Spinal Cord—(See Brain, Dura Mater; "Cord" under Spine). The Meninges, or Brain Coverings, are ruled by ♅ and the ♋ sign.

Cerebral Meningitis—Inflammation of the Cerebral Meninges—The ☉ or ♅ afflicted in ♈; the ☽ in the 6th H., and much afflicted at B., and by dir., and espec. if ☿ also be afflicted and not in the Asc.; Subs at AT and CP. (See Cerebral).

Cerebro-Spinal Meningitis — (See Brain, Cerebro-Spinal, Dura Mater).

Leptomeningitis—Inflammation of the Pia and Arachnoid Membranes—♅ afflicted in ♈; Subs at AT.

Spinal Meningitis—♅ afflicted in ♌ or ♒; ♌ on the Asc.; a ♌ disease; ♆ ☌ the ☉ and ♄ in ♌, and afflicted by ♅; Subs at AT, AX, CP, and KP. (See Spine). Case of Spinal Meningitis—Birth Data, etc.—See Chap. XIV in Daath's Medical Astrology.

MENKAR—Whale's Jaw—(See Ceti).

MENOPAUSE — The Change of Life — Menses Stopped — (See "Menopause" under Menses).

MENORRHAGIA — (See "Profuse" under Menses).

MENS SANA—(See "Sound Mind" under Mind).

MENSES—The Monthly Flow from the Womb — Menstrues — Periodics — Courses—Catamenia — Feminine Functions, etc.—The Menses are an excrementitious fluid ruled by the ♏ sign. (See Excretion). The Menses begin when the Prog. ☽ reaches the sign and degree opposite to her radical place. This time may be earlier or later in different individuals according to the signs of long or short ascension thru which the ☽ must pass. This is equivalent to the Full ☽, or the 2nd Quarter of the ☽ by progression from her place at the birth of the native. The Change of Life occurs at the progressed Third Quarter of the ☽ from her radical place. (See "Menopause" in this section). The natural female functions are ruled by the ☽. (See Functions, Moon).

Abnormal Menses — (See Imperfect, Irregular, Painful, Profuse, and the various paragraphs in this section).

Absence Of—Arrested—Amenorrhoea —(See Irregular, Never Occur, Suppressed, in this section).

Amenorrhoea — Irregularity or Suppression of the Menses—(See "Absence" in this section).

Change of Life—(See "Menopause" in this section).

Chlorosis—Anaemia In Young Women, and Attended with Menstrual Disturbances—(See Chlorosis).

Courses Overflowing—Copious—(See Flooding, Profuse, in this section).

Delayed—(See "Puberty" in this section).

Deranged Menses — (See "Puberty Weakened", and the various paragraphs in this section).

Difficult and Slow — (See Painful, Slow, in this section).

Disturbances Of — (See "Irregular", and the various paragraphs in this section).

Dysmenorrhoea—(See "Painful" in this section).

Effusion Of — (See Flooding, Hemorrhage, Profuse, in this section).

Excessive—(See Flooding, Hemorrhage, Menorrhagia, Profuse, in this section).

Flooding Hemorrhages—Menorrhagia —Metrorrhagia — Excessive Menses—♂ afflicting ♀, and ♀ also afflicting the ☽; ♀ afflicted in ♏; Subs at PP. (See "Profuse" in this section).

Functions—The Menstrual Functions Disordered—The ☽ hyleg in ♏, and afflicted. (See Irregular, Suppressed, and the various paragraphs in this section).

Hastened—Earlier Manifestation of— (See the Introduction, "Puberty" in this section).

Headache—At Time of Periods—(See "Periodic" under Headache).

Hemorrhage—(See Flooding, Profuse, in this section; "Hemorrhage" under Womb).

Immoderate Discharges—(See Flooding, Hemorrhage, Profuse, in this section).

Imperfect Menstruation—The ☉ in ♏ in evil asp. to ♆, ♅, or ♄; the ☉ in ♉, ♌, or ♒, and afflicted by ♄, ♅, or ♆. (See Irregular, Suppressed, in this section).

Incoordination—At Time of Menses— ♅ afflicted in ♉ or ♏ at B., and especially at times when ♅ is also afflicted by direction, or afflicting planets in ♉; Subs at PP. (See Incoordination).

Irregular Menses—A ♉ and ♏ disease, and afflictions in these signs; the ☽ or ♀ afflicted by ♄; the ☽ □ or ♉ ♀, and ♄ also afflicting ♀; the ☽ to the ill-asps. ♀ by dir., and ♀ in a water sign at B.; the ☽ or ♀ afflicted in ♏; the Prog. ☽ in the sign and degree in ♉ to her place at B., and afflicted by malefics; ♂ in ♏, ♂, or ill-asp. the ☉; ♀ afflicted by ♄; ♀ in ♋ in the 6th H., and afflicted; ♀ in ♋ and afflicting the ☽ or Asc. (See Painful, Suppressed, in this section; "Irregular" under Functions).

Irritating and Painful — (See "Painful" in this section; "Hour Glass Contraction" under Womb).

Lungs—Menstruation Thru the Lungs —(See "Vicarious" in this section).

Menidrosis — Vicarious Menstruation Thru the Sweat Glands — (See "Menidrosis" under Sweat).

Menopause — The End of the Menstrual Life — The Change of Life In Women — Menstruation begins when the ☽ by progression reaches the sign and degree in ♉ to her radical place, on her first course around after birth of the native, which is usually about the 14th year of life. The Menses stop, and are discontinued, when the ☽ by progression reaches her 3rd Quarter from her radical place, on her second course around thru the 12 Signs. The beginning or ending of the Menses may be earlier or later in life according to the nature of the signs thru which the ☽ passes, whether they be signs of long or short ascension. (See "Ascension" under Long). The Menopause takes place at from the 43rd to 48th years of life.

Menorrhagia — An Excessive Menstrual Flow — Metorrhagia — (See Flooding, Profuse, in this section).

Menstrual Trouble—Deranged Menses —Catamenial Disorders—The ☽ hyleg in ♏, and afflicted; ☽ diseases; the ☽ afflicted at B., and by dir.; the ☽ affl. by ♀; the ☽ to the ill-asp. ♀ by dir.; the ☽ afflicted in ♉ or ♏; ♂ or ♀ afflicted in ♏; ♂ in ♏ in the 6th H., and afflicted; ♂ in ♏ and afflicting the ☽ or Asc.; a ♏ disease; malefics and afflictions in ♉ tend to by reflex action to the ♏ sign. (See Imperfect, Irregular, Profuse, and the various paragraphs in this section).

Never Occur — Entirely Absent — Menses May Never Occur—♀ afflicted by the ☽ and ♄, and ♀ in a sign of ♄. This may also lead to sterility. (See the ♀ influences under Barrenness).

Nose—Menstruation Thru the Nose— (See "Vicarious" in this section).

Obstruction — Of the Menses — (See Painful, Suppressed, in this section; Obstructions).

Overflowing — Of the Courses — (See Flooding, Hemorrhage, Profuse, in this section).

Painful Menstruation—Irritating— Difficult and Slow—Dysmenorrhoea— Painful Catamenial Discharges — The ☉ or ☽ in ♏, ♂, or ill-asp. any of the malefics as promittors; the ☉ in ♉ and afflicted by one or more malefics; the ☽ □ or ♉ ♀, and ♄ also afflicting ♀; the ☽ in a fixed sign, and espec. in ♏, and afflicted by malefics; ♄, ♂, ♀, or ♀ afflicted in ♏; ♂ afflicting ♀ and ♀ evilly aspected by the ☽; ♀ afflicted in ♏, and especially with ♀ in the 6th H., or ♀ afflicting the ☽ or Asc. (See Imperfect, Restricted, Suppressed, in this section).

Profuse Menses—Excessive—Overflowing — Flooding — Menorrhagia — Metorrhagia— Immoderate and Copious Discharges — Menstrual Effusions — Catamenia Profuse and Weakening — The ☉ in ♉, ♌, ♏, or ♒, and afflicted by any of the malefics; afflictions in the fixed signs, and espec. in ♏; the ☽ afflicted in ♏; the ☽ □ or ♉ ♀; the ☽ to the ill-asps. ♀ by dir., and ♀ in a water sign at B.; the ☽ □ or ♉ ♂; ♂ afflicting ♀ and ♀ also afflicting the ☽; ♂ in ♉ or ♏, and afflicting the ☽ or ♀; ♂ ♂ or ill-asp. the ☽; ♂ in ♏, ♂, or ill-asp. the ☉; caused by ♂ as ♂ rules hemorrhages and rupture of blood vessels; ♀ afflicted in ♏; ♀ afflicting the ☽, and espec. when both are in water signs. (See "Women" under Anaemia; Leucorrhoea, Plethora; "Flooding", "Vicarious", in this section).

Puberty Weakened — Ill-Health At Puberty—The Menses Hastened or Delayed — Sensuous Imaginations At Adolescence — Suppressed Menses— Painful Menses—The ☽ afflicted by ♀; afflictions in ♉ or ♏. The removal of the tonsils in childhood (tonsils ruled by ♉) tends to make the puberty period more disturbed, and also increased disturbances later in parturition and childbirth. (See Puberty, Tonsils; Irregular, Menopause, Suppressed, in this section).

Restricted Menses — ♄ afflicted in ♉ or ♏; ♄ ♂ ♆ in ♉. (See "Suppressed" in this section).

Scanty Menses — (See Imperfect, Irregular, Painful, Suppressed, in this section).

Sick with Menses—In Hor'y Maps if the ☽ is in the 6th H., in ill-asp. to ♀ in ♏, it denotes that the patient is sick with Menses if a female.

Slow and Difficult—The ☽ in a fiery sign at B., the female functions are slow and difficult. (See "Fire Signs" under Fire; "Impeded" under Functions).

Stomach — Hemorrhages Thru — (See "Vicarious" in this section).

Suppressed Menses — Amenorrhoea — Arrested Menses — The Menses Obstructed — Suppression of the Catamenia — The influence of ♄ tends to delay, suppress, and hinder the functions of the body, and espec. when afflicting the ☉, ☽, or Asc. The ☉ and ♄ in ♏ when they are the afflictors in the disease; the ☉ or ☽ in ♏, ☌, or ill-asp. ♄, or any of the malefics; the ☉ in ♉, ♌, or ♒, and afflicted by ♄, ♅, or ♆ as promittors; the ☽ in any of the fixed signs, and especially ♏, and afflicted by ♄, ♅, or ♆; the ☽ affl. by ♀; the ☽ or ♀ affl. by ♄; the ☽ □ or ☍ ♀, and ♄ also afflicting ♀; ♄ affl. in ♏; ♀ in the 6th H., and affl. by ♄; ☿ affl. in ♏, and espec. when he is afflicted by ♄, or is of the nature of ♄; many planets in fixed signs at B. (See Imperfect, Irregular, Never Occur, Painful, Restricted, in this section).

Tonsils — Removal of In Childhood Disturbs the Menses at Puberty and In Later Life—(See "Puberty" in this section).

Vicarious—Vicarious Menstruation—The Menses Thru Some Other Passage Than the Womb—Menstrual Effusions—The blood must have an outlet, and when the ♏, or womb sign, is badly afflicted at B., as by ♄ in ♏, the outlet of blood is suppressed thru the womb, and is diverted thru the Nose, Lungs, Stomach, or Sweat Glands. Mars in ♏, and afflicted by ♄ and the ☽, tends to hemorrhage thru the Nose at the time of the period. Afflictions in □ tend to hemorrhage thru the lungs at such times. Afflictions in ♋, hemorrhage thru the stomach. Afflictions which cause vicarious menstruation may also cause death by excessive hemorrhages, and espec. if the afflictions come from the 8th H., the house of death. (See "Hemorrhage" under Lungs, Stomach; "Epistaxis" under Nose; Sweat, Vicarious; "Blood" under Vomiting).

Weakened—The Puberty Weakened—(See "Puberty" in this section).

Young Females — Weakness Incident to Young Females At Adolescence — (See "Females" under Puberty).

MENTAL—Mentally—Mentality—Pertaining to the Mind—This Article, or section, is a part of, and supplementary to the Article on "Mind", but arranged under "Mental" for convenience of reference, as there are so many references in the Textbooks of Astrology as "Mental". For subjects not found in this section see Intellect, Mind, and also look in the alphabetical arrangement for the subject you have in mind. The Cardinal Signs are Mental in Temperament. Mercury has relation to the Mind, and all Mental Diseases. The Mentality is ruled by the Pineal Gland, presided over by ♆.

Abilities—Mental Abilities—Many of these are listed in the Article on Mind, and also in this section. (See Elegant, Examinations, Genius; "Great Abilities" under Great; Learning, Mathematical, Mechanical, Mind, Reading, Scholar, Study, etc. Also look in the alphabetical arrangement for the subject you have in mind).

Abnormal Mental Trouble—♆ afflicted in the 3rd or 9th H., and especially when in □ or ☍ to ♄ or ♂ from these houses. (See Abnormal).

Action—Excessive Mental Action—(See "Over-Active Mind" under Active). For the opposite conditions of Mind see Apathy, Dull, Indifferent, etc.

Activity—Mental Activity—An Active Mind—♂ ☌ ☿ gives, and the capacity for hard mental work unless in ♓; the ☽ to the good asps. ☿ by dir., and ☿ strong at B.; the signs ♊, ♍, and ♐ all tend to great mental activity, and this activity is greatly increased if the ☽ or ☿ be aspected by ♅ or ♂. (See "Active Mind" under Active; Effervescent; "Mental Energy" under Energy; "Quickened" in this section).

Acute Mentality — (See Activity, Quickened, in this section; "Good" under Mind).

Affliction — Mental Affliction — Affliction of Mind—The ☉ to the ill-asps. ☿ by dir., loses interest in studies, and is averse to learning for the time; the ☉ or ☽ to the ☌ or ill-asps. ♄; the ☽ to the ☌ or ill-asps. the ☉ or ♄ by dir., afflicted in mind and body; ♆ afflicted in the 9th H.; ♄ passing over the place of the radical ☽, or ♄ at a Solar Rev. ☌ the ☉ or ☽. (See Anguish, Distress, Disturbances, Infirmities, in this section; "Mental Afflictions" under Affliction; Examinations; "Affliction of Mind", "No Peace of Mind", "Troubled In Mind", and other paragraphs under Mind).

Anguish — Mental Anguish — (See Anguish).

Anxiety — Mental Anxiety — (See Anguish, Anxiety, Cares, Fears, Worry).

Arrested Mental Powers—Retarded—Inhibited — The ☉ or ☽ in the 6th or 12th H., and afflicted by malefics; ♃, ♏, or ♑ on the Asc.; the malefics are usually closely associated; ♅, ♄, or ♂ in ☌ or ☍ in fixed signs; rays, or bodies of malefics, are in or directed upon the 5th, 6th, or 12th Houses, or their cusps, or to the ascending degree; many planets in ♍, and the 6th or 12th H. These same influences may also retard the growth of the body, or cause deformities, dwarfed conditions, hunchback, etc. (See Arrested, Backwardness, Deformities, Dwarfed; "Mind" under Growth; Humpback (see Spine); Idiocy, Imbecility, Insanity; "Weak Mind" under Mind; Childlike, Deficiency, Derangement, Retarded, Weak, Weakened, in this section).

Bad Mental Traits — (See "Undesirable" under Mind).

Blindness—From Mental Exertion, or Too Much Reading and Study — (See "Mental Exertion" under Blindness).

Breakdown Mentally — (See "Brain Fag" under Brain; "Mind" under Exercise; "Over-Exertion" under Exertion; "Mind" under Fatigue; Insanity, Reading, Study, etc.).

Chaotic Mental States—(See Chaotic).

Childlike Mentality—Mental Suppression — Never Grew Up — Case — (See "Mind" under Children).

Clouded Mentality—(See Clouded).

Combative — (See Anger, Choleric, Quarrelsome; "High Temper" under Temper; etc.).

Complaints—Mental Complaints—(See the various paragraphs in this Article, and also under Faculties, Intellect, Mind, Perception, Reason, etc.).

Confusion — Mental Confusion — Clouded Mind — Chaotic — Mixed Ideas, etc. — (See "Mental Chaos" under Chaotic; Clouded, Confusion; "Dreamy Mind" under Dreams; Ideas, Memory; "Absent-Minded" under Mind).

Conservation — Of Mental Powers — (See Conservation).

Craziness — Mental Deficiency — (See "Deficiency" in this section; Insanity, Madness, Mania).

Curable Mental Diseases — (See "Curable" under Brain; Conspicuous, Curable, Epilepsy, Incurable, Insanity).

Death — From Mental Disorders — (See "Death" under Epilepsy, Madness, Melancholy).

Debility — Mental Debility — (See "Mental Debility" under Debility; "Weak Intellect" under Intellect; "Debility" under Mind).

Decanates and Mentality — (See Decanates).

Defects — Mental Defects — (See "Deficiency" in this section; "Foolish Mind" under Foolish; Idiocy, Imbecility, Insanity; "Weak Mind" under Mind).

Deficiency — Mentally Deficient — The Mind Afflicted — The affliction of ♄ to the 3rd H., ♄ in the 3rd, or afflicting the ruler of the 3rd, is usually at the bottom of mental deficiency. Mercury and the ☽ may be strong at the same time, and also the ☉ or Asc. not afflicted. Also the water signs are usually on the 3rd H., or intercepted in this house, and containing malefics. Venus is often afflicted by the □ or 8 of ♄ or ♂. The Mutable Signs are often involved, and espec. the 22° of the Mutables; ♅ in the 3rd H., and afflicted, tends to; ♄ and ♂ afflicting the cusp of the 3rd H.; the ☉ ruler of the 3rd H., in ♓, and afflicted by ♄. Cases — See Chap. VIII, in Daath's Medical Astrology; also see "Mentally Defective", No. 408, and "Defective Mentally", No. 670, both in 1001 N.N. (See Idiocy, Imbecility, Insanity; "Diseased Mind", "Weak Mind", under Mind; Arrested, Derangement, Unbalanced, in this section).

Demoniac — Mental Obsession — (See Demoniac, Insanity, Obsessions; Spirit Controls).

Depression — Mental Depression — (See Dejected, Depressed; "Low Spirits" under Low; Melancholy, etc.).

Derangement — Mental Derangement — ☿ and the ☽ weak at B., and unconnected with each other or the Asc.; the ☽ hyleg at B., and to the ♂ or ill-asps. ♄ by dir.; ♃ to the ill-asps. ☿ by dir., and ☿ weak and afflicting at B.; ♈ denotes, and afflictions in ♈; cardinal signs on the cusp the 6th H.; the 30° ♍ on the Asc. Temporary mental derangement may be caused by the ☽ being in the 6th H. at B., and much afflicted at B., and by dir., and especially if ☿ also be afflicted, not in the Asc., or connected with the Asc. or ☽. (See Deranged, Epilepsy, Fears, Hallucinations, Hypochondria, Idiocy, Imaginations, Insanity, Madness, Mania; "Diseased Mind" under Mind). Case — See Chap. XIII, in Daath's Medical Astrology.

Desirable Mental Traits — (See "Desirable" under Mind).

Destructive — Mental Destructiveness — (See Destructiveness).

Development — The Mental Development Arrested, Obstructed, Precocious, Premature, etc. — (See Arrested; "Mind" under Growth; Incomplete, Precocious, Premature, Prodigies; "Suppressed" in this section).

Deviations — Deviation of the Mental Faculties — (See Aversions, Deviations).

Disabilities — Mental — ☿ diseases and afflictions to ☿ at B., and by dir. (See "Mental" under Disabilities; Intellect, Mind; the various paragraphs in this section).

Diseases — Mental Diseases — Mental Disorders — Danger of — Causes of — The ☉ afflicted in the 6th H., and with ☿ also weak and afflicted at B.; the ☽ afflicted by ♅; the ☽ afflicted by ☿; the ☽ and ☿ weak and afflicted at B., and unconnected with each other or the Asc.; the ☽ affl. by ♄ at B., and to the ♂ or ill-asp. ♄ by dir.; ♅ in the 3rd or 9th H., and afflicting the ☽ and ☿; ♅ afflicting the 3rd, 6th, 9th, or 12th H.; born under strong and adverse ♄ influence, liable to mental disorders and infirmities; ☿ afflicted at B., and to the ill-asps. the ☽, or the hyleg by periodic revolution, or by dir., often causes mental diseases or Epilepsy; ☿ in the 6th H. in ♊, ♐, or ♓, and afflicted, mental diseases to be feared; ☿ afflicting the ☽, and the ☽ afflicted by the ♂ or ill-asps. the malefics. (See "Mental" under Infirmities; "Diseased Mind" under Mind; the various paragraphs in this Article).

Disorders — Mental Disorders — ☿ has relation to all nervous and mental disorders; ☿ afflicted in ♈; ☿ □ or 8 the Asc. (See "Diseases", and the various paragraphs in this section, and under Mind).

Distress — Mental Distress — (See Anguish, Anxiety, Despondent; "Hopeless" under Hope; Melancholy; "Tormented In Mind" under Mind; Worry).

Disturbances — Mental Disturbances — (See "Irritations", and the various paragraphs in this section, and under Mind).

Effervescent — Effervescent Mental Activity — (See Effervescent).

Ego — Exaggerated Ego — (See Ego).

Energy — Mental Energy — An Active, Energetic Mind — (See "Active Mind" under Active; "Mental" under Energy; "Quickened" in this section). For the opposite conditions of mind see Apathy, Dull, Idle, Lassitude, Lethargy, etc.

Excessive Mental Action — (See "Over-Active Mind" under Active).

Exertion — Mental Over-Exertion, Blindness, and Other Ills From — (See "Mental Exertion" under Blindness; "Over-Exertion" under Exertion; "Mind" under Fatigue).

Extremes — Goes to Mental Extremes — (See Anger, Choleric, Cruel, Extremes, Fury, Ideals, Madness, Riotous; "High Temper" under Temper; Violent, etc.).

Face — The Mental Type Face — (See Decanates; "Narrow" under Face).

Faculties—The Mental Faculties Endangered—Signs of Danger To—The ☽, ☿, and the Asc. in no relation to each other, and at the same time ☿ be afflicted by the ☌ or ill-asp. the malefics. (For other conditions concerning the Faculties see the various paragraphs under Faculties).

Fantasies — Mental Fantasies — (See "Dreamy Mind" under Dreams).

Feeble Mentality—(See Feeble; "Foolish Mind" under Foolish; Idiocy, Imbecile; "Weak" in this section).

Force — Mental Force — The ♈ sign gives much mental force, and with the ☉ or ♂ in this sign in the Asc. (See "Mind" under Force; "Quickened" in this section).

Forces—Conservation of the Mental Forces—(See Conservation).

Freaks; Genius—Mental Genius—(See Genius).

Good Mental Traits—(See "Desirable" under Mind).

Growth—Mental Growth Accelerated or Retarded — (See "Mind" under Growth; Arrested, Quickened, Retarded, in this section).

Healing — Mental Healing — (See "Psychic Healing" under Healers).

Illusions; Imaginations—(See Imagination).

Imbecile; Impaired Mentality — (See "Diseases" under Mind; "Mental Faculties" under Impairment; Affliction, Arrested, Deficiency, Derangement, in this section).

Impediments—Mental Impediments—(See Impediments).

Incapacity—Profound Mental Incapacity — (See Dementia, Demoniac, Idiocy, Imbecile; "Mental Faculties Impaired" under Impaired; Insanity; "Incapable" under Learning; Incompetency, Shallow, Weak, in this section).

Incompetency—Mental—The ☉ ☌ ☿, combust, and in □ or 8 Ħ or ♂, lack of judgment and forethought; the ☽ and ☿ weak, and unconnected with each other or the Asc.; ♄ or the ☽ □ or 8 ☿ at B.; ♃ Sig. □ or 8 the ☽, mind weak and foolish; ♃ □ or 8 ☿. (See Foolish, Forethought, Idiocy, Imbecile, Insanity; "Bad" under Judgment; Incapacity, Shallow, Weak, in this section).

Inferior Mentality — (See Arrested, Dwarfed, Examinations, Foolish, Imbecile, Judgment, Learning; "Weak Mind" under Mind; Incapacity, Incompetency, Weak, and the various paragraphs in this section).

Infirmities—Liable to Mental Infirmities—(See "Mental" under Infirmities; "Diseases", and the various paragraphs in this section).

Ingenious Mentality — (See "Ingenious" under Genius).

Inhibited Mentality — (See Arrested, Retarded, Weak, in this section; "Mental" under Inhibitions).

Intellect — (See Faculties, Intellect, Mind, Perception, Reason, Understanding, and also note the various paragraphs in this section).

Inventive Mentality — (See Genius; "Inventive" under Learning; Mathematical).

Irritability—Mental—(See Irritable).

Irritations—Mental Irritations and Disturbances — Mental Indisposition— Affliction of Mind — Troubled In Mind —The Mind Disturbed—The ☉ or ☽ to the ☌ or ill-asps. ♄ by dir., mental troubles and afflictions; the ☉ to the ill-asps. ☿ by dir.; the ☽ to the ill-asps. Ħ or ♄ by dir., the mind is troubled and anxious; the bad asps. of the ☽ by dir. to the ☉, ♄, Ħ, or the Asc.; Ψ afflicted in the 9th H., danger of mental trouble; caused by the afflictions of Ħ to the ☉, ☽, or ☿; Ħ by transit ☌ ♂, troubled almost to violence; Ħ by tr. in ☌ the ☽ may tend even to a mild form of Idiocy for the time; ♄ ☌ or ill-asp. the ☉, ☽, ☿, or the Asc. by dir.; ♃ to the ill-asps. ☿ by dir.; ♂ in the Asc. at decumb., or the beginning of an illness; the M.C. to the ☌ or ill-asps. the ☽ by dir., troubled in both mind and body; afflictions to ♀ or the ≏ sign, or to any of the airy signs, generally cause discord, inharmony, a troubled mind, and disturbed emotions. (See "Mental" under Afflictions; Anguish, Anxiety, Dejected, Distress, Emotions, Irrational, Irritable, Idiocy; "No Peace" under Mind; Misery, Trouble, Worry, etc.).

Limitations—Mental Limitations— (See Foolish, Idiocy, Imbecile, Limitations, Twelfth House).

Low Mentality — (See "Low Mentality" under Mind).

Melancholic—(See Melancholy).

Mentality Not So Good—When ☿ rises after the ☉, or is combust, but the mind is brightened when ☿ rises before the ☉. (See "Weakened" in this section).

Moisture of the Brain — Mental Diseases Arising From—(See "Brain" under Moisture).

Morbid Deviations — (See "Morbid" under Mind; Morbid, Unsavory).

Never Grew Up—The Mentality of a Child In An Adult—Case—(See "Mind" under Children).

Obsessions—(See Delirium, Demoniac, Insanity, Mediumship, Obsessions, Spirit Controls).

Over-Exertion—Mental—(See "Exertion" in this section; Reading, Study).

Over-Study—(See "Exertion" in this section; "Brain Fag" under Brain; "Eyestrain" under Eyes; "Mind" under Fatigue; Reading, Study).

Perversions—Mental—(See Delusions, Hallucinations, Illusions; "Morbid" under Imaginations; Perversions, etc.).

Pineal Gland—And the Pituitary Body — As Related to the Mentality — (See Pineal, Pituitary).

Planets—The Mental Planets—Ħ and ☿ are termed the Mental Planets. (See Mercury, Uranus).

Poor and Shallow—(See "Shallow" in this section; "Fails In" under Examinations; "Weak" under Mind; "Aversion" under Study).

Powers Retarded—(See Arrested, Inhibited, Retarded, Weak, in this section).

Premature—The Mental Development Premature — (See Genius, Precocious, Premature, Prodigies).

Profound Mentality—Depth of Mind —(See Learning; "Deep and Profound" under Mind; Reading, Scholar, Science, Study; Activity, Quickened, in this section).

Qualities—The Mental Qualities—The Mental Traits—Many of these are considered and listed in this book. Look in the alphabetical arrangement for the subject you have in mind. See the list under Conduct, Expression, Habits, Manners, Mental, Mind, Morals, Temper, Temperament, etc. Especially see the paragraphs, "Desirable Mental Traits", "Undesirable Mental Traits" in the Article on Mind.

Quality—The Mental Quality — (See "Quality of the Mind" under Mind).

Quickened Mentality—Forceful Mentality—Presence of Mind—Quick and Sharp Mind—Forethought—Acuteness of Mind—Good Mental Capacity—Good Mental Energy — Great Discernment, etc.—The ☽ or ♂ to the good aspects ☿ by dir.; the ☽ on the Meridian, or coming to it, and at the same time in ✳ or △ ☿, quick-witted and clever; ☿ rising in the East at B., before the ☉, well-aspected by the ☽, and also in good relation to the Asc.; ☿ rising in ♊, ♍, or ♐, well-aspected by ♃, and espec. in ☌ or P. dec. ♃; ☿ ☌ or good asp. the ☽, and free from the affliction of ♄; ☿ ☌ or any aspect ♂; ☿ Sig. ✳ or △ ♂, presence of mind, and an acute and ready wit; ♅ well-aspected in the 3rd H., the mental faculties are enhanced; ♅ or ♂ well-aspected in ♊ or ♍; ♄ in ♒ and not afflicting the ☉, ☽, ☿, Asc., Hyleg, or M.C.; ♂ well-asp. in ♐ or ♑; ♂ Sig. ✳ or △ ☿, acute and penetrating mind; ♂ to the good asps. ☿ by dir.; the ♋ and ♑ influences strong at B. give an acute mind. (See Comprehension, Discernment, Intellect, Judgment; "Sound Mind", "Strong Mind", under Mind; Perception, Reason, Understanding; "Mental" under Vitality; "Activity" in this section).

Rest—Mental Rest—(See Rest).

Retarded Mentality—☿ badly afflicted during the Prenatal Period, or at birth, or after birth, may tend to retard the mental growth; ☿ afflicted in the 12th H., the house of limitations and restraints; also the ♄ influence tends to retard both mind and body by his afflictions, to limit the Senses, etc., and especially when in the 12th H. at B. Cases of congenital Deafness, Dumbness, Idiocy, Imbecility, Foolish Mind, etc., indicate retarded mentality from some cause from the time of conception, on down to birth, and also influences at B., and after birth, may contribute to the condition. (See Arrested, Childlike Mentality, Inhibited, Limitations, Weak, in this section; Congenital; "Weak Mind" under Mind; Saturn, Thyroid, Twelfth House).

Scattered—The Mental Energies Scattered—(See "Scattered" under Energy).

Shallow Mentality — Mean and Shallow Abilities—Superficial Mind—Narrow-Minded—Contracted Mind—Little Depth of Mind—The ☽ □ or ☌ ☿, but little ability; ♀ Sig. ☌ the ☽, not a very deep mind, and promises more than the native is capable of rendering unless ☿ is strong and well-fortified; ☿ Sig. ☌ and combust the ☉, and with no assistance from benefics, little ability for learning or Science, and has a contracted and superficial mind; ☿ affl. in ♐ or ♓; ☿ afflicted in ♐, has a flow of speech, but of little depth; ☿ affl. in ♋, a shallow mind; ☿ setting in the West, in a weak sign, afflicted by the ☽, following after the ☉, and in no aspect to the Asc., has little power for study or concentration, and tends also to bad judgment, lack of foresight. (See Apathy, Dull, Examinations, Idle, Imbecility, Impairment, Improvident, Judgment, Knowledge; "Void Of" under Learning; "Weak Mind" under Mind; Prejudiced; "Incompetency" in this section).

Signs of Zodiac — The Mental Signs are ♈, ♊, ♍, ♒. The airy signs are called Mental Signs.

Strain—Mental Strain—Danger of—☿ afflicted in ♍, ♐, or ♓, warns against over-study and mental strain; ☿ □ or ☌ ☽; ☿ afflicted in the 6th H.; the ☽ afflicted in an airy sign. (See "Exertion" in this section; Reading, Strain, Study).

Strengthened — The Mental Faculties Strengthened — (See Activity, Quickened, in this section).

Studious Mentality—(See "Good" under Intellect; Knowledge; "Studious" under Learning; "Strong Mind" under Mind; Occult, Reading, Science, Study; "Activity", "Quickened", in this section).

Suffering — Mental Suffering — (See Anguish, Anxiety, Dejected, Depression, Despondency, Discontentment, Disgrace, Distress, Fears, Gloom, Hope; "Low Spirits" under Low; Melancholy; "No Peace" under Mind; Misery, Restlessness, Reverses, Ruin, Sadness, Sorrow, Trouble, Unhappy, Worry, Wretched; the various paragraphs in this Article).

Superficial Mentality—(See "Shallow" in this section; "Light" under Mind).

Suppressed Mentality—(See Arrested, Childlike, Inhibited, Limitations, Retarded, in this section; Idiocy, Imbecile, Suppressons).

Temperament—The Mental Temperament—Born under ☿. (See Decanates; "Nervous Temperament" under Nerves).

Temporary—Temporary Mental Afflictions or Deviations—(See Derangement, Irritations, in this section; "Brain Storms" under Brain; Dementia, Demoniac, Idiocy, Insanity, Temper, Temporary, Violence, etc.).

Troubles—Mental Troubles and Afflictions—(See the various paragraphs and references in this Article, and under Mind).

Turbulent Mentality — (See Anarchists, Anger, Brutish, Choleric, Criminal, Cruel, Emotions, Erratic, Feelings, Fierce, Fighting, Irascible, Irresponsible, Irritable, Jealousy, Murderous, Perverse, Quarrelsome, Rebellious, Revengeful, Riotous; "High Temper" under Temper; Vicious, Violent, etc.).

Unbalanced Mentality—Unbalanced Mind—Diseases of the ☽ and ☿, and by afflictions to these bodies at B., and by dir.; ♅ □ or ⚷ ☿, mental unbalance. Brain balance is controlled largely by the secretions of the Thyroid Gland, which gland is ruled by ☿. (See "Derangement" in this section; Coordination, Dementia, Demoniac, Frenzy, Fury, Idiocy, Incoordination, Insanity, Madness, Mania, Paranoia, Thyroid, etc.).

Undesirable Mental Traits—Many of these are listed and considered in this book. Look in the alphabetical arrangement for the subject you have in mind. See "Qualities" in this section. See such subjects as Anger, Cheating, Conduct, Criminal, Debauched, Deceitful, Dishonest, Forgers, Gamblers, Hate, Hypocritical, Infamous, Jealousy, Liars, Love Affairs, Morals, Quarrelsome, Revengeful, Selfish, Sensuous; "High Temper" under Temper; Thieving, Treacherous, Vicious, Violent, etc. (See "Undesirable Mental Traits" under Mind).

Undeveloped — (See Arrested, Inhibited, Limitations, Retarded, Weak, in this section).

Ungovernable—Mentally Undefinable and Ungovernable—♂ influence, and ♂ afflicting the mental rulers. (See "Wild Delirium" under Delirium; Demoniac, Frenzy, Fury; "Outrageous" under Insanity; Irrational, Madness, Mania; "Void of Reason" under Reason).

Unusual Mental Faculties — ♅ well-aspected in the 3rd H., or in ♊ and ♍; ♅ strong at B., ascending, rising and elevated; ♅ ☌ the ☉ or ☿ in the 10th H. (See Genius, Intuitions; "Great Learning" under Learning; Mathematical, Prodigies, Scholar; "Scientific Mind" under Science).

Weak Mentality—The ☽ and ☿ in no aspect to each other or the Asc. at B., and afflicted by malefics; the ☽ and ☿ afflicting the Asc.; the ruler of the Asc. in a fixed sign, and afflicting the ☽ and ☿ by □ or ⚷ aspect. (See "Weak Mind" under Mind; Arrested, Retarded, in this section).

Weakened Mental Faculties—The ☉ ☌ or P. ☿; ☿ rising after the ☉; ♒ on the 6th H. (See "Mental Faculties" under Impairment; Shallow, Weak, in this section).

Weaknesses—Mental Weaknesses and Disabilities—In judging of mental weaknesses, and the liability to Insanity, Epilepsy, and various other mental afflictions, the positions and aspects of ☿ and the ☽ should be considered, their relation to each other and the Asc.; their aspects to the malefics, etc. The ☽ and ☿ in no aspect or relation to each other or the Asc. tends to result in mental weakness, and inability to understand or comprehend things. The ♋ sign on the Asc. at B., and afflicted, and with other conditions of ☿ and the ☽, as just stated, tend to weakness of both mind and body. (See

Weak, Weakened, and the various paragraphs in this section, and under Intellect, Mind).

Weariness—Mental Weariness—Ennui—Lack of Interest In Life—(See Ennui, Lassitude, Lethargy, Weariness).

Well-Balanced Temperament — (See Well-Balanced).

Worry—Mental Worry—(See Anxiety, Dejected, Depressed, Despair, Despondent, Gloom, Hope, Hypochondria; "Low Spirits" under Low; Melancholy, Worry, etc.).

MENTHA—Mint—Peppermint—A Typical Plant and Drug of ♃. (See "Jupiter Group" under Herbs).

MEPHITIC—Mephitic Air—(See "Corrupt Air" under Air; "Winds" under Pestilence).

MERCILESS—(See Cruel, Pity).

Merciful—Kind—Humane—Compassionate—♒ influence; ♃ well-aspected in ♒; ♃ strong and well-aspected at birth. (See Humane, Kind, Noble).

MERCURY—The Planet Mercury—Hermes—Also known as "The Messenger of The Gods." This planet is the principal ruler of the Mind, and is known as the planet of Mind, Reason, Logic, etc. Also ☿ rules the Nerves and Nervous System in general. Mercury well placed and aspected at B. gives a good and well-balanced mind, but when weak and afflicted at B., and by dir., various disorders of the Mind and Reason develop, mental diseases and disturbances, shallowness of mind, poor reasoning powers, bad judgment, madness, insanity, epilepsy, nervous diseases, etc. Mercury is strongest at B. when found in the airy signs, as in ♊, ♎, and ♒, and is also strong in ♍. Mercury rules the two signs ♊ and ♍, and is said to be exalted in ♍ or ♒, to have his detriment in ♐, and fall in ♓. Mercury stirs the vocal cords into action, and rules the air which vibrates them. Also the vibrations which give Sight are originated by ☿. The aspects and position of ☿ sometimes express the Features. Mercury exerts a dry influence when masculine, and moisture when feminine, and is considered a variable, varying, or irregular planet, and partakes largely for the time of the planet, or planets, with which he is in aspect. When with ♄ he becomes like ♄ in influence, and tends to cause the same kind of diseases as does ♄, and so with each planet. Mercury is called the Hermaphrodite planet, owing to his dual nature, as he may be either masculine or feminine, according to the nature of the planet with which he is aspected, or associated for the time, or his position. He is masculine when oriental of the ☉, and feminine when occidental. He is masculine when in a masculine sign, and feminine when in a feminine sign; is masculine when with a masculine planet, and feminine when with a feminine planet; is masculine or feminine according to the number of his aspects with masculine or feminine planets, and the sign he is in, or as he is ori. or occi.; is masculine or feminine, diurnal or nocturnal, good or evil in influence, lucky or unlucky, according to the nature of the planets with which he is aspected. Mercury is considered as being ordinarily a cold planet, cold in influence, cold and dry when masculine, and cold and moist when feminine. He is considered a cold, dry, earthy, and melancholic planet, and is also nervous, impulsive, egotistical, malefic when with malefics, and benefic in influence when with the benefics. Mercury when well-aspected and dignified gives a strong mind and memory, active, and subtle. When afflicted he tends to cause overwork, sleeplessness, insomnia, restlessness, nervous diseases, and is indicative of a lack of spiritual calm. Also when afflicted, ill-dignified, or combust, he tends to produce a mean person, a liar, thief, gambler, swindler, etc. He may also be taken for the Anareta when strongly afflicted at B. He is considered by Max Heindel to be the lower octave of ♆, and by most other Authors as the lower octave of ♅. For convenience of reference this Article is divided into three Sections, as follows: Section One, The Influence of Mercury; Section Two, Mercury Rules, and Section Three, The Diseases and Afflictions of Mercury.

— SECTION ONE —

THE INFLUENCE OF MERCURY—The influences of ☿ have been partly considered in the Introduction to this Article.

Action of Mercury—☿ action is nervous, excitable, quivering, subtle, and ceaseless motion. Is also variable, varying, and causes an irregular course in disease. (See "Qualities" in this section).

Affinity—☿ has affinity with the Mind, the Nervous System, the Ears, Tongue, Hearing, Speech.

Anareta—May become Anareta when badly afflicted at B. (See Anareta).

Angel Of—Raphael.

Blind Spot of Retina — Is blind because it does not respond to the vibrations of ☿. (See "Blind Spot" under Retina).

Causes—☿ causes Nervous Disorders, Mental Disturbances, Various Diseases, those which vary in course and are iregular, and also those which return periodically, as in Mental Diseases. (See the Diseases of ☿ in Sec. 3 of this Article).

Classification—A cold planet, cold and dry when masculine, cold and moist when feminine, a variable planet, earthy, melancholic, nervous, egotistical, malefic with malefics, and benefic when with benefics, etc. (See the Introduction to this Article).

Colors—(See "Color" in Sec. 2 of this Article).

Combust—☿ when combust, in close ☌ with the ☉ at B., or afflicted and ill-dignified, tends to produce a mean person, liars, thieves, gamblers, swindlers, etc., and also to weaken the mind for hard study, but usually to give good commercial instincts. Our best students usually have ☿ separated from the ☉ by from 15 to 25 degrees.

Convertible—☿ is a convertible and variable planet, and may be masculine or feminine, benefic or malefic, etc., according to the nature of the sign, position, or planet with which he is associated. (See the Introduction to this Article).

Denotes—☿ denotes mental worry, restlessness, nervous complaints, sleeplessness, over-worked brain, and irregularities in food. (See "Qualities" in this section; Diseases in Sec. 3 of this Article).

Diathesis—(See Cranium).

Dignified—☿ when dignified, rising and elevated in the East, in one of his strong signs, and well-aspected, gives a strong mind and memory, good judgment, a happier state of mind, good reasoning powers, etc., and also aids the health. This planet is dignified when in the ♊, ♍, or ♒ signs.

Directions—Of Mercury—The adverse primary directions of ☿ are especially evil from the 4th to 10th years of life, the period when ☿ exerts a strong influence for good or ill over the native. (See Directions, Periods).

Diseases—Of Mercury—(See Sec. 3 of this Article).

Drugs—Of Mercury—(See Herbs, Metal, Plants, Typical Drugs, in this section).

Dry Influence—☿ exerts a cold and dry influence when masculine. (See the Introduction to this Article).

Ears—☿ has special affinity with the Ears. (See the Introduction under Ears).

Elementary Qualities—Cold and Dry.

Eyes—The Influence of ☿ over the Eyes and Vision—(See the Introduction under Sight).

Feminine—When ☿ is Feminine—(See Introduction to this Article).

Foetus—The Influence of ☿ in the Development of the Foetus—(See Foetus).

Food Stuffs—☿ represents Food in a general way. (See Food).

Functions—Of Mercury—The special functions of ☿ are in connection with the Brain, Mind, and Nerves.

Herbs—Mercury Group of Herbs—(See "Mercury Group" under Herbs).

Hour—☿ Hour—(See "Hours" under Planets).

Ill-Dignified—And Combust—(See "Combust" in this section).

Lower Octave—(See "Octave" in this section).

Masculine—When ☿ is Masculine—(See "Convertible" in this section; Variable).

Memory—The Memory and Mercury—(See "Dignified" in this section; Memory; "Good Mind" under Mind).

Metal of Mercury—Quicksilver—(See Therapeutics).

Mind—The Mind and Mercury—(See the Introduction to this Article; "Dignified", "Ill-Dignified", in this section; Intellect, Mental, Mind).

Moist—☿ exerts a cold and moist influence when feminine. (See Introduction to this Article).

Octave—☿ is said by most Authorities to be the lower octave of ♅. Max Heindel says ☿ is the lower octave of ♆, as ♆ rules the Higher, or Spiritual Mind. Read about this subject in the book, "Message of the Stars", by Max Heindel, the Chapter on Neptune.

Physiological Action—Of ☿ Plants and Herbs—Through the Solar Plexus they tend to innervation of the Gastro-Abdominal Region. Thru the Brachial Plexus they tend to Pulmonary Innervation, and Pulmonary Haematosis. They also tend to the Nervous Influx, and Periodicity. The general action of the ☿ Group of Plants is Nervine and Periodic.

Plant Group Of—Plant Remedies of—Bryonia Alba, Horehound, Licorice, May Apple, Mandrake, Parsley, etc. (See "Mercury Group" under Herbs).

Presides Over—☿ especially presides over Cellular Irritation and Periodicity, and also over the Mental Faculties. (See Cells).

Principle Of—Reason—(See Reason).

Quality—In Quality ☿ is relative, subtle, ingenious, witty, persuasive, and restless.

Qualities—The following special Qualities, Influences, and Actions are attributed to ☿—Abstractive, Active, Alterative, Anti-periodic, Benefic, Ceaseless Motion, Cephalic, Changeable, Cholagogue, Cold, Cold and Dry, Cold and Moist, Comprehensive, Connective, Convertible, Coordinating, Corrosive, Critical, Debili'' ting, Defective, Depressive, Dist ng, Diurnal, Dry, Duel, Earthy, Egotistical, Evil, Excitable, Fanciful, Feminine, Flighty, Gambling, Good, Hurried, Imaginative, Impeding, Impulsive, Incoordinative, Ingenious, Intellectual, Intelligent, Introspective, Irrational, Irregular, Irritable, Irritating, Jerky, Lethargic, Logical, Loquacious, Lucky, Lying, Maddening, Masculine, Melancholic, Moderately Fruitful, Moist, Nervine, Nervous, Neurotic, Nocturnal, Obsessive, Obstructive, Periodic, Persuasive, Quivering, Rational, Reasoning, Reflective, Relative, Restless, Spasmodic, Sterterous, Subtle, Swindling, Thieving, Torpid, Unbalanced, Unlucky, Unreasonable, Variable, Vibratory, Wakeful, Witty, Worrisome, etc. These influences and qualities are very opposing in some cases, as ☿ is a variable planet, masculine, feminine, malefic, benefic, etc., according to his aspects. This is explained in the Introduction to this Article.

Reason—☿ is known as the Planet of Reason, and also Reason is the Principle of ☿. (See Reason).

Remedies Of—(See Herbs, Metal, Plant Group, Therapeutic, Treatment, Typical, in this section).

Represents—☿ represents Food Stuffs in general. Also represents the Mind, Reason, and Mental Endeavor, etc. (See Food, Mental, Mind, Reason).

Signs Ruled By—♊ and ♍. The day sign, or house, of ☿ is ♊, and ♍ his night sign. Also ☿ is strong and exalted in ♒; has his fall, and is weakest in the ♓ sign.

Tall Body—☿ gives. (See Tall).

Temperament—☿ rules the Nervous Temperament. Also called the Mental Temperament. (See "Nervous Temperament" under Temperament).

Therapeutic Qualities—Alterative, Antiperiodic, Cephalic, Cholagogue, Nervine. (See Therapeutics).

Tongue—☿ has special affinity with the Tongue and Speech, and afflictions to ☿ tend to defects of speech, as stammering, tongue-tied, etc. (See Speech, Tongue).

Treatment—Treatment by ☿ Drugs, Herbs, Plants, and the Metal of ☿— These remedies tend to combat the diseases of ♃, as ☿ and ♃ rule opposite signs. (See "Planetary Opposites" under Opposites).

Typical Drugs—Apiol, Avena, Calomel, Mercury, Petroselinum, Podophyllin.

Typical Plants—(See "Mercury Group" under Herbs).

Variable—☿ is a variable and convertible planet according to his aspects, etc. (See "Convertible" in this section).

Vibrations Of—The vibrations which give Sight are originated by ☿. (See the Introduction under Sight).

Well-Dignified—(See "Dignified" in this section).

— SECTION TWO —

MERCURY RULES—See the following subjects in the alphabetical arrangement—Acquaintances; Air (the Air which stirs the Vocal Cords to action); Arms (Nerves of); Azure Color; Bile; Blue (Light Blue Color—Sky Blue Color—Blue in the Solar Spectrum—Bluish Colors); Bowels (Nerves and Nerve Fibers of); Brachial Plexus; Brain as a Whole—Brain Functions and Substance (ruled by the ☽ and ☿); Breath and Air Cells; Bronchial Tubes; Cellular Irritation and Periodicity; Cerebral Hemisphere (Right); Cerebral Nerves; Cerebro-Spinal Nervous System; Chylification; Chylopoiesis (see Chyle); Circulation (Pulmonary); Clothing; Color—Bluish Colors—Azure—Light Blue Color—Sky Blue Color—Blue in the Solar Spectrum—Lemon Color—Shot Lemon—Orange—Violet—Yellow, says H.P.B. in her Secret Doctrine (see Colors); Comprehension; Coordination in the Body, and between the Mind and Body; Dryness (when Masculine); Ears (Hearing); Eustachian Tubes; Excitement of Muscles to Action by Nerve Impulses, which Impulses are carried out by Mars; Faculties (the Mental, Rational and Reasoning Faculties); Fancy (The Fancy, Fancies); Features; Feeling; Feet; Fibers of the Nerves; Fluid (the Invisible Vital Fluid in the Nerves); Food (Food Stuffs); Functions (the Voluntary Nervous Functions); Fundament (the Fundament of the Body); Gall (see Bile); Gamblers; Genito-Urinary Organs (Nerves of); Gland (the Thyroid); Hair; Hands (Nerves of); Hearing; Heart (Nerves of); Hemisphere (Right Cerebral); Herbs (Mercury Group); Imagination; Impulses (Nervous Impulses to Muscular Action—See Excitation); Innervation; Intellect; Intelligence; Intestines (Small); Invisible Vital Fluid (in the Nerves); Irritability; Irritation (Cellular); Journeys by Land; Land Journeys (Short Journeys); Larynx; Legs (Nerves of); Lemon Color (Shot Lemon); Letters (Correspondence and Writings); Liars; Life from 7 to 15 Years of Age; Light Blue and Azure Color; Lips; Limbs; Lungs; Meanness; Memory; Mental Faculties and Forces (along with ♅, ♆, and ☽); Mercury (Quicksilver); Mind; Moisture (when feminine); Mother's Relatives; Motion in the Body; Motor Segment of the Spinal Cord; Mouth; Moving Parts of the Body; Nerves — (Nerve Impulses to Muscular Action — Nerve Tissue Building along with ♅ — The Telegraphic System of the Body—Nervous Influx (♂ adds to or subtracts from)— Nervous System as a Whole, along with ♅ — the Cerebro-Spinal Nervous System — Nerve Fibers Over the Body —The Voluntary Nervous Functions— Sensory Nerves, etc.); Nervous Temperament (along with ♅, ♄, and the Earthy Signs); Optic Nerve; Orange Color; Perception, and all Sense Perception; Periodicity (Cellular); Plexus (Brachial); Pulmonary Circulation and Innervation; Quicksilver; Rational and Reasoning Faculties; Reason; Relatives (of the Mother); Respiration; Right Cerebral Hemisphere; Sense Perceptions; Sensory Nerves; Servants; Short Journeys (Inland, and by Land); Shot Lemon Color; Shoulders; Sickness (from Worry, Nervousness, and Diseases Arising in the Mind); Sight; Sky Blue Color; Small Intestines; Speech (Nerves of); Spine (Motor Segment of the Spinal Cord—Spinal and Cerebral Nervous System); Stomach (Nerves of); Subtleness; Telegraphic System of the Body (Nerves); Texture of the Tissues of the Body; Thieves; Thyroid Gland; Tissue Building (Nerve Tissue Building, along with ♅ — Texture of the Tissues of the Body); Tongue; Touch (Sense of); Trachea; Understanding; Vibration (the Air which Stirs the Vocal Cords to Vibration); Violet Color; Vital Fluid (the Invisible Vital Fuid in the Nerves); Vocal Cords and Vocal Organs; Voluntary Nervous Functions; Wednesday (Day of Week); Windpipe; Writings (Letters and Correspondence); Years of Life (4 to 10, says Daath—7 to 15, general—See Periods); Yellow in the Solar Spectrum (see Colors).

— SECTION THREE —

MERCURY DISEASES — Mercury in the different Signs rules the Nerves in the parts of the body ruled by the sign he is in at birth, and if ☿ is badly afflicted at B., and also by dir., the nerves of such part, or parts, are apt to give more trouble. Thus ☿ in ♈ tends to nerve troubles in the head, headaches, brain-fag, etc. Mercury in ♋, disorders of the nerves of the stomach, etc. Mercury is a convertible planet, and produces diseases of the nature of the planet, or planets, with which he is joined and configurated, and also according to the nature of the sign in which he is posited. Mer-

cury causes, and has relation to nervous and mental disorders which affect the nerve fibres of the various organs and parts of the body. Mercury brings danger of Consumptions, Madness, Fits, when badly afflicted, and according to the afflictions, and the signs from which it occurs. Mercury has special affinity with the Ears and Tongue, and in causing Deafness, and disorders of Speech. Mercury may become Anareta, or the Killing Planet, when strongly afflicted at birth. The following is a classified list of the Diseases and Afflictions of Mercury. See these subjects in the alphabetical arrangement when not more fully considered here—

Accidents—And Death By—Death or Injury by Robbers, or In Exercise and Sports — (See Exercise, Robbers, Sports).

All Nervous Complaints — (See "All Nervous Disorders", and the various paragraphs under Nerves).

Apoplexy; Arms — ☿ afflicted in the signs which rule the Arms, Hands, and Legs, tends to Cramps, Neuralgic Pains, and Paralysis in these parts. Also the ☿ and ♄ afflictions tend to cause Gouty Pains, and Rheumatism in the Arms. (See these subjects under Arms).

Asthma; Back—Pains In—Weakness In—(See Back).

Bile—Gall — Disorders of—Bilious Flatulency—(See Bile).

Blindness — From Eye-strain, Over-Study, and Too Much Reading—(See "Over-Study" under Blindness).

Blood—Disordered Blood—Impure Blood—Wind In the Blood—(See Impure; "Blood" under Wind).

Body — Incoordination Between Mind and Body—(See Incoordination).

Bowels—Diseases of—Obstructions In —Pains In—Wind In—(See Bowels).

♥ Brain—All Complaints Caused by Diseases of—Disorders of, and Death By —Diseases of from Over-Work and Over-Study—Brain Fag—Disorders of the Brain Functions and Substance— Incoordination Between the Brain, Mind and Body — Lightness In the Brain—Dizziness—Over-Worked Brain —Violent Brain Storms, etc. — (See Brain).

Breath — Breathing — Disorders and Disturbances of — Rapid Breathing — Shortness of Breath, etc.—(See Breath).

Bronchial Disorders—Bronchitis— (See Bronchial, Lungs).

Calm—Lack of Spiritual Calm—(See Spiritual; the Introduction to this Article).

Cellular Irritation—(See Cells).

Cholera; Cold—(1) Cold and Dry Diseases — (See "Cold and Dry" under Dry); (2) Cold In the Knees and Legs —(See Knees, Legs); (3) Cold In the Stomach—Stomach Offended with Cold —(See "Raw Humours" under Indigestion).

Colds — Colds Caught In the Feet — (See Colds; "Cold Taken" under Feet).

Colic—In the Bowels—Flatulent Colic —Wind Colic—(See Colic).

Consumption; Convulsions; Corrosion — Of the Nervous System — (See Corrosion).

Cough —Coughs—Death by Cough—Dry Cough—(See Cough).

Course of Disease—Variable and Irregular Course—(See Course).

Cramps — In the Arms, Shoulders, Hands, Legs, and Feet—(See "Arms" under Cramps).

Deafness — Deaf and Dumb — (See Hearing, Mutes).

Death By—Mercury Causes Death by Accidents (if Violence Attend); Brain Diseases; Cough; Despair; Dry Habit and All Diseases Proceeding From; Epilepsy; Frenzy; Fury; Grief; Lethargy; Madness; Melancholy; Nervous Diseases; Obstructions; Phrenitis; Phthisis; Robbers (Attacks By); Sports; Stomach Disorders, etc. (See "Death" under these subjects).

Debility—Nervous Diseases Due To—(See Debility; "Debility" under Nerves).

Defects of Memory—(See Memory).

Delirium; Depletion — (See "Depletion" under Nerves).

Depression—(See "Mental" under Depressed).

Despair; Distempers — In Reins and Secret Parts—(See Reins, Secrets).

Distillation — Of Rheum — (See Rheum).

Dizziness; Dry Cough—Dry and Cold Diseases—(See Cough; "Cold and Dry" under Dry).

Dryness — ☿ produces Dryness when masculine. Also tends to Diseases from Superabundance of Dryness, and Immoderate Heat. (See "Dry Habit", "Superabundance", under Dryness).

Dumbness—(See Mutes).

Epilepsy; Excitement—Mental—Neurotic — Reflected — Nervous Diseases Arising From—(See Excitement).

Eyestrain — (See "Eyestrain" under Eyes).

Faculties—Disturbed Mental Faculties — (See "Faculties" under Mental; "Diseases of the Mind" under Mind).

Fag—Fatigue—(See "Brain Fag" under Brain; "Mind" under Fatigue).

Falling Fits—(See Fainting).

Fancy—Disorders of—(See Fancies).

Feet—Colds Caught In the Feet—Diseases of the Feet—Gout In—Pains In—Weakness In—(See Feet).

Fits; Flatulency — Flatulent Colic — Bilious Flatulency—(See Flatulence).

Flightiness; Fluxes; Flying Humours —Flying Pains—(See Flying).

Food—Irregularities In—(See Eating, Food).

Foul Tongue—(See Breath, Tongue).

Frenzy; Fundament — Disorders of — (See Fundament).

Fury; Gall—Diseases of—(See Gall).

Gastro-Abdominal Troubles — (See Gastro).

Giddiness—In the Head—(See Fainting, Vertigo).

Gonorrhoea; Gout—Gouty Pains—Goutish Humours—Gout In the Arms,

Shoulders, Hands, Head, Feet, Hips, Thighs, Knees—(See Gout).

Grief—Death By—(See Grief).

Gripings; Habit — Dry Habit and All Diseases Proceeding From, and Death By—(See "Dry Habit" under Dry).

Hands—Diseases In—(See Hands).

Hay Fever; Head—Disorders In—Dizziness In — Gouty Pains In — Humours In—Stoppages In—Pains In—Headaches — Spasms In — Snuffling In Nose—(See Head, Headaches, Nose).

Headaches; Heart—Trembling of—Nerve Troubles of — Neuralgia of — Wind Around—(See Heart).

High Strung — (See "Strung" under High).

Hips—Gout In—Swellings In—(See Hips).

Hoarseness; Humours — In the Head — In the Nose — Flying Humours — Goutish Humours—(See Humours).

Hurried Breathing—(See Breath).

Hyperaesthesia; Imagination—Disorders of—(See Imagination).

Impediments — In Speech — (See Impediments, Inarticulate, Speech, Tongue).

Imperfections — Of the Fancies — Of the Speech, etc.—(See Fancies, Impediments, Imperfections, Mental, Mind, Speech).

Incoordination; Influx—The Nervous Influx — ☿ adds to or subtracts from. (See Innervation; "Influx" under Nerves).

Innervation; Insanity; Insomnia—(See Sleep).

Intellect — (See the various paragraphs under Intellect).

Irregular Diseases — Diseases with a Variable Course — (See Course, Intermittent, Interrupted, Irregular, Remittent, Variable, Various, etc.).

Irregularities — (See "Irregularities" under Food).

Irritation—Cellular Irritation—Sympathetic Irritation—(See Cells, Irritation, Sympathy).

Kidneys—Neuralgia In—Obstructions In—(See Kidneys).

Knees — Cold In — Goutish Humours In—Lameness In—(See Knees).

Lameness—In Knees and Legs—(See Knees, Lameness, Legs).

Legs — Cramps In — Cold In — Lameness In—Humours In—Lameness In—(See Legs).

Lesions—Of the Nervous System—(See Lesions).

Lethargy; Lightness In Brain — (See Dizziness, Fainting, Vertigo).

Liver—(See "Torpid" under Liver).

Locomotor Ataxia; Lunacy; Lungs—Afflicted—Diseases of—(See Lungs).

Madness; Mania; Melancholy;

Memory—All Defects In—(See Memory).

Mental—Various Mental Disorders—(See Mental, Mind).

Mind — Disorders of — (See Comprehension, Intellect, Mental, Mind, Perception, Reason, Understanding, etc.).

Mouth—Diseases of—(See Mouth).

Mutes; Nerves — Nervous System — Disorders of — (See the various paragraphs under Nerves).

Neuralgia; Neurasthenia — (See Nerves).

Neurotic Excitement — (See "Nerves" under Excitement).

Nose—Disorders of—Sniffling—(See "Snuffling" under Head, Nose).

Obsessions; Obstructions—In Bowels, Kidneys, Nerves — Death by Obstructions—(See Obstructions).

Over-Study—Blindness, or Disease From—(See "Eyestrain" under Eyes).

Over-Work — Nervous Debility By — (See "Over-Active Mind" under Active; "Over-Worked" under Brain; "Inordinate" under Exercise; "Eyestrain" under Eyes; "Debility" under Nerves; Reading, Study).

Pains — In the Back — In the Feet — Gouty Pains In the Head, Arms, Shoulders, Knees, Feet — Rheumatic Pains In the Arms and Shoulders— Running and Flying Pains Over the Body—Spasmodic Pains In the Stomach—Neuralgic Pains, etc.—(See these subjects, and the various paragraphs under Pain).

Palpitation—(See Heart).

Paralysis — Of the Nervous System — In the Arms, Hands, Legs—(See Paralysis).

Periodical Diseases — (See Epilepsy, Fainting, Insanity, Periodic, Periodicity, Vertigo, etc.).

Phrenitis — (See "Inflammation" under Brain).

Phthisic — (See Asthma; Consumption).

Phthisis; Psychic Disorders — (See Psychic).

Pulmonary Diseases — (See Lungs, Pulmonary).

Quivering — Of the Body — (See Tremors).

Quotidian Fevers—(See Quotidian).

Rapid Breathing—(See Breath).

Rational Faculties—Disorders of—(See Rational).

Reading—Blindness, Eyestrain, Brain Fag, Mental Fatigue, etc., from Too Much Reading and Study—(See Brain; "Eyestrain" under Eyes; Fatigue, Reading, Study).

Reason—Disorders of—(See Reason).

Reflected Excitement—(See Reflected).

Reflex Action—(See Reflected).

Reins—Affected— Diseases In—Distempers In—(See Reins).

Respiration— Disorders of— Hurried —(See Breath, Bronchial, Lungs).

Restlessness; Retention—Of Urine—(See Urine).

Rheum—Distillation of—(See Rheum).

Rheumatic Pains— In Arms and Shoulders — (See Arms, Rheumatism, Shoulders).

Robbers—Accident, Injury, or Death By—(See Robbers).

Running Pains—(See Flying).

Saliva—Too Much—(See Saliva).

Secret Parts — Distempers In — (See Secrets).

Senitiveness; Shallow Mind — (See "Shallow" under Mental).

Short Breath—Hurried—Rapid—(See Breath).

Shoulders— Diseases In — Rheumatic Pains In—(See Shoulders).

Sickness — Arising from Mental Disturbances and Worries—(See Invalids; "Irritations" under Mental; "Neurasthenia" under Nerves; "Slow" under Recuperation; Trouble, Worry, etc.).

Sight — The Sight Affected — (See "Eyesight" under Eyes).

Signs—Diseases of ☿ in the 12 Signs of the Zodiac—☿ in each sign tends to nervous disorders of the part ruled by the Sign, Pains, Neuralgic conditions when ☿ is afflicted, and also if ☿ partake of the nature of ♄, to suppression, retention, etc. For classified lists of the Diseases of Mercury in the different Signs, see the Textbooks and Dictionaries of Astrology.

Sleeplessness—(See "Insomnia" under Sleep).

Sniffling—In the Head and Nose—(See "Snuffling" under Head).

Spasmodic Pains—In the Stomach and Other Organs and Parts—(See Colic, Gripings; "Gripings" under Stomach).

Spasms—Fits—Convulsions—Spasms In the Head—(See Convulsions, Fits; "Spasms" under Head; Spasmodic).

Speech—Disorders of—Stammering— Tongue-Tied — Impediments In — (See Speech, Tongue).

Spiritual Calm—Lack of—(See "Calm" in this section).

Spittle—Excess of—(See Saliva).

Sports—Accidents, Injuries, or Death By—(See Exercise, Sports).

Stammering—(See Speech).

Stertorous Breathing—Hurried—(See Breath).

Stomach—Cold Stomach—Gripings In —Spasmodic Pains In—Stoppage At— Raw Humours In — (See "Raw Humours" under Indigestion; Belching, Gripings, Obstructions, Pains, Worms, under Stomach).

Stoppage—In the Head, Nose, Stomach, Urine—(See "Obstructions" under Head, Nose, Stomach, Urine).

Storms—Violent Brain Storms—(See "Brain Storms" under Brain).

Strain—Eyestrain—Nervous Diseases Arising from Stress and Strain — (See "Eyestrain" under Eyes; "High Strung" under High; "Nervousness" under Nerves; "Nervous Strain" under Strain).

Study—Eye Trouble, Mental Fatigue, from Over-Study and Too-Much Reading—(See "Eyestrain" under Eyes; "Mind" under Fatigue; Reading, Study).

Stuttering—(See Speech).

Superabundance — Of Dryness — Diseases Arising From — (See "Superabundance" under Dryness).

Suppression—Of Urine—(See Supressions, Urine).

Swellings—In the Hips, Neck, Thighs — (See "Swellings" under these subjects).

Swindlers; Sympathetic Irritation — (See "Irritation" in this section).

Thieves; Thighs—Swellings In—(See "Swellings" under Hips).

Throat—Defects In—(See Throat).

Thyroid Gland — Disorders of — (See Thyroid).

Tongue—Foul Tongue—Tongue-Tied —(See "Foul" under Breath; Tongue; "Impediments" in this section).

Torpid Liver—(See Liver).

Trembling—Of the Heart—Tremors— (See Heart, Tremors).

Unbalanced Mind—(See Frenzy, Fury, Idiocy, Insanity, Madness, Mania; "Unbalanced" under Mind).

Urine—Obstruction of—Suppression of—(See Urine).

Uterus—Diseases of—(See Womb).

Vain Imaginations—(See Imagination).

Variable Diseases — (See Variable; "Irregular" in this section).

Vertigo; Violent Brain Storms — (See Brain).

Vital Fluid—Of the Nerves—Lowered or Exhausted — (See "Neurasthenia" under Nerves).·

Vitality — (See "Mental Vitality" under Vitality).

Vocal Disorders — (See Inarticulate, Larynx, Speech, Tongue, Voice).

Voice—Loss of—(See Voice).

Water Brash—(See Belching).

Weakness—In the Back, Legs, Feet— (See "Weakness" under these subjects).

Wind — In the Blood, Bowels — Wind Around Heart — Wind Colic — (See "Wind" under Blood, Bowels, Heart, Colic; also see Wind).

Womb—Disorders of—(See Womb).

Worms — In Bowels — In Stomach — (See Worms).

Worry—Mental Worry—Nervous Diseases Arising From—(See Worry).

MERCY—(See Merciless, Pity).

MERIDIAN— Medium Coeli —The Midheaven — Zenith — Tenth House — The Meridian is the highest point, or place of the ☉ each day at Noon, Sun Time, and the ☉ is very powerful at this time. After passing the Zenith, the ☉ begins to set, and is not as powerful in nativities. (See Elevated, Majority, Rising, Setting, Tenth House).

MERRY DISPOSITION—(See Cheerfulness, Contentment, Happiness, Joy).

MESENTERY— The Peritoneal Attachment of the Small Intestines — Ruled by ♍. The Mesenteric Glands are also ruled by ♍. (See "Small Intestines" under Bowels; "Splanchnic" under Ganglion; Peritoneum).

MESMERISM— A Mesmerizer—The 2nd face of ♓ on the Asc., and ♂ therein. Case—See "Moores", No. 816, in 1001 N.N. (See Healers, Hypnotism, Magnetism, Suggestion). Mesmerism was first put into practice by a man named Frank Mesmer, born in 1733, died in 1815. Mesmerism is now identified with Hypnotism.

MESOCOLON—Meso-Rectum—The Mesentery of the Colon—Ruled by ♍. (See Colon, Mesentery, Rectum).

METABOLISM — A Constructive or Destructive Change in the Intimate Condition of Cells or Tissues.

Cells—The Alteration and Metabolism of Cells—(See Alterations; "Alterations" under Cells; Constructive, Destructive, Metamorphosis, Structural, Transformation).

Digestive Tract — Metabolism of Disturbed — (See "Metabolism" under Digestion).

Tissues—Metabolism In—(See "Alterations" under Cells; the various paragraphs under Tissues). Also for further study see Absorption, Alterations, Assimilation, Catabolism; "Chemistry of the Body" under Chemistry; Crystallization, Decay, Decomposition, Degeneration, Diathesis, Digestion, Disintegration, Dissolution, Emaciation, Energy, Gangrene, Growth, Growths, Hardening, Nutrition, Processes, Putrefaction, Resolution, Secretion, Softening, Solution, Structural, Wasting, etc.

METACARPUS—(See Hands).

METALS—Alloys—The ☉ rules Gold; ☽ rules Silver; ♄ rules Lead; ♃ rules Tin; ♂ Iron; ♀ Copper; ☿ Quicksilver, also called Mercury. These are the seven metals used in treatment. (See "Metal" under each of the Planets. Also see Drugs, Medicines, Minerals, Remedies, Therapeutics).

Dross of Metals—Ruled by ♄.

Work In Metals — As a Business or Vocation—The ☽ rules work in Metals, Silver, Silver Plated Articles, etc.

METAMORPHOSIS—Transformation — Structural Change—Largely the work of the ☽. Venus presides over the Cellular Retrogressive Metamorphosis. The Five Processes, known as the Nervous Influx, the Renal Process, the Hepatic Process, the Thoracic Process, and the Splenic Process, form the basis for all Organic and Structural changes undergone by the Cell, and according to the zones occupied in the Zodiac by the heavenly bodies. (See Cells, Diathesis, Metabolism, Organic, Processes, Structural, Tissues, Transformation).

METAPHYSICS — Fond of — Given to Study of—(See "Metaphysical Healing" under Healers; "Metaphysics" under Learning; Ninth House, Occult; "Metaphysical" under Religion; Science).

METATARSUS — (See "Bones" under Feet).

METEORISM — Gas In the Abdominal Cavity—(See "Abdomen" under Gas).

METHODICAL — (See "Methodical" under Habits).

METHODS — Methods Used In the Attainment of Ends—(See Cheating, Conduct, Deceitful, Dishonest, Gambling, Honest, Liars, Motives, Thieves, Treachery, etc.). Look in the alphabetical arrangement for the subject you have in mind.

METONIC CYCLE — (See this subject under Moon).

METORRHAGIA — (See "Flooding" under Menses).

METRITIS—(See "Inflammation" under Womb).

MIASMA — A Noxious Emanation—Air-Borne Germs — Miasmic Ailments — Moonlight and the night air are especially noxious, and tend to Miasmic Troubles and Diseases. The exhalations of the vegetables at night, the prevalence of carbonic acid, and the chemical action of the Moon's rays, become very deleterious at night. The day time is less evil, as the heat tends to absorb the vapors and exhalations. (See Ague; "Corrupt Air" under Air; Carbon, Day, Germs, Malaria; "Moonlight" under Moon; Night, Noxious, Vapors, Vegetation).

MICROBES—(See Germs, Microzymasis, Virus).

MICROCEPHALUS — A Person with a Small Head—Microcephalic Idiot—(See "Small" under Head; Idiocy).

MICROZYMASIS — Microzyma — Micro-organisms Giving Rise to Disease — Principally the physiological action of the ☽, and the Moon Group of Herbs. (See Fermentation, Germs; "Moon Group" under Herbs; Miasma; "Physiological Action" under Moon; Zymosis).

MICTURITION—Painful and Difficult—(See "Strangury" under Urine).

MIDDLE — Middle Parts of Organs — Medium Stature — Middle Stature — Middling—For Middle Life and its conditions see the next Article after this one.

Above Middle Stature—♃ Sig. ✳ or △ ♄ and ♄ well-dignified; ♈, ♌, ♐, or ♒ on the Asc. (See Giants, Growth, Height, Tall).

Below Middle Stature — (See "Body Diminished" under Diminished; Dwarf; "Arrested" under Growth; "Body" under Short, Small).

Cervical Ganglion — (See "Middle Cervical" under Ganglion).

Complexion — (See "Middling" under Complexion).

Corpulent and Middle-Sized—(See the various influences under Corpulent, Fleshy, and also under "Middle Stature" in this section).

Fleshy and Full—Middle-Sized, Fleshy and Full Body—(See Fleshy).

Fleshy and Middle-Sized—(See Corpulent, Fleshy; "Middle Stature" in this section).

Full — Full, Fleshy, and Middle-Sized —(See Fleshy).

Lean and Middle-Sized—(See "Middle-Sized" under Lean).

Mean Stature — (See "Mean Stature" under Mean; "Medium Stature" under Medium; "Middle Stature" in this section).

Middle Life — (See Article following this one).

Middle Stature—Middle-Sized Body— Mean Stature—Medium Stature— Middling Stature—The ☉ Sig. in ♋, ♑, or ♒; the ☉ Sig. in ♋ or ♑, a mean stature, ill-formed and ill-made body; the ☽

Sig. in ♈, ♉, ♋, ♏, ♑, ♒, or ♓; indicated by ♄; when ♄ forms the body he gives a middle-sized stature; ♄ in the Asc.; ♄ lord of the Asc., and ori., as from the Asc. to the M.C., or from the Desc. to Nadir, gives middle stature; ♄ in ♈, ♉, ♏, ♑, or ♓, partile the Asc.; in Hor'y Q., ♄ Sig. in ♉, ♋, ♏, ♑, ♒, or ♓, indicates one of middle stature; ♃ occidental; ♃ ruler of the Asc., and occi.; ♃ in ♉, ♋, ♒, or ♓, partile the Asc.; ♃ in ♒, partile Asc., compact, corpulent, middle-sized; ♃ in ♏ or ♓, partile Asc., full, fleshy, middle-sized; ♂ ruler of the horoscope; ♂ Sig. in ♈, ♉, ♍, ♑, ♒, or ♓; ♂ in ♈, partile Asc., middle, well-set, and large bones; ♂ ♍, partile Asc., middle, well-proportioned; ♂ in ♏ or ♒, partile Asc., well-set, corpulent, but middling, but with ♂ in ♒ some Authorities say a tall body; ♂ ruler of the Asc., and occi.; ♀ in the Asc., fair, medium, and not usually tall; ♀ Sig. in ♈, ♉, or ♓; ♀ ♈, partile Asc., middle, but slender; ♀ ♓, partile Asc., middle, but rather plump and fleshy; ☿ Sig. in ♈, ♉, ♏, ♑, or ♒; ☿ ♉, partile Asc., middle, corpulent, and well-set; ♈, ♉, ♍, ♎, ♏, ♑, ♒, or ♓ on the Asc. tend to produce middle stature; ♉ on the Asc., middle or short, thick, strong, well-set body; ♍ on Asc., middle, but in no way handsome, says Lilly; ♏ on Asc., middle, strong and corpulent; ♒ on Asc., middle, and rarely tall; ♓ on Asc., middle, fleshy and corpulent, but sometimes pale, sickly and short. (See Corpulent, Fleshy; "Mean Stature" under Mean; "Medium Stature" under Medium).

Moderate In Stature—(See Moderate).

Organs—Middle Parts of Organs—Are shown by the middle parts of Signs, from 10 to 20 degrees, the middle or second decanate, and planets and afflictions in this decanate show Moles, Marks, Scars, Blemishes, or afflictions to the middle parts of organs under the rule of such Signs. (See "Parts of Body" under Accidents; Blemishes, Decanates; "Marks" under Face; "Organs" under Lower; Marks, Moles, Navamsa, Organs, Parts of Body, Scars, Upper, etc.).

Parts — Middle Parts of Body or Organs—(See "Organs" in this section).

Plump — Plump, Fleshy, and Middle-Sized—(See Fleshy, Plump).

Short or Middle-Sized—♉ on Asc. (See "Middle Stature" in this section; "Body" under Short).

Slender —And Middle-Sized —(See "Middle-Sized" in this section; Slender).

Stature—Middle Stature—(See "Middle" in this section).

Strong — Strong, Corpulent and Middle-Sized—♏ on the Asc. at B. The opposite sign ♉ on the Asc. tends to give a middle-sized or short, strong, thick, and well-set body. (See "Middle Stature" in this section; Strong, Thick, Well-Set).

Thick and Middle-Sized—Thick, Middle-Sized, or Short, etc.—♉ on the Asc. (See "Strong" in this section).

Well-Formed—And Middle Size—Corpulent—The ☉ or ☽ in ♒, partile the Asc., well-formed and well-made.

Well-Made—And Middle-Sized— (See "Well-Forméd" in this section; Well-Formed, Well-Made, Well-Proportioned, Well-Set).

Well-Proportioned—And Middle-Sized —☽ in ♋ partile Asc., middle, fleshy, well-proportioned; ♂ in ♍ partile the Asc. (See Well-Proportioned).

Well-Set—And Middle-Sized—The ☽ in ♑, partile the Asc., but may also be rather short; ♂ in ♏ partile Asc., but corpulent; ♂ in ♒ partile Asc., middle-sized, corpulent and well-set, but some Authorities say Tall. (See Well-Set).

MIDDLE LIFE—Middle Age—People of Middle Age are described by ♃. The full effects of ♃, for good or ill, are not felt until middle life, and espec. when he is in ♋, or in the 4th H. Mars rules the years of life from 41 to 56. (See Periods).

Corpulent—At Middle Life—The ☽ in ♓ at B.; ♍ on the Asc., and attended with a prominent abdomen; ♎ on the Asc. Stoutness in later years is caused by ♃ in the Asc. at B., and well-aspected, or ♃ in ♋ on the Asc., and afflicted. (See "Prominent" under Abdomen; Corpulent; "Body" under Fat; Stoutness).

Death At Middle Life — Danger of — The ☉ in the 8th H., and afflicted, or afflicting the hyleg.

Death Before Middle Life—Danger of —Dies Young—Death In Youth—Lord of the 10th H. in the 5th, thru feasting and dissipation; the 27° ♐ on the Asc.; the 5° ♒ on Asc.; the 9° ♓ on Asc.; thru dissipation and passional excesses; the 11° ♓ on the Asc. (See Adults; "Early Death" under Early; Maturity; "Death In Youth" under Youth).

Eclipses — Solar Eclipses At Middle Life — The ruling places at a Solar Eclipse occurring in the Midheaven tend to affect middle-aged people for good or ill according to the aspects, and signs occupying such places, etc. (See Eclipses).

Fifty-Six—Dies At 56 Years of Age— Case and Birth Data — See "Thrice Married", No. 108, in 1001 N.N.

Friends Die—At Middle Life or Before—(See "Short Life" under Friends).

Lives to Middle Life—(See "Death At Middle Life" in this section; Adults, Maturity, Old Age).

Pimples At Middle Life — (See Pimples).

Solar Eclipse—At Middle Life—(See "Eclipses" in this section).

MIDGETS — A Small Dwarf — (See Dwarf).

MIDHEAVEN—Medium Coeli (M.C.)— The Meridian—Zenith—Tenth House— (See "Passive Planets" under Passive; Tenth House).

MIDRIFF—(See Diaphragm).

MIDWIVES—A Woman Obstetrician— The ☽ rules and signifies Midwives. The ☽ ruler of the horoscope tends to make successful Midwives, and espec. when the ☽ is in the 10th H., or ruler of the 10th, in a female nativity. (See Nurses, Obstetricians).

MIGRAINE — Megrims—A Paroxysmal Headache, generally unilateral, and may be attended with Visual and Gastric Disturbances — An ♈ disease, and caused by the ☉ or ☽ afflicted in ♈; caused by afflictions to the ☉; a ♂ disease and affliction, and caused by afflictions to ♂; Subs at AT. (See Headache).

MILD—Mild Diseases—Mild Disposition —The influence of ♃ is mild, kindly, and benevolent, and espec. when well-placed and aspected at B., and tends to a mild and good disposition, better health and stronger vitality.

Disease Is Mild — Lord of the 6th H. cadent at B. Also the disease is minimized when the attributes are conflicting, as with the ☉ and ♄ when they are the afflicters in the disease, as these are opposing forces and tend to neutralize the influence of each other. (See Colds, Ephemeral; "Non-Malignant" under Growths; Indisposition, Minor, Opposites, Slight).

Mild Disposition— Quiet—Harmless— Even Temper—People born under the strong and good influence of ♀ tend to be mild and quiet in disposition; ♃ Sig. in ♎; ♀ Sig. in ♒ or ♓; ♎ on the Asc., a mild and even temper, as a rule; the ☉ Sig. ✶ or △ ♃; ♂ rather weak at B., and not badly aspected by malefics; many planets in airy signs. (See Cheerfulness, Contentment, Elegant, Excellent; "Many Friends" under Friends; Genteel, Gentle, Happy, Harmless, Humane, Joyful, Kind; "Amiable", "Obliging", under Manners; Quiet; "Popular" under Reputation).

Mild Epidemics — (See "Mild" under Epidemics).

Mild Fevers — (See "Mild" under Fevers).

Syphilis—Mild Form of—(See Syphilis).

MILITARY LIFE—Danger of Injury or Death In—The ☉ or ☽ to the ♂, or P. Dec. Antares; the ☽ to the ♂ or P. Dec. Aldebaran. (See "Battle" under Abroad; Foreign Lands, Maritime, Officers, Sailors, Ships, Soldiers, War).

Officer Killed—A Military Officer Murdered by His Soldiers—Mutiny—Danger of—The ☽ to the ♂ the South Star in the Lion's Neck. Also at such a time the Officer may become violent, and very intemperate in diet and disposition.

MILK—Milk Glands—Lacteals—Mammary Glands—Lactation—Breasts— Milky, etc. — The Milk is ruled by the ☽, ♀, the ♋ sign, and the 4th H. The ☽ rules the basic fluid in Milk. Jupiter adds the fatty constituents. The ☉ adds Casein, the clotted proteid of Milk, and ♄ adds the Salts. Lactation, Nursing of the Child, is ruled by the ♋ sign.

Caked Breasts—(See Breasts).

Child Could Not Nurse — Death of — Case—(See "Nursing" under Children; "Incapable of Nurture" under Nutrition).

Diseases of Lacteals—Afflictions in ♋; ♄ afflicted in ♋; Subs at Lu.P. (4D), KP.

Dry Breasts—No Milk for Nursing—Scanty Supply of—♄ afflicted in ♋; ♄ in ♋ and afflicting the ☽ or ♀; ♄ affl. in ♋ in the 4th H.

Sympathetic Lactation — Case — (See "Sympathetic Lactation", No. 810, in 1001 N.N.

Urine—Milky Urine—(See Urine). See Breasts, Fluids, Glands, Juices, Secretions.

MIND—The Mind—Intellect—Reason—Understanding—The Mentality, etc.—The planet ☿ is the principal ruler of the Mind. The Mind is ruled by ☿, the ☽ and the Asc., and the relation between these three at B. largely determine the Mentality. The ☽, taken separately from ☿ and the Asc., has only partial rule over the Mind. The Hebrew letter Vau (V) is related to the ♉ sign, and is predominant in Mind and Hearing, and the transformation of Thought into Speech. Thus ♈ (Intellect), and ♉ (Speech) are closely related, and the organ of Coordination is located in ♉. An afflicted ☿ tends to disturbances of the Mind, and to Brain and Nerve Disorders. The 3rd and 9th Houses also rule the Mind, and planets therein tend to show afflictions or benefits to the Mind. Mercury and the ☽ are Significators of Mind, and any evil aspect between them tends to weaken and injure the Mind, and its expression. Uranus and ☿ are called the Mental Planets. This subject of Mind is also largely considered under the subjects of Intellect, Mental, Perception, Reason, and Understanding, in this book, and quite lengthy under "Mental" for convenience of reference, as so many of the references in the Textbooks of Astrology use the word "Mental" in giving the influences about the Mind. (See the various paragraphs under Mental). This Article is divided into two Sections: Section One, General Considerations About the Mind; Section Two, Diseases and Afflictions of the Mind.

— SECTION ONE —

GENERAL CONSIDERATIONS—Divisions and Sub-Divisions of the Mind—Qualities—Manifestations and Expressions of the Mind, etc. See the following subjects in the alphabetical arrangement—

Abilities—(See "Abilities" under Mental).

Accomplished Mind — (See "Accomplished" under Manners).

Acquired Tendencies—(See Acquired).

Action of the Mind — Action of the Mind Upon the Body—☿, the ruler of the ♍ sign, the sign of health, and also the influences of the 6th H. at B., the house of health, and the house of ☿, indicate the action of the mind upon the body, and especially as related to the causes and origins of disease, as the ☿, ♍, and 6th H. influences connect mind and body, and afflictions to these important centers in the radical map tend to physical disorders arising from a mental cause. (See "Mind" under Action; Mercury, Sixth House, Virgo; "Principle" under Vital).

Active Mind—Acute Mind—(See "Active Mind" under Active; "Mental Energy" under Energy; "Quickened" under Mentality).

Acute Mind — (See "Active" in this section).

Affections—The Affections—(See Affections, Desire, Love Affairs, Marriage).

Afterthought — (See "Lack Of" under Forethought).

Aims — Intentions — Purposes — (See Ambitions, Ideals, Motives, Purposes).

Ambitions; Animal Propensities—(See "Animal Instinct" under Animal; Beastly, Fear, Fierce, Hunger, Instincts, Passion, Savage, Self-Preservation, Violent, Wild, etc.).

Apprehension — (See Comprehension, Discernment, Perception, Senses, Understanding).

Attention—(See "Attention" in Sec. 2 of this Article).

Blushing; Body — Action of the Mind Upon the Body—(See "Action" in this section).

Boyishness; Brain — (See the various paragraphs under Brain, Cerebral)

Brightened — The mind is brightened when ☿ rises before the ☉, and gives forethought, precision, concentration, and better powers of mind. (See "Active" in this section).

Capacity—Of the Mind—Is governed largely by the 3rd and 9th Houses, and planets in these houses at B., as these are the houses of mind. (See Ninth House, Third House).

Ceaseless Motion In—(See Motion).

Cells—Each Cell of the body is a center of Intelligence. (See the various paragraphs under Cells).

Cerebral —Cerebellum — Cerebrum—(See Brain, Cerebral).

Character; Cheerfulness; Choices — (See Discrimination, Forethought, Judgment, Reason, Will, etc.).

Clear and Incisive — ☿ well-aspected in ♊; ♂ a strong ruler at B. (See "Good" under Intellect; "Sound Mind" in this section).

Comprehension; Concentration;

Conduct; Congenital—Innate Mental Tendencies—(See Congenital, Heredity, Nativity, Prenatal).

Conscience — The Inner Voice which approves or disapproves of various lines of action and conduct. The predominating planet, or planets at birth, and the majority influences, as well as the degree of knowledge and spiritual advancement, determine the action of Conscience. Born under ♄, the Conscience approves revenge, secretiveness, greed, covetousness, miserliness, etc. Born under ♃, the native is more kind, honest, and his conscience says to do right, and be religious, etc., and so on with each of the planets, according to their nature.

Consciousness; Contentment;

Coordination; Countenance — Reflection of Mental States In—(See Countenance, Expression, Eyes, Face, Glances, Look).

Cultivation—Of the Mind— ☿ strong at B., and well-aspected, leads to, and makes cultivation, learning, and mental growth easier. (See Learning, Reading, Scholar, Science, Study).

Deep and Profound—Depth of Mind— (See "Active Mind" under Active; "Good" under Intellect; Knowledge, Learning, Scholar, Study; Brightened, Clear, Cultivation, Penetrating, Sound, Strong, in this section).

Deportment— (See Conduct, Habits, Love Affairs, Morals, Passion, Religion, etc.).

Desirable Mental Traits — The More Fortunate Traits of Mind—Admirable Physical Traits—As a contrast to the less desirable traits and characteristics of mind and body, some of the more fortunate qualities, and not of a pathological nature, have been introduced into this book for the study of students. See the following subjects in the alphabetical arrangement—Active Mind, Agile, Ambitions, Animated, Balanced, Beautiful, Brisk, Careful, Cheerfulness, Cleanly, Clear Intellect, Comely, Commanding, Comprehension Good, Concentration (Good Powers of); Constructive, Contented, Courage, Determined, Dexterity, Dimples, Discernment Good, Duty (Faithful In); Elegant Mind, Even Temper (see Temper); Excellent, Faculties Quickened, Fair, Favored Mind, Fine, Forethought (Good Powers of); Fortunate, Friendly, Fruitful, Generous, Genius, Genteel, Gentle, Good, Graceful, Handsome, Harmless, Harmonious, Healers, Health Good, Healthy, Honest, Honorable, Hopeful, Humane, Improved Mind, Independent, Inoffensive, Intuitive, Inventive, Joyful, Judgment Good, Just, Juvenility, Keen, Kind, Knowledge (Acquires Easily); Learning (Fond of); Lively, Lovely, Lucky, Magnetic, Manly, Manners (Good, etc.); Marriage (Happy In); Mathematical, Mechanical, Memory Good, Mentality Good, Mild, Mind Strong, Moderate, Modesty, Morals Good, Motives Good, Musical, Mystical, Natural Abilities, Nature (Active, Good, etc.); Neat, Noble, Normal, Opinions Good, Optimistic, Overcoming, Passion (Free From); Patient, Peaceful, Perception Good, Perfect, Perfection of Mind, Persevering, Philanthropic, Philosophical, Pious, Pity, Pleasant, Poised, Polite, Popular, Practical, Prepossessing, Presence of Mind, Proficient, Prophetic, Prudent, Quick Mind, Quiet, Rescue Work (see Rescue); Responsible, Riches (Acquires); Ruddy, Sagacious, Sanguine Temperament, Scholar, Self-Confident, Self-Controlled, Self-Reliant, Sensible, Sincere, Sober, Sound Mind, Strong Mind, Study (Fond of); Sweet Disposition (see Sweet); Sympathetic, Tastes (Good); Temperate, Thinking (Good); Trustworthy, Truthful, Understanding (Good); Vital Force (Plenty of); Wealthy, Well-Disposed, Well-Favored, Youthful, Zealous, Zest, etc. For subjects which may be overlooked here, look in the alphabetical arrangement. (See "Undesirable Mental Traits" in Sec. 2 of this Article).

Desires; Dexterity; Discernment;

Discretion—(See Balance; "Good" under Judgment; Prudence, etc.).

Discrimination; Disposition — (See Decanates, Disposition, Mental, Temper, Temperament, etc.).

Dull Mind—(See Dull).

Educational Mind — Ruled by the 3rd H. and its conditions. A strong 3rd H. gives a good mind for education and learning, and especially along material and worldly lines. The 9th H. strong and well-aspected at B. gives more desire for Philosophy, Truth, Religion, and the recognition of the Higher Mind.

Ego—The Ego—(See Ego).

Elegant Mind—(See Elegant).

Emotions; Exalted Mind— (See Ecstasy; "Mind" under Exaltation).

Excellent Mind—(See Excellent).

Expression; Faculties—(See the various paragraphs under Faculties).

Fancies; Favored Mind — (See Elegant, Favored).

Fears; Feelings; Fickle-Minded—(See "Fickle" under Love Affairs).

Fixed Mind—(See "Fixed Ideas" under Ideas).

Flexible Mind — (See Changeable, Flexible, Mutable, Negative, Susceptible, Receptive, etc.).

Forethought; Fruitful Mind — (See Fruitful, Inventive).

Ganglion — Note the various paragraphs under Ganglion).

Genius; Good Mind—(See "Good" under Intellect; Active, Deep, Elegant, Excellent, Sound, Strong, in this section).

Great Mind—(See "Great Ability" under Great; "Abilities" in this section).

Habits; Happiness; Harmless;

Harmony Disturbed—(See Harmony).

Healing Powers—(See Healers).

Health of Mind—(See "Active Mind" under Active; Cheerfulness, Contentment, Happy; "Good" under Intellect; "Peace of Mind" in this section).

Hearing; Heredity; Higher Mind— (See Conscience, Educational, Individuality, in this section; Ego, Soul, Spirit).

Honesty; Houses of Mind — The 3rd and 9th H. (See Ninth, Third).

Hypnotism; Ideals; Ideas;

Idiosyncrasies; Imagination;

Impulses; Inclinations—(See Conduct, Desires, Disposition, Habits, Ideals, Morals, Motives, Purposes, Temperament, etc.).

Independent; Individuality;

Infertile Mind — (See "Unfertile" in this section).

Ingenious — (See Genius; "Inventive" under Learning).

Innate—(See "Congenital" in this section).

Instincts; Intellect—(See the various paragraphs under Intellect, Mental, and in this Article).

Intentions—(See Character, Conduct Evil, Good, Motives, Purposes, etc.).

Introspection; Intuition; Jealousy;

Judging the Mind — To judge of the mind, consider the sign on the Asc., planets in the 1st H., or Asc., if any, and the aspects of planets to the Asc. The ☽ and ☿ are chiefly to be considered, and the aspects to them, their relation to each other and to the Asc. Also, before judging of the effect of any planet upon the ☽, ☿, or Asc., note how that planet itself is aspected and affected by other planets, as every planet acts upon every other planet by its aspects, except the ☽ and ☿, which are passive. Any planet in the 3rd or 9th H. has a powerful influence upon the mind for good or evil. Uranus and ☿ are termed the Mental Planets, and their aspects, positions, and influences tend to greatly determine the quality, state, and conditions of the mind. (See "Mental Faculties" under Faculties; "Good", "Weak", under Intellect; "Weaknesses" under Mental; Prenatal Epoch; "Quality", and the various paragraphs in this section).

Judgment—Good or Bad Judgment—(See Judgment).

Light In Mind—Little Mind—Credulous — Narrow-Minded — Easily Convinced—Negative—Vacillating—♃ Sig. ☌ ☉; ☿ weak at B., and often in a watery sign, and espec. in ♓, and afflicted; ♋ on the Asc., and the ☽ remote in a common sign, light, credulous, and inconstant. (See Inconstant, Influenced; "Shallow" under Mentality; Mutable, Negative, Prejudiced, Pretender, Reason, Receptive, Restless, Susceptible, Vacillating; "Weak Mind" in this section).

Likes and Dislikes—(See Likes).

Little Mind—(See "Light" in this section).

Look—Intellectual Look—(See Look).

Lower Mind—Instinctive Mind—Ruled by ♄ and ♑. Also ruled by ♂ and ♀ when these planets are afflicted, or afflicting each other. (See Amorous; "Animal Instincts" under Animal; Appetites, Desires, Drink, Excesses, Gluttony, Passion, Personality, etc.).

Manners; Mathematical; Meditative—(See Grave, Introspection, Reserved, Sad, Serious).

Memory—(See the various paragraphs under Memory).

Mesmerism; Methods; Moods; Morals;

Motion — (See Action, Coordination, Energy, Motion, Motor, Movement, Muscles, Walk, etc).

Motives; Movement; Narrow-Minded (See "Light" in this section).

Natural Abilities—(See Natural).

Normal Mind—(See Normal).

Notions; Novelties—Fond of—(See Novelties).

Opinions; Optimism;

Over-Active Mind — (See "Over-Active" under Active).

Peace of Mind—Contentment—Happiness—Joy—Confident—Not Swayed by Fears or Anxieties—A Calm and Tranquil Mind—The ☉ or ☽ to the ☌ or good aspect ♃ or ♀ by dir.; the ☽ to

the ☌ or good asp. ♀ by dir., peace of mind espec. to females; the ☽ at a Solar Rev. well-aspected by the ☉, ♃, or ♀, and passing her own place at B.; the Asc. to the ⚹ or △ the ☉ or ☽ by dir.; lord of the Asc. in the 1st H.; the 14° ♓ on the Asc.; good aspects of planets to ♀ and the ♎ sign; ♎ on the Asc. at B. tends to give poise and balance. (See Balance, Contentment; "Good Fate" under Fate; Gentle, Happy, Harmless; "Good Health" under Health; Joyful; "Mild Disposition" under Mild; Optimistic; "Sanguine Temperament" under Sanguine; Spiritual, etc.).

Pedestrianism; Penetrating Mind—♂ Sig. in ♑; ♂ Sig. ⚹ or △ ☿. (See "Active Mind" under Active; "Quickened" under Mental).

Perception—Acute Perceptive Faculties—(See Perception).

Perfection—Of Mind and Body—Given by the ♒ sign. (See Beautiful, Harmony; "Good Mind" in this section).

Personality; Phantasies;

Pineal Gland—(See Pineal).

Pituitary Body—(See Pituitary).

Planets—The Mental Planets—♅, ☿, and the ☽. The Asc. is also strongly mental, along with the ☽ and ☿. (See "Judging the Mind" in this section).

Plexuses; Positive Mind — (See Individuality, Positive, Powerful, Self-Confidence, Self-Reliant, etc.).

Prejudiced; Prenatal Epoch;

Presence of Mind—(See "Active Mind" under Active; "Good" under Judgment; "Quickened" under Mental).

Pretenses—(See Character, Cheating, Deceitful, Dual, Honest, Hypocritical, Motives, Pretender, Purposes).

Principles; Propensities; Prophetical;

Prudence; Psychic Powers; Purposes;

Quality of the Mind— ☿ and the ☽, their sign and house positions, aspects, dignity, etc., tend to determine the quality of the mind. Mercury well-aspected by the ☽, ♄, ♃, and the Asc. tend to give a good quality to the mind, and with ☿ also not combust. Mercury combust, in no aspect, or in evil aspect to the ☽, ♅, ♄, ♃, and the Asc. tends to weaken the quality of the mind, give poor abilities, bad judgment, lack of foresight, and many mental ills. (See Intellect, Mental; "Abilities", and the various paragraphs in this section).

Qualities of the Mind—(See "Qualities" under Mental; the various paragraphs in this section). The Qualities of the Mind are legion. Many of them are listed in this book, both the good and the less desirable ones. Look in the alphabetical arrangement for the subject you have in mind. (See "Desirable" in Sec. 1 of this Article; "Undesirable" in this section).

Quickened—The Mind Quickened—(See "Quickened" under Mental; "Active", "Brightened", in this section).

Rational Mind—Rational Faculties—(See Rational, Reason).

Reason—(See the various paragraphs under Reason).

Refined Mind—(See Elegant).

Religion; Rulers of the Mind—(See the Introduction to this Article).

Satisfaction of Mind—(See Cheerful, Contentment, Fortunate, Happy, Joyful; "Peace of Mind" in this section; "Popular" under Reputation).

Scruples—(See Ideals, Ideas, Love Affairs, Morals, Motives, Purposes, Principles).

Senses; Sentient Faculties—(See Sentient).

Sentiments—(See Emotions, Feelings, Ideals, Ideas, Notions, etc.).

Shallow Mind—(See "Shallow" under Mentality; "Light" in this section).

Sharpened—The Mind Sharpened— (See "Quickened" under Mentality; Active, Brightened, Clear, Penetrating, in this section).

Sight—Vision—(See Sight).

Significators of Mind—The ☽ and ☿.

Signs of Mind—The airy signs ♊, ♎, ♒. Also ♍, the sign of ☿, and ♈, the head and brain sign.

Smell; Solar Plexus — (See "Solar" under Plexus).

Solidarity of Mind — Given by any aspect of ♄ to ☿. (See "Good" in this section).

Soul—The Soul—(See Soul).

Sound Mind — A Sound Mind In a Sound Body — Mens Sana In Corpore Sano—The ☽ and ☿ must be strong, connected with each other, the Asc., or with ♃, ♂, or ♀, and free from affliction. The mutual configurations between the ☽ and ☿ are very desirable. Mercury in the Asc., well-aspected, and in his own signs ♊ and ♍. (See Active, Brightened, Clear, Deep, Good, Quality, Quickened, Strong, in this section).

Speculative Mind—(See Speculative).

Speech—(See the various paragraphs under Speech).

Spirit—The Spirit—(See Spirit).

Spirituality—(See Spiritual).

States of the Mind—Are largely ruled by the aspects to the ☽ and ☿ each day and hour of life. Self-control, knowledge, wisdom, foresight, discrimination, and a highly developed spiritual nature, etc., tend to give more poise, balance, and control under the various conflicts and emotions to which the mind is subject daily under the planetary aspects, transits, and directions. (See Anger, Balance, Despondency, Emotion, Fear, Feelings, Grief, Hope, Joy, Melancholy, Optimism, Sadness, Worry, etc.).

Strong Mind—Good Mind—Powerful Mind—Sound Mind—Good aspects of ♃ to the ☽, ☿, and the Asc. tend to give a strong mind and body, and espec. when ☿ and the ☽ are in good relation to each other, and to the Asc., and both ☿ and the ☽ dignified and strong. (See "Good" under Intellect; "Quickened" under Mentality; "Sound" in this section).

Studious Mind — (See "Studious" under Learning; Reading, Scholar, Science, Study).

Subconscious Mind—(See "Animal Instincts" under Animal; the Introduction under Habits; Hypnotism, Reason, Subconscious).

Superconscious Mind — (See Superconscious).

Superficial Mind—(See "Fails In" under Examinations; "Shallow" under Mentality; Pretender; "Light" in this section).

Susceptibility; Suspicious—(See Fears, Suspicion).

Talented Mind — (See Genius, Inventive, Knowledge, Learning, Mathematical; "Abilities" under Mental; Oratorical, Reading, Scientific, Study, Talents; Elegant, Excellent, Good, in this section).

Taste; Tastes; Telepathy; Temper; Temperament; Tendencies; Thinking —Thought—(See Thinking).

Thyroid Gland; Understanding;

Unfertile Mind—♄ in the 3rd H., and afflicting the mental rulers. (See "Little Depth" under Learning; "Shallow" under Mentality; "Light" in this section).

Vagaries; Views — (See Anarchists, Ideals, Ideas, Materialism, Notions, Opinions, Reformers, Religion).

Vision—(See Accommodation, Sight).

Visions; Volition;

Well-Balanced Mind—The ☉ in a fiery sign, and the ☽ in a watery sign.

Will; Wisdom; Worry; Young Mind—(See Juvenility). There are many other subjects about the Mind, too numerous to list here. Look in the alphabetical arrangement for the subject you may have in mind.

— SECTION TWO —

DISEASES OF THE MIND — Mental Disorders, Afflictions, and Deviations — Disturbances of the Mind — Mental Excesses or Limitations, etc.—See the following subjects in the alphabetical arrangement when only listed here—

Absent-Minded — Chaotic Mental State—Flightiness—Confusion of Mind —Dreamy Mind—A ♆ affliction; ♆ ♂ ☿; ☿ in a ♃ sign at B., as in ♐ or ♓, or ☿ afflicted by ♃ or ♆; Subs at AT. (See Flightiness).

Activity—Effervescent Mental Activity—(See Effervescent).

Adult—With Mind of a Child—Never Grew Up—Case—(See "Mind" under Children).

Affects the Mind — ☿ afflicted at B., and by dir. (See the various paragraphs in this section, and under Mental).

Afflicted In Mind and Body — (See "Mind and Body" in this section).

Affliction of Mind—The ☉ to the ill-asps. ☿ by dir.; the ☉ to the ♂ or ill-asps. ♄ by dir.; the ☽ to the ♂ or ill-asps. the ☉ or ♄ by dir., afflicted in mind and body; ♄ passing over the place of the radical ☽, or at a Solar Rev. ♂ the ☽; planets afflicted in the 3rd or 9th H.; ☿ ♂ or ill-asp. ♄ by dir. (See Anguish, Anxiety, Brooding, Dejected, Depressed, Despondent, Gloom;

"Mental" under Infirmities; "Weak" under Intellect and Mentality; "Diseased Mind", and the various paragraphs in this section).

Alcoholism—(See Alcoholism, Drink; "Delirium Tremens" under Delirium; Intoxication).

Alzheimer's Disease—(See "Atrophy" under Brain).

Analgesia; Anguish; Anxiety; Apathy of Mind—(See Apathy).

Aphasia — (See "Aphasia" under Speech).

Aphonia — (See "Aphonia" under Voice).

Apologetic Attitude—(See "Inferiority Complex" under Inferior).

Apparitions — (See Phenomena, Psychic, Visions).

Appetites — Abnormal — Perverted — (See Appetites, Perversions).

Apprehension Dull—(See Dull).

Arrested Mental Powers — (See "Arrested" under Mental; "Weak Mind" in this section).

Attention — Not Able to Fix the Attention — (See Flightiness; "Absent-Minded" in this section).

Aversions; Backwardness; Balance— Lack of—(See Balance).

Bashfulness; Beside Oneself — (See Excitable, Frenzy, Fury).

Blind Impulses—(See Impulses).

Blindness—From Over-Study— (See "Over-Study" under Blindness).

Blues; Body and Mind Afflicted—(See "Mind and Body" in this section).

Bomb Plotters—(See Anarchists).

Brain — Disorders of — (See Brain, Cerebral).

Breakdown Mentally — (See "Breakdown" under Mental).

Brooding; Capacity of the Mind — Limited Capacity — Suppressed — (See Foolish, Idiocy, Imbecile, Insanity; "Arrested", "Weak Mind", in this section).

Catalepsy; Centered On Disease—The Mind Centered On Disease—The ☉ or ☽ afflicted in ♉ or ♍; the ☉ or ♄ afflicted in ♍; ♉ or ♍ on the Asc. It is said the ♉ people fear disease, and the ♍ people court and nurse it. (See "Afflicted" under Body; Taurus, Virgo; "Mind and Body" in this section).

Chaotic Mind — (See "Mental Chaos" under Chaotic).

Child—Adult Has the Mind of—Never Grew Up—(See "Mind" under Children).

Clairaudience; Clairvoyannce;

Claustrophobia; Clogging — Of the Mind—(See Clogging).

Clouded Mind—☿ in the 12th H. at B., combust, or afflicted by ♄ or ♂. (See Chaotic, Confused, Dreamy, Flightiness, Insanity; "Absent-Minded" in this section).

Colds — From Over-Exertion of the Mind—(See "Colds" under Exercise).

Coma; Complaints—Mental Complaints — (See "Complaints" under Mental; the various paragraphs in this section).

Comprehension Dull — (See Comprehension; "Mind" under Dull; "Weak" under Understanding).

Concentration — Inability to Concentrate—(See Concentration).

Conduct—Abnormalities, Excesses, and Perversions In—(See Conduct).

Confusion; Consciousness — Clouding of—Loss of—(See Consciousness).

Conspicuous Mental Diseases — (See Conspicuous).

Contracted Mind — (See Imbecile; "Shallow", "Weak", under Mentality; "Arrested", "Light", "Weak", in this Article).

Control — The Mind Should Be Kept Under Good Control—♅ afflicted in ♒. For Lack of Control over the Mind, see references under Control.

Convulsions; Coordination—Disorders of—(See Coordination, Incoordination).

Cravings; Crazy—(See Frenzy, Fury, Insanity, Madness, Mania).

Cretinism; Criminal Tendencies—(See Criminal).

Cruel; Curable Mental Diseases—(See "Curable" under Mental).

Darkened Mind—A Mind of Darkened Desires—♄ afflicted by ♄. The mind tends to be darkened thru fear when ♄ or ♋ are in the Asc. in ♂ the ☉, ☽, or ☿. (See Desires, Fears).

Darkness—Fear of—(See Darkness).

Deafness—A Mental Limitation—(See Deafness, Limitations, Twelfth House).

Death—(See "Death" under Mental).

Debased In Mind—(See Debased).

Debility—Mental Debility—(See "Debility" under Mental; "Diseased Mind", and the various paragraphs in this section).

Deficient Mentally—(See "Deficiency" under Mental).

Deformed—In Mind and Body—♀ Sig. ☐ or ☌ ♄. (See "Mind and Body" under Deformities).

Dejected; Delirium; Delusions;

Dementia; Demoniac; Depraved;

Depression; Depth of Mind — Little Depth of Mind—(See "Fails In" under Examinations; "Shallow" under Mentality; "Light In Mind" in Sec. 1 of this Article).

Derangement — Of the Mind — (See "Derangement" under Mental).

Desires—A Mind of Darkened Desires —(See "Darkened" in this section; Depraved; "Low Desires" under Low; Perversions).

Despondency; Development — Of the Mind—Premature, Precocious, Arrested, Late, or Slow — (See Genius, Idiocy, Incomplete; "Arrested" under Mental; Precocious, Premature, Prodigies; "Weak Mind" in this section).

Deviations; Dipsomania; Directions —The Mind Affected By—(See Directions)

Disabilities—Mental—(See "Disabilities" under Mental; the various paragraphs in this section).

Discomfort; Discord — Inner Discord and Inharmony In Mind and Emotions —Afflictions to the Airy Signs, and to ♎ especially. Also afflictions to ♀. (See "Mind and Emotions" under Emotions).

Disease—The Disease Is More In the Mind Than In the Body—Is of Psychic Origin—Is Chiefly In the Mind—(See "Diseases" under Psychic; "Centered On Disease", "Mind and Body", in this section).

Diseased Mind—Diseases of the body act upon the mind thru the Vital Principle, and diseases of the mind upon the body thru the same medium, which medium is ruled by the ☉. (See "Principle" under Vital). Also caused by the ☉ or ☿ in a common sign, and afflicted by the ♂ or ill-asps. of malefics; the ☽ or ☿ affl. by ♅, unhealthy states of the mind; ♄ afflicted in ♍; ♃ or the ☽ to the ill-asps. ☿ by dir.; the 30° ♍ on the Asc. (See "Action of the Mind", and the various paragraphs in this section; Frenzy, Fury, Insanity, Madness, Mania, Melancholy, etc.).

Dishonesty; Disordered Mind—(See "Diseased", and the various paragraphs in this section, and under Intellect, Mental).

Dispersions; Disspirited; Distempers —Distempered Fancies—Distempers of the Mind — Melancholic Distempers — (See Distempers, Fancies; "Dry and Melancholic" under Melancholy; the various paragraphs in this section, and under Intellect, Mental, Psychic).

Distracted; Distress; Disturbances — (See "Irritations" under Mental; the various paragraphs in this section).

Doubts and Fears — (See Doubts, Fears, Gloomy, Melancholic, Morbid, Reserved, Secretive, Suspicious).

Dreads; Dreams — Dreamy — (See Dreams).

Drink—Craving For—(See Dispomania, Drink, Drunkenness, Intoxication).

Drowsiness — Stupor — Dull — (See "Drowsiness", "Heaviness", "Stupor", under Sleep).

Dual-Minded—(See Dual).

Dull—(See "Mind" under Dull, Heavy).

Dumb; Dwarfed — In Mind and Body —(See "Mind" under Children; Diminished, Dwarfed, Growth; "Arrested" under Mental).

Eccentric; Ecstasy; Effeminate;

Effervescent— Over-Active Mind— (See "Over-Active Mind" under Active; Effervescent).

Ego—Exaggerated Ego—Ego Mania —(See Ego).

Elation—(See "Exaltation" under Emotions).

Emotions—Disorders of—(See Emotions; "Discord" in this section).

Ennui—(See "Weariness" under Mental).

Enthusiasm—The Fury of—(See Enthusiasm).

Epilepsy; Equilibrium—Loss of— (See Equilibrium).

Erotic; Erratic; Erring; Evil — Evil Qualities of Mind—Mind Disturbed by

Evil Thoughts—(See "Thoughts", and the various paragraphs under Evil; "Unclean" in this section).

Exaggerated Ego—(See Ego).

Exaltation — (See "Mind and Body" under Exaltation).

Examinations—Fails In—(See Examinations).

Excitable; Exhibitionism; Extremes —(See "Mental Extremes" under Extremes).

Faculties—Disorders of—(See Faculties).

Fag—(See "Brain Fag" under Brain; "Mind" under Fatigue).

Fainting; Fanatical; Fancies—Disorders of—(See Fancies).

Fear—Fears—Phobias—(See Fear).

Feeble-Minded — (See "Mind" under Feeble; Foolish; "Weak" in this section).

Feelings — Disorders of — (See Feelings, Emotions).

Filthy Mind — (See "Mind" under Filthy).

Fits; Flighty Mind — (See Flightiness).

Folly; Foolhardy; Foolish; Force — Dissipation of Mental Force—(See Effervescent).

Forebodings; Forethought — Lack of —(See Forethought).

Forgetfulness—(See Memory).

Foul Mind—(See "Mind" under Filthy; Lewd, Obscene, Shameless, etc.).

Frantic; Frenzy; Fright; Fury; Gambling; Gloom; Grief;

Growth of the Mind — Growth Arrested—(See "Arrested" under Mental; "Weak Mind" in this section).

Hallucinations; Hatred; Hauntings;

Headaches—From Much Reading and Study—(See "Ocular" under Headache).

Health of Mind — (See "Health of Mind" in Sec. 1 of this Article).

Heavy Mind—Drowsiness—(See Dull; "Mind" under Heavy; "Drowsiness" under Sleep).

Hebetude—Dulling of the Mind and the Senses—(See Dull, Hebetude).

High Temper — (See "High" under Temper).

Homicidal; Homosexuality; Horrors;

Hyperactivity—Of the Psychic Powers — (See "Over-Active Mind" under Active; Effervescent, Excitable; "Mind" under Hyperactivity; Psychic).

Hyperaesthesia; Hypersensitive;

Hypochondria; Hysteria; Idealism — Extremes of—(See Ideals).

Ideas — Chaotic—Confused — Incoordinated—(See Ideas).

Identity—Loss of — Disorientation — (See Identity).

Idiocy; Idiopathy — Morbid State of Mind — (See Idiopathy; "Mind" under Morbid).

Idle and Dull—(See Dull, Idle).

Illness — From Over-Exertion of the Mind—(See "Exertion" under Mental; Reading, Study).

Illusions; Imaginations; Imbecility;

Impaired Mental Faculties— (See Faculties; "Mental" under Impairment).

Imperfections — All Imperfections of the Intellectual Parts—All Evils of— (See Imperfections; "All Evils" under Intellect; the various paragraphs under Mental, and in this section).

Impractical; Improvident; Impulses— Blind Impulses — Morbid — (See Impulses).

Inactive Mind—(See Inactive).

Incendiarism; Incoherence—Of Ideas — (See Chaotic, Confused, Ideas, Incoherent).

Incompetency—Mental—(See Inability, Incapable; "Incompetency" under Mental).

Incomplete; Incomposed;

Incoordination; Incurable — (See "Mental" under Incurable).

Indifferent — (See "Mind" under Indifferent).

Indisposition; Inefficiency;

Inferior Mentality—Inferiority Complex—(See Inferior; "Inferior" under Mental).

Infirmities—(See "Mental" under Infirmities).

Inharmony — (See Inharmony; "Discord" in this section).

Inhuman and Wild—(See Inhuman).

Injured—The Mind Injured—Caused by an evil aspect between the ☽ and ☿, and also when ☿ and the ☽ are disconnected with each other or the Asc. (See Forethought, Imbecile, Insanity, Judgment; "Weak" under Mental, and in this section).

Injuries—Mindful of—Retains Anger —(See "Mindful" under Injuries).

Inner Discord—(See "Discord" in this section).

Insanity; Insensibility; Insomnia— (See Sleep).

Instability—Of Mind—The ☽ afflicted in the Asc.; ☿ afflicted by ♂; ☿ afflicted in ♋ or ♓ unless ♄ be in good aspect to ☿. (See Instability, Mutable, Negative, Restless, Roaming, Vacillating, Wandering, etc.).

Instincts—Disorders of—(See Instincts).

Intellect—Disorders of—(See the various paragraphs under Intellect, Mental, and in this Article).

Intemperance; Introspection;

Intuitions—Disorders of—(See Intuition).

Involuntary Disorders—Loss of Control—(See Involuntary).

Irrational; Irresponsible; Irritable;

Irritations—(See "Irritations" under Mental).

Jealousy; Judgment—Disorders of— (See Judgment).

Kleptomaniac; Knavish; Knowledge —A Pretender to All Manner of Knowledge—(See Knowledge; "Void Of" under Learning; Pretender).

Lack Of — Mental Deficiencies — (See the various paragraphs under Lack Of).

Languishing; Lapsing — Moral Lapsing—(See Lapsing, Morals).

Lascivious; Lassitude; Laxity;

Learning—Incapable of—(See Learning).

Left-Handed—(See Left, Right).

Lesions—Tending to Affect the Mind, and the Expression of Mind—(See Cortical, Lesions, Paralysis; "Aphasia" under Speech).

Lethargy; Lewd; Liable To — Liable to Mental Disorders and Disturbances —(See the various paragraphs under Intellect, Mental, and in this section).

Liars; Libelers; Licentious;

Light In Mind—(See "Light In Mind" in Sec. 1 of this Article; "Weak Mind" in this section).

Limitations — Upon the Mind — (See Limitations).

Lisping; Listless; Locomotion — Disorders of — (See Gait, Locomotion, Motion, Movement, Walk).

Loneliness; Longings; Loose—Loose Habits—Loose Morals—(See Loose).

Loss Of—Loss of Faculties—Loss of Reason—(See "Loss Of" under Faculties, Reason; also see the various subjects under "Loss Of").

Love Affairs—Abnormalities In—(See Amorous, Excesses, Love Affairs, Marriage, Passion, Perversions).

Low Mentality—Mind of a Low Order—♅ afflicted at B., and especially in the 3rd H.; ☿ □ or ☍ ♅. (See "Low and Base", and the various paragraphs under Low).

Low Morals — (See "Loose Morals" under Morals).

Low Spirits—(See Low).

Lower Mind — Lives Much In— (See Appetites, Conduct, Debauched, Depraved, Habits, Lewd, Love Affairs, Morals, Passion, etc.).

Lowering—Lowering Tendency—(See Dejected, Depressed, Despondent; "Low Spirits" under Low; Melancholy).

Lunacy—(See Insanity, Lunacy).

Lustful; Luxuries — Fond of, and Health Injured By — (See Extravagance; "Rich Food" under Food; Luxuries, etc.).

Madness; Magical Powers — (See Magic).

Malefic Planets — Adverse Influences of Over the Mind—(See Malefics).

Malevolent— (See Evil, Malefic, Malevolent).

Malice; Mania; Masochism;

Materialism; Mean-Spirited — (See Mean).

Mechanical; Mediumship — Dangers Thru—(See Clairvoyance, Mediumship).

Melancholy; Memory — Defects In — (See Memory).

Men—Mental Abnormalities In—(See the various paragraphs under Men).

Mental Disorders — (See the various paragraphs under Faculties, Intellect, Mental, Mind, Perception, Reason, Understanding, and also in this Article).

Merciless; Mercury—Mental Disorders Caused by ☿ — (See the various paragraphs under Mercury).

Methods; Mind and Body — Afflicted In—(a) The Disease Is Chiefly In the Mind—Of Psychic Origin—(See "Diseases" under Psychic; "Centered On Disease" in this section). (b) The Disease Is More In the Body Than In the Mind—(See "Afflicted" under Body). (c) The Disease Is In Both Mind and Body—The ☽ to the ♂ or ill-asp. the ☉ or ♄ by dir.; ♀ Sig. □ or ☍ ♄, deformed in body and mind; the M.C. to the ♂ or evil asps. the ☽ by dir., and espec. if the ☽ be afflicted at B.; malefics in the Asc., afflicting the lord of the Asc. or either the ☉ or ☽, both body and mind are diseased. (See "Body" under Disease; "Affliction of Mind" in this section).

Mind Centered Upon Disease— (See "Centered" in this section).

Mind Threatened—The ☉ ♂ ♄ in ♍; ♅ □ or ☍ ♀; ♄ ♂, □ or ☍ ♀; ♂ afflicted in ♈. (See Frenzy, Fury, Insanity, Madness, Mania, Melancholy).

Mind Unsettled — (See Changes; "Inability" under Concentration; Discontentment, Home, Journeys, Location, Removals, Residence, Scattering, Travel, Vagabond, Wanderer; "Light In Mind" in Sec. 1 of this Article; "Instability" in this section).

Mindful of Injuries—(See "Mindful" under Injuries).

Moisture of Brain—Mental Disorders From—(See "Brain" under Moisture).

Monomania—(See Mania).

Moods; Morals — Disorders of — (See Morals).

Morbid Mind — Morbid Deviations — Morbid Imaginations, etc. — (See the various paragraphs under Morbid. Also see Anxiety, Brooding, Dejection, Depressed, Despondency, Deviations, Fears, Hallucinations, Hypochondria, Idiopathy, Imaginations, Insanity, Introspection, Low Spirits (see Low); Nymphomania, Unsavory, Worry).

Moroseness; Muddled—Muddled Condition of Mind—☿ afflicted by ♅. (See Chaotic, Confused, Eccentric, Erratic, Misunderstood, Peculiar).

Murderous; Mutable—A Mutable, Changeable, Restless, Negative, and Scattering Mind — (See Mutable; "Instability" in this section).

Mute; Mysterious Sayings—Given To — Mysterious States of Mind — (See Catalepsy, Demoniac, Insanity, Mysterious, Trance, Weird).

Nakedness — Wandering In — (See "Outrageous" under Insanity).

Nerves — Mental Disturbances from Disordered Nerves — (See Anguish, Anxiety; "Brain Storms" under Brain; Depression, Despair, Excitable, Gloom; "High Strung" under High; Hope, Hypochondria, Hysterical; "Low Spirits" under Low; Melancholy; "Psychic Storms" under Psychic; Restlessness, Sensitive, Worry, etc.).

Neuroses — Anxiety Neuroses — (See Anxiety).

No Peace of Mind—♆ □ or ☍ ♅ at B.,
no peace of mind, and full of fears and dreads. (See Discontentment; "Signs of Fear" under Fear).

Noisome Diseases—(See Noisome).

Obscene; Obscure Mind—(See "Mind" under Obscure).

Obsessions; Obstructed Mind—♄ ♂ ☿ in ♈. (See "Mind" under Dull; "Weak" in this section).

Organic Disabilities—Tending to Affect the Mind — Are indicated by the ☽ and Asc., their relation to each other, and afflictions to them. (See Organic).

Out-of-Sorts—(See Irritable).

Outrageous — (See "Outrageous" under Insanity).

Over-Active Mind—(See "Over-Active" under Active).

Over-Exertion of Mind—(See "Mind" under Exercise; "Exertion" under Mental).

Pain — Insensibility To — (See Analgesia, Insensibility).

Paranoia; Passion—Perversions of— (See Passion, Perversions).

Passive Faculties—Deviations of— (See Deviations).

Peculiar — Peculiar Appetites and Tastes—(See Appetites, Eccentric, Peculiar, Tastes).

Peevish; Pensive; Perceptive Powers —Impaired—(See Perception).

Perjury—Given To—(See Perjury).

Persecution—Delusions of—(See Paranoia, Persecution).

Personality—Dual or Triple Personality—(See Personality).

Perverse; Perversions; Pessimistic— (See Doubts, Fears, Mistrustful, Morbid, Suspicious).

Pettifogging—Tricky—(See Deceitful, Dishonest, Pettifogging).

Petulant; Phantasies — (See "Prejudiced" under Fancies).

Phobias—(See Fears).

Phrenitic Man — (See "Wild" under Delirium).

Phrenitis — (See "Inflammation" under Brain; "Wild" under Delirium).

Phrenzies—(See Frenzy).

Physical Condition — Often Tends to Clogging of the Mind—(See Clogging).

Pilfering; Pity — Without Pity or Mercy—(See Pity).

Pleasure—Abnormally Fond of—(See Pleasure).

Plodding; Polluted Mind — (See Polluted).

Poor Mentality — (See "Poor" under Mental; "Weak" in this section).

Practices; Precipitate Actions—Fancies—(See Fancies, Precipitate).

Precocious; Prejudiced—Narrow-Minded—(See "Shallow" under Mentality; Prejudiced).

Premature—(See "Premature Mental Development" under Premature; Prodigies).

Premonitions—(See Forebodings, Premonitions).

Presentiments—(See Forebodings).

Pretender; Pretenses— B r a g g i n g— Conceited, etc.—(See "Pretenses" under Pretender).

Pride; Primitive Instincts Strong — (See "Animal Instincts" under Animal).

Principles — S c r u p l e s — (See Principles).

Procrastination; Prodigal; Prodigies; Profane; Professions—Declarations— Avowals—(See Professions).

Profligate; Projects—Confusion of— (See Projects).

Promises — Profuse In — (S e e Promises).

Propensities — Evil — Sensual — (See the references under Propensities).

Proud; Prudence — E x c e s s of — Imprudent—(See Prudence).

Psychic Diseases — (See Psychic; the various paragraphs u n d e r Intellect, Mental, and in this section).

Purposes; Pyromania — (S e e Incendiarism).

Qualities of the Mind — (See "Qualities" u n d e r Mental; "Desirable" in Sec. 1 of this Article; "Undesirable" in this section. Also look in the alphabetical arrangement for the subject you have in mind).

Quick-Tempered — (See Choleric; "High Temper" under Temper).

Rambling In Speech—(See Speech).

Rape—An Attacker of Women—(See Rape).

Rash Thinking—(See Rashness).

Rationalism; Rattle - Brained — (S e e "Rapid" under Speech).

Raving; Reactionary; Reality—The Imagination Runs Away from the Limitations of Reality—(See Ideals; "Imagination Runs Away" under Imagination).

Reason—Disorders of—Void of—(See Reason).

Recklessness; Recluse; Reformers; Religion—Religious Mania—Religious Ecstasy—(See Religion).

Remorse; Renunciation; Reserved; Restlessness; Retarded Mental Powers —(See "Arrested", "Retarded", under Mental; "Obstructed", "Weak", in this section).

Retrospection; Revengeful; Revolutionary; Riotous; Roaming; Robbers; Romantic; Rough; Sadism— (See "Violence" under Passion; Sadism).

Sadness; Sarcasm; Satire; Savage; Scandalmongers; Scattering — Of the Mental Forces—(See Scattering).

Scepticism; Scornful; Scruples; Seclusive; Secretive; Self-Indulgent; Sensational; Sensitive; Sensuous; Serious-Minded—(See Serious).

Severe; Sex Addict — (S e e Addicts; "Addict" under Sex).

Shallow Mind—(See "Shallow" under Mental; "Light" in Sec. 1 of this Article).

Shameless; Simple-Minded — (See Foolish, Idiocy, Imbecile; "Weak Mind" in this section).

Sleepiness—Drowsiness—(See Sleep).

Sleep-Walking—(See Sleep).

Slow Mental Development — Slow of Speech—(See "Arrested" under Mental; "Slow" under Speech).

Sluggish Mind—(See Dull; "Persons" under Sluggish).

Solitude—Fond of—(See Solitude).

Somnambulism—(See Sleep).

Sorrowful Spirit — (See Grief, Sad, Sorrow).

Speech—Disorders of—(See Speech).

State of Mind — D i s o r d e r s Arising From — The ☉ a f f l i c t e d in ♒. (See "State of the Mind" under Disease; "Mind" under Indifferent; "Mind and Body" in this section).

Stopped—Growth of the Mind Stopped —Retarded—Arrested — (See Dwarfed, Growth, Idiocy, Imbecile; "Arrested" under Mental; "Weak" in this section).

Storms—Brain and Psychic Storms— (See "Brain Storms" u n d e r Brain; Psychic).

Strain — The Mind Should Be Kept Free from Over-Strain—☿ afflicted in ♓. (See "Strain" under Mental).

Strange Terrors — (See "Terrors" in this section).

Strong Fits—(See Fits).

Studies—Loses Interest In Studies— Fails In Examinations—(See Examinations; "Void Of" under Learning; "Shallow" under Mental; "Light In Mind" in Sec. 1 of this Article).

Stupor—Mental Stupor—(See Apathy; "Brain Fag" under Brain; Dull, Fatigue, Idle, Lassitude, Lethargy; "Drowsiness", "Stupor", under Sleep).

Stuttering — (See "Stammering" under Speech).

Suffering In Mind — (See Anguish, Anxiety; "Hopeless" under Hope; Melancholy; "Irritations" u n d e r Mental; Worry; "No Peace of Mind" in this section).

Suggestion—Easily Affected By—(See Suggestion).

Suicidal Mania—(See Suicide).

Superficial Mind — (See "Superficial" in Sec. 1 of this Article).

Supersensitive; Swindler; Tact—Lack of—(See "Bad" under Judgment).

Tastes — Disorders of — Perverted — (See Tastes).

Temper—(See Anger, Choleric; "High" under Temper).

Terrors — Strange Terrors of Mind — (See "Terrors" under Strange).

Thieves; Thinking—Rash and Uncontrolled Thinking—(See Anger, Brutish, Choleric, Cruel, Jealousy, Rashness; "High Temper" under Temper; Uncontrolled, etc.).

Thoughtless — (See Foolhardy, Forethought, Judgment, Rashness, Reckless; "Absent-Minded" in this section).

Threatened—The Mind Threatened— (See "Mind Threatened" in this section).

Thyroid Gland—Disorders of—Relation of To the Mind—(See Thyroid).

Tormented—In Mind — (See Anguish, Anxiety, Dejected, Depressed, Despondency, Disgrace, Gloom, Grief, Melancholy, Misery, Misfortune, Pain, Reverses, Ruin, Scandal, Sorrow, Suffering, Tormented, Worry, Wretched).

Torpid Mind—(See Torpid).

Trance; Treatment — Of Mental Disorders — (See Colors, Cure, Healers, Hypnotism; "Treatment" under Insanity; Mesmerism, Suggestion, Treatment).

Triple Personality—(See Personality).

Trouble—In the Mind—In the Mind and Body — Troubled In Mind — (See "Mental" under Infirmities; "Irritations" under Mental; "Mind and Body", "Tormented", in this section).

Turbulent Mind — (See "Turbulent" under Fancies; Riotous).

Twelfth House — Mental Disorders Caused By—(See Limitations, Twelfth House).

Unbalanced Mind—(See "Unbalanced" under Mental).

Uncanny Feelings—(See Uncanny).

Uncertain—The Mind Uncertain—(See Chaotic, Changeable, Confused, Mutable, Negative, Removals, Restless, Scattering, Vacillating, Worry, etc.).

Unclean Mind — (See Debauched, Depraved, Dissipated, Evil, Lewd, Licentious; "Loose Morals" under Morals; Obscene, Perversions, Shameless, Wanton, Wicked, etc.).

Unconsciousness — (See the subjects and references under Unconsciousness).

Uncontrolled Thinking—(See "Thinking" in this section; Uncontrolled).

Understanding — (See "Weak" under Understanding).

Undesirable Mental Traits—
The following subjects have to do with the Mind, its Afflictions, Deviations, Abnormalities, and Undesirable Traits of Mind. See these subjects in the alphabetical arrangement—Agitation, Agony, Ambition (Of No Ambition); Amorous, Anarchists, Anger, Artifice, Assassins, Astral Body, Asylums, Ataxia, Atony, Atrabile, Austere, Aversions, Awkwardness, Bachelors, Backwardness, Begging, Binding, Bold, Brutish, Careless, Cares (Full of); Celibacy, Cheating, Clumsiness, Coarse, Complaining, Countenance, Critical, Curious, Dangerous, Debauched, Deceitful, Denegerate, Dirty, Disagreeable, Discomposed, Discontentment, Disgraceful, Dishonorable, Dislikes, Disorderly, Disorganized, Disrespectful (see Respect); Disputes, Dissatisfied, Dissipated,. Dissolute, Divination, Doleful, Downcast, Drunkenness, Ease (Fond of); Enemy (His Own Worst Enemy); Enmity (Strong In); Environment (Much Affected By); Epicureans; Expense (Prodigal of); Explosive Manner; Extravagant, Fading, Failure, Fate, Fault-finding, Feasting, Ferocious, Fierce, Fiery, Fighting, Forgers, Free Love (see Free); Fretfulness, Frivolous, Grave,

Gross, Hard Nature (see Hard); Harmful, Harsh, Hasty, Helplessness, Honour (Loss of); Hope (Lack of); Hurtful, Hypocritical, Ignoble, Ill-Disposed, Illicit Appetites (see Appetites); Immoderate, Immodest, Immoral (see Morals); Impetuous, Improper, Imprudent, Impure Morals (see Morals); Incest, Incompatibility, Inconstant, Indecent, Indigent, Indiscreet, Indisposition; Indolent, Indulgent, Inertia, Infamous, Inflexible, Influenced, Inharmony, Injudicious, Inordinate, Insatiable, Intercourse, Intoxication, Intractable, Introversion, Irascible, Irregular, Joy (No Joy); Lamenting, Lazy, Libidinous, Lugubrious, Materialistic, Mean-Spirited (see Mean); Meddlers, Misanthropic, Mischievous, Miserable, Miserly, Mistrustful, Misunderstood, Mockery, Moping, Mournful, Murmuring, Nasty Temper (see Temper); Neglectful, Notoriety, Obstinate, Odd, Offended Easily, Outrageous, Over-Indulgent, Penurious, Perverse, Precipitate, Prejudiced, Prudery, Quarrelsome, Queer, Rakishness, Rapacious, Rebellious, Refractory, Regretful, Repining, Resentful, Resigned, Roving, Salacious, Sanctimonious, Saucy, Scheming, Scolding, Scornful, Seclusive, Sedate, Selfish, Servile, Shrewd, Shy, Slothful, Superstitious, Suspicious, Taciturn, Treacherous, Ugly Disposition, Uncertain, Uncleanly, Uncontrolled, Unhappy, Untidy, Vacillating, Vicious, Wanton, Wicked, Wrangling, Wrathful, etc. (See "Desirable Mental Traits" in Sec. 1 of this Article; "Undesirable" under Mental).

Uneasiness of Mind—(See Uneasiness).

Unfertile Mind — (See "Unfertile" in Sec. 1 of this Article).

Ungovernable—Intractable—Insubordinate—(See Ungovernable).

Unhealthy—Unhealthy State of the Mind—(See "Diseased Mind", and the various paragraphs in this section, and under Mental).

Unmanageable — (See "Outrageous" under Insanity; Ungovernable, Unmanageable).

Unnatural Acts — (See Perversions, Unnatural).

Unreasonable—(See Reason).

Unrefined—A Coarse Body and Mind (See Coarse, Unrefined).

Unreliable—(See Deceitful, Dishonest, Mutable, Unreliable, Vacillating; Light, Shallow, Superficial, in this section).

Unruly—(See Rebellious, Ungovernable, Unmanageable, Unruly).

Unsavory Subjects—The Mind Morbid Upon—(See Unsavory).

Unsettled Mind—And Habits — (See "Unsettled" under Habits; "Instability" in this section).

Unsound Mind—(See "Derangement", "Unbalanced", under Mental; Unsound; "Diseased", and the various paragraphs in this section).

Unstable—Unstable and Weak Mind —Unsteady — (See Chaotic, Confused; "Shallow" under Mentality; Mutable, Negative, Restless, Unsettled, Unstable, Vacillating; Instability, Light, Uncertain, Weak, in this section).

Vagabond; Vagaries—Mind Full of—(See Vagaries).

Vague; Vain Fears—(See Fears).

Vapors—Low Spirits—(See Low, Vapors).

Vehement; Vertigo; Vexations; Vibrations—Mental Vibrations Stopped—(See Vibrations).

Vices; Vile Wretch—(See Vile).

Violent Tendencies—(See Violent).

Virgo Sign—A Sign Ruled by ☿, and the Diseases of ♍ are closely related to the Mind. (See Virgo).

Visions—Visionary Mind—(See Visions).

Vitiated—In Mind and Body—(See Vitiated).

Void Of—Void of Reason—Void of Solid Learning, etc.—(See Learning, Reason, Void Of).

Volition—Loss of—(See Volition, Will).

Voluntary Power—Excessive—(See Voluntary).

Voracious; Vulgar—(See Unrefined).

Wakefulness—(See Sleep).

Wandering Mind—(See Chaotic; "Inability" under Concentration; Dreamy, Wandering, etc.).

Warlike—(See War).

Wayward State of Mind—(See Conduct, Criminal, Debauched, Dissipated, Drink, Drunkenness, Morals, Prodigal, Recklessness, etc.).

Weak Mind—Weak and Unstable—Very Weak Mind—Weak-Minded—The ☉ Sig. ✳ or △ ♄, and ♄ be weak and ill-dignified at B.; ☿ ill-dig. and ☌ ♄ as Significator. (See Foolish, Idiocy, Imbecile, Intellect; "Weak" under Mental; Prenatal; "Diseased", and the various paragraphs in this section). Case of Weak Mind—Birth Data, etc. —See "Weak Mind", No. 145 in 1001 N.N.

Weakened—The Mental Faculties Weakened—(See "Weakened" under Mental; "Weak" in this section).

Weaknesses—Mental Weaknesses—Tendency To—Observe the positions of the ☽, ☿, and the Asc. These unconnected with each other, and afflicted by ♄ and ♂, tend to mental diseases and weaknesses. (See "Weaknesses" under Mental).

Weariness—Of Mind and Body—(See Weariness).

Weeping—Crying Spells—(See the Introduction under Emotions).

Weird Mind—(See Weird).

Wench; Wife—Mind Unsound In—(See "Mind" under Wife).

Wild Delirium—Wild Nature—(See Delirium, Wild).

Will—Weak Will—(See Will).

Wisdom—Lacking In—(See Wisdom).

Wishes—Thwarted—Perverted, etc.—(See Ambitions, Desires, Hopes, Wishes).

Witchcraft; Women—Mental Disorders of—(See Fainting, Hysteria; "Mad Mother" under Madness; Nymphomania; "Mania" under Puerperal).

Words—Loss of—(See "Aphasia" under Speech).

Worry; Wretched; Wrong-Thinking—Wrong Habits—(See Wrong).

Zeal—Intemperate Zeal—Fanatical—Irrational—(See Anarchists, Erratic; "Mental Extremes" under Extremes; Fanatical, Irrational, Irresponsible, Reformers, Religion, Zeal).

MINERAL—Minerals—Mineral Salts—The Minerals of the body are connected with the Earthy Signs ♉, ♍, ♑. (See "Earth Signs" under Earth). The earthy minerals carried by the blood, which are used to form the bony structures, and also the concretions in soft tissues, are ruled by ♄ and the ♑ sign. Saturn rules the bones, and supplies the minerals to the bones, and an afflicted, weak, and ill-dignified ♄, will tend to weaken his action and influence in this regard, and to cause disorders of the bones. (See Bones).

Blood—The Mineral Salts of the Blood Deficient—The Prog. ☽ in ♍, ☌, ☐, or ☍ ♄ and other malefics; ♄ afflicted in ♍, thru the obstruction of intestinal digestion and assimilation, and indirectly denying the bones and muscles the necessary minerals for their strength, and often resulting in Rickets or Tetanus. (See Rickets; "Influence Of" under Saturn; Tetanus).

Deposits of Minerals—Excess Mineral Deposits Over the Body, Causing Disease—Caused by ♄ and his afflictions, and tend to such ailments as Stone, Calculus, Sand, Gravel, Gout, Rheumatism, Hardening of the Arteries, Deformities, Contortions, the Retention of Wastes, Suppression of the Functions, and the Retarding of Elimination and the Secretions. Leukocytes, ruled by ♄, form a nucleus for mineral deposits. (See these subjects just mentioned. Also see Chalk, Concretions, Crystallization, Deposits, Hardening, Hyperacidity, Impure, Leukocytes, Lime, Retention, Suppression, Tumors, Urea, Uric Acid, Wastes, etc).

Mineral Waters—(See "Mineral Waters" under Healers).

Planets and Minerals—Each Planet has rule over a Mineral, Minerals or Metal—(See Metals; "Drugs", "Metal", Minerals", "Typical Drugs", under each of the Planets).

Zodiac Mineral Salts—(See "Salts" under Zodiac). See Antipathy; "Cure of Disease" under Cure; Drugs, Herbs, Medicines, Opposites, Remedies, Salts, Sympathy, Treatment.

MINES—Mines and Mining Concerns are ruled by ♄, and great riches are often gained if the native has ♃ at B. in ✳ or △ ♄, and espec. with ♃ in the 2nd H.

Death In Mines—Danger of Accident, Injury, or Death In Mines—♄ ☌ ♂ in ♉, ♊, ♌, or ♏ in the 4th H., and upon the lower Meridian; the 19° ♑ upon the Asc. at B.

MINIMIZING—Of the Disease—The disease is weakened, minimized, and largely neutralized, when the attributes of the afflicting planets are conflicting and opposing, as when the ☉ and ♄ are the afflictors, as the ☉ opposes ♄, and are opposites in influence. (See Abatement, Amelioration, Antipathy, Crises; "Minimizing" under Disease; Mild, Minor, Moderation, Opposites, Sympathy).

MINISTERS — Clergymen — Priests — Anxiety To—(See Clergymen).

MINOR—Minor Ailments—Minor Bodily Disorders—The Disease Is Not So Important—Mild Disorders—Minor Ailments are ruled by the ☽. These disorders usually occur from the ☽ being posited in a Tropical or Equinocial Sign, which are the cardial signs. (See Cardinal, Equinoxes, Minimizing, Slight, Tropical). The Benefic Planets in a sign, and also the absence of a malefic from a sign, tend to lessen the diseases to the parts of the body ruled by such signs, and to give minor, mild, and slight disorders to that part, and not as malignant or severe.

Minor Fevers—(See "Slight" under Fevers).

Minor Planets—♀ and ☿. (See Major, Mercury, Venus).

Minor Spasm—(See Twitchings).

Minor Throat Ailments—(See "Minor" under Throat).

Women—Minor Disorders of—(See "Minor" under Women).

MINT—Peppermint—(See Mentha).

MIRTH — Mirthful — Joyful — ♃ and ♀ are the planets of Mirth, Joy, Good Cheer, Happiness, Peace and Contentment, when they are strong and well-aspected at B., and the rulers of the horoscope. The Hebrew letter Qoph (K) is connected with the ♓ sign, the sign of ♃, and is predominant in Mirth. For the value of the Hebrew letters of the alphabet, and their connection with Astrology, every student should read the book, "The Tarot of the Bohemians" by Papus. (See Joy).

MISANTHROPIC — Distrust — Mistrustful—Hatred of Mankind—Suspicious— ♄ influence; the ☽ to the ☌ or ill-asp. ♄ by dir., and ♄ weak, ill-dig., and afflicted at B. (See Aversions, Hatred, Miserly, Mistrustful, Penurious, Recluse, Seclusive, Secretive, Selfishness, Suspicious).

MISCARRIAGE—Abortion—Premature Birth—Death by Miscarriage—(See "Death by Miscarriages" under Abortion; "Death" under Hemorrhage; Parturition). Cases of Death by Miscarriage—(See "Cases" under Abortion; "Premature Birth" under Premature). Cases of Miscarriage and Premature Birth are often caused when several of the Moon's librations do not return to, and cross the central line of impulse at the monthly period during gestation, thus causing a lack of equilibrium, and an unbalanced condition of the Foetus. (See Prenatal Epoch).

MISCHANCES—Mishaps—Misfortune—"Bad Luck", etc.—(See Accidents, Danger, Fate; "Malice of Fortune" under Fortune; Injury, Luck, Misfortune, Perils, Unfortunate, Wounds, etc.).

MISCHIEF — Mischievous — Pranks — Evil—Damage—Vexations—Injury, etc. —Mischief is usually the result of ♂ being strong in a nativity, and ♂ aspecting ☿. Mischief mixed with the element of covetousness, envy, malice, or revenge, is associated with ♄.

Active to Do Mischief—Mischievous—Tricky—Artful—The ☽ applying to ♂, or conjoined with him in a nocturnal geniture; ♄ Sig. in ♓, active to do mischief; in Hor'y Q. ♄ Sig. in ♏; ♄ Sig. □ or ♂ ☿; ♂ Sig. in ♓; ♂ strong at B., and afflicting ☿; ♀ Sig. □ or ♂ ♄ or ♂, full of mischief. (See Artifice, Cheating, Deceitful, Dishonest, Enemies, Evil, Forgers, Gamblers, Knavish, Liars, Libelers, Malevolent, Malicious, Pettifogging, Poisoner, Scandalmonger, Thieves, Treachery, Trickery, Vicious, Violent, etc.).

Common People—Mischief To—(See Public).

Danger from Mischief—The ☽ to Castor, Cauda, Lucida, and Caput Algol; the ☽ to the place of Hydra's Heart, and espec. for women; ♅ passing over the place of ♂ at B. by tr., or at a Solar Rev., some sudden and serious mischief to the native; ♂ at a Solar Rev. passing the radical ♅, and espec. if the ☉, ☽, Asc., or M.C. were afflicted by ♅ at B.

Dryness—Mischief and Destruction from Dryness—(See Drouth, Dryness, Famine, Heat, etc.).

Enemies—Mischief By—(See Enemies).

Every One—Mischief to Every One—An eclipse of the ☽ in the 2nd Decan. of ♎, mischief and trouble to every one. (See Prevalent, Public, Trouble).

Fevers—Mischievous Fevers—(See Fever).

Full of Mischief—♀ Sig. ☌, □, or ♂ ♄; ♂ Sig. in ♓ if in terms of ☿. (See "Active" in this section).

Mischief At Hand—The ☽ or lord of the 1st H. in the 6th, 8th, or 12th H., afflicted, combust, ☌, □, or ♂ lords of the 4th, 6th, 8th, or 12th H., slow in motion, out of dignity, and with no assistance from benefics. These influences at B., and the ☽ or lord of the 1st afflicted by dir., tend to bring some calamity, mischief, misfortune, and suffering upon the native. (See Accidents, Air, Blows, Burns, Calamity, Danger, Death, Disgrace, Drowning, Earthquakes, Epidemics, Events, Falls, Famine, Fire, Flood, Grief, Heat, Highwaymen, Honour, Hurt, Injury, Misfortune, Murdered, Perils, Pestilence, Pirates, Public, Reputation, Reverses, Robbers, Ruin, Scandal, Shipwreck, Sickness, Sorrow, Storms, Thieves, Travel, Trouble, Vehicles, Violence, Weather, Wind, Wounds, etc. Also look in the alphabetical arrangement for the subject you have in mind).

MISERABLE—Misery—Miseries—Full of Afflictions—All manner of afflictions, and miseries, are ruled by the 12th H., and with ♄ or ♂ afflicted in this house; lord of the 12th in the 1st H., much misery, or illness from folly; the ☽ or ♃ Sig. □ or ♂ ♄. (See Affliction, Folly, Indiscretions, Misfortune, Sorrow, Suffering, Trouble, Twelfth House).

Dies a Miserable Death—(See Beheaded; "Miserable" under Death; Execution, Hanging, Murdered, Painful, Poison Death (see Poison); Tragical).

Has Many Miseries—(See "Many Afflictions" under Affliction).

Much Misery Everywhere—Much Misery Generally—♄ in ♍ at a Solar Ingress, or an Eclipse, in □ to ♂ in ♑, and the ☽ in ♐ in aspect with both ♄ and ♂, much misery, destruction of Kingdoms, and Revolutions, and espec. if the New ☽ immediately preceding or following these aspects should happen to be an eclipse, and the Countries affected most will be those ruled by the signs containing the malefics and the darkened Luminary. In cases of a Solar Eclipse, the miseries will be especially felt in places over which the central line of the eclipse passes. Saturn in ♎, ♀, and in ☍ the ☉, and the ☉ at the same time in evil configuration with ♂ ♀ at a Solar Ingress or Eclipse, there will be misery upon misery. (See Accidents, Affliction, Calamity, Casualties, Cholera, Comets, Crime, Dangers, Drought, Earthquakes, Eclipses, Epidemics, Events, Evils, Famine, Floods, Grief, Heat (Excessive); Humanity, Lightning, Lynching, Mankind, Mischief, Misfortune, Mobs, Mortality Great, Murders, Pestilence, Plague, Prevalent, Prisons, Public, Railroads, Riots, Robberies, Sadness, Seas, Ships, Shipwrecks, Sorrow, Storms, Suffering, Travel, Trouble, Twelfth House, Vernal Equinox, Violence, Volcanoes, Voyages, War, Water, Weather, Wind, etc.).

MISERLY—Avaricious—Covetous—Niggardly—Rapacious—Envious—Sordid—Selfish, etc.—A ♄ characteristic, and caused by ♄ afflictions; ♄ ruler of the Asc., or the horoscope, at B., and afflicted; ♄ Sig. in ♑; ♄ in ☍ or ♍, avaricious; ♄ in ♑, covetous; ♄ or ☿ in the Asc. or 10th H.; in Hor'y Q. ♄ as Sig. of the person; the ☉ Sig. □ or ☍ ♄; the ☽ Sig. ☌ ♄, extremely covetous; the ☽ Sig. in ♍; ♃ Sig. in ♍, ♏, or ♑; ☿ Sig. ☌ ♄; many influences in fixed signs at B.; ♋ and ♄ combinations in the 2nd H. (See Misanthropic, Penurious, Recluse, Secretive, Selfishness, Solitude).

MISFORTUNE—Adversity—Ill-Fortune —Calamity, etc.— The 12th H. is the house of sorrow, disgrace, and misfortune. The quality and time of the misfortune are usually denoted by the Map of Birth, and by the afflictions to that map by transits, directions, and progressions.

Causes His Own Misfortunes—Causes His Own Illnesses—(See "Brings Disease Upon Himself" under Disease; Disgrace; "His Own Worst Enemy" under Enemies; "Ruined by Women" under Love Affairs; Ruin, Self-Undoing).

Child of Misfortune—The Complete Child of Misfortune—♄ on the Meridian at B., or coming to it, and ill-aspected and ill-dignified; ♄ on or near the Nadir, the cusp of the 4th H., is almost as unfortunate.

Children—Misfortune To—(See "Accidents", and the various paragraphs under Childhood, Children, Infancy. Also for Misfortunes and Afflictions to members of the family, see the various paragraphs under Aunts, Brother, Daughter, Family, Father, Females, Friends, Grandparents, Husband, Males, Men, Mother, Relatives, Sister, Son, Uncles, Wife, Women).

Common People—Misfortune To—(See Public).

Face — Misfortune To — (See Cuts, Hurts, and the various paragraphs under Face. Also for misfortune and affliction to the various parts of the body, look in the alphabetical arrangement for the part you have in mind, such as Arms, Eyes, Feet, Hands, Head, Hips, Legs, Shoulders, etc.).

Liable to Misfortune — Subject To — Danger of — The ☉ rising at B., and afflicted by the ☌, □, or ☍ ♄; the ☉ Sig. □ or ☍ ♄; the ☽ to the ☌, □, or ☍ ♄ or ♂ by dir.; the ☽ to Deneb, misfortune by water or vehicles; the ☽ to the ☌ or P. Dec. South Scale; the ☽ decr. in light, sepr. from ♃ and apply. to ♄; the ☽ sepr. from ♂ and apply. to the ☉; ♄ rising or setting at B.; ♄ near the Meridian, or coming to, or on or near the Nadir; ♄ in the 10th H. in detriment or fall, sudden disgrace and irretrievable ruin; ♄ in the 10th H. in a Solar Rev., and elevated above the Lights; ♄ to his own bad aspects by dir.; ♃ and ♀ cadent and under the Earth; ♂ in detriment and ☍ the Asc.; malefics in the 10th H., and afflicted; malefics elevated above the Lights, and afflicted (see Elevated); malefics rising and in angles, and the benefics setting and ill-dignified; lord of the 12th H. in the 8th, and usually ends in a miserable death; the M.C. to the ☌ or P. Dec. the ☉ if the ☉ is afflicted at B. by malefics, or is in ☌ violent fixed stars. In Hor'y Q. the lord of the 12th H. also being lord of the Asc. Almost every subject in this book has to do with some affliction, or misfortune to the native. See the following subjects, and also look in the alphabetical arrangement for other subjects along this line you may have in mind. (See Accidents, Affliction, Air, Assassinated, Bathings, Blows, Burns, Calamity, Cuts, Destiny, Detriment, Directions, Disease, Disgrace, Drowning, Earth, Events, Evils, Execution, Exile, Falls, Fate, Fire, Folly, Fortune (see "Evil", "Ill-Fortune", "Malice of Fortune", under Fortune); Grief, Highwaymen, Honour (Loss of); Ill-Fortune (see Fortune); Ill-Health, Imprisonment (see Prison); Indiscretions, Injury, Malice of Fortune (see Fortune); Mischief, Miseries, Murdered, Pirates, Poverty, Recklessness, Reputation (Loss of); Reverses, Robbers, Ruin, Scandal, Sea, Ships, Sickness, Sorrow, Stabs, Thieves, Trouble, Tragical, Twelfth House, Unfortunate, Untimely, Vehicles, Violence, Water, Weather, Wind, Wounds, etc., and various other subjects too numerous to list here).

Malice of Fortune—(See "Malice" under Fortune).

Mankind—Misfortune To—(See "Much Misery Everywhere" under Miseries).

Much Misfortune Generally — (See Calamity, Drought, Eclipses, Epidemics, Famine, Grief, Humanity, Mankind, Mischief, Miseries, Panics, Pestilence, Plague, Prevalent, Public, Sorrow, Suffering, Trouble; "Liable to Misfortune" in this section).

Public Misfortune — (See Calamity, Drought, Earthquakes, Epidemics, Famine, Floods; "Much Misery Everywhere" under Misery; Pestilence, Plague, Public, Storms, etc.).

Remarkable Misfortunes — ♅ ascending at B., or with the chief Significator. (See Extraordinary, Mysterious, Peculiar, Strange, Sudden, Tragical, Uncommon, Untimely, etc.).

Some Misfortune Near — Mischief At Hand — (See "Threatened" under Calamity; "Near Some Danger" under Danger; Imminent; "Mischief At Hand" under Mischief; Perils, Public; "Near Relatives" under Relatives; Sudden, Tragedy, etc.).

Time of Misfortune—(See "Time" under Accidents; Directions, Disease, Events, Time; "Some Misfortune Near" in this section).

Vehicles—Misfortune By—(See Journeys, Railroads, Ships, Travel, Vehicles, Voyages).

Water — Misfortune By — (See Bathings, Drowning, Floods; "Hot Liquids" under Heat; Moisture, Rain, Scalds, Sea, Water, etc.).

Women — Much Misfortune, Sickness, Sorrow, and Trouble to Women — The ☽ incr. at B., and apply. to ♄; the ☽ to the ill-asps. the ☉, ♄, or ♀ by dir.; ♂ in ♉ at the Vernal Equi., occi., and Lord of the Year; ♄ in ♍ at the Vernal, ori., and Lord of the Year; ♎ ascending at a Vernal Equi., and ♀ afflicted, tends to much suffering, ill-health and trouble for women during the following Quarter. (See the various paragraphs under Females, Women).

Wounds — Hurts — Injuries—Misfortune By — (See Accidents, Ambushes, Assaults, Bloodshed, Blows, Burns, Cuts, Crushed, Duels, Enemies, Gunshot, Hurts, Injury, Instruments, Iron, Mobs, Operations, Plots, Poison, Robbers, Stabs, Stones (see "Flying Stones" under Stones); Sword, Trampled, Treachery, Weapons, Wounds, etc.).

MISHAPS—(See Accidents, Injury, Mischances, Misfortune, Wounds, etc.).

MISSHAPED — Misshaped Body — (See Contortions, Crooked, Deformities, Distortions; "Ill-Formed" under Ill; Malformations, Missing, Monsters, Twins, Ugly, etc.).

Misshaped Bones — (See "Misshaped" under Bones).

Misshaped Legs—(See Bad, Bent, Bow Legs, Crooked, Ill-Formed, Knock-Knees, One Leg Shorter, Strikes Legs Together, and the various paragraphs under Legs).

Organs Misshaped — Or Undersized — (See Diminished, Enlargements; "Misshaped" under Organs; Undersized, Undeveloped).

MISSING—Missing Members, or Parts Thereof — (See "Missing" under Arms, Feet, Forearm, Hands, Legs, Toes). The case of the famous Frog Child, with both forearms missing from birth, and both legs missing below the knees, is given under Forearm. There are cases of record born with both arms and both legs completely missing. I saw such a case, a lady, with a Circus,

but failed to get her birth data. These cases are caused by Prenatal afflictions. (See Prenatal Epoch). The case of the Frog Child is illustrated and written up in the book, "The Prenatal Epoch", by Mr. Bailey, Editor of the British Journal of Astrology.

MISTRUSTFUL—Mistrustful of Others —Misanthropic—Suspicious—Cautious —The ☉ Sig. ♂ ♄; the ☉ ♂, □, 8, or P. ♄; the ☽ Sig. ♂ ♄, much suspicious caution; ♄ to the ill-asps. his own place by dir. or tr.; ♄ Sig. ✳ or △ the ☽; ♄ Sig. in ♓; the evil directions of ♄ to the ☉, ☽, ♀, the Asc. or M.C.; ♃ afflicted in ♍; ♀ ill-dig. at B.; ♂ or ♀ Sig. ✳ or △ ♄. (See Jealousy, Misanthropic, Selfishness, Suspicious).

MISUNDERSTOOD—Misjudged—Misunderstandings—Not Easy to Understand —Eccentric—The ☉ ♂ ♅ at B.; the ☽ applying to the ♂ or any asp. of ♆ or ♅, difficult to understand; ♆ or ♅ in the Asc. or M.C.; ♂ afflicting the ☉ or ☽, apt to have many disputes and misunderstandings; afflictions between ♀ and ♃; the bicorporeal sign influence strong at B., on angles, and containing many planets; born when there are many □ aspects to a planet, and espec. to ♀ or ♀, or planets ascending at B. (See Eccentric, Fancies, Ideals, Ideas, Independent, Notions, Occult, Metaphysics, Mystical, Peculiar, Persecution, Quarrels, Reformers, Religion).

MITRAL DISORDERS — (See "Mitral" under Heart).

MIXED—Blends—Combinations—

Mixed Colors—Spotted Colors— (See "Clothing", "Mixed", under Colors).

Mixed Diseases—(See "Complications" under Disease).

Mixed Fevers — (See "Mixed" under Fever).

Mixed Fracture—Fracture with Laceration — (See "Compound" under Fracture).

Mixed Ideas — Mixed and Confused Ideas—(See Chaotic, Confused, Ideas).

MOBILITY—(See Action, Gait, Locomotion, Motion, Movement, Walk).

MOBS—Death or Injury By—Death by Mob Violence—Violent Death By—The ☉ □ or 8 ♂ by dir. in a map where violent death is indicated; the □ and 8 aspects of the ☽ to the Significators, death or injury by the Common People in Mobs or Riots; ♅ in the 8th H. and afflicting the hyleg by dir., and other testimonies concurring for a violent death; ♄ in a fixed sign, □ or 8 the ☉, and contrary in condition, or with ♄ occi., and the ☽ be succedent to him. (See "Burned At Stake" under Burns; Common People (see Common); Crushed, Hanging, Impalement, Lynched, Riots; "Assaults" under Stone; Trampled).

MOCKERY — Shams — A False Show — Derisive—Delusive—♂ ruler at B., and afflicted. (See Deceitful, Dual-Minded, Hypocritical, Liars, Pretender, Sardonic, Scornful).

MODERATE—Moderate In Size—Moderate and Temperate In Habits, etc.—

Drink — Moderate Drinker — (See "Moderate" under Drink).

Eating—(See "Moderate" under Eating).

Habits—Moderate In—(See "Habits" under Temperance).

Hair — Moderate Growth of Hair — Moderate Curling — (See "Moderate" under Hair).

Immoderate—(See "Eating", "Habits", under Immoderate).

Stature—Moderate Stature—The ☉ in ♋, or ♋ on the Asc.; ♂ occi. at B.; ♄ in ♌ partile asp. the Asc.; ♈, ♉, ♎, or ♏ on the Asc., moderate in stature but rather long; ♈ on the Asc., a spare, dry, moderate-sized, strong body; ♑, ♒, or ♓ on the Asc., or the ☉ or ☽ in these signs. (See "Mean Stature" under Mean; "Medium Stature" under Medium; Middle; "Stature" under Moderately).

Vitality — Moderate Vitality — (See "Medium" under Vitality).

MODERATELY — Fairly Good — Medium—

  Complexion — Moderately Good Complexion—Moderately Fair— (See Fair, Middling, Moderately, Tolerably, under Complexion).

  Fortunate — (See "Moderately Fortunate" under Fortune).

  Fruitful — (See "Moderately" under Fruitful).

  Good Health—Moderately Good—(See "Tolerably Healthy" under Health).

  Moderately Large Body — ♄ in ♌ in partile asp. the Asc. (See "Middle Stature" under Middle; "Stature" under Moderate).

  Proportioned—Moderately Proportioned Stature—♍, ♎, ♓, and the first parts of ♒ give a moderately proportioned body when on the Asc., but the latter part of ♒ on the Asc., a spare and thin body. (See Well-Proportioned).

  Signs — Moderately Strong Signs of the Zodiac—(See "Moderately Strong" under Signs).

  Stature — Moderately Large Body — (See "Moderately Large" in this section).

  Temperate—Moderately Temperate—(See Temperate).

MODERATION — Amelioration — Under Better Control—Abatement—

  Habits and Affairs—Exercises Moderation In — (See "Moderate" under Drink, Eating, Habits; Temperance).

  Moderation of Disease — Abatement or Amelioration of—The ☉ or ☽ angular, ori., and elevated above the malefics, and also the benefics in a strong position and well-aspected; a Solar Eclipse falling on the place of the radical ♃; the ☽ coming to the ✶ or △ the lords of the Asc., 9th, 10th, or 11th H. brings an interval of ease and amendment; the Prog. ☽ ☌, ✶, or △ ♃ or ♀ in the radical map; ♃ or ♀ ori., and elevated above the malefics; a good aspect of ♃ or ♀ to the ☉, ☽, Asc., or hyleg at the same time there are evil aspects from the malefics, tends to moderate the disease. Also ☿ configurated with ♃ gives the addition of skillful Healers, or the proper remedies and treatment. When a malefic applying to the ☽ at decumbiture passes the ☽, the patient gets better. Any disease will tend to be mitigated, ameliorated, or curable if the benefics be elevated above the malefics which produce it, and the more angular, ori., and elevated above the malefics the benefics may be, the more they assist in the cure and amelioration of the disease. When a train of evil directions and aspects indicate ill-health or death, the course of disease is modified and ameliorated when the good asps. of ♃ or ♀ to the hyleg intervene. A strong map of birth tends to modify disease and give greate: powers of resistance, no matter how evil the directions. If an afflicted planet causing the disease is well-aspected by the benefics, as by ☌ or P. asp., then the evil will be mitigated. The afflicting planet turning ℞ tends to modify the disease. Planets passing from cardinal to common signs tend to a falling off in the power and degree of morbid action in disease, and to moderation and improvement. (See Amelioration, Antipathy, Continuity, Course, Crises, Curable; "Better" under Disease; Duration, Ease; "Disease" under Force; "Improved" under Health; Minimizing, Modification, Opposites, Prognosis, Recovery, Recuperation, Remission, Resistance, Retrograde; "Illnesses" under Short; Termination, Treatment; "Good" under Vitality; Worse, etc.).

MODESTY — ♃ is the author of; ♀ Sig. ✶ or △ ♄, modest, shy, and retiring. (See Backwardness, Bashfulness, Blushing; "Chaste" under Females; Gentle, Immodest, Manners, Meek, Prudery, Quiet, Reserved, Retiring, Shy, etc.).

MODIFICATION OF DISEASE—The horoscope as a whole should be studied in judging of the force or outcome of a disease, and not any one aspect, as the good aspects from the benefics, the ☉ or ☽, will tend to modify the disease in a fortunate map. If the radical map is generally weak, the disease would tend to be more severe. Each planet imparts a special type of disease to an organ, but the disease may become disguised, modified, or changed by cross aspects from other planets, by the afflicting planet passing from one sign or house to another, or turning ℞. Also at the crisis time in a disease, if it is acute, it will either resolve itself, or go into a chronic form, and especially if the disease has progressed for about 28 days, one revolution of the ☽ from the time it began. (See the references under Moderation. Also see "Crises" under Acute; "Long Chronic Distempers" under Chronic; Complications, Diagnosis; "Complications" under Disease; Fatal; "Disease" under Force, Judgment, Nature, Quality, Severity; Polarity, Worse, etc.).

MOISTURE—Moist—Dampness—Vapors —Humidity—Wet—Water, etc.—Moisture is a feminine quality and passive, and is a benefic influence given by the ☽, and the benefics ♃ and ♀, and also by the watery signs ♋, ♏, and ♓. The airy signs ♊, ♎, and ♒, are next in degree of moisture. Dryness and moisture are passive qualities, and heat and cold are active qualities. The ☽ is moist in quality, and generates moisture, dampness, and vapors. The ☽ rules largely over the radical moisture of the body, and its distribution, and contributes moisture of temperament to the body. The ☽ makes the constitution moist from the New ☽ to the 1st Quarter. Jupiter is warm and moist, being temperate in nature, and produces moisture when occidental. Venus gives off much moisture, gathers the moist vapors from the Earth, and causes moisture when occidental. Venus denotes death by epidemics, rottenness, and putrefactions which proceed from too much moisture. White, the color ruled by the ☽, is passive, and is the sign of radical moisture. The colors of ♃ and ♀ combined are signs of heat and moisture combined, as blue and yellow. Mercury produces moisture when femininely constituted, and dryness when masculine. Moisture is prolific and nutritive. Heat and Moisture combined are positive and tend to fermentation. (See Zymosis). The feminine signs of the Zodiac, the even signs, predominate in moisture. The elementary qualities of moist and dry alternate in the signs of the Zodiac, one being moist, and the next one dry, etc., on around thru the 12 Signs. The ☽ and ♀ Groups of Herbs and Plants have a cold and moist action, but some Authors say that the Herbs of ♇ have a moist and warm influence. Moisture largely predominates in the female sex, and is a female and passive quality. Moisture is more feeble in the left side of the body, as the left side is ruled by Cold. Damp vapors are caused by the nearness of the ☽ to the Earth, thus tending to cause putrefaction and relaxation of animal bodies. Humidity is ruled by the ☽. The following subjects have to do with Moisture, its influences and action, the diseases caused by, and its general effects upon Humanity.

Abundance of Moist Humours — And Suffering From—Over-Moist Air—Excess of Rain and Floods—The ♒ sign ascending at a Vernal Equi., and espec. in places ruled by this sign. (See Floods, Rain; "Moist" in this section).

Air—Over-Moist Air and Suffering From — (See "Abundance" in this section).

Bodily Temperament — Moist Bodily Temperament — The ☉, ☽, and many planets in watery signs, and abounds especially in ♏; a watery sign on the Asc.; ♃ or the ☽ occi.; those born in cold climates and the Arctics. (See "Body" under Cold).

Body — Moist Body — Moist and Cold Body—Hot and Moist Body—(See Bodily Temperament, Cold and Moist Body, Hot and Moist Body, in this section).

Brain—Moisture of—The ☽ coming to the ☌ ☉, and ruled by ♄, or the ☽ at her Full being ruled by ♂, and espec. when it may happen in ♎, ♐, or ♓. Under these conditions if the malefics be in Eastern Parts and in angles, and the benefics in the West, tend to demoniacal affections, and ♄ and the ☽ cooperating in the scheme contribute

to moisture of the brain; the ☽ and ☿ unconnected with each other or the Asc., ♄ and ♂ angular and ori., and with ♃ and ♀ setting and occidental. (See "Wild" under Delirium; Demoniac; "Outrageous" under Insanity).

Clothing—Damp Clothing and Linen, Illness and Colds From—(See "Colds" in this section; "Linen" under Wet).

Clouds — Excessive Rain From, and Suffering to Humanity — (See Clouds, Floods, Rain).

Cold and Moist Body—Cold and Moist Bodily Temperament—The Phlegmatic, or Lymphatic Temperament — The watery signs ♋, ♏, or ♓ predominant at B., or upon the Asc.; ♄ produces, and espec. when ori.; given by the Quadrant from the Winter Tropic to the Vernal Equi.; characteristic of those born in cold climates and in the Arctics. The ☽ and ♀ groups of plants and herbs are cold and moist. (See "Body" under Cold; "Temperament" under Lymphatic, Phlegmatic).

Cold and Moist Diseases—Distempers, or Humours — (See "Cold and Moist" under Humours).

Cold and Moisture — Dampness and Cold, and Diseases or Fevers Arising From—Caused by ♄ or ♅; ♄ diseases. (See "Cold and Dampness" under Exposure; "Humours" under Watery).

Colds—Colds Taken from Wet Linen, Wet Feet, or from Living In Cold and Damp Places—Afflictions in ♓, and are ♓ diseases. (See Exposure; "Cold Taken" under Feet; Pneumonia; "Linen" under Wet).

Constitution—A Moist Body and Constitution—(See "Bodily Temperament" in this section).

Corruption of Moisture—Diseases Arising From—Caused by ♀. (See Corruption; "Superabundance" in this section).

Damp and Cold Places—Diseases from Living In — (See "Colds" in this section).

Damp Vapors—Caused by the ☽, and tend to Putrefaction and Relaxation of Animal Bodies. (See Putrefaction, Relaxation, in this section).

Dampness and Cold—Diseases Arising From—(See "Cold and Moisture" in this section).

Death — From Diseases Arising from Moisture — ♀ denotes death by Epidemics, Rottenness, and Putrefaction which proceed from too much moisture. (See "Superabundance" in this section).

Diseases — Diseases Proceeding from Moisture—Water signs on the Asc. or 6th H. at B., or at decumb., or the Sig. of the disease in a watery sign at the beginning of an illness. (See "Cold and Moist" under Humours; "Superabundance" in this section).

Distempers—(a) Cold and Moist Distempers — ♓ diseases. (See "Cold and Moist" under Humours). (b) Hot, Moist, and Putrid Distempers — (See "Hot and Moist Diseases" under Heat).

Epidemics—From Too Much Moisture —Caused by ♀. (See Epidemics; "Death" in this section).

Exposure to Dampness—Diseases Arising From—(See "Cold and Dampness" under Exposure; "Colds" in this section).

Eyelids—Excessive Moisture of—(See "Watery Eyes" under Tears).

Feet—Moist Humours In—(See "Humours" under Feet).

Fermentation — (See Fermentation; "Hot and Moist Body" in this section).

Fevers—Arising from Dampness and Cold—(See "Cold and Moisture" in this section).

Fluids of the Body—Disorders of—(See Fluids).

Head—Moist and Watery Humours In—(See "Moist Humours" under Head).

Hips—Moist Humours In—(See "Cold and Moist" under Hips).

Hot and Moist Body—Hot and Moist Bodily Temperament — The Sanguine Temperament—This is a positive temperament, and tends to produce fermentation. Is given by the Quadrant from the Asc. to the Nadir, the Summer Tropic, or during the passage of the ☉ thru the ♈, ♉, and ♊ Signs. Also the Airy Signs are hot and moist, and with the ☉ and many planets in these signs, or with an airy sign upon the Asc., and especially the ♒ sign. The New ☽ is hot and moist. Also ♃ when ori. tends to produce this temperament. (See "Hot and Moist Diseases" under Heat, and in this section; "Sanguine Temperament" under Sanguine).

Hot and Moist Diseases—Hot, Moist, and Putrid Diseases—Distempers—(See "Hot and Moist" under Heat). The body abounds in heat and moisture with ♈, ♉, or ♊ on the Asc., or with the ☉ or ☽ in these signs; ♃ ruler of the Asc., a hot and moist constitution. (See Humidity).

Humidity — Much Affected By — (See Humidity).

Humours — Abundance of Moist Humours — Moist Diseases and Humours — (See Abundance, Diseases, Distempers, Moist Diseases, Superabundance, in this section; "Moist Humours" under Head, Humours).

Journeys—Danger from Dampness On—(See "Travel" under Exposure, Health; "Wet" under Journeys; "Dampness" under Voyages).

Lack of Moisture — Diseases Arising From — (See Drought; "Superabundance" under Dryness; "Heat" under Epidemics; Famine, Fountains; "Extreme Heat" under Heat; Pestilence, Scarcity).

Left Side of Body—Suffers from Lack of Moisture—Cold and Moist Humours In — (See "Cold and Moist Humours" under Humours; "Feeble" under Left).

Linen — Colds and Disease from Wet Linen—(See "Colds" in this section).

Liquids—(See Liquids).

Living In Damp Places — Colds and Diseases From — (See "Colds" in this section).

Moist Body — (See "Bodily Temperament" in this section).

Moist and Cold Body—(See "Cold and Moist Body" in this section).

Moist and Cold Diseases—Distempers — Humours — (See "Cold and Moist" under Humours).

Moist Constitution — (See "Bodily Temperament" in this section).

Moist Diseases and Humours — Moist Distempers—The Body Over-Charged with Moist Humours — The ☽ afflicted in ♓; the ☽ to the ☌, P., □ or 8 ♄, cold and moist humours; ♓ diseases; watery signs on the Asc. at B., moist humours; many planets in watery signs. (See "Moist Humours" under Feet, Head; "Cold and Moist" under Humours; "Abundance", "Diseases", "Distempers", in this section).

Moist and Hot Body — (See "Hot and Moist Body" in this section).

Moist and Hot Diseases — (See "Hot and Moist" in this section).

Moist Humours—(See "Moist Diseases" in this section).

Moist Signs—(See "Signs" in this section).

Moist Warmth—Moist and Warm Diseases—The physiological action of the ☽, and in Nature tending to rottenness and putrefaction. In the human body afflictions to the ☽, or by the ☽, and especially when the ☽ is ☌ ♂, tend to warm and moist, or hot and moist diseases. Also warm and moist diseases are diseases of ♆, ♃, and ♀. (See "Hot and Moist Diseases" in this section; "Moist and Warm" under Heat).

Moisture — Diseases Which Proceed From—(See "Diseases" and the various paragraphs in this section).

Moisture of the Brain—(See "Brain" in this section).

Odors—Foul Odors or Vapors—(See Foul, Odors; "Foul" under Vapors).

Over-Moist Air—(See "Abundance" in this section).

Places—Locations—Diseases Arising from Living In Damp Places — (See "Colds" in this section).

Planets—The Moist Planets—♃, ♀, ☽, and also ☿ when femininely constituted. Also ♆ is classed as moist, as ♓ is the strong sign of ♆, and ♆ rules the Sea. These planets, along with ♆, tend to cause moist diseases, or moist and warm diseases.

Putrefaction—Putrid Diseases—Death By — (See "Hot and Moist Diseases" under Heat; the various paragraphs under Putrid; "Relaxation" in this section).

Rain—Excess of, and Suffering From —(See Rain).

Relaxation and Moisture—Relaxation of Animal Bodies—Damp vapors caused by the nearness of the ☽ to the Earth, tend to cause putrefaction and relaxation of animal bodies. Also ☽ and ♀ tend to relaxation of the body and tissues, and to bring on moist diseases. (See Decay; "Moist and Warm" under Heat; Putrefaction, Relexation).

Residence—Colds and Disorders from Living In Damp Places—(See "Colds" in this section).

Rivers—Rivers Fail—Corruption of—(See Rivers).

Rottenness—♀ denotes death by rottenness which proceeds from too much moisture. (See Rottenness).

Sanguine Temperament—A Moist Temperament. (See "Temperament" under Sanguine).

Sea—(See the various paragraphs under Ocean, Sea, Ships, Voyages).

Signs—The Moist Signs of the Zodiac —The watery signs ♋, ♏, ♓. The airy signs ♊, ♎, and ♒ are next in degree of moisture. Libra and ♒ are warm and moist signs.

Sudden Exposure—To Dampness, and Diseases Arising From — (See "Exposure" in this section).

Superabundance — Of Moisture — Suffering and Disease From—♀ influence tends to when the dominion of death is vested in her. (See Abundance, Air, Colds, Death, Diseases, Epidemics, Fevers, Moist Diseases, in this section; Floods, Rain, Storms, Water).

Temperament—(See Bodily Temperament, Cold and Moist Body, Hot and Moist Body, Sanguine, in this section).

Thighs and Hips—Cold and Moist Humours In—(See "Cold and Moist" under Hips).

Too Much Moisture—Diseases Arising From—(See Colds, Death, Superabundance, in this section).

Vapors — Damp Vapors — (See Damp Vapors, Relaxation, in this section; Vapors).

Voyages—Danger from Dampness On —(See "Dampness" under Voyages).

Warm and Moist Diseases—(See Hot and Moist Diseases, Moist Warmth, Relaxation, in this section).

Warmth—(See Moist Warmth, Relaxation, Warm and Moist, in this section).

Water—(See Water).

Watery Signs — (See "Signs" in this section).

White Color—Ruled by the ☽, and is the sign of radical moisture. (See White).

MOLECULAR NUTRITION—Under the rule of ♃. (See Nutrition).

MOLES — A Small, Brown, Cutaneous Spot — Marks tend to be Moles when the part is not afflicted by ♂. The ☉ alone in a sign, away from ♂, tends to a Mole rather than a Scar or Wound. (See Blemishes, Defects, Freckles, Marks, Scars). For the influences which cause Moles on the various parts of the body, see "Moles" under the part you have in mind. See "Moles" under such parts as Arms, Back, Breast, Face, Feet, Front, Knees, Left Side (see Left); Legs, Neck, Right Side (see Right); Shoulders, Thighs, Throat, etc. Many of the rules as to the location of Moles are given in the Articles on Marks and Scars, and also in this section in what follows.

Location of Moles — Examples of —
(1) A masculine sign on the Asc., and a masculine planet in the Asc., as ♎ on the Asc., and ♃ in the Asc., tends to a mole on the right side of the face. (See "Left Side", "Marks", under Face).

(2) The latter degrees of ♎ on the Asc. would indicate a mole on the lower part of the Reins near the Haunches.

(3) The first part of ♈ on the 6th H., a mole on the head near the hair, or on scalp. The middle part of ♈ on the cusp of the 1st or 6th, a mole near the middle of the right side of the face.

(4) ♂ lord of the 6th, in ♐, near the middle of the sign, and under the earth, shows a mole on the back part of the right thigh, near the middle of the thigh, and not as noticeable. If ♂ had been prominent and above the earth, the mole would be on the front of the thigh and more prominent.

(5) The ☽ in a female sign, and under the earth, indicates a mole on the left foot, under and near the extremity of the foot.

(6) ♓, a feminine sign, on the Asc. would denote a mole on the left cheek, as the Asc. rules the head and face. Also as ♓ rules the feet there would be a mole on the left foot.

(7) ♌, a masculine sign, on the 10th denotes a mole, scar, or mark on the right side, below the breast, as ♌ rules the Sides. Other examples might be mentioned. Learn the rules and you can apply them to any case. (See "Moles" under Left; "Organs" under Lower, Middle; Naevus; "Lower Part" under Organs; Right; "Organs" under Upper).

MOMENT—The Time of Events—
Moment of Action — Hesitates In — (See Chaotic, Confused, Dreamy; "Doubts" under Fears; Inconstant, Mutable, Negative, Restless, Vacillating, etc.).

Moment of Birth—The time when the child takes in its first breath, and makes the first cry, for it is at this time that the magnetic forces and vibrations of the Planets, Aspects, and Universe, etc., are stamped upon the native, and not when the cord is cut. The cord may be cut some minutes after the first cry and intake of breath. However, some Authorities take either time as the Moment of Birth, as Wilson does in his Dictionary of Astrology under the subject of "Nativity". The Moment of Birth, and the actual Map of Birth intended for the native, are usually a fixed time, and predetermined, and interferences with normal birth may change the map, and thus considerably interfere with, or change and modify the destiny of the individual. (See "Planetary Baptism" under Baptism; "Causes of Birth", "Moment of Birth", under Birth; Calamity; "Born" under Children; "Map of Birth" under Map; Nativity).

Moment of Conception—(See "Moment" under Conception; Prenatal Epoch). See Events, Time.

MONARCHS—(See Kings, President, Queens, Rulers).

MONDAY—Ruled by the ☽. (See Week).

MONEY—Reckless and Extravagant In the Use of — Disease and Suffering From, etc. — (See Appetites, Conduct, Debauched, Dissipated, Dress, Drink, Eating, Excesses, Expense, Extravagant, Feasting, Food, Fortune, Gambling, Generous, Gluttony, Habits,

Harlots, Love Affairs, Luxuries, Men (see "Health Injured" under Men); Passion, Pleasures, Poverty, Prodigal, Property, Prosperity, Recklessness, Resources, Reverses, Riches, Ruin, Social Life, Sports, Travel, Wealth, Women, etc.).

MONOMANIA—(See this subject under Mania).

MONSTERS—Monstrosities—Monstrous Births — Teratism — An Anomaly of Conformation, and Usually Congenital —Too Many Parts or a Deficiency of— Abnormalities — Unnatural Conformations—Freaks of Nature—Congenital Conformations, etc.—Teratology is the Science, or Study of Monsters. The subject of Monsters, and especially of Congenital Monsters, is one largely for Prenatal study, and the conditions which existed at Conception and during Gestation, the aspects, position, and condition of the ☽ at her monthly return to the central line of impulse during pregnancy. The Map of Birth also may show conditions which indicate Monstrosity, if not at birth, that which may be acquired, and develop at some time later in life when certain directions and influences culminate. The Map of Birth is also apt to contain influences, aspects, and indications which supplement prenatal conditions. The Occult side of Monstrosities, and their relation to the Laws of Cause and Effect, and the Law of Karma, etc., are discussed in the book, "Cosmo-Conception", by Max Heindel.

Animal Forms — Resembles Animals or Fowls—The Luminaries in Bestial or Quadrupedal Signs at B., and the malefics in the Asc. or M.C. at the New or Full ☽ previous to birth, the birth will not be fully human. If the Lights in such case are supported by no benefic, but greatly afflicted by malefics, the person so born will be of a wild, savage, or indocile nature. In features such births often resemble the animals in appearance, as cats or dogs. Aspects from ☿ at the same time tend to bird features, or those of cattle or swine. Mercury in the foregoing configurations tends to a disposition agreeable to nature, but with an unnatural body, and not conforming altogether to human form. The Luminaries disconnected with the Asc. at a New or Full ☽ just previous to birth, and being in bestial signs, with no support from benefics, and afflicted by ♄ and ♂ at the same time, the offspring will then be like dogs, cats, or other creatures held in religious veneration, and used in worship. (See "Beastly Form", "Beastly Signs", under Beasts; "Dogs" under Children; Inhuman).

General Causes — General Considerations — Map of Birth and Prenatal Considerations—Monsters are often caused by an over-production of the secretion of the Pineal Gland under an afflicting influence of ♅, which planet rules this Gland. If at conception the Lights are in the 6th or 12th H., and the malefics angular, or if the place of the last Full ☽, or its lord, and the disposer of the Luminaries have no aspect to the Asc., monsters are gen-

erated. Also may occur when the ruler of the last New or Full ☽ before birth, and the rulers of the ☉ and ☽ are unconnected with the preceding New or Full ☽. The Luminaries at the time of a New or Full ☽, or just previous to birth, are usually unconnected with the Asc. by aspect. In these cases the Luminaries at B. have been found cadent from the Asc., and forming no aspect to the Asc., and also with the malefics in angles, and espec. in the Asc. or M.C. Also the malefics in angles, and the ☉ and ☽ in ☍ in the 6th and 12th H., which would indicate great limitations. Are also said to be produced by the common sign influence predominant at conception, and at birth, the common signs on the angles, or the common signs much afflicted during gestation. Other influences along this line are given in the other paragraphs of this Article.

Monstrous In Quality—But with Proper Conformation of Body—The ☉ and ☽ in ♊, ♍, ♐, or ♒; the ruling planets discordant; the Luminaries in signs of human shape, and the other circumstances in the scheme of the nativity existing as before described, the body will be human, partake of human nature, but be defective in some peculiar quality. In order to ascertain the nature of the defect the shape and form of the signs containing the ☉ and ☽, and those on the angles occupied by malefics, should be considered. (See "Void Of" under Reason). For further and collateral study along this line see Abnormalities, Acquired, Armless Wonder (see Arms); Birth, Body, Born Blind (see Blindness); Congenital, Contortions, Cyclops, Deaf and Dumb (see Hearing, Mutes); Deaf, Dumb and Blind (see Deafness); Defects, Deficient, Deformities, Demoniac, Diminished, Distortions, Dwarfed, Enlarged, Eunuchs, Eyes Fused (Cyclops); Foetus, Freaks, Frog Child (see Forearm); Gestation, Giants, Growth, Heredity, Hermaphrodites, Idiots, Imbecile, Incomplete, Insanity, Irrational, Legs Missing Below Knees (see Forearm); Malformations, Mind (Weak Mind); Mutes, Organic, Perversions, Pineal Gland, Pregnancy, Prenatal Epoch, Reason, Savage, Structural, Twins (see United Twins); Undersized, Undeveloped, Unnatural, Virile, Void Of, Wild, etc.

MOODS — Moody—Moodiness—Melancholic Moods are given by ♄.

Subject to Moods—The ☉, ☽, or ☿ in ♑; the ☉ or ☽ to the ☌, P., □, or ☍ ♄ by dir.; the ☉, ☽, or ☿ afflicted by ♄ at B.; ♎ or ♑ on the Asc. The influences of the watery signs tend to moodiness, and espec. the ♓ sign, and also attended by a lack of cardinal influences strong at B., and the mutable signs predominant. The fiery signs strong at B. tend to emotional instability, but with greater power to throw off moods. (See Anxiety, Brooding, Dejected, Depressed, Despair, Despondent, Emotions, Fears, Gloom, Hope, Hypochondria, Introspection, Melancholy, Morbid, Morose, Obsessions, Regretful, Repining, Sadness, Serious, Sorrowful, Taciturn, Worry).

MOON—Lunar—The ☽ is one of the principle influences to be considered in Astrology, as her aspects, positions, influences, and progressed positions, tend to bring into action the vibrations of the ☉ and planets for good or ill over human life, as well as over the animal and vegetable kingdoms. The ☽ is the collector of the Solar forces, and reflects the heat and light of the ☉, and by her rapid course around thru the 12 Signs each month she is the distributor and conveyer of the forces of the ☉, and other planets she passes and aspects. The ☽ was thrown off from the Earth because it became a hard crystal and was holding back the evolution of the Earth. The bones in man's body were soft and cartilaginous before the ☽ was thrown off. The distant action of the ☽ now is to harden and crystallize, and after the ☽ was thrown off in the Hyperborean Epoch the bones of man began to harden, and a stronger skeleton was formed. The action of the ☽ today is to harden and crystallize man's body, and to bring on death. If man were to live on the ☽ his body would turn into stone and he would soon die. There is no plant, vegetable or animal life on the ☽. The ☽ is a corpse and gives off corpse-like emanations which makes her influence obnoxious. (See Decay, Moonlight). See the book, "Cosmo-Conception" by Max Heindel, for a full discussion of the origin of the ☽, and her present influences and destiny. The ☽ is feminine in quality, and along with ♀, a feminine planet, and is the general Significator of health in a female nativity, and also rules the female functlions. The ☽ is the planet of Fecundation, the planet of fertilization and impregnation, and the ☽ stands at the head of the functional group, and is the chief index of functional activity. The ☽ rules the night, and the ☉ the day time. The ☽ has special affinity with the eyes, and when afflicted at B., and by dir., tends to eye disorders and blindness. The period of Gestation in man and beast is measured by the ☽. The ☽ is magnetic, and also an indicator of disease. She generates moisture, and causes putrefaction, rottenness, and relaxation of animal bodies by generating damp vapors. The ☽ has the greatest effect in infancy, and affects both mind and body. The ☽ weak and afflicted at B. rarely brings good health, and especially in females. In quality the ☽ is negative, feminine, magnetic, cold, moist, fruitful, changeful, lymphatic, plastic, romantic, and wandering. Her influence tends to change, and also to act as an expulsive, cleansing, and alterative agency. She is a receiver, and the preparer, and has strong influence over the breasts, stomach, and womb, and is of powerful import in a female nativity. A ☽ person is ever inconstant, restless, changeable, variable, and a rover. As the ☉ is typical of Spirit, so the ☽ represents Matter, organic decay, and transitory experience. (See Matter). What she represents is of an illusive nature, and has to do with present existence on the Earth Plane. The ☽ influence implies fate, thraldom of the flesh, and bondage to Matter. The ♋ sign is the home and only sign of the ☽. She has her exaltation in ♉, her fall in ♏, and her detriment in ♑. The ♋ and ♓ signs are the two best signs for the ☽, and the airy signs. The fire signs are not favorable for the ☽, and also ♏ and ♑ are considered bad signs for the ☽, as she has her fall and detriment in these signs. In order to get the ☽ influences in shape for more ready reference, this Article has been arranged into three Sections. Section One—Influences of the Moon, and General Considerations. Section Two—The Moon Rules. Section Three—Diseases and Afflictions of the Moon.

— SECTION ONE —

INFLUENCES OF THE MOON—

Above the Earth—The ☽ to be powerful should be above the Earth in a night nativity, and below the Earth in a day geniture. When the ☽ is above the Earth in a night map, the functional activities of the body are more normal and regular. The influence and power of the ☽ are weakened when above the earth by day, or below the horizon by night. (See "Below the Earth" in this section).

Absorbent Vessels—The ☽ rules the Absorbent Vessels, and when in the watery signs ♋ and ♓ is most at home and gives efficient and strong functions, and the action of the absorbent vessels and lymphatic system are regular and normal. (See Absorption; "Strong" under Functions; Lymph).

Action of the Moon—The Moon's action is reflective, and she has no basic nature of her own, but focuses the planetary influences upon the mind and body. The action of the ☽ by her different positions and aspects becomes chemically convertive, metamorphic, assimilating, integrative, and secreting. The Moon's action is periodic, mutational, changing, fluidic, and of the ebb and flow order, and traceable for the most part among the fluids. The action of the ☽ also is to harden and crystallize the body with age. (See the Introduction, "Qualities", and the various paragraphs in this Article).

Acts as a Medium—The ☽ acts as a medium of relationship between the ☉, planets, and human, animal and vegetable life and mundane affairs. She rapidly takes up the magnetic force from the other planets and distributes it, and quickly lets go, thus producing change and a great variety of conditions over mind and body.

Afflictions of the Moon—The ☽ afflicts by her □ and ☍ aspects, and by her progressed evil aspects to the radical ☉, planets, Asc., M.C., or hyleg. (See "Aspects" in this section).

Air Signs—Next to the watery signs, the airy signs are rather congenial to the ☽. (See "Air Signs" under Air).

Anareta—The ☽ as Anareta—(See Anareta).

Angel Of—Gabriel.

Appearance—The ☽, her sign and house position, have considerable influence over the personal appearance, and the positions of her nodes are also said to partly determine the height of the body. (See Appearance, Decanates, Height).

Aspects—Aspects and Position of the ☽—These tend to bring events to pass, as she is the time marker in human affairs and World conditions, the minute hand on the clock of destiny, and the ☉ is the hour hand. (See Events). The aspects and position of the ☽ affect and react on the general health, and also the aspects of the other planets to the ☽ have much to do with the general health. The ☽ is fortunate or evil in her influences according to the planets with which configurated, and in many respects is the most powerful of all the planets in health and other matters, the ☉ not even excepted. She afflicts by her □ and ☍ aspects, and tends to benefit the mind and body by her favorable aspects to the ☉, planets, Asc., M.C., and hyleg. (See Afflictions Of, Evil Aspects, in this section).

Below the Earth—The ☽ rules by night, and the ☉ by day, and the ☽ to be more powerful should be above the Earth in a night nativity, and below the earth in a day geniture. The influence and power of the ☽ are weakened when above the earth by day, or below the earth by night. Also when the ☽ is below the earth by day or night the functional activities are not as strong and regular as when the ☽ is above the earth, rising, elevated, dignified, and in a watery sign, as in ♋ or ♓. This is the rule with all the planets that they are more powerful when rising and elevated, and weaker when setting, or below the earth, or horizon at B. (See "Above the Earth" in this section).

Benefic—The action of the ☽ is more benefic in influence when increasing in light, and to some extent malefic and weaker in her action on the functions when in her decrease.

Best Signs—For the ☽—The watery signs ♋ and ♓.

Bodily Forces Weakest—At the New ☽. (See "New Moon" in this section).

Changeable and Variable—In the 12 Signs the influence of the ☽ is variable and changeable, and does not follow the same arrangement as the ☉ and Asc. The ☽ and ☿ are considered variable planets and take on much of the nature and attributes of the planets with which configurated. Thus the ☽ with ♄ gives a very serious, grave and despondent nature and personality, and also retarded and suppressed functions. The ☽ with ♃ gives a more fortunate and buoyant nature, and aids the functions, etc. (See Variable).

Changes of the Moon—The ☽ at her changes, as the New and Full ☽, has a very strong influence over Epileptics, Lunatics, Hysterical and Nervous people, and such people are very sensitive to these changes, and at the Full ☽ especially are very restless, and should never sleep in the open moonlight. (See "Full Moon", "New Moon", in this section).

Character and the Moon—The sign position of the ☽ at B. represents the personal character, the personality, the personal habits, and the functional activities, and to react on the general health according to the nature of the sign, house position, and aspects to the ☽.

Chemical Action Of—Is more deleterious at night by blending with the carbonic acid exhalations of the vegetable kingdom. (See Moonlight, Night, in this section).

Chief Index Of—The ☽ is the chief index of functional activity. (See Functions).

Children—The ☽ is the Sig. of children in Hor'y Q. The ☽ is classed as fruitful, and a giver of children. Females born at the time of an eclipse of the ☽, at a New ☽, are apt to die at birth, or soon after. (See "Death At Birth" under Birth; Eclipses, Fruitfulness).

Classification Of—The ☉ and ☽ are both reckoned as planets in Astrology. The ☽ is classified as a feminine, negative, passive, nocturnal, cold, moist, magnetic, fruitful, phlegmatic body. (See "Qualities" in this section).

Colors—The ☽ rules Green in the Solar Spectrum. Also rules white, or white spotted, or a light mixed color, silver, violet, spotted and mixed colors. The color of the ☽ has a passive power, and white is the sign of radical moisture. (See Colors).

Conduct and the Moon—The ☽ has much to do with the conduct and habits of life, the growth, the functional activities, and the general health.

Constitution—The Constitution Strengthened—(See "Strengthened" under Constitution).

Contracts Disease Easily—(See Contracts).

Crises In Disease—Ruled by the ☽. (See Crises).

Critical Days—Of the ☽ Influence—(See "Crises" under Acute; Amelioration; Crises, Critical, Decrease; "Disease" under Increase, Severe; Moderation; Full Moon, New Moon, Quarters, in this section).

Cycle of the Moon—(See "Metonic" in this section).

Damp Vapors—(See "Damp Vapors" under Moisture).

Dark of the Moon—(See "Decrease" in this section).

Day—The ☽ Above the Earth by Day —(See Above, Below, Night, in this section).

Death and the Moon—(See the Introduction, "Death" in Sec. 3 of this Article).

Decrease of the Moon—The vitality is usually less during the decr. of the ☽, and the body often loses two pounds in weight, and then regains it again during the light, or increase of the ☽. Sickness begun in the decr. of the ☽ is more apt to be depressing and weakening until after the New ☽. During the decr. of the ☽ the fluids of the body are at low ebb, and rise again, and fill the vessels of the body to a greater fullness during the incr. of the ☽. Goiter and Tumors decrease in size during the decr. of the ☽. The ☽ is more malefic during her decr. (See Benefic, Fluids, Last Quarter, in this section).

Diastole and Systole—Of the ☽—(See Full Moon, New Moon, in this section).

Diathesis—(See "Fifth Thoracic" under Ganglion).

Directions Of—The evil directions of the ☽ are especially dangerous during the Lunar Period of life in infancy, and from the 1st to 4th years especially. The directions of the ☽ along thru life bring to a climax other directions culminating and operating, and which are released by the ☽ entering into the configurations. Thus the time of crises in disease, and the critical times, months, and periods of life, can largely be predetermined by the movements of the ☽, and her aspects to the planets in the radical map. (See "Directions" under Children; Crises, Critical, Directions, Periods, Prognosis, Secondary).

Diseases Of—(See Section 3 of this Article).

Domain—Of the ☽—Is over Fluids. (See Fluids).

Dragon's Head—And Tail—The Nodes of the ☽. (See Dragon's Head).

Drugs Of—(See Herbs, Metal, Typical Drugs, in this section).

Earthy Signs—And the ☽—The ☽ is more fortunate in ♉, which is the sign of her exaltation, and tends to good health, regular functions, fixed and methodical habits. In ♍ the ☽ is not as fortunate, and tends to irregular bowel action, irregular functions, and digestive disorders. In ♑ the ☽ has her detriment, and is tinged with ♄ influence. (See "Earthy Signs" under Earth).

Eclipses Of—(See Eclipses, Lunations; "Full Moon", "New Moon", in this section).

Elementary Qualities—At the New ☽ the ☽ is hot and moist; at the 1st Quarter is hot and dry; at her Full is cold and dry, and the 3rd Quarter, cold and moist. (See First Quarter, Full, Last Quarter, New Moon, in this section).

Epoch—The sign the ☽ is in at the Epoch, or time of conception, or the opposite sign, is the Asc. at birth, as a rule. (See Prenatal Epoch).

Equivalent To—The ☽ is equivalent to a ♃ planet when slow in motion, and moving less than 13° 11′ in 24 hours. (See Retrograde).

Events and the Moon—(See Events; Aspects, Directions, in this section).

Evil Aspects Of—The ☽ Fortunate or Evil In Her Influences—(See Afflictions Of, Aspects, in this section). The evil aspects of the ☽ indicate the ailments which arise after birth, and to the detriment and injury of the native's health. (See Asquired).

Exaltation Of—The ☽ has her exaltation in ♉. (See "Earthy Signs" in this section).

Eyes—The ☽ has special affinity with the Eyes. (See Blindness, Eyes, Nebulous, Sight).

Fall—The ☽ has her fall in the ♏ sign. (See Scorpio).

Fecundation—Is the most salient characteristic of the ☽. (See Fecundation).

Females and the Moon—The ☽ is the principal ruler over the health of females, and the female functions, and is usually taken as the hyleg in female nativities when strong and well-aspected at B. Also ♀ is a ruler over females. (See Females, Functions, Menses, Women).

Fevers—The motion of the ☽ regulates fevers, and hot and dry diseases. (See Better, Crises, Fevers, Moderation, Recovery, Resolution, Worse).

Fire Signs and the Moon—The ☽ is not congenial in fiery signs and tends to disturbed functions and many disorders when in such signs, and also to give a hasty and excitable nature. (See "Fire Signs" under Fire).

First Quarter—Exerts a hot and dry influence, and acts especially on the Bile. The 1st Quarter of the ☽ is also concerned with the revitalization of the fluids and functions of the body, and with organic development.

Fluids—The ☽ rules the white fluids of the body, or the body oil; the lymph, chyle, synovial fluid, etc. (See Fluids).

Foetus—The ☽ Influence Over the Foetus—(See Foetus).

Fortunate or Evil—(See "Aspects" in this section).

Friendly To—The ☽ is friendly to all our planets except ♄ and ♂. (See Antipathy, Opposites, Sympathy).

Fruitfulness—The ☽ is fruitful and a giver of children. (See Fruitful).

Full Moon—The Full ☽ is of a cold and dry nature, and affects the Innervation. The Full ☽ corresponds to the Lunar Diastole, and is the Lunar expiration, while the New ☽ typifies the Lunar inspiration, preparation for a new cycle, and is the Lunar Systole. The Full ☽ is typical of maturity, or maturation, of the fullness or plenitude of fluids, the high tide, high tension, fruition, etc. Discharges are more profuse at the Full ☽. The Brain is largest at the Full ☽ and smallest at the New. Fits of nervousness are worse at the New and Full ☽, and also Lunatics are more affected, agitated or raving at these times, and the Insane, Hysterical, Nervous, and Epileptic patients are worse at the Full ☽, and should not sleep exposed to the Moonlight. At the New or Full ☽ the ☽ influence is not so manifest except with Lunatics, whose fluids are more violently disturbed at these times. A child born at the instant of the Full ☽, and especially females, usually dies at the next New ☽, and a child born at the New or Full ☽ rarely lives unless ♃ give a favorable aspect. The exact time of the Full ☽ is very dangerous for a surgical operation. White is the symbol of the Full ☽, which is the symbol of Initiation. (See Changes, First Quarter, Last Quarter, New Moon, in this section; Brain; "Death At Birth" under Children; Discharges;

Dropsy, Eclipses, Emissions, Entozoons, Evacuations; "Nervous Affections" under Fits; Fluids, Fluxes, Haemoptysis; "Profuse" under Hemorrhage; "Discharges" under Hemorrhoids; Insanity, Itching, Scabs, etc.).

Functions—The ☽ has rule over the Functions and the natural powers of the body, and especially over the female functions, childbirth, the menses, etc. (See Functions).

General Health—The ☽ has rule over the general health and habits. (See Habits; "General Health" under Health).

Generates—The ☽ generates moisture and damp vapors. (See "Damp Vapors", and the various paragraphs under Moisture).

Gestation — The period of Gestation for Man and Beast is measured by the ☽. (See Gestation).

Gives Life—The ☽ reflects the Solar Forces which helps to give life.

Growth—The ☽ has much to do with the growth and development of the body. (See Growth).

Habits of Life—The ☽ has an important influence over the personal habits. (See Habits).

Health—The ☽ weak at B., and afflicted tends to ill-health, and espec. in females. The ☽ strong at B., hyleg, and well-aspected, tends to good health in females, good vitality, and prospect of long life. (See Females, Health, Women).

Height of the Body—The Nodes of the ☽ have influence over. (See Height).

Herbs of the Moon — (See "Moon Group' under Herbs).

Home—The ☽ is at home in the watery signs ♋ and ♓, and also in her exalted sign ♉.

Horas—Lunar Horas—(See Horas).

Hour—☽ Hour—(See "Hours" under Planets).

House Position Of—The ☽ tends to disturb the functions more severely when in the 6th H., or ruler of the 6th, and afflicted by lords of the 1st, 6th, or 8th H.

Hyleg—The ☽ is hyleg in female nativities when she is strong, and can be taken for such. (See Hyleg).

Identified With—The ☽ is identified with the negative, passive, magnetic, and feminine forces in Nature.

Implies—The ☽ influence implies fate, thraldom of the flesh, and bondage to matter.

Increase Of— (See Benefic, Decrease, First Quarter, New Moon, in this section).

Indicator Of — The ☽ is an indicator of events, and of disease or health, and espec. in females.

Infancy — The ☽ has greatest effects over Infants, as Infancy is the Lunar Period of life. (See Infancy; "Directions" in this section).

Influence and Power Of—(See "Above the Earth", and the various paragraphs in this section).

Last Quarter — Third Quarter of the ☽—Is cold and moist, and acts especially on the Lymph. This Quarter is typical of the reaping period, the reaping of the harvest, and the application of power already generated. Sleep is more quiet during the last Quarter. (See "Quarters" in this section).

Life — (See "Gives Life" in this section).

Light of the Moon—Increase of—(See Benefic, Gives Life, Increase, Moonlight, in this section).

Lunar — Lunar Horas — Solar Lunar Forces — (See Horas; "Solar-Lunar" under Solar).

Lunations—(See Lunations).

Lymphatic System — Ruled by the ☽. (See Lymphatic).

Magnetic—The ☽ is a magnetic and negative body. (See Magnetic, Negative).

Mars and the Moon—The ☽ ☌ ♂ tends to cause the same diseases as does ♂ in the Asc. at B.

Malefic—When the ☽ is more Malefic— (See Benefic, Decrease, in this section).

Matter — The ☽ is typical of Matter. (See Matter; "Implies" in this section).

Mental Qualities — Given by the ☽ — The ☽ tends to make one timid and imaginative. (See Imagination, Timidity).

Metals—Ruled by the ☽—Aluminum, Silver. (See Therapeutics).

Metonic Cycle—Cycle of the ☽—The Nodes of the ☽ complete one revolution in about 1000 weeks, or 19 years, and the ☽ forms her ☌ with the ☉ on the same day every 19 years. The Eclipse at this time is very powerful for good or ill in health matters, according to her sign, aspects, etc., as related to the map of birth, and for People and Countries falling under the shadow of such an Eclipse. (See Eclipse).

Minerals Of—Emerald, Marcassite, Moonstone, Selenite. (See Minerals).

Moisture — The ☽ generates moisture and damp vapors. (See "Damp Vapors" under Moisture).

Moon People—A Moon person is ever inconstant, restless, changeable, variable, and a rover. Moon people, and with the ☽ afflicted at B., tend to contract disease easily, and usually have less vitality. The ☽ sign ♋ on the Asc. at B. tends to give a weak constitution. (See Cancer Sign; "Contracts Disease Easily" under Contracts; Restless; "Weak" under Vitality).

Moonlight — The night air and moonlight are noxious and tend to produce miasmic ailments, malaria, etc. (See "Full Moon", "Sleep", in this section; Malaria, Miasma, Noxious).

Moonstone—A Mineral ruled by the ☽.

Motion of the Moon—(See Equivalent, Fevers, in this section; "Planets" under Motion; "Motion" under Planets).

Mutation of Fluids—(See "Mutation" under Fluids).

Natural Powers—(See "Functions" in this section; "Natural Forces" under Natural).

Nebulous Spots — And the ☽ — The ☽ with at B. tends to Eye Trouble and Blindness. (See Blindness, Eyes, Nebulous).

Negative — The ☽ is a negative and magnetic body. (See Negative; "Classification" in this section).

New Moon—The New ☽ is the systole, or the low ebb of her influence, and implies death, disintegration, and the preparation for a new Cycle. The New ☽ is hot and moist in influence. The functional activities are lower at this time, and the bodily forces are weakest. A male child born at the time of the New ☽, which may also be a total eclipse of the ☉, may not survive. Much infant mortality is referable to the New ☽, which is a critical time with infants, and tends not only to weaken the constitution, but to make any contemporaneous malefic aspects and influences more powerful in their action upon the body. (See "New Moon" under Children). At the New and Full ☽ the ☽ influence is not so manifest except with Lunatics, whose fluids are more violently disturbed at these times. The New ☽ just previous to an event, an accident, or the beginning of a disease, has much to do with precipitating the event, and even before it would otherwise occur, and the aspects of a New ☽, or a Progressed ☽, tend to focus the hidden forces. Thus a New ☽ may hasten an event if it occurs previous to the natural time of a possible event, or tend to retard an event when it occurs soon after, or immediately after the time of the culmination of an event, accident, or the beginning of a disease. In a train of evil directions the focus of their action is often guided by a New ☽ at or near the time of their culmination. The influence of a New ☽ just previous to birth often tends to congenital malformations and monstrosities. (See Changes, Full Moon, in this section; Directions, Eclipses, Events; "Nervous" under Fits; Irritable; "Low Spirits" under Low; Lunations, Misery, Monsters, Prenatal Epoch).

Night Action Of — The ☽ by Night — The ☽ being magnetic helps to keep up the morbid action of germs at night, and make disease worse. The action of the ☉ being electric tends to destroy and overcome the morbid action of germs during the day, and to equalize the deteriorating action of the ☽ at night, and thus save life. (See Above the Earth, Chemical, Moonlight, in this section; Day, Electric, Germs, Magnetic, Night, Noxious).

Nodes — Of the ☽ — (See "Height" in this section; Dragon's Head).

Noxious — (See Chemical, Damp Vapors, Moonlight, Night Action, in this section).

Operations — Surgical Operations and the ☽—(See Operations).

Organic Development — The position, aspects, and influence of the ☽ at B. show the quality of the organic development. (See "First Quarter" in this section; Organic).

Origin of the Moon — (See the Introduction to this Article).

Pathological Action—Of the ☽—Tends to Atonicity, Critical Epochs, Dropsy, Disease Contracted Easily, Fluidic Secretions, Transudation; is also Sedative and Soporific.

Perigee Of — The ☽ in perigee tends to cause pains in various parts of the body. Also nightmares and dreams usually occur about 48 hours before the Moon's perigee, and when the ☽ is about an hour high. (See Perigee).

Personal Appearance—(See "Appearance" in this section).

Personality—(See "Represents" in this section).

Physiological Action—Of the ☽ — Influences the Tears and Mutation of Fluids; influences the stomach; makes the womb receptive to the seminal fluid; rules and influences impregnation, inspiration, the animal instincts, and tends to inertia and sedentary habits. Movement in the body is a physiological action of the ☽. Moisture is a physiological action of the ☽, and tending to rottenness and putrefaction. The ☽ is classed as a physiological planet, and not pathological. The physiological action of the ☽ Group of Herbs has a cold and moist action, and tends to Mycrozymasis, Zymotic Periodicity, and to affect the Sympathetic Nervous System. (See "Moon Group" under Herbs; Microzymasis, Zymotic).

Plants Of—The general action of the ☽ plants tends to periodicity, and to be intermittent and zymotic. (See "Physiological Action" in this section).

Position Of—(See Above, Aspects, Below, House, Sign, in this section).

Power Of — (See Above, Below, Increase, and the various paragraphs in this section).

Principle of the Moon—Change, Harmony, Receptivity.

Quadratures—The 1st and 3rd Quarters of the ☽, and are very important in health matters. (See First Quarter, Last Quarter, in this section).

Quality Of—In quality the ☽ is moist, secreting, receptive, generating, mutational, relaxing, and pacific. (See "Qualities" in this section).

Qualities Of—The following Qualities are attributed to the ☽ — Alterative, Apathetic, Assimilative, Atonic, Attenuant, Binding, Changeful, Cleansing, Cold, Cold and Dry at the Full ☽; Cold and Moist at the 3rd Quarter; Collective, Convertive, Crystallizing, Decaying, Decomposing, Diluting, Dissipating, Dissolving, Distributing, Dreamy, Dry and Hot at the 1st Quarter; Dry and Cold at the Full ☽; Emetic, Emotional, Expulsive, Fecundating, Feminine, Fermenting, Fertilizing, Flaccid, Fluidic Fructifying, Fruitful, Functional, Generating, Hardening, Harmonious, Hot and Moist at the New ☽; Hot and Dry at the 1st Quarter; Illusory, Imaginative, Impregnating, Impressionable, Inconstant, Inertia, Instinctive, Integrative, Intermittent, Lethargic, Lymphatic, Magnetic, Materialistic, Metamorphic, Moist, Mutational, Negative, Neurasthenic, Nocturnal, Nutritive, Pacific,

Passive, Periodic, Phlegmatic, Plastic, Putrefying, Receptive, Reflective, Relaxing, Remittent, Restless, Rhythmic, Roaming, Romantic, Roving, Scattering, Secreting, Sedative, Sedentary, Self-Indulgent, Sensitiveness, Sequential, Sleep-Producing, Soporific, Timorous, Tumorous, Vacillating, Variable, Visionary, Wandering, Watery, Worrisome, Zymotic, etc. (See Classification, Elementary, in this section).

Quarters of the Moon — At the 1st Quarter, the Full ☽, and 3rd Quarter of the ☽ the Solar-Lunar forces are disturbed, and the functions and the constitution tend to be disordered. (See Decrease, First Quarter, Full Moon, Increase, Last Quarter, New Moon, Solar-Lunar, in this section).

Reflects—The ☽ reflects and collects the·Solar Forces and the influences of the other planets as she passes around thru the 12 Signs. (See Action of the Moon, Acts As a Medium, Aspects, in this section).

Regulates—The ☽ regulates the period of gestation and time of; the female functions and menses, and also the course of disease, crises in disease, etc., and also the time of events. (See "Indicator" in this section).

Represents—The ☽ represents matter, organic decay, and transitory experiences. What she represents is of an illusory nature, and has to do with the present existence on the Earth Plane. The ☽ sign in the map of birth represents the Personality, the Lower Mind, the mind which denotes the contacts with the outer world, environment, externals, disease, pain, suffering, worry, social relations, etc. (See Personality).

Retrograde—(See "Equivalent" in this section).

Salient Characteristic—(See "Fecundation" in this section).

Scorpio Sign—Sign of the fall of the ☽, and in this sign at B. tends to disturbed functions, ill-health, sex disorders, etc. (See Scorpio).

Secretions — The ☽ and Secretions — The secretions are more normal and regular with the ☽ in ♋ or ♓ at B. In an airy sign also the secretions are more regular and normal, but with the ☽ in a fiery sign the functions and secretions are greatly disturbed. Of the earthy signs the ☽ in ♉ has the most favorable influence over the secretions. (See Secretions).

Shows the Quality Of—(See "Organic" in this section).

Sign Position—The ☽ is strong in ♉, ♋, and ♓; has her fall in ♏, and detriment in ♑. Is rather strong in the airy signs, but incongenital in fiery signs.

Significator Of—The ☽ is the general Sig. of the health in female nativities.

Sixth House — And the ☽ — (See "House" in this section; Sixth House).

Sleep—The ☽ is Sleep-producing. Hysterical and Nervous people should not sleep exposed to the Moonlight. (See Full Moon, Moonlight, in this section; "Sleep-Inducing" under Sleep).

Slow In Motion—(See "Equivalent" in this section).

Solar Forces — The ☽ reflects them. (See "Reflects" in this section).

Solar-Lunar Influences — (See "Solar-Lunar" under Solar).

Source Of—The ☽ is the source of the Natural Forces in the body. (See "Natural" in this section).

Strengthens Constitution—(See "Strengthened" under Constitution).

Strongest—The ☽ is strongest in the watery signs ♋ and ♓. Is weakest in ♏ and ♑. (See "Signs" under Water).

Systole Of—(See "Full Moon" in this section).

Temperament—(See Lymphatic).

Therapeutic Affinities — Ipecac has a strong affinity with the ☽, and is used as an emetic in stomach troubles. (See Emetics, Ipecac).

Therapeutic Qualities—Alterative, Attenuant, Emetic. (See these subjects).

Third Quarter — (See "Last Quarter" in this section).

Tides—The ☽ rules the Tides, and the ebb and flow. The Full ☽ is the high tide of fluids, and the New ☽ the low ebb. (See Full, New, in this section).

Time — The ☽ a Time Marker — (See "Aspects" in this section).

Typical Drugs Of—Agaricus, Argentum, Colocynth, Pellitory.

Typical Plants — (See "Moon Group" under Herbs).

Vapors—The ☽ generates moisture and damp vapors. (See "Damp Vapors" under Moisture).

Variable — (See Acts As a Medium, Changeable, in this section).

Vital Center — The ☽ is one of the three Vital Centers of the Map of Birth, along with the ☉ and Asc. The ☽ is usually hyleg in a female nativity. (See "Centers" under Vital).

Vitality — (See "Vitality" under Females).

Water Signs — The ☽ is strongest in the watery signs ♋ and ♓, and when in these signs at B. tends to more regular functions, and to good health. (See "Signs" under Water).

Weakened — Weaker — The Power of the ☽ Weakened — (See Below the Earth, Decrease, Fire Signs, in this section).

Weakest — The Bodily Forces are weakest at the time of the New ☽, and also when the ☽ is afflicted in ♏ or ♑ with females. (See "New Moon" in this section).

Weather and the Moon—(See Floods, Rain, Weather).

White Fluids—The ☽ rules the white fluids of the body. (See "Fluids" in this section; "Fluids" under White).

Women and the Moon — (See "Females" in this section).

— SECTION TWO —

THE MOON RULES—See the following subjects in the alphabetical arrangement — Abdomen and Abdominal Cavity; Absorbent Vessels; Acquired Diseases; Acute Diseases; Air, and the

Tidal Air in the Lungs; Alimentary Canal; Aluminum; Animal Lusts and Passions; Animal Propensities; Apathy; Atonicity; A u t o m a t i c Action; Belly; Birth Place; Bladder; Blood—Flow of, or Rush of Blood to the Head; Body Oil; Bondage to Matter; Bowels; Brain Functions and S u b s t a n c e; Breasts; Canal (Intestinal); Cancer Sign; Cavities of Body; Cellular Tissue Building; Cerebellum; Changes in Life; Childbirth; Children — P e r i o d of Infancy; Chyle and Chylification; Cleansing of the Body; C o l o r l e s s Lymph in the Body; Colors (see "Colors" in Sec. 1 of this Article); Common People; Constitutional Functions; Constructive Functions; Corpulency; Crises in Disease; Critical Days, Epochs and Years (see Critical); Crystallization; Day of the Week — Monday; Death; Decay (Organic; Decomposition; D e g l u t i t i o n; Deluges; Digestive Activity and Juices; Dilution; Disintegration; Dissolution; Dissolving P r o c e s s e s in the Body; Dropsical Swellings; Drugs of the ☽ (see "Drugs" in Sec. 1 of this Article); Ebb and Flow (see "Tides" in Sec. 1 of this Article); E m e r a l d; Emissions; Emotions; Epileptics; Epochs; Etheric Double of Man (see Astral); Experiences (Transitory — See "Represents" in Sec. 1 of this Article); Expulsory Forces in the Body; Eyes—Left Eye in a Male and Right Eye in the Female; Faculties (the S e n t i e n t Faculties); Fate; Fecundation; Feelings; Female Functions; Female Relatives (see Relatives); Female—Right Eye in; Female Signs of Zodiac—The ☽ rules the first half of Female Signs, and the second half of Masculine Signs (see "Signs" under Female); Fermentation; Fertilization; First Seven Years of Life (Infancy Period); First Half of Life in General, and the ☉ Rules the 2nd Half of Life; Fleshiness (see Fleshy); Fluids of the Body and the White Fluids; Forces (E x p u l s o r y Forces); F r u i t f u l n e s s; Functions— Brain Functions — Constitutional and Constructive Functions—Female Functions — Organic Functions and Development — S e c r e t i n g Functions (see Functions); Gall Bladder as a Receptacle; Gastric Juices in General; General Health and General Habits of Life; Gestation; Glands of the Body and the Glandular Processes; Green Color; Habits of Life — Due to Automatic Action—Sedentary Habits (see Habits); Hardening; Health—The General Health, and especially among Females; Heart—Functions of; Herbs of the Moon (see "Moon Group" under Herbs); Home (the Home); Humidity; Humours; Humus; Impregnation; Inertia; Infancy (Period of); Inspiration (see Breath); Instincts; Intercellular Fluids (see Cells); Intermittent Action on the Body; Intermittent Fevers; Intestinal Canal; Irrational Faculties; Journeys by Water (see Voyages); Juices in the Body; Lachrymal Apparatus; Lacteals; Lassitude; Left Eye in a Male; Left Side of the Body (see Left); Lethargy; Life (Period of Infancy, from 1 to 7 Years); Light Mixed Colors; Liquids of the Body in General; Lower Mind (see "Represents" in Sec. 1 of this Article); Lunations;

Lungs—Tidal Air in Lungs; Lusts and Animal Passions; Lymph — Lymphatic System—Lymphatic T e m p e r a m e n t; Mammae (see Breasts); M a r c a s s i t e; Marriage Affairs; Masculine S i g n s — 2nd Half of (see "Masculine" under Signs); Maternity; Matter in General on the Earth Plane; M e n o p a u s e; Menses; Metal (Silver); Metamorphosis; Miasma; Microzymasis; Midwives; Milk; Mind—The I n s t i n c t i v e Mind; Mixed Light Colors; Moisture — Moist Warmth; Monday; Moonlight; Moonstone; Mother (d u r i n g Pregnancy); Motion; Movement; Mucous Surfaces; Mutation of Fluids; N a t i v e Place (Birthplace); Natural Functions in the Female — Natural Faculties — Natural Forces in the Body (see N a t u r a l); Nerves — Nerve Sheaths — Nervous People — Nerves in a General Way — Sympathetic Nervous System (see Nerves); Night (see Miasma, Moonlight, Night, Noxious); Obstetricians; Ocean; Oesophagus; Oils — Body Oils and White Fluids — Oozings; Organic Functions — Organic Decay; Osmosis; Ovaries; Palate; Parturition; Passions (the Animal Passions and Lusts); Pericardium; Periodic Action — Periodic Disease; Peristalsis; Personality; Perspiration; Physique; Plants (see "Moon Group" under Herbs); Powers (the Natural Powers of the Body); Pregnancy; Processes—The Dissolving Processes in the Body — The G l a n d u l a r Processes; Putrefaction; Receptacles of the Body (see Cavities, Receptacles); Reception of S e m e n (see Semen); Relatives (Female Relatives); Remittent Action; Residence (Place of); Respiratory S y s t e m (Absorbent and Lymphatic Vessels of); Restlessness; Returning Diseases; Rhythm; Right Eye in the Female; Right Side of the Body (see Right); Rivers; Saliva; Secretions; Sedatives; Sedentary Habits; Seeds, Selenite; Semen (Reception of); Sensation; Sensitive Faculties; Sensitives; S e n s u o u s Faculties; Sentient Faculties; Serous S u r f a c e s; Sheaths (Nerve Sheaths); Shot Violet Color; Signs of Zodiac — Rules the ♋ sign; Silver Cord and Silver Metal; Sleep-Inducing Drugs, Herbs and Habits (see Narcotics; "Drugs" under Sleep); Soft Tissues; Stamina; Stomach (Functions and Glands of); Surfaces (Mucous and Serous); Swallow (see Deglutition); S w a m p s; Sweat; Swellings (Dropsical); S y m p a t h e t i c Nervous System; Synovial Fluid; Tears; Temperament (the Lymphatic); Testicle (the Left); Thoracic Cavity; Thraldom of the Flesh (see "Implies" in Sec. 1 of this Article); Throat; T h y r o i d Gland; Tidal Air in Lungs; Tides— Ebb and Flow of — D r o p s i c a l and Fluidic Tides in the Body, Swellings, etc.; Tissue—Tissue Building—Cellular —Soft Tissues; T o n s i l s; Transitory Diseases and Experiences (see "Represents" in Sec. 1 of this A r t i c l e); Transudation of Fluids; Travel; Urine (as a Liquid); Uterus; Uvula; Vessels in General, and as Receptacles; Violet Color — Shot Violet Color; V i t a l i t y (Low, L o w e r e d); Voyages; Water; Watery Tides in the Body; Weather; White — White Fluids of the Body — White Spotted Colors; Womb; Worldly

Conditions (see Acts As a Medium, Implies, Represents, in Sec. 1 of this Article); Zymotic Action.

— SECTION THREE —

DISEASES OF THE MOON—Diseases and Afflictions Ruled by the Moon — The ☽, by reflecting the aspects and influences of the ☉ and planets, tends to produce and regulate disease, and eventually to bring death. Her Quarters from the time of the beginning of a disease are the crises times. (See Crises). The ☽ rules and causes all Acute and Acquired Diseases. The ☽ joined with ♂ at B. causes the same diseases as ♂ does when in the Asc. The ☽ rules such diseases as return after a time, as Periodic Diseases. The ☽ rules the Functions and Health matters in females, and an afflicted and ill-dignified ☽ at B. tends to disturbed and irregular female functions. The ☽ is the Significator of Health in a female horoscope. Moon people contract disease easily. Over the body the ☽ normally represents a cleansing, alterative, and expulsive influence, and also with age to harden and crystallize the body, and the ☽ being a cold, ashy and cinder-like body, the body of man would quickly turn into stone if he lived upon the Moon, and death quickly result, as vegetable and animal life cannot exist on the ☽. See the following subjects in the alphabetical arrangement when not more fully considered here—

Abdomen — Gaseous Distention of — (See Abdomen, Flatulence, Tympanites).

Abscesses; Accommodation — Disorders of Vision — (See Accommodation).

Aches; Acute Diseases; Adaptation—Defective Powers of In the Eyes—(See Accommodation, Sight).

Alimentary Canal—Diseases of—(See Alimentary).

Anaemia; Aneurysm; Anxiety;

Apathy; Apoplexy; Arms—Gout In—Weakness In—(See Arms).

Arterial Blood—Defects In—(See Arteries).

Asthma; Astigmatism; Atonicity;

Back—Weakness In—(See Back).

Belly—Bellyache—Fluxes of the Belly —(See Belly, Fluxes).

Birth—Premature—(See Premature).

Bladder—Disorders of—(See Bladder).

Blemishes; Blindness; Blood—Cold Blood—Thin Blood—Defective Red Blood—(See Blood).

Boils; Bowels—Disorders of—Distempers In—Fluxes In—Disturbed Functions—Obstructions In—Pains In —(See Bowels).

Brain — Disorders of the Brain Substance—Inflammation of—(See Brain).

Breasts—Disorders of—See Breasts).

Bronchial Disorders—Bronchial Catarrh and Oedema—(See Bronchial).

Calculi—(See Stone).

Cancer Disease—(See Carcinoma).

Carcinoma; Carditis—(See Heart).

Catarrhs; Cellular Zymosis—(See Cells, Zymosis).

Children—Disorders of—Worms In— —(See Childhood, Children, Infancy).

Chlorosis; Cholic; Cold — Cold Diseases — Cold Blood — Cold and Moist Diseases—Cold, Phlegmatic Diseases—Taking Cold—Indigestion from Taking Cold—Cold Taken In the Feet—Cold, Rheumatic Diseases—Cold Stomach—Cold and Raw Humours In the Stomach—(See Cold).

Colds; Colic; Colliquative Sweats — (See Colliquative, Sweat).

Conjunctivitis—(See Conjunctiva).

Consumptions; Convulsions; Coughs —Rotten Coughs—(See Cough).

Crises In Disease—(See Crises).

Critical Days — In Disease — (See Crises, Critical).

Crystallization; Cysts; Death—The ☽ causes Death by Cold and Moist Diseases; Crystallization; Hardening; Drowning; Cold, Phlegmatic Diseases. (See these subjects).

Debauchery; Decay; Decomposition;

Defluxions; Delirium Tremens — (See Delirium).

Diarrhoea; Digestive Disorders—(See Digestion, Indigestion).

Dilutions; Discharges — Menstrual, Mucous, Serous—(See Discharges).

Dissipation; Dissolution;

Distempers — In Bowels — Genitals— Reins — Secret Parts—Sex Organs— (See Distempers).

Distension—Of the Abdomen—(See Abdomen, Distentions).

Dizziness; Drink; Dropsies;

Drowning; Drowsiness—(See Sleep).

Drunkenness; Dry Bellyache — (See Belly).

Duration of Disease—(See Duration).

Dyspepsia; Effusions; Epilepsy;

Eruptions—(See Eruptions, Face).

Excess—Of Mucous and Phlegm—(See Mucous, Phlegm).

Eyes—Disorders of—(See Accommodation, Blindness, Eyes, Nebulous, Sight).

Face—Eruptions On—(See Face).

Faintings—Falling Fits—(See Fainting).

Feet—Cold Taken In—Gout In— Lameness In—Pains In—Weakness In —(See Feet).

Female Complaints — (See Females, Women).

Fermentation; Fevers—The Motion of the ☽ Regulates Fevers—(See Fevers).

Fits—(See Fainting, Fits).

Flabbiness; Fluids—Of the Body— Disorders of—(See Fluids, Osmosis).

Fluor Albus—(See Leucorrhoea).

Fluxes; Functions—Disorders of— (See Females, Functions, Menses).

Gaseous Distentions—(See Abdomen, Distensions, Flatulence, Gas).

Generation—Diseases of Organs of— (See Generation).

Genitals—Diseases of—(See Genitals).

Genito-Urinary Disorders—(See Genito-Urinary).

Giddiness; Glands—Disorders of—(See Glands).

Gluttony; Goiter; Gout—In the Arms, Hands, Wrists, Legs, Joints, Feet, Knees—(See Gout).

Habits of Life—Diseases By—(See Habits).

Haemoglobin—Defects In—(See Haemoglobin; "Blood" under Red).

Hands—(See "Gout" under Hands).

Hardening; Head—(Defluxions of Rheum From).

Heart—(Inflammation of—Trembling of—Palpitation of).

High Strung—And Nervous—(See High, Nerves).

Hot and Dry Diseases—(See "Dry and Hot" under Heat; "Fevers" in this section).

Humours; Hurts to Eyes—(See Eyes).

Hydrocephalus; Hyperopia—(See Sight).

Hysteria; Imaginations; Indigestion; Infancy—(Disorders of).

Infiltrations; Inflammation—Of the Heart—(See Heart).

Injuries—To the Eyes—(See Blindness, Eyes).

Insanity; Intoxication;

Irregularities—Of the Bowels—Of the Female Functions—Of the Stomach—(See Bowels, Females, Fluids, Functions, Irregular, Menses, Stomach).

Joints—(Gout In).

Kidneys—Disorders of—Stone In—(See Kidneys).

King's Evil—(See Scrofula).

Knees—(See "Gout", "Pain", under Knees).

Lachrymal Apparatus—Disorders of—(See Tears).

Lacteals—Diseases of—(See Milk).

Lameness—(In Feet and Thighs).

Larynx—Disorders of—Laryngitis—(See Larynx).

Left Eye—Defects In—Hurts To—Blindness In—(See "Left" under Eyes; "Eyes" under Left).

Left Side of Body—Cold In—Disorders In—(See Left).

Legs—(Gout In—Pains In—Swellings In—Dropsy In).

Lethargy; Leucorrhoea; Limbs—(Obstructions In).

Liver—(Disorders of).

Lunacy; Lunar Diseases—Suffers from ☽ Diseases—The ☽ afflicted at B., and to the evil aspects the Asc. by dir.; the Asc. to the ☌, P., or ill-aspect the ☽ by dir. (See Lunar; also note the various paragraphs in this section).

Lungs—(Obstructions In).

Lymphatics—(Disorders of).

Mammae—Disorders of—(See Breasts).

Measles; Membranes—Diseases of the Mucous and Serous Membranes—(See Membranes, Mucous, Serous).

Menorrhagia—(See Menses).

Menses—Disorders of—(See Menses).

Mental Strain—(See "Strain" under Mental).

Miasma; Milk—(Disorders of).

Minor Ailments—(See Mild, Minor, Slight).

Miscarriage—(See Abortion, Miscarriage).

Moist and Cold Diseases—(See "Cold and Moist" under Humours; "Cold" in this section).

Moist Humours—Body Over-Charged With—(See Humours).

Morbid Action—Of Germs At Night—(See "Night Action Of" in Sec. 1 of this Article).

Mucous—Mucus—Mucous Discharges—Excess of Mucus and Phlegm—(See Discharges, Mucous, Phlegm).

Myopia—(See Sight).

Nausea; Near-Sighted—(See Sight).

Nervousness—(See "High Strung" under High; Hysterical; "Nervousness" under Nerves).

Neuralgia—In the Head—(See Head).

Night Diseases—(See Night).

Night Sweats—(See Phthisis).

Obstructions—(In Bowels, Limbs, Lungs).

Oedema—In Lungs—(See Lungs, Oedema).

Oesophagus—(Disorders of).

Oozings; Operations—Surgical—Influence of the ☽ Over—(See "Rules" under Operations).

Ophthalmia—(See Conjunctiva).

Osmosis; Pains—In Bowels—Feet—Knees—Legs—In Secret Parts—Painful Female Functions—(See "Pain" under these subjects; Menses, Pain).

Palsy; Periodic Irregularities—(See Irregularities, Periodic).

Periodical Diseases—(See Intermittent, Menses, Periodical, Returning).

Periods of Women—Disorders of—(See Menses).

Phlegmatic Diseases—Excess of Phlegm and Mucus—(See Mucous, Phlegm).

Phthisic; Phthisis—Night Sweats of—(See Phthisis).

Pimples; Pleurisy; Poison—Sickness From—(See Poison).

Premature Births—(See Premature).

Presbyopia—(See Sight).

Profluvial Effusions—(See Effusions).

Putrefaction; Quinsy; Raw Humours—(See Indigestion).

Red Blood—Defective—(See Haemoglobin; "Blood" under Red).

Reins—(Distempers In).

Relaxation—Of Animal Bodies—(See "Damp Vapors" under Moisture).

Renal Stone—(See "Kidneys" under Stone).

Respiratory Disorders—(See Breath, Bronchial, Lungs).

Restlessness; Returning Diseases—(See Periodical, Returning).

Rheum—(Defluxions of).

Rheumatism — (Cold, Rheumatic Diseases).

Right Eye—Of a Female—Hurts To, etc.—(See "Right" under Eyes; "Right Eye" under Females; "Eyes" under Right).

Ringworm; Salivation—(See Saliva).

Scrofula; Scurvy; Secret Parts—(Diseases In — Distempers In — Pains — Swellings).

Sedative Conditions — In the Body — (See Sedative).

Serous Membranes—Disorders of—(See Serous).

Severity of Disease — (See "Severe" under Disease; Duration, Severity).

Serum—(Disorders of—Infiltration of).

Sex Organs—Diseases of—Distempers In—(See Generation, Genitals, Genito-Urinary, Privates, Reproduction, Secret Parts, Sex, etc.).

Shingles—Herpes Zoster—(See Herpes).

Shoulders—(Weakness In).

Sight—Disorders of—(See Blindness, Eyes, Nebulous, Sight).

Signs—Diseases of the ☽ in the various Signs of the Zodiac — (See the Classified Lists in the various Textbooks and Dictionaries of Astrology).

Sixth House—The House of Health—Weakening Influence of the ☽ In—(See Sixth House; "House Position Of" in Sec. 1 of this Article).

Skin Diseases—Tendency To—(See Herpes, Pimples, Scrofula, Scurvy; "Tendency To" under Skin).

Sleep-Inducing—(See Lethargy, Sedative; "Drowsiness" under Sleep).

Smallpox; Soft Tissues—Disorders of —(See Tissues).

Somnambulism—(See Sleep).

Soporific — (See "Soporific" under Sleep).

Sore Throat—(See Throat).

Stomach— (Cold Stomach—Indigestion—Raw Humours In—Stomachache).

Stone—(In Kidneys).

Stoppage—In Throat—(See Throat).

Suffocation—(Death By—Drowning).

Surfaces—Disorders of the Mucous and Serous Surfaces — (See Mucous, Serous).

Surfeits; Sweats—Night Sweats—(See Phthisis, Sweat).

Swellings—(In Throat—Legs—Secret Parts—Dropsical).

Swoonings—(See Fainting).

Sympathetic Nervous System—Disorders of—(See Sympathetic).

Synovial Fluid—And Membranes—Disorders of—(See Synovial).

Tears—(Disorders of).

Tetters; Thighs — (Lameness In—Weakness In).

Thin Blood—(See Blood).

Throat—(Sore Throat—Stoppage In—Swellings In).

Transudations; Tumors — (Oedematous).

Tympanites; Ulcers—(In Arms—Legs—Throat).

Uterus—Disorders of—(See Womb).

Uvulitis; Varicose Veins — (See Varicose).

Vertigo; Vesicles—(Disorders of).

Vision—Disorders of—Errors of—Defects of—(See Blindness, Eyes, Sight).

Vitality—(Lowered).

Vomiting; Weakness—Weak—Weakness and General Debility—Weakness In the Arms, Back, Eyes, Feet, Shoulders and Thighs — Weak Sight — (See "Weakness" under Arms, Back, etc.; "General Debility" under Debility; "Ill-Health All Thru Life" under Ill-Health; "Weak" under Sight; "Low" under Vitality).

Whites In Women — (See Leucorrhoea).

Wind — In Bowels or Stomach — (See Wind).

Women—Diseases of—Liver Trouble In—Functional Disorders—Periodic Illnesses—Whites In—(See Females, Functions, Leucorrhoea, Liver, Menses, Women).

Worms—In Children—(See Worms).

Worry; Wrists—(Gout In).

Zymosis—(See Fermentation, Zymosis).

MOPING—Listless—Spiritless—♄ ruler at B., and characteristic of a ♄ person. (See Despondent, Dull, Listless; "Low Spirits" under Low; Melancholy, etc.).

MORALS—The Moral Faculties—The Moral Conduct—The Map of Birth may indicate a tendency to moral delinquency, or moral turpitude, but the native does not have to yield to them. It depends upon the age of the Soul as to how the influences of a map manifest, or do not manifest themselves. To get certain important influences in the birth map, many very Advanced Souls have an evil map in many ways, but the real and inner character of Advanced Souls cannot be told by the birth map. Only those who are drifting, or who may be young Souls, follow their maps, and especially where the evils are indicated. The following subjects have to do with the moral life, the principles, the motives, and conduct of the native. See these subjects in the alphabetical arrangement when not more fully considered here—

Abandoned—An Abandoned Person—(See Depraved, Profligate).

Adulterous — (See "Adultery" under Love Affairs).

Bad Company — Bad Courses — (See "Conduct" under Bad; Conduct, Courses, Evil, Harlots, Low; "Loose Morals" in this section).

Balance—Lack of Moral Balance—The lower influences and vibrations of ♅ tend to; ♅ in the ♀ signs ♉ or ♎, and afflicted by ♄, ♂, or ♀; ♅ ♂, □, or ☍ ♀. (See Balance; the various paragraphs in this section).

Chaotic Acts—Unnatural Acts—(See Chaotic, Perversions, Unnatural).

Character; Chastity — (See "Chaste", "Virgin", under Females).

Cheating; Conduct; Cravings — (See Cravings, Drink, Narcotics, Thirst).

Criminal; Debased; Debauched; Deceitful; Depraved; Desires; Deviations; Disgraceful—(See Disgrace, Lewd, Shameless).

Dishonest; Dissipated; Dissolute; Drunken; Endurance — Moral Endurance — The fixed signs, and especially ♏, and also the planet ♄, tend to give moral endurance when well-aspected. The ♉ sign also gives endurance when strongly placed, occupied, and aspected. Venus when ill-aspected by malefics tends to give very little moral stamina or endurance. Uranus, ♂, and the masculine signs signify only sudden, temporary, or spasmodic efforts at moral endurance. The feminine signs give greater perseverance and patience in moral efforts. (See Endurance; "Moral Stamina" in this section).

Evil-Minded — Wicked — (See Evil, Lewd, Licentious, Obscene, Perversions, Shameless, etc.).

Excesses — Indulges In — (See Excesses).

Filthy Morals — (See "Loose" in this section; Filthy, Lewd, Obscene, Shameless, Wanton).

Flirting — (See "Unwomanly" in this section).

Folly — Moral Folly — (See "Free-Living" under Free; Folly; "High Living" under High; "Clandestine" under Sex; "Loose Morals" in this section).

Fornicators—(See "Clandestine" under Sex).

Free Love—(See Free).

Freedom—Unwomanly Freedom—(See "Unwomanly" in this section).

Gamblers; Good Morals—♄ Sig. ♂ ♃, extremely moral and grave; in Hor'y Q. ♃ Sig. of the person; ♀ ⚹ or △ ♄. (See "Chaste" under Females; Honest, Honorable, Sincere, etc.).

Habits—Loose Habits — (See Habits; "Habits" under Loose).

Harlots; Homesexuality; Honest; Honour—(Loss of).

Husband—The Morals of—(See Husband).

Hypocritical; Imbecility—Moral Imbecile — (See Debauched, Depraved, Lascivious, Lewd, Obscene; "Loose Morals", and the various paragraphs in this section).

Immodest; Immoral—(See Conduct, Evil, Habits, Indecent, Lewd, Love Affairs, Lust, Passion, Perversions, Sex, Shameless, Vices; "Loose", and the various paragraphs in this section).

Imprisonment—(See Prison).

Improper; Impure Conduct — (See Lewd, Loose; "Amours", "Liaisons", under Love Affairs; Lust; "Impure" under Sex; Shameless; "Loose" in this section).

Incestuous—(See "Incest" under Perversions).

Indecent; Indiscretions; Indulgent; Infamous; Inimical to Himself—(See Inimical).

Inhuman; Inordinate; Intemperate; Intercourse—(Criminal In).

Intoxication; Introversion—(Moral).

Irresponsible; Judicial Condemnation —(See Judges).

Knavish; Lapsing—(Moral).

Lascivious; Law—Disregards Moral Laws—(See "Moral Laws" under Love Affairs).

Laxity—Lax Morals—(See Laxity; "Loose Morals" in this section).

Lewd; Liaisons—(See Love Affairs).

Liars; Libelers; Libidinous; Licentious; Light-Fingered — (See Kleptomaniac).

Liquors—Indiscriminate Use of—(See Liquors).

Living — (See "Free Living" under Free).

Look—(Debauched, Dissipated, Wanton Look).

Loose Morals—Loose Living—Immorality—The ☉ ♂ ♀ in ♏, and afflicted; the ☉ to the bad aspects ♀ or the ☽ by dir.; ♆ affl. in the 5th or 7th H.; a ♆ disease and affliction; ♆ ♂, □, or ☍ ☽; ♆ by tr. in ♂ the radical ☽ or ♀ if ♆ is afflicted at B., tends to an unclean and polluted mind; the bad aspects of ♆ to the Sigs. tend to moral introversion, as the perverted influence of this planet is seductive; ♆ afflicted in ♏; the violent oppositions of ♆ and ♅ from the ♉ and ♏ signs, and affecting the 5th or 7th H.; ♅ by tr. ♂ ♀; the influence of ♅ by his afflictions and lower vibrations is to pervert the moral nature, lead to free love, unconventionalities, sex freedom, and clandestine love affairs; ♅ in the 5th or 7th H., and afflicting ♀; ♄ Sig. □ or ☍ ♀; ♄ in ♓, □ ♃ in ♐; ♃ □ ♄; ♂ ruler of the horoscope, and afflicted; ♂ ♂ or ill-asp. ♀ or the ☽; ♂ to the ill aspects ♀ by dir.; no direction of ♂ to ♀ is good for the morals; ♂ affl. in ♏, or afflicting ♀ from this sign, tends to sex diseases from sex abuses and sex immoralities; ♀ in ♏ and afflicted by ♆, ♅, ♄, ♂, or the ☽; ♀ afflicted at B., and to the ♂ or ill-asps. the Asc. by dir.; ♀ progressed, ♂, P., □ or ☍ ♅ or ♆ in the radical map, or vice versa; ♀ to the ♂ ♂ by dir.; ♀ or the ☽ to the ♂ or ill-asp. ♆, ♅, or ♂ by dir., and espec. if the ☽ or ♀ are afflicted by malefics at B., tends to loose morals, especially in women; ☿ progressed in □ or ☍ the radical ♅, a wayward state of mind; ☿ prog. to the □ or ☍ the radical ♆, if such is shown in the radix; the 3rd face of ♓ on the Asc. (See "Free Living" under Free; Infamous, Intercourse; "Loose Habits" under Loose; Love Affairs, Lust, Passion, Perverse, Perversions, Sex; the various subjects in this section).

Love Affairs—(See the various paragraphs under Love Affairs).

Low— (Low and Base—Low Character—Low Women).

Lower Nature — (See "Nature" under Lower).

Lustful; Luxuries—Fond of—(See Expense, Extravagance, Luxuries).

Malevolent; Malicious;

Manly and Sober—(See Manners).

Manners — (See the various paragraphs under Manners).

Marriage—Marriage Partner—(See the various paragraphs under these subjects).

Men—(See "Addicted to Women", and the various paragraphs under Men).

Methods — (See the subjects under Methods).

Mockery; Modest; Money — (Prodigal In the Use of).

Moral Folly—(See "Folly" in this section).

Moral Insensibility—(See Debased, Debauched, Depraved, Infamous, Loose, Low, Obscene, Perversions, Shameless, Virtue, Wanton; the various paragraphs in this section).

Moral Lapses—(See Lapsing).

Moral Laws—Little Respect For— (See "Moral Laws" under Love Affairs).

Moral Nature Suffers—The moral nature tends to suffer under the evil aspects of ♅, as this planet is seductive. (See "Loose Morals" in this section).

Moral Perversions — ♅ diseases; ♀ ruler of the horoscope and afflicted by malefics. (See Deviations, Perversions, Shameless, Unnatural).

Moral Stamina Weakened—The ☉ afflicted by ♄; ♄ ☌ ♀; ♀ ☌ ♂ or ill-asp. ♂; ♅ ☌ ♀; ♅ □ or ☍ ♀. (See Endurance, Loose, and the various paragraphs in this section).

Morally Ruined — (See Debased, Depraved, Dishonest, Infamous, Love Affairs, Murderers, Passion, Profligate, Shameless, Thieves, Wanton, Wench, Wicked; "Loose" in this section).

Morbid Desires—Morbid Deviations— (See Desires, Deviations, Morbid, Nymphomania, Passion, Sex, etc.).

Motives; Murderers; No Moral Sense —Case—See "Mentally Defective", No. 408 in 1001 N.N. Also see Cases under Nymphomania.

Nymphomania; Obscene; Passion — (See the various paragraphs under Passion).

Perverse; Perversions—Moral and Sex Perverts—(See Passion, Perversions, Sex; "Moral Perversions" in this section).

Pious; Poisoners—(See Poison, Treachery).

Polluted; Principles; Prodigal;

Profligate; Promiscuity—(See "Clandestine" under Sex).

Rape; Respect — Little Respect for Moral Laws — (See "Moral Laws" under Love Affairs).

Riotous; Robbers; Ruined — By the Opposite Sex—(See Disgrace, Excesses; "Ruined" under Love Affairs, Women; "Injured" under Men; "Health Suffers" under Opposite Sex; "Poison Death" under Poison; Scandal, Tragical, Treachery).

Salacious—(See Effeminate, Lust).

Saloons—Frequenter of—(See Drink, Drunkenness, Harlots, Taverns).

Scandal; Scruples — (See Anarchists, Cheating, Conduct, Criminal, Deceitful, Dishonest, Hypocritical, Ideals, Ideas, Liars, Libelers, Motives, Principles, Thieves, etc., and also note the various paragraphs in this Article).

Seduction—(Liable To).

Sensuous—(See Amorous; Lascivious, Lewd, Licentious, Obscene; "Passional Excesses" under Passion; Perversions, Sensuality, Sex, etc.).

Sex Life — Given To — Excesses In — Sex-Perverts—(See Amorous, Excesses, Intercourse; "Amours" under Love Affairs; Passion; "Clandestine" under Sex, etc.).

Shameless; Sober and Manly — (See "Manly" under Manners).

Social Relations — (See Companions, Environment, External, Harlots; "Low Company" under Low; Social, Women).

Sodomists; Sordid; Stamina — (See "Moral Stamina" in this section).

Temptations—(See Influenced, Negative Nature, Temptation).

Thieves; Treacherous; Turpitude;

Unbridled Passion—(See Passion).

Unchaste—(See Immodest, Shameless; "Without Virtue" under Virtue).

Unclean; Unconventional—(See Love Affairs).

Unfaithful—(See Love Affairs).

Unnatural Practices—(See Depraved, Perversions, Unnatural).

Unrestrained—(See Inordinate).

Unwomanly Freedom — Flirtatious — The ☽ afflicted by ♄, and ♂ at the same time above the ☽ or ♀; ♂ ☌ or bad aspect the ☽; ♂ in any aspect to ♀ disposes to flirtation, intense affections, and without stability in love affairs with either sex. (See "Free Love" under Free; "Fickle" under Love Affairs; Nymphomania).

Upright—(See Honest; "Good Morals" in this section).

Vagabond; Venery; Vices; Virtue;

Wanton; Wayward—(See "Wayward" under Mind).

Weak Morals—(See "Loose", and the various paragraphs in this section).

Wench; Whoremongers — (See Harlots).

Wicked; Wife—The Morals of—(See Wife).

Women—Loose Morals In—(See Loose Morals, Unwomanly Freedom, in this section; Harlots, Imprudent, Nymphomania; "Unchaste" under Women).

Worldliness; Wrong — Has Many Temptations to Do Wrong—(See Evil, Habits, Love Affairs, Men, Passion, Sex, Temptations, Women). For other subjects along the line of Morals you may think of, and which are not listed here, look for the subject in the alphabetical arrangement.

MORBID — Pertaining to Disease — An Abnormal State—Saturn is responsible for morbid conditions generally, both of mind and body. (See Saturn).

Action — Morbid Action — The power and degree of morbid action shows a falling off as the planets pass from the cardinal to common signs. (See "Better" under Disease).

Anxiety—Morbid Anxiety About the Health—(See Hypochondria).

Blood—Morbid Blood Conditions— Morbid Changes In the Blood — (See "Morbid" under Blood).

Chronic Diseases—Those caused, and under the rule of ♄ are morbid. (See Chronic).

Compulsions—Morbid Compulsions— Morbid and Uncontrolled States of Mind Which May Lead to Crime, Death, Hallucinations, Insanity, Mania, Murder, Suicide, Violence, etc.—(See these subjects. Also see Fears; "Fixed Ideas" under Ideas; Jealousy; "Morbid" under Mind; Obsessions, Revenge, Spirit Controls, Treachery, etc.).

Deaths—Morbid Deaths—The Anareta In—(See Anareta).

Debility — Morbid Debility is caused by ♄. (See Debility).

Depression—Morbid Depression and Anxiety — (See Anxiety, Depressed, Hypochondria).

Desires — Morbid Sex Desires — (See Amorous; "Morbid", "Sensuous", under Imagination; "Erotic" under Mania; "Morbid" under Passion; Unsavory).

Deviations—Morbid Deviations—(See Deviations, Perversions, Unnatural, Unsavory).

Discharges—Morbid—(See "Offensive" under Discharges).

Diseases — Morbid Diseases and Distempers—Caused by ♄. Due to inhibited functions in the different organs governed by the sign ♄ is in at B., or the sign he occupies temporarily by tr. or dir., as ♄ action tends to a lack of vital activity, or circulation of the vital force in such parts of the body. Chronic diseases also tend to become morbid under ♄ action. (See Chronic).

Distempers—Morbid—(See "Diseases" in this section).

Enlargements — (See "Morbid" under Enlarged).

Evacuations—Morbidly Frequent— (See Diarrhoea, Dysentery, Evacuations).

Exudations — Morbid Exudations of Mucous Membranes—(See Exudations).

Face—(See "Morbid Red" under Face).

Fears—(See "Morbid" under Fears).

Fixed Ideas — Tending to Morbid States of Mind — (See "Morbid" under Fears; "Fixed" under Ideas; Obsessions).

Fluids—Morbid Oozing of—(See Exudations, Osmosis).

Germs—(See "Morbid" under Germs).

Growths—(See "Morbid" under Growths; "Vegetable Growths" under Vegetable).

Health—Morbid Anxiety Concerning— (See Hyponchondria).

Heart — (See "Morbid Action" under Heart).

Humours— Morbid — (See "Offensive" under Humours).

Hyponchondria — Morbid Anxiety About the Health—(See Hypochondria).

Imaginations — (See "Morbid" under Imagination).

Impulses — (See "Morbid" under Impulses).

Manifestations— Morbid manifestations are caused by ♄ and the ♄ sign ♑. (See Capricorn; "Peripheral Nerves" under Peripheral; Saturn).

Mind — (See Idiopathy; "Morbid" under Mind).

Mortification — (See Death, Decay, Gangrene, Mortification).

Obscure — Obscure Morbid Manifestations—(See "Morbid" under Obscure).

Particles—Collections of Morbid Particles In the Body—(See Deposits).

Product — Virus a Morbid Product — (See "Virus" under Pestilence; Virus).

Red Face—(See "Morbid Red" under Face).

Sadness—Morbid Sadness—(See Despair, Gloom, Hope, Hypochondria; "Low Spirits" under Low; Melancholy, Worry, etc.).

Secretions—Morbid Secretions—(See Discharges, Secretions).

Sensations—(See Paraesthesia).

Sex Desires—Morbid—(See "Desires" in this section).

Softening—Morbid Softening of Tissues—(See Malacia).

Stealing—A Morbid Desire to Steal— (See Kleptomania).

Throat—Morbid Exudations In—(See Diphtheria; "Exanthematous" under Throat; "Quinsy", "Tonsilitis", under Tonsils).

Tremors—Morbid Tremors and Twitchings — A ♅ disease. (See Subsultus; "Morbid" under Tremors).

Twitchings—Morbid—(See "Tremors" in this section).

Unclassified—Unclassified Morbid Conditions—The diseases caused by ♆ and ♅. (See Extraordinary, Mysterious, Obscure, Peculiar).

Unsavory Subjects—The Mind Morbid Upon—(See "Morbid" under Mind; Unsavory; "Desires" in this section).

Virus — A Morbid Product — (See "Virus" under Pestilence; Virus).

Vitality—(See "Morbid" under Vitality. For other conditions which may not be listed here, and which involve morbid conditions, look for the subject in the alphabetical arrangement.

MORGUES—A Place Where Corpses Are Kept—Are ruled by the 12th H. (See Corpse, Twelfth House).

MOROSE — Moroseness — Sullen and Austere—Fretful—Surly Temper—Bitter—Particular—The ☉ conciliated with the ruler of the mind, and being cadent and occidentally posited; the ☽ applying to ♄; ♄ ☌ ☿, a heavy mind, dejected, morose and dull; ♄ ruler of the Asc. at B., and afflicted; the 30° ♎ on the Asc. (See Austere, Dejected, Dull, Fears, Fretful; "Mind" under Heavy; Melancholy, Reserved, Rouse, Suicide, Taciturn, etc.).

MORPHINE HABIT—(See Narcotics).
Apomorphine—(See Emetics).

MORTAL ILLNESS—(See "Arguments for Death", "Sure Death", under Death; Fatal).

MORTALITY—The Death Rate—
Aged People—Much Mortality Among —(See "Mortality" under Old Age).

Children — Much Mortality Among — (See "Mortality" under Children).

Common People—Many Deaths Among —(See "Public Mortality Great" under Public).

Death Rate Augmented—The months of April and November tend to an increased death rate, as the action of the ☉ upon our planet is weaker during those months. In the intervals between these months the death rate is diminished.

Death Rate Diminished—(See "Death Rate Augmented" in this section; "Public Health Good" under Public).

Death Rate High — ♂ gives a high death rate when supreme at the Equinoxes or Solstices. (See "Public Mortality Great" under Public).

Depopulation—Great Mortality—Much Mortality, Slaughter and Bloodshed— ♄ ☌ ♂ in the first three degrees of the ♋ sign. (See "Shedding of Blood" under Blood; Epidemics, Famine, Pestilence, War).

Eastern Parts—Much Mortality In— ♂ in ♑ and Lord of the Year at the Vernal Equi. Comets appearing in ♈ or ♌ tend to much bloodshed in Eastern Parts. (See "Aries Rules" under Nations).

Great — Much Mortality Among The Great—(See "The Great" under Great).

Great Mortality — (See "Death Rate High" in this section).

Grievous Mortalities — Grievous and Petulant—An Eclipse of the ☉ in the 2nd Decan. of ♋. (See Grievous).

Infants — Much Mortality Among — (See "Mortality Great" under Children).

Just Men — Much Mortality Among— The ☉, ☽, and ♃ conjoined in ♎.

Many Deaths Generally — (See Death Rate Augmented, Death Rate High, in this section).

Men — Death of Many Men — (See "Death of Men" under Men).

Persons About to Die—(See Dying).

Petulant Mortalities—(See "Grievous" in this section).

Public Health Bad — Many Deaths Generally—(See "Death Rate High" in this section; Cholera, Drought, Epidemics, Famine, Pestilence, Plague; "Public Health Bad", "Public Mortality Great", under Public).

Public Mortality Great—(See "Death Rate High" in this section).

Summer — A Sickly Summer — (See "Excessive Heat" under Heat; Summer).

Women — Much Mortality Among — (See "Mortality" under Women).

Young Men — Much Mortality Among —(See "Young Men" under Young).

MORTICIANS—(See Undertakers).

MORTIFICATION—♂ causes death by. (See "Death" under Mars).
Foetus—Mortification of—(See Foetus).
Granulations — When Attended by Mortification—(See Granulations).
Soft Tissues—Mortification of—(See Gangrene, Tissues).

MOSSES—Ruled by ♆. (See Neptune).

MOTHER—The Mother—Motherhood— The ☽, ♀, and the 10th H. are allotted to the Mother. In Hindu Astrology the 4th H., the house of the ☽, always rules the mother. Also in European Astrology there is a finer ruling which says that the 4th H. rules the mother in a male nativity, and the 10th H. the mother in a female nativity, and this rule seems to work out in its practical application. The 10th H. is said to rule the affairs of the mother in a general way, and the 4th H., the affairs of the father. By day the ☉ and ♀ are the chief representatives of the parents, and the ☽ and ♄ by night. In Hor'y Q. the ☽ and ♀ are Significators of the mother. (See Father). The following influences are to be noted in the map of the child, and especially in the map of the first-born, if living. However, the influences may exist in the maps of any of the children. Also the map of the mother should be studied in regard to some of the paragraphs, which give influences which especially apply to her map, and show her indications. For the various conditions which affect the mother see the following paragraphs herein, and in the alphabetical arrangement—

Abortions—Miscarriage—Mother May Die By—(See Abortion).

Accidents To — Hurts, Injuries, or Wounds To—Death By—Danger of— The ☽ to the ☌ or ill-asp. ♂ by dir.; the ☽ in the 4th or 7th H., and afflicted by ♂; ♄ □ or ☍ ♂; ♄ or the ☽ cadent, and in □ or ☍ aspect each other; ♄ or the ☽ void of course, and espec. if ♄ is ℞; ♄ cadent, ℞, slow of motion, and afflicting the ☽; ♂ □ or ☍ the ☽ or ♀; ♂ and the ☽ angular, swift in motion, and ♂ □ or ☍ the ☽ and the ☽ ori.; ♂ succedent to the ☽ or ♀, and in □ or ☍ to them, the ☽ void of course, and both ♂ and ♀ ℞; ♂ in evil asp. to the ☽ or ♀, and in angular or succedent houses, and ♄ cadent, ℞ and slow of motion, and afflicting the ☽. An eclipse falling on the ☽ in a child's map. (See Eclipses).

Afflicted—The Mother Afflicted— The ☽ and ♀ in occi. angles or succedent houses denote her afflictions. The ☽ and ♀ in occi. angles and in □ or ☍ ♂; the ☽ ruler of the 4th or 10th H., and afflicted by ♄ or ♂, or malefics; ♄ and the ☽ in angles, swift in motion, and in □ or ☍ each other; ♂ succedent to the ☽ or ♀, or in □ or ☍ to them, and both swift in motion and in angles. (See "Short Life", and the various paragraphs in this section).

Ague — The Mother Afflicted With — (See "Mother" under Ague).

Breasts—Disorders of—(See Breasts, Milk).

Burns—The Mother Dies by Burns—The ☽ in the 4th or 7th H., and afflicted by ♂.

Caesarian Operation—(See "Excision" under Foetus).

Childbed Fever—(See Puerperal).

Childbirth—Danger In — Death In—Accidents In—(See Parturition, Puerperal).

Children—Sex of Her Children—(See "First-Born Child" under Children; "Birth of a Female" under Females; "Births" under Male; Predetermination; "Birth of a Son" under Son).

Cold—Diseases or Death By—♄ ori., and in □ or 8 ☽. (See Cold).

Confinement — Bad Time During, and After—Danger In—(See Parturition).

Consumption—Afflicted With—Death By—The ☽ occi., and in □ or 8 ♄; the ☽ in the 1st or 10th H., and affl. by ♄. (See Consumption).

Danger To—The ☽ eclipsed near the time of a Solar Rev., and afflicted by ♅, ♄, or ♂, and espec. if the place of the malefic at B. ascends at the Solar Rev.; the ☽ to the ☌ or P. Dec. Regulus if the ☽ be hyleg; ♄ in the 10th H. in a female nativity, or in the 4th H. in a male geniture, and afflicted by the ☉ or ☽; the M.C. to the ill-asps. the ☽; the M.C. to the ☌ or P. Dec. the ☉ if the ☉ be afflicted at B., or in ☌ violent stars; an eclipse falling on the place of the radical ☽ in the child's horoscope. (See "Disease", and the various paragraphs in this section; "Danger" under Parturition).

Death Of—Indications of Death—Possible Time of Death of the Mother—Manner of Death of—The ☉ in the 10th or 4th H. at B., (according to the sex of the nativity) or ruler of these houses, and to the ☌ or ill-asp. ♅; the ☉ ruler of the 5th H. at B., and afflicted, and to the ☌ or P. Dec. the M.C. by dir.; the ☽ to the ill-asps. ♄ by dir., death from Colds or Cold Diseases; the ☽ in the 10th H., □ or 8 ♄ from an angle; the ☽ weak and affl. at B., and to the ☌ the Asc. M.C., ♄ or ♂ by dir.; afflictions to the ☽ or ♀ in the map of the child; the ☽ afflicted at B., and to the ☌ or P. asp. the Asc. by dir.; the ☽ to the place of Rigel or Cor Scorpio; ♄ in the 10th H., □ or 8 ☽; ♄ by dir. □ or 8 the degree on the M.C. at B. The day of death may also occur when ☽ is in □ or 8 the M.C. at B. by transit; ♄ passing over the place of the ☽ or ♀ at B. by tr., or at a Solar Rev.; ♄ in the 4th H. in a male nativity, or in the 10th H. in a female, and afflicted by the ☉ or ☽; the M.C. to the ☌ or P. Dec. the ☉ by dir. when the ☉ rules the 5th H. at B. (See "Death" under Sister, Wife). For death by Abortion, Accidents, Burns, Childbirth, Cold, Consumption, Early Death, Fevers, Miscarriage, Sudden Death, see these paragraphs in this section.

Detriment To—(See the various paragraphs in this section).

Disease — Diseases Will Attend the Mother—The Mother Diseased — The Mother Subject to Many Diseases—The Mother May Suffer, etc.—In considering the question of the sickness of the mother, the nature of her diseases, the property of the signs in which the afflicting planets are posited should be noted. The ☉ and ♀ by day should be observed, and ♄ and ☽ by night. There is a close bond of sympathy in these matters between the horoscope of the child and that of the mother, and by making a study of the child's map, the principle concerns of the parents may be ascertained. Evil directions in the child's map may not injure the child, but will tend to affect the parents or guardian. In such study the map of the first-born is preferable, then the map of the second child, etc. Along this line, the following influences are to be noted in the map of the child as to the causes of disease in the mother—The ☽ ori., and afflicted by ♄; the ☽ to the ☌ or ill-asp. ♄ or ♂ by dir.; the ☽ in the 1st or 10th H., and afflicted by ♄, the mother is diseased; the ☽ in the 10th H., □ or 8 ♄ from an angle; the ☽ at a Solar Rev. passing the place of ♄ at B.; the ☽ to the □ or 8 the ☉ or ♀ by dir.; the ☽ to the ☌ or P. Dec. Regulus if the ☽ be hyleg; an eclipse falling on the radical ☽ in a child's map; ♄ passing over the place of the ☽ or ♀ at B. by tr., or at a Solar Rev.; ♄ affl. in the 10th H. at B.; ♄ in the 10th H., □ or 8 ☽; ♄ or ♂ ☌ or evil asp. the ☽ in the 4th, 5th, 7th, or 8th H., the mother is subject to many diseases; ♄ in the 4th H. in a male nativity, or in the 10th H. in a female, and afflicted by the ☉ or ☽; ♄ cadent, slow in motion, ℞, and afflicting the ☽; ♂ in evil asp. the ☽ or ♀, and in angular or succedent houses; ♂ succedent to the ☽ or ♀, and in □ or 8 to them, and with ♂ and ♀ ℞; the Asc. to the □ or 8 the ☽ or ♀ by dir.; the M.C. to the ☌, P., or evil asp. the ☽ or ♀ if either be weak or afflicted at B.; lord of the 6th in the 4th or 10th H., the mother is afflicted or sickly. (See Afflicted, Early Death, Fevers, Short Life, Sudden Sickness, and the various paragraphs in this section).

Early Death Of—♆, ♅, or ♄ in the 10th H., and afflicted by the □ or 8 of planets; lord of the 10th a malefic in the 8th, and afflicted. These influences may also apply to the 4th H., according to the sex of the child, as the 4th H. rules the mother in a male nativity, and the 10th H. the mother in a female horoscope. (See Short Life, Sudden Death, in this section).

Eyes—Or Face—Hurts To—The ☽ in the 1st or 10th H., and afflicted by ♂; the ☽ to the ☌ or ill-asp. ♅ or ♂ by dir.; the ☽ ori. and angular, and □ or 8 ♅ or ♂; ♅ or ♂ angular, □ or 8 ☽. (See "Eyes" under Father).

Face—Injury To—(See "Eyes" in this section).

Fevers—Liable To—Death by Fevers—The ☽ or ♀ to the ☌ or ill-asp. ♂ by dir.; the ☽ ori., □ or 8 ♄, tends to death from slow fevers; the ☽ in the 1st or 10th H., and afflicted by ♄ or ♂; ♂ □ or 8 ♀, with ♂ angular and ♀ occidental. (See "Fevers" under Father).

Foetus — Caesarian Operation—(See "Excision" under Foetus).

Gestation—(See the various paragraphs under Conception, Gestation, Pregnancy, Prenatal Epoch).

Good Health For—Happiness For the Mother—♃ ☌, ✶, or △ the ☽ or ♀; ♀ ☌, ✶, or △ the ☽; the M.C. to the ☌, P., ✶, or △ ♀; the M.C. to the ☌ or P. the ☉ except when the ☉ is ruler of the 5th H. at B., which may cause her death. (See "Long Life" in this section).

Grandmother—Death of—(See Grandparents).

Grievously Afflicted—(See "Afflicted" in this section).

Happiness To—(See "Good Health" in this section).

Health Of—(See Afflicted, Good Health, and the various paragraphs in this section).

Hemorrhages—Floodings—(See Menses).

Hurts To—(See Accidents, Eyes, in this section).

Hysteria—(See "Mother" under Hysteria).

Ill-Fortune To—The ☽ to the place of Hydra's Heart. (See "Ill-Fortune" under Wife).

Ill-Health Of—Illness To—(See Afflicted, Disease, and the various paragraphs in this section; "Ill-Health" under Wife).

Inflammations To—The Possible Death of the Mother by Inflammations or Wounds—The ☽ to the ☌ or ill-asps. ♂ by dir.; the ☽ occi., and angular, and in □ or ☍ ♂. (See Accidents, Fevers, in this section).

Injuries To—(See Accidents, Eyes, Inflammations, in this section).

Kindred—On the Mother's Side—(See "Relatives" in this section).

Latent Disease—Illness or Death of the Mother From—♂ □ or ☍ the ☽ and ♀, with ♂ angular, and with the ☽ and ♀ occi. in the map of the child. (See Latent, Organic).

Leucorrhoea; Life Shortened—For the Mother—The ☽ Sig. □ or ☍ ♄, and caused at times by the evil ways of children. (See "Worries Thru Children" under Children; "Death of a Parent" under Parents; Early Death, Short Life, in this section).

Long Life For—The ☉ configurated with the ☽ or ♀, or ♀ in good asp. to the ☽; ♃ favorably configurated with the ☽ or ♀; ♀ ☌, ✶, or △ the ☽. (See "Good Health" in this section; "Long Life" under Females).

Mad Mother—The Mother a Lunatic—(See "Cases of Madness" under Madness).

Mammae—Disorders of—(See Breasts, Milk).

Mania—Puerperal Mania—(See Puerperal).

Many Diseases—Subject To—(See "Disease" in this section).

Maternal Instincts—(See Maternity).

Matricide—(See "Patricide" under Father).

Menses—Disorders of—(See Menses).

Milk—Disorders of—(See Breasts, Milk).

Miscarriage—Danger of Death By—(See Abortion, Miscarriage).

Misfortune To—(See Accidents, Affliction, Eyes, and the various paragraphs in this section; "Women" under Misfortune).

Mother Fixation—(See this subject under Marriage).

Mother-In-Law—Governed by the 4th H. in a male nativity, and by the 10th H. in a female. (See "Father-In-Law" under Father).

Mother May Suffer—(See Affliction, Disease, and the various paragraphs in this section).

Nervous Complaints—The ☽ in the 4th or 7th H., and afflicted by ♄. (See "Mother" under Hysteria; Neurasthenia, Nervousness, under Nerves).

Organic Trouble—(See "Latent" in this section).

Parents—(See the various paragraphs under Parents).

Parturition—Childbirth—Danger or Death In—(See Parturition, Puerperal).

Pregnancy—(See the paragraphs under Conception, Gestation, Pregnancy).

Puerperal Fever—Puerperal Mania—(See Puerperal).

Relatives—Of the Mother—(See "Aunts and Uncles" under Maternal).

Sex of Her Children—(See "Children" in this section).

Short Life For—The ☽ and ♀ in oriental angles or succedent houses, and in □ or ☍ ♂; ♄ and the ☽ in angles, swift in motion, and in □ or ☍ each other; ♄ and ♂ both afflicting the ☽; ♂ □ or ☍ the ☽ or ♀; ♂ succedent to the ☽ and ♀, or in □ or ☍ to them, and both swift in motion and in angles; lord of the 6th H. in the 8th, and afflicted, and espec. if the lord of the Asc. apply to the □ or ☍ the lord of the 6th. (See "Short Life" under Females).

Shortened—(See "Life Shortened" in this section).

Sickly—The Mother Sickly—(See Affliction, Disease, and the various paragraphs in this section).

Sickness Of—The Mother Suffers—Is Diseased—Sudden Sickness of—(See Afflicted, Disease, Sudden, and the various paragraphs in this section).

Significator Of—A planet in the 10th or 4th H., according to the sex of the child, is the Sig. of the mother if the ☉ or ☽ be not in these houses at B. (See the Introduction to this Article).

Slow Fevers—Death By—(See "Fevers" in this section; "Slow Fevers" under Fever).

Strangles Her Baby—Case—(See "Strangled", No. 922, in 1001 N.N.

Sudden Death Of—The ☽ in the 1st or 10th H., and afflicted by ♂; the ☽ or ♀ to the ☌ or ill-asp. ♅ or ♂ by dir.; the ☽ ori., and angular, and □ or ☍ ♅ or ♂; ♅ or ♂ angular, □ or ☍ the ☽, or to ♀ occidental. (See "Death" under Sudden).

Sudden Sickness Of—♂ in □ or 8 the ☽ or ♀, with ♂ angular, and the ☽ and ♀ occidental.

Suffers—The Mother Suffers—(See Afflicted, Disease, and the various paragraphs in this section).

Swoonings—(See Fainting).

Time of Death—(See "Death" in this section).

Widows; Wife—(See the various paragraphs under Wife).

Womb Trouble—Possible Death From —The ☽ occi., in □ or 8 ♄ in map of child. (See Womb).

Women—(See the various paragraphs under Women). Also see such subjects as Family, Fifth House, Fourth House, Fruitful, Home, Husband, Love Affairs, Marriage, Marriage Partner; "Influence Of" under Moon, Venus; Ovaries, Prenatal Epoch, Sister, Tenth House).

Wounds To—(See "Injuries" in this section).

MOTION — Mobility — Motility — Movement—Moving—Action—Kinetic Force, etc.—Mercury rules motion, as the influence of ☿ is excitable, quivering, and tends to ceaseless motion in mind and body. Life manifests as motion and vibration. Motion corresponds to the Mutable Signs, to the Legs, and to the Motive Temperament.

Accelerated Motion—Augmented Mobility—♂ influence. Mars when afflicted tends to tear the body apart and rupture organs and vessels. Augmented mobility is a plus condition, or tonic action of the ♂ influence. (See Action, Augmented, Exaggerated, Hernia; "Tonic" under Mars; Quick, Rapid, Rupture, Tonic, etc.).

Action—(See the various paragraphs under Action).

Amoeboid Action—(See "Amoeboid" under Cells).

Augmented Motion—(See Augmented).

Body—Motion In the Body—(See Action, Gait, Locomotion, Movement, Quick, Slow, Walk; the various paragraphs in this section).

Ceaseless Motion—In Mind and Body —(See the Introduction to this Article).

Energy—(See the subjects under Energy).

Exaggerated Motion—(See Exaggerated).

Excitability—(See Excitable).

Force—(See the paragraphs under Force).

Gait—(See Gait, Walk).

Increased Motion—(See Augmented, Exaggerated, Excitable, Increased, Motion, Movement, Tonic, etc.).

Kinetic Motion—(See Kinetic).

Locomotion; Mind—Motion In—(See Introduction to this Article).

Moon—Motion of—The motion of the ☽ has to be considered in cases of sickness, as the duration and severity of disease, and the crises and critical days, especially in fevers and acute diseases, depend upon her motion. (See Acute, Crises, Critical, Duration;

"Motion Of" under Moon; Severity; "Planets" in this section).

Motor—Motor Nerves—Motor Disturbances—(See Motor).

Movement—(See the paragraphs under Motion, Movement).

Muscles—Action and Movement of— (See Locomotion, Muscles).

Nebuloid Motion—(See "Amoeboid" under Cells).

Planets—Motion of—(See "Motion Of" under Planets; "Moon" in this section).

Quick In Motion — Rapid—Active— Quick In Action—Nimble—Quick Walk, etc.—In Hor'y Q. when the Significator is in S. Lat., a quick and nimble person is indicated, and when the Sig. is in N. Lat., a person slow in motion and movement. (See Action, Active, Energy, Gait, Locomotion, Movement, Quick, Rapid, Walk; "Slow" in this section).

Rapid Motion—(See Rapid; "Quick" in this section).

Retarded Motion — (See Lameness, Legs, Paralysis, Retarded, Slow, Suppressed).

Rotational Motion—Rotary—Vortex Motion—♀ influence.

Slow Motion—Retarded Motion—♄ tends to slow motion of body, and to hinder and retard action and movement. (See Accelerated, Quick, in this section; Clumsiness, Dull, Idle, Impeded, Retarded, Slow).

Spasmodic Motion — (See Irregular, Jerky, Spasmodic).

Vibration; Vortex Motion—(See "Rotary" in this section).

Walk—(See the paragraphs under Gait, Locomotion, Walk).

Weak—Weak Motion and Action In the Body—Feeble Action—(See Debility, Feeble, Infirm, Lassitude, Lethargy, Malaise; "Weak Body" under Weak). There are many subjects which have to do with Motion, as related to the body, and to change the motion, as by disease, deformities, defects, habits, acquired tendencies, etc., and also which may be natural. See such subjects as Automatic, Brisk, Contortions, Coordination, Crippled, Defects, Deformities, Dexterity, Disturbed, Dynamic, Erratic, Feet, Graceful, Harmony, Incoordination, Inharmony, Knees, Lameness, Legs, Muscles, Paralysis, Tremblings, etc. For other subjects which you may have in mind look in the alphabetical arrangement. Especially see the subjects of Action, Gait, Locomotion, Motor, Movement, Muscles, Spasmodic, Walk, etc.

MOTIVE—

Motive Signs—□, ♐, ♓. The ♐ sign especially gives motive force.

Motive Temperament—Motion corresponds to the Motive Temperament. The Common Signs are motive in temperament. Also indicated by ♄, and the 2nd face of the ♄ sign ♑ rising on the Asc. at B. The head in the motive temperament is flatter at the sides and square shaped. (See Decanates, Motion; "Mutable Signs" under Mutable).

MOTIVES—Purposes—Intentions—

Evil Motives — (See Cheating, Conduct, Criminal, Deceitful, Dishonest, Enemies, Evil, Forgers, Hatred, Liars, Libelers, Plots, Poison, Revenge, Thieves, Treachery, Wicked, etc.).

Good Motives—(See Character, Good, Honest, Humane, Kind; "Good Morals" under Morals; Noble, Pious, Purposes, Sincere, etc.).

Misunderstood—Motives Misunderstood—(See Misunderstood).

MOTOR—Motory—Motor Nerves—Motor Functions—Pertaining to Motion —Kinetic Force, etc.—The Motor Nerves are ruled by ♂, and also influenced strongly by ♅.

Arms—♅ in signs which rule the Arms, Hands, Legs, and Feet tends to affect the motor nerves of these parts, causing cramp, spasm, and paralysis.

Brain—Diseases of the Brain Affecting the Motor Functions—♅ afflicted in ♈ or ♉; Subs at AT. (See Brain).

Disturbances—Motor Disturbances— (See Coordination; "Movements" under Erratic; Incoordination).

Erratic Movements—(See Erratic).

Eyes—Oculo Motor Paralysis—(See "Motor" under Eyes).

Functions — Exalted Excito-Motory Functions — (See "Functions" under Exaltation).

Motor Nerves—Disorders of—♅ diseases and afflictions; ♅ afflicted in the 6th H.; ♅ ☌ ♂ in the 6th H.; ♅ afflicted by ♂. Uranus in any sign tends to disturbances of the motor nerves of the part, or parts, ruled by such sign. (See "Arms" in this section; "Motor Nerves" under Arms, Feet, Hands, Legs, Speech, Throat; "Disorders Of" under Coordination; "Nerve Action" under Incoordination).

Motor Vehicles—Death, Accident, or Injury By—Caused by the afflictions of ♅. (See Vehicles).

Neuroses — Motor Neuroses—(See "Movements" under Erratic).

Spinal Cord—Lesions of the Motory Columns Within the Spine—(See "Cord", "Lesions", under Spine).

Vaso-Motor System—(See Vaso). For disorders and diseases which are attended by disturbances of the motor nerves and functions see such subjects as Antiperistalsis, Ataxia, Colic, Contortions, Contractions, Coordination, Cramps, Deformities, Distortions, Energy, Epilepsy, Fits, Gait, Hiccough, Hysteria, Involuntary, Irregular, Jerkings, Kinetic, Locomotion, Motion, Movement, Muscles, Nausea, Nodding (see Head); Nystagmus (see Eyeballs); Paralysis, Saint Vitus Dance, Spasmodic Diseases, Speech (Impediments In); Tetanus, Tics, Tremors, Twistings, Twitching, Vomiting, Walk, Winking (see Eyelids); Wry Neck (see Neck).

MOUNTAIN FEVER—Rocky Mountain Fever—A ♌ disorder, and afflictions in ♌; ♂ afflicted in ♌; Subs at CP and KP. (See Fevers).

MOURNFUL—(See Bereavement, Complaining, Rejected, Depressed, Despond-

ent, Gloom, Grief, Lamenting, Low Spirits (see Low); Melancholic, Murmuring, Regretful, Repining, Sad, Sorrowful, Worry, etc.).

MOUTH—The Mouth—The Cavity At the Entrance to the Alimentary Canal —The Mouth is under the external rulership of the ♈ sign. Also ruled by ☿ and the ♎ sign. Mercury in ♈ has special rule and influence over the mouth, and its diseases when afflicted.

Affections—Of the Mouth—All Diseases of the Mouth—☉ diseases; the ☉ afflicted in ♈; the ☉ tends to cause all diseases of the mouth; ☿ afflicted in ♈; afflictions in ♈ or ♉, as ♉ rules the lower teeth and gums; afflictions in ♎ by reflex action; afflictions in the 1st House; Subs at MCP, LCP, CP, SP(7D), and KP (11D). (See the various paragraphs in this section).

All Diseases In—Signified by the 1st House. (See "Affections" in this section).

Aphthous Ulcers—Canker — Gangrenous Sores—Stomatitis—Thrush—Sore Mouth—(See "Mouth" under Aphthae, Gangrene).

Breathing—Mouth Breathing—(See "Mouth" under Breathing).

Broad Mouth—A Great Mouth—Large Mouth—Wide Mouth—The ☉ Sig. in ♉; the ☉ or ♂ in ♉ in partile asp. the Asc.; the ☉ in ♍; ♂ Sig. in ♉; ♉ gives, and with ♉ on the Asc.

Cankers—Aphthae—Mouth Sores— Cancrum Oris, etc.—(See "Mouth" under Aphthae, Gangrene).

Cleft Palate—Case—(See Palate).

Cystic Tumor—Under the Tongue—♀ afflicted in ♉. (See Ranula, Tongue).

Dentition—(See Teeth).

Dry Mouth—(See Fauces).

Foot and Mouth Diseases—(See "Foot and Mouth" under Feet).

Frothing At Mouth—(See Epilepsy, Fits, Hydrophobia, Saliva).

Gangrenous Sores — Cancrum Oris — (See Aphthae, Gangrene).

Glands — Glands of the Mouth Disordered—The ☽, ♆, or ☿ afflicted in ♈ or ♉; Subs at SP (7D). (See Glands, Saliva).

Great Mouth — (See "Broad" in this section).

Heat — Extreme Heat In the Mouth and Throat—(See "Heat" under Throat).

Infants — Sore Mouth In — Thrush — (See Aphthae).

Inflamed Mouth — Stomatitis — Aphthous Stomatitis—(See Aphthae).

Large Mouth — (See "Broad" in this section).

Lips — (See the paragraphs under Lips).

Lovely Mouth — ♀ in the Asc., and well dignified at B. (See "Lovely" under Face).

Mucous Membranes—Of the Mouth— Disorders of—Dryness of—♄ afflicted in ♈ or ♉; ♂ afflicted in ♉; Subs at LCP and SP. (See Fauces; "Heat" under Throat).

Muscles — Nervous Catching of the Muscles of the Mouth — ♄ afflicted in the Asc. at B.

Nervous Disorders—Of the Muscles of the Mouth—(See "Muscles" in this section).

Palate — Roof of the Mouth — (See Palate).

Posterior Part — Of the Mouth — Disorders In—Dry Conditions In—Sore In, etc.—Caused by afflictions in the latter degrees of ♈, and in ♏; Subs at LCP (6, 7C). (See Diphtheria, Fauces; "Heat" under Throat; Tonsils).

Pyorrhoea—(See Gums, Pyorrhoea).

Ranula—(See "Cystic Tumor" in this section).

Roof of Mouth—Palate—Cleft Palate —(See Palate).

Salivation—(See Saliva).

Sordes — Fetid Accumulations About the Teeth—(See "Sordes" under Teeth).

Sore Mouth — Sores In — Inflamed Mouth — Aphthous Stomatitis — (See Aphthae, Gangrene).

Stomatitis—Aphthous Stomatitis— (See "Mouth" under Aphthae).

Teeth — (See the paragraphs under Teeth).

Throat — (See the paragraphs under Fauces, Pharynx, Throat, Tonsils).

Thrush — Cankerous Sores In Mouth of Infants—Aphthous Stomatitis—(See Aphthae, Thrush).

Tongue — (See the subjects under Tongue).

Tumor—Under the Tongue—Epulis— (See "Cystic" in this section; Ranula).

Ulcers — Small, White Ulcerous Patches—Cankerous Sores—Aphthae— (See Aphthae, Gangrene, Thrush).

Uvula—Disorders of—(See Uvula).

Wide Mouth — (See "Broad" in this section).

MOVEABLE SIGNS—(See Cardinal).

MOVEMENT — Movements — Mobility — Motion—

Accelerated — (See "Accelerated" under Motion).

Arms—Inability to Move Arms—(See "Movement" under Arms).

Balance of Movement—In the Body— (See Balance, Coordination, Dexterity, Harmony).

Body—Movement In the Body—The Physiological Action of the ☽. Also caused by ♂. (See Action, Energy, Gait, Locomotion, Motion, Muscles).

Brisk Movements—(See Brisk).

Crippled—The Movements Crippled— (See Crippled, Deformities, Paralysis).

Erratic Movements—(See Erratic).

Gait — (See the paragraphs under Gait, Locomotion, Walk).

Jerky Movements—(See Jerkings).

Muscular Movements — Ruled by ♂. (See Muscles).

Quick In Movement — (See "Full of Action" under Action; "Active Body" under Active; "Choleric Temperament" under Choleric; "Abundance" under

Energy; "Energetic" under Gait; "Accelerated" under Motion; Quick, Rapid).

Retarded Movements—(See Retarded, Slow, under Motion; Retarded, Slow, Suppressed).

Slow Movements—(See "Retarded" in this section; "Slow Gait" under Gait; Slow).

Spasmodic Movements — (See Spasmodic).

MOVING PARTS — Of the Body — Such as the Arms, Extremities, Feet, Hands, Legs, Limbs, etc., are, as such, ruled by ☿ in a general way. (See these subjects).

MUCH—Abundant— Excessive—Along this line see such subjects as Abundance, Accelerated, Augmented; "Much" under Beard; "Too Much" under Blood; "Much Sickness" under Cattle; "Suffers Much" under Disease; "Great" under Energy; Enlargements; "Much Evil" under Evil; Excessive, Great; "Abundance" under Hair; Hyperacidity, Hyperactivity, Increased, Large, Many; "Too Much" under Moisture; "Great Mortality" under Mortality; Over (see the various subjects under Over); Plethora; "Much Rheum" under Rheum; "Much Sickness" under Sickness; "Much Suffering" under Suffering; Superabundance, Swellings; "Much Vitality" under Vitality, etc.).

MUCILAGINOUS—(See Demulcent).

MUCIPAROUS GLANDS — Producing Mucus—(See "Glands" under Mucus).

MUCOUS — Mucus — Muciparous — Mucous Surfaces — Mucous Membranes — Mucous Discharges and Exudations— The Mucous System—Phlegm—Sputum, etc.—Mucous Discharges are ruled in general, and as a fluid, by the ☽. The ♓ sign, and the watery signs in general, also rule over, and greatly influence the secretion, flow, and production of, and especially in pathological and disease conditions. Mucus is also strongly influenced and acted upon by the ♍ sign, which sign rules the Skin and Surfaces, and the ☉ and ☽ acting thru this sign tend to greatly influence mucous secretions, and especially those associated with skin disorders. (See what is said about the Mucous System, the ♍ sign, and the Splenic Diathesis, in the Introduction under Knees). The Saturn Group of Metals tends to have a pathological action on the Mucus, Cutaneous, and Osseous Systems, and especially the metal Lead, which is a ♄ metal. Sulphur, a strong ♄ remedy, also tends to greatly influence the mucous membranes and secretions, and to modify their action and functions. Arsenic, a ♂ remedy, when given in large doses, acts as a powerful irritant to the mucous membranes, and especially the bronchial membranes. Phlegm is mucus from the Bronchial Tubes, and a number of paragraphs concerning Mucus are considered in the Article on Phlegm.

Bowels—Mucus In the Bowels—(See "Mucus" under Bowels).

Catarrh — And with Mucous Discharges—(See Catarrh).

Colds — (See the paragraphs under Colds).

Colic—Mucous Colic—(See "Colic" under Bowels).

Conjunctiva — Mucous Membrane of the Eye—Inflammation of—(See Conjunctiva).

Cough — (See Cough, Expectoration, Spitting).

Discharges — Mucous Discharges — A ♓ disease, and afflictions in ♓. (See "Catarrhal" under Discharges).

Diseases—Mucous Diseases—Diseases of the Mucous Membranes — Largely under the rule of ♄ and ♑, and of which Eczema is typical. (See Eczema; the various paragraphs in this section).

Dropsy — (See "Mucus-Like Dropsy" under Dropsy).

Excessive Secretion Of—(See Catarrh; "Excessive", "Great Expectoration", under Phlegm).

Expectoration—(See "Great Expectoration" under Phlegm).

Exudations — Morbid Discharges On Mucous Membranes—(See Exudations).

Fluids—Mucous Fluids—(See "Mucous Membranes" in this section).

Glands— The Muciparous Glands— Those of the Generative Organs are ruled by the ♏ sign. Also the Muciparous Glands, the Mucus-Producing Glands of any part or organ, are ruled by the sign which rules the part. (See Glands).

Head—Mucous Discharges From— (See Catarrh; "Mucus" under Head; Nose).

Inflammation — Of the Mucous Membranes — Catarrhal Disorders are Inflammations of the Mucous Membrane of the part involved. Acute Inflammations of Mucous Membranes may be caused by ♂ in the sign ruling the part, as ♂ in ♊ tends to colds on the lungs. Saturn in signs tends to a chronic form of irritation and inflammation, as ♄ in ♊ to consumption, continued and morbid expectoration, etc. (See such subjects as Bronchitis, Catarrh, Conjunctivitis, Colds, Consumption, Defluxions, Diphtheria, Discharges; "Catarrh" under Nose; Pneumonia; "Inflammation", "Sore Throat", under Throat, etc.).

Larynx—Phlegm Collections In—(See "Phlegm" under Larynx).

Lungs — (See Catarrh, Consumption, Mucus, Obstructions, under Lungs).

Morbid Exudations—On Mucous Surfaces — (See Diphtheria, Exudations, Throat, Tonsils).

Mouth—(See Aphthous, Mucous Membranes, under Mouth).

Mucous Membranes—Mucous Surfaces and Fluids—Diseases of—The ☽ rules the internal mucous surfaces in a general way, and the ♑ sign rules the outer mucous surfaces, and the comparatively dry Epidermis. Arsenic, a ♂ drug, is an irritant to mucous membranes. The mucous membranes and vascular tissues are influenced by ♀ in such diseases as result from Impure Blood, Poisoning of the System, and Sloughing Sores resulting from Pustular Diseases. Afflictions to the ☽, and the ☽ ☌ or ill-asp. ♄, and af-

flictions in ♑, tend to disorders of the mucous membranes, surfaces, and the normal secretion of mucus. (See "Exudations", and the various paragraphs in this section).

Nose—Nasal Discharges of Mucus— (See Catarrh, Discharges; the various paragraphs under Nose).

Phlegm—Phlegmatic Diseases— Phlegmatic Temperament — (See Phlegm).

Respiratory Membranes—Deficient Secretion of Mucus On the Respiratory Membranes — ♄ ☌ or ill-asp. ☿. (See "Dry Cough" under Cough).

Rheum—(See Rheum).

Stomach — (See Irritations, Mucous Membrane, Obstruction, under Stomach).

Surfaces—The Mucous Surfaces—(See Exudations, Mucous Membranes, in this section).

Throat—Mucus Falling Into—(See "Mucous" under Throat).

Urine—Mucus In—(See "Mucus" under Urine).

Watery Humours — (See Defluxions, Fluxes, Rheum; "Humours" under Watery).

MUDDLING CREATURE — (See "Ill-Formed" under Ill).

MUDDY COMPLEXION — (See "Dull" under Complexion).

MULES—Hybrids—(See the Introduction under Barren; Horses, Hybrids).

MULATTO COMPLEXION—(See "Complexion" under Yellow).

MULLEIN—A Typical Drug of ♄. (See "Saturn Group" under Herbs; "Drugs" under Saturn).

MULTIPLE BIRTHS — (See Double-Bodied Signs, Fruitful, Quadruplets, Triplets, Twins).

MULTITUDE — The Multitude — (See "Common People" under Common; Humanity, Lynching, Mankind, Mobs, Public, Riots, Trampled, Tumults).

MUMPS — Parotiditis — (See "Mumps" under Parotid).

MUNDANE ASTROLOGY — This has to do with Events in the World At Large, and treats of the influence of the Planets, their Aspects, Conjunctions, Sign and House positions, as they affect different Countries, Nations, Cities, and Divisions of the World. This subject has much to do with the study of Calamities, Catastrophies, Cholera, Disasters, Drought, Earthquakes, Epidemics, Famine, Floods, Excessive Cold or Heat, Pestilence, The Plague, Wars, their causes and predetermination, etc. (See these subjects). Every student should make a study of Mundane Astrology, and a convenient Textbook is "Raphael's Mundane Astrology." Also see Pearce's Textbook of Astrology. (See "Planetary Aspects" under Aspects; Humanity, Mankind, Nations, Parallel, Perigee, Perihelion, Planets, Prevalent, Public).

Mundane Parallel Aspect — (See Parallel).

MURDER—Murders—Murderers—Murdered—Murderous—Mars and his afflicting aspects are the principal causes of murder, and of causing people to do things under sudden, exciting, and rash impulses. The afflictions of ♄ over the mind tend to premeditated murder, as resulting from malice, hatred, revenge, plots, jealousy, suspicion, treachery, etc., and especially when ♄ is conjoined with Mars. Murders which are committed under very sudden impulses are usually caused by ♅, and are of the unexpected and unpremeditated class, extraordinary, and unusual, tragical, etc.

A Murderer—Murderous Tendencies—An Assassin—A Potential Murderer—Has the Murder Complex—Not Averse to Shedding Blood—Homicidal—Ready to Rush Into Bloodshed — Criminally Inclined—Bloodthirsty—Violent Tendencies, etc.—The ☉ Sig. □ or 8 ♂; the ☉ Sig. to the ♂ or ill-asp. ♂ by dir., if the map shows a tendency to violence, and ♂ be much afflicted and ill-dignified at B.; the ☉ joined to Hyades, Castor, Pollux, Pleiades, Ascelli, or Praesepe, danger of being a murderer, or being murdered, and espec. when the ☉ is with Praesepe; the ☉ conjoined with Caput Algol in an angle, and to come to an untimely end; the ☉ with Caput Algol in an angle, or with the hyleg, or if ♂ be there elevated above the Lights when Caput Algol is angular, denotes a murderer and an untimely end; the ☉ directed to all Nebulous Stars, and to Castor and Pollux; the ☉ or ☽ Sig. ♂ ♂, and ♂ ill-dignified; the ☽ in ♍ and afflicted by ♄ or ♂; the ☽ Sig. □ or 8 ♂; the ☽ to the place of Caput Algol; ♅ afflicted in ♈; ♅ ♂ or ill-asp. ♂; ♅ afflicted in the 9th H.; ♅ ♂ ♂ in ♈; ♅ influence often provides the impulse to do wrong, and commit murder, or have moral lapses; ♅ ♂ or ill-asp. ♄; ♄ Sig. □ or 8 ♂; ♄ Sig. to the ♂ or ill-asp. ♂ by dir., and especially if ♄ or ♂ were in the 1st, 3rd, 9th, or 10th H. at B.; ♂ Sig. ♂ ♄, and ♂ ill-dignified; the □ and 8 aspects of ♂ are the aspects of cruelty and murder; ♀ Sig. □ or 8 ♃, often a secret murderer or thief; ♀ ill-posited and □ or 8 ♄ or ♂; ♀ Sig. ♂ or ill-asp. ♂, and espec. when in evil asp. to ♄ also; the M.C. to Algol or Hydra's Heart; the 3rd decan. ♌, or 1st dec. ♏ on the Asc. (See Anarchists, Assassins, Criminal, Cruel, Dangerous, Destructiveness, Execution; "Patricide" under Father; Homicidal, Malicious, Manslaughter, Poisoner; "Imprisonment" under Prison; Revengeful, Riotous, Robbers, Thieves, Treachery; "Tendency To" under Violence). Cases and Birth Data of Murderers—All taken from 1001 N.N. See "Wife Murderer", No. 189; "Holloway", No. 189; "Beach Murder", No. 134; "Schauman", A Political Murderer, No. 209; "H. G. R.", Shot and Killed a Man, No. 337; "Thaw Case", Murder of Stanford White, No. 340; "Who Was This?", Homicide, No. 560; "Pressed to Death", No. 626; "Murderer", No. 636; "Boy Murderers", No. 079.

Death by Murder—Murdered to Death —Danger of Being Murdered—Threatened with Murder — Meets with an Untimely End by Violence—The ☉ hyleg, and to the □ or 8 ♂ by dir.; the ☉ to the place of Praesepe; the ☽ to the ♂ ♂ by dir., and especially if ♂ be Anareta; the ☽ to the place of Caput Algol or the Pleiades; the ☽ hyleg, and to the ♂, P., □ or 8 ♂ by dir.; ♅ ♂ ♂ in the 7th H.; ♂ is Significator of; ♂ afflicted in fiery signs, and ♂, P., □ or 8 the Asc. by dir.; ♂ in a human sign and afflicted by other malefics; ♂ ♂ the Asc. by dir.; ♂ ori., □ or 8 ☉ from fixed signs, or ♂ occi., □ or 8 ☽ from fixed signs, or death by Suicide, and caused by women if ♀ be with ♂; the Asc. □ or 8 ♂ by dir., if in an earthy sign; cardinal signs show when strong at B., and containing several malefics, and the hyleg badly afflicted; the 26° ♊ on the Asc. Cases of Death by Murder—In 1001 N.N. See "Peasenhall", No. 170; "Whiteley", No. 336; "Prince", No. 744; "Russia", No. 763. (For further study along this line see Ambushes, Assassinated, Assaults, Attacks, Blows, Burning, Cuts, Duels; "Murdered" under Enemy; Executed, Feuds, Guillotine, Guns, Hanging, Highwaymen, Lynching; "Hand of Man" under Man; Mobs, Mutilation, Pirates, Plots, Poisoning, Public Death, Quarrelsome, Robbers, Ruffians, Stabs; "Flying Stones" under Stones; Suicide, Sword, Thieves, Tragical; "Treachery" under Women; "Untimely End" under Untimely; "Death" under Violence).

Great Men—Murder of—(See "Assassination" under Kings).

Journey—Murdered While On a Journey—Murdered During Travel—Lord of the 8th in the 3rd or 9th H., and afflicted; lord of the 3rd or 9th in evil asp. the ☽, or in the 7th or 8th H. (See Abroad, Assassination, Highwaymen, Journeys, Pirates; "Murder" under Ships; Travel, Voyages).

Many Murders Prevalent—Murderous Pandemics — The ☉ directed to all Nebulous Clusters, and to Castor and Pallux, threatens Murders, Rapes, and Quarrels, both committed upon, and by the native; an eclipse of the ☉ or ☽ in a fiery sign; an eclipse of the ☉ in ♍; the ☽ in the 8th H. at the Vernal Equinox, and Lady of the Year, and especially if in ♈, ♏, or ♑, and afflicted; ♂ sole ruler of an eclipse of the ☉; ♂ in ♏ at the Vernal, and Lord of the Year; ♂ ♂ the ☉ tends to many murders; ♂ elevated above and configurated with ♀ at a Solar Ingress or Eclipse; ♂ ♂ or P. ♀ near the Equator or Tropics; caused by fixed stars of the nature of ♂; caused by ♂ when he is in Perigee, nearest the Earth; ♀ in ♊ ♂ ♂ at the Vernal, and Lord of the Year; a maximum of planetary influences, as the ♂ of three or four of the superior planets in the signs of ♂, as in ♈ or ♏, tend to murderous pandemics. (See "Much Crime Prevalent" under Crime; Mobs; "Murderous Outrages" under Outrages; Robberies; "Much Slaughter Everywhere" under Slaughter; "Outbreaks of Violence" under Violence).

Murdered to Death—(See "Death" in this section).

Murderous Outrages—♂ in 8th H. at a Solar Ingress of ☉ into ♈, and afflicting the ☽ or planet ascending; ♂

in 7th H. at a Solstice, many murders, and criminals very active for the ensuing Quarter.

Noblemen—Murders of—(See Nobles).

Slaughter — M u c h Slaughter Everywhere—(See "Shedding of Blood" under Blood; Slaughter, War).

Travel — M u r d e r e d D u r i n g — (See "Journey" in this section).

Women—Many Murders of Women— ☿ in ♋ at the Vernal Equi., Lord of the Year, and ☌ ♂ or ♀. (See Cases of Wife Murder under Wife. Also for cases of Men murdered by Women, see "Poison Death" under Poison; Tragical; "Female Treachery" under Treachery).

MURMURING. — Regretful — Complaining—Lamentations—The ☽ Sig. □ or ☍ ♄; ♄ Sig. □ or ☍ ☽; many planets in double-bodied signs. (See Anguish, Complaining, D e j e c t e d, Discontentment, Exhibitionism, Grief, Lamentations, M i s e r y, P e e v i s h, Regretful, Repining, Sadness, Sorrowful, etc.).

Endures Disease Without Murmuring —Lord of the 5th in the 6th H. (See Complaining).

M U S C A E V O L I T A N T E S — Floating Specks Before the Eyes—(See "Muscae" under Eyes).

MUSCLES — The Muscular System — Muscular — The Muscles, Tendons and Sinews are ruled principally by ♂. Also ruled by the ☽. Certain Groups of Muscles are ruled by other planets. Mars in any sign rules the muscles of the part, or organ, ruled by such sign. Thus, ♂ in ♈ rules the muscles of the head; ♂ in ♉, ♊, ♋, the Intercostal muscles; ♂ in ♋, the muscles of the stomach; ♂ in ♌, the muscles of the heart; in ♍, the abdominal muscles; in ♐, the thighs. Also ♐ rules the locomotor muscles of the hips and thighs. Mars in ♑, ♒, and ♓, the muscles of the knees, calves, feet, etc., and ♂ afflicted in any of these signs tends to affect and disturb the muscular action in the part. The Motor Nerves, which supply the muscles, are also ruled by ♂, and influenced by ♅, and afflictions to ♂ and ♅, or by them, tend to disturbed m u s c u l a r action, cramps, spasms, paralysis, etc. The muscles of the Genito-Urinary Organs and System, as a whole, are ruled by ♂, as ♂ rules the external Genital Organs.

GENERAL CONSIDERATIONS—

Activity — Muscular Activity — Mars draws upon the Glycogen in the liver for fuel for the muscles during muscular activity. Also during m u s c u l a r activity, ♄ deposits Uric Acid over the body, causing Gout and Rheumatism. (See Deposits, Glycogen, Gout, Rheumatism, Urea, Uric, Wastes).

Body—A Muscular Body—Athletic— The ☉ Sig. in ♉, proud of his physical strength; the ☽ in ♍; ♂ rising at B., more muscular than corpulent; ♂ in ♌ or ♍; given by ♂; ♄ in ♍. (See Athletics, Exercise, Sports; "Body" under Strong; "Strength" in this section).

Bony and Muscular — (See "Bony, Lean and Muscular", "Bony and Muscular", under Bones).

Cardiac Muscle—(See "Jupiter Group" in this section).

Coordination — Coordinated Muscular Action — (See Coordination, Dexterity, Harmony, Incoordination).

Dexterity—Harmonious Muscular Action—(See Coordination, D e x t e r i t y, Harmony).

Fibers and Filaments—Of the Muscles —Ruled by ♂. (See Fibers, Filaments, Ligaments).

Fuel for Muscles—(See "Activity" in this section).

Glycogen — The Fuel for Muscles — (See "Activity" in this section).

Harmony—Harmonious Muscular Action—(See "Coordination" in this section).

Jupiter Group—Of Herbs—This Group of Herbs tends to have a pathological action on the cardiac muscle, and also the Muscular, and Fibro-Ligamentous Systems, the Gastro-Intestinal Tunics, the Vesical Muscle (Bladder), and the Pulmonary Parenchyma. (See "Impar" under Ganglion; "Jupiter Group" under Herbs; "Pathological Action" under Jupiter).

Large Muscles — ♄ in ♌, partile asp. the Asc.

Lean, B o n y, and M u s c u l a r — (See "Bony" in this section).

Ligaments—(See Ligaments).

Locomotor Muscles — Of the Hips — Ruled by ♐. (See Locomotion).

Motion In—(See Gait, Motion, Movement, Walk).

Motor Nerves — W h i c h S u p p l y the Muscles—(See Motor).

Movements — Muscular Movements — Are ruled by ♂. (See Action, Motion, Motor, Movement).

Muscular Activity—(See "Activity" in this section).

Muscular Body—(See "Body" in this section).

Muscular and Bony — (See "Raw-Boned" under Bones; "Bony" in this section).

Muscular Energy—Muscular Power— Ruled by ♂. (See Energy, Physical, Power, Strength, Strong; "Weak Body" under Weak; "Strength" in this section).

Muscular Movements — (See "Movements" in this section).

Muscular System—Ruled by ♂. (See Mars).

Nerve Supply—To the Muscles—(See "Motor Nerves" under Motor).

Power — Muscular Power — (See Activity, Energy, Muscular, Strength, in this section).

Sinews—(See Sinews).

Strength — M u s c u l a r Strength a n d Power — Strong Muscles — Given by ♂ and the ♂ signs ♈ and ♍. Also assisted by the good aspects of ♅ to ♂, and with the ☉ and ☽ in favorable asp. to ♂ also. The bad aspects of ♅, the ☉ or ☽ to ♂ tend to give strength, but with more danger of disease, strain, or accident. Neptune, ♄, ♀, and the ☽ tend to less muscular strength and power.

The ☳ and ♒ sign people often have strong and muscular bodies, and also ♍ develops muscular strength by exercises and physical culture. The ☉ Sig. in ☳, proud of his physical strength. The mutable signs do not tend to give much muscular strength, and especially ♓, which is weak, and tends to corpulency. The mutable signs tend to give agility rather than muscular strength, except ♓, which is a rather weak sign physically, and tends to dissipation, drink, lethargy, slovenliness, lassitude, etc. Some general aspects which give muscular strength are—♂ in the 6th H. in ♍, and well-aspected by the ☉ and ☽; ♂ rising at B. in ♈ or ♏, and well-aspected by the ☉, ☽, and ♄; ♂ ☌ ♅ in ♏ in the 6th H.; ♂ ✳ or △ the Asc., great muscular strength; the ☽ ☌ ♅ in ♉, and well-aspected by the ☉ and ♂. (See "Body" in this section).

Strong Muscles — (See "Strength" in this section; "Body" under Strong).

Tendons—(See Tendons).

Tensity—The muscles are rendered tense and trembling by ♂. (See Contractions, Spasmodic).

DISEASES OF THE MUSCLES—

Abdominal Muscles—Disorders of— Afflictions in ♍; ♂ in ♍, inflammation of; ♅ in ♍, cramps of; ♄ affl. in ♍, spasm of; Subs at PP (3L). (See Abdomen; "Ileac Passion" under Ileac).

Action — Incoordinated Muscular Action — Ataxia — ♅ influence and afflictions; ♅ afflicted in ☳, the organ of coordination. (See Action, Ataxia, Catalepsy, Contractions, Coordination, Erratic, Gait, Incoordination, Jerky, Lameness, Locomotion, Locomotor Ataxia, Motion, Motor, Movement, Spasmodic, Tics, Twitchings, Walk).

Arms—Muscular Rheumatism In— (See Muscles, Rheumatism, under Arms).

Arthritic Muscular Atrophy — (See "Arthritis" under Legs).

Ataxia—Incoordination—(See Ataxia; "Action" in this section).

Atrophy — (See Atrophy; "Arthritis" under Legs; "Progressive" in this section).

Catalepsy — With Loss of Muscular Activity—(See Catalepsy).

Back—Muscular Rheumatism In— (See Back).

Clonic Spasm—Of Muscles—(See Alternating, Involuntary, Myoclonia, Paramyoclonus; "Clonic" under Spasmodic).

Collapse—Muscular Collapse—Case— (See "Muscular" under Collapse; Flabby, Laxity, Relaxation, in this section).

Contortions—(See Contortions).

Contractions — Of the Muscles — ♅ in any sign, and afflicted, tends to erratic and spasmodic contractions in the part ruled by the sign. Also ♄ tends to contractions due to cold, deposits, impeded functions, as his influence is to hinder, suppress, and interfere with the nerve supply to a part, and as indicated by the sign he is in at B.

An alternating contraction is called a clonic spasm of the muscle. A continued rigid contraction is known as a tonic spasm. There are various movements in the muscles, due to contractions, such as jerkings, tremors, tremblings, irregularities, etc., due to the nature and aspects of the afflicting planet or planets. An exaggerated muscular contraction is often caused by ♂ ☌ of ♂ with ♅, known as Hyperkinesia. ~~Irregular, Alternate, and~~ Spasmodic Contractions are the work of ♅, while a continued contraction is more apt to be caused by ♄, and to become chronic, which may result in a deformity. In intensified muscular contractions ♂ combines his influence in the configuration. (For Contractions in the various parts of the body see Contractions; "Contractions" under Anus, Arms, Face, Feet, Limbs, Neck; "Muscles and Limbs" under Father. Also see Action, Clonic, Cramps, Hyperkinesia, Involuntary, Myoclonic, Opisthotonos, Paramyoclonus, Spasmodic, Tetanus, and the various paragraphs in this section).

Control — Lack of Control Over the Muscles — A weak ♂ at B. (See "Muscles" under Control; "Involuntary" in this section).

Cramps—(See Cramps).

Crystallization — Of the Eye Muscles —(See "Crystallization" under Eyes).

Degeneration—Fatty Degeneration of the Muscles — Caused by ♃. (See Degeneration; "Fatty Degeneration" under Fat).

Diaphragm—Erratic Action of—(See Diaphragm).

Erratic Action — (See "Movements" under Erratic).

Exaggerated Contractions—(See Contractions, Exaggerated; "Hyperkinesia" in this section).

Excitement—Involuntary Muscular Excitement — (See Contractions, Control, Involuntary, in this section).

Exercise — Inordinate Exercise — (See Exercise, Sports).

Extremities—Disorders of Muscles of —(See "Muscles" under Arms, Extremities, Feet, Hands, Legs; Atrophy, Progressive, and the various paragraphs in this section).

Eyes—Congestion and Crystallization of the Muscles of — (See "Crystallization" under Eyes).

Father — (See "Muscles and Limbs" under Father).

Fatty Degeneration—(See "Degeneration" in this section).

Flabby Muscles—(See "Muscular" under Collapse; Flabby).

Gout — In the Muscles — (See Gout, Rheumatism).

Hands—(See "Muscles" under Hands).

Head—(See "Muscles" under Head).

Heart Muscle—Inefficiency of—(See "Inefficiency" under Heart).

Hurts — To the Muscles — (See the various paragraphs under Blows, Bruises, Cuts, Hurts, Injuries, Stabs, Wounds, etc.).

Hyperkinesia—Exaggerated Muscular Contraction — ♂ ☌ or ill-asp. ♅. (See "Contractions" in this section).

Incoordination — Of Muscular Action —(See "Action" in this section).

Inefficiency — (See "Heart Muscle" in this section).

Inflammation—Of Muscles—Myostitis —May be caused by ♄, by excess deposits of acid wastes, as in Gout, Rheumatism, etc. Also caused by ♂, by excess heat in a muscle, or from hurts, etc. (See Gout, Inflammation, Rheumatism).

Intensified—Muscular Contractions Intensified—(See Contractions, Hyperkinesia, in this section).

Intercostal Muscles—(See Intercostal).

Involuntary Contractions — Involuntary Action of Muscles — Involuntary Muscular Excitement — ♅ or ♂ afflictions; ♂ ☌ ♅. (See Action, Clonic, Contractions, Control, Spasm, Tetanus, and the various paragraphs in this section; Involuntary, Nausea, Vomiting).

Jerkings; Laxity—Of Muscular Tissue —Caused by a weak ♂ at B. Also caused by ♀, and is classed as a ♀ disease. (See Flabby, Laxity, Relaxation).

Legs—(See "Muscles" under Legs).

Ligaments—(See Ligaments).

Limbs — Muscles of — (See Atrophy, Muscles, under Limbs).

Lock-Jaw—Spasm of the Muscles of Jaw—(See Lock-Jaw).

Locomotion—Disorders of Muscles of —(See "Muscular Spasm" under Feet; Gait, Locomotion; "Muscles" under Hips, Legs, Thighs; Walk).

Locomotor Ataxia—(See Ataxia, Locomotor Ataxia; "Action" in this section).

Mastication — Spasm of Muscles of — (See Lock-Jaw).

Mineral Salts — Deficiency of In the Muscles — (See "Blood" under Minerals).

Mouth—(See "Muscles" under Mouth).

Movements — Incoordinated Muscular Movements — ♅ influence. (See Gait, Incoordination, Locomotion, Motion, Motor, Movements, Walk; "Action" in this section).

Myoclonus—(See "Paramyoclonus" in this section).

Myostitis — (See "Inflammation" in this section).

Neck—Contractions and Cramps In— (See Neck).

Opisthotonos—(See Opisthotonos, Trunk).

Pain—In the Muscles—(See Inflammation, Rheumatism, in this section).

Paramyoclonus Multiplex—Myoclonus —A Nervous Disease with Clonic Spasms of the Voluntary Muscles—A ♅ disease and affliction; Subs at AT and AX. (See "Clonic" under Spasmodic).

Power—Lack of Muscular Power—A weak ♂ at B. (See Collapse, Control, Flabby, in this section; "Strength" in the first Division of this Article; "Weak Body" under Weak).

Progressive Muscular Atrophy — Tabes—A ♄ disease and affliction. (See Atrophy, Emaciation, Tabes, Thin, Wasting). Case Of—See "Living Skeleton", No. 053, in 1001 N.N.

Quiverings; Relaxation—Of Muscles —(See Collapse, Flabby, Laxity, Relaxation).

Rheumatism — Muscular Rheumatism —Pain In the Muscles—Caused by the afflictions of ♄, and the retention of wastes and Uric Acid in the tissues. Also caused by ♂ afflictions. (See "Muscular Rheumatism" under Back, Neck; "Rheumatism" under Arms, Feet, Hands, Legs, Limbs, Shoulders; Gout, Rheumatism).

Rigidity—Stiffness—(See Rigidity).

Saint Vitus Dance—(See Saint).

Shoulders — (See "Muscles" under Shoulders).

Sinews—(See Sinews).

Spasm of Muscles—Caused by ♅. (See Abdominal, Clonic, Contractions, Lock-Jaw, Saint Vitus, Tonic, and the various paragraphs in this section; Spasmodic).

Sphincter Ani Muscle—Contraction of —(See Anus).

Stabs—Muscles Wounded By—(See Stabs).

Sterno-Mastoid Muscle—Disorders of —(See Mastoid).

Stiffness—(See Rigidity).

Strain—(See "Muscular Strain" under Strain).

Strength—(See "Strength" in the first Division of this Article; Flabby, Power, Weak, in this section).

Tabes—(See "Progressive" in this section).

Tendons—(See Tendons).

Tetanus — Spasmodic and Continued Contraction of the Muscles — (See "Blood" under Minerals; Spasmodic, Tetanus; "Tonic Spasm" under Tonic).

Tissues — Muscular Tissues—Inflammation of—Laxity of—(See Collapse, Flabby, Inflammation, Laxity, Rheumatism, in this section; Tissues).

Tonic Spasm of Muscles—(See "Tonic" under Spasmodic; Tetanus, Tonic).

Tremors; Trismus—(See Lock-Jaw).

Twistings—(See Twistings).

Twitchings—(See Saint Vitus, Spasmodic, Tics, Twitching; "Involuntary" in this section).

Voluntary Muscles—Clonic Spasm of —Myoclonus — (See Clonic, Paramyoclonus, Spasm, in this section).

Wasting of Muscles—(See Consumptions, Emaciation, Tabes, Wasting; "Progressive" in this section).

Weak Muscular Action—♂ weak at B. (See Collapse, Flabby, Laxity, Power, Relaxation, in this section).

Wounds To—(See "Hurts" in this section). For other subjects along this line which may have been overlooked, and not listed here, look in the alphabetical arrangement for what you have in mind.

MUSHROOMS—Ruled by ♆.

MUSIC—Musicians—

Fond of Music—Has Musical Ability —Denoted by ♀ and Ψ strong at B. Venus especially rules music, and when well-aspected with Ψ gives the higher and inspirational musical genius. The ♊ sign favorably placed and occupied gives manual dexterity, and a good touch in musical work and piano playing. The fire and water elements are also strong in the map, as they rule strongly over the emotions. Taurus and ♎, the signs of ♀, are musical signs, but ♉ gives better executive ability than ♎. The ♋ and ♒ signs also give musical ability. The special areas of the signs which give musical ability and genius are the 16° ♉ and ♏; the 15° of the cardinal signs, and espec. of ♈ and ♋, and also the 24° of cardinal signs; the latter degrees of ♌ and ♒, and the first few degrees of ♍ and ♓. As ♄ rules the hearing, this planet when well configured with ♀ and Ψ, and otherwise favorably placed, tends to give a good ear for music, and to detect all in-harmony. Other general influences found in the maps of musical people are the ☉, ☽, or ☿ in ♉ or ♎; ♃ and ♀ configurated with ☿; ♀ in ♉ or ♎; ♀ in the Asc. near the horizon, or ♀ in ♑ gives a musical voice; ☿ Sig. ⚹, ☌, or △ ♀; ♉ or ♎ on the Asc. or M.C.; many planets in bicorporeal signs. (See Geniuses, Prodigies; "Influence Of" under Libra, Taurus, Venus).

Music Halls—Case—Killed In a Fire In a Music Hall—See "Lafayette", No. 812, in 1001 N.N. (See Amusements, Theatres).

Singers—♀ ruler at B., rising in the Asc., and well-aspected, tends to make good singers, and espec. with ♀ rising in ♉. Also, ♉ or ♎ on the Asc., the signs of ♀. Loud singing and straining of the voice should be avoided when ☿ is afflicted in ♉ at B., as ☿ here often tends to nerve disorders of the larynx and vocal cords. (See "Hoarseness" under Larynx; "Musical Voice" under Voice).

MUSTARD—Sinapis—(See Rubefacient, Sinapis, Vesicant).

MUTABLE—Changeable—The Mutable Signs, etc.—

Diseases of the Mutable Signs—Diseases Ruled By — The Common Signs show Asthma, Blood (Poor Blood, Spitting of Blood); Bowel Disorders, Bronchial Disorders, Consumption, Cough, Dejection (Mental); Depression (Mental); Diabetes, Dropsy, Extremities (Diseases In); Kidney Disorders, Lung Diseases, Melancholy, Negative States of Mind, Nervous Diseases, Neurasthenia, Respiratory Disorders, Sciatica, Scurvy, Spasms, Tuberculosis, Worry, etc. (See these subjects).

Mutable Disposition — A Changeable, Vacillating, Restless, and Negative Nature — Given by the mutable signs, such signs on the angles at B., or many planets in them; the 3rd Decan. of ♓ on the Asc. (See "Lack Of" under Concentration; "Mind" under Instability; "Negative Nature" under Negative; Plastic, Restless, Vacillating, etc.).

Mutable Signs of Zodiac—Also called Common Signs, Flexed Signs, and Acute Signs. These signs are ♊, ♍, ♐, and ♓, and are closely allied with the cadent houses, the 3rd, 6th, 9th, and 12th Houses. (See Cadent). These signs relate to Thought. Flexibility is the main characteristic of the mutable signs, and people born with many planets in them are more amenable to suggestion and treatment. These signs form the Mutable Cross, and are all in ♌ or ♉ aspect to each other, and planets and afflictions in any of them tend to affect or afflict parts or organs ruled by all the common signs. (See "Disease" under Nature). These signs are ruled by ♃ and ☿. Resistance to disease is low with many planets in common signs at B., and especially if the planets are out of dignity, setting, ℞, below the horizon, and badly afflicted, and the mutable signs are more identified with disease than the cardinal and fixed signs. The ♍ people especially court disease, and think and brood much about their health conditions. (See Virgo). The ♍ and ♓ signs, and the 6th and 12th Houses, both have to do with matters of health and sickness, hospitals, asylums, etc. (See Asylums, Hospitals, Pisces, Sixth House, Twelfth House). People born under these signs are more passive, amenable to suggestion, and are subject to many diseases, but easily cured if under the right treatment, but disease may also be greatly prolonged with them, and become chronic, if under evil influences, and bad suggestions as to their condition and cure. People born with all four of the common signs on angles are more vacillating, changeable, and difficult to cure, as they are apt to change Healers frequently, go from one Healer, or System of Healing, to another, and for this reason they often become chronic invalids, and die an early death. Common signs on the angles also increase the chances of Insanity unless the mind is well controlled, and especially if the ☽, ☿, and the Asc. are badly afflicted at B. Pisces is considered the weakest of the common signs, and this sign on the Asc. at B. tends to give a very weak constitution, and also to corpulency, flabbiness of muscle and tissue, a watery constitution, and less vitality. Afflictions in ♓ tend to affect the lungs, bowels, thighs, and feet. (See Pisces). Gemini is the strongest of the common signs, is a positive and highly intellectual sign, and gives more power to resist and fight off disease. (See Gemini). Also, ♐ is a strong, fiery, masculine, and vital sign, and when on the Asc. at B. gives good vitality. (See Sagittarius). The mutable signs are Motive in Temperament, and correspond to the legs, and motion. Gemini, ♐, and ♓, are also called double-bodied signs, and tend to produce Twins, Monsters, and Hermaphrodites. (See Double-Bodied).

Rulership of the Common Signs—The Common, or Mutable signs, bear rule especially over the Arms, Bowels, Digestion, Extremities, Feet, Glandular System, Hands, Legs, Limbs, Lungs, Nervous System, Thighs. (See these subjects). For further study see Angles, Cardinal, Curable, Fixed Signs, Incurable, Mutation, Ninth House, Residence, Sixth House, Suicide, Third House, Twelfth House.

MUTATION — Mutations—Changes— Mutability—Mutations and changes are especially under the rule of the ☽.

Body—Mutations In—(See "Body" under Change).

Fluids — (See "Mutation" under Fluids).

Mind—The Mutability of the Mind Increased—(See "Instability" under Mind; "Mutable Disposition" under Mutable).

MUTE — Mutes — Dumb — Without the Power of Speech—Mute Signs, etc.—

Deaf and Dumb — Deaf Mute — (See "Deaf and Dumb" under Hearing).

Deaf, Dumb and Blind—(See this subject under Hearing).

Deaf, Dumb and Idiot—(See this subject under Hearing).

Mute or Dumb Signs — ♋, ♏, and ♓. Also known as the Reptilian Signs. Called Dumb, or Mute, because the creatures ruled over by these signs make no audible sound. (See Dumb).

Mutes — Dumbness — Deprived of Speech—(See Dumb).

MUTILATED — Mutilations — ♂ is Significator of Mutilations.

Death by Mutilation—♂ in the 7th H., and afflicted at a Solstice, as the ☉ is coming into ♋, or at a Solar Ingress. (See Beheaded; "Burned At Stake" under Burns; "Death By" under Cuts; Hanging, Lynching, Maimed, Mangled, Mobs; "Murdered" under Murder; Stabs; Tortured, etc.).

Degrees — The Mutilated Degrees of the Zodiac—♉ 6th to 10th degrees; ♋ 9th to 15th degrees; ♌ 18, 27, 28; ♏ 18, 19; ♐ 1, 7, 8, 18, 19; ♑ 26 to 29; ♒ 18, 19. These degrees on the Asc. at B., or when such degrees contain malefics, are supposed to cause Deformities, Distortions, Lameness, Mutilations, and especially Lameness. (See "Signs" in this section; "Azimene Degrees" under Azimene; Deformities; "Zodiac" under Degrees; Distortions, Lameness, etc.).

Foetus—Mutilation of At Birth—(See Foetus).

Limb—Mutilation of—(See Beheaded).

Mutilated Beyond Recognition—Case —Fell Under a Train—(See "Strafford", No. 814, in 1001 N.N.

Mutilated Degrees—(See "Degrees" in this section).

Mutilated Signs—(See "Signs" in this section).

Signs — The Mutilated Signs of the Zodiac—The Broken Signs—Imperfect Signs—These signs are ♌, ♏, and ♓. (See "Broken Signs" under Broken; "Causes Of" under Distortions; Imperfect).

MUTINY — Death In Abroad — (See "Battle" under Abroad; "Officer Killed" under Military).

MYDRIASIS—Abnormal Dilation of the Pupils—(See "Mydriasis" under Iris).

MYELITIS—Inflammation of the Spinal Cord—(See "Inflammation" under Spine).

MYOCARDITIS — Inflammation of the Heart—(See Heart).

MYOCLONUS — Myoclonia— (See "Myoclonia" under Arms; "Paramyoclonus" under Muscles; "Clonic", "Myoclonia", under Spasmodic).

MYOPIA — Nearsightedness — (See Accommodation; "Myopia" under Sight).

MYOSTITIS — (See "Inflammation" under Muscles).

MYSTERIOUS — Strange— Extraordinary—Peculiar—Vague—Obscure, etc.

Mysterious Death—Mysterious and Sudden Death—Caused by ♆ or ♅; ♆ the afflicting planet; ♆ afflicted in the 8th H.; ♅ afflicted in the 8th H., or afflicting the hyleg, tends to a strange and mysterious death, and in an uncommon, sudden, and extraordinary manner; the evil aspects of ♆ or ♅ to the hyleg at B., and by dir. (See "Mysterious Death" under Children; Curious, Extraordinary, Remarkable; "Death" under Strange, Sudden; Trance, Untimely, etc.). Case of Mysterious Death—See "Mysterious Death", No. 362, in 1001 N.N.

Mysterious Diseases—Obscure Diseases — Vague — Having a Psychic Rather Than a Physical Origin—♆ diseases. (See Extraordinary; "Imaginary Diseases" under Imagination; Obscure; "Diseases" under Peculiar; Praeincipients, Pseudo, Psychic).

Mysterious Sayings—(See Demoniac).

Mystery—Fond of Mystery, Mysterious Doctrines and Studies, and of The Mysteries—(See Metaphysics, Mystical, Neptune, Occult, Philosophy, Perception, Psychic, Science, Truth; "Influence Of" under Uranus).

MYSTICAL — Inclined to Mystical Studies and Practices — Having the Power of Spiritual Sight and Illumination—Intuitive—People who are mystical usually have the Pineal Gland more fully developed than the ordinary person. This Gland is ruled by ♆, the planet of Spiritual Sight, and mystical people are born under the strong influence of ♆, and have ♆ in ♓, the Asc., M.C., 9th H., or ♆ ☌ ☿. Mystical people are in greater danger of obsessions by evil spirits, and Spirit Controls. Uranus is the planet of Occultism, rather than Mysticism, but ♅ conjoined with ♆ aids in giving mystical power, and a desire for Illumination and greater spiritual power and sight. Also ♄, when powerful in the nativity, or conjoined with ☿, renders one mystical, and a confederate in secrecy. (See Hypnotism, Magic, Metaphysics, Neptune, Ninth House, Occult, Philosophy, Psychic, Religion, Science, Spiritual, Truth, etc.).

MYXOEDEMA — Cretinism—Caused by afflictions to ☿, the ruler of the Thyroid Gland; Subs at AT, AX, LCP, SP. This is a disease with mucus-like dropsy, and also is often accompanied by spade-like hands, and with Idiocy, Goiter, and an undeveloped body. (See Cretinism, Dwarf, Goiter, Idiocy, Undeveloped).

N

NADIR — This is the point below the Earth, directly opposite to the Midheaven, or Zenith, and is the beginning of the cusp of the 4th H., and planets occupying the Nadir at B. are considered very strong in their influences to cause disease, and especially when malefics are so situated. The Nadir in a map of the Northern Hemisphere becomes the Midheaven if the native removes to the Southern Hemisphere. Therefore, if a group of malefic planets occupy the Nadir and the 4th H. at B., the native should remain in the Northern Hemisphere where they have less power to cause disease or misfortune, for if he removes to the Southern Hemisphere, he brings these planets to the Midheaven, and makes them powerful for disease, misfortune, or loss of vitality, according to their nature and aspects at B., etc. For this reason, people crossing the Equator, changing Hemispheres, tend to greatly change their fate in life, have misfortune, illness, early death, or good fortune, according to the conditions of their natal map. People born with ♃ ♂ ♀ on the Nadir would thus tend to have better fortune by crossing the Equator, and living in the Southern Hemisphere. If the malefics were all elevated at B., and near the Midheaven, they also would tend to benefit in health if they removed to the Southern Hemisphere, for they would then be on the Nadir of their map, and the polarity changed. Thus, in disease, and the cure of disease, and to change one's fate in life, the map of birth should be carefully studied along this line, and a proper location chosen according to the rules for location and residence. (See Abroad, Foreign Lands, Fourth House, Location, Misfortune, Nations, Native Land; "Place of Birth" under Place; Polarity, Residence, Travel, etc.).

NAEVUS—Nevus—Birthmarks—A Congenital Cutaneous Blemish—Birthmarks are supposed to correspond with the planetary positions at the time of birth.

Face—Naevus On—(See "Naevus" under Face. For further influences along this line see Blemishes, Congenital, Defects, Disfigurements, Freckles, Imperfections, Marks, Moles, Prenatal Epoch, Scars, etc.

NAILS—Nails of the Fingers and Toes—The Nails are connected with the ♍ sign, and are supplied by the Virgo Salt, Potassium Sulphate. Different kinds and shapes of Nails are given by the various Temperaments. In diagnosis, and as an index of disease, health, and the state of the constitution, the Nails make an interesting study. Thus pink nails indicate a good circulation, and a white background under the nails, an anaemic state, low vitality, etc. When there are many planets in one sign at B. the nails change shape as the native gets older. People born under ♀ tend to have beautiful nails, to harmonize with the comeliness, grace and shapeliness of the rest of the body. Born under ♂ tends to make the nails strong, durable, and with resisting and fighting power when they are used in self-defense. When born under ♄, the nails are dryer, more brittle, lacking in vitality, circulation, etc., and break more easily, and are also more ugly and ill-shaped, and partake of the qualities of ♄. The nails of a ☿ person are usually thin, long, may have ridges and crack easily, and such characteristics are a strong sign of intellectuality, and of a studious and philosophical temperament. And so on with each of the planets. Judge the nature of the nails according to the characteristics of the ruling planet, and the predominating signs and planets at B. Note the following paragraphs about the Nails—

Blue Discolorations—The Half-Moons Dark—The sign of heart trouble, bad circulation, and caused by afflictions in the heart sign ♌, and especially ♄ in ♌. Also caused by ♌ on the Asc., and afflicted. (See Cyanosis; "Nails" under Heart).

Brittle Nails—Dry Nails—Caused by ♄, and also by ☿ when he partakes of the nature of ♄.

Broad Nails—Given by ♌, and ♌ on the Asc.; many planets in fixed signs, and fixed signs on the Asc. and angles. Also, ♌ on the Asc. gives large, broad nails.

Dark Discolorations — (See "Blue" in this section).

Discolorations — (See "Blue" in this section).

Distorted Fingers and Nails — (See "Distorted" under Fingers).

Eats Nails — Eats Glass, Nails, Iron, etc.—(See "Human Ostrich", No. 986, in 1001 N.N.).

Falling Out—Of the Nails—Whitlows —(See "Nails" under Toes).

Felon—Inflammation About the Nails —(See "Felon" under Fingers).

Fingers—(See the various paragraphs under Fingers). The description of the fingers, as clubbed, long, short, slender, etc., will also apply to the Nails.

Half Moons—Discolored—(See "Blue" in this section).

Horny Growths — Instead of Nails — (See "Horny" under Fingers).

Inflammation—About the Nails—(See "Felon" in this section).

Ingrowing Nails — Turned Down On the Sides—♌ influence, and afflictions in ♌.

Large and Long—Large and Broad—♌ influence. Such nails usually indicate afflictions in ♌ or the 5th H., and heart trouble.

Long Nails—Long, Slender and Well-Shaped—The Psychic Type of Nails—

Many planets in the common and watery signs at B.; □ on the Asc. (See "Long" under Hands; Psychic).

Neck Of—Slender—□ on the Asc.

Pallor Of—Pale or White Background —Lack of Circulation In—♄ influence; ♄ affl. in signs which rule the fingers and toes. (See Emaciation, Invalids, Pale, Sickly; "Weak Body" under Weak).

Phlegmonous Suppuration—Whitlows —(See "Nails" under Toes).

Psychic Type Nails—(See "Long" in this section).

Ridged Lengthwise— ☿ influence; born under ☿; □ or ♌ on the Asc., and often indicates weak lungs or heart trouble.

Rounded Nails—Well-Shaped—Beautiful— ♀ influence, and born under ♀; the ♀ signs ♉ or ♎ on the Asc.

Shape—The nails change shape with age when there are many planets in one sign at B.

Sides Turned Up—Or Down—♌ influence, and is indicative of heart trouble; afflictions in ♌, or ♌ on Asc.

Slender—(See "Long", "Neck", in this section).

Small Nails—With Slender Neck—□ on the Asc.

Suppuration—About the Nails—Whitlows — (See "Felons" under Fingers; "Nails" under Toes).

Toes—(See "Nails" under Toes).

Turned Up or Down On Sides—♌ influence. (See Ingrowing, Sides Turned Up, in this section).

Well-Shaped—(See "Rounded" in this section).

White— Pallor of — (See "Pallor" in this section).

Whitlows—(See "Suppuration" in this section).

Yellowish — Indicative of Jaundice — ♌ influence; ♌ on the Asc.; ♃ influence; ♃ afflicted at B., and especially by ♂. (See Jaundice).

NAKEDNESS—Wandering In Nakedness—(See "Outrageous" under Insanity).

NARCOTICS—Narcotic Drugs—Hypnotic Drugs—The Drug Habit—Drug Taking—Desire for Drugs and Opiates —Drug Addicts—The Cocaine, Heroin, Morphine and Opium Habits.—Sleep-Producing Drugs — Soporifics —Stimulant Drugs, etc.—Neptune in general rules Narcotics, Opium, Soporifics, Sleep-Producing, Hypnotic, and Stimulant Drugs of this class. Narcotics are also partly ruled by ♄. (See Xanthalin). These drugs affect the Pineal Gland, which Gland is ruled by Ψ, and the use of such drugs as Morphine, Cocaine, Heroin, Opiates, Alcohol, and other Narcotics, cause a supernormal rate of vibration of the Pineal Gland, causing, in many cases, Delirium Tremens and Demoniacal affections. (See "Delirium Tremens" under Delirium; Demoniac, Pineal).

Addicted to Narcotics—Has the Drug Habit—Addicted to the Use of Cocaine, Morphine, Heroin, or An Opiate In

Some Form — The Inordinate Use of Drugs and Opiates — Ψ influence, and Ψ weak and afflicted at B.; people born under the strong influence of Ψ are predisposed to; Ψ afflicted in ♈, brain disorders from the inordinate use of narcotics; Ψ afflicted in ♌, suspension of the heart action thru drugs, opiates, and narcotics; Ψ affl. in ♍, bowel disorders due to drugs and opiates; Ψ to the ☌, ⚹, or △ ♅ arouses the Pineal Gland, and to cause cravings and soul hunger which is often satisfied by narcotics with the weaker souls; Ψ ☌, P., □, or 8 the ☉ or Asc., all ailments arising from injudicious use of drugs and narcotics; Ψ ☌, □, or 8 ☽; Ψ in a weak sign at B., and especially in ♍ and afflicted; Ψ □ or 8 ♄, ill-health by use of narcotics; Ψ afflicted in ♎, ♍, or ♓; Ψ afflicted in the 6th H., and espec. when in ♍ in this house; Ψ affl. in the 8th H.; progressed planets in ☌ Ψ tend to form the habit; Ψ in ♓ in the 12th H., and afflicted; Ψ afflicting the hyleg; the ☽ afflicted in ♓, the sign of Ψ; the ☽ or ☿ afflicted by Ψ; the Prog. ☽ to the ☌, P., □, or 8 Ψ, and espec. if Ψ is weak and afflicted at B., and in a watery sign; ♓ on the Asc. at B.; lord of the 6th or 12th H. in ♓; Subs at AT, AX, SP, KP. Cases of Narcotic Addiction— See "Marriage", No. 256; "Spendthrift", No. 262; "Opium Eater", No. 286; "Opium", No. 288, in 1001 N.N. Also in the book, "Astro-Diagnosis", by the Heindels, see Figures 18H, and 20B. (See the various paragraphs in this section).

Alcohol and Opium Habit — Ψ in a watery sign, and especially in ♓ in the 6th or 12th H., and afflicted, tends to both inclination for Drink and Narcotics; ♓ on the Asc. Cases—See Nos. 262 and 288 in 1001 N.N. (See Neptune, Pisces).

Bowels Affected By—Ψ affl. in ♍, and espec. in 6th H. (See "Opiates" under Bowels).

Brain Affected—By Alcohol or Opiates —(See "Drugs", "Softening", under Brain; "Delirium Tremens" under Delirium).

Cigarettes—And Narcotics—Given to Use of—Case—See Fig. 18H in "Astro-Diagnosis." Also see Case, "Self-Indulgence", No. 229, in 1001 N.N. (See Tobacco).

Cocainism—(See "Addicted To" in this section).

Craving for Narcotics — (See "Addicted To" in this section).

Death from Drug Habit—Ψ setting in 8 to the Luminaries indicates danger of death by taking Drugs, Opiates, Poisons; Ψ afflicted in the 8th H. (See "Death by Poison" under Poison).

Delirium Tremens—From Alcoholism and Narcotics — (See Delirium; Introduction to this Article).

Demoniacal Affections—From Use of Narcotics — (See Demoniac; Introduction to this Article).

Diseases from Drug Taking — Ψ afflicted in ♍ or ♎; Ψ affl. in the 6th H. (See Addicted, Bowels, Brain, Heart, in this section).

Drink — (See the various paragraphs under Drink, Drunkenness, Intoxication).

Drug Habit—Drug Taking—Influences Causing — Toxic Psychoses — Principally Ψ influence and affliction; Ψ afflicting the hyleg. Also caused by ♓, the sign of Ψ. (See "Addicted To" in this section).

Heart—Drug Heart—Ψ affl. in ♌. (See "Drug Heart" under Heart; Tobacco).

Heroin—Use of—(See "Addicted To" in this section).

Hypnotic Drugs — (See "Hypnotic Drugs" under Hypnotic; "Soporifics", and the various paragraphs in this section).

Ill Habits of Body—Thru the Use of Narcotics—Ψ diseases.

Injudicious Use Of — All Ailments Arising From—Ψ ☌, □, ☍, or P. the ☉. (See "Addicted To" in this section).

Inordinate Use of Opiates—(See "Addicted To" in this section).

Morphine Habit—Morphomania—A Ψ disease and affliction; ♃ in ☍, □, or ☍ ☉, and especially if given first to alleviate pain and suffering; Subs at AT, AX. Cases—Death from An Overdose of Morphine—See "Marriage", No. 256, in 1001 N.N. Also see Fig. 20B in "Astro-Diagnosis". (See "Addicted To" in this section).

Narcotic Drugs — Ruled by Ψ and ♄, and ♄ configurated with Ψ tends to make their daily use more deadly, debilitating, and with greater danger of death.

Narcotic Troubles — And Diseases Arising from Their Inordinate Use—Ψ diseases; Ψ afflicted by ♄ at B., and by dir. (See "Addicted To", and the various paragraphs in this section).

Obsessions from Narcotics—Ψ □ or ☍ ♄ at B., bad for the health thru obsessions, and by taking narcotic drugs, medicines, and poisons. (See Medicines, Obsessions, Poisons).

Opium Habit—Addicted to Opiates— Ψ diseases; Ψ in ♌ tends to heart trouble from taking opiates; Ψ setting, and in ☍ the ☉ and ☽, tends to death by opiates; Ψ afflicted in ♎ tends to diseases arising from taking opiates, diseases such as weaken, debilitate, and emaciate the constitution, and which usually end in death unless the opiate is discontinued. Cases — See "Opium Eater", No. 286; "Spendthrift", No. 288, in 1001 N.N. (See "Addicted To" in this section; Opium).

Pain and Suffering — Morphine and Opiates should not be used to relieve pain and suffering when ♃ is in ☍, □ or ☍ ☉, and especially if also afflicted by Ψ, as such subjects tend to become addicts to morphine, or some form of opiate. (See "Morphine Habit" in this section).

Pineal Gland — Stimulated by Narcotics—(See Pineal; the Introduction to this Article).

Poisoning by Drugs—And Narcotics— Ψ, when afflicting, induces to the habit of taking drugs, opiates, hypnotic drugs, narcotics, and is also symptomatic of poisoning by drugs. (See Medicines, Poisons; "Obsessions" in this section).

Predisposed to Use Of—Ψ afflicted at B.; Ψ afflicted in the 6th H. (See "Addicted To" in this section).

Sedatives—Given to Opium Sedatives and Sleep-Producing Drugs — Ψ afflicted at B.; Ψ □ or ☍ ♅; Ψ ☌ or ill-asp. ☿. (See "Addicted To" in this section; Drugs, Soporifics, under Sleep).

Sleeping Potions — Suffers Injury By —(See "Drug Heart" under Heart; Drugs, Sleeping Potions, Soporifics, under Sleep).

Smoking Habit — (See "Tobacco" in this section; "Drug Heart" under Heart).

Snuff — Pulverized Tobacco Snuffed Into the Nose—A habit fostered by Ψ influence. (See "Tobacco" in this section).

Soporifics—Narcotics—Sleep-Producing Drugs—Anaesthetics—Ruled by Ψ, and Ψ influence and afflictions tend to their use. (See Anaesthetics, Sedatives, Soothing; "Soporifics" in this section and under Sleep).

Stimulants — All narcotic stimulants are under the rule of Ψ. Cocaine, Morphine, Heroin, etc., have a stimulating and exhilarating effect for a time, then depression sets in, and weakness, calling for more. (See "Addicted To" in this section).

Suffering and Pain—Alleviation of by Narcotics—(See "Pain" in this section).

Therapeutics—Narcotics, Soporifics, Habit-Producing Drugs, Opiates, etc., are a Therapeutic Property of Ψ. (See "Therapeutic" under Neptune).

Tobacco Habit—Snuff Habit—Under the rule of Ψ, and Ψ influence and afflictions tend to make great smokers, and especially when Ψ is in the 6th H. (See "Cigarettes" in this section; Tobacco). See Debauched, Dissipated; "His Own Worst Enemy" under Enemies; Indulgent, Prodigal, Sensuous, Self-Indulgent).

NARES—The Nostrils—(See Nose).

NARROW—Narrowing—

Narrow Breast—(See "Narrow" under Chest).

Narrow Chest—Hollow Chest — (See "Narrow" under Chest).

Narrow Chin—(See "Narrow" under Chin).

Narrow Escapes — From Injury or Death—(See "Death" under Escapes).

Narrow Face—(See Decanates; "Narrow" under Face).

Narrow-Minded — Shallow Mind— Little Depth of Mind—(See "Shallow" under Mental).

Narrow Sides—(See Sides).

Narrow Sympathies — Not Humane — The Mind Narrow In Its Sympathies— ♄ influence in general. Also caused by the afflictions of ♂. (See Apathy, Cruel, Indifferent; "Shows No Pity" under Pity; Selfish, Treacherous, Vicious, Violent, etc.).

Narrowing of Parts—(See Constrictions, Contractions, Stenosis, Strictures).

NASAL — Nasal Bones — Nasal Duct — Nasal Fossae—Nares—Nostrils—Naso-Pharynx—Nasal Catarrh—Nasal Disorders, etc.—(See Nose).

NASTY—Foul—Disagreeable, etc.—(See Conduct, Corrupt, Dirty, Disagreeable, Discharges, Filthy, Foul, Habits, Immoral (see Morals); Indecent, Knavish, Lewd, Obscene, Odors, Offensive, Rotten, Temper, Unclean, etc.).

NATAL—Natal Place—The Birth Place — Native Land — (See "Moment of Birth" under Birth; Location, Native, Nativity; "Place of Birth" under Place; Residence, etc.).

NATES—(See Buttocks).

NATIONS—Countries—Peoples—Races —Rulership of the Various Nations— A list of the Rulership of Countries and Nations can be found in Lilly's Grammar of Astrology. A list will also be given here, as far as I have been able to gather up to this time. The ♍ sign is said to rule North America, and the benefic planets in ♍ at B. would make America more fortunate for residence. If a person born in England, ruled by ♈, should have ♃ and ♀ in ♍ at B., he would be apt to have more good fortune in North America than in England, and especially if he had malefics in ♈ at B. However, before removing from one's Native Land, the conditions over the 4th and 9th Houses should be noted, and to know whether the map is fortunate, or unfortunate, for Foreign Residence or Travel. For these rules see Fourth House, Location, Native Land, Ninth House; "Place of Birth" under Place; Residence, Removals, Travel, etc. The following paragraphs give the rulership of the Signs of the Zodiac over the various Nations, and in choosing residence Abroad, see what signs you have ♃ and ♀ in at B., and choose a Country ruled by such signs, if you leave your Native Land. Also it is well to travel and locate in the direction of the benefic planets in your map, provided there are no malefics with them at B., and in the same direction.

ARIES RULES—Great Britain, England, Wales, Germany, Denmark, Galatia, Lithuania, Spain, Portugal; Part of France; Lesser and Lower Poland; Morocco, Eastern Parts; Syria and Judea, and especially Lebanan and Damascus; Palestine, Iceland and adjoining Islands; Northern Soudan, New Zealand; a Small Part of Australia; Part of the Australasian Archipelago; Peru. The Cities and Towns of Lebanon, Damascus, Brunswick, Capua, Cracow, Florence, Leicester, Marseilles, Naples, Padua, Saragossa, Utrecht.

TAURUS RULES — Ireland, Persia, Italy, Great Poland, Asia Minor, The Archipelago, South Russia, Holland, Cypress, Samos, Greenland, Labrador, Newfoundland, Tasmania, New Guinea; the Main Body of Australia; the Atlantic Ocean Base—the Site of the Ancient Atlantis, and a number of small Islands, and a corner of South America; Aderbijan, Caucasus, Georgia, Media, Mozendaran, White Russia. The Cities and Towns of Dublin, Leipsic, St. Louis, Franconia, Mantua, Palermo, Parma.

GEMINI RULES—North America as a whole; Eastern Canada; the United States east of the Mississippi River in particular; Belgium; West of England, Lower Egypt, Lombardy, Sardinia, West Indies, Colombia, Venezuela; Central America north to the Peninsula of Yucatan; the Southern Half of the Dutch West Indies; a Small Portion of Australia; Northern Ecuador and Islands Adjacent; Indian Ocean. The Cities and Towns of London, Versailles, Louvaine, Melbourne, New York City, San Francisco, Mentz, Nuremburg.

CANCER RULES—Holland, Scotland, Zealand, China, Africa, Armenia, Central Canada; the United States west of the Mississippi River and to the Eastern Part of California; Southern California, Lower California, the Greater Part of Mexico; Indian Ocean and Small Islands; Africa (North and West); Anatolia (near Constantinople); some Writers say Germany. The Cities and Towns of Constantinople, Algiers, Amsterdam, Venice, Genoa, Milan, Bern, Cadiz, Lubeck, Manchester (29th and 30th degrees); St. Andrews, Tunis, York. Some say New York City.

LEO RULES—France, Italy, Bohemia; Northern Part of Roumania; Sicily, Chaldea, Australia, the Alps, Madagascar, Zanzibar, East Africa; Part of Rhodesia; Western Canada; Washington and Oregon States; the Extreme Western Part of the United States; the Northern Half of California; Eastern and Central Alaska; a Large Area of the Pacific Ocean and Numerous Islands; Coast of Tyre and Sidon; Puglia, Cappadocia. Cities and Towns of Prague, Bath, Damascus, Bristol, Philadelphia, Rome, Taunton, Bolton-le-Moors; Ravenna, Chicago.

VIRGO RULES—Turkey in Europe and Asia; Switzerland, Mesopotamia, West Indies, Babylonia; Extreme Southern Siberia; Greece, Assyria, Thessaly, Uraguay, Western Alaska, Hawaiian Islands, Aleutian Islands, Pacific Ocean Basin, Rhodesia, The Congo, Babylon, Candia, Corinth, Croatia; the Country Between the Euphrates and Tiber; Lavadia, Morea, Lower Silesia, Brazil, Crete, New England States, State of Virginia. Cities and Towns of Jerusalem, Paris, Basil, Bagdad, Heidelberg, Cheltenham, Lyons, Navarre, Padua, Reading, Boston, East Side of Los Angeles; Corinth, Norwich, Strasburg, Brindisi.

LIBRA RULES — China, Japan, and Parts of India near them; Austria, Upper Egypt, Livonia, Tibet, Argentine, Siberia, South Pacific Islands, Savoy, Pacific Ocean (the South Pacific); Islands of the South Pacific. Cities and Towns of Lisbon, Vienna, Antwerp, Frankfort On Main; Charlestown, Fribourg, Speyer, Plasencia.

SCORPIO RULES—Barbary, Morocco, Norway, Bavaria, Transvaal, Brazil; Part of East Indies; Siberia, Korea, Manchuria, Philippines, Japan, China, Halifax, Algeria, Catalona, Judea, Uruguay, Paraguay, Eastern Bolivia, Eastern Argentine and Small Islands. Cities and Towns of Frankfort On Oder; Ghent, Algiers, Fez, Liverpool, Messina; Washington, D.C.; Baltimore, Cincinnati, New Orleans.

SAGITTARIUS RULES—Arabia, Spain, Hungary, Tuscany, Dalmatia, Moravia, Siberia, Mongolia, Siam, Burma, Tibet, Borneo, Northern Sumatra; China, Indo-China, Bolivia, Argentine, Chile, South Eastern Peru, Eastern Ecuador, Western Brazil, Southern Colombia, Cape Finisterre; France between Masien and La Garon; Italy (especially Tarante); Provence, Slavonia. Cities and Towns of Singapore, Cologne, Avignon, Toronto, Toledo, Buda, Narbonne, Naples, Sheffield (in Toledo).

CAPRICORN RULES—India, Thrace, West Saxony; Siberia, China, Tibet, Persia, Bulgaria, Afghanistan, Mexico, Orkney Islands, New Zealand; Small Islands in the Antarctic Region; the South Pacific Ocean Region; Bosnia, Circars, Hesse, Illyria, Morea, Khorassan, Lithuania, Macedonia, Mecklenburg, Punjab, Thrace, Styria, Saxony. Cities—Brandenburg, Brussels.

AQUARIUS RULES—Arabia, Russia, Prussia, Tartary, Poland, Siberia, Asiatic Turkey; Sweden, Lithuania, Muscovy, Abyssinia, the Holy Land, Syria, Persia, Cyprus, the Red Sea, the Black and Caspian Seas, Westphalia; Part of the Polynesian Islands; the South Pacific Ocean; Circassia; Lower Sweden, Piedmont. Cities and Towns of Hamburg, Bremen, Trent, Salsburg, Ingoldstadt.

PISCES RULES—Russia, Portugal, Galicia In Spain, Calabria, Scandinavia; Europe as a Whole; Algeria; a Small Part of England; Tripoli, Normandy, Cilicia, Egypt, Nubia, Tunis, the Mediterranean Basin, Polynesia, Samoa, Islands of the Antarctic Ocean, Southern Asia, North Africa, Desert of Sahara; Small Islands of the Mediterranean; Judea. Cities and Towns — Alexandria, Ratisbon, Seville, Worms, Tiverton, Cilicia, Compostella.

NATIVE—Natal—Native Country—Native Land, etc.—

Native Country—The Native Land— The Country of Birth—Hereditary tendencies, and also the nature of the individual environment, are indicated by the sign which rules the Country of Birth. If it is a positive sign, an electro-positive environment is indicated. If a negative sign, an electronegative environment, etc. In long and chronic diseases the Native Land is often a curative agency in disease if the environment is suited to the constitution. The male is positive by nature, and the female negative. A male, or positive person, being born with the ☉ in ♓, a negative ♃ sign having a potentiality contrary to his own, would be out of place in a Country ruled by the ♓ sign, but such conditions would benefit a female. Thus ♃, ruler of ♓, may thus be evil for a male, but good for a female. Health conditions will tend to be better when a male having the ☉ in a positive sign at B. lives and locates in a Country

ruled by a positive sign, as ♈, ♊, ♌, etc., which location gives a potentiality similar to his own, etc. A female with the ☉ in a negative sign at B. would tend to thrive better in a Country ruled by a negative sign, as one ruled by ♉, ♋, ♍, etc. By following these illustrations up, and applying them to all the Signs, and choosing a Country for residence accordingly, the magnetic conditions over each individual may be better balanced. (See Location, Nations, Polarity, Residence; "Native Land" in this section).

Dangers and Perils—Many Dangers and Perils to the Native—(See "Many Dangers" under Danger; "Narrow" under Escapes; Perils).

Native Land—Should Remain In— Should Not Remain In—

(a) Should Remain In—The ☉, ☽, ♃, or ♀ well-aspected in the 3rd or 4th H.; Planets well-aspected in the 4th H., or Benefics in the 4th in good aspect to the ☉ or ☽; the ☉, ☽, ♃, or ♀ in the Asc., and well-aspected, will tend to give the native success and good health either at Home or Abroad.

(b) Should Remove from Native Land —Malefics in the sign ruling his Native Land; ♃ or ♀ in the 9th H., or rulers of the 9th, and with no malefics in the 9th, and also with the 4th H. badly afflicted by malefics. (See Abroad, Foreign Lands, Location, Nadir; "Place of Birth" under Place; Residence; "Fortunate In Travel", and the various paragraphs under Travel).

Native Place—(See "Place of Birth" under Place).

NATIVITY—Chart of Birth—Figure of the Heavens for the Moment of Birth —The Horoscope of Birth—The Time When the Child Draws the First Breath—The Nativity, or Horoscope of Birth, shows the tendencies and temperament of the native, the environment and external conditions he will encounter, and how he will manifest during the present Incarnation if he drifts with the influences shown. In every nativity there are the good and evil influences. The good should be allowed to manifest, and the evils overcome and transmuted. In every map of birth lies the secret of God's Will over the native, his place and work in life, the niche he is to fill if he finds out what it is. The Nativity shows what line of work to follow for success, advancement, and usefulness; shows the possible health conditions, the parts of the body weakest, most sensitive and ill-fated, and the prospects along health lines; the map shows the financial indications, the relation of the native to neighbors, relatives, children, friends, the Public, etc., for good or ill; shows the marriage conditions, the sign and birthday of the type of person to marry; the prospects of a happy or unhappy marriage; shows who will be the friends, and his possible enemies, and the signs they are born under. In fact, the Nativity deals with every possible condition that will be apt to confront the native, and the nature of the Personality, and the Lower Mind, and what he will have to contend with along moral lines. Man is born with Free Will to use this map as he will, and as he sows, so will he reap. Libraries have been written along this line, and the nature of the Chart of Birth, what it shows and indicates, and every student will have to make a deep and thorough study of the Elements of Astrology in order to understand life, himself, and destiny, and to obey the Axiom, "Man Know Thyself." More is said along this line under the following subjects. (See "Planetary Baptism" under Baptism; "Moment of Birth" under Birth; Character, Destiny, Environment, External, Fate, Heredity, Horoscope; "Map of Birth" under Map, Radix, etc.). Almost every subject in this book has to do with the Map of Birth, the Nativity, and your relation to it Mentally, Physically, and Spiritually. Look in the alphabetical arrangement for the subject you have in mind.

NATURAL—The ☽ rules the Natural and Expulsive Energies over the body, and also the Natural Functions, and especially the natural functions in the female. The ☽ is the source of the natural powers of the body, as the natural powers of each organ, or part, are maintained by the regular and proper functions of such part. (See Energy, Expulsion, Females, Functions; "Influence of the Moon" under Moon).

Natural Abilities—Innate—Inborn—Hereditary, etc.—

(a) Great Natural Abilities—(See the various paragraphs under Ability, Active, Ambition, Energetic, Excellent, Genius, Gifted, Good, Great, Inventive, Learning, Mathematical, Mechanical, Metaphysics; "Good" under Mind; Music, Orator, Philosophy, Prodigies, Qualities, Reading, Scholar, Speech, Study, Talents, Vocation, etc.).

(b) Poor Natural Abilities — Not Highly Gifted—(See Ambition, Chaotic, Concentration, Defects, Dreamy, Dull, Examinations, Idle, Imbecile, Impairments, Inability, Inactive, Incapable, Indifferent, Lack Of, Lazy, Learning, Limitations; "Shallow" under Mentality; "Light In Mind", "Quality", under Mind; Vacillating, Vagabond, Void Of, Wanderer, etc.).

Natural Death—Ordinary Death—Death from Natural Causes—Death In the Ordinary Course of Nature, and Not by Accident, Violence, or by Extraordinary Means—When a natural death is judged to ensue, the 6th and 8th H. are taken into consideration, and the signs in which the malefics are placed. Note the hyleg, the 8th H., and the nature of any planets in the 8th, and also the ruler of the 8th. A benefic planet well-aspected in the 8th H., as ♃ or ♀ in the 8th, or ruler of the 8th, and with no malefic influences in the 8th H., indicate a natural and easy death, and to die in comfort, and in order, and usually at home; ♃ or ♀ in the 8th H., and not afflicted by malefics; ♃ or ♀ in the 4th H., and not afflicted, and with no malefics in the 8th; ♃, ♀, ☿, or the ☽, in the 8th H., well-aspected, and the Asc. hyleg also

favorably aspected; ♄ in the 8th H., well-aspected, or in ♑ or ♎ in the 8th; in Hor'y Q. a natural death is indicated when ♃ or ♀ are lords of the 8th, or in the 8th, or aspecting the cusp of the 8th H. by a ⚹ or △, and the death will be by such diseases as shown by the sign they are in, and the part of the body they govern; the lords of death possessing their own natural and peculiar properties, and the malefics ♅, ♄, or ♂ elevated above them, tend to death in the ordinary course of Nature; lord of the 8th in the 8th; lord of the 1st in good aspect to, or stronger than lord of the 8th, or planets in the 8th, or if the benefics be lord of the 8th, or in the 8th, or if there be translation by good aspect. (See "Easy Death" under Death; "Death" under Home).

Natural Defects—In Body or Mind—(See the various references and subjects under Blemishes, Body, Congenital, Defects, Mind).

Natural Faculties—Are ruled by the ☽. (See Faculties).

Natural Forces—In the Body—The Natural Powers—The ☽ is the source of the Natural Forces and Powers of the body. The ☉ and ♂ also tend to endow the bodily forces with life and greater activity. The ☽ afflicted in ♍ tends to lower the natural powers of the body, the vitality and tone, and especially the functions in females. Saturn tends to weaken, subdue, destroy, and to cause death and decay of the natural forces by his afflictions. (See Active, Diminished, Energies, Forces, Functions, Hindrances, Increased, Powers, Retarding, Suppressions, etc.).

Natural Functions—In the Female—Under the rule of the ☽. (See "Functions" under Females; Functions, Menses).

Natural Habits—(See "Natural" under Habits).

Natural Powers — (See "Natural Forces" in this section).

Natural Temperament — The Bodily Temperament—The Physical Temperament—This Temperament is ruled by the Asc., the sign rising, and especially by the Decanate of the rising sign. (Note the various paragraphs under Temperament which refer to the body, such as Cold, Cold and Moist, Hot, Hot and Dry, etc. Also see Decanates).

Unnatural—Contrary to Nature—(See Abnormal, Unnatural).

NATURE—

Active Nature — (See Active, Ambition, Angles, Brisk, Cardinal, Energy, Force, Movement, Motion, Positive, Powers, Quick, Rapid, Walk, etc.).

Curing—Nature-Curing—Nature Cure —♓ is the sign of, and this sign strong at B., and well-occupied, tends to give the magnetic forces which enable one to effect cures along Natural lines. Uranus strong at B. also tends to make Natural Healers, Magnetic Healers, Chiropractors, Naturopaths, Masseurs, Drugless Healers, Faith Healers, Spiritual Healers, Christian Science

Healers, etc. (See "Nature Cure", and the various paragraphs under Healers).

Death—Nature, Kind and Quality of the Death—The Terminus Vitae—Species of the Death—The nature and quality of the death are ruled over by the 8th H., the house of death, and indicated by the 8th H. and the nature of the planets in this house, or ruler of the 8th. The kind of death depends chiefly upon the nature of the planets which by direction tend to cause death, and also to forecast the nature of the final illness, the signs in which such planets were located at B. must be considered, and to know the part of the body liable to be attacked. The nature of the death is to be judged principally by the Directions in operation at the time. If ♄ is the afflictor, death will most likely be from some ♄ disease, as from Cold, Cough, Consumption, Rheumatism, etc., or by a blow or fall if violence is indicated. Saturn when afflicting the hyleg at B., or by dir., or holding the dominion of death, causes death by ♄ diseases, and so with each of the planets when they hold the dominion of death in the natal map, and afflict the hyleg at B., and by dir. Even the Benefics cause death when so situated. When the planet is known which afflicts the hyleg, see the diseases ruled by that planet for the one which may cause death, and the disease under that planet most likely indicated by the map of birth. The nature and kind of the death is also chiefly denoted by the planet which most afflicts the ☉ or ☽, and the sign and house in which placed, and also by the 6th H. conditions. (See "Death" in the Disease Section under each of the planets, where the kind and nature of death are noted under each planet. Also see Anareta; "Quality" under Death; "Death" under Kind, Quality, Species; "Kind of Death" under Old Age).

Disease—Nature of the Disease—Quality and Type of the Disease—The nature and state of the planet from which the ☽ is separating at decumb. shows the cause and nature of the disease, and the state of the sick. (See Sick). The nature and cause of the disease, or sickness, illness, fever, etc., are shown and indicated by the signs on the 6th H. and the Asc., and also by the position of the Significators. Also note the sign in which the majority of the planets are posited at B., and especially the signs which contain the malefics. Shown by the planets which afflict the ☉, ☽, or Asc. The nature of the disease is said to be known from the signs containing the lords of the 1st and 6th H., and the ☽, and whether they are fiery, airy, earthy, or watery signs, as each of these classes produce diseases of a different nature. (See "Signs" under Air, Earth, Fire, Water). In Hor'y Q., to judge of the nature of the disease, take the sign containing the ☽ for the nature and place of the disease. If not the ☽ take the sign on the cusp of the 6th H., and next to it the signs containing the Dispositors of the ☉ and ☽, and there can be little doubt

of the nature of the disease if all, or nearly all, of these agree. If they disagree it is an indication that the Querent has no particular anxiety in the matter. Cardinal Signs show Mental Derangement, Weak Stomach, Kidney and Liver Complaints, Fevers, Indigestion, Vertigo. The Fixed Signs indicate Heart Trouble, Diseases of Throat, of the Urinary Organs, Bronchitis, Stone, Gravel. The Common Signs show Poor Blood, Dropsy, Spitting of Blood, Consumption, Sciatica, Bowel Disorders. (See Ascendant, Cardinal; "Fixed Signs" under Fixed; "Mutable Signs" under Mutable; Parts, Rising Sign; "Quality" under Sickness; Sixth House, Species, Type).

Disposition—Mind—Temperament—Nature of—(See Conduct, Disposition, Evil, Good, Habits, Manners, Mentality; "Quality of the Mind" under Mind; Personality, Temper, Temperament).

Events—Nature of—(See Directions, Events).

Freaks of Nature—(See Freaks).

Healing Powers of Nature—(See Vis Conservatrix).

Magnetic Nature—(See Magnetism).

Nature Cure—(See "Curing" in this section).

Nature's Laws—(See Laws).

Naturopathy—(See this subject under Healers).

Operations—The Four Operations of Nature—These are based upon the four great Elements, Water, Air, Fire, and Earth, and are known respectively as Congelation, Volatilization, Combustion, and Condensation. These four fundamental and essential operations of Nature are synthetized by Hydrogen, Nitrogen, Oxygen, and Carbon. Hydrogen and Congelation are related to the Watery Signs of the Zodiac, ♋, ♏, ♓. Volatilization and Nitrogen are related to the Airy Signs, ♊, ♎, ♒. Oxygen and Combustion are related to the Fiery Signs ♈, ♌, ♐. Condensation and Carbon are related to the Earthy Signs ♉, ♍, ♑, and the fundamental operations in Nature result from the combinations of the elements in various degrees. Heat, Light, Electricity, and Magnetism are the forces which animate the elements of Water, Air, Fire, and Earth, and bring them into correlation with the Universe. (See Air, Earth, Fire, Water, and "Signs" under these subjects; also see Carbon, Combustion, Condensation, Congelation, Electricity, Ether, Heat, Hydrogen, Light, Magnetism, Nitrogen, Oxygen, Rhythm, Volatilization, etc.).

Planets—Nature of—(See each of the planets in the alphabetical arrangement, as Mars, Mercury, Moon, Saturn, etc. Also see Benefics, Malefics, Planets).

Requirements—Nature's Requirements, such as the Care of the Mind, Body, Health, etc.—♄ in ♏ tends to a laxness in attending to Nature's wants, and also ☿ afflicted in ♏, and forgetfulness and carelessness of Nature's requirements should be guarded against when these influences are in the star map of birth. (See Carelessness).

Weak Nature—The 6th Face of ♌ on the Asc. (See Apathy, Environment, External, Indifferent, Lassitude; "Shallow" under Mentality; "Weak Mind" under Mind; Mutable, Negative, Receptive, Suggestion, Susceptibility; "Weak" under Will, etc.).

NATUROPATHY—(See this subject under Healers; Medical Astrology; "Nature Cure" under Nature).

NAUSEA—Sickness At the Stomach—A Desire to Vomit—Caused by ♄ and the ♌ influences, rulers of the peripheral nerves, and tending to morbid manifestations; a ♋ and ♌ disease; the ☽ afflicted in ♋ or ♌; the ☽ in ♋ or ♌ and afflicted by ♂; the ☽ in ♌, and afflicted by the ☉ or ♂ when taken ill, nausea abounds; ♅, ♄, ♂, or ♀ afflicted in ♋ or ♌; ♀ afflicted in ♋ in the 6th H. Physic tends to nauseate if given when the ☽ is in ♈, ♉, or ♌, the Ruminant Signs. (See Antiperistalsis, Emetics, Incoordination, Peripheral, Physic, Ruminant; "Irritations" under Stomach; Vomiting, etc.).

Bilious Nausea—♂ in ♋, or in ♑ or ill-asp. the ☽. (See "Biliousness" under Bile).

NAVAMSA—This is a term used in Hindu Astrology, and is much discussed and mentioned in the British Journal of Astrology, and some mention of it will be given here. (See Hindu). The Navamsa is a division of each Sign of the Zodiac into nine parts of 3.20° each, and each part having a sub-influence of the 12 Signs in strict rotation. Thus ♈ from 0° to 3.20° is the ♈ Navamsa; from 3.20° to 6.40° is the ♉ Navamsa, etc., and so on around thru the Signs. By following this out you can erect and complete your own Table of Navamsas. Navamsa is a Sanscrit term, and means nine-fold division. This is a Hindu division of the Signs, and is not spoken of in European Astrology, but should be studied by Western students, as these sub-influences have been able to account for many diseases and conditions not found or explained in our Western Textbooks. The parts of an organ afflicted are shown by the Navamsa. Thus ♈ rules the head as a whole, but the subdivisions, as Eyes, Nose, Lips, Forehead, etc., would be indicated by the Navamsa. In the heart, the valves, pericardium, endocardium, auricles and ventricles, etc., would be shown by the Navamsa subdivisions of the ♌ sign, to show the rulership of the various parts. Consumption is an affliction of the common signs, and the common sign subdivisions of such signs. Thus the 28° of ♑ and ♐ govern Consumption, as they are in the ♑ and ♐ Navamsa of these signs. (See Consumption, Convulsions, Decanates).

NAVEL—Umbilicus—Under the external rulership of the ♍ sign. Also ruled by ♀ and the 7th H.

Diseases—Of the Umbilicus—♀ diseases, and caused by afflictions to ♀.

Umbilical Hernia—♄ or ♂ afflicted in ♍, and especially in the 6th H.; Subs at Spl.P.

NAVIGATION—Dangers In—**Injury or** Death In—Sickness In—

Dangers In—Danger In Travel by Water—Troubles by Sea—An eclipse of the ☉ or ☽ in ♓; malefics in the 9th H. in weak signs and afflicted; Comets appearing in ♓. (See "Dangers" under Seas, Ships, Voyages).

Much Loss of Life—Among Seamen and Maritime People—(See Maritime).

NEAR—Nearly—

Near Relatives—(See "Near" under Relations).

Near-Sighted—(See "Myopia" under Sight).

Near Some Danger—Near Some Misfortune—(See "Near Some Danger" under Danger).

Nearly Blind—(See this subject under Blindness).

NEAT—Orderly—Cleanly—Tidy—

Neat Appearance—Neat In Dress—Tidy—Fond of Dress—♂ Sig. in ♌ or ♎; ♀ in the Asc., and dignified at B.; ☿ ✶ or △ ♀; ☿ Sig. in ♓ tends to make the native a Dandy, foppish, and fond of frivolous ornaments. (See Cleanliness, Dress, Extravagance, Luxuries).

Neat Body—♍ gives a neat and well-formed body; ♍ on the Asc., neat, compact, and well-formed; the ☽ in ♍; ♀ in the Asc. and dignified; ♀ ori., neatly composed, and not too tall or corpulent; ♂ Sig. in ♎. (See Beautiful, Compact, Handsome, Well-Formed, Well-Proportioned).

Neat and Cleanly—(See Cleanliness, Dress).

NEBULOID MOTION—Under the rule of ♇. (See "Amoeboid" under Cells).

NEBULOUS STARS—Nebulae—Nebulous Clusters—Nebular Areas—Nebular Spots—The principal Nebulous Stars mentioned in the Textbooks of Astrology are the Pleiades, Antares, the Ascelli, Hyades, Castor, Pollux, Praesepe, Cloudy Spot of Cancer, Mane of Leo, Sting of Scorpio, Arrow Head of Sagittarius. These Nebulous influences, and their places and degrees, signs, etc., as they appear thru the Zodiac, are given in the front Glossary of Simmonite's Arcana of Astral Philosophy, and also you can find them listed in the various Textbooks and Dictionaries of Astrology. They are listed in this book. Look for them in the alphabetical arrangement. The Nebulous Stars, when directed to the ☉, ☽, or Asc., or rising with the ☉ or ☽ in the Asc. or 10th H., tend to Banishment, Blindness, Cataracts, Decapitation, Disgrace, Dreadful Diseases; Bad Eyes, and Hurts to Eyes; Evils, and every Evil that can befall Humanity; Hurts to Face, Violent Fevers (see Fever); Glaucoma, Imprisonment (see Prison); Miseries, Murders, Quarrels, Rape, Ruin, Sickness, Stabs, Violent Death (see Violent); Wounds, Wretchedness, etc. (See these subjects). These Clusters impair the physical sight by interfering with the etheric vibrations sensed by the retina of the eye, and greatly afflict the sight, and especially when these Nebulous Areas are in ♂ or bad aspect the

⊙ or ☽ at B., or in angles with the Luminaries. The ☽ in an angle, afflicted, and with Nebulous Stars, tends to a defect in the Sight. The ⊙ or ☽ in a Nebulous place at B., and afflicted by a malefic, tend to eye trouble. Also if the malefic be in one of these places, and afflict the ⊙ or ☽, there is danger to the eyes. The influence of ♆ is said to be with these Areas. The Nebulous Areas are mostly of the nature of ♂ and the ☽ combined. (See Blindness, Eyes, Optic, Retina, Sight; "Fixed Stars" under Stars).

NECK—The Part of the Body Between the Head and Trunk—The Cervical Region—The Neck is under the external rulership of the ♉ sign. Is also ruled by ♀. The Bones of the Neck are under the structural rulership of ♉. Also the Neck, and the hinder part towards the shoulders, are represented by the 2nd H. The Nerves and Blood Vessels of the Neck are under the internal rulership of ♉.

DESCRIPTIONS OF THE NECK—

Adam's Apple—(See "Long" in this section).

Bull Neck—Short and Thick—♉ on the Asc.

Fat Neck—Fat and Thick—(See "Thick", and the various paragraphs in this section).

Fleshy Neck—Fleshy and Full About the Neck—Thick Neck—The ⊙ in ♉; ♉ or ♏ on the Asc. (See "Thick" in this section).

Full Neck—♉ on the Asc.

Hollow Neck—(See "Long and Thin" in this section).

Long Neck — Long and Thin — Long and Scraggy—Hollow—Long and Small —♈ gives a long, scraggy neck, and with ♈ on the Asc.; ♑ gives a long and small neck, a hollow, ill-shaped, ungainly, or disfigured neck, and especially with ♑ on the Asc. at B. Also ♈ or ♑ on the Asc. at B. usually give a prominent Adam's Apple.

Marks or Moles On—Scars On—Malefics in ♉ or the 2nd H., or very low in the Asc. at B.; ♂ affl. in ♉ in the Asc. tends to hurts, and a scar on the neck from a wound. (See Marks, Moles, Scars).

Moles—(See "Marks" in this section).

Scars On — (See "Accidents To", "Marks", in this Article).

Scraggy and Long — (See "Long" in this section).

Short Neck—♃ in the Asc.; ♉ or ♏ on the Asc.; ♉ on the Asc., short and thick. (See "Thick" in this section).

Small and Long — Scraggy — (See "Long" in this section).

Thick Neck—Fat Neck—Muscular Neck—Strong Neck—Full Neck—♉ or ♏ give, and espec. when on the Asc. at B.; ♂ well-aspected in ♉, and with this sign on the Asc., tends to a strong and muscular neck; ♃ affl. in ♉ may cause more fat than real muscular strength unless ♂ enters favorably into the configuration.

Thin Neck—Long and Scraggy—(See "Long" in this section).

DISORDERS OF THE NECK—Afflictions to the Neck—See the following subjects in the alphabetical arrangement when not more fully considered here—

Abscess Of—A ♉ disease, and afflictions in ♉; afflictions in or about the 16° ♉ or ♏; ♀ in ♉ in the 6th H., afflicted, or afflicting the ☽ or Asc.; ♃ afflicted in ♉. These same influences also tend to abscesses of the throat. Case of Abscess — See "Imperfectly Formed", No. 303, in 1001 N.N. (See Abscesses; "Abscesses" under Throat).

Accidents To — Hurts, Injuries, or Wounds To—♄ or ♂ affl. in ♉ at B.; the ♄ influence tends to blows, bruises, broken neck, etc., while the ♂ influence tends to cuts, stabs, incised wounds, flow of blood, or suicide by razor cuts to the throat.

Affected—The Neck tends to be affected when the ⊙ is in ♏; ♄ in ♒ or ♓; ♃ in ♉ or ♑. (See Table 196 in Simmonite's Arcana. Also see "Affected" under Head).

Back Part of Neck—Lower Back Part — Disorders In — Afflictions and malefics in the 2nd H. at B., and especially when in ♉ in this house; afflictions in the latter degrees of ♉; Subs at AX.

Barber's Itch—Of the Face and Neck —(See Barbers).

Boils — Carbuncles On — (See "Neck" under Boils).

Bronchocele—(See Goiter).

Burns — To Face and Neck — (See "Face" under Burns).

Carbuncles—(See Carbuncles; "Neck" under Boils).

Cervical Region—Disorders of—(See Cervical).

Chronic Distempers—About the Neck —♄ in ♉ when he is the afflictor in the disease.

Contractions In — Muscles of Contracted — Spasmodic Contractions — ♅ afflicted in ♉. (See "Wry Neck" in this section; Contortions, Contractions, Coordination, Incoordination; "Contractions" under Throat).

Cramps In—♅ affl. in ♉; Subs at MCP (3C). (See "Contractions" in this section; Cramps).

Diseases of the Neck—The Neck Disordered—Neck Complaints—The ⊙ and ☽ acting thru the Paryngeal Plexus, and the Superior Cervical Ganglion, tend to affect the neck, Eustachian Tubes, the Throat and their dependencies, and give way to the Renal Diathesis (see "Cervical Ganglion" under Ganglion); caused by afflictions in ♉ or ♏; the ⊙ in ♏—♄ in ♒ or ♓—♃ in ♈, ♉, or ♑, and ♀ in ♓, indicate and signify troubles about the neck when these planets are taken as Significators in Hor'y Questions (see Table "A" in Lilly's Astrology); ♃ affl. in ♐; a ♀ disease. (See the various paragraphs in this section).

Dislocations—Caused by ♄ afflicted in ♉, and death by hanging, and especially when the nativity shows violence, or a violent death. (See Dislocations, Hanging).

Distempers—(See "Chronic" in this section).

Enlarged Veins—(See "Veins" in this section).

Fever In—(See Glands, Inflammation, in this section).

Glands—Glandular Swellings—Glandular Fever—(See Goiter; "Mumps" under Parotid; "Glandular Swellings" under Throat; "Swellings" in this section).

Goiter—(See Goiter).

Guillotined; Hanging; Hurts To—(See "Accidents" in this section).

Inflammation In—♂ afflicted in ♉, and also to feverish conditions in neck; the ☽ in ♉ and afflicted by the ☉ or ♂ when taken ill, tends to inflammation in the neck, or hinder part thereof (Hor'y); ♂ affl. in ♉. (See "Swellings" in this section).

Injuries To—(See "Accidents" in this section).

Larynx—Disorders of—(See Larynx).

Left Side of Neck—Burns To—Case—(See "Face" under Burns).

Marks, Moles Scars—(See "Marks" in the first Division of this Article).

Men Suffer with Neck—♂ in ♐ and ♑ at the Vernal Equinox, and lord of the year.

Moles—(See "Marks" in the first part of this Article).

Muscles Of—Cramps and Contractions In—Stiffness of—Pains In—(See Contractions, Cramps, Inflammation, Pains, Rheumatism, Stiff, in this section).

Nervous Disorders Of—♅ or ☿ afflicted in ♉; ♅ ☌ ☿ in ♉, and afflicted by the □ and ♉ aspects of other planets.

Obscure Diseases In—♆ affl. in ♉. (See Obscure).

Obstructions In—♄ affl. in ♉. (See "Obstructions" under Throat).

Pains In—Pains In Neck and Throat —♂ affl. in ♉, extreme pain in the neck when taken ill, and ♂ the afflictor in the disease. (See Inflammation, Rheumatism, Stiff, in this section).

Parotid Gland—Inflammation of— Mumps—(See "Mumps" under Parotid).

Rheumatism — Muscular Rheumatism In—♂ affl. in ♉.

Scars On—(See "Marks" in the first part of this Article).

Scrofula—King's Evil—♉ denotes, and afflictions in ♉; a ♉ disease when in the neck. (See Scrofula).

Stiff Neck—Rigidity—♄ causes stiff neck from cold, and from the deposit of minerals and wastes in the muscles of the neck, and espec. when ♄ is afflicted in ♉ or ♍. Mars causes stiff neck from inflammation of the tissues, or by Mumps, and espec. when afflicted in ♉. (See Inflammation, Parotid, Rheumatism, in this section).

Subluxations—Of the Cervical Vertebrae—(See Subluxations; "Cervical Vertebrae" under Vertebrae).

Swellings In—The ☉ or ♂ affl. in ♉; the ☉ or ☽ in ♉, and afflicted by ♄ or ♂; the ☉ afflicted in ♍ when the ☉ is the afflictor in the disease; ♄ affl. in ♉, from deposits, wastes, or subdued functions; ♂ affl. in ♉, from inflammations of an acute nature; ♀ affl. in ♉, and generally from moist humours in the head when ♀ is the afflictor in the disease (see "Moist Humours" under Head); ☿ affl. in ♉; a ♉ disease and with ♉ on the Asc. Glandular swellings in the neck are signified by the 2nd H., and by afflictions in ♉. (See Glands; "Swellings" under Throat).

Throat—(See the various paragraphs under Throat).

Thyroid Gland—Disorders of—(See Thyroid).

Torticollis—(See "Wry Neck" in this section).

Tumors In—In Neck or Throat—The ☽ affl. in ♉, or afflicting the hyleg therefrom; ♄ affl. in ♉, from deposits of minerals and wastes of the body; ♃ or ♀ afflicted in ♉; ♂ ☌ ♃ in ♉. (See Tumors).

Various Disorders—Of the Neck—The ☽ hyleg in ♉, and afflicted, in a female nativity; the ☉, ☽, and malefics afflicted in ♉ or ♍.

Veins—Veins, Arteries, and Blood Vessels of the Neck Affected—Enlarged Veins—♃ or ♀ afflicted in ♉, or ☌ ♄ or ♂ in ♉. (See Arteries, Veins).

Voice—Vocal Organs—Disorders of— (See Larynx, Voice).

Wens—In the Neck—(See Wens).

Wounds To—(See "Accidents" in this section).

Wry Neck—Torticollis—Contraction of Muscles of the Neck—♅ affl. in ♉; ♄ ☌ ♅ in ♉. (See Contortions, Contractions, Spasmodic).

For disturbances of the Neck of the Bladder and Womb see "Neck" under Bladder, Womb.

NECROMANCY—Given To—☿ ill-dignified and afflicted at B. (See Magic).

NECROPHILISM—Necrophilia—The Desire To Have Sexual Congress with a Dead Body—♄ afflicted in ♏; ♄ ☌ ♆ in ♏; ♄ affl. in ♏ in the 8th H., the house of death. (See "Sex Perversions" under Perversions).

NECROSIS—The Death of a Circumscribed Piece of Tissue—♄ influence; ♄ in ♈ or ♉ tends to Necrosis of the bony sockets of the teeth; ♄ in any sign tends to necrosis, death, decay, or gangrene of the part. (See Decay, Gangrene, Pyorrhoea).

NEGATIVE—Negative Nature — Negative Signs—Negative Planets—

Negative Horas—(See Horas).

Negative Houses—The 2nd, 4th, 6th, 8th, 10th and 12th H. (See "Negative Houses" under Houses. Also see each of these Houses in the alphabetical arrangement, as Second House, Fourth House, Sixth House, etc.).

Negative Nature—The □ and ♉ aspects to the ☽ tend to make one negative and indifferent; the ☽ □ or ♉ ♆; the Prog. ☽ to the ☌, P., or ill-asp. ♆ if ♆ is afflicted at B., tends to negativeness and lassitude; the ☽ or ♀ strong and predominant at B., the native tends to be negative, more easily influenced, and more susceptible to disease, have less will power, live more in the feelings and emotions; give up more easily in the face of obstacles, disease and difficulties, and also be more easily hypnotized; Ψ and ♄, negative planets, tend to negative states of mind thru Psychic and Spiritual causes, Melancholy, Depression, Dejection, etc.; the majority of planets at B. in earthy and watery signs, the negative signs. (See Apathy; "Gives Up Easily" under Disease; Dull; "Fond Of" under Ease; Environment, External; "Hypnotic Subject" under Hypnotism; Improvident, Inactive, Indifferent, Influenced, Instability, Lassitude, Lethargy, Listless; "Low Spirits" under Low; Melancholy; "Shallow" under Mentality; "Light" under Mind; "Mutable Nature" under Mutable; Obsessions, Plastic, Psychic, Receptive; "Low" under Resistance; Spirit Controls, Susceptible, Vacillating; "Weak" under Will, etc.).

Negative Planets — The Magnetic Planets—Ψ, ♄, ♀, and the ☽, and they render the mind more negative, timid, receptive, susceptible to environment and outside influence, and the mind and body liable to a variety of diseases. They also tend to acidity in the body. (See Acid, Environment, External, Hyperacidity, Magnetic, Receptive. See these planets in the alphabetical arrangement, and note their special influences, and the diseases they foster. See the paragraphs in this Article).

Negative Psychism—(See Psychic).

Negative Signs—Of the Zodiac—Nocturnal Signs—Unfortunate Signs—Receptive Signs—Feminine Signs—♉, ♋, ♍, ♏, ♑, ♓, the earthy and watery signs. The fiery and airy signs are positive. The negative signs predominant at B., and well-occupied by planets, tend to make the native negative, weaker-willed, timid, receptive, somewhat lacking in daring, courage and individuality, and to be more easily influenced and persuaded, or dominated by others; to worry and brood over the troubles of life; to be more anxious and morbid along health lines, and to give up more easily to obstacles and difficulties. These signs on the Asc. at B. tend to give a weaker constitution and less vitality, except ♏, and the ♋ and ♓ signs on the Asc. at B. are considered the weakest of all the Signs when on the Asc., and to give low vitality and resistance, unless counteracted by many other favorable and powerful influences in the radix. Scorpio on the Asc. is considered the best of the negative signs for greater vitality and stamina. Taurus is next to ♏ in giving strength when on the Asc. at B. The negative signs are acid, and the positive signs alkaline. (See Acid, Alkaline, Deceitful, Dishonest; "Signs" under Feminine; Horas, Introspection; "Negative" under Magnetic; "Negative Nature" in this section. Also see each of the Negative Signs in the alphabetical arrangement, and note their influences, characteristics, diseases, qualities, and what they rule).

Polarity—Negative Polarity—(See Polarity).

NEGLECT—Neglectful—Privation—

Native is Neglectful—Is Negligent—Indifferent to Duty—Given to Laxity—Nothing Careful of the Things of This Life—(See Carelessness, Conduct, Debauched, Disgrace, Dissipated, Drink, Drunkenness; "Free Living" under Free; Habits, Idle, Imprisonment (see Prison); Improvident, Inactive; Indifferent; "Fear of Work" under Labor; Lassitude, Laxity, Lazy, Poverty, Procrastination; "Hard to Arouse" under Rouse; Vagabond, etc.).

Privation and Neglect—Diseases Arising From—♄ diseases; the ☉ or ☽ afflicted by ♄. (See "Internal Diseases" under Chill; Famine, Poverty, Privation, Starvation).

NEGRO—

Negro Lips—(See "Thick Lips" under Lips).

Negro Race—(See "Black Skin" under Black; Dark, Races).

NEIGHBORS—Are ruled by the 3rd H. Malefics in this house at B. tend to bad relations with, and possibly injury or hurt by neighbors. Benefics in this house, well-aspected, and with no malefic influence over the 3rd H., tend to benefits by neighbors. (See Brothers, Journeys, Sisters, Third House).

NEOPLASM—A New Growth or Tumor —(See "New Growths" under Growths; Tumors, Warts, Wens, Xanthoma).

NEPHEWS—(See Nieces).

NEPHRITIS—Inflammation of the Kidney—(See Kidneys).

NEPHROLITHIASIS — (See "Kidneys" under Stone).

NEPHROPTOSIS—Prolapse of the Kidney—(See Kidneys).

NEPTUNE—This planet was discovered in 1846. Some Writers say this planet does not belong to our Solar System, but is an outside planet exerting more of a psychic and spiritual influence over Humanity, and tending to Involuntary Clairvoyance, Mediumship, Psychic Diseases, Weird States of Mind, etc. The older Textbooks of Astrology, as Lilly's Astrology, do not mention this planet. Some Writers say that Ψ is the higher octave of ♀. Max Heindel says it is the higher octave of ♀, and exerts an inspirational influence over the mind, and corresponds to the higher vibrations of ♀ rather than those of ♀. Also Ψ is considered the higher octave of ♀ because he acts so strongly upon the Nervous System. (See the book, "Cosmo-Conception", by Max Heindel). At this writing not much is found about this planet in the Textbooks of Astrology, but the Magazines are well-filled with Articles on his nature and influence. Max Heindel, in his book, "The Message of the Stars", has given considerable information about Ψ, and information given by the Rosicrucians, and The Elder Brothers of Humanity. In this Article, the information and influences of Ψ have been collected and arranged, both from Books and Magazine Articles. Neptune is especially affiliated with the 12th sign ♓, the sign which rules the Ocean, and the Seas, and also with the 12th House. Neptune is considered strongest in his influence when in ♓. He is said to have his exaltation in the ♋ sign. From observation the influence of ♆ is said to be similar to that of ♄, and is Astringent and Contracting. (See Astringent, Contractions, Ocean, Pisces, Sea, Twelfth House, Waters). This Article has been arranged into three Sections as follows: Section One—General Considerations. Section Two—Neptune Rules. Section Three—Diseases and Afflictions of Neptune. See the following subjects in the alphabetical arrangement when they are merely listed in any of the three divisions of this Article—

— SECTION ONE —

GENERAL CONSIDERATIONS—Also see the Considerations in the Introduction to this Article.

Abstract—♆ in the abstract is semi-spiritual, occult, supra-material, ensnaring, and illaqueative.

Action Of—The action of ♆ is aesthetic, magnetic, negative, moist, warm, fruitful, mysterious, inconstant, seductive, ensnaring, treacherous, etc. (See the various paragraphs in this Article).

Acts Upon—Acts upon the Nervous System, and also upon the Moral and Spiritual Nature, and the Psychic Powers. Acts strongly upon the Pineal Gland, which Gland it rules, which is the Spiritual and Intuitive center in the brain, and also greatly influences the Emotions, and especially in Religious matters. See Emotions, Intuition, Morals, Nerves, Pineal, Psychic, Religion, Spiritual).

Afflictions Of—Evil Aspects of—♆ afflicts by his ☌, P., □ and ☍ aspects. This planet is seductive by his evil aspects, and tends to greatly deprave the moral nature, and also lead to the Drug and Narcotic Habit. His afflictions tend to a chaotic mind, false fears, weird states of mind, obsessions, spirit controls, and Astral disturbances, etc. For the influence of his good aspects see "Aspects" in this section. (See the Diseases of ♆ in Sec. 3 of this Article).

Anareta—♆ may become the Anareta when powerful at B., and afflicting the hyleg, and he usually disposes to death in a riotous manner, by assassination, violence, etc., when Anareta. (See Anareta).

Aspects Of—Good Aspects of—The good aspects of ♆, his ⚹, △, etc., to the ☉, ☽, and ☿ tend to greatly enhance the psychic, spiritual and intuitive powers, and to give true and genuine clairvoyance, spiritual sight and foresight, and power to discern Truth. For his Evil Aspects see "Afflictions" in this section).

Chaos—The Planet of Chaos, Doubt and Fear—♆ is the planet of Fear, and Chaos, and Doubt, to ordinary Humanity, as, it is said, the Human Race is not yet very responsive to the higher and better influences of this planet. (See Chaos, Doubt, Fear).

Colors—Lavender. (See Colors).

Discovered—In 1846. See the Article on Neptune, Chap. XVIII, in Pearce's Textbook of Astrology.

Doubt—The Planet of—(See Doubts, Fears).

Drugs—♆ has association with drugs and narcotics, such as Cocaine, Morphine, Heroin, Opiates, and other soporifics and stimulants. (See Narcotics).

Emotions—Influence of ♆ Over—(See Emotions).

Environment—The lower vibrations of ♆ are ensnaring, enticing, and often lead to passional excesses, and an immoral environment. (See Environment, External; "Morbid" under Imagination).

Evil Aspects Of—(See "Afflictions" in this section).

External Influences—The negative and afflicting influences of ♆ tend to unwise entanglements, sex excesses, and to lead the native astray, and into low and bad company. (See Companions, Environment, External, Licentiousness, Morbid, Nymphomania, Sensuality, etc.).

Eyesight and Neptune—(See "Nebulous" in this section).

Fear—♆, the planet of Chaos, Doubt, Fear, Timidity, etc.—(See these subjects).

Herbs Of—(See Herbs).

Hyleg and Neptune—♆ in evil asp. to the hyleg at B., and by dir., helps to destroy life, and to act as Anareta. (See Anareta, Hyleg).

Inclines To—♆ inclines to secrecy and hidden methods of work, deceit, treachery, etc., when afflicted at B., and by dir. (See Deceitful; "Secretive" under Secret; Treachery; "Tends To" in this section).

Indicates—♆ indicates Anaemia, Necrosis, Depletion, and Catalysis. (See Diseases in Sec. 3 of this Article).

Influence Of—The influences of ♆ by his afflictions are not always physical, but tend to be psychic, and to act upon the mind. The good aspects of ♆ to the ☉ tend to benefit the constitution psychically rather than in a physical way. Example of the Influence of ♆. Case—See "Neptune", No. 283 in 1001 N.N. (See the various paragraphs in this Article).

Inimical—The influence of ♆ is said to be inimical to the great majority of the Earth's inhabitants at this time, due to their materialistic tendencies, and lack of spiritual development. Neptune is attributed as the planet which will rule strongly over the new Sixth Sub-Race, and the Sixth Race, the foundations of which Races are now being formed. At this Stage and Era of the Evolution of the Earth, and of Humanity, people tend to respond more to the lower, or evil vibrations of ♆ than to his higher and spiritual ones, and to be greatly disturbed thereby, and especially along moral and sex lines, and to have chaotic, morbid, weird and sensuous states of mind. (See Chaos, Sixth Sub-Race, in this section).

Magnetic—Ψ is a magnetic and negative planet, and tends to render the mind and body negative, timid, and subject to a variety of affections, and susceptible to external influences and environment. In this regard Ψ has an influence similar to ♄. (See Magnetic, Negative, Receptive, Susceptibility).

Mars and Neptune—These planets when in ♂ tend to make one lawless, unrestrained, self-indulgent, and to possibly become an Atheist or Anarchist, and go to extremes in whatever they do, and also to be more subject to obsessions, and the influences of discarnate spirits, and the influences on the Astral Planes. (See Anarchists, Astral; "Atheistical" under Religion; Self-Indulgent, Unrestrained, etc.).

Mental Qualities—Ψ tends to make the native psychic, romantic, intuitive, spiritual, imaginative, and inspirational, according to his aspects. (See Aspects, Qualities, and the various paragraphs in this section).

Metals and Minerals—Ψ is said to rule Potassium, and such substances as Ambergris and Meerschaum.

Morals and Neptune—His afflictions and lower vibrations tend to loose morals, and morbid sex desires, and especially when afflicting the ☉, ☽, or ♀ at B. (See Aspects, Inimical, Tends To, and the various paragraphs in this section; "Loose Morals" under Morals).

Most Evil In—Ψ is most evil in his afflictions when in the 6th or 12th H. at B., or afflicted in ♍ or ♓. The 6th H. and ♍ are indicators of disease, while the 12th H. and ♓ tend to bring sorrow, self-undoing and trouble. (See Sixth House, Twelfth House).

Nebulous Areas—And Ψ—The influence of Ψ is largely with the Nebulous Areas, which afflict the Eyes and the Eyesight. (See Blindness, Eyes, Nebulous, Sight).

Negative Planet—(See "Magnetic" in this section).

Neptune Persons—The Ψ person is often unconsciously deceptive, and without malice or predetermination. (See Inclines To, Tends To, and the various paragraphs in this section).

Nervous System—Ψ acts strongly upon the Nervous System, and for this reason is considered the higher octave of ☿. (See Nerves).

Occult Influence Of—Ψ is a Mystical Planet fundamentally, but Occult in the abstract. (See "Abstract" in this section).

Octave Of—(See the Introduction to this Article).

Orbit Of—It takes Ψ approximately 164½ years to make one revolution in his orbit, and he is about 14 years passing thru one Sign of the Zodiac, which tends to prolong his afflictions over the various Signs and Classes of people, as Ψ in any sign tends, more or less, to afflict the people born under that sign unless they are Advanced and highly spiritualized. (See the Diseases in Sec. 3 of this Article).

Pathological Action Of—(See the opening statements in Sec. 3 of this Article).

Period Of—(See "Orbit" in this section).

Persons—(See "Neptune Persons" in this section).

Physical Effects Of—(See "Influence Of" in this section).

Principle Of—Involution.

Qualities Of—As given by the Higher or Lower vibrations and influences of this planet—Abstract, Aesthetic, Analgesic, Astringent, Cataleptic, Changeable, Chaotic, Clairvoyant, Comatic, Confusing, Conserving, Constrictive, Contracting, Debilitating, Deceitful, Defensive, Delusive, Depraving, Destroying, Dissipating, Doubtful, Ecstatic, Effeminate, Elusive, Emotional, Ensnaring, Entrancing, Estranging, Exciting, Fearful, Fomenting, Frenzical, Fruitful, Generative, Habit-Forming, Hallucinating, Hidden, Hyperactive, Hypnotic, Illaqueative, Illusive, Imaginative, Immoral, Inconstant, Indulgent, Inimical, Inspirational, Intuitive, Lapsing, Lascivious, Lawless, Lethargic, Lewd, Licentious, Lustful, Lymphatic, Magnetic, Maniacal, Mediumistic, Misleading, Moist, Morbid, Mysterious, Mystical, Narcotic, Negative, Nervous, Neurotic, Obscuring, Obsessional, Occult (in the Abstract); Passional, Perverting, Poisonous, Producing, Protean, Psychic, Receptive, Relaxing, Religious, Romantic, Sardonic, Seclusive, Secretive, Sedative, Seductive, Self-Indulgent, Semi-Spiritual, Sensuous, Solitary, Somnambulistic, Soothing, Soporific, Speculative, Spiritual, Stimulant, Storing, Strange, Stupefying, Suffocating, Suggestive, Supra-Material, Susceptible, Timorous, Trance-Producing, Transforming, Treacherous, Unrestrained, Warm, Wasting, Weird, etc.

Revolution Of—(See "Orbit" in this section).

Sensitives—Ψ has the most effect on Sensitives. (See "Sensitives" under Sensitive).

Shows—Ψ shows distinct Nebuloid and Amoeboid motion, and is more relaxed, changeable, protean, and elusive than ♀, which planet is said by some Authors to be the lower octave of Ψ. Also Ψ shows Depletion and Wasting diseases. (See "Amoeboid" under Cells; Depletion, Nebuloid, Wasting).

Sicknesses Caused By—(See the Diseases in Sec. 3 of this Article).

Sign Of—♓ is the strong and home sign of Ψ. (See Pisces).

Signifies—(See the various paragraphs in this section).

Sixth Sub-Race—Sixth Race—Ψ will be the strong ruler over them. The Pineal Gland, the center of Ψ in the brain, will be more highly developed in the future Ages to come, and people will have more Spiritual Sight, Intuition, Voluntary Clairvoyance, and the power to see and recognize Truth, Doctrine, and things as they are, and not as they seem to be, and when illusion, superstition, and fear will be done away with. (See "Inimical" in this section; Pineal, Pituitary).

Spiritual Influence Of—Is very great in his higher vibrations, and with those who are sufficiently advanced and developed spiritually to respond to his better influences. (See Inimical, Sixth Sub-Race, in this section; Retina).

Strong—Ψ is strong in ♓, and also in the 12th H.

Temperament — (See "Temperament" under Lymphatic).

Tends To—Inclines To—Predisposes To—The lower vibrations of Ψ tend to moral lapses, perverted and loose sex morals, depravity, and to chaotic and morbid states of mind, obsessions, hallucinations, delusions, psychic diseases and disturbances, religious excitement and extremes, disturbances from 'the Astral Planes, Spirit Controls; peculiar, Mysterious and unusual diseases, weird and uncanny feelings, secrecy and hidden methods of work, etc. (See "Inclines To", and the various paragraphs in this section and Article).

Therapeutic Properties—Analgesic, Anodyne, Hypnotic, Soporific, Suggestive. (See these subjects).

Typical Drugs Of—Chloroform, Ether, Iodine, Narcotics, Opiates, Poppy. (See Anaesthetics, Narcotics).

Vitality Benefitted By—Ψ ⚹ or △ the ☉, in a psychic way rather than physical. (See "Influence Of" in this section).

— SECTION TWO —

NEPTUNE RULES—See the following subjects in the alphabetical arrangement—Ambushes; Amoeboid Motion (see "Amoeboid" under Cells); Anodynes; Appendix Vermiformis (see Appendix); Arms (Glands of when Ψ is in signs which rule the Arms); Assassinations; Astral Influences (see Astral, Spirit Controls); Asylums (see Insanity); Azoth; Blue Color; Brain (the Cerebral Ventricles and Pineal Gland); Canal (Spinal); Cells (Cell Development—Cell Reproduction—Cellular Tissue Building); Cerebral Ventricles; Clairaudience; Clairvoyance; Colors (Indigo and Blue); Conjunctiva; Conservation of the Functions (see Conservation); Cytoplastema; Death (see "Death" in Sec. 3 of this Article); Deceptions; Depressor Nerve (of the Heart); Disguises (see Deceptions) Dishonesty, Enemies, Plots, Treachery); Drowning; Ecstasy (Religious); Exiles; Eyes (The Eyesight—See Nebulous, Sight); Feet (Glands of); Fibers (Nerve Fibers); Fluidic System (Fluids—Spinal Fluids); Frauds (In Business—Deceptions—Defalcations—Thefts—See Dishonesty, Liars, Plots, Thieves, Treachery); Functions (The Conserving, Storing and Transforming Functions—The Telepathic Functions); Fungus Growths (Vegetable); Genito-Urinary System and Organs (Glands of); Glands (Glands of Arms, Hands, Feet—Glands of Genito-Urinary System—Pineal Gland); Growths (Fungus Growths—Vegetable Growths); Hands (Glands of); Heart (Depressor Nerve of); Higher Religious Experiences (see Religion); Hospitals; Humming; Hypnotic Powers; Ideals (Impractical Ideals); Impositions (see "Disguises"

in this section); Indigo Color; Insane Asylums; Intuition (the Higher Intuitions); Kidnappings; Laughter; Lavender Color; Legs (Glands of); Life (the Period from 84 to 99 Years—See Periods); Lymphatic Temperament; Mediumship; Meerschaum; Metals and Minerals (see "Metals" in Sec. 1 of this Article); Methods Given By (see "Inclines To" in Sec. 1 of this Article); Minerals (see "Metals" in Sec. 1 of this Article); Mosses (Fungus Growths); Mushrooms; Mysterious Happenings (see Mysterious); Narcotics; Nebuloid Motion; Nerves (Nervous System—Depressor Nerves of Heart—Nerve Fibers—Optic Nerve—See "Nervous System" in Sec. 1 of this Article); Nutrition; Ocean; Odic Force (see Hypnotism); Odors from Man, Animals and Plants (see Odors); Optic Nerve; Period of Life from 84 to 99 Years; Pineal Gland; Pisces Sign; Plastic Fluid (see Cytoplastema); Poisons; Potassium; Prisons; Psychic States (see Psychic); Radium; Religious Experiences (see Ecstasy, Religion); Reproduction of Cells (see Cells); Respiratory System (Tissues of); Seas; Secret Societies; Secretions of Stomach (see "Secretions" under Stomach); Secrets of Life (see "Secrets" under Secret); Seduction; Soporifics; Spine (Spinal Canal and Azoth In—Spinal Cord—Spinal Fluids—Spinal Gas—Spinal Spirit Fire); Spirit Controls; Spiritual Nature and Spiritual Sight; Sponges; Stomach (Glands and Secretions of); Strange Conditions (see Mysterious, Strange); Sudden, Mysterious, Quick, and Unexpected Deaths; Talking to Oneself (see Speech, Talk); Tears; Telepathic Functions (see Telepathy); Throat (Tissues of); Tissues of the Throat and Respiratory System; Trance; Treachery; Twelfth House; Unusual Conditions in Mind and Body (see Extraordinary, Mysterious, Peculiar, Strange, Unusual); Vegetable and Fungus Growths; Ventricles (Cerebral); Vermiform Appendix (see Appendix); Wanderings (see Roving; "Given To" under Travel; Wandering); Waters (see Ocean, Sea, Water); Whistling.

— SECTION THREE —

DISEASES OF NEPTUNE—The Afflictions of Neptune—Neptune acts principally upon the Mind and Nervous System, the Emotions, the Psychic Powers, the Passions by his lower vibrations, and tends to chaotic and morbid conditions. The strong pathological action of Ψ over the Nervous System is considered a strong argument in favor of Ψ being the higher octave of ☿, as ☿ is the ruler of the Nervous System in general. Neptune has more of a Psychic and Mental effect than physical in causing disease. Also the vitality of the physical body is increased by the good aspects of Ψ thru psychic and mental effects, and by creating greater poise, and intensifying the Spiritual Powers, the Higher Intuitions, and Spiritual Sight. Neptune is closely related to the Nebulous Areas, and tends to affect the Eyes and Eyesight of Man. Neptune tends to strange and mysterious diseases and afflictions, hard to explain without a knowledge of the Occult and Mystical Sciences. Neptune has the most effect in a pathological way upon Sensitives, those very susceptible to Astral influences, and people who are nervous and high strung. The sicknesses caused by ♆ are chiefly of a depressive nature, and of a nervous tendency. The pathogenic and disease-producing influences of this planet are stronger when he is in the 6th or 12th H., or afflicted in the ♍ or ♓ signs, the signs affiliated with these two houses. (See "Most Evil In" in Sec. 1 of this Article). In a general way the pathological action of ♆ tends to Analgesia, Involuntary Clairvoyance and Mediumship, Obsessions, Spirit Controls, Psychic Disturbances; Dissipation of Functional Energy, and Atrophy of Process thru the cessation of functions; also causes laxity, relaxation, and lack of cohesion of parts. His pathological action is suggestive, delusive, ensnaring, hypnotic, analgesic, soporific, sleep-producing, anodyne, and with a feeling of torpor, lassitude, and a dreamy, chaotic, and weird state of mind, and even to demoniacal demonstrations, as in Obsessions and Spirit Controls. The following is a list of the Diseases and Afflictions of ♆, as far as I have been able to gather from my reading, study, observation, and the careful examination of nearly 10,-000 Maps of Birth of people, and their letters setting forth their diseases and complaints, during my career as a Physician Astrologer. See the following subjects in the alphabetical arrangement—

Absent-Minded—(See Chaotic, Dreamy; "Absent-Minded" under Mind; Visionary).

Accidents—♆ produces accidents, such as by Drowning, Water, Suffocation, in Sleep-Walking, and those of a Mysterious, Strange and Unusual Nature. (See these subjects, and also note the various paragraphs in this section).

Ambushes—Attacks By—Death or Injury In—(See Ambushes).

Anaemia; Analgesia; Appendicitis—(See Appendix).

Arms—Wasting of the Tissues of—(See "Arms" under Wasting).

Assassination; Astral Influences—Disorders, Obsessions, or Death From—(See Astral, Obsessions, Spirit Controls).

Asylums—Insanity and Confinement In An Asylum—(See "Asylums" under Insanity).

Atrophy—Of Function—(See "Atrophy" under Functions).

Beside Oneself—(See Excitable, Frenzy, Fury).

Blindness—(See Causes, Day Blindness, under Blindness).

Brain—Disorders of—(See Brain, Cerebral, Pineal).

Brooding; Cancer—(See Carcinoma).

Carcinoma; Carus—(See Carus, Coma).

Catalepsy; Catalysis; Cataphora;

Chaotic Mind—(See Chaotic).

Clairaudience; Clairvoyance;

Claustrophobia; Cocainism—(See Narcotics).

Cohesion—Lack of Cohesion of Parts—(See Cohesion).

Coma; Confusion of Mind—(See "Mental Chaos" under Chaotic).

Conjunctivitis—(See Conjunctiva).

Consumption — (See "Consumptive" under Consumption).

Crying Spells—(See Emotions).

Dark—Fear of—(See Claustrophobia).

Day Blindness—(See Blindness).

Day Dreaming—(See "Dreamy" under Dreams).

Death—♆ causes death by Ambushes, Assassination, Drowning, the Drug and Narcotic Habit, Obsessions, Poison, Riots, Spirit Controls, Trance, Treachery, and by Mysterious, Strange, Sudden, Unexpected, and Unusual Causes and Events. (See these subjects).

Debility—As General Debility, Depletion of the Vital Fluids, Fears, Nervous Complaints, etc. (See these subjects, and also note the various paragraphs in this section).

Deformities; Delirium — Delirium Tremens — The Delirium of Typhus Fever—(See Delirium, Typhus).

Demoniacal Affections — (See Demoniac).

Depletion — Of the Tissues and Vital Forces—(See Depletion).

Depravity; Depression—Mental—(See Depressed).

Destroys Life—By afflicting the hyleg at B., and by dir. (See Anareta).

Dispersions; Dissipation — Of Functional Energy—(See Dispersions).

Dreams—Dreamy—(See Dreams).

Drink Habit — (See Drink, Drunkenness).

Dropsy—(See "Dropsy" under Bowels; "Abdomen" under Dropsy).

Drowning; Drowsiness—Sleepiness—Stupor—(See Sleep).

Drug Habit—Drug Taking—(See Narcotics).

Ecstasy; Emissions—(See Semen).

Emotions—Disturbances of—(See Emotions).

Energy—Dissipation of Functional Energy — (See Dispersions; "Dissipation" under Functions).

Excesses—(See "Passional Excesses" under Passion).

Excitement—Religious—(See "Religious" under Excitement).

Extraordinary Diseases—Or Death—(See Extraordinary, Mysterious, Peculiar, Strange).

Eye Troubles—(See Blindness, Eyes, Nebulous, Sight).

Faculties—Disorders of the Spiritual Faculties — (See Ecstasy; "Religious" under Excitable; Pineal, Religion, Spiritual).

Faintings; Fears—False and Morbid Fears—(See Fears, Obsessions, Spirit Controls).

Feet — Wasting of the Tissues of — (See "Tissues" under Feet).

Fingers—Horny Nails On—(See Fingers).

Fluids—Disorders of—(See Fluids).

Forgetfulness—(See Memory).

Frenzy; Functional Energy—Dissipation of—(See Atrophy, Energy, in this section). •

Fungus Growths—In the Body—(See Fungus).

Glands—(See Swelling, Wasting, under Glands).

Growths — (See Carcinoma, Fungus, Tumors).

Habits — (See Drink, Narcotics, Tobacco).

Hallucinations; Hands — (See "Wasting" under Hands).

Heart — (See Depressor, Drug Heart, Sleeping Potions, Stoppage, under Heart).

Hypnotic Disturbances — (See Hypnotism).

Hypochondria; Hysteria;

Infantile Paralysis—(See "Infantile" under Paralysis).

Influenza; Insanity; Insensibility—(See Analgesia, Carus, Coma, Insensibility).

Intemperance; Intoxication;

Intuitions Impaired—(See Intuition).

Involuntary—(See "Involuntary" under Clairvoyance, Mediumship).

Lapsing of Morals—(See Lapsing).

Legs—(See "Legs" under Wasting).

Lethargy; Limbs — Shrinking, Wasting and Withering of — (See "Arms" under Limbs).

Loose Morals—(See Morals).

Mania—(See All Forms Of, Neurotic, Religious, under Mania).

Mediumship; Mind — Diseases Originating In the Mind—(See Fears, Hallucinations, Imaginations, Insanity, Obsessions; "Diseases" under Psychic; Spirit Controls, etc.).

Moisture — (See "Moist and Warm" under Heat; "Relaxation and Moisture" under Moisture).

Morals—Moral Lapsing—Loose Morals — Moral Perversions — (See Lapsing; "Loose" under Morals; Perversions).

Morbid Manifestations—Of the More Obscure Types — (See "Morbid" under Mind, Obscure; "Unclassified" under Morbid).

Morphine Habit—(See Narcotics).

Myopia—(See Sight).

Mysterious Death — And Diseases — (See Mysterious, Peculiar, Strange).

Nails — Horny Nails — (See "Horny" under Fingers).

Narcotics—Use of—(See Narcotics).

Necrosis; Nervous Diseases—Nervous Depletion—Neuroses—Neurotic Affections—(See Depletion, Nerves).

Nightmare — (See Dreams; "Nightmare" under Sleep).

Noisome Diseases—(See Noisome).

Nyctalopia—(See "Day Blindness" under Blindness).

Obscure Diseases—(See Obscure).

Obsessions; Opium Habit—(See Narcotics).

Pain — Insensibility To — (See Analgesia, Insensibility).

Paralysis—(See "Infantile" under Paralysis).

Passional Desires—Excesses—Perversions — (See "Passional Excesses" under Passion; Perversions).

Peculiar Diseases — Or Death — (See Extraordinary, Mysterious, Obscure, Peculiar, Strange, Unusual).

Phenomena — Referable to Psychic Causes — (See Hallucinations, Obsessions, Psychic, Spirit Controls).

Pockmarks—(See Smallpox).

Poisoning — By Drugs and Opiates — (See Narcotics; "Death" under Poison; "Septic" in this section).

Psychic Powers — Disorders of — Hyperactivity of—(See Psychic).

Pus Diseases—(See Pus, Pyorrhoea).

Puzzling Diseases — (See Mysterious, Obscure, Peculiar, Strange).

Pyorrhoea; Relaxation of Tissues — (See Relaxation).

Religion—Religious Mania—Religious Ecstasy—Religious Excitement—(See Ecstasy, Excitable; "Religious" under Mania; Religion).

Saint Vitus Dance—(See Saint).

Self-Abuse—Solitary Vice—(See "Solitary" under Vice).

Self-Undoing—(See Self-Undoing, Twelfth House; "Most Evil In" in Sec. 1 of this Article).

Seminal Losses—(See Semen).

Sensitiveness—Hypersensitive—Sensitives—(See Sensitive).

Septic Poisonings—(See Septic; "Septic" under Throat).

Sex Abuses — Sex Perversions — Sex Excesses — (See "Loose Morals" under Morals; "Passional Excesses" under Passion; Perversions, Sex).

Shrinking Limbs—(See Shrinking).

Sleep — Disorders of — Drowsiness — Sleepiness — Soporifics — Nightmare — (See Dreams, Narcotics, Sleep).

Sleeping Sickness—(See Sleep).

Smoking — Disorders From — (See "Drug Heart" under Heart; Narcotics, Tobacco).

Snuff Habit—(See Narcotics).

Solitary Vice—(See "Solitary Vice" under Vice).

Sonambulism—(See Sleep).

Soothing Drugs — Use of — (See Narcotics, Sedatives; "Sleeping Potions" under Sleep; Soothing).

Soporific Drugs — Use of — (See Anodynes, Narcotics; "Soporifics" under Sleep).

Spirit Controls—Obsessions and Death By—(See Obsessions, Spirit Controls).

Spiritual Causes — Disease or Death By — (See Astral; "Religious" under Mania; Obsessions, Psychic, Spirit Controls, Spiritual).

Spiritual Faculties—Disorders of—(See "Faculties" in this section).

Strange Affections—Strange Death—(See Mysterious, Peculiar, Strange, Unusual).

Stupor—(See Sleep).

Suffocation — (See Drowning, Gases, Suffocation).

Suspended Heart Action—(See Heart).

Swellings—Glandular—(See Glands).

Talking to Oneself — (See Speech, Talk).

Therapeutic Properties — (See "Therapeutic" in Sec. 1 of this Article).

Throat — Septic Poisonings In — (See "Septic" under Throat).

Tissues—Wasting of—(See "Tissues" under Wasting).

Tobacco Habit — (See "Drug Heart" under Heart; Narcotics, Tobacco).

Trance—And Death By—(See Trance).

Treachery—Death or Injury By—(See "Death" under Poison; Treachery).

Treatment — The treatment of Ψ diseases should be mostly Psychic and Spiritual, and thru the Will Power, and also by proper knowledge of Astral Influences, the Astral Planes, and the Entities thereon; a knowledge of Spirits, Elementals, etc., and how to deal with them, drive out evil Spirits, and to bring relief to those who are under Obsessions and Spirit Controls. The use of Suggestion to patients in the Hypnotic State has proven very valuable in these cases to effect cures, but the Operator must know the nature of the Forces he is dealing with, and how to rid the patient of them. Evil Spirits do not linger long in the presence of a Master who knows and recognizes them, and gives them their orders. (See "Psychic Healers", "Spiritual Healers", under Healers; "Treatment" under Hypnotism).

Tumors; Typhomania — The Delirium of Typhus Fever—(See Typhus).

Unclassified Diseases — (See Extraordinary, Mysterious, Obscure, Peculiar, Strange, Uncommon, Unusual, etc.).

Unexplainable Diseases — (See Mysterious, Obscure, Strange, etc.).

Venereal Diseases—(See Venereal).

Vision—Eyesight—Disorders of—(See Blindness, Nebulous, Sight).

Warm and Moist Diseases — (See "Moist and Warm" under Heat; "Relaxation" under Moisture).

Wasting Diseases—(See Wasting).

Withering of Limbs—(See "Arms" under Limbs).

NERVES—Nervous System—Mercury is said to rule the Nerves in general, as ☿ rules the right Cerebral Hemisphere and the Motor Segment of the Spinal Cord. Neptune, as the higher octave of ☿, also rules over, and strongly influences the Nerves, and acts upon the Nerves thru the Brain Centers, the Mind, the Psychic and Spiritual Powers, the Emotions, and acts especially upon the Pineal Gland, which Gland is ruled by Ψ. Uranus also has a very remarkable influence over the Nervous System, and especially upon the Motor

Nerves, disturbing their action, and tending to Erratic, Spasmodic, and Jerky Movements over the body. The Motor Nerves are ruled by ♅ and ♂. Mercury exerts a nervous influence, and is usually badly afflicted in nervous and mental disorders. The Airy Signs are Nervous Signs, and on the Asc. at B. tend to nervousness. The ☉ is also said to rule strongly over the Nerves and the Brain. The Nerves, acting as sinews, or wires of transmission for nerve force and nerve impulses and messages from the Brain and other centers, are ruled by the ☉. The nerves of the brain are fed by the rays of the ☉. The Common, or Mutable Signs, also strongly influence the Nervous System, and especially ♍ and ♐. The Nerve Sheaths are connected with the ♌ sign, and are also under the rule of the ☽. The Third House also rules and influences the Nerves, and the conditions of the 3rd House, the house of ☿, should be studied in connection with Nervous Complaints. The Nerve Fibers are said to be under the internal rulership of the ♍ sign, the 3rd H. sign. The ♒ sign, the strong sign of ♅, also is a strong ruler over the Nervous System. For convenience of reference this Article is divided into two Sections. Section One — General Considerations. Section Two—Diseases of the Nervous System. See these subjects in the alphabetical arrangement when they are not more fully considered in this Article.

— SECTION ONE —

GENERAL CONSIDERATIONS—

Airy Signs — Are classed as Nervous Signs. (See "Air Signs" under Air).

Augmented — The Nerve and Vital Forces Augmented — ♅ ⚹ or △ the ☉ (See "Augmented" under Vital).

Blue Color — Blue Color is a nerve Palliative, and nervous patients benefit in a Blue Room. (See Blue).

Brain—Disorders of—(See "Nervous Disorders", and the various paragraphs under Brain; Cerebellum, Cerebral, Cerebrum).

Capillary — The Cutaneous Capillary Vaso-Constrictor Nerves—(See "Vaso-Constrictor" under Vaso).

Cells—Nerve Cells—(See Cells).

Centers—Nerve Centers—Are said to be under the internal rulership of the ♈ Sign. (See "Centers" in Sec. 2 of this Article).

Cerebellum; Cerebral Nerves — (See Cerebral).

Cerebro-Spinal Nerves—(See Cerebro-Spinal).

Cerebrum; Cervical Nerves—Cervical Ganglion—(See Cervical, Ganglion).

Color—(See "Blue Color" in this section).

Constrictor Nerves — (See Constrictions; "Vaso-Constrictor" under Vaso).

Control — The Nerves, Nervous System, and the Mind, should be kept under good control when ♅ is in ♒ at B., and afflicted.

Cranial Nerves—(See Cranial).

Depressor Nerves—(See Depressor).

Dilator Action — (See "Vaso-Dilator" under Vaso).

Discharge of Nerve Force — (See Innervation).

Disposition—The Nervous Disposition —(See "Temperament" in this section).

Dorsal Nerves—(See Dorsal).

Energy — Nervous Energy — (See "Nervous" under Energy).

Fibers — The Nerve Fibers are under the internal rulership of the ♂ sign.' Also ruled by ♅ and ♆, and by the Anterior Lobe of the Pituitary Body, which Body is ruled by ♆. (See "Nerve Fibers" under Organs).

Filaments — The Nerve Filaments — (See Filaments).

Fluids — The Nerve Fluids are ruled by ♆. (See "Nerve Fluids" under Depletion; "Fluids" under Vital; "Depletion" in Sec. 2 of this Article).

Force — Nerve Force — (See "Nerve Force" under Force; "Fluid", "Force", under Vital).

Function — Of the Nerves — (See Innervation).

Ganglion—Nerve Centers—(See Centers, Ganglion).

Genito-Urinary System—Nerves of— (See Genito-Urinary).

Heart—Nerves of—(See Heart).

Impulses—The Nerve Impulses—(See Innervation; the Introduction to this Article).

Influx—The Nervous Influx— ☿ adds to or subtracts from. (See Innervation).

Innervation—The Discharge of Nerve Force—(See Innervation).

Kinetic Force—(See Energy, Kinetic, Motion, Motor).

Lumbar Nerves—(See Lumbar).

Medulla Oblongata—(See Medulla).

Motor Nerves—(See Motor).

Nerve Centers—(See "Centers" in this section).

Nerve Fibers—(See Fiber; "Fibers" in this section).

Nerve Filaments—(See Filaments).

Nerve Fluids — (See "Fluids" in this section).

Nerve Force—(See "Life Force" under Force; "Force" in this section).

Nerve Sheaths—(See "Sheaths" in this section).

Nerve Tissue Building—(See "Tissue" in this section).

Nervine—An Agent Calming Nervous Excitement. A Therapeutic Property of ☿. Also the Blue Color is a Nervine, and soothing to nervous patients.

Optic Nerve—(See Optic).

Palliative — Nerve Palliative — Blue Color. (See Blue, Nervine, in this section).

Peripheral Nerves—(See Peripheral).

Plantar Nerves — (See Ligaments, Plantar).

Plexuses—(See Ganglion, Plexuses).

Pneumogastric Nerve — Vagus Nerve —(See Pneumogastric).

Pudic Nerves—(See Genitals, Pudic).

Renal Nerves—(See Kidneys).

Respiratory System—Nerves of—(See the Introduction under Breathing; "Nerves" under Lungs).

Sacral Nerves—(See Sacral).

Salt—The Nerve-Building Salt—Magnesium Phosphate, the Salt ruled by the ♌ sign. (See "Salts" under Zodiac).

Sciatic Nerves—(See Sciatic).

Secretory Nerves—(See Secretions).

Sensory Nerves — (See "Sensory Nerves" under Sensation).

Sheaths—The Nerve Sheaths—Ruled by the ☽. They are also connected with the ♌ sign, and the ♌ Salt, Magnesium Phosphate. Mercury rules the invisible rose-colored vital fluid which flows in the visible nerve sheath. (See "Fluid" under Vital).

Signs — The Nervous Signs of the Zodiac—The Airy Signs. Also ♉, ♍, ♎, ♏, ♑, are generally listed as the Nervous Signs, those which contribute to Nervousness.

Sinews—Nerve Sinews—Ruled by the ☉. (See the Introduction to this Article).

Solar Plexus — (See "Solar" under Plexus).

Speech—Nerves of—(See Speech).

Spinal Nerves—(See Spine).

Sympathetic Nervous System — (See Peripheral, Sympathetic).

Temperament — The Nervous Temperament — Melancholic Temperament —Cold and Dry Bodily Temperament— Ruled by ♆, ♄, ☿, and the Earthy Signs. Also influenced by the Airy Signs, as ♄ rules strongly over ♎ and ♒. This temperament is also said to be an exaggeration of the Bilious Temperament. The Nervous Temperament is one of thinking and feeling, and tends to Neurasthenia, restlessness, and a hurried, alert, and agitated manner. (See "Cold and Dry Body" under Dry; "Disposition" under Melancholy; Restlessness; "Temperament" under Saturn; "Neurasthenia" in Sec. 2 of this Article).

Tissue — Nerve Tissue-Building—The work of ♆ and ☿. (See Tissues).

Treatment — Of Nervous Disorders — Onions are nerve builders. The Blue Color is soothing to nervous and excitable patients. The Herbs of ☿ are Nervine. (See Blue, Nervine, Palliative, in this section; "Mercury Group" under Herbs; Onions).

Upper Dorsal Nerves—(See Dorsal).

Vagus Nerve—(See Pneumogastric).

Vaso-Constrictor Nerves—Vaso-Dilator—Vaso-Motor—(See Vaso).

Vital Fluid — In the Nerves — Vital Force—(See Augmented, Fluids, Force, in this section).

Voluntary Nervous System — (See Voluntary).

Weakest Part — The Nervous System the Weakest Part—The ☉ affl. in ♐.

— SECTION TWO —

DISEASES OF NERVOUS SYSTEM—
See the following subjects in the alphabetical arrangement when not considered here—

Absorption Of—(See Resolution).

Acute Nervous Diseases—♄ diseases. (See the Introduction under Acute).

Affections—Nervous Affections—(See "Disordered", and the various paragraphs in this section).

Ailments—Arising from Nervous Conditions — The ☽ hyleg in ♈, and afflicted, and especially with females. (See "Disordered" in this section).

All Nervous Disorders—Diseases of ♄ and ☿; caused by the afflictions of ♄.

Anaemia; Analgesia; Apprehensive—Nervously Apprehensive—Afflictions to ☿; ☿ afflicted by ♄. (See Suspicious, Worry).

Arms—Nerves of Afflicted—(See "Motor Nerves" under Arms).

Ataxia; Attacked—The Nervous System Chiefly Attacked—The ☽ hyleg in ♐, and afflicted, in females.

Auditory Nerve—Clogging of—(See "Auditory" under Hearing).

Blue Color—A Nerve Palliative—(See "Blue" in Sec. 1 of this Article).

Bowels—(See "Nerves Of" under Bowels).

Brain—Disorders of—(See Brain Fag, Brain Storms, Nervous Disorders, and the various paragraphs under Brain).

Breakdown—Nervous Breakdown—(See "Prostration" in this section).

Burning Sensations—(See "Sensations" under Burning).

Centers—The Nerve Centers—Excitement and Irritation of—(See Erethism, Neuritis, in this section).

Chills—Nervous Chills—Caused by the strong afflictions of ♄ to the hyleg, and accompany Nervous Debility, Neurasthenia, etc. (See Debility, Neurasthenia, in this section).

Collapse—Complete Nervous Collapse—(See Collapse; "Prostration" in this section).

Color—In the Treatment of Nervous Disorders—(See "Blue" in Sec. 1 of this Article).

Complaints—(See "Disordered", and the various paragraphs in this section).

Constipation—(See "Nervous" under Constipation).

Contortions; Control—(See "Control" in Sec. 1 of this Article).

Convulsions—Convulsive Movements—(See Convulsions, Fits, Spasmodic).

Corrosions—Of the Nerves—(See Corrosion, Lesions, Paralysis).

Cramps; Crystallization—Of the Nerves and Muscles of the Eyes—(See "Crystallization" under Eyes).

Death—From Nervous Disorders—♅ afflicted in the 8th H., and afflicting the hyleg by dir.; ☿ denotes; ☿ afflicted at B., and especially by malefics, and ☿ afflicting the hyleg by dir., or taking part in a train of fatal

directions. (See Case of Death under "Strain" in this section).

Debility—Nervous Debility—The ☽ hyleg, and to the ♂, P., □ or ☍ ♆ or ♅ by dir.; the ☽ in ♍ or ♒, and to the ♂ or ill-asp. any of the malefics as Promittors; the ☽ in fire signs, from haste and excitement, and espec. when afflicted in ♐; ♆, ♅, or ♄ in ♉ or ♏, and affl. the ☉ or ☽; ♄ diseases; ♄ affl. in ♐; a ☿ disease; ☿ affl. in ♍; ☿ affl. in the 6th H., from worry, overwork, or overstudy; ☿ afflicted in ♒, general debility of the Nervous System. Debility arising from nervous diseases is denoted by ☿. (See Depletion, Depression, Disordered, Neurasthenia, and the various paragraphs in this section).

Defects—In the Nervous System—Denoted by ☿, and with ☿ afflicted at B.

Depletion—Nervous Depletion—☿ afflicted by ♆; ♅ □ or ☍ the Asc. or ☿, depletion of the nerve and vital fluids. (See Depletion; "Depletion" under Vital; Debility, Depression, Disordered, Fluids, Neurasthenia, in this section).

Depression—Nervous Depression—♅, ♆, or ♄ in ♉ or ♏, and afflicting the ☉ or ☽; ☿ affl. by ♄, depression and brain fag. (See "Brain Fag" under Brain; "Mental" under Depressed; "Debility" in this section).

Derangement—Of the Nervous System—☿ diseases; ☿ ♂ ♂, and in □ or ☍ the ☽ or ♄. (See Debility, Disordered, Neurasthenia, and the various paragraphs in this section).

Diplegia—(See Paralysis).

Discharge—Excessive Discharge of Nerve Force—(See "Excessive" in this section).

Diseased Nervous System—(See "Disordered", and the various paragraphs in this section).

Disordered Nervous System—Deranged Nervous System — Predisposition to Nervous Complaints and Disorders—Liable To—Nervous Susceptibility, etc.—The ☉ affl. in □, ♐, or ♒; the ☉ in □ or ♐, and to the ♂ or ill-asp. ♄ or ♂ by dir.; the ☉ ♂ or ill-asp. ♅; a ☉ disease; the ☉ in any aspect to ♅, or vice versa; the ☉ or ☽ in the 6th H. in cardinal signs, and afflicted; the ☉ and ☿ affl. in ♓; the ☽ in ♒, ♂ or ill-asp. any of the malefics as Promittors; the ☽ to the ♂ or ill-asp. ♄ by dir.; the ☽ hyleg in □ or ♐ in female nativities, and afflicted; the ☽ to the ♂ or ill-asp. ☿ by dir., and ☿ afflicted at B.; the ☽ in ♐ in ♉ ♃ in □; the ☽ hyleg in ♈, and afflicted; ♆ ruler of the horoscope, and afflicted; ♆, ♅, ☿, and the ☽ when afflicted tend to make one nervous and high strung; ♆ afflicting ☿; ♆ in ♒ and afflicted; ♆ in ♒ and afflicting the Asc. or hyleg; ♆ afflicted in ♒ in the 6th H.; ♆ in the 3rd or 9th H., and afflicting the ☽ or ☿; ♆ in a prominent position at B., and afflicted; ♆ afflicting the Asc. at B., and by dir.; ♆ afflicted in ♐; ♅ in any asp. to the ☉ at B., and by dir.; ♅ afflicted in the 6th H.; ♅ afflicting the Asc. at B., and by dir.; ♅ ♄, or ♆ in ♏, and afflicting the ☉ or ☽; ♄ in ♌, ♍, ♎, or ♏, and afflicted; ♄ and ♂ in □; ♄ afflicted in a ☿ sign; born under strong ♄ influence; ♄ ruler of the horoscope, and afflicted; ♄ is one of the rulers of the Nervous Temperament, along with ♅, ☿, and the earthy signs; ♄ and ☿ combined in their influences, and afflicting the hyleg; ♃ afflicted in ♒; ♃ in perihelion when there is a Sun Spot tends to greatly aggravate the nerves of people generally; ♂ ☌, □, or ☍ the ☽ or ☿; ♂ Progressed, ☌ or ill-asp. ♆, or vice versa; ♂ afflicted in ♍; denoted by ☿, and is a ☿ disease; afflictions to ☿ or the ☽ by planets, as ☿ rules the sensory nerves; ☿ in a weak sign at B., and afflicted; ☿ afflicted in the 6th H., and usually from overwork or over-study; ☿ affl. in ♓; ☿ afflicted by ♅; ☿ in ♐, ☌, or ill-asp. any of the malefics as promittors; ☿ afflicted by ♆; ☿ prog., ☌ or ill-asp. ♅, and vice versa; ☿ ruler of the horoscope, and afflicted by malefics; ☿ ill-dignified at B., and afflicted; ☿ ☌ or ill-asp. ♂; ☿ in the 1st H., and afflicted by ♄; □, ♐, ♑, or ♒ on the Asc. at B.; common signs show, and especially afflictions in □, ♐, or ♓; the malefics, or afflicting planets, in the flexed, or common signs; many planets, a Stellium, in the 3rd H. at B.; many planets in earthy signs; airy signs tend to worry and nervous disorders; the combined influence of two planets whose nature is cold and dry tends to nervousness, as that of ♄ and ☿; common signs on the cusp the 6th H. (For other influences along this line see the various paragraphs in this section. Also see "Mutable Signs" under Mutable; Perihelion; "Sun Spots" under Spots; Stellium). Cases of Disordered Nervous System, Maps, etc.— See Figures 1A, 14A, B, C, D, E, F, in the book, "Astro-Diagnosis" by the Heindels.

Dissolving Of—(See Resolution).

Disturbances — Of the Nervous System — Caused especially by afflictions in ♒, as this sign rules the nervous system. (See "Disordered",. and the various paragraphs in this section).

Dreads and Fears — Nervous and Anxious Fears—(See Fears).

Drowsiness—Stupor—Sleepiness— (See Sleep).

Dyspepsia — (See "Nervous" under Dyspepsia).

Ears — Lack of Nerve Force to the Ears—(See Deafness).

Energy — Nervous Energy is upheld by ☿, and suppressed by ♄. (See "Suppression" in this section).

Enervation—A Weakening—(See Enervation; "Depletion" in this section).

Epilepsy; Erethism — Of the Nerve Centers—Abnormal Increase of Nervous Irritability—(See Erethism).

Erratic Movements—(See Erratic).

Excessive Nervous Power — Over-Activity of the Nervous System—Neurosthenia—The ☽ in ♐ and coming to the ☍ of ♃ at B. (See Highly Neurotic, Over-Activity, in this section).

Excitability— Nervous Excitability — (See "Nerves" under Excitable; "High Strung" under High; "Highly Neurotic" in this section).

Excitement—Nervous Diseases Arising from Excitement — Denoted by ☿; ☿ afflicted by ♅ or ♂. (See Excitable; Debility, Neurasthenia, Prostration, in this section).

Exhaustion — Of the Nerve Force — (See "Neurasthenia" in this section).

Eyes — (See "Crystallization" in this section).

Facial Nerve — Disorders of — (See "Nerves" under Face).

Fear — (See "Nervous Fears" under Fear).

Feet—(See "Feet" under Cramps; "Motor Nerves" under Feet).

Fibers — (See "Nerve Fibers" under Organs).

Fibroma — A Fibroma On a Nerve — Neuroma — Nerve Tumor—(See "Neuroma" in this section).

Fits — (See "Nervous Affections" under Fits).

Fluids—Depletion of Nerve Fluids— (See "Depletion" in this section).

Force — Lack of Nerve Force — (See "Force" under Vital; Collapse, Depletion, Loss Of, Nerve Force, Neurasthenia, Prostration, in this section).

Functional Disorders—Of the Nerves —(See Enervation; "Nerves" under Excitable; Hindered, Impeded, under Functions).

Gastric Neuroses — (See "Neuroses" under Stomach).

Genitals — Genito-Urinary System — Nervous Disorders of — (See "Nervous Affections" under Genitals, Genito-Urinary).

Gripings; Hands — Nerve Pains In — (See "Nerves" under Hands).

Hardening — Of Nerves — (See Corrosions, Crystallization, Lesions, Paralysis, in this section; "Nerves" under Hardening; Sclerosis).

Haste and Excitement — Nervous Debility From — (See Debility, Excitement, in this section).

Head — Nervous Disorders of — (See "Nervous Affections" under Head; Headaches).

Headaches — Nervous Headaches — (See Headaches).

Heart — Nervous Affections of — (See Cardialgia, Depressor, Nervous Affections, Neuralgia, under Heart).

Hemiplegia; Hiccough; High Strung —(See "Strung" under High).

High Tension—High Nervous Tension —(See "Nerves" under Excitable; "High Strung" under High; "High Nervous Tension" under Tension; "Highly Neurotic" in this section).

Highly Neurotic — Excessively Neurotic — Extremely Nervous — ♆ in a prominent position at B., and afflicting the ☽ or ☿; ♆ in the 3rd or 9th H. at B., and in adverse asp. to the ☽ or ☿; ♂ afflicting ♆ at B., and by dir.; ☿ afflicted in the 6th H. (See "Brain Storms" under Brain; Erethism; "Nerves" under Excitable; Frenzy, Fury; "High Strung" under High; Hyperaesthesia, Mania; Nervousness, Neurasthenia, Neurotic, in this section).

Hips—Nervous Pains In—(See Hips).

Horrors — Nervous Horrors — (See Horrors).

Hot Flashes — (See "Sensations" under Burning; Paraesthesia).

Hyperaesthesia; Hysteria;

Incoordination; Increase—Of Nervous Irritability — (See Erethism; "Nerves" under Excitable).

Indigestion—Nervous Indigestion—(See Indigestion).

Inflammation — Of a Nerve — (See "Neuritis" in this section).

Influx—The Nervous Influx—Mercury adds to or subtracts from. The ☿ Group of Herbs by their physiological action tend to modify the nervous influx and periodicity. (See "Alterations" under Cells).

Inhibition — ♄ has an inhibitory action over the Nervous System by his afflictions. (See Inhibitions, Retarded, Suppressions).

Insensibility—To Pain—(See Anaesthetics, Analgesia, Insensibility).

Irritability — Abnormal Increase of Nervous Irritability—The ☽ in P. asp. to ♄ in the Zodiac. (See Erethism, Irritability; Highly Neurotic, Neurasthenia, in this section).

Jerky Movements—(See Jerky).

Kidneys—Nervous Disorders of—(See Kidneys).

Lack of Nerve Force — (See Depletion, Neurasthenia, in this section; "Force" under Vital).

Leakage—Nervous Leakage—♆ strong at B., and holding a dominant position, or afflicting ☿ or the ☽. (See Depletion, Loss Of, Neurasthenia, in this section).

Legs—(See Motor Nerves, Nerves, under Legs).

Lesions—Of the Nerves—Denoted by ♅; ☿ afflicted by ♅. (See Corrosions, Lesions, Paralysis).

Locomotion—Nervous Disorders of—(See "Stoppage" under Gait; "Paralysis" under Legs; Locomotor Ataxia; "Incoordinated" under Walk).

Locomotor Ataxia—(See Locomotor).

Loss of Nerve Power—Denoted by ♐, and afflictions in this sign. (See Collapse, Depletion, Lack Of, Neurasthenia, Prostration, in this section).

Lumbar Nerves — Obstructions In — (See "Fifth Lumbar" under Lumbar).

Mania—Neurotic Mania—(See Mania).

Manners—(See "Nervous" under Manners).

Marriage Partner — (See "Neurotic" under Marriage Partner).

Medullary Substance — Inflammation of—Neuromyelitis—(See Medulla).

Mental Over-Strain — Nervous Diseases Arising from—☿ afflicted in the 6th H.; ☿ or ♅ afflicted in ♈; ♅ in ♊. (See "Exertion" under Mental; "Nerves" under Mind; Reading, Study).

Mother—(See "Nervous Complaints" under Mother).

Motion—Nervous Disorders of—(See "Spasmodic" under Motion).

Motor Nerves—Disturbances of—(See "Motor Nerves" under Motor).

Movements—Nervous Disorders of—(See Ataxia, Erratic, Incoordination, Jerky, Movement, Paralysis, Spasmodic; "Equilibrium" under Walk).

Neck and Throat—(See "Nervous Disorders" under Neck, Throat).

Nerve Force — Disturbances of the Circulation of the Nerve Force—♃ or ♀ □ or ♂ ☉. (See Fluids, Force, in this section; Fluid, Force, under Vital).

Nerve Power—Loss of — (See "Loss Of" in this section).

Nerveless—Lacking In Courage—♃ afflicted in ♓; ♂ weak and afflicted at B. (See Dejection, Depression; "Low Spirits" under Low; Timidity).

Nervine—(See "Nervine" in Sec. 1 of this Article).

Nervously Apprehensive — (See "Apprehensive" in this section).

Nervousness—Nervous—Neurotic—Unsettled Condition of the Nerves—Nervous Susceptibility—The Prog. ☉ or ☽ ☌, □, or ☌ ♅; the ☽ in P. asp. to ♄; nervous patients tend to be worse at the Full ☽, and more restless; ♆ and ♅ afflicted; ♆ □ or ☌ ♅; ♅ or ♂ afflicted in ♒ in the 6th H.; ♅ ☌ ♂; ♅ afflicted in ♉; ♅ in ♊ in □ or ☌ ♃ in ♍; denoted by an afflicted ☿; ☿ badly afflicted in ♈; a □ and ♒ disorder, and afflictions in these signs. (See Disordered, Excitability, Highly Neurotic, Neurasthenia, in this section).

Neuralgia—(See "Pain" in this section).

Neurasthenia—Exhaustion of Nerve Force—Nervous Depletion—Enervation—Nervous Debility—The Vital Fluid and Vital Forces Lowered, etc.—The ☉ to the ☌ or ill-asps. ♅ by dir., and with the ☉ affl. by ♅ at B.; ♆ afflicting ☿ predisposes to, and to nervous depletion; ♆ in a prominent position at B., and afflicting the ☽ or ☿, tends to depletion of the nervous energy and complete nervous collapse; ♅ ☌, □, or ☌ the Asc. at B., and by dir., nervous exhaustion from excessive excitement; a ☿ disease, and with ☿ afflicted by malefics at B., and by dir.; ☿ in a ♄ sign and afflicted; the Asc. to the ☌ or ill-asp. ♅ by dir.; a disease of the Nervous Temperament, ruled by ♅, ♄, ☿, and the earthy signs. The degrees usually involved are 10° ♉, the 25° ♑ and ♐, and the 26° ♒, and the ☉, ☽, or planets in these degrees at B. tend to greatly deplete the nervous system under evil directions; Subs at AT and PP. (See Collapse, Debility, Depletion, Enervation, Excitability, Highly Neurotic, Nervousness, Prostration, in this section).

Neuritis—Inflammation of a Nerve—Neuromyelitis—The bad aspects of ♆ to ☿, or to the Significators, the ☉, ☽, Asc., or M.C.; ♂ afflicted in ♊; ♂ afflicting ☿; ♂ in a ☿ sign, and afflicting ☿; ☿ afflicted by malefics, and especially by ♅ or ♂; those having the 29° ♌ or ♒ involved at B. are liable to this disease. Neuritis in the lower extremities is caused by ♆ in ♓ and afflicting the ☉ or ☽; ♂ in ♑, ♒, or ♓, ☌, or ill-asp.

☿, or with malefics afflicted in these lower signs at B., and by dir. Neuritis may occur in the nerves of any part of the body, according to the sign positions of the malefics and ☿ at B. (See Erethism, Medullary Substance, in this section; "Nerves" under Excitable).

Neuroma—A Nerve Tumor—Fibroma On a Nerve—♂ ☌ or ill-asp. ☿. (See "Fibroma" under Fiber).

Neuromalacia—Softening of Nerve Tissue—A ♀ and ♓ disease; ♀ afflicted in ♓. (See "Softening" under Brain; Malacia, Softening).

Neuromyelitis — (See Inflammation, Medullary, in this section).

Neurosis—Neuroses—Neurotic—Nervous Affection Without Lesion—A ♅ disease. (See "Anxiety Neuroses" under Anxiety; Catalepsy; "Movements" under Erratic; "Neuroses" under Motor, Stomach).

Neurosthenia — (See "Excessive" in this section).

Neurotic—Nervous—Pertaining to Neuroses—A ♅ disease and affliction. (See Erethism, Highly Neurotic, Mania, Marriage Partner, Nervousness, Neurasthenia, Neurosis, Sexual, Wasting, in this section).

Nodding Spasm—(See "Nodding" under Head).

Numbness of Nerves—Tingling of Nerves—(See Numbness, Paraesthesia, Tingling).

Nystagmus — Oscillating Eyeballs — Quivering of—(See Eyeballs).

Obstructed—The Nerves Obstructed— Vital Force Obstructed—The ☉ ☌ ♄ at B., and by dir.; ☉ ☌ ♄ in 6th H.; ♃ in the Asc., or in ☐ or ☍ to the Asc.; ♃ in ☐ in the Asc. or M.C., and afflicted by ♄; the Prog. ☽ ☌, P., ☐, or ☍ ♂ and ☿, planets which rule the motor and sensory nerves, tends to obstruct the vital flow along the nerves, and often results in paralysis; ♄ in ☐ ☌ ♃, ♅, or ☿. (See Fluid, Force, Nerves, under Vital; Lumbar, Pneumogastric, Sacral, in this section).

Operations—When Not to Sever a Nerve—Do not cut a nerve when the ☽ is passing thru the sign which rules the part. (See "Rules" under Operations).

Optic Nerve—Disorders of—(See Optic).

Over-Activity—Of the Nerves—Neurosthenia — (See Erethism, Excessive, Excitable, Highly Neurotic, in this section; "Over-Active" under Active; "Over-Activity" under Brain, Lungs, Stomach).

Over-Strain—Mental and Nervous Diseases Arising From—♅ or ♂ ☌ or bad asp. ☿; ♅ in ☐ at B. warns against over-strain of the mind and nervous system; the ☽ afflicted by ♅. (See "Brain Fag" under Brain; Fatigue; "Strain" in this section).

Over-Study—Nervous Diseases Arising From—♅ afflicted in ☐. (See Reading, Study).

Over-Work—Nervous Diseases Arising From—(See "Over-Worked" under

Brain; "Inordinate", "Mind", under Exercise; Reading, Study; Over-Strain, Over-Study, Strain, in this section).

Pain In Nerve—Neuralgia—Caused by an afflicted ☿, and usually in the part ruled by the sign ☿ is in at B. Also caused by the afflictions of ♅ to ☿. (See Headaches, Neuralgia, Pain; Hands, Hips, Insensibility, Neuritis, Numbness, in this section).

Palliative—A Nerve Palliative—(See "Blue Color" in Sec. 1 of this Article; Anaesthetics, Anodyne, Sedatives).

Palsy; Paraesthesia; Paralysis—(See Paralysis; "Lesions" in this section).

Paramyoclonus—(See Muscles).

Paroxysms—Of Nervous Excitation— (See Collapse, Excitable, Prostration, in this section).

Peculiar Nervousness—Peculiar Nervous Diseases—Caused by ♅; ☿ in evil asp. to ♅. (See Peculiar).

Periodicity—Nervous Periodicity— (See Innervation; "Influx" in this section).

Pneumogastric Nerve—Obstruction of —(See Pneumogastric).

Power—Loss of Nerve Power—(See Depletion, Loss Of, in this section).

Pressure—Upon the Nerves—(See Pressure, Spine, Subluxations, Vertebrae).

Prickling Sensations—(See Burning, Numbness, Tingling, in this section).

Privy Parts—Disorders of Nerves of —(See "Genitals" in this section).

Prostration—Nervous Prostration— Nervous Breakdown—Complete Nervous Collapse—A ☉ disease; afflictions to the ☉ by ♅, ♆, or ♄; ♅ afflicting ☿ or the hyleg at B., and by dir.; ♄ ☌ the ☉ in ☐ or ♒; ♂ or ☿ in the 6th or 12th H., and in ☍ each other; ☿ weak and ill-dig. at B., and afflicted by malefics. The Mercurial man tends to exhaust his nervous energies due to the restless activity of Modern Life. Cases —See Fig. 14A and 14B in "Astro-Diagnosis". (See Collapse; "Nerves" under Excitable; Depletion, Neurasthenia, in this section).

Puffing—Puffing Up of the Sinews of the Nerves—The ☽ in ♑ and afflicted by the ☉ or ♂ when taken ill (Hor'y).

Quick and Nervous—(See "Quick and Nervous" under Speech, Walk).

Quiverings; Resolution—Of the Nerves —A ♄ disease. (See "Nerves" under Resolution).

Respiratory System—Nervous Disorders of—(See "Nerves" under Lungs).

Restlessness—Nervous Diseases Arising From—☐ on the Asc. (See Restlessness).

Sacral Nerves—Obstructed—(See Sacrum).

Saint Vitus Dance—(See Saint).

Sensations; Sensibility — Excessive Sensibility or Sensitiveness—Sensitive Nerves—♅ ☌ ☿. (See Hyperaesthesia, Sensibility, Sensitive; Excessive, Excitable, Highly Neurotic, Neurasthenia, in this section).

Sexual Neurotic—(See "Neurotic" under Sex).

Shock and Strain—(See Shock; "Strain" in this section).

Sinews—Puffing Up of Nerve Sinews —(See "Puffing" in this section).

Sleep — Nervous Disorders of — (See "Insomnia", and the various paragraphs under Sleep).

Softening—Of the Nerve Tissue—(See "Neuromalacia" in this section).

Somnolence — (See "Drowsiness" under Sleep).

Spasmodic Diseases—Spasmodic Movements—Spasms—(See Convulsions; "Movements" under Erratic; Fits, Jerky, Spasmodic, Tics, Twitchings).

Speech — (See "Quick and Nervous" under Speech).

Spinal Cord — Disorders of — (See "Cord" under Spine).

Stomach—Nervous Disorders of—(See Nerve Pains, Nerve Terminations, Nervous Indigestion, Neuralgia, Neuroses, under Stomach).

Storms—Psychic Storms—Violent Brain Storms—(See "Brain Storms" under Brain; Frenzy, Madness, Mania; "Psychic Storms" under Psychic).

Strain—High Nervous Strain and Tension, and Diseases Arising From—The ☽ afflicted by ♅; caused by afflictions to ☿; ♅ afflicted in ♈; airy signs on the Asc.; Aldebaran or Antares directed to the angles of the horoscope, the Asc., or M.C., tend to terrible periods of stress and nervous strain, the worst which may occur in a lifetime. (See Aldebaran, Antares; "Nerves" under Excitable; "Nervous Strain" under Headaches; "High Strung" under High; Strain, Stress; Highly Neurotic, Nervousness, Neurasthenia, Over-Strain, Stress, in this section). Case of Death from Nervous Strain and Shock—See "Leland", No. 813 in 1001 N.N.

Stress and Strain—Nervous Diseases Arising From, and from Over-Work and Worry—Denoted by ☿, and this planet afflicted by malefics at B., and by dir. (See Over-Strain, Over-Study, Over-Work, Strain, Worry, in this section).

Stupor—(See "Stupor" under Sleep).

Suppression — Of Nervous Energy — Caused by ♄ afflictions to ☿. (See Energy, Inhibition, in this section).

Susceptibility—Nervous Susceptibility —♄ afflicted in ♎. (See Disordered, Nervousness, Neurasthenia, in this section).

Swallowing — Deglutition Difficult — Dysphasia—(See Deglutition).

Sympathetic Nervous System—Disorders of—(See Peripheral, Sympathetic).

Tension—High Nervous Tension— (See "Nerves" under Excitable; "High Strung" under High; Tension; High Tension, Highly Neurotic, Strain, in this section).

Throat and Neck—(See "Neck" in this section).

Tics—Spasmodic Twitching—(See Spasmodic, Tics, Twitching).

Tingling — (See "Numbness" in this section).

Tissues—Wasting of Nerve Tissues— ♆ disease and affliction. (See Wasting).

Treatment—Of Nervous Disorders— (See "Treatment" in Sec. 1 of this Article).

Tremors — Tremblings—(See Tremors).

Tumor — Of the Nerve — (See "Neuroma" in this section).

Twitchings—(See Tics, Twitching).

Unsettled—The Nerves Unsettled— (See "Nervousness" in this section).

Urinary System — Nervous Disorders of—(See "Nervous Affections" under Urine).

Vascular Excitement—Of the Nerve Centers—(See Erethism).

Violent Brain Storms — (See "Brain Storms" under Brain).

Vital Flow — Obstructed — (See "Obstructed" in this section).

Vital Fluid—Vital Force—Exhaustion of—Lack of—(See Depletion, Exhaustion, Fluids, Force, Neurasthenia, Prostration, in this section).

Walk—(See "Quick and Nervous" under Walk).

Wasting—Neurotic Wasting—(See "Neurotic" under Marriage Partner; Wasting; "Neurotic" in this section).

Weakest Part—The Nervous System the Weakest Part—The ☉ afflicted in ♐.

Weakness—Nerve Weakness—♅ ☌, P., □, or ☍ the Asc., nerve weakness and depletion of nerve fluids; ☿ □ or ☍ Asc. (See Collapse, Enervation; Depletion, Exhaustion, Neurasthenia, Prostration, in this section).

Women—Nervous Disorders of—Afflictions to the ☽ and ☿; the ☽ ☌, □, or ☍ ♅. (See Emotions; "Women" under Headaches; Hysteria; "Disordered" in this section).

Worry — Nervous Disorders From — Afflictions to ☿, and especially ☿ afflicted by ♄; ☿ affl. in 6th H. (See Apprehensive, Depletion, Enervation, Fears, Strain, Stress, in this section; Dejection, Depressed; "Low Spirits" under Low; Melancholy; "Morbid" under Mind; Worry, etc.).

NERVINE—A Therapeutic Property of ☿. (See "Nervine" under Nerves).

NETTLE RASH—Urticaria—(See Hives, Itch, Urticaria).

NEURALGIA—Pain In a Nerve—Neuralgia may occur in any part, or organ of the body, and is caused principally by ☿ afflicted in the sign which rules the part or organ. Also ♄ causes Neuralgia, and lingering pains in a part due to the deposit of wastes and minerals in the part, and interfering with function, elimination, secretion, excretion, etc. Uranus also contributes to Neuralgia when configurated with Mercury. Mars causes acute neuralgic pains in a part; darting, sharp, shooting, or violent pains and Neuralgia in those parts ruled by the sign he may be in at B., as ♂ in any sign tends to draw heat to the part ruled by the sign, and to cause disturbances at times, pains, and an acute form of Neuralgia. The Neuralgia of ♄ is more chronic, dull, lingering, throbbing, more like an ache, but very severe and painful at times. Mercury afflicted in ♈ tends to Neuralgia and pains in the head, and headaches; ☿ in ♉, Neuralgia of the neck and throat; ☿ in ♊, of the chest and lungs; ☿ in ♋, of the stomach; ☿ in ♍, Neuralgia in the bowels and abdomen; ☿ in ♎, of the kidneys; ☿ in ♏, of the generative organs, womb, bladder, etc.; ☿ in ♐, in the hips and thighs; ☿ in ♑, in the knees and legs; ☿ in ♒, in the calves, ankles, and lower legs; ☿ in ♓, Neuralgia and pains in the feet, etc. For additional influences which may cause Neuralgia in the different parts and organs, see "Nerves", "Neuralgia", "Pains", under Arms, Bladder, Bowels, Face, Feet, Hands, Head, Heart, Intercostal, Kidneys, Legs, Stomach, Teeth, Womb, etc., and in other parts or organs which may not be mentioned here. Also note the various paragraphs in the Article on Pain, as the parts afflicted by Pains and Neuralgia are listed there, and also the various kinds of Neuralgic Pains, such as Darting, Sharp, Shooting, Violent, etc. In the treatment of Neuralgia the tonic remedies of ♂ will often relieve the Neuralgia caused by ♄, and where ♄ has caused a weak circulation, as ♂ opposes ♄, on the theory of opposites. (See Antipathy, Opposites; "Medicines" under Tonic).

NEURASTHENIA—(See Nerves).

NEURITIS—Inflammation of a Nerve—(See "Neuritis" under Nerves).

NEUROMA—Nerve Tumor—(See "Neuroma" under Nerves).

NEUROMALACIA—Softening of Nerve Tissue—(See this subject under Nerves).

NEUROMYELITIS—Inflammation of Nerve Tissue, or of the Medullary Substance—(See Medulla; "Inflammation" under Nerves).

NEUROSIS—Nervous Affection without Lesion—(See "Neurosis" under Nerves).

NEUROSTHENIA—Over-Activity of the Nervous System—(See this subject under Nerves).

NEUROTIC—Nervous—Pertaining to Neuroses—(See "Neurotic" under Nerves).

NEUTRAL—Neutral Planets—☿ is a neutral, or variable planet, and partakes of the nature of the planet with which configurated. This is important to note in making a study of the map of birth along health lines. Mercury with ♄ becomes like ♄, and causes the same diseases as ♄. Mercury with ♀ adds to the power of ♀ in musical and artistic matters. Mercury with ♂ adds to the hasty and impulsive tendencies of the mind, and to excitability of the nerve centers, etc. The ☽ is also variable, and takes on the nature of other planets when configurated with them, the same as does ☿. The ☽ ☌ ♄ gives a very depressed and despondent nature, or personality, and often leads to an increase of ♄ diseases, and to add to their power. (See Variable. Also study the Articles on the Moon and Mercury, and note their neutral, and variable influences).

NEW BORN—(See Birth, Children, Infancy, Parturition, Puerperal).

NEW GROWTHS—Neoplasm—Tumors—(See "New Growths" under Growths"; Tumors).

NEW MOON—(See "New Moon" under Moon).

NEWSMONGER—A Gossip—Busy-Body—Prattler—Meddler—Tale-Bearer—♃ affl. in ♋.

NEWTON—Sir Isaac Newton—Born Dec. 25, 1642. Died March 20, 1727. He came to be a great believer in Astrology. On one occasion, when upbraided by Mr. Halley, the discoverer of Halley's Comet, for his belief in Astrology, answered, "I have studied the subject, Mr. Halley, you have not". The only way to understand Astrology is to study it, observe the effects of the planetary influences over individuals, and not persecute what God has ordained as fixed Laws over His Universe. (See Kepler, Map, Medical Astrology, Nativity, Paracelsus, Star Map).

NICOTINE—(See Tobacco).

NIECES—Nephews—Ruled by the 3rd H., and come under the same rules as for the brothers and sisters of the native. (See "Case" under Aunt; Brothers, Sisters).

NIGHT—Nocturnal—The Night is ruled by the ☽, and the ☉ rules the Day. The night is magnetic, while the day is electric. At night the ☽ tends to keep up the action of morbid germs, while the electric action of the ☉ by day tends to destroy them. The night is less vitalizing than the day. Saturn is more malignant at night as the moisture of the night adds to his cold. Mars is less malignant by night as the moisture of the night moderates his heat and dryness. Thus ♄ is more malignant in night nativities, and ♂ less so. However, as Anareta, ♄ and ♂ are equally destructive to life whether they be diurnal or nocturnal. In a night nativity the ☽ is more powerful when elevated above the Earth, and tends to better functions. (See Day, Elevated). The planetary causes of disease, and even in the same disease, as in Insanity, tend to differ in a day and night nativity, due to the degree of malignancy of the afflicting planet. Thus in Insanity ♄ may cause and rule the scheme in a day nativity, and ♂ in a night nativity. (See Insanity). Moonlight and night air are noxious, and tend to Miasmic diseases. The exhalations of the vegetables at night, the prevalence of carbonic acid, and the chemical action of the Moon's rays, become very deleterious at night. People should not sleep with the Moonlight directly upon them. The Insane, Epileptics, the Hysterical and Nervous, are more affected by Moonlight, and at the Full Moon, and should not be allowed to sleep under the Moon's rays. (See Electric, Magnetic, Malignant, Miasma; "Full Moon", "Moonlight", "Night Action of the Moon", under Moon; Noxious). The following subjects have to do with the Night, and the Planetary Influences over Disease at Night.

Air—The Night Air Noxious, and Causing Miasma, etc.—(See Miasma, Noxious).

Danger to Life—In a Night Nativity—Influences Tending To—(See "Danger to Life" under Danger).

Diseases by Night—(a) Disease More Prevalent At Night—The ☽ in ♓, and afflicted by the ☉ or ♂ when taken ill (Hor'y). (b) The Disease Worse by Night—The Disease is worse at night if the ☽ was badly afflicted at B., as the ☽ rules the night, and also the ☽ be afflicted by direction at the time. The ☉ being more afflicted than the ☽ at B. tends to make the disease worse by day, as the ☉ rules the day. Females tend to suffer more at night in disease, as the ☽ rules strongly over female disorders, and the ☽ rules the night. Fevers and diseases which are strongly influenced by Miasmic conditions are usually worse at night. Also Chronic and Low Fevers usually get worse towards Sunset, and at night. (See "Chronic" under Fever; Miasma; "Night Action" under Moon).

Epilepsy—♂ ruling the scheme by day and ♄ by night. (See Epilepsy, Insanity).

Father—(See "Mother" in this section).

Fits—♄ by Day, and ♂ by Night, and Their Influences In Tending to Cause Fits—(See "Causes" under Fits).

Insanity—♄ Ruling the Scheme by Day and ♂ by Night. (See Insanity).

Insomnia—Loss of Sleep by Night—(See "Insomnia" under Sleep).

Losses—Night Losses—Wet Dreams—(See "Emissions" under Semen).

Malignant—♄ More Malignant In a Night Nativity—(See Malignant"; the Introduction to this Article).

Mars—(See Day, Night, under Mars).

Miasma—Noxious Night Air—(See Miasma).

Moonlight—Influence of—(See "Full Moon", "Moonlight", "Night Action", under Moon; the Introduction to this Article).

Mother—Disease In—In studying the diseases of the mother note the positions and aspects of Venus in a day nativity, and the ☽ in a night nativity. (See "Disease" under Mother). With the father the ☉ is to be noted in a day nativity, and ♄ by night. Thus the ☉ and ♀ represent the parents in a day geniture, and the ☽ and ♄ by night.

Nativity—Night Nativity—(See the Introduction, and the various paragraphs in this Article).

Nightmare—Horrible Dreams—(See Dreams; "Nightmare" under Sleep).

Night Study—(See "Night Study" under Study).

Night Sweats—Of Phthisis—(See Phthisis).

Night Vision—Vision Best At Night—(See "Night Vision" under Sight).

Nocturnal Life—Night Life—Disposed To—The 3rd Decan. of ♒ on the Asc. at B. More common among people born between Sunset and Midnight, and with the ☽ in this Quarter and afflicted by malefics, and also with the ☽ and many planets in watery signs in this Quarter, which influences may lead to dissipations of various kinds. Also people born between Noon and Midnight may be inclined to a night life. People born between Midnight and Noon, and with the ☉ and many planets rising in the East, are more active during the day, and inclined to rest and relax at night.

Nocturnal Signs—The Feminine Signs —♉, ♋, ♍, ♏, ♑, ♓, and called nocturnal because they excel in dryness or moisture. These are also the night signs, or night houses, of the planets, except ♋, which is the only sign of the ☽, and serves as the home and strong sign by day or night. The diurnal signs are ♈, ♊, ♌, ♎, ♐, ♒, as their rulers are stronger in them by day than at night. The ☉ has only one sign, that of ♌, and the ☉ is equally strong in this sign, day or night.

Noxious Air At Night—(See Miasma).

Pain Greater At Night—The ☽ ☌ or ill-asp. ♄ (or ☿ if he be of the nature of ♄) at the beginning of an illness, or at decumbiture (Hor'y). (See "Diseases by Night" in this section).

Parents—Significators of the Parents In a Night Nativity—(See "Mother" in this section).

Patient Worse At Night — (See "Disease" in this section).

Saturn by Night — ♄ is more malignant when afflicting in a night nativity. (See Introduction to this section).

Study At Night—(See "Night Study" under Study).

Vision At Night — Better At Night Than In Day—(See "Night Vision" under Sight).

Worse — Disease Worse At Night—(See "Diseases by Night" in this section).

NIMBLE BODY — Nimble Step — (See "Energetic" under Gait; "Quick" under Motion).

NINTH HOUSE—The house of ♃ and ♐, and a masculine house. Denotes the Fundament, the Hips, Thighs, Hams. This is the House of Religion, Philosophy, the Higher Mind, Dreams, Dream Consciousness, Visions, Kindred of the Marriage Partner, Long Journeys, Foreign Travel, Voyages, Residence Abroad. In the body this House rules the Hips, Thighs, and Fundament, and signifies all diseases of these parts. Malefics in the 9th H. at B. tend to disturb and unbalance the mind, or cause Religious Excitement, Religious Fanaticism, Distorted Religious Views, Religious Mania, Unorthodox Views, and trouble with Religious Authorities. Malefics in the 9th H. also tend to dangers in Foreign Travel, Injury, loss or death at Sea, and ill-health, dangers, or death Abroad. Mars afflicted in this House at B. tends to dangers at Sea by Lightning, Fire, or Shipwreck, and also to cause many conflicts with the Clergy and Orthodox Leaders. Neptune or ♅ well-aspected in this house at B. tend to give an Occult and Mystical mind, Advanced Views, and with good powers to comprehend and appreciate Truth wherever found. People having malefics in this house at B., and afflicted, and with no benefics in the house, or favorably influencing the house, should remain in their Native Land, and not take voyages, or go Abroad, as such might bring them disease, ill-health, accident, injury, capture, death, failure, or disaster. The benefics ♃ and ♀ in this house, and with no malefic in, or ruling, the house, tend to give a religious and devotional mind, and with greater success along Orthodox lines and the Ministry, and to have more success in ordinary Church work. Uranus here tends to make the native soon rebel against the Orthodox interpretations of the Bible, and to study into the Mysteries, and the Esoteric explanations of Christianity, and of all Religions, and to delve into the Secret Doctrines of the Ages. These tendencies for Esoteric study are also given by the ☉ or ☿ ☌ ♅ at B., or with ♅ rising in the Asc. or M.C. Neptune well-aspected in the 9th H. gives strong Psychic, Clairvoyant, Mediumistic, and Spiritual Powers. The Colors ruled by this house are Green and White. (See Abroad, Foreign Lands, Jupiter, Religion, Sagittarius, Third House, Voyages, etc.).

NIPPLES—Paps—Ruled by the ♋ sign. Afflictions in ♋, and Subs at Lu.P. (3D), tend to Imperfections in, Disorders of, and Injuries to, etc.

Pain Under Nipples—♅ or the ☽ in ♋, ☌, or ill-asp. ♄ (or ☿ if he be of the nature of ♄) at the beginning of an illness or at decumbiture; the ☽ ☌ ♄ in ♓ (or ☌ ☿ in ♓ if he is of the nature of ♄) at the beginning of an illness, or at decumb., tends to pain under the Nipples, and in the chest, and caused by wet feet or damp linen; ♂ affl. in ♋, or in ♋ in the Asc. (See "Pain" under Breast, Chest).

Sore Nipples—♄ or ♂ afflicted in ♋.

Suppurative Inflammation — Of the Areola About the Nipple—Phlegmon—♄ affl. in ♋. (See "Phlegmon" under Pus). See Milk, Nursing.

NITROGEN—Ozote—A Gaseous Element and Constituent of the Air—Is the base of a number of compounds ruled by ♅. Nitrogen is ruled by ♅ and the Airy Signs, and is a dominant element of the Airy Signs. Nitrogen is unstable, highly explosive, and tends to explosions and accidents, and death by explosions when ♅ is afflicted in the 8th H. at B., and by dir. Hydrogen, Nitrogen, Oxygen and Carbon correspond to the four elements of Nature, as Water, Air, Fire, and Earth respectively, and the four fundamental and essential Operations of Nature are synthetized by their qualities, namely—Congelation, Volatilization, Combustion, and Condensation. (See these subjects. Also see Air, Carbon, Explosions, Gases, Hydrogen; "Operations" under Nature; Oxygen, Uranus, Urea).

NOBLE—Noble-Minded—A Just Mind and Disposition—The ☉ Sig. in ♈, ♌, ♎, or ♑; the ☽ Sig. in ♉; the ☽ Sig. ✳ or △ ♃; ♄ Sig. ✳ or △ the ☉; ♃ Sig. in ♈, ♌, ♎, ♐, or ♒; a ♃ trait; ♃ well-aspected in the Asc.; ♃ ✳ or △ the ☉; ♂ Sig. ☌ ♃; ♀ Sig. in ♐ or ♓; ☿ Sig.

in ♎; ♎ on the Asc.; many influences in fixed signs. (See Honest, Humane, Kind, Philanthropic, Royal, Sincere, Sympathetic, etc.).

NOBLES—Noblemen—Grandees—The ☉ rules Nobles and Noblemen.

Death Of—Suffering or Evils To—♃ or ♂ conjoined in ♓; Comets appearing in ♌; Comets appearing in ♈, detriment and evils to Grandees and Nobles in Eastern Parts. (See Famous; "Great Men" under Great; Kings, Rulers).

Injury To — ♃, ♂, ♀, and the ☽ conjoined in ♉.

Murders Of — ☿ in ♋ at the Vernal Equi., Lord of the Year, and ☌ ♂ or ♀. (See Assassination).

Sickness and Infirmities — ♄ Lord of the Year at the Vernal, in ♊, and ori., tends to much sickness to Nobles or Grandees.

Suffer — Nobles, Grandees, and the Associates Suffer — ♄, ♃, and ♂ conjoined in ♓; ♃ and ♂ conjoined in ♎; Comets appearing in ♌.

NOCTURNAL—(See Night).

Nocturnal Signs—(See "Signs" under Night).

NODDING SPASM—Of the Head—(See "Nodding" under Head).

Nods Head to One Side—When Speaking—(See Skippish).

Nodding of the Eyeballs—Rolling of—(See "Nystagmus" under Eyeballs).

NODES — The points where planets cross the Ecliptic from South Latitude into North Latitude, and also where they cross again from N. Lat. to S. Lat. The Nodes of the ☽ are the ones mostly used and studied. The North Node of the ☽, when she crosses the Ecliptic going North, is called Caput Draconis, or the Dragon's Head, and is considered a fortunate influence in health, and other matters, when falling on the place of the Asc., or M.C. in a nativity. (See Dragon's Head). The South Node of the ☽, where she crosses the Ecliptic going South, is called the Dragon's Tail, and is considered unfortunate, and to have an influence similar to ♄ in health matters when it falls in the Asc., M.C., and other vital centers of the map of birth. (See "Nodes" under Moon). However, in the consideration of the power and force of the planets in disease, the Nodes of all the planets should be considered, and their Latitudes. A planet is stronger in its influence when near its node, and on or near the Ecliptic, and the further from the Ecliptic the afflicting planet may be, the less is its power to cause affliction and disease. Also the aspects between planets which have a wide difference in Latitude are not as important to consider as those which are in aspect in and near the same degree of Latitude, either North, or South. If several planets are on the Ecliptic at B., near their Nodes, and afflicting the hyleg, their power is greater to cause disease, or great suffering and affliction. It is very important, therefore, for every student and Diagnostician in Astrology to have an Ephemeris which gives the Latitudes of the planets, and to study their positions as to Latitude and Declination, as well as Longitude. (See Latitude). Declination is the distance of a planet North or South of the Equator, and planets with the same Declination, or within 1° of the same, are said to be in Parallel Aspect, which is a very strong aspect for good or evil in health matters, according to the nature of the planets so aspected. (See Parallel).

Nodules — Tubercles — Tophus — A ♄ disease. (See "Nodes" under Ears; "Adiposa Dolorosa" under Fat; Tubercles).

NOISE—Noisy—Noisome—

Noise In the Head — Rumbling or Ringing Noises In the Head — (See "Noises" under Head).

Noisome Diseases — ♆ afflicted in the 12th H., and bordering on Fury or Insanity. (See Fury, Insanity, Madness, Mania).

Noisy Breathing—(See "Noisy" under Breathing).

Noisy and Contentious—A Brawler— A Scold—A ♄ characteristic. (See Harlots, Riotous, Scolding).

NON—The Latin word for "Not".

Non-Malignant Growths—(See "Non-Malignant" under Growths).

Non-Oxygenation—Of the Blood—(See Oxygen).

Non-Sensitives — (See Dull, Indifferent, Inertia, Lethargy, Mild; "Dulling of the Senses" under Senses).

NORMAL—According to Rule or Type—

Normal Births—(See "Normal Birth" under Parturition).

Normal Constitution — (See Good, Sound, Strong, under Constitution).

Normal Functions — (See "Normal" under Functions).

Normal Growth — Of the Body — (See "Normal" under Growth).

Normal Health — (See "Abundance", "Good Health", under Health; Immunity; "Good" under Vitality).

Normal Mind — ☿ strong, dignified, and well-aspected at B., and free from the affliction of malefics; ☿ in good aspect to the ☽ and Asc., and otherwise free from the afflictions which tend to an unbalanced mind. (See "Quickened" under Mentality; "Good Mind" under Mind).

Planets — Normal Action of — (See "Perverted" under Planets).

NORTH—Northern—

North Scale — A Star of the second magnitude, of the nature of ♃ and ♂, in the 17° ♏. The Asc. ♂ this star at B. tends to unusual melancholy. (See "Tendency To" under Melancholy).

North-Western Parts — War and Bloodshed In—☿ in ♋ and afflicted by ♂ at the Vernal Equi., and Lord of the Year.

Northern Parts — Effusion of Blood Prevalent In Northern Parts — (See Effusions).

Northern Signs — Of the Zodiac — Called Commanding Signs—♈, ♉, ♊, ♋,

♌, ♍. Planets in these signs are said to command, and those in opposite signs to obey. The Southern Signs are ♎, ♏, ♐, ♑, ♒, ♓, and a planet in these signs, in direct ☍ to a planet in a Northern sign, and with the same Declination, is weaker, and is said to obey the northern planet, and the Southern Signs are called Obeying Signs.

NOSE—Nostrils—Nares—Nasal Fossae —Nasal Bones — Nasal Septum — Turbinated Bones—The Nose, taken as a whole, is ruled by the ♏ Sign. It is also said to be under the external rulership of the ♈ sign, and influenced by ♈, and planets in this sign, and especially by ♂ in ♈, as ♂ rules both the ♈ and ♏ signs. The Nose has special affinity with the ♏ sign, and is one of the organs of Excretion. The nasal bones, and the nasal orifice, are ruled by ♏. Ptolemy says the Nostrils are ruled by ♀. Wilson, in his Dictionary, says the Olfactory Nerves are ruled by ♀. The Nerves to the Nose pass thru the 3rd, 4th and 5th Cervical Vertebrae, known as MCP, Middle Cervical Place, and these nerves when impinged tend to nasal disorders. The Naso-Pharynx is especially affected when planets are in both the ♈ and ♉ signs, or with ♂ in ♉. The Nasal Duct is the Tear Duct, or Lachrymal Duct. (See Aries, Excretion, Scorpio, Tears).

DESCRIPTIONS OF THE NOSE—

Broad Nose—☿ Sig. in ♌, broad and high. (See Thick, Wide, in this section).

Conspicuous — And High — ♊ on the Asc.

Great Nose—(See "Large" in this section).

Grecian Nose — ☿ in ♐, or ♐ on the Asc.

High Nose—♃ Sig. in ♈; ☿ Sig. in ♌, high and broad; ♊ on the Asc., high and conspicuous.

Large Nose—The ☉ Sig. in ♉, or in ♉ in partile asp. the Asc.; ♄ Sig. in ♎, or in ♎ in partile asp. the Asc.; ☿ Sig. in ♐ or ♑; ☿ in ♐ partile asp. the Asc.; ♉ on the Asc., large or wide.

Long Nose — Long and Straight — ☿ gives when strong at B., or the ruler.

Pointed Nose — (See "Sharp" in this section).

Prominent Nose—♄ in ♎, ♏, or ♐; ☿ in ♊ or ♌; ☿ in ♐, a prominent Grecian Nose; ♈ on the Asc., a prominent Roman Nose. (See "Large" in this section).

Roman Nose—♈ on the Asc., prominent Roman Nose.

Rounded and Short—♋ on the Asc.

Sharp Nose—Pointed—A ☿ person has a long, thin, and sharp nose; ☿ Sig. in ♋, or in this sign in partile asp. the Asc.

Short Nose — Short and Rounded — ♋ on the Asc.

Smell—Sense of—(See Smell).

Straight Nose—Straight and Long— ☿ gives; ☿ ascending at B., and free from the rays of other planets; ♐ gives a straight, Grecian nose.

Thick Nose — Thick Nostrils — Given by ♄ when he forms the body; ♄ ascending at B.

Thin Nose— ☿ gives a long, straight, thin, and sharp nose; ☿ ascending at B., and free from the rays of other planets.

Wide Nose — �808 gives, and with this sign on the Asc. (See "Broad" in this section).

DISEASES OF THE NOSE—Afflictions to the Nose — See the following subjects in the alphabetical arrangement when not more fully considered here—

Abscess — Frontal — (See "Frontal" under Abscesses).

Accidents To — Hurts — Wounds To — Injuries To—♄ or ♂ afflicted in ♏, and especially when in the 1st H. at B.; ♂ afflicted in ♈ tends to accidents to the head, which may involve the nose. (See "Accidents" under Face, Head).

Adenoids; All Diseases—In the Nose—Signified by planets in the 1st H., or by afflictions in ♈, �8, or ♏.

Asthma—Hay Asthma—(See Asthma; "Hay Fever" in this section).

Bleeding — At the Nose — (See Epistaxis, Vicarious, in this section).

Capillaries — Of the Nose — Red and Swollen—Obstructed—Red Nose—Usually caused by ♄ influence, and ♄ afflicted in ♈ or ♏, due to deposits, or afflictions to ♃ or ♀ if these planets also are in ♈ or ♏; ♃ in ♈, ♂, or ill-asp. ♄; ♂ afflicted in ♈ tends to a general redness of the face. Is also caused by Alcoholism, and gives the Toper's Nose when there are many planets in watery signs at B., and especially in ♏ or ♓. (See Capillaries, Drink, Drunkenness; "Red Face" under Face).

Caries—Of the Cartilage of the Nose —♄ afflicted in ♏. (See Caries).

Cartilage — Caries of — (See "Caries" in this section).

Catarrh—Nasal Catarrh—Foul Odors of—Catarrhal Headaches—A ♏ disease, and afflictions in ♏; the ☉ afflicted in ♈ or �8; ♄ afflicted in ♈, �8, ♎, or ♏; ♃ afflicted in �8; Subs at MCP. (See Catarrh, Colds, Defluxions, Discharges; "Noises In" under Head; "Catarrhal" under Headaches; "Coryza" in this section).

Cold Nose — Coldness and Whiteness of—A ♄ disease. (See "Raynaud's Disease" under Fingers).

Colds — (See Colds; Coryza, Rhinitis, in this section).

Constrictions In—Stenosis of—Stricture of the Nasal Passage—♄ afflicted in ♏; Subs at MCP (3, 4C).

Coryza—Catarrhal Inflammation of the Nose—♄, ♃, or ♂ afflicted in �8; a ☿ disease. Subs at MCP (4C), and KP. (See Colds; "Colds" under Head; Hay Fever, Rhinitis, in this section).

Cut Off — The Nose Nearly Cut Off — Case—See Chap. XIII in Daath's Medical Astrology).

Destroyed — The Nose Partially Destroyed by Lupus—Case—See "Lupus", No. 363, in 1001 N.N. (See Lupus).

Discharges — Much Discharge At the Nostrils—The ☽ in ♈, □ or ☍ ♄ (or ☿

if he be of the nature of ♄) at the beginning of an illness, or at decumb. (Hor'y). (See Catarrh, Colds, Discharges, Rheum; "Coryza" in this section).

Diseased Nose—The ☉ afflicted in ♏; ♂ diseases; ♂ affl. in ♏; afflictions in ♏. (See the various paragraphs in this section).

Disorders—Nasal Disorders—♂ afflicted in ♈; Subs at MCP (4C). (See the various paragraphs in this section).

Ducts — Nasal Ducts — (See "Ducts" under Tears).

Epistaxis—Nose Bleed—Hemorrhage from the Nose—A ♃ disease, due to fullness and plethora of blood vessels; ♃ afflicted in ♈, �8, or ♏; ♂ affl. in �8 or ♏; ♂ afflicted in ♏ in the Asc. or 6th H.; ♏ on the cusp the 6th H.; Subs at MCP (4C). (See Hemorrhage, Plethora; "Vicarious" in this section).

Epithelioma — Of the Nose — ♂ afflicted in ♏; ♂ in ♏ and afflicting the Asc.; ♂ in ♏ in the 7th H., angular, and in �8· the Asc.; the ☽ in ♑, afflicted by malefics, and conjoined with afflictions in ♏, and especially ♂ afflicted in ♏ at the same time, and with ♂ in the Western angle. Case — See "Epithelioma", in Chap. XIII, in Daath's Medical Astrology. (See Epithelioma).

Eustachian Tubes—Disorders of—(See Eustachian).

Fluids—Regurgitation of Fluids Thru the Nose — ♄ influence; ♄ afflicted in ♈, �8, or ♏; Subs at MCP (4C). (See "Obstruction" in this section).

Floor of Nose—(See Palate).

Fossae Diseased—Disorders of the Nasal Fossae — ♏ diseases, and afflictions in ♏; malefics in ♏.

Foul Odors From — ♄ afflicted in ♈, �8, ♎, or ♏. (See "Catarrh" in this section; "Foul Breath" under Breath; Foul).

Frontal Bones—Frontal Sinuses—Abscess In—(See "Frontal" under Abscesses).

Growths In — (See "Polypus" in this section).

Hay Fever—Hay Asthma—Rose Cold —A Microbic Disease of the Nasal Mucous Membrane, and accompanied by Inflammation, Coryza, and Lacrimation—Caused by afflictions in �8, ♓, or ♏; the ☽ afflicted in �8 or ♏; ♀ afflicted in ♓, due to disturbances of the bronchioles from breathing Pollen in the Summer time; ♄ or ♂ ♂ ♃ or ♀ in ♏; ♅ afflicted in ♏; ♂ afflicted in ♏; ♀ in �8, ♂, □, or ☍ ♂; Subs at MCP (4C), LCP (6C), and AP (1D). (See Asthma, Hay Fever; "Sneezing" in this section).

Hemorrhage Of—(See Epistaxis, Vicarious, in this section).

Humours In—A ☿ disease; ☿ afflicted in ♈, �8, or ♏. (See "Humours" under Head).

Hurts To — (See "Accidents" in this section).

Hypertrophy — Of the Nasal Membranes—♃ or ♂ afflicted in ♈, �8, or ♏. (See Hypertrophy).

Inflammatory Action—In the Nose— ♂ afflicted in ♈, ♉, or ♏; ♀ in ♉, ♎, □, or ♉ ♂. (See Coryza, Hypertrophy, Polypus, Rhinitis, in this section).

Influenza—The Nose Affected By—Afflictions in ♉ or ♏ prevailing at the time; ♃ in ♉ or ♏ in ♂ or ill-asp. ♄; Subs at MCP (4C), CP, and KP. (See Influenza, La Grippe).

Injuries To—(See "Accidents" in this section).

Lachrymal Disorders—And of the Nasal Duct—(See Tears).

Lupus—(See "Destroyed" in this section).

Menses—Menstruation Thru the Nose—(See "Vicarious" under Menses).

Mucous Membranes—Of the Nose—Inflammation of—(See "Inflammation" in this section).

Mucus—In the Nose and Head—The ☽ or ♀ afflicted in ♈. (See Catarrh, Discharges, in this section; "Mucus" under Head; "Humours" under Throat).

Nares—(See "Nostrils" in this section).

Nasal Catarrh—Nasal Disorders—(See "Catarrh", and the various paragraphs in this section).

Naso-Pharynx—Disorders In—♂ afflicted in ♉. (See Pharynx).

Noises In Head—(See "Noises" under Head).

Nose Bleed—(See "Epistaxis" in this section).

Nostrils — Nares — Much Discharge From—Stenosis of—Stricture of—(See Constriction, Discharges, Obstruction, in this section).

Obstruction—In the Nasal Passages— An afflicted ♄ in ♏ tends to, and to growths, such as Adenoids and Polypus, and especially when the mutable signs are also prominent. Throat troubles usually result, and enlarged Tonsils. (See Adenoids; "Obstructions" under Head; Tonsils; Constrictions, Fluids, Hypertrophy, Polypus, Spurs, in this section).

Odors—(See "Foul" in this section).

Olfactory Nerve—Disorders of—Loss of Smell—Anosmia—(See Smell).

Palate—(See Palate).

Passages—Nasal Passages—Disorders In—(See Catarrh, Colds, Constriction, Discharges, Inflammation, Nostrils, and the various paragraphs in this section).

Pharynx—The Naso-Pharynx—Disorders of—(See "Naso-Pharynx" in this section).

Polypus—Nasal Polypus—The ☉ afflicted in ♉; ♄ afflicted in ♉ or ♏, obstructions and growths; ♂ afflicted in ♉; an ♈ and ♉ disease, and afflictions in these signs; ♀ in ♉, ♎, □, or ♉ ♂; Subs at MCP (4C). Case—See Fig. 18B in "Astro-Diagnosis" by the Heindels. (See Hypertrophy, Inflammatory, Obstruction, Turbinated Bones, in this section; Adenoids, Polypus).

Posterior Nares—Disorders In—♄ or ♂ afflicted in ♉; afflictions in ♉; Subs at MCP (4C). (See Adenoids, Pharynx; "Naso-Pharynx" in this section).

Raynaud's Disease — Coldness and Whiteness of the Nose and Fingers— (See "Raynaud" under Fingers).

Red Nose—(See "Capillaries" in this section).

Regurgitation—Of Fluids—(See "Fluids" in this section).

Rheum In—(See Rheum).

Rhinitis—Inflammation of the Nasal Mucous Membrane—Acute Rhinitis— Coryza—Cold In the Head—♂ afflicted in ♉. (See Colds, Coryza, Inflammation, in this section; "Colds" under Head).

Rose Cold—(See "Hay Fever" in this section).

Sneezing—♅ or ☿ afflicted in ♈ or ♉, from nerve irritations and excitement; ♄ in ♈, ♉, ♎, or ♑, from chill and cold; ♄ rising at B., in evil asp. the hyleg, and also with many planets in the earthy or watery signs, are subject to a cold body, chill, to take cold easily, and to sneezing spells, and should dress warmly, and wear wool next to the skin. (See Chill; "Body" under Cold; "Causes of Colds" under Colds; "Hay Fever" in this section).

Snuffling — Snaffling — Snuffles—A ☿ disease, and with ☿ badly afflicted at B. Usually exaggerated in Infancy and Childhood.

Spurs — Elongated Projections from the Septum—Projected Turbinated Bone—♄ afflicted in ♉ or ♏, tending to obstruction of the passage; many afflictions in fixed signs, fixed signs on the angles, and many afflictions in or to ♏ especially. (See Hypertrophy, Obstruction, Polypus, in this section).

Stenosis — Of the Nares — (See Constrictions, Obstruction, in this section).

Stoppage—Caused principally by the ♄ influence, and ♄ afflicted in ♈, ♉, or ♏. (See Catarrh, Colds, Constrictions, Polypus, Rhinitis, Spurs, in this section; Stenosis, Strictures, Stoppages).

Stricture—Of the Nares, and Nasal Passage—(See Constrictions, Stoppage, in this section).

Throat—All Inflammations In the Throat and Naso-Pharynx—♂ afflicted in ♉. (See Throat, Tonsils).

Turbinated Bones—Swelling and Inflammation of — Projection of — (See "Spurs" in this section).

Ulcers—Venereal Ulcers In the Nose— ♂ afflicted in ♏. (See Ulcers, Venereal).

Venereal Ulcers—In the Nose—(See "Ulcers" in this section).

Vicarious Menstruation — Thru the Nose—(See "Vicarious" under Menses).

Whiteness and Coldness—Of the Nose —(See "Raynaud" in this section).

Wounds To—(See "Accidents' in this section).

NOTABLE PEOPLE—Death of—(See "Great Men", "The Great", under Great; "Death" under Famous, Kings, Nobles, Princes, Rulers, etc.).

NOTIONS—Conceptions—Ideas—Intentions—Opinions, etc.—

Chaotic Notions—Chaotic and Fanciful—♅ afflicted in ♊; ☿ affl. in ♒, fanciful notions should be guarded against. (See Chaotic, Dress, Fancies, Food, Ideas).

Impractical Notions—Notions Which Outrage Common Sense—Ψ afflicted in ♈. (See Confusion, Erratic, Ideals, Ideas, Impractical; "Bad" under Judgment).

Wrong Notions — In General — ☿ afflicted by the ☽ or ♃ at B., and by dir. (See Delusions, Expense, Imaginations, Improvident, Impulses, Opinions, Purposes, Recklessness, etc.).

NOTORIETY—Of the Passions—Exposure of the Passions—Exhibitionism— (See "Sex Organs" under Exhibition; "Notoriety" under Passion).

NOTORIOUS DEATH—(See "Notorious" under Death).

NOURISHMENT—(See Absorption, Assimilation, Digestion, Nutrition).

NOVELTIES—Novelty—

Fond of Novelties—The ☽ ascending at B., fond of novelties, and roaming about.

Many Novelties — Strikes Out Many Novelties—♅ strong at B., ascending, and well-dignified. (See Eccentric, Genius; "Inventive" under Learning; "Influence Of" under Uranus).

NOXIOUS—Poisonous—Harmful — Destructive—Obnoxious—Mephitic— Moonlight and Night Air are noxious. Also cold and dryness are noxious and destructive. (See "Obnoxious" under Air; Cold, Dryness, Epidemics, Foul, Gases, Malaria, Miasma; "Moonlight" under Moon; Obnoxious, Pestilence, Poisonous, Putrefaction, Stagnant, Venomous, Vermin, etc.).

Noxious Growths—(See Growths).

NUCLEUS — Nucleolations — Nuclei — Neucleolus — The Nucleus of Cells is ruled and supported by the ☉ influence. Neucleolations are the work of ♄ and the ♋ sign. (See "Nucleus" under Cells; Protoplasm).

NUMBNESS—Tingling of a Nerve— Lack of Feeling In a Part—Caused by an afflicted ♄ in the sign ruling the part, or in a sign in □ or 8; ♄ ♂ or ill-asp. ☿; also caused sometimes by ♅, and ♅ ♂ ☿ in the sign ruling the part. This is generally due to pressure upon a nerve, and the spine and vertebrae should be relieved of subluxations. Also caused by poor circulation, due to the cold, restraining and suppressing influence of ♄, and ♄ ♂ ☿, ♃, or ♀ tends to considerable numbness, and disturbance in the part ruled by the sign so occupied. (See Analgesia; "Poor Circulation" under Circulation; "Raynaud's Disease" under Fingers; Paraesthesia, Tingling).

Arms—Numbness In—♄ in ♊, ♂ ♃ or ♀; ♄ afflicted in common signs; ♃ in ♊ 8 ♄; ♅ afflicted in ♊, as ♅ in any sign, if afflicted, tends to a numbness and peculiar prickling sensation in the part ruled by the sign.

Legs—Numbness In—(See "Cold and Numb", "Numbness", under Legs). Saturn in the signs which rule the Legs, as in ♐, ♑, ♒, or ♓, tends to a coldness of the legs, which often is accompanied by numbness, slow and disturbed circulation, lack of sensation in the lower limbs, etc. (See "Body", "Temperament", under Cold).

NURSES—Trained Nurses—Practical Nurses—The ☉ in ♍, or ♍ on the Asc., is not as favorable for a Nurse, as ♍ is too negative, susceptible, and takes on the diseases of others. (See Virgo).

Successful As a Nurse—Fortunate In the Care of the Sick—The ☉ well-aspected in ♍; the ☽ ruler of the horoscope, or ☽ well-aspected in the 10th H.; influences in ♍, the sign of health, or in the 6th H., the house of health, or in the 12th H., the house of Confinement, Asylums, Hospitals, Prisons, etc.; the 6th H. well-aspected at B.; ♃ or ♀ well-aspected in the 6th or 12th H., and especially when in ♓, the home sign of ♃, and the exalted sign of ♀; ♃ well-aspected in ♓ in the 10th H.; ♂ well-aspected in ♍; common signs on angles. For a Nurse to be compatible with the patient, the places of the malefics in her nativity should not fall in the 6th H. of the patient, or her vibrations and magnetism would tend to injure, worry, and weaken the patient. This is also true of the Healer and patient. The same influences which are good for the work of a Healer, Physician, Midwife, etc., may also be good for Nursing and the care of the sick. (See "Compatibility", and the various paragraphs under Healers; Hospitals, Midwives, Obstetricians).

NURSING—The Nursing of Infants— (See Breasts; "Nursing" under Children; Milk, Nipples, Weaning).

NUTRITION—Nutriment—Nurture— Nourishment—Sustenance—Nutritive— Nurturing—Alimentation, etc.—The ☽ is nurturing, and nourishment and alimentation are ruled largely by the ☽ and the ♋ sign. The influences of Ψ, ♃, and ♀ are also nutritive, and are concerned with the nourishment, sustenance, conservation, preservation, and the aphetic processes in the body. The functions of growth and nutrition are ruled by ♀ and ♅. Venus rules growth and nutrition until puberty and adolescence, and then the ♅ influence takes charge of growth and assimilation. The Kidneys, being under the rule of ♀, tend to play an important part in the nutrition of the body, as well as to eliminate wastes and poisons. Physiologically ♂ acts thru the demands of sustenance and evolution. Heat and moisture are nutritive. The Venus Group of Planets are nutritive. Fermentation, which is produced by heat and moisture, plays and important part in nutrition and alimentation. Venus rules the fermentative, or nutritive process, and also the distillatory processes in the body. Molecular Nutrition is under the special rule of ♃. (See Alimentary, Assimilation, Conservation, Diet, Digestion, Distillation, Eating, Fermentation, Food, Growth, Heat, Jupiter, Moisture, Neptune, Pituitary, Preservation, Processes, Venus, Zymosis, etc.). The following are Diseases and Disorders of Nutrition, and conditions which tend to disturb Nutrition. See these subjects in the alphabetical arrangement when not considered here—

Absorption—Disorders of—(See Absorption).

Alimentary Tract—Alimentation—Disorders of—(See Alimentary).

Alteratives—Drugs which change the Process of Nutrition—(See Alterative).

Assimilation—Disorders of—(See Assimilation; "Malnutrition" in this section).

Atrophy; Blood Disorders—From Improper or Excessive Nutrition—(See "Poor", "Thin", under Blood; "Impure Blood" under Impure).

Cachexia—A Depraved Condition of Nutrition—(See Cachexia; "Malnutrition" in this section).

Defective Nutrition—Dystrophia—Faulty—Imperfect—(See "Imperfect" under Assimilation; "Malnutrition", and the various paragraphs in this section).

Diet—Ailments from Improper Diet—(See Diet).

Digestion—Disorders of—(See Digestion, Indigestion).

Eating—Excesses In—Fast Eating—(See Eating).

Emaciation; Embryo Not Nourished—(See "Nourishment" under Foetus).

Faulty Nourishment—(See "Defective" in this section).

Food—(See "Indigestible Food" and the various paragraphs under Food).

Growth and Nutrition—(See Abnormal, Arrested, Increase, and the various paragraphs under Growth).

Illness—From Want of Proper Nutrition—The ☉ afflicted in ♍; ♄ afflicted in the 6th H. (See Ailments, Evil Diet, under Diet; Meat, Starches, Sugar, Sweets, Unnatural, Wrong, under Food).

Imperfect Nutrition—(See Defective, Illness, in this section).

Incapable of Nurture—Dies Immediately After Birth—Either the ☉ or ☽ in an angle in ☌ a malefic, and a malefic equally distant from the ☉ or ☽, and no benefic configurated with the ☉ or ☽, and the rulers posited in a place ruled by the malefics, the child then born will not be susceptible to nurture, and will immediately die. The ☉ or ☽ in an angle, and the malefics be succedent to the Lights, or in ☍, or with one malefic succedent, and the other in ☍ to the ☉ or ☽, and with no good aspects from ♃ or ♀, then no duration of life is allotted. All the Significators of life afflicted, as the ☉, ☽, Asc., and lord of the Asc., and with no assistance from benefics. The ☽ besieged between ♄ and ♂, or between ♅ and ♂, and the hyleg severely afflicted by malefics. Uranus, ♄, or ♂ ☌ ☊ in the 4th H., and the hyleg afflicted also by malefics. (See "Imperfect" under Assimilation; Emaciation; "Death Soon After Birth" under Infancy; "Malnutrition" in this section).

Indigestion; Infants—Not Capable of Nurture—(See "Incapable" in this section).

Lack of Nutrition—Illness from Lack of Proper Nourishment and Assimilation—(See "Imperfect" under Assimilation; Atrophy, Famine, Neglect, Poverty, Starvation; "Illness" in this section).

Malnutrition—Mal-Assimilation—Starved Condition of the Body—Imperfect Assimilation—Afflictions in ♋, ♍, or ♎; the ☉ afflicted in ♍; the ☽ in ♋ or ♍ in the 6th H., and afflicted; ♆ afflicted in ♋ or ♍; ♆ in ♋, □, or ☍ the ☉ or ♀; ♆ afflicted in the 6th H.; ♆ in ♍ and afflicting the ☉, ☽, Asc., or hyleg; ♄ or ♃ afflicted in ♍, due to over-eating, and great energy required to eliminate wastes; ♄ afflicted in ♋ or ♎; caused by ♄ through decay of the teeth; ♄ ☌ ♃ or ♀, by impeding the circulation, retention of carbonic acid, and insufficient oxygenation; ♂ in ♋, □, or ☍ ♃ or ♀, which latter governs the circulation; a ♍ disease. (See "Imperfect" under Assimilation; Atrophy, Emaciation, Tabes, Wasting; "Incapable" in this section).

Mastication—Does Not Masticate Food Sufficiently—(See "Fast Eater" under Eating).

Molecular Nutrition—Under the rule of ♃. Interferences with this function may occur when ♃ is weak and afflicted at B.

Not Susceptible To Nurture—(See "Incapable" in this section).

Nurture—Infants Incapable of—(See "Incapable" in this section).

Nutritive Process—Ruled by ♀, and ♀ weak and afflicted at B., and by dir., tends to disorders of, and especially when ♄ afflicts ♀.

Obesity; Perverted Nutrition—♅ diseases, and this planet afflicting the hyleg.

Plants—The ♀ Group of Plants are nutritive. (See "Venus Group" under Herbs).

Process—(See "Nutritive Process" in this section).

Stomach Disorders—From Improper Nutrition—(See Indigestion, Stomach).

Superfluous Nutriment—A ☉ and ♃ affliction. (See "Abnormal" under Appetite; Epicureans, Fat, Feasting; "Rich Food" under Food; Gluttony, Plethora).

Textural Nutrition—Changes In the Process of Textural Nutrition—♀ diseases.

Tissues—Nutrition of the Tissues Affected—The ☉ and ☽ acting thru the ♒ sign. (See the Introduction under Lymph).

Venus Group of Herbs—And Plants—Are nutritive. (See "Plants" in this section).

Wasting Diseases—From Imperfect Assimilation, or Disorders of Nutrition—(See Anaemia, Cachexia, Emaciation, Tabes, Wasting; "Malnutrition" in this section). For other subjects along this line, and which may have to do with Nutrition, look in the alphabetical arrangement for the subject you have in mind.

NUTS—For the various rulership of Nuts, Seeds, Plants, etc., and the Planetary influences over them, see Fruit, Herbs, Seeds, etc.

Nut Butters—Successful Makers of As a Specialty—(See "Specialties" under Healers).

NUX VOMICA — Is one of the typical Polycrest Remedies, corresponding to the ♍ sign, the sign ruled by ☿. Some Writers, therefore, class it as an Herb of ☿. The Herbs of ☿ are Nervine, and tend to calm nervous excitement. Nux Vomica, and its alkaloid, Strychnine, are, on the other hand, stimulant, supporting, tonic, and exciting, and have the action of ♂. This Writer has, therefore, taken the liberty of classing Nux Vomica as a ♂ Drug, even though it is assigned to the ♍ sign in the Polycrest classification. However, ☿ may also have some rule over Nux Vomica, as excitability and irritation are ☿ qualities, and a few drops of the Tincture of Nux Vomica given before meals excite the nerves of the stomach, increase the appetite, and aid digestion. Mercury is a variable planet, and partakes much of the nature of ♂

at times, and ☿ and ♂ can both have rulership over Nux Vomica. (See "Polycrest" under Zodiac).

NYCTALOPIA — (See "Day Blindness" under Blindness).

NYMPHOMANIA—Unbridled Passion In Women—Sexual Obsession In Women —Excessive Sexual Desire—The ☽ to the ill-asps. ♀ by dir., and the ☽ or ♀ afflicted by ♂ or ♅ at B.; ♂ Sig. ♂ or ill-asp. ♀, and especially with ♀ in ♍ and also afflicted by ♄; ♀ Sig. ♂ or ill-asp. ♂; ♀ ruler of the horoscope and afflicted by malefics. Cases—See "Nymphomania", Nos. 289 and 306, in 1001 N.N. (See Amorous, Erotic; "Morbid" under Imagination; Lascivious, Licentious, Lust; "Abnormal" under Passion; "Solitary" under Vice, etc.).

NYSTAGMUS—(See Eyeballs).

O

OBESITY—Fatness—Corpulence — Excess of Corpulence—The ☉ or ☽ in the ♋ sign tends to direct the mind to the stomach, causing over-eating or gluttony, and resulting in Obesity; the ☽ afflicted in ♋; the ☽ afflicted in ♏, an impure kind of obesity in females; the ☉ or ☽ afflicted in the first few degrees of ♒; ♃ conduces to blood changes and accumulation of fluid, either in the form of obesity or tumors; ♃ afflicted in the 6th H., from over-eating; ♃ is usually found in ♍, and afflicted by ♅ or ♄; ♃ ♂ ♅ or ♄; ♃ badly aspected by the ☉, ☽, or any of the planets except ♂; ♀ influences and an afflicted ♀ tends to, and especially brought on by bad habits, lack of exercise, sedentary habits, and gastonomical indiscretions; the fixed signs are usually prominent, except ♏; ♉ influence tends to, and with ♉ on the Asc., and ♀ as ruler, and afflicted; ♋ on the Asc., and the ☽ □ or ☍ the Asc., tends to bad results from over-eating; Subs at AT, CP, and KP (11D). (See "Abnormal" under Appetite; "Accumulation" under Blood; Corpulent; "Excesses" under Diet, Eating, Food; "Lack Of" under Exercise; Fat, Feasting, Fleshy; "Large Quantities" under Food; Gluttony, Plethora, Puffing, Sedentary, Stout, Surfeits, Tumors, etc.).

OBEYING SIGNS—Southern Signs—(See "Northern Signs" under North).

OBNOXIOUS—Offensive—Odious—Poisonous—Noxious—

Obnoxious Air—(See "Obnoxious" under Air; Noxious).

Obnoxious Creatures — Bites, Stings, Injury, or Death By—(See Adder, Bites, Reptiles, Serpents, Stings, Venomous).

Obnoxious Signs—Of the Zodiac—(See "Hurtful Signs" under Hurtful).

OBSCENE—Obscenity—Foul Mind — A Filthy Mind — Infamous — Immoral — Shameless—Lewd—♄ ill-dignified at B. tends to a foul mind; ♄ afflicted in ♋ or ♓; ♅ and ♂ afflictions involving the 5th H.; ♂ ill-dig. at B., and afflicted; ♀ Sig. □ or ☍ ♂, if a female, and often

becomes a harlot; in male nativities affliction of malefics to the ☽, and tend to coarsen the nature; afflictions in the 5th H., and in the earthy and watery signs. (See Depraved; "Sex Organs" under Exhibition; "Habits" under Filthy; Harlots, Immodest, Infamous, Knavish, Lewd, Lust; "Loose Morals" under Morals; "Notoriety Of" under Passion; Perversions; "Women" under Scandalous; Shameless, Vices, etc.).

Obscene In Speech — (See "Obscene" under Speech).

OBSCURE—Obscuration—Obscurity—

Air—(See "Obscuration" under Air).

Complexion — (See "Obscure" under Complexion).

Diseases—Obscure Diseases—Vague—Puzzling—Unclassified—Having a Psychic Rather Than a Physical Origin—♅ diseases; ♅ afflicted in ♉, obscure diseases of the neck or throat; ♅ in any sign tends to obscure diseases in the part, parts, or organs ruled by such sign; ♅ afflicted in the 6th H.; ♅ has dominion over certain vague and obscure diseases of Psychic origin; ♄ ♂ or ill-asp. ♅ tends to obscure ailments, puzzling, and difficult to explain. (See Extraordinary, Mysterious, Peculiar, Praeincipients, Pseudo, Psychic, Strange, Vague, etc.).

Marks—Moles—(See "Obscure" under Marks).

Mind — Obscure Mind — (See Chaotic, Confusion, Delusions; "Dreamy" under Dreams; Dull, Fears, Hallucinations, Ideas, Imaginations, Obsessions, Psychic, Vague, Weird, Worry, etc.).

Morbid Manifestations—Obscure Morbid Manifestations are due to the influences of ♅ and ♇, and afflictions to the ☉, ☽, ☿, Asc., M.C., and Significators by these planets; caused by ♄ and the ♑ sign influences; ♄ afflicting the ☉, ☽, Asc., M.C., or hyleg. Morbid Mental Manifestations are caused, and complicated, and made more mysterious, extraordinary, obscure and peculiar by the afflictions of ♅ and ♇, in addition to the ♄ configurations, and especially when afflicting ☿, the mental ruler. (See Dejected, Depression, Despondency, Gloom, Hope, Hypochondria; "Low Spirits" under Low; Melancholy, Morbid, Obsessions, Spirit Controls, Worry, etc.).

Obscure In Life—Dies In Obscurity— The ☽ separating from ♄ and applying to ☿, and the ☽ increasing in light; the ☉ or ☽ far below the horizon, afflicted by malefics, and no benefics angular; ♃ Sig. ☌ ♄, dies in obscurity.

OBSESSIONS—Possessed by a Demon, or An Evil Spirit—Obsessed with Fears, Hallucinations, Wrong Ideas—

Cases of Obsession—See "Obsession", No. 130 in 1001 N.N. See Fig. 16B and 10C in "Astro-Diagnosis" by the Heindels.

Demoniacal Obsession—Principally caused by ♆ and his afflictions. The ♅ afflictions also tend to, and especially when configurated with ♆, ♄, or ☿; ♆ afflicted in ♓; ♆ in ♓ in the 6th H., and afflicted; ♆ in the 6th H., afflicting the Asc. or hyleg, liable to death from obsessions; ♆ afflicted in the 1st, 3rd, 6th, 8th, 9th, 10th, or 12th H.; ♆ □ or ☍ ♅ or ♄, and ill-health by obsession; ♆ afflicted in ♈ in the 12th H.; ♆ ☌ ☽ in the 12th H.; ♆ ☌ ♄ in the 8th H., and in □ asp. to ☿; ♆ afflicted in ♍ or the opposite sign ♓; ♆ afflicted in the 1st H., tends to spirit obsession; ♆ afflicted in a water sign; ♆ ruler of the horoscope and afflicted; ♆ in ♒ in the 6th H., and afflicting the Asc. or hyleg; ♆ afflicting the hyleg, and adding his influence to that of ♄ or ♂; ♅ afflicted in the 6th H.; the ☽ or ☿ afflicted by ♆; ♓ on the Asc., and especially the 27° ♓; the Prog. ☉ to the ☌, P., □ or ☍ ♆; Subs at AT or AX. (See Darkness; "Wild" under Delirium; Dementia, Demoniac, Fears, Forebodings, Hallucinations, Horrors, Madness, Mania, Mediumship, Premonitions, Psychic, Spirit Controls, Terrors, Visions, Weird, etc.).

Fears—Obsessed With—(See "Obsessions" under Fears).

Fits of Obsession—The ☽ ☌, □, or ☍ ♄ at B., and by dir. (See Depressed, Despondent; "Low Spirits" under Low; Melancholy, Prophetic, Worry, etc.).

Medicines and Obsessions—♆ □ or ☍ ♄ at B., bad for the health through obsessions by taking medicines.

Narcotics and Obsessions—(See "Obsessions" under Narcotics).

Sexual Obsession In Women—(See Lewd, Nymphomania, Shameless).

OBSTETRICIANS—The ☽ as ruler of the horoscope tends to make good Obstetricians. (See Healers, Midwives, Nurses).

OBSTINATE—Stubborn—Resisting—

Obstinate Diseases—Stubborn Diseases—Tedious—Prolonged—(See Chronic, Consumptions, Lingering; "Diseases" under Long; Prolonged, Tedious, Wasting, etc.).

Obstinate Nature—Headstrong—Stubborn—Tenacious—Resisting—The ☉ Sig. ☌ ♂; the ☉ in the Asc. □ ♂ in the 10th; the ☉ or ☽ afflicted in ♉; ♂ afflicted in the 1st H.; ♂ affl. in ♉, ♏, ♑,

or ♒; many planets in fixed signs at B., and with fixed signs on the angles; ♉ on the Asc., the sign of "The Bull", especially obstinate in nature. (See "Fixed Signs" under Fixed; Inflexible, Rebellious).

OBSTRUCTIONS—Stoppages—Hindrances—Occlusions—Obstruction is the keynote, and the most salient characteristic of ♄. Also Cauda (☋) is of the nature of ♄, and tends to obstructions when in ☌ the ☉, ☽, Asc., M.C., or hyleg at B., and to especially obstruct and afflict the part of the body, or matters ruled by the sign ☋ is in at B. (See "Dragon's Tail" under Dragon; "Influence Of" under Saturn). Saturn tends to obstructions in the body, in the tissues, blood vessels and organs, by retaining the wastes and poisons of the system, hindering and suppressing elimination, functional activity, secretion, and by causing hardening of the tissues, crystallization, retardation, deposit of mineral wastes, and the deposit of too much Urea over the body. The good aspects of ♄ tend to obstruct when coming to the other planets. Saturn in an angle, occi. of the ☉, and ori. of the ☽, tends to obstruct. Caused by ♄ or ☿ when the dominion of death is vested in them. Signified by ♄ in ♈ when ♄ is the afflictor in the disease. Saturn in any sign tends to obstructions in the part, parts, or organs ruled by the sign so occupied, and even ♄ in his own signs ♑ and ♒ tends to afflict the knees and lower legs, and make them subject to cold, obstructions, etc. Saturn causes all diseases proceeding from obstructions in any part of the body. In this regard the influence of ♄ is normal, as it is necessary for the planetary influences to be balanced, otherwise the influence of any one planet in excess, as that of ♂, would tend to tear people apart, or bring instant death, if not opposed and balanced by ♄, ♃, and ♀. To grow old in the body here is normal, natural, and the only way to progress, as continued life in the body on Earth would be a hindrance to the evolution and progress of the Soul. Also the ☉ in the 6th H. has an obstructing influence in health matters, and invites disease; the ☉ or ☽ afflicted by ♄; the ☽ afflicted in ♍, or afflicting the hyleg therefrom. The ☽ afflicted in ♓ tends to great obstructions; the ☽ or ☿ afflicted in ♍ or ♎. Obstructions may take place in any part of the body, and go under the names of various diseases. A few of these conditions are listed as follows. See these subjects in the alphabetical arrangement when not commented upon here, as they are all caused by the obstructing work of ♄, and by his deposits, or work of suppression, retardation of function, etc.

Arms—Circulation In Obstructed—(See "Circulation" under Arms).

Arterial Circulation—Obstruction of—(See "Arterial" under Circulation).

Bile Passages—Obstruction of—(See Bile).

Bladder—Obstructions In—(See Gravel, Stone, Stricture, under Bladder).

Blindness—(See Blindness, Cataracts; "Growths" under Eyes).

Blood — Circulation of Obstructed — Oxygenation Obstructed — (See "Obstructions" under Circulation; "Non-Oxygenation" under Oxygen).

Blood Vessels Obstructed—(See Clots).

Body—Obstructions Over the Body— The ☽ in ⊓ and afflicted by the ☉ or ♂ when taken ill (Hor'y).

Bowels Obstructed — (See "Obstructions" under Bowels).

Brain—(See "Obstructions" under Brain).

Breasts — (See Adenoma; "Obstructions" under Breasts).

Breathing—(See "Obstructions" under Breathing).

Bronchial Tubes—(See "Obstructions" under Bronchial, Lungs).

Calculus—Obstruction By—(See Calculus).

Capillaries Obstructed — (See Capillaries; "Capillaries" under Lungs).

Cataracts; Circulation—(See Blood, Fluids, in this section).

Clots; Cold—The Body Obstructed By —(See the various paragraphs under Cold, Colds).

Colon — (See "Obstructions" under Colon).

Congestions—Obstructions By—(See Congestion).

Constrictions; Contractions;

Crystallization—(See Crystallization, Hardening, Petrifaction, Stone).

Death from Obstructions—♄ (or ☿ if he be of the nature of ♄) afflicting the hyleg at B., and by dir., if either hold the dominion of death; ♄ Anareta, and to the ♂ or ill-asp. his own place by dir., and especially if the direction fall in the 8th H.

Deformities; Digestion Obstructed — (See "Hindered" under Digestion).

Diseases—Arising from Obstructions —♄ diseases; ♄ in the 6th H., or afflicting the hyleg or the Asc.

Dropsy; Ducts—Obstruction of—(See the subjects under Ducts).

Ears—Obstructions In—(See "Circulation" under Ears; "Auditory", "Deafness", under Hearing).

Elimination—(See "Hindered" under Elimination).

Embolism; Excretion—(See "Obstructions" under Excretion).

Eyes Obstructed — (See Blindness, Cataracts; "Growths" under Eyes; Optic; Sight).

Fevers—Obstructions From—(See "Fever" under Heart, Liver).

Fluids Obstructed — (See "Obstructions" under Fluids, Gastric, Juices, Secretions, Spine; "Fluids" under White).

Functions— (See Hindered, Impaired, Impeded, Inhibited, Obstructed, Retarded, Slow, Stagnation, Suppressed, under Functions).

Gall Ducts Obstructed—(See Bile).

Gas — Spinal Gas Obstructed — (See Gas, Obstructed, under Spine).

Gastric Juices Obstructed — (See Digestion, Gastric, Indigestion, Juices; "Obstructions", "Stopped", under Stomach).

Generative Organs — (See "Obstructions" under Generative).

Goiter; Gout; Great Obstructions — The ☽ afflicted in ⊓. (See "Body" in this section).

Growths; Hardening; Head — (See "Obstructions" under Head).

Hearing Obstructed — (See "Ears" in this section).

Heart Obstructed—(See Blood, Fever, Obstructions, Valves, under Heart).

Hindrances; Hydronephrosis—(See "Dropsy" under Kidneys).

Ileum — (See "Obstructions" under Ileum).

Impairments; Impediments; Infarcts —(See Clots, Embolus, Infarcts, Thrombus).

Inhibitions; Interferences; Intestines —(See "Bowels" in this section).

Intussusception—(See Bowels).

Jaundice — (See "Obstructive" under Jaundice).

Judgment—The Judgment Obstructed —(See "Bad" under Judgment).

Juices Obstructed — (See "Fluids" in this section).

Kidneys Obstructed — (See "Obstructions" under Kidneys).

Legs — (See "Obstruction" under Legs).

Life Forces Obstructed — (See "Obstructed Life Forces" under Life; "Obstructed" under Nerves, Vital).

Limbs — (See "Obstructions" under Limbs).

Limitations; Liver — (See Deranged, Fever, Infirmities, Obstructions, under Liver).

Lower Limbs—Obstructions In—Circulation Obstructed — (See Blood, Obstruction In, under Legs).

Lungs — (See "Obstructions" under Breathing, Lungs; Bronchial, Consumption, Oxygen, Phthisis, Tuberculosis).

Lymph Obstructed—(See Lymph).

Menses Obstructed — (See "Obstruction" under Menses, Womb)

Mind Obstructed—(See Fears, Idiocy, Imbecile, Insanity, Obsessions; "Obstructed" under Mind; Spirit Controls, Worry, etc.).

Mucus — Obstructions By — (See Mucus; "Mucus" under Bowels, Head, Nose, Stomach, Throat).

Neck and Throat Obstructed — (See Goiter; "Obstructions" under Neck, Throat).

Nerves Obstructed—Nerve Force Obstructed—(See "Obstructed" under Nerves; "Nerves" under Pressure; "Life Forces" in this section).

Nose Obstructed—(See "Obstruction" under Nose).

Oesophagus Obstructed—(See "Stricture" under Oesophagus).

Oxygenation—Of the Blood Obstructed —(See "Non-Oxygenation" under Oxygen).

Phlegm—Obstructions By—(See the various paragraphs under Humours, Mucus, Phlegm).

Plugs; Pneumogastric Nerve—Restricted Action of—(See Pneumogastric).

Poisons and Wastes—In the Body—Obstructions Caused By—(See Deposits, Elimination, Excretion, Fevers, Filth, Gout, Hyperacidity, Impure, Inflammation, Inhibition, Minerals, Poisons, Retention, Rheumatism, Stoppages, Suppressions, Urea, Uric Acid, Wastes).

Pressure; Private Parts—(See "Obstructions" under Generative; "Diseases" under Private).

Prohibitions; Prolapse; Reason—(See "Impaired" under Reason).

Recovery Obstructed—(See Incurable; "Slow" under Recovery).

Rectum—(See "Obstructions" under Rectum).

Reins—(See "Obstructions" under Reins).

Renal Obstructions—(See Circulation, Dropsy, under Kidneys).

Respiration Obstructed—(See Interrupted, Labored, Obstructions, under Breath).

Restraints; Restrictions; Retarded; Retentions; Rheum—Obstructions By—(See Rheum).

Rheumatic Obstructions—(See Rheumatism).

Rigidity—Stiffness—(See Rigid).

Secretions Obstructed—(See Secretions).

Senses Obstructed—And Inhibited—(See Senses).

Sex Organs—(See "Obstructions" under Generative).

Slow—(See "Slow" under Motion, Speech; Slow).

Sluggish Conditions—(See Sluggish).

Smell Obstructed—(See "Loss Of" under Smell).

Speech—(See Halting, Impediment, under Speech).

Spine—(See "Obstructions" under Spine).

Stagnation; Stamina Obstructed—(See "Void Of" under Stamina).

Stammering—(See Speech).

Stiffness; Stomach—Obstructions In—(See "Inability" under Digestion; Indigestion; "Obstructions" under Stomach).

Stones—Calculi—(See Gravel, Sand, Stone).

Stoppages; Strictures; Suppressions; Throat Obstructed—(See "Neck" in this section).

Thrombus; Too Much Blood—Obstructions From—(See "Too Much" under Blood).

Trachea Obstructed—(See Trachea).

Transverse Colon—Obstructions In—(See Colon).

Tumors—Causing Obstructions—(See Abscesses, Boils, Carbuncles, Carcinoma, Growths, Swellings, Tumors).

Urea—Urates—Uric Acid—Deposit of, and Causing Obstruction—(See Deposits, Gout, Hyperacidity, Minerals, Poisons, Rheumatism; "Influence Of" under Saturn; Urates; Urea, Uric Acid, Wastes).

Ureters Obstructed—(See Ureters).

Urethra Obstructed—(See Urethra).

Urine Obstructed—(See "Obstructions" under Urine).

Venous Circulation—Obstruction of—(See "Obstruction" under Veins).

Viscera Obstructed—(See Viscera).

Vision Obstructed—(See Blindness, Cataract; "Growths", "Obstructions", under Eyes; Sight).

Walk—Obstructions To—(See Crippled, Deformities, Feet, Gait, Lameness, Legs, Locomotion, Locomotor Ataxia, Paralysis, Walk).

Wastes of System—Obstructions Caused by Deposit and Retention of—(See Deposits, Gout, Minerals, Wastes).

White Fluids Obstructed—(See "Fluids" under White).

Womb Obstructed—(See "Obstructions" under Womb). The subject of Obstructions in the Mind and Body is a large one, and the conditions too numerous to list here. Nearly all disease is caused by some obstruction, limitation, hindrance, suppression, excess, etc. For subjects along this line which may not be listed here, look in the alphabetical arrangement for the subject you have in mind.

OCCASIONAL INDISPOSITION—(See Indisposition).

OCCIDENTAL—Planets Occidental—The ☉, ☽, and planets in the Occidental Quarters of the Heavens at birth show disease, and in the Oriental Quarters indicate Acute Pains and Accidents. Malefics occi., and afflicting the ☉ or ☽, tend to cause disease. Planets are considered Occidental, in a general way, when setting in the West between the M.C. and Nadir, and Oriental when rising between the Nadir and Midheaven. The Occidental Quarters of the Heavens are those from the Nadir to the Asc., and from the M.C. to the Descendant, and the ☉ or ☽ found in these Quarters at B. are said to be Occidental. Also planets are said to be occidental when rising and setting after the ☉, and oriental when rising and setting before him. (See the lengthy Article on "Oriental" in Wilson's Dictionary of Astrology, which also deals with Occidental conditions). In Health matters, and in judging of the effects of disease, or the liability to the predisposition to disease or accidents, it is necessary for the student to understand these differences between Oriental and Occidental in order to be able to more accurately diagnose ailments, and to know the severity or mildness of the complaint, its nature, prospects, and possible outcome. Mercury rising before the ☉ tends to give a keener and better mind, but rising after the ☉, to dull the mentality. The ☽ in an Oriental Quarter at B., indicates an early marriage, and a late marriage when in an Occidental Quarter, etc. Jupiter oriental, and rising before the

⊙, or elevated above the ⊙, is more powerful in health matters than when he is occidental, or rising after the ⊙. In this book, many references are made to oriental and occidental, and such influences listed under the various diseases, and it is very important to note these causes in making a planetary study of disease, accidents, affliction, etc., as well as in matters of joy, happiness, abundance, good health, success, long life, etc. (See Elevated, Majority, Oriental, Quadrants, Quarters, Rising, Rouse, Setting).

OCCIPITAL REGION—Occiput—Ruled by the 8 Sign.

    Occipital Headache—(See Headache). See Brain, Head, Medulla, Skull.

OCCLUSION—Stopping Up of An Opening In the Body—Generally caused by ♄ influence. (See Anus, Canals, Clots, Constrictions, Contractions, Ducts, Growths, Hernia, Nipples, Nose, Obstructions, Orifices, Polypus, Stenosis; "Pylorus" under Stomach; Stricture, Tubes, Urethra, Valves, etc.).

OCCULT STUDY—Fond of—Given To—Occult Powers—♅ strong, dignified and well-aspected at B.; ♅ in the 1st, 9th, or 10th H. at B.; ♅ ☌ the ⊙ or ☿ at B. Also ♆ prominent, rising, elevated, and well-aspected, tends to give Occult, Mystical, and Spiritual Sight of a high order. (See Eccentric, Ideals, Independent, Magic, Metaphysics, Misunderstood; "Mystery" under Mysterious; Mystical, Ninth House, Reformers; "Occult Science" under Science).

OCCUPATION—The Employment or Vocation—

    Accidents In—Death or Injury In—(See Employment).

    Strange Occupational Diseases—♅ afflicted in the 6th H. (See Strange).

OCEAN—The Sea—Ocean Travel—The Salt Water—The ☽, ♆, and the ♓ Sign rule the Ocean and the Seas.

    Danger On—(See Maritime; "Danger" under Voyages).

    Fire On Ships At Sea—(See "Ships" under Fire).

    Fish—Death of In the Seas—(See Fish).

    Fortunate Upon the Ocean—(See Maritime; "Fortunate" under Seas).

    Good Time For Voyages—Bad Time For—(See Bad Time, Good Time, Long Journeys, under Journeys, Voyages).

    Misfortunes At Sea—(See Sea, Ships, Shipwreck).

    Unfortunate On the Sea—(See Sea). See Abroad, Bathings, Drowning, Events, Foreign Lands, Navigation, Sailors, Travel; "Perils by Water" under Water.

OCULAR—Pertaining to the Eyes—(See Accommodation, Blindness, Cataracts, Eyes, Nebulous, Sight).

    Ocular Defects—(See "Defects" under Eyes).

OCULUS TAURUS—Bull's South Eye—der) Headaches.

    Ocular Headaches—(See "Ocular" un-A Star in 6° 13′ ♊, and of the nature

of ♀. Men born with ♃ in ♊ near Oculus Taurus tend to be addicted to women. This star is mentioned only a few times in Astrological books, but is listed in the Tables of Stars in the various Textbooks of Astrology. Aldebaran is the North Eye of the Bull, and of the nature of ♂. (See Aldebaran, Bulls, Chances; "Addicted to Women" under Men; Stars).

ODD—Peculiar—Singular—Queer—Unusual, etc.—

    Odd Diseases—(See Extraordinary, Mysterious, Obscure, Peculiar, Psychic, Strange, Unusual).

    Odd Disposition—(See Eccentric, Fanatical, Fancies, Independent, Misunderstood, Occult, Peculiar, Recluse).

    Odd Signs—Of the Zodiac—The positive and masculine signs, as ♈, ♊, ♌, ♎, ♐, ♒. The Odd Houses also correspond to these signs, as the 1st, 3rd, 5th, 7th, 9th, and 11th H. Many planets in the Odd Signs at B. tend to give a strong will, determination, greater vitality, as a rule, and with greater power to resist and overcome disease. (See "Positive Signs" under Positive; "Masculine Signs" under Signs).

ODIC FORCE—(See Hypnotism, Magnetism; "Powers" under Psychic).

ODORS—A Scent or Smell—

    Foul Odors—(See "Sweating" under Axillae; "Foul" under Breath; Carcinoma, Corpse, Corruption, Dead, Decay, Discharges, Disintegration, Excrement, Faeces; "Fetid" under Feet, Sweat; Fetid, Foul, Gangrene, Gases, Leprosy, Noxious, Obnoxious, Offensive; "Stagnant" under Pools; Pungent, Pus, Putrid, Rottenness, Sores, Ulcers).

    Foul Vapors—(See Vapors).

    Man, Animals and Plants—Odors From—Ruled by ♆.

    Pungent Odors—Ruled by ♂. (See "Hot Acids" under Acids; Perfumes, Pungent).

OEDEMA—Edema—Oedematous Tumors—Accumulation of Serum In the Cellular Tissue—A ☽ disease, and the ☽ afflicted in watery signs. (See Accumulative; "Fluids" under Cells; Dropsy, Elephantiasis, Enlargements, Hypertrophy; "Oedema" under Lungs; Osmosis, Puffing, Resolvent, Serum, Swellings, Tissues, etc.).

OESOPHAGUS—Esophagus—Gullet—The Canal from the Pharynx to the Stomach—Ruled by the ☽ and the ♋ sign. Also under the internal rulership of 8, and is greatly influenced and affected when the ☽ is in 8. The upper part of the Oesophagus is more under the rule of 8.

    Disorders Of—♄ afflicted in 8; Subs at SP (7D), and KP.

    Obstruction Of—Stricture of—Sluggish Action of—♄ afflicted in ♋; the ☽ in ♋, □, or 8 ♄; Subs at SP.

    Stricture Of—(See "Obstruction" in this section).

OFFENDED—Offending—

    Easily Offended—♂ afflicting ☿. (See "High Strung" under High; Hyperaesthesia; "Sensitiveness" under Sensitive; "High Temper" under Temper).

Offending Humours — (See "Offending" under Humours).

Stomach Offended — (See "Raw Humours" under Indigestion).

OFFENSIVE—Peccant—Corrupt—Putrid—

Offensive Breath—(See "Foul" under Breath).

Offensive Discharges — (See "Offensive" under Discharges).

Offensive Manners — (See Disagreeable, Rough, Unpleasant, under Manners).

Offensive Odors — (See Decay, Odors, Pus, Putrid).

OFFICERS OF THE LAW — Killed by Police Officers—♂ Sig. □ or ⚺ the ☉, and also ☿ □ ♂ concurring. (See Judge, Law).

Officer Killed—(See Military).

OFFSPRING—Issue—(See Children).

OFTEN AILING—(See "Many Diseases" under Disease; "Ill-Health All Thru Life" under Ill-Health; "Much Infirmity" under Infirmity; "Much Sickness" under Sickness).

OIL—Oils—Oils of the Body—The Body Oil—Ruled largely by the ☽, ♃, and ♀. The White Fluids, or the Body Oil, are ruled by the ☽. The Oils of the body are connected with the ♍ sign, and Potassium Sulphate, the Virgo Salt. (See Fat; "Fluids" under White).

Emollients — Oils As An Emollient — (See Emollient).

Oily Face—Oily and Shining Skin—♃ gives. (See "Oily" under Face).

Oily Hair — Glossy and Shiny — (See "Glossy" under Hair).

OINTMENTS—Unguents—Ointments are principally ♄ remedies, and applied to combat the evil effects of Bruises, Injuries, Eruptions, Excoriations, Ulcers, Sores, Inflammations, Skin Diseases, etc. Treating on the basis of Antipathy, ♄ remedies are used in Ointments to combat the diseases, hurts, eruptions, and afflictions of ♂, and the remedies of ♂ in ointments to combat ♄ diseases. On the basis of Sympathy, the ♄ remedies in ointments are used to combat ♄ diseases, and ♂ remedies to combat ♂ diseases. The Oxide of Lead, a ♄ remedy, mixed with Olive Oil, is a common Lead Plaster. Also Zinc, ruled by ♅, is much used in Ointments where a mild astringent action is desired. (See Antipathy, Lead, Opposites, Sympathy, Zinc).

OLD—Mature—Old Maladies—

Old Aches—In Hips and Thighs—(See "Aches" under Hips).

Old Age—(See Old Age, the Article following this one).

Old Maladies Return—(See Return).

OLD AGE—Old People—Elderly People—Conditions Affecting the Aged—The Latter Part of Life—The conditions at the close of life, and in Old Age, are denoted by the 4th H. and its influences in the map of birth. The 4th H. is one of the Terminal Houses, along with the 8th and 12th H. (See Fourth House, Terminal). Saturn also rules Old Age, and is the Star of Old Age, and the planet which rules hoary hairs. In the Kabala, Old Age was dedicated to ♄. The 3rd Decan. of ♍ denotes Old Age, Weakness, Infirmity, Decay, and Dissolution. The ruling places situated in the West at a Solar Eclipse tend to affect the Aged, and persons about to die, for good or ill, according to the aspects and influences at B., and by Direction, Transit, or Progression. The following paragraphs give the planetary influences which affect Old Age, making it fortunate or unfortunate, and the conditions which the native is apt to meet with at the close of life.

Adult Life—(See Adults).

Aged Female Relative — Death of — (See "Female" in this section).

Aged People—Those of Frail Constitution—Death of—Caused by the ill-aspects of malefics to the ☉, ☽, Asc., M.C., or Hyleg, by dir.; the ☉ to the bad aspects ♆, ♅, ♄, or ♂ by dir. with males, or the ☽ to these bad aspects in females.

Aged Person In the Family—Death of—(See Grandparents).

Asylum—Ends Life In An Asylum or Institution — ♆ afflicted in the 4th or 12th H. (See Confinement; "Asylums" under Insanity; Prison, Twelfth House).

Aunt—Death of An Aged Aunt—(See Aunts).

Bad End — Frequently Meets with a Bad End—The ☉ Sig. □ or ⚺ ♄; ♄ or ♂ afflicted in the 4th H. (See "Bad End" under End; "Sad" in this section).

Childish—In Old Age—☿ afflicted at B., in a weak sign, and afflicted by dir., and especially by ♄ and the ☽. (See "Weak Mentality" under Mental; "Weak Mind" under Mind).

Chronic Ill-Health — In Old Age — ♄ rising at B. tends to chronic ill-health in the latter part of life; ♄ afflicting the ☉, ☽, Asc., or Hyleg at B., and by direction in old age; the ill-asps. of the ☉ or ☽ to ♄ by dir. (See "Ill-Health" in this section).

Close of Life — (See "Close of Life" under Close; Death, End, Terminal; the paragraphs in this section).

Complexion — In Old Age — (See Pimples, Ruddy, in this section).

Dangerous Illness—In Old Age—Malefics in the 4th H., and afflicted at B., and by dir.; ♅ afflicted in the 4th H.; the hyleg afflicted by malefics by dir., and with little or no help from benefics; be the ☽ in ♊, □, or ⚺ ♄ (or ☿ if he be of the nature of ♄) at the beginning of an illness, or at decumbiture, if at decumb. the ☽ shall be under the beams of the ☉, or with ♄ or ♂, there is great peril even tho the ☽ be in ☌ a benefic.

Death of Aged People — (See "Aged People" in this section).

Decrepit Old Men—(See "Men" in this section).

Dies In Old Age — (See "Long Life" under Life).

Easy Death—Natural and Peaceful Death In Old Age—Benefics in the 4th or 8th H., and no malefic influences over these houses. (See "Easy Death" under Death).

Elderly People—Ill-Health of—(See "Ill-Health" in this section; Grand-parents).

Father—The Father Lives to Old Age —(See "Long Life" under Father).

Feebleness—Decrepitude—(See Men, Senility, in this section).

Female—Death of An Aged Female— (See Aunts, Grandparents).

Fortunate Old Age—The ☉ in the 4th H., and well aspected; ♄ in ♎ or ♑, and not afflicted; ♃ or ♀ in the 4th H., and well-aspected.

Good Health—In Old Age—The ☉, ♃, ♂, or ♀ in the 4th H., and well-aspected; the 19° ♓ on the Asc. at B., but sickly in youth.

Grandparents—Sickness and Death of —(See Grandparents).

Gray Hair—(See "Gray" under Hair).

Great Age—Will Live To—Will Not Live To — (See "Long Life", "Seldom of Long Life", "Short Life" under Life).

Health—The Health Good In Old Age — Health Bad — (See "Good", "Ill-Health", in this section).

Ill-Health—Of the Aged and Elderly People—The ill-asps. of the ☉ to malefics by dir., and the ☉ hyleg, even tho they did not aspect the ☉ at B., and especially among the Aged and Feeble, or others of frail constitution; the ill-asps. of malefics to the ☉ by dir.; ♄ rising at B., ill-health or chronic troubles in old age. (See Chronic, Dangerous Illness, Incurable, Senility, in this section).

Illness—(See "Dangerous Illness" in this section).

Incurable Infirmity—♅ afflicted in the 4th H. (See Incurable).

Infirmity—Incurable Infirmity In Old Age—(See "Incurable" in this section).

Kind of Death—The nature and kind of death in old age are largely determined, and modified, by the conditions over the 4th and 8th H. at B., the lord or ruler, of these houses, and their aspects towards the end of life, and also the nature of the directions, transits, or progressions which may be affecting the hyleg. (See "Quality Of" under Death; "Death" under Kind, Nature, Quality, Species).

Many Deaths — Of the Aged — (See "Mortality" in this section).

Meets With a Bad End — (See "Bad End" in this section).

Men—Decrepit Old Men—Ruled by ♄; ♄ in the 4th H. at B., and afflicting the ☉, and also ♄ afflicting the ☉ or hyleg by dir., tend to make old men more decrepit and feeble, or to suffer with a chronic ailment, lameness, gout, rheumatism, or paralysis. (See "Chronic", "Senility", in this section).

Mind—An Uneasy Mind In Old Age— ♅ afflicted in the 4th H.

Mortality—Much Mortality Among the Aged—The evil aspects of the ☉ to the malefics ♅, ♅, ♄, or ♂ by dir., many deaths of those who are under such

aspects, and especially among those of frail constitution; ♄ Lord of the Year at the Vernal Equi., and espec. in places ruled by ♄, as those ruled by ♑ and ♒, or in places ruled by the sign in which ♄ is located; ♄ sole ruler at an eclipse of the ☉; ♂ in ♍, and ori. at the Vernal, and Lord of the Year; the ruling places situated in the West at a Solar Eclipse. (See Mortality).

Mother — (See "Long Life" under Mother).

Natural Death—(See "Easy Death" in this section).

Paralysis—In Old Age—Danger of— ♅ afflicted in the 4th H. at B. (See Paralysis).

Peaceful End to Life—Benefics well-aspected in the 4th H. at B. (See "Easy Death" in this section).

Pimples — Usually Afflicted with Pimples At Middle Life and In Old Age — A Highly Colored Complexion and Pimples—Given by ♎; ♎ on the Asc. at B., and many planets in ♎, and giving a deep red color, with pimples, but the complexion is usually clear and fair in youth. (See "Ruddy" in this section; Pimples, Ruddy).

Premature Old Age—(See Juvenility; "Senility" in this section).

Recluse—In Old Age—♆ or ♄ in the 4th H. at B., and prefers to end life in seclusion. (See Recluse).

Relative—Death of An Aged Relative —(See Aunts, Grandparents). For influences indicating that Brethren do not live to Old Age, see "Old Age" under Relatives).

Ruddy Complexion — In Old Age — ♎ gives, and ♎ on the Asc. at B., and with pimples. (See "Pimples" in this section).

Sad Old Age—Sad and Unfortunate— ♆, ♅, ♄, or ♂ in the 4th H. at B., near the lower Meridian, and afflicted; adverse afflictions of the malefics falling in the 4th H. in old age, and especially of ♄. (See Sadness).

Seclusion — Ends Life In Seclusion — (See Asylum, Recluse, in this section).

Senility — The Weakness of Old Age, or Imbecility — Senile Feebleness — Tendencies in the body to dryness, contraction, decrepitude, and immobility, are the work of ♄. Also, ♄ tends to harden the tissues and blood vessels with age, and to increase the mineral deposits over the body, and with the powers of elimination weakened. (See Feeble, Imbecility, Infirm).

Shrinkage—Of the Limbs In Old Age — Withering of — ♆ or ♄ afflicted in signs which rule the Arms or Legs. (See Shrinking, Withering).

Stout In Later Years—♃ in the 1st H., and well-aspected; ♃ in ♋ on the Asc., and afflicted. (See "Corpulent" under Middle Life; Stoutness).

Uneasy Mind — In Old Age — (See "Mind" in this section).

Unfortunate—In Old Age—(See Bad End, Sad, and the various paragraphs in this section).

Vision—Old Age Vision—(See "Presbyopia" under Sight).

Vitality Good — In Old Age — (See "Good Health" in this section; "Long Life" under Life; "Good" under Vitality).

Weakness — In Old Age — (See Ill-Health, Senility, in this section).

Will Not Live to Old Age—(See "Seldom of Long Life" under Life).

Withering—(See "Shrinkage" in this section).

Wrinkles—(See Wrinkles).

OLFACTORY — Olfaction — Olfactory Nerves—(See Smell).

OLIVE—

Olive Complexion—Olive Brown Complexion — (See Olive, Sunburnt, under Complexion).

Olive Tree — Ruled by the ☉. (See "Sun Group" under Herbs).

OMENS — Ominous — Forebodings — A Prophetic Sign—(See Forebodings).

Ominous Fevers — (See "Portentous" under Fever).

OMENTUM—A Fold of the Peritoneum —(See Peritoneum).

ONANISM — Self-Abuse — (See "Solitary Vice" under Vice).

ONE—Single—

One Child At a Birth — (See "Single Births" under Children).

One Ear — Deafness In — (See "One Ear" under Hearing).

One Eye—Loss of One Eye—(See "One Eye" under Blindness, Eyes).

One Passage — A Common Outlet to the Rectum and Bladder—(See Cloaca).

One Side of Body—Paralysis In—(See "Hemiplegia" under Infancy, Paralysis).

ONION—Allium Cepa—A Bulb of the Lily Family—The Onion is classed as an Herb of Mars in most books, due to its pungent taste and odor, stimulating and nerve-building qualities. Other Authors list it as ruled by ♄, due to the fact that it opposes the excitability of ♅ and ♂, and as a poultice is excellent to relieve the inflammation of bruises, contusions, etc. On the theory of Antipathy or Sympathy in treatment, the Onion could be ruled by either ♄ or ♂, or both, as it is both building and soothing. Saturn tends to suppress the nerves, and as a nerve builder, ♂ is the more suitable ruler of this vegetable. Onions are very stimulating, a ♂ characteristic, while ♄ depresses. An onion sandwich taken at bed time is said to purify the kidneys and liver, and to build up the nervous system. (See "Treatment" under Nerves).

OOZING — Of Fluids — Oozings — (See Dropsy, Exudations, Oedema, Osmosis, Transudations).

OPEN—

Open Countenance—(See "Open" under Face).

Resentment—Open In—(See Resentment).

Sex Organs—Open Display of—(See "Sex Organs" under Exhibition).

Sores—Open Sores—Ulcers—(See Sores, Ulcers).

OPENING—Opening Medicine—Yellow Color acts as an opening medicine, the color ruled by ☿ in the Solar Spectrum. (See Physic, Yellow).

OPENLY—Openly Scandalous—Infamous—(See Exhibitionism, Harlots, Infamous, Lewd; "Women" under Scandalous; Shameless).

OPERATIONS — Surgical Operations — Incisions—Surgical Incisions are ruled by ♂, and this planet causes Operations and Violence.

Abdominal Operations—Avoid when the ☽ is passing thru ♍, ♎, or ♏. Good times for are when the ☽ is passing thru ♐, ♑, or ♒, when the ☽ is passing down and below the vital signs. Operations for Appendicitis, or upon the Womb, or any abdominal location, when the ☽ is in ♍, ♎, or ♏, are apt to result in inflammation, infection, and often result in death. (See "Appendicitis" under Appendix; "Operations" under Womb).

Amputations—Danger From—Danger of Death By—♂ in ♉ or ♏ and afflicting the hyleg; ♂ in ♉ near Caput Algol, or in ♉ aspect in ♏, and at the same time in □ or ☌ the ☉ or ☽, a dangerous time to operate, and especially if the radical map also shows this position of ♂; the ☽ under. the Sun's beams, and opposed by ♂, is considered a dangerous, or fatal time for amputations, and brings danger in the loss of a member at such a time. (See "Rules" in this section).

Death by Operations—Danger of—The ☉ to the ☌ or ill-asp. ♂ by dir.; ♂ in ♉ or ♏ and afflicting the hyleg; ♂ ori. in ♉ or ♏, □ or ☌ the ☉ at B., or ♂ occi. in ♉ or ♏, □, or ☌ the ☽ at B.; death may result if the ☽ is afflicted and passing thru the sign ruling the part to be operated upon, and also if the ☽ is in the same sign as at birth.

Eyes—Operations Upon—(See "Operations" under Eyes).

Hemorrhage—Greater Hemorrhage from An Operation—(See "Operations" under Hemorrhage).

Immediate Causes—For An Operation —♂ influence and affliction is usually the immediate cause for an operation, and resulting either from inflammation, infections, or an accident. Caused by the ☉ or ♂, which are the positive, electric, and heat-producing planets; caused by the evil directions, transits, or progressed positions of ♂ to the ☉ or ☽; the ☉ to the ☌ or ill-asp. ♂ by dir.; ♂ □ or ☌ the ☉ or ☽ by dir. (See "Certain" under Disease).

Liable to Operations—♂ strong at B., as in the Asc. or M.C., and afflicting the ☉ or ☽; ♂ afflicting the ☉, ☽, Asc., or hyleg by dir. tends to precipitate conditions making an operation necessary, or more likely; ♂ afflicted in the 6th H.; the ☽ in the 6th H., ☌ or □ ♂. (See "Immediate Causes" in this section).

Loss of Blood—Undesirable Elemental Spirits often are present at Operations to absorb the life force from the blood of the patient, introduce Astral infections, and prevent recovery. Every operation should be preceded with prayer to prevent the presence of Elementals, and to place an Aura of Protection about the patient.

Major Operations — Time and Rule For—(See "Rules" in this section).

Nature—The Four Operations of Nature—(See "Operations" under Nature).

Operations Dangerous—Performed when the ☉ is in the 12th H., in ♂ ♄ or ☋, and ♂ afflicted in the 6th H. at the same time. (See Death, Rules, in this section).

Ovariotomy—Rules For—(See Ovaries).

Pelvic Operations—(See "Operations" under Hips; Pelvis).

Rhythmic Operations—In the Body—(See Rhythm).

Rules for Operations—Statistics show that operations are more successfully performed when the ☽ is increasing in light, between the New and Full ☽, and heal more quickly, and are less liable to complications than when the ☽ is past the full and decreasing. Note the following Rules—

(1) Operate in the increase of the ☽ if possible.

(2) Do not operate at the exact time of the Full ☽, as the fluids are running high at this time.

(3) Never operate when the ☽ is in the same sign as at birth.

(4) Never operate upon that part of the body ruled by the sign thru which the ☽ is passing at the time, but wait a day or two until the ☽ passes into the next sign below, and especially if the ☽ be in ♂, □, or ☍ ♅, ♅, ♄, or ♂ at the time. This rule should be especially followed in major operations. Ptolemy says, "Pierce not with iron that part of the body which may be governed by the sign actually occupied by the Moon".

(5) Do not operate when the ☽ is applying closely to the □ or ☍ the ☉, ♄, or ♂.

(6) Let the ☽ be increasing in light, and in ⚹ or △ ♃ or ♀, and not afflicted by ♂.

(7) Let the ☽ be in a fixed sign, but not in the sign ruling the part to be operated upon, and such sign of the ☽ also not on the Asc.

(8) Do not operate when the ☽ is applying to any aspect of ♂, as such tends to danger of inflammation and complications after the operation.

(9) Avoid operation when the ☉ is in the sign ruling the part upon which the operation is to be performed.

(10) Never operate when the ☽ is combust, or within 17° of the ☉, and with the ☽ ☍ ♂ at the same time.

(11) The ☽ should be free from all manner of impediment.

(12) ♃, ♀, and the ruler of the Asc. should be in the Asc. or in the M.C., if possible, and free from ♂ affliction.

(13) Fortify the Sign ruling the part of the body to be operated upon.

(14) A ♂ hour is evil for surgical operations.

(15) Do not cut a nerve when ☿ is afflicted. (See Amputations, Death, and the various paragraphs in this section).

Surgeons—(See Surgeons).

Successful Operations—(See "Rules" in this section).

Times for Operations—(See "Rules" in this section).

Undergoes An Operation—(See Immediate Causes, Liable To, in this section).

Womb Operations—(See "Abdominal" in this section).

OPHIUCUS—Stars in the last part of ♏ and the first half of ♐, of evil import, and threaten disease, disgrace, ruin, sickness, every evil, and debauchery when with the ☉ or ☽ at B., or when the Lights are directed to them. The Right Knee and Leg, and the Left Hand of Ophiucus, are mentioned. (See Debauchery; "Threatened" under Disease; Disgrace).

OPHTHALMIA — (See "Conjunctivitis" under Conjunctiva; Xeroma).

OPINIONS—Views—Notions—

Distorted Opinions — Wrong Notions In General—Wrong Opinions—(See Anarchists, Confused, Eccentric, Erratic, Fanatical, Ideals, Ideas; "Bad" under Judgment; Notions; "Atheistical", and the various paragraphs under Religion).

Fixed Opinions—(See "Obstinate" in this section).

Forms Bad Opinions—Of Every One— ♄ Sig. □ or ☍ ☿. (See Mistrustful, Suspicious).

Inconstant In Opinions—Constant In No Opinion—☿ ill-dignified at B.; ☿ afflicted in ♓. (See Inconstant).

Independent Opinions—(See Independent).

Obstinate In Opinions—Fixed Notions and Opinions—Born under strong ♄ influence; many planets in fixed signs at B., or fixed signs on angles. (See "Fixed Signs" under Fixed; Inflexible, Misunderstood, Obstinate, Reformers, Riotous, etc.).

Opinionated of Himself—Egotistical —(See "Egotistical" under Ego).

OPISTHOTONOS—A Spasmodic Rigidity of the Body in which the Trunk is Thrown Backward and Arched Upward —A ♅ disease and affliction; ♅ afflicted in ♌; ♅ ♂ ♂ in ♌, or in fixed signs; ♆ ♂ ♄ in ♌. (See Contractions; "Movements" under Erratic; Incoordination; "Contraction" under Muscles; Rigidity, Spasmodic, Trunk).

OPIUM—Opiates—Poppy Plant—Papaver—Ruled by ♆. (See "Neptune Group" under Herbs; Narcotics).

OPPOSITE—Opposites—Opposition—

Aspect—The Opposition Aspect—The 180° aspect (☍)—In health, and other matters, this is a very evil aspect, and is of the same nature as the □ aspect, or 90° aspect, the ☍ being a double square. When the ☽ is in ☍ the ☉ at B., as at the exact time of Full ☽, the vitality tends to be weakened. Also malefics in ☍ the ☉, ☽, Asc., or hyleg, or in ☍ to each other, tend to weaken the nativity, invite more disease, affliction, and trouble. (See Aspects).

Fond of Opposition—The ☉ Sig. in ☍. (See Obstinate, Taurus).

Opposite Sex—(See the next Article after this one).

Opposite Signs—Of the Zodiac—The Opposite Signs, as ♈ and ♎, ♉ and ♏, etc., are complementary, or supplementary signs, and both rule and effect the same parts, or organs by their reflex action, and there is great sympathy between opposite signs, especially in health matters. Planets in ♏ not only affect the sex organs and nature, but also the throat, and vice versa. There is Polarity and affinity between opposite signs. These signs are 180° apart, and planets in them at B. are in ☍ aspect, if within orb of the aspect. Many planets in opposite signs at B., and in the signs which are in □ to each other, indicate weakened vitality, a more difficult fate, and many troubles and vicissitudes to be overcome. (See Kinetic; "Aspect", "Planetary Opposites", in this section).

Planetary Opposites—Planets ruling opposite signs oppose each other in their action. Mars, ruler of ♈, opposes ♀, the ruler of ♎. Saturn, ruler of ♒, opposes the ☉, the ruler of ♌. The remedies of the ☉ will cure the diseases caused by ♄, and on the theory of Antipathy. Jupiter, the ruler of ♐ and ♓, opposes ☿, the ruler of □ and ♏, the opposite signs, and ♃ remedies tend to offset and heal the diseases of ☿, etc. Mars is strong in ♈, and ♄ has his exaltation in ♎, the opposite sign, and also ♄ has his fall in ♈, and the remedies of ♂ tend to bring cure and relief to ♄ diseases, and the diseases and afflictions of ♂ are relieved by ♄ remedies. By observing this rule of Opposites, the student can soon quickly learn how to analyze and treat disease Astrologically and scientifically. In treating disease by sympathy, a ♄ remedy is used to relieve a ♄ disease, and a ♂ remedy to alleviate a ♂ disease, and this is the theory of Homeopathy. The Planetary Opposites are as follows—The ☉, ruler of ♌, opposes ♄, ruler of ♒. The ☽, ruler of ♋, opposes ♄, ruler of ♑. Mars, ruler of ♈ and ♏, opposes ♀, ruler of ♉ and ♎. Saturn, ruler of ♑ and ♒, opposes the ☉ and ☽, rulers of ♋ and ♌. Jupiter, ruler of ♐ and ♓, opposes ☿, ruler of □ and ♏. Venus, ruler of ♉ and ♎, opposes ♂, ruler of the opposite signs ♏ and ♈. Mercury, ruler of □ and ♏, opposes ♃, ruler of ♐ and ♓. (See Antipathy, Aspects, Chemical, Complications; "Allopathy" under Healers; Herbs, Homeopathy; "Disease" under Mild; Minimizing, Signature, Sympathy, Treatment).

OPPOSITE SEX—The Relations of the Opposite Sex and Their Dealings with Each Other—

Addicted to Women—(See Love Affairs, Marriage; "Addicted To", "Fascinating", under Men; Passion, Sex).

Aversions—To the Opposite Sex—Indifferent To—(See Apathy, Aversions, Bachelors, Celibacy, Deviations, Indifferent; "Aversion" under Marriage; "Free From" under Passion; Perversions).

Health Suffers—Through the Opposite Sex—Energies Wasted On the Opposite Sex—♂ diseases; ♂ ☌ or ill-asp. the ☽ or ♀; lord of the 6th in the 5th or 7th H. (See Amorous; "Energies Wasted" under Love Affairs; "Health Injured" under Lust, Men; "Passional Excesses" under Passion; Venereal).

OPPRESSED—Oppression—♄ influence, and ♄ in any sign tends to oppression, suppression, and affliction to the part ruled by the sign he is in at birth. (See Depressed; "Oppression" under Heart; "Oppressed" under Lungs; Saturn, Suppression).

OPTIC—Pertaining to Vision and Its Organs, the Eyes—

Decay of Optic Nerve—Atrophy of—Crystallization of—Hardening of—Inhibition of—Weakness of—Sight Destroyed or Dimmed By—The ☽ or Asc. in Nebulous Parts at B., and afflicted by ♄; the ☉ and ♅ in angles at B., and the ☉ afflicted by ♅, tends to weakness of the optic nerve; ♅ in the Asc. at B., near Nebulous Spots, and afflicted by the ☉, ☽, or ♃, tends to some affection of this nerve; Subs at MCP (3, 4C). (See Blindness; "Crystallization" under Eyes; Nebulous, Retina, Sight).

Optic Nerves—Ruled by ☿ and the ♈ sign. Also ruled and affected by ♅ when in ♈. Also strongly influenced by ♅.

OPTIMISM—Optimistic—Hopeful—Cheerfulness—People who are optimistic, cheerful, and hopeful, who have developed an inner vision of power, and who avoid worry, have better health, and avoid loss of nerve and vital force, while the pessimistic, negative, despondent, worrisome, melancholic Saturn person, full of fear, is apt to weaken, become a chronic sufferer, and die an earlier death. The following influences tend to Optimism and Good Health. The ☉ and ☽ well-aspected by ♃, and with ♃ in one of his own signs, and favorably aspected; the ☉ and ♂ strong and well-aspected at B., and especially when in ♈ or ♌; ♃ is considered the planet of optimism and hope, and this planet when in the Asc. or M.C. at B., and in favorable aspect to the ☉, ☽, ♀, or ☿, tends to optimism; ♀ alone does not tend to optimism as much as she does to resignation and contentment in life, when strong and well-aspected at B. However, ♀ in the 10th H. at B., and favorably aspected, tends to optimism, cheerfulness, and success in life, which favors better health. Mercury in the 3rd H., and well-aspected by the ☽, ♃, and ♀, tends to hopefulness, a cheerful and optimistic spirit; ☿ progressed, and to the ⚹ or △ ♂, favors an optimistic and enthusiastic state of mind for the time. (See Cheerfulness, Contentment; "Resigned" under Fate; Happiness, Hope, Joy; "Peace of Mind" under Mind; "Sanguine Temperament" under Sanguine).

Optimism Destroyed—A Pessimistic State of Mind—Fears—Doubts—Gloomy State of Mind—Saturn strong at B., rising in the Asc. or M.C., and afflicting the ☉, ☽, ☿, Asc., or Hyleg, tends to destroy hopefulness and optimism, and to bring grief, sorrow, sadness, gravity, a less hopeful outlook upon life, and to invite mental depression, ill-health, chronic diseases, loss of nerve and vital force, and with more of a desire for seclusion, separateness, and to lead a solitary life. Also ♆ is called the planet of Doubt and Fear. (See Doubts, Gloom; "Hopes Cut Off" under Hope; "Low Spirits" under Low; Melancholy, Misanthropic, Miserable, Miserly, Pessimistic, Recluse, Secretive, Selfishness, Unhappy, Worry, Wretched, etc.).

ORANGE COLOR—Saffron—This Color in the Solar Spectrum is ruled by the ☉. Orange Color tends to sharpen the appetite, and rooms papered with Orange tend to increase the appetite, and stimulate the forces of the body to better action, as Orange color is pregnant with the vital Sun forces. Gold, the orange-colored metal, is also ruled by the ☉. (See "Planets and Color" under Colors; "Saffron" under Complexion; Gold, Saffron).

Orange Fruit—Citrus Aurantium—The Gold-Colored Fruit or Berry—Ruled by the ☉. The juice of the Sun-kissed Orange contains the vital forces of the ☉, and is health-restoring, nerve building, a purifier and eliminator of the poisons, wastes, and over-acidity of the body. (See "Sun Group" under Herbs).

ORATOR—Oratorical Ability—A Good Voice—No Stammer or Defect of Speech—(See Eloquent, Fluency, under Speech; "Gifted" under Voice).

ORBS OF PLANETS—The planets in forming aspects with each other are said to be within orb of the aspect, and to cause the aspect to act, if within a certain number of degrees of the exact aspect. The Orbs of the planets are as follows: The ☉—17°; ☽—12°, 30'; ♆—8°; ♅—8°; ♄—10°; ♃—12°; ♂—7° 30'; ♀—8°; ☿—7°. Example—The orb of the ☉ plus the orb of the ☽ are equal to 29° 30'. One-half of this is 14° 45', the distance on either side of the exact aspect. The ☉ and ☽ to be in △ aspect each other at B. must be within the orb of 14°. The ☉ in 4° ♌, and the ☽ in 18° ♐ would still be within the orb of the △ aspect, and fortunate for good health. The smaller orbs of the other planets make the range of the aspects smaller. The student should study carefully the subject of Orbs in the Textbooks and Dictionaries of Astrology, and how to calculate aspects. (See Aspects, Reaction).

ORDINARY—(See "Ordinary" under Complexion, Death).

ORGANIC—Pertaining To, Or Having Organs—The Physical Body—Structural—

Organic Constitution—The ☉ is the chief index of the Organic Constitution. Also the Asc. rules largely over, and determines the nature and quality of the physical constitution. (See Constitution, First House, Structural).

Organic Decay—(See Decay).

Organic Defects—Those inherent in the body, and congenital. Caused by the ☉ afflicted in signs, and also by prenatal conditions. The ☽ rules Ac-

quired Defects. (See Acquired, Congenital, Defects, Heredity, Structural).

Organic Development—The ☽ shows the quality of Organic Development. (See "First Quarter" under Moon).

Organic Diseases—Constitutional Diseases—Structural Diseases—Inherent—Hereditary—Innate—Organic diseases are due to afflictions to the Signs of the Zodiac, while Functional Disorders are caused by afflictions to the Planets. The ☉ is the chief index of the organic constitution, and to determine organic diseases, note the nature of planets afflicting the ☉, and the signs they occupy, and the sign and house the ☉ is in at B. Organic diseases are denoted by conditions in the radical map, and by the afflictions to the ☉. The organic elements of the body, and the organic resistance against disease, are largely ruled by the sign on the Asc. at birth. Organic diseases are those which take a deeper hold upon the constitution, and tend to be chronic, slow, tedious, or fatal. The nature of structural and functional disorders can be inferred from the combination of the sign, planet, house and aspects of the ☉, ☽, and other planets. The Organs of the body are ruled by the different Signs, and a planet, or planets, in each sign will definitely affect the organs, and part, ruled by such sign. Also the position of the ☉ in the houses plays some part in the development of an organic disease, and whether the ☉ is rising, elevated, above, or below the horizon at B., and according to the degree of the power of the ☉ in the map of birth. The ☉ below the horizon at B., between the middle of the 6th H., and the middle of the 1st H., tends to a weakening of the constitution and vital powers, and if much afflicted to bring the danger of serious constitutional and organic diseases. The ☉ □ or ☍ the Asc. tends to organic diseases. Organic diseases which tend to mental disorders are indicated by the ☽ and Asc. (See "Organic" under Mind). The following influences are some of the principle causes of organic diseases. The ☉ in each sign, from ♈ on around to ♓, tends to organic diseases, and structural defects in those parts which are under the special rule of the ☉. Thus the ☉ in ♈ would tend to affect the Brain and Eyes; the ☉ afflicted in ♉, organic defects of the throat and neck; the ☉ afflicted in ♊, organic defects and weakness of the lungs; the ☉ afflicted in ♌, organic weakness of the heart, etc., and on around thru the Signs. Afflictions in the Fixed Signs tend to organic diseases. (See "Fixed Signs" under Fixed). The evil aspects between the ☉ and ☽ tend to disturbances of the organic functions ruled by the ☽. (For a list of Constitutional and Organic Diseases see "Constitutional Diseases" under Constitution; Structural; "Diseases of the Sun" under Sun).

Organic Force—(See Force).

Organic Functions—(See "Organic under Functions).

Organic Headaches—(See Headaches).

Organic Power—Given by the fire signs on the Asc. at B. (See "Fire Signs" under Fire).

Organic Resistance—The ☉ or ♂ ✳ or △ the Asc. (See "Abundance of Health" under Health; Immunity, Resistance; "Body" under Strong; "Good" under Vitality).

Organic Weakness — Structural Defects—Afflictions to the ☉ at B., and usually in the part or organ ruled by the sign the ☉ is in; the ☉ or ☽ in the 6th H., and afflicted by malefics. (See Congenital, Heredity; "Ill-Health All Thru Life" under Ill-Health; Organs; "Low" under Vitality; "Weak Body" under Weak).

ORGANS — Organs of the Body — The Organism—Members of the Body—In a general way the ☉ rules the structural organization of the organs of the body, and the organic functions are ruled by the ☽. The ☉ in the different signs tends to organic and structural diseases of the part, or organs, ruled by the sign the ☉ is in at B. Also the Organs are ruled by the different Signs, and a planet, or planets, in each sign will definitely affect only certain parts of an Organ. Thus ♈ rules the head and face, and the ☉ in ♈ affects the Brain and Eyes, and tends to organic Brain trouble. The ☽ in ♈ affects the Glands and Eyes. Venus in ♈, the Skin and Complexion. Jupiter in ♈, the Arteries and Right Ear. Saturn in ♈, the Skull, Teeth, and Left Ear (some Authorities say the Right Ear). Uranus in ♈, the Membranes of the Brain and the Pituitary Body. Neptune in ♈, the Optic Nerve and the Pineal Gland, etc. The various Organs of the body, and the planetary influences relating to them, and the Diseases of Organs, are listed alphabetically in this book, and only the general conditions tending to affect the Organs will be listed in this Article. Also see the Articles on Body, Constitution; "Left Side" under Left; Lower, Members, Middle, Parts; "Right Side" under Right; Upper. Also there are subjects which may include and deal with Parts containing several Organs, such as Abdomen, Chest, Head, Thorax, Trunk, etc. The following subjects have to do with the Organs of the Body—

Ablation of Organs — (See Remote, Removal, Suppression; "Ablation" under Tonsils).

Affected—The Organs affected in disease are denoted by the Sign occupied by the afflicting planet. The House position of the afflicting planet shows which part of the organ is affected, and whether on the right or left side of the body, according to the sex of the native. (See "Left Side" under Left; "Disease" under Members; Navamsa; "Right Side" under Right).

Atrophy of Organs—(See Atrophy).

Birth—Organs Afflicted from Birth— (See Birth, Blindness, Congenital, Crippled, Cyclops, Deafness, Deformities, Distortions, Dumb, Forearm, Frog Child, Hearing, Hermaphrodites, Idiocy, Lameness, Limitations, Maimed, Missing, Monsters, Mutes, Prenatal

Epoch, Twelfth House; "United" under Twins; Virile, etc.).

Bulky Organs—(See "Organs" under Enlarged; "Over-Developed" in this section).

Chest—Organs of, and Afflictions To —(See the subjects under Chest).

Cold Organs—♄ rules Cold, and the Organ, or Organs, ruled by the sign in which ♄ is posited at B., tend to be cold, and more subject to disease, poor circulation in, etc., and especially if it is a weak sign for ♄, and ♄ is badly afflicted by the ☉, ☽, or malefics. (See Cold, Saturn).

Compression of Organs—(See Compressed).

Conformity of Members—(See Conformity, Harmony, Well-Proportioned).

Coordinated Action—Of Organs—(See Coordination, Incoordination).

Deficient Development—Of the Organism—(See Cretinism, Deficient, Development, Diminished, Undersized, Undeveloped).

Degeneration Of—(See Decay, Degeneration).

Development Of—(See Cretinism, Development, Diminished, Enlarged, Growth; "Organic Development" under Organic; Overgrowth, Undersized, Undeveloped).

Digestion—Organs of—(See "Organs" under Digestion).

Diminished—In Size—(See "Body" under Diminished; "Arrested" under Growth; Undersized, Undeveloped).

Displacement—Of Organs—(See "Organs" under Dislocations; Displacements).

Elimination—Organs of—(See Elimination).

Enlarged Organs—(See "Organs" under Enlarged; "Over-Developed" in this section).

Erratic Action—Of Organs—Caused by ♅. (See Erratic, Spasmodic).

Excretion—Organs of—(See Excretion).

External Organs—(See "External" under Genitals).

Functions—Of Organs—(See Functions).

Generative Organs—External and Internal—(See External, Internal, under Generative; "External" under Genitals; Ovaries, Reproductive, Sex, Womb).

Glandular Organs — (See Glands, Secretion).

Hardening Of — (See Crystallization, Hardening, Sclerosis).

Head—Organs of—(See "Organs" under Head).

Heart—The Heart On the Right Side —(See "Right Side" under Heart).

Ill-Placed Organs — (See "Displacement" in this section; "Right Side" under Heart; Floating, Prolapsed, under Kidneys; "Falling Of" under Womb).

Incomplete Organs — (See "Born Incomplete" under Incomplete).

Incoordination—Of Organs—(See Incoordination).

Inhibition—Of Organs—(See Inhibition, Suppression; "Ablation" in this section).

Intermittent Action—Of Organs—(See Erratic, Intermittent, Irregular, Jerky, Spasmodic).

Internal Organs—(See Internal).

Irregular Action — Of Organs — (See "Intermittent" in this section).

Kidneys — (See Floating, Prolapsed, under Kidneys).

Left Side — Of the Body — Organs of Affected—(See Left).

Lower Part of Organs—Is shown by the latter part of a Sign, or the 3rd Decanate. The upper and lower parts of an organ may be ruled by a different sign. The ♋ Sign rules the upper part of the Stomach, while ♍ rules the lower part. Gemini rules the upper lobes of the Lungs, while ♋ rules the lower lobes. The upper lobes of the Liver are ruled by ♋, while ♍ rules the lower lobes, etc. Thus, ♄ in ♊ would tend to affect the upper lobes of the Lungs, and ♄ in ♋, the lower lobes, etc. (See "Lobes" under Liver, Lungs). The upper part of an organ is shown and indicated by the early degrees of a Sign, or the first Decanate, and planets in this decan. tend to affect the upper part. The middle part of an organ is shown by the second decan., or from 10 to 20° of the sign. Thus, to judge which part of an organ is the more afflicted, or diseased by the action of a malefic, or afflicting planet, note the position of the planet in the sign. (See Decanates; "Organs" under Lower, Middle, Upper; Navamsa).

Middle Parts of Organs—(See "Lower" in this section; "Organs" under Middle).

Misshaped Organs—♅ influence; ♅ afflicted by ♄, and in the part ruled by the sign ♅ is in at B. (See Misshaped; "Development Of" in this section).

Nerve Fibres — Of Organs — ☿ rules Complaints which affect the nerve fibers of organs; also diseases of the ☿ sign ♊; caused by the afflictions of ♅ and ♓ to ☿. (See "Fibers" under Nerves).

Organic Diseases—(See Organic).

Over-Activity Of—(See Over-Active).

Over-Developed Organs — Enlarged — Bulky—♅ influence; ♅ ☌ ☉, ♂, or ♀ in airy signs; ♅ afflicted by ♄, and the organ afflicted is that ruled by the sign containing ♅; ♂ □ or ☍ the ☉ and ♀, abnormally enlarged organs according to the sign containing the ☉ and ♀. Also the overgrowth of connective tissue, or an organ, often result from ♄ affliction, and the mineral deposits of ♄. (See Development; "Organs" under Enlarged; "Abnormal" under Growth).

Over-Growth — Of Organs — (See "Over-Developed" in this section).

Parenchyma Of—(See Parenchyma).

Part of Organ Afflicted—(See Lower, Middle, Upper, in this section).

Perversion—Of the Natural Function of An Organ—(See "Perversion" under Functions; Perversions).

Polarity of Changed—(See Polarity).

Prolapsus of Organs—(See Prolapse; "Ill-Placed" in this section).

Right Side—Of the Body—Organs of Affected—(See Right).

Rulership of Organs — Each Sign of the Zodiac rules over a different Organ, or part of the body, and also each of the Planets rules one or more organs. A Sign of the Zodiac may rule an organ as a whole, yet the different parts of an organ may be ruled by different Signs, as explained in the paragraph on "Lower Part Of" in this Article. Also the Decanate and Navamsa divisions of a sign indicate what part of an organ may be afflicted. (See Decanates, Navamsa; also see "Lower Part" in this section). The Head, as a whole, is ruled by the ♈ Sign, but the Nose is ruled by ♏. The ☉ and ♌ rule the Heart, yet the various forms of disease which attack the heart may be caused by the afflictions of other planets when in ♌, and especially the malefics in ♌. The different parts of the heart, as the auricles, ventricles, endocardium, pericardium, etc., and how to know which part of the heart is afflicted, is explained in the Article on Navamsa. The ☉ and the ♌ Sign also rule the Spine, taken as a whole, but the Spinal Canal is ruled by ♅, and the rulerships of the different parts of the Spine need to be studied carefully to diagnose Spinal Disorders. (See Spine). For the rulerships of the various organs of the body, see the Articles on each of the Planets, as Sun, Moon, Neptune, etc. Also see each of the 12 Signs, as Aries, Taurus, Gemini, etc. Also look in the alphabetical arrangement for each of the Organs of the body, as Brain, Ears, Eyes, Heart, Larynx, Liver, Lungs, Nose, Spleen, etc. (See "External Rulership" under Signs; the Introduction to this Article).

Rupture of Organs — (See "Accelerated" under Motion; Rupture).

Secretory Organs — (See Glands, Secretions).

Sensitive Organs—(See "Organs" under Sensitive).

Shrinkage Of—(See Shrinkage).

Spasmodic Action — Of Organs — (See "Organs" under Spasmodic).

Suppression—Of Organs—(See "Ablation" in this section).

Undersized Organs — Undeveloped — (See Atrophy, Diminished, in this section).

Upper Parts of Organs—(See "Lower" in this section; "Organs" under Upper).

Vital Organs — The Internal Organs, such as Bowels, Brain, Heart, Liver, Lungs, Stomach, etc.—(See these subjects).

Weak Organs—Weakened—♄ in any sign tends to weaken, and make more liable to disease, the part ruled by the sign he is in at B., and the sign so occupied is usually considered the most vulnerable part of the organism, or to cause death eventually thru disease and breakdown of the organ, organs, or parts, ruled by such sign. Thus ♄ afflicted in ♌ usually brings death by heart trouble; ♄ afflicted in ♎, by kidney disorder, etc., and especially if ♄ holds the dominion of death, and otherwise afflicts the ☉, ☽, Asc., or Hyleg. (See Saturn Diseases and Afflictions under Saturn).

ORIENTAL — Planets Oriental — The more oriental and angular a planet is at B., whether benefic or malefic, the more powerful will be its effects for good or ill. The ☉ and ☽ are oriental from the 1st to 10th H., and from the 7th to 4th House, and when in these Quarters at B. tend to have different effects in health matters. Planets rising between midnight and noon are considered oriental, and occidental when setting between noon and midnight. Planets in the Oriental Quarters at B. indicate Acute Pains and Accidents, and when in the Occidental Quarters tend to Disease. Planets are also said to be oriental when rising and setting before the ☉. Malefics ori., and afflicting the ☉ or ☽, tend to cause Blemishes. (See Benefics, Blemishes; "Total Blindness" under Blindness; Fits, Lunacy, Malefics, Occidental). The oriental influences of the planets are listed and mentioned many times in this book, under the different diseases and condtions, and the student should make a careful study of this subject in the Textbooks of Astrology, and thoroughly know the Elements of Astrology before he can expect to make a good Diagnostician, or Medical Astrologer. (See Quadrants).

ORIENTATION—Ability to Know Correctly One's Position In a Given Environment—(See Balance; "Coordinated Action" under Coordination; "Sound Mind" under Mind).

   Disorientation — Loss of Identity — (See Identity, Memory).

ORIFICES — Øf the Body — A Mouth, Opening, oʀ Entrance Into the Body from the Outside World. (See Ears, Eyes, Mouth, Navel, Nose, Rectum, Urethra, Vagina, etc). Also in Infancy the Fontanelle is an opening in the Skull, covered by a thin membrane. In Occult Literature considerable is said about the 12 openings into the human body, and their Mystical meaning. There are also many internal orifices in the body, as the Valves, the Pylorus, the Inguinal Canals, the Ducts, etc. The Orifices in the different parts of the body are under the rulership of the Signs ruling the part. In Ancient Times, it is said, there was a Third Eye in the human head, enabling one to see on all sides, and to avoid dangers when the Earth was in a more molten stage, but that opening has long since been closed. (See Pineal Gland).

ORION—Constellation of Orion—

   Orion's Belt—Cingular Orionis— Three stars, from 21° to 24° ♊, of 2nd magnitude, of the nature of ♄ and ♃. These stars are mentioned in the following subjects — (See Assassination; "Causes" under Blindness; Drowning; "One Eye" under Eye, as causing loss of one eye). Other references to subjects and diseases are given under Bellatrix and Rigel.

   Orion's Foot—(See Rigel).

   Orion's Left Shoulder—(See Bellatrix).

   Orion's Right Shoulder — Betelgeuse —A fixed star of the first magnitude in the last face of ♊, of the nature of ♂ and ☿. (See "Many Calamities" under Calamity; "Many Dangers" under Danger; Disgrace, Drowning; "Hot Diseases" under Heat; "Fevers" under Putrid; Ruin; "Danger Of" under Sickness; Trouble; "Death" under Violent).

ORNAMENTS— (See "Adornment" under Dress; Neat).

ORPHANS — (See Adoption; "Early Death", "Separated from Parents", under Parents).

ORTHOPEDIST—One who corrects Deformities—One with the Qualities of a Surgeon — ♂ strong at B., as in the Midheaven, makes good Orthopedists. (See Surgeons).

OS CALCIS—The Heel Bone—Ruled by ♓. (See Feet).

OS COCCYX — (See Coccyx, Sacrum, Spine).

OS SACRUM—(See Sacrum).

OSCILLATION— Of the Eyeballs— (See "Nystagmus" under Eyeballs).

OSMOSIS—The Transudation or Oozing of Fluids thru the Walls of Vessels, or thru Membranes — The Oozing of Fluids—Osmosis is a ☽ influence. Endosmosis is the transudation, or osmosis, of fluids inward, and is generally a ☽ influence. Exomis is the outward oozing, or transudation of fluids, and is under the rule of ♀, and in abnormal conditions is a ♀ disease. Osmosis may also be caused by ♄ affliction, due to stoppages, and with the ☽ afflicted by ♄, as in Dropsies. (See Dropsy, Effusions, Exudations, Fluids, Oedema, Serum, Transudations).

OSSEOUS—The Osseous System—Ossification—Resembling Bone—The Bones —Concretions, etc.—

   Osseous Deposits — Mineral Deposits —(See Calculus, Concretions, Crystallization, Deposits, Gravel, Hardening; "Fontanelles" under Head; Mineral, Sand, Sclerosis, Stone; "Influence Of" under Saturn; Urea, Uric, Wastes, etc.).

   Osseous System — The Bones — The Skeleton — Ruled generally by ♄ and the ♑ Sign. The Osseous System is especially affected with the ☉ and ☽ acting thru the ♑ sign. (See Bones; the Introduction under Knees; Minerals).

   Ossification — Bone-Building — Ruled and denoted by ♄, and is a ♄ process. (See "Ossification" in Sec. 1 under Bones; "Morbid Ossification" in Sec. 2 under Bones).

OSSICLES — The Small Bones of the Ears—Ruled by ☿, and also influenced by ♈. (See "Bony Parts" under Ears).

OSTEITIS — Inflammation of a Bone — (See "Bones" under Arms; "Inflammation" under Bones).

OSTEOMYELITIS—(See "Osteomyelitis" under Bones; "Marrow" under Femur; "Inflammation" under Marrow).

OSTEOPATHY — Osteopathic Physician —Good Influences For—Successful As An Osteopath—(See "Osteopathy" under Healers).

OSTRICH — A Human Ostrich — Swallows Glass, etc.—(See "Human Ostrich" under Human).

OUT—Words beginning with "Out"—

Outbreaks of Violence — (See "Outbreaks" under Violence).

Outbursts of Passion — (See "Outbursts" under Passion).

Outbursts of Rage — (See Anger, Choleric, Rashness; "High Temper" under Temper; "Becomes Violent" under Violent).

Outcaste — A Social Outcaste — ♂ afflicted in the 12th H. (See Social Relations).

Outcome of the Disease — (See "Outcome" under Disease).

Outdoor Sports—(See Exercise, Hunting, Sports).

Outlaw—(See Banishment, Exile).

Out-of-Sorts—(See Anguish, Anxiety, Irritable; "High Temper" under Temper; Worry, etc.).

Out-of-the-Way Places—Detention In—Detention In a Foreign Land—(See "Accidents" under Abroad; Banishment, Captivity, Exile).

Outgrowth—(See Exostosis).

Outrageous—The Patient Becomes Outrageous and Unmanageable — (See "Outrageous" under Insanity).

Outrageous Diseases — (See "Private Diseases" under Private; Scandalous, Venereal).

Outrages—(1) Murderous Outrages—(See "Murderous Outrages" under Murder). (2) Outrages Prevalent—Outrages Numerous—☿ in ♊, ♂ ♂ at the Vernal Equi., and Lord of the Year. (See "Much Crime" under Crime).

Outraging Nature's Laws—(See "Nature's Laws" under Laws).

Outside Influence Over Body — (See Contagions, Environment, External, Susceptibility).

Outward — The Blood and Fluids Drawn Outward to the Surface—(See Caustics, Centrifugal, Congestions, External, Irritations, Rubefacients, Surface).

OUTER PARTS—The Outer and Upper Part of the Kidney—(See Kidneys).

Outer Parts of the Body — (See External, Skin, Surface).

OVAL—Oval Face—(See "Oval" under Face).

OVARIES—Ova—Ruled by the ☽, ♀, ♎, and ♏. The ☉ rules the right ovary, and the ☽ the left. The Ovum is ruled by ♀. They are also affected by planets in the cardinal signs, as in ♈, ♋, ♎, or ♑.

⁎Ablation Of — Suppression of the Ovaries—♄ afflicted in ♉, by reflex action to ♏, from the opposite sign; ♄ ♈ afflicted in ♏. (See Ablation, Remote, Removal, Suppressions).

Abscess Of — ♂ afflicted in ♏. (See Abscess).

Afflicted Ovaries—Diseased Ovaries—The ☉ or ☽ afflicted in ♏; the ☽ afflicted, and especially when in ♉, ♏ and fixed signs; a ☽ disease; ♀ affl. in ♏; ♀ in ♏ and afflicting the ☽ or Asc.;

♀ afflicted in ♏ in the 6th H.; a ♏ disease, and afflictions in ♏; a ♉ disease by reflex action to ♏; Subs at PP.

Dropsy Of—The ☽ afflicted in ♏; ♄ ♂ ☽ in ♏; ♃ or ♀ ♂ ♄ in ♏; Subs at PP (2L). (See Dropsy).

Inflammation Of—Abscess of—Ovaritis — Ulceration of — ♂ afflicted in ♏; Subs at PP (2, 3, 4L).

Ovariotomy—Surgical Removal of the Ovaries—Never operate upon the Ovaries or Womb when the ☽ is in ♏, ♎, or ♏, and especially applying to ♄ or ♂, or other malefics, as death or inflammation may result. (See "Rules" under Operations).

Ovaritis—(See "Inflammation" in this section).

Oviducts—Fallopian Tubes—Disorders of—(See Fallopian).

Suppression Of — (See "Ablation" in this section).

Ulceration Of — (See "Inflammation" in this section; Ulcers). See Barren, Conception, Fallopian, Fecundation, Fruitful, Menses, Pregnancy, Reproduction, Womb.

OVER—Words Beginning with "Over"—

Over-Abundance — (1) Over-Abundance of Animal Heat, and Disease From—(See "High Fever" under Fever; "Animal Heat" under Heat). (2) Over-Abundance of Life Force—(See "Excess Of" under Force; "Force" under Vital; Vitality).

Over-Activity — Over-Active — Many planets in one sign at birth, and especially the ☽ and ♂ in the same sign, tend to over-activity of the organ, or organs ruled by such sign. (1) Over-Active Brain—(See "Over-Active" under Brain; "Over-Active Mind" under Active). (2) Over-Active Body — (See "Body" under Hyperactivity). (3) Over-Activity of the Lungs, Stomach and Nerves — (See "Over-Activity" under Lungs).

Over-Ardent — (See "Ardent" under Love Affairs).

Over-Braced Tonic Fibers — (See "Tonic Fibers" under Fiber).

Over-Charged—The Body Over-Charged with Moist Humours — (See "Moist Diseases" and Humours" under Moisture).

Overcoming—(1) Power to Overcome Evil Directions — (See "Overcoming" under Directions). (2) Overcomes Disease — (See "Overcoming" under Disease; Immunity; "Strong Resistance" under Resistance; "Good" under Vitality).

Over-Eating—(See "Over-Eating" under Eating; Feasting; Gluttony; "Over-Indulgence" in this section).

Over-Emotional — (See Ecstasy; "Intensified" under Emotions; Hysteria).

Over-Excitement—(See Excitement).

Over-Exercise — Disease or Fatigue From—(See "Inordinate" under Exercise; Fatigue, Sports).

Over-Exertion — Illness From — (See Exertion).

Overflowing—♃ is overflowing in action. (See Excesses, Flooding, Flow, Jupiter, Redundant).

Over-Growth—(See "Thickening" under Cells; "Abnormal" under Growth; Hypertrophy; "Over-Growth" under Organs; Sclerosis).

Over-Heated — (See "Over-Heated" under Blood, Heat; "Sunstroke" under Sun).

Over-Indulgence — (1) Appetites—Over-Indulgence of the Appetites and Sickness From—♃ afflicted in ♉; ♃ in ♋ on the Asc., and afflicted; ♃ afflicted in the 6th H.; ♂ afflicted in ♏; ☿ Sig., and to the ☌ ♀, and ♀ ill-dignified at B.; ♉ influence; the 11° ♊ on the Asc. (See Amorous; "Over-Indulgence" under Appetites; Desires, Epicureans; "Excesses" under Diet, Drink, Eating, Food, Passion, Pleasure; Excesses; "Inordinate" under Exercise; Feasting, Gluttony; "High Living" under High; Indiscretions, Indulgences, Living; "Health Injured" under Men; Plethora; "Intemperate" under Sports; "Over-Indulgence" under Sugar; Surfeits).

(2) Of the Passions—(See Amorous; "Health Suffers" under Opposite Sex; "Passional Excesses" under Passion).

Over-Loaded Stomach — (See "Over-Loaded" under Stomach).

Over-Secretion — (See the various paragraphs under Excess, Fluids, Secretion; "Excess" under Urates, Urine).

Over-Strain—Of the Mind and Body, and Diseases Resulting From — (See "Over-Active Mind" under Active; "Inordinate", "Mind", under Exercise; "Over-Exertion" under Exertion; "Mind" under Fatigue; Hyperactivity; "Exertion", "Strain", under Mental; "Over-Strain", "Strain", under Nerves; Reading, Strain, Stress, Study, etc.).

Over-Study — Disorders From — (See "Reading and Study" under Blindness; "Brain Fag" under Brain; "Eyestrain" under Eyes; "Mind" under Fatigue; Reading, Study, etc.).

Over-Time Children — (See Prenatal Epoch).

Over-Work—(See Over-Activity, Over-Exercise, Over-Exertion, Over-Strain" in this section; "Over-Work" under Nerves).

OVUM—Ruled by ♀. (See Ovaries).

OWN—Relating to the Individual—

(1) Causes His Own Death — (See "Causes His Own Death" under Death).

(2) Fears His Own Death — (See "Death" under Fear).

(3) His Own Worst Enemy—(See this subject under Enemies).

(4) Causes His Own Illnesses—(See "Brings Disease Upon Himself" under Disease).

(5) Causes His Own Misfortunes — (See this subject under Misfortune).

OXEN—Large Cattle—Death of Many Great Cattle—Injury or Attacks By—(See "Death", "Hurts By", under Animals; "Great Beasts", "Hurts", under Beasts; "Death", "Destruction", "Diseases", "Great Cattle", under Cattle; "Cattle" under Detriment; "Great Beasts", "Great Cattle", under Great; "Cattle" under Large; "Epidemics" under Sheep).

OXYGEN—Oxygenation—Non-Oxygenation, etc.—Oxygen is one of the Gaseous Elements, and the Supporter of Life, and is an important element in Heat and Combustion. Oxygen is essential in the four Operations of Nature. (See Combustion; "Operations" under Nature). The ☉ rules Oxygen, and also the oxygen in the blood is supplied and ruled by the ☉. The oxygen of the ☉, and the iron of ♂, maintain the heat of the blood. (See Haematopoiesis). Also, oxygen is ruled largely by the Fiery Signs of the Zodiac. Oxygenation of the blood is ruled by, and is a function of the ♊ sign, the sign which rules the Lungs, and people born under Airy Signs require more oxygen, and should sleep in well-ventilated rooms. The atmosphere about us is made up of about 23 per-cent of oxygen by weight, and Nature gives this gas to us freely, if we will breathe it in, to replenish, purify, and revitalize the blood. People who have ♄ afflicted in ♊, the lung sign, tend to shallow breathing, and for lack of sufficient oxygen, tend to Anaemia, and also to be more liable to go into Consumption. Sunlight, Oxygen, and the most of the vital, and life-giving forces about us, both in drink, and our food, are ruled by the ☉, as the ☉ is the Giver of Life. The fruits and vegetables which are ruled by the ☉ are strong with oxygen.

Non-Oxygenation of the Blood — Insufficient Oxygenation — Oxygenation Interfered With—Obstructed—Poor, etc.—The ☉ in ♊ ☌ ♅; the ☉ in ♊, □ or ☍ ♂ at B.; ♆, ♅, ♄ in ♊, □ or ☍ ♃ or ♀; ♆ in ♊ in the 12th H., □ or ☍ ♅, the capillaries are incapable of taking in sufficient oxygen for the blood; ♅ ☌ ♂ in ♊, and in □ or ☍ the ☉ or ☽; ♅ in ♊ on the Asc., and in ☍ ♃, ♀, or the ☽, oxygenation is spasmodic, and the capillaries contracted; ♅ or malefics in ♊, and afflicting ♃ or ♀, rulers of the Arterial and Venous circulation; ♄ in ♊, ☍ the ☽, insufficient tidal air and oxygen to cleanse the blood of carbon dioxide; ♄ in ♊, ♃, □, or ☍ ♃ or ♀; ♄ in ♊, □ ♂, ♀, or ☿, expulsion of carbonic acid, and proper oxygenation of the blood prevented; ♄ ☌ ♃ in the 6th H.; ♄ ☌ ♃, and □ ♅; ♄ afflicted in ♌, due to a weak heart; ♂ afflicted in ♊, the oxygen in the lungs is burned up too fast; ☿ afflicted in ♊; malefics in ♊ in the 12th H.; many afflictions in ♊ or common signs; common signs on the angles. Aquarius causes incomplete oxygenation, morbid blood conditions, blood poisoning, etc. Case of Insufficient Oxygenation — See Fig. 24 in the book, "Message of the Stars", by the Heindels. (See Air, Carbon, Combustion, Gases, Hydrogen, Iron, Nitrogen).

Sickness from Non-Oxygenation — Disease and Illness From — Afflictions and Disturbances By — (See Anaemia, Asphyxiation; "Labored", "Obstructions", under Breathing; "Delayed Birth" under Children; "General Causes" under Cough; Cyanosis; "Impure Blood" under Impure; "Blood Poisoning" under Poison; Suffocation; "Tidal Air" under Tidal).

P

PAIN — Pains — Painful — Painless—
Aches—Acute Suffering, etc.—The various parts of the body are more apt to
suffer with pains at the time of the
Moon's Perigee. Also Pains, Tumors, and
Fluxions follow a Solar Periodicity.
The afflictions of the malefic planets,
and especially of ♄ and ♂, are the
principal causes of pain and distress
in suffering, and especially when they
afflict the Asc., or are in the 6th H.,
or lords of this house. (See "Pain"
under Jupiter, Mars, Mercury, Moon,
Neptune, Saturn, Uranus, Venus).
Every part of the body is subject to
pain and disease at times, and each of
the planets when afflicted tends to
cause pain in the part, parts, or organ
ruled by the sign in which posited.
Mars tends to acute, sharp, darting
pains. Saturn gives dull pains and
aches. Uranus tends to spasmodic
pains. For pain in the various parts
and organs of the body see "Pain", or
"Pains", under the subject you have in
mind. In this Article a partial list of
the organs and parts affected by pain
are listed, and also general considerations and conditions concerning pain.
For subjects not listed here, look in
the alphabetical arrangement for what
you have in mind.

Abdomen — Pain In — (See Abdomen,
Appendicitis; "Pain" under Bowels;
Colic, Flatulence, Ileac Passion, Tym-
panies; "Bowels" under Wind).

Abscesses—Painful Abscesses — (See
Abscesses, Boils, Carbuncles).

Accidents—(See "Painful" under Accidents).

Aches—Heavy and Dull Pains — (See
"Heavy" under Aches; "Dull Pains"
under Head; Headaches, Neuralgia).

Acute Pains — Acute Nerve Pains —
Acute Pains In the Body—Caused principally by the afflictions of ♂; the ☉
or ☽ afflicted in the Oriental Quarters
of the map. (See "Suffering" under
Acute; "Acute Diseases" under Head;
Fierce, Sharp, Shooting, Violent, in
this section)

All Over the Body — Pains Over the
Whole Body—(See Whole).

Alleviated—The good aspects of the
benefic planets ♃ and ♀ to the afflicting planets tend to alleviate pain and
suffering. (See Amelioration, Moderation).

Analgesia — Insensibility to Pain —
(See Analgesia, Insensibility).

Angina Pectoris — Pain About the
Heart—(See Angina).

Anguish of Mind—(See Anguish).

Anodynes—A Drug Relieving Pain—
(See Anodyne; "Pain and Suffering"
under Narcotics).

Arms—Pains In—(See "Pains" under
Arms, Hands, Shoulders).

Arthralgia—(See "Pain" under Joints).

Asthenopia — Painful Vision — (See
Sight).

Back—(See "Pains" under Back).

Backbone —-Spine — Pains In — (See
"Pain" under Spine).

Bladder—(See "Pains" under Bladder,
Bile).

Boils; Bones — (See "Pain" under
Bones).

Bowels — (See "Pain" under Bowels;
Cholera, Colic, Dysentery, Enteralgia).

Breasts—(See "Pain" under Breast).

Burning Pains — Burning Sensations
—Burning Pains In the Chest or Stomach—(See Belching; "Heartburn" under Heart).

Catamenia Painful — (See "Painful"
under Menses).

Chest—(See "Pains" under Chest).

Children — (See "Pain" under Children).

Cholera Pains—(See Cholera).

Chordee—(See "Chordee" under Gonorrhoea).

Colic; Complaints—Painful Complaints
—(See "Diseases" in this section).

Consumptive Pains—(See "Consumptive Pains" under Knees, Thighs).

Cramps; Darting Pains — (See "Darting Pains" under Head; "Sharp" in this
section).

Day Time — Pains Less In the Day
Time, and Greater At Night — (See
"Pain" under Night).

Death—(1) Painful Death—♂ in the
8th H. at B., and afflicting the hyleg;
♂ lord of the 8th., or afflicting the
lord of the 8th H., or afflicting the
cusp of the 8th H. at B., or by dir.; ♂
having sole dominion at a Solar Eclipse,
many painful deaths; a malefic planet
in the 8th H., and when other testimonies do not show a violent death.
(See "Death" under Accidents, Blows,
Burns, Cuts, Duels, Hurts, Injuries,
Iron, Stabs, Sword, Wounds; "Diseases"
in this section). (2) Death Without
Pain — (See Comforts; "Easy Death"
under Death; "Natural Death" under
Natural). (3) Death of Females from
Pain and Long Illness—(See "Death"
under Females).

Delivery Painful—Childbirth Difficult
and Painful — (See "Painful" under
Parturition).

Dengue — Pain In the Bones — (See
Dengue).

Diseases — Painful Diseases—Suffers
Much Pain In Sickness—Distressful—
Poignant—Fierce—Sharp—Swift—Violent—Vehement, etc.—Caused by the ☉
and ♂, the positive, electric, and heat-
producing planets; the afflicting planets, or malefics, in the Oriental Quarters
tend to painful, short, and acute diseases; the ☽ afflicted by ♂ tends to
painful complaints and irregularities
due to rashness and want of forethought. At the time of a crisis in
disease, if the ☽ is ☌, □, or ☍ a planet
which afflicts the Asc., lord of the Asc.,
or if the ☽ is in evil aspect the lord

of the 6th H., the patient suffers much pain and distress, the disease runs high, and medicines do little good. (See "Suffering" under Acute; "Gall Stones" under Bile; Colic; "Worse" under Crises; Distressful, Fierce, Gnawing, Grievous; "High Fever" under High; "Mars Diseases" under Mars; Poignant, Quick, Severe, Sharp, Shooting; "Suffering" under Sickness; Swift, Terrible, Vehement, Violent, etc. Also for the various painful diseases note the paragraphs in this Article).

Distressful Maladies—(See "Diseases" in this section; Distressful).

Dull Pains—Dull Aches—Given by ♄ and ☿. (See "Pains" under Dull).

Dyspnoea — Painful Dyspnoea — (See Dyspnoea).

Ears—(See "Pain" under Ears).

Electric Pains — Caused by ♅. (See Electric).

Enteralgia—(See "Pain" under Bowels; Enteralgia).

Erections Painful — (See "Chordee" under Gonorrhoea; "Priapism" under Penis).

Extremities — (See "Pain" under Extremities).

Eyes—(See "Pain" under Eyes).

Father—(See "Pain" under Father).

Feet—(See "Pains" under Feet).

Females—Pains To—(See Accidents, Death, Functions, Painful, under Females).

Fierce and Painful — (See "Fierce Maladies" under Fierce).

Flying Pains—(See Flying).

Forethought—Pain and Disease from Lack of—(See Forethought).

Functions — (See "Painful" under Functions).

Gall Bladder—(See Cholic, Gall Stones, under Bile).

Generative System—(See "Pains" under Generative).

Genitals—(See "Pain" under Genitals).

Gnawing Pains—(See Gnawing).

Gouty Pains — (See "Pains" under Gout).

Groins—(See "Pain" under Groins).

Head—(See "Pains" under Head).

Headaches; Heart—(See "Pain" under Heart).

Heartburn—(See Heart).

Heavy Pains—(See "Heavy" under Aches).

Hips—(See "Pain" under Hips).

Hurts — Pains By — (See the paragraphs under Hurts).

Illness — Painful Illness and Death From—♂ in the 8th H., lord of the 8th, or afflicting the lord of the 8th, or cusp of the 8th, indicates death from a painful illness (Hor'y). (See Death, Diseases, in this section).

Increased—Pain Increased At Night— Pain and Suffering Increased — (See "Worse" under Crises, Disease; "Pain" under Night; "Suffering" under Sickness; "Diseases" in this section).

Inflammation—Painful Inflammations —(See Inflammation).

Injuries—Painful Injuries—(See Injuries).

Insensibility to Pain—(See Analgesia, Insensibility).

Irregularities—Painful Irregularities Due to Lack of Forethought—(See "Painful" under Forethought, Rashness).

Joints—(See "Pain" under Joints).

Kidneys—(See "Pain" under Kidneys).

Knees—(See "Pains" under Knees).

Left Ear—Pains In—(See "Left Ear" under Ears).

Legs—(See "Pain" under Legs).

Limbs—(See "Pain" under Limbs).

Lingering Pains—(See Aches; "Death" under Females; Headaches, Lingering, Neuralgia).

Liver—Pains In—(See Inflammation, Pain, under Liver).

Loins—(See "Pain" under Back, Loins; Lumbago).

Lumbago; Lumbar Region — Pain In — (See "Pain" under Back, Lumbar; Lumbago).

Mad with Pain — Almost Mad with Pain — The ☽ in ♈ and afflicted by the ☉ or ♂ when taken ill (Hor'y). (See Darting, Fierce, Sharp, Shooting, Violent, in this section).

Menses Painful — (See "Painful" under Menses).

Micturition Painful—(See "Strangury" under Urine).

Motor Functions—Pains and Cramps from Exalted Excito-Motory Function —(See "Functions" under Exaltation).

Muscles — Pains In — (See "Pain" under Muscles).

Neck—(See "Pains" under Neck).

Nerve Pains — Nervous Pains — (See "Pain In Nerve" under Nerves; "Acute" in this section).

Neuralgic Pains—(See Neuralgia).

Night—Pain Greater At Night—(See "Pain" under Night).

Nipples—(See "Pain" under Nipples).

Painful Diseases — (See "Diseases", and the various paragraphs in this section).

Painless—(See "Painless" under Functions).

Poignant and Painful—Severely Painful and Distressing—Keen—Cutting— (See Acute, Diseases, Distressful, Fierce, Severe, Sharp, Shooting, Violent, in this section; Poignant).

Priapism — Painful Erections — (See "Erections" in this section).

Private Parts — (See "Pain" under Generative, Genitals, Penis, Secrets).

Pyrosis—Burning Pains At the Stomach—(See Belching).

Rashness — Painful Diseases from Rashness and Lack of Forethought— (See Forethought, Rashness).

Reins—(See "Pain" under Reins).

Rheumatic Pains — (See "Pains", and the various paragraphs under Rheumatism).

Ribs — (See "Shooting Pains" under Ribs).

Running Pains — (See Flying, Running).

Secret Parts—(See "Private Parts" in this section).

Sharp Pains—(See Diseases, Poignant, in this section; "Pains" under Sharp).

Shooting Pains—(See Acute, Darting, Flying, Ribs, Running, in this section; Shooting).

Shoulders— (See "Pains" under Arms, Shoulders).

Sores—Painful Sores—(See Abscesses, Boils, Carbuncles, Pus, Sores, Ulcers).

Spasmodic Pains—(See Colic, Cramps, Gripings, Spasmodic).

Spine—(See "Pain" under Spine).

Stomach — (See "Pains" under Stomach).

Strangury—Painful Micturition—(See "Strangury" under Urine).

Suffers Much Pain—In Sickness—(See "Disease" in this section).

Swellings—Pain From—Painful Swellings — (See the paragraphs under Swellings).

Teeth — Pain In — (See "Toothache" under Teeth).

Thighs—(See "Pains" under Thighs).

Throat—(See "Pains" under Neck; the various paragraphs under Throat).

Urination Painful—(See "Strangury" under Urine).

Violent Pains — Caused by ♂. (See Fierce, Poignant, Sharp, Swift, Vehement, Violent).

Vision — Painful Vision — Asthenopia —(See "Painful" under Sight).

Whole Body—Pains Over the Whole Body—(See Gnawing, Shooting; "Pains" under Whole).

PAINTERS' COLIC—(See "Lead Colic" under Colic, Lead).

PALATE—The Roof of the Mouth and Floor of the Nose—Ruled by the ☽, ♀, and the ♉ sign, and the ☽ or ♀ afflicted in ♉ tend especially to affect the Palate. (See Mouth).

Cleft Palate—Case—Mouth a Series of Roofs, with none joining. Can return food out of nostrils. See "Cleft Palate", No. 679 in 1001 N.N.

PALE—Pallor—Pallid—Anaemic—Sickly-Looking — Ghastly-Looking — Wan Face—Pale Complexion—Pale Countenance—Unhealthy Countenance —White and Chalky Face—Cadaverous —Thin and Impoverished Blood, etc.— The ☽ and ♄ make the complexion paler and also darker; the ☉ Sig., and afflicted in ♋, ♑, or ♓, the weaker signs, and especially when these signs are upon the Asc. at B.; the ☉ in ♋ in partile aspect the Asc.; the ☉ in ♑, partile the Asc., pale and sickly; the ☽ and the ♋ sign tend to paleness; the ☽ gives a fair, pale countenance; the ☽, the planet ruling white, rising in the Asc., and afflicted, pale and white; the ☽ ascending at B.; the ☽ Sig. in ♋, ♑, or ♓; the ☽ in ♋, partile the Asc., pale, dusky complexion; the ☽ in ♓, partile the Asc., pale and sickly looking; the ☽ Sig. in ♓, a pale and bloated face; the ☽ Sig. □ or ♉ ♄; in Hor'y Q. the ☽

is Sig. of persons more white than red; the ☽ gives a whitely colored stature; the ☽ strong at B. gives a white and red mixed complexion, but tending to paleness; ♆ rising in the Asc. gives pallor; ♆ when setting at B. often gives a pallid complexion; ♅ afflicted in ♉, ♋, ♎, ♑, or ♓; ♄ influence tends to paleness, and especially when ♄ is in the Asc., or a ♄ sign on the Asc. at B.; in Hor'y Q. ♄ as Sig. indicates a pale and sickly-looking person; ♄ ascending at B.; ♄ Sig. in ♋ or ♓; ♄ in ♋, partile the Asc.; ♄ in ♓, partile the Asc., pale, but with dark hair; ♄ □ or ♉ the ☽; the two ♄ signs ♑ and ♒ tend to give a pale, tanned, and dusky complexion, even though the native is otherwise healthy; ♃ afflicted in ♋ or ♑; ♃ in ♋, partile the Asc., pale, sickly, and unwholesome countenance; ♃ in ♑, partile the Asc., a fragile appearance; ♃ afflicted in ♋ or ♑; ♂ in ♋ if afflicted by the ☉ and ☽; ♂ Sig. in ♋ or ♓; ♀ Sig. in ♋ or ♑; ♀ in power at B., pale and white, but with a dark hue; ♀ afflicted in ♋ or ♑; ♀ in ♋, partile the Asc., a sickly complexion; ♀ in ♑, partile the Asc., pale, thin, and sickly visage; ♀ Sig. ✶ or △ ♄, rather pale, but comely; ♀ Sig. in ♋; ♀ Sig. in ♓ when in the term of ♄; ☿ in ♓, partile the Asc., pale, sickly face; ♋ or ♓ on the Asc.; the ♋ sign gives a pale, sickly, and white complexion; ♓ gives a white, ghastly, chalky appearance, and a pale, large and bloated face; ♋ on the Asc., a round, pale, white face; ♓ on the Asc., pale, sickly, short, fleshy, crooked, and usually with stooping shoulders; ♑ or ♒, the signs of ♄, on the Asc.; ♒ on the Asc., rather pale complexion, delicate, but usually very beautiful, and with white hair early in life; a planet in the 1st H. which has the signification of white, as the ☽; given by the Lymphatic Temperament. People living in shaded and wooded places, or working in Mines, and who do not get the Sunshine, tend to paleness and anaemic conditions if such manner of living is continued over a long period of time. (See Anaemia; "Poor", "Thin", under Blood; "Bad", "Poor", "Sickly", under Complexion; "Weak Constitution" under Constitution; Delicate, Emaciation, Fading, Feeble; "Bad Health" under Health; Invalids, Sickly, Unhealthy; "Low" under Vitality; "Weak Body" under Weak; "Complexion" under White).

Fingers and Toes—The Fingers and Toes Pale, White, and Cold—(See "Raynaud's Disease" under Fingers).

Marks—Marks on the Body of a Pale, Lead Color—☿ influence. (See Marks).

PALLIATIVES—Mitigating and Relieving Remedies—(See Ameliorate, Anaesthetics, Anodynes, Antidotes, Antipathy, Blue Color, Cure, Drugs, Emollients, Healers, Medicines, Moderation, Modification, Opposites, Remedies, Sedatives, Soothing, Sympathy, Treatment, etc.).

PALMISTRY—The Birth Data of Cheiro. (See "Palmist", No. 083 in 1001 N.N. For planetary influences which incline to the study of Palmistry see "Occult Study" under Occult).

PALPITATION—Palpitations—The dynamic energy of ♂ causes palpitations. Also the influences of ♅ tend to tremblings, palpitations, spasmodic, and erratic movements, incoordination, etc. (See "Movements" under Erratic; Incoordination, Jerky, Spasmodic, Tremblings).

Heart—Palpitation of—(See "Palpitation" under Heart).

PALSY—Palsies—A ☽ disease; the ☽ afflicted at B., and by dir.; the ☽ hyleg, and to the ☌, P., □ or ☍ ♄ by dir.; a ♅ disease; a ♄ disease; ♄ in ♏, occi., and afflicting the ☉, ☽, or Asc.; denoted and caused by fixed stars of the nature of ♄; ♄ afflicted in the 6th H.; ♄ afflicting the hyleg or Asc.; an ♈ disease when malefics are in this sign. These influences may also cause death by Palsy. (See Paralysis).

Face—Palsy of—(See "Palsy" under Face).

Shaking Palsy—Paralysis Agitans—Trembling—Tremors—A ♅ and ♄ disease; ♅ afflicted in the sign ruling the part; ♅ or ♄ afflicted in ♓ tends to the peculiar walk in cases of Paralysis Agitans. (See Incoordination, Paralysis, Tremors; "Festination" under Walk). Subluxations in the Vertebrae, and pressure upon a Nerve, and improper distribution of nerve force, are often a contributing cause to these Shakings and Tremblings. (See Subluxations, Vertebrae).

PANARIS—(See "Whitlows" under Fingers, Toes).

PANCREAS—The Sweetbread—A Racemose Gland In the Abdomen—Ruled by ♋ and ♍ Signs. The Pancreatic Diastase is ruled by ♋.

Cancer of Pancreas—Caused by the afflictions of ♃.

Cyst Of—♀ afflicted in ♋, and especially in the 6th H.; Subs at SP (8D).

Inflammation Of—♂ afflicted in ♋ or ♍ in the 6th H.; Subs at LSP (8D).

PANDEMICS—Widespread Epidemics—Due to the maximum of planetary influence, as the ☌ of several superior planets in the airy signs. (See Epidemics).

Pandemic of Murders — (See "Many Murders" under Murder).

PAPAVER—The Poppy Plant—Opium—Ruled by ♆. (See Narcotics).

PAPILLAE—The Renal, or Kidney Papillae are ruled by ♀. (See Kidneys). The Papillae of the Tongue are ruled by ☿ and the ♉ sign. Also influenced by ♂. (See Taste, Tongue).

Papilloma—Hypertrophied Papillae of the Skin—♀ affl. in ♊.

PAPULES — Small Elevations on the Skin—Caused by ♄ and ♄ deposits. (See "Condyloma" under Anus; "Pustules" under Ears; Warts).

PARACELSUS—A Great Physician and Astrologer. Born Dec. 17, 1493, near Zurich. Died Sept. 23, 1541, at Salzburg. He was the first Physician to advocate giving Similars, and drugs to produce symptoms similar to those of the malady. Hahnemann afterwards demonstrated this principle in Homeopathy. (See Homeopathy. Sympathy). The ♈

and ♏ signs are called "The Poles of Paracelsus." Aries is the Cerebral Pole of Paracelsus, and Scorpio the Genital Pole. (See Aries, Cerebral, Genitals, Scorpio). Paracelsus said, "Man is related to the Stars by reason of his Sidereal Body." (See Astral, Sidereal).

PARAESTHESIA—A Morbid or Altered Sensation—May be caused by ♅, ♄, or ☿, and due to nerve irritations. (See "Sensations" under Burning; "Buzzing" under Ears; "Heartburn" under Heart; "Flushings" under Heat; Hyperaesthesia, Itch, Numbness, Sensations, Tingling).

PARALLEL ASPECT — The Mundane Parallel—In health matters this aspect is considered as evil as a ☌, □, or ☍, and should not be overlooked in calculating the influences of the star map of birth, and the aspects forming over it along thru life. Also all Progressed Parallels should be noted, as a Prog. P. aspect from a malefic to the ☉, ☽, Asc., or Hyleg, or Prog. P. aspects between two malefics, tend to cause great disturbances of the health or mind while such aspects last. The P. Aspects are strong factors in causing disease, as they are usually of long duration. Two planets are in P. aspect when they have the same Declination, North or South of the Equator, but of greater severity when both are North, or both South, and of the same Declination. P. Aspects between the malefics, or of the malefics to the ☉ or Hyleg, are very dangerous and annoying for the time, and may cause death, injury, or severe illness. P. Aspects between the Benefics, or of the Benefics to the ☉, ☽, Asc. or Hyleg, or very beneficial to the health and general prospects of the native. (See Aspects, Nodes).

PARALYSIS—Loss of Sensation or Voluntary Motion—Depressed Motility—Nerve Lesions—Corrosion and Hardening of the Nerves—Interference of the Nerve Force to a Part, or Parts of the Body, as by Vertebral Subluxations—

Agitans—Paralysis Agitans— (See "Shaking" under Palsy).

Arms—(See "Paralysis" under Arms).

Birth — Paralyzed from Birth — (See Distortions, Excrescences).

Blows—Paralysis From—(See Distortions).

Bulbar Paralysis—(See Medulla).

Cases of Paralysis—Birth Data, etc.—See "Tunnison", No. 113, and "Seventeen Years In Bed", No. 843, in 1001 N.N. See "Stone In Kidney", Case in Chap. XIII, Daath's Medical Astrology. See Figures 13A, 13B, 13C, 13D, 13F, 13G, 14A, in the book, "Astro-Diagnosis" by the Heindels.

Causes of Paralysis—The ☉ rising at B., and afflicted by ♄; the ☉ afflicted in ♐; the Prog. ☽ ☌, P., □, or ☍ ♂ and ☿; ♆ afflicting ☿ at B., and by dir.; ♅ and ☿ afflicted in signs which rule the part, or parts affected; ♅ brings danger of by corrosion of the nerves, and by nerve lesions; ♅ afflicting ☿; ♅ afflicting the Significators, as the ☉, ☽, Asc., or M.C.; ♄ afflicted in ♈; ♄ ☌ or ill-asp. the ☉; due to the atonic action of ♄; a ♄ disease; ♄ and ♃ combined afflictions to the Significators or the hyleg; ♄ affl. in the 6th H.; ♄ afflicting the hyleg or the Asc.; ☿ afflicted by ♆, ♅, or the ☽; ☿ affl. in ♐; many planets in ♉, ♋, ♏, or ♑; planets afflicted in and about the 8° ♋ or ♑; cardinal signs on the angles, more subject to paralysis. (See Corrosions, Distortions, Excrescences, Lesions; "Lesions" under Nerves; Spasmodic; the various paragraphs in this section).

Corrosion—Of the Nerves, and Resulting In Paralysis—(See Corrosion).

Cuts—Paralysis From—(See Distortions).

Death from Paralysis—The ☉ afflicted at B., and in □ or ☍ the ☽ or Asc., whichever may be hyleg, and the hyleg afflicted by a fatal train of directions; ♅ afflicted in the 8th H.; ♄ occi. at B., and afflicting the hyleg by dir.; ♄ in the 8th H. at a Solar Ingress into ♈, and afflicting the ☽ or planet ascending, tends to be very fatal according to the sign occupied by ♄; ♄ afflicting the hyleg by dir., and ♄ holding the dominion of death. (See Palsy).

Diaphragm — (See "Paralysis" under Diaphragm).

Diplegia—Double Symmetric Paralysis—Paralysis of both sides of the body may result in cases where both sides are afflicted by planets which cause paralysis, as ♄ in ♑, a feminine sign, and ♅ in ♐, a masculine sign, in cases with males. (See Left, Right). Also where the nerves which leave the Spine supply both sides, and are impinged in their exits thru the vertebrae, can cause a double Paralysis. Also Diplegia is caused by Subs at AT and AX, and by interferences with the Organ of Coordination situated in the ♉ sign. (See Coordination, Incoordination, Hemiplegia).

Distortions — Caused by Paralysis — (See Distortions).

Excrescences—Caused by Paralysis—(See Excrescences).

Eyes—(See "Paralysis" under Eyes).

Face—(See "Paralysis" under Face).

Falls—Paralysis From—(See Distortions, Excrescences).

Feet—(See "Paralysis" under Feet).

Hands — (See "Paralysis" under Hands).

Hemiplegia—Paralysis of One Side of the Body — The affliction of a single planet tends to this condition, or where the nerves leading out from the spine are only partially impinged. Caused by the afflictions of ♅ or ♄ to the ☉; ♄ in ♑, occi., and afflicting the ☉, ☽, or Asc.; Subs at AT, AX, or CP. (See "Hemiplegia" under Infancy).

High Places — Heights — Paralysis from Falls From — (See Distortions, Excrescences).

Infantile Paralysis—Poliomyelitis—♆ is the chief afflictor; ♆ in ♋ and afflicted by ♅ and ♄; ♅ in ♑ and afflicted by ♆ and ♄; ♅ afflicted in ♌ or ♒. (See "Paralysis" under Infancy; "Poliomyelitis" under Spine).

Injuries—Paralysis From— (See Distortions, Excrescences).

Lameness — From Paralysis — (See "Paralysis" under Feet, Legs, Limbs).

Legs—(See Locomotor Ataxia, Paralysis, under Legs).

Lesions—Paralysis from Nerve Lesions—(See Corrosions, Lesions; "Lesions" under Nerves).

Limbs — (See "Paralysis" under Limbs).

Locomotor Ataxia—(See Ataxia; "Argyll-Robertson Pupil" under Iris; "Knee Jerk" under Knees; Locomotion, Locomotor Ataxia).

Medulla—(See "Bulbar Paralysis" under Medulla)

Mobility Decreased—(See "Paralysis" under Feet, Legs; Gait, Locomotion, Locomotor Ataxia, Motion, Movement, Walk).

Moment of Birth—Paralysis from the Time of — (See Distortions, Excrescences, Prenatal Epoch).

Motor Nerves—Paralysis of—(See "Arms", and the paragraphs under Motor).

Nerve Lesions — (See Corrosions, Lesions; "Lesions" under Nerves).

Neuroses — (See "Neurosis" under Nerves).

Old Age—(See "Paralysis" under Old Age).

One Side of Body—Paralysis In—(See "Hemiplegia" in this section).

Ophthalmoplegia — (See "Paralysis" under Eyes).

Palsy—Shaking Palsy—(See Palsy).

Paraplegia—(See Legs).

Paresis—Slight Paralysis—Caused by the milder afflictions of ♅, and where the benefics give a favorable and saving aspect in the configuration. Also the subluxations are or a minor order, and not major, and the "Stroke" may be only temporary.

Partial Paralysis — Limited to One Organ or Part of the Body — Usually due to the affliction of one planet in a sign, and in the part, or organ, ruled by the sign, as ♅ afflicted in ♈ causes paralysis of an eye muscle. Also indicated in cases of Paralysis in the Arms, Hands, Feet, etc. Case—See No. 843 under "Cases" in this section.

Poliomyelitis — (See "Infantile" in this section).

Quadrupeds—Paralysis Due to Injury By—(See Distortions, Excrescences).

Robbers — Paralysis Resulting from Injuries By—(See Distortions, Excrescences).

Shaking Palsy — Paralysis Agitans — (See Palsy).

Shipwreck—Paralysis from Injury In —(See Distortions).

Slight Paralysis — (See "Paresis" in this section).

Speech — Paralysis of — Paralysis of Tongue — Loss of Power of Speech —(See "Deaf and Dumb" under Hearing; Mutes; "Aphasia" under Speech; "Paralysis" under Tongue).

Stabs—Paralysis From—(See Distortions).

Thought—Paralysis of—(See Chaotic, Confused, Delusions; "Dreamy" under Dreams; Hallucinations, Idiocy, Imbecility, Insanity; "Weak Mind" under Mind; Vague, etc.).

Walk—Interferred with by Paralysis — (See "Paralysis" under Feet, Legs; "Festination" under Walk).

PARAMYOCLONUS MULTIPLEX—(See Muscles).

PARANOIA—A Chronic Form of Insanity with Delusions—A Toxic Psychosis — Delusions of Persecution — Principally a ♇ disease and affliction; ♇ afflicted in ♈; ♇ in the 6th H. in ♈, and afflicted; ♇ in ♈, and afflicting the ☉, ☽, Asc., or Hyleg. (See Delusions, Hallucinations, Illusions, Insanity).

PARAPLEGIA — (See "Beriberi" under Dropsy; "Paraplegia"under Legs).

PARASITES—An Organism That Inhabits Another Organism, and Feeds Upon It.

  Contagious Parasitic Disease—Of the Skin—(See Favus).

  Intestinal Parasites—Caused by afflictions in ♍; ☿ or ♀ afflicted in ♍. (See Cestode, Entozoons, Taenia, Tapeworm, Worms).

  Parasitic Diseases—Caused by afflictions in ♑, and tend to the external form; afflictions in ♋ or ♍ tend to internal parasitic disorders, as in the stomach or bowels, such as worms. (See "Pruritis" under Itch; Scabies; "Worms" under Stomach; Worms).

  Worm Remedy—(See Anthelmintic).

PARCHED — Parched Body — The ☽ in ♌ and afflicted by the ☉ or ♂ when taken ill (Hor'y). (See "Hot and Dry Body" under Dry; "Liable to Fever" under Fever; "Animal Heat", "Excessive Bodily Heat", under Heat).

  Parching Diseases — (See "High Fever", "Parched", under Fever; "Dry and Hot Diseases" under Heat).

PARENCHYMA — Connective Tissue — Soft, Cellular Tissue — The Functioning or Secreting Structure of an Organ — The Pathological Action of the ♃ Group of Herbs tends to especially affect the Pulmonary Parenchyma. (See Cells, Glands, Secretions, Tissues).

PARENTS — The 10th and 4th Houses, and the planets in them, and their rulers, show the parents and the conditions affecting them. The ☉ and ♄ are allotted to the person of the father, and the ☽ and ♀ to the mother. The 10th H. rules the father in a male nativity, and the mother in a female horoscope. The 4th H. rules the father in a female nativity, and the mother in a male nativity. Guardians and Godfathers come under the rule of ♃. In diseases and afflictions to the parents the ☉ and ♀ should be principally observed by day, and the ☽ and ♄ by night. Many subjects in this book which have to do with parents are given in the Articles on Children, Family, Father, Husband, Mother, Wife. (See these subjects). The following planetary influences are to be considered in the map of the child, as the radical map and directions of the child show many of the conditions which will affect the parents, and show the nature of the possible events in the life of a parent, the diseases, afflictions, possible length of life, etc.

  Accident to a Parent — Danger to a Parent—Danger of Accidents, Hurts, Injuries, Wounds, etc.—♇ in the 10th H., and possibly by water, and during early youth or childhood; ♂ to the ♂, P., □ or ☍ the ☉, ♄, ☽, or ♀ by dir.; the Asc. to the ♂, P., □ or ☍ ♂ by dir.; malefics afflicted in the 4th or 10th H. at B., and by dir.; malefics in the 4th or 10th H. at a Solar Rev. (See "Accidents To" under Father, Mother).

  Adoption of Children—(See Adoption; "Death", "Separation", in this section).

  Affection—The Love and Affection of Parents for Children—(See "Love" in this section).

  Afflicted—Affliction to the Parents—Sickness—Illness—Indisposition—The Parents Suffer—The ☉ directed to Cor Leo; the ☉ afflicted in the 12th H.; the M.C. or Nadir to the ♂, P., □ or ☍ ♄ or ♂ by dir.; malefics in the 4th or 10th H. at a Solar Rev.; the 1st Decan. of ♓ on the Asc., affliction of a parent, or the early death of one. (See the various paragraphs in this section).

  Bad Children — Worries and Sorrows to Parents Thru Bad and Unfortunate Children—(See "Parents" under Children; "Injured" in this section).

  Benefits — To Parents — (See "Good Health" in this section).

  Creative Powers Of — (See Barren, Fruitful, which influences are in the map of the parent).

  Danger To—(See "Accidents" in this section).

  Day and Night Nativities — Diseases of the Parents In—(See "Mother" under Night).

  Death of Parents—Or a Parent—
  (1) Death of Parents—The ☉ or ☽ to the ♂ or ill-asp. ♄ by dir., and especially with women; ♄ or ♂ afflicting the ☉, ☽, Asc., M.C., or Nadir by dir., often kills or afflicts a parent; ♄ in the 4th or 10th H., and afflicted by the ☉ or ☽; the Asc. or M.C. afflicted by the malefics ♄ or ♂; the Asc. ♂ ♇, ♄, or ♂ by dir., often corresponds to the time of death of a parent; the M.C. to the ♂, P., □ or ☍ ♄, and espec. if the ☉ be elevated above the Earth, and ♄ be ori. of the ☉; the M.C. to the ♂ or ill-asp. ♂ by dir.; lord of the 8th H. in the 5th H., and caused by worries thru bad children; transits of malefics thru the 4th or 10th H. if they afflict these houses at B.; malefics in the 4th or 10th H. at a Solar Rev.; the Nadir afflicted by the ♂ or ill-asps. of ♄ or ♂ by dir.; ♀ by dir. afflicting the M.C. or Nadir, as by the □ aspect. (See "Early Death", and the various paragraphs in this section; "Directions", "Worries", under Children; "Early Death" under Early; "Death' under Father, Mother; "Short Life" under Life).
  (2) Death of Parents Before the Native—♄ afflicted in the 10th or 4th H., by disease; ♂ afflicted in the 10th or 4th, danger of, by an accident or swift fever. (See (1) in this paragraph).

(3) Death of Parents, or a Parent, Thru Bad Children—(See (1) in this paragraph).

(4) Death of Parents In the Youth of the Native—Case—See "Saturn in the Tenth", No. 831, in 1001 N.N. (See (1) in this paragraph).

Directions — Parents Affected by the Directions of Children — With young children, the directions of the M.C., the Nadir, and the ☉ and ☽ to the malefics, tend to affect the parents, and often cause their sickness, and in some cases their death, or the death of one parent, according to the rules of a male, or female nativity. (See "Directions" under Children).

Drink — Drunkenness — Parents, or a Parent, Liable to Drunkenness and Neglect of Children — The ☽ in ♓ in the 12th H., and afflicted. (See "Lewdness" in this section; "Father" under Drunkenness; "Drink" under Husband, Wife).

Early Death of Parents—Or of a Parent—Short Life For — Parents Do Not Live to be Old—Malefics in the 4th or 10th H. at B., and by dir., or at a Solar Rev., or by transit; the death of one parent is indicated by an affliction to the 4th or 10th H., and may be the father or mother, according to the sex of native; the death of both parents may take place at nearly the same time, or soon apart, if both the 4th and 10th H. are afflicted by malefics at B., and by dir., or at a Solar Rev.; the ☉, ☽, ♄, or ♀ severely afflicted at B. in map of child; the ☽ increasing, or at Full, sepr. from ♃ and applying to ♄; ♅ in the 10th H., and near the Meridian, early loss of one; ♄ in the 10th or 4th H., and afflicted; the Asc. or M.C. afflicted by ♄ or ♂; lord of the 8th or 11th H. a malefic, and in the 4th H., and afflicted; the 8° ♎ on the Asc; the 11° ♎ on the Asc., early death of the father, or the father unknown to him; the 1st Decan. of ♓ on the Asc., ruled by ♄. (See "Early Death" under Father, Mother; "Separation" in this section).

Family—(See the various paragraphs under Family).

Father—Illness of—Death of—Length of Life—(See the paragraphs under Father).

Females — (See "Parents" under Females).

Fever—Parents Suffer from Fevers—(See "Fevers" under Father, Mother).

Good Health—Benefits to the Parents—The ☉ and ☽ well-aspected at B., and free from serious afflictions; the progression of the benefics into the 4th and 5th H. of the child indicate a period of good health and good fortune for the parents if these houses are also free from the affliction of malefics, and the map of the child otherwise shows good health and long life for the parents; the M.C. to the ♂ or P. asp. the ☉ except when the ☉ is ruler of the 5th H. (See "Long Life" under Father, Mother).

Godfather—Godmother—(See Guardians).

Grandparents—(See Grandparents).

Guardians—Godfather—Godmother—(See Guardians).

Health Good—Health Bad—(See Afflicted, Early Death, Fever, Good Health, Long Life, Short Life, and the various paragraphs in this section).

Heredity—(See the various paragraphs and references under Heredity).

Hurts To—(See "Accident To" in this section; the various paragraphs under Father, Mother).

Husband—(See the various paragraphs under Husband).

Illness To—(See Afflicted, Fever, and the various paragraphs in this section).

Indisposition—(See "Afflicted" in this section).

Inflammatory Attacks — Fevers and Inflammations—(See "Infirmities" under Father; Fevers, Inflammations, under Mother).

Injured by Children—Lord of the 7th H. in the 5th, or lord of the 7th a malefic. (See Bad Children, Love, in this section).

Injured by Parents—Children Suffer Injury Thru Parents—Malefics in the 4th or 10th H., or lords of the 4th or 10th a malefic in map of child; lords of the 4th and 10th H. in □ or ☍ asp. each other. (See Drink, Love, Separation, in this section).

Injuries To—(See "Accident To" in this section).

Killing of a Parent—(See "Patricide" under Father).

Lewdness—Of Both Parents—♆ in the 10th H., ☍ ♄, ♀, and ☿ in the 4th; ♆ ☌ ☽ in the 10th H., and ♄ or ♂ ☌ ♀ in the 4th H. (See Lewd).

Life Endangered—♆ in the 10th H., according to the sex of the nativity, the father in a male horoscope, and the mother in a female nativity. (See "Accident To" in this section; "Danger To" under Father, Mother).

Long Life—(See "Long Life" under Father, Life, Mother).

Love and Affection — The Love and Affection of Parents for their Children is ruled and denoted by the 7th H. and its conditions. Benefics in this house tend to a greater love and affection, which is also strengthened by a benefic in the 5th H. of a parent, or a benefic ruling the 5th and 7th. Malefics in the 7th H. may make the parents cold and ill-disposed towards their children, which may be added to by the influence of malefics in the 5th or 11th H., causing the children to bring sorrow and misfortune upon the parents. Saturn weak and afflicted in the 7th H. of the child denotes antipathy from the father, and the ☽ so situated, antagonism from the mother. Also the conditions of the 10th and 4th H. should be noted, and judgment formed according to the sex of the native. (See Injured by Children, Injured by Parents, Separation, in this section; "Worries" under Children).

Matricide — (See "Patricide" under Father).

Mother—(See the various paragraphs under Mother).

Night Nativities—When the Parents are Afflicted In—(See "Mother" under Night).

Old Age—Parents Live To—Do Not Live To—(See Death, Early Death, Long Life, Short Life, in this section; "Death At Middle Life" under Middle Life).

Parents Die Before Native—(See Death, Early Death, in this section).

Patricide—(See "Patricide" under Father).

Relation of Children to Parents—Children a Blessing or Misfortune—(See Blessing, Parents, Worries, under Children; Eleventh House; "Drink", "Love and Affection", in this section).

Separation from Parents—The ☽ sepr. from ♃ and applying to the ☉, and especially if the ☽ be in ♈, ♏, ♑, or ♒; the ☽ sepr. from the ☉ and apply. to ♄ in a day geniture; the ☽ sepr. from ♀ and apply. to the ☉, separation from parents thru a bitter dispute; the ☽ increasing, or at Full, sepr. from ♃ and applying to ♄, separated and adopted by a stranger. (See Adoption; Death, Drink, Love and Affection, in this section).

Separation of Parents—A Separation In the Family—♅ afflictions and influences cause separations of all kinds; ♅ afflicted at B., and by dir., or ♅ afflicting the Midheaven, cusp of the 4th H., the Asc., ☉, ☽, or hyleg. (See "Death In the Family" under Family; "Unhappy Marriage" under Marriage; Death, Early Death, in this section).

Short Life—(See Death, Early Death, in this section).

Sickness of Parents—(See "Directions" under Children; Afflicted, Fever, and the various paragraphs in this section).

Significators of Parents—The ☉ and ♀ are Significators of the parents in a day nativity, and the ☽ and ♄ by night. The ☉ by day represents the father, and ♄ by night; ♀ by day, the mother, and the ☽ by night. In making a study of the diseases and afflictions to a parent, the severity, prognosis, nature of the disorder, etc., these distinctions should be noted.

Sorrow Thru Children—(See "Injured" by Children" in this section).

Suffer—The Parents Suffer—(See Afflicted, Directions, Fever, Injured, and the various paragraphs in this section).

Violent Death—Danger of—The ☽ sepr. from the ☉ and applying to ♂ in a day geniture. (See "Patricide" under Father; "Death" under Violent).

Wicked Children—(See Eleventh House).

Wife—(See the various paragraphs under Wife).

Worries Thru Children—(See "Injured" in this section; Parents, Worries, under Children).

Wounds To—(See "Accidents" in this section).

PARESIS—Slight Paralysis—(See "Paresis" under Paralysis).

PAROSMIA—(See this subject under Smell).

PAROTID GLAND—The Parotids—A large Salivary Gland in front of the Ear—Ruled by the ♉ Sign.

Diseases Of—Afflictions in ♉ or ♏. (See Bubo).

Mumps—Inflammation of—Parotiditis—Glandular Fever In the Neck—An Acute Infectious Disease Attended with Swelling of the Parotid Gland, and also Swollen Testes in some Cases—A ♉ disease, and afflictions in ♉; ♄, ♂, or ♀ afflicted in ♉; ♀ in ♉ in the 6th H., afflicted, or afflicting the ☽ or Asc.; Subs at LCP, SP (7D), and KP. (See Saliva).

PAROXYSMS—A Period of Increase, or Crisis of a Disease—A Spasm or Fit—

Asthma—Paroxysmal Dyspnoea—(See Asthma).

Coughing—Paroxysms of—(See "Convulsive" under Cough).

Crises In Disease—(See Crises).

Dyspnoea—Paroxysms In Breathing—(See "Labored" under Breathing; Dyspnoea).

Facial Paroxysms—(See "Paroxysms" under Face).

Headaches—Paroxysmal Headaches—(See Migraine).

Nervous Excitation—Paroxysms of—(See "Excitable" under Excitement).

Renal Paroxysms—(See "Paroxysms" under Kidneys).

Spasm or Fit—A ♅ disease, and caused by ♅ afflictions. (See Fits, Spasmodic).

Tachycardia—Heart Paroxysm—(See "Spasm" under Heart).

PARRICIDE—(See "Patricide" under Father).

PARROT FEVER—(See Psittacosis).

PARTIAL—

Partial Blindness—(See Gutta Serena).

Partial Deafness—(See "Partial" under Hearing).

Partial Paralysis—(See Paresis, Partial, under Paralysis).

PARTICULAR DISEASE—To Determine the Course Any Particular Disease May Follow—(See Amelioration, Continuity, Course, Crises, Decumbiture; "Better" under Disease; Duration, End, Fatal; "Course" under Irregular; Moderation, Prognosis, Termination, Worse).

PART OF FORTUNE—(⊕)—A point in the Horoscope where the rays of the ☉ and ☽ converge, and where the ☽ would be if the ☉ were exactly rising. Many Authors refer to the Part of Fortune as a benefic influence, and to indicate good fortune, good health, etc., when in favorable aspect to the Significators in the map. Wilson in his Dictionary says that the Part of Fortune is but a "Phantom hatched in the brain of Ptolemy", and has no influence whatever. Some Writers say the Part of Fortune may become Hyleg in a Nocturnal Horoscope if the ☽ be decreasing in light, and both the ☉ and ☽ are below the horizon, and not in a hylegiacal place. They also say the Part of Fortune may become Anareta when the ☉, ☽, or Asc. are hyleg.

The student should learn how to compute the place of the Part of Fortune, both in the Zodiac, and Mundane, and there are good Chapters and Articles on the subject in the various Textbooks and Dictionaries of Astrology. (See Anareta, Hyleg).

PARTNER—Companion—Associate—

Business Partner—Illness or Death of —♄ afflicted in the 12th H., from some lingering and chronic disease; ♂ afflicted in the 12th H., from some fever or inflammatory disease. Also malefics afflicted in the 7th H. tend to afflictions to, death of, or unfortunate relations with a business partner. (See "Lawsuits" under Public).

Marriage Partner—Illness or Death of—(See Husband; "Death", "Sickly", under Marriage Partner; Wife).

PARTS OF THE BODY—Members—Organs—

Absence of a Part—(See Missing).

Afflicted Parts—The Parts, Organs, or Members of the body usually afflicted are those ruled by the signs containing the malefics, or a badly afflicted ☉ or ☽. The Asc. denotes the part of the body liable to affliction from external causes. (See External). The Sign in which the Significator of disease is found indicates the Part, or Organs, principally affected. The Parts afflicted are also those containing the ☉ or ☽ if the Lights are in ♂ or ill-asp. with malefics. The places occupied by the malefics at B. are always considered places of affliction. (See Malefics). The Part of the Body afflicted is also shown by that part of the Sign, Face or Decanate of the Sign, which is rising upon the Eastern horizon at B., and especially if afflicted, or containing a malefic. (See "Locating the Disease" under Diagnosis). The Part of an Organ afflicted is denoted by the Face, Decanate, or Division of the Sign containing the afflicting planet, and which indicates whether the upper, middle, or lower part of the organ is afflicted. (See Decanates; "Organs" under Middle; Navamsa; "Lower Part" under Organs; "Organs" under Upper). The Asc. afflicted by a malefic tends to trouble in the head. (See "Disorders Of" under Head). For the influences causing diseases, infirmities, and afflictions to the various parts and organs of the body, see the Part, Organ, or Member in the alphabetical arrangement. The Sixth House should be noted, as this is the House of Health, and the Sign, Signs, and Planets ruling this house at B., and the parts of the body coming under these influences, are very subject to disease and weakness when the vitality becomes lowered for any reason, or thru worry and anxiety, bad thinking, and adverse planetary influences by Direction, Transit, or Progression, etc. Also observe the Sign and House containing the ☽, and especially with females, and the planets to which the ☽ may be applying, or from which she is separating, as such influence of the ☽ helps to form a judgment as to the part of the body afflicted, and also the nature of the disease. (See "Disease"

under Nature; Quality, Sixth House, Type, Vulnerable).

Blemishes — (See Blemishes, Defects, Deformities, Imperfections, Marks, Moles, Scars, etc.).

Conformity Between the Parts—Conformity In the Members—(See "Conformity" under Members).

Defects—(See "Blemishes" in this section).

Disease—Members or Parts Afflicted by Disease—(See "Afflicted Parts" in this section; Disease, Members, Organs).

Enlargement of Parts—(See Enlarged; "Abnormal Growth" under Growth; "Over-Developed" under Organs).

External Causes—Parts Afflicted By —Are denoted by the Asc., and the part, or parts, ruled by the Asc. at B. (See Ascendant, External).

Fever In a Part—Or Organ—(See the paragraphs under Fever).

Induration of a Part—(See Hardening, Hypertrophy, Sclerosis, Thickening).

Inflammation In a Part — (See the paragraphs under Inflammation).

Injury to a Part—(See Injuries).

Intellectual Parts—All Imperfections In—All Evils In—(See Intellect, Mental, Mind).

Internal Parts — Disorders In — (See Internal).

Irregular Action Of—(See Erratic, Irregular, Spasmodic).

Left Side Suffers—(See Left).

Lower Parts — (See Lower; "Lower Part" under Organs).

Marks, Moles, Scars—(See these subjects).

Members — (See the paragraphs and references under Members).

Middle Parts — (See "Organs" under Middle).

Missing Parts—(See Limbs, Missing).

Moving Parts—(See Moving).

Organs—(See the subjects under Organs).

Parts Liable to Suffer—(See Afflicted Parts, Disease, in this section; Ascendant, Malefics, Sixth House).

Right Side Suffers—(See Right).

Rush of Blood — To a Part — (See Rush).

Sensitive Parts—(See "Organs" under Sensitive).

Spasmodic Action of Parts—(See Erratic, Jerky, Spasmodic, Tics, Tremors, Twitchings).

Upper Parts—(See "Lower Part" under Organs; Upper).

Vulnerable Parts—(See Vulnerable).

Weak Parts — Those ruled by the Signs and Houses containing the malefics, and especially ♄, if afflicted. (See "Weak Spots" under Weak).

Weakest Part—The part ruled by the sign containing ♄, or several malefics. (See Vulnerable; "Weakest" under Weak).

PARTURITION — Childbirth — Delivery — Confinement — Accouchement — Puerpera — Puerperal — Pertaining to Child-Bearing, etc. — Ruled by the ☽ and the 5th H. conditions. The time of birth of a child is ruled by the movement of the ☽, but it is the influence of ♂ which ushers the child into the world. The rules of the Prenatal Epoch govern the time of the Accouchment. (See "Moment of Birth" under Moment; Prenatal Epoch). Normal births are ruled by ♃. Abnormal births, and dangerous and difficult parturition, are caused by the influences of the malefics at the time, or such influences in the 5th H. of the mother at B. The following subjects have to do with Parturition, Childbirth, and the normal, abnormal, dangerous, difficult, premature, or delayed entrance of the child into the world. See these subjects in the alphabetical arrangement when not more fully considered here—

Abortion; Accident At Birth—Extreme Danger In—Danger to the Mother and Child—The ☉ or ☽ to the ♂ or ill-asp. ♂ by dir. at the time; ♅ afflicted in the 5th H. at B., and afflicting the 5th H., or ruler of the 5th by dir.; ♅ afflicted in ♌ at B.; ♂ afflicted in the 5th or 11th H.; ♂ afflicted in ♌, the sign affiliated with the 5th H.; the afflictions of ♂ are very dangerous in cases of childbirth, and especially if ♂ is in the sex sign ♏ at B., or in ♏ by transit or direction at time of the Accouchment. These influences also often make it necessary for an instrumental delivery (and especially if ♄ is involved in the configuration causing delay), excision of the foetus (Caesarian Operation), or extraction of the foetus in mutilated parts. The ☽ or ♀ body afflicted by ♄ or ♂ during pregnancy at the times corresponding to the monthly periods, bring danger of an accident, or dangerous trouble to the mother during parturition. (See "Death At Birth" under Children; "Excision", "Mutilation", under Foetus; "Accidents At Birth" under Infancy; "Injured" in this section).

Almost Died In Confinement—Case—See "Four", No. 954 in 1001 N.N.

Asphyxiation—At Birth—(See "Birth" under Asphyxia; "Delayed Births" under Children).

Bad Time For Confinement—Bad Time for the Mother After Confinement—The ☽ afflicted at the time of birth of the child may cause death of the mother, puerperal fever, and dangerous complications. (See Accident, Death, Difficult, Excision, Fever, in this section).

Birth—(See the various paragraphs under Birth).

Born Before Time—Cases and Influences—(See Abortion; "Eight Months Children" under Children; Miscarriage, Premature).

Born Dead—(See Stillborn).

Breathing—Child Does Not Breathe Until Two Hours After Birth—Case—See "Foot", No. 106 in 1001 N.N.

Breech Presentation—Usually caused by ♄ in ♏ in the map of the mother.

Case—See "Breech Presentation", No. 075 in 1001 N.N.

Caesarian Operation—(See "Excision" under Foetus).

Caul—Child Born with Caul Over Face —(See "Caul" under Face).

Child—For the various conditions affecting the Child at birth, see the paragraphs under Birth, Children, Foetus, and in this Article.

Childbed Fever—(See "Puerperal Fever" under Puerperal).

Conception—(See the paragraphs under Conception).

Convulsions—(See "Convulsions" under Puerperal).

Danger In Childbirth—A Dangerous Event — (See Accident, Bad Time, Death, Difficult, Excision, Injury, and the various paragraphs in this section).

Dead—Child Born Dead—(See Stillborn).

Death—(1) Of Child—(See "Death of Children", Sec. 3, under Children). (2) Death of Mother In Childbirth—Danger of—The ☉ or ☽ to the ♂ or ill-asp. ♂ at time of delivery, and especially if ♂ afflict the ☉ at B., or occupy the 5th H.; the ☉ or ♂ in the 5th H. at B., and the ☉ to the ♂ or ill-asp. ♂ by dir. at delivery. Case—Death In Childbirth—See "Elizabeth", No. 562 in 1001 N.N. (See "Death by Miscarriage" under Abortion; "Death" under Hemorrhage, Mother; "Puerperal Fever" under Puerperal; Almost Died, Bad Time, Caesarian, Difficult, Hemorrhage, in this section).

Delayed Birth — (See "Birth" under Asphyxia; "Delayed Births" under Children; Prenatal Epoch; "Difficult" in this section).

Delivery—(See Danger, Delayed, Difficult, Excision, Premature, and the various paragraphs in this section).

Difficult Parturition—Birth Delayed— Extreme Danger In—A Dangerous Event—Painful and Difficult—The ☽ afflicted in ♏; the ☽ to the ♂ or ill-asp. ♂ by dir., and ♂ in the 5th H. at B., or afflicting the ☽; ♅ or ♂ afflicted in ♏; ♅ afflicted in ♌ or the 5th H.; ♂ afflicted in the 5th H.; ♀ in bad aspect to the ☽ at B., or at delivery. (See Delayed, Instrumental, Painful, and the various paragraphs in this section; "Danger To" under Wife).

Excision of Foetus—(See "Excision" under Foetus).

Feet First—Born Feet First—♄ afflicted in ♏ tends to malposition of the foetus, and to be born feet first, or breech. Case—See "Soraby", No. 089 in 1001 N.N.

Fever—Danger of Childbed Fever— (See "Puerperal Fever" under Puerperal).

Foetus—Excision of—(See Foetus).

Gestation — (See the various paragraphs under Gestation).

Hemorrhage—Flooding at Delivery— Great Loss of Blood—Danger of Death By—The ☉ or ☽ to the ♂ or ill-asp. ♂ by dir., and ♂ afflicting the ☉ or ☽ at

B., or in the 5th H.; the ☽ in the 8th H., and afflicted by ♂; ♂ afflicted in ♉ or ♏, and especially if in the 5th H. at B.; ♂ afflicted in the 8th H.; ♂ in the 8th H., and afflicting planets in the 5th H. Case—See Fig. 8-I, Chap. XIX, in the book, "Astro-Diagnosis", by the Heindels. (See "Death" under Hemorrhage; Miscarriage).

Incommodities—To Those Bearing Children—An Eclipse of the ☉ in the 2nd Decan. of ♉.

Infancy—(See the various paragraphs under Infancy).

Infant Dies At Birth—(See "Death At Birth" under Children, Infancy).

Infection At Birth—(See "Infections" under Infancy).

Injury At Birth—Instrumental Delivery—♅ afflicted in ♏ in map of the mother. (See Accident, Maimed, Mangled, in this section; "Death At Birth" under Children).

Instrumental Delivery—Necessity For —♅ afflicted in ♏; ♂ in the 8th H., and afflicting planets in the 5th H. Cases —See Fig. 8-I mentioned under "Hemorrhage" in this section. Also see "Four", Nos. 953 and 955, in 1001 N.N. (See Accidents, Injury, in this section; Prenatal Epoch).

Killed—Child Had to be Killed to Deliver—Case—See "Four", No. 952 in 1001 N.N. (See "Mangled" in this section).

Large At Birth—(See "Birth" under Large).

Lateral Position—Of Foetus—(See "Lateral" under Foetus).

Loss of Blood—In Childbirth—(See "Hemorrhage" in this section).

Maimed—Child Maimed At Birth, or Maimed from Birth—(See Accident, Injury, Instrumental, in this section; Maimed).

Mangled—Child Mangled or Mutilated At Birth—(See "Killed" in this section; "Mutilated" under Foetus).

Mania—Puerperal Mania—(See "Mania" under Puerperal).

Metritis—Inflammation of the Womb. Complications—(See "Metritis" under Womb).

Midwives—(See Midwives, Nurses, Obstetricians).

Miscarriage—(See Abortion, Miscarriage).

Mother—For the various conditions affecting the mother in childbirth see the subjects in this Article. Also see the paragraphs under Birth, Children, Congenital, Foetus, Gestation, Maternity, Mother, Pregnancy, Prenatal Epoch, Wife).

Nervous Shock—In Childbirth—Case —See Case mentioned under "Hemorrhage" in this section.

Normal Births—Are ruled by ♃; ♃ in ♌ or ♏, or in the 5th H. at B., and well-aspected. (See "Astral Body" under Astral; "Cause of Birth" under Birth; "Birth Of" under Foetus).

Obstetricians—(See this subject).

Painful Parturition—Painful and Se-

vere—♄ afflicted in ♌ or ♏; ♄ ♂ ♅ in ♌ or ♏; ♂ afflicted in ♏; afflictions in ♌ or ♏; Subs at PP. Case of Painful Delivery—See the Case under "Feet First" in this section. (See Difficult, Instrumental, in this section).

Pains—Suffers with After-Pains—♄ or ♂ afflicted in ♌ or ♏ at B.; Subs at PP.

Pregnancy—(See the various paragraphs under Conception, Gestation, Pregnancy, Prenatal Epoch).

Premature Birth—(See Abortion; "Eight Months Children" under Children; Miscarriage; "Premature Birth" under Premature).

Prevented—(See "Difficult" in this section; "Prevented" under Children; "Excision" under Foetus).

Puerperal Fever—Puerperal Convulsions — Puerperal Mania — (See Puerperal).

Quadruplets—(See Multiple).

Seven Months Children—(See "Seven Months Children" under Children. Also for Cases of, see Premature).

Severe and Painful—(See "Painful" in this section).

Shock—Suffers Great Nervous Shock In Childbirth—(See "Nervous Shock" in this section).

Single Births—(See "Single Births" under Children).

Stillborn—Cases—(See Stillborn).

Suffocation At Birth—(See "Asphyxiation" in this section).

Time of Delivery—To Know the Time Of—Time of Advent of a Child—When a pregnant person wishes to know the time of delivery, it is usual to direct the lord of the Asc., or the ☽, to the cusp of the 5th H. by oblique ascension, according to which of the two is nearer, and allow a day for every degree in the arc of direction. Or observe on what day ♃ or ♀ will transit the cusp of the 5th H., and look for the birth on that day. (Hor'y). (See "Cause of Birth", "Moment of Birth", under Birth; "Birth of a Child", "Born", under Children; "Moment of Conception" under Conception). The time of birth, or delivery, may be some days before, or after what would appear to be the normal time, according to the Order to which the case belongs in the Prenatal Epoch considerations. (See Prenatal Epoch; Delayed, Premature, in this section).

Triplets Born—(See Triplets, Twins).

Twins Born—(See Twins).

Two Weeks Premature—(See Case under Premature).

Unusual Diseases—At Childbirth— (See "Eyes", "Infections At Birth", under Infancy). For unusual complications to the mother see the various paragraphs in this section and under Puerperal.

When Will the Child Be Born?—(See Delayed, Premature, Time of Delivery, in this section).

Wife Benefits by Childbirth—♃ well-aspected in the 11th H. (See the various paragraphs under Wife).

PASSAGES—Channels—Canals—

    Narrowing Of — Caused by ♅ or ♄. (See Constrictions, Stricture).

    One Passage — A Common Outlet to the Rectum and Bladder—(See Cloaca).

    Sex Channels — Lack of Proper Sex Channels—(See Canals; "Channels and Vents" under Genitals).

PASSION — Intense Emotion — Intense Sexual Desire—Erotic Disturbances—Abuses of the Passional Nature—Morbid Passions—Excess of Passion—Passionate Diseases and Disorders from Passional Excesses, etc.—The Passions are ruled principally by ♂ and the ♏ sign. Are also ruled by the ☽ and the Asc. Animal Lust and Passion are ruled by the ☽ and ♂. The Liver is the seat of the passional desires. (See "Desire Body" under Desire; the Introduction under Liver. Also see Reins). The afflictions of ♂ tend to increase of the passion. Mars rules passion in men, and ♀ in women. The good aspects of ♂ stimulate the sex feelings along lawful lines, but the bad aspects of ♂ tend to destroy it by over-stimulation and excesses. In good aspect, ♄ tends to control passion, but in evil aspect perverts, destroys, or suppresses it. The ☉ also tends to give passion. Mercury in ♏ tends to center the mind upon sex and to give morbid sex desires. Since the separation of the sexes in the Lemurian Age, it is said the greatest problem of Earth life is to learn to properly control and use the creative force, avoid its abuse, perversion, waste. The creative function is at present under the control of Man, and to use at his will for pleasure or propagation, whereas in the earlier Races this function was under the control of the Higher Powers, and propagation was limited to certain times of the year when the planetary influences were favorable for such. The abuse of sex, sex excesses, and misuse of the creative power, is said to be the cause of sickness, suffering, sorrow, and earlier death upon the Earth today. From the Occult standpoint the question of Sex, its proper use, and how to transmute it to its proper use, is elaborately considered in the book, "The Key of Destiny", and other books by Dr. Homer and Mrs. Curtiss, Founders of the Order of Christian Mystics, or "The Order of the Fifteen." Passion is legitimate when properly used, and should not be killed out, but controlled. Each of us has within us much of the animal, but the Higher Mind should rule, and the animal in us guided, directed and controlled. From the human, or lower mind side, much is given in the Textbooks of Astrology along the lines of passion, its abuse, excesses, deviations, perversions, etc., and the following paragraphs and subjects have to do with such matters, as gathered, tabulated, and arranged from my Library of books. See the following subjects in the alphabetical arrangement when not more fully considered here—

    Abnormal Sex Desires—♂ ☌ or P. asp. the ☽; ♂ ☌ the ☽ or ♀ in ♏. (See Amorous, Venery; "Passional Excesses", and the various paragraphs in this section).

    Addict — A Sex-Addict — (See "Sex-Addict" under Marriage Partner; "Addict" under Sex).

    Adulterous—(See "Adulterous" under Love Affairs).

    Affection—Inordinate Affection—(See "Free Love" under Free; "Unlawful Affections" under Love Affairs).

    All Sensuous Enjoyments — Given To —(See "Sensuous" under Sensuality).

    Amativeness; Amorous; Amours — Illicit Amours—(See "Amours" under Love Affairs).

    Anaphrodisiacs — Remedies which Lessen Passional Desire—(See Anaphrodisiacs).

    Anger; Animal Propensities — (See "Animal Instincts" under Animal).

    Apathy—Lack of Passion — (See Apathy; "Free from Passion" in this section).

    Aphrodisiacs — Medicines Which Increase Passional Desire—(See Aphrodisiacs).

    Appetites — Over-Indulgence of the Sex Appetites—(See Amorous; "Over-Indulgence" under Appetites; "Love Affairs", "Sex Excesses", under Excesses; "Passional Excesses" in this section).

    Ardent Passion — Over-Ardent — (See "Ardent" under Love Affairs).

    Attackers of Women—(See Rape).

    Bohemian Pleasures — (See "Bohemian" under Pleasure).

    Celibacy; Chaotic Acts — Chaotic and Unnatural Acts—(See Unnatural).

    Chastity — (See "Chaste" under Females).

    Childhood—Unusual Passion In At Puberty—(See Puberty; "Young People" in this section).

    Choleric Passion—(See Choleric).

    Clandestine Relations—(See "Clandestine" under Sex).

    Command—Control—Has Great Command and Control Over the Passions—The ☉ exalted and dignified at B., and the ☽ well-aspected by ♃ and ♀. (See Apathy, Celibacy, Cohabitation, Self-Control; "Regulated" under Sex).

    Debauchery; Deportment — (See the subjects and references under Conduct, Love Affairs, Morals, Sex, and also in this Article).

    Depraved; Desires—(See the subjects under Desire).

    Deviations; Diseases — Arising from Sex Excesses or Irregularities — (See Amorous; "Diseases" under Excesses; "Health Injured" under Men; "Diseases" under Sex; Venery; Passional Excesses, Too Much Passion, Wastes Energies, in this section).

    Emotions—(See "Intensified" under Emotions).

    Enjoyments — All Sensuous Enjoyments—(See "Sensuous" under Sensuality; the various paragraphs in this section).

Erotic Mania—Morbid Sex Desires—(See "Erotic" under Mania).

Exaggerated Sex Desires—(See Amorous, Lewd; "Erotic" under Mania; Nymphomania; Abnormal, Passional Excesses, Unbridled, Violence, and the various paragraphs in this section).

Excess of Amorous Indulgence—(See Amorous).

Excess of Passion—The ☉, ☽, ♂, and ♀ in ♌ in the 5th H.; ♂ Sig. □ or ☍ ♀; ♀ Sig. □ or ☍ ♂; ♌ on the cusp of the 5th H. (See Abnormal, Morbid, Passional Excesses, Strong Passions, and other paragraphs in this section).

Excesses—(See "Passional Excesses" in this section).

Exhibitionism—Public Exposure of the Sex Organs—(See Exhibition; Notoriety" in this section).

Eyes—The Eyes Full of Amorous Enticements—(See "Amorous" under Eyes).

Flower—Passion Flower—(See "Sun Group" under Herbs).

Fornicators—(See "Clandestine" under Sex).

Free from Passion—Apathy—Little or No Passion—The ☽ Sig. in ♋; the ☽ in partile the Asc.; the ☉, ☽, and ♀ free from the affliction of malefics at B.; ♄ afflicted in ♈ or ♎. (See Apathy, Aversions, Bachelors, Celibacy, Cohabitation, Deviations; "Anchorite" under Husband; Indifferent; "Aversion" under Marriage).

Free Love—(See "Free Love" under Free).

Genitals—Diseased from Passional Excesses and Irregularities—(See "Diseases" under Genitals).

Gratification—Of the Passions—Men Prone to Violence In—(See "Violence" in this section).

Great Command—Of the Passions—(See "Command" in this section).

Habits—(See Bad Habits, Diseases, Sex Habits, under Habits).

Harlots—Becomes One—Injured By—(See Harlots).

Heart—Passion or Trembling of—(See "Passion" under Heart).

Homosexuality; Ileac Passion—(See Ileac).

Illicit Amours—(See "Amours" under Love Affairs).

Immodest; Immorality—In Sex Matters—(See "Free Love" under Free; Homosexuality; "Adulterous" under Love Affairs; "Loose Morals" under Morals; Perversions; "Clandestine" under sex; the various subjects in this Article).

Incest—(See "Incest" under Perversions).

Indulgence—Over-Indulgence of the Passions—Excesses In—(See Amorous, Lascivious, Lewd, Licentious, Lust, Venery; "Passional Excesses" in this section).

Infamous; Inflamed with Passion—(See Amorous; "Erotic" under Mania; Nymphomania; "Exaggerated" in this section).

Lack of Passion—(See "Free From" in this section).

Lascivious; Lewd; Liaisons—(See "Liaisons" under Love Affairs).

Libidinous; Licentiousness;

Love Affairs—(See the various paragraphs under Love Affairs).

Love Passion—(See "Love Passion" under Love Affairs).

Low and Base—(See Low).

Lower Passions—Carried Away By—(See Amorous, Lascivious, Licentiousness, Lust; "Low Pleasures" under Pleasures; "Excess of Passion" in this section).

Lust; Mania—Sex Mania—(See "Erotic" under Mania).

Marriage—(See the various paragraphs under Husband, Marriage, Marriage Partner, Wife).

Masturbation—Self-Abuse—(See "Solitary" under Vice).

Men—(See "Sex Gratification", and the various paragraphs under Men; "Violence" in this section).

Middle Life—Dies Before Middle Life from Sex Excesses—(See "Death Before Middle Life" under Middle Life).

Mind Absorbed with Passion—The ☉, ☽, ♀, ☿, and many planets in the sex sign ♏. (See Excess, Mania, Nymphomania, and the various paragraphs in this section).

Modesty; Morals—(See "Loose Morals", and the various paragraphs under Morals).

Morbid Passional Desires—Morbid Imaginations—(See "Morbid" under Imagination; "Erotic" under Mania; "Desires" under Morbid; Nymphomania, Perversions, Unsavory, Vice; the various paragraphs in this section).

Nakedness—Exposure of the Sex Organs—(See Exhibitionism, Notoriety, in this section; "Outrageous" under Insanity).

Notoriety of the Passions—Exposure of the Passions—Immodest—In male horoscopes, ♀ afflicted by ♄, ♂, and ☿, and ♀ be in the West at B., tends to make men wanton, licentious, and to display their passions publicly. In a female horoscope, the ☉, ☽, ♂, and ♀ in male signs, and ♀ sorely afflicted by ♄, ♂, and ☿, and with ♂ and ♀ oriental and diurnal, tend to notoriety of the passions, and to make women shameless. Saturn and ♀ in the Eastern Angles, in the Asc. or M.C., tend to a total exposure of the passions. (See Exhibitionism; "Outrageous" under Insanity; Perversions, Shameless).

Nymphomania—Unbridled Passion In Women—(See Nymphomania; "Unbridled" in this section).

Obscene; Obsessions—Sexual Obsessions In Women—(See Nymphomania; "Morbid" in this section).

Opposite Sex—Fond of—Addicted To—(See the paragraphs under Opposite Sex).

Outbursts of Passion—Should guard against when ♀ and ☿ are in ♌ at B.; ♂ ☌ ♀ in ♌ or ♏; the ☽ afflicted in ♏. (See Inflamed, Storms, in this section).

Outrages Nature's Laws — (See "Nature's Laws" under Nature; Perversions).

Over-Indulgence — Of the Sex Nature — (See "Passional Excesses" in this section).

Passional Excesses—Over-Indulgence of the Sex Nature—Excessive Venery — Excess of Amorous Indulgence — Caused principally by ♂, the ruler of the Genital Organs. Due also to ♥ and ♅ afflictions to ♀; the ⊙ in a weak sign at B., and afflicted; the ⊙ afflicted in ♐, the half man and half horse sign, and especially when other influences contribute to lowered moral standards; the ⊙, ☽, ♂, or ♀ in ♌ in the 5th H.; the ⊙ to the ill-asps. ♀ or the ☽ by dir.; the ☽ afflicted in ♍; the ☽ in ♍, □ or ☍ ♥; the Prog. ☽ to the ♂ or ill-asp. ♂; the ☽ to the ill-asps. ♀ by dir.; ♥ afflicted in ♍; ♥ ♂, □, or ☍ the ☽ or ♀ at B., and by dir.; ♅ afflicted in ♍; ♅ ♂, □, or ☍ ♀; ♄ Sig. □ or ☍ ♀; ♃ afflicted in ♉, ♎, or ♍; ♂ afflicted in ♍; ♂ in ♍ the 12th H., and afflicted; ♂ or ☿ Sig. to the ♂ ♀ and ♀ ill-dignified at B.; ♂ afflicted in the 5th H.; ♂ Sig. ♂, □, or ☍ ♀; ♂ Prog. to the ♂, P., □ or ☍ ♀, or vice versa; ♀ affl. in ♌ or ♍; ♀ in ♍, ♂ the ☽ or ♂; ♀ affl. at B., and to the ♂, P., or evil asp. the Asc. by dir.; ♀ in the ♂ ♂ by dir.; ♀ in the Asc. or M.C., and afflicted, prone to venery; ♀ Sig. □ or ☍ ♂; the tonic action of ♀ tends to venereal excesses; ♌ on the cusp of 5th H.; the 17° ♍ on the Asc, apt to be carried away by the lower passions. Remember that these influences apply only to unregenerate people, and those who may be drifting with their stars instead of ruling them. (See Amorous, Depraved, Dissipated, Dissolute; "Free Living", "Free Love", under Free; "Loose Morals" under Morals; Venery; Abnormal, Exaggerated, Excess, Too Much Passion, Unbridled, and the various paragraphs in this section).

Passional Violence — (See "Violence" in this section; "Violent" under Men).

Perversions; Pleasures—Given to Sexual Pleasures—(See Amorous, Pleasure; "Sensuous" under Sensuality; "Passional Excesses", and the various paragraphs in this section).

Prodigal; Profligate; Promiscuity— (See "Clandestine" under Sex).

Rape; Restraint — Unnatural Sex Restraint — ♄ influence and affliction; ♄ afflicting the ☽ or ♀ at B., and by dir. (See Apathy, Aversions, Bachelors, Celibacy, Indifferent). For influences which tend to lack of Restraint over the sex nature see Excess, and the various paragraphs in this section.

Salacious—(See Effeminate, Lust).

Same Sex—Sex Perversions with the Same Sex—Sodomy — (See Homosexuality).

Scheming and Underhanded—Resorts to Such Measures to Gratify Passion— ♀ ♂, □, or ☍ ♄.

Seduction; Self-Abuse — (See "Solitary" under Vice).

Sensuous Enjoyments—(See Amorous;

"Sensuous" under Sensuality; the various paragraphs in this section).

Sex-Conscious—(See Amative).

Sex Desires — Variations of — (See Amorous, Apathy, Desire, Love Affairs, Men, Sex, Women; the various paragraphs in this section).

Sex Gratification—Various Manners of —(See Rape, Scheming, Violence, and the various paragraphs in this section; Perversions, Sex, Venery).

Sex Perversions—(See Perversions).

Sex Relations—(See Cohabitation, Intercourse, Love Affairs, Morals, Sex; the various paragraphs in this section).

Sexual Immorality—(See "Free Love" under Free; "Loose Morals" under Morals; Perversions; "Clandestine" under Sex; the various paragraphs in this section).

Sexual Obsessions—(See "Morbid" under Imaginations; "Erotic" under Mania; Nymphomania, Perversions; "Sensuous" under Sensuality).

Shameless Practices — (See Exhibitionism, Perversions, Rape, Shameless; Notoriety, Violence, in this section).

Social Relations—(See Harlots, Love Affairs; "Low Company" under Low; Men, Social, Women).

Sodomy — (See Homosexuality, Perversions).

Solitary Vice — (See "Solitary" under Vice).

Storms — Sudden Storms of Passion, and with Violence—♂ ♂ the ☽ or ♀ in ♍; ♂ ♂ ♀ in ♈; ♂ afflicting ♅ or ♄ by dir., or ♄ to the ill-asps. ♂ by dir., and where other influences indicate great passion or sex perversions. (See Mania, Outbursts, Violence, in this section; "High Temper" under Temper).

Strengthened — The Passional Nature Strengthened—(See "Strong Passions" in this section).

Strong Passions — The Passional Nature Strengthened—The ☽ ♂ ♂ and ♀ in ♍; ♥ afflicted in ♉ or ♍; ♄ Sig. in ♌ or ♍ in Hor'y Q.; ♂ ♂ ♀ in any part of the map, and espec. in ♍; ♂ Sig. □ or ☍ ♀; ♂ in the 10th H.; ♀ in ♍; ♀ Sig. □ or ☍ ♂; the 3rd Decan. of ♈ on the Asc., ruled by ♀; the 3° ♋ on the Asc.; the 25° ♌ on the Asc.; the 3rd Decan. of ♐ on the Asc., ruled by ♄; the 3rd Decan. of ♓ on the Asc., ruled by ♂; the 30° ♓ on the Asc. (See Excess of Passion, Passional Excesses, in this section).

Sudden Storms of Passion — (See "Storms" in this section).

Too Much Passion—Diseases Arising From—Caused by ♂; ♂ Sig. □ or ☍ ♀, and vice versa. (See Diseases, Passional Excesses, in this section; Venery).

Unbridled Passion — Lustful — Profligate—The ☽ to the ill-asps. ♀ by dir.; ♂ afflicted in ♉, profligate; ♂ Sig. □ or ☍ ♀; ♀ ill-dignified at B.; ♀ ruler of the horoscope and afflicted by malefics; ♀ on the Meridian at B., and ill-aspected by ♂, tends to be unchaste; ♀ Sig. □ or ☍ ♃, void of virtue and prudence; ♀ Sig. □ or ☍ ♂; the 11° ♌

on the Asc., loss of virtue. (See Imprudent, Indecent, Infamous, Lust. Nymphomania, Obscene, Profligate, Shameless, Unchaste, Virtue, Wanton; "Passional Excesses", and the various paragraphs in this section).

Unnatural Desires — (See Aversions, Celibacy, Deviations, Homosexuality, Indifferent, Perversions, Unnatural; "Restraint" in this section).

Unsavory Subjects — Given To — (See Unsavory).

Unwomanly Freedom—(See "Unwomanly" under Morals; "Unchaste" under Women).

Vehement Passions—(See Vehement).

Venery; Vices; Violence — Violence Attending Passion—Men Prone to Violence In Sex Gratification — Sudden Storms of Passion with Violence—The ☉ □ or ☍ ♂; ♀ afflicted by ♂. (See Cruel, Libidinous, Lust, Masochism, Perversions, Rape, Sadism; "Shameless Practices" under Shameless; Vehement, Virile; "Storms" in this section). The lord of the 8th H. in the 7th H. tends to death from violent outbursts of passion.

Virtuous—Is Virtuous—Is Not Virtuous — (See "Chaste" under Females; Immodest, Modesty, Shameless, Virtue; "Unchaste" under Women; "Unbridled Passion" in this section).

Vitality Depleted — From Sex Excesses—(See "Wasted" under Vitality).

Voluptuous; Wanton; Wench — (See Harlots).

Women—Fond of—Given to Company of Lewd Women—Passional Excesses In Women—(See Addicted To, Fascinating, Harlots, under Men; Nymphomania, Opposite Sex, Women; "Virtuous" in this section).

Young People—Passion Strong In At Adolescence — (See "Passional Excesses under Children; Puberty).

PASSIVE—Unresisting—Cold is a negative and passive quality, and predominates in the left side of the body. (See Cold). Dryness is passive and feminine when acting alone. (See Dry). Moisture is a feminine and passive quality. (See Moisture). The Earthy and Watery Signs of the Zodiac are feminine, and considered more passive and negative than the fiery and airy signs, which are masculine and positive.

Passive Disposition — (See Apathy, Dull, Inactive, Influenced, Mutable, Negative, Receptive, Rouse, Susceptible).

Passive Faculties — Deviation of the Passive or Sensitive Faculties—(See Deviations; "Passive Faculties" under Faculties).

Passive Planets—The ☉, ☽, and ☿ are considered passive planets, and passive subjects of the other planets according to the nature of the aspects and planets with which configurated. In the Zodiac, the M.C. and the Asc. are considered passive points, and very strong for good or evil according to the aspects formed with them at B., and by direction. (See Ascendant, Mercury, Midheaven, Moon, Sun, Variable).

PAST EVENTS—(See "Past Events" under Events).

PASTIMES — (See Amusements, Exercise, Hunting, Journeys, Love Affairs, Pleasures, Reading, Recreations, Sports, Study, Theatres, Travel, Voyages, etc.).

PASTRIES—Fond of—(See "Pastries" under Food).

PATELLA—Knee Cap—(See Knees).

PATERNAL—Pertaining to the Father — Paternal Aunts and Uncles — Relatives On Father's Side—(See "Paternal" under Aunts; "Relatives" under Father).

PATHOLOGICAL—Pathogenic—Causing Disease—♄, ♃ and ♂ are considered the Pathological Planets, and their afflictions tend to cause disease. (See "Pathological Action" under each of the Planets).

Ganglion—Pathological Formation of —(See "Pathological" under Ganglion).

PATIENCE—Patient—This is a quality of ♄, and ♄ people are very patient in disease, suffering, and affliction, and have great power to wait tranquilly for events. The good aspects of ♄ to the ☉, ☽, and ☿ give patience, or any aspect of ♄ to ☿. Also given by many planets in the fixed signs at B. Uranus and ♂ more prominent at B. than ♄, or afflicting ♄, tend to give impatience. (See Contentment, Discontentment, Endurance, Fretful; "Peace of Mind" under Mind; Persevering, Resignation, Restless, Saturn).

PATIENT—The Patient—Condition of— —Conduct of—Prospects of—(See "Patient" under Disease).

PATRICIDE — (See this subject under Father).

PEACE—Peaceable—Peaceful—

Death — A Peaceful Death—(See "Peaceful" under Death, Old Age).

Lover of Peace—A Peaceful Disposition—(See Cheerfulness, Contentment, Gentle, Good, Harmless, Honest, Humane, Kind, Mild, Quiet, Sincere, etc.).

No Peace of Mind—(See "No Peace" under Mind).

Peace of Mind—(See "Peace of Mind" under Mind).

PECCANT HUMOURS—(See "Offensive" under Humours).

PECTORAL—Pectoral Affections—(See Breast, Chest, Lungs, Thorax).

PECTORIS—Angina Pectoris—(See Angina).

PECULIAR—Peculiarity—Peculiarities —Strange—Unusual, etc.—

Accidents—Peculiar and Sudden Accidents — (See "Extraordinary" under Accidents).

Appetites—Peculiar Appetites and Tastes—Capricious—Whimsical—Illusory—Fantastic—♅ in ♋ or the 6th H.; the ☽ in ♒, fantastic appetites. (See Appetites, Cravings, Diet, Eating, Fancies, Food, Ideals, Tastes, etc.).

Brain Diseases—(See "Peculiar" under Brain).

Clothing — Dress — Food—Peculiar Tastes In Food and Clothing — (See "Peculiar" under Dress, Food).

Course of Disease — Peculiar Course In Disease—Peculiar Symptoms— Caused principally by the afflictions of ♅ to the ☽ during the course of the disease. Also the afflictions of ☿ cause a various course in disease. (See Course, Erratic; "Disease" under Extraordinary; "Course of Disease" under Irregular; Mysterious, Strange, Symptoms, Unusual, Variable, etc.).

Death—Peculiar Death—(See "Death" under Extraordinary).

Diseases—Peculiar Diseases—Difficult to Understand—Ill-Health of a Peculiar Nature—The ☉ hyleg, and ♅ ♂ or P. the ☉ at a Solar Rev.; the ill-asps. of the ☽ by dir. to the hyleg; ♆ and ♅ diseases; ♆ or ♅ afflicted in the 6th H.; ♒ on the Asc. (See "Diseases" under Extraordinary; "Imaginary Diseases" under Imagination; Mysterious, Periodic, Praeincipients, Pseudo, Psychic, Strange, Uncommon).

Disposition—A Peculiar Disposition— (See Eccentric, Misunderstood).

Fears—Peculiar Fears—(See the various paragraphs under Fear).

Food and Clothing — (See Appetites, Clothing, in this section).

Forebodings—Peculiar Forebodings— (See Forebodings).

Head—(See "Peculiar Shaped" under Head).

Hurts—(See Extraordinary; "Strange" under Hurts).

Imaginations—(See "Peculiar" under Imagination).

Mind—A Peculiar Mind—(See Chaotic, Eccentric, Fancies, Ideals, Mentality, Mind, Misunderstood, Notions, Occult, Religion, Vagaries, Weird, etc.).

Nervous Diseases—A Peculiar Nervousness—(See "Peculiar" under Nerves).

Pleasures—Given to Peculiar Pleasures—(See "Peculiar" under Pleasure).

Symptoms — Peculiar Symptoms In Disease—(See "Peculiar" under Symptoms; "Course" in this section).

Tastes — Peculiar Tastes and Appetites—(See Appetites, Clothing, in this section).

Vagaries—(See "Peculiar" under Vagaries).

Vision—(See "Peculiarity of Vision" under Sight).

PEDESTRIANISM—A Fondness For Walking—A ♐ characteristic. Where ♄ is prominent, however, and afflicted, the Sagittarian may be averse to walking, exercise, out-door sports, or recreations. (See Exercise, Sports, Walk).

PEDUNCULATED TUMORS—(See "Polypus" under Nose; Polypus).

PEEVISH—Fretful—Irritable—Childish —Mostly a ♄ and ♑ influence; ♄ Sig. in ♋ or ♑; the ☽ ♂ or P. ♄ at B., and by dir., peevish and fearful; ♃ Sig. in ♑; ☿ Sig. in ♑ or ♓; ♏ upon the Asc. (See Dejected, Discontentment; "Brings Disease Upon Himself" under Disease; Fears, Fretful, Irritable; "Low Spirits" under Low; Murmuring, Patience, Regretful, Repining, Restlessness, Scolding, Worry, etc.).

PELLAGRA — An Endemic Erythematous Disease of Italy—Caused by the same general influences as given under Endemic and Erythema. (See Endemic, Erythema).

PELLITORY — Pyrethrum — A Typical Drug of the ☽. A Sialagog, increasing the flow of saliva. (See "Moon Group" under Herbs; Saliva).

PELVIS — Pelvic — The Bony Basin of the Trunk, formed by the Innominate Bones and the Sacrum—The Pelvis is ruled by the ♐ Sign. The Pelvic Bones are ruled by ♏. (See Hips, Innominate, Pubes, Sacrum).

Pelvic Operations—Are indicated by ♂ afflicted in ♐.

Pelvis of the Kidneys—Ruled by ♏. Stone is formed in the pelvis of the kidneys by the action of ♄. (See Kidneys).

PENETRATING—See "Penetrating" under Eyes, Mind; Pungent.

PENIS—Glans Penis—The Male External Sex Organ—The Organ of Copulation — Ruled by ♂. The Penis, the Urethra, and the Scrotum, are ruled by the ♏ Sign. The Muscles of Erection are ruled by ♏. The Uro-Genital Orifice is ruled by ♏.

Balanitis—Inflammation of the Glans Penis—♂ afflicted in ♏ or ♓.

Chancre — Hard Chancre — Accompanies Syphilis—(See Syphilis).

Chancroid—Soft Chancre—Accompanies Gonorrhoea—(See Gonorrhoea).

Channels and Vents—Lack of Proper Sex Channels—(See "Channels" under Genitals).

Chordee—Painful Down-Curved Erection—(See Gonorrhoea).

Circumcision Indicated—(See Circumcision).

Erections Painful — (See "Chordee" under Gonorrhoea; "Priapism" in this section).

Eunuchs — A Castrated Male — (See Eunuchs, Testes).

Genitals—Diseases of—(See Genitals).

Genito-Urinary Diseases—(See Genito-Urinary).

Glans Penis—Inflammation of—(See "Balanitis" in this section).

Gleet—(See "Chronic" under Gonorrhoea).

Gonorrhoea—(See Gonorrhoea).

Hermaphrodites—(See this subject).

Inflammation — (See "Balanitis" in this section).

Injuries To — (See "Mens' Genitals" under Genitals; Maimed).

Masturbation—(See "Solitary" under Vice).

Mens' Genitals—Diseases of—Injuries To—(See "Mens' Genitals" under Genitals; the various paragraphs in this section).

Natural Channels—(See "Channels" in this section).

Pain In—(See "Pain" under Genitals).

Painful Erections — (See "Priapism" in this section).

Prepuce—(See Circumcision).

Priapism—Painful Erection—A ♏ disease; a ♀ disease and caused by afflictions to ♀; ♂ influence at B. overlaid and intermixed with other planets, as ♄, ♅, and ♆; afflictions in ♏. (See "Chordee" under Gonorrhoea).

Scrotum — Complications Affecting — (See Scrotum, Semen, Testes).

Soft Chancre—(See Gonorrhoea).

Stricture of Urethra—(See Urethra).

Undeveloped — Sex Organs Undeveloped—(See Undeveloped).

Urethra—Disorders of—(See Urethra).

Venereal Diseases—(See Venereal).

PENSIVE—A Pensive or Sad Aspect— (See "Appearance" under Sadness).

PENURIOUS—Parsimonious—Sordid— Indigent—♄ ruler of the Asc. and the horoscope at B., and afflicted; ♄ in ♉, avaricious. (See Misanthropic, Miserly, Selfish).

PEOPLE — The People — The Public — Humanity—The Common People—Are ruled generally by the ☽. (See Common People, Humanity, Mankind, Mobs, Nations, Public).

Aged People—(See Grandparents, Old Age).

Middle-Aged People — (See Middle Life).

Young People—(See Children, Young, Youth).

PEPPER—Cayenne Pepper—Capsicum —Ruled by ♂. (See "Mars Group" under Herbs).

PEPPERMINT—Mentha—A Typical Drug of ♃. (See "Jupiter Group" under Herbs).

PEPSIN—Ruled by the ♋ Sign. (See "Fluids" under Digestion; "Juices" under Gastric; "Pepsin" under Stomach).

PERCEPTION — Perceptions — Perceptive Faculties—

Acute Perceptive Faculties — Saturn well-dignified at B., as in ♎, ♑, or ♒, and well-aspected by the ☽ and ☿; ♂ a strong ruler at B., well-aspected and dignified; ♂ Sig. in ♏, excelling in mystery. (See "Active Mind" under Active; Knowledge, Learning; "Quickened" under Mentality; "Good Mind" under Mind; Understanding, etc.).

Disorders of Perception—☿, the mental ruler, weak and afflicted at B.; ☿ in no aspect to the ☽ or Asc., and with ☿ otherwise weak and afflicted at B. (See Comprehension; "Mind" under Dull; Fears, Hallucinations, Illusions; "Mental" under Impaired; Inactive, Intuition; "Weak" under Intellect, Mentality, Mind, Senses, Smell, Understanding).

False Perceptions — (See Delusions, Hallucinations, Illusions).

Sense Perceptions—☿ rules all sense perceptions. (See Senses).

PEREGRINE—A Planet in a Sign having no essential dignity of any kind, and is reckoned a debility of five degrees. In Hor'y Q. a peregrine planet in an angle, or the 2nd H., is taken as the thief in matters of theft. (See Thieves). A benefic planet, when peregrine, also does not lend as much support in health matters, and a malefic

planet, when so situated, and afflicted, is more mischievous in causing disease, affliction, suffering, misfortune, and trouble. (See Benefics, Malefics).

PERFECT—Perfection—Physical Harmony—Perfection of Mind and Body— A "Perfect" Physical Body—(See "Perfect" under Eyes, Functions; Harmony; "Perfection" under Mind; "Free Will" under Will).

PERFORATED—Perforated Ear Drum —(See "Discharges" under Ears).

PERFUMES—Ruled by ♀. (See "Vocation" under Color; "Dealing In Medicines" under Medicine; Odors).

PERICARDIUM—The Membranous Sac Around the Heart — Ruled by the ♌ sign, and especially affected by the ☽ in ♌. (See Carditis, Endocarditis, Pericarditis, under Heart).

PERIGEE—A Planet in its Orbit nearest the Earth. Planets in Perigee tend to be very strong in causing disturbances, diseases, distempers, epidemics, etc. (See Cholera, Epidemics, Malefics; "Perigee" under Moon; Perihelion).

PERIHELION—A Planet in its Orbit nearest the Sun. The Superior Planets when in Perihelion tend to cause epidemics, weather and atmospheric disturbances, and many troubles upon the Earth. (See "Corrupt Air" under Air; Cholera, Dreams, Epidemics; "Disordered" under Nerves; Perigee, Pestilence; "Sun Spots" under Spots; Typhus, Volcanoes).

PERIHEPATITIS—(See "Inflammation" under Liver).

PERIL—Perils—Dangers—(See the various paragraphs under Accidents, Dangers, Death, Hurts, Injuries, Travel, Wounds, etc. Also look in the alphabetical arrangement for the subject you have in mind).

Danger and Peril—To the Native— The ☽ Sig. □ or ☍ ♂, passes thru innumerable dangers; the ☽ incr. in light, sepr. from ♃ and applying to ♂ in a nocturnal nativity; the ☽ with Antares or Aldebaran in the Asc. or M.C.; ♃ ruler of the 1st H., and to the ill-asps. ♄ by dir.; ♂ ☌ ☊. (See "Many Dangers" under Danger).

Great Perils Generally—Comets appearing in ♏. (See Abroad, Calamity, Comets, Drowning, Falls, Heights, Highwaymen, Pirates, Quadrupeds, Robbers, Shipwreck, Travel, Voyages, War, etc.).

PERINEUM — The Space between the Thighs from the Anus to the Genitals —Ruled by ♏. (See Fundament).

PERIODIC — Periodical — Recurrent — Returning—Intermittent, etc.—

Periodic Diseases—Periodic Sickness and Illness—Periodic Irregularities— The ☽ rules diseases and afflictions which return after a time, such as Vertigo, Epilepsy, Faintings, Falling Fits, Falling Sickness, Periodic Illnesses in Females, Giddiness, Gout, Swimming in the Head, etc. (See these subjects). Those who have the ☉ critically afflicted at B. tend to have peculiar trouble and serious illness every tenth year of life. The hyleg afflicted by ♄ at B., or ♄ in the Asc. or

M.C., or afflicting the ☉, ☽, or Asc., tends to cause the return of some chronic ailment, or cause some chronic disease every seven years when ♄ passes the evil aspects of □, ⚹, and ⚷ to his place at B., and also again when he reaches his place in the map of birth at from the 28th to 30th years of life, and also at about the 58th and 59th years of life, when ♄ finishes his second revolution in his orbit after birth. The ☽ in bad asp. to ♄ at B. tends to ill-health every seven years. The ☽ ruler of the 1st or 6th H. at B., and in bad asp. to ♀, tends to ill-health periodically, both by transit and the directions of ♀, when the ☽ is in bad asp. to ♀ at B.; the ☽ □ or ⚹ Asc., periodic illness. (See Climacteric, Critical Years, Cycles; "Periods of Bad Health" under Health; Periods; "Returning Diseases" under Return).

Periodic Fevers — (See Ague, Intermittent, Malaria, Quartan, Quotidian, Remittent, Semi-Tertian, Tertian, etc.).

Periodic Headache — (See "Periodic" under Headaches).

Periodic Insanity—Returning At Intervals — (See "Periodic" under Insanity).

Periodic Irregularities—Ruled by the ☽. (See Irregularities).

Periodic Lunations—The time the ☽ returns to her place each month in the map of birth, a period of 27d. 7h. 44m. This is a sensitive place for the ☽ in health matters, and also a very dangerous time for an operation. It may also be a crisis time in a fever, if the ☽ was on her place when the fever began, and when an acute disease will either resolve itself or go into a chronic form of disease, being the 28th day of the disease. (See Crises, Lunations; "Rules" under Operations).

Periodic Remedies — The Moon and Mercury Groups of Herbs are periodic in their general action. (See Antiperiodic; "Mercury Group", "Moon Group", under Herbs; Innervation).

Periodic Revolution—Of a Planet— The return of a planet to its place in the radix after making a revolution in its orbit. A planet at such times exercises considerable influence in health matters for good or ill according to the nature and aspects of the planet at the time. (See the ☿ influences in the paragraph, "General Causes" under Epilepsy; "Solar Revolution" under Revolution; "Periodic Lunations" in this section).

Periodic Vomiting—(See Vomiting).

Women—Periodic Illness In—(See Menses).

PERIODICITY—Regularly Recurrent— **Cellular Periodicity** — (See "Periodicity" under Cells).

Nervous Periodicity — Innervation — (See "Periodicity" under Nerves).

Solar Periodicity—(See "Periodicity" under Sun).

Zymotic Periodicity—(See Zymotic).

PERIODS—Periods of Life—Periods of Good or Bad Health— **Acute Diseases** — (See "Periods Of" under Acute).

Childhood—Periods of—(See Childhood).

Gestation — Period of — (See Gestation).

Good Health—Periods of—(See "Periods of Good Health "under Health).

Ill-Health — (See "Periods of Bad Health" under Health).

Infancy—Period of—(See Childhood, Infancy).

Life—Periods of Life Ruled by the Planets—Authorities seem to differ on the Periods of Life, as ruled over by the different Planets. The first four years of life are ruled by the ☽, and also it is generally understood that the ☽ rules the first seven years of life. Mercury rules from the 4th to 10th years. From the 10th to 18th years, by ♀. From the 18th to 37th years by the ☉. From the 37th to 52nd years by ♂. From the 52nd to 64th years by ♃. After the 64th year, by ♄. Another division given by some Authors is as follows: The ☽ rules the first seven years of life; ☿ from 7 to 15; ♀ from the 15th to 24th years; the ☉ from the 24th to 34th years; ♂ from the 34th to 45th; ♃ from the 45th to 57th; ♄ from the 57th to 70th. If a person lives beyond 70, then ♅ rules from 70 to 84, and ♆ from 84 to 99. When the ruler of any of these periods is severely afflicted at B., it indicates that that part of the life ruled by such planet will tend to be especially unfortunate, and filled with trouble, trials, misfortune, or illnesses of the nature attributed to such planet. The ☽ badly afflicted at B. tends to more danger in infancy. In the Kabala, Infancy was dedicated to the ☉; childhood to the ☽; youth to ♂ and ♀; mature age to ♃, and old age to ♄. (See Climacteric; "Critical Periods" under Critical; Cycles).

Middle Life—Period of—(See Middle Life).

Old Age — Period of — (See Fourth House, Old Age, Terminal).

Planetary Periods — Periods of the Planets — The revolution of ♄ takes 29y. 167d. 4h.; of ♃, 11y. 314d. 20h.; of ♂, 1y. 321d. 22h.; of ♀, 224d. 7h.; of ☿, 87d. 23h.; of ♅, about 84 years, or 7 years in a Sign; of ♆, 165 years, or about 14 years in one Sign of the Zodiac; of the ☽, 27d. 7h. 43m., her periodical course, but the period between her actual conjunctions is 29d. 12h. 44m. The ☉, about 365 days to pass thru the 12 Signs, as seen from the Earth. (See "Direct Motion" under Direct; Retrograde).

Seven-Year Periods—Every 7th year of life is said to be a changing, and more critical year in life, which years correspond to the Quarters of the ☽. Life is divided into seven-year periods, as 7, 14, 21, 28, 35, 42, 49, 56, 63, 70, etc., which are considered crisis years in life, or more dangerous years. Also every 7th year from birth corresponds to the ∠, □, ⚹, and ⚷ aspects of ♄ from his place in the radix, as his period is about 28 years, which makes every seventh year more critical for the health. The 49th and 63rd years of adult life are considerel dangerous years, being doubly climateric, and many deaths occur in such years of life. (See Aspects, Climacteric, Crises, Seven).

Youth—The Period of—(See Puberty, Young, Youth).

PERIOSTEITIS — Inflammation of the Periosteum—(See Bones).

PERIPHERAL — The Outer Boundary, Circumference, or Surface of the Body—

Peripheral Lesions — (See "Aphonia" under Voice).

Peripheral Nerves — Peripheral Sympathetic Nerves — Ruled by ♄ and ♅. Remedies used in the treatment of acute diseases begin their action at the peripheral nerves. These nerves also ruling the skin and mucous membranes, and also being ruled by ♄, tend to morbid diseases and manifestations. Cold, ruled by ♄, also affects these nerves, driving the blood inward, and causing internal congestions, and acute diseases start with disturbances in the peripheral nerves. (See Acute, Capillaries, Centripetal, Chilblain, Chill; "Blood' under Circulation; Cold, Colds, Congestion, Constrictions, Ganglion; "Congestion" under Internal; "Mydriasis" under Iris; the Introduction under Knees; Nausea, Saturn; "Arms" under Skin; "Sympathetic Nervous System" under Sympathetic).

PERISTALSIS—Peristaltic Action—The peristaltic action of the stomach is ruled by ♋, and of the bowels by ♍. Saturn when in these signs tends to impede this action. Antiperistaltic action is usually caused by the affliction of ♄ from an opposite sign, as from ♑ or ♓. (See Antiperistalsis; "Peristaltic Action" under Bowels, Stomach; Emetics, Expulsion, Nausea, Physic, Vomiting).

PERITONEUM— Mesentery— Omentum —Ruled by ♍. The Serum of the Peritoneum is connected with the ♓ sign. (See Mesentery, Omentum, Serous).

Diseases Of—Caused by afflictions in ♍.

Dropsy Of—Ascites—(See "Abdomen" under Dropsy).

Inflammation Of—Peritonitis—The ☉, ☽, or ♂ afflicted in ♍; ♂ afflicted in ♍ in the 6th H.; afflictions in ♍; Subs at PP. Cases—See Fig. 18E in "Astro-Diagnosis", by the Heindels. See "Marriage", No. 256, in 1001 N.N.

Rupture Of — ♂ afflicted in ♍. (See Rupture).

PERITYPHLITIS—Inflammation Around the Caecum—(See Caecum).

PERJURY—Perjured—Given to Perjury —♃ to the ill-asps. ☿ by dir.; ♂ ill-dignified at B., and afflicted; ☿ is the author of perjury; ☿ afflicted at B., and by dir. (See Deceitful, Dishonest, Liars; "Perjured" under Religion).

PERMANENT — Tending to Endure — More Lasting In Effects—Lingering—Chronic—

Permanent Diseases — These diseases proceed from ♄, and are generally regulated by the motion of the ☉. (See Chronic, Incurable, Lingering; "Diseases" under Long; "Incapable Of" under Remedy; Tedious, Wastings).

Permanent Habit In Disease—(See Diathesis, Hexis).

Permanent Habits—(See "Permanent" under Habits).

Permanent Hurts—Or Injuries—Those Tending to Cripple, Deform, Blemish, or Incapacitate—The ☉ in the 6th H., in cardinal signs, and afflicted by malefics. (See Blemishes, Crippled, Deformities; "Hurts" under Remedy).

PERNICIOUS — Fatal — Vehement — Highly Destructive—

Pernicious Anaemia—(See Anaemia).

Pernicious Diseases — Caused by ♂. (See Fierce, Quick, Sharp, Swift, Vehement, Violent).

Pernicious Fevers—(See "Destructive Processes" under Destructive; High, Violent, under Fever).

PERPLEXITIES — (See Affliction, Anguish, Anxiety, Cares, Disgrace, Gloom, Grief; "No Peace of Mind" under Mind; Miseries, Misfortune; "Loss Of" under Reputation; Reverses, Ruin, Sorrow, Trouble, Vexations, Worry, etc.).

PERSECUTION—Persecutions are ruled and denoted by the 12th H.

Delusions of Persecution — See Paranoia).

Religious Persecution — Persecuted Because of Religious Beliefs, or Advanced and Independent Views—☿ Sig. ☐ or ☍ ♃. (See Eccentric, Independent, Misunderstood, Occult, Opinions, Reformers, Religion, Revolutionary, etc.). Death from Religious Persecution may result when the lord of the 9th H. at B. is afflicted in the 8th H. (See "Injured" under Religion).

PERSEVERING — Perseverance — Persistent—Tenacious—Constant—Steady In Purpose — Unwavering — The ☉, ☽, and ☿ in fixed signs at B., and in angles; the ☉ influence strong at B.; ♄ strong at B.; ♃ to the ☌ and good asps. ♀, the mind is steady; many planets in fixed signs, or fixed signs on the angles. (See Constancy; "Fixed Habits", "Fixed Signs", under Fixed; Inflexible, Obstinate, Patience, Positive, Resolute, Self-Reliant, etc.).

PERSONAL—Pertaining to the Person—

Personal Appearance — (See Appearance, Beautiful, Body, Countenance, Crooked, Decanates, Deformities, Expression, Eyes, Face, Figure, Fleshy, Form, Hair, Height, Ill-Formed, Large, Look, Middle-Sized, Neat, Robust, Short, Sickly, Stature, Tall, Thin, Ugly, Weight, Well-Proportioned, etc.).

Personal Beauty — (See Beautiful, Comely, Complexion, Handsome, Harmony, Well-Proportioned, etc.).

Personal Cleanliness — (See Cleanly, Dress, Neat, etc.).

Personal Habits—The ☽ has an important influence over the personal habits, and represents the personal character. (See Character, Conduct, "Personal Habits" under Habits).

Personal Marks—(See Blemishes, Defects, Marks, Moles, Scars, etc.).

PERSONALITY—The Lower Mind — The Desires — The Animal Instincts — The Sense Mind—Denoted by the sign in which the ☽ is posited at B. The sign containing the ☉ indicates the Higher Mind, or the Individuality. (See Adrenals; "Animal Instincts" under Animal; Character, Desires, Habits, Individuality, Instincts; "Lower Mind" under Mind; Temperament).

Dual Personality—(See "Double-Bodied Signs" under Double-Bodied; "Dual-Minded" under Dual; Memory).

Erratic Personality—Caused by the □ and ⚹ of ♅ to planets; ♅ □ or ⚹ the ☉, ☽, ♃, ♂, ♀, or ☿; ♅ afflicted in ♊, ♍, ♐, ♑, ♒, or ♓; afflictions to the ☽; the ☽ □ or ⚹ ☿ or ♅; ☿ ruler of the horoscope and afflicted by malefics. (See Conduct, Eccentric; "Mind" under Erratic).

Good Personality—(See Pleasant).

Triple Personality — Case — (See "Triple", No. 369, in 1001 N.N.

PERSPIRATION—Sweating—(See Axillae, Excretion; "Bromidrosis" under Feet; Fetid, Sweat).

PERTUSSIS — Whooping Cough — (See "Convulsive Coughing" under Cough; Whooping).

PERUVIAN BARK—Cinchona—Quinine —(See Cinchona).

PERVERSE — Perversity — Perverted — An afflicted ♅ tends to make one perverse, and to rebel against established customs, and often unreasonably so. The good aspects of ♃ to ♅ tend to modify this, but with no good aspect from ♃, and ♅ also sorely afflicted, the perversity tends to be uncontrolled. Aquarius and ♓ when afflicted tend to perversity, and to be unconventional. Aquarius afflicted tends to perversions in sex relations, and to immorality. Saturn Sig. in ♊ tends to perversity; ♂ afflicted in ♒, perversity, and to be unruly and controversial. Also caused by the ☽ applying to the evil aspects of ♂. (See Anarchists, Eccentric, Erratic, Erring, Independent, Irrational; "Bad Judgment" under Judgment; Misunderstood, Perversions; "Unreasonable" under Reason; Rebellious, Riotous, Uncontrolled).

PERVERSIONS —Abnormal—Abnormalities of the Sexual Instincts — Perverted Action — Are due to the tonic action of ♅; ♅ afflicting the ☉, ♆, or ☿, a perverting agency, and disruptive.

Activity—Perverted Activity—Caused by the afflictions of ♅ and ♆, and especially when afflicting the ☉, ☽, ♀, or ☿. (See Action, Activity).

Appetites — Perverted Appetites — ♆ afflicted in ♋; ♆ afflicted in the 3rd or 12th H.; ♄ affl. in ♋. (See "Abnormal" under Appetites).

Contrary Manner—Men Seek Sex Connection In a Contrary Manner, but In Secret, and Not Openly — (See Homosexuality; "Licentious" under Men).

Desires — Perverted Desires — ♆ afflicted in the 5th H., perverted and depraved desires; ♆ afflicted in the 1st H.; ♅ ruler of the horoscope, and afflicted; ♀ afflicted at B., tends to faulty desires, dissipation, and debauchery. (See Debauchery, Depraved, Desires, Dissipation; "Low and Base" under

Low; "Loose Morals" under Morals; Perverse, Prodigal; the various paragraphs in this section).

Deviations—Deviations from the Usual Limits of Nature—(See Aversions, Deviations; "Nature's Laws" under Nature; Unnatural, Vices).

Easily Perverted — ☿ ill-dignified at B. (See Influenced).

Effeminate — Men Effeminate and Women Masculine—(See Effeminate).

Emotional Perversion — (See "Desire Body" under Desire; Emotions).

Food—(See "Perverted Tastes" under Food).

Functions — (See "Perversion" under Functions).

Homosexuality—Sodomy—(See Homosexuality).

Imagination Perverted — (See "Perverted" under Imagination).

Incest — Sex Connection with a Near Relative—♂ and ♀ both in masculine signs, and ori., inclines to, and with danger of; ♀ ill-dignified at B.

Judgment Perverted—(See "Bad" under Judgment).

Masochism—Cruel Treatment In Sex Relations—(See Masochism).

Men—Sex Perversions In—(See "Contrary", and the various paragraphs in this section).

Moral Perversions—(See "Adulterous" under Love Affairs; Loose Morals, Moral Perversions, under Morals; "Clandestine" under Sex; the various paragraphs in this section).

Morbid Perversions — (See Compulsions, Unsavory, and the various paragraphs under Morbid).

Necrophilism — Sex Congress with a Dead Body—(See Necrophilism).

Nutrition Perverted—(See "Perverted" under Nutrition).

Planets — Perverted Action of — (See "Perverted Action" under Planets).

Practices—Perverted Practices—♆ afflicted in the 1st, 3rd, 5th, 6th, 7th, 9th, or 12th H.; ☿ ruler of the horoscope, and afflicted by malefics. (See Practices).

Sadism — Sex Gratification Attended by Violence — (See "Violence" under Men, Passion; Sadism).

Sex Perversions — Largely caused by the afflictions and lower vibrations of ♅, which tend to make the unawakened and unspiritualized native careless, unconventional, and to believe in free love, and to disregard the laws of Society; ♅ and ☽ in ♏; ♅ afflicted in ♏; ♆ afflicted in the 1st, 3rd, or 12th H.; ♆ □ or ⚹ ☽; ♄ ♂, P., □, or ⚹ ♀, perverted sex desires, and usually directed against a younger person; ♀ in a female sign, and afflicted by ♂ in a male nativity, tends to make men wanton, and to seek connection contrary to nature, but privately, and not openly. If ♂ also be in a female sign, men will be shameless and public in their sex practices. The same conditions may exist in women if ♂, ♀, and the Lights are in masculine signs and sorely afflicted, and with ♄ also in evil configuration, tends to greater obscenity and impurity. (See Infamous, Lewd; "Low and Base" under Low; Obscene, Secret, Shameless, Unnatural; the various paragraphs in this section).

Shameless Practices—(See Shameless; "Sex Perversions" in this section).

Sodomy—Sex Connection by the Anus —(See Homesexuality).

Solar-Lunar Activity — Perversion of —(See "Solar-Lunar" under Solar).

Spiritual Perversions—(See Spiritual).

Talents — Perverted Talents — (See Talents).

Tastes — (See "Perverted" under Tastes).

Tonic Action—Perverted Tonic Action of Planets — (See "Perverted Action" under Planets; Tonic).

Violence—Men Given to Violence In Sex Gratification — (See Masochism; "Licentious" under Men; "Violence" under Passion; Sadism).

Vital Stimulus — Perversion of — (See "Stimulus" under Vital).

PESSIMISTIC—♄ strong at B., or born under ♄. (See Dejected, Despondent, Doubts, Fears, Gloom, Hope, Mistrustful; "Optimism Destroyed" under Optimism; Recluse, Reserved; "Secretive" under Secret; Suspicious, etc.).

PEST—

Black Pest—(See Pestilence, Plague).

Insect Pests—Vermin—(See Insects, Vermin).

Pest to Society — (See "Pest" under Society).

PESTILENCE—Pestilential—Deadly Epidemic Disease — Principally ♌, ♏, and ♐ diseases, and caused by afflictions in these signs. The Causes of Pestilence are discussed in the Article on Epidemics. (See "Causes" under Epidemics).

Air—Pestilential Air—(See "Corrupt Air" under Air; "Winds" in this section).

Danger by Pestilential Disease—The ☽ to the ☌ ☌ in ♌; the Asc. to the □ or ☍ ☌ by dir.; the ☽ directed to Antares or the Bull's Eye.

Death by Pestilence—Danger of—The ☉ directed to the Pleiades; ♂ ☌ the Asc. by dir. (See "Illness" in this section).

Eruptions — (See "Pestilential" under Eruptions).

Fevers — Pestilential Fevers — Pestilential Burning Fevers—The ☉ afflicted in ♉ when the ☉ is the afflictor in the disease; the ☽ in ♐ and afflicted by the ☉ or ♂ when taken ill; a ♂ disease and affliction; ♂ causes pestilential burning fevers; ♂ in the 6th H., or under the Sun's beams at a decumbiture, and if the ☉ or ♂, the planet signifying the disease, be in ♌ or ♏, the disease will be pestilential; ♂ in an earthy sign, and to the ill-asps. the Asc. by dir. (See "Epidemic Fevers" under Epidemics; "High" under Fever; "Illness" in this section).

Great Pestilence Signified—Pestilence Over the World—Pestilence Prevalent —A Solar Eclipse in the 2nd Decan. of

♍, and especially among People and Countries ruled by ♍. (See "Virgo" under Nations). An Eclipse of the ☉ or ☽ in airy signs, and especially in places ruled by the Signs in which it occurs; an eclipse of the ☉ in the 3rd Decan. ♉; an eclipse of the ☉ in ♎, and especially in the 1st Decan. of this sign, and due to corrupt air; an eclipse of the ☽ in the 2nd Decan. of ♈. or the 3rd Dec. of ♐; ♄ ☌ ♂ in the 6th or 8th H., in a human sign, and ♄ Lord of the Year at the Vernal Equinox (see "Human Signs" under Human); a malefic planet in power at a Summer Solstice, and afflicting the ☉ or ☽, or planets in the 6th H., and also a malefic in the 8th H.; caused by the ☌ of several superior planets in airy signs, and due to the maximum of planetary influence; coincident with the appearance of Comets; Comets appearing in ♋, ♑, or ♒. (See "Corrupt Air" under Air; Cholera, Comets, Drought; "Fountains" under Dry; Eclipses, Epidemics, Famine; "Extreme Heat" under Heat; Pandemics, Perihelion, Plague; Virus, Winds, in this section).

Illness by Pestilence—Pestilential Complaints — Danger of Death By — The ☉ afflicted in ♊; the ☉ directed to the Pleiades; the ☽ Sig. □ or ☍ ♂; the ☽ hyleg, and to the ☌ or ill-asp. ♂, and with ♂ in ♌ near the Ascelli, or if ♂ be near Cor Scorpio, there is danger of illness or death by pestilence, and especially if ♂ also be ill-aspected by the ☉ or ♄; ♄ ☌ ♂ in the 6th or 8th H., in a sign of human form, and ♄ Lord of the Year at the Vernal; ♂ afflicted in ♊ or ♍, and ☌, P., □ or ☍ Asc. by dir.; ♂ ☌ the Asc. by dir.; ♂ afflicted in earthy signs, and ☌ or ill-asp. the Asc. by dir. The crisis in any pestilential illness or fever may be terminated from the 3rd to 8th day after the beginning. (See Death, Fevers, in this section).

Immunity to Pestilence—Passes Thru Unharmed—(See Immunity).

Virus — Pestilential Virus — Eclipses of the ☉ or ☽ in airy signs, or in ♍, tend to develop pestilential virus, and to cause great Pestilences, afflicting humanity, as well as horses, cattle, sheep, goats, dogs, cats, fish, fowl, and also vegetables and fruits. (See Virus).

Winds — Pestilential Winds — The ☉ and ☿ conjoined in fiery signs, heat and pestilential winds; ♂ ☌ ♃, and ♂ have more Northern Latitude; ♂ in power, and Lord at Equinoxes and Solstices, or Lord of the Year at the Vernal Equinox. (See "Corrupt Air" under Air; "Fountains Dry Up" under Dry; Epidemics, Equinoxes, Solstices, Vernal, Wind).

PETIT MAL—A Mild Form of Epilepsy —(See Epilepsy).

PETRIFACTION — Conversion Into a Stony Substance — (See Calculus, Gravel, Hardening, Sand, Stone).

PETS — Domestic Pets — Ruled by ♃. Also Small Animals are ruled by the 6th H. (See "Small Animals" under Animals; Cats, Dogs; "Virus" under Pestilence).

PETTIFOGGING—Tricky—An Inferior Lawyer—☿ afflicted in □; ☿ □ or 8 ♄ indicates those who very seldom treat their clients honestly. (See Cheating, Deceitful, Dishonest, Liars, Libel, Mischief, Politics, Shrewdness, Thieves).

PETULANT—Fretful—Capricious—Captious — Fault-Finding — Vituperative—Hypercritical—The ☽ □ or 8 ☿; a ♄ characteristic; ♄ afflicted in ♏; ♂ afflicted in the 10th H.; ♀ Sig. in ♌; ♍ on the Asc. (See Fretfulness, Prejudice, Scolding, Virgo).

Petulant Mortalities—(See "Petulant" under Mortality).

PHAGOCYTES—Vis Conservatrix—Cells Which Have the Property of Absorbing — Healing Forces In the Body — Defensive Forces—Ruled by the ☉, ♃, ♂, and ♀. The planetary influences showing strong vitality also favor the power of the Phagocytes. In cases of a weak body the workings and power of the Phagocytes are hindered. (See Absorption, Defensive, Immunity, Preservation, Recuperation, Resistance, Stamina, Tone; "Good", "Low", under Vitality; "Weak Body" under Weak).

PHALANGES — The Bones of the Fingers and Toes — (See Feet, Fingers, Hands, Toes).

PHANTASIES—Fantasies—
Mental Fantasies — (See "Dreamy Mind" under Dreams).
The Phantasies Prejudiced — (See "Prejudiced" under Fancies).

PHARMACY — The Influences Which Favor Pharmacists—(See Chemists).

PHARYNX—The Musculo-Membranous Sac Behind the Mouth — The Naso-Pharynx—Ruled by the 8 sign.
Abscess—Retropharyngeal Abscess—Abscess Behind the Pharynx — ♀ afflicted in 8; Subs at LCP, SP, and KP.
Adenoids—(See Adenoids).
Diphtheria — Membranous Exudation On the Mucous Surface of the Pharynx —(See Diphtheria).
Diseases Of — Afflictions in 8. (See Fauces, Neck, Throat).
Mucous Surface Of — Infectious Disease of, with Membranous Exudation —(See Diphtheria).
Naso-Pharynx — Inflammation of—♂ afflicted in 8; Subs at MCP (4C). (See Nose).
Pharyngitis—Inflammation of—♂ afflicted in 8.
Plexus—The Pharyngeal Plexus—(See "Diseases of the Neck" under Neck).

PHENOMENA—Phenomenon—A Symptom—Uncommon Occurrences—
Apparitions In the Air — Eclipses of the ☉ or ☽ in fiery signs, and especially in those places ruled by the Signs in which the Eclipse occurs. Also caused by Comets appearing in ♓. (See Air, Illusions).
Psychic Phenomena—Phenomena Referrable to Psychic Causes—(See Psychic). See Dreams, Extraordinary, Fears, Forebodings, Imagination, Mysterious, Obsessions, Obscure, Spirit Controls, Strange, Symptoms, Vagaries, Weird, etc.).

PHILANTHROPIC—Humane—A Lover of Mankind—The ☉ in ♒, or ♒ on the Asc. at B. (See Humane).

PHILOSOPHY—Philosophical—Philosophy and Religion are ruled by ♐ and the 9th H.
Philosophical—♃ in ♐ in the 9th H., and well-aspected. (See Metaphysical, Occult, Religion, Renunciation, Science, Study).

PHILTRES—Love Potions—Ruled by ♀. (See Aphrodisiacs).

PHLEBITIS—Inflammation of a Vein—(See Veins).

PHLEGM — Phlegmatic — Watery Humour— Mucus — Phlegmonous — Mucus from the Bronchi — The Phlegmatic Signs are ♋, ♏, and ♓, the watery signs. Phlegm is ruled by ♄, and also by ☿ when this planet partakes of the nature of ♄. The ♓ sign produces Phlegm. Also the ☽ in aspect to ♄ or ♅ tends to produce phlegm, and to cause its excessive discharge.
Body—Phlegmatic Body—The ☽ gives a smooth, corpulent and phlegmatic body. (See Corpulent, Fleshy).
Breast — Much Afflicted with Tough Phlegm and Slimy Matter In the Breast, Chest, and Lungs, and the Trachea Obstructed—The ☽ in ♋, ♂, P., □, or 8 ♄ (or ☿ if he be of the nature of ♄) at decumbiture or the beginning of an illness. If the ☽ be decreasing, and near the body of ♄, the disease will continue a long time. (See Bronchial, Consumption, Cough, Lungs).
Catarrh—(See the various paragraphs under Catarrh).
Chest — Tough Phlegm In — (See "Breast" in this section).
Cold, Phlegmatic Diseases—And Death By—Caused by the ☽; by the ☽ and many planets afflicted in watery signs, and with a water sign on the Asc. The ☽ assists in causing death by phlegmatic diseases, when the ☉ or Asc. are hyleg, by her evil directions to the hyleg when she holds the dominion of death. (See Cold).
Colds — (See the paragraphs under Colds).
Cough — (See "Rotten Coughs", and the various paragraphs under Cough).
Defluxions—(See this subject).
Discharges of Phlegm — A ♄, ☽, and ☿ disease. Also a 8 disease. (See Discharges; "Discharges" under Mucous, Rheum).
Diseases — Phlegmatic Diseases — Caused by ♄, ☿, and the ☽, and by the 8 and ♓ Signs; the ☽ to the ☌ ♄ or ♅ by dir.; the Asc. to the ill-asps. ♄. (See the various paragraphs in this section).
Enteritis — Catarrhal and Phlegmonous Enteritis In Bowels—(See "Enteritis" under Catarrh).
Excessive Phlegm—Excess of—♄ in an angle, occi. of the ☉, and ori. of the ☽. (See "Throat" in this section).
Great Expectoration—Of Phlegm—The ☽ in ♓, and afflicted by the ☉ or ♂ when taken ill, great expectoration, and almost suffocated with phlegm. (See Bronchial, Cough, Lungs; "Humours", "Rheum", under Throat).

Humours—(See "Flow of Humours", and the various paragraphs under Humours).

Larynx — Collections of Phlegm and Mucus In—(See "Phlegm" under Larynx).

Legs—(See "Phlegmasia Alba Dolens" under Legs).

Lungs — Phlegm In — (See Breast, Great Expectoration, in this section; "Bronchitis" under Bronchial; Consumption; "Phlegm" under Lungs; Phthisis, Tuberculosis).

Melancholic Disease—Proceeding from Phlegm—(See "Diseases" under Melancholy).

Obstructions by Phlegm—♄ diseases and affliction. (See Breast, Great Expectoration, Larynx, Lungs, in this section; "Obstructions" under Bronchial, Lungs, Stomach).

Phlegmatic Dolens—(See "Milk Leg" under Legs).

Phlegmon—Suppurative Inflammation —(See Phlegmon, Pus).

Rheum — (See the paragraphs under Rheum).

Salt Phlegm — A ♋ sign disease, and caused by afflictions in this sign. (See "Salt Rheum" under Eczema).

Stomach — Phlegm In the Stomach — ☿ afflicted in ♋. (See Catarrh, Phlegm, under Stomach).

Suffocated — Almost Suffocated with Phlegm — (See "Great Expectoration" in this section).

Temperament—Phlegmatic Temperament—The Phlegmatic Attitude—The Lymphatic Temperament — Given by the ☽ in ♓; the ☽ ascending at B.; is also produced by ♄, and is a cold and moist bodily temperament. The Phlegmatic Attitude is especially caused by heavy ♄ afflictions at B., and by dir., and also by a preponderance of influences in the fixed signs. The ♉, ♋, and ♓ signs are phlegmatic. Given by ♓, and with ♓ on the Asc. (See "Dull Eyes" under Eyes; "Temperament" under Lymphatic; Pituitary).

Throat—Excess of Phlegm In—(See "Phlegm" under Throat).

Trachea—Windpipe Obstructed by Phlegm — (See "Breast" in this section).

Whitlows—Phlegmonous Inflammation About the Nails — (See "Nails" under Toes).

PHLEGMASIA ALBA DOLENS — (See "Milk Leg" under Legs).

PHLEGMON—Suppurative Inflammation of Areolar Tissue—(See Nipples; "Phlegmon" under Pus; Suppuration; "Whitlows" under Toes).

Phlegmonous Enteritis—(See "Inflammation" under Bowels).

Phlegmonous Ulcer—(See Ulcers).

PHOBIAS—Fears—Dreads—(See Fear).

PHONATION — The Emission of Vocal Sounds—(See Articulation, Dysphonia, Hoarseness, Larynx, Speech, Voice).

PHOSPHATE — Salts of Phosphoric Acid—

Phosphate of Iron—Ferrum Phosphate —Ruled by the ♓ Sign. (See "Iron Phosphate" under Iron).

Phosphate of Lime — Calcium Phosphate—Ruled by ♑. (See Lime).

Phosphate of Magnesia—Ruled by the ♌ sign. (See Magnesia).

Phosphate of Potassium—Ruled by ♈. (See Biochemistry, Potassium; "Salts" under Zodiac).

PHREN—Phrenic—(See Diaphragm).

Phrenasthenia—(See "Paralysis" under Diaphragm).

Phrenasthesia—(See Idiocy).

Phrenitic Man—(See "Wild Delirium" under Delirium).

Phrenitis—(See "Inflammation" under Brain).

Phrenologist — Case and Birth Data of a Phrenologist and Mesmerist—(See "Mesmerist" under Hypnotism; Mesmerism).

Phrenzy—(See Frenzy).

PHTHISIC — Consumptive — Asthma — (See Asthma, Consumption).

PHTHISIS—A Wasting or Consumption — Pulmonary Tuberculosis — Low and Hectic Fever—

Abdomen — Phthisis Abdominalis— Consumption of the Bowels—☉ in ♍ and afflicting the ☉, ☽, Asc., or Hyleg; ♆ afflicted in ♍ in the 6th H.; ♄ in ♍, occi., and afflicting the ☉, ☽, or Asc.; ♂ afflicted in ♍, inflammatory tubercular trouble in the bowels, and especially if ♂ is in a common sign division of ♍; many afflictions in common signs, and with these signs on the angles. (See "Inflammation" under Bowels; "Consumptive" under Consumption; Navamsa; "Acute" in this section).

Acute Phthisis—♂ in ♐ and afflicted by the ☉ in ♍, and by the ☐ aspect of ♄ or ♆; ♂ in ♐ at B., and afflicted by the ill-aspects of the ☉ by dir. Case— See Chap. XIII, page 90, in Daath's Medical Astrology.

Bowels—Phthisis In—Consumption of —(See "Abdomen" in this section).

Colliquative Sweats — Of Phthisis — (See "Night Sweats" in this section).

Death by Phthisis — Death by Consumption or Tuberculosis—The ☉ hyleg, and afflicted by ♄ from an angle; the afflictions of ♄ and ☿ to the hyleg denote death by Phthisis; ♄ afflicting the hyleg by dir., and holding the dominion of death; ♄ ☌ or evil asp. the Asc. by dir. when not the ruler of the Asc. at B.; ♄ in the 8th H. at B., and afflicting the hyleg; ♄ in the 8th H. at a Solar Ingress into ♈, and afflicting the ☽ or planet ascending, tends to be very fatal according to the sign occupied by ♄; ♅ ☌ ♄ in ♉ or ♐ in the 8th H. at B., and afflicting the ☉, ☽, Asc., or Hyleg; common signs show death by consumptions, and with many planets in these signs at B., with common signs on the angles, or a common sign on the cusp the 6th H., and especially with ♄ therein in the 6th H., and afflicting the hyleg. (See "Death By" under Consumption). For Cases of Death by Phthisis see the Cases at the end of the paragraph "Consumptive" under Consumption).

Fever—The Hectic Fever of Phthisis —(See "Hectic" under Fever).

Fibroid Phthisis — In Lungs — (See "Pulmonary" in this section).

Larynx—Phthisis of—(See "Consumption" under Larynx; "Tubercular" under Throat).

Night Sweats — Colliquative, Excessive, and Profuse Sweats of Phthisis— A ☽ and ♂ disease. A preparation of Lead (Tinct. Saturnina) is good for restraining the profuse sweats of hectic fevers, and in Phthisis. (See Lead, Sweat).

Pulmonary Phthisis—Pulmonary Consumption—Phthisis Pulmonalis—Consumption of the Lungs—Fibroid Phthisis — Pulmonary Tuberculosis — The ☉ ☌ ♄ in ♐ or ♐; the ☉ ☍ ♄ from ♐ or ♐; the ☉ ☌ or P. ♄ in ♐; the ☉ rising at B., and afflicted by ♄; the ☉ or ☽, or both, in common signs and in cadent houses, and especially in the 6th and 12th H., and afflicted by ♄ and ♂; the ☉ in ♒, ☌, P., or ill-asp. ♄, and espec. when ♄ is in the 12th H. and afflicting the ☽ in ♐ at the same time; the ☉ or ☽ in the 6th H., in common signs, and afflicted by ♄; the ☽ in ♐ or ♐, in a cadent house, and afflicted by ♄; ♄ in ♐ when ♄ is the afflictor in the disease; ♄ people become an easy prey to the germs of Phthisis from catching cold from drafts or wettings; a ♄ disease; ♄ afflicted in ♋ or ♓; ♄ in ♋, occi., and afflicting the ☉, ☽, Asc., or Hyleg; caused by ♀ when the dominion of death is vested in her; ♀ afflicted in ♓ or the 8th H.; ☋ in ♊; a ☍, ♊, ♋, and ♓ disease, and caused by afflictions in these signs; a ☍ disease, especially when there are malefics in this sign, and tend to bronchial consumption; planets in ♊, and afflicted by malefics in ♐; the Asc. ☌, P., ☐, or ☍ ♄ by dir., and ♄ occi. at B.; the 6th Face of ♒ on the Asc. if ♄ be there; the 6th Face of ♓ on the Asc.; Subs at Lu.P., CP, and KP. (See Consumption; "Diseased Lungs", "Pulmonary Affections", under Lungs; Pulmonary, Tuberculosis, Wastings). Case — See "Pulmonary Consumption", Chap. XIII, in Daath's Medical Astrology.

PHYSIC—A Purge — Cathartics — Laxatives—Medicine—An Opening Medicine —Yellow color acts as an opening medicine. Physic works less when the ☽ is in a fixed sign. Dr. Pearce, in his Textbook of Astrology, says, "Healthy Persons should never take Physic." In purging, the ☽ and lord of the Asc. should be descending and under the Earth. Do not give a physic when the ☽ is in a fixed sign, but give it when the ☽ is in a watery sign, as in ♋ or ♓, for the best and quickest results. A physic given when the ☽ is in ♈, ♉, or ♑, the Ruminant Signs, tends to nausea and vomiting. Avoid physic when the ☽ is in ♏, as this sign governs the Excretory System. (See Antiperistalsis; "Biliousness" under Bile; Constipation, Costiveness, Emetics, Enema, Faeces; "Organic" under Functions; "When to Give", "When Not to Give", under Medicine; Nausea, Peristalsis, Podophyllin, Vomiting, Xylostein; "Bowels" under Yellow).

PHYSICAL — Physique — Pertaining to the Physical Body—Physiological—The Physical Body is ruled largely by the sign on the Asc. at B., and the Asc. rules the physical strength, the body, and the organic force. Also as the Sign the ☽ is in at B. is either the Asc. or Descendant at Epoch, this sign should be considered in judging of the physique, as the ☽ is the Astral Mould upon which the body is built. When the ☽ is setting at B., or decr. in light, people come very much under the influence of the sign on the Descendant at B. (See Ascendant, Astral, Body, Descendant, First House; "Organic" under Force; Moon, Prenatal Epoch, Seventh House).

Activity — (1) The Physical Activity Increased — The cardinal signs and ♂ relate especially to physical activity. The ☉ and ☽ to the good aspects ♂ by dir., and ♂ in good asp. to the ☉ and ☽ at B. (See Action; "Active Body" under Active; "Body", "Strength", under Muscles; Strength, Strong). (2) Physical Activity Decreased — (See Apathy, Decrease, Diminished, Dull; "Bad Health" under Health; Inactive, Inertia, Sickly; "Low" under Vitality; "Weak Body" under Weak).

Ailments — (1) Many Physical Ailments—(See "Ill-Health All Thru Life" under Ill-Health; Sickly; "Much Sickness" under Sickness; "Weak Body" under Weak). (2) Physical Ailments Rare—(See "Abundance of Health" under Health; Immunity; "Good" under Vitality).

Appearance—Of the Physical Body— (See the paragraphs and subjects under Appearance, Body, Complexion, Countenance, Eyes, Face, Form, Hair, Height, Shape, Stature, Weight, etc.).

Aura—The Physical Aura—(See Aura).

Being — The Physical Being — The ☉ is the Soul of the Physical Being, and contains in itself every form of manifestation of Phenomena. (See Sun).

Body—The Physical Body—(See the subjects under Body; the various paragraphs in this section).

Comforts—Loss of Physical Comforts —(See Comforts).

Condition—The Physical Condition— Is denoted by the 1st H., and the Sign rising. (See Introduction to this Article; Body, Constitution; "Judging the Health" under Health).

Constitution—The Physical Constitution—(See Body, Constitution).

Debility—Physical Debility—(See Debility, Disease, Ill-Health, Sickly, Weak, etc.).

Defects—Physical Defects—(See Defects).

Degree of Physical Strength — (See Degree).

Derangements—(See Deranged).

Description Of — (See Description; "Appearance" in this section).

Development — Perfect Physical Development—(See Development).

Diseases Of—Disorders—(See the subjects under Disease).

Endurance—Physical Endurance—Strong or Weak, etc.—(See Endurance, Resistance, Stamina, Strength, Tone, Vitality, Weak).

Faculties — (See "Physical" under Faculties).

Feeble Physical Powers—(See Feeble).

Foetus—Physical Plasm of—(See Foetus).

Great Physical Powers—The ☉ in ♐, well-aspected by ♂; the ☉ ✶ or △ ♂; ♂ ✶ or △ ♅. (See Endurance; "Good Health" under Health; "Strength" under Muscles; "Increased" under Strength; "Body" under Strong; "Good" under Vitality, etc.).

Functions — (See the various paragraphs under Functions).

Harmony—Physical Harmony—(See Harmony).

Herbs — Physiological Action of—Therapeutic Action of—(See Herbs).

Judging the Physique—(See the Introduction, "Appearance", and the various paragraphs in this Article).

Limitations — Physical Limitations—(See Limitation).

Muscular Power—(See Muscles).

Planets—The Physiological Planets—(See "Physiological Planets" under Planets).

Resistance—The Physical Resistance Strong or Weak—The fiery signs give the greatest physical resistance and strength, while the watery signs are weakest when on the Asc. at B., and especially ♋ and ♓, and give little physical resistance. (See "Low", "Strong", under Resistance).

Restrictions—Physical Restrictions—(See Limitations).

Sensation; Senses — The Physical Senses—(See Senses).

Strain—Physical Strain—Over-Strain —(See "Body" under Strain).

Strength — The Physical Strength — Strong Body—Weak Body, etc.—(See Feeble; "Body", "Strength", under Muscles; Proud; "Body" under Strong; "Weak Body" under Weak).

Temperament—The Physical Temperament — (See "Natural Temperament" under Natural; the Bodily Temperaments under Temperament).

Vitality—The Physical Vitality—(See Vitality).

Weak—Weak Physical Constitution—(See "Weak" under Constitution; Debility, Feeble; "Low" under Vitality; "Weak Body" under Weak).

Wear and Tear—The Physical Body Able to Withstand Much Wear and Tear—(See Endurance, Immunity; "Strong" under Resistance; "Body" under Strong; "Good" under Vitality; Wear; "Resistance" in this section).

PHYSICIANS—Influences Which Make a Successful Physician—(See "Physicians" under Healers).

PIERCING—Darting—Penetrating—

Eyes—(See "Piercing" under Eyes).

Pains—(See Darting, Sharp, Shooting, under Pain).

PIETY—Pious—Much Given to Religion —(See "Pious" under Religion).

PIGMENT — Pigmentation — (See "Pigmentation" under Skin).

PILES—Hemorrhoids—(See Hemorrhoids).

PILFERING — (See Cheating, Dishonesty, Kleptomaniac, Thieves).

PIMPLES—Pimpled—A Small Pustule or Blotch — The ☉ in ♎, or ♎ on the Asc., tend to cause Pimples, and especially in Middle Life, and Old Age. Also caused by the ☽ in the Winter Tropic ♑ at B.; the ☽ afflicted in ♒ or ♓; ♃ afflicted in ♈, ♌, ♎, or ♑.

Face—Pimples On the Face—Rash On the Face—Face Eruptions—A disease of the ☉; the ☉ afflicted in ♈ or ♎; the ☉ in ♎ in partile asp. the Asc.; the ☽ afflicted in ♈, ♉, or ♊; the ☽ in the Winter Signs ♑, ♒, or ♓; ♃ Sig. in ♈ or ♎; ♃ in ♈ or ♎ in partile the Asc.; born under ♂, a breaking out on the face or skin; an ♈ and ♎ disease, and with these signs on the Asc.; ♎ on the Asc., inclined to pimples when old; the 6th face of ♈ on the Asc. at B.; the 4th face of ♉ on the Asc.; Subs at KP. (See Acne, Blemishes, Blotches; Eruptions; "Eruptions" under Face; Impetigo; "Pustules" under Pus; Skin).

Middle Life — Old Age — Pimples At Middle Life and In Old Age—The ☉ in ♎, or ♎ on the Asc.; many planets in ♎, but the complexion is usually clear and fair in youth. (See "Pimples" under Middle Life).

Red Face and Pimpled—♃ Sig. in ♈. (See "Red" under Face).

PINE—Pine Cone—Pineapple—Ruled by ♂. The Pineapple is a good digestive stimulant. (See "Mars Group" under Herbs).

PINEAL GLAND — The Hypophysis or Conarium—A Small, Reddish, Vascular Body In the Posterior Part of the Third Ventricle—The Third Eye—The Spiritual Center In the Body—The Organ of Spiritual Sight and Spirituality —The Seat of the Soul In the Body—The Organ of Thought Transference—This Gland, or Organ, is ruled by ♆, and ♆ in ♈ especially rules and affects this Gland. In the earliest Races of Humanity this organ is said to have been a Third Eye in the back of the head, so the people of that time, when the Earth was hot and full of dangers, could see in all directions at the same time for protection. In later Ages, when sight in so many directions became less necessary, this organ was withdrawn into the brain, and is now known as the Pineal Gland. (See Orifices.) This Gland in present Humanity is not very well developed, but is now becoming very well developed again in certain types of Humanity, and is especially connected with what is termed "The Sixth Sense". In the coming Sixth and Seventh Races, the Pineal Gland will be very highly developed, and be a powerful organ for high spiritual development and perception. The Pineal Gland is vibrated by the Ether, or Luminous Gas, in the Spinal Canal, and tends to produce Spiritual Sight and Religious Ecstasy.

A high rate of vibration of this gland tends especially to religious ecstasy. Drink, Drugs, and Narcotics produce a supernormal rate of vibration of the Pineal Gland, causing Delirium, and the seeing of Demoniacal Shapes, due to Ψ afflicted in the map of birth, and especially when Ψ is in the watery sign ♓, or in the 12th H. The Pineal Gland is stimulated and awakened also by the ⚹ and △ aspects between Ψ and ♅ at B. Also progressed planets, except ♄, in ☌, ⚹, or △ Ψ tend to awaken the Gland, and to cause unusual cravings and Soul hunger, and often to lead to the use of Narcotics. (See Delirium, Demoniac, Ductless Glands, Ecstasy, Monsters, Narcotics; "Sixth Sub-Race" under Neptune; Pituitary; "Canal" under Spine; Spiritual). See the Chapter on the Pineal Gland in .the book, "The Message of the Stars", by Mr. and Mrs. Max Heindel, of the Rosicrucian Fellowship at Oceanside, California.

PIOUS—Reverent—Religious—Godly— (See "Pious" under Religion).

PIRATES—Piracy—

Danger from In Travel—The Significators of Travel in evil aspect to ☿; the afflictor to the Sig. of Travel in the 12th H., and in ♊ or ♍. (See "Danger" under Travel).

Death by Pirates—Danger of—The ☉ conjoined with Antares, Hercules, Hyades, Regulus, Aldebaran, or any eminent star of the nature of ♂ at B., brings this danger. (See "Battle" under Abroad).

Piracy Prevalent—An eclipse of the ☉ or ☽ in ♓; an eclipse of the ☽ in the 3rd Decan. of ♓.

PISCES—The 12th Sign of the Zodiac, and closely related to the 12th H. (See Twelfth House). Symbol of—The Two Fishes. This Sign is the night house of ♃, the exaltation of ♀, and the fall of ☿. The planet Ψ is also strong in this Sign, as ♓ and Ψ rule the Sea. (See Neptune). Pisces is a double-bodied sign, and the most fruitful of all the signs, and tends to a large family when strong at B., and to the production of Twins, Triplets, and multiple births. This Sign is connected with the Hebrew letter Qoph (K), and is also predominant in mirth. Pisces is a sign of restraint and confinement, as symbolized by the Fishes joined together, and a sign of self-undoing. It is called "The Sign of Sorrows", and people born with the ☉ and ♄ in this sign are subject to great sorrows, tribulations, secret enemies, plots, treachery, self-undoing, restraints, confinement, isolation, as well as to reserve, and more of secrecy and seclusion. Pisces is classified as a bicorporeal, broken, changeable, cold, cold and moist, cold-blooded, common, crooked, double-bodied, effeminate, feminine, fruitful, humid, hyemal, imperfect, lymphatic, moist, motive, mutable, mute, negative, nocturnal, obeying, phlegmatic, plastic, relaxing, sickly, southern, torpid, unfortunate, watery sign. Also other qualities assigned to ♓, and which often characterize the Pisces people are — Brooding, clair-

voyant, compassionate, confining, consumptive, debauched, dissipated, erratic, fretful, generous, grievous, idle, indifferent, intoxicating, jovial, kind, loquacious, mediumistic, mirthful, obsessional, prodigal, psychic, receptive, reserved, restless, restraining, scattering, secretive, self-undoing, slothful, sorrowful, spiritual, stagnant, susceptible, sympathetic, treacherous, vacillating, weak and of low vitality, worrisome, etc. This sign, when on the Asc. at B., gives the least vitality of all the Signs. It tends to a softening and relaxing effect upon the tissues, and to produce phlegm and mucus. It has a torpid, lymphatic, plastic, and humid action, and leads to many ailments thru carelessness, forgetfulness, or dissipation. This sign, when afflicted at B., and containing the ☉ and malefics, tends to affect the lungs, and many Consumptives have the ☉ or ♄ in this sign, or ♓ upon the Asc. at B. Pisces is said by many Authors to be the most Spiritual Sign of the Zodiac in its higher vibrations, and being the last Sign of the Zodiac, denotes the end of material experiences, and the transition to a higher Spiritual State if the Soul is ready for it. However, with the unregenerate person, those who are drifting with Earth-life tendencies, and being dominated by Personality, it is considered a sign of Drink, Dissipation, Debauchery, and Self-Undong. Being a watery sign, it is restless, changeable, and vacillating, and tends to idleness, slothfulness, and indifference to life's duties in the unawakened person.

PISCES RULES—Externally, ♓ rules the feet and toes. Internally, ♓ rules the Glandular System, the Lymphatic System, the Synovial Fluids. Structurally, the Bones of the Feet, the Tarsus, Metatarsus, and Phalanges. Pisces rules the following matters, powers, subjects, habits, organs, functions, conditions, and parts of the body, which subjects see in the alphabetical arrangement — Abdomen and Abdominal Cavity, by reflex action in ♍; Asylums; Banishment; Blood (Fibrin of); Bones of Feet and Toes; Carelessness; Clairvoyance (Psychic and Mediumistic conditions); Cold; Cold and Moist Conditions; Color — Pure White or Glistening White; Confinement (Restraints and Limitations); Drink Habit (Alcoholic Liquors, Dissipation and Debauchery); Exiles; Feet—The Feet from the Ankles to the extremity of Toes; Ferrum Phosphate; Fibro-Ligamentous System and Fibrin of the Blood; Fluidic System; Forgetfulness; Gastro-Abdominal System, by reflex action in ♍; Glandular System; Hospitals; Idleness; Imprisonment; Indifference; Intestinal Mucus; Limitations, and especially those affecting the five Senses, thus restraining the expression of the Soul upon the Material Plane; Iron Phosphate Salt; Lost in out-of-the-way Places; Lymphatic System; Matrix and Secrets where Syphilitic contagion is involved; Mediumship; Misfortune; Moisture (Cold and Moist Conditions); Mucus (the Intestinal Mucus, and Mucus in the

Lungs); Nurses; Ocean; Peritoneal Serum; Phlegm; Pleural Serum; Prisons; Psychic and Spiritual Powers, which are normal, and strengthened by good influences in ♓, and perverted by afflictions in this sign); Relaxation of Tissues; Respiratory System; Restraints and Limitations of Life; Sea (The Seas); Secret Enemies; Secret Parts and the Matrix, and especially where Syphilitic Contagion is involved; Self-Undoing; Serum (the Pleural, Peritoneal, and Synovial); Slothfulness; Softening of Tissues; Sorrow; Spirituality (the Higher Spiritual Consciousness in Advanced and Highly Evolved Souls); Stagnant and Standing Pools of Water; Synovial Serum; Syphilitic Contagion; Tarsus Bones (the Tarsus, Metatarsus, and Phalanges of Feet); Toes; Torpidity; Trouble; Twelfth House; Veratrum Album (one of the 12 Polycrest Remedies); Water (the Ocean, Sea, and Standing and Stagnant Pools of Water); White, and Glistening White Color, etc.

PISCES DISEASES—The Morbid Action of Pisces—The Afflictions of Pisces—See the following subjects when not more fully considered here—

Abdominal Diseases — (See the paragraphs under Abdomen, Bowels).

Alcoholism; Blood — Putrefaction In —(See "Putrefaction" under Blood).

Blotches; Boils; Bowel Disorders— From Wet Feet, and Living In Damp and Cold Places—Colic—Mucus In the Bowels—(See Colic, Mucus, Wet Feet, and the various paragraphs under Bowels).

Breakings Out — (See Eruptions, Pimples, Skin).

Bunions; Carelessness — Ailments From—(See Carelessness).

Chilblains; Chronic Diseases—In the Lungs, such as Consumptions, Tuberculosis, etc.—(See Consumption, Lungs, Phthisis, Tuberculosis, Wastings, etc.).

Club Feet—(See Feet).

Cold and Moist Diseases—Cold, Phlegmatic Diseases—(See "Cold and Moist" under Humours; Phlegm).

Colds—Taken by Wet Feet, or Living In Cold and Damp Places—(See "Cold Taken" under Feet).

Consumptions; Contagious Diseases— Danger From — (See Contagions, Infections).

Corns; Corrupt Blood—(See "Impure Blood" under Impure).

Damp Feet — Colds By — (See "Cold Taken" under Feet).

Debauchery; Defluxions of Humours —(See "Flow Of" under Humours).

Deformities—Of the Feet and Toes— (See "Deformities" under Feet).

Delirium Tremens—(See Delirium).

Demoniacs; Dissipation; Drink Habit —(See Drink, Drunkenness).

Dropsy; Effeminate; Eruptions; Feet —All Diseases and Infirmities In—(See Feet).

Forgetfulness — Ailments Arising From — (See "Forgetfulness" under Memory).

Frenzy; Glandular Tissue—Softening of—(See "Softening" under Glands).

Gonorrhoea; Gout; Habits—The Drink and Narcotic Habits — (See Drink, Drunkenness, Narcotics).

Hallucinations; Humours—Defluxion of—(See Defluxions; "Flow Of" under Humours).

Imprisonment—(See Prison).

Insanity; Intestinal Diseases — (See "Bowel Disorders" in this section).

Intoxication; Itch—(See Scabies).

Lameness — (See "Lameness" under Feet).

Lungs —Consumption of — Tuberculosis—(See Consumption; "Pulmonary Affections" under Lungs; Phthisis, Tuberculosis, Wastings).

Mania — Alcoholic Mania — (See "Delirium Tremens" under Delirium).

Matrix — Womb — Syphilis of — (See "Syphilis" under Womb).

Moist and Cold Diseases—(See "Cold and Moist" in this section).

Mucus—Mucous Disturbances and Discharges—(See Mucous).

Narcotic Habit—(See Narcotics).

Obsessions; Pale and Sickly — (See Pale, Sickly; "Low" under Vitality; "Weak Body" under Weak).

Phlegmatic Diseases—(See Phlegm).

Phthisis; Putrid Blood—(See "Putrefaction" under Blood).

Relaxation of Tissue—(See "Tissues" under Relaxation; Softening).

Rheumatism; Scabies; Secrets — Private Parts — Diseases In—Contagions In—(See Gonorrhoea; "Distempers" under Secrets; "Syphilis" under Womb).

Self-Undoing; Sickly; Softening—Of the Glandular Tissues — (See "Softening" under Glands; "Tissues" under Relaxation; Softening).

Sores—Ulcerous Sores—(See Ulcers).

Spiritual Perversions — (See "Perversions" under Spiritual).

Swollen Feet—(See "Swelling" under Feet).

Syphilitic Contagion — (See Syphilis; "Syphilis" under Womb).

Tender Feet — (See "Tender" under Feet).

Toes —Diseases of—Deformities of— (See Toes).

Tuberculosis; Tumors; Ulcers;

Vitality Low—(See "Low" under Vitality; "Weak Body" under Weak).

Weak Body—(See "Weak Body" under Weak).

Weakness In the Feet—(See "Weakness" under Feet).

Wet Feet — Colds Taken By — (See "Cold Taken" under Feet).

PITCH-BLENDE — A Mineral ruled by ♅. It is a source of Uranium and Radium. (See Radium, Uranium; "Metals and Minerals" under Uranus).

PITTED DEGREES — Of the Zodiac — Pitted or Deep Degrees of the Zodiac —The Asc., or its lord, in any of these degrees makes the native subject to deep marks by scars or the pockmarks of smallpox. They also cause an impediment in the speech. These degrees are as follows—♈ 6, 11, 16, 23, 29; ♉ 5, 12, 24, 25; ♊ 2, 12, 17, 26, 30; ♋ 12, 17, 23, 26, 30; ♌ 6, 13, 15, 22, 23, 28; ♍ 8, 13, 16, 21, 22; ♎ 17, 20, 30; ♏ 9, 10, 22, 23, 27; ♐ 7, 12, 15, 24, 27, 30; ♑ 7, 17, 22, 24, 29; ♒ 1, 12, 17, 22, 24, 29; ♓ 4, 9, 24, 27, 28. (See "Face" under Smallpox).

PITUITARY BODY—Pituitary Gland—Hypophysis Cerebri—A Small Reddish Body in the Sella Turcica in the Pituitary Fossa of the Sphenoid Bone — Pertaining to Phlegm — The Pituitary Body is a Ductless Gland, and is ruled by ♅ and the ♏ Sign. Uranus in ♈ especially rules and affects this Gland. The Anterior Lobe of this Gland rules over the Creative, or Sex Force, and over the Nerve Fibers. (See "Fibers" under Nerves). The Posterior Lobe rules over the circulation of the Fluids of the body, and especially the circulation in the Kidneys. (See "Circulation" under Kidneys). The Pineal Gland, ruled by ♆, and the Pituitary Body, ruled by ♅, are closely related to the spiritual side of our natures. The Thyroid Gland acts as a connecting body between the Pineal and Pituitary Glands. The Pituitary Body, and also the Pineal Gland, are now more or less dormant and inactive in their workings in the majority of people, but are gradually becoming awakened in the more highly advanced and evolved Souls, and form the link between the Soul and the Spirit World about us. These Glands are gradually coming under the control of the Cerebro-Spinal Nervous System, which system rules the voluntary muscles. The Pineal and Pituitary Glands, acting as Spiritual Centers in our Being, rule over Voluntary and genuine Clairvoyance, Mediumship, Spiritual Sight, etc., and in a coming distant Age will be very highly developed, so that people can see and know what is going on in all parts of the Universe. These organs, or Glands, are not atrophied, as is usually thought by the Medical Profession, but are merely dormant, awaiting their future time and renewed development, and in the coming Sixth Race these Organs will be highly developed and very active. (See "Sixth Sub-Race" under Neptune). The Pituitary Body is awakened and stimulated by the ✶ and △ aspects of ♆ to ♅. Also progressed planets, except ♄, when in ☌, ✶, or △ ♅, tend to arouse and awaken the organ, and to cause unusual cravings and Soul hunger. Uranus acting too freely upon the Pituitary Body often causes too much Pituitary Secretion, and overgrowth of the body, Giants, and Freaks of Nature. (See Freaks, Giants; "Abnormal Growth" under Growth). Lethargy of the Pituitary Body is given by the Lymphatic Temperament. (See "Temperament" under Lymphatic). Uranus in ♉ also tends to diminish the Pituitary Secretion. The Pituitary Body supplies a secretion made up by the Uranus Alchemistry, which, by passing into the blood, aids the growth and nutrition of the body. The assimilation of food

is also regulated by ♅ through the Pituitary Body. (See Assimilation, Cerebro-Spinal, Clairvoyance, Ductless Glands, Dwarfed; "Basal Ganglia" under Ganglion; Glands, Leprosy, Mediumship, Nutrition, Phlegm, Pineal; "Creative Force" under Sex; Sphenoid, Spiritual, Thyroid, Uranus). See the Chapter on the Pituitary Body in the book, "The Message of the Stars", by the Heindels.

PITY—Compassion—Mercy—Sympathy—

Has Pity for Others — The watery signs tend to be more emotional, and to soften the nature and create sympathy for others. Venus in ♓ is a strong symbol of sympathy, but if ♄ or ♂ afflict ♀ in this sign, the sympathies and pity may be unwisely or foolishly bestowed. (Pisces is a strong sympathetic sign, being the sign of ♃, the planet of benevolence, and also ♃ in his exalted sign ♋ tends to pity and a sympathetic nature. The Airy Signs ♎ and ♒, when well-aspected at B., and occupied by benefics, are considered very sympathetic signs, and to make the native kind and pitiful of those in sorrow, trouble, illness, or distress. Aquarius is the sign of "The Water Pourer", and people born with the ☉ in ♒, or ♒ on the Asc., tend to be humane and full of mercy for others, and Emancipators, as was Abraham Lincoln, who was an Aquarian. (See Aquarius, Humane, Kind, Merciful, Sympathetic, Well-Disposed).

Shows No Pity — Cruel — Rough — Without Compassion—Merciless—Cold-Blooded, etc. — Born under the strong influence of ♂, and ♂ afflicted and ill-dignified at B. The ♂ signs ♈ and ♏, when afflicted tend to make the nature harder and more severe and cruel, and especially under provocation. The malefics, ♄ and ♂, when rising and elevated at B., and afflicting the mental ruler, ☿, tend to make the nature harder, more cruel, unsympathetic, revengeful, fierce and savage. The ☿ signs tend to be hard and self-occupied, and especially if ♄ be in the Asc., or afflicting the Asc. (See Brutish, Cruel, Fierce, Inhuman; "Rough", "Violent", under Manners; Merciless, Raving, Rough, Savage, Vicious, Violent).

PLACE—Location—Residence, etc.—

Place of Birth—Is ruled by the 4th H. When ♃ is in this house at B., and well-aspected, and with no malefics in this house, the place of birth is the most fortunate location for the native. The native should remain at the place of birth when the 3rd and 9th Houses, the Houses of Home and Foreign Travel, are afflicted by malefics, or ruled by them, as danger, injury, accident, sickness, or death, would be indicated by travel, making the place of birth the safest and most fortunate location. Also if the ☉, ☽, ♃, and ♀ are all above the Earth at B., remain at the place of birth. However, the native should remove from the place of birth when ♃ is in the 4th H. at B., and afflicted by malefics, or when there are malefics in the 4th H., and no benefics there, or when a malefic rules the 4th H., and is evilly aspected. Uranus or ♂ in the 4th H. at B., and afflicted, tend especially to make the birthplace very unfortunate and full of trouble. Also ♄ afflicted in the 4th H. tends to bring many sorrows, delays, hindrances, and disappointments if the native continues to live at the birthplace. (See Abroad, Environment, External, Foreign Lands, Fourth House, Location, Nadir, Native Land, Removals, Residence, Travel, etc.).

Place of Death—The Killing Place In the Map of Birth — The Anareta — Is indicated by the foremost, or most malevolent direction, in a train of evil directions to the hyleg. (See Anareta). For the actual place of the death, and the conditions under which death is apt to occur, see such subjects as Abroad, Accident, Desert, Exile, Foreign Lands, Home, Native Land, Prison, Shipwreck, Travel, Voyages, etc.).

Place of Residence — (See the paragraphs under Residence. Also see Abroad, Location, Native Land, Removals; "Place of Birth" in this section).

PLACENTA—(See "Placenta" under Womb).

PLAGUE—A Contagious, Malignant, Epidemic Disease — Pest — Pestilence, etc. — Plagues are usually coincident with the appearance of Comets in the sign ruling the different Countries and Nations. The appearance of Halley's Comet is usually followed by a Plague, and especially in the Country ruled by the Sign of the Zodiac in which the Comet appears. Plagues are also caused by afflictions in ♌, and are a ♌ and ☉ disease. Also caused by the ☌ of two or more Superior Planets. (See Comets, Eclipses, Epidemics, Pandemics, Perihelion, Pestilence).

Black Death — An Epidemic Disease with dark blotches upon the skin, and caused by the ☌ of several superior planets, and especially in airy signs. In March, 1866, this disease broke out in Dublin, Ireland, at a time when ♂ was badly afflicted in ♒, the sign which rules the blood, and when ♄ was also afflicting Ireland. Also the Black Death occurred in England in the 14th Century.

Bubonic Plague—(See Bubo).

Madness Plague—(See Madness).

Plague Sores—A ♂ disease, and caused by ♂ afflictions. (See Sores).

Spotted Fever—(See Spotted).

PLANETS—Planetary—Dominion of the Planets — From Ancient Times seven Planets have been referred to in Sacred Writings as belonging to, and making up our Solar System. In the Christian Bible, in Rev. 1:4, it speaks of the Seven Churches in Asia, and the Seven Spirits which are before the Throne. In Rev. 1:20 it says, "The Seven Stars are the Angels of the Seven Churches". Occult Writers refer to these verses as meaning our Planets, and the Seven Great Planetary Angels, the Planetary Hierarchies, the Seven Archangels, and that each Planetary Angel is an Aspect of God, and doing the work the Higher Powers have ordained to be done in our Universe. No Planet is, therefore, evil, but may have its disciplinary action for the good of Humanity, and to help Souls on in their Evolution. For the names of the Planetary Angels see "Angel" under each of the Planets. The seven Planets which make up our System are the ☉, ☽, ♄, ♃, ♂, ♀, and ☿. Neptune and ♅ are not spoken of by early Writers, and many Writers say that these two Planets are outside of our Solar System, but have a certain spiritual influence over us, acting thru the Pineal Gland, and the Pituitary Body, which influence is to gradually awaken Humanity to Powers which will be needed, and brought into greater manifestation in the people of the coming Sixth Race. (See Pineal, Pituitary; "Sixth Sub-Race" under Neptune; Pluto; "Influence Of" under Uranus). Much has been written upon the Occult and Mystical side of planetary influence, and the student can find these Teachings in the various Occult and Mystical Societies, such as The Rosicrucians, The Theosophical Society, The Order of Christian Mystics, etc. For the action and influence of the Planets, and the nature of their good and bad aspects over Humanity, see each of the Planets in the alphabetical arrangement. The Masters, Adepts, Initiates, and very Advanced and highly evolved Souls, have conquered the Planetary and Zodiacal influences, and are no longer affected by them, but ordinary Humanity, those who are still drifting with their Stars, and who may be still living in their lower minds, and who also may be breaking the Laws of God and Nature, are considerably affected by the Planetary influences for ill at times, which influences are placed over us for testings, training, education, experience, etc., and all which in the end are for our good and advancement. (See Aspects, Character, Destiny, Fate, Map; "Free Will" under Will). The following paragraphs have to do with the Planets, their Action, Classification, Influence, etc., and along lines which are generally spoken of in the Text-books of Astrology.

Accidents—And Planetary Influence— (See Accidents, Directions, Events).

Acid Action Of—(See Acids).

Action of the Planets—(See "Action", and the various paragraphs under each of the Planets. Also see Pathological, Perverted, Physiological, Polarity, Tonic, in this section).

Afflictions Of — The Planets may afflict by their evil aspects to the Significators in the Map of Birth, and benefit by their good aspects. The ☉, ♃, ♀, ☿, and the ☽ afflict only by their □ or ☍ aspects. The malefics afflict by their ☌, P., □, or ☍ aspects. However, any aspect of ♄ is considered an affliction in the life of the ordinary person, but his evil aspects are more inimical. Saturn in any part of the horoscope is considered an affliction to the Sign, House, and part of the body so ruled. Judgment cannot be based upon any one affliction, but the progressed planets, transits, directions, and the last New Moon, should be studied. (See Affliction, Aspects, Directions, Lunations).

Alkaline Action Of—(See Alkaline).

Angels—The Planetary Angels—These Angels have charge of the affairs, and various Departments in the rule of our Solar System. They are called "The Elohim" also in the Bible. They each manifest under a different Ray, or Color, and represent the seven principal Planetary Colors, or the seven Primary Colors of the Solar Spectrum. (See "Planets and Color" under Colors; "Angel" under each of the Planets).

Aspects Of—(See Aspects; Afflictions Of, Perverted Action, in this section).

Atonic Planets—(See Atonic).

Baptism — The Planetary Baptism — (See Baptism).

Barren Planets—(See Barren).

Benefic Planets—(See Benefics).

Chemical Action Of—(See Chemical).

Climacterical Years—Of the Planets—(See Climacteric, Cycles, Periods).

Clonic Action Of—(See Clonic).

Cold Planets—♄ is classed as the Cold Planet. The ☽ exerts a cold and moist influence. Mercury is cold when he partakes of the nature of ♄. (See Cold).

Colors and Planets — (See Colors; "Angels" in this section).

Conjunctions Of—(See Aspects; "Afflictions Of" in this section).

Cycles Of — (See Climacteric, Cycles, Periods, Years).

Daily Motion Of — This varies from time to time. A fast motion tends to make diseases more speedy and sharp, and to terminate more quickly. A slow, stationary, or ℞ motion, when such a planet is the afflictor in the disease, tends to make the ailment more protracted, and difficult to cure, and especially until such planet assumes a direct, faster, and more normal motion, as seen from the Earth. A Table of the standard Daily Motions of the Planets can be found in the Textbooks of Astrology. Also see the Article on the Motional Strength of the Planets in Chap. XI, in Daath's Medical Astrology.

Debilities Of—Dignities of—Exaltation of—Fall of—Detriment of, etc.— These are mentioned in the Articles on each of the Planets in this book. Also see the Tables of Dignities of the Planets in the various Textbooks of Astrology.

Dignities Of—(See "Debilities" in this section).

Direct Motion — The forward motion of a Planet, as seen from the Earth. The influence of a planet is more fortunate when direct in motion, and also more prompt and swift in disease. (See Direct).

Directional Strength—(See Directions. Also see the Article on "Directional Strength" in Chap. XI, in Daath's Medical Astrology).

Disease — The Planets and Disease — (See Complications, Course, Disease, Ill-Health, Sickness).

Dryness — Planets Exercising a Dry Influence—(See Dryness, Heat).

Electric Planets—(See Electric).

Elevated Planets—(See Elevated).

Exaltation Of — (See "Debilities" in this section).

Fall of Planets — Planets have their fall in the sign in 8 to the sign of their exaltation, and planets in their fall at B. tend to be more troublesome and evil in health, and other matters. (See "Debilities" in this section).

Feminine Planets—The ☽ and ♀.

Fiery Planets — The ☉ and ♂. (See "Fire Signs" under Fire).

Forms—Planetary Forms—(See Chap. III, on the Planets, in Sepharial's Manual of Astrology).

Fruitful Planets — The ☽, ♃, and ♀. (See Fruitful).

Functions Of—(See "Action", "Functions", and the various paragraphs under each of the Planets).

Geocentric System—Of the Planets—(See Geocentric).

Heliocentric System — Of the Planets —(See Heliocentric).

Herbs—Herbs Ruled by the Planets—(See Herbs).

Hot and Fiery Planets—The ☉ and ♂.

Hours—Planetary Hours—The Hours of the day are ruled by the Planets. There are 24 Planetary Hours in each day. The time from Sunrise to Sunset is divided by 12, which gives the time of the day-time planetary Hours. The Planetary Hours at night are from Sunset to Sunrise, and this time also divided by 12 gives the length of the night Planetary Hours. The Planets rule these hours, from sunrise to sunset, in the following order. On Sunday, the first hour after sunrise is ruled by the ☉; the 2nd planetary hour by ♀; the 3rd hour, by ☿; the 4th hour, by the ☽; the 5th hour by ♄; the 6th hour, by ♃; the 7th hour, by ♂, and the 8th hour by the ☉ again, etc., and in this order on thru the 24 hours. The first planetary hour of each day at sunrise is ruled by the planet which rules the day. Thus, Sunday, ruled by the ☉, the first hour at sunrise is ruled by the ☉. The ☽, ruling Monday, rules the first planetary hour after sunrise. Tuesday is ruled by ♂, and ♂ rules the first planetary hour after sunrise; ☿ the first hour after sunrise on Wednesday; ♃ the first hour after sunrise on Thursday; ♀ the first hour on Friday, and ♄ the first hour after sunrise on Saturday, etc. The planetary hours of each day of the week follow the same order of the planets as given for Sunday in this paragraph. The planetary hours are longer in the daytime in the Summer, as the days are longer, and shorter at night, with the shorter nights. In the Winter time, the night planetary hours are longer, due to the longer nights, and longer time between sunset and sunrise, and the daytime planetary hours shorter, etc. The happenings of each hour are said to be of the nature of the planet ruling the hour. Thus, the ♄ hour brings delays, trouble, hindrances, despondency, increased suffering, and is also known as the hour of death. To take sick in a ♄ hour tends to prolong the disease. (See Calm). The ♂ hour tends to accidents, injury, quarrels, etc., and so on with each of the planetary hours. The important planetary hours to be considered in connection with the health are the ♄ and ♂ hours, which are usually bad hours for the health, or for an operation. The ♃ and ♀ planetary hours also tend to bring alleviation and moderation in disease, and happier conditions. The student should make a study of Planetary Hours in the Textbooks of Astrology. In Dr. Broughton's book, "The Elements of Astrology", the subject is treated quite at length, and also a Perpetual Table of the Planetary Hours given for each of the 12 months of the year, and which can be used and adapted to any location. Also see the Articles on "Hours" in Wilson's Dictionary of Astrology, and in Alan Leo's Dictionary of Astrology. Also read the book, "The Silver Key", by Sepharial. (See "Order of the Planets" in this section; "Hour" under Saturn, Sun; "Days of the Week" under Week).

Houses — The House Position of the Planets—(See each of the 12 Houses, as First House, Second House, Third House, etc.).

Humid and Moist Planets — The ☽ especially rules Moisture. Also ♃ and ♀ give off moisture. (See Moisture).

Illnesses Caused By—(See the section on "Diseases" under each of the planets. Also see Disease, Ill-Health, Infirmities, Sickness).

Inferior Planets—♀, ☽, and ☿.

Influences Of — (See the section on "Influences" under each of the Planets).

Intrinsic Nature—Each planet has its own intrinsic and fundamental nature, rules over a certain Department of life and Human Affairs, and always acts in this manner unless modified by the aspects of other planets, and its sign or house position. Thus, ♄ is cold, contracting, suppressing, hindering, hardening, obstructing, etc. Mars is hot, fiery, hasty, combative, and tends to anger, fevers, inflammation, etc. The nature of the planets is given in the Articles on each of the Planets. Also good Articles on each of the Planets, and their nature, are given in the book, "The Message of the Stars", by the Heindels, and also in the Textbooks and Dictionaries of Astrology. Also see "Action", "Perverted", and the various paragraphs in this section).

Keywords—The Keywords, or the Intrinsic Principle of Each Planet—(See "Principle Of" under each of the Planets).

Kinetic Points — The Static and Kinetic Points for each planet are quite fully considered in Chap. XII, in Daath's Medical Astrology. These points have an effect upon the physical organism. The static point of a planet is its degree of Longitude in a Sign, while its kinetic points are those places in the map affected by its aspects. Thus ♄ in ♏ tends by his static

position to affect the sex nature and organs, and by his reflex aspect, or kinetic point in ♉, to greatly affect the throat and cause throat disorders. (See Ablation, Antipathy, Aspects, Opposites).

Life — The Period of Life Ruled by Each of the Planets—(See Periods).

Magnetic Planets—(See "Negative Planets" under Negative).

Major Planets—(See Major).

Majorities — Of the Planets — (See Majority).

Malefic Planets—(See Malefics).

Mars—(See Mars).

Masculine Planets — The ☉, ♅, ♄, ♃, and ♂ are classed as masculine planets. Also planets are classed as masculine when rising before the ☉ between the 1st and 10th Houses, or setting before the ☉ between the Descendant and Nadir. The ☽ and ♀ are classed as feminine. Mercury is variable according to the sex of the planet with which aspected and configurated.

Mental Planets—♅ and ☿.

Mercury—(See Mercury).

Metals—Metals Ruled by the Planets —(See Metals).

Mind and Planets — (See Intellect, Mental, Mind, Perception, Understanding, etc.).

Minerals — Minerals Ruled by the Planets—(See Metals, Minerals).

Minor Planets—Inferior—☽, ♀, ☿.

Moisture—Planets Exerting a Moist Influence—☽, ♃, ♀. (See Moisture).

Moon—(See Moon).

Motion of the Planets — The motion of the planets tends to modifications in health, disease, and states of the mind, and the planets have various effects in their vibrations over the mind and organism, according to their motion, whether slow, rapid, retrograde, or direct, and the aspects they form to each other, and their sign and house positions from time to time, by transit, direction, or progression. However, the motional strength of planets as related to disease is still considered an uncertain factor by some Authors. (See Daily Motion, Direct, Retrograde, Slow, Stationary, in this section; "Degree of Disturbance" under Disturbed).

Mystery Planet—(See Violet).

Nature Of — (See "Intrinsic" in this section).

Negative Planets—♆, ♄, ♀, and the ☽. (See "Negative Planets" under Negative).

Neptune—(See Neptune, Pineal).

Neutral Planets—(See Neutral).

Nutritive Planets—(See Nutrition).

Occidental—Planets Occidental—(See Occidental).

Orbs of the Planets—(See Orbs).

Order of the Planets—Esoteric Order of the Planets—The Planets considered in this order are as follows—☉, ♀, ☿, ☽, ♄, ♃, ♂. This is also the order of the Planetary Hours in their rotation. (See "Hours" in this section).

Oriental—Planets Oriental—(See Oriental).

Passive Planets—(See Passive).

Pathological Planets—(See Pathological).

Peregrine Planets—(See Peregrine).

Perigee — Planets In Perigee — (See Perigee).

Perihelion — Planets In — (See Perihelion).

Periods of Life—Ruled by the Planets —(See Periods).

Perverted Action Of—Each planet in its action is intrinsically normal, tonic, or above normal; atonic, or below normal; electric or magnetic, positive or negative. A planet in its fundamental nature is always the same. The action of the planets is changed, perverted, and mutated by the constantly new-forming polarizations formed by aspects to other planets. Also in a nativity there may be too much of the action of a planet, or an insufficiency or permutation, which may lead to disease, mental disorders, etc. Thus, the action and reaction of the planets upon each other is what causes the many contingencies of life, such as sin, suffering, misfortune, disease and death by their evil aspects, and good health, good fortune, peace of mind, etc., by their more favorable aspects, progressions, and directions after birth. (See Aspects, Atonic, Polarity, Tonic; Afflictions Of, Intrinsic Nature, and the various paragraphs in this section).

Physiological Action Of—(See "Physiological Action" under each of the Planets).

Physiological Planets — The ☉, ☽, ♀, and ☿.

Pluto—(See Pluto).

Polarization Of—(See Aspects, Polarity; "Perverted Action" in this section).

Positive Planets—☉, ♅, ♃, ♂. (See Electric, Positive).

Principle Of—(See "Principle Of" under each of the Planets).

Progression Of — (See Directions, Events, Progression).

Prolific Planets — (See "Fruitful" in this section).

Retrograde Planets — (See Retrograde; "Motion" in this section).

Rising Planets—(See Rising).

Rules — What Each Planet Rules — (See the section on "Rules" under each of the Planets).

Setting Planets—(See Setting).

Signs Ruled By—☉ rules ♌; ☽ rules ♋; ♄ rules ♑ and ♒; ♃ rules ♐ and ♓; ♂ rules ♈ and ♏; ♀ rules ♉ and ♎; ☿ rules ♊ and ♍. (See each of the Signs and Planets in the alphabetical arrangement; "Debilities" in this section).

Slow Motion Of—The slow motion of a planet which is the afflictor in the disease tends to make the disease more tedious, lingering, and prolonged, until the planet changes to a direct, or faster motion. (See "Motion" in this section; Slow).

Static Points Of — (See "Kinetic" in this section).

Stationary Position—Of Planets—Denotes constancy and duration of effects when such a planet is the afflictor in the disease, or in matters which it may rule. (See Stationary; "Motion" in this section).

Sun—(See Sun).

Superior Planets—(See Major, Superior).

Tempo and Daily Motion—(See "Daily Motion" in this section).

Therapeutic Properties Of — (See "Therapeutics" under each of the Planets).

Tonic Planets—Tonic Action of—(See "Planets" under Tonic; "Perverted Action" in this section).

Transits of Planets—(See Transits).

Uranus—(See Uranus).

Variable Planets—(See Variable).

Venus—(See Venus).

Vibrations Of—(See Vibration).

Violent Planets—The Malefics—(See Malefics; "Planets" under Violent).

Years—Planetary Years, Periods, and Cycles — (See Climacteric, Cycles, Periods, Years).

PLANTAR—Plantar Nerves—Ruled by ♓. (See Feet).

PLANTS — (See Fruits, Herbs, Odors, Rottenness, Trees, Vegetation; "Plants" in the Articles on each of the Planets, as "Plants" under Mars, Moon, etc.).

PLASM—Plasma—The Fluid Part of the Blood and Lymph—The physical Plasm of the Foetus is formed by ♄. (See Foetus). For Disorders of the Plasm of the Blood and Lymph, see the various paragraphs under Blood, Lymph.

PLASTIC—Capable of Being Moulded— The ☽ is plastic. Also the ♋ and ♓ Signs are plastic, which signs are very agreeable to the ☽, being of a plastic and watery nature. Cell development in a plastic fluid is presided over by ♆. (See Cancer Sign; "Cytoplastema" under Cells; External; "Flexible Mind" under Flexible; Influenced, Moon, Mutable, Negative, Pisces Sign, Receptive, Susceptible; "Signs' under Water).

PLAY — Injuries, Accidents, or Death While At Play, or At Some Amusement, or In Sports—(See Amusements; "Causes" under Blindness; Exercise, Hunting, Sports).

PLEASANT—Pleasing—

Companion—A Pleasant Companion— ☿ ⚹ or △ the ☽, because of his extensive knowledge, and sometimes a pleasant companion. (See Antipathy, Companions, Friends, Sympathy).

Disposition — Pleasant Disposition — (See Cheerfulness, Gentle, Happy, Harmless, Humane, Joy, Kind; "Amiable" under Manners; Mild, Quiet; "Popular" under Reputation; "Sanguine Temperament" under Sanguine).

Expression—A Pleasing Expression— (See "Pleasant" under Face).

Face—A Pleasing Face—(See Beautiful; "Beautiful" under Eyes; Beautiful, Pleasant, Smiling, under Face; Handsome).

Personality — A Pleasing Personality —Good Disposition—Pleasing Manner —A Good Personality— The ☉ well-aspected in ♎; the ☉ Sig. ☌ ♀, a pleasing address; the ☽ Sig. in ♋; ♃ or ♀ well-aspected in ♎; ♀ well-aspected in the Asc.; ☿ Sig. in ♎; ☿ Sig. in ♏, not in any way pleasing or elegant in manner. (See "Disposition" in this section).

Pleasing Address — (See "Pleasing" under Speech).

PLEASURE— Pleasures—Delights—Enjoyments—Amusements — Recreations —Sports—Pleasures, and the nature of the pleasures, are ruled by ♀, the ♌ sign, and the 5th H. Also ♐ is a pleasure-loving sign. The Animal and Worldly Pleasures are ruled over largely by ♂ and ♀, and by afflictions to the planets. The Higher, or Spiritual Pleasures, usually come from the good aspects to the ☉, ♆, ♅, ☿, or to any of the planets in the map of a more Advanced, Awakened, and Spiritualized Soul. Pleasures may be of a high or low nature, and the following subjects have to do with Pleasure in its various forms, and its effects upon the Native. See these subjects in the alphabetical arrangement—

Abandoned Persons—(See Debauched, Depraved, Profligate).

Abnormally Fond of Pleasure—Much Given to Pleasure and Enjoyment, and Especially of a Worldly Nature—Addicted to Pleasure—The ☉ Sig. in ♋, ♎, or ♓; the ☽ in the 5th H. at B.; the ☽ to the ☌ ♀ by dir.; the ☽ to the place of Canis Majoris; the ☽ at full in a nocturnal geniture, sepr. from ☿ and applying to ♀; ♄ Sig. ☌ ♀; ♄ to the ☌ or good asps. ♀; ♃ Sig. in ♌, ♎, or ♐; ♃ in ♐, fond of outdoor pleasures; ♂ ☌ ♀, and especially in ♏, fond of sexual pleasures; ♀ ascending at B., strong inclination for pleasure; ♀ in ♓; ♀ in ♋, a pleasure-loving disposition; ♀ by Periodic Rev. to the ☌ the radical ☉; ♀ in the Asc. near the horizon; ♀ to the good asps. her own radical place by dir.; ♀ Sig. in ♑, fond of enjoyment; ☿ in ♐; ☿ at a Solar Rev. passing the place of the radical ♀; ☿ to the good asps. ♀ by dir.; the 2nd Decan. 8 on the Asc., ruled by the ☽; the 1° or 6° ♍ on the Asc. at B.; the 6th face ♌ on the Asc. (See the various paragraphs in this section).

Accidents—While Seeking Pleasure— Accidents At Pleasure Parties—♂ in the 5th H., □ or 8 the ☉ or ☽. (See Amusements, Exercise, Play, Sports).

Addicted to Pleasure — (See "Abnormal", and the various paragraphs in this section).

Amusements—Given To—(See Amusements).

Appetites—Seeks Pleasure Thru Gratification of—(See the paragraphs under Appetites).

Averse to Pleasure—Seeks Very Few Pleasures—♄ in ♌ or the 5th H. (See Apathy, Aversions, Celibacy, Deviations, Miserly; "Free from Passion" under Passion; Recluse, Secretive, Selfishness).

Bohemian Pleasures — Given To — ♅ strong at B.; ♅ by transit ☌ the radi-

cal ♀; ♆ afflicted in the 5th H.; ♀ to the ☌ or ill-asp. ♅ or ♂ by dir.; ♀ afflicted at B., and to the ☌, □, 8, or P. the ☽, ♅, ♂, the Asc. or M.C. by dir.; ♀ by Periodic Rev. to the ill-asps. the radical ☉; ☿ strong at B. (See "Free Living", "Free Love", under Free; "Unconventional" under Love Affairs; "Loose Morals" under Morals; "Clandestine" under Sex).

Cruel Pleasures — (See Cruel, Masochism, Sadism; "Violence" under Passion).

Danger—In the Pursuit of Pleasure— ♅ afflicted in the 5th H. (See Accidents, Ill-Health, in this section).

Death—From Excess of Pleasures— Death In the Pursuit of Pleasure — (See "Causes His Own Death" under Death; "Death" under Bathings, Debauchery, Eating, Drink, Intoxication, Love Affairs, Sports, etc.).

Disease—From Excessive Pleasures— ♀ diseases; ♀ afflicted at B. by ♂, ♅, or ♆; ♀ or ♂ afflicted in the 5th or 6th H. (See Amorous; "Brings Disease Upon Himself" under Disease; Dissipation, Drink; "His Own Worst Enemy" under Enemies; Excesses, Gluttony, Intemperance, Lust; "Health Injured" under Men; Opposite Sex; "Diseases" under Passion, Sex; Venery).

Drink — Pleasure from Drink and Liquors—(See Drink).

Eating—The Pleasures of — (See Appetites, Cravings, Drink, Eating, Epicureans, Feasting, Food, Gluttony).

Energies Wasted—In Pleasure Seeking—♂ afflicted in the 5th H.; ♂ afflicting ♀. (See "Wasted" under Energies).

Enjoyment — Abnormally Fond of — (See "Abnormally" in this section).

Epicureans—Given to Pleasure, Luxury and Feasting—(See Epicureans).

Excessive Pleasures — Excesses In — The 6th face of 8 on the Asc. (See "Diseases", and the various paragraphs in this section).

Extravagant Pleasures — (See Dress, Eating, Expense, Extravagance; "Rich Food" under Food; Habits, Luxuries, Prodigal).

Feasting—Given To—(See Epicureans, Feasting, Gluttony).

Fond of Pleasure—(See "Abnormally Fond Of", and the various paragraphs in this section).

Food — Extravagant In — (See "Extravagant" under Food).

Free Living—Free Love—(See Free).

Given to Pleasure — (See "Abnormally", and the various paragraphs in this section).

Gluttony—Gormandizing—(See Gluttony).

Gratification — Of the Animal Appetites—Excesses In—(See Appetites, Excesses, Gratification, Indulgences, Self-Indulgent).

Habits—(See the various paragraphs under Habits).

Health Injured—By Lustful and Inordinate Pleasures—(See Amorous; "Wasted" under Energies; Excesses, Inordinate, Lust; "Health Injured" under Men).

Hedonism—(See Self-Indulgent).

High Living—(See High).

Ill-Health—Thru Inordinate Pleasures—(See Diseases, Health Injured, and the various paragraphs in this section).

Inclined to Pleasure—(See "Fond Of" in this section).

Indulgent — (See Indulgent, Self-Indulgent).

Injudicious Pleasures—Diseases From—♀ diseases. (See Imprudent, Indiscretions, Injudicious).

Injuries Thru Pleasure—(See "Accidents" in this section).

Inordinate Pleasures—(See Excesses, Inordinate).

Jovial—Joyous—(See Joy).

Lascivious; Lewd; Libidinous — (See Lewd).

Licentiousness; Loose Pleasures—Immorality—(See "Loose Habits" under Loose; "Adulterous" under Love Affairs; "Loose Morals" under Morals; "Clandestine" under Sex).

Love Affairs—(See the various paragraphs under Love Affairs).

Low Pleasures — Given to Low and Sensuous Pleasures—♅ afflicted in the 5th H.; denoted by the 5th H.; ♂ □ or ☍ ♀; ♀ to the � ♂ by dir.; ♀ afflicted at B., and to the ♂ or ill-asp. the Asc. by dir. (See Low Company, Low Public Houses, Low Women, under Low).

Lustful Pleasures — Given To — (See Amorous, Lust; "Passional Excesses" under Passion; "Sensuous" under Sensuality).

Luxuries; No Love of Pleasure—(See "Averse" in this section).

Opposite Sex—Seeks Pleasure With—(See Opposite Sex).

Outdoor Pleasures — Fond of — (See Exercise, Hunting, Sports).

Parties—Accidents At Pleasure Parties—(See "Accidents" in this section).

Passional Pleasures — (See Amorous, Love Affairs, Lust, Passion, Perversions, Sensuality, Sex).

Peculiar Pleasures—Given To—♅ in the 5th H. (See Peculiar).

Play — Accident or Death While At Play — (See Play; "Accidents" in this section).

Pleasure Parties—(See "Accidents" in this section).

Pleasure Seeking Generally — ♀ elevated above, and configurated with the ☽ at a Solar Ingress or Eclipse.

Plethora—From Excesses, Indulgences and Pleasure Seeking—(See Plethora, Surfeits).

Profligate—Profligate Love of Pleasure, and Sickness From—Lord of the 6th or 12th H. in the 5th H., and afflicted. (See Profligate).

Reckless—In the Pursuit of Pleasure—(See "Pleasure" under Recklessness).

Recreations; Religious Enjoyments—(See "Exaltation" under Emotions; "Devotion", "Ecstasy", and the various paragraphs under Religion).

Sensuous Pleasures—Sex Pleasures—

(See Amorous, Love Affairs, Lust, Passion, Sensuality, Sex, etc.).

Sex Pleasures — (See Passional, Sensuous, in this section).

Sickness—From Pleasurable Excesses—(See Disease, Health Injured, in this section).

Social Pleasures — (See Companions, Friends, Love Affairs; "Popular" under Reputation; Social Relations).

Study—Pleasure and Enjoyment In—(See Learning, Reading, Study).

Surfeits — From Excesses In Eating, Drink, and Pleasures — (See Plethora, Surfeits).

Table—Given to the Pleasures of the Table, and to Feasting—(See Diet, Eating, Epicureans, Feasting, Gluttony).

Temperate—Should Be Temperate and Moderate In Pleasure, and Excesses Avoided—When the 6th face of ♉ is on the Asc. at B. (See Temperate).

Theatre—A Lover of—(See Theatres).

Too Much Pleasure — Inclined To — (See "Abnormally Fond Of" in this section).

Travel — Takes Pleasure In — (See Travel).

Unfortunate Pleasures — Health Undermined By—♅, ♆, or ♂ afflicted in the 5th H.; ♂ ♂ or ill-asp. ♀; ♀ in the 5th H., and afflicted by malefics; ♀ afflicted in the Asc. at B.; ♀ afflicted at B., and to the ♂ or ill-asps. the Asc. by dir.; ♀ ascending at B., and afflicted or ill-dignified; ♀ by Periodic Rev. to the ill-asps. the ☽, ♂, or M.C. (See Amorous, Drink, Excesses, Indiscretions, Inordinate, Lust; "Health Injured" under Men; Passion, Sex, Venery, etc.).

Unrestrained Pleasures — (See Depraved, Dissipated, Dissolute, Drink, Drunkenness, Lewd, Licentiousness, Lust, Passion, Profligate, Venery, Wanton, etc.).

Venery; Vices; Vicious Pleasures — Fond of—(See Vicious).

Violence — Resorts to Violence In Seeking Sex Pleasures — (See "Violence" under Passion).

Vitality Wasted — And Lowered by Excessive Pleasures and Wasted Energies—(See "Wasted" under Energies; Excesses, Inordinate, Lust; "Passional Excesses" under Passion; "Waste" under Vitality).

Wanton Pleasures — (See Lust, Passion, Wanton).

Waste of Energies—In Seeking Pleasure—(See Disease, Energies Wasted, Health Injured, Vitality Wasted, in this section).

Whoremongers — (See Harlots; "Low Company" in this section).

Women—Fond of—(See "Addicted to Women", "Women", under Men).

PLEIADES—Lucida Pleiadum—A Nebulous Group of seven Stars in the 27° ♉, in the Bull's Neck, stars of the 5th magnitude, except the middle star, which is of the third magnitude. Many of the evils which befall Humanity are connected with the influences of these stars when they rise with the Lights, or are directed to the Asc. The Pleiades are of the nature of the ☽ and ♂, and have special affinity with the Eyes. Blindness is one of the principal afflictions caused by the Pleiades, and resulting from Accidents, Measles, or Smallpox complications. The Pleiades tend to injuries to the eyes, bad eyes, hurts and injuries to the face; illness, sickness, disgrace, ruin, imprisonment, violent death, and every evil that can befall Humanity. (See Nebulous). The Pleiades are mentioned many times in the Textbooks of Astrology, in connection with the Eyes, Disease, Calamity, and the various afflictions which come to Humanity. These influences have been gathered up and listed in this book under the subjects where the Pleiades have a part. These subjects are as follows, which see in the alphabetical arrangement—

Accidents to Eyes—(See "Accidents" under Eyes).

Arms—(See "Wounds" under Arms).

Bad Eyes—(See "Bad" under Eyes).

Beheaded; Blindness—In One or Both Eyes—Partial Blindness—(See Blindness).

Blows—(See "Death By" under Blows).

Both Eyes—Blindness or Injury To—(See "Total Blindness" under Blindness; Accidents, Injury, under Eyes).

Calamity — (See "Many Calamities" under Calamity).

Conjunctivitis; Controversies — (See "Quarrelsome" under Quarrels).

Cuts; Death — Violent Death — (See "Death" under Violent).

Defects In Eyesight—(See Defective, Weak, under Sight).

Disgrace; Evil—Every Evil Upon Humanity — (See "Every Evil" under Evil).

Exile—(See Banishment).

Eyes—Blindness In—Hurts and Accidents To—Diseases of—Defects In—Weak Eyes—Bad Eyes, etc. — (See Blindness, Conjunctivitis, Eyes; "Eyes" under Left, Right; Retina, Sight).

Face—(See "Hurts" under Face).

Fever—(See Death from Fever, High Fever, Violent Fever, under Fever).

Goiter; Hurts—To Eyes and Face—(See "Hurts" under Eyes, Face).

Imprisonment—(See Prison).

Injuries — To Eyes and Face — (See "Eyes" under Exercise; Accidents, Hurts, Injuries, under Eyes, Face; Sword).

Lustful—(See Lust).

Measles—(See "Measles" under Blindness).

Murder—(See A Murderer, Death by Murder, Many Murders Prevalent, under Murder).

Nearly Blind — (See "Nearly Blind" under Blindness).

Nebulous Stars—(See Nebulous).

One Eye—Blind In One Eye—Loss of One Eye—(See "One Eye" under Blindness).

Ophthalmia—(See Conjunctivitis).

Pestilence—(See "Death" under Pestilence).

Quarrels—(See "Quarrelsome" under Quarrels).

Ruin; Sharp Instruments—Death By —(See Instruments).

Shipwreck; Sickness; Sight—Defects In—Blindness—(See Blindness, Sight).

Smallpox — (See "Smallpox" under Blindness; "Face" under Smallpox).

Stabs; Throat — (See "Cuts" under Throat).

Total Blindness—(See "Total" under Blindness).

Tragical Death—(See Tragical).

Trouble — (See "Causes" under Trouble).

Unfortunate; Untimely Death — (See Untimely).

Violent Death—Violent Fevers—(See "Violent" under Fever; "Death" under Violent).

Weak Eyes—(See "Weak Eyes" under Eyes).

Women—Tragical Death by Means of —(See Tragical; "Female Treachery" under Treachery).

Wounds — To Eyes and Face — (See "Injuries" in this section).

PLENTY — Plentiful—Plenitude—Abundance—Fullness—

Fluidic Plenitude—(See "Full Moon" under Moon).

Hair—(See "Abundance" under Hair).

Health — (See "Abundance" under Health).

Heat — (See Abundant, Excessive, Plenty, under Heat).

Vitality—(See Good, Superabundance, under Vitality). See the subjects and paragraphs under Abundance, Exaggerated, Excess, Excesses, Hyper, Increase, Much, Over, Super, Tonic, etc.

PLETHORA—Abnormal Fullness of the Blood Vessels—Too Much Blood—The Plethoric Habit — Hyperaemia — Localized Swellings — Plethoric conditions in the body tend to be at their worst at the time of the Full Moon, when the fluids of the body are at high tide. Plethora tends to High Blood Pressure, Hyperaemia, Localized Swellings; Fullness at the Stomach, and Gas in Stomach from Gormandizing; Apoplexy; Epistaxis (Nose Bleed); Excessive Menses. Jupiter rules all diseases that arise from a Plethoric Habit. Plethora is a condition caused by the ☉, ♃, or ♀, and by afflictions to these bodies. Is a ☉ disease, and especially caused by superfluous nourishment; the ☉ afflicted by ♃; the ☉ to the □ or ☍ ♃ by dir.; a ♃ disease, as ♃ is plethoric, and tends to surfeits, fullness, thick and impure blood, and especially caused by gormandizing and bad habits in eating, and by gluttony, etc.; ♃ afflicted from high living; ♃ □ or ☍ the ☽, plethora and malaise; ♃ □ or ☍ Asc.; ♃ ♂ or P. ♂; the ☽ □ or ☍ ♃, ♅, or ♀; ♀ afflicting the ☉, ☽, or ♃; ♀ afflicted in the 6th H.; the Asc. to the □ or ☍ ♃ by dir.; the ☉ □ or ☍ ♃.

Asthenic Plethora—A ♀ disease, and due to the atonic action of ♀. This is a more feeble form of plethora. (See Asthenia, Atonic).

Sthenic Plethora — Sthenic Distentions—A ♃ disease and affliction, and caused by the plus, or tonic action of ♃. Jupiter causes plethora from too full a habit, over-eating, too much blood, etc., and especially when afflicted, or afflicted in the 6th H. (See "Too Much Blood", "Pressure", under Blood; "Excesses" under Eating; "Full Habit" under Habits; "Impure Blood" under Impure; Sthenic, Tonic). Also, for further study along this line, see Apoplexy, Carbuncles, Decay; "Complications" under Disease; Distentions, Excess, Excesses, Flatulence, Fullness; "Stomach" under Gas; Gluttony; "High Living" under High; Hyperaemia, Malaise; "Profuse" under Menses; "Full Moon" under Moon; "Epistaxis" under Nose; "Superfluous" under Nutrition; Pressure, Surfeits, Swellings; "Rupture" under Vessels, etc.).

PLEURA — The Serous Membrane Enveloping the Lungs—The Pleural Cavity—Pleurisy—The Pleura is ruled by the ☽, ♃, and the ♋ sign. Cancer also rules the Pleural Cavity. The Pleural Serum is connected with the ♓ sign. (See Serum; "Fifth Thoracic" under Ganglion). The Serous Membranes, Surfaces, and Fluids are under the rule of the ☽ generally.

Crisis In Pleurisy — May be terminated from the 3rd to 8th day after the beginning.

Death by Pleurisy — Denoted by the ☉; the ☉ to the ill-asps. ♃ by dir.; the ☽ in ☌, ☍, or ill-asp. any of the malefics as promittors; ♃ much afflicted at B., and afflicting the hyleg by dir.

Emphysema—Pleural Emphysema—A ♍ disease, and afflictions in ♍; a ♅ disease; ♅ in ♍; Subs at Lu.P. (See "Emphysema" under Chest; Emphysema).

Inflammation of the Pleura—Pleurisy — Pleuritis — The ☉ hyleg, and to the □ or 8 ♃ by dir.; the ☽ in ♐, 8 ♃ in ♍; the ☽ hyleg, and to the □ or 8 ♃, and ♃ afflicted at B.; the ☽ afflicted in ♎, and afflicting the hyleg therefrom; a ♃ disease; ♃ afflicted in 8, ♍, or ♋ tends especially to affect the pleura; ♃ afflicted in ♌ or ♎; ♃ afflicting the ☉ by dir; ♂ in ♍ and ☌ the Asc. by dir.; ♂ in watery signs, and ☌, □, or 8 the Asc. by dir.; a ♍ disease and afflictions in ♍; the Asc. to the □ or 8 ♃ by dir., and ♃ afflicted by ♂; the Asc. to any aspect ♃ by dir., and ♃ afflicted at B., and especially if ♃ be in ♌ or ♒; the Asc. to the ☌ ♃ by dir., and ♃ afflicted at B.; caused by afflictions in 8, ♍, ♋, ♌, ♎, or ♒; Subs at Lu.P. (See "Inflammation" under Lungs).

Pleurisies—The ☉ afflicted in ♍; the ☽ afflicted in ♎; ♄ afflicted in ♍; ♃ afflicted in ♍, ♌, ♎, or ♒; ♃ afflicting the ☉ by dir.; ♃ by direction in ♌ or ♒, and 8 the Asc.; ♂ afflicted in ♍ or ♐; ♂ in ♌ in the 6th H.; ♂ affl. in ♋; ☿ afflicted in ♍ or ♐; caused by afflictions in ♍, ♋, ♌, ♎, and ♒; a ♍, ♋, and ♌ disease.

Pleurisy—(See "Inflammation" in this section).

Pleurodynia—Pain—(See "Pain" under Intercostal).

Pleuro-Pneumonia — ♂ afflicted in ♍ in the Asc. or 6th H.; Subs at Lu.P. and KP. (See Pneumonia).

PLEXUS — Plexuses — A Network of Nerves or Veins—The seven great and important Nerve Plexuses are the Cardiac, Cavernous, Pharyngeal, Laryngeal, Solar, Prostatic, and Sacral.

Aortic Plexus—(See Hypogastrium).

Brachial Plexus—The action of the ☿ Group of Herbs tends to pulmonary innervation thru the Brachial Plexus. The ☉, ☽, and other planets, acting thru the ♍ sign tend to affect this Plexus and the Respiratory System. (See Brachial; "Middle Cervical" under Ganglion).

Cardiac Plexus — The Deep Cardiac Plexus—(See "Middle Cervical" under Ganglion).

Carotid Plexus—(See Carotid; "Ribes" under Ganglion).

Cavernous Plexus—(See "Ribes" under Ganglion).

Coronary Plexus—The Right and Left Coronary Plexuses—(See "Middle Cervical", "Fifth Thoracic", under Ganglion).

Diaphragmatic Plexus — (See Diaphragm).

Ganglion — (See the various paragraphs under Ganglion).

Gastric Plexus — (See "Fifth Thoracic" under Ganglion).

Hemorrhoidal Plexus — (See Ductless Glands).

Hepatic Plexus—(See Hepatic).

Hypogastric Plexuses—(See "Impar", "Lumbar", under Ganglion; Hypogastrium).

Intestinal Plexuses — (See the Introduction under Bowels; "External Humours" under Humours).

Laryngeal Plexus—(See Larynx).

Mesenteric Plexus—(See "Splanchnic" under Ganglion; Mesentery).

Pharyngeal Plexus—(See Pharynx).

Post-Pulmonary Plexuses — (See "Middle Cervical" under Ganglion; Pulmonary).

Prostatic Plexus—(See Prostate).

Renal Plexuses—(See Ductless Glands; "Lumbar" under Ganglion; Kidneys).

Sacral Plexus—(See Sacrum)

Solar Plexus — Is under the internal rulership of ♍, and is the seat of the Life Force, or Prana, in the physical body. Good descriptions of the nature and functions of the Solar Plexus are given in the books, "The Key to the Universe", by Dr. and Mrs. Homer Curtiss. Also in the book, "Cosmo-Conception", by Max Heindel. (See Ductless Glands; "Splanchnic" under Ganglion; "Innervation" under Gastric; "Force" under Vital).

Spermatic Plexus — (See Ductless Glands).

Splenic Plexus—(See "Fifth Thoracic" under Ganglion; Spleen).

Supra-Renal Plexus — (See Ductless Glands).

PLIABLE—(See Bending, Flexible, Influenced; "Mutable Disposition" under Mutable; "Negative Nature" under Negative).

PLODDING—A Plodding and Laborious Nature — (See "Laborious" under Labor).

PLOTS—Conspiracies—Secret Enmities—Caused by ♆ and the 12th H. influences, and afflictions in the 12th H., and especially malefics in this House.

Active In Plots — Schemes and Intrigues—☿ afflicted in the 12th H.

Death by Plots—Injury by Plots—♄ and ♂ elevated above, and in evil aspect to the ruler of the horoscope, enemies conspire against the native. (See "Death" under Ambushes, Enemies, Enmity, Murder, Poison, Treachery, Violence).

Many Plots Generally—An eclipse of the ☉ in the 1st Decan. of ♍; an eclipse of the ☽ in ♑; Comets appearing in ♎.

Prison — Imprisoned Thru the Plots of Relatives or Children—(See "Plots" under Prison).

Society—A Plotter Against Society—Bomb Plotters—(See Anarchists). For other influences along this line, which may lead to plots and treachery, see Artifice, Contests, Criminal, Dangerous, Destructive, Duels; "Secret Enemies" under Enemies; Hatred, Kidnapped, Libel, Malevolent, Malice, Mischief; "A Murderer" under Murder; Neptune; "Death by Poison" under Poison; Revengeful, Shrewdness, Treachery, Twelfth House, Vicious, Violent, etc.

PLUGS — Clots—Obstructions—(See Clots, Embolism, Infarcts, Obstructions, Thrombus).

PLUMBAGO—(See Graphite, Lead).

PLUMBUM—(See Lead).

PLUMP—Plump Body—Somewhat Fat—Distended—Filled Out—

Plump Body—The ☉ Sig. in ♓, plump and fleshy; the ☽ Sig. in ♈, rather plump; the ☽ in ♈ in partile asp. the Asc.; the ☽ Sig. in ♓, plump or fat; the ☽ in ♓, partile the Asc., plump or fat, and with a mean, short stature; the ☽ increasing causes a fat, plump, full, and tall body; ♄ Sig. in ♒, corpulent and plump; ♃ Sig. in ♓, plump and fleshy; ♃ Sig. in ♉, ♊, ♋, or ♓; ♃ Sig. in ♋, rather plump, but disproportioned; in Hor'y Q., ♃ as Sig. denotes a fat and plump person; ♀ Sig. in ♉, plump but not gross; ♀ Sig. in ♓, plump and fleshy; ♀ in ♓, partile the Asc., plump, middle-sized, and rather fleshy; ♀ rising in the Asc.; ♒ on the Asc., plump, robust, strong, well-set, healthy make; ♓ on the Asc.; given by the Sanguine Disposition. (See Compact, Corpulent; "Plump" under Face, Hands, Lips; Fat, Fleshy, Full, Lumpish, Sanguine, Stout).

PLUTO—The Planet Pluto—This planet will not be considered in this Edition of this book, as very little is known of it, and at present is considered by many Authorities to be a hypothetical planet. It is also doubted by some Writers as being a part of our Solar system, and is said to be outside of the Earth's Zodiac in the greater part of its orbit. (See Planets). Mr. E. H. Bailey, Editor of the British Journal of Astrology, writes in the October, 1931 issue of his Journal, and says—"I have no belief whatever in the alleged influence of this planet. It is a very great question whether it is a member of our Solar System . . . and I would warn my readers not to accept anything at the present time. It is far too early to lay down definite information with regard to a body which may, or may not, have any astrological influence." Also in the November, 1932 issue of the British Journal, Mr. Bailey further says—

"Several correspondents have written me asking for my opinion respecting this planet, and whether I consider it has any real influence in Astrology, and if so, in what way its influence will be felt. Also what sign it rules. To be quite candid, I must confess that I have little or no belief in this planet, and from the evidence which I have obtained personally, and what has been sent to me by students, I see no reason whatever to include it when dealing with horoscopes. It is far too early in the day for students to lay down any definite information as to its influence, real or imaginary, yet one would think from published statements that certain students were fully aware of its action in horoscopes, and knew nearly all there was to be known about it. A number of horoscopes have been sent to me from readers, in which they allege that certain events have been shown by this planet, but in all the cases sent, I have been able to detect the real cause without incorporating Pluto, or any other hypothetical planet."

PNEUMOCONIOSIS — Lungs Diseased by Dust Inhalation—(See this subject under Lungs).

PNEUMOGASTRIC NERVE—Vagus Nerve—Ruled by ♄. Saturn badly afflicted at B. tends to restrict and obstruct the action of this nerve, and to cause indigestion, irregular heart action, lung disorders, suppression of the urine, stools (faeces), and also to cause worry and fears. Case of Obstruction of this Nerve—See Fig. 14F in the book, "Astro-Diagnosis" by the Heindels. (See "Suppression" under Faeces; "Pneumogastric" under Fears; "Impeded" under Heart; Indigestion; "Obstructions" under Lungs, Nerves; Retentions, Suppressions, Urine, Worry, etc.).

PNEUMONIA—Inflammation In the Lungs—Lung Fever—The ☉, ☽, or ♄ afflicted in ♓, from catching cold, wet feet, or living in a damp place, and especially when these planets are in ♂ malefics in the 12th H.; the ☉ in ♓, □ the ☽ in ♐; the ☽ ☌ ♅ in ♓ in the 12th H., from catching cold; the ☽ afflicted in ♊; ♅ afflicted in ♊; ♅ in ♊ in the Asc., and afflicted by ♃, ♀, and the ☽; a ♄ disease; ♄ afflicted in ♊, and tending to consolidation; ♄ afflicted in ♓, from catching cold thru the feet; ♄ afflicted in ♐; ♄ in a strong sign of the ☽, and the ☽ in a ♄ sign; a ♃ disease, and due to surfeits caused by ♃, congested blood vessels, corrupt and impure blood, the result of gluttony and gormandizing, and Pleurisies also result from the afflictions of ♃; ♂ afflicted in ♉, ♉, ♍, or ♐; ♂ afflicted in ♍ in the Asc. or 6th H.; a ♍ disease, and afflictions in ♍; malefics in ♍ and common signs; malefics in ♍, and afflicting ♃ and ♀, the rulers of the circulation, and interfering with oxygenation, tends to colds, coughs, and even running into double pneumonia; the 3rd H. and ☿ are often involved with the afflictions which cause this disease; Subs at Lu.P., CP, and KP. Case—See "Pneumonia", in Chap. XIII, in Daath's Medical Astrology. (See "Pulmonitis" under Lungs; the paragraphs in this section).

Broncho-Pneumonia — (See "Pneumonia" under Bronchial).

Catarrhal Pneumonia—The ☽ afflicted in ♍. (See Catarrh).

Catching Cold — Pneumonia From — The ☉, ☽, or ♄ afflicted in ♓, from wet feet, or living in damp places. (See "Cold Taken" under Feet).

Consolidation In—♄ afflicted in ♍. (See Consolidation).

Croupous Pneumonia—Lung Fever— Generally caused by the same influences which lead to Croup, such as afflictions in ♉, which may also be combined with afflictions in ♍. (See Croup; "Lung Fever" under Lungs).

Death from Pneumonia—♂ afflicted in ♍ at B., occi., and also afflicting the hyleg by dir. (See "Death" under Bronchial, Lungs).

Delayed Resolution—♄ in ♍ and afflicting the ☉, ☽, Asc., or hyleg.

Pleuro-Pneumonia—(See Pleura).

Typhoid Pneumonia — Pneumonia accompanied by Typhoid Symptoms — Afflictions in ♍ combined with afflictions in ♍, ♐, and common signs at the same time; the ☽ afflicted in ♍. (See Typhoid).

POCK-MARKED—(See "Pitted Degrees" under Pitted; "Face" under Smallpox).

PODAGRA — Gout In the Feet — (See "Feet" under Gout).

PODOPHYLLIN — Podophyllum — May Apple—A Typical Drug of ☿. A Cathartic. (See "Mercury Group" under Herbs; Physic).

POIGNANT—Sharp—Severe—Poignant action over the body is ♂ action.

Poignant Diseases — And Maladies — Caused by the ☉ and ♂, the positive, electric, and heat-producing planets. (See "Poignant" under Diseases, Pain).

POINTED—(See "Pointed" under Chin; "Narrow" under Face; "Sharp" under Nose).

POISE — Balance — Equilibrium — (See Adrenals, Calm, Equilibrium; "Disposition" under Excellent; Harmony; "Mild Disposition" under Mild; "Even Temper" under Temper).

POISON—Poisons—Poisoning—Poisonous—Poisonings—Toxins—Virulent— Malignant—Noxious, etc.—Mars gov-

erns poison drugs, as a rule. Neptune rules poisons, as Narcotics and Opiates. The poisonous wastes and deposits in the system are ruled by ♄, and also ♄ tends to prevent the elimination of poisons from the body. Dealers in poisonous drugs are ruled by ♀, as a class. The following subjects have to do with poison, the poisons in the body, and the various uses and practices with poison.

Acidity — Excessive Acidity In the Body—(See Acids, Deposits, Gout, Hyperacidity, Rheumatism, Uric, Wastes).

Air—(See "Corrupt" under Air).

Alexipharmics — (See Alexipharmic, Antidotes).

Antidotes to Poisons — (See Alexipharmic, Antidotes, Antipathy, Opposites).

Arms—Blood Poisoning In—The ☉, ♃, or ♀ afflicted in signs which rule the Arms, Hands, Legs, and Feet tend to blood poisoning and blood impurities in these parts. (See "Blood In Arms" under Arms; "Disordered Blood" under Blood; "Corrupt Blood" under Hands; "Arms" under Impure).

Bites—Poisonous Bites—(See Bites).

Blood Poisoning—Septicemia—Toxic Blood—Impure Blood—Caused principally by afflictions in ♒, as this sign rules strongly over the blood. Also caused by afflictions to ♃, which planet rules the arterial blood. An ♒ disease, and ♒ causes blood poisoning, morbid blood conditions, and incomplete oxygenation of the blood; ♃ or the ☽ afflicted in ♒; the ☽ to the ☌ or ill-asps. ♂ by dir., and ♂ afflicting the ☽ at B., tends to death by blood poisoning; ♂ afflicted in ♒; ♂ afflicted in ♒ in the 6th H.; ♂ in ♒, and afflicting the ☽ or Asc.; caused by ♀ when the dominion of death is vested in her. (See Autointoxication; "Blood" under Impure; Septic, Toxaemia, Uremia).

Body — Poisoning of the System — Saturn obstructions retain the wastes of the body, retard the functions, weaken elimination and excretion, which tends to poisoning of the system. This surplus of poison and waste is burned out by ♂, and, if necessary, by high fevers and inflammation. Also an afflicted ♃ or ♀ tend to diseases which arise from poisoning of the system, and which may result from bad habits, gluttony, and indiscretions. (See Plethora, Pressure, Surfeits).

Carbonic Acid—Poisoning of the System By—(See Carbon).

Danger from Poisons — (See Death, Life Endangered, and the various paragraphs in this section).

Dealers In Poisons—Ruled by ♀. (See Chemists).

Death by Poison — Poison Death — Poison Death by Treachery — The ☽ hyleg, and to the ☌ or ill-asp. ♂ by dir., and especially if ♀ gives an evil aspect in the configuration; the ☽ hyleg, afflicted, and to the ☌ ☊ by dir.; the ☽ with Cor Hydra, ☌, □, or ☍ ♄ or ♂, death by poison, and especially if ♂ be angular; ♆ afflicting the hyleg, and elevated above it, indicates death by poison, and especially by Narcotics; Ψ afflicted in the 8th H., or afflicting the hyleg therefrom; Ψ setting in ☍ to the ☉ or ☽; ♄ in the Asc. in ☍ the ☉ or ☽, and ♀ attached to ♄ and ☿ combined; ♄ in ♏, afflicting the hyleg, and conjoined with ♀ by aspect, death by treachery or poison; ♄ afflicted in the 12th H.; ♄ Sig. of death, and in □ to ♀ (Hor'y); ♄ in ♏ in the 8th H., and both afflicting the hyleg at B., and by dir.; caused by ♄ and ♀ influences when these planets are conjoined, and thru the treachery of ♄; ♂ Sig. □ or ☍ ♄, if either be in the Asc., or ♄ in the M.C.; ♂ ☌ ♄ in ♏ in the 8th H., and both afflicting the hyleg at B., and by dir.; ♀ denotes death by; ♀ much afflicted at B., and afflicting the hyleg by dir., and taking part in a fatal train of directions to the hyleg; ♀ afflicting the hyleg, or giver of life, by dir.; ♀ or ☿ conjoined with ♄ and ♄ afflicting the hyleg; in a train of evil directions indicating death, if ♀ also cast a □ or ☍ to the hyleg, and ♀ be afflicted by malefics at B., danger of a poison death; ♀ afflicted at B., and afflicting the hyleg by dir., and holding the dominion of death, and especially if ♀ be in the 8th H., or afflicting the cusp of the 8th at the same time, and if the radical map also shows death by violence; ruled by the 8th H., and malefics in the 8th, or afflicting the lord of the cusp of the 8th, and ♀ in □ aspect to the Significator at the same time, death by poison, or from fear of a poison death; lord of the Asc. in ♏ in the 7th or 8th H., and afflicted by ♀ and malefics; Cor Hydra joined to ♂, and in evil asp. the ☉ or ☽. (See Enemy, Husband, Kings, Treachery, Women, in this section). Cases of Death by Poison—All in 1001 N.N. See "Husband", No. 162; "Allenby", No. 298; "Ladislaus", No. 450; "Medici", No. 525; "Hickman", No. 774.

Deposits — The System Poisoned by Mineral Deposits—(See Deposits).

Diseases Arising From—Sickness and Diseases Arising from Poisons In the System—Denoted by ♄ afflictions, retaining the wastes and poisons of the body. Also denoted by ♀. (See "Blood Poisoning", and the various paragraphs in this section; "Vascular Tissues" under Vascular).

Drugs—Poison Drugs are ruled by ♂, ♀, and the 8th H., and also poison death from such drugs.

Elimination — Of Poisons from the System—The elimination of the poisons from the body is done by ♂ in a normal way, but when there is too much surplus of poison and waste products, ♂ burns them out by causing high fevers and inflammations. (See Elimination, Fever, Inflammation; "Body" in this section).

Enemy — Poisoned by An Enemy — Danger of Secret Poisoning—Poisoned by Plots or Treachery—♄ afflicted in the 12th H.; lord of the 7th H. a malefic, in the 12th H., and afflicted. (See Death by Poison, Secret, Treachery, Women, in this section; "Death by An Enemy" under Enemies).

Fear of Poison Death — (See "Death by Poison" in this section).

Feet — Blood Poisoning In — (See "Arms" in this section).

Females — Poisoned by Treachery of —(See "Women" in this section).

Fevers—Purpose of to Burn up Poisons and Wastes—(See Body, Elimination, in this section).

Gases — Poison Gases — Death By — (See "Poisoning" under Gases).

Gastritis — The Toxic Form from Swallowing Poison — (See "Gastritis" under Gastric).

Gout — From Retention of Poisons — (See Gout).

Hands — Blood Poisoning In — (See "Arms" in this section).

Healer — Poisoned By — (See "Poisoned" under Healers).

Heart Afflicted by Poison—(See "Poison" under Heart).

Herbs—Poison Herbs—(See Herbs).

Husband—Commits Suicide by Poison — Case — (See "Poison" under Husband).

Illness from Poison—(See "Sickness" in this section).

Improper Medicines — Poisoned by Taking — (See "Improper Medicines" under Medicines).

Impure Blood — Poisoned By — (See "Blood Poisoning" in this section; "Blood" under Impure).

Inflammation—Poisons Eliminated By —(See Body, Elimination, in this section).

Ivy Poison—(See Ivy).

King—Death of a King by Poison— (See "Dethroned" under Kings).

Lead Poisoning—(See Lead).

Legs — Blood Poisoning In — (See "Arms" in this section).

Life Endangered—By Poison—The ☽ hyleg at B., afflicted, and to the ☌ ♄, ♂, or ☍ by dir., and especially if ♀ take part in the configuration; ♄ afflicted in ♌; ♄ afflicted in the 12th H. (See Death, Enemy, Treachery, in this section).

Malaise — From Poisons In the Body —(See Malaise).

Medicines — Poison Drugs and Medicines—(See Medicines, Remedies).

Metals—Poison Metals—(See Metals).

Minerals—Poison Minerals—(See Minerals).

Mineral Deposits — The System Poisoned and Injured By—(See Deposits, Gravel, Minerals, Sand, Stone, Wastes).

Mucous Membranes — Arsenic, a ♂ drug and poison, is a powerful irritant to the mucous membranes. (See Introduction under Mucous).

Narcotic Poisons—(See Narcotics).

Neutralization of Poisons—(See Alexipharmics, Antidotes, Antipathy, Opposites).

Noxious Poisons—(See Noxious).

Obstructions—From Poisons Retained In the Body—(See "Hindered" under Elimination; Obstructions, Retarded, Retentions, Suppressions).

Opiates — Poisoned By — (See Narcotics).

Oxygenation — The System Poisoned by Improper Oxygenation—(See Oxygen).

Physician—Healer—The Patient Poisoned By — (See "Poisoned" under Healers; "Improper Medicines" under Medicines).

Plots—Poisoned Thru Plots—(See Enemy, King, Women, in this section).

Poisoner—A Poisoner—The ♏ influence strong at B., and with afflictions in this sign; ♂ ill-dignified and afflicted at B., and adversely configurated with ♀; ♀ is usually badly afflicted at B., and in a weak sign, as in ♏, and also afflicted by ♄ and ♂, which leads to enmity, jealousy, hatred, revenge, etc. The same influences apply here as in the cases of murderers, but with ♀ strongly involved, if caused by some love affair, or where ♄, ♂, and ♀ are configurated in cases of business and financial grievances. (See "A Murderer" under Murder; "Tendency To" under Violence). Cases of a Poisoner—All in 1001 N.N. See "Poisoner", No. 271; "Horsford", No. 764; "Maybrick", No. 969.

Remedies — Poisons As Remedies — Poisons, such as Strychnine, when given in very small doses, act as a stimulant and tonic. Most drugs are poisonous if given in large doses. (See Cure, Drugs, Medicines, Remedies, Treatment; "Herbs", "Metals", "Minerals","Therapeutic Properties","Typical Drugs", under each of the Planets).

Retention of Poisons—In the System —(See Crystallization, Deposits, Hardening, Minerals, Retentions, Suppressions, Uric, Wastes; Blood Poisoning, Body, Elimination, in this section).

Rheumatism—From Retained Poisons and Wastes—(See Rheumatism, Uric).

Secret Poisoning — ♄ afflicted in the 12th H. (See Death by Poison, Enemy, King, Women, in this section).

Septic Poisoning — Septicemia — (See "Blood Poisoning" in this section; Putrefaction, Septic).

Sickness — From Poisoning — The ☽ afflicted in ♏; the ☽ to the ♂ or ill-asps. ♂ by dir.; ♅ setting in ♏ to the ☉ or ☽, sickness or death by; lord of the Asc. in ♏ in the 7th H., and afflicted by malefics. (See Death by Poison, Diseases Arising From, and the various paragraphs in this section).

Sloughings—Arising from Weakness and Poison—(See Sloughings).

Stings—Poisonous Stings—(See Bites, Stings, Venomous).

Suicide by Poison — ♅ in the 8th H., and afflicting the hyleg. (See "Poison" under Husband; Narcotics, Suicide).

Surplus Poisons—In the Body—Diseases or Death By—(See Blood Poisoning, Body, Death, Diseases, Elimination, Retention, Sickness, and the various paragraphs in this section).

Swallowing Poison — (See Gastritis, Suicide, in this section).

System—Diseases Arising from Poisons In the System — (See "Surplus" in this section).

Throat — Septic Poisoning In — (See "Septic" under Throat).

Toxaemia—Toxic Blood—(See "Blood Poisoning" in this section; Toxaemia).

Travel—Poisoned During Travel— ☿ in evil asp. to the Significators of Travel. (See Danger, Death, under Travel).

Treachery — Poison Death By — (See Death, Enemy, King, Women, in this section).

Uremia—Toxic Blood with Excess of Urea—(See Uremia).

Vegetable Poisons—(See Herbs, Vegetation).

Violent Death — By Poison — (See Death, Enemy, Women, in this section).

Virulent Poisons—(See Malignant, Noxious, Venomous).

Wastes and Poisons—In the Body—(See Body, Elimination, Retention, in this section).

Women — Poisoned Thru the Treachery of—The ☉ or ☽ afflicted in ♏, and ill-aspected by ♀; the ☽ hyleg, and to the ♂ or ill-asp. ♂ by dir., and ♀ throw in an aspect; ♄ in ♏, ♂, or evil asp. the Asc. by dir.; ♀ in ♏ and afflicting the ☉ or ☽; adverse ♀ influence at B. makes liable to, and afflictions in or from the ♏ sign. (See Death, Enemy, in this section; Enmity, Jealousy; "A Murderer" under Murder; Revengeful; "Female Treachery" under Treachery; Vicious; "Tendency To" under Violence).

Wrong Medicine—Poisoned By—(See "Improper Medicines" under Medicines).

POLARITY — Polarization — The fresh polarizations of the Planets cause their changing influences. Each planet has a certain and definite polarity in itself, and when unaspected will always act in a certain manner, and produce certain effects from the causes it generates. The aspects, and the changing and modified polarities of the planets, tend to produce the different diseases, different states of mind, and the afflictions and testings of life, according to the vibrations. Plants and Herbs gather the different properties given by the Planets, and individualize these properties, or vital forces, according to their form. The Plants contain particles of matter and colors corresponding to the seven planetary rays. The organs, tissues, and cells of the body also contain a polarity, and are ruled by planets, and when an herb is used as a remedy, by the law of antipathy or sympathy, such remedy can change the polarity of an organ or tissue, and thus modify, cure, or heal a disease, or make it worse, according to the reaction between the remedy and the organ. The location, or place of residence, also have a polarity which may, or may not agree with the native, and a change of residence in case of sickness often brings relief and a cure if the polarity of the new location is harmonious with the vibrations of the patient. Certain Adepts and Masters have the power to change their polarity, overcome the law of gravitation, cause their bodies to rise or float in the air in Levitation, and also to perform various unusual phenomenon. (See Antipathy,

Aspects; "Cure of Disease" under Cure; Location, Nadir; "Native Country" under Native; Negative, Opposites; "Action", "Polarity", under Planets; Positive, Residence, Sympathy; "Direction to Travel" under Travel, etc.).

POLES—The Cerebral and Genital Poles of Paracelsus—(See Paracelsus).

POLICE OFFICERS—Killed or Injured By—(See Officers).

POLIOCEPHALITIS—(See Brain).

POLIOMYELITIS—(See "Infantile" under Paralysis).

POLITE—Courteous—(See "Polite" under Manner).

POLITICS—Politician—Public Life—
   Fond of Political Life—Of Public Life —Born under the strong influence of the tropical signs ♋ and ♑.
   Political Murderer—Case—(See Murder).
   Political Strife—Much Public Discord —(See "Dissentions", and the various paragraphs under Public; "Discord" under Quarrels; Reformers, Religion, Revolutionary; "Civil War" under War).
   Public Life—Execrated by the Multitude In Public Life—(See Anarchists, Execrated).
   Subtle Politician — ☿ Sig. in ♊, and not afflicted. (See Pettifogging).

POLLUTION—Polluted—
   Polluted Blood — (See "Blood" under Impure).
   Polluted Mind — (S e e Amorous, Debased, Debauched, Degenerate, Depraved, Disgrace, Dissolute, Evil, Harlots, Infamous, Lascivious, Lewd, Licentious; "Loose Morals" under Loose; "Adulterous" under Love Affairs; "Low and Base" under Low; "Licentious" under Men; Obscene; "Pasional Excesses" u n d e r Passion; Perversions, Profligate; "Clandestine" under Sex; Shameless; "Solitary" under Vice; Vile, Wanton; "Dissolute Habits" under Women, etc.).

POLLUX—Hercules—Caput Hercules— One of the two stars known as "The Twins", Castor and Pollux. (See Castor). Pollux is a violent star of the 2nd magnitude, in the 4th face of ♋, and of the nature of ♂ and the ☽ combined, and denotes ruin, disgrace, death, and every calamity. The stars in the knees and feet of Castor and Pollux are equally injurious. The ☉ directed to the place of tends to cause blindness in one or both eyes, and if Praesepe be also with the ☉ and ☽ in an angle, or on the Asc., certain blindness is almost sure to result, or hurts to the face. The danger of a violent death is also denoted, and much evil to the native, if the ☉ is with Pollux at B. The ☽ to the place of Pollux often denotes blindness, or a great defect in the sight, and especially if the ☉ or ☽ at B. were with Nebulous Stars. The ☽ to the place of Pollux also tends to ill-health, danger of a violent death, or damage to the wife or daughter. Disgrace and ruin are also indicated if the ☉ or ☽ be with this star at B., or by dir. The ☽ directed to the Belly of the Twins, and the Knees of Castor and Pollux, tends

to danger by thieves. The star Pollux is mentioned many times in the Textbooks of Astrology, and these influences have been gathered up for this book. Pollux is referred to under the following subjects as Pollux, Hercules, Caput Hercules, The Twins, or Violent Fixed Stars. See Assassination, Banishment, Beheaded, Blindness, Blows, Calamity, Daughter; "Tragical", "Violent", under Death; Disease, Disgrace, Dreadful, Drowning; "Every Evil" under Evil; "Bad Eyes", "Accidents To", under Eyes; "Hurts To" under Face; "Death By", "Violent", under Fever; Ill-Health (see "Much" under Sickness); "A Murderer", "Many Murders", under Murder; Pirates, Prison; "Quarrelsome" under Quarrels; Rape, Ruin, Shipwreck, Shot to Death (see Gunshot); "Extreme Sickness", "Much Sickness", under Sickness; Stabs, Suffocation; "Danger By" under Thieves; "Tragical Death" under Tragical; "Death" under Violent; "Danger To" under Wife; "Danger Of" under Wounds; Wretchedness.

POLONIUM — A Radioactive Substance ruled by ♅, and closely related to Radium. (See Radium).

POLYCREST REMEDIES—(See "Polycrest" under Zodiac).

POLYPUS—A Pedunculated Tumor, and generally located in the Nose, Throat, Ear, or Rectum.
   Ear or Throat—Polypus In—An ♈ or ♉ disease; the ☉ or ☽ afflicted in ♈ or ♉; ♄ or ♂ in ♈ or ♉; Subs at AT.
   Nasal Polypus—(See "Polypus" under Nose).
   Rectal Polypus — The ☉, ☽, ♄, or ♂ afflicted in ♏; ♏ on the Asc. at B. (See Rectum).

POLYURIA — E x c e s s i v e Secretion of Urine—(See "Polyuria" under Urine).

POMPHOLYX — A Disease with Bullas of the Hands and Feet — (See Dysidrosis).

PONS VAROLII—Vital Knot, located at the base of the Brain. Ruled by the ☉ and ♉. (See Brain).

POOLS — Stagnant Pools — Ruled by ♓. Saturn sole ruler at an eclipse of the ☉ tends to diseases arising from stagnant pools. (See Foul, Odors).

POOR—Deficient—Lacking—Poorly—Indifferent—Not Up to Standard—Below Par—The Poor, etc.—
   Poor Abilities—Not Highly Gifted— (See "Fails In" under Examinations; Inability, Inactive; "Incapable", "Void Of", under Learning; "Shallow" under Mentality; "Light In Mind" under Mind; Talents, etc.).
   Poor Assimilation—(See Assimilation).
   Poor Blood — (See "Poor" u n d e r Blood).
   Poor Body—(See Crippled, Deformed; "Ill-Formed" under Ill; "Ill-Health All Thru Life" under Ill-Health; Invalid, Sickly; "Weak Body" under Weak).
   Poor Circulation—Of the Blood—(See "Poor" under Circulation).
   Poor Complexion—(See "Poor" under Complexion).

Poor Digestion — (See "Poor" under Digestion; Indigestion).

Poor Health — (See "Poor" under Health).

Poor Heart Action — (See "Poor Action" under Heart).

Poor Mentality—(See "Poor and Shallow" under Mental).

Poor Oxygenation — (See "Non-Oxygenation" under Oxygen).

Poor Vitality — (See "Low", "Weakened", under Vitality).

The Poor — The Poorer Classes, and the Common People are ruled by the ☽. Venus Sig. in ♋ at B. is in indication and influence in the map of a female that she may belong to the Poorer Classes. (See Common People, Humanity, Mankind, Poverty, Public).

POPPY PLANT—Opium—Ruled by Neptune. (See Narcotics, Opium).

POPULACE—The People—(See Common People, Humanity, Mankind, Public).

POPULAR—A Popular Person—Popularity — (See "Many Friends" under Friends; "Popular" under Reputation). For Unpopular, see "Many Adversaries" under Enemies; Execrated; "Hated by Others" under Hate; Recluse, Secretive).

POPULATION—The People—

Decreased — The Population Rapidly Decreased — (See "Death Rate High", "Depopulation", under Mortality).

Increased—The Birthrate Increased— (See "Birthrate" under Birth). See Common People, Mankind, Public.

PORES—(See "Pores" under Skin).

PORRIGO — Favus of the Scalp — (See Favus).

PORTAL BLOOD STREAM—The wastes of the Portal Blood Stream are converted into Glycogen in the Liver by ♃, to act as fuel for the body. (See Glycogen, Liver).

PORTENTOUS FEVERS—Dreadful— Ominous — (See "Portentous" under Fever).

PORTLY BODY—Full—Somewhat Stout —Commanding—♃ and ♀ make the body more portly and commanding. Also the ☉ Sig. in ♌, and especially with the ☉ in the Asc. in ♌, or elevated in the East in this sign; the ☉ ☌ ♃ and ♀ in ♌, and elevated in the East at B. (See Commanding, Corpulent; "Body" under Large; Stout, Tall).

POSITION IN LIFE—(See Low, Popular, Poverty, Reputation, Riches, Social, Vagabond, Wealth, etc.).

POSITIVE—

Positive Constitution—Positive Form —The ☉ in ♎, or ♎ on the Asc. at B. (See Constitution).

Positive Horas—(See Horas).

Positive Houses—(See "Positive" under Houses).

Positive Nature—Positive Disposition — A Firm, Ruling, and Commanding Nature—The ☉ rising and oriental at B. has a positive and electric influence upon the mind and body. A positive state of mind is given by the ☉,

♃, and ♂ when rising, elevated in the East, dignified, and well-placed at B.; ♂ well-aspected at B., and especially when rising and elevated; many planets in the masculine signs at B.; many planets elevated in the East at B., and more so if in masculine signs. (See Commanding, Electric; "Great Energy" under Energy; Environment; Independent, Majority, Resolute, Rule, Self-Assertive, Self-Confident, Self-Reliant; "Strong Will" under Will).

Positive Planets — Postive and Electric—(See Electric).

Positive Signs — Of the Zodiac — The masculine Signs, such as ♈, ♊, ♌, ♎, ♐, and ♒. The fiery signs ♈, ♌, and ♐ are extremely positive and fiery. The positive Signs are alkaline, and the negative, or female signs, are acid. (See Acid, Alkaline). Hot and Dry, and Hot and Moist combinations are positive. Hot and Dry are positive, and belong to the positive and fiery signs ♈, ♌, ♐. Also the Signs presiding over the right side of the body are positive, and especially in the female. (See Horas; "Hot and Dry", "Hot and Moist", under Heat; Left, Right; "Positive" under Signs).

POSTURE—Position—Attitude—

Awkward Posture — (See Awkwardness).

Body Bent Forward — Hooked Forward — Stooping — (See "Downward" under Look; Stooping).

Downward Look — (See "Downward" under Look; Stooping).

Erect Posture—(See Erect, Upright).

Stooping Head—(See Stooping).

Straight and Tall—(See Erect).

Walk—(See Gait, Walk). See Appearance, Body, Form, Shape, Stature.

POTASSIUM—Is ruled by ♄. Potassium Phosphate is ruled by the ♈ Sign, and supplies the Brain Tissues. Potassium Chloride is the Zodiac Salt, or Tissue Remedy, ruled by the ♊ sign, and is connected with the Animal Tissues. Potassium Sulphate is the Salt ruled by the ♍ sign. This Salt supplies the Hair, Nails, and Oils of the body. Injections of Potassium are said to cure Carcinoma, or Cancer. (See Carcinoma, Hair, Nails, Oils; "Salts" under Zodiac).

POTATO-LIKE CANCER — (See "Solanoid" under Carcinoma).

Potato Blight — Coincident with the appearance of Comets. (See Comets, Vegetation).

POTENTIALITY—Inherent Capacity— (See Heredity, Inherent, Innate; "Native Country" under Native; Polarity).

POTIONS—Love Potions—Philtres— Ruled by Venus. (See Philtres).

Sleeping Potions—Ruled by the ☽ and ♄. (See Narcotics; "Sleeping Potions" under Sleep).

POTT'S CURVATURE—Of the Spine— Pott's Disease — (See "Pott's" under Spine).

POUCH—A Pocket-Shaped Cavity—(See Cavities, Cysts, Sacs, Scrotum).

POULTICES — (See Emollient, Resolvent).

POVERTY — Neglect — Privation — Poor — Indigence — Poverty and Indigence are governed by ♄; ♄ in the 2nd H., and afflicting ♃; the ☉ and ☽ far below the horizon, with no benefic angular, and the Lights afflicted by malefics; the ☽ sepr. from the ☉, and applying to ♄, often in want and misery; the ☽ decr., sepr. from ♂ and applying to ♄; the ☽ sepr. from ♀ and applying to the ☉; the ☽ Sig. ☌ ♄, often poor and poverty stricken; the ☽ Sig. ☐ or ☍ ♀, tends to indigence and poverty; ♃ Sig. ☐ or ☍ ♀, becomes indigent thru lawsuits and losses; planets ℞ at B. are said to cause poverty and sickness, and especially ♄ and ♂ retrograde; the Ruler, or Significator, being in his own decanate or face signifies a person in want, and hardly able to support himself (Hor'y). (See Begging, Careless, Destiny, Dissolute, Dull, Failure, Famine, Fate, Fortune, Idle, Improvident, Indifferent, Indigent, Indolent; "Bad" under Judgment; Laborious, Lack Of, Lazy, Livelihood, Loss Of; "Shallow" under Mentality; Misery, Misfortune, Neglect, Poor, Privation, Property, "Many Changes" under Residence; Resources, Reverses, Riches, Ruin, Unfortunate, Vagabond, Void Of, Wretchedness, etc.).

Beggarly — Lives Beggarly and Carelessly — (See Begging).

Diseases — Diseases Arising from Neglect, Privation, and Poverty — ♄ diseases; the ☉ and ☽ afflicted by ♄.

Fear of Poverty — ♆ afflicted in the 2nd H. at B. (See Fear).

Indigent — (See Apathy, Careless, Dull; "Lack of Forethought" under Forethought; Idle, Indigent, Indifferent, Indolent, Lazy, Vagabond, etc.).

Journeys — Danger from Privations On Journeys or Voyages — (See "Privations" under Sea).

Property and Riches — Loss of — (See Expense, Money, Prodigal, Property, Reverses, Riches, Ruin, etc.).

Voyages — Privations On — (See Famine; "Privations" under Seas).

Want — Fear of Coming To — (See "Fear" in this section).

POWDER BURNS — (See Gunshot).

POWER — Powers — Powerful — Energy — Force — Strength, etc. — The ☉ and ♂ when strong at B., and supporting each other by aspect, tend to give the native more power, force, and energy on the physical plane, and in health matters, with increased vitality. The ☉ and ♂ weak and ill-dignified at B., and the ☉ not supported by ♂ by a good aspect, or no aspect, and at the same time with a weak sign rising in the Asc., tend to weaken the powers of the native, lower resistance to disease, etc. (See Mars, Sun).

Application of Power — (See "Last Quarter" under Moon).

Creative Powers — (See Creative).

Dynamic Power — ♂ is the planet of. (See Dynamic, Mars).

Energy — (See the various paragraphs under Action, Energy, Force, Life, Motion, Movement, Muscles, Physical).

Men In Power — (See "Power" under Men).

Mental Powers — (See Intellect, Mental; "Active Mind" under Mind; Perception, Understanding, etc.).

Natural Powers — (See "Natural Forces" under Natural).

Organic Power — (See Organic).

Physical Powers — (See Body, Physical, Strength, Strong, Weak, etc.).

Psychic Powers — (See Psychic).

Sources of Power — All of the Planets endow certain powers, according to their nature, sign and house positions, aspects, etc. For the nature and quality of the powers given by the Planets, see each planet in the alphabetical arrangement, and especially note the sections on "Influences", and the Qualities endowed by each planet. Also note the various paragraphs in this section.

Spiritual Power — (See Pineal, Pituitary, Spiritual).

Strength — (See the various paragraphs under Strength, Strong).

Vital Powers — (See "Life Force" under Life; Vital, Vitality).

Weak — The Powers Weakened — (See Diminished, Feeble, Lack Of, Loss Of, Void Of; the various paragraphs under Weak).

Will Power — (See Will).

POX — Syphilis — A Contagious, Eruptive, Pustular Disease — (See Eruptions, Pustular, Syphilis).

PRACTICAL — Utilitarian — The Earthy Signs strong at B. tend to make one practical, as these signs have more to do with the material, or Earth Plane. The Fiery Signs are also usually practical, and the ☽ influence, and the ♋ sign. Also ♅ when well dignified at B. tends to practicability in the business affairs of life, but with some dangers of going to extremes and being eccentric, peculiar, and misunderstood when ill-dignified and ill-aspected at B.

Impractical — The ♎, ♒, and ♓ signs do not tend to be as practical, and are usually more impractical and dreamy. The ♆ afflictions at B. also tend to make one less practical, and to be more liable to obsessions, hallucinations, dreamy ideas and notions, and to resort to strange, weird, uncanny, or unusual methods in their procedures. (See Chaotic, Dreamy, Eccentric, Erratic, Fanatical, Fancies, Ideals, Imaginations; "Bad" under Judgment; Notions, etc.).

PRACTICE OF MEDICINE — And Healing — (See "Physicians" under Healers).

PRACTICES — (See Conduct, Evil, Excesses, Good, Habits, Ideals, Ideas, Manners, Morals, Notions, Perversions, Religion, Vices, Wicked, Unnatural).

PRAEINCIPIENTS — In Disease — Incipients — ♅ and ♆, as related to disease, and as incipients and praeincipients in disease, are classed as planets which tend to obscure, extraordinary and mysterious causes in disease, and peculiar complications. Incipient diseases, those at their very beginnings, if taken when they first manifest themselves, as indicated by the diathesis and idiosyncrasies, habit in disease, etc., can usually be broken or neutralized by the proper remedy and treatment. Thus ♄ and ♂ in ☐ predispose to lung disorders, colds on the lungs, etc., and if this is known to the native who has such influences at B. he can safeguard these tendencies, remove the causes of nose, throat, and lung troubles in the body, and also have a remedy at hand always to quickly disseminate and break up the first symptoms of disease when they appear. Each person should make a study of his own case, know the tendencies of his body and mind, and then set out to control and rule conditions, and be Master of his Fate and Destiny, and thus avoid much unnecesary suffering, pain, sorrow, and tribulation. (See Antipathy; "Cure of Disease" under Cure; Diagnosis, Diathesis, Hexis, Opposites, Prevention, Prognosis, Remedies, Sympathy, Treatment, etc.).

PRAESEPE — The Cratch—The Crab's Claw—The Ascelli—A Nebulous Cluster in the first Decanate of ♌, of the nature of ♂ and the ☽, and said to cause blindness, or hurts to the face, when rising in ♂ the ☉ or ☽, and especially when in an angle. (See Ascelli). Also said to cause disgrace, diseases, and every calamity and evil upon humanity. The ☉ directed to Praesepe tends to blindness in one or both eyes, and if Praesepe be on the Asc., or with the ☉ or ☽ in an angle, certain blindness. The ☉ directed to the Cratch, in the 6° ♌, tends to danger to the head and eyes, injury by machinery, gunshot, falls, or bruises. The ☉ with Praesepe at B. also is indicative of evil, and the danger of a violent death. Also the ☉ and ☽ with Praesepe at B., and especially in an angle, tend to every kind of calamity upon the native, disgrace, and to cause diseases of various kinds. The ☽ to the place of tends to great defects in the sight, and often blindness, and especially if the Lights are with Nebulous stars at B. The ☽ with Praesepe, and espec. in an angle, tends to blindness, or injury to the eyes. The ☽ Sig. ♂ the ☉, and near Praesepe at B., the native is likely to be nearly blind. The Ascelli, Praesepe, and the Cratch, are all very close together in the first Decan. of the ♌ sign, and of the same nature, and make up a Nebulous Cluster, and in the Textbooks seem to be used interchangeably, and the influences given in the Article on The Ascelli in this book will also apply to those for Praespe, or Praesepe, as this word is spelled both ways in the books. Praesepe is mentioned many times in the Textbooks of Astrology. In this book Praesepe, the Cratch, or the Ascelli, are mentioned in the following subjects, and as taking a part in causing these diseases, afflictions, or injuries. See these subjects in the alphabetical arrangement — Arms (Wounds To); Banishment, Beheaded, Blindness, Bruises, Calamity, Conjunctivitis, Disgrace, Evil (Every Evil); Exercise (Death By); Eyes (Bad Eyes, Danger To); Face (Hurts To); Fevers (Violent); Fire (Death By); Gunshot

(Danger, Death, or Wounds By); Head (Danger To); Imprisonment (see Prison); Iron (Death By); Machinery (Accidents By); Murder (Death By); Nebulous Stars (see the Article on Nebulous); Ruin, Shipwreck, Shot to Death (see Gunshot); Sight (see Blindness, Sight); Stabs, Stars, Trouble, Untimely Death (see Untimely); Violent Death (see "Death", under Violent); Wounds, etc.

PRANA — The Hindu name for Vital Force, Life Force, etc. Ruled by the ☉. (See "Life Force" under Force; "Force" under Vital). Prana is Life Force in the Air, in Food and Drinking Water, and gives force, energy, strength, and nourishment to the body. It is an etheric force, and separate from the actual ingredients in air, food or water, and it is said that we absorb more of this Prana when we are conscious of its presence, and hold the thought that we are taking in this Force when breathing or eating. Orange is the color of the Pranic life forces in the blood. Occult books on the Science of Breath, and Breathing, deal with this subject quite fully. Read the Chapter on "Prana Absorption" in the book, "Hatha Yoga", by Yogi Ramacharaka (William Walter Atkinson). Prana is also said to increase the Spiritual Powers when taken in consciously, and directed by the thoughts and prayers to such Centers. (See "Fire Signs" under Fire; "Solar Plexus" under Plexus).

PRECARIOUS — Perilous — Uncertain — Subject to Dangers—(See "Many Dangers" under Danger; Escapes; "Precarious Life" under Life; Perils).

PRECIPICES—High Places—Falls From — (See Heights; "Dangers" under Travel).

PRECIPITATE — Hasty—Hurried — Without Due Deliberation—

Precipitate Actions — Accidents from Precipitate and Impulsive Actions—♂ in the 1st H., ☐ or ☍ the ☉ or ☽ at B. (See Foolhardy; "Lack Of" under Forethought; Hasty, Impulsiveness, Rashness, Recklessness, etc.).

Precipitate Fancies — (See "Foolish" under Fancies).

PRECIPITATION—The Throwing Down of Solids from Liquids—In the human body this is usually the work of ♄, thus causing excessive mineral deposits in the tissues, and resulting in disease, such as Gout, Rheumatism, Uric Acid Poisoning, etc. (See Deposits, Gout, Minerals, Rheumatism, Uric, Wastes, etc.).

PRECOCIOUS—Premature Development —Precocious Mental Development— (See Backwardness, Genius, Mathematician, Premature, Prodigies).

PREDETERMINATION — Of Sex — To Foretell Whether Male or Female During Pregnancy—Judgment of the 5th H. of a parent indicates whether the first child will be male or female. Also the time of conception, if known, and the planets in the signs at that time, are to be considered, and the nature of the signs and planets. The ☉, ☽, and Asc. are principally to be observed, and the planets which have prerogative over them. If the ☉, ☽, and Asc. are femininely constituted, then judge a female child. The masculine planets are the ☉, ♅, ♄, ♅, and ♂, and the ☽ and ♀ are feminine. Mercury partakes of both genders, according to his location and aspects with the masculine and feminine planets. The odd signs, as ♈, ♊, ♌, etc., are considered masculine, and the even signs, as ♉, ♋, ♍, etc., are feminine. The watery signs are very fruitful, and also feminine. In judging of the sex keep the gender of the planets, signs, and the degrees of the signs in mind. A Table of the Masculine and Feminine Degrees of the Zodiac is given in the book, "The Prenatal Epoch" by Mr. E. H. Bailey. Also see "Degrees" under Feminine, Masculine. For further consideration of this subject see "Female Children", "First-Born Child", under Children; Conception; "Birth of a Female" under Female; "Births" under Male; Prenatal Epoch, Quadrants, Quickening, Triplets, Twins).

PREDICTIONS—Predicting—(See Character, Curable, Destiny, Diagnosis, Directions, Events, Fatal, Fate, Foretold, Incurable, Judgment, Predetermination, Prognosis, Progressions, Prophetic, Quality, Secondary Directions, Transits, Type, Will, etc.).

PREDISPOSED — Predisposition — Inherent — Innate — Hereditary—Tendencies—Idiosyncrasies—Diathesis, etc.— The Signs occupied by planets at B., the rising sign, the signs on the Midheaven, and the 6th H., especially indicate what parts of the body are more predisposed to disease, afflictions, accidents, etc., and especially the signs occupied by malefics. The degree on the Asc. at B. gives predisposition to certain diseases and afflictions, according to the sign rising. (See the book, "Degrees of the Zodiac Symbolized", by Charubel). The part ruled by the sign occupied by the ☉ denotes a sensitive part, or organ, and more liable to disease if the ☉ is badly afflicted at B. (See Congenital, Constitutional, Diathesis; "Strong" under Disease; Environment, External, Heredity, Hexis, Inherent, Innate, Organic, Praeincipients, Prenatal, Propensities, Structural, Susceptibility, Temperaments, Tendencies, etc.).

PREGNANCY — Impregnation — Pregnant — Gestation — Prenatal Period — Fertilization—Conception, etc.—The ☽ and the 5th H. rule pregnancy, and the ☽ is the planet of impregnation and fertilization. (See Fifth House, Moon). The conditions for fruitfulness must exist, and the ☽ and watery influences strong and prominent at B., before impregnation can take place. Barren conditions in the map prevent pregnancy. Note the following subjects—

Barrenness—Not Capable of Becoming Pregnant—(See Barren).

Conception — Conception Has Taken Place — (See the paragraphs under Conception).

Delivery — To Know Time of — (See "Time of Delivery" under Parturition).

Fancy—A Pregnant and Ingenious Fancy—(See "Pregnant Genius" under Genius).

Fecundation—(See this subject).

Female — Male or Female During Pregnancy—(See Predetermination).

Fertilization—(See Fecundation, Fertilization).

Foetus — (See the paragraphs under Foetus).

Fruitful — May Often Become Pregnant — (See "Many Children" under Children; Fruitful).

Genius — A Pregnant Genius — (See Genius).

Gestation — (See the paragraphs under Gestation).

How Long Pregnant?—Observe the ☽ and lords of the Asc. or 5th H., and find the nearest past aspect they make to any planet. If separating from a ☌ of a planet, it is the first month of pregnancy; if sepr. from the ✶ aspect, judge she is in the 2nd or 6th month; from the □ aspect, in the 4th month; from the △ aspect, in the 3rd or 5th month; from an ☍ aspect, in the 7th month, etc. These are the rules for judging the matter in Hor'y Questions.

Male or Female — During Pregnancy —How to Judge the Matter—(See Predetermination).

Maternity — (See the paragraphs under Maternity, Mother).

Mother—Motherhood—(See Maternity, Mother).

Parturition — The Puerperal State — Childbirth—(See Parturition, Puerperal).

Party Has Just Conceived—(See this subject under Conception).

Period of Gestation—(See Gestation, Prenatal Epoch).

Prenatal Epoch—(See Prenatal).

Quickening—Of Foetus—(See Quickening).

Sign of Pregnancy—A Benefic in Cazimi. (See "Woman Is with Child" in this section).

State of a Woman With Child — This is judged by the 5th H. and its influences. Also the last application of the ☽, before she leaves the Sign she is in, denotes the state of the mother (Hor'y).

Uterus In Pregnant Women—Is especially affected and influenced by the ☉ and ☽ acting thru the ♎ sign.

Vexations During Pregnancy — Malefics in the 5th H. at B. and by dir.

When Will the Child Be Born?—(See "Born" in Sec. 1 of the Article on Children; "Time of Delivery" under Parturition).

Woman Is With Child—In Hor'y Q., the following influences indicate that she is with child—If the lord of the 5th H. behold a planet in an angle, and with reception; lords of the Asc., 5th, or 7th H., or the ☉, ☽, ♃, ♀, or ☿ be in the 5th H., and fortified, except when ☿ is in the 5th H. in aspect to a malefic, and with no aspect to a benefic, when ☿ cannot be relied upon; if translation of light has passed between the lords of the 1st and 5th, or if the ☽ be just separating from the latter in a fruitful sign, or in the 5th, 7th, or 11th H.; lords of the 1st and 5th, or the ☽, in reception to a planet angular; the ☽ and the lord of the triplicity she is in both be in fruitful signs, or if ♃ and ♀ be both angular and free from affliction, these are symbols of conception having taken place. If at the time any of these symptoms appear, ♃ be cadent, or afflicted, or ♄, ♂, or ☋ be present at the place of the aspect, or on the cusp the 5th H., there is either no conception, or there will be an abortion. It is the same if they afflict the ☽, ♀, or lord of the 1st or 5th H. (See "Signs of Children" under Children; Conception, Fruitfulness).

Woman Is Not With Child—Signs of No Conception In Hor'y Questions— Denoted when the ☽ is void of course; ♃ and ♀ afflicted; ♀ joined to ♄ or ♂, or to ♅ if he be afflicted, and these planets ℞, combust, or in ♌, ♍, or ♑; ♄ in the 11th H. frustrates hope; ♄ or ♂ in the 5th H., ☐ or ☍ the lord of the 5th; a barren sign on the Asc., or malefic planets there, or afflicting their lords or the ☽; a barren sign on cusp the 4th or 5th H.; lord of the Asc. joined to a ℞ planet, or to one in a cadent house, or received by a ℞ or combust planet, or if there be no translation of light or aspect between lords of the 1st or 5th, are all signs of no conception. (See Barren).

PREJUDICE—Prejudiced—
  Fancies—Prejudiced Fancies—(See Fancies).
  Heat or Fire — Prejudice By — (See "Danger" under Fire).
  Mind—Prejudiced Mind—Narrow-Minded — A characteristic of the fixed signs, and with ☿ and many planets in these signs at B.; ☿ afflicted by ♄ tends to prejudices and narrowness of mind; the ♍ sign and its influences tend to prejudice of mind, and to make one more critical and fault-finding, and less tolerant of the views and opinions of others. The ☐ and ♐ signs are more liberal. (See Doubts, Fears; "Shallow" under Mentality; "Light In Mind" under Mind; Mistrustful, Reason, Scepticism, Suspicious; "Weak" under Understanding, etc.).

PREMATURE—Precocious—
  Premature Baldness—(See "Early In Life" under Baldness).
  Premature Birth — Premature births may be attributed in some cases to the mother, and her tendency to habitual abortion. (See Abortion). In other cases the afflictions to the ☽ during the gestation period, when the ☽ crosses, or does not cross the central line of impulse at the monthly periods during the prenatal period, may cause it. If several of the Moon's librations do not return to, and cross the central line of impulse during pregnancy, there tends to be a lack of equilibrium, and an unbalanced condition of the foetus, which may lead to its expulsion. (See Prenatal Epoch). Diseases of the Foetus are also a cause.

CASES OF PREMATURE BIRTH—
  (1) Born Two Weeks Before Time—See "Weak Mind", No. 146, in 1001 N.N.
  (2) Born Three Weeks Too Soon—See "Deaf and Dumb", No. 166, in 1001 N.N.
  (3) Born At Eighth Month — (See "Eight Month's Children" under Children).
  (4) Born Six Weeks Too Soon—(See Chap. XIV, in Daath's Medical Astrology).
  (5) Born At the Seventh Month—See "Weak Mind", No. 145; "Twins", No. 681; "Sight Defective", No. 684, all in 1001 N.N. (See Abortion; "Eight Months Children" under Children; Miscarriage).

Premature Burial — Danger of Being Buried Alive—(See Burial).
Premature Death — (See "Death by Accident" under Accidents; Burial; "Death" under Childhood, Children, Early, Extraordinary, Hurts, Infancy, Injuries, Mysterious, Peculiar, Strange, Sudden, Untimely, Unusual, Violent, Wounds; "Short Life" under Life, etc. Also note the various paragraphs under Death).
Premature Decay — (See Decay; "Fluid" under Vital).
Premature Mental Development—Precocious—The favorable aspects of the ☉, ♅, ♂, or ☿ all tend to early mental development. (See "Active Mind" under Active; Backwardness, Genius; "Mind" under Growth; Mathematical; "Quickened" under Mentality; Precocious; Prodigies).
Premature Old Age—(See Juvenility; "Senility" under Old Age).
Premature Wrinkles—(See Wrinkles).

PREMONITIONS — Presentiments — Forebodings—(See "Impending" under Calamity; "Mental Chaos" under Chaotic; Dreams (Case of Strange Dreams and Premonitions); Fears, Forebodings; "Hallucinations, Hauntings, Imaginations, Obsessions, Spirit Controls; Terrors, Visions, Weird, etc.).

PRENATAL EPOCH—The Epoch—Conception — The time of conception is called The Epoch, and this time has a definite and fixed relation to the time and moment of birth, as these two points are connected by a fixed and determined arc, and when the time of birth is approximately known, the time of conception can be accurately determined by the proper astronomical calculations, and also when the time of conception is determined, the true time of birth can also be found, and the exact degree rising on the Asc. at the true moment of birth. Thus, by this method, the time of birth can be rectified, if such time is approximately known. Ptolemy, in his "Tetrabiblos", laid down many of the rules for the Epoch and its determination, which rules have been further worked out, amplified, and systematized by the Modern Astrologers Sepharial, and Mr. E. H. Bailey, Editor of the British Journal of Astrology. Read the books, "Sepharial's Manual of Astrology", and "The Prenatal Epoch", by Mr. E. H. Bailey. The fundamental rule of the Epoch is that the sign and degree of the ☽ at Epoch, or Conception, becomes the exact sign and degree on the Asc. or Descendant at the quickening, and at birth. (See Quickening). If at birth the ☽ is increasing and above the Earth, the place of the ☽ at conception becomes the Ascendant at B. If at birth the ☽ was below the Earth, and decreasing, the place of the ☽ at the Epoch becomes the Descendant at B. Thus, when the hour of birth is known approximately, the Prenatal Epoch calculations give us one of the best methods for rectifying the exact moment of birth, for when once the time of conception is determined, according to the Order, it is an easy matter to calculate the exact degree on the Ascendant or Descendant at the time of birth.

Orders of the Epoch—The Epoch may be regular or irregular, and the Epochs are classified into four Orders.

(1) The ☽ increasing and above the Earth at B., which gives a time of conception 273 days before birth, less the days for correction, which makes the period of gestation less than the ordinary time, or what we would call an "undertime" child.

(2) The ☽ above the Earth and decreasing, which makes the time of conception 273 days, plus the days for correction, and an "overtime" child. These two Orders of the Epoch have to do with the true Asc. at B., and the degree rising.

(3) The ☽ below the Earth and increasing at B., which gives a count back of 273 days, and plus the days for correction, and gives an "aparently overtime" child.

(4) The ☽ below the Earth and decreasing, which gives a pregnancy of 273 days, minus the days for correction, or an "undertime" child. In the book, "Prenatal Epoch", By Mr. Bailey, the Irregular Epochs are considered, and how they are calculated. The Index Date, or the ordinary day of conception, is found by counting back nine calendar months to the day and date when the ☽ is in the same sign and degree as at birth, or near the same degree. The distance in degrees of the ☽ from the Asc. in the first Order, and this distance divided by 13, gives the number of days for correction to the Index Date, to be subtracted, and the conception took place within 14 days following the Index Date. In the 2nd Order, the distance of the ☽ from the Asc. at B., divided by 13, gives the number of days to be added to the Index Date, and which may make the time of conception as much as 14 days before the Index Date, and an apparently overtime child. A knowledge of these Laws, and how to calculate the map for the time of conception, helps to clear away many of the mysteries of why children are not born on the exact times expected, some being born two weeks "ahead of time", and others two weeks late, etc. The time of birth is fixed by the arc of direction between conception and birth, and the child under normal conditions has to be born at the time fixed and set by Nature.

Therefore, birth should not be forced, or instruments used, if the mother seems to be in Labor too long, according to the Physician's views, or the opinions of the family. The child will be born when its time comes, if things are normal and allowed to have their way. This Article is not intended to be a full elaboration on the subject of the Pranatal Epoch, but only to give the student some ideas of the work, its importance, and then you must follow this up for yourself, and study the books mentioned. The Chart of Descent is a perpendicular line drawn from the place, sign and degree of the ☽ at Epoch to the degree of the Asc. at B. This line of descent is also known as "The Descent of the Monad." The date each month during Gestation when the ☽ is nearest to the ascending or descending degree at B. should be noted, and a line drawn on the Chart of Descent to this point. A Figure for a Chart of Descent is given on page 155 in Mr. Bailey's book. The ☽ at her return to this degree each month may come to the central line, fall short of it, or cross it. In a normal child, the ☽, at her return each month, should cross back and forth over the central line. If for several months the ☽ does not touch or cross this line at the time mentioned, it indicates an unbalanced condition of the child, lack of equilibrium, and when disease, malformation, idiocy, mental disorders, insanity, defects or even premature birth, abortion, or miscarriage may take place. Cases and illustrations of these unbalanced conditions are given in Mr. Bailey's book, such as The Frog Child, born minus a forearm and legs below the knees. Many weaknesses that exist in the child after birth, or at birth, such as deformity, malformation, tendency to certain diseases, etc., can be explained by the Prenatal Map, and by noting the descent of the ☽ thru gestation, and the relation of the ☽ to the line of central impulse, and also the aspects to the ☽ at these times. The Map of Birth is valuable to study in connection with the Epoch Map, and the maps for each month during the descent of the Monad. The map of the Epoch helps to explain many things. Infant Mortality is caused by afflictions to the ☽ at conception, or the Epoch. Procreation may be controlled, and even the sex of the child predetermined, if coitus and conception can take place at a time which will predetermine the Epoch map, which map is then reflected in the map of birth. Mr. Bailey deals with this subject, and many others, in his book, and it would take a whole volume to go into these matters here. The address of Mr. Bailey is 10 Red Lion Court, Fleet St., London, E. C. 4, England. The ☉, ☽, and Ascendant at birth are controlling factors in the calculation of a Prenatal Epoch Map. Also the gender of the degrees of the Zodiac have to be considered, and to ascertain the sex positions of the ☽ and Asc., and as given in the Table of Genders of Degrees, on page 40 of Mr. Bailey's book. The map for the time of conception also shows the nature of the incoming Ego, the innate character developed in previous Incarnations, the stage of the evolution of the native, etc., while the map of birth shows the environmental conditions, the contacts with the world which are laid out for the native in the present life; shows the Personality, tendencies of the mind and body, lessons and tests to be encountered, the diseases and afflictions apt to come to the native, and also his relation to Society, etc. In this Encyclopaedia, the Prenatal Epoch, its workings, and the conditions it causes in the body before birth, at birth, and after birth, are mentioned, or have to do with the following subjects, which see in the alphabetical arrangement, and the Epoch Map, and Chart of Descent, will help to explain the causes and presence of these diseases and conditions when such indications may be absent from the map of birth. Also the causes of many diseases, afflictions, defects, deformities, malformations, etc., are gone into quite fully in Mr. Bailey's book, and in Sepharial's Manual of Astrology. See Abortion; "Beastly Form" under Beasts; "Cause of Birth", "Moment of Birth", under Birth; "Born Blind" under Blindness; Character; "Born", "Delayed Births", "Eight Months Children", "Dogs", under Children; Conception, Congenital, Cyclops, Deafness, Deaf and Dumb; Defects, Deformities, Dumbness, Embryo, Fecundation, Fertilization, Foetus; "Foolish Mind" under Foolish; Forearm, Freaks, Gestation, Heredity, Idiocy; "Ill-Formed Body" under Ill; Imbecile, Imperfections, Incomplete; "Deformed from Birth", "Premature Birth", "Signs of Death", under Infancy; Inhuman, Insanity, Intellect; "Disease" under Judgment; Lameness; "No Limbs" under Limbs; Lunacy, Maimed, Miscarriage, Malformations; "Hereditary" under Mania; Map, Marks; "Mising Members" under Members; "Retarded" under Mental; "Weak Mind" under Mind; Missing; "Moment of Birth" under Moment; Monsters; "Epoch" under Moon; Mute, Naevus, Nativity; "Incapable Of" under Nutrition; Organic; "Birth" under Paralysis; Parturition, Personality, Perversions, Physical, Predetermination, Pregnancy, Premature, Ptolemy, Quadrants, Radix; "Void Of" under Reason; Rectification, Reproduction, Savage, Stillborn, Structural; "Birth" under Time; Triplets, Twins, etc.

PRESBYOPIA—(See Sight).

PRESENTIMENTS — (See Forebodings, Premonitions).

PRESERVATION—Preservatives—Preserved—Preservation is a Therapeutic Property of ♃, and this planet exerts a preservative and conserving influence over the body and tissues. The Sun Group of Herbs are preservative. In the physical world Sugar is a preservative, and is the result of ♃ action, and is ruled by ♃. (See "Substance" under Cells; Conservation, Defensive, Jupiter, Nutrition, Phagocytes, Prevention, etc.).

Life Preserved—(See Escapes; "Spared" under Life; "Disease Pre-

vented" under Prevented; "Patient Will Recover" under Recovery).

Preserves—Sweets—Sugars—Over-Indulgence In—♀ afflicted in ♎. (See Sugar).

Self-Preservation—(See this subject).

Well-Preserved—In Body—(See Juvenility).

PRESIDENT OF THE U. S. A.—Danger To — Danger of Assassination — Death or Injury To—These influences are the same as for Kings, Rulers, and Prominent People. (See Assassination, Famous; "Great Men" under Great; "Assassination" under Kings; Nobles, Princes, Queens, Rulers, etc.).

PRESSED TO DEATH—(See Crushed).

PRESSURE—Force—Weight—

Atmosphere—Excessive Atmospheric Pressure—Diseases Arising From—♀ diseases and influence. (See "Pressure" under Air, Gases; Caisson Disease, Compressed).

Blood Pressure—High or Low Blood Pressure — (See "Pressure" under Blood).

Nerves — Pressure Upon, and especially in the Spine, and as the Nerves make their exits thru the Vertebrae, as in Subluxations. (See Subluxations, Vertebrae). Undue, or abnormal pressures may be exerted upon any part, or organ of the body, due to diseased conditions, the deposit of minerals, poisons and wastes of the system by ♄ influence, as in Gout and Rheumatism. Pressure of the skull upon the brain by congenital defects, or by accidents to the head, is caused by ♂ in ♈ at B., or ♈ upon the Asc. There may be pressure upon the heart, due to stomach gases and indigestion, as caused by afflictions in ♋. Too much blood may cause undue pressure upon the blood vessels, resulting in rupture of the vessel, Apoplexy, Hemorrhage, Plethora, etc. Falls, caused by ♄, may result in too much pressure upon a part, causing a rupture of the tissues, as in Inguinal Hernia. (See these subjects).

PRETENDER—Pretenses—Pretended—Pretentions—

Pretended Ailments—♆ in evil asp. to ♀. (See Complaining, Delusions, Exhibition, Hysteria, Illusions, Imaginations, Lamentations, Mysterious, Neptune, Obscure, Obsessions, Peculiar, Spirit Controls, Strange, Weird, etc.).

Pretender—A Pretender to All Kinds of Knowledge—(See "Void Of" under Learning).

Pretenses — Outwardly of Great Decorum—♏ influence.

Pretensions — Pretentious — Ostentatious—

(1) Adornment — Fond of Personal Adornment, Fine Clothes, Jewelry, etc. —Governed by ♀; ♀ in the Asc., and dignified; ♂ Sig. in ♌ or ♎. (See Dress, Expense, Extravagance, Luxuries, Neat).

(2) Boastful—Bragging—Conceited— The ☉ ill-dignified at B., and afflicted; the ☉ Sig. ✶ or △ ♄; ♃ Sig. in ♏; ♂ Sig. in ♌ or ♎; in Hor'y Q. ♄ Sig. in ♈;

☿ ill-dignified at B.; ☿ Sig. in ♌, and apt to be full of idle words. (See "Exaggerated Ego" under Ego).

(3) Bombastic—Caused by the ☐ and ♀ aspects to ♃.

(4) Ostentatious — The ☉ Sig. in ♒; the ☉ Sig. ✶ or △ ♄; the ☐ and ♀ asps. to ♃; ♀ in the Descendant at B., and in a strong sign. (See Hypocritical, Proud, Religion).

PREVALENT — Prevailing Generally Among the People or Nations — The Mundane, or House positions of the Planets from day to day, rule over World Affairs, and tend to bring disease, epidemics, pestilence, famine, earthquakes, storms, calamity, catastrophy, public sorrow and distress, outrages, panics, etc., and the student should make a study of Mundane Astrology. Planetary influences at the Vernal Equinox, and at Solar Ingresses, tend to a general prevalence of World conditions, for good or ill. Comets, Eclipses, the conjunction of several Superior Planets, Planets in perihelion or perigee, etc., tend to unusual World conditions. (See Comets, Eclipses, Ingresses, Mundane, Perihelion, Vernal). Under the following subjects the planetary influences are given which tend to some of these prevailing conditions, and by which Mankind is afflicted in various ways. See these subjects in the alphabetical arrangement, and especially look for "Prevalent" in these Articles. See Abdominal Diseases; Aged — Great Mortality Among—(see Old Age); Bereavement; Bloodshed (see Blood); Boils, Calamity, Carbuncles, Catastrophy, Chest Diseases, Cholera, Colds, Colic, Conjunctivitis, Consumptions, Contempt for Religion (see Religion); Crime; Dangers (see Great Perils Generally" under Danger); Death (Painful Deaths Prevalent — see "Death" under Pain); Diarrhoea, Dissipation, Dropsy, Earthquakes; Effusion of Blood (see Effusions); Enemies (see "Fear Of" under Enemies); Epidemics, Eye Diseases, Famine, Fevers, Fluxes, Grief, Hatred; Head Diseases (see "Disorders" under Head); Heat (see "Extreme Heat" under Heat); Highwaymen, Incendiarism, Influenza, La Grippe, Lung Diseases, Mania, Measles; Melancholy (see "Much" under Melancholy); Mischief (see "Every One" under Mischief); Misery, Misfortune, Mortality, Murders, Nervous Diseases; Night (Diseases by Night); Outrages; Painful Deaths (see "Death" under Pain); Pandemics, Perils, Pestilence, Piracy, Plague, Pleasure Seeking, Plots; Public (see the paragraphs under Public); Railroad Accidents, Rapine; Reproductive Organs (Diseases of Prevalent); Robberies; Sadness (Much Sadness Generally); Sex Diseases (see "Diseases" under Sex); Shipwrecks; Skin Diseases, Slaughter, Smallpox; Sorrow (see "Sorrow" under Public); Suffering; Terrible Diseases (see Terrible); Trouble, Urinary Diseases, Violence, War, etc.

PREVENTED—Prevention—Averted—Preventive—

Birth Prevented — (See Abortion;

"Birth" under Asphyxia; Barrenness; "Delayed Births" under Children; "Excision" under Foetus; Miscarriages).

Death—Death In Sickness Averted—(See Averted).

Disease Prevented—Averted—"To be Forewarned is to be Forearmed", is an old saying. Much of the sickness, suffering, and sorrow in the world today could be prevented if people would live and think right. It is said the abuse of the sex nature is the cause of sickness, weakness, and premature death, and that by the proper use and conservation of the sex fluids and vital forces of the body, man would live to an extreme old age, as they did in Ancient Times. The greatest problem of Earth Life is to learn to control the creative force under the regime of the Separated Sexes, and to not abuse and misuse it for sensuous purposes. This question is discussed in the book, "The Voice of Isis" by Dr. and Mrs. Homer Curtiss. (See "Separation of the Sexes" under Sex). The more Advanced Souls are born with star maps which do not have the aspects which increase passion, and it is easier for such people to properly use their creative forces. People born with good and well-balanced maps, showing strong vitality and practical immunity to disease, have more power to prevent or throw off disease when it comes. (See Immunity; "Strong" under Resistance; "Body" under Strong; "Good" under Vitality). There are also Herbs, Remedies, and many Natural Methods, and the regulation of Diet, to combat and prevent disease. People who overeat, and clog the system, invite disease. Also worry, anxiety, fear, melancholy, despondency, depression, low spirits, etc., tend to bring on disease, and lower the vitality and powers of resistance. (See these subjects). The proper remedies, or treatment given at the beginning of a disease, can often scatter and prevent its progress, as remedies change the polarity of the disease. (See Polarity, Praeincipients, Remedies, Treatment). Many diseases originate in the Mind, and may be imaginary, and the power of Suggestion is a strong factor in the prevention or elimination of disease, if rightly used by the Healer. (See "Disease" under Fear; Healers, Hypnotism, Imaginations, Psychic, Suggestion). The Occult Masters teach that perfect health is the right of every one, and when we learn to think in terms of perfect health, and not in terms of disease, we will have health, for "As a Man Thinketh in His Heart, so is He". Spiritual Attainment and Spiritual Sight, the New Birth, and the proper use of our Forces, are essential to good health and the prevention of disease. The Masters, Adepts, and Initiates among us today in physical bodies have the spiritual power to control their health conditions, keep their bodies young, vigorous and healthy, and to renew their youth, and it is said they can renew their physical bodies, and keep them as long as they wish, and throw off the body also at their pleasure. Also Hygiene, Sanitation, and Cleanliness, play a large part in health, and the prevention of disease. (See these subjects. Also see Antipathy; "Cure of Disease" under Cure; Diathesis, Opposites, Medicines, Prognosis, Subluxations, Sympathy).

Events—Prevention of—(See Events).

Functions Prevented—Impeded—(See "Impeded" under Functions).

Preventive Remedies — (See Cleanliness, Diet, Discernment, Drugs, Healers, Hygiene, Knowledge, Power, Praeincipients, Remedies, Sanitation, Spirituality, Treatment, Wisdom, etc.).

PREY—Birds of Prey—(See "Birds of the Air" under Air; "Body Devoured" under Burial; Fowls, Vultures).

PRIAPISM — Painful Erections — (See Erections).

PRICKLING SENSATIONS—Ḥinfluence. (See "Sensations" under Burning; Numbness, Paraesthesia, Sensations, Tingling, etc.).

PRIDE—The ☉ in the Asc., or in aspect to the Asc.; the ☉ in ♒, tinctured with pride; the ☉ afflicted tends to; the ☉ ♂ or P. ☿; the Dispositors of the ☉ and ☽ weak and afflicted, and the ☽ □ the Asc.; ♃ in ♈, a becoming pride; ♀ in ♌, proper pride and dignity; ♂ Sig. □ or ☌ ♃. The Hebrew letter Ayin is connected with Pride and the ♑ sign. (See Ego, Pretender, Self-Esteem, Self-Laudation).

PRIESTS—The Clergy—Ministers—Churches—Sadness and Anxiety To—(See Clergyment).

PRIMARY DIRECTIONS — The Effects of — (See Directions). Rules for the working out of Primary Directions, and examples, etc., are given in Wilson's Dictionary of Astrology; Simmonite's Arcana of Astral Philosophy, and other standard Textbooks of Astrology. Simmonite's Arcana is considered the most complete work on the subject, as Tables, Formulae, various Examples and Helps are given in this book. Primary Directions are very powerful in their action, and especially when assisted by a Secondary Direction, a Revolution, or Transit. They are also enduring in their effects, slower to form, and slower to pass away, and the student of Diagnosis, Prognosis, and the Causes of Disease, should be well up in the Mathematics of Astronomy and Trigonometry to do this work when required. (See Progression; "Solar Revolution" under Revolution; Secondary, Transits).

PRINCES—Princes and Kings are signified by the 10th H., and also by the ♌ sign.

Death by Wrath Of — (See this subject under Kings).

Death of a Prince—An Eclipse of the ☉ in the 1st Decan. of ♌; Comets appearing in ♌, ♑, or ♒. (See "Death of a King" under Kings).

Has the Favor of Princes — Or the Favor of Kings and Rulers—♂ Sig. ♂ the ☉, and also it may be their frowns to the utter undoing of the native. (See Famous; "Great Men" under Great; Queens, Rulers).

PRINCIPLE—Principles—

Planets — Principle of the Planets — (See "Principle" under each of the Planets).

Principles—Scruples—There are many subjects listed in this book which have to do with the Mental Traits, Tendencies of Temperament, Scruples, Principles, Motives, Character, etc. Look in the alphabetical arrangement for the subject you have in mind. Many of these subjects and traits are listed in the Articles on Conduct, Habits, Love Affairs, Men, Mentality, Mind, Morals, Passion, Religion, Sex, Temperament, Women, etc.

PRISONS — Imprisonment — Places of Confinement and Retention — Detentions — Restraints, etc. — Prisons and places of Confinement are ruled by ♆ and the 12th H., which house rules confinement, limitations, restrictions, plots, treachery, misfortune, Institutions where people are confined, as Asylums, Sanitariums, Hospitals, Prisons, Exiles, Banishments, Seclusion, etc. If the influences at B. indicate the danger and liability of Imprisonment, the time of such confinement will be apt to come under the evil transits, directions, and afflictions to the 12th H. and its influences at B. The following subjects have to do with Prisons, Imprisonment, Loss of Liberty, Confinement, Restraints, Limitations, and Misfortunes which tend to imperil the life and liberty of the native. See these subjects in the alphabetical arrangement when they are not more fully considered here—

Abroad—Detention Abroad—(See "Detention" under Abroad; Captivity).

Absent Party In Prison—(See "Prison" under Absent Party).

Anarchists; Asylum — Confined In — (See "Asylum" under Insanity).

Banishment; Beaten In Prison — Put In Irons, Beaten, and Severely Punished—The ☽, or lord of the 1st H., in ♒ or ♌, and in ♒ ♄ or ♂; ♂ ascending, or ruler of the Asc., when put in prison (Hor'y). (See "Injured" in this section; Cruel).

Captivity; Confined In Prison — (See "Imprisonment" in this section).

Confinement; Crime — Imprisoned for Criminal Acts—(See Crime).

Danger of Imprisonment—Liable To — Subject To — The influences at B. will be given here, and the directions, progressed influences, etc., will indicate the time of, and the immediate danger of imprisonment, unless the character, life, conduct, and habits of the native are properly regulated. The SUN afflicted in the 12th H. at B., and to the ill-asps. the ☽ by dir.; the ☉ afflicted at B., and to the evil asp. the Asc. by dir.; the ☉ to the cusp the 10th H., and this house afflicted; the ☉ directed to the Ascelli, or to Caput Hercules; the ☉ progressed to the □ or ☍ the M.C.; the ☉ in the 12th H., and afflicted at the Vernal Equi., and lord of the year; the ☉ □ or ☍ ♂, falls a victim to the Law; the ☉ afflicted in the 12th H. at B.; the ☉ to the ill-asps. ♃ by dir.; the ☉ to the ☌ or ill-asp. ♅ by dir.; the MOON in the 12th H. at B., and to the ☌ or evil asp. ♅ by dir.; the ☽ to the ☌, ☐, or ☍ ♄ or ♂ by dir., and especially if the direction falls in the 8th or 12th H.; the ☽ at a Solar Rev. passing the place of the radical ♄; the ☽ to the ill-asps. ☿ if this planet be ruler of the 4th, 8th, or 12th H.; the ☽ at Full, or incr. in a day nativity, sepr. from ♀ and applying to ♂; the ☽ incr. in a night geniture, sepr. from ☿ and apply. to ♄, if malefic planets afflict them; the ☽ to the ill-asps. ☿ by dir., and ☿ afflicted at B.; the ☽ afflicted at B., and to the cusp the 12th H. by dir.; the ☽ or M.C. to the place of Algenib, thru Forgery and Writings; the ☽ to the place of the Pleiades or Praesepe; NEPTUNE or ♅ afflicted in the 12th H.; ♆ afflicted in ♈, and possibly to Anarchistic tendencies; ♆ afflicted in ♓; ♆ by transit ☌ the ☽ or ☿ in the radix, and thru crime if ♆ is afflicted at B.; URANUS afflicted in the 12th H.; ♅ ☌ ♂ in ♈, thru criminal acts; ♅ to the ☌ or ill-asp. ♄, for neglect of family; ♅ to the ☌ or ill-asp. ♂ by dir., and espec. if ♅ or ♂ were in the 12th H. at B.; ♅ ☌ ♄ in the 12th H.; ♅ in the 12th H., and afflicted by ♄; SATURN afflicted in the 10th or 12th H.; ♄ afflicted in ♓; ♄ ruler of the 12th H. at B., and afflicted, and ♄ ☌ or ill-asp. the Asc. by dir.; ♄ to the ☌ or ill-asp. ♂ by dir.; ♄ Sig. ☌ ♂, may end days in prison (Hor'y); ♄ Sig. ☌ the ☉, for contempt of the Law; ♄ in the 12th H., and affl. by ♅ or ♂; MARS to the ☌ or ill-asp. the ☉ by dir.; ♂ afflicted in ♓ or the 12th H.; ♂ in fiery signs, afflicted, and ☌ or evil asp. the Asc. by dir.; ♂ in the 12th H., and affl. by ♅ or ♄; ♂ ☌ the Asc. by dir.; ♂ afflicted at B., and to the ☌ the M.C.; ♂ lord of the 12th H. at B., and the M.C. to the ☌ ir ill-asp. ♂ by dir.; ♂ prog. to the ☌, ☐, or ☍ the radical ♄, or vice versa, the result of crime or murder; ♂ in the 12th H., but well-aspected, may be imprisoned, but escapes; the ASCENDANT to the ☐ or ☍ the ☉ by dir.; the 1st face of ♋, or the 7° ♎ on the Asc.; lord of the Asc. afflicted by lord of the 12th H. from bad houses; lord of the 1st in the 12th H.; the MIDHEAVEN to the cusp the 12th H. by dir.; the M.C. to the place of Procyon, the Pleiades or Pollux; the M.C. directed to Algenib, imprisonment thru writings, signings, forgery, bonds, libel; lord of the 10th a malefic, and in the 12th H.; the M.C. to the ☐ or ☍ the ☉; lord of the 10th in the 12th; the M.C. to the ☐ or ☍ ♂ by dir.; lord of the 3rd or 9th in the 12th H., imprisoned on a journey; lord of the 6th H. in the 10th H., and afflicted; lord of the 6th a malefic, and in the 12th H., and afflicted; lord of the 6th by transit over the cusp the 12th H.; lord of the 6th in the 12th H., sickness from imprisonment; the ruler of the 7th H. at B. in the 12th H. at a Solar Rev.; lord of the 8th a malefic, and in the 12th H., and afflicted; LORD OF THE 12TH in the 3rd or 9th, and especially while engaged in travel; lord of the 12th a malefic, and in the 12th, and afflicted, and afflicting the lords of the 1st or 4th, apt to end days in prison; lord of the 12th a malefic, and in the 1st H., thru his enemies; lord of the 12th a malefic, and in the

2nd H., thru money matters; lord of the 12th a malefic, and in the 3rd H., thru relatives; lord of the 12th a malefic, and in the 5th H., thru the influence of his children; lord of the 12th a malefic, in the 7th H., thru the wife's influence; lord of the 12th a malefic, and in the 10th, thru corrupt Judges, or his enemies in business swearing falsely; lord of the 12th a malefic, and afflicted in the 12th; lord of the 12th afflicted in ♓ in the Asc. (Hor'y); malefics, or a planet in the 12th H. at B., and afflicting the ☽; Fixed Stars of the nature of ♂ and the ☽ culminating at B., such as the Pleiades and other Nebulous stars of this character; the Ascelli, Pleiades, Hyades, Castor, Pollux, Praesepe, or Antares, directed to the Asc. or Lights, disgrace, imprisonment, and every evil that can befall the native; the Pleiades rising, or with the ☉ or ☽, or directed to the Asc. Cases of Imprisonment — All in 1001 N.N. See "Krishnananda", No. 225; "Tilak", No. 228, and "Scandals", No. 653. (See "Fixed Stars" under Stars; Twelfth House).

Danger to Those In Prison — Injured by Convicts or Other Prisoners—(See "Injured" in this section).

Death In Prison—Ends His Days In Prison—The ☉ or ☽ setting at B., and in ☍ to ♄ in the Asc.; the ☉ or ☽ rising and ♄ in ☍ to either; the ☉ Sig. ☐ or ☍ ♄, sometimes dies in prison; ♄ Sig. ☌ ♂, often ends days in prison; ♃ Sig. ☌ ♄, and especially if ♂ afflict ♃ and ☿ at the same time; lord of the Asc. in the 12th, and afflicted; lord of the Asc. disposed of by a malefic in the 8th (Hor'y); lord of the Asc. in the 4th, and afflicted by lords of the 7th, 10th, 11th, or 12th; lords of the 1st and 12th applying to a ☌ each other, and lord of the 12th stronger, or a malefic, denotes a fatal imprisonment; lord of the 1st also lord of the 12th; lord of the 1st, or the ☽, applying to the evil asps. ♄ or ♂, and especially if the malefic be lord of the 8th, or going into combustion without any good aspect of a benefic, or if ♄ and ♂ be in ☍ the ☉ or ☽, or the ☽ or lord of the 1st be near any violent fixed stars, as Caput Algol, it denotes that the whole will end in a violent death, or he will die in prison (Hor'y); lord of the 6th in the 12th, and afflicting the lords of the 1st, 4th, or 8th; lord of the 8th in the 12th, and afflicting the lord of the Asc., and with no benefics in the 12th; lord of the 8th in the 12th, or lord of the 12th in the 8th H.; afflictions in the 12th H.; lord of the 12th a malefic, and in the 12th, and afflicting the lords of the 1st or 4th; common signs show, and several malefics in them, and upon the angles.

Employment In Prisons — Successful In Prison or Hospital Work — (See "Employment" under Hospitals).

Ends Days In Prison—(See "Death" in this section;"Low Business" under Low).

Enemies—Imprisoned Thru Influence of Enemies—Lord of the 12th a malefic, and in the 1st or 10th H., and usually over money and business matters. (See Danger Of, Plots, in this section).

Escapes from Prison—♂ in the 12th H., and well-aspected. (See Fugitive).

Exile; Fear of Imprisonment—The ☽ afflicted at B., and to the cusp the 12th H. by dir. (See Fears).

Forgery—Imprisoned For—(See Forgers; "Danger Of" in this section).

Fugitive — The Fugitive Is Dead — Escaped from Prison—(See Fugitive; "Escapes" in this section).

Hospitals; Ill-Treated In Prison—(See Beaten, Injured, in this section).

Imprisonment — (See "Danger of" in this section).

Injured In Prison—By Convicts and Other Prisoners—♂ afflicted in fiery signs at B., and to the ☌, □, or ☍ the Asc. by dir.; a malefic ruler of the 12th at B., and at a Solar Rev. (See "Beaten" in this section).

Insanity — Confined In An Asylum — (See "Asylums" under Insanity).

Invalids; Irons — Put In Irons In Prison—(See "Beaten" in this section).

Judges—Imprisoned by Sentence of— (See Judges, Law).

Kidnapped; Liable to Imprisonment— (See "Danger Of" in this section).

Libel—Imprisoned For—(See Libel).

Limitations—(See this subject).

Long Imprisonment—In Prison Most of His Life—The ☽ disposed of by a malefic or lord of the 12th H.; the ☽ disposed of by a planet in an angle, and especially in the 4th H., and the planet ♃; the ☽ or lord of the 1st in the 8th or 12th H.; the ☽ or lord of the Asc. combust; the ☽ or lord of the Asc. in a fixed sign, or in ♓ at the time of arrest, or a fixed sign upon the Asc.; the ☽ in ♒ and afflicted by malefics, or a malefic in ♒, and espec. if the 12th H. is concerned and afflicted at the same time; ♄ or ☿ ascending, or ruling the Asc. at the time when imprisoned; a malefic in the 12th, and in evil asp. to the lord of the 1st or 10th; a fixed sign on the 12th, or lord of the 12th angular and in a fixed sign; lord of the Asc. in detriment or fall; lord of the 12th a malefic, and in the 12th H. (See "Fixed Signs" under Fixed).

Many Taken Prisoners—Held In Captivity—(See Captivity).

Murder — Imprisoned For — (See "A Murderer" under Murder).

Plots — Imprisoned Thru Plots and Treachery, as by Enemies, Children, Relatives, Competitors, etc.—The lord of the 12th H., and his position in the houses, and his afflictions, are the principal factors to be considered. (See the 12th H. influences in the paragraph "Danger Of", and also "Enemies" in this section; also see "Imprisonment" under Children; "Secret Enemies" under Enemies; "Asylums" under Insanity; Kidnapped, Plots, Revenge, Treachery).

Punishment—(See this subject).

Relatives — Imprisoned Thru Treachery of—(See Danger Of, Plots, in this section).

Restraints — Restrictions — (See Restraints).

Stealing—Imprisoned For—(See Kleptomaniac, Robbers, Thieves).

Surgeons In Prisons—Good Influences For—(See "Employment" under Hospitals).

Thieves — Imprisoned for Stealing — (See "Stealing" in this section).

Time of Imprisonment—Indicated by the directions, progressions, and transits to the 12th H., its lord, or to planets in the 12th at B.; also denoted by the ☌ or ill-asps. of lord of the 12th with malefics by dir. (See Directions, Events; the Introduction to this Article).

Travel—Danger of Being Held Captive, or Imprisoned During Travel—☿ in evil asp. to the Significator of Travel; the planets afflicting the Sigs. of Travel being in the 12th H. at the time; lord of the 12th a malefic, and afflicted in the 3rd or 9th H.; lord of the 3rd or 9th in the 12th, and afflicted. (See Captivity, Highwaymen, Pirates, Robbers, Travel; "Danger Of" in this section).

Treachery — Imprisoned By — (See Danger Of, Enemies, Plots, in this section).

Wife—Imprisoned by Influence of— Lord of the 12th a malefic in the 7th H. (See Marriage, Wife).

PRIVATE—Privacy—Secret—

Blindness by Private Injury — (See "Artifice", "Private Injury", "Treachery", under Blindness).

Loves Privacy and Seclusion — (See Grave; "Coldness" under Manner; Miserly; "Recluse" under Old Age; Recluse, Reserved, Retiring, Saturn, Seclusion; "Secretive" under Secret; Solitary, Suspicious).

Private Diseases—Diseases Connected with the Genitals and Organs of Sex and Reproduction—(See the subjects under Generative System; Genitals, Genito-Urinary, Penis, Reproduction, Secret Parts, Sex Organs, Venereal, Womb, etc.).

Private Enemies — (See "Secret Enemies" under Enemies; Enmity, Feuds, Hatred, Plots; "Death by Poison" under Poison; Revenge, Treachery, etc.).

Private Injury—Blindness By—Suffering By—(See Blindness, Private Enemies, in this section).

Private Parts — (See Genitals, Privates, Secrets, Sex Organs, etc.).

Private Sex Practices—(See "Liaisons" under Love Affairs; Perversions; "Clandestine" under Sex; "Solitary" under Vice).

PRIVATES — Secrets — Secret Parts — Private Parts—

Diseases In—(See "Private Diseases" under Private).

Injury To—The Asc. to the □ or ☍ ♄ by dir.; ♂ in ♏. (See "Mens' Genitals" under Genitals; Maimed, Testes; "Injuries To" under Womb).

Obstructions In—(See "Obstructions" under Generative). See the paragraphs under Generative, Genitals, Genito-Urinary, Penis, Ovaries, Reproduction, Secret Parts, Sex Organs, Vagina, Womb, etc.

PRIVATION—Privations—Poverty—Neglect—The strong afflictions of ♄ at B., and by dir., tend to privations, neglect, poverty, losses, or ruin, and especially when ♄ is afflicted in the 2nd H. (See Begging, Famine, Indifferent, Neglect; "Privation" under Seas; Starvation).

Functions Disordered—Thru Privation and Neglect—The ☽ afflicted by ♄. (See "Privation" under Functions).

Internal Disorders—Arising from Privation, Chill, Cold, and Neglect—(See "Internal Diseases" under Chill).

PROBABILITY—Probable—

Children—Probability of—(See "Promise of a Child" under Children; Fruitful).

Consumption—Probability of—(See "Consumptive" under Consumption).

Fainting — Probability of — (See Causes, Sudden, under Fainting).

Health — Probability of Good or Bad Health—(See Health, Stamina, Strength, Tone, Vitality, Weak, etc.).

Life—Probable Length of Life—(See "Probable Length" under Life).

Mental Disorders — Probability of — (See the paragraphs under Intellect, Judgment, Mental, Mind, Perception, Reason, Understanding).

Pleurisy — Probability of — (See Pleura). See the paragraphs under Danger, Diathesis, Disease, Health, Heredity, Idiosyncrasies, Ill-Health, Inherent, Liable, Receptivity, Susceptibility, Temperament, Tendencies, etc.

PROCEDURE—(See Action, Character, Conduct, Ideals, Ideas, Manners, Methods, Motives, Purposes, etc.).

PROCESS—Processes—

Alimentation—The Process of Nourishment—(See Alimentation, Nutrition).

Aphetic Process—(See Nutrition).

Asthenic Process—(See Asthenia).

Atrophy of Process—(See "Atrophy" under Functions).

Cell Processes—(See "Alteration" under Cells; Metabolism).

Coction Process — (See Combustion, Digestion).

Conservation Processes — (See Conservation).

Constructive Processes—In the Body — (See "Building the Body" under Build; Constructive).

Destructive Processes—(See Destructive).

Digestion—Process of—(See Alimentation, Assimilation, Diet, Digestion, Food, Nutrition).

Distillatory Process — (See Distillation).

Fermentation — (See Fermentation, Zymosis).

Gustatory Process — (See Gustativeness).

Hepatic Process—(See Hepatic).

Hypertrophic Process — (See Hypertrophy).

Inflammatory Process — (See Inflammation).

Metabolism; Metamorphosis;

Nerve Process — (See "Influx" under Nerves).

Preservative Processes—(See Preservation).

Renal Process—(See Kidneys, Renal).

Reproductive Processes — (See Conception, Fecundation, Fertilization, Foetus, Generative, Gestation, Parturition, Pregnancy, Prenatal Epoch; "Processes" under Reproduction).

Splenic Process—(See Spleen).

Sthenic Process—(See Mars, Sthenic).

Thoracic Process—(See Thorax).

PROCRASTINATION—Caused by the □ and ☍ aspects to ♃; ♃ □ or ☍ ☿. (See Dull, Idle, Inactive, Indifferent, Lassitude, Lazy, Lethargy, Negative, etc.).

PROCREATION—Ruled by the ☽ and ♀. (See Amativeness, Childhood, Conception; "Desire Body" under Desire; Fecundation, Fertilization, Fruitful, Gemmation, Puberty, Reproduction).

PROCYON—A violent star of the 1st magnitude in the 5th face of ♋, and of the nature of ♂ and ☿ combined. Tends to cause much evil in the life of the native, and dissipation. The ☽ to the ☌ Procyon tends to dissipation. The M.C. directed to brings danger of imprisonment, and many calamities. (See "Fixed Stars" under Stars).

PRODIGAL — Prodigality—Wasteful — Extravagant—Debauched—Dissipated —Prodigal of Expense—Fond of Luxuries—Diseases and Afflictions Arising from Prodigality, etc.—The ☉ to the ☌ ☽ by dir., and the ☽ badly afflicted at B.; the ☉ to the P. aspect the ☽; the ☉ or ☽ in a watery sign and afflicted; the ☉ Sig. □ or ☍ ♃; the ☉ and ♂ in the 1st H. in a fiery or airy sign; the ☽ strong at B. in the Asc., M.C., or ruler; the ☽ Sig. □ or ☍ ☉, ambitious but prodigal; ♄ or ♃ as Significators □ or ☍ ☉; ♄ Sig. ✳ or △ ♀; ♃ ☌ or illasp. ♂; ♃ afflicting the ☉ or ☽; ♂ diseases and affliction; ♂ in bad asp. to ♃; ♂ Sig. □ or ☍ ♀, or vice versa; ♀ afflicted at B.; water signs on the Asc. at B.; the 6th face of ♒ on the Asc., and ♀ therein; the 3rd face, or 3° ♓ on the Asc.; the cusp of the 2nd H., or its ruler, to the ill-asps. the ☉. (See Conduct, Debauched, Dissipated, Dissolute, Drink, Drunkenness, Eating, Excesses, Expense, Extravagance, Feasting, Food, Free Living, Gluttony, Habits, High Living, Imprudent, Indiscretions, Indulgent, Low Company, Luxuries, Morals, Profligate, Reckless, Riotous, Self-Indulgent, Wanton, etc.).

PRODIGIES—Genius—Evolved Types—Precocious Mental or Spiritual Development—Mental or Physical Prodigies —♆ and ♅ strong at B., and in good asp. to ☿, tend to Geniuses and youthful Prodigies. This subject is further explained in the Articles on Genius, and Mathematical.

Chess Players—In the case of Chess Players, Lightning Calculators, Inventors, Mechanical Geniuses, Cranks, etc., the fundamental responsibility depends upon the association of ♂ and ☿, and especially by the ☌ and ☍, and with these planets in angles or the 3rd or 9th H. Case—See Chap. XIII in Daath's Medical Astrology. (See Genius, Mathematical).

Child Prodigy—Case—Began to Read at three years of age, and read Darwin and Huxley at eight years of age—See "Wiener", No. 353, in 1001 N.N.

Does Two Things At Once—Writes a Letter and Solves a Problem at same time—Case—See "Neptune", No. 352 in 1001 N.N.

Genius— (See the subjects under Genius).

Inventive—(See Genius).

Lightning Calculator — (See "Chess Players" in this section; Genius, Mathematical). Cases — See Daath, Chap. XIII. Also see "Bidder", No. 787 in 1001 N.N.

Mathematical Mind — ☿ is especially associated with mathematical ability. Also ☿ aspected by ♂. (See Genius, Mathematical. See Cases under "Lightning Calculator" in this section).

Mechanical Genius—(See Mechanical). Case—See Daath, Chap. XIII.

Musical Genius—(See Music).

Performing Pig—Case—(See Hogs).

Physical Prodigies—The 26° ♐ on the Asc. tends to make physical or mental prodigies. (See Freaks, Giants; "Premature Mental Development" under Premature).

PROFANE — Given to Profanity — In coarse maps profanity is caused by severe ♂ affliction; ♂ afflicting ♃ or ☿; ♂ afflicted in the 9th H., the house of religion. (See Anger, Evil, Excitable, Filthy, Irritable, Quarrelsome, Rough; "High Temper" under Temper; Vicious, Violent, etc.).

PROFESSION—The Profession—The Employment or Vocation — Ruled by the 10th H. (See Business, Employment, Vocation).

PROFESSIONS—Declarations—Avowals —Claims—Pretenses, etc.—The Principles, Character, Temperament and Tendencies, etc.—There are many subjects in this book listed along this line. Look in the alphabetical arrangement for the subject you have in mind. See such subjects as Anarchists, Bad, Character, Conduct, Deceitful, Disgrace, Dishonest, Dual, Enemies, Evil, Fanatical, Fancies, Friends, Habits, Honest, Honor, Hypocritical, Ideals, Ideas, Liars, Libelers, Love Affairs, Low, Metaphysics, Mind, Morals, Motives, Occult, Pretender, Principles, Purposes, Reformers, Religion, Reputation, Revolutionary, Riotous, Science, Temperament, Visionary, etc.

PROFICIENT — Proficient In Learning and In the Arts and Sciences — (See Learning).

PROFILE—(See "Profile" under Face).

PROFIT — Profit and Support from the Exhibition of Maladies — (See Exhibitionism).

PROFLIGATE — An Abandoned Person —Debased—Debauched — Depraved— Dissolute — Drunken — Indecent — Immoral — Corrupt — Low — Prodigal — Vicious—Of Little or No Virtue, etc.— (See these subjects. Also see Conduct, Habits, Morals, Passion, Pleasures, Self-Indulgent, Wanton, etc.).

Husband a Profligate — (See "Profligate" under Husband).

Pleasure — Profligate Love of — (See "Profligate" under Pleasure).

Wife Profligate—Dissolute—(See Dissolute, Drink, under Wife).

PROFLUVIAL EFFUSIONS—(See Effusions).

PROFOUND—

Profound Mental Incapacity — (See "Incapacity" under Mental).

Profound and Deep Mind—(See "Deep and Profound" under Mind).

PROFUSE—Excessive—Colliquative—

Profuse Diarrhoea — (See Cholera, Diarrhoea, Discharges, Dysentery, Evacuations, Faeces, Fluxes, Watery).

Profuse Expectoration — (See Expectoration).

Profuse Functions — (See "Irregular" under Functions).

Profuse Hemorrhage—(See Effusions, Hemorrhage; "Flooding" under Menses; "Epistaxis" under Nose).

Profuse Living—(See Living).

Profuse Menses—(See Menses).

Profuse Sweats—(See "Night Sweats" under Phthisis; "Excessive" under Sweat). See Abundance, Defluxions, Excess, Excesses, Humours, Hyperidrosis, Increased, Much, Over-Abundance, Plenty, Superabundance, Too Much, etc.).

PROGENY—(See Children).

PROGNOSIS — Prognostication — Prediction of the Course and End of a Disease—Possible Outcome of the Disease—The Planetary influences operating over the lives of people at B., and by transit, progression, or direction, give a very important clue to the possible beginnings of disease, of affliction, misfortune, and the time, nature and outcome of events, and especially with people who are drifting with their stars, following their tendencies, and who are being dominated by their lower minds and the personality. By self-control, will-power, knowledge, wisdom, discretion, discrimination, spiritual sight, etc., it is usually possible to change the nature of events, or forestall them altogether, except in the case of ripe fate. (See Events, Fate; "Free Will" under Will). It is very difficult to give a correct prognosis as to the outcome of disease, suffering, or temporary affliction, in the case of Advanced Souls, Adepts, Initiates, etc., as the planetary influences have less power over them, and they have learned how to live more in harmony with Law, rather than to go against, and break them. (See "Disease Prevented" under Prevented). Predictions, therefore, and prognostications, may fail in proportion to your degree of spiritual attainment and development. The Art of Prediction has its foundations in Nature, and the movements of the Planetary Bodies. Events on the Earth Plane are but repetitions of similar occurrences, diseases, accidents, afflictions, trials, or sorrows of the Past, and which were produced by similar planetary aspects and influences in some remote Age of the World. Observations of these influences for thousands of years have enabled Astrologers to recognize, discover, and tabulate into a Science the Laws of Nature as they affect the destiny of the Individual, of Races, and Nations. Any possible event in a human life, from the cradle to the grave, can be reasonably foretold by the study of the coming aspects, conjunctions, and influences which will be culminating over the native and his map of birth, and even the time of death can ordinarily be predicted if the native drifts along, and follows the leadings of his planets, gives way to his weaknesses and tendencies, instead of controlling himself, and listening to the voice of Intuition and his Higher Mind. (See "Future Events" under Future).

Rules for Prognostication—

(1) Never predict the possible time of death.

(2) Never predict the actual future, or say what disease will actually come.

(3) Never predict that sickness, accident, or misfortune will actually come at a certain time.

(4) Do not say discouraging things to a patient.

(5) Do not tell the patient when crises are due.

(6) Never suggest sickness to a well person, or tell them they look pale and sickly, and especially to a Virgo person. (See "Time Of" under Accidents, Disease, Death; Calamity, Character, Danger, Diagnosis, Directions, Events, External, Fate, Future, Healers; "Good Health", "Periods of Bad Health", under Health; Individuality, Influenced, Map, Misfortune, Mutable Disposition, Nativity; "Death", "Disease", under Nature; Negative Disposition, Personality, Planets, Positive Nature, Predictions, Progressions, Prophetic, Receptive, Secondary, Spiritual, Susceptibility, Time, Transits, etc.). The following are a few subjects which have to do with Prognosis in Disease, either directly or indirectly.

Acute Diseases — Crises In — (See "Acute Diseases" under Crises).

Better — The Disease Will Turn for the Better — (See "Better" under Disease).

Course of the Disease—(See Course).

Crises In Disease—Favorable or Unfavorable—(See Crises).

Curable Diseases—(See Curable).

Death Almost Certain—(See "Certain Death" under Death; Fatal, Incurable).

Debility — Greater Debility and Continued Weakness In Disease—(See Debility, Duration, Lingering, Long Diseases, Prolonged, Protracted, Slow, Tedious).

Diagnosis — (See the paragraphs under Diagnosis).

Duration of the Disease—(See Duration, Long, Short, etc.).

End of the Disease—(See "End" under Disease).

Erratic Course — In Disease — (See "Course" under Erratic).

Favorable Prognosis — In Disease — (See "Disease" under Improved).

Fevers — Prognosis In — Fever Will Run High — The Fever Will Abate — (See "Curtailed", "High", under Fever).

Good — The Prognosis In Disease Is Good—(See "Disease" under Improved).

Incurable — The Disease Is Incurable — (See "Certain Death" under Death; Fatal, Incurable, Invalids, Wasting).

Judgment of the Disease—(See "Disease" under Judgment).

Long Diseases — (See "Diseases" under Long).

Moderation — Of the Disease — (See Moderation).

Modification — Of the Disease — (See "Better", "Complications", "Worse", under Disease; Modification).

Old Age — Prognosis of Disease In — (See "Health" under Old Age).

Peculiar Symptoms—In Disease—(See "Symptoms" under Peculiar).

Peril — Danger — The Disease Is Attended with Great Peril — (See "The Sick Will Hardly Escape" under Escape).

Prevention of Disease—(See Prevention).

Recovery In Disease—Will Recover— Will Not Recover—Recovery Doubtful —(See Curable, Fatal, Incurable, Recovery).

Resolution of Disease — (See Amelioration, Crises; "Better" under Disease; Moderation, Resolution, Termination).

Short Diseases — (See Acute; "Short" under Disease).

Suffering — Serious Suffering In Disease Forecasted—(See Grievous; "Diseases" under Pain).

Symptoms In Disease—(See Continuity, Course, Crises, Decumbiture, Diagnosis, Duration, Symptoms, etc.).

Tedious Diseases—(See Chronic, Consumption, Lingering, Long, Slow, Tedious, etc.).

Unfavorable Prognosis—(See "Worse" under Crises, Disease; "Illness" under Dangerous; "Certain Death" under Death; Fatal, Incurable, Majority, Malignant, Relapses).

Worse—The Disease Becomes Worse —(See "Worse" under Crises, Disease; Relapses).

PROGRESSION — Progressed—Progress — The Progressed Horoscope — Directions, etc.—According to the System of Primary Directions, the movements of the planets for each day after birth correspond to a year of life, or very close to a year. Thus, if ♂ be in the 1st degree of ♈ at B., and the Asc. in 6° ♈, we know that at about the 5th year of life ♂ will have progressed to the ☌ the Asc., and with the danger of an accident, injury, smallpox, hurts to the head or face, or a serious quarrel, etc. (See Primary). Secondary Directions, or Progressions, are based upon the movements of the ☽ on the days immediately after birth, and are calculated at the rate of two hours for every month, and the aspects thus formed by the ☽ to the positions of the radical planets are important to note, and tend to bring events, diseases, and afflictions, according to the nature of the planets, or planets aspected at such times. (See Secondary). The movements of the planets after birth are known as Progressions, Directions, Transits, etc., and the aspects, conjunctions, parallels, etc., formed to the radical planets by these progressions and movements of the planets after birth, indicate the possible time of events, disease, trouble, sorrow, misfortune, gloom, joy, happiness, good or bad health, prosperity, reverses, and possible death, etc., according to the nature of the planets aspected, and also the directions and transits which may be operating at the time. (See Aspects, Directions, Disturbances, Events, Fate; "Directions Of" under Moon; "Moon" under Motion; "Motion Of" under Planets; Prognosis, Progressive, Transits, etc.).

Disease—Progression In Disease— (See Chronic, Constancy, Continuity, Course, Crises, Duration, Progressive, Sequence, Slow, Tedious, Termination).

PROGRESSIVE—Gradually Extending—

Progressive Emaciation — (See Consumptions, Decay, Degeneration, Emaciation, Tabes, Wasting).

Progressive Muscular Atrophy — (See "Progressive" under Muscles).

Progressive Wasting — (See Emaciation, Tabes, Wasting, etc.).

PROHIBITION—Prohibitions—Prohibiting—In the human body, ♄ by his evil aspects and influences, tends to prohibit, retard and suppress function, secretion, elimination, excretion, etc., and to cause excess deposit of the poisons and wastes of the body, tending to hardening of the tissues, crystallization, thickening, stiffness, etc. In human affairs ♄ tends to bring limitations, confinement, sadness, sorrows, prohibitions, chastenings, testings, restraints, etc. (See Hardening, Limitations, Retentions, Suppressions).

Prohibition — The Prohibition of Intoxicating Liquors—Ruled over by ♃, and his good influences and aspects in Mundane Affairs. Also people born under the strong influence of ♃ tend to be sober and upright, religious, and not given to strong beverages. (See Temperance).

PROJECTING— Protruding— (See Protruding).

PROJECTS — Confusion of — Confusion of Mind — ♆ diseases and afflictions; the afflictions of ♆ to ☿, or to the Significators, the ☉, ☽, or Asc. at B., and by dir.; ♆ afflicted in ♒. (See Chaotic, Confusion; "Dreamy Mind" under Dreams; Ideas, Visionary, etc.).

PROLAPSE — Prolapsus — Prolapsed — Ptosis—A Falling Down of a Part—♅ and ♄ influence.

Abdominal Prolapsus — ♄ afflicted in ♍; Subs at PP (2L).

Bowels — (See "Prolapse" under Bowels).

Eyelid—(See "Ptosis" under Eyelids).

Hernia—The Prolapse and Protrusion of a Viscus—(See Hernia).

Kidneys—(See "Prolapsed" under Kidneys).

Spleen—(See "Prolapse" under Spleen).

Viscera — (See "Prolapse" under Viscera).

Womb — (See "Falling Of" under Womb).

PROLIFERATION — Cell Genesis—Reproduction — The general action of ♀ and her signs ♉ and ♎, and also of the ♀ Group of Herbs. (See "Gemmation" under Cells).

PROLIFIC—Fertile—Fruitful—♋ influence, and ♋ on the Asc., females are very prolific. (See "Many Children" under Children; Fertile, Fruitful).

Prolific Planets—(See "Fruitful" under Planets).

Unprolific—(See Barren).

PROLONGED — Prolongation —Protracted—Lengthened—

Disease Prolonged—The Disease Protracted—The Disease Will Continue— The ☉ or ☽ ill-aspected at B., or by dir., long and serious sicknesses; the ☉ or ♄ in the 6th H. in ♂, □, or ☍ denotes heavy affliction; the ☽ slow of motion, and in any asp. to the lord of the Asc., but with hope of a cure; the ☽ decr. in light, and near the body of ♄, the disease will continue a long time; ♅ ☌ ♄ in the 6th H., heavy and prolonged sickness; ♄ lord of the 6th H., in a fixed sign, ℞, and slow of motion; ♄ in the 6th H. and afflicted, or afflicting the hyleg, sad and heavy sickness; ♄ or ♂ occi. at B., between the 10th and 7th H., or in the 7th; to be taken sick in a ♄ hour tends to prolong the disease; lord of the 6th in the Asc., and lord of the Asc. in the 6th, the disease will continue until one of the Significators changes signs; lord of the 6th in the Asc., but the pain small at times; malefics in the occidental Quarters, the disease will be prolonged and tedious; signs of long ascension ascending. (See Chronic, Constancy, Continuity, Consumptions, Crises, Emaciation; "Hectic", "Low", under Fever; Grievous, Heavy; "Long Siege" under Ill-Health; Incurable, Invalids, Lingering; "Diseases" under Long; Serious Diseases, Severe, Slow Diseases, Tedious, Wastings, etc.).

Life Prolonged — The Life May Be Prolonged—The lord of the Asc. well-placed and free from affliction; ♃ or ♀ in the Asc. at B., and free from affliction; the hyleg well-aspected and free from the affliction of malefics. (See "Long-Lived", "Life Prolonged", under Children; Endurance; "Good Health" under Health; Immunity; "Long Life" under Life; Recuperation, Recovery, Resistance, Strength, Strong; "Good" under Vitality).

PROMINENT — Protruding —Conspicuous Parts of the Body—

Prominent Abdomen — (See "Prominent" under Abdomen).

Prominent Eyes — (See "Goggle" under Eyeballs; "Large", "Prominent", under Eyes; "Exophthalmic" under Goiter).

Prominent Forehead—(See Forehead).

Prominent Marks—Moles, or Scars—(See Marks, Moles, Scars).

Prominent Nose—(See Nose).

Prominent People — Death of — (See Famous; "Great Men", "The Great", under Great; Kings, Nobles, President, Rulers). See the subjects under Protruding.

PROMISCUITY — (See "Free Love" under Free; "Adulterous", "Liaisons", under Love Affairs; "Clandestine" under Sex; Shameless, Venery).

PROMISE—

Children—Promise of—(See "Promise of a Child" under Children; Fruitful).

Good Health—Promise of—(See "Good Health" under Health).

Long Life—Promise of—(See "Long" under Life).

Riches—Promise of—(See "Accumulates", "Confers", under Riches).

PROMISES—Profuse In Promises Thru Excess of Good Nature — ♄ well-aspected in ♐ at B.; ♃ influence; ♃ ruler, strong by sign, and well-aspected at B. (See Humane, Kind; "Obliging" under Manner).

Insincere Promises — (See Deceitful, Dual, Hypocritical).

PROMISSOR — Promittor — The Planet which promises, or indicates the kind or nature of the disease, affliction, or benefit, and to fulfill some event. The malefics, ♄ and ♂, tend to be evil Promittors, or the Anareta, when the hyleg is directed to them. The benefics, ♃ and ♀, promise good fortune, and are promittors of good when favorable directions to them are fulfilled. The planet signifying the event is the Promittor in Hor'y Questions. If the question is concerning health, take the lord of the 6th H. as the Promittor. If concerning marriage, the lord of the 7th, and its aspects, dignities, weaknesses, etc. If concerning money, the lord of the 2nd H. becomes the Promittor, etc. See the Articles on Promittor in Wilson's Dictionary of Astrology, and in Sepharial's New Dictionary of Astrology.

PROMOTED—

Health Promoted — (See "Improved" under Health).

Rheumatism Promoted — (See "Continued and Promoted" under Rheumatism). See Continuity, Crises; "Worse" under Disease; "Disease" under Increase).

PROMOTER — A Great Promoter — A Speculative Mind—(See Speculative).

PRONOUNCED — The Disease Is More Pronounced—(See Diathesis; "Certain" under Disease; "Disease" under Severity).

PROOF—Proof Against Attacks of Disease—(See "Good Health" under Health; Immunity; "Good" under Resistance; Robust; "Body" under Strong; "Good" under Vitality).

PROPAGATION — A Strong Desire to Propagate—(See Amativeness).

PROPENSITIES—Tendencies—

Animal Propensities — (See "Animal Instincts" under Animal).

Evil Propensities — (See Cheating, Conduct, Crime, Evil, Forgers, Gamblers, Liars, Murderous, Prodigal, Thieves, Wicked, Wanton, etc.).

Good Propensities — (See Good, Honest, Humane, Kind; "Good Morals" under Morals; Noble, Sincere, etc.).

Mental Propensities — (See the paragraphs and subjects under Mental, Mind).

Sensual Propensities—(See Amorous, Lascivious, Lewd, Licentious, Passion, Perversions, Sex, Vices, Wanton, etc.).

Tendencies—Of Mind and Body—(See Acquired, Character, Congenital, Constitution, Diathesis, Heredity, Intellect, Mind, Organic, Structural, Temperament, Tendencies, etc.).

PROPER STATURE — (See Beautiful, Comely, Handsome, Harmony, Well-Proportioned, etc.).

PROPERTY—Possessions—Riches—

Acquires Property—(1) By Honorable Means—(See Honest; "Confers" under Riches). (2) By Dishonest, Unfair, and Selfish Means—♃ Sig. ☌ ♄, and seldom enjoys it like other persons. (See Cheating, Deceitful, Dishonest, Forgers, Gambling, Thieves, etc.).

Duped of His Property — And Dies a Miserable Death—♃ Sig. ☌ ♄. (See Inheritance).

Loss of Property—Death from the Vexation of — Lord of the 8th in the 4th H. (See Misfortune, Resources, Reverses; "Losses" under Riches; Ruin, Wealth).

Property of Others—No Respect For —(See Respect).

Sickness—From Waste of Property— Lord of the 6th in the 2nd H. (See "Undermined" under Health; "Health Injured" under Men).

Wastes Property—By Riotous Living — (See Debauchery, Dissipation, Excesses; "Free Living" under Free; "High Living" under High; Indiscretions, Indulgences, Intemperance, Prodigal; "Property" under Religion; Riotous, Speculation).

PROPHETIC — Foretelling the Future — Seers — ♆ strong and well-aspected at B.; ♆ in the Asc. or M.C.; 4th face of ♍ on the Asc. (See Clairaudience, Clairvoyance, Dreams, Fears, Forebodings, Hypnotism, Intuition, Mediumship, Obsessions, Psychic, Religion, Seers, Spirit Controls, Visions, etc.).

PROPITIATIONS — (See the Introduction under Events).

PROPORTIONATE — (See Beautiful, Comely; "Fair Proportions" under Fair; Handsome, Harmonious; "Proportioned" under Moderately; Stature, Well-Proportioned).

PROPUS—Left Foot of Castor—In 29° ♊, of the nature of ♂. (See Castor).

PROROGATOR—Apheta—Hyleg—The Giver of Life—(See Hyleg).

PROSPECTS—

Good Fortune — Prospects of — (See Fortunate).

Good Health — Prospects of — (See "Good Health", "Prospects", under Health).

Ill-Fortune—Prospect of—(See "Ill-Fortune", "Malice of Fortune", under Fortune).

Ill-Health—Prospects of—(See "Bad Health", "Periods of Bad Health", under Health; "Ill-Health All Thru Life" under Ill-Health; "Much Sickness" under Sickness; "Low" under Vitality).

Long Life—Prospects of—(See "Long Life" under Life).

Short Life—Prospect of—(See "Death" under Childhood; "Early Death" under Early; "Death In Infancy" under Infancy; "Short Life" under Life).

Wealth—Prospect of—(See "Accumulates", "Confers", under Riches).

PROSPERITY—Success—The ☉, ☽, ♃, and ♀ rising and above the Earth, and especially when well-aspected in the 10th H.; ♃ ☌ ♀ in the 2nd H., well-aspected, and no malefics in this house. (See Contentment, Fortunate, Happiness; "Peace of Mind" under Mind; Property; "Prospers Anywhere" under Residence; Riches, Wealth, etc.).

PROSTATE GLAND—Ruled by the ♏ Sign.

Diseases Of—The ☉ afflicted in ♏; afflictions in ♏; Subs at LPP (4L).

Enlargement Of—Hypertrophy of—The ☉ ☌ ♄ or ♂ in ♎ or ♏, and affl. also by the □ or ☍ ♅; ♅ in ♏, ☌, □, or ☍ ♄; ♂ affl. in ♏. (See Enlarged, Hypertrophy).

Inflammation Of—Prostatitis—♂ afflicted in ♏.

Prostatic Plexus—Ruled by ♏.

Prostatic Stricture—A ♏ disease; ♅ or ♄ afflicted in ♏; ♄ ☌ ♅ in ♏. (See Stricture).

PROSTITUTES—(See Harlots).

PROSTRATION—Collapse—Fainting—Feeble—Weak—(See Collapse, Debility, Fainting, Feeble, Infirm, Languishing; "Low" under Resistance, Vitality; "Weakened" under Strength; "Weak Body" under Weak).

Heat Prostration—(See "Excessive Heat" under Heat; "Sunstroke" under Sun).

Nervous Prostration—(See Collapse; "Nerves" under Excitable; "Prostration" under Nerves).

PROTECTION—Protects—Protective Influence—The Benefics, ♃ and ♀, exert a protecting, saving and beneficial influence over the body and mind. Also the ☉ dignified, well-placed, and well-aspected at B. (See Benefics).

Protects the Health—The ☉ ☌ or P. ♃ or ♀ acts as a protective influence against the evil aspects of the other planets; the ☉ ☌, P., ✶ or △ ♃ is a protective influence, increases the vitality, strengthens the constitution, and helps to overcome disease; the benefics well-aspected in the 6th H., and with no malefics in the 6th, or ruling the 6th. (See Endurance; "Good Health" under Health; Immunity; "Good" under Recuperation, Resistance, Vitality).

PROTEIDS—An Albuminoid Constituent of An Organism—Ruled by the ☉. Also strongly influenced by the ♋ sign. The clotted Proteids of Milk are ruled by the ☉. (See Albumen, Casein; "Proteids" under Food).

Eats Excess Of—And of Starches and Sugars—(See "Proteids", "Sweets", under Food).

PROTOPLASM—Protoplasma—Germinal Matter—Primitive Organic Cell Matter—Ruled by the ☉, as the ☉ is the center of our Solar System, ruler of the Nucleus, or Germinal Center of Organisms. The irritation and activity of the Protoplasma are furnished by ☿, as ☿ is near the ☉, and less than 30° from the ☉ at all times. (See Cells, Nucleus).

PROTRACTED—Prolonged—Extended—Long Drawn Out—

Protracted Fevers—(See "Chronic", "Hectic", "Low", under Fever).

Protracted Illness—(See Chronic, Consumptions, Invalids, Lingering, Long Diseases, Phthisis, Prolonged, Slow Diseases, Tabes, Tedious, Tuberculosis, Wastings, etc.).

PROTRUDING—Protrusions—Projecting—Prominent—

Abdomen—A Protruding Abdomen—(See "Prominent" under Abdomen).

Breastbone—Protrusion of—(See "Breastbone" under Breast).

Chin—Protruding Chin—(See "Long" under Chin).

Ears—Protruding and Large Ears—(See the Introduction under Ears).

Eyeballs—Protruding—(See "Goggle Eyes" under Eyeballs).

Eyebrows—Bushy and Overhanging—(See "Beetle Brows", "Bushy", under Eyebrows).

Hernia—Hernia Protruding Thru the Abdominal Ring—(See "Inguinal" under Hernia).

Nose—Protruding Nose—(See "Long", "Prominent", under Nose).

Piles—Protruding Piles—(See "Blind Piles" under Hemorrhoids). See the subjects under Prominent.

PROUD—Haughty—Lofty-Minded—Disdainful—Lordly—Conceited—The ☉ rising in ♌; ♌ gives a haughty air, carriage and walk, and especially when the ☉ is rising in ♌; the ☉ Sig. in ♉, proud of his physical strength; the ☉ Sig. in ♐, lofty and proud-spirited; the ☉ Sig. in ♒; the ☉ ill-dignified at B., and afflicted; planets in ♌; the ☉ Sig. in ♌. lofty and proud; the ☽ Sig. ✶ or △ the ☉, proud and aspiring; ♄ Sig. in ♎; ♃ Sig. ☌ ♂; ♃ Sig. in ♌; ♃ Sig. □ or ☍ the ☉; ♂ in ♌; ♂ Sig. in ♈, ♌, ♏, or ♐; ♂ a strong ruler at B.; ♂ strong at B., and in the sign or house of the ☉; in Hor'y Q. ♂ Sig. of the person or querent; ♀ Sig. ☌ the ☉; ♀ Sig. in ♌ or ♐; ♀ Sig. ✶ or △ ♂; ☿ Sig. in ♌; the Ruler or Significator in its exalted sign, angular, and in no way impeded, the native is arrogant, haughty, and assuming to himself more than his due. (See Commanding; "Proud" under Gait; Pretender).

PROVISIONS—Scarcity of—(See Crops, Drought, Famine, Fountains, Privation, Scarcity).

PROWESS—Fearlessness—Daring In Battle—(See Bold; "Fearless" under Fear).

PRUDENT—Prudence—Cautious—Sagacious — Circumspect — Discreet—Good Judgment — Thoughtful—Thrifty, etc. —The good aspects of ♄ to the ☉, ☽, and ☿; the ☽ applying to the good asps. ♀ or ☿; ♃ in the Asc.; ♂ Sig. ✳ or △ ♄; ☿ Sig. in ♎; ☿ Sig. ✳ or △ ♄. (See "Good" under Judgment).

Excess of Prudence—The ☽ Sig. ♂ ♄, and doubts and deliberates too much in the moment of action. (See Doubts, Fears, Mistrustful, Suspicious).

Imprudent—Void of Prudence—(See Imprudent, Indiscretions, Foolhardy; "Bad" under Judgment; Recklessness).

PRUDERY— Excessive Modesty — Coyness—Most common with people born with the ☉ in ♋, ♏, ♎, and ♏, and especially with females. The fiery signs, and also ♉, ♑, and ♒, are devoid of exaggerated, or false modesty. The ♍ people especially have more sex modesty, this being the sign of the Virgin. (See Bashfulness; "Chaste" under Females; Modesty, Shy).

PRURITUS — Intense Itching — (See Itch).

PSEUDO—False—There are a number of conditions, or manifestations in mind and body, which may resemble a disease, and have its symptoms, but which may be false, unreal, and imaginary. The planets ♆ and ♅ are largely responsible for such conditions. Also the malefics in the Signs of the Zodiac which rule, or cause a disease, may for a time lead to false, or exaggerated conditions, and mental impressions. (See Curious, Extraordinary, False, Illusions; "Imaginary Diseases" under Imagination; Mysterious Diseases; "Diseases" under Obscure, Peculiar, Psychic, Strange, Uncommon; "Pretended Ailments" under Pretended; Vague, Weird, etc.).

Pseudo Angina—False Angina—(See "False Angina" under Angina).

Pseudo Ischuria — Spurious Ischuria —(See "False Ischuria" under Urine).

PSITTACOSIS — A Disease of Birds Communicable to Man, marked by High Fever and Pulmonary Disorders — Parrot Fever—A ♊ disease, and afflictions in ♊; the ☉, ☽, or ♄ afflicted in ♊, susceptible to if exposed to birds with the disease, as Parrots; ♊ on the Asc. at B.; Subs at Lu.P. (See Fowls).

PSORIASIS — A Chronic Inflammatory Skin Disease with Scale Formation — ♂ or ☿ afflicted in ♑. (See Scales, Skin Diseases).

Face—Psoriasis of—♄ or ♂ afflicted in ♈; Subs at MCP (4C), and KP. (See "Tetter" under Face).

PSYCHIC — Pertaining to the Mind — Psychic Powers—Psychic Conditions—Psychopathic — Psychosis — Psychoses —Psychism, etc.—The Psychic Powers and Psychic Mental Traits are largely ruled over by ♆, and this planet in his strong sign ♓ tends to enhance these powers, to make the native very psychic, clairvoyant and mediumistic, and to good advantage when ♆ is not sorely afflicted by malefics. The ♋ sign is a very Psychic Sign. The following subjects have to do, more or less, with the Psychic Powers and the

Mind. The Psychic Powers are also dealt with in this book in the Articles on the Intellect, Intuition, Mentality, Mind, Perception, Reason, Understanding, etc. See these subjects, and also see the following subjects in the alphabetical arrangement when only listed here—

Abeyance—Of the Psychic Powers— (See Coma, Consciousness, Delirium, Insensibility, Unconsciousness).

Apparitions—(See Phenomena).

Auto-Toxic Psychoses — (See "Psychoses" in this section).

Catalepsy; Chaotic Mind — (See Chaotic, Confusion).

Clairaudience; Clairvoyance; Coma;

Confusion; Consciousness;

Constitution — The Constitution and Vitality Benefitted Psychically—♆ ✳ or △ the ☉ at B.

Curious Diseases—(See Curious, Extraordinary, Pseudo, Strange, etc.).

Death—Of the Psychic Nature—Shown by the 12th H. and ♓ sign, as this is the last, or end of the signs and houses, when life on earth is finished, and the Soul is ready to pass out of the influence of the physical body. (See Terminal, Twelfth House).

Delirium; Delusions; Demoniac;

Diseases—Disorders—Psychic Diseases and Disturbances—Psychic Distempers—Psychic Origin of Disease— The Disease Originates In the Mind Rather Than In the Body — Caused principally by ♆; ♆ afflicted in the brain sign ♈; ♆ ♂, □, or 8 the Asc.; the ☽ afflicted by ♆; the ☽ □ or 8 lord of the 1st H.; ♄ ♂ or ill-asp. ♆; if ♄ afflict the Asc., the ☽, and dispositors of the ☉ and ☽ (as the 1st H. and the dispositors of the ☉ and ☽ signify the mind), and the trouble may be over some business loss; ☿ ♂ ♆; the Asc. afflicted by ♆ or ♅. (See "Centered on Disease", "Disease", "Diseased Mind", "Mind and Body", under Disease; "Imaginary Diseases" under Imagination; Mysterious Diseases, Obscure Diseases, Peculiar Diseases, Strange, Vague).

Dreams; Ecstasy; Emotions;

Experiences—Psychic Experiences— Predisposition To—♆ or ♅ in the 6th or 8th H. at B.; ♆ progressed, afflicting the ☉, ☽, ♀, ☿, or the Asc., and tends to undesirable phases of. (See "Involuntary" under Clairvoyance, Mediumship; Imaginations, Obsessions; Spirit Controls, Uncanny, Weird, etc.).

Fainting; Fears; Feelings; Functions —The Psychic Functions Strengthened —♆ ✳ or △ the Asc.

Hallucinations; Healing—Psychic Healing—(See "Psychic" under Healers).

Hyperactivity—Of the Psychic Powers —Over-Activity of—Caused by the afflictions of ♆ or ♅ at B.; these planets in the 8th H. at B., and afflicting the hyleg, the ☉, ☽, or Asc.; ♆ afflicting ☿, the mental ruler; ♆ in the Asc. or M.C., and afflicted by the ☉, ☽, ☿, or malefics. (See "Over-Active Mind" under Active; Coma, Effervescent, Excitable; "Mind" under Hyperactivity; Lethargy).

Hypnotism; Illusions; Imaginations; Insanity; Intellect; Introspection; Intuition; Low Grade — The Psychic Powers of a Low Grade—Ψ ruler of the horoscope and afflicted. Involuntary Clairvoyance, Undesirable Mediumship, Crystal Gazing, etc., are usually practiced by people with a low grade of Psychic Power, or who resort to Black Magic for commercial purposes. Neptune strong, dignified, and well-aspected at B. tends to give Psychic Powers of a very high grade, Spiritual Sight, and to use such powers only for the benefit of Humanity, and rarely for financial gain. (See Clairvoyance; "Practices Hypnotism" under Hypnotism; Magic, Mediumship).

Magic; Magnetic—(See "Healers" under Magnetism).

Mania—(See Madness, Mania, Fury).

Mediumship; Mental — (See the subjects under Mental, Mind).

Metempsychosis—(See Reincarnation).

Mind—The Disease Originates In the Mind—Of Psychic Origin—(See "Diseases" in this section).

Mysterious Diseases — (See Curious, Extraordinary, Mysterious, Obscure, Peculiar, Strange, Uncommon, etc.).

Nails—Psychic Type of—(See "Long" under Nails).

Negative Psychism—Ψ □ or ☍ ♃ tends to. (See Negative).

Obscure — Obscure and Psychic Diseases—(See "Diseases" under Obscure).

Obsessions; Over-Activity — Of the Psychic Powers—(See "Hyperactivity" in this section).

Passive — (See Influenced, Negative, Passive, Receptive, Susceptibility).

Perception; Phenomena— Psychic Phenomena—Phenomena Referable to Psychic Causes — ♂ ⚹ or ill-asp. Ψ. (See Catalepsy, Clairvoyance, Consciousness, Delirium, Delusions, Hallucinations, Hypnotism, Illusions, Magic, Mediumship, Obsessions, Spirit Controls, Trance).

Photographer—Psychic Photographer —Case—See "Psychic Photographer", No. 935, in 1001 N.N.

Pineal Gland — This Gland is closely related to the higher Psychic and Spiritual Powers, and is ruled by Ψ. (See Pineal, Pituitary).

Powers — Strong Psychic Powers— Odic Force—Ψ ⚹ or P. the ☽, and especially in ♋ or ♓; Ψ ⚹ or △ the Asc., the psychic functions strengthened; the 10° ♓ on the Asc. at B., tends to give much psychic power. (See "Active Mind" under Active; "Psychic" under Healers; Hypnotism, Intuition; "Quickened" under Mentality; Pineal, Spiritual; "Hyperactivity", "Low Grade", in this section).

Predisposition — To Psychic Experiences—(See "Experiences" in this section).

Predominance—Of the Psychic Powers Over the Physical—Ψ rising in the Asc. or M.C., and with the ☉, ♂, and many planets setting in the West; Ψ rising in ♋ or ♓. Also caused by the afflic-

tions of Ψ and ♅, and especially of the lower grade of psychic powers, and involuntary conditions. (See Experiences, Hyperactivity, Low Grade, Phenomena, Powers, Sensitive, in this section).

Premonitions; Pretended Ailments — (See Pretended).

Prophetic; Psychic Experiences—(See "Experiences", and the various paragraphs in this section).

Psychic Nature — Psychic Tendencies —Ψ and ♅ strong at B.; the 4th face of ♉ on the Asc., soft and negative; the 5th face of ♋, the 6th face of ♍, or the 5th face of ♓ on the Asc. (See Experiences, Powers, Predominance, and the various paragraphs in this section).

Psychic Storms—Afflictions to Ψ at B.; ☽ □ or ☍ ☿. (See "Brain Storms" under Brain; Emotions, Excitable, Hysteria).

Psychic Tendencies — (See Predominance, Psychic Nature, and the various paragraphs in this section).

Psychic World—Experimenting In, or Tampering with the Psychic Powers— (See "Tampering" in this section).

Psychism—Favorable To—Tendencies To—♅ in △ aspect to Ψ. Negative Psychism is caused by the □ or ☍ asp. of Ψ to ♃. Adverse Psychism and Obsessions are caused by Ψ □ ♄ in the 8th H., and in □ asp. to ☿ at the same time.

Psychoses—(1) Auto-Toxic Psychoses —(See Diabetes, Uremia). (2) Toxic Psychoses — Occurs in such disorders as Alcoholism, Dementia, Delirium Tremens, Mania, Narcotic Habit, Paranoia, etc. (See these subjects).

Reason—(See the paragraphs under Reason).

Religion—Ecstatic and Psychic Experiences In—(See "Religious Excitement" under Excitable; "Ecstasy" under Religion).

Seances—(See Spiritualism).

Sensitive — To Psychic and Spiritual Conditions—Ψ strong at B.; Ψ or ♅ in the 3rd, 6th, or 9th H. at B., and if these planets are afflicted in these houses, in an adverse manner, or to cause hyperactivity of the psychic powers, or involuntary conditions; the ☽ in ♋, and especially when aspected by Ψ or ♅, and for good or evil according to the aspect. (See Diseases, Experiences, Hyperactivity, Low Grade, Predominance, Psychic Nature, in this section).

Sensitives — The aspects and influences of Ψ along Psychic or Spiritual lines have the most effect upon Sensitives for good or ill. (See "Sensitives" under Sensitive).

Spirit Controls; Spiritualism — Is strongly ruled by Ψ. (See Spiritualism).

Spirituality — Spiritual Sight — (See Spiritual).

Storms—(See "Psychic Storms" in this section).

Strange Diseases—Of a Psychic Origin—Ψ and ♅ diseases. (See Strange).

Strengthened — The Psychic Powers Strengthened—(See Functions, Powers, in this section).

Strong Psychic Powers — (See Functions, Powers, in this section).

Subconscious Mind — (See "Subconscious" under Mind; Subconscious).

Tampering—With the Psychic Powers — Experimenting with the Psychic World—Born with ♆ in ♓, the Asc., 12th H., or in the 10th H.; ♆ ☌ ☿ or the ☽. The Psychic Powers should not be forced, or prematurely developed, but be allowed to unfold naturally, otherwise they bring great dangers to the native, danger of Obsessions, involuntary Clairvoyance or Mediumship, Spirit Controls, etc.

Telepathy; Tendencies—Psychic Tendencies—(See Experiences, Psychic Nature, and the various paragraphs in this section).

Undesirable Experiences—In Psychism—♆ afflicted by ♅ or the ☽. (See "Involuntary" under Clairvoyance, Mediumship; Spirit Controls; Experiences, Hyperactivity, Low Grade, Predominance, Tampering, in this section).

Vitality—The Vitality Benefitted Psychically—(See "Constitution" in this section).

PTOLEMY—Claudius Ptolemy was the Author of the great Textbook on Astrology, known as "The Tetrabiblos". This book is still considered the basis of our Modern Teachings on Astrology, and is quoted very much. Ptolemy was born 132 A.D., and passed out in A.D. 160. Ptolemy gave us the fundamental teachings and theories about the Prenatal Epoch, and its various Orders and Modifications, and of the close relationship between the time of conception, and the time of birth. His book is quite a valuable Treatise on Medical Astrology, and should be in the hands of every student of Astral Philosophy. Ptolemy's book has been translated by Mr. J. M. Ashmand in recent years, and is now available in the Occult and Metaphysical Book Stores. (See Prenatal Epoch).

PTOMAINES—A Putrefactive Alkaloid — (See "Offensive Humours" under Humours).

PTOSIS—A Falling—Drooping—Prolapsus—(See Prolapse).

PTYALISM—An Excess of Saliva—Salivation—(See Saliva).

PUBERTY — Adolescence — The Age of Capability of Reproduction — Adolescence is the age between Puberty and Maturity. In the Kabala, Puberty was dedicated to Mercury.

Delayed Puberty — ♄ afflicted in ♏; Subs at PP (2, 3, 4L). (See the Introduction under Menses; "Early", "Time Of", in this section).

Dementia Praecox—At Puberty—(See "Trouble" in this section).

Disturbed—The removal of the Tonsils in childhood (the Tonsils are ruled by ♉, the opposite and complementary sign to ♏, the sign which rules the sex organs) tends to make the puberty period more disturbed, and also to later make childbirth more difficult and painful. Afflictions in ♏ also tend to disturb the puberty period, as ♄ or ♂ afflicted in ♏. Also caused by afflictions in ♉ at B. (See "Puberty Weakened" under Menses; "Operations" under Tonsils; "Females", "Trouble", in this section).

Early Puberty — The ☽ progressing thru signs of short ascension after birth, and at a later age when passing thru signs of long ascension. (See the Introduction under Menses; "Time Of" in this section).

Females — Ill-Health In Females At Puberty—Weakness In Females At Time of—The ☽ ☌ ♄ in ♏, ♎, or ♏; the Asc. to the □ or ☍ the ☽ or ♀ when occurring near the age of adolescence. The regularity of the female system, and the health after puberty, will depend largely upon the conditions, positions, and affections of the ☽ and ♀. (See "Painful", "Profuse", under Menses).

Imaginations — Morbid and Sensuous Imaginations Upon Passion and Sex Life At Time of Adolescence—♆ in the 6th or 12th H., and especially if in ☍ to ♅, or if ♆ is ☍ ♅ from an angle. (See "Morbid" under Imagination; "Sensuous" under Sensuality).

Insanity—At Puberty—(See "Puberty" under Insanity).

Menses—The Menses Begin—(See Menses; Delayed, Early, Time Of, in this section).

Mental State—And Puberty—See Fig. 13 in "Message of the Stars" by the Heindels, page 630, and the comments on page 610 of the same book. Puberty usually occurs at about the 14th year of life, and at the beginning of the third seven-year cycle, and when the Mind begins to take a deeper hold upon the life. The voice in males also changes to a deeper tone at this time, due to the reflex action upon the Larynx (♉) from the ♏ sign, the sex sign. (See Larynx).

Morbid Brooding — On Sex Life At Time of Adolescence—(See "Imaginations" in this section).

Passion — The Passion Increased At Puberty, and Brooding Upon — (See "Imaginations" in this section).

Procreation — Strong Desire For At Puberty—(See Amativeness).

Sensuous Imaginations — At Puberty —(See "Imaginations" in this section).

Sex Activity—Great Sex Activity At Adolescence—Children who have ♆ in the 6th or 12th H. at B. tend to greater sex activity at adolescence and during puberty, and to have morbid sex desires, and should be carefully trained, advised, and watched at this time. (See "Imaginations" in this section).

Time of Puberty—The Menses Begin —The Voice Changes In Males—The ☽ by progression in ♉ to her place at B. tends to precipitate the adolescent period, and the menses begin in females, the voice changes in males. (See Childhood, Larynx; the Introduction under Menses; Delayed, Early, Mental State, in this section).

Trouble At Puberty—Danger of Dementia Praecox At Puberty—Afflictions in ♉ or ♏, or in both signs; ♄ ☌ ♅ in ♉ or ♏; ♄ afflicted in ♉ or ♏; ♃ ☌ ♅ or ♂ in ♉ or ♏; Subs at PP. (See Disturbed, Females, Insanity, and the various paragraphs in this section).

Voice Changes—In Males At Time of —(See Larynx; Mental State, Time Of, in this section).

Weakened—(See "Puberty Weakened" under Menses; Disturbed, Females, in this section).

Weakness Incident To — (See "Females" in this section).

Young Females — Weakness and Ill-Health In At Adolescence—(See "Females" in this section).

PUBES — The Anterior Portion of the Innominate Bone—Ruled by ♍. The Hair of the Pubic Region is also ruled by ♍. Some Writers also say that the ♏ sign rules the Pubic Bone. (See Innominate, Pelvis).

PUBLIC—The Public—The People—The Common People — The Community — The Multitude—Mankind—The Public Welfare—Public Benefits or Evils—Public Joys or Sorrows—Prevalent Conditions, etc.—The ☽ rules the Public, and especially the Common People. Also the Common People and Laboring Classes are ruled by the 6th H. (See Common People, Humanity, Mankind). The ☽, (unless ♋ be on the Meridian) and the planet ascending, or ruling the Asc., are the Significators of the People at a Vernal Ingress. The following subjects have to do with the Public, the State and Condition of the Public, as Accidents, Anxieties, Benefits, Births, Calamities, Crime, Dangers, Deaths, Discords, Diseases, Epidemics, Evils, Health, Pestilence, Pleasures, Punishments, Sufferings, etc. See these subjects in the alphabetical arrangement when not more fully considered here—

Abdominal Diseases—Prevalence of—(See "Diseases" under Abdomen).

Accidents Prevalent—♂ rising in the Asc. at the Vernal Equinox; ♂ ☌ the ☉ at an eclipse of the ☉. (See the paragraphs under Accidents; "Accidents" under Journeys, Railroads, Travel, Vehicles, Voyages, etc.).

Acute Fevers Prevalent—(See "Prevalent" under Acute, Fever; "High Fever" under Fever).

Aged — Much Mortality Among the Aged — (See "Mortality" under Old Age).

Air—Unhealthy Air Affects the Public—(See "Corrupt Air" under Air).

Assassinations;

Assaults and Batteries — (See Assaults).

Birth Rate—Increase of—Decrease of —(See "Birth Rate" under Birth).

Blood—Effusion of Blood Prevalent—Expectoration of Blood Prevalent—(See Effusions; "Expectoration" in this section).

Bloodshed Prevalent — (See "Bloodshed" under Blood; Shedding, Slaughter, War).

Boils Prevalent—(See Carbuncles).

Captivity—Many Taken Into Captivity—(See Captive).

Carbuncles Prevalent — (See Carbuncles).

Cattle—Loss of — (See Cattle, Goats, Sheep).

Cheating—Prevalence of—(See Cheating).

Chest Affections—Prevalence of—(See "Prevalent" under Chest).

Children — Much Mortality Among — (See "Mortality" under Children).

Cholera Prevalent—(See Cholera).

Civil War—Civil Revolution—Danger of—(See "Civil" under War).

Comets—Influence of on Humanity—(See Comets).

Common People — Mischief and Misfortune To—♃ ☌ ♂ in the Asc. at the Vernal E. (See Common, Mischief, Misfortune).

Conspiracies—Plots—(See Plots).

Controversies — Much Public Discord —(See "Discord" under Quarrels).

Countries — Nations — Rulerships of, and Conditions Over—(See Countries, Eastern Parts, Nations, Northern). Afflictions in the Signs which rule the different Nations, Comets appearing in such signs, or Eclipses, tend to bring afflictions upon such Countries. (See Comets, Eclipses).

Crime Prevalent—(See Crime).

Crushed — By Avalanches, Fall of Buildings, Mobs, etc. — (See Crushed, Trampled).

Cursed by the Multitude—(See Execrated).

Death—(See "Public Death" in this section).

Diarrhoea Prevalent—(See Diarrhoea).

Discord—Much Public Discord—(See "Discord" under Quarrels).

Disgrace—Public Disgrace—(See Disgrace).

Dissensions — Many Dissensions Generally—(See "Discord" under Quarrels).

Drought—Much Suffering From—(See Drought).

Earthquakes; Eclipses—Effects of—(See Eclipses).

Effusion of Blood — Prevalence of — (See Blood, Bloodshed, in this section).

Enemies—Much Fear of Generally—(See "Fear Of" under Enemies).

Epidemics; Events; Evil—Every Evil Upon Humanity — (See "Every Evil" under Evil).

Execrated — By the Multitude — (See Execrated).

Execution — Public Execution — (See Execution).

Exhibition—Public Exhibition of Maladies—(See Exhibition).

Expectoration of Blood — Prevalence of—☿ in ♋ at the Vernal E., lord of the year, and afflicted by ♂. (See Expectoration, Haemoptysis).

Eye Diseases — Prevalence of — (See "Males", "Prevalent", under Eyes).

Famine; Feuds; Fevers—(See High, Low, Prevalent, under Fever).

Public   679   **Public**

Fires—Great Fires—(See "Great Fires" under Fire; Incendiarism).

Floods; Fluxes—(See "Prevalent" under Fluxes).

Foes — (See "Enemies" in this section).

Great — Death to The Great — Much Mortality Among—(See Assassinations, Famous; "Great Men", "The Great", under Great; Nobles).

Grief—(See "Public" under Grief).

Grievous Infirmities—Among the People—(See "Public Health Bad" in this section).

Grievous State of the People—♄ ruler of the year at the Vernal Ingress, and ♄ ℞ in an angle.

Hatred Prevalent—(See Hatred).

Health—The Public Health—(See Public Health Bad, Public Health Good, and the various paragraphs in this section).

Health of the Nations — (See Countries, Public Health, in this section).

Heat — Much Suffering, and Many Deaths from Extreme Heat — (See Drought, Famine; "Extreme Heat" under Heat; Summer; "Hot Winds" under Wind).

Humanity — Suffering To — (See Humanity, Mankind; the various paragraphs in this section).

Incendiary Fires—(See Incendiarism).

Internal Revolutions — Civil War — Danger of—(See "Civil" under War).

Judges—Sentences By—(See Judges).

Kingdoms—Danger of Destruction of —(See Kingdoms).

Kings—Danger To—Death of—(See Kings).

Lamentations—♃ in aspect with, and elevated above ♄ at a Solar Ingress or Eclipse. (See Lamentations).

Lawsuits—Many Lawsuits Generally —Lawsuits are ruled by the 7th H. Malefic planets in this house at the time of the Vernal or Autumnal Equinox; an Eclipse of the ☉ falling in the 7th H. Also tends to much trouble between Partners in Business, and in the Marriage relation, causing separations and divorces. (See Quarrelsome).

Lightning—Many Deaths From—(See Lightning).

Low Fevers Prevalent — (See "Low Fevers" under Fevers).

Low Public Houses—Frequenters of— (See Harlots, Taverns).

Lynchings; Maladies—Public Exhibition of—(See Exhibition).

Mankind — Many Evils Upon — (See "Every Evil" under Evil; Mankind, Misery, Misfortune, Trouble).

Measles Prevalent—(See Measles).

Men—Diseases Among—Many Deaths Among — Men In Power — Men Suffer with Their Eyes—Young Men Suffer— (See "Males" under Eyes; the various paragraphs under Men; "Young Men" under Young).

Mischief and Misfortune—To the Common People—(See "Common People" in this section; Mischief; Misery, Misfortune, Poverty, Reverses, Ruin).

Misery—Much Misery Everywhere— (See Misery).

Misfortune—Public Misfortune—(See "Common People" in this section; "Much", "Public", under Misfortune).

Mobs—Mob Violence—(See Mobs).

Monarchs — Danger To — Death of — (See Kings, Monarchs, Princes, Rulers).

Mortality Great—(See Mortality).

Murders Numerous—(See "Many Murders" under Murder).

Nations—The Health of—(See "Countries" in this section).

Nobles—Noblemen—Death of—Murder of—(See Nobles).

Outrages Numerous—(See Outrages).

Pandemics; Pestilence; Piracy;

Plague; Pleasure Seeking Generally— (See Pleasure).

Plots; Politics—Political Strife—(See Politics).

Poor—The Poor—(See Poor).

Population—Increased—Decreased— (See Population).

Poverty; Power—Men In Power—(See "Power" under Men).

Prevalent — (See the subjects under Prevalent).

Priests—Clergymen—Churches—Anxieties To—(See Clergymen).

Princes—Death of—(See Princes).

Prisons; Privations; Prohibition;

Public Death—Death In the Streets— Death by Day—Death in a Public Resort—Death by Public Execution—The ☽ afflicted in the 8th H. at B., and by dir., death in the streets, in a public hospital, in the presence of strangers, and in a public place; ♅ afflicted in the 8th H., and afflicting the hyleg, denotes an extraordinary and unusual death, and one that may create much public interest and concern; ♄ or ♂ in the angles at B., or any malefic in an angle and afflicting the hyleg. (See "Notorious Death" under Death; Extraordinary, Hanging, Judges; "Death" under Journeys, Mobs, Railroads, Sea, Ships, Strangers, Tragical, Travel, Vehicles, Voyages; "Wild Beasts" under Wild).

Public Discord—(See "Discord" under Quarrels).

Public Disgrace—(See Disgrace; "Loss Of" under Honor; "Imprisonment" under Prison; Reputation, Ruin, Scandal, etc.).

Public Dissentions — (See "Discord" under Quarrels).

Public Execution — (See Execution; "Public Death" in this section).

Public Exhibition—Of Maladies—(See Exhibition).

Public Grief—(See Grief; "Much Sadness" under Sadness).

Public Health Bad—A Bad Year for the Health of the People Generally— An Unhealthy Season—Much Sickness Generally—The ☉ lord of the year at the Vernal, and afflicted; the ☽ lady of the year, and badly afflicted; the ☽ in the 6th H. at the Vernal E., or at a

Solstice, and afflicted by malefics; ♄ lord of the year and afflicted at the Vernal Ingress; ♄ near the cusp of the 4th H. at the Vernal; ♄ in ♊, direct in motion and angular at the Vernal, and tends to much lung trouble; ♄ in ♌, ori., and ruler of the year at the Vernal; ♄ in ♎, ℞, and ruler of the year at the Vernal; ♄ ☌ ♂ in a human sign at the Vernal, and especially if in the Asc., tends to many infirmities among men for the time; ♂ lord of the year at the Vernal, in ♈, and afflicted by ♄; ♂ lord of the year in ♉, and occidental; ♂ in ♍ in N. Lat., and lord of the year at the Vernal; ♂ in ♎ in S. Lat., or ℞, at the Vernal, and lord of the year; ♂ in ♏ at the Vernal, ori., and lord of the year, much sickness generally and ♏ diseases; ♂ in ♐ at the Vernal, lord of the year, and especially in places under the rule of ♐; ♀ in ♌ at the Vernal, afflicted, and lady of the year; ☿ in ♊, ☌ ♂ at the Vernal, and ☿ lord of the year; ☿ in ♎ at the Vernal, afflicted, and lord of the year; ☿ in ♐, ☌ ♄ at the Vernal, lord of the year, and otherwise afflicted; ☿ in ♓ at the Vernal, and afflicted; if the ☽ or the planet ascending at a Solar Ingress into ♈ be under the beams of the ☉, combust, and afflicted by one or more of the malefics; a malefic in the Asc. at the Vernal, and afflicting the lord of the year; lord of the year afflicted, and in evil asp. to the ruler of the sign in which located; lord of the year afflicted, unfortunate, and impeded at the Vernal; the ☌ of malefic planets in fiery signs at the Vernal or a Solar Ingress, and due to corruption of the air and the fruits of the Earth. (See "Corrupt Air" under Air; Famine; "Drying Up Of" under Fountains; "Corruption Of" under Fruit; "Bad Health", "Periods of Bad Health", under Health; "Extreme Heat" under Heat; "Sickly Summer" under Summer; "Public Mortality Great" in this section).

Public Health Good—A Healthy Year for the People—Death Rate Diminished—The 1st H., or the Asc., rules the Public Health generally. If the planet ascending be swift in motion, and more than 17° from the ☉, and well-aspected by ♃ or ♀, or both, or the ☽ so placed at a Solar Ingress into ♈, the Public Health tends to be good; the ☽ lady of the year and free from affliction; ♃ lord of the year at the Vernal, and well-aspected; ♃ in the Asc. at the Vernal, and well-aspected; the ☉ lord of the year at the Vernal, and free from affliction; ♂ in ♓, direct in motion at the Vernal, and lord of the year; ♀ lady of the year at the Vernal, in the Asc., and free from affliction; ♀ in ♉ or ♎ at the Vernal, lady of the year, and well-aspected; ☿ in ♍ at the Vernal, lord of the year, and in ✶ or △ ♃; ☿ in ♐, ☌ ♃ at the Vernal, lord of the year, and well-aspected; a benefic in the Asc., not afflicted by a malefic, and the ☽ applying to it by ☌, ✶, or △ aspect; lord of the year free from affliction, well-aspected and dignified at the Solar Ingress into ♈; lord of the year in good aspect to the planet ruling the sign in which it is located, and free from the affliction of malefics.

(See "Good Health" under Health; "Death Rate Diminished" under Mortality).

Public Life—Politics—Engaged In—(See Politics).

Public Mortality Great—Many Deaths Among the People—A Sickly Time—An eclipse of the ☉ or ☽ in watery signs; the ☽, or the planet ascending, afflicted by a malefic planet in the 8th H. at the Vernal; the ☽ in the 8th H. at the Vernal, afflicted, lady of the year, and espec. if the ☽ be afflicted in ♈, ♏, or ♑; an eclipse of the ☽ in the 3rd Decan. of ♏; ♄ in ♉ at the Vernal, afflicted by ♂ and the ☽, direct in motion, and in an angle; ♄ near the cusp the 4th H. in S. Lat. at the Vernal; ♄ ℞ in ♌, and ruler of the year at the Vernal; ♄ or ♂ supreme at the Vernal or Solar Ingresses; ♄ ☌ ♂ at the Vernal, or a Solar Ingress, afflicting the lord of the year, and espec. when in the first three degrees of ♋; ♄ in a fixed sign at the Vernal, or a Solar Ingress, and afflicting the lord of the year, and tends especially to the death of many men; ♂ ☌, □, or ☍ the lord of the year at the Vernal, and especially from angles, and being in a sign of human form; ♂ in ♉ at the Vernal, lord of the year, and occidental; ♀ in ♓ at the Vernal, lady of the year, and afflicted. (See the paragraphs under Mortality; "Public Health Bad" in this section).

Public Quarrels — (See "Discord" under Quarrels).

Public Sadness — (See "Public Grief" under Grief; "Much Sadness Generally" under Sadness).

Public Streets—Death In—(See "Public Death" in this section).

Quarrels Prevalent — (See "Discord" under Quarrels).

Railroad Accidents—(See Railroads).

Rapine Prevalent—(See Rapine).

Religion—Much Religious Intolerance—♄ lord of the year at the Vernal, and ♄ afflicted in the 9th H. Also ♅ falling in the 9th H. at the Vernal, or a Solar Ingress, rebellious against established Orthodoxy. (See "Intolerance" under Religion).

Revolution—Civil and Political—(See Politics; "Civil" under War).

Riots—Danger of—(See Riots).

Robberies Prevalent — (See Robberies).

Rulers—Danger To—Death of—(See Assassinations, Kings, Monarchs, Rulers).

Sadness—Public Sadness and Sorrow—(See "Public Sadness" in this section).

Scarlatina Prevalent—(See Scarlet).

Scorpio Diseases Prevalent — (See "Public Health Bad" in this section; "Prevalent" under Scorpio).

Secret Foes — Much Damage From Generally—(See "Fear Of" under Enemies; Plots, Poisonings, Treachery).

Sedition—Deadly Seditions—(See Sedition).

Sheep — Many Deaths Among — (See Sheep).

Shipwrecks; Sickness—Much Sickness Generally—(See "Public Health Bad", "Public Mortality", in this section).

Skin Diseases Prevalent—(See "Prevalent" under Skin).

Slaughter Everywhere—(See Slaughter. Also see "Bloodshed" in this section).

Smallpox Prevalent—(See Smallpox).

Society — Much Discord Between the Different Classes of Society—(See "Discord" under Quarrels; Revolutions, Riots; "Civil War" under War).

Sorrow — Public Sorrow and Grief — (See "Public" under Grief, Sorrow).

Stones — Many Injured by Flying Stones and Mob Violence — (See Assaults, Mobs; "Flying Stones" under Stones).

Storms—Much Suffering and Distress By — (See Floods, Lightning, Rain, Storms, Tornadoes, Wind).

Streets—Public Death In the Streets —(See "Public Death" in this section).

Thefts Prevalent — Thieves Active — (See Highwaymen, Piracy, Rapine, Robbers, Thefts, Thieves).

Throat Diseases Prevalent — (See "Prevalent" under Throat).

Tornadoes—Hurricanes—(See "Tornadoes" under Wind).

Trampled by Mob—(See Trampled).

Travel—Many Accidents In—Dangerous to Travel — (See Journeys, Railroads, Travel, Voyages).

Treachery Everywhere—(See Treachery).

Trouble Generally—(See Trouble).

Tumults; Unhealthy Year—Unhealthy Time—Unhealthy Air—(See "Corrupt", "Obnoxious", under Air; "Public Health Bad" in this section).

Untimely Deaths—(See Untimely).

Violence Everywhere—(See Highwaymen, Murders, Pirates, Robbers, Slaughter; "Mob Violence", "Outbreaks", under Violence; War).

Volcanoes Active—(See Volcanoes).

War; Weather—Much Suffering from Extremes of Heat or Cold—(See Blizzards, Cold; "Extreme Heat" under Heat; Lightning, Snow, Storms, Weather, Wind, etc.).

Welfare—The Public Welfare—(See the various paragraphs in this section).

Wind — High Winds — Hot, Blasting Winds — Much Suffering From — (See the paragraphs under Wind).

Women—Many Deaths Among—Much Suffering Among — Murders of Many Women—(See Females; "Women" under Misfortune; Murder; "Mortality", and the various paragraphs under Women).

Young Men—Great Mortality Among —(See Young, Youth).

PUDIC—Pertaining to the Genitals—

Pudic Nerves—Ruled by ♏. Disorders of these nerves are caused by ☿ afflicted in ♏. (See "Nervous Affections" under Genitals).

PUERPERAL — Pertaining to Child-Bearing—Puerpera—A Female In Labor—Parturition—The Puerperal State —This subject is considered in the Article on Parturition.

Puerperal Fever—Child-Bed Fever—Eclampsia — Danger of Death By—Puerperal Convulsions—♂ afflicted in the 5th H. of the mother; ♂ afflicted in ♋ in the 6th H.; Subs at AT, AX, and PP. (See "Death of Mother" under Parturition).

Puerperal Mania — The ☽ afflicted by ♄ and ♂ at childbirth; ♂ afflicted in the 5th H. of the mother. (See Foetus, Gestation, Maternity, Mother, Parturition, Pregnancy, Prenatal Epoch).

PUFFING—Puffy—Soft—

Puffing of the Body—Soft Body—The watery signs prominent at B.; a water sign on the Asc.; the ☉ and ☽ in water signs, due to excess of fluids in the body. (See Bloating; "Puffy" under Cheeks; Corpulent, Dropsy, Fat, Flabby, Flatulence, Fleshy, Fluids, Gases, Gluttony, Obesity, Oedema, Plethora, Surfeits; "Puffy" under Swellings; Water Signs, etc.).

Sinews—Puffing Up of—(See "Puffing" under Nerves).

PUGILIST—A Pugilist—Case—(See "Pugilist" under Athletics).

PULMONARY—Affecting the Lungs—

Pulmonary Affections—(See "Pulmonary Affections" under Lungs).

Pulmonary Apoplexy — (See "Pulmonary" under Apoplexy).

Pulmonary Circulation—Ruled by ☿. (See "Pulmonary" under Circulation; "Blood" under Lungs).

Pulmonary Congestion — (See "Congestion" under Lungs).

Pulmonary Consumption — (See Consumption; "Pulmonary" under Phthisis; Tuberculosis, Wasting).

Pulmonary Diseases—(See Bronchial, Consumption; "Pulmonary" under Lungs; Phthisis, Pleura, Tuberculosis; the various paragraphs in this section).

Pulmonary Haematosis — (See Haematopoiesis).

Pulmonary Hemorrhage—(See "Hemorrhage" under Bronchial, Lungs).

Pulmonary Inefficiency—(See "Lungs" under Inefficiency).

Pulmonary Innervation — (See Innervation).

Pulmonary Parenchyma—(See Parenchyma).

Pulmonary Phthisis—(See Phthisis).

Pulmonary Plexus — Post-Pulmonary Plexuses—(See "Middle Cervical" under Ganglion).

Pulmonary Stenosis—(See "Stenosis" under Lungs).

Pulmonary Tuberculosis — (See Consumption, Phthisis, Tuberculosis, Wastings).

Pulmonitis — Inflammation of the Lungs — (See "Pulmonitis" under Lungs).

PULSATILLA — An Alterative and Depressant Herb. A Typical Drug of ♀. Is also a Polycrest Remedy corresponding to the ♏ Sign. (See "Typical Drugs" under Venus; "Polycrest" under Zodiac).

PULSE—The Expansile Impulse of the Arteries—

Accelerated Pulse — (See "High" in this section).

Bradycardia—(See "Slow" in this section).

Failing, Weak Pulse — The ☽ ☌ ♂ in the Asc., and ♄ ruler of the 6th H. when taken ill (Hor'y). (See Faint, Rare and Weak, Slow, in this section).

Faint—Faint Pulse—Often Faint and Beats Slowly and Feebly—The ☽ in ♐, and afflicted by the ☉ or ♂ when taken ill (Hor'y). (See Faintings, Feeble, Weak, under Heart).

Feeble Pulse — (See Failing, Faint, Rare and Weak, Slow, in this section; "Weak Heart" under Heart).

High Pulse—High and Immoderate—Rapid—Accelerated Heart Action—The ☉ ☌ or ill-asp. ♂ when taken ill; the ☽ in ♈ or ♊, and afflicted by the ☉ or ♂ when taken ill (Hor'y); the ☽ in ♉, ☌, ☐, or ☍ ♄ (or ☿ if he be of the nature of ♄) when one is taken ill, or takes to his bed, which is generally due to high living, surfeits, etc., and is attended with high fever (Hor'y); the ☽ in ♎, afflicted by the ☉ or ♂ when taken ill, and due to too much blood (Hor'y); the ☽ in ♒, afflicted by the ☉ or ♂ when taken ill, and due to too much blood (Hor'y); the ☽ in ♒, afflicted by the ☉ or ♂ when taken ill, and the ☽ slow in motion and decreasing, and is usually attended with a hot and violent fever. (See High Pressure, Too Much Blood, under Blood; Accelerated, Palpitation, Pulse, Rapid, Spasm, under Heart).

Immoderate Pulse — (See "High" in this section).

Impeded Pulse—(See "Impeded" under Heart; "Slow" in this section).

Irregular Pulse — (See Interrupted, Irregular, Palpitation, Rhythm, Uncertain, under Heart).

Rapid Pulse—(See "High" in this section).

Rare and Weak—Weak Pulse—Afflictions in ♌ or ♒; the ☽ in ♌ ☌ ♄ at the beginning of an illness; ♄ afflicted in ♌. (See "Weak Heart" under Heart; Failing, Faint, Feeble, in this section).

Remits—(See "Remits" under Heart; "Slow" in this section).

Rhythm—Interrupted Rhythm — (See "Rhythm" under Heart).

Slow Pulse—The Pulse Remits and Is Slow—Bradycardia—The ☽ in ♑, and afflicted by the ☉, ♄, or ♂ when taken ill (Hor'y); ♄ afflicted in ♌; Subs at HP. (See "Slow" under Heart; Failing, Faint, in this section).

Suspended Pulse — (See "Suspended" under Heart).

Troubled Pulse—The ☽ in ♌, ☌, or ill-asp. ♄ (or ☿ if he be of the nature of ♄) at the beginning of an illness, or at decumbiture, and death may result if the ☽ comes to the ☍ ♄ during the sickness (Hor'y). (See "Troubled" under Heart; the various paragraphs in this section).

Uncertain — (See "Uncertain" under Heart).

Weak Pulse — (See Failing, Faint, Feeble, Rare and Weak, in this section).

PUNGENT—Acrid—Bitter—Penetrating —The Acrid, Bitter, and Pungent Drugs and Odors are ruled by ♂. (See "Hot Acids" under Acids; Astringent, Bitter, Odors).

PUNISHMENT — Penalties — Operation of the Law of Cause and Effect—Sowing and Reaping—Punishments, Chastenings, Afflictions, Suffering, Troubles, and Sorrows are usually brought upon us because we have broken some Law, and are not living right, or in harmony with the Laws of God, Man, or Nature. The Human Race is punished in thousands of ways, to adjust and restore the balance of harmony. Ill-Health is a punishment, and we usually bring sickness upon ourselves by our manner of living and thinking, and by engaging in excesses and indiscretions in some way. It is said that "Character is Destiny", and our fate in life is much as we make it by our character, innate and acquired tendencies, conduct, habits, etc. (See Character, Fate). Saturn is said to be "The Chastener", and it is principally into the hands of the Angel of Saturn that the chastenings, testings, and disciplinary measures have been given by the Higher Powers. (See Saturn). The Twelfth House also denotes sorrows, punishments, limitations, confinements, self-undoing, restraints, and if this house is badly afflicted at B., or had a malefic as its ruler, the native is apt to have his trials and afflictions considerably increased until he gets the New Birth, and learns how to live in harmony with the Law. (See Twelfth House). Our God is not an "Angry God", as is taught by some Creeds, nor does He seek revenge upon His Children, and, in the spiritual sense, there are no punishments inflicted upon us, but what we call punishments are merely trials, chastenings, suffering, and afflictions brought upon us to teach us lessons, increase our wisdom and understanding of life and destiny, and to show us the folly of sin, debauchery, wickedness, and an evil life. Good living always has its rewards and blessings, and the person who is living right, and in harmony with Law, and who has made conscious contact with his Higher Mind, and the Divine Within Himself, and who has learned to rule the animals within himself, and to not be dominated by personality and the lower mind — to such there are no "Punishments", but constant progress and attainment. Most every subject in this book deals in some way with the "Punishments" of life. Look in the alphabetical arrangement for the subject you have in mind. The following are a few of the important subjects along this line. See these subjects — Accidents, Affliction, Anguish, Anxiety, Assassination, Banishment, Beheaded, Bloodshed, Calamity, Casualties, Catastrophies, Confinements, Disaster, Discomforts, Discord, Disease, Disgrace, Dishonour, Distress, Early Death, Enemies, Events, Evils, Execrated, Executed, Exile, Failure, Fate, Fears, F o r t u n e, Gloom, Grief, Grievous, Hanging, H o r r o r s, Hurts, Ill-Fortune, Ill-Health, Imprisonment, Inharmony, Injuries, Insanity, Judges (Sentenced By); Lamentations, Limitations, Lingering Diseases, Madness, Mania, Mental Disorders, Mischief, M i s e r y, Misfortune, Murdered, Murmurings; "No Peace of Mind" under Mind; Pain, Plots (Victim of)); Poverty, Prison, Privations, Reputation (Loss of); Restraints, Reverses, Ruin, Sadness, Scandal, Self-Undoing, Sickness, Sorrow, Starvation, Suffering, Suicide, Tragedy, Treachery, Trials, Tribulations, Trouble, Unfortunate, Untimely End, Vexations, Violent Death, War, Worry, Wounds, etc., and many other subjects throughout this Encyclopaedia.

PUPILS—Pupils of the Eyes—The Aperture In the Iris of the Eye—For Disorders of the Pupils, see the various paragraphs in the Article on Iris.

PURE—Purity—Unalloyed—Unstained—**Air** — Pure Air — (See "Pure" under Air).

Blood — The Blood Should Be Kept Pure—(See "Pure" under Blood).

Morals — Pure Morals — Has Good Morals — (See "Good Morals" under Morals).

Skin—A Pure Skin—(See "Pure" under Skin).

PURGATION—Purging—(See Cleansing, Enema; "Organic" u n d e r Functions; Physic).

PURPLE—The Color of the ☉ is Yellow, or inclined to Purple. The Colors of ♀ are white and purple. Some Authors say ♃ rules Purple (or Violet) in the Solar Spectrum. (See Colors, Indigo, Violet). The Purple rays and color are valuable in the treatment of Blood and Liver Disorders. (See "Remedies" under Blood; "Treatment" under Liver).

Marks — Purple Marks on the body are given by ♃. (See Marks).

PURPOSES—Aims—I n t e n t i o n s—Motives, etc.—

Aims—Aiming At Great Things—The ☉, ☽, or ♀ Sig. in ♐. (See Ambition; "Elevated Planets" u n d e r Elevated; "Majorities of the Planets" under Majority; Positive Nature, Resolute; "Rising Planets" under Rising).

Constant In Nothing — (See Changes, Concentration, Discontentment, I d l e, Improvident, Indifferent, Instability, Location, Mutable Nature, Residence, Restlessness, Roamer, V a c i l l a t i n g, Vagabond, Wanderer, etc.).

Dishonest Purposes — (See Cheating, Criminal, Deceitful, Dishonest, Evil, Forgers, Hypocritical, Liars, Libelers, Plots, Thieves, Treachery, etc.).

Honest Purposes — (See Honest, Humane, Kind, Noble, Sincere, etc.).

Motives—Good—Evil—(See Motives).

Persevering — Steady In Purposes — (See "Good Powers Of" under Concentration; "Fixed Signs" under Fixed; Persevering, Positive Nature, etc.).

PURPURA—Hemorrhage Into the Cutis of the Skin—♄ afflicted in ♋. Scurvy

is a form of Purpura, and due to improper diet. (See Derma, Scurvy).

PURSUITS — Trades — Callings — Professions — Success In — Dangers In — (See Business, Chemists, Employment, Healers, Nurses, Occupation, Surgeons, Vocation, etc.).

PURULENT—Having the Character of Pus—(See Pus).

PUS—Purulent—Pus-Forming Diseases —Pustular— Pustules — Festering Diseases — S u p p u r a t i o n s—Phlegmon—Phlegmonous — Putrid—Putrefaction—Septic — Toxic — C o n t a g i o n s—Infections, etc.—Pus diseases are said to be caused especially by ♆. Also caused by afflictions to, or by the ☉, ☽, ♄, ♃, ♂, and ♀, depending upon the part, or parts of the body afflicted, and the parts ruled by the planet. The following diseases and conditions have to do with Pus, and where Pus is present in smaller or larger quantities. See these subjects in the alphabetical arrangement when only listed here—

Abscesses; Areolar Tissue—(See "Suppurative Inflammation" under Nipples).

Blood — (See "Putrefaction" u n d e r Blood).

Blotches; Bones — (See "Pus" under Bones).

Breast—(See "Abscess" under Breast).

Carbuncles; Carcinoma; Cavities—Pus Cavities—(See Cavities, Cloaca).

Chickenpox; Cloaca; Contagions;

Corruption; Decay; Decomposition;

Discharges — (S e e "Offensive" under Discharges; Fetid, Foul).

Ears—(See A b s c e s s e s, Discharges, Pustules, under Ears).

Eruptions; Festering; Fevers — (See "Fevers" under Putrid).

Finger Nails—Toe Nails—Pus Formations Around—(See "Whitlows" under Toes).

Free Surfaces—Suppuration of—Open Sores—(See Sores, Ulcers).

Gangrene—Malignant Gangrene with Pus—A ♄ disease; Subs at CP and KP. (See Gangrene, Malignant).

Granulations; Gums—Putrid Gums — (See Gums, Pyorrhoea).

Impetigo—Acute Pustular Inflammation of the Skin—(See Impetigo).

Kidneys—Pus In—(See "Pyonephrosis" under Kidneys).

Malignant — (See "Gangrene" in this section).

Measles; Morbid Discharges — (See "Offensive" under Discharges; Morbid).

Nails—Suppuration of—(See "Finger Nails" in this section).

Nipples — (See "Suppurative" u n d e r Nipples).

Offensive Discharges — (See Discharges, Odors, Offensive).

Osteomyelitis — (See "Pus" under Bones).

Papules; Phlegmon—Suppurative Inflammation of Areola Tissue, such as in the colored ring about the Nipple—Phlegmonous Suppuration About the

Nails—Phlegmonous Ulcers—(See Nipples; "Whitlows" under Toes; Ulcers).

Pimples; Pustular Diseases—Pustules—Pustular diseases arising from blood impurities and poisoning of the system are denoted by ♀. Acute pustular inflammation of the skin occurs in Impetigo, a ♐ disease. Mars is active in causing the pustules in eruptive diseases, as in Chickenpox, Smallpox, etc. Also ♄ causes Festerings. (See the various paragraphs in this section; Blotches, Chickenpox; "Pustules" under Ears; Impetigo, Measles, Pimples, Pox, Sloughing, Smallpox; "Vascular Tissues" under Vascular).

Pustules—A Small Purulent Papule—(See "Pustular Diseases" in this section; "Pustules" under Ears; Pimples).

Putrid Diseases—(See Putrid).

Pyemia; Pyorrhoea; Quinsy — (See Tonsils).

Septic Diseases—(See Putrid, Septic).

Skin — Pustular Inflammation of — (See Impetigo).

Sloughings; Smallpox; Sores;

Syphilis; Teeth—Suppuration Around —(See Gums, Pyorrhoea, Teeth).

Throat — Pus Sores In — Putrid Sore Throat — (See Diphtheria; Putrid, Ulcerated, under Throat; Tonsils).

Toe Nails—Suppuration About—(See "Whitlows" under Toes).

Tonsils — (See Quinsy, Suppuration, under Tonsils).

Ulcers; Urine — (See "Pus" under Urine).

Vascular Tissue — Suppuration of — (See Vascular).

Whitlows—(See Toes).

Xanthopsydracia — A Skin Disease with Yellow Pustules—(See this subject).

PUTRID— Putrefaction — Rottenness — Decay — Decomposition — Fetid—Offensive—Septic, etc.—The following subjects have to do with Putrefaction, Rottenness, Foul, Fetid, Offensive and Septic Conditions, which subjects see in the alphabetical arrangement when only listed here—

Abscesses; Animal Bodies—The putrefaction of animal bodies is caused by the damp vapors generated by the ☽, and caused by the nearness of the ☽ to the Earth. Putrefaction is also caused by ♄ or ♂ in the 1st or 7th H. in ♋, ♍, or ♓, and all signs ascribed to terrestrial animals or fishes. (See "Animal Signs" under Animal; Decay, Fish; "Damp Vapors", "Relaxation", under Moisture).

Blood—Putrefaction In—(See "Putrefaction" under Blood).

Bowels — Bowels Filled with Putrid Matter—(See "Putrid" under Bowels).

Breath — Putrid Breath—(See "Foul" under Breath).

Catarrh—Putrid Catarrh—Foul Odors of—(See "Catarrh" under Nose).

Cough—Rotten Cough—(See "Rotten" under Cough).

Death—Death from Putrid Diseases—♀ denotes death by, and by putrid sore throat, and from diseases arising from putrefaction and rottenness; ♀ afflictions at B., or afflicting the hyleg, and holding the dominion of death. (See "Death" under Moisture).

Decay; Decomposition; Dissolution;

Distempers — Putrid, Hot, and Moist Distempers—The ☉ or ☽ Sig. ♂ ♂. (See "Hot and Moist Diseases" under Heat).

Excretions; Faeces; Fermentation;

Fetid; Fevers—Putrid Fevers—The ☉ directed to Aldebaran, Deneb, Regulus, Antares, Bellatrix, or Frons Scorpio. The ☉ gives putrid fevers, and also ♃ and ♂; ♃ in fiery signs at a decumbiture, and ♂ behold him, and with the ☉ weak and afflicted; watery signs threaten putrid fevers if ♂ be in one of them at a decumbiture. (See "Eruptive Fevers", "Septic", under Fever; Septic).

Gums—(See "Putrid" under Gums).

Herbs—Rotten Herbs—Rottenness of Seeds—Putrid Condition of—(See "Seeds and Herbs" under Rotten).

Hot and Moist—Hot, Moist, and Putrid Distempers—(See "Distempers" in this section).

Moisture — Putrid Diseases From — (See Decay; "Hot and Moist Diseases" under Heat; "Damp Vapors", "Putrefaction", under Moisture; "Physiological Action" under Moon; Rottenness).

Odors—Offensive Odors—(See Odors).

Ptomaines; Pus Diseases—(See Pus).

Rottenness—(See Decay, Decomposition, Fermentation, Rotten, Zymosis).

Scrofula — When Attended with Putridity—(See Scrofula).

Septic Poison — Septic Fever — (See Septic).

Sores — Open Sores — (See Sores, Ulcers).

Sweat—Putrid and Fetid Sweat—(See "Fetid" under Sweat).

Throat — Putrid Sore Throat — (See "Putrid" under Throat).

Ulcers; Vegetation — Putrefaction of —(See Corruption, Fruit, Rotten, Vegetation).

Zymosis — Fermentation — (See Zymosis).

PUZZLING DISEASES—Obscure Diseases — Mysterious — (See Extraordinary, Mysterious, Obscure, Peculiar, Strange, Uncommon, etc.).

PYELITIS—Inflammation of the Pelvis of the Kidney—(See "Pyelitis" under Kidneys).

PYELONEPHRITIS—(See "Pyelitis" under Kidneys).

PYEMIA — Pyaemia — Septicemia with Abscess Formations—This condition is usually caused by afflictions to ♃ or ♀, and by acting upon the blood, causing impure blood, and blood poisoning. (See Abscesses; "Impure Blood" under Impure; "Blood Poisoning" under Poison; "Pustular Diseases" under Pus; Septic).

PYLORUS — The Opening of the Stomach Into the Duodenum—Constriction of—(See "Pylorus" under Stomach).

PYONEPHROSIS—Pus In the Kidney— (See this subject under Kidneys).

PYORRHOEA—A Discharge of Pus—

Alveolar Pyorrhoea — (See Necrosis; "Alveolar" under Teeth).

Pyorrhoea — Pus Around the Gums — A ♓ disease; ♄ afflicted in ♋ or ♑, and due to eating an excess of sugar and sweets. (See Gums).

PYRETHRUM—(See Pellitory).

PYREXIA—An Elevation of Temperature—(See Fever).

PYROMANIA—(See Incendiarism).

PYROSIS — A Gastric Burning Pain, with Eructations—(See Belching).

PYURIA—Pus In the Urine—(See "Pus" under Urine).

Q

QUADRANTS—Quarters of the Heavens —The three Houses, or the Quadrant from the Asc. to the Midheaven, and the three opposite Houses from the Descendant to the Nadir, are called the Male Quadrants, and are positive, and many planets in these Quadrants at B., and especially in the houses between the 1st and 10th H., tend to make the native very positive, forceful, energetic, and also to have more vitality, and greater resistance to disease. (See Quadratures, Quarters). The other Quadrants are the negative or feminine ones, those from the Nadir to the cusp of the 1st H., and from the Midheaven to the cusp of the 7th H., or Descendant. The Male Quadrants, and with the ☽ in such at conception, tend to produce male children, and with the ☽ in a female Quadrant at conception, the child conceived will usually be a female. These distinctions are important to note in connection with the study of the Prenatal Epoch, and the determination of sex. (See Predetermination, Prenatal Epoch). The Male Quadrants are also classed as Oriental as regards the position of the ☉ and ☽ at B., and the Female Quarters are Occidental, and the ☉ or ☽ in these Quarters at B., are oriental or occidental. With the other planets they are called oriental when in the Eastern Quadrants, occidental when in the Western half of the map. Planets are also called oriental when rising before the ☉. (See Occidental, Oriental). A planet rising before the ☉ is much more powerful over the mind and body, for good or ill, according to the nature of the planet, and its aspects, etc. (See Elevated, Majority, Rising, Setting). The ☽ in an oriental Quarter at B. indicates an early marriage, and a late marriage when in an occidental Quarter. (See "Early Marriage" under Marriage).

QUADRATURES — Quarters — This refers principally to the Quarters of the ☽, and to the position of planets in their orbits when the □, ☍, and ♊ aspects to their place in the map at B., and these aspects, or Quarters, are very important to note in health matters, as they usually precipitate some crisis in the life of the native. (See Crises; Decrease, First Quarter, Full Moon, Increase, New Moon, Quarters, Third Quarter, under Moon; "Planetary Periods" under Periods; Quadrants, Quarters).

QUADRUPEDS — Quadrupedal — Four-Footed — Four-Footed Beasts — The Four-Footed, Terrestrial, or Animal Signs of the Zodiac, are ♈, ♉, ♌, ♐, and ♑, all typical of the four-footed beasts which are symbolds of these signs. People born with malefics in these signs, and especially when they are on, or in the Asc., are more liable to attacks and injuries by Quadrupeds when under evil directions or transits. They also tend to have more of the animal nature in them, and to partake somewhat of the form, shape, and characteristics denoted by the animal symbol of the sign. (See "Animal Signs" under Animal; Beasts, Brutish, Four-Footed; "Human Signs" under Human; Hurtful, Ruminant. Also see each of these Signs in the alphabetical arrangement).

Animals — Injuries By — (See "Hurts By" under Animals, Beasts).

Attacks By—Malefics in the M.C., elevated above the Lights, or in ☍ to each other; ♄ in ♉, ♂, □, or ☍ the Asc. by dir., and probably an attack by a bull; ♂ in the 12th H., and afflicted by ♅ or ♄. (See Bites, Ferocious, Hurts, Kicks, Wild Animals, under Animals; "Attacks By", "Injury By", under Beasts; "Animals" under Bites; Cattle, Distortions, Elephants; "Great Beasts" under Great; Kicks; "Cattle" under Large).

Beasts—Attacks or Injury By—Death By—(See the various paragraphs under Animals, Beasts, Cattle; the paragraphs in this section).

Bull—Attack By—Malefics in the ♉ sign, and afflicted. (See "Attacks By" under Cattle, and also in this section).

Cattle—Attacks By—Danger or Death By—(See "Attacks By" under Cattle; "Great Beasts", "Great Cattle", under Great).

Death By — (See "Hurts By" under Animals; "Death By" under Beasts).

Distortions—Due to Injury by Quadrupeds—(See Distortions, Excrescences).

Elephants—Injuries, Hurts, or Death By—(See Elephants).

Excrescences — Due to Attacks of Quadrupeds—(See Excrescences).

Great Beasts — Great Cattle — Hurts, Injury, or Death By — (See Beasts, Cattle, Elephants; "Great Beasts", "Great Cattle", under Great; Horses; "Cattle" under Large).

Horses — Injury By — (See Horses, Kicks).

Injury By—Hurts By—(See "Attacks By", and the various paragraphs in this section).

Kicks—(See Horses, Kicks).

Lameness—Due to Injury By—(See Distortions, Excrescences).

Large Quadrupeds—Hurts By—(See "Great Beasts" in this section).

Paralysis — Due to Injury By — (See Distortions, Excrescences).

Signs—Quadrupedal Signs—(See the Introduction to this Article).

Thrusts—(See Kicks).

Wild Beasts—Attacks or Injury By—(See "Wild Animals" under Animals; "Wild Beasts" under Beasts; Wild).

QUADRUPLETS—Case—The four Doyle sisters, of Hollywood, Calif. Born August 10th, 1912. They are all living, and their picture appeared together in a Los Angeles paper in June, 1931. Hour and place of birth not known to me. (See Multiple, Triplets, Twins).

QUALITY—Qualities—Nature of—Type of—Attributes—Traits—Characteristics—

Body—Qualities of the Body—(See Body; "Body" under Cold; "Body", "Cold and Dry Body", under Dry; Elemental, Form, Good, Health; "Animal Heat", "Hot Bodily Temperament", "Hot and Dry Body", "Moist and Warm", under Heat; Height; "Cold and Moist", "Hot and Moist", under Moisture; Physical, Shape, Size, Stature, Strength, Strong; "Bodily Temperaments" under Temperament; "Weak Body" under Weak; Weight, etc. Also look in the alphabetical arrangement for the subject you have in mind).

Death—Quality of—(See Anareta; "Kind of Death", "Quality of the Death", under Death; Directions, Dominion, Events; "Death" under Nature, Species).

Disease—Quality of the Disease—(See "Causes", "Quality", under Disease; "Disease" under Nature, Species, Type; "Quality" under Sickness).

Disposition—Qualities of—Many of these Qualities are given and listed alphabetically throughout this book. Look for the subject you have in mind. A special list of the traits of Mind and Disposition are given in the Article on Mind. (See Conduct, Fancies, Habits, Ideals, Ideas, Mentality; "Desirable", "Undesirable", under Mind; Morals, Motives, Principles, Propensities, Purposes, Temperament, Tendencies, etc.

Eyes—(See "Quality Of" under Eyes).

Fever—(See "Quality Of" under Fever).

Intellect—Mind—Qualities of—(See Intellect, Mentality, Mind, Perception, Reason, Understanding; "Disposition" in this section).

Mind—Qualities of—(See Disposition, Intellect, in this section).

Passive Qualities—(See "Qualities" under Active; Negative, Passive).

Positive Qualities—(See Positive).

QUARRELS—Quarrelsome—Contentious—Discord—Disagreeable—Turbulent—Dissensions—Fights—Violent Outbreaks—Frays—Strife—Anger—Commotions—Dissimulations—Disputes—Misunderstandings, etc.—The planet ♂ is the principal author of quarrels and disputes, bloodshed, etc.,

and where violence may attend. For the general influences which tend to give a quarrelsome nature see "Quarrelsome" in this section. The following subjects have to do with Quarrels, the Causes leading to Quarrels, Attending Circumstances, States of Mind, and the Results of Quarrels. See these subjects in the alphabetical arrangement when merely listed here—

Ambushes; Anarchists; Anger;

Antipathy; Argumentative—(See Argumentative, Independent, Obstinate).

Assassinations; Assaults;

Banishment; Battle—(See Battle, Contests, Duels, Feuds, War).

Beside Oneself—(See Excitable).

Blackmailers—(See Libel).

Blasphemers—(See "Blasphemy" under Religion).

Bloodshed—(See "Bloodshed" under Blood; Murder, Shedding, Slaughter, War).

Bloodthirsty—(See Cruel; "A Murderer" under Murder; Vicious; "Tendency To" under Violence).

Bold; Causes of Quarrels—(See "Quarrelsome", and the various paragraphs in this section).

Chartering; Choleric; Contests;

Crime; Cruel; Cuts; Dangerous—To Society and the Community—(See Anarchists, Dangerous).

Death In Quarrels—Danger of—♂ holding dominion at B., and elevated above the Lights, and afflicting the hyleg; the ☉ Sig. ☌ ♂, death, or terribly wounded; ♃ Sig. ☌ ♂, sometimes wounded in a quarrel; ♀ Sig. ☌ ♂, and usually in a quarrel with a woman; the Asc. to the ☌, P., □, or ☍ ♂ by dir., and ♂ in a sign of human form at B.; lord of the 8th in the 7th H.; 26° ♉, or the 9° ♎ on the Asc. (See "Death" under Contests, Duels, Fighting, and under the various subjects mentioned in this Article).

Destructiveness; Disagreeable;

Discord—Much Public Discord Prevalent—Political Strife—Many Quarrels Prevail—Discord Between the Various Classes of Society—The ☽ elevated above, and configurated with ♄ at a Solar Ingress or Eclipse; an eclipse of the ☉ or ☽ in a fiery sign; an eclipse of the ☽ in ♍, or the 3rd Decan. of ♏; ♄ Lord of the Year at the Vernal Equi., direct in motion, and in an angle; ♄ ℞ in ♊, and angular at the Vernal; ♂ elevated above, and configurated with ☿ at a Solar Ingress or Eclipse, much discord everywhere. (See Anarchists, Politics, Prevalent, Public, Reformers, Revolutions, Sun Spots (see Spots); "Civil War" under War).

Disputes—Fond of War and Disputes—♂ strong at B.; ♂ Sig. in ♈ or ♏, and often gains by them; ♂ Sig. in ♌, ready for warlike occupations at any time; ♂ in the Asc. or 10th H. at B.; many cross aspects at B. to a planet, or planets ascending, and often not of their own seeking. (See "Quarrelsome", and the various paragraphs in this section).

Dissentions — Many Dissentions Generally—(See "Discord" in this section).

Dissimulation — (See "Quarrelsome" in this section).

Duels; Emotions—Disorders of—(See Anger, Emotions, Excitable, Feelings, Hatred, Jealousy, etc.).

Enemies—Quarrels With—Injury By —His Own Worst Enemy—Secret Enemies Active—(See Enemies).

Enmity; Excitable; Executed;

Exile; Family Quarrels—(See "Relatives" in this section).

Females—Quarrels With—(See Quarrels, Treachery, Vexations, under Females; "Injured Thru Women" under Men; "Death by Women" under Women).

Feuds; Fierce; Fiery; Fighting;

Fratricide; Gross—(See "Gross Manners" under Gross).

Gunshot Wounds — (See Gunshot; "Murdered" under Murder).

Hanging; Hasty; Hatred;

High Temper — (See "High" under Temper).

Highwaymen; His Own Death — (See "Causes His Own Death" under Death).

Homicide; Hot-Headedness — (See Anger, Choleric, Hasty, Irascible, Obstinate; "High Temper" under Temper; Vicious, Violent).

Hurts—(See "Quarrels" under Hurts).

Imprisonment—(See Prison).

Incised Wounds--(See Incised).

Incompatibility; Inhuman — (See "Inhuman Disposition" under Inhuman).

Injuries During Quarrels — (See Blows, Cuts, Duels, Gunshot, Stabs; the various paragraphs in this section).

Insanity — (See Dangerous, Outrageous, under Insanity).

Instruments—Injury By—(See Instruments).

Irascible; Irrational; Irresponsible;

Irritable; Jealousy; Judges—Sentenced By—(See Judges).

Kings—(See "Death By" under Kings).

Law—Killed by Officers of the Law—Sentenced by Law—(See Judges, Law, Officers).

Lawsuits—(See Law; "Lawsuits" under Public).

Libel; Love Affairs — Quarrels In — (See the paragraphs under Husband, Love Affairs, Marriage, Marriage Partner, Wife).

Lynchings; Madness — (See "Brain Storms" under Brain; "Beside Oneself" under Excitable; Frenzy, Fury, Madness; "Psychic Storms" under Psychic).

Maimed; Malicious—(See Malice).

Manners — (See "Rough" under Manners).

Manslaughter; Marriage—(See "Quarrels" under Marriage).

Mars — (See "Author of Strife", and the various influences under Mars).

Mean — (See "Mean-Spirited" under Mean).

Men — (See "Injured Thru Women" under Men).

Merciless; Military Life — Killed or Murdered In—(See Military).

Misanthropic; Mischief—(See "Active to Do Mischief" under Mischief).

Misunderstandings; Mob Violence — (See Mobs).

Monarchs—Death by Wrath of—(See ("Death by Wrath Of" under Kings).

Moods; Motives; Murder; Mutilations;

Neighbors; Obstinate; Offended—(See "Easily Offended" under Offended).

Officers—Killed by Officers of the Law —(See Officers).

Opinions; Opposite Sex—(See "Aversions" under Opposite Sex).

Outrages; Parents—(See "Injured by Children", "Killing of a Parent", under Parents).

Passion—(See "Violence" under Passion).

Patricide — (See this subject under Father).

Perils; Perplexities; Perverse;

Petulant; Pirates; Pity—(See "Shows No Pity" under Pity).

Plots; Poison Death — (See "Death" under Poison).

Politics—Much Strife In—(See "Discord" in this section; Politics).

Power — Ruined by Men In Power — (See "Power" under Men).

Prejudice—(See "Mind" under Prejudice).

Prevalent — (See the subjects under Prevalent).

Prison—(See "Beaten In Prison", "Injured", under Prison).

Profane; Propensities; Property—Disputes Over—(See "Duped of His Property" under Property).

Prowess — Daring In Battle — (See Bold, Prowess).

Public Discord — (See "Discord" in this section; the various paragraphs under Public).

Punishment; Purposes—(See Character, Motives, Principles, Purposes).

Quarrelsome—A Quarrelsome Nature —Warlike—Combative — Mars is the planet of War, and the ♂ influence must be strong at B., and the Significators afflicted by ♂, to give a warlike nature; ♂ ruler at B. and afflicted; ♂ afflicted in the 1st H. and near the cusp; ♂ afflicted and ill-dignified at B., and in his own signs or houses; people born under ♂, and with ♂ afflicted and ill-dignified at B., are always ready to rush into quarrels, disputes, war, and bloodshed; ♂ is the principal Sig. of strifes and contentions by his evil aspects and directions to the Significators, the ☉, ☽, Asc., or M.C.; ♂ Sig. in ♈, ♌, or ♏; ♂ afflicted in the Asc. or 10th H. at B.; ♂ to the ill-asps. ☿ by dir.; ♂ Sig. □ or ☍ the ☉; ♂ afflictions to the ☉, ☽, ♄, or ☿ at B.; ♂ afflicted in the 3rd H.; ♂ Sig., and afflicted in ♈, ♉, ♊, ♍, ♏, ♐, ♒, or ♓; ♂ ☌ the ☉ at a Solar Rev.; ♂ passing over the place of the ☽, ♃, or ☿ at a Solar Rev.; ♂ afflicted in ♊ or ♍, and

♂ or ill-asp. the Asc. by dir.; ♂ to the ☋ the North Node of the ☽ (☊); ♂ by Periodic Rev. to the ill-asps. the ☉; ♂ holding dominion at B., and elevated above the Lights; the ☉ afflicted at B., and the ☉ to the bad asps. the Asc. by dir.; the ☉, ☽, or ☿ to the ☌, P., □ or ☍ ♂; the ☉ to the □ or ☍ the ☽ by dir., or vice versa; the progressed ☉ or ☽ to the ☌ or ill-asps. ♅ or ♂; the ☉ Sig. □ or ☍ ♂; the ☉ afflicted at B. by malefics, or ☌ violent fixed stars; the ☉ ☌ ♂ at a Solar Rev.; the ☉ directed to all nebulous clusters, and to Castor and Pollux, threatens quarrels; the ☽ □ ♂; the ☽ afflicted in ♏, the ☽ to the ☌ or ill-asp. ♂ by dir.; the ☽ to the ☌ ♂ by transit, or passing the place of the radical ♂ by tr., progression or dir.; the ☽ Sig. ☌ ♂; the ☽ Sig. □ or ☍ the ☉; the ☽ to the □ or ☍ ☿ by dir., and the ☽ hyleg, and ☿ afflicted at B.; the ☽ to the □ or ☍ ♃ by dir.; the ☽ Sig. in ♈ or ♏; the ☽ ♂ in the Asc. or 10th H.; the ☽ to the ☌ the Pleiades, Ascelli, or Praesepe; ♄ to the ill-asps. ♂ by dir.; ♄ ☌ or ill-asp. ♂ at B.; ♄ ☍ ♂ at B. in angles; ♄ Sig. in ♈, ♎, ♏, or ♓; ♃ Sig. □ or ☍ ☿, involved in strife, contention, and lawsuits; ♃ Sig. ☌ ♂, loses much by strife and contention; ♀ afflicted in ♏, contentious and jealous; ☿ afflicted at B., and ☿ to the evil asps. the Asc. by dir.; ☿ Sig. □ or ☍ ♄, ♃, or ♂; ☿ Sig. ☌, P., □, or ☍ ♂; ☿ Sig. in ♈ or ♌; the Asc. to the ☌ ♂ by dir.; the M.C. to the place the Pleiades or Pollux; the M.C. to the ☌ or P. asp. the ☉ if the ☉ is afflicted at B. by malefics, or ☌ violent fixed stars; the M.C. to the □ or ☍ the ☽; the M.C. to the ☌, P., □, or ☍ ♂ by dir.; lord of the 6th in the 7th, sickness caused by quarrels and fighting; many influences in fixed signs at B.; the 16° ♓ on the Asc. at B.; the 7th H., and its influences rule and concern quarrels; malefics afflicted in the 7th H. (See "Disputes", and the various paragraphs in this section).

Quarrelsome Persons — Danger From —♂ badly afflicted at B., and ♄ passing over the place of the radical ♂ by transit, or at a Solar Rev. (See Cuts, Death, Injury, Maimed, Mutilated, Stabs; "Quarrelsome", and the various paragraphs in this section).

Rape; Rash Disposition — (See Rashness).

Ravings; Reactionary; Reason—(See "Void Of" under Reason).

Rebellious; Recklessness; Reformers;

Refractory; Relatives—Quarrels With —Indicated by malefics in, or ruling the 3rd, 6th, 7th, 9th, or 12th Houses, according to which class of relatives. (See Brethren, Brothers, Family, Husband, Relatives, Sisters, Third House, Wife, etc.).

Religious Quarrels—(See Clergymen; Fanatical, Intolerance, under Religion).

Resentful; Resisting—(See Obstinate, Rebellious).

Restraint—(See "Lack Of" under Restraint).

Retains Anger—(See Anger).

Revengeful; Revolutionary; Riotous; Robbers; Rough; Ruffians;

Ruling Nature — (See Commanding; "Positive Nature" under Positive; Rule).

Sanguinary; Sarcastic; Saucy;

Savage; Scolding; Scornful;

Secret Enemies—Injury or Death By —(See "Secret Enemies" under Enemies).

Seditions; Self-Control—Lack of—(See Self-Control).

Self-Undoing; Servants—Hurts By— (See Servants).

Seventh House — Rules Quarrels, etc. (See "Rules" under Seventh House).

Severe Disposition—(See Severe).

Sharp Instruments—Hurts By— (See Instruments).

Shedding of Blood—(See "Bloodshed" in this section).

Sickness from Quarrels—Lord of the 6th in the 7th H.

Slaughter; Social Relations — Much Trouble In—(See Execreted, Love Affairs, Marriage, Neighbors, Relatives, Social, Society, etc.).

Socialism; Society—Much Discord In —(See "Discord" in this section).

Stabs; Stones — Injured by Flying Stones—(See "Assaults" under Stones).

Strangulation; Strife—Fond of—(See "Quarrelsome" in this section).

Stubborn—(See Obstinate, Rebellious).

Suicide; Suspicious — (See Jealousy, Mistrustful, Suspicious).

Sword—Injury by During Quarrels— (See Duels, Stabs, Sword).

Temper—(See Choleric, Fierce, Fury; "High Temper" under Temper; Vicious, Violent).

Thieves; Tragical Death—(See Tragical).

Treachery; Trouble-Maker — (See "Quarrelsome", and the various paragraphs in this section).

Tumults; Turbulent; Unbalanced;

Uncompromising — (See Independent, Obstinate, Positive, Stubborn).

Uncontrolled; Ungovernable;

Unreasonable; Unreliable; Vicious;

Violent; War; Weapons; Wicked;

Wife—(See "Troublesome" under Wife).

Women — (See "Quarrels" under Women).

Wounds — Received During Quarrels —(See Death, Hurts, Injuries, and the various paragraphs in this section. Also see the paragraphs under Wounds).

Wrath—(See Anger, Wrath).

QUARTAN AGUE — Quartan Fever— Quarternaries—An Intermittent Fever with a Paroxysm Every Fourth Day— (See "Quartan Ague" under Ague; Intermittent, Malaria, Remittent, Semi-Tertian).

QUARTERS — Quadrants — Quadratures —Quarters of the Heavens—Quarters of the Year—Quarters of the Moon— (See "Fullness of Fluids" under Fluids; "Women" under Misfortune; "Quarters" under Moon; Occidental, Oriental, Quadrants, Quadratures; "Quarters of the Year" under Year).

QUARTZ—(See Silica).

QUEENS — Danger of Death of — The appearance of a Comet in ♒. An Eclipse of the ☽ in the 2nd Decan. of ♉, death of a Queen in a Country ruled by ♉. Comets, or an eclipse of the ☽, in the ruling sign of any Country tend to the death of a Queen over such a Country, while an eclipse of the ☉ in such a sign tends to the death, murder, or assassination of a male Ruler. (See Famous; "The Great" under Great; "Death" under Kings; Lady).

QUEER—Queer Ideas, Actions, and Disposition—(See Eccentric, Fanatical, Fancies, Ideals, Ideas, Independent, Misunderstood, Notions, Opinions, Peculiar, Persecution, Reformers; "Ranters" under Religion, etc.).

QUERENT—Quesited—In Hor'y Questions, the Querent is the person who asks the question. The Significator of the Querent is the Asc.,, lord of the Asc., or a planet in the Asc. The Quesited is the person or thing asked about by the Querent. The Significator of the Quesited varies, and is usually the planet, house, or lord of a house, which rules the matter about which the Querent asks. (See Horary).

QUICK — Quickness—Quickened—Quickening—Quickened Action—

Action — Quick In Action — ♂ people are usually quick and active, and move about freely; ☿ ⚹ or △ the Asc., quick, and with an active body; ☿ Sig. in Hor'y Q. denotes a quick walk. (See Acceleration, Action, Active, Energy, Motion, Movement; the various paragraphs in this section).

Death—A Quick Death—♂ afflicted in the 8th H., or afflicting the hyleg from this house; ♅ afflicted in the 8th H. tends to a quick death, as by explosion, accident, electricity, machinery, or on a Railroad, etc. (See "Death by Accidents" under Accidents; Assassination, Extraordinary, Gunshot, Heights (Falls From); Murdered; "Death" under Sudden, Tragical, Untimely, etc.).

Dexterity — Quickness of Mind and Body—(See Dexterity).

Diseases—Quick Diseases—The Disease Terminates Quickly — A Rapid Disease—♂ rules quick and rapid diseases. The afflictor, or afflictors, in cardinal signs tend to a quick disease, severe, and soon over. The ☽, or cusp of the 6th H. in a cardinal, or movable sign, the disease terminates quickly, either in death or recovery. (See Acute, Course, Curtailed; "Illness" under Dangerous; "End of the Disease" under End; Ephemeral; "High Fever" under Fever; Fierce, Fulminating; "Diseases" under Painful; Pernicious, Poignant, Rapid; "Rapid" under Recuperation; Severe, Sharp; "Illnesses" under Short; Slight, Swift, Termination, Vehement; "Diseases" under Violent, etc.).

Disposition — A Quick Disposition — (See Anger, Choleric, Excitable, Hasty, Impulsive, Irascible, Irritable, Rashness; "High Temper" under Temper; "Tendency To" under Violence, etc.).

Energy—(See "Abundance of Energy" under Energy).

Eyes — A Quick Eye — (See "Quick Eye" under Eyes).

Fevers—Quick Fevers—Fierce Fevers —Sharp—(See "High Fevers", "Pernicious", "Violent", under Fevers).

Foetus Quickened—(See "Quickening" in this section).

Light and Quick — In Action — (See "Action" under Light).

Mentality — (See "Quickened" under Mentality, Mind).

Mind—A Quick Mind—Quick-Witted —Clever—(See "Active Mind" under Active; "Quickened" under Mentality).

Motion—Movement—Quick In—(See "Quick" under Motion, Movement).

Muscular Action—Quick Action—(See "Action" under Light; "Quick" under Motion, Movement; "Movements" under Muscles).

Nervous and Quick—(See Excitable; "Energetic" under Gait; Hasty; "High Strung" under High; "Quick and Nervous" under Speech).

Quickening — Of the Foetus — The ☉ produces the Quickening of the foetus. The quickening occurs, as a rule, at about the end of the fourth month of pregnancy, and when the ☽ is passing the same sign and degree she will be found in at birth. The position of the ☽ at the quickening, and at birth, is also said to be the Ascendant at conception, and the position of the ☽ at conception becomes the ascendant or descendant at birth. Also the Ascendant at the time of the quickening is said to be the sign and degree position of the ☽ at conception, or very near it. By a study of the Prenatal Epoch, and the Chart of Descent, it is an easy matter for the student to determine beforehand the exact time of the quickening, as it is so closely related to the ☽ and Asc. at conception, and the positions of the ☽ and Asc. at birth. This matter is quite thoroughly discussed, and with illustrated Charts, in Chap. XXVIII, in the book, "The Prenatal Epoch" by Mr. E. H. Bailey. The quickening occurs approximately at the half-way point between conception and birth, and at the time of the fifth libration of the ☽, as shown in the Chart of Descent. In a Horary Map the Quickening has taken place if the Dispositor of the ☽, and the lord of the hour be angular, or ♄ in the 7th H. If ♃ be in the 7th H. a male is indicated. (See Conception, Foetus, Gestation, Pregnancy, Prenatal Epoch).

Quicksilver—(See "Metal" under Mercury; Therapeutics).

Rapid — (See the paragraphs under Rapid).

Recovery—Recuperation—Quick Recovery from Disease — (See "Throws Off Disease Quickly" under Disease; Recovery, Recuperation; "Strong Resistance" under Resistance).

Sight—Quick Sight—(See Keen, Penetrating, Quick, under Eyes).

Speech — (See "Quick and Nervous" under Speech).

Temper—Quick Temper—(See Anger, Choleric, Excitable, Hasty, Irascible; "High Temper" under Temper).

Walk — A Quick Walk — (See "Energetic" under Gait; "Quick" under Walk).

QUICKENING — Of the Foetus — (See "Quickening" under Quick).

QUICKSILVER—The Metal ruled by ☿. (See "Metal" under Mercury; Therapeutics).

QUIET—Calm—Peaceful—Without Excitement—Tranquil—

Quiet Body—Quieting Influences Over the Mind and Body—(See Anaesthetics, Anaphrodisiacs, Anodyne, Calm, Contentment, Emollient, Happiness, Insensibility, Narcotics; "Peace of Mind" under Mind; Palliatives, Poise; "Illumination" under Religion; Sedatives, Sleep, Soothing, etc.).

Quiet Death—(See "Quiet Death" under Death).

Quiet Disposition — Harmless — Inoffensive—(See Calm, Cheerfulness, Contentment, Easy-Going, Gentle, Grave, Harmless, Humane, Indifferent, Inoffensive, Kind; "Amiable" under Manners; "Mild Disposition" under Mild; Modesty, Patient, Peaceful, Pleasant, Poise, Recluse, Reserved, Retiring, Shy, Spiritual, Taciturn; "Even Temper" under Temper, etc.).

Quieting Remedies—(See Anaesthetics, Anaphrodisiacs, Anodynes, Narcotics, Palliatives, Sedatives, Soothing, Soporific, etc.).

Sleep More Quiet — (See "Quiet" under Sleep).

QUININE — (See Cinchona; "Typical Drugs" under Mars).

QUINSY—(See "Quinsy" under Tonsils).

QUIVERING — Tremor—Trembling — Jerkings—Thrills—Spasmodic—

Eyeballs—Quivering of—(See "Quivering" under Eyeballs).

Muscles — Quiverings of — Spasmodic Action of — (See Contractions, Coordination, Cramps; "Movements" under Erratic; Incoordination, Intermittent, Involuntary, Irregular, Jerkings; "Motor Nerves" under Motor; Muscles (see the paragraphs under Muscles); Palpitation, Palsy, Paralysis, Paroxysms, Saint Vitus Dance, Spasmodic, Tics, Tremors, Twitchings, etc.).

QUOTIDIAN FEVER—Intermittent, and with a Daily Paroxysm—☿ influence; ☿ afflicted by ♂; ☿ sole ruler at an eclipse of the ☉ tends to a greater prevalence of daily fevers. (See Ague; "Fever" under Intermittent; Malaria, Remittent, etc.).

R

RABIES—Rabid—(See Hydrophobia).

RACEMOSE GLAND — A Gland Resembling a bunch of Grapes. The Pancreas is such a Gland. Also the Meibomian Glands of the Eyelids. These Glands are also called Aggregate Glands, as they are composed of a number of vesicles arranged in groups, or globules, and their arrangement gives the largest amount of secreting surface in the smallest space. These Glands come under the rule of the Sign ruling the part in which located. The Racemose Glands of the Eyelids are ruled by the ♈ sign. The Pancreas by the ♋ and ♍ signs. (See Glands, Pancreas).

RACES—The different Races and Nations of the Earth come under the rulership of the various Signs of the Zodiac. These rulerships are given in the Article on Nations. Races, their color of skin, and their special characteristics, have been established in the various parts of the Earth, and adapted to their location, and to play their part in the Grand Plan of Humanity. There are Sixteen Races in all in the scheme of the Evolution of our Planet. For a good discussion of the Origin of Races, their time and endurance, destiny, etc., see the book, "Cosmo-Conception" by Max Heindel. (See Barrenness; "Black Skin" under Black; Complexion, Hair, Nations, Negro; "Sixth Sub-Race" under Neptune; Pigment, White; "Complexion" under Yellow).

RACHITIS—Rachitic—(See Rickets).

RADICAL MAP—(See Horoscope, Map, Nativity, Radix, Star Map).

RADICALISM—(See "Impractical Ideals" under Ideals; Reactionary, Religion).

RADIUM—Ruled by ♅. This planet has a radio-active influence. Pitch-Blende and Polonium, radio-active substances, and closely related to Radium, are also ruled by ♅. Some Writers also say Radium is ruled by ♆. (See Neptune, Pitch-Blende, Polonium, Uranus).

RADIUS—The Small Bone of the Forearm—The Radius is under the structural rulership of the ♌ sign, and also influenced by ♊, and disorders, or fractures to the bones of the forearm, as the Radius and Ulna, and also the Wrists, are caused by afflictions in ♌, and especially ♄ or ♂ afflicted in this sign, or in ♊. (See "Accidents", "Broken Arms", under Arms; Forearm). Case—Radius of Left Arm Fractured—See "Saturn in the Tenth", No. 831 in 1001 N.N.

Radius Missing — (See "Missing" under Forearm).

RADIX—The Radical Map—The Chart of Birth—The Nativity—Radix means "Root", and the Map of Birth is the Root Map, a foundation map upon which you are to build. The Radix Map shows the Permanent Habit, or Hexis, of the diseases to which you will be subject, your fundamental tendencies, and your relationship to external conditions, environment, etc. The Directions and Progressions of the planets over this map show the Diathesis, or Transient Disposition of the disease. Diseases indicated by the radical map tend to be constitutional, organic, structural, deep-seated, and if neglected and allowed to progress, to become chronic, morbid, malignant, and fatal. The Prenatal Epoch Map also shows fundamental conditions and tendencies, and should be studied in connection with the radical, or map of birth. (See Acquired, Character, Chronic, Diathesis, Directions, Fate, Fortune, Heredity, Hexis, Map, Nativity, Organic, Prenatal Epoch, Progressions, Star Map, Structural, etc.).

RAGE—Anger—Fury—Fierce—Raging — Raging Fevers, etc. — (See Anger; "Brain Storms" under Brain; "Beside Oneself" under Excitable; "High Fevers" under Fever; Fierce, Frenzy, Fury, Madness, Quarrels, Ravings, Riotous; "High.Temper" under Temper; Violent, Wrath, etc.).

RAILROADS — Public Conveyances — Vehicles — Street Railways, etc. — The Third House is the house of Short Journeys, Inland Journeys, as by Rail, or any class of Vehicle. Also ☿, the ruler of the 3rd H. influences fundamentally, and the ⊓ sign, which sign is affiliated with the 3rd H., have strong rule over short journeys and travel by land. Uranus is said to especially rule Railroads. Benefics in the 3rd H. at B., and with no malefics afflicting this house, make short journeys fortunate, and with less liability of accidents, injury, or death during inland travel. Malefics in, or ruling this house, make travel and short journeys, railroad, bus, automobile, or aeroplane travel very dangerous, and especially when the directions to the 3rd H., planets in this house at B., or to the ruler of the 3rd H., are bad. Before going on a journey by train, or other vehicle, every person should study the planetary conditions over them at the time, and be warned of impending dangers, or benefits, and by so doing travel could be reduced to a scientific basis, and many deaths and serious injuries avoided. In a serious railroad accident, those who are under bad directions are the ones who usually suffer, while the more fortunate escape. The opposite house, the 9th H., rules voyages, long journeys, and Foreign Travel. (See Journeys, Third House, Travel, Vehicles).

Accidents—Danger of Accidents, Injury, Misfortune, Delays, etc., on Short Journeys, Railroads, Vehicles, and Inland Travel—The ☽ in the 3rd H. at B., ♂, or evil asp. any of the malefic planets, and especially ♅; the ☽ in the 3rd H. at B., and to the ♂ or ill-asp. ♅ by dir.; the ☽ in the 3rd H. at the Vernal Equinox, and afflicted, greater danger in travel, and a prevalence of railroad accidents; ♅ afflicted in ⊓ or the 3rd H. at B.; ♃ afflicted in the 3rd H., but escapes injury, or serious hurt; ♄ ℞ by transit, and in ♂, □, or ☍ ☿ ℞; ♂ afflicted in ⊓ or the 3rd H. at B., and also ♂ afflicted by dir.; ♂ in the 1st H., and afflicted by ♃; ♂ to the cusp the 3rd H. by dir.; ♂ progressed to the ♂, P, □, or ☍ ☿, or vice versa; ♂ by Periodic Rev. to the ♂, □, or ☍ ♅, or to the ill-asps. the ☽, and especially if ♂ is in the 3rd H. at B.; ♂ in the 3rd H., in □ or ☍ the ☉ or ☽; ☿ afflicted in the 8th H.; malefics afflicted in the 3rd H.; lord of the 8th a malefic, in the 3rd H., and afflicted; lord of the 11th a malefic, and afflicted in the 3rd H. at B.; the 2nd Decan. of ⊓ on the Asc., which

decan. is ruled by ♂. (See "Short Journeys" under Journeys; "Accidents" under Travel; Vehicles; the various paragraphs in this section). Case—Injured In a Railroad Accident—See Fig. 21 in "Message of the Stars" by the Heindels. See "Strange Case, No. 405 in 1001 N.N. Also see Cases under Vehicles.

Death On Railways—Death On a Short Journey—Principally caused by the afflictions of ♅ to the hyleg if ♅ afflict the 3rd H. at B., and especially if this planet holds the dominion of death, and the radical map denotes a violent death; ♅ afflicting the hyleg by dir.; ♅ afflicted at B., and to the ♂, P, □ or ☍ the Asc. by dir., and especially if the Asc. be hyleg; the ☽ in the 3rd H. at B., and to the ♂ or P. asp. ♅ by dir.; the ☽ in the 3rd H. at the Vernal, lady of the year, and afflicted, many deaths on railroads; lord of the 8th H. a malefic, and afflicted in the 3rd H.; many afflictions in cardinal signs show. (See Avalanches; "Notorious Death" under Death; "Death" under Journeys, Travel, Vehicles). Cases of Death in Railroad Accidents—See "Luckless Youth", No. 390; "Run Over", No. 853; "Dey", No. 803; "Strafford", No. 814, all in 1001 N.N. Also see the Cases of Death under Vehicles.

RAIN—Moisture—Rain Storms—

Too Much Rain — Violent Rains — Floods — Excess of Rain, and Much Damage, Suffering, and Loss of Life by Rain, Storms, Water, etc.—An eclipse of the ☉ or ☽ in watery signs, and especially in places ruled by them; the ☽ applying to ♄; there tends to be more rain during the increase of the ☽; ♄ lord of the year at the Vernal, and with ♄ in an angle and direct in motion; ♄ in ⊓ at the Vernal, angular, and direct in motion; ♄ ♂ ♃ in a water sign; ♃ ♂ ♂, mischief by rains; malefics in the 3rd or 9th H., in watery signs, and afflicting the ☉ or ☽, the native is more apt to encounter floods and severe storms on journeys or voyages; coincident with the appearance of Comets, and especially Halley's Comet; Comets appearing in Western Quarters of the heavens tend to cause aqueous vapors; the ♒ sign ascending at the Vernal tends to over-moist air, excess of rain, and much damage and suffering, and espec. in places ruled by this sign; ♋ or ♏ ascending at the Vernal, and the ☽ weak and afflicted, Countries under these signs suffer much damage and sickness from excessive rains and floods. (See Clouds, Comets, Floods; "Wet Journeys" under Journeys; Lightning; "Abundance", "Superabundance", under Moisture; Storms, Thunder, Waters, Weather).

Not Enough Rain — (See Drought, Famine, Fountains).

RAKISHNESS—(See Debauched, Dissolute, Lewd, Prodigal, Profligate, etc.).

RAMBLING—

Rambling Nature — (See "Many Changes" under Residence; Vagabond, Wanderer).

Rambling Speech — (See "Mental Chaos" under Chaotic; "Mind" under Confusion; "Rambling" under Speech).

RANSOM—Held for Ransom—(See Captive).

RANULA — A Cystic Tumor Under the Tongue — (See "Cystic Tumor" under Tongue).

RAPACIOUS — Extortionate— Plundering—Grasping—Caused principally by a weak, afflicted, and ill-dignified ♄ at B., and when ♂ adds his adverse influences, violence in attaining ends may be added. (See Assassins; "Evilly Disposed" under Evil; Highwaymen, Miserly, Pirates, Rapine, Ravenous, Selfishness, Thieves, Violent, etc.).

RAPE — Attackers of Women — The ☉ directed to all Nebulous Clusters, and to Castor and Pollux, threatens the native with Rape, or to commit such; ♅, ♄, or ♂ in ♏; ♂ ☌ ♀ in ♏. (See Cruel, Degenerate, Depraved, Lewd; "Low and Base" under Low; "Violence" under Passion; Perversions, Seduction, Shameless).

RAPID—Accelerated—

 Rapid Action—(See Acceleration, Action, Active, Exaggerated, Quick).

 Rapid Breathing—(See "Rapid" under Breathing).

 Rapid Dyspnoea—(See Dyspnoea).

 Rapid Fevers — (See "High Fevers" under Fever).

 Rapid Heart Action — (See "Rapid" under Heart, Pulse).

 Rapid Motion — (See Motion, Movement, Quick).

 Rapid Physical Growth—(See Giants; "Abnormal Growth" under Growth).

 Rapid Planets — The Effect of the Planets When More Rapid, or Direct In Motion — (See Direct; "Degree of Disturbance" under Disturbance).

 Rapid Pulse — (See "Rapid" under Pulse).

 Rapid Recovery—From Disease—(See Recovery; "Rapid" under Recuperation; "Good" under Resistance).

 Rapid Respiration—(See "Rapid" under Breathing).

 Rapid Speech — (See "Rapid" under Speech).

 Rapid Walk—(See "Energetic" under Gait).

RAPINE—Thefts—Spoliation—Pillaging—Plundering—Rapacious, etc.—Prevalence of—An eclipse of the ☉ in the 3rd Decan. of ♌, or the 2nd Decan. of ♒; an eclipse of the ☽ in the 1st Decan. of ♊, the 1st Decan. of ♐, or the 3rd Decan. of ♓. (See Bandits, Highwaymen, Piracy, Rapacious, Robberies, Thefts, Thieves).

RARELY ILL — (See "Abundance of Health" under Health; Immunity; "Good" under Vitality).

RASHES—Eruptions—An Exanthematous Eruption on the Skin—Rashes are diseases of ♂, and also strongly ruled by the ♑ sign, and afflictions in ♑. (See Efflorescence; "Hot Eruptions" under Eruptions; Itch, Measles, Nettle Rash (see Hives, Urticaria); Pimples, Pruritis, Roseola, Rubefacient, Scarlatina, Skin Diseases).

RASHNESS—Rash Acts—Hasty—Rash Disposition — Self-Motived Acts — Precipitate — Turbulent — Inconsiderate — Foolhardy — Recklessness — Choleric — Lack of Forethought — Indiscreet — Lack of Judgment and Discrimination, etc.—Rashness is principally a ♂ influence, and with ♂ strong at B., in the Asc. or M.C., or afflicting the ☉, ☽, or Asc.; ♂ in an angle, and afflicted by the ☉, ☽, or other planets, by the □ or 8 aspects from angles; the ♂ signs ♈ and ♏ when strong, and especially with ♂ therein, tend to rashness; ♂ afflicted in the 1st H.; ♂ to the cusp of the 1st H. by dir.; ♂ ill-dignified at B., and afflicted; ♂ configurated with ☿; ♂ elevated above, and in evil asp. to the ruling planet; ♂ ☌ ☿ at B.; ♂ to the place of ☋ by dir.; ♂ afflicted in ♈, 8, ♏, ♐, ♑, or ♒; ♂ progressed to the ☌, □, or 8 ☿; fixed stars of the nature of ♂ and ☿ ascending at B.; the ☉ ☌, □, or 8 ♂ at B.; the ☉ to the ☌ or ill-asp. ♂ by dir. or progression; the ☉ rising at B., and afflicted by ♂; the ☉ in the Asc., and in □ to ♂ in the 10th; the ☉ □ or 8 ☽, and especially when the Lights are also afflicted by ♂ or ♅; the ☽ ☌ or ill-asp. ♂ at B. and by dir.; the ☽ Sig. ☌ the ☉ or ♂; the ☽ Sig. in ♈ or ♏; ♅ ☌, P, □ or 8 the ☽, ♂, or ☿ at B., and by dir.; ♃ afflicted in ♈; ♃ to the ☌ or ill-asp. ♂ by dir.; ♃ in □ near violent fixed stars; ♃ Sig. in ♏, rashness, and often resulting in serious losses; ♃ Sig. in □ near Aldebaran or the Bull's North Horn; ♄ Sig. ☌ ♂, or vice versa; ♀ Sig. ✶ or △ ♂, rash and inconsiderate; ☿ Sig. ☌, P, □, or 8 ♂; ☿ Sig. in ♐, rash to his own injury; the 16° ♌ on the Asc. Rashness is a characteristic of the Choleric, or Bilious Temperament, ruled by the ☉, ♂, and the Fiery Signs. (See Anarchists, Anger; "Animal Instincts" under Animal; Bold, Choleric, Cruel, Dangerous; "Causes His Own Death" under Death; Destructiveness, Duels; "His Own Worst Enemy" under Enemies; Emotions, Erratic, Excitable; "Mental Extremes" under Extremes; Feelings, Fierce, Fiery, Fighting, Folly, Foolhardy; "Lack Of" under Forethought; Frenzy, Fury, Hasty, Imprudent, Impulses, Indiscreet, Inordinate; "Bad" under Judgment; Madness, Malicious; "Unbalanced" under Mentality; Murderous, Obstinate, Perverse, Precipitate, Quarrelsome, Recklessness, Revengeful, Riotous, Savage, Self-Control, Self-Undoing, Severe Disposition; "High Temper" under Temper; Temperaments, Treachery, Turbulent, Unbridled, Uncontrolled, Ungovernable, Vicious, Violent, etc.).

 Death — From Rash Actions — (See "Causes His Own Death" under Death; Folly; "Death" under Imprudence).

 Disease or Injury — The Result of Rash Acts and Irregularities—Caused by the ☉ and ♂, the positive, electric, and heat-producing planets, and by afflictions to these bodies. (See "Brings Disease Upon Himself" under Disease; Folly; "Lack Of" under Forethought; Imprudent, Indiscretions, Intemperance; "Disease" under Irregularities; "Health Injured", "Injured Thru Women", under Men; Recklessness).

Free from Rash Actions—The ☽ Sig. in ♋, and well-aspected. (See Gentle, Harmless, Humane, Kind, Mild; "Even Temper" under Temper).

Painful Complaints—Due to Rashness—The Result of Self-Motivated Acts—Caused by the afflictions of the ☉ and ♂. (See "Painful Complaints" under Forethought; "Disease or Injury" in this section).

RATIONAL FACULTIES—The Reasoning Faculties—Ruled by ☿. (See Comprehension, Coordination, Faculties, Fears, Insanity, Intellect, Intuition, Irrational, Judgment, Mentality, Mind, Perception, Reason, Thinking, Understanding). Aquarius is classed as a Rational Sign of the Zodiac.

RATIONALISM — The Formation of Opinions from Reason Alone — Not Drawing Upon the Intuitive or Spiritual Powers to Reach Conclusions—The Earthy Signs strong, predominant, and well-filled with planets at B., and holding the Asc., angles, etc. Also ♄ strong and predominant at B., and in an earthy sign, tends to Rationalism. Also caused by ☿ when this planet partakes of the nature of ♄, and is in an earthy sign. The watery signs, when prominent and well-occupied at B., are quite free from Rationalism and Materialism. (See Materialism, Radicalism, Reactionary, Revolutionary).

RATTLE-BRAINED—Rapid and Noisy Talk—Talking Rapidly, Foolishly, and with Little Depth of Thought — (See "Shallow" under Mentality; "Light in Mind" under Mind; "Rapid" under Speech).

RAVENOUS — Furiously Rapacious or Hungry — Rapacious — Violent — ♂ ill-dignified at B., and afflicted. (See Rapacious, Rapine; "Tendency To" under Violence).

Ravenous Appetite—(See "Abnormal" under Appetite; Cravings, Gluttony, Hunger).

RAVING — Ravings — The ☽ in ♌ and afflicted by the ☉ or ♂ when taken ill (Hor'y). (See Cruel, Delirium, Demoniac, Drink, Fanatical, Fury; "Outrageous" under Insanity; Madness, Mania, Vicious, Violent, etc.).

RAW—Crude—Unrefined—Bleak—Chilling—Coarse—Caused by the ♄ and ♑ influences; ♄ rising in the Asc.; ♑ on the Asc.

Raw-Boned Body—(See "Raw-Boned" under Bones; Spare, Thin, Ugly, Ungainly).

Raw Food—(See "Cooked Foods" under Food; "Vegetarians" under Vegetables).

Raw Humours—In the Stomach—(See "Raw Humours" under Indigestion).

Raw, Tanned Appearance — Raw, Tanned, Leathery Appearance — (See "Tan" under Complexion).

RAYNAUD'S DISEASE—(See Fingers).

REACTION—Opposite Signs of the Zodiac, as ♉ and ♏, affect each other by reaction. Also signs in ☐ aspect to each other tend to have an unfavorable reactionaly influence upon each other, as ♈, ♋, ♎, and ♑. There is also the reaction of the Planets upon each other by their ☌, ☐, ☍, and other aspects, when within orb of aspect. The unfavorable reactions of Signs and Planets upon each other tend to produce affliction, discord, disease, and inharmony, except as they are ruled and transmuted. Planets in any of the fixed signs tend to react upon all of the fixed signs, and also with the cardinal and mutable signs. The stomach, ruled by the ♋ sign, is afflicted by planets in all the cardinal signs, or when these signs are on the Asc. Planets in ♏, the sex sign, also afflict the throat, ruled by the ♉ sign, etc. (See Action, Antipathy, Aspects, Opposites, Orbs, Removal, Sympathy).

REACTIONARY TENDENCY — Violent or Sweeping Methods of Procedure—The Fixed Sign influences, combined with a very strong ♄ influence at B., and with the cardinal and mutable signs in weaker positions; ♅ strong and prominent at B., as in the Asc. or M.C., and ☌ the ☉, ☽, or ☿, often tends to very radical characteristics, and a desire to bring about great Reforms, even tho resorting to violence. (See Anarchists, Fanatical, Radicalism, Rationalism, Reformers, Religion, Revolutionary, Sedition, Violence, etc.).

READAPTATION — In the System — ♏ influence. (See Recovery, Restoration, Scorpio).

READING—Study—

Blindness—Blindness from Over-Study and Too Much Reading—(See "Reading and Study" under Blindness).

Brain Fag—From Too Much Reading and Study — (See "Brain Fag" under Brain; "Mind" under Fatigue; "Ocular Headaches" under Headaches; "Over-Study" under Study).

Disease — And Ill-Health from Too Much Reading and Study—☿ afflicting the Asc., the ☽, and the Dispositors of the ☉ and ☽, causes disease from too intense application. (See "Over-Exertion" under Exertion).

Fond of Reading — (See Learning, Scholar, Study).

Myopia—From Too Much Reading—The ☽ Sig. ☌ the ☉, danger of. (See "Myopia" under Sight).

Reading Prodigy—Child Reads at Three Years of Age—Reads Darwin and Huxley at Eight Years of Age—(See "Child Prodigy" under Prodigies).

REAR PARTS — Of the Body — Hinder Parts — (See Back, Buttocks, Dorsal, Front, Loins; "Back Part" under Marks; Shoulders, Spine, Vertebrae, etc.).

REARED WITH DIFFICULTY — (See "Reared" under Children).

REASON — The Reasoning Faculties — The Rational Faculties—The Rational Mind—Ruled by ☿, and the Principle of ☿ is Reason. Uranus and ☿ are termed the Mental Planets, and greatly influence the Mind. Reason finds expression thru the planet ☿, and the good aspects to ☿ tend to a good mind, and to act as a check upon the lower nature. By many Authors ♅ is considered the higher octave of ☿. The Rational Mind corresponds to the Stars;

the Subconscious Mind to the ☽, and the Superconscious Mind to the ☉. (See "Influence Of" under Mercury, Uranus. Also see the paragraphs under Intellect, Mental, Mind, Perception, Rational, Thinking, Understanding). The following subjects and paragraphs have to do with the Reasoning Faculties, which see in the alphabetical arrangement when only listed here—

Detriments—To the Reasoning Faculties—(See "Mental Chaos" under Chaotic; Confusion, Idiocy, Insanity; "Bad" under Judgment; "Weak Mind" under Mind; "Weak" in this section).

Emotions—(See "Arrested Emotions" under Emotions).

Erratic Mind—(See "Mind" under Erratic).

Erring; Fears; Feelings — Predominance of Feeling Over Intellect—(See Feelings).

Forethought — Lack of — (See Forethought).

Ideals; Ideas; Idiocy; Imbecility;

Impaired — The Reasoning Faculties Impaired—The ☽ □ or ☍ ☿, and neither in any way connected with the Asc.; ♃ □ or ☍ the ☽. (See Idiocy, Insanity; "Bad" under Judgment; "Weak Mind" under Mind).

Impulses — (See "Blind" under Impulses).

Insanity; Intellect — (See the paragraphs under Intellect).

Irrational; Irresponsible; Judgment—(See "Bad" under Judgment).

Loss of Reason—(See Foolish, Idiocy, Imbecile, Insanity, Irrational; "Void Of" in this section).

Mental—Mind—(See the subjects under Mentality, Mind).

Monsters; Not Governed by Reason—(See Feelings, Foolhardy; "Impractical" under Ideals; Impulses, Irrational, Rashness, Recklessness, etc.).

Perception; Prejudiced;

Reasonableness—An Open Mind—The Airy Signs prominent at B., and ☿ strong and well-aspected, tend to give a reasonable mind, open to conviction, the study of Truth, and to gain new viewpoints. The ♊, ♍, ♎, and ♒ people are especially open to discussion and new points of view, while the watery signs strong at B. tend to prejudice, aversion to new ideas which disturb their fixed beliefs, while the earthy signs tend to give narrow and materialistic views and opinions. The planet ♅ strong at B. tends to give a wide mental outlook, and the ☉ influence the widest range for the emotions. (See Ideals, Ideas, Judgment, Materialism, Metaphysics, Occult, Opinions, Prejudiced, Rationalism, Reactionary).

Strengthened—The Reasoning Faculties Strengthened—♃ in good asp. to the ☽ and ☿; ☿ well-aspected by the ☽, and with ☿ in good aspect to the Asc.; ☿ free from the affliction of malefics. (See "Good" under Judgment; "Quickened" under Mental; "Strong Mind" under Mind).

Thought—Little Depth of Thought or Mature Reasoning — ☿ afflicted in ♋.

(See "Void Of" under Learning; "Shallow" under Mentality; "Light In Mind" under Mind; Pretender).

Unbalanced Mind—(See Balanced, Incoordination, Insanity, Irrational, Madness, Mania; "Unbalanced" under Mentality; "Void Of" in this section).

Understanding — (See "Weak" under Understanding).

Unreasonable—Not According to Reason — Irrational — (See Anarchists; "Mind" under Erratic; Erring; "Mental Extremes" under Extremes; Fanatical; "Fixed Signs" under Fixed; "Impractical" under Ideals; Ideas, Intractable, Irrational, Obstinate, Perverse, Radicalism, Rashness, Reactionary, Rebellious, Recklessness, Revolutionary, Ungovernable, Unruly).

Unsound Mind — (See "Unsound" under Mind).

Void of Reason — This condition is usually caused by prenatal conditions, and the afflictions during gestation, as in cases of Idiots, Imbeciles, Monsters, etc. Some important Prenatal causes are—The ☉ and ☽ at the time of the New or Full ☽ previous to birth forming no aspect to the Asc., and having no help from the Benefics ♃ and ♀, and also the angles, as the 1st and 10th H., occupied by malefics. Evil aspects to ☿ at the same time tend to unbalance the mentality, make void of reason, and the mind undefinable. If ♅, ♄, or ♂ give testimony in any of the foregoing positions, what is then generated will have ungovernable and irrational qualities. (See Foolish, Idiocy, Imbecile, Inhuman, Insanity, Monsters, Prenatal Epoch).

Weak Reasoning Faculties — (See "Mental Chaos" under Chaotic; Confusion; "Mind" under Erratic; Erring, Foolish; "Lack Of" under Forethought; Idiocy, Imbecile; "Mental" under Incompetency; Irrational; "Bad" under Judgment; "Weak Mind" under Mind; Precipitate; "Impaired", and the various paragraphs in this section).

Well-Balanced Mind—(See "Strengthened" in this section; "Good" under Judgment, Intellect, Understanding; "Quickened" under Mentality; "Good", "Strong", "Sound", "Talented", under Mind; "Acute" under Perception, etc.).

REBELLIOUS — Unruly — Refractory — Antagonistic—Contrary—Hostile—♂ is the author of rebellion, hostility, and of antagonism, war, etc. Caused by ☿ ill-dignified at B., and afflicted by the ☽ and ♂; many planets in fixed signs at B., and with these signs upon the angles; ♉ on the Asc., and ♂ afflicted in ♉. (See Erring; "Fixed Signs" under Fixed; Intractable, Irascible, Irritable, Obstinate, Perverse, Rashness, Reactionary, Reformers, Refractory, Revolutionary, Sedition; "High Temper" under Temper; Ungovernable, Unruly, etc.).

RECEPTACLES—The ☽ governs all Receptacles in the body, and the fluids in them, as the Stomach, Bladder, Uterus, etc. (See Cavities).

RECEPTIVITY—Reception—Receptive — The principle of the ☽ is receptivity, and people born under the strong influence of the ☽, the ☽ as ruler, or who have many planets in the negative and feminine signs of the Zodiac, are more receptive and susceptible to external and outside influences, and to environment. (See Environment, External, Hyperaesthesia, Influenced; "Influence Of" under Moon; Mutable, Negative, Susceptibility, etc.).

Semen—The Seed—The receptivity of the semen into the womb is ruled by the ☽. (See Fecundation, Fertile, Semen).

RECKLESSNESS — Wild — Hasty— Desperate— Foolhardy — Impulsive—Indiscreet, etc. — Caused principally by ♂ influences and afflictions; ♂ elevated above, and in evil asp. to the ruling planet; ♂ progressed to the ♂ or ill-asp. ♄, ♀, or ☿, or vice versa; ♂ afflicted in ♌, or afflicting the ☉, ☽, or Asc. from this sign; ♂ to the cusp the 11th H.; the ☉ in ♑ and afflicted by ♂, hasty and reckless at times; the ☉ to the ♂ or ill-asp. ♂ by dir.; the Prog. ☉ or ☽ to the ♂ or ill-asp. ♂; ♅ by transit to the ♂ ♂, ☿, or the ☽ in the radical map, or vice versa; ♃ to the ill-asps. ♂ by dir.; ♀ in ♌ and afflicted by ♂, hasty and reckless at times; ♀ afflicted at B., and to the ♂ or ill-asp. the Asc. by dir.; ☿ afflicted in ♈; ☿ ♂ or ill-asp. ♂ at B., or by dir.; the 4° ♋ or ♐, or 3° ♓ on the Asc. at B. (See Anger, Choleric, Erratic, Erring, Excitable, Explosive, Foolhardy; "Lack Of" under Forethought; Fury, Hasty, Imprudent, Impulsive, Indiscreet, Irascible, Judgment, Perverse, Precipitate, Quarrelsome, Rashness, Reactionary, Riotous; "High Temper" under Temper; Vicious, Violent, etc.).

RECLUSE — Secretive — Solitariness — Fond of Seclusion—Aversion to Society — Reserved — Retiring — Separateness, etc.—Caused by ♄, ♆, and the 12th H. influences; ♄ or ♆ in the 4th H., a recluse in old age, and usually ends life in seclusion; ♄ in the 1st H., shy and fond of solitude; ♄ ruler of the Asc., or horoscope, and afflicted; ♄ strong at B., and rising, a confederate in secrecy; ♄ afflicted in ♍; ♄ in the 12th H. leads to a secluded life; ♄ is the author of solitariness; born under ♄; ♄ ☐ or ☍ ☿ at B., and by dir.; the ☉ in the 4th H., and afflicted by ♄, inclined to secrecy; ☿ rising in ♍, contemplative, fond of retirement, and to dwell alone; ☿ ☐ or ☍ ♄; strong ☿ influence at B.; ruler of the Asc. in the 12th H.; the 15° ♉, the 13th and 30° ♎, the 12th and 21° ♑, or the 2nd and 3° ♒ on the Asc. at B.; the 1st Decan. of ♍, ruled by the ☉, on the Asc. (See Aversions, Backwardness, Bashfulness, Celibacy, Miserly, Mistrustful, Misunderstood, Modesty; "Asylum" under Old Age; "Free from Passion" under Passion; Renunciation, Reserved, Retiring, Saturn, Seclusion, Secretive, Self-Denying, Shy, Solitude, Suspicious, Twelfth House, etc.).

RECOLLECTION—(See Memory).

RECONDENSATION — (See Sublimation).

RECOVERY—Recovery from Disease— Convalescence — Recuperation — Pros-

pects of Recovery, etc. — See the following subjects in the alphabetical arrangement when not considered here—

Amelioration—The Abatement of the Disease — (See Amelioration; "Better" under Disease; Moderation).

Better—The Disease Changes for the Better—(See "Better" under Disease).

Certain— Recovery Is Certain—If at decumbiture the ☽ is applying to the ☉, or to benefics, and with small affliction to the hyleg from malefics, recovery is certain. (See "Rapid" under Recuperation; "Good" under Resistance, Vitality; "Will Recover" in this section).

Child Will Recover—The Child Sickly But Will Recover—(See "Sickly" under Children).

Complications; Continuity of Disease —(See Continuity).

Convalescence — (See Amelioration, Better, Moderation, Patient Will Recover, Resolution, in this section).

Crises In Disease—(See Crises).

Curable Diseases—(See Curable).

Cured, But Has Relapse — (See Relapse).

Dangerous Maladies — (See Dangerous).

Decrease—The Disease Will Decrease —The Disease Will Remove Shortly— Lord of the Asc. stronger than lord of the 6th; a malefic leaving the 6th H., the disease will remove shortly, in so many days or weeks, according to the nature of the sign; the ☽ sepr. from a malefic and applying to a benefic. (See Amelioration; "Better" under Disease; Moderation, Resolution).

Delayed Recovery—(See "Disease Delayed" under Delays; "Worse" under Disease; "Disease" under Increase; "Delayed" under Pneumonia; Relapse).

Denoted — Recovery Denoted — (See "Patient Will Recover" in this section).

Difficult to Cure—(See "Difficult" under Cure; Incurable, Obstinate).

Doubtful Recovery — The Illness Is Not Without Peril—Little Hope of Recovery—The ☽ at decumbiture under the Sun's beams, or ♂ ♄ or ♂, and with no assistance of the benefics to the ☽; lord of the Asc., or the ☽, combust, and applying to the ☉, and if not applying at the same time to a benefic, the danger is imminent (Hor'y); lord of the Asc., or the ☽, in ♂ lord of the 8th; lord of the Asc., or the ☽, applying by evil asp. to lord of the 8th, and if the latter be a malefic, death is considered certain; lord of the 1st in the 4th or 8th, and afflicted; lord of the 8th in an angle, and lord of the 1st cadent and afflicted; lord of the 8th in the 10th, or lord of the 1st in the 4th, 6th, or 7th H.; lord of the Asc., or the ☽, with violent fixed stars; an evil application to lord of the 8th is considered a fatal symptom; a malefic in the 6th H. (See "Arguments for Death", "Certain Death", under Death; Fatal).

Duration of Disease—(See Duration).

End of the Disease—(See "End of the Disease" under Disease, End; "Disease" under Termination).

Expected—Recovery Expected—(See "Patient Will Recover" in this section).

Hard to Cure — (See Chronic; "Difficult" under Cure; Incurable, Lingering, Long Diseases, Slow Diseases, Tedious, etc.).

Health Better — (See "Better" under Health).

Hopes of Recovery—(See "Doubtful", "Patient Will Recover", in this section; "Certain Death" under Death; Fatal, Incurable).

How Long Before Recovery? Used in Hor'y Questions—Observe the lord of the Asc. Observe what benefic planet is applying to an aspect of the lord of the Asc. Note what Signs and Houses they are in, whether in angles, moveable Signs, etc., and then frame the measure of time according to the quality of the disease. If the planet be angular, and the sign moveable, judge the time of recovery as many days as there are degrees to complete the aspect. If the planet be succedent, and the sign common, judge recovery in as many weeks as there are degrees to complete the aspect. If the planet be cadent, and the sign fixed, judge recovery to take place in as many months as there are degrees to complete the aspect. If the sign be common in which the application is, use discretion, according to the nature of the disease, and not by any fast rule of days, weeks, or months. The quick or slow motion of the ☽, the sign she is in, and her situation as to angles, often tends to hasten or retard the progress towards recovery. The patient often recovers very quickly when the lord of the Asc. quits the sign he is in, and enters one in which he has dignities. If a common sign be 28° on the cusp of the 6th H., judge that the disease will vary, or resolve itself in two weeks. (See Acute, Chronic, Continuity, Course, Crises, Curable; "Arguments for Death", "Certain Death", under Death; Duration, Fatal, Incurable, Lingering; "Long Diseases" under Long; "Short Diseases" under Short; Slow, Tedious, etc.).

Important — The Disease Is Not Important—(See "The Disease Will Soon End" under End; Mild, Slight).

Impossible—Recovery Almost Impossible—♄ afflicted in the 6th H. (See "Certain Death" under Death; "The Sick Will Hardly Escape" under Escape; Fatal, Incurable, Invalids, Wastings; "Doubtful" in this section).

Improved—The Sick Improved—(See Amelioration; "Better" under Disease; "Disease" under Improved; Moderation; "Rapid" under Recuperation; Resolution).

Increase — The Disease Will Increase —(See Crises; "Worse" under Disease; "Disease" under Increase).

Incurable; Little Hope of Recovery— (See Doubtful, Impossible, in this section).

Long Diseases — (See Chronic; "Diseases" under Lingering, Long, Prolonged, Slow, Tedious, etc.).

Moderation of Disease — The Disease Will Moderate—(See Amelioration, Crises; "Better" under Disease; Improved, Moderation, Modification).

Modification of Disease—(See Amelioration, Complications, Crises; "Better", "Worse", under Disease; Moderation, Modification, Relapse, etc.).

Old Diseases Return—(See Return).

Patient Will Recover—Testimonies of Recovery—Signs of Recovery—The ☽ leaving the ♑ the ☉, and applying to the ✶ or △ ♃ or ♀; the ☽ sepr. from malefics and applying to benefics, and without prohibition or frustration; the ☽ applying to a benefic in power, the former health is restored; the ☽ in the houses of ♃ or ♀, or in her own house, and free from the affliction of malefics; the ☽ applying to ♃ or ♀ by good aspect, or to the good asp. the ☉; the ☽ ☌ ♃ denotes recovery, but slower when in ♑; the ☽ incr. in light, in a good house, and applying to the good asp. the lord of the Asc.; the ☽ well-dignified, or in the Asc., or in ✶ or △ the Asc.; the ☽ applying to the lord of the Asc. by good asp., and not afflicted by lords of the 6th or 8th; the ☽ void of course at the beginning of the sickness, but at her next crisis forming a ✶ or △ to ♃ or ♀ in the exact degree which forms the perfect critical aspect; the ☉ or ☽ ruler of the Asc. at the beginning of a disease, and free from the evil asps. of malefics, or lord of the 8th; the ☉, ♃, or ♀ in the Asc., and in no way afflicted by the lord of the 6th or 8th, and especially if in the houses of the ☉, ☽, or benefics; lord of the Asc. a benefic, or the benefics angular and well-aspected; the lord of the Asc., or of the 6th, in good asp. or reception with the Lights, or with one of them, or if wholly free from affliction; reception by house and triplicity between the lords of the Asc. and 8th, and the benefics in good asp. to the degree ascending, or to the cusp of the 6th H., or in ☌, ✶, or △ the ☽, the sick will perfectly recover; lord of the 8th applying to the good asp. the benefics; fixed signs on the angles, and the ☉ and ♂ strong and well-aspected at B., and the ☉ ✶ or △ ♂. (See Curable; "Disease Not Dangerous" under Dangerous; "Disease Will Soon End" under End; Mild, Slight; "Rapid" under Recuperation; "Good" under Resistance; Resources, Vitality; "Certain" in this section).

Peril — Danger — The Illness Is Not Without Peril—(See Doubtful, Impossible, in this section).

Prognosis; Prolonged — The Disease Will Be Prolonged — (See Chronic, Lingering, Long, Prolonged, Slow, Tedious, etc.).

Quick Recovery—(See Immunity, Mild; "Rapid" under Recuperation; "Good" under Resistance; Slight).

Rapid Recovery—(See "Quick" in this section; "Recovery" under Quick).

Recuperation—(See "Rapid", "Slow", and the various paragraphs under Recuperation).

Readaptation; Relapses; Remission— The Remission of Disease — (See Remission).

Resolution — The Resolution of the Disease—(See Resolution).

Return — Old Maladies Return— (See Return).

Shifting—Of the Disease—(See "Shifting" under Disease).

Short Diseases — (See Acute; "High Fever" under Fever; Fierce, Mild, Quick, Rapid, Sharp, Short, etc.).

Signs of Recovery — (See "Patient Will Recover" in this section).

Slight Ailments — (See Colds, Mild, Slight).

Slow Recovery—(See Chronic, Lingering, Long Diseases, Prolonged, Slow, Tedious, etc.).

Solution of Disease—(See Amelioration, Moderation, Resolution, Solution).

Succumbs Easily to Disease — (See "Succumbs" under Disease).

Will Recover—(See "Patient Will Recover" in this section).

Worse — Patient Gets Worse — (See "Worse" under Disease).

RECREATIONS—Amusements—Sports —Exercise—Play, etc.

Death or Injury—Accident, Injury, or Death While Seeking Recreation, or Engaging In Sports — Caused principally by afflictions in the 5th H., and in the ♐ sign. (See Amusements, Athletics, Bathings, Exercise, Horses, Hunting, Play, Pleasures, Riding, Sports, Theatres, Travel, etc.).

Honest Recreations—Fond of—The ☉ Sig. in ♍; ♀ Sig. in ♐, fond of honest and innocent recreations.

Moderate—In Recreations—♃ Sig. in ♒. (See Moderate, Temperate).

Partial To—Partial to Recreation and Exercise—♃ Sig. in ♎ or ♐. (See "Fond Of" under Exercise).

Travel—(See "Love of Travel" under Travel).

RECTIFICATION — Of the Birth Hour and Moment of Birth—It is important in health matters to know, or determine, the exact moment of birth, as each degree rising upon the Eastern horizon at B. has a different meaning. Also the house positions of the planets at B. should be accurately known to give a proper prognosis or delineation. There are certain laws and rules, which if properly applied, make the science of Rectification practically certain and absolute, and the student should become familiar with these rules. Rectification is quite thoroughly discussed, and the principles given, in the various Textbooks and Dictionaries of Astrology. See the Articles on Rectification in Wilson's Dictionary of Astrology, and in Alan Leo's Dictionary of Astrology. Also the time of birth can be rectified by the Prenatal Epoch Method, as given in the book, "The Prenatal Epoch", by Mr. E. H. Bailey. When the time of birth is approximately known, the Prenatal Method is considered very accurate, as the Ascendant at conception is the degree and sign of the ☽ at B., and the place of the ☽ at conception is the sign and degree of the Asc. or Descendant at B. (See Prenatal Epoch).

RECTUM—The Lower Part of the Large Intestine—The Rectum is ruled by ♂, ♏, and the 6th and 8th H. The 6th H. denotes the Rectum. The Anus and the Meso-Colon are ruled by ♏. See the following subjects in the alphabetical arrangement when not considered here.

All Diseases In—In Hor'y Q., signified by the 8th H., and afflictions in the ♏ sign. (See "Diseases" in this section).

Anus — Disorders of — (See Anus; "Sphincter Ani" in this section).

Aphthae; Cancer Of—♄ afflicted in ♏; ♄ ☌ ♅ in ♏; Subs at LPP (4, 5L), and also at KP. (See Carcinoma).

Circulation Obstructed In—♄ afflicted in ♏; ♄ ☌ ♃ or ♀ in ♏.

Cloaca—A Common Outlet to the Rectum and Bladder—(See Cloaca).

Condyloma—(See Anus).

Contraction — Of the Anus Muscle — (See "Inbreathing" under Anus; "Sphincter" in this section).

Diseases In Rectum — Malefics in ♏, the 6th or 8th H., and afflicted; the ☽ in ♏, ☌, or ill-asp. ♄ (or ☿ if he be of the nature of ♄) at the beginning of an illness, or at decumbiture (Hor'y); ♄ or ♂ afflicted in ♏; Subs at PP, LPP. (See Fundament; the various paragraphs in this section).

Elimination—Rectal Elimination Obstructed—♄ afflicted in ♏; malefics in ♋ or ♏. (See "Rectal" under Elimination).

Fissure—(See Anus).

Fistula; Flux—Too Much Flux of the Hemorrhoids—(See Hemorrhoids).

Fundament—Disorders of—(See Fundament).

Hemorrhoids; Imperforate Anus—(See Anus).

Inbreathing—Thru the Rectum—(See Anus).

Inflammatory Diseases — Of the Rectum—♂ afflicted in ♋ or ♏; ♀ in ♋, ☌, □, or ☍ ♂. (See Hemorrhoids).

Meso-Rectum — Meso-Colon — (See Colon).

Nervous Trouble — In the Rectal Region—☿ afflicted in ♏.

Neuralgia In—Pains In—♄, ♂, or ☿ afflicted in ♏; ♅ ☌ ☿ in ♏; Subs at KP and LPP. (See Neuralgia).

No Rectum—Absence of—Case—See "Twins", No. 241, in 1001 N.N.

Obstructions—Obstructed Rectal Region—♄ afflicted in ♋ or ♏; Subs at PP and LLP. (See Anus, Constipation, Faeces; Circulation, Elimination, in this section).

One Passage — (See "Cloaca" in this section; Hermaphrodites).

Opening—A Common Opening to the Bladder and Rectum—(See Cloaca, One Passage, in this section).

Piles—(See Hemorrhoids).

Right Side — Rectum On the Right Side — Case — See "Heart", No. 981, in 1001 N.N.

Spasmodic Action—Of the Sphincter Ani—(See "Sphincter" in this section).

Sphincter Ani — The Anus Muscle — Contraction and Spasmodic Action of—

♄ in ♏ ☌ ♅; the ☽ in ♏ and afflicted by ♄. (See "Inbreathing" under Anus).

Syphilis Of—♂ ☌ ♀ in ♏; ♀ afflicted in ♏; Subs at KP and LPP. (See Syphilis).

Tumor In—♄ ☌ ♃ or ♀ in ♏; ♄ or ♂ afflicted in ♏. (See Tumors).

Ulcer In—♂ in ♏, and afflicted by ♄. (See Ulcers).

Wart-Like Growths — (See "Condyloma" under Anus).

RECUPERATION — The Recuperative Powers—

Augmented—The Recuperative Powers Augmented and Increased—The ☉ in the Asc. at B., and well-aspected; the ☉ well-aspected in ♈ or ♌; the ☉ ✶ or △ the ☽; ♃ or ♀ ☌, ✶, or △ the Asc.; ♈ or ♌ upon the Asc. at B. (See Augmented, Endurance; "Good Health" under Health; Immunity, Increased; "Good" under Resistance, Vitality; "Good", "Rapid", in this section).

Below Average—The Recuperative Powers Below Average — Arrested — Hindered—Low—The ☉ or ☽ in the 6th or 12th H., in a weak sign, and afflicted by malefics; a weak sign on the Asc., and a malefic in the rising sign; ♎, ♑, or ♓ on the Asc.; ♐ on the Asc., due to an over-active body, and using up the vital force too fast. (See Feeble; "Low" under Resistance, Vitality; "Weak Body" under Weak).

Fair Recuperative Powers — Medium —The ☽ hyleg in ♒ with females; the airy signs on the Asc., not as strong as the fiery signs for vitality. (See "Medium" under Vitality).

Functional Disorders — Well Able to Fight Against—(See "Resistance" under Functions).

Good Recuperative Powers — Resistance to Disease Strong—Good Vitality —Throws Off Disease Quickly—The ☉ well-aspected in the Asc.; the ☉ ✶ or △ the ☽; the ☉ rising in ♌, and not afflicted; the ☉ ✶ ♄ at B. gives persistence and tenacity of life; the ☉ ☌, P., ✶ or △ ♃; the greater the power of the ☉ at B., and the less the ☉ is afflicted, the stronger are the recuperative powers, and especially with males, and the ☽ likewise with females, but as the ☉ is the source of vital power, the resistance to disease is stronger in both sexes when the ☉ is strong and well-aspected at B.; the ☽ hyleg in ♍ or ♎ with females; the ☽ in the Asc. or M.C., well-aspected by benefics, and free from too much affliction of malefics; ♃ ascending at B., and well-aspected by the ☉ or ☽; ♃ or ♀ in the 6th H., and well-aspected; ♂ ☌, or in any aspect to the ☉ or ☽; ♂ in good asp. to the ☉ at B. especially tends to give a good store of vitality to draw upon when sick; ♈ or ♌ upon the Asc.; ♍ upon the Asc. if not too much afflicted, or containing malefics; lord of the 6th in the 6th, and well-aspected; a strong map of birth, and the hyleg well-aspected, good powers of recuperation, no matter how evil the directions, except in old age; fiery signs upon the Asc.; the airy signs upon the Asc. at B. are next in power to the fiery signs for good powers of recuperation; of the earthy

signs, the 3° ♑ is stronger for recuperation when on the Asc. at B. (See Endurance; "Abundance", "Good Health", under Health; Immunity; "Good" under Resistance, Vitality; "Rapid" in this section).

Inability to Throw Off Disease—The ☉ afflicted in ♍, or ♍ on the Asc., as it is said the ♍ people court disease, and spend much time in thinking of disease and the condition of their health; common signs on the angles at B. (See "Low" under Resistance, Vitality; Virgo; "Low", "Slow", in this section).

Increased — Powers of Recuperation Increased — (See Augmented, Good, Rapid, in this section).

Less Power to Throw Off Disease— (See Inability, Low, Slow, in this section).

Little Recuperative Power—(See Below Average, Inability, Low, Slow, in this section; Debility, Emaciation, Feeble; "Low" under Resistance, Vitality; "Weak Body" under Weak).

Lives Thru Disease — (See "Spared" under Life; ''Lives'' under Serious; "Good" under Resistance; "Good", "Rapid", in this section).

Low—Recuperative Powers Low—Inability to Throw Off Disease — Little Recuperative Power—Little Power to Throw Off Disease — Less Power to Throw Off Disease — Throws Off Disease With Difficulty — Resistance to Disease Low, etc. — The ☉ ☌ ♄ in a fixed sign; the ☉ afflicted in ♎, the sign of his fall; weak signs on the angles, as ♎, ♑, or ♓, and with the ☉ in a weak sign, and the ☉ in no aspect to ♂; ♄ afflicted in the 6th H.; many planets in fixed signs, or fixed signs on the angles, and especially the ♌ sign predominant; common signs on the angles, the patient is more passive, and hard to arouse from sickness; many afflictions in angles, and with common signs on the angles; ♎, ♑, or ♓ on the Asc.; afflictions in fixed signs, and mutable signs on the angles, succumbs easily to disease. (See Below Average, Inability, Less, Little, Slow, in this section; Diminished; "Gives Up Easily" under Disease; "Disease" under Inability; "Mutable Signs" under Mutable; "Slow" under Recovery; "Low" under Resistance, Vitality; "Weak Body" under Weak).

Makes Effort to Throw Off Disease— (See "Overcoming Disease" under Disease).

Males—Recuperative Powers Good In —The ☉ strong and well-aspected at B.; the ☉ rising and elevated in ♌; the ☉ in ♌ in the Asc., and with ♌ rising, strong recuperative powers. These powers tend to be weak in males when the ☉ is weak at B., and afflicted by ♄ and other malefics, and also when the ☉ is ☌ ♄ in common signs. (See Augmented, Below Average, in this section; "Health" under Males).

Medium Powers—Of Recuperation— (See "Fair" in this section).

Moderation of Disease—Recuperation Is Taking Place — (See Amelioration; "Better" under Disease; Moderation, Resolution, Solution).

Much Recuperative Power—(See Augmented, Good, Rapid, in this section).

Overcomes Disease—(See "Overcoming Disease" under Disease; "Good Health" under Health; Immunity; "Good", "Lives Thru Disease", "Rapid", in this section).

Poor Recuperative Powers—(See Below Average, Inability, Less, Little, Low, Slow, in this section).

Quickly Throws Off Disease — (See "Rapid" in this section).

Rapid Recuperation—Throws Off Disease Quickly — Strong Powers of Recuperation—Good Powers of Resistance to Disease—The ☉ or ♂ in the Asc. at B., and well-aspected; the ☉ well-aspected in ♈ or ♌, and especially when rising, or in the Asc. or M.C.; the ☉ in ♌, and with ♈ on the Asc.; the ☉ ✳ or △ ♂; ♅ ✳ or △ ♄ and ♂; ♂ ✳ or △ the ☉; ♂ in the 6th H., as ♂ by fever burns out the poisons quickly when in this house; ♂ well-aspected in ♍; taken sick in a ♃ hour, the patient soon recovers; born with fiery signs on the Asc., and with benefics in the 6th H., and the hyleg not badly afflicted; airy signs upon the Asc., as the airy signs tend to rapid recuperation thru mental rest and change of scenery; born under positive signs, and with many planets rising and elevated in positive, or masculine signs; positive signs on the Asc. at B.; cardinal signs on angles, and especially with a cardinal and positive sign on the Asc.; with the afflictions in common signs, and with fixed signs on the angles, the native overcomes disease. (See Augmented, Good, in this section; "Good" under Constitution, Resistance, Vitality; Immunity; "Body" under Strong).

Reserve Forces Large — (See Augmented, Good, Rapid, in this section).

Resistance to Disease—Good—Low— (See the paragraphs under Resistance).

Restoration to Health — (See "Lives Thru Disease" in this section).

Sickly, But Will Recover—(See "Sickly But Recovers" under Infancy).

Slow Recuperation — The Powers of Recuperation Low—The Recuperative Power Lessened — Resistance to Disease Low — Throws Off Disease with Difficulty—Little Power to Throw Off Disease—The Vitality Low, etc.—The ☉ or ☽ afflicted by malefics, and the malefics elevated above the Lights; the ☉ or ☽ afflicted in the 6th H. at B.; the ☉ □ ☽ at B.; the Prog. ☉ or ☽ to the ☌ or ill-asp. ♄ in the radix; the ☉ ☌ ♄ in a fixed sign; the ☽ hyleg in ♑ in a female nativity; ♄ ruler of the 6th H., or in the 6th H. at B., and afflicted; ♄ passing thru the 6th H. by transit or progression; ♄ ☌ ☿ in the 6th H.; ♄ rising at B., and afflicting the ☉ or ☽, and the ☉ badly aspected by the ☽; the ♄ sign ♑ upon the Asc. at B., weak during early years; the earthy signs on the Asc. at B., unless well aspected, tend to slow recovery or recuperation; ♋, ♑, or ♓ on the Asc.; many planets in fixed signs at B., or afflictions from fixed signs at the time of illness, the disease is pro-

longed. (See Below Average, Inability, Little, Low, in this section; Chronic, Consumptions, Emaciation, Feeble, Invalids, Lingering, Long Diseases, Prolonged; "Low" under Resistance, Vitality; Slow, Tuberculosis, Wastings; "Weak Body" under Weak).

Strong Powers of Recuperation—(See Augmented, Good, Rapid, in this section).

Throwing Off Disease — Much Power to Throw Off Disease—Little Power— (See "Throwing Off Disease" under Disease; the various paragraphs in this section).

Vitality—Good Vitality—Low Vitality—(See Vitality).

Weak—The Powers of Recuperation Weak—(See Below Average, Inability, Low, Slow, in this section).

Will Soon Recover—(See "Rapid" in this section; "Quick", "Rapid", under Recovery).

RECURRENT DISEASES—(See "Periods of Bad Health" under Health; Periodical; "Old Maladies Return" under Return).

RED—Red Color—Reddened—Reddish — Reddening — Red is the color ruled by ♂ in the Solar Spectrum. Red is ruled by ♂, the 3rd, 4th, and 10th Houses. The fiery red of ♂ is the result of intemperate heat and dryness. Red mixed with green is denoted by ♃. Aries denotes red and white; ♉ denotes red mixed with citrine; ♊, red and white mixed; ♌, red or green; ♎, dark crimson. (See Colors).

Beard—(See "Red" under Beard).

Blood—The Red Blood—The Arterial Blood — Red Blood Corpuscles — The Haemoglobin—Alterations In the Red Blood—Changes In the Blood Particles —The Red Blood Particles Defective— Red Blood Corpuscles Deficient, etc.— The afflictions of ♃ tend to cause alterations in the red blood, and such are considered ♃ diseases. Defects, deficiencies in the red blood corpuscles, or particles, are classed as ☽ diseases. Also such deficiency often exists in people born with the Lymphatic Temperament. For increase in the red blood corpuscles see "Red Blood Corpuscles" in this section. (See Anaemia, Arteries, Blood, Circulation, Haemoglobin, Iron, Jupiter Diseases; "Temperament" under Lymphatic; "Red Blood" in this section).

Body—Red Marks On— Given by ♂. (See "Red" under Marks).

Cheeks—Red Cheeks—♀ Sig. in ♋, in the Asc., and in the terms of ♂, a tinge of red color in the cheeks. (See Cheeks; "Red" under Complexion, Face).

Citrine and Red—♉ colors.

Color—Red Color and Combinations— (See the Introduction to this Article).

Complexion — (See "Red", "Ruddy", under Complexion, Face).

Enthusiasm—Red-Hot Enthusiasm— (See Enthusiasm).

Eyes—(See Fiery, Inflamed, Ophthalmia, Red Cast, under Eyes).

Face—Red Face—Morbid Red Face— (See "Red" under Complexion, Face, Nose; "Cheeks" in this section).

Gravel—Red Gravel—Voiding of Red Gravel—(See Gravel).

Haemoglobin — The Coloring Matter of Red Corpuscles—(See Haemoglobin, Iron; "Blood", "Red Blood", in this section).

Hair—(See "Red" under Hair).

Iron—The Red Metal of ♂—(See Iron; "Metal" under Mars).

Lips—(See "Red" under Lips).

Marks — Red Marks On the Body — (See "Red" under Marks).

Mars—Red is the Color of ♂, the Red Planet. (See "Color", "Red Planet", under Mars).

Nose—Red Nose—Morbid Red Nose—(See "Red" under Face, Nose). For the Toper's Red Nose see the influences under Drink, Drunkenness, Intoxication.

Red Blood Corpuscles—Increase of—Decrease of—♂ action increases them; ♂ ✻ or △ ♃. The afflictions of ♃ and the ☽ tend to decrease them. (See Blood, Haemoglobin, in this section; "Coloring Matter" under Blood; Corpuscles, Haemoglobin, Iron).

Red Pepper—(See Capsicum).

Reddening — Local Irritants — (See Rubefacients).

Rubefacients—An Agent that Reddens the Skin—(See Rubefacients).

Ruddy Complexion—(See Red, Ruddy, under Complexion).

Sandy Red Hair—(See "Sandy" under Hair).

Skin — Red Skin — (See "Red" under Cheeks, Complexion, Face; Pimples, Ruddy).

Treatment — The Treatment of Diseases by the Use of Red Color, Red Surroundings — Red Color is a tonic. Red color is used in the treatment of Inflammatory Skin Diseases, and Inflammatory Diseases of all kinds, and in the treatment of Lupus, Smallpox, Hypochondria, etc., and patients confined in a red room where all the colorings are red benefit when suffering with such diseases. The Herbs of ♂ are also used in the treatment and cure of diseases caused by ♂, on the basis of treatment by Sympathy. (See Antipathy; "Therapy", "Vibration", under Colors; "Mars Group" under Herbs; Hypochondria, Lupus; "Therapeutic Qualities" under Mars; Opposites, Skin, Smallpox, Sympathy, Tonic).

White and Red Colors — Ruled by ♈. (See the Introduction to this Article).

White and Red Complexion — (See "Red" under Complexion).

REDUCING — Reduced—Reducing Disorders are generally the work of ♄. The ☉ ☌ ♄ at B. tends to reduce males, and bring ill-health. The ☽ ☌ or P. asp. ♄ at B., and by dir. tends to reduce the system in females. (See Atrophy, Consumptions, Decay, Degeneration, Deterioration, Diminished, Emaciation; "Mal-Nutrition" under Nutrition; Phthisis, Tabes, Tuberculosis, Wastings, etc.).

REDUNDANT—Excessive—Overflowing —♀ in quality is redundant, excessive,

and overflowing. Also ♃ is overflowing, and an afflicted ♃ or ♀ tend to excesses, gluttony, dissipation, surfeits, etc. (See Dissipation, Excessive, Gluttony, Jupiter Influence, Overflowing, Surfeits, Venus Influence, etc.).

REFINED — Refinement—Elegant—Excellent—

Refined Body — The ☉ in airy signs, refined mind and body; airy signs on the Asc. at B. (See Beautiful, Comely, Elegant, Handsome; "Pure Skin" under Skin).

Refined Expression — (See "Intellectual Look" under Look).

Refined Manners—(See "Elegant" under Manners).

Refined Mind — An Elegant Mind — (See "Elegant Mind" under Elegant).

Refined Tastes—(See Tastes).

Unrefined Manners—And Body—(See Unrefined).

REFLECTED — Reflection — Reflexes — Reflex Action — Reflex Action is principally the work of ☿. Reflected Excitement is a ☿ disease and affliction. Planets and Signs of the Zodiac have a reflex, or supplemental action, upon each other. Opposite Signs of the Zodiac have an especially strong reflex action upon each other. (See Ablation, Action, Antipathy, Aspects, Excitement, Opposites, Planets, Signs of the Zodiac, Sympathy, etc.).

REFORMERS — The desire to reform Social, Civic, Political, or Religious conditions is usually due to the strong influences of ♅ in the map of birth, and especially when in ☌ ♃ strongly placed, as in the Asc. or M.C. An afflicted ♅ may lead to violence, rebelliousness, and indiscreet methods in working Reforms. (See Anarchists, Destructiveness, Fanatical, Hygiene, Ideals, Independent, Judgment, Misunderstood, Persecution, Quarrelsome, Rashness, Reactionary, Recklessness, Religion, Revolutionary, Riotous, Socialism, Uranus, Violent, etc.).

REFRACTORY—Rebellious—Unruly—Ungovernable, etc.—♂ influence; ♂ afflicted in the Asc. or M.C.; born under ♂, and with ♂ in the 10th H., and afflicted by ♄. (See Anger, Choleric, Erratic, Perverse; "Unreasonable" under Reason; "High Temper" under Temper; Ungovernable, Unruly, Vicious; "Tendency To" under Violence).

REFRESHMENT—Rest—Sleep—Illness from Lack of Rest or Sleep—The ☽ in ♒, ☌, or ill-asp. ♄ (or ☿ if he be of the nature of ♄) at the beginning of an illness, or at decumbiture (Hor'y). (See "Brain Fag" under Brain; Fatigue, Rest; "Insomnia" under Sleep; Weariness).

REFRIGERANT — Cooling — A Therapeutic Property of ♄ and ♄ Remedies. Aconite, a ♄ remedy, is used to combat and cool down the high fevers produced by ♂. (See Cold, Cooling; "Treatment" under Fevers; Saturn).

REFUSE—The Refuse, or Wastes of the System — The Elimination of — (See Cleansing, Elimination, Excretion, Faeces, Fevers, Inflammation, Mars Influence, Sweat, Urine, Wastes, etc.).

REGENERATION — The Organs of — The Regenerative Organs—The Reproductive System — The Generative Organs—(See Generation, Genitals, Genito-Urinary, Privates, Reproduction, Secrets, Sex Organs, Womb, etc.).

REGRETFUL — Murmuring — Repining —♄ influence. (See Anguish, Anxiety, Brooding, Complaining, Dejected, Depressed, Despondent, Discontentment, Ennui, Exhibitionism, Fears, Grief, Hypochondria, Imaginations, Lamentations, Low Spirits, Melancholy; "No Peace of Mind" under Mind; Obsessions, Peevish, Repining, Retrospective, Sadness, Sorrow, Worry, etc.).

REGULAR—Regularity—

Bowels—The Bowels Should Be Kept Regular—(See "Open" under. Bowels).

Features — (See "Regular" under Features).

Females—Regular Functions In—The ☽ hyleg in ♍ tends to give good regularity of the system and functions in females. The ☽ weak and afflicted, or in a fiery sign, tends to irregular and disturbed functions. The regularity of the female system and health after puberty depends almost entirely upon the conditions, positions, and affections of the ☽ and ♀. (See "Functions" under Females; "Irregular", "Regular", under Functions; Menses; Puberty).

Habits — Regular Habits Should Be Cultivated — (See "Regular" under Habits).

Health—Regularity of the Health In Females—(See "Functions" under Females; "Females" in this section). See Irregular, Periodical, Recurrent, Return.

REGULUS — Cor Leo — Cor Leonis — Lion's Heart—A violent fixed star of the nature of ♂, in the 28° ♌. Some Authors also say of the nature of ♅. It is said principally to give Military Honours, but to eventually end in ruin, disgrace, or a violent death, and especially if joined to either of the Luminaries. The influence of Regulus enters into many of the afflictions of life, and which have been listed and referred to. under various subjects in this book. See the following subjects for the various influences of this Star— Accidents (Causes, Death By); Acute Disease (see "Hot Diseases" under Acute); Apoplexy (Cerebral); Blindness (Total, One Eye); Danger (Many Dangers); Death (see "Death by Accident" under Accidents); Disease (Threatened); Disgrace; Exercise (Eyes Injured); Extreme Sickness (see "Extreme" under Sickness); Eyes (see "Total", "One Eye", under Blindness); Father (Violent Diseases To); Fevers (see "Fevers" under Putrid); Gunshot (Gunshot Wounds); Head — Rush of Blood To—(see "Blood" under Head); Health (Periods of Bad Health); Hot Diseases (see "Hot Diseases" under Heat); Ill-Health (Signs of); Inflammation (Causes of); Injuries (Danger of); Medicines (Care In Taking); Mother Suffers (see "Danger", "Disease", under Mother); Parents (Afflicted); Pirates (Death By); Putrid (Fevers); Ruin; Sickness (Extreme);

Total Blindness (see Blindness); Violence—Violent (Danger By, Death By, Diseases).

REGURGITATION — (See this subject under Heart, Nose).

REINCARNATION—Rebirth—Metempsychosis — The Doctrine that the Soul lives many times in a physical body upon the Earth Plane—This Doctrine is believed in by three-fourths of the people of the World today. In the New Testament, the doctrine is rather veiled, but is there. The Occult Masters teach the doctrine of Reincarnation, and that each life on Earth is but a day in School, and to gain experience, knowledge, and Soul-Growth. One life in a physical body is but a small time to learn, and to gain wisdom, and also one life would not account for the various inequalities between people, their many diseases, deformities, malformations, monsters, limitations, missing members, idiocy, deafness; born blind, deaf, or dumb, etc., or the death of children in infancy. Every Soul, in its Evolution, must travel in a Cycle, and alternately in the upper half of the Circle, which is the Heaven, or Astral World, and then again in the lower half of the Circle, which is the Physical, or Material World, and it takes repeated experiences in both Worlds to perfect the Soul, as well as to reach a more perfect body, and one which can be free from disease, suffering, and death. These matters, and the Secret Mysteries in general, are taught in the Theosophical and Rosicrucian Doctrines. Also in the books, "Cosmo-Conception", by Max Heindel; "The Key of Destiny", by Dr. and Mrs. Homer Curtiss, of the Order of Christian Mystics, and by many others. This subject would be too long to go into fully here, but if you are interested to know the Truth, you can find it. (See Baptism, Character, Conception, External; "Ripe Fate" under Fate; Heliocentric, Heredity; "Moment of Birth" under Birth, Moment; Nativity, Prenatal Epoch).

REINS—Inward Parts—Loins—Region of the Kidneys—The Seat of the Feelings, Affections, and Passions are sometimes referred to as being in the Reins. "I am He which searcheth the Reins and Hearts" (Revelation 2:23). There are a number of references to the Reins in the Bible, and in the various books and textbooks they are referred to sometimes in a spiritual way, but mostly in a physical and material way, and as having reference to the body. The following subjects refer to Diseases and Afflictions in the Reins. In Astrology, the Reins are ruled by ♃, ♂, ♀, ♎, the 7th H., and also affected by all the cardinal signs. (See Kidneys, Loins).

Abscesses In—Imposthumes—Ulcers —A ♎ disease, and afflictions in ♎. (See Abscesses, Ulcers).

Affected — The Reins are affected when the ☉ is in ♒; ☽ in ♑; ♄ ♎, ♌; ♃ ♊, ♍; ♂ ♉, ♎; ♀ ♈, ♍; ☿ ♐, ♓. (See "Affected" under Head. Also see Table 196, in Simmonite's Arcana).

All Diseases In—Signified by the 6th H., the House of Health, and also by the conditions of the 7th H. and the ≏ sign.

Back — Reins of the Back — All Diseases In—≏ diseases, and afflictions in ≏. (See Back, Kidneys, Stone).

Blood In—Inflammation and Obstructions In the Reins Thru Bad Blood—♃ affl. in ≏. (See "Impure Blood" under Impure).

Consumption—Of the Inward Parts—♄ in ♌ when ♄ is the afflictor in the disease. (See Consumption).

Diseases Of—Disordered Reins—Distempers In—Infirmities In—The ☉ afflicted in ≏ or ♒; the ☽ afflicted in ≏; the ☽ in ♉ and afflicted by the ☉ or ♂ when taken ill (Hor'y); the ☽ in ♋, ♂, or ill-asp. ♄ (or ☿ if he be of the nature of ♄) at the beginning of an illness, or at decumb., and if the ☽ be decr., and near the body of ♄, the disease may continue a long time; the ☽ afflicted in ♏; ♄ afflicted in ♋, ♌, or ≏; ♃ afflicted in ♊ or ♍; ♂ affl. in ≏; ♀ affl. in ♈, ≏, or ♏; caused by afflictions to ☿; ☿ affl. in ≏, ♐, or ♓; afflictions in ≏, and a ≏ disease; Subs at KP. (See the paragraphs in this section).

Distempers In—(See "Diseases Of" in this section).

Heat In—Heats In—The ☽ in ♌, and afflicted by the ☉ or ♂ when taken ill (Hor'y). (See "Heats" under Buttocks, Heat, Loins).

Imposthumes — (See "Abscesses" in this section).

Infirmities In—(See "Diseases" in this section).

Inflammation In—(See "Blood" in this section).

Inward Parts—(See "Consumption Of" in this section).

Kidneys—Reins of the Kidneys—All Diseases In — (See "All Diseases Of" under Kidneys).

Loins — (See the paragraphs under Loins).

Moles On — (See "Location Of" under Moles).

Obstructions In—(See "Blood" in this section).

Pain In—The ☽ in ♉, and assisted by the ☉ or ♂ when taken ill (Hor'y).

Passions — Disorders of — (See the paragraphs under Desire, Passion).

Running of the Reins — (See Gonorrhoea).

Stone In — (See "Kidneys" under Stone).

Tumors In—♃ afflicted in ≏; ♃ in ≏ in the 6th H., and afflicted; ♃ in ≏, and afflicting the ☽ or Asc. (See Tumors).

Ulcers In — (See "Abscesses" in this section; Ulcers).

RELAPSES — Relapsing — Relapse In Disease—Relapsing Fevers—Relapses tend to occur when the Significator of the disease at decumbiture is in a double-bodied sign, as in ♊, the first half of ♐, or in ♓. If there is not a relapse, the disease may, under such conditions, change into some other

form of disease, or disorder. The lord of the 1st H. in the 4th or 8th, ℞ or combust, the disease may be cured but afterwards relapse. (See Chronic, Complications, Continuity, Course, Crises; "Worse" under Disease; "Relapsing" under Fevers; Intermittent, Periodical, Prolongēd, Remittent, Remote, Return, Sympathy).

RELATIVES — Relations — Brethren — Kindred—The 3rd, 6th, 7th, 9th, and 12th Houses rule Kindred and Brethren, according to the relationship. Note the various paragraphs in this section for these rulerships. Male relatives are ruled by ♂, and the ☽ and ♀ rule female relatives. Also ♅ rules Relatives in general. The following subjects have to do with Relatives, which see in the alphabetical arrangement when only listed here—

Aged Female—Death of In the Family—(See Aunts, Grandparents).

Aunts—Death of—(See Aunts).

Brethren—(See the paragraphs under Brethren).

Brothers; Children; Cousins — (See Cousins, Third House).

Cursed By—(See Execrated).

Danger To—An eclipse of the ☉ falling on the place of the radical ♄; ♅ stationary, and near the place of the ☉ or ☽ at B., or in evil asp. to either.

Daughter; Death Among—The ☉ or ☽ to the ill-aspects ♅ by dir.; the ☉ by dir. to the ill-asps. the ☽, Asc., or M.C., or to the ill-asps. his own place; the ☉ hyleg, and· to the ♂ or ill-asps. ♄; the ☽ to the ill-asp. the ☉ or ♅ by dir.; the ☽ by periodic revolution to the ill-asp. the radical ♂; the ☽ at a Solar Rev. passing the place of the radical ♅; ♅ sta. near the place of the ☉ or ☽ at B., or in evil asp. to either; ♄ to the ill-asps. the ☉, ☽, ♀, or the M.C. by dir.; ♄ in the 3rd H. at B., and by dir. in evil asp. to the Asc.; ♄ in the 3rd H. at B., or ruler of the 3rd; the periodic direction of ♄ to the radical ☽; the ill-asps. of ♄ or ♂ to the hyleg, or to the ☉, ☽, Asc., or M.C.; ♄ to the ill-asps. ♀ by dir.; the Asc. to the bad asps. ☽ by dir.; the M.C. to the bad asps. ♀ by dir.; malefics in the 8th H. at a Solar Rev.; the transit of malefics thru the 8th H., and especially if they afflict the 8th H. at B., or lord of the 8th; lord of the 12th a malefic, in the 3rd H., and afflicted. (See "Death Of" under Loved Ones, and also under the various subjects listed in this Article).

Deceitful Relatives—Injured By—(See Deceitful; "Enemies" in this section).

Distant Relatives—Death Of—The ☉ or ♂ by Periodic Rev. to the ♂, □, or ♉ ♅ in the radix.

Early Death Of—(See "Sickly" in this section).

Enemies Among—♄ or ♂ in the 3rd. 6th, or 12th H., or malefics as rulers of these houses. (See Deceitful; "Secret Enemies" under Enemies; "Plots" under Prison; Treachery; "Significators" in this section).

Execrated By—(See Execrated).

Family—(See the subjects under Family).

Father—Relatives on the father's side are ruled by the 6th H., and on the mother's side by the 12th H. Also the father's relatives are ruled by ♃, and those of the mother by ☿. (See "Relatives", and the various paragraphs under Father; "Aunts and Uncles" under Maternal).

Female Relatives — Death of—Death of an Aged Female Relative — Ill-Health of—The ☽ and ♀ rule female relatives, and afflictions to these planets by direction in the map of the native tend to the death of a female relative, or their illness, as the wife, mother, sister, or daughter; the ☽ hyleg in a female nativity, and to the ♂ or ill-asp. ♄ by dir.; the ☽ afflicted at B., and to the evil asps. the Asc. by dir.; ♅ or ♄ passing the place of the ☽ or ♀ at B. by transit, or ☌ the ☽ or ♀ at a Solar Rev.; ♂ passing the place of the radical ☽ at a Solar Rev. (See "Death", "Ill-Health", or "Sickness", under Aunts, Daughter, Females, Grandparents, Mother, Sister, Wife).

Few Brethren — (See "Few" under Brothers, Children).

Godfathers; Grandparents; Guardians;

Hated by Relatives—(See "Enemies" in this section; Hatred).

Husband—(See the paragraphs under Husband).

Ill-Health Of — (See Death, Female Relatives, Sickly, and the various paragraphs in this section).

Imprisoned By — (See "Plots" under Prison).

Long Life For—(See "Long Life" under Brothers, Father, Life, Mother, Sister).

Love Affairs—(See the paragraphs under Love Affairs).

Loved Ones — Death of — (See Loved Ones).

Male Relatives—Ruled by ♂.

Marriage — (See the subjects under Fiance, Husband, Love Affairs, Marriage, Marriage Partner, Wife).

Maternal—Maternal Aunts and Uncles —(See Maternal).

Mother—Mother-In-Law—Relatives of the Mother—(See Maternal; the paragraphs under Mother; "Father" in this section).

Near Relatives—
(1) Die Early In Life—Lord of the 6th in the 3rd, 6th, or 12th H. of the native. (See "Sickly" in this section).
(2) Have Poor Health — Lord of the 6th in the 3rd H. of the native. (See "Sickly" in this section).
(3) Danger To—Death of—The ☉ or ☽ to the ill-asps. ♅ by dir.; ♅ passing over the place of ♄ at B. by transit; lord of the 6th, 8th, or 12th, a malefic, and in the 3rd, 4th, 5th, 7th, or 10th H., and afflicted. (See "Danger", "Death", under Brothers, Children, Father, Husband, Mother, Wife, Sister; "Danger To", "Death Among", and the various paragraphs in this section).

Nephews—Nieces—(See Nieces).

Old Age—Brethren Do Not Live To— Lord of the 3rd in the 8th or 10th; lord of the 6th, 8th, or 12th a malefic in the 3rd, 6th, or 9th H., and afflicted. (See "Short Life" under Life; "Death At Middle Life" under Middle Life; Death, Early Death, Sickly, in this section).

Outlives Relatives — (See "Death Among", "Sickly", in this section).

Paternal Aunts and Uncles—(See "Paternal" under Aunts; "Relatives" under Father; Uncles; "Father" in this section).

Plots—The Victim of Plots of Relatives—(See "Enemies" in this section).

Quarrels with Relatives—(See "Relatives" under Quarrels; "Enemies", "Significators", in this section).

Short Life Of—Death, Old Age, Sickly, in this section).

Sickly and Short-Lived—The malefics afflicting the ☽ or ♀ in map of the native; malefics in the 3rd H., and afflicting or over-powering the benefics, or surrounding the ☉; malefics afflicting the M.C. and the maternal places in the map, as afflicting ♀ by day, or the ☽ by night, or the paternal places, as the ☉ by day, or ♄ by night. Afflictions to the ☉, ♄, or ♂ in the map of the native tend to sickness, and ill-health to his male relatives, and afflictions to the ☽ and ♀, to his female relations. (See "Death", and the various paragraphs in this section).

Significators Of—The 3rd H. and its lord are considered Significators of Brethren, Brothers, and Sisters. Venus by day, and the ☽ by night, are also Sigs. of Brethren, and if the ☽ and ♀ be in dignities, well-aspected by many planets, and also in favorable asp. to each other, the brethren will love each other, but if in signs inconjunct, or in evil familiarity, they will hate or injure each other. (See Antipathy, Compatibility, Execrated, Sympathy; "Enemies", "Quarrels", in this section).

Sisters; Social Relations; Sons;

Terror to Relatives—(See Execrated).

Treachery Of — (See Enemies, Hated, Quarrels, Significators, in this section).

Uncles—(See Aunts, Maternal, Paternal, Uncles).

Wife; Woman's Horoscope — The Father and Mother In—The Father-In-Law, etc.—(See Father, Fourth House, Mother, Tenth House).

RELAXATION — Relaxed — Relaxing — Laxity — Laxness — Prolapse — Relaxation of Animal Bodies, etc.—♆ and ♀ tend to relaxation of the tissues. Neptune is more relaxing than ♀, and is more elusive, protean, formless, and changeable. Moisture and Moist Diseases, as given by ♆ and ♀, tend to relaxation of tissues. (See "Damp Vapors", "Relaxation", under Moisture; "Animal Bodies" under Putrefaction).

Cutis Relaxed—(See Derma).

Drooping Body—(See Limp).

Dull — (See Dull, Ease, Idle, Inertia, Labor, Lassitude, Lazy).

Energy — (See "Lack Of" under Energy; Feeble, Inactive, Inertia; "Weak Body" under Body).

Feeble — (See Debility, Dull, Feeble, Inactive, Inertia, Infirm, etc.).

Fiber—(See "Laxity" under Fiber).

Flabby—(See Flabby, Soft Tissues).

General Relaxation—A ♀ disease, and due to an afflicted ♀; ♓ on the Asc., or with the ☉, ☽, and many planets in this sign, as ♓ has a relaxing influence on the tissues. (See Dull; "Lack Of" under Energy; Lethargy; "Low" under Vitality; "Weak Body" under Weak).

Heat—Heat is relaxing, and cold is contracting. The heat of ♂ tends to relax the cutis and veins which have been contracted by the cold of ♄. (See Heat).

Lassitude—(See Lassitude, Listless).

Laxity — (See Laxity; the various paragraphs in this section).

Limp—Drooping—(See Limp).

Moisture — Moist Diseases—Moisture is relaxing. (See "Damp Vapors", "Relaxation", under Moisture).

Muscular Tissues — Laxity of — (See "Laxity" under Muscles).

Prolapse—(See the paragraphs under Prolapse).

Stimulus—Loss of—(See Dull; "Lack Of" under Energy; Lassitude, Lethargy; "General Relaxation" in this section).

Throat — Relaxed Throat—(See "Relaxed" under Throat).

Tissues—Relaxed Tissues—Softening of the Tissues—♅ and ♀ diseases; the ☽ in ♓, and ♓ influence; ♓ on the Asc. (See Emollient, Flabby, Malacia, Softening, Tissues; "General Relaxation" in this section).

Veins Relaxed—(See "Relaxation" under Veins; "Heat" in this section).

Viscera Relaxed—(See Viscera).

Weak and Relaxed Body — (See Debility, Feeble, Flabby, Infirm, Invalids; "Depletion" under Vital; "Low" under Vitality; "Weak Body" under Weak).

RELIABLE—Trustworthy—Honest— (See Character, Honest, Honorable, Humane; "Manly and Sober" under Manners; "Good Morals" under Morals; Noble, Religion, Responsibility, Sincere, etc.).

RELIEF IN DISEASE—(See Amelioration, Crises; "Better" under Disease; Ease, Moderation, Modification, Recovery, Recuperation, Resolution, etc.).

RELIGION—Piety—Devotion—Veneration—Adoration—Beliefs—Ecclesiastical Matters — Spiritual Matters — The Clergy — The Churches — The State of the Mind and the Relation of the Native to Such Matters, etc.—The Ninth House, the house of the Higher Mind, is classed as the House of Religion and Philosophy, and rules such matters, and also the ♐ sign, the 9th Sign, which Sign affiliates with the 9th H. Also ♃, the ruler of the ♐ Sign, rules Religion, along with ♐ and the 9th H. A powerful ♃ at B., and the 9th H. occupied by benefics at B., or ruled by a benefic, and free from the affliction of malefics, tend to make one very religious, pious, conscientious, honest, just, noble, sincere, generous, faithful, and to be more of the Orthodox type. The influence of ♅ in the 9th H., or afflicting ♃, tends to advanced, in-

dependent, occult, and metaphysical views of Truth, and with a desire to know the Mysteries and the Inner Truths of all Religions, and such Uranus characters are usually termed "Unorthodox." The following subjects have to do with Religion, Religious Views of the native, and the effects of such upon his mind, character, conduct, actions, and health, etc. See these subjects in the alphabetical arrangement when only listed here—

Advocates—Advocates Some Unpopular Religious Dogma—(See "Unpopular" in this section).

Anarchists; Anchorites — (See Celibacy; "Anchorite" under Husband).

Argumentative — In Religious and Other Matters — ♂ and ♅ in ♊, and especially when in the 3rd H., and afflicting ♀. (See Quarrelsome).

Ascetic—(See Self-Denying).

Atheistical — The ☽ separating from the ☉ and applying to ♀ in a day geniture; ♅ ☌ ♂; ♅ or ♂ in ♐, and afflicted; ♂ afflicted in the 9th H., and with frankness and freedom of expression. (See "Irreligious" in this section).

Awakening—Religious Awakening— (See "Exaltation" under Emotions).

Awe and Fear—(See "Religious" under Fears).

Banished—On Account of His Religion or Political Views—(See Banishment, Execrated, Exile, Imprisonment; "Unpopular" in this section).

Beside Oneself—(See Excitable).

Bigoted In Religion—♂ Sig. ✶ or △ ♄; ♂ afflicted in the 9th H. (See Fanatical, Hypocritical, Intolerance, in this section).

Blasphemy — Usually occurs in a coarse map, with many afflictions, and planets weak and out of dignity; ♂ afflicted in the 9th H., or ♂ ☌ ♃ in the 9th, and with ♃ also otherwise weak by sign, and afflicted by the ☉, ☽, and malefics. (See Atheistical, Bigoted, Intolerance, Irreligious, Scornful, in this section).

Cares Nothing for Religion — (See "Irreligious" in this section).

Ceremoniousness — Religious Ritualism—Fond of—Mania For—♃ strong at B., and well aspected, or in the 9th H.; the water signs predominant at B.; ♅ entering into the configuration gives desire for more show and ceremony where there is an occult purpose or meaning; ♄ and ♀ strong at B., little desire for ceremoniousness unless it be along the more stately and solemn lines; ♂ likes military ceremony; ♌, ♏, ♑ characteristics. Case—Mania for Religious Ceremony—See "Marriage", No. 834, in 1001 N.N. (See Magic).

Changeable — Inconstant In Religion —The ☽ afflicted in the 9th H. (See Credulity, Easy of Belief, in this section).

Chaotic Religious Mania — Chaotic Mind—(See "Mental Chaos" under Chaotic; "Religious Mania" under Mania).

Church Affairs — Fortunate In — Unfortunate In—(See Clergymen, Fortunate, Preferment, Unfortunate, in this section; Clergymen).

Churches—Cathedrals—Monasteries—Profanation of—An eclipse of the ⊙ in the 3rd Decan. of ♌, ruled by ♂.

Clergymen—Ministers—Priests—
(1) Anxiety and Sadness To — (See Clergymen).
(2) Enemies Among—Hated or Execrated by the Clergy — Trouble Thru the Clergy—♄ Sig. □ or ⚹ ♃; ♄ ☌ ♂ in the 9th H.; ♂ Sig. □ or ⚹ ♃, on account of Theological opinions; ♀ Sig. □ or ⚹ ♃, many enemies among the Clergy. (See Atheistical, Banished, Unfortunate, Unorthodox, Unpopular, in this section).
(3) Success As a Clergyman — Gains by Preaching—♄ Sig. ☌ ♃; ♃ Sig. ☌ ♀, a good Divine; ♂ Sig. ☌ ♃, success in the Church, and at Law. (See Fortunate, Pious, Preferment, in this section).

Contempt for Religion — Comets appearing in ♑, contempt for religion prevalent. (See Anarchists, Atheistical, Blasphemy, Irreligious, Scornful, in this section).

Cranks—Religious Cranks—(See Anarchists, Fanatical, Intolerance, Radicalism, Reformers, Unorthodox, and the various paragraphs in this section).

Credulity—Easy of Belief On Slight Evidence or Thought—(See Influenced; "Shallow" under Mentality; "Light in Mind" under Mind; "Mutable Disposition" under Mutable; Negative Nature, Receptive, Susceptible; "Changeable" in this section).

Curious Beliefs—♄ in the 9th H. at B., and afflicted, curious beliefs and superstitions.

Daring — In Expressing Religious Views—♂ in the 9th H.

Death — By Religious Persecution — (See Persecution).

Delusions; Desperate Sectarian—(See "Sectarian" in this section).

Destructiveness — (See "Iconoclasm" in this section).

Devils—Demons—Possessed of—(See Demoniac, Obsessions, Spirit Controls).

Devotion — Devout In Religion — ♃ governs devotion; ♃ well-aspected in ♐ or the 9th H.; ♃ in the Asc. or M.C. in ♐; the 2nd face of ♐ on the Asc. (See Emotions, Honest, Humane, Kind, Sincere, Spiritual; "Pious" in ths section).

Disease—Caused by Religion—♃ afflicting the ☾, Asc., and dispositors of the Lights, and especially if ♃ is lord of an evil house. (See "Disorders Of" under Emotions; Fears, Insanity, Madness; "Religious" under Mania; Obsessions, Spirit Controls).

Dishonest—In Religion—(See Deceitful, Dishonest, Dual, Hypocritical; "False" in this section).

Dogma — Advocates Some Unpopular Religious Dogma — (See "Unpopular" in this section).

Dreads—Religious Dreads and Fears —(See Dreads, Fears).

Easy of Belief — ☿ ill-dignified at B. (See "Changeable", "Credulity", in this section).

Ecstasy—Religious Ecstasy—A Ψ disease and affliction; caused by Ψ afflictions at B., and the result of religious excitement, and predominance of the psychic and spiritual powers. Also produced by the Ether, or Luminous Gas in the Spinal Canal, vibrating the Pineal Gland, and the greater the rate of vibration the more the native sees. A high rate of supernormal vibration of the Pineal Gland tends to religious ecstasy. (See "Exaltation" under Emotions; "Beside Oneself", "Religious Excitement" under Excitable; Happiness, Neptune, Pineal).

Egotistical Religious Notions — Ψ afflicted in the 9th H. (See Ego).

Elation — (See "Exaltation" under Emotions).

Emotionalism—(See Emotions).

Enemy To the Church — ♄ influence; ♄ ill-dignified and badly aspected in the 9th H. (See Contempt, Irreligious, in this section).

Established Religion—Fanatically Against—In Favor of—(See Atheistical, Contempt, Devotion, Faith, Fanatical, Fundamentalist, Irreligious, Orthodox, Unorthodox, and the various paragraphs in this section).

Enthusiasts—(See Fanatical, Sectarian, in this section; Enthusiasm).

Evil Spirits — Obsessed By — (See "Devils" in this section).

Exaltation— (See "Exaltation" under Emotions).

Excitement—(See "Exaltation", "Uncontrolled", under Emotions; "Religious" under Excitement; Frenzy).

Excommunicated—(See Banished, Clergymen, Persecution, Unpopular, in this section).

Exiled — On Account of Religious or Political Beliefs — (See Banishment, Execrated, Exile).

Faith—Strong Religious Faith—Given by ♃, ♐, and the 9th H. well-aspected; benefics in the 9th H., and well-aspected. Also given by the fiery signs, and especially ♌ and ♐. Aquarius gives strong religious leaders, Mystics, and Occultists. (See Devotion, Pious, in this section).

False Religionists—The ⊙ Sig. ☌ ♃, and ♃ ill-aspected and ill-dignified at B.; the ☾ ruler of the employment, in her decrease, in ♈, ♌, or ♎, and configurated with ☿, and with ♅ strong and aspected by ☿ or the ☾. (See Bigoted, Contempt, Cranks, Dishonest, Fanatical, Hypocritical, Iconoclasm, in this section).

Fanatical—Ranters—Intemperate or Irrational Zeal — The ⊙ in ♑ in an angle, and afflicting ♂ and ♀; the ⊙ Sig. ☌ ♃, and ♃ ill-aspected and ill-dignified at B.; the ☾ ruler of the employment, in her decrease, in ♈, ♌, or ♎, and with ♅ strong and aspected by ☿ or the ☾; Ψ or ♅ ☌, P., □ or ⚹ ♂; ♅ ruler of the horoscope and afflicted; ♅ afflicted in the 9th H., fanatical in whatever Cause they espouse; ♅ or ♂ in ♐, and afflicted, fanatical against Established Religion and Society; ♅ □ or ⚹ ♀, raving in public; ♅ afflicted in □ or ♐; ♅ □ or ⚹ ♀; ♄ afflicted in the

9th H. tends to a sombre kind of intolerance or bigotry; ♅ or ♂ afflicted in the 9th H., or giving their evil aspects to this house, or to the lord of the 9th H., and ♀ and the ♎ sign are also usually involved in such afflictions; caused by the □ or 8 aspects of ♅ to the 9th H., lord of the 9th, or planets in the 9th, or in ♐; ♂ ruler of the horoscope, and afflicted; ♂ afflicted in the 9th H.; ♂ afflicting ♃ tends to religious enthusiasm; ♀ in ♓, angular, and afflicted by the ☉ or ♂; ♀ ♂ or 8 ♂. (See Anarchists, Enthusiasm, Fanatical, Genius, Prodigies, Radicalism, Reactionary, Reformers; Argumentative, Bigoted, Cranks, Iconoclasm, Property, Sectarian, in this section).

Fanciful—Indulges In Fanciful Speculations About Religion — ♃ Sig. ♂ ☉, and the ☉ ill-aspected and ill-dignified at B. (See Chaotic, Confusion; "Dreamy" under Dreams; Fancies; "Bad" under Judgment; "Light In Mind" under Mind).

Fatalism—(See Scepticism).

Fears—Religious Fears—Ruled by ♆. (See Awe, Chaotic, Dreads, Demoniac, Dreads, Forebodings, Insanity, Mania, Obsessions, Spirit Controls, Superstition, Veneration, in this section; "Religious" under Fears).

Feelings—Inclined to Religious Feelings—The 6th face of ♋ on the Asc. (See Devotion, Pious, in this section).

Forebodings; Forms—Fond of Religious Forms and Ceremonial—(See "Ceremoniousness" in this section).

Fortunate—In Church Affairs—♄, ♂, ♀, or the ☽ ♂ ♃. (See "Clergymen" in this section).

Freedom of Thought — (See Daring, Independent, Misunderstood, Modernists, Persecuted, in this section).

Frenzy — (See "Religious" under Frenzy).

Fundamentalist — ♃ well-aspected in the 9th H., and with no malefics in the 9th, or afflicting the 9th, or lord of the 9th. (See Clergymen, Devotion, Faith, Fortunate, Orthodox, Pious, in this section).

Hallucinations; Hated by Clergymen —(See "Clergymen" in this section).

Healers—(See "Divine Healers" under Healers).

Heretical—(See Atheistical, Contempt, False Religionists, Freedom, Independent, Irreligious, Misunderstood, Persecuted, in this section).

Hypocritical—Insincere—(See Deceitful, Dishonest, Dual, Hypocritical; "False" in this section).

Iconoclasm—Image-Breaking—Radicalism — ♅ and ♂ are the destructive planets in religious or political matters. Violent configurations in the 9th H. tend to Iconoclasm in religious matters, such as ♅ ♂ ♂ in the 9th. Also ♅ or ♂ □ ☉, and with ♄ obscurely placed. (See Anarchists, Destructiveness, Radicalism, Reactionary, Reformers; Fanatical, Lawless, in this section).

Ideals; Ideas; Illumination — No certain judgment can be made from the Chart of Birth as to the degree and nature of illumination which proceeds from a spiritual source. Religion is an inherent aspiration of the Soul, and not a Man-made Institution, but is capable of transcending all external interests and affections, and the planetary influences at B. However, ♆, the ruler of the Pineal Gland, strong at B., tends to greater vibration of the Pineal, and to ecstasy, exaltation, and greater spiritual sight and illumination. (See Character, Intuition, Pineal, Spiritual).

Illusions; Image-Breaking — (See "Iconoclasm" in this section).

Imaginations; Inclined to Religion— (See Devotion, Feelings, Pious, in this section).

Inconstant—In Religion—(See Changeable, Credulity, Easy of Belief, in this section).

Independent — In Religious Matters and Thinking—(See Independent, Metaphysical, Misunderstood, Occult, Science, Truth; "Freedom" in this section)

Infidels — (See Heretical, Scepticism, in this section).

Injured—On Account of His Religion —Caused by fixed stars of the nature of ♃ if joined to the Anareta, or mixed with those of the nature of ♄ or ♂. (See Persecution; Banished, Clergymen, Unpopular, in this section).

Insanity; Intolerance — Self-Opinionated In Religious Matters — Religious Intolerance — Afflictions in or to the 9th H.; ♀ and ♅ in fixed signs, and in □ or 8; ♀ in a fixed sign and afflicted by ♄ or ♂ from fixed signs; ♀ and ♅ in 8 asp. from 8 and ♏; the ☉ and ☽ in fixed signs in □ or 8 asp., and with ♃ and the 9th H. afflicted. (See "Religion" under Public; Bigoted, Fanatical, Sectarian, in this section).

Intuition; Irreligious—Cares Nothing for Religion—The ☽ incr., or at Full, in a day geniture, sepr. from ♀ and apply. to ♂; strong ♄ characters, or with ♄ ruler at B., or ♄ in the 9th H. and afflicting the ☉, ☽, ♃, or ♀; ♃ or ♂ afflicting ♀; ♀ ill-dignified at B., cares little for religion. (See Atheistical, Contempt, Enemy, Heretical, Perjured, Scepticism, in this section).

Lawless — In Religious Matters—Afflictions to ♃; ♂ ♂, P., □, or 8 ♆. "Iconoclasm" in this section).

Leaders — Religious Leaders — (See Clergymen, Faith, Fortunate, in this section).

Magic; Mania—(See "Religious Mania" under Mania; "Ceremoniousness" in this section).

Mediumship; Melancholia—Case—See "Religious Melancholia", No. 976, in 1001 N.N.

Metaphysical—♆ and ♅ strong at B., and well-aspected. (See Metaphysics).

Ministers—Priests—(See "Clergymen" in this section).

Misunderstood—(See Independent, Metaphysics, Misunderstood, Occult, Opinions; Banished, Clergymen, Daring, Freedom, Heretical, Iconoclasm, Persecution, Unorthodox, Unpopular, in this section).

Mockery; Modernists—♅ or ♂ in the 9th H. (See Freedom, Independent, in this section).

Monasteries—(See "Churches" in this section).

Much Given to Religion—The ☉ Sig. ☌ ♃ if ♃ is strong and well-aspected at B. (See Devotion, Enthusiasts, Faith, Fanatical, Pious, in this section).

Mystics—Mysticism—(See Mystical).

Obsessions; Occultists—(See Occult).

Opinions—Beliefs—Persecuted On Account of — (See Banished, Clergymen, Execrated, Persecuted, Unpopular, in this section).

Orthodox—In Religious Views—(See Clergymen, Devotion, Faith, Fundamentalist, Pious, in this section).

Peculiar Beliefs—(See Anarchists, Atheistical, Cranks, Fanatical, Freedom, Heretical, Independent, Intolerance, Metaphysical, Misunderstood, Occult, and the various paragraphs in this section; Peculiar).

Perjured—The ☽ incr. or at full in a day geniture, sepr. from ☿ and apply. to ♂. (See Atheistical, Blasphemy, Dishonest, False Religionists, Hypocritical, Irreligious, in this section; Perjury).

Persecution—(See Banished, Clergymen, Death, Exiled, Metaphysical, Misunderstood, Occult, Opinions, Unpopular, in this section; Persecution).

Perversions—(See Perversions; "Perversions" under Spiritual).

Philosophical—(See Philosophy).

Pious — Piety — A Religious Disposition — Devotion — Veneration — Much Given to Religion and Worship—The ☉ Sig. ☌ ♃; the ☽ decr. in a day geniture, and applying to ♀ in the 10th H., tends to make Prelates, religious Leaders, builders of Churches, etc.; ♄ Sig. ✳ or △ ♃; ♃ well-aspected in the 9th H., and especially with ♃ in ♐; ♃ in the Asc., M.C., or 9th H., and well-aspected; ♃ strong at B., in one of his own signs or houses and well-aspected; ♃ well-aspected in ♐ or ♓; ♂, ♀, or ☿ Sig. ☌ ♃. (See Devotion, Faith, Feelings, Much Given, Spiritual, Veneration, in this section).

Popular In Religion — (See "Fortunate" in this section).

Preaching—Gains By—(See "Clergymen" in this section).

Preferment—Ecclesiastical Preferment—The ☽, ♄, ♂, or ♀ Sig. ☌ ♃. (See Clergymen, Fortunate, in this section).

Prelates — (See Clergymen, Pious, in this section).

Premonitions; Priests — (See Clergymen, Fortunate, Pious, in this section).

Profanation of Churches — (See "Churches" in this section).

Property — Property Is Impoverished by Hypocritical Fanatics—The ☽ Sig. □ or ☌ ♃. (See Property).

Prophetic; Psychic Powers — (See Psychic).

Rabid Sectarian—(See "Sectarian" in this section).

Radicalism; Ranters — (See "Fanatical" in this section).

Raving In Public — (See "Fanatical" in this section).

Reactionary; Reformers;

Renunciation; Revolutionary;

Ritualism — (See "Ceremoniousness" in this section; "Ceremonial Magic" under Magic).

Sanctimonious —Self-Righteousness— Caused by the afflictions of ♅ or ♄ to ☿; ♀ ☌ ♂ in ♓; ♄ in the 9th H., and especially in ♌; ♂ afflicted in ♉. (See Argumentative, Devotion, Pious, Self-Righteousness, in this section).

Scepticism — ♃ afflicted in ♊ or ♍. (See Argumentative, Atheistical, Heretical, in this section; Scepticism).

Scornful — (See Mockery, Scornful; Blasphemy, Contempt, Enemy, Iconoclasm, Irreligious, Profanation, in this section).

Sectarian—Rabid Sectarian—Desperate Sectarian—♄, ♂, or ☊ in the 9th H., a desperate Sectarian; ♂ afflicting ♃, and with other testimonies, a rabid Sectarian. (See Fanatical, Intolerance, in this section).

Seers—(See Prophetic, Seers).

Self-Exaltation—Of a Religious Kind —♆ or ♃ afflicting the ☉ or ☿. (See "Self-Righteousness" in this section).

Self-Opinionated — (See "Intolerance" in this section).

Self-Righteousness — Ego Exaltation —♓ influence; ♂ ☌ ♆ in ♓; ♌ influence; ♄ in ♌, and ruler of the 9th H.; ☿ affl. in ♓; many planets in □ asp. to the ♓ sign, and afflicting planets in ♓; ♂ in ♉ tends to obstinacy in religious matters, and a refusal to change beliefs, or admit one is wrong; ♄ and ♅ afflictions to ☿. (See Argumentative, Bigoted, Egotistical, Pious, Sanctimonious, Self-Exaltation, in this section).

Sincere—In Religion—(See Devotion, Faith, Pious, in this section).

Skepticism—(See Skepticism; "Unorthodox" in this section).

Socialism; Speculative—In Religion— (See Atheistical, Changeable, Credulity, Easy of Belief, Fanciful, Heretical, in this section).

Speech—Freedom of Speech In—(See Daring, Freedom, Hated, Independent, Intolerance, Misunderstood, Persecution, in this section).

Spirit Controls — (See Demoniac, Obsessions, Spirit Controls).

Spiritual Powers — (See Character, Ego, Individuality, Intuition; "Higher Mind" under Mind; Neptune, Pineal, Soul, Spirit, Spiritual, etc.).

Spiritualism—♆ strong at B. tends to the beliefs of Spiritualism, and to give the special powers and faculties for Spirit Communications, Mediumship, etc. (See Clairvoyance, Mediumship, Mystical, Psychic, Seances, Spirit Controls, Spiritualism).

Stoicism — Self - Abnegation — Given largely by the ♏ and ♒ Signs. Also indicated by the stubborn indifference of the ♉ sign, and especially when ♄ is strongly placed, and the negative signs predominant.

Strange Views—Strange and Chaotic Views Regarding Religion and the Higher Life—Ψ in the 9th H. (See Chaotic, Fancies, Metaphysics, Mysterious, Mystical, Occult, Spiritual, Strange, Superstitious, Visionary, Weird).

Superstitious — (See Awe, Dreads, Fears, Veneration, in this section; Forebodings, Horrors, Premonitions, Superstitious, Terrors, Uncanny, Visions, Weird, etc.).

Theological Opinions—Popular or Unpopular On Account of — (See Clergymen, Excommunicated, Fortunate, Unorthodox, Unpopular, and the various paragraphs in this section).

Truth — A lover and Seeker After Truth In Religious Matters—Ψ and ♅ influences strong and predominant at B. (See Knowledge, Learning, Metaphysics, Mysterious, Mystical, Neptune, Occult, Philosophy, Pineal, Psychic, Spiritual, Study, Truth, Uranus).

Unfortunate — In Religion or Church Work—Malefics in the 9th H., and afflicted, and especially ♄ or ♂ in this house. (See Banished, Clergymen, Execrated, Exile, Persecution, Unpopular, in this section).

Unorthodox — ♅ in the 9th H. (See Independent, Metaphysics, Misunderstood, Mystical, Occult, Skepticism, Science; Freedom, Truth, Unpopular, in this section).

Unpopular—Advocates Unpopular Religious Dogma — Lord of the 10th a malefic in the 12th H.; lord of the 12th H. a benefic in the 9th H.; ☿ Sig. □ or ☍ ♃, is persecuted because of his singular religious opinions. (See Unfortunate, Unorthodox, in this section).

Utopianism; Veneration — (See Awe, Fears, Pious, Superstitious, in this section).

Views — Beliefs — Opinions — (See Ideals, Ideas, Morals, Motives, Opinions, Principles, Purposes; the various paragraphs in this section).

Visions—Visionary—(See Visions).

Weird; Wicked—(See Evil, Wicked).

Zeal—(See Enthusiasts, Fanatical, Sectarian, in this section).

REMARKABLE— Unusual — Extraordinary—Singular—Sudden, etc.—

Remarkable Death — ♅ as the afflicting planet tends to death in some remarkable, extraordinary, sudden, unusual, or violent manner; ♄ and ♂ both in evil aspect to the ☉ and ☽, or even only one, and at the same time the Asc. be afflicted; the malefics in ♌ or ♒, and lords of the anaretic places, and if one or more malefics attack the ☉ or ☽. (See "Death" under Accidents, Extraordinary, Mysterious, Peculiar, Sudden, Untimely, Unusual, Violent).

Remarkable Misfortunes — (See Calamity, Disgrace, Dishonour, Events, Evils, Fortune, Misfortune, Prison, Property, Reputation, Reverses, Riches, Ruin, etc.).

Remarkable Persons—Remarkable Individuals represent a climax, or the greatest altitude in the family line, from whence the pendulum turns and moves in the opposite direction. (See Genius, Great, Heredity, Mathematician, Prodigies, etc.).

Remarkable Sickness — (See "Diseases" under Extraordinary).

REMEDIES—Remedy—Palliatives—The Modification, Cure, and Relief of Physical, Mental, or Spiritual Ailments—Therapeutics — Treatment, etc. — The main object of a remedy, as related to the human mind and body, is to counteract an undesirable condition. This can be done in manifold ways, and where spiritual, mental, and material means are used. Articles on the Therapeutic Properties of Remedies are listed in this book in the alphabetical arrangement. Also, in the Article on "Drugs", you will find quite a complete list of Remedies, and their Therapeutic actions, and this list will not be repeated here. Only the more abstract conditions about Remedies will be included in this Article. See the following subjects in the alphabetical arrangement—

Acid Conditions — In the Body — Require An Alkaline Remedy to Neutralize — A good remedy to use as a drink several times a day is the Granular Effervescent Citrocarbonate put up by Upjohn, which is alkaline, and tends to relieve Acidosis, Hyperacidity, Gout, Rheumatism, etc. (See Acids, Alkaline, Antipathy, Hyperacidity).

Alkalinity—(See "Acid Conditions" in this section; Acids, Alkalinity).

Antidotes; Antipathy—Remedies Which Oppose the Condition—(See Antipathy, Opposites, Polarity, Sympathy).

Colors As Remedies—(See Colors).

Cooling Remedies—Refrigerants—(See Cooling).

Cosmetics — Beautifying Remedies — (See Cosmetics).

Curable Diseases—Diseases Which Have a Remedy—(See Curable, Incurable).

Drugs As Remedies — Remedies by Drugs should be chosen according to the Temperament. Mars remedies should be used for ♂ people; ♄ remedies for ♄ people; ☉ remedies for ☉ people. This would be treating by Sympathy, or the Homeopathic principle. (See Homeopathy, Sympathy). By antipathy, ♂ people should use ♄ remedies, as ♄ opposes the diseases of ♂. This is the Allopathic Principle of treating by Opposites. (See the list of Therapeutic Properties of Drugs under Drugs. Also see Antipathy, Opposites). In every region of the Earth, and where the various maladies originate, there is also in that Region a Remedy, an Antidote, an Herb, a Metal, a Mineral, etc., all found in Nature, which has been placed there to relieve and combat the diseases of that locality, and the Native Medicine Men in the most obscure places are familiar with such remedies, and remedies which have been imported from other places, or Countries, may not be as efficacious as local ones. (See Drugs, Medicines, Praeincipients, Treatment).

Exciting Remedies—The remedies of ♂ are exciting, such as Aphrodisiacs,

Caustics, Rubefacients, Stimulants, Tonics, etc. (See these subjects. Also see Depressants; "Therapeutics Qualities" under Mars).

Healers—The Various Forms of Healing, and the Use of Remedies — (See the paragraphs under Healers).

Herbs As Remedies—(See Herbs).

Hurts—Hurts and Injuries Which Are Incapable of Remedy — Malefics in angles, well fortified, and preferably in fixed signs, elevated above the Luminaries and the Benefics, and the latter in weak signs, and in ♂, □, or 𝄞 the malefics. Such configurations in the Chart of Birth tend to permanent defects, and to make the effects of disease, hurts, and injuries more lasting, or to result in death. (See Events; "Remedy" under Hurts, Injuries; Incurable, Permanent).

Incapable of Remedy — (See "Hurts" in this section).

Incurable—(See "Hurts" in this section).

Injuries—Incapable of Remedy—(See "Hurts" in this section).

Medicines As Remedies—(See Drugs, Herbs, Medicines, Roots, Therapeutics, Treatment).

Mental Remedies—(See Healers, Hypnotism, Magic, Magnetic, Psychic, Spiritual, Suggestion).

Periodic Remedies—(See Periodic).

Planetary Remedies—(See Antipathy, Herbs, Medicines, Metals, Minerals, Opposites, Planets, Polarity, Praeincipients, Sympathy, Treatment, etc. Also see "Metal", "Remedies", "Therapeutical Qualities", "Typical Drugs", under each of the Planets).

Poisons As Remedies — (See "Remedies" under Poison).

Polycrest Remedies—(See "Polycrest" under Zodiac).

Proper Remedy Used—(See "Moderation of Disease" under Moderation). For the influences where improper remedies may be used see "Compatibility", "Death", "Poisoned", under Healers; "Care Taken", "Improper Medicines", under Medicines).

Quieting Remedies — (See Anaesthetics, Anaphrodisiac; "Quieting Remedies" under Quiet: Sedatives, Soothing, etc.).

Suggestion—Suggestive Therapeutics —Easily Affected by Suggestion—(See Environment, External, Influenced, Negative, Receptive, Suggestion, Susceptibility).

Sympathy—Remedies by Sympathy—(See Sympathy).

Therapeutics; Tissue Remedies—(See "Zodiac Salts" under Healers).

Treatment of Disease — (See Antipathy, Cure, Drugs, Events, Healers, Hygiene, Medicines, Opposites, Praeincipients, Prevention, Sanitation, Sympathy, Treatment, etc.).

Zodiac Remedies—(See Zodiac).

REMISSION—The Remission of Disease — Abatement — Amelioration — The period of abatement in fevers is under the rule of ♀. The remission of dis-

ease is associated with the common signs, and disease tends to fall off, and to be alleviated, as the afflicting planets leave the cardinal signs and pass into the mutable signs. Cardinal signs show the intensity of the disease. (See Abatement, Amelioration, Cataphora, Continuity, Course, Crises; "Better" under Disease; Duration, Ease, Intermittent, Moderation, Modification, Recovery, Recuperation, Remittent, Resolution, Solution, etc.).

REMITS — The Pulse Remits — (See "Slow" under Pulse).

REMITTENT—Alternately Abating and Returning — Remittent Fevers — The Daily Return of Fever—Intermittent— Irregular, etc. — These influences are discussed and given under the following subjects. (See Ague, Amelioration, Complications, Course, Crises, Ease, Epilepsy, Fever, Insanity, Intermittent, Irregular, Malaria, Moderation, Peculiar, Periodical, Quality, Quartan, Quotidian, Remission, Return, Semi-Tertian, Tertian, Various, etc.).

REMORSE — Remorselessness — (See Cruel, Gloom, Low Spirits, Merciless, Worry, etc.).

REMOTE ORGANS — A close relationship exists between the opposite signs of the Zodiac, as between ♈ and ♎, between ♉ and ♏, etc. Thus a disease in the Reproductive System, or the Genito-Urinary System, ruled by ♏, will be apt to affect the throat, voice, or neck, ruled by ♉. This is the cause of the shifting of disease. (See Ablation, Complications, Course, Crises; "Shifting" under Disease; "Ablation" under Ovaries, Tonsils; Relapse, Removal, Suppressions).

REMOVAL—Of Organs or Parts of the Body — Ablation — Suppression, etc.— Such organs as the Tonsils, Ovaries, or the Mammae, may be removed; suppressed, shrunken, or absorbed, by the influences in opposite signs of the Zodiac, and known as pairs of signs, such as ♉ and ♏, ♋ and ♑, etc. Afflictions in ♏ tend to affect the tonsils, throat, voice, and to cause defects in, loss of voice, abnormal changes in the voice, the shrinking up or loss of the tonsils, etc. Afflictions in ♏, by reflex action, may cause the shrinking up, ablation, loss of, or loss of function of the Mammae, the Milk Glands of the Breasts. Also afflictions in ♏, when not causing ablation, or removal of organs or parts ruled by ♉, may cause diseases in the parts ruled by ♉. Dr. Duz, the French Astrologer, in his book, "Astral Medicine", on page 80, discusses the theories of Ablation, and Removal of Organs by opposite sign influences. (See Remote, Suppression).

Operations — Removal of Organs or Parts by Surgical Operations, and Rules for Time of Operations, etc. — (See Operations).

REMOVALS—Changes of Residence or Location—(See Abroad, Foreign Lands, Location; "Native Land" under Native; "Place of Birth" under Place; Residence, Travel, Wanderer, etc.).

RENAL — Pertaining to the Kidneys — (See "Renal" under Kidneys).

RENDING OF PARTS — (See Bursting, Lacerations; "Accelerated" under Motion; Rupture).

RENEWALS—In the System—(See Conservation, Glycogen, Preservation, Readaptation, Recovery, Recuperation, Restoration, Revitalization).

RENOWN—Fame—Desire for Eminence and Distinction — Becomes Renowned —The ☉ Sig. in ♈, becomes famous; the ☉ strong at B., rising and elevated in the East, or in the M.C., and well-aspected; the ☉ Sig. in ♐, often becomes ennobled, or receives titles or honorary distinctions; ♃ approaching the Meridian at B., unless evil aspects counteract, the native becomes wealthy, and comes to distinction; ♃ Sig. ☐ or ☍ ☉, has a great desire to be distinguished, but rarely atains it; ♂ in ♐ tends to distinction; the ♋ and ♑ influences strong at B. (See Commanding, Famous; "The Great" under Great; Kings, Nobles, President, Princes, Rulers).

RENUNCIATION—Retirement from the World—Seclusion—Forsaking the World—A Recluse—The motive for renunciation should be considered. The afflictions of ♄ would cause retirement from a deep philosophical ambition, or disappointed ambitions. The influences of ♆ and the ♓ sign would tend to renunciation for religious reasons. Venus may cause retirement and seclusion because of failure to combat successfully with the trials or social conditions of life, or because of disappointment in love. The afflictions and influences of ♅ and ♂ tend to sudden retirement. Saturn afflicted in the 10th H. tends to downfall in business, loss of honour, and to seclusion and fondness for solitude. Scorpio influence tends to renunciation of the world due to some deep sorrow, or for emotional reasons, or in order to think deeply upon philosophical matters, and get at the root of things, and the truth about life and destiny. (See Aversions, Celibacy; "Anchorite" under Husband; "Recluse" under Old Age; Recluse, Reserved, Resignation, Retiring, Seclusion, Secretive, Solitude; "Release From" under Sorrow).

REPETITION — Habits Formed By — (See Automatic, Habits).

REPINING—Complaining—Murmuring —The ☉ or ☽ Sig. ☐ or ☍ ♄; the ☉ to the ♂, P, ☐, or ☍ ♄ by dir.; ♄ to the ill-asps. his own place by tr. or dir.; ♄ Sig. ☐ or ☍ the ☉ or ☽; ☿ Sig. in ♓; ☿ in ♓ in partile asp. the Asc.; the 3rd face of ♋, or the 3rd decan. of ♒ on the Asc. (See Anguish, Brooding, Complaining, Dejected, Discontentment, Exhibitionism, Fretful, Gloom, Grief; "Low Spirits" under Low; Melancholy; "No Peace of Mind" under Mind; Morbid, Miserable, Murmuring, Patience, Peevish, Regretful, Restlessness, Retrospective, Sadness, Sorrowful, Suffering, Trouble, Unhappy, Worry, Wretched).

REPLETION—The Condition of Being Full—(See Full, Gluttony).

REPRESSIONS—(See Confinements, Hindrances, Inhibitions, Limitations, Restraints, Retardation, Saturn Influence, Stoppages, Suppressions, Twelfth House).

REPRODUCTION—Reproductive Organs—Sex Organs—Secrets—Privates —Genitals—Generative System—Reins —Res Venereae—Procreative Organs— Members of Generation, etc.—This subject is largely considered in the Articles on Conception, Fecundation, Fertile, Foetus, Fruitful, Generative System, Genitals, Genito-Urinary, Gestation, Prenatal Epoch, Privates, Procreation, Proliferation, Secrets, Sex Organs. (See these subjects). The Reproductive Organs are ruled by ♂ and the ♏ sign. Also the ♌ sign and the 5th H. conditions show the power of reproduction, and the necessity for survival, and for offspring. The female reproductive organs, and especially the womb, are strongly influenced and ruled by the ♍, ♎, and ♏ signs. The external sex organs of males are ruled by ♂. The following subjects are related to the reproductive organs, which see in the alphabetical arrangement when not considered here—

Abscesses In — (See "Abscess" under Secrets).

Adolescence—(See Puberty).

All Diseases Of—(See "All Diseases" under Generative).

Barrenness; Castration—(See Testes).

Cell Reproduction — (See "Reproduction" under Cells).

Chancre—Hard Chancre—(See Syphilis).

Chancroid—(See Gonorrhoea).

Change of Life — In Women — (See "Menopause" under Menses).

Clitoris; Cohabitation; Conception;

Death—From Disorders of the Generative System—(See "Death" under Generation).

Deformities—Of the Sex Organs—(See "Deformities" under Generative).

Diseases In — (1) Diseases Incident To the Generative System—(See "Diseases" under Genitals; "Private Diseases" under Private; Venereal, Womb, etc.). (2) Diseases of the Reproductive Organs Prevalent — Comets appearing in ♏.

Fallopian Tubes—(See Fallopian).

Fecundation; Female Functions—(See "Functions" under Females).

Foetus; Fruitful; Gemmation — (See Cells, Gemmation, Proliferation).

Generative Organs — (See Generative, Genitals, Sex Organs).

Genitals; Genito-Urinary; Gestation;

Glands—Gonads—(See "Reproductive" under Glands).

Hermaphrodites; Impotent;

Injured In Privates — (See "Injuries" under Genitals; Maimed, Mutilated).

Intercourse; Leucorrhoea; Maimed;

Male Organs — (See "Mens' Genitals" under Genitals; "Male Organ" under Male).

Members of Generation—Disorders of — (See Generative, Genitals, Secret Parts, Sex. Also note the various paragraphs in this section).

Menses; Monsters; Offspring — (See Children).

Ovaries—Ovum—(See Ovaries).

Pain In—(See "Pain" under Genitals, Secrets).

Parturition; Passion; Penis; Perversions; Pregnancy; Prevalent—Diseases of Reproductive Organs Prevalent—(See "Diseases" in this section).

Private Diseases—(See Genitals, Private, Scandalous, Venereal).

Privates — Privy Parts—(See Privates).

Processes—Reproductive Processes—Ruled by ♏. (See "Reproductive Processes" under Processes).

Procreation—Ruled by the ☽ and ♀. (See Procreation).

Proliferation; Prolific; Puberty; Puerperal; Scandalous Diseases—(See Scandalous, Private, Venereal).

Secret Parts—(See Genitals, Privates, Secrets, Sex Organs).

Semen; Sex Organs—(See Sex).

Shameless Practices—(See Exhibition, Perversions, Rape, Shameless, Unnatural).

Sores—On Genitals—(See "Chancroid" under Gonorrhoea; "Abscesses" under Secrets; "Chancre" under Syphilis; "Genitals" under Ulcers).

Spermatic Cord—(See Spermatic).

Syphilis; Testes; Tubes—(See Fallopian; "Seminal Vesicles" under Semen).

Ulcers—(See "Genitals" under Ulcers).

Urethra; Uterus—(See Womb).

Vagina; Venereal; Voice—Changes In At Puberty — (See "Voice" under Puberty).

Vulva; Weakness—Of the Generative Organs—(See "Weakness" under Generative).

Whites—(See Leucorrhoea).

Womb — (See the paragraphs under Womb).

REPTILES — Reptilian — Serpents — Snakes—The Reptilian, or Dumb Signs of the Zodiac, are ♋, ♏, and ♓. (See Dumb, Mute).

Death or Injury By—The ☉ or ♂ with Fomahaut tends to bites by venomous animals; ♄ and ♂ in Terrestrial Signs, with ☿ concurring, and malefics afflicting the Luminaries; ♄ near the Constellation of the Serpent in the 4th face of ♏, configurated with ☿, and with ♄ in the 1st H. in ☍ to the ☉ or ☽ setting. (See Adder; "Journeys" under Bites; Fomahaut; "Bites To" under Kings; Obnoxious, Quadrupeds, Serpents, Stings, Terrestrial; "Danger" under Travel; Venomous).

REPULSIONS—Repulsive—(See Antipathy, Compatibility, Enemies, Hatred, Incompatibility, Opposites).

Repulsive Diseases — (See "Catarrh" under Head; Fetid, Foul, Gangrene, Odors, Offensive, Putrid, Rotten, Scandalous, Sores; "Fetid" under Sweat; Ulcers, Venereal).

REPUTATION—Public Estimation—

Abilities — Gains a Great Reputation from His Abilities—The ☽ Sig. ♂ ☿. (See Genius; "Great Ability" under Great; "Abilities" under Mental; "Good Mind" under Mind; Prodigies).

Bad Reputation—Of No Repute—Held In Low Esteem — Unpopular — The ☽ Sig. in ♑; ♀ ill-dignified at B. (See Banished, Conduct, Criminal, Debauched, Disgrace, Dishonest, Drink, Drunkenness; "Many" under Enemies; Execrated, Execution, Exile, Harlots; "Hated by Others" under Hatred; "Loss Of" under Honour; Infamous; "Low and Base" under Low; Loose Morals" under Morals; "Imprisonment" under Prison; Scandalous, Shameless; Unfortunate; "Vile Wretch" under Vile).

Good Reputation—(See "Popular" in this section).

Hated by Others—(See Hatred).

Loss of Reputation — (See Disgrace, Downfall; "Loss Of" under Honour; Sentence of Law (see "Death" under Judges; Prisons); Ruin, Scandal, etc.).

No Regard for Reputation—♀ ill-dignified at B.

Of No Repute — (See "Bad" in this section).

Popular — A General Favorite — Beloved and Esteemed—Highly Respected, etc.—The ☉ Sig. ✶ or △ ♃, always respected; the ☽ Sig. in ♉, gains in esteem and much respect; the ☽ Sig. in ♋, well-beloved; the ☽ Sig. in ♎ or ♐; ♃ rising at B., and well-aspected, held in high esteem; ♃ Sig. in ♎; ♃ Sig. ♂ ♀, admired and respected; ♀ Sig. in ♎, generally beloved; ♀ Sig. in ♐ or ♒; ♀ Sig. ♂ ♃. (See Pleasant, Popular).

Unpopular — (See "Bad Reputation" in this section).

REQUIREMENTS — Nature's Requirements—(See "Requirements" under Nature).

RES VENEREAE—Sex Diseases—(See "Diseases" under Generative, Genitals, Genito-Urinary, Private, Reproductive Organs, Sex, Venereal, etc.).

RESCUE WORK—Hazards His Life to Rescue Others—♄ in ♎, ♂, □, or ☍ the Asc. by dir., and ♄ ruling the 1st H., rescues others from impending danger. (See Danger).

RESEARCH — Fond of Study and Research Work—(See Knowledge, Learning, Metaphysics, Occult, Philosophy, Reading, Science, Study, Truth, etc.).

RESENTFUL—Indignant Displeasure—♄ Sig. ✶ or △ ♂, more open in resentment. (See Antipathy, Hatred, Jealousy, Offended, Revenge, Sensitive, Treachery, etc.).

RESERVATION — Of Cell Substances—(See "Substance" under Cells).

RESERVE FORCES — The Reserve Forces of the Body Strong or Weak—Reserve Forces Good — (See "Good" under Constitution, Health, Immunity, Recovery, Recuperation, Resistance, Stamina, Strength, Tone, Vitality).

Reserve Forces Low — (See Debility, Feeble, Infirm, Invalids; "Much Sickness" under Sickness; "Weak Body" under Weak).

RESERVED—Retiring—Quiet—Serious — Thoughtful—R e t i c e n t—Seclusive, etc. — The ☽ Sig. in ♍; ♄ influence strong at B.; ♄ in ♎, reserved and unsociable; ♄ Sig. in ♍ (Hor'y); ☿ strong at B.; ☿ Sig. ✳ or △ the ☽; ♏ on the Asc.; ♏ influence tends to make one thoughtful and reserved. (See Bashfulness, Grave, Mistrustful, Modesty, Mystical, Recluse, Retiring, Seclusion, Secretive, Serious, Shy, Solitude, Suspicious, etc.).

RESIDENCE—Place of Residence—Location—The Place of Residence is governed by the ☽ and the 4th H. The following subjects have to do with Residence, changes of, conditions over, its benefits or evils, etc. See the following subjects in the alphabetical arrangement when not considered here—

Abroad — Residence Abroad — Should Live Abroad—Should Not Live or Travel Abroad—The 9th H. containing benefics, and free from the affliction of malefics, is favorable for residence Abroad. If there are malefics in the 9th H. at B., in weak signs, and afflicted, avoid foreign residence or travel. In choosing a location Abroad for the best of health, or to benefit the health, if the map indicates life Abroad, choose a Country ruled by the Signs of the Zodiac containing ♃ or ♀ at birth if such signs are free from the presence, or severe affliction of the malefics. The native should live Abroad, or away from the Native Place or Land, if at birth the ☉, ☽, ♃, or ♀ were in the 1st, 9th, 10th, or 12th H., or if the ☉ or ☽ were afflicted in the 4th H., or malefics in the 4th. Malefics ruling the 4th H., or malefics in the 4th, always make it advisable for the native to remove from his place of birth. (See Abroad, Foreign Lands, Fourth House; "Native Land" under Native; Ninth House; "Place of Birth" under Place; Travel, Voyages).

Air Sign People — When the map of birth predominates with the airy sign influences, and with an air sign on the Asc., frequent changes of scenery or residence are good for such natives, and also to live in a high altitude where the air is lighter. The Air Signs tend to rapid recuperation thru mental rest and change of scenery. (See "Signs" under Air; Altitude).

Altitude — Should Reside In a High Altitude — (See Altitude; "Air Sign People" in this section).

Bad Time for Changes—Of Residence —The ☉ to the ♂, P, □, or ☍ ♅ by dir.; the ☉ to the ♂ or ill-asp. the ☽; the ☽ to the ill-asps. her own place by dir. (See "Bad Time" under Journeys, Travel; "Avoid" under Voyages).

Birthplace — Should Remain There — Should Remove—(See "Place of Birth" under Place; "Abroad" in this section).

Changes—Many Changes of Residence —Few Changes—People born under the strong influence of the Fixed Signs, and with the ☉, ☽, and many planets in these signs, or fixed signs on the Asc. or angles at B., are not given much to change, and often remain in one location for a lifetime. The Com-

mon Sign influences strong at B. tend to many changes, and inconstacy. The evil directions of ♅ tend to make one restless, notionate, and under this influence sudden and unwise changes of residence are apt to occur. (See Changes; "Fixed Habits", "Fixed Signs", under Fixed; Restlessness, Roaming; "Many Changes", "One Place", in this section).

Colds Taken—By Living In Cold and Damp Places — (See "Colds" under Moisture).

Comfort — Changes Which Interfere with Health and Comfort—♅ in the 6th H. at B. (See Comforts).

Constant In No Place—(See Changes, Many Changes, in this section).

Countries—Countries and Nations In Which To Reside—(See Countries, Location, Nations; Abroad, Prospers Anywhere, Where Not To Locate, and the various paragraphs in this section).

Damp Places — Living In, and Ill-Health From — (See "Colds" under Moisture).

Desire for Changes — (See Changes; "Inability" under Concentration; Discontentment, Patience, Restlessness, Roaming, Scattering, Vacillating, Vagabond, Wanderer; Discontentment, Many Changes, and the various paragraphs in this section).

Discontentment—Changes Due To—☿ to the good asps. the ☽ by Periodic Rev. tends to changes of residence if unsettled or discontented. (See Discontentment; "Instability"; "No Peace of Mind", under Mind; Restless; the various paragraphs in this section).

Fixed In Habits — And Opinions, and Not Given To Change—(See "Fixed In Habits" under Fixed; "Change", "One Place", in this section).

Foreign Lands — Residence Abroad— (See "Abroad" in this section).

Fortunate Locations—(See "Abroad", "Friends", in this section; "Native Land" under Native; "Place of Birth" under Place; "Directions To Travel" under Travel).

Friends — T h e Best Locations for Friends and Prosperity — Parts of the World Where To Meet the Most Friends —Signs containing ♃ and ♀, or the angles containing them, show the best directions and locations for the best prosperity, true, and helpful friends. (See Abroad, Birthplace, Native Land, Place of Birth, in this section).

Good Time To Remove—The ☽ to her own good aspects by dir. (See "Good Time" under Journeys, Voyages).

Health—The Best Location for Health —When Health is the object of travel, or a change of location, follow the lord of the Ascendant and the ☽. Also locate in places ruled by the signs which contain the Benefics at B., or in the direction of the Benefics. (See Abroad, Fortunate, Location, Friends, Where Not To Locate, in this section; "Location" under Health).

Home or Abroad — Whether To Live At Home or Abroad — (See Abroad, Liberty, in this section).

Ill-Health — Due To Location — (See Abroad, Altitude, Places to Avoid, Should Remove, Where Not to Locate, in this section).

Inconstant—(See Changes, Desire for Changes, Many Changes, in this section; Inconstant).

Leads Unsettled Life—(See Changes, Inconstant, Many Changes, Roamer, Unsettled, Wanderer, in this section).

Liberty — Can Travel or Locate Anywhere — (See "Prospers Anywhere" in this section; "Home or Abroad" under Travel).

Lives In One Place — (See Changes, One Place, in this section).

Location—Where To Locate—(See Location; "Native Land" under Native; "Place of Birth" under Place; "Direction To Travel" under Travel; Fortunate, Health, Ill-Health, Where Not To Locate, and the various paragraphs in this section).

Low Altitudes—Should Live In—(See Altitude).

Many Changes—Of Residence—Constant In No Place—Removes Constantly — Continually Shifting Their Situations—The ☉ Sig. ☌ ☽; the ☽ in the Asc., or ruler at B.; the ☽ in the 4th H.; ♄ or ♃ Sig. ☌ ☽; ♂ Sig. in ♊; ♂ Sig. ☌ ☽; ☿ ill-dignified at B.; ☿ Sig. ☐ or ☍ ☽, and especially if ☿ be in a movable sign; several planets conjoined with ☿, and also in configuration with the ☽; ☿ Sig. ☌ ☽, unsteady in his pursuits; a common sign on the cusp the 2nd H. at B., and ♄ in the 2nd by dir. (See Air Sign People, Changes, Desire for Changes, Discontentment, Inconstant, Mutable, in this section).

Military Life—Changes Caused By— (See Military, War).

Moisture — Colds and Ill-Health by Living In Moist and Damp Places — (See "Colds" under Moisture; "Ill-Health" in this section).

Mutable Signs — Their influence predominant at B. tends to many changes of residence. (See "Mutable Signs" under Mutable; "Many Changes" in this section).

Nations—The Rulerships of the Nations—(See Nations).

Native Land — Should Remain In — Should Leave—(See "Native Land" under Native; "Place of Birth" under Place; "Abroad" in this section).

Not Given To Changes—(See Changes, Fixed, One Place, in this section).

One Place—Lives In One Place for a Lifetime—Many influences in the fixed signs at B.; the ☉, ☽, and ☿ well-aspected by ♄; ♄ a strong ruler at B., may spend a lifetime in one place, and in one employment; ♄ afflicted in the 4th H. tends to tie the native down to one place to his detriment. (See Changes, Fixed, in this section; "Fixed Signs" under Fixed).

Place of Birth—Should Remain In— Should Remove — (See Fourth House, Nadir; "Native Land" under Native; "Place of Birth" under Place; "Abroad" in this section).

Places To Avoid—During the Current Year—When the ☉ or ☽ are hyleg, and the hyleg falls in the 8th H. at a Solar Rev., places and Countries ruled by the sign containing the hyleg at B. should be avoided, or ill-health, accident, or death might result. (See "Where Not To Locate" in this section; "Bad Time", "Current Year", under Travel). For places to avoid generally see Abroad; "Native Land" under Native; "Place of Birth" under Place).

Prosperity—Best Location For—(See "Friends" in this section).

Prospers Anywhere — At Home or Abroad — The ☉, ☽, ♃, or ♀ well-aspected in the Asc. (See Liberty, Prosperity).

Removals — Removes Constantly — Should Remain—Should Remove—(See Changes, Desire for Changes, Discontentment, Inconstant, Should Remain, Should Remove, in this section).

Roamer — (See Roamer, Vagabond, Wanderer; Changes, Desire for Changes, Many Changes, in this section).

Sailor — Travels About As a Sailor — (See Maritime, Navigation, Sailor, Sea, Ships).

Scenery—Change of Scenery Good — (See "Air Sign People" in this section).

Sea Level—Should Live At Sea Level —(See Altitude).

Shifting Here and There—(See Many Changes, Removals, in this section).

Should Remain—Should Not Move—A malefic in the 7th H., or the ☽ or lord of the 1st sepr. from a benefic, remain; lord of the Asc. and planets in the 1st stronger than the lord of the 7th, or planets in the 7th, should remain (Hor'y). (See Abroad, Nadir; "Native Land" under Native; "Place of Birth" under Place; "Abroad" in this section).

Should Remove—Caused by ♅ and his afflictions; the ☽ sepr. from a malefic, or ☋, or a benefic in the 7th H., should remove. (See "Should Remain" in this section).

Soldiers—Changes of Residence For, and For Sailors—(See Maritime, Military, Sailors, Ships, Soldiers, War).

Sudden Changes—Of Residence—♅ influence. (See "Sudden" under Changes).

Tied to One Place — (See Changes, Fixed, One Place, in this section).

Time—Best Time for Changes—Bad Time For—(See Bad Time, Good Time, in this section).

Travel — Good or Bad Time For — Travels Much—(See the various paragraphs under Travel; Vagabond, Wanderer; "Many Changes" in this section).

Unfortunate Locations — (See Places to Avoid, Where Not to Locate, and the various paragraphs in this section).

Unsettled Life—(See Changes, Desire For Changes, Discontentment, Inconstant, Many Changes, Removals, Roamer, Vagabond, Wanderer, in this section).

Vagabond — (See Roamer, Vagabond, Wanderer).

Wanderer—(See "Travels Much" under Travel; Vagabond, Wanderer; "Many Changes" in this section).

War — Causing Changes of Location or Residence — (See Army, Military, Ships, Soldiers, War).

Wet and Damp Locations—Colds and Illness From — (See "Colds" under Moisture).

Where Not to Locate—Signs containing malefics, and places and directions ruled by such signs, show the places and directions to avoid, and where the native would be apt to meet with inveterate opposition from public and private enemies, or suffer accident, ill-health, downfall, etc., unless the malefic itself be Significator, or the malefic well-aspected in his own sign, as ♄ in ♑, ♂ in ♈ or ♏, etc., and the malefic not ℞, combust, or badly afflicted. Avoid the direction of planets much afflicted, even though they be a benefic, as such afflictions tend to ill-health, misfortune, delays, execration, sorrows, suffering, enemies, downfall, losses, isolation, reversals, trouble, plots, treachery by others, loss of friends, etc. (See Abroad, Ill-Health, Location, Native Land, Place of Birth, Places to Avoid, in this section; "Countries to Avoid" under Travel).

RESIGNATION—

Resigned to Disease—Characteristic of the ♍ people. (See "Does Not Complain" under Complaining; Patience; Renunciation; the Introduction under Virgo).

Resigned to Fate — (See "Resigned" under Fate; Limitations, Recluse, Seclusion, Secretive, Solitude, Twelfth House).

RESINS—A Vegetable Exudate Soluble in Alcohol and Oils, but Insoluble in Water—Ruled mostly by ♅. (See Amber, Herbs, Shellac, Xylan).

RESISTANCE TO DISEASE — The degree of resistance, the vitality, and the powers of recuperation, vary in different individuals according to the conditions existing in the map of birth, or according to the degree of education, self-control, spiritual attainment, etc. The following subjects have to do with the powers to resist disease, which powers may be strong, medium, or weak. See these subjects in the alphabetical arrangement when not considered here—

Ascendant — Fiery signs on the Asc. give greater vitality, while the watery signs on the Asc. at B., and especially ♋ and ♓, tend to lower the resistance, and give a weaker body. (See Ascendant; "Fire Signs" under Fire; First House; "Body" under Strong; "Good", "Low", under Vitality).

Childhood — (See "Danger", "Death", "Fevers", under Childhood).

Children—Resistance to Disease Good In—A strong sign upon the Asc. at B., as ♈, ♌, or ♐, and the ruler of the Asc. well-placed and free from affliction. (See "Strong" under Children, Infancy).

Chronic Diseases—Poor Resistance— (See Chronic).

Debility Greater—(See "Chronic" under Debility).

Directions—(1) Overcomes Evil Directions — ♃ rising at B. in power and

dignity, and well-aspected. (See "Overcoming Directions" under Directions; Immunity; "Good" under Vitality; "Good" in this section). (2) Succumbs Easily Under Evil Directions — (See "Evil Directions" under Directions; "Directions Kill" under Infancy; "Low" in this section).

Early Death — (See "Death During Childhood" under Childhood; Early; "Death In Infancy" under Infancy; "Short Life" under Life).

Endurance; Feeble; Functions—Good, Strong, or Weak—(See Functions).

Gives Up Easily — To Disease — (See "Gives Up Easily" under Disease).

Good Powers of Resistance—The Resistance to Disease Increased—Throws Off Disease Easily—The ☉ ☌ or P. asp. ☿ increases and strengthens the Will, and gives the mind more power to resist disease, and to act against disorders; the ☉ or ☽ to the good asps. ♂ by dir.; the ☉ or ♂ ⚹ or △ the Asc., much organic resistance; the ☉ ☌, P., ⚹ or △ ♃ enables to overcome disease; the ☉ in a fire sign; the ☉ in the Asc. or M.C. at B., in a strong or fiery sign; the ☉ angular and diurnal at B.; the less the ☉ is afflicted at B. the greater is the vitality, and the more certain to ward off disease; the ☉ in ♈ or ♌, and well-aspected; the ☉ in ♌, and with ♈ on the Asc.; the ☽ free from affliction at B., and well-aspected by the benefics, and the Asc. free from the affliction of malefics; the ☽ hyleg in ♉ with females; ♄ on the Asc. at B. gives good resistance to disease, tenacity of life, and persistence against disease; ♃ and ♀ rising at B., and in good asp. to the ☉ and ☽; ♃ in the 6th H., and free from affliction, wards off disease easily; ♃ in the Asc. at B., and in good asp. to the ☉ and ☽; ♃ and ♀ in the Asc. at B., and free from the affliction of malefics; ♂ ⚹ or △ the ☉ at B.; ♂ in good asp. to the ☉ or ☽ at B.; fiery signs on the Asc. at B.; the 2° ♍ on the Asc. at B.; fixed signs on the angles, and the afflicting planets in common signs; many planets in fixed signs at B. give greater resistance and endurance, but tend to prolong the disease; born under the positive and masculine signs, and with many planets in such signs, will overcome, resist, and fight off disease; ♊ on the Asc., which is the strongest of the common signs to control illness. (See "Active Body" under Active; Defensive, Directions, Endurance; "Good Health" under Health; Immunity, Majority, Physical, Recovery, Recuperation, Resources, Stamina, Strength; "Body" under Strong; Tone; "Good" under Vitality, etc.).

Immunity from Disease—(See Immunity).

Inability — To Throw Off Disease — (See "Overcoming Disease", "Throwing Off Disease", under Disease; "Disease" under Inability; "Low" in this section).

Increased Resistance — To Disease — (See "Good" in this section).

Infancy — Powers of Resistance In — (See the paragraphs under Infancy).

Infirm; Invalids;

Less Liable to Disease—Proof Against Disease—(See "Less Liable" under Disease).

Less Power—To Throw Off Disease—(See "Less Power", "Overcoming", under Disease; "Low" in this section).

Lives Thru Sickness—(See "Good" under Recuperation; "Lives Thru Serious Illnesses" under Serious; "Good" in this section).

Long Illnesses—(See Chronic, Invalids; "Diseases" under Long; Prolonged; "Slow" under Recuperation; Tedious).

Long Life—(See "Long" under Life).

Low—Resistance Low—The ☉, ☽, or ♄ in the 6th H., and afflicted; the ☉ ♂ or P. ♄, and especially in common signs; the ☽ hyleg in ♏ and afflicted in female nativities; ♄ rising, and the ☉ afflicted by the ☽; a malefic afflicting the ☉ or ☽, and elevated above the Luminary; ♋, ♍, or ♓ on the Asc. (See "Low" under Recuperation, Vitality; "Weak Body" under Weak).

Majority—The majority of the planets rising, or rising and elevated at B., give greater resistance to disease. (See Elevated, Majority, Rising).

Makes Effort—To Throw Off Disease—(See "Overcoming" under Disease).

Middle Life—Dies Before or At Middle Life—(See Middle Life).

Offspring—(See "Children" in this section).

Old Age—Dies In Old Age—(See "Long Life" under Life; Old Age).

Organic Resistance—Has Much Organic Resistance—(See "Organic Resistance" under Organic; "Good" in this section).

Overcomes Disease—(See "Overcoming" under Disease; "Good" in this section).

Physical Resistance—(See "Resistance" under Physical; "Good", "Low", in this section).

Proof Against Disease—(See "Less Liable" under Disease; Immunity).

Protective Influences—(See Protection).

Receptive—More Open to Disease—(See Receptive, Susceptibility; "Inability", "Less Power", in this section).

Recovery Rapid—(See "Rapid" under Recovery).

Recuperative Powers—(See Defensive, Phagocytes, Protection, Recuperation, Vitality).

Rising Planets—Give Greater Resistance. (See Elevated, Majority, Rising, Setting).

Robust; Sickly; Sickness—(See "Much Sickness", and the various paragraphs under Sickness).

Stamina; Strong Resistance—To Disease—(See Immunity; "Good" under Recuperation, Vitality; "Good" in this section).

Stubborn Diseases—(See Chronic, Consumptions, Lingering; "Long Diseases" under Long; Prolonged, Slow, Tedious, Wastings; "Low" in this section).

Succumbs Easily—To Disease—(See "Succumbs Easily" under Disease; "Early Death" under Early; "Short Life" under Life; "Low" under Recuperation, Vitality; Sickly; "Weak Body" under Weak; Inability, Low, in this section).

Susceptibility—(See Contagions, Environment, External, Infections, Negative, Passive, Receptive, Susceptibility).

Tedious Diseases—(See Chronic, Long, Slow, Tedious, etc.).

Throwing Off Disease—(See this subject under Disease; Good, Inability, Low, Strong, in this section).

Tone; Treatment—Disease Resists Treatment Stubbornly—(See "Stubborn" in this section).

Vital Signs—Of the Zodiac—(See "Signs" under Vital).

Vitality—(See "Good", "Low", under Vitality).

Wards Off Disease Easily—(See "Over-coming", "Throwing Off", under Disease; Immunity; "Rapid" under Recovery; "Good" under Recuperation, Vitality; Strength, Strong, etc.).

Weak Constitution—(See Constitution, Feeble, Sickly; "Weak Body" under Weak).

Weak Will—Makes Little Effort to Resist Disease—(See "Overcoming" under Disease; Negative, Passive, Receptive, Susceptibility; "Weak" under Will, etc.).

Wear and Tear—Ability to Withstand—(See Wear).

Will-Power—Weak Will—Strong Will—(See "Weak Will" in this section; Positive, Power, Resolute, Will).

RESOLUTE—Resolution—Firmness—Determined—Daring—Resourceful—Valiant—Brave—Self-Reliant—Resolution of Disease or Tissues, etc.—Mars is the giver of resolution, resourcefulness, courage, boldness, daring, etc. In Hor'y Questions resolution, or a resolute temper, is denoted by ♄ Sig. in ♈, or ♃ Sig. in ♏; ♂ ruler of the horoscope, a resolute temper; the good aspects of ♂ to the ☉, ☽, or ☿; ♂ in ♈ or ♏; the ☉ strong at B.; the ♌ sign on the Asc. (See "Active Mind" under Active; Ambition; "Abundance", "Great", under Energy; Persevering, Positive, Rule, Self-Reliant; "Strong Will" under Will, etc.).

Lacking In Resolution—The ☉ Sig. in ♊; ♂ weak and ill-dignified at B.; born under the strong influence of ♀. (See Dull, Fears, Idle, Inactive, Indifferent, Indolent, Lassitude; "Mutable Disposition" under Mutable; "Negative Nature" under Negative; "Weak Ill" under Will).

Pneumonia—Delayed Resolution In—(See "Delayed" under Pneumonia).

Resolution of Disease—The Solution of Continuity In Disease—Abatement of Disease, etc.—(See Abatement, Amelioration, Cataphora, Continuity, Course, Crises; "Degree Of" under Disturbed; Duration; "Disease" under Force; Improved, Minimizing, Moderation, Modification, Prognosis, Recovery, Recuperation, Remission, Retrograde, Solution, etc.).

Resolution of the Nerves—Dissolving —Absorption, etc.—A ♄ disease; ☿ afflicted by ♄. (See "Resolution" under Nerves).

Resolution of Tissues — The Resolution, Absorption, or Analysis of Tissue Into Its Elements—The work of ♄, and a ♄ disease. (See Absorption, Dissolution, Solution; "Absorption" under Tissues).

RESOLVENT—That Which Causes Solution of Tissue — An Agent Removing Swelling or Effusion—Discutients—A Therapeutic Property of ♂. A Poultice of the fresh root of Bryonia Dioica is considered good to remove swellings from external injuries, to soften and promote absorption of oedematous and hard tumors, and to relieve rheumatic pains, etc. (See Absorption, Bryonia, Discutients, Emollient; "Remedies" under Inflammation; "Sugar of Lead" under Lead; "Therapeutic Properties" under Mars; Solution).

RESOURCE—Resourcefulness—

Lacking In Resourcefulness — (See Backwardness, Dull, Fears, Helplessness, Idle, Imprudent, Indifferent, Indolent, Inert, Inferior; "Bad" under Judgment; Lack Of; "Light In Mind" under Mind; Mutable, Negative, Purposes, Receptive, Resolution, Susceptibility, Timidity, Void Of, etc.).

Readiness Of — (See "Active Mind" under Active; Genius; "Good" under Judgment; "Inventive Mind" under Learning; "Abilities", "Quickened", under Mentality; "Good" under Mind; Positive, Resolute, Self-Reliant, etc.).

RESOURCES — Assets — Money — Property, etc.—The husbanding of financial and property resources is signified by ♄ and the ♑ sign. (See Property, Riches).

Bodily Resources — The resources, or strength of the human body, its vitality, recuperative powers, resistance to disease, etc., are strengthened and built up by the good influences of the ☉, ♂, ♃, and ♀, and also by a strong and powerful sign upon the Asc. at B. The influences of ♄, when afflicting, tend to tear down, retard, and hinder bodily processes. (See Immunity, Recuperation, Resistance, Strength; "Body" under Strong; Tone, Vitality).

RESPECT—Consideration For Others— ♂ Sig. □ or 8 ♃, or ♂ Sig. ☌ ☿, has little respect for the persons or possessions of others when advantage can be gained by sacrificing them to his own interests. (See Cheating, Cruel, Deceitful, Dishonest, Liars, Plots, Thieves, Treachery, etc.).

Respect For Others—Has Respect and High Regard for the Rights of Others —(See Honest, Humane, Kind, Sincere, Sympathetic, etc.).

RESPIRATORY SYSTEM—Respiration —Breathing—Organs of Respiration— Respiratory Tract—The Breathing Organs, etc. — (See Breath, Breathing, Bronchial, Lungs, Pulmonary).

RESPONSE — The Degree of Response Against Disease — (See "Response Against Disease" under Degree).

RESPONSIBILITY — The Sense of Responsibility—♄ strong and well-placed at B. gives a grave, serious, and thoughtful nature, and with a strong sense of responsibility, and indicates that many great responsibilities will be encountered along thru life. As to whether the native will be able to cope with them successfully and wisely, and overcome obstacles, will depend largely upon the strength of the horoscope as a whole, the judgment, the mental qualities, the spiritual sight and force, the state of the health, etc. (See Ambitions, Anxieties, Carelessness, Character, Destiny, Fate, Fortune, Honesty, Honour, Improvident, Indifferent, Irresponsible, Judgment, Morals, Motives, Purposes, Reliable, Reputation, etc.).

REST — Relaxation — Recuperation — Restoration — Sleep, etc. — Rest is signified by the 4th H., decay, death, and the end of things.

Mental Rest—The airy signs tend to rapid recuperation thru mental rest and change of scenery. (See "Signs" under Air; "Air Sign People" under Residence).

Sickness—Patient Has Very Little, or No Rest In Sickness—The ☽ in ♎, afflicted by the ☉ or ♂ when taken ill, and which is generally caused by too much blood (Hor'y); ♂ in ♈ when taken ill, and ♂ the afflictor in the disease. (See Aches; "Too Much Blood" under Blood; Delirium, Discomfort, Fatigue, Malaise, Pain, Plethora, Refreshment, Restlessness; "Insomnia" under Sleep; Suffering, Weariness, etc.).

Want of Rest — (See "Sickness" in this section).

RESTLESSNESS — Restless—Unsettled — Fretful — Discontented, etc. — The SUN ill-dignified at B., and afflicted; the ☉ Sig. ☌ ☽; the ☉ to the ☌ or P. asp. the ☽; the ☉ to the ill-asps. ♅ by dir., restless and unsettled; the MOON afflicted at B., and to the ☌ the M.C. by dir.; the ☽ ill-aspected by ♅ at B., and by dir.; the ☽ ☌ or P. asp. ♂; the ☽ to the ☌ or ill-asp. ♂ by dir., and ♂ in a sign or house of the ☽; the ☽ in the 3rd H. at B., perpetual restlessness; the ☽ in the 1st or 10th H.; the ☽ ruler of the horoscope and afflicted by malefics; the ☽ ascending at B.; the ☽ in ♍; the ☽ in ♑ unless well-aspected; the Progressed ☽ (or ☉) in ⚹ or △ asp. the radical ♂; the ☽ and ☿ configurated with several planets, restless, unsettled, and unstable; the ☽ afflicted in ♈; the ☽ in ♈, and afflicted by the ☉ or ♂ when taken ill (Hor'y); the ☽ ☌ the Asc. or M.C. by Secondary Direction, restless and unsettled; the ☽ to the ill aspects the Asc. or M.C., a restless and anxious time; the ☽ to the ☌ or ill-asp. ☿ by dir., and ☿ not dignified at B.; the ☽ to the ☌ or ill-asp. ♅ by dir.; the ☽ hyleg in ♈, and afflicted, and especially with females, and tends to ailments from restlessness; NEPTUNE afflicted in ♍; ♆ in transit over the place of the radical ☿; URANUS strong and ascending at B.; ♅ in the 1st, 3rd, or 9th H.; the place of the radical ♅, ☽, or ☿ ascending at a Solar Rev.; ♅ afflicting the ☽; SATURN Sig. □ or ☍ ☽, unsettled, wandering, and changeable; JUPITER Sig. ☌ ☽; ♃ afflicted in ♒; MARS Sig. in ♊; ♂ in a mutable sign; ♂ afflicted in ♈, extreme restlessness; ♂ Sig. ☌, ⚹, or △ ☽; ♂ in the 6th H. in ☍, ♌, or ♏, and afflicted by the ☉ or ☽; ♂ to the cusp the 1st H. by dir.; VENUS Sig. □ or ☍ ☽, an unsettled and changeable life; MERCURY ☌ ♂ or ♀ in ♈, and otherwise afflicted by □ or ☍ aspects of other planets; ☿ in the Asc. at B., and in no aspect with any planet, great restlessness and desire for change; ☿ afflicted at B., weak, and ill-dignified; ☿ progressed in ☌, P., □, or ☍ the radical ♅, and vice versa; ☿ configurated with several planets; ☿ afflicted in the 1st or 10th H., a restless spirit; a ☿ disease, and afflictions to ☿; ☿ Sig. □ or ☍ ☽; the Asc. or M.C. to the ☌ ☽ by dir.; the ASCENDANT to the □ or ☍ ☿ by dir.; characteristic of the nervous temperament, ruled by ♅, ♄, ☿, and the earthy signs; a common sign on the cusp of 2nd H. at B., and ♄ therein by dir.; □ on the Asc. at B. tends to nervous disorders brought on by restlessness and discontentment; the 3rd decan. of □ on the Asc., ruled by the ☉, a restless and anxious life; cardinal signs on angles, and many planets in them; an ♈ influence. (See Active, Anxiety, Cardinal, Changes, Crime, Dejected, Depressed, Despondent, Discontentment, Fretful, Influenced, Instability, Journeys, Love Affairs, Low Spirits, Marriage, Mutable, Negative, Novelties, Patience, Peevish, Receptive, Recklessness, Regretful, Removals, Repining, Residence, Roaming, Scattering, Travel, Vacillating, Vagabond, Wanderer, Worry, etc.).

RESTORATION — To Health — (See Crises, Cure; "Better" under Disease; "Spared" under Life; Recovery, Recuperation, Rest; "Good" under Vitality).

Restoratives—(See Analeptic, Drugs, Healers, Medicines, Recreations, Remedies, Rest, Sleep, Stimulants, Tonics, Treatment, etc.).

RESTRAINTS — Restrictions — Limitations—To Hold In Check—Hindrances, etc. — Caused generally by the influences and afflictions of ♄.

Bodily Restraints—Physical Restrictions — The influence of ♄ over the body is confining, restrictive, hindering and retarding. Also the 12th H. influences tend to confinement, limitations and restrictions. Saturn tends to restrain the action of the nerves, circulation, stop bodily functions, and retard and obstruct the proper action of the organs of the body, hinder elimination, excretion, secretion, etc. For the details and influences, aspects, etc., causing these restrictions and disturbances, note carefully the paragraphs under each of the organs, and parts of the body, as given in the alphabetical arrangement of this book. Also the various evil aspects between the planets at birth and at conception, the house positions of planets, the influences of the fixed stars and Constellations at birth, and the Prenatal influences during gestation, play their important part in bringing restrictions over both mind and body. (See Birth, Blindness, Circulation, Conception, Confinement, Congenital, Crystallization, Deafness, Deformities, Elimination, Excretion, Fluids, Foetus, Functions, Hardening, Hearing, Hindrances, Limitations, Malformations, Missing, Monsters, Mutes, Nerves, Obstructions, Organs, Parts, Prenatal Epoch, Prison, Retardation, Retentions, Saturn, Secretions, Senses, Stoppages, Suppressions, Twelfth House, etc.).

Lack of Restraint — The Evil Tendencies of the Temperament Unrestrained — The ☽ sepr. from ♀ and applying to ☿; ♆ rising, or in the 3rd or 9th H., and afflicted; ♂ ☌, P., □, or ☍ ♆, lack of restraint in almost everything. (See Anger, Conduct, Cruel, Debauched, Depraved, Drink, Drunkenness, Eating, Excesses, Free, Gluttony, Habits, High Living, Indiscretions, Indulgences, Lascivious, Lewd, Licentious, Loose, Love Affairs; "Low and Base" under Low; "Loose Morals" under Morals; Luxuries, Narcotics; "Passional Excesses" under Passion; Perversions, Pleasures, Rashness, Recklessness, Riotous, Self-Control, Sex; "High Temper" under Temper; Uncontrolled, Venery, Vices, etc.).

Mental Restraints—Restrictions Over the Mind — These are caused principally by afflictions to ☿ at birth, or before birth, the evil aspects to ☿, the house position of ☿, etc., as this planet is the general ruler of the mind. The afflictions of ♄ to ☿ tend to dull and retard the mind, and the afflictions of each of the planets to ☿ tend to affect the mind according to the nature of the afflicting planet. Also, ☿ weak and ill-dignified at B., and with no relation to the ☽ or Asc., tends to impair the action of the mind. (For influences along this line, see Chaotic, Confusion, Dull, Faculties, Fears, Foolish, Forethought, Idiocy, Imbecile, Insanity, Intellect, Judgment, Memory, Mentality, Mind, Obsessions, Perception, Reason, Understanding, etc. Especially note the paragraphs and subjects under Mental, Mind).

RESTRICTIVE—Restraining—Retarding—(See Restraints, Retardation).

RETAINS—Retains Anger—Retains a Wrong or Injury—Unforgiving—(See Anger, Enemies, Enmity, Hatred, Jealousy, Malevolent, Malice, Murderous, Plots, Revenge, Treachery, Vicious, Violent, etc.).

RETARDATION — Retarded — Retarding—

Retarded Action—Due to ♄ influence and affliction. (See "Lack Of" under Action; Arrested, Decrease, Diminished, Dull, Energy, Feeble, Functions, Growth, Hindrances, Inactive, Inertia, Lassitude, Lazy, Lethargy, Motion, Movement, Obstructions, Restraint, Slow, Stoppages, Suppression, etc.).

Retarded Mental Powers — (See Arrested; "Fails In" under Examinations; Foolish, Growth, Idiocy, Imbecile, Impediments, Inhibitions; "Arrested" under Mental; "Weak Mind" under Mind; "Mental Restraints" under Restraints; "Void Of" under Reason).

RETENTION—Retentive—Holding Back—Stoppage—In the body ♄ is the planet of retention, and rules the retentive faculty. By nature, ♄ is frigid, dry, and intropulsive, tending to retain and drive inward the wastes of the body. (See "Influences of Saturn", Qualities", under Saturn).

Faeces—Retention of—(See "Hardening" under Faeces).

Food — Retention of Difficult — (See "Retention" under Food).

Memory — (See "Retentive Memory" under Memory).

Poisons of the Body—Retention of—Retention of Wastes — Caused principally by the afflictions of ♄, the planet of retention; ♄ ☌ the ☉ or ☽ in ♏; ♅ in ♎, ☌, P., □, or ☍ ♂, due to spasmodic kidney action; caused by ♀ when the dominion of death is vested in her. (See Accumulative, Crystallization, Deposits, Elimination, Excretion, Filth, Gout, Hardening, Hyperacidity, Lameness, Local Parts; "Deposits Of" under Minerals; Poisons, Rheumatism, Stone, Stoppages, Suppression; "Lessened" under Sweat; Uric, Wastes, etc.).

Urea—Retention of—(See Gout, Urea).

Uric Acid Deposits—(See Uric).

Urine—(See "Retention" under Urine).

Wastes of Body—Retention of—(See "Poisons" in this section).

RETINA—The Expansion of the Optic Nerve, and the Internal Membrane of the Eye—Ruled by the ☉ and the ♈ Sign. The etheric vibrations sensed by the retina are often interfered with by the afflicted stellar rays from certain parts of the Zodiac, as from Nebulous Spots, the ☉ or ☽ in ☌ with Nebulous Stars and Clusters at B., and tend to blindness, or to impair the physical sight. (See Blindness; "Retina" under Eyes; Nebulous; "Optic Nerve" under Optic; Pleiades, Sight).

Blind Spot Of—This is blind because it is not responsive to the etheric Mercurial vibrations. However, the spiritual ray of ♆ makes this spot sensitive, and one who may be blind physically, or have weak sight, may have great spiritual sight under the influence of ♆. (See Neptune, Spiritual).

RETIRING—Retirement—Quiet—Modest—

Retirement—The ☽ P. ♄ at B., with females.

Retiring Nature—Reserved—Quiet—♄ and ♀ influence strong at B.; ♀ rising in ♏; ♀ Sig. ✶ or △ ♄, retiring in manner. (See Grave; "Retiring" under Manner; Quiet, Recluse, Renunciation, Reserved, Serious, Thoughtful, etc.).

RETRACTION—Retractive—Shortening—Drawing Backward—The retractive forces over the body are ruled by ♄. (See Contractions; "Retraction" under Eyeballs; Opisthotonos, Rigidity, Saturn Influences).

RETROGRADE PLANETS—A planet is retrograde (℞) when it appears to be moving backward in the Zodiac, as seen from the Earth. In Astrology, this condition of a planet is considered a debility, and to weaken the action of the planet over disease and human af-

fairs. This is because it denotes a solution of continuity, interrupted sequence, the same as the direct motion of a planet indicates continuity of influence. In health matters, a planet turning ℞ indicates a change in the disease, a possible breaking up and disorganization of the disease, while the disease may continue strong as long as the afflicting planet remains direct and rapid in motion. Planets are not as forceful over the life when ℞ at B., and a person born with many planets ℞ usually has a weaker constitution, more trouble in life, less energy, etc. It is said, however, that planets ℞ at B. have a direct spiritual effect upon the life, which, in the end, often leads to greater success by Soul Growth than when the nature is more dominated by merely materialistic ambitions. Planets ℞ tend to give the Intuitional Powers greater rule, rather than Reason and the Intellect. The ☉ and ☽ are never ℞ in motion, as seen from the Earth, but the ☽ is said to be equivalent to a ℞ planet when she is slow in motion, and moving less than 13° in the 24 hours. By some Authors planets ℞ at B. are said to bring poverty and sickness. (See Continuity, Direct; "Degree Of" under Disturbed; Interrupted, Poverty, Resolution, Sequence, Sickness, Solution, Stationary).

RETROGRESSIVE—The Cellular Retrogressive Metamorphosis is presided over by ♀. (See "Alterations" under Cells; Metamorphosis).

RETROPHARYNGEAL ABSCESS—(See "Abscess" under Pharynx).

RETROSPECTIVE—Retrospection—Brooding—Living In the Past—A special trait of the ♋, or mother sign, and to be much given to the memories of childhood; ♄ in ♋, or afflicting ♋ and ☿, unpleasant memories, brooding over the mistakes of life, repining, regrets, etc. (See Brooding, Introspection, Melancholy, Morbid, Regretful, Repining, etc.).

RETURN—Returning—Returning Diseases—The Return of Disease After a Time—Old Maladies Return, etc.—The ☽ causes diseases which return after a time, such as Epilepsy, Fits, Spasms, Vertigo, etc.; the evil directions of ♄ to the hyleg; ♂ rising at B., and again at a Solar Rev.; the Asc. to the ☌ or ill-asp. ♄ by dir. (See Complications, Course, Epilepsy, Insanity, Intermittent, Irregular, Periodic, Recurrent, Regular, Relapses, Vertigo, etc.).

REVENGEFUL — Revenge — Spiteful—Vindictive—Unforgiving—Malice, etc.—The ☉ □ or ☍ ♂; the ☉ Sig. □ or ☍ ♄, spiteful; the ☽ in ♏ and afflicted by ♂; ♄ as Sig. denotes such a person in Hor'y Q.; a strong ♄ characteristic; ♄ □ or ☍ ☿, and attended with secret revenge; ♂ Sig. □ or ☍ ♄, given to secret revenge; ♂ Sig. in ♏ or ♏; the evil aspects of ♂ to the Significators; the 28° ♏ on the Asc. (See Anger, Cruel; "Secret" under Enemies; Enmity, Feuds, Hatred, Jealousy, Knavish, Malevolent, Malice, Mean, Mischief, Murderous, Plots, Poison Death, Resentful, Suicide, Treachery, Unforgiving).

REVERSES — Reversals — Failure In Business — Misfortune — Bankruptcy — Discredit — Disgrace — Dishonour — Trouble — Miseries — Downfall — Failure of Desires, etc. — The ☽ to the ☌ or P. Dec. the ☉, if the ☽ be hyleg, and the ☉ afflicted at B.; the ☽ in the 2nd H. at B., and to the ☌ or ill-asp. ♄ by dir.; ♂ Sig. ☌ ☉, sudden failures and downfall. For other influences along this line see Ambitions, Ascelli, Calamity, Cares, Castor, Catstrophies; "Failure" under Desires; Disgrace, Downfall; "Own Worst Enemy" under Enemies; Evils, Failure, Fate; "Ill-Fortune" under Fortune; "Loss Of" under Honour; Inheritance, Loss Of, Mischief, Miseries, Misfortune, Plots, Pollux, Poverty, Prison, Property; "Diseases" under Psychic; Reputation, Riches, Ruin, Scandal, Sorrow, Treachery, Trials, Trouble, Unfortunate, Wretched, etc.).

Reversing Your Stars—(See Character, Fate, Nadir; "Free Will" under Will).

REVITALIZATION — Of Fluids and Functions — (See "First Quarter" under Moon).

REVOLUTION—

Civil Revolution — Civil War — (See Revolutionary; "Civil" under War).

Periodic Revolution — Of the Planets —(See Periodic).

Planets—Revolution of—(See Climacteric; "Metonic Cycle" under Moon; "Periods of the Planets" under Periods).

Solar Revolution—(See Solar).

REVOLUTIONARY—

Revolutionary Figure—(See "Planetary Periods" under Periods; "Solar Revolution" under Solar).

Revolutionary Ideas—♃ afflicted in ♒. (See Anarchists, Destructiveness, Radicalism, Reactionary, Reformers, Riotous, Sedition; "Civil War" under War).

Revolutions—Political Revolutions and Upheavals — Revolutionary — Civil War, etc.—☿ elevated above, and configurated with ♄ at a Solar Ingress or Eclipse. (See "Much Misery Everywhere" under Misery; "Public Discord" under Quarrels; Riotous, Riots; "Civil War" under War).

RHEUM—Any Watery Flux or Catarrhal Discharge—A Watery Discharge from the Mucous Membranes, Nose, Skin, etc.—Signified by ♄ in ♈ when ♄ is the afflictor in the disease; a ⚷ disease. (See Catarrh, Colds, Defluxions, Discharges, Fluxes, Humours; "Watery Humours" under Watery).

Defluxions of Rheum—The ☽ afflicted in ♈; ♄ in ♓; a ⚷ and ♓ disease. (See Defluxions; "Rheum" under Head).

Discharges of Rheum—♈ and ⚷ diseases. (See Catarrh, Colds, Defluxions; "Rheum" under Head; "Discharges" under Nose; "Humours", "Rheum", under Throat).

Distillation — Of Rheum — ☿ afflicted in ♋.

Eyes—(See "Rheum" under Eyes).

Head—(See "Rheum" under Head).

Much Rheum—The ☉ in a water sign, and ☌ the Asc. by direction

Salt Rheum—A Form of Chronic Eczema—(See Eczema).

Throat—(See "Rheum" under Throat).

RHEUMATISM—Rheumatic—Rheumatism is caused by ♄, and ♄ afflicting the ☉ and ☽, and is caused by the retention of the wastes and poisons of the body, by the deposit of mineral wastes, or the deposit of Urates, Uric Acid, Urea, etc. (See Precipitation). Rheumatism is also brought on by worry, lowered vitality and nerve force, by over-eating, irregular habits, excesses, surfeits, and by breaking the laws of health. (For further influences causing this disease see "Causes", "Tendency To", and the various paragraphs in this section. Also see Saturn).

Acute Rheumatism—♂ in the 6th H. in a cardinal sign, and afflicted by the ☉ or ☽.

Arms—Hands—Legs—Feet—♄ or ♂ in signs which rule the arms, hands, legs, and feet tend to rheumatism in these parts. (See "Rheumatism" under Arms, Feet, Hands, Legs).

Arthritis—(See Joints).

Articular Rheumatism — (See "Rheumatism" under Joints).

Back — (See "Muscular Rheumatism" under Back; Lumbago).

Bones—(See "Rheumatism" under Bones).

Cases of Rheumatism — Birth Data, etc.—See Figures 11G and 11H, in the book, "Astro-Diagnosis" by the Heindels).

Causes of Rheumatism—A ☽ disease, and by the afflictions of ♄ to the ☽; ♄ or ♂ ☌ ☽; ♄ afflicted in ♋ or ♑; a ☿ disease; a ♐, ♑, and ♒ disease; malefics angular, occi. to the ☽, and in the last degrees of ♊ or ♐, and if the benefics are with the malefics, or ori. or angular, and cast any ray to the Lights, the disease will be cured, and the rapidity and the certainty of the cure will be proportionate to their strength. If the benefics are weak, and do not assist, it will tend to be incurable, or greatly prolonged. (See the Introduction to this Article," Tendency To", and the various paragraphs in this section; Hyperacidity; "Impure Blood" under Impure).

Chronic Deformans—(See Ankylosis, Arthritis, Rheumatism, under Joints).

Chronic Rheumatism—♄ in the 6th H. at B., in a fixed sign, and afflicted by the ☉ or ☽.

Cold, Rheumatic Diseases—A ☽ disease, and afflictions to the ☽; the ☽ afflicted by ♄, and especially in earthy signs.

Continued and Promoted — ♄ or ☿ holding dominion at B., and in familiarity with each other; ♄ angular and elevated above the Lights, and in familiarity with ☿. (See "Tendency" in this section).

Curable — (See "Causes" in this section).

Death by Rheumatism — Death from Rheumatic Fever—♄ occi, and afflicting the hyleg by dir.; ♄ holding the dominion of death, and afflicting the hyleg by dir.; ♄ in the 8th H. at a Solar Rev. into ♈, and afflicting the ☽ or planet ascending, tends to be very fatal according to the sign occupied by ♄. (See Fever, Tendency, in this section).

Deformities From—(See "Ankylosis", and the various paragraphs under Joints).

Dengue — (See "Fever" in this section).

Deposits—Mineral and Waste Deposits Causing Rheumatism — (See Bile, Deposits, Minerals, Poisons, Uric, Wastes).

Extremities — Rheumatism In — (See "Rheumatism" under Arms, Extremities, Feet, Hands, Legs, Limbs).

Feet—(See "Rheumatism" under Feet).

Fever — Rheumatic Fever — Also Resembles Dengue—The ☽ hyleg, and to the ♂, P., □, or 8 ♄ by dir.; ♂ afflicted in ♑; ♂ in ♑ in the 6th H.; ♂ in ♑, and afflicting the ☽ or Asc.; Subs. at CP, KP. (See Dengue; "Death" in this section).

Gall Disturbances—(See Bile).

Gout—Rheumatic Gout—(See Gout).

Hands—(See "Arms" in this section).

Headaches—(See "Rheumatic" under Headaches).

Heart — (See "Rheumatic" under Heart).

Hips and Thighs—(See "Rheumatism" under Hips).

Incurable—(See "Causes" in this section).

Joints — (See Ankylosis, Arthritis, Rheumatism, under Joints).

Knees—(See "Rheumatism" under Knees).

Legs — (See "Arms" in this section; "Rheumatism" under Extremities, Legs).

Limbs—Rheumatism In—(See Arms, Extremities, Legs, in this section).

Melancholy—(See "Rheumatism" under Melancholy).

Mineral Deposits—(See Deposits, Minerals).

Muscular Rheumatism — (See "Rheumatism" under Muscles).

Pains — Rheumatic Pains — (See "Pains", "Rheumatism", under Arms, Extremities, Feet, Hands, Hips, Knees, Legs, Thighs; Gout, Resolvent).

Promoted and Continued—(See "Continued" in this section).

Remedy For—(See "Acid Conditions" under Remedies; Resolvent).

Rheumatic Fever — (See "Fever" in this section).

Rheumatoid Arthritis—(See "Arthritis" under Joints).

Shoulders—(See "Rheumatism" under Arms; "Pains", "Rheumatism", under Shoulders).

Tendency to Rheumatism — ♄ influence and affliction at B., and by dir., is the principal cause. Saturn deposits Urea and Gall over the body as Uric Acid, which is one of the principal causes of Rheumatism. (See Bile, Uric Acid). Caused by ♄, and especially when the dominion of death is vested in him; ♄ in an angle, occi. of the ☉, and ori. of the ☽, tends to promote the continuance of rheumatism, and especially if he is also in familiarity with ☿; ♄ afflicting the hyleg or Asc.; ♄ in ♎, ♑, or ♓, occi., and afflicting the ☉, ☽, or Asc.; ♄, ♅, or ♆ in ♒, and afflicting the ☉ or ☽; ♄ afflicted in the 6th H. in cardinal signs; a ♑ disease, the sign of ♄; afflictions in ♐ or ♑; afflictions in ♒, also the sign of ♄; ♑ on the Asc. or 6th H.; ♄ sole ruler of a Solar Eclipse; ♄ to the ♂ or ill-asps. the ☽ if the ☽ be hyleg, or ruler of the 6th or 8th H.; an ♒ disease, the day sign of ♄; ♄ afflicted in ♒; the ☉ to the ♂, P., □, or 8 ♄ by dir.; the ☉ to the ♂ ☋ by dir.; the ☉, ♄, ♂, or ☿ afflicted in ♑; the ☉, ♄, or ♂ in the 6th H., afflicted, and in a cardinal sign; the ☉ in ♋ and afflicted by ♄; the parallel or ♂ of ♄ and the ☉ in ♋, ♑, or ♒; the ☉ to the ♂ or ill-asp. ♄ by dir., and the ☉ and ♄ in ♋, ♑, or ♒ at B.; the ☽ hyleg, and to the ♂, P., □, or 8 ♄ by dir.; the ☽ hyleg in ♑, and afflicted, and especially with females; the ☽ sign ♋ upon the Asc., and afflicted by ♄; the ☽ ♂, □, or 8 ♄ at a Solar Rev.; ♆ in ♓ and afflicting the ☉; ♆ in ♒ and afflicting the ☉ or ☽; ♅ in ♒ and afflicting the ☉ or ☽; ♃ afflicted in ♐; a ♐ disease, and caused by afflictions in ♐; ♃ afflicted in ♉, ♋, or in the 6th H., and usually from over-eating and surfeits; ♂ and ♄ in signs which rule the arms, hands, legs and feet tend to rheumatism in these parts; ♂ in the 6th H. in cardinal signs, and afflicting the ☉ or ☽, tends to acute rheumatism; ☿ in ♏ or ♒, ♂, or ill-asp. any of the malefics as Promittors, tends to touches of rheumatism; a ♓ disease, and caused by afflictions in ♓. (For other influences see the various paragraphs in this Article).

Thighs — (See "Rheumatism" under Hips).

Treatment For — (See "Remedy" in this section).

Urea—Retention of—(See Urea).

Uric Acid Deposits—(See Uric). For collateral study, see such subjects as "Pressure", "Too Much Blood", under Blood; Diet, Eating, Excesses, Gluttony, Habits, Hyperacidity, Plethora, Surfeits, etc.

RHINITIS—Cold In the Head—Coryza —(See "Rhinitis" under Nose).

RHUS TOXICODENDRON—Poison Ivy —(See Ivy).

RHYTHM—Rhythmical—Symmetric Movement—

Arhythmia Cordis — (See "Rhythm" under Heart).

Breathing—Interference With Rhythmic Breathing — (See "Rhythmic Breathing" under Breath).

Diaphragm—Rhythmic Action of Disturbed—(See "Rhythm" under Diaphragm).

Heart—Rhythm of Disturbed—(See "Rhythm" under Heart).

Operations — The Rhythmical Operations In the Body — These depend largely upon the vital points in the Cranium and Encephalon, and ruled over by the first zone, or node of ♈. The ☉ in ♈ in this zone, and influenced by ☿, excites the nervous cell. The ☉ incites organic rhythm. The ☽ also excites the organismic rhythm according to the Zodiac zones she passes through, and gives way to Zymotic Periodicity. Venus also largely influences the harmony and rhythm in the system. In Nature, there is a rhythmic movement throughout the Universe, and everything moves in cycles of more or less regularity, and the pendulum swings back and forth in human, and other matters, in rhythmic order. The Planets also have their rhythm. The student should make a study of the subject of Rhythm in the Occult and Metaphysical books, as such books go into various details as to the rhythm in the Universe. (See Balance, Coalition, Coordination, Dexterity, Equilibrium, Harmony, Nature, Sympathy, Vibration, etc.).

RIBES—Ganglion of—(See "Ribes" under Ganglion).

RIBS—Costal—The Ribs are under the structural rulership of the ♋ sign. Gemini also rules over the upper Ribs. Also ♃ rules the ribs. Saturn in ♉, ♐, and ♋ rules and affects the ribs and bones connected with the Respiratory System. There are 24 Ribs, with 12 on each side, and their attachments to the vertebrae are given under the subject of Vertebrae.

All Diseases In—In and Around the Ribs—♌ diseases, and afflictions in ♌; diseases of ♃.

Broken Ribs—Fractures of—Caused generally by ♄ or ♂ afflicted in ♐ or ♋.

Shooting Pains—Under the Ribs—The ☽ in ♍, ♂, P., □, or ☍ ♄ (or ☿ if he be of the nature of ♄) at the beginning of an illness, or at decumb., and under this affliction the patient is generally ailing a long time (Hor'y).

Upper Ribs—The True Ribs—Ruled by ♐. The Lower, or False Ribs, are ruled by ♐ and the ♋ sign. (See Chest, Flanks, Intercostal, Sides, Sternum, Thorax, Vertebrae).

RICH—Abundant—Copious—

Blood Too Rich — Gross Blood — (See Gross, Rich, under Blood).

Food Too Rich—Love of Rich Food— (See "Rich" under Food). See Riches.

RICHES—Wealth—Property Interests— Real Estate—Lands—Fortune—Material Prosperity, etc.—

Accumulates Great Riches — The ☽ Sig. ♂ ♃, but is apt to lose it thru many impositions upon his kindness and generosity; ♃ aspecting the Meridian at B., unless evil aspects counteract, becomes extremely wealthy, and comes to distinction; ☿ Sig. ♂ ♃. (See "Confers", and the various paragraphs in this section).

Acquires Property—(See Property).

Bankruptcy — And Reverses — (See Failure, Loss Of, Reverses, Ruin).

Benevolent — Gives Money Freely — The ☽ ♂ ♃; ♃ in the Asc. or M.C., in

♐ or ♓, and well-aspected. (See Generous; "Accumulates" in this section).

Betting—(See "Gambling" in this section).

Buildings and Real Estate—Gains By —The ☽ on the Meridian at B., or coming to it, and well-aspected by ♄, and ♄ strong and dignified. (See Property).

Confers Riches—The ☉ Sig. ✶ or △ ♃, gains money rapidly; the ☉ Sig. ✶ or △ ☽, confers riches and honours; the ☽ on the Meridian at B., or coming to, and well-aspected by ♃; ♃ Sig. ♂, ✶, or △ ♀; ♀ Sig. ♂ ♃; fixed stars of a fortunate nature ascending, culminating, or with the ☉ or ☽, such as Arista, North Scale, Rigel, etc. (See "Accumulates", and the various paragraphs in this section).

Death — Thru Worry from Loss of Property—(See Property).

Disgrace—And Loss of Riches—(See Disgrace, Honour, Reverses, Ruin, Scandal; "Losses" in this section).

Duped of His Property — (See Property).

Extravagant—(See Expense, Extravagance, Luxuries, Prodigal, etc.).

Failure — In Business — (See Failure, Property, Reverses, Ruin).

Free Living — High Living — (See "Free Living" under Free; "Living" under High).

Gains Property—Often Gains Considerable Property, Although Unstable In Disposition—♀ Sig. ✶ or △ the ☽. (See Accumulates, Confers, in this section; Property).

Gambling—Losses By—Fond of Betting—♃ afflicted at B., and ♃ to the ill-asps. ♂ by dir. (See Gambling).

Generous With Money—(See "Benevolent" in this section; Money).

Great Riches—(See "Accumulates" in this section).

Honors Conferred — Confers Honors and Riches—The ☉ Sig. ✶ or △ the ☽ or ♃; ♃ strong, dignified, and well-aspected in the 10th H.; ♀ Sig. ♂ ♃. (See "Confers" in this section).

Hypocritical Fanatics — Impoverished By—(See "Impoverished" in this section).

Impoverished—Property Impoverished by Hypocritical Fanatics—The ☽ Sig. □ or ☍ ♃.

Indigent—(See Apathy, Dull, Indifferent, Indigent, Lazy, Poor, Poverty, Property).

Lawsuits — Losses By — Brings Lawsuits Over Money Matters — Lawsuits are ruled by the 7th H., and malefics passing thru this house by transit or direction tend to lawsuits; the ☉ to the ♂ or ill-asp. ♂ by dir.; the ☽ to the □ or ☍ ♂ by dir.; the ☽ hyleg, and ☿ afflicted at B.; ♃ Sig. □ or ☍ ☿, becomes indigent and poor; ☿ Sig. □ or ☍ ♄. (See Law, Libel; "Lawsuits" under Public; Quarrelsome).

Losses—Suffers Losses—The ☉ Sig. □ or ☍ the ☽ or ♃; ♄ in the 2nd H. at B., in a weak sign, and afflicted. (See Misfortune, Property, Reverses, Ruin; the various paragraphs in this section).

Luxuries—Waste of Fortune By—(See "Extravagant" in this section).

Merchandise—Gains a Fortune By—♄ Sig. ☌ ♃.

Mines—Riches From—(See Mines).

Miserly—(See Miserly, Penurious).

Misfortune—(See Fate, Fortune, Misery, Misfortune, Wretched).

Money—Makes Money—Loses Money — (See Money, Property, Reverses, Ruin, Wealth; the various paragraphs in this section).

Poverty and Indigence — (See "Indigent" in this section).

Preaching — Gains Riches By — (See "Clergymen" under Religion).

Profession—Gains Riches By—Loses By — (See Confers, Losses, and the various paragraphs in this section; "Fortunate" under Fortune; Prosperity).

Property—Gains Property—Losses of — (See Property; the various paragraphs in this section).

Prosperity—(See "Degrees", "Fortunate", under Fortune; Prosperity; "Confers" in this section).

Rapidly—Gains Money Rapidly—(See "Confers" in this section).

Real Estate—Gains By—(See "Buildings" in this section).

Reverses—(See Failure; "Ill-Fortune" under Fortune; Misfortune, Reverses, Ruin, etc.).

Rich—Becomes Rich—(See Accumulates, Confers, in this section).

Riotous Living—Wastes Riches By—(See Drink, Expense, Extravagant, Free, Loose, Luxuries, Prodigal, Riotous).

Ruined — Financial Ruin — (See Disgrace, Drink, Excesses, Failure, Free Living, Gambling, High Living, Honour, Loose Living, Prodigal, Ruin, Thieving, etc.).

Speculation—Loses By—The ☉ Sig. ☌ ♄; malefics afflicted in the 5th H., or a malefic lord of the 5th, and afflicted, and with no fortunate influences over the 5th H. (See Gambling).

Uncharitable — (See Cruel, Miserly, Mistrustful, Penurious, Pity, Selfish, Suspicious).

Unsettled—Not Settled Long Enough to Gain Wealth — ♃ Sig. ☌ ☽. (See Changes, Residence, Restless, Travel, Vacillating, etc.).

Vocation — Many Changes In — (See Vocation).

Waste of Fortune—(See "Riotous" in this section).

Wealth—Gains Wealth—Loses Wealth (See Accumulates, Confers, Losses, Reverses, Riotous, and the various paragraphs in this section).

RICKETS—Rachitis—A ♄ disease; ♄ afflicted in ♓; the ☉ afflicted by ♄ at B. This is a disease of childhood, and with increased cell growth of the bones, softening of the bones, lack of earthy matter, with deformity, and changes in the liver and spleen.

Case of Rickets—(See Fig. 13G in the book, "Astro-Diagnosis", by the Heindels).

Foetal Rickets — Due to Improper Formation of Cartilage — (See Cartilage).

Mineral Salts—Lack of In the Blood, Causing Rickets—(See "Blood" under Minerals).

RIDING—Horseback Riding—Fond of—(See "Riding" under Horses; "Outdoor" under Sports).

Injury By—(See "Injury", "Thrown", under Horses).

RIGEL—Orion's Foot—A star of the 1st magnitude in the 3rd face of ♊, and of the nature of ♃ and ♂. When rising or culminating at B. tends to bring honors, riches, and happiness. The ☉ to the place of gives boldness, and also tends to loss of blood. The ☽ to the place of brings danger of sickness, death of the wife or mother, or an aged female relative. The Asc. to the place of causes melancholy and timidity. (See "Death Of" under Aunts; Mechanical; "Tendency To" under Melancholy; "Death Of" under Mother, Wife, Timidity).

RIGHT—Right Side of the Body—Taken as a whole the ☉ is said to rule the right side of the body. It is also ruled by heat, and the hot and dry elements, and has more heat than the left side, and the left side is ruled by cold, and cold and moisture. The even, negative, and feminine signs of the Zodiac correspond to the right side of the body in the male, and the odd, positive, and masculine signs to the right side of the body in the female. Thus in the male the right side is ruled by the 2nd, 4th, 6th, 8th, 10th, and 12th Houses, corresponding also to the ♉, ♋, ♍, ♏, ♑, and ♓ signs. These influences would rule the left side of the female. In the female the right side is ruled by the positive signs and houses, as the 1st, 3rd, 5th, 7th, 9th, and 11th Houses, and by ♈, ♊, ♌, ♎, ♐, and ♒, etc. However, the ☉ and the masculine signs are said to rule the right side as a whole, regardless of sex, and the ☽ and feminine signs over the left side as a whole. However, in determining the degree of heat and cold in the different organs and parts of the right side of the body, it is well to be governed by the rules according to the sex of the nativity. (See "Houses", "Signs", under Feminine, Masculine, Negative, Odd, Positive; Houses; "Left Side of Body" under Left; Signs of the Zodiac).

Accidents to Right Side — Hurts and Injuries To—Malefics, and especially ♄ and ♂ in feminine signs. Thus ♄ in ♑ at B. tends to injuries to the right knee in a male, and to the left knee in a female, etc.

Auricle—Right Auricles of the Heart —(See "Auricles", "Right Side", under Heart).

Cerebral Hemisphere — The Right Cerebral Hemisphere—(See Cerebral).

Coronary Plexus—The Right Coronary Plexus—(See "Middle Cervical" under Ganglion).

Eyes — The Right Eye in a male is ruled by the ☉, and by the ☽ in a female. The ☉ afflicted by malefics, Nebulous Stars, or the ☉ afflicted in ♈

or the 1st H., or the ☉ to the evil asp. a malefic by dir., tends especially to accidents, blindness, impediments, marks, scars, diseases, or injuries to the right eye of a male, and the ☽ under similar conditions to the right eye of a female. Hurts, Blows, and Injuries to the right eye of a male are caused also by the ☉ afflicted at B., and to the ♂, P, or ill-asp. the Asc. by dir., and especially if the ☉ be in an airy sign. The ☉ to the ♂ ♄ by dir., or the ☉ to the place of Antares, tends to hurts to the right eye of a male by blows, injuries, or falls. The ☽ when afflicted under similar conditions tends to the same kind of afflictions, marks, or injuries to the right eye of a female. In Hindu Astrology the 2nd House rules the right eye. (See "Right Eye" under Eyes, Females, Males, Scars; "Eyes" under Left, Marks).

Face—Marks on Right Side of—(See "Marks" under Face).

Females—Right Eye In—Right Side of—(See the Introduction, and "Eyes" in this section).

Foot—Mark or Mole on the Right Foot—(See "Marks" under Feet).

Heat—The Right Side of the body is ruled by heat, and heat is the elemental quality. (See Heat; Introduction to this Article).

Injuries—To Right Side—(See "Accidents", "Eyes", and the Introduction in this section).

Lungs—(See "Right Lung" under Lungs).

Males—Right Side of—(See "Accidents", "Eyes", and the Introduction in this section; "Right Eye" under Males).

Marks—Moles—On Right Side of the Body—(See "Right Side" under Marks; the various paragraphs, and the Introduction in this section).

Right-Handedness—(See Dexterity).

RIGHTS OF OTHERS—Little Regard For—(See Cruel, Improvident, Indifferent, Respect).

RIGIDITY—Rigid—Stiffness—Immobility—Inflexible—Spastic, etc.—Caused by ♄, and the hardening of the synovial membranes. (See Contortions, Contractions, Crystallization, Deposits, Gout, Hardening, Immobility, Inflexible, Joints, Limbs, Minerals, Muscles, Opisthotonos, Retraction, Rheumatism, Spasmodic, Spine, Stiffness, Synovial, Tetanus, Tonic Spasm, etc.).

Rigid Parts—Contortion of—♄ ♂ or ill-asp. ♅. (See Contortions, Distortions, Twistings).

Rigid Self-Denial—(See Miserly, Penurious, Recluse, Renunciation, Self-Denial, Selfishness).

Rigors—(See Rigors).

Testicle—Right Testicle—(See Testes).

RIGORS—Coldness—Stiffness—Rigidity—♄ ♂ or ill-asp. the ☉. (See "Body" under Cold; Rigidity, Stiffness).

Rigor Mortis—The Rigidity of the Body After Death—Ruled over and produced by ♄. (See Death).

RINGWORM—The Circling Tinea or Herpes—Tetter—Ringworm is a ♀ disease, and results from Gormandizing and Gluttony, as a rule; a ♂ disease, and caused by ♂ afflictions; an ♈ disease when malefics are in this sign; ♂ afflicted in ♈, or ♂ in ♈ in the 6th H., and afflicted; the ☽ afflicted in ♋, ♌, or ♍; ♃ afflicted in ♉. (See "Barber's Itch" under Barbers; Eczema, Herpes, Tetter).

RIOTOUS—A Turbulent Mind—A ♂ quality; ♂ ♂ or ill-asp. ☿; ♂ ill-dignified at B., and afflicted; ♂ to the ill-asps. ☿ by dir.; ♂ □ or ☍ ☿, a sharp and turbulent mind; ♂ Sig. in ♒; the ☽ in ♋, and afflicted by ♂ or the ☉; ♄ Sig. ♂ ♂, rash and turbulent; ♀ ill-dignified at B.; Part of Fortune (⊕) to the ill-asps. ♀ by dir.; the M.C. to the place of Algol or Hydra's Heart; strong ♋ and ♑ influence at B. (See Anarchists, Destructiveness, Erratic, Foolhardy; "Impractical" under Ideals; Malevolent, Mischief, Quarrelsome, Radicalism, Rashness, Reactionary, Recklessness, Reformers; "High Temper" under Temper; Turbulent, Vicious, Violent, etc.).

Death—A Riotous Death—Death In a Riotous Manner—♆ and ♂ predispose to when they are Anareta, and holding the dominion of death. (See Anareta, Lynching, Mobs; "Death" under Neptune, Violent; Riots, etc.).

Fancies—Turbulent and Riotous Fancies—(See "Turbulent" under Fancies).

Riotous Living—The ☉ Sig. □ or ☍ ♃; ♀ diseases, and afflictions to ♀. (See Debauchery, Dissipation, Dissolute, Drunkenness; "Free Living" under Free; "High Living" under High; Living; "Loose Morals" under Morals).

Stomach Disordered—By Drink and Riotous Living—(See "Stomach" under Drink).

RIOTS—Danger of—Danger of Death In—♂ in the Asc. at the Vernal, lord of the year, and afflicted. (See Hanging, Lynching, Mobs; "Death" under Riotous, Violent; "Flying Stones" under Stones; Trampled, Tumults, War).

RIPE—Ripening—Maturation—

Ripe Fate—(See Fate).

Ripe Old Age—Lives To—(See "Long Life" under Life).

Ripening—(See Fruit, Maturation, Tubercle).

RISING—Rising Planets—Rising Sign—Risings—

A Rising—(See Abscesses, Boils, Carbuncles, Swellings, Tumors, etc.).

Rising Planets—Planets when rising at B., between Midnight and Noon, are more powerful for good or ill over the native than when setting between the time of Noon and Midnight. Children born in the morning hours, with the ☉ rising, tend to be leaders in the World, and have better health and vitality, while those born in the afternoon hours, with the ☉ setting in the West, tend, as a rule, to be followers, and especially if other conditions and majorities of the planets concur. (See Elevated, Majority; "Above the Earth" under Moon; Occidental, Oriental, Quarters, Setting, etc.).

Rising Sign—The Sign rising on the cusp of the First House at Birth—The

Ascendant—The Degree Rising on the Eastern Horizon at Birth—The Rising Sign rules largely over the life and the health. The most vital and sensitive part of the body is ruled by the Rising Sign, and when this part of the body is weakened, long illnesses often result. Also the Sign upon the Ascendant at B. shows the nature of the diseases the native is subject to during life. (See Ascendant; "Zodiac" under Degrees; First House).

RISKS — Perils — Has Endured Many Dangers — (See Dangers, Perils, Rescue).

RITUAL—Ritualism—(See "Ritualism" under Religion).

RIVERS—Streams—Running Water—
Corruption Of—Eclipses of the ☉ or ☽ in ♍ or ♓. (See Corruption, Fishes, Moisture, Waters).

Rivers Fail — Eclipses of ☉ in 1st Decan. of ♓. (See Drought; "Fountains" under Dry; Famine, Fountains; "Extreme Heat" under Heat).

ROAMING NATURE — A Roving and Wandering Nature—A ☽ influence; the ☽ in the Asc. or M.C. at B. (See Changes, Instability, Location, Novelties, Residence, Restlessness; "Travels Much" under Travel; Vacillating; Vagabond, Wanderer, etc.).

ROBBERS — Bandits — Robberies — Thieves—
A Robber—♂ and ☿ together lords of the employment; ♂ stronger, and in ill-asp. to the ☽; ☿ Sig. ☌ ♂. (See Cheating, Deceitful, Dishonest, Gambling, Highwaymen, Murderous, Pirates, Thieves, etc.).

Accidents—In Attacks by Robbers— (See "Death by Burns" under Burns).

Attacks By — Attacks or Injury by Robbers, Bandits, or Burglars — The malefics in the M.C., and elevated above the Lights, and ♂ holding dominion and afflicting the hyleg; ♅ afflicted in the 12th H.; ♄ and ♂ in human signs and controlling the Luminaries; ♂ afflicted in ♐ or ♍, and ☌, □, or ☍ the Asc. by dir.; ♂ in the 12th H., and afflicted by ♅ or ♄. (See Distortions, Excrescences, Highwaymen; "Dangers" under Travel; the various paragraphs in this section).

Burned to Death—During Attack by Robbers—(See "Death by Burns" under Burns).

Danger by Robbers—Or Thieves—Injury By—The ☽ passing over the place of the radical ♂ at a Solar Rev.; eclipse of ☽ in 3rd dec. of ♓; the Periodic Rev. of ♄ on the place of the radical ♂; the ⊕ to the ☌, P., or ill-asp. ♂ by dir.; the cusp of the 2nd H., or its ruler, to the ☌, P., or evil asp. ♂ by dir.; the ☉ to the ☌ ♂ by dir.; ♂ ☌ the Asc. by dir. (See the various paragraphs in this section).

Death by Robbers—Violent Death by Robbers, Highwaymen or Thieves — The ☽ passing over the place of the radical ♂ at a Solar Rev.; ♅ afflicted in the 12th H.; ♄ and ♂ in ♐, ♍, ♐, or ♒, and in □ or ☍ the ☉ or ☽, and ☿ also evilly configurated with ♂; ♃ Sig. □ or ☍ ♂; ♂ in signs of human form,

□ or ☍ the ☉ or ☽, and contrary in condition, and ☿ also configurated with them; ♂ by Periodic Rev. to the evil asps. ♅; ♂, (or ☿ afflicted by ♂), and either of them ruler of the 12th H. at B., and be found on the cusp the 7th H. in a Solar Rev., danger during the ensuing year; ♂ badly aspected at B., and ♄ passing over the place of ♂ by transit, or at a Solar Rev.; ♂ ori. in fixed signs, and □ or ☍ the ☉ at B., or ♂ occi., □ or ☍ the ☽ at B.; ♂ Sig. □ or ☍ ☉ if ☉ be lord of 7th H.; ☿ afflicted at B. by ♄ or ♂, and ♂ afflicting the hyleg by dir., and ☿ holding the dominion of death; ☿ occi. at B., ☌, □, or ☍ ♄ or ♂, and afflicting the hyleg by dir., and in a train of fatal directions; ☿ afflicting the hyleg, or giver of life, by dir. (See Bandits, Highwaymen, Murdered, Pirates, Thieves; "Danger" under Travel).

Distortions—Excrescences—The Result of Attacks by Robbers—(See Distortions, Excrescences).

Excrescences — (See "Distortions" in this section).

Eyes — Injury To by Robbers — (See "Robbers" under Eyes).

Gunshot Wounds By—(See Gunshot).

Highwaymen—Death or Injury By—(See Death, Prevalent, in this section; Highwaymen).

Hurts By—Injury By—(See "Attacks", and the various paragraphs in this section).

Injury By—(See Attacks, Distortions, and the various paragraphs in this section).

Journey—Hurts By On a Journey—♂ or ☋ in the 3rd H. in a fiery sign. (See "Accidents" under Journeys).

Killed By — (See "Death" in this section).

Many Robberies—(See Highwaymen, Prevalent, in this section).

Prevalent — Many Robberies Prevalent—An eclipse of the ☉ in 2nd decan. of □ or ♒; eclipse of ☽ in 2nd decan. ♐; ♂ in ♏ at the Vernal, and lord of the year. (See Crime, Highwaymen, Rapine, Thieves).

Rapine Prevalent—Plundering—(See Rapine, Thefts).

Thieves—Injury or Death By—(See Attacks, Death, and the various paragraphs in this section).

Travel—Attacks by Robbers or Highwaymen During Travel—The afflictor to the Sig. of travel being in the 12th H., and in □ or ♍, and especially if ♂ or ☿ be the afflictor. (See Highwaymen, Pirates; "Danger" under Travel; "Journey" in this section).

Violent Death By — (See "Death" in this section).

ROBUST—Robust Body—Strong Body—Wiry Body — Robust Constitution — Rugged—Ruddy—Hardy—Sturdy—Enduring Health and Strength, etc.—
Complexion—Robust and Ruddy Complexion—(See Complexion, Ruddy).

Constitution—Robust Constitution—♂ people tend to have a strong, robust, sturdy body; ♂ ascending at B.; born under the strong rule of ♂, and ♂ ruler; the ♂ signs ♈ or ♏ upon the Asc. at B.; the ☽ or ♃ in ♌; ♃ strong at B.; ♃ well-aspected in ♏; born under ♃; fiery signs on the Asc. at B.; born under the whole signs ♊, ♎, and ♒, strong and robust; ♏ on the Asc., strong, robust, and corpulent, and of middle size; ♒ on the Asc., robust, strong, well-set, healthy, plump, but usually not tall; the 19° ♍ on the Asc. at B. (See "Good" under Constitution; "Abundance", "Good", under Health; Immunity, Invigoration; "Great Physical Powers" under Physical; Ruddy, Stamina, Strength; "Body" under Strong; Tone; "Good" under Vitality).

Females Robust — (See "Robust" under Females).

Frame Strengthened—(See "Strengthening" under Bones).

Health Good — (See "Good" under Health).

Less Robust — (See Debility, Feeble, Ill-Health, Infirm, Invalids; "Much Sickness" under Sickness; "Low" under Vitality; "Weak Body" under Weak).

Men More Robust—(See "Good Health", "Robust", under Males).

Not Robust — (See "Bad Health" under Health; "Ill-Health" All Thru Life" under Ill-Health; Pale, Sickly; "Weakened" under Strength; "Not Strong" under Strong; "Less Robust" in this section).

Sports—Fond of Robust Sports—(See "Robust" under Sports).

Tone—(See "Good Tone" under Tone).

Vitality Good—(See "Good" under Vitality).

Weak Body—(See "Weak Body" under Weak).

ROCKS—Rocky—(See Metals, Minerals).

Rocky Mountain Fever—(See Mountain).

ROLLING STOCK—Accidents, Injuries, or Death By — (See Journeys, Railroads, Travel, Vehicles).

Rolling Eyes — (See "Rolling" under Eyes).

ROMAN EMPEROR—Should be Careful of Assassination by a Stab — ♂ in ♑, Ruler of the Year at the Vernal Equi., and ori., and especially if the ☽ is in the 8th H., or with the lord of the 8th, or with ♂ in an angle, and with no good aspect from ♃. (See Kings, Nobles, Princes, Rulers).

ROMANCE — Romantic — Love of Romance — Romantic Disposition — Given by ♆ and ♅; ♆ ☌ ☽ in ♓; ♅ strong and rising at B.; the 2° ♉ on the Asc., ruled by the ☽. The watery signs are also strongly connected with romance and emotionalism, and also the ♌ sign. (See Emotions, Feelings, Leo Sign; "Romance" under Love Affairs; Mental, Neptune, Temperament, Uranus, Watery Signs).

ROOTS — Root Vegetables which grow under the ground, such as carrots, turnips, potatoes, etc, are not as nourishing and life-giving as the leafy vegetables and fruits which grow above the ground, as the latter are Sun-kissed, and contain more of the vital power of the ☉. Roots are more governed by ♄, and grow in the dark and cold, as ♄ rules the ground. In illness, fruit juices are more vitalizing than roots. (See Drugs, Herbs, Medicines, Remedies, Treatment, Vegetables, etc.).

ROSE COLD—(See "Hay Fever" under Nose).

ROSE-COLORED—Rosy—

Rose-Colored Vital Fluid — (See "Fluid" under Vital). See Roseola.

Rosy Complexion—(See "Rosy" under Complexion).

ROSEOLA— A Rose-Colored Efflorescence on the Skin—A ♄ and ♑ disease; ♄ afflicted in ♑, or in the Asc.; ♑ on the Asc.; afflictions in ♑. (See Efflorescence, Skin).

ROTTEN — Rottenness — Putrid — Corruption—See the following subjects—

Abscesses; Breath—Rotten and Putrid Breath—(See "Foul" under Breath).

Corrupt; Coughs—(See "Rotten" under Cough).

Death—♀ denotes death from diseases arising from rottenness and putrefaction, and such as arise from too much moisture. (See "Death" under Moisture, Putrid).

Diseases—Arising from Rottenness— Death From—(See "Death" in this section).

Disintegration; Fetid; Food — (See "Rottenness" under Food).

Foul; Fruit; Gangrene; Herbs—Rottenness of—(See "Seeds" in this section).

Impure — Impurities — (See Corrupt, Impure).

Moisture — Moisture and Dampness are associated with rottenness. (See "Moist Warmth" under Moisture; "Physiological Action" under Moon; Vapors).

Mortification; Pus; Putrid;

Seeds and Herbs—Rottenness of—An eclipse of the ☉ or ☽ in ♎; an eclipse of the ☽ in ♒, seeds are injured; Comets appearing in ♑, detriment to seeds of the Earth. (See Comets, Eclipses, Fruit, Grain, Herbs, Putrefaction, Seeds, Vegetation, etc.).

Sores; Teeth — (See "Rotten" under Teeth).

Ulcers; Vegetation.

ROUGH— Not Smooth—Harsh—Rugged —Uncouth—Coarse—

Carriage—Rough In Carriage—(See "Rough" under Gait).

Gait—(See "Rough" under Gait).

Hair—(See "Coarse", "Rough", under Hair).

Manner—Rough In Manner—Rude— Unrefined — Vulgar — Coarse — The ☽ Sig. ☌ ♄; caused by the undesirable aspects and afflictions of ♄ and ♂ to the ☉, ☽, ♀, or Asc.; ♄ ☍ ♂ in angles. The signs of ♀ also tend to a lack of polish and refinement if ♀ is not strong and well-placed, but the strong and good aspects of ♃ and ♀ tend to counteract this. Neptune and the ☽ when well-aspected do not tend to roughness of manner, but give more refinement. (See Awkwardness, Coarse, Cruel, Gross; "Rough" under Manners; Merciless, Pity, Profane, Refined, Rugged, Unrefined, Vulgar, etc.).

Skin—Rough and Hard Skin—(See "Skin" under Hard; Scales; "Rough", "Thick", under Skin).

Voice—(See Hoarseness; "Rough" under Voice).

ROUND—Circular—(See "Round" under Eyes, Face, Head, Shoulders, Upper).

ROUSE—Arouse—Hard to Arouse—Difficult to Excite to Action—The occidental positions of the planets at B. tend to make the native less active, and difficult to arouse to action. Also, ♄ influence strong at B. tends to heaviness and moroseness. (See "Degree Of" under Activity; Apathy, Careless, Dull; "Lack Of" under Energy; Enervation, Heavy, Idle, Improvident, Inactive, Indifferent, Inertia, Labor, Lassitude, Lazy, Lethargy, Listless, Morose, Negative, Neglectful, Occidental, Procrastination, Sickly; "Arouse" under Sickness; "Low" under Vitality; "Weak Body" under Weak, etc.).

ROVING NATURE—A Roamer—A Wanderer—Many Changes of Residence, etc.—(See Changes, Location, Residence, Restlessness, Roaming, Travel, Vagabond, Wanderer).

ROYAL—Royalty—

Royal Disposition—The ☉ Sig. in ♌. (See Leo, Noble, Sincere, Temperament).

Royalty—(See Kings, Monarchs, Princes, Queens, Roman, Rulers).

RUBBING—Friction—Fremitus—Irritation—(See Friction).

RUBEFACIENT—Counter-Irritants—An Agent Which Reddens the Skin—The action of ♂ is rubefacient and reddening. Cantharides, a ♂ drug, is used as a rubefacient, and for blistering. Capsicum (Red Pepper) is used in strong Pain Liniments, a ♂ remedy. Sinapis Nigra and Alba (Mustard), ☉ remedies, are also strong rubefacients. (See Applications, Blisters, Cantharides, Capsicum, Caustics, Efflorescent, Liniments, Lotions, Mustard, Rashes, Sinapis, Stimulant, Tar, Vesicant).

RUBEOLA—(See Measles).

RUDDY—Healthy Appearance—

Ruddy Complexion—Florid Complexion—Ruddy Countenance—Ruddy Face—The ☉ and ♂ make the complexion more florid; the ☉ strong at B.; the ☉ Sig. in ♎; the ☉ rising in the Asc.; the ☽ in ♍, dark and ruddy; the ☽ Sig. in ♎, ♐, or ♒; ♄ in ♈ in Hor'y Q.; ♄ in ♈ in partile asp. the Asc., and in good aspect to the Asc.; ♃ ascending; ♃ Sig. in ♌ or ♐; ♃ in ♌ or ♐, partile asp. the Asc.; ♃ Sig. in ♍, ruddy but not clear or fair; ♂ occidental; characteristic of ♂ people; ♂ ascending; ♂ in the Asc. tends to increase the iron in the system, giving a ruddy color, red hair, etc.; in Hor'y Q., ♂ Sig. of the person; ♂ Sig. in ♉, or ♂ in ♉ in partile asp. the Asc., ruddy, but never fair; ♂ Sig. in ♈ or ♍, ruddy and smooth countenance if ♂ be ori.; ♂ in ♌; ♂ strong at B., and ruler; ♀ Sig.,

ruddy but not fair; ☿ Sig. in ♎, or ♐; ☿ in ♐ in partile asp. the Asc.; ♌, ♍, and ♐ on the Asc.; ♍ on the Asc., a dark, ruddy complexion; ♌ on the Asc., a ruddy, oval countenance; ♎ on the Asc., a ruddy complexion in youth, but with pimples in middle life and old age. (See "Ruddy Constitution" in this section; Beautiful; "Good" under Complexion, Constitution, Health, Vitality; "Red Face" under Face; Fresh, Handsome, Robust; "Body" under Strong; "Complexion" under Youth, etc.).

Ruddy Constitution—The ☉ rising in the Asc.; the ✳ and △ aspects of the ☉ to ♂ and the planets; the ☽ in ♍ in partile asp. the Asc., tall and rather ruddy; born under ♃; ♂ ruler of the Asc., and ori.; ♂ in ♈, partile the Asc. if ♂ be occi., the native will be more ruddy and smooth, but if ♂ be ori., tall and less swarthy; ♐ on the Asc., ruddy and handsome. (See "Good" under Constitution; "Abundance" under Health; Immunity, Resistance, Robust, Strong; "Good" under Vitality).

Ruddy Countenance—Ruddy Face—(See "Ruddy Complexion" in this section).

Ruddy Face—(See "Ruddy Complexion" in this section).

RUDE—In Manner—(See Rough).

RUFFIANS—Assaults By—The 15° ♑ on the Asc. at B. (See Assaults).

RUGGED—Rough—Unkempt—Sturdy—Robust, etc.—

Rugged Disposition—Overbearing—The ☉ afflicted in ♍; ♄ Sig. □ or ☍ the ☉. (See "Manner" under Rough).

Rugged Hair—(See "Rugged" under Hair).

Rugged Health—Rugged Stature—(See Robust, Ruddy).

RUIN—Ruined—

Ruined In Business—Reverses—Bankruptcy—In Hor'y Questions, ♄ is the Significator of Ruin and Disgrace; ♄ afflicted in the 2nd or 10th H., danger of periodical downfall, loss of position, and of the favor of employer; ♄ in the 10th H., in detriment or fall, and afflicted, almost irretrievable ruin to the average native so born, and difficult to get a permanent foothold in business until he finds his real place in life, and a master of his destiny; the ☉ to the □ ♀ by dir., thru marriage, love affairs, and women; the ☉ directed to Antares, Aldebaran, Deneb, Regulus, Betelgeuse, Bellatrix, South Scale, Frons Scorpio, threatens ultimate ruin; the ☉ or ☽ joined to the Whale's Jaw; the ☽ directed to Deneb, ultimate ruin and disgrace; the ☽ to the ☌ Cor Hydra, Bellatrix, Left Shoulder of Bootes; ♃ Sig. □ or ☍ ♄; ♂ afflicted in the 10th or 11th H.; the Asc. or M.C. to the □ or ☍ the ☉ or ♄ by dir.; the M.C. directed to Nebulous Stars, the Pleiades, Praesepe, Hyades, Shoulders of Orion, and the Twins, causes ruin and disgrace; the Hyades rising or setting with ☉; the M.C. directed to the Ascelli, Caput Hercules, Markab, Auriga's Right Shoulder, and Medusa's Head; lord of the 10th H. in the 12th; lord of the 12th in the 1st, 9th, or 10th; lord of the 12th in the 2nd, poverty and ruin; lord of the 12th in the 10th, ruin by envy. In order to prevent reverses, business failure, bankruptcy, etc., every person should early in life have their horoscope, and see what their limitations are, find out what their proper vocation is, whether they are calculated for leadership, or to be a follower in life, and then live within their means, and always be saving in times of prosperity, and be ready for the financial emergencies of life, and not be too much given over to the pleasures of this World. The pendulum is ever swinging back and forth, and unusual prosperity comes in cycles, and we must pass thru the Spring, Summer, Autumn, and Winter Periods of life. Seek balance, poise, self-control, and be prepared. (See Business, Disgrace, Downfall; "Own Worst Enemy" under Enemies; Evils, Fate; "Ill-Fortune", "Malice of Fortune", under Fortune; "Loss Of" under Honour; "Ill-Fortune" under Ill; Infamous; "Ruins Himself" under Intemperance; "Ruined" under Love Affairs, Women; Miseries, Misfortune, Neglect, Privation, Poverty, Property, Reputation, Restless, Reverses, Riches, Scandal, Unfortunate).

Ruined by Disgrace — By Dishonour, etc.—(See Disgrace, Dishonour; "Loss Of" under Honour; Scandal, etc.).

Ruined by Love Affairs—And Women —(See "Ruined" under Love Affairs; "Injured Thru Women" under Men).

RULE—Ruling—Ruling Nature—Fond of Rule and Authority—The ☉ Sig. in ♌ or ♒; the ☉ Sig. ♂ ♂ in ♈ or ♌, autocratic; the ☽ Sig. in ♌, and abhors servitude and dependence; ♃ Sig. in ♏, desirous to bear rule over his equals. (See Austere, Commanding, Cruel, Dynamic; "Abundance" under Energy; "Fearless" under Fears; Kings, Merciless; "Shows No Pity" under Pity; "Positive Nature" under Positive; Power, Self-Assertive, Self-Confidence, Self-Reliant; "Disposition" under Severe; "Strong Will" under Will, etc.).

RULERS—Kings—Monarchs—Princes—Death by the Wrath of Rulers—Death of, etc.—Rulers are ruled by the ☉, the ♌ sign, and also denoted by the 10th H. (See Famous; "Great Men", "The Great", under Great; Kings, Nobles, President, Princes, Queens, Roman).

RUMBLING—Noises—

Bowels — Rumbling In the Bowels — (See "Rumbling" under Bowels).

Head—A Rumbling Noise In the Head —(See "Noises" under Head).

RUMINANT SIGNS — Of the Zodiac — Symbolic of an animal which chews the cud, as ♈, ♉, and ♑. Medicines should not be given when the ☽ is passing thru one of these signs, as they tend to produce vomiting or nausea at such a time, and to have an emetic influence. The best time to give an emetic is when the ☽ is in one of these signs. (See Emetics, Nausea, Vomiting).

RUMP — Haunches — Buttocks — (See Buttocks).

RUNNING—

Running of the Reins — (See Gonorrhoea).

Running Pains — Shooting Pains — Flying Pains—Wandering Pains—(See "Running Pains" under Arms, Shoulders; "Flying Pains" under Flying; "Shooting Pains" under Shooting; "Pains" under Whole Body).

Running Sores — (See Discharges, Sores, Ulcers).

RUPTURE—Hernia—Bursting of Parts —Rending—Lacerations—A ♂ and ♏ disorder, and afflictions in ♏. Also caused by the tonic action of ♅, and ♂ ♂ ♅, and the exaggerated action of ♂. See the following subjects in the alphabetical arrangement—

Abdominal Rupture — (See "Abdominal", "Inguinal", "Umbilical", under Hernia).

Aneurysm — (See Aneurysm; "Aneurysm" under Hernia).

Blood Vessels—Rupture of—(See Apoplexy; "Rupture" under Vessels).

Brain—Rupture of Blood Vessels In—Hernia of the Brain — (See Apoplexy, Cerebral; "Brain" under Hernia).

Burstings; Death — By Rupture, and by Rupture of Blood Vessels — (See Apoplexy; "Death" under Hernia).

Exaggerated Action—Of the Planets, and Causing Rupture — The tonic action of ♅ and ♂. (See Exaggerated).

Groin—Rupture In—(See Groins; "Inguinal" under Hernia).

Head — Rupture of Vessels In — (See Apoplexy).

Hemorrhages—From Ruptures—(See Apoplexy; "Rupture" under Hemorrhage, Vessels).

Hernia—(See the various paragraphs under Hernia).

Inguinal Rupture — (See "Inguinal" under Hernia).

Lacerations; Motion — (See "Accelerated" under Motion).

Organs—Rupture of—(See "Accelerated" under Motion; Organs).

Peritoneum — (See "Rupture" under Peritoneum).

Rending — (See Bursting; "Exaggerated Action" under Exaggerated; Lacerations; "Accelerated" under Motion).

Scrotum—Rupture In—(See "Hernia" under Scrotum).

Strangulation—Of a Part Due to Rupture—(See the paragraphs under Hernia).

Tears—Tearing and Rending of Parts —(See "Rending" in this section).

Testicle—Rupture of—(See Testes).

Umbilical Rupture — (See "Hernia" under Navel).

Ventral Hernia — (See "Ventral" under Hernia).

Vessels — Rupture of — (See "Blood Vessels" in this section).

RUSH—Rush of Blood—Determination of Blood To a Part—Flow of Blood—

Head—Rush of Blood To the Head—(See "Blood" under Head).

Part—Rush of Blood To a Part—♂ influence. (See Centrifugal, Determination, Flow, Rubefacient).

RUSSET COLOR—Ruled by the ♋ and ♑ Signs. (See Colors).

RUTHLESSNESS — (See Cruel, Merciless, Pity).

S

SACRUM — Sacral Region—Sacral—Os Sacrum—Sacral Nerves—Sacral Plexus — Sacral Region of the Spine — Ruled by ♏ and ♐. The Bones of the Sacrum are under the structural rulership of the ♏ Sign, and also of ♄, as ♄ rules all the bones. The Sacral Region as a whole is said to be ruled by ♐. The Sacral Plexus is ruled by ♏. The Sacrum includes the large triangular bone above the Coccyx. (See Coccyx, Pelvis, Spine, Subluxations; "Sacrum" under Vertebrae).

Circulation Obstructed—In the Sacral Region—♄ afflicted in ♐; ♄ in ♐, ♂, □, or ☍ ♃ or ♀. (See "Nerves" in this section).

Disorders—In the Sacrum and Sacral Region—Afflictions in ♏ and ♐; ♄ afflicted in ♐; ♄ ♂ ♂ in ♐, and afflicted by ♅; ♂ afflicted in ♐, danger of inflammations and hurts to.

Nerves—The Sacral Nerves Obstructed —♄ afflicted in ♐, and in □ ♃; ♅ or ♀ afflicted in ♏ or ♐.

Obstruction — In the Sacral Circulation and Nerves — (See Circulation, Nerves, in this section).

Pelvis—Formed Partly by the Sacrum —(See Pelvis).

Spina Bifida—Cleft of the Spine Over the Sacrum—Case—(See "Spina Bifida" under Spine).

SACS — Pouch — (See Cavities, Cysts, Follicles, Pouch, Receptacles, Scrotum, Vesicles).

SAD — Sadness — Sad Expression — Sad Hair—Grief—Doleful—Pensive—Lugubrious — Sorrowful — Sad Appearance, etc.—The following subjects have to do with Sadness, which see in the alphabetical arrangement—

Appearance — A Sad Appearance — A Sad Countenance—Thoughtful Expression—A Pensive Aspect—♄ in ♋ gives a thoughtful and sad expression; ♀ afflicted in ♈, a pensive aspect. (See "Sadness" in this section).

Aspect—A Pensive Aspect—(See "Appearance" in this section).

Complexion — (See "Sad Brown" under Complexion).

Countenance — (See "Appearance" in this section).

Death — A Sad Death — Death from Sadness—The 23° ♓ on the Asc. (See the various paragraphs under Death).

Dejected; Depressed; Despondency;

Disgrace—Sad Disgrace—Lord of the 12th in the 10th H., sad disgrace. (See Disgrace).

Expression—(See Appearance" in this section).

Fears; Gloom; Grave; Grief — (See "Public Grief" under Grief).

Hair—Sad Black or Sad Brown Hair —(See "Sad" under Hair).

Hypochondria; Imaginations — (See Doubts, Fears, Imagination).

Low Spirits—(See Low, Melancholy).

Melancholy; Mournful;

Much Sadness Generally — ♄ Lord of the Year at the Vernal, and afflicted; Comets appearing in ♏ or ♎; an eclipse of the ☉ in the 3rd decan. of ♈. (See "Public Grief" under Grief; Highwaymen).

Old Age — (See "Sad Old Age" under Old Age).

Pensive Aspect — (See "Appearance" in this section).

Prevalent — (See the subjects under Prevalent).

Public Sadness — (See "Much Sadness" in this section).

Reserved; Sadism—(See Sadism).

Sadness — A Sad Disposition — A Sad Countenance and Expression — Caused principally by ♄ influence and afflictions, and by the signs of ♄ on the Asc. at B., or with ♄ in his own signs and afflicting the ☉, ☽, ♀, or the Asc.; ♄ in ♋; ♄ in the Asc. or M.C., and afflicting ♀, the mental ruler, or in evil asp. to the ☉ or ☽; ♄ ♂ the Asc. at B.; the ☉, ☽, or ♀ ♂ or ill-asp. ♄ at B., and by dir. or transit; the ☽ at a Solar Rev. passing over the place of ♄ at B.; ♀ Sig. in ♈, a pensive aspect; ♀ Sig. ♂ ♄; ♀ in ♑ and afflicted by ♄; ♑ or ♒ on the Asc., and with ♄ as ruler, and afflicted; lord of the 12th in the 10th, sad disgrace; the 3rd decan. of ♒ on the Asc., inclined to be lugubrious; the 4th face of ♋ on the Asc. at B. (See "Appearance", and the various paragraphs in this section).

Sickness—Sad and Heavy Sickness— (See "Heavy and Sad Sickness" under Heavy).

SADISM—Sex Gratification Attended by Violence — ♂ configurated with ♀. (See "Violent" under Men; "Violence" under Passion; Perversions).

SAFFRON — A Deep Orange Color — Ruled by the ☉ and the 11th H. (See Colors; "Saffron" under Complexion; Eleventh House, Orange).

SAGACIOUS — Sagacity — Shrewdness — Quick Discernment — Wisdom — (See Discernment; "Good" under Judgment; Shrewdness, Wisdom).

SAGITTARIUS — (♐). The Ninth Sign of the Zodiac, ruled by ♃, and is the day sign or house of ♃, and the joy of ♃. This is a fiery, hot, dry, positive, masculine, choleric, common, mutable, changeable, obeying, bicorporeal, quadrupedal, four-footed, autumnal, southern, half human and half mute, speaking, religious, philosophical, restless, adventurous, venturesome, motive, mental sign, and of long ascension. This Sign is affiliated with the Ninth House, the house of Religion, Philosophy, and of Foreign Residence or Travel. It is a rather fruitful sign because of its ♃ influence. The Symbol of this Sign is the Centaur, the Archer. Its influence is strongly for Sports and outdoor life, horseback riding, hunting, etc. When upon the Asc. at

B. it tends to enlarge the body, make the native tall, and many Giants have this sign rising at B. The sign when strong, or ruling at B., tends to give a ruddy complexion, oval face, fine clear eyes, chestnut colored hair, but apt to be bald, and especially about the temples, and with a high forehead. The native of this sign is usually strong, active, intrepid, and with plenty of motive force. Jupiter, the ruler of this sign, when in the Asc. at B., tends to give strong and well-proportioned hips, thighs, and legs. The Colors ruled by this sign are Light Green or Olive, Light Olive, Sanguine, Light Green and Blue, Yellow. For Countries and Nations ruled by this sign see "Sagittarius Rules" under Nations. The Hebrew Letter Samech (S) is connected with ♐, and also with the sense of Smell and Perception. Mercury (Mercurius) is the typical Polycrest Remedy assigned to this sign. (See "Polycrest" under Zodiac). The Pathological Qualities of this sign tend to cause accidents, fractures, restlessness, and venturesomeness. The following Qualities are assigned to this sign—Active, Autumnal, Bicorporeal, Bitter, Changeable, Choleric, Common, Confiding, Conscientious, Diurnal, Double-Bodied, Dry, Eastern, Excitable, Feral (the 2nd half); Fiery, Foolhardy, Fortunate, Frank, Fruitful, Hasty, Heedless, Honest, Hot, Intrepid, Masculine, Mental, Mutable, Obeying, Open-Minded, Philosophical, Pleasure-Loving, Quick, Receptive, Reckless, Religious, Restless, Southern, Speaking, Strong, Susceptible, (being a Common and Mutable Sign); Trusting, Venturesome, etc.

SAGITTARIUS RULES — Arterial System, and especially the Iliac Arteries; Bones (the Coccygeal and Sacral Bones, Pelvis); Buttocks; Coccygeal Region of the Spine, and Coccygeal Vertebrae; Colors — Light Green and Olive or Blue, Sanguine, Yellow; Externally, rules the Hips and Thighs; Femur; Fractures of the Hip and Thigh Bones; Gluteus Muscles; Green Color—Light Green; Hams; Haunches; Hips—Region around the Hips—Locomotor Muscles of the Hips and Thighs; Iliac Arteries and Veins; Ilium; Internally, rules Arterial System and Sciatic Nerve; Ischium; Light Green and Light Olive Colors; Liver; Lungs; Motive Force; Mind—The Higher Mind, a 9th H. influence; Muscles—Gluteus, Sartorius, Rectus Muscles, the Locomotor Muscles of the Hips and Thighs, and also considerable influence over the Muscular System generally; Nerves—The Sciatic Nerve, and has some rule over the Nervous System generally, along with the ♐ Sign; Olive Color (Light Olive); Os Sacrum; Pelvis; Physical Strength, and especially with ♐ on the Asc. at B.; Quartz; Rectus Muscles; Sacrum—The Os Sacrum — The Sacral Bones and Coccygeal Region of the Spine; Sanguine and Green Color; Sartorius Muscles; Sciatic Nerves; Silica; Spine—The Sacral and Coccygeal Region of; Structurally rules the Thigh Bone and Femur; Thighs — The Locomotor Muscles of Hips and Thighs; Veins — The Iliac Arteries and Veins; Yellow Color. (See Coccyx; "Fire Signs" under Fire; Jupiter; Mutable Signs (see Mutable); Ninth House, Pelvis, Philosophy, Religion, Sacrum, Spine, Vertebrae).

SAGITTARIUS DISEASES—And Afflictions—The ♐ people are usually easily cured of disease because of their confiding, trusting, frank, and open natures if good and positive suggestions are made, but evil and negative suggestions are also equally powerful with them in health matters. The ♐ sign belongs to the Mutable Cross, made up of ♊, ♍, ♐, and ♓, and afflictions and malefics in ♐, or any of these signs, tend to afflict the parts of the body ruled by ♐. The ♊ sign is in 8 to ♐, and supplemental, and afflictions in either sign tend to affect the lungs, hips, thighs, and sacral region. The diseases of ♐ are caused principally, however, by afflictions in ♐, or with ♐ on the Asc., afflicted, and containing malefics; caused by the ☉, ☽, or other planets afflicted in ♐; afflictions in the common, or mutable signs, and with such signs on the angles, and containing malefics. The following diseases and afflictions are ruled over, or influenced by the ♐ sign.

Accidents — Hurts or Injuries to the Hips or Thighs — The principal accidents of this sign are fractures, broken hips or thighs, femurs, etc., and caused by ♄ or ♂ afflicted in ♐, and especially with ♐ on the Asc., and malefics in ♐ in the 1st H. (See Femur, Fractures; "Accidents", "Hurts", under Hips; Thighs).

Aches — In Hips or Thighs — (See "Aches" under Hips).

All Diseases — In Hips or Thighs — (See "All Diseases" under Hips, Thighs).

Baldness—(See Baldness).

Bees Destroyed—(See Bees).

Blood — (See "Over-Heated" under Blood).

Bones—Broken Bones—Fractures of the Hip, Femur, and Bones of the Lower Extremities—(See Fractures).

Bowel Disorders—Enteric Diseases—(See "Disorders Of" under Bowels).

Broken Bones—(See Accidents, Bones, in this section).

Bronchitis—(See Bronchial).

Buttocks—Diseases In—Injuries To—(See Buttocks, Haunches).

Consumptive Pains—In the Thighs—(See Thighs).

Coxalgia—(See "Pain" under Hips).

Deformities — Of Hips and Thighs — (See "Deformity" under Thighs).

Dislocation—Of the Hip Joint—(See "Dislocation" under Hips).

Endemic Diseases—(See Endemic).

Enteric Diseases—(See "Disorders Of", and the various paragraphs under Bowels).

Eye—Loss of One Eye—The ☽ with the Arrow Head of ♐ tends to blindness in one eye. (See Arrow Head; "One Eye" under Blindness; Nebulous).

Falls from Horses—(See Horses).

Femur — Dislocation of—Fracture of (See Femur).

Fevers—(See "High Fevers", "Liable To", under Fever).

Fire — Danger or Injury By — (See Fire).

Fistulous Tumors — (See "Buttocks", "Thighs", under Fistula).

Four-Footed Beasts—Hurts By—(See Quadrupeds).

Fractures—Of the Hips or Thighs—(See Fractures).

Gout — In Hips and Thighs — (See "Hips" under Gout).

Gunshot Wounds—(See Gunshot).

Haunches—Disorders In—Injuries To —(See Buttocks, Haunches).

Heat—Fire—Danger or Prejudice By —(See Fire, Heat).

Heated Blood — (See "Over-Heated" under Blood).

Hemorrhoids — Piles — (See Hemorrhoids).

Hips—All Diseases In—Injuries To—(See the various paragraphs under Hips).

Horses—Hurts By—Falls From—(See Horses).

Hot Humours — (See "Hot" under Hips).

Humours—(See "Hot Humours", "Humours In", under Hips).

Hunting — Riding — Injuries In — (See "Riding" under Horses; Hunting).

Hurts—By Horses and Quadrupeds—(See Horses, Quadrupeds).

Injuries — (See Femur, Fractures; "Accidents", "Hurts", "Injuries", under Hips, Thighs).

Intemperateness—In Sports—(See Exercise; "Intemperate" under Sports).

Ischium—Disorders of—(See Ischium).

Itching — In Thighs — (See "Itching" under Thighs).

Knees—Pains In—(See Knees).

Legs—Disorders In—Fractures—(See Extremities, Femur, Fractures, Legs, Limbs, Thighs).

Locomotor Ataxia—Tabes Dorsalis—(See Locomotor).

Lower Extremities — Disorders In — Fractures In — (See Extremities, Femur, Fractures, Legs, Limbs, Lower, Thighs).

Lumbago; Lungs—Disorders of—(See Lungs).

Muscles—Disorders of—(See Muscles).

Nerve Power—(See "Loss Of" under Nerves).

Over-Heated Blood — (See "Over-Heated" under Blood).

Pains — (See "Pains" under Hips, Thighs).

Pestilence; Piles—(See Hemorrhoids).

Prejudice by Fire — (See "Danger", "Injury", under Fire; "Injuries By" under Heat).

Quadrupeds—Injuries By—(See Horses, Quadrupeds).

Respiratory Troubles — (See Breath, Bronchial, Lungs).

Rheumatism; Riding—Injured In Horseback Riding — (See "Riding", "Thrown", under Horses; Hunting).

Sciatica; Sports—Injuries In—Intemperate In—(See Exercise, Sports).

Tabes Dorsalis — (See Locomotor Ataxia).

Thighs—All Diseases In—Injuries To —(See Femur, Fractures, Hips, Thighs).

Tumors—(See "Tumors" under Hips, Thighs).

Ulcers — (See "Ulcers" under Hips, Thighs).

Volition—(See "Loss Of" under Volition).

Weakness — (See "Weakness" under Hips, Thighs).

SAILORS—The ☽ indicates, represents, and rules Sailors. For influences which indicate Injury to, or Death of, see Maritime, Military, Navigation, Seas, Ships, Shipwreck, Soldiers).

SAINT ANTHONY'S FIRE — (See Erysipelas).

SAINT VITUS DANCE—Chorea—Involuntary Muscular Twitchings — Spasmodic Muscular Contractions — An Irregular Minor Spasm — Involuntary Twitchings of Muscles—Incoordination — Caused by Incoordination, and the reflex influence of ♅ in ♐, in which sign the Organ of Coordination is situated. Also due to non-adjustment between the Vital Body and the Physical Body. In this disease, and also in Idiocy, the nerve centers are not properly adjusted, and there is mal-adjustment between the mind, brain, and body, which prevents the Ego from having full and proper control of its instrument, the human body. The general causes of this disorder are as follows—♆ in ♈, and □ ♅, and both afflicted by ♄ or ♂, and the progressed ☽ passing a radical malefic in this case, tends to attacks; ♅ afflicted in ♐; ♅ in ♏ tends, by reflex action, to afflict the ♐ sign, or planets in ♐; ♅ afflicted in the 6th H.; ♅ ☌, P, □, or ☍ the ☉; ♅ and ♃ afflicting ♀; ♄ or ♂ afflicting ♀; ☿ ☌ or P. ♂ in fixed signs, and with ☿ and the ☽ in mutual affliction at the same time; Subs at AT and AX. (See Contractions, Coordination; "Movements" under Erratic; Idiocy, Incoordination, Jerkings; "Contractions", "Involuntary", under Muscles; Spasmodic, Tics, Tremors, Twitchings; "Body" under Vital). Cases of Saint Vitus Dance, Map, Birth Data, etc.—See Figures 12, 13, and 15, in the book, "Message of the Stars", by the Heindels).

SALACIOUS—Lustful—Lecherous—Impure — (See Effeminate, Lewd, Licentious, Lust; "Loose Morals" under Morals; Shameless, Wanton, etc.).

SALICYLATE OF SODA—(See Sodium).

SALIVA — Spittle — Salivary Glands — Parotid Gland — The Parotid Gland, ruled by ♉, yields saliva. The Salivary Glands are ruled by the ♉ sign. The Saliva is ruled by the ☽ and ♋ sign. (See Parotid).

Inflammation—Of the Salivary Glands — Mumps — (See "Mumps" under Parotid).

Pellitory— An Agent increasing the flow of Saliva—(See Pellitory).

Salivation—Too Much Saliva—Ptyalism—Great Abundance of Spittle—A ☿ disease, and ☿ afflicted shows salivation; the ☽ in ♋, ♌, P, ♎, or ♏ ♄ (or ☿ if he be of the nature of ♄) at the beginning of an illness, or at decumb. (Hor'y); the ☽ afflicted in ♈ affects and disturbs the saliva; ♀ afflicted in ♏; Subs at LCP and SP. (See "Frothing" under Mouth).

Too Little—Dry Mouth—(See Fauces).

SALLOW—Sallow Complexion—A Jaundiced Look—Yellow Complexion—(See "Sallow" under Complexion; Pale, Sickly).

SALOONS—Frequenter of Taverns and Saloons—Saloons are ruled by the 5th H., the house of pleasures and dissipations. Venus afflicted in the 5th H. tends to such dissipations. (See Drunkenness, Taverns).

SALPINGITIS—(See Fallopian).

SALT— Salts — Sodium Chloride — The Salts of the Body—Zodiac Salts—

Salts of the Body—Are connected with the earthy signs and ♄. The Salts in Milk are ruled by ♄. (See "Earthy Signs" under Earth; Milk, Minerals, Saturn; "Salts" under Zodiac).

Salt Phlegm—Salt Rheum—(See "Salt Phlegm" under Phlegm).

Salt Rheum — (See "Salt Phlegm" in this section).

Salt Water—The Oceans—(See Ocean).

Sodium Chloride — Common Salt — Ruled by ♒. (See Sodium; "Salts" under Zodiac).

Zodiac Salts—(See Zodiac).

SANCTIMONIOUS — Self-Righteous — (See "Sanctimonious" under Religion).

SAND—Sandy—Gravel—Concretions—

Kidney and Bladder—Sand In—Urinary Sand — These deposits are the work of ♄, being the retention and crystallization of waste products, and also gravel; a ♄ disease; ♄ in ♎ or ♏; the ☽ to the ♂ or ill-asp. ♂ by dir.; the ☽ in ♎, and afflicted by the ☉ or ♂ when taken ill (Hor'y); ♂ in ♌ or ♏; a ♏ disease, and afflictions in ♏. (See Crystallization, Deposits, Elimination, Gravel, Retentions, Stone, Suppressions, etc.).

Sandy Hair—(See Hair).

SANE—Sanity—(See "Sound Mind" under Mind; Sanity).

SANGUINARY — Bloodthirsty — Generally a ♂ and ♏ influence, and the fiery signs. (See Assassins, Cruel, Merciless, Murderous, Pity, Revengeful, Treachery, etc.).

Sanguinary Fevers—♃ in fiery signs, and the ☉ weak and afflicted, causes them at decumbiture in Hor'y Q. (See "Blood", "Sanguinary", under Fever).

SANGUINE—Buoyant—Hopeful— Sanguineous—

Sanguine Color—Ruled by ♃ and the 5th H.

Sanguine Complexion—The ☉ strong at B., more sanguine than otherwise; the ☉ Sig. in ♊, ♌, or ♃; the ☉ or ☽ in ♈, ♉, or ♊; the ☉ in ♊, ♌, or ♃ in

partile asp. the Asc.; the ☉ as Sig. in Hor'y Q.; the ☽ Sig. in ♈, ♉, ♊, ♌, ♎, ♃, or ♒, or in these signs in partile the Asc.; ☽ in ♒ partile Asc., clear sanguine; ♄ in ♊, a dark sanguine; ♄ Sig. in ♊ in Hor'y Q.; ♄ in ♑ or ♒; ♃ strong at B.; born under ♃; ♃ oriental; ♃ Sig. in ♊, ♌, ♏, or ♃; ♃ in ♊, partile the Asc., sanguine, but of dusky complexion; ♂ Sig. in ♊, ♌, ♎, or ♃; ♂ in ♊, ♎, or ♃, partile the Asc.; ♀ Sig. in ♉, ♏, ♎, ♃, or ♒; ♀ in ♎, partile the Asc., a beautiful sanguine; ♀ in ♃, partile the Asc., fair sanguine; ☿ Sig. in ♎ or ♃; ☿ in ♎, partile the Asc.; ☿ ori., but if occi., lean and sallow; ☿ orientally posited as regards the ☉, except when ☿ is in ♊; ♊ or ♏ on the Asc., a dark sanguine; ♈, ♉, ♊, ♌, ♎, ♃, or ♒ on the Asc.; ♌ on the Asc., a ruddy, high sanguine; ♎ on the Asc., a fine sanguine complexion in youth, but with pimples in middle life and old age; given by the 5th H. influences strong at B., as this house rules sanguine color; ♃ and ♒ on the Asc., a clear sanguine, and especially when ♀ is rising in these signs; ♓ on Asc., sometimes sanguine if the ☉ be rising in ♓. (See "Red", "Rosy", under Complexion; "Ruddy" under Face; Robust, Ruddy; "Good" under Vitality).

Sanguine Signs—The Airy Signs ♊, ♎, and ♒. Also the fiery signs, and especially ♌ and ♃ when on the Asc.

Sanguine Temperament—Artistic Temperament—The Ardent, Buoyant, Confident, Enthusiastic, Hopeful, Optimistic Temperament or Disposition — Ruled by ♃ and the Airy Signs. This Temperament is moist in general, and not a hot and dry temperament. (See Air Signs, Moisture). The Choleric and Sanguine Temperament act, while the Lymphatic and Nervous Temperaments think and feel. This temperament gives a plump body, good circulation, fine complexion, jovial nature, good cheer, hopefulness, etc. The people of this temperament benefit by fasting. (See Cheerfulness, Fasting; "Diathesis" under Hemorrhage; "Hot and Moist Body" under Moisture; Optimistic, Plump).

Sanguineous Discharges—(See Blood, Discharges, Hemorrhage, Menses; "Epistaxis" under Nose).

Sanguineous System — The Blood — Blood Vessels—Arteries—Veins, etc.— Ruled principally by ♃ and ♀, and also greatly affected by the ♒ sign. (See Arteries, Blood, Capillaries, Circulation, Lymph, Veins, Vessels).

SANITARIUMS—(See "Sanitariums" under Healers; Hospitals).

SANITATION—Hygiene—Cleanly—Prevention of Disease — Sanitary, etc. — These matters are associated largely with the ♏ sign, the sign which rules over health matters. Mars well aspected in ♏ tends to give good success as a Sanitary Worker. (See Cleanly, Healers, Hygiene, Nurses, Prevention).

Neglects Sanitation—Unsanitary— Filthy In Habits and Surroundings—♄ afflicted in ♉; ♄ ☌ ♅ or ♂ in ♉. (See Careless, Cleanly, Filthy; "Careless" under Habits; Improvident, Knavish, Laxity, Neglect, Untidy, etc.).

SANITY—Sane—Insane—(See Insanity; "Sound Mind" under Mind).

SARCASM—Sarcastic—Bitter In Temper —Ironical — Vituperative— A strong characteristic of the ♏ sign, and ♂, its ruler; ♂ strong at B., and afflicting ☿; ♂ Sig. ☌ ☿, an acute, sarcastic wit; ♂ or ♅ to the ☌ or ill-asp. ☿ by dir.; ☿ in ♏ and afflicted by ♂; many planets in mutable signs. (See Anger, Choleric, Imprudent, Rashness, Satire; "High Temper", "Nasty", under Temper).

SARCOMA—A Fleshy Tumor—A Tumor of Modified and Embryonic Connective Tissue—

Adipose Sarcoma — A Fatty Tumor — Caused by ♃ and afflictions to ♃; ♂ ☌ or ill-asp. ♃. (See "Tumors" under Fat, Fleshy; "Fatty" under Tumors).

SARDONIC—Derisive—Sneering— Mocking—Unnatural—♆ rising in the Asc., a sardonic look. (See Mockery).

SARSAPARILLA—A Typical Drug of ♂. Is Alterative, Diuretic, Tonic.

SATIRE—Irony—Ridicule—Derisive— Sarcasm — A characteristic of the ♏ and ♐ signs. Also ♍ when strong at B. tends to satire and criticism. The Mercurial signs ♊ and ♍, and especially when afflicted, or joined with ♄ or ♂ influences, tend to satire, and along the lines of making fun, or light of people and things, or making lamentations over the evils and degeneracy of the Times, etc. The ♎ and ♑ signs are also given to satire. (See Sarcasm).

SATISFACTION OF MIND—(See Cheerfulness, Contentment; "Peace of Mind" under Mind).

SATURDAY — The day of ♄. For the significance of the Days of the Week see Week. (See Saturn; "Saturday" under Week).

SATURN — The Planet Saturn — Also known as Kronos, or Cronos—Known as a malefic, and "The Greater Infortune." However, Saturn, in himself, is not evil, but is chastening, corrective, and untiring in his efforts to arouse Humanity to better and right living, and by bringing sorrow, suffering, sickness, trials, and tribulations upon people that they may learn by their experiences, and reap what they sow. To the Angel of Saturn has been given the great task of the Redemption of Humanity, and He was one of the first of the Hierarchies upon the field at the Creation, the "Serpent" of Eden, and He will be at his work until the last human Soul is redeemed and perfected, and able to master all Earth and material conditions when in physical incarnation. Saturn is a masculine planet, and of a cold, dry, and barren nature, and his influence is of a steadying nature, and to restore the balance with those who need it. The afflictions of ♄ usually force people on, and out of ruts in life, and to a better environment if they are living in the wrong place, or engaging in a wrong and illegitimate business, or are much tortured by the aggressions of enemies, relatives, or business associates. Such changes usually conduce to greater happiness and usefulness in life, greater success, and better health.

Saturn is known as "The Reaper", "The Tester", "The Chastener", "The Initiator", and also as the Planet of Death. (See "Periods of Bad Health" under Health). This Planet is much written about in the Textbooks of Astrology, and I have spent considerable time gathering up, and arranging these influences so that they will be more readily available to students. This Article will be arranged into three Sections, as follows: Section One —General Influences of Saturn; Section Two—Saturn Rules; Section Three —The Diseases of Saturn, and the Afflictions of Saturn. In any of these three Sections, when subjects are listed without comment, see the subject in the alphabetical arrangement.

— SECTION ONE —

THE INFLUENCES OF SATURN—
Action of Saturn—His action is principally binding, chastening, chronic, cold, crystallizing, denuding, hardening, depleting, hindering, limiting, magnetic, obstructing, retarding, suppressing, etc. Also centripetal, driving the blood inwards from the surface, thru chill and cold. To those who have the New Birth, his action is also very helpful, spiritual, and leads to attainment and advancement. (Note the various paragraphs in this Article).

Afflictions—♄ afflicts by the ☌, P, □, and ☍ aspects. He afflicts any part of the map of birth, or by transit or direction, in which he may be located, and even when in his own signs ♑ and ♒, or in his exaltation sign ♎, but to a less extent when in signs of his debility, as in ♈, ♋, or ♌. His afflictions seem to be inimicable to the great masses of people of the Earth, due to their lack of self-control, spiritual sight and development, and materialistic tendencies, as they are as yet unable to respond to his higher vibrations. (See "Aspects" in this section).

Ameliorated—His afflictions are ameliorated and moderated when the benefics are favorably configurated with him, or when the progressed ☽ forms good aspects to him, or to ♃.

Angel Of—Casiel is known as the Angel of ♄. Also Orifiel is mentioned by some Authors. Mikael is said to be the Regent of Saturn. Also by some Satan is said to represent ♄, and to try the hearts of men, discover their weak points, bring temptations and testings, which, if the native can successfully meet, makes him all the stronger in the end.

Ascending at Birth—Makes the native liable to falls, bruises, blows, accidents, fractures, debility, catarrh, rheumatism, nervous affections, melancholy, etc.

Aspects — ♄ well-aspected and fortified in a map tends to have a beneficial influence over the planets he aspects, but afflicts the sign he is in, and the parts, or organs, ruled by such sign. The good aspects of ♄ are physically inimicable, but may help mentally and spiritually. The evil aspects of ♄ deplete and denude. (See Afflictions, Earth, Evil, Good, Jupiter, Mars, Moon, Sun, Venus, in this section).

Barren— ♄ is a barren planet, and tends to barrenness, and to deny children when in the houses of children at B. (See Barrenness).

Body—In the human body ♄ crystallizes, and makes bone, cartilage and the tendons.

Causes—♄ Causes—(See the various paragraphs and subjects in this Article).

Chaos—♄ is said to be the "Door to Chaos", and especially if you appropriate his afflicting vibrations and influences, and are not living a proper moral and balanced life.

Characteristics — His typical characteristics are coldness, gravity, and concretion. His influence is also depressing, cachectic, clotting, coagulating, etc. (See "Qualities", and the various paragraphs in this section).

Cheer—♄ takes the cheer out of life to many, and especially when rising at B., and afflicted, or afflicting ☿, the mental ruler. (See Cheerfulness).

Children — ♄ being a barren planet denies children when in the houses of children at B., and to cause their death if born, or to be less fortunate in life until awakened and spiritualized. (See Barrenness; "Death Of" under Children).

Chronic—♄ is chronic, enduring, and the principal cause of chronic diseases.

Church—♄ evilly aspected at B. tends to an evil mind, and to make one an enemy of Society, the Church, and the State.

Cold — ♄ produces dryness and cold, being remote from the ☉ and the vapors of the Earth, but he is more effective in producing cold than dryness. He causes excess of cold and dryness, and is malevolent. (See Cold, Dryness).

Colors — Black, Indigo, Green, Lead Color, Gray. In the Solar Spectrum ♄ rules Indigo. (See Colors).

Day and Night—♄ is less malignant by day, as his cold is modified by the heat of the ☉, but he is more malignant at night, and adds his cold influence to that of the cold, dampness, and moisture of the night. (See Day, Night).

Death —'♄ Causes Death By — (See "Death" in Sec. 3 of this Article).

Decay and Decrepitude — ♄ is the planet of. (See Decay, Decrepitude).

Delights In — ♄ delights in the 12th H., the house of self-undoing, prisons, imprisonment, confinement, limitations, hospitals, secret enemies, plots, treachery, chronic diseases, etc. (See Twelfth House).

Denotes—(See the various paragraphs and subjects in this Article).

Denudes and Depletes — (See these subjects. Also see "Aspects" in this section).

Depression of Mind—(See Depression).

Destructive—His influence in the human body is destructive, and he afflicts any part of the map he is in at B., or by transit or direction. (See Destructive; "Afflictions" in this section).

Diathesis—♄ adds or subtracts to the Splenic Diathesis, or the Splenic Process. (See the Introductions under Knees, Lymph).

Directions—The evil directions of ♄ tend to bring fears, jealousies, and mistrust. His good directions to the hyleg favor better health for the time, and more peace of mind, a better fate, etc. His evil directions are more pernicious and evil during old age, or during the period ruled by ♄, as from the 63rd to 77th years of life, when afflicting the hyleg. (See Directions).

Distress—♄ causes distress by colds, bruises, falls, and chronic diseases.

Dragon's Tail—And ♄—(See Dragon).

Drugs—Typical Drugs of ♄ are Aconite, Antimony, Astringents, Belladonna, Conium (Hemlock), Helleborus, Hyoscyamus, Hydrocyanic Acid, Indian Hemp, Lead, Mullein, Rhus Toxicodendron, Salicylate of Soda, Tincture Saturnina (see "Hectic Fever" under Fever); Styptics, Verbascum, etc. (See "Saturn Group" under Herbs; Lead).

Dry—♄ is dry and cold by nature, and his afflictions over the body tend to dry up the fluids and tissues. (See Cold, Dry).

Earth—His evil aspects and afflictions seem to be inimical to the inhabitants of the Earth, as the Earth is said to be the lowest in Materialism in our Solar System, and also the only planet where the sexes are separated, and where the Sex Problem, its control, and proper uses, are the great issues. (See "Afflictions" in this section).

Ends Life—♄ tends by his afflictions to end life in the physical body, to weaken and lower vitality, and opposes the life-giving ☉. (See Opposites).

Endurance — A principal of ♄, and strong ♄ people cling to life tenaciously in sickness, trouble, and adversity. (See Endurance).

Environment—♄ being a negative and magnetic planet renders the native more receptive and susceptible to external influences and environment. (See Environment, External, Negative, Receptive, Susceptibility).

Evil Lessened—The influence of ♄ for evil is lessened when he is occi. of the ☉ at B., and increased when ori., and rising before the ☉.

External Influences — (See "Environment" in this section).

Fears—Creates Fears—(See Fears).

Febrifuge — (See Antipyretic, Febrifuge).

Fixed Signs—♄ in a fixed sign tends to be a very evil afflictor, and to tend to chronic and lingering diseases. (See Fixed Signs).

Fluids of the Body—♄ adds the Salts to the Milk and Fluids of the body. (See Fluids).

Foetus — The physical plasm of the foetus is developed under ♄. (See Foetus).

Gall—♄ forms the Gall—(See Bile).

Gases—(See Hydrogen).

Gloom—♄ brings gloom and death by his afflictions. (See Gloom).

God — (See "Will of Providence" in this section).

Good Aspects—The good aspects of ♄ tend to obstruct when applying to other planets. (See "Aspects" in this section).

Gravity — A ♄ characteristic. (See Grave).

Hard—His influence is hard, hardening, and barren. (See Hard).

Health—♄ and Health—(See Health; the various paragraphs in this Article).

Heat—♄ is cold, of little heat, and with low caloric. The cold of ♄ is opposed to the heat of the ☉ and ♂. (See "Cold" in this section).

Herbs Of—(See "Saturn Group" under Herbs).

Hinders—♄ contracts, binds, hinders, restricts, while ♂ accelerates and burns up the wastes of the body by fevers and inflammations. (See Hindrances).

Hour—♄ Hour—(See "Hours" under Planets).

Husbanding—One great influence of ♄ is the husbanding of resources, and even to hoarding and miserliness. (See Miserly).

Hypocrites — In religious, and other matters, ♄ tends to breed hypocrites. (See Hypocritical).

Ills of Life—The ills of life are ascribed to ♄ and his afflictions, and to his chastenings. Saturn allows people to pursue their wicked courses, but calls them severely to account under his evil aspects, and to bring suffering, sorrows, disease, or death to those who are not living right. (See Affliction; "Afflictions" in this section; "Diseases" in Sec. 3 of this Article).

Infortune — ♄ is classed as "The Greater Infortune", due to his severe and prolonged periods of affliction, while Mars is known as "The Lesser Infortune". However, ♄ is not an Infortune to those who are living right, and striving to rule their lower natures, and the evils of life. The Planetary Hierarch which rules over ♄, is one of the Elohim, one of the "Seven Spirits Before the Throne", a Messenger of God, and assigned to the work of uplifting humanity, and working out their ultimate salvation and perfection. No planet is evil, but only seems evil from our viewpoint when we come under his afflictions and chastenings, which are not given as punishments or retribution, but only to make humanity better. (See Benefics, Malefics).

Intropulsive — ♄ is intropulsive, and tends to retain and drive inward the poisons and wastes of the body. By chilling the surface he drives the blood inward, causing internal congestions. His action is centripetal, towards the center, while the action of ♂ is centrifugal, away from the center. (See Centripetal, Intropulsion).

Jealousy—(See Jealousy; "Directions" in this section).

Joy—♄ tends to suppress life and joy, and take the cheer out of life in the ordinary, unawakened, and unspiritualized person. (See Cheer, Joy).

Jupiter and Saturn—In the treatment of ♄ diseases, the good aspects of ♃, or the remedies, herbs, or roots of ♃, help more than those of ♀. (See "Jupiter Group" under Herbs; Jupiter).

Keynote — The keynote of ♄ is obstruction. (See Obstruction).

Lasting Influence—The influence of ♄ by his aspects is the most lasting and malignant of all the planets.

Life—♄ suppresses life and joy. (See Suppressions).

Limitation — The Principle of ♄ is limitation, and he, therefore, rules the skin and bones, as these tend to define and limit the corporature. (See Limitations).

Liver—♄ forms Uric Acid, Urea, and Gall in the Liver, and during muscular activity these are deposited over the body and cause Gout and Rheumatism. Saturn is chronic and causes torpid liver and constipation. (See Bile, Constipation, Gout, Liver, Rheumatism, Urea, Uric).

Low Caloric—(See Cold, Dry, Heat, in this section).

Magnetic—♄ is a negative and magnetic planet. (See "Environment" in this section; Magnetic; "Negative Planets" under Negative).

Malefic — ♄ is considered malefic, or chastening in his influence. (See "Infortune" in this section).

Malevolent — ♄ is malevolent in his action upon the human body in that he produces an excess of cold and dryness. (See Cold, Dry, Malevolent).

Malignant — (See Malignant; "Lasting" in this section).

Mars and Saturn—♄ is the negative of ♂, and the opposite of ♂ action. Saturn is centripetal, and ♂ is centrifugal; ♄ is restrained, and ♂ is intensive. Together ♄ and ♂ act as heat and cold, acute and chronic. Saturn tends to offset the active life given by ♂, and to check, delay, repress, and smother the fiery spirit of ♂. Saturn tends to depress, and ♂ to enhance. What is given by ♂ is overcome by ♄. One is sudden, and the other is tardy. Saturn draws from the circumference to a center, along lines of radii, drawing the blood inward, contracting, crystallizing, restricting, binding, hampering, consolidating, etc., while the action of ♂ is the opposite. Saturn opposes the heat, life, energy, courage, and vital power given by ♂ and the ☉. The mind is considerably improved by the good aspects of ♂ to ♄. (See Mars).

Mercury and Saturn—(See the Introduction under Mercury).

Metals of Saturn — Lead is the principal Metal of ♄. (See Lead, Therapeutics; "Mineral" in this section).

Milk—♄ adds the Salts to Milk. (See Milk).

Mind—The afflictions of ♄ tend to afflict the mind, cause depression and melancholy, jealousy, hatred, revenge, and an evil mind. (See Mind; "Church" in this section).

Mineral World—Minerals of—In the mineral world ♄ crystallizes, such as coal, rock, lead, etc. Graphite and Lead are principal minerals of ♄.

Mischief—♄ is said to be the author of mischief, and especially when he is afflicted in the 12th H. (See Mischief).

Mistrusts — (See Mistrustful; "Directions" in this section).

Moon and Saturn—♄ is antagonistic to the ☽, and tends to aggravate all ☽ diseases by his ♂ and evil aspects to the ☽. The ☽, ruler of ♋, opposes ♄, ruler of ♑. (See Moon, Opposites).

Muscular Activity—The Action of ♄ During—(See "Liver" in this section).

Nature of Saturn—Cold and dry, contracting, obstructing, etc. (See "Qualities", and the various paragraphs in this Article).

Negation—♄ is the planet of negation.

Negative—♄ is a negative and magnetic planet and gives negative qualities, such as fear, worry, timidity, cowardice, pessimism, revenge, etc.

Nervous—♄ influence is nervous. (See Nerves).

Night — ♄ influence by Night — (See "Day" in this section).

Obstruction—Obstruction is the keynote, and the most salient characteristic of ♄. (See Obstructions).

Occidental and Oriental— (See "Evil Lessened" in this section).

Old Age—♄ is the planet of, and rules old age. (See Old Age).

Oriental—(See "Evil Lessened" in this section).

Part of Body—The Parts Afflicted by ♄—(See "Afflictions" in this section).

Pathological Action — ♄ is a pathological planet, and especially in his afflictions and lower vibrations. The pathological action of ♄ Herbs, Minerals, and Metals, and his own direct action over the body by his afflictions, is to disturb the Peripheral Nerves, the Connective Tissues, the Osseous, Mucous, and Cutaneous Systems, to cause the degeneration of tissues, and disturbances of vaso-constriction.

Period Of—(See "Planetary Periods" under Periods).

People — Saturn people are secretive, fond of solitude, melancholic, pessimistic, penurious, hypochondriac, but capable of great endurance; are strong in enmity, are austere, grave, often ascetic, and very stupid if ♄ afflict ☿. (See "Saturn Persons" in this section).

Places Ruled By—Graveyards, churchyards, the Desert, woods, obscure places, dens, caves, holes, mountains, coal mines, stinking and dirty places, sinks, cess pools, stagnant ponds, etc. For Places and Countries ruled by ♄ see "Capricorn Rules", "Aquarius Rules", under Nations).

Plants, Herbs, Roots — Of ♄ — (See "Saturn Group" under Herbs).

Principle Of—Limitation. (See Limitations).

Punishment — Chastisement — ♄ chastens and punishes our wayward natures, but what seem to be his evils are only good in the making. (See Punishment; "Afflictions", "Infortune", in this section).

Qualities—Qualities Given and Ruled Over by Saturn—These are here listed alphabetically, the most of which you can find in the alphabetical arrangement of this book—Abnormal, Abortive, Absorbing, Accumulative, Acquisitive, Afflicting, Anaphrodisiac, Antiperistaltic, Antiphlogistic, Antipyretic, Ascetic, Asphyxiating, Astringent, Atrophying, Austere, Avaricious, Barren, Beggarly, Binding, Blighting, Brooding, Cachetic, Careful, Catabolic, Cautious, Centripetal, Chaotic, Chastening, Checking, Checkmating, Cheerlessness, Chilling, Chronic, Clotting, Coagulating, Cold, Cold and Dry, Cold and Moist when Oriental, Compressing, Concretive, Condensing, Confining, Congealing, Consolidating, Constant, Constricting, Consumptive, Contemptous, Contentious, Contracting, Corrupting, Covetous, Cowardly, Cruel, Crushing, Crystallizing, Death-Dealing, Deathly, Debilitating, Decaying, Deceitful, Decrepitating, Defective, Defensive, Deforming, Degenerating, Dejecting, Delaying, Deluding, Delusive, Denuding, Depleting, Depressing, Deprivating, Despairing, Despondent, Destructive, Deteriorating, Devitalizing, Diminishing, Disagreeable, Dissoluting, Dissolving, Distressing, Distributing, Disturbing, Diuretic, Diurnal, Dry, Dull, Earth-bound, Earthy, Emaciating, Enduring, Enervating, Enlarging, Enmity, Envious, Eruptive, Evil, Excessive, Fearful, Fear-Producing, Febrifuge, Fretful, Frigid, Frugal, Gloomy, Granulating, Grasping, Grave, Greedy, Habit-Forming, Haemostatic, Hallucinating, Hampering, Hard, Hardening, Heaviness, Hindering, Hopelessness, Husbanding of Resources, Hypochondriac, Hypocritical, Ill (Evil); Illusive, Imaginative, Impairing, Impeding, Imposing, Induration, Inflaming, Ingenious, Inhibiting, Injurious, Intropulsive, Invalidating, Jealous, Lasting, Lessening, Limiting, Lingering, Long-Enduring, Lowering, Lumpy (Lump-forming); Lying, Maddening, Magnetic, Malefic, Malevolent, Malicious, Malignant, Malnutritive, Maniacal, Masculine, Materialistic, Melancholic, Miscarrying, Mischievous, Miserly, Mistrustful, Moody, Moping, Morbid, Mortifying, Motive, Mournful, Mystical, Mystifying, Narrowing, Nauseating, Negative, Neglectful, Nervous, Neurotic, Nodular (Node-forming); Nucleolating, Obsessing, Obstinate, Obstructing, Ossifying, Painful, Paralyzing, Pathological, Patient, Paucity, Penurious, Permanency, Pernicious, Persevering, Perverse, Perverting, Pessimistic, Petrifactive, Petulant, Phlegmatic, Pitiless, Poisonous, Privative, Procrastinating, Prolonging, Proud, Pus-forming, Quarrelsome, Reclusive, Reducing, Refrigerant, Regretful, Repining, Repressive, Resentful, Reserved, Resolving, Restraining, Restrictive, Retarding, Retentive, Retractive, Revengeful, Rheumatic, Rigid, Ruinous, Rupturing, Sad, Saddening, Scolding, Scybalous, Secretive, Sedate, Sedative, Sedentary, Selfish, Self-Undoing, Serious, Servile, Serving, Severe, Shrinking, Sickening, Skeptical, Slavish, Slow, Smothering, Sober, Solitary, Sorrowful, Souring, Speculative, Stagnating, Stenotic, Stiffening, Stopping, Strangulating, Styptic, Subduing, Subtle, Suffering, Suffocating, Suicidal, Sullen, Suppressing, Suspicious, Taciturn, Tactful, Tardy in Action, Tedious, Testing, Thickening, Thrifty, Timid, Tissue-Destroying, Torpid, Torturing, Toughening, Tremulous, Troublesome, Tuberculous, Tumorous, Ulcerating, Unmerciful, Unsociable, Vain, Vapourous, Visionary, Wasting, Wayward, Weakening, Wicked, Worrisome, Wrinkling, etc.

Recluse—(See Recluse, Reserved, Secretive, Solitude).

Remedies Of — (See Drugs, Herbs, Metals, Minerals, Therapeutic, Treatment, in this section. Also see Antipathy, Opposites, Remedies, Sympathy, Treatment).

Resources—Husbanding of—(See Resources).

Restraint — ♄ influence tends to restraints, confinements, and limitations. (See Restraints).

Roots and Herbs—(See "Saturn Group" under Herbs).

Ruin and Disgrace—♄ in the M.C. at B., and afflicted, danger of. (See Disgrace, Ruin).

Salts Of—(See Salts; "Fluids" in this section).

Saturday—Saturn's Day—(See Week).

Saturn Persons—The unawakened and drifting ♄ person frets, mopes, and worries, and thereby renders himself liable to suicidal mania, melancholia, liver disease, and chronic ailments in general, and to an earlier death. (See "People" in this section).

Senses and Saturn—♄ is not a builder to the Senses, but rather exerts a strong psychological and intellectual power. (See Senses).

Signifies—♄ signifies servitude, limitation, husbanding of resources, nucleolation, induration, etc.

Signs — ♄ rules the ♑ and ♒ signs. He is considered an affliction in any sign, and even in his own signs afflicts the knees, lower limbs, and ankles. (See "Afflictions", "Aspects" in this section).

Sixth House — ♄ when in the 6th H., or afflicting the hyleg or Asc., produces cold, lingering and chronic complaints.

Skin — ♄ rules the skin. (See Skin; "Limitation" in this section).

Society—An Enemy To—(See "Church" in this section).

Sours People — ♄ afflictions tend to sour people upon the World, and to make recluses and pessimists. (See Pessimistic, Recluse).

Spirituality — The good aspects of ♄ tend to help spirituality. (See Spiritual; "Aspects" in this section).

Splenic Diathesis — (See "Diathesis" in this section).

Stagnation—♄ is the planet of. (See Stagnation).

State—(See "Church" in this section).

Suicide — ♄ afflictions tend to — (See Suicide).

Sun — Relation of ♄ to — (See Cold, Evil, Heat, in this section; Opposites, Sun).

Suppresses Life—And Joy—(See Joy, Life, in this section).

Suppression — The planet of — (See Hindrances, Retarding, Retentions, Stagnation, Stoppages, Suppressions).

Symbol Of — The Reaper with his Scythe and Hour Glass in hand. Also the Black Vulture, or Raven.

Sympathizes With—In disease ♄ sympathizes with the ☽, and aggravates all diseases of the ☽. He also adds his sympathy to the other malefics in bringing oppression, suffering, and evils upon humanity in order to teach self-control thru varied experiences.

Temperament — ♄ gives the Nervous Temperament, and also the Melancholic Disposition, the Sad, Grave, Gloomy, and Pessimistic nature, and with reserve, suspicion, and selfishness. (See "Temperament" under Nerves).

Therapeutic Qualities—Antiphlogistic, Antipyretic, Astringent, Diuretic, Febrifuge, Refrigerant, Sedative, Styptic. (See Drugs, Remedies, in this section).

Treatment — In the treatment of ♄ diseases, the Herbs and Remedies ruled by Signs in ☍ to the signs of ♄ are best, as the ☉ and ☽ remedies of the ♋ and ♌ signs. Also, ♂ remedies oppose ♄, being opposite in effect, one cold, and the other hot, etc. (See Antipathy, Opposites, Remedies, Sympathy, Treatment).

Twelfth House — ♄ delights in this house, as he is the Author of Mischief. (See Mischief, Twelfth House).

Typical Drugs Of—(See "Drugs" in this section).

Urea—♄ forms Urea. (See Urea).

Uric Acid — ♄ forms Uric Acid and deposits it over the body. (See Uric).

Venus and Saturn — ♄ with ♀ at B. tends to lower and debauch the good influences of ♀. (See Love Affairs, Passion, Perversions, Venus; "Jupiter" in this section).

Victims of Saturn—The victims of ♄ are hard to reach, as they are usually full of fears, worries, are pessimistic, skeptical of a cure, and lack joy and cheer when unawakened and living in their lower minds.

Vocations of Saturn — Undertakers, Gravediggers, Dealers in Lead, Mines, Minerals; Agriculture, Building, etc.

Vulnerable Spots — (See "Weak" in this section).

Wastes of the Body — The afflictions of ♄ tend to retain the wastes and poisons of the body, and to deposit them over the system in the form of urea and uric acid, causing Gout, Rheumatism, etc. (See Deposits, Minerals, Wastes, etc.).

Waywardness—♄ tends to subdue our wayward natures, to correct the evils of our lives, and to "Punish", or chastise, for our sins, to restore our balance, and make us better. (See "Punishment" in this section).

Weak Spots—The position of ♄ at B., by transit, by direction, progression, shows the weak and vulnerable spots in our horoscope, and the parts or faculties under affliction along thru life.

Well-Aspected — (See Aspects, Good, Spirituality, in this section).

Wickedness — (See "Ills of Life" in this section).

Will of Providence—♄ is the cause of the greater part of human suffering, but subservient to the Will of Providence.

Worry—Tends To—(See Worry).

— SECTION TWO —

SATURN RULES—These subjects are merely listed here, and the most of them you will find in the alphabetical arrangement of this book — Abortion; Accumulations; Acquisitiveness; Afflictions; Aged People (see Old Age); Agnostics; Anaphrodisiacs; Animals (Small); Antiphlogistics; Antipyretics; Apoplexies; Aquarius Sign; Articulations (see Joints); Ash; Ashes; Astringents; Atheists; Atrophies; Auditory Organs (especially the Right Ear); Auricle (Left Auricle of Heart when ♄ is in ♌); Barrenness; Bindings, Black —Black Clothing—Black Color, Black Hair, the Black Raven; Bladder; Blood —The Composition of the Blood, and the Circulation of the Blood in the Tissues; Blows; Bones—The Bones in all Parts of the Body, and the Joints; Bruises; Burial Alive; Cachexia; Calcarea (Lime); Calces (Calcium); Caloric (Low Caloric); Calves of Legs; Capricorn Sign; Carbon; Cartilage; Cartilaginous Tissue Building; Catabolism; Catalysis; Caves; Centripetal Action; Cervical Vertebrae (♄ in ♍ rules and affects them); Cesspools; Chalk; Chaos; Chastisement; Checkmates; Chronic Diseases; Chyle; Chylification; Chylopoiesis; Circulation of the Blood in the Tissues; Clothing (Black); Clots; Clotting; Coagulation; Coal and Coal Mines; Cold (Intemperate Cold); Colds; Colors—Black, Lead, Green, Gray, Indigo; Composition of the Blood; Compressions; Concretions; Condensation; Confinements; Congelation; Consolidation; Constrictor Nerves; Consumptions; Contractions; Contusions; Covetousness; Cowardice; Cramps; Crushings (Death By); Crystallization; Cube (The Geometrical Cube); Cutaneous Capillary Vaso-Contrictor Nerves; Darkness; Death; Debility; Decay; Decomposition; Decrepitude; Defensiveness; Deficiencies; Degeneration; Dejection; Delays; Denuding; Depletions; Deposits; Depression; Deprivations; Desert (The Desert); Despair; Destruction; Dirty Places; Disease (Chronic); Dissolution; Distribution and Circulation of the Blood in the Tissues; Dross of Metals; Drugs (Narcotic); Dryness and Cold; Ear (Right Ear); Earthy Minerals Carried by the Blood; East Wind; Emaciations; End of Life (Old Age); Endocardium; Endurance; Enemies (Secret); Envy; Evils; Excretions; Faculty — The Retentive Faculty throughout the Body; Faeces;

Falls; Father (the Father); Fears; Febrifuges; Foetus (the Physical Plasm of); Foul Odors; Fractures; Fretfulness; Friendships and Long Ties; Frigidity; Frost and Snow (Atmospherically); Gall and the Gall Bladder; Genito-Urinary Organs (Bones of); Gloom; Grandfathers; Graphite; Grave (the Grave); Graveyards; Grave Diggers; Gravity (Grave Disposition); Green Color in the Solar Spectrum; Gristle; Habits; Hair (Black Hair); Hangings; Hardening and Hardness; Heart (Left Auricle and Endocardium); Heaviness; Hermits; Hindrances in Life; Holes (Holes in the Ground, Cesspools, etc.); Hopelessness, Humours; Husbanding of Resources; Hydrogen; Hypochondria; Hypocrites; Ice; Ills of Life; Impediments; Imprisonment; Indigo Color; Indurations; Intellectual Power; Intropulsion; Introspection; Invalidism; Jealousy; Joints; Knees; Lead and Lead Color; Left Auricle of the Heart; Leukocytes; Life from 56 to 70 Years; Ligaments; Lime; Limitations; Lingering Diseases and Lingering Death; Liver; Long Ties and Friendships; Low Caloric; Lower Mind; Lower Strata, as Coal and the Deposits in the Earth; Lumpy Faeces (Scybalum); Magnetism; Malignant Conditions; Melancholy; Memory; Metal — Lead; Metals (Dross of); Minerals (Earthy Carried by the Blood, and also Minerals in General; Mines; Mischief; Misers; Misfortunes; Mistrusts; Moping; Morbid Conditions and Morbid States of the Mind and Body; Mortification; Motive Temperament; Mountains; Mourning; Narcotic Drugs; Neck (Bones of); Negation; Negative Qualities; Neglect and Privation; Nerves— The Cutaneous Capillary Vaso-Constrictor Nerves—The Peripheral Sympathetic Nerves — The Pneumogastric Nerve; Nervous Temperament; Nucleolation; Obstacles; Obstructions; Old Age (and especially Decrepit Old Men); Onions; Ossification; Pathological Conditions; Peripheral Nerves and the Peripheral Sympathetic Nerves; Permanency; Pernicious Actions; Pessimism; Petrifactions; Phlegm; Plots; Plumbago (Lead); Pneumogastric Nerve; Poverty; Privation; Psychological Powers; Punishments (Chastisements); Putrefactions; Raven (the Black Raven, or Black Vulture); Recluses; Reducing Agencies and Drugs; Refrigerants; Regrets; Religious Hypocrites; Repining; Repression; Reserve; Resources (Husbanding of); Respiratory System (when ♄ is in ♊, ♍, or ♒); Restrictions; Retentions (and the Faculty of Retention in the Body); Retraction; Revenge; Reverses; Ribs; Right Ear; Rigidity; Rigors; Rocks; Ruin; Sand (in Kidneys or Bladder); Saturday; Scybalous Agencies and Matter; Secret Enemies; Secretive System Generally; Secretiveness; Sedatives; Sedentary Habits; Selfishness; Senility and Senile Feebleness; Servitude; Shrinkings; Sigmoid Flexure; Signs of the Zodiac—♑ and ♒; Shameless Practices; Skeptics; Skin; Skull (♄ in ♈); Slavery; Small Animals; Snow and Frost (Atmospherically); Solitudes; Soot; Soured Disposition; Spine (Vertebrae); Spleen; Splenic Diathesis and Splenic Process;

Stagnation and Stagnant Waters; Stiffness of Joints and Muscles, and Stiff and Rigid Conditions in the Body in General; Stinking Places (Foul Odors); Stones; Strata (Lower Strata in the Earth, as Coal, etc.); Strifes; Styptics; Subduings; Suffering; Suffocation; Suicides; Sullenness; Suppressions; Suspicions; Sympathetic Nerve and the Sympathetic Peripheral Nerves; Tabefaction; Teeth; Temperament (the Nervous Temperament); Tendons and their Crystallization; Throat (Bones of with ♄ in ♉); Ties (Long Ties and Friendships); Time (the Reaper); Timidity; Tissue Building (Cartilaginous); Tissues (the Blood Circulation In); Tortures; Treachery; Troubles; Urea; Uric Acid; Urinary Organs; Vagus Nerve; Vaso-Constrictor Cutaneous Nerves; Veneral Desire (Drugs which Lessen — Anaphrodisiacs); Vertebrae; Vulture (Black Vulture or Black Raven); Want and Neglect; Waste Products of the Body; Weakness; Wickedness; Woods; Worry, etc.

— SECTION THREE —

THE DISEASES OF SATURN — The Afflictions of Saturn—Diseases Ruled by ♄—Diseases which proceed from ♄ are more permanent, and are generally regulated by the motion of the ☉. His influence is destructive in the human body, and he tends to afflict any sign he is in, and to disturb the organs or parts ruled by such sign. He especially causes distress by bruises, colds, chronic diseases, by mineral deposits, urea, and uric acid over the system. He causes hindrances, disturbances of function, stoppages, retentions, suppressions, suspensions, stagnations, lowered vitality, melancholy, etc., and finally death of the physical body. In normal conditions he furnishes the lime, minerals, earthy salts for the body, and in the proper proportions, but as age creeps on, the minerals and wastes of the body are deposited more unevenly, retained, not properly eliminated, until the body becomes acid, hardened, crystallized, and unable to further carry on its work, and death results. The three score and ten years are assigned to man, and it is the work of ♄ to see to it that people do not live too long on the Earth at one time. When in a fixed sign at B., and by dir., ♄ tends to be a very evil afflictor, and to lead to long, lingering, chronic and tedious diseases. Saturn is depressing, antipyretic, and opposed to the action of ♂ and the Luminaries over the body. The most of his diseases are brought on by cold, exposure to cold, chill, and he specializes in cold and dry diseases, which are more destructive to the body. His influence over the mind is worrisome, pessimistic, depressing, melancholic, etc., which states of mind tend to lowered vitality, and earlier death. Saturn in the Signs and Houses at B. shows the weak spots in our map, and where we are liable to go wrong, and what parts of the body are more subject to disease and permanent affliction, the vulnerable parts of the body. Saturn afflicted in the 6th H., or afflicting the ☉, ☽, Asc., M.C., or Hyleg therefrom, is very evil in health matters. Also ♄ posited in the 12th H. tends to confinements, restraints, bodily defects, limitation of the five senses, and to chronic diseases. As it takes ♄ about 2½ years to pass thru one Sign or House, his afflictions tend to be prolonged, and people ignorant of Astrology, and of what vibration is working over them, causing worry and anxiety, fears, etc., usually begin to lose weight, vitality, and have no peace of mind, and to eventually go into some form of chronic disease until ♄ changes signs, and turns his affliction to other classes of people. It need not be so, however, if people knew of ♄ and his working, and the times of his increased afflictions over their lives, and then could relax, avoid worry, and go right along, and at the same time try to gain in Wisdom, Knowledge, and Spiritual Power.

Many of the influences of Saturn along the lines of disease and his afflictions are listed in Sec. 1 of this Article. The diseases and afflictions of ♄ are, perhaps, more numerous than those of any other planet, and more spoken of in the Textbooks of Astrology. In order to handle the great mass of material gathered about the afflictions of this planet, these subjects have been placed in the alphabetical arrangement of this book for quick reference, rather than to deal with them more fully here in this Article. Therefore, this Section is mostly an alphabetical Summary of the Saturn Diseases and Afflictions, to bring them to your attention, and you are requested to follow them up throughout the book. See the following subjects in the alphabetical arrangement—

Abeyance; Ablation; Abortion; Absorption; Accidents; Aches; Acute Nervous Diseases—(See "Acute Nervous" under Nerves).

Adynamia; Ague; Analysis of Tissues —(See Absorption, Tissues).

Antiperistalsis; Apoplexies; Arms— Infirmities In—(See Arms).

Arterio-Sclerosis—(See Arteries, Hardening).

Arthritis—(See Joints, Synovial).

Articular Rheumatism — (See Gout, Joints).

Articulations — Hardening of — (See Joints).

Asphyxia — Cutaneous — (See Asphyxia).

Assimilation—Imperfect—(See Assimilation).

Asthenia; Asthma; Ataxia; Atrophy; Auricular Disease—(See "Auricles" under Heart).

Back—Disorders In—(See Back).

Barrenness; Bellyache—Dry Bellyache —(See Belly).

Berberi—(See Anaemia, Dropsy).

Black Jaundice—(See "Black" under Jaundice).

Bladder Disorders; Blemishes; Blight; Blindness—By Cataracts, Colds, Decay of the Optic Nerve, and by Specks, Gutta Serena, etc.—(See Blindness).

Blood—Disorders of—Impure Blood— Blood Driven Inwards — Congestion —

Impeded Circulation—Blood Tumors—Blood Vessels — Constrictions, etc. — (See Blood, Centripetal, Circulation, Constrictions, Haematoma, Impeded, Impure, Vessels, etc.).

Blows; Bodily Energies—Bodily Fluids—Bodily Functions—Disorders of—(See Abeyance, Energy, Fluids, Functions, Impairments, Impeded, Suppressions, etc.).

Body—Debility of—Depressions In—(See Body, Debility, Depressions).

Bones—All Diseases In—Fractures—Pains In—(See Bones).

Bowels—Gripings In—Obstructions In—Peristaltic Action Impeded—Pains In—(See Bowels).

Breakings Out—(See Eruptions, Pimples).

Breasts—Bruises In—Cancer of—Obstructions In — Suppressions — (See Breast).

Breath—Foul Breath—(See Breath).

Breathing—Cutaneous Breathing Suppressed—(See "Cutaneous" under Asphyxia).

Bright's Disease—(See Bright's).

Broken Bones — Fractures — (See the various parts and subjects under Fracture).

Bronchitis — (See "Chronic" under Bronchial; Lungs, Pulmonary).

Bruises; Bunions; Cachexia; Calamity—Fear of—(See Calamity).

Calculus; Cancer Disease—(See Carcinoma).

Carcinoma; Caries; Cataract; Catarrh; Cavities—Pus In—Disorders of—(See Cavities, Pus, Receptacles, Sacs).

Celibacy; Cells — Disorders of — (See the various paragraphs under Cells).

Centripetal Action; Cerebral Disorders; Cessations; Chalk Stones—(See Calculus, Chalk, Lime, Stone).

Chest Disorders; Chilblain; Childhood—Disorders of—(See Childhood, Children, Infancy).

Childless—(See Barrenness, Impotent; "Unfruitful" under Wife).

Children—Afflictions To—Hurts To—Early Death of—(See Childhood, Children, Infancy).

Chill; Chlorosis; Chronic Diseases; Chyle Disordered; Circulation Disordered; Cirrhosis; Claw Hand; Cloaca; Clogging; Clots; Clouded Mind—Clouded Sight—(See Clouded).

Club Feet; Coagulation; Cold — Diseases Arising From — Cold and Dry Diseases—(See Cold, Dry).

Colds; Colic; Colon Disordered; Compressions; Concretions; Concussions; Condensations; Confinements; Congelation; Congenital Defects; Congestions; Consolidations; Constant Diseases; Constipation; Constitutional Disorders; Constrictions; Consumptions; Contractions; Contusions; Cord — Maladies of the Spinal Cord—(See "Cord" under Spine).

Corns—Bunions—(See Bunions).

Corrosions; Corruption; Costiveness; Coughs; Cramps; Cravings; Criminals; Crippled; Crooked Body; Crushings;

Crusts; Crystallization; Curvature—Of Spine—(See Spine).

Cutaneous Diseases—(See Cutaneous, Skin).

Cuticle (Thickening of); **Cutis**—Contraction of—(See Derma).

Cyanosis; Dead Tissue—(See Crusts; "Tissue" under Dead; Scales).

Deafness; Death—♄ causes death by Agues, Blows, Bruises, Chronic Diseases, Cold, Colds, Consumptions, Crushings, Dropsies, Drowning, Epilepsy, Falls, Fears, Fluxes, Fractures, Hysterics, Ileac Passion, Lingering Diseases, Melancholy, Phthisis, Slow Diseases, Suffocation, etc. (See these subjects, and also the paragraphs under Death).

Debauchery; Debility; Decay; Declines; Decreased Motility—(See Decrease).

Decrepitude; Deep-Seated Diseases; Defects; Deficiencies; Defluxions; Deformities; Degeneracy; Degeneration; Dejection; Delays; Delicacy; Delusions; Demoniac; Density; Dental Disorders—(See Dental, Teeth).

Denuding; Depletion; Deposits; Depravity; Depressed—Depressions—(See Depressed).

Derangements; Derma Disordered; Desires Abnormal; Despondency; Destructive Processes — (See Atrophy, Consumptions, Emaciations; "Low Fever" under Low; "Malnutrition" under Nutrition; Tabes, Tuberculosis, Wastings, etc.).

Deteriorations; Detriments; Deviations; Devitalization; Diarrhoea (Chronic); **Difficulties; Digestion** (Disorders of); **Dilatations; Diminishments; Disabilities; Disagreeable; Disaster; Discharges; Discolorations; Discomposed; Discontentment; Disease** (Chronic); **Disfigurements; Disgrace; Dishonesty; Disintegration; Dislocations; Disorders; Disorganization; Dispersions; Displacements; Disproportionate Body; Disputes; Dissipations; Dissolution; Distempers; Distortions; Distraction; Distress; Disturbances; Dizziness; Doubts; Downcast; Downfall**—(See Disgrace, Dishonour, Losses, Property, Reputation, Reverses, Ruin).

Dreads — (See Anxieties, Dreads, Fears).

Driving Blood Inwards—(See Centripetal, Chill, Cold).

Drooping; Dropsy; Drought; Drowning; Drowsiness—(See Sleep).

Drug Habit—(See Narcotics).

Dry and Cold Diseases — (See Cold, Dry).

Dullness—Dull Pains and Aches—(See Dull).

Durable Diseases—(See Chronic, Duration, Lingering, Long, Prolonged, Slow, Tedious).

Dwarfed; Dysmenorrhoea — (See Menses).

Dypspepsia; Dyspnoea; Ears—Impediments In—(See Ears; "Right Ear" under Right).

Eczema; Elimination (Disorders of); **Emaciation; Embolism; Emotions** (Disorders of); **Endocarditis**—(See Heart).

Enemies (Secret);

Energy (Abeyance of); **Enervation; Enlargements; Enmities; Ennui; Enteralgia; Enteric Fever** — (See Bowels, Typhoid).

Epidemics; Epilepsy; Epithelioma; Erratic; Eructations—(See Belching).

Eruptions; Erysipelas; Evil—Evils—King's Evil, Scrofula).

Excesses — Excessive Deposits — Excess of Urea and Uric Acid—(See Deposits, Minerals, Poisons, Urea, Uric, Wastes).

Excoriations; Excrescences; Excretion (Disorders of); **Exercise** (Lack of); **Exertion**—Lack of—(See "Sickly" under Exertion).

Exhaustion; Exposure; External Disorders — (See Eruptions, External, Pimples, Skin).

Extremities (Disorders of); **Eyes** — (See "Blindness" in this section; Eyeballs, Eyes).

Face (Disorders of—Red Face); **Faculties Inhibited**—(See Inhibitions).

Fading; Faeces (Disorders of); **Fag; Faint; Fainting; Falls; Family**—Death In — Sickness In — (See Family, Relatives).

Famine; Fancies (Distempered); **Fatal Illness; Fate** (Bad Fate); **Father** (Death or Illness of); **Fatigue; Fauces** (Dryness of); **Fears; Feeble; Feelings** (Disorders of); **Feet** (Distempered — Gout In); **Female Disorders** — (See Female, Menses, Ovaries, Womb, Women, etc.).

Festerings; Fetid Conditions; Fevers (Hectic, Low); **Fibrous Tumors; Filth; Fissure; Fistula; Fixed Habits** — (See "Habits" under Fixed).

Flesh (Loss of); **Fluids** (Disturbances of); **Fluxes**—(See Flux, Hemorrhoids).

Foetus (Disorders of); **Food**—Errors In Diet—(See Diet, Eating, Food).

Fools; Forebodings; Fortune (Ill-Fortune); **Foul Conditions; Fractures; Frail; Freaks; Fretfulness; Frictions; Friends** (Death of—Illness of); **Frigidity; Functions** (Atrophy of—Suppression of); **Fury** (Fits of); **Gait** (Disorders of); **Gall Disorders**—Gall Stones (See Bile).

Gangrene; Gas (In Stomach or Bowels); **Gastric Disorders; General Debility**—(See Debility).

Generative Organs — Disorders of — (See Generation, Genitals, Genito-Urinary).

Gestation (Disorders of); **Ghastly Look**—(See Pale, Sickly).

Giddiness; Glaucoma; Gloom; Goiter; Gout; Grandparents (Afflictions To — Death of); **Gravel; Grief; Grievous Diseases; Gripings; Gristle**—Disorders of—(See Cartilage).

Groins (Disorders In); **Growth** (Disorders of); **Growths** (Morbid, Obstructing); **Gutta Serena; Habits** (Fixed Habits, Evil Habits, Habitual Disorders); **Haematoma; Hair** (Little Hair); **Halitosis** — (See "Foul" under Breath).

Hallucinations; Hands (Gout In); **Hard; Hardening; Hatred; Head** (Colds In, Pains In); **Headaches; Health** (Bad Health, Periods of Bad Health); **Hearing** (Deafness, Impaired); **Heart** (Afflicted with Grief, Afflicted with Poison,

Action Impeded, Left Auricle Disordered); **Heavy Aches** — And Pains — (See Aches, Heavy).

Heights (Falls From); **Hematochromatosis; Hemiplegia; Hemorrhoids** (Too Much Flux of); **Hernia; Herpes; Hip Diseases** (Hip Joint); **Hoarseness; Homicide; Hopelessness; Horny Growths; Hospitals** (Death In); **Houses**—Death by Fall of—(See Buildings).

Humours (Gouty, Offensive); **Humpback**—(See "Curvature", "Humpback", under Spine).

Hunger; Hurts; Husband (Death of); **Hypochondria; Hysterics; Ignoble Death; Ileac Passion; Ileum** (Obstructions In); **Ill-Formed; Ill-Health; Imaginations; Imbecility; Impairments; Impediments; Impending Disaster** — Fear of—(See Calamity).

Imperfections; Imperforations; Impotency; Impoverishments; Imprisonment—(See Prison).

Impure Blood—(See "Corrupt" under Impure).

Inabilities; Inactive; Incapable; Incomplete; Increases (Dryness and Disease Increased); **Incurable Diseases; Incurvating Body; Indifference; Indigestion; Indisposition; Indurations; Infamous; Infancy** (Death In); **Infarcts; Inferiority Complex; Infirmities; Inflammation** (Chronic, and Lungs Inflamed); **Inflexibility; Inherent Diseases; Inhibitions; Inhuman Shape; Injuries** (By Blows, Depressions in Skull or Body, by Falls, Crushings, Fractures, but with no loss of Blood).

Insufficiencies; Internal Disorders (Congestions, Intropulsion); **Intestines**—Disorders of—(See Bowels).

Intropulsion; Invalidism; Inward—Blood Driven Inward — (See Centripetal, Chill).

Inward Parts — Disorders of — (See Reins).

Irregularities; Irremediable Diseases—(See Incurable, Permanent, Remedy).

Irritations; Ischium (Disorders of); **Ischuria**—(See Urine).

Itch; Ivy Poison; Jaundice (Black); **Jealousy; Jejunum** (Obstructions In); **Joints** (Disorders of); **Journeys** (Death During, Delays, Fatigue, Illness); **Joy** (Life Robbed of); **Judges** (Death by Sentence of); **Judgment Bad; Kidneys** (Bright's Disease, Distempered, Renal Colic, Stone In, etc.); **Killed** (By Blows, Falls, etc.); **King's Evil** — (See Scrofula).

Knees (Disorders of); **Knuckles** — Swollen—Enlarged—(See Fingers).

Lack Of—(See subjects under "Lack Of").

Lameness; Lamenting; Languid; Lapses; Larynx (Disorders of); **Lassitude; Latent Diseases; Lazy; Leakages; Leanness; Leathery Skin; Legs** (Crooked, Gout In); **Leprosy; Less**—Lessened—(See Less).

Lethargy; Leucorrhoea; Leukocytes (Increased); **Lewd; Liars; Life** (Short Life); **Ligaments** (Disorders of); **Limbs** (Disorders of); **Limitations; Limp Body; Limping; Lingering Diseases; Lisping; Listless; Lithemia; Little**—(See subjects under Little).

Liver (Disorders of); **Local Parts** (Disorders of); **Lock-Jaw; Locomotion** (Disorders of); **Locomotor Ataxia; Loneliness; Long Diseases; Longings; Look** (Downward Look); **Loose Morals;** —(See "Loose" under Morals).

Loss Of — (See subjects under "Loss Of").

Love Affairs (Troubles In); **Loved Ones** (Death of); **Low Fevers** — (See "Low" under Fever).

Lower Parts — Disorders In — (See Lower).

Lowered—Lowering—(See these subjects).

Lubrication (Disorders of); **Luck** (Bad Luck); **Lumbago; Lumbar Disorders; Lumps; Lungs** (Congestions, Consumption, Disorders of); **Lupus; Luxations**—(See Dislocations).

Lymph (Disorders of); **Lynching; Maiming; Maladies; Malaise; Males** Disorders In); **Malice; Malignant Diseases; Malnutrition**—(See Nutrition).

Mammae—Disorders of—(See Breasts).

Mania (Suicidal); **Marasmus; Marks; Marriage** (Disturbances In); **Marriage Partner** (Death of — Illness of); **Mastoid Abscess; Masturbation** — (See "Solitary" under Vice).

Materialism; Matrix—Disorders of—(See Womb).

Matter (Decay of); **Maturity** (Death Before); **Meagre Body; Mean Stature**—Mean-Spirited—(See Mean).

Meat (Ill-Digested); **Medicines** (Cooling); **Medium Vitality**—(See Vitality).

Medulla (Bulbar Paralysis); **Melancholy; Members of Body** (Disorders of); **Membranes** (Disorders of); **Memory** (Disorders of); **Men** (Disability To); **Menses** (Disorders of); **Mental Disorders** — (See Intellect, Mental, Mind).

Merciless; Metabolism (Disorders of); **Metamorphosis** (Disorders of); **Micturition** — Disorders of — (See "Strangury'" under Urine).

Middle Life (Disorders of, Death At); **Milk** (Disorders of); **Mind** (Disorders of); **Mineral Deposits**—(See Deposits, Minerals, Wastes).

Misanthropic; Miscarriages; Mischief; Miseries; Miserly; Misfortunes; Misshaped Body; Mistrustful; Mitral Diseases—(See Heart).

Mobs (Death By); **Moist and Cold Diseases**—(See "Cold and Moist" under Humours).

Moles; Monsters; Moods; Moping; Morals (Loose); **Morbid Diseases; Moroseness; Mortal Illness; Mortality** (Increased); **Mortification; Mother** (Death of, Affliction To); **Motion In Body** (Impeded); **Mournful; Mouth** (Disorders of); **Movement** (Slow); **Moving Parts** (Impediments In); **Much Sickness**—(See Sickness).

Mucous Membranes (Disorders of); **Muddling Creature**—(See "Ill-Formed" under Ill).

Mumps—(See Parotid).

Murderous; Murmuring; Muscles (Stiffness of, Contraction of); **Mutes; Mutilations; Mydriasis**—(See Iris).

Myopia—(See Accommodation, Sight).

Mystical; Nakedness — Wandering In —(See "Outrageous" under Insanity).

Narcotic Habit; Narrowing (Of Parts); **Nasal Diseases**—(See Catarrh, Nose).

Nasty Temper—(See Temper).

Nature (Nature of the Death — Disposition Ill-Natured); **Nausea; Navigation** (Dangers In); **Near** (Near Some Danger); **Neck** (Disorders In); **Necrosis; Negative Nature; Neglect and Privation** (Diseases Arising From); **Nerves** (Disorders of); **Neuralgia; Night Diseases**—(See Day, Night).

Night Sweats—(See Phthisis).

Nipples (Disorders of); **Nobles** (Infirmities To—Death of); **Nodules; Nose** (Disorders of); **Nourishment** — Disorders of—(See Nutrition).

Noxious Diseases; Numbness; Nutrition (Disorders of); **Obnoxious Diseases; Obscenity; Obsessions; Obstinate Diseases; Obstructions; Occlusions; Odors** (Foul); **Oesophagus** (Disorders of); **Offensive Diseases; Offspring**—Disorders of—Death of—(See Children).

Often Ailing—(See Often).

Old Age (Disorders of — Senility); **Operations** (Rules and Times for Surgical); **Ophthalmia**—(See Conjunctiva).

Opinions (Distorted); **Opposite Sex** (Aversions To); **Oppressions; Organic Diseases; Organs** (Diseases of); **Orifices** (Disorders of); **Orphans; Osseous Deposits; Ovaries** (Diseases of); **Own Death**—Fears Own Death—(See "Fears" under Death).

Oxygenation (Disorders of); **Pains** (Dull Pains and Aches); **Pale; Palsy; Paraesthesia; Paralysis; Parasitic Diseases; Parents** (Afflictions to, and especially to the Father or Grandfather); **Parotid Gland** (Disorders of); **Parts of the Body**—Afflictions To—(See Parts).

Parturition (Disturbances of); **Passages** (Narrowing of); **Passion**—Disorders of—Lack of—Perversion of—(See Apathy, Passion, Perversions).

Paternal Afflictions — (See Father, Paternal).

Pathological Conditions; Patricide — (See Father).

Peace of Mind—(See "No Peace" under Mind).

Peccant Humours—(See Humours).

Pectoral Affections; Peevishness; Pensiveness; Penurious; Perils; Periodic Diseases—The diseases of ♄ tend to return about every seven years, when ♄ afflicts his place in the radix, and tend to become chronic, due to the long period of ♄ in one sign, or house. (See Periodic, Returning).

Peripheral Nerves (Disorders of); **Peristalsis** (Impeded); **Permanent Diseases; Perplexities; Perversions; Perversity; Pessimism; Petrifaction; Pettifogging; Petulant; Phantasies; Phlegmatic Diseases; Phobias** — (See Fears).

Phthisis; Physical Disorders — (See "Ailments" under Physical).

Piles—(See Hemorrhoids).

Pimples; Pity (Without Pity); **Place** — Place of Birth Unfortunate — Place of Death In the Map of Birth — (See Anareta; "Place of Birth" under Place).

Plague; Planets—The Afflictions of ♄ as a Planet—(See "Afflictions Of" under Planets).

Pleasure (Aversion To); **Plodding**—(See "Laborious" under Labor).

Plots; Plugs; Pneumogastric Nerve (Disorders of); **Pneumonia** (Consolidation In); **Podagra**—(See "Feet" under Gout).

Poison (Heart Afflicted By—Retained Poisons); **Pollutions; Poor**—(See "Poor" under Circulation, Health; Poverty).

Posture (Defects of); **Poverty; Power** (Loss of); **Practices** (Evil); **Praecipients; Precipitation; Predispositions; Pregnancy** (Disorders of); **Prejudice; Premature** (Premature Birth—Death); **Premonitions; Presentiments; Pressure; Pretenders; Preventions** (Functions Prevented); **Prison** (Imprisonment); **Private** (Private Enemies—Private Sex Practices); **Processes** (Disturbances of); **Prodigal; Profligate; Prohibitions; Prolapsus; Prolonged Diseases; Promoted** (Rheumatism Promoted); **Prostrations; Protracted Diseases; Provisions** (Scarcity of); **Prudery; Psoriasis; Psychic Disturbances; Ptosis**—(See Eyelids, Prolapsus).

Public (Public Calamity—Public Sorrow); **Puerperal Disorders; Pulmonary Diseases; Pulse** (Feeble); **Punishments; Pupils Dilated**—(See Iris).

Pupura; Pus Diseases; Putrid Diseases; Pyorrhoea; Pyrosis—(See Belching).

Quadrupeds (Hurts By); **Quarrels; Quartan Ague; Rape; Rashes; Raw-Boned Body; Reason** (Disorders of); **Receptacles** (Disorders of); **Recklessness; Recluse; Recovery Slow; Rectum** (Disorders of); **Recuperation Slow; Recurrent Diseases; Red Face**—Morbid—(See Face).

Reducing Disorders; Refrigerant; Refuse of Body—Retention of—(See Elimination, Retention, Wastes).

Regeneration (Organs of Diseased); **Regretful; Reins** (Disorders of); **Relapses; Relatives** (Illness or Death of); **Relaxation; Religion** (Hypocites In); **Remarkable** (Remarkable Misfortunes); **Remedy** (Incapable of); **Remorse; Remote Organs** (Disorders of); **Removal of Organs**—By Ablation—(See Remote, Removal).

Renal Disorders—(See Kidneys).

Rending of Parts—(See Rupture).

Renunciation; Repining; Repressions; Reptiles (Death or Injury By); **Reputation** (Loss of); **Resentful; Reserved; Residence** (Place of Unfortunate); **Resignation** (To Fate); **Resistance Low; Resolution** (Of Tissues); **Resources** (Husbanding of—Loss of); **Respiratory Organs**—Disorders of—(See Breath, Bronchial, Lungs).

Rest (Lack of); **Restlessness; Restraints; Restrictions; Retardations; Retentions; Retiring; Retractions; Retrospective; Returning Diseases; Revengeful; Reverses; Rheum; Rheumatism; Rhythm In Body** (Disturbed Rhythm); **Ribs** (Fractures of); **Riches** (Loss of); **Rickets; Right Side of Body** —Disorders In—Right Ear Disordered—(See Right).

Rigidity; Rigors; Riotous; Robbers; Roseola; Rottenness; Rough (Rough Skin); **Rouse** (Hard to Arouse); **Ruin; Rupture; Sadness; Sailors** (Death or Injury To); **Saliva**—Too Little—(See Fauces, Saliva).

Sallow; Salts of Body (Disturbances of); **Sand** (In Kidneys); **Satire; Saturnine**—(See Melancholy).

Sciatica; Sclerosis; Scrofula; Scurvy; Scybalum—Hard Faeces—(See Faeces).

Secret Parts—Disorders In—(See Secrets).

Secretions (Disorders of); **Sedentary Habits; Selfishness; Self-Undoing; Senility**—(See Old Age).

Sensibility (Diminished); **Severe Diseases; Sex**—Disorders of Sex Organs—Sex Perversions—(See Perversions, Sex).

Shoulders (Infirmities In); **Shrinkages; Sickly; Sickness**—(See Chronic, Lingering, Long Diseases, Sickness, Tedious).

Signs—The Diseases of ♄ in the Signs of the Zodiac—♄ in any sign tends to hinder and restrict the functions and circulation in the part ruled by the sign he is in at B., or by direction, progression, or transit. For classified lists of the diseases of ♄ in the Signs, see the various Textbooks and Dictionaries of Astrology. (See the paragraph, "Pathological Qualities" in Sec. 1 of this Article).

Skin (Disorders of); **Skull** (Depressions In); **Slow Diseases; Sluggishness; Solitary Vice**—(See Vice).

Solitude (Fond of); **Sore Throat**—(See Throat).

Sorrow; Spare Body; Spasmodic Pains (In Bowels); **Specks Over Eyes**—(See Eyes, Specks).

Speech (Impediments In); **Spinal Cord**—Spine (Disorders of); **Spleen** (Disorders of); **Sprains; Stagnations; Stamina** (Low); **Stammering**—(See Speech).

Starvation; Stature Limited—(See Dwarfed, Growth, Limitations).

Stenosis; Stiffness; Stomach (Disorders of—Indigestion); **Stone In Kidneys**—Chalk Stones of Gout—(See Stone).

Stools—Lumpy and Hard—(See Faeces).

Stoppages; Strangulation; Strangury—(See Urine).

Strictures; Subluxations; Subnormalities; Suffocation; Suicidal Mania—(See Suicide).

Suppressions; Surface of Body—Chilling of—(See Centripetal, Chill, Constrictions).

Suspensions; Suspicious; Sweat (Disorders of); **Swellings** (In Joints, Neck, Secret Parts, Throat).

Swindler; Syncope; Synovial Membranes—And Fluids (Disorders of); **System Disordered**—(See System).

Tabefaction; Tabes; Tedious Diseases; Teeth (Decay of—Disorders of); **Tetter; Thickenings; Thighs** (Disorders of); **Thin Body; Throat** (Disorders of); **Thrombus; Thyroid Gland** (Disturbed); **Tidal Air** (Lack of in Lungs); **Tissues**

(Disorders of); **Tone** (Lack of); **Tongue** (Foul); **Tonsils** (Ablation of — Tonsilitis); **Toothache**—(See Teeth).

Torpidity; Toughening; Toxaemia; Travel (Dangers or Death In); **Treachery; Treatment**—Of ♄ Diseases—(See "Jupiter", "Treatment", in Sec. 1 of this Article).

Tremors; Trials; Trouble; Tubercles; Tuberculosis; Tumors; Typhus Fever; Ugly Body; Ulcers; Uncleanly; Uncles (Death or Illness of); **Undersized Body; Unfortunate; Ungainly; Unhappy; Unhealthy; Unrefined; Untimely Death; Urea** (Deposits of); **Uremia; Urethra** (Stricture of); **Uric Acid** (Deposits of); **Urine** (Disorders of); **Uterus**—Disorders of—(See Womb).

Vain Fears—(See Fears).

Valves (Disorders of); **Vapors** (Foul —Low Spirits); **Varicose Veins; Vaso-Constrictor Nerves** (Disorders of); **Veins;** (Disorders of); **Venereal Diseases; Vertebrae** (Subluxations of); **Vessels** (Disorders of); **Vexations; Vices** (Addicted To); **Vigor** (Lack of); **Violent Tendencies** — (See Revenge, Treachery, Violent).

Virulent Disorders; Vision—Disorders of—(See Sight).

Vital Activity (Lack of); **Vitality** (Lessened, Low); **Vitiated; Vocal Organs**—Voice (Disorders of); **Voluntary Power** (Diseased); **Vomiting; Voyages** (Danger On); **Vulnerable Parts** — (See "Weak Spots" in Sec. 1 of this Article).

Vultures (Body Devoured By); **Walk** (Disorders of); **Walls of Cells**—Thickening of—(See Cells).

Waning of Forces; Want (In Want); **Warts; Wastes of Body** (Retention of); **Wasting Diseases; Weak** — (Weak Body, Weak Back, Debility, Feeble); **Weariness; Weight** (Loss of); **Wife** (Danger To—Death of); **Womb** (Disorders of); **Women** (Diseases of—Female Weaknesses — Womb Disorders); **Worms; Worry; Wretched; Wrinkles; Wrists** (Fracture of); **Wrong Habits**—(See Habits).

Xanthanuria. For subjects, diseases, and afflictions which may involve the ♄ influences, and not listed or included in this Article, look in the alphabetical arrangement for the subject you have in mind.

SAUCY—Impudent—Independent—Disrespectful—Insolent—Insulting—♂ Sig. ♂ ☿; ♂ Sig. □ or ⚹ ♃; the ☽ in good aspect to ♂, but ♂ evilly aspected by other planets, and especially by ♅ or ♄, tends to make the native bold and impudent. (See Bold, Impudent, Independent, Respect).

SAVAGE—Savages—Wild—Indocile—Savage Disposition—(See "Beastly Form" under Beasts; Brutish; Cannibals; "Dogs" under Children; Cruel; Destructiveness, Fierce, Indocile, Inhuman, Merciless; "Animal Forms" under Monsters; "Shows No Pity" under Pity; Prenatal Epoch, Vicious, Violent, Wild, etc.).

SAVED — Life Will Be Saved — (See "Spared" under Life).

SAYINGS — Mysterious Sayings — (See Delirium, Demoniac, Dreams).

SCABS—Scabies—Scabs may be the result of Abrasions, Injuries, or from Sores, Pus conditions, Eruptions, etc. Scabs are more burstling at the Full ☽. (See Chickenpox, Crusts, Eruptions, Favus, Sloughings, Smallpox, etc.).

Scabbed Lips—(See Lips).

Scabies — The Itch — A Contagious, Parasitic Disease—A ♄ and ♓ disease, and caused by afflictions in these signs; ♂ afflicted in ♉, ♉, ♄, or ♓; ♂ afflicted in ♓, and ♂, □, or ♉ the Asc. by dir.; ♂ in ♉ when ♂ is the afflictor in the disease. (See Itch, Parasites).

SCALDS—Scalding — Scald — Burns by Hot Water or Hot Liquids—

Death by Scalds—The ☉ to the ♂ or ill-asp. ♂ by dir.; ♂ ori. at B., and afflicting the hyleg by dir.; ♂ afflictions dispose to; ♂ the afflicting planet, in violent signs, and afflicting the hyleg; ♂ in ♉ or ♏, and afflicting the hyleg; cardinal signs show. (See "Death" under Burns, Liquids; "Hot Liquids" under Heat; "Fire" under Home).

Liable to Scalds—Danger of—Caused by the ☉ and ♂, the positive, electric, and heat-producing planets; the ☉ or ☽ to the ♂ or ill-asp. ♂ by dir.; the ☉ hyleg, and the ☉ to the ♂ or ill-asp. ♂ by dir.; the progressed ☉ to the ♂ or ill-asp. ♂; the ☽ in water signs, and to the ♂ or ill-asp. ♂ by dir.; the ☽ Sig. ♂ the ☉, subject to; the ☽ Sig. ♂, □, or ⚹ the ☉, and especially if ♂ aspects the ☉; the ☽ ♂ ♂ in the M.C., and in evil asp. to Antares; ♂ afflictions predispose to, and born under ♂; ♂ diseases and afflictions; ♂ afflicted in ♈; ♂ in the 6th H., in a cardinal sign; ♂ afflicted in the 1st H.; ♂ afflicted in water signs, and ♂ or ill-asp. the Asc. by dir.; ♂ □ or ⚹ the ☉; ☿ Sig. ♂ the ☉, and the ☉ ill-dignified at B.; the Asc. to the place of the Ascelli or Capricornus. (See "Danger Of" under Burns; "Hot Liquids" under Heat).

Scald-Head—(See Favus).

Urine—(See "Scalding" under Urine).

SCALES—Scale Formation — Scaling— Desquamation — Scale Tetter—Caused principally by ♄. May also be caused by excess dryness of the skin, and due to the heat of the ☉ and ♂. (See Bunions, Crusts; "Body" under Dry; Eczema, Exudations; "Skin" under Hard; "Body" under Heat; Herpes, Horny; "Desquamative Nephritis" under Kidneys; Parched, Psoriasis; "Dry Skin" under Skin; Tetter, Xeransis, Xeroderma). See North Scale, South Scale.

SCALP — The Skin Over the Skull — Ruled by ♈, and the ☉ in ♈ tends to dry up the scalp, and cause Baldness. (See Baldness; "Loss of Hair" under Hair).

Favus of Scalp — Scald - Head — (See Favus).

Wounds To — ♂ afflicted in ♈. (See "Accidents", "Hurts", under Head; Skull).

SCANDAL—Scandalous Diseases—

Danger of Scandal—Loss of Honour— Disrepute — Loss of Reputation—Disgraced — Dishonoured, etc. — The ☉ by Periodic Rev. to the ill-asps. the radical ♅; the ☉ to his own ill-asps. by dir.; the ☉ to the bad aspects ♀; the ☽ to the P. Dec. South Scale; the ☽ to the bad asps. ♀ by dir., or transit; the ☽ decr. in light, and be carried or conjoined with ♀; ♅ or ♂ to the ill-asps. ♀ by dir.; ♄ to the ☍ ☋ by dir.; ♄ or ♂ passing over the place of ♀ at B., or by transit, or at a Solar Rev.; ♃ to the place of ☋; ♂ to the ☌ or ill-asp. ♀; ♂ by periodic rev. to the ill-asps. the ☉ tends to infamy; ♀ afflicted by malefics at B.; the M.C. to the □ or ♉ the ☽ or ♀ by dir. (See Disgrace; "Own Worst Enemy" under Enemies; Evils, Execrated, Harlots; "Loss Of" under Honour, Reputation; Infamous, Love Affairs, Misfortune, Passion, Reverses, Ruin, Sex, Shame, Sorrow, Trouble, Vile, Wanton; "Ruined" under Women, etc.).

Scandalmongers — Loves to Defame, Gossip, and Slander Others—Afflictions to the ☽ or ☿, and with ♂ entering into the configuration; ♆ and ♏ afflictions tend to the most treacherous attacks; the ☽ and the ♋ sign afflicted tend to domestic gossip. (See "Secret Enemies" under Enemies; Liars, Libelers; "Injured" under Men; Revenge, Treachery, etc.).

Scandalous Diseases — Danger of — Suspicion of—The ☽ in ♏ and afflicted by the ☉ or ♂ when taken ill, and especially if ♀ afflict the ☽ (Hor'y); ♀ or ☿ afflicted in ♏. (See Genitals, Gonorrhoea, Private Diseases, Syphilis, Venereal).

Women Openly Scandalous — The ☽ Sig. in ♏, infamous, obscene, and openly scandalous, and if the ☽ also be in □ or ♂ ♄ or ♂. (See Infamous, Lewd, Licentiousness, Obscene, Shameless, etc.).

SCANTY—

Scanty Hair On Head — (See Baldness).

Scanty Menses—(See Menses).

SCAPULA—The Shoulder Blade—Ruled by ♐. (See Shoulders).

SCAR—Scars—Scar Tissue—Scarred—Scarified Sores — Cicatrix — Dents — Blemishes—Marks, etc.—Scars on any part of the body are usually the result of ♂ affliction to that part of the body, and from wounds or injury. There tend to be scars on the right side of the body when masculine signs are upon the Asc., and a masculine planet in the Asc., or sign indicated, and on the left side of the body when feminine, etc. Mars on the Asc. tends to a scar or mark on that part of the body ruled by the sign ♂ is in at B. This does not indicate that the scar exists at B., but it may happen after birth from an accident or injury. (See "Scars" under Arms, Back, Breasts, Eyes, Face, Feet, Forehead, Head, Knees, Legs, Neck, Skin, Throat; Blemishes, Cuts, Dents, Left Side; "Organs" under Lower, Middle, Upper; Marks, Moles, Pitted, Right Side, Scarlet Fever; "Face" under Smallpox; Stabs, Wounds, etc.).

Scarified Sores—♄ and ♂ in an angle, occi. of the ☉, and ori. of the ☽, and ☿ in familiarity with ♂. (See "Face" under Smallpox).

SCARCITY—Lack of—Diminished Supply—

Corn Destroyed—An eclipse of the ☉ or ☽ in the earthy signs ♉, ♍, or ♑, and loss to grains such as are sown annually; an eclipse of the ☉ in ♎, and especially the 1st decan. of ♎; an eclipse of the ☉ in the 1st decan. of ♌, scarcity of corn and bread; ♄ in a fixed sign at the Vernal, and during the year, scarcity of grains and crops; Comets appearing in ♉; Comets in ♌ tend to worms and vermin, destroying grains and crops; Comets appearing in ♏. (See Drought, Earth, Famine, Fountains; "Extreme Heat" under Heat; Grain).

Famine—(See Famine).

Food — Scarcity of — (See Drought, Famine; "Scarcity" under Food).

Fruits—Scarcity of—(See Fruit).

Rain — Scarcity of — (See Drought; "Air", "Fountains", under Dry; Famine, Fountains, Rain, Rivers).

Seeds—(See "Scarcity" under Seeds).

Waters — (See "Scarcity" under Waters).

Wheat—(See "Scarcity" under Wheat; "Corn" in this section).

SCARF ·SKIN—The Cuticle—Epidermis —(See Cuticle, Epidermis, Skin).

SCARLET FEVER—Scarlatina—A Contagious, Epidemic, Exanthematous Disease, with Fever and a Scarlet Eruption—Caused by ♂ afflictions to the hyleg at B., and in such cases often proves quickly fatal. Those free from ♂ affliction to the hyleg at B., or ♂ in power at B., are usually immune to the disease, and also immune to smallpox. In such cases of natural immunity vaccination is unnecessary. (See "Immunity" under Smallpox). Mars afflicting the hyleg at B. tends to leave malignant scars resulting from this disease, or smallpox. Mars alone, his afflictions at B., and by transit or direction to the hyleg, and to the Asc., is said to be the cause of this disease. Mars rising at a Solar Eclipse; ♂ ☌ ♄ and ♃ at a Solar Eclipse; ♂ supreme at the Equinoxes or Solstices; ♂ is supreme in years of Scarlatina epidemics, afflicts the hyleg in those who succumb, or are attacked; ♂ in ♏ and afflicting the hyleg; ♂ coming to the ☌ or ill-asp. the Asc. early in life usually causes scarlet fever, scarlatina, smallpox, or measles; ♂ in ♉ at B., occi., and lord of the year at the Vernal E., many children die from scarlatina and smallpox; ♂ lord of the year at the Vernal, in ♈, and afflicted by ♄; ♂ predominating at a ☌ of three or four of the superior planets tends to epidemics of Scarlatina or Smallpox, and severe in type, with many deaths, but milder in form when ♂ is in ☌ or ♂ only one other superior planet, and ♂ holding power; ♂ in power at B., and to the ☌ or ill-asp. ♄ by dir., and especially liable to the disease in childhood; the ☉, ☽, or Asc. to the ☌, P, □, or ♂ ♂ by dir., and in power, and afflicting the hyleg at B.; the ☉ and ☽ □ the radical ♂ at a Solar eclipse; the ☉ at the Vernal ☌ or ill-asp. ♂; the ☉ or ☽ ☌ ♄ and ♂ at an eclipse of the ☽; the ill-asps. of the ☉ to the hyleg by tr. or dir. if the ☉ be afflicted by ♂ at B.; the ill-asps. of the ☉ or ♂ to the Asc. early in life; the ☉ or ☽ hyleg and afflicted by ♂; the ☽ sepr. from the ☉ and applying to ♂ at a Solar Ingress; the hyleg much afflicted at B. by ♂; the Asc. to the □ or ☍ ♃ by dir., and ♃ afflicted by ♂ at B.; the Asc. to the ♂ or ill-asp. ♂ by dir. if ♂ is in power at B., or afflicting the Asc. or hyleg; especially identified with the fixed signs, and especially ♉ and ♏, and also causes Diphtheria under these fixed sign afflictions; Comets appearing in □ tend to much mortality from scarlet fever; Subs at MCP, CP, SP, and KP. (See Chickenpox; "Mortality Great" under Children; Contagious, Diphtheria, Epidemics, Eruptive Fevers, Infections. Measles; "Mumps" under Parotid; Smallpox). Cases of Scarlet Fever—See Chap. XIII in Daath's Medical Astrology.

SCARS—(See Scar. Also see Blemishes, Marks, Moles, Naevus).

SCATTERING— Scattered—Dissipation of Mental and Bodily Forces — (See Changes, Chaotic, Concentration, Confusion, Diffusiveness, Dispersions, Dissipation, Dull, Effervescent; "Scattered" under Energy; Improvident, Indifferent, Influenced; "Shallow" under Mentality; Mutable, Negative, Receptive, Restless, Susceptibility, Vacillating, Vagabond, Wanderer, etc.).

SCENERY— Changes of Scenery Good for the Health — (See "Rapid" under Recuperation).

SCEPTICISM— Sceptical — Skeptic — Doubt — Indifference to Orthodox Religion—Caused principally by ♃ weak and afflicted at B.; ♃ afflicted in signs of his detriment, debility, or fall, as in ♊, ♍, ♑, incline to indifference, a more superficial and sceptical nature along religious and philosophical lines, and to selfishness, covetousness, and a more self-centered nature. The strong afflictions of ♃ at B., and especially to ☿, tend to indifference, fatalism, doubt, materialism, etc. Also ☿ prominent at B., and afflicted, or malefics in the signs of ☿. The 9th H. afflicted by malefics, and especially with ♄ there. (See Doubts, Fears, Independent, Materialism, Metaphysical, Occult; "Mind" under Prejudice; "Irreligious" under Religion; Science, etc.).

SCHEAT PEGASI— A Star of the 2nd magnitude, of the nature of ♄, in the last face of ♓, and produces danger of death by drowning. (See Drowning).

SCHEMES— Scheming — Calculating — (See Artifice, Cheating, Deceitful, Dishonest; "Secret Enemies" under Enemies; Evil, Feuds, Mischief, Plots, Poison Death, Quarrelsome, Revenge, Secret, Shrewdness, Treachery, etc.).

SCHOLAR—Scholarly—Studious—Smart In Books and Learning—Obtains Profound Knowledge—The ☽ Sig. ♂, ✶, or △ ☿; the good aspects of ♅ or ♄ to the 9th H., and lord of the 9th, or ♄ well-aspected in the 9th H., a deep desire to get at the philosophy of life, go into profound things, and get at ultimates; ♃ Sig. ✶ or △ ☿, gives great learning;

♂ Sig. ✶ or △ ☿; ☿ Sig. in ♏ and free from affliction; ☿ Sig. ✶ or △ the ☽; ♏ influence, and this sign on the Asc. at B.; the Asc. favorably aspected by the ☽ and ☿. (See Genius; "Great Ability" under Great; Intellect; "Good" under Judgment; Knowledge, Learning; "Abilities","Quickened", under Mental; Metaphysical; "Cultivation", "Deep and Profound", "Good", under Mind; Occult, Perception, Philosophy, Prodigies, Reading, Science, Study; "Good" under Understanding).

SCIATIC NERVES— Are under the internal rulership of the ♐ sign.

Fear of Sciatica—The ☽ in ♎, ♂, or ill-asp. ♄ (or ☿ if he be of the nature of ♄) at the beginning of an illness or at decumbiture (Hor'y). (See Fears).

Sciatica—Pains In the Sciatic Nerves —Principally a ♐ disease, and with afflictions in this sign and in the opposite sign ♊; the ☉ afflicted in ♐; the ☽ afflicted in ♐, or afflicting the hyleg therefrom; the ☽ hyleg in ♐, and afflicted, and especially with females; a ☽ disease, and afflictions to the ☽; the ☽ hyleg, and to the ♂ or ill-asp. ♄ by dir.; ♆, ♅, or ♄ in ♎ or ♐, and afflicting the ☉ or ☽; ♅ in ♐ and afflicting the ☉, ☽, or Asc.; ♅ in ♐; ♅ in ♐ in the 6th H.; ♄ in □ by reflex action; ♄ in ♐, occi., and afflicting the ☉, ☽, or Asc.; ♄ afflicted in ♐; ♄ in ♊, ♎, or ♐ and afflicting the ☉, ☽, or Asc.; ♄ in ♐ in the 6th H., and afflicted; ♃ afflicted in ♐, and especially in the 6th H.; ♂ in □ or ♐; ♂ in ♐ and afflicting the ☽; ♂ in ♐ in the 6th H., and afflicting the hyleg; ☿ afflicted in ♐; ♐ on the Asc.; afflictions in common signs. Subs at LLP (4, 5L). (See "Pains In" under Thighs).

SCIENCE—A Scientific Mind—The Applied Sciences—

Arts and Sciences— Proficient In — Fond of—(See "Arts and Sciences" under Learning).

Astrology—Studious of—♅ strong at B., rising, or in the M.C., and in favorable aspect to ☿; ♆ □ or ☍ ♅ at B. inclines to the study of Astrology, but in a more superficial way, and to make bogus Astrologers, or Charlatans; ☿ Sig. in any aspect of ♅, and if the ☽ assist ☿, tends to make a good, studious, honest and sincere Astrologer; the ♋ and ♑ influences strong at B. (See "Occult Study" in this section; "Metaphysics" under Learning; Metaphysics, Mystical, Occult, Philosophy, Reading, Study).

Learns Science Easily—(See "Learns Easily" under Learning).

Little Ability For Science—(See "Void Of" under Learning; "Shallow" under Mentality; "Light in Mind", "Weak Mind", under Mind; "Scientific Mind" in this section).

Occult Science—Fond of—♅ strong at B.; ♅ and ♄ conjoined with ☿; the ☽ Sig. in ♒, lover of the Curious and Scientific studies. (See "Astrology" in this section; Intuition, Perception, Psychic Powers, Spiritual Sight, Truth, Understanding).

Scientific Mind—The ♊, ♍, and ♒ Signs are highly scientific; the ☉ or ☿ in ♍

or ♒; ♅ ✳ or △ ♃, ♀, or ☿; ♃ Sig. in ♒; ☿ in ♊, ♍, or ♒, well-aspected, and especially by ♅. There is little ability for scientific learning when ☿ is combust and close to the ☉ at B. (See Genius; "Inventive Mind" under Learning, Prodigies; Mathematical, Mechanical).

Scientific Signs — Of the Zodiac — ♊, ♍, ♒.

SCIRRHUS—A Hard Form of Carcinoma —(See "Scirrhus" under Axillae, Tumors; "Breasts" under Carcinoma).

SCLEROSIS—Hardening of Tissue—Induration, Over-growth, and Hardening of the connective tissue of an organ, are the work of ♄ deposits. Also a ♋ and ♅ disease. (See "Thickening" under Cells; Cirrhosis, Congelation, Deposits, Hardening, Hypertrophy, Minerals; "Over-Growth" under Organs; Thickening).

Arteries—Hardening of—(See "Arterio—Sclerosis" under Arteries).

Lungs — (See "Hardening" under Lungs).

Spinal Cord—(See "Spinal Cord" under Hardening).

See "Earth Signs" under Earth; "Salts of the Body" under Salts; Saturn.

SCOLDING — Rebuking — Reproving — Fault-Finding—Critical—A ♄ characteristic. Also the ♍ people are given to much criticism, scolding, and faultfinding. (See Fretful, Noisy, Peevish, Petulant; "Mind" under Prejudice; Virgo, Worry, etc.).

SCOPE—Scope of the Disease Enlarged —(See "Scope" under Enlarged).

SCORNFUL—Contemptuous—Disdainful — Given To Mockery and Scoffing — ♂ ruler at B., and afflicted. In Hor'y Q. ♂ Sig. of the person. (See Mars Influence, Mockery; "Scornful" under Religion).

SCORPIO—The Scorpio Sign (♏)—The Eighth Sign of the Zodiac, and ruled by ♂. This Sign is affiliated with the 8th H., the House of Death. Scorpio is symbolized by both the Scorpion and the Eagle. Scorpio gives the death sting, and then the Soul soars away like an eagle into its airy home. This sign also gives features resembling an eagle. The Scorpion is the symbol of the lower mind, and the Eagle of the Higher Mind. This sign is the night sign, or house, of ♂, the exaltation of ♅, and the fall of the ☽, and the ☽ is most unfortunate in this sign, and especially with females, and tends to disturbed and irregular female functions. This sign belongs to the Fixed Cross, made up of ♉, ♌, ♏, and ♒, and is sympathetic with all the fixed signs, and planets in these signs tend to influence or afflict the parts, or organs ruled by all the fixed signs, and this thru sympathy or reflex action. Scorpio is a sign of long ascension and is classed as a cold, watery, feminine, fixed, negative, nocturnal, moist, fruitful, magnetic, vital, nervous, broken, hurtful, imperfect, mute, phlegmatic, unfortunate, obeying, southern, autumnal sign. The Scorpio people are said to be "The Salt of the Earth" when awakened, spiritualized, and living in

their Higher Minds, but when living in the lower mind, its influence is to make the natives of the sign more treacherous, deceptive, jealous, murderous, passionate, revengeful, deliberate in crime and evil, and to be selfish, and especially when the ♆ influence is involved. Taurus and ♏ are the strongest of the negative and feminine signs, and these signs when on the Asc. at B. give considerable vitality, and more strength than the other earthy or watery signs. Scorpio is known as the "Genital Pole of Paracelsus", while the other ♂ sign, ♈, is called the "Cerebral Pole of Paracelsus". This sign has to do with Procreation, Readaptation, and the Reproductive and Destructive Processes of Life. Scorpio tends to give an excess of magnetic power, and to attract disease, and especially infectious complaints, contagious diseases, and to fall easy victims to Epidemics. (See External). The ☽ in ♏ at B. gives the ♏ and ♂ personality, and often a very troublesome, warlike and combative nature, and if afflicted, to center the mind more upon passion and sex matters. Being a strong occult sign, and the exaltation of ♅, this sign when on the Asc. at B., or containing the ☉, ☿, and other planets, tends to make the native very fond of the Occult, Mystical, Metaphysical, and Astrological Sciences. The Sex Organs are ruled by ♏, and in the early stages of humanity, the opposite and complemental sign ♉ is said to have drawn the larynx and vocal organs from ♏, and this is the reason the larynx, throat, and vocal cords are so intimately related, and why the voice changes at puberty in males. (See Larynx). Scorpio has special affinity with the Nose, Nasal Bones, and the Bladder. When on the Asc. at B., ♏ gives a strong constitution, and the strongest of the watery signs. Excretion is a function of ♏ and ♂, and to burn out the wastes and poisons of the system by fevers and inflammation. This is a fruitful sign, but the least fruitful of the watery signs because of its ♂ influence. The Hebrew Letter "Nun", or "N", is connected with the ♏ sign, which rules the Generative Organs. The Pathological Qualities of this sign are Destructiveness, Reproduction, Tyranny, Worry. The Places denoted by ♏ are Drains, Sinks, Kitchens, Washhouses, Stinking Pools, Quagmires, Muddy Swamps, Marshes, Ruins near Water, and places where Reptiles and Vermin breed. Brown is the Color of ♏, and also red, and a reddish brown, as red is the color of ♂. Also rules dark brown color. People born with the ☉ in ♏, and especially if this sign, or ♂, are not in the Asc., often have very black eyes and black hair, and some of our most beautiful brunettes were born with the ☉ in this sign. (See "Black Hair" under Hair). The Star Antares, also known as "Cor Scorpio", or Scorpion's Heart, partakes of the nature of ♂ and ♃, and some Writers say of the nature of ♂ and ☿. (See Antares). Frons Scorpio is a fixed star in ♐. (See Frons Scorpio). The Zodiac Salt ruled by the ♏ sign is Calcium

Sulphate. The following are some of the principal Qualities assigned to this sign—Autumnal, Bold, Broken, Burning, Caustic, Cleansing, Cold, Combative, Constructive, Courageous, Crooked, Deceptive, Destructive, Excitable, Feminine, Feverish, Fiery in Temper, Fixed, Foolhardy, Fruitful, Harmful, Hasty, Hot-Tempered, Hurtful, Imperfect, Impetuous, Incisive, Irritable, Jealous, Lustful, Malicious, Military, Moist, Murderous, Mute, Negative, Nervous, Nocturnal, Obeying, Obstinate, Occult, Passionate, Phlegmatic, Pungent, Quarrelsome, Rash, Rebellious, Reckless, Red, Reproductive, Revengeful, Ruinous, Southern, Strong, Stubborn, Treacherous, Tyrannical, Unfortunate, Vicious, Violent, Vital, Warlike, Watery, Worrisome.

SCORPIO RULES—See the following subjects in the alphabetical arrangement—Anus (the Sphincter Ani Muscle); Appendix Vermiformis; Bladder—The Sphincter of—Stone in Bladder—Elimination of Urine Thru the Bladder; Blood (Red Coloring Matter of); Bones—the Nasal Bones—Brim of Pelvis—Pubic Bone; Bronchials; Brown Color; Calcium Sulphate; Calculi; Canal (the Inguinal); Capsules (Supra-Renal); Cervix of Uterus and the Glandular Portion of Cervix; Clitoris; Coccyx (the Os Coccyx); Colon (the Descending Colon, the Meso-Colon, and probably the whole of the Colon); Colors (Brown, Dark Brown, Red); Cowper's Gland; Descending Colon; Destructive Processes of Life; Ductless Glands; Elimination of Urine Thru the Bladder and Urethra; Excrementitious Fluids; Excretion (Excretory Bowels—Excretory System—Excretory Organs — The Lower Bowels — Excretory Vessels of the Testicles—Internal Excretory System—Excretion in the Kidneys); External Humoural Secretions; Female Functions (Menses); Fluids (Excrementitious); Functions (of Excretion, Reproduction, and the Female Functions); Fundament; Gall; Ganglia (the Intestinal); Generative Organs; Genitals; Genito-Urinary System; Glands (Cowper's Glands—Ductless Glands—Glans Clitoris—Glans Penis — Muciparous Glands—Glandular Portion of the Prostates — Glandular Portion of the Uterine Cervix — Thymus Gland—Thyroid Gland); Gravel; Groins; Healers (Magnetic); Humoural Secretions (the External and Internal); Iliac Region; Inguinal Canal and Region; Internally ♏ rules the Internal Generative and Excretory Systems, the Bladder, Appendix, and the Internal Humoural Secretions; Intestines (Large Intestine—Lower Excretory Bowels—Descending Colon); Ischium (Tuberosity of); Kidneys (Excretion In—Lower Portion of the Pelvis or Sinus); Large Intestine; Lime Sulphate; Liver; Lower Excretory Bowels; Magnetic Healers; Menses; Meso-Colon; Muciparous Glands of the Generative System; Nasal Bones and Nasal Orifice; Nose; Organs (Organs of Excretion — Sex and Reproductive Organs); Orifice (of Nose, Penis, and Rectum); Os Coccyx; Ovaries; Pasty Complexion; Pelvis (Pelvic Bones—Brim of Pelvis—Pelvis of Kidneys);

Penis (Glans Penis); Perineum; Pituitary Gland (or Body); Plexus (the Intestinal Ganglia and Plexus ruling the Internal and External Humoural Secretions—the Sacral Plexus); Private Members and Privy Parts; Procreation; Prostate Gland; Pubes and Pubic Bone; Pulsatilla; Readaptation; Rectum (the Anus and the Meso-Rectum); Red Coloring Matter of the Blood; Renal Capsules (Supra-Renals); Reproduction and Reproductive Organs; Sacrum and Sacral Plexus; Sand (in Kidneys and Bladder); Scrotum; Secret Parts (Stone In, and Disorders of); Secretions (the External and Internal Humoural Secretions); Sex Organs; Sigmoid Flexure; Sinus of Kidneys; Spermatic Cord; Sphincter Muscle (of Bladder and Anus); Spleen; Stone (in Bladder, Kidneys, or Secret Parts); Structurally ♏ rules the Nasal Bones, the Sacrum, Ischium, and Os Coccyx; Supra-Renal Capsules; Sweat; Symphysis Pubis; Testicles (Excretory Vessels of); Thymus Gland; Thyroid Gland; Tuberosity of the Ischium; Ureters, Urethra; Urine (Urinary Organs and the Elimination of Urine); Uro-Genital Orifice; Uterus (Glandular Portion of the Uterine Cervix); Vessels (Excretory Vessels of the Testicles); Womb, etc.

SCORPIO DISEASES—The Afflictions of Scorpio — Scorpio attracts disease, and especially contagious and infectious diseases. Scorpio has special affinity with the Nose and Bladder. The principal causes of diseases ruled by ♏ are afflictions in the ♏ sign, the presence of malefics in this sign, or with ♏ upon the Asc. at B., or on the cusp of the 6th H., and afflicted. Planets in ♉, the opposite sign, also tend to increase and aggravate ♏ diseases, as well as planets in ♌ and ♒, in evil aspect to ♏. The Fixed Signs, or the Fixed Sign Cross, when containing a preponderance of planets at B. tends to afflict all parts and organs ruled by the fixed signs, and the afflictions are even greater, and more lasting, when the fixed signs are found upon the four angles of the map at B. The following is an Alphabetical Summary of Diseases and Afflictions caused and ruled by the Scorpio Sign. See these subjects in the alphabetical arrangement—

Anus (Disorders of—Contraction of); **Appendicitis; Back** (Disorders of); **Bladder** (Diseases of—Stone In); **Blood** —Disorders of Red Coloring Matter of — (see Haemoglobin, Iron; "Blood" under Red); **Bow Legs** — (see Legs); **Bowels**—Disorders In the Lower, Excretory Bowels, In the Colon and Descending Colon — (see Bowels, Colon, Excretion, Faeces); **Bubo; Calculus; Caries**—Of the Cartilage of the Nose—(see "Caries" under Nose); **Catamenial Disorders**—(see Menses); **Cecum**—Inflammation of—(see Caecum); **Chronic** —Chronic Exanthematous Sore Throat —(see Throat); **Colon**—Disorders of—Colitis—(see Colon); **Contagions; Discharges** (Unnatural); **Drunkenness; Ductless Glands** (Disorders of); **Elimination** (Disorders of); **Emissions**—(see Semen); **Enlarged Prostate**—(see Prostate); **Epidemics; Exanthema; Excess; Excesses; Excretion** (Disorders of);

Falling of Womb—(see Womb); **Fissure** — (see Anus); **Fistula; Fluids** — Disorders of the Excrementitious Fluids—(see "Fluids" under Excretion); **Fossae of Nose** — Disorders of — (see Nose); **Functions** — Female Functions Irregular — (see Menses); **Fundament** (Disorders of); **Gall** — Disorders of — (see Bile, Gall); **Generative System** (Disorders of); **Genitals** (Disorders of); **Genito-Urinary System** (Disorders of); **Glands** — (see Parotid; "Cervix" under Womb); **Goiter; Gonorrhoea; Gout; Gravel; Groins** (Diseases In); **Heart** (Disorders of); **Hemorrhoids; Hernia** (Inguinal); **Humoural Secretions**—Disorders of—(see "External" under Humours); **Hydrocele; Infections** (Infectious Diseases); **Inflammations** — (see Genitals, Parotid, Secret Parts, Womb); **Inguinal Hernia**—(see Hernia); **Injuries** — To Sex Organs — (see Genitals, Maimed, Penis, Secret Parts, Sex Organs, Spermatic Cord, Testes, Womb); **Irregular Menses**—(see Menses); **Kidneys**—Stone In—(see "Kidneys" under Stone); **Larynx** (Disorders of); **Legs** (Ill-Formed); **Leucorrhoea; Liver** (Disorders of); **Lues**—(see Syphilis); **Magnetic Power** (Excess of); **Matrix**—Defects In—(see Womb); **Menses** (Disorders of); **Mucous Membranes**—Of the Nose — Disorders of — (see Nose); **Mumps**—(see Parotid); **Natural Powers** —Lowered In Females—(see "Natural Forces" under Natural); **Nose**—Disorders of — (see Catarrh, Colds, Nose); **Obstruction** — Of Urine — (see Urine); **Ovaries** (Diseases of); **Pain** — Pain In Groins—Painful Menses—(see Groins, Menses); **Parotid Gland** (Swelling of); **Parturition** (Disorders In); **Penis** (Diseases and Injury); **Perityphlitis**—(see Caecum); **Piles** — (see Hemorrhoids); **Prevalent**—Scorpio Diseases Prevalent —♂ in ♏, ori., and lord of the year at the Vernal. (See "Public Health Bad" under Public); **Priapism**—(see Penis); **Private Diseases; Prostate Gland** (Disorders of); **Puerperal Disorders; Rectum** (Disorders of); **Regenerative Organs** (Disorders of); **Renal Stone**—(see "Kidneys" under Stone); **Reproductive Organs** (Disorders of); **Retention**—Of Poisons—Of Urine—(see Poisons, Retention, Urine); **Rupture**—In Groins— (see "Inguinal" under Hernia); **Sand** (In Kidneys); **Scandalous Diseases; Scrotum** (Disorders of); **Scurvy; Secret Parts** (Distempers In—Stone In); **Secretions** (Disorders of); **Semen** (Emissions); **Sex Organs** (Disorders of—Injuries to); **Sigmoid Flexure** (Disorders of); **Sore Throat**—Exanthematous and Syphilitic — (see Throat); **Spasm** (of Bladder and Urethra); **Spermatic Cord** (Injuries To); **Sphincter Ani**—Contractions of—(see Anus); **Spleen** (Derangements of); **Stone**—In Bladder, Kidneys, or Secret Parts—(see Stone); **Strangury** (see Urine); **Stricture** (of Urethra); **Syphilis; Testicles** (Disorders of); **Throat** (Chronic Exanthematous Sore Throat — Syphilitic—Ulcerated); **Thyroid Gland** (Disorders of); **Ulceration** (Of the Throat In Syphilis); **Unnatural Discharges** (see Discharges); **Urethra** (Disorders of — Stricture — Urethritis); **Urine** (Disorders of — Retention—Obstructions); **Uterus** — Disorders of—(see Womb); **Vagina** (Dis-

orders of); **Venereal Diseases; Vitality Lowered** (see Vitality); **Vulva** (Disorders of); **Womb** (Disorders of). For subjects which may have been overlooked for this list, and which you have in mind, look for them in the alphabetical arrangement.

SCOURGE — Punished by the Lash or Whip—Death or Injury By—(See Assaults, Blows; "Beaten In Prison" under Prison).

SCROFULA — King's Evil — Struma — Scrofulous Tumors — A Constitutional Disease with Glandular Tumors, and a Tuberculous Tendency — A ☉ disease, and afflictions to the ☉; a ☽ disease, and afflictions to the ☽; the ☽ afflicted in ♌, or afflicting the hyleg therefrom; the ☽ hyleg in ♌, and afflicted, and especially among females; ♆, ♅, or ♄ in ♋ and afflicting the ☉ or ☽; ♄ afflicted in ♉ or ♓; ♄ in ♉, ♊, or ♓, occi., and afflicting the ☉, ☽, or Asc., and with a strong tubercular and wasting tendency; ♄ or ♂ in the Asc. or M.C., in ♋, ♑, or ♓, and signs ascribed to animals or fishes; ♄ in ♉ when Sig. of the disease; ♄ in ♋ and afflicting the ☉, ☽, or Asc.; ♄ and ♂ joined anywhere in the figure, and especially in angles, or in their own nodes, or in the Lunar nodes; a ♃ disease; ♂ afflicted in ♉; ♀ afflicted in ♊; a ♉ disease when malefics are in ♉ at B., and the disease appears in the neck; a ♊ disease; ♋ on the Asc.; a ♏ disease; malefics in ♋, ♑, and ♓, angular, ori. of the ☉ and occi. of the ☽, tend to scurvy or scrofula, and if the malefics be in the 1st or 7th H. tends to add putridity; ♉, ♏, and ♀ rulers of the 4th and 10th Houses, the houses of the parents, bring the danger of inheriting scrofulous blood; airy signs on the Asc. and 6th H. at B., or at decumb., or Sigs. at the beginning of an illness, indicate scrofula in Hor'y Q.; signified by the 2nd H. influences. (See Adenoma, Glands; "Scrofula" under Neck; Scurvy, Tuberculosis).

SCROTUM—The Pouch Containing the Testes—Ruled by ♏.

Hernia—Scrotal Hernia—The ☉ in ♏ in the 6th H., and afflicted by ♅ or ♂; the ☉ ☌ ☿ in ♏ in the 6th H., and afflicted by ♅, ♄, and the ☽; ♂ afflicted in ♏; ♂ in ♏ in the 6th H., and afflicted. Case of Scrotal Hernia — See Chap. XIII in Daath's Medical Astrology. (See Hernia, Rupture).

Hydrocele—(See this subject).

Varicocele—Dilated Veins In Scrotum —(See Testes, Varicocele).

SCRUPLES — Motives—Conduct, etc.— (See Cheating, Conduct, Deceitful, Dishonest, Gamblers, Honest, Liars, Libelers, Motives, Purposes, Sincere, Thieves, etc.).

SCURVY — A Form of Purpura Due to Deficient and Improper Diet — The ☉ afflicted in ♊; the ☽ afflicted in ♏, or ♐, the autumnal signs; ♄ in ♉ when ♄ is the afflictor in the disease; ♄ afflicted in ♋, due to improper and deficient diet; ♄ in an angle, occi. of the ☉ and ori. of the ☽; ♄ Sig. of the party in Hor'y Q., a scurvy face and countenance; ♃ affl. in ♋; ♃ in an earthy sign, peregrine, and ☌ the Asc.

by dir.; caused by ♀ when the dominion of death is vested in her; a ♏ disease, and afflictions in ♏; malefics in ♋, ♑, or ♓, angular, ori. to the ☉, and occi. to the ☽, and especially if the malefics be in the 1st or 7th H., which tends to putridity; Subs at CP, SP, and KP. (See Diet, Food, Purpura, Putrid, Scrofula).

SCYBALUM — Scybalous Matter—Hard and Lumpy Faeces—(See Faeces).

SEA—Seas—The Oceans—Salt Water— The Seas are ruled by the ☽, ♆, and the ♓ Sign. The ♋ Sign rules Rivers, Lakes, Fresh Water, and Running Streams. The ☽ and planets in the watery signs ♋, ♏, and ♓ at B. tend to bring events affecting Waters, Seas, Lakes and Rivers. The ☉, ☽, or ♂ cadent dispose to Sea Voyages. (See Voyages).

Accidents At Sea — (See Ships, Shipwreck).

Aground — (See "Foundering" under Ships).

Avalanches — Danger From On Voyages—(See Avalanches).

Bathing—Bathing In Sea Dangerous — (See Bathing; "Perils By" under Water).

Bites—Bitten by Animal On Sea Voyage—(See "Bites" under Voyages).

Burns—Suffers Burns On Sea Voyage —(See "Journeys" under Burns).

Calamities At Sea—(See Ships, Shipwreck; the various paragraphs in this section).

Corruption of the Seas—Death of Fish —(See Fish).

Cuts On Voyages—(See "Travel" under Cuts).

Danger By—Danger In Navigation— Peril by Waters — (See Drowning, Maritime, Navigation, Ships, Shipwreck; "Danger" under Travel; "Peril By" under Waters).

Death At Sea—Drowning At Sea—The ☽ afflicted in the 8th H.; ♄ or ♂ afflicted in the 9th H. at B., and by dir.; planets in ♋, ♏, or ♓, and afflicting the ☽ or hyleg. (See Drowning; "Death" under Shipwreck, Waters).

Drowning At Sea — (See "Death" in this section).

Events — Events On the Waters and Seas—(See "Nature Of" under Events).

Explosion At Sea—(See "Ships" under Explosions).

Falls On Voyages—(See "Travel" under Falls).

Famine On Voyages—(See Famine).

Fevers At Sea—(See "Health" under Journeys; "Fever" under Voyages).

Fire At Sea—(See "Ships" under Fire).

Fish — Death of In the Seas — (See Fish).

Foreign Travel—(See Abroad; "Long Journeys" under Journeys; Ocean; "Foreign Travel" under Travel; Voyages).

Fortunate Upon the Seas—Successful In Maritime Pursuits — Fond of the Water—The ☉ Sig. in ♏; ♃ Sig. in ♋, ♏, or ♓, or ♂ ☽); ♃ Sig. in ♓ if the ☽ is not afflicted. (See Maritime; "Fortunate" under Travel, Water).

Foundering of Ship—(See "Foundering" under Ships).

Good Time For Voyages—(See "Good Time" under Voyages).

Injury At Sea—Losses At Sea—♄ or ♂ afflicted in the 9th H. (See "Death", and the various paragraphs in this section).

Journeys by Sea—(See Abroad, Journeys, Maritime, Navigation, Sailors, Ships, Voyages).

Lightning At Sea — Death or Injury By—(See "Voyages" under Lightning).

Long Journeys—By Sea—(See Abroad; "Long Journeys" under Journeys; "Foreign Travel" under Travel; Voyages).

Losses At Sea—(See "Injury" in this section).

Maritime Affairs — (See Maritime, Navigation, Ships).

Misfortunes At Sea—An eclipse of the ☉ in the 1st decan. of ♓. (See Calamity, Danger, and the various paragraphs in this section; Shipwreck; "Danger" under Voyages; "Perils" under Water).

Navigation — (See Maritime, Navigation, Sailors, Ships, Voyages).

Near Water—Danger to Go Near Water—(See Bathing; "Petrils" under Water).

Ocean—(See Ocean).

Peril by Waters — (See Bathing, Drowning, Maritime, Navigation, Pirates, Ships, Shipwreck; "Danger" under Voyages; "Perils" under Waters).

Piracy; Privations — On Journeys or Voyages—Malefics in the 3rd or 9th H., in earthy signs, and afflicting the ☉ or ☽ at B., or by dir. (See Famine, Privation).

Sailing—Good Time For—(See "Good Time" under Voyages).

Sailors—Dangers To—(See Sailors).

Sea Level—Should Live There—(See Altitude).

Sea Sickness—(See "Sickness" under Voyages).

Sea Travel — (See "Long Journeys" under Journeys; Ships, Voyages).

Ships—Shipping—(See Ships).

Shipwreck—(See Ships, Shipwreck).

Sickness At Sea—(See "Sickness" under Voyages).

Stabs At Sea — (See "Travel" under Cuts).

Successful On the Sea — (See "Fortunate" in this section).

Tempests At Sea—Hurricanes—Lightning — (See "Fountains" under Dryness; "Voyages" under Lightning; Shipwreck; "Storms", "Tornadoes", under Wind).

Tidal Waves — (See "Tidal" under Water).

Travel—Sea Travel—(See Maritime, Navigation, Voyages).

Troubles by Sea—Danger In Navigation—Malefics in the 9th H. in water signs, weak and afflicted; an eclipse of the ☉ or ☽ in ♓; an eclipse of the ☽ in the 3rd decan. of ♓; Comets appearing in ♓. (See "Danger", and the various paragraphs in this section).

Unfortunate—On the Sea—Malefics in water signs in the 9th H., and afflicted. (See "Misfortunes", and the various paragraphs in this section; "Danger", "Death", under Voyages).

Voyages—(See the various paragraphs under Voyages).

Water Signs—♋, ♏, ♓.

Waters — Water — (See the subjects under Water).

SEANCES—(See Clairvoyance, Mediumship, Negative, Psychic, Spirit Controls, Spiritualism).

SEARING BURNS—(See "Burning" under Blindness; "Searing" under Burns).

SEASONS — The Four Seasons — (See Autumnal, Equinoxes, Ingresses, Solstices, Spring, Summer, Tropical, Vernal, Winter; "Lord of the Year" under Year, etc.).

Cold Winter—Much Suffering From—(See Snow; "Cold" under Weather; Winter).

Sickly Summer—(See "Extreme Heat" under Heat; Summer).

SEBACEOUS—Pertaining To Fat or Suet — Sebaceous Glands — Sebaceous Ducts—

Comedo — Blackheads — Sebaceous Ducts Obstructed — Afflictions to ♃ at B.; ♃ afflicted in ♈; ♃ ill-aspected by ♄; ♀ in signs which rule the arms, hands, legs and feet tends to blackheads in these parts due to wrong habits of living; Subs at CP and KP (11D). (See Fat, Sweat).

Cysts—Sebaceous Cysts—Steatoma—(See Wens).

Inflammation — Of the Sebaceous Glands—(See Acne).

Tumor — Sebaceous, Encysted Tumor —(See Wen).

SECLUSION—Secluded—Seclusiveness—

Ends Life In Seclusion—(See "Seclusion" under Old Age; Recluse).

Fond of Seclusion—♄ influence. (See Loneliness, Misanthropic, Miserly, Mistrustful, Recluse, Renunciation, Reserved, Retiring, Secretive, Shy, Solitude, Suspicious, Twelfth House).

Secluded by Law — (See Banishment, Exile; "Imprisonment" under Prison).

SECOND—

Second Death—(See the Introduction under Twelfth House).

Second Half of Life — (See Fourth House, Middle Life, Old Age).

Second House—This House is related to the ♉ Sign, the second sign of the Zodiac. This is a feminine and succedent house. Is known as the House of Finance. It rules the Neck, the back part of the Neck down to the Shoulders; the Vocal Organs; Throat, etc. It denotes the Throat and Ears. In material matters, rules Property, Wealth, and the Financial Condition of the Native. The Benefics in this house at B., and well-aspected, denote wealth and good business success. The Malefics here tend to losses, reversals of fortune, poverty, etc. Rules the Color

Green. In Hindu Astrology, the Second House rules the Eyes. This House signifies all diseases in the throat and neck, quinsy, glandular swellings, sore throat, scrofula, etc., and malefics in this house at B. tend to affect adversely the neck and throat, the eyes, and to cause diseases in these parts. (See Finance, Neck, Poverty, Property, Riches, Taurus, Throat, Wealth).

SECONDARY DIRECTIONS—These are the Progressed Moon directions, counting each day after birth as a year of life, and the aspects the ☽ forms to the radical planets on each day after birth are very important to study in connection with health matters. Ill-health, and other dangers, are apt to attend the native when the progressed ☽ thus forms evil aspects to the radical planets. An evil secondary direction, when combined with an evil periodic direction, may frustrate the good of a fortunate primary direction. Directions, Transits, or Solar Revolutions, cannot bring anything to pass not shown in the radical map. The subjects of Primary and Secondary Directions are discussed, and the methods of calculation given, in the various Textbooks of Astrology. See Lilly's Astrology, Sepharial's Manual of Astrology, Pearce's Textbook of Astrology, Simmonite's Arcana of Astral Philosophy, and others. (See Directions, Lunations, Periodic, Primary Directions, Prognosis, Progression, Transits).

SECRET—Secretly—Secrecy—Secretive —Secrets of Life, etc.—

Secret Bad Habits—The ☽ afflicted in ♏; ♄ in the 1st H.; ♄ ♂ or ill-asp. ♀, addicted to secret and unnatural practices; ♀ in bad aspect to ♄, secret and evil practices; ☿ in bad asp. to ♄. (See Habits, Perversions, Unnatural; "Solitary" under Vice, etc.).

Secret Dangers — (See "Secret Dangers" under Danger; "Secret Enemies" under Enemies; Plots, Poison Death, Treachery, etc.).

Secret Enemies—(See "Secret" under Enemies).

Secret Parts — Private Parts — (See Secrets).

Secret Revenge—(See Revengeful).

Secret Societies—Are ruled by ♅.

Secret Sorrow — (See "Secret" under Sorrow).

Secret Treachery—(See Ambushes; "Secret Enemies" under Enemies; Plots, Poison Death, Treachery).

Secret Vices—(See Perversions; "Solitary" under Vice).

Secretive—Secrecy—♄ people are very secretive; ♄ strong at B., and rising, a confederate in secrecy; ♄ in ♏; a quality of ♅; ♏ on the Asc. (See Recluse, Renunciation, Reserved, Retiring, Seclusion, Solitude, etc.).

Secretly Lascivious—(See Lascivious).

Secretly Vicious — (See Artifice, Lascivious, Malice, Plots, Poison Death, Revenge, Treachery, Vicious).

Secrets of Life — Are under the rule of ♅. (See Neptune).

SECRETIONS—Secretion—Secretory System—Secretory Organs—Glands— The Secretive System generally is ruled by ♄, and also the ☽ has influence over the secretions of the body. Also ♏ rules the Secretory Organs. The Secretory Nerves are ruled by ♏. The Bronchials, which are secretory organs, are ruled by the ♏ sign. (See Bronchial). Interferences, stoppages, diminishing, morbid conditions, stoppages, suppressions, and hindrances over the secretory organs and system, are under the general rule of ♄ and his afflictions. (See Tumors). For the Secretions of the various parts and organs of the body, and the influences controlling or disturbing them, look in the alphabetical arrangement for the part, or organ, you have in mind. A few subjects concerning the Secretions will be listed here. See the following subjects in the alphabetical arrangement—

Augmented; Bronchial Secretions— (See Bronchial).

Diminished; Discharges; Elimination; Excretion; Fluids; Follicles;

Functions; Glands; Hindrances;

Humoural Secretions—(See Humours).

Increased; Interferences;

Interrupted; Irregular; Juices;

Lack Of—(See the various paragraphs under "Lack Of").

Milk; Morbid Secretions—(See Morbid).

Mucous Membranes—Secretions of— (See Mucous).

Normal Secretions—The ☽ in the airy signs tends to normal and regular secretions, but liable to skin, blood, and kidney disorders. (See Abnormal, Augmented, Decreased, Diminished, Increased, Irregular, Normal, Regular).

Obstructions; Organs—The Secreting Structure of Organs—(See Parenchyma).

Over-Secretion—(See Abundance, Augmented, Excess, Flow, Increased, Over-Flowing, etc.).

Phlegm; Regular—(See Regular; "Normal" in this section).

Serum; Skin; Stomach—(See Glands, Secretions, under Stomach).

Stoppages; Suppressions; Sweat;

Synovial; Urates (Over-Secretion of); **Urine** (Secretion of Obstructed).

SECRETIVE—Inclined to Secrecy— (See "Secretive" under Secret).

Secretive System—(See Secretions).

SECRETS—Secret Parts—Private Parts — Sex Organs, etc. — This subject is largely considered in the Articles on Generative System, Genitals, Genito-Urinary System, Privates, Reins, Reproduction, Sex Organs, etc. However, in the Textbooks of Astrology the Sex Organs are often spoken of as the "Secret Parts", and for convenience of reference, such subjects are again listed alphabetically in this present Article. The Secret Parts are ruled in general by the ♏ sign and the 8th House, and also by ♂, the ruler of the ♏ sign. See the following subjects in the alphabetical arrangement when only listed here—

Abscess—In the Secret Parts—In the Private Parts—♃ afflicted in ♏; ♃ in ♏ and afflicting the ☽ or Asc.; ♃ in ♏ in the 6th H., and afflicted. (See Abscesses).

Affected—The Secret Parts are affected when the ☽ is in ♒; ♅ in ♍; ♄ in ♌ or ♍; ♃ in ♎; ♂ in ♉ or ♏; ♀ in ♉; ☿ in ♈ or ♑. (See Table 196 in Simmonite's Arcana).

Afflicted—In the Secret Parts—(See "Distempers", and the various paragraphs in this section).

All Diseases In—♏ diseases and afflictions in ♏, either in men or women; ☽ diseases and caused by afflictions to the ☽ at B.; the ☽ afflicted in ♏; ♂ diseases, and caused by afflictions of ♂ in either sex; ♂, and other malefics, afflicted in ♏; signified by the 7th H. (See "All Diseases In" under Generative System)..

Channels and Vents—Lack of Proper Sex Channels—(See "Channels" under Genitals).

Death—Arising from Diseases of the Secret Parts—(See "Death" under Generative).

Diseases In—(See "Distempers" in this section).

Distempers—In Secret Parts—Diseases In—Infirmities In—The ☉ or ☽ afflicted in ♏ or ♓, ♂, or ill-asp. any of the malefics as promittors; the ☉ afflicted in ♒; ☽ diseases; the ☽ afflicted in ♏, ♒, or ♓; ♄ affl. in ♋, ♌, ♍, or ♏; ♃ affl. in ♊, ♋, or ♎; ♂ diseases; ♂ afflicted in ♊, ♎, or ♏; ♂ in ♏, ♂, or ill-asp. the ☉; ☿ affl. in ♎ or ♏. (See "Diseases" under Generative, Genitals, Genito-Urinary, Reproduction, Sex, and also note the various paragraphs in this section).

Eunuchs; Eruptions—(See "Eruptions" under Generative).

Functional Disorders—(See "Functions" under Females; "Female Functions" under Functions; Menses).

Generation—Disorders of Organs of— (See Generative System).

Genitals—Disorders of—(See Genitals).

Hermaphrodites; Impotency;

Infirmities In—(See "Distempers" in this section).

Inflammatory Diseases—♂ afflicted in ♏, and especially in the Asc., 6th, or 8th H. (See "Inflammatory" under Generative; "Inflammation" under Genitals).

Injuries To—(See "Men's Genitals" under Genitals; Maimed).

Maimed; Matrix—Disorders of—(See Womb).

Members of Generation—Disorders of —(See the paragraphs under Generative, Genitals, Genito-Urinary, Ovaries, Penis, Privates, Reproduction, Sex Organs, Testes, Womb, etc.).

Mens' Genitals—Disorders of—Injury To—(See "Mens' Genitals" under Genitals; Penis; Scrotum, Testes).

Nerves—Of the Privy Parts—Disorders of—♅ or ☿ afflicted in ♏. (See Nerves).

Ovaries—Disorders of—(See Ovaries, Fallopian).

Pains In—Neuralgia In—The ☉ in ♓ when the afflictor in the disease, violent pains in; the ☽ afflicted in ♒; ♄ afflicted in ♓, violent pains in; ♂ in ♏, ☌, or ill-asp. the ☉; ♀ afflicted in ♉ or ♏; ☿ affl. in ♏. (See "Pain In" under Genitals).

Penis — Disorders of — (See Genitals, Gonorrhoea, Penis, Urethra).

Private Parts—Privy Parts—Privates — Disorders In — Injuries To — (See Genitals, Maimed, Penis, Privates, Reproduction, Sex Organs, Vagina, Womb).

Regenerative Organs—Disorders of— (See Regeneration).

Reins—Disorders of—(See the paragraphs under Reins).

Scandalous Diseases — (See Genitals, Gonorrhoea, Private, Scandalous, Syphilis, Venereal).

Scrotum—Disorders of—(See Scrotum).

Secret Enemy—Secret Diseases of— (See "Secret Enemies" under Enemies).

Sensitive — Sensitive Generative Organs—♏ on the Asc. (See Sensitive).

Sex Organs—Disorders of—(See the various paragraphs in this section, and under Sex Organs).

Spermatic Cord—Disorders of — (See Spermatic).

Stone In—(See "Secret Parts" under Stone).

Swellings In—The ☽ and ♂ afflicted in ♏; the ☽ afflicted in ♒; ♄ in ♏ when ♄ is the afflictor in the disease; ♃ afflicted in ♏. See "Swellings" under Generative; Hydrocele, Varicocele; "Swellings" under Womb).

Syphilis; Testicles — Disorders of — (See Testes).

Ulcers In — (See "Genitals" under Ulcers).

Urethra—Disorders of—(See Urethra).

Uterus—Disorders of—(See Womb).

Vagina—Disorders of—(See Vagina).

Violent Pains In — (See "Pains" in this section).

Vulva—Disorders of—(See Vulva).

Womb—Disorders of—(See Womb).

SEDATE—Sober—(See Harmless, Quiet, Reserved, Retiring, Serious, Sober, Thoughtful, etc.).

SEDATIVE—Sedatives—Soothing—Depressants — Quieting Remedies — A Therapeutic quality of ♄ and ♄ remedies. Also the ☽ has sedative and sleep-inducing influences. Sedatives do little good during the increase of the ☽, are weakest in effect then, and the dose should be increased. During the decrease of the ☽ sedatives work more rapidly, and can be given in smaller doses. (See Aconite, Anaesthetics, Anaphrodisiacs, Anodyne; "Sedative" under Heart; "Saturn Group" under Herbs; Narcotics; "Nervine" under Nerves; "Quieting Remedies" under Quiet; "Soporifics" under Sleep; Soothing, etc.).

SEDENTARY HABITS — A characteristic of ♄ people, and with ♄ ruler, or strong at B. Also ruled by the ☽, and caused by afflictions to the ☽. Mars weak and ill-dig. at B. tends to less

activity in the nature, and more liable to seek a life of ease. Also caused by ♀ weak and afflicted at B. (See "Of No Ambition" under Ambition; Apathy; "Lack Of" under Exercise; Inactive, Indifferent, Inertia, Lazy, Lethargy, Listless, Negative Nature, Obesity, Tumors, etc.).

SEDIMENTS — (See Deposits, Gravel, Minerals, Sand, Stone; "Brick Dust Deposits" under Urine).

SEDITION — Opposition to the Government—Treason—A Promoter of Sedition—

Deadly Sedition—An eclipse of the ☉ in ♈; an eclipse of the ☉ or ☽ in watery signs; an eclipse of the ☉ or ☽ in airy signs, and especially in Regions under such signs; a solar eclipse in the 2nd decan. of ♍, and enduring as many years as the eclipse lasted in hours, and especially with People and Countries under the rule of ♍; an eclipse of the ☉ in the 2nd decan. of ♎, or the 3rd decan. of ♓; an eclipse of the ☽ in ♍, ♏, or ♑, and affecting Countries ruled by these Signs; an eclipse of the ☽ in the 3rd decan. of ♏ or ♑; ♂ ill-dignified at B., and afflicted, tends to make one seditious and rebellious to established Laws, Government, and Social customs. (See Anarchists, Reactionary, Rebellious, Reformers, Revolutionary, etc.).

SEDUCTION—Danger of—Liable to Seductive Influences—Liable to Be Led Astray—The ☽ Sig. ☌ ♂, if a female; ♅ afflicted in the 5th H.; ♅ in aspect to ♀; ♅ in ♉ or ♏, □ ♂, or ♂ in ♉ or ♏ in □ to ♅, escape from seduction almost impossible unless warned, or the early training is good and restraining; ♅ □ ♂ in a woman's horoscope when occurring in any part of the map; ♄ ☌ the ☽, or afflicting the ☽, and ♂ also in bad aspect to the ☽; ♂ ☌ or bad asp. the ☽; ♀ with ♂ alone at B., and afflicted, women liable to be led astray. (See "Chaste", "Unchaste", "Virtue", under Females; "Free Love" under Free; Kidnapped; "Liaisons" under Love Affairs; Rape; "Clandestine" under Sex).

Seductive — The influence of ♆ is seductive, and under his evil aspects the moral nature tends to suffer. (See "Free Living" under Free; "Loose Morals" under Morals; Neptune).

SEED — Seeds — Seminal — The Seed is ruled by ♃. Earth and Plant Seeds are ruled by the ☽. The Semen is ruled by ♀. (See Semen).

Rottenness — Of Seeds and Herbs — (See "Seeds" under Rottenness).

Scarcity Of—An eclipse of the ☽ in the 2nd decan. of ♉, or in the 2nd decan. of ♒, the seeds of the Earth are hurt. (See Drought, Famine, Grain, Scarcity).

Seed Atom—(See Barren, Conception).

SEERS—Prophets—One Who Foresees the Future—The ♆ influence strong at B. tends to enhance this Faculty. Also the ♅ influence strong at B. gives a desire to study the laws of the Mental, Psychic, and Spiritual Worlds, and to develop Spiritual Faculties, and to know the Truth. (See Clairvoyance,

Magic, Mediumship, Metaphysical, Mystical, Occult, Prophetic, Religion, Spiritual, Visions).

SEGMENTS — Motor Segment of the Spinal Cord — (See "Cord", "Lesions", "Motor", under Spine).

SELDOM—Rare—Infrequent—

Seldom Healthy—(See "Ill-Health All Thru Life" under Ill-Health; "Much Sickness" under Sickness).

Seldom Ill—(See "Strong" under Constitution;"Good Health" under Health; Immunity; "Good" under Recuperation; Resistance, Vitality; Robust, Ruddy; "Increased" under Strength; "Body" under Strong).

SELECTION — Selection of Cell Substances—(See "Substance" under Cells).

SELENITE—A Mineral ruled by the ☽.

SELF—All words beginning with "Self" are listed in this section.

Self-Absorbed—Self-Contained—☿ in the 12th H.

Self-Abuse—(See "Solitary" under Vice).

Self-Approbation — Excessive Vanity —Principally ♀ influence, and the ♋ and ♓ signs prominent. Also ♌ is proud, vain at times, and fond of flattery. (See Vain).

Self-Assertive — Dogged — Fond of Rule and Authority—Positive—The ☉, ♅, and ♂ are all self-assertive; the ☉ Sig. in ♌, fond of rule and authority; ☿ Sig. in ♌; ♌ qualities. (See Commanding, Independent, Obstinate, Opinions, Positive Nature, Ruling).

Self-Centered — (See "Selfishness" in this section; Misanthropic, Penurious).

Self-Confidence — ♂ rising at B.; ♂ Sig. in ♈; the good asps. of ♂ to the ☉, ☽, or ☿; ♂ Sig. ✶ or △ ☿, extremely self-confident; the ☽, ♀, and ♆ influences tend to a lack of self-confidence. (See "Self-Reliant" in this section; "Inferiority Complex" under Inferior).

Self-Consciousness — The Airy Signs are Self-Conscious. (See "Signs" under Air; Egotistical).

Self-Contained—(See "Self-Absorbed" in this section).

Self-Control — Has good self-control when ♄ is strong at B., and in a fixed sign; ♄ well-aspected by ♅; ♄ in ♏ and well-aspected by ♅. In this matter, however, the star map of birth as a whole should be studied. The influences tending to lack of self-control are—♆ rising at B., or in the 3rd or 9th H., and afflicted; ♆ ☌ or ill-asp. ♂; the ☽ sepr. from ♀ and applying to ♀. (See Anger, Control, Disorderly, Harmless, Hasty, Immoderate, Impulsive, Inoffensive, Inordinate, Intemperance; "Command" under Passion; Restraints, Temperance, Uncontrolled, Violent).

Self-Debasement—♄ ☌ or ill-asp. ♀; the 11° ♌ on the Asc. (See Debauched, Depraved, Lewd, Obscene, Perversions, Profligate, Shameless, Wanton, etc.).

Self-Denying—Ascetic—Abstemious—Hermits — Reclusive — Reserved—♄ ruler of the horoscope, and of the Asc. at B.; ♄ ruler of the 12th H., and ♄ in the 12th and afflicted; ♄ people, and born under ♄, often ascetic; ♄ in any

aspect to ☿, and configurated with ♃; a strong ♄ influence in the 5th H., or ♄ afflicting the lord of the 5th. (See Celibacy, Misanthropic, Miserly, Penurious; "Averse To" under Pleasure; Recluse, Renunciation, Reserved, Retiring, Seclusion, Secretive, Solitude; "Selfishness" in this section).

Self-Esteem — Self-Approval—The ☉ and ♃ strong at B., but afflicted; ♃ afflicted by ♆; the ♌ sign prominent at B. (See Egotistical, Pretender, Pride; "Self-Approbation", "Self-Righteous", in this section).

Self-Exaltation—(See this subject under Religion).

Self-Flattery — (See Egotistical, Erratic; "Bad" under Judgment; "Light In Mind" under Mind; Pretender; "Self-Approbation", "Self-Esteem", in this section).

Self-Glorifying — (See "Self-Esteem" in this section).

Self-Indulgent — Hedonism — The ☉ afflicted in ♓; the ☽ afflicted in ♏ or ♐; ♆ ruler of the horoscope, and afflicted; ♆ afflicted in ♋; ♆ afflicted in the 6th H., self-indulgent manner of living; ♆ ☌ or ill-asp. ♂; due to the □ and ☍ aspects of ♆ to planets; ♆ in the 3rd or 9th H. in asp. to the ☽ or ☿; ♃ in the Asc. in ♋, and afflicted; ♃ afflicted in ♏, diseases arising from self-indulgence; afflictions to ♃; ♃ □ or ☍ the ☉ or ☉; ♃ afflicted in the 7th H., a self-indulgent marriage partner; ☿ Sig., and to the ☌ ♀, and ♀ ill-dignified at B.; ♂ afflicted in ♋ in the 1st H.; ♀ afflicted by ♂; ♀ affl. in ♎; the 10° ♉, the 8° ♋, the 11° ♌, or the 15° ♎ on the Asc. at B. Cases of Self-Indulgence—See "Self-Indulgence",No. 229, in 1001 N.N. Also Fig. 35 in the book, "Message of the Stars" by the Heindels. (See Conduct, Debauched, Diet, Drink, Drunkenness, Eating, Epicureans, Excesses, Feasting, Food, Gluttony, Habits, Indulgent; "Passional Excesses" under Passion; Pleasures, Vices, etc.).

Self-Inflicted Wounds — (See Demoniac, Suicide, Superstitious).

Selfishness—Careful of Own Interests — Not Easily Imposed Upon — Niggardly—Penurious—Frugal, etc.—A ♄ characteristic; ♄ strong at B., rising in the Asc. or M.C., and afflicting ♃; ♄ afflicted in the 6th H., ill-health thru selfish aims; ♄ afflicted in ♉; the ☽ or ☿ afflicted by ♄; ♃ Sig. ☌ ♄; ♃ or ♀ in ♑; ♃ Sig. in ♏, careful of own interests, and not easily imposed upon; ♃ Sig. in ♏; ☿ ori. at B., all for own interests; ☿ Sig. in ♐, understands own interests, and not easily deluded by the most cunning knave; ☿ Sig. in ♏, careful of own interests; many planets in ♑ at B.; ♑ influence; the 3rd decan. of ♑ on the Asc.; the 5th Face of ♒ on the Asc.; selfishness comes principally under ♈, ♏, and ♑. (See Misanthropic, Miserly, Mistrustful, Penurious, Scepticism, Secretive, Suspicious).

Self-Laudation—Self-Praise—The ☉ □ ♃ in fixed signs. (See "Self-Esteem", "Self-Flattery", in this section).

Self-Motivated Acts—Diseases or Injury From—(See "Disease or Injury" under Rashness).

Self-Opinionated— (See "Intolerance" under Religion).

Self-Preservation — The ♄ influence strong at B. gives tenacity to hold onto life, and to husband the resources, and for self-preservation. (See Careful, Miserly, Prudent; "Selfishness" in this section).

Self-Reliant—The ☉, ♅, and ♂ are all self-reliant; the ☉ Sig. in ♌; the ☉ well-aspected by ♂; ♂ Sig. in ♈; the good asps. of ♂ to the ☉, ☽, or ☿; ♂ Sig. ✳ or △ ☿; ♂ in ♐; the ♈ people usually have much self-reliance. (See Self-Assertive, Self-Confidence, in this section; Ambition; "Positive Nature" under Positive; Ruling).

Self-Righteous—(See "Sanctimonious" under Religion).

Self-Satisfaction—The ☉ weak in ♓, and afflicted; the ☽ weak in ♌, and ill-dignified; mutable signs on angles. (See "Of No Ambition" under Ambition; Contentment, Dull; "Fond of Ease" under Ease; Idle, Lassitude, Negative Nature, etc.).

Self-Sufficient—♅, ♏, and ♍ influence. (See "Self-Absorbed" in this section).

Self-Torture — Usually from a Religious Cause or Belief — Usually caused by afflictions to ♆ in the map of birth, and especially if ♆ is weak and ill-dignified, and due to spiritual causes, obsessions, narrow religious views, hallucinations, etc.; ♆ afflicted by ♅, ♄, or ♂; afflictions in the 12th H. at B. (See Obsessions, Religion, Spirit Controls; "Self-Denying" in this secton).

Self-Undoing—Ruled by the 12th H., its afflictions and influences; also largely characteristic of the ♓ sign, the 12th sign; the ☉ or ☽ ♂ ♄ in the 12th H., and espec. if in ♓; ♆ or ♄ afflicted in ♓ or the 12th H.; ♂ afflicted in the 12th H.; lord of the 12th H. a malefic, and in the 12th, and afflicting the lord of the Asc.; malefics afflicted in the 12th H.; the 12° ♋ on the Asc. at B. (See Disgrace; "Own Worst Enemy" under Enemies; Fate, Folly, Grief, Honour, Misery, Misfortune, Rashness, Recklessness; "Loss Of" under Reputation; Reverses, Ruin, Scandal, Sorrow, Trouble, Unfortunate).

Self-Willed—The 30° ♓ on the Asc. at B. (See Obstinate, Stubborn; "Strong Will" under Will).

SEMEN — Seminal — Seminal Fluid — Vital Fluid—The Seed—Spermatozoa— Seminal Vesicles, etc.—The Semen is ruled by ♃ and ♀, and also the seminal vesicles and their contents,. The reception of semen into the womb is ruled by the ☽. The seminal tubes, the Tubuli Seminiferi, or Vesicles, are ruled by ♀. (See "Fluid" under Vital).

Emissions — Loss of Seed — Involuntary Discharges of Semen — Night Losses—Wet Dreams—♆ afflicted in ♏; ♀ diseases, and afflictions to ♀; ♃ in ♏ and afflicted by ♂; Subs at PP (2, 3, 4L).

Seminal Complaints—♃ afflicted in ♏; ♃ in ♏ in the 6th H., and afflicted; ♃ in ♏ and afflicting the ☉ or ☽; ♀ diseases, and afflictions to ♀. (See Barrenness).

Seminal Signs—The Fruitful Signs— The watery signs, ♋, ♏, and ♓ are called the fruitful, or seminal signs. (See "Fruitful Signs" under Fruitful).

SEMI—

Semi-Lunar Ganglion — (See "Semi-Lunar" under Ganglion).

Semi-Spiritual — The abstract influence of ♆. (See Spiritual).

Semi-Square Aspect—The 45° aspect, or one-half of the □ aspect. Partakes of the nature of the □ aspect, but is milder. However, the ∠ aspect is evil in health, and other matters, and the ∠ asp. of the ☉ to ♀ tends to Intemperance and Indiscretions. (See Aspects).

Semi-Tertian Fevers—Have the characteristics of both a Tertian and Quaternary Fever. Caused by ♂ when the dominion of death is vested in him. (See Ague, Quartan, Tertian).

SEMINAL—(See Semen).

SENILITY — (See "Senility" under Old Age).

SENSATION—Sensations—Corporeal Feeling — Sensorial — Sensory—The Physical Sense of Feeling—The Sense of Touch, etc. — The Sensations are ruled by the ☽, ☿, and the Asc.

Altered Sensations — (See Paraesthesia).

Animal Sensations — Love of — ♆ rising, or in the 3rd or 9th H., and afflicted. (See "Animal Instincts" under Animal; Appetites, Astral Body, Cravings; "Desire Body" under Desire; Hunger, Passion, Thirst, etc.).

Burning Sensations—Burning Pains— (See Belching; "Heartburn" under Heart; "Hot Flashes" under Heat; Paraesthesia).

Crawling Sensations — Creeping Sensations — (See Hyperaemia, Hyperaesthesia, Paraesthesia).

Disorders Of—(See Senses; the various paragraphs in this section).

Easily Moved by Sensation—The 5th face of ♋ on the Asc. at B., very impressionable, and often reflecting others. (See Influenced, Negative Nature, Receptive, Susceptible, etc.).

Functions — The Sensorial Functions Impaired—♄ ♂ or ill-asp. the ☽. (See Functions, Senses).

Hot and Cold Sensations—Hot Flashes —Chill, etc.—(See Chill, Cold, Congestions, Fever, Heat, Paraesthesia, Rigors, etc.).

Hyperaesthesia; Morbid Sensations— (See Paraesthesia).

Numbness; Paraesthesia;

Physical Sensation — Represented by the watery signs, and as brought on by contact with, and stimulation from the external world, and such as give comfort, ease, or distress to the physical body. (See External, Physical).

Prickling Sensations—(See Prickling).

Senses—(See the various paragraphs under Senses).

Sensory Nerves — Ruled by ☿. (See "Elimination" under Urine).

Tingling—(See Numbness, Tingling). See Sensibility, Sensitive.

Touch—Sense of—Ruled by ☿. (See Touch, Senses).

SENSATIONAL— Sensationalism—Sensations — Along emotional and sensational lines the watery signs are excitable and sensational. Also the fiery signs love sensation, and in a positive way. The ♏ sign gives a love of sensationalism along lines of crime, adventure, and the Occult. Pisces along lines of trouble, sorrow, bereavement, etc. (See Astral Body; "Desire Body" under Desire; Emotions; Excitement).

SENSE NATURE—(See Amorous, Emotions, Feelings, Passion, Sensuality).

SENSES—The Five Senses—Sensorium —Sense Organs—☿ is the originator of the sense vibrations, and also rules all sense perceptions, as seeing, hearing, smelling, feeling, tasting, etc. Saturn is not a builder to the senses, but exerts rather a strong psychological and intellectual power. In the Hindu System the five physical Senses are attributed to the First House.

Acute — The Senses Made Acute — ☿ elevated and well-aspected, and the mind is keen. (See "Active Mind" under Active; "Quickened" under Mentality).

Animal Instincts—(See Animal).

Color—Sense of—(See Color).

Dulling of the Senses — Hebetude — Non-Sensitive—☿ afflicted at B.; ♄ influence; ♄ ☌ ☿, the mind is dull and heavy. (See "Mind" under Dull, Heavy; Hebetude, Hyperaesthesia, Inertia, Lassitude, Lethargy, etc.).

Feeling — (See Sensation, Sensibility, Touch).

Functions — The Sensorial Functions Impaired—(See "Functions" under Sensation).

Gratification — Of the Senses — (See Appetites, Conduct, Desires, Drink, Excesses, Food, Gluttony, Habits, Passion, etc.).

Hypersensitive—(See Hyperaesthesia).

Impaired Senses — (See "Dulling" in this section; "Functions" under Sensation).

Intuition—(See Intuition).

Limitations—Upon the Senses—(See Blindness, Deafness, Dull, Hearing, Hindrances, Impairments, Impediments, Limitations, Sight, Smell, Suppressions, Touch, Twelfth House, etc.).

Passion—(See the paragraphs under Passion).

Perception—(See the paragraphs under Perception).

Physical Sensations—(See "Physical" under Sensation).

Saturn and the Senses—(See the Introduction to this Article).

Sensation—Disorders of—(See Sensation).

Sense Mind—(See Personality).

Sensibility—(See this subject).

Sensory Nerves—(See "Sensory" under Sensation).

Sight — Sense of — (See Accommodation, Blindness, Eyes, Sight).

Sixth Sense—(See Pineal Gland).

Taste—(See paragraphs under Taste).

Touch—(See Sensation, Touch).

Vibrations — Sense Vibrations — (See Introduction to this Article; Vibration).

Vision—(See Sight).

SENSIBILITY — Susceptibility of Feeling—

Augmented Sensibility — Excessive Sensibility — A ♂ disease, and due to the tonic action of ♂. Also caused by afflictions to ☿. (See Hyperaesthesia).

Diminished Sensibility—A ♄ disease. (See Diminished).

Insensibility—(See this subject).

Sensible— (See "Good" under Judgment; "Sound" under Mind). See Sensation, Senses, Sensitive.

SENSITIVE—Sensitives—Sensitiveness — Sensibility — The part of the body ruled by the sign containing the ☽ at B. is always a very sensitive spot, and any part of the body ruled by the sign thru which the ☽ is passing for the time is made more sensitive, and operations should not be performed upon such a part, or parts, until the ☽ has passed into the next sign, or several signs further along. (See "Rules" under Operations). The Sensitive, or Irrational Faculties, are ruled by the ☽.

Augmented Sensibility — (See Sensibility).

Body — A Sensitive Body — ♆ ☌ the Asc.

Chart of Birth—Sensitive Places In— The parts or organs ruled by the Signs, Houses, and Degrees in which the ☉, ☽, and planets are found at B., and especially the ☉, ☽, and malefics, and also the parts ruled by the Asc., the Midheaven, the 4th, 6th, 8th, and 12th Houses, the cusps of these houses, or their lords, tend to be the sensitive parts of the body, and more subject to disease and affliction. (See Map, Nativity, Star Map).

Constitution—A Sensitive Constitution—The ☉ in ♍; ♍ on the Asc., and also very sensitive to suggestions of ill-health. (See Constitution; "Zodiac" under Degrees).

Degrees — Sensitive Degrees of the Zodiac—(See "Sensitive" under Zodiac).

Deviations — (See "Faculties" in this section).

Diminished Sensitiveness — A ♄ disease and affliction. (See Diminished).

Disposition — The ♋ sign influences give a sensitive disposition; the ☉ or ☽ in ♋ at B., or this sign on the Asc. (See "Sensitiveness" in this section).

Excessive Sensitiveness—(See Hyperaesthesia; "Augmented" under Sensibility).

Faculties—Deviation of the Sensitive Faculties—(See Deviations, Faculties).

Fright — Easily Frightened — (See Fright).

Generative Organs—Sensitive Generative Organs—♏ on the Asc.

High Strung — (See "Strung" under High).

Hypersensitive — (See "Excessive" in this section).

Ill-Health — Sensitive to Suggestions of Ill-Health—The ☉ in ♍, or ♍ on the Asc. at B. (See Virgo).

Mind—A Sensitive and Acute Mind— (See "Active Mind" under Active; "Quickened" under Mentality).

Nerves—Sensitive Nerves—High Strung—♅ ☌ ☿. (See "Strung" under High; "High Tension", "Neurasthenia", under Nerves).

Non-Sensitive—(See "Dulling" under Senses).

Organs—Sensitive Organs—Sensitive Parts—The more sensitive organs, or parts of the body, are those ruled by the sign upon the Asc. at B. Thus ♍ on the Asc. tends to make the Generative Organs, and the Excretory System more sensitive; ♊ on the Asc., the lungs sensitive; ♎ on the Asc., the kidneys sensitive, and more liable to disturbances, etc. (See Organs, Parts).

Psychic Conditions — Sensitive To — (See "Sensitive" under Psychic).

Sensitive Degrees — Of the Zodiac — (See Zodiac).

Sensitiveness—Highly Sensitive—Sensitives—The ☉ or ☽ afflicted in the ♋ sign tend to give a sensitive nature, to take offense easily, and to be greatly disturbed by adverse environment; the ☉ in ♍, a sensitive constitution; the ☽ in the 1st H. in ♋ or ♓, and afflicted; the ☽ in the 1st H.; the ☽ ruler of the Asc. or M.C., and not strongly supported by aspects; the aspects of ♆ tend to greatly affect the native for good or ill, but only the sensitive people in the World today feel the rays of ♆ and ♅; ♆ has the most effect upon sensitives; ♆ ☌ ☿; ♅ in ♋; ♄ afflicting ♀; ♀ in ♈, ♍, or ♐; many cross, or ☐ aspects to a planet, or planets ascending at B.; ♑ on the Asc.; the 3rd decan. of ♉ on the Asc., ruled by ♄; common to all the watery signs, and especially to ♋, which sign makes the native more susceptible to external influences and environment; a ♓ influence; the negative, or feminine signs, are negative and receptive, with the exception of ♉; ♍ is rather sensitive, critical, and quickly resents slights or injury; ♎ is quickly offended, and over-sensitive, but does not retain the memory of insult very long; ♊, ♌, ♐, and ♒ do not feel injury, slight, or insult as easily, as they are more mental than emotional. (See Augmented, Emotions, Environment, External, Feelings; "High Strung" under High; Hyperaesthesia, Negative Nature; "Sensitive" under Psychic; Receptive; "Augmented" under Sensibility; Susceptibility, etc.).

Sensitives — (See "Sensitiveness" in this section).

Skin—(See "Sensitive" under Skin).

Slights—Sensitive to Real or Fancied Slights — The ☽ afflicted in ♑. (See Imaginations, Offended).

Spirit Controls — Sensitive To — (See Clairvoyant, Mediumistic, Spirit Controls).

Suggestion—Sensitive To — (See "Ill-Health" in this section; Hypnotism, Influenced, Negative Nature, Receptive, Suggestion, Susceptible).

Super-Sensitive—♄ influence; a ♑ and ♒ disease, and afflictions in these signs. (See Hyperaesthesia).

Troubles and Worries — Sensitive to the Conditions of Others, etc.—☿ afflicted in the 6th H. (See Brooding, Despondency, Environment, External, Hyperaesthesia, Hypochondria, Servants, Suicide, Worry, etc.).

Zodiac — Sensitive Degrees of — (See "Sensitive Degrees" under Zodiac).

SENSORIAL—Sensory—

Functions—Sensorial Functions—(See "Functions" under Sensation).

Sensory Nerves — (See "Sensory Nerves" under Sensation). See Senses, Sensibility, Sensitive.

SENSUALITY — Sensuous — Sensuous Mind—Sensuous Appetites—Sense Nature—The Passional Nature Predominant—The ☽ rules the sensual faculties. Also ♆, ♂, and ♀ when configurated together, or with ♆ or ♂ ☌, or afflicting ♀ and the ☽, licentiousness is increased. In a general way ♂ is king and ruler of the sense nature, and of the passions and emotions. See the following subjects in the alphabetical arrangement when only listed here—

Amorous; Amours — (See "Amours" under Love Affairs).

Animal Instincts—(See Animal).

Death — Early Death from Passional Excesses — (See "Dies Before Middle Life" under Middle Life).

Debauched; Depraved; Diseases — From Sensuality—♀ afflicted at B., and by dir. (See Venery; "Death" in this section).

Dissolute; Early Death—From Excessive Sensuality—(See "Death" in this section).

Emotions; Energies Wasted — Thru the Opposite Sex—(See "Injured" under Men; "Health Suffers" under Opposite Sex; "Unfortunate Pleasures" under Pleasure).

Enjoyments—Given to Sensuous Enjoyments—All Sensuous Enjoyments—Denoted by the 5th H.; ♆ afflicted in the 5th H.; ♂ ☌ ♀ in the 5th H. (See Energies, Sensuous, in this section; "Sensuous" under Pleasures).

Excesses—(See "Passional Excesses" under Passion).

Fits — Fits of Sensuality or Drink — (See "Fits" under Drink).

Gratification—Sensual Gratification— (See "Sensuous", and the various paragraphs in this section; Gratification).

Harlots; Highly Sensuous—♆ afflicted in ♌, the 5th H., or afflicting the ☽ or ♀. (See Lewd, Licentious, Nymphomania, Passion, Perversions, Sex, etc.).

Imaginations—(See "Sensuous" under Imagination).

Lascivious; Lewd; Liaisons — (See "Liaisons" under Love Affairs).

Licentiousness; Low Pleasures—Given To—(See "Low" under Pleasures).

Lust; Men—Sensuous Gratifications In —(See "Licentious", "Violent", under Men).

Opposite Sex—Wastes Vital Energies On—(See "Energies" in this section).

Passion — (See "Passional Excesses" under Passion).

Perversions; Pleasures — Given to Sensuous Pleasures — (See Amorous, Excesses, Passion; "Unfortunate" under Pleasure; Venery, etc.).

Profligate; Prostitutes—(See Harlots).

Puberty—Sensuous At Time of—(See "Imaginations" under Puberty).

Self-Indulgent; Sensualist—(See "Sensuous" in this section).

Sensuous—A Sensuous Mind—A Sensualist — Sensuous Gratification — Sex Addict—Sensuality—Sensual Appetites —A Passionate Nature—Voluptuous— Given to Sensuous Pleasures and Enjoyments, etc.—The ☽ to the ill-asps. ♀ by dir.; the ☽ Sig. in ♎; the ☽ in ♓, danger of a sensuous mind if afflicted by ♄ or ♀; ♆ afflicted in the 5th or 6th H.; ♆ afflicted in ♌, supersensual; ♆ afflicted in ♉ or ♏; ♆ ☌ or ill-asp. ♂, coarse and sensual; ♆ progressed to the ☌ or ill-asps. the radical ♀, or vice versa; ♓ ruler of the horoscope and afflicted; ♃ afflicted in ♌; ♃ in the Asc. in ♏, and afflicted; afflictions to ♃; ♂ ☌ or ill-asp. the ☽ or ♀; ♂ afflicted in ♎, voluptuous; ♂ □ or ☍ ♀; ♀ weak at B., and afflicted by ♄; ♀ in the Asc. and afflicted by ♄ or ♂; ♀ afflicted at B., weak, and ill-dignified; ♀ afflicted by the □ or ☍ ♆, ♓, ♄, ♂, and the ☽; ♀ □ or ☍ ☽); ♀ ruler of the horoscope and afflicted by malefics; ♀ afflicted at B., and to the ☌ or evil asp. the Asc. by dir., voluptuous; ☿ affl. in ♌; the transit of malefics thru the 5th H. if they afflict the 5th at B., and other indications show sensuality; the 1st decan. of ♏ on the Asc., ruled by ♂; the 4° ♋ on the Asc.; 22nd and 29° ♍ on the Asc.; the 3rd dec. of ♏ on the Asc., ruled by ♀; the 17° ♏ on the Asc.; ♓ on the Asc.; the 9° ♓ on the Asc., apt to die young thru passional excesses. (See Amorous, Licentious; "Passional Excesses" under Passion; the various paragraphs in this section).

Sex Addict—(See Amorous, Lewd, Licentious; "Unbridled" under Passion; "Sensuous" in this section).

Supersensual—♆ afflicted in ♌. (See Highly Sensuous, Sensuous, in this section).

Voluptuous—(See "Sensuous" in this section).

Wanton; Wench; Women—Sensuality In—(See "Sex Gratification" under Females; Nymphomania, Women).

SENTENCE OF LAW—Death By—(See Judges).

SENTIENT FACULTIES—The Faculties of Consciousness, Feeling, Knowing, Perception, Sensation, etc. — Ruled by the ☽, ☿, and the Asc. Also the ☉, his positions and aspects, are essential factors in our conscious life. (See Consciousness, Emotions, Faculties, Feeling, Feelings, Intellect, Knowledge, Learning, Mental, Mind, Perception, Sensation, Senses, Sensibility, Understanding, Volition, Will, etc.).

SENTIMENTS—Sentimental—(See Effeminate, Emotions, Feelings, Ideas, Motives, Notions, Philosophy, Principles, Purposes, Religion, Truth, etc.).

SEPARATION—Separations—Separateness—Separating—

Aspects — In health matters the aspects of planets when separating from the exact aspect are less evil, and indicate some relief and amelioration of the disease. (See Aspects).

Family—Separation In—(See "Separation of Parents" under Parents).

Parents — Separation of Parents — Separation from Parents—(See Adoption, Orphans, Parents).

Separateness—♄ influence. (See Loneliness, Recluse, Renunciation, Reserved, Retiring, Secretive, Solitude).

Sexes—Separation of—(See "Separation" under Sex).

SEPTIC—Septic Poisoning—Relating to Putrefaction—Septicaemia—

Blood Poisoning—Septicaemia—(See "Impure Blood" under Impure; "Blood Poisoning" under Poison).

Pyemia—Septicaemia with Abcess Formations—(See Pyemia).

Septic Fevers — Septic Poisoning — ♂ in ♏; ♂ in ♏ in the 6th H.; ♂ in ♏ and afflicting the ☽ or Asc. (See "Fevers" under Putrid).

Septicemia — (See "Blood Poisoning" under Poison).

Throat — Septic Poisoning In — (See "Septic" under Throat). See Abscesses, Festering, Infections, Odors, Poison, Pus, Putrid, Sloughings, Suppuration, Toxaemia.

SEPTUM—Nasal Septum—(See Nose).

SEQUENCE — Interrupted Sequence In Disease—Sequence of Progression In Disease—Planets ℞ tend to interrupted sequence in disease, and solution of continuity, just as planets direct, swift, and rapid in motion denote continuity and sequence of progression. (See Amelioration, Constancy, Continuity, Course, Direct, Duration, Interrupted, Moderation, Modification, Resolution, Retrograde, Solution, Stationary).

SERIOUS — Dangerous — Severe — Important—Serious-Minded—

Accidents — Serious Accidents — (See "Dangerous" under Accidents).

Constitutional Diseases—Serious Constitutional Disorders and Defects—(See "Constitutional Diseases" under Constitution).

Lives Thru Serious Illnesses — The fiery and airy signs, or with ♍ or ♏ upon the Asc. at B., and with the hyleg favorably aspected, the native will live thru serious illnesses which would prove fatal to those born under the weaker signs, as ♋ and ♓; born with strong signs upon the Asc., and especially the fiery signs ♈ or ♌; ♃ or ♀ in the Asc., in good aspect to the hyleg, and the lord of the Asc. well-placed and free from affliction. (See "Good" under Constitution, Recuperation, Resistance, Stamina, Strength, Tone, Vitality; "Body" under Strong).

Organic Diseases — Serious Organic, Constitutional, and Structural Diseases —(See Chronic, Congenital; "Constitutional Diseases" under Constitution; Consumptions, Hereditary; "Organic Diseases" under Organic; Structural, Tuberculosis, Wastings, etc.).

Serious Illnesses—Long and Tedious Diseases — Difficult to Cure — Apt to Prove Fatal — (See Chronic; "Arguments for Death", "Sure Death", under Death; "The Sick Will Hardly Escape" under Escape; Fatal; "High" under Fever; Fierce, Fulminating, Grievous; "Bad Health" under Health; "Heavy and Sad Sickness" under Heavy; Incurable, Invalids, Lingering, Long Diseases, Pernicious, Quick, Severe, Sharp, Slow Diseases, Swift Diseases, Tedious Diseases, Vehement, Violent Diseases, etc.).

Serious Mind—♄ strong at B.; ♄ ☌ ☿; the ☉, ☽, or ☿ in ♑ and afflicted by ♄; the 4th face of ♍ on the Asc., ♑ on the Asc. (See Dejected, Depressed, Despondency, Gloom, Grave, Hypochondria; "Low Spirits" under Low; Melancholy, Recluse, Regretful, Renunciation, Repining, Reserved, Responsibility, Retiring, Sad, Secretive, Solitude, Sorrowful, Taciturn, Thoughtful, etc.).

Suffering—Forebodes Serious Suffering—(See Grievous; "Painful Diseases" under Painful; Severe, Sharp, Violent Diseases, etc.).

SEROUS—Serous Membranes—(See Serum).

SERPENTS—Venomous Creatures—Obnoxious Creatures—Snakes—Death or Wounds from Bites of — (See Adder; "Journeys", "Venomous", under Bites; Obnoxious, Reptiles, Stings, Venomous).

Cruelty On Serpents—Prevalence of—An eclipse of the ☽ in the 3rd decan. of ♋.

SERUM—Serous—Serous Membranes—The Serum, the fluid constituent of the blood, is ruled principally by the ☽. The Serous Membranes, Surfaces, and Fluids are under the rule of the ☽. Also the Serum of the Blood is ruled by the ♋ sign. (See Blood). The Pericardium, Peritoneum, Pleura, Synovial Membranes, Tunica Vaginalis, etc., are classed as Serous Membranes. (See these subjects).

Serous Circulation—(See Circulation).

Serous Collections — Serous Effusions — In Various Parts of the Body — ☽ diseases, and afflictions to the ☽. Connected with the watery signs, and the ☽ afflicted in such signs, and especially in ♓. (See Blisters, Blood, Circulation, Cysts, Dropsy, Effusions, Fluids, Hydrocele, Hydrocephalus, Hydrothorax, Infiltration, Oedema, Osmosis, Peritoneum, Puffing, Synovial, Vesicles, Watery, etc.).

Serous Discharges — And Effusions — ☽ diseases, and afflictions to the ☽, and are especially characteristic of the Lymphatic Temperament.

Serous Diseases—☽ diseases, and afflictions to the ☽ at B., and by dir. The inherent disposition to serous diseases is characteristic of the Lymphatic Temperament. (See Lymphatic).

Serous Infiltrations — Infiltration of Serum—A ☽ disease. (See Dropsy, Osmosis).

Serous Stools — (See "Serous" under Faeces).

SERVANTS—Subordinates—Dependents —Ruled by ☿. Also the 6th H. is the house of Servants. Benefics in the 6th

H. at B. make the relations and dealings with servants pleasant and fortunate. The malefics in this house give servants are rebellious, insubordinate, and tend to bring misfortune to the master. (See Sixth House).

Hurts By—Danger of Being Killed by a Servant—Lord of the 8th H. a malefic, and afflicted by lord of the 6th or 12th, and especially if the hyleg, or lord of the Asc. are also afflicted.

Sickness Of — Disability or Sickness Among—The ☽ in the 6th H., or in ♋ to the lord of the 6th (Hor'y); ♄ ruler of the year at the Vernal E., in ♎, and ℞ planets in the 6th H., afflicted, or themselves afflicting the Significators, the ☉, ☽, Asc., or M.C.

Worries Thru Servants—Or Subordinates—Malefics in the 6th H. at B., or lord of the 6th a malefic, and with no favorable influences over the 6th H.; ☿ afflicted in the 6th H., and tending to mental stress and ill-health thru worries brought on by servants.

SERVILE — Dependent — Enslaved — ♃ Sig. ☌ the ☉; ♂ Sig. in ♋; ♂ Sig. ⚹ or △ the ☽; ♂ weak and ill-dignified at B. (See Dull, Energy (Lack of); Fears, Inactive, Indifferent, Indolent, Inertia, Labor (Fear of); Languid, Lassitude, Lazy, Lethargy, Limitations, Mean (Mean Creature); Resolution (Lack of); Servitude, Timidity; "Weak Will" under Will, etc.).

SERVITUDE — Bondage — Subjection — Limitations, etc.—Servitude is signified by ♄, the ♑ sign, and the 12th H. conditions. The ☽ decr. in light, sepr. from ♃, and applying to ♄; the ☉, ☽, or ♄ afflicted in the 12th H., and in a negative horoscope; lord of the Asc. in the 12th H., and afflicted; ♂ weak, afflicted, and ill-dignified at B. Uranus, ♂, and the ☉ are courageous, and never servile. (See Confinements, Fears, Limitations, Negative, Prison, Rule, Servile, Twelfth House).

SETTING PLANETS—Planets setting in the West are less powerful than when rising, as a rule. Planets setting in an occidental quarter show disease, but setting in an oriental quarter indicates accidents and injuries. The health is not as good when the ☉ and many planets are setting in the West, and also the nature is less forceful, and not as capable of leadership. Mercury setting also somewhat impairs the mind for hard study and school life, but tends to enhance the mind for success in commercial enterprises, and where the native learns in the school of experience rather than out of books. When the hyleg sets on the Western horizon, death usually results. (See Elevated, Majority, Occidental, Oriental, Rising).

SEVEN—Seven-Year Periods of Life—Seven Months Children—Life from the cradle to the grave is divided into periods of seven years, and certain and definite changes come into the life at every 7th year, as the 7th, 14th, 21st, 28th, 35th, etc. Every 7th year tends to be a more critical year, and especially in health and other matters, as every 7th year begins a new cycle in life. More deaths occur in these cycle years, as a rule, than during the years in between them in the life of the native. The cycle of ♅ is 84 years, and every seven years he changes signs of the Zodiac, thus tending to changes in the life of the native. Also every seven years the planet ♄ is at the quarter points in his journey thru his orbit from the place where he was at the birth of the native, and at these seven-year places he forms the ∠, □, ⚹, and ☍ aspects to his place in the radical map, and tends to bring on disease, worries, sorrows, anxieties, and to chasten the native who is not living right, and who may be living a life of sin and wickedness, until thru worry, disgrace, financial disaster, etc., he may weaken and go into some form of chronic disease, or even meet with death of the physical body. It is said also that the particles of the body are entirely changed and renewed once in every seven years. These 7th year places in life also correspond to the Quarters of the ☽, and are years of affliction, and correspond to the □ aspect and its divisions. The number 7 is said to be the number of Perfection, and is mentioned many times in the Bible, and in Occult Literature. There are the Seven Days of the Week, the Seven Planetary Angels, the Seven Churches in Asia, the Seven Spirits Before the Throne, etc. Read about the number "7" in the book, "The Key To the Universe" by Dr. and Mrs. Homer Curtiss. Also see the Seventh Card in the Tarot of the Bohemians. (See Cycles, Periods).

Seven Months Children—Born At the Seventh Month—(See "Seven Months Children" under Children).

SEVENTH HOUSE—Known as the Descendant, or Angle of the West. (See Descendant). This House is closely affiliated with the ♎ Sign, the 7th Sign of the Zodiac, and also with ♀, the ruler of this sign. It is known as the House of Marriage, Partnerships, Agreements, Disagreements, Contracts, Litigation, Public and Open Enemies, the Marriage Partner, Sweetheart, Fiance or Fiancee, the Husband in a female nativity, the Wife in a male horoscope. It denotes the Physician or Healer in health matters; gives the description, shape, and condition of the Sweetheart or Marriage Partner; indicates quarrels, contests, thieves, thefts, separations, divorce, losses thru business partners, the aggression of open and public enemies if afflicted by malefics. The Ingress of the ☉ into this house may be indicative of War, if War is threatened, and of Peace, if War is raging. This is a masculine house, and positive. The ☉ in this house is indicative of good health, but gives a good and honorable wife. Saturn in this house at B. tends to short life. Mars here, a bad wife and sickness.

Color—The Colors ruled by this house are Blue, Brown, Black, or Dark Black.

Diseases Ruled By—This house signifies all diseases in the Hams, Flanks, Bladder, Small Intestines, Members of Generation, the Kidneys, Lower Part of the Back, in the Reins, Haunches, Loins, Navel, Diseases of the Womb or Matrix; Diseases and afflictions in any parts of the body ruled by this house or the ♎ sign; diseases and afflictions of the Marriage Partner, or of Public Enemies, etc.

Seventh House Rules—Agreements; Back (Lower Part of); Bladder; Business Partners; Buttocks (the Haunches to the Buttocks); Colors (Blue, Brown, Black, and Dark Black); Contests; Contracts, Duels, Enemies (Open and Public); Flanks; Generation (Members of); Grandfather; Hams, Haunches (Down to the Buttocks); Healers; Husband; Kidneys; Law (the Law); Lawsuits; Litigation; Loins; Marriage; Marriage Partner; Matrix of the Womb; Navel; Paternal Love and Affection; Partners; Physician in the Case; Public Affairs and Public Enemies; Quarrels; Reins; Small Intestines; Sweethearts; Theft; Thieves; Veins; Wife; Womb, etc. (See Libra Sign).

SEVERE—Severity—Severely—

Accidents — (See "Dangerous" under Accidents).

Blows—(See "Severe" under Blows).

Bruises — (See "Death By" under Bruises).

Cuts—(See "Severe" under Cuts).

Disease—The Disease More Severe—Severe Illness — The Severity of the Disease—The severity and intensity of the disease depend upon the power of the aspecting bodies, aspect configurations, and other impressions of celestial influences. Intensity and severity are associated with the cardinal signs, while remission is related to the mutable signs. The motion of the ☽ indicates the duration and severity of the disease by the nature of the critical days which accompany every attack. The afflictions of the major planets cause the disease to be more severe and fulminating, while the minor planets tend to milder and slight disorders. (See Major). The following aspects and influences indicate severity of the disease—The SUN and ☽ afflicted by malefics at B., and the malefics elevated above them; the ☉ and ☽ cadent, and their dispositors unfortunate; the ☉ and ☽ with malefics, or in ☌ with them at the beginning of an illness, the sick will hardly escape; the ☉ and ☽ afflicting each other at B., or by dir., long and severe illness; the ☉ in fiery signs with males, but it is soon over; the ☉ causes death by slow and severe illnesses, and feverish disorders in females; the ☉ or ♄ in the 6th H., in ☌, □, or ☍ asp. to each other, heavy and serious illness; to be taken sick in a ☉ Hour, the disease tends to be severe (see "Hours" under Planets); the ☉ or ☽ to the ☌ or ill-asps. ♄ by dir.; the ☉ hyleg, and to the ☌ or ill-asp. ♄ by dir.; the ☉ to the ill-asps. the ☽ by dir., and the ☽ hyleg or afflicted at B., according to the sign the ☉ is in; the ☉ hyleg, and the ☉ to the ☌ or P. asp. ☿ by dir., and ☿ afflicted and unfortunate at B.; the MOON at decumbiture, or first taking sick, be under the beams of the ☉, or ☌ ♅, ♄, or ♂ if the party be old, or even her ☌ with ♃, ♀, or ☿, the disease is not without peril; if the ☽ is in a sign occupied by a malefic at B. at the beginning of an illness, is apt to prove severe and dangerous; the ☽ to the ♂ or P. dec. the ☉ at B. if the ☽ be hyleg, and the ☉ afflicted at B.; the ☽ to the ♂ or ill-asp. ♄ or ♂ by dir., or in their place at the beginning of an illness; the ☽ decr. in light, and apply. to the ♂, □, or ☍ ♄, very dangerous unless the disease is already leaving the patient; the ☽ in the Asc., ♂, □, or ☍ ♄, ♂, ♅, or ♆, severe, and with danger unless in mutual reception with the afflicting planet; URANUS ♂ ♄ in the 6th H., and afflicting the hyleg, heavy and prolonged illness; SATURN in the 6th H., and afflicted, or afflicting the hyleg, sad and heavy sickness; ♄ and ♂ between the 10th and 7th H. at B., or in the 7th, and afflicted, heavy and prolonged illness; MARS in the 6th H., and afflicting the ☉ or ☽; malefics in the 1st or 7th H., or near the cusps of other angles, and more severe if the Lights be angular; the fiery sign ♌ on the Asc., suffers severely when ill; earthy signs give long and severe illnesses; the Asc. to the ♂ or P. Dec. ☿ by dir. if ☿ be much afflicted at B. (See Acute, Angles, Cardinal, Consumptions, Course, Crises, Dangerous; "Arguments For" under Death; Destructive, Diathesis, Direct Motion, Directions, Escape, Fatal; "High" under Fever; Fierce, Force, Fulminating, Grievous, Heavy, Increase, Incurable, Intensity, Invalids, Killing, Malignant; "Moon" under Motion; Mortal; "Disease" under Nature; Painful, Pernicious, Prognosis, Quick, Rapid, Serious, Sharp, Sudden, Swift, Terrible, Vehement, Violent, Virulent, Wastings, Worse, etc.).

Disposition—The Disposition Severe, Stern, and Austere—The ☉ Sig. in ♐; ♄ in ♑ or ♒, austere; characteristic of ♄ people; ♄ ruler of the Asc. and horoscope, and afflicted; ♄ Sig. ⚹ or △ the ☉, austere in behavior; ♄ well-dignified in ♎, ♑, or ♒; ♂ influence is sudden, severe, and fulminating. (See Austere).

Epidemics—(See "Severe" under Epidemics).

Fevers — Severe Fevers — (See "High Fever" under Fever).

Fulminating—Sudden Severity of Disease—(See Fulminating).

Headaches—Severe Headaches—(See "Shooting Pains", "Violent", under Headaches).

Illnesses—Severe Illness—(See "Disease" in this section).

Injuries—Severe Injuries—(See Accidents, Cuts, Blows, in this section; "Serious" under Injuries).

Punishment — Severe Punishments — (See Punishment).

Sudden Severity of Disease — (See Fulminating).

Temper—Severe In Temper and Disposition — (See Anger, Cruel, Fierce, Merciless, Pity; "High Temper" under Temper; "Tendency To" under Violence; "Disposition" in this section).

Women—Fevers, Severe and Painful Diseases To — (See "Females" under Fever).

SEX—Sex Organs—Sex Diseases—Sexual — Sex Deformities — Sex Desires—Sex Functions — Sex Relations — Sex Powers — Sex Perversions — Sex Passions—Sexual Instincts—Sex Abuses—Sexual Deportment—Sex Excesses, etc. —The subject of Sex is also considered under the subjects of Generative Organs, Genitals, Genito-Urinary, Privates, Reproduction, and Secrets. The Sex Organs are ruled principally by the Scorpio Sign. The Hebrew Letter "Nun", or "N", is connected with the ♏ sign, the sign which rules the Sex Organs and Nature. The following subjects have to do with Sex, the Sex Nature, Sex Diseases, the Uses of Sex, the Sex Organs, etc., which subjects see in the alphabetical arrangement when only listed here—

Abandoned Persons—(See Profligate).

Abnormalities—(See Abnormal, Apathy, Aversions, Celibacy, Deformities, Desire, Deviations, Genitals; "Anchorite" under Husband; Passages, Passion, Perversions, Unnatural, etc.).

Abortion; Abuses Of — (See Amorous, Excesses; "Passional Excesses" under Passion; Perversions, Venery, Vices).

Addicts—Sex Addicts—(See Amorous, Excesses; "Sex Addict" under Marriage Partner; "Licentious" under Men; Nymphomania, "Passional Excesses" under Passion; Perversions, etc.).

Adolescence—Disorders At Time of—(See Puberty).

Adulterous—(See Love Affairs).

Affections—Disorders of—(See Affections).

Amorous; Amours — (See Love Affairs).

Anaphrodisiacs; Animal Propensities —(See Animal).

Apathy; Aphrodisiacs; Appetites — (See "Sexual Appetites" under Appetites).

Ardent—(See Love Affairs).

Aversions; Bachelors; Barrenness; Bashful; Bisexual—(See Hermaphrodites).

Bohemian Pleasures—(See Pleasure).

Bubo; Cancer of Sex Organs — (See "Generative Organs" under Carcinoma).

Cases of Sex Disorders—See "Sexual", No. 285 in 1001 N.N.; Fig. 34 in the book, "Message of the Stars" by the Heindels; Figures 8A, 8B, 8C, 8D, 8F, 8G, 8H, 8I, 8J, in the book, "Astro-Diagnosis" by the Heindels. Also see Cases under Nymphomania.

Castration—(See Testes).

Celibacy; Chancre—(See Syphilis).

Chancroid—(See Gonorrhoea).

Channels and Vents—(See "Channels" under Genitals).

Chaotic Sex Relations — (See "Adultery", "Liaisons", under Love Affairs; "Clandestine", "Relations", in this section).

Chaste — (See "Chaste" under Females).

Childbirth—(See Parturition).

Children; Clandestine Relations—Love Intrigues—Fornication—Unlawful Intercourse — Adultery — Promiscuity —

The ☉ to the ♂ ♀ by dir. if ♀ be weak and afflicted at B.; the ☽ in any aspect to ♅; the ☽ afflicted in the 12th H.; the ☽ to the ♂ or ill-asps. ♀ or ♅ by dir.; ♆ or ♅ □ or ☍ ♀; ♆ afflicted in ♎, or in the 7th or 12th H.; ♅ afflicted in ♌ or ♎; the strong afflictions of ♅ tend to, and to perversion of the generative function; ♅ to the ill-asps. ♀ by dir.; ♅ afflicted in the 5th or 7th H.; ♅ ♂ or P. the ☽; ♂ afflicted in ♓; ♀ in the 7th H. in ♏ or ♑, and afflicted; in a male horoscope ♀ in a masculine sign, and ♂ in a feminine sign; ♀ ♂ ♄ or ♂ in ♏. (See "Free Love" under Free; Harlots, Lewd, Licentious; "Adultery", "Amours", "Liaisons", under Love Affairs; Lust; "Loose Morals" under Morals; Obscene, Perversions, Scandalous, Shameless, Venery, etc.).

Cohabitation—Little or No Desire For —Excessive Cohabitation—(See Cohabitation, Intercourse; "Married Women", "Single Persons", in this section).

Conception; Confinement— (See Parturition, Puerperal).

Conscious — Sex-Conscious — (See Amative; "Erotic" under Mania; Nymphomania; "Solitary" under Vice; "Sex-Conscious" in this section).

Control—Good Control Over the Passions and Sex Nature—Little Control Over — (See "Command", "Unbridled", under Passion).

Conventions—Disregard of Sex Conventions—Unconventional—♆ afflicted in ♎; ♅ afflicted in ♌ or ♎, or in the 5th or 7th H.; the ☽ ♂ ♂ in ♏; ♀ afflicted in ♒. (See "Free Love" under Free; "Liaisons" under Love Affairs; "Clandestine" in this section).

Creative Force — The Sex Force — Is ruled over by the Anterior Lobe of the Pituitary Body, ruled by ♅. (See Creative, Pituitary).

Criminal Intercourse — (See Intercourse; "Adultery" under Love Affairs; Rape; "Clandestine" in this section).

Death—From Sex Disorders and Dissipations — (See "Causes His Own Death" under Death; "Brings Disease Upon Himself" under Disease; "His Own Worst Enemy" under Enemies; "Death" under Generative, Syphilis, Womb, etc.).

Debauched; Deformities—Sex Deformities—(See "Channels" under Genitals; Hermaphrodites; "Deformity" under Womb).

Degeneracy; Deportment — Sex Deportment—(See the various paragraphs in this Article).

Depraved; Depressant—A Sex Depressant—(See Anaphrodisiacs).

Desires—Sex Desires—(See Amorous, Desire, Love Affairs, Passion, Perversions, Venery; the various paragraphs in this section).

Development Of — Sex Organs Not Fully Developed—(See "Undeveloped" in this section).

Deviations; Diseases—Sex Diseases— Are caused principally by afflictions in ♏, which sign rules the Sex Organs and Genitals. Uranus, said to be exalted in ♏, tends to produce Venereal Diseases, Sex Disorders, and deep-seated when in ♏ at B., or afflicting that sign. Also caused by many planets, a Stellium, in ♏, or the 8th H. Diseases from inordinate lust and sex excesses are caused by ♀. Comets appearing in ♏ tend to a prevalence of sex diseases. (See Excesses, Generation, Genitals, Genito-Urinary; "Health Injured" under Men; Opposite Sex, Passion, Private, Scandalous, Venereal, etc.; "Cases" in this section).

Early Death—From Sex Excesses and Venery — (See Early; "Dies Before Middle Life" under Middle Life).

Emissions—(See Semen).

Emotions; Enjoyments—Given to Sex Enjoyments—(See Amorous, Excesses, Harlots, Licentiousness, Love Affairs, Lust, Passion, Venery, etc.).

Entanglements — (See "Free Love" under Free; Love Affairs; "Clandestine" in this section).

Erections—Painful—(See Penis).

Erotic Mania—(See Mania).

Erratic—In Sex Life—(See Amorous, Free Love, Love Affairs, Passion, Venery; "Clandestine", and the various paragraphs in this section).

Eunuchs; Excesses — (See "Sex Excesses" under Excesses; Passion; the various paragraphs in this section).

Exhibitionism; Expression — Sex Expression—(See "Freedom" in this section).

Fallopian Tubes—(See Fallopian).

Fecundation; Feelings—Sex Feelings —(See Control, Regulated, Restraint, and the various paragraphs in this section).

Females — Female Sex Organs — Sex Gratification In — (See "Sex Gratification" under Females; Ovaries, Vagina, Womb, etc.).

Foetus; Force—Sex Force—(See "Creative" in this section).

Fornication — (See "Clandestine" in this section).

Free from Passion—(See "Free From" under Passion).

Free Love—(See Free).

Freedom of Sex Expression—♂ ♂ or ill-asp. ♀, or ♀ in a ♂ sign. (See Amorous; "Free Love" under Free; "Unwomanly Freedom" under Morals; "Passional Excesses" under Passion).

Fruitful; Generation — Organs and Members of—(See Generative).

Generative Function—Abuse of—(See "Clandestine" in this section; Perversions; "Passional Excesses" under Passion).

Genitals; Genito-Urinary System;

Gestation; Glands—(See "Sex Glands" under Glands).

Gonorrhoea; Gratification;

Great Command — Of the Passions — (See "Control" in this section).

Habits—Sex Habits—(See Amorous; "Licentious" under Men; "Unbridled", "Violence", under Passion; Perversions, Sadism; "Solitary" under Vice; the various paragraphs in this section).

Harlots; Hermaphrodites;

Highly Sexed—♂ in the 5th H. in any aspect to ♀. (See "Strong" under Passion).

Homosexuality; Husband; Hydrocele;

Illegitimate Sex Relations—(See "Free Love" under Free; "Adultery", "Liaisons", under Love Affairs; "Clandestine" in this section).

Illicit Amours — (See "Amours", "Adultery", "Liaisons", under Love Affairs; "Clandestine" in this section).

Immodest; Immorality — (See "Loose Morals" under Morals).

Impotent; Impurity—In Sex Relations —(See Illegitimate, Illicit, Immorality, in this section).

Incest—(See Perversions).

Indecent; Indiscretions — (See "Sex Life" under Indiscretions).

Indulgences; Infamous;

Inflamed with Passion — (See "Inflamed With" under Passion).

Intemperate — (See "Sex Life" under Intemperance).

Intercourse; Lack of Passion — (See "Free From" under Passion).

Larynx — The Larynx As Related to the Sex Force—(See Larynx).

Lascivious; Leucorrhoea; Lewd;

Liaisons—(See Love Affairs).

Libidinous—(See Lewd).

Licentiousness; Life Force—(See Life).

Little Sex Desire—(See Apathy, Celibacy, Indifferent; "Free From" under Passion).

Loose Morals—(See Morals).

Loss of Sex Desire—(See "Little Sex Desire" in this section).

Love Affairs; Love Passion—(See this subject under Love Affairs).

Low and Base — Low Women — Fond of Low Company—Low Public Houses —(See Harlots, Low).

Lower Passions—Carried Away By— (See "Lower Passions" under Passion; Venery, etc.).

Lues—(See Syphilis).

Lust; Male Sex Organs — (See "Sex" under Male; Penis, Scrotum, Testes).

Mania—Sex Mania—(See "Erotic" under Mania; "Licentious" under Men; Nymphomania).

Marriage; Marriage Partner;

Married Women—Cohabits With—The ☽ ☌, □, or 8 ♅. (See "Adultery" under Love Affairs; "Single Persons" in this section).

Masochism; Masturbation—(See "Solitary" under Vice).

Maternity; Men — (See Genitals, Licentious, Sex, under Men).

Menses; Middle Life — (See "Early Death" in this section).

Mind—The Mind Absorbed with Passion—(See "Mind" under Passion).

Miscarriages; Mixture of Sex — (See Hermaphrodite, Virile).

Modesty; Monsters; Morals — (See "Loose" under Morals).

Morbid Sex Desires — (See "Desires" under Morbid).

Mother—Motherhood—(See Maternity, Mother, Parturition).

Nakedness — Wandering In — (See "Outrageous" under Insanity).

Necrophilia—Sexual Congress with a Dead Body—(See Necrophilism).

Neurotic—A Sexual Neurotic—Case— See "Sexual Neurotic", No. 285, in 1001 N.N.

Notoriety — Of the Passions — (See Notoriety).

Nymphomania; Obscene; Obsessions— Sexual Obsessions—(See "Erotic" under Mania; Nymphomania, Perversions).

Obstructions — In the Sex Organs — (See "Obstructions" under Generative).

Offspring—(See Children).

Opposite Sex; Outbursts—Of Passion —(See Outbursts, Storms, under Passion).

Outrages Nature's Laws — (See "Nature's Laws" under Nature; Obscene, Perversions, Shameless).

Ovaries; Over-Indulgence—Of the Sex Passion—(See Amorous, Excesses, Indulgence, Licentiousness; "Passional Excesses" under Passion; Venery).

Ovum; Pain — In Sex Organs — (See "Pain" under Generative, Genitals, Penis, Secrets).

Parturition; Passion — (See "Free From", "Passional Excesses", and the various paragraphs under Passion).

Penis; Perverse; Perversions;

Pleasures—Sex Pleasures—(See Amorous, Lewd, Licentious, Passion, Sensuality; the various paragraphs in this section).

Powers—The Sex Powers—(See Control, Creative, Highly Sexed, Strong, Weak, and the various paragraphs in this section; Barrenness, Fruitfulness, Generative, Impotent, Reproduction).

Predetermination—Of the Sex Before Birth — (See "First-Born Child" under Children; Predetermination).

Pregnancy; Prenatal Epoch;

Prevalent—Sex Diseases Prevalent— (See "Diseases" in this section).

Privates — Private Diseases — (See Privates, Venereal).

Profligate; Promiscuity—(See "Clandestine" in this section).

Prostitutes—(See Harlots).

Prudery; Puberty—Sex Activity At— (See Puberty).

Puerperal; Rape; Regeneration;

Regulated — The sex feeling is regulated, moderated, and better controlled by the good aspects of ♄ or ♃ to the ☽ and ♀. (See "Control" in this section).

Relations — The Sex Relations — Legitimate — Illegitimate — Controlled — Uncontrolled, etc. — (See the various paragraphs in this section).

Reproduction; Restraint — Unnatural Sex Restraint — Lack of Restraint — (See "Passional Excesses", "Restraint", under Passion).

Sadism; Salacious—(See Lust).

Same Sex — Unnatural Sex Relations With—(See Homosexuality).

Scandalous Diseases; Scheming—Underhanded In Measures to Gratify Passion—(See "Scheming" under Passion).

Scorpio Sign—The Sex Sign—Diseases Ruled By—(See Scorpio).

Scrotum; Secret Vices — (See Secret, Solitary, under Vices).

Secrets (Secret Parts); **Seduction; Self-Abuse**—(See "Solitary" under Vice).

Semen — Seminal Vesicles — (See Semen).

Senility—(See Old Age).

Sensuality; Separation of the Sexes— The First Two Races of Mankind are said to have been Bisexual, or Androgynous, Hermaphroditic, but during the Third, or Lemurian Race, the sexes were separated into two bodies, male and female, and Adam and Eve are considered the first types of the separated sexes. The separation of the sexes was not sudden, but took place gradually over a long period of time. It is said that the ♍ and ♏ signs were separated at the time of the separation of the sexes, and the ♎ sign inserted between them. This subject is considered, and its history given, in the books, "Cosmo-Conception", by the Heindels; in the "Key of Destiny", by Dr. and Mrs. Homer Curtiss. Also see the subject of "Scales" in Sepharial's New Dictionary of Astrology.

Sex Addicts—(See "Addicts" in this section).

Sex Appetites — (See "Sexual" under Appetites).

Sex Channels — (See "Channels" under Genitals).

Sex-Conscious — ♂ in the 5th H. in aspect to ♀, and especially if ♀ is in ♏ or ♑. (See "Conscious" in this section).

Sex Desires — (See "Desires" in this section).

Sex Excesses—(See "Excesses" in this section).

Sex Expression—(See "Freedom" in this section).

Sex Feelings—(See "Feelings" in this section).

Sex Force—(See "Creative Force" in this section).

Sex Gratification—(See Gratification, Indulgent, Love Affairs, Marriage, Passion, Self-Indulgent, Venery; the various paragraphs in this section).

Sex Indiscretions — (See "Sex Life" under Indiscretions; the various paragraphs in this section).

Sex Organs — (See Generative, Genitals, Ovaries, Penis, Privates, Reproduction, Secrets, Testes, Vagina, Womb; the various paragraphs in this section).

Sex Passion—(See Amorous, Love Affairs, Passion; the various paragraphs in this section).

Sex Perversions—(See Perversions).

Sex Powers—(See Apathy, Aversions, Imbecile, Impotent, Passion; "Powers" in this section).

Sex Relations — (See Adultery, Clandestine, Illegitimate, Illicit, Intemperate, Relations, Trouble, Unfaithful, and the various paragraphs in this section; Husband, Love Affairs, Marriage, Marriage Partner, Men, Passion, Venery, Wife, Women, etc.).

Shameless; Single Persons—Cohabits With—♅ ☌, ▢, or ☍ ♀. (See "Married Women" in this section).

Social Relations—(See Social).

Society—Aversions To—(See Celibacy, Recluse, Renunciation, Reserved, Retiring, Secretive, Solitude).

Sodomy—(See Homesexuality).

Solitary Vice — (See "Solitary" under Vice).

Spermatic Cord—(See Spermatic).

Spermatozoon—(See Semen).

Spinsters; Sterility—(See Barren).

Stimulated—The Sex Feelings Stimulated—(See Aphrodisiacs).

Storms—Sudden Storms of Passion— (See "Outbursts" in this section).

Strangury—(See Urine).

Strengthened—The Passional Nature Strengthened — (See "Strong" under Passion).

Stricture — Of the Urethra — (See Stricture, Urethra).

Strong Passions — (See "Strong" under Passion).

Strong Sex Powers — (See Fruitful; Highly Sexed, Powers, in this section).

Sudden Storms — Of Passion — (See "Outbursts" in this section).

Syphilis; Testes; Trouble—Thru Sex Relations—♆ or ♅ ▢ or ☍ ♀. (See "Adultery", "Liaisons", under Love Affairs; "Health Injured" under Men; Opposite Sex; "Clandestine" in this section).

Unbridled Passion — Uncontrolled— (See Nymphomania; "Unbridled" under Passion).

Unconventional—In Sex Relations— (See "Free Love" under Free; "Amours", "Liaisons", under Love Affairs; Clandestine, Conventions, Illicit, in this section).

Undersized — The Sex Organs Undersized and Undeveloped—(See "Sex Organs" under Undersized, Undeveloped).

Undeveloped Sex Organs—(See Undersized, Undevloped).

Unfaithful—In Sex Relations—♆ afflicted in ♎; ♅ afflicted in ♌ or ♎. (See Adulterous, Clandestine, Conventions, Illegitimate, Illicit, Sex Relations, in this section).

Unnatural Desires—Unnatural Restraint Over the Sex Nature—Unnatural Sex Desires — (See Chaotic, Depraved, Desires; "Restraint" under Passion; Perversions, Unnatural).

Unwise Entanglements — (See "Entanglements" in this section).

Urethra; Uterus—(See Womb).

Vagina; Varicocele; Varicose;

Vehement Passion — (See Outbursts, Storms, Unbridled, Violence, under Passion; Vehement, Venery).

Venereal Diseases; Venery;

Vents and Channels—(See "Channels" under Genitals).

Vices — Sex Vices — (See Lewd, Obscene, Perversions, Shameless; "Solitary" under Vice).

Violence—(See "Violence" under Passion).

Virile Members—(See Virile).

Virtue — Virtuous — Not Virtuous — (See "Chaste" under Females; Modesty, Nymphomania; "Unbridled" under Passion; "Unchaste" under Women).

Vital Fluid—(See "Fluid" under Vital; "Creative Force" in this section).

Vitality—Depletion of Thru Sex Excesses — (See "Health Injured" under Men; Opposite Sex; "Lessened", "Wasted", under Vitality).

Voice—The Voice and the Sex Force —(See Larynx, Puberty).

Voluptuous; Vulva; Wanton;

Wastes Energies—On Opposite Sex— (See Amorous, Harlots; "Health Injured" under Men; Opposite Sex; "Passional Excesses" under Passion; "Wasted" under Vitality).

Weak Sex Powers — ♄ afflicted in ♏ usually tends to an earlier breakdown sexually, and especially if the native has been given over to sexual excesses. (See Impotent; "Senility" under Old Age).

Wench; Wife; Womb; Women—(See "Women" under Passion; "Sex Gratification" under Women).

SEXTILE ASPECT—The 60 degree aspect (✳). This aspect is based upon the trine (△) aspect and is very fortunate in health, and other matters. (See Aspects).

SHAGGY—Bushy—(See "Bushy" under Eyebrows, Hair).

SHAKING — (See Chill, Concussion, Palsy, Paralysis, Spasmodic, Tremors).

SHALLOW—Not Deep—
Shallow Breathing — (See "Shallow" under Breath).
Shallow Mind — Shallow Intellect — (See "Shallow" under Intellect, Mentality, Mind; "Bad" under Judgment; "Void Of" under Learning; Pretender).

SHAME—Shameless—
Sense of Shame—And Bashfulness— ♄ strong and well-dignified tends to give a sense of shame and bashfulness; ♄ to the ☌ ☋. (See Bashful, Blushing, Modesty, Reserved, Shy).

Shameless Practices — Shameless and Immodest Sex Practices—

(1) **In Men**—♂ in a female sign, and ♀ in a masculine sign, and ♄ configurated with them, makes men more prone to violence, unnatural desires, impurity, and obsenity. Mercury adds to their lusts and gives a greater variety of contrivances to give vent to lasciviousness and shameless practices. Jupiter taking part in the configuration tends to moderate the desires and make either sex more circumspect, and less vicious or open in their practices. The ☽ sepr. from ♀ and applying to ☿, and the ☽ decreasing, tends to shameless viciousness. (See "Licentious" under Men; Obscene; "Violence" under Passion; Perversions, etc.).

(2) **In Females**—The ☽ afflicted in ♏; ♀ ☌ ♂ in ♏; ♀ Sig. ☐ or ☍ ♂, and often becomes a harlot. (See Harlots, Immodest, Nymphomania, Virile).

Sickness from Shame—Or Disgrace— Lord of the 6th H. in the 10th. (See

Disgrace, Downfall; "Ruined by Women" under Love Affairs; Reputation, Reverses, Ruin, Scandal). See Debased, Depraved; "Sex Organs" under Exhibition; Infamous, Lascivious, Lewd, Licentiousness; "Loose Morals" under Morals; "Notoriety of the Passions" under Passion; Profligate, Wanton, Wench.

SHANKS—Shin Bone—(See Tibia).

SHAPE OF THE BODY — For the description of the form, shape, and appearance of the various parts of the body, see in the alphabetical arrangement the part, or organ, you have in mind. Thus see such subjects as Abdomen, Arms, Cheeks, Chest, Chin, Ears, Extremities, Eyes, Face, Feet, Forehead, Hands, Head, Hips, Jaws, Knees, Legs, Limbs, Lips, Mouth, Nails, Neck, Nose, Shoulders, Thighs, etc. Also under the following subjects you will find lists of the descriptions of the form and shape of the body—

Appearance, Beautiful, Body, Coarse, Comely, Compact, Corpulent, Decanates, Deformities, Diminished, Dwarfed, Elegant, Enlarged, Fat, Features, Figure, Fleshy, Form, Frame, Freaks, Full, Good, Handsome, Height, Ill-Formed, Large, Lean, Long, Malformations, Mean, Medium, Members, Middle, Misshaped, Missing, Monsters, Oval, Posture, Rough, Round, Short, Size, Skeleton, Slender, Small, Smooth, Square, Stature, Stooping, Stout, Tall, Thick, Thin, Ugly, Weight, Well-Formed, Well-Proportioned, Wide, etc. Nearly all the adjectives describing the form and shape of the body are listed in the alphabetical arrangement of this book, and with the planetary influences causing them. Look for the subject you have in mind.

SHARP—

Diseases—Sharp Diseases—Sharp, Sudden, Violent, and Short Attacks of Sicknesses—Caused by ♂. (See Acute, Dangerous; "High" under Fever; Fierce; Fulminating, Painful, Pernicious, Poignant, Quick, Rapid, Sudden, Swift, Vehement, Violent, etc.).

Eyes — Sharp Eyes — Sharp Sight — Quick Sight — (See "Sharp" under Eyes).

Face—Sharp Face—Sharp Features— (See "Sharp" under Face).

Features — Sharp Features — (See "Sharp" under Face).

Fevers—(See "Sharp" under Fever).

Instruments — Sharp Instruments — Cuts and Injury By—(See Cuts, Instruments).

Look—Sharp Look—(See Look).

Males — Sharp Illnesses for Males — (See "Sharp Illnesses" under Males).

Mind — A Sharp, Active, and Acute Mind—(See "Active Mind" under Active; "Good" under Intellect; "Quickened" under Mentality; "Sharpened" under Mind; "Good" under Understanding).

Nose—(See "Sharp" under Nose).

Pains—Sharp Pains—Denoted by ♂, and are ♂ diseases and afflictions. (See "Sharp" under Pains; Poignant).

Sicknesses — Short and Sharp Sicknesses—(See "Diseases" in this section).

Sight — Sharp Sight — Sharp Eyes — (See "Eyes" in this section).

Violent—And Sharp Affections—(See "Diseases" in this section).

SHEATHS — The Nerve Sheaths — (See "Sheaths" under Nerves).

Synovial Sheaths—(See Synovial).

SHEDDING—Sheds—

Shedding of Blood—Bloodshed—Loss of Blood—♂ is the planet of Bloodshed, and of War. Injuries with the loss of blood are caused by ♂, while ♄ rules hurts and injuries without loss of blood. Compound injuries, with possible fracture and loss of blood, are caused by the combined influences of ♄ and ♂ in the configuration. (See Assassins; "Loss Of", "Shedding", under Blood; Criminals, Cuts, Duels, Effusions; "Patricide" under Father; Feuds, Gunshot, Hemorrhage, Homicide, Hurts, Incised, Injuries, Instruments, Menses; "Depopulation" under Mortality; Murder; "Epistaxis" under Nose; Rigel, Slaughter, Stabs, Suicide, Sword, War, Weapons, Wounds, etc.).

Sheds Tears Easily—(See Tears).

SHEEP—Rams—Lambs—Ruled by the ♈ Sign, the sign of "The Ram". (See Aries). Also ruled by the 6th H., the house of Small Animals.

Diseases Among — Many Will Die — Afflictions or eclipses in ♈ at a Solar Ingress; Comets appearing in ♈. (See "Small Animals" under Animals; "Small Cattle" under Cattle; Goats).

Epidemics Among—Sheep and Cattle Will Die—The ☽ in the 6th H. at the Vernal E., lady of the year, and afflicted; ♄ Lord of the Year at the Vernal, and afflicted by ♂; ♂ in ♉, ♎, ♌, or ♐, direct in motion, ori., Lord of the Year, and afflicted, many cattle, oxen, and sheep die. Many eclipses occurring in the same year tend to the death of many small animals, small cattle, sheep, goats, etc., and especially if they occur in four-footed signs, and in the territory afflicted by the eclipse. (See "Small" under Animals, Cattle; Comets, Eclipses, Epidemics, Horses, Oxen; "Virus" under Pestilence; Pets, Swine, Virus; "Cold" under Weather).

SHELLAC—A Resinous Substance ruled by ♅. (See Resins).

SHIFTING — Of the Disease — (See "Shifting" under Complications).

SHIN BONE—Shins—(See Tibia).

SHINGLES — Herpes Zoster — (See "Herpes Zoster" under Herpes).

SHINY—Shining—Glossy—

Shiny Face—(See "Shiny" under Face).

Shining Hair — (See "Glossy" under Hair).

Shiny Skin—Oily Skin—♃ gives. (See "Oily" under Face; Glossy, Oils).

SHIPS — Shipping — Shipwreck — Maritime Affairs—Navigation, etc.—The ☽ in general rules Ships, Shipping, the Ocean and Seas. Also these matters are influenced by ♆, the ♓ sign, and 9th H., the house of Foreign Travel and Long Journeys. The following subjects have to do with Ships, Shipping, Ocean Voyages, etc., and the dangers or benefits which may attend them.

Abroad — Journeys Abroad — (See Abroad).

Accidents On Ships — Or To Ships — (See Fire, Foundering, and the various paragraphs in this section). Case—An Accident On Trial Trip—See "Launching", No. 852, in 1001 N.N.

Best Time to Sail—When ♃ or ♀ are in the Asc., the M.C., 2nd or 9th H., and no malefics in the angles. (See "Good Time" under Journeys, Voyages; "Fortunate" under Travel).

Burning of Ship—(See "Ships" under Fire).

Collide — Ships Collide — Case — 300 drowned. See "Launching", No. 711, in 1001 N.N.

Crew Sickly — Sickness On Board — Lord of the Asc., or the ☽ combust, or if they be in the 6th or 12th H., and in evil aspect their lords, denotes sickness, or great calamity (Hor'y); if the Asc. and ☽ be fortunate, and lord of the Asc. unfortunate, the ship is safe, but the crew sickly (Hor'y). See Death, Sickness, in this section).

Death On Ship — Danger of — (See "Long Journeys" under Journeys; "Death At Sea" under Sea; Shipwreck; "Death" under Voyages, Water).

Drowning At Sea — (See Drowning). Case — Fell Overboard and Was Drowned—See "Died In Harness", No. 802, in 1001 N.N.

Explosion On Ship—(See "Ships" under Explosions).

Fell from Ship—And Was Drowned— (See "Drowning" in this section).

Fire On Ship — (See "Ships" under Fire).

Foreign Travel — (See Abroad, Foreign; "Long Journeys" under Journeys; Travel, Voyages).

Foundering — Danger of Running Aground — Malefics in the 9th H., afflicting the ☉ or ☽ at time of sailing, or during the voyage, and especially if the configurations are in earthy signs. (See Shipwreck).

Hurricanes At Sea—(See "Fountains" under Dry; "Voyages" under Lightning; Shipwreck; "Storms" under Travel).

Launching of Ships — Good Time For —The ☽ in ♓ and free from affliction. The ☽ should not be afflicted by malefics. (See "Best Time to Sail" in this section). Cases of Launchings — See "Launching", No. 711, and No. 852, in 1001 N.N.

Lightning — Ships At Sea Injured or Burned By—♂ in a fiery sign on cusp the 10th H., and near violent fixed stars. (See "Sea", "Voyages", under Lightning).

Long Journeys — (See "Long" under Journeys; Maritime, Navigation, Travel, Voyages).

Lost — The Ship Is Probably Lost — Lord of the Asc. or the ☽ combust (Hor'y); lord of the 8th in the 1st H., or lord of the 1st in the 8th in evil asp. with its lord; or lord of the 1st in the 4th H. in evil asp. with its lord, or with lord of the 8th if the aspect be separating, and if the lords of the 4th are malefics the danger is more imminent (Hor'y). (See "Sunk", in this section; Shipwreck).

Maritime Affairs — (See Maritime, Navigation, Ocean, Sailors, Sea, Voyages; "Shipping" in this section).

Murder On Ship — Danger of — ♂ afflicted in ♏, ♐, or ♒ denotes in Hor'y Questions.

Navigation—(See Navigation).

Navy—The Army and Navy—Attains Considerable Rank In—The ☉ Sig. ♂ ♂; ♂ Sig. ♂ ♃ or ☿, or ⚹ or △ the ☉. (See Army, Sailors, War).

Officer — Death of a Principal Officer of Ship—Lord of the Asc. only in the 8th H., or in evil asp. with its lord (Hor'y).

Runs Aground—(See "Foundering" in this section).

Sailing Time — (See "Best Time" in this section).

Sailors — Seamen — (See Maritime, Sailors).

Sea—(See the paragraphs under Sea).

Shipping—Successful In—♃ Sig. ♂ ☽. (See Maritime).

Shipwreck—(See Shipwreck).

Sickness On Ship—(See Crew, Death, in this section).

Submersion of Ship — (See Burning, Lightning, Sunk, in this section; Shipwreck).

Successful—In Maritime Affairs—(See Maritime; "Shipping" in this section).

Sunk—The Ship Has Sunk—Lord of the Asc. under the Earth, and in the 4th H. (Hor'y).

Travel — (See the paragraphs under Travel).

Trial Trip—Accident On—Case—See "Launching", No. 852, in 1001 N.N.

Voyages—(See the paragraphs under Voyages).

Waters—(See Danger, Death, Fortunate, Perils, and the various paragraphs under Water).

"One ship sails East, and another sails West
With the selfsame winds that blow,
'Tis the set of the sail,
And not the gale,
Which determines the way they go.

"Like the winds of the Sea are the ways of Fate,
As we voyage along through life,
'Tis the act of the Soul
That determines the goal,
And not the calm or the strife."

SHIPWRECK—Calamities At Sea—

Danger of Shipwreck—The following influences may exist in the chart of birth of the individual; have reference to the time of launching or sailing, and also exist at the time of the calamity. The following influences tend to cause shipwreck, or involve the native in such a misfortune. Good influences in the 9th H. at B., such as ♃ or ♀, or both benefics in this house,

and in ♂, even though there may also be malefics in this house at B., usually save the native from death of injury, or bring about his escape and rescue. The general influences causing shipwreck are — The SUN afflicted at B., and the ☉ by dir. in evil asp. the Asc.; the ☉ hyleg, and to the ♂, P., □ or ☍ ♄ by dir.; the ☉ to the cusp the 9th H., and if any of the malefics afflict this house at B., and by dir.; the ☉ to the ♂ or ill-asp. ♄ by dir. in water signs; the ☉ near Argo; the ☉ joined with the Ascelli, Castor, Pollux, Hyades, Pleiades, or Praesepe, and danger of death by; an eclipse of the ☉ or ☽ in ♓, the sign which rules the Ocean; an eclipse of the ☉ or ☽ in ♑, shipwreck and submersion of ships, and especially in places ruled by ♑; the MOON in ♋, ♏, or ♓ in the 3rd or 9th H., and afflicted by malefics; the ☽ to the □ or ☍ ♂ by dir.; the ☽ afflicted at B., and to the evil asp. the Asc. by dir.; NEPTUNE in tr. over the radical ♂, or ♆ ♂ ♂ at a Solar Rev.; ♆ in ♓ in the 9th H., and afflicted by malefics; URANUS or ♄ in ♋, ♍, ♏, or ♓, and afflicting the ☽, and if ♅ or ♄ be near Argo; ♅, ♄, or ♂ afflicted in the 9th H.; SATURN ascending at B., and the ☉ to the ♂ or ill-asp. ♄ by dir.; ♄ near Argo, and afflicting the ☽ hyleg; ♄ in ♋ at B., and afflicted by ♂ at the Vernal E., and ♄ Lord of the Year; ♄ afflicted in the 10th H.; ♄ afflicting the Asc. and the ☽; ♄ sole ruler at an eclipse of the ☉; ♄ Lord of the Year at the Vernal, and occi., destruction of ships and loss of life of sailors; ♄ ascending in ♓ at departure; ♄ in the Asc. when the ship leaves port, or a fiery sign on the Asc., which usually places a watery sign on the 8th H.; ♄ and ♂ in watery signs, controlling the Lights, and when ♄ and ♂ are distant from each other, and not active in concert; ♄ in water signs, or in ♍, configurated with the ☽, and near Argo; ♄ angular at B., and holding dominion, and elevated above the Lights; JUPITER in ♏ and afflicted or ℞, and lord of the year at the Vernal; MARS sole ruler at an eclipse of the ☉; ♂ in power and lord of the year at the Equinoxes or Solstices; ♂ in ♋ and lord of the year at the Vernal; ♂ in the Asc. when the ship sails, and also danger of fire on ship; ♂ in the 9th H. in a water sign, and afflicted; planets in ♋, ♏, or ♓, and afflicting the ☽, or afflicting the Sigs. of travel; lord of the ASC. in the 9th H., and afflicted; malefics in the 9th H. in water signs, afflicted, or afflicting the ☉ or ☽; the Asc. to the □ or ☍ the ☉ by dir.; malefics in the M.C., elevated above the Luminaries, and ♄ holding dominion; lord of the 12th H. in the 9th; the 11° ♋ on the Asc.; common signs show. (See "Long Journeys" under Journeys; Maritime, Navigation, Ocean, Sea, Ships; "Danger" under Travel; Voyages, Waters; the various paragraphs in this section).

Death At Sea—Death In Shipwreck—The ☽ in the 9th H. at the Vernal, lady of the year, and afflicted; ♆ in the 8th H., and afflicting the hyleg by dir.; ♅ in the 8th H., and afflicting the hyleg by dir., and other testimonies concurring; ♅ or ♄ in ♋, ♍, ♏, or ♓, and afflicting the ☽, and if ♅ or ♄ be near Argo; planets in ♋, ♏, or ♓, and afflicting the ☽ and hyleg. (See "Fountains" under Dry; "Death" under Sea, Ships, Voyages, Waters).

Distortions — From Injury In Shipwreck—(See Distortions).

Drowning At Sea — By Shipwreck — (See Drowning; "Death" in this section).

Explosion — Shipwreck By — (See "Ships" under Explosion).

Fire At Sea—(See "Ships" under Fire).

Foundering — (See "Foundering" under Ships).

Hurricanes — Shipwreck By—(See "Hurricanes" under Ships).

Injury — In Shipwreck — (See Distortions).

Lightning — Shipwreck By — (See "Ships" under Fire; "Lightning" under Ships).

Long Journeys — Ocean Voyages — Danger of Shipwreck On—(See "Danger" in this section; "Long" under Journeys; "Danger" under Voyages).

Maritime—Much Loss of Life Among Maritime People by Shipwreck — (See Maritime, Navigation, Ocean, Sailors, Sea, Ships; "Danger" under Travel, Voyages, Water).

Misfortunes At Sea — (See "Misfortunes" under Sea).

Navigation—Danger In—(See Navigation).

Ocean—Much Danger On—(See Ocean, Sea, Ships, Voyages).

Paralysis—From Injury In Shipwreck —(See Distortions).

Prevalent—Shipwrecks Prevalent—♄ lord of the year at the Vernal, and occi.; ♃ in ♍, and afflicted or ℞, and lord of the year at the Vernal; ♂ in ♋ and lord of the year at the Vernal; ☿ in ♋ and afflicted by ♂ at the Vernal, and ☿ lord of the year; ☿ in ♓ at the Vernal, afflicted, and lord of the year or Quarter; ☿ in an angle at an Equinox or Solstice; an eclipse of the ☉ or ☽ in ♓.

Runs Aground — (See "Foundering" under Ships).

Sailors—Seamen—Loss of Life Among by Shipwreck—(See "Maritime" in this section).

Sea — Troubles by Sea — (See Ocean; "Troubles" under Sea; Ships, Voyages; the various paragraphs in this section).

Ships — Loss of by Shipwreck — (See Ships; the various paragraphs in this section).

Storms At Sea—Shipwreck By—(See Hurricanes, Lightning, in this section).

Travel — Danger In Ocean Travel — (See "Danger" under Travel; the various paragraphs in this section).

Troubles by Sea—(See "Sea" in this section).

Voyages—Danger In—(See "Danger" under Voyages; the various paragraphs in this section).

Water — Accidents and Dangers On the Water—(See the paragraphs under Ocean, Voyages, Water, and in this section).

Wind Storms — Danger of Shipwreck By — (See "Hurricanes" under Ships; "Storms" under Wind).

SHOCK — Shocks — Shocks from any cause are usually due to ♅ influence and affliction. (See Ether). Uranus afflicted in ♌ tends to make shocks very harmful to the system due to disturbance of the heart action, circulation, and nerves. Saturn in ♌ tends to make sudden shocks harmful. Mars tends to shock by cuts, hurts, and injuries.

Brain Disorders—From Shock—(See "Shocks" under Brain).

Childbirth—Nervous Shock In—(See "Nervous Shock" under Parturition).

Died from Shock — Due to Fire and Loss of Family—Case—See "Leland", No. 813 in 1001 N.N.

Electricity—Shocks By—Death By—Caused by ♅; ♅ ☌ or ill-asp. the ☉; ♅ afflicted by ♂; the Asc. afflicted by ♅. (See Electricity, Lightning).

Fright—Shocks By—(See Fright).

Lightning — Shock By — (See Lightning).

Nervous Shock — (See "Shock and Strain" under Nerves; "Childbirth" in this section).

Violent Shocks—The work of ♂ or ♅, or their combined influences. Death or serious injury may result from shocks according to the degree and power of the shock, and the planetary influences operating at the time. (See Accidents, Blows, Bruises, Concussion, Employment, Exaggerated Action, Explosions, Extraordinary, Falls, Hurts, Injuries, Lightning, Machinery, Railroads, Sudden, Uranus, etc.).

SHOOTING—

Fond of Shooting—Fond of Hunting, Riding, Robust Sports, etc.—♂ Sig. in ♌. (See Hunting, Sports).

Shooting Pains — Darting Pains — Sharp Pains—Flying Pains, etc.—Denoted by ♂; ☿ afflicted in ♒; common signs on the cusp of 6th H.; sharp, shooting pains generally. (See Acute, Fierce, Flying, Gnawing, Headaches, Pain, Poignant; "Shooting Pains" under Ribs; Sharp, Violent; "Pains" under Whole Body).

SHORT—Shortened—Shortening—

Arms—(See "Short" under Arms).

Ascension—Signs of Short Ascension —♑, ♒, ♓, ♈, ♉, ♊.

Body — Short Body — The ☽ in ♉ in partile asp. the Asc., rather short and well-set; ♄ in ♏, partile the Asc.; ♄ in ♑, partile the Asc., rather short than otherwise; ♄ in S. Lat. makes the body shorter; ♄ occi., a shorter body than when oriental; born under ♃, and ♃ occi., the body is somewhat shorter; ♂ in ♉, partile the Asc., rather short, compact, well-set, corpulent, but rather ugly; born under ♂, short, strong, and well-set; ♀ or ☿ in their signs of fall or detriment causes shortness; ♀ Sig. in Hor'y Q., rather short than tall; ♉,

♋, ♏, ♑, or ♓ on the Asc.; ♉ on the Asc., short and well-set; ♏ on the Asc., short, strong, corpulent, able body; ♓ on the Asc., short or medium, and usually crooked and stooped. (See Diminished, Dwarfed, Low, Mean, Medium, Middle, Small, Squab, Stature).

Breath—(See "Short" under Breath).

Chest—(See "Short and Wide" under Chest).

Chin—(See "Short" under Chin).

Coarse—Coarse, Short, and Hairy Body —♏ on the Asc. (See Coarse; "Body" under Hairy).

Compact—Short, Corpulent, and Compact—♂ in ♉, partile the Asc. (See Compact, Corpulent).

Corpulent — Corpulent, Short, and Compact—(See "Compact" in this section).

Crooked — Short, Crooked, and Ill-Made—(See Crooked).

Diseases—Short Diseases—(See "Illnesses" in this section).

Face—Short, Small, and Round Face —(See "Short" under Face).

Fat—Short, Mean, Fat, Plump Stature —(See "Body" under Fat).

Father—Short Life For—(See "Short Life" under Father).

Feet—(See "Short and Fleshy" under Feet).

Fleshy — Short and Fleshy — (See "Fleshy Body" under Fleshy).

Full and Short — (See "Body" under Full).

Hair—(See "Short and Thick" under Hair).

Hairy Body — Short, Coarse, Hairy Body—(See "Body" under Hair).

Hands—(See "Short" under Hands).

Ill-Formed — Ill-Formed, Lean and Short—(See "Ill-Formed Body" under Ill).

Illnesses — Short Diseases and Illnesses—Signs of a Short Disease—The Disease Is of Short Duration — The Disease Terminates Quickly — Brief Diseases — Short and Sudden — Quick Diseases — The Disease Is Curtailed — The Disease Will Remove Shortly — Will the Disease Be Short?, etc.—Diseases beginning in the Summer are usually shorter than those beginning in Winter. The ☉, ♃, and ♂ cause short diseases. Hot and Dry diseases brought on by the ☉ and ♂ are usually short, and regulated by the motion of the ☽. Long and chronic diseases brought on by ♄ are regulated by the motion of the ☉. (See Chronic; "Diseases" under Long). The predomination of diseases is usually attended with a fever, and acute in nature, and many of the influences which tend to cause short illnesses are considered in the Articles on Acute Diseases, Fevers, Fierce, Fulminating, Rapid, Swift, etc. The following are general influences which tend to cause Short Diseases— The ☉, ♃, and ♂ cause short diseases, but ♂ is the most acute of all; the ☽ in a fiery sign, or a fire sign on the Asc. or 6th H. at decumbiture; the ☽ ☌ an oriental planet which is direct and swift in motion; the ☽ swift in motion and aspecting the lord of the Asc.;

the ☽ applying to the ☌, P, ⚹ or △ a benefic at decumb.; the ☽ in a common sign, and a common sign on the cusp of 6th H.; the ☽ or cusp of the 6th H. in a moveable sign, the disease terminates quickly either in recovery or death; the ☽ in a movable sign; in sickness when the ☽ applies to a planet contrary to the nature of the disease, and especially if it be a benefic, the disease will soon be changed for the better; ♆ in the 8th H. at B. tends to short illnesses, and of a watery nature; ♄ lord of the Asc., strong and well-qualified, not ℞, and fast in motion; ♂ ☌, □, or ☍ the ☉, short but sharp attacks of sickness; ♂ afflictions tend to death after a short or sudden illness; planets oriental signify short attacks of sickness; afflictions from cardinal signs, the disease is more acute, transient, and more quickly broken; malefics in ori. quarters, the illness will be acute, short, and painful; afflictions from common signs are more amenable to treatment; a benefic in the 6th H., judge that the disease will be short; the last degrees of a sign on the cusp of 6th H., the disease is almost at an end; lord of the Asc. swift in motion, and going out of his own sign or house into another, except into the sign of the 6th or 12th H.; lord of the Asc. or 6th, or the ☽, be in ☌, ⚹, or △ a benefic, or with the lord of the 10th, or the last degree of a sign be on the cusp the 6th H., the disease is not of long duration; a movable sign, or ♓, on the cusp the 6th H.; lord of the 6th a benefic in the 6th; lord of the Asc. stronger than lord of the 6th; a malefic leaving the 6th, the disease will remove shortly, and in so many days, weeks, or months, according to the nature of the sign; lord of the 6th H. cadent; lords of the 1st and 6th H., and the cusp of the 6th and the ☽ in movable signs. (For further influences along this line see Acute, Cardinal, Course, Crises, Curtailed; "Arguments For" under Death; Duration, Fatal; "High" under Fever; Fierce, Fulminating, Grievous, Mars Diseases, Mild, Painful Diseases, Pernicious, Quick Diseases, Rapid Diseases; "Rapid" under Recovery, Recuperation; "Good" under Resistance; Severe Diseases, Sharp Diseases, Slight, Sudden Diseases, Swift, Termination, Transient, Vehement, Violent Diseases, etc.).

Journeys — (See "Short" under Journeys).

Lean—Lean, Short, and Ill-Formed— (See "Ill-Formed" under Ill).

Legs—(See "Short" under Legs).

Life—Short Life—Early Death—(See "Short Life" under Life).

Long or Short Diseases—Will the Disease Be Long or Short?—Indicated by the 6th H. conditions at B., and at decumbiture. Diseases beginning in Summer are shorter than those which start in the Winter. (See "Illnesses" in this section).

Low—Low, Short and Squat Stature —(See "Low Stature" under Low).

Lower Parts—Short and Small—(See "Parts" under Lower).

Mean, Short Stature — (See "Short Stature" under Mean).

Medium Stature—(See Medium).

Members—(See "Brevity" under Members).

Middle-Sized—Short, Thick, and Strong Body — (See "Middle Stature" under Middle).

Mother — (See "Short Life" under Mother).

Neck—(See "Short" under Neck).

Nose—(See "Short" under Nose).

Pale—Sickly, Pale, Short, and Fleshy —♓ on the Asc. (See Pale).

Plump — Short, Mean, Plump, Fat Stature—(See Plump).

Rather Short Body — (See "Body" in this section).

Short Body — Short Stature — (See "Body" in this section).

Shortened—The Disease Is Shortened — (See Curtailed; "Illnesses" in this section).

Sickly—Sickly, Pale, and Short—(See "Pale" in this section).

Sight—Short-Sighted—(See "Myopia" under Sight).

Slender — Short and Slender — (See Slender).

Squab—Short, Squab Figure—☿ in ♋ in partile asp. the Asc., short, squab stature. (See "Low Stature" under Low; "Parts" under Lower; Plump, Squab, Squatty).

Squat—Short, Low, and Squat Body— (See "Low Stature" under Low; Squab, Squat).

Stature—Short Stature—(See "Body" in this section; Fat; "Low Stature" under Low; Mean, Plump, Squab, Squatty).

Strong — Short, Strong, Middle-Sized, Thick Body—♉ on the Asc. (See "Middle Stature" under Middle).

Temper — A Short Temper — (See "Short" under Temper).

Thick — Thick, Short Body — (See "Fleshy Body" under Fleshy; "Middle Stature" under Middle; Thick).

Well-Set and Short — Born under ♂. (See Well-Set).

SHOTGUN WOUNDS—Shot To Death— Injury by Gunshot — Danger by Fire Arms—(See Gunshot).

SHOULDERS — Shoulder Joint — The Arms and Shoulders are ruled by ☿, ♈, and the 3rd H.. The Shoulders are under the external rulership of ♊. The Scapula, or Shoulder Blade, is under the internal rulership of the ♊ Sign. The hinder part of the Shoulders is ruled by the 5th H. Many of the influences mentioned in this Article also apply to the Arms. (See Arms).

Accidents — All Accidents and Hurts To—♊ signifies; ♂ afflicted in ♊. (See "Accidents" under Arms).

Affected—According to Table 196 in Simmonite's Arcana, the shoulders are affected when the ☉ is in ♎; the ☽ in ♊, ♌, ♍; ♄ in ♓; ♃ in ♉; ♂ in ♑; ♀ in ♋ or ♐.

All Diseases In—Signified by the 3rd H. All diseases in the hinder part of the shoulders are signified by the 5th H.

Arms — (See the various paragraphs under Arms).

Auriga's Right Shoulder — (See Auriga).

Bent Forward—(See Stooping).

Broad Shoulders—Strong Shoulders— Thick and Powerful Shoulders — ♈ gives; ♈ on the Asc., thick, broad, and powerful; ♉ gives, and with ♉ on the Asc.; ♌ on the Asc., broad and well-set, and powerful; ♏ on the Asc.; ♄ ascending at B.; ♄ in ♌ or ♏ in Hor'y Q.; ♄ in ♏ in partile asp. the Asc.; ♄ in ♌, partile the Asc., broad, round shoulders; ♃ in the Asc.; ♂ Sig. of the person in Hor'y Q.; characteristic of ♂ people; ☿ Sig. in ♏. (See "Large" in this section).

Clavicle—(See the paragraphs under Clavicle).

Cramp In—♅ in ♊. (See Cramps).

Crooked Shoulders—♄ ascending at B. (See Crooked).

Cuts To—(See "Arms" under Cuts).

Diseases In — (See "All Diseases In", "Diseases Of", under Arms; "All Diseases In", and the various paragraphs in this section).

Dislocation — ♄ afflicted in ♊. (See Dislocations).

Eruptions On—♂ afflicted in ♊ in the 6th H. (See Eruptions).

Gout In — (See "Shoulders" under Gout).

Granulations — In Shoulder Joint—♄ afflicted in ♊ or ♐. (See Granulations; "Hardening" under Joints; Synovial).

Hardening—In Shoulder Joint—(See "Hardening" under Joints; "Granulations" in this section).

Hinder Part — Of the Shoulders — All Diseases In—Signified by the 5th H.

Hurts To — (See "Accidents" in this section).

Infirmities In—(See "Diseases In" in this section).

Joint—Shoulder Joint—(See Dislocation, Gout, Granulations, Pain, in this section).

Lameness In—♄ afflicted in ♊ or the 3rd H. (See Gout, Rheumatism, in this section).

Large Shoulders — Large and Uncomely — ♉ on the Asc. gives large shoulders; ♊ gives large and uncomely shoulders if ♄ or ♃ also be setting. (See "Broad" in this section).

Marks On—Moles On—Malefics in ♊ or the 3rd H. (See Marks, Moles).

Muscles Of — Disorders In — (See "Muscles" under Arms; Pains, Rheumatic, in this section).

Nerve Pains In—☿ afflicted in ♊. (See "Pains" under Arms; "Nerves", "Pains", under Hands).

Orion—Shoulders of—(See Orion).

Pains In—☉ ☌ ♂ in ♊; ♄ or ♂ in ♊; ☿ afflicted in ♊, nerve pains in. (See Gout, Granulations, Joint, Lameness, Nerve Pains, Rheumatic, Stiffness, in this section).

Rheumatic Pains In—(See "Rheumatism" under Arms).

Round Shoulders — ♓ influence tends to unless the ☉ be rising; ♓ on the Asc.; 1st face of ♉ on the Asc.; in Hor'y Q. ♄ Sig. in ♌, broad and round. (See "Downward Look" under Look; Stooping; "Stoop" in this section).

Running Pains—(See "Running" under Arms; "Flying Pains" under Flying).

Scapula—Fracture of—♂ afflicted in ♉.

Scars On—(See "Marks" in this section).

Stiffness In—Stiffness and Pain—♄ or ♂ afflicted in ♉.

Stoop Shoulders — Stooping Body — ♄ ascending at B., and afflicted, the head and shoulders stooping; ♄ Sig. in ♌ Hor'y); the * or △ aspects to the ☉ tend to round shoulders and stooping; the 2nd face of ♉ on the Asc.; ♓ influence tends to a stooping gait, and to hold the head downward when walking; ♓ on the Asc., round and stooped, with crooked body, head bent forward, the shoulders thick and round, and with an ill figure. (See "Round" in this section).

Strong Shoulders — (See "Broad" in this section).

Thick Shoulders — Thick and Powerful—Broad—♈ on the Asc., thick and powerful; ♓ on the Asc., thick and round. (See Broad, Round, in this section).

Uncomely — Large and Uncomely — (See Broad, Large, Round, Stoop, in this section).

Warts On—(See "Arms" under Warts).

Weakness In—The ☽ afflicted in ♉ or ♍. (See "Weakness" under Arms).

Well-Set — (See "Broad" in this section).

SHREWDNESS—Shrewd—Sagacious—Artful—Cunning—Sly, etc.—Are strong characteristics of the ♋ sign, and ☿, and often used for all purposes when ♋ and ☿ are sorely afflicted by malefics at B., and by dir.; the ☽ Sig. in ♉, crafty and subtle to excess; the ☽ Sig. □ or ☍ ☿, a low cunning, and often applied to debauched purposes; ♄ Sig. □ or ☍ ♀ or ☿; ♄ Sig. ☌ ☿, subtle and crafty; ♂ Sig. ☌, □, or ☍ ♄; ♂ Sig. in ♑; ♂ Sig. in ♓, sly and artful if in terms of ☿; ♂ Sig. * or △ ☿, crafty; ♀ Sig. ☌, □, or ☍ ♄; ☿ Sig. in ♉, cunning; ☿ Sig. in ♈; ♂ Sig. ☌ ♄, calculating and covetous; ☿ in the 12th H., active in schemes, plots, and intrigues; ☿ Sig. □ or ☍ ♄; ☿ or ♂ afflicted in ♉. (See Cheating, Deceitful, Dishonest, Gambling, Pettifogging, Plots, Schemes, Thieves, Treachery, etc.).

SHRINKAGE — Shrinking—Due to the atonic action of ♄. Also caused by ♆.

Arms—♆ or ♄ in signs which rule the Arms, Hands, and Legs tends to shrinking and withering of these parts. (See Withering).

Brain—(See "Shrinkage" under Brain).

Limbs—Withering and Shrinkage of —(See "Arms" in this section; "Arms" under Limbs).

Organs or Tissues — Shrinkage of — ♄ influences and afflictions, and with ♄ in the sign or house ruling such

parts. (See Atrophy, Contractions, Diminished, Emaciation, Hardening, Old Age, Remote, Removal, Undersized, Undeveloped, Wasting, Withering, Wrinkles, etc.).

SHUFFLING GAIT—(See Gait, Walk).

SHY—Bashful—A ♄ influence; ♄ in the 1st H. at B. (See Bashfulness).

SIALAGOG—(See Pellitory, Saliva).

SICCATION—Drying Up—Lack of Moisture—(See Xeransis).

SICK—The Sick—

Care and Cure Of — Success In — ♃ well-aspected by the ☽; ♃ well-aspected in ♓; lord of the employment in ♍, and well-aspected; the 6th face of ♋ culminating on the M.C. (See the various paragraphs under Healers).

Escape—The Sick Will Hardly Escape —(See "Sick" under Escape).

Headaches — (See "Sick Headache" under Headache).

Improved—The Sick Improved—(See Amelioration; "Better" under Disease; Moderation, Recovery, Recuperation).

Industries — Success In Industries Connected with the Sick — ♂ well-aspected in ♍. (See "Health Foods" under Food; "Specialties" under Healers; Hospitals, Hygiene, Sanitation).

Sick Bed — Confined In — (See "Sick Bed" under Confinement).

Sickly—(See Invalids, Sickly).

Sickness—(See Disease, Sickness).

State of the Sick — The nature and state of the planet from which the ☽ is separating at decumbiture shows the cause and nature of the disease, and the state of the sick. (See Acute, Chronic, Curable, Grievous; "Heavy and Sad Sickness" under Heavy; Incurable, Long Diseases, Quality, Recovery, Relapse, Resolution, Short Diseases, Worse, etc.).

Worse — The Sick Become Worse — (See Worse).

SICKLY — Sickly Looking—Pale—Debilitated and Wan Look—An Unhealthy Aspect — Sickly Persons — Vitality Low, etc.—

Body—Sickly Body—(See "Constitution" in this section).

Brothers Sickly—(See "Health Poor" under Brothers).

Children — (See "Sickly" under Children).

Complexion — (See "Sickly" under Complexion).

Constitution — Sickly Constitution — Sickly Body—Weak Body—Low Vitality—Debilitated Look—Ill-Health All Thru Life — The Quadrant from the Autumnal Equinox to the Winter Solstice, tends to produce weak and sickly persons; the ☉ or ☽ in the Autumnal Signs ♎, ♏, or ♐, or with these signs upon the Asc., the constitution is inclined to be weak and sickly; the ☉ or ☽ □ or ☍ ♄ at B., and by dir.; the ☉ or ☽ Sig. to the ☌ or ill-asps. ♄ by dir.; the ☉ Sig. □ or ☍ ♄ and ♄ in the Asc.; the ☉ afflicted by ♄ in a male horoscope; the ☉ ☌ ♄ in the 1st H. in ♋ or ♑ with males; the ☉ afflicted in the 6th H.; the ☉ Sig. in ♋, an un-healthy aspect; the ☉ Sig. in ♑; the ☽ Sig. ♂ ☉; the ☽ combust, applying to the ♂ ☉, sickly and short-lived; the ☽ Sig. □ or 𝄖 ☉, and especially if the ☽ be sepr. from the 𝄖; the ☽ Sig. □ or 𝄖 ♄ at B.; the ☽ carried to, or con-joined with the ☉ at B. in any part of the horoscope; the ☽ decr. in light, sepr. from ♄ and applying to ☿; ☽ sepr. from ♃ and applying to ♂ in a nocturnal nativity, and the ☽ incr. in light; ☽ decreasing, separating from ♂, and apply. to ♃; the ☽ afflicted in ♋; the ☽ or ☉ ♂ ♄ or ♂ in the 8th H., and the hyleg afflicted by malefics; ♄ in the 10th H., and afflicting the hy-leg; ♄ Sig. ♂ ☉ or ☽ at B.; ♄ Sig. in ♋; ♄ in ♋, partile asp. the Asc., thin, pale face; ♄ in an angle, occi. of the ☉ and ori. of the ☽; ♃ Sig. in ♋ or ♑; ♃ in ♑, partile Asc., weak, small and sickly; ♀ Sig. to the ♂ ☉ and the ☉ ill-dignified at B.; born under ♀ in-fluence the constitution is usually not strong, and the habits of living tend to ill-health and short life; ♀ Sig. in ♋ or ♑; ♀ Sig. ♂ ☉, too sickly to make much exertion; ♀ in ♑ in partile the Asc., pale, sickly, and thin visage; ☿ Sig. in ♑, sickly and feeble due to worry and melancholy; ☿ in ♑ or ♓ in partile asp. the Asc.; ♋ on the Asc., and the ☽ in her fall; ♋, ♎, ♐, ♑, or ♓ on the Asc.; a ♓ disease, as ♓ is classed as a sickly sign; lord of the 1st H. applying to the ♂, □, or 𝄖 a malefic (Hor'y); lords of the 1st and 6th being in each other's houses, or afflicting each other, or if lord of the 1st be disposed of by lord of the 6th, or be in □ or 𝄖 ♄ or ♂, or be combust in the 6th, 7th, or 12th houses; malefics elevated above, and in evil asp. to the ruling planet. (See Anaemia; "Poor Blood" under Blood; Consumptions, Debility, Delicate; "Early Death" un-der Early; Emaciated, Feeble, Fragile, Frail; "Bad Health" under Health; "Ill-Favored Body" under Ill; "Ill-Health All Thru Life" under Ill-Health; "Short Life" under Life; "Mal-nutrition" under Nutrition; Pale; "Low" under Recuperation, Resistance, Vitality; "Red Blood" under Red; "Much Sickness" under Sickness; Un-healthy, Wastings; "Weak Body" un-der Weak; "Complexion" under White).

Face — Sickly Looking Face — (See "Sickly" under Face; Pale; "Complex-ion" under White).

Father—(See "Sickly" under Father).

Females Sickly — (See "Ill-Health", "Short Life", under Females).

Fleshy and Sickly Looking—♓ on the Asc. at B. (See Fleshy, Pale).

Males Sickly—(See "Bad Health For" under Males).

Men Sickly—(See "Ill-Health" under Men).

Mother—(See "Sickly" under Mother).

Pale and Sickly — (See Complexion, Constitution, in this section; Pale).

Relatives—(See "Sickly" under Rela-tives).

Secret Enemy Sickly — (See "Secret Enemies" under Enemies).

Short, Pale, and Sickly — ♓ on the Asc. at B. (See "Pale" under Short).

Sickly But Recovers — (See "Reared with Difficulty" under Children; "Sickly But Recovers" under Infancy).

Sister Sickly—(See Sister).

Summer—Sickly Summer—(See Sum-mer).

Thin, Pale, and Sickly — ♀ in ♑ in partile asp. the Asc. (See "Thin Face" under Face; Pale, Thin).

Visage — Sickly Visage — (See "Face" in this section).

Women Sickly—(See "Ill-Health" un-der Women).

Youth — Sickly In Youth — (See "Sickly" under Youth).

SICKNESS — Illness — Maladies — Ill-Health — Disease — Bodily Disorders, etc.—Sickness and health are largely determined by the conditions of the 4th, 6th, 8th and 12th houses and the planets therein at B., and the aspects to the ☉, ☽, Asc., M.C., and hyleg. The 6th H. and its lord signify the sick-ness, its nature, and the part, or parts of the body afflicted. Sickness, or ac-cidents, usually come, or begin, when the ☉ or ☽ are transiting the place of the radical ♄ or ♂, or when ♄ or ♂ are on the places of the radical ☉, ☽, Asc., or in □ or 𝄖 to them by transit, or when a malefic is transiting the 6th H., and at these times more care and caution are necessary, and especially if the hyleg was afflicted at the pre-vious New or Full ☽. A Total Eclipse of the ☉ falling on the place of the ☉ at B. is indicative of sickness. (See the paragraphs under Acute, Chronic, Disease, Distempers, Health, Ill-Health, Infirmities, etc.). The following sub-jects have to do with sickness, which see in the alphabetical arrangement when not considered here—

Abroad—(See "Sickness Abroad" un-der Abroad).

Absent Party—(See "Sick" under Ab-sent Party).

Ailments; Amelioration; Animals — (See "Sickness Of" under Animals).

Appetites — Sickness from Over-In-dulgence of — (See "Sickness" under Eating; "Disease" under Excesses; In-dulgences; "Health Injured" under Men; "Passional Excesses" under Pas-sion, etc.).

Arouse — Difficult to Arouse from Sickness — Many planets in common signs, or such signs on the angles at B. (See Rouse).

Begins—Sickness Begins When, etc.— (See the Introduction to this Article; "Time of the Disease" under Disease).

Better—(See "Better" under Disease).

Blood — Sickness from Corrupt Blood —(See "Sickness" under Impure).

Body—The Body Alone Is Afflicted— (See "Afflicted" under Body).

Causes of Sickness — (See "Causes" under Disease).

Changes — Changes To Another Dis-ease—(See "Changes" under Disease).

Children — Sickness of — Sickness Caused By — (See Parents, Sickness, Unhealthy, Worries, under Children).

Chronic Sickness — (See Chronic, Incurable, Invalids, Lingering Diseases, Long Diseases, Prolonged, Slow, Tedious, etc.).

Colds—Sickness From—(See Colds).

Complications; Continued Sickness — (See Chronic, Consumptions, Continuity, Course, Duration; "Low Fevers" under Fever; Incurable, Invalids, Long Diseases, Permanent, Tedious, Wastings, etc.).

Course of the Disease—(See Course).

Crises; Curable; Danger of Sickness — Liable To — Sickness Threatened — Weak Body—Vitality Low—The ☉ to the mundane ☌ ♄ may cause great sickness, and especially with males; the ☉ to the ☌ ♄ by dir. in the Zodiac, or mundane; the ☉ to the ☌, □, or ☍ the ☽ by dir.; the ☉ joined with Antares, Aldebaran, Bellatrix, Caput Algol, Hercules, Regulus, South Scale, or any eminent star of the nature of ♂, extreme sickness; the ☉ directed to stars in the Lion, Goat's Back, the South Scale, Knee and Right Leg of Ophiucus, Left Shoulder and Right Arm of Aquaries causes sickness; the ☉ ☌ the Asc. by dir.; malefics elevated above the ☉ or ☽ (see Elevated); the ☽ to the □ or ☍ ☉ in Zodiac or mundane; the ☽ weak and afflicted at B., and ☌ the Asc. by dir.; the ☽ to the □ or ☍ ♂ by dir., all kinds of sickness; the ☽ to the ☌ the ☉ or Asc. by dir.; the ☽ to the place of Hercules; the ☽ to the □ or ☍ the ☉, ♄, or ♂ by dir.; the Lights joined to the Whale's Jaw; ♄ ☌ ♃ at B.; ♄ ☌ the Asc. by dir.; ♄ afflicted in the 6th H.; ♃ Sig. ☌ the ☉, and ♃ combust, is an evil familiarity and denotes sickness; ♂ and ☿ both ℞ are a mark of sickness, says Placidus; ♂ afflicted in the 7th H.; denoted by the 6th H.; lord of the 5th in the 6th, thru worries by children; lord of the 6th in the 2nd, sickness thru financial losses and waste of property; lord of the 6th by transit over the cusp the Asc.; the Pleiades rising, or with the ☉ or ☽, or directed to the Asc.; Pleiades, Hyades, Praesepe, Castor, Pollux, or The Ascelli directed to the Asc. or Lights; Antares, Aldebaran, Regulus, Frons Scorpio, Deneb, and the Shoulders of Orion, when directed to the ☉, ☽, or Asc., tend to sickness, trouble, and danger of violence; the Asc. to the □ or ☍ the ☉ or ♄ by dir. (See "Danger", "Liable To", "Threatened", under Disease; "Liable To" under Ill-Health; "Much Sickness" in this section).

Dangerous Sickness—(See Dangerous; "Arguments for Death" under Death; Fatal; "High Fever" under Fever; Grievous, Pernicious, Severe, Vehement, Violent, etc.).

Death—Death Averted—Illness Ends In Death — (See Averted; "Certain Death" under Death; Fatal).

Debility — (See "Sickness" under Debility).

Delirium; Disease—(See the various paragraphs under Disease).

Disgrace—Sickness From—(See Disgrace).

Disordered System—(See Disordered; "Disordered" under System).

Distempers; Distressful Sicknesses—(See Distress).

Duration; Eating — (See "Sickness" under Eating).

Elevated Planets—And Sickness—(See Elevated).

Endures Sickness — Does Not Complain—(See Complaining, Endures).

Enemy—Sickness of Secret Enemy—(See "Secret Enemies" under Enemies).

Escape—Little Escape from the Sickness — (See Escape, Fatal, Grievous, Prolonged, Tedious, etc.).

Excesses—Sickness From—(See "Sickness" under Excesses).

Exposure—Sickness From—(See Exposure).

Extraordinary Sickness — (See Extarordinary, Mysterious, Obscure, Peculiar, Strange, Unusual, etc.).

Extreme Sickness — The ☉ joined with Antares, Aldebaran, Bellatrix, Caput Algol, Hercules, Regulus, or any eminent star of the nature of ♂. (See Extreme).

Falling Sickness—(See Fainting).

Fatal Sickness—(See Fatal).

Father — (See "Sickness To" under Father).

Fatigue — Sickness From — (See Fatigue).

Feeble; Females—Sickness of—(See "Ill-Health" under Females).

Fevers; Fighting—Sickness From—(See Fighting).

Food — Sickness From — (See "Sickness" under Eating; "Rich Food" under Food).

Friends — Sickness On Account of — (See "Sickness" under Friends).

Fruit—Sickness from Eating Corrupt Fruit—(See Fruit).

Gluttony—Sickness From—(See Gluttony).

Great — The Great — Much Sickness Among — (See "The Great" under Great).

Greatness — Sickness by Aiming At and Striving For — (See "Greatness" under Great).

Grievous Sickness—(See Grievous).

Habits — Sickness From — (See "Bad Habits", "Diseases", under Habits).

Headache—(See "Sick Headache" under Headaches).

Health Bad — (See "Bad Health", "Periods of Bad Health", under Health).

Heavy Sickness—(See Heavy).

Humours; Hurts—Incurable Hurts—(See Incurable, Permanent).

Husband — (See "Sickness Of" under Husband).

Ill-Health — (See the paragraphs under Ill-Health).

Ill Treatment—Sickness From—Lord of the 6th in the 11th H. (See Cruel; "Poisoned" under Healers; "Beaten" under Prison).

Immunity from Sickness — (See Immunity).

Impairments; Imprisonment — Sickness From—Lord of the 6th in the 12th H. (See "Imprisonment" under Prison).

Increase — Sickness Will Increase — (See "Disease" under Increase).

Incurable; Indiscretions — Sickness From—(See Indiscretions).

Indisposition; Infirmities; Inheritance — Sickness from Loss of — (See Inheritance. Also for Hereditary Sicknesses see Heredity).

Invalids; Irregularities — (See "Sickness" under Irregularities).

Journeys—Sickness On—(See "Sickness" under Journeys, Travel, Voyages).

Less Liable — To Sickness — The ☉ angular, free from affliction, and also the hyleg not afflicted by malefics at B. (See Angles, Immunity; "Good" under Resistance, Vitality).

Life Spared — (See "Spared" under Life).

Lingering Sickness—(See Chronic, Lingering, Long Diseases, Prolonged, Slow Diseases, Tedious, Wastings).

Little Sickness — (See "Abundance", "Good Health", under Health; Immunity; "Good" under Resistance, Vitality).

Location — Sickness Due To — (See "Ill-Health" under Residence).

Long Sicknesses — (See "Lingering" in this section).

Long or Short Illnesses—(See "Long or Short" under Short).

Many Sicknesses—Lord of the Asc. in the 6th H., afflicted by lord of the 6th, and coming to combust, which will be apt to cling until death. Death will be more certain if the ☽ and lords of the 1st and 8th be in the 6th H. (See "Ill-Health All Thru Life" under Ill-Health; "Much Sickness" in this section).

Medicines — The Medicines Given In Sickness—(See "Sickness" under Medicines).

Melancholy — Sickness From — (See "Death By", "Diseases", under Melancholy).

Mental Disturbances—Sickness From —(See Anguish, Cares, Despondency, Disgrace, Distress, Melancholy; "Irritations" under Mental; Reverses, Ruin, Vexations, Worry, etc.).

Moderation; Mortal Illness — (See "Certain Death" under Death; Fatal).

Mortality — (See "Death Rate Augmented" under Mortality).

Mother—Sickness of—(See Mother).

Much Sickness — Much Sickness All Thru Life — Much Sickness Generally — Frequent Sicknesses — Many Sicknesses—The ☉ in ♋ or ♌ and much afflicted, and not well-placed in the houses in the map; the ☉ afflicted in the 6th H., and the ☽ afflicted in ♋ at the same time; the ☉ or ☽ □ ♄ at B.; the ☉ or ☽ Sig. □ or ⚹ ♄ and ♄ be in the Asc.; the ☉ joined with Hercules, Antares, Hyades, Regulus, Aldebaran, or any eminent star of the nature of ♂; the ☉ or ☽ in the 6th or 12th H. in weak signs, and afflicted by malefics; the ☽ afflicted in ♑; the ☽ sepr. from ♄ and applying to ♂; the ☽ decr. and sepr. from ♃ and apply. to ♄; the ☽ sepr. from the ☉ and apply.

to ♄ in a nocturnal geniture; ♅ afflicted in the 6th or 12th H.; ♄ afflicted in the 6th H., or afflicting the hyleg from this house; the Knee of Castor and Pollux, the Whale's Jaw, Little Bear, or Cynosura, joined with the ☉ in an angle, much sickness, disgrace, and great affliction and trouble; lord of the 1st in the 6th; lord of the 6th in the 1st, by the native's irregularities; lord of the 12th in the 6th; lord of the 6th ℞, combust, in ☌, □, or ⚹ ♄ or ♂, or the lord of the 4th or 8th, there will be much sickness and great danger. (See Chronic; "Bad Health" under Health; "Ill-Health All Thru Life" under Ill-Health; Infirmities, Invalids; "Public Health Bad" under Public; Sickly; "Low" under Recuperation, Resistance, Vitality; "Weak Body" under Weak; "Many Sicknesses" in this section).

Nature of the Sickness — (See "Disease" under Nature; "Quality" in this section).

Nausea—Sickness At Stomach—(See Nausea).

Nobles—(See "Sickness" under Nobles).

Old Age — Dangerous Sickness In — (See "Dangerous" under Old Age).

Old Maladies Return—(See Return).

Over-Eating — Sickness From — (See "Sickness" under Eating).

Over-Indulgence—Of the Appetites— Sickness From — (See "Over-Indulgence" under Appetites; "Diseases" under Excesses; Indulgences).

Painful Sickness—(See "Diseases" under Pain).

Passional Nature — Sickness from Over-Indulgence of — (See Amorous; "Health Injured" under Men; "Health Suffers" under Opposite Sex; "Passional Excesses" under Passion; "Diseases" under Sex; Venery, etc.).

Past Sicknesses — The times of possible past sicknesses, or great affliction, can be obtained by looking back thru the Planetary Tables, and noting the times when the vital centers of the map, such as the ☉, ☽, Asc., M.C., Hyleg, or 6th H., were under the serious afflictions of the malefics by transit, direction, or progression, and also by noting the general strength or weakness of the radix. (See "Judgment of the Disease", "Time of the Disease", under Disease; "Periods of Bad Health" under Health).

Peculiar Sicknesses—(See Peculiar).

Periodic Sicknesses—(See Periodic).

Periods of Bad Health—(See this subject under Health).

Pleasure — Sickness by Excess of — (See "Disease", "Sickness", under Pleasure).

Poison—Sickness From—(See Poison).

Prolonged Sickness — (See Chronic, Heavy, Lingering, Prolonged, Tedious).

Property — Waste and Loss of Property, and Sickness By—(See "Sickness" under Property).

Public Health Bad — (See this subject under Public).

Quality of the Sickness — Nature of the Disease — Indicated by the 6th H.

and its conditions. In Hor'y Q. the Significators in fiery signs, and a fire sign on the Asc. and 6th H., indicate feverish and hot complaints, hectic fevers, erysipelas, etc. The Sigs. in earthy signs, and an earthy sign on the Asc. and 6th H., signify chronic, tedious and long diseases, intermittent fevers, ague, and such diseases as proceed from consumptions or melancholy. Airy signs on the Asc. and 6th H. at B., or decumb., qr the Sigs. in airy signs, indicate cutaneous diseases, gout, corrupt blood, scrofula, etc. Water signs on the Asc. and 6th H. at B., or at decumb., or with the Sigs. in watery signs at the beginning of an illness, show coughs, stomach disorders, and diseases which proceed from moisture and cold. The planet from which the ☽ is sepr. at decumb. shows the nature and quality of the disease, the state of the sick, and also the cause of the sickness. The sign descending at B., or on the cusp the 6th H., shows the nature and quality of the disease. Thus if the sign be ♈, the head is affected; if ♉, the neck and throat, etc. The 6th H., its lord, and planets in the 6th H. at B., if any, describe the nature of the disease, and especially if they afflict the ☉, ☽, or lord of the Asc. The lord of the 6th H. afflicted indicates the nature of the disease. (See "Causes" under Disease; Directions, Events, First House, Hyleg, Malefics; "Disease" under Nature; Quality, Sixth House, Transits, Type, Virgo, etc.).

Quarrels—Sickness From—(See "Sickness" under Quarrels).

Raving During Sickness — (See Raving).

Recovery — Will Recover — Will Not Recover—(See Recovery).

Recuperation; Relapses;

Remarkable Features — Of the Sickness—(See "Diseases" under Extraordinary).

Resistance; Rest — Has No Rest In Sickness—(See Rest).

Sad and Heavy Sickness—(See "Heavy and Sad" under Heavy).

Sea — Sickness At Sea — (See "Sickness" under Voyages).

Secret Enemy — Sickness of — (See "Secret Enemies" under Enemies).

Serious Sickness—(See Serious).

Servants — Sickness of — (See Servants).

Severe Sickness—(See Severe).

Shame and Disgrace—Sickness From —(See Disgrace).

Short Sicknesses — Short or Long Sicknesses — Sickness On Short Journeys—(See "Sickness" under Journeys; "Illnesses", "Long or Short", under Short).

Sick—The Sick—State of the Sick— (See Sick).

Sick Bed — Confined In — (See "Sick Bed" under Confinement; Invalids).

Sick Headache—(See Headaches).

Sickly — Pale — Weak — (See Feeble, Sickly, Pale; "Weak Body" under Weak).

Significators of Sickness — The ☉, ☽, Asc., lord of the Asc., and lords of the 6th and 12th Houses. The lords of the 4th and 8th H. are more the Sigs. of Death. In Hor'y Q. in rendering judgment as to the disease, its nature, etc., the 1st and 6th Houses, their lords, the Lights and their disposition, are to be taken. (See "Significators" under Disease).

Signs of Sickness—(See "Signs of Ill-Health" under Ill-Health).

Stomach—Sickness At—(See Nausea; "Sickness" under Stomach; Vomiting).

Strange Sicknesses—(See Strange).

Succumbs Easily—To Disease—♋, ♑, or ♓ on the Asc. at B., and the hyleg severely afflicted by malefics. (See Feeble, Frail; "Low" under Recuperation, Resistance, Vitality; Succumbs; "Weak Body" under Weak).

Suffers Much—In Sickness—♌ on the Asc. at B. (See Anguish; "High Fever" under Fever; Fierce, Painful Disease, Poignant, Sharp, Severe, Suffering, Violent Diseases, etc.).

Sure to Come — The Sickness Almost Sure to Come — The ☽ hyleg, and to the ☌, □, or ☍ ♄ by dir., and especially if the direction fall in the 6th H. (See Directions; "Certain", "Time Of", under Disease; Events; "Periods of Bad Health" under Health; "Periods of Ill-Health" under Ill-Health).

Tedious Sickness — (See Chronic, Lingering, Long Diseases, Prolonged, Slow, Tedious, Wastings, etc.).

Terminates Quickly — (See "Disease Will Soon End" under End; Quick Diseases, Short Diseases, Termination).

Threatened — Sickness Threatened — (See "Threatened" under Disease; "Danger Of" in this section).

Thrives and Lives — Thru Serious Sickness—(See "Stamina Good" under Infancy; "Good" under Recuperation, Resistance, Vitality; "Lives Thru" under Serious).

Time of the Sickness — (See Directions; "Time Of" under Disease).

Travel — Sickness During — Sickness Resulting From — (See Fatigue; "Health" under Journeys; "Sickness" under Ships, Travel, Voyages).

Treatment—Of Sickness—(See Antipathy, Cure; "Treatment" under Disease; Drugs, Healers, Ill-Health, Incurable, Medicines, Operations, Remedies, Subluxations, Sympathy, Treatment, etc.).

Uncommon Sicknesses—(See Extraordinary, Mysterious, Obscure, Peculiar; "Diseases" under Psychic; Strange, Uncommon).

Vehement Sickness—(See Vehement).

Vexations—Sickness From—(See Vexations).

Violent Sickness—(See "High Fevers" under Fever; Fierce, Fulminating, Painful Diseases, Severe, Sharp, Swift, Vehement, Violent, etc.).

Vitality Low—Sickness From—(See Anaemia, Debility, Emaciation, Feeble, Infirm, Invalids, Malignant, Morbid; "Malnutrition" under Nutrition; "Low" under Recuperation, Resistance, Stamina, Vitality; "Weakened" under Strength; "Lack Of" under Tone; Wastings; "Weak Body" under Weak).

Vulnerable Spots—Parts Predisposed to Disease—(See Vulnerable).

War—Much Sickness and Want In—(See War).

Weak Body—(See "Weak Body" under Weak).

Wife—(See "Sickness" under Wife).

Women—Sickness of—Sickness Caused By—(See "Sickness" under Women).

Worry — Sickness Caused By — (See Worry).

Worse — The Sickness Worse — (See Worse).

Young Men—Sickness of Prevalent—(See "Young Men" under Young; "Death" under Youth).

SIDEREAL BODY—The Astral Body—Paracelsus says "Man is related to the Stars by reason of his Sidereal Body", called the Astral Body by Modern Astro-Psychologists. (See Astral Body; "Desire Body" under Desire).

SIDES — Sides of the Body — Strongly ruled by ♌ and the 5th H. The Sides are denoted by the 5th H. Dr. Broughton says the Sides are ruled by ♃.

All Diseases In—Afflictions in ♌, the 5th H., and are signified by the 5th H.; ♌ diseases.

Narrow Sides — ♌ gives. (See Ribs, Trunk).

SIGHING—Yawning—A Prolonged Deep Inspiration — (See "Sighs" under Breathing).

SIGHT—Eyesight—Vision—The Sense of Vision — The Sight is ruled by the ☉, ☽, ♅, ♄, ♀ and ☿, and is also under the internal rulership of the ♒ sign. The ether, thru which light is transmitted, is ruled by ♅ and ♒. The vibrations which give sight are originated by ☿, and the Blind Spot in the eye is blind because it is not responsive to the etheric Mercurial vibrations. The ♒ sign has affinity with the sense of Sight, and it is the sign which corresponds to the etheric vibrations, and this sign when on the Asc. at B. is especially closely connected with Sight. The Nebulous Areas greatly afflict the Sight of Man, and the influence of ♆ is said to be largely with these Areas, as his vibration is very ethereal. The Pleiades especially are a Nebulous Cluster which tend to blindness, and many disorders of Sight, when with the ☉ or ☽ at B., or by dir. In the Hindu System of Astrology the 2nd H. rules the Eyes and Sight. (See Aquarius, Ether, Eyes; "Rays" under Light; Nebulous, Neptune, Uranus). The following subjects have to do with Sight, or Disorders of Sight, which see in the alphabetical arrangement when not more fully considered here—

Accommodation—Errors of—(See Accommodation, Hyperopia, Myopia, Presbyopia, in this section).

Affliction to Sight—The ☽ to the ☉ or ill-asp. ♂, and ♂ in ♌ aspected by the ☉ or ♄, or ♂ be near Cor Scorpio. (See the various paragraphs in this section).

Artifice—Blindness By—(See "Artifice" under Blindness).

Asthenopia—(See "Painful", "Weak", in this section).

Astigmatism; Bad Eyes — (See "Bad Eyes" under Eyes).

Blepharitis—(See Eyelids).

Blindness; Both Eyes—Loss of—Injury To—(See "Both Eyes" under Eyes).

Bloodshot Eyes — (See "Bloodshot" under Eyes).

Cataracts; Clouded Sight—The ☉ or ☽ with Nebulous Stars and Clusters at B. (See "Film" under Blindness; Cataracts; "Cornea" under Eyes; Specks; the various paragraphs in this section).

Cornea—Disorders of—(See Cornea).

Crossed Eyes—(See "Strabismus" under Eyes).

Crystallization — Of the Muscles and Nerves of the Eyes — The ☉ or ☽ ☌ Nebulous Stars, and at the same time in ☐ or ⚼ ♄, tends to, and to destroy the sight. (See Crystallization).

Danger to Sight — The ☉ and ☽ with Nebulous Stars at B., and especially in ☌ or ⚼ Antares, Aldebaran, The Ascelli, or the Pleiades. The central degrees of the mutable signs afflicted, and when the Lights, or those areas are much involved by malefics, or with Nebulous Stars, and especially in angles, there is much danger to the sight. Afflictions to ☿ tend to endanger the sight, as ☿ is ruler of the nervous system, and also ☿ originates the vibrations which give sight. The ♒ sign on the Asc., and when the ruler of the Decan. on the Asc. is in the 2nd H. and afflicted by malefics. In the Hindu System of Astrology, the 2nd H. rules the eyes and sight. (See the various paragraphs in this section).

Day Blindness — Nyctalopia — Vision Best At Night — Caused by ♆. (See "Day Blindness" under Blindness).

Defective Sight—Or Vision—Bad Vision—The ☉ and ☽ in signs of their fall, as the ☉ in ♎, and the ☽ in ♏, and afflicted; the ☉ or ☽ with, or near the Pleiades, Ascelli, or Antares, and afflicted by any planet, the cause differing according to the afflicting planet; the ☽ unfortunate, and with Nebulous Stars; the ☽ to the place of Praesepe, great defect in the sight, and often blindness, and especially if the Lights are with Nebulous Stars. Defects in sight are especially ☽ diseases. Case of Defective Sight—See "Sight Defective", No. 684, in 1001 N.N. (See the various paragraphs in this section).

Destroyed — Sight Destroyed — (See Blindness; "Decay Of" under Optic; "Crystallization" in this section).

Dim Sight—Dim Vision—Nearly Blind —(See "Nearly Blind" under Blind; "Dim Eyes" under Eyes).

Diplopia — Double Vision — May be caused by afflictions in ♋, and due to indigestion. Caused by Subluxations at SP (7D). Also caused by Crossed Eyes. (See "Muscae", "Strabismus", under Eyes).

Disordered Sight—(See Affliction To, Defective, and the various paragraphs in this section).

Disturbances—Visual Disturbances—(See Migraine; "Diplopia" and the various paragraphs in this section).

Dots and Specks—Before the Eyes—(See "Muscae Volitantes" under Eyes).

Double Vision—(See "Diplopia" in this section).

Effective Sight—(See "Good" in this section).

Eyelids — Eyelashes — Sight Injured by Inverted Lashes—(See "Blepharitis" under Eyelids).

Eyes—(See "Sight", and the various paragraphs under Eyes).

Eyestrain — Tending to Blindness — (See "Eyestrain" under Eyes).

Far-Sighted — (See "Hyperopia" in this section).

Father — Injury To Sight of — (See "Eyes" under Father).

Feeble Vision — (See "Weak" in this section).

Film—Blindness from White Film—(See "Film" under Blindness).

Focus — Defect of Focus — Usually caused by □ influence. (See Accommodation, Unequal, and the various paragraphs in this section).

Glaucoma—Blindness By—(See Glaucoma).

Good Sight — Effective Sight — Keen Vision—Perfect Sight—A Quick Eye—Sharp Eyes, etc.—□, ♒, or ♍ on the Asc. (See "Good Eyes" under Eyes).

Hemianopia — Blindness of One-Half the Visual Field—Defective Vision In the Outer Half of the Eyes—Afflictions in ♈ and ♉, and with subluxations at MCP (4C).

Hyperopia—Hypermetropia—Far-Sighted—A ☽ disease; the ☽ afflicted in ♈; ♅ and ♀ afflictions to the ☉ or ☽, a relaxing action on the tissues, tendons and muscles, tending to a flattened crystalline lens, relaxed Ciliary muscles, and a distant focus. Myopia is the opposite condition to this. (See "Myopia" in this section).

Infants—Sight of—(See "Sight" under Infancy).

Infirmities of Sight — (See Defective, Weak, and the various paragraphs in this section).

Injury to Sight — (See Accidents, Artifice, Burning, under Blindness; "Accidents To" under Eyes).

Keen Vision — □ gives when on the Asc., and not afflicted. (See "Good" in this section).

Left Eye — Sight of Affected — (See "Left Eye" under Eyes).

Loss of Sight—Danger of—The ☽ to the ◌ ♂ by dir. (See Blindness; "Accidents" under Eyes; "Decay" under Optic; Crystallization, Danger, and various paragraphs in this section).

Migraine—Causing Visual Disturbances—(See Migraine).

Muscae Volitantes—Specks or Threads Before the Eyes—(See "Muscae" under Eyes).

Muscles of Eyes—Crystallization of, and Impairing the Sight—(See "Crystallization" in this section).

Myopia—Short Sight—Near-Sighted—The ☉ in any part of the heavens conjoined with the Pleiades; the ☉ rising in the Asc. in ♉ ☽ decreasing in the 7th H., and in the ♋ and ♍ signs; the ☽ in ♈ or ♉, and afflicted by ♆; a ☽ disease; the ☽ Sig. ◌ ☉, myopia from too much reading; the ☽ rising in ♍, □ the ☉ and ♂, and applying to ◌ ♅, existed in a case; ♆ in ♈; ♆ in ♈ in the 6th H.; ♆ in ♈, and afflicting the ☽, Asc., or hyleg; strong afflictions to ♀, the ruler of the nervous system; many planets in ♋ and ♍ in ◌ or ♉, and these signs on the Asc. and Desc., tends to extreme myopia and astigmatism. Also caused by Subs at MCP (4C). Cases of Myopia — See "Sight Defective", No. 684, and "Spinal Curvature", No. 838, in 1001 N.N. Case No. 684 is Myopic in one eye, and Hyperopic in the other. Also see Cases in Chap. XIII in Daath's Medical Astrology.

Near-Sighted—(See "Myopia" in this section).

Nearly Blind — (See "Nearly Blind" under Blindness; Cataracts; "Defects In", "Dim Eyes", under Eyes).

Nebulous Stars—Sight Impaired By—(See Nebulous).

Nerves of Eyes—Sight Affected By—(See "Decay" under Optic; Retina; "Crystallization" in this section).

Night Vision—Vision Best At Night—(See "Day Blindness" under Blindness).

Nyctalopia — (See "Day Blindness" under Blindness).

Obstructions To Sight — (See "Film" under Blindness; Cataracts; "Growths", "Obstructions", under Eyes; Glaucoma; Crystallization, Muscae, and the various paragraphs in this section).

Old Age Vision — (See "Presbyopia" in this section).

One Eye—Blindness In—Myopia In—(See "One Eye" under Blindness; "Myopia" in this section).

One-Half Vision—(See "Hemianopia" in this section).

Ophthalmia—(See Conjunctivitis; "Ophthalmia" under Infancy).

Optic Nerve—Decay of—(See Optic).

Painful Vision — Asthenopia — Afflictions in ♉; Subs at MCP (4C). (See "Weak" in this section).

Peculiarity of Vision—Caused by ♆; ♆ afflicting the ☉ or ☽; ♆ with one of the Nebulous Clusters and afflicting the ☉ or ☽.

Penetrating Sight — (See "Penetrating" under Eyes).

Perfect Sight—(See "Good Sight" in this section).

Pleiades — Sight Affected By — (See Pleiades).

Presbyopia — Old Age Vision — Lack of the Power of Accommodation — Failure of the Ciliary Muscle to Contract for Accommodation—♄ influence, and due to the deposits and crystallizing influences of ♄, which take place over the whole body with age; ♄ afflicted in ♈, especially aggravated cases, and require a strong convex glass. Presbyopia may be considered an aggravated condition of Hyperopia, and the conditions tending to cause Hyperopia will also apply here. (See Crystallization, Hyperopia, in this section).

Quick Sight — (See "Good Eyes", "Quick Eye", under Eyes; "Good Sight" in this section).

Reading—Sight Disordered By—(See "Reading and Study" under Blindness; "Eyestrain" under Eyes).

Retina—Disorders of—(See Retina).

Right Eye—Sight of Impaired—Loss of—(See "Right Eye" under Right).

Sharp Sight—(See "Sharp Eyes" under Eyes).

Short Sight — (See "Myopia" in this section).

Specks Over Eyes — (See "Muscae" under Eyes; Specks).

Squint — Crossed Eyes — (See "Strabismus" under Eyes).

Stomach — Disturbances of Vision from Stomach Disorders—(See "Muscae" under Eyes; "Diplopia" in this section).

Strabismus — Crossed Eyes — (See "Strabismus" under Eyes).

Study—Sight Impaired by Too Much Reading and Study — (See "Reading" in this section).

Threads Before Eyes — Dots and Specks—(See "Muscae Volitantes" under Eyes).

Total Blindness — (See "Total" under Blindness).

Unequal Sight—Caused by the ☉ and ☽ in strong mutual affliction to each other. Also as the right and left eyes are under different planetary rulership, the planetary afflictions to these rulers may cause inequalities in the sight so that the two eyes do not focus in harmony. Thus there may be myopia in one eye, and hyperopia in the other. Case—See "Myopia" in this section. This is also caused by Strabismus, and where one eye loses its power for want of proper use. Can also be caused by decay of optic nerve, and various disease conditions which may affect only one side of the body. (See "Strabismus" under Eyes; "Eyes" under Left, Right; "Decay" under Optic).

Weak Sight—Weak Vision—Asthenopia—Feeble Vision—Weak or Painful Vision—A ☽ disease, and caused by afflictions to the ☉; the ☉ or ☽ with Nebulous Stars at B., and afflicted by malefics or ☋; the ☉ or ☽ in the Western Angle, and conjoined with the Pleiades, or the ☉ in any part of the heavens conjoined with the Pleiades; the ☉ and ☽ in signs of their fall, as the ☉ in ♎, and the ☽ in ♏; the ☉ afflicted in ♎ or ♒; the ☉ ☌ ♄ in ♒; the ☉ ☌ ☋ in ♐ near Antares; the ☉ or ☽ afflicted by ♄, and at the same time the ☉ and ☽ afflict each other; the ☉ in ♎, and ♄ in ♈, weak eyes; one or both Lights afflicted by Nebulous Stars or malefics; the affliction of the ☉ or ☽ from angles by the malefics, and especially if the ☉ or ☽ be near the Pleiades; the ☉ or ☽ in □ or

☍ each other from angles; the ☉ and ☽ in ☍ from ♈ and ♎; the ☉ or ☽ in ♈, and afflicted by ♂; the ☽ occi. at B., and in evil asp. to ♂; the ☽ sepr. from the ☉ and applying to ♂ in a day nativity; the ☽ afflicted in ♈, or afflicting the hyleg therefrom; the ☽ afflicted in ♏; the Full ☽ rising at B.; ♅ ☌ Nebulous Stars, and in □ or ☍ the ☉ or ☽; ♅ afflicted in ♈; ♄ to the ☌ or ill-asps. the ☉ by dir.; the periodic direction of ♄ to the radical ☉; Fixed Stars of the nature of ♂ and the ☽ ascending at B.; malefics with Nebulous Stars in the 6th or 12th H., and afflicting the ☉ or ☽; in Hor'y Q., the Sig. with Nebulous Stars; the 3rd Decan. of ♒ on the Asc., ruled by the ☽; afflictions in ☋, and Subs at MCP (4C). (See Defective, Dim, Painful, and the various paragraphs in this section; Blindness; "Bad Eyes", "Weak Eyes", under Eyes).

Yellow Vision—(See Xanthopsia).

SIGMOID FLEXURE — The S-shaped portion of the Colon above the Rectum —Ruled by ♏. Some Authors also say it is ruled by ♄.

Disorders Of — ♄ or ♂ afflicted in ♏; Subs at PP (3, 4L). (See Colon).

SIGNATURE — Correspondences — The Law of—There are many resemblances in the Material World to parts and shapes in the human body, and also affinity between herbs, roots, minerals, metals, etc., and parts of the body. Thus the kidney-bean resembles the kidneys in shape. The convolutions of nuts resemble the convolutions of the brain. The coffee seed resembles the two cerebral lobes, etc. The bitterness of Nux Vomica is a good remedy in bile disorders. The subject of Signatures is considered quite fully in the book, "Astral Medicine", by Dr. Duz. (See Antipathy, Opposites, Remedies, Sympathy, Treatment, etc.).

SIGNIFICATORS—In the horoscope of birth the ☉, ☽, Asc., and Midheaven, are called Significators, as they are the vital points, or centers of the map, and afflictions to them mean more than to other places, and in the diagnosis and prognosis of disease the Significators should be examined first as to their strength or weakness. (See "Significators" under Disease, Form, Health. Also see Indicators).

SIGNS—Indicators—Symbols—

Children — Signs of — (See "Signs Of" under Children; Fruitful).

Death — Signs of — (See "Arguments For", "Certain Death", under Death).

Health—Signs of Good or Bad Health —(See "Bad Health", "Good Health", under Health).

Long Diseases—Signs of—(See "Diseases" under Long).

Pregnancy — Signs of — (See Conception, Pregnancy).

Recovery—Signs of—(See "Signs Of" under Recovery).

Short Diseases—Signs of—(See "Illnesses" under Short).

Zodiac—Signs of—(See the next Article).

SIGNS OF THE ZODIAC — There are twelve Signs of the Zodiac, as listed and divided today. In the early stages of Humanity, before the separation of the sexes, the ♍ and ♏ signs were united into one sign, but when the sexes were separated, these signs were separated and ♎ inserted between them. (See "Separation of the Sexes" under Sex). Each Sign of the Zodiac has a certain influence on the Mental and Physical Constitution of Man, and each sign rules a certain part, parts, or organs of the body, and with chief attention to the Sign rising upon the Eastern Horizon at B., which is called the Rising Sign. (See Ascendant, First House). The Signs are also closely affiliated with their corresponding Houses. Thus ♈ is in close sympathy with the First House; ♉ with the 2nd H.; ♊ with the 3rd H., etc. The following is a classified list of the Signs, showing their different qualities, characteristics, functions, and their various classifications, etc. Each Sign of the Zodiac is considered in an Article in the alphabetical arrangement of this book. See the following subjects in the alphabetical arrangement when they are only listed here—

Acid Signs — (See Acids; "Negative Signs" under Negative).

Air Signs — (See "Signs" under Air).

Alkaline Signs — (See Alkaline; "Positive Signs" under Positive).

Animal Signs — (See "Animal Signs" under Animal; Quadrupeds).

Aquarius Sign; Aries Sign;

Articulate Signs — (See Articulate).

Autumnal Signs — (See Autumnal).

Barren Signs — (See "Barren Signs" under Barrenness).

Bestial Signs — (See Beasts).

Bicorporeal Signs — (See Double-Bodied).

Bilious Signs — (See Bile).

Birds — Signs Which Give Forms Resembling Birds or Animals — (See "Animal Forms" under Monsters).

Bitter Signs — (See Bitter).

Brevity — Signs of — ♋, ♑, and ♓, and when on the Asc. at B. tend to make the body shorter. (See Brevity).

Broken Signs — (See Broken).

Brutish Signs — (See Brutish; "Human Signs" under Human).

Cancer Sign; Capricorn Sign;

Cardinal Signs — (See Cardinal).

Changeable Signs — ♊, ♌, ♍, ♎, ♐. (See Changeable; "Mutable Signs" under Mutable).

Choleric Signs — (See Choleric).

Cold Signs — The Earthy and Watery Signs — (See Cold).

Colors — The Colors ruled by the Signs are given under each Sign. (See "Colors" under Aries, Taurus, etc. Also see Colors).

Commanding Signs — (See Commanding).

Common Signs — (See "Mutable Signs" under Mutable).

Conditional Signs — (See "Constitutional" in this section).

Constitutional Signs — Conditional Signs — (See the Introduction under Constitution).

Crooked Signs — (See Broken, Crooked).

Cud-Chewing Signs — (See Ruminant).

Debility — Signs of Debility of the Planets — A Planet is in debility and detriment when in the opposite sign to its home sign at B. (See Lists of Debilities and Dignities of the Planets in the various Textbooks of Astrology. See "Debilities" under Planets in this book).

Decanates of Signs — (See Decanates).

Deformed Signs — Broken Signs — Imperfect Signs — (See Broken, Deformities, Imperfect).

Detriment — Planets In Detriment In Signs — (See "Detriment" under Planets).

Dignities — Of the Planets In the Signs — (See "Dignities" under Planets).

Distorted Signs — (See Broken, Crooked, Distortions).

Diurnal Signs — (See "Nocturnal Signs" under Night).

Domestic Signs — ♋ and ♑. (See Cancer, Capricorn).

Double-Bodied Signs; Dry Signs — (See "Signs" under Dry).

Dumb Signs — Mute Signs — (See Dumb).

Earth Signs — (See "Earthy Signs" under Earth).

Eastern Signs — (See Eastern).

Effeminate Signs — (See "Signs" under Effeminate).

Electro-Negative Signs — Electro-Positive Signs — The masculine signs are electro-positive, and alkaline. The feminine signs are acid, and electro-negative.

Elemental Signs — Temperamental Signs — (See Elements).

Equinoctial Signs — (See Equinoxes).

Estival Signs — (See Summer).

Even Signs — The Feminine Signs — (See "Signs" under Female).

Exaltation — Planets Exalted In Signs — (See "Planets" under Exaltation; "Debilities" under Planets).

External Rulership — Of Signs — Each Sign of the Zodiac exerts an external, internal, and structural rulership over the part, or parts of the body ruled by such sign. Thus ♈ rules the head and face externally, the brain internally, and the cranium and facial bones structurally, and so on with each of the signs. These rulerships are given in each of the Articles on the Signs in this book. (See "Aries Rules" under Aries; "Taurus Rules" under Taurus).

Faces of Signs — There are six Faces of five degrees in each sign. (See Chap. IV, on "Faces of the Signs", in Simmonite's Arcana).

Fall of Planets — In Signs — (See "Debilities", "Fall of Planets", under Planets).

Feminine Signs — (See "Signs" under Female).

Feral Signs — Bestial Signs — (See Beasts).

Fire Signs—(See "Fire Signs" under Fire).

Fixed Signs—(See "Fixed Signs" under Fixed).

Flexed Signs — (See "Mutable Signs" under Mutable).

Food — The Food Adapted to People Born Under Each Sign—(See "Signs of Zodiac" under Food).

Fortunate Signs—(See "Signs of Zodiac" under Fortune).

Foundation Signs—(See "Fixed Signs" under Fixed).

Four-Footed Signs — (See Quadrupeds).

Fowls — Resembling Fowls — (See "Birds" in this section).

Fruitful Signs—(See Fruitful).

Gemini Sign; Half Feral Sign—♐.

Hoarse Signs—(See Hoarseness).

Horas — The Positive and Negative Halves of Signs—(See Horas).

Hot Signs—The fiery signs. Also the airy signs are classed as moist and warm. (See "Signs" under Heat).

Human Form—Signs of—(See Articulate; "Human Form" under Human).

Human Signs — (See "Human Signs" under Human).

Humane Signs—The Airy Signs, and especially ♒. (See Humane).

Hurtful Signs—(See Hurtful).

Hyemal Signs — Winter Signs — (See Winter).

Idle Sign—♓ is classed as an idle and dull sign. (See Idle).

Imperfect Signs—(See Imperfect).

Inarticulate Signs—(See Inarticulate).

Indifferent Signs—Neither Fruitful nor Barren—♎, ♑, and ♒.

Internal Rulership — Of Signs — (See "External" in this section. Also see Internal).

Jacob—The 12 Sons of Jacob—Each son is said to have been born with the ☉ in a different Sign of the Zodiac, and being typical of the 12 fundamental classes of Humanity. See the book, "Bible Astrology" by Lyman Stowe. To get this book, address Mildred K. Stowe, 1325 Madison Ave., Detroit, Michigan, U. S. A. Lyman Stowe was one of the great Writers of his day on Biblical and Medical Astrology, and gave the World many new interpretations of the Bible, and also did much to help explain the causes of disease, and the Philosophy of Life, and every student should have a copy of this book.

Leo Sign; Libra Sign;

Life-Giving Signs — The fiery signs, and especially ♌.

Long Ascension—Signs of—(See "Ascension" under Long).

Luxuriant Sign—(See Luxuriant).

Lymphatic Signs—(See Lymphatic).

Magnetic Sign — (See "Signs" under Magnetic).

Masculine Signs—The positive signs, the odd signs, as ♈, ♊, ♌, ♎, ♐, ♒. The ☉ rules the first half of masculine

signs, and the ☽ the second half. (See "Odd Signs" under Odd).

Melancholic Signs—(See "Signs" under Melancholy).

Members of Body—Members ruled by Signs—(See each Sign in the alphabetical arrangement).

Mental Signs — (See "Signs" under Mental).

Mineral Signs—(See Earth, Signs).

Moderately Strong Signs — ♉, ♊, ♍, ♏, ♒.

Moist Signs — (See "Signs" under Moisture).

Motive Signs—(See Motive).

Movable Signs—(See Cardinal Signs).

Mutable Signs — (See Common, Mutable).

Mute Signs—(See Dumb, Mute).

Mutilated Signs—(See Mutilated).

Navamsa—Navamsa Division of Signs —(See Navamsa).

Negative Signs—(See Negative; "Electro-Negative" in this section).

Nervous Signs — (See "Signs" under Nerves).

Nocturnal Signs—(See "Signs" under Night).

Northern Signs—(See Northern).

Obeying Signs—Southern Signs—(See "Northern Signs" under North).

Obnoxious Signs—(See "Hurtful Signs" under Hurtful).

Odd Signs—(See Odd, Positive).

Opposite Signs—(See Opposite).

Organs Ruled by Signs—(See the Introduction under Organs).

Parts of the Body—Ruled by Signs—(See Parts).

Pestilential Signs—(See Pestilence).

Phlegmatic Signs—(See Phlegm).

Pisces Sign; Planets and Signs—(See "Signs Ruled By" under Planets).

Positive Signs—(See Positive; "Electro-Negative" in this section).

Psychic Signs—(See the Introduction under Psychic).

Quadrupedal Signs — (See Quadrupeds).

Rational Signs—(See Rational).

Receptive Signs—(See Receptivity).

Reptilian Signs—(See Reptiles).

Right Side of Body—And the Signs—(See Left, Right).

Rising Sign—(See Ascendant, Rising).

Ruminant Signs—(See Ruminant).

Sagittarius Sign; Sanguine Signs — (See Sanguine).

Scientific Signs—(See Science).

Scorpio Sign; Seminal Signs — (See Semen).

Short Ascension—Signs of—(See "Ascension" under Long, Short).

Sickly Signs—♎ and ♓, and especially when upon the Asc. at B. (See Sickly; "Low" under Vitality).

Slow of Voice—Signs of—(See "Slow of Voice" under Voice).

Southern Signs—(See Northern, Southern).

Speaking Signs—(See Speaking).

Strong Signs—(See "Fixed Signs" under Fixed).

Structural Rulership—Of Signs—(See "External" in this section).

Sub-Divisions of Signs — (See Decanates, Faces, Horas, Navamsa).

Summer Signs—(See Summer).

Sweet Signs—Air Signs—(See Sweet).

Symbols of the Signs — (See the Introduction under each of the Signs, as Aries, Taurus, etc.).

Sympathetic Signs—Signs in Sympathy with Each Other—(See Sympathy). Aquarius is said to be the most sympathetic and humane sign.

Taurus Sign; Temperamental Signs—(See "Elemental" in this section).

Terminal Signs—(See Terminal).

Terrestrial Signs—(See Quadrupeds).

Torpid Sign—(See Pisces, Torpid).

Tropical Signs—(See Tropical).

Unfortunate Signs — (See Unfortunate).

Vernal Equinox Sign—(See Vernal).

Violent Signs — (See "Signs" under Violent).

Virgo Sign; Vital Signs—(See "Signs" under Vital).

Voice—Signs of—(See "Signs" under Voice).

Warm and Moist Signs—(See "Signs" under Moisture).

Water Signs — (See "Signs" under Water).

Weak Signs — ♋, ♑, and ♓ are considered the weak signs when upon the Asc. at B., and tend to lower vitality, and ♋ and ♓ especially, as they correspond to the terminal houses, the 4th and 12th houses. (See "Low" under Recuperation, Resistance, Vitality; "Weak Body" under Weak).

Western Signs—(See Western).

Whole Signs — (See "Signs" under Whole).

Winter Signs—(See Winter).

Zodiac—Signs of—Zodiac Salts—(See Zodiac).

SILENT — (See Dumb, Hermaphrodites, Mutes; "Silent" under Speech).

SILICA—Quartz—Ruled by ♃. Silica is called "The Surgeon of the Body".

SILVER — Argentum — Ruled by the ☽, and is a typical drug and metal of the ☽. (See Metals, Therapeutics).

Silver Cord—The Cord which connects the Soul to the body. When this Cord is snapped, disintegration of the physical body begins. This happens usually about 3½ days after the apparent death of the body, and during that time there is hope that the body may be revived. Therefore, the body should not be embalmed, disturbed, buried, or cremated until this period has elapsed. Saturn and ♂ cut the Cord. (See Death). What we call the death of the body is not death, as the body becomes more alive than ever when its Captain and Leader, the Ego, has left it, as the atoms and particles then begin their disorganized battle in earn-

est to free themselves in order to enter into new combinations. Cremation sets the particles free immediately, and without the long period of decay and disintegration. The physical body is but a wrapping for the Soul, a physical vehicle to work with and through on the Earth Plane, and when we have finished our "Day in School" here, we are thru with this body, and should forget it, burn it up, the same as we would do to some old worn out cloak or garment. By setting the particles of the body free by fire, the Soul also is more free to depart to the Heaven World, and to have nothing to hold it back, or worry about except the loved ones and relatives left behind. Graveyards are a menace to the health of a Community, and constantly give off foul vapors, and a stench of decaying bodies, and the Astral Shell, or counterpart of the physical body, haunts the grave about its corpse, and appears to those who are psychic enough to see them as an Apparition, or "Ghost", at times until the body is finally disposed of. The questions of the Silver Cord, of Cremation, and other subjects about Death, etc., are quite fully considered in the book, "Cosmo-Conception", by Max Heindel. In the Bible the Silver Cord is spoken of in Eccl. 12:6. (See "Astral Shells" under Astral).

SIMILAR—Similars — Treatment By— (See Homeopathy, Sympathy).

SIMPLE—

Simple Fevers — (See "Non-Contagious" under Fevers).

Simple Fractures—(See "Simple" under Fractures).

Simple-Minded—(See Foolish, Idiocy, Imbecility, Insanity; "Weak Mind" under Mind, etc.).

SIMULATION—Simulated—

Simulated Death — (See Catalepsy, Trance).

Simulation of Disease—A ♍ trait. (See Virgo).

SINAPSIS NIGRA — Mustard — Sinapsis Alba—Typical Plants of the ☉. (See Mustard).

SINCERE — Honest — Conscientious — ♅ and ♂ influences tend to sincerity unless they are badly afflicted. Aries and ♌ are sincere and open-minded, also the ♒ people. Sagittarius is sincere unless ♃, its ruler, is ill-aspected by malefics. Also the 5th face of ♌, the 1st face of ♍, or the 6th face of ♐, when on the Asc. at B. tend to make the nature sincere. The afflictions of ♅ and ♄ to the mental rulers tend to Deception and Hypocrisy. (See Character, Cheating, Deceitful, Dishonest, Gambling, Honest, Hypocritical, Motives, Noble, Purposes, Reputation).

SINEWS—Tendons—Ligamentous Tissues—(See Achilles, Fiber, Ligaments, Muscles; "Sinews" under Nerves; Tendons).

SINGING—(See "Speech" under Breath; Humming, Larynx; "Singers" under Music; "Injudicious Use", "Speaking Signs", under Speech; "Melodious", "Musical", under Voice).

SINGLE—

Single Births — (See "Single Births" under Children).

Single People—(See Aversions, Bachelors, Celibacy, Deviations; "Aversion" under Marriage; Spinsters).

SINGULAR—

Singular Death—(See "Death" under Extraordinary, Murder, Mysterious, Notorious, Peculiar, Poison, Public, Remarkable, Strange, Sudden, Suicide, Tragical, Uncommon, Untimely, Unusual, Violent, etc.).

SINISTER — Situated on the Left Side, or Left Hand — Evil — Perverse — Wicked, etc.—

Aspects — Sinister Aspects — Evil Aspects—(See Aspects).

Left-Handed—(See "Left-Handed" under Left).

Perverse—(See Conduct, Evil, Morals, Perverse, Prodigal, Wanton, Wicked).

SINKING—Sunken—

Sinking of Parts—Of the Body—Depressions, etc.—Caused by ♄ afflictions. (See "Sunken" under Chest; Compression, Contractions, Depressions, Eyeballs; "Sunken" under Face; Hollow; Saturn Influence, Skull, Sunken).

Sinking Spells—(See Collapse, Fainting; "Faintings" under Heart; Prostration, Weak, etc.).

SINUS—Sinuses—(See Fossae, Frontal).

Sinus of Kidneys—(See Kidneys).

SIRIUS—The Dog Star—Of the nature of ♃ and ♂, and situated in 12° ♋. Produces glory, renown, and great wealth. The Asc. to the place of tends to good health. Sirius also tends to bring some evils when with the ☽, and the danger of death by Soldiers or Wild Beasts. Also Dog Days were originally named after Sirius. (See "Corrupt Air" under Air; "Dog Days" under Dogs; "Death" under Soldiers; "Wild Animals" under Wild).

SISTER—Sisters—Are ruled by the 3rd H., and also indicated by the ☽ and ♀. Happenings to them, dangers, ill-health, death, etc., are indicated by afflictions to the ☽, ♀, or 3rd H. (See Brethren).

Danger To—Accident or Injury To—The ☽ hyleg and to the ♂, P, □ or ☍ ♅ by dir.; the M.C. to the ill-aspects of ☽ or ♀ by dir.; an eclipse falling on ♀ in a child's map.

Death or Illness Of—The ☽ to the □ or ☍ the ☉ or ♀ by dir.; ♄ passing over the place of the ☽ or ♀ at B., by transit, or at a Solar Rev., and the ☽ or ♀ afflicted at B., or at a Solar Rev. by malefics; the M.C. to the □ or ☍ the ☽ or ♀ by dir.; the M.C. to the ♂, P, □, or ☍ the ☽ or ♀ if either be weak or afflicted at B.; the Asc. to the □ or ☍ the ☽ or ♀ by dir.; the Asc. to the ♂ ♂ by dir. (See "Sickness Among" under Brethren).

Long Life For — And Good Relations With—Benefics in, or ruling, the 3rd H., and no malefic influences over this house at B.; the ☽ and ♀ well-aspected at B., and free from affliction in the map of a brother. (See "Long Life" under Females. Mother).

Short Life For—Evil Relations With —Malefics in or ruling the 3rd H. of the native; the ☽ and ♀ badly afflicted at B., and by dir., and with no good influences over the 3rd H.; the Asc. to the □ or ☍ the ☽ or ♀ by dir., and the ☽ and ♀ sorely afflicted at B. (See "Short Life" under Females, Mother, Relatives).

Sisters Indicated — Stars femininely constituted, which promise brethren, indicate sisters. (See Brothers Indicated" under Brothers; "First-Born Child", "Many Children", under Children).

SITUATION IN LIFE—Location, etc.— (See Abroad, Altitude, Changes, Foreign Lands, Journeys, Location; "Native Land" under Native; "Place of Birth" under Place; Residence, Travel, Voyages, etc.).

SITUATIONS—(See Ambition, Business, Employment, Fortune, Idle; "Ill-Fortune" under Ill; Improvident, Poverty, Reputation, Riches, Vocation, etc.).

SIXTH HOUSE — This is a feminine house, and is known as the House of Health, and also of Sickness, and is affiliated with the 6th Sign, Virgo. The 6th H. and ♍ are indicators of disease, and the Sign on the cusp of this house indicates the part of the body more liable to disease and affliction. (See "Action of the Mind" under Mind; Virgo; "Principal" under Vital). Disease is apt to come from the 6th H. conditions, and this house shows the natural and ordinary state of the health. Benefic influences in and ruling this house show better health, while malefics in the 6th H. at B. tend to ill-health, and also indicate the nature of the disease most liable to afflict the body or mind. Malefics in the 6th H. indicate an evil end to the disease. This house shows disease, its cause and quality; it shows the principal humour or disease offending, and whether curable or incurable, and whether the disease will be long or short. The 6th H., in a broad sense, governs disease, and especially if there are planets in this house at B. (See Majority). Diagnosis is more remote, and less accurate, when considering only the lord of the 6th. Wilson in his Dictionary says, "Not to depend too much upon the 6th H. to judge of the disease unless it is very conspicuous in influence." The ☉ in this house at B. tends to lower the vitality, and to cause mental diseases. The ☽ here tends to diseases of the head. Jupiter, ♂, or ♀ here denote a good Physician. Also ♀ afflicted in this house at B. tends to Venereal Diseases. Mercury here tends to bad breath, and a disordered brain. Mars here tends to fevers, evil servants, and destruction of cattle.

Colors Ruled By—Dark, or Black.

Denotes — This house denotes the Lower Belly, the Solar Plexus, the Intestines, and the Rectum.

Diseases Ruled By—Signifies all diseases in the lower part of the Abdomen, in the Intestines, Liver, and Reins. Also tends to General Ailments. Rules the sicknesses of Servants, Dependents, and also malefic influences over this house tend to the destruction of the small cattle, and small animals of the native.

Rules — The Sixth House Rules the Abdomen, Belly, the inferior part of the Belly and the Intestines, even to the Rectum; the Womb; the Climatic and other conditions affecting the health; Food; Clothing; Ritual; the Colors Black or Dark; the physical Comforts of Life; the Common People and the relation of the native to them; the Mother's brothers and sisters in a male horoscope; Aunts and Uncles, and Kindred on the father's side; Aunts and Uncles in a female nativity, or the Father's brothers and sisters; Enemies (in the Hindu System); General Ailments; Healers; Physicians; Sickness, and the nature of the Sickness; rules the Health; Servants, Slaves, Dependents, Persons in employ; Small Animals, such as Ponies, small Cattle, Sheep, Hogs, Goats, Rabbits, etc. The Sixth House influences are referred to many times throughout his Book, and under the various diseases and conditions. See the Sixth House influences in the paragraph "Arguments for Death" under Death; "Indicators of Health", "Judging the Health", under Health; "Signs of Ill-Health" under Ill-Health; "Judgment of the Disease" under Judgment; "Nature of the Disease" under Nature; "Quality of the Sickness" under Sickness; the subjects and diseases under Virgo.

SIXTH RACE — Sixth Sub-Race — (See Neptune, Pineal Gland).

SIXTH SENSE—(See Pineal Gland).

SIZE—Measurements—Volume, etc.—

Body—Size and Weight of the Physical Body — (See Body, Commanding, Corpulent, Diminished, Dwarfed, Enlarged, Fat, Figure, Fleshy, Form, Frame, Full, Giants, Growth, Heavy, Height, High, Large, Lean, Little, Low, Mean, Medium, Middle, Moderate, Portly, Round, Shape, Short, Skeleton, Small, Stature, Stout, Tall, Thin, Undersized, Undeveloped, Weight, etc.).

Brain—Size and Weight of the Brain —(See the Introduction under Brain).

Good Habit and Size — (See "Good Habit" under Habit).

SKELETON — The Framework of the Body—The Bones—Ruled by ♄. The skeletone is built up by deposits formed by ♄, and from earthy minerals carried by the blood. (See Bones, Deposits, Minerals).

A Living Skeleton — Case — See "Living Skeleton", No. 053 in 1001 N.N.

Well-Framed Body—The ☽ Sig. in ♊; ♀ Sig. in ♒; ☿ Sig. in ♉ or ♐; the ♍ influences give a neat, well-formed, and well-framed body; ♐ gives a tall, well-formed, and well-framed body. (See "Large" under Bones; Well-Proportioned, Well-Shaped).

Whole Frame Disordered — (See "Frame" under Whole).

SKEPTICISM—Doubt In Religious Matters—Unorthodox—Due usually to ☿ and the ☿ signs ♊ and ♍ prominent at B.; caused by ♄ affliction; ♄ in the 9th

H.; ♃ afflicted in ♊; malefics in ♊ and ♍ in □ asp. to each other; ♅ afflicted in the 9th H. (See Independent, Misunderstood, Occult, Metaphysical; "Unorthodox" under Religion; Science).

SKIN — Cutis — Derma — The External Covering of the Body—The Cuanteous Surface—Epidermis—Cuticle—Corium — The True Skin — Epithelium, etc. — The Skin is under the external rulership of the ♑ sign, and also ruled by ♄. The Skin is also largely influenced by the ♎ sign, the exalted sign of ♄. By internal government the skin is influenced by all the cardinal signs, and planets in these signs. Cardinal signs denote the skin. The external layer of the skin is called the Epithelium, the Epidermis, the Cuticle, or Scarf Skin. The Derma is the deep layer of the Skin, known as the Corium, Cutis, or True Skin. (See Cutis, Derma). The principle of ♄ is Limitation, and he, therefore, rules the skin and bones, as these tend to define and limit the corporature. (See Capricorn, Saturn Influence). The planets tend to affect the skin according to their nature. Venus tends especially to affect the complexion, and the skin of the face, and to cause disorders thru the wrong use of Cosmetics. Mars causes inflammations of the skin. The afflictions of ♅ and ☿, disorders of the nerves of the skin. Saturn tends to hardening, thickening, scaling, dryness, and chilling of the skin, etc. (See Centripetal). This Article is divided into Two Sections. Section One—Characteristics of the Skin. Section Two—Diseases of the Skin.

— SECTION ONE —

CHARACTERISTICS OF THE SKIN— These are also largely considered in the Articles on Appearance, Blemishes, Complexion, Face, Marks, Moles, Scars.

Black Skin—Black Personal Figure— (See "Dark Complexion" under Complexion; "Figure" under Dark; Races).

Brown Skin—(See "Complexion" under Brown).

Chalky and White—♓ gives, and especially when on the Asc. at B.; ♅ or ☿ rising in the Asc., white skin. (See Pale, Sickly; "Complexion" under White).

Clear Skin — Clear and Lucid — (See "Clear" under Complexion).

Color of the Skin—The First House has signification of the color of the skin, the complexion, form, shape, etc. (See the various paragraphs in this section, and under Color, Complexion, Face, Races).

Complexion—(See the paragraphs under Complexion).

Dark Skin—(See "Dark" under Complexion; "Figure" under Dark).

Delicate Skin—♍, ♒, and ♓ give when on the Asc. at B. (See "Delicate" under Complexion).

Face—Skin of—(See the various paragraphs under Face).

Fair Skin—(See "Fair", "Light", under Complexion; "Degrees" under Light).

Flabby Skin—(See Flabby, Wrinkles).

Glossy Skin — O i l y — S h i n y — (See Shiny).

Hard and Rough Skin—Denoted by ♄. (See "Skin" under Hard; "Thick" in this section).

Negro Race—(See Negro, Races).

Oily Skin—(See Oils, Shiny).

Pigment In—(See Sulphur; "Pigmentation" in Sec. 2 of this Article).

Pure Skin—♒ gives. (See "Pure" under Complexion).

Race Color—(See "Color" in this section).

Rough and Hard—(See "Hard" in this section; "Rough" in Section Two of this Article).

Shiny and Oily—(See Oils, Shiny).

Soft Skin — ♍ gives a soft, velvety skin, and pure, delicate, thin, and easily broken or injured. (See "Delicate" in this section).

Sulphur Pigment—(See Sulphur).

Tender Skin—White and Tender Skin —The ☉ strong at B., and produced by the ☉ influence.

Thick Skin—♄ gives; ♄ ascending at B. (See "Skin" under Hard).

Thin Skin — (See "Soft" in this section).

Vaso-Constrictor Nerves—Of the Skin —(See "Vaso-Constrictor" under Vaso).

White and Chalky—(See "Chalky" in this section).

White and Tender—(See Chalky, Delicate, Tender, in this section).

Yellow Skin — (See "Yellow" under Complexion, Face; "Jaundiced Look" under Jaundice).

— SECTION TWO —

DISEASES OF THE SKIN—See "Tendency to Skin Diseases" in this section for the general influences which make one more liable to skin diseases. The following subjects have to do with the diseases, afflictions, hurts and injuries to the skin. See these subjects in the alphabetical arrangement when only listed here—

Abrasions; Abscesses; Acne;

Acute Diseases Of — A c u t e Pustular Inflammation — (See Eruptions; Impetigo; "Inflammation" in this section).

All Cutaneous Diseases—♍ diseases.

Anthrax—(See Carbuncles).

Arms — ♀ in signs which rule the arms, hands, legs, and feet tends to skin eruptions of these parts, and skin affections due to wrong habits of living, and also tends to blackheads. Mars in signs which rule these parts tends to skin diseases of an inflammatory nature. Saturn in such signs tends to chill the skin, disturbances of the capillary circulation, the nerves of the skin, and to dryness, shrinking, hardening, contractions, defects, and various impediments. These influences also may apply to the skin of any part of the body. (See "Eruptions" under Arms).

Asphyxia—Cutaneous Asphyxia—(See "Cutaneous" under Asphyxia).

Barber's Itch—(See Barbers).

Bathing; Birthmarks—(See Naevus).

Blackheads—(See "Comedo" under Sebaceous; "Arms" in this section).

Bleeding; Blemishes; Blisters; Blood —(See "Skin" under Blood).

Blotches; Blows; Blue Discolorations— (See Cyanosis; "Bluish" under Marks).

Boils; Breakings Out—(See Breakings Out, Eruptions, Pimples).

Breathing—Skin Breathing Interfered With—(See "Cutaneous" under Asphyxia).

Bruises; Bunions; Burns; Cancer— (See Carcinoma).

Capillaries—Disturbances of'—(See Capillaries, Centripetal, Constrictions; "Vaso-Constrictor" under Vaso; "Arms" in this section).

Carbuncles; Carcinoma; Chickenpox; Chilblain; Chill—The Surface Chilled —(See Capillaries, Centripetal, Chill, Constrictions; "Vaso-Constrictor" under Vaso).

Chloasma—(See "Pigmentation" in this section).

Chlorosis — Greenish Discoloration— (See Chlorosis).

Chronic Skin Trouble—(See Psoriasis).

Coarse and Rough Skin—(See "Rough" in this section).

Cold Skin—♄ in ♑. (See "Chill" in this section; the Introduction under Cold; Hemachromatosis).

Color Of—Discolorations—(See Discolorations, Pigmentation, Red, White, Yellow, in this section; "Color" in Sec. 1 of this Article).

Comedo—(See "Blackheads" in this section).

Complexion—Disorders of—(See Complexion, Cosmetics; "Lotions" under Face).

Compound Fractures—Breaking Thru the Skin—(See Fractures).

Congestions—Caused by Chill of the Skin—(See "Chill" in this section; Congestions).

Constrictions—Due to Chill—(See "Chill" in this section).

Contractions—Due to Cold and Chill —(See Centripetal, Chill, Constrictions, Contractions; Arms, Chill, in this section).

Contusions—(See Bruises).

Cornification; Corns; Cosmetics—Disorders from Wrong Use of—(See Cosmetics).

Crusts; Cutaneous Disorders—All Cutaneous Diseases—♍ diseases, and afflictions in ♑. (See "Tendency To", and the various subjects in this section).

Cuticle—Epidermis—Scarf Skin—Epithelium—Disorders of—♍ diseases, and afflictions in ♑; ♄ diseases, causing hardening, thickening, etc.; ♂ causes inflammatory conditions of. (See the various paragraphs in this section).

Cutis—D e r m a—Corium—The True Skin—Disorders of—♄ and ♑ diseases; ♂ diseases, with inflammations, abscesses, etc. (See the various paragraphs in this section).

Cuts; Cyanosis Discolorations— (See Cyanosis).

Dead Tissue—(See Crusts, Scales, Sloughing; "Dry" in this section).

Defects—(See Blemishes, Blotches, Defects, Marks, Moles, Naevus, Scars; "Arms" in this section).

Dermatitis—(See "Cutis", "Inflammation", in this section).

Discharges; Discolorations— (See Chlorosis, Cyanosis, Marks, Moles, Naevus, Scabs, Scars; Pigmentation, Red, Yellow, in this section).

Dry Skin—♄ the afflicting planet; ♄ ✶ or △ the Asc.; ♍ on the Asc. (See Crusts; "Body" under Dry; Hardening, Hemachromatosis, Psoriasis, Scales, Shrinkage, Tetter, Withering, Wrinkles, Xeransis, etc.).

Ducts— (See Ducts, Follicles, Sebaceous).

Eczema; Efflorescence; Elephantiasis;

Ephemeral Skin Eruption—(See Urticaria).

Epidermis—Disorders of—(See "Cuticle", and the various paragraphs in this section).

Epithelioma; Eruptions; Erysipelas;

Exanthema; Excoriations—(See Abrasions).

Excrescences; Exudations; Face—Skin Disorders of — (See Acne, Cosmetics; "Lotions" under Face; Pimples).

Favus; Feet—Skin Disorders of—(See "Eruptions", and the various paragraphs under Feet; "Arms" in this section).

Flabby; Fluids — (See Elimination, Excretion; "Skin" under Fluids; Osmosis, Sebaceous, Sweat).

Follicles; Freckles; Gangrene; Glands —(See "Skin" under Glands).

Glossy Skin—(See Oils, Shiny).

Greenish Discoloration—(See Chlorosis).

Growths; Gunshot Wounds — (See Gunshot).

Habits — Skin Diseases from Wrong Habits of Living — (See Cosmetics; "Eruptions" under Face; Pimples; "Arms" in this section).

Hair—Hairy Body—(See "Body" under Hair).

Hands — (See "Skin" under Hands; "Arms" in this section).

Hardening—(See "Skin" under Hard; Hemachromatosis; Rough, Thick, in this section).

Hemorrhage — Into the Skin — (See Purpura, Scurvy).

Herpes; Hives; Horny; Hot Skin — (See Fevers; "Body" under Heat).

Hurts To—(See Blows, Bruises, Burns, Cuts, Hurts, Injuries, Instruments, Stabs, Weapons, Wounds, etc.).

Hyperaemia; Hypertrophy;

Icthyosis—(See Xeroderma).

Impediments — (See Impediments; "Arms", and the various paragraphs in this section).

Impetigo; Incised Wounds—(See Cuts, Instruments, Stabs).

Indurations; Infections; Inflammation —Inflammatory Skin Complaints—Dermatitis—Cutaneous Inflammations— Caused by ♂; ♂ afflicted in ♍. Mars in any sign tends to inflammation of the skin of the part ruled by such sign. Red color, red rays, or to be confined in a red room, are good in the treatment of inflammatory skin diseases. Chilblains are cutaneous inflammation due to cold. (See Chilblain, Impetigo, Inflammation, Psoriasis; "Treatment" under Red; Swellings, etc.).

Injuries to Skin—(See "Hurts" in this section).

Itch; Ivy Poisoning—(See Ivy).

Jaundiced Skin—(See "Yellow" under Complexion; Jaundice).

King's Evil—(See Scurvy).

Lead Color—(See Lead).

Leathery Skin—(See Hemachromatosis; Hardened, Rough, Thick, in this section).

Legs — (See "Skin Diseases" under Legs; "Arms" in this section).

Leprosy; Lips—(See "Scabbed" under Lips).

Liver Spots—(See "Spots" under Liver).

Lotions—Bad Effects of Face Lotions — (See Cosmetics; "Lotions" under Face).

Lupus; Marks; Measles; Membranes;

Moisture—Of the Skin—(See Exudations, Oils, Sweat).

Moles; Naevus; Nails; Nerves of Skin —(See Peripheral; "Arms" in this section).

Nettle Rash — (See Hives, Itch, Urticaria).

Nodules — (See "Nodules" under Nodes).

Nose—Morbid Red Nose—(See "Morbid Red" under Face; "Capillaries" under Nose).

Numbness; Obstructions—In the Skin —(See Comedo, Elimination, Eruptions, Excretion, Growths, Hardening, Inflammations, Pores, Swellings, and the various paragraphs in this section).

Oedema; Oily Skin—(See Oils, Shiny).

Oozing of Fluids—(See Oozing).

Operations — Surgical Incision—Best Time For—(See "Rules" under Operations).

Pale Skin—(See Pale, Sickly).

Papilloma; Papules; Paraesthesia;

Parched; Pigmentation—Chloasma— The color of the pigment in the skin, as in the different Races, is largely regulated by climatic conditions and the heat of the ☉. In the hottest Countries the pigment is dark, or black, as black does not absorb the heat as readily, and gives a cooler body. (See Races). Saturn contributes Sulphur for the pigment of the skin. (See Sulphur). People born under ♄, and with ♍ or ♒ on the Asc., or the ☉ and many planets in the signs of ♄, tend to white hair earlier in life, and due to the influence of ♄ in withdrawing the pigment, and also due to lower vitality. Various colorings of the skin are also caused by deposits from disease, as in Jaundice, or Chlorosis, Green Sickness.

(See Chlorosis; "Yellow Complexion" under Complexion; "Figure" under Dark; Yellow; Red, Yellow, in this section).

Pimples; Poison Ivy—Skin Susceptible To—(See Ivy).

Pores—(See Ducts, Glands; "Comedo" under Sebaceous; Sweat).

Porrigo—Scald-Head—(See Favus).

Prevalent—Skin Diseases Prevalent—♂ in ♐, ori., lord of the year at the Vernal).

Prickling Sensations—(See Prickling).

Pruritis—Intense Itching—(See Itch).

Psoriasis; Purpura; Pus—Pustules—Pustular Inflammation — (See "Pustular Diseases" under Pus).

Putrefaction—(See Putrid).

Rashes; Reddish Color—(See "Red Complexion" under Complexion; "Red" under Face; "Cheeks" under Red; "Ruddy Complexion" under Ruddy).

Remedies—Skin Remedies—(See Collyria, Lead, Lotions, Ointments, Zinc).

Rheum; Ringworm; Rose-Colored Skin —(See "Rosy" under Complexion).

Roseola; Rough Skin—Denoted by ♄; ♄ in ♌; ♄ in ♑, partile asp. the Asc., rough and coarse. (See Hardening, Thick, in this section; Hemachromatosis, Psoriasis, Scales).

Rubefacients; Rubeola—(See Measles).

Ruddy Looking — (See "Reddish" in this section).

Rush of Blood—To the Skin—♂ influence. (See Caustic, Centrifugal; "Action of Mars" under Mars; Rubefacient).

Saint Anthony's Fire — (See Erysipelas).

Sarcoma; Scabbed Lips—(See Lips).

Scabs—Scabies—(See Scabs).

Scald-Head—Porrigo—(See Favus).

Scalds; Scales; Scalp; Scarlatina; Scarlet Fever; Scars; Scrofula;

Scurvy; Searing—(See "Searing" under Burns).

Sebaceous Glands—Of Skin—(See Sebaceous).

Sensation; Senses—Sense of Touch—(See Feeling, Sensation, Sensibility, Touch).

Sensitive Skin — ♒ gives. Extreme sensitiveness of the skin is an ♒ disease, and afflictions in ♒. (See "Delicate" in Sec. 1 of this Article).

Shingles—(See "Herpes Zoster" under Herpes).

Shiny Skin—(See Oils, Shiny).

Shrinkage; Sickly Looking — (See Pale, Sickly; "Complexion" under White).

Sloughings; Smallpox; Soft Skin — (See Delicate, Soft, in Sec. 1 of this Article; Flabby, Laxity, Soft).

Sores; Stabs; Subcutaneous Diseases —(See Abscesses, Boils, Carbuncles).

Sudorifics; Suppressions—Suppression of Skin Breathing, or Elimination, Excretion, Sweat, etc.—(See "Cutaneous" under Asphyxiation; "Hindered" under Elimination; "Obstructions" under Excretion; Suppressions; "Lessened" under Sweat).

Surface Chilled — (See "Chill" in this section).

Sweat; Swellings; Syphilis;

Tendency to Skin Diseases—Liable to Cutaneous Disorders — The ☉ afflicted in ♎ or ♑; the ☽ hyleg in ♌, ♍, or ♑, and especially with females; the ☽ afflicted in airy signs; ☽ diseases, and the ☽ afflicted at B.; the ☽ in ♊ or ♍, afflicted by the ☉ or ♂ when taken ill, or the ☽ in ♑ (Hor'y); ♇ in ♑; ♇ in ♑ in the 6th H., and especially when afflicting the Asc. or hyleg; ♄ in ♋ or ♑, and especially when afflicting the ☉, ☽, Asc., or hyleg; ♃ afflicted in ♑, from indiscretions; ♃ afflicted in ♑ in the 6th H.; ♃ afflicted in ♋; ♂ afflicted in ♓, and ♂, P., □, or ☍ the Asc. by dir.; ♂ in ♑; ♀ afflicted in ♈, ♎, or ♑ in the 6th H., or afflicting the ☽ or Asc.; ♀ affl. in ♑; ♀ afflicted at B., and to the evil asp. the Asc. by dir.; the Asc. to the ill-asps. ♀ by dir., and ♀ afflicted at B.; ♎ or ♑ on the Asc.; a ♎ and ♑ disease; cardinal signs show, and especially afflictions in ♑; the malefics, or afflicting planets in cardinal signs; afflictions in ♌ or ♒, due to blood disorders; airy signs on the Asc. and 6th H. at B., or at decumb., or the ☽ in an airy sign at such times, indicate corrupt blood, gout, or cutaneous diseases. (See the various paragraphs in this section).

Tetters; Thickening—Of the Cuticle—♄ influence; a ♄ disease and affliction. (See "Skin" under Hard; Hemachromatosis, Thickening).

Tinea—(See Ringworm, Worms).

Tingling; Tissues; Touch — Disorders of Sense of — (See "Senses" in this section).

Toughening—Of the Skin—Caused by ♄, and brought about gradually with age. (See "Thickening" in this section).

Transudations—(See Exudations, Oozing, Osmosis).

Treatment — Of Skin Diseases — Red color, red rooms, red rays, red clothing, etc., are beneficial, as ♂ rules red, and ♂ color and remedies oppose the influence of ♄ in skin disorders. The acute and inflammatory skin conditions caused by ♂ are treated and opposed by the remedies of ♄, as Lead Ointments or solutions. (See Remedies, Water, in this section; Antipathy, Remedies, Treatment).

Tubercles; Tubercular Skin Diseases —(See Lupus, Scrofula).

Tumors; Ulcers; Urticaria;

Varicose Ulcers—(See Varicose).

Various Forms — Of Skin Diseases — (See "Tendency To", and the various paragraphs in this section).

Venereal Eruptions — (See "Chancroid" under Gonorrhoea; "Chancre" under Syphilis; Venereal).

Warts; Water—Water on the skin is Man's best friend to keep the skin clean, and prevent skin diseases. Hydrant water is good for external use, but after middle life, distilled water should be used exclusively for drinking purposes, as it is free from minerals, and helps to take up and absorb the excess of mineral deposits laid down by ♄, and to aid the kidneys in elimination, and prevent skin disorders. Max Heindel says, in the book, "Cosmo-Conception", — "Undistilled water, taken internally, is Man's worst enemy, but used externally on the skin, is his best friend." (See Bathing; "Mineral Waters" under Healers).

Wens; White Skin—(See "Chalky and White" in Sec. 1 of this Article).

Withering; Women — The Skin and Complexion In — (See "Skin" under Women).

Wounds; Wrinkles; Yellow Skin — Yellow Discoloration — (See "Yellow" under Complexion; "Yellow" under Face; "Jaundiced Look" under Jaundice; "Complexion" under Yellow; "Pigmentation" in this section).

Zoster — (See "Herpes Zoster" under Herpes). For subjects which may have been overlooked in this Article, look in the alphabetical arrangement for what you have in mind.

SKIPPISH MANNER — Jumps Forward When Speaking — Nods Head to One Side—(See "Nodding" in Sec. 1 under Head).

SKULL—Cranium—The Cranial Bones —The Bony Framework of the Head— The Bones of the skull are ruled by ♄, as ♄ rules the bones in general. Also the bones of the skull are under the structural rulership of the ♈ sign. Saturn in ♈ tends to especially affect the bones of the skull, and also the teeth and left ear. The Base of the Skull, or the Occipital Region, is ruled by the ♉ sign. (See Cranium, Occipital).

Depression In—Malformation—The ☉ or ☽ in the Asc., ill-aspected by ♅ or other malefics; malefics in the Asc.; ♈ on the Asc. and containing malefics, and especially ♄ or ♅. (See "Skull" under Excrescences; "Deformities", "Malformations", under Head; Idiocy).

Excrescences—Hemispherical Excrescences on the Skull — Case — (See "Skull" under Excrescences).

Fontanelles—Slow Closure of—(See "Fontanelles" under Head).

Fracture—♄ or ♂ afflicted in ♈ in the Asc.; a ♓ affliction, and afflictions in ♊. Case—See "Run Over", No. 853, in 1001 N.N. (See "Accidents To" under Head).

Longitudinal Depression—In Central Part of Head — (See "Malformation" under Head).

Malformation — (See "Skull" under Excrescences; "Deformities", "Malformation", under Head; Hydrocephalus, Idiocy).

Pressure — Upon the Brain — (See "Nerves" under Pressure).

Skin Over Skull — (See Forehead, Scalp, Temples).

Soft Water Excrescences — Of the Skull — (See "Skull" under Excrescences).

SLANDEROUS—Slander—(See Disgrace, Libel; "Scandalmongers" under Scandal).

SLAUGHTER — Bloodshed — Murders— Killed In Battle and War—

A Lover of Slaughter—♂ ill-dignified at B., and afflicted. (See "Shedding of Blood" under Blood; Cruel; "Murderous" under Murder; Vicious, Violent).

Great Men—Slaughter of—(See Assassination, Famous; "Great Men" under Great; "Assassination" under Kings; President).

Much Slaughter Everywhere—Slaughter Prevalent—An eclipse of the ☉ in ♏; an eclipse of the ☉ in the 2nd decan. of ♊, the 3rd dec. of ♌ or ♍, or in the 1st dec. of ♏; ♄ ☌ ♂ in the first three degrees of ♎; ♃ ☌ ♂ in the Asc. at the Vernal, and ♂ ℞ and in perigee; ♂ elevated above, and configurated with ☿ at a Solar Ingress or Eclipse; Comets appearing in ♈, ♊, ♋, ♌, ♎, ♏, ♐, ♒, or ♓. (See "Shedding of Blood" under Blood; "Blood" under Effusions; "Many Murders Prevalent" under Murder; "War and Bloodshed" under War).

Slaughter's Disease—(See "Knee Cap" under Knees).

War — Slaughter In — (See "War and Bloodshed" under War).

SLAVISH — Enslaved — Servile — (See "Morbid Fears" under Fears; "Negative Nature" under Negative; Servile, Servitude, etc.).

SLEEP — Drowsiness — Stupor — Soporifics — Sleeping Sickness — Insomnia, etc.—The Twelfth House rules and governs Sleep. (See Twelfth House). The following paragraphs and subjects have to do with Sleep, and Disorders of Sleep, or Consciousness, which see in the alphabetical arrangement when only listed here—

Anaesthetics; Analgesia; Anodynes; Brain Fag—(See Brain).

Broken Sleep — Sleep Disturbed — Sleeps Unquietly — Wakefulness — Insomnia, etc.—The ☽ in ♉, and afflicted by ♂ or the ☉ when taken ill, or the ☽ ☌ ♂ in the Asc. when taken ill (Hor'y). (See Illness, Insomnia, Refreshment, Rest, in this section).

Catalepsy; Cold Feet — Wakefulness By—(See "Cold Feet" under Feet).

Coma; Consciousness; Deep Sleep — (See Catalepsy, Coma, Trance).

Died During Sleep—Case—See "Sarasto", No. 329, in 1001 N.N.

Disorders of Sleep—Caused especially by afflictions in ♈. (See the various paragraphs in this section).

Disturbed Sleep — (See Broken, Cold Feet, Coma, Insomnia, Rest, and the various paragraphs in this section).

Dreams; Drowsiness—Inclined to Sleep — Somnolence — Sleepiness — Stupor— The ☽ in ♌ and afflicted by the ☉ or ♂ when taken ill (Hor'y); a ♅ disease; ♄ ☌ the Asc. by dir., a lethargic drowsiness; ♃ afflicted in ♈. (See "Brain Fag" under Brain; "Mind" under Dull; "Sleepy Eyes" under Eyes; Fatigue, Lassitude, Lethargy, Narcotics, Refreshment, Rest; "Heaviness of Mind" in this section).

Drugs — Sleep - Producing Drugs — Soporifics—Narcotics—Ruled by the ☽ and ♅. (See Narcotics; "Sleep-Inducing" in this section).

Epilepsy; Eyes — (See "Sleepy Eyes" under Eyes).

Fainting; Fatigue; Heart Action— Sleeping Potions Harmful To — (See "Sleeping Potions" under Heart).

Heaviness of Mind—Dull—Drowsiness —The ☽ in ♈, □ or ☍ ♄ (or ☿ if he be of the nature of ♄) when taken ill, or at decumbiture (Hor'y). (See "Mind" under Heavy; "Drowsiness" in this section).

Horrors During Sleep—(See Dreams; "Nightmare" in this section).

Hypnotic Sleep—(See Hypnotism).

Illness—From Want of Sleep or Due Refreshment—(See Refreshment, Rest; "Insomnia" in this section).

Inclined to Sleep—(See "Drowsiness" in this section).

Insensibility; Insomnia—Inability to Sleep — Broken Sleep — Nervous Disorders of Sleep—Wakefulness—Sleeplessness — The ☽ afflicted in ♈ or ♎; the ☽ hyleg in ♈, and afflicted, and especially with females; any ill-aspects to the ☽ or ☿ tend to by affecting the emotions, but the evil is less when the cadent houses are not involved; ♆ ☌ the ☽ in ♈, and afflicted by the □ or ☍ of ♅ and ♂; ♅ or ☿ afflicted in ♈; ♂ in ♈, and especially when in ☌ or, ill-asp. the ☉; denoted by ☿; a ☿ disease; ☿ afflicted in ♈; ☿ ☌ ♂ in ♈; ☿ ☌ ♀ in ♈, and in □ or ☍ ♆, ♃, or the ☽; an ♈ and ♎ disease, and especially when these signs are on angles, or strongly occupied at B.; many planets in ♈ at B.; a 12th H. influence, and planets therein; afflictions to the 12th H. from other cadent houses; afflictions in ♓, and especially ♄ in ♓, tends to Insomnia from cold feet. (See "Cold Feet" under Feet; Refreshment, Rest; Broken Sleep, Wakefulness, in this section).

Lack of Sleep—(See "Diseases" under Pain; Refreshment, Rest; "Suffers Much" under Sickness; Broken Sleep, Insomnia, Wakefulness, in this section).

Mind — Heavy Drowsiness of Mind — (See "Brain Fag" under Brain; "Mind" under Dull, Heavy; Drowsiness, Heaviness, in this section).

Moonlight and Sleep — (See "Sleep" under Moon; "Sleep-Inducing" in this section).

Narcotics; Neptune — (See "Influence Of" under Neptune).

Nervous Disorders — Of Sleep — (See Insomnia, Wakefulness, in this section).

Nightmare—Horrible Dreams During Sleep—♆ in ♈, □ or ☍ the ☽ at B., and ♆ afflicted by dir. (See Dreams, Obsessions, Spirit Controls). Nightmare occurs mostly about 48 hours before the Moon's perigee, and when the ☽ is about an hour high.

Potions — Sleeping Potions — (See "Sleeping Potions" under Heart; Potions).

Quiet — Sleep tends to be more quiet during the Last Quarter of the ☽. (See "Last Quarter" under Moon).

Refreshment — Illness from Lack of Refreshing Sleep—(See Refreshment, Rest).

Rest — Sickness from Lack of Rest and Sleep — (See Refreshment; "Sickness" under Rest; "Insomnia" in this section).

Restoring Sleep — Sleep is more restoring from midnight to sunrise. (See "Quiet" in this section).

Sedatives; Sleep-Inducing Drugs — (See Drugs, Potions, in this section; Anaesthetics, Narcotics, Sedatives, Soothing). Moonlight has a soothing, sleep-inducing effect, but tends to decay in the vegetable kingdom. It is advised that people do not sleep with the moonlight directly upon them, as it is depleting and weakening. (See Decay; "Sleep" under Moon).

Sleep-Walking—Somnambulism—The ☽ rising at B., and afflicted by ♆; the ☽ in the 1st H., and afflicted, and especially afflicted by ♆ at B., and by dir.; caused by planets in the 6th and 12th H., and in ☍ aspect, and especially where the ☽, ☿, and ♆ are involved; a ♆ disease, and caused primarily by ♆ afflictions to the ☽ or ☿ at B., and by dir., and occurs at times of such evil directions. Also caused by Subs at AT and AX. (See Hypnotism, Neptune, Obsessions, Spirit Controls).

Sleepiness—(See "Drowsiness" in this section).

Sleeping Dropsy—(See "Sleeping Sickness" in this section).

Sleeping Potions — (See Drugs, Potions, in this section).

Sleeping Sickness—Also called Sleeping Dropsy—Lethargic Encephalitis— A Peculiar Disease of West Africa, and characterized by increasing Drowsiness—A ♆ disease; afflictions of ♆ to the ☉, ☽, Asc., or hyleg at B., and by dir., and especially if ☿ is also involved in the configuration; ♆ ☌, □, or ☍ the ☉; ♆ afflicted in the 8th H. (See "Encephalitis" under Encephalon; Epidemics, Influenza, La Grippe, Lethargy; "Drowsiness" in this section).

Sleeplessness—(See Broken Sleep, Insomnia, Wakefulness, in this section).

Sleepy Eyes — (See "Sleepy" under Eyes; "Drowsiness" in this section).

Snoring — (See "Snoring" under Breathing).

Somnambulism—(See "Sleep Walking" in this section).

Somnolence — (See "Drowsiness" in this section).

Soothing Drugs — (See "Sleep-Inducing" in this section; Soothing).

Soporifics — (See "Sleep-Inducing" in this section; "Soporifics" under Narcotics; Soothing).

Stupor—Caused by ♆ afflictions; Subs at AT and AX. (See "Drowsiness" in this section; Analgesia, Anodyne, Coma, Consciousness, Delirium; "Mind" under Dull; Lethargy).

Swoonings—(See Fainting).

Trance; Unconsciousness — (See Consciousness).

Unquietly — Sleeps Unquietly — (See Broken, Insomnia, Wakefulness, in this section).

Walking In Sleep—(See "Sleep-Walking" in this section).

Wakefulness—The 3rd H. is said to rule wakefulness, and caused especially by malefics in this house afflicting the ☽, ☿, the hyleg, or Asc. at B., and by dir. (See Broken, Insomnia, in this section; "Cold Feet" under Feet; Refreshment, Rest).

Want of Sleep — Illness From — (See Refreshment, Rest; Broken, Insomnia, Wakefulness, in this section).

SLENDER—Thin Body—Lean Make—

Body—Slender Body—Slender Make— The ☉ in ♍; ♅ and ☿ make tall and thin, tall and slender; ♅ on the Asc., or in close aspect thereto, tends to give a slender body and long limbs; ♀ in ♈ or ♊; a ☿ person; ♍ on the Asc., slender, well-made, and of medium stature, but with females tends to give a slender little body; ♑ on the Asc., slender make, and with long, thin visage; the Autumnal Signs ♎, ♏, and ♐ on the Asc., or the ☉ or ☽ in these signs, the body is inclined to be lean and slender, and especially if ☿ is also oriental; the Quadrant from the Autumnal Equinox to the Winter Solstice makes slender. (See Lean, Tall, Thin).

Extremities—(See "Long and Slender" under Extremities).

Face—(See "Slender" under Face).

Graceful and Slender—(See Graceful).

Legs—(See "Slender" under Legs).

Limbs—(See "Slender" under Limbs).

Little, Slender Body — ♍ on the Asc., and especially with females.

Make—Slender Make, and with Long, Thin Visage—♑ on the Asc.

Medium Stature—Slender, Medium, and Well-Made—♍ on the Asc. (See Medium).

Middle Stature—And Slender—♀ in ♈ in partile asp. the Asc. (See Middle).

Short and Slender—♑ on the Asc., and tending to be ill-formed.

Tall and Slender — The ☉ or ☿ in ♍, partile the Asc.; the ☉ Sig. in ♎; ♅ and ☿ make tall and slender; ♀ in ♊, partile the Asc., tall, slender, and well-made; ♍ on the Asc., tall, slender, and well-proportioned; ♎ on the Asc., tall, slender, and graceful. (See Tall).

Thin, Tall, and Slender—The ☉, ♄, or ☿ in ♍, partile asp. the Asc.; indicated by ☿, and characteristic of ☿ people. (See Tall, Thin).

Upright and Slender—♃ in ♎ in partile asp. the Asc. (See Erect, Upright).

Visage—Slender Visage—(See "Slender" under Face).

Well-Proportioned — And Slender — The ☉ or ☿ in ♍, partile the Asc.; ♍ on the Asc. (See Well-Proportioned).

Youth—Slender In Youth—♍ or ♎ on the Asc.

SLIGHT—

Slight Build—(See "Little Body" under Little; "Body" under Small).

Slight Cuts—(See Cuts).

Slight Deafness—(See "Slight" under Hearing).

Slight Deformities — A Little Deformed In Body—♄ or ♉ in the Asc.; ♑ on the Asc. (See Deformities).

Slight Disorders—(See Colds, Ephemeral; "Slight" under Excesses, Fevers,

Indiscretions; Indisposition, Mild, Minor, Transient).

Slight Fevers — (See "Slight" under Fever).

Slight Indisposition — (See Indisposition; "Quick Recovery" under Recovery).

Slights—Sensitive To—(See "Slights" under Sensitive). For further influences, such as slight cuts or injury to the face, head, and hands see "Cuts To" under Hands; "Accidents To" under Head).

SLIMY MATTER—The Breast Affected By—(See "Slimy" under Breast).

SLOTHFUL — ♂ weak and ill-dignified at B.; ♓ influence, and ♂ afflicted in ♓. (See Apathy, Careless, Dull, Idle, Indifferent, Indolent, Inertia, Labor, Lassitude, Lazy, Procrastination, Rouse, Slovenly, Uncleanly, etc.).

SLOUGHING — Dry Slough — Eschar — Ruled by ♂. (See Crusts; "Eschar" under Escharotic; "Crusts" under Tissue).

Sloughings — Denoted by ♀, those arising from weakness and poison. (See "Vascular Tissues" under Vascular).

Sloughing Sores—Denoted by ♀, such as arise from pustular diseases, as smallpox, measles, etc. (See Pus, Scabs, Smallpox, Sores, Ulcers, etc.).

SLOVENLY—Generally caused by ♄ influence, and ♄ afflicting ☿. (See Careless, Dirty, Dress, Filth; "Bad Habits" under Habits; Improvident, Indifferent, Knavish, Lazy, Neglectful, Slothful, Sluggish, Uncleanly, Untidy, etc.).

SLOW—Retarded—Hindered—Sluggish — Impeded — Arrested, etc. The influence of ♄ is to slow up conditions and functions in the body, and to hinder and retard. (See Hindrances, Impediments, Limitations, Obstructions, Retarded, Saturn, Stoppages, Suppressions, etc.).

Slow Death—(See "Lingering" under Death).

Slow Diseases—Are diseases of the ☉ and ♄. The course of chronic and permanent diseases is regulated by the motion of the ☉. (See Carcinoma, Chronic, Consumptions, Continuity, Duration; "Fixed Signs" under Fixed; Incurable, Inhibitions, Invalids, Lingering Diseases, Long Diseases, Low Fevers, Permanent Diseases, Phthisis, Prognosis, Prolonged, Saturn Influences, Tabes, Tedious, Tuberculosis, Wastings, etc.).

Slow Fevers—(See 'Slow" under Fevers).

Slow Functions — In Females — (See "Functions" under Females; "Slow" under Functions).

Slow Growth — (See "Arrested", "Retarded", under Growth).

Slow Mental Development—(See "Arrested", "Retarded", under Mentality; "Contracted", "Weak", under Mind).

Slow Motion—(See "Slow" under Gait, Motion, Movement, Planets; Impediments, Locomotion, Retarded, Sluggish, Stoppages, Suppressions).

Slow Pulse—(See "Slow" under Heart, Pulse).

Slow Recovery—Slow Recuperation—(See "Slow" under Recovery, Recuperation).

Slow of Speech — (See Halting, Impediment, Slow, Stammering, under Speech; "Slow of Voice" under Voice).

Slow of Voice—(See "Slow of Speech" in this section).

SLUGGISH—Slow —Inactive—Torpid—Dull—♄ influence.

Blood — (See "Sluggish Circulation" under Circulation).

Body—Sluggish Body—♄ afflicted in ♎. Also given by the water signs, and especially ♋ or ♓ on the Asc. Those parts of the body tend to be more sluggish which are ruled by the signs containing ♃ and ♀ at B. (See Dull, Idle, Inactive, Indifferent, Inertia. Lassitude, Lethargy, Listless, etc.).

Bowels — (See "Sluggish" under Bowels).

Circulation — (See "Sluggish" under Circulation).

Ears—Sluggish Circulation In—(See "Circulation" under Ears).

Eczema — Skin Diseases and Eczema from Sluggish Circulation—♃ afflicted in ♍. (See Eczema, Skin).

Fluids of the Body—Sluggish Condition of —. (See "Restricted", and the various paragraphs under Fluids).

Gastric Juices — Sluggish Production of—(See "Juices" under Gastric).

Heart — Sluggish Action of — (See "Slow Action" under Heart).

Kidneys—(See "Sluggish" under Kidneys).

Liver—(See "Sluggish" under Liver).

Oesophagus — Sluggish Action of — (See Oesophagus).

Parts of the Body — The Sluggish Parts—(See "Blood" in this section).

Peristaltic Action—Sluggish and Impeded—(See Peristalsis).

Persons — Sluggish Persons — Dull People—The ☽ separating from ♂ and applying to ♄. (See Dull, Heavy, Inactive, Inertia, Labor, Lassitude, Lazy, Lethargy, Slothful, Slovenly, etc.).

Secretions Sluggish—(See Secretions).

Skin Diseases—From Sluggish Circulation—(See "Eczema" in this section).

Spinal Fluids — Sluggish and Obstructed — (See "Obstruction" under Spine).

Stomach — Sluggish Action of — (See "Peristaltic Action", "Sluggish", under Stomach). For further study see Hindrances, Retarded, Retention, Stagnant, Stoppages, Suppressions.

SLY — (See Cheating, Deceitful, Dishonest, Hypocritical, Petifogging, Shrewdness, etc.).

SMALL—Diminutive—Little—

Animals — (See "Small" under Animals).

Body—Small Body—♄ influence tends to a small body and small features; ♄ rising in ♑ tends to reduce the stature; ♄ lord of the Asc. and occi.,

as between the Nadir and Asc., or between the M.C. and Descendant, gives a small, thin body, and with dark complexion; ♋ on the Asc. gives short, small persons; the second half of ♌ on Asc., smaller than when first half is rising; ♑ on the Asc., short, slender, and ill-formed. (See "Body" under Diminished; Dwarfed; "Mean Stature" under Mean; "Body" under Short) .

Bones — (See "Small" under Bones; "Body" in this section).

Bowels—The Small Intestines—(See "Small Intestines" under Bowels).

Eyes—(See "Small" under Eyes).

Face—(See "Narrow", "Small", under Face).

Features — (See "Small", "Thin", under Features).

Fever — (See "Small Fevers" under Fever).

Finger Nails—(See "Small Nails" under Nails).

Head — (See "Little", "Small", under Head).

Hips—(See "Small" under Hips).

Intestines — (See "Small" under Bowels).

Lean, Small and Thin — (See "Small" under Lean).

Legs—(See "Small" under Legs).

Mean, Small Figure — (See "Mean Stature" under Mean).

Mind—A Small Mind—(See "Light In Mind" under Mind).

Neck—(See "Small" under Neck).

Shrill, Small Voice—(See Voice).

Slender, Small Body—Slender, Small Legs — (See "Slender" under Legs; "Little" under Slender).

Smaller and Weaker Bodies—Planets oriental, and in their second orientality, cause smaller and weaker bodies. (See "Weak Body" under Weak).

Smallpox; Thighs — Small Hips and Thighs — (See "Small" under Hips, Thighs).

Thin, Small and Lean—(See "Small" under Lean; Thin).

Voice—(See "Small" under Voice).

Weak, Small Figure — (See "Mean Stature" under Mean).

Weaker and Smaller Bodies — (See "Smaller and Weaker" in this section).

Weakly, Small and Sickly—♃ in ♍, partile the Asc. (See "Constitution" under Sickly).

SMALLPOX — Variola — Varioloid Diseases—Caused principally by ♂, and ♂ too much in evidence at B.; ♂ afflicted in the Asc. at B., and ♂ in the Asc. tends to precipitate the disease when ♂ reaches the ☌ the rising degree at B.; ♂ ☌ the Asc. by dir.; ♂ in ♈ or ♑; ♂ afflicted in ♈ tends to blindness by smallpox; ♂ in ♈ in the 6th H.; ♂ exactly rising or setting at B., and especially in ♈, ♉, or ♍; ♂ afflicted in ♊ or ♍, and ♂ ☌, P., or evil asp. the Asc. by dir.; ♂ afflicted in ♓, and ☌, P., □, or ☌ the Asc. by dir.; this disease is peculiar to ♂, and often happens when ♂ is □ the Asc. in the

Zodiac; the ☉ afflicted in ♋; the ☉ to the ☐ or ☍ the ☽ by dir., and the ☽ afflicted by ♂ at B.; the ill-asps. of the ☉ to the hyleg or Asc. by transit or dir. tend to if the ☉ be afflicted by ♂ at B.; the ☉, ☽, or Asc. to the ☌, P., ☐, or ☍ ♂ by dir.; a ☽ disease; the ☽ afflicted in ♋ or ♏; the ☽ afflicted in ♏, and afflicting the hyleg therefrom; the ☽ in an earthy sign, and to the ☌, P., or ill-asp. ♂ by dir., and the ☽ hyleg; the ☽ afflicted in a watery sign, and to the ill-asps. ♀ by dir.; caused by afflictions to the ☽; the ☽ to the ill-asps. ♀ by dir., and ♀ in a watery sign at B.; ♄ in ♋, ♏, or ♓, and ☌, P., or evil asp. the Asc. by dir.; ♃ in an airy or watery sign, peregrine, and ☌ the Asc. by dir.; a pustular disease denoted by ♀; the Asc. to the ☌ or ill-asp. ♂ by dir., and ♂ in ♉ at B.; the Asc. to the ☐ or ☍ ♃ by dir., and ♃ afflicted by ♂ at B.; attacks are liable when the ☉, ☽, Asc., or hyleg, come to the ☌, P., or ill-asps. ♂ by dir.; the Asc. to the place of ☋ by dir.; the hyleg much afflicted at B. by ♂; an ♈ disease when malefic planets are in ♈ at B.; a ♌ disease, and caused by afflictions in ♌; the 6th face of ♉ on the Asc., and with the Pleiades in the Asc.; Subs at MCP 4, 5C), and at CP, or KP (11D). (See Chickenpox, Measles, Scabs, Scarlatina; Face, Pitted, Pock-Marked, and the various paragraphs in this section).

Blindness By—(See "Smallpox" under Blindness).

Children Die—From Smallpox—(See "Mortality Great" under Children).

Children Suffer—From Smallpox, but May Not Die—♂ coming to the ☌ or ill-asp. the Asc. early in life tends to smallpox, measles, or scarlatina. The ☽ to the ☐ or ☍ ♀ by dir. tends to smallpox in children.

Death by Smallpox — Great Danger of—♂ afflicting the ☉, ☽, Asc., or hyleg by dir.; ♂ in ♉ or ♏, and afflicting the hyleg; ♂ denotes. Case of Death By—See "Prince", No. 651, in 1001 N.N. (See Measles, Scarlet Fever).

Epidemic of Smallpox — Smallpox Prevalent — ♂ is supreme in years of smallpox epidemics, and afflicts the hyleg in those affected; ♂ supreme at the Equinoxes and Solstices; ♂ ☍ the ☉ at the Vernal; ♂ predominating at a ☌ of three or four superior planets, and severe in type, but milder when ♂ is in ☌ or ☍ only one other superior planet, and ♂ holding power; ♂ in the 8th H. at a Solar Ingress into ♈, and afflicting the ☽ or planet ascending; ♃ in perigee tends to a great epidemic of smallpox, and which spreads and proves fatal in spite of vaccination. (See Epidemics).

Eyes — Blindness In by Smallpox — (See "Smallpox" under Blindness).

Face—Smallpox In—Pock-Marked—Pitted Face — A ♂ affliction; ♂ in ♈, and especially in the Asc.; caused by ♅ afflictions, and with ♅ in ♈ or the 1st H., and configurated with ♂ at B.; ♅ ☌ ♂ at B., and especially in the Asc.; in Hor'y Q. indicated by the ☽ with ♄ in ♈; ♀ Sig. in ♈, and especially if ♀ is afflicted by ♂; the 5° ☐ on the Asc.; the first face of ♓ on the Asc.,

and ♂ therein; the Asc. or its lord in one of the pitted degrees of the Zodiac at B. (See Pitted, Scars).

Immunity from Smallpox — There is little danger of taking smallpox unless ♂ afflicts the ☉, ☽, or Asc. at B., or in a train of evil directions. Vaccination is not needed in cases immune from this disease from birth. Also, in cases destined to fatality by the afflictions of ♂ to the ☉, ☽, Asc., or hyleg at B. vaccination is of little, or no avail. (See Immunity; "Epidemic" in this section).

Pitted Degrees—Of the Zodiac—The Asc., or its lord, in one of these degrees at B. tends to leave pitted scars on the face. (See Pitted; "Face" in this section).

Pock-Marked — (See "Face" in this section).

Prevalent—Smallpox Prevalent—(See "Epidemic" in this section).

Treatment—Of Smallpox—Red color, the color ruled by ♂, and to be confined in a red room, or have red rays and lights about the patient, is said to help alleviate the severity of the disease. This is on the theory of treatment by Similars and Sympathy. Also on this basis Vaccination often proves beneficial and preventive, which is the introduction of the lymph from the cow-pox vesicle into the human body, which lymph is under the rule of ♂, the same as ♂ rules the vesicle in the human. There is also a tablet remedy, known as "Double Sulphide", discovered and advocated by Dr. William Burgess, of the New Field Laboratory, Chattanooga, Tenn. Dr. Burgess is now deceased, and the address of this Laboratory is now P. O. Box 52, Lawrence, Long Island, New York. This remedy is a combination of Lime, Sulphur, and Magnesia, and quickly raises the resistance of the body, and overcomes the disease in a short time. Also, it is claimed, if these tablets are taken immediately after exposure to smallpox, the disease does not develop in the patient. Every family should have a box of these tablets in the house for emergencies in Chickenpox, Measles, Smallpox, Rashes, and Epidemic Diseases. This tablet is made up of materials ruled by ♄, ♂, and ♅, and represents a combination of both Antipathy and Sympathy in the treatment. The remedies of ♄ oppose the diseases of ♂. (See Antipathy, Opposites, Red, Remedies, Sympathy, Treatment).

Vaccination—(See "Immunity" in this section).

Varioloid Diseases—♂ afflicted in ♑.

Vascular Tissues—Affected by Smallpox — (See "Vascular Tissues" under Vascular).

Young People—Many Die of Smallpox —(See "Mortality Great" under Children).

SMART—

Smart Appearance—Smart and Active Appearance—☐ on the Asc. at B. (See "Body" under Active; Brisk, Energetic, Quick, etc.).

Smart In Learning — (See Learning; "Quickened" under Mentality; "Good Mind" under Mind; Reading, Scholar, Study, etc.).

Smart and Quick Step — (See "Energetic" under Gait).

SMELL—The Sense of Smell—Olfaction—Olfactory Nerves—The etheric vibrations of ☿ give Smell. Also ruled by ♂. Wilson, in his Dictionary, says the Olfactory Nerves are ruled by ♀. Smell is also influenced by the ♏ sign, which sign rules the nose, and ♄ or ♂ afflicted in this sign tend to affect the smell, and cause various disorders of smell. Loss of Smell (Anosmia), and Perversions of Smell (Parosmia), are caused by ♄ afflicted in ♏, and also by Subs at AT, AX, and MCP (3, 4C). (See Nose). The Hebrew Letter Samech (S) is connected with the sense of Smell.

SMILES—Smiling Face—Pleasing Smiles —♀ in the Asc., or ruler of the Asc., well-aspected and dignified, gives dimples, and a pleasing, smiling face; ♀ Sig. in ♎, pleasing smiles; in Hor'y Q., ♀ Sig. of the person. Also, the ☽ Sig. in ♒, gives a smiling, cheerful, kind, humane, and benevolent countenance. People born under ♄ are not much given to smiles, as they are of a more serious, melancholic and taciturn nature. (See Cheerfulness, Contentment, Countenance, Dimples, Expression; "Smiling" under Face; Happiness, Humane, Joyful, Ҝind, Laughter; "Peace of Mind" under Mind; Mirth, Optimistic, Pleasant; "Sanguine Temperament" under Sanguine).

SMOKING — (See "Drug Heart" under Heart; Narcotics, Tobacco).

SMOKY — The Smoky Degrees of the Zodiac—If the Asc., or its lord, are in any of these degrees at B., the native is more dun and swarthy of complexion, and with a dull intellect. These degrees are as follows—0° ♈; 0° ♉; 0° ♊; 20° ♋; 20° ♌; 22° ♍; 0° ♎; 24° ♏; 23° ♐; 15° ♑; 4° ♒; 0° ♓. (See "Swarthy" under Complexion; "Mind" under Dull).

SMOOTH—

Body—Smooth Body—The ☽ gives a smooth, corpulent, and phlegmatic body; the ☽, when oriental, gives a smooth, corpulent, and tall body; ♄ in S. Lat. tends to a smooth and fleshy body, but in N. Lat. to one more lean, hairy, and bony; ♂ in ♈, partile the Asc., and occi., the native will be more ruddy and smooth, but if ♂ be ori., tall and less swarthy.

Face—(See "Smooth" under Face).

Hair—(See "Smooth" under Hair).

SMOTHERED — Smothering — Smothering Sensation — Danger of Being Smothered — (See Angina, Asphyxia, Cyanosis, Fainting; "Faintings" under Heart; "Non-Oxygenation" under Oxygen; Strangulation, Suffocation).

SNAKES—(See Reptiles, Serpents).

SNEEZING—(See "Hay Fever", "Sneezing", under Nose).

SNORING—(See "Snoring" under Breathing).

SNOW—Snow is ruled by ♄.

Suffering From—Extremes of Snow— ♃ ☌ ♂, mischief by snow. The ♉ sign

ascending at the Vernal E., and ♀ afflicted, and especially in Countries ruled by ♉. (See Blizzards, Cold, Frost, Hail, Ice, Saturn, Storms, Weather, Wind, Winter).

SNUFF—(See "Snuff" under Narcotics).

SNUFFLES — Snuffling — Snaffling — (See "Snuffling" under Nose).

SOBER—Well-Balanced—Self-Possessed — Dispassionate — Even-Tempered — Grave—Seriously Thoughtful, etc.—

Sober and Commanding—Born under ♃. (See Commanding).

Sober and Manly—(See "Manly" under Manner).

Sober and Serious—(See Despondent, Grave, Melancholic; "Serious Mind" under Serious, etc.).

SOCIAL RELATIONS — Social Life — Society — Social Diseases, etc. — The following subjects have to do with the Social Life, and the Social Relations of the native, his dealings with others, etc., and also with the dealings of the Social Classes with each other. The position, strength, power, weakness, and afflictions to the planet ♀ in the map of birth indicate to a large degree the kind and nature of the dealings of the native with the World socially, and his fate in such matters. A strong ♃ at B. also will help the native to be fortunate and well-received by the people. Each of the planets in their own sphere, and their positions, aspects, and strength in the radical map, will play their part in the conduct of the native, for better or worse, and in accordance with the character, attainments, conduct, morals, motives, purposes, and self-control manifested. Many of the subjects in this book have a bearing upon social relations, and which would be too numerous to list here, but the following are a few of the more important ones. See the following subjects in the alphabetical arrangement when only listed here—

Amusements; Anarchists;

Aversion to Society—(See Aversions, Recluse, Renunciation, Seclusion, Secretive, Solitude, etc.).

Banishment; Busy-Body — (See Meddlers).

Character; Classes of Society — Much Discord Between—(See "Discord" under Quarrels).

Common People — Injured By — (See Common).

Companions — Companionships — (See Companions).

Conduct; Crime—Criminal Tendencies —(See Crime).

Dangerous; Deception; Destiny;

Destructiveness; Discord — Discord Between the Classes of Society—(See "Discord" under Quarrels).

Diseases — Social Diseases — (See "Scandalous Diseases" under Scandal; Venereal).

Enemies; Environment; Execrated;

Exile; External Influences—Reaction of the Native To—(See Environment, External, Influenced, Negative, Positive, Receptive, Ruling, Susceptibility).

Family Life—(See Family).

Fanatical—Fanatical Against Established Religion and Society—(See "Fanatical" under Religion).

Fate; Friends; Government — Rebellious Against the Government — (See Anarchists, Mutiny, Sedition).

Hand of Man—Injury or Death By—(See Hand of Man).

Hatreds; Honesty; Humanity—Every Evil Upon—(See Humanity).

Hypocrisy; Ideals; Imprisoned — (See Prison).

Jealousies; Judge — Sentenced By — (See Judges).

Laws—Disregard for Social or Moral Laws—(See "Moral Laws" under Love Affairs; "Loose Morals" under Morals).

Libelers; Love Affairs — (Note the various paragraphs under Love Affairs).

Marriage — (See the subjects under Husband, Marriage, Marriage Partner, Wife).

Men—The Many Conditions Affecting Men—(See the subjects under Men).

Mistrustful; Misunderstood;

Mob Violence—Victim of—(See Lynching, Mobs; "Flying Stones" under Stones; Trampled).

Money—Reckless In Use of—(See Expense, Money, Prodigal).

Morals — (See "Good", "Loose", and the various paragraphs under Morals).

Murderers; Neighbors; Outcaste — A Social Outcaste—♂ afflicted in the 12th H. (See Disgrace, Execrated; "Hated by Others" under Hatred; "Loss Of" under Reputation).

Pest to Society—(See Execrated).

Pleasures; Politics; Popularity;

Prattlers—(See Meddlers).

Property; Public — The Public — (See Public).

Quarrelsome; Radicalism;

Reactionary; Rebellious; Recluse;

Reformers; Relatives; Religion;

Renunciation; Reputation; Reserved;

Residence; Reverses; Revolutionary;

Riches; Riotous; Roamer; Ruin;

Secret Societies—(See Secret).

Secretive; Sedition; Sex Relations — (See Amorous, Cohabitation, Intercourse; "Adultery", "Liaisons", under Love Affairs; Marriage, Morals, Opposite Sex; "Passional Excesses" under Passion; Sensuality; "Clandestine" under Sex; Wanton, Wench, etc.).

Socialism; Suspicious;

Terror to Society—(See Execrated).

Thieves; Treachery; Treason — (See Sedition).

Unruly; Vagabond; Violent;

Wanderer; Wealth; Women — Conditions Affecting Women Socially—(See the various paragraphs under Women). For other subjects along this line, which may not be listed in this Article, look in the alphabetical arrangement for the subject you have in mind.

SOCIALISM—Socialism is said to be under the rule of ♅ and the ♒ sign, and is one of the New Movements now being brought into manifestation for the establishment of the Aquarian Age, Fraternity, and Justice, and the overthrow of the old Political Bosses. The Movement seems to be peculiar, and somewhat misunderstood, due to its Uranian character. Some of the influences in the radical map which indicate Socialistic tendencies are the ☉ ♂ or ill-asp. ♅; ♅ ♂ or ill-asp. ♂; ♅ afflicted in the 9th H.; lord of the 10th a malefic, and afflicted in the 12th H. Mars strong at B., rising and elevated, and configurated with ♅ and ☿, tends to make Extremists in any Cause of Reformation. (See Ideals, Ideas, Independent, Misunderstood, Politics, Radicalism, Reactionary, Rebellious, Reformers; "Fanatical" under Religion; Revolutionary).

SOCIETY—(See Social Relations).

SODIUM—Soda—Sodium is an alkaline metal, and the base of Salt. Being alkaline it is used internally to counteract over-acidity in the system, caused by the deposits, retentions, and suppressions of ♄. The Alkaline Salts in the body also help to keep the balance between acidity and alkalinity when they are normal. (See Acidity). Alkaline substances are under the rule of the positive planets, and the positive Signs of the Zodiac. The planet ♂ is, therefore, a strong ruler over Sodium, and tends to counteract the diseases of ♄ in the system, and to restore the balance of alkalinity in the body. The ☉, ♅, and ♃, being positive planets, also have a strong influence over Sodium, and its various forms. (See Alkalinity).

Sodium Chloride — Common Salt — Ruled by the ♒ sign, and is connected with the control of water in the system.

Sodium Hydrate — Caustic Soda — Is said to be strongly ruled by ♂, due to its caustic and escharotic qualities. (See Caustic).

Sodium Phosphate—The Salt ruled by the ♎ Sign, and is said to be connected with the acids of the body, and is a combination of Sodium and Phosphoric Acid. Libra is the exalted sign of ♄, and Sodium Phosphate is partly ruled by ♄, and also by ♀, negative planets which rule the acids in the body.

Sodium Salicylate—Partly ruled by ♄, due to the combination of Sodium with Salicylic Acid, and is strongly antipyretic, and opposes the fevers of ♂ when given internally in large doses. Also, due to its positive qualities, it is cholagogue and diaphoretic.

Sodium Sulphate — The Salt ruled by the ♉ Sign, and is connected with the elimination of water in the system. Internally Sodium Sulphate stimulates the liver, pancreas, and also the intestinal secretions, and acts as a purgative. (See "Salts" under Zodiac).

SODOMY — (See Homosexuality, Perversions).

SOFT—Softening—

Agents — Softening Agents — (See Emollient, Ointments, Resolvent).

Body—A Soft Body—(See Flabby).

Bones—Softening of—(See Rickets).

Brain—(See "Softening" under Brain).

Cellular Tissue—Soft Cellular Tissue —(See Parenchyma).

Chancre—Soft Chancre—Chancroid— (See Gonorrhoea).

Complexion—(See "Soft" under Complexion).

Effeminate and Soft — (See Effeminate).

Excrescences — Soft, Watery Excrescences—(See Excrescences).

Glandular Tissues — Softening of — (See "Softening" under Glands).

Hair—(See "Soft" under Hair).

Nature—Soft and Effeminate Nature —(See Effeminate).

Nerve Tissue — Softening of — (See "Softening" under Nerves).

Parts—Soft Parts—Enlargement and Thickening of — Acromegaly — (See "Acromegaly" under Enlargements; "Enlargements" under Extremities).

Skin—(See "Soft" under Skin).

Thickening — Of Soft Parts — (See "Parts" in this section).

Tissues—The Soft Tissues—Disorders of—(See Elephantiasis, Fiber, Flabby, Gangrene; "Softening" under Glands; Hypertrophy, Malacia, Mortification, Muscles, Parenchyma, Relaxation, Thickening; "Soft Tissues" under Tissues; Wastings; "Agents" in this section).

Tubercles — Softening of — (See Tubercles).

SOLANOID CANCER — (See "Solanoid" under Carcinoma).

SOLAR—Pertaining to the Sun—

Solar Eclipse—(See Eclipse).

Solar Forces—The Spleen is the gateway to the Solar Forces. (See "Forces" under Sun).

Solar Horas—(See Horas).

Solar Ingresses—(See Ingresses).

Solar Life Currents—The Vital Fluid —(See "Fluid" under Vital).

Solar-Lunar Activities—The combined influences of the ☉ and ☽ at B. represent the constitution and the health, and according to the harmony or adverse aspects existing between the ☉ and ☽ at B., so will the vitality, the efficiency of the functions, and the general health be. Dr. Duz. in his book, "Astral Medicine", discusses the Solar-Lunar System, and the Solar-Lunar Chart, from quite a new and advanced standpoint, and somewhat different from anything seen in the regular Textbooks of Astrology, and every student should read this book by Dr. Duz. (See Constitution, Functions, Health; "Quarters of the Moon" under Moon; "Moon and the Sun" under Sun; "Depletion", "Force", under Vital; "Good", "Low", under Vitality).

Solar Orb—(See "Forces" under Sun).

Solar Periodicity—(See "Periodicity" under Sun).

Solar Plexus — (See "Solar" under Plexus).

Solar Revolution—This is the return of the ☉ each year to the same degree of Longitude as in at B. These times are important to note in connection with health matters, as the malefics falling upon the places of the radical ☉, ☽, Asc., or hyleg, at the Solar Revolution tend to many evils, disturbances in the constitution or mind, and in the general affairs of the native, according to the nature of the afflicting planet, or planets. Solar Revolutions, Transits, or Directions, cannot bring anything to pass which is not shown in the map of birth. Chapter XXXVI in Pearce's Textbook of Astrology gives a good Treatise on Solar Revolutions, their various influences and aspects, and as related to disease. (See "Birthday" under Birth). The influences of Solar Revolutions are mentioned many times under the various diseases and afflictions in this book. The following are some of the subjects in which the Solar Rev. influence is mentioned. See these subjects in the alphabetical arrangement — Abroad; Anguish; "Causes" under Chronic; Contentment; "Causes" under Disease; Disgrace; Dissipation; Eclipses; "Conduct" under Evil; "Accidents To", "Eye Trouble", under Eyes; "Death In" under Family; "Danger To" under Father; "Death Of" under Friends; "Periods of Bad Health" under Health; Imbecility; Influenza; "Abroad" under Journeys; "Danger To" under Life; "Chronic Diseases" under Malignant; "Affliction Of", "Peace of Mind", under Mind; "Liable To" under Misfortune; "Danger To" under Mother; "Death Of" under Parents; "Periodic Revolution" under Periodic; "Danger of Imprisonment" under Prison; "Death By" under Rheumatism; "Birth Of" under Son).

Solar Spectrum — (See "Planets and Color" under Colors).

SOLDIERS—Military People—

Assaults By — Prevalence of — An eclipse of the ☽ in the 2nd decan. of ♑.

Bloodshed — Many Soldiers Killed — (See "Shedding" under Blood; "Shedding of Blood" under Shedding; Slaughter; "War and Bloodshed" under War).

Cruelty Of—Inhumanity of—Furiousness of—An eclipse of the ☉ in the 3rd decan. of ♓.

Danger To—The ☽ to the ☌ Aldebaran by dir. (See Army, Military; "Navy" under Ships; War).

Death by Soldiers—The ☽ with Sirius or ♄, or with Markab and ♂.

Death In the Service — (See "Battle" under Abroad; Military Life; "Death" under War).

Injury by Soldiers—The ☉ to the ☌ ♂ by dir. (See Assaults, Cruelty, Death By, in this section).

Killed In Battle—(See "Death In War" under War).

Officer Killed — (See "Officer Killed" under Military).

Slaughter — (See "Much Slaughter Everywhere" under Slaughter).

War—Death or Injury In—(See War).

Wounded In Battle—The ☉ Sig. ☌ ♂; the ☉ to the ☌ ♂ by dir. if ♂ afflict the

⊙ or hyleg at B.; ♂ in the Asc. at B., and ill-dignified, may be dangerously wounded; ♂ □ or ☍ the Asc., and if he is also in ☍ to the ⊙ or ☽, danger of a violent death, and if applying and near the exact ☍, killed on the spot. (See "Death or Injury In" under War).

SOLID—

Solid Constitution — Given by the earthy signs, and able to withstand much wear and tear. (See "Good" under Constitution; Endurance, Wear and Tear).

Solid Countenance—(See "Solid Countenance" under Face).

Solid Intellect—(See "Solidarity" under Intellect).

Solid Judgment—Void Of—(See "Bad Judgment" under Judgment).

Solid Learning—Void of—(See "Void Of" under Learning).

Solid Sense — (See "Good Judgment" under Judgment).

Solidification—Of the Body—(See Cirrhosis, Crystallization, Density, Deposits, Hardening, Lime, Minerals, Precipitation, Sclerosis, Stone, etc.).

SOLITARY VICE — Self-Abuse — (See "Solitary" under Vice).

SOLITUDE—

Fear and Dread Of — (See Darkness; "Solitude" under Fear).

Fond Of—Propensity to Solitude and Retirement—The ☽ P ♄ at B., and especially with females; ♄ inclines to solitude, and retirement from the World, which they equally fear and detest. (See Misanthropic, Mistrustful, Recluse, Renunciation, Reserved, Resignation, Retiring, Saturn, Seclusive, Secretive, Serious, Shy, Suspicious, Twelfth House, etc.).

SOLSTICES — The Summer and Winter Solstices—The Summer Solstice is when the ⊙ passes into the ♋ sign, usually on June 21st. At the Winter Solstice the ⊙ passes into the ♑ sign, usually on Dec. 21st or 22nd. These Solstice Points constitute the beginning of Angles in the map, and the cusps of the 4th and 10th Houses, and have an important bearing in health matters over the World in General, and also over the individual whose map of birth they may strongly affect. The influences of the configurations at the time of the Solstices are mentioned quite a number of times in this book under various diseases and conditions, and the following are a few of them. Also read the Chapter on "Equinoxes and Solstices" in Pearce's Textbook of Astrology, Chapter 2, of Book 2. The times of the Solstices are also Ingresses of the ⊙ into the ♋ and ♑ signs, known as the Tropical Signs. (See Equinoxes, Ingresses, Tropical, Vernal. Also see Angles, Cancer Sign, Capricorn Sign, Cardinal, Crime; "Air" under Dryness; "Dog Days" under Dogs; Epidemics; "Prevalent" under Fluxes; Fourth House, Hail; "Nil" under Mars Diseases; "Minor Disorders" under Minor; "Death" under Mutilated; "Great Pestilence" under Pestilence; "Sickly Summer" under Summer; Tenth House; "Dry" under Winter).

SOLUTION — Disintegration—The Termination of a Disease—A Crisis—Resolution In Disease, etc.

Disease — The Solution of Continuity In Disease—(See the Introduction under Continuity. Also see Abatement, Amelioration, Course, Crises; "Better" under Disease; "Degree of Disturbance" under Disturbed; Duration, Interrupted, Moderation, Modification, Recovery, Recuperation, Resolution, Retrograde, Sequence, etc.).

Tissue—Solution of—(See Decay, Disintegration, Resolution, Resolvent; "Solution" under Tissues).

SOMNAMBULISM — (See "Sleep-Walking" under Sleep).

SON—Sons—

Birth of a Son — The ⊙ to the ☌ or good aspect ♃ by dir.; the ☽, lords of the Asc. and 5th H., and the signs on the Asc. and 5th H. being masculine, denote a male, but female if such conditions are feminine; the ☽ to the ✶ or △ ♂ by dir.; ♃ at a Solar Rev. ☌ the place of the radical ⊙; the M.C. to the ☌ or good asp. the ⊙ in a female nativity; the M.C. to the good asp. the ☽, as the ☽ may be aspected; the Asc. to the ✶ or △ the ⊙ or ♂ by dir.; the majority of the planets in masculine signs and houses, and with the Asc. and sign on the 5th H. masculine. (See "Female Children", "First-Born Child", "Male Children Born", under Children; "Births" under Male; Predetermination).

Death of a Son — (See "First-Born Child", "Son Born May Die", under Children; Eclipses; "Death of a Male" under Males).

Health of Sons—(See "Good Health", "Ill-Health", under Males).

SOOTHING—Mitigating—Calming — Blue is a soothing color in the treatment of the sick.

Disease Soothed — (See Amelioration, Calm, Convalescence, Ease; "Disease" under Improved, Solution; Moderation, Recovery, Recuperation).

Soothing Drugs—The drugs of ♆ are especially soothing, as Opiates and Narcotics. Also ♄ remedies are soothing, and act as sedatives, and tend to relieve the excitement and irritability of ♂ diseases. (See Anaesthetics, Anodyne, Narcotics, Sedatives; "Soporifics" under Sleep).

Soothing Influences—Over the Body— The Adrenal Secretions, under the rule of ♃, when scattered over the body, tend to exert a soothing, quieting, and peaceful effect when the nature is disturbed by the evil aspects of the malefics, and especially by ♄ and ♂. The influence of ♀ is also soothing. The benefics, ♃ and ♀, are both soothing and beneficent in their action upon the body. Moonlight has a soothing influence over the body. Blue color is soothing. (See Blue, Calm; "Moonlight" under Moon; Sedatives; "Soothing Drugs" in this section).

SOPORIFIC DRUGS—Ruled by ♆. (See Narcotics, Neptune; "Soporifics" under Sleep).

SORCERY—Witchcraft—Black Magic—(See "Practices Hypnotism" under Hypnotism; "Black Magic" under Magic; Pretender, Witchcraft).

SORDES—(See "Sordes" under Teeth).

SORDID — (See Depraved; "Low and Base" under Low; Vile).

SORE—Soreness—Inflamed—

  Eyes—Sore Eyes—(See "Inflamed" under Eyes).

  Sore Gums — (See "Inflamed" under Gums).

  Sore Mouth—(See "Sore" under Mouth).

  Sore Nipples—(See Nipples).

  Sore Throat — (See "Sore" under Throat).

For further influences along this line see the various paragraphs under Blows, Bruises, Burns, Cuts, Hurts, Inflammation, Injuries, Swellings, Wounds, etc.).

SORES—Any Ulcer, Chafe, or Wound—Sores resulting from feverish disturbances, epidemics, violence, or an injury, are denoted by ♂, and brought on by ♂ in an angle, occi. of the ☉, and ori. of the ☽. Sores from impure blood, plethora, surfeits, etc., are usually the result of ♃ afflictions. Venereal sores are brought on by ♀. Sores caused by deposits, retention of poisons and wastes in the system, etc., are ruled by ♄. The ☽ also rules sores brought on by disturbance of the fluids and functions of the body. Sores are also considered ♎ diseases, and by afflictions in ♎, due to disturbed kidneys, and improper elimination. Also the ♓ sign relates to sores and ulcers. The ☉ and ♂, the fiery and electric planets, tend to bring on sores by excess of heat in a part, as bed sores, etc. For the general influences along this line see the following subjects — Abscesses, Apthae, Boils, Canker, Carbuncles, Carcinoma; "Offensive" under Discharges; Eruptions; "Chancroid" under Gonorrhoea; "Sores On" under Face, Legs; Foul, Gangrene, Impure, Malignant, Pimples; "Plague Sores" under Plague; Pus Sores, Putrid Sores, Scabs; "Scarified Sores" under Scars; Skin Disorders, Sloughing, Smallpox; "Chancre" under Syphilis; Ulcers, Venereal, etc. For other subjects which may have to do with Sores, and which are not listed here, look in the alphabetical arrangement for the subject you have in mind.

SORREL COLOR — Ruled by the Third House. (See Colors).

SORROW — Grief — Miseries—Afflictions — Anxieties — Losses, etc. Saturn is generally looked upon as the planet which brings sorrows into our lives, chastenings, afflictions, etc., but for our own good, in the end, and to test us, and burn the dross from our natures. Also ♂ brings sorrow thru violence, injuries, fevers, quarrels, disputes, etc. The 12th H. is called the House of Sorrows and Self-Undoing. All of the malefic planets by their afflictions tend to bring more or less of sorrow, affliction, disappointment, anxiety, and grief into our lives until we learn to transcend them, become spiritualized, and live more in our Higher Minds. For the general influences which tend to bring sorrows see "Much Sorrow" in this section.

  Abundance of Sorrow — (See "Many Sorrows" in this section).

  Aries—Sorrow to People Under Aries —(See "Sorrow" under Aries).

  Dies of Sorrow—And a Broken Heart —The 29° ♑ on the Asc. at B. (See "Broken Heart" under Broken).

  Face — Sorrowful Face — (See "Sad Face" under Face).

  Life Robbed of Its Joy — (See Joy, Melancholy, Sadness).

  Many Sorrows — Has Much Sorrow — The ☉ or ☽ afflicted by ♄ at B., and to the ♂ ♄ by dir.; the ☉ to the ill-asps. the ☽ by dir., and the ☉ afflicted by the ☽ at B.; the ☽ to the ♂ or ill-asps. ♄ or ♂ by dir.; the ☽ to the cusp the 12th H. by dir.; ♅ afflicted in ♓; ♅ □ or ☍ ♀; ♅ afflicted in ♎, ♑, ♒, or in the 10th H.; ♄ in the 1st H. at B., much sorrow and melancholy; ♄ ruler of the 12th H. at B., and to the ♂ or ill-asp. the Asc. by dir.; ♄ to his own ill-asps. by dir.; given by the □ and ☍ aspects of ♄ to the planets at B., and by dir., and also by his ♂ with the Lights; ♄ in ♎, ♂, □, or ☍ the Asc. by dir., and ♄ ruler of the 1st H. at B.; in Hor'y Q. ♄ afflicting the Significator of the person; ♄ to the ♂, or ill-asps. the ☉, ☽, or Asc. by dir.; ♃ ruler of the 1st H., and to the ill-asps. ♄ by dir.; ♃ by periodic revolution to the ♂ ♄ in the radix; ♂ to the ♂ or ill-asp. ♄ by dir.; ♂ afflicted in the 12th H.; ♀ by periodic rev. to the ill-asps. the ☽ or M.C. in the radix, and produced by previous pleasures; ♀ progressed in ♂, P, □, or ☍ ♄ in the radix, or vice versa; lord of the Asc. in the 12th H., and afflicted at B., and by dir.; the M.C. to the cusp the 12th H. by dir.; the 2nd H., or its ruler, to the ♂, P, □, or ☍ ♄ by dir.; the 2nd face of ☍ on the Asc. at B.; the 2nd decan. of ♐ on the Asc. shows afflictions, distress of mind, suspicion, woe, mistrust, and sorrow. (See Affliction, Anguish, Anxiety, Brooding, Cares, Dejected, Depressed, Despair, Despondent, Discontentment, Disgrace, Distress; "Own Worst Enemy" under Enemies; Evils, Fate, Fears; "Ill-Fortune" under Fortune; Gloom, Grief; "Hopes Cut Off" under Hope; "Low Spirits" under Low; Melancholy; "No Peace of Mind" under Mind; Miserable, Regretful, Renunciation, Repining; "Loss Of" under Reputation; Reverses, Ruin, Sadness, Scandal, Self-Undoing, Suffering, Trouble, Twelfth House, Worry, etc.).

  Periods of Sorrow—The ☉ or ☽ to the ♂, P, □, or ☍ ♄ or ♂ by dir. (See "Periods of Bad Health" under Health).

  Prevalent—Much Sorrow Prevalent— (See "Public Grief" under Grief).

  Public Sorrow — Public Sorrow and Grief—Much Sorrow Generally—♄ lord of the year, and afflicted at the Vernal Equinox; ☿ in ♑ at the Vernal, lord of the year, and afflicted, and especially to Peoples and Countries under the rule of ♑. (See Casualties; "Much Grief Generally", "Public Grief", under

Grief; "Much Misery Everywhere" under Misery; "Much Misfortune Generally" under Misfortune; Prevalent, Public).

Release from Sorrow—Through Resignation and Atonement—The ☉ or ☽ to the ♂, or ill-asps. ♄ by dir. (See Renunciation).

Secret Sorrows—The ☽ in the 12th H., and to the ♂ or ill-asp. ♅ or ♄ by dir.; ♄ ruler of, or in the 12th H. at B., and afflicted; ♃ to the ill-asps. ♄ by dir., and the direction falling in the 12th H.; ruler of the Asc. in the 12th H.; the Asc. or M.C. to the cusp the 12th H. by dir.

Sorrowful Spirit — ♄ afflicting the ☉, ☽, ☿, Asc., or hyleg at B., and by dir. (See Sad).

Suffering — A Life of Suffering and Sorrow—(See "Life of Suffering" under Suffering; "Many Sorrows" in this section).

Women — Much Sorrow To — (See "Women" under Misfortune).

SOTTISHNESS — Dull — Stupid—Foolish — Senseless — Danger of Excesses In Drink, etc.—The ☽ afflicted in ♑, ♏, or ♓; ♂ Sig. in ♋ or ♓; ♂ Sig. in water signs unless well-aspected by the ☉, ☽, or ♃; ♀ Sig. ♂ ♂; ♀ afflicted in ♓; ☿ afflicted in ♋ or ♓; a ♓ influence, and with the ☉, ☽, ♂, or ☿ afflicted in ♓, or with ♓ on the Asc. at B.; many planets in watery signs at B., and especially in ♓. (See "Habitual Drunkard" under Drunkenness; "Mind" under Dull; "Lack Of" under Energy; Idle, Improvident, Inactive, Indifferent, Inertia, Lazy, Taverns, etc.).

SOUL—The Soul is said to be governed by the 5th H., and corresponds to the ♌ Sign. (See Ego, Heliocentric, Pineal Gland, Spirit).

Physical Being — The Soul of — (See "Being" under Physical).

SOUND—

Sound Constitution—(See "Sound" under Constitution).

Sound Intellect—(See "Sound" under Intellect, Mind).

Sound Judgment—(See "Good" under Judgment).

Sound Mind—(See "Sound" under Intellect, Mind).

SOURCE—The ☉ is the chief source and regulator of the life forces. (See "Life Force" under Life; Sun; "Fluid", "Force", under Vital).

SOUTH SCALE—A Star of the nature of ♄ and ♀, in the 13° ♏, violent in nature, and productive of every species of disease and misfortune when rising or with the Lights, and especially in female nativities. The ☉ with at B. is indicative of trouble and disgrace. The ☉ or ☽ to the ♂ of tends to scandal, disgrace, misfortune, and ill-health. The influences of this star are listed a number of times in the various Articles in this book. The following are some of them—See "Threatened With" under Disease; Disgrace; "Every Evil" under Evil; "Liable To" under Misfortune; Ruin; "Danger Of" under Sickness; "Disease" under Species.

SOUTHERN SIGNS — (See "Northern Signs" under North).

SPACES — Intercellular Spaces — (See "Intercellular" under Cells).

SPARE BODY—Indicated by ♄; ☿ in ♐, partile the Asc., spare, tall, well-shaped, and large-boned; born under ♈, spare, dry, strong, moderate-sized body, as with ♈ on the Asc.; ♍ on the Asc., spare, tall, well-made, but compact body; the first half of ♐ rising, a spare body; the second half of ♒ on the Asc., spare and thin body. (See "Raw-Boned" under Bones; Lean, Slender, Thin).

SPARED — The Life Spared — (See "Spared" under Life; "Patient Will Recover" under Recovery; "Good Powers of Resistance" under Resistance; "Good" under Vitality).

SPASMODIC DISEASES — Spasms— Spasmodic Movements — Convulsive Movements — Erratic Movements—Increased Motility — Paroxysms — Motor Neuroses—Jerky and Irregular Movements—Involuntary Movements—Tonic Action—Spastic Action—Rigidity, etc. The planet ♅ is spasmodic, and spasmodic action is largely ruled by this planet, and also by the ♒ sign, the strong sign of ♅. Uranus in any sign tends to spasmodic action over that part of the body, and its opposite. Both ♅ and ♆, when afflicted, indicate spasmodic action. Uranus in signs which rule the arms, hands, legs, and feet tends to spasm and cramps in these parts. Spasmodic diseases are further caused by ♅ in the 6th H., or afflicting the ☉, ☽, Asc., or hyleg from this house; the ☉ afflicted in ♒; ☿ afflicted in ♒, spasmodic action arising from debility, and called "Wind in the Blood" by the Ancients; ♒ diseases, and afflictions in ♒; ♒ on the Asc. or 6th H. Also caused especially by Subs at the Atlas, the 1st Cervical Vertebra. The following subjects have to do with Spasmodic Diseases, which see in the alphabetical arrangement when only listed here—

Abdomen — Spasm of Muscles of — Spasmodic Pains In — (See "Colic", "Cramps", "Pain", under Bowels; Ileac Passion; "Abdominal" under Muscles).

Acute and Spasmodic Pains — In the Head—(See "Pains" under Head).

Alternating Spasm — (See "Clonic" in this section).

Angina Pectoris—(See Angina).

Antispasmodic Remedies—(See Antispasmodic).

Aorta — Spasmodic Gushing of Blood Thru—(See Aorta).

Arms — (See "Cramps", "Spasm", under Arms).

Arterial Circulation—Spasmodic Disturbance of — (See "Arterial" under Circulation).

Asthma — (See "Spasmodic" under Asthma).

Bladder — (See "Spasm" under Bladder).

Blood—Spasmodic Gushing of—(See "Aorta" in this section).

Bowels—(See "Spasm" under Bowels).

Brain—(See "Spasmodic Diseases" under Brain).

Breathing — (See "Spasmodic" under Breath).

Ceaseless Motion — (See Excitable, Motion).

Cheyne-Stokes Breathing—(See "Cheyne-Stokes" under Breathing).

Chorea—(See Saint Vitus Dance).

Clonic Spasm—Spasm with Alternating Relaxations — Myoclonus — Paramyoclonus Multiplex — Involuntary Muscular Contractions — A ♄ disease and affliction; Subs at AT and AX. Uranus in any sign tends to cause clonic spasms in the part, or parts, ruled by such sign. (See "Myoclonia" under Arms; Contractions, Epilepsy; "Movements" under Erratic; "Nystagmus" under Eyeballs; Incoordination; "Contractions" under Involuntary, Muscles; "Clonic Spasm" under Iris; Jerkings; "Paramyoclonus" under Muscles; Quivering; Saint Vitus Dance, Tremors, Twitching; "Tonic" in this section).

Colic; Constrictions; Continued Spasm —(See "Tonic" in this section).

Contortions; Contractions — Involuntary Muscular Contractions — Caused by the afflictions of ♄ in the sign which rules the part. (See Contractions, Coordination, Hyperkinesia; "Contractions" under Involuntary, Muscles; Tetanus, Twitchings; "Clonic", "Tonic", and the various paragraphs in this section).

Convulsions; Convulsive Movements— (See "Movements" under Convulsions).

Coordination; Cough; Cramps;

Dancing Spasm—(See "Saltatory" in this section).

Death by Spasms — (See "Death" under Fits).

Diaphragm—(See "Spasmodic" under Diaphragm).

Diseases—Spasmodic Diseases—(See the Introduction, and the various paragraphs in this Article).

Distortions; Dyspnoea; Eclampsia — (See Eclampsia, Epilepsy).

Emotions — (See "Spasmodic" under Emotions).

Epilepsy; Erratic Movements — (See "Movements" under Erratic).

Exaggerated Action; Eyeballs — (See "Clonic Spasm", "Nystagmus", under Eyeballs).

Face—(See "Spasmodic Diseases" under Face).

Feet—(See "Spasms In" under Feet).

Fits; Fluttering — (See "Fluttering" under Heart).

Gait—The Peculiar Walk of Paralysis Agitans — (See "Festination" under Walk).

Glottis—Involuntary Closure of—(See Glottis).

Gripings; Hands — (See "Cramps", "Spasms", under Hands).

Head — (See "Spasmodic Pains", "Spasms In", under Head).

Headache — (See "Spasmodic" under Headache).

Heart—(See "Spasm" under Heart).

Hiccough; Hippus — (See "Clonic Spasm" under Eyeballs).

Hyperkinesia—(See Muscles).

Hysteria; Ileac Passion;

Incoordination; Infancy—(See "Colic", "Cramps", "Convulsions", "Paralysis", "Paroxysms", under Infancy).

Inspiration—(See "Spasmodic" under Breath).

Intermittent; Interrupted; Intestines —(See "Spasm" under Bowels).

Introversion; Involuntary; Iris—(See "Clonic Spasm" under Iris).

Irregular Spasm—(See Colic, Cramps, Saint Vitus Dance; "Clonic" in this section).

Jerkings; Jumping Spasm — (See "Saltatory" in this section).

Kidney Action—(See "Spasmodic" under Kidneys).

Larynx — (See "Spasmodic" under Larynx).

Leaping Spasm—(See "Saltatory" in this section).

Legs—(See "Spasms In" under Legs).

Lock-Jaw; Lumbago — Spasmodic Lumbago—(See Lumbago).

Lungs — (See "Spasmodic" under Lungs).

Minor Spasm—(See Saint Vitus Dance, Twitchings).

Motion — (See "Spasmodic" under Motion).

Motor Disturbances — (See "Arms", "Disturbances", "Neuroses", and the various paragraphs under Motor).

Movements—Spasmodic Movements— (See the various paragraphs in this section).

Muscles — (See "Spasm Of" under Muscles).

Myoclonia — (See "Myoclonia" under Arms; "Paramyoclonus" under Muscles; "Clonic" in this section).

Nerves — (See "Spasmodic Diseases" under Nerves).

Neuralgia—Spasmodic Neuralgia— (See "Neuralgia" under Face; Neuralgia).

Nodding Spasm—(See "Nodding" under Head).

Oesophagus—(See "Stricture Of" under Oesophagus).

Opisthotonos; Organs—Spasmodic Action—Note the various Organs in this section. Also see Erratic, Intermittent, Irregular, Organs, Palpitation, etc.).

Oscillation—(See Eyeballs).

Oxygenation—Spasmodic Oxygenation —(See "Non-Oxygenation" under Oxygen).

Pains—(See "Spasmodic" under Pain).

Palpitations; Paralysis;

Paramyoclonus Multiplex — (See "Paramyoclonus" under Muscles; "Clonic" in this section).

Paroxysms; Prickling;

Puerperal Convulsions — (See Puerperal).

Quiverings; Reflexes; Remedies—(See Antispasmodic).

Remittent; Respiration — (See "Spasmodic" under Breathing).

Retraction; Rhythm — Interferences With—(See Rhythm).

Rigidity; Saint Vitus Dance;

Saltatory Spasm — Dancing Spasm — Jumping Spasm — Leaping Spasm — ♅ afflicted in signs which rule the lower extremities; Subs at PP (2, 3, 4L). (See "Clonic" in this section).

Shaking; Sneezing—(See Nose).

Spasms—Spasm—Spasms are due to incoordination, and afflictions of ♅ to the Organ of Coordination in the ♍ sign; ♅ influence by reflex from the ♏ sign, in which sign he is exalted. The afflictions of ♅ tend to cause spasms, and in the part of the body ruled by the sign he is in at B., or the part ruled by the opposite sign; ♅ in the 6th H.; ♄ angular, holding dominion, elevated above the Lights, and afflicting the hyleg; caused by ♃ when the dominion of death is vested in him; ♃ afflicted in ♍; ☿ afflicted in ♋. For Death by Spasms see "Death" under Fits. Spasms and muscular contractions are directly the result of nervous disturbances, and dominated by ♅. A clonic spasm is alternating, while a tonic spasm is continued. Case of Spasms—See Fig. 20A in "Astro-Diagnosis" by the Heindels. (See "Spasm" under Bladder, Heart, Urethra; Convulsions, Epilepsy; "Death" under Fits; "Clonic", "Tonic", and the various paragraphs in this section).

Spastic Action — Spasmodic Action — Rigidity — (See Rigidity; the various paragraphs in this section).

Squint—Crossed Eyes—(See "Strabismus" under Eyes).

Stomach—(See "Pains", "Spasm", under Eyes).

Strictures—Spasmodic Stricture of the Bladder or Urethra—(See "Stricture" under Bladder, Urethra; Stricture).

Subluxations; Subsultus — Morbid Tremors or Twitching—(See Subsultus, Tremors, Twitching).

Suffocation—Spasmodic Suffocating Attacks—(See Angina Pectoris, Cyanosis, Dyspnoea; "Non-Oxygenation" under Oxygen; Suffocation).

Tetanus; Throat — (See "Spasmodic Disorders" under Throat).

Tics—Tic Dourouleux—(See Tics).

Tonic Spasm—A Continued Rigid Muscular Spasm — This form of Spasm occurs in the more serious and chronic cases, and where ♅ is configurated with other malefics, as ♄ and ♂, and also when the subluxations of vertebrae may be more severe. The occasional, or alternating form of spasm, the clonic spasm, may be only temporary, and more easily remedied, as in twitchings, Saint Vitus Dance, etc. Also, in tonic spasm, the organ of coordination in ♍ is more permanently afflicted, and which may be caused by ♅ or ♄ badly afflicted in ♍. Epilepsy and Tetanus are typical forms of tonic

spasm. (See Contractions, Convulsions, Epilepsy, Incoordination, Rigidity, Tetanus, Tonic; "Clonic" in this section).

Torsion; Torticollis—(See "Wry Neck" under Neck).

Tremblings; Tremors; Trismus—(See Lock-Jaw).

Twistings; Twitching;

Uranus Diseases—(See Uranus).

Uremia; Urethra — (See "Spasmodic", "Stricture", under Urethra).

Venous Circulation — Spasmodic Disturbance of — (See "Spasmodic" under Veins).

Vomiting; Walk — (See "Incoordinated", "Twisted", under Walk).

Will — Spasmodic Will — (See "Weak Will" under Will).

Wind Spasm — (See "Spasm" under Wind).

Winking—(See Eyelids).

Writer's Cramp — (See "Cramps" under Hands).

Wry Neck — (See "Wry Neck" under Neck). For subjects along this line which may have been omitted in this Article, look in the alphabetical arrangement for the subject you have in mind.

SPASTIC ACTION—(See Rigidity, Spasmodic).

SPEAKING—

Loud Speaking—Should be Avoided— (See "Loud" under Speech; "Injudicious Use" under Voice).

Speaking Signs—Human Signs—Signs of Voice—♊, ♍, ♎, ♐, ♒. (See "Human Signs" under Human; "Signs Of" under Voice).

SPECIES — Kind — Nature of — Quality of—

Death — Species of the Death — This depends upon the one malefic planet which occupies an Anaretic Place. The quality of the death is indicated by the nature of the least prominent, or least powerful directions, in a train of directions to the hyleg, and by the nature of the sign, or signs containing them. These directions, even though benevolent, show the quality, and when acting with the major killing directions. (See Anareta; "Immediate Cause Of", "Quality Of", under Death; Directions; Dominion; Events; "Death" under Nature, Quality).

Disease—Species of Disease—Causes Every Species of Disease — Species of the Disease—The South Scale, a violent star, when joined to the ☉ or ☽, or afflicting the vital places of the map, is said to cause every species of disease. (See South Scale). For the influences which tend to define the Species, Type, and Quality of the disease, see "Disease" under Nature, Quality; "Quality Of" under Sickness; Type).

SPECKS—Specks Over the Eyes—Blindness By—Vision Impaired By—The ☉ directed to Praesepe, Hyades, Castor and Pollux, and other stars of the nature of ♂ and the ☽ combined, and especially if Praesepe be on the Asc., or with the ☉ or ☽ in an angle, which tends to certain blindness. Specks are also caused by ♄, and with ♄ the afflicting planet. (See Cataract; "Defects", "Film", "Total", under Blindness; "Muscae", "Specks", under Eyes).

SPECTRUM — Solar Spectrum — (See "Planets and Color" under Colors).

SPECULATION — Speculative — Visionary—

Mind — A Speculative Mind — A Promoter—♄, ♃, or ☿⚹ in ♍; ♋ and ♑ influence. (See Gambling).

Property — Loses Property by Speculation—The ☉ Sig. ♂ ♄. (See Expense, Property, Riches).

Religion—Fanciful Speculations About Religion and Other Matters— (See "Fanciful" under Religion).

SPEECH—Utterance—Talk—Language — Sound — Communication — Words — Tone—Conversation—Phonation—Voice —Delivery—Signs—Gesticulation, etc. The planet ☿ rules Speech, and the nerves of Speech. Also ruled by the ♈, ♉, and ♊ Signs. Uranus rules the motor nerves of speech. Mercury in ♉ especially rules and affects the nerves of speech, and ♅ in ♉ rules and affects the motor nerves of speech. The Hebrew letter "He" (E) is connected with speech, and the ♈ sign, which sign rules the intellectual faculties, of which speech is the natural expression. The ♉ sign is closely connected with speech, as the center where thought is transformed into speech is under the rule of ♉. The following subjects have to do with speech, its normal and abnormal expression, defects in, suppression of, etc.

Amnesia—Loss of Memory for Words —(See "Amnesia" under Memory).

Aphasia—Loss of Power of Speech— The ☉ afflicted in ♈; Subs at Atlas. (See "Loss of Speech" in this section).

Aphonia — (See "Aphonia" under Voice).

Articulation Bad—(See "Impediment", "Inarticulate", "Stammering", in this section; Articulation, Inarticulate).

Backwardness of Speech — ☿ afflicted in the 6th or 12th H., and if also afflicted by the ☽, ♄, or ♂, there may be an impediment of speech. Under these conditions if ☿ be in a mute sign, and afflicted by ♄, the native may be born dumb. (See Dumb, Mutes; "Impediment" in this section).

Breathing—Improper Breathing In Speaking or Singing — (See "Speech" under Breath).

Cannot Talk — Case — A Dwarf and Hunchback — See Chap. 8 in Daath's Medical Astrology.

Clear Voice — (See "Clear" under Voice).

Coarse Voice — In Women — (See "Coarse" under Voice).

Coprolalia — (See "Obscene" in this section).

Deaf Mute — (See "Deaf and Dumb" under Hearing).

Deep Voice — (See "Deep" under Voice).

Defects In Speech—Caused principally by afflictions to ☿; the ☽ Sig. □ or ☍

☿; the ☉ in an angle, ♂ ♄ and ☿, especially if ☿ be occi., and both ♄ and ☿ configurated with the ☽. The defect in the tongue, or speech, may be removed if ♂ be found with them, after the ☽ by direction or progression passes her ♂ with ♂, or completes her approach to him. (See "Impediments", "Stuttering", and the various paragraphs in this section).

Disconnected Speech—(See Dysphasia, Halting, Incoordination, Stammering, in this section).

Disorders of Speech—Afflictions to ☿ at B.; ☿ diseases; ☿ in the 6th H., ♂ ☉ and afflicted by ♄ or ♂; ☿ in any of the first six degrees of ♍, and in ♉ the ☽; afflictions in or to the ♈, ♉, or ♏ signs. (See the various paragraphs in this section).

Drawling Speech — The 3rd face of ♋ on the Asc.; ♎ influence.

Dumb—(See Dumb, Hearing, Mute).

Dysphasia—Disconnected speech from loss of words, or faulty arrangement of words — This is due to a ♄ limitation over the mind, a mind slow to think, and can be caused by ♄ ♂ the ☽ or ☿ in the 12th H., and otherwise afflicted by malefics; ♄ and the ☽ disconnected, and also having no relation to the Asc. (See "Bad Judgment" under Judgment; "Amnesia" under Memory; "Weaknesses" under Mental; "Weak Mind" under Mind; "Halting", "Rambling", "Stammering", in this section).

Dysphonia—Difficulty In Phonation— (See "Hoarseness" under Larynx).

Easy and Gentle Address—The ☽ Sig. ♂ ♀.

Effeminate Voice In Men — (See Effeminate).

Eloquent of Speech — A Good Orator and Linguist—♀ in ♍; ♀ Sig. in ♍; ☿ ⚹ ♃ and ♀; ☿ ascending at B., and free from affliction, and especially when ☿ is in ♍, a great orator. (See "Fluency" in this section; "Gifted Vocally", "Great Voice", under Voice).

Esperanto—Inventor of—See "Zamenhof", No. 432 in 1001 N.N.

Excited Manner—In Speaking — (See "Excitable" under Excitement; "Rapid", "Speaking", in this section).

Expression Good — (See "Expression" under Voice).

Fluency of Speech—Oratorical Ability —☿ angular at B., in the 1st, 7th, or 10th H., well-aspected, or in ♈, ♎, or ♑, signs corresponding to these houses. The 16° ♉ and ♏ are closely associated with voice control and tone. The 17° ♈ and ♎, and 7° ♑ and ♓ give fluency of expression. Power to sway the masses is given by ♋. Aries incites to anger and martial action, and ♏ excites powerful emotions. (See "Eloquent" in this section).

Functional Disorders — Of Speech — Caused by afflictions to ☿.

Gentle and Easy Address — (See "Easy" in this section).

Gestures—(See Gesticulation).

Gifted Vocally — (See "Eloquent", "Fluency", in this section).

Good Voice Expression — (See "Expression" under Voice; "Eloquent" in this section).

Great Orator—(See "Eloquent", "Fluency", in this section).

Halting—Hesitating Speech—♄ in ♎, a sign of voice, and ☿ in ♌, a bestial sign, tend to, and to obstruct perfect vocalization; many planets in mutable signs. (See "Dysphasia", "Impediment", "Stammering", in this section).

Has Never Talked—Case—See "Defective Mentality", No. 670, in 1001 N.N.

Head — Nods Head to One Side In Speaking — (See "Nodding" in Sec. 1 under Head).

Hearing and the Speech—(See "Deaf and Dumb" under Hearing).

High Voice—Tenor Voice—(See "Men" under Effeminate).

Hoarseness — (See "Hoarseness" under Larynx).

Humming—Droning—(See Humming).

Hurried Speech — (See "Excited" "Rapid", in this section).

Impediment In Speech — Defects In Utterance — Slow of Speech — Speaks with Difficulty — Impediment On the Tongue—The ☉ ♂ ♄ and ☿ in the 1st or 7th H., and especially when in the 7th, and ☿ P., □, or 8 the ☽, and the impediment is worse when ☿ is in a mute sign, as in ♋, ♏, or ♓. If ♂ be with them the speech becomes better when the ☽ by dir. leaves the aspect to ☿; the ☽ decr., and sepr. from ♄, and applying to ☿; the ☽ □ or 8 ♄ if the ☽ is otherwise much afflicted; the ☽ incr. in a day geniture, sepr. from ☿, and applying to ♄; the ☽ sepr. from ☿ and applying to the ☉; the ☽ Sig. □ or 8 ☿; ♅ afflicted in 8, the organ of coordination; ☿ diseases; ☿ Sig. ♂ ♄; ☿ ruler of the 6th H., in a watery sign, and afflicted by ♄ or ♂; ☿ afflicted in ♓; ☿ and the ☽ afflicted, and ♂, P., □, or 8 ♄; ♄ ♂ or ill-asp. ☿; ♄ ♂ in ♈; ♄ ascending in a bestial sign, as ♈, 8, ♌, or ♑, or in a mute sign, as ♋, ♏, and ♓; the native of ♄ usually has an impediment of speech; ♄ afflicting ☿, and the ☽ also afflicted; ♃ Sig. in a water sign, and in □ or 8 ☿; ☿ ill-dignified, and ♂ ♄; ☿ in 8, □ ♄ in ♌; caused by the □ or 8 aspects of ☿; ruler of the Asc. in a mute sign; ♑ on the Asc. (See Articulation, Inarticulate, Lisping; "Pitted Degrees" under Pitted; "Defects" under Tongue; Backwardness, Defects, Dumb, Halting, Incoordination, Slow, Stammering, and the various paragraphs in this section).

Imperfections of Speech — (See Defects, Impediment, and the various paragraphs in this section; "Defects" under Tongue).

Inarticulate Speaking—Planets, or ☿ in the inarticulate signs ♈, 8, ♌, or ♑. (See Inarticulate, Mute; "Defects" under Tongue; "Impediment In", and the various paragraphs in this section).

Incoordination of Speech — (See Dysphasia, Impediment, Stammering, in this section; Incoordination).

Injudicious Use—Of the Voice—Loud Speaking or Singing should be avoided when ☿ is in 8 and afflicted by malefics. (See "Hoarseness" under Larynx; "Injudicious" under Voice).

Jumps Forward — When Addressing or Speaking—Skippish Manner — (See "Nodding" in Sec. 1 under Head).

Larynx—Disorders of—(See "Hoarseness", and the various paragraphs under Larynx).

Linguist — (See "Eloquent" in this section).

Lisping—(See Lisping).

Logorrhoea — (See "Rapid" in this section).

Loss of Speech — Inability to Talk — Unable to Talk — Loss of the Power of Speech — Loss of Voice — Aphasia — The ☉ afflicted in ♈; ♆ in □ in 8 ♄ and ☿; ♅ ♂ ♄ in 8 or ♏; ♅ or ♄ afflicted in 8 or ♏; ♄ afflicted in 8 tends to loss of voice, and usually due to some chronic laryngeal and throat trouble, hoarseness, etc.; ☿ afflicted in 8; afflictions to ☿, to a ☿ sign, or the ☉ in the ☿ signs □ or ♍, and afflicted by malefics; Subs at Atlas. (See "Hoarseness" under Larynx; Mute, Removal; "Aphonia" under Voice; Aphasia, Cannot Talk, Has Never Talked, in this section). Cases of Loss of Speech—See Fig. 3G in the book, "Astro-Diagnosis", and Fig. 1 in "Message of the Stars", by the Heindels.

Loud Speaking — Should Avoid Loud Speaking or Singing—(See "Injudicious Use" in this section).

Manner — Skippish Manner In Speaking — Jumps Forward — Nods Head to One Side—(See "Nodding" in Sec. 1 under Head).

Men—Effeminate Voice In—(See Effeminate; Bass, High, Low, Tenor, under Voice).

Moans — Unable to Articulate — (See "Deaf and Dumb" under Hearing; Idiocy, Inarticulate, Insanity, Mute).

Motor Nerves of Speech — Disorders of — ♅ afflicted in 8. (See "Motor Nerves" under Motor).

Musical Voice—(See "Singers" under Music; "Musical" under Voice).

Mutes—(See Dumb; "Deaf and Dumb" under Hearing; Mute).

Nerves of Speech — Ruled by ☿, and are especially affected and disturbed by ☿ or ♅ afflicted in 8.

Nervous Manner—In Speaking—Quick and Nervous Speech—(See Jumps Forward, Quick and Nervous, Rapid, in this section).

Obscene Use of Words—Coprolalia—Caused by the afflictions of ♄ and ♂ to ♀ and ☿; Subs at AT. (See Obscene, Profane).

Orator — A Good Orator — (See Eloquent, Fluency, in this section).

Paralysis of Speech — Danger of — ♅ afflicted in 8, ♏, or the 2nd H.; ♅ □ or 8 ☿. (See "Speech" under Paralysis; Cannot Talk, Has Never Talked, Loss of Speech, in this section).

Peculiarities of Speech—(See the various paragraphs in this section. For the peculiarities of speech, as given by each Sign of the Zodiac, see the subject of "Speech" in Carter's Encyclopaedia of Psychological Astrology.

Phonation—Difficulty In—(See Articulation, Inarticulate; "Hoarseness" under Larynx; Lisping, Mute; Defects, Impediment, Imperfections, Stammering, in this section).

Pitted Degrees — Of the Zodiac — Effects of Upon Speech — (See "Pitted Degrees" under Pitted).

Pleasing Address — The ☉ Sig. ☌ ♀. (See "Easy Address" in this section).

Power to Sway Masses — The ♋ sign strong and well-occupied at B. (See "Eloquent" in this section).

Quick and Nervous Speech—☿ in the 1st H., and afflicted by ♅. (See "Rapid" in this section).

Rambling Speech — Afflictions in ♓, and involving the 3rd H., the ♐ sign, and ☿. (See "Mind" under Chaotic; "Inability" under Concentration; Confusion; "Light In Mind" under Mind).

Rapid Speech — Logorrhoea — Speaks Rapidly and Hastily—Rattle-Brained— The ☽ in a fiery sign, and ☌ or ill-asp. ☿; ♅ or ♂ in ♈ at B., and ♅ □ or ☍ ♂, rattle-brained. (See Excited, Quick and Nervous, in this section). Case of Curiously Rapid Utterance — See "Puzzle Horoscopes". No. 347, in 1001 N.N.

Refuses to Talk—Prefers Silence—In the radix of such a case, ☿ was in ♉, □ ♄ in a fixed sign. Birth Data not available.

Shrill, Small Voice—(See "Shrill" under Voice).

Signs of Voice — Speaking Signs — (See "Speaking Signs" under Speaking; "Signs of Voice" under Voice).

Silent — Refuses to Talk — (See "Refuses to Talk" in this section).

Singing—(See "Singers" under Music; Singing; "Singing" under Voice; "Injudicious Use" in this section).

Skippish Manner—In Speaking—(See "Nodding" in Sec. 1 under Head).

Slow of Speech — (See Halting, Impediment, Stammering, in this section; "Slow of" under Voice).

Small, Shrill Voice—(See "Shrill" under Voice).

Speaking—Manner of Speaking—(See the various paragraphs in this section).

Speaking Signs — (See "Signs of Voice" in this section).

Speechless — (See Dumb; "Deaf and Dumb" under Hearing; Mute; Cannot Talk, Has Never Talked, Loss of Speech, Refuses to Talk, in this section).

Stammering—Stuttering—Hesitating Speech — Slow of Speech — Halting — Impediment In Speech—Bad Articulation—The ☉ in an angle, ☌ ♄ and ☿, especially if ☿ be occi., and both ♄ and ☿ configurated with the ☽; the ☽ incr. in a day geniture, sepr. from ☿ and applying to ♄; the ☽ and ☿ afflicted, and P., ☌, □, or ☍ ♄; caused by the □ and ☍ aspects of the ☽; ♄ gives the stammer and ♂ the lisp; ♄ ☌ ☿, and

in □ or ☍ the ☽; a ☿ disease; ☿ afflicted at B.; ☿ in a weak sign, as in ♋, ♐, or ♓, and afflicted by ♄; ☿ afflicted in ♉ or ♏; ☿ in the 1st H., and afflicted by ♄; ☿ ruler of the 6th H., in a water sign, and afflicted by ♄ or ♂; ☿ in a water sign anywhere in the map; ☿ afflicted by ♄ or ♂, and with the ♐ sign involved, and with one of the planets in the 12th H.; a mute sign, as ♋, ♏, or ♓ on the Asc., or the ☽ or lord of the Asc. in one of these signs; many planets afflicted in mute signs. (See Halting, Impediment, in this section; "Pitted Degrees" under Pitted; "Defects" under Tongue).

Straining the Voice—Should Avoid— (See "Injudicious Use" in this section; "Singers" under Music).

Strong Voice — (See "Strong" under Voice; "Eloquent" in this section).

Stuttering — (See Impediment, Stammering, in this section).

Taciturn—Not Inclined to Converse— Quiet — Silent — Reserved—Born under ♄, and with ♄ rising in the Asc.; ♄ ☌ or ill-asp. ☿. (See Grave; "Taciturn" under Manner; Recluse, Renunciation, Reserved, Secretive, Taciturn).

Talk—(See Cannot Talk, Has Never Talked, Refuses to Talk, in this section).

Talking to Oneself — A ♆ influence, and ♆ strong at B.; ♆ in ♈; ♆ ☌ ☿. (See Humming).

Tenor Voice — (See "Men" under Effeminate).

Tone and Voice Control—(See "Fluency" in this section; "Control" under Throat).

Tongue—Imperfections In—(See Impediment, Stammering, in this section; "Defects" under Tongue).

Unable to Talk — (See Cannot Talk, Has Never Talked, Loss of Speech, in this section; Dumb; "Deaf and Dumb" under Hearing; Mute).

Utterance—(See Rapid, Slow, and the various paragraphs in this section).

Vertical Larynx—And Speech—(See "Vertical" under Spine).

Vocal Cords — Disorders of — (See Larynx; "Vocal Cords" under Voice).

Vocalization—(See Lisping; Articulation, Defects, Impediment, Inarticulate, Stammering, in this section).

Voice—Disorders of—Signs of Voice —(See "Disorders", "Signs of Voice", and the various paragraphs under Voice).

Weak Voice — (See "Weak" under Voice).

Whispering Voice — (See "Aphonia" under Voice).

Whistling — Whistling Sound to the Voice—(See Whistling).

Women—Coarse Voice In—(See "Coarse", "Deep", under Voice; "Masculine Women" under Women).

Words—Loss of Memory for Words— (See "Amnesia" under Memory).

SPENDTHRIFT—Wastefully Lavish of Money—(See Expense, Improvident, Money, Prodigal).

SPERMATIC CORD—
　Injuries To — ♏ diseases, and afflictions in ♏; ♂ afflicted in ♏. (See Testes).
　Spermatic Plexus — (See "Ductless Glands" under Ductless).

SPHENOID BONE—Is under the structural rulership of the ♈ Sign. It is through this bone that food odors, and other impressions, reach the Pituitary Body, and start the Uranus Alchemistry. For a discussion of this subject see the Chapter on "Ductless Glands" in the book, "The Message of the Stars" by the Heindels.

SPHINCTER ANI MUSCLE—(See Anus, Rectum).

SPICA VIRGO—A Star. (See Arista).

SPICE—
　A Spice of Gout — (See "Feet" under Gout).
　Spices — Ruled by ♀. (See "Condiments" under Food).

SPINE — Spinal Cord — Spinal Canal — Backbone — Spinal Vertebrae — The Spine is ruled by the ☉, ♅, and the ♌ sign. The vertebrae of the Spine are ruled and influenced by the Signs of the Zodiac, according to the distribution of the nerves to the various parts and organs of the body. The Spinal Cord, taken as a whole, is said to be ruled by the ☉ and the ♌ Sign. The Cord is also strongly influenced by ♅ and ♀. The Motor Segment of the Spinal Cord is ruled by ♂. Some Writers say by ☿. The membranes of the Cord are ruled by ♅. The Spinal Canal is ruled by ♅, and this canal is filled with a force called "Spinal Spirit Fire." The Spinal Fluid, called "The River of Life", is ruled by ♅ and the ♌ sign, and connects the organs ruled by ♉ and ♏. The different parts of the Spine, and their rulerships, are considered under the subject of Vertebrae. (See Vertebrae). The Cerebro-Spinal Nervous system is ruled by ☿. The following subjects have to do with the Spine, its Divisions, functions, anatomy, defects, disorders, injuries to, etc.

Accidents To—Injuries To—The ☉ afflicted by malefics at B., and by dir.; malefics afflicted in ♌, and especially ♄ and ♂; malefics in the 5th H. and afflicting the ☉, and especially if in ♌ in this house; malefics in ♏, injuries to the lower part of the spine, and the lumbar region. (See "Injuries To" under Back).

Adjustments Of—(See Subluxations).
All Diseases In—Signified by the 8th H. in Hor'y Q.
Ankylosis — (See Adhesions, Ankylosis, Joints).
Arm Place—In the Spine—(See "First Dorsal", "Seventh Cervical", under Vertebrae).
Atlas Vertebra — (See Atlas; "First Cervical" under Vertebrae).
Atrophy of Cord — ♄ afflicted in ♌. (See Atrophy; "Inability to Walk" under Walk).
Axis Vertebra — (See "Second Cervical" under Vertebrae).
Azoth — In the Spinal Canal — (See Azoth).

Backbone—(See Ankylosis, Curvature, Humpback, Malformed, Pains In, Rigid, Spina Bifida, Subluxations, in this section).
Bifida — (See "Spina Bifida" in this section).
Bulbar Paralysis—(See Medulla).
Canal—The Spinal Canal—Is ruled by ♅. Is said to be filled with Ether during life, which becomes fluid when exposed to the air. The Spinal Spirit Fire which fills the Canal is a luminous gas. (See "Azoth", "Fluids", "Obstruction", "Spinal Spirit Fire", in this section). The theories about the Canal, the Spinal Spirit Fire, etc., are discussed in the book, "The Message of the Stars", by Max Heindel.
Caries—Of the Spine—♄ afflicted in ♌ or ♒.
Cases of Spinal Trouble — (See Deformed, Diseases of Spine, Potts, Spina Bifida, Weakness, in this section).
Centers—The Spinal Centers Affected and Weakenetd—♄ ☌ or ill-asp. the ☉.
Central Place — In the Spine — (See "Fifth Dorsal" under Vertebrae).
Cerebro-Spinal System—Disorders of —(See Cebro-Spinal).
Cervical Region—Of the Spine—Cervical Vertebrae — (See Cervical; "Cervical Vertebrae" under Vertebrae).
Cleft In—(See "Spina Bifida" in this section).
Coccyx—Coccygeal Region—(See Coccyx; "Coccyx" under Vertebrae).
Columns — (See "Motor" in this section).
Compression — Of the Cord — (See "Spinal Cord" under Compressed).
Cord—The Spinal Cord—Ruled by the ♌ Sign. Salt, Sulphur, Mercury, and Azoth are found in the spinal cord. Azoth is ruled by ♅. The Motor Segment of the Cord is ruled by ♂, and ♂ afflicted in ♌ tends to disorders of this part of the Cord. Some Writers say the Motor Segment is ruled by ☿. Maladies of the Cord are frequent when ♄ afflicts the ☉, or when ♄ is afflicted in ♌, or when there are malefics in ♌ at B. For the various afflictions to the Cord see Atrophy, Compression, Dura Mater, Inflammation, Leptomeningitis, Lesions, Motor, Myelitis, Sclerosis, Spinal Meningitis, Tabes, and other paragraphs in this section).
Crevice — (See "Spina Bifida" in this section).
Curvature of Spine—Malformed Spine — Pott's Curvature — Pott's Disease — (See "Pott's Curvature" in this section). See Case — "Spinal Curvature", No. 838, in 1001 N.N.
Death—From Spinal Complaints—☉ diseases; the ☉ badly afflicted in ♌ or ♒, and especially when in the 5th, 6th, or 12th H. at B. Fixed Signs dispose to, and many planets in such signs, and especially in ♌ or ♒.
Defects In Spine — The ☉ afflicted in ♌ or ♒; ♄ in ♌ on the cusp of the 12th H., and in □ asp. the ☉, and both in fixed signs. (See the various paragraphs in this section).

Deformed Spine—Afflictions in ♌, and especially ♄ in ♌. Case — See "Deformed", No. 689, in 1001 N.N. (See Humpback, Pott's Curvature, Spina Bifida, in this section).

Diseases of Spine — Diseased Spine — Spinal Complaints — Spinal Trouble — Spinal Affections—♌ diseases, and afflictions in ♌; ♌ on the Asc., and afflicted; the ☉ afflicted in ♌ or ♒; the ☉ ☌ ♄ or ♆ in ♌ or ♒; a ☉ disease; the ☉ afflicted in ♐ sometimes affects the spine; malefics in ♌ and the hyleg much afflicted at B.; the ☽ afflicted in ♌, or afflicting the hyleg therefrom; a ♆ affliction; ♆ in □ in ♉ to ♃ or ♂; ♆ afflicted in ♌; ♆ □ or ♉ ♅, ♄, or ♂; ♆ ☌ ♄ in ♌; caused by ♄ and ♄ afflictions at B., and by dir.; ♄ afflicted in ♌ or ♒, and afflicting the hyleg therefrom; ♄ in ♌, occi., and afflicting the ☉, ☽, or Asc.; ♄ afflicting the hyleg or Asc. at B., and by dir.; ♄ afflicted in the 6th H., and especially when in ♌, and also afflicting the hyleg; ♀ diseases; ♀ afflicted in ♌. Cases of Spinal Trouble—See Figures 9A, 9B, 9C, 9D, 18G, in the book, "Astro-Diagnosis", by the Heindels. Also see Chap. 13, in Daath's Medical Astrology. See Case under "Deformed" in this section. (See the various paragraphs in this Article for other influences along this line).

Dislocations — Partial Dislocation of Vertebrae—(See Subluxations).

Dorsal Region — Of the Spine — (See Dorsal. Also see "Dorsal Vertebrae" under Vertebrae).

Dura Mater—Of the Cord—(See Dura Mater).

Dwarfed Hunchback — (See "Humpback" in this section).

End of Backbone — Disorders in Region of — (See Buttocks, Coccyx, Lumbar, Sacrum).

Ether—In Spinal Canal—(See Azoth, Ether).

Fire — The Spinal Spirit Fire — (See "Spirit Fire" in this section).

Fissure—Of the Spine— (See "Spina Bifida" in this section).

Fluids—The Spinal Fluids—Obstruction of — Lack of — (See Canal, Obstruction, Synovial, in this section; the Introduction to this Article).

Ganglion — (See "Spinal" under Ganglion).

Gas — The Spinal Gas — The Spinal Fluid — The Spinal Spirit Fire — (See Canal, Obstruction, Spirit Fire, in this section; Azoth, Ether).

Gray Matter — Of the Cord—Inflammation of — (See Inflammation, Myelitis, Poliomyelitis, in this section).

Haematomyelia — Hemorrhage Into the Cord — (See "Spine" under Hemorrhage).

Hardening—Of the Cord—(See "Sclerosis" in this section).

Heart Place — In the Spine — (See "Second Dorsal" under Vertebrae).

Hemorrhage — Into the Cord — (See "Spine" under Hemorrhage).

Humpback—Hunchback — Kyphosis — Curvature of the Spine — Dwarfed Hunchback — Deformed Spine — The ☉

in ♌ or ♒ on the cusp the 6th or 12th H., and □ ♆; the ☉ and ☽ in the 6th or 12th H., and afflicted by malefics; ♅, ♄, and ♂ in fixed signs in ☌ or ♉; the bodies or rays of ♅, ♄, and ♂ in, or directed upon, the 5th, 6th, or 12th H., or cusps of these houses, or the cusp of the Asc.; ♄ afflicted in ♌; ♂ in ♌, □ the Asc.; ♂ or the ☽ ☌ ♄ or ♉ in the 12th H., and the ☉ and ♃ in the 4th H.; ♉ on the Asc., and the rising degree □ ♂ in ♌; ♉, ♏, or ♑ on the Asc.; many planets in ♍ in the 6th or 12th H. Cases of Humpback — See "Hunchback", No. 685; "Spinal Curvature", No. 838, both in 1001 N.N. See Chap. 8, Case of a Female, in Daath's Medical Astrology. See Fig. 20 in the book, "Message of the Stars", by Max Heindel. (See Defects, Deformed, Pott's Curvature, in this section; "Arrested Mental Powers" under Mental).

Incomplete Spine — (See "Deformed", "Spina Bifida", in this section).

Infantile Paralysis — Accompanied by Poliomyelitis, or Inflammation of the Gray Matter of the Spine—(See "Infantile Paralysis" under Paralysis; Inflammation, Poliomyelitis, in this section).

Inflammation — Of the Spinal Cord — Myelitis—Leptomeningitis—Poliomyelitis—♂ afflicted in ♌ or the 5th H.; Subs at AT, AX, CP. (See "Infantile Paralysis" in this section).

Kidney Place — In the Spine — (See "Eleventh Dorsal", "Tenth Dorsal", "Twelfth Dorsal", under Vertebrae).

Kyphosis—(See "Humpback" in this section).

Leptomeningitis—Inflammation of the Pia and Arachnoid Membranes of the Brain and Cord—(See this subject under Meninges).

Lesions — Lesions of the Motory Columns Within the Spine—♄ ☌ or ill-asp. the ☉; ♅, ♄, or ♂ afflicted in ♌. (See Lesions, Locomotor Ataxia; "Motor Nerves" under Nerves; "Lesions" under Paralysis).

Ligaments — Of the Spine — Loss of Strength In—♄ afflicted in ♌. (See Ligaments).

Liver Place — In the Spine — (See "Fourth Dorsal" under Vertebrae).

Lumbar Region—Of the Spine—(See Lumbar; "Lumbar Vertebrae" under Vertebrae).

Lung Place — In the Spine — (See "Third Dorsal" under Vertebrae).

Luxations—(See Dislocations, Subluxations).

Malformed Spine — (See Defects, Humpback, Pott's Curvature, Spina Bifida, in this section).

Marrow — Spinal Marrow Diseased — ♀ afflicted in ♌. (See Marrow).

Medulla Oblongata — Disorders of — (See Medulla).

Meningitis—Spinal—(See Meninges).

Motor Segment — Motory Columns of the Cord—Disorders of—(See Cord, Lesions, in this section).

Myelitis—Inflammation of the Cord— (See "Inflammation" in this section).

Nerves—Pain In the Spinal Nerves— ☿ afflicted in ♌; ☿ affl. in ♏, pains in the upper spinal nerves. (See "Pain In Nerve" under Nerves; "Pain", and the Introduction in this Article).

Obstruction — Of the Spinal Fluids — Of the Spinal Gas—The Vital Fluids of the Spine Obstructed—The Spinal Fluid Sluggish and Restricted—The ☉ in ♌ or ♒, ☌ or ☍ ♄; the ☉ ☌ ♆ or ♄ in ♌; ♆ ☌ ♄ in ♌, ♒, or the 5th H.; ♆ ☌, □, or ☍ the ☉ or ♄; ♆ in ♏, ☌, □, or ☍ the ☉ or ♄; ♅ in ♌ or ♒, □, or ☍ the ☉ and ♄, the functions of the spinal canal are interfered with. (See Canal, Fluids, Gas, Spirit Fire, Synovial, in this section; the Introduction to this Article).

Operations—Avoid surgical operations on the spine when the ☽ is in ♌. (See "Rules" under Operations).

Os Coccyx—(See "Coccyx" in this section).

Pain — In the Spine — Pains In the Backbone—A ♃ disease. (See "Nerves" in this section).

Paralysis — Bulbar Paralysis — (See Medulla).

Poliomyelitis — Inflammation of the Gray Matter of the Cord — Occurs in Infantile Paralysis. (See "Inflammation" in this section; "Infantile Paralysis" under Paralysis).

Pott's Curvature — Of the Spine — Pott's Disease—Spondylitis—Tubercular Spine — Vertebral Arthritis Deformans—The ☉ or ♄ afflicted in ♌; the ☉ or ♄ in the 6th H. in ♌, or other fixed signs, and afflicted by several malefics; ♄ afflicted in ♌, tubercular spine; malefics conjoined in the 5th H., and afflicted by others from the 11th H.; ♌ and ♒ are signs which greatly affect the heart and spine, and especially when afflicted, or containing the Lights or malefics, or when on angles, or on the cusps of the 5th or 6th H. Cases— See "Pott's Disease", No. 224 in 1001 N.N. See Fig. 9C in "Astro-Diagnosis" by the Heindels. See Case in Chap. 8 in Daath's Medical Astrology. (See "Humpback", "Tubercular", in this section).

Private Place — In the Spine — The Lumbar Vertebrae — (See Lumbar; "Lumbar Vertebrae" under Vertebrae).

Rigid Spine — Stiff Spine—Caused by ♄, and the hardening of the synovial membranes by ♄ influence; ♄ afflicted in ♌ tends to restrict and to dry up the synovial fluids in the joints of the spine. (See Joints, Rigidity, Synovial).

Sacrum — The Sacral Region of the Spine — (See Sacrum; "Sacrum" under Vertebrae; "Spina Bifida" in this section).

Sclerosis—Of the Cord—(See "Spinal Cord" under Hardening).

Segment—Motor Segment of the Cord —(See "Motor Segment" in this section).

Spina Bifida—Cleft of the Spine Over Sacrum — Crevice — Fissure — The ☉ or ☽ in ♌, and afflicted by malefics; the ☽ in ♌, □ or ☍ ♅ and ♀, and applying to, or afflicted by ♄. Case — Male, born Nov. 22, 1853, 5:40 p.m., in Lat. 53° 23' N., and 10' 12" W. L. Also see case under "Deformed" in this section).

Spinal Canal — (See "Canal" in this section).

Spinal Centers—(See "Centers" in this section).

Spinal Cord—(See "Cord" in this section).

Spinal Diseases—(See "Diseases", and the various paragraphs in this section).

Spinal Marrow — (See "Marrow" in this section).

Spinal Meningitis—(See Meninges).

Spinal Nerves—(See "Nerves" in this section).

Spinal Spirit Fire—(See "Spirit Fire" in this section).

Spinal Trouble — (See "Diseases" in this section).

Spirit Fire — Spinal Spirit Fire — The Force which fills the Spinal Canal, and called by the Heindels, "The Life of the Father". Also this Force is said to be ruled by ♆, and spoken of as "The Spinal Spirit Fires of Neptune", which represent the Will. The Spinal Spirit Fire, by vibrating the Pineal Gland, produces Spiritual Sight. See Chap. 29, on "The Pathogenic Effects of Neptune", in the book, "Message of the Stars", where this matter is discussed. The Spinal Spirit Fire tends to be obstructed when the ☉ is in ♌ or ♒ in ☌ or ☍ ♄. (See Canal, Obstructions, in this section; Pineal Gland).

Spleen Place — In the Spine — (See Spleen; "Ninth Dorsal" under Vertebrae).

Spondylitis—(See "Tubercular" in this section).

Stiff Spine—(See "Rigid" in this section).

Stomach Place — In the Spine — (See "Sixth Dorsal" under Vertebrae).

Subluxations — (See Subluxations, Vertebrae).

Synovial Fluid—Lack of In Joints of Spine—(See "Rigid" in this section).

Tabes Dorsalis — Progressive Degeneration of the Posterior Columns of the Cord—(See Tabes).

Tubercular Spine—Spondylitis—♄ afflicted in ♌. Case — See Fig. 9C in "Astro-Diagnosis", by the Heindels. (See "Pott's Curvature" in this section).

Upper Spinal Nerves—Are ruled by ♏, and affected when there are malefics afflicted in ♏, or pains in with ☿ afflicted in ♏.

Vertebrae—Disorders of—(See "Backbone" in this section; Subluxations, Vertebrae).

Vertical Spine—Vertical Larynx and Spine In Man—The Ego can work only thru a vertical spine, as in Man. The animals, with a horizontal spine, are under the direction of Group Spirits, and are subject to the horizontal currents of the Desire World. See Chap. X in the book, "Cosmo-Conception", by Max Heindel, in which chapter the Evolution of the Spine in Man is discussed. The vertical larynx, as in man, is the only larynx capable of speech. The Parrot has a vertical larynx, and can utter and imitate human speech.

Vital Fluids — Obstruction of In the Spine—(See "Obstruction" in this section).

Weakness—Case of Spinal Weakness —See "Seventeen Years in Bed", No. 843 in 1001 N.N.

SPINSTERS—Women Who Have Never Married—Unmarried Elderly Women— The ☉ ☌ or ill-asp. ♄ at B.; the ☉ in ♏, ♌, P, ☐, or ☍ ♄; ♄ afflicted in ♏. (See Bachelors, Celibacy; "Aversion from Marriage", "Delayed", "Denied", under Marriage).

SPIRIT — The Spirit — The Soul — The Ego—The ☉ is typical of Spirit, and the ☽ of Matter. The Spirit is especially ruled by the ☉, the ♌ sign, and the 5th H., the house of the ☉ and the ♌ Sign. Also the Fiery Signs predominate in Spirit. The Pineal Gland is said to be the Seat of the Soul in the body, and the direct point of contact of the Ego. (See Astral Body, Aura, Character, Ego, Intuition, Pineal Gland, Soul, Will). Planets ℞ at B. are conducive to more rapid Soul Growth. (See Retrograde). The Spiritual Faculties are especially ruled over by ♆, the ruler of the Pineal Gland. (See Neptune, Spirit Controls, Spiritual).

SPIRIT CONTROLS— Obsessions—Controlled by Elemental Spirits—Demoniacal Obsession—Caused principally by ♆ and his afflictions; ♆ ☌ the ☉ or ☽ in the 9th H., and afflicted; ♆ ☌ ♄ in the 8th H., and afflicted by the ☐ aspect of ☿; ♆ afflicted in the 12th H., liable to be preyed upon by Spirit Controls, and assuming demoniacal shapes; ♆ ruler of the horoscope, and afflicted; ♆ ☌ the Asc., or afflicted in the 1st H., spirit obsessions; ♆ afflicted in the 6th H., or in ♏ or ♓, or in a watery sign; ♆ ☐ or ☍ ♄; ♆ ☌, P, ☐ or ☍ ♂; ♆ ☌ the ☽, and in ☐ ♅; ♆ ☍ Antares; ♆ ☐ ♅ at B., and the Prog. ☽, or Lunations, forming a ☐ aspect to them; caused by the evil aspects of ♆; the ☽ in the 9th H., ☐ or ☍ ♅; the ☽ in ♓, ☐ or ☍ ♆; ♅ ☌ the ☽ in the 9th H., and in ☐ or ☍ ♆ and ♂; ♓ on the Asc., the tool of low spirits; the 27° ♓ on the Asc. The subject of Spirit Controls is discussed quite fully in the book, "The Message of the Stars", by Max Heindel. Cases of Spirit Controls—See Fig. 16A, 16B, in "Astro-Diagnosis"; Fig. 2 in "Message of the Stars", both books by the Heindels. (See Antares, Astral Body; "Involuntary" under Clairvoyance; Demoniac, Fears, Horrors, Insanity; "Black Magic" under Magic; Mania; "Dangers" under Mediumship; Obsessions, Sensitives; "Terrors" under Strange; Visions).

SPIRITED—Animated—Full of Life— Vigorous—Active—Lively—Given by the fiery signs, many planets in a fiery sign, or a fiery sign on the Asc. and angles. Also ♂ rising in ♈ or ♏, and well-aspected by the ☉; many planets elevated in the East in positive, or fiery signs at B. (See Active, Brisk, Energetic; "Fire Signs" under Fire; Lively, Quick; "Good" under Vitality).

SPIRITS — Obsessed by Evil Spirits — (See Demoniac, Obsessions, Spirit Controls).

SPIRITUAL — Spirituality—Spiritual Faculties—Spiritual Sight—The Religious Faculties — Religion, Philosophy, and the Spiritual Faculties, are ruled by ♃ and the 9th H. Also by the ☉, ♆, ♅, ♄, and the ♐ and ♒ Signs. In fact, all of the Planets by their higher vibrations, have to do with the Evolution and Spiritual advancement of the Race, and the Seven Planetary Angels, or the Seven Spirits Before The Throne, are ever on the alert to help the individual who wants help, and it is only those who are living in their lower minds, and are dominated by personality, materialism, and the lower things of this Earth, who do not progress under the various planetary influences, but become stragglers and laggards in the scheme of life. The following subjects have to do with the Spiritual Side of Man, his Spiritual Faculties, his Higher Mind, and with Spiritual Forces and Influences in the Universe which affect Man. See these subjects in the alphabetical arrangement when only listed here—

Aquarius Sign — Considered the most spiritual of all the Signs. (See Aquarius).

Astral Body—(See Astral).

Aura; Aversions; Beside Oneself—(See Excitable).

Calm—Lack of Spiritual Calm—☿ afflicted by ♄ or ♆. (See Despondent, Fears; "Low Spirits" under Low; Melancholy; "No Peace of Mind" under Mind; Worry, etc.).

Centers—The Spiritual Centers of the Body — (See Pineal Gland, Pituitary Body).

Chaotic Mind — (See "Mind" under Chaotic).

Character; Clairaudience;

Clairvoyance; Color — The Spiritual Color—Indigo. (See Blue, Indigo).

Confusion of Mind—(See "Mind" under Chaotic, Confusion, Ideas).

Contentment; Death—Spiritual Causes of—♆ influences; ♆ in the 8th H. at B. (See Catalepsy, Catalysis, Coma, Delirium, Demoniac, Insanity, Madness, Mania, Obsessions, Spirit Controls, Trance).

Desires—Desire Body—(See Desire).

Deviations; Dreams; Ecstasy; Ego;

Emotions; Exaltation — Emotional Exaltation—(See Exaltation).

Excitement — (See "Religious" under Excitement).

Faculties—The Spiritual Faculties are ruled by ♅ and ♆, and thru the centers of the Pineal Gland and the Pituitary Body. (See Neptune, Pineal, Pituitary, Uranus).

Fanaticism — (See "Fanatical" under Religion).

Fate; Fears — (See "Religious" under Fears).

Feelings; Forebodings; Free-Will — (See Will).

Genius; Good — Good and Evil — (See Good, Evil).

Hallucinations; Happiness; Healing— (See "Spiritual Healers" under Healers).

Health — Good Health Thru Spiritual Power—Ψ and ♅ strong at B., dignified, and well-aspected, and by attainment, and knowledge of the great Truths of the Universe, the Plan of Things, and the Destiny of the Soul.

Higher Mind—(See Ego, Soul, Spirit).

Honesty; Honor; Hope, Humane;

Hypocrisy; Ideals; Ideas;

Illumination—(See this subject under Religion).

Indigo Color — The Spiritual Color — (See Indigo).

Individuality; Insanity; Intuition;

Joy; Jupiter — (See the influences of this planet).

Justice; Kind; Lower Mind — (See "Mind" under Lower).

Mathematical; Mediumship;

Mentality — (See the various paragraphs under Mentality).

Mind—The Spiritual Mind—Indigo is the Color of the Spiritual Mind. (See Ego; "Higher Mind" under Mind; Soul, Spirit).

Morals; Motives; Negative — (See "Negative Nature" under Negative).

Neptune — (See the influences under Neptune).

New Birth — (See "Exaltation" under Emotion; "Ecstasy" under Religion).

Ninth House—The House of Religion and the Higher Mind — (See Ninth House).

Noble; Obsessions; Opinions;

Optimism; Peace of Mind — (See this subject under Mind).

Personality; Perversions—Spiritual Perversions — Usually caused by the afflictions and lower vibrations of Ψ. (See "Mind" under Chaotic; "Involuntary" under Clairvoyance; Delusions, Fears, Hallucinations, Hypnotism, Illusions, Insanity, Magic, Mediumship; "No Peace of Mind" under Mind; Obsessions, Perversions; "Fanatical", "Intolerance", under Religion; Spirit Controls).

Pineal Gland — The Spiritual Center in the Body—(See Pineal).

Pituitary Body—(See Pituitary).

Positive — (See Individuality; "Positive Nature" under Positive; Ruling).

Power—Spiritual Power—Given especially by the higher vibrations of Ψ and ♅, and through the Pineal Gland and Pituitary Body. (See Pineal, Pituitary, Retrograde, Soul, Spirit, Will).

Prana; Premonitions; Pretender;

Pretenses; Principles; Prophetic;

Psychic; Purposes; Qualities—Spiritual Qualities—(See the various paragraphs in this section; "Desirable Mental Traits" under Mind).

Radicalism; Ranters — (See "Fanatical" under Religion).

Rationalism; Reactionary; Rebellious;

Reformers; Religion — (See the various paragraphs under Religion).

Renunciation; Resignation;

Revolutionary; Ruling; Sagittarius— (See the Influences under Pisces, Sagittarius, the Signs of ♃).

Seers; Sensitive—Sensitive To Psychic and Spiritual Influences — (See Clairvoyance, Mediumship, Obsessions; "Sensitive" under Psychic; Receptive, Sensitive, Spirit Controls, Susceptibility).

Sensitives — (See this subject under Sensitive).

Sincere; Sleep—(See "Nightmare", "Somnambulism", under Sleep).

Soul; Spirit; Spirit Controls;

Spiritual Sight — (See Antares, Neptune, Pineal Gland).

Spirituality — The Different Degrees of—(See the various paragraphs in this section, and also under Religion).

Sun—(See the Influences under Sun).

Sympathetic; Truth — Lover of—(See Truth).

Twelfth House — (See the influences under Twelfth House).

Uncanny Feelings—(See Uncanny).

Uranus — (See the influences under Uranus).

Veneration; Visions; Weird. Look in the alphabetical arrangement for subjects along this line, and which may not be listed here.

SPIRITUOUS LIQUORS—Excessive Use of—(See Dipsomania, Drink, Intoxication).

SPITEFUL — (See Revengeful, Treachery).

SPITTING—Spittle—

Spitting of Blood—(See Haemoptysis).

Spittle—(See Expectoration, Saliva).

SPLANCHNIC — Pertaining to the Viscera — (See "Splanchnic Ganglia" under Ganglion; Viscera).

SPLAY FOOT—Flat Foot—(See "Splay Foot" under Feet).

SPLEEN—Splenic—Milt—The Spleen is under the internal rulership of the ♍ sign. Also ruled by the ☉, ♄, and the ♏ sign. Saturn in ♍ especially rules and affects the activities of the Spleen. The Solar Forces enter the body thru the Spleen, and are then circulated thru the body as the Vital Etheric Fluid, which fluid is ruled by the ☉. The Spleen is called the Gateway of the Solar Forces. (See "Fluid" under Vital). The focal point of the Astral Body in the physical body is in the Spleen, and the Spleen contains the center which connects the physical body with the Astral World, and to coordinate with its activities requires much balanced power of understanding. (See Astral Body). The Liver is the great central vortex of the Desire Body. (See "Desire Body" under Desire). The Spleen Place in the Spine is the 9th Dorsal Vertebra. (See "Ninth Dorsal" under Vertebrae).

Afflicted with Spleen—(See Anger).

Calculi of Spleen — (See "Stone" in this section; Stone).

Cancer Of—Carcinoma—♄ afflicted in ♍; ♄ ☌ ♃ or ♀ in ♍; Subs at Spl.P., and at KP. (See Carcinoma).

Catarrh Of — The ☉, ☽, or ♄ afflicted in ♍; ♄ ☌ the ☉ or ☽ in ♍; Subs at SP, Spl.P., and KP. (See Catarrh).

Death—By Disordered Spleen—Caused by ♄ when the dominion of death is vested in him; ♄ afflicted in ♍ at B., and afflicting the hyleg therefrom.

Diseases Of—Disorders of—The ☉ and ♄ diseases; the ☉ afflicted in ♌, or ♌ on the Asc.; the ☉ or ♄ afflicted in ♍; afflictions in ♌, ♍, or ♏; Subs at Spl.P. (See the various paragraphs in this section).

Enlarged Spleen—Weil's Disease, and attended with Jaundice or Malaria Fever—A ♄ disease; ♄ and ♂ afflicted in ♍, and especially in the 6th H.; ♄ ☌ ♃ in ♍; Subs at CP, Spl.P., and KP. (See Ague, Jaundice, Malaria).

Flexure—Of the Spleen—Splenic Flexure—A ♄ disease; ♄ afflicted in ♍, and due to weakening of the supports and attachments; ♄ afflicted in ♏; Subs at PP. (See Flexure).

Hyperaemia — Of the Spleen, and usually attended with Fever — The ☉ or ♂ afflicted in ♍; ♂ ☌ the ☉ or ♃ in ♍; Subs at SP (8D). (See Hyperaemia).

Hypertrophy — ♃ or ♂ afflicted in ♍; Subs at SP (8D), and at Spl.P. (See Hypertrophy).

Inflammation Of—♂ afflicted in ♍; ♂ ☌ the ☉ in ♍; Subs at SP (8D), and Spl.P.

Leukemia—(See Leukocytes).

Malaria Fever—Enlarged Spleen In—(See "Enlarged" in this section).

Prolapsus—Splenoptosis—♅ or ♄ afflicted in ♍; Subs at Spl.P. (See Prolapse).

Rickets — Due to Changes in the Spleen—(See Rickets).

Right Side—The Spleen On the Right Side — Case — See "Heart", No. 981, in 1001 N.N.

Splenic Diathesis—(See the Introductions under Knees, Lymph).

Splenic Humour—The Splenic Humour has dominion from 3 P.M. to 9 P.M. of each day, and is more active during this time. (See "Astral Medicine", by Dr. Duz, page 74. Also see Humours).

Splenic Plexus—(See "Fifth Thoracic" under Ganglion).

Splenic Process—♄ adds or subtracts to the Splenic Process. (See "Alterations" under Cells; Metamorphosis. Also see Chap. VI in "Astral Medicine", by Dr. Duz).

Splenoptosis—(See "Prolapsus" in this section).

Stone In—Calculi—A ♄ affliction; ♄ afflicted in ♍; Subs at SP and Spl.P. (See Stone).

Symptoms of Spleen — (See "Symptoms Of" under Consumption).

Treatment—By Sympathy diseases of the Spleen are treated by ♄ remedies. By Antipathy, use the remedies and Herbs of ♂. (See Antipathy, Opposites, Sympathy). Also the Spleen Place in the Spine (Spl.P.) should be adjusted, to see that the nerve forces thru the spine to the Spleen are not impinged. (See Treatment).

Tuberculosis—Of the Spleen—A ♄ disease; ♄ afflicted in ♍; ♄ in ♍ in the 6th H.; Subs at SP and Spl.P. (See Tuberculosis).

Upper Spleen—Disorders of—The ☉, ♄, or ♂ afflicted in the first degrees of the ♍ sign; Subs at SP (8D).

Weil's Disease — (See "Enlarged" in this section).

White Blood Corpuscles—Excess of—(See Leukocytes).

SPONGES — Ruled by ♆. (See Fungus; "Vegetable Growths" under Vegetable).

Spongy Gums—(See Gums).

SPONTANEOUS—Sudden—♅ and ♂ influences tend to sudden and spontaneous events. (See Accidents, Events, Explosions, Hurts, Injuries, Sudden, Unexpected, Untimely; "Spontaneous" under Wounds).

SPORADIC CHOLERA — (See "Cholera Morbus" under Cholera).

SPORTS—Athletics— Exercise—Recreations—Pastimes—Amusements—Play—Games—Muscular Exercises—Hunting —Fishing, etc. There are many dangers in connection with Sports, and attended with accidents, disease, death, injuries, etc., and some of these conditions, and their planetary causes, are listed here.

Amusements — Death or Injury In — ♂ in the 5th H., □ or ☍ the ☉. (See Amusements; "Blindness" in this section).

Athletics—Injury or Death In—(See Athletics; "Death", "Injury", under Exercise; "Death", "Injuries", in this section).

Blindness—From Injury in Sports or Amusements — (See Amusements; "Amusements" under Blindness; "Eyes" under Exercise).

Blood — Over-Heated Blood Thru Sports and Violent Exercise — (See "Blood Over-Heated" under Exercise).

Burned to Death — From Accident During Sports—(See "Death by Burns" under Burns).

Care—Lack of Care In Sports—♂ in ♐.

Colds—From Over-Exercise and Over-Exertion — (See "Colds" under Exercise).

Dancing—The ☉ Sig. in ♎, spends his time in Sports, Pastimes, and Dancing.

Death by Sports—By Accidents or Injuries In Sports—The ☉ afflicted in ♐; ☿ afflicted by ♄ or ♂ at B., and ♂ holding the dominion of death; ☿ afflicting the hyleg by dir., and ☿ or the hyleg badly afflicted by malefics at B. (See Amusements; "Death" under Exercise).

Exercise — Excesses In — Injury or Death In — Hurts to Eyes During — (See the paragraphs under Exercise; "Amusements" in this section).

Falls During Sports—The ☉ afflicted in ♐.

Fatigue—Fatigue from Sports or Exercise—(See "Exercise" under Fatigue).

Fishing—Fond of—The ☉ or ☽ in ♓ at B.; ♓ upon the Asc.; many planets in watery signs at B.; the ♃ signs ♐ or ♓ strong at B. (See "Outdoor Exercise" in this section).

Fond of Sports—♃ Sig. in ♎ or ♐.

Horses—Injury by Horseback Riding —(See "Riding" under Horses).

Hunting—Injury or Death In—(See Gunshot, Hunting, Shooting).

Hurts—And Injuries During Sports—The ☉, ☽, ♅, or ♂ afflicted in ♐; afflictions in ♐. (See the various paragraphs in this section).

Indiscretions—In Sports, and Warning Against—♂ or ♀ afflicted in ♐, and especially with females. (See "Intemperate" under Exercise).

Injuries—Hurts or Accidents In Sports—The ☉, ♄, ♂, or ♅ afflicted in ♐; afflictions in ♐. (See Amusements, Death, Injury, and the various paragraphs in this section).

Inordinate Exercise—Fatigue or Illness From—(See "Inordinate" under Exercise; Fatigue).

Intemperate—In Sports—The ☉ afflicted in ♐; a ♐ disorder, and afflictions in ♐. (See "Intemperate" under Exercise; Intemperance).

Lack of Exercise—(See "Lack Of" under Exercise; Obesity, Sedentary).

Muscular Body—Athletic Body—(See Athletics; "Body" under Muscles, Strong).

Outdoor Exercise—And Sports—Fond of—♐ is primarily the Sportsman Sign, and the ☉, ☽, ♃, ♂, and ☿ in this sign favor outdoor sports, riding, hunting, fishing, etc.; ♃ in ♐ makes one fond of horses, riding, hunting, etc.; ♂ in ♌, fond of robust sports. (See "Riding" under Horses, Hunting; "Fishing" in this section).

Over-Exercise—Over-Exertion—Disease, Illness, Fatigue, or Colds From—(See "Colds", "Inordinate", under Exercise; Fatigue).

Pleasure—(See "Abnormally Fond Of" under Pleasure).

Rash Actions—In Sports, and Warns Against Injury By—♂ afflicted in ♐. (See Hasty; "Sudden Impulses" under Impulses; "Painful Complaints" under Rashness).

Recreations—Death or Injury In—(See Recreations).

Riding—(See "Riding" under Horses; "Outdoor Exercise" in this section).

Robust Sports—(See "Outdoor" in this section).

Shooting—(See Gunshot, Hunting, Shooting).

Theatres—Death or Injury In—(See Theatres).

Travel—(See "Love of Travel", and the various paragraphs under Travel).

Vicious Pleasures—Vicious Sports—Fond of—♀ Sig. in ♏. (See Pleasures).

Wrestling—(See "Pugilist", "Wrestler", under Athletics).

SPOTS—Spotted—

Nebulous Spots—(See Nebulous).

Skin Spots—(See Blemishes, Blotches; "Spots" under Liver; Marks, Moles, Naevus, Scars; "Pock-Marked" under Smallpox. Also note the various paragraphs under Skin).

Sun Spots—A number of Spots appear upon the Sun when ♃ is in perihelion, and disappear when ♃ is in aphelion. They tend to affect the Nerv-ous System, make men irritable, quarrelsome, and given to War. These spots disturb the gases of our atmosphere, and tend to epidemics, tornadoes, cyclones, cloudbursts, and atmospheric disturbances. (See Epidemics, Perihelion; "Tornadoes" under Wind).

SPOTTED—

Spotted Colors—Mixed Colors—(See "Mixed" under Colors).

Spotted Fever—Cerebro-Spinal Fever—Cerebro-Spinal Meningitis with Fever and Eruption—The ☉ afflicted in ♌; the ☉ in ♌ when the afflictor in the disease. Coincident with the appearance of Comets. Halley's Comet has brought it, and been followed by Plague. It very frequently accompanies Cerebro-Spinal Meningitis, and also Herpes. (See "Cerebro-Spinal Meningitis" under Cerebro-Spinal; Comets, Herpes, Plague).

SPRAINS—Strains—The accidents of ♑ are Sprains, Dislocations, and Broken Limbs. Caused by ♑ on the Asc. at B. Also caused by ♄, the ruler of the ♑ Sign.

Ankles—Sprains In—(See "Sprains" under Ankles).

Knees—(See "Strains In" under Knees).

Lower Parts—Sprains In—The ☽ afflicted in ♑; ♄ in ♑ or ♒. (See "Parts" under Lower).

Wrists—Sprains In—(See "Sprains" under Wrists). See Strains.

SPREAD OF DISEASE—(See "Corrupt Air" under Air; Cholera, Comets, Endemic, Epidemics, Noxious, Obnoxious, Pandemics, Perihelion, Pestilence, Plague; "Sun Spots" under Spots).

SPRING EQUINOX—The Vernal Equinox—(See Equinoxes, Vernal).

SPRINGS DRY UP—(See Drought; "Fountains Dry Up" under Dry; Famine, Fountains; "Extreme Heat" under Heat; "Hot Blasting Winds" under Wind).

SPURIOUS ISCHURIA—(See this subject under Urine. Also see False).

SPUTUM—(See Expectoration, Mucus, Phlegm, Saliva, Spitting, etc.).

SQUAB BODY—Fat and Short—Low and Bulky—Lumpish—Plump—Well-Trussed—Squat—Short and Thick—The ☽ in her decrease causes a short, low, squat stature; ♄ Sig. in ♍ in Hor'y Q.; ☿ in ♋ or ♓; ☿ Sig. in ♋, short, squab body; ☿ in ♓, partile the Asc., a short squab figure, but some Authorities say thin; ♋, ♍, or ♓ on the Asc.; some Authorities say that ♒ on the Asc. gives a squab figure, and especially if there are many planets in watery signs. (See "Body" under Fat; "Fleshy Body" under Fleshy; Lumpish; "Low Stature" under Low; Plump; "Body" under Short, Thick; Well-Trussed, etc.).

SQUARE—

Aspect—The Square Aspect (□)—The 90° Aspect, and very evil and afflicting. This is the cross aspect of crucifixion, and many of these aspects between the planets at B. tend to a life of trouble, sorrow, and ill-health for the native, and a more turbulent career. (See Aspects).

Body — Square-Built Body — S q u a r e Make—The ☉ in ♏, square and fleshy; the ☉ or ☽ in ♑, ♒, or ♓, or these signs upon the Asc., square make; ♄ in ♈ in good aspect the Asc.; ♃ Sig. in a fiery sign, the body is square made and strong. (See "Body" under Fat; "Fleshy Body" under F l e s h y ; Squab).

Face—(See "Square" under Face).

Head—(See "Square" under Head).

SQUAT STATURE—(See Fat, Squab).

SQUINTING — S q u i n t Eyes — Crossed Eyes—(See "Strabismus" under Eyes).

STABS — Cuts — Wounds by Knife or Sword—Caused by ♂, as ♂ is the instigator of quarrels, disputes, contests, and violence; ♂ ☐ or ☍ the ☉ at B., and by dir.; ♂ afflicted in the 1st H. at B.; born under ♂, and with ♂ ruler of the Asc., and afflicted; ♂ in the 1st or 10th H., and afflicting the hyleg; ♂ afflicting the ☉, ☽, or hyleg at B., and elevated above them in a violent map; ♂ with Aldebaran, and especially in angles, and afflicting the ☽; the ☉ or ☽ to the ♂ or ill-asps. ♂ by dir.; the ☉ joined with the Ascelli, Castor, Pollux, Hyades, Praesepe, or the Pleiades; the ☽ directed to Capella; the Asc. to the ♂ or evil asp. ♂ by dir., and especially if ♂ be in a fiery sign; the M.C. to the place of Pollux or the Pleiades; the Ascelli, Pleiades, Hyades, Castor, Praesepe, directed to the Asc. or Lights. (See Blows, Cuts, Duels, Instruments, Sword).

Contests—Killed or Injured In—(See Chartering, Contests, Duels, Quarrels).

Cuts — (See the various paragraphs under Cuts).

Death by Stabs—♂ causes death by; ♂ with Aldebaran, and ♂ in ☐ or ☍ the ☉, and ♂ just setting at B.; ♂ the afflicting planet, in a violent sign, and afflicting the hyleg; ♂ in the 10th H., and ☐ the Asc., and the ☉ afflicted; the ☽ to the ♂ or ill-asp. ♂ by dir.; the ☽ directed to Capella, danger of death by stabs or blows; the ☽ Sig. ♂, ☐, or ☍ ♂; the ☉ to the place of Praesepe. Case of Death by Stabs—See "Terris", No. 789, in 1001 N.N. (See Assassination; "Death" under Blows, Cuts, Duels, Sword; Roman Emperor).

Distortions — Lameness, or Paralysis Resulting from Stabs — (S e e Distortions).

Duels — Death or Injury In — (See Duels).

Incised Wounds—(See Cuts, Incised).

Instruments—Stabs by Sharp Instruments, and Edged Tools — (See Cuts, Duels, Instruments, Iron, Sword; the various paragraphs in this section).

Journeys — S t a b s or Cuts During — (See "Travel" under Cuts).

Lameness—From Stabs—(See Distortions; "Lameness" under Cuts; "Stabs" under Lameness).

Paralysis—From Stabs—(See Distortions).

Quarrels—(See "Death", "Injury", under Quarrels).

Sharp Instruments — Stabs By — (See Cuts, Duels, Instruments, Sword; the various paragraphs in this section).

Spinal Curvature—From Stabs—Case —See "Spinal Curvature", No. 838, in 1001 N.N.

Travel—Journeys—Voyages—Stabs or Cuts D u r i n g — (See "Travel" under Cuts).

Violent Death—By Cuts or Stabs—In a violent map, ♂ elevated above, and afflicting the ☉, ☽, or hyleg at B., and by dir. (See "Death" in this section).

Voyages — S t a b s or Cuts On — (See "Travel" under Cuts).

War — Stabs In — Death In — (See "Death or Injury In" under War).

Weapons — Stabs by Sharp Weapons —(See Cuts, Duels, Instruments, Sword; the various paragraphs in this section).

STAGES OF LIFE—(See Childhood, Infancy, Middle Life, Old Age; "Life" under Periods; Youth).

STAGGERING WALK — (See Drunkenness; "Staggering" under Gait; Intoxication).

STAGNATION—Stagnant—

Air — Stagnant Air — (See "Corrupt" under Air).

Blood—(See "Stagnant" under Blood).

Functions — (See "Stagnation" under Functions).

Pools—Stagnant Pools—(See Pools).

STAKE—Burned At Stake—Case—(See "Stake" under Burns).

STAMINA—Vital Stamina—Tone—Vitality, etc. The bodily Stamina is ruled by the Asc. The Fiery Signs on the Asc. at B. give the best stamina, and next to these the Airy Signs, and the Watery Signs ♋ and ♓ give the least stamina. Of the earthy and watery signs the ♉, ♍, and ♏ signs give good stamina when on the Asc. at B. The ☽ has much to do with the stamina of the constitution at all times, and the health will not be as good if the ☽ is badly afflicted in a female nativity, or the ☉ weak and afflicted in a male nativity, and also the fate and fortune of the native is less favorable.

Stamina Good—The Stamina Increased —The ☉ ✳ or △ ♂ or the Asc., and also the organic resistance is increased; ♈, ♌, ♎, or ♐ upon the Asc. at B. (See "Good" under Resistance, Tone, Vitality; "Increased" under Strength; "Body" under Strong).

Stamina In Infancy—(See "Stamina" under Infancy).

Stamina Low — The ☉ in ♑, ♋, ♑, or ♓ on the Asc. at B. (See "Low" under Recuperation, Resistance, Vitality).

Stamina Reduced — (See ''S t a m i n a Low" in this section; "Lessened" under Vitality; "Weak Body" under Weak).

Stamina Strengthened — Increased — (See "Stamina Good" in this section).

Void of Stamina — The ☉ or ☽ in an angle at B., and ♂ a malefic. (See "Weakest Constitution" under Constitution; "Early Death" under Early; Feeble, Infirm, Invalids; Sickly; "Low" under Resistance, Vitality).

STAMMERING—(See "Stammering" under Speech).

STANDING — Standing On the Feet — (See "Standing" under Feet).

STANNUM—Tin—A Typical Metal of ♃. (See Metals).

STARCH — Starches—Amylum—Starch-Like—Amyloid—Starches are ruled by ♃, and are the physiological action of ♃. (See Hydrocarbonates, Jupiter, Sugar).

Animal Starch—This is the Glycogen found in the Blood and Liver, and is ruled by ♃. (See Glycogen).

Desire for Starches—Tendency to Excess of Starches In the Food — (See "Starches", "Sweets", under Food).

Kidneys—(See "Amyloid Kidney" under Kidneys).

STARING EYES—(See "Large", "Staring" under Eyes).

STAR MAP OF BIRTH—(See Map, Nativity, Radix, Will).

STARS—Fixed Stars—Constellations— The Stars outside of our Solar System, and which are not our Planets, are called Fixed Stars. Only the Stars near the Ecliptic will be considered here. (See Planets). The Constellations make up a Group of Stars. These stars have much effect upon Humanity when in the Asc. or Angles at B., when near the ☉ or ☽, and also when directed to the Angles. Fixed Stars operate only by ☌, P., or ☍ aspects in the Zodiac, or Mundane, and not by ✶, ☐, or △. The Fixed Stars have various natures after the order of our Planets, and tend to cause good fortune, calamity, sickness, disease, pestilence, misfortune, accidents, injuries, blindness, eye troubles, drowning, disgrace, imprisonment, violent death, etc., according to their nature. Some Fixed Stars are of the nature of ♂, or of ♂ and the ☽ combined, of ♂ and ♀, or of ♂ and ♀ combined, etc. Other stars are of the nature of ♅, ♄, ♃, ♀, and ☿, and their various combined influences. Fixed stars of the nature of ♂ tend to fevers, accidents, injuries, violent death, etc. Those of the nature of ♄, chronic disorders, and ill-fortune. Those of the nature of ♃ and ♀, good fortune, etc. The violent fixed stars are of the nature of ♂ and ♂ combinations, and are the most dangerous to Humanity, and when joined with the ☉ at B., threaten a violent death or extreme sickness. (See "Violent Stars" in this section). Stars of the nature of ♃ and ♀, or ♃ and ♀ combined influences, are more fortunate in their influences, and tend to bring good fortune, good health, honors, renown, happiness, etc. Arista, of the nature of ♂ and ♀, is said to be one of the most fortunate of the fixed stars. Algol is said to be the most evil of all the Fixed Stars. Lists of the Fixed Stars are to be found in the various Textbooks and Dictionaries of Astrology. In this Article you will find an alphabetical list of the Fixed Stars referred to in the various Textbooks, as related to, and causing disease, and other conditions over Humanity. See these Stars in the alphabetical arrangement for further information about them, their position, influences, etc. Also in this Article the various Groups of Fixed Stars are given.

Fixed Stars—Alphabetical List of the Fixed Stars mentioned in the Textbooks in relation to Disease, Accidents, Misfortunes, Violence, etc. — Acquirius, Aldebaran, Algenib, Algol, Alphard, Altair, Andromeda, Antares, Aquaries, Arcturus, Argo, Arista, Ascelli, Auriga (Capella); Bellatrix, Betelgeuse, Bootes, Bull's Eyes and Horns, Canis Majoris, Capella (Auriga); Capricornus, Caput Algol, Caput Andromeda, Caput Hercules (Pollux); Castor, Cauda Lucida (Deneb, Lion's Tail); Cepheus, Ceti, Cor Hydra (Alphard, Hydra's Heart); Cor Leonis (Regulus, Lion's Heart); Cor Scorpio (Antares); Cratch (Ascelli); Crater, Cynosura (Little Bear, Ursa Minor); Deneb (Lion's Tail); Dorsa Leonis (Lion's Back); Eagle (Attair, Scorpio); Fomahaut, Frons Scorpio, Gemini (Twins); Goat (Capricorn); Gorgon's Head (Algol); Hercules (Pollux); Hircus, Hyades, Hydra's Heart (Alphard, Cor Hydra); Lion (Cor Leonis, Dorsa Leonis, Mane of Leo, etc. — See Lion); Little Bear (Cynosura); Lucida Maxilla (Ceti, Menkar, Whale's Jaw); Lucida Pleiadum (Pleiades); Markab, Medusa's Head (Algol); Menkar (Ceti, Whale's Jaw); Nebulous Spots (see Nebulous); North Scale; Oculus Taurus (Bull's Eye); Ophiucus, Orion, Pleiades, Pollux (Hercules); Praesepe, Procyon, Propus, Regulus, Rigel, Scales (North and South Scale); Scheat Pegasi, Scorpion's Heart (Cor Scorpio, Antares); Sirius, Twins (Castor and Pollux, Gemini); Urn of Aquarius, Ursa Minor (Little Bear, Cynosura); Vega, Vindemiatrix, Virgin's Spixe (Arista); Vulture (Altair); Whale's Jaw — Whale's Belly (Ceti, Menkar); Zona Andromeda (Andromeda).

Fortunate Stars — Arista (Spica Virginus), of the nature of ♂ and ♀, is said to be the most fortunate in influence of the Fixed Stars. Also the stars of the ♃ and ♀ Group in this section.

Jupiter and Mars Group — Arcturus, Antares, North Scale, Rigel, Sirius. Fixed Stars of the nature of ♃, or of ♃ and ♂, when joined to the Anareta, denote injuries to arise from Religion, or some one in Power.

Jupiter and Venus Group—Caput Andromedae, Crater. Stars of the nature of ♃ and ♀ can do little injury unless mixed with those of ♄ and ♂.

Mars Group—The principal group of ♂ stars, listed as purely of ♂ influence, are Aldebaran, Bull's North and South Horns, Cor Leo (Regulus), Propus, and Pollux. Fixed stars of the ♂ nature denote sudden fevers, accidents, or murders. (See "Stars of Mars Nature" under Mars).

Mars and Mercury Group — Algenib, Antares (Cor Scorpio), Bellatrix (Orion's Left Shoulder); Betelgeuse (Orion's Right Shoulder); Capella (In Auriga's Left Shoulder); Hircus, Procyon.

Mars and Moon Group — Ascelli, Hyades, Nebulous Spots and Clusters, Pleiades, Praesepe. This group also acts like the ♂ group, but especially on the eyes, and to cause eye troubles, blindness, and also fevers, accidents, injuries, and violent death. (See Hyades, Nebulous, Pleiades, etc.).

Mars and Venus Group—Arista (Virgin's Spixe); Markab, Serpentis.

Moon Group—The Constellation Argo is typical of the ☽ group, and tends to drowning. Fixed stars of the nature of the ☽ tend to drowning, colic, cold and watery diseases. There are practically no stars listed in the Textbooks of Astrology as being distinctly of a ☽ nature, but those referred to in Astrology are the ♂ and ☽ combination, such as the Nebulous Clusters, Pleiades, etc. (See "Mars and Moon Group" in this section. Also see Argo, Drowning, Shipwreck).

Ruling Your Stars — (See Character, Fate, Hospitals, Map, Medical Astrology; "Treatment" under Melancholy; Occult, Science, Spiritual, etc.).

Saturn Group—Cauda Lucida (Lion's Tail, Deneb);Scheat Pegasi, Ceti (Menkar, Whale's Jaw); Whale's Belly, Whale's Tail, Capricornus. Afflictions of the ♄ group tend to Agues, Cold Diseases, Palsies, and denote Falls.

Saturn and Jupiter Group — Algol, Orion's Belt (Orion). Algol is considered the most evil and malign of all the fixed stars. (See Algol).

Saturn and Mars Group — Left Hand of Ophiucus, Ram's Head, Frons Scorpio. Wilson, in his Dictionary of Astrology, gives Frons Scorpio as of the nature of ♄ and ♀. Simmonite gives it as of the nature of ♄ and ♂.

Saturn, Mars and Venus—Castor.

Saturn, Mercury, and Venus — Lion's Tail (Deneb); Vindemiatrix, both as given in Wilson's Dictionary of Astrology.

Saturn and Venus — Dorsa Leonis (Lion's Back); Hydra's Heart, Frons Scorpio, Right Knee of Ophiucus, South Scale, Vindemiatrix.

Sun and Mars Group — The Ascelli, Capricornus. Tend to Blindness, Eye Disorders, Fevers, etc.

Unfortunate Stars—The principal unfortunate stars are Aldebaran (♂); Algol (♄ and ♃); Antares (♂ and ☿); Castor (♄, ♂, ♀); Deneb (♅); Dorsa Leonis (♄ and ♀); Hyades (♂ and ☽); Pleiades (♂ and ☽); Praesepe (♂ and ☽); Whale's Jaw (♄). Fixed Stars of the nature of the malefics ♅, ♄, and ♂, and some of the combinations with these malefics, are very unfortunate over human affairs when found with the ☉ or ☽ at B.

Uranus Group — Acquirius, Aquaries, Altair, Deneb (Lion's Tail, listed as of ♅ influence in Simmonite). These stars tend to sudden mishaps, sudden death, and violence.

Venus Group—Bull's South Eye (Oculus Taurus), Canis Majoris, Zona Andromeda. In the lists of Fixed Stars in the Textbooks Wilson gives the Bull's North Eye as Oculus Taurus, and of the nature of ♀. Wilson gives the Bull's South Eye as Aldebaran, and of the nature of ♂. Simmonite gives the Bull's South Eye as of ♀, and the North Eye (Aldebaran) as of ♂. Pearce gives Oculus Taurus as of ♀, and Aldebaran as of ♂. Alan Leo's Dictionary of Astrology gives the same as in Pearce's Textbook, and Wilson's Dictionary seems to stand alone in giving Aldebaran as the Bull's South Eye.

Violent Fixed Stars — Fixed Stars of the nature of ♂, and of ♂ combinations, tend to be violent in their nature and effects. Also some stars of ♄ influence are violent in nature. In addition to those listed in the Mars Group in this section, the following stars are considered violent in nature: Aldebaran (♂); Algenib (♂ and ☿); Algol (♄ and ♃); Antares (♂ and ☿); Bellatrix (♂ and ☿); Castor (♄, ♂, and ♀); Markab (♂ and ♀); Procyon (♂ and ☿); South Scale (♄ and ♀). (See "Mars Group" in this section).

STARVATION—Want of Food—Famine—♄ and ♂ in ♌ aspect, in Equinoctial Signs, and controlling the Luminaries. (See "Lost In" under Desert; Drought, Famine, Neglect, Poverty; "Dangers" under Travel).

Desert — Danger of Starvation In — (See Desert).

Starved to Death—Case—See "Popejoy", No. 771 in 1001 N.N.

Tissues—Starvation of—(See Emaciation; "Incapable Of", "Malnutrition", under Nutrition; Wastings).

STATIONARY PLANETS — The afflicting planet in disease when stationary in the Zodiac tends to prolong the disease, make it more constant and enduring in its effects. (See Constancy, Continuity, Course, Direct Motion; "Degree Of" under Disturbed; Duration, Lingering Diseases, Prolonged, Retrograde, etc.).

STATURE—Form—Shape of the Body—Figure—Height—Weight, etc. The Sign ascending, and the First House, have significance of the Stature of Man. The matter of determining the stature from the horoscope is not an easy task, and it requires considerable knowledge of the nature and qualities of the Planets, Signs, Houses, Aspects, etc., and of Synthesis, to form a reasonable judgment of the appearance, build, complexion, height, weight, etc., without seeing the native. However, the influences given in connection with the following subjects have proven very accurate along these lines. Planets ascending, the sign ascending, the degree ascending at B., the Ascendant, lord of the Ascendant, the nature and position of the majorities of the planets, the dignities of the planets, planets rising, setting, elevated, below the Earth, the combinations and aspects of the planets, and the general synthesis of the map, have to be carefully examined in order to form a judgment about the appearance of the native. These rules are further set forth in the Articles on Appearance, Complexion, Form, Height, Shape, Weight, etc. When the ☉ or ☽ are ascending at B., judge from the quality of the sign they are in. When ☿ is ascending he gives a stature according to the lord of the Ascendant. In the Articles on each of the planets something is said about the kind of a form and stature such planet tends to give when predominant at B. By making a study of the following subjects the student will get a very good idea of the various causes and influences which tend to produce the different types of body and physique. See these subjects in the alphabetical arrangement when they are only listed here—

Abdomen ᵥ Prominent — (See "Prominent" under Abdomen).

Abnormally Tall — (See Enlarged, Giants, Height, Tall).

Above Average Height—(See Giants, Height, Tall).

Above Middle Height — (See Height, Middle).

Advantageous Stature — (See "Good Constitution" under Constitution).

Appearance — (See the various subjects and references under Appearance).

Arms — (See "Long", "Short", under Arms).

Awkward; Badly Made — And Ugly — (See Crooked; "Not Handsome" under Handsome; "Ill-Formed" under Ill; Ugly).

Beautiful; Bent Forward—(See "Body Bent Forward" under Bending).

Best-Formed Body — ♌ on the Asc. (See Beautiful, Form, Handsome, Well-Formed).

Big Head and Face—(See "Big" under Face; "Large" under Head; "Body" under Large).

Body—(See the various subjects and references under Body).

Broad; Build; Chest — (See Hollow, Narrow, Wide, and the various descriptions under Chest).

Coarse; Comely; Commanding;

Compact; Conformity of Members — (See Well-Proportioned).

Constitution — (See Good, Strong, Weak, and the various paragraphs under Constitution).

Contracted Body—Small—(See Diminished, Dwarfed, Small Body).

Corpulent; Crooked;

Decent-Made and Compact—(See Compact).

Deformed; Diminished — (See Diminished, Dwarfed, Low, Short Body, Small).

Discomposed; Disproportioned;

Distorted; Dwarfed; Elegant;

Enlarged; Erect; Face—(See Angular, Broad, Long, Oval, Round, Thin, and the various descriptions under Face).

Fair; Fat; Fine; Fleshy; Form of Body —(See Form).

Full Stature—(See Full).

Giants; Good Stature—(See Beautiful, Comely, Elegant, Fine, Good, Handsome, Well-Proportioned).

Hands — (See Broad, Fleshy, Long, Short, and the various descriptions under Hands).

Handsome; Harmonious; Head—(See Large, Round, Small, and the various descriptions under Head).

Healthy Make—(See Healthy).

Height—(See the various paragraphs and references under Height).

Hips—(See Narrow, Small, Well-Proportioned, under Hips).

Hooked Forward — (See Bending; "Downward" under Look; "Stoop Shoulders" under Shoulders; Stooping).

Horary Questions—Stature In—Indicated by the Sign ascending.

Ill-Formed Body—(See Crooked, Deformed; "Ill-Formed" under Ill; Incurvating, Malformations, Misshaped, Ugly).

Incurvating—Crooked—Not Straight —(See Incurvating).

Indifferent Stature — (See "Stature" under Indifferent).

Knees—(See Crooked, Ill-Made, Knock-Knees, under Knees).

Large Stature — (See Full, Giants, Large).

Lean; Legs—(See the descriptions under Legs).

Limbs — (See Crooked, Large, Long, Short, Small, Stout, and the various paragraphs under Limbs).

Little Stature — (See Diminished, Dwarfed, Short, Small).

Low Stature—(See "Low Stature" under Low).

Lumpish; Mean Stature—(See Mean).

Medium Stature—(See Medium).

Members — (See Brevity Of, Long, Missing, under Members).

Middle-Sized—(See Medium, Middle).

Misshaped; Moderate Stature — (See Moderate).

Monsters; Muscular Body—(See Athletic; "Body" under Muscles).

Not High — (See Diminished, Dwarf, Low, Short, Small).

Not Well-Made—(See "Ill-Formed" in this section).

Obesity; Physique—(See Physical).

Plump; Positive Form — (See Positive).

Posture; Prepossessing Stature—(See Commanding).

Proper Stature—(See Proper).

Proportionate — (See "Fair Proportions" under Fair).

Raw-Boned — (See "Raw-Boned" under Bones).

Robust Looking—(See Robust).

Rugged; Shape — (See the references under Shape).

Shapely—(See Beautiful, Handsome).

Short Body—(See "Body" under Short).

Shoulders—(See Broad, Round, Stoop, Thick, under Shoulders).

Sickly Looking—(See Sickly).

Size; Skeleton; Slender; Small Body— (See "Body" under Small).

Squab Body—(See Squab).

Square-Built—(See Square).

Squatty—(See Fat, Squab; "Short and Thick" under Thick).

Stooped—(See "Hooked Forward" in this section).

Stout; Straight—(See Erect, Straight, Upright).

Strong Body — (See "Body" under Strong).

Sturdy—(See Robust, Rugged).

Tall; Thick Body—(See Thick).

Thighs — (See Long, Short, Small, Strong, under Thighs).

Thin Body—(See Lean, Slender, Thin).

Trunk; Ugly; Undersized; Undeveloped; Ungainly; Unrefined; Upright; Weak and Small — (See "Smaller and Weaker" under Small).

Weight; Well-Built; Well-Favored; Well-Formed; Well-Framed; Well-Made; Well-Proportioned; Well-Set; Well-Shaped; Well-Trussed;

Youthful Looking — (See "Youthfulness" under Youth). For other subjects along this line, and which may be omitted here, look in the alphabetical arrangement for what you have in mind.

STEALING — (See Kleptomaniac, Robbers, Thieves).

STEATOMA — Steatomatous Tumor — (See Cysts, Fat, Sebaceous, Wen).

STEEL—The Metal Steel is ruled by ♂. Wounds By—(See Iron).

STELLAR BAPTISM — (See "Planetary Baptism" under Baptism; "Moment of Birth" under Moment).

STELLIUM—An Over-Cargo of Planets in a Sign or House. A Stellium, or group of Stars, in a house, tends to cause disease, and corresponding to the Sign ordinarily ruling the House. Thus many planets in the 2nd H. denote throat trouble. A Stellium in ♌ or the 5th H., heart disturbances. A Stellium in ♓ or the 12th H., humours in the feet. A Stellium in ♊ or the 3rd H., Lung and Nervous Disorders. (See Majority).

STENOSIS—A Narrowing or Constriction—A Contraction—Stenosis is presided over by ♄. Cold, ruled by ♄, is a strong factor in contractions.

Bile Ducts—Stenosis of—(See "Ducts" under Bile).

Blood Vessels—Stenosis of—(See Constrictions).

Cells—(See "Stenosis" under Cells).

Mitral Stenosis—(See "Mitral" under Heart).

Nose—Nares—(See "Stenosis" under Nose).

Pulmonary Stenosis—(See "Stenosis" under Lungs).

Pylorus—Stenosis of—(See "Pylorus" under Stomach).

Vaso-Constriction — (See Constrictions, Vaso).

Vessels—Stenosis of Blood Vessels—(See Constrictions, Vaso, Vessels). See Capillaries, Centripetal, Cold, Colds, Congestions, Constrictions, Contractions, Spasmodic Diseases, Stricture).

STEP—Gait—Walk—For the different variations in Step see Gait, Walk).

Step Children — (See "Step Children" under Children).

STERILITY—(See Barren, Impotent).

Sterilization — Forcible Castration — Danger of—(See Maimed; "Violent Castration" under Testes).

STERN — Stern Expression—(See Austere).

STERNUM—The Flat Bone of the Breast — Manubrium — Ensiform Cartilage — Xiphisternum—Is under the structural rulership of the ♋ Sign. (See "Breastbone" under Breast).

Pain In—(See Xiphodynia).

Sterno-Mastoid Region—Sterno-Mastoid Muscle—Disorders of—(See Mastoid).

STERTOROUS — Sonorous — Stertorous Breathing — (See "Snoring", "Stertorous", under Breathing).

STHENIA—Sthenic—Strong—Active—

Sthenic Inflammation—(See "Sthenic" under Inflammation).

Sthenic Plethora—(See "Sthenic" under Plethora).

Sthenic Process—Is presided over by ♂. (See "Active Body" under Active; Asthenic, Dynamic, Energetic, Mars, Strength, Strong).

STIFFNESS — Stiff — Rigid — Stiff and rigid conditions in the body are caused by ♄, and by Cold, which is ruled by ♄. They also occur during Spasmodic conditions. (See Cold, Rigidity, Saturn, Spasmodic).

Stiff Body—Caused by ♄ deposits, retention of the wastes of the body, excess of Uric Acid, etc. (See Crystallization, Deposits, Gout, Hardening, Retentions, Rheumatism, Sand, Stone, Wastes, etc.).

Stiff Hair—(See "Stiff" under Hair).

Stiff Joints—(See Adhesions, Ankylosis; "Stiff" under Joints; Rheumatism).

Stiff Muscles — (See "Contractions" under Muscles; Rigidity, Rigors).

Stiff Neck—(See "Stiff" under Neck).

Stiff Shoulder Joint—(See "Stiffness" under Shoulders).

Stiff Spine—(See "Stiff" under Spine).

STILLBORN — Stillbirth — Born Dead — Child Dies In the Womb — Child Thought Born Dead—♅ afflicted in ♏ in the map of the mother; all of the Significators afflicted, as the ☉, ☽, Asc., lord of the Asc., and with no assistance from Benefics; the Benefics in the 1st, 5th, or 11th H., and sorely afflicted by malefics; ♄ exactly on the cusp of the 1st or 7th H., born dead, or breathes only a few times and dies. (See Abortion; "Death at Birth" under Children; "Mutilation Of" under Foetus; Miscarriage). Cases of Stillbirth — See "Breech Presentation", No. 075 in 1001 N.N. Case — Thought Born Dead, and does not breathe until two hours after birth—See "Foot", No. 106 in 1001 N.N. Prenatal conditions, and afflictions to the ☽ during Gestation, are usually the causes of a stillbirth, and which kill the foetus in utero. (See Prenatal Epoch).

STIMULANTS — Stimulant — Stimulation —Tonics—Stimulus—Mars is stimulant, and the drugs of ♂ are used in Tonics and Stimulant Remedies. The ☉ Group of Plants are stimulant. Neptune is associated with Drugs, and especially Narcotic Stimulants, as Opiates, Tobacco, etc. The Adrenals, ruled by ♃, are the organs which stimulate the body. The Glycogen in the liver is drawn upon by ♂ for fuel during muscular activity. (See Adrenals, Glycogen).

Avoid Stimulants—Stimulants should be avoided when the ☽ is ☌ ♂, and especially ♂ in ♈, the Asc., or strong at B. Also avoid stimulants during the decrease of the ☽. (See "Best Time to Give Medicine" under Medicines).

Digestive Stimulants — (See "Stimulated" under Digestion).

Disordered Stimulation—In the Body —Caused by afflictions to ♃, and interference with the Adrenal Secretions. (See "Diminished Secretion" under Adrenals).

Dosage of Stimulants — Should be smaller during the increase of the ☽, and larger dosage during the decrease of the ☽. (See "Decrease", "Increase", under Moon).

Given to Stimulants — To Liquors or Narcotics—The ☉, ☽, and many planets in watery signs at B., more desire for drink; ♆ in a watery sign; ♆ afflicted in the 6th H., or in ♍; ♄ in the Asc., and afflicted by ♆. (See Drink, Drunkenness; "Sugar" under Food; Intoxicants, Narcotics, Wine).

Greatest Effect—Stimulants have the greatest effect when the ☽ is increasing in light, and sedatives do little good. The ☽ ☌ ♄ causes stimulants to have little effect. (See Sedatives).

Heart Stimulants—Cautions In Using —(See "Stimulants" under Heart).

Of Little Effect — See Avoid, Dosage, Greatest Effect, in this section).

Rubefacients — Local Stimulants— Caustics — External Stimulants — The remedies of ♂ are stimulant when applied to the skin, and may cause blistering, and are used to stimulate the local circulation which has been impeded by ♄. Cantharides is a typical ♂ rubefacient and caustic. The remedies of the ☉, such as Mustard, are stimulant locally on the skin. (See Applications, Cantharides, Caustics, Mustard, Rubefacients, Sinapis, Vesicant).

Stimulus—Incentive—Ambition—Energy—Lack of—Loss of—(See "Of No Ambition" under Ambition; Apathy, Dull; "Lack Of" under Energy; "Mind" under Heaviness; Inactive, Indifferent, Inertia, Languid, Lassitude, Lazy, Lethargy, Listless, Malaise, Morose, Relaxation, Rouse; "Drowsiness" under Sleep; Slothful, Slovenly, Torpid, etc.).

Tonic Medicines — (See "Liquids", "Stimulants", under Drink; Narcotics, Poisons; "Medicines" under Tonic; Wine, etc.).

STINGS—Venomous Stings—Wounds or Death By Obnoxious Creatures—♄ or ♂ in the Terrestrial, or Quadrupedal Signs (see Quadrupeds); ♄ near the Constellation of the Serpent, and with ♄ in the 1st H., configurated with ☿, and in ♉ the ☉ or ☽ setting, and also tends to death from such; ♄ and ♂ conjoined in ♏; ♂ causes bites and stings, and with swellings and eruptions; the star Fomahaut conjoined with ♂. (See Adder, Bites, Insects, Obnoxious, Reptiles, Serpents, Venomous).

STINKING — Foul — Offensive — Loathsome—Obnoxious—Unpleasant Odors— (See "Foul" under Breath; Corruption, Decay, Decomposition, Fetid, Foul, Odors, Offensive; "Stagnant" under Pools; Putrefaction; "Fetid" under Sweat).

STOCK BODY—Stocky and Short—The ☉ in ♉, or ♉ on the Asc. at B. (See Corpulent, Fat Body, Fleshy; "Body" under Short).

STOICISM — Self-Abnegation — (See "Stoicism" under Religion).

STOMACH—Gastric—The Chief Digestive Organ of the Body—The stomach is under the internal rulership of the ♋ sign. Also ruled by the ☽ and the 4th H. The 5th H. denotes the stomach. The Cardinal Signs influence and affect the stomach, and especially ♋ and ♑.

— SECTION ONE —

GENERAL CONSIDERATIONS — Organs and Matters Related to the Stomach—See the following subjects in the alphabetical arrangement—

Abdomen; Acids — Of the Stomach — (See Gastric, Juices; "Juices" in this section).

Alimentation—Alimentary Canal— (See Alimentary).

Appetite; Arteries—Of the Stomach— Ruled by ♃, and ♃ in ♋.

Assimilation; Cardinal Signs — The cardinal signs denote the Head, Stomach, Kidneys, and Skin. (See Cardinal).

Diet; Digestion; Drink; Duodenum; Eating; Emetics; Epigastrium;

External Lining—Of the Stomach—Is ruled by ♋, and ♄ in ♋.

Fluids Of—(See Acids; "Fluids" under Digestion; Gastric, Hydrochloric, Juices, etc.).

Food; Functions — Of the Stomach — Ruled by the ☽ and the ☽ in ♋. (See Assimilation, Digestion; "Functions" under Stomach).

Gastric — Gastronomical — Gastro-Abdominal—(See Gastric).

Glands — The Glands of the Stomach are ruled by the ☽, and the ☽ in ♋. Also the glands and secretions in the stomach are ruled by ♆, and ♆ in ♋.

Gustativeness; Hydrochloric Acid — (See Hydrochloric).

Juices — The Juices of the Stomach are under the rule of the ☽. (See Fluids, Glands, in this section).

Lining — Of the Stomach — (See "External" in this section).

Lower Part—Of the Stomach—Ruled by ♍. (See "Splanchnic" under Ganglion).

Membranes—Of the Stomach—Ruled, and largely influenced by ♅, and ♅ in ♋.

Muscles—Of the Stomach—Ruled by ♂, and ♂ in ♋. (See Muscles).

Nerves—Of the Stomach—Ruled by ☿, and ☿ in ♋. (See Nerves).

Oesophagus; Pepsin; Peristalsis — In the Stomach—Ruled by ♋. (See Peristalsis).

Pylorus—Pyloric Valve—Ruled by ♍, the sign which rules the lower part of the Stomach.

Receptacle—The Stomach as a receptacle is ruled by the ☽ and the ♋ sign.

Secretions — Of the Stomach — (See Acids, Fluids, Glands, Hydrochloric, Juices, Pepsin, in this section).

Stomach Place—In the Spine—Known as "S.P.", and consists of the 6th, 7th, and 8th Dorsal Vertebrae. (See Subluxations; "Dorsal Vertebrae" under Vertebrae).

Structure—Of the Stomach—Ruled by the ☉, and the ☉ in ♋. (See Organic, Structural).

Tunics—The Gastro-Intestinal Tunics —(See "Impar" under Ganglion).

Upper Part—Of the Stomach—Ruled by the ♌ sign. (See the Introduction under Heart).

Veins—Of the Stomach—Ruled by ♀ and ♀ in ♋.

— SECTION TWO —

DISEASES OF THE STOMACH — See these subjects in the alphabetical arrangement when only listed here—

Abnormal Functioning—Of the Stomach—♅ afflicted in ♋ or the 4th H.

Abscess—(See "Ulcer" under Gastric).

Ache—Stomachache—A ☽ disease; the ☽ afflicted in ♋. (See Aches; Neuralgia, Pain, in this section).

Acidity — (See "Gastric Acidity" under Acids).

Acute Catarrh—Of the Stomach—(See "Gastritis" under Gastric; "Inflammation" in this section).

Affected — The Stomach tends to be affected when the ☽ is in ♋ or ♍; ♀ in ♍, or ☿ in ♎ or ♑. See Table 196 in Simmonite's Arcana.

Alimentation — Alimentary Canal — Disorders of—(See Alimentary).

Antiperistalsis — (See Antiperistalsis, Nausea, Peristalsis, Vomiting; "Peristalsis" in this section).

Anxiety—Stomach Disorders Due To —(See "Anxiety" under Digestion).

Appetite — Excess or Lack of — (See "Abnormal", "Loss Of", under Appetite).

Arteries of Stomach — Disorders of — ♃ afflicted in ♋. (See Arteries).

Assimilation—Disorders of—(See Assimilation).

Asthma—(See "Stomach Asthma" under Asthma).

Belching; Bilious Vomiting — (See Nausea, Vomiting).

Bloating; Blood — Stomach Disorders from Corrupt Blood—The ☉, ♄, ♃, or ♀ afflicted in ♋. (See "Impure Blood" under Impure). For the influences which cause vomiting of blood see Haemoptysis; "Blood" under Vomiting).

Cancer—Of the Stomach—(See "Stomach" under Carcinoma).

Carcinoma — (See "Stomach" under Carcinoma).

Cases—Of Stomach Disorders—Maps and Birth Data — See Figures 6A, 6B, 6C, 6D, in "Astro-Diagnosis", and also Figures 17 and 18 in "Message of the Stars", by the Heindels. Also see Seventeen Years in Bed", No. 843 in 1001 N.N., Case of Weak Stomach.

Catarrh — Of the Stomach — Gastric Catarrh—A ♋ disease, and afflictions in ♋; ♄ afflicted in ♋; the ☽ afflicted in ♋ or ♍; Subs at SP (7D), and at KP. (See "Gastritis" under Gastric; "Inflammation" in this section).

Cestode—(See "Worms" in this section).

Chronic Disorders—Of the Stomach— Chronic Gastritis — Chronic Catarrh — Chronic Indigestion—The ☉ hyleg, and to the ☌, P, □, or ☍ ♄ by dir., according to the sign ♄ is in at B.; ♄ afflicted in ♋ tends to chronic stomach troubles, chronic catarrh, and chronic indigestion. (See "Gastritis" under Gastric; "Chronic" under Indigestion; "Catarrh" in this section).

Circulation—Of the Stomach Impeded —♄ in ♋ or ♑, ☌, □, or ☍ ♃ or ♀; ♃ or ♀ in ♋, ☌, □, or ☍ ♄; ♀ in ♋, □, or ☍ ♄ or ♂; Subs at SP. (See "Impeded" under Circulation).

Cold Stomach—Cold Humours In—Indigestion from Taking Cold — (See "Cold", "Raw Humours", under Indigestion).

Colic In Stomach—Due to Worry and Anxiety—The ☽, ♅, or ☿ afflicted in ♋. (See Colic; Cramps, Pain, Wind, in this section).

Congestion—In Stomach—♄ afflicted in ♋. (See Congestion).

Contraction — Of the Pylorus — (See "Pylorus" in this section).

Corrupt Blood — Stomach Trouble From—(See "Blood" in this section).

Cough — Stomach Cough—(See "Dry, Hard Cough", "Stomach Cough", under Cough).

Cramps In — ♅ afflicted in ♋ or the 4th H. (See Cramps).

Death — By Stomach Trouble — ♃ causes death by foul stomach and foul blood; ♀ afflicted at B., and afflicting the hyleg in a train of fatal directions; denoted by ☿; cardinal signs dispose of.

Defects In — Born under ♃, some defect in digestion.

Deglutition; Deranged Stomach—(See "Disordered", and the various paragraphs in this section).

Diet—Ailments Due to Wrong Diet— (See "Ailments", "Excesses", under Diet).

Digestion—Disorders of—(See Digestion, Indigestion).

Dilatation—Of the Stomach—♃ or ♀ afflicted in ♋. (See Dilatations, Distentions, Flatulence; "Distended" in this section).

Diseased Stomach—(See "Disordered", and the various paragraphs in this section).

Disordered Stomach—Diseased Stomach—Stomach Trouble—Gastric Disorders—The Stomach Offended—Digestive Disorders, etc.—Afflictions in ♋, ♍, in the cardinal signs, or in the 4th H.; ♋ on the Asc., and afflicted; Subs at SP. (See the various paragraphs in this section, and under Gastric. Also see Digestion, Indigestion).

Distended Stomach — ♃, ♂, or ♀ afflicted in ♋; ♂ afflictions to the stomach. (See Belching, Dilatations, Distentions, Flatulence; "Stomach" under Gas; Inflation, Tympanites; Fermentation, Wind, in this section).

Dizziness — From Stomach Trouble — Afflictions in ♈ and ♋; a ☽ disease; the ☽ afflicted in ♋; ♃ or ♀ afflicted in ♋; Subs at SP (7D), and at KP. (See Dizziness, Vertigo).

Drink — Stomach Trouble from Too Much Drink and Riotous Living—(See "Stomach" under Drink).

Dry Stomach Cough—(See "Cough" in this section).

Dyspepsia; Dystrophia—(See "Defective Nutrition" under Nutrition).

Eating—(See the various paragraphs under Eating).

Eats Nails—Eats Glass, etc.—Case—(See "Human Ostrich" under Human).

Emetics; Enlarged Stomach—(See Dilated, Distended, in this section).

Epicureans; Epigastrium;

Eructations—(See Belching).

External Lining — Of the Stomach — Disorders of—♄ afflicted in ♋.

Eyes — Floating Specks Before the Eyes from Stomach Trouble — (See "Muscae" under Eyes).

Faecal Vomiting—(See Ileac Passion).

Feasting; Fermentation—In the Stomach—♋ influence; ♋ sign on the cusp the 6th H.; the ☽ hyleg in ♋ with females. (See "Putrid Matter" under Bowels; "Stomach" under Gas).

Fever In Stomach — Gastric Fever — (See "Fever" under Gastric; "Hot" in this section).

Flatulence; Fluids—Of the Stomach—Disordered and Retarded — ♄ afflicted in ♋ or ♍. (See "Fluids" under Gastric; Hydrochloric).

Food — Retention of Difficult — (See "Retention", and the various paragraphs under Food).

Foul Stomach—♃ afflicted in ♋; ♃ ♂ ♄ in ♋. Also ♃ causes death by foul stomach. (See "Foul" under Breath; "Raw Humours" under Indigestion).

Fullness—At the Stomach—(See Flatulence; "Stomach" under Gas).

Functions Disordered — Functional Weakness of the Stomach—Digestive Functions Disturbed—♄, ♅, or ♆ afflicted in ♋; the ☽ afflicted in ♋ with females; the ☽ afflicted by ♄; ♃ afflicted in ♋ or ♍; Subs at SP. (See "Functions" under Digestion; "Juices" under Gastric; Abnormal, Impeded, Obstructions, Stopped, in this section).

Gas In Stomach — (See Belching; "Stomach" under Gas).

Gastralgia—(See Neuralgia, Pains, in this section).

Gastric Disorders — (See Digestion; "Stomach" under Gas; "Disorders" under Gastric; Indigestion; the various paragraphs in this section).

Gastritis—(See "Inflammation" in this section).

Gastro-Abdominal Disorders — (See "Gastro-Abdominal" under Gastric).

Gastronomical Indiscretions—(See "Indiscretions" under Gastric).

Gastroenteritis—(See this subject under Gastric).

Glands—Glands of the Stomach Disordered—(See "Stomach" under Glands; Fluids, Functions, Sluggish, Spasmodic, Undersized, in this section).

Glass — Eats Glass and Nails — (See "Eats Nails" in this section).

Gluttony; Gormandizing; Gripings—☿ afflicted in ♋. (See Gripings; "Cramps" in this section).

Haematemesis — (See "Blood" under Vomiting).

Haemoptysis — (See "Blood" in this section).

Hard and Dry Cough—(See "Cough" in this section).

Head Affected—By Stomach Disorders —(See "Noises In", "Stomach", under Head; Headaches).

Heated Stomach—(See Fever, Hot, in this section).

Heaviness—Of the Stomach—The ☽ ♂ or ill-asp. ♄ (or ☿ if he be of the nature of ♄) at the beginning of an illness, or at decumbiture. (See Heaviness).

Hemorrhage—♂ afflicted in ♋; ♂ in ♋ in the 6th H. (See Haemoptysis; "Blood" under Vomiting).

Hiccough; High Living — Disorders From—(See "Living" under High).

Hindered — The Stomach Fluids Hindered — (See Fluids, Obstructions, Stopped, in this section).

Hot Stomach — Over-Heated Stomach —Feverish Stomach—The ☉ ♂ ♂ in ♋, and ♋ on the Asc., tends to degeneration of the stomach walls, ulceration, and an over-heated stomach if over-eating is indulged in. (See Fever, Irritable, Ulcer, in this section).

Human Ostrich—Eats Nails and Glass —Case—(See "Human Ostrich" under Human).

Humours—(See "Raw Humours" under Indigestion).

Hydrochloric Acid — (See Hydrochloric).

Hypochondria; Illnesses—Arising from Indigestion, Anxiety, and Worry —(See "Anxiety" under Digestion; Indigestion).

Impeded—Functions of the Stomach Impeded — Peristaltic Action Impeded —(See Fluids, Functions, Obstructions, Peristaltic Action, in this section).

Imperfections—In Stomach—♋ gives when afflicted; a ♋ disease, and afflictions in ♋; the malefics afflicted in ♋; Subs at SP. (See Imperfections).

Imposthumes—Abscess—Ulcer—(See "Ulcer" under Gastric; "Hot Stomach" in this section).

Impurities of System — Stomach Diseases Arising From—The ☉ afflicted in ♓; the ☽ affl. in ♓ with females. (See "Blood" in this section).

Indigestion; Indiscretions—In Diet— Diseases From—(See "Evil Diet" under Diet; Starches, Sugar, Sweets, under Food; Gluttony; "Living" under High; Obesity, Plethora, Surfeits, etc.).

Inflammation—Of the Stomach—The ☉ or ♂ afflicted in ♋; ☉ ☌ ♂ in ♋. (See "Gastritis" under Gastric; "Hot Stomach" in this section). The Mucous Membranes of the stomach tend to become inflamed when the ☽ is in ♋ and afflicted by ♂. (See "Irritations" in this section).

Injuries—To the Stomach—Afflictions in ♋; ♂ afflicted in ♋.

Interfered With—(See Fluids, Functions, Impeded, Obstructions, Stopped, and the various paragraphs in this section).

Intestinal Indigestion—(See "Intestinal" under Indigestion).

Irregularities—Stomach Irregularities —Afflictions in ♋; the ☽ afflicted in ♋. (See Fluids, Functions, Impeded, Obstructions, and the various paragraphs in this section).

Irritable Stomach—Irritable Stomach Walls—The ☉ and ♂ action in ♋; the ☉ ☌ ♂ in ♋; ♂ afflicted in ♋. These influences also tend to difficulty in retaining food, and to hemorrhage and acute gastritis. (See "Retention" under Food; "Gastritis" under Gastric; Nausea).

Irritations — Of the Stomach — ♄ afflicted in ♋ or ♑; the ♄ and ♑ influences, and with ♄ or afflictions in ♑, tend to irritate the nervous terminations of the mucous membranes of the stomach by their action on the peripheral nerves, and afflicting the ♋ sign by reflex action, and tending to nausea or vomiting. (See Nausea, Vomiting; "Peristaltic Action" in this section).

Juices Retarded—(See "Fluids" under Digestion; "Juices" under Gastric; Hydrochloric; Fluids, Obstructions, in this section).

Lining of Stomach — Irritation of — (See External Lining, Inflammation, Irritable, Irritations, in this section; Nausea, Vomiting).

Liver—Enlarged Liver Resulting from Indiscretions In Diet—(See "Enlarged" under Liver).

Lower Part—Of the Stomach Affected —Afflictions in ♍. (See "Splanchnic" under Ganglion; "Pylorus" in this section).

Malnutrition—(See Nutrition).

Meat—Ill-Digested Meat—(See "Raw Humours" under Indigestion; Meat).

Membranes—Of the Stomach—Disorders of—♅ afflicted in ♋. (See Lining, Mucous Membranes, in this section).

Menstruation — Vicarious Thru the Stomach — (See "Vicarious" under Menses).

Mucous Membranes—Of the Stomach —Irritation and Inflammation of—(See Inflammation, Irritations, Lining, Mucus, Phlegm, in this section).

Mucus In Stomach—Phlegm In—The Stomach Obstructed By—(See Catarrh, Irritations, Mucous, Obstructions, Phlegm, in this section).

Muscae Volitantes—(See "Muscae" under Eyes).

Muscles Disordered—♂ afflicted in ♋ tends to afflict and disorder the muscles of the stomach.

Nails — Swallows Nails — Case — (See "Human Ostrich" under Human).

Nausea; Nerves of Stomach — Nerves of Disordered—Nerve Terminations Irritated—Nerve Pains In—Nervous Indigestion—Neuroses — (See Irritations, Neuralgia, Neuroses, Pains, in this section; "Nervous Indigestion" under Indigestion).

Neuralgia—Of Stomach—Nerve Pains In—☿ afflicted in ♋. (See Neuralgia).

Neuroses—Of Stomach—Gastric Neuroses—☿ afflicted in ♋.

Nutrition Faulty — (See "Defective" under Nutrition).

Obesity; Obstructions—In Stomach— Stoppages At the Stomach—The ☉ afflicted in ♋, ♍, or ♏; the ☽ afflicted in ♋, ♎, or ♑; ♄ afflicted in ♋ or ♑; ☿ afflicted in ♐; Subs at SP. (See "Stopped" under Digestion; "Juices" under Gastric; Fluids, Functions, Impeded, Peristaltic, Phlegm, Pylorus, in this section).

Oesophagus—Disorders of—Stricture of—(See Oesophagus).

Offended — The Stomach Offended — (See "Disordered Stomach" in this section).

Operations — Avoid Surgical Operations upon the Stomach when the ☽ is in ♋, and also when ♂ is in ♋, or afflicting the ☽ in ♋. (See "Rules" under Operation).

Organic Disease — Of the Stomach — Structural Defects—The ☉ afflicted in ♋. (See Organic, Structural).

Ostrich — The Human Ostrich — Eats Nails and Glass—(See "Eats Nails" in this section).

Over-Activity—Of the Stomach—The ☽ afflicted in ♐, and especially if the ☽ is coming to the ☍ of ♃ in ♊, which tends to over-activity of the stomach, lungs, and nerves. (See Over-Activity).

Over-Indulgence—Of Food—(See "Excesses In Eating" under Eating; Gluttony, Gormandizing, Over-Indulgence, Self-Indulgent).

Over-Loaded Stomach — (See "Over-Indulgence" in this section).

Pains In—Nerve Pains In—Neuralgia —Burning Pains In—Spasmodic Pains In—☿ in ♋, nerve pains and neuralgia in stomach; ♅ and ☿ afflicted in ♋, spasmodic pains in; ♂ afflicted in ♋, eructations, belching, and burning pains in stomach; ♂ in ♋ when ♂ is the afflictor in the disease, or ♂ in ♋, ☌ or ill-asp. the ☉ or ☽. (See Belching; "Gastralgia" under Gastric).

Pepsin—Lack of—♄ afflicted in ♋ or ♑. (See Pepsin).

Periodic Vomiting—(See Vomiting).

Peristaltic Action—Peristalsis Interrupted, Impeded, and Obstructed—Antiperistaltic Action of the Stomach — The peristaltic action of the stomach is ruled by the ♋ sign, and afflictions in ♋ or ♑ tend to interfere with this action; the ☽ afflicted in ♑ tends to antiperistaltic action in the stomach, as ♑, the sign in 8 to ♋, tends to reverse and oppose the stomach processes, and to cause nausea or vomiting; also caused by ♄ afflicted in ♋ or ♑. (See Antiperistalsis, Nausea, Peristalsis, Vomiting; "Obstructions" in this section).

Phlegm — In the Stomach — Mucus — Stomach Obstructed By—♄ afflicted in ♋; ☿ afflicted in ♋, and especially when ☿ partakes of the nature of ♄. (See Catarrh, Inflammation, Mucous Membranes, Obstructions, in this section).

Plethora; Poor Digestion—(See "Poor" under Digestion).

Pylorus—Constriction of—Contraction of—Stenosis of—Undersized—♄ in the latter degrees of ♋, or the first degrees of ♍, and in ☐ or 8 ♅, the pylorus tends to. be constricted, or undersized, so that the food cannot pass, but is vomited; ♅ afflicted in ♋; Subs at SP (7D). Case—See Fig. 6C in "Astro-Diagnosis" by the Heindels. (See Pylorus; Obstructions, Undersized, in this section).

Pyrosis—(See Belching).

Raw Humours—In the Stomach—(See "Raw Humours" under Indigestion).

Retarded—Retarded Fluids and Juices —Retarded Functions—Peristalsis Retarded—♄ afflicted in ♋ or ♑. (See Fluids, Functions, Impeded, Obstructions, Peristalsis, Pylorus, Stopped, in this section).

Retention of Food—Difficulty In Retaining Food—(See "Retention" under Food; Nausea, Vomiting; "Pylorus" in this section).

Secretions Disordered—The ☽, ♄, or ♅ afflicted in ♋. (See "Stopped" under Digestion; "Juices" under Gastric; Hydrochloric; Fluids, Impeded, Obstructions, in this section).

Sickness at Stomach—The ☽ afflicted in ♑. (See Nausea, Vomiting; Peristaltic Action, Pylorus, in this section).

Sluggish Action—Of the Glands of the Stomach—♄ afflicted in ♋ or ♑; ♅ in ♋, ☐, or 8 ♄. (See Fluids, Glands, in this section).

Spasmodic Action—In the Stomach— Wind Spasm — Spasmodic Pains In — Spasmodic Action of the Glands—♅ afflicted in ♋ or ♑, wind spasm in, and spasmodic action; ♅ and ☿ afflicted in ♋, spasmodic pains in. (See Colic, Cramps, Gas, Gripings, Pains, Wind, in this section).

Spitting of Blood—(See Haemoptysis; "Blood" under Vomiting).

Spots and Specks — Before the Eyes from Stomach Trouble—(See "Muscae Volitantes" under Eyes).

Stenosis—Of the Pylorus—(See "Pylorus" in this section).

Stomachache—(See "Ache" in this section).

Stomach Trouble — (See "Disordered Stomach", and the various paragraphs in this section).

Stomatitis—(See "Mouth" under Aphthae).

Stopped — Digestion Stopped — Stoppages At the Stomach—♄ afflicted in ♋ or ♑. (See "Stopped" under Digestion; Fluids, Functions, Impeded, Obstructions, in this section).

Structural Disorders—(See "Organic" in this section).

Surfeits — From Over-Eating — ♃ afflicted in ♋. (See "Excesses" under Eating; Obesity, Plethora, Surfeits).

Swallowing—Difficulty In—(See Deglutition).

Swollen Stomach—(See Dilatation, Distended, in this section).

Trouble — Stomach Trouble — (See "Disordered", and the various paragraphs in this section).

Tumor — In Stomach — (See "Tumor" under Gastric; Tumors).

Tympanites; Ulcer—(See "Ulcer" under Gastric; "Hot Stomach" in this section).

Undersized Stomach — Undersized Glands — The Pylorus Undersized and Contracted — ♅ and ♄ influence, and with these planets afflicted in ♋; ♅ in ♋ and in ☐ or 8 ♄ and ♅. (See "Pylorus" in this section; Undersized).

Undigested Humours — In Stomach — (See "Raw Humours" under Indigestion).

Upper Part — Of Stomach — Affected and Disordered when there are afflictions in the latter degrees of ♌, and the first face of ♋; Subs at SP (6D). (See "Upper Part" in the first part of this Article).

Veins of Stomach — Tend to be disordered when ♀ is afflicted in ♋. (See Veins).

Vertigo — From Stomach Trouble — The afflicting planets in the cardinal signs, and especially with ♈ and ♋ involved. (See Dizziness, Vertigo).

Vomiting — (See Nausea, Vomiting; "Pylorus" in this section).

Walls of Stomach — (See Irritable, Irritations, Lining, in this section).

Water Brash — Pyrosis — Belching — (See Belching, Pyrosis).

Weak Stomach—The Digestion Weak —(See "Weak", "Weakest", under Digestion; "Cases" in this section).

Wind In Stomach—♅, ☿, or the ☽ afflicted in ♋; ♅ afflicted in ♋, wind spasm in stomach. (See Colic, Cramps, Distended, Gas, Gripings, Spasmodic, in this section; Belching, Flatulence, Indigestion, Tympanites).

Women—Stomach Disorders In—(See "Women" under Digestion).

Worms In—Cestode—☿ afflicted in ♋; Subs at SP (7D). (See Worms).

Worry — Stomach Trouble Due To — (See "Anxiety" under Digestion).

Wrong Diet — Stomach Disorders From — (See "Ailments Due to Diet", "Evil Diet", "Excesses in Diet", under Diet; "Dainty Foods", "Rich Food", "Starches", "Sweets", under Food; Gluttony).

STOMATITIS — (See "Mouth" under Aphthae).

STONE—Stones—Concretions—Calculus — Lithiasis — Osseous Deposits — Mineral Deposits In the Body—Calcareous Matter—Gravel—Sand—Chalk—Lime—Stone Blindness — Birth Stones — Violence with Stones, etc.—The following subjects have to do with the various forms of Concretions and Stone in the body, and also in some of the other senses in which the word Stone is used, as "Assaults by Stones", "Stone Blind", etc.

Assaults by Stones—Injuries by Flying Stones — (See "Flying Stones" in this section).

Back—Stone In the Reins of the Back —A ♎ disease, and afflictions in ♎; ♅ or ♄ afflicted in ♎. (See "Kidneys" in this section).

Biliary Calculi — (See "Gall Stones" under Bile).

Birth Stones — The following are the Birthstones of the various Signs of the Zodiac when these signs are rising upon the Ascendant at birth. This does not especially apply to the ☉ in Signs unless you are born at Sunrise, and with the ☉ in the rising sign. It is said that a birthstone which vibrates in harmony with your ruling planet, and when worn as a Talisman, is favorable for good health, good fortune, peace of mind, and also protection against dangers. The Birthstones of the Signs are as follows—♈, Diamond and Amethyst; ♉, Emerald and Moss Agate; ♊, the Aqua Marine and Crystal; ♋, the Emerald and Black Onyx; ♌, the Diamond and Ruby; ♍, the Hyacinth and Pink Jasper; ♎, the Opal and Diamond; ♏, the Topaz and Malachite; ♐, the Turquoise and Carbuncle; ♑, the Moonstone and White Onyx; ♒, the Opal and Sapphire; ♓, the Chrysolite and Moonstone. (See Amulets). Considerable valuable information is given about Birthstones, Amulets, and Talismans, in the book, "Message of the Stars", by Max Heindel.

Bladder—Stone In—Gravel In—Death from Stone In—The ☉, ☽, ♄, or ♂ in the 6th H., and afflicted, in fixed signs; the ☉ afflicted in ♏; the ☽ to the ill-asps. ♂ by dir.; the ☽ in ♏, and to the ☌, P., □, or 8 ♄ (or ☿ if he be of the nature of ♄) at the beginning of an illness, or at decumbiture, is an indication of stone or gravel existing in the bladder; ♆, ♅, or ♄ in ♍, and afflicting the ☉ or ☽; ♄ in ♏ in the 6th H., and afflicted; a ♄ disease; caused by ♂ afflictions; ♂ in ♏ and afflicting the ☽ or Asc.; ♂ denotes death from; ♂ in ♉ or ♏ in the 6th H., and afflicted; a ♎ disease, and afflictions in ♎; a ♏ disease, and with afflictions in ♏; ♏ on the Asc. and the ☽ in ♒ (Hor'y). People of the melancholic type, and who suffer from Hypochondria, a ♄ disease, are more subject to Stone or Gravel, as ♄ tends to crystallize and deposit the solid substances of the urine in such subjects. Cases—Of Stone In the Bladder — See Chap. XIII in Daath's Medical Astrology. (See Gravel; the various paragraphs in this section).

Body Turns Into Stone—(See "Petrifaction" in this section).

Calces—(See Chalk).

Calculus—A stone-like concretion in the body, and usually formed by the mineral deposits of the body as thrown down, deposited, and accumulated by the work of ♄. (See Concretions; the various paragraphs in this section).

Causes of Stone—In the Body—Stone, Sand, Gravel, and Concretions in the body, are principally the work of ♄, and his afflictions to the ☉ and ☽, or to both at the same time, and where the signs of ♄ may also be strongly occupied, or many planets in the earthy signs at B.; ♄ afflicted in ♏; the ☽ to the □ or 8 ♂ by dir. tends to the formation of stone if other conditions in the radical map concur. Also the afflictions of ♅ to the ☉ and ☽, from a ♄ sign, tend to stone formation. Stone in the kidney is usually the result of afflictions from cardinal signs. In Gall Stones, the afflictions are from mutable signs. Lilly says Stones in the body are mostly limited to diurnal maps. These Causes are further discussed in the Articles on Concretions, Deposits, Minerals, and also in the different paragraphs of this Article.

Chalk—(See Chalk, Lime).

Chololithiasis—(See "Gall Stones" under Bile).

Cold—Cold As a Cause of Stone—(See Cold, Concretions).

Concretions—Osseous Deposits—Stone —(See Concretions; the various paragraphs in this section).

Crystallization — Hardening In the Body — (See Crystallization, Hardening).

Death from Stone—In the Kidneys or Bladder—Denoted by ♂, and especially when ♂ is afflicted in the 6th H. in a fixed sign, as in ♏; fixed signs, and many planets in these signs, and especially in the 6th H., dispose to death from stone, sand, or gravel in the bladder; many planets in cardinal signs, to death from stone in the kidneys, and many planets in mutable signs to death from Gall Stones.

Deposits—Calcareous Deposits—♄ in ♏ tends to stone by obstructing the elimination of urine, and causing calcareous deposits. (See Chalk, Concretions, Deposits, Minerals).

Ductless Glands—As Related to Stone —(See "Petrifaction" in this section).

Elimination—Faulty Elimination As a Cause of Stone—(See "Faulty" under Elimination).

Excretion—Obstructions of, and Tending to Stone—(See "Obstructions" under Excretion).

Fixed Signs—Many afflictions in these signs at B. tend to stone, sand, or gravel in the bladder, and death by such disorders. (See "Fixed Signs" under Fixed; "Death" in this section).

Flying Stones—Injury or Death by Flying Stones In Mob Violence—♂ afflicted in ♊ or ♍, and ☌, P., □, or 8 the Asc. by dir. (See Mobs). Wounds by wood or stones are indicated in Hor'y Q. when ♄ is in the 1st H. at B., and a malefic planet with the lord of the 1st. When ♂ is lord of the year at the

Vernal, and afflicted, many people tend to be injured by flying stones and mob violence.

Gall Stones — (See "Gall Stones" under Bile).

Goiter—This disease is a Crystallization. (See Goiter).

Gout—Chalk Stones of—(See Chalk).

Gravel — Gravel In the Kidneys or Bladder—Voiding of Red Gravel—(See Gravel).

Hardening — (See Cirrhosis, Crystallization, Hardening, Sclerosis; the various paragraphs in this section).

Injury by Stones — (See "Flying Stones" in this section).

Kidneys—Stone, Sand, or Gravel In—Renal Stones—Nephrolithiasis—Stone In the Reins of the Back—Death from Stone In Kidneys — Gravel and Renal Stones are formed in the peduncles, or pelvis of the kidneys, which part is ruled by ♏, and the ♏ sign has more to do with stone in the kidneys than the ♎ sign for this reason. However, the ♎ influence is also responsible, as the stone is crystallized in the kidney by ♄, and by virtue of his exalted power in ♎. Stone in the kidney is ruled principally, or fundamentally, by ♏ and the 8th H. Is caused by the ☉ afflicted in ♏; the ☉ or ☽ afflicted by ♄ or ♅ from a ♄ sign; the ☉ afflicted in ♌, ♎, or ♒; the ☽ afflicted in ♏ or ♐, or afflicting the hyleg therefrom; the ☽ afflicted in ♑; the ☽ to the ☌, P., □, or ☍ ♂ by dir.; the ☽ in ♌, ☌, P., or ill-asp. ♄ (or ☿ if he be of the nature of ♄) at the beginning of an illness, or at decumbiture, and the patient may die when the ☽ comes to the ☍ aspect of ♄, and if no good aspect prevent it (Hor'y); the ☽ in ♎, and afflicted by the ☉ or ♂ when taken ill (Hor'y); ♆, ♅, or ☿ in ♏, ♎, or ♏, and especially in the 6th or 8th H., and afflicting the ☉ or ☽; ♄ afflicted in the 6th H. in a fixed sign; ♄ afflicted in ♈, ♍, ♎, or ♏; ♄ in ♏ tends to stone by obstructing the elimination of urine, and causing calcareous deposits; ♄ in the Asc. in ♎; ♂ in ♌ or ♏, and afflicting the hyleg at B.; caused by ♂ afflictions; ♂ afflicted in ♈, ♌, ♎, or ♏; ♂ in the 6th H. in a fixed sign, and afflicted, and this influence also denotes death by stone; a ♎ and ♏ disease, and afflictions in these signs; Subs at KP (11D). (See Deposits, Elimination; Back, Bladder, and the various paragraphs in this section).

Lime — Limestone Deposits — ♄ afflicted in ♓ tends to lime deposits, and to petrifaction, crystallization, and hardening of the body, or ♄ in ♍ by reflex action. Also caused by ♄ afflicted in ♒. (See Chalk, Deposits, Lime, Minerals; "Petrifaction" in this section).

Lithiasis — The Formation of a Calculus, or Stone in the Body. For causes, see Calculus, Chalk, Concretions, Crystallization, Deposits, Hardening, Minerals, etc. Also note the various paragraphs in this section).

Liver—In Cirrhosis of the liver there is a hardening and thickening process, the work of ♄, and which is along the same lines as the forming of stones.

(See "Hardening", "Hobnail Liver", under Liver).

Mineral Deposits — Tending to the Formation of Stone—(See Chalk, Concretions, Deposits, Gravel, Lime, Minerals, Osseous, Sand; the various paragraphs in this section).

Nephrolithiasis — (See "Kidneys" in this section).

Obstructions—Stone in the Body is an Obstruction, and caused by ♄. (See Impediments, Obstructions, Retentions, Saturn Influence, Suppressions).

Osseous Deposits—(See Osseous).

Pelvis of Kidneys — Stone In — (See "Kidneys" in this section).

Petrifaction — Turning of the Body Into Stone—♄ afflicted in ♒, and especially in the 6th or 8th H., and with many planets in fixed signs, have been recorded as existing in a case; ♄ afflicted in ♍ or ♓. Also the earthy and mineral signs, as ♉, ♍, and ♑, when well-filled with planets at B., and such a sign on the Asc. also, may cause, and with other stone-forming conditions concurring. Some Physicians attribute Petrifaction to disorders of the Ductless Glands, which are largely ruled by the ♏ sign. (See Ductless Glands; "Earthy Signs" under Earth; Hardening, Lime, Minerals; "Lime", and the various paragraphs in this section).

Red Gravel—Voiding of—(See Gravel).

Reins—Stone In Reins—In Reins of the Back—(See "Kidneys" in this section).

Remedy for Stone—Docoction of Geranium Robertianum (Daath).

Renal Stone — Renal Calculi — (See "Kidneys" in this section).

Retentions — (See "Poisons of the Body" under Retention).

Sand—Sand In Kidneys—(See Sand).

Secret Parts—Stone In—A ♏ disease, and afflictions in ♏; ♏ on the Asc., and the ☽ in ♒ (Hor'y). (See Bladder, Kidneys, in this section).

Spleen—(See "Stone In" under Spleen).

Stone—The Stone—The following influences indicate Stone in Hor'y Q., and that Stone may exist at the beginning of an illness, and at decumbiture. The ☉ afflicted in ♒; the ☉ in ♌ when the afflictor in the disease; the ☽ in ♑ signifies the Stone when the afflictor in the disease; the ☽ in ♉ and afflicted by the ☉ or ♂ when taken ill. (See the various paragraphs in this section).

Stone Blind — (See "Total" under Blindness).

Stones — Injury by Flying Stones — (See "Flying Stones" in this section).

Suppressions — Tending to Stone — (See Concretions, Deposits, Hindrances, Impediments, Retentions, Suppressions, Wastes, etc.).

Thickening — (See Cirrhosis, Hardening, Thickening).

Touch of Stone—The ☽ to the ill-asps. ♂ by dir.

Urea—Urates—Uric Acid—Excess of —Retention of—(See these subjects).

Urinary Calculi—(See "Calculi" under Urine).

Wastes—Retention of—(See Deposits; "Faulty", "Hindered", under Elimination; Retention, Suppression, Wastes).

Xanthic Calculus—(See Xanthic).

STOOLS — Bowel Discharges — (See Faeces).

STOOPING — Stooping Posture — Body Hooked Forward—Body Bent Forward —♓ gives a stopping, heavy gait, and holding the head downward when walking, and especially with ♓ on the Asc. at B.; ♄ ascending at B., and afflicted; ♄ Sig. in ♌; ♄ in ♌, partile the Asc.; ♄ Sig. in ♑, a stooping, awkward posture in walking; ♄ Sig. □ or ☍ ☽. (See Bending; "Crooked Body" under Crooked; Limp; "Downward" under Look; "General Relaxation" under Relaxation; "Stoop Shoulders" under Shoulders).

STOPPAGES—Obstructions—Impediments—Inhibitions—Hindrances—

Bowels—Stoppages In— (See "Intussusception", "Obstructions", under Bowels; Constipation; "Hardening" under Faeces).

Circulation—Stoppages In—(See "Interferred With", "Sluggish", under Circulation; Clots, Embolus, Infarct, Thrombus, etc.).

Digestion Stopped—(See "Stopped" under Digestion).

Elimination — (See "Hindered" under Elimination).

Functions — (See "Stoppage" under Functions).

Gait—(See "Stoppage Gait" under Gait).

Gall Ducts — Stoppage In— (See "Ducts", "Gall Stones", under Bile).

Growth — (See "Arrested" under Growth).

Head—(See "Stoppages" under Head).

Heart—(See "Stoppage" under Heart).

Menses—(See "Suppressed" under Menses).

Nose—(See "Stoppage" under Nose).

Secretions Stopped—(See Secretions).

Speech—(See "Halting" under Speech).

Stomach — Stoppages In — (See "Pylorus", "Stopped", under Stomach).

Throat—(See "Stoppages", "Swellings", under Throat; "Swollen" under Tonsils).

Urethra — (See "Stricture" under Urethra).

Urine—(See "Stoppage" under Urine).

Vibration—Mental Vibrations Stopped —(See Vibration). For further study along this line see Arrested, Clogging, Congestions, Constrictions, Contractions, Crystallization, Dropsy, Growth, Hardening, Hindrances, Hyperacidity, Impediments, Impure, Inflammation, Inhibitions, Interrupted; "Obstructive" under Jaundice; Limitations, Obstructions, Retarded, Retentions, Slow, Stenosis, Stone, Strictures, Suppressions, Suspensions, Swellings, Thickening, Tumors, etc.

STORING—Storing Functions of the Body—(See Conservation).

STORMS—

Brain Storms — (See "Brain Storms" under Brain; "Psychic Storms" under Psychic).

Hail Storms—(See Hail).

Rain Storms—(See Rain, Storms).

Snow Storms—(See Blizzards, Snow).

Thunder Storms — (See Lightning, Thunder).

Wind Storms — (See "Storms" under Wind).

STOUT — Stoutness — A Stout Person— Corpulent—Fleshy—Lords of Nativity of stout people have great Latitude as a rule. Oriental planets in their first orientation cause large, stout bodies. The Quadrants from the Summer Tropic to the Autumnal Equinox, and from the Winter Tropic to the Vernal Equinox, tend to give stout bodies, and with the ☉, ☽, and many planets in these Quarters at B.; ♄ ori. at B. makes the body more stout, tall and hairy than when he is occi., and also gives a stout chest; ♃ Sig. in ♉, ♏, ♒, or ♓; ♃ in ♉, partile the Asc., stout, well-set, but not handsome; ♃ Sig. in ♉, compact and well-set; ♃ in ♏, partile the Asc., or ♃ Sig. in ♏, stout and compact, ♃ in the Asc., stout, and with a stout chest; ♃ in ♒, partile the Asc., stout, compact, and of middle stature; ♂ in ♌, partile the Asc., stout limbs; ♀ Sig. in ♏; ♀ in ♏, partile the Asc., stout, corpulent, and well-set; ♉, ♏, or ♒ on the Asc.; the last few degrees of ♎ on the Asc. give a shorter and stouter body, but the most of the sign tends to a tall, graceful, and slender body; ♐ on the Asc., a stout, athletic frame. Case — Stout In Build — See "Jaaskelainen", No. 213, in 1001 N.N. (See Athletic, Compact, Corpulent, Fat Body, Fleshy, Muscular, Portly; "Body" under Strong; Thick Body, Well-Set).

STRABISMUS — Crossed Eyes — (See "Strabismus" under Eyes).

STRAIGHT—Straight Body—Erect and Upright Body—The ☉ in ♎, partile the Asc., tall, straight, and upright; the ☽ in ♊, partile the Asc., tall, straight, upright, comely, and well-made; born under strong ♃ influence, tall, fine, straight, and well-made; ♃ in ♐, partile the Asc., tall, straight, fine, and well-made; born under ♀, and ♀ ori., tall, straight, and upright; ♀ in ♊, partile the Asc., tall, straight, and well-made; ♊ on the Asc., tall, fine, and straight; ♎ on the Asc., straight, tall, and handsome if ♀ is also oriental. (See Erect, Tall, Upright).

Forehead — The Forehead Straight, Deep, and Tall — (See "Deep" under Forehead).

Nose—(See "Straight" under Nose).

STRAIN—Stress and Strain—Tension—

Body—The Constitution—Over-Straining of — Physical Strain — Muscular Strain — Stress and strain of the body are caused by ♂ activities, and often from anger, which stress is relieved by the release of Glycogn in greater quantity by the Adrenals to restore the equilibrium. Physical strain is harmful when ♄ is in ♌ at B., and afflicting the ☉, ☽, Asc., or hyleg, due to weakened heart action at times, and unsustained circulation of the blood during severe exercise. When the airy signs are upon the Asc. at B. the constitution becomes easily run down under strain, and subject to nervous disorders. (See Adrenals, Anger, Excitable; "Inordinate" under E x e r c i s e ; "Over-Exertion" under Exertion; Fatigue, Glycogen; "Intemperate" under Sports).

Excretory System—(See "Strain" under Excretion).

Eyestrain — (See "Eyestrain" under Eyes).

Headaches — From Nervous Strain — (See "Nervous Headaches" under Headaches).

Heart Strain —'(See "Strain" under Heart).

Knees — (See "Strains In" under Knees).

Mental Strain — (See "Strain" under Mental, Mind).

Muscular Strain — And of Ligaments and Tendons—(See Exercise, Exertion, Ligaments, Sports, Tendons, Tension; "Body" in this section).

Nervous Strain—(See "Strain" under Nerves).

Over-Strain—Of Mind and Body—(See Over-Strain; the various paragraphs in this section).

Physical Strain—(See Body, Muscular, in this section).

Sprains—(See Sprains).

STRANGE—Unusual—Extraordinary—Mysterious, etc. — The influences of ♆ and ♅ in a configuration tend to produce strange, extraordinary, mysterious, obscure, u n u s u a l, and curious events, which would be unexplainable to the ordinary mind, and without a knowledge of Astrology. (See Neptune, Uranus).

Accidents—Strange Accidents—♅ afflicted by ♂, or ♂ ill-aspected by ♅. (See "Extraordinary" under Accidents).

Ailments—Strange Ailments—Strange Diseases—♅ afflicted in ♍; ♅ afflicted in the Asc.; ♅ ☌, □, or ☍ the Asc.; ♆ diseases, and of a psychic origin. (See "Diseases"·under Extraordinary, Mysterious, Obscure, P e c u l i a r, Psychic, Sudden, Uncommon; "Imaginary Diseases" under Imagination; Incurable, Praeincipients, P s e u d o, Remarkable, Unusual).

Anxieties — Strange Anxieties — (See Anxiety; "Impending Calamity" under Calamity; "Fears; "Low Spirits" under Low; Worry, Fears).

Calamities — Strange Calamities or Catastrophies — (See "Strange" under Calamity).

Conduct—Strange Conduct—The ☉ by dir. to the ☌ or P. aspect ♅.

Death—Death from Strange Causes—♆ the afflicting planet. (See "Mysterious Death" under Mysterious).

Diseases — S t r a n g e Diseases — (See "Ailments" in this section).

Dreams — S t r a n g e Dreams — (See Dreams).

Events—(See "Strange" under Events).

Fancies — (See "Distempered" under Fancies).

Fears—Strange Fears—(See "Morbid", "Solitude", under Fears; Forebodings, Spirit Controls; Terrors, Visions, in this section).

Growth — Strange and Abnormal Growth — (See "Abnormal" under Growth).

Hurts—(See "Strange" under Hurts).

Imaginations — (See "Strange" under Imagination).

Injuries—Strange Injuries—(See Accidents, Hurts, in this section).

Land — Death In a Strange Land — (See "Accidents" under Abroad).

Mysterious—(See the paragraphs under Mysterious).

Occupations —Strange Occupational Diseases—(See Occupation).

Premonitions — (S e e Dreams, Forebodings, Premonitions).

Sayings—Strange Sayings—(See Demoniac, Insanity).

Sicknesses — (See "Ailments" in this section).

Spirit Controls—The Strange Terrors of—(See Obsessions, Spirit Controls).

Tastes—Strange Tastes—(See Tastes).

Terrors — Strange Terrors of Mind — The 3rd decan. of ♒ on the Asc. (See Obsessions, Spirit C o n t r o l s, Terrors, Visions).

Vagaries—(See "Peculiar" under Vagaries).

Views—Strange Views—(See Eccentric, Ideals, Ideas, Independent, Metaphysical, Misunderstood, Occult, Reformers; "Fanatical" under Religion).

Visions — S t r a n g e Visions — (See Dreams, Forebodings, Horrors, Obsessions, Premonitions; "Nightmare" under Sleep; Spirit Controls, Visions).

STRANGERS — Death In the Presence of Strangers—The ☽ in the 8th H. at B. (See "Public Death" under Public).

STRANGULATION—Strangulated—Suffocated—A ♎ disease and affliction.

Birth—Strangled At Birth—Cases—(See "Birth" under Asphyxia).

Death By—Death by Strangulation or Suffocation—♄ exactly on the Asc. at B., danger of at B.; ♄ in a fixed sign, □ or ☍ the ☉, and contrary in condition, or ♄ be occidental, and the ☽ be succedent to him; ♄ in ♉, and evil fixed stars and ♄ afflicting the hyleg; ♄ to the ☌ or ill-asp. ♂ by dir.; ♄ and many planets in fixed signs show; earthy signs strong, prominent, and well-occupied at B. tend to; malefics in ♉. Cases—See "Beach Murder", No. 134; "Morrison", No. 188; "Child Strangled", No. 252; "Strangled", No. 922, all in 1001 N.N. (See Asphyxia, Drowning, Execution, Halter, Hanging; "Death" under Suffocation).

Hernia — (See "Strangulated Hernia" under Hernia).

Wife—Strangles His Wife—Case—See "Beach Murder", No. 134, in 1001 N.N.

STRANGURY—Painful Urination—(See "Strangury" under Urine).

STRATEGY—Injury or Death By—(See Artifice; "Death By" under Enemies; Plots, Poison Death, Treachery, etc.).

STREETS—Public Death In the Streets —(See "Public Death" under Public).

STRENGTH — Power — Force — Activity —Energy—The Asc. rules the physical strength, the body, and the organic force. The strength of the body, and the organic resistance to disease, are largely shown and revealed by the sign rising upon the Asc. at B. Mars in any aspect to the ☉ produces strength, and a stronger constitution. Also ♂, known as the planet of dynamic power and energy, is the planet of courage, boldness, and physical prowess. The Mind and Mental Faculties are strengthened when ☿ is strong and well-fortified at B., as ☿ is the ruler of the mind, the planet of mental power, and especially when rising in the Asc. at B., well-aspected, and not combust with the ☉. The following subjects have to do with the strength of the Mind and Body, which subjects see in the alphabetical arrangement when only listed here—

Active — Active Mind — Active and Strong Body — (See "Full of Action" under Action; "Active Body", "Active Mind", under Active; Dynamic; "Quickened" under Mentality; "Strong Mind" under Mind; "Strength" under Muscles; "Activity" under Physical; "Body" under Strong).

Adynamia — Loss of Vital Power — (See Adynamia).

Asthenia — Loss of Strength — (See Asthenia; "Weakened" in this section).

Athletic — Pugilist — Wrestler — (See Athletics).

Body — Strong Body — The Body Strengthened—Great Physical Powers —The body is strengthened when ♃ is ✶ or △ the Asc. The fiery signs rising on the Asc. give a strong body, and especially ♈ or ♌ on the Asc. at B. (See Endurance; "Abundance" under Energy; Immunity; "Good" under Resistance; Robust, Ruddy, Stamina; "Body" under Strong; Tone; "Good" under Vitality).

Bones Strengthened—(See "Strengthening Of" under Bones).

Collapse; Constitution—(See Strength, Strong, Weak, under Constitution; "Good", "Low", under Vitality).

Debility; Degree of Strength — (See Degree).

Depletion; Diminished Strength — (See Diminished, Lessened).

Dissipated—The Strength Dissipated —The ☉ in ♌ in the Asc., ✶ or △ ♂ gives great energy, but a tendency to dissipate it; the ☉ and ♀ in the Asc. in ♑, and afflicted by ♆, ♃, or ♂, the strength is dissipated; ♂ in ♌ in the Asc., and afflicted by ♃ or ♀; ♂ in ♌ on the Asc., and the ☉ ruler of the Asc., and afflicted; weak signs on the Asc., and containing afflicting planets. (See "Energy Dissipated" under Dissipation; "Wasted" under Energy; "Health Suffers" under Opposite Sex).

Early Years—Little Strength In—(See "Early Years of Life" under Early).

Emaciation; Endurance; Energy; Exhaustion; Fatigue; Feeble; Force; Functions Strengthened — Or Weakened—(See Functions).

Health — (See "Bad Health", "Good Health", under Health).

Immunity from Disease—(See Immunity; "Abundance of Health" under Health; "Good" under Vitality).

Increased—The Strength Increased— The upper and anterior parts of ♈, ♉, and ♌ increase the strength, and also the posterior parts of ♓, ♏, and ♐; ♃ or ♀ in the Asc., or the ☉, ☽, ♃, ♀·in the Asc. or M.C., and well-aspected; ♃ and ♀ ☌ or good aspect the Asc.; ♂ in good aspect to the ☉ assists the bodily strength. (See "Strength" under Increased; "Improved" under Health; Robust, Ruddy; "Increased" under Vitality).

Infancy — (See "Strength Increased", "Vitality", under Infancy).

Infirm; Injured—The Strength of the Constitution Injured — (See "Weakened" in this section).

Intellect—Strength of Intellect—(See the paragraphs under Intellect).

Invalids; Less Muscular Strength — (See "Strength" under Muscles).

Life Force—(See "Life Force" under Force).

Little Sickness — Rarely Ill — (See "Little Sickness" under Sickness).

Loss of Strength — (See Diminished, Lessened, Loss Of; "Lessened" under Vitality; "Dissipated" in this section).

Males—The Strength of—(See "Males Nearly Impotent", "Strength", and the various paragraphs under Males).

Mind — Strength of Mind — (See the various paragraphs under Intellect, Mental, Mind, Perception, Understanding).

Muscular Strength—(See Muscles).

Not Very Strong—(See Debility, Feeble; "Bad Health" under Health; Infirm, Invalids, Sickly; "Much Sickness" under Sickness; "Low" under Resistance, Vitality; "Weak Body" under Weak).

Physical Strength — Degree of — (See Action, Active, Degree, Feeble, Muscles, Physical, Stamina, Strong, Tone, Vitality, Weak; the various paragraphs in this section).

Powerful—Powerful Body—Powerful Mind—(See "Powerful" under Intellect; "Strong" under Mind; Power; "Body" under Strong).

Prostration; Proud — Proud of His Physical Strength—(See Proud).

Pugilist—(See Athletics).

Recuperative Power—Strong—Weak —(See Recuperation).

Resistance—Powers of Resistance to Disease—(See Endurance, Feeble, Immunity, Resistance; "Body" under Strong; "Good", "Low", under Vitality; "Weak Body" under Weak).

Restoratives—Of Health and Strength —(See Analeptic, Restoratives).

Robust; Ruddy; Stamina;
Strong Body — (See "Body" under Strong).

Tone; Vital Force—(See "Force" under Vital).

Vitality—(See "Good", "Low", and the various paragraphs under Vitality).

Wasting of the Body — (See Tabes, Wasting).

Weak Body—(See "Weak Body" under Weak).

Weakened — Strength of the Body Weakened—Loss of Strength—Asthenia—The lower and posterior parts of ♈, ♉, and ♌ tend to make the body weaker, and also the anterior parts of ♊, ♍, and ♐; the ☉ or ☽ ☌ a malefic planet tends to injure and weaken the constitution; the ☉ or ☽ in weak signs and afflicted; the ☉ or ☽ to the ☌ or ill-asps. ♄ by dir.; the ☉ to the evil aspects ♃ by dir.; ♄ in the 6th H., and conjoined with the ☉; ♄ afflicted in ♒; ♃ afflicting the ☉; the Asc. ruled by ♄; the 3rd decan. of ♉ on the Asc. (See Adynamia, Asthenia, Dissipation, Dull, Emaciation, Feeble; "Bad Health" under Health; Inactive, Inertia, Languishing, Lassitude, Lethargy, Listless, Loss Of; "Low" under Resistance, Vitality; "Weakened" under Vitality; "Weak Body" under Weak).

Wrestler—(See Athletics). For subjects along this line which may have been overlooked, and not included in this Article, see the alphabetical arrangement.

STRESS AND STRAIN — (See "Strain" under Nerves; Strain, Tension).

STRICTURE—A Narrowing — Contraction—Stenosis—A ♅ disease, and due to the tonic action of ♅; ♅ in the 6th H.; a ♄ disease; ♄ ☌ or ill-asp. ♅. (See Adhesions, Constrictions, Contractions, Obstructions, Spasmodic, Stenosis).

Bladder—(See "Stricture" under Bladder).

Nose—Nares—(See "Stricture" under Nose).

Oesophagus — (See "Stricture" under Oesophagus).

Prostatic Stricture — (See Prostate Gland).

Pylorus—Constriction of—(See "Pylorus" under Stomach).

Throat — (See "Stricture" under Throat).

Urethra — Spasmodic Stricture of— (See Urethra).

Womb—Stricture of the Neck of the Womb—(See "Stricture" under Womb).

STRIFE — Injuries or Death By — (See Contests, Duels, Enemies, Feuds, Hatred, Jealousy, Murdered, Plots, Poison Death, Quarrels, Revenge, Sword, Treachery, War, etc.).

STROKES — Blows — (See Assaults; "Strokes" under Blindness; Blows, Stabs, Sword, etc.).

Paralytic Strokes—(See Paralysis).

STRONG — Active — Sthenic — Strong Body and Mind—Good Powers of Resistance and Vitality—Stronger— Strongest—Strength—Virile, etc.—

Body—Strong and Active Body—Able Body — Strong Constitution — Healthy

Appearance—Robust—Vigorous, etc.— The SUN rising at B., and especially in a fiery or airy sign, or in ♉ or ♏, and well aspected, and more so if the ☉ be hyleg; the ☉ strong and well-dignified at B.; the ☉ in ♉ if not afflicted; the ☉ gives a large, strong, and bony body; the ☉ in ♈ or ♌, partile the Asc., strong and well-made; the ☉ in ♐ unless the hyleg be afflicted; the ☉, ☽, and Asc. well-aspected by benefics, and free from the affliction of malefics; the ☉ in the Asc. or M.C. at B., and well-aspected; the ☉ in good asp. to ♃, ♂, or the ☽, and especially if the ☉ be rising, or in any house except the 6th, or 8th; the ☉ or ☽ in ♋, ♌, or ♍, signs of the Summer Quarter, or with these signs upon the Asc. if the ☉ is in them and free from affliction; the ☉ in the signs of the Winter Quarter, in ♑, ♒, or ♓, tend to give a square and strong make, or with these signs upon the Asc. if the ☉ is in them and well-aspected; the ☉ in signs of the Spring months, in ♈, ♉, ♊, tend to give a strong constitution, and stronger than when the ☉ is in the Winter signs; the MOON in ♉, partile the Asc., strong, corpulent, and well-set; the ☽ Sig. in ♉, strong and well-set; the ☽ in ♌, partile the Asc., tall, strong, and large-boned; the ☽ well-aspected in ♌, strong and robust; the ☽ in ♑, partile the Asc., never strong; the ☽ in the Asc., and well-aspected by the ☉, ♃, and ♀, and free from the affliction of malefics; the ☽ angular, and the Lights nearly free from affliction, tolerably healthy and strong; SATURN in N. Lat. makes the body more strong, corpulent and bony; ♄ ✶ or △ ♂; ♄ in ♏, partile asp. the Asc., strong, well-set, but short; ♄ well-aspected in ♒; JUPITER rising in the Asc. or M.C., in an airy sign, and well-aspected; ♃ Sig. in airy signs denotes the body is more strong and corpulent in Hor'y Q.; ♃ in ♉, partile the Asc., strong and compact; ♃ well-aspected in ♉; ♃ Sig. in ♌; ♃ in ♌, partile the Asc., strong, tall, large, and well-made; ♃ Sig. in a fiery sign, the body is strong and square-made; ♃ and ♀ in good asp. the hyleg, and free from the affliction of malefics; ♃ well-aspected in ♎, good and strong nature; ♃ rising at B. confers strength of constitution, and the power to overcome very evil directions; born under ♂ the body is strong, well-set, but short or medium-sized; MARS ✶ or △ the ☉, ☽, ♅, or ♄; ♂ in good asp. the ☉ gives great strength of constitution; ♂ ☌ or any asp. the ☉, the native is usually strong and healthy; the ♂ signs ♈ and ♏ upon the Asc. at B. tend to give great strength and vitality; ♂ rising at B., and well-aspected; ♂ in the Asc., and well-aspected in a fiery sign, or in ♑, or if evilly aspected in the Asc., tends to strengthen the constitution; ♂ well-aspected in the 4th H.; in Hor'y Q., ♂ Sig. of the person; ♂ rising in the Asc. in ♌; ♂ in ♌, partile the Asc., strong, large, and tall; given by the ✶ or △ aspects of ♂; VENUS when ☌ ♃ adds power to ♃, but ♀ of herself does not tend to give muscular power, or any very great physical strength; MERCURY rising and well-aspected in ♉, or Sig. in ♉, tends to make the native strong, thick and well-set; the ☿ sign ♊ when upon the Asc. at B. tends to give a strong and active body; the ☿ sign ♍ when on the Asc. gives fair vitality and endurance; many planets rising at B., well-aspected, and in their strong signs, give a strong body; fiery signs upon the Asc. at B. give the strongest constitutions, and the airy signs, along with ♉ and ♏, are the next in strength, while the watery signs ♋ and ♓ when upon the Asc. at B. give the weakest constitutions; fixed signs give a strong constitution when on the Asc., and many planets in them, and give stamina and endurance; many planets in succedent houses, corresponding to the fixed signs, give a strong constitution; ♉ on the Asc. gives a strong, thick, short, or middle-sized body; ♈ on the Asc., a strong, spare, dry, bony, moderate-sized body; born under ♈ tends to a strong body; ♌ on the Asc., a strong, large, athletic, ruddy body, and with broad shoulders; the first half of ♌ on the Asc. gives a stronger body than the second half when rising; ♏ on the Asc., a strong, able, athletic, heavy, corpulent, robust, middle-sized or short body; ♐ on the Asc., a strong, intrepid, well-formed, well-made, tall body; ♒ on the Asc., strong, athletic, robust, healthy, plump, well-set body, but not tall; born under the whole signs ♊, ♎, or ♒, strong and robust. (See "Full of Action" under Action; "Active Body" under Active; "Good" under Constitution; Corpulent, Dynamic, Endurance, Energy, Exertion, Force; "Abundance", "Good", under Health; Healthy, Immunity, Muscles, Physical, Power; "Good" under Recuperation, Resistance, Stamina, Tone, Vitality; Resources, Robust, Ruddy, Rugged, Stout, Strength, Vigor; "Force" under Vital).

Constitution — (See "Strong" under Constitution; "Body" in this section).

Drink—Given to Strong Drink—(See "Strong Drink" under Drink).

Fairly Strong — (See "Medium Vitality" under Vitality).

Females — Strong Constitution In — (See "Constitution", "Health Good", under Females).

Fits—Strong Fits—(See "Strong" under Fits).

Functions—(See "Strong" under Functions).

Health — The Health Stronger — (See "Abundance", "Good", "Stronger", under Health).

Hips—(See "Strong" under Hips).

Imagination — (See "Strong" under Imagination).

Intellect—(See "Strong" under Intellect, Mind).

Legs—(See "Strong" under Legs).

Limbs—(See "Strong" under Limbs).

Liquors — Strong Liquors — Craving For—(See "Strong Drink" under Drink; "Strong Intoxicants" under Intoxication).

Males — Men—(See "Strong Constitution" under Males, Men).

Medium Strong — (See "Medium" under Vitality).

Men—(See "Strong Constitution" under Men).

Mind—(See "Strong" under Mind).

Moderately Strong — (See "Tolerably Healthy" under Health; "Medium" under Vitality).

Never Strong—The ☽ in ♑, in partile aspect the Asc. (See Emaciated; Feeble; "Ill-Health All Thru Life" under Ill-Health; Infirm, Invalids; "Short Life" under Life; Pale, Sickly; "Much Sickness" under Sickness; "Low" under Resistance, Stamina, Tone, Vitality; "Weak Body" under Weak).

Not Strong — The Constitution Not Very Strong—The ☉ or ☽ to the ☌ or ill-asp. the malefics by dir.; born at the time of an eclipse of the ☉ or ☽; the ☽ nearly in ☌ with the ☉ tends to weaken the constitution; the ☽ applying to ♂, or conjoined with him in a day nativity; the ☽ in ♑ in partile the Asc.; the ☽ Sig. in ♑, thin, feeble, weak, and sickly; ♄ in ♌ unless the energies are conserved; ♃ or ♀ the ☉ when the ☉ is hyleg, as all planets combust are weakened; ♃ Sig. in ♑, a weakly person; ♂ weak and ill-dignified at B.; ♀ in the 6th H. tends to good health, and a harmonious constitution, as long as excesses are avoided, and good habits adhered to; ☿ Sig. in ♑; ♋ or ♓ on the Asc.; the ♋ influence tends to a weakly constitution. (See "Weak" under Constitution; Eclipses, Feeble; "Bad Health" under Health; "Ill-Health All Thru Life" under Ill-Health; Infirm, Invalids; "Short Life" under Life; Pale, Sickly; "Much Sickness" under Sickness; "Low" under Resistance, Vitality; "Weakened" under Strength; "Weak Body" under Weak).

Passions — (See "Strong" under Passion).

Plethora—(See "Sthenic" under Plethora).

Recuperative Powers—(See "Strong" under Recuperation).

Resistance—(See "Strong Resistance to Disease" under Resistance).

Robust — (See "Robust Constitution" under Robust).

Shoulders—(See "Strong" under Shoulders).

Signs of Zodiac—The Strong Signs—(See "Fixed Signs" under Fixed).

Sthenic Process—(See Sthenic).

Stronger—The Health Stronger—(See "Health" in this section).

Strongest Body—The strongest body is given by ♌ on the Asc., and with the ☉ hyleg, and many planets elevated in the East at B., and preferably in fiery signs.

Thighs—(See "Strong" under Thighs).

Very Strong Body — (See Athletic; "Body", "Strength", under Muscles; "Body" under Strength; "Body" in this section).

Vigorous Body—(See Vigor).

Voice—(See "Strong" under Voice).

Will Power — (See "Strong" under Will).

Women—Strong Constitution In—(See "Constitution" under Females).

STRUCTURAL—Organic—The ☉ rules the structural organization of the parts and organs of the body, while the ☽ rules the functions, habits, and general health. The ☉ afflicted, therefore, tends to structural deterioration, and to inherent, hereditary, and constitutional diseases. The Sign on the Asc. at B. rules the structure of the part, or organ signified, both internally and externally. The nature of structural and functional disorders can be inferred from the combination of Sign, Planet, House, and Aspects. The bones of each part of the body come under the structural rulership of the Sign ruling such part. Thus ♈, in a structural way, would rule the Cranium, the Facial Bones, bones of the skull, etc. Externally ♈ would rule the skin, face, muscles, hair of the head, etc. Internally ♈ rules the Brain, and the contents of the skull, etc. The structural rulership is given under each of the Signs. The question of Structural Influences is further considered in the Article on Organic. (See Organic).

Brain — Structural Defects In — (See "Defects" under Brain).

Cells — Structural Changes In — (See "Structural" under Cells; Metabolism, Metamorphosis, Transformation).

Changes — Structural changes are brought about principally by the ☉, and an afflicted ☉, while functional changes and disorders are due to ☽ influence.

Defects—Structural Defects—(See Defects; "Organic Weakness" under Organic).

Degeneration — Structural Deterioration of Tissues — (See Decay, Degeneration; "Degeneration" under Tissues).

Disorders — Structural Disorders— (See "Organic Diseases" under Organic).

Eyes — Structural Defects In — (See "Defects In" under Eyes).

Heart — (See "Structural Disorders" under Heart).

Lumbar Region — Organic and Structural Weakness In — (See "Organic" under Lumbar).

Lungs—(See "Structural Defects" under Lungs).

Metabolism — Metamorphosis — (See these subjects. Also see "Cells" in this section).

Organic Diseases — (See "Constitutional Diseases" under Constitution; "Organic Diseases" under Organic; the various paragraphs in this section).

Respiratory Organs — (See "Structural Defects" under Breathing, Lungs, Throat).

Stomach—(See "Structural Disorders" under Stomach).

Throat—(See "Structural Defects" under Throat).

Tissues — (See "Structural Defects" under Tissues). For further study along this line see Acquired, Chronic, Congenital, Diathesis, Directions, Heredity, Hexis, Idiosyncrasies, Organic, Praeincipients, Sun Influence. For a list of typical structural diseases see "Constitutional Diseases" under Constitution, and also note the paragraphs under Organic.

STRUMA—(See Scrofula).

STRUTTING GAIT — (See "Strutting" under Gait).

STRYCHNINE—Strychnin—Strychnia— An Alkaloid of Nux Vomica. (See Nux Vomica).

STUBBORN—Stubborn Diseases—Stubborn Nature — Obstinate — (See Obstinate).

STUDY—Mental Exertion — Reading— Studious—

Active Mind—(See "Active Mind" under Active; "Quickened" under Mentality; "Good Mind" under Mind).

Aversion to Study—The ☽ to the □ or ☌ by dir., and ☿ weak and afflicted at B.; ☿ setting in the West, and following after the ☉; ☿ ☌ ♄, and also afflicted by the ☽, and in no relation to the Asc. (See "Mental Chaos" under Chaotic; "Inability" under Concentration; "Mind" under Dull; "Fails In" under Examinations; Flightiness; "Mind" under Heavy; Idle; "Bad" under Judgment; "Incapable", "Void Of", under Learning; "Shallow" under Mentality; "Light In Mind" under Mind; Pretender; "Weak" under Understanding, etc.).

Blindness — From Too Much Reading and Study—(See "Reading and Study" under Blindness; "Eyestrain" under Eyes).

Disease — From Too Much Reading and Study—(See "Disease" under Reading).

Educational Mind—(See "Educational Mind" under Mind).

Examinations—Fails In—(See Examinations).

Fatigue—Mental Fatigue from Over-Study—(See "Brain Fag" under Brain; "Mind" under Fatigue).

Genius — (See Genius, Mathematical, Scholar).

Good Student — Scholar — Studious Mind—☿ rising, dignified, well-aspected by the ☽ and Asc., and ☿ in one of his own signs, as in ♊ or ♍, and not combust; ♍ on the Asc. at B. (See "Active Mind" under Active; Education, Genius; "Good", "Sound", under Intellect; "Good" under Judgment; Knowledge, Learning, Mathematical; "Quickened" under Mentality; Metaphysics; "Deep", "Educational", "Good", "Sound", under Mind; Occult, Perception, Philosophy, Scholar, Science; "Great Love Of" under Truth; "Good" under Understanding, etc.).

Learning—(See "Fond Of", "Incapable Of", and the various paragraphs under Learning).

Loses Interest — In Studies — (See "Fails In" under Examinations; "Mind" under Indifferent; "Aversion" in this section).

Mathematics—Fond of—(See Mathematical).

Mind Quickened — (See "Quickened" under Mentality; "Good", "Penetrating", under Mind; "Good Student" in this section).

Night Study—Avoid when ☿ is afflicted in ♈ at B.

Occult Study—Fond of—(See Occult; "Astrology", "Occult Science", under Science).

Over-Study—Injury From—☿ afflicted in ♈, and too much reading, study, and night study, should be avoided. (See "Brain Fag" under Brain; Cares; "Mind" under Fatigue; "Strain" under Mental; Blindness, Disease, in this section).

Poor Student—(See Aversion, Loses Interest, in this section).

Renowned—Becomes Famous by His Studies—Takes Degrees—(See Renown).

Scholar—(See Scholar; "Good Student" in this section).

Science—Fond of Scientific Study—(See Science).

Studious Mind—(See "Learns Easily", "Studious Mind", under Learning; "Good Student" in this section).

Unqualified—For Study—(See "Mental Abilities" under Impaired; "Shallow" under Mentality; "Light" under Mind; Aversion, Loses Interest, in this section).

STUPIDITY—Stupid—Slow of Wit—(See "Mind" under Dull, Heavy; Foolish, Idle, Improvident, Indifferent; "Bad" under Judgment; "Weak Mind" under Mind; "Disorders" under Perception; "Stupor" under Sleep; "Persons" under Sluggish; "Slow Mental Development" under Slow; Sottish; "Weak" under Understanding).

STUPOR—A Condition of Insensibility—(See Catalepsy, Coma, Consciousness, Delirium, Insensibility; "Stupor" under Sleep; Trance, Unconsciousness).

STURDY—Robust—Hardy—Enduring—(See "Good" under Constitution; Robust, Ruddy, Rugged; "Body" under Strong; "Good" under Vitality, etc.).

STUTTERING—(See "Stammering" under Speech).

STYPTIC—(See Haemostatics).

SUB-ACUTE DISEASES—(See Chronic).

SUBCONSCIOUS MIND—Corresponds to the ☽. (See "Subconscious" under Mind; Reason, Superconscious).

SUBCUTANEOUS DISEASES—(See Abscesses, Boils, Carbuncles; "Subcutaneous" under Skin).

SUBDUING—Repression—Suppression—A ♄ quality. (See Repressions, Suppression).

SUBJECTIVITY—(See Introspection).

SUBLIMATION—Vaporization and Recondensation—Implied by the ♎ sign. (See Distillation, Filtration, Libra, Vapor).

Urine—Sublimation of—(See Filtration" under Urine).

SUBLUXATIONS—A Partial Dislocation of a Vertebra, or a Partial Dislocation in a Joint in any Part of the Body. Under the pull and pressure of the planetary vibrations and afflictions, the vertebrae are easily diverted from their normal positions, become partially dislocated, and impinge upon the nerves passing thru them, tending to shut off the nerve supply to the various organs and parts of the body, and leading to disease and discomfort in the body. The Spine is the central keyboard of the body, and if the nerve currents to the different parts of the body are to be kept free, open, and unimpeded, the vertebrae must be kept in proper line. Palpation and X-Ray examinations discover these deviations, but there are other ways also of knowing when and in what part of the spine these subluxations exist, and that is by Astrology, as each vertebra is ruled by a Sign of the Zodiac, and the planets in the various Signs at B., and along thru life, tend to afflict the vertebra, or vertebrae, ruled by such sign, and to cause it to deviate. Thus, these subluxations are coming and going constantly in every human being, and many of the partial dislocations adjust themselves at night during sleep. Some subluxations are more serious and prolonged, and especially the vertebra ruled by the Sign in which ♄ is found at B., and if ♄ is also afflicting this sign by direction and his position in the Zodiac at the time of a chronic illness, and which also may involve and cause a major subluxation. Such subluxation tends to be the major one throughout life, and occurs about every seven years, and may endure for two years at a time. The ♎ sign rules the Kidneys, and if ♄ is in ♎ at B. the kidneys become the weakest and most afflicted organs of the body, and are subject to severe affliction when ♄ along thru life is passing thru any of the cardinal signs, for a period of 2½ years to a sign, as thru ♈, ♋, ♎, and ♑, but the most severe when ♄ is again passing thru the kidney sign ♎ in the 28th and 29th years of life, and again in the 56th, 57th, and 58th years of life when ♄ finishes his second cycle, and is back in the ♎ sign again, and considering that he was in ♎ at B. Thus we know in what years of life the Kidney Place (KP) in the spine is under affliction by ♄, and we know this without palpation or examination of the patient if we have his birth data. Also the ☉ in ♎ at B., or ♂, tend to afflict the kidneys, and the vertebrae thru which the nerves pass to the kidneys, and you can usually set it down that a person born with the ☉, ♄, ♂, ♅, or any planet in ♎ at B., or with ♎ rising upon the Eastern horizon, the Ascendant, that they are a kidney subject, and that from the standpoint of the vertebrae, the kidney place in the spine should be the first place to be adjusted. This rather lengthy illustration can be applied to any sign of the Zodiac. The ☉, ♄, or ♂ in the ♋ sign at B. would affect the stomach, and SP in the spine. If the ☉ and malefics are in ♋, the lungs would be affected, and the Lung Place (Lu.P.), the 3rd Dorsal vertebra, would be the major subluxation, and need constant attention for a time, and during the time the afflicting planet is afflicting the Lung vertebrae. The major subluxations tend to be brought on by the major planets, as ♅, ♆, ♄, and ♂, and also the ☉, and with several planets afflicting one vertebrae at the same time. The minor subluxations are caused usually by the minor planets, ♀ and ☿, and also by the less severe aspects of the other planets. Every Physician, Chiropractor, Osteopath, or Healer, who would understand his patients, what vertebrae and parts of the body, or organs, are afflicted, should understand Astrology, and how to erect a star map of birth, and to know the planetary influences that are working over his patient at birth, and at the time of illness. The subluxations caused by the slower moving planets are more prolonged. It takes ♄ over two years to pass thru one Sign of the Zodiac, and his afflictions last longer, and tend to a chronic disease. Mars will pass thru one sign usually in about six weeks, and tend to bring on an acute disease, or high fever during this period if the afflicted vertebra is not adjusted frequently. The ☉ passes thru one sign in about one month, and his afflictions tend to last for a month, by his transits. It takes ♅ seven years to pass thru one sign, and during this period he may cause frequent subluxations of the vertebra he is afflicting. By knowing these laws, the Physician, Chiropractor, or Healer, can have a proper knowledge of what vertebrae are afflicted, when they began to be afflicted, and when to stop giving adjustments. This subject is further discussed in the Article on Vertebrae, and each of the Vertebrae given, the parts and organs they supply, etc. At the end of the various Articles on the diseases throughout this book, the subluxations tending to cause the disease have been listed as an aid to Chiropractors who may be using this book. The writer of this Encyclopaedia is a graduate Chiropractor, with the degree of D.C., having taken a resident course at the Palmer School of Chiropractic, at Davenport, Iowa. Also later, in recognition of his Writings, and research work along the lines of Chiropractic, and the Spine, as related to Astrology, he was given the Honorary Degree of Ph.C. by the Mecca College of Chiropractic, located at 143 Roseville Ave., Newark, New Jersey, of which Dr. Frederick W. Collins, A.M., M.D., is the Dean and President. Also the Mecca College of Chiropractic has had a chair of Medical Astrology for some years now, and instructs its students in the Astrological Analysis of the Spine. (See Anatomical, Cervical, Coccyx, Compressed, Dorsal, Healers, Lumbar, Medical Astrology, Numbness, Pressure, Ribs, Sacrum, Spine, Vertebrae; "Fluid" under Vital, etc.).

SUBNORMAL—Subnormalities of the Mind and Body—Below Normal—Almost every subject in this book is dealing with some subnormal, or abnormal condition of the mind, or body, and will ask you to look in the alphabetical arrangement for the subject you have in mind. The planet ♄ tends principally to subnormal conditions by his inhibitions, retentions, and suppressions. Also the afflictions of ♇ tend to subnormal conditions, as lack of development, undersized body, or organs. The ☉, ♃, ♂, and ♀ tend, by

their good aspects, to keep the body and mind at normal. Afflictions during Gestation tend to subnormal conditions, and defective births. See the following subjects, which are suggestive along the lines of subnormalities, and the weaknesses and defects of body and mind. See Abeyance, Abnormal, Adynamia, Anaemia, Apathy, Arrested, Asthenia, Atonic, Atrophy, Aversions, Birth, Blemishes, Body, Congenital, Defects, Deficient, Deformities, Deviations, Diminished, Disease, Dull, Dwarfed, Enervation, Feeble, Foolish, Heredity, Idiocy, Ill-Health, Imbecile, Impairments, Imperfections, Impotent, Inactive, Inertia, Infirm, Insanity, Intellect, Lack Of, Lethargy, Listless, Loss Of, Malformations, Mind, Missing, Monsters, Perversions, Prenatal Epoch, Sickness; "Subnormal" under Temperature; Undersized, Understanding, Unnatural, Void Of, Weak, etc.

SUBSTANCE—Matter—(See "Substance" under Brain, Cells; Matter; "Medullary Substance" under Medulla).

SUBSULTUS—Any Morbid Tremor or Twitching—A ♅ disease. (See "Movements" under Erratic; Jerkings, Saint Vitus Dance, Spasmodic, Tremors, Twitchings).

SUCCEDENT HOUSES—The Houses Between the Cardinal and Cadent Houses —The Succedent Houses correspond to the Fixed Sign influence, and many planets in them tend to give a strong constitution. The qualities of these houses are much the same as those of the Fixed Signs. (See "Fixed Signs" under Fixed; "Succedent" under Houses).

SUCCESS—The benefic planets ♃ and ♀ when rising, strong, and well-aspected at B. tend to bring material success, honors, and good health, and especially when in the M.C. in an otherwise fortunate map. (See Ambition, Famous, Fate; "Fortunate" under Fortune; "Good Health" under Health; Optimism, Power, Prosperity, Renown, Reputation, Riches, etc.).

SUCCUMBS—

Disease—Succumbs Easily to Disease —♎, ♍, or ♓ on the Asc., and the hyleg heavily afflicted by malefics; afflictions in fixed signs, and with mutable signs on the angles. The ☽ people become easy subjects to contagions and infectious diseases. The ♍ people court disease, and give up easily to it, and bad suggestions along health lines should not be made to the ♍ people. The ♏ people, by their excess of magnetic power, attract disease, and especially contagious and infectious diseases, and fall easy victims in epidemics. (See Contagions, Directions; "Succumbs Easily" under Disease, Sickness; "Ill-Health All Thru Life" under Ill-Health; Infectious Diseases, Influenced; "Negative Nature" under Negative; Receptive; "Low" under Recuperation, Resistance, Vitality; "Much Sickness" under Sickness; Susceptibility, Virgo; "Weak Body" under Weak).

Does Not Succumb—Strong Resistance to Disease—(See "Abundance", "Good", under Health; Immunity; "Good" under Resistance, Stamina, Tone, Vitality; "Body" under Strong).

SUDDEN—Spontaneous—Unexpected—Untimely—Sudden Events, etc.—The action of ♂ is sudden, intense, fulminating, and severe. Also the action and influence of ♅ tends to sudden and unexpected diseases and events in the life of the native. See the following subjects in the alphabetical arrangement when only listed here—

Accidents—(See the various paragraphs under Accidents).

Blows; Burns; Calamities—(See "Sudden" under Calamity).

Casualties; Catastrophies; Chances;

Changes—(See "Sudden" under Changes).

Child—Sudden Death of—(See "Sudden Death Of" under Children).

Collapse—(See "Sudden" under Collapse).

Cramps; Cuts; Danger—Sudden Danger—The ☉ hyleg, ♅ in the 8th H. and Anareta, and the ☉ to the ♂ or ill-asp. ♅ by dir. (See the paragraphs under Danger).

Death—Sudden Death—Unexpected—Sudden and Extraordinary Death—Quick Death by Violence—The ☉ or ☽ afflicted by the □ or ☍ ♂, and ♂ elevated above the Lights; the ☉ in the 8th H., ♂, □, or ☍ ♂; the ☉ much afflicted in ☍; the ☉ hyleg, and with ♅ in the 8th H., and Anareta, and the ☉ to the ♂, P, □, or ☍ ♅; the ☉ to the ill-asps. ♂ or ♅ by dir.; the ☽ at Full, or increasing, sepr. from ♀, and applying to ♂ in a day geniture, sudden death thru a love affair; the ☽ sepr. from the ☉, and applying to ♂ in a day nativity; the ☽ in the 8th H., and afflicted by ♅, ♄, or ♂; the ☽ to the place of Caput Algol; ♅ afflicted in ♌, ♏, or in the 4th or 8th H.; ♅ and ♂ afflicted in the 8th H.; ♅ afflicted in ♏ in the 8th H.; ♅ and ♂ cause sudden deaths, and especially when in the 8th H., and afflicting the hyleg by dir.; ♅ does not kill by himself, but assists in destroying life by his evil espects, and when they concur in afflicting the hyleg is usually sudden, singular, and of an extraordinary nature; ♆ afflicted at B., and to the ♂ or ill-asp. the hyleg by dir., and it may be by drowning or suffocation; ♄, ♂, or ☊ in the 8th H.; ♂ afflicted in the 1st, 4th, or 8th H.; ♂ lord of the 1st, and in the 8th H.; ♂ in the 8th H., and afflicting the hyleg, death may be sudden and violent; ♂ ♂ or ill-asp. the ☉ at B., and by dir.; ♂ ♂ the ☉ or ☽ in the 1st, 6th, 8th, or 10th H., and especially if ♅ and ♄ add their evil testimony to ♂. There are many ways to meet with a sudden death, too numerous to list here. Look in the alphabetical arrangement for the subject, cause, and kind of death you have in mind. Especially see the following subjects—Accidents, Blows, Contests, Death, Drowning, Duels, Earthquake, Electricity, Enemies, Explosion, Extraordinary, Falls, Flood, Gases, Gunshot, Highwaymen, Hurts, Injury, Killed, Lightning, Murdered, Mysterious, Peculiar, Poison, Quarrels, Quick, Railroads, Remarkable, Shipwreck, Singular, Stabs, Storms, Strange, Suicide, Sword, Thieves, Tornadoes, Tragical, Travel, Treachery, Uncommon, Unexpected, Untimely, Unusual, Vehicles, Violent, Wind, Wounds, etc.).

Diseases—Sudden and Unexpected Diseases—Sudden Distempers—Mad and Sudden Diseases—Severe, Sharp, and Fulminating—♅ rules all sudden diseases, and afflicts the part of the body ♅ is in at B.; ♅ afflicted in the 6th H.; ♅ afflictions and influences show sudden attacks of disease, as by cramps, spasms, ruptures, shocks, etc.; ♅ □, ☍, or P. the ☉, sudden and incurable diseases; ♂ also shows sudden diseases, and death from them; ♂ in the 6th H., and afflicting the ☉ or ☽; ♂ diseases are sudden, and caused by an over-abundance of animal heat. (See Acute; "High" under Fever; Fierce, Fulminating; "Sudden Distempers" under Head; "Animal" under Heat; Painful Diseases, Pernicious, Quick Diseases, Severe, Sharp, Short Diseases, Swift, Vehement, Violent Diseases).

Disgrace—Sudden Disgrace—(See "Causes" under Disgrace).

Distempers—Sudden Distempers—Mad and Sudden—(See "Diseases in this section; "Sudden" under Distempers, Head; "Distempers" under Mad).

Downfall—Sudden Downfall—(See Downfall).

Drowning; Enthusiasms—(See "Sudden" under Enthusiasm).

Escapes; Events—(See "Sudden" under Events).

Evils—(See "Sudden" under Evils).

Explosions; Exposure—Illness from Sudden Exposure—(See Exposure).

Extraordinary—Sudden and Extraordinary Diseases—(See Extraordinary).

Failure—Sudden Failure—(See Disgrace, Downfall, Reverses, Ruin).

Fainting—(See "Sudden Swoonings" under Fainting).

Falls; Family—Sudden Death In—(See "Sudden Death" under Family).

Father—Sudden Death of—(See "Sudden Death" under Father).

Fever—(See "High", "Sudden", under Fever).

Fulminating; Good—Sudden Good or Ill—(See "Sudden Good" under Good).

Head—Sudden Distempers In—Sudden Headaches—(See "Sudden" under Head, Headache).

Heart—Sudden Death from Heart Trouble—(See "Sudden Death" under Heart).

Homicide; Hurts—(See "Strange", "Sudden", under Hurts).

Ill—Sudden Good or Ill—(See "Good" in this section).

Illnesses—Short and Sudden Illnesses—(See Acute; "High Fever" under Fever; Fierce Maladies, Pernicious; "Illnesses" under Short; "Diseases" in this section).

Impulses—(See "Sudden" under Impulses).

Incurable—(See "Sudden and Incurable Diseases" under Incurable).

Injuries—(See the various paragraphs under Injuries; "Accidents" in this section).

Journeys—(See "Sudden" under Journeys).

Lightning — Sudden Death By — (See Electricity, Lightning).

Mad Distempers—Mad and Sudden—(See "Distempers" in this section).

Marriage Partner — (See "Sudden Death Of" under Marriage Partner).

Mischief — Some Sudden Mischief — (See "Danger From" under Mischief).

Mother — (See "Sudden Death Of", "Sudden Sickness Of", under Mother).

Murder; Mysterious and Sudden—(See "Mysterious and Sudden Death" under Mysterious).

Paroxysms—Sudden Paroxysms—(See Convulsions, Epilepsy, Fainting, Fits, Paroxysms, Spasmodic Diseases).

Passion — (See "Sudden Storms Of" under Passion).

Peculiar and Sudden—(See "Extraordinary Accidents" under Accidents; "Death" under Extraordinary; Peculiar).

Perils; Remarkable and Sudden—(See Remarkable).

Reputation — (See "Loss Of" under Reputation).

Reverses; Ruin; Ruptures;

Severe and Sudden—Sudden Severity of Disease—(See Fulminating, Severe, Sharp; "Diseases" in this section).

Sharp and Sudden—(See Sharp).

Shocks; Short Diseases — Short and Sudden — (See Acute, Quick Diseases; "Illnesses" under Short).

Sickness — (See "Diseases" in this section).

Singular; Spontaneous; Stabs;

Strange and Sudden—(See Strange).

Strokes; Suffocation; Suicide;

Swoonings — (See "Fainting" in this secton).

Tragical Death—(See Tragical).

Troubles — Sudden Troubles — (See "Causes" under Trouble; the various paragraphs in this section).

Uncommon and Sudden — (See Uncommon).

Unexpected and Sudden — (See Unexpected).

Unlooked-For and Sudden — (See the various paragraphs in this section).

Untimely; Unusual and Sudden—(See Unusual).

Violent and Sudden — (See "Death", and the various paragraphs under Violence).

Wounds. If the subject you have in mind has been omitted in this Article, look for it in the alphabetical arrangement.

SUDORIFIC — Sudorifics—Diaphoretics —Remedies which Increase the Sweat —A Therapeutic Property of the ☉ remedies. (See Sweat).

SUFFERING—Suffers—Distress—Painful Experiences—Pains In the Body—Anguish of Mind—Anxiety—Sorrow—Trouble, etc. — Suffering is produced principally by the 12th H. influences, as this is the house of sorrow and self-undoing, of hindrances, limitations, and confinements. Suffering is also brought on by the ☐ and ☍ aspects of ♄, as ♄ is known as "The Chastener", and the Angel of Saturn is ever working with Humanity to right the wrongs, establish justice, and it is often necessary for the Gods Above to bring many afflictions, troubles, sorrows, suffering, or even death, to awaken and arouse the individual to a better life, more spiritual discernment, and to attainment. (See Punishment). The greater part of the suffering brought upon mankind is due to the abuse and improper use of the sex forces, and to use them for sensuous gratifications, lust, and venery, which brings on disease, and an earlier death. (See Passion, Sex). Nearly every subject in this book deals with the sufferings of Humanity in one form and another, and it will not be advisable to list in this Article all these subjects, but you can find them in the alphabetical arrangement. The following subjects will be listed here, however, which see in the alphabetical arrangement when not more fully considered here—

Abroad — Suffering and Distress Abroad — (See "Suffering" under Abroad).

Affliction; Anguish; Anxiety; Body — Suffering In—Physical Suffering—(See Disease; "Bad Health" under Health; Ill-Health, Infirm, Invalids, Sickness).

Death — Little Suffering At Death — (See "Easy Death" under Death).

Detriment; Disease—Suffers Much In Disease — The afflictions of ♄ tend to prolonged and chronic suffering, dull aches, weakness, and depression. Mars tends to high fevers, sharp pains, etc. (See Aches, Acute, Chronic; "High Fevers" under Fever; Fierce, Fulminating, Grievous; "Heavy and Sad Sickness" under Heavy; "Diseases" under Pain; Pernicious, Poignant; "Serious Illnesses" under Serious; "Disease" under Severe; "Diseases" under Sharp; Vehement, Violent Diseases, etc.).

Disgrace; Distress; Evils; Grief;

Illness—Suffers Severely When Ill— ♌ on the Asc. at B.

Ill-Health—(See "Ill-Health All Thru Life", and the various paragraphs under Ill-Health; "Much Sickness" under Sickness).

Life of Suffering—♄ ☌ the ☉ or ☽ in the 6th H.; ♄ afflicted in the 6th or 12th H.; malefic planets in the 12th H., and afflicting the hyleg; a weak sign on the Asc., and a malefic planet in the rising sign. (See "Many Afflictions" under Affliction; "Malice of Fortune" under Fortune; Miseries, Misfortune, Self-Undoing, Sorrow, Trouble, Twelfth House).

Mind — Suffering In — (See Anguish, Anxiety, Dejected, Despondent, Doubts, Fears; "Low Spirits" under Low; Melancholy; "No Peace of Mind" under Mind; Renunciation, Worry, etc.).

Miseries; Moderated — Suffering and Pain Alleviated — Moderation In Disease—(See Amelioration, Ease, Moderation; "Alleviated" under Pain; Recovery).

Much Suffering—The ☽ to the ☐ or 8 the ☉ by dir.; the ☽ to the place of Antares; ♃ Sig. ☐ or 8 ♄, ruin, disgrace, misery, and suffering; ♂ Sig. ☐ or 8 ♄, and especially if ♄ be stronger than ♂; lord of the 11th in the 12th H. (See "Every Evil" under Evil; "Much Misery Everywhere" under Misery; "Much Sickness" under Sickness; "Many Sorrows" under Sorrow; Trouble).

Pain—(See "Suffers Much Pain", and the various paragraphs under Pain).

Patience—Has Much Patience In Suffering—(See "Does Not Complain" under Complaining; Patience).

Plots — Suffers Much by Plots — (See "Secret Enemies" under Enemies; Plots, Treachery).

Poverty—Suffers From—(See Neglect, Poverty, Privation).

Quarrels—Suffers By—(See Quarrels).

Rash Actions—Suffers By—(See Rashness).

Religion—Suffers Because of His Religion—(See Persecution).

Rest—Has No Rest In Sickness—Suffers Much — (See "Sickness" under Rest).

Reverses; Ruin; Sadness;

Scandal — Suffers From — (See Scandal).

Serious Suffering—Forebodes Serious Suffering—(See Grievous; "Heavy and Sad Sickness" under Heavy; "Suffers Much Pain" under Pain; "Serious Illnesses" under Serious; "Disease" under Severe; Vehement, etc.).

Sickness—Suffers Much In—(See Disease, Illness, Pain, in this section).

Sorrow; Treachery—Suffers By—(See "Female Treachery", "Injury By", under Treachery).

Trouble; Vehicles—Suffers Injury or Death By — (See Railroads, Travel, Vehicles).

Wounds — Injury and Suffering By — (See Cuts, Hurts, Injuries, Instruments, Iron, Mobs, Stabs, Violence, Wounds, etc.).

SUFFOCATION—Suffocated—Stoppage of Respiration—Smothered—Strangulation—Asphyxiation—See the following subjects—

Angina—A Sense of Suffocation—(See Angina).

Asphyxiation—(See Asphyxiation; "Delayed Births" under Children; "Non-Oxygenation" under Oxygen).

Birth — Danger of Suffocation At Birth—(See "Asphyxiation", "Delayed Births", under Children).

Buried Alive—(See Burial).

Choking — (See Asphyxiation, Choking, Drowning, Hanging, Strangulation; "Stricture" under Throat).

Cutaneous Asphyxiation — (See "Cutaneous" under Asphyxia).

Danger of Suffocation—♄ in bad asp. the ☉; the Asc. to the ☌ or ill-asp. ♂ by dir., and ♂ in an earthy sign at B.; the Asc. to the ☌ or ill-asp. ♄ by dir., and ♄ in ♍ at B.

Death by Suffocation—Danger of—If the ☽ be with Antares in 8 to ♂ with Hercules or Arcturus, and especially in 8 from angles, threatens death by suffocation; ♄ ☐ or 8 the ☉ from a fixed sign, and ori., or when occi. in a fixed sign and ☐ or 8 the ☽, produces death by hanging, suffocation, or by being trodden or crushed to death in a tumult; ♄ in the M.C., or close to the Asc. at B., and afflicting the hyleg by dir.; ♄ afflicting the hyleg by dir., and holding the dominion of death, and especially with ♄ in ♍; ♄ in 8, and evil fixed stars and ♄ afflicting the hyleg, and are in mutual ☐ or 8; ♄ or ♅ in ♋, ♍, ♏, or ♓, and afflicting the ☽; ♄ in ♍ and afflicting the hyleg; ♄ ☌ or ill-asp. the ☉ in fixed signs; ♄ influences tend to; ♂ with Hercules or Arcturus, in angles, and afflicting the ☽; fixed signs dispose to. (See Asphyxia, Burial, Choking, Drowning; "Death" under Gas; Halter, Hanging, Strangulation).

Drowning; Dyspnoea; Gas—Death by Escaping Gas — (See "Death" under Gas).

Halter; Hanging; Hysterical Fits — Danger of Suffocation In — (See Hysteria).

Non-Oxygenation — Of the Blood — (See Oxygen).

Phlegm — Almost Suffocated With — (See "Great Expectoration" under Phlegm).

Smothering Sensation — (See Angina, Asphyxia, Cyanosis, Dyspnoea; "Non-Oxygenation" under Oxygen; Smothered).

Spasmodic Suffocation—(See Angina, Dyspnoea; "Non-Oxygenation" under Oxygen).

Strangulation — (See the paragraphs under Strangulation).

Trampled by Mob — Suffocation By — (See Trampled).

SUGAR—Sweets—Candies—Pastries—Preserves—Sugar is the physiological action of ♃. Sugar is also ruled by ♀, as strong ♀ influence at B. inclines to the use of sweets. (See Hydrocarbonates).

Abnormal Desire For — Heavy Sugar Eaters — (See "Pastries", "Starches", "Sugar", "Sweets", under Food; Starches).

Blood—Sugar In—A ♃ disease.

Pyorrhoea — From Eating Excess of Sugar—(See Pyorrhoea).

Urine—Sugar In—Diabetes Mellitus—(See Diabetes).

Xylan—Xylose—Wood Sugar—Wood Gum—(See Xylan, Xylose).

SUGGESTION—Easily Affected By—The ☉ in ♍, or with ♍ on the Asc.; characteristic of the ♍ people, and especially along health lines, as this is the sign which rules over the health. (See Virgo). The planet ♆ is suggestive, and people born under the very strong influence of this planet are very susceptible to suggestion, and especially along passional lines. (See "Attracts Disease" under Attracts; Contagions, Environment, External; "Hypnotic Subject" under Hypnotism; Infections,

Influenced, Magic, Magnetic, Mesmerism; "Mutable Disposition" under Mutable; "Negative Nature" under Negative; Neptune, Obsessions; "Morbid Passional Desires" under Passion; Passive, Receptive, Susceptible, Sympathy, Telepathy, Virgo).

SUICIDE — Suicidal Tendency—Suicide is ruled principally by the 12th House.

Cases of Suicide — Birth Data, etc. — See "Suicide", No. 137, and No. 171; "Husband", No. 162; "Schauman", No. 209; "Puzzle Horoscopes", No. 672; "Prince", No. 744; "Haydon", No. 818; "Allonby", and "Bavaria", No. 823, all in 1001 N.N. Also see Figures 12, 13, and 14 in "Message of the Stars" by the Heindels.

Causes of Suicide—Any of the planets may cause suicide when such planet is under the heavy affliction of malefics, and from causes due to the nature of the afflicting planet. The ☉ and ♂ tend to suicide thru haste, excitement, sudden impulses, and from quarrels. Saturn tends to suicide from worry, brooding, despondency, moping, etc., and to bring on Suicidal Mania. General Causes are—the SUN, ☽, and malefics in the 8th H. in common signs; the ☉ hyleg, and to the ☌ or ill-asp. ♄ by dir.; the ☉ and ☽ afflicted by malefics; the □ and ☍ aspects of the ☉ tend to cause; the ☉ or ☽ ☌ ♄ or ♂ in the M.C., may commit suicide to escape public execution; the MOON to the ☌ or ill-asp. ♅ by dir., and ♅ afflicting the ☽ at B., and especially thru intrigues with the opposite sex; the ☽ in ♏, □ ♄, and ☿ or ♀ □ ♅; the ☽ ☌ ♅, and in □ or ☍ ♄ or ♂, and with ♄ ☌ ☿; NEPTUNE □ or ☍ ♄ or ♀; ♆ afflicted in ♏; ♆ in and about the 16° or cardinal signs, and afflicting ☿; the afflictions of URANUS tend to; ♅ afflicting the Significators, the ☉, ☽, Asc., or M.C. when other indications point to mental derangement; ♅ afflicted in ♓; the transit of ♅ thru the 3rd or 9th H. if afflicting these houses at B.; in violent deaths ♅ disposes to; ♅ afflicting the hyleg; ♅ afflicted in the 8th H.; SATURN ruler of the 12th H. at B., and ♄ ☌ or ill-asp. the Asc. by dir.; ♄ in the Asc., and afflicted by cross aspects; ♄ people are often driven to suicide thru moroseness; ♄ and ♂ in ♊, ♍, ♐, or ♒, and in □ or ☍ the ☉ or ☽; the ♄ sign ♑ on the Asc., and with ♄ as ruler, and afflictions to the Asc. when ♄ is in the 8th H.; ♄ afflicted in the 12th H. at B., has thoughts of suicide; ♄ ☌ or ☍ ☿, and afflicting the hyleg; ♄ in the 3rd or 9th H., and afflicting the ☉, ☽, ☿, or the hyleg; JUPITER weak and afflicted by malefics at B., and especially if ♃ is afflicting the hyleg; ♃ ☌ ♄ and ♂, and otherwise afflicted, or afflicting the hyleg, and thru financial losses or bankruptcy, and the 2nd H. also badly afflicted at B.; MARS ori., □ or ☍ the ☉ from fixed signs, or ♂ occi., □ or ☍ the ☽ from fixed signs, and caused by women if ♀ be with ♂; ♂ ☌ ☿, and also □ or ☍ ♄; ♂ in signs of human form, and □ or ☍ the ☉ or ☽, and contrary in condition; ♂ Sig. □ or ☍ ♄, addicted to suicide or secret revenge; ♂ Sig. □ or ☍ ♄ if either be in the

Asc., or ♄ in the M.C.; ♂ afflicting the hyleg by dir., and holding the dominion of death, and especially when the radical map shows a violent death; ♂ in the Asc. in evil asp. to ♄ often leads to times of misfortune, or false accusation, and to suicide; ♂ ☌ the Lights in the 3rd or 9th H., and afflicted by ♄, and also afflicting the hyleg by dir.; VENUS ☌ ♄ or ♂, and ♀ badly afflicted by malefics by dir., it may be thru jealousy, or some love affair; MERCURY, the mental ruler, in the 8th H., and afflicted by the ☽ or malefics, gives some tendency to suicide, and especially when ☿ and the ☽ are in fixed signs; ☿ in the 6th H., and afflicted by ♅, ♄, or ♂; ☿ weak, afflicted, and unfortunate at B., and afflicted by the evil directions of one or more malefics, and especially by ♄, threatens to do away with himself, and especially with the mad or insane; ☿ in an earthy sign at decumbiture, and ♂ afflicting ☿, danger of suicide (Hor'y); many planets in common signs show, and with these signs on the angles, and containing malefics; lord of the Asc. in the 8th H., with lord of the 6th in the 8th, and especially if the lord of the Asc. apply to the □ or ☍ lord of the 6th; lord of the 8th in the 1st H., and from irregularities; lord of the 8th in the 7th, and usually due to mental troubles, or thru quarrels; lord of the 1st in the 8th, and lord of the 8th in the 1st H.; lord of the 1st H. also being lord of the 8th, and lord of the 8th also lord of the 1st; people born under ♎ are said to be prone to suicide, for with ♎ on the Asc., ♉, also ruled by ♀, is on the cusp of the 8th, or near it, which makes the lady of the Asc. also the lady of the 8th H., and such people usually cause their own death; also when ♈ is on the Asc. at B., ♏ is on cusp of the 8th, which may lead to self-destruction under evil aspects to ♂, or evil directions falling in the 8th H., and afflicting lord of the 1st and 8th; afflictions in the 8th H.; planets or malefics in and around the 15° of cardinal signs, the 25° of fixed signs, and the 26° of common signs, known as the more violent areas, or degrees, give suicidal tendencies. (See "Causes His Own Death" under Death.)

Cutting the Throat—Suicide By—(See "Cuts His Own Throat" under Throat).

Drowning—Suicide By—(See Drowning).

Fire Arms—Suicide By—(See "Death By" under Gunshot).

Husband—(See "Suicide" under Husband).

Insane — Commits Suicide While Insane—(See "Cases Of" under Insanity).

Poison—(See "Suicide By" under Poison).

Shot Himself—(See Nos. 209, 672, 818, under "Cases" in this section; "Death by Gunshot" under Gunshot).

Suicidal Mania — Caused by ♄; ♄ in the 3rd or 9th H., and afflicting the hyleg; ♄ ☌ ☿ in the 8th H., and afflicting the hyleg or the Asc.; ♄ ruler at B., and afflicting ☿ and the hyleg. (See "Of No Ambition" under Ambition;

Brooding, Dejection, Depressed, Despair, Despondent, Gloom; "Hopes Cut Off" under Hope; Hyperacidity, Hypochondria, Insanity; "Low Spirits" under Low; Melancholy; "No Peace of Mind" under Mind; Morose, Twelfth House; "Death" under Violent; Worry).

SULPHATES—Calcium Sulphate (Lime Sulphate) — Potassium Sulphate — Sodium Sulphate—(See Lime, Potassium, Sodium).

SULPHUR — Brimstone — Is one of the Twelve Polycrest Remedies, and corresponding to the ♍ sign. It is ruled by both ♄ and ♂. Daath mentions sulphur as a typical drug of ♂. The ♍ sign is the sign of ♄, and also ♂ has his exaltation in this sign. The hair is darkened by sulphur, and ♄ rising at B. tends to produce dark and black hair. (See Hair). When in aspect to the ascending degree ♄ contributes sulphur pigment to the skin, and makes the complexion dark and sombre. (See Complexion, Mucous; "Pigmentation" under Skin; "Polycrest" under Zodiac).

SUMMER—

Sickly Summer—♄ or ♂ in power at the Summer Solstice, in the 6th or 8th H., and afflicting the ☽. (See Drought; "Extreme Heat" under Heat; "Death Rate High" under Mortality; "Winds" under Pestilence; "Hot Blasting Winds" under Wind).

Summer Signs—Of the Zodiac—♋, ♌, ♍. Diseases which begin when the ☉ is in these signs are usually short, more fierce, sharp and severe for the time. (See "Illnesses" under Short).

Summer Solstices—(See Solstices).

Warm Summers — (See Drought; "Fountains Dry Up" under Dry; Famine, Fountains; "Extreme Heat" under Heat; Scarcity; "Sickly" in this section).

SUN—The Sun (☉)—Solar Influences—The ☉ is the central body of our Solar System, and around which the planets move. The ☉ is the source of the vital power, and is the regulator and principal source of the life forces. The ☉ stands at the head of the Vital Group. The ♌ Sign is the home Sign, and the only Sign of the ☉, and the ☉ and the ♌ Sign are closely affiliated with the 5th House, as ♌ is the 5th Sign of the Zodiac. The ☉ when strong and powerful at B. tends to make the life and general fate of the native much more favorable, and when weak, ill-dignified, and badly aspected, the health, vitality, fate and destiny of the individual are very trying, and unfavorable. The ☉ is typical of Spirit, and the ☽ of Matter. The ☉ is hot, dry, fiery, inflammatory, electric, positive, barren, masculine, diurnal, life-giving, constructive, expansive, tonic, variable, and vital in action. Much has been written in the Textbooks of Astrology about the various influences of the ☉, and in order that the student may have quicker and more systematic access to these influences, this Article will be arranged into three Sections, as follows: Section One—Influences of the Sun. Section Two—The Sun Rules. Section Three—Diseases Ruled by the Sun.

— **SECTION ONE** —

INFLUENCES OF THE SUN—The ☉ is a physiological planet (classed as a Planet in Astrology), and is called "The Light of Time". He gives principally the Brain and Heart in Man.

Above the Earth — The ☉ is more powerful in health matters when above the Earth, or horizon at B., and weaker when below, as the ☉ rules by day, and the ☽ by night. (See Elevated, Majority, Rising).

Action Of — The ☉ is hot, electric, vital, and positive in action, and acts upon the whole substance of the Globe, and not upon just any one part or element. (See "Qualities", and the various paragraphs in this section and Article).

Affinity—The ☉ has affinity with all the Planets.

Afflictions Of — Tend to Fevers and Inflammations.

Anareta—The ☉ may become Anareta when the ☽ or Asc. are hyleg. (See Anareta).

Angel Of—Michael.

Angular and Diurnal—The ☉ angular and diurnal exerts his strongest influence in health and other matters.

Ascendant — The ☉ tends to cause death by his evil aspects to the Asc. or ☽ if they are hyleg, in which case he acts like ♂, and produces death by fire if other testimonies concur.

Aspects—Aspects to the ☉ are necessary to give zest to life, and bad aspects are better than none at all. Planets in ☌ the ☉ are known as in Combust, and the ☉ in such an aspect tends to destroy the nature and influence of such planet, and appropriate its qualities to himself. In other aspects the ☉ afflicts only by his □ and ☍.

Beams Of — (See "Rays" in this section).

Below the Earth — (See "Above" in this section).

Benefic—The ☉ is reckoned as benefic, and a Fortune, when with, or in good aspect the Benefics, and not afflicted by malefics.

Blood—The ☉ supplies oxygen to the blood, and also presides over Blood Making. (See Haematopoiesis).

Body—In the body the ☉ concerns itself with the Brain, Heart, Circulation of the Blood, and the Vitality.

Bondage — The ☉ influence is ever clamoring for deliverance and freedom from the thraldom of matter and the flesh, the opposite to the ☽ influence, which gives bondage.

Brain — The rays of the ☉ feed the nerves of the Brain.

Caloric—(See "Heat" in this section).

Capricorn — The ☉ in the ♄ sign ♑ tends to give longevity, and great tenacity of life. (See Endurance).

Cellular Excitation — The ☉ presides over. (See "Excitation" under Cells).

Center — The ☉ is one of the vital centers in a star map, along with the ☽, Asc., M.C., and hyleg.

Chief Index Of— (See "Organic" in this section).

Chronic Type—The inflammatory action of the ☉ is of the chronic type. Also the motion of the ☉ regulates Chronic Diseases. (See Chronic).

Circulation of Blood—(See "Body" in this section).

Circumferential—The influence of the ☉ is circumferential, in circles, like the ripples on water when a stone is thrown into a pond.

Colors—Gold, Orange, Saffron, Golden Yellow, and inclined to Purple. (See Colors).

Combust Planets—(See "Aspects" in this section).

Combustion—A physical action of the ☉. (See Combustion).

Complexion—The ☉ gives a sunburnt complexion. (See Complexion).

Conjunction Aspect — (See "Aspects" in this section).

Constitution—The ☉ has strong rule over the constitution, and the strength of the constitution is at full when the ☉ is above the horizon at B., and hyleg. (See "Strongest Constitution" under Constitution).

Constructiveness — The Principle of the ☉.

Contains In Itself—The ☉ contains in itself all the inherent powers and qualities specialized in the other planets, and the planets abstract from the ☉ certain properties, and transmit them to the Earth Sphere in modified form. (See "Forces", "Phenomena", in this section).

Corresponds To — The ☉ corresponds to the heart and the right eye of a man. The ☉ in nature and action corresponds closely to ♂. (See Mars, Left, Right).

Crucified—The ☉ is crucified in the ♑ sign. (See "Saturn" in this section).

Cycle—The Cycle of the ☉ is 28 years.

Denotes—The ☉ denotes Hysterics in women; Fevers and Sunstroke when afflicting the Asc., arising from excess of heat. The ☉ denotes inherent tendencies, and hereditary transmissions, organic diseases, constitutional and structural defects, etc. (See Organic, Structural).

Detriment Of — (See "Dignities" in this section).

Dignities Of—The ☉ is at home and strongest in his own sign ♌; has his exaltation in ♈, his fall in ♎, and his detriment in ♒. (See Antipathy, Opposites).

Directions—The evil directions of the ☉ are more critical during the ☉ period of life, from the 18th to 37th years of life. (See "Life" under Periods). When the ☉ is afflicted at B. he becomes a malefic in nature, and his evil directions to the ☽ or Asc., if they be hyleg, tend to destroy life. (See "Anareta" in this section; Directions).

Disease — The ☉ is an Indicator of Disease, and his position, strength, and aspects should always be noted when forming a judgment of disease. (See "Significators" under Disease; "Indicators of Health" under Health).

Diurnal—(See "Angular" in this section).

Drugs—Of the ☉—The general action of Drugs and Herbs ruled by the ☉ are Stimulant, Tonic, and Preservative. By their physiological action they act upon the Cerebral-Spinal Nervous System, the Circulatory System, the Tonicity, and the Vital Force. Typical Drugs of the ☉ are Aurum (Gold), Chamomilla, and the Sun Flower (Helianthus). The Therapeutic Properties of ☉ Remedies are Anticachectic, Cardiac, and Sudorific. (See Gold; "Sun Group" under Herbs, and the other subjects mentioned in this paragraph).

Dryness — The ☉ produces heat and moderate dryness. The ☉ is classed as dry and hot.

Earth and Sun — The ☉ is the sole vital agent of the Earth, and therefore of our organism. (See "Action Of" in this section).

Ease In Disease—During the daytime the electric force of the ☉ tends to diminish fevers and ease disease. (See Magnetic).

Eclipses—Of the ☉—(See Eclipses).

Electric—The ☉ is identified with the positive, masculine, electric, active, and constructive forces of Nature. The ☉ is a positive and electric body, and tends to heat and expansion in the body, and a confident, forceful, and positive mind. The ☉ influence is electric, strong, fearless, inflammatory, vital, fiery, sanguine, dry, hot, and the rays rather fruitful. (See Electric).

Electricity—The energy of the ☉ is partly represented by electricity, which is ☉ force reflected thru the planet ♅. (See Electricity).

Energy Of—(See "Electricity" in this section).

Equinoxes—(See Equinoxes).

Exaltation Of — (See "Dignities" in this section).

Expansive—The influence of the ☉ is expansive, expanding, and circumferential, as denoted by the dot in the circle in its symbol. (See "Electric" in this section).

Experience—(See "Expressive Of" in this section).

Expressive Of — The ☉ is expressive of Infinity, Continuity, Life, and Enlargement of Experience.

Fall Of—(See "Dignities" in this section).

Father — The ☉ signifies the father and his affairs. (See Father).

First House—The ☉ well-aspected in the 1st H., and especially when in a fiery sign, gives a strong constitution. (See Constitution).

Foetus—(See Quickening).

Force—The ☉ in the Solar System has to do with the renewal and interchange of Force, Circulation, and the Conservation of Matter.

Forces—Of the ☉—The Forces of the ☉ are made of use to us by the reflective and refractive powers of the encircling planets, and the rays of the planets are combined in the Solar Orb, the same as white contains all the colors of the Solar Spectrum. The Spleen is the gateway of the Solar Forces which enter the body. The ☉ in the 4th H. at B. tends to deprive the native of the Solar Forces during a greater part of life, but is good for old age. The Solar Life Currents in the body are diminished when the ☉ is in ☌ ♄ at B. (See Forces, Solar; "Force" under Vital).

Fortune—A Benefic—The ☉ is equal to one of the Benefics for good when well-dignified at B. (See "Benefic" in this section).

Friendly To — The ☉ is said to be friendly to all the planets except ♄.

Haematopoiesis—Blood-Making—(See "Blood" in this section).

Health—The ☉ is general Significator of Health, and especially in a male nativity. (See "Indicators" under Health).

Heart—In Man the ☉ corresponds to the heart.

Heat—The ☉ is hot and dry by nature, and tends to produce dry and hot diseases. The ☉ is caloric, and heat-producing, but is also vitalizing and constructive. The ☉ is vital heat and energy. The rays of the ☉ are dry, hot, and rather fruitful, and sunlight is beneficial to growth, health, and vitality. Without sunlight and Solar Forces none could live. The ☉ and ♂, being hot by nature, tend to fevers and inflammations by their afflictions. The ☉ disseminates heat over the body, and gives heat to the part of the body ruled by the sign he is in at B. (See Dry, Electric, Sunlight, in this section).

Heliocentric—(See this subject).

Herbs of the Sun—(See "Sun Group" under Herbs).

Heredity — The ☉ is the Significator of Hereditary Transmissions—(See Heredity, Organic, Structural; "Organic" in this section).

Hot and Dry—(See Dryness, Heat, in this section).

Hour—☉ Hour—(See "Hours" under Planets).

Hyleg—The ☉ as Hyleg—(See Hyleg).

Identified With — (See "Electric" in this section).

Incites — (See "Rhythm" in this section).

Indicator Of—(See Disease, Health, in this section).

Infinity—(See "Expressive Of" in this section).

Ingresses—(See Ingresses).

Inherent Powers — (See "Contains In Itself" in this section).

Joined to Planets—(See "Aspects" in this section).

Jupiter and the Sun—Give Short Diseases. The ☉ is friendly to ♃, and the ☉ is equivalent to a Benefic in influence when dignified, and well-aspected at B. (See "Benefic" in this section).

Leo Sign—Ruled by the ☉. (See Leo).

Life—Life Forces—The ☉ is life and motion. The ☉ is the Life Giver, and

the Regulator of the Life Forces. (See Hyleg). The ☉ tends to destroy life when malefic. (See "Directions" in this section). The ☉ is Significator of life and health. (See "Health" in this section). The ☉ maintains life. The most salient characteristic of the ☉ is life, and the giving of life. The Life Forces are governed by the aspects and position of the ☉. (See "Life Force" under Force; "Force" under Vital).

Magnetic and Negative — When setting and occidental, the ☉ has a magnetic and negative influence. (See Magnetic; "Oriental" in this section).

Male Nativities — The ☉ is Sig. of Health in, and also taken as hyleg, when the ☉ is strong at B., and in a hylegiacal place. (See Hyleg; "Health" in this section).

Malefic—Malefics and the ☉—When in ☌ or evil asp. the malefics, the ☉ acquires their nature and operates as a malefic. Planets combust transfer their power to the ☉, good or evil. (See "Aspects" in this section).

Mars and the Sun — (See "Action of Mars", "Sun and Mars", under Mars; "Ascendant", "Corresponds To", in this section). The ☉ ☌ ♂ causes the same diseases as ♂ in the Asc. at B.

Masculine — The ☉ is classed as a masculine planet, positive and electric.

Matter — (See "Bondage", "Force", in this section. Also see Matter).

Mentality—Mentally, the ☉ gives stability, firmness, perseverance, and strong will power, and especially when strong, rising, and well-aspected at B.

Metals and Minerals—Ruled by the ☉ —Carbuncle, Chrysolite, Gold, Hyacinth.

Mind — (See "Electric", "Mental", in this section).

Minerals — (See "Metals" in this section).

Moon and the Sun — The ☉ is malignant to the ☽ when ☌ or ☍ the ☽. The ☉ is stronger during the decrease and waning of the ☽. (See Moon; "Ascendant", "Directions", in this section).

Motion of the Sun — (See "Chronic", "Life", in this section). The motion of the ☉ is always direct, and never retrograde.

Negative — (See "Magnetic" in this section).

Nerves—(See "Brain" in this section).

Occidental—(See "Magnetic", "Oriental", in this section).

Orb Of—(See Orbs).

Organic—The ☉ is organic, and the ☽ functional. The ☉ is the chief index of the organic constitution. The ☉, its position and influence, is looked to for structural, organic, and hereditary troubles, and the vital physiological history of the native's constitution. (See Heredity, Organic, Structural; "Denotes", "Earth", "Rhythm", in this section).

Oriental—The ☉ when rising and oriental, has a positive, or electric influence upon the mind and body.

Oxygen—(See "Blood" in this section).

Pathological Action — Pathologically, the ⊙ by his afflictions tends to feverish conditions, hemorrhage, plethora, superfluous nutriment, and syncope.

Periodicity — Many diseases follow a Solar Periodicity, such as Tumors, Pains and Fluxions, and increase in proportion to the Declination of the ⊙ towards the West. (See Periodicity).

Phenomena — The ⊙ is the Soul of Physical Being, and contains in itself every form of manifestation of Phenomena. (See "Contains In Itself" in this section).

Physical Being — (See "Phenomena" in this section).

Physiological Action—Of the ⊙ Plants, Herbs, and Remedies, tend to the generation of heat in the body, and to build up the Tone and Vital Force. They also act upon the Cerebro-Spinal Nervous System, and the Circulatory System. (See "Drugs" in this section).

Planets and the Sun — (See Aspects, Contains In Itself, Forces, Jupiter, Mars, Moon, Saturn, in this section).

Plant Remedies Of — (See Drugs, Physiological Action, in this section).

Plexus — The Solar Plexus — (See "Solar" under Plexus).

Positive — (See Electric, Oriental, in this section).

Powers of the Sun—(See "Contains In Itself", "Forces", "Phenomena", and the various paragraphs in this section).

Presides Over—(See "Cellular" in this section).

Principle Of—Constructiveness.

Produces—(See Electricity, Foetus, Force, Heat, Motion, and the various paragraphs in this section).

Qualities—Action of the ⊙—The most of these subjects appear in the alphabetical arrangement — Active, Anticachectic, Ardent, Autocratic, Barren, Benefic (when well-aspected and dignified), Caloric-Producing, Cardiac, Chronic, Circumferential, Combustive, Commanding, Confident, Constitutional, Constructive, Courageous, Destructive (when malefic), Diurnal, Dry, Dynamic, Electric, Enlarging, Eruptive, Expanding, Fearless, Feverish, Fiery, Forceful, Fruitful (rather fruitful), Hemorrhagic, Hot, Inflamatory, Kinetic, Life-Giving, Magnetic (when occidental), Malefic (when ill-dignified), Masculine, Muscular, Organic, Pernicious, Physiological, Positive, Preservative, Quickening, Ruling, Rhythmic, Sanguine, Spiritual, Strong, Structural, Sudorific, Supporting, Temperate, Tonic, Variable, Vital, Vitalizing, Vivifying, etc.

Quickened—The Foetus is quickened by the ⊙. (See Quickening).

Rays of the Sun—The Rays of the ⊙ are dry, hot, and fruitful. (See Brain, Electric, Heat, in this section).

Regulator Of—The Life Forces. (See "Life" in this section).

Resistance to Disease — Is stronger when the ⊙ is angular and diurnal. (See "Good" under Resistance).

Revolution — Solar Revolution — (See Solar).

Rhythm — The ⊙ incites organic rhythm. (See Rhythm).

Right Eye—(See "Corresponds To" in this section).

Rising — (See "Oriental" in this section).

Salient Characteristic—(See "Life" in this section).

Saturn and the Sun—The ⊙ is crucified in ♑, the sign ruled by ♄, and which is the exalted sign of ♂, and thus the ⊙ is crucified "Between the Two Thieves" of the Heavens in this sign. The ⊙ is opposed to ♄.

Sensitive Part — Of the Body — The Sign in which the ⊙ is posited at B, indicates an internal part of the body which is very sensitive, and if the ⊙ is also much afflicted, complaints of such organ, or part, usually result, and according to the sign and nature of the afflicting planet.

Setting—(See "Magnetic" in this section; Setting).

Seventh House—The ⊙ well-aspected in the 7th H. gives a strong constitution, and is also favorable for marriage.

Sign In At Birth — (See "Sensitive Part" in this section).

Significator Of — The ⊙ is Sig. of Honor, Credit, and accidentally of Health and Life. (See "Male Nativities" in this section).

Signifies—The ⊙ signifies the Father. (See Father). The ⊙ also signifies diseases of the Brain, and also Fevers and Sunstroke.

Solar—Solar Eclipse—Solar Forces—Solar Ingresses — Solar-Lunar Activities—Solar Orb—Solar Plexus—Solar Periodicity — Solar Revolution—Solar Spectrum—(See Eclipses, Ingresses, Orbs, Periodicity, Plexus, Revolution, Solar, Spectrum; "Forces" in this section).

Solstices—(See this subject.

Soul of Physical Being — (See "Phenomena" in this section).

Source Of—The ⊙ is the source of the Life Forces and the Vital Powers. (See Vital, Vitality; "Forces", "Life" in this section).

Spleen — The Gateway of the Solar Forces—(See Spleen; "Forces" in this section).

Spots—Sun Spots—(See Spots).

Strength—Of the ⊙ At Birth—Great care should be taken in judging of the strength of the ⊙ at B., as the physical powers, the constitution, the vitality, and the entire life, depend upon its aspects and position in the Signs and Houses. (See "Judging the Health" under Health).

Structural Rulership—(See "Organic" in this section).

Sunburnt Complexion — The ⊙ gives. (See "Sunburnt" under Complexion).

Sunday—(See Week).

Sunlight—People born under the fiery signs need more sunlight for the best of health. (See "Heat" in this section).

Sunrise and Sunset — Sunrise is the best time of the day to be born for a strong constitution. The ☉ in the 7th H. just before sunset also gives a strong constitution, but the ☉ becomes weaker for health and strength when he passes into the 6th H., after sunset, and especially if afflicted by, or ♂ a malefic. (See Ascendant, First House, Sixth House).

Sun Spots—(See Spots).

Symbol Of — The Dot within the Circle (☉). Chapter V in the book, "The Key To the Universe", by Dr. and Mrs. Homer Curtiss, is devoted to the Occult and Spiritual meaning of this symbol.

Tenth House — The Midheaven — The ☉ well-aspected in this house, and in a strong sign for the ☉, tends to give a strong constitution, honors, and good fortune in life. (See Tenth House).

Therapeutic Properties—(See "Drugs Of" in this section).

Typical Drugs Of — (See "Drugs" in this section).

Vital — The Vital Powers — Ptolemy says the ☉ is the source of Vital Power, and there would be no life without the ☉. The ☉ rules over the Vital Powers, the Constitution, and the Prana, no matter in what part of the map he is in at birth. The ☉ is one of the vital centers of the map, along with the ☽, Asc., M.C., and hyleg. The Vital Fluid, ruled by the ☉, enters the body thru the Spleen. The ☉ stands at the head of the Vital Group. The Vital Powers are at full when the ☉ is above the horizon at B., and hyleg. (See Center, Constitution, Forces, Life, Source Of, Strength, in this section; "Life Force" under Force; Prana; "Fluid", "Force", and the various paragraphs under Vital; "Life Force" under Vitality).

Weather and the Sun—(See Drought, Famine; "Extreme Heat" under Heat; "Winds" under Pestilence; "Warm Weather" under Weather; "Storms" under Wind).

Winter Solstice — Entrance of the ☉ into ♑. (See Equinoxes, Solstices).

Zest—(See "Aspects" in this section; Zest).

— SECTION TWO —

THE SUN RULES — Look for these subjects in the alphabetical arrangement — Ardency; Arms — The Blood in the Arms, Hands, Legs and Feet when the ☉ is in Signs ruling these parts; Arteries; Back; Barrenness; Bilious Temperament (see Choleric); Blood—Blood-Making—The Blood—Oxygen in the Blood (see Blood, Haematopoiesis, Oxygen); Brain (the Structure of); Casein; Cellular Excitation (see Cells); Choleric Temperament (see Choleric); Chronic Diseases (motion of the ☉ regulates); Circulation of the Blood (see Circulation); Colors (see "Colors" in Sec. 1 of this Article); Constitution and Constitutional Diseases; Constructive Energy; Creative Powers; Daytime (see Day); Diamonds; Dorsal Region of Spine (see Dorsal); Drugs (see "Drugs" in Sec. 1 of this Article); Emotional Nature in Women (see Emotions); Energy (see Constructive, Vital,

under Energy); Etheric Fluid (see "Fluid" under Vital); Eyes — Right Eye of Male and Left Eye of Female; Faculties (see "Physical" under Faculties); Father (the Father); Feet — (Blood in when ☉ is in ♓); Feminine Signs of Zodiac—Second Half of (see "Signs" under Female); Fires of Life (see "Fires" under Life); Gold; Grape (Vinus Vinifera); Hands (Blood in when ☉ is in Sign which rules Hands); Health Matters in Males; Heart (Structure of when ☉ is in ♌); Heat (Distribution of in the Body—Excess Heat in the Body—Heat in the Parts or Organs ruled by the Sign ☉ is in at birth); Herbs (see "Sun Group" under Herbs); Hereditary Complaints; Hot and Dry Diseases (see "Dry and Hot" under Heat); Hyleg in the Male (see Hyleg); Internal Diseases (and especially in the part or organs ruled by the Sign the ☉ is in at birth); Kings; Left Eye in Females; Legs (Blood in when ☉ is in Signs ruling the Legs); Leo Sign; Life Force (see "Life Force" under Force); Males (Health Matters in); Man (the Heart and Brain in); Masculine Signs of the Zodiac—First Half of—(see "Masculine Signs" under Signs); Memory; Mustard; Nobles; Nucleus of Cells; Orange Color; Organic Conditions in the Body—Organic Diseases—Organic and Structural Disorders — Organismic Rhythm; Ovary (the Right Ovary); Oxygen in the Blood and Body; Physical Faculties (see "Physical" under Faculties); Plant Remedies (see "Sun Group" under Herbs; "Herbs" in Sec. 1 of this Article); Pons Varolii; Prana; Proteids; Protoplasm; Remedies (see "Drugs" in Sec. 1 of this Article); Retentive Faculties (see Memory); Right Side of Body—Right Eye in the Male — Right Ovary — Right Testicle (see Right); Rulers; Rhythm (Organic); Saffron Color; Second Half of Life (see "Second Half" under Life); Sinews (see "Sinews" under Nerves); Solar Spectrum — Orange In (see Colors); Spine—Dorsal Region of (see Dorsal); Spleen (the Vital Etheric Fluid entering thru the Spleen); Stomach (the ☉ in ♋ rules the Structure of); Strength of Youth (see Youth); Structural and Organic Diseases — Structure of the Body; Sunday; Sun Flower; Sympathetic Nervous System (see Sympathetic); System (the Physical System in the Male); Temperament — Bilious Temperament (see Choleric); Testicle (Right); Vital Energy—Vital Force—Vital Body—Vital Etheric Fluid—Vital Parts—Vital Powers—Vital Principle —Vital Spirit in Women—Vital Group (see Vital; "Vital" in Sec. 1 of this Article); Vitality; Women—Emotional Nature In—Left Eye In—Vital Spirit In (see Women); Yellow Color; Youth —The Strength of Youth (see Youth).

— SECTION THREE —

DISEASES RULED BY THE SUN — Afflictions and Disturbances Caused by the Adverse Aspects and Influences of the Sun—Here are a few axioms, or concise statements, about the influences of the ☉ as related to health and disease, which the student and Diagnostician should keep in mind when forming judgment. The diseases of the ☉ are organic, constitutional, and structural. The chief diseases of the ☉ are of the Brain, Eyes, and Heart, and the ☉ has special affinity with the Eyes. The ☉ especially rules health matters in the male. The ☉ is more powerful in health matters when above the horizon, or hyleg, and weaker when below the horizon, and not hyleg, or dignified by sign and aspect, as the ☉ rules the day, and the ☽ the night. The sign the ☉ is in at B. indicates an internal part of the body which is very sensitive, and if the ☉ is also afflicted, complaints of such organ, or part, usually result, and according to the sign and nature of the afflicting planet. The ☉ angular and diurnal exerts his strongest influence in health matters, and gives greater resistance to disease. Chronic diseases are regulated by the motion of the ☉. Fevers and Inflammations produced by the ☉ are slow, but severe, while those of ♂ are quick, destructive, and contagious. The ☉ in whatever part of the map largely determines the strength of the constitution in both males and females. The ☉ joined with ♂ causes the same diseases as ♂ in the Asc. at B. In judging of the importance of the disease, note whether the ☉ is weak by sign and house. The ☉ cadent, and in a common sign, tends especially to ☉ diseases, but less so when the ☉ is in the 9th H., or in the ♐ sign. There is less liability to sickness and disease when the ☉ is angular, and the powers of immunity and resistance to disease are greater. As the ☉ is the source of the vital powers, his position, aspects, house position, and dignities in the map should be looked to first in determining the nature and prognosis of the disease, as a weak ☉ at B. usually means an earlier death, short life, while a strong and dignified ☉ at B. promises long life, stronger vitality, and good health. The following are classed as diseases of the ☉. See these subjects in the alphabetical arrangement when they are merely listed here—

Acne; Acute Fever — (See "Fevers" under Acute).

Apoplexy; Appendicitis; Arms—Pains In—(See Arms).

Arteries—Diseases of—(See Arteries).

Augmented Vitality — A Morbid Condition—(See "Augmented" under Vitality).

Back—Pains In—Weak Back—(See Back).

Barrenness; Bilious Affections — (See Bile).

Blood Disorders — Inflamed Blood — Disorders of the Blood in the Arms, Hands, Legs, and Feet — Blood Disorders—Blood Impurities—Blood Poisoning—(See Blood, Impure).

Bloody Flux—(See Flux).

Bowel Disorders—Cancer of—Inflammation of—Organic Diseases of—Humours In—(See Bowels).

Brain—Diseases of—Disordered Brain —Brain Fever—Organic Brain Trouble —Structural Defects of—(See Brain).

Breakings Out—On the Body—On the Face—In the Throat—(See Eruptions, Face, Pimples, Skin Diseases, Throat).

Breath—(See "Foul" under Breath).

Cancer—Carcinoma of the Bowels or Stomach—(See Carcinoma).

Cataract; Catarrhs; Choroiditis—(See Choroid).

Chronic Inflammation—(See "Chronic" under Inflammation).

Circulation—Of the Blood—Disorders of—(See Circulation).

Cold—Diseases Arising From—The ☉ afflicting the Asc. at B., and by dir. (See "Diseases Arising From" under Cold).

Combustion; Conjunctivitis—(See Conjunctiva).

Constitutional Diseases—(See Constitution, Organic, Structural).

Cramps; Cuts; Death — The ☉ causes death by Pleurisy, or some obstruction in the Viscera. Also death by fire if other testimonies concur. (See "Death" under Fire, Pleura; "Obstruction" under Viscera).

Defects—The ☉ causes structural defects, and with attending diseases. (See Defects; "Defects" under Eyes; Structural).

Defluxions; Deprived — Of the Solar Forces—(See "Forces" in Sec. 1 of this Article).

Destroys Life — (See "Anareta", "Ascendant", in Sec. 1 of this Article; "Death" in this section).

Diphtheria; Distempers — In Secret Parts — Venereal — (See "Distempers" under Secrets; Venereal).

Dizziness; Dropsy;

Dry and Hot Diseases—(See "Dry and Hot" under Heat).

Ease In Disease—(See "Ease" in Sec. 1 of this Article).

Epidemic Fevers—(See Epidemics).

Eruptions; Eyes—All Infirmities In—Defects—Disorders—Hurts To—Sore Eyes—Structural Disorders—The Right Eye In Males and the Left Eye In Females Affected—(See Eyes).

Face—Breakings Out—Pimples—(See "Eruptions" under Face; Pimples).

Faintings; Feet—Swellings In—Blood Disorders In—(See Feet).

Fevers—Acute Fevers—Epidemic Fevers — Fevers Generally — Putrid Fevers—Spotted Fever—The fevers produced by the ☉ are slow, but severe. (See "Fevers" under Acute; "Epidemic Fevers" under Epidemics; "Generally" under Fevers; "Fevers" under Putrid; Spotted).

Fire—Death By—(See "Death" under Fire).

Fistula; Flushings — Heated Flushings — Hot Flashes — (See Flushings; "Flushings" under Heat).

Fluxes; Foul Breath — (See "Foul" under Breath).

Fullness—Of the System—(See "System" under Fullness; Plethora).

Giddiness—In the Head—(See Dizziness).

Glaucoma; Gravel; Growths—Fungus, or Vegetable Growths In the Body — (See Fungus; "Growths" under Vegetable).

Head — Giddiness In — Headaches — Violent Pains In — (See "Dizziness; "Pains" under Head; Headaches).

Heart — Diseases of — Palpitations — Organic Heart Trouble—Trembling of —Weak Heart—(See Heart).

Heat—Diseases Arising from Excess of Heat, as Fever and Sunstroke—(See Fever; Flushings; "Extreme Heat", "Flushings", under Heat; "Sunstroke" in this section).

Heated Flushings — (See Flushings; "Heat" in this section).

Hemorrhage; Hereditary Diseases — (See Constitutional, Heredity, Organic, Structural).

Hips — Hot Humours In — (See "Hot Humours" under Hips).

Hoarseness—(See Larynx).

Hot and Dry Diseases—Hot Humours —(See "Dry and Hot Diseases" under Heat; "Hot Humours" under Hips; "Heat" in this section).

Hot Flashes — (See "Flushings" in this section).

Hour—The ☉ Hour—A critical hour to fall ill, as the sickness is liable to be violent and dangerous. (See "Hours" under Planets).

Humours — In the Bowels — Hot Humours In the Hips — (See "Hot Humours" under Hips; "Bowels" under Humours).

Hurts to Eyes — (See "Hurts To", "Left", "Right", under Eyes).

Hyperaemia; Hysteria; Impure — Impurities — Impure Blood — Impure Breath — (See "Foul" under Breath; Impure).

Inflammation—Of All Kinds—Chronic Inflammation — Inflamed Blood — Inflammation of the Lungs and Stomach —(See "Inflamed" under Blood; "All Kinds", "Chronic", under Inflammation; "Pulmonitis" under Lungs; "Inflammation" under Stomach).

Inherent Diseases—Innate Diseases— (See Constitutional, Heredity, Innate, Organic, Structural).

Internal Diseases—(See Internal).

Iritis—(See Iris).

Judgment of Sun Diseases — Rules For—(See the Introduction to this section).

Keratitis—(See "Cornea" under Eyes).

Knees—Lameness In—Tumors In— (See Knees).

Lameness — (See "Lameness" under Knees).

Left Eye — Defects In — Hurts To — (See "Left Eye" under Eyes; "Eyes" under Left).

Legs—Impure Blood In—Milk Leg— Pains In—Weakness In—(See Legs).

Life — Tends to Destroy Life When, etc.—(See Anareta, Ascendant, Directions, Life, in Sec. 1 of this Article; "Death" in this section).

Life Forces—Disorders of—Obstruc-

tion of—(See "Life Force" under Life; "Obstructed" under Vital; "Forces of the Sun" in Sec. 1 of this Article).

Lungs — (See "Hyperaemia", "Inflammation", under Lungs).

Mania — May be caused by afflictions to the ☉ at a Solar Ingress into ♈. (See Mania).

Measles; Megrims — Migraine — (See Migraine).

Milk Leg—(See Legs).

Mouth—All Diseases of—(See "Affections" under Mouth).

Neck — (See "Swellings In" under Neck).

Nervousness—Nervous Prostration— Neurasthenia—(See Nerves).

Nutriment—(See "Superfluous" under Nutrition).

Obstructions—In the Stomach—(See "Poor Digestion" under Digestion; "Obstructions" under Stomach).

Ophthalmia — (See "Conjunctivitis" under Conjunctiva).

Organic Diseases—Organic Defects— (See Organic, Structural; "Defects", "Eyes", in this section).

Pains—In the Arms, Back, Head, and Legs — (See "Pain" under these subjects; Headaches; "Periodicity" in Sec. 1 of this Article).

Palpitation—(See Heart).

Periodicity — Many Diseases Follow a Solar Periodicity—(See "Periodicity" in Sec. 1 of this Article).

Phlegmatic Dolens—(See "Milk Leg" under Legs).

Physical Disorders — (See Physical; "Disordered System" under System; the various paragraphs in this section).

Pimples; Plague; Plethora; Polypus;

Prostration — (See "Prostration" under Nerves).

Putrid Fevers—(See Putrid).

Quinsy—(See "Quinsy" under Tonsils).

Reins Disordered—(See Reins).

Remedies — Sun Remedies — (See "Drugs" in Sec. 1 of this Article; "Treatment" in this section).

Respiratory Troubles—(See the various paragraphs under Breathing, Bronchial; "Diseased", "Pulmonitis", under Lungs).

Right Eye—Disorders and Defects of In Males—Hurts To—(See "Right Eye" under Eyes; "Eyes" under Right).

Scrofula; Scurvy; Secret Parts—Distempers In — Violent Pains In — (See Secrets).

Sharpness of Urine—(See Urine).

Short Diseases—(See "Illnesses" under Short).

Shoulders — (See "Pains In" under Shoulders).

Sight—Weak Sight—Disorders of Vision—(See Sight).

Slow Diseases—(See "Slow Diseases" under Slow).

Smallpox; Solar Forces—Deprived of —(See "Forces" in Sec. 1 of this Article).

Sore Eyes — Sore Throat — (See Conjunctiva; "Inflamed" under Eyes; "Sore" under Throat).

Spine—Disorders of—(See Spine).

Spotted Fever—(See Spotted).

Stomach — Disorders of — Structural Defects of — Obstructions In — (See Stomach).

Stone; Strangury — (See this subject under Urine).

Structural Diseases — And Defects — (See Organic, Structural).

Sudden Swoonings—(See Fainting).

Sun Spots — As Causes of Disease — (See Spots).

Sunstroke—Heat Prostration—The ☉ denotes; the ☉ afflicting the Asc.; the ☉ or ♂ afflicted in ♈; a fiery sign on the Asc. at B., and many planets in a fiery sign; Subs at AT, AX, and KP. (See "Excessive Bodily Heat" under Heat; "Sunstroke" under Voyages; "Denotes", "Signifies", in Sec. 1 of this Article).

Superfluous Nutriment — An afflicted ☉ inclines to excesses in eating. (See Gluttony; "Superfluous" under Nutrition).

Swellings—In the Neck or Feet—(See "Dropsy" under Feet; "Swellings" under Neck).

Swoonings — (See "Falling Fits" under Fainting).

Syncope—(See Fainting).

Thighs — (See "Hot Humours" under Hips).

Throat — Breakings Out In — Sore Throat—Swellings In—All Diseases In —Organic Defects of—(See Throat).

Tissues—Combustion of—(See "Combustion" under Tissues).

Treatment—The diseases of the ☉ are combatted by ♄ remedies, as ♄ opposes the ☉. (See Antipathy, Opposites).

Tremblings — (See "Palpitation" under Heart; Tremblings).

Tumors—(See "Tumors" under Knees; "Periodicity" in Sec. 1 of this Article).

Tympanites; Urine — Sharpness of — Strangury—(See Urine).

Venereal Distempers—(See Venereal).

Violent Pains—In the Head—In the Secrets — (See "Violent Pains" under Head, Secrets).

Vision—Disorders of—(See Sight).

Vital Force—Vital Powers—Vitality —Disturbances of—Obstructions To— (See the various paragraphs under Vital, Vitality).

Vitality Augmented — A Morbid Plus Condition — (See "Augmented" under Vitality).

Weak — Weak Back — Weak Sight — (See "Weak" under Back, Sight).

Weakness—In the Heart—In the Legs —(See "Weakness" under Heart; "Weak Legs" under Legs).

Women — Hysterics In — (See Hysteria).

SUBCONSCIOUS MIND—Corresponds to the ☉. (See "Subconscious" under Mind).

SUNBURNT COMPLEXION—(See "Sunburnt" under Complexion).

SUNDAY—Ruled by the ☉. (See Week).

SUNKEN—Hollow—(See "Sunken" under Chest, Eyeballs, Face; "Falling In Of" under Cheeks; Hollow).

SUNRISE AND SUNSET—Effects of In Health Matters—(See "Sunrise" under Sun).

SUNSTROKE—Heat Prostration—(See "Sunstroke" under Sun).

SUPERABUNDANCE—Over-Abundance —Excessive—

Air — Death or Disease from Superabundance of Air—(See "Superabundance" under Air).

Animal Heat — Superabundance of — (See "Animal Heat" under Heat).

Blood—(See "Too Much Blood" under Blood; Plethora).

Cold — Disease or Death from Too Much Cold, or a Cold Body — (See "Superabundance" under Cold; "Cold" under Weather).

Energy — Superabundance of Energy, and of Vital Energy — (See "Superabundance" under Energy; "Energy" under Vital).

Heat — (See "Superabundance" under Heat; "High Fever" under Fever; "Sunstroke" under Sun).

Moisture—(See "Superabundance" under Moisture).

Passion — (See "Excess of Passion" under Passion).

Rain — (See "Too Much Rain" under Rain). See the subjects under Exaggerated, Excess, Excesses, Hyper, Increased, Over, Too Much).

SUPERFICIAL MIND — (See "Superficial" under Mind).

SUPERFLUOUS — (See "Superfluous" under Nutrition).

SUPERIOR—

Ganglion — The Superior Cervical Ganglion — (See "Cervical Ganglion" under Cervical).

Jaw—Superior Maxillary Bone—(See "Upper Jaw" under Jaws).

Superior Planets—The Major Planets —♅, ♆, ♄, ♃, ♂. Called Superior because their orbs are beyond those of ☿ and ♀, the Inferior Planets, and because they are more powerful in their effects. (See "Major Planets" under Major).

Superior Vena Cava—(See Veins).

SUPERSENSITIVE — (See Hyperaesthesia; "Supersensitive" under Sensitive).

SUPERSENSUAL—(See "Excess Of" under Passion; "Supersensuality" under Sensual).

SUPERSTITIOUS — (See Fears, Forebodings, Horrors, Obsessions, Premonitions; "Superstitious" under Religion; Spirit Controls, Strange, Terrors, Visions, etc.).

SUPPORTING — The Constitution Supported—A ♃ quality. Also the ☉ supports by giving the Vital Life Forces. Mars supports by giving energy, dynamic power, and also is constructive by helping to cleanse the body of impurities by fevers and inflammations. (See Conservation, Preservation).

SUPPRESSIONS—Inhibitions—Restrictions—Ablation or Removal of Organs or a Part of the Body—Suppressions are caused principally by ♄, and also by ☋. (See Dragon's Tail, Saturn).

Ablation of Organs — By Suppression —(See Removal).

Cutaneous Breathing—Suppression of —(See "Cutaneous" under Asphyxia).

Faeces — (See "Suppression" under Faeces).

Functions—(See "Suppressed" under Functions).

Gastric Juices — (See "Stopped" under Digestion; "Ailments Of" under Fluids; "Obstructions" under Stomach).

Growth Suppressed—(See "Arrested" under Growth).

Mammae — (See "Ablation" under Breasts).

Mental Powers — Mind — Suppression of—(See Idiocy, Imbecility; "Arrested Mental Powers", "Retarded", under Mentality; "Weak Mind" under Mind).

Nervous Energy — Suppression of — (See "Nervous Energy" under Nerves).

Organs — Suppression of — (See Remote, Removal; "Ablation" under Tonsils).

Ovaries — Ablation or Suppression of —(See "Ablation" under Ovaries).

Stools—(See "Faeces" in this section).

Sweat—(See "Lessened" under Sweat).

Tonsils—(See "Ablation" under Tonsils).

Urine — (See "Suppression" under Urine). For further study along this line see Ablation, Arrested, Atrophy, Cirrhosis, Clots, Concretions, Congelation, Congestions, Crystallization, Deafness, Decrease, Delayed, Diminished, Dropsy; "Hindered" under Elimination; "Arrested" under Emotions; Hardening, Hindrances, Hyperacidity, Impediments, Impure, Incurable, Inhibitions, Interrupted, Irregular, Lessened, Lethargy, Morbid, Mutes, Obstructions; "Osseous Deposits" under Osseous; Prevented, Restraints, Retarded, Rigidity, Sclerosis, Slow, Sluggish, Stone, Stoppages, Suspensions, Thickening, Tumors, Twelfth House.

SUPPURATION—The Formation of Pus —Pus Diseases—Festering Diseases— (See Pus).

SUPRA-RENAL CAPSULES — Supra-Renal Plexus—(See Adrenals).

SURE—

Sickness Sure — (See "Sure to Come" under Sickness).

Sure Death — (See "Certain" under Death; Fatal; "Death" under Immediate; "Time of Death" under Time).

SURFACE—Constrictions of the Blood Vessels of the Surface—(See Centripetal, Chill, Constrictions, External; "Chill" under Skin).

Rubbing of Surfaces—Fremitus—(See Friction).

Serous Surfaces—Mucous Surfaces— (See Mucous, Serum).

SURFEITS—A Surfeit—Excess—A Surplus—More Than Enough—Congestion —♃ denotes diseases arising from surfeits, congestion, over-functional activity of a part, parts, or organ ruled by the sign he is in at B., or by dir. Also caused by ♃ afflicted in ♋; ♃ afflicted in ♎, from too much blood; ♃, ♂, and ♀ cause degeneration thru excesses and surfeits; ♃ afflicted in ♉, ♋, or ♑, surfeits from wrong and evil diet; the ☉ afflicted in ♉, and especially by ♃; a disease of the ☽, and afflictions to the ☽ at B., and by dir.; the ☽ afflicted in ♋ or ♎; the ☽ afflicted in ♑, or afflicting the hyleg therefrom; the ☽ in ♉ or ♎, ♂, or ill-asp. ♄ (or ☿ if he be of the nature of ♄) when first taken ill, or at decumbiture, and occasioned by high living and surfeits; ♄ afflicted in ♋; ♂ afflicted in ♑ or ♒; ♂ by periodic revolution to the ♂ or ill-asps. ♃ or the ☽; ♀ afflicted in ♋ or ♐; ♀ afflicted in ♎, from too much eating and drinking; ♀ afflicted at B., and to the ♂, P, or evil asp. the Asc. by dir.; ♀ in ♋ in the 6th H., afflicted, or afflicting the ☽ or Asc.; the Asc. to the ill-asps. ♀ by dir. (See Appetite, Degeneration; "Evil Diet" under Diet; Drink; "Excesses In" under Eating; Epicureans, Feasting; "Excesses In", "Rich Food", under Food; Gluttony; "High Living" under High; Intoxication, Over-Indulgence, Plethora, Redundant).

Blood—Surfeit Arising from Too Much Blood—♃ afflicted in ♎. (See "Too Much Blood" under Blood).

Congestion — Surfeits From — (See Congestion).

Death from Surfeits—The ☽ occi. at B., and afflicting the hyleg by dir., and according to her familiarity with the malefics. (See "Death" under Indiscretions).

Degeneration — Thru Surfeits — (See Degeneration).

Diet — Surfeits Arising from Wrong and Evil Diet—(See "Evil Diet" under Diet; "Excesses In", "Rich Food", "Sweets", under Food).

Disease — Arising from Surfeit — Denoted by ♃. (See Jupiter, Toxaemia, Tumors).

Drinking and Eating—Surfeits From —(See Diet, Drink, Eating, Food, Wine).

Dropsy from Surfeits — (See the Introduction under Dropsy).

Eating — Surfeits by Excesses In — (See "Excesses" under Eating).

Excess—Excesses—Surfeits and Diseases From—(See "Excesses In" under Eating, Food; Excess, Excesses, Gluttony).

Fevers—From Surfeits—(See "Fever" under Heart, Liver; "Feverish" under Lungs).

Food — Surfeits from Excesses In — (See "Excesses In" under Food).

Fullness—From Surfeits — (See "Engorgement" under Fullness; Plethora).

Functions—The Functions Disordered by Surfeits—(See "Over-Activity" under Functions).

Gluttony—(See "Big Appetite" under Appetite; Gluttony).

Gout—From Surfeits—The ☉ or ♃ afflicted in ♉, and usually from over-eating, and excess of rich food. (See "Rich Food" under Food; Gout).

Impure Blood—Caused by Surfeits—(See "Too Much Blood" under Blood; Impure).

Over-Functional Activity—From Surfeits — (See "Over-Activity" under Functions).

Plethora—From Surfeit—(See Plethora).

Puffing—Of the Body—(See Inflation, Plethora, Puffing).

Rheumatism — From Surfeits — (See "Tendency To" under Rheumatsm).

Rich Foods — Surfeits From — (See "Dainty", "Rich", under Food).

Stomach — Afflicted with Surfeits — (See "Surfeits" under Stomach).

Wine—Surfeits from Excessive Use of —(See Wine).

SURGEONS — Surgical — Surgery— ♂ rules Surgeons and Surgical Operations.

Danger to Surgeons—The ☽ to the ♂ or P. Dec. Aldebaran by dir.; the M.C. to the ♂ ♂ if ♂ be afflicted at B.

Dealing with Surgeons — Good Time For—When the ☽ is applying to the good aspects ♂, but this is not a good time for a surgical operation. (See "Rules" under Operations).

Dishonest Surgeons—Tricky In Diagnosis—♅ or ♂ in ♏ or ♓, and especially if ♅ and ♂ form an evil asp. to each other at B.

Fame As Surgeon—♂ ☀ or △ the ☉ at B., and the stronger the position of ♂ the greater will be the success. (See "Honors" in this section).

Fortunate—As Surgeons—The ☉ Sig. in ♏; the ☽ Sig. ♂ ♂, and ♂ well-aspected by ♃; ♆ in good aspect ♂; ♃ Sig. ♂, ☀, or △ ♂; the 29° ♐ on the Asc. at B.; many planets in fiery signs, and especially if ♂ be strong, dignified, and well-aspected by the ☉, ☽, or ♃. (See "Good Surgeon", "Honors", in this section).

Good Surgeon—Makes a Good Surgeon —The ☉, ☽, or ♂ well-aspected in ♏; the ☽ Sig. ♂ ♂ and ♂ well-dignified; the ☽ on the Meridian, or coming to, and well-aspected by ♂; ♆ or ♅ in good aspect to ♂; ♃ Sig. ♂ ♂; ♃ in ♏, and especially when in ♂ or good asp. to ♂; ♂ strong at B., and well-dignified; ♂ in the 6th or 10th H., and well-aspected; ♂ well-aspected in ♍, ♏, or ♓; ♂ ruler of the horoscope; ♂ and ☿ together lords of the employment; ♂ ☀ or △ the ☉ at B., and especially when ♂ is otherwise strong; surgeons should have good aspects between the ☉, ♂, and ☿ to make good surgeons and be successful; ♂ ♂ ☿; ♂ in ♏ in the 10th H.; ♂ well-aspected in ♓, or ♂ in the 12th H., and especially in hospitals, prisons, or asylums; the ☀ or △ aspects of ♂, skillful in surgery; any aspect of ♂ to the ☽ or ☿; ♂ in good aspect to ♅; ♀ Sig. ♂ ♂ and ♂ well-dignified; ☿ and the Lights configurated with ♂; ☿ ♂ or good asp. ♂ at B.; ☿ joined with ♂ makes good surgeons; in Hor'y Q. ♂ Sig. of the party, or the Sig. in a fiery sign, or in ♏; born under ♏; the 6th face of ♋, the 1st face of ♌, or the 6th face of ♐ culminating on the M.C.; ruler of the

employment in ♏, strong and well-aspected; the majority of planets in fiery signs at B. (See Barbers, Chemists; "Physicians" under Healers).

Honours—Promotion and Honours for Surgeons—Periods of Success for Surgeons—The ☉, ☽, or ♃ Sig., and to the good asps. ♂ by dir.; the ☉ to the ♂ or P. Dec. Aldebaran, surgeons gain distinction for a time; the ☉ in the 11th H. in ♈, well-aspected by ♂ at the Vernal, and lord of the year; the Prog. ☽ ☀ or △ ♂ if ♂ is well-aspected at B.; ♂ ☀ or △ the Asc. or M.C. by dir.; lord of the Asc. in his own dignities if he apply to ♂ exalted, and in an angle.

Horary Questions—In Hor'y Q. ♂ Sig. of the party, or the Sig. in a fiery sign, or in ♏, denotes a Surgeon, Chemist, or Physician..

Hospitals — Prisons and Asylums — Successful as Surgeon In—♂ well-aspected in ♓ or the 12th H. (See Hospitals; "Asylums" under Insanity; Prisons, Twelfth House).

Operations—The Best Time for Surgical Operations — (See "Rules" under Operations).

Periods of Success — For Surgeons — (See "Honours" in this section).

Study of Surgery—Inclined To—Any aspect of ♂ to the ☽ or ☿ inclines to the study of Medicine or Surgery.

Surgeon of the Body—(See Silica).

Unfeeling Surgeons — Cruel — ♅ in ♉ or ♏ and □ ♂, or ♂ in ♉ or ♏ and □ ♅.

Unfortunate as Surgeons—♂ in a weak sign at B., and sorely afflicted by the ☉, ☽, and malefics, and tends to downfall or disgrace under the evil directions of ♂ to the Asc., M.C., ☉ or ☽ along thru life; an absence of the ☉, ☽, ♃, or ♂ in the ♏ sign at B., or strong ♂ influence in ♍, the 1st, 6th, 8th, or 12th H. at B. (See "Unfortunate" under Healers).

Vivisectionists—(See this subject).

SURLY—(See "Gruff" under Manners).

SURROUNDINGS—Much Affected By—The 4th face of ♋ on the Asc. (See Environment, External, Influenced, Negative Nature, Receptive, Susceptible).

SUSCEPTIBILITY — Susceptible—Idiosyncrasies—Predisposition—Receptivity—Sensitiveness, etc.—

Climate—Susceptibility to Changes In —(See Climate).

Cold or Colds — Susceptible To— (See Cold, Colds).

Contagious Diseases—Infectious Diseases — Susceptible To — (See Contagions, Epidemics, Infectious Diseases, Magnetism, Scorpio).

Disease — Susceptibility To — Predisposition To—(See Attracts; "Susceptibility" under Disease; Magnetism, Predisposed, Propensities; "Much Sickness" under Sickness; "Low" under Vitality; "Weak Body" under Weak).

External Influences — Susceptible To —(See Environment, External, Influenced; "Negative Nature" under Negative; Passive, Receptive).

Fever — (See "Susceptibility" under Fever).

Inflammation — (See "Susceptibility" under Inflammation).

Nervous Susceptibility—(See "Susceptibility" under Nerves).

Psychic Susceptibility — (See Clairvoyance, Emotions, Feelings, Hyperaesthesia, Hynotism, Magnetism, Mediumship, Psychic, Sensitives, Suggestion).

Women—More Susceptible to Disease and Outside Influences—(See "External Influences" under Women). For further study along this line see Diathesis, Flexible, Heredity, Idiopathy, Idiosyncrasies, Organic, Plastic, Structural.

SUSPENSIONS—

Animation — Suspended Animation — (See "Buried Alive" under Burial; "Suppressed" under Functions; Trance).

Breathing—(See "Suspension" under Breathing).

Digestion—(See "Stopped" under Digestion).

Functions—(See "Suppressed" under Functions).

Heart Action—(See "Stoppage" under Heart).

Stomach—(See "Stopped" under Digestion; "Obstructions" under Stomach). See Interrupted, Irregular, Obstructions, Retentions, Stoppages, Suppressions.

SUSPICION—Of Some Venereal Disease —(See Venereal).

SUSPICIOUS—♄ strong at B. tends to give a suspicious mind. (See Jealousy, Mistrustful; Scepticism; "Many Sorrows" under Sorrow).

SWALLOWING—Deglutition—Difficulty In—(See Deglutition).

Swallows Glass — Nails, etc. — Case — (See "Human Ostrich" under Human).

SWAMPS — Marshes — Ruled by the ☽. (See Dampness, Moisture, Moon).

SWARTHY — Swarthy Complexion — Swarthy Brown—(See "Swarthy" under Brown, Complexion).

SWEAT—Sudor—Sweating—Perspiration—Sweat is an excrementitious fluid and ruled by the ♏ sign. (See Excrement). It is also the work of the ☽, as the ☽ influences the fluids of the body. The ☉ exerts a sudorific action.

Anhidrosis — Anidrosis — (See "Lessened" in this section).

Axillae—Fetid Perspiration In—(See Axillae).

Bloody Sweat — (See Haematidrosis" in this section).

Bromidrosis — Fetid Perspiration — Caused by ♂ in signs; ♂ in ♓, fetid perspiration in axillae; ♂ in ♓, in feet. (See "Excessive" in this section; Axillae; "Bromidrosis" under Feet).

Chromidrosis — Colored Sweat — Observed in the attacks of Hysteria when the sweat may be blue, brown, yellow or red. Also in Jaundice the sweat may be yellow. (See Hysteria, Jaundice).

Colliquative Sweats—(See Phthisis).

Deficiency Of — (See "Lessened" in this section).

Diaphoretics — (See "Sudorifics" in this section).

Dysidrosis—Impaired Perspiration In Hands or Feet—♂ afflicted in ♍ or ♓. (See Dysidrosis; "Bromidrosis" in this section).

Excessive Sweating—Hyperidrosis— ♂, a hot planet, in any sign, tends to more heat and sweating in the part of the body ruled by such sign, and the perspiration to be more fetid if confined. (See "Bromidrosis" in this section; "Night Sweats" under Phthisis).

Excrement—Sweat is an excrementitious fluid, ruled by the ♏ sign. The Menses and Urine also belong to this class. (See Excrement).

Feet — Fetid Perspiration In — (See "Bromidrosis", "Excessive", in this section).

Fetid Perspiration — (See "Bromidrosis", "Excessive", in this section).

Frequent Perspirings — The ☽ in ♊ under the Sun's beams, or ☌ ♅, ♄, or ♂ at decumbiture, or at the beginning of an illness, tends to frequent attacks of perspiration (Hor'y).

Haematidrosis — Menidrosis — Bloody Sweat — Caused by the extravasation of blood into the cells and ducts of the sweat glands, capillary hemorrhages of nervous origin, or may be a species of vicarious menstruation known as Menidrosis. The ♒ sign rules strongly over the nerves and blood, and ♅, ♄, or ♂ badly afflicted in this sign, and also afflictions in ♑, the sign which rules the surface, are causes of these conditions, and along with other influences which tend to great nervousness, anxiety, stress or strain.

Hands—(See "Dysidrosis" in this section).

Hyperidrosis — (See "Excessive" in this section).

Impaired Sweating—(See the various paragraphs in this section).

Lessened—Anidrosis—Diminuation or Absence of—Occurs during the high fevers of ♂. Also ♄ in ♏ may cause it by hindering the excretion of sweat in a chronic condition. (See "Obstructions" under Excretion; "High Fever" under Fever).

Menidrosis — (See Haematidrosis" in this section).

Night Sweats—(See Phthisis).

Profuse Sweating—(See "Excessive", "Night Sweats", in this section).

Sudorifics—Diaphoretics—Agents Inducing Sweating — ☉ remedies. (See Sudorific).

Suppression Of — (See "Lessened" in this section).

Vicarious—Vicarious Menses Thru the Sweat Glands — (See "Haematidrosis" in this section).

Violent Sweating—Unseasonable—The ☽ in ♈, □ or ☍ ♄ (or ☿ if he be of the nature of ♄) when first taken ill, or at decumbiture (Hor'y).

SWEET—

Sweetbread—(See Pancreas).

Sweet Signs—Of the Zodiac—The Airy Signs, ♊, ♎, ♒, and are said to give a sweet disposition. (See "Amiable" under Manner).

Sweet Things — Sweets — Comfits — Ruled by ♃, and ♃ rules all sweet things in merchandise. Also ruled by ♀, and especially in their use, and afflictions to ♃ and ♀ tend to over-indulgence in sweets, sugars, and pastries. (See "Sugar", "Sweets", under Food).

SWELLINGS — Swelling — Swollen — Tumefactions—Morbid Enlargements — Various planetary influences may cause swellings, according to causes, habits, inherent tendencies, and the parts of the body afflicted. The following subjects have to do with swellings, which see in the alphabetical arrangement when only listed here—

Abdominal Swellings — (See "Swellings" under Abdomen).

Abscesses; Ankles — (See "Swollen" under Ankles).

Arms — ♃ in signs which rule the Arms, Hands, Legs and Feet tends to swellings in these parts. (See "Swelling Of" under Feet; "Swelling In" under Hands; "Swellings In" under Legs).

Blisters; Bloating; Body Swollen — Puffy Body—The ☽ in ♓ and afflicted by the ☉ or ♂ when taken ill (Hor'y). (See Puffing; "Fleshy" in this section).

Boils; Carbuncles; Carcinoma; Cysts; Death By—Caused by ♃.

Discutients — Resolvents — Agents Which Remove Swellings—♂ remedies. (See Discutients, Resolvents).

Distentions; Dropsy; Effusions; Emphysema; Enlargements; Extravasations—(See Effusions).

Face—(See "Bloated", "Swellings", under Face).

Feet—(See "Dropsy", "Swelling", under Feet; "Arms" in this section).

Fixed Points — Swellings At — ♀ diseases.

Flatulence; Fleshy—Fleshy and Swelling—♃ in watery signs; ♏ on the Asc.; ♓ on the Asc., fleshy and swelling. (See Bloating, Puffing; "Body Swollen" in this section).

Fluids — Swellings from Accumulations of — (See Accumulative, Cysts, Dropsy, Hydrocephalus, etc.).

Gas—Swellings By—(See Flatulence, Gas, Tympanites, etc.).

Glands — (See "Swellings" under Glands).

Gout; Hands — (See "Arms" in this section).

Head—(See "Swells" under Head).

Hips and Thighs — (See "Swellings" under Hips).

Hydrocele; Hydrocephalus; Hydrothorax; Hyperaemia;

Incurable Swellings — Those Arising from Structural Defects and Incurable Diseases — (See Aneurysm, Apoplexy; "Tumor" under Brain; "Valves" under Heart; Incurable, Inflation, Malignant, Morbid, Ruptures, etc.).

Inflammations; Inflation; Jaws—(See "Swollen" under Jaws).

Knees — (See "Swellings In" under Knees).

Knots; Larynx—(See "Swollen" under Larynx).

Legs—(See "Arms" in this section).

Localized Swellings—(See Local).

Lower Parts — Swellings In — The ☽ afflicted in ♑, ♒, or ♓. (See "Swellings" under Ankles, Feet, Knees, Legs).

Neck — (See "Swellings In" under Neck; "Glandular Swellings" under Throat).

Nodules; Painful Swellings—(See Abscesses, Boils, Carbuncles; the subjects under Pain; "Mumps" under Parotid; Sore, Sores, Testes, Throat, Tonsils, etc.).

Plethora; Puffing Up—Of the Sinews of the Nerves — (See "Puffing" under Nerves; Puffing).

Puffy Body—(See "Body Swollen" in this section).

Remedy—For Swellings—(See Discutients, Resolvents).

Resolvents — An Agent to Reduce Swelling — (See Discutients, Resolvents).

Ruptures; Scrotum — Swelling In — (See Hydrocele, Scrotum, Testes, Varicocele, Varicose).

Secret Parts—(See "Swellings" under Secrets).

Sharp Pains By—Caused by ♂. (See "Pains" under Sharp).

Sinews — (See "Puffing Up" in this section).

Skin — (See Eruptions, Inflammation, Rashes; the various paragraphs under Skin).

Sore Parts—(See Sore).

Sores; Testes — (See "Swollen" under Testes).

Thighs—(See "Hips" in this section).

Throat — (See Diphtheria, Neck; "Glandular", "Swellings", under Throat; Tonsils).

Tonsils—(See "Tonsilitis" under Tonsils).

Treatment Of — (See Discutients, Resolvents).

Tubercles; Tumors; Ulcers; Varicocele; Varicose Veins—(See Varicose).

Wind—In Stomach and Bowels—(See "Gas", "Wind", under Bowels; Flatulence; "Wind" under Stomach; Tympanites).

SWIFT DISEASES—Swift, Rapid, and Violent Fevers — Diseases tend to be swift and violent when ♂ is in the Asc., and death may follow if the ☉ and ☽, and their dispositors, be afflicted. (See Acute, Directions; "High" under Fever; Fierce, Fulminating, Pernicious, Quick, Rapid, Sharp, Severe, Vehement, Violent Diseases).

SWIMMING—

In the Head — (See Dizziness, Fainting, Vertigo).

In Water — Dangerous to Go Near Water—(See Bathing, Drowning).

SWINDLER—♄ Sig. □ or ☍ ☿, a swindler, cheat, or thief; ♂ Sig. in ♊, a mere swindler, but the good aspects of the ☉, ♃, or ♀ mitigate the evil; ☿ Sig. ☌

♂. (See Cheating, Deceitful, Dishonest, Forgers, Gambling, Liars, Pettifogging, Shrewd, Thieves, etc.).

SWINE—Pigs—Hogs—The interest of the native in hogs, swine, sheep, small animals, etc., for good or ill, profit or loss, is denoted by the 6th H. (See "Small Animals" under Animals; Hogs, Sheep, Sixth House).

Performing Pig—(See Hogs).

Resembles Swine — (See "Animal Forms" under Monsters).

SWOLLEN—(See Swellings).

SWOONINGS — Faintings — Sudden Swoonings—(See "Falling Fits" under Fainting).

SWORD—

Death By—Injury By—Severe Stabs or Cuts—The ⊙ or ☽ ori., and afflicted by ♄ or ♂; ♂ disposes to; ♂ afflicting the hyleg by dir., and holding the dominion of death, and especially when the radical map shows a violent death; the ☽ Sig. □ or ☍ ♂; in Hor'y Q. lord of the 1st H., or the ☽ in ♉ or ♌, and ♉ ♂, slain by the sword, or in a quarrel; the 5° ♎ on the Asc. (See Contests, Cuts, Duels, Murdered, Quarrels, War).

Eyes—Injury to the Eyes by a Stroke, Blow, the Sword, or Burning—The ⊙ in the Asc. or M.C., ♂ rising before him, and the ⊙ ☌ or ☍ the ☽, and may cause blindness; the ⊙ in an angle, in the same sign with the ☽, or in ☍, and with ♄ and ♂ ori. to the ⊙, ascending before him, and ♄ and ♂ occi. of the ☽; the ⊙ or ☽ afflicted by ♂ by dir., and the Lights with Nebulous Stars at B.; the ☽ to the ☌, P., or evil asp. ♂ by dir., and the ☽ afflicted at B. (See "Burning" under Blindness; "Hurts", "Injuries", under Eyes).

SYBARITES—(See Epicureans).

SYCOSIS — (See "Barber's Itch" under Barbers).

SYMBOLS—Signs—

Children — (See "Symbols Of" under Children).

Death — (See "Symbols Of" under Death).

Disease — (See "Indicators Of" under Disease).

Health—Signs of Good or Bad Health —(See "Signs Of" under Health).

Signs of Zodiac — Symbols of — (See each of the Signs in the alphabetical arrangement, as Aries, Taurus, etc.).

SYMMETRY OF FORM—(See Beautiful, Comely, Handsome, Harmonious, Well-Formed, Well-Proportioned, etc.).

SYMPATHY—Sympathetic—

Cured by Sympathy—Paracelsus was the first Physician to suggest giving Similars, and drugs to produce symptoms similar to those of the malady. Hahnemann afterwards demonstrated this principle in Homeopathy. Hippocrates also observed that diseases were sometimes cured by similars. The Astrological selection of remedies was based principally upon Sympathy and Antipathy. The diseases of ♄ were treated by the remedies of ♂, which is by sympathy, or ♂ diseases by ♄

remedies, as ♄ and ♂, both being malefics, work together in greater sympathy. Also ♄ diseases are treated by ♄ remedies; ♂ diseases by ♂ remedies; ♃ diseases by ♃ or ♀ remedies, etc., which is treatment by sympathy. It was also believed by the Ancients that every planet was capable of curing its own diseases, and by its own remedies. Thus remedies of the ⊙ and ☽ were used to cure Eye Diseases. Diseases of the Spleen were cured by ♄ remedies; of the Liver, by ♃ remedies, etc. Dr. Broughton, in his book, "The Elements of Astrology", on page 241, gives a Table of the Friendships and Enmities of the Planets. Planets which rule opposite Signs of the Zodiac are not in sympathy. Thus ♌, ruled by the ⊙, is in ☍ to ♒, ruled by ♄; the ♋ sign, ruled by the ☽, is in ☍ to ♑, ruled by ♄, and by this rule we can know that ♄ is opposed to the ⊙ and ☽, and not sympathetic with them, and that the diseases of ♄ can be mitigated by remedies of the ⊙ or ☽. The ♈ and ♌ signs are in △ aspect, and in harmony, and ♂, the ruler of ♈, is friendly with the ⊙, and the ⊙ has his exaltation in ♈, the sign of ♂, etc. Thus when the diseases of the ⊙ are treated by ♂ remedies, it is by sympathy, or vice versa. (For further influences along this line see Antipathy, Colors, Cure, Drugs, Harmony, Herbs, Hippocrates, Homeopathy, Medicines, Ointments, Opposites, Paracelsus, Polarity, Praeincipients, Remedies, Rhythm, Signature, Treatment, etc.).

Disease—Disease Caused by Sympathy —There is an analogy and sympathy between each Sign of the Zodiac and some definite zone of the body. If the afflicting planet governs the part diseased or afflicted, it is caused by sympathy. If the disease is in the bones, and ♄ is the cause of it, it is by sympathy, as ♄ rules the bones. If the disease is in the Arteries, Veins, and Circulation, it is usually caused by ♃ or ♀, the rulers of these matters, etc. If by the ⊙, diseases of the Brain, Eyes, or Heart, with which the ⊙ has affinity. (See Attracts, Complications; "Complications" under Disease; Magnetic, Polarity, Relapses, Zones).

Disposition—Sympathetic Disposition —(See "Nature" in this section).

Expression — A Sympathetic Expression On the Face—Born under ♃. (See Honest, Humane, Kind, Sincere, Smiling, etc.).

Irritation—Sympathetic Irritation—A ♀ disease and affliction.

Lactation—Case of Sympathetic Lactation—(See Lactation).

Narrow Sympathies—Cruel—Not Humane—(See Narrow).

Nature — A Sympathetic Nature and Disposition — Born under ♃ and ♃ strong at B.; the 5th face of ♌ on the Asc.; ♒ on the Asc., and with the ⊙, ☽, and several planets in ♒. (See "Expression" in this section).

Signs of Zodiac—The Signs In Sympathy with Each Other—The Signs in ✳ and △ relation to each other are in sympathy, or harmony. In matters of health and disease all the fixed signs are in sympathy, and form the Fixed Cross of ♉, ♌, ♏, and ♒, and afflictions in any of these signs tend to affect by sympathy all the parts, or organs, ruled by these signs, which is the fundamental cause of complications in disease. Thus afflictions in ♉ or ♏ tend to affect the throat and sex organs. So with the Cardinal and Common Signs. Afflictions in ♈, ♋, ♎, and ♑ tend to affect the Head, Stomach, Kidneys, and Skin. Afflictions in the Common Sign Cross, ♊, ♍, ♐, and ♓, to affect the Lungs, Bowels, Thighs and Feet. (See Complications).

Sympathetic Nervous System — This System is ruled by the ☽, ♄, ♂, and the ♍ Sign. It automatically takes care of the process of digestion ruled by ♍, and also pertains to the care of indvidual preservation. It begins with ♈, the Cerebral Pole of Paracelsus, and ends with ♏, the Genital Pole of Paracelsus. The Peripheral Sympathetic Nerves are ruled by ♄ and ♑. (See Cerebral, Genitals; "Pathological Action" under Mars). The ☽ Group of Herbs, by their physiological action, tend to act upon, and to especially affect the Sympathetic Nervous System. This system is also called the Involuntary Nervous System, and rules over the involuntary functions and actions of the body, such as Digestion, the Heart Action, etc. (See Cardia).

SYMPTOMS — Symptoms In Disease — The word "Symptoms" is not mentioned much in the Textbooks of Astrology, as Astrology deals more with the Causes and Philosophy of Disease rather than Symptoms. However, I have run across the following influences, which have been referred to as Symptoms—

Consumption — (See "Symptoms Of" under Consumption).

Peculiar Symptoms—In Disease—The ☽ ☌, □, or ☍ ♄, ♅, or ♂, or passing their place at B., or at the beginning of an illness, and especially when the ☽ is afflicted by ♅. (See "Course of Disease" under Peculiar).

Symptoms of Spleen—(See "Symptoms Of" under Consumption). For the symptoms which may attend the various diseases, and which may be caused by the planetary aspects and afflictions, see in the alphabetical arrangement the subject you have in mind.

SYNCOPE—Swooning or Fainting—(See Fainting).

SYNOCHA—(See "Continuous Fevers" under Fever).

SYNOVIAL—Synovial Fluid—Synovial Membrane — The Synovial Fluid is ruled by the ☽, and is also under the internal rulership of the ♓ Sign, and lubricates the joints. The Synovial Serum is connected with the ♓ Sign, and the ☉ and ☽ acting thru ♓ tend to affect the Synovial System. (See Ligaments).

Bursitis — In the Knee Joint — (See Bursa).

Hardening — Of the Synovial Membrane—Caused by ♄, and making the joints, limbs, and spine rigid. (See "Hardening" under Joints).

Hips and Thighs—Drying Up of Synovial Fluid In Joints of—♄ afflicted in ♐. (See "Synovial" under Hips; Lubrication).

Inflammation—Of the Synovial Membrane—Synovitis—Caused by ♂, and in the part of the body ruled by the sign he is in at B.; ♂ in ♐, in hips and thighs; ♂ in ♑, in the knees, etc.

Joints — Lack of Synovial Fluid In Joints — Drying Up of — ♄ influence. (See "Hardening" under Joints; Lubrication).

Knees—Bursitis In—Inflammation In —(See Bursa; "Inflammation", "Joint", "Synovitis", under Knees).

Lack of Synovial Fluid—In the Joints —Drying Up of—The ☽ afflicted in ♑; the work of ♄, as ♄ tends to dry up the bodily fluids. (See "Drying Up" under Fluids; Lubrication).

Synovial Troubles—The ☽ afflicted in ♑.

Synovitis — (See "Inflammation" in this section).

Thickening—Of the Synovial Membrane—A ♄ disease, and caused by retention of wastes. (See Hardening, Retention, Thickening).

Vertebrae — Lack of Synovial Fluid Between the Vertebrae—♄ afflicted in ♌. (See "Diseases" under Vertebrae).

SYPHILIS — Lues — Syphilic Blood — Pox—A ♀ disease, and caused by afflictions to ♀; ♀ denotes death by; ♀ afflicted in ♏; the ☽ in ♏ and afflicted by the ☉ or ♂ when taken ill (Hor'y); the ☽ in the 6th H., and afflicting ♀ in ♏; the ☽ to the ☌ or □ ♂ by dir.; ♅ in ♎, and with venereal eruptions on the skin; ♅ in ♏ and in □ or ☍ ♂ ♀; ♂ in ♎ when ♂ is the afflictor in the disease, Lues may be suspected; a ♎ disease and afflictions in ♎; when on the Asc., ♎ gives a milder form of syphilis; a ♏ disease and afflictions in ♏, and affecting also the throat (♉) by reflex action, and causing syphilitic ulcers of the throat; ♏ on the Asc. tends to the worst form of syphilis; a ♓ disease and afflictions in ♓, and tends to affect the Matrix and Secrets where syphilitic contagion is involved; caused by Fixed Stars of the nature of ♀; Subs at KP and PP.

Chancre — Called "Hard Chancre" to distinguish it from the Soft Chancre of Gonorrhoea. The Chancre is the primary sore, or ulcer, which may appear on the Privates, or other parts of the body in syphilis, and is caused by the foregoing influences.

Death by Syphilis — ♂ afflicting the hyleg, or Giver of Life, by dir.; ♀ denotes death by; ♀ afflicted in ♏ in the 8th H., holding the dominion of death, and afflicting the hyleg. (See Gonorrhoea, Private Diseases, Scandalous Diseases, Venereal).

Eruptions — Syphilitic Eruptions On the Skin — ♅ afflicted in ♎, and also afflictions in ♎, and due to greater disturbance of the action of the kidneys.

Rectum — (See "Syphilis" under Rectum).

Throat — Syphilitc Ulcers In — ♂ afflicted in ♏; afflictions in ♉ or ♏.

SYSTEM—The System—Systemic—The Constitution—The Physical Body—
Arterial System—(See Arteries, Blood, Circulation).
Assimilative System—(See Assimilation).
Cleansing — Of the System — (See Cleansing).
Clogging—Of the System—(See Clogging, Retentions, Suppressions, Wastes).
Cold—The System Affected Generally with Cold—(See "Body" under Cold).
Decayed System—(See "Death" under Decay).
Deranged System—(See "Disordered" in this section).
Digestive System — (See Digestion, Gastric, Indigestion, Stomach, etc.).
Disordered System—Deranged System — Physical Disorders — The ☉ in the 6th H. in cardinal signs, and afflicted by the ☽ or ♄; the ☉ to the ill-aspects ♄, ♃, or the ☽ in the radix; the ☽ to the bad aspects ♄, ♃, or ♀ by dir.; ♄, ♅, or ♆ in ♍, and afflicting the ☉ or ☽; ♄ or ♃ in the 6th H. in a cardinal sign, and afflicted by the ☉ or ☽; the appearance of Comets tends to a deranged system and many·evils upon Mankind. (See Deranged, Disease, Disordered; "Bad" under Health; Ill-Health; "Much Sickness" under Sickness; "Low" under Vitality; "Weak Body" under Weak).
Dry System—(See "Body" under Dry).
Excretory System—(See Elimination, Excretion).
Females — Regularity of the System In — (See "Functions In" under Females; "Females" under Regularity).
Fluidic System—(See Fluids).
Fullness—Of the System—(See "System" under Fullness).
Functional System—(See Functions).
Glandular System—(See Glands).
Hot System — (See "Animal Heat", "Excessive Bodily Heat", under Heat).
Impurities — Of the System — (See Elimination, Excretion, Faeces, Impure, Sweat, Urine, Wastes, etc.).

Inactive State—Of the System—(See Apathy, Dull, Inactive, Inertia, Lassitude, Lethargy, Listless, etc.).
Invigorated System — Strong System —(See "Active Body" under Active; "Abundance of Energy" under Energy; "Abundance of Health" under Health; Invigoration; "Good" under Resistance, Stamina, Tone, Vitality; Robust, Ruddy, Rugged; "Body" under Strength, Strong; "Vigorous Body" under Vigor).
Irregularities—Systemic Irregularities—(See Irregularities).
Lymphatic System—(See Lymphatic).
Moist System—(See "Bodily Temperament" under Moisture).
Muscular System—(See Muscles).
Nervous System—(See Nerves).
Preservation — Of the System — (See Conservation, Nutrition, Preservation).
Readaptation — In the System — (See Readaptation).
Regularity — Of the System — (See Regularity).
Relaxation—In the System—(See Relaxation).·
Vascular System — (See Arteries, Blood, Capillaries, Vascular, Vaso, Veins, Vessels).
Venous System—(See Veins).
Vitality—Of the System—(See Vitality).
Wastes — Of the System — (See "Impurities" in this section).
Wasting—Of the System—(See Consumptions, Emaciation; "Malnutrition" under Nutrition; Phthisis, Tabes, Tuberculosis, Wasting, etc.).
Weak System — (See Weak). For other subjects along this line, and not listed here, look in the alphabetical arrangement for what you have in mind.
SYSTOLE—The New Moon is the Lunar Systole. (See "New Moon" under Moon).
SYZYGES — The Times of the ☌ and ☍ of Planets. Also the New and Full Moon, or the ☌ and ☍ of the ☉ and ☽.

T

TABES — Tabefactions — Gradual and Progressive Emaciation — The ☽ afflicted in ♓; Subs at SP and KP. (See Atrophy, Consumptions, Emaciation, Lean; "Progressive Muscular Atrophy" under Muscles; "Malnutrition" under Nutrition; "A Living Skeleton" under Skeleton; Thin, Wasting, etc.).
TACHYCARDIA—(See this subject under Heart).
TACITURN—Habitually Silent and Reserved — Not Inclined to Converse — ♄ influence, and ♄ strong at B. (See Grave; "Taciturn" under Manner, Speech; Melancholic, Recluse, Renunciation, Reserved, Retiring, Seclusive, Serious, Solitude; "Refuses to Talk", "Taciturn", under Speech).
TACT—Tactful—(See "Good Judgment" under Judgment).

TAENIA—Tenia—A Parasitic Worm—Cestode—(See Cestode, Parasites, Tapeworm, Worms).
TAKING COLD — (See "Taking Cold" under Colds).
TALENTS—
Good Talents—Talented—(See Genius; "Great Ability" under Great).
Perverted Talents — (See Cheating, Criminal, Dishonest, Gambling, Pettifogging, Thieves, etc.).
Unused Talents—(See Dull, Idle, Improvident, Inactive, Indifferent, Lazy, Listless, Negative Nature, Passive, Procrastination, Slovenly, Vagabond, Wanderer, etc.).
TALIPES—Talipes Varus—Club Foot—(See "Club Feet" under Feet).
TALISMANS—(See Amulets).

TALK—Speech—(See "Talk", "Talking to Oneself", under Speech; Tongue, Voice).

TALL BODY—High Stature—♅ and ☿ lengthen the body, and make taller, and especially when rising in the Sign they rule. Uranus on the Asc. tends to tallness and the true Uranians are usually very tall people. The tallest people, and Giants, usually have the ♐ sign upon the Asc. at B. The ♌ sign rising is the next tallest. The fiery and airy signs upon the Asc. give a tall person, while the earthy and watery signs produce short people. For the general influences producing a tall body see "Tall Body" in this section.

Abnormally Tall—(See Giants; "Abnormal Growth" under Growth; "Above Average Height" under Height).

Bones — Large-Boned—(See "Large" under Bones).

Commanding and Tall — (See Commanding).

Compact and Tall—(See Compact).

Corpulent and Tall—(See Corpulent).

Elegant and Tall — (See "Tall and Elegant" under Elegant).

Enlarged Body — (See "Body" under Enlarged).

Erect and Tall—(See Erect).

Fair and Tall—(See Fair).

Fat and Tall — (See "Tall and Fat" under Fat).

Fine and Tall — (See "Body" under Fine).

Fleshy and Tall—(See "Fleshy Body" under Fleshy).

Forehead — A Deep and Tall Forehead—(See "Deep" under Forehead).

Full-Bodied and Tall — (See "Body" under Full).

Giants; Graceful and Tall — (See Graceful).

Growth — (See "Abnormal" under Growth).

Hairy and Tall — (See "Body" under Hair).

Handsome and Tall—(See "Tall and Handsome" under Handsome).

Height—(See "Above Average" under Height).

High Stature — (See Giants; "Tall Body" in this section).

Inclined to be Tall — ♍ influence; ♍ on the Asc.

Large and Tall—(See "Large Bones" under Bones; "Tall, Large and Strong" under Large).

Large-Boned and Tall—(See "Large" under Bones).

Long Body—(See "Body" under Long; "Tall" in this section).

Plump and Tall—(See Plump).

Rather Tall — ♒ influence; ♒ on the Asc., rather tall, and never short.

Slender and Tall — (See "Tall and Slender" under Slender).

Smooth, Tall Body—(See Smooth).

Spare and Tall—(See Spare).

Stature Above Average—(See "Above Average" under Height).

Stout and Tall—(See Stout).

Straight and Tall—(See Straight).

Strong and Tall — ♃ or the ☽ in ♌, partile the Asc. (See "Body" under Strong).

Swarthy and Tall — ♂ in ♈, partile the Asc. (See "Swarthy" under Complexion).

Tall Body — High Stature — In this paragraph is given a summary of the influences causing tallness, and with the accompanying characteristics — The SUN in ♊ or ♐, tall and well-proportioned; the ☉ strong and dignified, tall, fleshy, strong, and of large frame; the ☉ in ♍, partile the Asc., tall, slender, and well-proportioned; the ☉ in ♎, partile the Asc., tall, erect, straight, and upright; the MOON in ♊, partile the Asc., tall, well-made, well-formed, comely, and upright; the ☽ in ♌ in the Asc., or partile the Asc., tall, of fine proportions, strong, and large-boned; the ☽ in ♍, partile the Asc., tall and rather ruddy; the ☽ in ♎, partile the Asc., tall and of pleasing form; the ☽ in her increase gives a tall, fat, plump, and full body; the ☽ ori. gives a body more tall, corpulent, and smooth; URANUS on the Asc.; SATURN in ♊, in good asp. the Asc., tall and well-proportioned; ♄ in ♍, partile the Asc., tall and thin; ♄ in ♎, partile the Asc.; ♄ ori. makes the body taller than when he is occidental, and also with a stout and hairy body; born under JUPITER, tall, well-made, and upright; ♃ indicates a tall and commanding body; ♃ in ♊, partile the Asc., rather tall; ♃ in ♌, partile the Asc., tall, strong, well-made, and large-boned; ♃ in ♎, partile the Asc., tall, elegant, and handsome; ♃ in ♐, partile the Asc., tall, fine, upright, and well-made; MARS in ♈, partile the Asc., and ori., tall and less swarthy; ♂ in ♊, partile the Asc., tall, well-made, and well-formed; ♂ in ♎, partile the Asc., tall, commanding, and well-proportioned; ♂ in ♐, partile the Asc., tall, compact, and well-made; ♂ in ♒, partile the Asc., tall, well-set, and corpulent; VENUS or ☿ in their own signs or exaltation give tallness; the ✳ and △ aspects of ♀ give a tall and elegantly made body; ♀ in ♊, partile the Asc., tall, slender, but well-made; ♀ in ♌, partile the Asc., tall, well-boned; the ☽ in ♍, partile the Asc. tall made, and well-formed; ♀ in ♍, partile the Asc., tall and well-proportioned; ♀ in ♐, partile the Asc., well-made, tall, and well-formed; born under ♀ and ♀ ori., tall, handsome, elegantly made, erect, straight, and upright; MERCURY indicates tall and thin persons; ☿ in ♊, partile the Asc., tall, well-made and upright; ☿ in ♎, partile the Asc., tall, handsome, and not thin; ☿ in ♐, partile the Asc., tall, well-shaped, but rather spare and large-boned; ♊ on the Asc., tall, erect, straight, fair, well-formed; ♌ on the Asc., commanding and tall; ♍ on the Asc., compact, well-made, well-proportioned, rather slender, and inclined to be tall; ♎ on the Asc., tall, beautiful, graceful, handsome, elegantly made, well-framed; ♎ on the Asc. and ♀ ori., tall, straight, upright, and elegantly made; the last few degrees of ♎ rising tend to a shorter and stouter body due to the nearness of the ♏ influence; ♐ on the Asc., tall, strong, well-made, well-formed, and this sign on the Asc. produces the tallest people of all signs, as a rule; ♒ on the Asc., strong, healthy, robust, well-set, and rather tall. (See the various paragraphs in this article).

Tallest People—♐ on the Asc.

Thin and Tall—(See "Thin and Tall" under Thin).

Upright and Tall — (See Erect, Straight, Upright).

Well-Formed and Tall — (See Well-Formed).

Well-Made and Tall — (See Well-Made).

Well-Proportioned and Tall — (See Well-Proportioned).

Well-Set and Tall—(See Well-Set).

Well-Shaped and Tall — (See Well-Shaped).

TAN COMPLEXION —Tanned —Tawny — Bronzed — Brownish Color — (See "Tan" under Complexion).

TAPEWORM—One of the Cestoda—A Parasitic Worm In the Bowels—♀ or ☿ afflicted in ♍; afflictions in ♍; Subs at SP (8D), and at PP (2L). (See Worms).

TAR — Pix Liquida — Obtained by the destructive distillation of the wood of the Pine Tree. Pine Trees, Cone-bearing Trees, are ruled by ♂. Turpentine is also procured from the Yellow Pine, and other varities of Pine. The blistering, caustic, counter-irritant, and penetrating qualities of Tar Preparations, and of Turpentine, are qualities of Mars Remedies. (See Rubefacients).

Coal Tar—(See Xylene).

TARSUS — The Bones of the Instep of the Feet — Are under the structural rulership of the ♓ Sign, and correspond to the Carpal Bones in the Hands, ruled by ♍. (See Feet, Hands, Wrists).

TARTAR—On the Teeth—(See "Tartar" under Teeth).

TASTE—Gustatory—The Sense of Taste —The Sense by which Savors are Perceived — Ruled by ♂ and the ♉ sign. The Gustatory Process is ruled by ♉. The Hebrew Letter "Tzaddi", which is connected with the ♒ Sign, is also connected with the Sense of Taste. (See Gustativeness).

TASTES—

Abnormal Tastes—Along Food Lines — (See "Tastes", "Unnatural", under Food).

Appetites—Peculiar Tastes and Appetites — (See Appetites; "Peculiar" under Food; "Appetites" under Peculiar).

Clothing—Dress—Peculiar Tastes In —(See "Peculiar" under Dress).

Food—(See "Peculiar Tastes", "Sugar", "Sweets", under Food).

Perverted Tastes — ♀ afflicted in the 1st or 12th H.; ♅ ruler of the horoscope, and afflicted; ♀ ruler of the horoscope, and afflicted by malefics. (See Cravings, Depraved, Drink; "Per-

verted Tastes" under Food; Narcotics, Perversions).

Refined Tastes—Born under the Airy Signs. (See Genteel; "Elegant" under Manner; "Elegant Mind" under Mind; Refined).

Strange Tastes — And Fancies — (See "Distempered Fancies" under Fancies).

TAURUS—The Second Sign of the Zodiac, and ruled by ♀, and also affiliated with the 2nd H. This is the night Sign of ♀, and ♎ is the day Sign of ♀. The ☽ has her exaltation in ♉, and ♂ his detriment. Taurus is the Sign opposite to ♏, and is supplemental to the ♏ sign, and for this reason planets in either of these signs tend to affect the throat and sex organs, as this sign represents the sex organs, along with the ♏ sign. Taurus is the sign of "The Bull", and is symbolized by the Bull, and the sign partakes much of the animal nature of the Bull, being stubborn, obstinate, and easily maddened, as a rule. Also being the sign of ♀, the ♉ people have their artistic and musical side, and also strong desires for pleasure, gluttony, and excesses, which makes this the sign for Gout, Rheumatism, and earlier death thru over-eating, and the excessive use of rich foods. Statistics show that ♉ people are averse to taking baths, and cold baths especially. Taurus is a fixed sign, feminine, negative, cold, dry, bestial, brutish, hurtful, four-footed, animal, commanding, crooked, earthy, even, fruitful, hoarse, luxurious, melancholic, nocturnal, northern, vernal, vital, unfortunate, and a sign of short ascension. It is rather fruitful, belonging to ♀, one of the Givers of Children. The ♉ and ♏ signs are the strongest of the negative signs, and these signs upon the Asc. at B. give considerable vitality, and are next to the fiery and airy signs in degree of vitility. Being cold and dry the ♉ sign requires some energizing from without. Taurus is influenced by all the Fixed Signs, and belongs to the Fixed Sign Cross of ♉, ♌, ♏, and ♒, and planets in these signs at B. tend to affect all the organs and parts ruled by these signs, as the Throat, Heart, Sex Organs and Nature, and the Blood. Planets in these signs also tend to make disease more stubborn, enduring and permanent, and an afflicting planet in one of these signs at the beginning of an illness tends to keep the disease going until the planet changes signs, and enters a common sign. The ♉ people have a great fear of disease, and should never be told anything discouraging about their case when sick, as they are very susceptible to suggestion. They hold onto disease, and also tend to bring disease upon themselves due to their strong animal appetites, and tendency to excesses, and to suffer from Impure Blood, Gout, Rheumatism, and end with Paralysis or Heart Trouble. They are usually a materialistic class of people, earth-bound, covetous, of good business abilities, and the wealth of the world is largely in their hands. The ☽ well-aspected in ♉ is strong, and tends to regular functions, methodical habits, and good health. This sign has affinity with the Ears, Tongue, Bladder, and Sex Organs. The body given by ♉ is much like that of the ♏ sign. Taurus gives a strong neck and shoulders, and often stooped; full nostrils and thick lips, pensive brows, wavy or curling hair, dark eyes, full and broad forehead, heavy jaws, and a thick neck. The Colors ruled by this sign are red, and red mixed with citrine, and white mixed with lemon. For Countries ruled by this sign see "Taurus Sign" under Nations. The Pathological Qualities of this sign are anger, brooding, love of luxury, excessive stubbornness, and uncontrolled emotions. The Organ of Coordination is situated in ♉. (See Coordination). Also the Larynx, situated in ♉, was originally built up by the ♏ sign, and taken from ♏, and this is the reason why the voice and throat are so quickly affected by sex changes, as at puberty, or by sex diseases, as in the throat ulcers of syphilis. (See Larynx, Puberty, Voice).

TAURUS RULES—See the following subjects in the alphabetical arrangement—Arbor Vitae; Arteries and Veins of the Neck and Throat; Atlas Vertebra; Axis Vertebra; Base of the Brain; Beard; Belladonna; Bladder (has affinity with); Blood Vessels (Minor Blood Vessels of the Neck); Bones of the Neck; Brain (Base of); Carotid Arteries; Cerebellum; Cervical Nerves and Vertebrae; Chin, and Beard of Chin; Colors — White mixed with Lemon — Red mixed with Citrine; Coordinated Action (Organ of); Countries (see Nations); Drugs (Belladonna, Sodium Sulphate); Ears (has special affinity with); Eustachian Tubes; External Carotid Arteries; Externally rules the neck, throat, and lower back part of the head,'the occipital region; Fear of Sickness; Functions, and Disorders of the Functions when the ☽ is afflicted in ♉; Generative Organs (♉ represents these organs, along with ♏); Glands (the Parotids and Salivary Glands); Gullet; Gustatory Process; Head (lower back part of, and Occiput); Internally rules the Gullet, Larynx and Cerebellum; Jaw (Lower Jaw); Jugular Veins; Larynx; Lower Jaw and Lower Teeth; Neck (Bones of, Region of, Cervical Nerves of, Blood Vessels of, Carotid Arteries, Jugular Veins, Cervical Vertebrae); Nerves (the Cervical Nerves); Occipital Region; Occiput; Oesophagus (upper part of); Palate; Parotids; Passages Thru the Throat; Pharynx; Process (the Gustatory Process); Region of the Neck; Salivary Glands; Sex Organs (by reflex action to ♏); Sodium Sulphate; Structurally Rules the Cervical Vertebrae; Taste (Sense of); Teeth (Lower Teeth); Throat and All Passages Thru the Throat); Thyroid Gland and Cartilage; Tissues of the Throat; Tongue (has affinity with); Tonsils; Trachea; Tubes (Eustachian); Uvula; Veins of the Throat; Vertebrae (Cervical); Vessels (the Blood Vessels of the Neck, Carotid Arteries, Jugular Veins, Minor Blood Vessels, etc.); Vocal Cords and Vocal Organs; Windpipe.

TAURUS DISEASES—And Afflictions —The ☽ and the Benefics when in ♉, and well-aspected, tend to give greater immunity against diseases of the throat and neck, but the presence of malefics, or any planet afflicted in this sign, and also afflicted in the 2nd H., tend to disorders of the throat, neck, larynx, vocal cords, etc. The following subjects have to do with the diseases and afflictions presided over by the Taurus Sign. See these subjects in the alphabetical arrangement when only listed here—

Abscess — Of the Throat or Neck — (See "Abscess" under Neck, Throat).

Angina; Aphonia — (See this subject under Voice).

Apoplexy; Bladder Disorders — (See Bladder).

Bronchial Consumption — (See Bronchial).

Bronchocele—(See Goiter).

Collapse—Sudden Collapse—(See Collapse).

Constipation; Consumption—Bronchial and Laryngeal — (See Bronchial, Larynx).

Coordination—Disorders of Organ of —(See Coordination, Incoordination).

Cough; Countries under Taurus—Afflictions to People and Countries under the Rule of Taurus — Comets appearing in ♉; total eclipses of the ☉ or ☽ in ♉. (See Comets, Eclipses; "Taurus Rules" under Nations).

Croup; Death—♉ denotes death from Putrid Sore Throat. (See "Putrid" under Throat).

Defluxions of Rheum — Discharges of Rheum—(See Rheum; "Rheum" under Throat).

Diet—Disease from Erroneous Diet— (See "Evil Diet" under Diet).

Discharges—Of Phlegm—Of 'Rheum— (See Phlegm, Rheum).

Diphtheria; Ear Disorders — (See Ears).

Epistaxis — (See this subject under Nose).

Erratic Movements — (See "Movements" under Erratic; Incoordination).

Fluxes of Rheum — Falling Into the Throat—(See "Rheum" under Throat).

Functions — (See "Irregular" under Functions).

Glandular Swelling — In the Neck — (See "Glands" under Neck).

Goiter; Gout; Guillotine—Death By— (See Guillotine).

Halter—Death By—(See Halter).

Hanging—Death By—(See Hanging).

Heart Trouble—(See "Heart Trouble" under Heart).

Hoarseness—(See Larynx).

Impure Blood—(See Impure).

Incoordination; Inflammation—Of the Throat — (See "Inflammation" under Throat).

Irregular Functions—(See "Irregular" under Functions).

King's Evil—(See Scrofula).

Laryngitis—(See Larynx).

Melancholy; Menses Irregular — (See Menses).

Mumps—(See Parotid).

Neck — Various Disorders of — (See Neck).

Nose Bleed—(See "Epistaxis" under Nose).

Obscure Diseases—(See Obscure).

Occipital Region—Occiput—Disorders of—(See Occipital).

Pains—In the Neck and Throat—(See "Pains In" under Neck).

Palate—Disorders of—(See Palate).

Paralysis; Parotiditis—(See "Mumps" under Parotid).

Pharyngitis—(See Pharynx).

Phlegm—Discharges of—(See Phlegm).

Poisonings—Septic Poisoning In the Throat—(See "Septic" under Throat).

Polypus; Putrid Sore Throat — (See "Putrid" under Throat).

Quinsy—(See "Quinsy" under Tonsils).

Rheum — Discharges of — Fluxes of — Defluxions of—Rheum In the Throat— (See Rheum; "Rheum" under Throat).

Rheumatism; Scrofula — Of the Neck —(See "Scrofula" under Neck).

Septic Poisonings—(See "Septic" under Throat).

Sore Throat — (See "Purtid", "Sore Throat", under Throat).

Strangulation; Sudden Collapse—(See Collapse).

Suffocation; Swellings—(See "Glandular", "Swellings", under Throat; "Tonsilitis" under Tonsils).

Syphilis — In the Throat — (See "Throat" under Syphilis).

Throat—Various Disorders of—(See Throat).

Tonsilitis—(See Tonsils).

Tumors — Of the Neck or Throat — (See "Tumors" under Neck, Throat).

Ulcerated Throat — (See "Ulcerated" under Throat).

Venereal Diseases—(See Venereal).

Vocal Cords — Voice — Disorders of — (See Larynx, Voice).

Wens — In the Neck — (See Wens). See the Articles on Fixed Signs, Scorpio, Second House).

TAVERNS — Saloons — Ruled by the Fifth House.

Brawling In—♀ Sig. ☌ ♂; ♀ ill-dignified at B.; ♀ afflicted in the 5th H. If a female, ♀ afflicted in ♋ or ♏. (See Drink, Drunkenness, Harlots, Intoxication; "Low Character" under Low; Saloons, Sottishness).

TAWNY COMPLEXION — (See "Tan" under Complexion; "Tawny" under Hair).

TEARING OF PARTS — Tears — (See Bursting, Laceration, Rupture).

TEARS — The Lachrymal Apparatus — Lachrymal Canal — The Nasal Duct — The ☽ rules the Tears and Lachrymal Apparatus, and its diseases. Tears are the physiological action of the ☽. Tears are also ruled by ♆, which planet is strong in ♓ and the 12th H., the House of Sorrows.

Crying Spells — Due to Despondency, Sorrow, or Worry — Caused by ♄; ♄ afflicted in the 12th H., and also with many planets in watery signs; ♄ or ♆ afflicted in ♓ in the 12th H.; ♆ afflicted in the 12th H. (See Anguish, Bereavement, Despondency, Emotions, Gloom, Grief, Sad, Sorrow, Worry).

Ducts — The Nasal Ducts — The Tear Ducts — Disorders of — Stoppage In — Obstruction In—Tumor In—♄ afflicted in ♈; Subs at MCP (4C).

Epiphora — (See "Watery Eyes" in this section).

Excessive Flow of Tears — (See "Watery" in this section).

Hay Fever—The Lacrimation of—(See "Hay Fever" under Nose).

Humours — Lachrymal Humours — ♀ afflicted in ♈.

Obstruction—Of the Tear Ducts—(See "Ducts" in this section).

Overflow of Tears — (See "Watery Eyes" in this section).

Sheds Tears Easily—Many planets in watery signs at B., and the ☽ especially in such a sign, as in ♋, ♓, and afflicted by malefics. (See "Intensified Emotions" under Emotions; "Acute Feelings" under Feeling; "Sensitiveness" under Sensitive).

Stoppage — Of the Tear Ducts — (See "Ducts" in this section).

Tumor — Of the Tear Duct — (See "Ducts" in this section).

Watery Eyes — Epiphora — Excessive Flow of Tears — Overflow of Tears — The ☽ on ♀ afflicted in ♈; ♄ afflicted in ♈, due to stoppage of the Nasal Duct to drain away the tears; Subs at MCP (4C), and at KP (11D).

TEDIOUS — Slow — Lingering — Prolonged—

Tedious Death — (See "Lingering Death" under Death, Lingering).

Tedious Diseases — The ☉ occi., and afflicted by ♄; taken sick when the ☉, ☽, and many planets are in fixed signs; the ☉ in the 6th H. unless well-aspected; lord of the Asc. in the 6th H., afflicted by lord of the 6th, and coming to combust, and the disease will be apt to cling until death, and death be more certain if the ☽ and lords of the 1st and 8th are in the 6th H. (See Chronic; "Many Diseases" under Complications; "Disease" under Constancy; Consumption; "Continued Sickness" under Continuity; "Low Fevers" under Fever; "Long Siege" under Ill-Health; Incurable, Invalids, Lingering; "Diseases" under Long; Permanent Diseases, Phthisis, Prolonged, Relapses; "Incapable of Remedy" under Remedy; Slow Diseases, Tuberculosis, Wastings, etc.).

TEETH — Dentition — The Organs of Mastication—The Teeth are ruled by ♄, which planet rules the bones of the body. The upper teeth are ruled by the ♈ Sign, and ♉ rules the lower teeth and the lower jaw. (See Jaws). Also ♃ has influence over the teeth. Saturn affects the teeth, the skull, and the left ear. The teeth are concerned also with the ♋ Sign, and Calcium Fluoride, the ♋ Sign Salt, which supplies the calcium and lime to the teeth. (See Lime). The following subjects have to do with the teeth, which see in the alphabetical arrangement when not more fully considered here—

Absence of Teeth—No Teeth—Cannot Talk—Case—See Chap. IX in Daath's Medical Astrology.

Accidents To—Injuries To—♂ in ♈ or ♉, and afflicted, and especially with ♂ in the Asc.; ♄ in ♈ or ♉, and in the Asc., causes injuries to the teeth from blows or falls, knocking the teeth out, etc. (See "Accidents" under Head, Jaws).

Ailments Of—(See the various paragraphs in this section).

Alveolus — The Bony Socket of the Teeth—Necrosis, Decay, and Disorders of—♄ afflicted in ♈ or ♉. (See Necrosis, Pyorrhoea).

Bad Teeth—Rotten—Caries of—Erosions of — Decayed — Broken and Decayed—Indifferent Teeth—Those born under the rule of ♄ tend to, and earlier loss of the teeth; ♄ in ♈, decay of the upper teeth; ♄ in ♉, of the lower teeth; ♄ rising at B.; ♄ in the 1st H.; ♄ always gives bad teeth, decay of, and toothache, and ♄ as Sig. in Hor'y Q. indicates a party with bad and decayed teeth, or if an elderly party, one with false teeth; ♄ afflicted in ♓; the ☉ afflicted in ♏, or with this sign on the Asc. (See the various paragraphs in this section).

Beautiful Teeth—(See "Small" in this section).

Black and Rotten—Discolored—♃ Sig. in a watery sign, and especially if he be with ☋, or ill-aspected by ♄ or ♂, the teeth grow black and rotten, and tend to sudden decay; ♃ Sig. in an earthy sign tends to discoloration of the teeth. (See "Decayed" in this section).

Bony Sockets — Decay of — (See "Alveolus" in this section).

Broad Teeth—Well-Set—♃ strong at B. (See "Fore-Teeth" in this section).

Broken and Decayed — (See "Bad Teeth" in this section). Case—See "Unfortunate Case", No. 351 in 1001 N.N.

Carious Teeth—Erosion of—Ulcerous Inflammation of the Bony Structure—(See "Bad Teeth", "Toothache", in this section).

Convulsions—During Dentition—(See "Dentition" in this section).

Crooked Teeth—♄ in ♑ or ♒; ♃ Sig. in a fiery sign.

Death During Dentition—(See "Dentition" in this section).

Decay Of—Early Decay of—The ☉ afflicted in ♏, or this sign on the Asc. and afflicted; ♄ afflicted in ♈, ♉, or ♓; the 5th face of ♈ on the Asc.; the 3rd face of ♊ on the Asc. (See Alveolus, Bad, Black, Treatment, and the various paragraphs in this section; Acidity, Decay).

Defects—Dental Defects—♄ in ♌ on the cusp the 12th H., and □ the ☉, and both in fixed signs. (See the various paragraphs in this section).

Dental Maladies — (See "Diseases", and the various paragraphs in this section).

Dentated—If the edges of the teeth are dentated or furrowed it is an indication of malnutrition or scrofula. (See "Malnutrition" under Nutrition; Scrofula).

Dentist—Makes a Good Dentist—(See "Dentist" under Dental).

Dentition—Teething—Disorders of—Fits During — Convulsions During — Death From — Difficult Dentition — Paroxysms In—♉ on the Asc., with ♄ or ♂ therein tends to fits during dentition, and difficult dentition, and if the ☉ or ☽ be afflicted in a fixed sign, and the figure be a weak one generally, the child may die in a paroxysm. (See Fits).

Difficult Dentition—(See "Dentition" in this section).

Discolored—(See "Black" in this section).

Diseases Of—Dental Maladies—♄ and ♃ diseases; ♄ afflicted in ♈ affects the upper teeth and jaw, and ♄ in ♉, the lower teeth and lower jaw; ♄ afflicted in ♑, ♒, or ♓; ♄ rising at B., and especially when afflicted in the Asc. (See the subjects in this section).

Distorted Teeth — Irregular—Caused by the ☉ influence; ♄ afflicted in ♒ or ♓; ♄ Sig. in ♓ indicates such a person in Hor'y Q.; ♂ and the ♏ sign Significators of the party (Hor'y); the ♒ sign gives distorted teeth if ♄ also be ascending; the 5th and 6th faces of ♈ on the Asc.; the 2nd face of ♉, ♊, or ♌ on the Asc. Also in inherited syphilitic conditions, known as "Hutchinson's Teeth", "Screw Driver Teeth", etc., the teeth may be notched, widely separated, tapering, pointed, peg-like, and especially the two front upper incisors. (See Syphilis).

Early Decay Of—(See "Decay" in this section).

Erosion Of—(See "Bad", "Carious", in this section).

Evenly Set — (See "Regular" in this section).

Extraction Of—Avoid when the ☽ is passing thru ♈ or ♉. (See "Rules" under Operations).

Fits During Dentition — (See "Dentition" in this section).

Fore-Teeth — The Two Front Upper Teeth — The Incisors — In Hor'y Q. ♃ Sig. of the party, and in an airy sign, denotes broad upper front teeth. Also ♃ Sig. denotes some defect in the two upper front teeth, a mark of difference between them, either standing awry, or some imperfection or blackness in them. (See "Black", "Distorted", in this section).

Front Teeth — (See "Fore-Teeth" in this section).

Furrowed — (See "Dentated" in this section).

Good Teeth—Well-Preserved—♃ rising at B.; ♃ in the 1st H.; ♃ as Sig. of the party (Hor'y); ♎ gives, and with this sign on the Asc.

Grinding the Teeth — A Symptom of Worms in Children. (See Worms).

Gums—Disorders of—(See Gums).

Hutchinson's Teeth—(See "Distorted" in this section).

Ill-Placed Teeth—♄ afflicted in ♓; ♄ in ♓ in partile asp. the Asc. (See Crooked, Distorted, Fore-Teeth, in this section).

Impediments In—♄ in ♈ or ♉; a ♄ disease and affliction.

Incisors — (See "Fore-Teeth" in this section).

Indifferent Teeth—(See "Bad Teeth" in this section).

Irregular — (See "Distorted" in this section).

Jaws — (See the paragraphs under Jaws).

Knocked Out—(See "Accidents To" in this section).

Large Teeth—♏ gives; the ☉ in ♏, or this sign on the Asc.

Lime—The Lime Supply to the Teeth —(See the Introduction to this Article).

Lock-Jaw; Loosened—(See "Alveolus" in this section; Pyorrhoea).

Lower Teeth—Ruled by the ♉ sign, and ♄ afflicted in ♉ tends to decay and disorders of the lower teeth and lower gums.

Malnutrition Of—(See "Dentated" in this section).

Marks On — (See Distorted, Fore-Teeth, in this section).

Mastication; Mouth — Disorders of — (See Gums; "Affections" under Mouth).

Necrosis—(See "Alveolus" in this section).

Neuralgia Of — (See "Toothache" in this section).

No Teeth or Hair — Case — (See "No Hair" under Hair).

Notched—(See "Distorted" in this section).

Nutrition — Interfered With — (See "Dentated" in this section).

Obliquely Set—Caused by ☉ influence; the ☉ in ♈, ♉, or ♏, and afflicted by ♄.

Pain In — (See "Toothache" in this section).

Paroxysm — During Dentition — (See "Dentition" in this section).

Peg-Like — (See "Distorted" in this section).

Pitted Teeth—Caused by an Inflamed Mouth, or Stomatitis conditions. (See "Mouth" under Aphthae).

Pointed—(See "Distorted" in this section).

Projecting Teeth — (See "Prominent" in this section).

Prominent—Projecting—Given by ♒; the ☉ or ♄ afflicted in ♒; ♒ on the Asc. Also people conceived while the ☉ was in ♒ often have this defect.

Pulling Teeth—(See "Extraction" in this section).

Pyorrhoea; Regularly Set — Even Teeth—♃ strong at B., well-aspected, or in the Asc., and free from ♄ affliction.

Rotten and Black — (See "Black" in this section).

Screw Driver Teeth—(See "Distorted" in this section).

Scrofulous — (See "Dentated" in this section).

Separated — Widely Separated — (See "Distorted" in this section).

Small Teeth—Beautiful—Even—Given by ♃ strong and well-aspected at B.

Sockets—(See "Alveolus" in this section).

Sordes — Fetid Accumulations About the Teeth—Increased by ♄ in ♈ or ♉, and the teeth should be brushed after each meal.

Sudden Decay Of — (See "Black" in this section).

Syphilitic Teeth—(See "Distorted" in this section).

Tapering — (See "Distorted" in this section).

Tartar On—Caused by ♄, and with ♄ in ♈ or ♉.

Teething — (See "Dentition" in this section).

Toothache — Neuralgia of Teeth — Caused by ♄. Those born under the rule of ♄ suffer much with toothache and decayed teeth; ♄ occi. in ♈, ♉, or ♒, and afflicting the ☉, ☽, or Asc.; ♄ in ♈ or ♉ when he is the afflictor in the disease; ♆, ♅, or ♄ in ♈, and afflicting the ☉ or ☽; ♄ afflicted in ♓; ♄ in ♈ or ♎; ♄ in asp. the Asc., or in ill-asp. the lord of the Asc.; an ♈ and ♉ disease, and with malefics in these signs. (See "Bad Teeth" in this section).

Treatment—The decay of the teeth is due to the over-acid conditions in the body, due to ♄ influence. (See Acidity, Decay, Hyperacidity). A diet which keeps the body more alkaline tends to preserve the teeth, or to take an alkaline preparation daily, such as Upjohn's Citrocarbonate Effervescent drink. Natives on Islands, or in Countries where the drinking water is largely dominated with Lime and Alkali, usually have good teeth to old age, and rarely ever see or use a toothbrush. The cure for decaying teeth must be from within, and keeping down the acidity of the system, and tooth pastes and mouth washes do not remedy the trouble, altho they assist in keeping the mouth in a more antiseptic and clean condition, and to prevent Sordes. The planetary influences at birth largely determine the nature and life of the teeth regardless of treatment. People who have the positive Signs of the Zodiac prominent at birth, and well-filled with planets, are more alkaline, and have better teeth. (See Alkalinity).

Ulceration Of—Erosion of—(See "Carious" in this section).

Upper Teeth—Ruled by ♈. Disorders and decay of are caused by ♄ and other malefics afflicted in ♈. (See "Bad Teeth" in this section).

Well-Preserved—(See "Good", "Treatment", in this section).

Well-Set and Broad—(See "Broad" in this section).

Widely Separated — (See "Distorted", "Fore-Teeth", in this section).

TELEPATHY—The Telepathic and Psychometric Functions are ruled by ♆. The Telepathic Functions are also influenced by ♅, and especially in a pathological way. (See Psychic, Suggestion, Thought).

TELLURIC INFLUENCES—(See Earth).

TEMPER—Heat of Mind or Passion—Disposition to Become Angry—The Nature and Disposition—

Even Temper—Mild Temper—♎ gives, and with this sign on the Asc. at B., if the mental rulers are not otherwise badly afflicted. (See Excellent, Gentle, Harmless, Inoffensive, Kind; "Amiable" under Manner; Mild; "Lover of Peace" under Peace; Quiet, Sober).

Furious Temper— (See Cruel, Furious).

High Temper—Choleric—Excitable—Quick Temper—Goes to Mental Extremes of Anger and Fury—The ☉ or ☽ afflicted by ♂; ♄ and ♂ in angles, and in ☌ or ☍ each other; ♂ ☌ or ill-asp. ☿ at B.; due to the afflictions of ♂ at B., as ♂ is the planet of anger, fury, passion, and violence; ♂ in the 6th H. in ☍ ♀ in the 12th H.; ♋ on the Asc. (See Anger; "Choleric Temperament" under Choleric; "Destructiveness, Excitable; "Manner" under Explosive; Fury, Hasty, Impulsiveness, Irascible, Murderous, Profane, Quarrelsome, Rashness; "Tendency to Violence" under Violence, etc.).

Ill-Disposed—Ill-Tempered—A Mean Disposition—The ☽ Sig. in ♈, ♍, ♏, or ♓; the ☽ Sig. □ or ☍ ♄; in Hor'y Q. ♄ Sig. in ♈; ☿ afflicted at B., and in evil asp. the Asc. by dir.; ☿ Sig. in ♈, ♌, ♋, ♏, ♑, or ♓. (See Anger, Choleric, Cruel, Deceitful, Dishonest, Hatred; "Ill-Disposed", "Ill-Natured", under Ill; Irritable, Jealousy, Liars, Libelers, Malevolent, Malicious; "Abrupt", "Disagreeable", under Manner; "Mean Spirited" under Mean; "Active to Do Mischief" under Mischief; Revengeful, Selfish, Thieves, Vicious, etc.).

Mild Temper—(See "Even Temper" in this section).

Nasty Temper—Bitter—Short Temper—Sarcastic—♅ to the ill-aspects ☿ by dir.; ♄ ☌ or ill-asp. ♂, and especially in the 1st, 3rd, 9th, or 10th Houses. (See "Abrupt", "Disagreeable", under Manner; Sarcasm).

Quick Temper—(See "Temper" under Quick; "High" in this section).

Short Temper — (See "Nasty" in this section).

Surly Temper—(See "Gruff", "Rough", "Rude", under Manner; "Manner" under Rough).

Violent Temper — Terrible Temper When Enraged—The ☉ Sig. ☌ ♂; the ☽ ☌ ♂ in ♏; ♆ afflicted in ♏; ♅ ☌ ♄ in ♈, ♉, ♋, or ♎; ♅ ☌, ♄, P, □, or ☍ ♂; ♅ □ or ☍ ♄; ♂ afflicted in ♈, ♉, or ♎; ♂ Sig. ☌, □, or ☍ ♄, and especially in angles. (See Cruel, Fury, Madness; "Shows No Pity" under Pity; Raving; "Tendency to Violence" under Violence).

TEMPERAMENT—Temperaments—The Bodily Temperaments—In the matter of health, and in the diagnosis of disease, the subject of Temperament is an important one, as people born with a predominance of planets in the different Signs of the Zodiac, as in the fiery, airy, earthy, and watery signs, the cardinal, fixed, or mutable signs, etc., are subject to different classes of diseases, and each temperament tends to furnish its own list of diseases. Temperament is judged according to the grouping of the planets in the Chart of Birth. The four fundamental Temperaments are determined by the predominance of the planets at birth in the Temperamental Signs, the Fiery, Airy, Earthy, and Watery signs, and known as the Choleric, Sanguine, Nervous, and Lymphatic Temperaments respectively. The Constitutional, or Conditional Temperament, is determined by the predominance of planets in the Constitutional Signs, the Cardinal, Fixed, or Common Signs at birth. The Natural, or Bodily Temperaments, are determined by the Decanate of the Sign rising upon the Ascendant at birth. If the ☉, ☽, and ☿ were in ♌ at birth, ♃ and ♂ in ♈, ♅ and ♄ in ♐, and with a fiery sign on the Asc. at B., the predominating influences would be fiery, and indicate the Choleric, or Bilious Temperament. If the planets predominated in the earthy signs, and also with an earthy sign on the Asc., the temperament produced would be the Nervous Temperament, etc. If the majorities of the planets at B. were in the fiery and fixed signs, the temperament would be that of the Fixed-Fire Combination. If the majorities of planets at B. were in the cardinal and earthy signs, the combination would be Cardinal-Earth, etc. It is very difficult to determine the Temperament from any one group of Signs, but the majorities and combinations of the Temperamental and Constitutional Signs must be considered, along with the nature of the Sign and Decanate rising on the Ascendant at birth. The Ascendant, the sign on the Asc. at birth, rule and determine largely the nature of the physical body, and whether it is hot or cold, cold and dry, cold and moist, hot and dry, hot and moist, etc., and each of the four fundamental temperaments correspond to one of the bodily temperaments. Thus the Choleric Temperament has a hot and dry body. The Nervous Temperament, a cold and dry body. The Sanguine Temperament, a hot and moist body. The Lymphatic, or Phlegmatic Temperament, a cold and moist body, etc. The best balanced temperaments are those wherein the planets at birth are more equally divided between the different groups of signs, as to have all the planets in fiery signs at birth, would greatly unbalance the native. Thus the ☉ in a fiery sign, and the ☽ in a watery sign, help to balance the nature, and avoid extremes, as the fiery and watery elements oppose each other, etc. The Choleric Temperament produces anger, excitement, haste, fevers, etc., and is fiery. The Nervous Temperament leads to increased nervousness, neurasthenia, but with good mental abilities. The Sanguine Temperament is refined, artistic, intellectual, and also known as the Artistic

Temperament. The Lymphatic Temperament is dull, idle, lethargic, slow, slovenly, and with less vitality. (See "Air Signs" under Air; Ascendant, Cardinal; the Introduction under Constitution; Decanates; "Earthy Signs" under Earth; "Fire Signs" under Fire; First House; "Fixed Signs" under Fixed; "Mutable Signs" under Mutable; "Signs" under Water). The following paragraphs on the Temperaments are here arranged alphabetically for quicker reference—

Bilious Temperament—(See "Choleric Temperament" under Choleric).

Bodily Temperaments—Natural Temperaments—Physical Temperaments—(See Cold, Cold and Dry, Cold and Moist, Hot, Hot and Dry, Hot and Moist, in this section).

Choleric Temperament — (See "Choleric Temperament" under Choleric; "Hot and Dry Body" in this section).

Cold Bodily Temperament — (See "Body", "Temperament", under Cold).

Cold and Dry Body — (See "Cold and Dry Body" under Dry; "Nervous Temperament" in this section).

Cold and Moist Body—(See "Cold and Moist Body" under Moisture; "Temperament" under Lymphatic, Phlegmatic).

Constitutional Temperaments—Conditional Temperaments—(See the Introduction to this Article; the Introduction under Constitution).

Dry Bodily Temperament — (See "Body" under Dry).

Dry and Cold Body — (See "Cold and Dry Body" under Dry; "Nervous Temperament" in this section).

Dry and Hot Body — (See "Hot and Dry Body" in this section).

Hot Bodily Temperament — (See this subject under Heat).

Hot and Dry Body — (See "Choleric Temperament" under Choleric; "Heat and Dryness" under Dry; "Hot and Dry Body" under Heat).

Hot and Moist Body—(See "Hot and Moist Body" under Moisture; "Sanguine Temperament" under Sanguine).

Lymphatic Temperament—(See "Cold and Moist Body" under Moisture; "Temperament" under Lymphatic, Phlegmatic).

Melancholic Temperament — (See "Nervous Temperament" in this section).

Mental Temperament — (See Decanates; "Temperament" under Mental).

Moist Bodily Temperament — (See "Bodily Temperament" under Moisture).

Moist and Cold Body—(See "Cold and Moist Body" in this section).

Moist and Hot Body—(See "Hot and Moist" in this section).

Motive Temperament—(See Decanates, Motive).

Natural Temperaments—The Physical Temperaments — (See "Natural Temperament" under Natural; "Bodily Temperaments" in this section).

Nervous Temperament — The Melancholic Temperament—(See "Cold and Dry Body" under Dry; "Disposition" under Melancholy; "Temperament" under Nerves).

Phlegmatic Temperament—(See "Lymphatic" in this section).

Physical Temperament — (See "Natuarl" in this section).

Sanguine Temperament — (See "Hot and Moist Body" in this section).

Vital Temperament—(See Decanates; "Fixed Signs" under Fixed; the Introduction under Life).

Well-Balanced Temperament — (See Well-Balanced).

TEMPERANCE — Temperate — ♃ is the author of Temperance, and this planet is also mild and temperate in nature.

Eating and Drinking—Temperate In —(See "Moderate" under Drink, Eating).

Habits—Temperate In—♃ in the Asc., and well-aspected; ♃ ☌ ☿; ♃ Sig. in ♒; the ☽ to the ☌ ♀, the mind is more temperate. (See Control, Self-Control).

Intemperance—(See Intemperance).

Pleasure—Should be Temperate In— (See "Temperate" under Pleasure; "Moderate" under Recreations).

TEMPERATURE—

High Temperature—(See "High Fevers" under Fever).

Increase—Of Temperature—Due to the ☉ and ♂ influences. (See "Increased" under Fever).

Rapid Extremes — Of Temperature — ♂ with ♄, and both the afflictors at the same time.

Subnormal Temperature—(See "Body" under Cold; "Lack of Animal Heat" under Heat). As a pathological condition, persistent subnormal temperature may be present in cases of Consumption, Wasting Diseases, Tuberculosis, during convalescence from Fevers, in cases of Acute Alcoholism, poisoning from Carbolic Acid, or some other drug, Opiate, or Intoxicant; from loss of blood in Hemorrhage; from Melancholy, Cretinism, or Myxoedema; occurs during the intervals in Intermittent Fevers, and occurs in some cases of Starvation. See these subjects, and note the planetary influences causing them. The influence of ♄ tends to depress and suppress the heat of the body, and in most cases of subnormal temperature the ♄ afflictions are the fundamental causes of the disorder.

TEMPESTS—Danger, Injury, or Death In—(See Blizzards; "Tempests at Sea" under Sea; "Storms at Sea" under Shipwreck; Storms; "Tornadoes" under Wind).

TEMPLES — The Temporal Region — The Temples are ruled by ♃, and much affected by ♃ in ♐.

Bald About Temples—(See "Temples" under Baldness).

Hair — Light Brown Hair Near the Temples and Forehead—Born under ♃, and ♃ occidental. (See "Light Hair" under Hair).

Head—The Head Wide at the Temples—(See Decanates).

Headaches — (See "Temporal" under Headaches).

Temporal Bones—The Mastoid Bones are the protruding parts of the Temporal Bone, and subject to Mastoid Abscess. (See "Mastoid Abscess" under Mastoid).

TEMPORARY—Of Brief Duration—

Deafness—(See "Temporary Deafness" under Hearing).

Diseases—Temporary Diseases—(See Acute, Colds, Indisposition, Mild, Short Diseases, Slight).

Insanity—(See "Temporary Insanity", "Violent Forms", under Insanity).

Mental Derangement—(See "Temporary" under Mental).

TEMPTATIONS—

Many Temptations—Subject to Many Temptations to Do Wrong—Caused by the afflictions of ♂ and ♀, or of ♂ to ♀, and especially along moral and passional lines; ♂ ☌, P, □, or ☍ ♀ at B., and by dir. Also the ♂ afflictions to the ☉, ☽, ♄, ☿, or the Asc. tend to criminal acts. The afflictions of ♄ and ♂ to ☿ tend to dishonesty. The afflictions of � tend to deceit. (See Cheating, Criminal, Deceitful, Dishonest, Evil, Forgers, Gambling, Liars; "Illicit" under Love Affairs; "Loose Morals" under Morals; "Clandestine" under Sex; Thieves, etc.).

Resists Evil Temptations—(See Honest; "Good Morals" under Morals; Noble; "Popular" under Reputation; Sincere, etc.).

Yields to Temptation—(See Amorous, Debauched, Dissipated, Drink, Drunkenness, Excesses, Gluttony, Harlots, Lewd; "Promiscuity" under Love Affairs; Lust; "Immoral" under Morals; Opposite Sex, Prodigal, Recklessness; "Many Temptations" in this section).

TENACITY—

Tenacity of Life — (See Endurance; "Good Powers of Resistance" under Resistance; "Good" under Vitality; Wear and Tear).

Tenacious Nature—(See Obstinate).

TENDENCIES—The tendencies of each individual are largely shown and indicated by the Map of Birth, and also the Prenatal Epoch Map for the time of Conception. The tendencies of the Mind, the talents and abilities of the native, and the line of work most fitted for, and the various relationships he will have with the World, are indicated by the map of birth. The real inner character is indicated more by the map for the time of conception. The radical map also indicates the tendencies to disease, what diseases, and what parts of the body are more subject to affliction. The influence of the ☉ in the map shows the innate, hereditary, organic, and structural disorders to which the native is subject. The ☽ influence denotes acquired tendencies. It would take too much space here to list all the tendencies of mind and body, for good or ill, which are mentioned in this book, but will give a few suggestive subjects, and for other subjects not listed, look for it in the alphabetical arrangement. See Acquired, Animal Instincts, Attracts, Character, Conduct, Congenital, Constitution, Criminal, Depravity, Desires, Diathesis; "Tendency To" under Disease; Dishonest, Evil, Good, Habits, Health, Heredity, Honest, Idiosyncrasies, Inclined, Innate, Instincts; "Low and Base" under Low; Magnetism, Melancholic, Mind, Morals, Motives, Murderous, Nativity, Natural, Nature, Noble, Organic, Predisposition, Prenatal, Propensities, Purposes, Sickness, Sincere, Spiritual, Strong, Structural, Susceptibility, Temper, Temperaments, Violent, Vitality, Weak, Wicked, etc.

TENDER—Tenderness—

Axillae—Tenderness In—(See Axillae).

Feet—(See "Tender" under Feet).

Skin — (See "Delicate", "Tender", under Skin).

TENDONS — The Attachments of Muscles—Ruled by ♂. Are also ruled by ♄, as ♄ tends to harden, strengthen and solidify them, but ♂ brings them into action in connection with muscular activity. The Tendons are crystallized by ♄. The tendons and sinews should not be strained when ♅ is in ♎ at B. (See Achilles, Cartilage, Fiber, Ligaments, Muscles, Sinews).

TENIA—(See Taenia, Worms).

TENOR VOICE — (See "Tenor" under Voice).

TENSION—Tensity—Strain—

Body — Tension In — Produced by ♂ during muscular activity. (See "Activity", "Strength", "Tensity", under Muscles).

Eyes — Intraocular Tension — (See Glaucoma).

Fluids and Liquids — High tension with the fluids and liquids of the body is reached at the time of the Full Moon. (See "Full Moon" under Moon).

Mind—Mental Strain—The influences of ♅ and ☿ tend to bring the mind and nervous forces under greater tension. (See "Strain" under Mental, Mind; "Strain", "Stress and Strain", "Tension", under Nerves).

Muscular Strain—(See "Body" in this section; "Body", "Muscular Strain", under Strain).

Nervous Tension—High Nervous Tension—(See "High Strung", "High Tension", under Nerves; "Mind" in this section).

TENTH HOUSE — The House of the Midheaven—The M.C.—The Meridian—Medium Coeli—The Zenith, etc.—This House corresponds to the ♑ Sign, and is a feminine house, and is also the house of ♄. Planets culminate in this house, and are strong by accidental dignity if not otherwise in a strong sign, or dignified. This House rules the Knees, Hams, and Thighs, and signifies all diseases in the knees, and the upper part of the leg behind the knees. Planets in this house have a powerful influence in matters of health and disease, and especially malefic planets here, and which may be elevated above the Lights, or afflicting the hyleg from this position. This house signifies Kings, Rulers, Presidents, Princes, Judges, Magistrates, the Profession, the Employment, Vocation, Business, Honors, Preferment, Fame, Renown. Also signifies the Medicine given in sickness, the credit and honor of the native, and his business standing. In a male nativity, it rules the father, and in a female nativity, the mother, and the affairs of the mother. It also governs the hidden and Occult side of life. Saturn afflicted in this house at birth, or ruler of this house, tends to bring ruin, disgrace, self-undoing, sudden downfall, imprisonment, or an ignominious death. Also ♄ or ☌ here bring disgrace and ruin to Great Men. Mars afflicted in this house, or ruler of, tends to bring trouble with Judges, Magistrates, great misery, and also causes sickness, danger of accidents, a violent death, and much evil to a parent, according to the sex of the nativity. The malefic planets when coming to the ☌ the M.C., or the cusp of this house, and especially ♄ or ♂, indicate the danger of death, violence to the native, falls, blows, injury, or the death of a parent, as the cusp of this house is one of the very sensitive places of the map of birth, along with the Ascendant, and the ☉, ☽, and the Hyleg. The M.C. and the Ascendant are considered passive points in the map, and very strong for good or evil according to the aspects formed with them at birth and by direction. The Colors ruled by this house are Red and White. (See Nadir). For a list of the various influences of the Planets in this House, see Chapter VI in Sephar-ial's Manual of Astrology.

TERATOLOGY — The Science of Mon-sters—(See Monsters).

TERMINAL HOUSES — Terminal Signs —The Terminal Triangle—The triangle formed by the Fourth, Eighth, and Twelfth Houses have a close relation to death, the cause of death, the man-ner of death, the end of life in the physical body, and to old age. The 8th and 12th Houses have no affinity with the Ascendant. The Fourth House, which is affiliated with the ♋ sign, shows the death of the physical body, the end of life, and the fate in old age. (See Cancer Sign, Fourth House). The Eighth House, known as the House of Death, and which is af-filiated with the ♏ sign, shows the transition from the physical body to the spiritual. (See Eighth House, Scorpio). The Twelfth House, the last of the Houses, and affiliated with the ♓ sign, and last of the 12 Signs, is the house of privation, suffering, and limi-tation, and shows the death of the psychic nature. (See "Arguments For Death", "Certain Death", under Death; "End of Life" under Life; "Kind of Death" under Old Age; Pisces Sign; "Death" under Psychic; Twelfth House).

Terminal Signs—♋, ♏, ♓.

TERMINATION—The End—
Disease—Termination or the Disease —The last degrees of a sign on the cusp of the 6th H. during a sickness denote that the disease will soon end,

and when the sign on the cusp changes. The lord of the Asc. changing signs, and entering a sign in which he has dignity, also indicates the speedy termination of the disease. Benefics in the 6th H. help to end the disease, if they are free from affliction, and also not afflicting the hyleg. Malefics in the 6th H. tend to prolong the disease, or bring an evil ending to the disease. The lord of the 6th H. in the Asc., or lord of the Asc. in the 6th, the disease will continue until one of the Signifi-cators changes signs. When the ☽, or cusp of the 6th H., are in a cardinal sign, the disease tends to terminate quickly. When the afflictor is in a cardinal sign, the disease is severe, but soon over. (See Acute, Ameliora-tion, Chronic, Complications, Continu-ity, Crises, Curable; "Certain Death" under Death; "Better", "Worse", under Disease; Duration, Ease, End, Fatal; "Disease" under Force; Increase, In-curable, Lingering, Long Diseases, Minimizing, Moderation, Modification, Prognosis, Prolonged, Quick Diseases, Recovery, Recuperation, Relapse, Reso-lution, Short Diseases, Tedious, Worse).

Life—Termination of In the Physical Body—The Terminus Vitae—(See "Ar-guments for Death", "Certain Death", "Time of Death", under Death; Fatal; "Terminal Houses" under Terminal).

TERMINUS VITAE—(See Death; "Life" under Termination).

TERMS — There are certain degrees of the Zodiac, which are supposed to alter the nature of planets when they are in these degrees. Thus, a malefic in the terms of ♃ or ♀ is modified for good, and the evil of the malefic miti-gated. The word "Term" is mentioned much in Astrological Literature, and the student should be familiar with the subject. In the Article on "Terms" in Alan Leo's New Dictionary of As-trology, and also in Wilson's Diction-ary of Astrology, there are Tables of these Terms, and showing in what de-grees each planet is more powerful. A study of this subject will help stu-dents to understand better why a ma-lefic in a sign does not always act in the same way in disease. (See Degrees).

TERRESTRIAL — Of the Earth—Per-taining to the Earth—
Terrestrial Magnetism — Is ruled by ♅. (See Magnetism).
Terrestrial Signs—(See "Signs" un-der Quadrupeds).

TERRIBLE—Dreadful—Horrible—
Terrible Death — (See "Dreadful Death" under Death; Execution, Guil-lotine, Hanging, Judges, etc.).
Terrible Diseases Prevail—If ♄ and ♃ be in ☌, and ♄ have higher Latitude than ♃, terrible diseases, and Influ-enza prevail, but if the Lat. of ♃ be more Northern, the evil will be miti-gated. (See Carcinoma, Cholera, Dreadful, Epidemics; "Portentous" under Fever; Influenza, Leprosy, Ma-lignant, Outrageous, Pestilence, Plague, Smallpox, Sores, Syphilis, Ul-cers, etc.).
Terribly Wounded — In Battle — (See War).

TERRORS—Extreme Fright or Fear—
  Strange Terrors — (See Forebodings, Horrors, Obsessions, Premonitions, Spirit Controls; "Terrors", "Visions", under Strange; Visions).
  Terror to Society—(See Execrated).

TERTIAN FEVERS — (See "Tertian" under Ague).

TESTES—Testicles—The Testicles, and the Sac, or Scrotum, containing them, are ruled by ♂, as a unit. The Excretory Vessels of the Testes are ruled by the ♏ sign. The ☉ rules the right testicle, and the ☽ the left one. The Serum of the Tunica Vaginalis is ruled by the ☽. (See Serum).
  Castration—Should not be done when the ☽ is passing through the ♍, ♎, or ♏ signs. The ♉ and ♏ signs, being opposite and supplemental, castration affects the voice, and tends to make the voice effeminate, or into a tenor. (See Effeminate, Eunuchs, Voice).
  Hydrocele—A Collection of Serum in the Tunica Vaginalis — (See Hydrocele).
  Infirmities In — A ♍ disease, and afflictions in ♍; Subs at PP.
  Injuries To—Accidents To—Afflictions in ♏; ♂ afflicted in ♏. (See Scrotum, Spermatic).
  Rupture Of—Case—See "Imperfectly Formed", No. 303, in 1001 N.N.
  Scrotum—The Pouch Containing the Testes—Disorders of—(See Scrotum).
  Seminal Tubes — Tubuli Seminiferi — (See Semen).
  Spermatic Cord — Injuries To — (See Spermatic).
  Swollen Testes—(See "Mumps" under Parotid). See Generation, Genitals, Privates, Reproduction, Sex Organs, Varicocele, Varicose.

TETANUS — Tetany — Tonic Spasm — Tetanilla—A Disease with Spasmodic and Continuous Contractions of the Muscles—Caused by ♅ afflictions, and causing Incoordination. Also caused by Subs at AT, AX, MCP, and CP. This disease sometimes occurs as a result of a deficiency of the Mineral Salts in the Blood, and caused by ♄ afflicted in ♍, obstructing intestinal digestion and assimilation. Case of Tetanus — see Fig. 13G in the book, "Astro-Diagnosis", by the Heindels. (See Incoordination; "Blood" under Minerals; "Tonic Spasm" under Spasmodic).
  Fingers and Toes—Tetanic Spasm In —Tetanilla—♅ afflicted in ♍ or ♓.

TETTER — Tetters — A form of Ringworm, Herpes, Eczema—Dry Tetter—Scaly Tetter—Caused by the ☽ in the sign of the Summer Tropic at birth; the ☽ in ♋, ♌, or ♍; ♄ and ♂ in an angle, occi. of the ☉, and ori. of the ☽, and ☿ in familiarity with ♂; ♄ or ♂ in the 1st or 7th H. in ♋, ♑, or ♓, and signs ascribed to animals and fishes; ♂ or ☿ holding dominion at birth, and in familiarity with each other, and ♂ afflicting the hyleg, and elevated above the Luminaries, Tetters are increased. The Dry and Scaly forms of Tetter are caused more by ♄ and the earthy sign influences, and the

moisture forms where the ☽ and moist signs are involved. (See Eczema, Herpes, Psoriasis, Ringworm, Scales; "Dry Skin" under Skin).

TEXTURE—Of the Tissues of the Body —Ruled by ☿. (See Tissues).
  Textural Nutrition — Changes In the Processes of — (See "Textural" under Nutrition).

THEATRES — Music Halls — Places of Amusement—Ruled by the 5th H.
  Death or Injury In — Malefics in the 5th H.; ♂ in the 5th H., in □ or ☍ the ☉ or ☽. (See Amusements; "Music Halls" under Music; Pleasure, Recreations, Sports, Taverns).
  Loves the Theatre — ♀ in ♌ or the 5th H.
  Theatre Fire—Case—188 Lives Lost—See "Exeter", No. 717, in 1001 N.N. Also see Case under "Music Halls" under Music).

THEFTS—Thefts Prevalent—Rapine—Robberies—An eclipse of the ☉ in the 2nd Dec. of ♒, thefts and robberies; an eclipse of the ☉ in the 2nd Decan. of ♒, public thefts, robberies, and rapines; an eclipse of the ☽ in the 1st Dec. of ♐, thefts and rapines; an eclipse of the ☽ in the 2nd dec. of ♑; an eclipse of the ☽ in the 3rd dec. of ♓, rapines, robberies, and piracies. (See Highwaymen, Piracy, Rapine, Robbers, Thieves).

THERAPEUTICS — The Science of the Application of Remedies and the Treatment of Disease. The word Therapeutics means literally, "The Worship of the Gods, or Cure by Faith in the Divinities of Certain Planets." The seven Therapeutical Pioneers for the treatment of disease are Gold (☉), Silver (☽), Lead (♄), Tin (♃), Iron (♂), Copper (♀), and Mercury or Quicksilver (☿). For the Therapeutic Properties of the Planets see "Therapeutic Properties" under each of the Planets. (See Antipathy, Colors, Cure, Drugs, Healers, Herbs, Medicines, Metals, Minerals, Opposites, Poisons, Remedies, Sympathy, Treatment, Vibration).

THICK—Thick Body—
  Beard—(See "Thick" under Beard).
  Body—Thick Body—The ☉ Sig. in ♉, thick and well-set; the ☽ Sig. in ♉ or ♏; the ☽ Sig. in ♏, thick, short, well-set, ill-made; the ☽ in ♏, partile the Asc., thick, short, fleshy, ill-made; ♄ Sig. in ♏, thick, squat, well-trussed; ♄ in ♏, partile the Asc.; ♄ Sig. in ♍; ♂ in ♏, partile the Asc., thick and well-set; ♀ in ♋, partile the Asc., thick and short; ☿ Sig. in ♉, thick, strong, and well-set; ☿ Sig. in ♋, thick, squat, and well-trussed; ☿ in ♏, partile the Asc., thick and well-set; ♉ on the Asc., thick, well-set, strong, middle-sized, or short; ♏ on the Asc., thick, well-set, fleshy, middle stature. (See Corpulent, Fat, Fleshy, Full, Lumpish, Obesity, Plump, Short Body, Squat, Well-Set, Well-Trussed).
  Feet—(See "Thick" under Feet).
  Fleshy and Thick — (See Fleshy; "Body" in this section).
  Hair—(See "Thick" under Hair).
  Hands—(See "Thick" under Hands).

Ill-Made and Thick— (See "Ill-Formed" under Ill; "Body" in this section).

Legs—(See "Thick" under Legs).

Lips—(See "Thick" under Lips).

Middle-Sized and Thick—(See "Middle Stature" under Middle; "Body" in this section).

Neck—(See "Thick" under Neck).

Nose—Nostrils—(See "Thick" under Nose).

Short and Thick—(See "Thick" under Short; "Body" in this section).

Shoulders—(See "Thick" under Shoulders).

Skin—(See "Thick", "Thickening", under Skin).

Strong and Thick—(See "Body" in this section; "Body" under Strong).

Thick-Trussed—Well-Trussed—(See "Body" in this section; "Well-Trussed" under Well).

Thickening—(See the next Article after this one).

Well-Set and Thick—(See "Body" in this section; "Well-Set" under Well).

Well-Trussed and Thick—(See "Thick-Trussed" in this section).

THICKENING—Thickening of the Tissues—Saturn by his deposits tends to thickening of the cell walls and tissues.

Acromegaly—Enlargements by Thickening—(See "Acromegaly" under Enlargements, Extremities).

Cell Walls—(See "Thickening" under Cells).

Cirrhosis—Thickening of Connective Tissue—(See Cirrhosis, Connective).

Connective Tissue — (See "Cirrhosis" in this section).

Enlargements—(See "Acromegaly" in this section; Hypertrophy).

Extremities—(See "Enlargements" under Extremities).

Hypertrophy—(See this subject).

Kidneys—(See "Thickening" under Kidneys).

Liver—(See "Thickening" under Liver).

Sclerosis—Hardening and Thickening of Tissues—(See Sclerosis).

Skin—(See "Thickening" under Skin).

Soft Parts—Thickening of—(See "Parts" under Soft; "Acromegaly" in this section).

THIEVES—Thieving—The Seventh House rules Thieves, and is the Sig. of Thieves in Hor'y Q.

A Thief—The afflictions to ♂ and ☿ tend to make thieves; ♂ ill-dignified, Significator, and ◇ ♄; ♂ Sig. □ or 8 ☽; ♂ Sig. □ or 8 ☿, a thief and swindler; ♂ afflicted in ♊; ♀ Sig. □ or 8 ♃, often a secret thief or murderer; ☿ Sig. in ♋; ☿ afflicted by ♄ and ♂. Case—See "Marriage", No. 425 in 1001 N.N. (See Cheating, Criminal, Deceitful, Dishonest, Forgers, Gambling, Kleptomaniac, Liars, Peregrine, Swindlers, etc.).

Danger by Thieves—Death or Injury By—The ☽ directed to the Whale's Jaw, Knees of Castor and Pollux,

Belly of the Twins, or Cynosura; ♂ ori. in fixed signs, □ or 8 the ☉ at B., or ♂ occi., □ or 8 the ☽. (See Highwaymen, Murdered, Piracy, Rapine, Robbers, Thefts).

THIGHS—Hams—Hamstrings—The Thighs are under the external rulership of the ♐ sign. The Thigh Bones are under the structural rulership of ♐. (See Sagittarius). The Thighs are also ruled by the 9th H. (See Ninth House). Also ruled by ♃, and influenced by the 10th H. The Hams are ruled by ♃ and ♐. The Hamstrings are ruled by ♑ and the 10th H.

Accidents To—♅, ♄, or ♂ afflicted in ♐; ♄ ◇ ♂ in ♐; afflictions in ♐; ♐ on the Asc. (See "Accidents" under Hips, Legs).

Aches In—(See "Aches" under Hips).

Affected—The thighs are affected when the ☉ is in ♈ or ♓; the ☽ in ♊, ♐, ♑, ♓; ♅ in ♎; ♄ in ♍ or ♎; ♃ in ♋, ♌, or ♍; ♂ in ♍; ♀ in ♊ or ♐; ☿ in 8 or ♓. (See Table 196 in Simmonite's Arcana).

All Diseases In—Signified by the 9th H. (See "All Diseases In" under Hips).

Broken Femur—(See Femur).

Bruises To—Contusions—♄ in ♐.

Chill and Cold In—♄ in ♐.

Circulation Poor—♄ in ♐, ◇, □, or 8 ♃ or ♀.

Cold and Moist Humours—(See "Cold and Moist" under Hips).

Consumptive Pains In—♄ in ♎ or ♐ when ♄ is the afflictor in the disease.

Contusions—(See "Bruises" in this section).

Cramps In—♅ in ♐. (See Cramps).

Cuts To—(See "Cuts" under Hips).

Deformity—The ☽ in ♐, □ ♄ or ♅; ♄ in ♐ in the 6th H.

Diseases In—The ☉ afflicted in ♈ or ♓; the ☽ afflicted in ♊, ♐, ♑, or ♓; signified by ♄ in ♍, ♎, or ♃ afflicted in ♋, ♌, ♍, ♐, or ♓; ♂ afflicted in ♍ or ♓; ♀ afflicted in ♊, ♐, or ♑; ☿ afflicted in ♊, ♐, ♑, or ♓; ♐, ♑ and ♓ diseases. (See "Impar" under Ganglion; "Diseases In" under Hips).

Dislocation—Of the Femur—(See Femur).

Feverish Ailments In—♂ in ♐; ♂ in ♐ in the Asc. or 6th H.; ♐ on the Asc. (See "Feverish", "Hot Humours", under Hips).

Fistulous Tumor In — (See "Thighs" under Fistula).

Fracture—(See "Accidents To" under Femur; "Fracture" under Hips).

Gout In—(See "Hips and Thighs" under Gout).

Hamstrings—All Diseases In—Signified by afflictions in ♑, and in the 7th and 10th H.

Heats In — (See "Heats In" under Hips).

Hips — Many of the influences given in the subjects under Hips will also apply to the Thighs. (See the various subjects under Hips).

Hot Humours In — (See "Hot Humours" under Hips).

Humours In—(See "Humours" under Hips).

Hurts To—Injuries or Wounds—(See "Accidents To" under Femur, and in this section; "Hurts", "Injuries", under Hips).

Injuries To—(See "Accidents" "Hurts", in this section).

Itching—In the Thighs—The ☽ in ♎, ♂, P., □ or ☍ ♄ (or ☿ if he be of the nature of ♄) at the beginning of an illness, or at decumbiture (Hor'y).

Lameness In—(See "Lameness" under Hips).

Lean Thighs—Thin—♄ gives; ♄ ascending at B.

Legs—(See the various subjects under Legs).

Lightning—The Thigh Injured By—Case—See "Child" under Lightning.

Locomotor Ataxia—(See this subject).

Long Thighs—(See "Long" under Legs).

Men—Men Suffer With Thigh Diseases—(See "Men Suffer" under Hips).

Moist and Cold Humours—(See "Cold and Moist" under Hips).

Mole On—(See "Location of Moles" under Moles).

Muscles Of—Disorders of—Afflictions in ♐, ♑, the 9th and 10th H.; Subs at PP and Sacrum.

Neuralgia In—(See "Pains" in this section).

Old Aches In—(See "Aches" under Hips).

Operations On—Surgical—Avoid when the ☽ is passing thru the ♐ sign. (See "Rules" under Operations).

Pains In—Neuralgia In—Malefics in ♐ and afflicting the ☉ or ☽; ♄ afflicted in ♐, rheumatic pains in; ♃ afflicted in ♐, and especially with ♃ in the 6th H.; ♂ in ♐, pain or ulcers in the hips or thighs by humours settled in those parts; ☿ afflicted in ♐. (See "Pain" under Hips; "Consumptive", "Gout", "Rheumatism", in this section).

Restrictions—In Region of—♄ afflicted in ♐.

Rheumatism In—(See "Rheumatism" under Hips).

Sciatica—(See Sciatic).

Short Thighs—(See "Short" under Legs).

Shorter—Left Leg Shorter—Case—(See "Leg" under Left).

Small and Lean—(See "Slender" under Legs).

Strong—And Well-Proportioned Legs and Thighs—(See "Strong" under Hips).

Swellings In—(See "Swellings" under Hips).

Thick and Short—(See "Thick" under Legs).

Thin—(See "Lean" in this section).

Tumors In—(See "Thighs" under Fistula; "Tumors" under Hips).

Ulcers—(See "Ulcers" under Hips; "Pains" in this section).

Weakness In—(See "Weakness" under Hips).

Well-Formed—♐ on the Asc.

Well-Proportioned—♃ in the Asc.; ♐ on the Asc.

Wounds To—(See "Hurts" in this section).

THIN—Thinness—

Beard—(See "Thin" under Beard).

Blood—(See "Thin" under Blood).

Body—Thin Body—The Quadrant from the Autumnal Equinox to the Winter Solstice tends to produce thin, weak, and sickly people. Lords of thin people have little or no Latitude. The ☉ in ♍, partile the Asc., thin, tall and slender; the ☽ occi., and decr. at B.; the ☽ in ♑, partile the Asc., thin body and face; ♄ in ♑, partile the Asc., thin, raw-boned, and ungainly; ♄ occi., thin and small; ♄ lord of the Asc. and occi., as between the M.C. and Desc., and between the Nadir and Asc., a thin, small body; ♄ in So. Lat. makes the body thinner, and more corpulent when in N. Lat.; ♄ ascending at B.; ♄ in ♍, partile the Asc., thin and tall; ♂ in ♑, partile the Asc., thin, small, lean body; ☿ ascending at B., and free from the rays of other planets; ☿ indicates tall and thin persons; ☿ posited occidentally as regards the ☉ except when ☿ is in ♊; ☿ in ♈, partile the Asc., thin, mean stature; ☿ ruler of the Asc., and occidental; ☿ in ♌, partile the Asc., rather lean and thin, and not tall; ☿ in ♓, partile the Asc., thin and small, say some Writers; ♈ on the Asc.; the latter parts of ♈, ♉, or ♐ ascending, and the foreparts of ♊ or ♏, cause thinness; ♍ on the Asc., tall, well-made, and rather thin and slender; ♑ on the Asc. (See "Raw-Boned" under Bones; Lean, Slender, Spare; "Noted Thin Man" in this section).

Chin—(See "Thin" under Chin).

Face—(See "Thin" under Face).

Lean and Thin—(See Lean; "Body" in this section).

Legs—(See "Thin" under Legs).

Lips—(See "Thin" under Lips).

Living Skeleton—(See Skeleton).

Mean and Thin—(See "Mean Stature" under Mean; "Body" in this section).

Noted Thin Man—Case—(See "A Living Skeleton" under Skeleton).

Pale and Thin—(See "Thin Face" under Face; Pale, Sickly).

Raw-Boned and Thin—(See "Raw-Boned" under Bones).

Sickly and Thin—(See Emaciated; "Thin Face" under Face; Pale, Sickly, Wastings).

Skeleton—(See "Living Skeleton" under Skeleton).

Skin—(See "Thin" under Skin).

Slender and Thin—(See "Body" under Slender).

Small and Thin—(See "Body" under Small, and in this section; "Small" under Lean).

Spare and Thin—(See Spare).

Tall and Thin—♅ and ☿ make more tall and thin; the ☉ in ♍, partile the

Asc.; ♄ in ♍, partile the Asc.; ♍ on the Asc.; ♍ on the Asc., tall, well-made, and rather slender. (See "Body" under Slender, and in this section; "Tall Body" under Tall).

Thighs—(See "Lean" under Thighs).

Ungainly and Thin — (See "Raw-Boned" under Bones; Crooked; "Ill-Formed" under Ill; Ugly, Ungainly).

Visage—(See "Face", "Pale", "Sickly", in this section).

THINKING—Thought—Thoughts—

Disorders Of—(See Aversions, Dejected, Delusions, Depressed, Despondent, Deviations, Evils, Fears, Hallucinations, Ideals, Ideas, Illusions, Insanity; "Low Spirits" under Low; Melancholy, Negative, Obsessions, Opinions, Rashness, Spirit Controls, Temper, Uncontrolled, Worry, etc.).

Good Thinking—Right Thinking—A Good Thinker — (See Cheerfulness, Contentment, Gentle, Happiness, Honest, Humane, Joy, Kind; "Peace of Mind" under Mind; Noble, Optimistic, Positive, Sanguine, Sincere, etc.).

Thought—Little Depth of Thought or Mind — (See "Light In Mind" under Mind; "Thought" under Reason). For the opposite influences see "Deep and Profound" under Mind).

Thoughtful Expression — (See "Appearance" under Sadness). See Thought.

THIRD EYE—(See Pineal).

THIRD HOUSE — The House of Brethren, Brothers, Sisters, Cousins, Neighbors, Short Inland Journeys. This is a masculine and cadent house, and is affiliated with ☿ and the ♊ Sign. Denotes and rules the Neck, Arms, Shoulders, Hands, Fingers, Chest, Lungs, the Lower Mind, Wakefulness or Waking. It governs also the Mental Capacity, and the Educational Mind. The Third and Ninth Houses are the Houses of Mind, and malefics in these Houses tend to disturb and unbalance the Mind. Benefics and ☿ well-aspected and dignified in this house give a good mind. In the Hindu System of Astrology, this house rules the Ears. Its Colors are Red, Yellow, and Sorrel. For a Horoscope Example of a Stellium in this House at birth see "Pasteur", No. 950, in 1001 N.N. (See the subjects mentioned in this Article).

THIRST—Thirsty—

Craving for Liquids — The ☽ afflicted in ♓; the ☽ in water signs. (See Cravings).

Drinks — Desire for Strong Drinks, Strong Coffee, Hot Drinks, etc.—The ☽ afflicted in ♓; ♄ ☌ ♀ in ♋, and also afflicted by the ☽. (See Dipsomania, Drink, Drunkenness, Intoxication, Liquors, Wine, etc.).

Extreme Thirst — The ☽ in ♓ or ♈, and afflicted by the ☉ or ♂ when taken ill; ♂ ☌ or ill-asp. ☿. People born under the Hot and Dry Bodily Temperament often suffer from extreme thirst, and need to drink plenty of water to help keep the fluids of the body replenished. (See "Hot and Dry Body" under Heat).

Unquenchable Thirst — Many planets

in fiery signs at B., and with a fire sign upon the Asc.; the ☉ and ♂ in the Asc. at B. Also occurs in the high fevers of ♂. (See "High Fever" under Fever; "Excessive Bodily Heat" under Heat; "Extreme" in this section).

Vehement Thirst — A Violent Thirst and Craving, and Especially for Spirituous Liquors—(See Dipsomania). See Appetites, Bloodthirsty (see "A Murderer" under Murder); Drought, Eating, Epicureans, Excesses, Famine, Feasting, Food, Gluttony, Starvation.

THORAX — Thoracic—The Chest—The Cavity Above the Abdomen—Ruled by the ☽ and the ♋ Sign.

Diathesis—The Thoracic Diathesis—(See Fiber; "Impar" under Ganglion; Ligaments).

Dropsy Of — (See "Hydrothorax" under Chest).

Duct—Thoracic Duct—Ruled by the ♋ Sign. (See Lymph).

Ganglia — Thoracic Ganglia — (See "Fifth Thoracic", "Middle Cervical", under Ganglion).

Hydrothorax—Dropsy In Chest—(See "Dropsy" under Chest).

Mediastinum—Septum of the Thoracic Cavity—Tumor of—(See "Mediastinal" under Tumors).

Process — Thoracic Process — ♃ adds or subtracts to the Thoracic Process. (See "Alterations" under Cells; Metabolism, Metamorphosis).

Tumor — In Thoracic Cavity — (See "Mediastinum" in this section).

THORIUM — A Metal ruled by ♅. (See Uranus).

THOUGHT—Thoughts — Thoughtful — Thoughtless—

Evil Thoughts—(See Evil).

Expression — Thoughtful Expression —(See "Appearance" under Sad).

Little Depth — Of Thought — (See "Thought" under Thinking).

Thoughtful — Sober — Serious — ♄ influence; the 4th face of ♏ on the Asc. (See Austere, Grave, Melancholy, Reserved, Responsibility; "Sadness" under Sad; Serious, Sober).

Thoughtless — (See Excitable, Foolhardy; "Lack Of" under Forethought; Hasty; "Sudden Impulses" under Impulses; Rashness, Recklessness, etc.).

THREADS—Threads and Specks Before the Eyes—(See "Threads" under Eyes).

THREATS—Threatened—

Danger Threatened—(See "Near Some Danger" under Danger).

Death Threatened — (See "Threatened" under Death; "Death Imminent" under Imminent).

Disease Threatened—(See "Threatened" under Disease).

Misfortune Threatened — (See "Some Misfortune Near" under Misfortune).

THRILLS—(See "Thrills" under Heart).

THRIVES—And Lives Thru Serious Illness — (See Immunity; "Good" under Recuperation, Resistance, Vitality; "Lives Thru Serious Illnesses" under Serious).

THROAT — The Fauces — Larynx — Pharynx — The Throat is under the external rulership of the ♉ Sign. Also ruled by ♀, the 2nd H., and influenced by all the Fixed Signs. (See Fixed Signs, Second House, Taurus, Venus). Planets when in signs immediately following their own home signs affect the throat, and influence the ♉ sign. The ☉ is at home in ♌, and thus when he is in ♍ he affects the throat, and so on with all the planets. The ☉ also in ♉, ♌, ♏, or ♒, the fixed signs, affects the throat, in addition to his other sign influences, according to this rule. Table 196 in Simmonite's Arcana is worked out along this line. The following subjects have to do with the diseases and afflictions of the throat, which see in the alphabetical arrangement when only listed here—

Abscesses — Of the Throat or Neck — (See "Abscesses" under Neck).

Adenoids; Affected — The Throat or Neck Affected — The ☉ in ♍ and the fixed signs; the ☽ in ♌ and fixed signs; ♄ in ♒ or ♓; ♃ in ♑, ♈, and fixed signs; ♂ in ♉, ♐, and fixed signs; ♀ in ♊, ♍, and fixed signs; ☿ in ♋, ♎, and fixed signs. (See "Affected" under Head; the Introduction to this Article, and Table 196 in Simmonite's Arcana).

All Diseases Of—☉ diseases; signified by afflictions in ♉, the 2nd H., and the fixed signs, and especially ♉ and ♍.

Aphasia — (See "Aphasia" under Speech).

Arteries and Veins—Of the Throat— Ruled by ♃ and ♀, and these planets afflicted in ♉ tend to affect the blood vessels of the throat and neck.

Blood—Excess of Blood In the Throat —Ψ in ♉, ☌ the ☉ or ♂.

Breaking Out—In the Throat—The ☉ afflicted in ♉ when the ☉ is the afflictor in the disease; ♂ in ♍, by reflex action to ♉, as in Lues; a ♍ disease.

Breath Affected—By Catarrh In the Throat — ♄ afflicted in ♉. (See "Foul Breath" under Breath; "Catarrh" in this section).

Cases of Throat Diseases—(See Figures 3A, 3B, 3C, 3D, 3E, 3F, 3G, 8A, 8B, 16B, in the book, "Astro-Diagnosis" by the Heindels; Figures 9, 10, 11, and 34, in "Message of the Stars", by the Heindels; Chap. XIII in Daath's Medical Astrology.

Catarrh Of — ♄ afflicted in ♉; ♄ ☌ ☽ in ♉; the ☉ in ♉ and afflicted by ♄; Subs at MCP.

Cervical Region—Disorders In—(See Cervical).

Choking—♄ afflicted in ♉. (See Choking).

Chronic Distempers—About the Throat —♄ in ♉ when ♄ is the afflictor in the disease.

Circulation — The Circulation About the Throat Impaired—♄ ☌ ♃ or ♀ in ♉; ♃ or ♀ in ♉, □, or ☍ the ☉ or ♄. (See "Restricted" in this section).

Colds In—♄ afflicted in ♉.

Constrictions In — ♅ or ♄ afflicted in ♉. (See Constrictions).

Contractions In—Spasmodic Contractions of—Constrictions—♅ afflicted in ♉; ♄ or ♋ in ♉, and especially in the 6th H. (See Constrictions, Contractions, Spasmodic).

Control—Loss of Nervous Control of the Throat — Swallowing Difficult — (See Deglutition; "Nerves" in this section).

Cough — (See "Throat Cough" under Cough).

Croup; Crystallization—(See Goiter).

Cuts His Own Throat — Suicide By — ♂ afflicted in ♉, and with the Pleiades at B.; ♂ elevated above, and afflicting the hyleg. (See Suicide).

Death — By Throat Disorders — By Putrid Sore Throat — ♄ afflicted in ♉; ♀ afflicted in ♉, by putrid sore throat; afflictions in the fixed signs, and especially in ♉ or ♍.

Defects—In the Throat—The ☉, ♄, or ☿ afflicted in ♉. (See "Structural" in this section).

Deglutition Difficult—Swallowing Difficult — (See Deglutition; "Nerves" in this section).

Diphtheria; Diseased Throat — Distempers In — Throat Trouble — Disordered Throat—Afflictions in ♉, ♍, and the fixed signs; the ☉ or ☽ afflicted in ♉ or ♍, and ☌ malefics in these signs; the ☉ afflicted in ♍, throat trouble of a violent and inflammatory nature; the ☽ hyleg in ♉, and afflicted, throat trouble in females; Ψ, ♅, ♄, ♃, ♂, ♀, or ♍ afflicted in ♉ or ♍; a Stellium of planets in ♉, ♍, or the 2nd H., and afflicted, or containing malefics; planets in ♉ or ♍ in the Asc., 2nd, 6th, 8th, or 12th H., and afflicted; planets in fixed signs in the 6th H., and afflicted; malefics in ♉ and afflicting the hyleg; ♉ on the cusp the Asc. or 6th H., and afflicted by malefics; born under ♀ and ♀ badly afflicted at B., and by dir.; ♀ in ♉ in the 6th H., afflicted, or afflicting the ☽ or Asc.; ♍ on the cusp the Asc. or 6th H., and containing malefics; any planet afflicted in the 6th H. in a fixed sign; fixed signs on the cusp the 6th H., and afflicted, or containing malefics. The ♉ and ♍ signs are opposite and supplemental signs, and planets and afflictions in either of these signs tend to especially affect the throat and sex organs. This relationship is more fully explained in the Article on Larynx. Thus Syphilis, a ♍ disease, produces the ulcerated throat by reflex action in ♉. Also Subluxations of the Cervical Vertebrae, or MCP, and LCP, and at SP (7D), and at PP, tend to affect the throat. (See the various paragraphs in this section).

Distempers In—(See "Chronic", "Diseased Throat", in this section).

Dress — The Throat Disordered by Improper Dress—♀ afflicted in ♉. (See Dress).

Dryness—Dry and Feverish Throat— Dryness of the Throat Increased—Dry Fauces—♂ in ♉. (See Fauces).

Dysphonia—(See "Hoarseness" under Larynx).

Enlarged Tonsils—(See Tonsils).

Exanthematous Sore Throat — Afflictions in ♍. (See "Sore Throat" in this section).

Excess of Blood In—(See "Blood" in this section).

Expectoration — Great Expectoration of Phlegm—The ☽ afflicted in ♌, excess of mucus and phlegm in the throat; ♄ afflicted in ♈, much falling of mucus into the throat. (See "Great Expectoration" under Phlegm; "Humours", "Phlegm", in this section).

Exudations — Membranous Exudation In the Throat—(See Diphtheria, Exudations).

Fauces—Dryness of—(See "Dryness" in this section).

Fluids of Throat—Disorders of—Disturbance of—Restriction of—♄ afflicted in ♌ or ♏. (See "Ailments Of" under Fluids; "Dryness", "Restricted", in this section).

Fluxes — Of Rheum In the Throat — (See "Rheum" in this section).

Glandular Swellings — In Throat and Neck—A ♀ disease; afflictions in ♌ or ♏, and fixed signs; ♄ ☌ ♅ in ♌ or ♏; ♀ afflicted in ♌; signified by the 2nd H.; Subs at CP and KP. (See "Glands" under Neck; "Swellings" in this section).

Goiter; Heat — Extreme Heat In the Throat and Mouth—♂ in ♐ when ♂ is the afflictor in the disease; ♂ in ♐, ☌, or ill-asp. the ☉, and with ♂ as Promittor. (See "Heats" under Heat).

Hoarseness—(See Larynx).

Humours—Falling Into the Throat—The ☽ in ♈, ♑, or ♌ ♄ (or ☿ if he be of the nature of ♄) when first taken ill, or at decumbiture. (See "Expectoration", "Rheum", in this section).

Inflammation — All Inflammatory Action In the Throat — ♂ afflicted in ♌; ♌ diseases. (See "Sore Throat" in this section; Diphtheria; "Inflammation" under Larynx; "Pharyngitis" under Pharynx; "Tonsilitis" under Tonsils).

Influenza — Involving the Throat — (See Influenza).

Irritations — ♅, and other bodies afflicted in ♌. (See "Cough", "Spasmodic", in this section).

Larynx—Disorders of — (See Larynx; "Vocal Cords" under Voice).

Lymphatic Vessels Of—(See "Throat" under Lymphatic).

Membranes—Membranous Exudations —Membranous Deposits — (See Croup, Diphtheria, Exudations; "Mucous Membranes" in this section).

Minor Diseases—Of the Throat—The benefics in ♌; ♌ on the cusp of the Asc. or 6th H., and not severely afflicted; few planets in fixed signs at B.

Mole—Mole On the Throat or Neck—Malefics in ♌ or the 2nd H. (See "Moles" under Neck).

Motor Nerves—Of the Throat—Disorders of—♅ afflicted in ♌. (See Incoordination).

Mucous Membranes — Mucous Surfaces—Mucus—Mucus Falling Into the Throat—Exudations—Expectoration of Mucus and Phlegm, etc.—(See Croup, Diphtheria, Exudations; Expectoration, Humours, Phlegm, Rheum, in this section).

Mumps—(See Parotid).

Neck — (See the various paragraphs under Neck).

Nerves—Of the Throat—Disorders of —♅ afflicted in ♌, disturbances of the motor nerves of the throat; ☿ afflicted in ♌. (See "Control", "Deglutition", in this section; "Nervous Disorders" under Neck).

Obscure Diseases—Of the Throat and Neck—♆ afflicted in ♌. (See Obscure).

Obstructions In — The Throat Obstructed—♄ afflicted in ♌ or ♏; ♃ afflicted in ♑ when the afflictor in the disease. (See Stoppages, Swellings, Tumors, in this section; "Hoarseness" under Larynx; Tonsils).

Operations — Avoid surgical operations upon the throat when the ☽ is passing thru the ♈, ♌, or ♐ signs, and when the ☽ is in a fixed sign, if possible. (See "Rules" under Operations).

Pains In — (See "Pains In" under Neck).

Palate; Pertussis — (See "Convulsive" under Cough; Whooping).

Pharynx—(See the paragraphs under Pharynx).

Phlegm—An Excess of Phlegm In the Throat—The ☽ in ♌, ☌, P., ♑, or ♌ ♄ (or ☿ if he be of the nature of ♄) at the beginning of an illness, or at decumbiture; ♄ afflicted in ♌ or ♏. (See Expectoration, Humours, Mucous, Rheum, in this section; Phlegm).

Poisonings In — (See "Septic" in this section).

Polypus; Prevalent—Throat Disorders Prevalent—♂ in ♌ or ♋ at the Vernal Equinox, and lord of the year.

Putrid Sore Throat—The ☽ in ♌, and afflicted by the ☉ or ♂ when taken ill (Hor'y); ♀ afflicted in ♌, and denotes death by. (See "Death", "Septic", "Sore Throat", in this section).

Quinsy—(See Tonsils).

Relaxed Throat — A ♀ disease; ♀ afflicted in ♌; the ☽ and ♀ afflicted in ♌. (See Relaxation).

Restricted—The Circulation or Fluids of the Throat Restricted — ♄ afflicted in ♌ or ♏. (See "Circulation", "Fluids", in this section).

Rheum — Fluxes of Rheum Into the Throat — A ♌ disease, and afflictions in ♌; ♄ in ♈ when ♄ is the afflictor in the disease. (See Rheum; Expectoration, Humours, Mucous, Phlegm, in this section).

Scar—In the Throat, or On the Neck — Malefics in ♌ or the 2nd H. (See "Mole" in this section; Marks, Moles, Scars).

Septic Poisonings—Of the Throat—♆ afflicted in ♌. (See "Putrid", "Sore Throat", in this section).

Singing — Avoid Loud Singing—(See "Singers" under Music).

Sore Throat—Putrid Sore Throat—♌ diseases, and afflictions in ♌; malefics afflicted in ♌; ♀ afflicted in ♌, putrid sore throat and death by; afflictions in ♏; ♌ or ♏ on the Asc. or cusp the 6th H., and containing afflictions; afflictions in ♏ tend to exanthematous sore throat; the ☉ in ♉ or ♍, ♂, or ill-asp. any of the malefics as Promittors; the ☽ in ♉, ♏, or any of the fixed signs, and ♂ or ill-asp. ♄ (or ☿ if he be of the nature of ♄) at the beginning of an illness, or at decumbiture (Hor'y); ♆, ♅, or ♄ in ♒, and afflicting the ☉ or ☽; ♃ or ♀ ♂ ♄ in ♉, due to congestion and poor circulation; ♂ afflicted in ♉; ♂ in ♉ or fixed signs in the 6th H., and afflicted; signified by the 2nd H., and by malefics in this house at B. (See Hoarseness, Inflammation, Putrid, Quinsy, Septic, Swellings, Syphilitic, Tonsils, Ulcerated, and the various paragraphs in this section).

Spasmodic Disorders — In the Throat —♅ afflicted in ♉. (See Spasmodic; "Contractions" in this section).

Stoppages In—The ☽ or ♄ afflicted in ♉; ♄ ♂ the ☽ in ♉. (See "Obstructions" in this section).

Stricture Of — ♅ or ♄ afflicted in ♉. (See Stricture; "Contractions" in this section).

Structural Defects—The ☉ afflicted in ♉. (See Structural).

Suppurations — (See Exudations, Putrid, Septic, Sore, Tonsils, Ulcerated, in this section).

Swallowing Difficult — (See Control, Deglutition, Nerves, in this section).

Swellings In—The ☉, ☽, ♄, or ♃ afflicted in ♉; ♃ afflicted in ♈, and caused by ill-blood in the veins of the head. (See Glandular, Inflammation, Obstructions, Sore, Tumors, in this section).

Syphilitic Throat—Syphilitic Ulcers— (See "Throat" under Syphilis; "Ulcerated" in this section).

Taurus—(See "Diseases" under Taurus).

Throat Complaints Generally—The ☉ afflicted in ♉. (See "Prevalent" in this section).

Throat Trouble — (See "Diseased Throat", and the various paragraphs in this section).

Tissues—♆ has special rule over the tissues of the throat, and ♆ afflicted in ♉ or the 2nd H. tends to disorders, septic poisonings, and wastings of the tissues of the throat. (See "Wasting" under Tissues).

Tonsils—Disorders of—(See Tonsils).

Tubercular Throat—♄ affl. in ♉. (See "Consumption" under Larynx).

Tumors—(See "Tumors" under Neck).

Ulcerated Throat—A ♉ and ♏ disease; the ☽ afflicted in ♉; ♀ afflicted in ♉, ulceration and disorders due to improper protection of the throat, and indiscretions in dress; ♂ afflicted in ♏ tends to ulcerated throat, and the Venereal Ulcers of Lues, or Syphilis. (See Ulcers; "Sore Throat" in this section).

Veins—(See "Arteries" in this section).

Venereal Ulcers — In Throat — (See "Ulcerated" in this section).

Voice—Vocal Cords—Disorders of— (See Larynx, Speech, Voice).

Wasting — Of the Tissues of the Throat—(See "Tissues" in this section).

Whooping Cough—(See Whooping).

THROBBING—Pulsating— Beating— Throbbing in the different parts of the body may be caused by various planetary influences. Palpitation of the heart is usually caused by ♅ in the heart sign ♌. The throbbing from the fullness of blood vessels, and high blood pressure, is usually caused by ♃, and due to plethoric conditions. The ♂ influence over a part tends to draw too much blood to the part, due to his heating influence, and cause throbbing. The deposits and obstructions of ♄ often cause throbbing, pain, and aches in a part. For these various influences see "Throbbing" under Aches, Ears, Heart, Limbs; "Fullness of Blood", "High Blood Pressure", under Blood; "Rush of Blood" under Head; Pain, Plethora, Pulse, Surfeits, Tremors; "Beating" under Vessels).

THROMBUS—A Blood Clot In a Vessel —Embolism—Infarct—The influence of ♄ is clotting and obstructing; ♄ ♂ ♃ or ♀, rulers of the circulation, and affecting the part containing the affliction.

Brain—Thrombus In—(See "Clot On Brain" under Brain). See Clots, Embolism, Infarcts, Obstructions.

THRUSH — Aphthae — (See Aphthae; "Thrush" under Mouth).

THRUSTS — Thrusts with Weapons— Kicks by Animals, etc. — (See Duels, Instruments, Kicks, Stabs, Sword, War).

THUMBS — (See "Thumb" under Fingers).

THUNDER—Ruled by ♃.

Deaths—Many Deaths from Thunder and Lightning Storms—♄ in ♊, direct in motion, and angular at the Vernal Equinox; ♂ in ♊ and lord of the year at the Vernal; Eclipses of the ☽ in ♏; Comets appearing in ♊ or ♒. (See Clouds, Lightning, Storms, Wind).

Much Thunder—And Lightning—An eclipse of the ☽ in the 1st Decan. of ♏.

THURSDAY—Day of the Week. Ruled by ♃. (See "Days of the Week" under Week).

THYMUS GLANDS—A Glandular Organ at the Base of the Tongue—Ruled by ♀. Some Authors say it is also ruled by ♊ and ♏.

Disorders Of—♀ afflicted by malefics. Case—See Fig. 17C in the book, "Astro-Diagnosis", by the Heindels.

THYROID GLAND — Thyroid Cartilage —Ruled by ☿, and also by the ♉ and ♏ Signs. The ☽ when in ♉ rules and affects this Gland. The Thyroid Gland acts as a connecting link between the Pineal Gland and the Pituitary Body. (See Pineal, Pituitary). The Thyroid Cartilage is ruled by ♄ and the ♉ sign. Brain Balance is also under the rule of the Thyroid Gland, and is controlled largely by the secretions of this Gland.

Brain Balance—Disturbances of—Afflictions to ☿. (See "Unbalanced Mentality" under Mental).

Circulation Disturbed—Circulation and Functions of the Thyroid Disturbed—♆ afflicted by ♄; ♆ in ♉, ♂, □, or ♉ ♄; Subs at LCP (6C). Case—See Fig. 17B in "Astro-Diagnosis", by the Heindels.

Disturbed Thyroid — ♆ or ♅ afflicted in ♉; malefics in ♉; ♅ ☌ ♄ in ♉ or ♏.

Enlarged Thyroid — Goiter — ♆ in ♉, and afflicted by ♄; ♆ ☌ the ☉ and ♂ in ♉; ♀ afflicted in ♉. Case—See Fig. 17A in "Astro-Diagnosis", by the Heindels. (See Goiter).

Functions Disturbed — (See "Circulation" in this section).

Goiter — Enlarged Thyroid — (See Goiter; "Enlarged" in this section).

Mental Growth Retarded — Arrested Mental and Physical Growth — Caused by afflictions to ☿, the ruler of this Gland. (See Backwardness, Cretinism, Dwarfed, Idiocy, Imbecile, Myxoedema).

Physical Disorders—Diseases Which Often Accompany Disturbed Thyroid— (See Cretinism, Goiter; "Arrested" under Growth; Leprosy, Myxoedema; the various paragraphs in this section).

Thyroid Cartilage — Adam's Apple — Prominent Adam's Apple—(See "Long" under Neck).

TIBIA—The Shin Bone—Shank—Under the structural rulership of the ♒ Sign. Is opposite to, and corresponds to the Radius in the arm, ruled by ♌. All diseases in, infirmities or accidents to, fracture, etc., are signified by the 11th H., and also caused by afflictions in ♒. Dislocation of the head of the Tibia is caused by afflictions in ♑. (See Ankles, Fibula, Knees, Legs, Radius).

TICS—Spasmodic Twitchings—

Tic Dourouleux—Spasmodic Facial Neuralgia — (See "Movements" under Erratic; "Neuralgia", "Spasmodic", under Face; Jerkings, Saint Vitus Dance, Spasmodic Diseases, Tremors, Twitchings).

TIDAL AIR — In the Lungs — Ruled by the ☽.

Lack of In Lungs—Insufficient—♄ in ♊ and ♉ the ☽ tends to insufficient tidal air in the lungs, and lack of oxygenation. The tidal air in the lungs is almost stopped by ♄ or ♅ in ♊, and other afflictions in ♊; the ☉ in ♊ or ♐, interferences with the tidal air; ♄ afflicted in ♏, the tidal air in the bowels is disturbed, causing a weakened action of the diaphragm, and disturbed breathing. (See "Inbreathing" under Anus; "Labored" under Breathing; "Carbonic Acid Poisoning" under Carbon; "Non-Oxygenation" under Oxygen).

TIDES—(See "Tides" under Moon).

Tidal Waves — (See this subject under Water).

TIGHT—Tightness—

Tightness of Chest—(See "Tightness" under Chest).

Tightness of Feature — (See "Tightness" under Features).

Tight Lacing — Causing Respiratory Troubles — (See "Indiscretions" under Dress).

TIME—The Time Factor In Life—"To Everything There Is a Season, and a Time to Every Purpose under the Heaven; a Time to be Born, and a Time to Die." Eccl. 3:1, 2. These Times are governed by the Planetary movements, as the Planets are but the visible material bodies, or vehicles, thru which the Archangels of God work to carry out His Orders, and to administer, direct, and supervise Human Affairs on our Earth, and in other parts of our Solar System. The ☽ is the Time Marker in Human Affairs and World Conditions, the minute hand on the Clock of Destiny, and the ☉ is the Hour Hand. (See "Aspects" under Moon).

Accidents—(See "Time of Accidents" under Accidents).

Acute Diseases—The Time When Apt to Come—(See "Periods of Acute Disease" under Acute).

Birth—Time of—The Time of Birth is a fixed quantity, if not interfered with, and the child will be born when the heavens form the star map predetermined. Delivery, therefore, should not be hastened by drugs or instruments, except in emergencies to save the life of the mother or child, or both, and where abnormalities exist. (See "Causes of Birth", "Delayed Birth", "Moment of Birth", "Premature Birth", "Time of Birth", under Birth; "Birth of a Child", "Born", "Delayed Births", "Time of Advent", under Children; "Moment of Birth" under Moment; Premature, Prenatal Epoch).

Child Promised — (See "Birth of a Child" under Children).

Conception — (See "Time of Conception" under Conception).

Crises In Disease — Time of — (See Crises).

Death—Time of Death—In the ordinary course of events in the life of an individual, the planetary influences and directions, or progressions, reach a point where there is a checkmate, and when the game of life in the physical body must cease. This time can be ascertained if the student cares to work long enough, and hard enough to determine all the influences which may be afflicting the Hyleg in the train of fatal directions. However, it is unwise, and unethical for Astrologers to predict the time of death of people, even if they know, or to state openly when noted and famous people will die, due to the worry it might cause. The time of death, or what may seem to us to be the apparent time of death, can sometimes be put off, or prevented for the time, by right living, right thinking, spiritual attainment, and by obtaining wisdom and knowledge of the plan of things. However, most people die on scheduled time, and fit right into the scheme of things by drifting along with their stars, and by following their natural, or evil tendencies. The only proper way of discovering the probable time of death is by directing the Hyleg to the Anareta, and this can only be done when the true hour and moment of birth are known. One fatal direction to the Hyleg ordinarily does not kill, and death by disease is usually the result of the afflictions of a train of evil directions to the hyleg. When the hour of birth is not known a Horary Figure may be erected at the strong desire of the Querent, which figure tends to answer the purpose of a true map of birth for judgment in the matter. These rules for working out the time of death in Hor'y Questions would be too lengthy to list here, but they are given quite fully in Lilly's Astrology. Also a smaller and handy book is "Raphael's Horary Astrology." There are a number of standard books on Horary Astrology, and the student should own them, and make a study of this subject. For further rules and influences along this line in this book, see Anareta; "Death During Childhood" under Childhood; "Death of Children" under Children; Crises; "Arguments for Death", "Certain Death", "Day of Death", "Hour of Death", under Death; Directions; "Early Death" under Early; Events, Fatal, Hyleg; "Death In Infancy" under Infancy; "Long Life", "Probable Length of Life", "Short Life", under Life; "Death At Middle Life" under Middle Life; "Dies In Old Age" under Old Age; "Death In Youth" under Youth, etc.

Disease—Illness—Sickness—The Time When Due In the Ordinary Course of Life—(See "Time of the Disease" under Disease; "Periods of Bad Health" under Health; "Type of the Disease" under Type).

Energy—A Time of Great Energy—(See "Great Energy" under Energy).

Events—The Time of Events of Various Kinds—(See Events).

Evil—An Evil Time for the Native—(See "Time" under Evil).

Hurts—(See "Time Of" under Hurts).

Imprisonment—(See "Time Of" under Prison).

Injuries — (See "Time Of" under Injuries).

Life—The Time Factor In Life—(See Childhood, Climacteric; "Critical Days", "Critical Periods", under Critical; Cycles, Infancy, Middle Life, Old Age, Periodic; "Life", "Seven Year Periods", under Periods; Youth).

Misfortune — (See Disgrace, Dishonour; "Time Of" under Misfortune; "Loss Of" under Reputation; Reverses, Ruin, Scandal, Sorrow, Trouble, etc.).

Public Grief—A Time of—(See "Public Grief" under Public).

Recovery—The Time of—(See Amelioration; "Better" under Disease; Moderation; "How Long Before Recovery", "Signs of Recovery", under Recovery).

Sorrow—A Time of—(See Sorrow).

Travel—Good and Bad Times For—(See Travel).

Trouble—A Time of—(See Trouble). For other subjects along this line not listed here look in the alphabetical arrangement for the subject you have in mind.

TIMIDITY—A ☽ and ♋ Sign influence. Also caused by the afflictions of ♆. (See Backwardness, Bashfulness; "Mind" under Dull; Fears, Mistrustful, Modesty, Recluse, Reserved, Retiring, Rigel, Secretive, Sensitiveness, Shy, Solitude, Suspicious, etc.).

TIN—Stannum—A Typical Metal of ♃. (See Jupiter, Metals, Therapeutics).

TINEA—A Skin Disease from Fungi—(See "Barber's Itch" under Barbers; Herpes, Itch, Ringworm, Tetter, Worms).

TINGLING — Of the Nerves — Tingling Sensations—Numbness In a Nerve—♄ ♂ or ill-asp. ☿; ♅ ♂ ☿, and in the part ruled by the sign ♅ is in at B. (See Numbness, Paraesthesia).

TINNITUS AURIUM — (See "Ringing" under Ears).

TIRED FEELING—The ☽ afflicted in ♑; ♃ in ♑; ♄ or ♋ on the Asc. at B. (See Apathy, Dull, Fatigue, Inactive, Indifferent, Inertia, Lassitude, Lazy, Lethargy, Listless; "Low" under Vitality; "Weak Body" under Weak).

TISSUES—The Modern Writers say that ♆ has strong rule over the Tissues, and that ♆ afflicted in any sign tends to wasting of the tissues of the part involved. All of the planets affect the tissues in their own way. The ☉ and ♂ supply heat and force to the tissues, and also help to burn up wastes. Decay and disintegration, and the death of tissue, are the work of ♄ and the ☽. The conservation and preservation of tissue are the work of the benefics ♃ and ♀. The nerve tissues are supported by ☿. The following subjects have to do with the tissues, which subjects see in the alphabetical arrangement when only listed here—

Absorption of Tissue — Analysis of Tissue — Resolution of — A ♄ disease. (See Absorption).

Adipose Tissue—(See Fat).

Alterations In — (See "Alterations" under Cells).

Analysis Of — (See "Absorption" in this section).

Animal Tissue — The Animal Tissues are connected with the ♊ Sign, and the ♊ Salt, Potassium Chloride. (See Potassium; "Salts" under Zodiac).

Areolar Tissue—Connective, or Cellular Tissue—Inflammation of—Combustion of—(See Phlegmon; Cellular, Combustion, Connective, in this section).

Arms—Wasting of the Tissues of—♆ afflicted in signs which rule the arms, hands, legs, and feet tends to wasting of the tissues of these parts. (See "Wasting" in this section).

Atrophy Of—(See Atrophy).

Blood Circulation — And Distribution In the Tissues — Ruled and presided over by the ♒ Sign. (See Circulation).

Blood Vessels—Of the Tissues—(See "Blood Vessels" under Blood).

Bony Tissue—(See Bones).

Building—Cellular Tissue Building—(See "Tissue Building" under Cells).

Capillaries; Cartilage—Cartilaginous Tissue Building—The work of ♄. (See Cartilage).

Cells—Cellular Tissue Building—(See Cells).

Changes—Structural Changes In the Tissues—(See Lesions, Structural).

Circulation — In the Tissues — (See Circulation).

Cirrhosis; Cleansing—Of the Tissues —(See Cleansing).

Combustion — Of the Tissues — (See Combustion).

Connective Tissue—(See Connective).

Conservation Of—(See Conservation).

Contraction Of—(See Contractions).

Corrosion; Crusts—Of Dead Tissue—♂ diseases. (See Crusts).

Crystallization; Dead Tissue — (See "Crusts" in this section).

Decay Of — Decomposition of — The work of ♄ and the ☽. Urea is the principal nitrogenous product of tissue decomposition. (See "Tissues" under Decay; Decomposition, Urea).

Decomposition Of — (See "Decay" in this section).

Defects In —.Structural Defects are caused by afflictions to the ☉. Defects in the bony structure are ♄ afflictions. (See Bones, Defects, Organic, Structural).

Degeneration — Of the Tissues — Deterioration of — Presided over by ♄. (See Decay, Degeneration, Deterioration, Emaciation, Fatigue, Softening, Wasting, etc.).

Depletion—(See "Constitution" under Depletion).

Development—Of the Tissues—Is assisted greatly when ♆ is △ or ✶ the Asc. (See Assimilation, Nutrition).

Dissolution Of—(See Dissolution).

Drying Up — Of Tissues — ♄ diseases and afflictions. (See Atrophy, Crystallization; "Dry Diseases" under Dry; Scales, Shrinking, Withering).

Effusions Into—(See Effusions).

Elephantiasis; Emollients — Agents Which Soften the Tissues—(See Emollients).

Epithelioma; Expansion Of—(See Expansion).

Extravasations—(See Effusions).

Face—(See "Tissues" under Face).

Feet — (See "Tissues" under Feet; "Wasting" in this section).

Fibers — Fibrous Tissue Building — The work of ♂. (See Fiber).

Glandular Tissue—(See "Tissues" under Glands).

Hands—(See "Wasting" under Hands, and in this section).

Hardening; Hypertrophy; Induration; Inflammation Of—(See "Tissues" under Inflammation).

Intercellular Spaces—(See "Intercellular" under Cells).

Interstitial Tissues—(See "Intercellular" under Cells; Connective, Interstitial).

Laxity Of—(See Laxity, Relaxation).

Legs — Wasting of the Tissues of — (See "Arms" in this section).

Lesions; Ligaments; Lymphatics;

Malacia — Softening of Tissue — (See Malacia, Softening).

Metabolism; Metamorphosis; Muscles; Nerves—Nerve Tissue Building—The work of ☿ and ☿. Wasting of the Nerve Tissues is a ♆ disease and affliction. (See "Neurotic", "Tissues", under Nerves; "Wasting" in this section).

Nutrition—(See "Tissues" under Nutrition).

Obstruction — Of Tissues —(See Hindrances, Obstructions, Retarded, Stoppages, Suppressions).

Oedema; Organic Defects—(See Congenital, Organic, Structural).

Parenchyma—Soft Cellular Tissue—(See Parenchyma).

Polarity Of—(See Polarity).

Preservation Of — (See Conservation, Preservation).

Relaxed Tissues — (See Emollient, Laxity, Relaxation).

Resolution Of—(See "Absorption" in this section; "Resolution Of" under Resolution).

Resolvents — Agents Reducing the Swelling of Tissue—(See Resolvent).

Respiratory System — Tissues of Affected—(See "Tissues Affected" under Breathing).

Sclerosis—(See Hardening, Sclerosis).

Serum Collections—(See Serum).

Shrinking; Sinews; Soft Tissues—The Soft Tissues, taken as a whole, are under the rule of the ☽, and the ☽ afflicted tends to disorders of these tissues. (See Decay, Gangrene, Glands, Muscles, Parenchyma; "Tissues" under Soft).

Softening Agents — (See Emollients, Resolvent).

Softening of Tissues—♓ and ♀ influence. (See Malacia, Softening).

Solution of Tissue — (See Resolvent; "Tissue" under Solution; "Absorption", "Degeneration", in this section).

Structural Defects — (See Congenital, Defects, Hereditary, Innate, Organic, Structural).

Suppressions—Of Tissues—(See Ablation, Remote, Removal, Suppressions).

Suppurations — (See Phlegmon, Pus, Putrid).

Tendons; Texture—Of the Tissues—Ruled by ☿. (See Texture).

Thickening; Throat—Wasting of the Tissues of — (See "Tissues" under Throat).

Tissue Building — (See "Building" in this section).

Tissue Remedies—(See "Zodiac Salts" under Healers).

Tubes—Tubules—(See Tubes).

Vascular Tissues—(See Arteries, Capillaries, Vascular, Vaso, Veins, Vessels).

Vessels; Warmth — Of the Tissues — (See Electric, Heat).

Wasting — Of the Tissues — ♆ and ♄ influence. (See Atrophy, Consumptions, Emaciation; "Malnutrition" under Nutrition; Phthisis, Tabes, Tuberculosis, Wasting; "Arms", "Nerves", in this section).

Withering Of — (See Atrophy, Emaciation, Hardening, Infirm, Old Age, Scales, Shrinkage, Tabes, Withering, Wrinkles). For other subjects which have to do with the Tissues, and which may have been overlooked for this Article, look for the subject in the alphabetical arrangement.

TOBACCO — Tabacum — Nicotine— The Dried Leaves of Nicotiana Tabacum, and is a powerful Depressant. Tobacco is classed as an Herb of Mars. (See Mars Group under Herbs). The Herbs of ♂ are generally stimulant. Tobacco stimulates at first, but later, if its use is persisted in, it becomes a depressant, and paralyzes the motor nerves of the involuntary muscles, and of the secreting nerves of the glands, and also of the Spinal Cord, and the Vagus Nerve. It is also sedative and narcotic, and undoubtedly comes under the rulership of ♅ under its persistent and habitual use. The moderate use of tobacco, if it does not debilitate the system, is said to be a protection against infection. (See Infections).

Drug Heart — Tobacco Heart — (See "Drug Heart", "Tobacco Heart", under Heart).

Snuff Habit—(See "Snuff" under Narcotics).

Tobacco Habit—Smoking—Chewing—Cigarette Habit, etc.—♅ influence; ♅ afflicted in the 6th or 12th H.; ♅ ☌ ♄ in the 6th or 12th H.; ♅ afflicted in ♌ or the 5th H., tobacco heart. (See "Cigarettes", "Tobacco Habit" under Narcotics). Case—Addicted to the Use of Tobacco—See "Self-Indulgent", No. 229, in 1001 N.N.

TOES — Digits of the Feet — The Toes are under the structural rulership of the ♓ Sign, and are opposite to the fingers, which are ruled by the ♍ Sign. The Toes are also ruled by the 12th H.

Accidents To — Hurts, Injuries, or Wounds To—♄ or ♂ afflicted in ♓ or the 12th H. (See "Accidents", "Hurts", "Injuries", under Feet).

All Diseases In — Signified by afflictions in the 12th H., and in the ♓ Sign; the malefics afflicted in ♓.

Athetosis—Inability to Hold the Fingers or Toes in One Position—A Nervous and Spasmodic Affliction — ♅ afflicted in ♓ or the 12th H.; Subs at LPP. (See "Athetosis" under Palsies).

Coldness Of—Coldness and Whiteness of — (See "Raynaud's Disease" under Fingers).

Corns — Corns and Bunions — (See Bunions).

Cramps In — ♅ afflicted in ♓. (See "Cramps" under Feet).

Deformed Toes — Afflictions in ♓ or the 12th H.; ♄ or ♂ afflicted in ♓.

Diseases Of — Distempers In — Afflictions in ♍ or ♓; ♄ or ♂ afflicted in ♓; malefics in ♓. (See "Diseases In", "Distempers", under Feet).

Feet — (See the various subjects under Feet).

Fingers—(See the paragraphs under Fingers).

Gout In—(See "Feet" under Gout).

Ingrowing Nails — (See "Ingrowing" under Nails).

Joints — Gout In — (See "Feet" under Gout).

Left Foot — Two Toes Missing On — Case—See "Born Incomplete", No. 281, in 1001 N.N.

Missing—Two Toes Missing on Left Foot—(See "Left Foot" in this section).

Nails—Suppuration and Phlegmonous Inflammation About the Nails—Panaris — Whitlows — Falling Out of the Nails — ♅ afflicted in ♍, ♓, or in the Signs in the 6th or 12th H., and affecting the nails of the fingers or toes. (See "Felons" under Fingers; Phlegmon, Pus).

Raynaud's Disease — (See "Coldness" in this section).

Tetanic Spasm In—(See "Fingers and Toes" under Tetanus).

Two Toes Missing—On the Left Foot —(See "Left Foot" in this section).

Whitlows—(See "Nails" in this section).

Writes with Toes—Case—See "Armless Wonder", No. 054, in 1001 N.N.

TOMBOYISHNESS — (See this subject under Females).

TONE — Tonicity of the Body — Vital Tonicity—The Normal Activity or Vigor —The Pressure or Resistance of the Body to Disease, Wear and Tear—The Stamina and Vitality—

Good Tone—The ☉ or ☽ ☌, ⚹, or △ the Asc. at B.; the ☉ well-aspected by ♂ at B.; the ☽ to the ☌ or good aspect ♃ by dir. (See "Good" under Constitution, Health, Resistance, Recuperation, Stamina, Vitality; Invigoration, Robust; "Body" under Strong; Vigor, Zest).

Lack of Tone—The Tone Lowered—Atony—The ☉ or ☽ weak and afflicted at B.; the ☽ afflicted in ♑, lowers the tone and vitality thru worry and depression; the ☽ afflicted in ♏ lowers the whole tone and the vital and natural powers of the body; the ☽ to the ☌ or ill-asp. ♄ by dir., the health suffers from want of tone; the Asc. afflicted by the ☉ or ☽; afflictions in ♎ show disturbance in the system, causing want of tone; characteristic of the Lymphatic Temperament. (See Atony, Debility, Feeble, Infirm, Invalids, Lymphatic, Pale; "Low" under Resistance, Stamina, Vitality; Sickly; "Much Sickness" under Sickness; "Weak Body" under Weak).

TONGUE—Glossa—The Organ of Taste and Speech—Ruled by ☿. The ♉ sign and ☿ have special affinity with the tongue, and the papillae of the tongue. Dr. Duz says the tongue is ruled by the ♎ sign. When in ♈ the planet ☿ has strong rule over the tongue, and greatly affects the tongue for good or ill, according to his aspects.

Chronic Glossitis—(See "Glossitis" in this section).

Cystic Tumor — Under the Tongue — Epulis — Ranula — ♀ affl. in ♉. (See "Tumor" under Gums).

Defects In — Imperfections—Impediment On—The ☉ ☌ ☿ in angles. However, if ♂ is also with them, the defect will tend to be removed when the ☽ by progression reaches the place of ♂; the ☽ Sig. □ or ☍ ☿; a ☿ disease; ☿ afflicted at B.; ☿ affl. in ♓, an impediment in the tongue. (See Dumb, Inarticulate, Mute; "Impediment", "Stammering", under Speech; "Tongue-Tied" in this section).

Epulis—(See "Cystic" in this section).

Foul Tongue—Foul and Diseased—A ☿ disease, and afflictions to ☿ at B.; ♄ ☌ or ill-asp. ☿ at B., and by dir.; the ☽ in ♈, and afflicted by the ☉ or ♂ when taken ill (Hor'y); Subs at MCP and SP. (See "Foul" under Breath).

Glossitis—Inflammation of the Tongue — Swollen Tongue — ♂ afflicted in ♉; Subs at MCP and SP (7D). The chronic form is caused by ♄ affl. in ♉, or ♄ ☌ ♂ in ♉ at B. (See Aphthae; "Inflamed" under Gums).

Impediment On — (See "Defects" in this section).

Imperfections In—(See "Defects" in this section).

Paralysis Of—♅ or ☿ affl. in ♉; ♅ ☌ ☿ in ♉, and otherwise afflicted by malefics. (See Coordination, Incoordination, Paralysis).

Ranula — (See "Cystic" in this section).

Stammering—Stuttering—(See "Stammering" under Speech).

Tongue-Tied — Case — See "Born Incomplete", No. 281 in 1001 N.N. This defect is caused by afflictions to ☿ at B.; ☿ affl. by ♄; born under ☿; a ☿ sign rising on the Asc. at B., and ☿ badly afflicted.

Tumor Of—(See "Cystic" in this section).

Writes — With Aid of the Tongue — Case—See "Tunison", No. 113, in 1001 N.N.

TONIC—Tonic Action—Tonics—The ☉ and ♂ have a tonic influence over the body. (See Constructive, Electric, Energy, Exaggerated; "Life Force" under Force; Mars, Sun).

Color—Red is a tonic color, and to wear red colors, be confined in a red room, or be treated with red lights and rays, are stimulating and bracing to the weak. Red Color is ruled by ♂. (See Colors; "Treatment" under Red; Stimulant).

Disorders — Tonic Disorders — Perverted Tonic Action — The ☉ and ♂ weak and affl. at B., or afflicting each other.

Fibers—Over-Braced Tonic Fibers—A ♂ disease. (See Fiber).

Hair Tonics—Injury From—(See Cosmetics; "Tonics" under Hair).

Medicines—Tonic Drugs—The ☉ and ♂ drugs and plants are tonic. Tonic medicines are ruled by ♂. Medicinally ♂ is tonic, and rules Iron and iron tonics. The tonic remedies of ♂ relieve neuralgia from a weak circulation caused by ♄. (See "Drugs" under Mars, Sun; Medicines, Stimulants, Treatment).

Perverted Tonic Action — (See "Disorders" in this section).

Planets—Tonic Action of—Each planet in the map of birth, according to position and aspects, is intrinsically tonic or atonic, electric or magnetic, positive or negative, and exerts a normal, natural, unnatural, or perverted influence, a plus or minus influence over the body. Planets in great conflict with each other at B. by evil aspects, and being situated contrary to their natural influences, tend to perverted tonic disorders, such as enlargements, exaggerated action, hypertrophy, overactivity, tumors, growths, etc. (See these subjects. Also see "Perverted Action" under Planets). The Tonic Planets are the ☉, ♅, ♃ and ♂. The Atonic Planets are ♆, ♄, ☽, and ♀. (See Atonic). The planet ♅ exerts an alternate, or clonic action, as in spasms, spasmodic diseases, contractions, convulsions, etc. (See Aspects, Clonic; "Organs" under Enlargement; Exaggerated, Hyperactivity, Hypertrophy; "Action Of", "Tonic Action", under Mars; Motion; "Clonic", "Tonic", under Spasmodic; "Action Of" under Sun).

Spasms—Tonic Spasms—(See Convulsions, Epilepsy; "Spasms", "Tonic", under Spasmodic).

Stimulants — Tonic Medicines — (See "Medicines" in this section; Drugs, Medicines, Poisons, Rubefacients, Stimulants).

TONSILS — The Glandular Organ on Each Side of the Fauces—Ruled by the ♉ Sign. Also strongly influenced by the opposite sign ♏, and especially at the time of Adolescence. (See "Disturbed" under Puberty). The ☽ when in ♉ strongly rules over, and affects the tonsils for good or ill, according to her aspects.

Ablation—Suppression of the Tonsils —Removal by Suppression—♄ afflicted in ♉ or ♏. Case — Of Removal of the Tonsils by Ablation—See Chap. XIII in Daath's Medical Astrology. (See Ablation, Remote, Removal, Suppression).

Amygdalitis—(See "Tonsilitis" in this section).

Cases—Of Tonsils Affected—See Figures 3A, 3B, 3C, 3D, 16B, in the book, "Astro-Diagnosis" by the Heindels; Chap. XIII in Daath's Medical Astrology.

Diseased Tonsils — Afflictions in ♉; Subs at LCP (6C), and at SP (7D). (See the various paragraphs in this section).

Enlarged Tonsils—♂ affl. in ♉ or ♏; a ♀ disease, and caused by afflictions to ♀; ♀ afflicted in ♉. (See "Swollen", "Tonsilitis", in this section; Enlargements).

Exudation On—(See Diphtheria, Exudations).

Fauces — (See the paragraphs under Fauces).

Follicular Tonsilitis — (See "Tonsilitis" in this section).

Inflamed Tonsils — ♂ afflicted in ♉. (See "Tonsilitis" in this section).

Operations—For Removal of Tonsils —Do not operate when the ☽ is passing thru the ♈, ♉, or ♊ Signs. Removal of the Tonsils by an operation tends to affect the voice, and to interfere with the proper modulation and tone of the voice. Also as the ♉ and ♏ signs are opposite and supplemental signs, removal of the tonsils adversely affects the sex functions, disturbs the puberty, and also makes child-bearing more difficult. In reality, the tonsils should never be removed, but can be shrunken, diminished, and rendered of little trouble, by the application of strong nitrate of silver solution, or the nitrate of silver stick as a cautery. It is better to snare and pinch them off with a wire snare, than to cut them off suddenly, as extreme and dangerous hemorrhage often results, or even death, from the sudden severing of the blood vessels which supply the tonsils. (See "Rules" under Operations; "Disturbed" under Puberty).

Quinsy—An Acute, Severe Inflammation of the Tonsils, and with Fever—Suppurative Tonsilitis—A ♉ and ♍ disease; ♉ or ♍ on the cusp of the Asc. or 6th H., and containing malefics; the ☉ affl. in ♉; the ☉ in ♉, ♂, or ill-asp. any of the malefics; the ☉ ♂ ♂ in the 6th H., in fixed signs, and espec. in ♉ or ♍; the ☽ affl. in ♉ or ♌, or afflicting the hyleg therefrom; the ☽ hyleg in ♉, and afflicted, and espec. with females; the ☽ in the 1st face of ♉ on the Asc., and ♂ any of the malefics; ♄ or ♂ affl. in ♉ or ♍, and espec. when afflicted in the 6th H.; ♄ ♂ ♀ in ♉; ♄ in ♒, occi., and affl. the ☉, ☽, or Asc.; a ♃ disease; ♃ affl. in ♈, and chiefly from ill-blood in the head; ♃ affl. in ♉; ♃ ♂ ♄ or ♂ in ♉, due to disturbed and restricted circulation in the tonsils; ♃ causes death by Quinsy when he is the afflictor in the disease, holding the dominion of death, and affl. the hyleg by dir.; ♂ affl. in ♉; ♀ affl. in ♉ or ♍; ♀ in ♉ in the 6th H., and affl. the ☽ or Asc. (See "Tonsilitis" in this section).

Removal of Tonsils—(See "Ablation", "Operations", in this section).

Suppuration—Of the Tonsils—Suppurative Tonsilitis—♆ affl. in ♉; ♆ ♂ ♄ in ♉. (See "Quinsy", "Tonsilitis", in this section).

Swollen Tonsils—Enlarged—Bulky—♆ in ♉, and affl. by ♄; ♆ in ♉, and between the ☉ and ♀, gives bulk to the tonsils; ♂ in ♉. (See Enlarged, Quinsy, Tonsilitis, in this section).

Throat—(See "Sore Throat", and the various paragraphs under Throat).

Tonsilitis — Amygdalitis—Inflamed Tonsils—Follicular Tonsilitis—Suppurative Tonsilitis — Many of the influences under Quinsy in this section will also apply here. The ☉, ♄, ♂, or ♀ affl. in ♉ or ♍; ♆ ♂ ♄ or ♃ in ♉; ♆ ♂ ♄ in ♉, inflamed and suppurative; ♂ ♂ ♄ in ♉, inflamed, and follicular tonsilitis; ♂ in ♉ in the 6th H. (See Quinsy, Suppuration, Swollen, in this section; Putrid, Sore Throat, Swellings, under Throat).

Trouble with Tonsils—Caused mostly by afflictions in the ♉ and ♍ zones; ♎ or ♐ on the Asc., which ordinarily places ♉ on the cusp the 6th or 8th Houses; ♉ or ♍ upon the Asc. at B.; ♂ in ♉, and with the ☽ or ♀ in ♍. Also the nasal obstructions caused by afflictions in ♍ tend to disturb the throat and tonsils. In cases of Adenoids the tonsils often become involved. (See Adenoids, Nose, Throat; the various paragraphs in this section).

TOO MUCH — Excessive — Superabundance—(See "Too Much" under Blood, **Drink, Moisture, Passion, Pleasure,**

Rain. Also see Abundance, Excess, Excesses, Fullness; "Too Full a Habit" under Habit; Hyperactivity, Over-Abundance, Plethora, Superabundance, Surfeits, etc.).

TOOLS—Sharp Tools—Injury or Death By—(See Cuts, Duels, Incised, Instruments, Iron, Stabs, Sword, Weapons).

TOOTHACHE—(See this subject under Teeth).

TOPHUS—Nodes—Nodules—(See "Nodules" under Nodes).

TORMENTED—In Mind and Body—(See Anguish, Dejection, Fears, Grief, Grievous; "Hopes Cut Off" under Hope; Insanity; "Low Spirits" under Low; Melancholic; "No Peace" under Mind; Misfortune, Obsessions, Pain, Reverses, Ruin, Suffering, Trouble, Worry, etc.).

TORN — Mangled — Lacerations — (See "Wild Animals" under Animals; Explosions, Lacerations, Machinery, Mangled, Rupture, etc.).

TORNADOES — Injury or Death By — (See "High Winds", "Hurricanes", "Tornadoes", under Wind).

TORPID—Torpidity—Torpor—The principal torpid Sign is ♓, and this sign is low in vitality. (See Pisces). Torpor is also a ♄ influence, as ♄ by his afflictions tends to hinder and suppress the functions of the body, and also to dull the mind. (See Apathy, Dull, Idle, Inactive, Indifferent, Inertia, Lassitude, Lethargy, Malaise; "Drowsiness" under Sleep; Sluggish, Stupidity; "Low" under Vitality, etc.).

TORSALGIA — Painful Torsions — (See "Torsalgia" under Torsion).

TORSION — Twistings—Contortions—♅ influence; ♅ afflicted in signs which rule the part afflicted. (See Spasmodic, Twistings).

Torsalgia—Painful Torsion or Twisting—♅ ♂ ♂ or ♀ in the sign ruling the afflicted part. (See Contortions, Contractions, Cramps; "Twistings" under Feet, Legs; "Spasmodic" under Pain; Spasmodic).

Torticollis — (See "Wry Neck" under Neck; Torticollis).

TORTICOLLIS—Contraction and Twisting of the Muscles of the Neck, and with Bending of the Head—Wry Neck —♅ afflicted in ♉. (See Contortions, Contractions, Cramps, Distortions; "Wry Neck" under Neck; Torsion, Twistings).

TORTURE — Tortured — Tortured to Death—(See "Burned At Stake" under Burning; Execution, Hanging, Lynched, Mobs).

TOTAL—

Total Blindness—(See "Total" under Blindness; Cataracts; "Both Eyes" under Eyes; Gutta Serena; "Loss Of" under Sight).

Total Depravity — (See Degenerate, Depraved, Infamous, Lewd, Licentiousness; "Low and Base" under Low; Obscene, Perversions, Shameless, Sottishness, Vile, Wench, etc.).

Total Disability — (See Deformities, Disabilities, Helplessness, Incurable, Infirm, Insanity, Invalids, Paralysis; Weakly Person" under Weak. etc.).

TOUCH—The Sense of Touch—Feeling—Sensation—Ruled by ☿. (See Feeling; "Chiropractors" under Healers; Sensation).

Disorders Of—(See Feeling, Hyperaesthesia, Insensibility, Numbness, Paraesthesia, Paralysis, Sensation, Senses, Sensibility, etc.).

TOUGH—Toughening—

Phlegm—Tough Phlegm—(See "Breast" under Phlegm).

Skin—Toughening of—(See "Toughening" under Skin). See Hardening, Thickening.

TOXAEMIA—Toxic—Toxins—A Poisonous State of the Blood—

Auto-Toxic Psychoses—Caused by afflictions in ♎, and usually due to disordered kidneys. (See "Psychoses" in this section).

Blood—Toxic Blood—Poisonous Blood—(See Impure; "Blood Poisoning" under Poison; Urea, Uremia, Uric Acid).

Gastritis—The Toxic Form from Swallowing Poison—(See "Gastritis" under Gastric).

Headache—(See "Toxaemia" under Headaches).

Jaundice—(See "Toxaemic" under Jaundice).

Psychoses—Auto-Toxic Psychoses—Toxic Psychoses—(See Autointoxication, Diabetes; "Psychoses" under Psychic; Uremia).

Toxaemia—A Poisoned State of the Blood—Caused by ♄, due to the retention of the wastes of the system. Also the pathological action of ♃, due to excesses in diet, over-eating, plethora, etc. Also caused by afflictions in ♎, improper kidney action, and the accumulation of too much Urea in the blood. (See "Blood" in this section; Deposits; "Excesses" under Diet, Eating; Elimination, Excretion, Fatigue; "Diseased" under Kidneys; Plethora, Septic, Surfeits, Uremia, Wastes).

Toxins—(See "Offensive" under Humours).

Uremia—Toxic Blood from Urea—(See Uremia).

TRACHEA—Windpipe—Under the internal rulership of the ♉ sign. Also ruled by ♊. Also ☿ in ♉, ♊, or ♒ rules and affects the windpipe, the air cells, breath, and nerves of the Respiratory System.

Nervous Contraction Of—♄ in ♌, and affl. by the ☌ of ☿ in ♒.

Obstructed—The Trachea Obstructed with Phlegm—(See "Breast" under Phlegm).

Phlegm In—(See "Obstructed" in this section). Subluxations at LCP (7C) tend to disorders of the Trachea.

TRACHOMA—(See "Granulated Lids" under Eyelids).

TRACT—A Canal or Passage—

Alimentary Tract—(See Alimentary).

Genito-Urinary Tract—(See Genito-Urinary).

Respiratory Tract—(See Breathing, Bronchial, Lungs, Pulmonary).

TRADE—The Business—The Occupation—The Employment—Accidents, Injury, Illness, or Death In—(See Business, Employment, Machinery, Vocation).

TRAFFIC—Killed or Injured In—(See Journeys, Railroads, Travel, Vehicles).

TRAGEDIES—Tragical—The planet ♅ rules Tragedies, Sudden Events, Calamities, Catastrophies, Explosions, Accidents by Electricity, Machinery, etc. (See these subjects).

Tragical Death—(See "Tragical" under Death).

TRAMPLED—Trodden—Crushed—

Trampled to Death—Trampled by a Mob—Crushed By—Danger of—♄ ori. in a fixed sign, □ or ☍ the ☉ at B., or ♄ occi. in a fixed sign, and □ or ☍ the ☽, and ♄ in a contrary condition. (See Crushed, Mobs, Riots; "Death" under Suffocation; Tumults).

TRANCE—A Form of Catalepsy—Protracted Syncope—

Trance Conditions—Involuntary Trance—A ♆ disease and affliction, and afflictions to ♆; ♆ □ or ☍ ♃; ♆ afflicted in the 8th H., danger of premature burial, or being buried alive, due to trance conditions simulating death; ♆ the afflicting planet tends to trance, or simulated death, and ending in coma or death; ♆ afflicted in ♈, and espec. in the 8th H.; an ♈ disease and afflictions in ♈. (See "Buried Alive" under Burial; Catalepsy, Coma, Dreams, Emotions, Fainting, Sleep).

TRANQUILITY—A Tranquil Mind and Nature—(See Balance, Calm, Cheerfulness, Contentment, Equilibrium, Gentle, Happiness, Joy, Kind, Mild; "Peace of Mind" under Mind; Peaceful, Poise, Quiet; "Even Temper" under Temper).

TRANSFORMATION—Transforming—Metamorphosis—Structural Changes—Metabolism, etc.—

Cell Substance—Transformation of—(See "Substance" under Cells; Metabolism, Metamorphosis, Structural).

Functions—The Transforming Functions In the Body—(See "Substance" under Cells; Conservation).

Liver—Fatty Transformation of—Fatty Degeneration of—(See Liver).

TRANSFUSION—Of Blood—(See Bleeding).

TRANSIENT DISEASES—(See Acute, Colds; "Temporary" under Insanity; "Transitory" under Mania; Mild, Quick Diseases, Slight, Temporary, Transitory, etc.).

Transient Disposition—In Disease—(See Diathesis, Directions).

TRANSITORY—Of Short Duration—

Transitory Diseases—(See Cholera, Epidemics, Pestilence, Transient).

Transitory Experiences—Are represented by the ☽. (See Events; "Represents" under Moon).

Transitory Mania—(See Mania).

TRANSITS—Of the Planets—The transits of the planets are not, in themselves, as dangerous as the Progressed influences, or Primary Directions, but transits assist in bringing an evil direction into action. It is important to watch the evil transits of the malefics, especially in passing judgment upon a disease, and when it will tend to be worse, or get better, according to the nature of the transiting planet, whether it be benefic or malefic. When there are some very evil directions culminating over a person, the transit of ♄ or ♂, or other malefics, which may add their evil force to the directions, can usually be depended upon as causing a time of misfortune, accident, disaster, or ill-health in the life of the native, even though the life seemed to be moving along quietly until the transit came upon the scene. Also the transit of a malefic over a Stellium of planets in a sign is bound to cause considerable disturbance for the time, and also a transit by □ or 8 is evil in its effects, and helps to intensify other evils which may be culminating over the native, if a malefic, or to bring some great good if the transit of a benefic unites its force to that of good directions, or progressions. The transit of ♄ thru any sign tends to bring disease, lowered functions, and suppressions in the part ruled by the sign he is in for the time, and especially if he is passing his own radical place, or in signs in □ or 8 to his place in the map of birth. The transit of ♂ thru the signs tends to bring injury, fever, or inflammation to the part ruled by the sign he is transiting, and to draw more heat to that part for the time. And so on with each of the planets, as they all tend to carry their special benefits or afflictions along with them, according to their nature, and aspects for the time, and to affect each sign they pass thru for good or ill. Chap. XXXIX, in Pearce's Textbook of Astrology is devoted entirely to Transits, and the effects of each planet by transit. (See Directions, Primary Directions, Secondary Directions).

TRANSMISSION—Hereditary Transmission—(See Diathesis, Heredity, Innate, Organic, Structural).

TRANSUDATION—Of Fluids—☽ disorders. (See Dropsy, Exudations, Fluids, Oedema, Osmosis).

TRANSVERSE COLON—(See Colon).

TRAP ROCKS—Minerals ruled by ♂.

TRAUMATISM—(See Injuries, Wounds).

TRAVEL—The 3rd H. rules Short Journeys, Inland Journeys, as by Rail, Automobile, Bus, or Vehicle. The 9th H. rules Long Journeys, Ocean Voyages, and Travel Abroad. The conditions ruling these two houses in the map of birth, and also how the present planetary positions affect these radical houses and the hyleg by transit, direction, or progression, should be consulted before engaging in travel, and to know whether the native would be fortunate or unfortunate in these matters. It is better for the health and general affairs for some people to travel and seek change of location, while others should keep quiet, remain in one locality, or at their place of birth, and avoid travel. This subject of Travel is largely considered in the Articles on Abroad, Journeys, Rail-

roads, Ships, Vehicles, and Voyages, and will be further considered here. See the following subjects, and the paragraphs under them, when only listed here—

Abroad — Travel Abroad — Fortunate or Unfortunate—(See the various paragraphs under Abroad, Foreign Lands, Sea, Ships, Shipwreck, Voyages).

Accidents In—Malefics in the 3rd or 9th H. at B., and by tr. or dir., or the lords of these houses afflicted; malefics in the 3rd or 9th H. at a Solar Rev., travel should be avoided during the following year; the ☽ to the ☌ ♂ by dir., and either the ☽ or ♂ in the 3rd or 9th H. at B., or by dir. (See "Accidents" under Abroad, Journeys, Railroads, Ships, Vehicles, Voyages; Maritime, Navigation, Shipwreck. For Sickness from an Accident in Travel see "Sickness" in this section).

Altitude — Whether to Travel In a High or Low Altitude—(See Altitude).

Assassinated — During Travel — (See "Assassinated Abroad" under Assassination).

Avalanches — Hurt By — (See Avalanches).

Avoid Travel—When the malefics are in the 3rd or 9th H. at B., or the lords of these houses are seriously afflicted by malefics at B., and by dir. (See "Avoid" under Journeys, Voyages; Bad Time For, Current Year, Danger In, Death During, and the various paragraphs in this section).

Bad Time for Travel—Dangerous to Travel — When malefics are passing thru the 3rd or 9th H. of the radix by tr., dir., or progression, and espec. if these houses contained malefics at B.; do not travel at a time when the lords of the 3rd or 9th H. at B. are under severe affliction; ♂ to the cusp of the 3rd or 9th H. by dir. (See "Bad Time For" under Journeys; Avoid, Current Year, Danger, Death, and the various paragraphs in this section).

Bandits—Injured by During Travel—(See Bandits).

Beasts—Attacks by Wild Beasts During Travel—(See "Wild Beasts" in this section).

Beneficial—Travel Safe and Beneficial — Good Time For — ♃ and ♀ in good asp. to the ☽; ♃ or ♀ in the 3rd or 9th H. at B., and no malefics therein, and the benefics not affl. by malefics by dir.; lords of the 3rd and 9th H. at B. being benefics, and with no malefics in these houses, and the benefics well-aspected by dir. (See Fortunate, Good Time For, Health, in this section).

Bites During Travel—(See "Journeys" under Bites).

Burns—(See "Journeys" under Burns).

Cannibals—Attacks By—(See "Savages" in this section).

Captivity—Held In Captivity During Travel—(See Captivity).

Cattle—Attacks by During Travel—(See "Travel" under Cattle).

Change of Scenery — Good for the Health—(See "Air Sign People" under Residence).

Countries to Avoid—Places Unfavorable for Travel—Avoid Countries ruled by the Sign containing ♄ or ♂ at B.; avoid those ruled by ♃ and ♀ if they be lords of evil houses, as of the 6th, 8th, or 12th H.; avoid those Quarters and directions in the map of birth containing malefics unless the malefics be essentially dignified and strong, or lords of the 1st, 2nd, 10th, or 4th H. (See Countries, Location, Nations; "Native Land" under Native; "Place of Birth" under Place; "Abroad" under Residence; "Direction" in this section).

Current Year — Dangerous to Travel During—♅, ♄, or ♂ on the cusp of the 3rd or 9th H. at B., and these degrees of the malefics ascending at a Solar Rev. (See Accidents, Danger, Death, Drowned, Fire, and the various paragraphs in this section).

Cuts—(See "Travel" under Cuts).

Danger In Travel — Dangerous to Travel—The ☉ hyleg at B., and to the ☌ or ill-asp. ♄ or ♂ by dir., or other malefic, if such malefic were in the 3rd or 9th H. at B.; the ☉ to the ☌ or ill-asp. ♅ or ♂ by dir.; the ☉ to the ☌ ♄ by dir., either by Land or Sea, and if ♄ and ♂ govern the Lights, or oppose them, travel will be dangerous and unprofitable, and if these planets be in watery signs there is great danger of shipwreck or being lost in the Desert and uninhabitable places — if in fixed signs they tend to death or injury climbing precipices—if in cardinal signs, to be sickly and in want of food — if in human signs, to suffer danger from injury by robbers and bandits—if in earthy signs, to suffer injury or death in an earthquake, or by wild beasts, and if ☿ have dignity there also, there is danger of injury by venomous reptiles; the ☽ in the 3rd or 9th H. at B., and to the ☌ or ill-asp. ♅, ♄, or ♂ by dir.; the ☽ to the ☌ or ill-asps. the Asc. or M.C. by dir.; the ☽ to the □ or ☍ ☿ by dir., and the ☽ hyleg, and ☿ affl. at B.; the ☽ to the ☌ ♂ by tr. or dir.; ♆, ♅, ♄, or ♂ affl. in ♊ or ♐ at B., or in the 3rd or 9th H.; ♄ by tr., prog., or dir., or at a Solar Rev., affl. the places of the ☽ or ☿ at B., and espec. if ♄ affl. these planets at B.; ♄ ascending at B., and the ☉ to the ☌ or ill-asp. ♄ by dir.; ♃ affl. in ♊ or ♐, or in the 3rd or 9th H.; ♃ in ♐, ℞ and afflicted, and lord of the year at the Vernal, danger in travel generally; ♂ to the ☌ or ill-asp. ♄ by dir., and espec. if either rule the 3rd or 9th H. at B.; ☿ affl. in the 8th H. at B., and by dir.; the Asc. to the place of ♄ or ☋ in the 3rd H. at B.; the 2nd decan. of ♊ on the Asc. at B., ruled by ♂; malefics in the 3rd or 9th H. at B., and affl. the ☉ or ☽; the Sig. of travel in evil asp. to the ☉, ♅, ♄, or ♂, and these widely separated from each other, or ascend after the other Significators. (See Abroad, Bandits; "Lost In" under Desert; Foreign Lands, Highwaymen; "Danger" under Journeys, Voyages; Maritime, Navigation, Ocean, Pirates, Railroads, Robbers, Sea, Ships, Shipwreck, Vehicles; "Perils By" under Waters; the various paragraphs in this Article).

Death During Travel — Sickness or Death During Travel—Any of the malefics in the 3rd or 9th H. at B., and afflicted; ♄ ruler of the 3rd or 9th H. at B., and ♄ ☌ or evil asp. the Asc. by dir.; ☿ in the 8th H. and afflicted; malefics in the 3rd or 9th H., and affl. the ☉ or ☽; the afflictor to the Sig. of Travel being in the 12th H., and afflicted in ♈, ♎, or ♑; lord of the 6th H. in the 8th H., and afflicted. (See "Death" under Abroad, Falls, Heights, Journeys, Railroads, Sea, Ships, Voyages).

Desert — Lost In the Desert — In the Wilderness, or In Inaccessible Places —(See Desert).

Direction to Travel — For the Best Health and Success — Travel in the direction of the Benefics at B. if they are not rulers of evil houses, or severely afflicted by malefics at B., or by dir. Travel to Countries ruled by the Signs containing the Benefics at B. if they are not evilly disposed. (See "Friends" under Residence; the references in the paragraph, "Countries to Avoid", in this section).

Drowned During Travel—(See Drowning; "Drowning" under Sea; Ships, Shipwreck).

Earthquake—Injured by In Travel—(See "Danger" in this section).

Escapes — Has Narrow Escapes from Death or Injury During Travel—♃ in ♊ or the 3rd H., and afflicted, may be in wrecks, but escapes injury; ♃ in ♐ or the 9th H., and afflicted, may be in a shipwreck, or in railroad wrecks Abroad, but usually escapes injury, and is saved, and espec. if the ✶ or △ aspects of ♃ intervene, or the Benefics are elevated above the malefics or afflicting planet at the time. (See Escapes, Railroads).

Evil Time for Travel — (See "Bad Time" in this section).

Exposure In Travel — Health Suffers From—(See "Travel" under Exposure; Weather, Wet, in this section).

Falls — (See "Travel" under Falls, Heights; Accidents, Danger, Sickness, in this section).

Famine—Danger of During Travel—(See Famine; "Food" in this section).

Fatigue—Sickness From—(See "Sickness" in this section).

Fevers — (See "Health" under Journeys; "Sickness" in this section).

Fire — Danger From — (See "Ships" under Fire).

Food—Lack of—Danger of Starvation and Privation During Travel—Malefics in the 3rd or 9th H. in earthy signs, and afflicting the ☉ or ☽; the afflictor to the Sig. of Travel in the 12th H., and in ♈, ♎, or ♑. (See Desert, Famine).

Foreign Travel—Will prove favorable and benefit the health when there are benefics in the 9th H. at B., and not afflicted, and when the radix indicates that the Native Land is not beneficial. Malefics in the 9th H., and afflicted, and with a benefic in the 4th H., the native should remain in his Native Land. (See Abroad, Foreign, Nadir;

"Native Land" under Native; "Place of Birth" under Place; Countries to Avoid, Health, and the various paragraphs in this section).

Fortunate In Travel—Benefics in the 3rd or 9th H. at B., well-aspected, and with no malefics in these houses, and with many planets in watery signs; lords of the 3rd and 9th .H. well-placed and aspected, and with fortunate signs upon the cusps of the 3rd or 9th H.

Good Time For— (See "Good Time" under Journeys, Voyages; "Beneficial" in this section).

Health — Travels for Health — ☿ affl. in the 6th H., and usually on account of nervousness, nervous breakdown, overwork, worries and troubles. (See "Travel" under Health). For influences which tend to impair the health during travel see Exposure, Sickness, Wet Journeys, in this section.

Heights — Falls from During Travel —(See "Falls" in this section).

High Altitudes — Should Travel In — (See Altitude).

Home or Abroad—Travel Where You Will, At Home or Abroad—The ☉ or lord of the Asc. in no way unfortunate, and not afflicted by any planet. (See "Native Land" under Native; "Prospers Anywhere" under Residence).

Hurts—Or Injuries During Travel— Malefics in the 3rd or 9th H., and affl. the ☉ or ☽; ♄, ♂, and the ☽ conjoined in ♒; the 2nd decan. of ♓ on the Asc., ruled by ♂; ♂ afflicting the cusp of the 3rd or 9th H. by dir. The time of possible injury during travel is shown by the arcs of directions to the Sigs. of Travel. (See "Time Of" under Accidents; Accidents, Avalanches, Danger, Falls, Heights, Robbers, Stabs, and the various paragraphs in this section).

Illness — During Travel, or Due to Travel—(See Exposure, Fevers, Health, Sickness, and the various paragraphs in this section).

Imprisonment—During Travel—(See Captivity; "Travel" under Prison).

Inconveniences—Incommodities During Travel — An eclipse of the ☉ in the 2nd decan. of ♉.

Injuries—(See Accidents, Escapes, Falls, Fire, Hurts, Sickness, and the various paragraphs in this section).

Inland Travel — (See "Inland" under Journeys; Railroads, Vehicles).

Journeys — (See the subjects under Journeys).

Kicks—During Travel—(See Kicks).

Land Travel—Danger In—(See "Land Journeys" under Journeys; Railroads, Vehicles).

Location—Travel As Related To—(See Abroad, Location, Native Land, Place of Birth, Residence; Countries to Avoid, Direction, in this section).

Long Journeys — (See Abroad, Journeys, Ships, Voyages).

Losses — (See Bad Time, Robbers, Weather, and the various paragraphs in this section).

Love of Travel—♃ and ♐ prominent at B.; the ☉ in a cardinal sign in the 3rd or 9th H., and with a card. sign on the cusp of these houses. (See "Wanderer" in this section).

Low Altitudes—Should Live, or Travel In—(See Altitude).

Misfortunes—In Travel—(See Accidents, Danger, Death, Falls, Hurts, Imprisonment, Robbers, Sickness, and the various paragraphs in this section. Also see the subjects under Abroad, Foreign Lands, Journeys, Navigation, Railroads, Sea, Ships, Shipwreck, Vehicles, Voyages).

Much Travel — Travels Much — (See Love of Travel, Wanderer, in this section).

Murdered — During Travel — (See "Journey" under Murder).

Narrow Escapes—(See "Escapes" in this section).

Native Land — Should Remain In — Should Remove — (See "Native Land" under Native).

Ocean Travel — ♆ prominent at B. leads to. (See "Disposes To" under Voyages).

Parts of World—Fortunate and Unfortunate Parts for Travel — (See Countries to Avoid, Direction, in this section).

Pirates—Danger From—(See Pirates).

Place of Birth — Travel As Related To — (See "Place of Birth" under Place).

Poisoning—(See "Travel" under Poison).

Precipices—Falls From—(See "Travel" under Heights).

Privations—(See Desert, Food, Losses, Starvation, and the various paragraphs in this section).

Railroad Travel—(See Railroads).

Remains In One Place—The ☉, ☽, and many planets in fixed signs at B., or fixed signs upon the angles, not inclined to travel much, and such people often spend their entire lives in the community of their birth. (See "Good Powers Of" under Concentration; "Fixed Signs" under Fixed; Recluse; "Travels Little" in this section).

Removals; Reptiles—Injured by During Travel — (See Reptiles; "Danger" in this section).

Residence — (See the subjects under Residence).

Robbers — Attacks by During Travel —(See Robbers; "Danger" in this section).

Safe — Travel Safe and Beneficial — (See Beneficial, Fortunate, Good Time, in this section).

Savages — Attacks By — (See Cannibals).

Sea Travel — (See Abroad, Foreign Lands, Maritime, Navigation, Ocean, Sailors, Sea, Ships, Shipwreck, Voyages).

Shipwreck; Short Journeys — (See "Short" under Journeys; Railroads, Vehicles).

Should Never Travel—(See Avoid, Remains In One Place, in this section; "Place of Birth" under Place).

Sickness — During Travel — Sickly — Fatigue — Lord of the 6th H. in the 9th, and afflicted; ♄ or ♂ ruler of the 6th H. at B., and in the 3rd or 9th H. at a Solar Rev., or in the 3rd or 9th by tr. or dir., sickness from an accident, injury, fall, or misfortune; ♄ affl. in ♌ or ♐ tends to sickness from fatigue in travel. (See "Sickness" under Abroad, Ships, Voyages; "Ill-Health" under Foreign Lands; "Health" under Journeys; Danger, Death, Fevers, and the various paragraphs in this section).

Stabs and Cuts—(See "Travel" under Cuts).

Starvation—(See "Food" in this section; "Privations" under Sea).

Stings—(See "Journeys" under Bites; Stings).

Storms at Sea—(See "Tempests" under Sea; Shipwreck).

Thirst — May Suffer From — (See "Food" in this section; "Lost In" under Desert).

Time to Travel—Good and Bad Times —Time of Injury In—(See Accidents, Bad Time, Good Time, Hurts, Sickness, and the various paragraphs in this section).

Travel Where You Will—(See "Home or Abroad" in this section).

Travels Little—The ☽ cadent, and in a fixed sign, except when in ♏; the ☽ and ☿ in fixed signs, in angles, little disposition to travel; many planets in fixed signs, or fixed signs upon the angles. (See "Remains In One Place" in this section).

Travels Much — (See Love of Travel, Wanderer, in this section; "Many Changes" under Residence).

Trouble—In Travel—(See "Weather", and the various paragraphs in this section).

Unfortunate—In Travel—(See "Should Never Travel", and the various paragraphs in this section).

Vehicles—(See the subjects under Vehicles).

Venomous Creatures — Injured By — (See "Journeys" under Bites; Venomous; "Danger" in this section).

Voyages — (See the various subjects under Voyages).

Wanderer — Travels Much — Love of Travel—♅ strong and ascending at B.; ♄ or ♂ Sig. □ or ☍ ☽); ♂ Sig. ☌ ☽); the ☽ ascending at B.; the ☽ cadent in the 3rd or 9th H.; the ☽ ruler at B.; ♃ Sig. ☌ ☽); the 21° ♋ on the Asc. (See "Love Of" in this section; Roaming, Wanderer).

Water Travel — (See "Sea Travel" in this section; Voyages).

Weather—Meets with Losses, Trouble, or Bad Weather In Travel—The ☽ in the 3rd or 9th H. at B., and affl. by malefics; the malefics in evil asp. the ☽ at B. (See "Wet" under Journeys; "Tempests" under Sea; "Exposure", "Winds", in this section).

Wet Journeys — Health Suffers By — (See "Wet" under Journeys).

Wild Beasts — Attacks by During Travel — (See "Wild Animals" under Animals; "Danger" in this section).

Wilderness—Lost In—(See Desert).

Winds — Meets with Contrary Winds and Storms — (See "Weather" in this section; "Storms" under Wind).

TREACHERY—Treacherous—The ♆, ♓, and 12th H. influences tend to secret treachery. Deliberate treachery, and with malice, is usually ♏ influence. Treachery thru greed, covetousness, or for revenge, is ♄ influence. Also the ♂ element is usually configurated with the influences which lead to violent treachery. When ♀ adds her influence, women are usually involved, or a poison death. The ♆ and ♏ influences usually lead to the most treacherous attacks. Ambush attacks, plots, and the work of secret enemies, are denoted by the 12th H. The 8th H. shows the influences working over, and the fate of secret enemies. The Signs containing malefics at B. show the types and locations of the worst enemies. Private and secret enemies are ruled and indicated by the 12th H. and its conditions.

Blindness By—(See "Treachery" under Blindness).

Death or Injury By—Denoted by the 12th H., and malefics in the 12th, afflicting the 12th, or lord of the 12th a malefic, and afflicted; the ☉ to the ☌ ♂ by dir., and especially involving the 12th H.; the ☉ to the place of Antares, threatened with treachery; the ☽, ♄, or ♂ to the cusp the 12th H. by dir.; the ☽ to the ☌ or ill-asp. ♂ by dir.; the ☽ in the 12th H. at the Vernal, lady of the year, and afflicted, and with no gd. asp. of ♃ or ♀; ♆ the afflicting planet; ♆ affl. in the 1st or 12th H.; ♄ in ♏, ☌, or evil asp. the Asc. by dir.; ♄ and ♂ in signs of human form, and afflicting the Luminaries; lord of the 8th H. a malefic, in the 8th, and affl. by the lord of the 6th or 12th H.; lord of the 7th H. a malefic, and in the 12th H., and afflicted; lord of the 8th in the 12th, and affl. the hyleg or lord of the Asc., and with no benefics in the 12th H.; ruler of the 12th afflicting the Significator; the 20° ♍ on the Asc. (See Ambushes, Assassination; "Secret Enemies" under Enemies; Feuds, Jealousy; "Mischief at Hand" under Mischief; Murdered, Plots; "Death by Poison" under Poison; Revenge, Twelfth House; "Death" under Violence; the various paragraphs in this section).

Female Treachery—Death or Injury By—The ☽ hyleg, and to the ☌ or ill-asp. ♂ by dir., and ♀ throwing an ill aspect; ♄ in the Asc., ☍ the ☉ or ☽, and ♀ also be evilly configurated with both ♄ and ☿; ♄ in a brutal sign, ori., and □ or ☍ the ☉ at B., or occi., □ or ☍ the ☽ at B., and ♀ give testimony, and by poison; ♂ just setting in □ or ☍ the ☉ or ☽, and ♀ adding her testimony to ♂; ♀ and ☿ conjoined with ♄, and ♄ affl. the hyleg; the M.C. to the place of the Pleiades or Pollux. (See "Tragical Death" under Death; "Injured Thru Women" under Men; "Women" under Poison).

Imprisonment—By Treachery of Relatives or Enemies—(See "Plots" under Prison).

Insane Asylum — Confined In by the Work of an Enemy—(See "Asylums" under Insanity).

Treacherous — Given to Treachery — The ☉ Sig. □ or 8 ♄; the ☽ Sig. in ♏; the ☽, ♀, or ☿ Sig. □ or 8 ♂; ♅ □ or 8 ♄; ♄ Sig. □ or 8 ♂ or ☿; ♂ ill-dignified at B., and afflicted; ♂ Sig. in 8, and afflicted;· ♂ Sig. □ or 8 ♄; ☿ Sig. ☌ ♂, a treacherous miscreant; the 28° ♏, or the 13° ♓ on the Asc. (See Cheating, Deceitful, Dishonest, Forgers, Gambling, Liars, Libelers; "Low and Base" under Low; Malevolent, Malicious; "Active to Do Mischief" under Mischief; Pettifogging, Revengeful, Shrewd, Thieves; "Vile Wretch" under Vile; Wicked, etc.).

TREAD — The Step—Treading Walk— (See "Awry" under Gait. Note the various paragraphs under Gait, Walk).

TREASON—(See Sedition).

TREATMENT—The Treatment of Disease—This book is not intended to be a Treatise on the Treatment or Cure of Disease, but rather to go into the Planetary Causes of Disease. However, the true treatment of disease is based upon the planetary influences, and upon the Antipathy and Sympathy between the Planets, and what they rule. The Planets cause disease by their afflicting aspects, and according to their nature, and the diseases of one planet are combatted by the forces, herbs, and remedies of an opposing planet, or by the remedies of the afflicting planet itself. Thus arose the theories of Antipathy and Sympathy in the treatment of disease. The Allopathic School is based upon Antipathy, or contrary influences, in the treatment of disease. The Homeopathic School is based upon Sympathy, and Similars, in the treatment of disease. These Principles are discussed in the Articles on Antipathy, Cure, Healers, Homeopathy, Medicines, Opposites, Polarity, Praeincipients, Remedies, Sympathy, Therapeutics, etc. While there is in Nature a remedy for every disease in its locality, an Herb, Mineral, Root, or Plant, there are also various ways and means which Man has discovered to combat disease, and neutralize the afflicting forces. These are represented in the various Schools of Healing, and all are good, have their strong points, and their place in the cure and treatment of disease. This book is not intended to go into the merits of any School of Healing, but rather to give to all a Scientific explanation of the Philosophy and Causes of Disease, and they are left free to apply whatever treatment they desire, and in which they have faith, and in which the Patient also has faith. Wrong thinking and adverse mental states, are also the cause of many diseases, due to the afflictions in the Map of Birth, which often lead to Imaginary Diseases at first, and then to real ones, and lower the vital forces of the body. These can be combatted by the Mental, Psychic, and Spiritual Schools of Healing, to a large extent, for when the Mind is once set right, many of the evils of ill-health soon take their exit. (See "Treatment" under Melan-

choly). Good Health should be Man's heritage, and he should be taught to think in terms of perfect heatlh, and avoid thinking in terms of disease. In Ancient Times all Physicians were required to be Astrologers before they were allowed to Practice Medicine, or the Healing Art. They were required to know the Philosophy of each case, and how to go at the treatment on a planetary basis, and to properly combat the disease with the remedies at hand. But in the Middle Ages the Science of Medical Astrology was more or less suppressed by those in Authority, and this knowledge became a Lost Science, but it is now being revived, and soon should be a required study in the Curriculum of every School which teaches the Art of Healing. Each Physician, or Healer, should know something of the Elements of Astrology, and how to draw up a Star Map of Birth for his patients, or at least look up the Signs in which the planets were at birth, to know what parts of the body are most afflicted, and the vulnerable parts, or organs, be sure of your diagnosis, and then proceed with the treatment intelligently. The Temperament of the patient also should be studied from the star map of birth, as every patient is under one of the fundamental Temperaments, the Choleric, Nervous, Sanguine, or Lymphatic, and each of these Temperaments requires a different handling. Also Location plays an important part in treatment, and the Map of Birth shows the proper location, whether it should be in a high or low altitude, at the birthplace, in the Native Land, or to go Abroad, and in what direction to travel, and which Nation or Country will give the patient the best vibrations for healing. Also the compatibility, or incompatibility between Healer and Patient should be looked into, and the Radical Maps of each show this, as the wrong Healer often unknowingly kills his patient, and the right Healer sees him get well. Also the Map of Birth should be studied to know what the nature of the trials of the patient are, his peculiar weaknesses, his besetting sins, his wrong tendencies, which may be causing the disease, so as to give proper advice. A volume in itself could be written along these lines as to how to treat patients Scientifically, and according to the leadings and indications of Astrology, which shows God's Plan over each individual, and the relation of every one to Nature.

For further study along this line, see the following subjects in this book— Abroad, Acquired Diseases, Altitude, Antipathy, Aspects, Attraction, Character, Colors; "Compatibility" under Healers; Correspondences, Course of Disease, Crises in Disease; Death (Arguments For); Diagnosis, Diathesis, Directions, Disease, Drugs, Duration of Disease, Electricity (Healing By); Environment, Events, External Influences, Fate, Galen, Habits, Harmony, Healers, Health, Herbs, Heredity, Hippocrates, Homeopathy, Horoscope, Hypnotism, Idiosyncrasies, Ill-Health; "Incompatibility", "Injured By", under

Healers; Kepler, Location, Long Diseases, Magic, Magnetism, Map of Birth, Medical Astrology, Mind, Nations; "Native Land" under Native; Nativity; "Negative Nature" under Negative; Newton (Sir Isaac); Operations (Rules For); Opposites, Organic Diseases, Paracelsus, Parts of the Body; Physicians (see Healers); "Place of Birth" under Place; Planets, Polarity, Positive Nature, Praeincipients, Predisposition, Prevention of Disease; Prognosis, Psychic Diseases, Radix, Receptive, Remedies, Repulsions, Residence, Short Diseases, Sickness, Signature, Spiritual, Structural Diseases, Subluxations, Suggestion, Surgeons, Susceptibility, Sympathy, Temperaments, Tendencies, Therapeutics, Travel, Typical Drugs, Vertebrae, Vibration; "Days of the Week" under Week; Zodiac Salts, etc. These, and many other subjects listed in this book, have their place in a knowledge of the patient, the disease in hand, and its treatment. If the subject you have in mind is not mentioned in this Article, look for it in the alphabetical arrangement.

TREES—Corruption of the Fruit of— (See Corruption, Fig Trees, Fruit, Herbs, Plants, Roots, Rottenness, Seeds, Vegetation, Vines, etc.).

TREMBLINGS—(See Tremors).

TREMORS — Tremblings — Quivering — Twitching—Thrills—A ♅ affliction to ♒, which Sign rules the Organ of Co-ordination, and due to Incoordination and impeded nerve force to a part, or organ; a ♅ disease; ♅ affl. in ♒; ♅ afflicted in the 6th H.; a ☉ disease; a ♄ disease, due to deposits, hardening, and impaired functions; ♄ affl. in ♏, nervous trembling; a ☿ disease, and caused by afflictions to ☿. (See Contractions, Coordination; "Movements" under Erratic; Incoordination, Jerky, Motor, Palsy, Saint Vitus Dance, Spasmodic, Tics, Twitchings).

Eyeballs—Trembling of—(See "Nystagmus" under Eyeballs).

Heart — Trembling of — (See "Trembling" under Heart).

Morbid Tremors—(See Subsultus).

Muscles — Trembling of — (See "Tensity" under Muscles).

Subsultus — Morbid Tremors — (See Subsultus).

TRIALS — Tribulations — Troubles — Trouble and Sorrow are ruled by the 12th H.

Has Many Trials—And Tribulations— A total eclipse falling on the place of the ☉ at B.; ♄ Sig. □ or ☍ the ☽; the ☽ Sig. □ or ☍ ♄ or ♂. (See Fortune, Miseries, Misfortune, Renunciation, Reverses, Ruin, Self-Undoing, Sorrow, Trouble, Twelfth House, Vexations).

TRIANGLE — The Terminal Triangle— The Terminal Houses—(See Terminal). The Triangle is also the symbol of the Trine Aspect, one of the very fortunate aspects between the planets. (See Aspects, Trine, Triplicities).

TRIBULATIONS—(See Trials, Trouble).

TRICHIASIS—(See Eyelids).

TRICKY — (See Deceitful, Dishonest, Liars, Pettifogging, Shrewd).

TRINE ASPECT—(△)—The 120° Aspect between the planets, and one of the very fortunate aspects for harmony and good health. (See Aspects, Sextile, Triplicities).

TRIPLE PERSONALITY—(See Personality).

TRIPLETS—

Three Born—♃, ♀, or ☊ in a fruitful sign on the cusp of the 1st or 5th H., three may be born, and espec. if the ☽ have good aspect. Also ♃ or ♀ in the 10th or 11th H., in a watery sign, or in the 4th or 5th H. if there are no benefics in the 10th or 11th, there may be two or three children at one confinement, and espec. if in bicorporeal signs, but if in other places, only one child. (See "Single Births" under Children; Double Bodied Signs, Fruitful, Predetermination, Quadruplets, Twins). Cases of Triplets Born—See "Triplets", Numbers 333, 334, 335, in 1001 N.N.

Three Females—If the ☽, ♀, and ☿ at conception behold the ☉, ☽, or Asc. from bicorporeal signs, there will be three females conceived.

Three Males—If ♄, ♃, and ♂ behold the ☉, ☽, or Asc. at conception, from bicorporeal signs, there will be three males conceived. Also when ♄, ♃, and ♂ are in ♊, ♐, or ♓, and configurated with the ☉, ☽, Asc., or 1st H. Such conceptions very often are not complete, and children so born have deformities or imperfections.

Two Females, One Male—If two feminine planets, and one masculine planet at conception behold the ☉, ☽, or Asc. from bicorporeal signs, as ♊, ♐, ♓, two females and one male will be conceived.

Two Males, One Female—If two masculine planets, and one feminine planet at conception, as ♄, ♃, and ♀, behold the ☉, ☽, or Asc. from bicorporeal signs, two males and one female will be conceived. (See Conception, Congenital; "Predetermination of Sex" under Predetermination; Prenatal Epoch).

TRIPLICITY — Triplicities—These are the Fiery, Airy, Earthy, and Watery Signs, and there are three signs in each class. In the Fiery signs there are ♈, ♌, ♐. In the Airy Signs, ♊, ♎, ♒. In the Earthy Triplicity, ♉, ♍, ♑, and in the Watery triangle, ♋, ♏, ♓. The signs in each triplicity are in △ aspect, and in great harmony. People born with the majority of the planets in any one of these Triplicities, as many planets in ♈, ♌, and ♐, have better balance, a more even temper, whereas a mixture of planets, and occupying several of the Triplicities at B., tend to unbalance the native, cause more discord, strife, inharmony, and ill-health, as such mixtures involve the □ and ☍ aspects in the Map of Birth. (See "Airy Signs" under Air; Aspects; "Earthy Signs" under Earth; "Fire Signs" under Fire; Heredity; "Signs" under Water).

TRISMUS—(See Lock-Jaw).

TRODDEN—(See Crushed, Mobs, Trampled).

TROPICAL SIGNS—♋ and ♑. (See Angles, Blemishes, Cancer, Capricorn,

Cardinal, Equinoxes, Fourth House, Ingresses, Minor Ailments, Solstices, Tenth House).

TROUBLE — Troubled — Troublesome — Trials—Vexations—

A Time of Trouble—Causes of Trouble In the Life of the Native—Has Much Trouble—The SUN to the ☌ ♄ by dir.; the ☉ to the ill-asps. the ☽ by dir.; the ☉ or ☽ to the ☌ or ill-asp. the malefics; the ☉ □ or ☍ the ☽ at B., and by dir.; the ☉ with South Scale, or the Knee of Ophiucus at B.; an eclipse of the ☉ or ☽ falling close to the places of the ☉ or ☽ at B., or in ☍ thereto, or near the ☌ or ☍ a malefic, and espec. if such eclipse is visible at the birthplace, or falls on the place of the hyleg, there will tend to be much trouble or ill-health; the ☉ or ☽ in weak signs in the 3rd or 6th H., and afflicted; the MOON □ or ☍ ♄ at B., and by dir.; the ☽ hyleg, and afflicted, and to the ☌ or ill-asp. the ☉ by dir.; the ☽ to the ☌ or ill-asp. any of the malefics by dir.; the ☽ weak and afflicted at B., and to the ☌ the Asc. by dir., much trouble in mind and body; the ☽ directed to the Pleiades, Hyades, Praesepe, Deneb, or The Twins; the ☽ to the □ or ☍ the ☉ by dir.; the ☽ Sig. □ or ☍ ♄; the ☽ sepr. from ♀ and apply. to the ☉; the ☽ at a Solar Rev. passing over the place of ♄ or ♂ at B.; the Prog. ☽ ☌, P., or ill-asp. the place of ♄ at B.; the Prog. ☽ □ or ☍ the Asc. or M.C.; NEPTUNE □ or ☍ ♀ at B., much trouble all thru life, and espec. in love affairs; URANUS passing the place of ♄ at B. by tr., sudden troubles; ♅ affl. the ☉ or ☽ at B., and by dir.; ♅ afflicted in the 10th H.; ♅ affl. in ♎ or ♑; SATURN by tr. or dir. ☌ or ill-asp. the ☉, ☽, or any of the radical planets; ♄ in the 10th H. at a Solar Rev., and elevated above the Lights; ♄ ruler of the 12th H. at B., and ♄ ☌ or evil asp. the Asc. by dir.; ♄ elevated above, and in evil asp. the ruling planet; ♄ on the Meridian, or coming to it at B., perpetual trouble or disgrace; JUPITER Sig. □ or ☍ ☿; ♃ prog., and in □ or ☍ ♀, or vice versa; MARS affl. in the 12th H.; ♂ prog. ☌, □, or ☍, or vice versa, much trouble thru recklessness; ♂ at a Solar Rev. passing the places of the radical ☉, ☽, or planets; VENUS prog. ☌, P., □, or ☍ ♄ at B., or vice versa; ♀ ☌ the ☉ at a Solar Rev., and ☿ affl. by malefics at the same time; ♀ by periodic rev. to the ill-asps. the ☉ at B.; ♀ to the ☌ or ill-asp. ♄ by dir.; MERCURY affl. at B., and the ☽ to the ill-asps. ☿ by dir.; ☿ at a Solar Rev. passing the place of ♄ or ♂ at B.; ☿ affl. in the 7th, 10th, or 11th H., many worries and vexations; the ASC. to the place of Deneb; the Asc. to the ☌ or ill-asp. ♄ by dir.; the M.C. to the ☌ or P. the ☽, and espec. if the ☽ is affl. at B.; the M.C. to the ill-asps. the ☉ by dir.; the M.C. to the place of Algol or Hydra's Heart; a Lunation falling on the place of the malefics, and espec. if it occurs with evil primary directions; the 2nd decan. of ♉ on the Asc., ruled by ♂, tends to much grief, anxiety, and trouble; Fixed Stars of the nature of ♄ culminating at B.; an evil direction to the ☉, ☽. Hyleg, or Asc. signifies

trouble or illness; Antares, Aldebaran, Frons Scorpio, Deneb, and the Shoulders of Orion, when directed to the ☉, ☽, or Asc. tend to trouble and sickness. (For further influences along this line see Accidents, Affliction, Anguish, Anxiety, Cares, Dejected, Delays, Depressed, Despondency, Disgrace, Dishonor, Distress, Enemies (Secret); Evils, Fears, Females (Injuries by); Foolhardy, Fortune (Malice of); Gloom, Grief, Honor (Loss of); Imprudent, Indiscretions, Injury, Judgment Bad, Low Spirits (see Low); Melancholy, Men (Injured Thru Women); Miseries, Misfortune, Mind (No Peace of); Own Worst Enemy (see "His Own Worst Enemy" under Enemies); Plots, Poverty, Rashness, Recklessness, Reputation (Loss of); Reverses, Ruin, Scandal, Self-Undoing, Sickness, Sorrows, Suffering, Tears (Crying Spells); Trials, Twelfth House, Vexations, Women (Injuries by); Worries, etc.).

Appearance—Troubled Appearance— ♄ Sig. □ or ☍ the ☽, or vice versa.

Mind—Troubled Mind—(See Anguish, Anxiety, Dejected, Despondency, Distress, Doubts, Fears, Gloom, Grief, Hope (Hopes Cut Off); Lamenting; Low Spirits, Melancholy, Mournful, Recluse, Renunciation, Sad, Worry, etc.).

Person—A Troublesome Person—(See Anarchist, Assassin, Criminal, Destructiveness, Forgers, Gambler, Knavish; "Full of Mischief" under Mischief; Murderous, Newsmonger, Reactionary, Reformer; "Intolerance" under Religion; Revolutionary, Riotous, Thief, Violent, etc.).

Prevalent—Trouble Prevalent—Much Trouble Generally—An eclipse of the ☽ in the 3rd decan. of ♏; ♄ lord of the year at the Vernal, much trouble and tribulation generally; Comets appearing in ♎ or ♑, much trouble and distress generally. (For the various kinds of Troubles which may be prevalent, see the subjects and references under Humanity, Mankind, Prevalent, Public).

Pulse—(See "Troubled" under Pulse).

Women—Trouble To—(See "Women" under Misfortune). This Encyclopaedia is full of subjects and influences which deal with the Troubles of Humanity, which would be too numerous to list here. Look in the alphabetical arrangement for the subject you have in mind.

TRUE—

True Moment of Birth—(See "Moment of Birth" under Birth).

True Motives — And Purposes — (See Honest).

True Ribs—(See "Upper" under Ribs).

True Skin—(See Derma).

TRUNK — The Body Except the Head and Limbs — Ruled and influenced by the Fixed Signs. For Disorders of the Trunk, or parts thereof, see Bowels, Chest, Heart, Kidneys, Liver, Lungs, Pelvis, Ribs, Sides, Stomach, Thorax, and the various organs of the Trunk. Also see "Opisthotonos", a spasmodic disorder in which there is rigidity of the upper body, and the trunk is thrown backward and arched upward. (See "Fixed Signs" under Fixed).

TRUSTWORTHY—(See Honest, Honorable, Humane, Kind, Noble, Reliable, Responsibility, Sincere, etc.).

TRUTH—

Lover of Truth — Born under the strong influence of ♅. (See "Treatment" under Melancholy; Metaphysics, Occult, Philosophy; "Reasonableness" under Reason; "Truth" under Religion; "Astrology" under Science).

Truthful—(See Honest, Trustworthy).

Untruthful—(See Cheating, Deceitful, Dishonest, Liars, etc.). Case — See "Nymphomania", No. 306, in 1001 N.N.

TUBERCLES — A Small Eminence, or Nodule — Nodes — A ♄ disease. (See "Nodules" under Nodes).

Ears — Tubercles In — (See "Nodes" under Ears).

Fat — Tubercles In — (See "Adiposa Dolorosa" under Fat).

Maturation—And Softening of Tubercle—♄ ☌ or ill-asp. the ☽. (See Excrescences).

Xanthoma — Yellowish Tubercles On the Skin—(See Xanthoma).

TUBERCULOSIS—Tubercular Tendency —Tuberculosis is a wasting and depleting disease, and is classed fundamentally as a disease of ♄. It may occur in any part of the body, but is generally circumscribed, or limited to certain parts, or organs, altho the entire system feels its effects. Note the following subjects of Tuberculosis in the various parts of the body, and also see these subjects in the alphabetical arrangement when they are not more fully set forth here—

Addison's Disease—(See Adrenals).

Adrenals—Tuberculosis of—(See "Addison's Disease" under Adrenals).

Bladder — (See "Tuberculosis Of" under Bladder).

Bones—(See "Tuberculosis" under Bones).

Bowels — (See "Tuberculosis" under Bowels; "Abdomen" under Phthisis).

Brain — (See "Tuberculosis" under Brain).

Bronchial — (See "Consumption" under Bronchial).

Cases—Of Tuberculosis — Birth Data, etc.—See Figures 4A, 4B, 4C, 6A, 9C, 19C, in the book, "Astro-Diagnosis", by the Heindels. See Figures 15, 16, 25, 26, 35, in "Message of the Stars", by the Heindels. See Cases in Chap. XIV, in Daath's Medical Astrology. Also for other Cases see "Consumptive" under Consumption.

Consumptive—(See "Consumptive" under Consumption).

Death By—And Cases—(See "Death" under Consumption, Phthisis).

Foci — Tubercular Foci In the Lungs —♄ in ♑, ☌ or ill-asp. the ☉ or ☽.

Kidneys — (See "Tuberculosis" under Kidneys).

Larynx — (See "Consumption Of" under Larynx).

Liver—(See "Tuberculosis" under Liver).

Lungs — Tuberculosis of — Consumption of Lungs—The ☉ ☌ ♄ in ♊ or ♐, or the ☉ ☍ ♄ in these signs; the ☉ ☌ or P. ♄ in ♊; the ☉ in ♊ or ♐, □ or P. ♄; the ☉ rising at B., and affl. by ♄; the ☉ or ☽ in the 6th H. in common signs, and afflicted; the ☉ or ☽ in common signs, in cadent houses, and espec. in the 6th or 12th H., and affl. by malefics; the ☽ in ♊ or ♓ in the 8th H., and affl. by malefics; ♆ in ♊ in the 12th H., and affl. by malefics; ♄ or ☋ in ♊, and due to hardening of the lungs; ♄ affl. in ♊ or ♐; ♄ ☌ ♆ in ♌, ♊, or ♋; ♄ in ♊, and affl. by both ♃ and ♀; ♄ and ☋ ☌ ♃ or ♀ in ♊; a ♄ disease; ♄ in ♋, occi., and affl. the ☉, ☽, Asc., or hyleg; ♄ people become an easy prey to tuberculosis from catching cold from drafts or wettings; ♄ in ♊ when ♄ is the afflictor in the disease; ♄ affl. in ♓, and due to cold and wet feet; ♄ in ♓, occi., and affl. the ☉, ☽, Asc., or hyleg; ♃ in ♊ or ♐, and affl. by ♄ and ♀; caused by ♀ when the dominion of death is vested in her; ♀ affl. in ♓; the Asc. ☌, P., □, or ☍ ♄ by dir., and ♄ occi. at B.; ☋ in ♊, and espec. when ♄ is also in ♊, ♐, or ♓; a ♍ disease when there are malefics in ♍; a ♊ and ♋ disease, and afflictions in these signs; planets in ♍ in ♍ to planets in ♐; afflictions in ♓, the result of colds in the feet; many planets afflicted in common signs; the 6th face of ♒ on the Asc. if ♄ be there; the 6th face of ♓ on the Asc.; Subs at Lu.P. (See "Consumptive" under Consumption; "Pulmonary Phthisis" under Phthisis; Wastings; "Cases" in this section).

Lupus — Tubercular Skin Disease — (See Lupus).

Phthisis—Pulmonary Consumption— (See "Pulmonary" under Phthisis).

Reins—(See "Consumption" under Reins).

Scrofula—Tubercular Tendency In— (See Scrofula).

Skin—Tubercular Skin Disease—(See Lupus).

Spine — (See "Tubercular" under Spine).

Spleen — (See "Tuberculosis" under Spleen).

Supra-Renals—Tuberculosis of—(See "Addison's Disease" under Adrenals).

Tuberculosis—Tubercular Tendency— (See "Lungs", and the various paragraphs in this section). For further study along this line see Asthma, Atrophy, Crystallization, Deposits, Emaciation, Hardening, Saturn, Tabes, Wastings.

TUBES — Tubules — The Tubes and Canals of the body are ruled by the different Signs of the Zodiac, according to their location, and also by the various planets which may rule their special function. (See "Blood Vessels" under Blood; "Tubes" under Bronchial; Canals, Capillaries, Eustachian, Oesophagus, Receptacles, Trachea (Windpipe); Tubuli Seminiferi (see Semen); Ureters, Urethra, Vessels).

TUESDAY—The Day of the Week ruled by ♂. (See "Days of the Week" under Week).

TUMEFACTIONS—(See Swellings).

TUMORS— A Swelling—Abnormal Enlargement—Lumps—Neoplasm—A New Growth Not the Result of Inflammation—Tumors are mostly the work of ♃ and ♀, and result from excesses of various kinds, over-eating, sedentary habits, lack of exercise, poor circulation, stomach disorders, indiscretions, dissolute living, kidney trouble, etc., and are diseases resulting from an ill-dignified, weak, and afflicted ♃ or ♀ at birth. Tumors are of various kinds and types, and may occur in any part of the body wherever there is weakness, deposits, accumulations, and increase of leukocytes. The ♃ and ♀ afflictions pile up the excesses and accumulations, and then ♄ takes them up and does his work by impeding elimination, stopping of functions and secretions, and excess of mineral deposits in the weak and afflicted parts of the body, as shown by the Chart of Birth. Tumors are also a ☽ disease, a ♃, ♏, and ♓ disease. Recent Writers also say that ♆ causes tumors. The action of ♃ conduces to blood changes, and the accumulation of fluids, either in the form of a tumor, or obesity. Tumors follow a Solar Periodicity, and increase in size in proportion to the Sun's Declination towards the West. (See "Periodicity" under Sun). Tumors tend to decrease in size during the decrease of the ☽. (See "Decrease" under Moon. Also see Deposits, Excesses, Hardening, Leukocytes, Retentions, Stoppages, Suppressions, Wastes, etc.). The following subjects have to do with Tumors and Enlargements in the body, which see in the alphabetical arrangement when only listed here—

Abdomen — Tumors In — ♀ affl. in ♍, and usually due to bad habits, feasting, over-eating, etc. (See "Aqueous" in this section).

Abscesses; Adenoma; Aqueous Tumor — In the Abdomen — ♅ in ♍, and affl. by ♀. Case—See "Aqueous", No. 120, in 1001 N.N. (See Abdomen, Fluids, in this section).

Bag-Like Tumor—(See Cysts).

Blood Tumor—(See Haematoma).

Boils; Bowels—(See "Tumors" under Bowels).

Brain—(See "Tumor" under Brain).

Breast—(See "Tumors" under Breast).

Bubo—Inguinal Tumor—(See Bubo).

Cancer—(See Carcinoma).

Carbuncles; Carcinoma;

Cartilaginous Tumor—(See "Chondroma" under Cartilage).

Cysts; Death by Tumor — Caused by ♄ and ♃. (See "Malignant" in this section).

Elastic Tumor—(See "Tumor" under Gums).

Encysted Tumors—Steatoma—Encysted Sebaceous Tumors—(See Steatoma, Wens).

Enlargements; Epithelioma; Epulis—(See "Tumor" under Gums).

Fatty Tumor—(See Degeneration; "Tumors" under Fat; Lipoma).

Fibroid Tumor—Fibroma—(See "Fibroma" under Fiber).

Fibroma — (See "Fibroma" under Fiber).

Fistulous Tumor—(See Fistula).

Fleshy Tumors—(See Caruncle; "Tumors" under Fat, Fleshy; Sarcoma).

Fluids—Watery Tumors—(See "Tumors" under Fluids; "Aqueous" in this section).

Fungus Growths—(See Fungus).

Gastric Tumor—Tumor In the Stomach—(See "Tumor" under Gastric).

Generative Organs—(See "Tumors In" under Generative).

Glandular Tumor — (See Adenoma, Scrofula).

Goiter; Groins—(See Bubo; "Tumors" under Groins).

Gums—(See "Tumor" under Gums).

Haematoma; Hard Tumor — Scirrhus—Ruled and caused by ♄ as ♄ is the afflictor in the disease. Also caused by the mineral deposits of ♄. (See "Scirrhus" under Carcinoma; Deposits, Hard, Resolvent, Scirrhus).

Head — Tumorous Growth In — (See "Growths In" under Head).

Hips and Thighs—(See "Tumors" under Hips, Thighs).

Hollow Tumors — (See "Hollow" under Cysts).

Hypertrophy; Inguinal Tumor—(See Bubo).

Intestines — (See "Tumors" under Bowels).

Kidneys — (See "Tumor" under Kidneys).

Knees — (See "Tumors In" under Knees).

Larynx — (See "Tumors Of" under Larynx).

Legs—(See "Tumors In" under Legs).

Lipoma — (See "Fatty" in this section).

Lumps; Malignant Tumors — Deadly—Fatal—Caused when the ♄ influence enters into the configuration; ♄ ☌ ♃ or ♀. (See Carcinoma, Malignant).

Mediastinal — Tumor In the Chest or Thorax—♃ or ♀ affl. in ♏; Subs at SP. (See Chest, Thorax).

Neck — And Throat — (See "Tumors In" under Neck).

Neoplasm; Nerve Tumor—Neuroma—(See "Neuroma" under Nerves).

New Growths—Neoplasm—(See Neoplasm, Warts, Wens).

Obesity — ♃ causes Obesity and Tumors. (See Obesity).

Oedematous Tumors — (See Oedema, Resolvent).

Pedunculated Tumor—(See Polypus).

Polypus; Reins — (See "Tumors" under Reins).

Remedy for Tumors—(See Resolvent).

Resolvents — Remedies to Dissolve Tumors—(See Resolvents).

Sarcoma; Scirrhus Tumors—The Hard Form—♄ and ♇ diseases. (See Scirrhus; "Hard" in this section).

Scrofulous Tumors—(See Scrofula).

Sebaceous Tumors—Steatoma—Containing Fat or Suet — Lipoma — (See "Sebaceous", "Tumors", under Fat; Lipoma, Sebaceous, Steatoma, Wens).

Steatoma—(See Encysted, Sebaceous, in this section).

Stomach — (See "Tumor" under Gastric).

Thighs—(See "Thighs" under Fistula; "Tumors" under Hips).

Thorax — (See "Mediastinal" in this section).

Throat—(See "Tumors" under Neck).

Tongue—(See "Cystic Tumor" under Tongue).

Treatment Of—(See Resolvents).

Tumourous Complaints—(See the Introduction, and the various subjects in this Article).

Ulcers; Uterine Tumor—(See "Fibroid", "Tumors", under Womb).

Womb—(See "Tumors" under Womb).

TUMULTS—Injury or Death by Popular Tumult—The ☽ to the bad asps. the ☉ or ☿. (See Hanging, Lynching, Mobs, Riots; "Death" under Suffocation; Trampled). An eclipse of the ☉ in the 1st decan. of ♏ tends to stir up Tumults, War, and Slaughter. (See Riots, Slaughter, War).

TUNICS — An Enveloping or Lining Membrane—Tunica—

Gastro-Intestinal Tunics — (See "Impar" under Ganglion).

Tunica Vaginalis — (See Serum, Testes). Also for other membranes which are classed as Tunics, see Arteries, Conjunctiva, Membranes, Peritoneum).

TURBINATED BONES—(See Nose).

TURBULENT MIND—(See Anarchists; "Turbulent" under Fancies; Perverse, Quarrelsome, Rashness, Reactionary, Rebellious, Recklessness, Reformers, Revolutionary, Riotous; "High Temper" under Temper; Ungovernable, Vicious, Violent).

TURPENTINE—Tar—Pix Cones—Pine Tree—Ruled by ♂. (See Tar).

TURPITUDE—(See Debased, Depraved, Indecent, Lewd; "Low and Base" under Low; "Loose Morals" under Morals; Obscene, Perversions, Shameless, Unnatural, Vile, etc.).

TUSSIS—(See Cough).

Pertussis—(See Whooping Cough).

TWELFTH HOUSE—This is the last of the 12 Houses, and is affiliated with ♓, the 12th Sign of the Zodiac, and also with ♆. This house is a part of the Terminal Triangle, and is a terminal house, showing the end of life, the death of the Psychic Nature, and refers to the sundering of Soul and Spirit, and is what is called the "Second Death". The 8th and 12th Houses are bases of the Occult Triangle, with the 4th H. as the apex. (See Pisces, Terminal). This House was formerly supposed to be connected with the Elementals, the Evil Spirits, and obsessions by them, and is said to be the House of Witchcraft. The confining influences of life, the restraints, limitations, and restrictions, are ruled and represented by this house, and its influences tend to bring trouble, sorrow, privation, confinement, self-undoing, folly, grief, anxiety, suffering, impaired senses, anguish, affliction, misery, misfortune, distress of every kind, persecution, imprisonment, secret enemies, malice, assassination, suicide, treason, sedition, and every evil that can befall humanity, and especially when there are afflictions and malefics in this house at birth. Saturn delights in this house, and has his joy here, being the Author of Mischief. Saturn and ♂ in this house tend to bring every evil, except death, that Mankind can suffer. The planet ♆ also delights in this house, and when afflicted here tends to Obsessions, Spirit Controls, Involuntary Mediumship, and to unusual and detrimental Psychic and Spiritual conditions, unless the native is awakened, and can respond to the higher influences of ♆. The ☉ ♂ ☿ in this house tends to deafness, and to hinder and limit the Soul in its manifestations in the physical body, by deprivation or destruction of the five Senses, thus thwarting the Soul in its search for knowledge. This is one of the evil houses, along with the 6th and 8th H., and people born with many planets in these houses at B., or the lord of the Asc. in them, and afflicted, are considered quite unfortunate in life, and subject to many diseases and troubles, and to have a less favorable fate. Being an evil house, evil in a human sense, this house is also a favorable place for the Anareta, or killing planet, and the 12th H. also, when badly afflicted, can act as Anareta. (See Anareta). This is a feminine and passive house, and its conditions at B., and especially when malefic, tend to greatly affect negative and passive people, and to cause much worry and brooding, and often resulting in suicide in a moment of despair and despondency. This house denotes the feet, ankles, and toes, and all hurts and diseases incident to them.

Color — Green is the Color ruled by this house.

Denotes — The 12th H. denotes the ankles, feet, and toes, and all diseases and hurts incident to them.

Diseases Of—Diseases, Hurts, Injury, and Affliction to the Ankles, Feet, Toes, and also to impaired Senses, as Deafness, and other physical and mental limitations. Also Chronic Diseases in general are ruled by this house.

Rules — The 12th House rules Afflictions, Anarchists, Anguish of Mind, Animals (Large); Ankles, Anxieties, Assassinations, Asylums, Aunts and Uncles (On the father's side in a male nativity, and on the mother's side in a female nativity); Backbiters, Banishment, Bondage, Captivity, Cattle (Great and Large); Chronic Diseases, Clairvoyance, Color (Green); Confinements, Desert (The); Desolate Places, Distress, Enemies (Secret and Private); Envy, Exile, Feet, Folly, Great Cattle, Green Color, Hermits, Hospitals, Imprisonment, Insane Asylums, Institutions where people are confined; Invalids (Bed-ridden); Kidnappings, Large Animals, Limitations, Mediumship, Miseries, Misfortunes, Morgues, Obsessions, Oxen, Persecutions, Plots,

Prisons, Private Enemies, Psychic Powers and Experiences, Recluses, Relatives (see "Aunts and Uncles" in this paragraph); Revenge, Secret Enemies, Sedition, Seduction, Self-Undoing, Servitude, Sleep, Solitary Vice, Solitude (Desire for); Spiritual Powers and Experiences, Suffering, Suicide, Toes, Treachery, Treason, Trouble, Wilderness (The); Witchcraft, etc.
Stellium — In the 12th H. at birth — Case—Six Planets in ♍ in the 12th H. —See "Idiot from Birth", No. 742, in 1001 N.N.
TWINS—Double Births—Multiple Births — Triplets — Quadruplets — Twins are especially produced and given by the ♊ Sign influences, a double-bodied sign, and which is also known as the Sign of "The Twins", and of Castor and Pollux. When Twins are conceived, the bicorporeal Signs ♊, ♐, or ♓, are prominent at conception, and also usually at B., and contain the ☽, and planets dominant in the giving of children. A study of the Prenatal Epoch Map, the map for the time of conception, is very important to understand the causes of multiple conceptions, and to determine the facts as to sex and number, etc. (See Predetermination, Prenatal Epoch, Triplets). The Planets at B. are in harmony with Prenatal conditions, normally, and help to account for single or multiple births, but it must be understood that it is not altogether the positions of the planets at B. which produce children, but those at conception also play their part. There is a close dependency between the time of conception and the moment of birth, and when one of these times is known, the time of the other can be mathematically calculated, as is proven in the Prenatal Epoch work. The influences at the time of conception work with, and concur with the influences in the natal map, and that is why there is often much similarity in the planetary positions at conception, and at birth. The influences in the radix bring the child into the world at the time predetermined at conception, and concur with those at conception under normal conditions. Twins may be conceived near the same time, or as much as a month apart. When conceived several weeks apart, the older twin, being at maturity, forces the younger twin away, which may be only at eight months. In such a case the last one born is considered the older of the two, and for this reason it was the belief of the Ancients that Jacob was older than Esau, altho born after him, and this is, no doubt, the Occult reason why the father Isaac bestowed the blessing upon Jacob instead of the first-born Esau. Twins are very much alike in appearance when the same Sign is rising upon the Eastern Horizon, or Ascendant, but if the rising Signs differ, as when the first twin is born with ♓ upon the Asc., and the second one with ♈ rising, they will be under different rulerships, and differ much in form and disposition. The one born under Pisces will be shorter, and of less vitality, and if either of them die soon after birth, or

in infancy or childhood, it will be apt to be the ♓ one, as ♈ rising is one of the very strong and vital signs, and also produces a taller body than ♓. Thus one of these twins may be short, fleshy, and flabby in early life and youth, while the other will be tall, thin, and wiry, and possibly not as plump and handsome as the first-born, or ♓-born child. (See Appearance). Noting the influences at the time of conception, the planet which is connected with the ruling places indicates the number generated, and the planets which are configurated with the ☉, ☽, or Asc., determine the sex, or sexes. This subject of the number and sex of multiple conceptions is discussed in the Article on Predetermination, and also in the Article on Triplets. (See these Articles). The following are the general influences which tend to produce Twins, influences which predominate at conception, and also those which are known to exist at birth in cases of multiple births.
Birth of Twins — Twins Conceived — When only two of the Significators of children behold the ☉, ☽, or Asc. at conception, only two are conceived. If these Sigs. both be masculine planets, two males will be conceived. If they both be feminine planets, two females will be conceived. If one of the Sigs. be masculine, and the other feminine, one male and one female will be conceived. The masculine Significators are the masculine planets ♄, ♃, and ♂. The feminine Sigs. are the ☽, ♀, and ☿, if they behold the ☉, ☽, or Asc. at conception. (See "Three Males", "Three Females", and the other paragraphs in the Article on Triplets). If the planets which promise progeny be in feminine, or bicorporeal signs, double offspring is granted, and if in the prolific and seminal signs, as ♋, ♏, or ♓, they will grant twins, and even more. If the ☉, ☽, or Asc., or planet aspecting them, be in bicorporeal signs at conception, there will be twins, or more, and the same if both the ☉ and ☽ are in the South Angle; the ☉, ☽, and Asc. occupied by double-bodied signs, as ♊, ♐, or ♓, or many prolific stars cast a good aspect to them; twins occur when both the ☉ and ☽ are in the Midheaven in a bicorporeal sign; the ☉ and ☽ in bicorporeal signs, or lords of the Asc. or 5th H., in such signs; the ☽ in the 5th H. in ♓; ♃, ♀, or the ☽ in the 10th, 11th, 4th, or 5th H. in double-bodied or feminine signs; ♌ with ♃, ♀, or the ☽, and all of them in double-bodied signs; a double-bodied sign on the Asc. or 7th H., or their lords; the ☽, in these signs, as in ♊, ♓, or the first half of ♐; if the 1st or 5th H., or their lords, be in bicorporeal signs, twins are denoted in Hor'y Questions; a fruitful planet, or planets, in the 10th, 11th, 4th, or 5th H. in fruitful, feminine, bicorporeal, or water signs, there are two, or more, at a birth; a double-bodied sign on the Asc. or 5th H., and with ♃ or ♀ therein. (See "Single Births" in Sec. 1 in the Article on Children. Also see Birth, Conception, Foetus, Fruitful, Gestation, Parturition, Pregnancy, Prenatal Epoch).

Cases of Twin Births — See "Twins", Numbers 215, 216, 236, 241, 324, 325, 326, 327, 638, 639, 675, 676, 680, 681, 682, 683, 715, 716, 740, 955, all in 1001 N.N.

Had Twins Three Times—See "Twins", No. 740, in 1001 N.N.

One Male, One Female — (See "Birth of Twins" in this section).

Siamese Twins — United Twins — See "Twins", No. 236, 241, in 1001 N.N.

Two Females—(See "Birth of Twins" in this section).

Two Males—(See "Birth of Twins" in this section).

United Twins—(See "Siamese" in this section; Xyphodymus).

TWISTINGS—Torsion—A ♅ disease and affliction, and due to incoordination, or lack of proper nerve supply to a part, or organ. Twisting may occur in any part of the body, and especially in the part ruled by the sign ♅ is in at B. This is classed as a Spasmodic disorder. If the contraction and twisting become chronic, a deformity may result, lameness, or disability. (See Contortions, Contractions, Deformities, Distortions; "Wry Neck" under Neck; Spasmodic Diseases, Torsion, Torticollis).

TWITCHING — An Irregular Minor Spasm—A ♅ disease and affliction, and where ♅ may not be as severely afflicted as in twistings. Twitchings are an indication that the nerves are being overworked, or affected by systemic disorders, and are a signal that something is wrong, and that habits, or the manner of living are wrong, and that it is time to slow up a bit before the vital forces become lowered or dissipated. (See Contractions; "Movements" under Erratic; Jerkings, Saint Vitus Dance, Spasmodic Diseases, Tics, Tremors, etc.).

TYMPANIES—Tympanites—Gaseous Distention of the Abdomen — Caused by the ☉ afflicted; the ☽ affl. in ♋ or ♍; also a ♂ disease. (See "Gas" under Bowels; Distentions, Flatulence; "Abdomen" under Gas; Inflation).

TYMPANUM—Tympanitis—(See "Drum" under Ears).

TYPE OF THE DISEASE — The Time and Type of the disease are indicated by the nature of the Direction, or Directions, operating at the time, and the nature of the afflicting planet, or planets, but only such disease can be predicted, or consummated, as is contained, or foreshadowed in the radical map. (See "Disease" under Nature, Quality, Species).

TYPHLITIS—Inflammation of the Caecum—(See Caecum).

TYPHOID FEVER—Enteric Fever—Intestinal Lesions and Eruptions — A ♍ disease, and caused by afflictions in ♍; the ☉ afflicted in ♍ or the opposite sign ♓; a ♂ disease, and ♂ is usually the afflictor; ♂ affl. in ♍, and especialy in the 6th H.; ♂ affl. in ♋ in the 6th H.; ☿ affl. in ♍; afflictions in ♐; occurs mostly when ♍, ♎, or ♏ are on the Asc. (See "Fever" under Bowels; "Epidemics" under Cholera; Epidemics). Case — Death by Typhoid Fever—See "De", No. 226, in 1001 N.N.

Typhoid Pneumonia—(See "Typhoid" under Pneumonia).

TYPHUS FEVER—Camp Fever—This fever is more prevalent when the major planets, and especially ♄ and ♃, are in perihelion. Is caused by the vitiated and disturbed atmospheric conditions by planetary influence. Caused by ♂ and ♀. Venus denotes death by when the afflictor in the disease. (See "Corrupt Air" under Air; Epidemics, La Grippe, Perihelion).

Typhomania—The Delirium of Typhus —Caused by ♆, and ♆ afflicted at B., or afflicting the hyleg.

TYPICAL DRUGS — Of Each Planet — (See "Typical Drugs" under each of the Planets).

TYRANTS—(See Cruel; "Shows No Pity" under Pity).

U

UGLY — An Ugly Person — Not Handsome — Not Attractive — Ugliness is usually caused by malefics afflicting the Asc., causing defects in the features, complexion, and form of the body, and according to the nature of the planets and signs involved. The signs ♋ and ♑, when prominent at B., or upon the Asc., are said to give the least beauty of all the signs, and especially ♑. The ♑ sign especially causes a crooked, raw-boned, ill-shaped body, knock-knees, bow legs, and usually a pale and swarthy complexion. The ♎ and ♒ influences, and the ♀ influences, tend to give the most beautiful and comely bodies when upon the Asc. at B., or ♀ dignified in the Asc.

Ugly Disposition—Given especially by the afflictions of the malefics ♄ and ♂, and when these planets are prominent at B., in angles, and afflicting each other. (See Cruel; "Cross", "Rough", under Manners; "High Temper" under Temper).

Ugly Face—(See "Ugly" under Face).

Ugly In Person — Ugly Body — Not Handsome—The ☉ Sig. in ♉, a rather ugly person; the ☉ in ♉ in partile asp. the Asc., short, well-set, and rather ugly; the ☽ ill-dignified at B., not handsome, but a muddling creature; the □ and ☍ aspects of the ☽ tend to give an ugly, crooked, and badly made body; ♄ Sig. in ♉, in no wise comely; in Hor'y Q. ♄ Sig. in ♉, ♋, ♑, or ♓; ♄ Sig. in ♑, thin and ungainly; in Hor'y Q. ♄ denotes a person of a lean, crooked, and ill-made body; ♄ indicates a person of a black, earthy, brown complexion; ♄ Sig. in ♉ or ♓; ♄ in ♓, partile the Asc., generally very ugly; ♄ Sig. □ or ☍ ☿, not of a genteel form; ♂ Sig. in ♓, far from handsome;

♂ in ♓, partile the Asc., generally ugly; ♀ Sig. □ or 8 ♄, not very handsome; ☿ Sig. in ♏, not in any way elegant or pleasing; ☋ on the Asc., a crooked body. Also note the influences in the Introduction to this Article. (See Awkwardness, Bloated; "Raw-Boned" under Bones; "Bad" under Complexion; Commonplace, Crooked, Deformed, Distortions; "Ugly" under Face; Freckles; Ill-Formed" under Ill; Lean, Lumpish, Marks, Pimples, Scars; "Pock-Marked" under Smallpox; Spare, Thin, etc.).

ULCERS—Ulceration—Ulcerous Sores— Open Sores — Erosions — Suppuration Upon a Free Surface — Ulcerous Growths — For the main influences causing Ulcer see "Tendency To" in this section. The following subjects have to do with Ulcer in its various forms and manifestations. See these subjects in the alphabetical arrangement when only listed here—

Abscesses; Aneurysm; Anus — (See "Ulceration" under Anus).

Aphthous Ulcers—Of the Mouth—(See Aphthae).

Arms — Ulcers In the Arms, Hands, Legs and Feet — The ☽ affl. in signs which rule these parts. (See Aneurysm).

Bladder — (See "Ulcers" under Bladder).

Blood — Ulcers Proceeding from Corrupt Blood — A ♓ disease, and afflictions in ♓. (See Impure).

Bone—Ulcerous Inflammation of— (See "Ulcerous" under Bones).

Bowels—(See "Ulcers" under Bowels).

Breast—(See "Ulcers" under Breast).

Cancer—(See Carcinoma).

Cancrum Oris—(See "Mouth" under Gangrene).

Caries; Chancroid—(See Gonorrhoea).

Corrupt Blood—(See "Blood" in this section).

Crusts; Duodenum—(See "Ulcer" under Duodenum).

Dysentery—Ulcer of Bowels In—(See Dysentery).

Eyes—(See "Ulcer" under Eyes).

Face—(See "Ulcers" under Face).

Feet—(See "Ulcers" under Feet).

Forehead — (See "Ulceration" under Forehead).

Gangrene; Gastric Ulcer—(See "Ulcer" under Gastric).

Generally Some Ulcer—The ☽ in ♏, and affl. by the ☉ or ♂ when taken ill, patients generally have some ulcer (Hor'y).

Genitals—Ulcer of—♂ affl. in ♏ tends to ulcer in the Genitals, Secret Parts, Urethra, Vagina, Womb, Vulva, and to the Chancroid accompanying Gonorrhoea. (See "Ulceration" under Womb).

Growths — Ulcerous Growths — (See "Tendency To" in this section).

Gums—(See "Ulcerated" under Gums).

Hands—(See "Ulcers" under Hands).

Head—(See "Ulceration" under Head).

Hips and Thighs—(See "Ulcers" under Hips).

Imposthumes—(See Abscesses).

Increased—Ulcers Increased—♄ and ♂ in an angle, occi. of the ☉, and ori. of the ☽, and ♀ in familiarity with ♂; ♂ or ♀ holding dominion at B., and in familiarity with each other, and ♂ affl. the hyleg.

Inflamed Ulcers—(See "Phlegmonous" in this section).

Jaws — (See Gums, Necrosis, Pyorrhoea; "Ulceration" under Teeth).

Kidneys — (See "Ulceration" under Kidneys).

Legs—(See "Ulcers" under Legs).

Liver—(See "Ulcerated" under Liver).

Loins—(See "Ulcers" under Loins).

Lower Jaw—Ulcerated Gums of—(See Gums).

Lungs — (See "Ulceration" under Lungs).

Milk Leg — (See this subject under Legs).

Mortification—(See Gangrene, Granulations, Mortification).

Mouth—Ulcers In—(See Aphthae).

Nose—(See "Ulcers" under Nose).

Ovaries—(See "Ulceration" under Ovaries).

Phlegmonous Ulcer — Inflamed Ulcer — Putrefying Ulcer— ♂ in an angle, occi. of the ☉, and ori. of the ☽. (See "Pus" in this section).

Pus — Ulcers with Pus — (See "Phlegmon" under Pus; "Phlegmonous" in this section).

Putrefying Ulcers — (See Phlegmonous, Pus, in this section).

Pyorrhoea; Rectum—(See "Ulcer" under Rectum).

Reins—(See "Ulcers" under Reins).

Remedy for Ulcer — Lead Ointment. (See Lead).

Secret Parts—(See "Genitals" in this section).

Sloughing; Sores—Ulcerous Sores—A ♓ disease, and afflictions in ♓. (See Sores).

Stomach — (See "Ulcer" under Stomach).

Suppurative Ulcer—Ulcer with Pus— (See "Pus" in this section).

Syphilitic Ulcer—Sores of Syphilis— Throat Ulcer of—(See Syphilis).

Tendency to Ulcer — Afflictions in ♓; a ♓ disease; a ♋, ♏, and ♓ disease, and afflictions in these signs; the ☽ affl. in ♒; a ♄ disease; ♄, ♅, or ♆ in ♋, and affl. the ☉ or ☽; ♄ and ♃ in ♏, and affl. the ☉ and ♅ in ♊; a ♂ disease; ♂ in ♏ or ♐, ♂, or ill-asp. the ☉. (See Leukocytes; the various paragraphs in this section).

Thighs—(See "Ulcers" under Thighs).

Throat — (See "Ulcerated" under Throat).

Thrush—(See Aphthae).

Treatment Of—(See "Remedy" in this section).

Ulcerous Growths — (See "Tendency To", and the various paragraphs in this section).

Upper Jaw—Ulcerated Gums of—(See Gums).

Urethra—(See "Genitals" in this section; Urethra).

Vagina—(See "Genitals" in this section; Vagina).

Varicose; Venereal Ulcers—♂ afflicted in ♏. (See "Ulcers" under Venereal).

Vulva—(See "Genitals" in this section; Vulva).

Womb—(See "Ulceration" under Womb).

ULNA—The Large Bone of the Forearm—Under the structural rulership of the ♌ Sign. Is opposite to, and corresponds to the Fibula in the leg, ruled by the ♒ Sign. Mars afflicted in ♌ tends to fracture of the Ulna. (See Forearm, Radius).

UMBILICUS—(See Navel).

UNBALANCED MIND—(See "Unbalanced" under Mentality, Reason).

UNBRIDLED PASSION—(See Nymphomania; "Passional Excesses", "Unbridled", under Passion).

UNCANNY FEELINGS—(See Dreams, Fears, Forebodings, Mysterious, Premonitions, Strange, Superstitious, Visions, Weird, etc.).

UNCERTAIN—

Uncertain Action—To the Body—♓ on the Asc.

Uncertain Health—(See "Uncertain" under Health).

Uncertain Mind—(See "Uncertain" under Mind).

UNCHARITABLE—♄ influence. (See Miserly).

UNCHASTE—(See "Chaste" under Females; "Adultery", "Liaisons", under Love Affairs; "Loose Morals" under Morals; "Unbridled" under Passion; "Clandestine" under Sex; "Unchaste" under Women).

UNCLEANLY—Filthy Habits of Body and Mind—Dirty—Slovenly—Untidy—Careless About the Body—The ☽ affl.; ♀ at B.; ♄ ill-dignified at B., and affl.; in Horary Questions ♄ Sig. denotes a dirty person; ♄ ☌ ♀; ♄ and ♂ in the Asc., and affl. the ☽ and ♀; ♂ prominent at B., with many planets in earthy and watery signs, and ♂ without the strong support of the ☉, ♃ or ♀; ♂ affl. in ♓, slovenly in habits; ♀ weak and ill-dignified at B.; ♀ affl. the ☽; ♀ to the bad asps. ☿ by dir.; ♀ ♂ ☽ ☍, and □ ♂ ♑; ♓ on cusp 6th, or in the 6th H., tends to carelessness in personal cleanliness; ♓ when afflicted produces ailments thru carelessness and forgetfulness. These afflictions existing at B., often tend to ill-health thru lack of proper care of the body. (See Carelessness, Cleanliness, Filthy, Habits, Knavish, Leprosy, Neglect, Slovenly, Untidy, etc.).

Unclean Mind—(See Lewd, Lust; "Loose Morals" under Morals; Obscene, Profane, Shameless, Vile, Wanton, etc.).

UNCLES—The Aunts and Uncles on the father's side, when considering a female nativity, are ruled by the 6th H., but in a male nativity, they are ruled by the 12th H. The Aunts and Uncles on the mother's side, in a female nativity, are ruled by the 12th H., and in a male nativity, by the 6th H. By noting these distinctions, and the nature of the planets in, or influences affecting the 6th and 12th houses at birth, the native can get some idea of the events, destiny, health, illness, early or late death, etc., which are apt to overtake an Aunt or Uncle on either side of the house. The Uncles on the father's side are ruled by ♄, and on the mother's side, by ☿. Thus ♄ badly afflicted at B., and by direction, tends to affliction or trouble to an Uncle, on one side of the house, according to the sex of the native, and the transits, progressions, and arcs of direction of afflictions to ♄ will give the time of the events and afflictions. Also ☿ is to be treated in the same way to determine the time and nature of events and afflictions to Aunts and Uncles on the mother's side. (See Aunts, Brethren, Sixth House, Twelfth House).

Maternal Uncles—And Aunts—Death or Suffering To—(See "Aunts and Uncles" under Maternal).

Paternal Uncles—And Aunts—Death or Suffering To—♄ ruler of the 6th or 12th H. at B., and ♄ ☌ or ill-asp. the Asc. by dir., according to the sex of the native, and especially as related to the aunts and uncles on the father's side. On the mother's side, if ☿ should rule the 6th, or be in the 6th, and be much affl. at B., and by direction by ♄, and other malefics, or by an Eclipse, then judge that the affliction will occur to an aunt or uncle on the mother's side, and according to the sex of the native, as to whether the affliction is to be judged as from the 6th or 12th H. Some Authors ignore these finer distinctions, and others lay great stress upon them, the same as in the finer distinctions concerning the 10th and 4th houses, in the cases of the father and mother in a male or female nativity. Most Writers just take the general rule that the 6th H. rules the aunts and uncles on the father's side, in either a male or female nativity, and the 12th H. on the mother's side, and that afflictions in these houses, or to the Asc. by dir., whether they be of ♄, ☿, or any planet, tend to afflict an Uncle or Aunt accordingly. (See Aunts; "Relatives" under Father; Grandparents, Maternal, Mother, Parents, Paternal, Relatives).

UNCOMELY PERSON—♄ in ♉, partile the Asc. (See Crooked; "Ill-Formed" under Ill; Stooping, Ugly, etc.).

UNCOMMON—Unusual—

Uncommon Death—(See "Uncommon" under Death).

Uncommon Diseases—Unusual Diseases—Peculiar—Extraordinary—Strange—Mysterious—Caused by ♅. If there is also a mysterious element in them, ♆ helps to cause them, or may be the direct afflictor. (See Extraordinary, Mysterious, Obscure Diseases, Peculiar Diseases; "Diseases" under Psychic; Strange Diseases, Unusual).

Uncommon Occurrences—(See Phenomena).

Uncommon Persons—Born under the strong influence of ♅. (See Eccentric, Independent, Metaphysics, Misunderstood, Occult, Philosophy; "Truth" under Religion; "Astrology" under Science; "Lover of Truth" under Truth, etc.).

UNCOMPROMISING—Fixed Sign influence, and caused by many planets in these signs, or with fixed signs upon the Asc. and angles at birth. (See "Fixed Signs" under Fixed"; Inflexible, Obstinate).

UNCONSCIOUSNESS—Unconscious— (See Anaesthetics, Catalepsy, Coma, Consciousness, Delirium, Dreams, Epilepsy, Fainting, Fits, Hypnotism; "Sleep Walking" under Sleep; Trance).

Unconscious Behavior — (See the Introduction under Habits).

UNCONTROLLED—Unrestrained—

Emotions—(See "Uncontrolled" under Emotions).

Impulses—(See "Uncontrolled" under Impulses).

Passion — (See Nymphomania; "Unbridled" under Passion).

Thinking — Uncontrolled and Rash Thinking — Indicated by ♂ and the ♂ afflictions to the ☽, ♄, ☿, and the Asc. at B., and by dir. (See Anger; "Brain Storms" under Brain; Brutish, Control, Criminal, Cruel, Dejected, Despondency, Depressed, Excitable, Fear, Folly, Foolhardy, Fury, Hasty, Hatred, Insanity, Involuntary, Jealousy, Liars; "Low Spirits" under Low; Madness, Melancholy; "Thinking" under Mind; Murderous, Perverse, Prodigal, Quarrelsome, Rashness, Recklessness, Revenge, Suicide; "High Temper" under Temper; Unbalanced, Vicious, Violent, Worry, etc.).

UNDER—(See Lower).

UNDERMINED HEALTH — (See Excesses; "Undermined" under Health; "Health Injured" under Men; "Health Suffers" under Opposite Sex; "Passional Excesses" under Passion; "Thinking" under Uncontrolled; Venery; "Lessened" under Vitality).

UNDERSIZED BODY — Undersized Organs or Parts—Dwarfed—Undeveloped — Malformed — ♆ influence; ♆ affl. by ♄, and in the part of the body ruled by the sign containing ♆; ♆ □ or ☍ ♄; ♆ the afflictor, and assisted by ♄, tends to undersized or misshaped organs in the part, or parts afflicted; ♆ affl. in ♋ tends to an undersized stomach; ♆ affl. in ♍, to undersized sex organs, etc. (See Atrophy, Diminished, Dwarfed, Misshaped, Undeveloped).

UNDERSTANDING — Apprehension — Comprehension — Discernment — Perception — Reason — The Understanding of every one depends much upon the strength, and distance of ☿ from the ☉ at B., and the further ☿ is from the ☉, the better the understanding. Also ☿ rising or setting before the ☉ gives a better mind and understanding, and greater depth of thought. When ☿ is combust, the understanding is impaired.

Good Understanding — □ gives, and with □ on the Asc.; ♅ strong and well-

aspected at B.; ☿ in ♍, and with the ☽ in ♏; ☿ well-aspected by the ☽, and also the ☽ and ☿ in good relation to the Asc. (See "Good" under Comprehension, Intellect, Judgment, Mind; "Quickened" under Mentality; "Clear and Incisive", "Sound Mind", under Mind).

Weak Understanding—Comprehension Dull—The ☽ sepr. from ☿ and applying to the ☉; the ☽ □ or ☍ ☿, and the ☽ or ☿ afflicting the Asc.; ♃ Sig. □ or ☍ ☿; ♂ afflicted in ♓, a dull and stupid understanding; ☿ Sig. □ or ☍ ♃. (See "Mental Chaos" under Chaotic; "Mind" under Dull; "Bad" under Judgment; "Weak" under Mentality, Mind; "Disorders Of" under Perception; "Void Of" under Reason; "Smoky Degrees of the Zodiac" under Smoky).

UNDERTAKERS—Embalmers—Morticians—Good Influences For—♂ and ♀ joint rulers of the Profession, and ♄ also give testimony; ♄ joined with ♂ and ♀. (See "Silver Cord" under Silver).

UNDEVELOPED—Undevelopment—Undersized—♆ influence tends to lack of development of any part or organ.

Undeveloped Body—(See Diminished, Dwarfed, Malformations, Myxoedema, Undersized).

Undeveloped Mind — (See Foolish, Idiocy, Imbecility; "Undeveloped" under Mentality). Case—See "Never Grew Up", No. 720, in 1001 N.N.

UNDIGESTED HUMOURS — (See "Raw Humours" under Indigestion).

UNDOING — Self-Undoing — (See Debauched, Disgrace, Dissipation, Drunkenness; "His Own Worst Enemy" under Enemies; "Ruined by Women" under Love Affairs; "Loss Of" under Reputation; Self-Undoing).

UNEASINESS—A Feeling of Uneasiness and Discomfort — (See Discomfort, Malaise).

Old Age—Uneasy Mind In Old Age— (See "Mind" under Old Age).

UNEQUAL—Unequal Sight of the Eyes —(See "Unequal Sight" under Sight).

UNEXPECTED — Unlooked For — Sudden—♅ causes unexpected and sudden disorders, accidents, events, and disasters.

Death—Unexpected and Sudden Death —(See Extraordinary; "Death" under Sudden; Untimely).

Diseases—Unexpected Diseases—(See "Diseases" under Sudden).

Events—Unexpected, Strange and Sudden Events—(See Events).

Wounds — Unexpected and Spontaneous — (See Accidents, Explosions, Hurts, Spontaneous, Wounds).

UNFAVORABLE—Detriments—

Crises—Unfavorable Crisis in Disease —(See Crisis).

Journeys—Unfavorable Journeys— (See Journeys).

Prognosis—Unfavorable—(See Prognosis).

UNFORGIVING—Malefics in the Fixed Signs in angles, retains anger. (See Anger, Jealousy, Revengeful).

UNFORTUNATE—Unfortunate In Life—
Extremely Unfortunate — The ☉ affl. in ⊓ or ♑; the ☉ with South Scale at B.; the ☉ Sig. ☌ ♄; the ☽ carried to, or conjoined with the ☉ at B.; the ☽ Sig. ☌ ♄ or the ☉, or the ☽ □ or ☍ ♄, extremely unfortunate; the ☽ decr. and sepr. from ♃, and applying to ♄; the ☽ sepr. from ♄ and apply. to the ☉; the ☽ Sig. in ♈, ♌, or ♍, generally unfortunate; the ☽ Sig. in ⊓, ♏, ♑, or ♓; the ☽ Sig. in ♎ unless ♀ be strong and well-aspected; the ☽ to Hydra's Heart or Ceti; ♅ ascending at B., or with the chief Significator; ♅ or ♆ affl. the Asc.; ♄ in the 10th or 4th H., and affl. the ☉ or ☽, malice of fortune is certain; signified by ♄ and his afflictions; ♄ to ☌ ☋ by dir.; ♄ Sig. ☌ ☌ or ♂; ♃ ♑; ♃ Sig. □, ☍ ♄; ♂ Sig. in ☍ near Pleiades; ♂ ⊓, thru many changes in work or residence; ♂ Sig. in ⊓, ♋, ♍, ♒ or ♓; ♂ Sig. ☌ ♄, and especially if the Significators be under the Earth; ♂ Sig. □ or ☍ the ☉ or ☽; ♀ Sig. ☌ the ☉ or ♄; ♀ Sig. in ♈ unless ♀ have the good asp. of ♃; ♀ Sig. in ♏ or ♑; ♀ Sig. □ or ☍ the ☽ or ♄; ☿ Sig. in ♈, ♉, ♋, ♐, ♑, or ♓; ♑ on the Asc.; the Sig. in ♏ in Hor'y Q. (See Disgrace, Fate; "Ill-Fortune", "Malice of Fortune", under Fortune; Misfortune, Poverty, Reverses, Ruin; "Much Sickness" under Sickness; Sorrow, Trouble, etc.).

Unfortunate Signs — Of the Zodiac — The Feminine Signs, the Even Signs, as ♉, ♋, ♍, ♏, ♑, and ♓. These are also the Negative Signs. People born under these Signs tend to worry and brood more, invite ill-health, and the general events of their lives tend to be more unfortunate than is the case with the positive, and more individualized classes of people. The ♑ sign is said to be the most unfortunate of all the Signs, being the Sign of ♄. (See "Negative Signs" under Negative).

Unfortunate Star Maps — Those having many □ and ☍ aspects; the malefic planets strong, rising, and elevated above the Lights; many planets out of dignity, in weak signs, cadent, setting, or under the Earth at B.; the hyleg severely afflicted by malefics at B.; ♄ rising in the 1st or 10th H., and afflicted, or ruler of these houses; ♑ upon the Asc. Such maps are considered unfortunate with the average person who is not awakened or spiritalized, as such maps usually tend to more sorrow, trouble, and ill-health, or an earlier death, and often result in crime, murder, suicide, and an untimely or tragical end. (See Character, Fate, Horoscope, Map, Nativity).

UNFRUITFUL — Unprolific — (See Barrenness; "Cold and Dry Body" under Dry; "Anchorite" under Husband; Impotent; "Woman Is Not With Child" under Pregnancy; "Unfruitful" under Wife).

UNGAINLY BODY — ♄ Sig. in ♑, thin and ungainly; ♄ in ♑, partile the Asc.; ♑ on the Asc. (See Awkward; "Raw-Boned" under Bones; Crooked; "Ill-Formed" under Ill; Thin, Ugly).

UNGOVERNABLE— Unmanageable— ♂ rising and elevated at B., and afflicted by malefics. Also in irrational states

of mind, a patient may become ungovernable. In cases of defective, or monstrous births, the offspring may be ungovernable. (See Anger; "Beastly Form" under Beasts; Brutish; "Dogs" under Children; Cruel, Dangerous, Demoniac, Indocile, Insanity, Irrational, Irresponsible, Madness, Mania; "Animal Forms" under Monsters; Murderous; "Void Of" under Reason; Rebellious, Riotous, Savage; "High Temper" under Temper; Vicious, Violent, Wild).

UNGUENTS—(See Ointments).

UNHAPPY—Unhappiness—The 12th H. influences strong and malefic at B.; born under ♄, and with ♄ afflicted in the 12th H.; lord of the 1st H. in the 12th H.; the star Dorsa Leonis (Lion's Tail), when directed to the ☉, ☽, or Asc., tends to bring unhappiness and discontentment. (See Anguish, Anxiety, Cares, Contentment, Dejected, Depressed, Despair, Despondency, Discontentment, Fears, Fortune, Gloom, Grief, Happiness; "Hopes Cut Off" under Hope; Hypochondria; "Ill-Health All Thru Life" under Ill-Health; Introspection, Invalids; "Lion's Tail" under Lion; "Low Spirits" under Low; Melancholy; "Morbid" under Mind; Miseries, Misfortune, Restlessness, Sadness, Sorrow, Suicide, Trouble, Twelfth House, Unfortunate, Worry, Wretched, etc.).

Unhappy Time—(See Disgrace, Events; "Periods of Bad Health" under Health; "Loss Of" under Honour, Reputation; Misery, Reverses, Ruin, Scandal, Self-Undoing; "Much Sickness" under Sickness; Sorrow, Trouble, etc.).

UNHEALTHY—Pale—Sickly—Cadaverous — People who live in covered places, as in houses in the woods, where the sunshine does not enter, or in mines, caves, etc., tend to be unhealthy, and in places where vegetation does not grow, as all vegetation points to the Midheaven, or Zenith. The ♋ and ♑ signs are the weakest signs when upon the Asc. at B., and tend to the weakest bodies, and to be pale, sickly, and unhealthy. Also the ☉ in ♋, in partile asp. the Asc. tends to give an unhealthy countenance, pale and white. (See "Unhealthy" under Complexion; "Weak" under Constitution; Emaciated, Feeble; "Bad" under Health; "Ill-Health All Thru Life" under Ill-Health; Infirm, Invalids, Pale, Sickly; "Much Sickness" under Sickness; "Low" under Vitality; "Weak Body" under Weak).

Air—Unhealthy Air—(See "Corrupt" under Air).

Body—Unhealthy Body and Constitution—(See the first part of this Article).

Countenance—Unhealthy Countenance —(See "Unhealthy" under Complexion; "Unhealthy Aspect" under Face; Pale, Sickly; "Complexion" under White).

Imagination — (See "Unhealthy" under Imagination).

Mind—(See "Unhealthy" under Mind).

UNILATERAL—Affecting But One Side of the Body—
Ears — Deafness In One Ear — (See "One Ear" under Hearing).

Eyes — Blindness In One Eye — (See "One Eye" under Blindness, Eyes; "Eyes" under Left, Right).

Headache — Unilateral Headache — (See "Hemicrania" under Head; Migraine).

Hemianopia—Blindness In One-Half of the Visual Field—(See "Hemianopia" under Sight).

Hemicrania — Neuralgia of One-Half of the Head—(See "Hemicrania" under Head; Migraine).

Hemiplegia — Paralysis In One Side of the Body—(See "Hemiplegia" under Paralysis).

Neuralgia—In One Side of the Head —(See "Hemicrania" in this section).

Nutrition—Impaired Nutrition of One Side of the Face—(See "Hemiatrophy" under Face).

Paralysis—In One Side of the Body— (See "Hemiplegia" under Paralysis).

Vision—Blindness In One-Half of the Visual Field—(See "Hemianopia" under Sight).

UNION OF PARTS — (See Adhesions, Coalition).

UNKNOWN — Has Fears of An Unknown Danger—(See "Danger" under Fears).

UNLOOKED FOR—(See Extraordinary, Sudden, Unexpected, Untimely).

UNMANAGEABLE — (See "Outrageous" under Insanity; Ungovernable).

UNNATURAL—Abnormal—Contrary to the Laws of Nature—

Acts — Unnatural Acts — (See Aversions, Deviations, Perversions).

Appetites—Unnatural Appetites—The ☽ or ♀ afflicted by ♅. (See Appetites, Cravings, Drink, Eating, Excesses, Food, Gluttony, Passion, Perversions).

Chaotic Acts—Chaotic and Unnatural Acts—♅ influence; ♅ afflicting the ☽ or ♀; ♅ afflicted in the 5th H.; ♅ affl. in the 7th H., immoral and unnatural practices with others of the same sex. (See Chaotic, Deviations, Homosexuality, Perversions, Vices).

Conformations—Unnatural Conformations — Defective Births — (See "Beastly Form" under Beasts; "Defective" under Births; "Dogs" under Children; Cloaca, Cyclops, Inhuman, Malformations, Missing, Monsters, Virile).

Desires — Unnatural Desires — ♅ afflicted at B.; ♅ affl. in the 5th H.; ♄ ♂ or ill-asp. ♀. (See Chaotic, Depraved, Desires, Excesses, Gluttony; "Males Nearly Impotent" under Impotent; Nymphomania; "Passional Excesses" under Passion; Perversions).

Discharges — (See "Unnatural" under Discharges).

Foods—Desire for Unnatural Foods— (See "Unnatural" under Food).

Mind — Unnatural States of Mind — The ☽ or ☿ affl. by ♅. (See the various paragraphs in this section).

Secret Practices — Unnatural Secret Practices — (See Perversions; "Secret Bad Habits" under Secret; "Solitary" under Vice).

UNORTHODOX—(See Independent, Misunderstood, Ninth House, Occult; "Lover of Truth" under Truth).

UNPLEASANT—(See Fetid, Foul; "Unpleasant" under Manner; Odors, Offensive).

UNPRINCIPLED — (See Cheating, Deceitful, Dishonest, Forgers, Gamblers, Knavish, Liars, Libelers; "Low and Base" under Low; Pettifogging, Swindlers, Thieves, etc.).

UNPROLIFIC — (See Barrenness, Unfruitful).

UNREASONABLE — (See "Unreasonable" under Reason).

UNREFINED — A Coarse, Rough, Vulgar, and Unrefined Person—A Coarse Body and Mind—The ☽ ill-dignified at B.; the ☽ affl. in ♍, coarse, and often vulgar; the ☽ Sig. ☌ ♄; in Hor'y Q. the ☽ ill-dig. and afflicted, a very vulgar, coarse, and ill-mannered person; ♄ Sig. in ♉, unpolished; ♄ Sig. in ♌, rough in carriage (Hor'y); ♍ on the Asc., coarse body. (See Awkwardness, Coarse, Gross; "Unrefined" under Manners; Rough, Ugly).

UNRELIABLE—(See Deceitful, Dishonest, Irrational, Irresponsible, Liars, Swindlers, Thieves, Unprincipled, Vacillating, etc.).

UNRESTRAINED—(See Control, Debauched, Dissipation, Drink, Excesses, Gluttony, Inordinate; "Passional Excesses" under Passion; Prodigal, Profligate, Rebellious, Riotous, Self-Control, Self-Indulgent, Ungovernable, Vicous, Violent, etc.).

UNRULY—(See Erring, Perverse, Rebellious, Riotous, Sedition, Ungovernable, etc.).

UNSAVORY SUBJECTS—The Mind Morbid Upon—♅ affl. in the 5th H., along sex lines, and with passional cravings; ♅ in the 6th or 12th H., in ♌ ♓, and with ♌ or ♍ upon the cusps of the 6th and 12th H. (See Brooding; "Erotic" under Mania; "Morbid" under Mind; Nymphomania, Perversions).

UNSEASONABLE — Unseasonable Perspiration — (See "Violent" under Sweat).

UNSETTLED — (See Changes, Discontentment; "Unsettled" under Habits; Removals, Residence, Restlessness; "Unsettled" under Riches; Roaming, Travel, Vacillating, Vagabond, Wanderer, etc.).

UNSOUND—

Unsound Legs — (See "Unsound" under Legs).

Unsound Mind — (See Dementia, Demoniac, Foolish, Idiocy, Imbecile, Insanity; "Derangement" under Mental; "Unsound Mind", "Weak Mind", under Mind; "Unsound Mind" under Wife).

UNSTABLE—Common Signs on the Asc. and Angles at B.; many planets in the negative signs; ♍ on the Asc. (See Instability).

UNTIDY—Careless—Bad aspects to the ☽, ♀, or ☿, and espec. if they are in the Asc., or in cadent houses, but the good asps. to these planets so situated tend to tidiness. (See Carelessness, Cleanliness, Dress, Filthy, Habits, Improvident, Indifferent, Knavish, Slovenly, Uncleanly, etc.).

UNTIMELY DEATH—
   Untimely End—A Premature Death—The ☉ or ☽ Sig. ♂ ♂, and ♂ ill-dignified at B.; the ☉ Sig. □ or ☍ ♄, may meet with a bad end; the ☉ or ☽ afflicted, and the ☽, or lord of the 1st, be near violent fixed stars, or a malefic or violent stars ascending, and danger of death Abroad; ☉ to the place of Aldebaran; the ☽ ill-dignified at B., and ♂ ♄, and ♂ in evil asp. the ☽, and the ☉ also ill-dig.; an eclipse of the ☽ in 1st decan. of ♑; ☽ to the ♂ Pleiades or Praesepe, and with the ☉ ☍ Asc. or ♂ at same time; ♅, ♇, ♄, ♂ in violent signs at B., and affl. the hyleg; ♄ Sig. ♂ ☽, and the ☽ affl. by ♂, and ♂ ill-dig.; ♄ or ♂ affl. in the 4th H., danger of a bad end to life; ♂ Sig. □, ☍ ♄ if either be in the Asc., or ♄ in the M.C.; ♂ affl. by ♄ at B., and ♂ to the ♂ the M.C.; lord of the 6th in the 8th H.; ruler of the 8th, and the ☉ and ☽ affl. by malefics from angles; lord of the 12th in the 10th; the 29° ♋ on the Asc.; the 3rd Dec. ♑ on Asc., ruled by the ☉, premature death. There are many influences which tend to what we would call an untimely death, such as a high fever from contagion or infection; an accident, injury, wound, drowning, quarrels, duels, violence, murder, execution, hanging, tragedy, death in infancy or childhood, a bad end from drink or dissipation, immorality, etc. See these subjects in the alphabetical arrangement. For the various kinds of a premature and untimely death, note the lists in the Articles on Accidents, Death, Hurts, Injuries, Wounds. (See "Death" under Accidents, Childhood, Children, Fire, Infancy, Kings, Middle Life, Poison, Stabs, Storms, Tragical, Travel, Treachery, Violent, Voyages, Water, Wounds, Youth; also see Assassination, Drowning; "Early Death" under Early; Execution, Gunshot, Hanging, Highwaymen, Killed; "Short Life" under Life; Lightning, Murdered, Pirates; "Premature Death" under Premature; Robbers, Sea, Ships, Shipwreck, Vehicles, Weather, Wind, etc.).

UNTRUSTWORTHY — (See Unprincipled, Unreliable).

UNUSUAL—
   Unusual Death—(See "Unusual" under Death; "Death" under Extraordinary, Mysterious, Peculiar, Strange, Untimely).

   Unusual Diseases — (See "Unusual Diseases" under Children, Infancy; "Diseases" under Extraordinary, Mysterious, Obscure, Peculiar, Strange, Uncommon).

UNWHOLESOME—Unhealthy—
   Unwholesome Air — (See "Corrupt", "Pestilential", under Air).

   Unwholesome Complexion—(See "Unhealthy" under Complexion; Pale, Sickly, Unhealthy).

UPPER PARTS — Upper Parts of the Body — Upper Parts of Organs — The upper part of an organ is shown by the first degrees of a Sign, as the first face or decanate, and planets in this part of a sign tend to afflict the upper part of the organ; planets in the middle of a sign, the middle part of the organ; and planets in the last part of a sign, or the last part upon the cusp of an evil house, as on the 6th, 8th, or 12th, tend to affect the lower, or under part of an organ. Thus malefics in the first part of ♋ would tend to affect the oesophagus, the entrance and upper part of stomach. Planets in the middle of ♋ would affect more the main body of the stomach, its glands, juices, etc. Planets in the latter degrees of ♋, the lower end of the stomach, and the pylorus. (See "Parts of Body" under Accidents; "Organs" under Lower, Middle; "Upper Parts" under Organs). The following conditions have to do with the Upper Part of the body, the Upper, or Outer Part of Organs or Members.

   Arms—The Upper Arms—(See "Upper Arm" under Arms).

   Back Parts—Of the Body—(See Rear).

   Blood—Too Much Blood In the Upper Parts—The majority of planets at B. in signs ruling the upper parts. (See "Too Much Blood" under Blood).

   Body—Upper Part of—With ♋ on the Asc., the upper part, or upper half of the body, is rounder and larger than the lower part. With ♊ on the Asc., and many planets in ♊, the upper part of the body is longer than the lower part. (See "Parts" under Lower).

   Diseases—In the Upper Parts of the Body—♂ in the Asc. at the beginning of an illness, or at decumbiture.

   Dorsal Nerves—Upper Dorsal Nerves —(See Dorsal).

   Ears—(See "Upper Ears" under Ears).

   Extremities—Upper Extremities—(See Arms, Hands, Head).

   Forehead—(See "Upper" under Forehead).

   Front Part of Body—(See Front).

   Jaw—(See "Upper" under Jaws).

   Kidneys — (See "Upper Kidneys" under Kidneys).

   Large Upper Part—Of the Body—(See "Body" in this section).

   Legs — (See "Upper Parts Of" under Legs).

   Lip—(See "Upper" under Lips).

   Liver—Upper Lobes of—(See "Lobes" under Liver).

   Lobes — Upper Lobes — (See "Lobes" under Liver, Lungs).

   Long Upper Part—Of the Body—(See "Body" in this section).

   Lower Parts—(See Lower).

   Lungs—Upper Lobes of—(See "Lobes" under Lungs).

   Marks and Moles — On the Upper Parts of the Body, or a Member—(See Marks, Moles, Scars).

   Middle Parts — (See "Organs" under Middle).

   Moles — On the Upper Parts of the Body, or Members — (See "Location" under Moles).

   Organs — Upper Parts of—(See "Upper" under Organs; the Introduction to this section).

Ribs—(See "Upper" under Ribs).

Round Upper Body—(See "Body" in this section).

Scars—On the Upper Part of An Organ or Part—(See Marks, Moles, Scars, and especially read what is said under "Marks").

Spinal Nerves—The Upper Spinal Nerves—(See Spine).

Teeth—The Upper Teeth—(See Teeth).

Upper Half of Body—Larger and Longer Than Lower Half—(See "Body" in this section).

UPRIGHT—

Upright Body—Erect—Straight—The ☉ in ♎, in partile asp. the Asc., tall, straight, and upright; the ☽ in ♊, partile the Asc., tall, upright, well-made, and also comely; born under ♃ tends to give an erect, upright, tall, and well-made body; ♃ in ♎, partile the Asc., upright and slender; ♃ in ♐, partile the Asc., upright, tall, fine, and well-made; born under ♀, and ♀ ori., tall, straight, and upright; ☿ in ♊, partile the Asc., upright, tall, and well-made; ♊ on the Asc., tall, fair, erect, straight, and upright; ♎ on the Asc., and ori., tall and upright. (See Erect, Straight, Tall).

Upright Nature—And Disposition—(See Honest, Humane, Kind; "Good Morals" under Morals; Noble, Sincere).

URAEMIA—(See Urea, Uremia).

URANIUM—Uranite—Minerals ruled by ♅. (See Pitch-Blende, Radium).

URANUS—The planet ♅—Also called "Herschel", in honor of its Discoverer. Also called Georgium Sidus. This planet was discovered on March 13th, 1781, by Sir William Herschel. By careful observation of the workings and effects of this planet over human affairs, much has been written about it, and especially in recent years. This Article will be arranged into three Sections, as follows: Section One—Influence of Uranus. Section Two—Uranus Rules. Section Three—Uranus Diseases and Afflictions. For the special Characteristics and Qualities of ♅, see "Qualities" in Sec. 1 of this Article.

— SECTION ONE —

INFLUENCE OF URANUS—Uranus is said to be a Ruler Among Planets. His influence is of a sudden and spasmodic nature, and fundamentally has been observed and determined to be more Psychic and Mental than Physical. In the Brain he rules the Pituitary Body, one of the Spiritual Centers, and closely associated with the Pineal Gland, ruled by ♆, in Spiritual and Psychic Development. (See Neptune, Pineal, Pituitary). Very few people as yet are able to respond to his higher vibrations, and it is asserted that the influences of ♅ and ♆ will be more positive over Races yet to come in the distant future, as the Sixth Sub-Race, and the Sixth Race itself. The Occult Significance of Uranus is well set forth in the book, "Message of the Stars", by the Heindels.

Affinity—♅ has affinity with the Eyes, as this planet rules the Ether, and transmits the rays of Light. Also ♅ has affinity with the ♒ sign, which is a strong sign of this planet.

Afflicts—♅ afflicts by his ☌, P., □ and ☍ aspects.

Alchemistry Of—(See Pituitary).

Anareta—♅ may be Anareta, altho he does not kill by himself, but usually in with a train of evil directions to the hyleg. (See Anareta).

Aspects—(See "Afflicts" in this section). His favorable aspects to the ☉, ☽, ☿, and other planets, and to the Asc., tend to elevate the mind and nature, expand the Intuitions, make the native Altruistic and Humane, give a love of Truth, and to greatly increase the Spiritual Foresight and Perceptions.

Changes—The ♅ influence, and especially his afflictions, tend to many changes, removals, journeys, and to be restless and unsettled until the native becomes awakened to the Higher Things in life.

Colors—Deep Rich Blue.

Denotes—(See "Spasmodic" in this section).

Directions Of—(See "Directions" in Sec. Three of this Article).

Discovery Of—(See the Introduction to this Article).

Drugs Of—(See Metals, Typical Drugs of, in this section).

Ether—♅ rules the Ether. (See Ether).

Events—Tends to sudden and unexpected events.

Evils—His evils come suddenly, as well as the good he brings.

Eyes—♅ has special affinity with the Eyes, as he rules the Ether, thru which Light Rays are transmitted. (See Blindness, Ether, Eyes; "Rays" under Light).

Free Love—(See "Free Love" under Free).

Higher Rays Of—Not many respond to the higher rays of ♅, and tend to be adversely affected by his vibrations.

Horoscope—♅ affects the horoscope mostly by his influence upon the other planets, as he is a Ruler among Ruling Planets.

Impulses—(See "Sudden" in this section).

Indicates—♅ indicates eccentric and uncommon people, Bohemians, and those who are abrupt, original, and not of the ordinary type. (See Eccentric, Independent, Misunderstood, Occult).

Intuition—The Principle of ♅ is Intuition.

Journeys—Causes Many Journeys, Changes, and Removals. (See these subjects).

Laws of Society—♅ people rebel against these Laws, and desire freedom. They also tend to chafe under the vows and restraints of marriage.

Love Affairs—The afflictions of ♅ to ♀, or with ♅ in the 5th or 7th H., tend to much trouble in love affairs and marriage, and to separations and estrangements.

Magnetism—♅ has influence over the Animal Magnetism, and the Impulses. (See Impulses, Magnetism).

Marriage Happiness—(See "Love Affairs" in this section).

Mental Effects—Mental and Psychic effects are shown by ♅ rather than physical.

Mental Qualities—Eccentric, Unconventional).

Metals and Minerals Of—(See Sec. 2 of this Article).

Metaphysics—Gives a great love for, and of the Occult, and of Truth, and especially by his Higher Vibrations, and to those who are awakened and ready for it. '(See Metaphysics, Occult, Science).

Moral Lapses — His afflictions, and especially to ♀, tend to moral lapses, free love, clandestine love affairs, disregard of conventionalities, and to sex perversions.

Occult—His higher vibrations give a love of the Occult, the Metaphysical, and Truth.

Octave Of — Most Writers say he is the higher octave of ☿, but the Heindels, of the Rosicrucian Fellowship, say he is the higher octave of ♀.

Pathological Influence—Telepathic. (See Telepathy).

Physical Effects Of—The physical effects of this planet are not always shown, but rather a Mental and Psychic influence and effect. (See "Body", "Health", in Sec. 3 of this Article).

Principle Of—Intuition.

Province Of—The province of ♅ lies in his spasmodic, explosive, shock-producing, electric, and neuralgic influences.

Psychic — His influences are more Psychic and Mental than Physical.

Qualities—The following qualities are attributed to his higher and lower vibrations, and tend to affect the individual according to his degree of enlightenment and awakening. Some of these are also his abstract qualities—Abrupt, Accidental, Acute, Advanced, Afflicting, Airy, Alternating, Altruistic, Antiperistaltic, Arresting, Barren, Bereaving, Blinding, Bohemian, Breaking, Bursting, Cataclysmic, Changeable, Clandestine, Clonic, Cold, Compressing, Constructive, Contracting, Convertible, Convulsive, Corrosive, Cramping, Creative, Curious, Demoniacal, Disorganizing, Disruptive, Distorting, Distressing, Disturbing, Dry, Eccentric, Electric, Emotional, Enlarging, Erratic, Etheric, Exaggerating, Excitable, Explosive, Extraordinary, Fanatical, Fractious, Fracture-Producing, Freak-Producing, Free-Loving, Free-Thinking, Fretful, Gaseous, Hasty, Heedless, High-Strung, Hindering, Humane, Hurtful, Hysterical, Immoral, Impeding, Impulsive, Incoordinating, Independent, Injurious, Inquisitive, Intuitive, Inventive, Investigating, Involuntary, Irregular, Irresponsible, Irritating, Jeopardizing, Jerky, Lesional, Licentious, Lustful, Magnetic, Maniacal, Masculine, Mental, Metaphysical, Mis-

understood, Morbid, Motor-Disturbing, Murderous, Nauseating, Nervous, Neuralgic, Neurotic, Obscuring, Occult, Open-Minded, Original, Out-of-the Ordinary, Paroxysmal, Passional, Peculiar, Perverting, Phenomenal, Philosophical, Positive, Psychic, Quick in Action, Quivering, Radical, Radio-Active, Reactionary, Rebellious, Reckless, Reforming, Remarkable, Rending, Resisting, Resolute, Resourceful, Restless, Romantic, Ruling, Rupturing, Scientific, Shock-Producing, Spasmodic, Speculative, Stopping, Straining, Strange in Procedure, Strictural, Sudden, Suicidal, Tangential Action, Telepathic, Temperamental, Tempting, Tensional, Tragical, Trembling, Twisting, Twitching, Truth-Loving, Uncommon, Uncontrollable, Unconventional, Unexpected, Unordinary, Unorthodox, Unprejudiced, Unruly, Unusual, Variable, Vibratory, Violent, etc. (See these subjects).

Rays Of—(See "Higher Rays" in this section).

Removals — (See "Changes" in this section).

Romance — Gives Bohemian Tendencies and love of Romance.

Salient Characteristic—Altruism.

Sex—♅ being exalted in the sex sign ♏ has great influence over the sex nature and the sex organs, tending to great passion, unless controlled, and to perversions of the sex nature.

Sign—♅ has his home in the ♒ sign. Is exalted in ♏, and has his detriment in ♌.

Society—Disregard of Laws of—(See "Moral Laws" under Love Affairs).

Spasmodic—♅ is radio-active, and denotes spasmodic, tangential and eccentric action.

Strong—♅ is strong in ♒ 'and ♏.

Sudden—Sudden is the keynote to ♅ action. He tends to sudden impulses to do wrong; brings sudden good or ill, sudden diseases, accidents, explosions, shock, the unexpected, uncommon, the unusual, unlooked-for, etc.

Temptations — His afflictions to ♀ make the native very subject to many temptations, and especially along sex and passional lines, to free love, etc. (See "Free Love" under Free).

Therapeutic Action—Electric, Vibrational.

Typical Drugs — Croton Oil, Ether, Compressed Air and Gases.

Waves Of — The Waves of ♅ are neither continuous nor rounded, but broken and spasmodic.

— SECTION TWO —

URANUS RULES — The following is an alphabetical arrangement of the matters ruled over by ♅. See these subjects. Air (Compressed Air and Gases); Amber; Appendix; Aquarius Sign; Assimilation at Puberty and After; Aura (the Physical and Magnetic Aura); Bereavements; Blind Impulses; Brain (the Membranes of the Brain); Breathing (Respiratory Action); Catastrophes; Celluloid (Xylonite); Changes (Sudden Changes);

Circulation in the Kidneys; Compressed Air and Gases; Creative Force (Sex Force — see Pituitary); Dura Mater; Electricity; Erratic States of Mind; Ether (or Ethers); Etheric Body; Events (Sudden); Explosives (and tends to ignite them); Extraordinary Events; Eyes; Fluids of the Body—Nerve Fluids—(and acting thru the Pituitary Body); Gases; Genito-Urinary Organs (Nerves of); Growth (Abnormal); Heart (Valves of); Impulses (Animal and Blind Impulses); Jerky Movements; Kidneys (Circulation in); Lodestone; Magnetic Aura; Magnetism (Animal, and the Terrestrial Magnetism); Membranes (of the Brain and Stomach); Metals and Minerals (Amber, Actinium, Chalcolite, Lodestone, Pitch-Blende, Polonium, Radium, Shellac, Thorium, Uranite, Uranium, Zinc); Mind (Erratic States of); Motor Nerves of Speech; Murders; Nerves (of the Genito-Urinary Organs —the Nerve Fluids—Motor Nerves of Speech; Nervous Temperament; Nitrogen; Phenomena (Telepathic); Physical Body; Pitch-Blende; Pituitary Body; Public Affairs; Radio Activity; Radium; Reformers; Resins; Respiratory Action; Romances; Sex Force (Creative Force); Shellac; Sky (Amber Color of); Spasmodic Movements; Speech (Motor Nerves of); Spinal Cord (Membranes of); Stomach (Membranes of); Sudden (Sudden Changes and Events); Suicides; Tall Body; Telepathic Phenomena; Temperament (the Nervous); Terrestrial Magnetism; Tragedies; Uncommon People; Understanding; Unusual Events; Uranium; Valves (of the Heart); Vibration; Xanthin; Xenon; X-Ray; Xyloidin, Xylonite; Zinc.

— SECTION THREE —

URANUS DISEASES, AFFLICTIONS —The Diseases and Complaints of ♅ are somewhat similar to the combined effects of ♄, ♀, and ☿ in the 12 Signs. His diseases are usually of a nervous origin, and difficult to understand, and often incurable. His afflictions tend to sudden and unexpected complaints, accidents, suicide, peculiar diseases, spasmodic disorders, and sometimes cause numbness and electrical pains, shooting pains, neuralgia, etc. His afflictions also tend to abnormal and strange growth, freaks of nature, etc. See the following subjects in the alphabetical arrangement when only listed here—

Abnormal Growth—(See "Abnormal" under Growth).

Accidents—♅ causes illness or death as a result of accidents. He causes accidents, injury, or death by Electricity, Machinery in the Employment, or by Violence. (See "Illness" under Accidents; Electricity, Employment, Lightning, Machinery, Violence).

Acute Pains — (See "Head" in this section).

Appendicitis—(See Appendix).

Arms—(See "Legs" in this section).

Asthma; Bathings—Death At, or Illness From — (See Bathing; "Bathing" under Demoniac).

Bladder—Spasm of—(See Bladder).

Blindness; Body — ♅ has a peculiar influence in relation to the human body, and his diseases are not usually of the ordinary character, but of a spasmodic and sudden nature. (See Spasmodic; "Diseases" under Sudden; "Health" in this section).

Bowels—Cramp In—Spasm In—Wind Colic In — (See these subjects under Bowels).

Brain — Peculiar Brain Affections — (See Brain).

Breathing—Spasmodic Breathing—(See Breathing).

Burstings—(See Apoplexy, Bursting, Hemorrhage, Laceration, Rupture).

Calamities—Sudden and Strange Calamities—(See Calamity).

Chorea—(See Saint Vitus Dance).

Claustrophobia; Clonic Spasm — (See "Clonic" under Spasmodic).

Cold and Dampness—Diseases Arising from Sudden Exposure To—(See "Cold and Dampness" under Exposure).

Cold and Dry Diseases — (See "Cold and Dry" under Dry).

Colic—(See "Wind" under Colic).

Contortions; Contractions; Cough;

Cramps—In Arms, Hands, Legs, Feet, Bowels, Stomach, etc.—♅ in the Signs which rule these parts. (See Cramps).

Dampness — (See "Cold and Dampness" in this section).

Death — ♅ does not kill by himself but assists by his evil aspects and directions. (See Death; "Death" under Sudden; "Accidents", "Sudden", "Tragical", in this section).

Demoniac; Directions—(See "Death", "Relatives", in this section).

Disruptions — (See Bursting, Laceration, Rupture).

Drink—(See "Death" under Intoxication).

Dry and Cold Diesases — (See "Cold and Dry" under Dry).

Electrical Pains — (See "Electric Pains" under Electric).

Electric Shocks — (See Electricity, Lightning).

Emphysema; Employment—Injury In by Machinery—(See Employment, Machinery).

Erratic Movements—(See Erratic).

Exaggerated Action—(See Exaggerated).

Explosions—Blindness, Death, or Injury By—(See Explosions).

Eyeballs—Quivering of — (See "Nystagmus" under Eyeballs).

Eyes—Disorders of—(See Blindness, Eyes).

Feet — Cramps In — (See "Legs" in this section).

Fits—(See Convulsions, Fits).

Floating Kidney — (See "Floating" under Kidneys).

Fractures; Freaks of Nature — (See Freaks, Genius, Giants, Prodigies).

Functions Suppressed — (See "Suppressed" under Functions).

Giants; Growth — (See Giants; "Abnormal" under Growth).

Hallucinations; Hands—Cramps In—(See "Cramps" under Hands; "Legs" in this section).

Head—Acute and Spasmodic Pains In —Ḥ affl. in ♈. (See Head).

Health — Ḥ has little influence over the health, except as reflected by psychic and mental states, or which is the result of accident, sudden and unexpected causes, etc. (See "Body" in this section).

Heart—Spasm of—Stoppage, Valvular Disease—Palpitation—(See Heart).

Hiccough; High Strung — And Nervous—(See High).

Homosexuality; Human Body—Ḥ influence over—(See "Body" in this section).

Hurts — Strange and Unexpected — (See Hurts).

Hysteria; Illness—Due to Accidents, Nervous Strain, etc.—☽ affl. by Ḥ. (See "Nervous Strain" under Nerves).

Impediment—Of Speech—(See Speech).

Incoordination; Incurable Diseases— (See Incurable).

Injuries; Insanity—Violent Forms of —See "Outrageous", "Violent", under Insanity).

Intussusception — (See this subject under Bowels).

Involuntary Movements — (See Erratic, Involuntary, Spasmodic).

Irregular Action — (See Erratic, Irregular, Spasmodic).

Jerky Movements—(See Jerky).

Kidneys—(See "Floating" under Kidneys).

Killed — (See Electricity, Explosions, Lightning, Machinery; "Death" under Railroads, Sudden, Violent; Shock).

Legs — Ḥ in signs which rule the arms, hands, legs, feet, tends to cramps, spasms, paralysis, and disturbance of the motor nerves of these parts. (See Legs).

Lesions — Nerve Lesions — (See Lesions).

Lightning — Death or Injury By — (See Lightning).

Machinery—Death or Injury By—(See Machinery, Mangled).

Mobs — Death or Injury By — (See Mobs).

Monsters; Morals—Perverted Morals (See "Loose Morals" under Morals; "Moral Lapses" in Sec. 1 of this Article).

Morbid — Obscure Morbid Manifestations—(See "Obscure" under Morbid).

Motor Nerves—Disturbances of—(See Motor).

Muscular Action — (See Involuntary; "Involuntary Contractions" under Muscles).

Nausea; Neck — Motor Disturbances In—(See Neck).

Nerves—Various Disorders of—(See the subjects under Nerves. Also see Corrosion; "High Strung" under High; Lesions, Motor; "Nervous Strain" under Strain).

Neuralgia; Nodding Spasm — (See "Nodding" under Head).

Numbness; Nutrition—(See "Perverted" under Nutrition).

Nystagmus—(See Eyeballs).

Obscure Diseases — (See "Obscure" under Morbid; Obscure).

Opisthotonos; Pains — Acute and Spasmodic Pains In the Head—Electric Pains — (See "Electric Pains" under Electric; "Acute", "Darting", "Pains", "Spasmodic", under Head).

Palpitation — (See "Palpitation" under Heart; Palpitations).

Paralysis; Paroxysms;

Peculiar Diseases — (See "Peculiar" under Brain, Nerves; Peculiar).

Perversions; Physical Effects Of — See "Physical Effects" in Sec. 1 of this Article).

Pituitary Body — Disorders of — (See Pituitary).

Prolapsus; Ptosis; Quiverings;

Railroads—Death or Injury On—(See Railroads).

Relatives — Death of — (See "Death", "Distant", under Relations).

Remarkable Diseases—(See Extraordinary, Remarkable, Uncommon).

Rendings — (See Bursting, Lacerations, Rupture).

Respiratory Disorders—(See Asthma; "Spasmodic" under Breathing).

Rupture; Saint Vitus Dance;

Sex Disorders—(See Perversions, Sex, Venereal; "Sex" in Sec. 1 of this Article).

Shipwreck; Shock; Sight—Disorders of—(See Blindness, Sight).

Sodomy—(See Homosexuality).

Spasmodic Diseases—Spasms—Spasms In Arms, Hands, Legs, Feet—Spasm of Bladder—Spasmodic Breathing—Spasmodic Heart Action—Clonic Spasm—Nodding Spasm, etc.—(See "Spasmodic", or "Spasm", under Arms, Bladder Breathing, Feet, Hands, Heart, Legs; "Nodding" under Head; "Clonic" under Spasmodic).

Speech—Impediment In—(See Speech).

Stomach—Ḥ ♋ tends to Cramp, Colic, and Wind Spasms of the Stomach. (See Stomach).

Stoppage—Of the Heart—(See Heart).

Strange Diseases — Strange Hurts — (See Strange, Unexpected).

Strictures; Subsultus;

Sudden Diseases—Sudden Death—(See Sudden).

Suicide; Suppressions — (See "Suppressed" under Functions; Suppressions).

Telepathy—Pathological Disturbances of—(See Telepathy).

Tetanus; Throat — (See "Spasmodic Disorders" under Throat).

Tics; Torticollis — (See "Wry Neck" under Neck).

Trade—Death or Injury In the Trade or Employment — (See Employment, Machinery).

Tragical Death—(See "Tragical" under Death).

Tremors; Twitchings;

Uncommon Diseases — (See Uncommon)

Uncontrolled Action — (See Control, Incoordination, Involuntary, Spasmodic, Uncontrolled).

Unexpected Disorders — (See Sudden, Unexpected).

Unusual Diseases—(See Uncommon).

Urethra — Spasm and Stricture of — (See Urethra).

Valvular Disease — Of the Heart — (See Heart).

Venereal Disease—(See Venereal).

Violent—Violent Accidents—Violent Forms of Insanity — (See "Hurts and Injuries" under Accidents; "Outrageous", "Violent", under Insanity).

Wind—Wind In Bowels—Wind Spasm of Stomach -- (See "Wind" under Bowels, Colic, Stomach; "Bowels" under Wind).

Winking—(See Eyelids).

Wry Neck -- (See "Wry Neck" under Neck).

URATES — Excess of — Over-Secretion of—♃ affl. in ♏. (See Urea, Uric Acid).

UREA—Urea is the chief solid constituent of the Urine, and the principal nitrogenous product of tissue decomposition. Urea is formed in the liver by ♄, and also deposited by ♄ over the body as Uric Acid, causing Gout, Rheumatism, Arthritis Deformans in the Joints, Toxaemia, etc. (See these subjects. Also see Uremia, Uric Acid).

Excess of Urea—Over-Secretion of— ♀ affl. in ♎.

Retention Of—(See Deposits, Gout, Hyperacidity, Rheumatism, Toxaemia, Uremia).

UREMIA—Toxic Blood from Accumulation of Urea—Uremic Convulsions—An Auto-Toxic Psychoses—A ♎ disease; ♄ or ♀ affl. in ♎.

Uremic Coma—(See Coma).

Uremic Convulsions — (See the first part of this Article).

Uremic Headache—(See "Toxaemic" under Headache).

URETERS—Ruled by ♎ and ♏. Elimination of Urine thru the Ureters, Bladder, and Urethra is ruled by the ♏ sign.

Calculus In—Renal Colic—(See "Colic" under Kidneys).

Constriction Of—♄ affl. in ♎. (See Constrictions).

Inflammation Of—Ureteritis—♂ affl. in ♎ or ♏.

URETHRA—Is ruled by the ♏ Sign. Elimination of Urine thru the Bladder and Urethra is ruled by ♏. Cowper's Glands are ruled by ♏.

Abscess Of—♃ affl. in ♏.

Chordee—♂ affl. in ♏. (See "Chordee" under Gonorrhoea).

Cloaca—A Common Outlet to the Bladder and Rectum—♄ affl. in ♏. (See Cloaca).

Contraction Of—(See "Stricture" in this section).

Gonorrhoea—Running of the Reins— (See Gonorrhoea).

Inflammation Of—Urethritis—Chordee—Gonorrhoea—♂ affl. in ♏ tends to, and to aggravated cases; a ♏ disease. (See Gonorrhoea).

Spasmodic Stricture Of—(See "Stricture" in this section).

Strangury — (See this subject under Urine).

Stricture—Contraction of—Obstruction of—A ♏ disease, and afflictions in ♏; ♀ affl. in ♌ or ♏; ♂ in ♏; ♄ affl. in ♏, spasmodic stricture. Case of Stricture—See Chap. 13 in Daath's Medical Astrology. (See Constrictions, Contractions, Stricture).

Ulceration—♂ affl. in ♏.

Urethritis — (See "Inflammation" in this section).

URIC ACID—♄ forms Uric Acid in the liver, and also deposits Uric Acid over the body during muscular activity, causing Gout, Rheumatism, Enlarged Joints, etc.

Blood—Excess of Uric Acid In the Blood—Lithemia—♄ influence. (See Lithemia).

Deposits—Excess Deposits of In Blood, and Over the Body—♄ influence; ♄ affl. in ♋ or ♑. (See Aches, Deposits, Gout, Lithemia, Pains, Rheumatism).

Lithemia—(See "Blood" in this section).

System—Uric Acid In—♂ affl. in ♎.

Urine—Excess of Uric Acid In—♆, ♓, or ♄ in ♏, and afflicting the ☉ or ☽. (For collateral study see Gall, Gout, Hyperacidity, Impure, Joints, Minerals; "Rheumatism" under Muscles; Rheumatism, Toxaemia, Urates, Urea, Uremia, Urine, Wastes).

URINE—Urinary Organs—Urinary System—Urinary Diseases—Are under the rule of the watery sign ♏. As a liquid, the ☽ rules the Urine. The Elimination of Urine thru the Ureters, Bladder and Urethra is under the rule of ♏. The Secretion of the Urine is under rule of ♎. (See Kidneys). Urine is an Excrementitious Fluid under the rule of ♏. The external Urinary Organs are under the external rule of ♎. Note the following subjects here, and in the alphabetical arrangement—

Absence of Urine — Anuria — (See "Suppression" in this section).

Acid Urine—(See Acidity).

Albuminuria; Alkaline Urine — (See Acidity, Alkalinity).

Anuria — (See "Suppression" in this section).

Bed-Wetting—(See "Incontinence" in this section).

Bladder—Bladder Troubles and the Urine—(See Bladder).

Blood In Urine—Haematuria—Occurs from Ulcerated and other conditions in Kidneys, Bladder or Urethra, or from passage of Gravel, etc. — (See Bladder, Gravel, Kidneys, Stone, Urethra, etc.).

Bright's Disease—(See this subject; "Nephritis" under Kidneys).

Calculi—Urinary Calculi—♄ ♂ or ill-asp. ♀. (See Calculus).

Cloudy Urine — (See "Milky" in this section).

Copious—Excessive Quantity—Polyuria—(See Diabetes).

Diabetes; Difficult Urination—(See "Painful" in this section).

Diseases—Of the Urinary Organs—Disorders of—(See "Disturbances" in this section).

Distillation—Of Urine—Disturbances of—Afflictions in ♎; ♄ affl. in ♎. (See Distillation).

Disturbances—Urinary Disturbances and Complaints—Urinary Troubles—The ☉ or ☽ affl. in ♏; ☉ ♏, and affl. by ♃; ☉ or ☽ ♏, ♂ or ill-asp. ♄, ♅, ♆ or ♂ as Promittors (Hor'y); ☉ affl. in ♓; ☽ affl. in ♏, or affl. the hyleg therefrom; ☽ hyleg in ♎ or ♏, with females; ☽ □ ☿; ♄ or ♋ in ♎ or ♏; ♄ ♂ or ill-asp. the ☉ in fixed signs; ♄ ♎ in the Asc.; ♃ affl. in ♏; ♃ ♏ in the 6th H., and affl.; ♃ ♏ and affl. the ☽ or Asc.; ♂ ♏; ♋, ♏ or ♓ on the Asc.; fixed signs show; a fixed sign on cusp the 6th H. (See the various paragraphs in this section).

Diuresis—Excessive Secretion of Urine—(See Diabetes; "Polyuria" in this section).

Diuretics—Medicines Increasing the Flow of Urine—(See Diuretics).

Drops—Passes Urine In Drops—(See "Strangury" in this section).

Dropsy—Renal Dropsy—(See "Dropsy" under Kidneys).

Dysuria—(See "Strangury" in this section).

Elimination—Of Urine—Retarded and Disturbed—Faulty Elimination—Suppression—The ☽ □ ☿, as ☿ rules the sensory nerves, and ♂ the motor nerves; the ☽ in ♎, □, or ♋ ☿; ♄ affl. in ♎ or ♏; ♃ in ♎, ♂ □, or ♋ ♄; ♂ in ♏ and affl. by ♄; ♋ in ♏. The elimination of urine thru the bladder and urethra is ruled by the ♏ sign. (See Elimination; "Over-worked" under Kidneys).

Enuresis—(See "Incontinence" in this section).

Excess of Urine—♃ affl. in ♎. (See Diabetes; "Polyuria" in this section).

Excretion Suppressed—(See Excretion, Expulsion; "Suppressed" in this section).

False Retention—Of Urine—False Suppression—False Ischuria—Spurious Ischuria — A ♎ disease and affliction; ♄ affl. in ♎.

Filtration of Urine—Sublimation of—Ruled by ♎ and ♀. Imperfect Filtration tends to result when ☿ is in ♑, ♂ or ill-asp. any of the malefics as Promittors.

Frequent Urination—(See Acid, Hot, Painful, and other subjects in this section).

Genito-Urinary Diseases—☽ affl. in ♏. (See Genito-Urinary).

Glycosuria—Sugar In Urine—Usually is found in Diabetes—(See Diabetes).

Haematuria—(See "Blood" in this section).

Highly Acid Urine—♂ ♎, and affl. by ♄ in ♋ or ♑. Occurs in cases of Scanty Urine, and in Rheumatism, Gout, Lithemia, Fevers, etc.

Highly Colored—☿ affl. in ♎. (See "Acid", "Scanty", in this section. Also occurs in Gout, Rheumatism, etc.).

Highly Loaded—♄ ♂ or ill-asp. ♀.

Hot Urine—(See "Scalding" in this section).

Impeded Passage—Impeded Excretion —(See "Stone" under Bladder; Gravel; "Suppressed" in this section).

Imperfect Filtration—(See "Filtration" in this section).

Incontinence—Involuntary Discharges of—Enuresis—Bed-Wetting—♂ in ♏; a ♀ disease, and caused by afflictions to ♀.

Insufficient Urine—(See "Scanty" in this section).

Involuntary Discharges of—(See "Incontinence" in this section).

Ischuria—Retention or Suppression of Urine—(See "False", "Retention", "Suppression", in this section).

Kidneys—The Kidneys and the Urine —(See Kidneys).

Micturition—The Act of Passing Urine —Disturbances of—(See False, Impeded, Obstructions, Painful, Retention, Strangury, in this section).

Milky Urine—Cloudy—Chyluria—Usually caused by pus in the urine, and may be due to Gonorrhoea, Chyle, Cystitis, Pyelitis, Abscesses or Ulcerations in the Kidneys, Bladder, or Urethra. (See these subjects; "Pus" in this section).

Mucus In—♄ affl. in ♎; ♃ in ♏, and affl. by ♂; ♃ in ♏ in the 6th H., and afflicted. (See Mucous).

Nervous Affections—Of the Urinary Organs—☿ affl. in ♉ or ♏.

Obstructions—To the Urine—A ♏ disease, and afflictions in ♏; ☉ or ☽ ♏, ♂ ♄ or ♋; ♄ affl. in ♎ or ♏; ☿ ♎, ♂ or ill-asp. any of the malefics as Promittors, urinal obstructions. (See "Painful", "Retention", "Stricture", "Suppression", in this section; "Stone" under Bladder; Gravel).

Painful Urination—Strangury—Dysuria—Difficult Urination, etc.—(See "Strangury" in this section).

Passage Impeded—(See "Obstructions" in this section).

Polyuria—Excessive Secretion of Urine—Caused by afflictions in ♎; ♂ ♂ or ill-asp. ♀; ♃ or ♀ affl. in ♎. (See Diabetes).

Prevalent—Urinary Diseases Prevalent—♄ or ♂ in ♎ at the Vernal Equi., and lords of the year; Comets appearing in ♏.

Pus In Urine—Pyuria—Milky Urine—Especially denoted by ♀ affl. in ♎. Other planets may cause pus in the urine, as from urethritis, ulcerated kidneys or urethra, cystitis of the bladder, etc. (See "Milky" in this section).

Retarded Elimination — (See "Elimination" in this section).

Retention of Urine—Ischuria—Retention is a ♏ disease, while Suppression is a ♎ disorder. Caused by ♄ or ☿ affl. in ♏; ♄ ♏ in the 6th H.; ♏ on cusp 6th H. (See "False", "Suppression", in this section).

Sand—Urinary Sand—Sand In the Kidneys—(See Sand).

Scalding Urine — Hot Urine — Sharpness of Urine—The ☉ affl. in ♏ when the afflictor in the disease; ♂ affl. in ♉ or ♏; ♂ in ♎ or ♏, and affl. by ♄; ♄ ♎, scanty and scalding.

Scanty Urine—Scarcity of—Anuria— ♄ ♎; ☽ ♎, ♂ ♄; ☽ ♎ □ or ♉ ♅, ♃ and ☿.

Secretion Stopped — (See "Suppression" in this section).

Sediment In—Brick Dust Sediment— Deposits In—♂ affl. in ♎.

Sharpness — Of Urine — (See "Scalding" in this section).

Spurious Ischuria — (See "False" in this section).

Stoppage—Of Urine—(See "Suppression" in this section).

Strangury—Dysuria—Painful Urination In Drops—Painful Micturition— The ☉ in ♒ or ♓, ♂, or ill-asp. ♅, ♅, ♄, or ♂ as Promittors; the ☉ affl. in ♒; the ☽ in ♉ and affl. by the ☉ or ♂ when taken ill (Hor'y); the ☽ to the place of the Bull's Horns; ♃ affl. in ♏; a ♂ disease; ♂ affl. in ♉, ♉, or ♏; ♂ in ♉, ♂ or ill-asp. the ☉; ♏ on the Asc., and the ☽ in ♒ (Hor'y).

Sublimation—Of Urine—(See "Filtration" in this section).

Sugar In Urine — Glycosuria — ♃ affl. in ♎. (See Diabetes, Glycogen, Sugar).

Suppression—Of Urine—Anuria— Stoppage of—Ischuria—Faulty Secretion of—Suppression is a ♎ disease, while Retention is a ♏ disease. A ♎ affliction; the ☽ in ♎ ♂ ♄; ♄ affl. in ♎; Subs at KP. (See Elimination, False, Scanty, in this section).

Urates—(See Urates).

Uric Acid—Too Much In Urine—♄, ♅, or ♅ in ♏, and affl. the ☉ or ☽. (See Uric Acid).

Urinary Calculi — (See "Calculi" in this section; Stone).

Urinary Diseases — (See "Disturbances", and the various subjects in this Article).

Urinary Organs — Ruled by ♎ and ♏. (See the Introduction to this Article; Bladder, Kidneys, Ureters, Urethra).

Urination—Micturition—Disturbances of—(See "Micturition", "Strangury", in this section).

Xanthine—Excess of In Urine—(See Xanthin).

URN OF AQUARIUS — (See "One Eye" under Blindness).

URSA MINOR—(See Cynosura).

URTICARIA—Nettle Rash—Hives—An Ephemeral Skin Eruption with Itching—A Vesicular Cutaneous Eruption —A ♑ disease; ♑ on the Asc.; the ☽ hyleg, and afflicted in female nativities; ♂ affl. in ♑; Subs at KP (11D). (See Hives, Itch, Skin).

UTERUS—Disorders of—(See Womb).

UTOPIANISM — Impractical Ideals and Schemes—Caused by ♅ and his afflictions. The methods of attainment are more humanitarian when ♄ and ♂ are weak and obscurely placed at B., but if the malefics ♄ and ♂ are strong, and enter into the configuration, the native may become more radical, revolutionary, or violent in his methods to carry out his ideals. (See "Impractical" under Ideals; Radicalism, Reformers, Revolutionary, etc.).

UTTERANCE — (See Larynx, Speech, Tongue, Voice).

UVULA — Ruled by the ♉ sign, and is also much affected by the ☽ in ♉.

Inflammation Of—Uvulitis—The ☽ or ♂ affl. in ♉.

Long Uvula — (See "Snoring" under Breathing).

V

VACCINATION — (See "Immunity", "Treatment", under Smallpox).

VACILLATING — Unsteady—Wavering —Common Sign influence, and with these signs on the angles at B.; many planets in common signs, setting in the West, and out of dignity. (See Changes; "Mind" under Chaotic; Confusion; Influenced, Instability, Irresponsible, Location; "Light In Mind" under Mind; "Mutable Signs" under Mutable; "Negative Nature" under Negative; Receptive, Removals; "Many Changes" under Residence; Restlessness, Roamer, Susceptibility, Unstable, Wanderer, etc.).

VAGABOND—(See Degenerate; "No Home" under Home; Roamer, Wanderer).

VAGARIES—Peculiar Ideas—

Full Of—Wild Fancies—♅ in any asp. to the ☉, ☽, or ☿; ♅ affl. in ♊; ♅ affl. by ♀; the 28° ♊ on the Asc. (See "Wild" under Fancies).

Peculiar Vagaries—Strange Vagaries —♀ in bad asp. to ♅. (See Chaotic;

"Dreamy" under Dreams; Extravagance, Fancies, Fears, Hallucinations, Ideals, Ideas, Imaginations, Notions, Peculiar, Uncanny, Vague, Visionary, Weird).

VAGINA—Ruled by the ♏ Sign.

Diseases Of — Afflictions in ♏; ♀ affl. in ♏; ♀ in ♏ in the 6th H., and afflicted; ♀ in ♏ and affl. the Asc. (See Gonorrhoea, Leucorrhoea).

Fluids Of — Secretions of — Fluids Passing Thru—(See Leucorrhoea, Menses).

Hymen—Imperforate Hymen—♄ in ♏, and to thickening of the hymen.

Inflammation Of — Vaginitis—Ulceration of—♅ affl. in ♏.

Leucorrhoea—(See this subject).

Tunica Vaginalis — (See Serous, Testes).

Ulceration Of—♂ affl. in ♏.

Vulva—(See Vulva).

Whites—(See Leucorrhoea). See Clitoris, Hermaphrodites, Urethra).

VAGUE—Indistinct—

Vague Forebodings — (See Forebodings).

Vague Mental States — ♆ ♓. Caused also by the □ and ☌ aspects of ♆ to ☿, ☽ or Asc. (See "Mental Chaos" under Chaotic).

Vague and Obscure Diseases — (See "Diseases" under Obscure).

VAGUS NERVE—(See Pneumogastric).

VAIN—Vain Fears—Vain Imaginations —(See "Vain" under Fears, Imagination; Self-Approbation).

VALLEY — Should Live In a Valley — (See Altitude).

VALVES — ♄ tends to adversely affect the valves of the body, and when in, or afflicting the signs ruling the different valves. ♅ tends to cause spasmodic disturbances of the valves, and of the organs containing the valves. The valves of the heart are ruled by the ♌ sign. The Ileo-Caecal Valve is ruled by ♍, and ♄ in ♍ tends to obstruction of this valve.

Heart—Valves of—(See "Valves" under Heart).

Ileo-Caecal Valve — (See Caecum, Ileum).

VAPID—(See Dull, Listless).

VAPOR — Vapors — The Gaseous Form of a Substance—Aeriform—Airy—(See Air, Atmosphere, Gas, Miasma, Odors, Rain).

Damp Vapors — (See "Damp Vapors" under Moisture).

Foul Vapors — Danger of Sickness From—♄ and ♂ in watery signs, and afflicting the ☉ and ☽. (See Foul, Moisture).

Vaporization—Volatilization—Recondensation — (See "Operations" under Nature; Nitrogen, Sublimation, Volatilization).

VAPORS—Ennui—(See Ennui).

VARIABLE—

Variable Diseases — Caused by ☿, as ☿ is a variable planet. (See "Irregular Diseases" under Mercury; Various).

Variable Planets—The ☉, ☽, ☿. They tend to take on the nature of the planets with which they are in ☌, aspected, or configurated.

VARICELLA—(See Chicken Pox).

VARICOCELE—Dilatation of the Scrotal Veins—♄ affl. in ♍. (See Scrotum, Varicose).

VARICOSE VEINS—Varicosities — Enlarged Veins—Dilated Veins—Swollen and Knotted Veins—

Aneurysm—Varicose Aneurysm—(See Aneurysm).

Arms — Varicosities in the Arms, Hands, Legs, and Feet—The ☽ affl. in signs which rule these parts.

Legs—Varicose Veins In—An ♒ disease, and afflictions in ♒; the ☉, ☽, ♄, ♂, ♀, or ☿ affl. in ♒; the ☽ and ♀ affl. in ♒, and espec. if the ♂ influence is added; ♂ affl. in ♒ in the 6th H.; ♂ in ♒, and affl. the ☽ or Asc.; ♀ and ☿ in ♒, and affl. by the ☽ and ♂; ☿ in ♓, ♂, or ill-asp. any of the malefics as promittors (Hor'y); planets afflicted in ♒ in the 11th H.; a fixed sign affliction;

a fixed sign on the cusp the 6th H.; Subs at PP (2L). Cases—See Fig. 11D in the book, "Astro-Diagnosis", and Fig. 7 in "Message of the Stars", by the Heindels. Also see the Case in Chap. 13 in Daath's Medical Astrology. (See Hemorrhoids, Varicocele, Veins).

VARIETY—Of Diseases—Causes Every Variety and Species of Disease—(See "Disease" under Species).

VARIOLA — Varioloid Diseases — (See Smallpox).

VARIOUS—Varied—

Consumption — Various Forms of — (See "Various" under Consumption).

Course of Disease—A Various Course In Disease, and Not Uniform—Diseases caused by ☿, and where ☿ is the principal afflictor in the disease. (See Complications, Course, Crises, Erratic, Intermittent, Irregular, Peculiar, Relapses, Spasmodic, Symptoms, Variable).

Functions—The Various Functions— (See "Harmony" under Functions).

Injuries — Various Injuries—(See "Various" under Injuries).

VASCULAR—Pertaining To Vessels—

Vascular Excitement — Of the Nerve Centers—(See Centers, Erethism).

Vascular Fullness—Vascular Congestion—♃ diseases. (See Arteries; "Pressure", "Too Much Blood", under Blood; Dilatations, Distentions, Engorgement, Fullness, Gluttony; "Epistaxis" under Nose; Plethora).

Vascular Tissues — ♀ influences the condition of the vascular tissues, and also the mucous membrane, thru such diseases as smallpox, measles, sloughings, pustular diseases, and diseases arising from blood impurities and poisoning of the system. (See Mucous Membranes, Tissues, Vaso, Vessels).

Want of Vascular Action — Characteristic of the Lymphatic Temperament. (See Lymphatic).

VASO—Vessels—

Vaso-Constrictor Nerves — The Cutaneous Capillary Vaso-Constrictor Nerves are influenced by, and under the rule of ♄ and his two signs ♑ and ♒, and also of ♃ and his two signs ♐ and ♓, and afflictions to ♄, ♃, and these signs tend to produce pathological conditions and disturbances, such as congestions, colds, etc. (See Centripetal, Congestion, Constrictions). Also the pathological action of the ♄ Group of Herbs tends to vaso-constriction.

Vaso-Dilator Action — Is under the rule of ♂, and his two signs ♈ and ♏, acting thru the central ganglia, and in an opposite manner to ♄ in his vaso-constrictor action. The Herbs of ♂ in their pathological action, also tend to vaso-dilation. The vaso-dilator action of ♂ and his signs tend to produce diseases acting from within outwards, and the vaso-constrictor action of ♄ tends to diseases operating from the surface of the body, and acting inwards, or towards the center, as by chilling the surface, etc. (See Centrifugal).

Vaso-Motor System—Ruled by the ♎ Sign. Disorders of are caused by ♅ affl. in ♎.

VEGETABLES —Vegetation— Herbs— Roots — Plants, etc. — All Vegetation points to the Zenith.

Blight—A ♄ affliction. (See Blight).

Cannot Eat Vegetables — Or Fruit — (See Fruit).

Crops—Destruction of—(See Crops).

Decay Of—Humus—Moonlight tends to decay in the Vegetable Kingdom. Also Moisture and Dampness, ruled by the ☽, tend to decay and rottenness of fruit and vegetation. Also the influence of ♄ tends to decay of vegetation, as he does in the human body, and especially when he is lord of the year at the Vernal Equinox, and afflicted. (See "Destruction" in this section).

Destruction To—Eclipses of the ☉ or ☽ in ♓. (See Blight, Drought, Famine, Fruit; "Virus" under Pestilence; Scarcity).

Exhalations—Of Vegetables—(See Carbon, Miasma; "Chemical Action" under Moon).

Fruit—Corruption of—(See Fruit).

Fungus Growths—(See "Growths" in this section).

Growths—Vegetable Growths—Fungus and Morbid Growths In the Body —Ruled by ♅, and afflictions to ♅; a ☉ disease; a ♄ disease; ♄ affl. in ♑ or ♏; afflictions in fixed signs. (See Adenoids, Fungus; "Morbid" under Growths).

Herbs—(See Herbs).

Humus — (See "Decay" in this section).

Life — Vegetable Life In the Body — The Cerebellum, ruled by the ☽ and the ♑ sign, is a type. (See Cerebellum).

Mosses—Ruled by ♅.

Plants—(See Plants, Vegetation).

Potato Blight—(See Potato).

Roots—(See Herbs, Roots).

Rottenness — Of Vegetation— (See "Seeds and Herbs" under Rotten).

Seeds—Rottenness of—Scarcity of— (See Seeds).

Sponges — Sponges, Mosses, Mushrooms, and Vegetable Fungus Growths, are ruled by ♅.

Trees—(See Fruit, Trees).

Vegetarians—An exclusive vegetable diet is said to be better for the body and health, and to increase spiritual power, and especially to eat those fruits and vegetables which grow above the ground, and which are Sun-kissed. Most Advanced Occult students are Vegetarians. The eating of Meat is said to be contrary to the real needs of the human body, as Man is not a carniverous animal. The best working animals, such as the Horse, Elephant, Camel, etc., are fed on grains and vegetation. Meat-eating animals do not work. A vegetable diet gives real strength and endurance. However, meat is said to contain the vegetable extracts, and the minerals, worked over by the animal, and made assimilable for man. (See "Meat Eating" under Meat). For further study see "Epidemics" under Cholera; Diet; "Fountains" under Dryness; Eating, Food.

VEHEMENT — Furious — Pernicious — Violent—

Vehement Diseases—(See "Vehement Maladies" in this section).

Vehement Fevers—(See "High", "Pernicious", "Violent", under Fever).

Vehement Maladies—Vehement Diseases and Pains — Violent Diseases — Caused by the ☉ and ♂, the positive, electric, and caloric-producing planets; ☉ affl. in ♏, disorders of a violent and vehement nature; taken sick in a ☉ hour; ☽ in ♐, and affl. by the ☉ or ♂ when taken ill, and usually the result of gluttony or repletion; ☽ in ♒ and affl. by the ☉ or ♂ when taken ill, and the ☽ slow in motion and decr. in light, tends to all violent, vehement and hot diseases caused by ♂; ♂ in the Asc. at an illness causes the disease to be vehement, violent and swift; the ill-asps. of ♂ to the hyleg by dir., or to the ☉, ☽, Asc., or M.C.; Comets appearing in ♉; ♌ on the Asc.; the ☌ of several superior planets in airy signs. (See Acute, Fierce, Inflammatory, Painful, Pernicious, Quick, Rapid, Sharp, Severe, Short Diseases, Sudden, Swift, Violent).

Vehement Pains — Violent Pains — Caused by ♂. (See "Pains" under Sharp).

Vehement Passion — And Diseases Arising From—☽ ♒ and affl. by ♄ or ♂ when taken ill, and the ☽ slow in motion, decr. in light (Hor'y). (See "Violence" under Passion).

Vehement Signs—Violent Signs of the Zodiac—♈, ♏ and ♑, being the signs of the exaltation of the malefics.

Vehement Thirst—(See Thirst).

VEHICLES—Conveyances—

Accidents—For the various causes of accidents or injuries by vehicles and conveyances, see the different subjects in this Article. Malefics in the 3rd house tend to accidents by vehicles, or on railroads on short journeys. Malefics in the 9th house tend to accidents on long journeys, and on voyages.

Aeroplanes — Injury or Death By — (See Aeroplanes).

Automobiles — Death or Injury By — ♅ or ♂ in the 3rd H., and afflicting the ☉, ☽, Asc., or hyleg, and especially if ♅ is here, as this planet has to do with gas, gasoline, and explosives. However, any malefic in this house may cause accidents in vehicles of any kind, as carriages, in automobiles, or on railroads. (See Railroads. Also see Fig. 21 in "Message of the Stars", by the Heindels).

Boarding a Car—Killed While Trying to Board a Street Car—♂ ruler 3rd H., and with ♄ in 3rd H. Case—See "Dey", Birth Data, No. 893, in 1001 Notable Nativities.

Danger By—(See "Falls" in this section).

Death By—(See the various parts of this Article; "Death" under Railroads).

Falls From — Danger By — ☽ to the place of Cor Scorpio by dir. (See Antares).

Injuries By — (See the various parts of this Article).

Journeys—Injuries or Death On—(See Journeys).

Man's Finer Vehicles — (See Desire Body, Vital Body).

Misfortune By — ☽ to the place of Deneb. (See "Lion's Tail" under Lion; Misfortune).

Motorcycle — Death By — Case — See "Foretold His Own Death", Birth Data, No. 979, in 1001 N.N.).

Railroads—Death or Injury On—(See Railroads; "Boarding a Car", "Run Over", in this section).

Ships — (See Ships, Shipwreck, Voyages).

Short Journeys—Death or Injury On —(See this subject under Journeys).

Street Railways—Street Cars—Street Accident—Cases— (1) Run Over—See "A Luckless Youth", Birth Data, No. 393. (2) "Run Over", Birth Data, No. 853. (3) "Lockjaw", Birth Data No. 913. (4) "Strafford", Birth Data No. 814. (5) "Died In Harness", Birth Data No. 801, all five cases in 1001 N.N. (See "Automobiles", "Boarding a Car", "Motorcycle", "Truck", in this section).

Traffic—(See "Street" in this section).

Train — Killed by Falling Under a Train — (See Case, "Strafford", Birth Data, No. 814, in 1001 N.N.).

Travel — Killed or Injured In — (See Travel).

Truck—Killed by a Truck Falling On Him — See Case, "Died in Harness", Birth Data, No. 801, in 1001 N.N.

Water — Killed or Injured On Water Vehicles—(See Ships, Shipwreck, Voyages).

VEINS — The Veins — The Venous System—The Venous Blood—The Venous Circulation—Ruled by ♀, the ♎ Sign, and the 7th H. Dr. Broughton says ♃ rules the Veins. Ptolemy says ♂ rules them. All three of these planets have their part to play in the activity and functioning of the Veins. The Airy Signs are also connected with the veins, and especially the ♒ Sign. However, ♀ bears strong rule over the veins in any part of the body. Thus ♀ in ♉ rules the veins of the throat. ♀ in ♍ rules the veins of the bowels, etc. In some instances, as will be noted in this article, ♃ rules both the arteries and veins of the part, and assumes a co-rulership along with ♀. It is to be noted that ♃ rules the blood, as a whole. Mars rules over blood-making, and fibrous tissue building, and thus has his part in building up the tissues of the veins, and giving strength and quality to the blood which flows thru them. Note the following Diseases and Afflictions of the Veins, the Venous System, the Venous Circulation, and the rulership of the more important Veins.

All Diseases In Veins — All diseases lying in the veins are classed as diseases of ♃ and ♀, the two planets which rule the circulation of the blood.

Blood Letting—(See Bleeding).

Bowels — ♀ in ♍ rules the veins of the bowels.

Contracted—♄ and cold tend to contract the veins and capillaries of the surface, driving the blood inward, and causing internal congestions, colds, etc, while the heat of ♂ tends to relax the veins and blood vessels, and drive the blood outward from the center to the surface. (See Centrifugal, Centripetal).

Dilated Veins—(See Varicose).

Diseases of the Veins — ♀ diseases; afflictions in ♎; caused by afflictions in ♒. (See the various subjects in this section).

Ears—Obstruction of the Venous Circulation In—(See "Venous Circulation" under Ears).

Enlarged Veins—Swollen—Knotted— (See "Varicocele" under Scrotum; Varicose).

Fullness Of—(See Plethora).

Gastric Vein—Ruled by ♋. (See Gastric).

Genito-Urinary System—♃ rules the veins and arteries of. (See Genito-Urinary).

Head — Ill-blood In Veins of — (See "Blood" under Head).

Heart—♀ in ♌ rules the veins of the heart.

Iliac Veins—And Arteries, ruled by ♐.

Inflammation of Vein — Phlebitis—♂ ♂ or ill-asp. ♀.

Jugular Veins—Ruled by ♉.

Knotted Veins—(See Varicocele, Varicose).

Legs — Venus rules the veins of the legs. For Obstruction of the Veins of the Leg, see "Milk Leg" under Legs.

Lungs—Veins of are ruled by ♀, and ♀ in ♊. (See "Obstruction", "Respiratory", in this section).

Milk Leg—Obstruction of the Venous Circulation In Leg — (See "Milk Leg" under Legs).

Neck—(See "Veins" under Neck).

Obstruction—Of the Venous Circulation—♄ ♂ ♀ in any sign, and especially in the parts ruled by the sign containing this ♂; ♄ ♂ ♀ in ♊, obstruction in lungs; ♄ ♂, P., □, ☍ ♀; ♄ or ♅ ♂ ♀. (See Ears, Legs, Poor Circulation, in this section).

Phlebitis—(See "Inflammation" in this section).

Plexus — A Network of Veins — (See Plexus).

Poor Circulation—Poor Circulation of the Venous Blood—☉ ♂ ♄ or ☋, and □ or ☍ ♀; ☽ □ or ☍ ♀; ♅ ♂, □, ☍ ♀, spasmodic disturbance of the Venous Circulation; ♄ ♂, □, ☍ ♀. (See "Obstruction" in this section).

Portal Vein—Ruled by ♍.

Relaxation — Of the Veins — ♂ influence, and by the heat of ♂. (See "Contracted" in this section).

Respiratory System — ♃ and ♀ in ♉, □ or ♋ rule and affect the veins of the Respiratory System. (See Breathing).

Scrotal Veins—Enlarged and Dilated Veins of Scrotum—(See Varicocele).

Spasmodic Disturbance — Of the Venous Circulation—♅ ♂, □, ☍ ♀.

Stomach — ♀ in ♋ rules the veins of stomach.

Swollen Veins—(See Varicocele, Varicose).

Throat—♃ and ♀ in ♉ rule and affect the veins of the throat and neck.

Varicocele—(See this subject).

Varicose Veins—(See Varicose).

Vena Cava — The Superior and Inferior Vena Cava Veins are ruled by ♌.

Windiness In Veins—□ signifies; a □ disease. (See Wind). For collateral study see Arteries, Blood, Capillaries, Circulation, Vascular, Venus; "Blood Vessels" under Vessels).

VENERATION—Awe—Dreads—Reverence—Adoration—(See Dreads, Fears; "Devotion", "Pious", "Superstitious", under Religion).

VENEREAL DISEASES—Venery—Diseases from Sexual Intercourse — Venereal Distemper — Suspicion of Some Venereal Distemper — The ☉ in ♎, ♏, or ♓, ☌ or ill-asp. any of the malefics as promittors; ☽ to the □ or ☍ ♀ by dir.; ☽ to Bull's Horns; ☽ to ☌ or ill-asp. ♂ by dir.; ☽ ♏ ☌ or ill-asp. any of the malefics as promittors; ☽ affl. in ♏; ♇ affl. in ♏; caused by ♇; ♅ affl. by ♂, and especially from ♉ or ♏; ♅ ♏, ☌, □, or ☍ ♀; ♅ ♏, □ or ☍ ♂ and the ☽; ♄ ♏, □ or ☍ ♂; ♃ affl. in ♏; ♂ ♏ when ♂ is the afflictor in the disease; ♂ ☌ ♀, and especially when in ♏; ♂ ☌ ♀ and also afflicted by the ☽; ♂ in ♏, ☌, or ill-asp. the ☉, ☽, or ♀; ♂ in ♏ in the 6th H.; ♂ in ♏ and affl. the ☽ or Asc.; ♀ affl. in ♏; ♀ ill-dig. at B., and ☌ ♂; ♀ affl. by ♂; ♀ in ♏ in the 6th H., and afflicted; ♀ in ♏, and affl. the ☽ or Asc.; ♀ affl. by evil aspects tends to venereal diseases in males; ♀ affl. in the 6th H.; ♀ in the Asc., and affl. by ♇, ♅, or ♂; ♀ affl. in ♏; a ♏ disease, and caused by afflictions in ♏; ♏ on the Asc.; the Asc. to the □ or ☍ ♀ by dir.; malefics in ♏; malefics in the 4th or 5th H., and affl. ♀; many afflictions in watery signs; ♌ on the Asc., and affl. by malefics in ♏. Leprosy may follow severe and malignant venereal diseases. (See Amorous, Bubo, Generation, Genitals, Genito-Urinary, Gonorrhoea, Leprosy; "Ulcers" under Nose; "Passional Excesses" under Passion; Penis, Private, Scandalous; "Distempers" under Secrets; "Diseases" under Sex; Testes, Vagina, Vulva, etc.).

Cases—Of Venereal Disease—See Figures 8F, and 8G, in the book, "Astro-Diagnosis", by the Heindels.

Excess of Venery — (See Amorous; "Women" under Men; "Health Suffers" under Opposite Sex; "Passional Excesses" under Passion).

Horny Venereal Growths — ♄ affl. in ♏. Case—See Fig. 36, in "Message of the Stars", by the Heindels. (See Horny).

Nose—Venereal Ulcers In—(See "Ulcers" under Nose).

Ulcers — Venereal Ulcers — In Nose, Throat, or Genitals—♂ ♏.

VENERY—Sex Indiscretions—(See Venereal).

VENOMOUS—Poisonous—Noxious—Venomous Creatures—Poisonous Animals and Insects—Reptiles—Scorpions—Serpents—Snakes, etc.—

Afflictions — By Storms of Venomous Creatures—♏ ascending at the Vernal Equi. tends to Floods, and afflictions by storms of venomous creatures. (See Floods).

Bites By—Fomahaut with the ☉ or ♂ tends to bites by venomous animals and creatures. (See Adder, Bites, "Bites" under Kings; Obnoxious, Reptiles, Serpents, Stings; "Danger" under Travel).

Fevers — Venomous Fevers — (See "High Fever" under Fever; Pernicious, Vehement).

Stings — Venomous Stings — (See Stings).

Swarms — Afflicted by Swarms of Venomous Creatures—(See "Afflictions" in this section).

Travel—Bites or Stings During—(See "Journeys" under Bites; Reptiles; "Danger" under Travel).

VENOUS BLOOD — Venous Circulation—Venous System—(See Veins).

VENTRAL HERNIA—(See Hernia).

VENTRICLES—

Cerebral Ventricles—Ruled by ♇. (See Cerebral).

Heart — (See "Ventricles" under Heart).

VENTS — Channels and Vents — (See "Channels" under Genitals).

VENUS—The Planet Venus—A Benefic and Fortunate planet, and called "The Lesser Fortune." This planet is feminine, fruitful, passive, negative, benign. benefic in her higher vibrations, nocturnal, and rules the signs ♉ and ♎. (See "Qualities" in this section). Much has been said about this beautiful planet in the Textbooks of Astrology, and in order to make the information I have gathered more convenient for reference, this Article will be made into three Sections, as follows: Section One, The Influences of Venus; Section Two, Venus Rules; Section Three, Diseases Ruled by Venus).

— SECTION ONE —

THE INFLUENCES OF VENUS—

Action Of — The action of ♀ is not rapid and tends to such results as proceed from Intemperance. (See Intemperance). The action of ♀ is also of a rotational or vortex motion.

Angel—Anael is the Angel of Venus.

Aspects Of—Her good aspects to the planets tend to greatly benefit the health, and also to enrich and ennoble the mind, to give a love of the beautiful, of harmony, and also to bring good fortune. The ☌ of ♀ with ♃ at B. tends to make the native very fortunate in life. Her ☌ with ♄, however. tends to vitiate her good influences in health matters. Venus afflicts only by her □ and ☍ aspects.

Atonic Action Of — (See "Asthenic Plethora" under Plethora).

Author Of—♀ is the author of mirth and cheerfulness.

Benefic — ♀ is classed as a Benefic, and is known as the "Lesser Fortune".

Body — ♀, and with ♀ in ♉, gives beauty of form and body, and as one Author says, "A Venus de Milo Figure." (See Beautiful, Handsome).

Coalition — This is the Salient Characteristic of ♀. (See Coalition).

Colors — Rules Blue, Sky Blue to Green; Yellow in the Solar Spectrum; Indigo; Purple and White. (See Colors).

Denotes — (See the Introduction to Sec. 3 of this Article).

Detriment — The home and strong signs of ♀ are ♉ and ♎. She has her exaltation in ♓; her fall in ♍, and her detriment in ♈ and ♏, signs opposite to her home signs. In judging of her power or weakness in connection with disease, it is well to bear these distinctions in mind.

Directions—The evil Directions of ♀ during the ♀ period of life are more critical, as from 10 to 18 years of age, according to Daath, or from the age of 14 to 28, according to others. (See "Life" in Sec. 2 of this Article).

Drugs Of — (See Herbs, Physiological Action, Typical Drugs, in this section).

Evil Aspects—(See "Aspects" in this section).

Evils—Her evils are shown mostly in General Debility, and general Relaxation of the System. (See Debility, Relaxation).

Exaltation—Her Sign of—(See "Detriment" in this section).

External Influences — Being a negative and magnetic planet, ♀ influence tends to render the mind more negative, timid and susceptible to external influences, and a variety of affections. (See External).

Fall Of—(See "Detriment" in this section).

Foetus—Sex distinction in the Foetus is effected by ♀. (See Foetus).

Form of Body — (See "Body" in this section).

Friendly To—♀ is friendly to ♂, as ♂ rules strongly over the passions, and helps ♀ in forming alliances between the sexes, and to perpetuate the Race. The good aspects of ♂ to ♀ tend to a higher and truer form of love, while the ☌, □ and ☍ aspects of ♂ to ♀ tend to the lower forms of love, and to passional excesses, dissipation, etc.

Ganglion—(See "Pathological" under Ganglion).

Good Aspects Of — (See "Aspects" in this section).

Hair — ♀ gives light hair, and light complexion, and makes blondes. (See "Light" under Hair).

Harmony — (See "Influences" in this section).

Herbs Of—(See "Venus Group" under Herbs; "Physiological Action" in this section).

Hour Of — The Venus Hour — (See "Hours" under Planets).

House Of — ♀ is affiliated with the 2nd and 7th Houses, the houses corresponding to ♉ and ♎, the 2nd and 7th Signs.

Identified With—♀ is especially identified with the Egg, Ovum, the Ovaries. (See Ovaries).

Influence Of—The influence of ♀ is to establish rhythm and harmony in the system, in whatever sign or house found, and to bring about Coalition. (See all the various paragraphs in this Article).

Jupiter and Venus—♀ has more to do with Love and Social affairs, with Marriage, Sex Diseases, etc., than has ♃. In matters connected with the nutrition of cells, tissue building, etc., ♃ and ♀ both take part, and also ♆. (See Jupiter; "Cell", "Functions", "Nutrition", "Storing", "Tissue", "Transformation", in Sec. 2 of this Article; "Nourishing" in this section).

Love—♀ when afflicted tends to lack of an uplifted love, to faulty desires, and to weakness of the Generative System.

Magnetic—(See "External Influences" in this section).

Mars and Venus—(See "Friendly" in this section).

Mental Qualities—Artistic, Amorous, Convivial.

Metal Ruled By — Copper. (See Copper, Therapeutics).

Moist and Warm — ♀ is moist and warm by nature. Some Authors say she is cold and moist.

Motion Of—(See "Action" in this section).

Nature Of—♀ has a nutritive and relaxing nature. (See "Evils" in this section; Nutrition, Relaxation).

Negative—(See "External Influences" in this section).

Neptune and Venus — (See "Jupiter" in this section; Cells, Neptune).

Nourishing—♃ and ♀ both have to do with the Nourishing, Conserving and Aphetic Processes, the storing of various cell substances, and with Selection, Transformation, Filtration and Reservation. (See Cells, Jupiter, Neptune, Nutrition, Tissues).

Octave — The Heindels say that ♅ is the higher octave of ♀, while others say ♀ is. The indications are that ♅ and ♀ form a pair in their workings, and ♆ and ☿ a pair.

Ovaries — Ovum—(See "Identified With" in this section).

Pathological Action — Cysts, Erotic, Laxity, Remission, Swellings. (See these subjects. Also see "Pathological" under Ganglion).

Physiological Action — The ☉, ☽, ♀ and ☿ are classed as Physiological Planets, and not necessarily pathological, as are ♄, ♃ and ♂. The general physiological actions of ♀ are fermentation, nutrition, and proliferation. In a physiological way, the Plants and Herbs of ♀ tend to affect, or modify and act upon the the Humoural Secretions, the Kidneys or Renal System, and also the Glandular System. (See "Venus Group" under Herbs; "External" under Humours).

Plants Of—Plant Remedies of—(See "Physiological" in this section).

Presides Over — ♀ presides over the Cellular Retrogressive Metamorphosis. (See Metamorphosis).

Principle Of—Desire, Love, Sex.

Professions Of — ♀ as Ruler of the Profession disposes to dealing in Cordials, Medicines, Perfumes, Spices, Wines, etc., and if ♄ give testimony, to deal in Charms, Love Potions, Philtres, and Poisons.

Qualities — For the planetary influences concerning the most of these qualities, see the following subjects in the alphabetical arrangement — Amorous; Antinephritic; Aphetic; Artistic; Beautiful; Benefic; Benevolent; Benign; Careless; Cheerful; Clandestine; Clogging; Coalition; Cold and Moist (say some Authors); Comely; Congesting; Conserving; Convivial; Debilitating; Demulcent; Discontent; Dissolute; Diuretic; Emaciating; Emetic; Emotional; Enlarging; Erotic; Excessive; Feminine; Fertile; Folly-Loving; Free-Living; Fruitful; Gluttonous; Gormandizing; Graceful; Habit-Forming; Handsome; Harmonious; Hot and Moist; Hysterical; Immoral; Indiscreet; Indulgent; Inordinate; Intemperate; Irregular; Languid; Laxity; Lethargic; Lewd; Licentious; Lustful; Lymphatic; Magnetic; Mirthful; Moist and Hot (or Warm); Musical; Negative; Nocturnal; Non-Malignant; Nourishing; Nutritious; Nurturing; Overflowing; Pacific; Passional; Passive; Pleasure-Loving; Plethoric; Poisonous; Pustular; Putrid; Redundant; Relaxing; Rotational; Rhythmical; Sedentary; Sloughing; Softening; Soothing; Storing; Susceptible; Temperate (not cold); Timid; Transforming; Warm; Warm and Moist; Wasting. (For other Qualities not mentioned here, look for the subject in the alphabetical arrangement).

Remedies Of — (See Drugs, Herbs, Metal, Physiological Action, Typical Drugs, in this section).

Renal Process — ♀ adds or subtracts to. (See the Introduction under Kidneys; Process).

Salient Characteristic — Coalition — (See Coalition).

Saturn and Venus—(See "Aspects" in this section).

Signs Of—♉ and ♎. (See Libra, Taurus).

Temperament—Lymphatic.

Tends To — Tends to Gormandizing Habits, and to Clogging of the System. (See Clogging, Gluttony).

Therapeutic Properties—Antinephritic, Demulcent, Diuretic, Emetic. (See these subjects).

Tonic Action Of—(See Plethora).

Typical Drugs Of—Copper (Cuprum), Pulsatilla. (See these subjects).

Unfriendly With — (See Antipathy, Opposites).

Uranus and Venus — ♅ is the higher octave of ♀. The lower vibrations of ♅, and the ☌ and evil asps. of ♅ to ♀, tend to Free Love, Clandestine Love Affairs, and the danger of Sex Excesses and Diseases from, and also to Sex Perversions. ♅ and ♀ working together in their higher vibrations tend to a love of the Occult, a love of Truth and the Metaphysical, and to great Knowledge, Wisdom, and Spiritual Sight. (See Uranus; "Octave" in this section).

Warm and Moist — (See "Moist" in this section).

— SECTION TWO —

VENUS RULES — For the planetary influences concerning the majority of these subjects, see the subject in the alphabetical arrangement — Abdomen; Acephalocysts; Adornments; Amulets; Antinephritics; Aphetic Process (see Nutrition); Aphrodisiacs; Appetite — The Appetite; Arts—The Arts; Aural Ducts (see Ears); Beauty (see Beautiful); Bladder Worm (see Acephalocysts); Blood—The Venous Blood (see Veins); Blue—Blue Color in the Solar Spectrum; Breasts (of Women); Budding — The Process of — (see Gemmation); Cell Reproduction (see Cells, Gemmation); Cell Substances—Storing of—(see "Substance" under Cells); Cellular Retrogressive Metamorphosis— (see "Metamorphosis" under Cells; Metamorphosis); Cellular Tissue Building — (see "Tissue" under Cells); Charms (see Amulets); Cheeks; Cheerfulness; Chin; Chylification (see Chyle); Circulation — The Venous Circulation —(see Veins); Cohabitation; Coins (Money); Colors (see Sec. 1 of this Article); Comeliness; Complexion; Conserving Process in the Body—(see Conservation); Copper; Cordials; Cosmetics; Courtship; Cuprum; Demulcents; Dimples; Diuretics; Effeminate Matters; Egg (the Egg, or Ovum); Emetics; Eustachian Tubes; Exosmosis; Face; Fecundation; Female Relatives and Female Sex; Fermentation (see Fermentation, Nutrition); Fevers — The Period of Remission in Fevers; Filtration of Cell Substances— (see "Substance" under Cells); Flesh (the Flesh); Friday; Functions—The Nutritive Functions (see Nutrition); Gemmation; Generative Organs — Internal (see Generation); Gluttony; Growth; Gormandizing; Hair (Light Hair); Handsome Body; Harmony in the System; Herbs (see "Venus Group" under Herbs); Intercourse (Social and Sexual); Internal Generative Organs and System; Jewels; Kidneys; Learning; Libra Sign; Life—Life from 10 to 18 years (Daath)—Life from 15 to 24 years, or from 14 to 28 years, say other Authors; Light Hair and Complexion; Lip (Upper Lip); Liver; Love Affairs; Love Potions (Philtres); Lower Parts of the Body; Lymphatic Temperament; Marriage; Maternity; Medicines (Cordials, Lotions, Perfumes, Wines, etc.); Metal (Copper); Metamorphosis; Milk (The Milk); Mirth; Moisture—Excessive Atmospheric Moisture; Money (Coins); Mother (The Mother); Navel; Neck; Nerves (Olfactory); Nostrils; Nourishing Process (see Nutrition); Olfactory Nerve (see Smell); Ovaries; Ovum; Palate; Papillae (Renal); Pastries; Perfumes; Phenomena of Gemmation;

Philtres; Plants (see Venus Group under Herbs); Pleasures; Poisons; Processes of Nutrition (see Nutrition); Pulsatilla; Purple Color; Reins; Relatives (Female); Relaxation of Tissues (see Relaxation); Remedies — Venus Herbs — Cuprum (Copper), and Pulsatilla — (see "Therapeutic Properties", "Typical Drugs", in Sec. 1 of this Article); Remission (Periods of in Fevers); Renal Papillae; Renal Process; Reproduction by Gemmation (see Gemmation); Reproduction of the Species (see Reproduction); Res Venerae; Reservation (see "Substance" under Cells); Rhythm in the System; Selection of Cell Substance (see "Substance" under Cells); Semen; Seminal Vesicles (see Semen); Sensuality; Sex Desires; Sexual Intercourse (see Cohabitation, Intercourse); Sisters; Skin of Face (The Complexion); Spices; Spine; Stomach (Veins of); Storing Process (see "Substance" under Cells); Sugars; Sweets; Taurus Sign; Throat; Thymus Gland; Tissue Building—Cellular (see Cells); Tissue Relaxation (see Relaxation); Toilet Articles (see Cosmetics); Transformation of Cell Substance (see "Substance" under Cells); Tubuli Seminiferi (see Semen); Umbilicus (see Navel); Upper Lip; Uterus (see Womb); Veins—Venous Blood, Venous Circulation, Venous System (see Veins); Venery; White Color; Wines; Womb; Yellow Color; Youth—Periods of — (see "Life" in this section; Periods).

— SECTION THREE —

DISEASES RULED BY VENUS—Diseases and Afflictions of Venus — The diseases of ♀, when afflicted, are those affecting the Generative System, the Genitals, Matrix, Womb, Reins, Bladder, and Breasts. Also those arising from Excesses, Intemperance, Pleasures, Venery, Sensuality, etc. Also Smallpox, Measles, Sloughings, and diseases arising from Weakness, or injury by Poison. No aspect of ♃ or ♀ alone causes disease, but only as configurated with malefics. See the following Subjects and Diseases in the alphabetical arrangement when only listed here—

Abdomen — Disorders of — Pain In — Spasm of Abdominal Muscles — (See Abdomen).

Acephalocysts; Amorous Indulgence— Excess of, and Diseases From — (See Amorous).

Arms—(See "Eruptions" under Arms).

Asthenic Plethora—(See Plethora).

Atrophy — (See Atrophy, Emaciation, Wasting).

Back—Disorders of—(See Back).

Belly—Disorders of—(See Belly).

Bilious Flatulency—(See "Flatulency" under Bile).

Blackheads—Comedo—(See "Comedo" under Sebaceous).

Bladder Diseases — Bladder Worm — (See Bladder).

Blood—Corrupt and Impure, and Diseases Arising From — (See Blood, Impure).

Bowels — Distempers In — Flux In — Mucus In—(See Bowels).

Breasts—Disorders of—(See Breasts).

Breathing—The Breathing Distressed from Tight Lacing and Indiscretions In Dress—(See Lacing).

Brief Fevers—(See Ephemeral).

Bright's Disease—(See Bright's).

Cancer—Death By—(See Carcinoma).

Carelessness — Diseases and Irregularities From—(See Carelessness).

Cells—Cellular Congestion—Cellular Metamorphosis—(See Cells).

Chest — Burning Sensation In — (See "Heartburn" under Heart).

Chilblains; Children—Worms In—(See Worms).

Circulation — Of the Venous Blood Poor — (See "Poor Circulation" under Veins).

Clogging—Of the System—(See Clogging).

Cold — Head Disordered by Cold — Knees, Legs, or Stomach Affected by Cold—Cold and Moist Humours—(See "Cold" under these subjects).

Colds—In the Head—(See "Colds" under Head).

Comedo — Blackheads— (See Sebaceous).

Complexion—Disorders of by Wrong Use of Cosmetics—(See Cosmetics).

Congestion—Cellular—(See Cells).

Consumption—Caused by ♀ when the dominion of death is vested in her. (See Consumption, Tuberculosis, Wasting).

Contagious Diseases — (See Contagious, Venereal).

Corrupt Blood—(See Impure).

Cosmetics — Skin Eruptions From — (See Cosmetics).

Cysts; Death — ♀ denotes Death by Atrophy, Cancer, Diabetes, Dysentery; Epidemic Diseases such as proceed from too much Moisture; Fistulas, Flux, Gleets, Pestilential Diseases, Poisoning, Putrefaction, Putrid Diseases, Putrid Sore Throat, Rottenness and Diseases Arising from; Scurvy, Syphilis, Tabes Dorsalis, Typhus Fever, and Wasting Away.

Debility — General Debility of the System—(See Debility).

Desires—(See "Faulty", "Perverted", under Desires).

Diabetes; Diet—Indiscretions In, and Diseases From—(See "Evil Diet" under Diet).

Diphtheria; Discharges—Involuntary Discharge of Urine — Unnatural Discharges—(See Discharges, Gonorrhoea, Humours, Semen; "Incontinence" under Urine).

Discontentment; Displacements;

Dissolute Living—(See Dissolute).

Distempers—In Bowels—Venereal— (See Bowels, Venereal).

Dress—Disorders from Improper Dress —(See Dress, Lacing; "Dress", "Ulcerated Throat", under Throat).

Drink—Drinking—Surfeits from Too Much Drinking, and Excess In Eating —(See Diet, Drink, Food, Surfeits).

Dropsy; Dysentery; Eating—Sickness from Over-Eating—(See Eating).

Effeminate; Emaciation—With a Consumption—(See Emaciation).

Emission—Of the Vital Fluids—(See Semen).

Emotions—Disorders of—(See Emotions).

Enlarged Tonsils—(See Tonsils).

Ennui; Ephemeral Fevers — (See Ephemeral).

Epidemics—From Too Much Moisture —(See Epidemics, Moisture).

Epigastrium—Disorders In—(See Epigastrium; "Heartburn" under Heart).

Erotic Disturbances; Eruptions—Skin Eruptions Due to Impure Blood, Wrong Habits of Living, Excessive Use of Cosmetics, etc.—(See Cosmetics, Habits, Impure Blood).

Excess—Of Amorous Indulgence, and Diseases From—(See Amorous).

Excesses — Passional, and Over-Eating, and Diseases From—(See Eating, Excesses, Passion; "Disease" under Pleasure; Venereal).

Exercise — Lack of — (See Exercise, Sedentary).

External Influences—Susceptible To, and Diseases Arising From—(See External).

Eyes—Humorous Discharges From— ♀ affl. in ♍. (See Eyes).

Faecal Vomiting—(See Ileac Passion).

Feet—Lameness In—Skin Eruptions and Diseases In Feet Due to Wrong Habits of Living— (See "Eruptions", "Lameness", under Feet).

Fevers—The Period of Remission In —(See Fevers).

Fibre—Laxity of—(See Fibre).

Fistula—Death By—(See Fistula).

Flatulency—Bilious—(See Bilious).

Fluids — Escape of the Vital Fluid — (See Semen, Vital Fluids).

Flux—In Bowels—Flux of Rheum— (See Bowels, Flux).

Folly — Moral Folly — (See Folly, Morals).

Free Living — And Diseases From — (See Free Living).

Gastronomical Indiscretions—(See Gastro).

General Debility—General Relaxation —(See Debility, Laxity, Relaxation).

Generation—Diseases of Members of —Impotency In—Diseases of the Generative Organs—Weakness of the Generative System — (See Generation, Genitals, Impotent, Reproduction).

Genitals — Diseases of—Any Disease of—(See Genitals).

Glandular Swellings—(See Glands).

Gleets—(See Gonorrhoea).

Gluttony; Goitre; Gonorrhoea;

Gormandizing; Gout—In Hips, Knees, Thighs—(See Gout).

Growths— Non-Malignant — (See Growths).

Habits — Bad Habits and Diseases From—Sedentary Habits—(See Habits, Sedentary).

Hands — Skin Eruptions On Due to Wrong Habits of Living—♀ affl. in ♉ or ♍. (See Hands).

Head—Affected by Cold—Colds In— Diseases In—Moist Humours In—Pains In—(See Head).

Heart — The Heart Afflicted or Ill-Affected—(See Heart).

Heartburn — (See this subject under Heart).

Hernia; Hip—Gout In—(See Gout).

Hollow Tumor—(See Cysts).

Humours — Moist Humours In Head —Cold and Moist Humours—Raw and Undigested Humours In Stomach—Humoural Discharges from Eyes — (See Humours).

Hysteria; Ileac Passion; Impotency;

Impure Blood; Incontinence — (See Urine).

Indiscretions—Diseases From—Wrong Diet and Habits — Gastronomical — Carelessness—Irregularities, etc.—(See Indiscretions).

Indulgences — Diseases from Excess of—(See Indulgence).

Inordinate Lust — Diseases From — (See Inordinate Lust).

Intemperance; Irregularities—In Food —In Habits, and Diseases From—(See Diet, Food, Habits, Indiscretions).

Involuntary Discharge — (See Emissions, Semen; "Incontinence" under Urine).

Kidneys — Diseased Kidneys — (See Kidneys).

King's Evil—(See Scrofula).

Knees—Cold In—Gout In—Pains In— Swellings In—(See Knees).

Lacing—Injury from Tight Lacing— (See Lacing).

Lameness—In Feet—(See Feet).

Languor—(See Dull, Inactive, Inertia, Lassitude, Lethargy, Listless).

Laxity—Of Fibre—Of Muscular Tissue — (See Fibre; "Laxity" under Muscles).

Legs—Cold In—Pains In—Skin Eruptions—Swellings—(See Legs).

Lethargy; Leucorrhoea; Liver — (See "Deranged" under Liver).

Loins—(See "Disorders" under Loins).

Lotions—Diseases from Wrong Use of —(See Cosmetics).

Lower Parts—Of the Body—Disorders of—(See "Lower Parts" under Lower).

Lues—(See Syphilis).

Lust — Any Disease Arising From — (See Lust).

Malacia; Matrix — Diseases of — (See Womb).

Measles; Mechanical Displacements— (See Displacements).

Members—Of Generation—Disorders of—(See "Generation" in this section).

Metamorphosis; Minor Disorders — (See Mild, Minor, Slight).

Moist— Moist and Cold Humours — Moist Humours In the Head — Moist and Warm Diseases—(See Head, Moisture).

Moisture—Diseases Arising from the Corruption of Moisture—Diseases Arising from Lack of Moisture—Diseases Arising from Superabundance of Moisture — (See "Corruption", "Lack of", "Superabundance", under Moisture).

Moral Folly—(See "Folly" under Morals).

Mucous Membranes — (See this subject under Mucous).

Mucus In Bowels—(See "Bowels" under Mucous).

Muscles—Spasm of Abdominal Muscles—Laxity of Muscular Tissue—(See Ileac Passion; "Laxity" under Muscles).

Navel—Disorders of—(See Navel).

Neck—Disörders of—Swellings In—(See Neck).

Night Losses — (See Emissions, Semen).

Non-Malignant Growths — (See Growths).

Nutrition—Disorders of—(See Nutrition).

Obesity; Ovaries—Disorders of—(See Ovaries).

Over-Eating — Sickness From — Surfeits From — (See Eating, Food, Surfeits).

Pain—In the Head, Knees, Legs, Private Parts, Secret Parts—(See "Pain" under these subjects. Also see these subjects, and the references, under Pain).

Passion—Passional Excesses—Erotic Disturbances — (See Erotic, Passion, Sex).

Pathological Action — Of ♀. (See "Pathological" in Sec. 1 of this Article).

Perversions — Sex Perversions— (See Perversions).

Plant Remedies of ♀—(See "Physiological Action" in Sec. 1 of this Article).

Pleasures — Excessive, and Diseases Arising From — (See "Disease" under Pleasure).

Plethora—Asthenic—(See Plethora).

Poisoning—Poison Death—(See "Blood Poisoning", "Body", "Death by Poison", under Poison).

Priapism—(See Erections).

Private Parts—Diseases In—Pains In — (See Generation, Genitals, Private Parts, Reproduction, Secrets).

Poor Circulation—Of the Venous Blood (See "Poor" under Veins).

Process—(See "Renal Process" in Sec. 1 of this Article).

Pustular Diseases—(See Pus).

Putrid Diseases — Putrefaction — (See "Death" under Putrid; "Putrid" under Throat).

Raw Humours — In Stomach — (See "Raw" under Indigestion).

Reins — The Reins Afflicted — Disordered — Running of the Reins — (See Gonorrhoea, Reins).

Relaxation—Laxity of the Tissues— Relaxed Throat—(See Relaxation).

Remedies—Plant Remedies of ♀. (See "Plant" in Sec. 1 of this Article).

Remission—♀ rules the period of Remission in Fevers.

Renal Disorders — Renal Process — (See Kidneys; "Renal Process" in Sec. 1 of this Article).

Respiration Bad—(See "Breathing" in this Section).

Rheum—Flux of—(See "Rheum" under Flux; Rheum).

Ringworm; Rottenness — Diseases Arising From—(See Rotten).

Running of Reins—(See Gonorrhoea, Reins).

Rupture—Hernia—Inguinal Hernia— (See Hernia, Rupture).

Scandalous Diseases — (See Scandalous).

Scrofula; Scurvy; Secret Parts—Diseases In—Pains In—(See Secrets).

Sedentary Habits—(See Sedentary).

Seminal Losses—(See Semen).

Sensuality—Diseases Arising From— (See Sensuality).

Sex Passion — Passional Excesses — Erotic Disturbances—(See Erotic, Love Affairs, Passion, Sex).

Signs—Diseases of ♀ in Signs—You will find classified lists of the diseases of ♀ in the Signs in the various Textbooks and Dictionaries of Astrology. Venus in any sign tends to disorders of the veins and circulation in the part ruled by such sign, and this is a good rule to follow.

Skin — Eruptions from Cosmetics — Eruptions On the Arms, Hands, Legs and Feet from Wrong Habits of Living — (See "Eruptions" under these subjects; Cosmetics; "Bad Habits" under Habits; Skin).

Sloughings; Smallpox; Softening—Of the Tissues—(See Malacia).

Sore Throat — (See "Putrid" under Throat).

Sores—Sloughing Sores—(See Sloughings).

Spasm—Of the Abdominal Muscles— (See Ileac Passion).

Spinal Disorders—(See Spine).

Sterility — Due to the Atonic Action of ♀. (See Barren, Impotent).

Stomach — Afflicted with Cold — Diseases of—Raw Humours In—(See Diet, Food; "Raw" under Indigestion; Stomach).

Surfeits — From Over-Eating and Wrong Diet — (See "Evil Diet" under Diet; Food, Surfeits).

Swellings — Glandular Swellings — Swellings In Knees, Legs, Neck, Thighs—(See "Swellings" under these subjects).

Syphilis; Tabes Dorsalis;

Textural Changes—In Nutrition—(See Nutrition).

Therapeutic Properties — Of ♀. (See "Therapeutic" in Sec. 1 of this Article).

Thighs—Gout In—Swellings In—(See Thighs).

Thorax — Disorders In — (See Chest; "Heartburn" under Heart).

Throat—Diseases of—Putrid Sore Throat—Relaxed Throat—Ulcerated— (See Throat).

Tight Lacing—Breathing Disturbed By—(See Lacing, Tight).

Tonsils — Enlarged, Tonsilitis — (See Tonsils).

Tuberculosis; Tumors—Hollow—(See Cysts, Tumors).

Typhus Fever; Typical Drugs—Of ♀. (See "Typical Drugs" in Sec. 1 of this Article).

Ulceration—Of the Throat—(See Throat).

Umbilicus—Disorders of—(See Navel).

Undigested Humours — In Stomach — (See "Raw" under Indigestion).

Unnatural Discharges—(See Discharges).

Uremia; Urine—Involuntary Discharges of—(See "Incontinence" under Urine).

Vascular Tissues—Disorders of—(See Vascular).

Veins—Disorders of—(See Veins).

Venereal Diseases; Venous Blood— Venous Circulation — Disorders of— (See Veins).

Venus Diseases—Suffers From—⊙ to the ill-asps. ♀ by dir., according to the sign ♀ is in at B.; ☽ to the ill-asps. ♂ by dir.; ☽ ♏ and affl. by the ⊙ or ♂ when taken ill, and espec. if ♀ affl. the ☽ (Hor'y); the Asc. to the ♂ or ill-asps. ♀ by dir., and ♀ affl. at B.

Vital Fluids—Escape of—(See Emissions, Semen; "Fluids" under Vital).

Vomiting—Faecal Vomiting from Wrong Diet—(See Ileac Passion).

Warm and Moist Diseases — (See "Warm and Moist" under Moisture).

Wasting Away—Death By—(See Wasting).

Weariness—(See Ennui, Lassitude, Weariness).

Windy Disorders—(See Wind).

Womb—Disorders of—(See Womb).

Women — Minor Disorders of — (See Leucorrhoea, Menses, Mild, Minor, Slight, Women).

Worms—In Children—(See Worms).

VERATRUM—Veratrum Album—Ruled by ♓, and is one of the Twelve Typical Polycrest Remedies, as ruled by the 12 Signs of the Zodiac. (See "Polycrest" under Zodiac).

VERBASCUM — A Typical Drug of ♄. (See "Typical Drugs" under Saturn).

VERMIFORM APPENDIX — (See Appendix).

VERMIN — Pests, Insects, Rats, Mice, Noxious, Obnoxious Animals, Worms, etc. (See "Scarcity of Corn" under Scarcity).

VERNAL EQUINOX—The Spring Equinox—The entry of the ⊙ into the ♈ Sign. The Vernal Signs of the Zodiac are ♈, ♉, ♊. The entrance of the ⊙ into ♈ is a very sensitive time in World Affairs, and the planetary influences operating at the time tend to make the year a good, healthy, and fortunate one for the People, or for individuals who may be affected by it,

or an unfortunate year, and tend to distress, evils, public ill-health, strife, etc. The Vernal Equinox is mentioned many times in this book, and in connection with various diseases, afflictions, the weather, World Conditions, etc. (See Air, Aries, Dry; "Inflammation" under Ears; Epidemics, Equinoxes; "Prevalent" under Eyes; "Eruptions" under Face; "Extreme Heat" under Heat; Ingresses, Lightning, Pestilence, Prevalent, Solstices, etc.).

VERSATILE — (See Genius, Learning, Metaphysics, Occult, Philosophy, Reading, Science, Study, etc.).

VERTEBRAE — The Bony Segments of the Spine. The Nerves which pass thru the Vertebrae supply the various Organs, and parts of the Body, from the Brain to the Feet. By making a study of the Signs of the Zodiac which rule the various Organs and Parts, and by knowing which Signs rule the different Vertebrae, it is a comparatively easy matter to know what Vertebrae, or Vertebra, are affected, or subluxated, when the symptoms of the various diseases of the Mind and Body manifest themselves. (See Subluxations). The Spinal Column is made up of seven Cervical Vertebrae, twelve Dorsal Vertebrae, and five Lumbar Vertebrae. The Sacrum is classed as No. 25, and the Coccyx as No. 26. (See Spine). The Vertebrae are also called the Zones of the Spine.

Abbreviations — For the Vertebrae —

At.P.—Atlas—1st Cervical—Ruled by ♈, ♉.

Ax.P.—Axis—2nd Cervical—♈, ♉.

M.C.P. — 3rd, 4th, 5th Cervicals — All ruled by ♉, and influenced by ♈.

L.C.P.—6th Cervical (♉)—7th Cervical (♉, and 1st Dec. ♊).

A.P.—7th Cervical (♉, first 10° ♊)— 1st Dorsal (♉, ♊).

H.P.—2nd Dorsal (♌ and the ⊙)—3rd Dorsal (♊, ♌).

Lu.P.—3rd Dorsal (♊, ♌)—4th Dorsal (♊, ♋, ♍, ♎, ♏).

Li.P.—4th Dorsal (♊, ♋, ♍, ♎, ♏)— 5th Dorsal (♌).

C.P.—5th Dorsal (♌).

S.P.—6th Dorsal (♋)—7th Dorsal (♋) —8th Dorsal (♋, ♍).

Spl.P.—9th Dorsal (♍, ♏).

K.P. — 10th Dorsal (♎) — 11th Dorsal (♎)—12th Dorsal (♎, ♏).

U.P.P. — 1st Lumbar (♍, ♎, ♏) — 2nd Lumbar (♍, ♏, ♐, ♑, ♒).

P.P.—2nd Lumbar (♍, ♏, ♐, ♑, ♒)— 3rd Lumbar (♍, ♏, ♐, ♑)—4th Lumbar (♍, ♏, ♐, ♑, ♒, ♓).

L.P.P.—4th Lumbar (♍, ♏, ♐, ♑, ♒, ♓)—5th Lumbar (♎, ♏, ♐).

Sac.—Sacrum—(♎, ♏, ♐).

Coc.—Coccyx (♏, ♐).

Cervical Vertebrae—Taken as a whole, these Vertebrae are ruled by the ♉ Sign, the Sign which rules the throat and neck and the upper Cervicals, and are also strongly dominated by the ♈ Sign, the Sign which rules the Brain and Head. Also planets and afflictions in the opposite signs, ♏ and ♎, and also in any of the Fixed Signs, as in ♉, ♌, ♏ or ♒, tend to affect the Cervical Vertebrae. The ♉ and ♏ signs, being opposite and supplemental to each other, both strongly influence the throat and sex organs. The Larynx and the Sex Organs are so closely related that the voice in the male changes at Adolescence. (See Puberty). Any of the planets when in ♉, afflicted in this sign, or afflicting the ♉ sign by their evil aspects, tend to subluxations of these vertebrae. Planets when in the first third of the ♉ sign will afflict the upper Cervicals; when in the middle part of ♉, will afflict the middle Cervicals, and when in the latter third of ♉ at birth, or by direction, transit, or progression, will afflict the lower Cervicals. (See Cervical, Lower, Middle, Upper).

First Cervical — Atlas — Ruled by ♈ and ♉. The tissues and organs affected by the nerve supply passing thru this vertebra are the Brain, Scalp, Atlas, Optic Tract as far as the Commissure, the Cranial Bones, the Upper Ear, Ossicles, and the Upper Forehead. Subluxations at the Atlas tend to diseases which affect the substance of the brain; to diseases of the Brain which affect the Mind, the Motor Functions; to cause Spasmodic Diseases, diseases of the Head, Scalp, Ears, Eyes, Spinal Cord, etc. (See these subjects in the alphabetical arrangement).

Second Cervical—Also called the Axis. Ruled by ♈ and ♉. The nerves passing thru this vertebra supply the Brain, Ears, a part of the Face, and the back part of the Neck, and planetary afflictions in ♈ or ♉, or the opposite signs, ♎ or ♏, tend to disorders in these parts. (See these subjects. Also see "Diseases of Aries" under Aries; "Diseases of Taurus" under Taurus).

Third Cervical—The 3rd, 4th and 5th Cervicals are called The Middle Cervical Place (M.C.P.). Ruled by ♈ and ♉. The nerves which pass thru the 3rd Cervical vertebra supply the Retina, the Teeth, Cheeks, Nasal Passages, the Face, and planetary afflictions in ♈ and ♉ tend to subluxations of this vertebra, and to disease in these parts. (See these subjects).

Fourth Cervical—Ruled by ♈ and ♉. Nerves passing thru this vertebra pass to the Eyes, Cornea, Retina, Mouth, Gums, Teeth, Bones and Tissues of the Face; the Jaw, Eustachian Tubes, the Outer Ear, the Posterior Nares, Nasopharynx, and the Hyoid Bone, and afflictions in these signs at birth tend to subluxations of this vertebra, and to afflict these parts of the body. (See these subjects).

Fifth Cervical — Ruled by ♈ and ♉. Also strongly influenced by the ♏ sign. The nerves which pass thru this vertebra go to the Face, Nose, Eyes, Lower Jaw and Teeth; the Hyoid Bone, and to the Lateral and Posterior Muscles of the Neck, and planets afflicted in these signs tend to disturb these parts of the body, and cause subluxations of this vertebra. (See these subjects).

Sixth Cervical—Ruled by ♉, and especially affected by planets in the last Decanate of ♉. The 6th and 7th Cervicals, taken together, are known as the Lower Cervical Place (L.C.P.). Nerves passing thru this vertebra supply the Larynx, Vocal Cords, and the surrounding tissues; the Thyroid Gland, Palate, Posterior part of the Mouth, Tonsils, upper parts of Shoulders, Anterior parts of the Arms, Lower parts of the Neck, Sterno-Mastoid Region, and Upper Parts of the Bronchii, and afflictions in ♉, ♏, and fixed signs, tend to subluxations of this vertebra, and to cause Throat, Sex, and Uterine Disorders. (See these subjects. Also see Puberty).

Seventh Cervical — Ruled by ♉, and also the first part of ♊. The 7th Cervical, and the 1st Dorsal, are called The Arm Place (A.P.). The Nerves passing thru the 7th Cervical vertebra pass to the Trachea (Windpipe), Radius, Upper Part of Arms, Muscles on back of Neck, and to Deltoid Muscles of the Shoulders, and afflicting planets in ♉ tend to subluxations of this vertebra, and to cause disorders in these parts. (See these subjects. Also see Cervical).

Coccyx—The Coccyx consists of four or five rudimentary vertebrae coalesced into one, and articulates with the apex of the Sacrum above. The Os Coccyx is ruled by the ♏ Sign, and the Coccygeal Region also influenced by the ♐ sign, and afflictions in these signs tend to Pain, Inflammation, or disease in this region, or to deviation of the Coccyx. (See Coccyx).

Diseases of the Vertebrae—Ankylosis, and the drying up of the Synovial Fluid, are the principal diseases of the vertebrae. Ankylosis is caused by the combined heat of the ☉ and ♂ in ♂ in the ♌ sign principally, as ♌ is also a hot sign. The Synovial Fluid is dried up by the presence of the cold and dry planet ♄, and especially ♄ affl. in ♌. (See Anatomical Changes, Ankylosis, Fractures; "Diseases of the Spine" under Spine; Synovial).

Dorsal Vertebrae—The ♌ Sign rules the Dorsal Region of the Spine. The Dorsal Vertebrae are under the structural rulership of ♌. They are also ruled by the ♐ Sign. However, as these Vertebrae cover a wide field of the vital organs, their range of rulership includes the last part of ♉, all of ♊, ♋, ♌, ♍, ♎, and the first degrees of ♏, according to the parts, or organs supplied by nerves passing thru these vertebrae.

First Dorsal—The 7th Cervical, and the 1st Dorsal are called the Arm Place (A.P.). The 1st Dorsal is ruled by ♉ and ♐. Nerves which pass thru this vertebra supply the Muscles of the Arms, the Humerus, Ulna, Bones of the Hands; the Clavicle, Scapula and Shoulders, the 1st Rib, the Manubrium, and the Upper Bronchii, and afflictions in the last degrees of ♉, and in ♐ tend to cause subluxations of this vertebra, and to bring diseases in these parts, and to tend to Aneurism of the Aorta, Asthma, Dyspnoea, Hay Fever, Bronchial Disorders, Disorders of the Sternum, and also Diseases in the Shoulders, Arms, Hands and Fingers. (See these subjects).

Second Dorsal—Ruled by ♌ and the ☉. The 2nd and 3rd Dorsals, taken together, are known as the Heart Place (H.P.). Nerves passing thru this vertebra supply the Heart, its Vessels and Covering, the Pericardium, the Aorta, the Bronchii, 2nd Rib, Hands, and Muscles of the Lower Arms, and planetary afflictions in ♌ at birth tend to subluxations of this vertebra, and to all Heart Disorders, Bronchial Disturbances, and to various diseases and afflictions to the Arms and Hands. (See these subjects).

Third Dorsal—Ruled by the last degrees of ♌, and by the ♊ Sign. The 3rd and 4th Dorsals taken together, are known as Lung Place (Lu.P.). Nerves passing thru this vertebra supply the Chest, Breast, Nipples, Lower Sternum, the 3rd Pair of Ribs, the lower Heart, the Lungs and Pleura, and subluxations at this vertebra tend to diseases in these parts, and to Consumption, Tuberculosis, Chest Deformities, and to various diseases of the Breasts, Heart and Lungs. (See these subjects).

Fourth Dorsal — Ruled by the last degrees of ♊, and by ♋, ♍, ♎ and ♏. This vertebra has a wide field of action, as the nerve supply passing thru it goes to the Lower Lungs, the 4th Pair of Ribs, and to the Liver, Gall Bladder and Bile Ducts. The 4th and 5th Dorsals are known as the Liver Place (Li.P.). Planets in these signs at birth tend to diseases in these parts and Organs, and to all Diseases of the Liver especially. (See these subjects).

Fifth Dorsal — A part of the Liver Place, and is also known as Center Place (C.P.). Under the strong rule of the ♌ Sign. Nerves passing thru this vertebra supply the 5th Pair of Ribs, and being the General Heat Center, subluxations at this vertebra tend to Diseases of the Brain and Spinal Cord, to Nervous Diseases, High and Burning Fevers, Impaired Nutrition, Cold Diseases, Cold Feet, Gout, Rheumatism, Dropsy, Influenza, Rashes, Scarlet Fever, Anaemia, Chills, Obesity, and a variety of Diseases. (See these subjects. Also see "Center" under Heat).

Sixth Dorsal — The 6th, 7th and 8th Dorsals are grouped together, and known as Stomach Place (S.P.). Is ruled principally by the ♋, or Stomach Sign, and also, in conjunction with the 7th and 8th Dorsals, influenced by the ♍ Sign. Subluxations at this vertebra tend to disorders in the upper part of the Stomach, and in the Oesophagus, in and about the 6th Pair of Ribs, and being nearly identical with the 7th Dorsal, tends to nearly all the same diseases as caused by subluxations at the 7th Dorsal. (See Oesophagus, Stomach).

Seventh Dorsal—Ruled principally by the ♋ Sign. The following Organs and Parts of the Body receive nerve supply and impetus thru the opening in this vertebra, namely, the Stomach, Oesophagus, the Mucous Membrane of the Mouth and Stomach; the Tonsils, Uvula, Pharynx, Palate, Throat,

Tongue, Gums, Salivary Glands, Glands of the Mouth and Stomach; the 7th Pair of Ribs; the Omentum, and also the Eyeballs, Pupils, Iris and Cornea of the Eyes, and afflictions in the ♋ Sign tend to subluxations of this vertebra, and to cause diseases in these parts and organs. (See these subjects).

Eighth Dorsal—A part of the Stomach Place in the Spine, and ruled by the ♋ sign, and also by ♍. The nerve supply thru this vertebra passes to the lower parts of the Stomach, the Pylorus, Duodenum, the Upper Spleen, the Pancreas, Diaphragm, and the 8th Pair of Ribs, and subluxations of this vertebra tend to diseases and ailments in these parts. (See these subjects).

Ninth Dorsal—Ruled by ♍ Sign, and also strongly influenced by the ♏ Sign. Is known as Spleen Place (Spl.P.). The nerve supply passing thru this vertebra goes to the Spleen, Omentum, Duodenum, and the 9th Pair of Ribs, and subluxations at this vertebra tend to diseases in these parts and organs, and also to Intestinal Worms. (See these subjects).

Tenth Dorsal — The 10th, 11th and 12th Dorsals are called the Kidney Place (K.P.). This vertebra is ruled by the ♎ Sign. The nerve supply passing thru this vertebra goes to the Upper Kidneys, the Supra-Renal Capsules, the 10th Pair of Ribs, and also to the Eyelids, and subluxations of this vertebra tend to diseases in these parts. (See these subjects).

Eleventh Dorsal — Ruled by the ♎ Sign. The nerve supply passing thru this vertebra is to the same parts and organs as mentioned under the 10th Dorsal, but this vertebra when subluxated, and being the middle one in the Kidney Place, tends to the more serious Kidney Diseases, and to a greater variety of them, such as Bright's Disease, Diabetes, Nephritis, Stone, Gravel, the Suppression of Urine, Uremia, Blepharitis, Granulated Lids, and also to Skin Rashes, Dropsy, Dysentery, Rheumatism, etc. (See these subjects).

Twelfth Dorsal — Ruled by ♎. Also the ♏ Sign influence begins to be felt at this vertebra. The nerve supply passing thru this vertebra goes to the lower portion of the Kidneys, the Ureters, the 12th Pair of Ribs, the end of the Spine, and also rules the Serous Circulation, and subluxations here tend to diseases and disorders of these parts and functions. (See these subjects. Also see Dorsal).

Lumbar Vertebrae—In the Astrological Textbooks, the ♎ Sign is given as general Ruler of the Lumbar Vertebrae, and Lumbar Region of the Spine. However, as the Sex Organs, the Reproductive Nature, the Bladder, Rectum, Lower Limbs, and Feet, get their nerve supply thru the Lumbar Vertebrae, the rest of the Signs of the Zodiac after ♎ must also have their influence over these vertebrae, and especially over those below the 1st Lumbar.

First Lumbar—This vertebra is ruled by the ♍, ♎ and ♏ Signs, and together with the 2nd Lumbar is known as the Upper Private Place (U.P.P.). The nerve supply thru this vertebra passes to the Ureters, Loins, Peritoneum, and to the Upper Small Intestines, and planetary afflictions in these Signs tend to subluxations of this vertebra, and to diseases in these parts. (See these subjects).

Second Lumbar — The 2nd, 3rd and 4th Lumbar Vertebrae, taken together as a unit, are known as the Private Place (P.P.). Considering the parts and organs supplied by nerves passing thru this vertebra, it is ruled by the middle third of the ♏ sign, and also by ♏, ♐, ♑, and the ♒ sign, as the nerve supply passing thru this opening goes to the Small Intestines, the Vermiform Appendix, the Ovaries, Caecum, Peritoneum, and the Muscles of the Legs, and subluxations of the vertebra must necessarily lead to diseases of these parts, and cause Abdominal Diseases, Bowel Disorders, Peritonitis, Varicose Veins in the Leg, Lameness, and various other disorders.

Third Lumbar—According to the organs supplied by nerves passing thru this vertebra, it is ruled by the latter third of ♏, and by ♏, ♐, and ♑, as the nerve supply goes to the Abdominal Muscles, to the lower Small Intestines, the Caecum, Colon, Appendix, the Hepatic and Splenic Flexures, the Ovaries and Broad Ligaments, the Bladder, Testicles, Sexual Organs, the Anterior Muscles of the Thighs, and to the Knees, and subluxations of this vertebra will tend to diseases and afflictions in these parts and organs. (See these subjects).

Fourth Lumbar — The 4th and 5th Lumbars, taken together, are known as the Lower Private Place (L.P.P.). This vertebra is ruled and influenced by the ♏, ♏, ♐, ♑, ♒ and ♓ Signs, as the nerve supply going thru it passes to the Womb, Vagina, Bladder, Prostate Gland, Large Intestines, Colon, Rectum, Pelvis, Hip Bone, Buttocks, Femur, Posterior Thighs, Tibia, Fibula, and the Feet, and subluxations of this vertebra tend to ailments and afflictions in these parts. (See these subjects).

Fifth Lumbar — Astrological writers give ♎ and ♐ as rulers of this vertebra, but ♏ should also be included, as the nerve supply thru this opening goes to the Uterus, Rectum, and the Buttocks, and planetary afflictions in these signs tend to subluxations of this vertebra, and to ailments and diseases in these parts, and in the lower abdominal region, and especially to Piles, Falling of the Womb, and Menstrual Disorders. (See these subjects. Also see Lumbar).

Sacrum—The nerve supply going out thru the foramen of the Sacrum passes to the Womb, Buttocks, the Posterior parts of the Thigh, and to the Anus and Rectum, and therefore this vertebra is ruled and influenced by the ♎, ♏ and ♐ Signs, and planets afflicted in these Signs tend to disorders in these parts and organs, and to deviations of the Sacrum. (See these subjects. Also see Sacrum).

VERTIGO — Giddiness — Dizziness — Lightness In the Brain—Swimming In the Head, etc.—The ☉ affl. in ♈; ☉ ☐, ♂ ☽ or Asc. at B., or by dir.; ☉ in 6th H. in a cardinal sign, and afflicted; a disease of the ☽, and afflictions to the ☽, as the ☽ causes diseases which return after a time, such as Vertigo; ♃ affl. in ♈ or ♎; ♂ affl. in ♍ or ♍, and ♂ or evil asp. the Asc. by dir.; a ☿ disease; ☿ affl. in ♈, and in ♎ by reflex action; ☿ in ♈, ♂, or ill-asp. any of the malefics as Promittors; ♄ ☌ ♃ in the Asc.; ♄ ☌ ♃ or ♀ in ♈; an ♈ disease; Subs at Li.P., SP. (7D), and at KP. (See Brain, Cerebral, Dizziness, Fainting).

Death from Vertigo — Afflictions in cardinal signs.

VESICA — Vesical — (See Bladder; "Jupiter Group" under Muscles).

VESICANT—An Agent Producing a Bleb or Blister—♂ influence and remedies. (See Blisters, Cantharides, Caustic, Mustard, Rubefacients).

VESICLES — Vesicle—A Small Sac—A Small Blister—The ☽ and ♃ in Signs which rule the Arms, Hands, Legs and Feet affect the Vesicles and Glands of these parts, causing Cysts, Ulcers, Aneurysm, and Varicose Veins. (See Aneurysm, Bladder, Blisters, Carbuncles, Cavities, Cysts; "Foot and Mouth Disease" under Feet; Herpes, Hives, Malignant, Pustules, Receptacles, Sacs, Seminal, Serum, Varicose, Vesicant).

VESSELS—Blood Vessels—Tubes—Sacs —Receptacles—Vascular—Vaso, etc. — See the following subjects in the alphabetical arrangement when only listed here. These subjects have to do with the vessels of the body, their contents, and disorders.

Absorbent Vessels—(See Absorption).

Action — Want of Vascular Action — Characteristic of the Lymphatic Temperament. (See Lymph).

Aneurysm; Aorta; Apoplexy; Arteries — Various Disorders of — (See Arteries).

Beating Of — Increased Beating and Throbbing of Blood Vessels—A ♃ disease. (See "Vascular Fullness" under Vascular).

Bile—(See "Ducts" under Bile).

Bladder; Blisters; Blood Vessels—Obstructions In—High Pressure In—Rupture of—Diseases of—(See Apoplexy; Arteries; "Pressure" under Blood; Capillaries, Clots, Embolism, Infarct, Rupture, Thrombus, Veins; "Rupture" in this section).

Bowels; Brain — Bursting of Blood Vessel In—(See Apoplexy).

Bursting — Of a Blood Vessel — (See "Blood Vessels" in this section).

Canals; Capillaries; Carotids;

Centrifugal; Centripetal; Cerebral;

Clots; Cold — The Action of Cold on Surface Blood Vessels—(See Centripetal).

Congestion; Constrictions—(See Constrictions, Contractions, Stenosis, Vaso).

Cysts; Dilatations — (See Aneurysm; "Pressure", "Too Much Blood", under Blood; Dilatation, Distentions, Varicose; "Vascular Fullness" under Vascular).

Ducts; Embolism; Fullness Of—(See Apoplexy; "Pressure", "Too Much Blood", under Blood; Dilatations, Distentions, Plethora; "Vascular Fullness" under Vascular).

Hardening; Heart; Hemorrhage;

High Blood Pressure—(See Apoplexy; "Pressure", "Too Much Blood", under Blood; Plethora; "Vascular Fullness" under Vascular).

Iliac Arteries—(See Ilium).

Infarcts; Inflammation Of—(See "Arteritis" under Arteries; "Phlebitis" under Veins).

Injuries To—(See "Hemorrhages" in this section).

Jugular; Lachrymal—(See Tears).

Lacteals—(See Breasts, Milk).

Low Blood Pressure—(See "Pressure" under Blood).

Lungs—Absorbent Vessels of—Other Vessels of — (See Absorption, Lungs, Lymph).

Lymphatic Vessels—(See Lymph; "Action" in this section).

Membranous Sacs—(See Cysts).

Mineral Deposits—(See Minerals).

Obstructions — (See Clots, Infarcts, Thrombus).

Peripheral—Vessels and Nerves—(See Peripheral).

Plethora; Plugs—(See Clots, Infarcts, Thrombus).

Portal Vein—(See Veins).

Pressure—High and Low Blood Pressure—(See "High Blood Pressure" in this section).

Pulse; Receptacles;

Respiratory System — Absorbent and Lymphatic Vessels of — (See Absorption, Breathing, Bronchial, Lungs, Lymph, Pulmonary).

Rupture—Of Blood Vessels—Bursting of — Caused by ♂, and apt to come when ♂ is exactly rising or setting; a ♂ disease; ♂ ☌ ♃ at B., and ♂ affl. the hyleg; ♂ ☌, □, or ☍ the ☽; ♂ affl. the ☉ or ☽ at B., and by dir., and also the ☉ or ☽ to the ☌ or ill-asp. ♂ by dir., or ♂ affl. the hyleg by dir., tend to death by the rupture of blood vessels; the ☉ to the ill-asps. ♃ by dir., and afflicted, and espec. if the ☉ or ☽ be affl. at B. by ♄ or ♂. The tonic action of ♂ tends to disruptions, rending, and bursting of parts or vessels. (See Apoplexy; "Pressure" under Blood; Bursting, Cerebral; "Accelerated" under Motion; Plethora, Rending; "Vascular Fullness" under Vascular).

Seminal Vesicles—(See Semen).

Stenosis — (See Constrictions, Stenosis).

Stomach; Surface Vessels—(See Centripetal, Constrictions).

Throat — Absorbent Vessels of — (See Absorbent, Lymphatic).

Throbbing — (See "Beating" in this section).

Thrombus; Too Much Blood — (See this subject under Blood).

Tumors; Valves; Varicocele; Varicose; Vas Deferens—(See Testes).

Vascular Action — (See "Action" in this section).

Vascular Fullness—(See Vascular).

Vaso-Constriction — Vaso-Dilation — Vaso-Motor—(See Vaso).

Veins; Ventricles.

VETERINARY SURGEON — Makes a Good Veterinary—Ruler of the 10th H., or of the Employment, strong in ♈, or ♌, makes a good Veterinary, or Cow Doctor. The ♐ sign strong at B., and well-occupied, makes the native fortunate with horses and large animals, and if at the same time ♂ also be strong in ♏, or in ♏ in the 1st, 6th, or 12th H. at B., the native should make a successful Veterinary Surgeon; the ☉ or ☽ well-aspected in ♐; born under ♐, and with this sign on the Asc. (See Cattle, Horses, Surgeons).

VEXATIONS—A Time of Trouble, Sorrow, or Ill-Health—The ☉ or ☽ transiting the place of the malefics at B., and espec. if the ☉ and ☽ be □ their own place at the same time, or the preceding New ☽ be in an evil place; the ☉ ☍ a radical malefic, and the ☽ □ a radical malefic at same time; ☽ Sig. □, ☍ ♄; the ☽ at a Solar Rev. passing over her own place at B., and affl. by malefics, or the ☽ passing the place of the radical ♄ at such a time; ♄ Sig. □, ☍ ☽; ♃ Sig. □, ☍ ☿; caused by the evil directions of ♂ to the ☉, ☽, or asc.; ☿ affl. in 7th H.; Asc. to the □, ☍ ☿; lord of the 6th in the 12th H., sickness from deep vexation; lord of the 8th H. in the 4th, possible death from vexation over loss of property, or loss of inheritance; malefics in the 5th H., vexations and sorrows thru children; the Asc. to the □ or ☍ ☿; Fixed Stars of the nature of ♄ ascending. (See Anguish, Anxiety, Cares; "Parents", "Worries", under Children; Disgrace, Evil, Fate; "Vexations" under Females; Fortune, Honour, Inheritance, Love Affairs, Marriage, Mischief, Miseries, Misfortune, Perplexities, Property, Reputation, Reverses, Riches, Ruin, Sickness, Sorrow, Trouble, Twelfth House, Women, Worry, etc. Also look in the alphabetical arrangement for the subject you have in mind).

Death By—Lord of the 8th H. in the 4th H.

Sickness—From Deep Vexation—Lord of the 6th H. in the 12th H., and afflicted.

VIBRATION—Vibrational—Life manifests itself as Motion and Vibration. Vibration is a Therapeutic Property of ♅. (See Uranus). Also ☿ is vibrational, and the originator of vibratory movement, and afflictions to ☿ at B. tend to stop mental vibrations, and to dull the Senses. However, all the planets have their rate of vibration, and tend to cause disease when their vibrations reach the individual adversely, and as caused especially by the □, or ☍ aspects, which aspects and vibrations are contracting and afflicting, while the △ aspects to the Significators at B. tend to be benevolent and expanding. Disease and suffering are but rates of vibration, and a change to the proper vibrations in mind and body often cures the disease. (See Antipathy, Aspects, Attracts; "Vibration" under Colors; Compatibility; Discord, Ether, Harmony; "Compatibility", "Incompatibility", under Healers; Hearing, Hyperaesthesia, Lethargy, Life; "Rays" under Light; Motion, Movement, Opposites, Planets, Polarity, Repulsions, Rhythm, Sympathy, etc.).

Healing by Vibration—In disease, when the rates of vibration are weakening and detrimental, any means, or remedy, to restore the normal rate of vibration is beneficial. This may be done by the use of drugs, by suggestion, by diet, natural means and remedies, by massage, adjustments of the spine, by electricity, baths, and in a thousand various ways as used and practiced by the various Schools of Healing. From the planetary standpoint, when a patient is suffering from a ♂ disease, the remedies of ♄, which oppose the fiery action of ♂, tend to slow down the ♂ vibrations, and bring ease, relief, or a cure to the patient, and the vibration of the disease or affliction has been changed. (See Antipathy, Opposites, Sympathy). Also if the rates of vibration of the Healer blend with those of his patient, the patient will benefit, and make a quicker cure, but if the innate vibrations of the Healer antagonize and worry the patient, and their Star Maps of Birth are not in harmony, the patient may weaken, die, or make slow progress unless he changes Healers, and gets one who is fortunate for him. (See "Compatibility", "Death", "Enemies", "Incompatibility", "Poisoned", under Healers).

VICARIOUS—The Assumption of the Functions of One Organ by Another—(See "Vicarious" under Menses; "Blood" under Vomiting).

VICE—Vices—

Addicted to Vices—Given to Many Vices—Inclined to Vice—The ☉ ill-dig. at B., and afflicted, prone to many vices; the ☽ sepr. from the ☉, and apply. to ♀ in a day geniture; the ☽ to Capella, ruins himself by vices and with infamous women; the ☽ to the ♂ or ill-asp. ♂ by dir., addicted to vices, according to the sign ♂ is in; ♄ ♂ or ill-asp. ♀, secret and solitary vices; ♃ affl. in ♓; ♂ prog., ♂, or ill-asp. the radical ♄, or vice versa, all the vices of the character tend to be prominent and active; ♀ affl. by ♄; ♀ by Periodic Rev. to the ill-asps. the radical ☉; ♀ affl. in the 5th H., dissolute vices. (See Conduct, Debauched, Depraved, Dissolute, Drink, Gluttony, Habits, Homosexuality, Lascivious, Lewd, Lust, Narcotics, Obscene, Passion, Perversions, Self-Indulgent, Sex, Shameless, Tobacco, Women; "Solitary" in this section).

Solitary Vice—Secret Vice—Self-Abuse—Masturbation—Defilement—The ☉ in ♏, and affl. by ♀; principally a ♀ affliction; ♀ in the 12th H. in ☍ to

the ☽ in ♏ in the 6th H., and espec. when ♀ is in ♉; ♀ affl. in ♏; ♀ affl. in the 6th or 12th H., sex activity and abuses during adolescence; ♀ afflicted at B.; ♅ ♂ ♄ in ♏, or these two planets otherwise afflicted in ♏; ♄ ♂ or ill-asp. ♀; ♂ ♂ ♀, an inflammatory sex condition; ♂ affl. in ♏; ♀ or ☿ in bad asp. to ♄; ♉ or ♏ on the cusp of the 6th or 12th H.; a 12th H. influence. (See Aversions, Deviations, Passion, Perversions; "Secret Bad Habits" under Secret; Self-Indulgence). Case of Insanity From Self-Abuse—(See "Self-Abuse" under Insanity).

VICIOUS—Depraved—Wicked, etc.—The influences of the malefic planets ♄ and ♂, when these planets are strong at B., rising in the Asc., or M.C., and afflicted, and espec. when ♄ is ♂ or ☍ ♂ in angles, tend to make the native vicious, high tempered, unruly, and violent at times, and apt to do some desperate things in life until he becomes awakened. (See Anarchists, Anger, Conduct, Dangerous, Depraved, Destructiveness, Evil, Hatred, Infamous, Irascible, Jealousy; "Low and Base" under Low; Malevolent, Malicious, Murderous, Plots; "Poisoner" under Poison; Rebellious, Revengeful, Riotous, Treachery, Unruly, Vile, Violent, Wicked, etc.).

Pleasures—Fond of Vicious Pleasures—♀ Sig. in ♋. (See Pleasure, Sports).

Secretly Vicious—Caused by ♄ afflictions. (See "Secret Enemies" under Enemy; Hatred, Malice, Plots; "Poisoner" under Poison; Revenge, Treachery).

VIEWS—(See Ideals, Ideas, Materialism, Metaphysics, Morals, Motives, Notions, Occult, Philosophy, Purposes, Religion, Science, Spiritual, Thinking).

VIGOR—Vim—Force—Energy—

Vigorous Body—The fiery signs ♈, ♌, or ♐ upon the Asc. tend to give the most vigorous bodies, and the greatest vitality; given by the ⚹ and △ aspects of ♂ to the ☉, hyleg and Asc.; the ☉ or ☽ in the signs of the Summer Quarter, as in ♋, ♌ or ♍, or when these signs are upon the Asc., and well-aspected, tend to give a vigorous body, but the ♋ sign on the Asc., if badly afflicted, and the map otherwise weak, would tend to a low vitality. The vigor and force of the constitution tend to become weakened and unbalanced when there are many evil aspects to the ☉, ☽, hyleg, or Asc., and the planets at birth at variance with each other by their □ and ☍ aspects. The △ aspects between the planets tend to give the best vigor, and espec. when the ☉ and ♂ favorably aspect each other. (See Action, Active; "Good Constitution" under Constitution, Females; "Abundance Of" under Energy; "Good Health" under Health, Males; Immunity; "Males Nearly Impotent" under Impotent; Invigorated; "Vigor and Strength" under Males; "Good" under Recuperation, Resistance, Stamina, Tone, Vitality; Robust, Ruddy; "Body" under Strong, etc.).

VILE—Sordid—Loathsome—Base—

Artifice—Blindness by Some Vile Artifice—(See "Blindness" in this section).

Blindness — By Some Vile Artifice — (See Artifice; "Total Blindness" under Blindness).

Diseases — Vile and Loathsome Diseases—(See Carcinoma, Leprosy, Private, Putrid, Sores, Syphilis, Ulcers, Venereal, etc.).

Vile Wretch—♂ Sig. ☐ or ♉ ☽; ♀ Sig. ☐ or ♉ ♂; ☿ Sig. ♂ ♂. (See Debased, Depraved, Infamous; "Low and Base" under Low; Obscene, Perversions, Shameless, Vagabond, Wanton, etc.).

VIM—Force—Energy—Spirit—(See Active, Energy, Force, Power, Stamina, Strong, Vigor, Vitality, Zest, etc.).

VINDEMIATRIX—A Star—(See "Fixed Stars" under Stars; Widows).

VINDICTIVE—(See Malice, Revenge).

VINES—Vineyards—(See Fruit, Trees, Vegetation).

VIOLENT—Violence—Forcible—Severe—Sharp—Fierce—Vehement—Furious, etc—Mars is the planet of violence. Also sudden violence, as in explosions, is caused by ♅. Violence by bruises, falls, etc., is caused by ♄. Any of the malefics, when afflicted, or even the ☉, and other planets, may cause violence, accidents, injuries, wounds, etc., by their evil aspects and directions, but ♂ is the principal planet causing violent diseases, violent, sharp and fierce fevers, or a violent death. See the following subjects in the alphabetical arrangement, which subjects have to do with violence in its various phases, whether it be violence and hurts to the body, or violent actions. Under these subjects look for such paragraphs as "Accidents", "Danger", "Death", "Hurts", "Injuries", Violent", "Wounds", etc.

Abroad; Accidents — The subject of Violence is largely dealt with in the Article on Accidents, and where Accidents are attended with Violence. (See the various paragraphs under Accidents).

Actions; Affections — Violent Affections and Diseases—(See "High" under Fever; Fierce, Painful Diseases, Pernicious, Poignant, Severe Diseases, Sharp Diseases, Vehement, etc.).

Ambushes; Anarchists; Anger;

Animals — Hurts By — (See Animals, Beasts, Bites, Cattle, Kicks, etc.).

Areas—Violent Areas In the Map of Birth—The 15° of cardinal signs; the 25° of fixed signs, and the 26° of the common signs, are known as violent degrees and areas, and people with the ☉ or ☽, or the malefics, in or very near these degrees at B., are more subject to violence in some form, or to commit suicide. (See "Causes" under Suicide).

Assassination; Assaults; Battle—(See War).

Becomes Violent—Given to Violence— ♂ ☌ or ill-asp. ♄ at B., and espec. in the Asc., 10th H., and angles; the ☉ to the place of Antares; the 2nd decan. or face of ♉ on the Asc.; the 1st decan. of ♌ on the Asc., ruled by ♄; the 3rd decan. of ♌ on the Asc., ruled by ♂; the 1st decan. of ♏ on the Asc., ruled by ♂. (See "Tendency to Violence" in this section).

Beheaded; Bites; Blindness—By Violence—(See Artifice; "Total Blindness" under Blindness).

Blows; Bomb Plotters—(See Anarchists).

Brain Storms—(See Brain).

Bruises; Burning—Searings—(See the Calamities; Catastrophies; Cattle;

Chances — Endures Many Violent Chances—(See Chances).

Conduct; Contractions — Violent Invarious paragarphs under Burns). voluntary Contractions—(See Convulsions).

Cough—(See "Violent" under Cough).

Countenance — (See "Violent Countenance" under Face).

Cruel; Crushed; Cuts;

Danger from Violence—☉ to the place of Antares; ♂ ☌ ☉, ☽, Asc. or hyleg at B., and by dir.; Aldebaran, Antares, Regulus, Frons Scorpio, Deneb, and the Shoulders of Orion when directed to the ☉, ☽, or Asc. (See Danger).

Dangerous — Dangerous Accidents — Dangerous Destructiveness—(See Accidents, Destructiveness).

Death—Violent Death—Death by Violence—Danger of Violent Death—Violent Death Threatened — In death by violence, observe the Genethliacal positions of the ☉ and ☽, how they are affected by the malefics, and how the ☉ and ☽ are concerned by Directions in the quality of death. In Countries where Wars and Violence are unknown, people born with maps indicating a violent death usually die a natural death, but in Countries where Wars and Violence predominate, they usually meet an untimely death, and even under slight afflictions. The most desperate men and worthless of people are generally the most anxious to engage in violent, hazardous, and dangerous enterprises. The ☐ and ☍ asps. of the ☉ to the Significators are the aspects of infamy and contempt, and lead often to a violent death, suicide, or public execution. The ☐ and ☍ asps. of the ☽, to a violent death by mobs, riots, etc. The following influences tend to a violent death—The SUN or ☽ to the ☌ or ill-asp. ♂ by dir., and the radix be a violent one, and the Lights affl. by ♂ at B.; the ☉ or ☽ to the ☌ or ill-asps. ♂ by dir., and affl. the hyleg, or ♂ affl. the ☉ or ☽ at B.; the ☉ or ☽ ☐ or ☍ ♂ from angles, and espec. from the 10th or 4th; the ☉ and ☽ affl. by a malefic, and with no assistance from ♃ or ♀; the ☉ affl. by one malefic, and the ☽ by another; the ☉ or ☽ in violent signs, as in ♈, ♏, or ♑, or the afflicting planets be in violent signs; the ☉ or ☽ alone affl. by more than one malefic, and no assistance from the benefics; ☉ Sig. ☌ ♄ or ♂, and these malefics ill-dig. at B.; ☉ Sig. ☐ or ☍ ♂; the ☉ near violent fixed stars, or having their declination, and affl. at same time by ♄ or ♂, great danger if the benefics do not interfere; the ☉ or ☽ affl. by malefics in the 1, 4, 6, 8, or 10th houses; the ☉ or ☽ affl. by one or more malefics, and one of the Luminaries, or one of the malefics be in a violent sign; both the ☉

and ☽ affl. by a malefic, and one Luminary oriental; ☉ Sig. □ ♂, and if ♄ or ♅ also add their testimony by disposing of the ☉ at the same time, the danger is greater, and almost certain death; the ☉ or ☽ affl. by ♂, and ♂ elevated above the Lights; the ☉ and ☽ affl. by anaretic bodies; the ☉ in the 8th H. ☌ or ill-asp. ♂; ☉ joined with Aldebaran, Antares, Ascelli, Bellatrix, Castor, Pollux, Caput Algol, Hercules, Hyades, Pleiades, Praesepe, or Regulus, or any eminent star of the nature of ♂, threatens a violent death, or extreme sickness; the MOON sepr. from ♂, and applying to the ☉; ☽ sepr. from the ☉, and applying to ♂ in a day geniture; ☽ decr., sepr. from ♂, and applying to ♄; ☽ decr., sepr. from ♃ and applying to ♄ or ♂, and espec. in a nocturnal nativity; ☽ applying to ♂ at B., or conjoined with him in a day nativity; ☽ Sig. ☌ ♂; ☽ Sig. □, ☍ ♄ or ♂; ☽ with Antares, and in ☍ ♄ and Aldebaran; the ☽ to the □ or ☍ the ☉ if the radix show a violent death; the ☽ in the 8th H., and affl. by ♅, ♄, or ♂; the ☽ conjoined with Antares, Aldebaran, Caput Algol, Cor Leo, Bellatrix, or Pollux; the full ☽ sepr. from ♂ and apply. to ☿ in a day nativity; NEPTUNE affl. in the 8th H., and may be by drowning or suffocation, or in a riotous manner if Ψ is Anareta; URANUS affl. in the 8th H., violent death, as by explosion, gas, machinery, lightning, or electricity; SATURN or ♂ in the 8th H., and affl. the ☉, ☽, or hyleg; ♄ Sig. to the ☌ or ill-asps. the ☉ or ♂ by dir.; ♄ with Regulus; ♄ and ♂, and evil or violent fixed stars affl. the hyleg; ♄ and ♂ in ♊, ♍, ♒, or ♐, and in □ or ☍ the ☉ or ☽; ♄ ☌ or ☍ the ☉ or ☽ from card. signs, and ♂ conjoined to ♄; ♄ Sig. □ or ☍ the ☉ or ♂; ♄ and ♂ having dignities in Anaretic Places, or □ or ☍ the ☉ or ☽ at B.; ♄ and ♂ both attacking the ☉ or ☽, or one of them, by dir., and at the same time the malefics or Asc. be afflicted, and with a malefic in the 8th H. as additional testimony; ♄ Sig., ill-dig., and ☌ ♂; ♄ or ♂ in the 4th or 10th H., and in □ or ☍ the ☉ or ☽; JUPITER Sig. □ or ☍ ♂, a violent death by blows, wounds, or resistance to robbers; MARS ☌ or ill-asp. the ☽, and ♄ in like asp. to the ☉ from angles; ♂ and ♄ in the 8th H., and affl. the hyleg; ♂ ☌, □, or ☍ ♄, and espec. when neither are essentially dignified; ♂ the ruling planet, or ruler of the Asc.; ♂ affl. in the 8th H.; ♂ sole ruler at a Solar Eclipse, many violent deaths generally; ♂ ☌, □, ☍ ☽, and at same time ♄ be in angle in ☌ or ill-asp. the ☉; ♂ affl. the ☉ or ☽, or one Light only, by ☌ or ill-asp., and be elevated above it; ♂ in a violent sign at B., and affl. the hyleg; ♂ ☌ or ill-asp. the ☉; ♂ ☌ the ☉ or ☽ in the 1st, 6th, 8th, or 10th H., and espec. if ♅ or ♄ add their evil testimony to ♂; ♂ with the Pleiades; ♂ on the Asc. at B., and affl.; ♂ in angles and affl. the ☉ or ☽, and espec. the ☉; ♂ and ♄ both having dignities in the Anaretic Place, or when □ or ☍ the ☉ and ☽ at B.; ♂ affl. the ☉, and the ☉ be weak and ill-dig.; MERCURY mixing his beams with ♂ is an argument for a violent death; lord of the

Asc. affl. by ♄ or ♂ at B., or by dir.; ♉ in the 8th H.; the Asc. affl. by the □ or ☍ of ♄ and ♂ at B., or by dir., and espec. if the Asc. be hyleg; the M.C. to the ☌, P., □, or ☍ ♂, and espec. if ♂ be lord of the 8th H. at B., and the radix promotes it; the M.C. directed to Nebulous Stars, the Pleiades, Praesepe, the Ascelli, Hyades, The Twins, Shoulders of Orion, Auriga's Right Shoulder, Medusa's Head, Hercules, and Markab; Lion's Heart joined to the ☉ or ☽ at B.; Markab, a violent star, joined to the ☉, ☽, or ♂ at B.; eminent FIXED STARS of the nature of ♂ in an angle with the ☉ at B.; Aldebaran ☌ ♄, ♂, ☉, or ☽, and espec. in the Asc.; the MALEFICS in ☌ or ☍ lords of the anaretic places, and if one or more malefics attack the ☉ or ☽; a malefic being Anareta, and elevated above the Lights; a malefic planet in the 8th H. and afflicted; in Horary Questions, malefic planets lord of the 8th, or in the 8th, or affl. the cusp of the 8th by □, ☌, or ☍; a malefic on the cusp of the 7th, or in the 1st or 8th, and affl. the ☉ or ☽, or both; lord of the 8th a malefic, and in the 8th, or afflict cusp of 8th; malefics in ☍ asp. from angles, and in cardinal or violent signs; two malefics in ill-asp. to, and attacking the same Luminary; violent planets, as Ψ, ♅, ♄ and ♂, in violent signs at B., and affl. the hyleg; malefics affl. the ☉ or ☽, and elevated above the Lights; lord of the 8th affl. by malefics; lord of the 8th a malefic, and in the 8th, and affl. by lord of the 6th or 12th, and espec. if the lord of the Asc. or the hyleg, are afflicted; lord of the 8th in the 10th, and lord of the 8th, a malefic, and lord of the 10th affl. by lord of the 8th; lord of the 8th in the 6th; the malefics having dignity in the anaretic places, or in □ or ☍ the ☉ or ☽ at B.; the hyleg affl. by planets angular, and elevated above them; the sign on cusp the 8th a violent sign, or if the ☉, ☽, or lord of the 8th be in a violent sign, or malefics in the 8th in evil asp. to lord of the Asc., the ☉ or ☽ from violent signs; malefics in the 10th H., or the Significators evilly disposed; lord of the 10th in the 8th; the 2nd Dec. of ♉ on the Asc. denotes violence; 28° ♐ on the Asc.; the 15° of cardinal signs, the 25° of fixed signs, and the 26° of mutable signs, are classed as violent areas, and malefics, or planets in these degrees at B. tend to a violent death, as by murder or suicide. (See "Causes His Own Death" under Death; "Own Worst Enemy" under Enemies; the various paragraphs in this section). Cases of Violent Death—See "Medici", No. 527; "Sebastian", No. 576; "Villiers", No. 647, all in 1001 N.N.

Decapitation; Deportment—(See Conduct).

Desires — Violent Desires — (See Impotent; "Violent" under Men; "Violence" under Passion; Virile).

Diseases — Violent Diseases — (See "High Fevers" under Fevers; Fierce, Painful, Quick, Sharp, Swift, Vehement).

Dislocations; Dispersals — (See "Violent" under Dispersions).

Disposition — Violent Nature—(See "Tendency to Violence" in this section; Inhuman, Savage).

Drowning; Duels; Effusions of Blood —(See Effusions).

Electricity; Enemies; Eruptions—(See "Violent" under Eruptions).

Evil; Excretory Sytsem—Violent Disorders of—(See "Disorders" under Excretion).

Execution—(See Execution, Hanging, Judges).

Exercise; Explosions; Extraordinary; Falls; Famine; Father—Violent Diseases To—(See Father).

Females — Violently Libidinous—(See Lewd, Nymphomania, Virile).

Ferocious; Fevers—Violent and Burning — (See "High", "Violent", under Fevers).

Fierce — Violent and Fierce Maladies —Fierce Nature—(See Fierce, Savage, Sharp, Vehement, Wild).

Fire—(See Burns, Fire, Heat, Scalds).

Fixed Stars—The Violent Fixed Stars —(See Stars).

Fluxes; Foreign Lands — Danger of Violence In—(See Abroad).

Fractures; Frenzy; Gas;

Given to Violence — (See "Becomes Violent", "Tendency To", in this section).

Guillotine; Gunshot; Hand of Man — Death By—(See "Hand of Man" under Man).

Hanging; Head—(See "Pains" under Head).

Headaches — (See "Violent" under Headaches).

Heart—Violent Palpitation of—(See "Palpitation" under Heart).

Heat—(See "Extreme" under Heat).

Heights—Falls From—(See Heights).

Hemorrhages; High Fevers — High, Fierce and Violent—(See "High" under Fever).

Highwaymen; Hurts; Ignoble Death —(See Ignoble).

Incendiarism; Inflammation—Violent Inflammation—(See Inflammation).

Injuries; Insanity—(See "Violent" under Insanity).

Involuntary — (See "Contractions" in this section).

Iron—Or Steel—Hurts By—(See Iron).

Journeys—(See "Accidents" under Journeys).

Kicks; Killed; Libidinous — Violently Libidinous—(See Lewd, Virile).

Lightning; Lunatics — (See "Violent" under Insanity).

Lust; Lynching; Machinery; Maladies —(See "Violent" under Disease).

Man — Death by Hand of Man — (See Man).

Mania—(See "Violent" under Mania).

Manners—(See "Violent" under Manner).

Marriage Partner — (See "Violent Death" under Marriage Partner).

Men — Men Become Violent In Sex Gratification — (See "Violent" under Men; "Violence" under Passion; Shameless).

Mob Violence—(See Mobs).

Murder; Nature—A Violent Nature— (See "Given To", "Tendency To", in this section; Cruel; "Shows No Pity" under Pity; "High Temper" under Temper; Vicious).

Outbreaks of Violence — Generally — ♄ ♅ ♂, direct in motion and angular at the Vernal Equinox; ♂ in the 7th H. at a Solstice and Ingresses into ♋ or ♑.

Pains—(See "Violent" under Pain).

Palpitation—Violent—(See "Palpitation" under Heart).

Parents—Violent Death of—(See "Violent" under Parents).

Passion—(See "Violence" under Passion).

Perspiration — (See "Violent" under Sweat).

Planets — The Violent Planets — The Malefics, ♅, ♅, ♄, ♂.

Poison Death—(See Poison).

Prevalent—Violence Prevalent—(See Crime, Highwaymen, Pirates, Prevalent, Rapine, Robbers, Thieves).

Prison—(See "Beaten", "Injured", under Prison).

Public — (See "Public Death" under Public).

Quadrupeds; Quarrels; Railroads;

Rains—Violent Rains—(See Rain).

Rash; Reformers; Remarkable;

Reptiles; Riots; Robbers; Savage;

Scalds; Sex Passion—(See "Violence" under Passion).

Shedding of Blood—(See "Shedding" under Blood).

Shocks; Sicknesses — (See "Violent" under Disease, Sickness).

Signs—Violent Signs—♈, ♏, ♑.

Slaughter; Stabs; Stars — (See "Violent" under Stars).

Stings; Stones — (See "Assaults" under Stone).

Strangulation; Sudden — (See "Chances", "Death", "Diseases", "Hurts", "Severe", "Wounds", "Violent", and other paragraphs under Sudden).

Suffers from Violence — The ☉ hyleg, ruler of the 10th H., and to the ♂ or ill-asp. ♄, and espec. if an eclipse fall on the ♂ of the ☉ with ♄ by dir., and generally of a public nature; the evil directions of ♂ to the ☉, ☽, Asc., or hyleg, if ♂ be afflicted and strong at B. (See the various paragraphs in this section).

Suffocation; Suicide; Sweating—(See "Violent" under Sweat).

Swift; Sword; Temper—(See Furious, Temper).

Tendency to Violence—The ☉ and ♂ in the 1st H., in fiery or airy signs; the ☉ or ☽ to the ♂ or ill-asp. ♂ by dir., and ♂ affl. at B.; ☉ Sig. □, ☍ ♂; the ☉ in bestial or violent signs, and afflicted by malefics; ☽ applying to ♂, or conjoined with him in a nocturnal nativity; ☽ to the place of Medusa; ☽ sepr. from the ☉ and applying to ♂ in a nocturnal geniture; ☽ Sig. ☌ ☉; ♅ by transit ☌ the radical ♂; ♄ to the ill-asps. ♂ by dir.; ♄ Sig. in ♍, one who undertakes violent and dangerous actions; ♃ Sig. in ♊, with the Bull's North Horn, rash and violent; ♃ Sig. ☐, 8 ♂ at B.; ♂ and ☿ together lords of the employment, and with ♂ stronger; ♂ ♃, and to the cusp the 11th H. by dir; the evil asps. of ♂ to the Significators; ♂ ill-dig. at B., and affl.; ♂ Sig. ☐, 8 ☉; ♂ to the ill-asps. ♄ by dir.; ♂ in evil asp. ☿; ♂ to the ill-asps. ☿ by dir.; ♂ by tr. thru the Asc. or M.C. if in these houses at B.; ☿ ☌, ☐, 8 ♂; ☿ affl. by ♅ or ♂, and espec. when ☿ is in the 12th H.; ☿ Sig. ☐ or 8 ♂; the ♈ sign when affl. by malefics tends to give an angry disposition, and as violent as the Ram; 8 on the Asc., and afflicted, violent and furious as the Bull when provoked; the M.C. to Algol or Hydra's Heart. (See Algol, Anarchists, Anger, Dangerous, Destructiveness, Fierce, Fury, Impulses; "A Murderer" under Murder; "Poisoner" under Poison; Profane, Rapacious, Rashness, Ravenous, Raving, Recklessness, Savage; "High Temper" under Temper; Vicious; "Becomes Violent", "Passion", and the various paragraphs in this section).

Thieves; Tragical; Trampled; Travel — Meets with Violence During — (See "Hurts", "Injuries", and the various paragraphs under Travel).

Untimely; Vehement; Vehicles; Vicious; Violent Death—(See "Death" in this section).

War; Wild; Wounds.

VIOLET COLOR — Violet Rays — (See "Planets and Color", "Vibration", under Colors).

VIRGIN'S SPICA—(See Arista).

VIRGO — The sixth Sign of the Zodiac, and the second of the Common, or Mutable Signs. Ruled by ☿. This sign is affiliated with the 6th House, and is the sign which rules principally over Health Matters, Diet, Hygiene, Sanitation, and also over Servants, Small Animals, etc. (See Sixth House). This Sign is classed as a cold, dry, barren, earthy, feminine, common, mutable, nocturnal, mental, human, speaking, critical, melancholic, unfortunate, petulant, estival, northern, changeable, nervous, commanding sign, and a sign of long ascension. It is especially associated with the Bowels, Duodenum, Jejunum, Ileum, and Chylification. (See "Organic Functions" under Functions). Its functions are Assimilation, Absorption, Selection and Utilization of food products. The sign is commonly spoken of as the "Virgin Sign", and is considered a sign of great virtue and chastity. The Symbol of this sign is a Virgin. It is identified with Argo, the Ship, and with Zebulon, one of the sons of Jacob, of whom it was written in Scripture that he "Shall be a Haven for Ships". Being the sign of Health, the natives of this sign tend to center

their minds much upon matters of health, diet, and disease, and even to court disease, and to give up more easily to disease, being a negative and susceptible sign. (See Mutable, Negative). They tend to take on the disease conditions of others, and for this reason should not be Physicians or Nurses. They often become chronic invalids, and imagine they have all kinds of diseases, and Healers, in dealing with them should avoid any adverse suggestions about their health, or impending crisis, as they are greatly weakened by fear. This sign acts strongly upon the mind and digestive organs. As a class, they seem to enjoy bad health, and to be always looking for sympathy, and to tell others of their many diseases. Simulation of disease is also a ♍ trait. (See "Unfortunate" under Healers). However, the ♍ people, as a class, should enjoy good health, if they will think properly, and it is said of them that they should never take medicines, and especially physics, as their bowels are more tender and susceptible to drugs. (See Eczema). When once sick, and in the grasp of disease, and poor thinking, they are usually very difficult to treat, or to see a cure effected. They should early be taught to think in terms of health, and not in terms of disease, and also to obey the laws of health. Virgo is said to be the most critical of all the Signs, and people born under ♍, with ♍ rising, or the ☉, ☽, and ☿ in this sign, are much given to criticism, fault-finding, and intolerance of the views and opinions of others, which often tends to adversely affect the health thru worry, fretfulness, and peevishness. This sign gives very thin, delicate and tender skin. The Colors ruled by this sign are Amber, Black or Brown Spotted with Blue. The Qualities of this sign are as follows—Barrenness, Changeableness, Chastity, Cold, Commanding, Common, Critical, Dry, Earthy, Fault-Finding, Feminine, Human, Intolerant, Long Ascension (one of the Signs of); Melancholy, Mental, Mutable, Negative, Nocturnal, Northern, Receptive, Selfishness, Speaking, Summer (a Summer Sign); Susceptibility, Unfortunate, Unsympathetic, Vituperative, etc.

VIRGO RULES — See the following subjects in the alphabetical arrangement — Abdomen, Abdominal Organs and Region; Absorption of Nourishment, Amber Color, Assimilation, Belly, Black Color speckled with Blue; Carpus Bones, Chastity; Chyle, Chylification, Chylopoiesis; Colors — Black spotted with Blue; Criticism, Diaphragm, Diet, Dorsal Nerves (the lower Dorsal); Duodenum; Externally ♍ rules the Abdominal Region, the Umbilicus and Hands; Food; Gastro-Abdominal System; Generative Organs, and especially when there is a malefic afflicted in this sign, and in the 6th House; Hands; Hygiene; Ileum; Internally ♍ rules the Bowels, Pyloris, Spleen, Solar Plexus, Duodenum, Jejunum, Ileum, Small Intestines, Mesenteric Glands, the Assimilative System; Intestinal Canal, Intestines—the Large and Small Intestines; Jejunum; Large Intestines; Liver (Lower Lobes of); Mesentery; Mesenteric Glands; Metacarpus; Nails; Nerves (the Lower Dorsal); Nutrition; Nux Vomica; Pancreas; Peristaltic Action of the Bowels; Peritoneum; Portal Veins; Potassium Sulphate Salt; Pylorus; Sanitation; Satire; Selection of Food; Selfishness; Servants; Sixth House (affiliated with); Small Animals; Small Intestines; Solar Plexus; Spine (part back of the ♍ Region); Spleen; Stone in Body; Sympathetic Nervous System; Umbilical Region (Externally); Uterus; Utilization of Food; Veins (Vena Portae); Virginity; Womb.

VIRGO DISEASES—Diseases and Afflictions of Virgo—The ☉ well-aspected in ♍ tends to natural habits. The ☽ is not as strong in ♍, and afflicted in this sign tends to digestive disorders, and irregularities of the bowels, and of the intestinal functions. See the following subjects in the alphabetical arrangement when only listed here—

Abdomen—Diseases and Injuries of—(See Abdomen).

Appendicitis; Assimilation—Disorders of—(See Assimilation).

Barrenness; Belly—Any Disease In—(See Belly).

Bowels — All Diseases, Disorders and Injuries of—(See Bowels).

Catarrh of Bowels — (See "Catarrh" under Bowels).

Cholera; Chronic Invalids — (See Invalids).

Chyle—Disorders of—(See Chyle).

Colic; Constipation; Cramps; Croakings — (See "Croakings" under Bowels).

Diarrhoea; Digestion—Digestive Disorders — Intestinal Indigestion — (See Digestion, Indigestion).

Dysentery; Enteralgia — Pain In the Bowels — (See "Enteralgia", "Pain", under Bowels).

Enteric Fever — (See "Fever" under Bowels. Also see Typhoid).

Flatulence; Functions — Irregular Bowel Functions—(See "Irregular" under Bowels; "Organic" under Functions).

Generative Organs — Disorders of — (See the Introduction under Generation).

Hernia; Ileac Passion; Indigestion — Intestinal—(See Indigestion).

Infirmities—All Infirmities In the Intestines — (See "All Diseases" under Bowels).

Injuries—To Abdomen and Intestines — (See "Injuries" under Abdomen, Bowels).

Intestines — All Disorders In — (See "All Diseases" under Bowels).

Invalids—Chronic Invalids—(See Invalids).

Irregular Bowels — (See "Irregular" under Bowels).

Malnutrition; Melancholia; Neuralgia — Of Intestines — (See "Pain" under Bowels).

Obstructions In Bowels — (See "Obstructions" under Bowels).

Peritonitis—(See Peritoneum).

Simulation of Disease—A ♍ trait.

Spleen—Disorders of—(See Spleen).

Sterility—(See Barrenness).

Tapeworm; Testicles — Infirmities In —(See Testes).

Treatment — Of ♍ Diseases — (See Enema).

Tympanites; Typhoid; Wind In Bowels —(See "Colic" under Bowels; Colic, Wind).

Womb Disorders—(See Womb).

Worms—(See Cestode, Tinea, Worms).

VIRILE MEMBERS — Excessive Virile Members — Excessive In Males, and Hermaphrodites In Females — The ☉ and ☽ both in masculine signs, and configurated together, and both configurated with ♂ and ♀ in any way, males then born will have excessive virile members, and females be quite, or nearly, Hermaphrodites. If ♂ and ♀ be also in masculine signs, males will have a mixture of sex, and females be violently libidinous. If ♀ only be in a masculine sign, they will conceal their desires, and be more discreet. (See Eunuchs, Hermaphrodites, Lewd, Nymphomania).

VIRTUE—Virtuous—Chaste—

Females Virtuous—(See "Chaste" under Females; Honest; "Good" under Morals; "Popular" under Reputation; Sincere).

Void of Virtue—(See Harlots, Imprudent; "Adultery", "Liaisons", under Love Affairs; "Low and Base" under Low; Shameless, Unchaste; "Unchaste" under Women).

VIRULENT—Noxious—Malignant—(See Fatal, Malignant, Noxious, Poisonous).

VIRUS—A Morbid Product—A Pathogenic Microbe—

Pestilential Virus — (See "Virus" under Pestilence. Also see "Death" under Animals, Cattle, Fish, Fowls, Horses; Contagions, Eclipses, Epidemics; "Scarcity" under Fruit; Infections, Microbes, etc.).

VIS CONSERVATRIX — The Healing Powers of Nature — Are ruled by the ☉, ♂, ♃, and ♀. (See Absorption, Cleansing, Conservation, Cure, Defensive, Phagocytes, Preservation, Recuperation, Resistance, Restoration; "Good" under Vitality, etc.).

VISAGE — The Face — Countenance — Look — Expression—Aspect, etc.—This subject is mostly considered in the Article on Face. (See Appearance, Aspect, Cheeks, Chin, Complexion, Countenance, Cruel, Ears, Expression, Eyebrows, Eyes, Face, Forehead, Glances, Hair, Jaws, Lips, Look, Mouth, Nose, Pleasant, Profile, Smiling, Teeth, Temples, etc.).

VISCERA — The Contents of the Body Cavities—Splanchnic—Splanchnic Ganglia—♃ rules all the Viscera, and all diseases seated in these parts.

Death — By Some Obstruction In — (See "Obstruction" in this section).

Obstruction—Death by Some Obstruction In—Denoted by the ☉.

Prolapse Of — Splanchnoptosis — Relaxation of the Viscera—♅ and ♀ influence. (See Prolapse, Relaxation).

VISCUS — Organs Enclosed within the Cavities of the Body, as in the Cranium, Thorax, Abdomen, Pelvis, etc.— (See Abdomen, Bowels, Brain, Chest, Heart, Kidneys, Lungs, Pelvis, Stomach, Thorax, etc.).

Prolapse of a Viscus—(See Hernia).

VISION — Sight — Eyesight — The Sense of Vision—The Disorders of Vision are listed in the Article on Sight. See such subjects as Dim Vision, Double Vision, Feeble, Keen Vision, Night Vision, Old Age Vision, One-Half Vision, Painful Vision, Weak Vision, and the various paragraphs under Sight. Also see Accommodation, Blindness, Eyes.

VISIONS—Visionary—

A Dreamy Mind—(See "Dreamy Mind" under Dreams; "Visionary" in this section).

Hanging — Haunted by Visions of Hanging — (See "Fears of Hanging" under Hanging).

Visionary Mind — ♅ affl. at B.; ♅ affl. in ♊, or in the 1st, 9th, or 10th H. (See Chaotic, Concentration, Confusion; "Dreamy Mind" under Dreams; "Mind" under Erratic; Fancies; "Impractical" under Ideals; Imaginations, Vacillating, Vagaries, etc.).

Visions — Tendency to Visions — Visions are ruled by ♅ and the 9th H., and ♅ in one of the Houses of Mind, as in the 3rd or 9th H., tends to visions, and unusual psychic, clairvoyant, and mediumistic faculties; ♅ ✳ or △ ☽, prophetic visions; ♅ ✳, △ ♅, ♃, ☽; ♅ affl. in ♐, visions of distress; ♅ by tr. ☌ ☽ or ☿ in radical map; ♅ to the ☌, □ or ☍ Antares, may have visions, or hear spirit voices; the ☽ in the 9th H., and aspected by ♅; ☽ in ♒ and well-asp. by ☊; the Pr. ☽ ☌, P., □, ☍ the radical ♅ if ♅ affl. at B.; ♅ ♐; ♅ ✳ or △ ♅, prophetic and inspirational nature; ♄ in the 9th H., and well-asp. by the ☽; the 3rd Dec. of ♒ on the Asc., ruled by the ☽. (See Clairvoyance, Delirium, Delusions, Demoniac, Dreams, Fancies, Fears, Forebodings, Hallucinations, Ideals, Ideas, Illusions, Imagination, Insanity, Intuition, Mediumship, Mind, Neptune, Ninth House, Notions, Obsessions, Premonitions, Prophetic, Psychic, Religion; "Sensitiveness" under Sensitive; "Nightmare" under Sleep; Spirit Controls, Third House, Vagaries, etc.).

VITAL — Vital Force — Vital Power — Vital Fluid—Vital Centers—Solar Life Currents — Pertaining to Life—Vitality, etc. — The subject of Vitality is considered in the next Article after this one. The ☉ is Vital, and stands at the head of the Vital Group. (See "Vital" under Sun). The ☉ rules the Vital Force, the Vital Body, the Vital Fluid, and has affinity with the Vital Centers in the body. The Vital Fluid in the Nerves is ruled by ☿. The Fixed Signs are Vital in Temperament. (See "Fixed Signs" under Fixed). The following subjects have to do with the Vital Power, Vital Force, etc.

Activity—Lowered Vital Activity—It

is lowered by ♄, and affecting the part ruled by the sign he is in at B., or in by Dir. or Tr. (See Activity; "Lowered" under Vitality).

Adynamia — Asthenia — Loss of Vital Power — (See Adynamia, Asthenia; "Lessened" under Vitality; "Weak Body" under Weak).

Asthenia — (See "Adynamia" in this section).

Augmented — The Vital Forces Augmented—The ☉ ✳ or △ ☽, ♅ or ♂. (See Vitality).

Body—The Vital Body—Ruled by the ☉. The ☉ affl. at B. tends to diseases of the Vital Body. The Vital Body is one of Man's finer vehicles, and is made of Ether, and interpenetrates the physical body. The Blood and the Glands are the special manifestation of the Vital Body, and its function is to build up and restore the tone of the body when it is tired and worn thru its activities and from the emotions of the mind. (See Astral Body, Childhood, Desire Body).

Centres — The Vital Centres in the Star Map are the ☉, ☽, Asc., and Hyleg, and the ☉, ☽, or Asc. are usually taken as the Hyleg, or Life Giver, according to their strength, power, and aspects at B. (See Hyleg). The ☉ has special affinity with the Vital Centers. (See "Centers" under Nerves; Solar, Sun).

Currents — (See "Solar" in this section).

Deficiency — Of Vital Power — Vital Forces Depleted—Loss of Vital Power —The ☽ to the ☌ or ill-asps. ♅ by dir.; the circulation of the vital forces to the different organs is lowered and impeded by ♄, and that part suffers which is ruled by the sign containing ♄ at B., or temporarily by dir. or tr. (See Depletion, Lowered, Waste, Weak, in this section).

Depletion — Of the Vital Fluid and Vital Forces — Depletion of the Nerve Force—The evil asps. of the ☉ and ☽ to each other tend to deplete and lower the vital powers and forces, and also to disturb the organic functions ruled by the ☽; caused by the ☉ □ or ☍ ☽; ♅ □ or ☍ Asc. (See Energy, Vitality; "Deficiency" in this section).

Diminished — The Vital Solar Life Currents Diminished—The ☉ ☌ ♄ at B., and the ☉ affl. by ♄ by dir. (See Diminished).

Diseases—Vital Diseases—In all Vital Diseases the influence of the ☉ at B., and all afflictions to the ☉ by dir., should be carefully studied, to give a proper judgment, diagnosis, and prognosis upon the case, and the part of the body most afflicted.

Ears—Vital Fluid Lacking In—(See "Circulation" under Ears; Hearing).

Energy—Vital Power—Vital Heat— Vital Energy is connected with the ♓ Sign, and with Iron Phosphate, the ♓ Sign Salt. (See "Iron Phosphate" under Iron). For Increase of the Vital Energy, see "Augmented", "Force", in this section. For Decrease of, see Depletion, Diminished, Fluid, Nerves, in this section; "Lessened" under Vitality.

Etheric Fluid—The Vital Etheric Fluid—(See "Fluid" in this section).

Face—The Vital Type Face—(See Decanates).

Flow—The Vital Flow Along the Nerves Obstructed—(See "Vital Flow" under Nerves).

Fluid—The Vital Fluid—Prana—Vital Force—Nerve Force—Vital Etheric Fluid—The Vital Fluid is ruled by the ☉, and is made up of the Solar Force. It is concentrated and drawn in thru the Spleen, and passes from there to the Solar Plexus, and is distributed over the body. (See "Solar Plexus" under Plexus; Spleen). It is an invisible, rose-colored fluid, the vitalizing force of the body, and corresponds to the electric current going over the wires. Obstruction of this flow results in disease and disturbed functions. The Vital Fluid which flows in the Nerve Sheath is ruled by ☿. This flow of the Solar Life Currents is obstructed and diminished when the ☉ is afflicted by ♄; the ☉ ☌ ♄; the ☉ affl. by any of the malefics at B., and by dir.; the ☉ affl. in the 6th H.; ♆ in the Asc., or □ or ☍ the Asc., tends to a wasting away, depletion, escape of, loss of, or sapping of the Vital Fluids, causing premature decay, wrinkling, etc. (See the various paragraphs in this section. Also see Blood, Creative, Ears, Energy, Force; "Obstructed" under Nerves, Spine; Power, Prana, Semen; "Force" under Sex; Wrinkles).

Force—Vital Force—Vital Power—Prana—Nerve Force—Life Force—The ☉ rules the Vital Force, or the Prana, as it is called in the Hindu Philosophy. (See "Life Force" under Force; Prana). Also the planet Mars aids the Sun in giving Life Force, Energy, Zest, and Zeal to Humanity. (See Mars). The Sun Group of Plants also act on the Vital Force. (See "Sun Group" under Herbs). Plenty of Vital Force is given when the ☉ is in ♈, ♌ or ♏, and with females when the ☽ is hyleg in ♌. Aries on the Asc., and ♂ in ♈ in the Asc., tends to an excess of Life Force, and to augmented Vital Powers. These Powers are also augmented and increased, and with a superabundance of Vital Energy, when the planets ♅ and ♂ are in ⚹ or △ asp. to the ☉, and espec. when the ☉ is in a fiery sign, or with such a sign upon the Asc. (See Augmented, Depleted, Fluid, Power, and the various paragraphs in this section).

Full—The Vital Powers and the Constitution are at their full, and greatest, when the ☉ is above the horizon at B., and espec. when the ☉ is rising in the East in the 1st or 10th H., or when in the 7th H., and in a Hylegiacal Place. (See "Good" under Recuperation, Resistance, Stamina, Tone, Vitality). The next strongest Vital Powers are given when the ☉ is in the 9th or 11th H., and the weakest when in the 4th, 6th, 8th, or 12th H., and afflicted.

Functions—The Vital Functions Suspended—(See "Vital Functions" under Functions).

Greatest—Vital Powers Greatest—(See "Full" in this section).

Heat—Vital Heat—Given when ♂ is in any asp. to the ☉ or ☽. Is also connected with the fiery signs, ♈, ♌, and ♐, and with these signs upon the Asc. at B. The ☉ and ♂ are the fiery, hot, and electric planets, and supply vital heat to the body. (See Electric; "Fire Signs" under Fire; "Energy" in this section).

Inhibition—Of Vital Power—♄ influence. (See Inhibition; Diminished, Depletion, in this section).

Iron Phosphate—The Vital Salt—Ruled by the ♓ Sign. (See Iron).

Knot—The Vital Knot—(See Pons Varolii).

Loss of Vital Power—(See Adynamia, Deficient, Depletion, Fluid, Force, Lowered, Obstructed, in this section).

Lowered—Vital Force Lowered—(See Activity, Depletion, Force, Loss Of, and the various paragraphs in this section).

Lowering—(See Depletion, Loss Of, in this section).

Lowest—(See "Lowest" under Vitality).

Medium Vital Power—The ☉ in the 9th or 11th H. at B. (See "Full" in this section).

Nerves—The Vital Fluid of the Nerves is ruled by ☿. The Vital Flow along the nerves is obstructed when the ☉ is affl. at B., and espec. when in ☌ ♄. (See Inhibition, Obstructed, in this section).

Obstructed—The Vital Forces and Vital Flow Obstructed—(See Fluid, Inhibition, Loss Of, Nerves, in this section).

Organs—The Vital Organs—(See Organs).

Part—The Most Vital Part of the Body—The Rising Sign, the Sign on the Eastern horizon at B., indicates the most vital and sensitive part of the body. (See "Weak Parts" under Parts; "Organs" under Sensitive; Vulnerable).

Perversion—Of the Vital Stimulus—(See "Stimulus" in this section).

Plenty—Of Vital Force—(See "Force" in this section).

Pons Varolii—The Vital Knot—(See Pons).

Power—The Vital Power—The ☉ and ♌ signify Vital Power. (See Augmented, Depletion, Diminished, Fluid, Force, Full, Heat, Loss Of, Obstructed, and the various paragraphs in this section; Vitality).

Prana—The Hindu Term for Vital Power and Vital Force—(See Prana).

Principle—The Vital Principle—Ruled by the ☉. The diseases of the body act upon the Mind thru the Vital Principle, and also the diseases of the mind act upon the body thru the same medium. This occurs largely thru the 6th House, known as the house of health, and ruled by ☿, a mental ruler, and it is thru this house that matter acts upon mind, and mind upon matter, thus tending in the unenlightened, and the unawakened native to generate diseases of both the mind and body. (See "Action of Mind" under Mind; Sixth House).

Processes — The Vital Processes of the body are ruled by the ☉, the Giver of Life, and are largely kept up by the power of the ☉, and aided by ♂ in giving iron and haemoglobin to the blood for fuel. The Vital Processes tend to be arrested when ♄, ♍, or ♆ are upon the Asc. at B., and thru fear of disease. (See "Disease" under Fear).

Salt—The Vital Salt—Iron Phosphate, the ♓ Salt. (See "Energy" in this section).

Signs—The Vital Signs of the Zodiac —The Fiery and Airy Signs, and also ♄ and ♏ are among the most vital of the signs when upon the Asc. at B., and well-aspected. The Fixed Signs are vital in temperament.

Solar — Solar Vital Life Currents — (See "Fluid" in this section; Solar).

Spark — The Vital Spark of Life is maintained by the ☉ and ♂, the ☉ as life-giver, and ♂ as giver of the iron and haemoglobin.

Spine — The Vital Flow Obstructed Through — (See "Obstruction" under Spine).

Spirit—The Vital Spirit in Women is ruled by the ☉, and denotes Hysterics. (See Hysteria).

Spleen—The Vital Fluid, ruled by the ☉, is drawn in thru the Spleen. (See Spleen).

Stamina—Vital Stamina—(See Stamina).

Stimulus — Perversion of the Vital Stimulus—A General Action of the ♃ Group of Herbs and Plants. (See "Jupiter Group" under Herbs).

Strength—The Vital Strength—(See Strength).

Sun—The ☉ is vital, and the source of Vital Power. (See Sun).

Superabundance — Of Vital Energy— (See Augmented, Energy, Force, in this section; "Excess", "Superabundance", under Vitality).

Suspended—The Vital Functions Suspended — (See "Suppressed" under Functions; "Processes" in this section).

Temperament — The Vital Temperament — When ♀ is strong at B., the Vital Temperament abounds; ♀ in the 1st H. (See Decanates; "Fixed Signs" under Fixed; the Introduction under Life; Temperament).

Tonicity—Vital Tonicity—(See Stamina, Tone, Vitality).

Vital Body—(See "Body" in this section).

Vital Type — Of Temperament — (See "Temperament" in this section).

Vitality—(See Vitality).

Waste — Of the Vital Force — The ☉ affl. in weak signs; the ☽ to the ill-asps. ♆ by dir.; the 1st Dec. of ♌ on the Asc., ruled by ♄; ♄ affl. in ♒; ♀ diseases. (See Adynamia, Depletion, Fluid, in this section; Debauched, Dissipated; "Passional Excesses" under Passion; "Wasted" under Vitality).

Weak Vital Powers—(See "Depleted" in this section; Impotent, Sickly; "Low", "Weak", under Vitality; "Weak Body" under Weak).

Weakened Vital Power—(See Activity, Adynamia, Depletion, Fluid, Force, Power, in this section; "Weakened" under Vitality).

Weaker — The Vital Powers tend to be weaker when the ☉ is in the 8th or 12th H.

Weakest—The Vital Powers are weakest when the ☉ is on the cusp of the 4th H. at B. (See Fourth House, Nadir).

VITALITY—Vital Tonicity—Vital Power —The Vital Principle of Life—Strength — Energy — The ☉ rules the Vitality, and is the source of vital energy. The Solar Force focussed thru the ☽ gives vitality. The less the ☉ is afflicted at B., the greater is the vitality. The ☉ is vitalizing, and concerns itself with the vitality in the human frame. The ☉ rules the vitality in both sexes. The vitality is governed by the aspects and position of the ☉. The vitality is not weakened by functional disorders and derangements when there is no aspect between the ☉ and ☽ at B. The following paragraphs have to do with the Vitality—See these subjects in the alphabetical arrangement when not considered here.

Abundance—Of Vitality—(See "Good", "Superabundance", in this section).

Active; Adynamia — Loss of Vital Power—(See Adynamia).

Amorous Indulgence—Vitality Sapped By—(See Amorous).

Arrested — (See "Lessened" in this section).

Ascendant—A Vital Center—(See Ascendant, First House).

Asthenia—Loss of Vital Power—(See Asthenia).

Atony — Low Vitality — (See Atony; "Low" in this section).

Augmented Vitality — A Morbid Plus Condition—A ☉ disease. In a normal way the vitality is increased and augmented when the ☉ at B. is well-asp. by ♅ and ♂. (See Excess, Good, Increased, Superabundance, in this section).

Bad Vitality—(See "Low" in this section).

Benefitted — (See Augmented, Good, Increased, in this section).

Better — The Vitality Better — The ☉ in ♈ or ♌; born in the increase of the ☽; fiery signs upon the Asc.; the majority of planets rising and elevated at B. (See "Increased" in this section).

Children — Vitality Bad In — (See "Sickly" under Children; "Early Years" under Early; "Vitality", "Weak", under Infancy).

Considerable Vitality — (See "Females", "Good", "Males", in this section).

Constitution Good—(See Constitution; "Good Health" under Health; "Body" under Strong).

Degree of Vitality — Of Physical Strength—Is largely determined by the rising sign in both sexes. (See Degree).

Depletion—Of the Vitality—Sapped— Undermined — (See "Lessened", "Wasted", in this section; Amorous; "Depletion" under Vital).

Devitalization—A ♄ disease. (See "Lessened" in this section).

Dissipation Of—(See "Wasted" in this section).

Dynamic Energy—(See Dynamic)

Early Death—(See Early).

Easily Weakened—By Illness or Excesses—The ☉ affl. by the ☽, ♄ and malefics at B.; the ☽ hyleg in ♍, and afflicted with females. (See Lessened, Low, Wasted, in this section).

Endurance; Energy—Vital Energy—(See Dynamic, Electric, Energy).

Excess of Vitality—A Morbid or Plus Condition—The ☉ □ or ☍ ♂, and tending to increased excitability and nervousness. (See "Augmented" in this section).

Excesses—Loss of Vitality By—(See Amorous; "Health Injured" under Men; "Health Suffers" under Opposite Sex; "Easily Weakened" in this section).

Fair Vitality—(See "Medium" in this section).

Females — (See "Vitality In" under Females; "Low", "Not Very Strong", in this section).

Force — Plenty of Vital Force — (See "Force" under Vital).

Good Vitality—Abundance—Considerable—Plenty—Fullness of—Much Vitality—Strong Vitality—The ☉ in the Asc., M.C., or 7th H. at B., and hyleg; the ☉ ✶ or △ ♄ at B., good tenacity of life; the ☉ ☌ and good asp. ♂ at B.; the ☉ in a fiery sign, and espec. in ♈ or ♌; the ☉ in airy signs, but of more refined and mental nature than physical; the ☉ ☌ ♃ or ♀ in the Asc. at sunrise; the ☉ or ♂ in the Asc., and well-asp.; the ☉ rising in ♌ and not affl.; the ☉ ☌ or good asp. ♃; the ☉ in ♉ or ♏ in the Asc. at sunrise and not affl.; the ☉ ✶ or △ ♃ at B., and the ☉ hyleg; the ☉ well-asp. in ♐ if the hyleg is not affl.; the ☉ or ☽ in good asp. ♂ at B., and by dir.; the ☉ strong by sign at B.; the ☉ well-asp. by ♂, ☽, or the benefics at B., and the ☉ essentially dignified, as exalted or elevated, in a male horoscope, and the ☽ similarly placed in a female nativity; the ☉ in ♈, plenty of vital force; the ☉ in ♌, and with ♈ on the Asc.; the ☉ above the horizon at B. gives the greatest vital power, and when in the 1st, 10th, or 7th houses, and the constitution and the vital powers are at their full when the ☉ at B. is in one of these places, a hylegiacal place, and the ☉ hyleg; the ☽ ✶ or △ ♂ at B., and by dir.; the ☽ to the good asps. the ☉, ♃, ♂ or ♀ by dir.; the Pr. ☽ ✶ or △ ♂ if ♂ is well-asp. at B.; the ☽ hyleg in ♉, ♋, ♌, ♎, or ♐ with females; ♃ in ♌, rising and well-asp., abundance of vitality; ♃ ascending at B., and in good asp. the ☉ and ☽); ♃ and ♀ both rising, and in good asp. the ☉ and ☽; ♂ ✶ △ the ☉ or ☽; ♂ ☌ ☉; ♂ in good asp. the ☉ at B., the spark of vitality is not easily put out; ♈, ♉, ♌, ♍, or ♐ on the Asc.; the 3rd face of ♐ on the Asc.; the 3° ♑ on the Asc.; the 6th face of ♒ on the Asc. (For additional influences along this line see "Good" under Constitution, Health, Recuperation, Resistance, Stamina, Tone; En-

durance, Hyleg, Immunity, Invigoration; "Long Life" under Life; Resources, Robust, Ruddy; "Little Sickness" under Sickness; "Increased" under Strength; "Body" under Strong; Vigor, etc.).

Hyleg; Immunity; Impaired;

Increased — The Vitality Increased — Benefitted—Augmented—Strengthened —The Health Improved—The Constitution Strengthened—The ☉ or ♂ in the 1st H., and well-asp.; the ☉ well-asp. in any sign; the ☉ rising in ♋; the ☉ rising and above the horizon in any sign; the ☉ ✶ or △ ☽; the ☉ ☌ or good asp. ♂; the ☉ and ☽ to the good asps. ♂ by dir.; the ☉ rising in ♍; the ☉, ☽, and planets above the horizon; the ☉ ☌ and good asp. ♃; ☉ ✶ or △ ♆, benefits the vitality and constitution psychically; good asps. to the ☉ in a male horo., and good asps. to the ☽ in a female horo.; ♃ in the Asc. increases the vitality and gives bulk to the body; ♂ ☌ and good asp. the ☉; ♂ in the 6th H., and well-asp.; ♂ Promittor to the good asps. the ☉ or ☽ by dir.; ♂ in good asp. the Asc., the system is invigorated; ♂ ☌ and good asp. ♃; the good asps. of ♃ and ♀ to the ☽; any asp. of the benefics, good or bad, to the hyleg at B. tend to strengthen the constitution rather than to weaken, but the good asps. are better. (See "Augmented", "Good", in this section; "Periods of Good Health" under Health; "Augmented", "Force", "Full", under Vital).

Infancy—Vitality Low In—(See "Vitality" under Infancy).

Invalids; Invigorated—(See Invigorated, Vigor).

Lack of Vitality—The ☉ ☌, □, ☍ ♄ at B.; ☉ ☌ ♄ in the 6th H.; ☉ □, ☍ ♄ at B.; ☉ in a weak sign and affl. by ♄; ♅ in ♑ or ♋ on the Asc.; ♄ affl. in the Asc. in a weak sign; ♄ the afflictor in disease and ♄ affl, the ☉, ☽, Asc. or hyleg at B.; ♃ □, ☍ ♄.; ruler of the Asc. in the 8th H. in a weak sign and afflicted. (See "Lessened", "Low", in this section; "Depletion", "Lowered", under Vital).

Large Body—Large and Strong—(See "Body" under Large, Strong).

Lessened—The Vitality Lessened— Lowered—Vitality Sapped—Wasted— Weakened—Impaired—Arrested—The ☉ in the 6th or 12th H., in a weak sign and affl.; the ☉ in the 6th H. ill-dig. and affl. by ♄ or ♂ at B.; the ☉ setting and below the horizon; the ☉, ☽ and many planets below the horizon at B.; the ☉ or ☽ hyleg, and to the ☌ or ill-asp. ♄ or ♂ by dir.; the ☽ affl. in 6th H., the vital forces depleted; the ☽ affl. in ♍, and hyleg with females; the ☽ to the ☌ or ill-asp. ♆ or ♄ by dir.; ♆, ♅, or ♄ in ♊, and affl. the ☉ or ☽; ♄ in 6th H. at B., and ☌ or ill-asp. the ☉ or ☽; ♄ ☌, P, □ or ☍ ☉; a ♄ disease, and ♄ affl. the ☉, ☽, Asc., or hyleg at B., and by dir.; a weak sign on the Asc. at B., and a malefic in the rising sign; ♀ ♍, ☌ ☽ or ♂, and thru sex excesses or abuses. (See Debauched, Depraved, Dissipation, Drink; "Wasted" under Energies; "Bad Habits" under Habits; Majority; "Health

Injured" under Men; "Health Suffers" under Opposite Sex; Excesses, Lack Of, Low, Wasted, Weakened, in this section).

Life Force—(1) Overabundance of—♈ on the Asc., and ♂ in ♈ in the Asc.; ♌ on the Asc. (See "Life Force" under Life; "Force" under Vital; Augmented, Excess, Superabundance, in this section). (2) Impeded and Obstructed — (See "Inhibition", "Obstructed", under Vital; Lessened, Low, Weakened, in this section).

Loss of Vitality — And Early Death From — (See "Early Death" under Early; "Easily Weakened", "Low", "Wasted", in this section).

Low Vitality — Weak Vitality — Poor Vitality—Vitality Bad—Weak Constitution—The Vitality Reduced—The ☉ or ☽ in the 6th H. in weak signs, and affl. by malefics; the ☉ in ♋, or ♋ on the Asc.; the ♋ person as a rule has the least vitality of any person; ♋, ♑, or ♓, the signs of low vitality, on the Asc.; the ☉ in ♑ and affl.; the ☉ affl. in the 1st, 4th, 6th, 8th or 12th houses; the ☉ in ♋ on the Nadir, and affl.; the ☉ ☌ ☽ if closer than three degrees; the ☉ affl. by ♄; the ☉ or ☽ to the ☌ or ill-asp. ♄ by dir.; the Pr. ☉ or ☽ to the ☌ or ill-asp. ♄ by dir.; the ☉ affl. in a sign of low vitality; the ☉ affl. in ♓, the vital powers are weak; the ☉ □, ☍ ☽, and at same time the hyleg affl. by malefics, and a weak sign on Asc.; the ☽ in bad asp. the ☉; the ☽ affl. in ♏; ☽ in 6th or 12th H., and affl. by malefics; the Pr. ☽ to the ☌ or ill-asps. ♅ if ♅ affl. at B.; the ☽ ♑, partile the Asc., never strong; the ☽ affl. in ♑; the ☽ hyleg in ♑ with females; ♄ ☌ or ill-asp. the ☉ or ☽; ♄ culminating and affl. the ☉ or ☽; ♄ by tr. in ☌ or bad asp. the ☉, ☽, ♃ or ♀; ♄ by dir. affl. the ☉, ☽, Asc. or hyleg; ♄ in the 6th H. and conjoined with the ☉; ♄ in evil asp. the ☉ from common signs; ♄ or ♂ affl. the ☉, ☽, or Asc. by body or asp.; ♄ in the 10th H., affl. the hyleg, and ♄ also rendered more evil by afflictions from ♅ and ♂; ♀ affl. in ♏; a weak sign on the Asc., and a malefic in the rising sign; bodies near the cusps of angles, and espec. in infancy; ♋ on the Asc. tends to give the least vitality unless containing the ☉ and benefics, and free from the affliction of malefics. (See Adynamia, Asthenia, Atonic; "Death" under Childhood, Children, Infancy, Middle Life, Youth; Consumptions, Debility; "Contracts Disease Easily" under Disease; "Early Death" under Early; Emaciation, Feeble; "Bad Health" under Health; "Offensive" under Humours; "Ill-Health All Thru Life" under Ill-Health; Infirm, Invalids; "Short Life" under Life; "Low" under Recuperation, Resistance, Stamina; Sickly; "Much Sickness" under Sickness; "Weakened" under Strength; "Lack Of" under Tone; Vitiated, Wasting; "Weak Body" under Weak).

Lowered Vitality — (See Lessened, Low, Wasted, Weakened, in this section; "Lowered" under Vital).

Lowest Vitality — The Vital Powers are at their lowest when the ☉ is on cusp the 4th H. at B., or in this house;

the ☉ affl. in ♑, or with ♋, ♑, or ♓ on the Asc. (See "Low" in this section).

Males Vigorous—(See "Good Health" under Males; "Good", "Not Very Strong", in this section).

Mars Influence—(See Mars).

Medium Vitality — Vitality Fair — Moderately Vital—Fairly Strong—The Moderately Vital Signs are ♉, ♊, ♍, ♒ and ♏, and these signs on the Asc. at B. usually bring the native to mature life. The 3° ♑ on the Asc. is the strongest of the ♑ degrees, and usually gives fair vitality and recuperative powers. The ☽ hyleg in ♊, ♒, or ♓ gives fair vitality, and espec. with females. Earthy signs on the Asc. are classed as of medium vitality; the fiery signs the strongest, and the watery signs the weakest, and espec. ♋ and ♓, but ♏ on the Asc. is strongly vital. (See "Tolerably Healthy" under Health).

Mental Vitality—With the ♊ sign, the sign of ☿, the vitality is more mental than physical. (See Gemini).

Morbid Vitality—The ☉ and ♄ in the 6th H. at B. tend to give a lowered and morbid vitality all thru life, much sickness, and with slow powers of recuperation. (See Morbid; Lessened, Loss Of, Low, in this section).

Nerve Force—(See "Nerve Force" under Force; "Fluid", "Force", under Vital).

Not Very Strong — The Vitality Not Very Strong—The ☉ affl. in signs of low vitality with males; the ☽ affl. in ♈ or ♏ with females. (See Females, Low, Males, Medium, in this section).

Over-Abundance—Of Vitality and Life Force—(See "Superabundance" in this section, and under Vital).

Periods — Of Increased Vitality, and of Lowered Vitality—(See "Improved", "Loss of Health", "Periods of Bad Health", "Periods of Good Health", under Health).

Physical Vitality — (See "Mental" in this section).

Plenty of Vitality—(See Good, Superabundance, in this section; "Force" under Vital).

Poor Vitality—(See Low, Weakened, in this section).

Powers — The Vital Powers — Read carefully all the paragraphs under "Vital", and in this section).

Prodigal Of — (See "Wasted" in this section).

Recovery; Recuperation; Reduced — The Vitality Reduced—The ☉ or ♄ in the 6th H. (See Low, Lessened, Wasted, in this section; "Depletion" under Vital).

Resistance; Restored—The ☉ restores vitality by day. (See Day).

Revitalization; Robust, Sapped—(See "Depletion", "Lessened", "Reduced", "Wasted", in this section).

Signs—The Vital Signs—(See "Signs" under Vital; "Medium" in this section).

Stamina; Sthenic; Strength;

Strengthened Vitality — (See "Increased" in this section).

Strong; Strong Vitality—(See "Good" in this section; "Body" under Strong).

Sun Influence—(See Sun).

Superabundance—Of Vitality—The ☉ ♂ ♂ in ♈, and with ♈ on the Asc., but tends to burn up the body faster, and danger of breakdown earlier in life; ☉ ♂, P, ⚹, △ ♂; ♌ on the Asc.

System Invigorated — (See Invigorated, Vigor).

Tone; Undermined Vitality — (See "Wasted" in this section; Debauched, Dissipation, Drink, Habits; "Passional Excesses" under Passion).

Vigorous Body—(See Robust; "Strong Body" under Strong; Vigor; "Good Vitality" in this section).

Vital Fluid—(See "Fluid" under Vital).

Vital Force—(See "Force" under Vital).

Vital Stamina—(See Stamina).

Vitality Low—(See "Low" in this section).

Vitiated; Wasted Vitality — Waste of the Vital Forces—The ☉ or ☽ in weak signs at B., and affl.; the ☽ to the ill-asps. ♀ by dir., prodigal of the vitality; the ☉ or ☽ affl. in the 5th, 6th, or 12th H., the vitality wasted thru dissipation; ♂ affl. in ♌ or the 5th H., waste of thru prodigality, and with the opposite sex; ♂ ♂ ♀ in ♍; the 1st decan. of ♌ on the Asc. (See Amorous, Conduct, Debauched, Dissipation, Drink; "Wasted" under Energy; Excesses, Gluttony, Habits, Narcotics; "Passional Excesses" under Passion; Prodigal; "Easily Weakened", "Lessened", in this section).

Weak Vitality — (See "Low" in this section).

Weakened Vitality—The ☉ affl. by the ☽, ♄, and malefics at B.; the ☉ or ♄ in the 6th H., and tend to give a weakened vitality all thru life; the ☽ affl. in ♑ lowers the vital tonicity thru worry and mental depression; the evil asps. between the ☉ and ☽ at B., and by dir. act as a disturbing and retarding agent upon the functions and vital forces; ♄ ♂, P, □, or 8 ☉. (See Depletion, Easily Weakened, Lessened, Low, Wasted, in this section; "Weakened" under Strength).

VITAMINES — (See "Vitamines" under Food).

VITIATED—In Mind and Body—♄ or ☋ in the Asc., and ♑ on the Asc.

Atmosphere — The Atmosphere Vitiated — (See "Corrupt Air" under Air; Cholera, Epidemics, Pestilence).

VITREOUS HUMOR — (See "Danger", "Muscae", "Vitreous", under Eyes).

VITUPERATIVE — (See Petulant, Sarcasm, Scolding; "Nasty Temper" under Temper; Virgo).

VIVACITY — Vivacious — Full of Life and Spirits—Lively—Active—(See Active, Buoyant; "Abundance" under Energy; "Full" under Expression; Lively, Quick, etc.).

VIVISECTIONISTS — Favored by Surgeons who have ♅ or ♂ in ♍ or ♓ at B., and these planets affl. each other; ☿ affl. by ♂, and with no good asps. from ♃ or ♀. (See Surgeons).

VOCAL ORGANS — Vocal Cords — The Voice—Larynx—Speech, etc.—This subject is considered in the Article on Voice. (See Voice. Also see Larynx, Speech).

VOCATION—The Business—The Occupation—The Employment—The Vocation—The Profession—Pursuits, etc.— The Vocation is ruled by the 10th H., and the Planets, or Planet in, or the ruler of this House, etc., determine the natural vocation, and where the native fits into the scheme of life. The indications of the 10th H. at B. show the natural Calling, and which, if the native follows it up, will tend to bring him success, happiness, and usefulness in life. For this reason every young person should have his, or her, horoscope cast early in life, to know what they are fitted for, and what the Higher Powers have ordained for them, so that they will not waste many years drifting, and trying to get into their right calling, after, perhaps, many failures and loss of time, effort and money. Many of the various Vocations are listed throughout this book, and the planetary influences which tend to bring success in them. See such subjects as Chemists, Healers, Nurses, Surgeons. Look in the alphabetical arrangement for the Vocation you have in mind. This subject is also considered in the Articles on Business, Employment, Occupation.

Accidents — In the Vocation — (See "Accidents" under Employment; Machinery, Pursuits).

Changes In—Makes Many Changes In Vocation — (See Changes, Instability, Restless, Unstable, Vacillating).

Death In — (See "Death" under Employment, Explosions, Machinery, Mines, Railroads).

Extraordinary Pursuits—Ruled by ♅; born under the strong influence of ♅, and with ♅ in the 10th H. (See Ideas; "Unusual" under Mental; Occult, Science, etc.).

Liquid Pursuits—Ruled and indicated by the ☽; many planets in watery signs at B., and espec. in the 10th H., or a watery sign upon the Asc.; the ♓ influence strong at B. (See "Pursuits" under Liquids).

Low Business — Follows Some Low Business—(See Crime, Gambling, Harlots, Highwaymen; "Low Business" under Low; Pettifogging, Robbers, Saloons, Taverns, Thieves, etc.).

Strange Diseases In — ♅ affl. in the 6th H. (See Occupation).

VOICE—The Voice—The Vocal Cords— The Larynx—Speech—The Vocal Organs, etc.—The Vocal Organs are ruled by ☿ and the ♉ sign. The larynx, as a whole, is ruled by ♉. The Vocal Cords are ruled by ☿, and ☿ rules the air which stirs the vocal cords into action. The vocal organs are also strongly ruled and influenced by the ♍ sign, as ♉ and ♍ are supplemental signs, and form a unit. The subjects concerning the Voice and Vocal Organs are also largely considered under Larynx, Speech, Tongue, and if the subject you have in mind is not listed here, look for it under these headings. The 2nd H., the house affiliated with ♉, also rules and influences the vocal organs, cords, voice, etc. Also influences in the 3rd H., the house of ☿, tend to influence and modify the speech and tones of the voice. See the following subjects in the alphabetical arrangement when not considered here—

Abused—The Voice Abused—(See "Injudicious" in this section).

Affections Of—(See "Disorders", and the various paragraphs in this section).

Aphasia—(See "Aphasia", "Loss of Speech" under Speech).

Aphonia—Loss of Voice—Whispering Voice—♅ or ☿ affl. in ♉; Subs at AT and LCP. (See "Hoarseness" under Larynx; Removal).

Articulation; Bass Voice—(See "Deep" in this section).

Beautiful Voice—(See "Melodious" in this section).

Breathing; Change of Voice—In Males At Puberty—(See Larynx, Puberty).

Clear Voice—The ☉ strong at B.; the ☉ well-asp. in ♉.

Coarse Voice — Rough — Strong — Coarse and Masculine Voice In Women — Contralto Voice — Afflictions in ♏, and due to debauchery or sex excesses; ♎ gives, and ♎ on the Asc.; ♍ on the Asc. The removal of any part of the sex organs in women tends to make the voice more masculine, and in men, more effeminate. (See Coarse, Deviations, Effeminate; "Hoarseness" under Larynx; "Deep" in this section).

Contralto Voice — (See Coarse, Deep, in this section).

Control — Tone and Voice Control — Largely influenced and controlled by the 16° of ♉ and ♏. (See "Fluency" under Speech; "Control" under Throat).

Cords — The Vocal Cords — Are ruled by the ♉ sign, and disorders of the Cords are caused by afflictions in ♉, and also by Subs at LCP (6C). (See Larynx; the various paragraphs in this section).

Cultivated Voice—Cultured—Refined — Pleasant — Given by ♒. (See Melodious, Musical, in this section).

Deep Voice — Bass Voice — ♄ in ♈ or ♉; ♏ influence, and espec. in women; ♎ on the Asc. tends to give a deep and strong voice. (See "Coarse" in this section).

Diaphragm; Disorders — Vocal Disorders—Afflictions in ♉; the ☽ hyleg in ♉ with females; ♅ affl. in ♉; ☿ affl. in ♉; afflictions to ☿; ☿ affl. in the 12th H. Cases—See Fig. 3F, 3G, in the book, "Astro-Diagnosis", by the Heindels. (See "Disorders" under Speech; the various paragraphs in this section).

Dumbness—Mutes—(See Dumb; "Deaf and Dumb" under Hearing; Mutes).

Effeminate Voice—Tenor Voice—(See Effeminate).

Expression—Good Voice Expression— ☿ well-placed in a sign of voice. (See Larynx; "Signs" in this section).

Females—Masculine, or Coarse Voice In—(See "Coarse" in this section).

Feminine Voice—In Males—(See Effeminate).

Fluency In Speaking—(See "Fluency" under Speech).

Functions — Functional Disability of the Vocal Cords—☿ in a weak sign and affl., and espec. affl. by ♄.

Gifted Vocally — ♀ or ☿ in ♉, or the 2nd H., and free from affl., or if a sign of voice be on the cusp of the 2nd, as ♉, ♎, or ♒, then the native tends to be eloquent, a great singer, or endowed with some special vocal gift. (See "Eloquent", "Fluency", under Speech).

Great Voice—Good Orator—Eloquent —☿ ascending in ♍ and well-asp.; ☿ in ♉ or ♍; ♀ Sig. in ♍, a linguist; ☿ Sig. in ♉, a good orator; ☿ in the Asc., and well-dig.; a sign of voice on the Asc.; ♀ Sig. in ♍, eloquent. (See "Gifted", "Strong", and other paragraphs in this section).

Hears Voices—(See Clairaudience).

Hoarseness — (See Hoarseness; "Hoarseness" under Larynx).

Inarticulate; Injudicious Use—Of the Voice In Speaking or Singing—Danger of Injury to the Voice — ☿ in ♉, and affl. by malefics, and loud singing or speaking should be avoided. (See "Singers" under Music).

Larynx—Afflictions of—(See Larynx).

Linguist — (See "Gifted", "Great Voice", in this section; "Eloquent", "Fluency", under Speech).

Loss of Voice—(See "Aphonia" in this section; Ablation, Hoarseness, Removal, Remote; "Loss of Speech" under Speech).

Loud Speaking — Should Be Avoided —(See "Injudicious" in this section).

Masculine Voice In Women—(See Effeminate; "Coarse" in this section).

Melodious Voice—Beautiful Voice—A Sweet Voice—Born under ♀; ♀ in the Asc.; ♀ in ♉ in the Asc., and ♂ ☿; ♉ influence, and with ♉ on the Asc. (See "Musical" in this section; "Music" under Singers).

Men — Effeminate Voice In — Tenor Voice—Deep Voice—(See Effeminate; "Deep" in this section).

Musical Voice—♀ in the Asc. near the horizon; ♀ well-asp. in ♍. The ♍ sign gives an unmusical voice. (See Melodious" in this section; "Singers" under Music).

Mutes—(See Dumb; "Deaf and Dumb" under Hearing; Mutes).

Orator — A Good Orator — (See Fluency; Gifted, Great Voice, in this section).

Organic Afflictions — Of the Vocal Cords—The ♉ or ♏ signs afflicted by malefics at B., or by tr., dir., or progression; the ☉ affl. in ♉ or ♏, as the ☉ is organic. (See Organic, Structural).

Over-Straining—Of the Vocal Cords— (See "Injudicious" in this section).

Paralysis—Of the Vocal Cords—♅ or ♄ affl. in ♉.

Phonation Difficult — (See "Hoarseness" under Larynx; "Aphonia" in this section).

Puberty—Voice Changes At Puberty—(See Larynx, Puberty).

Refined Voice — (See "Cultivated" in this section).

Resonant Voice—♏ influence.

Ringing and Sharp Voice — ♈ infl; ♈ on the Asc.

Rough Voice—♑ on the Asc. tends to a weak voice, and with a kind of a whistling roughness. (See "Coarse" in this section; Hoarseness; "Hoarseness" under Larynx).

Sharp and Ringing—Incisive Voice—♈ influence.

Shrill Voice — Shrill and Small — ♏ produces; ♏ on the Asc.

Signs of Voice—Speaking Signs—♊, ♏, ♎, ♒, and the first half of ♐.

Singing—(See "Speech" under Breath; "Singers" under Music; "Gifted", "Melodious", "Musical", in this section).

Slow of Voice—Slow of Speech—Produced by the ☉ influence; in Hor'y Q. the ☉ as Sig.; ♄ in ♉; born under ♋, as ♋ is a mute sign, and slow of voice.

Small Voice—(See "Shrill" in this section).

Soprano Voice — High Voice — Born under ♀; the ☉, ☽, or ☿ well-aspected in ♉, and not afflicted by ♄; ♉ or ♎ on the Asc., and free from ♄ affliction, as ♄ tends to hamper, restrict, bind, and limit the vocal powers.

Sound—Tone Control—(See "Control", "Cords", in this section).

Speaking — Avoid Loud Speaking — (See "Injudicious" in this section; "Speaking" under Speech).

Speech—(See the various paragraphs under Speech).

Speechless—Mute—Cannot Talk—Refuses to Talk—(See "Deaf and Dumb" under Hearing; Mute; "Speechless" under Speech).

Stammering—(See Speech).

Straining the Voice — (See "Injudicious" in this section).

Strong Voice — Great Voice — Strong Vocal Organs — The ☉ in ♉ and not afflicted. (See Coarse, Deep, Great, Orator, in this section).

Stuttering—(See Speech).

Sways the Masses — (See Fluency; "Power to Sway" under Speech).

Sweet Voice—(See Gifted, Melodious, Musical, in this section).

Talk—Cannot Talk—Refuses to Talk — Mute — Dumb, etc. (See these subjects under Speech).

Tenor Voice—(See Effeminate, Testes).

Throat — Disorders of, and Affecting the Voice—(See the various paragraphs under Throat).

Tone Control—(See "Control" in this section).

Tongue — Impediments In — (See Tongue).

Unmusical Voice — (See "Musical" in this section).

Vocal Cords — Disorders of — (See Cords, Functions, Organic, Straining, and the Introduction to this section; Larynx).

Voice — (See the various paragraphs in this section).

Weak Voice—♋ gives; ♋ on the Asc.; ♑ on Asc. (See "Aphonia", "Rough", in this section; "Hoarseness" under Speech).

Weakness Of — Loss of Voice — Dysphonia — (See "Hoarseness" under Larynx; "Paralysis", "Speechless", in this section).

Whispering Voice — (See "Aphonia" in this section).

Whistling Sound — (See "Rough" in this section).

Women—Masculine Voice In—Coarse Voice In — (See Coarse, Deep, in this section; Deviations, Effeminate).

VOID—Void of—Devoid of—

Course—Planets Void of Course—A Planet is void of course when it forms no aspect to other planets during the remainder of its course thru the sign in which it is posited. This is considered a debility, and such a planet when the afflictor in the disease tends to have less effect upon the disease for the time, and the disease is more or less at a standstill, and lingers along, as it takes the aspects of the planets to the afflicting planet, for good or ill, to cause the disease to get better, worse, relapse, or resolve itself. (See Aspects, Course, Direct, Planets, Retrograde, Stationary).

Void Degrees — Of the Zodiac — The Asc., or its lord, in any of these degrees at B. tend to render the native empty and void of knowledge. The Void Degrees are ♈ 24°, 30°; ♉ 12°, 30°; ♊ 16°, 30°; ♋ 18°, 30°; ♌ 25°; ♍ 10°, 17°; ♎ 30°; ♏ 14°, 29°; ♐ 0°; ♑ 25°; ♒ 25°; ♓ 25°. (See Knowledge; "Void Of" under Learning; "Shallow" under Mentality).

Void Of—There are many things every individual is void of, or has a lack of, and such subjects would be too numerous to list here. Look in the alphabetical arrangement for the subject you have in mind. In the Articles on "Lack Of", "Loss Of", you will find many subjects listed along this line. Also see "Void Of" under Energy, Learning, Reason, Stamina. Also see such subjects as Aversions, Collapse, Depletion, Deviations, Diminished; "Fails In" under Examinations; Exhaustion, Idiocy, Irrational; "Free From" under Passion; "Shows No Pity" under Pity; Pretender; "Weak" under Understanding, etc.

VOLATILIZATION — (See "Operations" under Nature; Nitrogen, Sublimation, Vapor).

VOLCANOES—Volcanic Eruptions—Coincident with an eclipse of the ☉ in a watery sign; coincident with the appearance of Comets, and especially of Halley's Comet; due to major planets in perihelion. (See "Epidemics" under Cholera; "Earthquakes" under Earth).

VOLITION — The Will to Act—Willing —Ruled by ☿.

Loss of Volition—Indiscretions From —Denoted by ♐; ♆ affl. in ♐. (See "Mind" under Chaotic; Hypnotism, Influenced, Involuntary, Negative Nature (see Negative); Obsessions, Passive; "Negative Psychism" under Psychic; Self-Control, Spirit Controls, Suggestion, Voluntary; "Weak Will" under Will).

VOLUNTARY — Under the Control of the Will—The Voluntary Nervous System is under the rule of ☿.

Clonic Spasm — Of the Voluntary Muscles—(See "Paramyoclonus Multiplex", "Voluntary", under Muscles).

Diseased Voluntary Power — ♄ ♂ or ill-asp. the ☉. (See Volition).

Excessive Voluntary Power — Given by ♂, and is a ♂ disorder; the ☉ to the ♂ or ill-asp. ♂ by dir. It is relieved by the ♄ remedy, Antimony, and by the application of cold to the head.

Muscles — (See "Clonic" in this section).

Will—(See "Free Will" under Will).

VOLUPTUOUS—(See Amorous, Beautiful; "Voluptuous" under Face; "Sensuous" under Sensuality).

VOMITING—Antiperistalsis—Nausea—Sickness At the Stomach—

Bilious Vomiting — ♂ affl. in ♋. (See Nausea).

Blood—Vomiting of—Haematemesis—The ☽ affl. in ♍; ♂ affl. in ♋, and also affl. the hyleg; ♂ ori. at B., and affl. the hyleg. (See "Ulcer" under Gastric; "Vicarious" under Menses).

Desire to Vomit—(See Nausea).

Diet — Vomiting from Wrong Diet — (See "Ailments" under Diet).

Emetics — Agents Producing Vomiting—(See Antiperistalsis, Emetic, Medicines, Ruminant).

Expulsion—(See Expulsion).

Faecal Vomiting — (See Faeces, Ileac Passion).

Haematemesis—(See "Blood" in this section).

Nausea — A Desire to Vomit — (See Nausea).

Periodic Vomiting — The ☽ affl. in ♋; the ☽ in ♋ and affl. by ♄; evil asps. of the ☽ to ♋ if the ☽ was in ♋ at B.; Subs at SP (7D), and at PP.

Pylorus Constricted—Causing Vomiting—(See "Pylorus" under Stomach).

Ruminant Signs — ♈, ♉, ♑. To give medicine when the ☽ is passing thru one of these signs tends to produce nausea or vomiting. (See Ruminant).

Stomach — (See "Peristalsis" under Stomach).

VORACIOUS—Voracity—Having An Insatiable Appetite—(See Appetite, Eating, Epicurean, Feasting, Food, Gluttony).

VOYAGES—Long Journeys by Water—Sea Travel—Are ruled by the 9th House, the house of Foreign Travel, or Foreign Residence. Are also ruled by the ☽. Long Voyages are also ruled and influenced by ♐, the 9th sign affiliated with the 9th H., and also by ♃, the ruler of this sign. The subject of Voyages is partly considered under such subjects as Journeys, Ships, Shipwreck, Travel, etc. The following subjects also have to do

with Voyages, which see in the alphabetical arrangement when not considered here—

Abroad — Avoid Journeys Abroad — (See Abroad).

Accidents—Accidents In Foreign Travel — (See "Accidents" under Abroad).

Advisability — Of Voyages — Benefic planets in the 9th H., and malefics in the 4th H. at B., make it advisable to go Abroad, take voyages, and leave the Native Land. (See Abroad; "Long Journeys" under Journeys; "Native Land" under Native; "Home or Abroad" under Travel).

Avoid Voyages—When there are malefics in the 9th H. at B., or the ruler of the 9th H. a malefic, and with no benefics in the 9th H. (See "Avoid" under Abroad; "Abroad" under Journeys; the various paragraphs under Travel).

Bad Time — For Voyages — (See "Avoid" under Journeys; "Bad Time" under Travel).

Bites, Kicks, or Fevers—On Journeys or Voyages—Fevers on Journeys—Malefics in the 3rd or 9th H., in fire signs, and affl. the ☉ or ☽. (See Bites).

Burns — On Journeys or Voyages — (See "Journeys" under Burns).

Calamities — At Sea — (See "Calamities" under Sea; Ships, Shipwreck).

Cuts — Stabs — On Voyages — (See "Travel" under Cuts).

Dampness—Suffers From on Voyages or Journeys — Malefics in the 3rd or 9th H., in watery signs, and affl. the ☉ or ☽. (See Moisture).

Danger On Voyages—Dangerous Voyages—Danger In Navigation—The ☉ to the ♂ ♄ by dir.; ☽ in the 9th H. at B., and to the ♂ or ill-asp. ♅ by dir.; ☽ affl. in the 8th H.; ♆, ♅, ♄, or ♂ in the 9th H., and affl.; ♄ affl. in ♏; ♄ or ♂ affl. in the 9th H., in watery signs; malefics in the 9th H., and affl. the ☉ or ☽; the transit of malefics thru the 9th H., if in the 9th at B., or affl. the lord of the 9th; the Asc. by dir. to the evil asps. the ♂ at B. (See Drowning, Journeys; "Dangers" under Navigation, Ocean; "Death At Sea" under Sea; Ships, Shipwreck; Travel; "Peril" under Waters; "Bad Time" in this section).

Death At Sea — (See Abroad, Drowning, Journeys; "Death" under Sea; Ships, Shipwreck, Travel, Water, etc.).

Directions — (See "Disposes To" in this section).

Disposes To Voyages—A Voyage Indicated—Primary Directions falling due in a watery sign; the ☉, ☽, or ♂ cadent, occidental, and in mutable signs at B. Many planets in fixed signs, or fixed signs on angles, do not dispose to travel or voyages. The passage of the ☽ or a benefic thru the 9th H. disposes to. (See "Good Time" in this section).

Drowning; Events — (See "Nature of Events" under Events).

Falls — On Voyages — (See "Travel" under Falls).

Famine On—(See Famine).

Fatal Voyages — (See "Bad Time", "Danger", "Death", in this section).

Fever — On a Voyage or Journey — (See "Bites" in this section).

Fire—On a Voyage—(See "Ships" under Fire).

Fixed Signs — (See "Disposes To" in this section).

Foreign Lands—Foreign Travel—(See "Advisability", "Avoid", in this section; Abroad).

Fortunate — Upon the Seas — (See "Fortunate" under Seas).

Foundering—(See Ships, Shipwreck).

Good Time—For Sea Voyage—The ☉ to the good asps. the 9th H. if the cusp of the 9th be ♋, ♏ or ♓, and the 9th be not affl. by malefics; the ☉ to the good asps. ♂, and the ☉ or ♂ ruler of the 9th; the ☽ to the good asps. the ☉, and espec. if the direction fall in the 9th H. and in a watery sign; the ☽ to the good asps. the Asc. by dir. if the ☽ was well-asp. at B.; the ☽ in the 9th H., and to the good asps. ♅ by dir.; the ☽ to the ☌ ☿ by dir., and ☿ in the 9th H. in ♋, or if the ☽ or ☿ be in the 3rd or 9th H. at B.; when the ☽, ♂, or ☿ are in the 9th H. at B. a voyage is usually made when the ☽, or planet, by primary dir. in mundo comes to the cusp of the 9th H.; when ♃ or ♀ are in the Asc., M.C., 2nd, or 9th houses, and malefics not in angles, a good time; M.C. to the ☌ ☽ if the ☽ rule the 9th H. at B.; M.C. to the good asps. the ☽; M.C. to the cusp the 9th, or to the good asps. ruler of the 9th H. (See "Good Times" under Journeys).

High Places — Falls From During Travel or Voyages—(See "Death" under Heights).

Indicated—A Voyage Indicated—(See "Disposes To" in this section).

Injury on Voyages — Malefics in the 9th H., and affl. the ☉ or ☽. (See Ships, Shipwreck; "Accidents", "Hurts", under Travel).

Journeys — Long Journeys — (See Abroad, Journeys; the various paragraphs in this section).

Kicks—On Voyages—(See "Bites" in this section; Kicks).

Lightning—Danger By On Voyages—(See "Voyages" under Lightning).

Long Journeys—(See Journeys, Ships, Travel; the various paragraphs in this section).

Maritime Affairs—(See Maritime, Navigation, Sailors, Sea; "Shipping" under Ships, Voyages, etc.).

Misfortunes At Sea — (See "Misfortunes" under Sea).

Moisture — Suffers From In Travel — (See "Dampness" in this section).

Nations—Where to Go On Voyages—(See Location, Nations, Native Land, Residence, Travel).

Native Land—Should Leave—Should Remain—(See Native Land).

Navigation; Ocean; Piracy;

Poisoning — During Travel — (See "Travel" under Poison).

Privations — (See Famine; "Privations" under Seas; "Food" under Travel).

Sailors; Sea Sickness—(See "Sickness" in this section).

Ships; Shipwreck; Sickness—On Voyages—Sea Sickness—☽ affl. in 8th H.; ♄ Sig. in the 9th H.; ♄ in 8th H. in a watery sign, and affl. the hyleg; the ship leaving Port in a ♄ hour, or with ♄ in the Asc., danger of, or some disaster; lord of the 6th in the 9th H., and affl.; malefics in the 9th H., or the tr. of malefics thru the 9th, if in the 9th at B., or affl. the lord of the 9th. (See "Health" under Journeys; "Sickness" under Travel). Seasickness is caused usually by ♄ in ♋, or in cardinal signs, and by the ☉, ☽, and many planets in card. signs; ♋ or card. signs upon angles, as the card. signs all afflict the stomach region. Also malefics in ♍ tend to disturb the organ of coordination.

Storms At Sea—(See "Voyages" under Lightning; Ships, Shipwreck; "Tempests" under Sea; Wind).

Sunstroke—During Travel, or At Sea —Malefics in the 3rd or 9th H., in fiery signs, and affl. the ☉ or ☽; the ☉ in ♌ in the 9th H., and ☌, or ill-asp. ♂ at B., and the ☉ affl. by ♂ by dir.

Tempests — (See "Tempests" under Sea).

Travel—Note the various subjects under Journeys, Maritime, Navigation, Sea, Ships, Travel, etc.).

Trouble by Sea—(See "Troubles" under Sea).

Unfortunate—On the Sea—(See "Unfortunate" under Sea).

Voyage Soon Follows—♆ ☌, or P. the ☉ at a Solar Rev., and the ☉ in a watery sign; the M.C. to the ✶ or △ ♂. (See "Disposes To" in this section).

Water—Danger On—Danger By—(See Drowning, Sea, Water, etc.).

Where to Go — On Voyages — (See Abroad, Nations, Native Land, Residence).

Wind Storms—At Sea—(See Wind).

VULGAR—A Vulgar and Unrefined Body —(See Rough, Unrefined).

VULNERABLE — The vulnerable spots in the horoscope are the ☉, ☽, Asc. and Hyleg, when affl. by malefics. Also the degree and sign occupied by ♄ at B. denote a weak and vulnerable place, and the part of the body so ruled is always subject to more or less of affliction and weakness, in the ordinary course of life, and espec. when ♄ afflicts this degree by tr. or dir. All the malefics tend to weaken and afflict the part of the body ruled by the sign containing them at B. (See Malefics; "Weak Spots" under Saturn). With the Signs of the Zodiac, the ♋, ♑ and ♓ signs are the weakest and most vulnerable to bodily affliction and disease. (See "Vitality Low" under Vitality; "Weak Body" under Weak). The Nebulous Stars and Clusters are also quite dangerous and vulnerable when with the ☉ or ☽ at B. (See Nebulous).

VULTURES—Fowls—Birds of the Air—Vultures Eat the Body—The Body, or Corpse, may be devoured by beasts and birds if ♅, ♄ and ♂ all three occupy anaretic places, and be in signs similar in form to birds and beasts, and espec. if the benefics give no good asps. to the anaretic places or to the 4th H. (See "Birds of the Air" under Air; "Body Devoured" under Burial; Buzzards).

VULVA—Ruled by ♏.

Abscess Of—Ulceration of—♂ affl. in ♏; ♂ ☌ ♃ or ☽ in ♏; ♂ ☌ ♀ in ♏. (See Abscesses, Vagina). Subluxations of the Lumbar Vertebrae, at PP, tend to disorders of the Vulva, Vagina, and Sex Organs.

W

WADDLING GAIT—(See Gait).

WAKEFULNESS—(See "Cold Feet" under Feet; "Insomnia" under Sleep).

WALK—Gait—Carriage—Tread—Step—Locomotion, etc.—This subject is also considered in the Articles on Action, Gait, Locomotion, Motion, Movement. See these subjects, and also the following subjects in the alphabetical arrangement when not considered here—

Ankles Knock—When Walking—(See Ankles).

Awkward Walk—(See Gait).

Awry Walk — (See "Awry" under Gait).

Bad Gait—(See Gait).

Brisk Walk—(See Brisk; "Energetic" under Gait).

Carriage — Free In — Born under ♃. (See Carriage).

Child—Nine Years of Age Has Never Walked—Case—See "Defective Mentality, No. 670 in 1001 N.N.

Clumsy Walk—(See Clumsiness).

Commanding Walk — (See Commanding; "Majestic" under Gait).

Could Not Walk — Child Could Not Walk Before Six Years of Age—Case —See "Datas", No. 896 in 1001 N.N.

Defective Walk—The ☉ ☌ ♅ or ♄ in ♐; ♄ in the Asc. at B.; caused by ♄ afflictions; ♄ affl. in ♓; ♄ in ♑, □ or ☍ ♆. For Cases of Defective Walk see Figures 14C, 14D, in the book, "Astro-Diagnosis", by the Heindels. (See "Defective" under Gait).

Distorted Walk—(See "Distorted" under Gait).

Dragging Walk — (See "Dragging" under Gait).

Energetic Walk — (See "Energetic" under Gait).

Equilibrium Disturbed—Incoordinated Walk—Pitches Forward In Walking—♄ affl. in ♉; many planets, and malefics in ♉, afflicting the organ of Co-ordination. (See Balance, Coordination, Equilibrium, Incoordination).

Feet — (See "Club Feet", "Lameness In", and the various paragraphs under Feet; "Feet" under Gait).

Festination — The Peculiar Walk In Paralysis Agitans—♅ or ♄ affl. in ♓; Subs at LPP. (See "Shaking" under Palsy).

Firm Walk—Firm Step—♌ gives, and ♌ on the Asc. at B. (See "Commanding" under Gait).

Forward — Pitches Forward — (See "Equilibrium" in this section).

Free In Carriage—(See "Carriage" in this section).

Gait — (See the various paragraphs under Gait).

Genteel Walk—(See "Genteel" under Gait).

Has Never Walked — Case — (See "Child" in this section).

Heavy Walk—♓ influence; ♓ on the Asc. at B. (See Dull; "Heavy", "Stooping", under Gait; Heavy).

Inability to Walk — Unable to Walk or Stand—♆ in □ or ♌, and affl. by ♄, and due to obstruction of the spinal fluids; ♄ affl. in ♌, due to Spinal Sclerosis, and lack of synovial fluid in the vertebrae, and to atrophy of the spine; ♄ affl. in ♐, due to hip trouble; ♄ affl. in ♑, and espec. if ♄ afflict ♆ at the same time; ♄ affl. in ♓, due to chronic foot disorders, or deformed feet. Inability to walk is also due to afflictions to ☿, or a ☿ sign, or planets in a ☿ sign. Case—See Fig. 1 in "Message of the Stars", and Fig. 9D, in "Astro-Diagnosis", books by the Heindels. (See "Club Feet", "Paralysis", under Feet; "Hip Joint Disease" under Hips; "Paraplegia" under Legs; "Child", "Stand", in this section).

Incoordinated Walk — (See "Equilibrium" in this section).

Lameness; Legs — (See Club Feet, Crippled, Lameness, Missing, Paraplegia, under Legs).

Light Walk — Nimble — (See "Energetic" under Gait).

Limping — (See "Limping" under Gait).

Locomotion — Defects of — (See Gait, Locomotion, Motion, Movement; the various paragraphs in this section).

Lower Extremities—Disabilities In—(See "Extremities" under Lower).

Majestic Walk — Proud Walk — ♌ gives, and with ♌ on the Asc. (See "Commanding" in this section).

Motion — Movement — (See "Motion" under Gait).

Nervous and Quick Walk — ♅ or ☿ affl. by ♂. (See "Energetic" under Gait).

Paralysis of Legs — (See "Paralysis" under Legs, Limbs; "Festination" in this section).

Peculiar Walk — (See "Festination" in this section).

Pedestrianism; Pitches Forward — When Walking—(See "Equilibrium" in this section).

Proud Walk—♌ gives. (See "Majestic" in this section).

Quick Walk—Quick and Nervous Walk — (See "Nervous" in this section).

Rough Walk — (See "Rough" under Gait).

Shuffling Walk — Drags Feet — (See "Dragging" under Gait).

Six Years of Age — Could Not Walk Before this Age — Case — (See "Could Not Walk" in this section).

Smart and Quick Walk—(See "Energetic" under Gait).

Staggering Walk—Tottering—Swaying — (See "Staggering" under Gait; "Equilibrium" in this section).

Stand — Unable to Stand or Walk — See "Deformed", No. 689 in 1001 N.N. (See "Inability" in this section).

Step Firm and Majestic—(See "Firm", "Majestic", in this section).

Stooping Gait — (See "Stooping" under Gait; "Festination" in this section).

Strutting Walk—(See "Strutting" under Gait).

Swaying Walk—(See "Staggering" in this section).

Tottering Walk — (See "Staggering" under Gait; "Equilibrium" in this section).

Treading Walk — (See "Awry" under Gait).

Twisted Walk — (See "Awry" under Gait).

Unable to Walk — Or Stand — (See "Paralysis", "Stand", in this section).

Unsteady Walk — (See "Staggering" in this section).

Waddling Gait—(See "Waddling" under Gait).

Walking—Fondness For—(See Pedestrianism).

WALLS — Of the Stomach Irritable — (See "Irritable" under Stomach).

WAN FACE—(See Pale, Sickly).

WANDERER—Wandering—Roaming—Scattering—Vacillating—

Affections — Wandering Affections — (See "Fickle" under Love Affairs).

Diseases—Wandering Diseases—(See Flying; "Wandering" under Gout; "Whole Body" under Pain; Running, Whole Body).

Gout—Wandering Gout—(See "Wandering" under Gout).

Mind—Wandering Mind—(See "Mental" under Chaotic; "Inability" under Concentration; Confusion; "Dreamy" under Dreams; Vacillating, Vagaries, Weird).

Nature — A Wandering Nature — A Roamer — An Itinerant — (See "No Home" under Home; "Instability" under Mind; "Many Changes" under Residence; Restlessness, Roaming; "Wanderer" under Travel; Vacillating, Vagabond).

WANING FORCES — Brought on by ♄ influence and afflictions. (See Anaemia, Consumptions, Debility, Emaciation, Feeble, Ill-Health, Infirm, Invalids, Sickly; "Much Sickness" under Sickness; "Low" under Vitality; Wastings; "Weak Body" under Weak).

WANT—In Want and Misery—(See Miseries, Misfortune, Neglect, Poverty, Reverses, Ruin, Starvation, Wretched).

WANTON—Extravagant—Without Restraint—Libidinous—Lewd—Licentious—Loose, etc.—(See these subjects).

Destructiveness — Wanton Destructiveness—(See Destructiveness).

Disgrace — Thru Wantonness — (See Disgrace).

Wanton Look — □ gives. (See Debauched, Depraved, Effeminate, Immodest; "Licentious" under Men; "Notoriety" under Passion; Perversions, Shameless, etc.).

WANT AND MISERY — (See Miseries, Misfortune, Neglect, Poverty, Wretched).

WANTS—Nature's Wants and Requirements — (See "Requirements" under Nature).

WAR—Battle—Strife—♂ is the planet of War and Bloodshed.

Battle—(See "Death" in this section).

Civil War—Danger of—♂ in the Asc. at the Vernal Equi., lord of the year, weak and afflicted; Comets appearing in the Ruling Sign of a Country. (See Politics; "Discord" under Quarrels; Revolutionary).

Death In Battle—Death or Injury In War — Killed In Battle — Wounded In Battle—Signs of Death In Battle—The ☉ Sig. to the ☌ ♂ by dir. if ♂ afflict the ☉ or hyleg at B., and the map be a violent one, or show a violent death, danger of being terribly wounded, or killed in battle; the ☉ in the 8th H., or with the lord of the 7th; the ☉ to the ☌ or P. Dec. Antares; the ☽ to the ☌ or P. Antares or Aldebaran; an eclipse of the ☉ or ☽ in a fiery sign, terrible slaughter in war; ♂ in signs of human form, and in □ or ☍ the ☉ or ☽, and contrary in condition; ♂ the afflicting planet, death in war; ♂ in the 8th H. at B., and afflicted; □ or ☍ the Asc., and if he is also in ☍ the ☉ or ☽, there is danger of a violent death, and if applying, and near the exact ☍, to be killed on the spot; ♂ in the Asc., afflicted, and ill-dignified, may be dangerously wounded in battle; leaving for war in a ♂ hour tends to death in battle; malefics aff. in the 8th H.; malefics in the 9th H. at B., danger of death in a Foreign War; lord of the Asc. in the 8th, or with lord of the 8th, or lord of the 8th in the Asc.; the Asc. to the ☌ or ill-asp. ♂ by dir., and ♂ in a sign of human form at B.; the 6th face of ♈, or the 5th face of ♋ culminating on the M.C. (See "Battle" under Abroad; Captivity, Contests, Duels, Feuds, Military, Shedding of Blood (see Shedding); Slaughter, Soldiers).

Excites and Stirs Up War—An eclipse of the ☽ in the 1st decan. of ♋. (See "Sun Spots" under Spots).

Fond of War — And Disputes — (See "Disputes" under Quarrels).

Killed In War—(See "Death" in this section).

Kings — Overthrow or Assassination of In War—(See Kings).

Military Officer—Death of—(See "Officer Killed" under Military).

Quarrels—Given To—(See "Discord", "Disputes", under Quarrels).

Radicalism; Reactionary; Rebellious; Reformers; Revolutionary; Riotous; Soldiers—Death By—(See Soldiers).

Stirs Up War—(See "Excites" in this section).

Sun Spots—Tending to Cause War— (See "Sun Spots" under Spots).

Terribly Wounded — In War — (See "Death" in this section).

Violent Death In — (See "Death" in this section).

War and Bloodshed—An eclipse of the ☉ in the 1st decan. of ♏ stirs up wars, tumults, and slaughter; coincident with the appearance of Comets; Comets appearing in the ♈ sign, and espec. in Countries under the rule of ♈; Comets appearing in ♈, ♊, ♋, ♌, ♏, ♐, ♑, ♒, or ♓, and espec. in Countries ruled by these signs. (See "Shedding" under Blood; "Blood" under Effusions; Public; "Discord" under Quarrels; Seventh House, Slaughter, Strife, etc.).

Warlike—(See "Disputes" under Quarrels; Revolutionary, Riotous, Violent).

Wounded In War—Injured In Battle —(See "Death" in this section).

WARDS OFF DISEASE — (See Immunity; "Good" under Recuperation, Resistance).

WARM—Warmth—Heat—♃ and ♀ are warm, and exert a warm influence over the body, but not hot. Libra and ♒ are warm and moist signs.

Air—(See "Warm" under Air).

Body — Warm Body — (See "Animal Heat", "Hot Bodily Temperament", under Heat).

Functions — Warmth and Expansion of—(See Electric).

Heat—(See "Warm", and the various paragraphs under Heat).

Moist and Warm Diseases—(See "Moist and Warm" under Heat).

Summers Warm—(See Summer).

Warm-Hearted—(See Good, Humane, Kind).

Warm Weather—(See "Warm" under Weather).

WARTS—Verruca—An Excrescence—

Anus — Wart-Like Growth On — Condyloma—♄ affl. in ♏; Subs at LPP (4, 5L). (See Anus, Rectum).

Arms — Hands or Shoulders — Warts On — Afflictions in signs which rule these parts; ♄ affl. in ♋, ♌, or ♍; Subs at AP (1D), and also at UHP (1D).

Eyelids—Warts On—♄ affl. in ♈; Subs at KP (11D). (See Eyelids).

Face—Warts On—(See "Marks" under Face).

Hands — Warts On—(See "Arms" in this section).

Head—(See "Warts" under Head).

Rectum—(See "Anus" in this section).

Shoulders—(See "Arms" in this section). See Blemishes, Marks, Moles, Naevus, Scars.

WASTE—Wastes—Waste Products of the Body—Retention of Wastes—Improper Elimination of—Wasted— Wasteful, etc.—The following subjects have to do with the Wastes of the body, their retention or excess in the body, and also of their elimination. See these subjects in the alphabetical arrangement when not considered here—

Accumulation of Wastes—(See Accumulative).

Acids — Over-Acidity of the Body — (See Acids, Hyperacidity).

Bathing—(See Bathing; "Water" under Skin).

Carbonic Acid Poisoning — (See Carbon).

Cleansing the Body — Of Wastes and Impurities—(See Cleansing, Elimination, Fever, Inflammation, Mars Action; "Bathing" in this section).

Crusts; Deposits; Dirty; Elimination —(See "Stopped" under Elimination).

Energies Wasted—(See Amorous; Debauched, Dissipation; "Wasted" under Energies; Excesses, Intemperate, Opposite Sex, Passion, Pleasure, Sports; "Sex Forces" in this section).

Eruptions; Excess; Excesses;

Excretion Disordered — (See Excretion).

Expulsion of Wastes — Carried on by the ☽ and ♂. The afflictions of ♄ to the ☽, and with ♄ affl. in ♍, ♎, ♏, or ♑, tend to disorders of expulsion and elimination. (See Elimination, Excretion, Expulsion, Faeces, Retention, Stoppages, Suppression, Sweat, Urine).

Exudations—(See Excretion, Exudations, Faeces, Sweat, Urine).

Faeces; Fevers — The fevers and inflammations of ♂ help to burn up and eliminate wastes, and in this regard are constructive and purifying forces if not too violent, and the life is saved. (See Fever; "Cleansing the Body" in this section).

Filth; Gout; Gravel; Hindered—Elimination of Wastes Hindered — (See Hindrances).

Hyperacidity; Impeded—(See the various paragraphs under Impeded).

Impurities—(See Excretions, Faeces, Hyperacidity, Impure; "Blood Poisoning" under Poison; Sweat, Urine, etc.).

Inflammation—A Cleanser of the Body from Impurities — (See "Cleansing", "Fevers", in this section).

Jaundice — (See "Obstructive" under Jaundice).

Leukocytes—As a Nucleus for Wastes —(See Leukocytes).

Menses; Mineral Deposits — (See Deposits, Gravel, Minerals, Sand, Stone).

Obstructions; Paralysis;

Poisons Retained—(See Impure, Poisons).

Portal Blood Stream—The Wastes of —(See Portal).

Retardations; Retention of Wastes— (See Hyperacidity, Retention).

Rheumatism; Sand; Secretions — The Secretions Hindered by Wastes — (See Secretion).

Sex Forces Wasted — (See Amorous; "Health Injured" under Men; "Health Suffers" under Opposite Sex; "Passional Excesses" under Passion).

Stone — Calculus — (See Gravel, Sand, Stone).

Stoppages; Suppressions; Sweat;

Toxaemia; Urea; Uric Acid; Urine — Suppression of—(See Urine).

Vital Fluid—Waste of—(See "Fluid", "Waste", under Vital).

Wasteful — (See Expense, Extravagant, Improvident, Luxuries, Money, Prodigal).

Wasting Diseases—(See Wasting).

WASTING DISEASES — Wasting Processes In the Body—Tabefaction—Marasmus—Consumptions, etc.—The influences and afflictions of ♆ and ♄ tend to wasting processes in the body. (See Neptune, Saturn). The following subjects have to do with the Wasting Processes in the body, which see in the alphabetical arrangement when not considered here—

Arms—Wasting of the Tissues of the Arms, Hands, Legs and Feet—Shrinking and Withering of the Limbs — ♆ influence, and caused by ♆ afflicted in the signs which rule these parts, and to cause shrinking and withering of such parts, and of the Limbs.

Assimilation — Wasting Due to Improper Assimilation of Food — (See "Imperfect" under Assimilation; "Incapable", "Malnutrition", under Nutrition).

Atrophy — Wasting of a Part — (See Atrophy; "Atrophy" under Feet, Hands).

Body—Wasting of the Body—Wasting Diseases—Tabefactions—A ♆ and ♄ disease; ♆ affl. in ♏; ♆ in ♏ in the 6th H., and affl. the Asc. or hyleg; the ☉ affl. by ♄; the ☽ in ♑, and affl. by the ☉ or ♂ when taken ill, the body extremely wasted (Hor'y); ♄ affl. the hyleg, and ♄ the afflictor in the disease; ♄ in ♓, occi., and affl. the ☉, ☽, or Asc. (See Atrophy, Consumption, Corrosion, Decay, Degeneration, Destructive, Emaciation, Marasmus, Phthisis, Tabes, Tuberculosis, etc.).

Bowels—♆ affl. in ♍, wasting of the glands of the bowels.

Chronic Low Fevers—(See "Chronic", "Hectic", under Fever).

Consumptions; Decay;

Destructive Processes—In the Body—(See "Destructive Processes" under Destructive).

Diabetes; Diseases—Wasting Diseases—These diseases are worse at sunset, and at night. They are caused principally by the afflictions of ♆ and ♄. (See the various paragraphs in this section).

Emaciation; Feet—Wasting of—(See "Arms" in this section).

Glands of Bowels—Wasting of—(See "Bowels" in this section).

Hands—Wasting of Tissues of—(See "Arms" in this section).

Hectic Fever—Low, Wasting Fevers —(See "Hectic" under Fever, Phthisis).

Legs — Wasting of — (See "Arms" in this section; "Wasting" under Legs).

Leprosy; Limbs—(See "Arms" in this section).

Liver—(See "Wasting" under Liver).

Locomotor Ataxia; Low Fevers—(See "Hectic", "Low", under Fever).

Malnutrition—(See Nutrition).

Marriage Partner—Neurotic Wasting of—(See Marriage Partner).

Neurotic Wasting — (See "Wasting" under Nerves).

Phthisis — Pulmonary Consumption— (See Phthisis).

Respiratory System — (See "Tissues Affected" under Breathing).

Scrofula — Tubercular a n d Wasting Tendency In—(See Scrofula).

Shrinking; Tabes; Throat — Wasting of Tissues of—♆ affl. in ♉.

Tissues—Wasting of—♆ □ or ⚹ the Asc.; ♆ affl. in signs which rule the part; ♄ influence. (See "Wasting" under Tissues).

Tuberculosis; Wasting Away—Death By—Tabefaction—♄ affl. at B., holding the dominion of death, and affl. the ☉, ☽, Asc., or hyleg; ♀ affl. at B., holding the dominion of death, and affl. the hyleg by dir. (See Consumptions, Emaciation, Phthisis, Tabes, Tuberculosis).

Withering; Worse—Wasting diseases are worse at sunset, and at night. (For other diseases along this line, and which may not be listed here, look in the alphabetical arrangement for what you have in mind).

WATER—Waters—Watery — Fluids— Aqueous — Hydro, etc. — Waters and Fluids are ruled by the ☽, ♆, and the watery signs. (See "Operations" under Nature; "Signs" under Water). The following subjects have to do with Water, Waters, Liquids, and Fluids inside and outside the human body. See these subjects in the alphabetical arrangement when not considered here—

Accidents by Water—Injury By— ☽ □, ♄ ♂; ♆ affl. in the 8th, 9th or 10th H.; ♆ affl. in ♏; ♂ affl. in watery signs and ♂ or ill-asp. the Asc. by dir. (See Bathing, Drowning, Navigation, Scalds, Shipwreck, Ships, Sea; the various paragraphs in this section).

Bathing; Blood—Watery Blood—(See "Thin" under Blood).

Brain—Water On—(See Hydrocephalus).

Brash—Water Brash—(See Belching).

Burns — By Hot Water — (See "Hot Liquids" under Heat; Scalds).

Chest—Water In—(See "Dropsy" under Chest).

Children—Watery Diseases In—(See "Watery" under Children).

Cold Water—Craving For In Illness —(See "Cold Water" under Cravings).

Cold, Watery Diseases — (See "Cold and Moist" under Humours).

Control of Water — In the System — (See "Sodium Chloride" under Sodium).

Corruption of Waters — (See Fish, Rivers).

Dampness — (See Linen, Moisture, Wet).

Danger by Water — (See Bathing, Drowning; "Hot Liquids" under Heat; Navigation, Scalds, Sea, Ships, Shipwreck, Voyages).

Death—By Means of Water—The ☉ to the ill-asps. ♄ by dir., and one or both in watery signs; the ☽ in a watery sign at B., and affl. by ♄, and affl. the hyleg by dir., or taking part in a fatal train of directions; ♆ affl. in the 8th H. at B., and also affl. the hyleg; ♅ or ♄ in ♋, ♍, ♏ or ♓ and affl. the ☽; ♄ ♍ and affl. the ☽ hyleg; ♄ in a watery sign and affl. the Asc. or hyleg by dir. (See Bathing, Drowning, Scalds, Ships, Shipwreck, Voyages, etc.).

Diarrhoea — Profuse Watery — (See Diarrhoea).

Discharges — Watery Discharges — (See Discharges).

Distilled—(See "Water" under Skin).

Drinks Much Water—(See Cravings, Thirst).

Dropsies; Drowning;

Elimination of Water—From the System—Carried on by the ♉ sign, and the Sodium Sulphate Salt.

Epiphora—Watery Eyes—(See Tears).

Events—Affecting the Waters—(See "Nature" under Events; Navigation, Sea, Ships, Shipwreck, Voyages, etc.).

Excrescences — Watery Excrescences —(See "Skull" under Excrescences).

Eyes — Watery Eyes — Overflow of Tears—(See Tears).

Fallopian Tubes — Water In — (See Fallopian).

Fear of Water—(See Hydrophobia).

Fish—Destruction of In the Waters— (See Fish).

Fluids — Watery Fluid Collections — (See "Water" under Fluids; Serum).

Floods — (See Floods, Rain, Venomous).

Fond of the Water—The ☽ or ♆ in ♓; many planets in watery signs at B. (See "Fortunate" in this section).

Fortunate On the Water—Fond of the Water—♃ Sig. in ♋ or ♓, or ♃ ♂ ☽, fortunate on, and fond of the water, if the ☽ is not ill-asp.; the ☉ Sig. in ♏, and well-asp., fortunate on the Seas. (See "Fortunate" under Seas).

Fountains—Drying Up of—(See Fountains).

Fresh Water—(See "Running" in this section).

Head—Watery Excrescences of—(See "Excrescences" in this section; "Malformations" under Head).

Hot Water—Accidents and Injuries By — (See "Hot Liquids" under Heat; Scalds).

Humours—Watery Humours—☽ ♂ the Asc. by secondary dir.; ♆ in the 8th H.; ♄ sole ruler of a Solar Eclipse; ♃ affl. in ♍, and with possible discharges of blood; many planets in watery signs at B.; ♀ water sign on the Asc. or 6th H. at B. The watery humours of the body are dried up by ♄ and ♂ as the native declines in life. Also the ☉ in the Asc. at B. tends to dry them up after middle life. (See Defluxions, Discharges; "Humours" under Father; Humours, Mucus, Phlegm, Rheum).

Hurts By — (See Bathing, Drowning; "Hot Liquids" under Heat; Scalds, Shipwreck; "Accidents" in this section).

Hydrocephalus; Hydrophobia;

Hydrosalpinx—(See Fallopian).

Hydrothorax — (See "Water" under Chest).

Injury — By Means of—(See "Hurts" in this section).

Liquids; Maritime; Mineral Waters— (See this subject under Healers; "Distilled Water" under Skin).

Misfortune — By Water — (See Accidents, Death, Perils, in this section).

Moisture; Navigation; Neptune;

Ocean; Perils by Water—The ☽ in a watery sign, and to the ill-asps. the Asc. by dir.; ☽ to the ♂ or ill-asps. ♅ by dir., dangerous to go near bodies of water; ☽ to Deneb, misfortunes by water; ☽ at a Solar Rev. passing over the place of ♄ at B.; ♆ in tr. over the radical ♂, and ♂ in ♋, ♏, or ♓ at B.; ♆ and other malefics affl. in the 8th H., and espec. when in a watery sign, and also affl. the hyleg; ♂ affl. in watery signs, and to the ♂ or ill-asp. the Asc. by dir.; ♂ in evil asp. ♆, and ♆ in the 8th H. in a watery sign, and espec. in ♓; the Asc. to the ♂ or P. the ☽, and the ☽ affl. at B.; malefics in the 9th H. in water signs, and affl. (See "Accidents" in this section; Bathing, Sea, Ships, Shipwreck, Voyages).

Plastic; Pools; Pyrosis—Water Brash —(See Belching).

Rain; Running Water — Streams — Rivers—Fresh Water—Ruled by the ♋ sign. (See Rivers).

Sailors; Salt Water—(See Ocean, Sea).

Scalds; Scarcity of Waters — Comets appearing in ♏. (See Drought, Famine, Fountains, Scarcity).

Seas; Ships; Shipwreck; Signs — The Water Signs of the Zodiac—♋, ♏, ♓. The watery signs dispose to drowning, scalds, fluxes, colds, dropsy, catarrh, hydrocephalus, and to excess of fluid in the body. They give the Lymphatic, or Indolent Temperament. They rule and influence the Blood, and are connected with fluids, both in the body, and outside. The watery signs have much to do with the emotions, desires, romance, the physical sensations, self-protection, and self-preservation, and along emotional and sensational lines are excitable. (See Desires, Emotions, Excitable, Feelings, Imaginations, Romance, Sensation). They are also fruitful, and have much to do with reproduction, the sustaining and preservation of the Race. The ♋ sign has to do with the stomach, assimilation, and digestion. The ♏ sign with elimination, excretion, sex, and reproduction. The ♓ sign with the Lymphatics, and the Lymphatic Temperament. These signs are related to Hydrogen. (See Hydrogen). The ☉ in water signs tends to give a weak constitution, and lowered vitality, except when in ♏, or rising in the Asc. in a watery sign, and also tends to diseases of the glands, fluids, and Lymphatic System. Also the ♋ and ♓ signs when upon the Asc. tend to give low vitality. The ♏ sign gives both vitality and constitutional power, but attracts disease, and infectious diseases. When upon the Asc. at B., the ♏ sign gives the strongest vitality of the water signs, and a hardy and ruddy constitution. The ♏ sign is the worst position for the ☽, having her fall in this sign, which tends to painful and irregular functions, espec. in females, and to lower the natural powers, the vitality, and the whole tone of the body. The ☽ is very strong in ♋ and ♓, and in these signs tends to good and regular functions, and also the absorbent and lymphatic systems and vessels are regular in their respective functions and actions. These signs are also called the Dumb, or Mute Signs, and are said, under certain conditions, to cause impediments of speech, and espec. when ☿ is also afflicted at the same time. The Water Signs are also known as the Terminal Signs, being related to the 4th, 8th, and 12th Houses. (See Cancer, Events, External, Introspection, Lymphatic, Majority, Pisces, Pity, Plastic, Scorpio, Seas, Terminal; "Low" under Vitality. Also see the various subjects mentioned in this paragraph).

Springs — (See Fountains, Rivers, Springs).

Stagnant Pools—(See Pools).

Storms; Streams—(See Rivers; "Running" in this section).

Suffering by Water — (See Bathing, Drowning, Floods; "Hot Liquids" under Heat; Maritime, Navigation, Rain, Scalds, Sea, Ships, Shipwreck, Storms, Voyages, etc.; "Accidents", "Death", "Perils", in this section).

Superabundance of Waters — (See Floods, Rain).

Tears; Tidal Waves — An eclipse of the ☉ in watery signs, overflowing of the Sea banks; coincident with the appearance of Comets, and espec. Halley's Comet. (See "Tides" in this section).

Tides — (See "Tides" under Moon; "Tidal Waves" in this section).

Tumor—Watery Tumor—(See "Aqueous" under Tumor).

Urine; Voyages; Watery Diseases — Watery and Cold Diseases—(See Blood, Children, Cold, Diarrhoea, Discharges, Excrescences, Eyes, Fluids, Head, Humors, and the various paragraphs in this section).

Waves—(See "Tidal" in this section).

Wet Feet—(See Feet).

Wet Journeys — (See "Wet" under Journeys; Ships, Voyages).

Wetting—Bed Wetting—(See "Incontinence" under Urine).

WAXY—Fatty—

Ambergris—(See this subject).

Cancer—Waxy Cancer—(See "Fatty" under Carcinoma).

Fingers — (See "Raynaud's Disease" under Fingers).

Liver — (See "Waxy" under Liver). See Fat.

WAYWARD—(See Criminal, Debauched, Dissipated, Drink, Expense; "Free Living" under Free; "Loose Morals" under Morals; Perverse, Prodigal, Recklessness, etc.).

WEAK—Weaker—Weakest—Weakened — Weakening — Weakly — Weakness — Faint, etc.—Some parts of the human organism are usually weak from birth, and especially the part, or organ, ruled by the sign containing ♄ at B. Some charts of birth are considered weak and unfortunate while others may be termed strong and fortunate. Note the following subjects in the alphabetical arrangement when only listed here—

Action of the Body—Weak and Feeble—(See Action, Feeble; "Weak Body" in this section).

All Weaknesses—Of the Body—♄ diseases, and caused by ♄ afflictions.

Anaemia; Ankles—Weakness In—(See Ankles).

Arms—Weakness In—(See Arms).

Asthenia; Atrophy; Back—Weak Back —(See Back).

Beard—Weak and Thin—(See Beard).

Bladder — Weakness of — (See Bladder).

Blood — The Weakest Blood — Thin Blood—Blood Circulation Weak—(See Blood, Circulation, Rupture, Vessels).

Bodies — Weaker and Smaller Bodies — (See "Smaller", "Weaker", under Small).

Body—Weak Body—Feeble Action to the Body—Strength of the Body Rendered Weaker — (See Feeble; "Bad Health" under Health; "Much Sickness" under Sickness; Strength; "Low" under Vitality; "Weak Body" in this section).

Bones—Weak Bones—(See Bones).

Bowels—Weaknesses of—(See Bowels).

Breakdown; Chest—Weak Chest and Lungs—(See Chest, Lungs).

Children — Weak and Sickly — (See Children).

Chronic Diseases—Thru Weakness— ♄ diseases; ♄ affl. in the Asc. (See Chronic).

Circulation—Weak Circulation of the Blood—(See "Poor" under Circulation).

Collapse; Constitution—Weak Constitution—Frail—The Constitution Weakened — The Weakest Constitutions — The weakest constitutions are given by the water signs, except ♏. (See "Lessened" under Vitality; "Weak Body" in this section).

Consumptions; Death — Of the Frail and Weak—Caused by the evil asps. of the malefics to the ☉ at B., and by dir.; born under ♋, ♑, or ♓. (See "Aged People" under Old Age).

Debility; Decay; Decrepitude;

Degeneration; Degrees — The Weak and Lame Degrees of the Zodiac—(See Azimene).

Delicate; Digestion Weak—(See Digestion, Indigestion; "Weak" under Stomach).

Dull; Ears—The Hearing Weak—(See "Weak" under Hearing).

Emaciation; Energy—Lack of—(See Energy).

Enervation; Exhaustion; Eyes—Weak Eyes—Weak Sight—(See Eyes, Sight).

Faint; Feeble; Feet—Weakness In—(See Feet).

Females—Weaknesses In—(See Females).

Feminine Signs—Of the Zodiac—The Weaker Signs—(See "Signs" under Female).

Figure — Small and Weak Figure — (See "Mean Stature" under Mean; "Smaller and Weaker" under Small).

Frame—A Weak Frame—♋, ♑, or ♓ on the Asc. at B. (See Frame).

Functions — Impaired and Weakened —(See Functions).

General Weakness — (See Fatigue, Feeble; "General Ill-Health" under Ill-Health; "Much Sickness" under Sickness; "Low" under Vitality).

Generative System — Weakness of — (See Generation).

Health — Weak Health — (See "Bad Health" under Health; Invalids, Sickly; "Weak Body" in this section).

Hearing Weak—(See Hearing).

Heart Weak—(See Heart).

Hips—Weakness In—(See Hips).

Horoscope—A Weak Map of Birth— (See Aspects, Fate, Horoscope, Malefics, Map, Saturn, Vulnerable; "Free Will" under Will).

Inactive; Infirm; Infirmities;

Insufficiency; Intellect Weak — (See Intellect, Mind, Understanding).

Intestines — Weaknesses In — (See Bowels, Intestines).

Invalidism; Kidneys—Weak Kidneys — Kidneys the Weakest Part — (See Kidneys).

Knees—Weakness In—(See Knees).

Lassitude; Laxity; Leakages; Legs—Weakness In—(See Legs).

Lessened; Lethargy; Limbs—Weak Limbs—(See Limbs).

Limitations; Limp; Listless; Loins — Weak Loins—(See Loins).

Low Vitality—(See Vitality).

Lowest; Lungs — Weak Lungs — (See Lungs).

Malacia; Malaise; Males — Health In Males Weak—(See Males).

Malefics — The Weakening Influences of—(See Malefics).

Map of Birth — Weak Map — (See "Horoscope" in this section).

Mean—Mean and Weak Stature—(See Mean, Stature).

Memory—Weak—(See Memory).

Men—Weaknesses In—(See Men).

Menses — Profuse and Weakening — (See Menses).

Mental Weakness — (See Intellect, Mental, Mind).

Middle Life—Death At—Weaknesses At—(See Middle Life).

Mind—Weak Mind—(See "Weak Mentality" under Mental; "Feeble", "Weak", under Mind).

Morals—Weak Morals—(See "Loose Morals" under Morals).

Much Weakness—Of Body—(See "Ill-Health All Thru Life" under Ill-Health; "Much Sickness" under Sickness).

Muscles — Weakened Condition of — (See Muscles).

Nature—Weak Nature—The 6th face of ♑ on the Asc. (See Influenced; "Negative Nature" under Negative; Passive, Vacillating).

Nerves—(See "Weakest Part", "Weakness", under Nerves).

Old Age — Weaknesses In — (See Old Age).

Organic Weakness—(See Organic).

Organs — Weak Organs — (See Organs).

Ovaries—Weaknesses In—(See Ovaries).

Pale; Parts of the Body—Weak Parts — Weakest Parts — (See Malefics, Organs, Parts, Saturn).

Passion — The Passions Weak — (See "Lack Of" under Passion).

Person — A Weakly Person — (See Feeble, Imbecility; "Weak Mind" under Mind; "Weak Body" in this section).

Peristaltic Action — Weakened — (See Peristaltic).

Physical Body—Weak—(See "Weak Body" in this section).

Poor — Poor Health — (See "Bad Health" under Health; Poor, Vitality Low; "Weak Body" in this section).

Prostration; Puberty Weakened—(See Puberty).

Pulse—Weak Pulse—(See Pulse).

Reason — The Reasoning Powers Weakened—(See Reason).

Recuperative Powers — Weak — (See Recuperation, Resistance, Vitality Low).

Regenerative Organs — (See "Weakness" under Generation).

Reins—Weakness and Disorders In— (See Reins).

Relaxation; Reproductive System — (See "Weakness" under Generation).

Resistance — To Disease — Low and Weak—(See "Low" under Resistance).

Respiratory System—Weakness of— (See the various paragraphs under Breathing, Lungs, Respiratory).

Ruptures; Saturn—(See "Influence of Saturn" under Saturn).

Secretory System—Weaknesses of— (See Secretions).

Sex Powers Weak—(See "Weak" under Sex).

Short Life—(See Short).

Shoulders — Weakness In — (See Shoulders).

Sickly; Sickness; Sight—Weak Sight —(See Sight).

Signs — Of the Zodiac — The Weak Signs—(See "Weak" under Signs).

Sloughings—From Weakness—(See Sloughing).

Slow—Slow and Weak Conditions In the Body—(See Slow).

Small—Small and Weak Body—(See Mean, Small).

Spine—Weaknesses of—(See Spine).

Stomach—Weak Stomach—(See Stomach).

Strength — (See "Weakened" under Strength).

Structure—The Structural Organization of the Body Weakened — (See Structural).

Suppressions; Suspensions; System—The System Weakened — (See Constitution, System, Vitality Lessened).

Thighs—Weakness In—(See Thighs).

Thin and Weak — (See Emaciated; "Thin Body" under Thin; Wasting).

Throat—Weak and Afflicted Throat— (See the various paragraphs under Throat).

Tone—The Tone of the Body Weak— (See Tone).

Trouble—Weakened Thru Trouble— (See Miseries, Misfortune, Reverses, Ruin, Sorrow, Trouble).

Understanding — (See "Weak" under Understanding).

Urinary Organs—Weaknesses of— (See Urine).

Valves—Weak Valves—(See Valves).

Vessels—Weakened Blood Vessels— (See Apoplexy, Hardening, Rupture, Vessels).

Vices—Weakened By—(See Vice).

Vigor — The Vigor Weakened — (See Vigor).

Vision—Weak Vision—(See Sight).

Vitality Weak—Weakened—(See Vitality).

Voice—(See "Weak Voice" under Voice).

Volition — The Powers of Volition Weakened—(See Volition, Will).

Wasting; Weak Body—Weak Constitution — Weakness — Feeble Constitution — Not Robust — The Constitution Not Very Strong, etc.—Vitality Low— The ☉ affl. in ♋, ♑, or ♓, or with these signs upon the Asc. at B.; the ☉ hyleg, and to the ☌ or ill-asp. ♄ by dir.; the ☉ or ☽ in the Asc., and hyleg, affl. by malefics in angles, and no good asps. from ♃ or ♀ to the hyleg, a weak constitution, and may die in infancy, or under the first train of evil directions, but the good asps. of the benefics to the hyleg will tend to prolong life under these conditions and strengthen the constitution; the ☉ or ☽ to the ☌ or ill-asps. ♄ or ♂, the constitution is weakened; the ☉ or ☽ in ☌ or ill-asp. the malefics; born at the time of a total eclipse of the ☉, and under its shadow, and males so born may die soon after birth; the ☽ decr. in light, sepr. from ♄ and applying to the ☉, ♂, or ☿; the ☽ nearly in ☌ with the ☉ at B., or at a total eclipse of the ☉; the ☽ affl. in ♑; ☽ ♑ partile Asc., never strong; the ☽ Sig. in ♑, thin, weak, feeble and sickly; the ☽ applying to ♂, or conjoined with him in a day nativity; ♄ affl. in ♋, a weak and infirm body; ♄ ascending at B.;

♄ in his second station at B.; ♄ in 6th H., and conjoined with the ☉ at B.; ♄ in S. Lat., the body weaker than when in N. Lat.; ♄ affl. in ♌ unless the energies are conserved; ♃ Sig. in ♑, a weakly person; ♃ or ♀ in ☌ with the ☉ when the ☉ is hyleg, as all planets combust are weakened; ♃ Sig. ☌ ☉; ♂ ♐; ♀ affl. in the 6th H., but the health may be good, and the constitution harmonious as long as excesses are avoided, and good habits adhered to; ☿ Sig. in ♑; many planets setting in weak signs or positions, and many evil asps. among them; ♎ on the Asc., the body weaker in old age; the lower and posterior parts of the ♈, ♉ and ♌ signs tend to make the body weaker, and also the anterior parts of ♊, ♏ and ♐; malefics in angles, and the ☉, ☽, and Asc. affl.; the Asc. hyleg, and ☌ or ill-asp. one or more malefics; the hyleg ☌ ♄ or ♂; the earthy and watery signs on the Asc., except ♉ or ♏, give a weaker body. (For other influences along this line see Debility; "Early Death" under Early; Emaciation, Enervation, Fatigue, Feeble, Infancy (Death In); "Health Bad" under Health; Malnutrition, Pale; "Much Sickness" under Sickness; "Low" under Resistance; "Short Life" under Short; Sickly; "Thin and Weak" under Thin; "Low" under Vitality, etc.).

Weak-Minded—(See Feeble, Impaired, Light, Shallow, Weak, Weakened, under Mind).

Weak Spots — In the Body and Star Map of Birth — (See "Horoscope" in this section; "Weak Parts" under Parts; Vulnerable).

Weakened — The Functions, Organs, and Vitality Weakened — The Disease Is Weakened—(See Diminished, Functions, Lessened, Minimizing, Moderation, Organs, Strength; "Lessened" under Vitality).

Weakening—Weakening Conditions and Diseases In the Mind and Body— (See Debauchery, Disease, Dissipation, Emaciation, Excesses, Habits, Hemorrhage; Insanity; "Profuse" under Menses; Passion, Venery, Vices, Waste, Wasting, Worry, etc.).

Weaker — The Strength of the Body Rendered Weaker — (See Breakdown, Collapse; "Weaker" under Constitution; "Wasted" under Energy; Exhaustion, Feeble, Prostration; "Weak" under Signs; "Weakened" under Strength; "Lessened" under Vitality; Worse, etc.).

Weakest—The Weakest Blood—The Weakest Constitution — The Weakest Organs—The Weakest Parts, etc.—The parts ruled by the signs containing the malefics at B. tend to be the weakest and most afflicted parts, and the part ruled by the sign containing ♄ at B. is always very sensitive to disease, weakness, breakdown, and affliction, whether ♄ is afflicted or not. (See "Weakest" under Blood, Constitution, Part; "Weak" under Organs; Saturn, Vulnerable; "Kidneys", "Parts", "Signs", in this section).

Weakly Person—(See Fatigue, Feeble; "Bad Health" under Health; "Ill-Health All Thru Life" under Ill-Health;

Infirm, Invalids; "Low" under Recuperation, Resistance, Vitality; Sickly; "Much Sickness" u n d e r S i c k n e s s ; "Weak Body" in this section).

Weakness—Debility — Feeble — General Weakness — Female Weakness — Weakness In Children, Females, and Males, etc.—(See Childhood, Children, Debility, F e m a l e s, Functions; "General Ill-Health" under Ill-Health; Infancy, Males, Men, Resistance, Sloughing, Stamina, Tone, Vitality, Women).

Will—A Weak Will—(See Influenced; "Negative Nature" u n d e r Negative; Passive, Vacillating, Volition; "Weak" under Will).

Women — Weakness In — (See Aunts, Daughter, Females, Functions, Menses, Mother, Sister, Wife, Women).

WEALTH—Money—Riches—Property—Assets—Wealth is ruled by the 2nd H., and benefics in this house at B., and fortunate conditions over this house, tend to the accumulation of wealth. (See Money, Property, P r o s p e r i t y, Riches).

Loss of Wealth—A malefic ruling, or in the 2nd H. at B., and with no benefics in, or good influences, over this house at B. (See Disgrace, Expense, Extravagance, Honour, Loss Of, Luxuries, Miseries, M i s f o r t u n e, Money, Pleasure, Poverty, Property; "Loss Of" under Reputation; Reverses; "Riotous Living" under Riotous; Ruin, Starvation, Wretched, etc.).

Promise of Wealth — ♃ or ♀ in the 2nd H. at B., well-aspected, and with no malefic afflicting this house; ♃ well-aspected in the 8th H., thru legacy; ♃ well-aspected in the 4th or 10th H., thru inheritance. (See Money, Property, Prosperity, Riches, Success).

WEANING—Wean Infants after the ☽ has passed out of the ♏ sign. (See Breast, Infancy, Milk, Nursing).

WEAPONS—Injury or Death By—(See Cuts, Duels, E x e c u t i o n, Gun-Shot, Hurts, Injury, Instruments, Iron, Mobs, Sharp Instruments; "Flying Stones" under Stone; Sword, War, etc.).

WEAR AND TEAR—On the Body—The earthy signs, when s t r o n g, well-occupied, and well-aspected at B., and espec. ♉ on the Asc., give a solid constitution, and able to withstand much wear and tear on the physical body; the ☉ in an earthy sign at B., and well-aspected, gives much endurance to the constitution, and able to withstand much wear and tear; fiery signs on the Asc., great vitality, and resistance to disease. (See Endurance, Immunity; "Good" under Recuperation, Resistance, Stamina, Tone, Vitality; "Increased" under Strength; "Body" under Strong).

WEARINESS—Of Mind and Body—Ennui—Generally caused by ♄ influence. (See Apathy; "Brain F a g" under Brain; Dull, E n n u i; "Dull" under Eyes; Fatigue, Inactive, Inertia, Languid, Lassitude, Lazy, Lethargy; "Low Spirits" under Low; R e f r e s h m e n t, Rest; "Drowsiness" under Sleep).

WEATHER — The Weather and atmospheric conditions are closely related to disease, suffering, as well as to human comforts and well-being. Millions have died, or been made sick thru weather conditions. See the following subjects in the alphabetical arrangement when only listed here—

Air—(See Air, Atmosphere).

Aqueous Vapors—(See Rain).

Blizzards; Changes—In the Weather — Susceptible To — People born when the L u m i n a r i e s are afflicting each other. (See Colds).

Cold — Much Suffering from Extreme Cold—Severe Winters—The ☉ ♂ ♄ in ♑ at the Winter Solstice; ♅ in an angle at the Winter Solstice; ♅ or ♄ crossing the Equator in Winter; ♄ lord of the year at the Vernal, direct in motion, in an angle, and affl. by ♂ and the ☽, severe cold, and loss of cattle and sheep; ♀ in an angle at the Winter Solstice, and espec. when in asp. with ♅; an earthy sign, as ♉, ♍, or ♑, ascending at the Vernal, and the lord of the rising sign affl., tends to extremely cold weather, and much suffering from cold, diseases in the parts of the body ruled by such sign, and especially in Countries ruled by the sign rising. (See Cold).

Colds; Corrupt Air—(See Air).

Drought; Dry Weather — Dryness — Suffering From — (See Drought, Epidemics, Famine, F o u n t a i n s, Heat, Pestilence, etc.).

Epidemics; Exposure — To the Elements — To Cold and Dampness, and Illness From — ♄ affl. in the 6th H. (See Exposure).

Famine; Floods; Frost; Hailstorms—Furious and Tempestuous Hailstorms —(See Hail).

Heat — Extreme H e a t and Suffering From—(See "Extreme Heat", "Warm", under Heat).

High Temperature—Hot Weather—♃ and ♂ act to produce higehr temperatures, being positive planets, while ♅ and ♄ produce a lower temperature.

High Winds—(See Winds).

Hot—Hot and Dry Air—Hot, Blasting Winds—Hot Weather—(See Drought; "Weather" under Heat; Winds).

Hurricanes—(See Winds).

Inundations—(See Floods, Rain).

Journeys—Wet Journeys—(See Journeys, Travel, Voyages).

Lightning; Low Temperatures — (See "Cold", "High", in this section).

Over-Moist Air—Suffering From—(See Rain).

Perihelion; Pestilential Air — (See "Corrupt" under Air).

Rain; Ships; Shipwreck; Snow; Storms — (See Blizzards, Rain, Shipwreck, Snow, Storms, Wind).

Susceptible — To Changes In the Weather—(See "Changes" in this section).

Temperature—(See Cold, Heat, High, in this section).

Tempests—(See "T e m p e s t s" under Sea; Wind).

Thunder — (S e e Lightning, Thunder, Wind).

Travel—(See "Weather" under Travel).

Volcanic Eruptions—(See Volcanoes). Many of the same influences which tend to disturbed weather conditions, with suffering to humanity, also tend to Earthquakes, Volcanic Eruptions, Tidal Waves, Pestilence, Plague, etc., and to much destruction of property and human life.

Voyages—(See "Dampness" under Voyages).

Warm Weather—The ☉ ♂, or any asp. ♃ except when the ☉ is also in asp. with ♅ or ♄. (See "Fountains" under Dry; "Extreme", "Warm", under Heat; "Hot Winds" under Wind).

Wet Journeys—(See Journeys).

Wind Storms—(See Wind).

Winter — Severe and Cold Winters — (See "Cold" in this section). For further study of Astro-Meteorology, see Book III in Pearce's Text Book of Astrology; the Articles on "Weather" in Wilson's Dictionary of Astrology, and in Sepharial's New Dictionary of Astrology.

WEDNESDAY — The day of the week ruled by ☿. The first hour at sunrise on Wednesday is ruled by ☿. (See "Hours" under Planets; Weak).

WEEK — Days of the Week — In considering matters of health and disease, it is an advantage to know something of the planetary rulership of the days of the week, and of the planetary hours of each day.

Sunday — Ruled by the ☉. Patients suffering from slow and lingering ♄ diseases benefit most by treatments on Sunday, as the ☉ and ♄ rule opposite signs of the Zodiac, as ♌ and ♒. Sunday is named after the Sun, being "Sun's Day". The first hour at sunrise on Sunday is a ☉ hour, and treatment given in the three ☉ hours of Sunday are more beneficial than in other hours. (See "Hours" under Planets).

Monday — The day ruled by the ☽, being "Moon's Day". Monday is also a good day to treat ♄ diseases, and in the ☽ hours of this day, as the ☽ opposes ♄, the ☽ ruling ♋, and ♄ the opposite sign ♑. The ☽ moves fast, and people born on Monday tend to be restless, and fond of travel and change, and also to be more subject to ☽ diseases, and to be strongly affected at the Quarters of the ☽.

Tuesday — Ruled by ♂, and people born on Tuesday tend to be more hasty, excitable, and impetuous, and also to be more susceptible to accidents, injuries, wounds, fevers, inflammations, and to quarrels. Tuesday is a good day to give the remedies of ♂, as tonics and stimulants, and espec. in the three ♂ hours of the day, as at sunrise, the 8th and 16th hours after sunrise. Tuesday is a good day to apply poultices to draw out suppurations, or to draw boils to a head, as pus is a ♄ formation.

Wednesday — The day ruled by the planet ☿, the mental ruler. Wednesday people tend to be studious, and to suffer more from mental disorders,

brain-fag, fatigue from over-study, or too much reading. They need periods of mental rest, and to relax the nerves. Mercury rules the ♊ and ♍ signs, and opposes the ♃ signs ♐ and ♓, and the diseases of ♃ tend to be benefitted on Wednesday, and to be treated by the Herbs and remedies of ☿, and to apply such in the ☿ hours of Wednesday. (See "Mercury Group" under Herbs).

Thursday — Ruled by ♃, and Thursday people tend to partake of the ♃ qualities, and to be more kindly and generous, or religiously inclined. Mental, nervous, and chronic disorders tend to rapid relief when treated on Thursday, in the ♃ hours of this day, and to be treated by the remedies of ♃ or the ☽, as the ♃ signs ♐ and ♓ oppose the ☿ signs ♊ and ♍, and also the ♋ sign, the exalted sign of ♃, opposes the ♄ sign ♑. Thursday is a good day for religious devotion, quietude, peace of mind, relaxation, etc.

Friday—The day ruled by ♀. A good day for pleasure, recreation, amusement, travel, etc. Also a good day to treat the diseases of ♂, as the ♂ and ♀ signs in the Zodiac are in ♉ aspect, as ♈ and ♎, or ♉ and ♏. Friday is a good day, and in the ♀ hours of Friday, to treat diseases of the head, ruled by ♈, and sex disorders, ruled by ♏ and ♂. The diseases of ♀ are apt to be more aggravated on Friday, or to have their incipiency thru dissipation, excesses, pleasures, or venery.

Saturday — Ruled by ♄, being "Saturn's Day". Is the day of rest in Nature, or the Sabbath Day. Is also the day of death, relaxation of tissue, of decay and degeneration. People born on Saturday tend to be more melancholic, serious, and grave, and to have delays, disappointments, and misfortunes in life. The inflammations and fevers of ♂ are greatly benefitted when treated on Saturday, and by the remedies of ♄, and by cold applications, as ♄ opposes ♂, one being cold by nature, and the other hot and inflammable. Poultices and applications to reduce a swelling, as from an injury caused by ♂, have greater effect when used on Saturday, and in a ♄ hour. (See the ♄ hour in the paragraph, "Hours" under Planets).

In prolonged and lingering diseases, the patient also tends to make more rapid progress when treated on the day, or days, ruled by the planets which have the best aspects in the map of birth, for to treat a patient on the days, or in the planetary hours, ruled by planets which are badly afflicted at B., not much progress is made, and even harm may be done, or a relapse occur. (See Antipathy, Opposites, Remedies, Treatment).

WEEPING—

Eczema—Weeping Eczema—(See Eczema). See Emotions, Tears.

WEIGHT—

Body—Weight of the Body—The body usually gains one or two pounds in the increase of the ☽, and falls off in weight during the decr. of ☽. The fluids of the body, and the weight, are at their height at Full ☽. The body tends to be lighter in weight, thin and small when ♄ is on the Asc. at B., and a watery sign on Asc. tends to a fleshy and corpulent body, and with less vitality, except ♏, which is a more vital sign. (See Corpulent, Fat, Fleshy, Giants, Mean, Short, Small, Thin, Emaciated, Wasted).

Brain — Weight of the Brain — (See "Weight" under Brain).

Gains Weight Rapidly— ☽ in ♋ at B.

Loses Weight — (See Anaemia, Atrophy, Consumptions, Emaciation; "Malnutrition" under Nutrition; Tuberculosis, Wasting).

WEIL'S DISEASE—(See Spleen).

WEIRD—

Weird Mind — Weird Experiences — Uncanny Feelings—♅ affl. in the 3rd or 9th houses; the Pr. ☽ to the ☌ or ill-asp. ♅ if ♅ be affl. at B.; the 3rd decan. of ♒ on the Asc., strange terrors of mind. (See Chaotic, Confusion, Delirium, Delusions; "Dreamy Mind" under Dreams; Fears, Forebodings, Hallucinations, Illusions, Imagination, Insanity; "Low Spirits" under Low; Melancholy, Obsessions, Premonitions, Solitude, Spirit Controls, Visions).

WELL—Words beginning with "Well".

Well-Balanced — (1) Well-Balanced Body—(See Beautiful, Comely, Handsome, Harmony). (2) Well-Balanced Mind—(See "Well-Balanced" under Mind).

Well-Built Body—Well-Built Person —Indicated by ♂ and the ♌ sign; ♌ on the Asc.

Well-Composed Body—Good Make— The ☉ gives; the ☽ Sig. in ♎; ♄ Sig. in ♐; ♃ in ♐; ♃ Sig. in an earthy sign; in Hor'y Q., ♃ Sig. of the party; ♂ Sig. in ♒; ☿ ori. at B.; ♍ and ♒ give, and espec. when on the Asc. (See Beautiful, Handsome).

Well-Descended Body—♃ in an earthy sign; the ruler, or the Sig., in his own triplicity. (See Heredity).

Well-Disposed Mind—The 6th face of ♎ on the Asc. (See Humane, Kind, Noble; "Even Temper" under Temper).

Well-Favored Body — ♍ gives, and with ♍ on the Asc., but not necessarily beautiful or handsome.

Well-Formed Body — The ☉ or ☽ in ♒, in partile asp. the Asc., well-formed, middle-sized, and corpulent; the ☽ Sig. in ♍; the ☽ in ♍ or ♎, partile the Asc., well-formed and tall; ♄ ori. of the ☉; ♃ in ♍ or ♎; ♂ in ♍, partile the Asc., well-formed and tall; ♀ ori., or in the Asc.; ♀ in ♉, ♍, or ♎; ♀ in ♌ or ♐, partile the Asc., well-formed and tall; ♀ Sig. in ♒; ☿ Sig. in ♍ or ♐; ♍ on the Asc., well-formed, neat, and compact; ♍ or ♐ on the Asc., well-formed and tall; ♐ on the Asc., well-formed, rather tall and strong. (See Corpulent, Skeleton; "Well-Made" in this section).

Well-Framed Body — Tall and Elegantly Made — ♎ on the Asc. (See Skeleton).

Well-Jointed Body—(See Joints).

Well-Made Body — The ☉ gives; the ☉ as ruler; the ☉ in the Asc., rising, and well-aspected; the ☉ Sig. in ♈, ♌, or ♒; the ☉ in ♈ or ♌, partile the Asc.,

well-made and strong; the ☉ in ♑, partile the Asc., not very well made, and of mean stature; the ☉ or ☽ in ♒, partile the Asc., well-made, middle-sized, and corpulent; the ✶ or △ asps. of the ☉ to the planets when the ☉ is strong and dignified at B., well-made, ruddy, and of good stature; the ☽ in ♍ or ♎, partile the Asc., well-made and tall; the ☽ in ♍, partile the Asc., well-made, tall, upright and erect; the ☽ Sig. in ♒; ♃ in ♍, ♌, ♍, or ♐; ♃ in ♌, partile the Asc., well-made, tall, and strong; ♃ in ♍, partile the Asc., well-made and handsome; ♃ in ♐, partile the Asc., well-made, fine, tall, and upright; born under strong ♃ influence, well-made, tall, and upright; ♂ ruler of the Asc., and ori.; ♂ Sig. in ♍, ♌, ♍, or ♐; ♂ in ♍, partile the Asc., well-made and tall; ♂ in ♐, partile the Asc., well-made, tall, and compact; ♀ Sig. in ♍, ♌, ♍, ♎, or ♐; ♀ in ♉, partile the Asc., well-made and fleshy; ♀ in ♍, partile the Asc., well-made, tall, and slender; ♀ in ♌ or ♐, partile the Asc., well-made and tall; ♀ in ♑, partile the Asc., well-made, handsome, and rather corpulent; ☿ in ♍, partile the Asc., well-made, tall, erect and upright; ☿ Sig. in ♎; ♍, ♍, ♎, or ♐ on the Asc.; ♍ on Asc., well-made, compact, but may be tall, slender, and of spare body; ♐ on the Asc., well-made, tall and strong. The body is usually not well-made when ♑ or ♓ are on the Asc. (See Comely, Corpulent, Crooked, Handsome, Ill-Formed; Well-Composed, Well-Favored, in this section).

Well-Preserved Body — Young Looking—Youthfulness—The ☉ hyleg, and ☌ or good asp. ♃. (See Juvenility, Preservation; "Youthfulness" under Youth).

Well-Proportioned Body—Conformity of Members—The ☉ or ☽ in the Summer Quarter Signs, as in ♋, ♌, or ♍, or these signs on the Asc.; the ☉ Sig. in ♊, ♌, ♍, ♐, or ♒; the ☉ or ☿ in ♍, partile the Asc., well-proportioned, tall, and slender; the ☽ in ♋, partile the Asc., fleshy, well-proportioned, and middle-sized; the ☽ Sig. in ♋, ♌, or ♐; ♄ ori. at B.; ♄ Sig. in ♊ or ♐, and in partile asp. the Asc.; ♄ in ♊, in good asp. the Asc., well-proportioned and tall; ♄ in ♐, partile the Asc.; ♃ in ♎, symmetry of form, and good stature; ♃ in the Asc.; ♃ Sig. in ♌; ♂ Sig. in ♊, ♌, ♍, ♎, or ♐; ♂ in ♎, partile the Asc., well-proportioned and tall; ♂ in ♍, partile the Asc., well-proportioned, middle-sized, and slender; ♂ in ♐, partile the Asc.; ♀ in the Asc., dignified, and well-aspected; ♀ Sig. in ♌, ♍, or ♒; ♀ in ♍, partile the Asc., well-proportioned and tall; ☿ Sig. in ♌ or ♍; ♌ on the Asc., well-proportioned and tall; ♍ on the Asc., well-proportioned, tall, slender, or compact; people born in temperate climates, with alternate heat and cold; the Quarters from the Summer Tropic to the Autumnal Equi., and from the Winter Tropic to the Vernal Equi., tend to give. (See Comely, Compact, Elegant, Handsome, Harmony; "Well-Proportioned" under Legs; "Proportioned" under Moderately; Proportionate; "Well-Shaped" in this section).

Well-Set Body — Thick Body—The ☉ or ☽ Sig. in ♉ or ♏, well-set, thick body; the ☉ in ♉, well-set, thick body; the ☉ in ♉, partile the Asc., well-set, short, and rather ugly; the ☽ in ♉, partile the Asc., well-set, strong, corpulent, and rather short; the ☽ Sig. in ♏, thick, stout, well-set, and rather ill-shaped; ♄ in ♏, partile the Asc., well-set and strong body; ♃ in ♉, partile the Asc., well-set, stout, but not handsome; ♃ in ♒, compact and well-set; born under ♂ gives a well-set, strong, short body; ♂ rising at B.; ♂ in ♈, partile the Asc., middle stature, with well-set body; ♂ in ♏, partile the Asc., well-set, middling stature; ♂ in ♐, partile the Asc., compact, well-set, and fleshy; ♂ in ♒, partile the Asc., well-set, middling, and corpulent, and some Authors say tall; ♀ Sig. in ♉ or ♏; ♀ in ♉, partile the Asc., well-set, corpulent, and of middling stature; ♀ in ♏, partile the Asc., well-set, stout, and corpulent; ☿ Sig. in ♉, thick, stout, and well-set; ☿ in ♉, partile the Asc., well-set, corpulent, and middle stature; ☿ in ♏, partile the Asc., full, well-set, and with broad shoulders; ♉ or ♏ on the Asc.; ♒ on the Asc., well-set, strong, robust, plump, and healthy make. (See Compact, Corpulent, Muscular, Stout, Thick; "Well-Trussed" in this section).

Well-Shaped Body — Good Shape— Handsome— ♀ in the Asc., or ruler of the Asc.; ♀ Sig. in Hor'y Q.; ♀ Sig. ☌ ☿; ☿ in ♐, partile the Asc., well-shaped, tall, but spare and large-boned; the ✶ or △ asps. of ☿, and ☿ well-dignified. Also ♄ lord of the Asc., and occi., as between the M.C. and Desc., or between the Nadir and Asc., is said to give a good shape. (See Handsome; "Well-Proportioned" in this section).

Well-Trussed — Squab — Squat — Fat and Short — Thick-Trussed — In Hor'y Q., ♄ Sig. in ♏, squat and well-trussed; ☿ Sig. in ♋, squab and well-trussed; ☿ Sig. in ♓, short, squab, well-trussed, and dumpy; ♏ and ♒ give. (See Corpulent, Fleshy, Lumpish, Plump, Stout; "Well-Set" in this section).

WENCH — (See Harlots, Lewd; "Low Company" under Low; "Harlots" under Men; Shameless).

WENS—A Sebaceous Cyst—Steatoma— A Sebaceous Encysted Tumor—♂ ☌ or ill-asp. ♃; ♂ ☌ ♃ in ♈, in the head; ♂ ☌ ♃ in ♉, in the neck; a ♉ disease. (See Cysts, Sebaceous).

WESTERN SIGNS — Of the Zodiac — ♊, ♎, ♒. (See Eastern, Northern, Signs of the Zodiac, Southern).

WET—Damp—Moist—

Bed Wetting — (See "Incontinence" under Urine).

Dreams — Wet Dreams — (See Emissions, Semen).

Feet—Wet Feet— (See "Bowel Complaints", "Cold Taken", "Damp", under Feet).

Journeys — (See "Wet" under Journeys).

Linen—Wet Linen or Clothing—Colds Taken By—The ☽ in ♓, ☌ or ill-asp. ♄ (or ☿ if he be of the nature of ♄) at the beginning of an illness, or at decumb., from wet feet or damp linen. (See "Colds Taken" under Feet; Linen; "Colds" under Moisture).

WHALE—

Sperm Whale—(See Ambergris).

Whale's Belly — Influences of — (See "Danger" under Blows; Falls).

Whale's Jaw—Ceti—Menkar—Influences of—(See Ceti, Disgrace; "Every Evil" under Evil; Menkar; "Much Sickness" under Sickness; Thieves).

WHEAT — Scarcity of — An eclipse of the ☉ in ♌; an eclipse of the ☉ or ☽ in earthy signs, and such grain as is sown Annually. (See Corn, Drought, Famine, Fruit, Grain; "Corn" under Scarcity; Vegetation).

WHEEZING—A Sibliant Respiration— (See "Labored" under Breathing).

WHIMS—Whimsical—Capricious—Eccentric—The ☽ affl. in ♒; ♃ ill-dig. at B.; ♅ influence tends to make the native whimsical, witty, and subtle; the 7° ♑ on the Asc., carried away with foolish whims. (See Eccentric; "Foolish Fancies" under Fancy).

WHISPERING—Whispering Voice— (See "Aphonia" under Voice).

Whistling Roughness — To the Voice —A Whistling Sound In the Voice— (See "Hoarseness" under Larynx; "Rough" under Voice).

WHITE — White is ruled by the ☽. White is the Symbol of the Full Moon, which is also the Symbol of Initiation. The 1st H. has signification of white, and espec. if a planet in the 1st at B. has signification of white, as the ☽. White is also ruled by the 5th, 9th and 10th houses. Ruled by ♀ and ♓. In Hor'y Q., ♀ rules white. All the colors are contained in white. White, the color signified by the ☽, has a passive power, and is the sign of radical moisture. The ☽ also denotes a white-spotted, or light mixed color. White and purple mixed are denoted by ♀. White and red are denoted by ♈. Also ♊ denotes white and red mixed. Pure white, or glistening white, is ruled by ♓. (See Colors).

Blindness—From White Film—(See "Film" under Blindness).

Blood—White Blood Corpuscles—(See Leukocytes).

Color—White Color—(See the Introduction to this section).

Complexion — A White Complexion — Clear—Fair—Pale, etc.—☉ strong at B., a white and tender skin; the ☉ generally denotes an obscure white color, mixed with red; ☉ Sig. in ♒, clear and white; ☽ Sig. in Hor'y Ques., face more white than red; ☽ gives a whitely-colored stature; ☽ ascending at B., a whitish complexion; ☽ in Asc., pale and white; ☽ strong at B. gives a red and white mixed, but tending to paleness; ☽ Sig. in ♊, between a white and red complexion; ☽ Sig. in ♎, partile Asc., a fine, red and white complexion; ☽ Sig. in ♏, white skin; ☽ Sig. in ♒, clear and white; ♅ and ☿ rising in the Asc., a white skin; ♄ Sig. of the party, a pale and white complexion; ♃ strong at B., or ♃ Sig. of the person, a white and red mixture; ♃ ori., clear and white, or between a white and red complexion; ♃ ruler of the Asc., and ori., fair and white; ♂ ori. at B., and Martialists, some white mixed with red; ♀ ori., clear and white; ♀ in power at B., pale and white, but with a dark hue; ♀ Sig. in ♈, ♉, ♌, ♎, ♐, ♒, fair and white; ♀ Sig. in ♓ with females gives a clear, lucid skin, but very white; ☿ Sig. in ♒, clear and white; ♋ gives white and pale; ♎ infl. tends to neither excess of red nor white in youth, but pimpled or ruddy in old age; ♒ gives clear, white and delicate except when ♄ is in ♒; ♓ in females gives a clear, lucid and white, and ordinarily a chalky skin appearance; being born in cold climates, with alternating hot and cold Seasons, a whitish complexion. (For other influences see Cadaverous; "Good Complexion" under Complexion; Face, Fair, Light, Pale, Sickly, Skin).

Corpuscles — White Blood Corpuscles —(See Leukocytes).

Eyes—White Film Over—(See "Film" under Blindness; "Blindness" under Cold).

Face — White Face — (See "Complexion" in this section; Pale, Sickly).

Females—Complexion White and Lucid In—♓ gives. (See "Complexion" in this section).

Film — White Film Over Eyes — (See "Film" under Blindness).

Fingers—The Fingers Cold and White —(See "Raynaud" under Fingers).

Fluids—The White Fluids of the Body —The Body Oil—Ruled by the ☽. These fluids are obstructed when ♄ is in ♋ or ill-asp., the ☽ at B., and by dir.

Hair — The Hair Turns White In a Night—A Case Record—(See "White" under Hair).

Leprosy—White Leprosy—(See Leprosy).

Magic—White Magic—(See Magic).

Marks—White Marks On the Body— Indicated by the ☽, and the sign containing the ☽. (See Marks).

Nose — Whiteness of — (See "Cold Nose" under Nose).

Pale and White — (See Pale; "Complexion" under Poor; Sickly; "Complexion" in this section).

Red and White — A Mixed Red and White Complexion—(See "Complexion" in this section).

Skin—White Skin—(See "White" under Skin; "Complexion" in this section).

Toes—Whiteness of—(See "Raynaud" under Fingers).

WHITES — In Women — (See Leucorrhoea).

WHITLOWS — Panaris — Phlegmonous Inflammation About the Nails — (See "Whitlows" under Toes).

WHOLE—The Whole Body—The Entire Body—Whole Signs, etc.—

Abscesses—Over the Body, and Due to Bad Blood—♃ affl. in ♉. (See Abscesses).

Aches and Pains — Over the Entire Body—(See Aches; "Pains" in this section).

Disordered — The Whole Frame Disordered—The Disease Is Thru the Entire Body—The ☉, ☽, and Asc. afflicted; the ☽ in ♉, and affl. by the ☉ or ♂ when taken ill (Hor'y).

Dropsy — Over the Body — General Dropsy — (See "Anasarca" under Dropsy).

Entire Body Disordered — (See "Disordered" in this section).

Fever — In the Whole Body — The ☉ directed to Cor Scorpio. (See Fever).

Frame—The Whole Frame Disordered —(See "Disordered" in this section).

General—The Distemper Is General— Over the Whole Body—The ☽ in ♉, and to the evil asps. the Asc. by dir. (See General).

Gnawing Pains — Over the Entire Body — (See "Pains" in this section; "Flying", "Gnawing", "Shooting", under Pain).

Heaviness — Over the Body — (See Aches, Dull, Feeble, Heavy Malaise).

Humours — The Whole Body Full of Gross Humours—(See Gross; "Gross" under Humours).

Imperfections — All Over the Body — Given by the ♋ sign, and afflictions in ♋. (See Imperfections).

Inflammation — All Over the Body — (See "All Over" under Inflammation).

Joints — Pain In the Joints All Over the Body—(See "Pain" under Joints).

Pains—Gnawing and Shooting Pains Over the Whole Body—The ☽ to the ♂ or ill-asp. ♄ by dir., the whole body suffers from aches and pains; the ☽ in ♉, and affl. by the ☉ or ♂ when taken ill (Hor'y); the ☽ ♂ ☉, combust, or the ☽ ♂ ♅, ♄, or ♂ at the beginning of an illness, or at decumb., and espec. if the party be old (Hor'y). (See "Gnawing" in this section).

Shooting Pains—Over the Body—(See "Pains" in this section).

Signs—The Whole Signs of the Zodiac —The Airy Signs, ♊, ♎, and ♒, and those born under these signs tend to be more robust, strong, and also more immune from accidents. (See "Air Signs" under Air).

Tone — The Tone of the Whole Body Lowered—The ☽ affl. in ♏. (See Tone).

WHOLESOME AIR—Pure and Good Air —(See Air).

WHOOPING COUGH—Pertussis—A Violent Convulsive Cough — A ♊ and ♐ disease; ♊ on cusp of 6th H.; ☿ affl. at B. by malefics, and the hyleg also afflicted; ☿ occi. at B., affl. by malefics, and ☿ affl. the hyleg by dir., and taking part in a train of fatal directions, tends to death by whooping cough; the Asc. to the □ or 8 ☿ and ☿ affl. at B.; the hyleg much afflicted at B. Subs at LCP (6, 7C), and at SP. Coral Necklaces, or Amulets, are worn against Whooping Cough, and the drug, Corallium Rubrum, a Calcium Carbonate, Chalk, or Lime preparation, is useful in its cure. (See Amulets, Chalk; "Convulsive" under Cough; Talisman).

WICKED—Evil—Depraved—Vicious—Sinful—

Children— Wicked Children — (See Eleventh House; "Bad Children", "Injured", under Parents).

Countenance— Wicked and Cruel Countenance—♂ rising in the Asc. or M.C. at B., and afflicted by ♄. (See Abandoned, Cruel, Depraved, Evil; "Shows No Pity" under Pity; Profane, Vicious).

WIDE—Broad—

Chest—(See "Wide" under Chest).

Face — The Face Wide Across the Cheeks — (See Decanates; "Wide" under Face).

Head — The Head Wide Between the Temples—(See Decanates).

Mouth—(See "Wide" under Mouth).

Nose—(See "Wide" under Nose).

Shoulders—(See "Broad" under Shoulders).

WIDOWERS—The ☽ ori. in an angle in ♊, ♐, or ♓; the ☽ in this situation, and applying to several planets in oriental signs, indicates two or three marriages for men, by death of wife, or divorce. (See Fiancee; "Death" under Marriage Partner; "Death of Wife" under Wife).

WIDOWS—Often Becomes a Widow—The ☉ in an angle, ori., and in asp. to many planets oriental in ♊, ♐, or ♓; the ☽ incr. in light at B., and applying to ♄; the evil asps. of ♄ and malefics to the ☉, or ♄ in the 7th H. of the wife's horoscope; the 2nd face of ♍ on the Asc., which face contains the unfortunate star Vindemiatrix. Case — See "Princess", No. 851, in 1001 N.N. (See "Death of Husband" under Husband).

WIFE—The ☽ rules the wife in a male nativity, and afflictions to the ☽, and in the 7th H. in the husband's map of birth indicate her fate and the state of her health.

Accident To—♅ or ♂ affl. in ♎ or the 7th H. in a male nativity.

Afflicted — The Wife Afflicted — The directions of the ☽ in the husband's horoscope afflict and affect the wife for good or ill; ♄ in 7th H. of husband's map, and affl. by the ☉ or ☽; to marry when ♄ or ♂ are in the Asc. or 7th H., or the planet signifying the wife being combust in the husband's horo., indicates a life of affliction or sorrow to the wife. (See the various paragraphs in this section).

Barren—(See Barren).

Childbirth—The Wife Benefits By—♃ in the 11th H., and well-asp. (See Parturition).

Danger to Wife—☽ hyleg and to the ☌ or ill-asp. ♅ by dir.; ☽ to the place of Hercules by dir.; ☽ in 7th H., and eclipsed at a Solar Rev., and affl. by ♅, ♄, or ♂, and especially if the place of a malefic planet at B. ascends, or if ♄ ascends also at the time; ♄ in the 7th H. at B., and again in the 7th at a Solar Rev.; M.C. to the ill-asps. the ☽ or ♀ by dir.

Death of Wife—Death of Wife Threatened—These influences are to be noted in the husband's horoscope—The ☉ or ☽ to the ☌ or ill-asp. ♄, ♅, or ♂ by dir.; the ☉ to the ill-asps. the ☽ by dir.; the ☽ applying first to ♃, and then to ♅, and ♅ or ♄ be in the 7th H.; the ☽ to the ill-asps. the ☉ or ♀ by dir.; the ☽ to the place of Rigel or Cor Scorpio; ♅ or ♄ affl. in the 7th H. in husband's horo.; ♄ ruler of the 7th H. at B., and to the ☌ or ill-asp. the Asc. by dir.; ♄ passing over the place of the ☽ or ♀ at B. by tr. or at a Solar Rev.; ♄ to the ☌ or ill-asp. the ☽ or ♀ by dir.; the M.C. to the ill-asps. the ☽ or ♀ by dir.; lord of the 7th in the 2nd, wife does not live to be old. (See "Early Death" in this section; "Death" under Marriage Partner.

Dies Before Husband—Malefics in the 7th in husband's map, or lord of 7th a malefic, and with benefic influences over the 7th in the wife's horo. In Horary Questions, the lord of the 1st H. and the ☽ are taken for the man, and the lord of the 7th and the ☉ for the woman, and judge of the nature of the aspects to them. Another method is to measure the distance in degrees between the lords of the 1st and 7th, and the lord of the 8th, and then predict that the one will die first whose Sig. is nearer the lord of the 8th; the planet to which the ☽ first applies being a malefic; malefics affl. the ☽ in husband's horo.; the ruler of the 7th a malefic and ♃. (See Fiancee; "Dies Before Wife" under Husband; Widowers, Widows).

Directions — (See "Afflicted" in this section).

Dissolute Habits — Wife Given To — Profligate—☽ □ or ☍ ♀ in husband's horo. (See "Drink" in this section).

Drink—Given To—Influences in husband's map—☽ □, ☍ ♀; ♂ ☌ or ill-asp. ☽; ♂ in 7th H. in ♋, ♏, or ♓, and affl. the ☽.

Early Death—Wife May Die Soon After Marriage—Lord of the 6th in the 7th, and espec. if ♂ be in the 7th; malefics in the 7th H. in the husband's map. (See "Early Death" under Husband; "Death", "Early Death", under Marriage Partner.

Father—Wife's Father Afflicted—Lord of the 6th in the 10th H. (See Father).

Fiancee — Ill-Health, or Death of — (See Fiancee; "Ill-Health" in this section).

Fruitful—Wife Will Be Fruitful—♃ in the 11th H. of the husband's map if the map of the wife is also fruitful. (See Fruitful; "Fruitful" under Husband).

Grave and Morose—The ☽ apply. to ♄ in the husband's map of birth.

Habits—(See Dissolute, Drink, in this section).

Has Children — By Other Men — (See Bastards; "Untrue" in this section).

Husband—Suffers Thru Wife—Sickness Caused by Wife—Lord of the 7th in the 6th, 8th, or 12th houses in husband's map.

Ill-Fortune To—☽ to the place of Hydra's Heart.

Ill-Health Of—Wife May Suffer—Illness of Wife or Fiancee — The Wife

Sickly—The ☽ applying to any asp. of ♄ in a man's horo., and ♄ be in the 7th H.; the ☽ or ♀ in the 7th H. at a Solar Rev. and ☌ or ☍ ♅, ♄, or ♂; the ☽ at a Solar Rev. passing over the place of ♄ at B.; ☽ to the □ or ☍ ☉ or ♀ by dir.; the ☽, or Pr. ☽, to the ☌ or ill-asp. ♄; ♄ passing over the place of the ☽ or ♀ at B. by tr.; M.C. to the ☌ or ill-asp. the ☽ or ♀ if either be weak and affl. at B. (See Improvident; "Dissipated", "Drink", in this section).

Infamous—The Wife Infamous—The ☽ at Full, or incr. in a nocturnal sign, sepr. from ♀, and apply. to ♄. (See Infamous).

Jealous of Wife—(See "Jealousy" under Love Affairs).

Marriage Partner—(See this subject).

Mind Unsound — Has Nervous Disorders—☿ in 7th H. in husband's horo., and affl. by ♅ or ♂.

Murdered—By Husband—(See "Murders His Wife", "Strangles", under Husband).

Nervous Disorders Of — (See "Mind Unsound" in this section).

Plurality of Wives—(See "Plurality" under Husband).

Relatives—The Wife's Relatives—Ill-Health of — Lords of the 6th, 8th, or 12th a malefic, and in the 9th H., and affl.; lord of the 9th a malefic and affl.; malefics in the 9th H., and affl. (See "Relatives" under Husband, Marriage Partner).

Self-Indulgent—(See "Self-Indulgent" under Marriage Partner; "Dissipation", "Drink", in this section).

Seventh House—(See Marriage, Marriage Partner, Seventh House).

Several Wives—(See "Plurality" under Husband).

Sickness of Wife — (See "Ill-Health" in this section).

Sterile—(See Barren).

Strangled—By Husband—(See "Murdered" in this section).

Sudden Death Of—♅ or ♂ affl. in the 7th H. in the husband's map. (See "Death" in this section).

Suffers—Wife May Suffer—(See "Ill-Health", and other paragraphs in this section).

Time of Marriage—A Bad Time, and Consequent Suffering—(See "Afflicted" in this section).

Troublesome—The Wife Troublesome—(See "Grave" in this section).

Unfruitful — The Wife May Be Unfruitful—♄ in the 11th H. (See Barren, Maimed).

Unsound Mind — (See "Mind" in this section).

Untrue — Wife Unfaithful — ♅ in the 7th H., □ or ☍ the ☽ in the husband's map.

Widows—(See Widows).

WILD—Feral—Untamed—Savage—
Wild Animals—Attacks By—Death or Injury By—The ☽ with ♄ and Sirius, or with ♂ and Markab. (See "Wild Animals" under Animals; Ferocious; "Dangers" under Travel).

Wild Conduct — (See Conduct, Debauched, Dissipated, Evil, Loose, Low, Morals, Perverse, Prodigal, Riotous).

Wild Delirium—(See Delirium).

Wild Fancies — (See Fancies, Vagaries).

Wild Nature—Indocile—Savage—(See "Dogs" under Children; "Inhuman"; "Animal Forms" under Monsters; Savage).

WILDERNESS—Lost In—(See Desert).

WILL — The Will — Will Power—Volition—The Power of Willing—The Stars do not rule the Will, and the powers of the Will, and what people will do, is not always revealed in the horoscope. The Will is Divine, and by taking control of the life can, by the proper efforts, largely change the limitations and afflictions indicated in the map of birth, and the Will can be asserted to such an extent as to largely overcome the indications of the birth map. However, it takes knowledge, and an increased consciousness of power to do this, a realization of your own Divinity, of your Higher Self, of the God within you. Many people are endowed with great powers, but are unconscious of them, and drift along thru life half asleep, and then when awakened, the Will Power can lead them on to new achievements, to good health, to greater usefulness, even tho they were passive and negative by birth. Astrology is a good study to show and explain the causes of things, the philosophy of life, but it may not teach you how to think, and for this you need Metaphysics, Philosophy, Religion, Psychology, and the Mental and Spiritual Sciences. We are not here upon this Earth Plane merely to hunt for happiness, worldly pleasures, but to overcome the world, to achieve, and to gain Soul Growth from the experiences of life, and our Will Power is given us to help us to do these things, rather than to go thru life as weaklings, sufferers, invalids, failures, misfits, etc. The study of your star map will show you your natural fitness, your tendencies, the lines of least resistance for you for the best success, and then it is within your power to follow up these leadings, and make a success of your life, talents and powers.

Disorders of Volition — Affl. in ♐; ♆ affl. in ♐ or 9th H.

Free Will—The stars do not rule the human Will, and Man is a free moral agent to do and act according to his degree of advancement, enlightenment, knowledge, and self-control. Man is held responsible for the influences stamped upon him at B., and if his Chart of Birth predominates in evil aspects and tendencies, he is expected to master the evils, transcend, and allow the good to predominate, and to seek to perfect his nature and character, as perfection is the ultimate goal of all life on Earth. We are all Gods in the making, all Children of God at various stages in our Evolution. Some cannot keep up with the procession, and fall out of line, become laggards, stragglers, all because in the use of their free will they have chosen the downward path of sin, wickedness, debauchery, and dissipation, instead of the upward path which leads to God. The Higher Mind is The God, or The Christ within us, and when this Super Mind is awakened, and we become conscious of our Inner Divine Powers, then we direct the Free Will within us to higher attainments, self-control, and the attainment of knowledge, wisdom, discretion, discrimination, spiritual power, and to conquer and overcome the World. Be careful how you use this gift of Free Will. The Animals do not have free will, but are under the power and direction of Group Spirits, and act according to Instinct. Man is above Instinct, and can be ruled by his own Spirit, his Higher and Divine Mind, when he allows his Mind and Body to be used for good and high purposes, and not to live just for the gratification of his animal nature, or to carry out selfish and unholy purposes. (See Character, Fate, Negative Nature, Positive Nature, Self-Control, Spiritual; "Positive", "Strong", "Weak", in this section).

Insistent Will — ♂ influence. (See Bold, Folly, Foolhardy, Quarrelsome, Recklessness, Riotous, Violent, etc.).

Loss of Volition—♐ influence, and afflictions in this sign; ♅ affl. in ♐. (See Catalepsy, Clairvoyance, Hypnotism, Influenced, Involuntary, Mediumship, Negative Nature, Obsessions, Passive, Spirit Controls, Volition, Voluntary; "Weak" in this section).

Negative — Passive — (See "Negative Nature" under Negative; "Weak" in this section).

Positive — A Positive and Strong-Willed Person—(See "Positive Nature" under Positive; "Strong" in this section).

Self-Willed — The 30° ♓ on the Asc. (See Obstinate, Rebellious, Stubborn).

Spasmodic Will—(See "Weak" in this section).

Spirit Fire—The Spinal Spirit Fires of ♅ are said to represent the Will. (See "Spirit Fire" under Spine).

Strengthened—The Will Strengthened — The ☉ ☌ or P ☿ increases and strengthens the Will, and gives the mind more power to resist disease, and act against disorders. (See "Strong" in this section).

Strong Will—Powerful Will—The Will Strengthened—The ☉, ♅, and ♄ tend to give strong will-power when strongly placed at birth; the ☉ ✶ or △ ♂; the ☉ ☌ or P ☿; ♅ ✶ or △ ♅; many planets in fixed signs, or in masculine signs at B.; many planets elevated in the east at B.; a Stellium in the Asc. or midheaven, in a masculine sign; cardinal or fixed signs on the angles, and with many planets in positive signs; the first face of ♏ on the Asc. (See Elevated, Majority; "Positive Nature" under Nature; Rising, Rule; "Strengthened" in this section).

Weak Will—Spasmodic Will—Planets in ♐, and opposed by malefics in ♐, the Will is weak or spasmodic; ♓ on the Asc., devoid of much will-power; the 3° of ♋ on Asc. The weakest-

willed signs are ♎ and ♓. The mutable signs tend to indecision, and the watery signs to emotion, susceptible to external influences, to environment, and to be more easily influenced. Courage, self-confidence, and determination, are given by ♂ rising and strong at B. (See "Will-Power" under Drink; Influenced, Involuntary; "Weak Nature" under Nature; "Negative Nature" under Negative, Obsessions, Passive; "Lacking In" under Resolution; Spirit Controls, Vacillating; "Loss Of" in this section).

WIND—Winds—The following subjects have to do with Wind, Gas, or Air, both in the body and outside, and with Windy Diseases, and also Windy Weather. See these subjects in the alphabetical arrangement when only listed here—

Abdomen — Wind In — (See "Bowels" in this section).

Air; All Diseases—Arising from Wind In Bowels—♍ diseases, and afflictions in ♍; ♅ or ☿ affl. in ♍. (See Colic, Flatulence, Gas, Tympanites).

Atmosphere; Blasting Winds—Blasts of Wind — Death or Injury By — (See Air; "Fountains" under Dry; Heat; "Tempests", "Tornadoes", in this section).

Blizzards; Blood—Wind In the Blood —♃ affl. in ♒; ☿ affl. in ♊ or ♒. (See Flatulence; the Introduction under Spasmodic; "Windiness" under Veins).

Bowels—Wind In—Wind Colic—Flatulent Colic—Afflictions in ♍; a ♍ disease; ♍ on Asc.; a ☽ disease; ☽ ♍, and affl. by the ☉ or ♂ when taken ill; the ☽ or ♂ in ♍, and ♄ ruler of the 6th H. when taken ill; ♅ affl. in ♍, wind spasm, spasmodic pains and cramps from wind in bowels; ☿ lord of the Asc., and applying to the □ or ☍ a malefic; ☿ affl. in ♍, much wind in bowels; ☿ ♍ ☌ or ill-asp. any of the malefics as promittors; afflictions in ♒. (See "Cramps" under Bowels; Colic, Flatulence, Gas, Tympanites).

Cramps; Danger from Winds — (See the various paragraphs in this section).

Death or Injury — By Winds — (See "Storms", "Tornadoes", in this section).

Disorders — Windy Disorders — (See Blood, Bowels, Colic, Spasm, Stomach, in this section).

East Winds—Caused and ruled by ♄. (See Eastern).

Flatulence; Gas; Heart—Wind Around the Heart—☿ in ♌.

High Winds—Hurricanes—Tornadoes —Suffering From—♊ ascending at the Vernal Equi., and ☿ afflicted, and in places and Countries ruled by ♊; comets appearing in ♊; ☿ in an angle at an Equinox or Solstice; ☉ ☌ ☿; ♒ ascending at the Vernal Equinox, and places under ♒ suffer; ♂ in power at the Vernal, and lord of the year; ♂ in power at an Equinox or Solstice. (See "Corrupt Air" under Air; "Fountains" under Dry; "Storms", "Tornadoes", in this section).

Hot Blasting Winds — Parched and Hot — Much Suffering From — ♂ in power, and lord of the year at the

Vernal. (See Drought, Famine; "Excessive Heat" under Heat; "Winds" under Pestilence).

Hurricanes—(See "High Winds", "Tornadoes", in this section).

Loss of Life — From High Winds — (See High Winds, Storms, Tornadoes, in this section; Sea, Ships, Shipwreck, Voyages).

Pestilential Winds—(See "Winds" under Pestilence).

Shipwreck—(See "Hurricanes" under Shipwreck).

Snow Storms—(See Blizzards, Snow).

Spasm—Wind Spasms—(See Bowels, Stomach, in this section).

Stomach—Wind Spasm In—♅, ☿ or ☽ affl. in ♋. (See Colic, Flatulence; "Stomach" under Gas).

Storms—Danger from Wind Storms— An eclipse of the ☉ or ☽ in airy signs; ☉ hyleg, and to the ☌ or ill-asp. ♄ by dir.; ♄, ♂ and ☿ conjoined, great loss of life from wind storms and tempests; the afflictor to the Significators of travel in the 12th H. in a fixed sign, great danger from wind storms during travel; ♎ ascending at the Vernal, and ♀ also be afflicted; malefics in the 9th H., and affl. the ☉ or ☽ in airy signs, danger from wind storms on voyages and long journeys. (See "Tornadoes" in this section; Floods, Sea, Ships, Shipwreck, Travel, Voyages).

Strong Winds — (See "Tornadoes" in this section).

Tempests—(See "Storms" in this section; "Tempests" under Sea).

Tornadoes — Strong Winds — Hurricanes—♄ and ♂ in fixed signs, widely separated, and controlling the Luminaries. (See "Fountains" under Dry; "Sun Spots" under Spots; "High Winds", "Storms", in this section).

Travel—Suffers from Wind Storms In Travel—(See "Storms" in this section).

Tympanites; Veins — Windiness In — (See "Blood" in this section).

Voyages—Wind Storms—Tempests— (See "Storms" in this section).

Weather; Wind Colic—(See "Bowels" in this section).

WINDPIPE — Trachea—The Cartilaginous Tube extending from the Larynx to the Bronchi—Ruled by the ♊ and ♉ signs. For Disorders of, see Trachea.

WINE—

Addicted To — A Craving For — ☽ ♓; ☽ in ♉ or ♓, and affl. by the ☉ or ♂ when taken ill; ☿ Sig. in ♓. (See Drink, Food, Thirst).

Surfeit of Wine — Diseases Arising From—☽ ♎ ♄ (or ☿ if he be of the nature of ♄), at the beginning of an illness, or at decumbiture. (See "Excesses" under Diet).

WINKING—Spasmodic and Involuntary —(See Eyelids).

WINTER — Those born in the Winter months have a weaker constitution than those born in the Spring months. Diseases beginning in Winter are longer than those beginning in Summer, and are more apt to run into a chronic form.

Cold Winter— (See Blizzards, Frost, Ice, Snow; "Cold" under Weather).

Dry Winter — ♂ in ♌ at the Winter Solstice.

Winter Signs — Of the Zodiac — The Hyemal Signs—♑, ♒, ♓.

Winter Solstice—The time when the ☉ enters ♑. (See Solstice).

WIRY BODY—Wiry Constitution—♐ on the Asc. (See Endurance; "Good" under Resistance, Stamina, Tone, Vitality; "Body" under Strong).

Wiry Hair—Wiry and Rough—♈ on the Asc. (See Hair).

WISDOM—Discretion—Good Judgment — Understanding — Discrimination — Power, etc.—

Lacking In Wisdom—(See Foolhardy, Imprudent, Indiscreet; "Bad" under Judgment; Recklessness, etc.).

Seeker After Wisdom—(See Independent, Knowledge, Learning, Metaphysical, Misunderstood, Occult, Philosophy, Religion, Science, Spiritual, Truth).

WISHES — The Hopes, Wishes, Ambitions, Desires, are ruled by the 11th H. (See Ambition, Desire, Hope).

WIT—Comprehension—Reason—Judgment—

Acute Wit—Ready Wit—(See "Quickened" under Mentality).

Dull Wit—(See "Mind" under Dull).

WITCHCRAFT—Ruled and denoted by the 12th H.

Tendency To — ♆ ☌ ☿ in the 12th H. (See "Black Magic" under Magic; Sorcery, Spirit Controls).

WITCH-HAZEL — Ruled by ♂. (See "Mars Group" under Herbs).

WITHERING—Blight—Fading—Decay —Withered—(See Blight). ♆ in signs which rule the Arms, Hands, Legs, and Feet, tends to withering, shrinking, and wasting of these parts. (See Atrophy, Decay, Dry, Old Age, Shrinkage, Wasting, Wrinkles).

WOE — Affliction — Grief — Sorrow — Usually brought on by the afflictions and testings of ♄, and as a result of wrong living and thinking. (See Affliction, Disgrace, Grief, Miseries, Misfortune, Reputation, Reverses, Ruin, Sorrow, Suffering, Trouble, etc.).

WOMB—Uterus—Matrix—The Womb is ruled by the ☽ and ♀ among the planets. Ruled to some extent by the ♋ sign, the sign of the ☽. Ruled by the 6th H. and the ♍ sign. By their internal government, ruled by the ♊, ♋, ♍, ♏, ♐ and ♓ signs, and influenced by planets in these signs. The Matrix is under the rule of ♓, especially when Syphilitic contagion is involved. The Womb as a receptacle is ruled by the ♋ sign. The Cervix, the Glandular portion of the Womb, the Neck, is ruled by the ♏ sign. The following subjects have to do with the Womb, which see in the alphabetical arrangement when not considered here—

Abortions; All Diseases—Of the Womb —Signified by the 7th H.

Barren; Birth; Broad Ligaments — A fold of the Peritoneum—Ruled by ♍. Disorders of, affl. in ♍, and also caused by subluxations at PP, the 3rd lumbar vertebrae. (See Vertebrae).

Cancer Of—Carcinoma—(See "Generative System" under Carcinoma).

Catamenial Disorders—(See Menses).

Catarrh—Mucus In—The ☽ in ♎ or ♑, ♂, or ill-asp. any of the malefics as promittors; ♄ affl. in ♏; Subs at PP 2, 3, 4L), and at KP. (See Leucorrhoea).

Cervix — (See Cervix; "Contraction", "Neuralgia", in this section).

Change of Life — (See "Menopause" under Menses).

Child Dies In Womb—(See Stillborn).

Childbed Fever—(See Parturition).

Childbirth—(See Parturition).

Chronic — Chronic Womb Trouble—♄ affl. in ♋ or ♏ in the 8th H.

Conception; Contraction Of — Hour-Glass Contraction of — Case — (See "Hour-Glass", No. 240 in 1001 N.N.).

Death—Death by Womb Trouble—☽ occi., □ or 8 ♄ in map of child; ♄ affl. in ♏ in map of the mother. Case of Sudden Death by Womb Trouble—See "Uterine", No. 985 in 1001 N.N. (See Abortion, Cancer Of, Hemorrhage, Tumors, in this section).

Death In the Womb—(See Stillborn).

Defects Of—Affl. in ♏, and ♏ diseases.

Deformity Of—♅ affl. in ♏.

Disordered Womb—Diseased—Uterine Affections — Matrix Disordered, etc. — The ☉ or ☽ affl. in ♏; ♏ diseases; afflictions in ♏; ☉ affl. in ♓; ☽ to the ill-asps. ♀ by dir., and espec. if the ☽ or ♀ be in the 5th H., or ruler of the 5th, or in 8 or ♏; ☽ to the ill-asps. ♀ by dir., and ♀ in a water sign at B., and espec. in ♏; ☽ ♏ ☌ or ill-asp. ♄ (or ☿ if he be of the nature of ♄) at the beginning of an illness, or at decumbiture; the ☽ afflicted; ♅ affl. in ♏; ♄ ☌ ♆ and ♂ in 8 or ♏; ♄ in an angle, occi. of the ☉ and ori. of the ☽; ♄ affl. in ♋ or ♏; ♂ affl. in ♏; ♀ affl. in ♈ or ♏; ♀ diseases are principally those of the matrix and members of generation, and espec. if ♀ be ruler of the 5th H., and throw an evil asp. to the ☽ or Asc.; ♀ affl. by evil aspects; ♀ in ♏ and affl. the ☽ or Asc.; ♀ in ♏ in the 6th H., and afflicted; ♀ affl. by ♄ or ♂; ☿ affl. in ♈; afflictions in ♍; ♍ diseases, and espec. when malefics are in ♍ in the 6th H. at B., and afflicted; malefics in 8 or ♏; ♏ on the Asc.; Subs at PP (2, 3, 4L). Case of Disordered Womb—See Fig. 8H in the book, "Astro-Diagnosis" by the Heindels. (See the various paragraphs in this section).

Embryo—Disorders of—(See Foetus).

Excessive Menses—(See Menses).

Falling Of—Prolapsus—Afflictions in ♏; a ♏ disease; the ☽, ♄, ♂ or ♀ affl. in ♏; Subs at LPP (5L). (See Prolapsus).

Fallopian Tubes—(See Fallopian).

Fecundation; Fibroid Tumor—♄ affl. in ♏; ♄ ☌ ☽ in ♏; ♂ ☌ ♀ or ☿ in ♏; malefics in 8 or ♏.

Flexion — Bending of the Uterus — ♄ affl. in ♏; Subs at PP (4, 5, 6L).

Flooding—(See Menses).

Fruitful; Generation—Disorders of—(See Generation, Reproduction, Sex).

Gestation; Hemorrhage—Of the Womb —♂ affl. in ♏; ♂ in ♏, and affl. the ☉, ☽, or Asc.; ♂ in ♏ in the 6th H. (See Abortion; "Childbirth" under Hemorrhage; "Flooding" under Menses; Miscarriage).

Hour-Glass Contraction—Irregular Contraction of the Womb—Contracted Cervix—♅ or ♄ affl. in 8 or ♏. (See "Contraction" in this section).

Impregnation—(See Conception, Fecundation).

Inflammation — Metritis — The ☽ affl. by ♂ at the birth of child often tends to; ♄ or ♂ affl. in ♏; ♂ ♏ in 6th H.; ♂ ♏ and affl. the ☽ or Asc.; afflictions in ♏; a ♏ disease; a ♍ disease, and espec. when malefics in ♍ in the 6th H. at B., and afflicted.

Injuries To—A ♏ affliction; malefics in ♍ or ♏, and espec. when in the 6th H. at B., and afflicted; ♂ affl. in ♏ in 6th or 8th H. (See "Excision" under Foetus).

Leucorrhoea; Maternity; Matrix—Defects of—Disorders of—(See "Defects", "Disorders", and other subjects in this section).

Menopause; Menses; Metritis — (See "Inflammation" in this section).

Miscarriage; Mother—Womb Trouble In—(See "Womb" under Mother).

Mucous In — (See "Catarrh" in this section).

Neck Of—Cervix—Disorders of—Neuralgia of — (See Cervix, Hour-Glass, Neuralgia, Stricture, in this section).

Obstruction In—♄ in ♏. (See "Hour-Glass" in this section).

Operations On—Avoid when the ☽ is in ♍, ♎, or ♏. (See "Rules" under Operations).

Ovaries—Ovum—(See Ovaries).

Pains In—♅, ♄, ♂, or ♀ affl. in ♏.

Parturition; Placenta — Ruled by ♏. Abnormalities of, attachments, delayed delivery of, caused by ♄ affl. in ♏.

Pregnancy; Prenatal Epoch — (See Prenatal).

Prolapsus—(See "Falling" in this section).

Puberty; Regeneration; Reproduction; Semen—Reception of—(See Semen).

Sex Disorders—(See Sex, Generation, Genitals, Reproduction).

Single Births—(See Children).

Sterility—(See Barren).

Stillborn; Stricture of Neck Of—♅ affl. in ♏. (See Cervix, Hour-Glass, in this section).

Swellings Of—(See Inflammation, Tumors, in this section).

Syphilis Of—Afflictions in ♓. (See the Introduction to this section).

Triplets; Tumors—Ulceration of—Fibroids — ♃ or ♀ affl. in ♏, tumors, and resulting from surfeits, too rich food, over-eating; ♄ affl. in ♏, fibroids; ♂ affl. in ♏, ulcers or ulceration. (See "Fibroid" in this section). The tumors are also caused by subluxations at PP (2, 3, 4L), and disturbances at KP. (See Swellings, Tumors).

Twins; Ulceration—(See "Tumors" in this section).

Uterine Disorders—(See "Disordered", and the various paragraphs in this section).

Vagina; Version — Of the Foetus — Caused by subluxations at PP, LPP, the 2, 3, 4, 5 lumbar vertebrae, and malefics in the signs which rule these vertebrae. (See Foetus).

Whites — In Women — (See Leucorrhoea).

WOMEN — Woman—Ladies—Females— This subject is partly considered in the Article on Females. In this section the subjects will be listed which apply more specifically to adult females. The ☽ and ♀ rule strongly over the health and affairs of women, and of females of all ages. The ☽ rules the adult female functions, such as the Menses, Maternity, Reproduction, etc. In a woman's horoscope, the ☽ is the Sig. of Health, and the ☉ in a male nativity. The ☽ is taken as hyleg in a woman's map, when possible, and the ☽ is favorably situated as hyleg. An afflicted ☽ in a woman's horoscope tends to disease, and disturbed functions. In female horoscopes, after puberty, the regulation of the health, the regularity of the system, and the function of maternity, depend upon the ☽ and ♀. The ☽ in the Asc. has much effect upon the health of the female sex, according to the aspects to the ☽. Women are denoted by the 5th H., and this is the house of women in the native's horoscope, and his relations to them. See the following subjects in the alphabetical arrangement, or under "Aunts", "Daughter", "Female", "Mother", "Sister", "Wife", when not considered here—

Abortion; Accidents To—Hurts To— The ☽ or ♀ to the ☌ or ill-asp. ♂ by dir.; malefics to the ☌ or ill-asp. the ☽ or ♀. (See "Children" under Hurts).

Active Mind and Body—(See "Active Body", "Active Mind", under Active).

Addicted to Women—(See "Addicted" under Men; "Addict" under Sex).

Aged Women—Illness or Death of— (See Aunts, Grandparents, Old Age).

Anaemia—(See Anaemia, Chlorosis).

Anxieties—Mental Anxieties—Mental Anxieties to Women—The ☽ to the ☌ the ☉ by dir.

Assaults By — Attacks By — Malefics in ♌ or the 5th H. in a man's map, or lord of the 5th a malefic, and placed in the 8th or 12th houses; lord of the 5th a malefic, and affl. by other malefics.

Astray — Women Liable To Be Led Astray—(See Seduction).

Attackers of Women—(See Rape).

Aunts; Bad Health For — (See "Ill-Health" under Females; "Health" in this section).

Bad Women — Loss and Waste of Property Thru — The M.C. to the evil asps. the ☽ by dir. (See "Free Living" under Free; Lewd; "Low Company" under Low; Riotous, etc.).

Barren; Beautiful; Bereavement; Births To — (See Birth, Children, Fruitful).

Blind — In Left Eye — The ☉ to the evil asps. a malefic by dir. (See "Eyes", "Left Eye", under Left).

Blondes — (See "Light Complexion" under Light).

Blood—Irregular Circulation of—The Blood Corrupted — Dropsical Blood — The ☽ to the ill-asps. ♃ by dir.; the ☽ affl. in ♏, impurities in the blood and system; the ☽ hyleg in ♓, and afflicted, dropsical blood. (See Blood, Circulation, Impure).

Breasts In — Ruled by the ☽ and ♀. (See Breasts).

Brunettes — (See "Dark Complexion" under Dark; "Black Hair", "Brunettes", under Hair).

Cerebral Functions — Disorders of — (See Brain; "Cerebral Functions" under Cerebral).

Cervix—(See Cervix, Womb).

Change of Life — (See "Menopause" under Menses).

Chaste—The ☽ and ♀ free from the affl. of malefics.

Child — The Woman Is With Child — Is Not With Child—(See Pregnancy).

Childbed Fever—(See Parturition).

Childbirth—(See Parturition).

Children; Chills—Women Suffer With Fever from Chills and Cold — (See Chills).

Chlorosis; Chronic Diseases—Women Suffer By — Death By — (See "Death" under Chronic).

Circulation Irregular — (See "Blood" in this section).

Clitoris; Coarse — Coarse Body — Coarse Voice — (See Coarse; Effeminate; "Coarse" under Voice).

Cohabitation; Cold—Suffers from Cold and Chills—(See Chills).

Complexion; Conception—The Woman Will Conceive — Will Not Conceive — (See Barren, Conception, Fruitful).

Conduct—(See Conduct; "Chaste" under Females; Harlots, Immodest, Imprudent, Lewd, Loose; "Loose Morals" under Morals; Nymphomania, Shameless).

Constitution—Good Constitution— Strong Constitution—Constitution Deranged—(See "Constitution" under Females).

Courses—(See Menses).

Dangers to Women — (See Abortion, Births, Miscarriage, Parturition, Rape, Seduction).

Daughter Born—(See Daughter).

Death — Of a Female Friend — (See "Female Friend" under Friends).

Death — Of a Female Relative — (See "Female" under Relations).

Death—Of Women by Fevers and Severe Illnesses—(See "Females" under Fever).

Death by Women—By Female Treachery — (See "Women" under Poison; "Tragical Death" under Tragical; "Female" under Treachery).

Death of Women—Danger of Death To —The ☉ causes death to women by fevers and severe illnesses; the ☉ to the ☌ ☽ by dir., and the ☽ affl. at B.; ☽ to the ill-asps. ♅, ♄, or ♂ by dir.; the ☽ to the ☌ ☉ by dir., and espec. if in the 6th or 8th H. (See "Death" under Aunts, Females, Fever, Mother, Sister).

Debilitated—(See "Constitution" under Female).

Depraved; Deranged—(See Deranged; "Constitution" under Female).

Detriment To — The ☉ in the 5th H. at the Vernal, lord of the year and afflicted; ☽ to the ☌ ☉ by dir.; ♄, ♂, and ☿ conjoined in ♍.

Digestive Disorders — (See "Women" under Digestion).

Disappointments To — The ☽ to the ill-asps. ♀ by dir.; ♄ to the ☌ or ill-asps. the ☽ or ♀. (See Love Affairs, Marriage; "Women" under Misfortune; Wife).

Diseases of Women—(See the various paragraphs in this section, and under Females).

Disgrace For — (See "Women" under Disgrace; Harlots, Immodest, Scandalous, Seduction, Shameless; "Unchaste" in this section).

Dissolute Habits — The ☽ affl. in ♍. (See Dissolute; "Drink" in this section).

Drink—Fond of—Women Crave Drink —♄ to the ☌ or ill-asp. the ☽ by dir. (See Drink).

Dropsy — Dropsical Condition of the Blood—(See "Blood" in this section).

Eminent Lady—Death of Some Eminent and Prominent Woman—Comets appearing in ♒. (See Famous; "Great Women" under Great; Queens).

Emotions In—(See Emotions).

Evil—Sudden Evil For—♀ to the body of ♅ by dir.

Evil — Women Very Evil — Of Evil Qualities—The Asc., ☽, ♂, ♀ and ☿ in double-bodied signs. (See Evil).

External Influences — Susceptible To —The ☽ hyleg in ♏ or ♓. (See External).

Eyes—Fine and Beautiful—Left Eye Affected—(See "Fine", "Women", under Eyes; "Left Eye" under Left; "Blind" in this section).

Face—A Plump Face—♓ gives.

Father—Death of—(See "Death" under Father).

Female — Females — (See the various paragraphs under Females, which Article is supplemental to this one).

Female Child Promised—(See "Birth of a Female" under Female).

Female Complaints—Functional Disorders — (See the various paragraphs under Females, Functions, and in this Article).

Females—(See "Female" in this section).

Fever — Danger of — Death By—Suffers From—(See Chills; "Death", "Females", under Fever).

Fiancee—Death of—(See Fiancee).

Flooding—(See Menses).

Fluids — Of the System — (See "Ailments" under Fluids).

Foetus; Fond of Women — (See "Addicted" under Men).

Freedom—Unwomanly Freedom—(See "Unwomanly" under Morals).

Friend—Death of a Woman Friend— (See "Female" under Friend).

Fruitful; Functions — The Female Functions Disordered—(See "Female" under Functions).

Generation; Genitals; Gestation;

Good Constitution—Good Health For —(See "Good" under Constitution; "Health" under Females).

Grandmother—(See Grandparents).

Great Women—Death of—An eclipse of the ☉ in the 3rd decan. of ♈. (See Famous; "The Great" under Great; Queens).

Grief—Thru Women—(See "Females", "Grief", under Men). The ☽ to the ill-asps. ♀ by dir. tends to grief to women thru men. (See "Women" under Misfortune; Opposite Sex, Sorrow).

Habits—Dissolute Habits—(See "Dissolute", "Drink" in this section).

Hair; Harlots; Hatred of Women — Hated by Some Female — (See "Females" under Hatred).

Headaches In — (See "Pains" under Head; "Women" under Headaches).

Health — The ☽ is Sig. of health in women.
(1) Health Bad — (See "Ill-Health" under Females).
(2) Health Better—(See "Health" under Females).
(3) Health of the Female Sex — Is much affected when the ☽ is in the Asc., according to the aspects to the ☽.
(4) Health Good—(See "Health" under Females).
(5) Health Injured by Women—Sickness Caused by Women—Lord of the 6th in the 5th or 7th H.
(6) Health a Source of Trouble—(See "Constitution" under Female).
(7) Health Strengthened — (See "Health" under Females).
(8) Health Weaker — (See "Health" under Females).

Hermaphrodites; Hurts To—(See "Accidents" in this section).

Husband; Hyleg; Hysteria; Ill-Health — (See "Health", "Ill-Health", under Females; "Women" under Misfortune).

Impurities—Of the System—☽ affl. in ♏ tends to impurities in the female system. (See Impure).

Infamous — (See Harlots; "Women" under Scandal; Shameless).

Inflammations — (See "Females" under Inflammation).

Injuries To — (1) Injuries to Women —(See "Accidents" under Females, and in this section). (2) Injuries by Women —(See "Injured" under Men; Treachery).

Internal Complaints—(See "Women" under Internal).

Irregularities—Of the Functions, and of the System—☽ affl. in ♏. (See Functions, Irregularities).

Left—(1) Left Eye—Blind In—Hurts To—(See "Left Eye" under Left). (2) Left Side of the Body—(See Left).

Length of Life — (See "Length" "Long", "Short", under Females).

Leucorrhoea; Libidinous—Violently Libidinous—(See Lewd, Lust, Virile).

Licentious; Life—(See "Long", "Short", under Life; "Length of Life" in this section).

Liver Disordered—(See "Women" under Liver).

Long — (1) Long Diseases In and Death By — (See Chronic Diseases; "Death" under Females; "Females" under Fever). (2) Long Life — (See "Long" under Life).

Loose Morals In — (See "Unchaste" under Females; Harlots, Immodest; "Loose" under Morals; Shameless).

Lower Order of Women — (See Harlots).

Lust In—Unbridled Lust—(See Lewd, Lust, Nymphomania, Shameless, Virile).

Male Child Promised — (See "First-Born" under Children; "Births" under Male).

Marriage — (See the various paragraphs under Husband, Love Affairs, Marriage, Marriage Partner, Wife; "Free from Passion" under Passion; Spinsters, Widows).

Masculine Women — (See Deviations, Effeminate; "Coarse" under Voice; "Degrees" under Whole).

Maternity; Matrix—(See Womb).

Men Injured By—(See "Injured Thru Women" under Men; "Health Suffers" under Opposite Sex; Treachery).

Menopause; Menses; Midwives;

Minor Disorders—(See Colds, Leucorrhoea, Menses, Mild, Minor, Slight).

Miscarriage; Misfortune To—(See "Women" under Misfortune; Sorrow).

Moon — The Moon Influences Over Women — The Moon As Hyleg — (See "Female" under Functions; Hyleg, Menses, Moon).

Mortality — Much Mortality Among Women—The ☉, ☽, and ♃ conjoined in ♎; the ☽ or ♀ lady of the year at the Vernal, weak, and afflicted; ♂ in ♏ at the Vernal, and lord of the year. (See "Death" under Females; Mortality).

Mother; Murders—Many Murders of —(See "Women" under Murder).

Natural Functions Of—Ruled by the ☽. (See Functions, Maternity, Menses, Mother, Parturition).

Nervous Disorders — (See Emotions; "High Strung" under High; Hysteria; "Disordered" under Nerves).

Nurses; Nymphomania; Opposite Sex; Ovaries; Painful Diseases—(See "Females" under Fever).

Parents — (See "Parents" under Females).

Parturition; Passion In—Ruled by ♀, and the afflictions of ♂ to ♀. (See "Passion" under Females; Lewd, Licentious, Nymphomania; "Passional Excesses", "Women", under Passion; Shameless, Virile).

Peace of Mind—(See Contentment, Happiness; "Peace of Mind" under Mind).

Periodic Illness—(See Menses).

Periods Of—(See Menses).

Poisoned—By Treachery of Women—(See "Women" under Poison; "Female" under Treachery).

Pregnancy; Property—Waste of Thru Bad Women — (See "Bad Women" in this section).

Prostitutes—(See Harlots).

Puberty—Ill-Health at Time of—(See Puberty).

Puerperal Fever — (See Parturition, Puerperal).

Quarrels—With Women—M. C. to the □ or ☍ ♀ or the ☽ by dir. (See "Women" under Quarrels).

Rape; Regularity—Of the Health and Functions — (See "Females" under Regular).

Relatives — Female Relatives — (See "Female" under Relatives).

Reproduction; Right Eye—Defects In —Blindness In—Hurts To—(See "Right Eye" under Right).

Ruined by Women — Ruins Himself Among—(See "Ruined" under Love Affairs).

Salacious — (See Lust; "Masculine Women" under Masculine; Nymphomania).

Scandalous — (See "Women" under Scandal).

Seduction; Severe Diseases—(See "Females" under Fever; Severe).

Sex Diseases In—(See Venereal).

Sex Gratification In — (See Amorous, Cohabitation, Lewd, Lust, Nymphomania; "Women" under Passion; "Secret Bad Habits" under Secret; "Married Women" under Sex; Shameless, Virile).

Sex Organs Of—(See Fallopian, Ovaries, Vagina, Vulva, Womb, etc.).

Shameless; Sickness — Caused by Women—Much Sickness Among Women —(See "Ill-Health" under Females; "Health Injured" under Men; "Much Sickness" under Sickness).

Single Women—Not Inclined to Marry —(See Celibacy; "Aversion" under Marriage; "Free From Passion" under Passion; Spinsters).

Sister; Skin—The Skin and Complexion In — (See the various paragraphs under Complexion, Face, Skin).

Sorrows To — (See "Women" under Misfortune).

Spinsters; Sports—Indiscretions In— (See "Indiscretions" under Sports).

Sterility In — (See Barrenness; "Unfruitful" under Wife).

Stomach Disorders In—(See "Women" under Digestion; Gastric, Indigestion, Stomach).

Sudden Evil For — (See Disgrace, Rape, Scandal, Seduction; "Evil" in this section).

System — Disorders of — (See Functions; "Impurities", "Irregularities", in this section).

Tomboyishness — Caused by positive signs being prominent, and with the ☉, ☽, ♅, ♈, ♃, and ♀ obscurely placed.

Tragical Death — By Women — (See Tragical).

Treachery—Suffers by Treachery of— (See "Injured" under Men; "Women" under Poison; "Female" under Treachery).

Trouble — For Women — Through Women—(See "Women" under Misfortune; Poisoned, Tragical, Treachery, in this section).

Unbirdled Lust—(See Nymphomania; "Unbridled" under Passion).

Unchaste—♂ affl. in the 7th H. with females; ♄ or ♂ ☌ ♀ in ♏, danger of. (See "Chaste" under Females; Nymphomania; "Unbridled" under Passion).

Unmarried Women — (See Aversions, Celibacy; "Single Persons" under Sex; Single, Spinsters).

Unwomanly Freedom — (See Immodest; "Unwomanly" under Morals; "Unchaste" in this section).

Uterus—Disorders of—(See Womb).

Vagina; Venus Figure — (See "Brunettes" under Hair).

Vexations—Annoyances—
(1) By Women—☽ to place ♋ by dir. or tr.; ☽ Sig. □ or ☍ ♀; ♀ by periodic revolution to the ill-asps. the ☉ in the radix. (See "Women" under Men; Poisoned, Treachery, Trouble, in this section).
(2) To Women—(See "Women" under Misfortune; Sorrows, Trouble, Vexations).

Virgin — (See "Chaste" under Females).

Virile Members—(See Virile).

Virtue In — (See "Chaste" under Females; Harlots, Lewd, Immodest; "Good Morals", "Loose Morals", under Morals; Perversions, Shameless).

Vital Spirit In — Governed by the ☉. (See "Spirit" under Vital).

Vitality In—(See "Good" under Constitution; "Health" under Females; Vitality).

Voice In—(See Effeminate; "Coarse", "Deep", under Voice; "Masculine Women" in this section).

Vulva; Weak Constitution — (See "Constitution" under Females; "Weak Body" under Weak).

Whites—(See Leucorrhoea).

Widows; Wife; Woman With Child— Is Not With Child—(See "Woman" under Pregnancy).

Womanish—(See Effeminate).

Womanly — (See "Chaste" under Females; Modesty).

Womb; Young Women—(1) Chlorosis In—(See Chlorosis). (2) Weakness In at Puberty—(See Puberty).

WOOD — Hurts and Wounds by Wood or Flying Stones—(See "Flying Stones" under Stone).

WORDS—Loss of Memory for Words— (See "Amnesia" under Memory).

WORK—Labor—Exertion—

Fear of Work—Lazy—Not Inclined to Work—Ergophobia—(See Idle, Labor. Lazy).

Over-Work — Health Injured By — Fatigue From—(See "Brain Fag" under Brain; Exercise, Exertion, Fatigue, Reading, Study).

WORLDLINESS — Earth-Bound — Absorbed In Pleasure, Material Gains, and Selfish Purposes—The earthy signs strong and predominant at B., and espec. the ♍ sign, and with this sign upon the Asc.; ♄ influence; ♄ in the Asc. or M.C., and espec. when in ♍; ♂ rising and strong at B.; ♂ or ♀ affl. in the 5th H.; ♂ affl. in ♍, and in □ to the ☉ in ♈; ♀ influence, and with ♀ affl. by ♄ or ♂. The fiery and airy signs predominate more in spirit and intellect. The watery signs are more emotional, dreamy, scattering, and vacilating in seeking worldly gains and pleasures, and espec. ♋ and ♓. (See Amusements, Conduct, Excesses, Expense, Luxuries, Materialism, Passion, Pleasure, Prodigal, Riches, Sports).

WORMS—Cestode—Parasites—The ☉ to the evil asps. the ☽ by dir., and the ☽ affl. at B.; a ☽ disease, and the ☽ affl. in ♋ or ♍; ♂ affl. in ♍; a ♀ disease when ♀ is the afflictor in the disease, and espec. when affl. in ♍; ♀ in ♍ in the 6th H.; ♀ in ♍ or ♍, and affl. the ☽ or Asc.; ☿ affl. in ♍; a ♍ disease, and afflictions in ♍; Subs at SP (8D), and at PP (2L).

Anthelmintic — A Remedy Expelling Worms—A Therapeutic Property of ♃.

Bladder Worm—(See Acephalocyst).

Bowels—Worms In—♂, or ♀ affl. in ♍. (See Entozoons, Parasites, Tapeworm).

Children — Worms In — A ☽ disease, and afflictions to the ☽; the ☽ affl. in ♋ or ♍; ♂ affl. in ♍; ♂ in ♍, ☌ or ill-asp. the ☉; ♀ affl. in ♍; a ♍ disease.

Corn and Grain—Destroyed by Worms — (See "Corn Destroyed" under Scarcity).

Expulsion of Worms—(See "Anthelmintic" in this section).

Remedy for Worms—Anthelmintics— The Herbs and Remedies of ♃. (See "Jupiter Group" under Herbs).

Ringworm—(See Herpes, Ringworm).

Stomach—(See "Worms" under Stomach).

Tapeworm—(See Tapeworm).

WORRY — Fears—Fretfulness—Anxiety —Peevishness—The ☉ or ☽ affl. in ♍; the ☽ □ or ☍ ♀; the ☽ affl. in airy signs, and to cause irregularity of the functions thru worry, anxiety, and mental strain; ♄ strong and rising at B.; ♄ affl. in the Asc. or M.C.; ♄ ☌ or ill-asp. ♀; ♄ affl. in ♍; ♀ □ or ☍ ☽; ☿ ☌, □, or ☍ ♄; ☿ affl. in ♈, ♍, or ♓; ☿ ☌ ♄ in ♍; many planets in earthy signs at B., and with an earthy sign upon the Asc.; ♍ upon the Asc. (See Anxiety, Dejection, Depressed, Despondency, Downcast, Fears, Fretfulness, Gloom, Grief; "Life Robbed of Its

Joy" under Joy; "Low Spirits" under Low; Melancholy; "No Peace of Mind" under Mind; Misery, Peevishness, Sadness, Sorrow, Trouble, Vexations, etc.).

Business Cares—Many Worries By— (See Business, Cares, Property, Reverses, Riches, Ruin).

Children—Parents Worried Thru Children—(See "Parents" under Children; "Injured" under Parents).

Enemies—Worried By—(See "Secret Enemies" under Enemies; Plots, Treachery).

Females—Worries To and By—(See the various paragraphs under Females, Women; "Health Suffers", "Injured", under Men; Treachery).

Functions—The Functions Disturbed Thru Worry—The ☽ affl. in airy signs. (See Functions).

Gout from Worry—☿ in ♑, ♂, or ill-asp. any of the malefics as promittors. (See "Melancholy" under Gout).

Ill-Health from Worry—☿ affl. in the 6th H., and espec. when in ♑. (See Ill-Health).

Nervous Disorders—From Over-Work and Worry—(See "Worry" under Nerves).

Parents—Worries to Thru Children— (See "Children" in this section).

Servants—(See Hyperaesthesia; "Worries Thru Servants" under Servants).

Stomach Disorders—Due to Worry— (See "Anxiety" under Digestion).

Women—Worries Thru—(See the various paragraphs under Females, Husband, Jealousy, Love Affairs, Men, Treachery, Wife).

The diseases and disturbances of mind and body, which may be brought on by Worry, are legion, and too numerous to list here. Look in the alphabetical arrangement for the subject you have in mind. Especially see the following subjects, in addition to the references made in this Article— Anguish, Banishment, Bereavement, Brooding, Disease, Disgrace, Dishonour, Distress, Execrated, Exile, Family, Fortune, Imprisonment (see Prison); Injury, Judges, Marriage, Misfortune, Neglect, Neighbors, Obsessions, Poverty, Relatives, Reputation, Responsibility, Restraints, Scandal, Sickness, Spirit Controls, Suffering, Suicide, Terrors, Travel, Unfortunate, Vehicles, Visions, etc.

WORSE—Aggravated—Less Favorable —The Disease Worse, etc.—

Chronic Disease—A Turn for the Worse In—(See "Chronic Disease" under Crisis).

Crisis In Disease—The Disease Worse At—(See "Worse" under Crisis).

Disease Worse—The disease tends to be worse at crises days, as on the 7th, 14th, and 21st days after the beginning of the disease. Also when the planet which is the afflictor in the disease meets the evil aspect of a malefic, or of the ☉ or ☽, or when the afflictor changes from a common sign, and passes into a cardinal sign, the

disease turns to run higher. Also the afflictor passing into the 4th, 6th, 8th, or 12th Houses, the disease may take a turn for the worse, or prove fatal. This subject is more fully discussed in paragraphs in the following Articles. (See "Worse" under Crises, Disease; "Arguments for Death", "Certain Death", under Death; Fatal; "High" under Fever; "Disease Will Increase" under Increase; "Disease Prolonged" under Prolonged; Relapse, etc.).

Dropsy Worse—(See "Increased" under Dropsy).

Epilepsy Worse—(See "Worse" under Epilepsy).

Eye Diseases Worse—Crisis Worse In—(See "Crisis" under Eyes).

Fever Worse—The Disease Runs High —Protracted Fever—(See Hectic, High, under Fever; "Fever" under Inflammation).

Fluxes Worse—Are worse at the Full Moon. (See "Bloody Flux" under Flux; "Full Moon" under Moon).

Health Worse—Health Weaker—Malefics elevated above the ☉ or ☽ tend to make the health worse than when the Lights are elevated above the malefics; the ☉ setting at B. (See Chronic, Complications, Consumptions; "Worse" under Disease; Emaciated; "Enlarged Scope" under Enlarged; Feeble; "Low Fever" under Fever; "Weakened" under Health; "Ill-Health All Thru Life" under Ill-Health; Infirm, Invalids, Relapses; "Much Sickness" under Sickness; "Low" under Vitality; "Weak Body" under Weak).

High—The Disease Runs High—(See "High Fever" under Fever; Poignant, Severe, Sharp, Swift, Violent Diseases).

Night—The Disease Worse at Night — (See "Diseases by Night" under Night; "Night Sweats" under Phthisis).

Relapse—The Disease Takes a Relapse—(See Complications, Increased, Prolonged, Relapse, Tedious). For further study see Continuity, Course; "Better" under Disease; "Degree" under Disturbance; Duration, Hospitals, Polarity, Praeincipients, Prevention, Remedies, Treatment, etc.

WOUNDS—Wounding—Hurts—Injuries —Traumatism—Wounds, such as Cuts, Stabs, Loss of Blood, and those due to violence against the person, Maiming, etc., are caused by ♂. The subject of Wounds is largely considered under Cuts, Hurts, Injuries, in this book, in which sections you will find subjects not listed here. The following subjects have to do with Wounds, and Wounds to the different parts of the body, which see in the alphabetical arrangement when not considered here. See "Accidents", "Hurts", "Injuries", "Wounds", under subjects which relate to Parts, Organs, or Members of the Body.

Abdomen; Abrasions; Accidents;

Ambushes; Animals—Hurts and Wounds By—(See Animals, Beasts, Bites, Kicks, Quadrupeds, Wild).

Arms; Assassins; Assaults; Battle— (See Bloodshed, War).

Beasts; Bites; Blindness; Blood — Loss of—(See Cuts, Effusions, Hemorrhage, Instruments, Iron, Menses, Shedding, Stabs, Sword, etc.).

Blows; Bones—(See Fractures).

Burns — (See Burns; "Hot Liquids" under Liquids; Scalds).

Buttocks—(See Haunches).

Chest; Contests; Cuts;

Danger of Wounds—Wounds Threatened—☉ affl. by ♂; ☉ hyleg, and ☉ to the ☌ or ill-asp. ♂ by dir.; the ☉ as Sig., or the Pr. ☉ to the ☌ or ill-asps. ♂; ☽ to the ☌ or ill-asps. ♂ by dir.; ☽ to the ☍ ♂ in mundo; ☽ to the ☌ or P. Dec. Aldebaran or Antares; ☽ to the ☌ Regulus if the ☽ be hyleg; ♅ to the ☌ or ill-asps. ☽ by dir. (See Electricity, Explosions, Machinery, Railroads); ♄, ♂, and ♀ conjoined in ♏ at B.; ♄ ascending at B., and the ☉ to the ☌ or ill-asp. ♄ by dir.; ♂ affl. in the Asc. at B.; ♂ ☌ or ill-asp. the ☉ or ☽ at B., and by dir.; a ♂ affliction, and liable to occur especially to ♂ people, those who have ♂ as ruler of the Asc., or ♂ in the Asc. or M.C.; ♂ in ♌ □ or ☍ ☉; ♂ in evil asp. ♄ at B.; ♂ affl. in ♊ or ♍, and to the ☌ or ill-asp. the Asc. by dir.; malefics in the M.C. elevated above the Luminaries, and ♂ holding dominion; fiery signs in the Asc. or 6th H., or the ☽ in a fiery sign at B., threatens wounds under the evil directions of ♂ to the Asc. or 6th H., or when ♂ is in the Asc. or 6th H. by tr. or dir.; ♂ coming to the Asc. early in life usually causes hurts and wounds; the 14° ♍, or the 1° ♎ on the Asc.; the Ascelli, Hyades, Castor, Pollux, Pleiades, Praesepe, directed to the Asc. or Lights; those born under the hurtful signs, ♈, ♉, ♋, ♏, or ♑, are more liable to wounds and hurts. (See the various paragraphs in this section, and under Hurts, Injuries).

Death by Wounds—Danger of—The ☉ to the ☌ or ill-asp. ♂ by dir. in a violent map; ☉ to the place of Praesepe; ☽ hyleg and to the ☌ or ill-asps. ♂ by dir.; ♃ Sig. □ or ☍ ♂; ♃ Sig. ☌ ♂, and ♂ ill-dig., and usually the result of folly; ♂ denotes death by; ♂ affl. the hyleg by dir., and ♂ holding the dominion of death, and espec. if ♂ be in the 8th H.; ♂ ori. at B., and affl. the hyleg by dir. (See "Death" under Hurts, Injuries, Violent; the various paragraphs in this section, as Cuts, Lightning, Machinery, Stabs, Sword).

Demoniacs — Wound Themselves — (See Demoniac).

Directions — Designate Events and Time of—(See Directions, Events).

Duels; Ears; Earthquakes;

Electricity; Enemies — Wounds or Death By—(See Enemies).

Events; Excoriations — (See Abrasions).

Explosions; Extremities; Eyes—(See Blindness; "Accidents" under Eyes).

Face; Falls; Father; Feet; Feuds;

Fire; Fire Arms—(See Gunshot).

Flying Stones—(See Stones).

Folly—(See "Death" in this section).

Fractures; Genitals — (See "Mens' Genitals" under Genitals).

Groins; Gunshot; Hands; Haunches; Head; Heat; Heights; Hemorrhages;

Highwaymen; Himself — Brings Wounds Upon Himself—♂ people. (See Demoniac).

Hips; Hurts — Hurtful Signs — (See Hurts).

Incised Wounds — (See Cuts, Instruments, Iron, Stabs, Sword, etc.).

Injuries; Instruments; Iron; Kicks; Kings; Knees; Lacerations; Legs; Lightning; Limbs; Loins;

Loss of Blood — (See "Blood" in this section).

Machinery; Maiming; Mayhem — (See Maiming).

Mens' Genitals—(See Genitals, Penis).

Mobs; Mother; Mouth; Murder; Muscles; Neck; Nose; Officers;

Parents; Pirates; Plots; Prison — Wounded In—(See Prison).

Privates — (See "Men's Genitals" under Genitals).

Quadrupeds; Quarrels; Railroads; Reptiles; Revenge; Robbers, Ruffians; Ruptures; Scalds; Scalp; Sea;

Secret Parts — (See "Injuries" under Secrets).

Self-Inflicted—(See Demoniac, Suicide; "Himself" in this section).

Serpents; Sharp Instruments — (See Instruments).

Ships; Shipwreck; Shoulders;

Soldiers; Skin—(See Abrasions, Bites, Blows, Cuts, Hurts, Injuries, Kicks, Stabs, Stings, Sword, etc.).

Sorely Wounded—But Will Not Die— (See "Badly Injured" under Injuries).

Spine—(See "Accidents" under Spine).

Spontaneous Wounds — Sudden — ♂ causes when the dominion of death is vested in him. On the other hand, ♅ causes sudden accidents. (See Accidents, Sudden).

Sports; Stabs; Steel—(See Iron).

Stings; Stones—(See "Flying Stones" under Stones).

Storms—(See Weather, Wind).

Strokes—(See Blows, Stabs).

Sudden; Sword; Teeth — (See Gums; "Accidents" under Teeth).

Testicles; Thieves — (See Highwaymen, Robbers, Thieves).

Thighs; Thorax—(See Chest).

Threatened—(See "Danger Of" in this section).

Time Of — (See Directions, Events; "Time" under Hurts, Injuries).

Tornadoes—(See Wind).

Total Blindness — By Wounds — (See "Total" under Blindness).

Travel; Treachery; Venomous;

Violence; Voyages; War; Weapons;

Wild Animals—(See Wild).

Wind; Wood — (See "Assaults" under Stone).

Women — (See Assaults, Injuries, Tragical, Treachery, under Women).

WRANGLINGS — Suffering, Injury, or Death By—(See Contests, Duels, Feuds, Fighting, Quarrels, Revenge; "Shedding of Blood" under Shedding; War).

WRATH—Wrathful—

Death by a King—Death by Wrath of —(See Kings).

Wrathful—(See Anger, Hatred, Jealousy, Malice; "A Murderer" under Murder; Revengeful, Unforgiving, etc.).

WRESTLING—A Champion Wrestler— (See "Wrestler" under Athletics).

WRETCHED — Wretchedness — Miserable—Unhappy—Sunk In Dejection— The ☉ or ♃ Sig. ☐ or ⚹ ♄; the ☉ directed to all Nebulous Clusters, and to Castor and Pollux; the 3rd Dec. of ♉ on the Asc., ruled by ♄, the face of poverty, slavery, and wretchedness. (See Dejected, Gloom, Misery, Unhappy).

WRINKLES—Wrinkled—Deep Lines In Skin—Ψ in the 1st H. tends to premature wrinkling of the face, due to a wasting and sapping of the vital forces; ♄ influence and afflictions, and ♄ rising in the Asc., tends to dry up the skin and cause wrinkles; ♅ on the Asc. (See "Cold and Dry Body" under Dry; Juvenility, Old Age; "Dry Skin" under Skin; Withering).

WRISTS—Carpus—Carpal Bones—The Wrists in the upper extremities correspond to the ankles in the lower limbs, and are ruled by opposite Signs of the Zodiac. The ankles are ruled by ♒, and the wrists by ♌, the opposite sign as ruler of the arms, wrists, and hands. (See Ankles).

Ankylosis In—Danger of—The ☉ ☌ ♂ in ♌. (See Ankylosis, Joints).

Dislocation Of — ♅ or ♄ affl. in ♊; malefics in ♌ or ♒; afflictions in fixed signs, and espec. with fixed signs on angles. Case—See "Wrist", No. 150, in 1001 N.N. (See Dislocations).

Fracture—Colles Fracture—♄ affl. in ♊, ♌, ♍, or ♒; malefics in ♌ or ♒. (See Fractures).

Gout In—The ☽ affl. in ♊, ♌, or ♍; a ☽ disease. (See "Arms", "Hands", under Gout).

WRITING—Transcribing—

Writer's Cramp—(See "Cramps" under Hands).

Writes With Toes — Case — (See "Writes With Toes" under Toes).

Writes With Tongue—Case and Birth Data—(See "Writes" under Tongue).

WRONG—Erratic—

Wrong Conduct — (See the various subjects under Conduct, Females, Habits, Love Affairs, Men, Morals, Passion, Sex, Women).

Wrong Diet—♃ and ♀ disorders. (See "Evil Diet" under Diet; "Wrong Diet" under Food).

Wrong Habits — (See "Bad Habits" under Habits).

Wrong Living — (See "Conduct" in this section; "Free Living" under Free; "High Living" under High; "Loose Living" under Loose; "Loose Morals" under Morals; "Passional Excesses" under Passion; "Riotous Living" under Riotous, etc.).

Wrong Thinking — (See "Mental Chaos" under Chaotic; "Mind" under Erratic; "Bad" under Judgment; "Shallow" under Mentality; "Light In Mind" under Mind; Perversions; "Disorders Of" under Thinking; Thought, Uncontrolled, etc.).

WRY NECK — Torticollis — (See Contortions; "Wry Neck" under Neck).

X

The subjects in "X" have been very much neglected in Astrological Literature, and in all my reading of the Textbooks of Astrology, I have not been able to record a single subject for the "X" Section of this book. However, by a careful research thru the Dictionaries, and the Medical Dictionaries, some very important subjects have been discovered which should be recorded in this book, and their Planetary relationships and correspondences given. This section of the book, therefore, is entirely creative on my part, and if I make mistakes, or assign wrong planetary influences to any subject, the student will bear with me, and suggest the proper influences, and also further subjects, for later Editions of this Encyclopaedia. This Section of the book has not been correlated with the rest of the book, as it has only recently been prepared, and after the entire manuscript has been finished, and for this reason there will not be many references in the first half of this book to see subjects in the "X" Section, as the first half of the book at this writing has already been set up by the Linotyper. The following subjects are herewith submitted for your study.

XANTHALIN—Xanthaline—An Alkaloid from Opium — Ruled by Ψ, and also may come under the rule partly of ♄, as Opium products are very depressing. (See Narcotics).

XANTHELASMA—(See Xanthoma).

XANTHIC — Yellow Color — Having a Yellow Color, and In Which Yellow Predominates — The Yellow Color is ruled by the ☉, and the Sun Fruits, such as the Orange, etc., have a yellow, or golden color, and are life-giving. Saturn also rules yellow in disease conditions, as in Jaundice, Stone, and the yellow skin of sickness, due to uric acid and urea deposits, hyperacidity, etc. In the Solar Spectrum the yellow ray is ruled by ☿. (See Yellow).

Xanthic Calculus — A Urinary Calculus composed of Xanthin—A ♄ disease and affliction. (See Stone, Xanthin).

Xanthic Oxide—(See Xanthin).

XANTHIN—Xanthine—Xanthinine—A thin, white, crystalline, nitrogenous compound, contained in blood, urine, and other secretions, and also present in the liver, spleen, pancreas, urinary calculi, and is closely related to uric acid. The nitrogenous element is ruled by ♅. (See Nitrogen). Also being a poisonous mineral deposit, when in excess, it also partakes of the ♄ nature. (See Uric).

XANTHINURIA — An Excess of Xanthine in the Urine—A ♄ disease and affliction. It is also undoubtedly true that the tonic action of ♅ in the ♎ sign, or ♅ ☌ ♂ in ♎, will tend to an excess of Xanthin in the urine, and to a pathological and unbalanced kidney action. (See "Calculi" under Urine; Xanthin).

XANTHOCHROIA — Xanthochrous — Xanthocroid—A Yellowness of the Skin —Under normal conditions the ☉ gives a yellowish tint to the skin, as in the Mongolian Races, as the Sun Color is yellow and golden, as indicated also in the fruits ruled by the ☉. In pathological and disease conditions a yellowish skin, and resembling Jaundice, is generally the result of ♄ action, and from hyperacidity, and excess deposits of Urea and Uric Acid. (See Jaundice, Yellow, Xanthin, Xanthochromia, Xanthoderma).

XANTHOCROID — Having a Yellowish or Fair Complexion, and with Xanthocroid Traits — (See Xanthic, Xanthocroia).

XANTHOCHROMIA—Yellowish Discoloration of the Skin, Resembling Jaundice—Also caused by a yellowish discoloration of the Cerebro-Spinal Fluid, from hemorrhage of the Spinal Cord. May be caused by ♄ and ♂ affl. in ♌, and espec. ♄ ☌ ♂ in this sign, or the ☌ of these planets in the 5th H., the house of ♌, the sign which rules the Spine, the Heart, and Circulation. (See "Spine" under Hemorrhage).

XANTHOCYANOPSIA—Color Blindness in which only Yellow and Blue can be distinguished. (See "Color Blindness" under Blindness).

XANTHODERMA — Xanthodermia — A Yellowness of the Skin, and no doubt a disease condition caused by the afflictions of ♄, and excess of mineral deposits, and espec. of the Xanthin variety. (See Xanthin).

XANTHODONT — Xanthodontous — Yellow discoloration of the teeth, and espec. of the Incisors—Caused by the afflictions of ♄ or ♃ in ♈ or ♉. The Incisors come especially under the rule of ♃, and ♃ afflicted by ♅ or ♄ may cause an excess of yellow mineral deposits in the teeth, of the yellow and Xanthic variety. (See "Fore-Teeth" under Teeth).

XANTHOMA—Xanthelasma— Xanthomatous—Yellow Tubercles of Neoplastic Growths — Yellowish Patches On the Skin and Eyelids—A Disease often associated with Diabetes Mellitus. On the Eyelids it may occur with ♄ affl. in ♈. When on the skin, or appearing as a tubercle, or neoplastic growth, ♄ is found strong at B., or affl. in a cardinal sign, and espec. in ♎ or ♑. (See Diabetes, Neoplasm, Tubercles, Xanthoderma).

XANTHOPATHY—A Morbid Yellowness of the Skin—Caused by ♄, and due to excess of mineral deposits, excess of Urea and Uric Acid over the body, torpid liver, and usually accompanied with lowered vitality. (See Deposits, Minerals, Saturn, Urea, Uric, Wastes, Xanthin, Xanthoderma).

XANTHOPICRINE—Berberine—A form of bitter yellow crystals from the root of the Barberry, Goldthread, and used as an antiperiodic and tonic, and is ruled by ♂. (See "Mars Group" under Herbs; Mars, Stimulant, Tonic).

XANTHOPSIA — Yellow Vision, as In Jaundice — Objects Appear Yellow— A ♄ disease and affliction; ♄ affl. in ♈. (See Jaundice).

XANTHOPSYDRACIA—A Skin Disease, and attended with small Yellow Pustules—♄ and the ♑ sign rule the skin, and skin diseases with yellow pustules are the work principally of ♄. Caused by ♄ in ♑, ♎, or in the Asc. or 6th H. in these signs; ♑ on cusp the Asc. or 6th H. Mars and ♀ also aid in causing pus, and pus diseases, and these planets entering into the configuration with ♄, or being with ♄ in ♑, would lend aid to the disease. (See Pus, Skin Diseases).

XANTHOSIS — Yellow Discoloration In Cancerous Tumors — Carcinoma (Cancer) tends to result in that part of the body ruled by the Sign ♄ is in at B., and the excess deposits of Urea, Uric Acid, and Xanthin, are brought to this part of the organism, tending to the yellowish discoloration which is so frequently seen in Carcinoma. Also ♄ ☌ ♃ or ♀, the rulers of the circulation, tends to such discolorations, and to cause stoppage of the circulation, lack of proper elimination, and unusual yellowish and poisonous deposits in the part ruled by the sign containing ♄ at B. (See Carcinoma).

XANTHOUS — Having a Yellow Skin — The Mongolian Races — People with Yellow, Red, Auburn, Blonde, or Brown Hair—Given principally by the ☉. If the ♂ influence is also strong at B., there is auburn, or red hair. (See Blondes, Light, Saffron, Yellow, under Complexion; "Light", "Yellow", under Hair; "Yellow" under Skin; "Complexion" under Yellow, Xanthochroia).

XANTHOXYLUM — Xanthoxylin — The Ash Tree—Prickly Ash—A Stimulant and Aromatic Bitter, and ruled by the ☉. Extracts from the Powdered Bark of this tree are used much by Physicians as a tonic, diuretic, and stimulant, and in the treatment of Chronic Rheumatism.

XENOGENESIS—Monsters—The Generation of Something Foreign—The Offspring Varying In Character and Life-Cycle from the Parents — Caused by Prenatal conditions, and afflictions to the ☽ at the monthly periods during Gestation. The afflictions of ♅, the ruler of the Pineal Gland, to the ☽ and other vital centers during the prenatal period, is assigned as a predominating cause. In such cases also, the past, the stage in Evolution, and many things, would have to be considered. (See Heredity, Inhuman, Monsters, Prenatal Epoch).

XENOMANIA — Attachment to Foreign Customs and Institutions—♅ well-aspected in the 9th H. at B., and also this house containing benefics, and free from the influences and afflictions of ♄ and ♂. (See Abroad, Foreign Lands, Location, Ninth House, Residence).

XENOMENIA — Xeromenia — Vicarious Menstruation—(See "Vicarious" under Menses).

XENON—A Heavy, Inert, Gaseous Element in the Atmosphere, discovered by Ramsay and Travers in 1898 — Ruled by ♅. (See Air, Atmosphere, Ether, Gases).

XENOPHOBIA—A Hatred of Foreigners — Malefics afflicted in the 9th H., and espec. ♄ or ♂. In such cases the native should also avoid Foreign Travel. (See Abroad, Foreign, Native Land; "Place of Birth" under Place; Residence, Travel).

XENOPHTHALMIA—Conjunctivitis Due to a Foreign Body In the Eye — Malefics afflicted in ♈, and espec. ♂ in ♈, which makes the eyes more susceptible to accident, injury, and the entrance of foreign and irritating bodies from without. (See Conjunctivitis, Xeroma).

XERANSIS—Xerantic—A Drying Up—Desiccation—Siccation—Lack of Moisture—Dry Skin and Body—A ♄ influence and affliction. Also caused by the ☉ and ♂, due to excessive heat in a part. (See "Body" under Dry; "Excessive Bodily Heat" under Heat; Parched, Scales; "Dry Skin" under Skin; Xeroderma, Xerosis, Xerotes, Xerotripsis).

XERASIA—Morbid Dryness of the Hair, and Cessation of Growth of—♄ affl. in ♈. (See Baldness; "Dry and Brittle" under Hair).

XEROCOLLYRIUM—A Dry Collyrium—An Eye-Salve — An Astringent Eye Remedy—Such preparations are ruled by ♄, and intended to allay the inflammations of ♂. Sugar of Lead, ruled by ♄, is usually the base of such preparations. (See Collyria, Lead).

XERODERMA — Dryness of the Skin — Roughness of, with Desquamation — A Mild Form of Ichthyosis — A ♄ disease and affliction. (See Scales; "Dry Skin" under Skin; Xeransis).

XEROMA—Xerophthalmia—Chronic Inflammation and Dryness of the Eyeball—Atrophy of the Conjunctiva—♄ affl. in ♈. (See Atrophy, Conjunctivitis, Eyeballs, Xenophthalmia).

XEROMENIA—(See Xenomenia).

XEROPHTHALMIA—(See Xeroma).

XEROSIS—Xerotic—Dryness—Marked by Dryness—Abnormal Dryness of the Skin or Eyes—Caused by ♄; ♄ affl. in cardinal signs; ♄ in ♈, of the eyes; ♄ in ♎ or ♑, of the skin. (See Xeransis, Xeroderma, Xeroma, Xerotes).

XEROSTOMA — Xerostomia— Abnormal Dryness of the Mouth, Due to Suppression of the Secretions—Dryness of the Mouth—(See Fauces).

XEROTES — Dryness — Dry Habit of Body — ♄ influence; many planets in earthy signs at B., and with an earth sign on the Asc. (See Xeransis, Xerosis).

XEROTIC—Dryness—(See Xerosis).

XEROTRIPSIS—Dry Friction—A Rubbing—Fremitus—Caused by ♄, and due to a suppression of the secretions, and espec. on the mucous surfaces. May also be caused by the ☉ and ♂, due to too much heat in a part, or by the afflictions of ♃, from lack of proper circulation. (See Friction, Xeransis).

XIPHICOSTAL—Relating to the Xiphoid Cartilage, and the Ribs — (See Ribs, Sternum, Xiphisternum, Xyphodynia, Xiphoid).

XIPHISTERNUM—The Metasternum, or Ensiform Cartilage — (See Sternum, Xiphicostal, Xiphodynia, Xiphoid).

XIPHODYMUS — A Double Monster, with United Pelvic and Thoracic Cavities, and Two Legs — This class of United Bodies comes under the same class of influences as given in the Article on Monsters. They are also due to irregular conceptions, and afflictions, and an unbalanced condition during the prenatal period. (See Conception, Monsters, Prenatal; "United" under Twins; Xiphopagus).

XIPHODYNIA — Pain In the Ensiform Cartilage—♅, ♄, ♂, or ☿ affl. in ♋. (See Sternum).

XIPHOID — Sword-Like — The Xiphoid Appendix, or Cartilage—The Third and Lowest Part of the Sternum — Ruled by the ♋ sign. (See Chest, Sternum, Thorax, Xiphicostal, Xiphisternum, Xiphodynia, Xiphopagus).

XIPHOPAGUS — A Double Monster United by the Xiphoid Cartilage, or the Epigastrium — (See Xiphodymus, Xiphoid).

X-RAYS—Röntgen Rays—Discovered in 1895 by Prof. Röntgen, of Würzburg. These Rays are produced by passing a high voltage of electricity thru a vacuum tube, and thru resisting substances, causing efflorescence. These Rays have the power of penetrating opaque substances, such as the bones and interior of the body, and from which Photographs, Shadowgrams, Skiagrams, etc., can be produced. These Rays are ruled by the planet Uranus, as ♅ rules Electricity, the Ether, Light, Rays, etc. (See Air, Atmosphere; "Vibration" under Colors; Electricity, Ether, Explosions, Light, Uranus, etc.).

XYLAN — Tree Gum — Wood Gum — A Gummy Substance of the Pentosan Class—A Gum which yields Xylose, a non-fermentable sugar, on hydrolysis. Pentose products, such as Xylan, Xylose, etc., and all Sugars and Sweets, are ruled by ♃. Xylan and Xylose contain five carbon atoms to the molecule, and being strong in carbon, which is ruled by ♄, they may also come strongly under the rule of ♄. Sugars, and substances of the Pentose class, are acid-forming in the system, if used to excess, and tend to the deposit of wastes, hyperacidity, etc., which matters are ruled by ♄. (See Carbon, Hydrocarbonates, Sugar, Xylite, Xylose).

XYLANTHRAX—Charcoal—Ash—Ruled by ♄. The Ash in the human body is also ruled by ♄. (See Ash).

XYLENE — Xylol — Xyloquinone — An Antiseptic Hydrocarbon from Coal Tar, and used in the treatment of Smallpox. Ruled by ♄, and opposes the diseases of ♂, such as Smallpox, and other Eruptive Diseases, Rashes, etc. Coal Tar Preparations, when taken internally, are very depressing, pain-killing, anodyne, and soothing for a time, and are generally used in Headache Tablets, and in Tablets to relieve pain, high fever, over-excitement, etc., matters ruled by ♂. The vegetable Tar taken from the Pine Tree, when applied externally, has a caustic and rubefacient effect, which qualities are ruled by ♂. (See Tar, Xylic Acid).

XYLIC ACID — A Tar and Petroleum Substance found in Coal and Wood Tar, and is obtained principally from Xylene. Ruled by ♄, as ♄ rules the mineral products of the ground. (See Xylene).

XYLITE—A Syrupy Liquid obtained by the reduction of Xylose — A Pentahydric Alcohol — Also contains five atoms of carbon to the molecule. Ruled by ♃. People born under the strong rule of ♃ tend to have a craving for alcohol, drink, intoxicants, sweets, etc., and especially those born under the ♃ sign ♓. (See Alcohol, Carbon, Drink, Jupiter, Sugar, Xylan, Xylose).

XYLOBALSAMUM — Balsamea Meccanensis—The Dried Twigs of the Balm of Gilead Tree — Balms and Balsams are ruled by ♃. (See "Jupiter Group" under Herbs). Also Balm (or Melissa)

is listed in the Mercury Group under Herbs.

XYLOIDIN—An Explosive Substance— Prepared by the action of Nitric Acid on Starch, or Wood Fiber. Ruled by ♅, as this planet rules explosive substances, and explosions. (See Explosions, Uranus, Xylonite).

XYLOL—(See Xylene).

XYLONITE—Celluloid—A Substance composed essentially of Camphor and Soluble Guncotton—Explosive and Inflammable. Ruled by ♅. (See Xyloidin).

XYLOPHONE — A Musical Instrument made up of a series of wooden bars, graduated in length to the musical scale, and sounded by striking with two wooden bars. Musical Instruments in general are ruled by ♀. (See Music, Venus).

XYLOQUINONE—(See Xylene).

XYLOSE — A Sugar obtained from Beechwood—Wood Sugar—A Non-fermentable Sugar of the Pentose Class. Ruled by ♃. (See Xylan, Xylite).

XYLOSTEIN—A Toxic Glucoside from the Berries of Lonicera Xylosteum — Honeysuckle — Ruled by the ☽. Is Emetic and Cathartic. (See Emetic; "Moon Group" under Herbs; "Therapeutic Qualities" under Moon; Physic).

XYLOTOMOUS — Having the Power of Boring, or Cutting into Wood—A quality possessed by many insects. A ♂ quality. (See Instruments, Mars).

XYSMA — Pseudo, or False Membrane, seen in the Stools of Diarrhoea—A ♍ disease, and afflictions in ♍; ♂ affl. in ♍. (See "Disorders Of" under Bowels; Cholera, Diarrhoea, Dysentery, False, Pseudo, Typhoid).

XYSTER—A Surgeon's Rasp. Surgeons, and the tools used by them, are ruled by ♂. (See Operations, Surgeons).

Y

YAWNING—(See "Sighs" under Breath).

YEARS—Year—

Critical Years — Critical Periods of Life—These are the years when the ☽ by progression finishes her first cycle, as at the 28th to 30th years of life, and also when by progression the ☽ is at her Quarters, or □ and ☍ aspects to her place at B. These times of the ☽ also nearly correspond to the evil aspects of ♄ every seven years over the life, and tend to be evil, critical, and changing years for the native, and also when ill-health may come, or some calamity, or misfortune, unless the native is forewarned, relaxes, keeps quiet, and avoids worry, anxiety, and despondency. (See Climacteric, Crises, Critical; "Periods of Bad Health" under Health; Periodic, Periods, Square).

Favorable Years of Life—These years, or periods, are based upon the trine (△) aspects of the progressed ☽, and are multiples of the No. 9, as the 18th, 27th, 36th, 45th years, etc. Also the years in life when ♄, and other plan-

ets, form their △ aspects to their radical places tend to be fortunate years if not offset by a train of evil Directions to the Hyleg. (See Aspects, Climacteric, Critical; "Periods of Good Health" under Health; Periods, Sextile, Trine).

Lord of the Year—The nature of the ruler of the year at the Vernal Equinox has much to do with the health of the Public during the year. Much mortality, and a prevalence of chronic diseases, are indicated when ♄ is lord of the year. When ♂ is lord of the year, many accidents, injuries, much bloodshed, and danger of War, and especially in Countries ruled by the Sign rising, etc. (See Vernal).

Public Health Good — Public Health Bad — Good and Bad Years for the Health of the People — (See "Public Health Bad", "Public Health Good", under Public. Also note the various paragraphs and subjects in the Article on Prevalent).

Quarters of the Year—Those born in the First Quarter of the year, between the times of the Vernal Equinox and the Summer Solstice, and especially in March, when the ☉ is passing thru his exalted sign ♈, have a stronger constitution, and are of longer life than those born in the Winter months when the ☉ is in the South and passing thru the ♄ Signs ♑ and ♒, and the 12th House sign ♓. The two Northern Quarters of the year, from the Vernal Equinox to the Autumnal Equinox, tend to give greater vitality when the ☉ is passing thru these Northern Signs, and especially if the fiery signs ♈ or ♌ are also upon the Asc. at B., while the Southern Signs, below the Equator, are not as strong for vitality unless there is a strong and vital sign rising on the Asc. at B., such as ♈, ♌, ♏, or ♐. (See Quarters).

YEAST—(See Fermentation, Zymosis).

YELLOW—Yellow Color—Yellowish—Xanthic—The ☉ denotes Yellow, or inclined to purple. Yellow color is ruled by the ☉, ♀, ☿, the 3rd H., and by the ♐ Sign. In the Solar Spectrum the Yellow Color is ruled by ☿. Deep Yellow, and Saffron, are ruled by the 11th H. (See Colors). The Sun-Kissed fruits, with the yellow, or golden yellow skin, such as the Orange, are ruled by the ☉, and denote strength, vitality, and health. In disease conditions the skin may have a yellow tinge due to the pathological action of ♄, and the deposits of poisons, wastes, minerals, Uric Acid, Urea, and Xanthin. Also in Jaundice, the skin may be yellow. (See Jaundice, Xanthin, Xanthoderma).

Bowel Disorders — The yellow color acts as an opening medicine in bowel disorders, and is somewhat of a Physic. Cathartic tablets should be coated with yellow color. (See Physic).

Complexion — Yellow Complexion — Yellowish — Sallow — Saffron — Mulatto — Unhealthy Yellowish Hue — The ☉ gives a yellowish, saffron complexion; ♄ in ♉; ♄ ♑, sallow; ♄ ori. at B.; ♂ Sig. in ♑; ♀ in ♈ in the 6th H., afflicted, or affl. the ☽ or Asc.; ☿ oriental at B.; a ☿ person is usually of a dark, yellow color, or a sad brown; ☿ posited occi. of the ☉, except when ☿ is in ♊; ♈ on the Asc.; the Quadrant from the Autumnal Equinox to the Winter Solstice causes a yellowish complexion. (See "Yellow" under Complexion; Jaundice, Xanthous).

Eyes — A Yellow Tinge — ♂ people— (See "Yellowish" under Eyes).

Face—Yellow Face—Face Yellowish In Sickness — (See "Yellow" under Face; Jaundice).

Fever — Yellow Fever — A ♌ disease, and afflictions in ♌. Also caused by vitiated and disturbed atmospheric conditions by planetary influences. Also contributed to by subluxations at CP, SP and KP. (See Epidemics, Immunity, Vertebrae).

Hair—Yellow—Yellowish—Yellowish Brown—(See "Yellow" under Hair).

Jaundice — (See "Yellow" under Jaundice).

Marks — Yellow Marks On Body — ♀ tends to give a yellow mark on the part of the body ruled by the sign she is in at B. (See Marks).

Opening Medicine — (See "Bowel Disorders" in this section).

Races—Yellow Races—Mulatto—Mongolian—(See Races, Xanthous; "Complexion" in this section).

Skin — Yellow Skin — (See "Yellow" under Complexion, Face, Jaundice, Skin; Xanthoderma, Xanthous; "Complexion" in this section).

Vision — Yellow Vision — (See Jaundice, Xantopsia).

YOGI BREATHING—(See "Yogi" under Breath).

YOUNG—Immature—The Early Period of Life—

Dies Young — (See "Death" under Childhood, Children, Infancy; "Early Death" under Early; "Short Life" under Life; "Dies Before Middle Life" under Middle Life; Untimely; "Death In Youth" under Youth).

Females—Young Females At Puberty —(See "Females" under Puberty).

Young Men — Much Mortality Among —♂ in ♌ at the Vernal Equi., and lord of the year; Comets appearing in ♊. (See "Death of Men" under Men).

Young Mind — Youthful — (See Juvenility).

Young People — (See "Young" under Females, Women; "Young Men" in this section).

Young Women — (See "Young" under Women).

YOUTH—Youthful—Young People—The ☉ rules Youth, and when one is at the strongest. Also ♂ rules the flourishing time of youth. In the Kabala, youth was dedicated to ♂ and ♀. The period of youth from 14 to 28 years of age is said to be ruled by ♀, which is the mating time. In Hor'y Questions, youth, and a youthful person are indicated by ☿ as Sig. The following subjects have to do with youth, young men and women, and the period before middle life. See these subjects in the alphabetical arrangement when not considered here—

Boyishness — (See "Youthfulness" in this section).

Complexion—In Youth—♎ on the Asc. tends to a fair complexion in youth, and rather ruddy, with no excess of red or white, but tends to pimples and a high color toward old age.

Death In Youth — ♂ sole ruler at an eclipse tends to the death of many young people. The 9° ♓ on the Asc., many young people die thru dissipation and passional excesses. (See "Early Death" under Children, Early; Directions; "Death" under Females, Men, Women; "Dies Before Middle Life" under Middle Life; Untimely; "Early Youth" in this section).

Directions — The Effects of Primary Directions In Youth, and Over Youth — (See "Directions" under Childhood, Infancy, Parents).

Early Years — Not Strong or Robust In Early Years — Much Sickness In — Death During — (See "Early Death", "Early Years", under Early).

Early Youth—Death In—Not Apt to Live Until Adult Age — Rarely Lives to Maturity—The ☽ sepr. from ♄ and applying to ♂ if the ☽ be hyleg; ♅ in the M.C., elevated above, and affl. the ☉, ☽, or hyleg; ♄ in the 11th, and ♂ in the 5th, or □ the cusp of the 5th, not apt to live to adult age; the 5° ♒, or the 11° ♓ on the Asc. at B. (See "Death In Youth" in this section; "Young Men" under Young).

Excesses—Dies Young Thru Excesses —(See "Death In Youth" in this section; "Passional Excesses" under Passion).

Fevers In Youth — And Childhood — (See "Fevers" under Childhood).

Health—State of In Youth—♄ in the Asc., or ☋ upon the Asc., are bad for the health during the earlier years and in youth, and more so when the ☉, ☽, Asc. or hyleg are afflicted by malefics. Fiery signs upon the Asc., and with the ☉, ☽, Asc., and hyleg strong and well-asp. tend to good health in youth, strong vitality, and little sickness in life. (See Constitution, Vitality).

Hurts In — Injuries In — (See "Accidents" under Childhood, Children, Infancy; "Early Years of Life" under Early).

Juvenility — Young Looking — Well-Preserved—(See Juvenility, Well-Preserved; "Youthfulness" in this section).

Men — Young Men — Great Mortality Among — Much Sickness Among — Comets appearing in ♊. (See "Death" under Men; "Young Men" under Young; "Death" in this section).

Middle Life—(See "Dies Before Middle Life", and other paragraphs under Middle Life).

Passional Excesses—(See "Excesses" in this section).

Perpetual Youth — There is no such thing in the human body, and such is not intended by the Higher Powers for the masses of Humanity. The Adepts and great Masters, however, have learned the secrets of keeping the body young, or to take on, or throw off, a physical body at will, which matters are discussed in the Occult Books, and in the Rosicrucian and Theosophical Societies. After middle life, ♄ begins to get in his work, deposit wastes and excess minerals over the body, hardens the arteries, the muscles and tendons become less tense and more brittle, the functions of the body become lowered, and Man's time comes to pass out of

the physical body. It is not so much how long we live in the physical body, but how we use it, how we occupy our time for the good and uplift of Humanity, and for our own growth, advancement, spiritual attainment, etc. Some physical bodies are not destined to endure very long, due to low vitality, and a very afflicting map of birth, while others are endowed with great vitality, and powers of endurance. (See "Youthfulness" in this section).

Planetary Periods—Of Childhood and Youth—(See Childhood, Periods).

Puberty; Robust—(See "Early Years" in this section; Robust).

Ruddy In Youth—(See Robust, Ruddy; "Good" under Vitality; "Complexion" in this section).

Scarlatina—Scarlet Fever—Smallpox — Many Young People Die of — (See "Mortality" under Children; Scarlatina, Smallpox).

Sickly During Youth—And Childhood —The 19° ♓ on the Asc. at B., but good health in old age. (See "Health" in this section; "Much Sickness" under Childhood; "Ill-Health" under Females; "Health Worse" under Men).

Slender In Youth—(See Slender).

Smallpox — (See "Scarlatina" in this section; Smallpox).

Strong In Youth — Not Strong — (See "Health" in this section).

Thin In Youth — ☋ infl.; ☋ on Asc. (See Slender).

Tomboyishness—Due to obscure positions of the ☉, ☽, ♆, ♅, ♃, ♂ and ♀, and with the positive signs prominent in a female nativity.

Vitality — Strong — Weak — (See "Health" in this section; Vitality).

Women—Chlorosis In—Ill-Health At Puberty—(See Chlorosis, Puberty).

Youthfulness—Youthful Looking—Boyishness—Given by the ♐ sign when this sign is strong, upon the Asc., well-aspected. Also given by the ♊ sign, the opposite and complementary sign to ♐, when well-placed and aspected. Venus tends to give prolonged youthfulness if dissipations and excesses are avoided. Saturn when strong and well-placed at B., and not severely afflicting the hyleg, tends to keep the native younger looking for some years in late life, and to give tenacity of life. (See Juvenility, Well-Preserved; "Pereptual Youth" in this section).

Z

ZEAL — Intemperate or Irrational Zeal —(See Ideals, Intemperate, Irrational, Reactionary; Reformers; "Fanatical" under Religion; Revolutionary).

ZENITH—(See Meridian, Tenth House).

ZEST — Given by planets in cardinal signs, and such signs on angles; planets rising and elevated in masculine signs. Aspects to the ☉ and ♂ are necessary to give zest, activity, and energy, and even bad asps. to the ☉

and ♂, or of ♂ to the ☉, are better than no aspects at all. (See Active, Energy, Exercise, Stamina, Tone).

ZINC—Ruled by ♅. A good Skin Remedy in Ointments. (See Actinium).

ZINZIBER — Zingiber — Ginger — Ruled by ♂. Is Tonic, Stimulant, and Counter-irritant.

ZODIAC—The Twelve Signs of the Zodiac constitute the Grand Man, and rule the different parts of the body from the head to the feet, ♈ ruling the head, ♉ the throat and neck, ♊ the lungs, shoulders, arms; ♋ the breasts; ♌ the heart; ♍ the bowels and abdomen; ♎ the kidneys; ♏ the sex organs and reproductive system; ♐ the hips, thighs; ♑ the knees; ♒ the calves and ankles; ♓ the feet. The planets in the signs tend to affect, for good or ill, the parts of the body, organs, or functions, ruled by such signs, and by knowing what signs were occupied by planets, and their nature, at the birth of a person, the diagnosis of the possible diseases of the native are made easier. (See Diagnosis, Prognosis, Subluxations, Vertebrae).

Aspects—Zodiacal Aspects—(See Aspects).

Azimene Degrees Of—(See Azimene).

Body—Zodiacal Rulership Over—This is three-fold, and is external, internal and structural. The external rulership relates to the external organs, the external parts and anatomy. The Internal rulership relates to the internal construction and internal organs. The structural rulership relates to the skeleton and bony structure. (See the various signs, as Aries, Taurus, etc., and also the various organs. Also see External, Internal, Structural).

Constellations—Many Fixed Stars in the Constellations are noted in Astrology as having influence in matters of health, disease, and the affairs of Humanity. (See Nebulous, Stars).

Critical Degrees — Of the Zodiac — (See "Sensitive" in this section).

Dark Degrees — Of the Zodiac — ♈ 3, 16; ♉ 3, 30; ♊ 7, 27; ♋ 14; ♌ 10; ♍ 5, 30; ♎ 10, 21; ♏ 3, 30; ♐ 12; ♑ 7, 22, 30; ♒ 13; ♓ 6, 18, 30. If the Asc., or its lord, be in any of these degrees at B., the native is more dark of complexion. (See "Dark" under Complexion''; Dark).

Degrees of the Zodiac—(See Azimene; "Zodiac" under Degrees; "Dark", "Sensitive", in this section).

Food—The Food Adapted to People Born under Each Sign of the Zodiac—(See "Signs of the Zodiac" under Food).

Monsters of the Zodiac—Many of the Signs of the Zodiac have Animals as Symbols, and the forces of the Zodiac which work over Humanity are intended to try, test, and examine into every trait of human character, and until Man is able to conquer these forces, and not allow his lower nature to dominate him, he is far from perfection. In the Writings of the Occult Masters, we are admonished to conquer these "Monsters of the Zodiac", rule and control them, otherwise they will rule us, and lead us astray for a time, and into many difficulties and trying situations. (See "Periods of Bad Health" under Health).

Negative Signs—Of the Zodiac—The Feminine Signs, as ♉, ♋, ♍, etc. (See "Signs" under Feminine; "Negative Signs" under Negative; "Negative" under Signs of the Zodiac).

Pitted Degrees—Of the Zodiac—(See Pitted; "Face" under Smallpox).

Polycrest Remedies—Of the Signs of the Zodiac — These Remedies correspond to the Twelve Signs of the Zodiac as follows—♈, Aconite Napellus; ♉, Belladonna; ♊, Bryonia Alba; ♋, Ipecac; ♌, Chamomilla; ♍, Nux Vomica; ♎, Rhus Toxicodendron; ♏, Pulsatilla; ♐, Mercurius; ♑, Sulphur; ♒, Arsenicum Album; ♓, Veratrum Album. There are also 12 Salts assigned to the 12 Signs of the Zodiac. (See "Salts" in this section).

Positive Signs—Of the Zodiac—(See Positive; "Electro-Positive" under Signs).

Remedies — Zodiac Remedies — (See "Polycrest", "Salts", in this section).

Salts—The Zodiac Salts—Cell Salts—Also known as the Schuessler Tissue Remedies — Each Sign of the Zodiac rules a different cell salt in the body, and these 12 salts make up the general chemical structure of the body, any one of which, when lacking, tends to disturb the chemical balance of the system. Dr. Schuessler, a Homeopathic Physician, prepared these 12 salts, finely triturated, in tablet form, so as to give the proper dosage, and in a form most easily assimilated. The Science of Biochemistry gives special attention to the use of these 12 Remedies, and to prescribe which are needed, and as indicated by the star map of birth. These Remedies are as follows, one for each Sign of the Zodiac — ♈, Potassium Phosphate; ♉, Sodium Sulphate; ♊, Chloride of Potassium; ♋, Fluoride of Lime (Calcium Fluoride); ♌, Phosphate of Magnesia; ♍, Potassium Sulphate; ♎, Sodium Phosphate; ♏, Sulphate of Lime (Calcium Sulphate); ♐, Silica (called the "Surgeon of the System"); ♑, Phosphate of Lime; ♒, Sodium Chloride; ♓, Phosphate of Iron (Ferrum Phosphate). (See these subjects).

Example—People born with the ☉ in the ♌ sign are apt to use up the Phosphate of Magnesia of the body faster, and in illness should receive this Salt to supply the need of the body, and the birthday, and the sign born under would indicate what salt is especially needed in an increased quantity, and more than has been taken in normally in the food. And so on with all the Signs, the Rising Signs at birth, the Signs containing the ☽ and malefics, and all the aspects, etc., should be considered in determining what Salts are needed. These Salts are Inorganic, and as Inorganic Salts in their raw forms are not as easily assimilated, or as beneficial for the system, but tend to be deposited as minerals in the body, these Salts should be taken in their vegetable forms, and taken from the food. All of these Salts are contained in vegetables, and food of various kinds, and the student, or patient, should make a study of the Diet question, of food values, and then take those special foods, meats, nuts, vegetables, or fruit juices, which predominate in the Salt needed. Mineral waters containing these Salts are not good for the system, as the minerals in water are inorganic. People should drink distilled water after middle life, and get their Salts and Minerals from their food, and not from their drink, or from Medicines. These are the views of the Occult Masters, and the best Authorities upon the subject. (See Chemistry; "Signs of the Zodiac" under Food; "Biochemistry" under Healers; Minerals; "Water" under Skin).

Sensitive Degrees — Of the Zodiac — Critical Degrees — The Sensitive, and more Critical Degrees of the Zodiac are the 13° and 26° of cardinal signs; the 9° and 21° of fixed signs; and the 4° and 17° of the common signs, and planets when in these degrees at birth tend to affect the native greatly, for good or ill, in health, or other matters, according to the nature of the planets, their power, and the aspects to them. (See Sensitive).

Signs—Signs of the Zodiac, their nature, qualities, rulership, etc. (See Aries, Taurus, etc.; Signs; the Introduction to this Article).

Vulnerable Spots—In the Zodiac—In the Horoscope—(See Vulnerable).

Zones—Zodiac Zones—(See Zones).

ZONES—Zone—

Zone Diseases — Zones of the Body Afflicted — Shown by the planets in Signs, as each Sign rules a certain Zone of the body. (See the Section on "Rules" under each of the Signs, as "Aries Rules" under Aries; "Taurus Rules" under Taurus, etc. Also see the Article, "Signs of the Zodiac").

Zones of the Spine—(See "Vertebrae" under Cervical, Dorsal, Lumbar; Spine, Subluxations, Vertebrae).

Zones of the Zodiac—Denoted by the Twelve Signs, as Aries, Taurus, Gemini, etc. (See each of the Signs in the alphabetical arrangement, as Aries, Taurus, etc.).

ZOSTER—Herpes Zoster—(See Herpes).

ZYMOSIS — Zymotic — The Process of Fermentation — To Ferment, Boil or Agitate—Yeast, etc.—Fermentation is the work of the ☽, and also ruled by the ♋ Sign. Heat and Moisture combined are positive, and tend to fermentation. Thru the different Processes of the body, the ☽ carries on the work of Cellular Zymosis, while the ☉ acts for Cellular Excitation. (See "Excitation" under Cells; Fermentation, Processes).

Bowels — Fermentation of Food In — (See "Putrid" under Bowels).

Break-Bone Fever—(See Dengue).

Dengue — Break-Bone Fever — A Zymotic Disease, with Fever, Pain in the Bones, Eruptions, etc. (See Dengue).

Diseases—Zymotic Diseases—Zymotic Fevers—Germ Diseases—Diseases with Fermentation — The Fermentative, or Nutritive Processes, are ruled by ♀, and ♀ afflicted, or an afflicted ☽, tend to zymotic disorders. Also an afflicted ♂ tends to zymotic skin disorders, such as Measles, and other forms of skin germ diseases, rashes, etc. (See Dengue, Germs, Measles, Moisture, Nutrition; "Fermentation" under Stomach).

Periodicity — Zymotic Periodicity — Fermentation—Ruled by the ☽. The general and physiological action of the ☽ Group of Herbs are zymotic in their influence, and also tend to Zymotic Periodicity. (See Microzymasis, Periodicity).

Stomach — Fermentation In—(See "Fermentation" under Stomach). See Assimilation, Diet, Digestion, Food, Indigestion, Nutrition.